Bill James presents

THE GREAT AMERICAN BASEBALL STAT BOOK

Library of Congress Catalog Card Number: 86-92043

ISBN: 0-345-34570-3

Cover design by Dale R. Fiorillo

Manufactured in the United States of America

First Edition: April 1987

10 9 8 7 6 5 4 3 2 1

Bill James presents

THE GREAT AMERICAN BASEBALL STAT BOOK

by
Bill James, John Dewan, and Project Scoresheet

with
Editors

Geoff Beckman	Mark Podrazik
Dennis Bretz	Gary Skoog
Gary Gillette	Craig Wright
Michael O'Donnell	Don Zminda

Susan Dewan, Computer Consultant

Ballantine Books • New York

Contents

Acknowledgments

If you flip through the pages of this book, you will see the names of many people who contributed their writing, time, and effort to making this book a reality. But there are still many more who worked behind the scenes, either within Project Scoresheet, or directly on this book. They make up a large group of people scattered around the country, loosely connected by their enchantment with the game of baseball and by the U.S. Postal Service and a variety of phone companies. Listed below, is my attempt to acknowledge these people.

Let's start with Project Scoresheet.

Board of Directors

This board of nine baseball enthusiasts meets several times a year to set the direction for improving the project. Their guidance has helped the Project progress by leaps and bounds.

Dennis Bretz (AL West Captain)
John Dewan (Director)
Gary Gillette (AL East Captain)
Bill James
Kenneth Miller
Pete Palmer
Gary Skoog (NL West Captain)
Mark Podrazik (NL East Captain)
Craig Wright

1986 Team Captains

These 26 people are responsible for coordination of the scoring of all games played by their respective teams. By keeping in contact with the scorers, they are (in a sense) the lifeblood of the project.

Geoff Beckman	Mike Marrero
Russell Bell	Clint Mueller
Dennis Bretz	Susan Nelson
Richard Carter	Chris Pohl
Craig Christmann	Mark Podrazik
Clem Comly	Greg Pryor
Joe Cook	Jim Rogde
Gord Fitzgerald	Steve Russell
Gary Gillette	Ira Saltz
Dave Gordon	Scott Segrin
Mike Kopf	John Ungashick
Brent MacInnes	Jay Walker
Don Malcolm	Chuck Waseleski

1986 Scorers

What would the project have without all these scoresheets? Listed below are those who scored a large number of games during the 1986 season. There are many others who have scored fewer games during the season, but nonetheless, their scoresheets are just as valuable. Thanks to all, and congratulations on scoring all the games. (This may look like a lot of names, but remember, there is always room for more scorers.)

Paul Adomites	Dennis Bretz
Sunil Agarwal	David Broughton
Bob Bailey	Paul Brown
Brick Barrientos	Jack Carlson
Diana Barnum	Richard Carter
Geoff Beckman	Chris Chew
John Beisner	Craig Christmann
Tom Benner	Paul Collett
Mark Blume	Clem Comly
Terry Bohn	Joe Cook
Marc Bowman	Steven Copley
David Bradley	Carmen Corica

Bruce Cox
Luke DalFiume
Paul Debbas
Jay Demarest
Mr. Derrait
David Driscoll
Jessie Drucker
Jeff Eby
Roger Ellam
Bernie Esser
Frank Fincken, Jr.
Gord Fitzgerald
Michael Fitzgerald
Greg Funk
Mike Galbreath
Jim Gartung
Kirk Gibson
Gary Gillette
Dave Gordon
Jay Gregory
Rick Guzman
Jon Heinlen
Bryan Holliman
William F. Hugo
Tom Idziak
Bill James
Bill Jensen
Darwin Johnson
Dennis Johnson
Tom Jones
Stacy Kaneshiro
Michael Klobas
Steve Kolk
Mike Kopf
Luke Kraemer
Theo Lambos
Ward Larkin
Bob Leeper
Rollie Loewen
Steve Lysogorski
Brent MacInnes
Gary Magee
Don Malcolm
Frank Markotich
Mike Marrero
Rick Martinez
Michael Mathon
Steve Mattan
Welford McCaffrey
Pat McCann
Susan McCarthy
Pat McCormick
John Mitchell
Brian T. Morris
Clint Mueller
Tim Mulligan
Susan Nelson
Tom Nester
Jim Netter
Bob Newton
David Nichols
Joe Nunziata III

Joe O'Connell
Michael O'Donnell
Dennis Orr
Robert Ostrove
Pete Palmieri, Jr.
Mark Pankin
Charlie Pavitt
Fred Percival
Richard Perrotti
Tom Peters
David Pinto
Bud Podrazik
Mark Podrazik
Chris Pohl
Cindy Pohl
Greg Pryor
Mark Prysant
Doug Ranny
Rita Ann Reimer
Fred W. Reisser
John Rickert
David Robinson
Jim Rogde
Ira Saltz
Martin Schneider
Jeff Schwarze
Paul Schwarzenbart
Phil Scott
Skip Seeger
Scott Segrin
Chris Shanklin
Stuart Shea
Sanford Sklansky
James Skelly II
Chris Smith
James A. Smith, Jr.
Jeff Smith
Mike Sopp
Jeff Sosnowski
Pat Steininger
Page Stephens
Tim Swindle
Al Them
Bill Thomas
Kirk Thomas
Antoinette Tomczak
Wayne Townsend
John Unghishick
Bill Venski
Chuck Waseleski
Bob Webb
Jeff Welch
Bob Wertzberger
Bob Whitemore
Dean Williams
Wendy Wilson
Dave Wolfe
Barry Wolven
Donald A. Yeager
Don Zminda

1986 Computer Inputters

These people add value to scoresheet data by entering it into personal computers, where it can be easily manipulated, totaled, and reported on. It's a big job! Thank goodness they were there to help.

Diana Barnum
Tom Benner
Andrew Berman
Dennis Bretz
John Buehler
Norman Clearfield
Dick Craig
Reg Delperdang
Bill Disney
William Dozier
David Driscoll
Vicki Driscoll
Bill Farley
Robert Fegley
Dan Feinstein
Shellie Garrett
Gary Gillette
Don Gunning
Steve Hamburg

Tim Hedquist
Arthur Kimes
Steve Kolk
Ward Larkin
Bob Levittan
Mark Loomis
Jim Lowder
Jana McBride
Ken McKusick
John A. Marr
Mark Pankin
Tom Peters
David Pinto
Mark Podrazik
John Stryker
Rich Szilagyi
Tom Tippett
Jeff Yaguda
Don Zminda

1986 League Coordinators

The league coordinators receive mail from scorers, and lots of it. Their responsiblity is to keep track of all the scoresheets at Project Scoresheet Central and keep them flowing between the scorers and inputters. The coordinator for the American League is *Bud Podrazik*. I keep track of the mail for the National League. By the way, I'm *Sue Dewan*. I won the job of writing these acknowledgments because as a league coordinator I had the pleasant opportunity (like Bud) to correspond with many of the people whose names appear on these pages.

Then there are those who put in additional effort on this book:

Editorial Board

Read, edit, read, edit. . . For a couple of weeks this became the daily routine and sole activity of our editorial board. Thanks to these people, who did such a fine job of editing the manuscripts submitted by project members. Their knowledge of the game of baseball is an invaluable asset.

Geoff Beckman
Dennis Bretz
John Dewan
Bill James
Gary Gillette

Michael O'Donnell
Mark Podrazik
Gary Skoog
Craig Wright
Don Zminda

Computer System

Computers were an indispensable tool in cranking out the statistics in this book. The programs which ran for hours, grinding and formulating the numbers were created by myself and *John Dewan*. But we had some help, too. Thanks to *Dennis Bretz* and *Mark Podrazik* who contributed some of their programming expertise. Thanks also to *Gary Skoog*, whose technical knowledge helped us set up the equipment necessary to process so many numbers.

Data Verification

In order to assure accuracy, many people spent days bent over computer listings and boxscores to verify our data. We hope their eyes have recovered.

Joe Baird	Patrick Hoye
Andrew Berman	Bill Jensen
Alan Boodman	Scott Johnson
Tom Bradley	Sharon Jones
Dennis Bretz	Robert Kasier
Dennis Bronstein	Keith Knopf
Jack Carlson	Martin LaCoste
Steven Carter	Frank Markotich
Clem Comly	Don McKennan
Greg Crouse	Tim Mulligan
Russ Eagle	Michael O'Donnell
Tom Eckel	Dennis Orr
Bernie Esser	Bud Podrazik
Joni Fabiano	Mark Podrazik
Daniel Feinberg	Steve Russell
Frank Fincken, Jr.	Steven Scott
Mike Galbreath	Rory Shaw
Jay Gregory	Russell Shipe
John Gregory	James Smith
Stuart Hall	Steve Stephenson
Jeff Held	Thomas Stillman
Thomas J. Henry	Peggy Sykes
George Hines	Rich Szilagyi
Bryan Holliman	

Data Editing

Once an error was uncovered, someone had to find the source of it and fix it. That job was in the capable hands of *Mark Podrazik* along with *John Dewan*. Possibly the largest job in the entire project, this took countless hours, days, and weeks to assure accuracy.

Career Data

Thanks to *Dr. Richard Cramer* and STATS Inc. for their assistance in compiling the player career register.

Writers

Last, but not least, there are the many writers. You can find their names throughout the book. We regret that we could not include all of the essays and commentaries that were submitted. All added extra insight into the players and the game.

Finally, special acknowledgements to those who gave that extra special help in the compilation of the book.

Sarah Teeling, was the renaissance person in the project. She did everything and anything, from inputting data, to verifying numbers, to bringing over her special dinners to keep us going as we worked late. What a friend!

Thanks to *Geoff Beckman*, for all the extra help during the critical final weeks. And to *Don Zminda* for use of his extensive research material, hereupon known as The Official Don Zminda Baseball Library. (Library cards can be obtained by . . . oops, only kidding Don.)

Thanks also to *David Nichols* who has revised our scoring form for 1987. And also, thanks for the extra effort:

Andrew Berman	Steven Scott
Sharon Jones	Rich Szylagyi
Marge Morra	

Now that I have finished the acknowledgments, I realize why I really got this job. Because it's a hard one. But then again it's very rewarding. When we sent out the word that Project Scoresheet would be producing a book, we received responses from many members who wanted to help. As I wrote these acknowledgments, I browsed through my binder of letters from these same people. I was once again reminded of the large number of people who offered their time and baseball expertise. Regrettably, it seemed almost impossible to coordinate the efforts of all in such a short timeframe, and so, as personnel coordinator (a fancy name for general gofer) I took the easier way out, and coordinated the efforts of a subset of these people (albeit still many, many people). Let me now express our sincere appreciation to everyone who responded to the book survey. Even if we could not coordinate everyone's help, your responses provided support and encouragement.

My sincere apologies to anyone I inadvertently omitted in the above list.

—Sue Dewan

I

INTRODUCTION

INTRODUCTION

Hi. My name is Bill James. I make my living by analyzing baseball games. I pick up things that people say and try to figure out whether or not they are true. I write a book every year about the research I have done and anything else that pops into my head, which is not this book but another one.

When I started doing this eleven years ago, I wrote to the league offices and asked about getting access to the scoresheets of major-league games. I got very evasive answers, as if they weren't really sure that I was a legitimate person with a legitimate need to see the scoresheets. Over the following years, I encountered many questions that I wanted to research for which I needed to have access to actual game accounts. Occasionally, as my reputation grew and the frequency of people taking potshots at me in *The Sporting News* increased, I would figure that now maybe the league offices would know which idiot I was and would let me see their precious scoresheets, and I would write back and ask if I could study the official scoresheets of the games.

Well, they never exactly told me to get lost, but it eventually dawned on me that they didn't intend to ever let me see the scoresheets, so what then?

What I decided to do then was just to start collecting them myself. Fortunately, I went into this the same way I go into everything, which is to say with no idea of what I was doing. When I decided to collect fan's scoresheets of all major-league games, I had no concept of the difficulty of the task, no plan as to how I was going to get them and only a sort of loose idea of what my goals were. I didn't have any idea what it would cost or how I would recoup that cost. It is fortunate that I didn't have any of these things, or I quite certainly would never have had the heart to begin.

Project Scoresheet is a loose organization of a few hundred baseball fans, who score each and every major-league game. They do more than that, but to explain what would be getting ahead of the story. In the spring of 1984 I put out the word through every source that I could think of that I was going to start an organization to collect scoresheets. Maybe a hundred or one hundred fifty people responded.

The first director of Project Scoresheet was Kenneth Miller, a bright, well-organized gentleman whom I met when he was trying to put together a computer baseball game, which eventually became the computer version of APBA, which is marketed through Random House. Anyway, Kenneth ran Project Scoresheet, sort of, through its first summer in 1984. Kenneth was too busy with other projects, like making a living, to provide the kind of hands-on supervision that the infant organization needed, but in his role as the first director he performed an invaluable service: he located the person who did have the desire and ability to pull the organization together.

That person was John and Sue Dewan. John Dewan is a Chicago actuary who, like a lot of young men, loves baseball and has always wanted to work with baseball statistics. It is an interesting question (I will have to ask him sometime) as to whether or not, if John had had a clear idea of the load that he was picking up, he would have felt equal to it. Another interesting question is whether, if Sue had known what they were getting into, she would have gone along so graciously. Anyway, in late summer 1984, John agreed to take on the task of organizing Project Scoresheet.

And a hell of a task it was. Here's what has to be done for each game:

1) Somebody has to make sure the game is being scored.

2) Somebody has to score the game, write down what happens on every play.

3) The scoresheet has to be copied and sent to a central location.

4) The account of the game has to be entered on computer.

5) The account of the game on computer has to be checked for accuracy.

6) The accounts of all the games have to be joined together for analysis.

Behind each of these requirements, there is a whole array of needs. Before somebody can assign the game, you have to construct a nationwide network of volunteers and a structure by which their work is organized.

Before the game can be scored, you have to develop a standard scoring method. You have to instruct all of your scorers in the method that you're using.

Before you can get the game entered on computer, you have to design the software to enter the game. Before you can use the software, you have to buy the computers. When you buy computers, you almost always have to pay for them; computer stores are explicit about this.

The idea that I would be capable of doing all of these things is laughable to anyone who knows me. My basic function in the organization is to beat the tom-toms and get the scorers to gather. After that, it's up to John and the organization's workhorses.

John has, in this work, two advantages, one of which he shares with me and the other of which he doesn't. Like me, he has a wonderful wife who is willing to devote a great deal of time and effort to the project. Unlike me, he is very well-organized.

So when John joined the organization, we began to set goals. And we began to meet them. We have a board of directors which meets in John's kitchen every few months and talks about what needs to be done and how to do it. It's a good board, bright people who thrash through difficult issues in an orderly manner. I suppose that to those of you in the business community this wouldn't seem rare, but it's been a real pleasure for me to be associated with these people.

So ever since John joined the organization, we have been making steady strides toward the attainment of our generel goal: to get all of the scoresheets of all of the games, and to make them as available to the public as is humanly possible.

Let me back up half a sentence and emphasize that: we are a volunteer, nonprofit organization whose goal is to gather the scoresheets of all major-league games and make them available as cheaply as we can to whoever wants to study them. We have accounts of every game played in the major leagues since 1984, and we can make them available to you on disk or on paper. The cost varies according to the form and whether you want up-to-date service, which obviously is more expensive. If you want information on availability of scoresheets, contact Project Scoresheet, P.O. Box 46074, Chicago, Illinois, 60646.

Anyway, having assembled all of this information, the idea occurred to us to produce a book, which you are now reading. Drawing on the resources of the organization, we felt we could (and we feel we have done so) produce a book of research and analysis about major league baseball the like of which had never been seen before.

We have tried, in selecting the information to present to you, to concentrate on presenting *meaningful* information. We have tried to concentrate on *building up* information, rather than breaking it down. Not meaning to put anyone down, but you know that there have been other books presenting some similar data that have concentrated on breaking down performance into categories so small and so specific that, to be honest, the published data is obviously meaningless.

Now, I'm skeptical about the entire notion of clutch performance, but I'm willing to take a look at the data. It is difficult for me to understand how a player who is not a good hitter can magically become a good hitter when the game or the pennant is on the line. Nonetheless, there is

such a thing as clutch *performance,* whether resulting from clutch ability or from random fluctuations in data.

But while I *might* believe that there is an ability to hit with runners in scoring position, and while I *might* believe that there is an ability to hit in the late innings of close games, does anyone really believe that there is an ability to hit with runners in scoring position in the late innings of close games, as distinguished from merely an ability to hit in one situation or the other?

Even if there was such an ability, unlikely as that seems, a player faces that specific situation, as a full-time regular, only 15 or 20 times a season. Even if the hitter hits .400 in that situation that means nothing, there being a 15 or 20% chance that an average hitter would go 6-for-15 anyway, just in the nature of things. To get a meaningful data sample, you would have to look at such information over a period of at least ten years—during which the player's abilities would change so much as to render the grouping useless.

So as we see it, it's silly to break the player's performance down into specific situations so small that no ability is being measured. What we have tried to do instead is make some sensible, systematic breakdowns of player performance, and then look at performance in those categories over a period of years, so that you have a chance to distinguish meaningful tendencies from random fluctuations.

There are some evident patterns in the data. It is quite apparent in the data that many hitters are situation-responsive in ways that I would not have anticipated. The assumption of table games or computer games is, in the main, that play happens randomly, that if a player hits .275 then he hits .275 no matter what the game situation. That's not only the assumption of table games, but the assumption with which most of us watch the game: if we see a .275 hitter at the plate, we figure that he's going to hit .275 unless he's got an advantage on the pitcher or the pitcher has an advantage on him. This data makes it clear that that assumption is not true in certain systematic ways. A few examples:

Leading off the inning, it is obvious that the number of walks issued decreases. The pitcher doesn't want to walk the leadoff hitter.

Further, it is obvious that *disciplined* hitters tend to increase their *power* quite dramatically when leading off the inning. The reason for this is that when a disciplined hitter gets ahead of the pitcher leading off the inning, the pitcher will risk a home run to avoid walking the leadoff man. For example, over the last three years Bill Doran has 40% of his at bats leading off in the innings, but has hit 50% of his homers in that situation. Mike Scioscia has 23% of his at bats, but 59% of his homers. Those kind of ratios are not uncommon.

Less disciplined hitters have a smaller advantage in that situation than do disciplined hitters, and to the extent that they do the edge tends to be in average, rather than in power. A free swinger, hitting leadoff, tends to see a strike early in the count and will hit it, lifting his average. For example, Damaso Garcia in the last three years has 37% of his at bats leading off an inning, has hit 37% of his homers leading off an inning, and has a .274 average when leading off, as opposed to .283 overall.

With runners on first base (only), a good many left-handed hitters and some right-handers increase their batting averages substantially because of the hole created by holding the runner on first.

As pitchers tend to try to avoid the walk when facing the leadoff hitter and will risk the home run, in the late innings of close games they try to avoid the home run and will risk the walk. For that reason, there are many hitters whose on-base percentages increase, but whose slugging percentages decrease, in the late innings of close games—in fact, you might even say that this is "standard," the norm more than the exception. (I just checked ten players at random, and over a three-year period all ten had lower slugging percentages in the late innings of close games than overall. Seven of the ten had higher on-base percentages.)

These things make sense, but we didn't know them before. It's knowledge that you can take with you to the ballgame. It seems to me, at a glance, that there are definite types of players who do and do not take advantage of the positives in these situations, but we'll have to study that. This book will make it possible to study those kinds of situation effects.

Another thing that has been done before, which we've tried to avoid, is to present the same information three or four times in different forms. We didn't, for example, go in big for rankings and listings. If a guy hits .177 in the late innings of close games, no baseball fan needs to be told that this isn't a very good performance. I mean, maybe it's nice to know whether he ranks 108th or 117th out of 126 American League regulars, but it's not really essential for the understanding or interpretation of the material, and since we are dealing with far more information than we can pack into a book, it didn't seem to us like a real good idea to repeat data.

Batting breakdowns against right-handed and left-handed pitching have been a staple topic of conversation for years. We thought it would make sense to look at them over a period of years, trying to distinguish real splits in ability from statistical flukes. Other things we're doing on a more experimental basis, looking at how each hitter has hit against groundball pitchers and flyball pitchers, how he has hit against power pitchers and finesse pitchers. There are many options for how to cut the data, and in time we plan to try all of them.

Within Project Scoresheet, there are a great many talented, intelligent, wonderful people. We have tried, in putting together this book (the brunt of which has fallen, again, upon John and Sue Dewan) to create a form which gives you as much information as possible, but which also allows those people to share with you some of their knowledge, some of their research, some of their insights, and some of their wit. We hope you like it, and in fact we hope you like it so much that you'll join us and help with the Project next year.

Project Scoresheet has been getting every game, but in some places, most notably California, it's a real struggle. We can't figure out what the problem is in California, because the attendance shows that there are a lot of good baseball fans out there. We've had a great deal of trouble reaching them and getting them involved in the effort. There are a few other areas, like St. Louis, which have been difficult to organize—but wherever you are, your help would be valued. We don't ask you to do anything too difficult or painful, just learn a new scoring system, which is a good scoring system and easy to learn, and score a few baseball games. You score games anyway, don't you?

One of the rewards of getting involved with this project is that, in the areas where the organization is strong, you get to know some other hard-core baseball fans, which is fun. To make this thing go, a lot of people have given an immense amount of time and effort, and we'll try to mention most of them somewhere in the book, but I wanted to single out here about five of the hardest-working volunteers. Dennis Bretz is a tireless scorekeeper, division captain, computer volunteer and writer for this book. Gary Skoog's understanding of the infernal machines is invaluable to us, as are his services as a division captain, business organizer, and scoresheet scrounger. Mark Podrazik is a delightful person, comfortable as an old shoe and twice as much fun, and his gifts of time, work, worry, computer knowledge, wit, and balance are beyond assessment, even by a pack of numbers-crazed zombies such as the rest of us. Bud Podrazik is his brother and much like him, without being too much like him. Gary Gillette shows up at every meeting with fresh ideas and refreshing enthusiasm; he, too, is appreciated for his services as division captain and board member. Many, many other people have devoted large blocks of valuable talent to the project. Without any of these people and their diverse talents, if a clod be washed away by the sea, as well as if a promontory were . . . no, wait a minute; that's not right. To learn that we could all work together, being so different, has been one of the most satisfying experiences of my life. And you're talking to a man who's got a baby.

5

NUMBERS, NUMBERS ... EVERYWHERE!

Of all the channels of effort necessary for the production of this book, one quite justifiably has received a disproportionate amount of time and toil: the quest for accuracy. Over three seasons, the Project has generated scoresheets for well over 6,000 major-league games. If each game consists of 75 or so distinct game "events," then we have the unenviable task of keeping more than 450,000 events in order. How do we do the best we can? Well, perhaps we should start with an explanation of our methods.

When a game is played, it is common for several Project Scoresheet scorers to be keeping a play-by-play account; we usually receive three or more scoresheets for each game (a lot of paper!). It is unlikely that any of these scorers were sitting in the press box at the game, but the fact that they each score the game from a different vantage point—a broadcast or maybe a seat down the leftfield line—helps ensure a certain degree of accuracy and completeness. Their accounts check and balance each other, and in that respect, they are superior to the single-game account from the perspective of the pressbox.

Once the scoresheets are received, the next task is to put the game account into a computer-manageable form. The game is coded into a computer much as it had transpired. An input routine (program) prompts the inputter for each game event; if our standard scoring system was used, the game is entered almost verbatim from the scoresheet. Typically a game can be input in about ten minutes.

By this point, however, the possibility of human error has greatly increased. Perhaps the scoresheet chosen for input was flawed; even if the scoresheet used by the inputter was perfect in every way, typographical errors may have been introduced during the input process. Occasionally, obscure events such as foul-ball errors may be mistakenly omitted by the inputter. It may seem a futile task to weed out these types of errors. It turns out just to be very time intensive.

Since the game account at this point exists in a form accessible by computer—stored on a floppy diskette—it exists in a form that can be viewed and manipulated. A simple but effective check for accuracy is the comparison of our game account with other, published accounts of the game. Experience indicates that something like 90% of the errors and discrepancies in our data can be resolved using this method.

So we generate standard box scores from our data and print them. Thousands of them. Each is checked against a published box score and compared in every way: players involved, positions played, statistical totals. Discrepancies are marked, and the task is now one of resolution. The game accounts exist on computer in a form easily edited. With the box score mark-up in one hand and a stack of scoresheets in the other, the game editor confronts his time-consuming but essential task; we affectionately refer to it as "cleaning the data." After many hours, the editing is done, so what do we do?

We print standard box scores. Thousands of them. Each one is checked against a published box score and compared in every way. Inevitably, this second check uncovers more skewed data, and a second edit takes place. Having many scoresheets for a game is invaluable here. Only one of them may indicate the missing or proper game event, but since it does, the editor knows exactly how to handle it. Just when the editor thinks his job is done, he prints ... box scores ... thousands of them. However, this time he checks just his last corrections to make sure they took.

Even after this enormous task, we face a horrifying fact: the game data may still have errors. Solution: generate the weekly cumulative statistics for each player and check them against published totals. More corrections are required as the errors are located. It is a lot of work, but the results are good, and allow us to present our data—as statistically correct information—in an enlightening and descriptive fashion.

The information presented to you in this book is accurate, at least in the sense of being meaningful, and we are confident that the efforts of the Project will continue to advance the analysis of this information as it makes it increasingly available to the public.

Baseball statistics, like the game itself, are for the fans.

—Mark Podrazik

II

PLAYER CAREER REGISTER

INTRODUCTION TO THE PLAYER REGISTER

If an infinite number of monkeys sat down at an infinite number of personal computers with an infinite number of official statistic listings from the Official Don Zminda Baseball Library, how long would it take to turn out the year-by-year career statistics for 650 major-league baseball players? Well, the answer is that it takes forever! And, that's almost exactly how we did it.

Fortunately, we did get a head start thanks to Dick Cramer at STATS, Inc. who provided a large part of the seasonal statistics going back to 1963. Then the infinite number of Project Scoresheet enthusiasts got to work—adding missing players, filling in missing data items, checking, rechecking, and re-rechecking completed info. Until, finally, you get the exceptionally comprehensive compilation of stats which follows in the next section.

There are 650 players included in this section (and throughout this book). Our basis of selection was to take players who were active and played a significant amount of time in 1986. For batters, we include every player who had at least 100 at bats in 1986. For pitchers, any pitcher who pitched at least 30 innings AND pitched in at least 15 games is included. The 650 represents an average of 25 players for each major league team.

The format of the Player Register may look familiar to you. It is taken from The Bill James Historical Abstract with slight modifications. Virtually every official batting and pitching statistic is included. Our intent was to provide a comprehensive statistical picture of the baseball player. We also hope that it facilitates research by including as much info as possible all in one convenient place.

—John Dewan

LEGEND TO PLAYER REGISTER

PITCHING AND BATTING: G-Games, H-Hits, R-Runs, HR-Home Runs, TBB-Total Bases on Balls, IBB-Intentional Bases on Balls, SO-Strikeouts

BATTING ONLY: AB-At Bats, 2B-Doubles, 3B-Triples, Hm-Home Runs at Home, Rd-Home Runs on the Road, TB-Total Bases, RBI-Runs Batted In, HBP-Hit By Pitch, SH-Sacrifice Hits, SF-Sacrifice Flies, SB-Stolen Bases, CS-Caught Stealing, SB%-Stolen Base Percentage SB/(SB+CS), GIDP-Grounded Into Double Play, AVE-Batting Average, OBP-On Base Percentage, SLG-Slugging Percentage

PITCHING ONLY: GS-Games Started, CG-Complete Games, GF-Games Finished in Relief, IP-Innings Pitched, BFP-Batters Faced Pitcher, ER-Earned Runs, HB-Hit Batsmen, WP-Wild Pitches, Bk-Balks, W-Wins, L-Losses, Pct-Winning Percentage, ShO-Shut Outs, Sv-Saves, ERA-Earned Run Average

DON AASE

Pitches Right-handed, Bats Right-handed

Turns Age 33 in 1987, Born 09/08/54

Year	Team	League	G	GS	CG	GF	IP	BFP	H	R	ER	HR	SH	SF	HB	TBB	IBB	SO	WP	Bk	W	L	Pct	ShO	Sv	ERA
					HOW MUCH HE PITCHED							WHAT HE GAVE UP											THE RESULTS			
1977	Boston	A	13	13	4	0	92	373	85	36	32	6	2	3	1	19	1	49	0	0	6	2	.750	2	0	3.13
1978	California	A	29	29	6	0	179	773	185	88	80	14	5	1	2	80	1	93	3	0	11	8	.579	1	0	4.02
1979	California	A	37	28	7	4	185	817	200	104	99	19	8	8	1	77	7	96	5	0	9	10	.474	1	2	4.82
1980	California	A	40	21	5	6	175	761	193	83	79	13	12	9	1	66	3	74	2	1	8	13	.381	1	2	4.06
1981	California	A	39	0	0	31	65	265	56	17	17	4	1	1	0	24	2	38	1	0	4	4	.500	0	11	2.35
1982	California	A	24	0	0	18	52	212	45	20	20	5	4	0	0	23	2	40	2	0	3	3	.500	0	4	3.46
1984	California	A	23	0	0	1	39	160	30	7	7	1	3	2	0	19	5	28	0	0	4	1	.800	0	8	1.62
1985	Baltimore	A	54	0	0	43	88	366	83	44	37	6	5	3	1	35	7	67	0	1	10	6	.625	0	14	3.78
1986	Baltimore	A	66	0	0	58	81.2	337	71	29	27	6	3	2	0	28	2	67	4	0	6	7	.462	0	34	2.98
9 YEARS			325	91	22	161	956.2	4064	948	428	398	74	43	29	6	371	33	552	17	2	61	54	.530	5	75	3.74

JIM ACKER

Pitches Right-handed, Bats Right-handed

Turns Age 29 in 1987, Born 09/24/58

Year	Team	League	G	GS	CG	GF	IP	BFP	H	R	ER	HR	SH	SF	HB	TBB	IBB	SO	WP	Bk	W	L	Pct	ShO	Sv	ERA
					HOW MUCH HE PITCHED							WHAT HE GAVE UP											THE RESULTS			
1983	Toronto	A	38	5	0	8	97.2	426	103	52	47	7	1	2	8	38	1	44	1	0	5	1	.833	0	1	4.33
1984	Toronto	A	32	3	0	9	72	313	79	39	35	3	4	1	6	25	3	33	5	0	3	5	.375	0	1	4.38
1985	Toronto	A	61	0	0	26	86.1	370	86	35	31	7	1	2	3	43	1	42	2	0	7	2	.778	0	10	3.23
1986	2 Teams		44	19	0	9	155	661	163	81	69	13	12	9	3	48	6	69	5	1	5	12	.294	0	0	4.01
4 YEARS			175	27	0	52	411	1770	431	207	182	30	18	14	20	154	11	188	13	1	20	20	.500	0	12	3.99
1986	Toronto	A	23	5	0	6	60	259	63	34	29	6	6	5	2	22	3	32	3	1	2	4	.333	0	0	4.35
1986	Atlanta	N	21	14	0	3	95	402	100	47	40	7	6	4	1	26	3	37	2	0	3	8	.273	0	0	3.79

LUIS AGUAYO

Bats Right-handed, Throws Right-handed

Turns Age 28 in 1987, Born 03/13/59

Year	Team	League	G	AB	H	2B	3B	HR	(Hm	Rd)	TB	R	RBI	TBB	IBB	SO	HBP	SH	SF	SB	CS	SB%	GIDP	AVE	OBP	SLG
						BATTING															BASERUNNING			PERCENTAGES		
1980	Philadelphia	N	20	47	13	1	2	1	(0	1)	21	7	8	2	0	3	0	0	1	1	1	.50	0	.277	.300	.447
1981	Philadelphia	N	45	84	18	4	0	1	(0	1)	25	11	7	6	0	15	2	2	0	1	0	1.00	0	.214	.283	.298
1982	Philadelphia	N	50	56	15	1	2	3	(2	1)	29	11	7	5	1	7	1	1	0	1	1	.50	1	.268	.339	.518
1983	Philadelphia	N	2	4	1	0	0	0	(0	0)	1	1	0	1	0	2	0	0	0	0	0	.00	0	.250	.400	.250
1984	Philadelphia	N	58	72	20	4	0	3	(1	2)	33	15	11	8	2	16	0	0	0	0	0	.00	1	.278	.350	.458
1985	Philadelphia	N	91	165	46	7	3	6	(4	2)	77	27	21	22	5	26	6	4	3	1	0	1.00	7	.279	.378	.467
1986	Philadelphia	N	62	133	28	6	1	4	(3	1)	48	17	13	8	0	26	3	0	2	1	1	.50	3	.211	.267	.361
7 YEARS			328	561	141	23	8	18	(10	8)	234	89	67	52	8	95	12	7	6	5	3	.63	12	.251	.325	.417

RICK AGUILERA

Pitches Right-handed, Bats Right-handed

Turns Age 26 in 1987, Born 12/31/61

Year	Team	League	G	GS	CG	GF	IP	BFP	H	R	ER	HR	SH	SF	HB	TBB	IBB	SO	WP	Bk	W	L	Pct	ShO	Sv	ERA
					HOW MUCH HE PITCHED							WHAT HE GAVE UP											THE RESULTS			
1985	New York	N	21	19	2	1	122.1	507	118	49	44	8	7	4	2	37	2	74	5	2	10	7	.588	0	0	3.24
1986	New York	N	28	20	2	2	141.2	605	145	70	61	15	6	5	7	36	1	104	5	3	10	7	.588	0	0	3.88
2 YEARS			49	39	4	3	264	1112	263	119	105	23	13	9	9	73	3	178	10	5	20	14	.588	0	0	3.58

MIKE ALDRETE

Bats Left-handed, Throws Left-handed

Turns Age 26 in 1987, Born 01/29/61

Year	Team	League	G	AB	H	2B	3B	HR	(Hm	Rd)	TB	R	RBI	TBB	IBB	SO	HBP	SH	SF	SB	CS	SB%	GIDP	AVE	OBP	SLG
						BATTING															BASERUNNING			PERCENTAGES		
1986	San Francisco	N	84	216	54	18	3	2	(1	1)	84	27	25	33	4	34	2	4	1	1	3	.25	3	.250	.353	.389

DOYLE ALEXANDER

Pitches Right-handed, Bats Right-handed.   Turns Age 37 in 1987, Born 09/04/50

			HOW MUCH HE PITCHED						WHAT HE GAVE UP													THE RESULTS					
Year	Team	League	G	GS	CG	GF	IP	BFP	H	R	ER	HR	SH	SF	HB	TBB	IBB	SO	WP	Bk	W	L	Pct	ShO	Sv	ERA
1971	Los Angeles	N	17	12	4	0	92	395	105	45	39	6	2	2	1	18	0	30	1	0	6	6	.500	0	0	3.82
1972	Baltimore	A	35	9	2	1	106	393	78	36	29	5	5	2	1	30	8	49	7	1	6	8	.429	2	2	2.46
1973	Baltimore	A	29	26	10	16	175	674	169	85	75	19	7	5	7	52	5	63	3	0	12	8	.600	0	0	3.86
1974	Baltimore	A	30	12	2	9	114	497	127	65	51	7	8	4	4	43	4	40	6	0	6	9	.400	0	0	4.03
1975	Baltimore	A	32	11	3	12	133	561	127	47	45	7	7	1	1	47	5	46	6	0	8	8	.500	1	1	3.05
1976	2 Teams		30	25	7	4	201	812	172	81	75	12	5	9	0	63	2	58	6	2	13	9	.591	3	0	3.36
1977	Texas	A	34	34	12	0	237	995	221	103	96	24	9	5	2	82	2	82	3	0	17	11	.607	1	0	3.65
1978	Texas	A	31	28	7	3	191	822	198	84	82	18	10	8	1	71	1	81	4	0	9	10	.474	1	0	3.86
1979	Texas	A	23	18	0	3	113	508	114	65	56	3	5	7	1	69	3	50	4	0	5	7	.417	0	0	4.46
1980	Atlanta	N	35	35	7	0	232	981	227	120	108	20	12	4	4	74	5	114	3	0	14	11	.560	1	0	4.19
1981	San Francisco	N	24	24	1	0	152	646	156	51	49	11	5	2	2	44	2	77	4	1	11	7	.611	1	0	2.90
1982	New York	A	16	11	0	3	66.2	293	81	52	45	14	4	3	0	14	2	26	1	4	1	7	.125	0	0	6.07
1983	2 Teams		25	20	5	3	145	603	157	76	71	20	1	4	1	33	1	63	4	0	7	8	.467	0	0	4.41
1984	Toronto	A	36	35	11	1	261.2	1061	238	99	91	21	5	11	3	59	1	139	2	0	17	6	.739	2	0	3.13
1985	Toronto	A	36	36	6	0	260.2	1090	268	105	100	28	6	3	6	67	0	142	9	0	17	10	.630	1	0	3.45
1986	2 Teams		34	34	5	0	228.1	966	255	114	105	27	11	4	4	37	2	139	2	0	11	10	.524	0	0	4.14
16 YEARS			467	370	82	56	2708.1	11297	2693	1228	1117	242	102	74	38	803	45	1199	65	8	160	135	.542	13	3	3.71
1976	Baltimore	A	11	6	2	4	64	265	58	27	25	3	2	4	0	24	2	17	0	1	3	4	.429	0	0	3.52
1976	New York	A	19	19	5	0	137	547	114	54	50	9	3	5	0	39	0	41	6	1	10	5	.667	3	0	3.28
1983	New York	A	8	5	0	2	28.1	121	31	21	20	6	1	1	0	7	0	17	0	0	0	2	.000	0	0	6.35
1983	Toronto	A	17	15	5	1	116.2	482	126	55	51	14	0	3	1	26	1	46	4	0	7	6	.538	0	0	3.93
1986	Toronto	A	17	17	3	0	111	470	120	56	55	18	3	3	4	20	1	65	1	0	5	4	.556	0	0	4.46
1986	Atlanta	N	17	17	2	0	117.1	496	135	58	50	9	8	1	0	17	1	74	1	0	6	6	.500	0	0	3.84

ANDY ALLANSON

Bats Right-handed, Throws Right-handed.   Turns Age 26 in 1987, Born 12/22/61

			BATTING																	BASERUNNING				PERCENTAGES		
Year	Team	League	G	AB	H	2B	3B	HR	(Hm	Rd)	TB	R	RBI	TBB	IBB	SO	HBP	SH	SF	SB	CS	SB%	GIDP	AVE	OBP	SLG
1986	Cleveland	A	101	293	66	7	3	1	(0	1)	82	30	29	14	0	36	1	11	4	10	1	.91	7	.225	.260	.280

NEIL ALLEN

Pitches Right-handed, Bats Right-handed.   Turns Age 29 in 1987, Born 01/24/58

			HOW MUCH HE PITCHED						WHAT HE GAVE UP													THE RESULTS					
Year	Team	League	G	GS	CG	GF	IP	BFP	H	R	ER	HR	SH	SF	HB	TBB	IBB	SO	WP	Bk	W	L	Pct	ShO	Sv	ERA
1979	New York	N	50	5	0	27	99	431	100	46	39	4	5	6	0	47	13	65	6	0	6	10	.375	0	8	3.55
1980	New York	N	59	0	0	47	97	407	87	43	40	7	6	4	0	40	9	79	2	1	7	10	.412	0	22	3.71
1981	New York	N	43	0	0	35	67	286	64	26	22	4	10	3	0	26	8	50	3	0	7	6	.538	0	18	2.96
1982	New York	N	50	0	0	42	64.2	279	65	22	22	5	3	1	1	30	5	59	4	0	3	7	.300	0	19	3.06
1983	2 Teams		46	22	5	12	176	762	179	84	77	12	9	2	1	84	9	106	8	1	12	13	.480	3	2	3.94
1984	St Louis	N	57	1	0	18	119	495	105	54	47	6	4	2	0	49	9	66	6	0	9	6	.600	3	3	3.55
1985	2 Teams		40	1	0	23	58.1	259	58	31	27	4	1	3	1	30	6	26	3	1	2	4	.333	0	3	4.17
1986	Chicago	A	22	17	2	1	113	466	101	50	48	8	5	7	2	38	1	57	1	0	7	2	.778	2	0	3.82
8 YEARS			367	46	7	205	794	3385	759	356	322	50	43	28	5	344	60	508	36	3	53	58	.477	5	75	3.65
1983	New York	N	21	4	1	9	54	246	57	29	27	6	4	1	0	36	5	32	2	0	2	7	.222	1	2	4.50
1983	St Louis	N	25	18	4	3	122	516	122	55	50	6	5	1	1	48	4	74	6	1	10	6	.625	2	0	3.69
1985	New York	A	17	0	0	10	29.1	124	26	9	9	1	0	0	0	13	0	16	2	0	1	0	1.000	0	1	2.76
1985	St Louis	N	23	1	0	13	29	135	32	22	18	3	1	3	1	17	6	10	1	1	1	4	.200	0	2	5.59

BILL ALMON

Bats Right-handed, Throws Right-handed.   Turns Age 35 in 1987, Born 11/21/52

			BATTING																	BASERUNNING				PERCENTAGES		
Year	Team	League	G	AB	H	2B	3B	HR	(Hm	Rd)	TB	R	RBI	TBB	IBB	SO	HBP	SH	SF	SB	CS	SB%	GIDP	AVE	OBP	SLG
1974	San Diego	N	16	38	12	1	0	0	(0	0)	13	4	3	2	0	9	0	0	0	1	0	1.00	0	.316	.350	.342
1975	San Diego	N	6	10	4	0	0	0	(0	0)	4	0	0	0	0	1	0	0	0	0	0	.00	0	.400	.400	.400
1976	San Diego	N	14	57	14	3	0	1	(0	1)	20	6	6	2	0	9	0	1	0	3	1	.75	0	.246	.271	.351
1977	San Diego	N	155	613	160	18	11	2	(1	1)	206	75	43	37	1	114	0	20	0	20	9	.69	14	.261	.303	.336
1978	San Diego	N	138	405	102	19	2	0	(0	0)	125	39	21	33	10	74	0	3	1	17	5	.77	6	.252	.308	.309
1979	San Diego	N	100	198	45	3	0	1	(0	1)	51	20	8	21	7	48	0	5	2	6	5	.55	1	.227	.299	.258
1980	2 Teams		66	150	29	4	3	0	(0	0)	39	15	7	9	1	32	0	0	1	2	1	1.00	2	.193	.238	.260
1981	Chicago	A	103	349	105	10	2	4	(1	3)	131	46	41	21	0	60	2	2	3	16	6	.73	4	.301	.341	.375
1982	Chicago	A	111	308	79	10	4	4	(2	2)	109	40	26	25	0	69	1	1	1	10	8	.56	4	.256	.313	.354
1983	Oakland	A	143	451	120	29	1	4	(3	1)	163	45	63	26	3	67	2	5	11	26	8	.76	5	.266	.302	.361
1984	Oakland	A	106	211	47	11	0	7	(5	2)	79	24	16	10	0	42	0	0	4	5	7	.42	3	.223	.253	.374
1985	Pittsburgh	N	88	244	66	17	0	6	(3	3)	101	33	29	22	0	61	1	4	3	10	7	.59	6	.270	.330	.414
1986	Pittsburgh	N	102	196	43	7	2	7	(4	3)	75	29	27	30	2	38	0	1	3	11	4	.73	4	.219	.319	.383
13 YEARS			1148	3230	826	132	25	36	(19	17)	1116	376	290	238	24	604	6	42	29	127	60	.68	53	.256	.305	.346
1980	Montreal	N	18	38	10	1	1	0	(0	0)	13	2	3	1	0	5	0	0	1	0	0	.00	2	.263	.275	.342
1980	New York	N	48	112	19	3	2	0	(0	0)	26	13	4	8	1	27	0	0	0	2	0	1.00	0	.170	.225	.232

LARRY ANDERSEN

Pitches Right-handed, Bats Right-handed

Turns Age 34 in 1987, Born 05/06/53

			HOW MUCH HE PITCHED						WHAT HE GAVE UP												THE RESULTS					
Year	Team	League	G	GS	CG	GF	IP	BFP	H	R	ER	HR	SH	SF	HB	TBB	IBB	SO	WP	Bk	W	L	Pct	ShO	Sv	ERA
1975	Cleveland	A	3	0	0	1	6	23	4	3	3	0	0	1	0	2	0	4	2	0	0	0	.000	0	0	4.50
1977	Cleveland	A	11	0	0	7	14	62	10	7	5	1	3	0	0	9	3	8	1	0	0	0	.000	0	0	3.21
1979	Cleveland	A	8	0	0	4	17	77	25	14	14	3	1	2	0	4	0	7	0	0	0	0	.000	0	0	7.41
1981	Seattle	A	41	0	0	23	68	273	57	27	20	4	0	3	3	18	2	40	0	0	3	3	.500	0	5	2.65
1982	Seattle	A	40	1	0	14	79.2	354	100	56	53	16	2	3	4	23	1	32	2	0	0	0	.000	0	0	5.99
1983	Philadelphia	N	17	0	0	4	26.1	106	19	7	7	0	1	1	0	9	1	14	1	1	1	0	1.000	0	0	2.39
1984	Philadelphia	N	64	0	0	25	90.2	376	85	32	24	5	4	4	0	25	6	54	2	1	3	7	.300	0	4	2.38
1985	Philadelphia	N	57	0	0	19	73	318	78	41	35	5	3	1	3	26	4	50	1	1	3	3	.500	0	3	4.32
1986	2 Teams		48	0	0	8	77.1	323	83	30	26	2	10	5	1	26	10	42	1	0	2	1	.667	0	1	3.03
9 YEARS			289	1	0	105	452	1912	461	217	187	36	24	20	11	142	27	251	10	3	12	15	.444	0	14	3.72
1986	Houston	N	38	0	0	7	64.2	268	64	22	20	2	8	4	1	23	10	33	1	0	2	1	.667	0	1	2.78
1986	Philadelphia	N	10	0	0	1	12.2	55	19	8	6	0	2	1	0	3	0	9	0	0	0	0	.000	0	0	4.26

ALLAN ANDERSON

Pitches Left-handed, Bats Left-handed

Turns Age 23 in 1987, Born 01/07/64

			HOW MUCH HE PITCHED						WHAT HE GAVE UP												THE RESULTS					
Year	Team	League	G	GS	CG	GF	IP	BFP	H	R	ER	HR	SH	SF	HB	TBB	IBB	SO	WP	Bk	W	L	Pct	ShO	Sv	ERA
1986	Minnesota	A	21	10	1	3	84.1	371	106	54	52	11	2	3	1	30	3	51	2	2	3	6	.333	0	0	5.55

DAVE ANDERSON

Bats Right-handed, Throws Right-handed

Turns Age 27 in 1987, Born 08/01/60

			BATTING																	BASERUNNING				PERCENTAGES		
Year	Team	League	G	AB	H	2B	3B	HR	(Hm	Rd)	TB	R	RBI	TBB	IBB	SO	HBP	SH	SF	SB	CS	SB%	GIDP	AVE	OBP	SLG
1983	Los Angeles	N	61	115	19	4	2	1	(1	0)	30	12	2	12	1	15	0	4	0	6	3	.67	1	.165	.244	.261
1984	Los Angeles	N	121	374	94	16	2	3	(2	1)	123	51	34	45	4	55	2	7	5	15	5	.75	8	.251	.331	.329
1985	Los Angeles	N	77	221	44	6	0	4	(1	3)	62	24	18	35	3	42	1	4	1	5	4	.56	4	.199	.310	.281
1986	Los Angeles	N	92	216	53	9	0	1	(0	1)	65	31	15	22	1	39	0	2	1	5	1	.83	11	.245	.314	.301
4 YEARS			351	926	210	35	4	9	(4	5)	280	118	69	114	3	151	3	17	7	31	13	.70	24	.227	.311	.302

RICK ANDERSON

Pitches Right-handed, Bats Right-handed

			HOW MUCH HE PITCHED						WHAT HE GAVE UP												THE RESULTS					
Year	Team	League	G	GS	CG	GF	IP	BFP	H	R	ER	HR	SH	SF	HB	TBB	IBB	SO	WP	Bk	W	L	Pct	ShO	Sv	ERA
1986	New York	N	15	5	0	4	49.2	201	45	17	15	3	2	4	0	11	3	21	1	1	2	1	.667	0	1	2.72

JOAQUIN ANDUJAR

Pitches Right-handed, Bats both Right and Left-handed

Turns Age 35 in 1987, Born 12/21/52

			HOW MUCH HE PITCHED						WHAT HE GAVE UP												THE RESULTS					
Year	Team	League	G	GS	CG	GF	IP	BFP	H	R	ER	HR	SH	SF	HB	TBB	IBB	SO	WP	Bk	W	L	Pct	ShO	Sv	ERA
1976	Houston	N	28	25	9	1	172	729	163	74	69	8	9	4	1	75	2	59	1	5	9	9	.474	4	0	3.61
1977	Houston	N	26	25	4	1	159	678	149	80	65	11	10	6	4	64	3	69	2	2	11	8	.579	1	0	3.68
1978	Houston	N	35	13	2	11	111	470	88	45	42	3	11	5	4	58	6	55	3	5	5	7	.417	0	1	3.41
1979	Houston	N	46	23	8	9	194	825	168	86	74	7	9	6	2	88	6	77	5	0	12	12	.500	0	4	3.43
1980	Houston	N	35	14	0	5	122	529	132	59	53	8	7	3	0	43	2	75	2	0	3	8	.273	0	3	3.91
1981	2 Teams		20	11	1	0	79	336	85	41	36	6	2	2	0	23	1	37	2	1	8	4	.667	0	0	4.10
1982	St Louis	N	38	37	9	1	265.2	1056	237	85	73	11	8	4	7	50	7	137	3	2	15	10	.600	5	0	2.47
1983	St Louis	N	39	34	5	3	225	943	215	112	104	23	12	3	3	75	7	125	5	6	6	16	.273	2	1	4.16
1984	St Louis	N	36	36	12	0	261.1	1052	218	104	97	20	12	6	7	70	13	147	6	4	20	14	.588	4	0	3.34
1985	St Louis	N	38	38	10	0	269.2	1127	265	113	102	15	11	4	11	82	12	112	2	0	21	12	.636	2	0	3.40
1986	Oakland	A	28	26	7	2	155.1	647	139	70	66	23	1	4	4	56	1	72	2	4	12	7	.632	1	1	3.82
11 YEARS			369	282	67	33	2014	8392	1859	869	781	135	92	50	43	684	60	965	33	29	122	108	.530	19	9	3.49
1981	Houston	N	9	3	0	0	24	113	29	17	13	2	1	2	0	12	0	18	0	0	2	3	.400	0	0	4.87
1981	St Louis	N	11	8	1	0	55	223	56	24	23	4	1	0	0	11	1	19	2	1	6	1	.857	0	0	3.76

TONY ARMAS

Bats Right-handed, Throws Right-handed   Turns Age 34 in 1987, Born 07/02/53

								BATTING													BASERUNNING				PERCENTAGES		
Year	Team	League	G	AB	H	2B	3B	HR	(Hm	Rd)	TB	R	RBI	TBB	IBB	SO	HBP	SH	SF	SB	CS	SB%	GIDP	AVE	OBP	SLG
1976	Pittsburgh	N	4	6	2	0	0	0	(0	0)	2	0	1	0	0	2	0	0	0	0	0	.00	0	.333	.333	.333
1977	Oakland	A	118	363	87	8	2	13	(7	6)	138	26	53	20	2	99	0	1	8	1	2	.33	8	.240	.274	.380
1978	Oakland	A	91	239	51	6	1	2	(0	2)	65	17	13	10	2	62	2	6	1	1	2	.33	5	.213	.250	.272
1979	Oakland	A	80	278	69	9	3	11	(4	7)	117	29	34	16	2	67	1	0	2	1	0	1.00	6	.248	.290	.421
1980	Oakland	A	158	628	175	18	8	35	(17	18)	314	87	109	29	4	128	2	2	5	5	3	.63	22	.279	.310	.500
1981	Oakland	A	109	440	115	24	3	22	(13	9)	211	51	76	19	6	115	2	0	1	5	1	.83	6	.261	.294	.480
1982	Oakland	A	138	536	125	19	2	28	(14	14)	232	58	89	33	5	128	1	0	8	2	2	.50	14	.233	.275	.433
1983	Boston	A	145	574	125	23	2	36	(17	19)	260	77	107	29	0	131	2	0	8	0	1	.00	31	.218	.254	.453
1984	Boston	A	157	639	171	29	5	43	(21	22)	339	107	123	32	9	156	1	0	7	1	3	.25	13	.268	.300	.531
1985	Boston	A	103	385	102	17	5	23	(10	13)	198	50	64	18	4	90	2	0	5	0	0	.00	14	.265	.298	.514
1986	Boston	A	121	425	112	21	4	11	(5	6)	174	40	58	24	1	77	2	0	2	0	3	.00	12	.264	.305	.409
11 YEARS			1224	4513	1134	174	35	224	(108	116)	2050	542	727	230	35	1055	15	9	47	16	17	.48	131	.251	.287	.454

ALAN ASHBY

Bats both Right and Left-handed, Throws Right-handed   Turns Age 36 in 1987, Born 07/08/51

								BATTING													BASERUNNING				PERCENTAGES		
Year	Team	League	G	AB	H	2B	3B	HR	(Hm	Rd)	TB	R	RBI	TBB	IBB	SO	HBP	SH	SF	SB	CS	SB%	GIDP	AVE	OBP	SLG
1973	Cleveland	A	11	29	5	1	0	1	(0	1)	9	4	3	2	0	11	0	0	0	0	0	.00	0	.172	.226	.310
1974	Cleveland	A	10	7	1	0	0	0	(0	0)	1	1	0	1	0	2	0	0	0	0	0	.00	0	.143	.250	.143
1975	Cleveland	A	90	254	57	10	1	5	(1	4)	84	32	32	30	1	42	1	16	0	3	2	.60	10	.224	.309	.331
1976	Cleveland	A	89	247	59	5	1	4	(1	3)	78	26	32	27	4	49	0	6	3	0	2	.00	6	.239	.310	.316
1977	Toronto	A	124	396	83	16	3	2	(1	1)	111	25	29	50	3	51	2	10	1	0	2	.00	14	.210	.301	.280
1978	Toronto	A	81	264	69	15	0	9	(6	3)	111	27	29	28	4	32	1	4	1	1	1	.50	10	.261	.333	.420
1979	Houston	N	108	336	68	15	2	2	(1	1)	93	25	35	26	10	70	2	3	3	0	0	.00	6	.202	.262	.277
1980	Houston	N	116	352	90	19	2	3	(1	2)	122	30	48	35	12	40	0	2	5	0	0	.00	11	.256	.319	.347
1981	Houston	N	83	255	69	13	0	4	(3	1)	94	20	33	35	6	33	0	3	2	0	2	.00	9	.271	.356	.369
1982	Houston	N	100	339	87	14	2	12	(5	7)	141	40	49	27	4	53	1	2	3	2	0	1.00	7	.257	.311	.416
1983	Houston	N	87	275	63	18	1	8	(2	6)	107	31	34	31	4	38	0	1	4	0	0	.00	12	.229	.303	.389
1984	Houston	N	66	191	50	7	0	4	(0	4)	69	16	27	20	2	22	1	4	3	0	0	.00	9	.262	.330	.361
1985	Houston	N	65	189	53	8	0	8	(3	5)	85	20	25	24	2	27	1	1	1	0	0	.00	9	.280	.363	.450
1986	Houston	N	120	315	81	15	0	7	(1	6)	117	24	38	39	9	56	0	1	6	1	0	1.00	7	.257	.333	.371
14 YEARS			1150	3449	835	156	12	69	(25	44)	1222	321	414	375	61	526	9	53	32	7	9	.44	104	.242	.315	.354

PAUL ASSENMACHER

Pitches Left-handed, Bats Left-handed   Turns Age 27 in 1987, Born 12/10/60

			HOW MUCH HE PITCHED						WHAT HE GAVE UP											THE RESULTS					
Year	Team	League	G	GS	CG	GF	IP	BFP	H	R	ER	HR	SH	SF	HB	TBB	IBB	SO	WP	Bk	W	L	Pct	ShO	Sv	ERA
1986	Atlanta	N	61	0	0	27	68.1	287	61	23	19	5	7	1	0	26	4	56	2	3	7	3	.700	0	7	2.50

KEITH ATHERTON

Pitches Right-handed, Bats Right-handed   Turns Age 28 in 1987, Born 02/19/59

			HOW MUCH HE PITCHED						WHAT HE GAVE UP											THE RESULTS					
Year	Team	League	G	GS	CG	GF	IP	BFP	H	R	ER	HR	SH	SF	HB	TBB	IBB	SO	WP	Bk	W	L	Pct	ShO	Sv	ERA
1983	Oakland	A	29	0	0	21	68.1	277	53	22	21	7	2	5	1	23	4	40	1	1	2	5	.286	0	4	2.77
1984	Oakland	A	57	0	0	24	104	453	110	51	50	13	4	6	2	39	8	58	3	0	7	6	.538	0	2	4.33
1985	Oakland	A	56	0	0	21	104.2	435	89	51	50	17	3	4	0	42	8	77	2	0	4	7	.364	0	3	4.30
1986	2 Teams		60	0	0	36	97	431	100	47	44	11	6	6	1	46	4	67	2	0	6	10	.375	0	10	4.08
4 YEARS			202	0	0	102	374	1596	352	171	165	48	15	21	4	150	24	242	8	1	19	28	.404	0	19	3.97
1986	Minnesota	A	47	0	0	31	81.2	356	82	37	34	9	5	4	1	35	3	59	2	0	5	8	.385	0	10	3.75
1986	Oakland	A	13	0	0	5	15.1	75	18	10	10	2	1	2	0	11	1	8	0	0	1	2	.333	0	0	5.87

WALLY BACKMAN

Bats both Right and Left-handed, Throws Right-handed   Turns Age 28 in 1987, Born 09/22/59

								BATTING													BASERUNNING				PERCENTAGES		
Year	Team	League	G	AB	H	2B	3B	HR	(Hm	Rd)	TB	R	RBI	TBB	IBB	SO	HBP	SH	SF	SB	CS	SB%	GIDP	AVE	OBP	SLG
1980	New York	N	27	93	30	1	1	0	(0	0)	33	12	9	11	1	14	1	4	1	2	3	.40	3	.323	.396	.355
1981	New York	N	26	36	10	2	0	0	(0	0)	12	5	0	4	0	7	0	2	0	1	0	1.00	0	.278	.350	.333
1982	New York	N	96	261	71	13	2	3	(1	2)	97	37	22	49	1	47	0	2	0	8	7	.53	6	.272	.387	.372
1983	New York	N	26	42	7	0	1	0	(0	0)	9	6	3	2	0	8	0	1	0	0	0	.00	0	.167	.205	.214
1984	New York	N	128	436	122	19	2	1	(0	1)	148	68	26	56	2	63	0	5	2	32	9	.78	13	.280	.360	.339
1985	New York	N	145	520	142	24	5	1	(0	1)	179	77	38	36	1	72	1	14	3	30	12	.71	3	.273	.320	.344
1986	New York	N	124	387	124	18	2	1	(1	0)	149	67	27	36	1	32	0	14	3	13	7	.65	3	.320	.376	.385
7 YEARS			572	1775	506	77	13	6	(2	4)	627	272	125	194	6	243	2	42	9	86	38	.69	30	.285	.355	.353

13

SCOTT BAILES

Pitches Left-handed, Bats Left-handed   Turns Age 26 in 1987, Born 12/18/61

Year Team League		HOW MUCH HE PITCHED						WHAT HE GAVE UP												THE RESULTS					
		G	GS	CG	GF	IP	BFP	H	R	ER	HR	SH	SF	HB	TBB	IBB	SO	WP	Bk	W	L	Pct	ShO	Sv	ERA
1986 Cleveland	A	62	10	0	22	112.2	500	123	70	62	12	7	4	1	43	5	60	4	2	10	10	.500	0	7	4.95

MARK BAILEY

Bats both Right and Left-handed, Throws Right-handed   Turns Age 26 in 1987, Born 11/04/61

Year Team League		BATTING																	BASERUNNING				PERCENTAGES		
		G	AB	H	2B	3B	HR	(Hm	Rd)	TB	R	RBI	TBB	IBB	SO	HBP	SH	SF	SB	CS	SB%	GIDP	AVE	OBP	SLG
1984 Houston	N	108	344	73	16	1	9	(7	2)	118	38	34	53	4	71	2	1	3	0	1	.00	7	.212	.318	.343
1985 Houston	N	114	332	88	14	0	10	(4	6)	132	47	45	67	13	70	1	1	1	0	2	.00	16	.265	.389	.398
1986 Houston	N	57	153	27	5	0	4	(1	3)	44	9	15	28	6	45	0	0	1	1	1	.50	7	.176	.302	.288
3 YEARS		279	829	188	35	1	23	(12	11)	294	94	94	148	23	186	3	2	5	1	4	.20	30	.227	.344	.355

HAROLD BAINES

Bats Left-handed, Throws Left-handed   Turns Age 28 in 1987, Born 03/15/59

Year Team League		BATTING																	BASERUNNING				PERCENTAGES		
		G	AB	H	2B	3B	HR	(Hm	Rd)	TB	R	RBI	TBB	IBB	SO	HBP	SH	SF	SB	CS	SB%	GIDP	AVE	OBP	SLG
1980 Chicago	A	141	491	125	23	6	13	(3	10)	199	55	49	19	7	65	1	2	5	2	4	.33	15	.255	.281	.405
1981 Chicago	A	82	280	80	11	7	10	(3	7)	135	42	41	12	4	41	2	0	2	6	2	.75	6	.286	.318	.482
1982 Chicago	A	161	608	165	29	8	25	(11	14)	285	89	105	49	10	95	0	2	9	10	3	.77	12	.271	.321	.469
1983 Chicago	A	156	596	167	33	2	20	(12	8)	264	76	99	49	13	85	1	3	6	7	5	.58	15	.280	.333	.443
1984 Chicago	A	147	569	173	28	10	29	(16	13)	308	72	94	54	9	75	0	1	5	1	2	.33	12	.304	.361	.541
1985 Chicago	A	160	640	198	29	3	22	(13	9)	299	86	113	42	8	89	1	0	10	1	1	.50	23	.309	.348	.467
1986 Chicago	A	145	570	169	29	2	21	(8	13)	265	72	88	38	9	89	2	0	8	2	1	.67	14	.296	.338	.465
7 YEARS		992	3754	1077	182	38	140	(66	74)	1755	492	589	263	60	539	7	8	45	29	18	.62	97	.287	.331	.468

DOUG BAIR

Pitches Right-handed, Bats Right-handed   Turns Age 38 in 1987, Born 08/22/49

Year Team League		HOW MUCH HE PITCHED						WHAT HE GAVE UP												THE RESULTS					
		G	GS	CG	GF	IP	BFP	H	R	ER	HR	SH	SF	HB	TBB	IBB	SO	WP	Bk	W	L	Pct	ShO	Sv	ERA
1976 Pittsburgh	N	4	0	0	1	6	28	4	4	4	0	0	0	0	5	1	4	0	0	0	0	.000	0	0	6.00
1977 Oakland	A	45	0	0	28	83	377	78	39	32	11	6	6	0	57	9	68	6	0	4	6	.400	0	8	3.47
1978 Cincinnati	N	70	0	0	56	100	416	87	23	22	6	6	3	0	38	3	91	1	0	7	6	.538	0	28	1.98
1979 Cincinnati	N	65	0	0	42	94	430	93	47	45	7	10	3	3	51	12	86	3	0	11	7	.611	0	16	4.31
1980 Cincinnati	N	61	0	0	38	85	377	91	40	40	7	4	4	1	39	10	62	5	0	3	6	.333	0	6	4.24
1981 2 Teams		35	0	0	20	55	234	55	34	31	5	2	0	0	19	4	30	3	0	4	2	.667	0	1	5.07
1982 St Louis	N	63	0	0	33	91.2	372	69	27	26	7	4	4	1	36	13	68	2	0	5	3	.625	0	8	2.55
1983 2 Teams		53	1	0	19	85.1	355	75	38	34	12	3	1	1	32	7	60	1	0	8	4	.667	0	5	3.59
1984 Detroit	A	47	1	0	12	93.2	387	82	42	39	10	3	4	0	36	2	57	3	0	5	3	.625	0	4	3.75
1985 2 Teams		23	3	0	5	51	232	55	38	34	3	2	4	1	27	5	30	6	1	2	2	1.000	0	6	6.00
1986 Oakland	A	31	0	0	17	45	189	37	15	15	5	3	3	0	18	0	40	2	0	2	3	.400	0	4	3.00
11 YEARS		497	5	0	271	789.2	3397	726	349	322	73	43	32	7	358	66	596	32	1	51	40	.560	0	80	3.67
1981 Cincinnati	N	24	0	0	12	39	174	42	28	25	5	2	0	0	17	4	16	3	0	2	2	.500	0	0	5.77
1981 St Louis	N	11	0	0	8	16	60	13	6	6	0	0	0	0	2	0	14	0	0	2	0	1.000	0	1	3.37
1983 Detroit	A	27	1	0	10	55.2	233	51	27	24	8	2	0	1	19	4	39	0	0	7	3	.700	0	4	3.88
1983 St Louis	N	26	0	0	9	29.2	122	24	11	10	4	1	1	0	13	3	21	1	0	1	1	.500	0	1	3.03
1985 Detroit	A	21	3	0	4	49	224	54	38	34	3	2	4	1	25	5	30	6	1	2	0	1.000	0	6	6.24
1985 St Louis	N	2	0	0	1	2	8	1	0	0	0	0	0	0	2	0	0	0	0	0	0	.000	0	0	0.00

DUSTY BAKER

Bats Right-handed, Throws Right-handed   Turns Age 38 in 1987, Born 06/15/49

Year Team League		BATTING																	BASERUNNING				PERCENTAGES		
		G	AB	H	2B	3B	HR	(Hm	Rd)	TB	R	RBI	TBB	IBB	SO	HBP	SH	SF	SB	CS	SB%	GIDP	AVE	OBP	SLG
1968 Atlanta	N	6	5	2	0	0	0	(0	0)	2	0	0	0	0	1	0	0	0	0	0	.00	0	.400	.400	.400
1969 Atlanta	N	3	7	0	0	0	0	(0	0)	0	0	0	0	0	3	0	0	0	0	0	.00	0	.000	.000	.000
1970 Atlanta	N	13	24	7	0	0	0	(0	0)	7	3	4	2	0	4	0	0	1	0	0	.00	0	.292	.333	.292
1971 Atlanta	N	29	62	14	2	0	0	(0	0)	16	2	4	1	1	14	0	1	0	0	1	.00	1	.226	.238	.258
1972 Atlanta	N	127	446	143	27	2	17	(10	7)	225	62	76	45	2	68	4	2	6	4	7	.36	9	.321	.383	.504
1973 Atlanta	N	159	604	174	29	4	21	(10	11)	274	101	99	67	8	72	5	1	9	24	3	.89	14	.288	.359	.454
1974 Atlanta	N	149	574	147	35	0	20	(11	9)	242	80	69	71	9	87	1	3	7	18	7	.72	12	.256	.335	.422
1975 Atlanta	N	142	494	129	18	2	19	(9	10)	208	63	72	67	7	57	0	1	5	12	7	.63	10	.261	.346	.421
1976 Los Angeles	N	112	384	93	13	0	4	(3	1)	118	36	39	31	3	54	1	1	4	2	4	.33	15	.242	.298	.307
1977 Los Angeles	N	153	533	155	26	1	30	(18	12)	273	86	86	58	6	89	6	2	5	2	6	.25	9	.291	.364	.512
1978 Los Angeles	N	149	522	137	24	1	11	(5	6)	196	62	66	47	2	66	3	4	3	12	3	.80	10	.262	.325	.375
1979 Los Angeles	N	151	554	152	29	1	23	(14	9)	252	86	88	56	0	70	1	2	3	11	4	.73	16	.274	.340	.455
1980 Los Angeles	N	153	579	170	26	4	29	(14	15)	291	80	97	43	4	66	3	1	12	12	10	.55	11	.294	.339	.503
1981 Los Angeles	N	103	400	128	17	3	9	(4	5)	178	48	49	29	1	43	1	1	5	10	7	.59	9	.320	.363	.445
1982 Los Angeles	N	147	570	171	19	2	23	(7	16)	261	80	88	56	5	62	3	2	5	17	10	.63	7	.300	.361	.458
1983 Los Angeles	N	149	531	138	25	1	15	(8	7)	210	71	73	72	2	59	2	4	7	7	1	.88	9	.260	.346	.395
1984 San Francisco	N	100	243	71	7	2	3	(2	1)	91	31	32	40	1	27	0	0	4	4	1	.80	5	.292	.387	.374
1985 Oakland	A	111	343	92	15	1	14	(5	9)	151	48	52	50	0	47	0	0	3	2	1	.67	12	.268	.359	.440
1986 Oakland	A	83	242	58	8	0	4	(1	3)	78	25	19	27	1	37	0	0	2	0	1	.00	8	.240	.314	.322
19 YEARS		2039	7117	1981	320	23	242	(121	121)	3073	964	1013	762	52	926	30	27	85	137	73	.65	158	.278	.347	.432

STEVE BALBONI

Bats Right-handed, Throws Right-handed — Turns Age 30 in 1987, Born 01/16/57

Year	Team	League	G	AB	H	2B	3B	HR	(Hm	Rd)	TB	R	RBI	TBB	IBB	SO	HBP	SH	SF	SB	CS	SB%	GIDP	AVE	OBP	SLG
1981	New York	A	4	7	2	1	1	0	(0	0)	5	2	2	1	0	4	0	0	0	0	0	.00	0	.286	.375	.714
1982	New York	A	33	107	20	2	1	2	(0	2)	30	8	4	6	0	34	0	0	1	0	0	.00	1	.187	.228	.280
1983	New York	A	32	86	20	2	0	5	(0	5)	37	8	17	8	0	23	0	0	1	0	0	.00	2	.233	.295	.430
1984	Kansas City	A	126	438	107	23	2	28	(10	18)	218	58	77	45	5	139	4	0	1	0	0	.00	9	.244	.320	.498
1985	Kansas City	A	160	600	146	28	2	36	(17	19)	286	74	88	52	4	166	5	0	5	1	1	.50	14	.243	.307	.477
1986	Kansas City	A	138	512	117	25	1	29	(10	19)	231	54	88	43	2	146	1	0	6	0	0	.00	8	.229	.286	.451
6 YEARS			493	1750	412	81	7	100	(37	63)	807	204	276	155	11	512	10	0	14	1	1	.50	34	.235	.299	.461

JAY BALLER

Pitches Right-handed, Bats Right-handed — Turns Age 27 in 1987, Born 10/06/60

Year	Team	League	G	GS	CG	GF	IP	BFP	H	R	ER	HR	SH	SF	HB	TBB	IBB	SO	WP	Bk	W	L	Pct	ShO	Sv	ERA
1982	Philadelphia	N	4	1	0	1	8	35	7	4	3	1	1	0	1	2	0	7	0	1	0	0	.000	0	0	3.37
1985	Chicago	N	20	4	0	4	52	223	52	21	20	8	4	1	1	17	7	31	2	0	2	3	.400	1	1	3.46
1986	Chicago	N	36	0	0	16	53.2	248	58	37	32	7	4	3	2	28	4	42	2	4	2	4	.333	0	5	5.37
3 YEARS			60	5	0	21	113.2	506	117	62	55	16	9	4	4	47	11	80	4	5	4	7	.364	0	6	4.35

CHRIS BANDO

Bats both Right and Left-handed, Throws Right-handed — Turns Age 31 in 1987, Born 02/04/56

Year	Team	League	G	AB	H	2B	3B	HR	(Hm	Rd)	TB	R	RBI	TBB	IBB	SO	HBP	SH	SF	SB	CS	SB%	GIDP	AVE	OBP	SLG
1981	Cleveland	A	21	47	10	3	0	0	(0	0)	13	3	6	2	0	2	0	1	1	0	0	.00	1	.213	.240	.277
1982	Cleveland	A	66	184	39	6	1	3	(1	2)	56	13	16	24	1	30	0	1	3	0	0	.00	6	.212	.299	.304
1983	Cleveland	A	48	121	31	3	0	4	(4	0)	46	15	15	15	0	19	0	1	1	0	1	.00	6	.256	.336	.380
1984	Cleveland	A	75	220	64	11	0	12	(5	7)	111	38	41	33	5	35	0	3	4	1	2	.33	8	.291	.377	.505
1985	Cleveland	A	73	173	24	4	1	0	(0	0)	30	11	13	22	0	21	0	2	2	0	1	.00	5	.139	.234	.173
1986	Cleveland	A	92	254	68	9	0	2	(1	1)	83	28	26	22	0	49	1	10	3	0	1	.00	8	.268	.325	.327
6 YEARS			375	999	236	36	2	21	(11	10)	339	108	117	118	6	156	1	18	14	1	5	.17	34	.236	.314	.339

SCOTT BANKHEAD

Pitches Right-handed, Bats Right-handed — Turns Age 24 in 1987, Born 07/31/63

Year	Team	League	G	GS	CG	GF	IP	BFP	H	R	ER	HR	SH	SF	HB	TBB	IBB	SO	WP	Bk	W	L	Pct	ShO	Sv	ERA
1986	Kansas City	A	24	17	0	2	121	517	121	66	62	14	5	5	3	37	7	94	1	0	8	9	.471	0	0	4.61

FLOYD BANNISTER

Pitches Left-handed, Bats Left-handed — Turns Age 32 in 1987, Born 06/10/55

Year	Team	League	G	GS	CG	GF	IP	BFP	H	R	ER	HR	SH	SF	HB	TBB	IBB	SO	WP	Bk	W	L	Pct	ShO	Sv	ERA
1977	Houston	N	24	23	4	0	143	622	138	70	64	11	2	4	4	68	1	112	6	2	8	9	.471	1	0	4.03
1978	Houston	N	28	16	2	3	110	502	120	59	59	13	7	3	1	63	4	94	7	2	3	9	.250	2	0	4.83
1979	Seattle	A	30	30	6	0	182	792	185	92	82	25	5	3	4	68	4	115	1	0	10	15	.400	2	0	4.05
1980	Seattle	A	32	32	8	0	218	918	200	96	84	24	8	5	4	66	6	155	7	0	9	13	.409	0	0	3.47
1981	Seattle	A	21	20	5	0	121	522	128	62	60	14	2	0	3	39	0	85	7	1	9	9	.500	2	0	4.46
1982	Seattle	A	35	35	5	0	247	1022	225	112	94	32	10	5	3	77	0	209	6	0	12	13	.480	3	0	3.43
1983	Chicago	A	34	34	5	0	217.1	902	191	88	81	19	4	4	7	71	3	193	8	1	16	10	.615	2	0	3.35
1984	Chicago	A	34	33	4	0	218	936	211	127	117	30	3	10	6	80	2	152	10	0	14	11	.560	0	0	4.83
1985	Chicago	A	34	34	4	0	210.2	928	211	121	114	30	9	8	4	100	5	198	11	0	10	14	.417	1	0	4.87
1986	Chicago	A	28	27	6	0	165.1	688	162	81	65	17	7	5	2	48	0	92	5	0	10	14	.417	1	0	3.54
10 YEARS			300	284	49	3	1832.1	7832	1771	908	820	215	57	47	31	680	25	1405	68	6	101	117	.463	14	0	4.03

JESSE BARFIELD

Bats Right-handed, Throws Right-handed — Turns Age 28 in 1987, Born 10/29/59

Year	Team	League	G	AB	H	2B	3B	HR	(Hm	Rd)	TB	R	RBI	TBB	IBB	SO	HBP	SH	SF	SB	CS	SB%	GIDP	AVE	OBP	SLG
1981	Toronto	A	25	95	22	3	2	2	(1	1)	35	7	9	4	0	19	1	0	0	4	3	.57	4	.232	.270	.368
1982	Toronto	A	139	394	97	13	2	18	(11	7)	168	54	58	42	3	79	3	6	1	1	4	.20	7	.246	.323	.426
1983	Toronto	A	128	388	98	13	3	27	(22	5)	198	58	68	22	0	110	4	1	5	2	5	.29	5	.253	.296	.510
1984	Toronto	A	110	320	91	14	1	14	(10	4)	149	51	49	35	5	81	2	1	2	8	2	.80	5	.284	.357	.466
1985	Toronto	A	155	539	156	34	9	27	(15	12)	289	94	84	66	5	143	4	0	3	22	8	.73	14	.289	.369	.536
1986	Toronto	A	158	589	170	35	2	40	(16	24)	329	107	108	69	5	146	8	0	5	8	8	.50	9	.289	.368	.559
6 YEARS			715	2325	634	112	19	128	(75	53)	1168	371	376	238	18	578	22	8	16	45	30	.60	47	.273	.344	.502

MARTY BARRETT

Bats Right-handed, Throws Right-handed
Turns Age 29 in 1987, Born 06/23/58

Year	Team	League	G	AB	H	2B	3B	HR	(Hm	Rd)	TB	R	RBI	TBB	IBB	SO	HBP	SH	SF	SB	CS	SB%	GIDP	AVE	OBP	SLG
1982	Boston	A	8	18	1	0	0	0	(0	0)	1	0	0	0	0	1	0	0	0	0	0	.00	1	.056	.056	.056
1983	Boston	A	33	44	10	1	1	0	(0	0)	13	7	2	3	0	1	0	0	0	0	0	.00		.227	.271	.295
1984	Boston	A	139	475	144	23	3	3	(1	2)	182	56	45	42	2	25	1	4	4	5	3	.63	9	.303	.358	.383
1985	Boston	A	156	534	142	26	0	5	(3	2)	183	59	56	56	3	50	2	12	4	7	5	.58	14	.266	.336	.343
1986	Boston	A	158	625	179	39	4	4	(4	0)	238	94	60	65	0	31	1	18	4	15	7	.68	13	.286	.353	.381
5 YEARS			494	1696	476	89	8	12	(8	4)	617	216	163	166	5	108	4	34	13	27	15	.64	38	.281	.344	.364

KEVIN BASS

Bats both Right and Left-handed, Throws Right-handed
Turns Age 28 in 1987, Born 05/12/59

Year	Team	League	G	AB	H	2B	3B	HR	(Hm	Rd)	TB	R	RBI	TBB	IBB	SO	HBP	SH	SF	SB	CS	SB%	GIDP	AVE	OBP	SLG
1982	2 Teams		30	33	1	0	0	0	(0	0)	1	6	1	1	0	9	0	1	0	0	0	.00	1	.030	.059	.030
1983	Houston	N	88	195	46	7	3	2	(2	0)	65	25	18	6	1	27	0	4	1	2	2	.50	2	.236	.257	.333
1984	Houston	N	121	331	86	17	5	2	(1	1)	119	33	29	6	1	57	3	2	0	5	5	.50	2	.260	.279	.360
1985	Houston	N	150	539	145	27	5	16	(9	7)	230	72	68	31	6	63	1	4	2	19	8	.70	10	.269	.309	.427
1986	Houston	N	157	591	184	33	5	20	(5	15)	287	83	79	38	11	72	6	1	4	22	13	.63	15	.311	.357	.486
5 YEARS			546	1689	462	84	18	40	(17	23)	702	219	195	82	19	228	10	12	7	48	28	.63	30	.274	.310	.416
1982	Milwaukee	A	18	9	0	0	0	0	(0	0)	0	4	0	1	0	1	0	1	0	0	0	.00	0	.000	.100	.000
1982	Houston	N	12	24	1	0	0	0	(0	0)	1	2	1	0	0	8	0	0	0	0	0	.00	1	.042	.042	.042

BILL BATHE

Bats Right-handed, Throws Right-handed
Turns Age 27 in 1987, Born 10/14/60

Year	Team	League	G	AB	H	2B	3B	HR	(Hm	Rd)	TB	R	RBI	TBB	IBB	SO	HBP	SH	SF	SB	CS	SB%	GIDP	AVE	OBP	SLG
1986	Oakland	A	39	103	19	3	0	5	(4	1)	37	9	11	2	0	20	1	6	0	0	0	.00	2	.184	.208	.359

DON BAYLOR

Bats Right-handed, Throws Right-handed
Turns Age 38 in 1987, Born 06/28/49

Year	Team	League	G	AB	H	2B	3B	HR	(Hm	Rd)	TB	R	RBI	TBB	IBB	SO	HBP	SH	SF	SB	CS	SB%	GIDP	AVE	OBP	SLG
1970	Baltimore	A	8	17	4	0	0	0	(0	0)	4	4	4	2	0	3	0	0	1	1	1	.50	0	.235	.300	.235
1971	Baltimore	A	1	2	0	0	0	0	(0	0)	0	0	1	0	1	1	0	0	0	0	0	.00	0	.000	.600	.000
1972	Baltimore	A	102	320	81	13	3	11	(3	8)	133	33	38	29	0	50	9	2	3	24	2	.92	9	.253	.330	.416
1973	Baltimore	A	118	405	116	20	4	11	(4	7)	177	64	51	35	3	48	13	0	6	32	9	.78	11	.286	.357	.437
1974	Baltimore	A	137	489	133	22	1	10	(3	7)	187	66	59	43	6	56	10	3	4	29	12	.71	10	.272	.341	.382
1975	Baltimore	A	145	524	148	21	6	25	(10	15)	256	79	76	53	8	64	13	4	4	32	17	.65	12	.282	.360	.489
1976	Oakland	A	157	595	147	25	1	15	(5	10)	219	85	68	58	4	72	20	1	11	52	12	.81	11	.247	.329	.368
1977	California	A	154	561	141	27	0	25	(17	8)	243	87	75	62	7	76	12	2	8	26	12	.68	15	.251	.334	.433
1978	California	A	158	591	151	26	0	34	(21	13)	279	103	99	56	9	71	18	0	12	22	9	.71	15	.255	.332	.472
1979	California	A	162	628	186	33	3	36	(17	19)	333	120	139	71	6	51	11	0	12	22	12	.65	10	.296	.371	.530
1980	California	A	90	340	85	12	2	5	(0	5)	116	39	51	24	4	32	11	0	5	6	6	.50	9	.250	.316	.341
1981	California	A	103	377	90	18	1	17	(10	7)	161	52	66	42	1	51	7	0	6	3	3	.50	13	.239	.322	.427
1982	California	A	157	608	160	24	1	24	(13	11)	258	80	93	57	7	69	7	0	8	10	4	.71	18	.263	.329	.424
1983	New York	A	144	534	162	33	2	21	(10	11)	264	82	85	40	11	53	13	2	8	17	7	.71	10	.303	.361	.494
1984	New York	A	134	493	129	29	1	27	(10	17)	241	84	89	38	6	68	23	1	3	1	1	.50	10	.262	.341	.489
1985	New York	A	142	477	110	24	1	23	(12	11)	205	70	91	52	6	90	24	1	10	0	4	.00	10	.231	.330	.430
1986	Boston	A	160	585	139	23	1	31	(9	22)	257	93	94	62	8	111	35	0	5	3	5	.38	12	.238	.344	.439
17 YEARS			2072	7546	1982	350	28	315	(144	171)	3333	1141	1179	726	86	966	227	16	106	280	116	.71	176	.263	.341	.442

BILLY BEANE

Bats Right-handed, Throws Right-handed
Turns Age 25 in 1987, Born 03/29/62

Year	Team	League	G	AB	H	2B	3B	HR	(Hm	Rd)	TB	R	RBI	TBB	IBB	SO	HBP	SH	SF	SB	CS	SB%	GIDP	AVE	OBP	SLG
1984	New York	N	5	10	1	0	0	0	(0	0)	1	0	0	0	0	2	0	0	0	0	1	.00	0	.100	.100	.100
1985	New York	N	8	8	2	1	0	0	(0	0)	3	0	1	0	0	3	0	0	0	0	0	.00	0	.250	.250	.375
1986	Minnesota	A	80	183	39	6	0	3	(0	3)	54	20	15	11	0	54	0	0	0	2	3	.40	6	.213	.258	.295
3 YEARS			93	201	42	7	0	3	(0	3)	58	20	16	11	0	59	0	0	0	2	4	.33	6	.209	.250	.289

STEVE BEDROSIAN

Pitches Right-handed, Bats Right-handed Turns Age 30 in 1987, Born 12/06/57

			HOW MUCH HE PITCHED						WHAT HE GAVE UP											THE RESULTS					
Year	Team	League	G	GS	CG	GF	IP	BFP	H	R	ER	HR	SH	SF	HB	TBB	IBB	SO	WP	Bk	W	L	Pct	ShO	Sv	ERA
1981	Atlanta	N	15	1	0	5	24	106	15	14	12	2	0	1	1	15	2	9	0	0	1	2	.333	0	0	4.50
1982	Atlanta	N	64	3	0	30	137.2	567	102	39	37	7	9	2	4	57	5	123	0	0	8	6	.571	0	11	2.42
1983	Atlanta	N	70	1	0	52	120	504	100	50	48	11	8	4	4	51	8	114	2	0	9	10	.474	0	19	3.60
1984	Atlanta	N	40	4	0	28	83.2	345	65	23	22	5	1	1	1	33	5	81	4	0	9	6	.600	0	11	2.37
1985	Atlanta	N	37	37	0	0	206.2	907	198	101	88	17	6	7	5	111	6	134	6	0	7	15	.318	0	0	3.83
1986	Philadelphia	N	68	0	0	56	90.1	381	79	39	34	12	3	3	0	34	10	82	5	2	8	6	.571	0	29	3.39
6 YEARS			294	46	0	171	662.1	2810	559	266	241	54	27	18	15	301	36	543	17	2	42	45	.483	0	70	3.27

BUDDY BELL

Bats Right-handed, Throws Right-handed Turns Age 36 in 1987, Born 08/27/51

						BATTING															BASERUNNING				PERCENTAGES		
Year	Team	League	G	AB	H	2B	3B	HR	(Hm	Rd)	TB	R	RBI	TBB	IBB	SO	HBP	SH	SF		SB	CS	SB%	GIDP	AVE	OBP	SLG
1972	Cleveland	A	132	466	119	21	1	9	(7	2)	169	49	36	34	8	29	3	1	1		5	6	.45	5	.255	.310	.363
1973	Cleveland	A	156	631	169	23	7	14	(8	6)	248	86	59	49	2	47	6	0	3		7	15	.32	13	.268	.325	.393
1974	Cleveland	A	116	423	111	15	1	7	(4	3)	149	51	46	35	1	29	3	8	2		1	3	.25	14	.262	.322	.352
1975	Cleveland	A	153	553	150	20	4	10	(6	4)	208	66	59	51	6	72	1	10	4		6	5	.55	11	.271	.332	.376
1976	Cleveland	A	159	604	170	26	2	7	(3	4)	221	75	60	44	3	49	2	5	6		3	8	.27	12	.281	.329	.366
1977	Cleveland	A	129	479	140	23	4	11	(3	8)	204	64	64	45	5	63	1	8	5		1	8	.11	14	.292	.351	.426
1978	Cleveland	A	142	556	157	27	8	6	(3	3)	218	71	62	39	1	43	0	9	2		1	3	.25	24	.282	.328	.392
1979	Texas	A	162	670	200	42	3	18	(9	9)	302	89	101	30	4	45	3	7	10		5	4	.56	16	.299	.327	.451
1980	Texas	A	129	490	161	24	4	17	(8	9)	244	76	83	40	11	39	0	4	0		3	1	.75	16	.329	.379	.498
1981	Texas	A	97	360	106	16	1	10	(2	8)	154	44	64	42	10	30	3	0	10		3	3	.50	6	.294	.364	.428
1982	Texas	A	148	537	159	27	2	13	(3	10)	229	62	67	70	8	50	2	0	5		5	4	.56	13	.296	.376	.426
1983	Texas	A	156	618	171	35	3	14	(8	6)	254	75	66	50	5	48	4	0	6		3	5	.38	24	.277	.332	.411
1984	Texas	A	148	553	174	36	5	11	(6	5)	253	88	83	63	8	54	3	2	9		2	1	.67	21	.315	.382	.458
1985	2 Teams		151	560	128	28	5	10	(6	4)	196	61	68	67	3	48	1	1	6		3	3	.50	24	.229	.309	.350
1986	Cincinnati	N	155	568	158	29	3	20	(14	6)	253	89	75	73	4	49	5	3	6		2	8	.20	14	.278	.362	.445
15 YEARS			2133	8068	2273	392	53	177	(90	87)	3302	1046	993	732	79	695	37	58	75		50	77	.39	227	.282	.341	.409
1985	Texas	A	84	313	74	13	3	4	(2	2)	105	33	32	33	1	21	1	0	4		3	2	.60	14	.236	.308	.335
1985	Cincinnati	N	67	247	54	15	2	6	(4	2)	91	28	36	34	2	27	0	1	2		0	1	.00	10	.219	.311	.368

GEORGE BELL

Bats Right-handed, Throws Right-handed Turns Age 28 in 1987, Born 10/21/59

						BATTING															BASERUNNING				PERCENTAGES		
Year	Team	League	G	AB	H	2B	3B	HR	(Hm	Rd)	TB	R	RBI	TBB	IBB	SO	HBP	SH	SF		SB	CS	SB%	GIDP	AVE	OBP	SLG
1981	Toronto	A	60	163	38	2	1	5	(3	2)	57	19	12	5	1	27	0	0	0		3	2	.60	1	.233	.256	.350
1983	Toronto	A	39	112	30	5	4	2	(1	1)	49	5	17	4	1	17	2	0	0		1	1	.50	4	.268	.305	.438
1984	Toronto	A	159	606	177	39	4	26	(12	14)	302	85	87	24	2	86	8	0	3		11	2	.85	14	.292	.326	.498
1985	Toronto	A	157	607	167	28	6	28	(10	18)	291	87	95	43	6	90	8	0	8		21	6	.78	8	.275	.327	.479
1986	Toronto	A	159	641	198	38	6	31	(15	16)	341	101	108	41	3	62	2	0	6		7	8	.47	15	.309	.349	.532
5 YEARS			574	2129	610	112	21	92	(41	51)	1040	297	319	117	13	282	20	0	17		43	19	.69	42	.287	.327	.488

RAFAEL BELLIARD

Bats Right-handed, Throws Right-handed Turns Age 26 in 1987, Born 10/24/61

						BATTING															BASERUNNING				PERCENTAGES		
Year	Team	League	G	AB	H	2B	3B	HR	(Hm	Rd)	TB	R	RBI	TBB	IBB	SO	HBP	SH	SF		SB	CS	SB%	GIDP	AVE	OBP	SLG
1982	Pittsburgh	N	9	2	1	0	0	0	(0	0)	1	3	0	0	0	0	0	0	0		1	0	1.00	0	.500	.500	.500
1983	Pittsburgh	N	4	1	0	0	0	0	(0	0)	0	1	0	0	0	1	0	0	0		0	0	.00	0	.000	.000	.000
1984	Pittsburgh	N	20	22	5	0	0	0	(0	0)	5	3	0	0	0	1	0	0	0		4	1	.80	0	.227	.227	.227
1985	Pittsburgh	N	17	20	4	0	0	0	(0	0)	4	1	1	0	0	5	0	0	0		0	0	.00	0	.200	.200	.200
1986	Pittsburgh	N	117	309	72	5	2	0	(0	0)	81	33	31	26	6	54	3	11	1		12	2	.86	8	.233	.298	.262
5 YEARS			167	354	82	5	2	0	(0	0)	91	41	32	26	6	61	3	11	1		17	3	.85	8	.232	.289	.257

BRUCE BENEDICT

Bats Right-handed, Throws Right-handed Turns Age 32 in 1987, Born 08/18/55

						BATTING															BASERUNNING				PERCENTAGES		
Year	Team	League	G	AB	H	2B	3B	HR	(Hm	Rd)	TB	R	RBI	TBB	IBB	SO	HBP	SH	SF		SB	CS	SB%	GIDP	AVE	OBP	SLG
1978	Atlanta	N	22	52	13	2	0	0	(0	0)	15	3	1	6	2	6	0	0	0		0	0	.00	0	.250	.328	.288
1979	Atlanta	N	76	204	46	11	0	0	(0	0)	57	14	15	33	3	18	0	2	2		1	3	.25	4	.225	.331	.279
1980	Atlanta	N	120	359	91	14	1	2	(1	1)	113	18	34	28	8	36	1	13	1		3	3	.50	11	.253	.308	.315
1981	Atlanta	N	90	295	78	12	1	5	(2	3)	107	26	35	33	4	21	3	5	3		1	1	.50	8	.264	.341	.363
1982	Atlanta	N	118	386	95	11	1	3	(2	1)	117	34	44	37	9	40	3	7	3		4	4	.50	10	.246	.315	.303
1983	Atlanta	N	134	423	126	13	1	2	(1	1)	147	43	43	61	16	24	1	4	3		1	3	.25	12	.298	.385	.348
1984	Atlanta	N	95	300	67	8	1	4	(2	2)	89	26	25	34	3	25	1	1	4		1	2	.33	9	.223	.301	.297
1985	Atlanta	N	70	208	42	6	0	0	(0	0)	48	12	20	22	1	12	1	4	1		0	1	.00	9	.202	.279	.231
1986	Atlanta	N	64	160	36	10	1	0	(0	0)	48	11	13	15	1	10	2	4	1		1	0	1.00	9	.225	.298	.300
9 YEARS			789	2387	594	87	6	16	(8	8)	741	187	230	269	47	192	12	40	19		12	17	.41	71	.249	.326	.310

JUAN BENIQUEZ

Bats Right-handed, Throws Right-handed   Turns Age 37 in 1987, Born 05/13/50

								BATTING								BASERUNNING				PERCENTAGES		
Year	Team	League	G	AB	H	2B	3B	HR	(Hm | Rd)	TB	R	RBI	TBB	IBB	SO	HBP	SH	SF	SB	CS	SB%	GIDP	AVE	OBP	SLG
1971	Boston	A	16	57	17	2	0	0	(0 | 0)	19	8	4	3	0	4	0	3	0	3	1	.75	3	.298	.333	.333
1972	Boston	A	33	99	24	4	1	1	(1 | 0)	33	10	8	7	0	11	0	0	2	2	0	1.00	2	.242	.287	.333
1974	Boston	A	106	389	104	14	3	5	(3 | 2)	139	60	33	25	2	61	1	7	1	19	11	.63	9	.267	.313	.357
1975	Boston	A	78	254	74	14	4	2	(1 | 1)	102	43	17	25	1	26	2	6	1	7	10	.41	7	.291	.358	.402
1976	Texas	A	145	478	122	14	4	0	(0 | 0)	144	49	33	39	1	56	3	5	1	17	6	.74	10	.255	.315	.301
1977	Texas	A	123	424	114	19	6	10	(5 | 5)	175	56	50	43	0	43	1	8	2	26	18	.59	13	.269	.336	.413
1978	Texas	A	127	473	123	17	3	11	(5 | 6)	179	61	50	20	1	59	3	10	4	10	12	.45	10	.260	.292	.378
1979	New York	A	62	142	36	6	1	4	(0 | 4)	56	19	17	9	0	17	2	1	4	3	3	.50	5	.254	.299	.394
1980	Seattle	A	70	237	54	10	0	6	(5 | 1)	82	26	21	17	0	25	0	3	1	2	3	.40	10	.228	.278	.346
1981	California	A	58	166	30	5	0	3	(2 | 1)	44	18	13	15	0	16	1	4	1	2	1	.67	6	.181	.251	.265
1982	California	A	112	196	52	11	2	3	(1 | 2)	76	25	24	15	1	21	1	16	0	3	0	1.00	4	.265	.321	.388
1983	California	A	92	315	96	15	0	3	(1 | 2)	120	44	34	15	0	29	4	6	1	4	2	.67	9	.305	.343	.381
1984	California	A	110	354	119	17	0	8	(5 | 3)	160	60	39	18	0	43	3	4	3	0	3	.00	12	.336	.370	.452
1985	California	A	132	411	125	13	5	8	(6 | 2)	172	54	42	34	3	46	5	9	1	4	3	.57	16	.304	.364	.418
1986	Baltimore	A	113	343	103	15	0	6	(4 | 2)	136	48	36	40	1	49	3	2	6	2	3	.40	12	.300	.372	.397
15 YEARS			1377	4338	1193	176	29	70	(39 | 31)	1637	581	421	325	10	506	29	84	28	104	76	.58	128	.275	.328	.377

JUAN BERENGUER

Pitches Right-handed, Bats Right-handed   Turns Age 33 in 1987, Born 11/30/54

			HOW MUCH HE PITCHED						WHAT HE GAVE UP												THE RESULTS					
Year	Team	League	G	GS	CG	GF	IP	BFP	H	R	ER	HR	SH	SF	HB	TBB	IBB	SO	WP	Bk	W	L	Pct	ShO	Sv	ERA
1978	New York	N	5	3	0	1	13	65	17	12	12	1	0	1	1	11	0	8	0	0	0	2	.000	0	0	8.31
1979	New York	N	5	5	0	0	31	126	28	13	10	2	1	1	1	12	0	25	0	0	1	1	.500	0	0	2.90
1980	New York	N	6	0	0	0	9	46	9	9	6	1	0	0	1	10	2	7	0	0	0	1	.000	0	0	6.00
1981	2 Teams		20	14	1	4	91	405	84	62	53	11	2	7	5	51	1	49	2	0	2	13	.133	0	0	5.24
1982	Detroit	A	2	1	0	0	6.2	34	5	5	5	0	0	0	0	9	1	8	0	0	0	0	.000	0	0	6.75
1983	Detroit	A	37	19	2	7	157.2	650	110	58	55	19	1	2	6	71	3	129	3	1	9	5	.643	1	1	3.14
1984	Detroit	A	31	27	2	0	168.1	720	146	75	65	14	2	6	5	79	2	118	7	2	11	10	.524	1	0	3.48
1985	Detroit	A	31	13	0	9	95	424	96	67	59	12	1	4	1	48	3	82	4	1	5	6	.455	0	0	5.59
1986	San Francisco	N	46	4	0	17	73.1	314	64	23	22	4	2	1	2	44	2	72	4	2	2	3	.400	0	4	2.70
9 YEARS			183	86	5	42	645	2784	559	324	287	64	9	22	21	335	15	498	20	8	30	41	.423	2	5	4.00
1981	Kansas City	A	8	3	0	4	20	97	22	21	19	4	0	3	2	16	0	20	1	0	0	4	.000	0	0	8.55
1981	Toronto	A	12	11	1	0	71	308	62	41	34	7	2	4	3	35	1	29	1	0	2	9	.182	0	0	4.31

DAVE BERGMAN

Bats Left-handed, Throws Left-handed   Turns Age 34 in 1987, Born 06/06/53

								BATTING								BASERUNNING				PERCENTAGES		
Year	Team	League	G	AB	H	2B	3B	HR	(Hm | Rd)	TB	R	RBI	TBB	IBB	SO	HBP	SH	SF	SB	CS	SB%	GIDP	AVE	OBP	SLG
1975	New York	A	7	17	0	0	0	0	(0 | 0)	0	0	0	2	0	4	0	0	0	0	0	.00	0	.000	.105	.000
1977	New York	A	5	4	1	0	0	0	(0 | 0)	1	1	1	0	0	0	0	0	0	0	0	.00	0	.250	.250	.250
1978	Houston	N	104	186	43	5	1	0	(0 | 0)	50	15	12	39	9	32	0	1	2	2	0	1.00	5	.231	.361	.269
1979	Houston	N	13	15	6	0	0	1	(0 | 1)	9	4	2	0	0	3	0	0	0	0	0	.00	0	.400	.400	.600
1980	Houston	N	90	78	20	6	1	0	(0 | 0)	28	12	3	10	2	10	0	3	0	1	0	1.00	1	.256	.341	.359
1981	2 Teams		69	151	38	9	0	4	(1 | 3)	59	17	14	19	3	18	0	2	1	2	0	1.00	1	.252	.333	.391
1982	San Francisco	N	100	121	33	3	1	4	(2 | 2)	50	22	14	18	3	11	0	0	1	3	0	1.00	1	.273	.364	.413
1983	San Francisco	N	90	140	40	4	1	6	(3 | 3)	64	16	24	24	2	21	1	2	0	2	1	.67	5	.286	.394	.457
1984	Detroit	A	120	271	74	8	5	7	(4 | 3)	113	42	44	33	2	40	3	3	6	3	4	.43	12	.273	.351	.417
1985	Detroit	A	69	140	25	2	0	3	(2 | 1)	36	8	7	14	0	15	0	1	2	0	0	.00	6	.179	.250	.257
1986	Detroit	A	65	130	30	6	1	1	(0 | 1)	41	14	9	21	0	16	0	0	0	0	0	.00	3	.231	.338	.315
11 YEARS			732	1253	310	43	10	26	(12 | 14)	451	151	130	180	21	170	4	12	12	13	5	.72	29	.247	.341	.360
1981	Houston	N	6	6	1	0	0	0	(0 | 0)	4	1	1	0	0	0	0	0	0	0	0	.00	0	.167	.167	.667
1981	San Francisco	N	63	145	37	9	0	3	(1 | 2)	55	16	13	19	3	18	0	2	1	2	0	1.00	4	.255	.339	.379

TONY BERNAZARD

Bats both Right and Left-handed, Throws Right-handed   Turns Age 31 in 1987, Born 08/24/56

								BATTING								BASERUNNING				PERCENTAGES		
Year	Team	League	G	AB	H	2B	3B	HR	(Hm | Rd)	TB	R	RBI	TBB	IBB	SO	HBP	SH	SF	SB	CS	SB%	GIDP	AVE	OBP	SLG
1979	Montreal	N	22	40	12	2	0	1	(0 | 1)	17	11	8	15	0	12	1	2	0	1	2	.33	2	.300	.500	.425
1980	Montreal	N	82	183	41	7	1	5	(2 | 3)	65	26	18	17	4	41	0	1	1	9	2	.82	3	.224	.289	.355
1981	Chicago	A	106	384	106	14	4	6	(3 | 3)	146	53	34	54	6	66	2	9	1	4	4	.50	7	.276	.367	.380
1982	Chicago	A	137	540	138	25	9	11	(1 | 10)	214	90	56	67	0	88	2	16	5	11	0	1.00	9	.256	.337	.396
1983	2 Teams		139	533	141	34	3	8	(6 | 2)	205	65	56	55	3	97	2	9	7	23	9	.72	9	.265	.332	.385
1984	Cleveland	A	140	439	97	15	4	2	(1 | 1)	126	44	38	43	0	70	2	7	6	20	13	.61	10	.221	.290	.287
1985	Cleveland	A	153	500	137	26	3	11	(4 | 7)	202	73	59	69	2	72	1	5	4	17	9	.65	11	.274	.361	.404
1986	Cleveland	A	146	562	169	28	4	17	(9 | 8)	256	88	73	53	5	77	6	7	8	17	8	.68	6	.301	.362	.456
8 YEARS			925	3181	841	151	28	61	(26 | 35)	1231	450	342	373	20	523	16	56	32	102	47	.68	57	.264	.341	.387
1983	Chicago	A	59	233	61	16	2	2	(2 | 0)	87	30	26	17	0	45	0	4	5	2	1	.67	5	.262	.306	.373
1983	Seattle	A	80	300	80	18	1	6	(4 | 2)	118	35	30	38	3	52	2	5	2	21	8	.72	4	.267	.351	.393

DALE BERRA

Bats Right-handed, Throws Right-handed   Turns Age 31 in 1987, Born 12/13/56

								BATTING											BASERUNNING				PERCENTAGES		
Year	Team	League	G	AB	H	2B	3B	HR	(Hm	Rd)	TB	R	RBI	TBB	IBB	SO	HBP	SH	SF	SB	CS	SB%	GIDP	AVE	OBP	SLG
1977	Pittsburgh	N	17	40	7	1	0	0	(0	0)	8	0	3	1	0	8	0	0	0	0	0	.00	0	.175	.195	.200
1978	Pittsburgh	N	56	135	28	2	0	6	(4	2)	48	16	14	13	3	20	2	0	1	3	1	.75	2	.207	.285	.356
1979	Pittsburgh	N	44	123	26	5	0	3	(1	2)	40	11	15	11	2	17	0	2	2	0	0	.00	5	.211	.272	.325
1980	Pittsburgh	N	93	245	54	8	2	6	(3	3)	84	21	31	16	6	52	1	4	2	2	0	1.00	6	.220	.269	.343
1981	Pittsburgh	N	81	232	56	12	0	2	(1	1)	74	21	27	17	4	34	3	2	0	11	1	.92	3	.241	.302	.319
1982	Pittsburgh	N	156	529	139	25	5	10	(4	6)	204	64	61	33	12	83	4	8	9	6	6	.50	15	.263	.306	.386
1983	Pittsburgh	N	161	537	135	25	1	10	(5	5)	192	51	52	61	19	84	0	7	2	8	5	.62	10	.251	.327	.358
1984	Pittsburgh	N	136	450	100	16	0	9	(7	2)	143	31	52	34	8	78	1	6	9	1	3	.25	11	.222	.273	.318
1985	New York	A	48	109	25	5	1	1	(1	0)	35	8	8	7	0	20	0	2	0	1	1	.50	2	.229	.276	.321
1986	New York	A	42	108	25	7	0	2	(2	0)	38	10	13	9	0	14	1	2	1	0	0	.00	0	.231	.294	.352
10 YEARS			834	2508	595	106	9	49	(28	21)	866	233	276	202	54	410	12	33	26	32	17	.65	54	.237	.294	.345

KARL BEST

Pitches Right-handed, Bats Right-handed   Turns Age 28 in 1987, Born 03/06/59

			HOW MUCH HE PITCHED						WHAT HE GAVE UP											THE RESULTS					
Year	Team	League	G	GS	CG	GF	IP	BFP	H	R	ER	HR	SH	SF	HB	TBB	IBB	SO	WP	Bk	W	L	Pct	ShO	Sv	ERA
1983	Seattle	A	4	0	0	0	5.1	36	14	9	8	2	0	0	2	5	0	3	1	0	0	1	.000	0	0	13.50
1984	Seattle	A	5	0	0	2	6	25	7	2	2	0	0	1	0	0	0	6	0	0	1	1	.500	0	0	3.00
1985	Seattle	A	15	0	0	7	32.1	128	25	9	7	1	0	0	1	6	0	32	0	0	2	1	.667	0	4	1.95
1986	Seattle	A	26	0	0	15	35.2	163	35	19	16	3	2	2	1	21	2	23	2	1	2	3	.400	0	1	4.04
4 YEARS			50	0	0	24	79.1	352	81	39	33	6	2	3	4	32	2	64	3	1	5	6	.455	0	5	3.74

BUDDY BIANCALANA

Bats both Right and Left-handed, Throws Right-handed   Turns Age 27 in 1987, Born 02/02/60

								BATTING											BASERUNNING				PERCENTAGES		
Year	Team	League	G	AB	H	2B	3B	HR	(Hm	Rd)	TB	R	RBI	TBB	IBB	SO	HBP	SH	SF	SB	CS	SB%	GIDP	AVE	OBP	SLG
1982	Kansas City	A	3	2	1	0	1	0	(0	0)	3	0	0	1	0	0	0	0	0	0	0	.00	1	.500	.667	.500
1983	Kansas City	A	6	15	3	0	0	0	(0	0)	3	2	0	0	0	7	0	0	0	1	0	1.00	0	.200	.200	.200
1984	Kansas City	A	66	134	26	6	1	2	(0	2)	40	18	9	6	0	44	0	5	0	1	2	.33	2	.194	.229	.299
1985	Kansas City	A	81	138	26	5	1	1	(1	0)	36	21	6	17	0	34	0	5	0	1	4	.20	1	.188	.277	.261
1986	Kansas City	A	100	190	46	4	4	2	(0	2)	64	24	8	15	0	50	0	4	0	5	1	.83	3	.242	.298	.337
5 YEARS			256	479	102	15	7	5	(1	4)	146	65	23	39	0	135	0	14	0	8	7	.53	7	.213	.272	.305

MIKE BIELECKI

Pitches Right-handed, Bats Right-handed   Turns Age 28 in 1987, Born 07/31/59

			HOW MUCH HE PITCHED						WHAT HE GAVE UP											THE RESULTS					
Year	Team	League	G	GS	CG	GF	IP	BFP	H	R	ER	HR	SH	SF	HB	TBB	IBB	SO	WP	Bk	W	L	Pct	ShO	Sv	ERA
1984	Pittsburgh	N	4	0	0	1	4.1	17	4	0	0	0	1	0	0	0	0	1	0	1	0	0	.000	0	0	0.00
1985	Pittsburgh	N	12	7	0	1	45.2	211	45	26	23	5	4	0	1	31	1	22	1	1	2	3	.400	0	0	4.53
1986	Pittsburgh	N	31	27	0	0	148.2	667	149	87	77	10	7	6	2	83	3	83	7	5	6	11	.353	0	0	4.66
3 YEARS			47	34	0	2	198.2	895	198	113	100	15	12	6	3	114	4	106	8	7	8	14	.364	0	0	4.53

DANN BILARDELLO

Bats Right-handed, Throws Right-handed   Turns Age 28 in 1987, Born 05/26/59

								BATTING											BASERUNNING				PERCENTAGES		
Year	Team	League	G	AB	H	2B	3B	HR	(Hm	Rd)	TB	R	RBI	TBB	IBB	SO	HBP	SH	SF	SB	CS	SB%	GIDP	AVE	OBP	SLG
1983	Cincinnati	N	109	298	71	18	0	9	(7	2)	116	27	38	15	3	49	1	2	4	2	1	.67	9	.238	.274	.389
1984	Cincinnati	N	68	182	38	7	0	2	(2	0)	51	16	10	19	3	34	1	4	0	0	1	.00	6	.209	.287	.280
1985	Cincinnati	N	42	102	17	0	0	1	(1	0)	20	6	9	4	1	15	1	1	0	0	0	.00	5	.167	.206	.196
1986	Montreal	N	79	191	37	5	0	4	(1	3)	54	12	17	14	3	32	0	7	0	1	0	1.00	5	.194	.249	.283
4 YEARS			298	773	163	30	0	16	(11	5)	241	61	74	52	10	130	3	14	4	3	2	.60	25	.211	.262	.312

BUD BLACK

Pitches Left-handed, Bats Left-handed   Turns Age 30 in 1987, Born 06/30/57

			HOW MUCH HE PITCHED						WHAT HE GAVE UP											THE RESULTS					
Year	Team	League	G	GS	CG	GF	IP	BFP	H	R	ER	HR	SH	SF	HB	TBB	IBB	SO	WP	Bk	W	L	Pct	ShO	Sv	ERA
1981	Seattle	A	2	0	0	0	1	7	2	0	0	0	0	0	0	3	1	0	1	0	0	0	.000	0	0	0.00
1982	Kansas City	A	22	14	0	2	88.1	386	92	48	45	10	4	3	3	34	6	40	4	7	4	6	.400	0	0	4.58
1983	Kansas City	A	24	24	3	0	161.1	672	159	75	68	19	4	5	2	43	1	58	4	0	10	7	.588	0	0	3.79
1984	Kansas City	A	35	35	8	0	257	1045	226	99	89	22	6	1	4	64	2	140	2	2	17	12	.586	1	0	3.12
1985	Kansas City	A	33	33	5	0	205.2	885	216	111	99	17	8	4	8	59	4	122	9	1	10	15	.400	2	0	4.33
1986	Kansas City	A	56	4	0	26	121	503	100	49	43	14	4	4	7	43	5	68	2	2	5	10	.333	0	9	3.20
6 YEARS			172	110	16	28	834.1	3498	795	382	344	82	26	17	24	246	19	428	22	12	46	50	.479	3	9	3.71

VIDA BLUE

Pitches Left-handed, Bats both Right and Left-handed — Turns Age 38 in 1987, Born 07/28/49

Year	Team	League	HOW MUCH HE PITCHED						WHAT HE GAVE UP												THE RESULTS					
			G	GS	CG	GF	IP	BFP	H	R	ER	HR	SH	SF	HB	TBB	IBB	SO	WP	Bk	W	L	Pct	ShO	Sv	ERA
1969	Oakland	A	12	4	0	1	42	173	49	34	31	13	4	0	0	18	1	24	1	0	1	1	.500	0	1	6.64
1970	Oakland	A	6	6	2	0	39	135	20	12	9	0	2	0	1	12	0	35	0	0	2	0	1.000	2	0	2.08
1971	Oakland	A	39	39	24	0	312	1119	209	73	63	19	9	3	4	88	3	301	10	1	24	8	.750	8	0	1.82
1972	Oakland	A	25	23	5	0	151	558	117	55	47	11	7	6	1	48	3	111	2	0	6	10	.375	4	0	2.80
1973	Oakland	A	37	37	13	0	264	978	214	108	96	26	8	10	4	105	2	158	15	2	20	9	.690	4	0	3.27
1974	Oakland	A	40	40	12	0	282	1159	246	118	102	17	7	12	1	98	7	174	9	0	17	15	.531	1	0	3.26
1975	Oakland	A	39	38	13	1	278	1153	243	103	93	21	15	6	5	99	4	189	4	2	22	11	.667	2	1	3.01
1976	Oakland	A	37	37	20	0	298	1205	268	90	78	9	13	5	1	63	3	166	5	1	18	13	.581	6	0	2.36
1977	Oakland	A	38	38	16	0	280	1184	284	138	119	23	12	9	1	86	5	157	11	0	14	19	.424	1	0	3.83
1978	San Francisco	N	35	35	9	0	258	1042	233	87	80	12	16	8	0	70	4	171	5	0	18	10	.643	4	0	2.79
1979	San Francisco	N	34	34	10	0	237	1041	246	143	132	23	11	12	1	111	11	138	8	0	14	14	.500	0	0	5.01
1980	San Francisco	N	31	31	10	0	224	914	202	79	74	14	13	6	0	61	8	129	3	2	14	10	.583	3	0	2.97
1981	San Francisco	N	18	18	1	0	125	513	97	40	34	7	9	3	1	54	3	63	7	0	8	6	.571	0	0	2.45
1982	Kansas City	A	31	31	6	0	181	773	163	80	76	20	5	3	0	80	3	103	4	0	13	12	.520	2	0	3.78
1983	Kansas City	A	19	14	1	4	85.1	382	96	62	57	12	4	5	2	35	0	53	6	2	0	5	.000	0	0	6.01
1985	San Francisco	N	33	20	1	5	131	574	115	70	65	17	11	3	1	80	1	103	8	2	8	8	.500	0	0	4.47
1986	San Francisco	N	28	28	0	0	156.2	663	137	65	57	19	7	6	0	77	3	100	5	1	10	10	.500	0	0	3.27
17 YEARS			502	473	143	11	3344	13566	2939	1357	1213	263	153	97	23	1185	61	2175	103	13	209	161	.565	37	2	3.26

BERT BLYLEVEN

Pitches Right-handed, Bats Right-handed — Turns Age 36 in 1987, Born 04/06/51

Year	Team	League	HOW MUCH HE PITCHED						WHAT HE GAVE UP												THE RESULTS					
			G	GS	CG	GF	IP	BFP	H	R	ER	HR	SH	SF	HB	TBB	IBB	SO	WP	Bk	W	L	Pct	ShO	Sv	ERA
1970	Minnesota	A	27	25	5	1	164	628	143	66	58	17	8	2	2	47	6	135	2	3	10	9	.526	1	0	3.18
1971	Minnesota	A	38	38	17	1	278	1067	267	95	87	21	12	3	5	59	1	224	5	1	16	15	.516	5	0	2.82
1972	Minnesota	A	39	38	11	1	287	1089	247	93	87	22	14	6	10	69	7	228	7	1	17	17	.500	3	0	2.73
1973	Minnesota	A	40	40	25	0	325	1254	296	109	91	16	11	13	9	67	4	258	7	2	20	17	.541	9	0	2.52
1974	Minnesota	A	37	37	19	0	281	1149	244	99	83	14	13	5	9	77	3	249	3	0	17	17	.500	3	0	2.66
1975	Minnesota	A	35	35	20	0	276	1104	219	104	92	24	10	8	4	84	2	233	7	0	15	10	.600	3	0	3.00
1976	2 Teams	A	36	36	18	0	297	1225	283	106	95	14	18	6	12	81	6	219	7	2	13	16	.448	6	0	2.88
1977	Texas	A	30	30	15	0	235	935	181	81	71	20	10	5	7	69	1	182	8	0	14	12	.538	5	0	2.72
1978	Pittsburgh	N	34	34	11	0	244	1011	217	94	82	17	13	2	6	66	5	182	6	2	14	10	.583	4	0	3.02
1979	Pittsburgh	N	37	37	4	0	237	1018	238	102	95	21	14	9	6	92	8	172	9	0	12	5	.706	0	0	3.61
1980	Pittsburgh	N	34	32	5	1	217	907	219	102	92	20	10	2	0	59	5	168	2	1	8	13	.381	2	0	3.82
1981	Cleveland	A	20	20	9	0	159	644	145	52	51	9	3	3	5	40	1	107	3	1	11	7	.611	1	0	2.89
1982	Cleveland	A	4	4	0	0	20.1	89	16	14	11	2	0	2	0	11	0	19	0	0	2	2	.500	0	0	4.87
1983	Cleveland	A	24	24	5	0	156.1	660	160	74	68	8	2	5	10	44	4	123	5	1	7	10	.412	0	0	3.91
1984	Cleveland	A	33	32	12	0	245	1004	204	86	78	19	6	8	6	74	4	170	6	0	19	7	.731	4	0	2.87
1985	2 Teams	A	37	37	24	0	293.2	1203	264	121	103	23	5	8	9	75	1	206	4	1	17	16	.515	5	0	3.16
1986	Minnesota	A	36	36	16	0	271.2	1126	262	134	121	50	5	4	10	58	4	215	4	0	17	14	.548	3	0	4.01
17 YEARS			541	535	216	3	3987	16113	3605	1532	1365	317	154	91	110	1072	62	3090	85	15	229	197	.538	54	0	3.08
1976	Minnesota	A	12	12	4	0	95	406	101	39	33	3	7	3	4	35	5	75	0	0	4	5	.444	0	0	3.13
1976	Texas	A	24	24	14	0	202	819	182	67	62	11	11	3	8	46	1	144	7	0	9	11	.450	6	0	2.76
1985	Cleveland	A	23	23	15	0	179.2	743	163	76	65	14	4	4	7	49	1	129	1	1	9	11	.450	4	0	3.26
1985	Minnesota	A	14	14	9	0	114	460	101	45	38	9	1	4	2	26	0	77	3	0	8	5	.615	1	0	3.00

BRUCE BOCHTE

Bats Left-handed, Throws Left-handed — Turns Age 37 in 1987, Born 11/12/50

Year	Team	League	BATTING																		BASERUNNING				PERCENTAGES		
			G	AB	H	2B	3B	HR	(Hm	Rd)	TB	R	RBI	TBB	IBB	SO	HBP	SH	SF	SB	CS	SB%	GIDP	AVE	OBP	SLG
1974	California	A	57	196	53	4	1	5	(2	3)	74	24	26	18	0	23	1	4	2	6	3	.67	6	.270	.332	.378
1975	California	A	107	375	107	19	3	3	(2	1)	141	41	48	45	5	43	2	3	3	3	4	.43	6	.285	.362	.376
1976	California	A	146	466	120	17	1	2	(0	2)	145	53	49	64	11	53	2	6	5	4	5	.44	12	.258	.346	.311
1977	2 Teams	A	137	492	148	23	1	7	(3	4)	194	64	51	47	3	42	0	8	5	6	4	.60	20	.301	.358	.394
1978	Seattle	A	140	486	128	25	3	11	(8	3)	192	58	51	60	3	47	1	7	6	3	4	.43	12	.263	.342	.395
1979	Seattle	A	150	554	175	38	6	16	(11	5)	273	81	100	67	8	64	2	3	10	2	2	.50	27	.316	.385	.493
1980	Seattle	A	148	520	156	34	4	13	(10	3)	237	62	78	72	13	81	0	4	7	2	3	.40	16	.300	.381	.456
1981	Seattle	A	99	335	87	16	0	6	(4	2)	121	39	30	47	5	53	2	1	0	1	3	.25	5	.260	.354	.361
1982	Seattle	A	144	509	151	21	0	12	(7	5)	208	58	70	67	5	71	3	4	3	8	5	.62	15	.297	.380	.409
1984	Oakland	A	148	469	124	23	0	5	(1	4)	162	58	52	52	3	59	0	4	8	2	5	.29	12	.264	.333	.345
1985	Oakland	A	137	424	125	17	1	14	(6	8)	186	48	60	49	6	58	0	0	1	3	1	.75	14	.295	.367	.439
1986	Oakland	A	125	407	104	13	1	6	(3	3)	137	57	43	65	3	68	0	0	1	3	2	.60	17	.256	.357	.337
12 YEARS			1538	5233	1478	250	21	100	(57	43)	2070	643	658	653	65	662	13	44	51	43	41	.51	156	.282	.360	.396
1977	California	A	25	100	29	4	0	2	(1	1)	39	12	8	7	0	4	0	1	0	3	2	.60	3	.290	.336	.390
1977	Cleveland	A	112	392	119	19	1	5	(2	3)	155	52	43	40	3	38	0	7	5	3	2	.60	17	.304	.364	.395

BRUCE BOCHY

Bats Right-handed, Throws Right-handed   Turns Age 32 in 1987, Born 04/16/55

Year	Team	League	G	AB	H	2B	3B	HR	(Hm	Rd)	TB	R	RBI	TBB	IBB	SO	HBP	SH	SF	SB	CS	SB%	GIDP	AVE	OBP	SLG
																								BATTING						BASERUNNING				PERCENTAGES		
1978	Houston	N	54	154	41	8	0	3	(0	3)	58	8	15	11	4	35	0	0	2	0	0	.00	8	.266	.311	.377
1979	Houston	N	56	129	28	4	0	1	(1	0)	35	11	6	13	4	25	1	0	0	0	0	.00	5	.217	.294	.271
1980	Houston	N	22	22	4	1	0	0	(0	0)	5	0	0	5	1	7	1	0	0	0	0	.00	0	.182	.357	.227
1982	New York	N	17	49	15	4	0	2	(1	1)	25	4	8	4	0	6	0	0	0	0	0	.00	1	.306	.358	.510
1983	San Diego	N	23	42	9	1	1	0	(0	0)	12	2	3	0	0	9	0	0	2	0	0	.00	2	.214	.205	.286
1984	San Diego	N	37	92	21	5	1	4	(0	4)	40	10	15	3	0	21	0	1	1	0	1	.00	2	.228	.250	.435
1985	San Diego	N	48	112	30	2	0	6	(4	2)	50	16	13	6	1	30	0	2	0	0	0	.00	1	.268	.305	.446
1986	San Diego	N	63	127	32	9	0	8	(6	2)	65	16	22	14	3	23	0	1	0	1	0	1.00	3	.252	.326	.512
8 YEARS			320	727	180	34	2	24	(12	12)	290	67	82	56	13	156	2	4	5	1	1	.50	22	.248	.301	.399

MIKE BODDICKER

Pitches Right-handed, Bats Right-handed   Turns Age 30 in 1987, Born 08/23/57

Year	Team	League	G	GS	CG	GF	IP	BFP	H	R	ER	HR	SH	SF	HB	TBB	IBB	SO	WP	Bk	W	L	Pct	ShO	Sv	ERA
					HOW MUCH HE PITCHED								WHAT HE GAVE UP										THE RESULTS			
1980	Baltimore	A	1	1	0	0	7	34	6	6	5	1	0	0	0	5	0	4	0	0	0	1	.000	0	0	6.43
1981	Baltimore	A	2	0	0	1	6	25	6	4	3	1	0	0	0	2	0	2	0	0	0	0	.000	0	0	4.50
1982	Baltimore	A	7	0	0	4	25.2	110	25	10	10	2	1	0	0	12	2	20	0	0	1	0	1.000	0	0	3.51
1983	Baltimore	A	27	26	10	1	179	711	141	65	55	13	4	3	0	52	1	120	5	0	16	8	.667	5	0	2.77
1984	Baltimore	A	34	34	16	0	261.1	1051	218	95	81	23	2	7	5	81	1	128	6	0	20	11	.645	4	0	2.79
1985	Baltimore	A	32	32	9	0	203.1	899	227	104	92	13	9	2	5	89	7	135	5	0	12	17	.414	2	0	4.07
1986	Baltimore	A	33	33	7	0	218.1	934	214	125	114	30	5	6	11	74	4	175	7	0	14	12	.538	0	0	4.70
7 YEARS			136	126	42	6	900.2	3764	837	409	360	83	19	18	21	315	15	584	25	1	63	49	.563	11	0	3.60

WADE BOGGS

Bats Left-handed, Throws Right-handed   Turns Age 29 in 1987, Born 06/15/58

Year	Team	League	G	AB	H	2B	3B	HR	(Hm	Rd)	TB	R	RBI	TBB	IBB	SO	HBP	SH	SF	SB	CS	SB%	GIDP	AVE	OBP	SLG
														BATTING							BASERUNNING				PERCENTAGES		
1982	Boston	A	104	338	118	14	1	5	(4	1)	149	51	44	35	4	21	0	4	4	1	0	1.00	9	.349	.406	.441
1983	Boston	A	153	582	210	44	7	5	(2	3)	283	100	74	92	2	36	1	3	7	3	3	.50	15	.361	.444	.486
1984	Boston	A	158	625	203	31	4	6	(5	1)	260	109	55	89	6	44	0	8	4	3	2	.60	13	.325	.407	.416
1985	Boston	A	161	653	240	42	3	8	(6	2)	312	107	78	96	5	61	4	3	2	2	1	.67	20	.368	.450	.478
1986	Boston	A	149	580	207	47	2	8	(3	5)	282	107	71	105	14	44	0	4	4	0	4	.00	11	.357	.453	.486
5 YEARS			725	2778	978	178	17	32	(20	12)	1286	474	322	417	31	206	5	22	21	9	10	.47	68	.352	.435	.463

BARRY BONDS

Bats Left-handed, Throws Left-handed   Turns Age 23 in 1987, Born 07/24/64

Year	Team	League	G	AB	H	2B	3B	HR	(Hm	Rd)	TB	R	RBI	TBB	IBB	SO	HBP	SH	SF	SB	CS	SB%	GIDP	AVE	OBP	SLG
														BATTING							BASERUNNING				PERCENTAGES		
1986	Pittsburgh	N	113	413	92	26	3	16	(9	7)	172	72	48	65	2	102	2	2	2	36	7	.84	4	.223	.330	.416

BOBBY BONILLA

Bats both Right and Left-handed, Throws Right-handed   Turns Age 24 in 1987, Born 02/23/63

Year	Team	League	G	AB	H	2B	3B	HR	(Hm	Rd)	TB	R	RBI	TBB	IBB	SO	HBP	SH	SF	SB	CS	SB%	GIDP	AVE	OBP	SLG
														BATTING							BASERUNNING				PERCENTAGES		
1986	2 Teams		138	426	109	16	4	3	(2	1)	142	55	43	62	3	88	2	5	1	8	5	.62	9	.256	.352	.333
1986	Chicago	A	75	234	63	10	2	2	(2	0)	83	27	26	33	2	49	1	2	1	4	1	.80	4	.269	.361	.355
1986	Pittsburgh	N	63	192	46	6	2	1	(0	1)	59	28	17	29	1	39	1	3	0	4	4	.50	5	.240	.342	.307

JUAN BONILLA

Bats Right-handed, Throws Right-handed   Turns Age 31 in 1987, Born 02/12/56

Year	Team	League	G	AB	H	2B	3B	HR	(Hm	Rd)	TB	R	RBI	TBB	IBB	SO	HBP	SH	SF	SB	CS	SB%	GIDP	AVE	OBP	SLG
														BATTING							BASERUNNING				PERCENTAGES		
1981	San Diego	N	99	369	107	13	2	1	(1	0)	127	30	25	25	5	23	2	9	2	4	9	.31	7	.290	.337	.344
1982	San Diego	N	45	182	51	6	2	0	(0	0)	61	21	8	11	0	15	1	3	0	0	1	.00	2	.280	.325	.335
1983	San Diego	N	152	556	132	17	4	4	(3	1)	169	55	45	50	11	40	3	3	5	3	0	1.00	19	.237	.301	.304
1985	New York	N	8	16	2	1	0	0	(0	0)	3	0	2	0	0	3	0	0	0	0	0	.00		.125	.125	.188
1986	Baltimore	A	102	284	69	10	1	1	(0	1)	84	33	18	25	0	21	3	4	0	0	0	.00	14	.243	.311	.296
5 YEARS			406	1407	361	47	9	6	(4	2)	444	139	98	111	16	102	9	19	7	7	10	.41	42	.257	.314	.316

BOB BOONE

Bats Right-handed, Throws Right-handed   Turns Age 40 in 1987, Born 11/19/47

									BATTING											BASERUNNING				PERCENTAGES		
Year	Team	League	G	AB	H	2B	3B	HR	(Hm	Rd)	TB	R	RBI	TBB	IBB	SO	HBP	SH	SF	SB	CS	SB%	GIDP	AVE	OBP	SLG
1972	Philadelphia	N	16	51	14	1	0	1	(0	1)	18	4	4	5	2	7	0	0	1	1	0	1.00	2	.275	.333	.353
1973	Philadelphia	N	145	521	136	20	2	10	(4	6)	190	42	61	41	8	36	0	5	8	3	4	.43	7	.261	.311	.365
1974	Philadelphia	N	146	488	118	24	3	3	(3	0)	157	41	52	35	9	29	4	9	5	3	1	.75	16	.242	.295	.322
1975	Philadelphia	N	97	289	71	14	2	2	(0	2)	95	28	20	32	6	14	1	6	1	1	3	.25	8	.246	.322	.329
1976	Philadelphia	N	121	361	98	18	2	4	(3	1)	132	40	54	45	14	44	1	4	7	2	5	.29	10	.271	.348	.366
1977	Philadelphia	N	132	440	125	26	4	11	(7	4)	192	55	66	42	5	54	2	3	8	5	5	.50	8	.284	.343	.436
1978	Philadelphia	N	132	435	123	18	4	12	(8	4)	185	48	62	46	10	37	1	5	8	2	5	.29	13	.283	.347	.425
1979	Philadelphia	N	119	398	114	21	3	9	(4	5)	168	38	58	49	9	33	2	4	1	1	4	.20	9	.286	.367	.422
1980	Philadelphia	N	141	480	110	23	1	9	(5	4)	162	34	55	48	12	41	1	4	2	3	4	.43	9	.229	.299	.338
1981	Philadelphia	N	76	227	48	7	0	4	(2	2)	67	19	24	22	2	16	0	2	2	2	2	.50	6	.211	.279	.295
1982	California	A	143	472	121	17	0	7	(5	2)	159	42	58	39	2	34	0	23	5	0	2	.00	9	.256	.310	.337
1983	California	A	142	468	120	18	0	9	(6	3)	165	46	52	24	1	42	0	10	7	4	3	.57	19	.256	.289	.353
1984	California	A	139	450	91	16	1	3	(1	2)	118	33	32	25	1	45	0	6	5	3	3	.50	11	.202	.242	.262
1985	California	A	150	460	114	17	0	5	(0	5)	146	37	55	37	2	35	3	16	4	1	2	.33	12	.248	.306	.317
1986	California	A	144	442	98	12	2	7	(1	6)	135	48	49	43	1	30	0	12	6	1	0	1.00	15	.222	.287	.305
15 YEARS			1843	5982	1501	252	24	96	(49	47)	2089	555	702	533	84	497	15	109	70	32	43	.43	154	.251	.310	.349

RICH BORDI

Pitches Right-handed, Bats Right-handed   Turns Age 28 in 1987, Born 04/18/59

			HOW MUCH HE PITCHED						WHAT HE GAVE UP											THE RESULTS					
Year	Team	League	G	GS	CG	GF	IP	BFP	H	R	ER	HR	SH	SF	HB	TBB	IBB	SO	WP	Bk	W	L	Pct	ShO	Sv	ERA
1980	Oakland	A	1	0	0	0	2	10	4	1	1	0	0	0	0	0	0	0	0	0	0	0	.000	0	0	4.50
1981	Oakland	A	2	0	0	2	8	8	1	0	0	0	0	0	1	0	0	0	0	0	0	0	.000	0	0	0.00
1982	Seattle	A	7	2	0	2	13	60	18	12	12	4	0	0	1	1	0	10	0	0	0	2	.000	0	0	8.31
1983	Chicago	N	11	1	0	1	25.1	119	34	15	14	2	1	0	0	12	1	20	0	0	0	2	.000	0	1	4.97
1984	Chicago	N	31	7	0	10	83.1	347	78	37	32	11	2	3	0	20	4	41	0	0	5	2	.714	0	4	3.46
1985	New York	A	51	3	0	16	98	415	95	41	35	5	6	3	3	29	4	64	1	0	6	8	.429	0	2	3.21
1986	Baltimore	A	52	1	0	22	107	464	105	56	53	13	2	3	4	41	5	83	1	0	6	4	.600	0	3	4.46
7 YEARS			155	14	0	53	330.2	1423	335	162	147	35	11	9	6	104	14	218	2	0	17	18	.486	0	10	4.00

THAD BOSLEY

Bats Left-handed, Throws Left-handed   Turns Age 31 in 1987, Born 09/17/56

									BATTING											BASERUNNING				PERCENTAGES		
Year	Team	League	G	AB	H	2B	3B	HR	(Hm	Rd)	TB	R	RBI	TBB	IBB	SO	HBP	SH	SF	SB	CS	SB%	GIDP	AVE	OBP	SLG
1977	California	A	58	212	63	10	2	0	(0	0)	77	19	19	16	0	32	1	4	2	5	4	.56	4	.297	.346	.363
1978	Chicago	A	66	219	59	5	1	2	(1	1)	72	25	13	13	1	32	0	2	2	12	11	.52	4	.269	.308	.329
1979	Chicago	A	36	77	24	1	1	1	(1	0)	30	13	8	9	0	14	0	0	0	4	1	.80	1	.312	.384	.390
1980	Chicago	A	70	147	33	2	0	2	(2	0)	41	12	14	10	3	27	0	4	1	3	2	.60	5	.224	.272	.279
1981	Milwaukee	A	42	105	24	2	0	0	(0	0)	26	11	3	6	0	13	0	1	0	2	1	.67	4	.229	.270	.248
1982	Seattle	A	22	46	8	1	0	0	(0	0)	9	3	2	4	0	8	0	0	1	3	1	.75	1	.174	.240	.196
1983	Chicago	N	43	72	21	4	1	2	(1	1)	33	12	12	10	1	12	0	0	1	1	1	.50	0	.292	.373	.458
1984	Chicago	N	38	98	29	2	2	2	(0	2)	41	17	14	13	2	22	0	0	1	5	1	.83	1	.296	.375	.418
1985	Chicago	N	108	180	59	6	3	7	(4	3)	92	25	27	20	1	29	0	0	2	5	1	.83	3	.328	.391	.511
1986	Chicago	N	87	120	33	4	1	1	(0	1)	42	15	9	18	3	24	0	1	0	3	0	1.00	3	.275	.370	.350
10 YEARS			587	1276	353	37	11	17	(9	8)	463	152	121	119	11	213	1	12	9	43	23	.65	26	.277	.337	.363

DARYL BOSTON

Bats Left-handed, Throws Left-handed   Turns Age 24 in 1987, Born 01/04/63

									BATTING											BASERUNNING				PERCENTAGES		
Year	Team	League	G	AB	H	2B	3B	HR	(Hm	Rd)	TB	R	RBI	TBB	IBB	SO	HBP	SH	SF	SB	CS	SB%	GIDP	AVE	OBP	SLG
1984	Chicago	A	35	83	14	3	1	0	(0	0)	19	8	3	4	0	20	0	0	0	6	0	1.00	0	.169	.207	.229
1985	Chicago	A	95	232	53	13	1	3	(1	2)	77	20	15	14	1	44	0	1	1	8	6	.57	3	.228	.271	.332
1986	Chicago	A	56	199	53	11	3	5	(1	4)	85	29	22	21	3	33	0	3	1	9	5	.64	4	.266	.335	.427
3 YEARS			186	514	120	27	5	8	(2	6)	181	57	40	39	4	97	0	4	2	23	11	.68	7	.233	.286	.352

DENNIS BOYD

Pitches Right-handed, Bats Right-handed   Turns Age 28 in 1987, Born 10/06/59

			HOW MUCH HE PITCHED						WHAT HE GAVE UP											THE RESULTS					
Year	Team	League	G	GS	CG	GF	IP	BFP	H	R	ER	HR	SH	SF	HB	TBB	IBB	SO	WP	Bk	W	L	Pct	ShO	Sv	ERA
1982	Boston	A	3	1	0	0	8.1	37	11	5	5	2	0	0	0	2	0	2	1	0	0	1	.000	0	0	5.40
1983	Boston	A	15	13	5	2	98.2	413	103	46	36	9	1	5	1	23	0	43	3	1	4	8	.333	0	0	3.28
1984	Boston	A	29	26	10	2	197.2	835	207	109	96	18	4	8	1	53	5	134	5	1	12	12	.500	3	0	4.37
1985	Boston	A	35	35	13	0	272.1	1132	273	117	112	26	9	7	4	67	3	154	1	1	15	13	.536	3	0	3.70
1986	Boston	A	30	30	10	0	214.1	893	222	99	90	32	3	6	2	45	1	129	3	0	16	10	.615	0	0	3.78
5 YEARS			112	105	38	4	791.1	3310	816	376	339	87	17	26	8	190	9	462	13	3	47	44	.516	6	0	3.86

PHIL BRADLEY

Bats Right-handed, Throws Right-handed   Turns Age 28 in 1987, Born 03/11/59

Year	Team	League	G	AB	H	2B	3B	HR	(Hm	Rd)	TB	R	RBI	TBB	IBB	SO	HBP	SH	SF	SB	CS	SB%	GIDP	AVE	OBP	SLG
1983	Seattle	A	23	67	18	2	0	0	(0	0)	20	8	5	8	0	5	0	1	1	3	1	.75	0	.269	.342	.299
1984	Seattle	A	124	322	97	12	4	0	(0	0)	117	49	24	34	2	61	3	11	0	21	8	.72	6	.301	.373	.363
1985	Seattle	A	159	641	192	33	8	26	(15	11)	319	100	89	55	4	129	12	4	2	22	9	.71	14	.300	.365	.498
1986	Seattle	A	143	526	163	27	4	12	(5	7)	234	88	50	77	1	134	8	1	2	21	12	.64	9	.310	.405	.445
4 YEARS			449	1556	470	74	16	38	(20	18)	690	245	167	174	7	329	23	17	5	67	30	.69	29	.302	.379	.443

SCOTT BRADLEY

Bats Left-handed, Throws Right-handed   Turns Age 27 in 1987, Born 03/22/60

Year	Team	League	G	AB	H	2B	3B	HR	(Hm	Rd)	TB	R	RBI	TBB	IBB	SO	HBP	SH	SF	SB	CS	SB%	GIDP	AVE	OBP	SLG
1984	New York	A	9	21	6	1	0	0	(0	0)	7	3	2	1	0	1	0	0	0	0	0	.00	0	.286	.318	.333
1985	New York	A	19	49	8	2	1	0	(0	0)	12	4	1	1	0	5	1	0	0	0	0	.00	2	.163	.196	.245
1986	2 Teams		77	220	66	8	3	5	(4	1)	95	20	28	13	4	7	4	2	2	1	2	.33	13	.300	.347	.432
3 YEARS			105	290	80	11	4	5	(4	1)	114	27	31	15	4	13	5	2	2	1	2	.33	15	.276	.321	.393
1986	Chicago	A	9	21	6	0	0	0	(0	0)	6	3	0	1	0	0	2	0	0	0	2	.00	1	.286	.375	.286
1986	Seattle	A	68	199	60	8	3	5	(4	1)	89	17	28	12	4	7	2	2	2	1	0	1.00	12	.302	.344	.447

GLENN BRAGGS

Bats Right-handed, Throws Right-handed   Turns Age 25 in 1987, Born 10/17/62

Year	Team	League	G	AB	H	2B	3B	HR	(Hm	Rd)	TB	R	RBI	TBB	IBB	SO	HBP	SH	SF	SB	CS	SB%	GIDP	AVE	OBP	SLG
1986	Milwaukee	A	58	215	51	8	2	4	(2	2)	75	19	18	11	0	47	1	2	3	1	1	.50	6	.237	.274	.349

MICKEY BRANTLEY

Bats Right-handed, Throws Right-handed   Turns Age 26 in 1987, Born 06/17/61

Year	Team	League	G	AB	H	2B	3B	HR	(Hm	Rd)	TB	R	RBI	TBB	IBB	SO	HBP	SH	SF	SB	CS	SB%	GIDP	AVE	OBP	SLG
1986	Seattle	A	27	102	20	3	2	3	(2	1)	36	12	7	10	0	21	0	1	0	1	1	.50	3	.196	.268	.353

SID BREAM

Bats Left-handed, Throws Left-handed   Turns Age 27 in 1987, Born 08/03/60

Year	Team	League	G	AB	H	2B	3B	HR	(Hm	Rd)	TB	R	RBI	TBB	IBB	SO	HBP	SH	SF	SB	CS	SB%	GIDP	AVE	OBP	SLG
1983	Los Angeles	N	15	11	2	0	0	0	(0	0)	2	0	2	2	0	2	0	0	0	0	0	.00	1	.182	.308	.182
1984	Los Angeles	N	27	49	9	3	0	0	(0	0)	12	2	6	6	2	9	0	1	2	1	0	1.00	1	.184	.263	.245
1985	2 Teams	N	50	148	34	7	0	6	(2	4)	59	18	21	18	5	24	0	3	2	0	2	.00	4	.230	.310	.399
1986	Pittsburgh	N	154	522	140	37	5	16	(5	11)	235	73	77	60	5	73	1	1	7	13	7	.65	14	.268	.341	.450
4 YEARS			246	730	185	47	5	22	(7	15)	308	93	106	86	12	108	1	5	11	14	9	.61	20	.253	.329	.422
1985	Los Angeles	N	24	53	7	0	0	3	(2	1)	16	4	6	7	3	10	0	2	1	0	0	.00	0	.132	.230	.302
1985	Pittsburgh	N	26	95	27	7	0	3	(0	3)	43	14	15	11	2	14	0	1	1	0	2	.00	4	.284	.355	.453

ROBERT BRENLY

Bats Right-handed, Throws Right-handed   Turns Age 33 in 1987, Born 02/25/54

Year	Team	League	G	AB	H	2B	3B	HR	(Hm	Rd)	TB	R	RBI	TBB	IBB	SO	HBP	SH	SF	SB	CS	SB%	GIDP	AVE	OBP	SLG
1981	San Francisco	N	19	45	15	2	1	1	(0	0)	22	5	4	6	0	4	1	0	0	0	1	.00	1	.333	.423	.489
1982	San Francisco	N	65	180	51	4	1	4	(1	3)	69	26	15	18	4	26	1	1	2	6	2	.75	2	.283	.348	.383
1983	San Francisco	N	104	281	63	12	2	7	(5	2)	100	36	34	37	6	48	2	1	2	10	7	.59	12	.224	.317	.356
1984	San Francisco	N	145	506	147	28	0	20	(6	14)	235	74	80	48	3	52	3	4	6	6	9	.40	14	.291	.352	.464
1985	San Francisco	N	133	440	97	16	1	19	(9	10)	172	41	56	57	5	62	2	4	2	1	4	.20	6	.220	.311	.391
1986	San Francisco	N	149	472	116	26	0	16	(8	8)	190	60	62	74	10	97	3	5	3	10	6	.63	4	.246	.350	.403
6 YEARS			615	1924	489	88	5	67	(29	37)	788	242	251	240	28	289	12	15	15	33	29	.53	39	.254	.338	.410

GEORGE BRETT

Bats Left-handed, Throws Right-handed

Turns Age 34 in 1987, Born 05/15/53

			BATTING										BASERUNNING				PERCENTAGES		
Year Team	League	G	AB	H	2B	3B	HR	(Hm Rd)	TB	R	RBI	TBB	IBB	SO	HBP	SH	SF	SB	CS	SB%	GIDP	AVE	OBP	SLG

Year Team	League	G	AB	H	2B	3B	HR	(Hm	Rd)	TB	R	RBI	TBB	IBB	SO	HBP	SH	SF	SB	CS	SB%	GIDP	AVE	OBP	SLG
1973 Kansas City	A	13	40	5	2	0	0	(0	0)	7	2	0	0	0	5	0	1	0	0	0	.00	0	.125	.125	.175
1974 Kansas City	A	133	457	129	21	5	2	(0	2)	166	49	47	21	3	38	0	6	2	8	5	.62	9	.282	.313	.363
1975 Kansas City	A	159	634	195	35	13	11	(2	9)	289	84	89	46	6	49	2	9	6	13	10	.57	8	.308	.353	.456
1976 Kansas City	A	159	645	215	34	14	7	(6	1)	298	94	67	49	4	36	1	2	8	21	11	.66	8	.333	.377	.462
1977 Kansas City	A	139	564	176	32	13	22	(9	13)	300	105	88	55	9	24	2	3	3	14	12	.54	12	.312	.373	.532
1978 Kansas City	A	128	510	150	45	8	9	(4	5)	238	79	62	39	6	35	1	3	5	23	7	.77	6	.294	.342	.467
1979 Kansas City	A	154	645	212	42	20	23	(11	12)	363	119	107	51	14	36	0	1	4	17	10	.63	8	.329	.376	.563
1980 Kansas City	A	117	449	175	33	9	24	(13	11)	298	87	118	58	16	22	1	0	7	15	6	.71	11	.390	.454	.664
1981 Kansas City	A	89	347	109	27	7	6	(2	4)	168	42	43	27	7	23	1	0	4	14	6	.70	7	.314	.361	.484
1982 Kansas City	A	144	552	166	32	9	21	(9	12)	279	101	82	71	14	51	1	0	5	6	1	.86	12	.301	.378	.505
1983 Kansas City	A	123	464	144	38	2	25	(7	18)	261	90	93	57	13	39	1	0	3	0	1	.00	9	.310	.385	.563
1984 Kansas City	A	104	377	107	21	3	13	(6	7)	173	42	69	38	6	37	0	0	7	0	1	.00	11	.284	.344	.459
1985 Kansas City	A	155	550	184	38	5	30	(15	15)	322	108	112	103	31	49	3	0	9	9	1	.90	12	.335	.436	.585
1986 Kansas City	A	124	441	128	28	4	16	(8	8)	212	70	73	80	18	45	4	0	4	1	2	.33	6	.290	.401	.481
14 YEARS		1741	6675	2095	428	112	209	(92	117)	3374	1072	1050	695	147	489	17	25	67	141	73	.66	119	.314	.377	.505

GREG BROCK

Bats Left-handed, Throws Right-handed

Turns Age 30 in 1987, Born 06/14/57

Year Team	League	G	AB	H	2B	3B	HR	(Hm	Rd)	TB	R	RBI	TBB	IBB	SO	HBP	SH	SF	SB	CS	SB%	GIDP	AVE	OBP	SLG
1982 Los Angeles	N	18	17	2	1	0	0	(0	0)	3	1	1	1	1	5	0	0	0	0	0	.00	0	.118	.167	.176
1983 Los Angeles	N	146	455	102	14	2	20	(14	6)	180	64	66	83	12	81	1	0	4	5	1	.83	13	.224	.343	.396
1984 Los Angeles	N	88	271	61	6	0	14	(8	6)	109	33	34	39	3	37	0	0	3	2	0	1.00	6	.225	.319	.402
1985 Los Angeles	N	129	438	110	19	0	21	(7	14)	192	64	66	54	4	72	0	2	2	4	2	.67	9	.251	.332	.438
1986 Los Angeles	N	115	325	76	13	0	16	(5	11)	137	33	52	37	5	60	0	1	4	2	5	.29	5	.234	.309	.422
5 YEARS		496	1506	351	53	2	71	(34	37)	621	195	219	214	25	255	1	3	13	19	8	.70	33	.233	.326	.412

TOM BROOKENS

Bats Right-handed, Throws Right-handed

Turns Age 34 in 1987, Born 08/10/53

Year Team	League	G	AB	H	2B	3B	HR	(Hm	Rd)	TB	R	RBI	TBB	IBB	SO	HBP	SH	SF	SB	CS	SB%	GIDP	AVE	OBP	SLG
1979 Detroit	A	60	190	50	5	2	4	(3	1)	71	23	21	11	0	40	2	4	1	10	3	.77	3	.263	.309	.374
1980 Detroit	A	151	509	140	25	9	10	(7	3)	213	64	66	32	3	71	1	2	7	13	11	.54	10	.275	.315	.418
1981 Detroit	A	71	239	58	10	1	4	(3	1)	82	19	25	14	0	43	2	4	6	5	3	.63	5	.243	.284	.343
1982 Detroit	A	140	398	92	15	3	9	(4	5)	140	40	58	27	0	63	0	2	5	5	9	.36	9	.231	.277	.352
1983 Detroit	A	138	332	71	13	3	6	(5	1)	108	50	32	29	2	46	2	5	6	10	4	.71	3	.214	.276	.325
1984 Detroit	A	113	224	55	11	4	5	(4	1)	89	32	26	19	0	33	1	8	1	6	6	.50	2	.246	.306	.397
1985 Detroit	A	156	485	115	34	6	7	(3	4)	182	54	47	27	0	78	0	9	1	14	5	.74	8	.237	.277	.375
1986 Detroit	A	98	281	76	11	2	3	(2	1)	100	42	25	20	0	42	1	6	2	11	8	.58	4	.270	.319	.356
8 YEARS		927	2658	657	124	30	48	(31	17)	985	324	300	179	5	416	9	40	29	74	49	.60	44	.247	.294	.371

HUBIE BROOKS

Bats Right-handed, Throws Right-handed

Turns Age 31 in 1987, Born 09/24/56

Year Team	League	G	AB	H	2B	3B	HR	(Hm	Rd)	TB	R	RBI	TBB	IBB	SO	HBP	SH	SF	SB	CS	SB%	GIDP	AVE	OBP	SLG
1980 New York	N	24	81	25	2	1	1	(0	1)	32	8	10	5	0	9	2	1	0	1	1	.50	1	.309	.364	.395
1981 New York	N	98	358	110	21	2	4	(2	2)	147	34	38	23	2	65	1	1	6	9	5	.64	9	.307	.345	.411
1982 New York	N	126	457	114	21	2	2	(1	1)	145	40	40	28	5	76	5	3	5	6	3	.67	11	.249	.297	.317
1983 New York	N	150	586	147	18	4	5	(4	1)	188	53	58	24	2	96	4	7	3	6	4	.60	14	.251	.284	.321
1984 New York	N	153	561	159	23	2	16	(12	4)	234	61	73	48	15	79	2	0	2	6	5	.55	17	.283	.341	.417
1985 Montreal	N	156	605	163	34	7	13	(4	9)	250	67	100	34	6	79	5	0	8	6	9	.40	20	.269	.310	.413
1986 Montreal	N	80	306	104	18	5	14	(3	11)	174	50	58	25	3	60	2	0	5	4	2	.67	11	.340	.388	.569
7 YEARS		787	2954	822	137	23	55	(26	29)	1170	313	377	187	33	464	21	12	29	38	29	.57	83	.278	.323	.396

CHRIS BROWN

Bats Right-handed, Throws Right-handed

Turns Age 26 in 1987, Born 08/15/61

Year Team	League	G	AB	H	2B	3B	HR	(Hm	Rd)	TB	R	RBI	TBB	IBB	SO	HBP	SH	SF	SB	CS	SB%	GIDP	AVE	OBP	SLG
1984 San Francisco	N	23	84	24	7	0	1	(0	1)	34	6	11	9	0	19	1	0	1	2	1	.67	4	.286	.358	.405
1985 San Francisco	N	131	432	117	20	3	16	(5	11)	191	50	61	38	4	78	11	1	0	2	3	.40	19	.271	.345	.442
1986 San Francisco	N	116	416	132	16	3	7	(3	4)	175	57	49	33	4	43	9	0	5	13	9	.59	9	.317	.376	.421
3 YEARS		270	932	273	43	6	24	(8	16)	400	113	121	80	8	140	21	1	6	17	13	.57	32	.293	.360	.429

MIKE C. BROWN

Bats Right-handed, Throws Right-handed   **Turns Age 28 in 1987, Born 12/29/59**

									BATTING										BASERUNNING				PERCENTAGES		
Year	Team	League	G	AB	H	2B	3B	HR	(Hm	Rd)	TB	R	RBI	TBB	IBB	SO	HBP	SH	SF	SB	CS	SB%	GIDP	AVE	OBP	SLG
1983	California	A	31	104	24	5	1	3	(0	0)	40	12	9	7	0	20	0	0	0	1	0	1.00	2	.231	.279	.385
1984	California	A	62	148	42	8	3	7	(0	0)	77	19	22	13	1	23	0	2	0	0	2	.00	8	.284	.342	.520
1985	2 Teams		117	358	109	27	3	9	(0	0)	169	52	53	29	4	48	1	6	3	2	3	.40	16	.304	.355	.472
1986	Pittsburgh	N	87	243	53	7	0	4	(1	3)	72	18	26	27	3	32	0	0	3	2	3	.40	9	.218	.293	.296
4 YEARS			297	853	228	47	7	23	(1	3)	358	101	110	76	8	123	1	8	6	5	8	.38	35	.267	.326	.420
1985	California	A	60	153	41	9	1	4	(0	0)	64	23	20	7	0	21	1	3	0	0	1	.00	9	.268	.304	.418
1985	Pittsburgh	N	57	205	68	18	2	5	(0	0)	105	29	33	22	4	27	0	3	3	2	2	.50	7	.332	.391	.512

MIKE G. BROWN

Pitches Right-handed, Bats Right-handed   **Turns Age 28 in 1987, Born 03/04/59**

			HOW MUCH HE PITCHED						WHAT HE GAVE UP												THE RESULTS					
Year	Team	League	G	GS	CG	GF	IP	BFP	H	R	ER	HR	SH	SF	HB	TBB	IBB	SO	WP	Bk	W	L	Pct	ShO	Sv	ERA
1982	Boston	A	3	0	0	3	6	24	7	0	0	0	0	0	0	1	0	4	0	0	1	0	1.000	0	0	0.00
1983	Boston	A	19	18	3	0	104	454	110	62	54	12	5	6	2	43	1	35	4	4	6	6	.500	1	0	4.67
1984	Boston	A	15	11	0	2	67	326	104	63	51	9	1	3	3	19	1	32	4	2	1	8	.111	0	0	6.85
1985	Boston	A	2	1	0	0	3.1	22	9	8	8	0	0	1	0	3	0	3	0	1	0	0	.000	0	0	21.60
1986	2 Teams		21	12	0	2	73	334	91	49	47	14	3	3	1	36	1	41	4	1	4	6	.400	0	0	5.79
5 YEARS			60	42	3	7	253.1	1160	321	182	160	35	9	13	6	102	3	115	12	8	12	20	.375	1	0	5.68
1986	Boston	A	15	10	0	2	57.1	260	72	35	34	10	3	3	1	25	1	32	3	0	4	4	.500	0	0	5.34
1986	Seattle	A	6	2	0	0	15.2	74	19	14	13	4	0	0	0	11	0	9	1	1	0	2	.000	0	0	7.47

TOM BROWNING

Pitches Left-handed, Bats Left-handed   **Turns Age 27 in 1987, Born 04/28/60**

			HOW MUCH HE PITCHED						WHAT HE GAVE UP												THE RESULTS					
Year	Team	League	G	GS	CG	GF	IP	BFP	H	R	ER	HR	SH	SF	HB	TBB	IBB	SO	WP	Bk	W	L	Pct	ShO	Sv	ERA
1984	Cincinnati	N	3	3	0	0	23.1	95	27	4	4	0	1	0	0	5	0	14	1	0	1	0	1.000	0	0	1.54
1985	Cincinnati	N	38	38	6	0	261.1	1083	242	111	103	29	13	7	3	73	8	155	2	0	20	9	.690	4	0	3.55
1986	Cincinnati	N	39	39	4	0	243.1	1016	225	123	103	26	14	12	1	70	6	147	3	0	14	13	.519	2	0	3.81
3 YEARS			80	80	10	0	528	2194	494	238	210	55	28	19	4	148	14	316	6	0	35	22	.614	6	0	3.58

TOM BRUNANSKY

Bats Right-handed, Throws Right-handed   **Turns Age 27 in 1987, Born 08/20/60**

									BATTING										BASERUNNING				PERCENTAGES		
Year	Team	League	G	AB	H	2B	3B	HR	(Hm	Rd)	TB	R	RBI	TBB	IBB	SO	HBP	SH	SF	SB	CS	SB%	GIDP	AVE	OBP	SLG
1981	California	A	11	33	5	0	0	3	(1	2)	14	7	6	8	0	10	0	0	0	1	0	1.00	0	.152	.317	.424
1982	Minnesota	A	127	463	126	30	1	20	(10	10)	218	77	46	71	0	101	8	1	2	1	2	.33	12	.272	.377	.471
1983	Minnesota	A	151	542	123	24	5	28	(8	20)	241	70	82	61	4	95	4	1	3	2	5	.29	13	.227	.308	.445
1984	Minnesota	A	155	567	144	21	0	32	(14	18)	261	75	85	57	2	94	0	0	4	4	5	.44	15	.254	.320	.460
1985	Minnesota	A	157	567	137	28	4	27	(12	15)	254	71	90	71	7	86	0	0	13	5	3	.63	12	.242	.320	.448
1986	Minnesota	A	157	593	152	28	1	23	(15	8)	251	69	75	53	4	98	1	1	7	12	4	.75	15	.256	.315	.423
6 YEARS			758	2765	687	131	11	133	(60	73)	1239	369	384	321	17	484	13	3	29	25	19	.57	67	.248	.326	.448

T.R. BRYDEN

Pitches Right-handed, Bats Right-handed   **Turns Age 28 in 1987, Born 01/17/59**

			HOW MUCH HE PITCHED						WHAT HE GAVE UP												THE RESULTS					
Year	Team	League	G	GS	CG	GF	IP	BFP	H	R	ER	HR	SH	SF	HB	TBB	IBB	SO	WP	Bk	W	L	Pct	ShO	Sv	ERA
1986	California	A	16	0	0	7	34.1	159	38	25	25	4	1	4	2	21	0	25	2	0	2	1	.667	0	0	6.55

BILL BUCKNER

Bats Left-handed, Throws Left-handed　　　　　　　　　　　　　　　　　　　　Turns Age 38 in 1987, Born 12/14/49

Year	Team	League	G	AB	H	2B	3B	HR	(Hm	Rd)	TB	R	RBI	TBB	IBB	SO	HBP	SH	SF	SB	CS	SB%	GIDP	AVE	OBP	SLG
1969	Los Angeles	N	1	1	0	0	0	0	(0	0)	0	0	0	0	0	0	0	0	0	0	0	.00	0	.000	.000	.000
1970	Los Angeles	N	28	68	13	3	1	0	(0	0)	18	6	4	3	1	7	0	0	0	0	1	.00	6	.191	.225	.265
1971	Los Angeles	N	108	358	99	15	1	5	(2	3)	131	37	41	11	4	18	5	7	2	4	1	.80	6	.277	.306	.366
1972	Los Angeles	N	105	383	122	14	3	5	(1	4)	157	47	37	17	2	13	1	3	1	10	3	.77	13	.319	.348	.410
1973	Los Angeles	N	140	575	158	20	0	8	(4	4)	202	68	46	17	5	34	3	6	5	12	2	.86	15	.275	.297	.351
1974	Los Angeles	N	145	580	182	30	3	7	(3	4)	239	83	58	30	10	24	4	4	2	31	13	.70	13	.314	.351	.412
1975	Los Angeles	N	92	288	70	11	2	6	(3	3)	103	30	31	17	7	15	2	4	4	8	3	.73	11	.243	.286	.358
1976	Los Angeles	N	154	642	193	28	4	7	(4	3)	250	76	60	26	6	26	1	6	5	28	9	.76	8	.301	.326	.389
1977	Chicago	N	122	426	121	27	0	11	(7	4)	181	40	60	21	2	23	1	2	7	7	5	.58	16	.284	.314	.425
1978	Chicago	N	117	446	144	26	1	5	(3	2)	187	47	74	18	5	17	0	1	5	7	5	.58	16	.323	.345	.419
1979	Chicago	N	149	591	168	34	7	14	(8	6)	258	72	66	30	6	28	2	1	4	9	4	.69	16	.284	.319	.437
1980	Chicago	N	145	578	187	41	3	10	(3	7)	264	69	68	30	11	18	0	0	6	1	2	.33	13	.324	.353	.457
1981	Chicago	N	106	421	131	35	3	10	(7	3)	202	45	75	26	9	16	1	0	5	5	2	.71	17	.311	.349	.480
1982	Chicago	N	161	657	201	34	5	15	(9	6)	290	93	105	36	7	26	5	1	10	15	5	.75	14	.306	.342	.441
1983	Chicago	N	153	626	175	38	6	16	(6	10)	273	79	66	25	5	30	5	4	5	12	4	.75	10	.280	.310	.436
1984	2 Teams		135	482	131	21	2	11	(6	5)	189	54	69	25	6	39	6	0	4	2	2	.50	12	.272	.313	.392
1985	Boston	A	162	673	201	46	3	16	(6	10)	301	89	110	30	5	36	2	2	11	18	4	.82	16	.299	.325	.447
1986	Boston	A	153	629	168	39	2	18	(8	10)	265	73	102	40	9	25	4	0	8	6	4	.60	25	.267	.311	.421
18 YEARS			2176	8424	2464	462	46	164	(80	84)	3510	1008	1072	402	100	395	42	41	84	175	69	.72	221	.292	.325	.417
1984	Boston	A	114	439	122	21	2	11	(6	5)	180	51	67	24	5	38	5	0	3	2	2	.50	11	.278	.321	.410
1984	Chicago	N	21	43	9	0	0	0	(0	0)	9	3	2	1	1	1	1	0	1	0	0	.00	1	.209	.239	.209

STEVE BUECHELE

Bats Right-handed, Throws Right-handed　　　　　　　　　　　　　　　　　　　　Turns Age 26 in 1987, Born 09/24/61

Year	Team	League	G	AB	H	2B	3B	HR	(Hm	Rd)	TB	R	RBI	TBB	IBB	SO	HBP	SH	SF	SB	CS	SB%	GIDP	AVE	OBP	SLG
1985	Texas	A	69	219	48	6	3	6	(5	1)	78	22	21	14	2	38	2	0	1	3	2	.60	11	.219	.271	.356
1986	Texas	A	153	461	112	19	2	18	(6	12)	189	54	54	35	1	98	5	9	3	5	8	.38	10	.243	.302	.410
2 YEARS			222	680	160	25	5	24	(11	13)	267	76	75	49	3	136	7	9	4	8	10	.44	21	.235	.292	.393

TIM BURKE

Pitches Right-handed, Bats Right-handed　　　　　　　　　　　　　　　　　　　　Turns Age 28 in 1987, Born 02/19/59

Year	Team	League	G	GS	CG	GF	IP	BFP	H	R	ER	HR	SH	SF	HB	TBB	IBB	SO	WP	Bk	W	L	Pct	ShO	Sv	ERA
1985	Montreal	N	78	0	0	31	120.1	483	86	32	32	9	8	3	7	44	14	87	7	0	9	4	.692	0	8	2.39
1986	Montreal	N	68	2	0	25	101.1	451	103	37	33	7	6	2	4	46	13	82	4	0	9	7	.563	0	4	2.93
2 YEARS			146	2	0	56	221.2	934	189	69	65	16	14	5	11	90	27	169	11	0	18	11	.621	0	12	2.64

RICK BURLESON

Bats Right-handed, Throws Right-handed　　　　　　　　　　　　　　　　　　　　Turns Age 36 in 1987, Born 04/29/51

Year	Team	League	G	AB	H	2B	3B	HR	(Hm	Rd)	TB	R	RBI	TBB	IBB	SO	HBP	SH	SF	SB	CS	SB%	GIDP	AVE	OBP	SLG
1974	Boston	A	114	384	109	22	0	4	(3	1)	143	36	44	21	0	34	2	3	5	3	3	.50	13	.284	.320	.372
1975	Boston	A	158	580	146	25	1	6	(3	3)	191	66	62	45	1	44	3	17	9	8	5	.62	18	.252	.305	.329
1976	Boston	A	152	540	157	27	1	7	(3	4)	207	75	42	60	2	37	5	8	3	14	9	.61	15	.291	.365	.383
1977	Boston	A	154	663	194	36	7	3	(2	1)	253	80	52	47	1	69	2	3	6	13	12	.52	15	.293	.338	.382
1978	Boston	A	145	626	155	32	5	5	(3	2)	212	75	49	40	2	71	4	10	5	8	8	.50	16	.248	.295	.339
1979	Boston	A	153	627	174	32	5	5	(4	1)	231	93	60	35	0	54	3	9	8	9	5	.64	13	.278	.315	.368
1980	Boston	A	155	644	179	29	2	8	(3	5)	236	89	51	62	0	51	2	6	4	12	13	.48	24	.278	.341	.366
1981	California	A	109	430	126	17	1	5	(2	3)	160	53	33	42	2	38	3	11	4	4	6	.40	8	.293	.357	.372
1982	California	A	11	45	7	1	0	0	(0	0)	8	4	2	6	2	3	0	2	0	0	0	.00	2	.156	.255	.178
1983	California	A	33	119	34	7	0	0	(0	0)	41	22	11	12	0	12	0	2	1	0	0	.00	5	.286	.348	.345
1984	California	A	7	4	0	0	0	0	(0	0)	0	2	0	0	0	2	0	1	0	0	0	.00	0	.000	.000	.000
1986	California	A	93	271	77	14	0	5	(2	3)	106	35	29	33	2	32	1	6	1	1	3	.25	2	.284	.363	.391
12 YEARS			1284	4933	1358	242	22	48	(25	23)	1788	630	435	403	12	447	25	78	46	72	66	.52	131	.275	.330	.362

RAY BURRIS

Pitches Right-handed, Bats Right-handed   Turns Age 37 in 1987, Born 08/22/50

| | | | HOW MUCH HE PITCHED | | | | | | WHAT HE GAVE UP | | | | | | | | | | THE RESULTS | | | | | |
Year	Team	League	G	GS	CG	GF	IP	BFP	H	R	ER	HR	SH	SF	HB	TBB	IBB	SO	WP	Bk	W	L	Pct	ShO	Sv	ERA
1973	Chicago	N	31	1	0	12	65	282	65	22	21	4	2	0	0	27	7	57	3	0	1	1	.500	0	0	2.91
1974	Chicago	N	40	5	0	14	75	344	91	61	55	8	7	4	4	26	6	40	10	3	3	5	.375	0	1	6.60
1975	Chicago	N	36	35	8	1	238	1020	259	121	109	25	13	9	4	73	6	108	2	2	15	10	.600	2	0	4.12
1976	Chicago	N	37	36	10	0	249	1053	251	102	86	22	18	5	5	70	5	112	7	1	15	13	.536	4	0	3.11
1977	Chicago	N	39	39	5	0	221	970	270	132	116	29	11	4	3	67	9	105	8	0	14	16	.467	1	0	4.72
1978	Chicago	N	40	32	4	3	199	870	210	112	105	15	7	7	10	79	11	94	6	3	7	13	.350	1	1	4.75
1979	3 Teams		33	4	0	10	71.1	323	84	49	42	7	4	3	2	31	5	43	2	0	1	5	.167	0	0	5.30
1980	New York	N	29	29	1	0	170	726	181	86	76	20	8	7	4	54	5	83	5	2	7	13	.350	0	0	4.02
1981	Montreal	N	22	21	4	0	136	554	117	56	46	9	6	6	3	41	3	52	6	1	9	7	.563	0	0	3.04
1982	Montreal	N	37	15	2	9	123.2	550	177	77	65	14	8	6	2	53	7	55	3	0	4	14	.222	0	2	4.73
1983	Montreal	N	40	17	2	6	154	641	139	68	63	13	9	5	2	56	4	100	2	1	4	7	.364	1	0	3.68
1984	Oakland	A	34	28	5	3	211.2	900	193	84	74	15	4	6	8	90	1	93	6	1	13	10	.565	1	0	3.15
1985	Milwaukee	A	29	28	6	0	170.1	738	182	95	91	25	6	3	3	53	0	81	7	0	9	13	.409	0	0	4.81
1986	St Louis	N	23	10	0	5	82	361	92	52	51	13	4	0	4	32	4	34	0	0	4	5	.444	0	0	5.60
14 YEARS			470	300	47	63	2166	9332	2277	1117	1000	217	109	70	54	752	73	1057	67	14	106	132	.445	10	4	4.16
1979	New York	A	15	0	0	7	28	132	40	22	19	5	3	2	0	10	1	19	1	0	1	3	.250	0	0	6.11
1979	Chicago	N	14	0	0	3	21.2	98	23	17	15	0	0	1	1	15	1	14	0	0	0	0	.000	0	0	6.23
1979	New York	N	4	4	0	0	21.2	93	21	10	8	2	1	0	1	6	3	10	1	0	0	2	.000	0	0	3.32

RANDY BUSH

Bats Left-handed, Throws Left-handed   Turns Age 29 in 1987, Born 10/05/58

| | | | BATTING | | | | | | | | | | | | | | | | BASERUNNING | | | | PERCENTAGES | | |
Year	Team	League	G	AB	H	2B	3B	HR	(Hm	Rd)	TB	R	RBI	TBB	IBB	SO	HBP	SH	SF	SB	CS	SB%	GIDP	AVE	OBP	SLG
1982	Minnesota	A	55	119	29	6	1	4	(2	2)	49	13	13	8	0	28	3	0	1	0	0	.00	1	.244	.305	.412
1983	Minnesota	A	124	373	93	24	3	11	(4	7)	156	43	56	34	8	51	7	0	1	0	1	1.00	7	.249	.323	.418
1984	Minnesota	A	113	311	69	17	1	11	(8	3)	121	46	43	31	6	60	4	0	10	1	2	.33	1	.222	.292	.389
1985	Minnesota	A	97	234	56	13	3	10	(5	5)	105	26	35	24	1	30	5	0	2	3	0	1.00	3	.239	.321	.449
1986	Minnesota	A	130	357	96	19	7	7	(6	1)	150	50	45	39	2	63	4	1	1	5	3	.63	7	.269	.347	.420
5 YEARS			519	1394	343	79	15	43	(25	18)	581	178	192	136	17	232	23	1	15	9	6	.60	19	.246	.320	.417

JOHN BUTCHER

Pitches Right-handed, Bats Right-handed   Turns Age 30 in 1987, Born 03/08/57

| | | | HOW MUCH HE PITCHED | | | | | | WHAT HE GAVE UP | | | | | | | | | | THE RESULTS | | | | | |
Year	Team	League	G	GS	CG	GF	IP	BFP	H	R	ER	HR	SH	SF	HB	TBB	IBB	SO	WP	Bk	W	L	Pct	ShO	Sv	ERA
1980	Texas	A	6	6	1	0	35	152	34	19	16	2	2	0	0	13	0	27	1	0	3	3	.500	0	0	4.11
1981	Texas	A	5	3	1	1	28	106	18	6	5	0	1	0	0	8	1	19	0	0	1	2	.333	1	0	1.61
1982	Texas	A	18	13	2	3	94.1	406	102	53	51	10	2	4	2	34	4	39	0	0	1	5	.167	0	1	4.87
1983	Texas	A	38	6	1	14	123	522	128	50	48	8	4	2	1	41	4	58	4	0	6	6	.500	1	5	3.51
1984	Minnesota	A	34	34	8	0	225	944	242	98	86	18	1	9	4	53	5	83	3	0	13	11	.542	1	0	3.44
1985	Minnesota	A	34	33	8	0	207.2	893	239	125	115	24	6	10	6	43	4	92	5	1	11	14	.440	2	0	4.98
1986	2 Teams		29	18	2	5	120.2	554	168	93	88	17	2	6	4	37	1	45	6	0	1	8	.111	1	0	6.56
7 YEARS			164	113	23	23	833.2	3577	931	444	409	79	18	31	17	229	19	363	19	1	36	49	.424	6	6	4.42
1986	Cleveland	A	13	8	1	4	50.2	246	86	43	39	6	1	3	3	13	0	16	2	0	1	5	.167	1	0	6.93
1986	Minnesota	A	16	10	1	1	70	308	82	50	49	11	1	3	1	24	1	29	4	0	0	3	.000	0	0	6.30

SAL BUTERA

Bats Right-handed, Throws Right-handed   Turns Age 35 in 1987, Born 09/25/52

| | | | BATTING | | | | | | | | | | | | | | | | BASERUNNING | | | | PERCENTAGES | | |
Year	Team	League	G	AB	H	2B	3B	HR	(Hm	Rd)	TB	R	RBI	TBB	IBB	SO	HBP	SH	SF	SB	CS	SB%	GIDP	AVE	OBP	SLG
1980	Minnesota	A	34	85	23	2	0	0	(0	0)	24	4	2	3	0	6	1	1	1	0	0	.00	4	.271	.300	.282
1981	Minnesota	A	62	167	40	7	1	0	(0	0)	49	13	18	22	0	14	0	3	2	0	0	.00	6	.240	.325	.293
1982	Minnesota	A	54	126	32	2	0	0	(0	0)	34	9	8	17	0	12	1	2	0	0	0	.00	8	.254	.347	.270
1983	Detroit	A	4	5	1	0	0	0	(0	0)	1	1	0	0	0	0	0	0	0	0	0	.00	0	.200	.200	.200
1984	Montreal	N	3	3	0	0	0	0	(0	0)	0	0	0	1	0	0	0	0	0	0	0	.00	0	.000	.250	.000
1985	Montreal	N	67	120	24	1	0	3	(0	3)	34	11	12	13	1	12	1	3	1	0	0	.00	1	.200	.281	.283
1986	Cincinnati	N	56	113	27	6	1	2	(0	2)	41	14	16	21	3	10	0	2	1	0	0	.00	5	.239	.356	.363
7 YEARS			280	619	147	17	2	5	(0	5)	183	52	56	77	4	54	3	11	5	0	0	.00	24	.237	.322	.296

BRETT BUTLER

Bats Left-handed, Throws Left-handed   Turns Age 30 in 1987, Born 06/15/57

| | | | BATTING | | | | | | | | | | | | | | | | BASERUNNING | | | | PERCENTAGES | | |
Year	Team	League	G	AB	H	2B	3B	HR	(Hm	Rd)	TB	R	RBI	TBB	IBB	SO	HBP	SH	SF	SB	CS	SB%	GIDP	AVE	OBP	SLG
1981	Atlanta	N	40	126	32	2	3	0	(0	0)	40	17	4	19	0	17	0	0	9	1	.90	0	.254	.352	.317
1982	Atlanta	N	89	240	52	2	0	0	(0	0)	54	35	7	25	0	35	0	3	21	8	.72	1	.217	.291	.225
1983	Atlanta	N	151	549	154	21	13	5	(4	1)	216	84	37	54	3	56	2	5	39	23	.63	5	.281	.344	.393
1984	Cleveland	A	159	602	162	25	9	3	(1	2)	214	108	49	86	1	62	4	11	52	22	.70	6	.269	.361	.355
1985	Cleveland	A	152	591	184	28	14	5	(1	4)	255	106	50	63	2	42	1	8	47	20	.70	3	.311	.377	.431
1986	Cleveland	A	161	587	163	17	14	4	(0	4)	220	92	51	70	1	65	4	17	32	15	.68	8	.278	.356	.375
6 YEARS			752	2695	747	95	53	17	(6	11)	999	442	198	317	7	277	11	42	200	89	.69	28	.277	.353	.371

ENOS CABELL

Bats Right-handed, Throws Right-handed   Turns Age 38 in 1987, Born 10/08/49

Year	Team	League	G	AB	H	2B	3B	HR	(Hm	Rd)	TB	R	RBI	TBB	IBB	SO	HBP	SH	SF	SB	CS	SB%	GIDP	AVE	OBP	SLG
1972	Baltimore	A	3	5	0	0	0	0	(0	0)	0	0	1	0	0	0	0	0	0	0	0	.00	0	.000	.000	.000
1973	Baltimore	A	32	47	10	2	0	1	(1	0)	15	12	3	3	0	7	0	1	2	1	3	.25	1	.213	.250	.319
1974	Baltimore	A	80	174	42	4	2	3	(0	3)	59	24	17	7	1	20	0	1	1	5	3	.63	6	.241	.269	.339
1975	Houston	N	117	348	92	17	6	2	(1	1)	127	43	43	18	1	53	3	1	4	12	3	.80	9	.264	.303	.365
1976	Houston	N	144	586	160	13	7	2	(1	1)	193	85	43	29	1	79	2	3	2	35	8	.81	13	.273	.309	.329
1977	Houston	N	150	625	176	36	7	16	(7	9)	274	101	68	27	2	55	3	2	3	42	22	.66	8	.282	.313	.438
1978	Houston	N	162	660	195	31	8	7	(2	5)	263	92	71	22	1	80	5	3	4	33	15	.69	14	.295	.321	.398
1979	Houston	N	155	603	164	30	5	6	(1	5)	222	60	67	21	7	68	3	2	1	37	18	.67	18	.272	.299	.368
1980	Houston	N	152	604	167	23	8	2	(0	2)	212	69	55	26	6	84	1	1	5	21	13	.62	13	.276	.305	.351
1981	San Francisco	N	96	396	101	20	1	2	(0	2)	129	41	36	10	0	47	1	4	2	6	7	.46	6	.255	.274	.326
1982	Detroit	A	125	464	121	17	3	2	(2	0)	150	45	37	15	2	48	1	2	2	15	6	.71	10	.261	.284	.323
1983	Detroit	A	121	392	122	23	5	5	(1	4)	170	62	46	16	2	41	1	5	6	4	8	.33	14	.311	.335	.434
1984	Houston	N	127	436	135	17	3	8	(2	6)	182	52	44	21	5	47	1	3	3	8	11	.42	12	.310	.341	.417
1985	2 Teams		117	335	91	19	1	2	(1	1)	118	40	36	30	1	36	0	2	0	9	3	.75	5	.272	.332	.352
1986	Los Angeles	N	107	277	71	11	0	2	(2	0)	88	27	29	14	2	26	2	2	3	10	4	.71	5	.256	.294	.318
15 YEARS			1688	5952	1647	263	56	60	(21	39)	2202	753	596	259	31	691	23	32	38	238	124	.66	134	.277	.308	.370
1985	Houston	N	60	143	35	8	1	2	(1	1)	51	20	14	16	0	15	0	0	0	3	1	.75	5	.245	.321	.357
1985	Los Angeles	N	57	192	56	11	0	0	(0	0)	67	20	22	14	1	21	0	2	0	6	2	.75	0	.292	.340	.349

IVAN CALDERON

Bats Right-handed, Throws Right-handed   Turns Age 25 in 1987, Born 03/19/62

Year	Team	League	G	AB	H	2B	3B	HR	(Hm	Rd)	TB	R	RBI	TBB	IBB	SO	HBP	SH	SF	SB	CS	SB%	GIDP	AVE	OBP	SLG
1984	Seattle	A	11	24	5	1	0	1	(0	1)	9	2	1	2	0	5	0	0	0	1	0	1.00	3	.208	.269	.375
1985	Seattle	A	67	210	60	16	4	8	(6	2)	108	37	28	19	1	45	2	1	1	4	2	.67	10	.286	.349	.514
1986	2 Teams		50	164	41	7	1	2	(0	0)	56	16	15	9	1	39	1	0	0	3	1	.75	1	.250	.293	.341
3 YEARS			128	398	106	24	5	11	(6	3)	173	55	44	30	2	89	3	1	1	8	3	.73	14	.266	.322	.435
1986	Chicago	A	13	33	10	2	1	0	(0	0)	14	3	2	3	1	6	0	0	0	0	0	.00	0	.303	.361	.424
1986	Seattle	A	37	131	31	5	0	2	(0	0)	42	13	13	6	0	33	1	0	0	3	1	.75	1	.237	.275	.321

ERNIE CAMACHO

Pitches Right-handed, Bats Right-handed   Turns Age 31 in 1987, Born 02/01/56

| | | | HOW MUCH HE PITCHED | | | | | WHAT HE GAVE UP | | | | | | | | | | | | THE RESULTS | | | | | |
Year	Team	League	G	GS	CG	GF	IP	BFP	H	R	ER	HR	SH	SF	HB	TBB	IBB	SO	WP	Bk	W	L	Pct	ShO	Sv	ERA
1980	Oakland	A	5	0	0	2	12	61	20	9	9	2	0	1	5	0		9	2	0	0	0	.000	0	0	6.75
1981	Pittsburgh	N	7	3	0	2	22	96	23	13	12	0	1	2	0	15	1	11	2	3	0	1	.000	0	0	4.91
1983	Cleveland	A	4	0	0	1	5.1	23	5	3	3	1	0	1	2	0		2	0	1	0	1	.000	0	0	5.06
1984	Cleveland	A	69	0	0	49	100	411	83	31	27	6	7	4	1	37	5	48	3	1	5	9	.357	0	23	2.43
1985	Cleveland	A	2	0	0	1	3.1	15	4	3	3	0	0	2	0	1	0	2	1	0	0	1	.000	0	0	8.10
1986	Cleveland	A	51	0	0	37	57.1	267	60	26	26	1	5	6	2	31	6	36	3	1	2	4	.333	0	20	4.08
6 YEARS			138	3	0	92	200	873	195	85	80	10	13	14	5	91	12	108	11	5	7	16	.304	0	43	3.60

BILL CAMPBELL

Pitches Right-handed, Bats Right-handed   Turns Age 39 in 1987, Born 08/09/48

| | | | HOW MUCH HE PITCHED | | | | | WHAT HE GAVE UP | | | | | | | | | | | | THE RESULTS | | | | | |
Year	Team	League	G	GS	CG	GF	IP	BFP	H	R	ER	HR	SH	SF	HB	TBB	IBB	SO	WP	Bk	W	L	Pct	ShO	Sv	ERA
1973	Minnesota	A	28	2	0	20	52	198	44	20	18	5	2	0	1	20	1	42	2	0	3	3	.500	0	7	3.12
1974	Minnesota	A	63	0	0	55	120	514	109	37	35	4	5	1	2	55	4	89	5	1	8	7	.533	0	19	2.62
1975	Minnesota	A	47	7	2	28	121	512	119	58	51	13	6	4	2	46	2	76	3	0	4	6	.400	1	5	3.79
1976	Minnesota	A	78	0	0	68	168	703	145	63	56	9	9	7	5	62	11	115	7	0	17	5	.773	0	20	3.00
1977	Boston	A	69	0	0	60	140	583	112	48	46	13	13	4	5	60	10	114	3	1	13	9	.591	0	31	2.96
1978	Boston	A	29	0	0	20	51	226	62	25	22	3	8	0	0	17	3	47	1	1	7	5	.583	0	4	3.88
1979	Boston	A	41	0	0	23	55	239	55	28	26	5	5	0	1	23	6	25	7	0	3	4	.429	0	9	4.25
1980	Boston	A	23	0	0	11	41	180	44	26	22	1	0	3	0	22	0	17	3	0	4	0	1.000	0	0	4.83
1981	Boston	A	30	0	0	23	48	208	45	23	17	5	2	2	0	20	4	37	2	0	1	1	.500	0	7	3.19
1982	Chicago	N	62	0	0	39	100	421	89	44	41	6	10	7	0	40	13	71	3	1	3	6	.333	0	8	3.69
1983	Chicago	N	82	0	0	46	122.1	530	128	65	61	4	10	5	1	49	18	97	6	1	6	8	.429	0	8	4.49
1984	Philadelphia	N	57	0	0	24	81.1	351	68	43	31	2	9	4	0	35	13	52	3	1	6	5	.545	0	1	3.43
1985	St Louis	N	50	0	0	18	64.1	270	55	30	25	5	3	2	1	21	9	41	1	0	5	3	.625	0	4	3.50
1986	Detroit	A	34	0	0	19	55.2	229	46	26	24	5	4	3	1	21	5	37	1	0	3	6	.333	0	3	3.88
14 YEARS			693	9	2	454	1219.2	5164	1121	538	475	80	88	40	20	491	99	860	47	6	83	68	.550	1	126	3.51

CASEY CANDAELE

Bats both Right and Left-handed, Throws Right-handed

Year	Team	League	G	AB	H	2B	3B	HR	(Hm	Rd)	TB	R	RBI	TBB	IBB	SO	HBP	SH	SF	SB	CS	SB%	GIDP	AVE	OBP	SLG
1986	Montreal	N	30	104	24	4	1	0	(0	0)	30	9	6	5	0	15	0	0	1	3	5	.38	3	.231	.264	.288

JOHN CANDELARIA

Pitches Left-handed, Bats both Right and Left-handed
Turns Age 34 in 1987, Born 11/06/53

			HOW MUCH HE PITCHED					WHAT HE GAVE UP												THE RESULTS				
Year	Team	League	G	GS	CG	GF	IP	BFP	H	R	ER	HR	SH	SF	HB	TBB	IBB	SO	WP	Bk	W	L	Pct	ShO	Sv	ERA
1975	Pittsburgh	N	18	18	4	0	121	497	95	47	37	8	6	4	2	36	9	95	1	0	8	6	.571	1	0	2.75
1976	Pittsburgh	N	32	31	11	1	220	881	173	87	77	22	13	6	2	60	5	138	0	0	16	7	.696	4	1	3.15
1977	Pittsburgh	N	33	33	6	0	231	917	197	64	60	29	9	6	2	50	2	133	1	2	20	5	.800	1	0	2.34
1978	Pittsburgh	N	30	29	3	1	189	796	191	73	68	15	8	2	5	49	6	94	3	3	12	11	.522	1	1	3.24
1979	Pittsburgh	N	33	30	8	2	207	850	201	83	74	25	4	7	3	41	6	101	2	0	14	9	.609	0	0	3.22
1980	Pittsburgh	N	35	34	7	1	233	969	246	114	104	14	14	12	3	50	4	97	0	2	11	14	.440	0	1	4.02
1981	Pittsburgh	N	6	6	0	0	41	168	42	17	16	3	1	1	0	11	1	14	0	0	2	2	.500	0	0	3.51
1982	Pittsburgh	N	31	30	1	1	174.2	704	166	62	57	13	5	6	4	37	3	133	1	0	12	7	.632	1	1	2.94
1983	Pittsburgh	N	33	32	2	0	197.2	797	191	73	71	14	5	4	2	45	3	157	3	2	15	8	.652	0	0	3.23
1984	Pittsburgh	N	33	28	3	4	185.1	751	179	69	56	19	10	6	1	34	3	133	1	1	12	11	.522	1	2	2.72
1985	2 Teams		50	13	1	26	125.1	530	127	56	52	14	7	7	4	38	3	100	2	1	9	7	.563	1	9	3.73
1986	California	A	16	16	1	0	91.2	365	68	30	26	4	3	3	3	26	2	81	2	1	10	2	.833	1	0	2.55
12 YEARS			350	300	47	36	2016.2	8225	1876	775	698	181	84	64	31	477	47	1276	16	12	141	89	.613	11	15	3.12
1985	California	A	13	13	1	0	71	301	70	33	30	7	4	3	3	24	1	53	2	0	7	3	.700	1	0	3.80
1985	Pittsburgh	N	37	0	0	26	54.1	229	57	23	22	7	3	4	1	14	2	47	0	1	2	4	.333	0	9	3.64

TOM CANDIOTTI

Pitches Right-handed, Bats Right-handed
Turns Age 30 in 1987, Born 08/31/57

			HOW MUCH HE PITCHED					WHAT HE GAVE UP												THE RESULTS				
Year	Team	League	G	GS	CG	GF	IP	BFP	H	R	ER	HR	SH	SF	HB	TBB	IBB	SO	WP	Bk	W	L	Pct	ShO	Sv	ERA
1983	Milwaukee	A	10	8	2	1	55.2	233	62	21	20	4	0	2	2	16	0	21	0	0	4	4	.500	1	0	3.23
1984	Milwaukee	A	8	6	0	0	32.1	147	38	21	19	5	0	0	0	10	0	23	1	0	2	2	.500	0	0	5.29
1986	Cleveland	A	36	34	17	1	252.1	1078	234	112	100	18	3	9	8	106	0	167	12	4	16	12	.571	3	0	3.57
3 YEARS			54	48	19	2	340.1	1458	334	154	139	27	3	11	10	132	0	211	13	4	22	18	.550	4	0	3.68

JOHN CANGELOSI

Bats both Right and Left-handed, Throws Left-handed
Turns Age 24 in 1987, Born 03/10/63

			BATTING																	BASERUNNING				PERCENTAGES		
Year	Team	League	G	AB	H	2B	3B	HR	(Hm	Rd)	TB	R	RBI	TBB	IBB	SO	HBP	SH	SF	SB	CS	SB%	GIDP	AVE	OBP	SLG
1985	Chicago	A	5	2	0	0	0	0	(0	0)	0	2	0	0	0	1	1	1	0	0	0	.00	0	.000	.333	.000
1986	Chicago	A	137	438	103	16	3	2	(1	1)	131	65	32	71	0	61	7	6	3	50	17	.75	5	.235	.349	.299
2 YEARS			142	440	103	16	3	2	(1	1)	131	67	32	71	0	62	8	7	3	50	17	.75	5	.234	.349	.298

JOSE CANSECO

Bats Right-handed, Throws Right-handed
Turns Age 23 in 1987, Born 07/02/64

			BATTING																	BASERUNNING				PERCENTAGES		
Year	Team	League	G	AB	H	2B	3B	HR	(Hm	Rd)	TB	R	RBI	TBB	IBB	SO	HBP	SH	SF	SB	CS	SB%	GIDP	AVE	OBP	SLG
1985	Oakland	A	29	96	29	3	0	5	(4	1)	47	16	13	4	0	31	0	0	0	1	1	.50	1	.302	.330	.490
1986	Oakland	A	157	600	144	29	1	33	(14	19)	274	85	117	65	1	175	8	0	9	15	7	.68	12	.240	.318	.457
2 YEARS			186	696	173	32	1	38	(18	20)	321	101	130	69	1	206	8	0	9	16	8	.67	13	.249	.320	.461

STEVE CARLTON

Pitches Left-handed, Bats Left-handed
Turns Age 43 in 1987, Born 12/22/44

			HOW MUCH HE PITCHED					WHAT HE GAVE UP												THE RESULTS				
Year	Team	League	G	GS	CG	GF	IP	BFP	H	R	ER	HR	SH	SF	HB	TBB	IBB	SO	WP	Bk	W	L	Pct	ShO	Sv	ERA
1965	St Louis	N	15	2	0	5	25	104	27	7	7	3	1	0	1	8	1	21	5	0	0	0	.000	0	0	2.52
1966	St Louis	N	9	9	2	0	52	223	56	22	18	2	2	3	0	18	1	25	2	1	3	3	.500	1	0	3.12
1967	St Louis	N	30	28	11	1	193	802	173	71	64	10	9	3	2	62	1	168	6	0	14	9	.609	2	1	2.98
1968	St Louis	N	34	33	10	1	232	954	214	87	77	11	11	9	3	61	4	162	6	0	13	11	.542	5	0	2.99
1969	St Louis	N	31	31	12	0	236	968	185	66	57	15	9	4	4	93	6	210	7	0	17	11	.607	2	0	2.17
1970	St Louis	N	34	33	13	0	254	1086	239	123	105	25	14	7	2	109	16	193	14	1	10	19	.345	2	0	3.72
1971	St Louis	N	37	36	18	0	273	1171	275	120	108	23	10	8	5	98	11	172	12	0	20	9	.690	4	0	3.56
1972	Philadelphia	N	41	41	30	0	346	1351	257	84	76	17	9	9	1	87	8	310	8	2	27	10	.730	8	0	1.98
1973	Philadelphia	N	40	40	18	0	293	1262	293	146	127	29	17	3	3	113	12	223	7	0	13	20	.394	3	0	3.90
1974	Philadelphia	N	39	39	17	0	291	1227	249	118	104	21	13	8	5	136	8	240	11	4	16	13	.552	1	0	3.22
1975	Philadelphia	N	37	37	14	0	255	1063	217	116	101	24	15	12	2	104	5	192	5	7	15	14	.517	3	0	3.56
1976	Philadelphia	N	35	35	13	0	253	1031	224	94	88	19	8	4	1	72	4	195	8	3	20	7	.741	2	0	3.13
1977	Philadelphia	N	36	36	17	0	283	1135	229	99	83	25	9	4	4	89	5	198	3	7	23	10	.697	2	0	2.64
1978	Philadelphia	N	34	34	12	0	247	1006	228	91	78	30	10	5	3	63	7	161	3	7	16	13	.552	3	0	2.84
1979	Philadelphia	N	35	35	13	0	251	1029	202	112	101	25	9	5	5	89	11	213	10	11	18	11	.621	4	0	3.62
1980	Philadelphia	N	38	38	13	0	304	1228	243	87	79	15	14	8	2	90	12	286	17	7	24	9	.727	3	0	2.34
1981	Philadelphia	N	24	24	10	0	190	763	152	59	51	9	12	4	1	62	3	179	9	4	13	4	.765	1	0	2.42
1982	Philadelphia	N	38	38	19	0	295.2	1193	253	114	102	17	11	5	1	86	5	286	9	9	23	11	.676	6	0	3.10
1983	Philadelphia	N	37	37	8	0	283.2	1183	277	117	98	20	20	4	3	84	10	275	13	9	15	16	.484	3	0	3.11
1984	Philadelphia	N	33	33	1	0	229	964	214	104	91	14	8	7	0	79	7	163	11	7	13	7	.650	0	0	3.58
1985	Philadelphia	N	16	16	0	0	92	401	84	43	34	6	9	1	4	53	4	48	3	2	1	8	.111	0	0	3.33
1986	3 Teams		32	32	0	0	176.1	792	196	120	100	25	8	5	1	86	4	120	7	2	9	14	.391	0	0	5.10
22 YEARS			705	687	251	7	5054.2	20936	4487	2000	1749	385	228	118	49	1742	145	4040	176	83	323	229	.585	55	1	3.11
1986	Chicago	A	10	10	0	0	63.1	259	58	30	26	6	2	2	0	25	0	40	2	1	4	3	.571	0	0	3.69
1986	Philadelphia	N	16	16	0	0	83	393	102	70	57	15	2	3	0	45	4	62	3	0	4	8	.333	0	0	6.18
1986	San Francisco	N	6	6	0	0	30	140	36	20	17	4	4	0	1	16	0	18	2	1	1	3	.250	0	0	5.10

DON CARMAN

Pitches Left-handed, Bats Left-handed   Turns Age 28 in 1987, Born 08/14/59

Year Team League	G	GS	CG	GF	IP	BFP	H	R	ER	HR	SH	SF	HB	TBB	IBB	SO	WP	Bk	W	L	Pct	ShO	Sv	ERA
1983 Philadelphia N	1	0	0	1	1	3	0	0	0	0	0	0	0	0	0	0	0	0	0	0	.000	0	1	0.00
1984 Philadelphia N	11	0	0	9	13.1	61	14	9	8	2	0	0	0	6	4	16	3	0	0	1	.000	0	0	5.40
1985 Philadelphia N	71	0	0	33	86.1	342	52	25	20	6	5	5	2	38	3	87	1	0	9	4	.692	0	7	2.08
1986 Philadelphia N	50	14	2	13	134.1	545	113	50	48	11	5	3	3	52	11	98	6	2	10	5	.667	1	1	3.22
4 YEARS	133	14	2	56	235	951	179	84	76	19	10	8	5	96	18	201	10	2	19	10	.655	1	9	2.91

GARY CARTER

Bats Right-handed, Throws Right-handed   Turns Age 33 in 1987, Born 04/08/54

Year Team League	G	AB	H	2B	3B	HR	(Hm	Rd)	TB	R	RBI	TBB	IBB	SO	HBP	SH	SF	SB	CS	SB%	GIDP	AVE	OBP	SLG
1974 Montreal N	9	27	11	1	1	1	(1	0)	16	5	6	1	0	2	0	0	1	2	0	1.00	0	.407	.414	.593
1975 Montreal N	144	503	136	20	1	17	(9	8)	209	58	68	72	8	83	1	10	4	5	2	.71	7	.270	.360	.416
1976 Montreal N	91	311	68	8	1	6	(5	1)	96	31	38	30	2	43	1	2	3	0	2	.00	7	.219	.287	.309
1977 Montreal N	154	522	148	29	2	31	(22	9)	274	86	84	58	5	103	5	3	7	5	5	.50	9	.284	.356	.525
1978 Montreal N	157	533	136	27	1	20	(7	13)	225	76	72	62	11	70	5	2	5	10	6	.63	10	.255	.336	.422
1979 Montreal N	141	505	143	26	5	22	(12	10)	245	74	75	40	3	62	5	2	7	3	2	.60	11	.283	.338	.485
1980 Montreal N	154	549	145	25	5	29	(12	17)	267	76	101	58	11	78	1	1	8	3	2	.60	9	.264	.331	.486
1981 Montreal N	100	374	94	20	2	16	(7	9)	166	48	68	35	4	35	1	3	6	1	5	.17	6	.251	.313	.444
1982 Montreal N	154	557	163	32	1	29	(16	13)	284	91	97	78	11	64	6	4	8	2	5	.29	16	.293	.381	.510
1983 Montreal N	145	541	146	37	3	17	(6	11)	240	63	79	51	7	57	7	2	8	1	1	.50	14	.270	.336	.444
1984 Montreal N	159	596	175	32	1	27	(14	13)	290	75	106	64	9	57	6	0	3	2	2	.50	8	.294	.366	.487
1985 New York N	149	555	156	17	1	32	(12	20)	271	83	100	69	16	46	6	0	3	1	1	.50	18	.281	.365	.488
1986 New York N	132	490	125	14	2	24	(13	11)	215	81	105	62	9	63	6	0	15	1	0	1.00	21	.255	.337	.439
13 YEARS	1689	6063	1646	287	26	271	(136	135)	2798	847	999	680	96	763	50	29	78	36	33	.52	136	.271	.346	.461

JOE CARTER

Bats Right-handed, Throws Right-handed   Turns Age 27 in 1987, Born 03/07/60

Year Team League	G	AB	H	2B	3B	HR	(Hm	Rd)	TB	R	RBI	TBB	IBB	SO	HBP	SH	SF	SB	CS	SB%	GIDP	AVE	OBP	SLG
1983 Chicago N	23	51	9	1	1	0	(0	0)	12	6	1	0	0	21	1	0	1	1	0	1.00	1	.176	.176	.235
1984 Cleveland A	66	244	67	6	1	13	(9	4)	114	32	41	11	0	48	1	0	1	2	4	.33	2	.275	.307	.467
1985 Cleveland A	143	489	128	27	0	15	(5	10)	200	64	59	25	2	74	2	3	4	24	6	.80	9	.262	.298	.409
1986 Cleveland A	162	663	200	36	9	29	(14	15)	341	108	121	32	3	95	5	1	8	29	7	.81	8	.302	.335	.514
4 YEARS	394	1447	404	70	11	57	(28	29)	667	210	222	68	5	238	8	5	13	56	17	.77	20	.279	.313	.461

CHUCK CARY

Pitches Left-handed, Bats Left-handed   Turns Age 27 in 1987, Born 03/03/60

Year Team League	G	GS	CG	GF	IP	BFP	H	R	ER	HR	SH	SF	HB	TBB	IBB	SO	WP	Bk	W	L	Pct	ShO	Sv	ERA
1985 Detroit A	16	0	0	6	23.2	95	16	9	9	2	0	1	2	8	1	22	0	0	0	1	.000	0	2	3.42
1986 Detroit A	22	0	0	6	31.2	140	33	18	12	3	2	2	0	15	4	21	1	1	1	2	.333	0	0	3.41
2 YEARS	38	0	0	12	55.1	235	49	27	21	5	2	3	2	23	5	43	1	1	1	3	.250	0	2	3.42

CARMEN CASTILLO

Bats Right-handed, Throws Right-handed   Turns Age 29 in 1987, Born 06/08/58

Year Team League	G	AB	H	2B	3B	HR	(Hm	Rd)	TB	R	RBI	TBB	IBB	SO	HBP	SH	SF	SB	CS	SB%	GIDP	AVE	OBP	SLG
1982 Cleveland A	47	120	25	4	0	2	(2	0)	35	11	11	6	2	17	2	1	0	0	0	.00	2	.208	.258	.292
1983 Cleveland A	23	36	10	2	1	1	(1	0)	17	9	3	4	0	6	1	0	0	1	1	.50	0	.278	.366	.472
1984 Cleveland A	87	211	55	9	2	10	(7	3)	98	36	36	21	0	32	2	0	3	3	3	.25	7	.261	.329	.464
1985 Cleveland A	67	184	45	5	1	11	(4	7)	85	27	25	11	0	40	3	0	0	3	0	1.00	6	.245	.298	.462
1986 Cleveland A	85	205	57	9	0	8	(4	4)	90	34	32	9	0	48	1	1	1	2	1	.67	9	.278	.310	.439
5 YEARS	309	756	192	29	4	32	(18	14)	325	117	107	51	2	143	9	2	4	7	5	.58	24	.254	.307	.430

BILL CAUDILL

Pitches Right-handed, Bats Right-handed   Turns Age 31 in 1987, Born 07/13/56

Year Team League	G	GS	CG	GF	IP	BFP	H	R	ER	HR	SH	SF	HB	TBB	IBB	SO	WP	Bk	W	L	Pct	ShO	Sv	ERA
1979 Chicago N	29	12	0	6	90	402	89	57	48	16	4	4	4	41	5	104	3	2	1	7	.125	0	0	4.80
1980 Chicago N	72	2	0	27	128	528	100	37	31	10	10	9	1	59	12	112	2	4	4	6	.400	0	1	2.18
1981 Chicago N	30	10	0	4	71	331	87	50	46	9	5	4	2	31	2	45	3	1	1	5	.167	0	0	5.83
1982 Seattle A	70	0	0	64	95.2	380	65	25	25	9	1	1	3	35	4	111	2	0	12	9	.571	0	26	2.35
1983 Seattle A	63	0	0	54	72.2	317	70	39	38	10	1	4	2	38	6	73	4	1	2	8	.200	0	26	4.71
1984 Oakland A	68	0	0	62	96.1	394	77	30	29	9	5	4	0	31	4	89	1	0	9	7	.563	0	36	2.71
1985 Toronto A	67	0	0	51	69.1	297	53	26	23	9	4	2	2	35	6	46	0	0	4	6	.400	0	14	2.99
1986 Toronto A	40	0	0	20	36.1	163	36	25	25	6	2	0	2	17	1	32	0	1	2	4	.333	0	2	6.19
8 YEARS	439	24	0	288	659.1	2812	577	289	265	78	35	30	14	287	40	612	15	9	35	52	.402	0	105	3.62

RICK CERONE

Bats Right-handed, Throws Right-handed   Turns Age 33 in 1987, Born 05/19/54

Year	Team	League	G	AB	H	2B	3B	HR	(Hm	Rd)	TB	R	RBI	TBB	IBB	SO	HBP	SH	SF	SB	CS	SB%	GIDP	AVE	OBP	SLG
1975	Cleveland	A	7	12	3	1	0	0	(0	0)	4	1	0	1	0	0	0	1	0	0	0	.00	0	.250	.308	.333
1976	Cleveland	A	7	16	2	0	0	0	(0	0)	2	1	1	0	0	2	0	0	0	0	0	.00	0	.125	.125	.125
1977	Toronto	A	31	100	20	4	0	1	(0	1)	27	7	10	6	0	12	0	1	0	0	0	.00	3	.200	.245	.270
1978	Toronto	A	88	282	63	8	2	3	(2	1)	84	25	20	23	0	32	1	4	0	0	3	.00	7	.223	.284	.298
1979	Toronto	A	136	469	112	27	4	7	(3	4)	168	47	61	37	1	40	1	3	4	1	4	.20	5	.239	.294	.358
1980	New York	A	147	519	144	30	4	14	(7	7)	224	70	85	32	2	56	6	8	10	1	3	.25	14	.277	.321	.432
1981	New York	A	71	234	57	13	2	2	(2	0)	80	23	21	12	0	24	0	4	4	0	2	.00	10	.244	.276	.342
1982	New York	A	89	300	68	10	0	5	(1	4)	93	29	28	19	1	27	1	4	5	0	2	.00	12	.227	.271	.310
1983	New York	A	80	246	54	7	0	2	(0	2)	67	18	22	15	1	29	1	4	0	0	0	.00	5	.220	.267	.272
1984	New York	A	38	120	25	3	0	2	(0	2)	34	8	13	9	0	15	1	2	0	1	0	1.00	5	.208	.269	.283
1985	Atlanta	N	96	282	61	9	0	3	(3	0)	79	15	25	29	1	25	1	0	4	0	3	.00	15	.216	.288	.280
1986	Milwaukee	A	68	216	56	14	0	4	(3	1)	82	22	18	15	0	28	1	5	5	1	1	.50	5	.259	.304	.380
12 YEARS			858	2796	665	126	12	43	(21	22)	944	266	304	198	6	290	13	36	32	4	18	.18	81	.238	.288	.338

JOHN CERUTTI

Pitches Left-handed, Bats Left-handed   Turns Age 27 in 1987, Born 04/28/60

			HOW MUCH HE PITCHED						WHAT HE GAVE UP										THE RESULTS				
Year	Team	League	G	GS	CG	GF	IP	BFP	H	R	ER	HR	SH	SF	HB	TBB	IBB	SO	WP	Bk	W	L	Pct	ShO	Sv	ERA
1985	Toronto	A	4	1	0	1	6.2	36	10	7	4	1	0	0	1	4	0	5	2	0	0	2	.000	0	0	5.40
1986	Toronto	A	34	20	2	3	145.1	616	150	73	67	25	4	5	1	47	2	89	8	0	9	4	.692	1	1	4.15
2 YEARS			38	21	2	4	152	652	160	80	71	26	4	5	2	51	2	94	10	0	9	6	.600	1	1	4.20

RON CEY

Bats Right-handed, Throws Right-handed   Turns Age 39 in 1987, Born 02/15/48

Year	Team	League	G	AB	H	2B	3B	HR	(Hm	Rd)	TB	R	RBI	TBB	IBB	SO	HBP	SH	SF	SB	CS	SB%	GIDP	AVE	OBP	SLG
1971	Los Angeles	N	2	2	0	0	0	0	(0	0)	0	0	0	0	0	2	0	0	0	0	0	.00	0	.000	.000	.000
1972	Los Angeles	N	11	37	10	1	0	1	(1	0)	14	3	3	7	0	10	1	0	0	0	0	.00	0	.270	.400	.378
1973	Los Angeles	N	152	507	124	18	4	15	(6	9)	195	60	80	74	7	77	2	4	8	1	1	.50	19	.245	.338	.385
1974	Los Angeles	N	159	577	151	20	2	18	(8	10)	229	88	97	76	13	68	7	3	10	1	1	.50	17	.262	.349	.397
1975	Los Angeles	N	158	566	160	29	2	25	(18	7)	268	72	101	78	15	74	7	3	8	5	2	.71	15	.283	.372	.473
1976	Los Angeles	N	145	502	139	18	3	23	(12	11)	232	69	80	89	13	74	3	2	4	0	4	.00	11	.277	.386	.462
1977	Los Angeles	N	153	564	136	22	3	30	(14	16)	254	77	110	93	6	106	2	3	7	3	4	.43	11	.241	.347	.450
1978	Los Angeles	N	159	555	150	32	0	23	(10	13)	251	84	84	96	9	96	7	2	7	2	5	.29	13	.270	.380	.452
1979	Los Angeles	N	150	487	137	20	1	28	(17	11)	243	77	81	86	8	85	2	0	4	3	3	.50	11	.281	.389	.499
1980	Los Angeles	N	157	551	140	25	0	28	(16	12)	249	81	77	69	5	92	5	4	1	2	2	.50	16	.254	.342	.452
1981	Los Angeles	N	85	312	90	15	2	13	(9	4)	148	42	50	40	3	55	3	1	3	0	2	.00	7	.288	.372	.474
1982	Los Angeles	N	150	556	141	23	1	24	(10	14)	238	62	79	57	6	99	4	2	8	3	2	.60	13	.254	.323	.428
1983	Chicago	N	159	581	160	33	1	24	(11	13)	267	73	90	62	11	85	5	1	9	0	0	.00	20	.275	.346	.460
1984	Chicago	N	146	505	121	27	0	25	(12	13)	223	71	97	61	10	108	6	0	8	3	2	.60	10	.240	.324	.442
1985	Chicago	N	145	500	116	18	2	22	(15	7)	204	64	63	58	9	106	4	0	2	1	1	.50	10	.232	.316	.408
1986	Chicago	N	97	256	70	21	0	13	(4	9)	130	42	36	44	1	66	3	1	2	0	0	.00	5	.273	.384	.508
16 YEARS			2028	7058	1845	322	21	312	(163	149)	3145	965	1128	990	116	1203	61	26	81	24	29	.45	181	.261	.354	.446

CHRIS CHAMBLISS

Bats Left-handed, Throws Right-handed   Turns Age 39 in 1987, Born 12/26/48

Year	Team	League	G	AB	H	2B	3B	HR	(Hm	Rd)	TB	R	RBI	TBB	IBB	SO	HBP	SH	SF	SB	CS	SB%	GIDP	AVE	OBP	SLG
1971	Cleveland	A	111	415	114	20	4	9	(5	4)	169	49	48	40	1	83	2	2	0	2	0	1.00	9	.275	.341	.407
1972	Cleveland	A	121	466	136	27	2	6	(3	3)	185	51	44	26	2	63	0	3	4	3	4	.43	8	.292	.327	.397
1973	Cleveland	A	155	572	156	30	2	11	(8	3)	223	70	53	58	8	76	3	1	2	4	8	.33	14	.273	.342	.390
1974	2 Teams		127	467	119	20	3	6	(4	2)	163	46	50	28	2	48	0	2	2	0	1	.00	10	.255	.296	.349
1975	New York	A	150	562	171	38	4	9	(4	5)	244	66	72	29	9	50	1	4	6	0	1	.00	19	.304	.336	.434
1976	New York	A	156	641	188	32	6	17	(10	7)	283	79	96	27	1	80	3	1	3	1	0	1.00	15	.293	.323	.441
1977	New York	A	157	600	172	32	6	17	(11	6)	267	90	90	45	5	73	2	0	5	4	0	1.00	22	.287	.336	.445
1978	New York	A	162	625	171	26	3	12	(6	6)	239	81	90	41	3	60	5	1	5	2	1	.67	6	.274	.321	.382
1979	New York	A	149	554	155	27	3	18	(10	8)	242	61	63	34	4	53	5	1	5	3	2	.60	11	.280	.324	.437
1980	Atlanta	N	158	602	170	37	2	18	(12	6)	265	83	72	49	6	73	4	2	4	7	3	.70	11	.282	.338	.440
1981	Atlanta	N	107	404	110	25	2	8	(2	6)	163	44	51	44	10	41	1	2	3	4	1	.80	11	.272	.343	.403
1982	Atlanta	N	157	534	144	25	2	20	(11	9)	233	57	86	57	13	57	0	0	6	7	3	.70	11	.270	.337	.436
1983	Atlanta	N	131	447	125	24	3	20	(9	11)	215	59	78	63	15	68	0	0	3	2	7	.22	8	.280	.366	.481
1984	Atlanta	N	135	389	100	14	0	9	(6	3)	141	47	44	58	12	54	1	0	6	1	2	.33	10	.257	.350	.362
1985	Atlanta	N	101	170	40	7	0	3	(1	2)	56	16	21	18	4	22	0	0	0	0	0	.00	5	.235	.307	.329
1986	Atlanta	N	97	122	38	8	0	2	(2	0)	52	13	14	15	4	24	0	0	1	0	0	.00	2	.311	.384	.426
16 YEARS			2174	7570	2109	392	42	185	(104	81)	3140	912	972	632	99	925	27	19	56	40	35	.53	166	.279	.334	.415
1974	Cleveland	A	17	67	22	4	0	0	(0	0)	26	8	7	5	1	5	0	0	0	0	1	.00	1	.328	.375	.388
1974	New York	A	110	400	97	16	3	6	(4	2)	137	38	43	23	1	43	0	2	2	0	0	.00	9	.243	.282	.343

JIM CLANCY

Pitches Right-handed, Bats Right-handed   Turns Age 32 in 1987, Born 12/18/55

Year	Team	League	G	GS	CG	GF	IP	BFP	H	R	ER	HR	SH	SF	HB	TBB	IBB	SO	WP	Bk	W	L	Pct	ShO	Sv	ERA
				HOW MUCH HE PITCHED								WHAT HE GAVE UP											THE RESULTS			
1977	Toronto	A	13	13	4	0	77	346	80	47	43	7	6	7	0	47	1	44	4	0	4	9	.308	1	0	5.03
1978	Toronto	A	31	30	7	0	194	846	199	96	88	10	8	10	1	91	1	106	10	0	10	12	.455	0	0	4.08
1979	Toronto	A	12	11	2	0	64	278	65	44	39	8	3	5	0	31	0	33	2	0	2	7	.222	0	0	5.48
1980	Toronto	A	34	34	15	0	251	1075	217	108	92	19	9	4	2	128	4	152	10	0	13	16	.448	2	0	3.30
1981	Toronto	A	22	22	2	0	125	556	126	77	68	12	2	4	5	64	0	56	12	0	6	12	.333	0	0	4.90
1982	Toronto	A	40	40	11	0	266.2	1100	251	122	110	26	5	4	2	77	1	139	6	0	16	14	.533	3	0	3.71
1983	Toronto	A	34	34	11	0	223	955	238	115	97	23	4	12	1	61	0	99	3	0	15	11	.577	1	0	3.91
1984	Toronto	A	36	36	5	0	219.2	966	249	132	125	25	4	4	3	88	2	118	10	0	13	15	.464	0	0	5.12
1985	Toronto	A	23	23	1	0	128.2	527	117	54	54	15	0	5	0	37	0	66	2	0	9	6	.600	0	0	3.78
1986	Toronto	A	34	34	6	0	219.1	913	202	100	96	24	5	9	4	63	0	126	4	0	14	14	.500	3	0	3.94
10 YEARS			279	277	64	0	1768.1	7562	1744	895	812	169	46	64	18	687	9	939	63	0	102	116	.468	10	0	4.13

JACK CLARK

Bats Right-handed, Throws Right-handed   Turns Age 32 in 1987, Born 11/10/55

Year	Team	League	G	AB	H	2B	3B	HR	(Hm	Rd)	TB	R	RBI	TBB	IBB	SO	HBP	SH	SF	SB	CS	SB%	GIDP	AVE	OBP	SLG
							BATTING														BASERUNNING				PERCENTAGES	
1975	San Francisco	N	8	17	4	0	0	0	(0	0)	4	3	2	1	0	2	0	0	1	1	0	1.00	0	.235	.263	.235
1976	San Francisco	N	26	102	23	6	2	2	(2	0)	39	14	10	8	0	18	0	3	2	6	2	.75	0	.225	.277	.382
1977	San Francisco	N	136	413	104	17	4	13	(7	6)	168	64	51	49	2	73	2	1	3	12	4	.75	7	.252	.332	.407
1978	San Francisco	N	156	592	181	46	8	25	(10	15)	318	90	98	50	8	72	3	3	9	15	11	.58	15	.306	.358	.537
1979	San Francisco	N	143	527	144	25	2	26	(10	16)	251	84	86	63	6	95	1	1	6	11	8	.58	9	.273	.348	.476
1980	San Francisco	N	127	437	124	20	8	22	(8	14)	226	77	82	74	13	52	2	1	10	2	5	.29	12	.284	.382	.517
1981	San Francisco	N	99	385	103	19	2	17	(7	10)	177	60	53	45	6	45	1	0	4	1	1	.50	12	.268	.341	.460
1982	San Francisco	N	157	563	154	30	3	27	(9	18)	271	90	103	90	7	91	1	0	5	6	9	.40	20	.274	.372	.481
1983	San Francisco	N	135	492	132	25	0	20	(11	9)	217	82	66	74	6	79	1	0	7	5	3	.63	14	.268	.361	.441
1984	San Francisco	N	57	203	65	9	1	11	(4	7)	109	33	44	43	7	29	0	0	3	1	1	.50	9	.320	.434	.537
1985	St Louis	N	126	442	124	26	3	22	(8	14)	222	71	87	83	14	88	2	0	5	1	4	.20	10	.281	.393	.502
1986	St Louis	N	65	232	55	12	2	9	(4	5)	98	34	23	45	4	61	1	0	1	1	1	.50	4	.237	.362	.422
12 YEARS			1235	4405	1213	235	35	194	(80	114)	2100	702	705	625	73	705	14	9	58	62	49	.56	112	.275	.363	.477

WILL CLARK

Bats Left-handed, Throws Left-handed   Turns Age 23 in 1987, Born 03/17/64

Year	Team	League	G	AB	H	2B	3B	HR	(Hm	Rd)	TB	R	RBI	TBB	IBB	SO	HBP	SH	SF	SB	CS	SB%	GIDP	AVE	OBP	SLG
							BATTING														BASERUNNING				PERCENTAGES	
1986	San Francisco	N	111	408	117	27	2	11	(7	4)	181	66	41	34	10	76	3	9	4	4	7	.36	3	.287	.343	.444

MARK CLEAR

Pitches Right-handed, Bats Right-handed   Turns Age 31 in 1987, Born 05/27/56

Year	Team	League	G	GS	CG	GF	IP	BFP	H	R	ER	HR	SH	SF	HB	TBB	IBB	SO	WP	Bk	W	L	Pct	ShO	Sv	ERA
				HOW MUCH HE PITCHED								WHAT HE GAVE UP											THE RESULTS			
1979	California	A	52	0	0	37	109	481	87	48	44	6	7	5	3	68	5	98	9	1	11	5	.688	0	14	3.63
1980	California	A	58	0	0	41	106	461	82	51	39	2	8	3	5	65	9	105	4	0	11	11	.500	0	9	3.31
1981	Boston	A	34	0	0	20	77	346	69	36	35	11	4	0	2	51	2	82	6	0	8	3	.727	0	9	4.09
1982	Boston	A	55	0	0	44	105	467	92	39	35	11	7	5	7	61	6	109	1	1	14	9	.609	0	14	3.00
1983	Boston	A	48	0	0	33	96	448	101	71	67	10	1	6	3	68	5	81	2	0	4	5	.444	0	4	6.28
1984	Boston	A	47	0	0	27	67	318	47	38	30	2	3	6	2	70	3	76	6	0	8	3	.727	0	8	4.03
1985	Boston	A	41	0	0	30	55.2	259	45	26	23	1	2	2	5	50	10	55	8	0	1	3	.250	0	3	3.72
1986	Milwaukee	A	59	0	0	52	73.2	306	53	23	18	4	1	4	1	36	2	85	8	2	5	5	.500	0	16	2.20
8 YEARS			394	0	0	284	689.1	3086	576	332	291	47	33	31	28	469	42	691	44	4	62	44	.585	0	77	3.80

ROGER CLEMENS

Pitches Right-handed, Bats Right-handed   Turns Age 25 in 1987, Born 08/04/62

Year	Team	League	G	GS	CG	GF	IP	BFP	H	R	ER	HR	SH	SF	HB	TBB	IBB	SO	WP	Bk	W	L	Pct	ShO	Sv	ERA
				HOW MUCH HE PITCHED								WHAT HE GAVE UP											THE RESULTS			
1984	Boston	A	21	20	5	0	133.1	575	146	67	64	13	2	3	2	29	3	126	4	0	9	4	.692	1	0	4.32
1985	Boston	A	15	15	3	0	98.1	407	83	38	36	5	1	2	3	37	0	74	1	3	7	5	.583	0	0	3.29
1986	Boston	A	33	33	10	0	254	997	179	77	70	21	4	6	6	67	0	238	11	3	24	4	.857	1	0	2.48
3 YEARS			69	68	18	0	485.2	1979	408	182	170	39	7	11	9	133	3	438	16	6	40	13	.755	3	0	3.15

PAT CLEMENTS

Pitches Left-handed, Bats Right-handed — Turns Age 25 in 1987, Born 02/02/62

			HOW MUCH HE PITCHED						WHAT HE GAVE UP											THE RESULTS				
Year	Team	League	G	GS	CG	GF	IP	BFP	H	R	ER	HR	SH	SF	HB	TBB	IBB	SO	WP	Bk	W	L	Pct	ShO	Sv	ERA
1985	2 Teams		68	0	0	19	96.1	400	86	37	37	6	6	1	2	40	5	36	3	0	5	2	.714	0	3	3.46
1986	Pittsburgh	N	65	0	0	19	61	256	53	20	19	1	7	4	2	32	6	31	2	0	0	4	.000	0	2	2.80
2 YEARS			133	0	0	38	157.1	656	139	57	56	7	13	5	4	72	11	67	5	0	5	6	.455	0	5	3.20
1985	California	A	41	0	0	12	62	247	47	23	23	4	4	0	2	25	2	19	1	0	5	0	1.000	0	1	3.34
1985	Pittsburgh	N	27	0	0	7	34.1	153	39	14	14	2	2	1	0	15	3	17	2	0	0	2	.000	0	2	3.67

BRYAN CLUTTERBUCK

Pitches Right-handed, Bats Right-handed — Turns Age 28 in 1987, Born 12/17/59

			HOW MUCH HE PITCHED						WHAT HE GAVE UP											THE RESULTS				
Year	Team	League	G	GS	CG	GF	IP	BFP	H	R	ER	HR	SH	SF	HB	TBB	IBB	SO	WP	Bk	W	L	Pct	ShO	Sv	ERA
1986	Milwaukee	A	20	0	0	7	56.2	250	68	32	27	8	1	1	2	16	2	38	2	0	0	1	.000	0	0	4.29

JAIME COCANOWER

Pitches Right-handed, Bats Right-handed — Turns Age 30 in 1987, Born 02/14/57

			HOW MUCH HE PITCHED						WHAT HE GAVE UP											THE RESULTS				
Year	Team	League	G	GS	CG	GF	IP	BFP	H	R	ER	HR	SH	SF	HB	TBB	IBB	SO	WP	Bk	W	L	Pct	ShO	Sv	ERA
1983	Milwaukee	A	5	3	1	0	30	118	21	8	6	1	0	0	1	12	0	8	1	0	2	0	1.000	0	0	1.80
1984	Milwaukee	A	33	27	1	6	174.2	771	188	99	78	13	5	6	9	78	3	65	13	3	8	16	.333	0	0	4.02
1985	Milwaukee	A	24	15	3	2	116.1	534	122	72	56	6	4	4	8	73	2	44	13	0	6	8	.429	1	0	4.33
1986	Milwaukee	A	17	2	0	2	44.2	205	40	29	22	1	3	1	2	38	0	22	5	0	0	1	.000	0	0	4.43
4 YEARS			79	47	5	10	365.2	1628	371	208	162	21	12	11	20	201	5	139	32	3	16	25	.390	1	0	3.99

CHRIS CODIROLI

Pitches Right-handed, Bats Right-handed — Turns Age 29 in 1987, Born 03/26/58

			HOW MUCH HE PITCHED						WHAT HE GAVE UP											THE RESULTS				
Year	Team	League	G	GS	CG	GF	IP	BFP	H	R	ER	HR	SH	SF	HB	TBB	IBB	SO	WP	Bk	W	L	Pct	ShO	Sv	ERA
1982	Oakland	A	3	0	0	0	16.2	70	16	8	8	1	0	0	4	0	5	0	0	1	2	.333	0	0	4.32
1983	Oakland	A	37	31	7	3	205.2	884	208	115	102	17	10	6	7	72	4	85	2	2	12	12	.500	2	1	4.46
1984	Oakland	A	28	14	1	5	89.1	406	111	67	58	16	2	2	3	34	4	44	2	0	6	4	.600	0	1	5.84
1985	Oakland	A	37	37	4	0	226	975	228	125	112	23	4	8	3	78	2	111	8	1	14	14	.500	0	0	4.46
1986	Oakland	A	16	16	1	0	91.2	406	91	54	41	15	1	1	2	38	2	43	4	0	5	8	.385	0	0	4.03
5 YEARS			121	101	13	8	629.1	2741	654	369	321	72	18	17	15	226	12	288	16	3	38	40	.487	2	2	4.59

VINCE COLEMAN

Bats both Right and Left-handed, Throws Right-handed — Turns Age 27 in 1987, Born 09/22/60

			BATTING																	BASERUNNING				PERCENTAGES		
Year	Team	League	G	AB	H	2B	3B	HR	(Hm	Rd)	TB	R	RBI	TBB	IBB	SO	HBP	SH	SF	SB	CS	SB%	GIDP	AVE	OBP	SLG
1985	St Louis	N	151	636	170	20	10	1	(1	0)	213	107	40	50	1	115	0	5	1	110	25	.81	3	.267	.320	.335
1986	St Louis	N	154	600	139	13	8	0	(0	0)	168	94	29	60	0	98	2	3	5	107	14	.88	4	.232	.301	.280
2 YEARS			305	1236	309	33	18	1	(1	0)	381	201	69	110	1	213	2	8	6	217	39	.85	7	.250	.311	.308

DARNELL COLES

Bats Right-handed, Throws Right-handed — Turns Age 25 in 1987, Born 06/02/62

			BATTING																	BASERUNNING				PERCENTAGES		
Year	Team	League	G	AB	H	2B	3B	HR	(Hm	Rd)	TB	R	RBI	TBB	IBB	SO	HBP	SH	SF	SB	CS	SB%	GIDP	AVE	OBP	SLG
1983	Seattle	A	27	92	26	7	0	1	(0	1)	36	9	6	7	0	12	0	1	0	0	3	.00	8	.283	.333	.391
1984	Seattle	A	48	143	23	3	1	0	(0	0)	28	15	6	17	0	26	2	3	0	2	1	.67	5	.161	.259	.196
1985	Seattle	A	27	59	14	4	0	1	(0	1)	21	8	5	9	0	17	1	0	2	0	0	1.00	0	.237	.338	.356
1986	Detroit	A	142	521	142	30	2	20	(12	8)	236	67	86	45	3	84	6	7	8	6	2	.75	8	.273	.333	.453
4 YEARS			244	815	205	44	3	22	(12	10)	321	99	103	78	3	139	9	11	10	8	7	.53	21	.252	.320	.394

DAVE COLLINS

Bats both Right and Left-handed, Throws Left-handed

Turns Age 35 in 1987, Born 10/20/52

Year	Team	League	G	AB	H	2B	3B	HR	(Hm	Rd)	TB	R	RBI	TBB	IBB	SO	HBP	SH	SF	SB	CS	SB%	GIDP	AVE	OBP	SLG
1975	California	A	93	319	85	13	4	3	(1	2)	115	41	29	36	1	55	1	3	3	24	10	.71	4	.266	.340	.361
1976	California	A	99	365	96	12	1	4	(1	3)	122	45	28	40	2	55	0	7	1	32	19	.63	2	.263	.335	.334
1977	Seattle	A	120	402	96	9	3	5	(2	3)	126	46	28	33	0	66	3	6	3	25	10	.71	2	.239	.299	.313
1978	Cincinnati	N	102	102	22	1	0	0	(0	0)	23	13	7	15	0	18	0	1	2	7	7	.50	2	.216	.311	.225
1979	Cincinnati	N	122	396	126	16	4	3	(0	3)	159	59	35	27	2	48	2	3	1	16	9	.64	6	.318	.364	.402
1980	Cincinnati	N	144	551	167	20	4	3	(3	0)	204	94	35	53	2	68	3	3	3	79	21	.79	5	.303	.366	.370
1981	Cincinnati	N	95	360	98	18	6	3	(1	2)	137	63	23	41	1	41	6	3	2	26	10	.72	6	.272	.355	.381
1982	New York	A	111	348	88	12	3	3	(2	1)	115	41	25	28	3	49	5	9	3	13	8	.62	6	.253	.315	.330
1983	Toronto	A	118	402	109	12	4	1	(0	1)	132	55	34	43	1	67	2	2	2	31	7	.82	6	.271	.343	.328
1984	Toronto	A	128	441	136	24	15	2	(2	0)	196	59	44	33	0	41	9	6	3	60	14	.81	0	.308	.366	.444
1985	Oakland	A	112	379	95	16	4	4	(1	3)	131	52	29	29	2	37	1	5	4	29	8	.78	6	.251	.303	.346
1986	Detroit	A	124	419	113	18	2	1	(0	1)	138	44	27	44	0	49	2	9	2	27	12	.69	9	.270	.340	.329
12 YEARS			1368	4484	1231	171	50	32	(13	19)	1598	612	344	422	14	594	34	57	29	369	135	.73	54	.275	.340	.356

DAVE CONCEPCION

Bats Right-handed, Throws Right-handed

Turns Age 39 in 1987, Born 06/17/48

Year	Team	League	G	AB	H	2B	3B	HR	(Hm	Rd)	TB	R	RBI	TBB	IBB	SO	HBP	SH	SF	SB	CS	SB%	GIDP	AVE	OBP	SLG
1970	Cincinnati	N	101	265	69	6	3	1	(0	1)	84	38	19	23	5	45	3	3	2	10	2	.83	10	.260	.324	.317
1971	Cincinnati	N	130	327	67	4	4	1	(0	1)	82	24	20	18	2	51	0	8	1	9	3	.75	10	.205	.246	.251
1972	Cincinnati	N	119	378	79	13	2	2	(1	1)	102	40	29	32	8	65	2	5	4	13	6	.68	11	.209	.272	.270
1973	Cincinnati	N	89	328	94	18	3	8	(1	7)	142	39	46	21	3	55	1	2	5	22	5	.81	7	.287	.327	.433
1974	Cincinnati	N	160	594	167	25	1	14	(10	4)	236	70	82	44	10	79	6	5	4	41	6	.87	20	.281	.335	.397
1975	Cincinnati	N	140	507	139	23	1	5	(2	3)	179	62	49	39	4	51	2	6	4	33	6	.85	17	.274	.326	.353
1976	Cincinnati	N	152	576	162	28	7	9	(4	5)	231	74	69	49	11	68	1	4	6	21	10	.68	11	.281	.335	.401
1977	Cincinnati	N	156	572	155	26	3	8	(5	3)	211	59	64	46	6	77	0	6	6	29	7	.81	15	.271	.322	.369
1978	Cincinnati	N	153	565	170	33	4	6	(3	3)	229	75	67	51	4	83	1	3	4	23	10	.70	14	.301	.357	.405
1979	Cincinnati	N	149	590	166	25	3	16	(10	6)	245	91	84	64	5	73	0	6	6	19	7	.73	18	.281	.348	.415
1980	Cincinnati	N	156	622	162	31	8	5	(4	1)	224	72	77	37	2	107	1	2	6	12	2	.86	20	.260	.300	.360
1981	Cincinnati	N	106	421	129	28	0	5	(4	1)	172	57	67	37	1	61	1	2	7	4	5	.44	13	.306	.358	.409
1982	Cincinnati	N	147	572	164	25	4	5	(3	2)	212	48	53	45	4	61	0	2	4	13	6	.68	20	.287	.337	.371
1983	Cincinnati	N	143	528	123	22	0	1	(0	1)	148	54	47	56	9	81	0	2	7	14	9	.61	21	.233	.303	.280
1984	Cincinnati	N	154	531	130	26	1	4	(3	1)	170	46	58	52	5	72	0	8	9	22	6	.79	9	.245	.307	.320
1985	Cincinnati	N	155	560	141	19	2	7	(1	6)	185	59	48	50	3	67	3	3	4	16	12	.57	23	.252	.314	.330
1986	Cincinnati	N	90	311	81	13	2	3	(0	3)	107	42	30	26	1	43	0	5	4	13	2	.87	13	.260	.314	.344
17 YEARS			2300	8247	2198	365	48	100	(51	49)	2959	950	909	690	83	1139	21	72	83	314	104	.75	252	.267	.322	.359

TIM CONROY

Pitches Left-handed, Bats Left-handed

Turns Age 27 in 1987, Born 04/03/60

			HOW MUCH HE PITCHED						WHAT HE GAVE UP											THE RESULTS					
Year	Team	League	G	GS	CG	GF	IP	BFP	H	R	ER	HR	SH	SF	HB	TBB	IBB	SO	WP	Bk	W	L	Pct	ShO	Sv	ERA
1978	Oakland	A	2	2	0	0	5	28	3	6	4	0	1	1	1	9	0	0	1	0	0	0	.000	0	0	7.20
1982	Oakland	A	5	5	1	0	25.1	110	20	13	10	1	1	0	1	18	0	17	1	0	2	2	.500	0	0	3.55
1983	Oakland	A	39	18	3	6	162.1	715	141	89	71	17	3	4	2	98	2	112	8	1	7	10	.412	1	0	3.94
1984	Oakland	A	38	14	0	6	93	418	82	58	54	11	0	4	2	63	0	69	8	1	1	6	.143	0	0	5.23
1985	Oakland	A	16	2	0	7	25.1	110	22	15	12	3	0	1	1	15	1	8	4	0	0	1	.000	0	0	4.26
1986	St Louis	N	25	21	1	2	115.1	513	122	72	67	15	0	10	3	56	7	79	7	0	5	11	.313	0	0	5.23
6 YEARS			125	62	5	21	426.1	1894	390	253	218	47	5	21	9	259	10	285	29	2	15	30	.333	1	0	4.60

CECIL COOPER

Bats Left-handed, Throws Left-handed

Turns Age 38 in 1987, Born 12/20/49

Year	Team	League	G	AB	H	2B	3B	HR	(Hm	Rd)	TB	R	RBI	TBB	IBB	SO	HBP	SH	SF	SB	CS	SB%	GIDP	AVE	OBP	SLG
1971	Boston	A	14	42	13	4	1	0	(0	0)	19	9	3	5	1	4	1	0	1	1	0	1.00	0	.310	.388	.452
1972	Boston	A	12	17	4	1	0	0	(0	0)	5	0	2	2	1	5	0	0	0	0	0	.00	0	.235	.316	.294
1973	Boston	A	30	101	24	2	0	3	(3	0)	35	12	11	7	1	12	0	0	1	1	2	.33	1	.238	.284	.347
1974	Boston	A	121	414	114	24	1	8	(5	3)	164	55	43	32	3	74	1	5	2	2	5	.29	3	.275	.327	.396
1975	Boston	A	106	305	95	17	6	14	(6	8)	166	49	44	19	6	33	3	3	3	1	4	.20	5	.311	.355	.544
1976	Boston	A	123	451	127	22	6	15	(9	6)	206	66	78	16	6	62	1	9	6	7	1	.88	3	.282	.304	.457
1977	Milwaukee	A	160	643	193	31	7	20	(9	11)	298	86	78	28	4	110	0	1	7	13	8	.62	13	.300	.326	.463
1978	Milwaukee	A	107	407	127	23	2	13	(5	8)	193	60	54	32	3	72	0	5	4	4	5	.43	5	.312	.359	.474
1979	Milwaukee	A	150	590	182	44	1	24	(13	11)	300	83	106	56	10	77	0	6	8	15	3	.83	14	.308	.364	.508
1980	Milwaukee	A	153	622	219	33	4	25	(12	13)	335	96	122	39	15	42	2	7	8	17	6	.74	16	.352	.387	.539
1981	Milwaukee	A	106	416	133	35	1	12	(5	7)	206	70	60	28	2	30	3	1	5	5	4	.56	16	.320	.363	.495
1982	Milwaukee	A	155	654	205	38	3	32	(12	20)	345	104	121	32	7	53	0	4	6	2	3	.40	4	.313	.342	.528
1983	Milwaukee	A	160	661	203	37	3	30	(14	16)	336	106	126	37	7	63	1	3	8	2	1	.67	17	.307	.341	.508
1984	Milwaukee	A	148	603	166	28	3	11	(3	8)	233	63	67	27	6	59	2	0	3	8	2	.80	12	.275	.307	.386
1985	Milwaukee	A	154	631	185	39	8	16	(6	10)	288	82	99	30	3	77	2	1	10	10	3	.77	24	.293	.322	.456
1986	Milwaukee	A	134	542	140	24	1	12	(6	6)	202	46	75	41	2	87	1	1	4	1	2	.33	15	.258	.310	.373
16 YEARS			1833	7099	2130	402	47	235	(108	127)	3331	987	1089	431	77	860	17	46	76	88	48	.65	146	.300	.338	.469

DOUG CORBETT

Pitches Right-handed, Bats Right-handed

Turns Age 35 in 1987, Born 11/04/52

Year	Team	League	HOW MUCH HE PITCHED						WHAT HE GAVE UP												THE RESULTS					
			G	GS	CG	GF	IP	BFP	H	R	ER	HR	SH	SF	HB	TBB	IBB	SO	WP	Bk	W	L	Pct	ShO	Sv	ERA
1980	Minnesota	A	73	0	0	63	136	531	102	31	30	7	7	2	1	42	8	89	3	0	8	6	.571	0	23	1.99
1981	Minnesota	A	54	0	0	45	88	377	80	29	25	5	3	5	0	34	13	60	2	0	2	6	.250	0	17	2.56
1982	2 Teams	A	43	0	0	23	79	334	73	45	45	11	3	0	0	35	6	52	4	2	1	9	.100	0	11	5.13
1983	California	A	11	0	0	7	17.1	80	26	10	7	1	1	0	1	4	2	18	0	0	1	1	.500	0	0	3.63
1984	California	A	45	1	0	30	85	353	76	22	20	2	5	4	2	30	12	48	2	1	5	1	.833	0	4	2.12
1985	California	A	30	0	0	11	46	203	49	33	25	7	2	1	1	20	3	24	0	0	3	3	.500	0	4	4.89
1986	California	A	46	0	0	32	78.2	312	66	36	32	11	1	2	1	22	2	36	2	0	4	2	.667	0	10	3.66
7 YEARS			302	1	0	211	530	2190	472	206	184	44	22	14	6	187	46	327	13	3	24	28	.462	0	65	3.12
1982	California	A	33	0	0	18	57	234	46	32	32	8	3	0	0	25	5	37	2	1	1	7	.125	0	8	5.05
1982	Minnesota	A	10	0	0	5	22	100	27	13	13	3	0	0	0	10	1	15	2	1	0	2	.000	0	3	5.32

ED CORREA

Pitches Right-handed, Bats Right-handed

Turns Age 21 in 1987, Born 04/29/66

Year	Team	League	HOW MUCH HE PITCHED						WHAT HE GAVE UP												THE RESULTS					
			G	GS	CG	GF	IP	BFP	H	R	ER	HR	SH	SF	HB	TBB	IBB	SO	WP	Bk	W	L	Pct	ShO	Sv	ERA
1985	Chicago	A	5	1	0	3	10.1	51	11	9	8	2	0	0	0	11	0	10	1	0	1	0	1.000	0	0	6.97
1986	Texas	A	32	32	4	0	202.1	886	167	102	95	15	4	3	3	126	2	189	19	2	12	14	.462	2	0	4.23
2 YEARS			37	33	4	3	212.2	937	178	111	103	17	4	3	3	137	2	199	20	2	13	14	.481	2	0	4.36

JOE COWLEY

Pitches Right-handed, Bats Right-handed

Turns Age 29 in 1987, Born 08/15/58

Year	Team	League	HOW MUCH HE PITCHED						WHAT HE GAVE UP												THE RESULTS					
			G	GS	CG	GF	IP	BFP	H	R	ER	HR	SH	SF	HB	TBB	IBB	SO	WP	Bk	W	L	Pct	ShO	Sv	ERA
1982	Atlanta	N	17	8	0	4	52.1	221	53	27	26	6	3	1	1	16	2	27	0	0	1	2	.333	0	0	4.47
1984	New York	A	16	11	3	2	83.1	356	75	34	33	12	0	2	2	31	1	71	2	1	9	2	.818	1	0	3.56
1985	New York	A	30	26	1	2	159.2	684	132	75	70	29	1	4	6	85	2	97	5	1	12	6	.667	0	0	3.95
1986	Chicago	A	27	27	4	0	162.1	692	133	81	70	20	6	4	3	83	1	132	4	0	11	11	.500	0	0	3.88
4 YEARS			90	72	8	8	457.2	1953	393	217	199	67	10	11	12	215	6	327	11	2	33	21	.611	1	0	3.91

DANNY COX

Pitches Right-handed, Bats Right-handed

Turns Age 28 in 1987, Born 09/21/59

Year	Team	League	HOW MUCH HE PITCHED						WHAT HE GAVE UP												THE RESULTS					
			G	GS	CG	GF	IP	BFP	H	R	ER	HR	SH	SF	HB	TBB	IBB	SO	WP	Bk	W	L	Pct	ShO	Sv	ERA
1983	St Louis	N	12	12	0	0	83	352	92	38	30	6	6	1	0	23	2	36	2	0	3	6	.333	0	0	3.25
1984	St Louis	N	29	27	1	0	156.1	668	171	81	70	9	10	5	7	54	6	70	2	4	9	11	.450	1	0	4.03
1985	St Louis	N	35	35	10	0	241	989	226	91	77	19	12	9	3	64	5	131	3	1	18	9	.667	4	0	2.88
1986	St Louis	N	32	32	8	0	220	881	189	85	71	14	8	3	2	60	6	108	3	4	12	13	.480	0	0	2.90
4 YEARS			108	106	19	0	700.1	2890	678	295	248	48	36	18	12	201	19	345	10	9	42	39	.519	5	0	3.19

STEVE CRAWFORD

Pitches Right-handed, Bats Right-handed

Turns Age 29 in 1987, Born 04/29/58

Year	Team	League	HOW MUCH HE PITCHED						WHAT HE GAVE UP												THE RESULTS					
			G	GS	CG	GF	IP	BFP	H	R	ER	HR	SH	SF	HB	TBB	IBB	SO	WP	Bk	W	L	Pct	ShO	Sv	ERA
1980	Boston	A	6	4	2	1	32	142	41	14	13	3	0	0	0	8	2	10	0	0	2	0	1.000	0	0	3.66
1981	Boston	A	14	11	0	2	58	257	69	38	32	10	3	4	3	18	0	29	2	0	0	5	.000	0	0	4.97
1982	Boston	A	5	0	0	4	9	41	14	3	2	0	0	0	0	0	0	2	0	0	1	0	1.000	0	0	2.00
1984	Boston	A	35	0	0	19	62	268	69	31	23	6	1	4	1	21	5	21	2	0	5	0	1.000	0	3	3.34
1985	Boston	A	44	1	0	26	91	394	103	47	38	5	6	3	0	28	8	58	5	0	6	5	.545	0	12	3.76
1986	Boston	A	40	0	0	15	57.1	248	69	29	25	5	3	2	0	19	7	32	2	0	0	2	.000	0	4	3.92
6 YEARS			144	16	2	67	309.1	1350	365	162	133	29	13	13	4	94	22	152	11	0	14	12	.538	0	17	3.87

JOSE CRUZ

Bats Left-handed, Throws Left-handed

Turns Age 40 in 1987, Born 08/08/47

Year	Team	League	G	AB	H	2B	3B	HR	(Hm	Rd)	TB	R	RBI	TBB	IBB	SO	HBP	SH	SF	SB	CS	SB%	GIDP	AVE	OBP	SLG
1970	St Louis	N	6	17	6	1	0	0	(0	0)	7	2	1	4	0	1	0	0	0	0	0	.00	1	.353	.500	.412
1971	St Louis	N	83	292	80	13	2	9	(4	5)	124	46	27	49	6	35	1	1	3	6	3	.67	6	.274	.377	.425
1972	St Louis	N	117	332	78	14	4	2	(0	2)	106	33	23	36	3	54	1	2	3	9	3	.75	4	.235	.309	.319
1973	St Louis	N	132	406	92	22	5	10	(5	5)	154	51	57	51	4	66	1	6	7	10	4	.71	8	.227	.310	.379
1974	St Louis	N	107	161	42	4	3	5	(3	2)	67	24	20	20	5	27	0	0	1	4	2	.67	3	.261	.341	.416
1975	Houston	N	120	315	81	15	2	9	(3	6)	127	44	49	52	6	44	1	3	6	6	3	.67	6	.257	.358	.403
1976	Houston	N	133	439	133	21	5	4	(1	3)	176	49	61	53	5	46	0	2	2	28	11	.72	6	.303	.377	.401
1977	Houston	N	157	579	173	31	10	17	(8	9)	275	87	87	69	13	67	0	3	10	44	23	.66	4	.299	.368	.475
1978	Houston	N	153	565	178	34	9	10	(7	3)	260	79	83	57	9	57	0	2	3	37	9	.80	9	.315	.376	.460
1979	Houston	N	157	558	161	33	7	9	(2	7)	235	73	72	72	16	66	0	1	5	36	14	.72	5	.289	.367	.421
1980	Houston	N	160	612	185	29	7	11	(4	7)	261	79	91	60	13	66	0	0	8	36	11	.77	11	.302	.360	.426
1981	Houston	N	107	409	109	16	5	13	(3	10)	174	53	55	35	4	49	0	0	7	5	7	.42	7	.267	.319	.425
1982	Houston	N	155	570	157	27	2	9	(3	6)	215	62	68	60	12	67	1	3	6	21	11	.66	11	.275	.342	.377
1983	Houston	N	160	594	189	28	8	14	(3	11)	275	85	92	65	10	86	1	1	3	30	16	.65	4	.318	.385	.463
1984	Houston	N	160	600	187	28	13	12	(0	12)	277	96	95	73	10	68	0	2	10	22	8	.73	8	.312	.381	.462
1985	Houston	N	141	544	163	34	4	9	(1	8)	232	69	79	43	10	74	0	0	3	16	5	.76	11	.300	.349	.426
1986	Houston	N	141	479	133	22	4	10	(5	5)	193	48	72	55	12	86	0	0	2	3	4	.43	9	.278	.351	.403
17 YEARS			2189	7472	2147	372	90	153	(52	101)	3158	980	1032	854	138	958	7	26	79	313	134	.70	113	.287	.358	.423

JULIO CRUZ

Bats both Right and Left-handed, Throws Right-handed

Turns Age 33 in 1987, Born 12/02/54

Year	Team	League	G	AB	H	2B	3B	HR	(Hm	Rd)	TB	R	RBI	TBB	IBB	SO	HBP	SH	SF	SB	CS	SB%	GIDP	AVE	OBP	SLG
1977	Seattle	A	60	199	51	3	1	1	(0	1)	59	25	7	24	1	29	0	7	0	15	6	.71	2	.256	.336	.296
1978	Seattle	A	147	550	129	14	1	1	(1	0)	148	77	25	69	0	66	1	10	4	59	10	.86	8	.235	.319	.269
1979	Seattle	A	107	414	112	16	2	1	(1	0)	135	70	29	62	0	61	0	4	3	49	9	.84	7	.271	.363	.326
1980	Seattle	A	119	422	88	9	3	2	(1	1)	109	66	16	59	0	49	1	13	2	45	7	.87	6	.209	.306	.258
1981	Seattle	A	94	352	90	12	3	2	(1	1)	114	57	24	39	0	40	3	4	3	43	8	.84	4	.256	.332	.324
1982	Seattle	A	154	549	133	22	5	8	(8	0)	189	83	49	57	1	71	3	6	2	46	13	.78	6	.242	.316	.344
1983	2 Teams	A	160	515	130	19	5	3	(1	2)	168	71	52	49	1	66	4	5	7	57	12	.83	12	.252	.318	.326
1984	Chicago	A	143	415	92	14	4	5	(1	4)	129	42	43	45	0	58	0	4	5	14	6	.70	9	.222	.295	.311
1985	Chicago	A	91	234	46	2	3	0	(0	0)	54	28	15	32	0	40	2	1	1	8	5	.62	6	.197	.297	.231
1986	Chicago	A	81	209	45	2	0	0	(0	0)	47	38	19	42	0	28	0	2	3	7	2	.78	4	.215	.343	.225
10 YEARS			1156	3859	916	113	27	23	(14	9)	1152	557	279	478	3	508	14	56	30	343	78	.81	64	.237	.321	.299
1983	Chicago	A	99	334	84	9	4	1	(0	1)	104	47	40	29	0	44	2	4	5	24	6	.80	9	.251	.311	.311
1983	Seattle	A	61	181	46	10	1	2	(1	1)	64	24	12	20	1	22	2	1	2	33	6	.85	3	.254	.332	.354

KAL DANIELS

Bats Left-handed, Throws Right-handed

Turns Age 24 in 1987, Born 08/20/63

Year	Team	League	G	AB	H	2B	3B	HR	(Hm	Rd)	TB	R	RBI	TBB	IBB	SO	HBP	SH	SF	SB	CS	SB%	GIDP	AVE	OBP	SLG
1986	Cincinnati	N	74	181	58	10	4	6	(3	3)	94	34	23	22	1	30	2	1	1	15	2	.88	4	.320	.398	.519

RON DARLING

Pitches Right-handed, Bats Right-handed

Turns Age 27 in 1987, Born 08/19/60

			HOW MUCH HE PITCHED						WHAT HE GAVE UP										THE RESULTS					
Year	Team	League	G	GS	CG	GF	IP	BFP	H	R	ER	HR	SH	SF	HB	TBB	IBB	SO	WP	Bk	W	L	Pct	ShO	Sv	ERA
1983	New York	N	5	5	1	0	35.1	148	31	11	11	0	3	0	3	17	1	23	3	2	1	3	.250	0	0	2.80
1984	New York	N	33	33	2	0	205.2	884	179	97	87	17	7	6	5	104	2	136	7	1	12	9	.571	2	0	3.81
1985	New York	N	36	35	4	1	248	1043	214	93	80	21	13	4	3	114	1	167	7	1	16	6	.727	2	0	2.90
1986	New York	N	34	34	4	0	237	967	203	84	74	21	10	6	3	81	2	184	7	3	15	6	.714	2	0	2.81
4 YEARS			108	107	11	1	726	3042	627	285	252	59	33	16	14	316	6	510	24	7	44	24	.647	6	0	3.12

DANNY DARWIN

Pitches Right-handed, Bats Right-handed

Turns Age 32 in 1987, Born 10/25/55

			HOW MUCH HE PITCHED						WHAT HE GAVE UP										THE RESULTS					
Year	Team	League	G	GS	CG	GF	IP	BFP	H	R	ER	HR	SH	SF	HB	TBB	IBB	SO	WP	Bk	W	L	Pct	ShO	Sv	ERA
1978	Texas	A	3	1	0	2	9	36	11	4	4	0	0	1	0	0	0	8	0	0	1	0	1.000	0	0	4.00
1979	Texas	A	20	6	1	4	78	313	50	36	35	5	3	6	5	30	2	58	0	1	4	4	.500	0	0	4.04
1980	Texas	A	53	2	0	35	110	468	98	37	32	4	5	7	2	50	7	104	3	0	13	4	.765	0	8	2.62
1981	Texas	A	22	22	6	0	146	601	115	67	59	12	8	3	6	57	5	98	1	0	9	9	.500	2	0	3.64
1982	Texas	A	56	1	0	41	89	394	95	38	34	6	10	5	2	37	8	61	2	1	10	8	.556	0	7	3.44
1983	Texas	A	28	26	9	0	183	780	175	86	71	9	7	7	3	62	3	92	2	0	8	13	.381	2	0	3.49
1984	Texas	A	35	32	5	2	223.2	955	249	110	98	19	3	3	4	54	2	123	3	0	8	12	.400	1	0	3.94
1985	Milwaukee	A	39	29	11	8	217.2	919	212	112	92	34	7	9	4	65	4	125	6	0	8	18	.308	1	2	3.80
1986	2 Teams	A	39	22	6	6	184.2	759	170	81	65	16	6	9	3	44	1	120	7	1	11	10	.524	1	0	3.17
9 YEARS			295	141	38	98	1241	5225	1175	571	490	105	49	50	29	399	32	789	24	3	72	78	.480	7	17	3.55
1986	Milwaukee	A	27	14	5	4	130.1	537	120	62	51	13	5	6	3	35	1	80	5	0	6	8	.429	1	0	3.52
1986	Houston	N	12	8	1	2	54.1	222	50	19	14	3	1	3	0	9	0	40	2	1	5	2	.714	0	0	2.32

DARREN DAULTON

Bats Left-handed, Throws Right-handed   Turns Age 25 in 1987, Born 01/03/62

Year	Team	League	G	AB	H	2B	3B	HR	(Hm	Rd)	TB	R	RBI	TBB	IBB	SO	HBP	SH	SF	SB	CS	SB%	GIDP	AVE	OBP	SLG
1983	Philadelphia	N	2	3	1	0	0	0	(0	0)	1	1	0	1	0	1	0	0	0	0	0	.00	0	.333	.500	.333
1985	Philadelphia	N	36	103	21	3	1	4	(0	4)	38	14	11	16	0	37	0	0	0	3	0	1.00	1	.204	.311	.369
1986	Philadelphia	N	49	138	31	4	0	8	(4	4)	59	18	21	38	3	41	1	2	2	2	3	.40	1	.225	.391	.428
3 YEARS			87	244	53	7	1	12	(4	8)	98	33	32	55	3	79	1	2	2	5	3	.63	2	.217	.361	.402

ALVIN DAVIS

Bats Left-handed, Throws Right-handed   Turns Age 27 in 1987, Born 09/09/60

Year	Team	League	G	AB	H	2B	3B	HR	(Hm	Rd)	TB	R	RBI	TBB	IBB	SO	HBP	SH	SF	SB	CS	SB%	GIDP	AVE	OBP	SLG
1984	Seattle	A	152	567	161	34	3	27	(15	12)	282	80	116	97	16	78	7	0	7	5	4	.56	7	.284	.391	.497
1985	Seattle	A	155	578	166	33	1	18	(11	7)	255	78	78	90	7	71	7	0	7	1	2	.33	14	.287	.381	.441
1986	Seattle	A	135	479	130	18	1	18	(14	4)	204	66	72	76	10	68	3	2	2	0	3	.00	11	.271	.373	.426
3 YEARS			442	1624	457	85	5	63	(40	23)	741	224	266	263	33	217	12	2	16	6	9	.40	32	.281	.382	.456

CHILI DAVIS

Bats both Right and Left-handed, Throws Right-handed   Turns Age 27 in 1987, Born 01/17/60

Year	Team	League	G	AB	H	2B	3B	HR	(Hm	Rd)	TB	R	RBI	TBB	IBB	SO	HBP	SH	SF	SB	CS	SB%	GIDP	AVE	OBP	SLG
1981	San Francisco	N	8	15	2	0	0	0	(0	0)	2	1	0	1	0	2	0	0	0	2	0	1.00	1	.133	.188	.133
1982	San Francisco	N	154	641	167	27	6	19	(6	13)	263	86	76	45	2	115	2	7	6	24	13	.65	13	.261	.308	.410
1983	San Francisco	N	137	486	113	21	2	11	(7	4)	171	54	59	55	6	108	2	3	9	10	12	.45	9	.233	.305	.352
1984	San Francisco	N	137	499	157	21	6	21	(7	14)	253	87	81	42	6	74	1	2	2	12	8	.60	13	.315	.368	.507
1985	San Francisco	N	136	481	130	25	2	13	(7	6)	198	53	56	62	12	74	0	1	7	15	7	.68	16	.270	.349	.412
1986	San Francisco	N	153	526	146	28	3	13	(7	6)	219	71	70	84	23	96	1	2	5	16	13	.55	11	.278	.375	.416
6 YEARS			725	2648	715	122	19	77	(34	43)	1106	352	342	289	49	469	4	15	29	79	53	.60	63	.270	.339	.418

ERIC DAVIS

Bats Right-handed, Throws Right-handed   Turns Age 25 in 1987, Born 05/29/62

Year	Team	League	G	AB	H	2B	3B	HR	(Hm	Rd)	TB	R	RBI	TBB	IBB	SO	HBP	SH	SF	SB	CS	SB%	GIDP	AVE	OBP	SLG
1984	Cincinnati	N	57	174	39	10	1	10	(3	7)	81	33	30	24	0	48	1	0	1	10	2	.83	1	.224	.320	.466
1985	Cincinnati	N	56	122	30	3	3	8	(1	7)	63	26	18	7	0	39	0	2	0	16	3	.84	1	.246	.287	.516
1986	Cincinnati	N	132	415	115	15	3	27	(12	15)	217	97	71	68	5	100	1	0	3	80	11	.88	6	.277	.378	.523
3 YEARS			245	711	184	28	7	45	(16	29)	361	156	119	99	5	187	2	2	4	106	16	.87	8	.259	.349	.508

GLENN DAVIS

Bats Right-handed, Throws Right-handed   Turns Age 26 in 1987, Born 03/28/61

Year	Team	League	G	AB	H	2B	3B	HR	(Hm	Rd)	TB	R	RBI	TBB	IBB	SO	HBP	SH	SF	SB	CS	SB%	GIDP	AVE	OBP	SLG
1984	Houston	N	18	61	13	5	0	2	(1	1)	24	6	8	4	0	12	0	2	1	0	0	.00	0	.213	.258	.393
1985	Houston	N	100	350	95	11	0	20	(8	12)	166	51	64	27	6	68	7	2	4	0	0	.00	12	.271	.332	.474
1986	Houston	N	158	574	152	32	3	31	(17	14)	283	91	101	64	6	72	9	0	7	3	1	.75	11	.265	.344	.493
3 YEARS			276	985	260	48	3	53	(26	27)	473	148	173	95	12	152	16	4	12	3	1	.75	23	.264	.335	.480

JODY DAVIS

Bats Right-handed, Throws Right-handed   Turns Age 31 in 1987, Born 11/12/56

Year	Team	League	G	AB	H	2B	3B	HR	(Hm	Rd)	TB	R	RBI	TBB	IBB	SO	HBP	SH	SF	SB	CS	SB%	GIDP	AVE	OBP	SLG
1981	Chicago	N	56	180	46	5	1	4	(4	0)	65	14	21	21	3	28	1	3	2	0	1	.00	6	.256	.333	.361
1982	Chicago	N	130	418	109	20	2	12	(6	6)	169	41	52	36	4	92	1	4	7	0	1	.00	6	.261	.316	.404
1983	Chicago	N	151	510	138	31	2	24	(15	9)	245	56	84	33	5	93	2	0	5	0	2	.00	16	.271	.315	.480
1984	Chicago	N	150	523	134	25	2	19	(13	6)	220	55	94	47	15	99	1	1	7	5	6	.45	20	.256	.315	.421
1985	Chicago	N	142	482	112	30	0	17	(10	7)	193	47	58	48	5	83	0	2	4	1	0	1.00	14	.232	.300	.400
1986	Chicago	N	148	528	132	27	2	21	(14	7)	226	61	74	41	4	110	0	4	8	0	1	.00	14	.250	.300	.428
6 YEARS			777	2641	671	138	9	97	(62	35)	1118	274	383	226	36	505	5	14	33	6	11	.35	76	.254	.310	.423

JOEL DAVIS

Pitches Right-handed, Bats Left-handed   Turns Age 22 in 1987, Born 01/30/65

Year	Team	League	G	GS	CG	GF	IP	BFP	H	R	ER	HR	SH	SF	HB	TBB	IBB	SO	WP	Bk	W	L	Pct	ShO	Sv	ERA
1985	Chicago	A	12	11	1	0	71.1	307	71	34	33	6	1	2	1	26	0	37	1	0	3	3	.500	0	0	4.16
1986	Chicago	A	19	19	1	0	105.1	468	115	64	55	9	3	2	1	51	0	54	4	1	4	5	.444	0	0	4.70
2 YEARS			31	30	2	0	176.2	775	186	98	88	15	4	4	2	77	0	91	5	1	7	8	.467	0	0	4.48

MIKE DAVIS

Bats Left-handed, Throws Left-handed Turns Age 28 in 1987, Born 06/11/59

									BATTING										BASERUNNING				PERCENTAGES		
Year	Team	League	G	AB	H	2B	3B	HR	(Hm	Rd)	TB	R	RBI	TBB	IBB	SO	HBP	SH	SF	SB	CS	SB%	GIDP	AVE	OBP	SLG
1980	Oakland	A	51	95	20	2	1	1	(0	1)	27	11	8	7	0	14	0	4	1	2	1	.67	2	.211	.262	.284
1981	Oakland	A	17	20	1	1	0	0	(0	0)	2	0	0	2	0	4	0	0	0	0	0	.00	1	.050	.136	.100
1982	Oakland	A	23	75	30	4	0	1	(1	0)	37	12	10	2	0	8	0	0	0	3	2	.60	0	.400	.416	.493
1983	Oakland	A	128	443	122	24	4	8	(3	5)	178	61	62	27	1	74	5	5	4	32	15	.68	9	.275	.322	.402
1984	Oakland	A	134	382	88	18	3	9	(4	5)	139	47	46	31	2	66	1	2	7	14	9	.61	5	.230	.285	.364
1985	Oakland	A	154	547	157	34	1	24	(12	12)	265	92	82	50	8	99	2	3	2	24	10	.71	10	.287	.348	.484
1986	Oakland	A	142	489	131	28	3	19	(11	8)	222	77	55	34	2	91	1	4	5	27	4	.87	7	.268	.314	.454
7 YEARS			649	2051	549	111	12	62	(31	31)	870	300	263	153	13	356	9	18	19	102	41	.71	34	.268	.319	.424

MARK DAVIS

Pitches Left-handed, Bats Left-handed Turns Age 27 in 1987, Born 10/19/60

			HOW MUCH HE PITCHED						WHAT HE GAVE UP												THE RESULTS				
Year	Team	League	G	GS	CG	GF	IP	BFP	H	R	ER	HR	SH	SF	HB	TBB	IBB	SO	WP	Bk	W	L	Pct	ShO	Sv	ERA
1980	Philadelphia	N	2	1	0	0	7	30	4	2	2	0	0	0	0	5	0	5	0	0	0	0	.000	0	0	2.57
1981	Philadelphia	N	9	9	0	0	43	194	49	37	37	7	2	4	0	24	0	29	1	1	1	4	.200	0	0	7.74
1983	San Francisco	N	20	20	2	0	111	469	93	51	43	14	2	4	3	50	4	83	8	1	6	4	.600	2	0	3.49
1984	San Francisco	N	46	27	1	6	174.2	766	201	113	104	25	10	10	5	54	12	124	8	4	5	17	.227	0	0	5.36
1985	San Francisco	N	77	1	0	38	114.1	465	89	49	45	13	13	1	3	41	7	131	6	1	5	12	.294	0	7	3.54
1986	San Francisco	N	67	2	0	20	84.1	342	63	33	28	6	5	5	1	34	7	90	3	0	5	7	.417	0	4	2.99
6 YEARS			221	60	3	64	534.1	2266	499	285	259	65	32	24	12	208	30	462	26	7	22	44	.333	2	11	4.36

RON DAVIS

Pitches Right-handed, Bats Right-handed Turns Age 32 in 1987, Born 08/06/55

			HOW MUCH HE PITCHED						WHAT HE GAVE UP												THE RESULTS				
Year	Team	League	G	GS	CG	GF	IP	BFP	H	R	ER	HR	SH	SF	HB	TBB	IBB	SO	WP	Bk	W	L	Pct	ShO	Sv	ERA
1978	New York	A	4	0	0	2	2	12	3	4	3	0	0	0	0	3	0	0	0	0	0	0	.000	0	0	13.50
1979	New York	A	44	0	0	21	85	357	84	29	27	5	4	3	1	28	9	43	1	0	14	2	.875	0	9	2.86
1980	New York	A	53	0	0	29	131	544	121	50	43	9	10	6	5	32	3	65	5	1	9	3	.750	0	7	2.95
1981	New York	A	43	0	0	22	73	285	47	22	22	6	4	3	0	25	3	83	1	1	4	5	.444	0	6	2.71
1982	Minnesota	A	63	0	0	53	106	459	106	53	52	16	2	2	1	47	12	89	5	1	3	9	.250	0	22	4.42
1983	Minnesota	A	66	0	0	61	89	382	89	34	33	6	6	6	3	33	3	84	4	1	5	8	.385	0	30	3.34
1984	Minnesota	A	64	0	0	56	83	364	79	44	42	11	3	6	2	41	9	74	8	0	7	11	.389	0	29	4.55
1985	Minnesota	A	57	0	0	50	64.2	285	55	28	25	7	3	4	4	35	6	72	8	1	2	6	.250	0	25	3.48
1986	2 Teams		53	0	0	33	58.2	289	86	60	56	10	2	2	4	32	8	40	4	1	2	8	.200	0	2	8.59
9 YEARS			447	0	0	327	692.1	2977	670	324	303	70	34	32	20	276	53	550	36	6	46	52	.469	0	130	3.94
1986	Minnesota	A	36	0	0	28	38.2	198	55	42	39	7	2	1	4	29	8	30	4	0	2	6	.250	0	2	9.08
1986	Chicago	N	17	0	0	5	20	91	31	18	17	3	0	1	0	3	0	10	0	1	0	2	.000	0	0	7.65

STORM DAVIS

Pitches Right-handed, Bats Right-handed Turns Age 26 in 1987, Born 12/26/61

			HOW MUCH HE PITCHED						WHAT HE GAVE UP												THE RESULTS				
Year	Team	League	G	GS	CG	GF	IP	BFP	H	R	ER	HR	SH	SF	HB	TBB	IBB	SO	WP	Bk	W	L	Pct	ShO	Sv	ERA
1982	Baltimore	A	29	8	1	9	100.2	412	96	40	39	8	4	6	0	28	4	67	2	1	8	4	.667	0	0	3.49
1983	Baltimore	A	34	29	6	0	200.1	831	180	90	80	14	5	4	2	64	4	125	7	2	13	7	.650	1	0	3.59
1984	Baltimore	A	35	31	10	3	225	923	205	86	78	7	7	9	5	71	6	105	6	1	14	9	.609	2	1	3.12
1985	Baltimore	A	31	28	8	0	175	750	172	92	88	11	3	1	1	70	5	93	2	1	10	8	.556	1	0	4.53
1986	Baltimore	A	25	25	2	0	154	657	166	70	62	16	3	2	0	49	2	96	5	0	9	12	.429	0	0	3.62
5 YEARS			154	121	27	12	855	3573	819	378	347	56	22	24	8	282	21	486	22	5	54	40	.574	4	1	3.65

BILL DAWLEY

Pitches Right-handed, Bats Right-handed Turns Age 29 in 1987, Born 02/06/58

			HOW MUCH HE PITCHED						WHAT HE GAVE UP												THE RESULTS				
Year	Team	League	G	GS	CG	GF	IP	BFP	H	R	ER	HR	SH	SF	HB	TBB	IBB	SO	WP	Bk	W	L	Pct	ShO	Sv	ERA
1983	Houston	N	48	0	0	37	79.2	304	51	26	25	9	5	0	1	22	4	60	1	0	6	6	.500	0	14	2.82
1984	Houston	N	60	0	0	27	98	402	82	24	21	5	10	6	0	35	9	47	2	1	11	4	.733	0	5	1.93
1985	Houston	N	49	0	0	19	81	347	76	35	32	7	12	4	0	37	7	48	2	0	5	3	.625	0	2	3.56
1986	Chicago	A	46	0	0	23	97.2	405	91	38	36	10	5	3	1	28	3	66	5	0	0	7	.000	0	2	3.32
4 YEARS			203	0	0	106	356.1	1458	300	123	114	31	32	13	2	122	23	221	10	1	22	20	.524	0	23	2.88

ANDRE DAWSON

Bats Right-handed, Throws Right-handed

Turns Age 33 in 1987, Born 07/10/54

										BATTING										BASERUNNING				PERCENTAGES		
Year	Team	League	G	AB	H	2B	3B	HR	(Hm	Rd)	TB	R	RBI	TBB	IBB	SO	HBP	SH	SF	SB	CS	SB%	GIDP	AVE	OBP	SLG
1976	Montreal	N	24	85	20	4	1	0	(0	0)	26	9	7	5	1	13	0	2	0	1	2	.33	0	.235	.278	.306
1977	Montreal	N	139	525	148	26	9	19	(7	12)	249	64	65	34	4	93	2	1	4	21	7	.75	6	.282	.326	.474
1978	Montreal	N	157	609	154	24	8	25	(12	13)	269	84	72	30	3	128	12	4	5	28	11	.72	7	.253	.299	.442
1979	Montreal	N	155	639	176	24	12	25	(13	12)	299	90	92	27	5	115	6	8	4	35	10	.78	10	.275	.309	.468
1980	Montreal	N	151	577	178	41	7	17	(7	10)	284	96	87	44	7	69	6	1	10	34	9	.79	9	.308	.358	.492
1981	Montreal	N	103	394	119	21	3	24	(9	15)	218	71	64	35	14	50	7	0	5	26	4	.87	6	.302	.365	.553
1982	Montreal	N	148	608	183	37	7	23	(9	14)	303	107	83	34	4	96	8	4	6	39	10	.80	14	.301	.343	.498
1983	Montreal	N	159	633	189	36	10	32	(10	22)	341	104	113	38	12	81	9	0	18	25	11	.69	14	.299	.338	.539
1984	Montreal	N	138	533	132	23	6	17	(6	11)	218	73	86	41	2	80	2	1	6	13	5	.72	12	.248	.301	.409
1985	Montreal	N	139	529	135	27	2	23	(11	12)	235	65	91	29	8	92	4	1	7	13	4	.76	12	.255	.295	.444
1986	Montreal	N	130	496	141	32	2	20	(11	9)	237	65	78	37	11	79	6	1	6	18	12	.60	13	.284	.338	.478
11 YEARS			1443	5628	1575	295	67	225	(95	130)	2679	828	838	354	71	896	62	23	71	253	85	.75	97	.280	.326	.476

KEN DAYLEY

Pitches Left-handed, Bats Left-handed

Turns Age 28 in 1987, Born 02/25/59

			HOW MUCH HE PITCHED						WHAT HE GAVE UP											THE RESULTS					
Year	Team	League	G	GS	CG	GF	IP	BFP	H	R	ER	HR	SH	SF	HB	TBB	IBB	SO	WP	Bk	W	L	Pct	ShO	Sv	ERA
1982	Atlanta	N	20	11	0	3	71.1	313	79	39	36	9	7	5	0	25	2	34	2	0	5	6	.455	0	0	4.54
1983	Atlanta	N	24	16	0	3	104.2	436	100	59	50	12	3	3	2	39	2	70	3	0	5	8	.385	0	0	4.30
1984	2 Teams		7	6	0	1	23.2	124	44	28	21	6	4	0	1	11	1	10	0	0	0	5	.000	0	0	7.99
1985	St Louis	N	57	0	0	27	65.1	271	65	24	20	2	4	2	0	18	9	62	4	0	4	4	.500	0	11	2.76
1986	St Louis	N	31	0	0	13	38.2	170	42	19	14	1	4	1	1	11	3	33	0	0	0	3	.000	0	5	3.26
5 YEARS			139	33	0	47	303.2	1314	330	169	141	30	22	11	4	104	17	209	9	0	14	26	.350	0	16	4.18
1984	Atlanta	N	4	4	0	0	18.2	92	28	18	11	5	3	0	1	6	1	10	0	0	0	3	.000	0	0	5.30
1984	St Louis	N	3	2	0	1	5	32	16	10	10	1	1	0	0	5	0	0	0	0	0	2	.000	0	0	18.00

DOUG DECINCES

Bats Right-handed, Throws Right-handed

Turns Age 37 in 1987, Born 08/29/50

										BATTING										BASERUNNING				PERCENTAGES		
Year	Team	League	G	AB	H	2B	3B	HR	(Hm	Rd)	TB	R	RBI	TBB	IBB	SO	HBP	SH	SF	SB	CS	SB%	GIDP	AVE	OBP	SLG
1973	Baltimore	A	10	18	2	0	0	0	(0	0)	2	2	3	1	0	5	0	0	0	0	0	.00	0	.111	.158	.111
1974	Baltimore	A	1	1	0	0	0	0	(0	0)	0	0	0	1	0	0	0	0	0	0	0	.00	0	.000	.500	.000
1975	Baltimore	A	61	167	42	6	3	4	(3	1)	66	20	23	13	2	32	1	0	2	0	1	.00	3	.251	.306	.395
1976	Baltimore	A	129	440	103	17	2	11	(5	6)	157	36	42	29	1	68	2	3	1	8	4	.67	11	.234	.284	.357
1977	Baltimore	A	150	522	135	28	3	19	(11	8)	226	63	69	64	6	86	2	0	5	8	8	.50	14	.259	.339	.433
1978	Baltimore	A	142	511	146	37	1	28	(14	14)	269	72	80	46	2	81	2	0	2	7	7	.50	12	.286	.346	.526
1979	Baltimore	A	120	422	97	27	1	16	(10	6)	174	67	61	54	5	68	3	0	5	5	3	.63	11	.230	.318	.412
1980	Baltimore	A	145	489	122	23	2	16	(7	9)	197	64	64	49	5	83	3	4	4	11	6	.65	20	.249	.319	.403
1981	Baltimore	A	100	346	91	23	2	13	(10	3)	157	49	55	41	2	32	1	1	2	0	3	.00	12	.263	.341	.454
1982	California	A	153	575	173	42	5	30	(17	13)	315	94	97	66	7	80	1	4	9	7	5	.58	18	.301	.369	.548
1983	California	A	95	370	104	19	3	18	(10	8)	183	49	65	32	2	56	0	1	8	2	0	1.00	13	.281	.332	.495
1984	California	A	146	547	147	23	3	20	(10	10)	236	77	82	53	4	79	0	0	12	4	1	.80	16	.269	.327	.431
1985	California	A	120	427	104	22	1	20	(12	8)	188	50	78	47	11	71	2	5	7	1	4	.20	17	.244	.317	.440
1986	California	A	140	512	131	20	3	26	(14	12)	235	69	96	52	4	74	2	2	4	2	2	.50	19	.256	.325	.459
14 YEARS			1512	5347	1397	287	29	221	(123	98)	2405	712	815	548	51	815	19	20	61	55	44	.56	166	.261	.329	.450

JOSE DELEON

Pitches Right-handed, Bats Right-handed

Turns Age 27 in 1987, Born 12/20/60

			HOW MUCH HE PITCHED						WHAT HE GAVE UP											THE RESULTS					
Year	Team	League	G	GS	CG	GF	IP	BFP	H	R	ER	HR	SH	SF	HB	TBB	IBB	SO	WP	Bk	W	L	Pct	ShO	Sv	ERA
1983	Pittsburgh	N	15	15	3	0	108	438	75	36	34	5	4	3	1	47	2	118	5	2	7	3	.700	2	0	2.83
1984	Pittsburgh	N	30	28	5	0	192.1	795	147	86	80	10	7	7	3	92	5	153	6	2	7	13	.350	1	0	3.74
1985	Pittsburgh	N	31	25	1	5	162.2	700	138	93	85	15	7	4	3	89	3	149	7	1	2	19	.095	0	3	4.70
1986	2 Teams		22	14	1	5	95.1	408	66	46	41	9	5	1	5	59	3	79	7	0	5	8	.385	0	1	3.87
4 YEARS			98	82	10	10	558.1	2341	426	261	240	39	23	15	12	287	13	499	25	5	21	43	.328	3	4	3.87
1986	Chicago	A	13	13	1	0	79	325	49	30	26	7	4	1	4	42	0	68	6	0	4	5	.444	0	0	2.96
1986	Pittsburgh	N	9	1	0	5	16.1	83	17	16	15	2	1	0	1	17	3	11	1	0	1	3	.250	0	1	8.27

JEFF DEDMON

Pitches Right-handed, Bats Left-handed

Turns Age 27 in 1987, Born 03/04/60

			HOW MUCH HE PITCHED						WHAT HE GAVE UP											THE RESULTS					
Year	Team	League	G	GS	CG	GF	IP	BFP	H	R	ER	HR	SH	SF	HB	TBB	IBB	SO	WP	Bk	W	L	Pct	ShO	Sv	ERA
1983	Atlanta	N	5	0	0	0	4	23	10	6	6	1	1	0	0	0	0	3	0	0	0	0	.000	0	0	13.50
1984	Atlanta	N	54	0	0	19	81	354	86	39	34	5	5	2	2	35	9	51	3	0	4	3	.571	0	4	3.78
1985	Atlanta	N	60	0	0	15	86	377	84	52	39	5	8	1	1	49	14	41	2	1	6	3	.667	0	0	4.08
1986	Atlanta	N	57	0	0	22	99.2	424	90	43	33	8	7	2	4	39	5	58	3	2	6	6	.500	0	3	2.98
4 YEARS			176	0	0	56	270.2	1178	270	140	112	19	21	5	7	123	28	153	8	3	16	12	.571	0	7	3.72

ROB DEER

Bats Right-handed, Throws Right-handed

Turns Age 27 in 1987, Born 09/29/60

Year	Team	League	G	AB	H	2B	3B	HR	(Hm	Rd)	TB	R	RBI	TBB	IBB	SO	HBP	SH	SF	SB	CS	SB%	GIDP	AVE	OBP	SLG
1984	San Francisco	N	13	24	4	0	0	3	(2	1)	13	5	3	7	0	10	1	0	0	1	1	.50	0	.167	.375	.667
1985	San Francisco	N	78	162	30	5	1	8	(5	3)	61	22	20	23	0	71	0	0	2			.00	1	.185	.283	.377
1986	Milwaukee	A	134	466	108	17	3	33	(19	14)	230	75	86	72	3	179	3	2	3	5	2	.71	4	.232	.336	.494
3 YEARS			225	652	142	22	4	44	(26	18)	304	102	109	102	3	260	4	2	5	6	4	.60	4	.218	.325	.466

RICK DEMPSEY

Bats Right-handed, Throws Right-handed

Turns Age 38 in 1987, Born 09/13/49

Year	Team	League	G	AB	H	2B	3B	HR	(Hm	Rd)	TB	R	RBI	TBB	IBB	SO	HBP	SH	SF	SB	CS	SB%	GIDP	AVE	OBP	SLG
1969	Minnesota	A	5	6	3	1	0	0	(0	0)	4	1	0	1	0	0	0	0	0	0	0	.00	0	.500	.571	.667
1970	Minnesota	A	5	7	0	0	0	0	(0	0)	0	1	0	1	0	1	0	0	0	0	0	.00	0	.000	.125	.000
1971	Minnesota	A	6	13	4	1	0	0	(0	0)	5	2	0	1	0	1	0	0	0	0	0	.00	1	.308	.357	.385
1972	Minnesota	A	25	40	8	1	0	0	(0	0)	9	0	0	6	0	8	0	1	0	0	0	.00	2	.200	.304	.225
1973	New York	A	6	11	2	0	0	0	(0	0)	2	0	0	1	0	3	0	1	0	0	0	.00	1	.182	.250	.182
1974	New York	A	43	109	26	3	0	2	(1	1)	35	12	12	8	0	7	0	1	1	1	0	1.00	5	.239	.288	.321
1975	New York	A	71	145	38	8	0	1	(0	1)	49	18	11	21	1	15	0	3	1	0	0	.00	5	.262	.353	.338
1976	2 Teams		80	216	42	2	0	0	(0	0)	44	12	12	18	0	21	2	4	0	1	1	.50	7	.194	.263	.204
1977	Baltimore	A	91	270	61	7	4	3	(1	2)	85	27	34	34	1	34	2	5	3	2	3	.40	9	.226	.314	.315
1978	Baltimore	A	136	441	114	25	0	6	(4	2)	157	41	32	48	2	54	0	3	6	7	3	.70	11	.259	.327	.356
1979	Baltimore	A	124	368	88	23	0	6	(1	5)	129	48	41	38	1	37	0	3	4	0	1	.00	12	.239	.307	.351
1980	Baltimore	A	119	362	95	26	3	9	(5	4)	154	51	40	36	1	45	3	4	1	3	1	.75	11	.262	.333	.425
1981	Baltimore	A	92	251	54	10	1	6	(4	2)	84	24	15	32	1	36	1	3	0	0	1	.00	5	.215	.306	.335
1982	Baltimore	A	125	344	88	15	1	5	(2	3)	120	35	36	46	1	37	0	7	5	0	3	.00	10	.256	.339	.349
1983	Baltimore	A	128	347	80	16	2	4	(3	1)	112	33	32	40	1	54	3	5	5	1	1	.50	9	.231	.311	.323
1984	Baltimore	A	109	330	76	11	0	11	(6	5)	120	37	34	40	0	58	1	5	4	1	2	.33	11	.230	.312	.364
1985	Baltimore	A	132	362	92	19	0	12	(4	8)	147	54	52	50	0	87	1	5	2	1	2	.33	2	.254	.345	.406
1986	Baltimore	A	122	327	68	15	1	13	(7	6)	124	42	29	45	0	78	3	7	0	1	0	1.00	5	.208	.309	.379
18 YEARS			1419	3949	939	183	12	78	(38	40)	1380	438	380	466	9	576	16	57	32	17	17	.50	102	.238	.318	.349
1976	Baltimore	A	59	174	37	2	0	0	(0	0)	39	11	10	13	0	17	2	3	0	1	1	.50	2	.213	.275	.224
1976	New York	A	21	42	5	0	0	0	(0	0)	5	1	2	5	0	4	0	1	0	0	0	.00	0	.119	.213	.119

JOHN DENNY

Pitches Right-handed, Bats Right-handed

Turns Age 35 in 1987, Born 11/08/52

Year	Team	League	G	GS	CG	GF	IP	BFP	H	R	ER	HR	SH	SF	HB	TBB	IBB	SO	WP	Bk	W	L	Pct	ShO	Sv	ERA
1974	St Louis	N	2	0	0	0	2	11	3	2	0	0	0	0	0	0	0	1	0	0	0	0	.000	1	0	0.00
1975	St Louis	N	25	24	3	0	136	591	149	73	60	5	1	3	3	51	6	72	8	1	10	7	.588	2	0	3.97
1976	St Louis	N	30	30	8	0	207	861	189	71	58	11	9	1	8	74	3	74	5	0	11	9	.550	3	0	2.52
1977	St Louis	N	26	26	3	0	150	664	165	85	75	9	7	3	5	62	0	60	6	1	8	8	.500	0	0	4.50
1978	St Louis	N	33	33	11	0	234	936	200	81	77	13	9	7	6	74	4	103	8	4	14	11	.560	2	0	2.96
1979	St Louis	N	31	31	5	0	206	900	206	116	111	24	15	3	3	100	7	99	6	1	8	11	.421	2	0	4.85
1980	Cleveland	A	16	16	4	0	109	464	116	54	53	4	1	3	5	47	2	59	4	1	8	6	.571	2	0	4.38
1981	Cleveland	A	19	19	6	0	146	623	139	62	51	9	2	5	3	66	3	94	10	0	10	6	.625	3	0	3.14
1982	2 Teams		25	25	5	0	160.2	703	144	92	87	12	4	3	6	83	3	113	5	2	6	13	.316	0	0	4.87
1983	Philadelphia	N	36	36	7	0	242.2	983	229	77	64	9	8	3	4	53	5	139	6	1	19	6	.760	1	0	2.37
1984	Philadelphia	N	22	22	2	0	154.1	612	122	53	42	11	6	3	4	29	2	94	0	0	7	7	.500	0	0	2.45
1985	Philadelphia	N	33	33	6	0	230.2	998	252	112	98	15	11	8	3	83	5	123	8	0	11	14	.440	2	0	3.82
1986	Cincinnati	N	27	27	2	0	171.1	731	179	89	80	15	9	4	4	56	9	115	2	1	11	10	.524	1	0	4.20
13 YEARS			325	322	62	0	2149.2	9077	2093	967	856	137	82	46	54	778	49	1146	68	12	123	108	.532	18	0	3.58
1982	Cleveland	A	21	21	5	0	138.1	609	126	80	77	11	3	3	6	73	2	94	5	2	6	11	.353	0	0	5.01
1982	Philadelphia	N	4	4	0	0	22.1	94	18	12	10	1	1	0	0	10	1	19	0	0	0	2	.000	0	0	4.03

BOB DERNIER

Bats Right-handed, Throws Right-handed

Turns Age 30 in 1987, Born 01/05/57

Year	Team	League	G	AB	H	2B	3B	HR	(Hm	Rd)	TB	R	RBI	TBB	IBB	SO	HBP	SH	SF	SB	CS	SB%	GIDP	AVE	OBP	SLG
1980	Philadelphia	N	10	7	4	0	0	0	(0	0)	4	5	1	1	0	0	0	0	0	3	0	1.00	0	.571	.625	.571
1981	Philadelphia	N	10	4	3	0	0	0	(0	0)	3	0	0	0	0	0	0	0	0	2	1	.67	0	.750	.750	.750
1982	Philadelphia	N	122	370	92	10	2	4	(3	1)	118	56	21	36	0	69	1	3	2	42	12	.78	6	.249	.315	.319
1983	Philadelphia	N	122	221	51	10	0	1	(0	1)	64	41	15	18	0	21	0	5	1	35	7	.83	2	.231	.288	.290
1984	Chicago	N	143	536	149	26	5	3	(2	1)	194	94	32	63	0	60	2	11	0	45	17	.73	5	.278	.356	.362
1985	Chicago	N	121	469	119	20	5	1	(1	0)	148	63	21	40	1	44	3	7	2	31	8	.79	7	.254	.315	.316
1986	Chicago	N	108	324	73	14	1	4	(2	2)	101	32	18	22	1	41	0	5	0	27	2	.93	7	.225	.275	.312
7 YEARS			636	1931	491	80	11	13	(8	5)	632	291	108	180	2	235	6	31	5	185	47	.80	27	.254	.319	.327

JIM DESHAIES

Pitches Left-handed, Bats Left-handed   Turns Age 27 in 1987, Born 06/23/60

Year	Team	League	G	GS	CG	GF	IP	BFP	H	R	ER	HR	SH	SF	HB	TBB	IBB	SO	WP	Bk	W	L	Pct	ShO	Sv	ERA
1984	New York	A	2	2	0	0	7	40	14	9	9	0	1	0	1	7	0	5	0	0	0	0	.000	0	0	11.57
1985	Houston	N	2	0	0	0	3	10	1	0	0	0	0	0	0	0	0	2	0	0	0	0	.000	0	0	0.00
1986	Houston	N	26	26	1	0	144	599	124	58	52	16	4	3	2	59	2	128	0	7	12	5	.706	1	0	3.25
3 YEARS			30	28	1	0	154	649	139	67	61	17	4	4	2	66	2	135	0	7	12	6	.667	1	0	3.56

BO DIAZ

Bats Right-handed, Throws Right-handed   Turns Age 34 in 1987, Born 03/23/53

Year	Team	League	G	AB	H	2B	3B	HR	(Hm	Rd)	TB	R	RBI	TBB	IBB	SO	HBP	SH	SF	SB	CS	SB%	GIDP	AVE	OBP	SLG
1977	Boston	A	2	1	0	0	0	0	(0	0)	0	0	0	1	0	0	0	0	0	0	0	.00	0	.000	.000	.000
1978	Cleveland	A	44	127	30	4	0	2	(1	1)	40	12	11	4	0	17	0	2	0	0	0	.00	1	.236	.260	.315
1979	Cleveland	A	15	32	5	2	0	0	(0	0)	7	0	1	2	0	6	0	1	0	0	0	.00	1	.156	.206	.219
1980	Cleveland	A	76	207	47	11	2	3	(2	1)	71	15	32	7	3	27	0	5	2	1	0	1.00	12	.227	.250	.343
1981	Cleveland	A	63	182	57	19	0	7	(5	2)	97	25	38	13	2	23	1	1	2	2	2	.50	7	.313	.359	.533
1982	Philadelphia	N	144	525	151	29	1	18	(11	7)	236	69	85	36	5	87	3	1	7	3	6	.33	20	.288	.333	.450
1983	Philadelphia	N	136	471	111	17	0	15	(9	6)	173	49	64	38	4	57	2	4	1	1	4	.20	10	.236	.295	.367
1984	Philadelphia	N	27	75	16	4	0	1	(1	0)	23	5	9	5	0	13	0	1	2	0	0	.00	4	.213	.256	.307
1985	2 Teams		77	237	58	13	1	5	(4	1)	88	21	31	21	0	25	1	2	2	0	0	.00	11	.245	.307	.371
1986	Cincinnati	N	134	474	129	21	0	10	(8	2)	180	50	56	40	0	52	0	2	3	1	1	.50	11	.272	.327	.380
10 YEARS			718	2331	604	120	4	61	(41	20)	915	246	327	166	14	308	7	19	19	8	13	.38	78	.259	.308	.393
1985	Cincinnati	N	51	161	42	8	0	3	(2	1)	59	12	15	15	0	18	1	2	2	0	0	.00	6	.261	.324	.366
1985	Philadelphia	N	26	76	16	5	1	2	(2	0)	29	9	16	6	0	7	0	0	0	0	0	.00	5	.211	.268	.382

MIKE DIAZ

Bats Right-handed, Throws Right-handed   Turns Age 27 in 1987, Born 04/15/60

Year	Team	League	G	AB	H	2B	3B	HR	(Hm	Rd)	TB	R	RBI	TBB	IBB	SO	HBP	SH	SF	SB	CS	SB%	GIDP	AVE	OBP	SLG
1983	Chicago	N	6	7	2	1	0	0	(0	0)	3	2	1	0	0	0	0	0	0	0	0	.00	0	.286	.286	.429
1986	Pittsburgh	N	97	209	56	9	0	12	(6	6)	101	22	36	19	0	43	2	0	3	0	1	.00	5	.268	.330	.483
2 YEARS			103	216	58	10	0	12	(6	6)	104	24	37	19	0	43	2	0	3	0	1	.00	5	.269	.329	.481

FRANK DIPINO

Pitches Left-handed, Bats Left-handed   Turns Age 31 in 1987, Born 10/22/56

Year	Team	League	G	GS	CG	GF	IP	BFP	H	R	ER	HR	SH	SF	HB	TBB	IBB	SO	WP	Bk	W	L	Pct	ShO	Sv	ERA
1981	Milwaukee	A	2	0	0	2	2	10	0	0	0	0	0	0	0	3	3	3	0	0	0	0	.000	0	0	0.00
1982	Houston	N	6	6	0	0	28.1	122	32	20	19	1	3	2	0	11	1	25	0	0	2	2	.500	0	0	6.04
1983	Houston	N	53	0	0	32	71.1	279	52	21	21	2	1	3	1	20	5	67	3	0	3	4	.429	0	20	2.65
1984	Houston	N	57	0	0	44	75.1	329	74	32	28	3	5	2	1	36	11	65	3	1	4	9	.308	0	14	3.35
1985	Houston	N	54	0	0	29	76	329	69	44	34	7	3	3	3	43	6	49	4	1	3	7	.300	0	6	4.03
1986	2 Teams		61	0	0	26	80.1	345	74	45	39	11	9	3	2	30	6	70	3	0	3	7	.300	0	3	4.37
6 YEARS			233	6	0	133	333.1	1414	301	162	141	24	21	13	6	143	29	279	13	2	15	29	.341	0	43	3.81
1986	Chicago	N	30	0	0	12	40	178	47	27	23	6	4	2	0	14	5	43	3	0	2	4	.333	0	0	5.17
1986	Houston	N	31	0	0	14	40.1	167	27	18	16	5	5	1	2	16	1	27	0	0	1	3	.250	0	3	3.57

KEN DIXON

Pitches Right-handed, Bats both Right and Left-handed   Turns Age 27 in 1987, Born 10/17/60

Year	Team	League	G	GS	CG	GF	IP	BFP	H	R	ER	HR	SH	SF	HB	TBB	IBB	SO	WP	Bk	W	L	Pct	ShO	Sv	ERA
1984	Baltimore	A	2	2	0	0	13	56	14	6	6	1	0	0	0	4	0	8	2	0	0	1	.000	0	0	4.15
1985	Baltimore	A	34	18	3	7	162	683	144	68	66	20	8	2	2	64	7	108	5	2	8	4	.667	1	1	3.67
1986	Baltimore	A	35	33	2	1	202.1	874	194	111	103	33	5	6	1	83	6	170	7	3	11	13	.458	0	0	4.58
3 YEARS			71	53	5	8	377.1	1613	352	185	175	54	13	8	3	151	13	286	14	5	19	18	.514	1	1	4.17

BILL DORAN

Bats both Right and Left-handed, Throws Right-handed   Turns Age 29 in 1987, Born 05/28/58

Year	Team	League	G	AB	H	2B	3B	HR	(Hm	Rd)	TB	R	RBI	TBB	IBB	SO	HBP	SH	SF	SB	CS	SB%	GIDP	AVE	OBP	SLG
1982	Houston	N	26	97	27	3	0	0	(0	0)	30	11	6	4	0	11	0	0	1	5	0	1.00	0	.278	.304	.309
1983	Houston	N	154	535	145	12	7	8	(1	7)	195	70	39	86	11	67	0	7	1	12	12	.50	6	.271	.371	.364
1984	Houston	N	147	548	143	18	11	4	(2	2)	195	92	41	66	7	69	2	7	3	21	12	.64	6	.261	.341	.356
1985	Houston	N	148	578	166	31	6	14	(5	9)	251	84	59	71	6	69	0	3	5	23	15	.61	10	.287	.362	.434
1986	Houston	N	145	550	152	29	3	6	(3	3)	205	92	37	81	7	57	2	4	5	42	19	.69	10	.276	.368	.373
5 YEARS			620	2308	633	93	27	32	(11	21)	876	349	182	308	31	273	4	21	15	103	58	.64	32	.274	.359	.380

RICHARD DOTSON

Pitches Right-handed, Bats Right-handed

Turns Age 28 in 1987, Born 01/10/59

Year	Team	League	HOW MUCH HE PITCHED						WHAT HE GAVE UP												THE RESULTS					
			G	GS	CG	GF	IP	BFP	H	R	ER	HR	SH	SF	HB	TBB	IBB	SO	WP	Bk	W	L	Pct	ShO	Sv	ERA
1979	Chicago	A	5	5	1	0	24	107	28	13	10	0	1		6	0	13	0	0	2	0	1.000	1	0	3.75
1980	Chicago	A	33	32	8	1	198	863	185	105	94	20	15	7	6	87	2	109	6	2	12	10	.545	0	0	4.27
1981	Chicago	A	24	24	5	0	141	599	145	67	59	13	4	5	4	49	0	73	3	2	9	8	.529	4	0	3.77
1982	Chicago	A	34	31	3	3	196.2	867	219	97	84	19	7	6	5	73	4	109	2	1	11	15	.423	1	0	3.84
1983	Chicago	A	35	35	8	0	240	997	209	92	86	19	4	7	8	106	1	137	7	0	22	7	.759	1	0	3.23
1984	Chicago	A	32	32	14	0	245.2	1035	216	110	98	24	8	10	7	103	5	120	4	1	14	15	.483	1	0	3.59
1985	Chicago	A	9	9	0	0	52.1	226	53	30	26	5	1	2	3	17	1	33	0	0	3	4	.429	0	0	4.47
1986	Chicago	A	34	34	3	0	197	861	226	125	120	24	4	4	2	69	2	110	10	0	10	17	.370	1	0	5.48
8 YEARS			206	202	42	4	1294.2	5555	1281	639	577	124	44	43	35	510	15	704	32	6	83	76	.522	9	0	4.01

BRIAN DOWNING

Bats Right-handed, Throws Right-handed

Turns Age 37 in 1987, Born 10/09/50

Year	Team	League	BATTING																	BASERUNNING				PERCENTAGES		
			G	AB	H	2B	3B	HR	(Hm	Rd)	TB	R	RBI	TBB	IBB	SO	HBP	SH	SF	SB	CS	SB%	GIDP	AVE	OBP	SLG
1973	Chicago	A	34	73	13	1	0	2	(1	1)	20	5	4	10	1	17	0	2	0	0	0	.00	3	.178	.277	.274
1974	Chicago	A	108	293	66	12	1	10	(6	4)	110	41	39	51	3	72	2	4	0	0	1	.00	11	.225	.344	.375
1975	Chicago	A	138	420	101	12	1	7	(5	2)	136	58	41	76	5	75	3	11	6	13	4	.76	2	.240	.356	.324
1976	Chicago	A	104	317	81	14	0	3	(0	3)	104	38	30	40	0	55	1	4	3	7	3	.70	2	.256	.338	.328
1977	Chicago	A	69	169	48	4	2	4	(1	3)	68	28	25	34	0	21	2	5	4	1	2	.33	1	.284	.402	.402
1978	California	A	133	412	105	15	0	7	(2	5)	141	42	46	52	2	47	6	4	2	3	2	.60	14	.255	.345	.342
1979	California	A	148	509	166	27	3	12	(3	9)	235	87	75	77	4	57	5	3	2	3	3	.50	17	.326	.418	.462
1980	California	A	30	93	27	6	0	2	(2	0)	39	5	25	12	1	12	0	1	2	0	2	.00	5	.290	.364	.419
1981	California	A	93	317	79	14	0	9	(6	3)	120	47	41	46	1	35	4	3	0	1	1	.50	11	.249	.351	.379
1982	California	A	158	623	175	37	2	28	(15	13)	300	109	84	86	1	58	5	3	8	2	1	.67	14	.281	.368	.482
1983	California	A	113	403	99	15	1	19	(10	9)	173	68	53	62	4	59	5	1	2	1	2	.33	6	.246	.352	.429
1984	California	A	156	539	148	28	2	23	(9	14)	249	65	91	70	3	66	7	3	9	0	4	.00	18	.275	.360	.462
1985	California	A	150	520	137	23	1	20	(10	10)	222	70	85	78	3	61	13	5	4	5	3	.63	12	.263	.371	.427
1986	California	A	152	513	137	27	3	20	(13	7)	232	90	95	90	2	84	17	3	8	4	4	.50	14	.267	.389	.452
14 YEARS			1586	5201	1382	235	17	166	(83	83)	2149	763	734	784	30	719	70	52	50	40	32	.56	142	.266	.366	.413

DOUG DRABEK

Pitches Right-handed, Bats Right-handed

Turns Age 25 in 1987, Born 07/25/62

Year	Team	League	HOW MUCH HE PITCHED						WHAT HE GAVE UP													THE RESULTS					
			G	GS	CG	GF	IP	BFP	H	R	ER	HR	SH	SF	HB	TBB	IBB	SO	WP	Bk	W	L	Pct	ShO	Sv	ERA
1986	New York	A	27	21	0	2	131.2	561	126	64	60	13	5	2	3	50	1	76	2	0	7	8	.467	0	0	4.10

DAVE DRAVECKY

Pitches Left-handed, Bats Right-handed

Turns Age 31 in 1987, Born 02/14/56

Year	Team	League	HOW MUCH HE PITCHED						WHAT HE GAVE UP													THE RESULTS					
			G	GS	CG	GF	IP	BFP	H	R	ER	HR	SH	SF	HB	TBB	IBB	SO	WP	Bk	W	L	Pct	ShO	Sv	ERA
1982	San Diego	N	31	10	0	11	105	426	86	37	30	8	9	0	1	33	3	59	0	1	5	3	.625	0	2	2.57
1983	San Diego	N	28	28	9	0	183.2	756	181	78	73	18	13	4	3	44	4	74	2	1	14	10	.583	1	0	3.58
1984	San Diego	N	50	14	3	17	156.2	631	125	53	51	12	9	4	4	51	0	71	3	2	9	8	.529	2	8	2.93
1985	San Diego	N	34	31	7	1	214.2	876	200	79	70	18	13	3	1	57	5	105	2	2	13	11	.542	2	0	2.93
1986	San Diego	N	26	26	3	0	161.1	677	149	68	55	17	12	5	1	54	7	87	0	1	9	11	.450	1	0	3.07
5 YEARS			169	109	22	29	821.1	3366	741	315	279	73	56	16	10	239	19	396	7	7	50	43	.538	6	10	3.06

MARIANO DUNCAN

Bats both Right and Left-handed, Throws Right-handed

Turns Age 24 in 1987, Born 03/13/63

Year	Team	League	BATTING																	BASERUNNING				PERCENTAGES		
			G	AB	H	2B	3B	HR	(Hm	Rd)	TB	R	RBI	TBB	IBB	SO	HBP	SH	SF	SB	CS	SB%	GIDP	AVE	OBP	SLG
1985	Los Angeles	N	142	562	137	24	6	6	(1	5)	191	74	39	38	4	113	3	13	4	38	8	.83	9	.244	.293	.340
1986	Los Angeles	N	109	407	93	7	0	8	(2	6)	124	47	30	30	1	78	2	5	1	48	13	.79	6	.229	.284	.305
2 YEARS			251	969	230	31	6	14	(3	11)	315	121	69	68	5	191	5	18	5	86	21	.80	15	.237	.289	.325

SHAWON DUNSTON

Bats Right-handed, Throws Right-handed

Turns Age 24 in 1987, Born 03/21/63

Year	Team	League	BATTING																	BASERUNNING				PERCENTAGES		
			G	AB	H	2B	3B	HR	(Hm	Rd)	TB	R	RBI	TBB	IBB	SO	HBP	SH	SF	SB	CS	SB%	GIDP	AVE	OBP	SLG
1985	Chicago	N	74	250	65	12	4	4	(3	1)	97	40	18	19	3	42	0	1	2	11	3	.79	3	.260	.310	.388
1986	Chicago	N	150	581	145	37	3	17	(10	7)	239	66	68	21	5	114	3	4	2	13	11	.54	5	.250	.278	.411
2 YEARS			224	831	210	49	7	21	(13	8)	336	106	86	40	8	156	3	5	4	24	14	.63	8	.253	.288	.404

LEON DURHAM

Bats Left-handed, Throws Left-handed
Turns Age 30 in 1987, Born 07/31/57

Year	Team	League	G	AB	H	2B	3B	HR	(Hm	Rd)	TB	R	RBI	TBB	IBB	SO	HBP	SH	SF	SB	CS	SB%	GIDP	AVE	OBP	SLG
1980	St Louis	N	96	303	82	15	4	8	(3	5)	129	42	42	18	1	55	1	3	5	8	5	.62	3	.271	.309	.426
1981	Chicago	N	87	328	95	14	6	10	(8	2)	151	42	35	27	6	53	0	0	0	25	11	.69	6	.290	.344	.460
1982	Chicago	N	148	539	168	33	7	22	(9	13)	281	84	90	66	14	77	2	0	2	28	14	.67	11	.312	.388	.521
1983	Chicago	N	100	337	87	18	8	12	(9	3)	157	58	55	66	12	83	3	0	3	12	6	.67	4	.258	.381	.466
1984	Chicago	N	137	473	132	30	4	23	(19	4)	239	86	96	69	11	86	1	0	5	16	8	.67	8	.279	.369	.505
1985	Chicago	N	153	542	153	32	2	21	(15	6)	252	58	75	64	24	99	0	0	1	7	6	.54	5	.282	.357	.465
1986	Chicago	N	141	484	127	18	7	20	(13	7)	219	66	65	67	16	98	1	0	5	8	7	.53	6	.262	.350	.452
7 YEARS			862	3006	844	160	38	116	(76	40)	1428	436	458	377	84	551	8	3	21	104	57	.65	43	.281	.360	.475

JIM DWYER

Bats Left-handed, Throws Left-handed
Turns Age 37 in 1987, Born 01/03/50

Year	Team	League	G	AB	H	2B	3B	HR	(Hm	Rd)	TB	R	RBI	TBB	IBB	SO	HBP	SH	SF	SB	CS	SB%	GIDP	AVE	OBP	SLG
1973	St Louis	N	28	57	11	1	1	0	(0	0)	14	7	0	1	0	5	0	0	0	0	0	.00	4	.193	.207	.246
1974	St Louis	N	74	86	24	1	0	2	(1	1)	31	13	11	11	2	16	1	0	2	4	1	.80	1	.279	.360	.360
1975	2 Teams		81	206	56	8	1	3	(3	0)	75	26	21	27	0	36	0	12	2	4	1	.80	1	.272	.353	.364
1976	2 Teams		61	105	19	3	1	0	(0	0)	24	9	5	13	2	11	0	0	1	0	0	.00	3	.181	.269	.229
1977	St Louis	N	13	31	7	1	0	0	(0	0)	8	3	2	4	0	5	2	0	0	0	0	.00	0	.226	.351	.258
1978	2 Teams		107	238	53	12	2	6	(3	3)	87	30	26	37	4	32	1	3	4	7	0	1.00	2	.223	.325	.366
1979	Boston	A	76	113	30	7	0	2	(2	0)	43	19	14	17	1	9	1	0	2	3	1	.75	7	.265	.361	.381
1980	Boston	A	93	260	74	11	1	9	(1	8)	114	41	38	28	5	23	2	1	1	3	2	.60	4	.285	.357	.438
1981	Baltimore	A	68	134	30	0	1	3	(3	0)	41	16	10	20	0	19	0	0	3	0	2	.00	2	.224	.318	.306
1982	Baltimore	A	71	148	45	4	3	6	(4	2)	73	28	15	27	4	24	0	1	2	2	0	1.00	2	.304	.407	.493
1983	Baltimore	A	100	196	56	17	1	8	(3	5)	99	37	38	31	3	29	0	1	1	1	1	.50	3	.286	.382	.505
1984	Baltimore	A	76	161	41	9	1	2	(1	1)	58	22	21	23	0	24	0	5	6	0	2	.00	2	.255	.337	.360
1985	Baltimore	A	101	233	58	8	3	7	(1	6)	93	35	36	37	2	31	1	2	1	0	2	.00	5	.249	.353	.399
1986	Baltimore	A	94	160	39	13	1	8	(5	3)	78	18	31	23	1	31	2	0	4	0	2	.00	2	.244	.339	.488
14 YEARS			1043	2128	543	95	16	56	(27	29)	838	304	268	299	24	295	10	25	29	20	14	.59	36	.255	.345	.394
1975	Montreal	N	60	175	50	7	1	3	(3	0)	68	22	20	23	0	30	0	11	2	4	1	.80	0	.286	.365	.389
1975	St Louis	N	21	31	6	1	0	0	(0	0)	7	4	1	4	0	6	0	1	0	0	0	.00	1	.194	.286	.226
1976	Montreal	N	50	92	17	3	1	0	(0	0)	22	7	5	11	1	10	0	0	1	0	0	.00	3	.185	.269	.239
1976	New York	N	11	13	2	0	0	0	(0	0)	2	2	0	2	1	1	0	0	0	0	0	.00	0	.154	.267	.154
1978	St Louis	N	34	65	14	3	0	1	(0	1)	20	8	4	9	1	3	1	0	0	1	0	1.00	1	.215	.320	.308
1978	San Francisco	N	73	173	39	9	2	5	(3	2)	67	22	22	28	3	29	0	3	4	6	0	1.00	1	.225	.327	.387

LENNY DYKSTRA

Bats Left-handed, Throws Left-handed
Turns Age 24 in 1987, Born 02/10/63

Year	Team	League	G	AB	H	2B	3B	HR	(Hm	Rd)	TB	R	RBI	TBB	IBB	SO	HBP	SH	SF	SB	CS	SB%	GIDP	AVE	OBP	SLG
1985	New York	N	83	236	60	9	3	1	(0	1)	78	40	19	30	0	24	1	4	2	15	2	.88	4	.254	.338	.331
1986	New York	N	147	431	127	27	7	8	(4	4)	192	77	45	58	1	55	0	7	2	31	7	.82	4	.295	.377	.445
2 YEARS			230	667	187	36	10	9	(4	5)	270	117	64	88	1	79	1	11	4	46	9	.84	8	.280	.363	.405

MIKE EASLER

Bats Left-handed, Throws Right-handed
Turns Age 37 in 1987, Born 11/29/50

Year	Team	League	G	AB	H	2B	3B	HR	(Hm	Rd)	TB	R	RBI	TBB	IBB	SO	HBP	SH	SF	SB	CS	SB%	GIDP	AVE	OBP	SLG
1973	Houston	N	6	7	0	0	0	0	(0	0)	0	1	0	2	1	4	0	0	0	0	0	.00	0	.000	.222	.000
1974	Houston	N	15	15	1	0	0	0	(0	0)	1	0	0	0	0	5	0	0	0	0	0	.00	0	.067	.067	.067
1975	Houston	N	5	5	0	0	0	0	(0	0)	0	0	0	0	0	1	0	0	0	0	0	.00	0	.000	.000	.000
1976	California	A	21	54	13	1	1	0	(0	0)	16	6	4	2	1	11	0	1	2	1	1	.50	1	.241	.259	.296
1977	Pittsburgh	N	10	18	8	2	0	1	(1	0)	13	3	5	0	0	1	0	0	0	0	0	.00	0	.444	.421	.722
1979	Pittsburgh	N	55	54	15	1	1	2	(1	1)	24	8	11	8	0	13	0	0	0	5	9	.36	0	.278	.371	.444
1980	Pittsburgh	N	132	393	133	27	3	21	(9	12)	229	66	74	43	7	65	0	0	9	5	9	.36	10	.338	.396	.583
1981	Pittsburgh	N	95	339	97	18	5	7	(4	3)	146	43	42	24	7	45	0	0	6	4	7	.36	10	.286	.328	.431
1982	Pittsburgh	N	142	475	131	27	2	15	(9	6)	207	52	58	40	12	85	6	1	4	1	1	.50	11	.276	.337	.436
1983	Pittsburgh	N	115	381	117	17	2	10	(2	8)	168	44	54	22	1	64	3	1	1	2	1	.67	10	.307	.349	.441
1984	Boston	A	156	601	188	31	5	27	(16	11)	310	87	91	58	4	134	4	1	2	1	1	.50	15	.313	.376	.516
1985	Boston	A	155	568	149	29	4	16	(4	12)	234	71	74	53	1	129	3	0	7	0	0	.00	15	.262	.325	.412
1986	New York	A	146	490	148	26	2	14	(6	8)	220	64	78	49	13	87	0	2	5	3	2	.60	17	.302	.362	.449
13 YEARS			1053	3400	1000	179	25	113	(52	61)	1568	445	491	301	46	644	16	6	37	19	25	.43	80	.294	.351	.461

DENNIS ECKERSLEY

Pitches Right-handed, Bats Right-handed   Turns Age 33 in 1987, Born 10/03/54

Year	Team	League	G	GS	CG	GF	IP	BFP	H	R	ER	HR	SH	SF	HB	TBB	IBB	SO	WP	Bk	W	L	Pct	ShO	Sv	ERA
					HOW MUCH HE PITCHED							WHAT HE GAVE UP											THE RESULTS			
1975	Cleveland	A	34	24	6	5	187	794	147	61	54	16	6	7	7	90	8	152	4	2	13	7	.650	2	2	2.60
1976	Cleveland	A	36	30	9	3	199	821	155	82	76	13	10	4	5	78	2	200	6	1	13	12	.520	3	1	3.44
1977	Cleveland	A	33	33	12	0	247	1006	214	100	97	31	11	6	7	54	11	191	3	0	14	13	.519	3	0	3.53
1978	Boston	A	35	35	16	0	268	1121	258	99	89	30	7	8	7	71	8	162	3	0	20	8	.714	3	0	2.99
1979	Boston	A	33	33	17	0	247	1018	234	89	82	29	10	6	6	59	4	150	1	1	17	10	.630	2	0	2.99
1980	Boston	A	30	30	8	0	198	818	188	101	94	25	7	8	2	44	7	121	0	0	12	14	.462	0	0	4.27
1981	Boston	A	23	23	8	0	154	649	160	82	73	9	6	5	3	35	2	79	0	0	9	8	.529	2	0	4.27
1982	Boston	A	33	33	11	0	224.1	926	228	101	93	31	4	4	2	43	3	127	1	0	13	13	.500	3	0	3.73
1983	Boston	A	28	28	2	0	176.1	787	223	119	110	27	1	5	6	39	4	77	1	0	9	13	.409	0	0	5.61
1984	2 Teams		33	33	4	0	225	932	223	97	90	21	11	9	5	49	9	114	3	2	14	12	.538	0	0	3.60
1985	Chicago	N	25	25	6	0	169.1	664	145	61	58	15	6	2	3	19	4	117	0	3	11	7	.611	2	0	3.08
1986	Chicago	N	33	32	1	0	201	862	226	109	102	21	13	10	3	43	3	137	2	5	6	11	.353	0	0	4.57
12 YEARS			376	359	100	8	2496	10398	2401	1101	1018	268	92	74	56	624	65	1627	24	14	151	128	.541	20	3	3.67
1984	Boston	A	9	9	2	0	64.2	270	71	38	36	10	3	3	1	13	2	33	2	0	4	4	.500	0	0	5.01
1984	Chicago	N	24	24	2	0	160.1	662	152	59	54	11	8	6	4	36	7	81	1	2	10	8	.556	0	0	3.03

MARK EICHHORN

Pitches Right-handed, Bats Right-handed   Turns Age 27 in 1987, Born 11/21/60

Year	Team	League	G	GS	CG	GF	IP	BFP	H	R	ER	HR	SH	SF	HB	TBB	IBB	SO	WP	Bk	W	L	Pct	ShO	Sv	ERA
					HOW MUCH HE PITCHED							WHAT HE GAVE UP											THE RESULTS			
1982	Toronto	A	7	7	0	0	38	171	40	28	23	4	1	2	0	14	1	16	3	0	0	3	.000	0	0	5.45
1986	Toronto	A	69	0	0	38	157	612	105	32	30	8	9	2	7	45	14	166	2	1	14	6	.700	0	10	1.72
2 YEARS			76	7	0	38	195	783	145	60	53	12	10	4	7	59	15	182	5	1	14	9	.609	0	10	2.45

NICK ESASKY

Bats Right-handed, Throws Right-handed   Turns Age 27 in 1987, Born 02/24/60

Year	Team	League	G	AB	H	2B	3B	HR	(Hm	Rd)	TB	R	RBI	TBB	IBB	SO	HBP	SH	SF	SB	CS	SB%	GIDP	AVE	OBP	SLG
							BATTING													BASERUNNING				PERCENTAGES		
1983	Cincinnati	N	85	302	80	10	5	12	(5	7)	136	41	46	27	1	99	3	0	3	6	2	.75	5	.265	.328	.450
1984	Cincinnati	N	113	322	62	10	5	10	(5	5)	112	30	45	52	3	103	0	3	5	1	2	.33	6	.193	.301	.348
1985	Cincinnati	N	125	413	108	21	0	21	(7	14)	192	61	66	41	3	102	4	3	3	3	4	.43	9	.262	.332	.465
1986	Cincinnati	N	102	330	76	17	2	12	(9	3)	133	35	41	47	0	97	1	1	4	0	2	.00	8	.230	.325	.403
4 YEARS			425	1367	326	58	12	55	(26	29)	573	167	198	167	7	401	8	7	15	10	10	.50	28	.238	.322	.419

DARRELL EVANS

Bats Left-handed, Throws Right-handed   Turns Age 40 in 1987, Born 05/26/47

Year	Team	League	G	AB	H	2B	3B	HR	(Hm	Rd)	TB	R	RBI	TBB	IBB	SO	HBP	SH	SF	SB	CS	SB%	GIDP	AVE	OBP	SLG
							BATTING													BASERUNNING				PERCENTAGES		
1969	Atlanta	N	12	26	6	0	0	0	(0	0)	6	3	1	1	0	8	0	0	1	0	0	.00	0	.231	.250	.231
1970	Atlanta	N	12	44	14	1	1	0	(0	0)	17	4	9	7	0	5	1	0	0	0	0	.00	2	.318	.423	.386
1971	Atlanta	N	89	260	63	11	1	12	(8	4)	112	42	38	39	4	54	1	0	5	2	3	.40	6	.242	.338	.431
1972	Atlanta	N	125	418	106	12	0	19	(12	7)	175	67	71	90	4	58	4	0	9	4	2	.67	6	.254	.384	.419
1973	Atlanta	N	161	595	167	25	8	41	(24	17)	331	114	104	124	8	104	3	3	8	6	3	.67	9	.281	.403	.556
1974	Atlanta	N	160	571	137	21	3	25	(14	11)	239	99	79	126	9	88	6	4	3	4	2	.67	11	.240	.381	.419
1975	Atlanta	N	156	567	138	22	2	22	(12	10)	230	82	73	105	5	106	2	2	5	12	3	.80	10	.243	.361	.406
1976	2 Teams		136	396	81	9	1	11	(4	7)	125	53	46	72	4	71	0	1	2	9	1	.90	5	.205	.326	.316
1977	San Francisco	N	144	461	117	18	3	17	(12	5)	192	64	72	69	3	50	3	1	5	9	6	.60	5	.254	.351	.416
1978	San Francisco	N	159	547	133	24	2	20	(7	13)	221	82	78	105	12	64	0	6	10	4	5	.44	5	.243	.360	.404
1979	San Francisco	N	160	562	142	23	2	17	(8	9)	220	68	70	91	14	65	2	1	5	6	7	.46	5	.253	.356	.391
1980	San Francisco	N	154	556	147	23	0	20	(8	12)	230	69	78	83	6	65	2	6	6	17	5	.77	12	.264	.359	.414
1981	San Francisco	N	102	357	92	13	4	12	(6	6)	149	51	48	54	8	33	2	3	3	2	3	.40	4	.258	.356	.417
1982	San Francisco	N	141	465	119	20	4	16	(8	8)	195	64	61	77	7	64	2	3	6	5	4	.56	4	.256	.360	.419
1983	San Francisco	N	142	523	145	29	3	30	(16	14)	270	94	82	84	12	81	2	0	2	6	6	.50	6	.277	.378	.516
1984	Detroit	A	131	401	93	11	1	16	(6	10)	154	60	63	77	10	70	0	1	4	2	2	.50	7	.232	.353	.384
1985	Detroit	A	151	505	125	17	0	40	(21	19)	262	81	94	85	12	85	1	1	2	4	0	.00	6	.248	.356	.519
1986	Detroit	A	151	507	122	15	0	29	(15	14)	224	78	85	91	5	105	1	0	2	3	2	.60	6	.241	.356	.442
18 YEARS			2286	7761	1947	294	35	347	(181	166)	3352	1175	1152	1380	123	1191	32	32	78	91	58	.61	116	.251	.363	.432
1976	Atlanta	N	44	139	24	0	0	1	(1	0)	27	11	10	30	0	33	0	0	0	3	0	1.00	3	.173	.320	.194
1976	San Francisco	N	92	257	57	9	1	10	(3	7)	98	42	36	42	4	38	0	1	2	6	1	.86	2	.222	.329	.381

DWIGHT EVANS

Bats Right-handed, Throws Right-handed
Turns Age 36 in 1987, Born 11/03/51

										BATTING										BASERUNNING				PERCENTAGES		
Year	Team	League	G	AB	H	2B	3B	HR	(Hm	Rd)	TB	R	RBI	TBB	IBB	SO	HBP	SH	SF	SB	CS	SB%	GIDP	AVE	OBP	SLG
1972	Boston	A	18	57	15	3	1	1	(1	0)	23	2	6	7	0	13	0	0	0	0	0	.00	2	.263	.344	.404
1973	Boston	A	119	282	63	13	1	10	(6	4)	108	46	32	40	2	52	1	3	2	5	0	1.00	8	.223	.320	.383
1974	Boston	A	133	463	130	19	8	10	(7	3)	195	60	70	38	2	77	2	6	5	4	4	.50	9	.281	.335	.421
1975	Boston	A	128	412	113	24	6	13	(8	5)	188	61	56	47	3	60	4	5	2	3	4	.43	10	.274	.353	.456
1976	Boston	A	146	501	121	34	5	17	(9	8)	216	61	62	57	4	92	6	3	4	6	7	.46	11	.242	.324	.431
1977	Boston	A	73	230	66	9	2	14	(9	5)	121	39	36	28	0	58	0	6	1	4	2	.67	3	.287	.363	.526
1978	Boston	A	147	497	123	24	2	24	(13	11)	223	75	63	65	2	119	2	6	2	8	5	.62	15	.247	.336	.449
1979	Boston	A	152	489	134	24	1	21	(12	9)	223	69	58	69	7	76	1	3	1	6	9	.40	14	.274	.364	.456
1980	Boston	A	148	463	123	37	5	18	(11	7)	224	72	60	64	6	98	5	6	4	3	1	.75	5	.266	.358	.484
1981	Boston	A	108	412	122	19	4	22	(15	7)	215	84	71	85	1	85	1	3	3	3	2	.60	8	.296	.415	.522
1982	Boston	A	162	609	178	37	7	32	(19	13)	325	122	98	112	1	125	1	3	2	3	2	.60	17	.292	.402	.534
1983	Boston	A	126	470	112	19	4	22	(12	10)	205	74	58	70	5	97	2	0	2	3	0	1.00	12	.238	.338	.436
1984	Boston	A	162	630	186	37	8	32	(15	17)	335	121	104	96	2	115	4	1	7	7	2	.78	19	.295	.388	.532
1985	Boston	A	159	617	162	29	1	29	(14	15)	280	110	78	114	4	105	5	1	7	7	2	.78	16	.263	.378	.454
1986	Boston	A	152	529	137	33	2	26	(8	18)	252	86	97	97	4	117	6	2	6	3	3	.50	11	.259	.376	.476
15 YEARS			1933	6661	1785	361	57	291	(159	132)	3133	1082	949	989	43	1289	40	48	48	61	42	.59	160	.268	.364	.470

STEVE FARR

Pitches Right-handed, Bats Right-handed
Turns Age 31 in 1987, Born 12/12/56

			HOW MUCH HE PITCHED						WHAT HE GAVE UP											THE RESULTS					
Year	Team	League	G	GS	CG	GF	IP	BFP	H	R	ER	HR	SH	SF	HB	TBB	IBB	SO	WP	Bk	W	L	Pct	ShO	Sv	ERA
1984	Cleveland	A	31	16	0	4	116	488	106	61	59	14	2	3	5	46	3	83	2	2	3	11	.214	0	1	4.58
1985	Kansas City	A	16	3	0	5	37.2	164	34	15	13	2	1	2	2	20	1	36	3	0	2	1	.667	0	1	3.11
1986	Kansas City	A	56	0	0	33	109.1	443	90	39	38	10	3	2	4	39	8	83	4	1	8	4	.667	0	8	3.13
3 YEARS			103	19	0	42	263	1095	230	115	110	26	6	7	11	105	15	202	9	3	13	16	.448	0	10	3.76

MIKE FELDER

Bats both Right and Left-handed, Throws Right-handed
Turns Age 25 in 1987, Born 11/18/62

										BATTING										BASERUNNING				PERCENTAGES		
Year	Team	League	G	AB	H	2B	3B	HR	(Hm	Rd)	TB	R	RBI	TBB	IBB	SO	HBP	SH	SF	SB	CS	SB%	GIDP	AVE	OBP	SLG
1985	Milwaukee	A	15	56	11	1	0	0	(0	0)	12	8	0	5	0	6	0	1	0	4	1	.80	2	.196	.262	.214
1986	Milwaukee	A	44	155	37	2	4	1	(0	0)	50	24	13	13	1	16	0	1	5	16	2	.89	2	.239	.289	.323
2 YEARS			59	211	48	3	4	1	(0	0)	62	32	13	18	1	22	0	2	5	20	3	.87	4	.227	.282	.294

SID FERNANDEZ

Pitches Left-handed, Bats Left-handed
Turns Age 25 in 1987, Born 10/12/62

			HOW MUCH HE PITCHED						WHAT HE GAVE UP											THE RESULTS					
Year	Team	League	G	GS	CG	GF	IP	BFP	H	R	ER	HR	SH	SF	HB	TBB	IBB	SO	WP	Bk	W	L	Pct	ShO	Sv	ERA
1983	Los Angeles	N	2	1	0	0	6	33	7	4	4	0	0	0	1	7	0	9	0	0	0	1	.000	0	0	6.00
1984	New York	N	15	15	0	0	90	371	74	40	35	8	5	5	0	34	3	62	1	4	6	6	.500	0	0	3.50
1985	New York	N	26	26	3	0	170.1	685	108	56	53	14	4	3	2	80	3	180	3	2	9	9	.500	0	0	2.80
1986	New York	N	32	31	2	1	204.1	855	161	82	80	13	9	7	2	91	1	200	6	0	16	6	.727	1	1	3.52
4 YEARS			75	73	5	1	470.2	1944	350	182	172	35	18	15	5	212	7	451	10	6	31	22	.585	1	1	3.29

TONY FERNANDEZ

Bats both Right and Left-handed, Throws Right-handed
Turns Age 25 in 1987, Born 08/06/62

										BATTING										BASERUNNING				PERCENTAGES		
Year	Team	League	G	AB	H	2B	3B	HR	(Hm	Rd)	TB	R	RBI	TBB	IBB	SO	HBP	SH	SF	SB	CS	SB%	GIDP	AVE	OBP	SLG
1983	Toronto	A	15	34	9	1	1	0	(0	0)	12	5	2	2	0	2	1	1	0	0	1	.00	1	.265	.324	.353
1984	Toronto	A	88	233	63	5	3	3	(1	2)	83	29	19	17	0	15	0	2	2	5	7	.42	3	.270	.317	.356
1985	Toronto	A	161	564	163	31	10	2	(1	1)	220	71	51	43	2	41	2	7	2	13	6	.68	12	.289	.340	.390
1986	Toronto	A	163	687	213	33	9	10	(4	6)	294	91	65	27	0	52	4	5	4	25	12	.68	8	.310	.338	.428
4 YEARS			427	1518	448	70	23	15	(6	9)	609	196	137	89	2	110	7	15	8	43	26	.62	24	.295	.335	.401

CHUCK FINLEY

Pitches Left-handed, Bats Left-handed

			HOW MUCH HE PITCHED						WHAT HE GAVE UP											THE RESULTS					
Year	Team	League	G	GS	CG	GF	IP	BFP	H	R	ER	HR	SH	SF	HB	TBB	IBB	SO	WP	Bk	W	L	Pct	ShO	Sv	ERA
1986	California	A	25	0	0	7	46.1	198	40	17	17	2	4	0	1	23	1	37	2	0	3	1	.750	0	0	3.30

MIKE FISCHLIN

Bats Right-handed, Throws Right-handed

Turns Age 32 in 1987, Born 09/13/55

Year	Team	League	G	AB	H	2B	3B	HR	(Hm	Rd)	TB	R	RBI	TBB	IBB	SO	HBP	SH	SF	SB	CS	SB%	GIDP	AVE	OBP	SLG
1977	Houston	N	13	15	3	0	0	0	(0	0)	3	0	0	0	0	2	0	0	0	0	0	.00	0	.200	.200	.200
1978	Houston	N	44	86	10	1	0	0	(0	0)	11	3	0	4	1	9	1	4	0	1	0	1.00	1	.116	.165	.128
1980	Houston	N	1	1	0	0	0	0	(0	0)	0	0	0	0	0	1	0	0	0	0	0	.00	0	.000	.000	.000
1981	Cleveland	A	22	43	10	1	0	0	(0	0)	11	3	5	3	0	6	0	1	1	3	2	.60	0	.233	.277	.256
1982	Cleveland	A	112	276	74	12	1	0	(0	0)	88	34	21	34	0	36	2	9	1	9	5	.64	3	.268	.351	.319
1983	Cleveland	A	95	225	47	5	2	2	(2	0)	62	31	23	26	0	32	2	11	2	9	2	.82	2	.209	.294	.276
1984	Cleveland	A	85	133	30	4	2	1	(0	1)	41	17	14	12	0	20	0	5	0	2	2	.50	2	.226	.290	.308
1985	Cleveland	A	73	60	12	4	1	0	(0	0)	18	12	2	5	0	7	0	4	0	0	1	.00	2	.200	.262	.300
1986	New York	A	71	102	21	2	0	0	(0	0)	23	9	3	8	0	29	0	5	1	0	1	.00	3	.206	.261	.225
9 YEARS			516	941	207	29	6	3	(2	1)	257	109	68	92	1	142	5	39	5	24	13	.65	11	.220	.291	.273

BRIAN FISHER

Pitches Right-handed, Bats Right-handed

Turns Age 25 in 1987, Born 03/18/62

Year	Team	League	G	GS	CG	GF	IP	BFP	H	R	ER	HR	SH	SF	HB	TBB	IBB	SO	WP	Bk	W	L	Pct	ShO	Sv	ERA
1985	New York	A	55	0	0	23	98.1	391	77	32	26	4	3	2	0	29	3	85	3	0	4	4	.500	0	14	2.38
1986	New York	A	62	0	0	26	96.2	424	105	61	53	14	5	2	1	37	2	67	2	0	9	5	.643	0	6	4.93
2 YEARS			117	0	0	49	195	815	182	93	79	18	8	4	1	66	5	152	5	0	13	9	.591	0	20	3.65

CARLTON FISK

Bats Right-handed, Throws Right-handed

Turns Age 40 in 1987, Born 12/26/47

Year	Team	League	G	AB	H	2B	3B	HR	(Hm	Rd)	TB	R	RBI	TBB	IBB	SO	HBP	SH	SF	SB	CS	SB%	GIDP	AVE	OBP	SLG
1969	Boston	A	2	5	0	0	0	0	(0	0)	0	0	0	0	0	2	0	0	0	0	0	.00	0	.000	.000	.000
1971	Boston	A	14	48	15	2	1	2	(0	2)	25	7	6	1	0	10	0	0	0	0	0	.00	1	.313	.327	.521
1972	Boston	A	131	457	134	28	9	22	(13	9)	246	74	61	52	6	83	4	1	0	5	2	.71	11	.293	.370	.538
1973	Boston	A	135	508	125	21	0	26	(16	10)	224	65	71	37	2	99	10	1	2	7	2	.78	11	.246	.309	.441
1974	Boston	A	52	187	56	12	1	11	(5	6)	103	36	26	24	2	23	2	2	1	5	1	.83	5	.299	.383	.551
1975	Boston	A	79	263	87	14	4	10	(6	4)	139	47	52	27	4	32	2	0	2	4	3	.57	7	.331	.395	.529
1976	Boston	A	134	487	124	17	5	17	(10	7)	202	76	58	56	3	71	6	3	5	12	5	.71	11	.255	.336	.415
1977	Boston	A	152	536	169	26	3	26	(15	11)	279	106	102	75	3	85	9	2	10	7	6	.54	9	.315	.402	.521
1978	Boston	A	157	571	162	39	5	20	(8	12)	271	94	88	71	6	83	7	3	6	7	2	.78	10	.284	.366	.475
1979	Boston	A	91	320	87	23	2	10	(5	5)	144	49	42	10	0	38	6	1	3	3	0	1.00	9	.272	.304	.450
1980	Boston	A	131	478	138	25	3	18	(12	6)	223	73	62	36	0	62	13	0	3	11	5	.69	12	.289	.353	.467
1981	Chicago	A	96	338	89	12	0	7	(4	3)	122	44	45	38	3	37	12	1	5	3	2	.60	9	.263	.354	.361
1982	Chicago	A	135	476	127	17	3	14	(7	7)	192	66	65	46	7	60	6	4	4	17	2	.89	12	.267	.336	.403
1983	Chicago	A	138	488	141	26	4	26	(17	9)	253	85	86	46	3	88	6	2	3	9	6	.60	8	.289	.355	.518
1984	Chicago	A	102	359	83	20	1	21	(11	10)	168	54	43	26	4	60	5	1	4	6	0	1.00	7	.231	.289	.468
1985	Chicago	A	153	543	129	23	1	37	(20	17)	265	85	107	52	12	81	17	2	6	17	9	.65	14	.238	.320	.488
1986	Chicago	A	125	457	101	11	0	14	(5	9)	154	42	63	22	2	92	6	0	6	2	4	.33	10	.221	.263	.337
17 YEARS			1827	6521	1767	316	42	281	(154	127)	3010	1003	977	619	63	1006	111	23	60	115	49	.70	141	.271	.342	.462

MIKE FITZGERALD

Bats Right-handed, Throws Right-handed

Turns Age 27 in 1987, Born 07/13/60

Year	Team	League	G	AB	H	2B	3B	HR	(Hm	Rd)	TB	R	RBI	TBB	IBB	SO	HBP	SH	SF	SB	CS	SB%	GIDP	AVE	OBP	SLG
1983	New York	N	8	20	2	0	0	1	(0	1)	5	1	2	3	1	6	0	0	0	0	0	.00	0	.100	.217	.250
1984	New York	N	112	360	87	15	1	2	(2	0)	110	20	33	24	7	71	1	5	4	1	0	1.00	17	.242	.288	.306
1985	Montreal	N	108	295	61	7	1	5	(3	2)	85	25	34	38	12	55	2	1	5	5	3	.63	8	.207	.288	.288
1986	Montreal	N	73	209	59	13	1	6	(1	5)	92	20	37	27	6	34	1	4	2	3	2	.60	4	.282	.364	.440
4 YEARS			301	884	209	35	3	14	(6	8)	292	66	106	92	26	166	4	10	11	9	5	.64	29	.236	.308	.330

MIKE FLANAGAN

Pitches Left-handed, Bats Left-handed

Turns Age 36 in 1987, Born 12/16/51

Year	Team	League	G	GS	CG	GF	IP	BFP	H	R	ER	HR	SH	SF	HB	TBB	IBB	SO	WP	Bk	W	L	Pct	ShO	Sv	ERA
1975	Baltimore	A	2	1	0	0	10	42	9	4	3	0	0	0	0	6	1	7	0	0	0	1	.000	0	0	2.70
1976	Baltimore	A	20	10	4	7	85	358	83	41	39	7	2	4	0	33	0	56	2	1	3	5	.375	0	0	4.13
1977	Baltimore	A	36	33	15	2	235	974	235	100	95	17	10	7	2	70	5	149	5	0	15	10	.600	2	1	3.64
1978	Baltimore	A	40	40	17	0	281	1160	271	128	126	22	10	5	3	87	2	167	8	1	19	15	.559	2	0	4.04
1979	Baltimore	A	39	38	16	0	266	1085	245	107	91	23	9	4	3	70	1	190	6	0	23	9	.719	5	0	3.08
1980	Baltimore	A	37	37	12	0	251	1065	278	121	115	27	10	12	2	71	3	128	12	1	16	13	.552	2	0	4.12
1981	Baltimore	A	20	20	3	0	116	482	108	55	54	11	0	4	2	37	1	72	6	0	9	6	.600	2	0	4.19
1982	Baltimore	A	36	35	11	1	236	991	233	110	104	24	5	6	4	76	5	103	9	2	15	11	.577	1	0	3.97
1983	Baltimore	A	20	20	3	0	125.1	528	135	53	46	10	4	2	2	31	2	50	1	0	12	4	.750	1	0	3.30
1984	Baltimore	A	34	34	10	0	226.2	947	213	103	89	24	8	6	1	81	5	115	8	1	13	13	.500	0	0	3.53
1985	Baltimore	A	15	15	1	0	86	379	101	49	49	14	7	2	2	28	0	42	3	0	4	5	.444	0	0	5.13
1986	Baltimore	A	29	28	2	0	172	747	179	95	81	15	10	6	1	66	4	96	8	1	7	11	.389	0	0	4.24
12 YEARS			328	311	94	10	2090	8758	2090	966	892	194	75	58	22	656	29	1175	68	6	136	103	.569	17	1	3.84

TIM FLANNERY

Bats Left-handed, Throws Right-handed Turns Age 30 in 1987, Born 09/29/57

Year	Team	League	G	AB	H	2B	3B	HR	(Hm	Rd)	TB	R	RBI	TBB	IBB	SO	HBP	SH	SF	SB	CS	SB%	GIDP	AVE	OBP	SLG
1979	San Diego	N	22	65	10	0	1	0	(0	0)	12	2	4	4	1	5	2	1	1	0	2	.00	3	.154	.222	.185
1980	San Diego	N	95	292	70	12	0	0	(0	0)	82	15	25	18	4	30	0	4	1	2	2	.50	5	.240	.283	.281
1981	San Diego	N	37	67	17	4	1	0	(0	0)	23	4	6	2	1	4	0	1	2	1	0	1.00	1	.254	.268	.343
1982	San Diego	N	122	379	100	11	7	0	(0	0)	125	40	30	30	10	32	2	6	6	1	0	1.00	4	.264	.317	.330
1983	San Diego	N	92	214	50	7	3	3	(1	2)	72	24	19	20	8	23	5	2	4	2	2	.50	4	.234	.309	.336
1984	San Diego	N	86	128	35	3	3	2	(2	0)	50	24	10	12	1	17	3	2	1	4	1	.80	1	.273	.347	.391
1985	San Diego	N	126	384	108	14	3	1	(1	0)	131	50	40	58	1	39	9	3	2	2	5	.29	1	.281	.386	.341
1986	San Diego	N	134	368	103	11	2	3	(1	2)	127	48	28	54	4	61	5	3	2	3	6	.33	8	.280	.378	.345
8 YEARS			714	1897	493	62	20	9	(5	4)	622	207	162	198	30	211	26	22	19	15	16	.48	30	.260	.335	.328

SCOTT FLETCHER

Bats Right-handed, Throws Right-handed Turns Age 29 in 1987, Born 07/30/58

Year	Team	League	G	AB	H	2B	3B	HR	(Hm	Rd)	TB	R	RBI	TBB	IBB	SO	HBP	SH	SF	SB	CS	SB%	GIDP	AVE	OBP	SLG
1981	Chicago	N	19	46	10	4	0	0	(0	0)	14	6	1	2	0	4	0	0	0	0	0	.00	0	.217	.250	.304
1982	Chicago	N	11	24	4	0	0	0	(0	0)	4	4	1	4	0	5	0	0	0	1	0	1.00	0	.167	.286	.167
1983	Chicago	A	114	262	62	16	5	3	(1	2)	97	42	31	29	0	22	2	7	2	5	1	.83	8	.237	.315	.370
1984	Chicago	A	149	456	114	13	3	3	(2	1)	142	46	35	46	2	46	8	9	2	10	4	.71	5	.250	.328	.311
1985	Chicago	A	119	301	77	8	1	2	(0	1)	93	38	31	35	0	47	0	11	1	5	5	.50	9	.256	.332	.309
1986	Texas	A	147	530	159	34	5	3	(2	1)	212	82	50	47	0	59	4	10	3	12	11	.52	10	.300	.360	.400
6 YEARS			559	1619	426	75	14	11	(5	6)	562	218	149	163	2	183	14	37	8	33	21	.61	32	.263	.334	.347

TOM FOLEY

Bats Left-handed, Throws Right-handed Turns Age 28 in 1987, Born 09/09/59

Year	Team	League	G	AB	H	2B	3B	HR	(Hm	Rd)	TB	R	RBI	TBB	IBB	SO	HBP	SH	SF	SB	CS	SB%	GIDP	AVE	OBP	SLG
1983	Cincinnati	N	68	98	20	4	1	0	(0	0)	26	7	9	13	2	17	0	2	0	1	0	1.00	1	.204	.297	.265
1984	Cincinnati	N	106	277	70	8	3	5	(2	3)	99	26	27	24	7	36	0	1	2	3	2	.60	2	.253	.310	.357
1985	2 Teams		89	250	60	13	1	3	(2	1)	84	24	23	19	8	34	0	0	0	2	3	.40	2	.240	.294	.336
1986	2 Teams		103	263	70	15	3	1	(1	0)	94	26	23	30	6	37	0	2	4	10	3	.77	4	.266	.337	.357
4 YEARS			366	888	220	40	8	9	(5	4)	303	83	82	86	23	124	0	5	6	16	8	.67	9	.248	.312	.341
1985	Cincinnati	N	43	92	18	5	1	0	(0	0)	25	7	6	6	1	16	0	0	0	1	0	1.00	0	.196	.245	.272
1985	Philadelphia	N	46	158	42	8	0	3	(2	1)	59	17	17	13	7	18	0	0	0	1	3	.25	2	.266	.322	.373
1986	Montreal	N	64	202	52	13	2	1	(1	0)	72	18	18	20	5	26	0	2	3	8	3	.73	3	.257	.320	.356
1986	Philadelphia	N	39	61	18	2	1	0	(0	0)	22	8	5	10	1	11	0	0	1	2	0	1.00	1	.295	.389	.361

RAY FONTENOT

Pitches Left-handed, Bats Left-handed Turns Age 30 in 1987, Born 08/08/57

Year	Team	League	G	GS	CG	GF	IP	BFP	H	R	ER	HR	SH	SF	HB	TBB	IBB	SO	WP	Bk	W	L	Pct	ShO	Sv	ERA
1983	New York	A	15	15	3	0	97.1	408	101	41	36	3	2	1	1	25	0	27	0	0	8	2	.800	1	0	3.33
1984	New York	A	35	24	0	1	169.1	720	189	77	68	8	5	4	3	58	4	58	4	2	8	9	.471	0	0	3.61
1985	Chicago	N	38	23	0	5	154.2	661	177	86	75	12	12	2	0	45	4	70	3	2	6	10	.375	0	0	4.36
1986	2 Teams		57	0	0	18	72.1	322	84	49	42	8	6	0	2	25	3	34	6	1	3	5	.375	0	2	5.23
4 YEARS			145	62	3	24	493.2	2111	551	253	221	31	25	7	6	153	11	216	13	5	25	26	.490	1	2	4.03
1986	Minnesota	A	15	0	0	7	16.1	81	27	19	18	3	0	0	2	4	0	10	2	0	0	0	.000	0	0	9.92
1986	Chicago	N	42	0	0	11	56	241	57	30	24	5	6	0	0	21	3	24	4	1	3	5	.375	0	2	3.86

CURT FORD

Bats Left-handed, Throws Right-handed Turns Age 27 in 1987, Born 10/11/60

Year	Team	League	G	AB	H	2B	3B	HR	(Hm	Rd)	TB	R	RBI	TBB	IBB	SO	HBP	SH	SF	SB	CS	SB%	GIDP	AVE	OBP	SLG
1985	St Louis	N	11	12	6	2	0	0	(0	0)	8	2	3	4	0	1	0	0	0	1	0	1.00	0	.500	.625	.667
1986	St Louis	N	85	214	53	15	2	2	(0	2)	78	30	29	23	2	29	0	1	2	13	5	.72	1	.248	.318	.364
2 YEARS			96	226	59	17	2	2	(0	2)	86	32	32	27	2	30	0	1	2	14	5	.74	1	.261	.337	.381

BOB FORSCH

Pitches Right-handed, Bats Right-handed

Turns Age 37 in 1987, Born 01/13/50

Year	Team	League	G	GS	CG	GF	IP	BFP	H	R	ER	HR	SH	SF	HB	TBB	IBB	SO	WP	Bk	W	L	Pct	ShO	Sv	ERA
1974	St Louis	N	19	14	5	0	100	408	84	38	33	5	4	4	1	34	4	39	6	0	7	4	.636	2	0	2.97
1975	St Louis	N	34	34	7	0	230	958	213	89	73	14	6	7	3	70	8	108	10	1	15	10	.600	4	0	2.86
1976	St Louis	N	33	32	2	0	194	844	209	112	85	17	9	6	3	71	8	76	9	0	8	10	.444	0	0	3.94
1977	St Louis	N	35	35	8	0	217	915	210	97	84	20	4	4	3	69	2	95	9	1	20	7	.741	2	0	3.48
1978	St Louis	N	34	34	7	0	234	981	205	110	96	15	9	8	5	97	9	114	8	3	11	17	.393	3	0	3.69
1979	St Louis	N	33	32	7	0	219	894	215	102	93	16	6	13	3	52	1	92	6	0	11	11	.500	1	0	3.82
1980	St Louis	N	31	31	8	0	215	878	225	102	90	12	8	9	4	33	6	87	7	0	11	10	.524	0	0	3.77
1981	St Louis	N	20	20	1	0	124	501	106	47	44	7	7	4	4	29	3	41	3	1	10	5	.667	0	0	3.19
1982	St Louis	N	36	34	6	0	233	962	238	95	90	16	8	7	4	54	7	69	6	2	15	9	.625	2	1	3.48
1983	St Louis	N	34	30	6	3	187	790	190	104	89	23	11	8	3	54	2	56	4	1	10	12	.455	0	0	4.28
1984	St Louis	N	16	11	1	2	52.1	233	64	38	35	6	1	2	0	19	0	21	5	0	2	5	.286	0	0	6.02
1985	St Louis	N	34	19	3	4	136	567	132	63	59	11	5	1	2	47	4	48	4	0	9	6	.600	1	2	3.90
1986	St Louis	N	33	33	3	0	230	939	211	91	83	19	5	9	2	68	11	104	7	0	14	10	.583	0	0	3.25
13 YEARS			392	359	64	10	2371.1	9870	2302	1088	954	181	83	82	37	697	65	950	84	9	143	116	.552	17	3	3.62

TERRY FORSTER

Pitches Left-handed, Bats Left-handed

Turns Age 35 in 1987, Born 01/14/52

Year	Team	League	G	GS	CG	GF	IP	BFP	H	R	ER	HR	SH	SF	HB	TBB	IBB	SO	WP	Bk	W	L	Pct	ShO	Sv	ERA
1971	Chicago	A	45	3	0	15	50	196	46	23	22	5	2	2	1	23	3	48	1	1	2	3	.400	0	1	3.96
1972	Chicago	A	62	0	0	45	100	375	75	31	25	0	7	5	3	44	3	104	5	0	6	5	.545	0	29	2.25
1973	Chicago	A	51	12	0	29	173	666	174	69	62	7	7	5	0	78	6	120	6	1	6	11	.353	0	16	3.23
1974	Chicago	A	59	1	0	49	134	560	120	57	54	6	9	6	8	48	3	105	9	0	7	8	.467	0	24	3.63
1975	Chicago	A	17	1	0	12	37	155	30	12	9	0	4	0	0	24	4	32	2	0	3	3	.500	0	4	2.19
1976	Chicago	A	29	16	1	8	111	486	126	61	54	7	6	1	1	41	4	70	7	0	2	12	.143	0	1	4.38
1977	Pittsburgh	N	33	6	0	7	87	378	90	47	43	7	5	5	2	32	5	58	3	1	6	4	.600	0	1	4.45
1978	Los Angeles	N	47	0	0	40	65	266	56	19	14	2	3	0	0	23	4	46	2	1	5	4	.556	0	22	1.94
1979	Los Angeles	N	17	0	0	8	16	73	18	11	10	0	0	1	0	11	4	8	1	0	1	2	.333	0	2	5.63
1980	Los Angeles	N	9	0	0	7	12	49	10	4	4	0	0	0	0	4	0	2	0	0	0	0	.000	0	0	3.00
1981	Los Angeles	N	21	0	0	6	31	137	37	14	14	1	2	0	0	15	3	17	3	0	0	1	.000	0	0	4.06
1982	Los Angeles	N	56	0	0	13	83	349	66	38	28	3	10	5	4	31	9	52	2	0	5	6	.455	0	3	3.04
1983	Atlanta	N	56	0	0	29	79.1	316	60	19	19	3	7	0	2	31	9	54	2	0	3	2	.600	0	13	2.16
1984	Atlanta	N	25	0	0	14	26.2	113	30	9	8	1	4	1	0	7	3	10	2	0	2	0	1.000	0	5	2.70
1985	Atlanta	N	46	0	0	19	59.1	253	49	22	15	7	2	2	0	28	4	37	1	0	2	3	.400	0	1	2.28
1986	California	A	41	0	0	17	41	182	47	18	16	2	3	1	3	17	1	28	0	0	4	1	.800	0	5	3.51
16 YEARS			614	39	5	318	1105.1	4554	1034	454	397	51	71	34	24	457	63	791	46	4	54	65	.454	0	127	3.23

GEORGE FOSTER

Bats Right-handed, Throws Right-handed

Turns Age 39 in 1987, Born 12/01/48

Year	Team	League	G	AB	H	2B	3B	HR	(Hm	Rd)	TB	R	RBI	TBB	IBB	SO	HBP	SH	SF	SB	CS	SB%	GIDP	AVE	OBP	SLG
1969	San Francisco	N	9	5	2	0	0	0	(0	0)	2	1	1	0	0	1	0	0	0	0	0	.00	0	.400	.400	.400
1970	San Francisco	N	9	19	6	1	1	1	(1	0)	12	2	4	2	1	5	0	8	1	0	0	.00	1	.316	.364	.632
1971	2 Teams		140	473	114	23	4	13	(9	4)	184	50	58	29	3	120	7	1	4	7	7	.50	20	.241	.292	.389
1972	Cincinnati	N	59	145	29	4	1	2	(1	1)	41	15	12	5	1	44	1	0	1	2	1	.67	6	.200	.230	.283
1973	Cincinnati	N	17	39	11	3	0	4	(0	4)	26	6	9	4	0	7	0	0	0	0	1	1.00	1	.282	.349	.667
1974	Cincinnati	N	106	276	73	18	0	7	(3	4)	112	31	41	30	5	52	4	2	2	3	2	.60	8	.264	.343	.406
1975	Cincinnati	N	134	463	139	24	4	23	(15	8)	240	71	78	40	11	73	3	0	5	2	1	.67	14	.300	.356	.518
1976	Cincinnati	N	144	562	172	21	9	29	(13	16)	298	86	121	52	4	89	4	0	8	17	3	.85	11	.306	.364	.530
1977	Cincinnati	N	158	615	197	31	2	52	(21	31)	388	124	149	61	10	107	5	0	8	6	4	.60	17	.320	.382	.631
1978	Cincinnati	N	158	604	170	26	7	40	(25	15)	330	97	120	70	16	138	7	0	6	4	4	.50	18	.281	.360	.546
1979	Cincinnati	N	121	440	133	18	3	30	(20	10)	247	68	98	59	7	105	3	0	11	3	0	1.00	11	.302	.386	.561
1980	Cincinnati	N	144	528	144	21	5	25	(14	11)	250	79	93	75	14	99	1	0	4	1	0	1.00	13	.273	.362	.473
1981	Cincinnati	N	108	414	122	23	2	22	(8	14)	215	64	90	51	5	75	3	0	4	4	0	1.00	12	.295	.373	.519
1982	New York	N	151	550	136	23	2	13	(7	6)	202	64	70	50	9	123	2	0	6	1	1	.50	13	.247	.309	.367
1983	New York	N	157	601	145	19	2	28	(17	11)	252	74	90	38	5	111	4	0	4	1	1	.50	19	.241	.289	.419
1984	New York	N	146	553	149	22	1	24	(11	13)	245	67	86	30	9	122	6	0	6	2	2	.50	14	.269	.311	.443
1985	New York	N	129	452	119	24	1	21	(9	12)	208	57	77	46	5	87	2	0	4	1	1	1.00	9	.263	.331	.460
1986	2 Teams		87	284	64	6	3	14	(10	4)	118	30	42	24	1	61	0	0	2	1	1	.50	9	.225	.284	.415
18 YEARS			1977	7023	1925	307	47	348	(184	164)	3370	986	1239	666	106	1419	52	11	69	51	31	.62	196	.274	.338	.480
1971	Cincinnati	N	104	368	86	18	4	10	(8	2)	142	39	50	23	2	93	7	1	3	7	6	.54	16	.234	.289	.386
1971	San Francisco	N	36	105	28	5	0	3	(1	2)	42	11	8	6	1	27	0	0	1	0	1	.00	4	.267	.304	.400
1986	Chicago	A	15	51	11	0	2	1	(1	0)	18	2	4	3	0	8	0	0	0	0	0	.00	4	.216	.259	.353
1986	New York	N	72	233	53	6	1	13	(9	4)	100	28	38	21	1	53	0	0	2	1	1	.50	7	.227	.289	.429

JOHN FRANCO

Pitches Left-handed, Bats Left-handed

Turns Age 27 in 1987, Born 09/17/60

Year	Team	League	G	GS	CG	GF	IP	BFP	H	R	ER	HR	SH	SF	HB	TBB	IBB	SO	WP	Bk	W	L	Pct	ShO	Sv	ERA
1984	Cincinnati	N	54	0	0	30	79.1	335	74	28	24	3	4	4	2	36	4	55	2	0	6	2	.750	0	4	2.61
1985	Cincinnati	N	67	0	0	33	99	407	83	27	24	5	11	1	1	40	8	61	4	0	12	3	.800	0	12	2.18
1986	Cincinnati	N	74	0	0	52	101	429	90	40	33	7	8	3	2	44	12	84	4	2	6	6	.500	0	29	2.94
3 YEARS			195	0	0	115	279.1	1171	247	95	80	15	23	8	5	120	24	200	10	2	24	11	.686	0	45	2.58

JULIO FRANCO

Bats Right-handed, Throws Right-handed   Turns Age 26 in 1987, Born 08/23/61

							BATTING												BASERUNNING				PERCENTAGES		
Year	Team	League	G	AB	H	2B	3B	HR	(Hm	Rd)	TB	R	RBI	TBB	IBB	SO	HBP	SH	SF	SB	CS	SB%	GIDP	AVE	OBP	SLG
1982	Philadelphia	N	16	29	8	1	0	0	(0	0)	9	3	3	2	1	4	0	1	0	0	2	.00	1	.276	.323	.310
1983	Cleveland	A	149	560	153	24	8	8	(6	2)	217	68	80	27	1	50	2	3	6	32	12	.73	22	.273	.306	.388
1984	Cleveland	A	160	658	188	22	5	3	(1	2)	229	82	79	43	1	68	6	1	10	19	10	.66	23	.286	.331	.348
1985	Cleveland	A	160	636	183	33	4	6	(3	3)	242	97	90	54	2	74	4	0	9	13	9	.59	26	.288	.343	.381
1986	Cleveland	A	149	599	183	30	5	10	(4	6)	253	80	74	32	1	66	0	0	5	10	7	.59	28	.306	.338	.422
5 YEARS			634	2482	715	110	22	27	(14	13)	950	330	326	158	6	262	12	5	30	74	40	.65	100	.288	.330	.383

TERRY FRANCONA

Bats Left-handed, Throws Left-handed   Turns Age 28 in 1987, Born 04/22/59

							BATTING												BASERUNNING				PERCENTAGES		
Year	Team	League	G	AB	H	2B	3B	HR	(Hm	Rd)	TB	R	RBI	TBB	IBB	SO	HBP	SH	SF	SB	CS	SB%	GIDP	AVE	OBP	SLG
1981	Montreal	N	34	95	26	0	1	1	(1	0)	31	11	9	5	1	6	1	3	0	1	0	1.00	1	.274	.317	.326
1982	Montreal	N	46	131	42	3	0	0	(0	0)	45	14	9	8	0	11	0	5	0	2	3	.40	2	.321	.360	.344
1983	Montreal	N	120	230	59	11	1	3	(1	2)	81	21	22	6	2	20	0	0	2	0	2	.00	7	.257	.273	.352
1984	Montreal	N	58	214	74	19	2	1	(1	0)	100	18	18	5	3	12	1	1	2	0	0	.00	4	.346	.360	.467
1985	Montreal	N	107	281	75	15	1	2	(0	2)	98	19	31	12	4	12	1	2	0	5	5	.50	1	.267	.299	.349
1986	Chicago	N	86	124	31	3	0	2	(0	2)	40	13	8	6	0	8	1	0	2	0	1	.00	3	.250	.286	.323
6 YEARS			451	1075	307	51	5	9	(3	6)	395	96	96	42	10	69	4	11	6	8	11	.42	17	.286	.313	.367

GEORGE FRAZIER

Pitches Right-handed, Bats Right-handed   Turns Age 33 in 1987, Born 10/13/54

				HOW MUCH HE PITCHED						WHAT HE GAVE UP										THE RESULTS					
Year	Team	League	G	GS	CG	GF	IP	BFP	H	R	ER	HR	SH	SF	HB	TBB	IBB	SO	WP	Bk	W	L	Pct	ShO	Sv	ERA
1978	St Louis	N	14	0	0	3	22	96	22	14	10	2	0	2	0	6	2	8	1	0	0	3	.000	0	0	4.09
1979	St Louis	N	25	0	0	14	32	143	35	19	16	3	3	1	1	12	2	14	0	0	2	4	.333	0	0	4.50
1980	St Louis	N	22	0	0	12	23	96	24	10	7	2	1	0	0	7	3	11	0	0	1	4	.200	0	3	2.74
1981	New York	A	16	0	0	9	28	117	26	7	5	1	0	0	0	8	1	17	1	0	0	1	.000	0	3	1.61
1982	New York	A	63	0	0	26	111.2	466	103	51	43	7	8	6	5	39	1	69	1	0	4	4	.500	0	1	3.47
1983	New York	A	61	0	0	30	115.1	479	94	44	44	5	6	10	3	45	4	78	5	0	4	4	.500	0	8	3.43
1984	2 Teams		59	0	0	34	108	463	98	49	47	7	5	3	1	40	12	82	4	0	9	5	.643	0	4	3.92
1985	Chicago	N	51	0	0	17	76	357	88	57	54	11	7	1	3	52	9	46	4	2	7	8	.467	0	2	6.39
1986	2 Teams		50	0	0	22	78.1	362	86	49	44	7	3	6	1	50	5	66	4	0	3	5	.375	0	6	5.06
9 YEARS			361	0	0	167	594.1	2579	576	300	270	45	33	29	14	262	44	391	20	2	30	38	.441	0	27	4.09
1984	Cleveland	A	22	0	0	17	44.1	190	45	19	18	3	2	0	0	14	4	24	0	0	3	2	.600	0	1	3.65
1984	Chicago	N	37	0	0	17	63.2	273	53	30	29	4	3	3	1	26	8	58	4	0	6	3	.667	0	3	4.10
1986	Minnesota	A	15	0	0	10	26.2	119	23	13	13	2	1	3	0	16	1	25	1	0	1	1	.500	0	6	4.39
1986	Chicago	N	35	0	0	12	51.2	243	63	36	31	5	2	3	1	34	4	41	3	0	2	4	.333	0	0	5.40

GARY GAETTI

Bats Right-handed, Throws Right-handed   Turns Age 29 in 1987, Born 08/19/58

							BATTING												BASERUNNING				PERCENTAGES		
Year	Team	League	G	AB	H	2B	3B	HR	(Hm	Rd)	TB	R	RBI	TBB	IBB	SO	HBP	SH	SF	SB	CS	SB%	GIDP	AVE	OBP	SLG
1981	Minnesota	A	9	26	5	0	0	2	(1	1)	11	4	3	0	0	6	0	0	0	0	0	.00	1	.192	.192	.423
1982	Minnesota	A	145	508	117	25	4	25	(15	10)	225	59	84	37	2	107	3	4	13	0	4	.00	16	.230	.280	.443
1983	Minnesota	A	157	584	143	30	3	21	(7	14)	242	81	78	54	2	121	4	0	8	7	1	.88	18	.245	.309	.414
1984	Minnesota	A	162	588	154	29	4	5	(2	3)	206	55	65	44	1	81	4	3	5	11	5	.69	18	.262	.315	.350
1985	Minnesota	A	160	560	138	31	0	20	(10	10)	229	71	63	37	3	89	7	3	1	13	5	.72	15	.246	.301	.409
1986	Minnesota	A	157	596	171	34	1	34	(16	18)	309	91	108	52	4	108	6	1	6	14	15	.48	18	.287	.347	.518
6 YEARS			790	2862	728	149	12	107	(51	56)	1222	361	401	224	12	512	24	11	33	45	30	.60	77	.254	.311	.427

GREG GAGNE

Bats Right-handed, Throws Right-handed   Turns Age 26 in 1987, Born 11/12/61

							BATTING												BASERUNNING				PERCENTAGES		
Year	Team	League	G	AB	H	2B	3B	HR	(Hm	Rd)	TB	R	RBI	TBB	IBB	SO	HBP	SH	SF	SB	CS	SB%	GIDP	AVE	OBP	SLG
1983	Minnesota	A	10	27	3	1	0	0	(0	0)	4	2	3	0	0	6	0	0	2	0	0	.00	0	.111	.103	.148
1984	Minnesota	A	2	1	0	0	0	0	(0	0)	0	0	0	0	0	0	0	0	0	0	0	.00	0	.000	.000	.000
1985	Minnesota	A	114	293	66	15	3	2	(0	2)	93	37	23	20	0	57	3	3	3	10	4	.71	5	.225	.279	.317
1986	Minnesota	A	156	472	118	22	6	12	(10	2)	188	63	54	30	0	108	6	13	3	12	10	.55	4	.250	.301	.398
4 YEARS			282	793	187	38	9	14	(10	4)	285	102	80	50	0	171	9	16	8	22	14	.61	9	.236	.286	.359

ANDRES GALARRAGA

Bats Right-handed, Throws Right-handed   Turns Age 26 in 1987, Born 06/18/61

							BATTING												BASERUNNING				PERCENTAGES		
Year	Team	League	G	AB	H	2B	3B	HR	(Hm	Rd)	TB	R	RBI	TBB	IBB	SO	HBP	SH	SF	SB	CS	SB%	GIDP	AVE	OBP	SLG
1985	Montreal	N	24	75	14	1	0	2	(0	2)	21	9	4	3	0	18	1	0	0	1	2	.33	0	.187	.228	.280
1986	Montreal	N	105	321	87	13	0	10	(4	6)	130	39	42	30	5	79	3	1	1	6	5	.55	8	.271	.338	.405
2 YEARS			129	396	101	14	0	12	(4	8)	151	48	46	33	5	97	4	1	1	7	7	.50	8	.255	.318	.381

JIM GANTNER

Bats Left-handed, Throws Right-handed   Turns Age 33 in 1987, Born 01/05/54

										BATTING												BASERUNNING				PERCENTAGES		
Year	Team	League	G	AB	H	2B	3B	HR	(Hm	Rd)	TB	R	RBI	TBB	IBB	SO	HBP	SH	SF	SB	CS	SB%	GIDP	AVE	OBP	SLG
1976	Milwaukee	A	26	69	17	1	0	0	(0	0)	18	6	7	6	0	11	1	3	0	1	0	1.00	1	.246	.316	.261
1977	Milwaukee	A	14	47	14	1	0	1	(0	1)	18	4	2	2	0	5	0	0	0	2	1	.67	1	.298	.327	.383
1978	Milwaukee	A	43	97	21	1	0	1	(0	1)	25	14	8	5	0	10	2	1	0	2	0	1.00	0	.216	.269	.258
1979	Milwaukee	A	70	208	59	10	3	2	(0	2)	81	29	22	16	1	17	2	5	3	3	5	.38	3	.284	.336	.389
1980	Milwaukee	A	132	415	117	21	3	4	(1	3)	156	47	40	30	5	29	1	8	3	11	10	.52	8	.282	.330	.376
1981	Milwaukee	A	107	352	94	14	1	2	(0	2)	116	35	33	29	5	29	3	9	4	3	6	.33	6	.267	.325	.330
1982	Milwaukee	A	132	447	132	17	2	4	(2	2)	165	48	43	26	3	36	2	7	3	6	3	.67	6	.295	.335	.369
1983	Milwaukee	A	161	603	170	23	8	11	(5	6)	242	85	74	38	5	46	6	11	4	5	6	.45	11	.282	.329	.401
1984	Milwaukee	A	153	613	173	27	1	3	(0	3)	211	61	56	30	0	51	3	2	10	6	5	.55	16	.282	.314	.344
1985	Milwaukee	A	143	523	133	15	4	5	(4	1)	171	63	44	33	7	42	3	10	4	11	8	.58	13	.254	.300	.327
1986	Milwaukee	A	139	497	136	25	1	7	(4	3)	184	58	38	26	2	50	6	6	7	13	7	.65	13	.274	.313	.370
11 YEARS			1120	3871	1066	155	23	40	(16	24)	1387	450	367	241	28	326	29	62	38	63	51	.55	78	.275	.320	.358

GENE GARBER

Pitches Right-handed, Bats Right-handed   Turns Age 40 in 1987, Born 11/13/47

			HOW MUCH HE PITCHED						WHAT HE GAVE UP											THE RESULTS					
Year	Team	League	G	GS	CG	GF	IP	BFP	H	R	ER	HR	SH	SF	HB	TBB	IBB	SO	WP	Bk	W	L	Pct	ShO	Sv	ERA
1969	Pittsburgh	N	2	1	0	0	5	20	6	3	3	3	1	0	0	1	0	3	0	0	0	0	.000	0	0	5.40
1970	Pittsburgh	N	14	0	0	5	22	94	22	13	13	4	1	1	2	10	1	7	0	0	0	0	.000	0	0	5.32
1972	Pittsburgh	N	4	0	0	1	6	29	7	5	5	3	0	0	0	3	0	3	0	0	0	0	.000	0	3	7.50
1973	Kansas City	A	48	8	4	26	153	594	164	78	72	14	7	6	2	49	15	60	4	0	9	9	.500	0	11	4.24
1974	2 Teams		51	0	0	20	76	337	74	36	26	4	12	2	2	44	24	41	5	1	5	2	.714	0	5	3.08
1975	Philadelphia	N	71	0	0	47	110	448	104	48	44	13	8	2	2	27	11	69	1	0	10	12	.455	0	14	3.60
1976	Philadelphia	N	59	0	0	33	93	384	78	33	29	4	4	4	4	30	8	92	2	0	9	3	.750	0	11	2.81
1977	Philadelphia	N	64	0	0	55	103	406	82	30	27	6	6	3	2	23	8	78	1	0	8	6	.571	0	19	2.36
1978	2 Teams		65	0	0	50	117	454	84	32	28	12	5	0	5	24	6	85	3	4	6	5	.545	0	25	2.15
1979	Atlanta	N	68	0	0	55	106	461	121	66	51	10	1	3	5	24	9	56	0	0	6	16	.273	0	25	4.33
1980	Atlanta	N	68	0	0	31	82	359	95	42	35	6	4	1	0	24	5	51	0	0	5	5	.500	0	7	3.84
1981	Atlanta	N	35	0	0	17	59	251	49	23	17	2	2	0	0	20	9	34	1	1	4	6	.400	0	2	2.59
1982	Atlanta	N	69	0	0	56	119.1	480	100	40	31	4	9	5	2	32	16	68	1	0	8	10	.444	0	30	2.34
1983	Atlanta	N	43	0	0	29	60.2	277	72	37	31	8	6	6	2	23	7	45	2	1	4	5	.444	0	9	4.60
1984	Atlanta	N	62	0	0	42	106	443	103	45	36	7	4	7	2	24	9	55	1	1	3	6	.333	0	11	3.06
1985	Atlanta	N	59	0	0	31	97.1	409	98	41	39	8	9	1	2	25	8	66	1	0	6	6	.500	0	1	3.61
1986	Atlanta	N	61	0	0	48	78	319	76	23	22	3	5	1	1	20	7	56	4	0	5	5	.500	0	24	2.54
17 YEARS			843	9	4	546	1393.1	5765	1335	595	509	111	84	42	33	403	143	869	26	8	88	99	.471	0	194	3.29
1974	Kansas City	A	17	0	0	4	28	132	35	21	15	3	6	0	1	13	9	14	2	0	1	2	.333	0	1	4.82
1974	Philadelphia	N	34	0	0	16	48	205	39	15	11	1	6	2	1	31	15	27	3	1	4	0	1.000	0	4	2.06
1978	Atlanta	N	43	0	0	36	78.1	302	58	26	22	11	3	0	2	13	3	61	3	2	4	4	.500	0	22	2.53
1978	Philadelphia	N	22	0	0	14	38.2	152	26	6	6	1	2	0	3	11	3	24	0	2	2	1	.667	0	3	1.40

DAMASO GARCIA

Bats Right-handed, Throws Right-handed   Turns Age 30 in 1987, Born 02/07/57

										BATTING												BASERUNNING				PERCENTAGES		
Year	Team	League	G	AB	H	2B	3B	HR	(Hm	Rd)	TB	R	RBI	TBB	IBB	SO	HBP	SH	SF	SB	CS	SB%	GIDP	AVE	OBP	SLG
1978	New York	A	18	41	8	0	0	0	(0	0)	8	5	1	2	0	6	0	0	1	1	0	1.00	1	.195	.227	.195
1979	New York	A	11	38	10	1	0	0	(0	0)	11	3	4	0	0	2	0	0	0	2	0	1.00	1	.263	.263	.289
1980	Toronto	A	140	543	151	30	7	4	(2	2)	207	50	46	12	2	55	3	4	3	13	13	.50	14	.278	.296	.381
1981	Toronto	A	64	250	63	8	1	1	(1	0)	76	24	13	9	1	32	0	3	1	13	3	.81	6	.252	.277	.304
1982	Toronto	A	147	597	185	32	3	5	(3	2)	238	89	42	21	1	44	5	5	1	54	20	.73	7	.310	.338	.399
1983	Toronto	A	131	525	161	23	6	3	(1	2)	205	84	38	24	3	34	2	5	5	31	17	.65	9	.307	.336	.390
1984	Toronto	A	152	633	180	32	5	5	(2	3)	237	79	46	16	1	46	9	3	4	46	12	.79	6	.284	.310	.374
1985	Toronto	A	146	600	169	25	4	8	(4	4)	226	70	65	15	2	41	4	5	3	28	15	.65	13	.282	.302	.377
1986	Toronto	A	122	424	119	22	0	6	(3	3)	159	57	46	13	0	32	4	2	3	9	6	.60	14	.281	.306	.375
9 YEARS			931	3651	1046	173	26	32	(16	16)	1367	461	301	112	10	292	27	27	21	197	86	.70	71	.286	.311	.374

PHIL GARNER

Bats Right-handed, Throws Right-handed   Turns Age 38 in 1987, Born 04/30/49

										BATTING												BASERUNNING				PERCENTAGES		
Year	Team	League	G	AB	H	2B	3B	HR	(Hm	Rd)	TB	R	RBI	TBB	IBB	SO	HBP	SH	SF	SB	CS	SB%	GIDP	AVE	OBP	SLG
1973	Oakland	A	9	5	0	0	0	0	(0	0)	0	0	0	0	0	3	0	0	0	0	0	.00	0	.000	.000	.000
1974	Oakland	A	30	28	5	1	0	0	(0	0)	6	4	1	1	0	5	0	1	0	1	1	.50	0	.179	.207	.214
1975	Oakland	A	160	488	120	21	5	6	(3	3)	169	46	54	30	1	65	5	21	3	4	6	.40	12	.246	.295	.346
1976	Oakland	A	159	555	145	29	12	8	(6	2)	222	54	74	36	1	71	2	6	4	35	13	.73	11	.261	.307	.400
1977	Pittsburgh	N	153	585	152	35	10	17	(9	8)	258	99	77	55	4	65	2	7	2	32	9	.78	13	.260	.325	.441
1978	Pittsburgh	N	154	528	138	25	9	10	(4	6)	211	66	66	66	12	71	5	3	7	27	14	.66	18	.261	.345	.400
1979	Pittsburgh	N	150	549	161	32	8	11	(6	5)	242	76	59	55	15	74	3	2	3	17	8	.68	6	.293	.359	.441
1980	Pittsburgh	N	151	548	142	27	6	5	(3	2)	196	62	58	46	12	53	2	7	7	32	7	.82	12	.259	.315	.358
1981	2 Teams		87	294	73	9	3	1	(0	1)	91	35	26	36	2	32	0	6	4	10	8	.56	4	.248	.326	.310
1982	Houston	N	155	588	161	33	8	13	(6	7)	249	65	83	40	4	92	3	0	7	24	13	.65	11	.274	.320	.423
1983	Houston	N	154	567	135	24	2	14	(4	10)	205	76	79	63	8	84	5	3	6	18	12	.60	4	.238	.317	.362
1984	Houston	N	128	374	104	17	6	4	(1	3)	145	60	45	43	2	63	4	5	4	3	2	.60	9	.278	.355	.388
1985	Houston	N	135	463	124	23	10	6	(2	4)	185	65	51	34	3	72	2	1	5	4	4	.50	12	.268	.317	.400
1986	Houston	N	107	313	83	14	3	9	(2	7)	130	43	41	30	2	45	1	0	3	12	6	.67	14	.265	.329	.415
14 YEARS			1732	5885	1543	290	82	104	(46	58)	2309	751	714	535	66	795	34	62	55	219	103	.68	126	.262	.324	.392
1981	Houston	N	31	113	27	3	1	0	(0	0)	32	13	6	15	1	11	0	4	1	6	2	.75	1	.239	.326	.283
1981	Pittsburgh	N	56	181	46	6	2	1	(0	1)	59	22	20	21	1	21	0	2	3	4	6	.40	3	.254	.327	.326

SCOTT GARRELTS

Pitches Right-handed, Bats Right-handed   Turns Age 26 in 1987, Born 10/30/61

			HOW MUCH HE PITCHED							WHAT HE GAVE UP									THE RESULTS					
Year Team League	G	GS	CG	GF	IP	BFP	H	R	ER	HR	SH	SF	HB	TBB	IBB	SO	WP	Bk	W	L	Pct	ShO	Sv	ERA
1982 San Francisco N	1	0	0	1	2	11	3	3	3	0	0	0	0	2	0	4	0	0	0	0	.000	0	0	13.50
1983 San Francisco N	5	5	1	0	35.2	154	33	11	10	4	3	0	2	19	4	16	4	1	2	2	.500	1	0	2.52
1984 San Francisco N	21	3	0	5	43	206	45	33	27	6	5	2	1	34	1	32	3	0	2	3	.400	0	0	5.65
1985 San Francisco N	74	0	0	44	105.2	454	76	37	27	2	6	3	3	58	12	106	7	1	9	6	.600	0	13	2.30
1986 San Francisco N	53	18	2	27	173.2	717	144	65	60	17	10	7	2	74	11	125	9	1	13	9	.591	0	10	3.11
5 YEARS	154	26	3	77	360	1542	301	149	127	29	24	12	8	187	28	283	23	3	26	20	.565	1	23	3.17

STEVE GARVEY

Bats Right-handed, Throws Right-handed   Turns Age 39 in 1987, Born 12/22/48

							BATTING												BASERUNNING				PERCENTAGES		
Year Team League	G	AB	H	2B	3B	HR	(Hm	Rd)	TB	R	RBI	TBB	IBB	SO	HBP	SH	SF	SB	CS	SB%	GIDP	AVE	OBP	SLG
1969 Los Angeles N	3	3	1	0	0	0	(0	0)	1	0	0	0	0	1	0	0	0	0	0	.00	0	.333	.333	.333
1970 Los Angeles N	34	93	25	5	0	1	(1	0)	33	8	6	6	0	17	0	0	1	1	1	.50	3	.269	.310	.355
1971 Los Angeles N	81	225	51	12	1	7	(5	2)	86	27	26	21	2	33	0	1	2	1	2	.33	6	.227	.290	.382
1972 Los Angeles N	96	294	79	14	2	9	(5	4)	124	36	30	19	3	36	1	0	3	4	2	.67	3	.269	.312	.422
1973 Los Angeles N	114	349	106	17	3	8	(6	2)	153	37	50	11	4	42	3	0	3	0	2	.00	8	.304	.328	.438
1974 Los Angeles N	156	642	200	32	3	21	(8	13)	301	95	111	31	4	66	3	1	8	5	4	.56	8	.312	.342	.469
1975 Los Angeles N	160	659	210	38	6	18	(9	9)	314	85	95	33	6	66	3	3	6	11	2	.85	19	.319	.351	.476
1976 Los Angeles N	162	631	200	37	4	13	(6	7)	284	85	80	50	11	69	1	5	9	19	8	.70	20	.317	.363	.450
1977 Los Angeles N	162	646	192	25	3	33	(16	17)	322	91	115	38	10	90	1	7	4	9	6	.60	15	.297	.335	.498
1978 Los Angeles N	162	639	202	36	9	21	(15	6)	319	89	113	40	9	70	1	1	8	10	5	.67	17	.316	.353	.499
1979 Los Angeles N	162	648	204	32	1	28	(20	8)	322	92	110	37	16	59	2	4	6	3	6	.33	25	.315	.351	.497
1980 Los Angeles N	163	658	200	27	1	26	(16	10)	307	78	106	36	6	67	3	3	4	6	11	.35	17	.304	.341	.467
1981 Los Angeles N	110	431	122	23	1	10	(5	5)	177	63	64	25	6	49	1	1	3	3	5	.38	8	.283	.322	.411
1982 Los Angeles N	162	625	176	35	1	16	(5	11)	261	66	86	20	10	86	1	5	9	5	3	.63	10	.282	.301	.418
1983 San Diego N	100	388	114	22	0	14	(8	6)	178	76	59	29	11	39	3	0	5	4	1	.80	16	.294	.344	.459
1984 San Diego N	161	617	175	27	2	8	(5	3)	230	72	86	24	3	64	1	1	10	1	2	.33	25	.284	.307	.373
1985 San Diego N	162	654	184	34	6	17	(10	7)	281	80	81	35	7	67	3	1	6	0	0	.00	25	.281	.318	.430
1986 San Diego N	155	557	142	22	0	21	(11	10)	227	58	81	23	5	72	1	0	3	1	2	.33	18	.255	.284	.408
18 YEARS	2305	8759	2583	438	43	271	(151	120)	3920	1138	1299	478	113	993	28	33	90	83	62	.57	248	.295	.330	.448

RICH GEDMAN

Bats Left-handed, Throws Right-handed   Turns Age 28 in 1987, Born 09/26/59

							BATTING												BASERUNNING				PERCENTAGES		
Year Team League	G	AB	H	2B	3B	HR	(Hm	Rd)	TB	R	RBI	TBB	IBB	SO	HBP	SH	SF	SB	CS	SB%	GIDP	AVE	OBP	SLG
1980 Boston A	9	24	5	0	0	0	(0	0)	5	2	1	0	0	5	0	0	0	0	0	.00	1	.208	.208	.208
1981 Boston A	62	205	59	15	0	5	(3	2)	89	22	26	9	1	31	1	1	3	0	0	.00	9	.288	.317	.434
1982 Boston A	92	289	72	17	2	4	(1	3)	105	30	26	10	2	37	2	4	0	0	1	.00	13	.249	.279	.363
1983 Boston A	81	204	60	16	1	2	(0	2)	84	21	18	15	6	37	1	3	0	0	1	.00	4	.294	.345	.412
1984 Boston A	133	449	121	26	4	24	(16	8)	227	54	72	29	8	72	1	2	5	0	0	.00	5	.269	.312	.506
1985 Boston A	144	498	147	30	5	18	(9	9)	241	66	80	50	11	79	3	3	2	2	0	1.00	12	.295	.362	.484
1986 Boston A	135	462	119	29	1	16	(2	14)	196	49	65	37	13	61	4	1	5	1	0	1.00	15	.258	.315	.424
7 YEARS	656	2131	583	133	12	69	(31	38)	947	244	288	150	41	322	12	14	15	3	2	.60	59	.274	.323	.444

KIRK GIBSON

Bats Left-handed, Throws Left-handed   Turns Age 30 in 1987, Born 05/28/57

							BATTING												BASERUNNING				PERCENTAGES		
Year Team League	G	AB	H	2B	3B	HR	(Hm	Rd)	TB	R	RBI	TBB	IBB	SO	HBP	SH	SF	SB	CS	SB%	GIDP	AVE	OBP	SLG
1979 Detroit A	12	38	9	3	0	1	(0	1)	15	3	4	1	0	3	0	0	0	3	3	.50	0	.237	.256	.395
1980 Detroit A	51	175	46	2	1	9	(3	6)	77	23	16	10	0	45	1	1	2	4	7	.36	0	.263	.303	.440
1981 Detroit A	83	290	95	11	3	9	(4	5)	139	41	40	18	1	64	2	1	2	17	5	.77	9	.328	.369	.479
1982 Detroit A	69	266	74	16	2	8	(4	4)	118	34	35	25	2	41	1	1	1	9	7	.56	2	.278	.341	.444
1983 Detroit A	128	401	91	12	9	15	(5	10)	166	60	51	53	3	96	4	5	4	14	3	.82	2	.227	.320	.414
1984 Detroit A	149	531	150	23	10	27	(11	16)	274	92	91	63	6	103	8	3	6	29	9	.76	4	.282	.363	.516
1985 Detroit A	154	581	167	37	5	29	(18	11)	301	96	97	71	16	137	5	3	10	30	4	.88	5	.287	.364	.518
1986 Detroit A	119	441	118	11	2	28	(15	13)	217	84	86	68	4	107	7	1	4	34	6	.85	8	.268	.371	.492
8 YEARS	765	2723	750	115	32	126	(60	66)	1307	433	420	309	32	596	28	15	29	140	44	.76	30	.275	.352	.480

DAN GLADDEN

Bats Right-handed, Throws Right-handed   Turns Age 30 in 1987, Born 07/07/57

							BATTING												BASERUNNING				PERCENTAGES		
Year Team League	G	AB	H	2B	3B	HR	(Hm	Rd)	TB	R	RBI	TBB	IBB	SO	HBP	SH	SF	SB	CS	SB%	GIDP	AVE	OBP	SLG
1983 San Francisco N	18	63	14	2	0	1	(1	0)	19	6	9	5	0	11	0	3	1	4	3	.57	3	.222	.275	.302
1984 San Francisco N	86	342	120	17	2	4	(4	0)	153	71	31	33	2	37	2	6	1	31	16	.66	3	.351	.410	.447
1985 San Francisco N	142	502	122	15	8	7	(6	1)	174	64	41	40	1	78	7	10	2	32	15	.68	10	.243	.307	.347
1986 San Francisco N	102	351	97	16	1	4	(1	3)	127	55	29	39	3	59	5	7	0	27	10	.73	5	.276	.357	.362
4 YEARS	348	1258	353	50	11	16	(12	4)	473	196	110	117	6	185	14	26	4	94	44	.68	21	.281	.347	.376

DWIGHT GOODEN

Pitches Right-handed, Bats Right-handed   Turns Age 23 in 1987, Born 11/16/64

			HOW MUCH HE PITCHED						WHAT HE GAVE UP											THE RESULTS					
Year	Team	League	G	GS	CG	GF	IP	BFP	H	R	ER	HR	SH	SF	HB	TBB	IBB	SO	WP	Bk	W	L	Pct	ShO	Sv	ERA
1984	New York	N	31	31	7	0	218	879	161	72	63	7	3	2	2	73	2	276	3	7	17	9	.654	3	0	2.60
1985	New York	N	35	35	16	0	276.2	1065	198	51	47	13	6	2	2	69	4	268	6	2	24	4	.857	8	0	1.53
1986	New York	N	33	33	12	0	250	1020	197	92	79	17	10	8	4	80	3	200	4	4	17	6	.739	2	0	2.84
3 YEARS			99	99	35	0	744.2	2964	556	215	189	37	19	12	8	222	9	744	13	13	58	19	.753	13	0	2.28

GOOSE GOSSAGE

Pitches Right-handed, Bats Right-handed   Turns Age 36 in 1987, Born 07/05/51

			HOW MUCH HE PITCHED						WHAT HE GAVE UP											THE RESULTS					
Year	Team	League	G	GS	CG	GF	IP	BFP	H	R	ER	HR	SH	SF	HB	TBB	IBB	SO	WP	Bk	W	L	Pct	ShO	Sv	ERA
1972	Chicago	A	36	1	0	7	80	308	72	44	38	2	10	2	4	44	3	57	7	0	7	1	.875	0	2	4.28
1973	Chicago	A	20	4	1	4	50	195	57	44	41	9	5	4	3	37	2	33	6	0	0	4	.000	0	0	7.38
1974	Chicago	A	39	3	0	19	89	397	92	45	41	4	6	4	2	47	7	64	2	1	4	6	.400	0	1	4.15
1975	Chicago	A	62	0	0	49	142	582	99	32	29	3	15	0	5	70	15	130	3	0	9	8	.529	0	26	1.84
1976	Chicago	A	31	29	15	1	224	956	214	104	98	16	8	7	9	90	3	135	6	0	9	17	.346	0	1	3.94
1977	Pittsburgh	N	72	0	0	55	133	523	78	27	24	9	7	6	2	49	6	151	2	0	11	9	.550	0	26	1.62
1978	New York	A	63	0	0	55	134	543	87	41	30	9	9	8	2	59	8	122	5	0	10	11	.476	0	27	2.01
1979	New York	A	36	0	0	33	58	234	48	18	17	5	4	0	0	19	4	41	3	0	5	3	.625	0	18	2.64
1980	New York	A	64	0	0	58	99	401	74	29	25	5	8	4	1	37	3	103	4	0	6	2	.750	0	33	2.27
1981	New York	A	32	0	0	30	47	173	22	6	4	2	1	1	1	14	1	48	1	0	3	2	.600	0	20	0.77
1982	New York	A	56	0	0	43	93	356	63	23	23	5	5	2	0	28	5	102	1	0	4	5	.444	0	30	2.23
1983	New York	A	57	0	0	47	87.1	367	82	27	22	5	5	6	1	25	5	90	0	0	13	5	.722	0	22	2.27
1984	San Diego	N	62	0	0	51	102.1	412	75	34	33	6	4	3	1	36	4	84	2	2	10	6	.625	0	25	2.90
1985	San Diego	N	50	0	0	38	79	308	64	21	16	1	3	4	1	17	1	52	0	0	5	3	.625	0	26	1.82
1986	San Diego	N	45	0	0	38	64.2	281	69	36	32	7	2	4	2	20	0	63	4	0	5	7	.417	0	21	4.45
15 YEARS			725	37	16	528	1482.1	6036	1196	531	473	89	92	55	34	592	67	1275	46	3	101	89	.532	0	278	2.87

BOBBY GRICH

Bats Right-handed, Throws Right-handed   Turns Age 38 in 1987, Born 01/15/49

			BATTING																BASERUNNING				PERCENTAGES		
Year	Team	League	G	AB	H	2B	3B	HR	(Hm	Rd)	TB	R	RBI	TBB	IBB	SO	HBP	SH	SF	SB	CS	SB%	GIDP	AVE	OBP	SLG
1970	Baltimore	A	30	95	20	1	3	0	(0	0)	27	11	8	9	0	21	0	0	0	1	1	.50	2	.211	.279	.284
1971	Baltimore	A	7	30	9	0	0	1	(0	1)	12	7	6	5	0	8	0	0	0	1	0	1.00	0	.300	.400	.400
1972	Baltimore	A	133	460	128	21	3	12	(6	6)	191	66	50	53	3	96	7	3	5	13	6	.68	8	.278	.358	.415
1973	Baltimore	A	162	581	146	29	7	12	(7	5)	225	83	50	107	3	91	7	3	2	17	9	.65	7	.251	.373	.387
1974	Baltimore	A	160	582	153	29	6	19	(11	8)	251	92	82	90	6	117	20	7	8	17	11	.61	15	.263	.376	.431
1975	Baltimore	A	150	524	136	26	4	13	(5	8)	209	81	57	107	4	88	8	9	7	14	10	.58	9	.260	.389	.399
1976	Baltimore	A	144	518	138	31	4	13	(8	5)	216	93	54	86	1	99	3	7	1	14	6	.70	8	.266	.373	.417
1977	California	A	52	181	44	6	0	7	(4	3)	71	24	23	37	4	40	1	3	3	6	6	.50	5	.243	.369	.392
1978	California	A	144	487	122	16	2	6	(4	2)	160	68	42	75	1	83	7	19	3	4	3	.57	6	.251	.357	.329
1979	California	A	153	534	157	30	5	30	(15	15)	287	78	101	59	10	84	2	12	2	1	0	1.00	14	.294	.365	.537
1980	California	A	150	498	135	22	2	14	(9	5)	203	60	62	84	2	108	4	5	5	3	7	.30	16	.271	.377	.408
1981	California	A	100	352	107	14	2	22	(7	15)	191	56	61	40	4	71	4	5	3	2	4	.33	5	.304	.378	.543
1982	California	A	145	506	132	28	5	19	(8	11)	227	74	65	82	3	109	8	6	3	3	3	.50	13	.261	.371	.449
1983	California	A	120	387	113	17	0	16	(8	8)	178	65	62	76	2	62	7	4	3	2	4	.33	11	.292	.414	.460
1984	California	A	116	363	93	15	1	18	(9	9)	164	60	58	57	3	70	2	6	4	2	5	.29	11	.256	.357	.452
1985	California	A	144	479	116	17	3	13	(7	6)	178	74	53	81	3	77	3	8	0	3	5	.38	18	.242	.355	.372
1986	California	A	98	313	84	18	0	9	(5	4)	129	42	30	39	1	54	3	10	1	1	3	.25	9	.268	.354	.412
17 YEARS			2008	6890	1833	320	47	224	(109	115)	2919	1034	864	1087	50	1278	86	107	50	104	83	.56	157	.266	.371	.424

KEN GRIFFEY

Bats Left-handed, Throws Left-handed   Turns Age 37 in 1987, Born 04/10/50

			BATTING																BASERUNNING				PERCENTAGES		
Year	Team	League	G	AB	H	2B	3B	HR	(Hm	Rd)	TB	R	RBI	TBB	IBB	SO	HBP	SH	SF	SB	CS	SB%	GIDP	AVE	OBP	SLG
1973	Cincinnati	N	25	86	33	5	1	3	(2	1)	49	19	14	6	0	10	0	0	0	4	2	.67	0	.384	.424	.570
1974	Cincinnati	N	88	227	57	9	5	2	(2	0)	82	24	19	27	2	43	1	4	0	9	4	.69	2	.251	.333	.361
1975	Cincinnati	N	132	463	141	15	9	4	(1	3)	186	95	46	67	2	67	1	6	3	16	7	.70	10	.305	.391	.402
1976	Cincinnati	N	148	562	189	28	9	6	(2	4)	253	111	74	62	0	65	1	0	3	34	11	.76	3	.336	.401	.450
1977	Cincinnati	N	154	585	186	35	8	12	(4	8)	273	117	57	69	2	84	0	1	2	17	8	.68	12	.318	.389	.467
1978	Cincinnati	N	158	614	177	33	8	10	(7	3)	256	90	63	54	1	70	0	9	3	23	5	.82	6	.288	.344	.417
1979	Cincinnati	N	95	380	120	27	4	8	(3	5)	179	62	32	36	3	39	1	0	3	12	5	.71	7	.316	.374	.471
1980	Cincinnati	N	146	544	160	28	10	13	(9	4)	247	89	85	62	4	77	1	3	5	23	1	.96	9	.294	.364	.454
1981	Cincinnati	N	101	396	123	21	6	2	(0	2)	162	65	34	39	6	42	1	2	4	12	4	.75	9	.311	.370	.409
1982	New York	A	127	484	134	23	2	12	(8	4)	197	70	54	39	1	58	0	1	3	10	4	.71	10	.277	.329	.407
1983	New York	A	118	458	140	21	3	11	(8	3)	200	60	46	34	3	45	2	3	2	6	1	.86	3	.306	.355	.437
1984	New York	A	120	399	109	20	1	7	(5	2)	152	44	56	29	2	32	1	3	4	2	2	.50	7	.273	.321	.381
1985	New York	A	127	438	120	28	4	10	(6	4)	186	68	69	41	4	51	0	0	8	7	7	.50	2	.274	.331	.425
1986	2 Teams		139	490	150	22	3	21	(14	7)	241	69	58	35	4	67	1	1	5	14	9	.61	9	.306	.350	.492
14 YEARS			1678	6126	1839	315	73	121	(71	50)	2663	983	707	600	34	750	10	30	45	189	70	.73	84	.300	.361	.435
1986	New York	A	59	198	60	7	0	9	(5	4)	94	33	26	15	0	24	1	1	4	2	2	.50	7	.303	.349	.475
1986	Atlanta	N	80	292	90	15	3	12	(9	3)	147	36	32	20	4	43	0	0	1	12	7	.63	2	.308	.351	.503

ALFREDO GRIFFIN

Bats both Right and Left-handed, Throws Right-handed

Turns Age 30 in 1987, Born 03/06/57

									BATTING											BASERUNNING				PERCENTAGES		
Year	Team	League	G	AB	H	2B	3B	HR	(Hm	Rd)	TB	R	RBI	TBB	IBB	SO	HBP	SH	SF	SB	CS	SB%	GIDP	AVE	OBP	SLG
1976	Cleveland	A	12	4	1	0	0	0	(0	0)	1	0	0	0	0	2	0	0	0	0	1	.00	0	.250	.250	.250
1977	Cleveland	A	14	41	6	1	0	0	(0	0)	7	5	3	3	0	5	0	0	0	2	2	.50	1	.146	.205	.171
1978	Cleveland	A	5	4	2	1	0	0	(0	0)	3	1	0	2	0	1	0	0	0	0	0	.00	0	.500	.667	.750
1979	Toronto	A	153	624	179	22	10	2	(2	0)	227	81	31	40	0	59	5	16	4	21	16	.57	10	.287	.333	.364
1980	Toronto	A	155	653	166	26	15	2	(1	1)	228	63	41	24	0	58	4	10	5	18	23	.44	8	.254	.283	.349
1981	Toronto	A	101	388	81	19	6	0	(0	0)	112	30	21	17	1	38	1	6	2	8	12	.40	6	.209	.243	.289
1982	Toronto	A	162	539	130	20	8	1	(0	1)	169	57	48	22	0	48	0	11	4	10	8	.56	7	.241	.269	.314
1983	Toronto	A	162	528	132	22	9	4	(2	2)	184	62	47	27	0	44	3	11	3	8	11	.42	5	.250	.289	.348
1984	Toronto	A	140	419	101	8	2	4	(1	3)	125	53	30	4	0	33	1	13	4	11	3	.79	5	.241	.248	.298
1985	Oakland	A	162	614	166	18	7	2	(0	2)	204	75	64	20	1	50	0	5	7	24	9	.73	6	.270	.290	.332
1986	Oakland	A	162	594	169	23	6	4	(1	3)	216	74	51	35	6	52	2	12	6	33	16	.67	5	.285	.323	.364
11 YEARS			1228	4408	1133	160	63	19	(7	12)	1476	501	336	194	10	390	16	84	35	135	101	.57	53	.257	.289	.335

KEVIN GROSS

Pitches Right-handed, Bats Right-handed

Turns Age 26 in 1987, Born 06/08/61

			HOW MUCH HE PITCHED						WHAT HE GAVE UP											THE RESULTS					
Year	Team	League	G	GS	CG	GF	IP	BFP	H	R	ER	HR	SH	SF	HB	TBB	IBB	SO	WP	Bk	W	L	Pct	ShO	Sv	ERA
1983	Philadelphia	N	17	17	1	0	96	418	100	46	38	13	2	1	3	35	3	66	4	1	4	6	.400	1	0	3.56
1984	Philadelphia	N	44	14	1	9	129	566	140	66	59	8	9	3	5	44	4	84	4	4	8	5	.615	0	1	4.12
1985	Philadelphia	N	38	31	6	0	205.2	873	194	86	78	11	7	5	7	81	6	151	2	0	15	13	.536	2	0	3.41
1986	Philadelphia	N	37	36	7	0	241.2	1040	240	115	108	28	8	5	8	94	2	154	2	1	12	12	.500	2	0	4.02
4 YEARS			136	98	15	9	672.1	2897	674	313	283	60	26	14	23	254	15	455	12	6	39	36	.520	5	1	3.79

JOHN GRUBB

Bats Left-handed, Throws Right-handed

Turns Age 39 in 1987, Born 08/04/48

									BATTING											BASERUNNING				PERCENTAGES		
Year	Team	League	G	AB	H	2B	3B	HR	(Hm	Rd)	TB	R	RBI	TBB	IBB	SO	HBP	SH	SF	SB	CS	SB%	GIDP	AVE	OBP	SLG
1972	San Diego	N	7	21	7	1	1	0	(0	0)	10	4	1	1	0	3	0	0	0	0	1	.00	1	.333	.364	.476
1973	San Diego	N	113	389	121	22	3	8	(6	2)	173	52	37	37	2	50	2	3	1	9	3	.75	6	.311	.373	.445
1974	San Diego	N	140	444	127	20	4	8	(3	5)	179	53	42	46	2	47	4	4	5	4	0	1.00	4	.286	.355	.403
1975	San Diego	N	144	553	149	36	2	4	(1	3)	201	72	38	59	4	59	5	3	5	2	7	.22	7	.269	.342	.363
1976	San Diego	N	109	384	109	22	1	5	(2	3)	148	54	27	65	10	53	4	6	2	1	2	.33	5	.284	.391	.385
1977	Cleveland	A	34	93	28	3	3	2	(1	1)	43	8	14	19	2	18	1	0	0	0	3	.00	3	.301	.425	.462
1978	2 Teams		134	411	113	19	6	15	(7	8)	189	62	67	70	5	65	2	8	2	6	2	.75	5	.275	.381	.460
1979	Texas	A	102	289	79	14	0	10	(4	6)	123	42	37	34	3	44	1	2	2	2	4	.33	6	.273	.350	.426
1980	Texas	A	110	274	76	12	1	9	(6	3)	117	40	32	42	5	35	2	2	3	2	3	.40	11	.277	.374	.427
1981	Texas	A	67	199	46	9	1	3	(1	2)	66	26	26	23	0	25	2	1	1	0	3	.00	6	.231	.316	.332
1982	Texas	A	103	308	86	13	3	3	(2	1)	114	35	26	39	2	37	6	2	3	0	3	.00	5	.279	.368	.370
1983	Detroit	A	57	134	34	5	2	4	(3	1)	55	20	22	28	1	17	2	0	1	0	0	.00	1	.254	.388	.410
1984	Detroit	A	86	176	47	5	0	8	(1	7)	76	25	17	36	5	36	2	1	1	1	0	1.00	1	.267	.395	.432
1985	Detroit	A	78	155	38	7	1	5	(4	1)	62	19	25	24	0	25	1	0	4	0	1	.00	5	.245	.342	.400
1986	Detroit	A	81	210	70	13	1	13	(8	5)	124	32	51	28	0	28	2	0	3	0	1	.00	0	.333	.412	.590
15 YEARS			1365	4040	1130	201	29	97	(49	48)	1680	544	462	551	41	542	36	32	33	27	33	.45	70	.280	.368	.416
1978	Cleveland	A	113	378	100	16	6	14	(6	8)	170	54	61	59	5	60	2	8	2	5	1	.83	5	.265	.365	.450
1978	Texas	A	21	33	13	3	0	1	(1	0)	19	8	6	11	0	5	0	0	0	1	1	.50	0	.394	.545	.576

KELLY GRUBER

Bats Right-handed, Throws Right-handed

Turns Age 25 in 1987, Born 02/26/62

									BATTING											BASERUNNING				PERCENTAGES		
Year	Team	League	G	AB	H	2B	3B	HR	(Hm	Rd)	TB	R	RBI	TBB	IBB	SO	HBP	SH	SF	SB	CS	SB%	GIDP	AVE	OBP	SLG
1984	Toronto	A	15	16	1	0	0	1	(0	1)	4	1	2	0	0	5	0	0	0	0	0	.00	1	.063	.063	.250
1985	Toronto	A	5	13	3	0	0	0	(0	0)	3	0	1	0	0	3	0	0	0	0	0	.00	0	.231	.231	.231
1986	Toronto	A	87	143	28	4	1	5	(4	1)	49	20	15	5	0	27	0	2	2	2	5	.29	4	.196	.220	.343
3 YEARS			107	172	32	4	1	6	(4	2)	56	21	18	5	0	35	0	2	2	2	5	.29	5	.186	.207	.326

CECILIO GUANTE

Pitches Right-handed, Bats Right-handed

Turns Age 27 in 1987, Born 02/02/60

			HOW MUCH HE PITCHED						WHAT HE GAVE UP											THE RESULTS					
Year	Team	League	G	GS	CG	GF	IP	BFP	H	R	ER	HR	SH	SF	HB	TBB	IBB	SO	WP	Bk	W	L	Pct	ShO	Sv	ERA
1982	Pittsburgh	N	10	0	0	1	27	117	28	16	10	1	0	4	2	5	0	26	0	0	0	0	.000	0	0	3.33
1983	Pittsburgh	N	49	0	0	19	100.1	431	90	45	37	5	7	2	2	46	6	82	3	0	2	6	.250	0	9	3.32
1984	Pittsburgh	N	27	0	0	15	41.1	166	32	12	12	3	2	3	2	16	2	30	0	1	2	3	.400	0	2	2.61
1985	Pittsburgh	N	63	0	0	31	109	445	84	34	33	5	4	3	5	40	9	92	5	0	4	6	.400	0	5	2.72
1986	Pittsburgh	N	52	0	0	24	78	326	65	32	29	11	3	2	3	29	3	63	2	1	5	2	.714	0	4	3.35
5 YEARS			201	0	0	90	355.2	1485	299	139	121	25	16	14	14	136	20	293	10	2	13	17	.433	0	20	3.06

MARK GUBICZA

Pitches Right-handed, Bats Right-handed   Turns Age 25 in 1987, Born 08/14/62

			HOW MUCH HE PITCHED				WHAT HE GAVE UP											THE RESULTS					
Year	Team	League	G	GS	CG	GF	IP	BFP	H	R	ER	HR	SH	SF	HB	TBB	IBB	SO	WP	Bk	W	L	Pct	ShO	Sv	ERA
1984	Kansas City	A	29	29	4	0	189	800	172	90	85	13	4	9	5	75	0	111	3	1	10	14	.417	2	0	4.05
1985	Kansas City	A	29	28	0	0	177.1	760	160	88	80	14	1	6	5	77	0	99	12	0	14	10	.583	0	0	4.06
1986	Kansas City	A	35	24	3	2	180.2	765	155	77	73	8	4	8	5	84	2	118	15	0	12	6	.667	2	0	3.64
3 YEARS			93	81	7	2	547	2325	487	255	238	35	9	23	15	236	2	328	30	1	36	30	.545	4	0	3.92

LEE GUETTERMAN

Pitches Left-handed, Bats Left-handed   Turns Age 29 in 1987, Born 11/22/58

			HOW MUCH HE PITCHED				WHAT HE GAVE UP											THE RESULTS					
Year	Team	League	G	GS	CG	GF	IP	BFP	H	R	ER	HR	SH	SF	HB	TBB	IBB	SO	WP	Bk	W	L	Pct	ShO	Sv	ERA
1984	Seattle	A	3	0	0	1	4.1	22	9	2	2	0	0	0	0	2	0	2	1	0	0	0	.000	0	0	4.15
1986	Seattle	A	41	4	1	8	76	353	108	67	62	7	3	5	4	30	3	38	2	0	0	4	.000	0	0	7.34
2 YEARS			44	4	1	9	80.1	375	117	69	64	7	3	5	4	32	3	40	3	0	0	4	.000	0	0	7.17

RON GUIDRY

Pitches Left-handed, Bats Left-handed   Turns Age 37 in 1987, Born 08/28/50

			HOW MUCH HE PITCHED				WHAT HE GAVE UP											THE RESULTS					
Year	Team	League	G	GS	CG	GF	IP	BFP	H	R	ER	HR	SH	SF	HB	TBB	IBB	SO	WP	Bk	W	L	Pct	ShO	Sv	ERA
1975	New York	A	10	1	0	6	16	69	15	6	6	0	0	1	1	9	0	15	1	0	0	1	.000	0	0	3.37
1976	New York	A	7	0	0	2	16	72	20	12	10	1	0	0	0	4	0	12	0	0	0	0	.000	0	0	5.63
1977	New York	A	31	25	9	4	211	850	174	72	66	12	5	3	0	65	2	176	6	0	16	7	.696	5	1	2.82
1978	New York	A	35	35	16	0	274	1057	187	61	53	13	13	2	1	72	1	248	7	1	25	3	.893	9	0	1.74
1979	New York	A	33	30	15	3	236	946	203	83	73	20	9	5	0	71	0	201	9	0	18	8	.692	2	2	2.78
1980	New York	A	37	29	5	4	220	929	215	97	87	19	9	12	1	80	1	166	5	0	17	10	.630	3	1	3.56
1981	New York	A	23	21	0	1	127	497	100	41	39	12	1	1	1	26	0	104	6	0	11	5	.688	0	0	2.76
1982	New York	A	34	33	6	0	222	935	216	104	94	22	9	6	1	69	3	162	6	1	14	8	.636	1	0	3.81
1983	New York	A	31	31	21	0	250.1	1024	232	99	95	26	4	9	2	60	3	156	4	2	21	9	.700	3	0	3.42
1984	New York	A	29	28	5	1	195.2	841	223	102	98	24	7	11	2	44	3	127	1	0	10	11	.476	1	0	4.51
1985	New York	A	34	33	11	0	259	1033	243	104	94	28	3	8	0	42	3	143	3	1	22	6	.786	2	0	3.27
1986	New York	A	30	30	5	0	192.1	809	202	94	85	28	5	4	1	38	2	140	3	0	9	12	.429	0	0	3.98
12 YEARS			334	296	93	21	2219.1	9062	2030	875	800	205	65	62	10	580	18	1650	51	5	163	80	.671	26	4	3.24

OZZIE GUILLEN

Bats Left-handed, Throws Right-handed   Turns Age 23 in 1987, Born 01/20/64

							BATTING											BASERUNNING				PERCENTAGES		
Year	Team	League	G	AB	H	2B	3B	HR	(Hm | Rd)	TB	R	RBI	TBB	IBB	SO	HBP	SH	SF	SB	CS	SB%	GIDP	AVE	OBP	SLG
1985	Chicago	A	150	491	134	21	9	1	(0 | 1)	176	71	33	12	1	36	1	8	1	7	4	.64	5	.273	.291	.358
1986	Chicago	A	159	547	137	19	4	2	(1 | 1)	170	58	47	12	1	52	1	12	5	8	4	.67	14	.250	.265	.311
2 YEARS			309	1038	271	40	13	3	(1 | 2)	346	129	80	24	2	88	2	20	6	15	8	.65	19	.261	.278	.333

BILL GULLICKSON

Pitches Right-handed, Bats Right-handed   Turns Age 28 in 1987, Born 02/20/59

			HOW MUCH HE PITCHED				WHAT HE GAVE UP											THE RESULTS					
Year	Team	League	G	GS	CG	GF	IP	BFP	H	R	ER	HR	SH	SF	HB	TBB	IBB	SO	WP	Bk	W	L	Pct	ShO	Sv	ERA
1979	Montreal	N	1	0	0	1	1	4	2	0	0	0	0	0	0	0	0	0	0	0	0	0	.000	0	0	0.00
1980	Montreal	N	24	19	5	1	141	593	127	53	47	6	3	4	2	50	2	120	5	0	10	5	.667	2	0	3.00
1981	Montreal	N	22	22	3	0	157	640	142	54	49	3	5	2	4	34	4	115	4	0	7	9	.438	2	0	2.81
1982	Montreal	N	34	34	6	0	236.2	990	231	101	94	25	9	6	4	61	2	155	11	3	12	14	.462	0	0	3.57
1983	Montreal	N	34	34	10	0	242.1	990	230	108	101	19	4	7	4	59	4	120	4	1	17	12	.586	1	0	3.75
1984	Montreal	N	32	32	3	0	226.2	919	230	100	91	27	8	4	1	37	7	100	5	0	12	9	.571	0	0	3.61
1985	Montreal	N	29	29	4	0	181.1	759	187	78	71	8	12	8	1	47	9	68	1	1	14	12	.538	1	0	3.52
1986	Cincinnati	N	37	37	6	0	244.2	1014	245	103	92	24	12	13	2	60	10	121	3	0	15	12	.556	2	0	3.38
8 YEARS			213	207	37	2	1430.2	5909	1394	597	545	112	53	44	18	348	38	799	33	5	87	73	.544	8	0	3.43

DAVE GUMPERT

Pitches Right-handed, Bats Right-handed   Turns Age 29 in 1987, Born 05/05/58

			HOW MUCH HE PITCHED				WHAT HE GAVE UP											THE RESULTS					
Year	Team	League	G	GS	CG	GF	IP	BFP	H	R	ER	HR	SH	SF	HB	TBB	IBB	SO	WP	Bk	W	L	Pct	ShO	Sv	ERA
1982	Detroit	A	5	1	0	2	2	13	7	6	6	1	1	0	0	2	0	0	0	0	0	0	.000	0	1	27.00
1983	Detroit	A	26	0	0	17	44.1	179	43	16	13	1	1	4	0	7	3	14	2	0	0	2	.000	0	2	2.64
1985	Chicago	N	9	0	0	3	10.1	52	12	7	4	0	0	2	0	7	1	4	0	0	1	0	1.000	0	0	3.48
1986	Chicago	N	38	0	0	12	59.2	259	60	32	29	4	4	1	1	28	7	45	3	0	2	0	1.000	0	2	4.37
4 YEARS			78	1	0	34	116.1	503	122	61	52	6	6	7	1	44	11	63	5	0	3	2	.600	0	5	4.02

JACKIE GUTIERREZ

Bats Right-handed, Throws Right-handed   Turns Age 27 in 1987, Born 06/27/60

							BATTING													BASERUNNING				PERCENTAGES		
Year	Team	League	G	AB	H	2B	3B	HR	(Hm	Rd)	TB	R	RBI	TBB	IBB	SO	HBP	SH	SF	SB	CS	SB%	GIDP	AVE	OBP	SLG
1983	Boston	A	5	10	3	0	0	0	(0	0)	3	2	0	1	0	1	0	0	0	0	1	.00	1	.300	.364	.300
1984	Boston	A	151	449	118	12	3	2	(2	0)	142	55	29	15	0	49	0	12	4	12	5	.71	18	.263	.284	.316
1985	Boston	A	103	275	60	5	2	2	(0	2)	75	33	21	12	0	37	0	9	1	10	2	.83	9	.218	.250	.273
1986	Baltimore	A	61	145	27	3	0	0	(0	0)	30	8	4	3	0	27	1	2	1	3	1	.75	3	.186	.207	.207
4 YEARS			320	879	208	20	5	4	(2	2)	250	98	54	31	0	114	1	23	6	25	9	.74	31	.237	.262	.284

JOSE GUZMAN

Pitches Right-handed, Bats Right-handed   Turns Age 24 in 1987, Born 04/09/63

			HOW MUCH HE PITCHED						WHAT HE GAVE UP										THE RESULTS					
Year	Team	League	G	GS	CG	GF	IP	BFP	H	R	ER	HR	SH	SF	HB	TBB	IBB	SO	WP	Bk	W	L	Pct	ShO	Sv	ERA
1985	Texas	A	5	5	0	0	32.2	140	27	13	10	3	0	0	0	14	1	24	1	0	3	2	.600	0	0	2.76
1986	Texas	A	29	29	2	0	172.1	757	199	101	87	23	7	4	6	60	2	87	3	0	9	15	.375	0	0	4.54
2 YEARS			34	34	2	0	205	897	226	114	97	26	7	4	6	74	3	111	4	0	12	17	.414	0	0	4.26

TONY GWYNN

Bats Left-handed, Throws Left-handed   Turns Age 27 in 1987, Born 05/09/60

							BATTING													BASERUNNING				PERCENTAGES		
Year	Team	League	G	AB	H	2B	3B	HR	(Hm	Rd)	TB	R	RBI	TBB	IBB	SO	HBP	SH	SF	SB	CS	SB%	GIDP	AVE	OBP	SLG
1982	San Diego	N	54	190	55	12	2	1	(0	1)	74	33	17	14	0	16	0	4	1	8	3	.73	5	.289	.337	.389
1983	San Diego	N	86	304	94	12	2	1	(0	1)	113	34	37	23	5	21	0	4	3	7	4	.64	9	.309	.355	.372
1984	San Diego	N	158	606	213	21	10	5	(3	2)	269	88	71	59	13	23	2	6	2	33	18	.65	15	.351	.410	.444
1985	San Diego	N	154	622	197	29	5	6	(3	3)	254	90	46	45	4	33	2	1	1	14	11	.56	17	.317	.364	.408
4 YEARS			452	1722	559	74	19	13	(6	7)	710	245	171	141	22	93	4	15	7	62	36	.63	46	.325	.376	.412

JERRY HAIRSTON

Bats both Right and Left-handed, Throws Right-handed   Turns Age 35 in 1987, Born 02/16/52

							BATTING													BASERUNNING				PERCENTAGES		
Year	Team	League	G	AB	H	2B	3B	HR	(Hm	Rd)	TB	R	RBI	TBB	IBB	SO	HBP	SH	SF	SB	CS	SB%	GIDP	AVE	OBP	SLG
1973	Chicago	A	60	210	57	11	1	0	(0	0)	70	25	23	33	0	30	1	0	1	0	0	.00	3	.271	.371	.333
1974	Chicago	A	45	109	25	7	0	0	(0	0)	32	8	8	13	0	18	0	3	0	0	2	.00	2	.229	.311	.294
1975	Chicago	A	69	219	62	8	0	0	(0	0)	70	26	23	46	3	23	1	6	2	1	0	1.00	4	.283	.407	.320
1976	Chicago	A	44	119	27	2	2	0	(0	0)	33	20	10	24	0	19	0	2	2	1	1	.50	0	.227	.352	.277
1977	2 Teams		64	78	18	4	0	2	(0	2)	28	8	10	11	0	17	0	0	1	0	0	.00	3	.231	.322	.359
1981	Chicago	A	9	25	7	1	0	1	(1	0)	11	5	6	2	0	4	1	0	1	0	0	.00	3	.280	.345	.440
1982	Chicago	A	85	90	21	5	0	5	(2	3)	41	11	18	9	0	15	0	1	3	0	0	.00	3	.233	.294	.456
1983	Chicago	A	101	126	37	9	1	5	(3	2)	63	17	22	23	4	16	0	0	2	0	1	.00	1	.294	.397	.500
1984	Chicago	A	115	227	59	13	2	5	(3	2)	91	41	19	41	3	29	1	0	2	2	1	.67	3	.260	.373	.401
1985	Chicago	A	95	140	34	8	0	2	(0	2)	48	9	20	29	3	18	2	0	4	0	0	.00	0	.243	.371	.343
1986	Chicago	A	101	225	61	15	0	5	(3	2)	91	32	26	26	3	26	1	0	1	0	0	.00	9	.271	.348	.404
11 YEARS			788	1568	408	83	6	25	(12	13)	578	202	185	257	16	215	7	12	19	4	5	.44	31	.260	.363	.369
1977	Chicago	A	13	26	8	2	0	0	(0	0)	10	3	4	5	0	7	0	0	0	0	0	.00	2	.308	.419	.385
1977	Pittsburgh	N	51	52	10	2	0	2	(0	2)	18	5	6	6	0	10	0	0	1	0	0	.00	1	.192	.271	.346

MEL HALL

Bats Left-handed, Throws Left-handed   Turns Age 27 in 1987, Born 09/16/60

							BATTING													BASERUNNING				PERCENTAGES		
Year	Team	League	G	AB	H	2B	3B	HR	(Hm	Rd)	TB	R	RBI	TBB	IBB	SO	HBP	SH	SF	SB	CS	SB%	GIDP	AVE	OBP	SLG
1981	Chicago	N	10	11	1	0	0	1	(1	0)	4	1	2	1	0	4	0	0	0	0	0	.00	0	.091	.167	.364
1982	Chicago	N	24	80	21	3	2	0	(0	0)	28	6	4	5	1	17	2	0	1	0	1	.00	0	.263	.318	.350
1983	Chicago	N	112	410	116	23	5	17	(6	11)	200	60	56	42	6	101	3	1	2	6	6	.50	4	.283	.352	.488
1984	2 Teams		131	407	108	24	4	11	(7	4)	173	68	52	47	8	78	2	0	7	3	2	.60	5	.265	.339	.425
1985	Cleveland	A	23	66	21	6	0	0	(0	0)	27	7	12	8	0	12	0	0	1	0	1	.00	2	.318	.387	.409
1986	Cleveland	A	140	442	131	29	2	18	(8	10)	218	68	77	33	8	65	2	0	3	6	2	.75	8	.296	.346	.493
6 YEARS			440	1416	398	85	13	47	(22	25)	650	210	203	136	23	277	9	1	14	15	12	.56	19	.281	.345	.459
1984	Cleveland	A	83	257	66	13	1	7	(4	3)	102	43	30	35	5	55	2	0	5	1	1	.50	3	.257	.344	.397
1984	Chicago	N	48	150	42	11	3	4	(3	1)	71	25	22	12	3	23	0	0	2	2	1	.67	2	.280	.329	.473

JEFF HAMILTON

Bats Right-handed, Throws Right-handed   Turns Age 23 in 1987, Born 03/19/64

							BATTING													BASERUNNING				PERCENTAGES		
Year	Team	League	G	AB	H	2B	3B	HR	(Hm	Rd)	TB	R	RBI	TBB	IBB	SO	HBP	SH	SF	SB	CS	SB%	GIDP	AVE	OBP	SLG
1986	Los Angeles	N	71	147	33	5	0	5	(2	3)	53	22	19	2	1	43	0	0	2	0	0	.00	3	.224	.232	.361

TERRY HARPER

Bats Right-handed, Throws Right-handed   Turns Age 32 in 1987, Born 08/19/55

Year	Team	League	G	AB	H	2B	3B	HR	(Hm	Rd)	TB	R	RBI	TBB	IBB	SO	HBP	SH	SF	SB	CS	SB%	GIDP	AVE	OBP	SLG
1980	Atlanta	N	21	54	10	2	1	0	(0	0)	14	3	3	6	0	5	0	1	0	2	1	.67	1	.185	.279	.259
1981	Atlanta	N	40	73	19	1	0	2	(2	0)	26	9	8	11	0	17	0	0	1	5	1	.83	2	.260	.353	.356
1982	Atlanta	N	48	150	43	3	0	2	(0	2)	52	16	16	14	0	28	1	0	2	7	4	.64	3	.287	.347	.347
1983	Atlanta	N	80	201	53	13	1	3	(2	1)	77	19	26	20	1	43	1	1	1	6	5	.55	6	.264	.332	.383
1984	Atlanta	N	40	102	16	3	1	0	(0	0)	21	4	8	4	0	21	1	0	1	4	1	.80	6	.157	.194	.206
1985	Atlanta	N	138	492	130	15	2	17	(9	8)	200	58	72	44	4	76	3	1	2	9	9	.50	13	.264	.327	.407
6 YEARS			367	1072	271	37	5	24	(13	11)	390	109	133	99	4	190	7	2	7	33	21	.61	31	.253	.318	.364

TOBY HARRAH

Bats Right-handed, Throws Right-handed   Turns Age 39 in 1987, Born 10/26/48

Year	Team	League	G	AB	H	2B	3B	HR	(Hm	Rd)	TB	R	RBI	TBB	IBB	SO	HBP	SH	SF	SB	CS	SB%	GIDP	AVE	OBP	SLG
1969	Washington	A	8	1	0	0	0	0	(0	0)	0	4	0	0	0	0	0	0	0	0	0	.00	0	.000	.000	.000
1971	Washington	A	127	383	88	11	3	2	(0	2)	111	45	22	40	3	48	0	2	3	10	9	.53	8	.230	.300	.290
1972	Texas	A	116	374	97	14	3	1	(0	1)	120	47	31	34	1	31	0	5	6	16	7	.70	3	.259	.316	.321
1973	Texas	A	118	461	120	16	1	10	(6	4)	168	64	50	46	2	49	2	7	3	10	3	.77	11	.260	.328	.364
1974	Texas	A	161	573	149	23	2	21	(11	10)	239	79	74	50	2	65	2	8	6	15	14	.52	14	.260	.319	.417
1975	Texas	A	151	522	153	24	1	20	(8	12)	239	81	93	98	3	71	1	6	4	23	9	.72	7	.293	.403	.458
1976	Texas	A	155	584	152	21	1	15	(4	11)	220	64	67	91	5	59	3	5	5	8	5	.62	17	.260	.360	.377
1977	Texas	A	159	539	142	25	5	27	(13	14)	258	90	87	109	7	73	10	9	6	27	5	.84	12	.263	.393	.479
1978	Texas	A	139	450	103	17	3	12	(6	6)	162	56	59	83	3	66	2	9	3	31	8	.79	8	.229	.349	.360
1979	Cleveland	A	149	527	147	25	1	20	(15	5)	234	99	77	89	2	60	8	7	4	20	9	.69	8	.279	.389	.444
1980	Cleveland	A	160	561	150	22	4	11	(7	4)	213	100	72	98	3	60	7	2	7	17	2	.89	16	.267	.379	.380
1981	Cleveland	A	103	361	105	12	4	5	(3	2)	140	64	44	57	4	44	1	0	8	12	1	.92	5	.291	.382	.388
1982	Cleveland	A	162	602	183	29	4	25	(17	8)	295	100	78	84	7	52	12	7	3	17	3	.85	13	.304	.398	.490
1983	Cleveland	A	138	526	140	23	1	9	(7	2)	192	81	53	75	1	49	7	4	3	16	10	.62	13	.266	.363	.365
1984	New York	A	88	253	55	9	4	1	(0	1)	75	40	26	42	2	28	2	0	2	3	0	1.00	9	.217	.331	.296
1985	Texas	A	126	396	107	18	1	9	(5	4)	154	65	44	113	2	60	4	2	6	11	4	.73	4	.270	.432	.389
1986	Texas	A	95	289	63	18	2	7	(3	4)	106	36	41	44	0	53	2	3	3	2	5	.29	7	.218	.322	.367
17 YEARS			2155	7402	1954	307	40	195	(105	90)	2926	1115	918	1153	51	868	63	76	72	238	94	.72	155	.264	.365	.395

GREG HARRIS

Pitches Right-handed, Bats both Right and Left-handed   Turns Age 32 in 1987, Born 11/02/55

			HOW MUCH HE PITCHED						WHAT HE GAVE UP												THE RESULTS				
Year	Team	League	G	GS	CG	GF	IP	BFP	H	R	ER	HR	SH	SF	HB	TBB	IBB	SO	WP	Bk	W	L	Pct	ShO	Sv	ERA
1981	New York	N	16	14	0	2	69	300	65	36	34	8	4	1	2	28	2	54	3	2	3	5	.375	0	1	4.43
1982	Cincinnati	N	34	10	1	9	91.1	398	96	56	49	12	5	3	2	37	1	67	2	2	2	6	.250	0	1	4.83
1983	San Diego	N	1	0	0	0	1	9	2	3	3	0	1	0	1	3	2	1	0	0	0	0	.000	0	0	27.00
1984	2 Teams		34	1	0	14	54.1	226	38	18	15	3	2	3	4	25	1	45	3	0	2	2	.500	0	3	2.48
1985	Texas	A	58	0	0	35	69.2	450	74	35	31	7	3	2	5	43	3	111	2	1	5	4	.556	0	11	2.47
1986	Texas	A	73	0	0	63	111.1	462	103	40	35	12	3	6	1	42	6	95	2	1	10	8	.556	0	20	2.83
6 YEARS			216	25	1	123	440	1845	378	188	167	42	18	15	15	178	15	373	12	6	22	25	.468	0	36	3.42
1984	Montreal	N	15	0	0	4	17.2	68	10	4	4	0	1	0	2	7	1	15	0	0	0	1	.000	0	2	2.04
1984	San Diego	N	19	1	0	10	36.2	158	28	14	11	3	1	3	2	18	0	30	3	0	2	1	.667	0	1	2.70

RON HASSEY

Bats Left-handed, Throws Right-handed   Turns Age 34 in 1987, Born 02/27/53

Year	Team	League	G	AB	H	2B	3B	HR	(Hm	Rd)	TB	R	RBI	TBB	IBB	SO	HBP	SH	SF	SB	CS	SB%	GIDP	AVE	OBP	SLG
1978	Cleveland	A	25	74	15	0	0	2	(1	1)	21	5	9	5	0	7	1	1	2	2	0	1.00	1	.203	.256	.284
1979	Cleveland	A	75	223	64	14	0	4	(2	2)	90	20	32	19	2	19	0	4	3	1	0	1.00	8	.287	.339	.404
1980	Cleveland	A	130	390	124	18	4	8	(5	3)	174	43	65	49	3	51	1	1	6	0	2	.00	13	.318	.390	.446
1981	Cleveland	A	61	190	44	4	0	1	(0	1)	51	8	25	17	0	11	2	3	3	0	1	.00	5	.232	.297	.268
1982	Cleveland	A	113	323	81	18	0	5	(2	3)	114	33	34	53	5	32	1	3	2	3	2	.60	10	.251	.356	.353
1983	Cleveland	A	117	341	92	21	0	6	(4	2)	131	48	42	38	2	35	2	2	5	2	2	.50	11	.270	.342	.384
1984	2 Teams		67	182	49	5	1	2	(1	1)	62	16	24	19	3	32	0	0	1	1	1	.50	5	.269	.337	.341
1985	New York	A	92	267	79	16	1	13	(3	10)	136	31	42	28	4	21	3	0	0	0	0	.00	7	.296	.369	.509
1986	2 Teams		113	341	110	25	1	9	(0	0)	164	45	49	46	3	27	3	1	2	1	1	.50	15	.323	.406	.481
9 YEARS			793	2331	658	121	7	50	(18	23)	943	249	322	274	22	235	13	15	24	10	9	.53	75	.282	.358	.405
1984	Cleveland	A	48	149	38	5	1	0	(0	0)	45	11	19	15	2	26	0	0	1	1	0	1.00	4	.255	.321	.302
1984	Chicago	N	19	33	11	0	0	2	(1	1)	17	5	5	4	1	6	0	0	0	0	1	.00	1	.333	.405	.515
1986	Chicago	A	49	150	53	11	1	3	(0	0)	75	22	20	22	2	11	1	0	1	0	0	.00	7	.353	.437	.500
1986	New York	A	64	191	57	14	0	6	(0	0)	89	23	29	24	1	16	2	1	1	1	1	.50	8	.298	.381	.466

BILLY HATCHER

Bats Right-handed, Throws Right-handed   Turns Age 27 in 1987, Born 10/04/60

Year	Team	League	G	AB	H	2B	3B	HR	(Hm	Rd)	TB	R	RBI	TBB	IBB	SO	HBP	SH	SF	SB	CS	SB%	GIDP	AVE	OBP	SLG
1984	Chicago	N	8	9	1	0	0	0	(0	0)	1	1	0	1	0	0	0	0	0	2	0	1.00	0	.111	.200	.111
1985	Chicago	N	53	163	40	12	1	2	(2	0)	60	24	10	8	0	12	3	2	2	2	4	.33	9	.245	.290	.368
2 YEARS			61	172	41	12	1	2	(2	0)	61	25	10	9	1	12	3	2	2	4	4	.50	9	.238	.285	.355

MICKEY HATCHER

Bats Right-handed, Throws Right-handed   Turns Age 32 in 1987, Born 03/15/55

Year	Team	League	G	AB	H	2B	3B	HR	(Hm	Rd)	TB	R	RBI	TBB	IBB	SO	HBP	SH	SF	SB	CS	SB%	GIDP	AVE	OBP	SLG
1979	Los Angeles	N	33	93	25	4	1	1	(0	1)	34	9	5	7	0	12	1	1	0	1	3	.25	5	.269	.327	.366
1980	Los Angeles	N	57	84	19	2	0	1	(1	0)	24	4	5	2	1	12	0	4	0	1	2	.00	6	.226	.244	.286
1981	Minnesota	A	99	377	96	23	2	3	(3	0)	132	36	37	15	2	29	2	5	3	3	1	.75	10	.255	.285	.350
1982	Minnesota	A	84	277	69	13	2	3	(2	1)	95	23	26	8	1	27	0	0	1	0	2	.00	12	.249	.269	.343
1983	Minnesota	A	106	375	119	15	3	9	(6	3)	167	50	47	14	0	19	1	3	2	2	0	1.00	12	.317	.342	.445
1984	Minnesota	A	152	576	174	35	5	5	(4	1)	234	61	69	37	3	24	2	1	8	0	1	.00	17	.302	.342	.406
1985	Minnesota	A	116	444	125	28	0	3	(1	2)	162	46	49	16	1	23	2	3	2	0	0	.00	15	.282	.308	.365
1986	Minnesota	A	115	317	88	13	3	3	(1	2)	116	40	32	19	2	26	0	0	4	2	1	.67	8	.278	.315	.366
8 YEARS			762	2543	715	133	16	28	(18	10)	964	269	270	118	10	182	8	17	20	8	10	.44	85	.281	.313	.379

BRAD HAVENS

Pitches Left-handed, Bats Left-handed   Turns Age 28 in 1987, Born 11/17/59

Year	Team	League	G	GS	CG	GF	IP	BFP	H	R	ER	HR	SH	SF	HB	TBB	IBB	SO	WP	Bk	W	L	Pct	ShO	Sv	ERA
1981	Minnesota	A	14	12	1	1	63.2	323	76	33	31	6	1	1	1	24	4	43	1	2	3	6	.333	1	0	3.58
1982	Minnesota	A	33	32	4	1	208.2	893	201	112	100	32	6	4	0	80	4	129	3	0	10	14	.417	1	0	4.31
1983	Minnesota	A	16	14	1	0	80.1	378	110	75	73	11	1	9	0	38	3	40	6	0	5	8	.385	0	0	8.18
1985	Baltimore	A	8	1	0	3	14.1	70	20	14	14	4	0	0	0	10	1	19	0	0	0	1	.000	0	0	8.79
1986	Baltimore	A	46	0	0	19	71	294	64	37	36	7	6	1	0	29	1	57	6	0	3	3	.500	0	1	4.56
5 YEARS			117	59	6	24	452.1	1958	471	271	254	60	14	15	1	181	13	288	16	2	21	32	.396	2	1	5.05

ANDY HAWKINS

Pitches Right-handed, Bats Right-handed   Turns Age 27 in 1987, Born 01/21/60

Year	Team	League	G	GS	CG	GF	IP	BFP	H	R	ER	HR	SH	SF	HB	TBB	IBB	SO	WP	Bk	W	L	Pct	ShO	Sv	ERA
1982	San Diego	N	15	10	1	2	63.2	281	66	33	29	4	6	5	2	27	3	25	2	3	2	5	.286	0	0	4.10
1983	San Diego	N	21	19	4	1	119.2	501	106	50	39	8	10	4	5	48	4	59	4	1	5	7	.417	1	0	2.93
1984	San Diego	N	36	22	2	9	146	650	143	90	76	13	10	4	2	72	2	77	1	2	8	9	.471	1	0	4.68
1985	San Diego	N	33	33	5	0	228.2	953	229	88	80	18	13	12	4	65	8	69	3	3	18	8	.692	2	0	3.15
1986	San Diego	N	37	35	3	0	209.1	905	218	111	100	24	7	6	5	75	7	117	6	2	10	8	.556	1	0	4.30
5 YEARS			142	119	15	12	767.1	3290	762	372	324	67	46	31	18	287	24	347	16	11	43	37	.537	5	0	3.80

VON HAYES

Bats Left-handed, Throws Right-handed   Turns Age 29 in 1987, Born 08/31/58

Year	Team	League	G	AB	H	2B	3B	HR	(Hm	Rd)	TB	R	RBI	TBB	IBB	SO	HBP	SH	SF	SB	CS	SB%	GIDP	AVE	OBP	SLG
1981	Cleveland	A	43	109	28	8	2	1	(0	1)	43	21	17	14	1	10	2	4	2	8	1	.89	2	.257	.346	.394
1982	Cleveland	A	150	527	132	25	3	14	(3	11)	205	65	82	42	3	63	4	8	2	32	13	.71	10	.250	.310	.389
1983	Philadelphia	N	124	351	93	9	5	6	(3	3)	130	45	32	36	7	55	3	0	2	20	12	.63	11	.265	.337	.370
1984	Philadelphia	N	152	561	164	27	6	16	(10	6)	251	85	67	59	4	84	0	0	2	48	13	.79	10	.292	.359	.447
1985	Philadelphia	N	152	570	150	30	4	13	(12	1)	227	76	70	61	6	99	0	2	4	21	8	.72	6	.263	.332	.398
5 YEARS			621	2118	567	99	20	50	(28	22)	856	292	268	212	21	311	9	14	12	129	47	.73	39	.268	.335	.404

ED HEARN

Bats Right-handed, Throws Right-handed   Turns Age 27 in 1987, Born 08/23/60

Year	Team	League	G	AB	H	2B	3B	HR	(Hm	Rd)	TB	R	RBI	TBB	IBB	SO	HBP	SH	SF	SB	CS	SB%	GIDP	AVE	OBP	SLG
1986	New York	N	49	136	36	5	0	4	(4	0)	53	16	10	12	0	19	0	2	1	0	1	.00	4	.265	.322	.390

MIKE HEATH

Bats Right-handed, Throws Right-handed   Turns Age 32 in 1987, Born 02/05/55

Year	Team	League	G	AB	H	2B	3B	HR	(Hm	Rd)	TB	R	RBI	TBB	IBB	SO	HBP	SH	SF	SB	CS	SB%	GIDP	AVE	OBP	SLG
1978	New York	A	33	92	21	3	1	0	(0	0)	26	6	8	4	0	9	1	1	1	0	0	.00	1	.228	.265	.283
1979	Oakland	A	74	258	66	8	0	3	(2	1)	83	19	27	17	1	18	3	3	5	1	0	1.00	14	.256	.304	.322
1980	Oakland	A	92	305	74	10	2	1	(1	0)	91	27	33	16	2	28	0	7	1	3	3	.50	7	.243	.280	.298
1981	Oakland	A	84	301	71	7	1	8	(4	4)	104	26	30	13	1	36	1	5	1	3	3	.50	9	.236	.269	.346
1982	Oakland	A	101	318	77	18	4	3	(3	0)	112	43	39	27	3	36	0	2	4	8	3	.73	3	.242	.298	.352
1983	Oakland	A	96	345	97	17	0	6	(5	1)	132	45	33	18	4	59	1	1	1	3	4	.43	9	.281	.318	.383
1984	Oakland	A	140	475	118	21	5	13	(8	5)	188	49	64	26	2	72	1	2	4	7	4	.64	14	.248	.287	.396
1985	Oakland	A	138	436	109	18	6	13	(8	5)	178	71	55	41	0	63	1	10	4	7	7	.50	13	.250	.313	.408
1986	Detroit	A	30	98	26	3	0	4	(3	1)	41	11	11	4	0	17	0	0	1	4	1	.80	1	.265	.291	.418
9 YEARS			788	2628	659	105	19	51	(34	17)	955	297	300	166	13	338	8	31	22	36	25	.59	71	.251	.295	.363

NEAL HEATON

Pitches Left-handed, Bats Left-handed

Turns Age 27 in 1987, Born 03/03/60

Year	Team	League	HOW MUCH HE PITCHED						WHAT HE GAVE UP												THE RESULTS					
			G	GS	CG	GF	IP	BFP	H	R	ER	HR	SH	SF	HB	TBB	IBB	SO	WP	Bk	W	L	Pct	ShO	Sv	ERA
1982	Cleveland	A	8	4	0	0	31	142	32	21	18	1	1	2	0	16	0	14	4	0	0	2	.000	0	0	5.23
1983	Cleveland	A	39	16	4	19	149.1	637	157	79	69	11	3	5	1	44	10	75	1	0	11	7	.611	3	7	4.16
1984	Cleveland	A	38	34	4	2	198.2	880	231	128	115	21	6	10	0	75	5	75	3	1	12	15	.444	1	0	5.21
1985	Cleveland	A	36	33	5	2	207.2	921	244	119	113	19	7	8	7	80	2	82	2	2	9	17	.346	1	0	4.90
1986	2 Teams		33	29	5	2	198.2	850	201	102	90	26	6	5	2	81	8	90	4	0	7	15	.318	0	1	4.08
5 YEARS			154	116	18	25	785.1	3430	865	449	405	78	23	30	10	296	25	336	14	3	39	56	.411	5	8	4.64
1986	Cleveland	A	12	12	2	0	74.1	324	73	42	35	8	2	0	1	34	4	24	2	0	3	6	.333	0	0	4.24
1986	Minnesota	A	21	17	3	2	124.1	526	128	60	55	18	4	5	1	47	4	66	2	0	4	9	.308	0	1	3.98

DANNY HEEP

Bats Left-handed, Throws Left-handed

Turns Age 30 in 1987, Born 07/03/57

Year	Team	League	BATTING																BASERUNNING				PERCENTAGES		
			G	AB	H	2B	3B	HR	(Hm	Rd)	TB	R	RBI	TBB	IBB	SO	HBP	SH	SF	SB	CS	SB%	GIDP	AVE	OBP	SLG
1979	Houston	N	14	14	2	0	0	0	(0	0)	2	0	2	1	4	0	0	2		0	0	.00	0	.143	.176	.143
1980	Houston	N	33	87	24	8	0	0	(0	0)	32	6	6	8	0	9	1	0	1	0	0	.00	0	.276	.340	.368
1981	Houston	N	33	96	24	3	0	0	(0	0)	27	6	11	10	2	11	0	0	0	0	0	.00	3	.250	.321	.281
1982	Houston	N	85	198	47	14	1	4	(1	3)	75	16	22	21	3	31	1	0	2	0	2	.00	2	.237	.311	.379
1983	New York	N	115	253	64	12	0	8	(6	2)	100	30	21	29	6	40	1	1	5	3	3	.50	5	.253	.326	.395
1984	New York	N	99	199	46	9	2	1	(1	0)	62	36	21	27	3	22	1	1	5	3	1	.75	9	.231	.319	.312
1985	New York	N	95	271	76	17	0	7	(2	5)	114	26	42	27	1	27	1	0	6	2	2	.50	12	.280	.341	.421
7 YEARS			474	1118	283	63	3	20	(10	10)	412	120	116	123	16	144	5	2	21	8	8	.50	34	.253	.324	.369

DAVE HENDERSON

Bats Right-handed, Throws Right-handed

Turns Age 29 in 1987, Born 07/21/58

Year	Team	League	BATTING																BASERUNNING				PERCENTAGES		
			G	AB	H	2B	3B	HR	(Hm	Rd)	TB	R	RBI	TBB	IBB	SO	HBP	SH	SF	SB	CS	SB%	GIDP	AVE	OBP	SLG
1981	Seattle	A	59	126	21	3	0	6	(5	1)	42	17	13	16	1	24	1	1	1	2	1	.67	4	.167	.264	.333
1982	Seattle	A	104	324	82	17	1	14	(8	6)	143	47	48	36	2	67	0	1	1	2	5	.29	5	.253	.327	.441
1983	Seattle	A	137	484	130	24	5	17	(9	8)	215	50	55	28	1	93	1	2	6	9	3	.75	5	.269	.306	.444
1984	Seattle	A	112	350	98	23	0	14	(8	6)	163	42	43	19	0	56	2	2	1	5	5	.50	4	.280	.320	.466
1985	Seattle	A	139	502	121	28	2	14	(8	6)	195	70	68	48	2	104	3	1	2	6	1	.86	11	.241	.310	.388
1986	2 Teams		139	388	103	22	4	15	(0	0)	178	59	47	39	4	110	2	2	1	2	3	.40	6	.265	.335	.459
6 YEARS			690	2174	555	117	12	80	(38	27)	936	285	274	186	12	454	9	9	12	26	18	.59	35	.255	.315	.431
1986	Boston	A	36	51	10	3	0	1	(0	0)	16	8	3	2	0	15	0	1	0	1	0	1.00	1	.196	.226	.314
1986	Seattle	A	103	337	93	19	4	14	(0	0)	162	51	44	37	4	95	2	1	1	1	3	.25	5	.276	.350	.481

RICKEY HENDERSON

Bats Right-handed, Throws Left-handed

Turns Age 29 in 1987, Born 12/25/58

Year	Team	League	BATTING																BASERUNNING				PERCENTAGES		
			G	AB	H	2B	3B	HR	(Hm	Rd)	TB	R	RBI	TBB	IBB	SO	HBP	SH	SF	SB	CS	SB%	GIDP	AVE	OBP	SLG
1979	Oakland	A	89	351	96	13	3	1	(1	0)	118	49	26	34	0	39	2	8	3	33	11	.75	4	.274	.338	.336
1980	Oakland	A	158	591	179	22	4	9	(3	6)	236	111	53	117	7	54	5	6	3	100	26	.79	6	.303	.420	.399
1981	Oakland	A	108	423	135	18	7	6	(5	1)	185	89	35	64	4	68	2	0	4	56	22	.72	7	.319	.408	.437
1982	Oakland	A	149	536	143	24	4	10	(5	5)	205	119	51	116	2	94	2	0	5	130	42	.76	5	.267	.398	.382
1983	Oakland	A	145	513	150	25	7	9	(5	4)	216	105	48	103	8	80	4	1	1	108	19	.85	11	.292	.414	.421
1984	Oakland	A	142	502	147	27	4	16	(7	9)	230	113	58	86	1	81	5	1	3	66	18	.79	7	.293	.399	.458
1985	New York	A	143	547	172	28	5	24	(8	16)	282	146	72	99	1	65	3	0	5	80	10	.89	8	.314	.419	.516
1986	New York	A	153	608	160	31	5	28	(13	15)	285	130	74	89	2	81	2	0	2	87	18	.83	12	.263	.358	.469
8 YEARS			1087	4071	1182	188	39	103	(47	56)	1757	862	417	708	24	562	25	16	23	660	166	.80	60	.290	.397	.432

GEORGE HENDRICK

Bats Right-handed, Throws Right-handed   Turns Age 38 in 1987, Born 10/18/49

Year	Team	League	G	AB	H	2B	3B	HR	(Hm	Rd)	TB	R	RBI	TBB	IBB	SO	HBP	SH	SF	SB	CS	SB%	GIDP	AVE	OBP	SLG
1971	Oakland	A	42	114	27	4	1	0	(0	0)	33	8	8	3	0	20	0	3	1	0	1	.00	6	.237	.254	.289
1972	Oakland	A	58	121	22	1	1	4	(3	1)	37	10	15	3	0	22	1	2	2	3	2	.60	3	.182	.205	.306
1973	Cleveland	A	113	440	118	18	0	21	(14	7)	199	64	61	25	1	71	2	2	4	7	6	.54	9	.268	.308	.452
1974	Cleveland	A	139	495	138	23	1	19	(12	7)	220	65	67	33	4	73	1	0	5	6	4	.60	17	.279	.322	.444
1975	Cleveland	A	145	561	145	21	2	24	(13	11)	242	82	86	40	2	78	0	4	8	6	7	.46	25	.258	.304	.431
1976	Cleveland	A	149	551	146	20	3	25	(11	14)	247	72	81	51	6	82	0	1	8	4	4	.50	16	.265	.323	.448
1977	San Diego	N	152	541	168	25	2	23	(13	10)	266	75	81	61	8	74	2	1	2	11	6	.65	9	.311	.381	.492
1978	2 Teams		138	493	137	31	1	20	(9	11)	230	64	75	40	1	60	2	1	4	2	1	.67	11	.278	.332	.467
1979	St Louis	N	140	493	148	27	1	16	(7	9)	225	67	75	49	5	62	0	0	6	2	3	.40	17	.300	.359	.456
1980	St Louis	N	150	572	173	33	2	25	(13	12)	285	73	109	32	9	67	4	1	4	6	1	.86	14	.302	.342	.498
1981	St Louis	N	101	394	112	19	3	18	(6	12)	191	67	61	41	7	44	4	0	2	4	2	.67	10	.284	.356	.485
1982	St Louis	N	136	515	145	20	5	19	(10	9)	232	65	104	37	8	80	1	1	14	3	2	.60	13	.282	.323	.450
1983	St Louis	N	144	529	168	33	3	18	(10	8)	261	73	97	51	15	76	2	0	11	3	4	.43	12	.318	.373	.493
1984	St Louis	N	120	441	122	28	1	9	(2	7)	179	57	69	32	2	75	1	0	5	0	2	.00	13	.277	.324	.406
1985	2 Teams		85	297	64	16	0	4	(0	4)	92	28	31	22	2	50	0	0	4	1	0	1.00	15	.215	.266	.310
1986	California	A	102	283	77	13	1	14	(8	6)	134	45	47	26	5	41	1	4	3	1	1	.50	11	.272	.332	.473
16 YEARS			1914	6840	1910	332	27	259	(131	128)	3073	915	1067	546	75	975	21	20	83	59	46	.56	201	.279	.331	.449
1978	St Louis	N	102	382	110	27	1	17	(7	10)	190	55	67	28	1	44	2	1	4	1	0	1.00	9	.288	.337	.497
1978	San Diego	N	36	111	27	4	0	3	(2	1)	40	9	8	12	0	16	0	0	0	1	1	.50	2	.243	.317	.360
1985	California	A	16	41	5	1	0	2	(0	2)	12	5	6	4	1	8	0	0	1	0	0	.00	4	.122	.196	.293
1985	Pittsburgh	N	69	256	59	15	0	2	(0	2)	80	23	25	18	1	42	0	0	3	1	0	1.00	11	.230	.278	.313

TOM HENKE

Pitches Right-handed, Bats Right-handed   Turns Age 30 in 1987, Born 12/21/57

Year	Team	League	G	GS	CG	GF	IP	BFP	H	R	ER	HR	SH	SF	HB	TBB	IBB	SO	WP	Bk	W	L	Pct	ShO	Sv	ERA
1982	Texas	A	8	0	0	6	15.2	67	14	2	2	0	1	0	1	8	2	9	0	0	1	0	1.000	0	1	1.15
1983	Texas	A	8	0	0	5	16	65	16	6	6	1	0	0	0	4	0	17	0	0	1	0	1.000	0	1	3.37
1984	Texas	A	25	0	0	13	28.1	141	36	21	20	0	1	4	1	20	2	25	2	2	1	1	.500	0	2	6.35
1985	Toronto	A	28	0	0	22	40	153	29	12	9	4	2	2	0	8	2	42	0	0	3	3	.500	0	13	2.02
1986	Toronto	A	63	0	0	51	91.1	370	63	39	34	6	2	6	1	32	4	118	3	1	9	5	.643	0	27	3.35
5 YEARS			132	0	0	97	191.1	796	158	80	71	11	6	12	3	72	10	211	5	3	15	9	.625	0	43	3.34

KEITH HERNANDEZ

Bats Left-handed, Throws Left-handed   Turns Age 34 in 1987, Born 10/20/53

Year	Team	League	G	AB	H	2B	3B	HR	(Hm	Rd)	TB	R	RBI	TBB	IBB	SO	HBP	SH	SF	SB	CS	SB%	GIDP	AVE	OBP	SLG
1974	St Louis	N	14	34	10	1	2	0	(0	0)	15	3	2	7	0	9	0	0	0	0	0	.00	1	.294	.415	.441
1975	St Louis	N	64	188	47	8	2	3	(0	3)	68	20	20	17	2	26	0	0	2	0	1	.00	5	.250	.309	.362
1976	St Louis	N	129	374	108	21	5	7	(4	3)	160	54	46	49	5	53	3	2	0	4	2	.67	8	.289	.376	.428
1977	St Louis	N	161	560	163	41	4	15	(5	10)	257	90	91	79	11	88	1	3	2	7	7	.50	17	.291	.379	.459
1978	St Louis	N	159	542	138	32	4	11	(4	7)	211	90	64	82	11	68	2	1	6	13	5	.72	12	.255	.351	.389
1979	St Louis	N	161	610	210	48	11	11	(5	6)	313	116	105	80	5	78	1	0	7	11	6	.65	9	.344	.417	.513
1980	St Louis	N	159	595	191	39	8	16	(8	8)	294	111	99	86	4	73	4	1	4	14	8	.64	14	.321	.408	.494
1981	St Louis	N	103	376	115	27	4	8	(4	4)	174	65	48	61	6	45	2	0	5	12	5	.71	9	.306	.401	.463
1982	St Louis	N	160	579	173	33	6	7	(4	3)	239	79	94	100	19	67	2	1	12	19	11	.63	10	.299	.397	.413
1983	2 Teams		150	538	160	23	7	12	(10	2)	233	77	63	88	14	72	2	2	3	9	5	.64	7	.297	.396	.433
1984	New York	N	154	550	171	31	0	15	(10	5)	247	83	94	97	12	89	1	0	9	2	3	.40	9	.311	.409	.449
1985	New York	N	158	593	183	34	4	10	(4	6)	255	87	91	77	15	59	2	0	10	3	3	.50	14	.309	.384	.430
12 YEARS			1572	5539	1669	338	57	115	(58	57)	2466	875	817	823	104	726	20	10	60	94	56	.63	115	.301	.390	.445
1983	New York	N	95	320	98	8	3	9	(8	1)	139	43	37	64	9	42	2	2	1	8	4	.67	5	.306	.424	.434
1983	St Louis	N	55	218	62	15	4	3	(2	1)	94	34	26	24	5	30	0	0	2	1	1	.50	2	.284	.352	.431

WILLIE HERNANDEZ

Pitches Left-handed, Bats Left-handed   Turns Age 32 in 1987, Born 11/14/55

Year	Team	League	G	GS	CG	GF	IP	BFP	H	R	ER	HR	SH	SF	HB	TBB	IBB	SO	WP	Bk	W	L	Pct	ShO	Sv	ERA
1977	Chicago	N	67	1	0	23	110	437	94	42	37	11	4	2	1	28	9	78	8	3	8	7	.533	0	4	3.03
1978	Chicago	N	54	0	0	21	60	264	57	26	25	6	8	3	1	35	7	38	3	0	8	2	.800	0	3	3.75
1979	Chicago	N	51	2	0	19	79	359	85	50	44	8	7	6	4	39	12	53	3	1	4	4	.500	0	0	5.01
1980	Chicago	N	53	7	0	13	108	473	115	58	53	8	6	3	2	45	4	75	6	1	1	9	.100	0	0	4.42
1981	Chicago	N	12	0	0	3	14	62	14	7	6	0	2	0	2	8	2	13	2	0	0	0	.000	0	2	3.86
1982	Chicago	N	75	0	0	30	75	312	74	26	25	3	8	4	1	24	11	54	0	0	4	6	.400	0	10	3.00
1983	2 Teams		74	1	0	31	115.1	478	109	47	42	9	7	0	1	32	8	93	5	0	9	4	.692	0	8	3.28
1984	Detroit	A	80	0	0	68	140.1	548	96	30	30	6	9	3	4	36	8	112	2	0	9	3	.750	0	32	1.92
1985	Detroit	A	74	0	0	64	106.2	415	82	38	32	13	4	5	1	14	2	76	2	0	8	10	.444	0	31	2.70
1986	Detroit	A	64	0	0	58	88.2	376	87	35	35	13	1	3	5	21	1	77	2	1	8	7	.533	0	24	3.55
10 YEARS			604	11	0	325	897	3724	813	359	329	77	56	30	20	282	64	669	33	6	59	52	.532	0	114	3.30
1983	Chicago	N	11	1	0	4	19.2	80	16	8	7	0	2	0	0	6	1	18	0	0	1	0	1.000	0	1	3.20
1983	Philadelphia	N	63	0	0	27	95.2	398	93	39	35	9	5	0	1	26	7	75	5	0	8	4	.667	0	7	3.29

LARRY HERNDON

Bats Right-handed, Throws Right-handed | Turns Age 34 in 1987, Born 11/03/53

Year	Team	League	G	AB	H	2B	3B	HR	(Hm	Rd)	TB	R	RBI	TBB	IBB	SO	HBP	SH	SF	SB	CS	SB%	GIDP	AVE	OBP	SLG
1974	St Louis	N	12	1	1	0	0	0	(0	0)	1	3	0	0	0	0	0	0	0	0	0	.00	0	1.000	1.000	1.000
1976	San Francisco	N	115	337	97	11	3	2	(1	1)	120	42	23	23	0	45	2	3	0	12	10	.55	4	.288	.337	.356
1977	San Francisco	N	49	109	26	4	3	1	(0	1)	39	13	5	5	1	20	1	2	0	4	2	.67	4	.239	.278	.358
1978	San Francisco	N	151	471	122	15	9	1	(0	1)	158	52	32	35	2	71	1	13	1	13	8	.62	12	.259	.311	.335
1979	San Francisco	N	132	354	91	14	5	7	(2	5)	136	35	36	29	5	70	1	3	2	8	6	.57	3	.257	.313	.384
1980	San Francisco	N	139	493	127	17	11	8	(3	5)	190	54	49	19	1	91	1	4	4	8	8	.50	10	.258	.284	.385
1981	San Francisco	N	96	364	105	15	8	5	(4	1)	151	48	41	20	2	55	1	3	3	15	6	.71	12	.288	.325	.415
1982	Detroit	A	157	614	179	21	13	23	(9	14)	295	92	88	38	3	92	1	2	4	12	9	.57	20	.292	.332	.480
1983	Detroit	A	153	603	182	28	9	20	(7	13)	288	88	92	46	6	95	3	0	6	9	3	.75	20	.302	.351	.478
1984	Detroit	A	125	407	114	18	5	7	(3	4)	163	52	43	32	1	63	2	1	3	6	2	.75	8	.280	.333	.400
1985	Detroit	A	137	442	108	12	7	12	(7	5)	170	45	37	33	1	79	1	1	1	2	1	.67	9	.244	.298	.385
1986	Detroit	A	106	283	70	13	1	8	(4	4)	109	33	37	27	2	40	1	0	5	2	1	.67	3	.247	.310	.385
12 YEARS			1372	4478	1222	168	74	94	(40	54)	1820	557	483	307	24	721	15	32	29	91	56	.62	105	.273	.320	.406

TOM HERR

Bats both Right and Left-handed, Throws Right-handed | Turns Age 31 in 1987, Born 04/04/56

Year	Team	League	G	AB	H	2B	3B	HR	(Hm	Rd)	TB	R	RBI	TBB	IBB	SO	HBP	SH	SF	SB	CS	SB%	GIDP	AVE	OBP	SLG
1979	St Louis	N	14	10	2	0	0	0	(0	0)	2	4	1	2	0	2	0	0	0	1	0	1.00	0	.200	.333	.200
1980	St Louis	N	76	222	55	12	5	0	(0	0)	77	29	15	16	5	21	1	1	2	9	2	.82	8	.248	.299	.347
1981	St Louis	N	103	411	110	14	9	0	(0	0)	142	50	46	39	3	30	1	6	5	23	7	.77	9	.268	.329	.345
1982	St Louis	N	135	493	131	19	4	0	(0	0)	158	83	36	57	2	56	2	3	5	25	12	.68	5	.266	.341	.320
1983	St Louis	N	89	313	101	14	4	2	(1	1)	129	43	31	43	2	27	1	8	3	6	8	.43	7	.323	.403	.412
1984	St Louis	N	145	558	154	23	2	4	(1	3)	193	67	49	49	2	56	2	10	3	13	7	.65	11	.276	.335	.346
1985	St Louis	N	159	596	180	38	3	8	(4	4)	248	97	110	80	5	55	2	5	13	31	3	.91	6	.302	.379	.416
7 YEARS			721	2603	733	120	27	14	(6	8)	949	373	288	286	19	247	9	33	31	108	39	.73	46	.282	.351	.365

OREL HERSHISER

Pitches Right-handed, Bats Right-handed | Turns Age 29 in 1987, Born 09/16/58

Year	Team	League	G	GS	CG	GF	IP	BFP	H	R	ER	HR	SH	SF	HB	TBB	IBB	SO	WP	Bk	W	L	Pct	ShO	Sv	ERA
1983	Los Angeles	N	8	0	0	4	8	37	7	6	3	1	1	0	0	6	0	5	1	0	0	0	.000	0	1	3.37
1984	Los Angeles	N	45	20	8	10	189.2	771	160	65	56	9	2	3	4	50	8	150	8	1	11	8	.579	4	2	2.66
1985	Los Angeles	N	36	34	9	1	239.2	953	179	72	54	8	5	4	6	68	5	157	5	0	19	3	.864	5	0	2.03
1986	Los Angeles	N	35	35	8	0	231.1	988	213	112	99	13	14	6	5	86	11	153	12	3	14	14	.500	1	0	3.85
4 YEARS			124	89	25	15	668.2	2749	559	255	212	31	22	13	15	210	24	465	26	4	44	25	.638	10	3	2.85

JOE HESKETH

Pitches Left-handed, Bats Left-handed | Turns Age 28 in 1987, Born 02/15/59

Year	Team	League	G	GS	CG	GF	IP	BFP	H	R	ER	HR	SH	SF	HB	TBB	IBB	SO	WP	Bk	W	L	Pct	ShO	Sv	ERA
1984	Montreal	N	11	5	1	2	45	182	38	12	9	2	2	2	0	15	3	32	1	3	2	2	.500	1	1	1.80
1985	Montreal	N	25	25	2	0	155.1	618	125	52	43	10	8	2	0	45	2	113	3	3	10	5	.667	1	0	2.49
1986	Montreal	N	15	15	0	0	82.2	362	92	46	46	11	2	2	2	31	4	67	4	3	6	5	.545	0	0	5.01
3 YEARS			51	45	3	2	283	1162	255	110	98	23	12	6	2	91	9	212	8	9	18	12	.600	2	1	3.12

TED HIGUERA

Pitches Left-handed, Bats both Right and Left-handed | Turns Age 29 in 1987, Born 11/09/58

Year	Team	League	G	GS	CG	GF	IP	BFP	H	R	ER	HR	SH	SF	HB	TBB	IBB	SO	WP	Bk	W	L	Pct	ShO	Sv	ERA
1985	Milwaukee	A	32	30	7	2	212.1	874	186	105	92	22	5	10	3	63	0	127	4	3	15	8	.652	2	0	3.90
1986	Milwaukee	A	34	34	15	0	248.1	1031	226	84	77	26	7	11	3	74	5	207	3	0	20	11	.645	4	0	2.79
2 YEARS			66	64	22	2	460.2	1905	412	189	169	48	12	21	6	137	5	334	7	3	35	19	.648	6	0	3.30

DONNIE HILL

Bats both Right and Left-handed, Throws Right-handed | Turns Age 27 in 1987, Born 11/20/60

Year	Team	League	G	AB	H	2B	3B	HR	(Hm	Rd)	TB	R	RBI	TBB	IBB	SO	HBP	SH	SF	SB	CS	SB%	GIDP	AVE	OBP	SLG
1983	Oakland	A	53	158	42	7	0	2	(1	1)	55	20	15	4	0	21	0	5	2	1	1	.50	3	.266	.280	.348
1984	Oakland	A	73	174	40	6	0	2	(0	2)	52	21	16	5	0	12	0	4	2	1	1	.50	3	.230	.249	.299
1985	Oakland	A	123	393	112	13	2	3	(0	3)	138	45	48	23	2	33	0	16	4	9	4	.69	9	.285	.321	.351
1986	Oakland	A	108	339	96	16	2	4	(0	4)	128	37	29	23	1	38	0	4	0	5	2	.71	9	.283	.329	.378
4 YEARS			357	1064	290	42	4	11	(1	10)	373	123	108	55	3	104	0	29	8	16	8	.67	22	.273	.306	.351

GUY HOFFMAN

Pitches Left-handed, Bats Left-handed   Turns Age 31 in 1987, Born 07/09/56

			HOW MUCH HE PITCHED					WHAT HE GAVE UP											THE RESULTS				
Year	Team	League	G	GS	CG	GF	IP	BFP	H	R	ER	HR	SH	SF	HB	TBB	IBB	SO	WP	Bk	W	L	Pct	ShO	Sv	ERA
1979	Chicago	A	24	0	0	9	30	142	30	18	18	0	3	0	1	23	5	18	3	1	0	5	.000	0	2	5.40
1980	Chicago	A	23	1	0	8	38	161	38	12	11	1	1	1	0	17	2	24	1	0	1	0	1.000	0	1	2.61
1983	Chicago	A	11	0	0	4	6	32	14	5	5	1	0	1	0	2	0	2	0	0	1	0	1.000	0	0	7.50
1986	Chicago	N	32	8	1	6	84	357	92	37	36	6	4	3	2	29	7	47	5	1	6	2	.750	0	0	3.86
4 YEARS			90	9	1	27	158	692	174	72	70	8	8	5	3	71	14	91	9	2	8	7	.533	0	3	3.99

AL HOLLAND

Pitches Left-handed, Bats Right-handed   Turns Age 35 in 1987, Born 08/16/52

			HOW MUCH HE PITCHED					WHAT HE GAVE UP											THE RESULTS				
Year	Team	League	G	GS	CG	GF	IP	BFP	H	R	ER	HR	SH	SF	HB	TBB	IBB	SO	WP	Bk	W	L	Pct	ShO	Sv	ERA
1977	Pittsburgh	N	2	0	0	0	2	10	4	2	2	0	0	0	0	0	0	1	0	0	0	0	.000	0	0	9.00
1979	San Francisco	N	3	0	0	0	7	29	3	0	0	0	0	0	0	5	0	7	0	0	0	0	.000	0	0	0.00
1980	San Francisco	N	54	0	0	31	82	349	71	21	16	2	5	4	1	34	8	65	1	3	5	3	.625	0	7	1.76
1981	San Francisco	N	47	3	0	23	101	431	87	31	27	4	7	5	2	44	11	78	3	0	7	5	.583	0	7	2.41
1982	San Francisco	N	58	7	0	10	129.2	546	115	56	48	12	4	3	1	40	6	97	6	1	7	3	.700	0	5	3.33
1983	Philadelphia	N	68	0	0	53	91.2	371	63	26	23	8	5	1	0	30	12	100	0	0	8	4	.667	0	25	2.26
1984	Philadelphia	N	68	0	0	61	98.1	404	82	38	37	14	5	4	1	30	6	61	0	3	5	10	.333	0	29	3.39
1985	3 Teams		56	0	0	28	87	355	70	28	28	9	6	4	0	31	9	62	1	1	1	5	.167	0	5	2.90
1986	New York	A	25	1	0	10	40.2	177	44	29	23	5	1	3	0	9	2	37	0	0	1	0	1.000	0	0	5.09
9 YEARS			381	11	0	216	639.1	2672	539	231	204	54	33	24	5	223	54	508	12	8	34	30	.531	0	78	2.87
1985	California	A	15	0	0	6	24.1	99	17	4	4	4	1	0	0	10	1	14	1	0	0	1	.000	0	0	1.48
1985	Philadelphia	N	3	0	0	3	4	21	5	2	2	0	1	1	0	4	2	1	0	0	0	1	.000	0	1	4.50
1985	Pittsburgh	N	38	0	0	19	58.2	235	48	22	22	5	4	3	0	17	6	47	0	1	1	3	.250	0	4	3.37

RICK HONEYCUTT

Pitches Left-handed, Bats Left-handed   Turns Age 33 in 1987, Born 06/29/54

			HOW MUCH HE PITCHED					WHAT HE GAVE UP											THE RESULTS				
Year	Team	League	G	GS	CG	GF	IP	BFP	H	R	ER	HR	SH	SF	HB	TBB	IBB	SO	WP	Bk	W	L	Pct	ShO	Sv	ERA
1977	Seattle	A	10	3	0	3	29	125	26	16	14	7	0	2	3	11	2	17	2	1	0	1	.000	0	0	4.34
1978	Seattle	A	26	24	4	0	134	594	150	81	73	12	9	7	3	49	5	50	3	0	5	11	.313	1	0	4.90
1979	Seattle	A	33	28	8	2	194	839	201	103	87	22	11	6	6	67	7	83	5	1	11	12	.478	1	0	4.04
1980	Seattle	A	30	30	9	0	203	871	221	99	89	22	11	7	3	60	7	79	4	0	10	17	.370	1	0	3.95
1981	Texas	A	20	20	8	0	128	509	120	49	47	12	5	0	0	17	1	40	1	0	11	6	.647	2	0	3.30
1982	Texas	A	30	26	4	3	164	728	201	103	96	20	4	8	3	54	4	64	3	1	5	17	.227	1	0	5.27
1983	2 Teams		34	32	6	0	213.2	865	214	85	72	15	5	6	8	50	6	74	1	3	16	11	.593	2	0	3.03
1984	Los Angeles	N	29	28	6	0	183.2	762	180	72	58	11	6	5	2	51	11	75	1	2	10	9	.526	2	0	2.84
1985	Los Angeles	N	31	25	1	2	142	600	141	71	54	9	5	4	1	49	7	67	2	0	8	12	.400	0	1	3.42
1986	Los Angeles	N	32	28	0	2	171	713	164	71	63	9	6	4	3	45	4	100	4	1	11	9	.550	0	0	3.32
10 YEARS			275	244	46	12	1562.1	6606	1618	750	653	139	62	46	32	453	54	649	26	9	87	105	.453	10	1	3.76
1983	Texas	A	25	25	5	0	174.2	693	168	59	47	9	3	6	6	37	2	56	1	2	14	8	.636	2	0	2.42
1983	Los Angeles	N	9	7	1	0	39	172	46	26	25	6	2	0	2	13	4	18	0	1	2	3	.400	0	0	5.77

BOB HORNER

Bats Right-handed, Throws Right-handed   Turns Age 30 in 1987, Born 08/06/57

			BATTING																BASERUNNING				PERCENTAGES		
Year	Team	League	G	AB	H	2B	3B	HR	(Hm	Rd)	TB	R	RBI	TBB	IBB	SO	HBP	SH	SF	SB	CS	SB%	GIDP	AVE	OBP	SLG
1978	Atlanta	N	89	323	86	17	1	23	(19	4)	174	50	63	24	2	42	2	1	9	0	0	.00	7	.266	.313	.539
1979	Atlanta	N	121	487	153	15	1	33	(21	12)	269	66	98	22	6	74	3	0	3	0	2	.00	9	.314	.346	.552
1980	Atlanta	N	124	463	124	14	1	35	(23	12)	245	81	89	27	3	50	1	0	4	3	1	.75	16	.268	.307	.529
1981	Atlanta	N	79	300	83	10	2	15	(9	6)	138	42	42	32	3	39	1	0	4	2	3	.40	6	.277	.345	.460
1982	Atlanta	N	140	499	130	24	0	32	(25	7)	250	85	97	66	3	75	4	0	3	3	5	.38	13	.261	.350	.501
1983	Atlanta	N	104	386	117	25	1	20	(12	8)	204	75	68	50	2	63	1	0	2	4	2	.67	14	.303	.383	.528
1984	Atlanta	N	32	113	31	8	0	3	(0	3)	48	15	19	14	2	17	0	0	2	0	0	.00	6	.274	.349	.425
1985	Atlanta	N	130	483	129	25	3	27	(13	14)	241	61	89	50	4	57	1	0	6	1	1	.50	18	.267	.333	.499
8 YEARS			819	3054	853	138	7	188	(122	66)	1569	475	565	285	25	417	13	1	32	13	14	.48	86	.279	.340	.514

RICKY HORTON

Pitches Left-handed, Bats Left-handed   Turns Age 28 in 1987, Born 07/30/59

			HOW MUCH HE PITCHED					WHAT HE GAVE UP											THE RESULTS				
Year	Team	League	G	GS	CG	GF	IP	BFP	H	R	ER	HR	SH	SF	HB	TBB	IBB	SO	WP	Bk	W	L	Pct	ShO	Sv	ERA
1984	St Louis	N	37	18	1	7	125.2	537	140	53	48	14	3	3	1	39	2	76	5	6	9	4	.692	1	1	3.44
1985	St Louis	N	49	3	0	10	89.2	382	84	30	29	5	8	3	3	34	13	59	3	2	3	2	.600	0	1	2.91
1986	St Louis	N	42	9	1	12	100.1	387	77	25	25	7	3	3	1	26	7	49	1	0	4	3	.571	0	3	2.24
3 YEARS			128	30	2	29	315.2	1306	301	108	102	26	14	9	5	99	22	184	9	8	16	9	.640	1	5	2.91

CHARLIE HOUGH

Pitches Right-handed, Bats Right-handed   Turns Age 39 in 1987, Born 01/05/48

			HOW MUCH HE PITCHED					WHAT HE GAVE UP											THE RESULTS					
Year	Team	League	G	GS	CG	GF	IP	BFP	H	R	ER	HR	SH	SF	HB	TBB	IBB	SO	WP	Bk	W	L	Pct	ShO	Sv	ERA
1970	Los Angeles	N	8	0	0	5	17	79	18	11	10	7	0	0	0	11	0	8	0	0	0	0	.000	0	2	5.29
1971	Los Angeles	N	4	0	0	3	4	19	3	3	2	1	1	0	0	3	0	4	0	0	0	0	.000	0	0	4.50
1972	Los Angeles	N	2	0	0	2	3	13	2	1	1	0	0	0	1	2	0	4	0	0	0	0	.000	0	0	3.00
1973	Los Angeles	N	37	0	0	18	72	309	52	24	22	3	4	3	6	45	2	70	2	0	4	2	.667	0	5	2.75
1974	Los Angeles	N	49	0	0	16	96	389	65	45	40	12	6	8	4	40	2	63	4	0	9	4	.692	0	1	3.75
1975	Los Angeles	N	38	0	0	24	61	266	43	25	20	3	3	0	8	34	0	34	4	1	3	7	.300	0	4	2.95
1976	Los Angeles	N	77	0	0	55	143	600	102	43	35	6	4	1	8	77	3	81	9	0	12	8	.600	0	18	2.20
1977	Los Angeles	N	70	1	0	53	127	551	98	53	47	10	10	4	7	70	6	105	8	0	6	12	.333	0	22	3.33
1978	Los Angeles	N	55	0	0	31	93	390	69	38	34	6	0	0	5	48	4	66	6	0	5	5	.500	0	7	3.29
1979	Los Angeles	N	42	14	0	10	151	662	152	88	80	16	9	4	5	66	2	76	9	1	7	5	.583	0	4	4.77
1980	2 Teams		35	3	2	12	93	426	91	51	47	6	7	4	5	58	2	72	11	0	3	5	.375	1	1	4.55
1981	Texas	A	21	5	2	9	82	330	61	30	27	4	1	1	3	31	1	69	4	0	4	1	.800	0	1	2.96
1982	Texas	A	34	34	12	0	228	954	217	111	100	21	7	4	7	72	5	128	9	0	16	13	.552	2	0	3.95
1983	Texas	A	34	33	11	1	252	1030	219	96	89	22	5	5	3	95	0	152	6	1	15	13	.536	3	0	3.18
1984	Texas	A	36	36	17	0	266	1133	260	127	111	26	5	7	9	94	3	164	12	2	16	14	.533	1	0	3.76
1985	Texas	A	34	34	14	0	250.1	1018	198	102	92	23	4	7	7	83	1	141	11	3	14	16	.467	1	0	3.31
1986	Texas	A	33	33	7	0	230.1	958	188	115	97	32	9	1	9	89	2	146	16	0	17	10	.630	2	0	3.79
17 YEARS			609	193	65	239	2168.2	9127	1838	963	854	198	72	49	90	918	33	1383	111	8	131	115	.533	10	61	3.54
1980	Texas	A	16	2	2	7	61	270	54	30	27	2	4	1	3	37	2	47	8	0	2	2	.500	1	0	3.98
1980	Los Angeles	N	19	1	0	5	32	156	37	21	20	4	3	3	2	21	0	25	3	0	1	3	.250	0	1	5.63

JAY HOWELL

Pitches Right-handed, Bats Right-handed   Turns Age 32 in 1987, Born 11/26/55

			HOW MUCH HE PITCHED					WHAT HE GAVE UP											THE RESULTS					
Year	Team	League	G	GS	CG	GF	IP	BFP	H	R	ER	HR	SH	SF	HB	TBB	IBB	SO	WP	Bk	W	L	Pct	ShO	Sv	ERA
1980	Cincinnati	N	5	0	0	1	3	19	8	5	5	0	0	1	1	0	0	1	0	0	0	0	.000	0	0	15.00
1981	Chicago	N	10	2	0	1	22	97	23	13	12	3	1	1	2	10	2	10	0	0	2	0	1.000	0	0	4.91
1982	New York	A	6	6	0	0	28	138	42	25	24	1	0	2	0	13	0	21	1	0	2	3	.400	0	0	7.71
1983	New York	A	19	12	2	3	82	368	89	53	49	7	1	5	3	35	0	61	2	1	1	5	.167	0	0	5.38
1984	New York	A	61	1	0	23	103.2	426	86	33	31	5	3	3	0	34	3	109	4	0	9	4	.692	0	7	2.69
1985	Oakland	A	63	0	0	58	98	414	98	32	31	5	3	4	1	31	3	68	4	1	9	8	.529	0	29	2.85
1986	Oakland	A	38	0	0	33	53.1	230	53	23	20	3	3	1	1	23	4	42	4	0	3	6	.333	0	16	3.38
7 YEARS			202	21	2	119	390	1692	399	184	172	24	11	17	8	146	12	312	15	2	26	26	.500	0	52	3.97

JACK HOWELL

Bats Left-handed, Throws Right-handed   Turns Age 26 in 1987, Born 08/18/61

			BATTING																	BASERUNNING				PERCENTAGES		
Year	Team	League	G	AB	H	2B	3B	HR	(Hm	Rd)	TB	R	RBI	TBB	IBB	SO	HBP	SH	SF	SB	CS	SB%	GIDP	AVE	OBP	SLG
1985	California	A	43	137	27	4	0	5	(2	3)	46	19	18	16	2	33	0	4	1	1	1	.50	1	.197	.279	.336
1986	California	A	63	151	41	14	2	4	(1	3)	71	26	21	19	0	28	0	3	2	2	0	1.00	1	.272	.349	.470
2 YEARS			106	288	68	18	2	9	(3	6)	117	45	39	35	2	61	0	7	3	3	1	.75	2	.236	.316	.406

KEN HOWELL

Pitches Right-handed, Bats Right-handed   Turns Age 27 in 1987, Born 11/28/60

			HOW MUCH HE PITCHED					WHAT HE GAVE UP											THE RESULTS					
Year	Team	League	G	GS	CG	GF	IP	BFP	H	R	ER	HR	SH	SF	HB	TBB	IBB	SO	WP	Bk	W	L	Pct	ShO	Sv	ERA
1984	Los Angeles	N	32	1	0	19	51.1	207	51	21	19	1	2	4	1	9	4	54	0	0	5	5	.500	0	6	3.33
1985	Los Angeles	N	56	0	0	31	86	356	66	41	36	8	4	0	0	35	3	85	4	2	4	7	.364	0	12	3.77
1986	Los Angeles	N	62	0	0	36	97.2	437	86	48	42	7	8	3	3	63	9	104	4	0	6	12	.333	0	12	3.87
3 YEARS			150	1	0	86	235	1000	203	110	97	16	14	7	4	107	16	243	8	2	15	24	.385	0	30	3.71

LAMARR HOYT

Pitches Right-handed, Bats Right-handed   Turns Age 32 in 1987, Born 01/01/55

			HOW MUCH HE PITCHED					WHAT HE GAVE UP											THE RESULTS					
Year	Team	League	G	GS	CG	GF	IP	BFP	H	R	ER	HR	SH	SF	HB	TBB	IBB	SO	WP	Bk	W	L	Pct	ShO	Sv	ERA
1979	Chicago	A	2	0	0	1	3	10	2	0	0	0	0	0	0	0	0	0	0	0	0	0	.000	0	0	0.00
1980	Chicago	A	24	13	3	5	112	496	123	66	57	8	8	7	2	41	3	55	3	0	9	3	.750	1	0	4.58
1981	Chicago	A	43	1	0	30	91	371	80	40	36	10	5	2	3	28	1	60	3	0	9	3	.750	0	10	3.56
1982	Chicago	A	39	32	14	2	239.2	995	248	104	94	17	6	7	2	48	3	124	4	0	19	15	.559	2	0	3.53
1983	Chicago	A	36	36	11	0	260.2	1034	236	115	106	27	4	8	1	31	4	148	1	1	24	10	.706	0	0	3.66
1984	Chicago	A	34	34	11	0	235.2	975	244	127	117	31	4	5	5	43	3	126	0	0	13	18	.419	1	0	4.47
1985	San Diego	N	31	31	8	0	210.1	839	210	85	81	20	9	3	2	20	2	83	0	4	16	8	.667	3	0	3.47
1986	San Diego	N	35	25	1	2	159	699	170	100	91	27	10	3	3	68	8	85	2	2	8	11	.421	0	0	5.15
8 YEARS			244	172	48	40	1311.1	5419	1313	637	582	140	46	35	18	279	24	681	13	7	98	68	.590	8	10	3.99

KENT HRBEK

Bats Left-handed, Throws Right-handed   Turns Age 27 in 1987, Born 05/21/60

							BATTING													BASERUNNING				PERCENTAGES		
Year	Team	League	G	AB	H	2B	3B	HR	(Hm	Rd)	TB	R	RBI	TBB	IBB	SO	HBP	SH	SF	SB	CS	SB%	GIDP	AVE	OBP	SLG
1981	Minnesota	A	24	67	16	5	0	1	(0	1)	24	5	7	5	1	9	1	0	0	0	0	.00	0	.239	.301	.358
1982	Minnesota	A	140	532	160	21	4	23	(11	12)	258	82	92	54	12	80	0	1	4	3	1	.75	17	.301	.363	.485
1983	Minnesota	A	141	515	153	41	5	16	(7	9)	252	75	84	57	5	71	3	0	7	4	6	.40	12	.297	.366	.489
1984	Minnesota	A	149	559	174	31	3	27	(15	12)	292	80	107	65	15	87	4	1	6	1	1	.50	17	.311	.383	.522
1985	Minnesota	A	158	593	165	31	2	21	(10	11)	263	78	93	67	12	87	2	0	4	1	1	.50	12	.278	.351	.444
1986	Minnesota	A	149	550	147	27	1	29	(18	11)	263	85	91	71	9	81	6	0	7	2	2	.50	15	.267	.353	.478
6 YEARS			761	2816	815	156	15	117	(61	56)	1352	405	474	319	54	415	16	2	28	11	11	.50	73	.289	.362	.480

GLENN HUBBARD

Bats Right-handed, Throws Right-handed   Turns Age 30 in 1987, Born 09/25/57

							BATTING													BASERUNNING				PERCENTAGES		
Year	Team	League	G	AB	H	2B	3B	HR	(Hm	Rd)	TB	R	RBI	TBB	IBB	SO	HBP	SH	SF	SB	CS	SB%	GIDP	AVE	OBP	SLG
1978	Atlanta	N	44	163	42	4	0	2	(1	1)	52	15	13	10	1	20	2	4	0	2	1	.67	2	.258	.309	.319
1979	Atlanta	N	97	325	75	12	0	3	(0	3)	96	34	29	27	2	43	1	2	2	0	6	.00	3	.231	.290	.295
1980	Atlanta	N	117	431	107	21	3	9	(6	3)	161	55	43	49	2	69	0	2	5	7	5	.58	7	.248	.322	.374
1981	Atlanta	N	99	361	85	13	5	6	(4	2)	126	39	33	33	2	59	2	3	1	4	2	.67	7	.235	.302	.349
1982	Atlanta	N	145	532	132	25	1	9	(7	2)	186	75	59	59	5	62	3	20	4	4	3	.57	5	.248	.324	.350
1983	Atlanta	N	148	517	136	24	6	12	(6	6)	208	65	70	55	2	71	4	9	7	3	8	.27	12	.263	.334	.402
1984	Atlanta	N	120	397	93	27	2	9	(3	6)	151	53	43	55	6	61	4	2	3	4	1	.80	8	.234	.331	.380
1985	Atlanta	N	142	439	102	21	0	5	(3	2)	138	51	39	56	2	54	4	7	6	4	3	.57	11	.232	.321	.314
1986	Atlanta	N	143	408	94	16	1	4	(4	0)	124	42	36	66	14	74	4	6	4	3	2	.60	5	.230	.340	.304
9 YEARS			1055	3573	866	163	18	59	(34	25)	1242	429	365	410	36	513	24	55	32	31	31	.50	60	.242	.322	.348

CHARLES HUDSON

Pitches Right-handed, Bats Right-handed   Turns Age 28 in 1987, Born 03/16/59

			HOW MUCH HE PITCHED						WHAT HE GAVE UP											THE RESULTS					
Year	Team	League	G	GS	CG	GF	IP	BFP	H	R	ER	HR	SH	SF	HB	TBB	IBB	SO	WP	Bk	W	L	Pct	ShO	Sv	ERA
1983	Philadelphia	N	26	26	3	0	169.1	701	158	73	63	13	6	4	0	53	6	101	4	3	8	8	.500	0	0	3.35
1984	Philadelphia	N	30	30	1	0	173.2	748	181	101	78	12	4	8	2	52	4	94	1	4	9	11	.450	1	0	4.04
1985	Philadelphia	N	38	26	3	7	193	833	188	92	81	23	8	4	1	74	7	122	4	3	8	13	.381	0	0	3.78
1986	Philadelphia	N	33	23	0	2	144	638	165	87	79	20	10	3	0	58	1	82	2	2	7	10	.412	0	0	4.94
4 YEARS			127	105	7	9	680	2920	692	353	301	68	28	19	3	237	18	399	11	12	32	42	.432	1	0	3.98

MARK HUISMANN

Pitches Right-handed, Bats Right-handed   Turns Age 29 in 1987, Born 05/11/58

			HOW MUCH HE PITCHED						WHAT HE GAVE UP											THE RESULTS					
Year	Team	League	G	GS	CG	GF	IP	BFP	H	R	ER	HR	SH	SF	HB	TBB	IBB	SO	WP	Bk	W	L	Pct	ShO	Sv	ERA
1983	Kansas City	A	13	0	0	5	30.2	135	29	20	19	1	1	1	0	17	3	20	4	1	2	1	.667	0	0	5.58
1984	Kansas City	A	38	0	0	23	75	324	84	38	35	7	3	5	1	21	3	54	3	0	3	3	.500	0	3	4.20
1985	Kansas City	A	9	0	0	6	18.2	70	14	4	4	1	1	2	0	3	0	9	0	0	1	0	1.000	0	1	1.93
1986	2 Teams		46	1	0	19	97.1	408	98	47	41	19	0	3	1	25	0	72	5	0	3	4	.429	0	5	3.79
4 YEARS			106	1	0	53	221.2	937	225	109	99	28	5	11	2	66	6	155	12	1	9	8	.529	0	8	4.02
1986	Kansas City	A	10	0	0	5	17.1	74	18	8	8	1	0	1	0	6	0	13	1	0	0	1	.000	0	1	4.15
1986	Seattle	A	36	1	0	14	80	334	80	39	33	18	0	2	1	19	0	59	4	0	3	3	.500	0	4	3.71

TIM HULETT

Bats Right-handed, Throws Right-handed   Turns Age 27 in 1987, Born 01/12/60

							BATTING													BASERUNNING				PERCENTAGES		
Year	Team	League	G	AB	H	2B	3B	HR	(Hm	Rd)	TB	R	RBI	TBB	IBB	SO	HBP	SH	SF	SB	CS	SB%	GIDP	AVE	OBP	SLG
1983	Chicago	A	6	5	1	0	0	0	(0	0)	1	0	0	0	0	0	0	0	0	1	0	1.00	0	.200	.200	.200
1984	Chicago	A	8	7	0	0	0	0	(0	0)	0	1	0	1	0	4	0	0	0	1	0	1.00	0	.000	.125	.000
1985	Chicago	A	141	395	106	19	4	5	(2	3)	148	52	37	30	1	81	4	4	3	6	4	.60	8	.268	.324	.375
1986	Chicago	A	150	520	120	16	5	17	(7	10)	197	53	44	21	0	91	1	6	4	4	1	.80	11	.231	.260	.379
4 YEARS			305	927	227	35	9	22	(9	13)	346	106	81	52	1	176	5	10	7	12	5	.71	19	.245	.287	.373

TOM HUME

Pitches Right-handed, Bats Right-handed | Turns Age 34 in 1987, Born 03/29/53

		HOW MUCH HE PITCHED					WHAT HE GAVE UP												THE RESULTS					
Year	Team	League	G	GS	CG	GF	IP	BFP	H	R	ER	HR	SH	SF	HB	TBB	IBB	SO	WP	Bk	W	L	Pct	ShO	Sv	ERA
1977	Cincinnati	N	14	5	0	2	43	197	54	36	34	5	2	1	0	17	3	22	0	0	3	3	.500	0	0	7.12
1978	Cincinnati	N	42	23	3	8	174	750	198	89	80	12	7	5	4	50	9	90	6	1	8	11	.421	0	1	4.14
1979	Cincinnati	N	57	12	2	33	163	669	162	54	50	12	9	9	0	33	9	80	2	0	10	9	.526	0	17	2.76
1980	Cincinnati	N	78	0	0	62	137	554	121	44	39	6	7	1	3	38	14	68	2	0	9	10	.474	0	25	2.56
1981	Cincinnati	N	51	0	0	40	68	281	63	27	26	7	4	2	1	31	9	27	0	0	9	4	.692	0	13	3.44
1982	Cincinnati	N	46	0	0	37	63.2	263	57	24	22	2	5	3	1	21	8	22	0	0	2	6	.250	0	17	3.11
1983	Cincinnati	N	48	0	0	33	66	301	66	40	35	8	3	4	3	41	11	34	1	0	3	5	.375	0	9	4.77
1984	Cincinnati	N	54	8	0	23	113.1	518	142	83	71	14	11	6	1	41	9	59	3	0	4	13	.235	0	3	5.64
1985	Cincinnati	N	56	0	0	15	80	331	65	33	29	7	2	1	3	35	5	50	3	1	3	5	.375	0	3	3.26
1986	Philadelphia	N	48	1	0	9	94.1	402	89	37	29	5	5	7	3	34	5	51	6	0	4	1	.800	0	4	2.77
10 YEARS			494	49	5	262	1002.1	4266	1017	467	415	78	55	39	19	341	82	503	23	2	55	67	.451	0	92	3.73

CLINT HURDLE

Bats Left-handed, Throws Right-handed | Turns Age 30 in 1987, Born 07/30/57

			BATTING																	BASERUNNING				PERCENTAGES		
Year	Team	League	G	AB	H	2B	3B	HR	(Hm	Rd)	TB	R	RBI	TBB	IBB	SO	HBP	SH	SF	SB	CS	SB%	GIDP	AVE	OBP	SLG
1977	Kansas City	A	9	26	8	0	0	2	(2	0)	14	5	7	2	0	7	0	0	0	0	0	.00	0	.308	.357	.538
1978	Kansas City	A	133	417	110	25	5	7	(3	4)	166	48	56	56	1	84	1	1	6	1	3	.25	6	.264	.348	.398
1979	Kansas City	A	59	171	41	10	3	3	(1	2)	66	16	30	28	4	24	1	0	4	0	1	.00	4	.240	.343	.386
1980	Kansas City	A	130	395	116	31	2	10	(3	7)	181	50	60	34	5	61	2	2	5	0	0	.00	11	.294	.349	.458
1981	Kansas City	A	28	76	25	3	1	4	(0	4)	42	12	15	13	3	10	0	0	0	0	0	.00	2	.329	.427	.553
1982	Cincinnati	N	19	34	7	1	0	0	(0	0)	8	2	1	2	2	6	1	0	0	0	1	.00	1	.206	.270	.235
1983	New York	N	13	33	6	2	0	0	(0	0)	8	3	2	2	0	10	0	0	0	0	0	.00	1	.182	.229	.242
1985	New York	N	43	82	16	4	0	3	(2	1)	29	7	7	13	3	20	1	1	0	0	1	.00	4	.195	.313	.354
1986	St Louis	N	78	154	30	5	1	3	(0	3)	46	18	15	26	0	38	1	1	2	0	0	.00	2	.195	.311	.299
9 YEARS			512	1388	359	81	12	32	(11	21)	560	161	193	176	18	260	7	5	17	1	6	.14	31	.259	.341	.403

BRUCE HURST

Pitches Left-handed, Bats Left-handed | Turns Age 29 in 1987, Born 03/24/58

			HOW MUCH HE PITCHED						WHAT HE GAVE UP												THE RESULTS					
Year	Team	League	G	GS	CG	GF	IP	BFP	H	R	ER	HR	SH	SF	HB	TBB	IBB	SO	WP	Bk	W	L	Pct	ShO	Sv	ERA
1980	Boston	A	12	7	0	2	31	147	39	33	31	4	0	2	2	16	0	16	4	2	2	2	.500	0	0	9.00
1981	Boston	A	5	5	0	0	23	104	23	11	11	1	0	2	1	12	2	11	2	0	2	0	1.000	0	0	4.30
1982	Boston	A	28	19	0	3	117	535	161	87	75	16	2	7	3	40	2	53	5	0	3	7	.300	0	0	5.77
1983	Boston	A	33	32	6	0	211.1	903	241	102	96	22	3	4	3	62	5	115	1	2	12	12	.500	2	0	4.09
1984	Boston	A	33	33	9	0	218	958	232	106	95	25	3	4	6	88	3	136	1	1	12	12	.500	2	0	3.92
1985	Boston	A	35	31	6	0	229.1	973	243	123	115	31	6	4	3	70	4	189	3	4	11	13	.458	1	0	4.51
1986	Boston	A	25	25	11	0	174.1	721	169	63	58	18	5	3	3	50	2	167	6	0	13	8	.619	4	0	2.99
7 YEARS			171	152	32	5	1004	4341	1108	525	481	117	19	26	21	338	18	687	22	9	55	54	.505	9	0	4.31

PETE INCAVIGLIA

Bats Right-handed, Throws Right-handed | Turns Age 23 in 1987, Born 04/02/64

			BATTING																	BASERUNNING				PERCENTAGES		
Year	Team	League	G	AB	H	2B	3B	HR	(Hm	Rd)	TB	R	RBI	TBB	IBB	SO	HBP	SH	SF	SB	CS	SB%	GIDP	AVE	OBP	SLG
1986	Texas	A	153	540	135	21	2	30	(17	13)	250	82	88	55	2	185	4	0	7	3	2	.60	9	.250	.320	.463

DANE IORG

Bats Left-handed, Throws Right-handed | Turns Age 37 in 1987, Born 05/11/50

			BATTING																	BASERUNNING				PERCENTAGES		
Year	Team	League	G	AB	H	2B	3B	HR	(Hm	Rd)	TB	R	RBI	TBB	IBB	SO	HBP	SH	SF	SB	CS	SB%	GIDP	AVE	OBP	SLG
1977	2 Teams		42	62	15	2	0	0	(0	0)	17	5	6	6	0	7	0	0	1	0	1	.00	1	.242	.304	.274
1978	St Louis	N	35	85	23	4	1	0	(0	0)	29	6	4	4	1	10	0	0	1	0	0	.00	2	.271	.300	.341
1979	St Louis	N	79	179	52	11	1	1	(0	1)	68	12	21	12	1	28	1	2	1	1	2	.33	5	.291	.337	.380
1980	St Louis	N	105	251	76	23	1	3	(1	2)	110	33	36	20	2	34	0	0	4	1	1	.50	5	.303	.349	.438
1981	St Louis	N	75	217	71	11	2	2	(1	1)	92	23	39	7	0	9	0	0	3	2	0	1.00	7	.327	.344	.424
1982	St Louis	N	102	238	70	14	1	0	(0	0)	86	17	34	23	3	23	0	0	3	0	1	.00	11	.294	.352	.361
1983	St Louis	N	58	116	31	9	1	0	(0	0)	42	6	11	10	2	11	1	0	4	1	0	1.00	6	.267	.321	.362
1984	2 Teams		93	263	64	18	2	5	(3	2)	101	30	33	15	4	21	0	0	6	0	1	.00	9	.243	.278	.384
1985	Kansas City	A	64	130	29	9	1	1	(0	1)	43	7	21	8	2	16	0	0	0	0	1	.00	6	.223	.268	.331
1986	San Diego	N	90	106	24	2	1	2	(0	2)	34	10	11	2	0	21	0	0	1	0	0	.00	2	.226	.239	.321
10 YEARS			743	1647	455	103	11	14	(5	9)	622	149	216	107	15	180	2	2	24	5	7	.42	54	.276	.317	.378
1977	Philadelphia	N	12	30	5	1	0	0	(0	0)	6	3	2	1	0	3	0	0	0	0	0	.00	0	.167	.194	.200
1977	St Louis	N	30	32	10	1	0	0	(0	0)	11	2	4	5	0	4	0	0	1	0	1	.00	1	.313	.395	.344
1984	Kansas City	A	78	235	60	16	2	5	(3	2)	95	27	30	13	3	15	0	0	6	0	1	.00	7	.255	.287	.404
1984	St Louis	N	15	28	4	2	0	0	(0	0)	6	3	3	2	1	6	0	0	0	0	0	.00	2	.143	.200	.214

GARTH IORG

Bats Right-handed, Throws Right-handed

Turns Age 33 in 1987, Born 10/12/54

Year	Team	League	G	AB	H	2B	3B	HR	(Hm	Rd)	TB	R	RBI	TBB	IBB	SO	HBP	SH	SF	SB	CS	SB%	GIDP	AVE	OBP	SLG
1978	Toronto	A	19	49	8	0	0	0	(0	0)	8	3	3	3	0	4	1	0	2	0	0	.00	3	.163	.218	.163
1980	Toronto	A	80	222	55	10	1	2	(1	1)	73	24	14	12	0	39	0	3	0	2	1	.67	5	.248	.286	.329
1981	Toronto	A	70	215	52	11	0	0	(0	0)	63	17	10	7	1	31	1	2	0	2	3	.40	3	.242	.269	.293
1982	Toronto	A	129	417	119	20	5	1	(1	0)	152	45	36	12	2	38	4	2	7	3	2	.60	6	.285	.307	.365
1983	Toronto	A	122	375	103	22	5	2	(1	1)	141	40	39	13	3	45	1	2	3	7	0	1.00	10	.275	.298	.376
1984	Toronto	A	121	247	56	10	3	1	(1	0)	75	24	25	5	1	16	1	3	1	1	3	.25	7	.227	.244	.304
1985	Toronto	A	131	288	90	22	1	7	(5	2)	135	24	37	21	3	26	0	2	1	3	6	.33	6	.313	.358	.469
1986	Toronto	A	137	327	85	19	1	3	(1	2)	115	30	44	20	0	47	1	1	2	2	0	1.00	7	.260	.303	.352
8 YEARS			809	2140	568	114	16	16	(10	6)	762	216	208	93	9	246	9	15	16	21	15	.58	47	.265	.297	.356

DANNY JACKSON

Pitches Left-handed, Bats Right-handed

Turns Age 25 in 1987, Born 01/05/62

Year	Team	League	G	GS	CG	GF	IP	BFP	H	R	ER	HR	SH	SF	HB	TBB	IBB	SO	WP	Bk	W	L	Pct	ShO	Sv	ERA
1983	Kansas City	A	4	3	0	0	19	87	26	12	11	1	1	0	0	6	0	9	0	0	1	1	.500	0	0	5.21
1984	Kansas City	A	15	11	1	3	76	338	84	41	36	4	3	0	5	35	0	40	3	2	2	6	.250	0	0	4.26
1985	Kansas City	A	32	32	4	0	208	893	209	94	79	7	5	4	6	76	2	114	4	2	14	12	.538	3	0	3.42
1986	Kansas City	A	32	27	4	3	185.2	789	177	83	66	13	10	4	4	79	1	115	7	0	11	12	.478	1	1	3.20
4 YEARS			83	73	9	6	488.2	2107	496	230	192	25	19	8	15	196	3	278	14	4	28	31	.475	4	1	3.54

REGGIE JACKSON

Bats Left-handed, Throws Left-handed

Turns Age 41 in 1987, Born 05/18/46

Year	Team	League	G	AB	H	2B	3B	HR	(Hm	Rd)	TB	R	RBI	TBB	IBB	SO	HBP	SH	SF	SB	CS	SB%	GIDP	AVE	OBP	SLG
1967	Kansas City	A	35	118	21	4	4	1	(0	1)	36	13	6	10	0	46	5	1	1	1	1	.50	1	.178	.269	.305
1968	Oakland	A	154	553	138	13	6	29	(9	20)	250	82	74	50	5	171	5	4	2	14	4	.78	3	.250	.316	.452
1969	Oakland	A	152	549	151	36	3	47	(26	21)	334	123	118	114	20	142	12	1	1	13	5	.72	6	.275	.410	.608
1970	Oakland	A	149	426	101	21	2	23	(8	15)	195	57	66	75	11	135	8	2	3	26	17	.60	10	.237	.359	.458
1971	Oakland	A	150	567	157	29	3	32	(17	15)	288	87	80	63	5	161	6	0	6	16	10	.62	7	.277	.352	.508
1972	Oakland	A	135	499	132	25	2	25	(16	9)	236	72	75	59	7	125	8	4	2	9	8	.53	5	.265	.350	.473
1973	Oakland	A	151	539	158	28	2	32	(18	14)	286	99	117	76	20	111	7	0	7	22	8	.73	13	.293	.383	.531
1974	Oakland	A	148	506	146	25	1	29	(14	15)	260	90	93	86	20	105	4	0	8	25	5	.83	8	.289	.391	.514
1975	Oakland	A	157	593	150	39	3	36	(18	18)	303	91	104	67	5	133	3	0	6	17	8	.68	10	.253	.329	.511
1976	Baltimore	A	134	498	138	27	2	27	(12	15)	250	84	91	54	7	108	4	0	2	28	7	.80	17	.277	.351	.502
1977	New York	A	146	525	150	39	2	32	(11	21)	289	93	110	74	4	129	3	0	4	17	3	.85	3	.286	.375	.550
1978	New York	A	139	511	140	13	5	27	(17	10)	244	82	97	58	2	133	9	0	3	14	11	.56	7	.274	.356	.477
1979	New York	A	131	465	138	24	2	29	(15	14)	253	78	89	65	3	107	2	0	5	9	8	.53	17	.297	.382	.544
1980	New York	A	143	514	154	22	4	41	(16	25)	307	94	111	83	15	122	2	0	1	1	2	.33	7	.300	.398	.597
1981	New York	A	94	334	79	17	1	15	(7	8)	143	33	54	46	2	82	1	0	1	0	3	.00	5	.237	.330	.428
1982	California	A	153	530	146	17	1	39	(21	18)	282	92	101	85	12	156	2	0	4	4	5	.44	10	.275	.375	.532
1983	California	A	116	397	77	14	1	14	(7	7)	135	43	49	52	5	140	4	0	5	0	2	.00	5	.194	.290	.340
1984	California	A	143	525	117	17	2	25	(15	10)	213	67	81	55	6	141	3	1	0	8	4	.67	10	.223	.300	.406
1985	California	A	143	460	116	27	0	27	(15	12)	224	64	85	78	12	138	1	0	2	1	2	.33	16	.252	.360	.487
1986	California	A	132	419	101	12	2	18	(11	7)	171	65	58	92	11	115	3	0	3	1	1	.50	14	.241	.379	.408
20 YEARS			2705	9528	2510	449	48	548	(273	275)	4699	1509	1659	1342	163	2500	92	13	67	226	114	.66	180	.263	.358	.493

ROY LEE JACKSON

Pitches Right-handed, Bats Right-handed

Turns Age 33 in 1987, Born 05/01/54

Year	Team	League	G	GS	CG	GF	IP	BFP	H	R	ER	HR	SH	SF	HB	TBB	IBB	SO	WP	Bk	W	L	Pct	ShO	Sv	ERA
1977	New York	N	4	4	0	0	24	116	25	16	16	2	1	1	3	15	1	13	2	0	0	2	.000	0	0	6.00
1978	New York	N	4	2	0	0	13	61	21	13	13	2	3	1	2	6	0	6	1	0	0	0	.000	0	0	9.00
1979	New York	N	8	0	0	0	16	61	11	4	4	1	0	1	1	5	0	10	1	0	1	0	1.000	0	0	2.25
1980	New York	N	24	8	1	4	71	299	78	37	33	4	3	4	0	20	4	58	4	1	1	7	.125	0	0	4.18
1981	Toronto	A	39	0	0	21	62	266	65	23	18	5	3	1	1	25	7	27	5	0	1	2	.333	0	7	2.61
1982	Toronto	A	48	2	0	24	97	394	77	37	33	7	3	4	2	31	4	71	1	0	8	8	.500	0	6	3.06
1983	Toronto	A	49	0	0	19	92	402	92	48	46	6	7	7	3	41	2	48	0	0	8	3	.727	0	7	4.50
1984	Toronto	A	54	0	0	29	86	355	73	40	34	12	4	2	1	31	4	58	4	0	7	8	.467	0	10	3.56
1985	San Diego	N	22	2	0	6	40	163	32	13	12	4	2	1	1	13	1	28	0	1	2	3	.400	0	2	2.70
1986	Minnesota	A	28	0	0	6	58.1	249	57	29	25	7	5	5	3	16	0	36	1	3	0	1	.000	0	1	3.86
10 YEARS			280	18	1	111	559.1	2366	531	260	234	50	31	27	17	203	23	351	20	4	28	34	.452	0	34	3.77

BROOK JACOBY

Bats Right-handed, Throws Right-handed

Turns Age 28 in 1987, Born 11/23/59

Year	Team	League	G	AB	H	2B	3B	HR	(Hm	Rd)	TB	R	RBI	TBB	IBB	SO	HBP	SH	SF	SB	CS	SB%	GIDP	AVE	OBP	SLG
1981	Atlanta	N	11	10	2	0	0	0	(0	0)	2	0	0	0	0	3	0	0	0	0	0	.00	1	.200	.200	.200
1983	Atlanta	N	4	8	0	0	0	0	(0	0)	0	0	0	0	0	1	0	1	0	0	0	.00	0	.000	.000	.000
1984	Cleveland	A	126	439	116	19	3	7	(2	5)	162	64	40	32	0	73	3	2	7	3	2	.60	13	.264	.314	.369
1985	Cleveland	A	161	606	166	26	3	20	(9	11)	258	72	87	48	3	120	0	1	7	2	3	.40	17	.274	.324	.426
1986	Cleveland	A	158	583	168	30	4	17	(10	7)	257	83	80	56	5	137	0	1	1	2	1	.67	15	.288	.350	.441
5 YEARS			460	1646	452	75	10	44	(21	23)	679	219	208	136	8	334	3	5	15	7	6	.54	46	.275	.328	.413

BOB JAMES

Pitches Right-handed, Bats Right-handed

Turns Age 29 in 1987, Born 08/15/58

			HOW MUCH HE PITCHED						WHAT HE GAVE UP													THE RESULTS					
Year	Team	League	G	GS	CG	GF	IP	BFP	H	R	ER	HR	SH	SF	HB	TBB	IBB	SO	WP	Bk	W	L	Pct	ShO	Sv	ERA
1978	Montreal	N	4	1	0	0	4	19	4	4	4	1	0	0	0	4	0	3	1	0	0	1	.000	0	0	9.00
1979	Montreal	N	2	0	0	1	2	11	2	3	3	0	0	0	0	3	1	1	0	0	0	0	.000	0	0	13.50
1982	2 Teams		19	1	0	7	28.2	131	32	19	17	4	0	0	2	16	1	31	6	1	0	2	.000	0	0	5.34
1983	2 Teams		31	0	0	19	54	227	42	22	21	5	6	0	3	26	2	60	2	1	1	0	1.000	0	7	3.50
1984	Montreal	N	62	0	0	33	96	430	92	47	39	6	6	8	4	45	7	91	4	2	6	6	.500	0	10	3.66
1985	Chicago	A	69	0	0	60	110	436	90	31	26	5	7	5	2	23	4	88	3	2	8	7	.533	0	32	2.13
1986	Chicago	A	49	0	0	40	58.1	263	61	36	34	8	4	4	4	23	4	32	5	1	5	4	.556	0	14	5.25
7 YEARS			236	2	0	160	353	1517	323	162	144	29	23	19	13	140	18	306	21	7	20	20	.500	0	63	3.67
1982	Detroit	A	12	1	0	6	19.2	87	22	13	11	4	0	0	0	8	0	20	4	0	0	2	.000	0	0	5.03
1982	Montreal	N	7	0	0	1	9	44	10	6	6	0	0	2	0	8	1	11	2	1	0	0	.000	0	0	6.00
1983	Detroit	A	4	0	0	3	4	19	5	5	5	2	0	0	0	3	0	4	0	0	0	0	.000	0	0	11.25
1983	Montreal	N	27	0	0	16	50	208	37	17	16	3	6	0	3	23	2	56	2	1	1	0	1.000	0	7	2.88

STAN JAVIER

Bats both Right and Left-handed, Throws Right-handed

Turns Age 22 in 1987, Born 01/09/65

			BATTING																BASERUNNING				PERCENTAGES		
Year	Team	League	G	AB	H	2B	3B	HR	(Hm | Rd)	TB	R	RBI	TBB	IBB	SO	HBP	SH	SF	SB	CS	SB%	GIDP	AVE	OBP	SLG
1984	New York	A	7	7	1	0	0	0	(0 | 0)	1	1	0	0	0	1	0	0	0	0	0	.00	0	.143	.143	.143
1986	Oakland	A	59	114	23	8	0	0	(0 | 0)	31	13	8	16	0	27	1	0	0	8	0	1.00	2	.202	.305	.272
2 YEARS			66	121	24	8	0	0	(0 | 0)	32	14	8	16	0	28	1	0	0	8	0	1.00	2	.198	.297	.264

STEVE JELTZ

Bats both Right and Left-handed, Throws Right-handed

Turns Age 28 in 1987, Born 05/28/59

			BATTING																BASERUNNING				PERCENTAGES		
Year	Team	League	G	AB	H	2B	3B	HR	(Hm | Rd)	TB	R	RBI	TBB	IBB	SO	HBP	SH	SF	SB	CS	SB%	GIDP	AVE	OBP	SLG
1983	Philadelphia	N	13	8	1	0	1	0	(0 | 0)	3	0	1	1	0	2	0	1	0	0	0	.00	2	.125	.222	.375
1984	Philadelphia	N	28	68	14	0	1	1	(0 | 1)	19	7	7	7	1	11	0	1	1	2	1	.67	3	.206	.276	.279
1985	Philadelphia	N	89	196	37	4	1	0	(0 | 0)	43	17	12	26	4	55	0	5	1	1	1	.50	6	.189	.283	.219
1986	Philadelphia	N	145	439	96	11	4	0	(0 | 0)	115	44	36	65	9	97	1	3	2	6	3	.67	9	.219	.320	.262
4 YEARS			275	711	148	15	7	1	(0 | 1)	180	68	56	99	14	165	1	10	4	9	5	.64	20	.208	.304	.253

CLIFF JOHNSON

Bats Right-handed, Throws Right-handed

Turns Age 40 in 1987, Born 07/22/47

			BATTING																BASERUNNING				PERCENTAGES		
Year	Team	League	G	AB	H	2B	3B	HR	(Hm | Rd)	TB	R	RBI	TBB	IBB	SO	HBP	SH	SF	SB	CS	SB%	GIDP	AVE	OBP	SLG
1972	Houston	N	5	4	1	0	0	0	(0 | 0)	1	0	0	2	0	0	0	0	0	0	0	.00	0	.250	.500	.250
1973	Houston	N	7	20	6	2	0	2	(2 | 0)	14	6	6	1	0	7	1	0	0	0	0	.00	0	.300	.364	.700
1974	Houston	N	83	171	39	4	1	10	(5 | 5)	75	26	29	33	1	45	3	0	3	0	1	.00	5	.228	.357	.439
1975	Houston	N	122	340	94	16	1	20	(10 | 10)	172	52	65	46	5	64	5	1	1	1	0	1.00	7	.276	.370	.506
1976	Houston	N	108	318	72	21	2	10	(5 | 5)	127	36	49	62	6	59	4	0	0	0	0	.00	9	.226	.359	.399
1977	2 Teams		107	286	85	16	0	22	(10 | 12)	167	46	54	43	2	53	10	0	0	0	2	.00	3	.297	.407	.584
1978	New York	A	76	174	32	9	1	6	(2 | 4)	61	20	19	30	1	32	1	0	0	0	0	.00	6	.184	.307	.351
1979	2 Teams		100	304	82	16	1	20	(11 | 9)	158	48	67	34	5	46	5	1	6	2	0	1.00	6	.270	.347	.520
1980	2 Teams		122	370	86	11	1	16	(10 | 6)	147	53	62	54	10	65	1	0	5	0	1	.00	12	.232	.328	.397
1981	Oakland	A	84	273	71	8	0	17	(11 | 6)	130	40	59	28	2	60	3	0	6	5	3	.63	3	.260	.329	.476
1982	Oakland	A	73	214	51	10	0	7	(4 | 3)	82	19	31	26	2	41	2	0	2	1	2	.33	3	.238	.324	.383
1983	Toronto	A	142	407	108	23	1	22	(10 | 12)	199	59	76	67	8	69	5	1	4	0	1	.00	10	.265	.373	.489
1984	Toronto	A	127	359	109	23	1	16	(3 | 13)	182	51	61	50	4	62	3	0	3	0	1	.00	4	.304	.390	.507
1985	2 Teams		106	369	96	17	1	13	(9 | 4)	154	35	66	40	2	59	3	1	4	0	0	.00	4	.260	.334	.417
1986	Toronto	A	107	336	84	12	1	15	(11 | 4)	143	48	55	52	1	57	4	0	2	0	1	.00	3	.250	.355	.426
15 YEARS			1369	3945	1016	188	10	196	(103 | 93)	1812	539	699	568	53	719	50	4	36	9	12	.43	86	.258	.355	.459
1977	New York	A	56	142	42	8	0	12	(3 | 9)	86	24	31	20	0	23	6	0	0	0	1	.00	2	.296	.405	.606
1977	Houston	N	51	144	43	8	0	10	(7 | 3)	81	22	23	23	2	30	4	0	0	0	1	.00	1	.299	.409	.563
1979	Cleveland	A	72	240	65	10	0	18	(10 | 8)	129	37	61	24	1	39	5	0	5	2	0	1.00	6	.271	.343	.538
1979	New York	A	28	64	17	6	0	2	(1 | 1)	29	11	6	10	4	7	0	1	1	0	0	.00	0	.266	.360	.453
1980	Cleveland	A	54	174	40	3	1	6	(4 | 2)	63	25	28	25	5	30	0	0	4	0	1	.00	8	.230	.320	.362
1980	Chicago	N	68	196	46	8	0	10	(6 | 4)	84	28	34	29	5	35	1	0	1	0	0	.00	4	.235	.335	.429
1985	Texas	A	82	296	76	17	1	12	(8 | 4)	131	31	56	31	2	44	3	1	3	0	0	.00	3	.257	.330	.443
1985	Toronto	A	24	73	20	0	0	1	(1 | 0)	23	4	10	9	0	15	0	0	1	0	0	.00	1	.274	.349	.315

HOWARD JOHNSON

Bats both Right and Left-handed, Throws Right-handed

Turns Age 27 in 1987, Born 11/29/60

			BATTING																BASERUNNING				PERCENTAGES		
Year	Team	League	G	AB	H	2B	3B	HR	(Hm | Rd)	TB	R	RBI	TBB	IBB	SO	HBP	SH	SF	SB	CS	SB%	GIDP	AVE	OBP	SLG
1982	Detroit	A	54	155	49	5	0	4	(1 | 3)	66	23	14	16	1	30	1	1	0	7	4	.64	3	.316	.384	.426
1983	Detroit	A	27	66	14	0	0	3	(2 | 1)	23	11	5	7	0	10	1	0	0	0	0	.00	1	.212	.297	.348
1984	Detroit	A	116	355	88	14	1	12	(4 | 8)	140	43	50	40	1	67	1	0	2	10	6	.63	6	.248	.324	.394
1985	New York	N	126	389	94	18	4	11	(5 | 6)	153	38	46	34	10	78	0	1	4	6	4	.60	6	.242	.300	.393
1986	New York	N	88	220	54	14	0	10	(5 | 5)	98	30	39	31	8	64	1	1	0	8	1	.89	2	.245	.341	.445
5 YEARS			411	1185	299	51	5	40	(17 | 23)	480	145	154	128	20	249	4	7	6	31	15	.67	18	.252	.326	.405

JOHN HENRY JOHNSON

Pitches Left-handed, Bats Left-handed Turns Age 31 in 1987, Born 08/21/56

Year	Team	League	G	GS	CG	GF	IP	BFP	H	R	ER	HR	SH	SF	HB	TBB	IBB	SO	WP	Bk	W	L	Pct	ShO	Sv	ERA
1978	Oakland	A	33	30	7	1	186	789	164	81	70	18	13	5	0	82	6	91	5	0	11	10	.524	2	0	3.39
1979	2 Teams		31	25	2	1	167	729	168	95	86	25	7	7	2	72	3	96	4	1	4	14	.222	0	0	4.63
1980	Texas	A	33	0	0	17	39	154	27	12	10	2	1	1	1	15	4	44	2	0	2	2	.500	0	4	2.31
1981	Texas	A	24	0	0	15	24	94	19	7	7	2	2	3	1	6	1	8	1	0	3	1	.750	0	2	2.62
1983	Boston	A	34	1	0	19	53.1	234	58	28	22	3	3	5	1	20	4	51	1	0	3	2	.600	0	1	3.71
1984	Boston	A	30	3	0	9	63.2	275	64	26	25	7	2	0	0	27	1	57	4	1	1	2	.333	0	1	3.53
1986	Milwaukee	A	19	0	0	5	44	184	43	15	13	2	3	0	0	10	1	42	5	0	2	1	.667	0	1	2.66
7 YEARS			204	59	9	67	577	2459	543	264	233	59	31	21	5	232	20	389	22	2	26	32	.448	2	9	3.63
1979	Oakland	A	14	13	1	0	85	372	89	45	41	13	2	2	1	36	0	50	1	0	2	8	.200	0	0	4.34
1979	Texas	A	17	12	1	1	82	357	79	50	45	12	5	5	1	36	3	46	3	1	2	6	.250	0	0	4.94

JOE JOHNSON

Pitches Right-handed, Bats Right-handed Turns Age 26 in 1987, Born 10/30/61

Year	Team	League	G	GS	CG	GF	IP	BFP	H	R	ER	HR	SH	SF	HB	TBB	IBB	SO	WP	Bk	W	L	Pct	ShO	Sv	ERA
1985	Atlanta	N	15	14	1	0	85.2	367	95	44	39	9	4	3	3	24	5	34	2	0	4	4	.500	0	0	4.10
1986	2 Teams		33	30	2	1	175	758	195	97	86	11	7	5	5	57	5	88	3	1	13	9	.591	0	0	4.42
2 YEARS			48	44	3	1	260.2	1125	290	141	125	20	11	8	8	81	10	122	5	1	17	13	.567	0	0	4.32
1986	Toronto	A	16	15	0	0	88	368	94	39	38	3	4	4	3	22	1	39	2	0	7	2	.778	0	0	3.89
1986	Atlanta	N	17	15	2	1	87	390	101	58	48	8	3	1	2	35	4	49	1	1	6	7	.462	0	0	4.97

WALLACE JOHNSON

Bats both Right and Left-handed, Throws Right-handed Turns Age 31 in 1987, Born 12/25/56

Year	Team	League	G	AB	H	2B	3B	HR	(Hm	Rd)	TB	R	RBI	TBB	IBB	SO	HBP	SH	SF	SB	CS	SB%	GIDP	AVE	OBP	SLG
1981	Montreal	N	11	9	2	0	1	0	(0	0)	4	1	3	1	1	1	0	0	0	1	1	.50	1	.222	.300	.444
1982	Montreal	N	36	57	11	0	2	0	(0	0)	15	5	2	5	0	5	0	0	0	4	1	.80	0	.193	.258	.263
1983	2 Teams	N	10	10	2	0	0	0	(0	0)	2	1	1	1	0	0	0	0	0	1	0	1.00	0	.200	.273	.200
1984	Montreal	N	17	24	5	0	0	0	(0	0)	5	3	4	5	0	4	0	0	0	0	0	.00	0	.208	.345	.208
1986	Montreal	N	61	127	36	3	1	1	(1	0)	44	13	10	7	0	9	0	0	0	6	3	.67	2	.283	.321	.346
5 YEARS			135	227	56	3	4	1	(1	0)	70	23	20	19	1	19	0	0	0	12	5	.71	3	.247	.305	.308
1983	Montreal	N	3	2	1	0	0	0	(0	0)	1	1	0	1	0	0	0	0	0	1	0	1.00	0	.500	.667	.500
1983	San Francisco	N	7	8	1	0	0	0	(0	0)	1	0	1	0	0	0	0	0	0	0	0	.00	0	.125	.125	.125

BARRY JONES

Pitches Right-handed, Bats Right-handed Turns Age 24 in 1987, Born 02/15/63

Year	Team	League	G	GS	CG	GF	IP	BFP	H	R	ER	HR	SH	SF	HB	TBB	IBB	SO	WP	Bk	W	L	Pct	ShO	Sv	ERA
1986	Pittsburgh	N	26	0	0	10	37.1	159	29	16	12	3	2	1	0	21	2	29	2	0	3	4	.429	0	3	2.89

ODELL JONES

Pitches Right-handed, Bats Right-handed Turns Age 34 in 1987, Born 01/13/53

Year	Team	League	G	GS	CG	GF	IP	BFP	H	R	ER	HR	SH	SF	HB	TBB	IBB	SO	WP	Bk	W	L	Pct	ShO	Sv	ERA
1975	Pittsburgh	N	2	0	0	1	3	10	1	0	0	0	0	0	0	0	0	2	0	0	0	0	.000	0	0	0.00
1977	Pittsburgh	N	34	15	1	9	108	466	118	63	61	14	5	3	3	31	2	66	4	2	3	7	.300	0	0	5.08
1978	Pittsburgh	N	3	1	0	1	9	38	7	3	2	0	0	0	0	4	0	10	0	0	2	0	1.000	0	0	2.00
1979	Seattle	A	25	19	3	2	119	553	151	90	80	16	10	6	3	58	8	72	6	0	3	11	.214	0	0	6.05
1981	Pittsburgh	N	13	8	0	1	54	232	51	23	20	3	4	1	0	23	6	30	1	1	4	5	.444	0	0	3.33
1983	Texas	A	42	0	0	33	67	281	56	28	23	4	4	2	2	22	1	50	1	0	2	4	.333	0	10	3.09
1984	Texas	A	33	0	0	24	59	254	62	28	24	7	6	2	2	23	3	28	3	0	2	4	.333	0	2	3.66
1986	Baltimore	A	21	0	0	12	49.1	219	58	22	21	4	2	4	0	23	6	32	2	0	2	2	.500	0	0	3.83
8 YEARS			173	43	4	83	468.1	2053	504	257	231	48	31	18	10	184	26	290	17	3	19	35	.352	0	12	4.44

RUPPERT JONES

Bats Left-handed, Throws Left-handed — Turns Age 32 in 1987, Born 03/12/55

Year	Team	League	G	AB	H	2B	3B	HR	(Hm	Rd)	TB	R	RBI	TBB	IBB	SO	HBP	SH	SF	SB	CS	SB%	GIDP	AVE	OBP	SLG
1976	Kansas City	A	28	51	11	1	1	1	(0	1)	17	9	7	3	0	16	0	0	0	0	2	.00	0	.216	.259	.333
1977	Seattle	A	160	597	157	26	8	24	(17	7)	271	85	76	55	3	120	2	3	6	13	9	.59	7	.263	.324	.454
1978	Seattle	A	129	472	111	24	3	6	(4	2)	159	48	46	55	2	85	0	8	5	22	6	.79	15	.235	.312	.337
1979	Seattle	A	162	622	166	29	9	21	(17	4)	276	109	78	85	4	78	3	2	4	33	12	.73	19	.267	.356	.444
1980	New York	A	83	328	73	11	3	9	(5	4)	117	38	42	34	3	50	3	5	3	18	8	.69	5	.223	.299	.357
1981	San Diego	N	105	397	99	34	1	4	(2	2)	147	53	39	43	2	66	0	4	7	7	9	.44	7	.249	.318	.370
1982	San Diego	N	116	424	120	20	2	12	(6	6)	180	69	61	62	11	90	1	3	3	18	15	.55	4	.283	.373	.425
1983	San Diego	N	133	335	78	12	3	12	(5	7)	132	42	49	35	4	58	0	2	0	11	11	.50	8	.233	.305	.394
1984	Detroit	A	79	215	61	12	1	12	(6	6)	111	26	37	21	0	47	0	0	1	2	4	.33	5	.284	.346	.516
1985	California	A	125	389	90	17	2	21	(10	11)	174	66	67	57	2	82	0	8	2	7	4	.64	5	.231	.328	.447
1986	California	A	126	393	90	21	3	17	(10	7)	168	73	49	64	5	87	3	7	3	10	3	.77	8	.229	.339	.427
11 YEARS	—		1246	4223	1056	207	36	139	(82	57)	1752	618	551	514	36	779	12	42	34	141	83	.63	83	.250	.331	.415

WALLY JOYNER

Bats Left-handed, Throws Left-handed — Turns Age 25 in 1987, Born 06/16/62

Year	Team	League	G	AB	H	2B	3B	HR	(Hm	Rd)	TB	R	RBI	TBB	IBB	SO	HBP	SH	SF	SB	CS	SB%	GIDP	AVE	OBP	SLG
1986	California	A	154	593	172	27	3	22	(11	11)	271	82	100	57	8	58	2	10	12	5	2	.71	11	.290	.348	.457

BOB KEARNEY

Bats Right-handed, Throws Right-handed — Turns Age 31 in 1987, Born 10/03/56

Year	Team	League	G	AB	H	2B	3B	HR	(Hm	Rd)	TB	R	RBI	TBB	IBB	SO	HBP	SH	SF	SB	CS	SB%	GIDP	AVE	OBP	SLG
1979	San Francisco	N	2	0	0	0	0	0	(0	0)	0	0	0	1	0	0	0	0	0	0	0	.00	0	.000	1.000	.000
1981	Oakland	A	1	0	0	0	0	0	(0	0)	0	0	0	0	0	0	0	0	0	0	0	.00	0	.000	.000	.000
1982	Oakland	A	22	71	12	3	0	0	(0	0)	15	7	5	3	0	10	2	0	2	0	0	.00	1	.169	.218	.211
1983	Oakland	A	108	298	76	11	0	8	(4	4)	111	33	32	21	1	50	4	4	1	1	4	.20	11	.255	.312	.372
1984	Seattle	A	133	431	97	24	1	7	(6	1)	144	39	43	18	0	72	2	9	4	7	5	.58	7	.225	.257	.334
1985	Seattle	A	108	305	74	14	1	6	(2	4)	108	24	27	11	1	59	4	1	1	1	1	.50	7	.243	.277	.354
1986	Seattle	A	81	204	49	10	0	6	(4	2)	77	23	25	12	1	35	0	9	1	0	2	.00	6	.240	.281	.377
7 YEARS			455	1309	308	62	2	27	(16	11)	455	126	132	66	3	226	12	27	9	9	12	.43	32	.235	.277	.348

TERRY KENNEDY

Bats Left-handed, Throws Right-handed — Turns Age 31 in 1987, Born 06/04/56

Year	Team	League	G	AB	H	2B	3B	HR	(Hm	Rd)	TB	R	RBI	TBB	IBB	SO	HBP	SH	SF	SB	CS	SB%	GIDP	AVE	OBP	SLG
1978	St Louis	N	10	29	5	0	0	0	(0	0)	5	0	2	4	2	3	0	0	0	0	0	.00	2	.172	.273	.172
1979	St Louis	N	33	109	31	7	0	2	(2	0)	44	11	17	6	2	20	0	0	1	0	0	.00	2	.284	.319	.404
1980	St Louis	N	84	248	63	12	3	4	(1	3)	93	28	34	28	3	34	0	1	4	0	0	.00	9	.254	.325	.375
1981	San Diego	N	101	382	115	24	1	2	(1	1)	147	32	41	22	6	53	2	4	2	0	2	.00	7	.301	.341	.385
1982	San Diego	N	153	562	166	42	1	21	(10	11)	273	75	97	26	9	91	5	3	8	1	0	1.00	10	.295	.328	.486
1983	San Diego	N	149	549	156	27	2	17	(7	10)	238	47	98	51	15	89	2	1	9	1	3	.25	10	.284	.342	.434
1984	San Diego	N	148	530	127	16	1	14	(8	6)	187	54	57	33	8	99	2	0	5	1	2	.33	16	.240	.284	.353
1985	San Diego	N	143	532	139	27	1	10	(7	3)	198	54	74	31	10	102	0	0	2	0	0	.00	19	.261	.301	.372
1986	San Diego	N	141	432	114	22	1	12	(7	5)	174	46	57	37	7	74	2	4	1	0	3	.00	10	.264	.324	.403
9 YEARS			962	3373	916	177	10	82	(43	39)	1359	347	477	238	62	565	13	13	32	3	10	.23	82	.272	.319	.403

MATT KEOUGH

Pitches Right-handed, Bats Right-handed — Turns Age 32 in 1987, Born 07/03/55

Year	Team	League	G	GS	CG	GF	IP	BFP	H	R	ER	HR	SH	SF	HB	TBB	IBB	SO	WP	Bk	W	L	Pct	ShO	Sv	ERA
1977	Oakland	A	7	6	0	0	43	183	39	25	23	4	1	1	1	22	0	23	0	0	1	3	.250	0	0	4.81
1978	Oakland	A	32	32	6	0	197	837	178	90	71	9	7	3	4	85	2	108	12	3	8	15	.348	0	0	3.24
1979	Oakland	A	30	28	7	2	177	800	220	115	99	18	7	9	2	78	2	95	13	0	2	17	.105	1	0	5.03
1980	Oakland	A	34	32	20	0	250	1041	218	94	81	24	12	6	5	94	3	121	13	2	16	13	.552	2	0	2.92
1981	Oakland	A	19	19	10	0	140	579	125	56	53	11	8	2	0	45	0	60	5	2	10	6	.625	2	0	3.41
1982	Oakland	A	34	34	10	0	209.1	946	233	144	133	38	10	9	1	101	5	75	10	3	11	18	.379	0	0	5.72
1983	2 Teams		26	16	0	3	99.2	456	109	71	59	19	2	2	3	51	1	54	3	1	5	7	.417	0	0	5.33
1985	St Louis	N	4	1	0	0	10	43	10	5	5	0	2	0	1	4	1	10	0	0	0	1	.000	0	0	4.50
1986	2 Teams		29	7	0	5	64	272	58	31	28	3	1	2	1	30	4	44	6	2	5	4	.556	0	0	3.94
9 YEARS			215	175	53	10	1190	5157	1190	631	552	132	52	34	23	510	18	590	62	13	58	84	.408	7	0	4.17
1983	New York	A	12	12	0	0	55.2	246	59	42	32	12	1	1	2	20	0	26	1	0	3	4	.429	0	0	5.17
1983	Oakland	A	14	4	0	3	44	210	50	29	27	7	1	2	0	31	1	28	2	1	2	3	.400	0	0	5.52
1986	Chicago	N	19	2	0	3	29	129	36	17	16	4	2	0	1	12	2	19	4	2	2	2	.500	0	0	4.97
1986	Houston	N	10	5	0	2	35	143	22	14	12	1	1	1	1	18	2	25	2	0	3	2	.600	0	0	3.09

CHARLIE KERFELD

Pitches Right-handed, Bats Right-handed   Turns Age 24 in 1987, Born 09/28/63

			HOW MUCH HE PITCHED						WHAT HE GAVE UP										THE RESULTS					
Year	Team	League	G	GS	CG	GF	IP	BFP	H	R	ER	HR	SH	SF	HB	TBB	IBB	SO	WP	Bk	W	L	Pct	ShO	Sv	ERA
1985	Houston	N	11	6	0	2	44.1	193	44	22	20	2	1	3	0	25	2	30	1	0	4	2	.667	0	0	4.06
1986	Houston	N	61	0	0	29	93.2	390	71	32	27	5	6	7	2	42	3	77	7	2	11	2	.846	0	7	2.59
2 YEARS			72	6	0	31	138	583	115	54	47	7	7	10	2	67	5	107	8	2	15	4	.789	0	7	3.07

JIMMY KEY

Pitches Left-handed, Bats Right-handed   Turns Age 26 in 1987, Born 04/22/61

			HOW MUCH HE PITCHED						WHAT HE GAVE UP										THE RESULTS					
Year	Team	League	G	GS	CG	GF	IP	BFP	H	R	ER	HR	SH	SF	HB	TBB	IBB	SO	WP	Bk	W	L	Pct	ShO	Sv	ERA
1984	Toronto	A	63	0	0	24	62	285	70	37	32	8	5	2	1	32	8	44	3	1	4	5	.444	0	10	4.65
1985	Toronto	A	35	32	3	0	212.2	856	188	77	71	22	5	5	2	50	1	85	6	1	14	6	.700	0	0	3.00
1986	Toronto	A	36	35	4	0	232	959	222	98	92	24	10	6	3	74	1	141	3	0	14	11	.560	2	0	3.57
3 YEARS			134	67	7	24	506.2	2100	480	212	195	54	20	13	6	156	10	270	12	2	32	22	.593	2	10	3.46

SAMMY KHALIFA

Bats Right-handed, Throws Right-handed   Turns Age 24 in 1987, Born 12/05/63

						BATTING								BASERUNNING		PERCENTAGES	
Year	Team	League	G	AB	H	2B	3B	HR	(Hm | Rd)	TB	R	RBI	TBB	IBB	SO	HBP	SH	SF	SB	CS	SB%	GIDP	AVE	OBP	SLG
1985	Pittsburgh	N	95	320	76	14	3	2	(1 | 1)	102	30	31	34	8	56	0	9	4	5	2	.71	9	.238	.307	.319
1986	Pittsburgh	N	64	151	28	6	0	0	(0 | 0)	34	8	4	19	6	28	0	3	0	0	2	.00	5	.185	.276	.225
2 YEARS			159	471	104	20	3	2	(1 | 1)	136	38	35	53	14	84	0	12	4	5	4	.56	14	.221	.297	.289

ERIC KING

Pitches Right-handed, Bats Right-handed   Turns Age 23 in 1987, Born 04/10/64

			HOW MUCH HE PITCHED						WHAT HE GAVE UP										THE RESULTS					
Year	Team	League	G	GS	CG	GF	IP	BFP	H	R	ER	HR	SH	SF	HB	TBB	IBB	SO	WP	Bk	W	L	Pct	ShO	Sv	ERA
1986	Detroit	A	33	16	3	9	138.1	579	108	54	54	11	6	1	8	63	3	79	4	3	11	4	.733	1	3	3.51

MIKE KINGERY

Bats Left-handed, Throws Left-handed   Turns Age 26 in 1987, Born 03/29/61

						BATTING								BASERUNNING		PERCENTAGES	
Year	Team	League	G	AB	H	2B	3B	HR	(Hm | Rd)	TB	R	RBI	TBB	IBB	SO	HBP	SH	SF	SB	CS	SB%	GIDP	AVE	OBP	SLG
1986	Kansas City	A	62	209	54	8	5	3	(1 | 2)	81	25	14	12	2	30	0	0	2	7	3	.70	4	.258	.296	.388

DAVE KINGMAN

Bats Right-handed, Throws Right-handed   Turns Age 39 in 1987, Born 12/21/48

						BATTING								BASERUNNING		PERCENTAGES	
Year	Team	League	G	AB	H	2B	3B	HR	(Hm | Rd)	TB	R	RBI	TBB	IBB	SO	HBP	SH	SF	SB	CS	SB%	GIDP	AVE	OBP	SLG
1971	San Francisco	N	41	115	32	10	2	6	(3 | 3)	64	17	24	9	0	35	1	0	3	5	0	1.00	2	.278	.328	.557
1972	San Francisco	N	135	472	106	17	4	29	(17 | 12)	218	65	83	51	2	140	4	0	4	16	6	.73	9	.225	.303	.462
1973	San Francisco	N	112	305	62	10	1	24	(0 | 0)	146	54	55	41	0	122	0	0	0	8	0	1.00	0	.203	.298	.479
1974	San Francisco	N	121	350	78	18	2	18	(12 | 6)	154	41	55	37	2	125	3	2	1	8	8	.50	8	.223	.302	.440
1975	New York	N	134	502	116	22	1	36	(14 | 22)	248	65	88	34	5	153	4	1	2	7	5	.58	13	.231	.284	.494
1976	New York	N	123	474	113	14	1	37	(16 | 21)	240	70	86	28	4	135	5	0	3	7	4	.64	11	.238	.286	.506
1977	4 Teams		132	439	97	20	0	26	(10 | 16)	195	47	78	28	4	143	7	3	4	5	6	.45	6	.221	.276	.444
1978	Chicago	N	119	395	105	17	4	28	(18 | 10)	214	65	79	39	8	111	6	2	6	3	4	.43	3	.266	.336	.542
1979	Chicago	N	145	532	153	19	5	48	(25 | 23)	326	97	115	45	7	131	4	0	8	2	2	.50	7	.288	.343	.613
1980	Chicago	N	81	255	71	8	0	18	(6 | 12)	133	31	57	21	3	44	0	0	4	2	2	.50	10	.278	.329	.522
1981	New York	N	100	353	78	11	3	22	(11 | 11)	161	40	59	55	5	105	1	1	2	6	0	1.00	9	.221	.326	.456
1982	New York	N	149	535	109	9	1	37	(19 | 18)	231	80	99	59	9	156	4	3	6	2	1	.67	11	.204	.285	.432
1983	New York	N	100	248	49	7	0	13	(8 | 5)	95	25	29	22	1	57	1	1	1	2	1	.67	2	.198	.265	.383
1984	Oakland	A	147	549	147	23	1	35	(19 | 16)	277	68	118	44	8	119	6	0	14	2	1	.67	7	.268	.321	.505
1985	Oakland	A	158	592	141	16	0	30	(14 | 16)	247	66	91	62	6	114	2	2	8	3	2	.60	17	.238	.309	.417
1986	Oakland	A	144	561	118	19	0	35	(15 | 20)	242	70	94	33	3	126	3	0	7	3	3	.50	16	.210	.255	.431
16 YEARS			1941	6677	1575	240	25	442	(207 | 211)	3191	901	1210	608	69	1816	51	15	73	85	44	.66	131	.236	.302	.478
1977	California	A	10	36	7	2	0	2	(0 | 2)	15	4	4	1	0	16	1	1	0	0	0	.00	0	.194	.237	.417
1977	New York	A	8	24	6	2	0	4	(0 | 4)	20	5	7	2	0	13	1	0	0	0	1	.00	0	.250	.333	.833
1977	New York	N	58	211	44	7	0	9	(5 | 4)	78	22	28	13	3	66	3	0	1	3	2	.60	3	.209	.263	.370
1977	San Diego	N	56	168	40	9	0	11	(5 | 6)	82	16	39	12	1	48	2	2	3	2	3	.40	3	.238	.292	.488

BOB KIPPER

Pitches Left-handed, Bats Right-handed

Turns Age 23 in 1987, Born 07/08/64

			HOW MUCH HE PITCHED						WHAT HE GAVE UP											THE RESULTS					
Year	Team	League	G	GS	CG	GF	IP	BFP	H	R	ER	HR	SH	SF	HB	TBB	IBB	SO	WP	Bk	W	L	Pct	ShO	Sv	ERA
1985	2 Teams		7	5	0	1	28	124	28	24	22	5	1	3	0	10	0	13	0	0	1	3	.250	0	0	7.07
1986	Pittsburgh	N	20	19	0	1	114	496	123	60	51	17	3	3	2	34	3	81	3	3	6	8	.429	0	0	4.03
2 YEARS			27	24	0	2	142	620	151	84	73	22	4	6	2	44	3	94	3	3	7	11	.389	0	0	4.63
1985	California	A	2	1	0	0	3.1	20	7	8	8	1	0	2	0	3	0	0	0	0	0	1	.000	0	0	21.60
1985	Pittsburgh	N	5	4	0	1	24.2	104	21	16	14	4	1	1	0	7	0	13	0	0	1	2	.333	0	0	5.11

RON KITTLE

Bats Right-handed, Throws Right-handed

Turns Age 29 in 1987, Born 01/05/58

					BATTING														BASERUNNING				PERCENTAGES		
Year	Team	League	G	AB	H	2B	3B	HR	(Hm	Rd)	TB	R	RBI	TBB	IBB	SO	HBP	SH	SF	SB	CS	SB%	GIDP	AVE	OBP	SLG
1982	Chicago	A	20	29	7	2	0	1	(0	1)	12	3	7	3	0	12	0	0	0	0	0	.00	0	.241	.313	.414
1983	Chicago	A	145	520	132	19	3	35	(18	17)	262	75	100	39	8	150	8	0	3	8	3	.73	10	.254	.314	.504
1984	Chicago	A	139	466	100	15	0	32	(17	15)	211	67	74	49	5	137	6	0	4	3	6	.33	7	.215	.295	.453
1985	Chicago	A	116	379	87	12	0	26	(12	14)	177	51	58	31	1	92	5	0	2	1	4	.20	12	.230	.295	.467
1986	2 Teams		116	376	82	13	0	21	(6	15)	158	42	60	35	1	110	3	0	8	4	1	.80	10	.218	.284	.420
5 YEARS			536	1770	408	61	3	115	(53	62)	820	238	299	157	15	501	22	0	17	16	14	.53	39	.231	.299	.463
1986	Chicago	A	86	296	63	11	0	17	(5	12)	125	34	48	28	0	87	3	0	6	2	1	.67	10	.213	.282	.422
1986	New York	A	30	80	19	2	0	4	(1	3)	33	8	12	7	1	23	0	0	2	2	0	1.00	0	.238	.292	.413

BOB KNEPPER

Pitches Left-handed, Bats Left-handed

Turns Age 33 in 1987, Born 05/25/54

			HOW MUCH HE PITCHED						WHAT HE GAVE UP											THE RESULTS					
Year	Team	League	G	GS	CG	GF	IP	BFP	H	R	ER	HR	SH	SF	HB	TBB	IBB	SO	WP	Bk	W	L	Pct	ShO	Sv	ERA
1976	San Francisco	N	4	4	0	0	25	104	26	9	9	0	3	0	0	7	1	11	2	0	1	2	.333	0	0	3.24
1977	San Francisco	N	27	27	6	0	166	710	151	73	62	14	7	4	3	72	2	100	6	0	11	9	.550	2	0	3.36
1978	San Francisco	N	36	35	16	0	260	1062	218	85	76	10	11	9	4	85	11	147	6	0	17	11	.607	6	0	2.63
1979	San Francisco	N	34	34	6	0	207	926	241	117	107	30	10	3	3	77	8	123	6	1	9	12	.429	2	0	4.65
1980	San Francisco	N	35	33	8	1	215	943	242	114	98	15	9	5	4	61	10	103	2	1	9	16	.360	1	0	4.10
1981	Houston	N	22	22	6	0	157	617	128	41	38	5	6	3	4	38	1	75	0	0	9	5	.643	5	0	2.18
1982	Houston	N	33	29	4	1	180	770	193	100	89	14	6	6	3	60	4	108	8	0	5	15	.250	0	1	4.45
1983	Houston	N	35	29	4	2	203	867	202	93	72	12	9	8	4	71	3	125	3	2	6	13	.316	3	0	3.19
1984	Houston	N	35	34	11	0	233.2	954	223	93	83	26	7	4	1	55	5	140	2	0	15	10	.600	3	0	3.20
1985	Houston	N	37	37	4	0	241	1016	253	119	95	21	15	9	3	54	5	131	4	0	15	13	.536	0	0	3.55
1986	Houston	N	40	38	8	1	258	1053	232	100	90	19	22	5	4	62	13	143	5	0	17	12	.586	5	0	3.14
11 YEARS			338	322	73	6	2145.2	9022	2109	944	819	166	105	56	37	642	63	1206	44	4	114	118	.491	27	1	3.44

RAY KNIGHT

Bats Right-handed, Throws Right-handed

Turns Age 35 in 1987, Born 12/28/52

					BATTING														BASERUNNING				PERCENTAGES		
Year	Team	League	G	AB	H	2B	3B	HR	(Hm	Rd)	TB	R	RBI	TBB	IBB	SO	HBP	SH	SF	SB	CS	SB%	GIDP	AVE	OBP	SLG
1974	Cincinnati	N	14	11	2	1	0	0	(0	0)	3	1	2	1	0	2	0	0	0	0	0	.00	1	.182	.250	.273
1977	Cincinnati	N	80	92	24	5	1	1	(0	1)	34	8	13	9	1	16	0	1	1	1	1	.50	0	.261	.324	.370
1978	Cincinnati	N	83	65	13	3	0	1	(0	0)	19	7	4	3	0	13	0	2	6	0	0	.00	4	.200	.216	.292
1979	Cincinnati	N	150	551	175	37	4	10	(4	6)	250	64	79	38	4	57	3	4	8	4	4	.50	20	.318	.360	.454
1980	Cincinnati	N	162	618	163	39	7	14	(6	8)	258	71	78	36	9	62	4	5	4	1	2	.33	24	.264	.307	.417
1981	Cincinnati	N	106	386	100	23	1	6	(1	5)	143	43	34	33	3	51	4	3	3	2	4	.33	18	.259	.322	.370
1982	Houston	N	158	609	179	36	6	6	(0	6)	245	72	70	48	9	58	5	1	13	2	5	.29	16	.294	.344	.402
1983	Houston	N	145	507	154	36	4	9	(3	6)	225	43	70	42	9	62	4	3	11	0	3	.00	17	.304	.355	.444
1984	2 Teams		115	371	88	14	0	3	(2	1)	111	28	35	21	2	43	2	0	4	0	3	.00	5	.237	.279	.299
1985	New York	N	90	271	59	12	0	6	(4	2)	89	22	36	13	1	32	1	0	5	1	1	.50	17	.218	.252	.328
1986	New York	N	137	486	145	24	2	11	(7	4)	206	51	76	40	2	63	4	3	8	2	1	.67	19	.298	.351	.424
11 YEARS			1240	3967	1102	230	25	67	(27	39)	1583	410	497	284	40	459	27	22	63	13	24	.35	141	.278	.326	.399
1984	Houston	N	88	278	62	10	0	2	(1	1)	78	15	29	14	1	30	1	0	4	0	3	.00	4	.223	.259	.281
1984	New York	N	27	93	26	4	0	1	(1	0)	33	13	6	7	1	13	1	0	0	0	0	.00	1	.280	.337	.355

WAYNE KRENCHICKI

Bats Left-handed, Throws Right-handed

Turns Age 33 in 1987, Born 09/17/54

					BATTING														BASERUNNING				PERCENTAGES		
Year	Team	League	G	AB	H	2B	3B	HR	(Hm	Rd)	TB	R	RBI	TBB	IBB	SO	HBP	SH	SF	SB	CS	SB%	GIDP	AVE	OBP	SLG
1979	Baltimore	A	16	21	4	1	0	0	(0	0)	5	1	1	0	0	0	0	2	0	0	0	.00	1	.190	.190	.238
1980	Baltimore	A	9	14	2	0	0	0	(0	0)	2	1	0	1	0	3	0	0	0	0	0	.00	0	.143	.200	.143
1981	Baltimore	A	33	56	12	4	0	0	(0	0)	16	7	6	4	0	9	0	0	0	0	0	.00	1	.214	.267	.286
1982	Cincinnati	N	94	187	53	6	1	2	(0	2)	67	19	21	13	1	23	0	1	4	5	3	.63	3	.283	.324	.358
1983	2 Teams		110	210	58	9	0	1	(1	0)	70	24	27	19	2	31	2	2	3	0	0	.00	3	.276	.338	.333
1984	Cincinnati	N	97	181	54	9	2	6	(2	4)	85	18	22	19	3	23	0	0	4	0	1	.00	4	.298	.358	.470
1985	Cincinnati	N	90	173	47	9	0	4	(2	2)	68	16	25	28	4	20	0	2	0	0	0	.00	3	.272	.369	.393
1986	Montreal	N	101	221	53	6	2	2	(1	1)	69	21	23	22	3	32	0	2	4	2	2	.33	2	.240	.306	.312
8 YEARS			550	1063	283	44	5	15	(6	9)	382	107	124	106	13	141	2	9	15	7	8	.47	17	.266	.330	.359
1983	Detroit	A	59	133	37	7	0	1	(1	0)	47	18	16	11	0	27	1	2	2	0	0	.00	1	.278	.333	.353
1983	Cincinnati	N	51	77	21	2	0	0	(0	0)	23	6	11	8	2	4	1	0	1	0	0	.00	2	.273	.345	.299

JOHN KRUK

Bats Left-handed, Throws Left-handed

Turns Age 26 in 1987, Born 02/09/61

						BATTING															BASERUNNING				PERCENTAGES		
Year	Team	League	G	AB	H	2B	3B	HR	(Hm	Rd)	TB	R	RBI	TBB	IBB	SO	HBP	SH	SF		SB	CS	SB%	GIDP	AVE	OBP	SLG
1986	San Diego	N	122	278	86	16	2	4	(1	3)	118	33	38	45	0	58	0	2	2		2	4	.33	11	.309	.403	.424

MIKE KRUKOW

Pitches Right-handed, Bats Right-handed

Turns Age 35 in 1987, Born 01/21/52

			HOW MUCH HE PITCHED						WHAT HE GAVE UP											THE RESULTS						
Year	Team	League	G	GS	CG	GF	IP	BFP	H	R	ER	HR	SH	SF	HB	TBB	IBB	SO	WP	Bk	W	L	Pct	ShO	Sv	ERA
1976	Chicago	N	2	0	0	0	4	20	6	4	4	0	0	0	0	2	0	1	0	0	0	0	.000	0	0	9.00
1977	Chicago	N	34	33	1	0	172	767	195	96	84	16	5	3	3	61	8	106	6	4	8	14	.364	1	0	4.40
1978	Chicago	N	27	20	3	3	138	582	125	62	60	11	6	4	5	53	4	81	1	0	9	3	.750	0	0	3.91
1979	Chicago	N	28	28	0	0	165	722	172	84	77	13	9	4	3	81	12	119	5	1	9	9	.500	0	0	4.20
1980	Chicago	N	34	34	3	0	205	884	200	117	100	13	9	13	6	80	5	130	5	2	10	15	.400	0	0	4.39
1981	Chicago	N	25	25	2	0	144	622	146	68	59	11	7	6	2	55	6	101	8	1	9	9	.500	1	0	3.69
1982	Philadelphia	N	33	33	7	0	208	893	211	87	72	8	11	10	3	82	10	138	13	1	13	11	.542	2	0	3.12
1983	San Francisco	N	31	31	2	0	184.1	816	189	95	81	17	9	3	3	76	8	136	8	1	11	11	.500	1	0	3.95
1984	San Francisco	N	35	33	3	1	199.1	903	234	117	101	22	5	7	5	78	5	141	3	3	11	12	.478	1	1	4.56
1985	San Francisco	N	28	28	6	0	194.2	804	176	80	73	19	10	3	3	49	10	150	10	3	8	11	.421	1	0	3.37
1986	San Francisco	N	34	34	10	0	245	987	204	90	83	24	10	5	4	55	4	178	4	0	20	9	.690	2	0	3.05
11 YEARS			311	299	37	4	1859.1	8000	1858	900	794	154	81	58	39	672	72	1281	63	16	108	104	.509	10	1	3.84

RANDY KUTCHER

Bats Right-handed, Throws Right-handed

Turns Age 27 in 1987, Born 04/20/60

						BATTING															BASERUNNING				PERCENTAGES		
Year	Team	League	G	AB	H	2B	3B	HR	(Hm	Rd)	TB	R	RBI	TBB	IBB	SO	HBP	SH	SF		SB	CS	SB%	GIDP	AVE	OBP	SLG
1986	San Francisco	N	71	186	44	9	1	7	(5	2)	76	28	16	11	0	41	0	6	0		6	5	.55	3	.237	.279	.409

MIKE LACOSS

Pitches Right-handed, Bats Right-handed

Turns Age 31 in 1987, Born 05/30/56

			HOW MUCH HE PITCHED						WHAT HE GAVE UP											THE RESULTS						
Year	Team	League	G	GS	CG	GF	IP	BFP	H	R	ER	HR	SH	SF	HB	TBB	IBB	SO	WP	Bk	W	L	Pct	ShO	Sv	ERA
1978	Cincinnati	N	16	15	2	0	96	420	104	56	48	5	6	6	1	46	9	31	2	1	4	8	.333	1	0	4.50
1979	Cincinnati	N	35	32	6	0	206	868	202	92	80	13	12	6	2	79	8	73	3	3	14	8	.636	1	0	3.50
1980	Cincinnati	N	34	29	4	1	169	762	207	101	87	9	7	3	1	68	8	59	3	2	10	12	.455	2	0	4.63
1981	Cincinnati	N	20	13	1	3	78	354	102	55	53	7	4	5	1	30	4	22	1	0	4	7	.364	1	1	6.12
1982	Houston	N	41	8	0	11	115	488	107	41	37	3	5	0	4	54	6	51	5	1	6	6	.500	0	2	2.90
1983	Houston	N	38	17	2	6	138	590	142	81	68	10	6	6	2	56	11	53	9	1	5	7	.417	0	1	4.43
1984	Houston	N	39	18	2	6	132	565	132	64	59	3	3	2	0	55	5	86	9	1	7	5	.583	1	3	4.02
1985	Kansas City	A	21	0	0	7	40.2	193	49	25	23	2	3	0	0	29	6	26	2	0	1	1	.500	0	1	5.09
1986	San Francisco	N	37	31	4	1	204.1	842	179	99	81	14	16	3	6	70	8	86	5	5	10	13	.435	1	0	3.57
9 YEARS			281	163	21	35	1179	5082	1224	614	536	66	62	31	17	487	65	487	39	14	61	67	.477	7	6	4.09

LEE LACY

Bats Right-handed, Throws Right-handed

Turns Age 38 in 1987, Born 04/10/49

						BATTING															BASERUNNING				PERCENTAGES		
Year	Team	League	G	AB	H	2B	3B	HR	(Hm	Rd)	TB	R	RBI	TBB	IBB	SO	HBP	SH	SF		SB	CS	SB%	GIDP	AVE	OBP	SLG
1972	Los Angeles	N	60	243	63	7	3	0	(0	0)	76	34	12	19	0	37	0	3	1		5	3	.63	4	.259	.312	.313
1973	Los Angeles	N	57	135	28	2	0	0	(0	0)	30	14	8	15	1	34	0	0	0		2	3	.40	2	.207	.287	.222
1974	Los Angeles	N	48	78	22	6	0	0	(0	0)	28	13	8	2	0	14	0	1	2		2	0	1.00	3	.282	.293	.359
1975	Los Angeles	N	101	306	96	11	5	7	(4	3)	138	44	40	22	1	29	0	5	3		5	9	.36	10	.314	.356	.451
1976	2 Teams		103	338	91	11	3	3	(2	1)	117	42	34	22	3	25	1	4	2		3	4	.43	12	.269	.314	.346
1977	Los Angeles	N	75	169	45	7	0	6	(3	3)	70	28	21	10	0	21	0	0	1		4	0	1.00	3	.266	.306	.414
1978	Los Angeles	N	103	245	64	16	4	13	(10	3)	127	29	40	27	4	30	1	1	2		7	4	.64	4	.261	.335	.518
1979	Pittsburgh	N	84	182	45	9	3	5	(3	2)	75	17	15	22	2	36	1	0	3		6	1	.86	1	.247	.327	.412
1980	Pittsburgh	N	109	278	93	20	4	7	(4	3)	142	45	33	28	3	33	2	2	4		18	9	.67	3	.335	.394	.511
1981	Pittsburgh	N	78	213	57	11	4	2	(1	1)	82	31	10	11	2	29	1	1	0		24	3	.89	1	.268	.307	.385
1982	Pittsburgh	N	121	359	112	16	3	5	(2	3)	149	66	31	32	4	57	1	2	1		40	15	.73	7	.312	.369	.415
1983	Pittsburgh	N	108	288	87	12	3	4	(1	3)	117	40	13	22	2	36	0	3	0		31	13	.70	2	.302	.352	.406
1984	Pittsburgh	N	138	474	152	26	3	12	(6	6)	220	66	70	32	2	61	0	12	2		21	11	.66	10	.321	.362	.464
1985	Baltimore	A	121	492	144	22	4	9	(3	6)	201	69	48	39	0	95	2	1	6		10	3	.77	10	.293	.343	.409
1986	Baltimore	A	130	491	141	18	0	11	(5	6)	192	77	47	37	2	71	0	4	5		4	6	.40	12	.287	.334	.391
15 YEARS			1436	4291	1240	194	39	84	(44	40)	1764	615	430	340	26	608	9	39	32		182	84	.68	81	.289	.340	.411
1976	Atlanta	N	50	180	49	4	2	3	(2	1)	66	25	20	6	1	12	1	3	0		2	2	.50	5	.272	.299	.367
1976	Los Angeles	N	53	158	42	7	1	0	(0	0)	51	17	14	16	2	13	0	1	2		1	2	.33	7	.266	.330	.323

PETE LADD

Pitches Right-handed, Bats Right-handed

Turns Age 31 in 1987, Born 07/17/56

			HOW MUCH HE PITCHED						WHAT HE GAVE UP												THE RESULTS					
Year	Team	League	G	GS	CG	GF	IP	BFP	H	R	ER	HR	SH	SF	HB	TBB	IBB	SO	WP	Bk	W	L	Pct	ShO	Sv	ERA
1979	Houston	N	10	0	0	4	12	56	8	5	4	1	1	0	2	8	0	6	2	0	1	1	.500	0	0	3.00
1982	Milwaukee	A	16	0	0	12	18	75	16	8	8	5	1	1	0	6	3	12	1	0	1	3	.250	0	0	4.00
1983	Milwaukee	A	44	0	0	40	49.1	194	30	17	14	3	0	3	1	16	2	41	3	0	3	4	.429	0	25	2.55
1984	Milwaukee	A	54	1	0	37	91	397	94	58	53	16	1	4	1	38	6	75	2	0	4	9	.308	0	3	5.24
1985	Milwaukee	A	29	0	0	13	45.2	202	58	26	23	5	0	6	2	10	0	22	1	0	0	0	.000	0	2	4.53
1986	Seattle	A	52	0	0	33	70.2	294	69	33	30	10	0	6	3	18	3	53	2	0	8	6	.571	0	6	3.82
6 YEARS			205	1	0	139	286.2	1218	275	147	132	40	3	20	9	96	14	209	11	0	17	23	.425	0	39	4.14

DENNIS LAMP

Pitches Right-handed, Bats Right-handed

Turns Age 35 in 1987, Born 09/23/52

			HOW MUCH HE PITCHED						WHAT HE GAVE UP												THE RESULTS					
Year	Team	League	G	GS	CG	GF	IP	BFP	H	R	ER	HR	SH	SF	HB	TBB	IBB	SO	WP	Bk	W	L	Pct	ShO	Sv	ERA
1977	Chicago	N	11	3	0	4	30	137	43	21	21	3	1	1	2	8	4	12	0	1	0	2	.000	0	0	6.30
1978	Chicago	N	37	36	6	0	224	928	221	96	82	16	10	3	4	56	8	73	2	2	7	15	.318	3	0	3.29
1979	Chicago	N	38	32	6	3	200	843	223	96	78	14	9	5	5	46	9	86	1	0	11	10	.524	1	0	3.51
1980	Chicago	N	41	37	2	3	203	921	259	123	117	16	17	4	1	82	7	83	10	0	10	14	.417	1	0	5.19
1981	Chicago	A	27	10	3	5	127	514	103	41	34	4	5	0	1	43	1	71	4	1	7	6	.538	0	0	2.41
1982	Chicago	A	44	27	3	11	189.2	817	206	96	84	9	12	2	6	59	3	78	5	0	11	8	.579	2	5	3.99
1983	Chicago	A	49	5	1	31	116.1	483	123	52	48	6	2	1	4	29	3	44	0	0	7	7	.500	0	15	3.71
1984	Toronto	A	56	4	0	37	85	387	97	53	43	9	7	1	1	38	7	45	2	0	8	8	.500	0	9	4.55
1985	Toronto	A	53	1	0	11	105.2	426	96	42	39	7	5	6	1	27	3	68	5	0	11	0	1.000	0	2	3.32
1986	Toronto	A	40	2	0	11	73	329	93	50	41	5	4	1	0	23	6	30	2	0	2	6	.250	0	2	5.05
10 YEARS			396	157	21	116	1353.2	5785	1464	670	587	89	72	24	24	411	55	590	31	4	74	76	.493	7	33	3.90

KEN LANDREAUX

Bats Left-handed, Throws Right-handed

Turns Age 33 in 1987, Born 12/22/54

			BATTING																	BASERUNNING				PERCENTAGES		
Year	Team	League	G	AB	H	2B	3B	HR	(Hm	Rd)	TB	R	RBI	TBB	IBB	SO	HBP	SH	SF	SB	CS	SB%	GIDP	AVE	OBP	SLG
1977	California	A	23	76	19	5	1	0	(0	0)	26	6	5	5	1	15	0	0	0	1	1	.50	0	.250	.296	.342
1978	California	A	93	260	58	7	5	5	(4	1)	90	37	23	20	4	20	2	1	0	7	3	.70	5	.223	.284	.346
1979	Minnesota	A	151	564	172	27	5	15	(8	7)	254	81	83	37	4	57	4	10	8	10	3	.77	13	.305	.347	.450
1980	Minnesota	A	129	484	136	23	11	7	(4	3)	202	56	62	39	4	42	2	6	5	8	6	.57	13	.281	.334	.417
1981	Los Angeles	N	99	390	98	16	4	7	(3	4)	143	48	41	25	3	42	1	3	1	18	4	.82	6	.251	.297	.367
1982	Los Angeles	N	129	461	131	23	7	7	(1	6)	189	71	50	39	2	54	4	8	6	31	10	.76	9	.284	.341	.410
1983	Los Angeles	N	141	481	135	25	3	17	(10	7)	217	63	66	34	5	52	2	2	5	30	11	.73	9	.281	.328	.451
1984	Los Angeles	N	134	438	110	11	5	11	(5	6)	164	39	47	29	3	35	1	3	7	10	9	.53	7	.251	.295	.374
1985	Los Angeles	N	147	482	129	26	2	12	(2	10)	195	70	50	33	2	37	1	3	8	15	5	.75	3	.268	.311	.405
1986	Los Angeles	N	103	283	74	13	2	4	(1	3)	103	34	29	22	1	39	1	0	4	10	5	.67	5	.261	.313	.364
10 YEARS			1149	3919	1062	176	45	85	(38	47)	1583	505	456	283	31	393	18	36	43	140	57	.71	74	.271	.320	.404

TITO LANDRUM

Bats Right-handed, Throws Right-handed

Turns Age 33 in 1987, Born 10/25/54

			BATTING																	BASERUNNING				PERCENTAGES		
Year	Team	League	G	AB	H	2B	3B	HR	(Hm	Rd)	TB	R	RBI	TBB	IBB	SO	HBP	SH	SF	SB	CS	SB%	GIDP	AVE	OBP	SLG
1980	St Louis	N	35	77	19	2	2	0	(0	0)	25	6	7	6	0	17	1	0	1	3	2	.60	3	.247	.306	.325
1981	St Louis	N	81	119	31	5	4	0	(0	0)	44	13	10	6	0	14	1	5	2	4	2	.67	2	.261	.297	.370
1982	St Louis	N	79	72	20	3	0	2	(0	2)	29	12	14	8	0	18	1	3	0	0	1	.00	1	.278	.358	.403
1983	2 Teams		32	47	14	2	1	1	(0	1)	21	8	4	2	0	13	0	0	1	1	2	.33	1	.298	.320	.447
1984	St Louis	N	105	173	47	9	1	3	(2	1)	67	21	26	10	1	27	0	1	3	3	4	.43	8	.272	.306	.387
1985	St Louis	N	85	161	45	8	2	4	(2	2)	69	21	21	19	1	30	0	1	0	1	4	.20	5	.280	.356	.429
1986	St Louis	N	96	205	43	7	1	2	(2	0)	58	24	17	20	2	41	1	1	3	3	1	.75	5	.210	.279	.283
7 YEARS			513	854	219	36	11	12	(6	6)	313	105	99	71	4	160	4	11	10	15	16	.48	23	.256	.313	.367
1983	Baltimore	A	26	42	13	2	0	1	(0	1)	18	8	4	1	0	11	0	0	0	0	2	.00	1	.310	.318	.429
1983	St Louis	N	6	5	1	0	1	0	(0	0)		1	0	1	0	2	0	0	0	1	0	1.00	0	.200	.333	.600

RICK LANGFORD

Pitches Right-handed, Bats Right-handed

Turns Age 35 in 1987, Born 03/20/52

			HOW MUCH HE PITCHED						WHAT HE GAVE UP												THE RESULTS					
Year	Team	League	G	GS	CG	GF	IP	BFP	H	R	ER	HR	SH	SF	HB	TBB	IBB	SO	WP	Bk	W	L	Pct	ShO	Sv	ERA
1976	Pittsburgh	N	12	1	0	5	23	105	27	17	16	2	2	1	0	14	0	17	0	1	0	1	.000	0	0	6.26
1977	Oakland	A	37	31	6	2	208	901	223	107	93	18	3	6	2	73	3	141	4	1	8	19	.296	1	0	4.02
1978	Oakland	A	37	24	4	5	176	741	169	77	67	15	7	7	3	56	8	92	2	0	7	13	.350	2	0	3.43
1979	Oakland	A	34	29	14	0	219	934	233	114	104	22	12	9	4	57	6	101	16	1	12	16	.429	1	0	4.27
1980	Oakland	A	35	33	28	2	290	1166	276	119	105	29	5	12	1	64	6	102	1	0	19	12	.613	2	0	3.26
1981	Oakland	A	24	24	18	0	195	823	190	81	65	14	8	3	2	58	2	84	1	0	12	10	.545	2	0	3.00
1982	Oakland	A	32	31	15	1	237.1	1006	265	121	111	33	6	5	2	49	1	79	4	0	11	16	.407	2	0	4.21
1983	Oakland	A	7	7	0	0	20	112	43	28	27	4	1	3	2	10	1	2	0	0	0	4	.000	0	0	12.15
1984	Oakland	A	3	1	0	0	8.2	43	15	8	8	2	0	0	0	7	0	6	0	0	0	0	.000	0	0	8.31
1985	Oakland	A	23	3	0	7	59	247	60	24	23	8	2	0	0	15	2	21	2	0	1	3	.375	0	0	3.51
1986	Oakland	A	16	11	0	1	55	251	69	49	45	13	0	2	1	18	0	30	2	0	1	10	.091	0	0	7.36
11 YEARS			260	195	85	24	1491	6329	1570	745	664	160	46	53	18	416	29	671	38	4	73	106	.408	10	0	4.01

MARK LANGSTON

Pitches Left-handed, Bats Right-handed

Turns Age 27 in 1987, Born 08/20/60

			HOW MUCH HE PITCHED						WHAT HE GAVE UP												THE RESULTS					
Year	Team	League	G	GS	CG	GF	IP	BFP	H	R	ER	HR	SH	SF	HB	TBB	IBB	SO	WP	Bk	W	L	Pct	ShO	Sv	ERA
1984	Seattle	A	35	33	5	0	225	965	188	99	85	16	13	7	8	118	5	204	4	2	17	10	.630	2	0	3.40
1985	Seattle	A	24	24	2	0	126.2	577	122	85	77	22	3	2	2	91	2	72	5	3	7	14	.333	0	0	5.47
1986	Seattle	A	37	36	9	1	239.1	1057	234	142	129	30	5	8	4	123	1	245	10	3	12	14	.462	0	0	4.85
3 YEARS			96	93	16	1	591	2599	544	326	291	68	21	17	14	332	8	521	17	8	36	38	.486	2	0	4.43

CARNEY LANSFORD

Bats Right-handed, Throws Right-handed

Turns Age 30 in 1987, Born 02/07/57

			BATTING																	BASERUNNING				PERCENTAGES		
Year	Team	League	G	AB	H	2B	3B	HR	Hm	Rd	TB	R	RBI	TBB	IBB	SO	HBP	SH	SF	SB	CS	SB%	GIDP	AVE	OBP	SLG
1978	California	A	121	453	133	23	2	8	4	4	184	63	52	31	2	67	4	5	7	20	9	.69	4	.294	.339	.406
1979	California	A	157	654	188	30	5	19	5	14	285	114	79	39	2	115	3	12	4	20	8	.71	16	.287	.329	.436
1980	California	A	151	602	157	27	3	15	8	7	235	87	80	50	2	93	0	7	11	14	5	.74	12	.261	.312	.390
1981	Boston	A	102	399	134	23	3	4	1	3	175	61	52	34	3	28	2	1	2	15	10	.60	6	.336	.389	.439
1982	Boston	A	128	482	145	28	4	11	4	7	214	65	63	46	2	48	2	1	8	9	4	.69	15	.301	.359	.444
1983	Oakland	A	80	299	92	16	2	10	4	6	142	43	45	22	4	33	3	0	4	3	8	.27	8	.308	.357	.475
1984	Oakland	A	151	597	179	31	5	14	7	7	262	70	74	40	6	62	3	2	9	9	3	.75	12	.300	.342	.439
1985	Oakland	A	98	401	111	18	2	13	7	6	172	51	46	18	1	27	4	4	5	2	3	.40	7	.277	.311	.429
1986	Oakland	A	151	591	168	16	4	19	10	9	249	80	72	39	2	51	5	1	4	16	7	.70	16	.284	.332	.421
9 YEARS			1139	4478	1307	212	30	113	50	63	1918	634	563	319	24	524	26	33	54	108	57	.65	95	.292	.339	.428

DAVE LAPOINT

Pitches Left-handed, Bats Left-handed

Turns Age 28 in 1987, Born 07/29/59

			HOW MUCH HE PITCHED						WHAT HE GAVE UP												THE RESULTS					
Year	Team	League	G	GS	CG	GF	IP	BFP	H	R	ER	HR	SH	SF	HB	TBB	IBB	SO	WP	Bk	W	L	Pct	ShO	Sv	ERA
1980	Milwaukee	A	5	3	0	1	15	75	17	14	10	2	2	0		13	1	5	0	1	1	0	1.000	0	1	6.00
1981	St Louis	N	3	2	0	0	11	45	12	5	5	1	1	0		2	0	4	0	0	1	0	1.000	0	0	4.09
1982	St Louis	N	42	21	0	6	152.2	656	170	63	58	8	9	5	3	52	8	81	4	2	9	3	.750	0	0	3.42
1983	St Louis	N	37	29	1	1	191.1	832	191	92	84	12	17	11	4	84	7	113	11	4	12	9	.571	0	0	3.95
1984	St Louis	N	33	33	2	0	193	827	205	94	85	9	8	3	1	77	8	130	15	3	12	10	.545	1	0	3.96
1985	San Francisco	N	31	31	2	0	206.2	886	215	99	82	18	7	5	0	74	6	122	10	0	7	17	.292	1	0	3.57
1986	2 Teams		40	12	0	6	129	588	152	86	72	19	9	2	1	56	7	77	3	5	4	10	.286	0	0	5.02
7 YEARS			191	131	5	14	898.2	3909	962	453	396	69	53	28	10	358	37	532	43	15	46	49	.484	2	1	3.97
1986	Detroit	A	16	8	0	2	67.2	314	85	49	43	11	4	1	0	32	3	36	2	1	3	6	.333	0	0	5.72
1986	San Diego	N	24	4	0	4	61.1	274	67	37	29	8	5	1	1	24	4	41	1	4	1	4	.200	0	0	4.26

BARRY LARKIN

Bats Right-handed, Throws Right-handed

Turns Age 23 in 1987, Born 04/28/64

			BATTING																	BASERUNNING				PERCENTAGES		
Year	Team	League	G	AB	H	2B	3B	HR	Hm	Rd	TB	R	RBI	TBB	IBB	SO	HBP	SH	SF	SB	CS	SB%	GIDP	AVE	OBP	SLG
1986	Cincinnati	N	41	159	45	4	3	3	3	0	64	27	19	9	1	21	0	0	1	8	0	1.00	2	.283	.320	.403

TIM LAUDNER

Bats Right-handed, Throws Right-handed

Turns Age 29 in 1987, Born 06/07/58

			BATTING																	BASERUNNING				PERCENTAGES		
Year	Team	League	G	AB	H	2B	3B	HR	Hm	Rd	TB	R	RBI	TBB	IBB	SO	HBP	SH	SF	SB	CS	SB%	GIDP	AVE	OBP	SLG
1981	Minnesota	A	14	43	7	2	0	2	2	0	15	4	5	3	1	17	1	0	0	0	0	.00	0	.163	.234	.349
1982	Minnesota	A	93	306	78	19	1	7	2	5	120	37	33	34	2	74	0	2	1	0	2	.00	6	.255	.328	.392
1983	Minnesota	A	62	168	31	9	0	6	2	4	58	20	18	15	0	49	0	0	1	0	0	.00	2	.185	.250	.345
1984	Minnesota	A	87	262	54	16	1	10	3	7	102	31	35	18	0	78	1	1	2	0	4	.00	4	.206	.258	.389
1985	Minnesota	A	72	164	39	5	0	7	5	2	65	16	19	12	0	45	1	4	1	0	1	.00	2	.238	.292	.396
1986	Minnesota	A	76	193	47	10	0	10	9	1	87	21	29	24	0	56	3	1	2	1	0	1.00	5	.244	.333	.451
6 YEARS			404	1136	256	61	2	42	23	19	447	129	139	106	3	319	6	8	7	1	3	.25	19	.225	.293	.393

MIKE LAVALLIERE

Bats Left-handed, Throws Right-handed

Turns Age 27 in 1987, Born 08/18/60

			BATTING																	BASERUNNING				PERCENTAGES		
Year	Team	League	G	AB	H	2B	3B	HR	Hm	Rd	TB	R	RBI	TBB	IBB	SO	HBP	SH	SF	SB	CS	SB%	GIDP	AVE	OBP	SLG
1984	Philadelphia	N	6	7	0	0	0	0	0	0	0	0	2	2	0	2	0	0	0	0	0	.00	2	.000	.222	.000
1985	St Louis	N	12	34	5	1	0	0	0	0	6	2	6	7	0	3	0	0	3	0	0	.00	2	.147	.273	.176
1986	St Louis	N	110	303	71	10	2	3	1	2	94	18	30	36	5	37	1	0	10	0	1	.00	7	.234	.318	.310
3 YEARS			128	344	76	11	2	3	1	2	100	20	36	45	5	42	1	10	3	0	1	.00	9	.221	.310	.291

RUDY LAW

Bats Left-handed, Throws Left-handed

Turns Age 31 in 1987, Born 10/07/56

Year	Team	League	G	AB	H	2B	3B	HR	(Hm	Rd)	TB	R	RBI	TBB	IBB	SO	HBP	SH	SF	SB	CS	SB%	GIDP	AVE	OBP	SLG
1978	Los Angeles	N	11	12	3	0	0	0	(0	0)	3	2	1	1	0	2	0	0	0	3	1	.75	0	.250	.308	.250
1980	Los Angeles	N	128	388	101	5	4	1	(1	0)	117	55	23	23	1	27	3	3	1	40	13	.75	2	.260	.306	.302
1982	Chicago	A	121	336	107	15	8	3	(0	3)	147	55	32	23	0	41	0	3	1	36	10	.78	5	.318	.361	.438
1983	Chicago	A	141	501	142	20	7	3	(1	2)	185	95	34	42	2	36	2	4	2	77	12	.87	4	.283	.340	.369
1984	Chicago	A	136	487	122	14	7	6	(4	2)	168	68	37	39	6	42	3	4	1	29	17	.63	9	.251	.309	.345
1985	Chicago	A	125	390	101	21	6	4	(4	0)	146	62	36	27	0	40	3	6	1	29	6	.83	4	.259	.311	.374
1986	Kansas City	A	87	307	80	26	5	1	(1	0)	119	42	36	29	0	22	2	2	1	14	6	.70	5	.261	.327	.388
7 YEARS			749	2421	656	101	37	18	(11	7)	885	379	199	184	9	210	13	22	7	228	65	.78	29	.271	.325	.366

VANCE LAW

Bats Right-handed, Throws Right-handed

Turns Age 31 in 1987, Born 10/01/56

Year	Team	League	G	AB	H	2B	3B	HR	(Hm	Rd)	TB	R	RBI	TBB	IBB	SO	HBP	SH	SF	SB	CS	SB%	GIDP	AVE	OBP	SLG
1980	Pittsburgh	N	25	74	17	2	2	0	(0	0)	23	11	3	3	0	7	0	1	0	2	0	1.00	2	.230	.260	.311
1981	Pittsburgh	N	30	67	9	0	1	0	(0	0)	11	1	3	2	0	15	0	1	1	1	1	.50	2	.134	.157	.164
1982	Chicago	A	114	359	101	20	1	5	(2	3)	138	40	54	26	1	46	1	7	5	4	2	.67	10	.281	.327	.384
1983	Chicago	A	145	408	99	21	5	4	(1	3)	142	55	42	51	1	56	1	6	5	3	1	.75	7	.243	.325	.348
1984	Chicago	A	151	481	121	18	2	17	(11	6)	194	60	59	41	2	75	1	6	4	4	1	.80	13	.252	.309	.403
1985	Montreal	N	147	519	138	30	6	10	(5	5)	210	75	52	86	0	96	2	8	6	6	5	.55	11	.266	.369	.405
1986	Montreal	N	112	360	81	17	2	5	(3	2)	117	37	44	37	1	66	1	2	2	3	5	.38	9	.225	.298	.325
7 YEARS			724	2268	566	108	19	41	(22	19)	835	279	257	246	5	361	6	31	23	23	15	.61	54	.250	.322	.368

RICK LEACH

Bats Left-handed, Throws Left-handed

Turns Age 30 in 1987, Born 05/04/57

Year	Team	League	G	AB	H	2B	3B	HR	(Hm	Rd)	TB	R	RBI	TBB	IBB	SO	HBP	SH	SF	SB	CS	SB%	GIDP	AVE	OBP	SLG
1981	Detroit	A	54	83	16	3	1	1	(0	0)	24	9	11	16	1	15	0	1	1	0	1	.00	5	.193	.320	.289
1982	Detroit	A	82	218	52	7	2	3	(0	0)	72	23	12	21	2	29	0	4	2	4	0	1.00	5	.239	.303	.330
1983	Detroit	A	99	242	60	17	0	3	(0	0)	86	22	26	19	1	21	1	0	0	2	2	.50	6	.248	.305	.355
1984	Toronto	A	65	88	23	6	2	0	(0	0)	33	11	7	8	0	14	0	0	1	0	0	.00	0	.261	.320	.375
1985	Toronto	A	16	35	7	0	1	0	(0	0)	9	2	1	3	1	9	0	0	0	0	0	.00	0	.200	.263	.257
1986	Toronto	A	110	246	76	14	1	5	(4	1)	107	35	39	13	3	24	0	0	7	0	0	.00	6	.309	.335	.435
6 YEARS			426	912	234	47	7	12	(4	1)	331	102	96	80	8	112	1	5	11	6	3	.67	22	.257	.314	.363

TIM LEARY

Pitches Right-handed, Bats Right-handed

Turns Age 29 in 1987, Born 12/23/58

			HOW MUCH HE PITCHED						WHAT HE GAVE UP										THE RESULTS					
Year	Team	League	G	GS	CG	GF	IP	BFP	H	R	ER	HR	SH	SF	HB	TBB	IBB	SO	WP	Bk	W	L	Pct	ShO	Sv	ERA
1981	New York	N	1	1	0	0	2	7	0	0	0	0	0	0	0	1	0	3	1	0	0	0	.000	0	0	0.00
1983	New York	N	2	2	1	0	10.2	53	15	10	4	0	1	1	0	4	0	9	0	1	1	1	.500	0	0	3.37
1984	New York	N	20	7	0	3	53.2	237	61	28	24	2	1	2	2	18	3	29	2	3	3	3	.500	0	0	4.02
1985	Milwaukee	A	5	5	0	0	33.1	146	40	18	15	5	2	0	1	8	0	29	1	0	1	4	.200	0	0	4.05
1986	Milwaukee	A	33	30	3	2	188.1	817	216	97	88	20	4	6	7	53	4	110	7	0	12	12	.500	2	0	4.21
5 YEARS			61	45	4	5	288	1260	332	153	131	27	8	9	10	84	7	180	11	4	17	20	.459	2	0	4.09

CRAIG LEFFERTS

Pitches Left-handed, Bats Left-handed

Turns Age 30 in 1987, Born 09/29/57

			HOW MUCH HE PITCHED						WHAT HE GAVE UP										THE RESULTS					
Year	Team	League	G	GS	CG	GF	IP	BFP	H	R	ER	HR	SH	SF	HB	TBB	IBB	SO	WP	Bk	W	L	Pct	ShO	Sv	ERA
1983	Chicago	N	56	5	0	10	89	367	80	35	31	13	7	0	2	29	3	60	2	0	3	4	.429	0	1	3.13
1984	San Diego	N	62	0	0	29	105.2	420	88	29	25	4	4	6	1	24	1	56	2	2	3	4	.429	0	10	2.13
1985	San Diego	N	60	0	0	24	83.1	345	75	34	31	7	7	1	0	30	4	48	2	0	7	6	.538	0	2	3.35
1986	San Diego	N	83	0	0	36	107.2	446	98	41	37	7	9	5	1	44	11	72	1	1	9	8	.529	0	4	3.09
4 YEARS			261	5	0	99	385.2	1578	341	139	124	31	27	12	4	127	19	236	7	3	22	22	.500	0	17	2.89

CHARLIE LEIBRANDT

Pitches Left-handed, Bats Right-handed

Turns Age 31 in 1987, Born 10/04/56

			HOW MUCH HE PITCHED						WHAT HE GAVE UP										THE RESULTS					
Year	Team	League	G	GS	CG	GF	IP	BFP	H	R	ER	HR	SH	SF	HB	TBB	IBB	SO	WP	Bk	W	L	Pct	ShO	Sv	ERA
1979	Cincinnati	N	3	0	0	1	4	16	2	2	0	0	1	0	2	0	1	0	0	0	0	0	.000	0	0	0.00
1980	Cincinnati	N	36	27	5	3	174	754	200	84	82	15	12	2	2	54	4	62	1	6	10	9	.526	2	0	4.24
1981	Cincinnati	N	7	4	1	0	30	128	28	12	12	0	4	2	0	15	2	9	0	0	1	1	.500	1	0	3.60
1982	Cincinnati	N	36	11	0	10	107.2	484	130	68	61	4	10	2	2	48	9	34	6	1	5	7	.417	0	0	5.10
1984	Kansas City	A	23	23	0	0	143.2	621	158	65	58	11	3	7	2	38	2	53	5	1	11	7	.611	0	0	3.63
1985	Kansas City	A	33	33	8	0	237.2	983	223	86	71	17	8	5	2	68	3	108	4	3	17	9	.654	3	0	2.69
1986	Kansas City	A	35	34	8	0	231.1	975	238	112	105	18	14	5	4	63	0	108	2	1	14	11	.560	1	0	4.09
7 YEARS			173	132	22	14	928.1	3961	979	429	389	65	51	24	13	288	20	375	18	12	58	44	.569	7	2	3.77

DAVID LEIPER

Pitches Left-handed, Bats Left-handed
Turns Age 35 in 1987, Born 06/18/52

			HOW MUCH HE PITCHED					WHAT HE GAVE UP												THE RESULTS					
Year	Team	League	G	GS	CG	GF	IP	BFP	H	R	ER	HR	SH	SF	HB	TBB	IBB	SO	WP	Bk	W	L	Pct	ShO	Sv	ERA
1984	Oakland	A	8	0	0	2	7	39	12	7	7	2	0	0	0	5	0	3	1	0	1	0	1.000	0	0	9.00
1986	Oakland	A	33	0	0	9	31.2	136	28	17	17	3	2	3	2	18	4	15	2	0	2	2	.500	0	1	4.83
2 YEARS			41	0	0	11	38.2	175	40	24	24	5	2	3	2	23	4	18	3	0	3	2	.600	0	1	5.59

CHET LEMON

Bats Right-handed, Throws Right-handed
Turns Age 32 in 1987, Born 02/12/55

						BATTING														BASERUNNING				PERCENTAGES		
Year	Team	League	G	AB	H	2B	3B	HR	(Hm	Rd)	TB	R	RBI	TBB	IBB	SO	HBP	SH	SF	SB	CS	SB%	GIDP	AVE	OBP	SLG
1975	Chicago	A	9	35	9	2	0	0	(0	0)	11	2	1	2	0	6	0	1	0	1	0	1.00	0	.257	.297	.314
1976	Chicago	A	132	451	111	15	5	4	(2	2)	148	46	38	28	0	65	7	7	4	13	7	.65	9	.246	.298	.328
1977	Chicago	A	150	553	151	38	4	19	(11	8)	254	99	67	52	1	88	11	4	7	8	7	.53	7	.273	.343	.459
1978	Chicago	A	105	357	107	24	6	13	(8	5)	182	51	55	39	2	46	8	8	4	5	9	.36	11	.300	.377	.510
1979	Chicago	A	148	556	177	44	2	17	(7	10)	276	79	86	56	6	68	13	3	4	7	11	.39	15	.318	.391	.496
1980	Chicago	A	147	514	150	32	6	11	(5	6)	227	76	51	71	6	56	12	4	3	6	6	.50	12	.292	.388	.442
1981	Chicago	A	94	328	99	23	6	9	(4	5)	161	50	50	33	0	48	13	5	4	5	8	.38	10	.302	.384	.491
1982	Detroit	A	125	436	116	20	1	19	(12	7)	195	75	52	56	2	69	15	4	1	1	4	.20	13	.266	.368	.447
1983	Detroit	A	145	491	125	21	5	24	(14	10)	228	78	69	54	1	70	20	4	4	0	7	.00	11	.255	.350	.464
1984	Detroit	A	141	509	146	34	6	20	(12	8)	252	77	76	51	9	83	7	2	4	5	5	.50	16	.287	.357	.495
1985	Detroit	A	145	517	137	28	4	18	(9	9)	227	69	68	45	3	93	10	0	3	0	2	.00	5	.265	.334	.439
1986	Detroit	A	126	403	101	21	3	12	(7	5)	164	45	53	39	3	53	8	3	4	2	1	.67	15	.251	.326	.407
12 YEARS			1467	5150	1429	302	48	166	(91	75)	2325	747	666	526	33	745	124	45	42	53	67	.44	124	.277	.356	.451

DENNIS LEONARD

Pitches Right-handed, Bats Right-handed
Turns Age 36 in 1987, Born 05/08/51

			HOW MUCH HE PITCHED					WHAT HE GAVE UP												THE RESULTS					
Year	Team	League	G	GS	CG	GF	IP	BFP	H	R	ER	HR	SH	SF	HB	TBB	IBB	SO	WP	Bk	W	L	Pct	ShO	Sv	ERA
1974	Kansas City	A	5	4	0	0	22	105	28	15	13	0	5	0	3	12	0	8	0	0	0	4	.000	0	0	5.32
1975	Kansas City	A	32	30	8	1	212	916	212	98	89	18	7	4	9	90	4	146	4	0	15	7	.682	0	0	3.78
1976	Kansas City	A	35	34	16	0	259	1072	247	113	101	16	12	12	11	70	5	150	7	1	17	10	.630	2	0	3.51
1977	Kansas City	A	38	37	21	1	293	1186	246	117	99	18	8	8	8	79	0	244	14	2	20	12	.625	5	1	3.04
1978	Kansas City	A	40	40	20	0	295	1218	283	125	109	27	11	6	9	78	7	183	12	0	21	17	.553	4	0	3.33
1979	Kansas City	A	32	32	12	0	236	966	226	117	107	33	11	5	2	56	3	126	8	0	14	12	.538	5	0	4.08
1980	Kansas City	A	38	38	9	0	280	1172	271	127	118	30	13	8	1	80	5	155	12	1	20	11	.645	3	0	3.79
1981	Kansas City	A	26	26	9	0	202	837	202	79	67	15	5	6	3	41	5	107	5	1	13	11	.542	2	0	2.99
1982	Kansas City	A	21	21	2	0	130.2	579	145	82	74	20	6	5	2	46	3	58	4	0	10	6	.625	0	0	5.10
1983	Kansas City	A	10	10	1	0	63	270	69	29	26	3	0	2	0	19	1	31	1	0	6	3	.667	0	0	3.71
1985	Kansas City	A	2	0	1	2	2	7	1	0	0	0	0	0	0	0	0	0	0	0	0	0	.000	0	0	0.00
1986	Kansas City	A	33	30	5	0	192.2	821	207	106	95	22	4	9	4	51	6	114	6	1	8	13	.381	2	0	4.44
12 YEARS			312	302	103	3	2187.1	9149	2137	1008	898	202	82	65	52	622	39	1323	73	6	144	106	.576	23	1	3.69

JEFF LEONARD

Bats Right-handed, Throws Right-handed
Turns Age 32 in 1987, Born 09/22/55

						BATTING														BASERUNNING				PERCENTAGES		
Year	Team	League	G	AB	H	2B	3B	HR	(Hm	Rd)	TB	R	RBI	TBB	IBB	SO	HBP	SH	SF	SB	CS	SB%	GIDP	AVE	OBP	SLG
1977	Los Angeles	N	11	10	3	0	1	0	(0	0)	5	1	2	1	0	4	0	0	0	0	0	.00	1	.300	.364	.500
1978	Houston	N	8	26	10	2	0	0	(0	0)	12	2	4	1	0	2	0	0	0	0	1	.00	0	.385	.407	.462
1979	Houston	N	134	411	119	15	5	0	(0	0)	144	47	47	46	7	68	2	3	5	23	10	.70	11	.290	.360	.350
1980	Houston	N	88	216	46	7	5	3	(3	0)	72	29	20	19	2	46	0	1	2	4	1	.80	8	.213	.274	.333
1981	2 Teams		44	145	42	12	4	4	(0	4)	74	21	29	12	3	25	1	1	1	5	2	.71	5	.290	.346	.510
1982	San Francisco	N	80	278	72	16	1	9	(4	5)	117	32	49	19	2	65	2	0	5	18	5	.78	11	.259	.306	.421
1983	San Francisco	N	139	516	144	17	7	21	(9	12)	238	74	87	35	2	116	1	0	6	26	7	.79	10	.279	.323	.461
1984	San Francisco	N	136	514	155	27	2	21	(13	8)	249	76	86	47	3	123	0	0	5	17	7	.71	13	.302	.357	.484
1985	San Francisco	N	133	507	122	20	3	17	(8	9)	199	49	62	21	5	107	1	1	1	11	6	.65	19	.241	.272	.393
1986	San Francisco	N	89	341	95	11	3	6	(2	4)	130	48	42	20	1	62	3	1	3	16	3	.84	4	.279	.322	.381
10 YEARS			862	2964	808	127	31	81	(39	42)	1240	379	428	221	25	618	10	7	28	120	42	.74	82	.273	.322	.418
1981	Houston	N	7	18	3	1	1	0	(0	0)	6	1	3	0	0	4	0	0	0	1	0	1.00	0	.167	.158	.333
1981	San Francisco	N	37	127	39	11	3	4	(0	4)	68	20	26	12	3	21	1	1	1	4	2	.67	5	.307	.371	.535

TIM LOLLAR

Pitches Left-handed, Bats Left-handed

Turns Age 31 in 1987, Born 03/17/56

Year	Team	League	HOW MUCH HE PITCHED						WHAT HE GAVE UP												THE RESULTS					
			G	GS	CG	GF	IP	BFP	H	R	ER	HR	SH	SF	HB	TBB	IBB	SO	WP	Bk	W	L	Pct	ShO	Sv	ERA
1980	New York	A	14	1	0	5	32	144	33	14	12	3	4	2	0	20	2	13	2	1	1	0	1.000	0	2	3.37
1981	San Diego	N	24	11	0	4	77	361	87	56	52	4	8	2	3	51	8	38	7	4	2	8	.200	0	1	6.08
1982	San Diego	N	34	34	4	0	232.2	962	192	82	81	20	9	4	4	87	4	150	8	3	16	9	.640	2	0	3.13
1983	San Diego	N	30	30	1	0	175.2	758	170	98	90	22	9	2	4	85	1	135	5	1	7	12	.368	0	0	4.61
1984	San Diego	N	31	31	3	0	195.2	836	168	89	85	18	8	4	1	105	2	131	10	0	11	13	.458	2	0	3.91
1985	2 Teams		34	23	1	7	150	669	140	85	77	19	4	5	2	98	1	105	10	2	8	10	.444	0	1	4.62
1986	Boston	A	32	1	0	4	43	211	51	35	33	7	2	4	3	34	3	28	5	1	2	0	1.000	0	0	6.91
7 YEARS			199	131	9	20	906	3941	841	459	430	93	44	23	17	480	21	600	47	12	47	52	.475	4	4	4.27
1985	Boston	A	16	10	1	4	67	291	57	37	34	9	1	1	1	40	0	44	5	0	5	5	.500	0	1	4.57
1985	Chicago	A	18	13	0	3	83	378	83	48	43	10	3	4	1	58	1	61	5	2	3	5	.375	0	0	4.66

STEVE LOMBARDOZZI

Bats Right-handed, Throws Right-handed

Turns Age 27 in 1987, Born 04/26/60

Year	Team	League	BATTING																BASERUNNING				PERCENTAGES		
			G	AB	H	2B	3B	HR	(Hm | Rd)	TB	R	RBI	TBB	IBB	SO	HBP	SH	SF	SB	CS	SB%	GIDP	AVE	OBP	SLG
1985	Minnesota	A	28	54	20	4	1	0	(0 | 0)	26	10	6	6	0	6	0	4	1	3	2	.60	0	.370	.426	.481
1986	Minnesota	A	156	453	103	20	5	8	(6 | 2)	157	53	33	52	2	76	1	9	0	3	1	.75	8	.227	.308	.347
2 YEARS			184	507	123	24	6	8	(6 | 2)	183	63	39	58	2	82	1	13	1	6	3	.67	8	.243	.321	.361

DAVEY LOPES

Bats Right-handed, Throws Right-handed

Turns Age 41 in 1987, Born 05/03/46

Year	Team	League	BATTING																BASERUNNING				PERCENTAGES		
			G	AB	H	2B	3B	HR	(Hm | Rd)	TB	R	RBI	TBB	IBB	SO	HBP	SH	SF	SB	CS	SB%	GIDP	AVE	OBP	SLG
1972	Los Angeles	N	11	42	9	4	0	0	(0 | 0)	13	6	1	7	0	6	0	0	0	4	0	1.00	1	.214	.327	.310
1973	Los Angeles	N	142	535	147	13	5	6	(2 | 4)	188	77	37	62	6	77	5	7	6	36	16	.69	14	.275	.352	.351
1974	Los Angeles	N	145	530	141	26	3	10	(4 | 6)	203	95	35	66	3	71	4	10	3	59	18	.77	10	.266	.350	.383
1975	Los Angeles	N	155	618	162	24	6	8	(2 | 6)	222	108	41	91	3	93	2	13	2	77	12	.87	4	.262	.358	.359
1976	Los Angeles	N	117	427	103	17	7	4	(4 | 0)	146	72	20	56	1	49	4	2	2	63	10	.86	8	.241	.333	.342
1977	Los Angeles	N	134	502	142	19	5	11	(5 | 6)	204	85	53	73	3	69	2	6	6	47	12	.80	3	.283	.372	.406
1978	Los Angeles	N	151	587	163	25	4	17	(10 | 7)	247	93	58	71	3	70	0	6	1	45	4	.92	9	.278	.355	.421
1979	Los Angeles	N	153	582	154	20	6	28	(15 | 13)	270	109	73	97	4	88	4	6	3	44	4	.92	8	.265	.372	.464
1980	Los Angeles	N	141	553	139	15	3	10	(5 | 5)	190	79	49	58	2	71	1	9	4	23	7	.77	8	.251	.321	.344
1981	Los Angeles	N	58	214	44	2	0	5	(3 | 2)	61	35	17	22	1	35	3	4	0	20	2	.91	7	.206	.289	.285
1982	Oakland	A	128	450	109	19	3	11	(5 | 6)	167	58	42	40	1	51	1	2	3	28	12	.70	14	.242	.304	.371
1983	Oakland	A	147	494	137	13	4	17	(10 | 7)	209	64	67	51	7	61	2	4	10	22	4	.85	9	.277	.341	.423
1984	2 Teams		88	247	63	12	1	9	(6 | 3)	104	37	36	37	1	41	1	2	3	15	0	1.00	8	.255	.351	.421
1985	Chicago	N	99	275	78	11	0	11	(6 | 5)	122	52	44	46	1	37	0	1	3	47	4	.92	14	.284	.383	.444
1986	2 Teams		96	255	70	10	3	7	(4 | 3)	107	49	35	43	0	25	2	2	2	25	8	.76	9	.275	.381	.420
15 YEARS			1765	6311	1661	230	50	154	(81 | 73)	2453	1019	608	820	36	844	31	74	48	555	113	.83	126	.263	.348	.389
1984	Oakland	A	72	230	59	11	1	9	(6 | 3)	99	32	36	31	1	36	1	2	3	12	0	1.00	8	.257	.343	.430
1984	Chicago	N	16	17	4	1	0	0	(0 | 0)	5	5	0	6	0	5	0	0	0	3	0	1.00	0	.235	.435	.294
1986	Chicago	N	59	157	47	8	2	6	(4 | 2)	77	38	22	31	0	16	2	0	1	17	6	.74	6	.299	.419	.490
1986	Houston	N	37	98	23	2	1	1	(0 | 1)	30	11	13	12	0	9	0	2	1	8	2	.80	3	.235	.315	.306

AURELIO LOPEZ

Pitches Right-handed, Bats Right-handed

Turns Age 39 in 1987, Born 10/05/48

Year	Team	League	HOW MUCH HE PITCHED						WHAT HE GAVE UP														THE RESULTS					
			G	GS	CG	GF	IP	BFP	H	R	ER	HR	SH	SF	HB	TBB	IBB	SO	WP	Bk	W	L	Pct	ShO	Sv	ERA
1974	Kansas City	A	8	1	0	5	16	76	21	12	10	0	3	2	0	10	0	5	1	0	0	0	.000	0	0	5.63
1978	St Louis	N	25	4	0	4	65	279	52	35	31	4	3	4	1	32	2	46	5	0	4	2	.667	0	4	4.29
1979	Detroit	A	61	0	0	49	127	519	95	37	34	12	8	5	3	51	3	106	3	0	10	5	.667	0	21	2.41
1980	Detroit	A	67	1	0	59	124	534	125	56	52	15	7	3	3	45	5	97	6	1	13	6	.684	0	21	3.77
1981	Detroit	A	29	3	0	19	82	338	70	34	33	8	1	4	2	31	2	53	0	1	5	2	.714	0	3	3.62
1982	Detroit	A	19	0	0	9	41	176	41	27	24	8	2	2	0	19	4	26	4	0	3	1	.750	0	5	5.27
1983	Detroit	A	57	0	0	46	115.1	473	87	36	36	12	4	5	1	49	7	90	7	1	9	8	.529	0	18	2.81
1984	Detroit	A	71	0	0	41	137.2	559	109	51	45	16	6	6	2	52	6	94	3	1	10	1	.909	0	14	2.94
1985	Detroit	A	51	0	0	22	86.1	379	82	50	46	15	3	6	1	41	9	53	4	0	3	7	.300	0	3	4.80
1986	Houston	N	45	0	0	22	78	321	64	32	30	6	3	4	0	25	1	44	0	0	3	3	.500	0	7	3.46
10 YEARS			433	9	0	276	872.1	3654	746	370	341	96	40	41	13	355	39	614	33	4	60	35	.632	0	92	3.52

DWIGHT LOWRY

Bats Left-handed, Throws Right-handed

Turns Age 30 in 1987, Born 10/23/57

Year	Team	League	BATTING																BASERUNNING				PERCENTAGES		
			G	AB	H	2B	3B	HR	(Hm | Rd)	TB	R	RBI	TBB	IBB	SO	HBP	SH	SF	SB	CS	SB%	GIDP	AVE	OBP	SLG
1984	Detroit	A	32	45	11	2	0	2	(1 | 1)	19	8	7	3	0	11	0	4	0	0	0	.00	3	.244	.292	.422
1986	Detroit	A	56	150	46	4	0	3	(1 | 2)	59	21	18	17	0	19	4	3	0	0	0	.00	4	.307	.392	.393
2 YEARS			88	195	57	6	0	5	(2 | 3)	78	29	25	20	0	30	4	7	0	0	0	.00	7	.292	.370	.400

GARY LUCAS

Turns Age 33 in 1987, Born 11/08/54

Pitches Left-handed, Bats Left-handed

			HOW MUCH HE PITCHED					WHAT HE GAVE UP										THE RESULTS					
Year	Team	League	G	GS	CG	GF	IP	BFP	H	R	ER	HR	SH	SF	HB	TBB	IBB	SO	WP	Bk	W	L	Pct	ShO	Sv	ERA
1980	San Diego	N	46	18	0	14	150	614	138	59	54	8	12	7	1	43	14	85	6	2	5	8	.385	0	3	3.24
1981	San Diego	N	57	0	0	40	90	369	78	26	20	1	9	5	3	36	15	53	1	1	7	7	.500	0	13	2.00
1982	San Diego	N	65	0	0	39	97.1	407	89	42	35	5	8	5	1	29	7	64	1	0	1	10	.091	0	16	3.24
1983	San Diego	N	62	0	0	41	91	391	85	38	29	9	7	3	0	34	11	60	1	0	5	8	.385	0	17	2.87
1984	Montreal	N	55	0	0	22	53	225	54	20	16	4	1	2	0	20	5	42	2	1	0	3	.000	0	8	2.72
1985	Montreal	N	49	0	0	18	67.2	284	63	29	24	6	7	2	0	24	8	31	5	0	6	2	.750	0	1	3.19
1986	California	A	27	0	0	11	45.2	185	45	19	16	1	0	1	0	6	0	31	5	0	4	1	.800	0	2	3.15
7 YEARS			361	18	0	185	594.2	2475	552	233	194	34	44	25	5	192	60	366	21	4	28	39	.418	0	60	2.94

ED LYNCH

Turns Age 31 in 1987, Born 02/25/56

Pitches Right-handed, Bats Right-handed

			HOW MUCH HE PITCHED					WHAT HE GAVE UP										THE RESULTS					
Year	Team	League	G	GS	CG	GF	IP	BFP	H	R	ER	HR	SH	SF	HB	TBB	IBB	SO	WP	Bk	W	L	Pct	ShO	Sv	ERA
1980	New York	N	5	4	0	0	19	86	24	12	11	0	0	1	1	5	0	9	0	0	1	1	.500	0	0	5.21
1981	New York	N	17	13	0	0	80	336	79	32	26	6	2	1	1	21	2	27	3	1	4	5	.444	0	0	2.92
1982	New York	N	43	12	0	11	139.1	585	145	57	55	9	4	7	3	40	4	51	2	3	4	8	.333	0	2	3.55
1983	New York	N	30	27	1	1	174.2	749	208	94	83	17	9	7	3	41	10	44	3	2	10	10	.500	0	0	4.28
1984	New York	N	40	13	0	14	124	556	169	77	62	14	2	5	4	24	3	62	0	0	9	8	.529	0	2	4.50
1985	New York	N	31	29	6	1	191	777	188	76	73	19	9	5	1	27	1	65	0	0	10	8	.556	1	0	3.44
1986	2 Teams		24	13	1	3	101.1	416	107	48	42	10	5	3	1	23	6	58	0	0	7	5	.583	0	0	3.73
7 YEARS			190	111	8	30	829.1	3505	920	396	352	72	36	26	12	181	26	316	10	6	45	45	.500	2	4	3.82
1986	Chicago	N	23	13	1	3	99.2	409	105	48	42	10	5	3	1	23	6	57	0	0	7	5	.583	1	0	3.79
1986	New York	N	1	0	0	0	1.2	7	2	0	0	0	0	0	0	0	0	1	0	0	0	0	.000	0	0	0.00

FRED LYNN

Turns Age 35 in 1987, Born 02/03/52

Bats Left-handed, Throws Left-handed

			BATTING											BASERUNNING				PERCENTAGES		
Year	Team	League	G	AB	H	2B	3B	HR	(Hm | Rd)	TB	R	RBI	TBB	IBB	SO	HBP	SH	SF	SB	CS	SB%	GIDP	AVE	OBP	SLG
1974	Boston	A	15	43	18	2	2	2	(1 | 1)	30	5	10	6	2	6	1	0	1	0	0	.00	0	.419	.490	.698
1975	Boston	A	145	528	175	47	7	21	(9 | 12)	299	103	105	62	10	90	3	6	6	10	5	.67	11	.331	.401	.566
1976	Boston	A	132	507	159	32	8	10	(4 | 6)	237	76	65	48	2	67	1	0	10	14	9	.61	9	.314	.367	.467
1977	Boston	A	129	497	129	29	5	18	(10 | 8)	222	81	76	51	2	63	3	5	8	2	3	.40	14	.260	.327	.447
1978	Boston	A	150	541	161	33	3	22	(11 | 11)	266	75	82	75	11	50	1	4	6	3	6	.33	2	.298	.380	.492
1979	Boston	A	147	531	177	42	1	39	(28 | 11)	338	116	122	82	4	79	4	0	5	2	2	.50	9	.333	.423	.637
1980	Boston	A	110	415	125	32	3	12	(6 | 6)	199	67	61	58	3	39	0	0	5	12	0	1.00	10	.301	.383	.480
1981	California	A	76	256	56	8	1	5	(3 | 2)	81	28	31	38	4	42	3	1	4	1	2	.33	7	.219	.322	.316
1982	California	A	138	472	141	38	1	21	(13 | 8)	244	89	86	58	4	72	3	5	7	7	8	.47	9	.299	.374	.517
1983	California	A	117	437	119	20	3	22	(14 | 8)	211	56	74	55	10	83	2	0	6	2	2	.50	7	.272	.352	.483
1984	California	A	142	517	140	28	4	23	(16 | 8)	245	84	79	77	9	97	2	2	2	2	2	.50	14	.271	.366	.474
1985	Baltimore	A	124	448	118	12	1	23	(14 | 9)	201	59	68	53	6	100	1	0	6	7	3	.70	7	.263	.339	.449
1986	Baltimore	A	112	397	114	13	1	23	(13 | 10)	198	67	67	53	1	59	2	0	4	2	2	.50	20	.287	.371	.499
13 YEARS			1537	5589	1632	336	40	241	(142 | 99)	2771	906	926	716	68	847	26	23	70	64	44	.59	119	.292	.371	.496

STEVE LYONS

Turns Age 27 in 1987, Born 06/03/60

Bats Left-handed, Throws Right-handed

			BATTING											BASERUNNING				PERCENTAGES		
Year	Team	League	G	AB	H	2B	3B	HR	(Hm | Rd)	TB	R	RBI	TBB	IBB	SO	HBP	SH	SF	SB	CS	SB%	GIDP	AVE	OBP	SLG
1985	Boston	A	133	371	98	14	5	5	(4 | 1)	133	52	30	32	0	64	1	2	3	12	9	.57	2	.264	.322	.358
1986	2 Teams		101	247	56	9	3	1	(0 | 0)	74	30	20	19	2	47	1	4	4	4	6	.40	4	.227	.280	.300
2 YEARS			234	618	154	23	6	6	(4 | 1)	207	82	50	51	2	111	2	6	7	16	15	.52	6	.249	.305	.335
1986	Boston	A	59	124	31	7	2	1	(0 | 0)	45	20	14	12	2	23	0	1	2	2	3	.40	3	.250	.312	.363
1986	Chicago	A	42	123	25	2	1	0	(0 | 0)	29	10	6	7	0	24	1	3	2	2	3	.40	1	.203	.248	.236

MIKE MADDUX

Turns Age 26 in 1987, Born 08/27/61

Pitches Right-handed, Bats Right-handed

			HOW MUCH HE PITCHED					WHAT HE GAVE UP										THE RESULTS					
Year	Team	League	G	GS	CG	GF	IP	BFP	H	R	ER	HR	SH	SF	HB	TBB	IBB	SO	WP	Bk	W	L	Pct	ShO	Sv	ERA
1986	Philadelphia	N	16	16	0	0	78	351	88	56	47	6	3	3	3	34	4	44	4	2	3	7	.300	0	0	5.42

BILL MADLOCK

Bats Right-handed, Throws Right-handed

Turns Age 36 in 1987, Born 01/12/51

Year	Team	League	G	AB	H	2B	3B	HR	(Hm	Rd)	TB	R	RBI	TBB	IBB	SO	HBP	SH	SF	SB	CS	SB%	GIDP	AVE	OBP	SLG
1973	Texas	A	21	77	27	5	3	1	(1	0)	41	16	5	7	0	9	1	0	0	3	2	.60	0	.351	.412	.532
1974	Chicago	N	128	453	142	21	5	9	(7	2)	200	65	54	42	8	39	5	3	6	11	7	.61	15	.313	.374	.442
1975	Chicago	N	130	514	182	29	7	7	(6	1)	246	77	64	42	5	34	3	1	5	9	7	.56	11	.354	.402	.479
1976	Chicago	N	142	514	174	36	1	15	(11	4)	257	68	84	56	15	27	11	3	4	15	11	.58	21	.339	.412	.500
1977	San Francisco	N	140	533	161	28	1	12	(6	6)	227	70	46	43	14	33	6	1	2	13	10	.57	25	.302	.360	.426
1978	San Francisco	N	122	447	138	26	3	15	(5	10)	215	76	44	48	11	39	3	9	2	16	5	.76	6	.309	.378	.481
1979	2 Teams		154	560	167	26	5	14	(3	11)	245	85	85	52	11	41	1	3	7	32	11	.74	17	.298	.355	.438
1980	Pittsburgh	N	137	494	137	22	4	10	(7	3)	197	62	53	45	12	33	4	0	3	16	10	.62	15	.277	.341	.399
1981	Pittsburgh	N	82	279	95	23	1	6	(2	4)	138	35	45	34	7	17	3	0	4	18	6	.75	5	.341	.413	.495
1982	Pittsburgh	N	154	568	181	33	3	19	(13	6)	277	92	95	48	16	39	4	1	13	18	6	.75	12	.319	.368	.488
1983	Pittsburgh	N	130	473	153	21	0	12	(8	4)	210	68	68	49	10	24	2	1	5	3	4	.43	16	.323	.386	.444
1984	Pittsburgh	N	103	403	102	16	0	4	(1	3)	130	38	44	26	5	29	1	1	4	3	1	.75	11	.253	.297	.323
1985	2 Teams		144	513	141	27	1	12	(6	6)	206	69	56	49	2	53	8	3	4	10	4	.71	15	.275	.345	.402
1986	Los Angeles	N	111	379	106	17	0	10	(4	6)	153	38	60	30	4	43	5	1	6	3	3	.50	7	.280	.336	.404
14 YEARS			1698	6207	1906	330	34	146	(80	66)	2742	859	803	571	120	460	57	27	65	170	87	.66	176	.307	.367	.442
1979	Pittsburgh	N	85	311	102	17	3	7	(2	5)	146	48	44	34	8	22	1	2	5	21	8	.72	14	.328	.390	.469
1979	San Francisco	N	69	249	65	9	2	7	(1	6)	99	37	41	18	3	19	0	1	2	11	3	.79	3	.261	.309	.398
1985	Los Angeles	N	34	114	41	4	0	2	(0	2)	51	20	15	10	0	11	3	0	1	7	1	.88	3	.360	.422	.447
1985	Pittsburgh	N	110	399	100	23	1	10	(6	4)	155	49	41	39	2	42	5	3	3	3	3	.50	12	.251	.323	.388

MICKEY MAHLER

Pitches Left-handed, Bats both Right and Left-handed

Turns Age 35 in 1987, Born 07/30/52

Year	Team	League	G	GS	CG	GF	IP	BFP	H	R	ER	HR	SH	SF	HB	TBB	IBB	SO	WP	Bk	W	L	Pct	ShO	Sv	ERA
1977	Atlanta	N	5	5	0	0	23	109	31	19	16	4	1	3	1	9	0	14	1	0	1	2	.333	0	0	6.26
1978	Atlanta	N	34	21	1	3	135	597	130	82	70	16	9	6	7	66	6	92	12	3	4	11	.267	0	0	4.67
1979	Atlanta	N	26	18	1	1	100	470	123	72	65	11	7	9	3	47	7	71	4	1	5	11	.313	0	0	5.85
1980	Pittsburgh	N	2	0	0	1	1	10	4	7	7	1	0	0	0	3	0	1	0	0	0	0	.000	0	0	63.00
1981	California	A	6	0	0	6	6	20	1	0	0	0	0	0	0	2	0	5	0	0	0	0	.000	0	0	0.00
1982	California	A	6	0	0	2	8	37	9	1	1	0	1	0	0	6	1	5	0	0	2	0	1.000	0	0	1.12
1985	2 Teams		12	9	1	2	69	287	59	30	23	5	3	1	1	28	3	46	7	0	2	6	.250	1	1	3.00
1986	2 Teams		31	5	0	8	64	284	72	31	29	3	1	4	4	29	2	28	5	0	0	2	.000	0	3	4.08
8 YEARS			122	58	3	23	406	1814	429	242	211	40	22	23	16	190	19	262	29	4	14	32	.304	1	4	4.68
1985	Detroit	A	3	2	0	0	20.2	84	19	8	4	2	1	0	0	4	2	14	4	0	1	2	.333	0	0	1.74
1985	Montreal	N	9	7	1	2	48.1	203	40	22	19	3	2	1	1	24	1	32	3	0	1	4	.200	1	1	3.54
1986	Texas	A	29	5	0	8	63	278	71	31	29	3	1	4	3	29	2	28	5	0	0	2	.000	0	3	4.14
1986	Toronto	A	2	0	0	0	1	6	1	0	0	0	0	0	1	0	0	0	0	0	0	0	.000	0	0	0.00

RICK MAHLER

Pitches Right-handed, Bats Right-handed

Turns Age 34 in 1987, Born 08/05/53

Year	Team	League	G	GS	CG	GF	IP	BFP	H	R	ER	HR	SH	SF	HB	TBB	IBB	SO	WP	Bk	W	L	Pct	ShO	Sv	ERA
1979	Atlanta	N	15	0	0	5	22	101	28	16	15	4	0	0	0	11	2	12	1	0	0	0	.000	0	0	6.14
1980	Atlanta	N	2	0	0	0	4	13	2	1	1	0	0	0	0	1	0	1	0	0	0	0	.000	0	0	2.25
1981	Atlanta	N	34	14	1	10	112	478	109	41	35	5	8	3	1	43	5	54	3	1	8	6	.571	0	2	2.81
1982	Atlanta	N	39	33	5	0	205.1	857	213	105	96	18	6	6	1	62	5	105	8	2	9	10	.474	2	0	4.21
1983	Atlanta	N	10	0	0	1	14.1	66	16	8	8	0	1	2	0	9	1	7	0	0	0	0	.000	0	0	5.02
1984	Atlanta	N	38	29	9	1	222	918	209	86	77	13	13	8	3	62	7	106	3	1	13	10	.565	1	0	3.12
1985	Atlanta	N	39	39	6	0	266.2	1110	272	116	103	24	10	5	2	79	8	107	3	1	17	15	.531	1	0	3.48
1986	Atlanta	N	39	39	7	0	237.2	1056	283	139	129	25	10	8	3	95	10	137	5	1	14	18	.438	1	0	4.88
8 YEARS			216	154	28	17	1084	4599	1132	512	464	89	48	32	10	361	38	529	23	7	61	59	.508	5	2	3.85

CANDY MALDONADO

Bats Right-handed, Throws Right-handed

Turns Age 27 in 1987, Born 09/05/60

Year	Team	League	G	AB	H	2B	3B	HR	(Hm	Rd)	TB	R	RBI	TBB	IBB	SO	HBP	SH	SF	SB	CS	SB%	GIDP	AVE	OBP	SLG
1981	Los Angeles	N	11	12	1	0	0	0	(0	0)	1	0	0	0	0	5	0	0	0	0	0	.00	0	.083	.083	.083
1982	Los Angeles	N	6	4	0	0	0	0	(0	0)	0	0	0	1	1	2	0	0	0	0	0	.00	0	.000	.200	.000
1983	Los Angeles	N	42	62	12	1	1	1	(1	0)	18	5	6	5	0	14	0	1	0	0	0	.00	1	.194	.254	.290
1984	Los Angeles	N	116	254	68	14	0	5	(1	4)	97	25	28	19	0	29	1	1	3	0	3	.00	6	.268	.318	.382
1985	Los Angeles	N	121	213	48	7	1	5	(2	3)	72	20	19	19	4	40	0	2	1	1	1	.50	3	.225	.288	.338
1986	San Francisco	N	133	405	102	31	3	18	(6	12)	193	49	85	20	4	77	3	0	4	4	4	.50	12	.252	.289	.477
6 YEARS			429	950	231	53	5	29	(10	19)	381	99	138	64	9	167	4	4	8	5	8	.38	22	.243	.291	.401

RICK MANNING

Bats Left-handed, Throws Right-handed   Turns Age 33 in 1987, Born 09/02/54

Year	Team	League	G	AB	H	2B	3B	HR	(Hm	Rd)	TB	R	RBI	TBB	IBB	SO	HBP	SH	SF	SB	CS	SB%	GIDP	AVE	OBP	SLG
1975	Cleveland	A	120	480	137	16	5	3	(2	1)	172	69	35	44	2	62	2	7	2	19	11	.63	9	.285	.347	.358
1976	Cleveland	A	138	552	161	24	7	6	(2	4)	217	73	43	41	1	75	0	7	6	16	10	.62	11	.292	.337	.393
1977	Cleveland	A	68	252	57	7	3	5	(0	5)	85	33	18	21	0	35	0	6	4	9	5	.64	4	.226	.282	.337
1978	Cleveland	A	148	566	149	27	3	3	(1	2)	191	65	50	38	1	62	1	8	3	12	12	.50	10	.263	.309	.337
1979	Cleveland	A	144	560	145	12	2	3	(1	2)	170	67	51	55	3	48	1	9	7	30	8	.79	13	.259	.323	.304
1980	Cleveland	A	140	471	110	17	4	3	(3	0)	144	55	52	63	11	66	2	10	9	12	6	.67	12	.234	.321	.306
1981	Cleveland	A	103	360	88	15	3	4	(2	2)	121	47	33	40	2	57	0	2	2	25	3	.89	4	.244	.318	.336
1982	Cleveland	A	152	562	152	18	2	8	(1	7)	198	71	44	54	5	60	0	2	1	12	8	.60	11	.270	.334	.352
1983	2 Teams	A	158	569	140	20	4	4	(2	2)	180	60	43	38	5	62	1	3	4	18	5	.78	13	.246	.292	.316
1984	Milwaukee	A	119	341	85	10	5	7	(1	6)	126	53	31	34	1	32	1	3	1	5	7	.42	7	.249	.318	.370
1985	Milwaukee	A	79	216	47	9	1	2	(1	1)	64	19	18	14	0	19	0	1	0	1	0	1.00	2	.218	.265	.296
1986	Milwaukee	A	89	205	52	7	3	8	(4	4)	89	31	27	17	2	20	1	1	3	5	3	.63	5	.254	.310	.434
12 YEARS			1458	5134	1323	182	42	56	(20	36)	1757	643	445	459	33	598	9	59	42	164	78	.68	101	.258	.317	.342
1983	Cleveland	A	50	194	54	6	0	1	(0	1)	63	20	10	12	1	22	0	2	1	7	3	.70	5	.278	.319	.325
1983	Milwaukee	A	108	375	86	14	4	3	(2	1)	117	40	33	26	4	40	1	1	3	11	2	.85	8	.229	.279	.312

MIKE MARSHALL

Bats Right-handed, Throws Right-handed   Turns Age 27 in 1987, Born 01/12/60

Year	Team	League	G	AB	H	2B	3B	HR	(Hm	Rd)	TB	R	RBI	TBB	IBB	SO	HBP	SH	SF	SB	CS	SB%	GIDP	AVE	OBP	SLG
1981	Los Angeles	N	14	25	5	3	0	0	(0	0)	8	2	1	1	0	4	1	0	0	0	0	.00	1	.200	.259	.320
1982	Los Angeles	N	49	95	23	3	0	5	(2	3)	41	10	9	13	1	23	1	0	1	2	0	1.00	1	.242	.336	.432
1983	Los Angeles	N	140	465	132	17	1	17	(9	8)	202	47	65	43	4	127	5	0	5	7	3	.70	8	.284	.347	.434
1984	Los Angeles	N	134	495	127	27	0	21	(11	10)	217	68	65	40	6	93	3	1	2	4	3	.57	12	.257	.315	.438
1985	Los Angeles	N	135	518	152	27	2	28	(15	13)	267	72	95	37	6	137	3	2	4	3	10	.23	8	.293	.342	.515
1986	Los Angeles	N	103	330	77	11	0	19	(13	6)	145	47	53	27	3	90	4	0	1	4	4	.50	5	.233	.298	.439
6 YEARS			575	1928	516	88	3	90	(50	40)	880	246	288	161	20	474	17	3	13	20	20	.50	35	.268	.328	.456

BUCK MARTINEZ

Bats Right-handed, Throws Right-handed   Turns Age 39 in 1987, Born 11/07/48

Year	Team	League	G	AB	H	2B	3B	HR	(Hm	Rd)	TB	R	RBI	TBB	IBB	SO	HBP	SH	SF	SB	CS	SB%	GIDP	AVE	OBP	SLG
1969	Kansas City	A	72	205	47	6	1	4	(2	2)	67	14	23	8	2	25	0	1	0	0	0	.00	4	.229	.258	.327
1970	Kansas City	A	6	9	1	0	0	0	(0	0)	1	1	0	2	0	1	0	0	0	0	0	.00	1	.111	.273	.111
1971	Kansas City	A	22	46	7	2	0	0	(0	0)	9	3	1	5	0	9	0	1	1	0	1	.00	1	.152	.231	.196
1973	Kansas City	A	14	32	8	1	0	1	(1	0)	12	2	6	4	0	5	0	1	0	0	0	.00	2	.250	.333	.375
1974	Kansas City	A	43	107	23	3	1	1	(0	1)	31	10	8	14	0	19	2	0	0	0	1	.00	1	.215	.317	.290
1975	Kansas City	A	80	226	51	9	2	3	(1	2)	73	15	23	21	0	28	1	6	1	1	0	1.00	4	.226	.293	.323
1976	Kansas City	A	95	267	61	13	3	5	(2	3)	95	24	34	16	1	45	0	9	3	0	0	.00	8	.228	.269	.356
1977	Kansas City	A	29	80	18	4	0	1	(1	0)	25	3	9	3	0	12	0	2	0	0	1	.00	1	.225	.253	.313
1978	Milwaukee	A	89	256	56	10	1	1	(0	1)	71	26	20	14	1	42	0	12	4	1	1	.50	4	.219	.255	.277
1979	Milwaukee	A	69	196	53	8	0	4	(0	4)	73	17	26	8	0	25	0	8	2	0	1	.00	3	.270	.296	.372
1980	Milwaukee	A	76	219	49	9	0	3	(1	2)	67	16	17	12	0	33	1	5	1	1	0	1.00	3	.224	.266	.306
1981	Toronto	A	45	128	29	8	1	4	(3	1)	51	13	21	11	0	16	1	3	3	1	0	1.00	6	.227	.287	.398
1982	Toronto	A	96	260	63	17	0	10	(6	4)	110	26	37	24	1	34	0	2	5	1	1	.50	10	.242	.301	.423
1983	Toronto	A	88	221	56	14	0	10	(5	5)	100	27	33	29	0	39	0	1	2	0	1	.00	7	.253	.337	.452
1984	Toronto	A	102	232	51	13	1	5	(2	3)	81	24	37	29	2	49	2	1	9	0	3	.00	3	.220	.301	.349
1985	Toronto	A	42	99	16	3	0	4	(2	2)	31	11	14	10	0	12	1	0	3	0	0	.00	3	.162	.239	.313
1986	Toronto	A	81	160	29	8	0	2	(1	1)	43	13	12	20	0	25	0	4	1	0	0	.00	5	.181	.271	.269
17 YEARS			1049	2743	618	128	10	58	(27	31)	940	245	321	230	5	419	8	56	35	5	10	.33	59	.225	.284	.343

CARMELO MARTINEZ

Bats Right-handed, Throws Right-handed   Turns Age 27 in 1987, Born 07/28/60

Year	Team	League	G	AB	H	2B	3B	HR	(Hm	Rd)	TB	R	RBI	TBB	IBB	SO	HBP	SH	SF	SB	CS	SB%	GIDP	AVE	OBP	SLG
1983	Chicago	N	29	89	23	3	0	6	(2	4)	44	8	16	4	0	19	0	0	1	0	0	.00	3	.258	.287	.494
1984	San Diego	N	149	488	122	28	2	13	(6	7)	193	64	66	68	4	82	4	0	10	1	3	.25	7	.250	.340	.395
1985	San Diego	N	150	514	130	28	1	21	(15	6)	223	64	72	87	4	82	3	2	4	0	4	.00	10	.253	.362	.434
1986	San Diego	N	113	244	58	10	0	9	(6	3)	95	28	25	35	2	46	1	1	2	1	1	.50	9	.238	.333	.389
4 YEARS			441	1335	333	69	3	49	(29	20)	555	164	179	194	10	229	8	3	17	2	8	.20	29	.249	.344	.416

DAVE MARTINEZ

Bats Left-handed, Throws Left-handed   Turns Age 23 in 1987, Born 09/26/64

Year	Team	League	G	AB	H	2B	3B	HR	(Hm	Rd)	TB	R	RBI	TBB	IBB	SO	HBP	SH	SF	SB	CS	SB%	GIDP	AVE	OBP	SLG
1986	Chicago	N	53	108	15	1	1	1	(1	0)	21	13	7	6	0	22	1	0	1	4	2	.67	1	.139	.190	.194

DENNIS MARTINEZ

Pitches Right-handed, Bats Right-handed   Turns Age 32 in 1987, Born 05/14/55

Year	Team	League	G	GS	CG	GF	IP	BFP	H	R	ER	HR	SH	SF	HB	TBB	IBB	SO	WP	Bk	W	L	Pct	ShO	Sv	ERA
1976	Baltimore	A	4	2	1	1	28	106	23	8	8	1	1	0	0	8	0	18	1	0	1	2	.333	0	0	2.57
1977	Baltimore	A	42	13	5	19	167	709	157	86	76	10	8	8	8	64	5	107	5	0	14	7	.667	0	4	4.10
1978	Baltimore	A	40	38	15	0	276	1140	257	121	108	20	8	7	3	93	4	142	8	0	16	11	.593	2	0	3.52
1979	Baltimore	A	40	39	18	0	292	1206	279	129	119	28	12	12	1	78	1	132	9	2	15	16	.484	3	0	3.67
1980	Baltimore	A	25	12	2	8	100	428	103	44	44	12	1	3	2	44	6	42	0	1	6	4	.600	0	1	3.96
1981	Baltimore	A	25	24	9	0	179	753	173	84	66	10	2	5	2	62	1	88	6	1	14	5	.737	2	0	3.32
1982	Baltimore	A	40	39	10	0	252	1093	262	123	118	30	11	7	7	87	2	111	7	1	16	12	.571	2	0	4.21
1983	Baltimore	A	32	25	4	3	153	688	209	108	94	21	3	5	2	45	0	71	2	0	7	16	.304	0	0	5.53
1984	Baltimore	A	34	20	2	4	141.2	599	145	81	79	26	0	5	5	37	2	72	13	0	6	9	.400	0	0	5.02
1985	Baltimore	A	33	31	3	1	180	789	203	110	103	29	0	11	9	63	3	68	4	1	13	11	.542	0	0	5.15
1986	2 Teams		23	15	1	2	104.2	449	114	57	55	11	8	2	3	30	4	65	3	2	3	6	.333	1	0	4.73
11 YEARS			338	258	70	38	1873.1	7960	1925	951	870	198	54	65	42	611	28	916	58	8	111	99	.529	11	5	4.18
1986	Baltimore	A	4	0	0	1	6.2	33	11	5	5	0	0	1	0	2	0	2	1	0	0	0	.000	0	0	6.75
1986	Montreal	N	19	15	1	1	98	416	103	52	50	11	8	1	3	28	4	63	2	2	3	6	.333	1	0	4.59

MIKE MASON

Pitches Left-handed, Bats Left-handed   Turns Age 29 in 1987, Born 11/21/58

Year	Team	League	G	GS	CG	GF	IP	BFP	H	R	ER	HR	SH	SF	HB	TBB	IBB	SO	WP	Bk	W	L	Pct	ShO	Sv	ERA
1982	Texas	A	4	4	0	0	23	96	21	13	13	3	1	0	0	9	1	8	1	0	1	2	.333	0	0	5.09
1983	Texas	A	5	0	0	2	10.2	50	10	7	7	0	2	0	1	6	0	9	0	0	0	2	.000	0	0	5.91
1984	Texas	A	36	24	4	6	184.1	750	159	78	74	18	6	9	2	51	4	113	5	1	9	13	.409	0	0	3.61
1985	Texas	A	38	30	1	1	179	806	212	113	96	22	4	10	3	73	4	92	4	1	8	15	.348	1	0	4.83
1986	Texas	A	27	22	2	2	135	587	135	71	65	11	3	3	0	56	3	85	5	1	7	3	.700	1	0	4.33
5 YEARS			110	80	7	11	532	2289	537	282	255	54	16	22	6	195	12	307	15	3	25	35	.417	2	0	4.31

GREG MATHEWS

Pitches Left-handed, Bats both Right and Left-handed   Turns Age 24 in 1987, Born 05/17/63

Year	Team	League	G	GS	CG	GF	IP	BFP	H	R	ER	HR	SH	SF	HB	TBB	IBB	SO	WP	Bk	W	L	Pct	ShO	Sv	ERA
1986	St Louis	N	23	22	1	1	145.1	591	139	61	59	15	7	1	2	44	3	67	5	6	11	8	.579	0	0	3.65

GARY MATTHEWS

Bats Right-handed, Throws Right-handed   Turns Age 37 in 1987, Born 07/05/50

Year	Team	League	G	AB	H	2B	3B	HR	(Hm	Rd)	TB	R	RBI	TBB	IBB	SO	HBP	SH	SF	SB	CS	SB%	GIDP	AVE	OBP	SLG
1972	San Francisco	N	20	62	18	1	1	4	(2	2)	33	11	14	7	2	13	0	1	1	0	1	.00	1	.290	.357	.532
1973	San Francisco	N	148	540	162	22	10	12	(5	7)	240	74	58	58	7	83	1	3	3	17	5	.77	12	.300	.367	.444
1974	San Francisco	N	154	561	161	27	6	16	(7	9)	248	87	82	70	5	69	3	2	2	11	9	.55	15	.287	.368	.442
1975	San Francisco	N	116	425	119	22	3	12	(4	8)	183	67	58	65	5	53	2	0	2	13	4	.76	13	.280	.377	.431
1976	San Francisco	N	156	587	164	28	4	20	(11	9)	260	79	84	75	3	94	1	2	6	12	5	.71	8	.279	.359	.443
1977	Atlanta	N	148	555	157	25	5	17	(14	3)	243	89	64	67	3	90	2	2	1	22	8	.73	13	.283	.362	.438
1978	Atlanta	N	129	474	135	20	5	18	(10	8)	219	75	62	61	2	92	2	1	4	8	7	.53	16	.285	.366	.462
1979	Atlanta	N	156	631	192	34	5	27	(18	9)	317	97	90	60	5	75	0	1	3	18	6	.75	6	.304	.363	.502
1980	Atlanta	N	155	571	159	17	3	19	(9	10)	239	79	75	42	2	93	0	1	5	11	3	.79	16	.278	.325	.419
1981	Philadelphia	N	101	359	108	21	3	9	(5	4)	162	62	67	59	2	42	3	1	6	15	2	.88	8	.301	.398	.451
1982	Philadelphia	N	162	616	173	31	1	19	(10	9)	263	89	83	66	1	87	2	0	6	21	4	.84	23	.281	.349	.427
1983	Philadelphia	N	132	446	115	18	2	10	(3	7)	167	66	50	69	3	81	0	4	7	13	9	.59	8	.258	.352	.374
1984	Chicago	N	147	491	143	21	2	14	(8	6)	210	101	82	103	2	97	3	1	10	17	8	.68	10	.291	.410	.428
1985	Chicago	N	97	298	70	12	0	13	(8	5)	121	45	40	59	2	64	0	0	3	2	1	1.00	8	.235	.362	.406
1986	Chicago	N	123	370	96	16	1	21	(11	10)	177	49	46	60	1	59	0	0	2	3	2	.60	15	.259	.361	.478
15 YEARS			1944	6986	1972	315	51	231	(125	106)	3082	1070	955	921	45	1092	21	19	61	183	73	.71	172	.282	.365	.441

DON MATTINGLY

Bats Left-handed, Throws Left-handed   Turns Age 26 in 1987, Born 04/20/61

Year	Team	League	G	AB	H	2B	3B	HR	(Hm	Rd)	TB	R	RBI	TBB	IBB	SO	HBP	SH	SF	SB	CS	SB%	GIDP	AVE	OBP	SLG
1982	New York	A	7	12	2	0	0	0	(0	0)	2	0	1	0	0	1	0	1	0	0	0	.00	2	.167	.154	.167
1983	New York	A	91	279	79	15	4	4	(0	4)	114	34	32	21	5	31	1	2	2	0	0	.00	5	.283	.333	.409
1984	New York	A	153	603	207	44	2	23	(12	11)	324	91	110	41	8	33	1	8	9	1	1	.50	15	.343	.381	.537
1985	New York	A	159	652	211	48	3	35	(22	13)	370	107	145	56	13	41	2	2	15	2	2	.50	15	.324	.371	.567
1986	New York	A	162	677	238	53	2	31	(17	14)	388	117	113	53	11	35	1	1	10	0	0	.00	17	.352	.394	.573
5 YEARS			572	2223	737	160	11	93	(51	42)	1198	349	401	171	37	141	5	13	37	3	3	.50	57	.332	.375	.539

LEN MATUSZEK

Bats Left-handed, Throws Right-handed   Turns Age 33 in 1987, Born 09/27/54

									BATTING										BASERUNNING				PERCENTAGES		
Year	Team	League	G	AB	H	2B	3B	HR	(Hm	Rd)	TB	R	RBI	TBB	IBB	SO	HBP	SH	SF	SB	CS	SB%	GIDP	AVE	OBP	SLG
1981	Philadelphia	N	13	11	3	1	0	0	(0	0)	4	1	1	3	1	1	0	0	0	0	1	.00	0	.273	.429	.364
1982	Philadelphia	N	25	39	3	1	0	0	(0	0)	4	1	3	1	0	10	1	0	1	0	1	.00	3	.077	.119	.103
1983	Philadelphia	N	28	80	22	6	1	4	(2	2)	42	12	16	4	1	14	0	2	1	0	1	.00	1	.275	.306	.525
1984	Philadelphia	N	101	262	65	17	1	12	(5	7)	120	40	43	39	4	54	4	0	4	4	3	.57	7	.248	.350	.458
1985	2 Teams		105	214	46	8	3	5	(1	4)	75	33	28	19	2	38	1	1	7	2	2	.50	5	.215	.274	.350
1986	Los Angeles	N	91	199	52	7	0	9	(7	2)	86	26	28	21	1	47	1	0	1	2	2	.50	3	.261	.333	.432
6 YEARS			363	805	191	40	5	30	(15	15)	331	113	119	87	9	164	7	3	14	8	10	.44	19	.237	.312	.411
1985	Toronto	A	62	151	32	6	2	2	(1	1)	48	23	15	11	0	24	0	0	4	2	1	.67	5	.212	.259	.318
1985	Los Angeles	N	43	63	14	2	1	3	(0	3)	27	10	13	8	2	14	1	1	3	0	1	.00	0	.222	.307	.429

LEE MAZZILLI

Bats both Right and Left-handed, Throws Right-handed   Turns Age 32 in 1987, Born 03/25/55

									BATTING										BASERUNNING				PERCENTAGES		
Year	Team	League	G	AB	H	2B	3B	HR	(Hm	Rd)	TB	R	RBI	TBB	IBB	SO	HBP	SH	SF	SB	CS	SB%	GIDP	AVE	OBP	SLG
1976	New York	N	24	77	15	2	0	2	(1	1)	23	9	7	14	0	10	1	0	1	5	4	.56	0	.195	.323	.299
1977	New York	N	159	537	134	24	3	6	(3	3)	182	66	46	72	6	72	3	4	2	22	15	.59	4	.250	.340	.339
1978	New York	N	148	542	148	28	5	16	(8	8)	234	78	61	69	6	82	1	2	5	20	13	.61	7	.273	.353	.432
1979	New York	N	158	597	181	34	4	15	(6	9)	268	78	79	93	5	74	0	0	3	34	12	.74	6	.303	.395	.449
1980	New York	N	152	578	162	31	4	16	(10	6)	249	82	76	82	11	92	3	0	5	41	15	.73	8	.280	.370	.431
1981	New York	N	95	324	74	14	5	6	(1	5)	116	36	34	46	3	53	2	0	4	17	7	.71	5	.228	.324	.358
1982	2 Teams		95	323	81	10	0	10	(5	5)	121	43	34	43	0	41	2	0	0	13	9	.59	6	.251	.342	.375
1983	Pittsburgh	N	109	246	59	9	0	5	(1	4)	83	37	24	49	1	43	2	4	4	15	5	.75	8	.240	.365	.337
1984	Pittsburgh	N	111	266	63	11	1	4	(3	1)	88	37	21	40	2	42	1	1	1	8	1	.89	5	.237	.338	.331
1985	Pittsburgh	N	92	117	33	8	0	1	(0	1)	44	20	9	29	1	17	0	1	0	4	1	.80	3	.282	.425	.376
1986	2 Teams		100	151	37	5	1	3	(1	2)	53	28	15	38	2	36	2	0	1	4	4	.50	3	.245	.401	.351
11 YEARS			1243	3758	987	176	23	84	(39	45)	1461	514	406	575	37	562	17	12	26	183	86	.68	55	.263	.361	.389
1982	New York	A	37	128	34	2	0	6	(3	3)	54	20	17	15	0	15	1	0	0	2	3	.40	2	.266	.347	.422
1982	Texas	A	58	195	47	8	0	4	(2	2)	67	23	17	28	0	26	1	0	0	11	6	.65	4	.241	.339	.344
1986	New York	N	39	58	16	3	0	2	(1	1)	25	10	7	12	1	11	2	0	0	1	1	.50	1	.276	.417	.431
1986	Pittsburgh	N	61	93	21	2	1	1	(0	1)	28	18	8	26	1	25	0	0	1	3	3	.50	2	.226	.392	.301

KIRK McCASKILL

Pitches Right-handed, Bats Right-handed   Turns Age 26 in 1987, Born 04/09/61

			HOW MUCH HE PITCHED						WHAT HE GAVE UP										THE RESULTS					
Year	Team	League	G	GS	CG	GF	IP	BFP	H	R	ER	HR	SH	SF	HB	TBB	IBB	SO	WP	Bk	W	L	Pct	ShO	Sv	ERA
1985	California	A	30	29	6	0	189.2	807	189	105	99	23	2	5	4	64	1	102	5	0	12	12	.500	1	0	4.70
1986	California	A	34	33	10	1	246.1	1013	207	98	92	19	6	5	5	92	1	202	10	2	17	10	.630	2	0	3.36
2 YEARS			64	62	16	1	436	1820	396	203	191	42	8	10	9	156	2	304	15	2	29	22	.569	3	0	3.94

BOB McCLURE

Pitches Left-handed, Bats Right-handed   Turns Age 35 in 1987, Born 04/29/52

			HOW MUCH HE PITCHED						WHAT HE GAVE UP										THE RESULTS					
Year	Team	League	G	GS	CG	GF	IP	BFP	H	R	ER	HR	SH	SF	HB	TBB	IBB	SO	WP	Bk	W	L	Pct	ShO	Sv	ERA
1975	Kansas City	A	12	0	0	4	15	66	4	0	0	0	0	0	0	14	2	15	0	2	1	0	1.000	0	1	0.00
1976	Kansas City	A	8	0	0	4	4	22	3	4	4	0	0	0	0	8	0	3	0	0	0	0	.000	0	0	9.00
1977	Milwaukee	A	68	0	0	31	71	302	64	25	20	2	5	5	1	34	5	57	1	2	2	1	.667	0	6	2.54
1978	Milwaukee	A	44	0	0	29	65	283	53	30	27	8	7	2	6	30	4	47	1	0	2	6	.250	0	9	3.74
1979	Milwaukee	A	36	0	0	16	51	229	53	29	22	6	2	3	3	24	0	37	5	0	5	2	.714	0	3	3.88
1980	Milwaukee	A	52	5	2	23	91	390	83	34	31	6	1	5	2	37	2	47	0	2	5	8	.385	1	10	3.07
1981	Milwaukee	A	4	0	0	1	8	34	7	3	3	1	0	0	0	4	1	6	0	0	0	0	.000	0	0	3.37
1982	Milwaukee	A	34	26	5	5	172.2	734	160	90	81	21	6	4	4	74	4	99	5	5	12	7	.632	0	4	4.22
1983	Milwaukee	A	24	23	4	0	142	625	152	75	71	11	0	4	5	68	1	68	4	6	9	9	.500	0	0	4.50
1984	Milwaukee	A	39	18	1	5	139.2	616	154	76	68	9	8	8	2	52	4	68	1	3	4	8	.333	0	1	4.38
1985	Milwaukee	A	38	1	0	12	85.2	370	91	43	41	10	3	2	3	30	2	57	5	0	4	1	.800	0	3	4.31
1986	2 Teams		65	0	0	22	79	332	71	29	28	4	4	3	1	33	3	53	1	1	4	6	.400	0	6	3.19
12 YEARS			424	73	12	148	924	4003	895	438	396	78	36	36	27	408	28	557	23	22	48	48	.500	1	41	3.86
1986	Milwaukee	A	13	0	0	7	16.1	75	18	7	7	2	1	1	0	10	1	11	0	0	2	1	.667	0	0	3.86
1986	Montreal	N	52	0	0	15	62.2	257	53	22	21	2	3	2	1	23	2	42	1	1	2	5	.286	0	6	3.02

LANCE McCULLERS

Pitches Right-handed, Bats Left-handed   Turns Age 23 in 1987, Born 03/08/64

			HOW MUCH HE PITCHED						WHAT HE GAVE UP										THE RESULTS					
Year	Team	League	G	GS	CG	GF	IP	BFP	H	R	ER	HR	SH	SF	HB	TBB	IBB	SO	WP	Bk	W	L	Pct	ShO	Sv	ERA
1985	San Diego	N	21	0	0	11	35	142	23	15	9	3	7	0	1	16	3	27	0	1	0	2	.000	0	5	2.31
1986	San Diego	N	70	7	0	29	136	550	103	46	42	12	8	3	4	58	9	92	5	3	10	10	.500	0	5	2.78
2 YEARS			91	7	0	40	171	692	126	61	51	15	15	3	5	74	12	119	5	4	10	12	.455	0	10	2.68

ODDIBE MCDOWELL

Bats Left-handed, Throws Left-handed — Turns Age 25 in 1987, Born 08/25/62

Year	Team	League	G	AB	H	2B	3B	HR	(Hm	Rd)	TB	R	RBI	TBB	IBB	SO	HBP	SH	SF	SB	CS	SB%	GIDP	AVE	OBP	SLG
1985	Texas	A	111	406	97	14	5	18	(10	8)	175	63	42	36	2	85	3	5	2	25	7	.78	6	.239	.304	.431
1986	Texas	A	154	572	152	24	7	18	(8	10)	244	105	49	65	5	112	1	3	2	33	15	.69	12	.266	.341	.427
2 YEARS			265	978	249	38	12	36	(18	18)	419	168	91	101	7	197	4	8	4	58	22	.73	18	.255	.326	.428

ROGER MCDOWELL

Pitches Right-handed, Bats Right-handed — Turns Age 27 in 1987, Born 12/21/60

Year	Team	League	G	GS	CG	GF	IP	BFP	H	R	ER	HR	SH	SF	HB	TBB	IBB	SO	WP	Bk	W	L	Pct	ShO	Sv	ERA
1985	New York	N	62	2	0	36	127.1	516	108	43	40	9	6	2	1	37	8	70	6	2	6	5	.545	0	17	2.83
1986	New York	N	75	0	0	52	128	524	107	48	43	4	7	3	3	42	5	65	3	3	14	9	.609	0	22	3.02
2 YEARS			137	2	0	88	255.1	1040	215	91	83	13	13	5	4	79	13	135	9	5	20	14	.588	0	39	2.93

ANDY MCGAFFIGAN

Pitches Right-handed, Bats Right-handed — Turns Age 31 in 1987, Born 10/25/56

Year	Team	League	G	GS	CG	GF	IP	BFP	H	R	ER	HR	SH	SF	HB	TBB	IBB	SO	WP	Bk	W	L	Pct	ShO	Sv	ERA
1981	New York	A	2	0	0	0	7	31	5	3	2	1	1	2	0	3	0	2	0	1	0	0	.000	0	0	2.57
1982	San Francisco	N	4	0	0	2	8	30	5	1	0	0	0	0	1	1	0	4	0	0	1	0	1.000	0	0	0.00
1983	San Francisco	N	43	16	0	11	134.1	560	131	67	64	17	5	2	1	39	5	93	8	7	3	9	.250	0	2	4.29
1984	2 Teams	N	30	6	0	10	69	282	60	28	27	4	2	1	0	23	2	57	1	2	3	6	.333	0	1	3.52
1985	Cincinnati	N	15	15	0	2	94.1	392	88	40	39	4	4	0	3	30	4	83	2	0	3	3	.500	0	0	3.72
1986	Montreal	N	48	14	1	8	142.2	583	114	49	42	9	10	5	2	55	8	104	5	4	10	5	.667	1	2	2.65
6 YEARS			142	51	3	31	455.1	1878	403	188	174	35	22	10	6	151	19	343	16	14	20	23	.465	1	5	3.44
1984	Cincinnati	N	9	3	0	2	23	98	23	14	14	2	2	0	0	8	0	18	0	0	0	2	.000	0	0	5.48
1984	Montreal	N	21	3	0	8	46	184	37	14	13	2	0	1	0	15	2	39	1	2	3	4	.429	0	1	2.54

WILLIE MCGEE

Bats both Right and Left-handed, Throws Right-handed — Turns Age 29 in 1987, Born 11/02/58

Year	Team	League	G	AB	H	2B	3B	HR	(Hm	Rd)	TB	R	RBI	TBB	IBB	SO	HBP	SH	SF	SB	CS	SB%	GIDP	AVE	OBP	SLG
1982	St Louis	N	123	422	125	12	8	4	(2	2)	165	43	56	12	2	58	2	2	1	24	12	.67	9	.296	.318	.391
1983	St Louis	N	147	601	172	22	8	5	(4	1)	225	75	75	26	2	98	0	1	3	39	8	.83	8	.286	.314	.374
1984	St Louis	N	145	571	166	19	11	6	(2	4)	225	82	50	29	1	80	1	0	3	43	10	.81	12	.291	.325	.394
1985	St Louis	N	152	612	216	26	18	10	(3	7)	308	114	82	34	2	86	0	1	5	56	16	.78	17	.353	.384	.503
1986	St Louis	N	124	497	127	22	7	7	(7	0)	184	65	48	37	7	82	1	0	4	19	16	.54	8	.256	.306	.370
5 YEARS			691	2703	806	101	52	32	(18	14)	1107	379	311	138	15	404	4	4	16	181	62	.74	54	.298	.331	.410

SCOTT MCGREGOR

Pitches Left-handed, Bats both Right and Left-handed — Turns Age 33 in 1987, Born 01/18/54

Year	Team	League	G	GS	CG	GF	IP	BFP	H	R	ER	HR	SH	SF	HB	TBB	IBB	SO	WP	Bk	W	L	Pct	ShO	Sv	ERA
1976	Baltimore	A	3	2	0	1	15	63	17	7	6	0	0	0	0	5	0	6	2	0	0	1	.000	0	0	3.60
1977	Baltimore	A	29	5	1	11	114	480	119	57	56	8	4	7	7	30	2	55	2	0	3	5	.375	0	4	4.42
1978	Baltimore	A	35	32	13	2	233	936	217	98	86	19	9	5	1	47	3	94	3	3	15	13	.536	4	1	3.32
1979	Baltimore	A	27	23	7	3	175	706	165	70	65	19	10	6	2	23	0	81	1	1	13	6	.684	2	0	3.34
1980	Baltimore	A	36	36	12	0	252	1037	254	101	93	16	9	9	2	58	3	119	3	2	20	8	.714	4	0	3.32
1981	Baltimore	A	24	22	8	2	160	664	167	63	58	13	7	6	0	40	5	82	3	1	13	5	.722	3	0	3.26
1982	Baltimore	A	37	37	7	0	226.1	957	238	126	116	31	5	6	1	52	6	84	3	0	14	12	.538	1	0	4.61
1983	Baltimore	A	36	36	12	0	260	1072	271	101	92	24	8	10	1	45	2	86	0	0	18	7	.720	2	0	3.18
1984	Baltimore	A	30	30	10	0	196.1	840	216	93	86	18	4	5	5	54	2	67	1	0	15	12	.556	3	0	3.94
1985	Baltimore	A	35	34	8	0	204	884	226	118	109	34	10	8	1	65	2	86	2	1	14	14	.500	1	0	4.81
1986	Baltimore	A	34	33	4	1	203	868	216	110	102	35	3	6	3	57	0	95	5	0	11	15	.423	2	0	4.52
11 YEARS			326	290	82	20	2038.2	8507	2106	944	869	217	70	68	23	476	25	855	25	8	136	98	.581	22	5	3.84

JOEL MCKEON

Pitches Left-handed, Bats Left-handed — Turns Age 24 in 1987, Born 02/25/63

Year	Team	League	G	GS	CG	GF	IP	BFP	H	R	ER	HR	SH	SF	HB	TBB	IBB	SO	WP	Bk	W	L	Pct	ShO	Sv	ERA
1986	Chicago	A	30	0	0	5	33	129	18	10	9	2	1	2	0	17	2	18	0	0	3	1	.750	0	1	2.45

CRAIG MCMURTRY

Pitches Right-handed, Bats Right-handed   Turns Age 28 in 1987, Born 11/05/59

			HOW MUCH HE PITCHED						WHAT HE GAVE UP											THE RESULTS					
Year	Team	League	G	GS	CG	GF	IP	BFP	H	R	ER	HR	SH	SF	HB	TBB	IBB	SO	WP	Bk	W	L	Pct	ShO	Sv	ERA
1983	Atlanta	N	36	35	6	0	224.2	943	204	86	77	13	9	5	1	88	1	105	1	2	15	9	.625	3	0	3.08
1984	Atlanta	N	37	30	0	1	183.1	811	184	100	88	16	12	9	1	102	4	99	4	3	9	17	.346	0	0	4.32
1985	Atlanta	N	17	6	0	3	45	220	56	36	33	6	7	2	1	27	1	28	3	0	0	3	.000	0	1	6.60
1986	Atlanta	N	37	5	0	5	79.2	356	82	46	42	7	0	2	2	43	5	50	2	0	1	6	.143	0	0	4.74
4 YEARS			127	76	6	9	532.2	2330	526	268	240	42	28	18	5	260	11	282	10	5	25	35	.417	3	1	4.06

HAL MCRAE

Bats Right-handed, Throws Right-handed   Turns Age 41 in 1987, Born 07/10/46

								BATTING												BASERUNNING				PERCENTAGES		
Year	Team	League	G	AB	H	2B	3B	HR	(Hm	Rd)	TB	R	RBI	TBB	IBB	SO	HBP	SH	SF	SB	CS	SB%	GIDP	AVE	OBP	SLG
1968	Cincinnati	N	17	51	10	1	0	0	(0	0)	11	1	2	4	0	14	0	0	0	1	0	1.00	0	.196	.255	.216
1970	Cincinnati	N	70	165	41	6	1	8	(5	3)	73	18	23	15	2	23	1	0	1	0	2	.00	4	.248	.313	.442
1971	Cincinnati	N	99	337	89	24	2	9	(6	3)	144	39	34	11	0	35	2	3	1	3	2	.60	8	.264	.291	.427
1972	Cincinnati	N	61	97	27	4	0	5	(2	3)	46	9	26	2	0	10	2	0	4	0	0	.00	5	.278	.295	.474
1973	Kansas City	A	106	338	79	18	3	9	(2	7)	130	36	50	34	2	38	6	1	3	2	2	.50	7	.234	.312	.385
1974	Kansas City	A	148	539	167	36	4	15	(9	6)	256	71	88	54	6	68	5	5	4	11	8	.58	12	.310	.375	.475
1975	Kansas City	A	126	480	147	38	6	5	(2	3)	212	58	71	47	7	47	4	6	10	11	8	.58	18	.306	.366	.442
1976	Kansas City	A	149	527	175	34	5	8	(4	4)	243	75	73	64	7	43	8	2	8	22	12	.65	13	.332	.407	.461
1977	Kansas City	A	162	641	191	54	11	21	(8	13)	330	104	92	59	5	43	13	2	5	18	14	.56	12	.298	.366	.515
1978	Kansas City	A	156	623	170	39	5	16	(8	8)	267	90	72	51	6	62	6	1	11	17	8	.68	15	.273	.329	.429
1979	Kansas City	A	101	393	113	32	4	10	(5	5)	183	55	74	38	0	46	4	1	7	5	4	.56	6	.288	.351	.466
1980	Kansas City	A	124	489	145	39	5	14	(6	8)	236	73	83	29	4	56	8	0	6	10	2	.83	13	.297	.342	.483
1981	Kansas City	A	101	389	106	23	2	7	(2	5)	154	38	36	34	3	33	2	3	5	3	4	.43	11	.272	.330	.396
1982	Kansas City	A	159	613	189	46	8	27	(12	15)	332	91	133	55	7	61	5	1	2	4	4	.50	8	.308	.369	.542
1983	Kansas City	A	157	589	183	41	6	12	(5	7)	272	84	82	50	7	68	10	0	5	2	3	.40	18	.311	.372	.462
1984	Kansas City	A	106	317	96	13	4	3	(2	1)	126	30	42	34	3	47	1	0	9	0	3	.00	10	.303	.363	.397
1985	Kansas City	A	112	320	83	19	0	14	(7	7)	144	41	70	44	3	45	1	2	2	0	1	.00	12	.259	.349	.450
1986	Kansas City	A	112	278	70	14	0	7	(1	6)	105	22	37	18	4	39	1	0	2	0	0	.00	9	.252	.298	.378
18 YEARS			2066	7186	2081	481	66	190	(86	104)	3264	935	1088	643	66	778	79	27	85	109	77	.59	183	.290	.351	.454

KEVIN MCREYNOLDS

Bats Right-handed, Throws Right-handed   Turns Age 28 in 1987, Born 10/16/59

								BATTING												BASERUNNING				PERCENTAGES		
Year	Team	League	G	AB	H	2B	3B	HR	(Hm	Rd)	TB	R	RBI	TBB	IBB	SO	HBP	SH	SF	SB	CS	SB%	GIDP	AVE	OBP	SLG
1983	San Diego	N	39	140	31	3	1	4	(3	1)	48	15	14	12	1	29	0	0	3	2	1	.67	1	.221	.277	.343
1984	San Diego	N	145	525	146	26	6	20	(10	10)	244	68	75	34	8	69	0	3	9	3	6	.33	14	.278	.317	.465
1985	San Diego	N	152	564	132	24	4	15	(6	9)	209	61	75	43	6	81	3	2	4	4	0	1.00	17	.234	.290	.371
1986	San Diego	N	158	560	161	31	6	26	(14	12)	282	89	96	66	6	83	1	5	9	8	6	.57	9	.288	.358	.504
4 YEARS			494	1789	470	84	17	65	(33	32)	783	233	260	155	21	262	4	10	25	17	13	.57	41	.263	.319	.438

LARRY MCWILLIAMS

Pitches Left-handed, Bats Left-handed   Turns Age 33 in 1987, Born 02/10/54

					HOW MUCH HE PITCHED						WHAT HE GAVE UP									THE RESULTS					
Year	Team	League	G	GS	CG	GF	IP	BFP	H	R	ER	HR	SH	SF	HB	TBB	IBB	SO	WP	Bk	W	L	Pct	ShO	Sv	ERA
1978	Atlanta	N	15	15	3	0	99	417	84	38	31	11	5	0	2	35	4	42	2	0	9	3	.750	1	0	2.82
1979	Atlanta	N	13	13	1	0	66	287	69	41	41	4	6	1	4	22	2	32	2	0	3	2	.600	1	0	5.59
1980	Atlanta	N	30	30	4	0	164	715	188	97	90	27	8	2	7	39	2	77	5	1	9	14	.391	1	0	4.94
1981	Atlanta	N	6	5	2	0	38	147	31	13	13	2	2	2	0	8	0	23	0	0	2	1	.667	1	0	3.08
1982	2 Teams		46	20	2	6	159.1	678	158	79	68	12	9	3	6	44	6	118	3	1	8	8	.500	2	1	3.84
1983	Pittsburgh	N	35	35	8	0	238	1002	205	99	86	19	13	6	3	87	7	199	9	4	15	8	.652	4	0	3.25
1984	Pittsburgh	N	34	32	7	1	227.1	957	226	86	74	18	12	6	2	78	7	149	3	3	12	11	.522	2	1	2.93
1985	Pittsburgh	N	30	19	2	2	126.1	568	139	70	66	16	4	3	7	62	11	52	4	0	7	9	.438	0	0	4.70
1986	Pittsburgh	N	49	15	0	11	122.1	545	129	75	70	16	8	1	7	49	5	80	5	0	3	11	.214	0	0	5.15
9 YEARS			258	184	29	20	1240.1	5316	1229	598	539	118	67	23	38	424	44	772	33	9	68	67	.504	11	2	3.91
1982	Atlanta	N	27	2	0	5	37.2	185	52	30	26	3	3	1	2	20	5	24	1	1	2	3	.400	0	0	6.21
1982	Pittsburgh	N	19	18	2	1	121.2	493	106	49	42	9	6	2	4	24	1	94	2	0	6	5	.545	2	1	3.11

BOBBY MEACHAM

Bats both Right and Left-handed, Throws Right-handed   Turns Age 27 in 1987, Born 08/25/60

								BATTING												BASERUNNING				PERCENTAGES		
Year	Team	League	G	AB	H	2B	3B	HR	(Hm	Rd)	TB	R	RBI	TBB	IBB	SO	HBP	SH	SF	SB	CS	SB%	GIDP	AVE	OBP	SLG
1983	New York	A	22	51	12	2	0	0	(0	0)	14	5	4	4	0	10	1	0	0	8	0	1.00	0	.235	.304	.275
1984	New York	A	99	360	91	13	4	2	(1	1)	118	62	25	32	0	70	3	14	9	9	5	.64	2	.253	.312	.328
1985	New York	A	156	481	105	7	2	1	(1	0)	128	70	47	54	1	102	5	23	3	25	7	.78	7	.218	.302	.266
1986	New York	A	56	161	36	7	1	0	(0	0)	45	19	10	17	0	39	3	4	0	3	6	.33	6	.224	.309	.280
4 YEARS			333	1053	244	38	7	3	(2	1)	305	156	86	107	1	221	12	41	12	45	18	.71	15	.232	.307	.290

BOB MELVIN

Bats Right-handed, Throws Right-handed   Turns Age 26 in 1987, Born 10/28/61

Year	Team	League	G	AB	H	2B	3B	HR	(Hm	Rd)	TB	R	RBI	TBB	IBB	SO	HBP	SH	SF	SB	CS	SB%	GIDP	AVE	OBP	SLG
1985	Detroit	A	41	82	18	4	1	0	(0	0)	24	10	4	3	0	21	0	2	0	0	0	.00	1	.220	.247	.293
1986	San Francisco	N	89	268	60	14	2	5	(2	3)	93	24	25	15	1	69	0	3	3	3	2	.60	7	.224	.262	.347
2 YEARS			130	350	78	18	3	5	(2	3)	117	34	29	18	1	90	0	5	3	3	2	.60	8	.223	.259	.334

ORLANDO MERCADO

Bats Right-handed, Throws Right-handed   Turns Age 26 in 1987, Born 11/07/61

Year	Team	League	G	AB	H	2B	3B	HR	(Hm	Rd)	TB	R	RBI	TBB	IBB	SO	HBP	SH	SF	SB	CS	SB%	GIDP	AVE	OBP	SLG
1982	Seattle	A	9	17	2	0	0	1	(1	0)	5	1	6	0	0	5	0	0	0	0	0	.00	0	.118	.118	.294
1983	Seattle	A	66	178	35	11	2	1	(1	0)	53	10	16	14	0	27	1	2	2	2	2	.50	3	.197	.256	.298
1984	Seattle	A	30	78	17	3	1	0	(0	0)	22	5	5	4	0	12	1	1	0	1	0	1.00	1	.218	.265	.282
1986	Texas	A	46	102	24	1	1	1	(1	0)	30	7	7	6	0	13	1	1	2	0	1	.00	5	.235	.279	.294
4 YEARS			151	375	78	15	4	3	(3	0)	110	23	34	24	0	57	3	4	4	3	3	.50	9	.208	.259	.293

EDDIE MILNER

Bats Left-handed, Throws Left-handed   Turns Age 32 in 1987, Born 05/21/55

Year	Team	League	G	AB	H	2B	3B	HR	(Hm	Rd)	TB	R	RBI	TBB	IBB	SO	HBP	SH	SF	SB	CS	SB%	GIDP	AVE	OBP	SLG
1980	Cincinnati	N	6	3	0	0	0	0	(0	0)	0	1	0	0	0	0	0	0	0	0	0	.00	0	.000	.000	.000
1981	Cincinnati	N	8	5	1	0	0	0	(0	0)	2	0	1	1	0	0	0	0	0	0	0	.00	0	.200	.333	.400
1982	Cincinnati	N	113	407	109	23	5	4	(1	3)	154	61	31	41	1	40	2	2	0	18	12	.60	7	.268	.338	.378
1983	Cincinnati	N	146	502	131	23	6	9	(3	6)	193	77	33	68	2	60	1	12	1	41	12	.77	11	.261	.350	.384
1984	Cincinnati	N	117	336	78	8	4	7	(5	2)	115	44	29	51	3	50	2	4	4	21	13	.62	2	.232	.333	.342
1985	Cincinnati	N	145	453	115	19	7	3	(1	2)	157	82	33	61	3	31	1	2	3	35	13	.73	3	.254	.342	.347
1986	Cincinnati	N	145	424	110	22	6	15	(8	7)	189	70	47	36	2	56	0	1	1	18	11	.62	3	.259	.317	.446
7 YEARS			680	2130	544	96	28	38	(18	20)	810	335	174	258	11	238	6	21	9	133	61	.69	26	.255	.336	.380

GREG MINTON

Pitches Right-handed, Bats both Right and Left-handed   Turns Age 36 in 1987, Born 07/29/51

	HOW MUCH HE PITCHED						WHAT HE GAVE UP												THE RESULTS					
Year Team League	G	GS	CG	GF	IP	BFP	H	R	ER	HR	SH	SF	HB	TBB	IBB	SO	WP	Bk	W	L	Pct	ShO	Sv	ERA
1975 San Francisco N	4	2	0	0	17	79	19	14	13	1	1	0	1	11	3	6	2		1	1	.500	0	0	6.88
1976 San Francisco N	10	2	0	5	26	117	32	18	14	0	1	2	1	12	1	7	3	1	0	3	.000	0	0	4.85
1977 San Francisco N	2	2	0	0	14	57	14	8	7	0	2	0	0	4	0	5	2	1	1	1	.500	0	0	4.50
1978 San Francisco N	11	0	0	3	16	76	22	14	14	3	1	1	1	8	1	6	0		0	1	.000	0	0	7.87
1979 San Francisco N	46	0	0	18	80	314	59	25	16	0	9	1	2	27	7	33	8	2	4	3	.571	0	4	1.80
1980 San Francisco N	68	0	0	38	91	377	81	28	25	0	8	1	0	34	6	42	7	1	4	6	.400	0	19	2.47
1981 San Francisco N	55	0	0	44	84	359	84	28	27	0	6	2	0	36	8	29	2	2	4	5	.444	0	21	2.89
1982 San Francisco N	78	0	0	66	123	496	108	29	25	5	6	4	2	42	17	58	7	0	10	4	.714	0	30	1.83
1983 San Francisco N	73	0	0	52	106.2	476	117	51	42	6	10	5	0	47	13	38	5	0	7	11	.389	0	22	3.54
1984 San Francisco N	74	1	0	43	124.1	556	130	60	52	6	7	6	0	57	20	48	5	0	4	9	.308	0	19	3.76
1985 San Francisco N	68	0	0	36	96.2	424	98	42	38	6	6	4	0	54	18	37	2	0	5	4	.556	0	4	3.54
1986 San Francisco N	48	0	0	28	68.2	296	63	35	30	4	7	3	1	34	15	34	3	0	4	4	.500	0	5	3.93
12 YEARS	537	7	0	333	847.1	3627	827	352	303	31	62	29	8	366	109	343	46	8	44	52	.458	0	124	3.22

KEVIN MITCHELL

Bats Right-handed, Throws Right-handed   Turns Age 25 in 1987, Born 01/13/62

Year	Team	League	G	AB	H	2B	3B	HR	(Hm	Rd)	TB	R	RBI	TBB	IBB	SO	HBP	SH	SF	SB	CS	SB%	GIDP	AVE	OBP	SLG
1984	New York	N	7	14	3	0	0	0	(0	0)	3	0	0	0	0	3	0	0	0	0	1	.00	0	.214	.214	.214
1986	New York	N	108	328	91	22	2	12	(4	8)	153	51	43	33	0	61	1	1	1	3	3	.50	6	.277	.344	.466
2 YEARS			115	342	94	22	2	12	(4	8)	156	51	44	33	0	64	1	1	1	3	4	.43	6	.275	.340	.456

DALE MOHORCIC

Pitches Right-handed, Bats Right-handed   Turns Age 31 in 1987, Born 01/25/56

	HOW MUCH HE PITCHED						WHAT HE GAVE UP												THE RESULTS					
Year Team League	G	GS	CG	GF	IP	BFP	H	R	ER	HR	SH	SF	HB	TBB	IBB	SO	WP	Bk	W	L	Pct	ShO	Sv	ERA
1986 Texas A	58	0	0	20	79	325	86	25	22	5	1	0	1	15	6	29	1	0	2	4	.333	0	7	2.51

PAUL MOLITOR

Bats Right-handed, Throws Right-handed | Turns Age 31 in 1987, Born 08/22/56

Year	Team	League	G	AB	H	2B	3B	HR	(Hm	Rd)	TB	R	RBI	TBB	IBB	SO	HBP	SH	SF	SB	CS	SB%	GIDP	AVE	OBP	SLG
1978	Milwaukee	A	125	521	142	26	4	6	(4	2)	194	73	45	19	2	54	4	7	5	30	12	.71	6	.273	.301	.372
1979	Milwaukee	A	140	584	188	27	16	9	(3	6)	274	88	62	48	5	48	2	6	5	33	13	.72	9	.322	.372	.469
1980	Milwaukee	A	111	450	137	29	2	9	(2	7)	197	81	37	48	4	48	3	6	5	34	7	.83	9	.304	.372	.438
1981	Milwaukee	A	64	251	67	11	0	2	(1	1)	84	45	19	25	1	29	3	5	0	10	6	.63	3	.267	.341	.335
1982	Milwaukee	A	160	666	201	26	8	19	(9	10)	300	136	71	69	1	93	1	10	5	41	9	.82	9	.302	.366	.450
1983	Milwaukee	A	152	608	164	28	6	15	(9	6)	249	95	47	59	4	74	2	7	6	41	8	.84	12	.270	.333	.410
1984	Milwaukee	A	13	46	10	1	0	0	(0	0)	11	3	6	2	0	8	0	0	1	1	0	1.00	0	.217	.245	.239
1985	Milwaukee	A	140	576	171	28	3	10	(6	4)	235	93	48	54	6	80	1	7	4	21	7	.75	12	.297	.356	.408
1986	Milwaukee	A	105	437	123	24	6	9	(5	4)	186	62	55	40	0	81	0	2	3	20	5	.80	9	.281	.340	.426
9 YEARS			1010	4139	1203	200	45	79	(39	40)	1730	676	390	364	23	515	16	50	34	231	67	.78	69	.291	.348	.418

BILL MOONEYHAM

Pitches Right-handed, Bats Right-handed | Turns Age 27 in 1987, Born 08/16/60

Year	Team	League	G	GS	CG	GF	IP	BFP	H	R	ER	HR	SH	SF	HB	TBB	IBB	SO	WP	Bk	W	L	Pct	ShO	Sv	ERA
1986	Oakland	A	45	6	0	18	99.2	456	103	53	50	4	3	2	3	67	4	75	2	0	4	5	.444	0	2	4.52

CHARLIE MOORE

Bats Right-handed, Throws Right-handed | Turns Age 34 in 1987, Born 06/21/53

Year	Team	League	G	AB	H	2B	3B	HR	(Hm	Rd)	TB	R	RBI	TBB	IBB	SO	HBP	SH	SF	SB	CS	SB%	GIDP	AVE	OBP	SLG
1973	Milwaukee	A	8	27	5	0	1	0	(0	0)	7	0	3	2	1	4	0	0	0	0	0	.00	0	.185	.241	.259
1974	Milwaukee	A	72	204	50	10	4	0	(0	0)	68	17	19	21	1	34	0	0	0	3	4	.43	4	.245	.316	.333
1975	Milwaukee	A	73	241	70	20	1	1	(0	1)	95	26	29	17	0	31	0	3	1	1	5	.17	6	.290	.336	.394
1976	Milwaukee	A	87	241	46	7	4	3	(1	2)	70	33	16	43	0	45	1	3	2	1	2	.33	4	.191	.314	.290
1977	Milwaukee	A	138	375	93	15	6	5	(2	3)	135	42	45	31	0	39	1	9	2	1	7	.13	13	.248	.306	.360
1978	Milwaukee	A	96	268	72	7	1	5	(4	1)	96	30	31	12	0	24	0	5	0	4	2	.67	4	.269	.300	.358
1979	Milwaukee	A	111	337	101	16	2	5	(2	3)	136	45	38	29	1	32	1	3	2	8	5	.62	11	.300	.335	.404
1980	Milwaukee	A	111	320	93	13	2	2	(1	1)	116	42	30	24	2	28	0	8	2	10	5	.67	7	.291	.336	.363
1981	Milwaukee	A	48	156	47	8	3	1	(1	0)	64	16	9	12	0	13	0	3	0	1	4	.20	4	.301	.351	.410
1982	Milwaukee	A	133	456	116	22	4	6	(3	3)	164	53	45	29	2	49	1	4	2	2	10	.17	11	.254	.299	.360
1983	Milwaukee	A	151	529	150	27	6	2	(1	1)	195	65	49	55	5	42	4	14	3	11	4	.73	14	.284	.354	.369
1984	Milwaukee	A	70	188	44	7	1	2	(1	1)	59	13	17	10	0	26	1	3	1	0	4	.00	6	.234	.275	.314
1985	Milwaukee	A	105	349	81	13	4	0	(0	0)	102	35	31	27	0	53	1	8	1	4	0	1.00	12	.232	.288	.292
1986	Milwaukee	A	80	235	61	12	3	3	(2	1)	88	24	39	21	1	38	0	4	3	5	5	.50	6	.260	.317	.374
14 YEARS			1283	3926	1029	177	42	35	(18	17)	1395	441	401	333	12	458	10	67	21	51	57	.47	102	.262	.320	.355

DONNIE MOORE

Pitches Right-handed, Bats Left-handed | Turns Age 33 in 1987, Born 02/13/54

Year	Team	League	G	GS	CG	GF	IP	BFP	H	R	ER	HR	SH	SF	HB	TBB	IBB	SO	WP	Bk	W	L	Pct	ShO	Sv	ERA
1975	Chicago	N	4	1	0	0	9	42	12	4	4	1	0	0	0	4	0	8	0	0	0	0	.000	0	0	4.00
1977	Chicago	N	27	1	0	5	49	207	51	27	22	1	7	3	0	18	7	34	2	4	4	2	.667	0	0	4.04
1978	Chicago	N	71	1	0	24	103	450	117	55	47	7	5	4	2	31	11	50	7	2	9	7	.563	0	4	4.11
1979	Chicago	N	39	1	0	12	73	330	95	46	42	8	5	2	2	25	7	43	3	0	1	4	.200	0	1	5.18
1980	St Louis	N	11	0	0	3	22	93	25	15	15	1	2	1	1	5	1	10	0	1	1	1	.500	0	0	6.14
1981	Milwaukee	A	3	0	0	2	4	19	4	3	3	0	0	1	0	4	0	2	1	0	0	0	.000	0	0	6.75
1982	Atlanta	N	16	0	0	5	27.2	121	32	13	13	1	2	1	2	7	3	17	0	1	3	1	.750	0	1	4.23
1983	Atlanta	N	43	0	0	16	68.2	276	72	30	28	6	3	5	0	10	3	41	0	1	2	3	.400	0	6	3.67
1984	Atlanta	N	47	0	0	29	64.1	271	63	27	21	3	6	2	1	18	6	47	1	0	4	5	.444	0	16	2.94
1985	California	A	65	0	0	57	103	417	91	28	22	9	10	2	0	21	3	72	2	0	8	8	.500	0	31	1.92
1986	California	A	49	0	0	42	72.2	295	60	28	24	10	7	3	0	22	4	53	4	1	4	5	.444	0	21	2.97
11 YEARS			375	4	0	195	596.1	2521	622	276	241	47	47	24	8	165	45	377	20	10	36	36	.500	0	80	3.64

MIKE MOORE

Pitches Right-handed, Bats Right-handed | Turns Age 28 in 1987, Born 11/26/59

Year	Team	League	G	GS	CG	GF	IP	BFP	H	R	ER	HR	SH	SF	HB	TBB	IBB	SO	WP	Bk	W	L	Pct	ShO	Sv	ERA
1982	Seattle	A	28	27	1	0	144.1	651	159	91	86	21	8	4	2	79	0	73	6	0	7	14	.333	1	0	5.36
1983	Seattle	A	22	21	3	1	128	556	130	75	67	10	1	6	3	60	4	108	7	0	6	8	.429	2	0	4.71
1984	Seattle	A	34	33	6	0	212	937	236	127	117	16	5	6	5	85	10	158	7	2	7	17	.292	0	0	4.97
1985	Seattle	A	35	34	14	0	247	1016	230	100	95	18	2	7	4	70	2	155	10	3	17	10	.630	3	0	3.46
1986	Seattle	A	38	37	11	1	266	1145	279	141	127	28	10	6	12	94	6	146	4	1	11	13	.458	1	1	4.30
5 YEARS			157	152	35	3	997.1	4305	1034	534	492	93	26	29	26	388	22	640	34	6	48	62	.436	6	1	4.44

KEITH MORELAND

Bats Right-handed, Throws Right-handed   Turns Age 33 in 1987, Born 05/02/54

Year	Team	League	G	AB	H	2B	3B	HR	(Hm	Rd)	TB	R	RBI	TBB	IBB	SO	HBP	SH	SF	SB	CS	SB%	GIDP	AVE	OBP	SLG
1978	Philadelphia	N	1	2	0	0	0	0	(0	0)	0	0	0	0	0	0	0	0	0	0	0	.00	0	.000	.000	.000
1979	Philadelphia	N	14	48	18	3	2	0	(0	0)	25	3	8	3	0	5	0	0	0	0	0	.00	1	.375	.412	.521
1980	Philadelphia	N	62	159	50	8	0	4	(1	3)	70	13	29	8	2	14	0	1	3	3	1	.75	6	.314	.341	.440
1981	Philadelphia	N	61	196	50	7	0	6	(4	2)	75	16	37	15	1	13	1	0	3	1	2	.33	10	.255	.307	.383
1982	Chicago	N	138	476	124	17	2	15	(8	7)	190	50	68	46	8	71	3	1	6	0	6	.00	9	.261	.326	.399
1983	Chicago	N	154	533	161	30	3	16	(8	8)	245	76	70	68	8	73	3	5	10	0	3	.00	16	.302	.378	.460
1984	Chicago	N	140	495	138	17	3	16	(13	3)	209	59	80	34	5	71	3	2	5	1	4	.20	16	.279	.326	.422
1985	Chicago	N	161	587	180	30	3	14	(11	3)	258	74	106	68	7	58	1	2	9	12	3	.80	14	.307	.374	.440
1986	Chicago	N	156	586	159	30	0	12	(8	4)	225	72	79	53	10	48	0	2	11	3	6	.33	15	.271	.326	.384
9 YEARS				887	3082	880	142	13	83	(53 | 30)	1297	363	477	295	41	353	11	13	47	20	25	.44	87	.286	.345	.421

OMAR MORENO

Bats Left-handed, Throws Left-handed   Turns Age 34 in 1987, Born 10/24/53

Year	Team	League	G	AB	H	2B	3B	HR	(Hm	Rd)	TB	R	RBI	TBB	IBB	SO	HBP	SH	SF	SB	CS	SB%	GIDP	AVE	OBP	SLG
1975	Pittsburgh	N	6	6	0	0	0	0	(0	0)	1	1	0	1	0	1	0	0	0	0	1	1.00	0	.167	.286	.167
1976	Pittsburgh	N	48	122	33	4	1	2	(0	2)	45	24	12	16	0	24	1	1	1	15	5	.75	0	.270	.357	.369
1977	Pittsburgh	N	150	492	118	19	9	7	(3	4)	176	69	34	38	5	102	1	0	2	53	16	.77	4	.240	.295	.358
1978	Pittsburgh	N	155	515	121	15	7	2	(1	1)	156	95	33	81	4	104	3	1	5	71	22	.76	5	.235	.339	.303
1979	Pittsburgh	N	162	695	196	21	12	8	(1	7)	265	110	69	51	9	104	3	6	2	77	21	.79	7	.282	.333	.381
1980	Pittsburgh	N	162	676	168	20	13	2	(1	1)	220	87	36	57	11	101	2	3	7	96	33	.74	9	.249	.306	.325
1981	Pittsburgh	N	103	434	120	18	8	1	(0	1)	157	62	35	26	3	76	3	1	4	39	14	.74	1	.276	.319	.362
1982	Pittsburgh	N	158	645	158	18	9	3	(1	2)	203	82	44	44	2	121	1	10	6	60	26	.70	6	.245	.292	.315
1983	2 Teams	A	145	557	136	21	12	1	(1	0)	184	65	42	30	3	103	1	3	1	37	16	.70	6	.244	.284	.330
1984	New York	A	117	355	92	12	6	4	(2	2)	128	37	38	18	1	48	1	4	4	20	11	.65	3	.259	.294	.361
1985	2 Teams	A	58	136	30	5	4	3	(2	1)	52	21	16	4	0	24	1	1	1	1	2	.33	2	.221	.246	.382
1986	Atlanta	N	118	359	84	18	6	4	(3	1)	126	46	27	21	2	77	0	6	0	17	16	.52	2	.234	.276	.351
12 YEARS				1382	4992	1257	171	87	37	(16 | 21)	1713	699	386	387	41	885	17	52	33	487	182	.73	45	.252	.306	.343
1983	New York	A	48	152	38	9	1	1	(1	0)	52	17	17	8	0	31	0	3	0	7	3	.70	4	.250	.288	.342
1983	Houston	A	97	405	98	12	11	0	(0	0)	132	48	25	22	3	72	1	0	1	30	13	.70	2	.242	.282	.326
1985	Kansas City	A	24	70	17	1	3	2	(2	0)	30	9	12	3	0	8	1	0	1	0	1	.00	1	.243	.280	.429
1985	New York	A	34	66	13	4	1	1	(1	0)	22	12	4	1	0	16	0	1	0	1	1	.50	1	.197	.209	.333

MIKE MORGAN

Pitches Right-handed, Bats Right-handed   Turns Age 28 in 1987, Born 10/08/59

Year	Team	League	G	GS	CG	GF	IP	BFP	H	R	ER	HR	SH	SF	HB	TBB	IBB	SO	WP	Bk	W	L	Pct	ShO	Sv	ERA
1978	Oakland	A	3	3	1	0	12	60	19	12	10	1	1	0	1	8	0	0	0	0	0	3	.000	0	0	7.50
1979	Oakland	A	13	13	2	0	77	368	102	57	51	7	4	4	3	50	0	17	7	0	2	10	.167	0	0	5.96
1982	New York	A	30	23	2	2	150.1	661	167	77	73	15	2	4	2	67	5	71	6	0	7	11	.389	0	0	4.37
1983	Toronto	A	16	4	0	2	45.1	198	48	26	26	8	0	1	0	21	0	22	3	0	0	3	.000	0	0	5.16
1985	Seattle	A	2	2	0	0	6	33	11	8	8	2	0	0	0	5	0	2	1	0	1	1	.500	0	0	12.00
1986	Seattle	A	37	33	9	2	216.1	951	243	122	109	24	7	3	4	86	3	116	8	1	11	17	.393	1	1	4.53
6 YEARS			101	78	14	6	507	2271	590	302	277	55	14	12	9	237	8	228	25	1	21	45	.318	1	1	4.92

RUSS MORMAN

Bats Right-handed, Throws Right-handed   Turns Age 25 in 1987, Born 04/28/62

Year	Team	League	G	AB	H	2B	3B	HR	(Hm	Rd)	TB	R	RBI	TBB	IBB	SO	HBP	SH	SF	SB	CS	SB%	GIDP	AVE	OBP	SLG
1986	Chicago	A	49	159	40	5	0	4	(1	3)	57	18	17	16	0	36	2	1	2	1	0	1.00	5	.252	.324	.358

JACK MORRIS

Pitches Right-handed, Bats Right-handed   Turns Age 32 in 1987, Born 05/16/55

Year	Team	League	G	GS	CG	GF	IP	BFP	H	R	ER	HR	SH	SF	HB	TBB	IBB	SO	WP	Bk	W	L	Pct	ShO	Sv	ERA
1977	Detroit	A	7	6	1	0	46	189	38	20	19	4	3	1	0	23	0	28	2	0	1	1	.500	0	0	3.72
1978	Detroit	A	28	7	0	10	106	469	107	57	51	8	8	9	3	49	5	48	4	0	3	5	.375	0	0	4.33
1979	Detroit	A	27	27	9	0	198	806	179	76	72	19	3	6	4	59	4	113	9	1	17	7	.708	1	0	3.27
1980	Detroit	A	36	36	11	0	250	1074	252	125	116	20	10	13	4	87	5	112	6	2	16	15	.516	2	0	4.18
1981	Detroit	A	25	25	15	0	198	798	153	69	67	14	8	9	2	78	11	97	2	2	14	7	.667	1	0	3.05
1982	Detroit	A	37	37	17	0	266.1	1107	247	131	120	37	4	5	0	96	7	135	10	0	17	16	.515	3	0	4.06
1983	Detroit	A	37	37	20	0	293.2	1204	257	117	109	30	8	9	3	83	5	232	18	0	20	13	.606	1	0	3.34
1984	Detroit	A	35	35	9	0	240.1	1015	221	108	96	20	5	3	2	87	7	148	14	0	19	11	.633	1	0	3.60
1985	Detroit	A	35	35	13	0	257	1077	212	102	95	21	11	7	5	110	7	191	15	3	16	11	.593	4	0	3.33
1986	Detroit	A	35	35	15	0	267	1092	229	105	97	40	7	3	0	82	7	223	12	0	21	8	.724	6	0	3.27
10 YEARS			302	280	110	10	2122.1	8831	1895	910	842	213	67	65	23	754	58	1327	92	8	144	94	.605	19	0	3.57

JOHN MORRIS

Bats Left-handed, Throws Left-handed   Turns Age 26 in 1987, Born 02/23/61

								BATTING											BASERUNNING				PERCENTAGES		
Year	Team	League	G	AB	H	2B	3B	HR	(Hm | Rd)	TB	R	RBI	TBB	IBB	SO	HBP	SH	SF	SB	CS	SB%	GIDP	AVE	OBP	SLG
1986	St Louis	N	39	100	24	0	1	1	(1 | 0)	29	8	14	7	2	15	0	0	1	6	2	.75	2	.240	.287	.290

JIM MORRISON

Bats Right-handed, Throws Right-handed   Turns Age 35 in 1987, Born 09/23/52

								BATTING											BASERUNNING				PERCENTAGES		
Year	Team	League	G	AB	H	2B	3B	HR	(Hm | Rd)	TB	R	RBI	TBB	IBB	SO	HBP	SH	SF	SB	CS	SB%	GIDP	AVE	OBP	SLG
1977	Philadelphia	N	5	7	3	0	0	0	(0 | 0)	3	3	1	1	0	1	0	0	0	0	0	.00	0	.429	.500	.429
1978	Philadelphia	N	53	108	17	1	1	3	(3 | 0)	29	12	10	10	1	21	1	4	0	1	1	.50	2	.157	.235	.269
1979	Chicago	A	67	240	66	14	0	14	(9 | 5)	122	38	35	15	0	48	4	7	3	11	3	.79	2	.275	.324	.508
1980	Chicago	A	162	604	171	40	0	15	(5 | 10)	256	66	57	36	2	74	8	12	6	9	6	.60	19	.283	.329	.424
1981	Chicago	A	90	290	68	8	1	10	(3 | 7)	108	27	34	10	0	29	2	9	4	3	2	.60	9	.234	.261	.372
1982	2 Teams		95	252	61	11	4	11	(5 | 6)	113	27	34	18	0	29	0	3	3	2	1	.67	9	.242	.289	.448
1983	Pittsburgh	N	66	158	48	7	2	6	(2 | 4)	77	16	25	9	1	25	2	4	1	2	6	.25	3	.304	.347	.487
1984	Pittsburgh	N	100	304	87	14	2	11	(6 | 5)	138	38	45	20	1	52	1	2	4	0	1	.00	9	.286	.328	.454
1985	Pittsburgh	N	92	244	62	10	0	4	(2 | 2)	84	17	22	8	1	44	1	1	3	3	0	1.00	3	.254	.277	.344
1986	Pittsburgh	N	154	537	147	35	4	23	(11 | 12)	259	58	88	47	5	88	4	0	5	9	8	.53	6	.274	.334	.482
10 YEARS			884	2744	730	140	14	97	(46 | 51)	1189	302	351	174	11	411	23	42	29	40	28	.59	63	.266	.312	.433
1982	Chicago	A	51	166	37	7	3	7	(3 | 4)	71	17	19	13	0	15	0	1	0	0	1	.00	5	.223	.279	.428
1982	Pittsburgh	N	44	86	24	4	1	4	(2 | 2)	42	10	15	5	0	14	0	2	3	2	0	1.00	4	.279	.309	.488

LLOYD MOSEBY

Bats Left-handed, Throws Right-handed   Turns Age 28 in 1987, Born 11/05/59

								BATTING											BASERUNNING				PERCENTAGES		
Year	Team	League	G	AB	H	2B	3B	HR	(Hm | Rd)	TB	R	RBI	TBB	IBB	SO	HBP	SH	SF	SB	CS	SB%	GIDP	AVE	OBP	SLG
1980	Toronto	A	114	389	89	24	1	9	(4 | 5)	142	44	46	25	4	85	4	10	2	4	6	.40	11	.229	.281	.365
1981	Toronto	A	100	378	88	16	2	9	(3 | 6)	135	36	43	24	3	86	1	5	4	11	8	.58	4	.233	.278	.357
1982	Toronto	A	147	487	115	20	9	9	(4 | 5)	180	51	52	33	3	106	8	3	2	11	7	.61	10	.236	.294	.370
1983	Toronto	A	151	539	170	31	7	18	(13 | 5)	269	104	81	51	4	85	5	3	6	27	8	.77	10	.315	.376	.499
1984	Toronto	A	158	592	166	28	15	18	(10 | 8)	278	97	92	78	9	122	8	3	7	39	9	.81	8	.280	.368	.470
1985	Toronto	A	152	584	151	30	7	18	(11 | 7)	249	92	70	76	4	91	4	1	5	37	15	.71	12	.259	.345	.426
1986	Toronto	A	152	589	149	24	5	21	(11 | 10)	246	89	86	64	3	122	6	2	7	32	11	.74	7	.253	.329	.418
7 YEARS			974	3558	928	173	46	102	(56 | 46)	1499	513	470	351	30	697	36	27	33	161	64	.72	62	.261	.331	.421

JOHN MOSES

Bats both Right and Left-handed, Throws Left-handed   Turns Age 30 in 1987, Born 08/09/57

								BATTING											BASERUNNING				PERCENTAGES		
Year	Team	League	G	AB	H	2B	3B	HR	(Hm | Rd)	TB	R	RBI	TBB	IBB	SO	HBP	SH	SF	SB	CS	SB%	GIDP	AVE	OBP	SLG
1982	Seattle	A	22	44	14	5	1	1	(1 | 0)	24	7	3	4	0	5	0	0	0	5	1	.83	0	.318	.375	.545
1983	Seattle	A	93	130	27	4	1	0	(0 | 0)	33	19	6	12	0	20	1	0	0	11	5	.69	4	.208	.280	.254
1984	Seattle	A	19	35	12	1	1	0	(0 | 0)	15	3	2	2	0	5	1	1	0	1	0	1.00	0	.343	.395	.429
1985	Seattle	A	33	62	12	0	0	0	(0 | 0)	12	4	3	2	0	8	0	1	0	5	2	.71	3	.194	.219	.194
1986	Seattle	A	103	399	102	16	3	3	(2 | 1)	133	56	34	34	3	65	0	5	4	25	18	.58	7	.256	.311	.333
5 YEARS			270	670	167	26	6	4	(3 | 1)	217	89	48	54	3	103	2	7	4	47	26	.64	14	.249	.305	.324

DARRYL MOTLEY

Bats Right-handed, Throws Right-handed   Turns Age 27 in 1987, Born 01/21/60

								BATTING											BASERUNNING				PERCENTAGES		
Year	Team	League	G	AB	H	2B	3B	HR	(Hm | Rd)	TB	R	RBI	TBB	IBB	SO	HBP	SH	SF	SB	CS	SB%	GIDP	AVE	OBP	SLG
1981	Kansas City	A	42	125	29	4	0	2	(0 | 2)	39	15	8	7	0	15	1	1	1	1	3	.25	2	.232	.276	.312
1983	Kansas City	A	19	68	16	1	2	3	(2 | 1)	30	9	11	2	0	8	1	0	1	2	1	.67	3	.235	.264	.441
1984	Kansas City	A	146	522	148	25	6	15	(5 | 10)	230	64	70	28	2	73	1	2	4	10	12	.45	23	.284	.319	.441
1985	Kansas City	A	123	383	85	20	1	17	(6 | 11)	158	45	49	18	2	57	2	0	5	6	4	.60	17	.222	.257	.413
1986	2 Teams		77	227	46	10	1	7	(3 | 4)	79	23	20	12	2	32	0	1	0	0	2	.00	8	.203	.243	.348
5 YEARS			407	1325	324	60	10	44	(16 | 28)	536	156	158	67	6	185	5	4	11	19	22	.46	53	.245	.281	.405
1986	Kansas City	A	72	217	44	9	1	7	(3 | 4)	76	22	20	11	1	31	0	1	0	0	2	.00	8	.203	.241	.350
1986	Atlanta	N	5	10	2	1	0	0	(0 | 0)	3	1	0	1	1	1	0	0	0	0	0	.00	0	.200	.273	.300

JAMIE MOYER

Pitches Left-handed, Bats Left-handed

			HOW MUCH HE PITCHED						WHAT HE GAVE UP											THE RESULTS					
Year	Team	League	G	GS	CG	GF	IP	BFP	H	R	ER	HR	SH	SF	HB	TBB	IBB	SO	WP	Bk	W	L	Pct	ShO	Sv	ERA
1986	Chicago	N	16	16	1	0	87.1	395	107	52	49	10	3	3	3	42	1	45	3	3	7	4	.636	1	0	5.05

TERRY MULHOLLAND

Pitches Left-handed, Bats Right-handed — Turns Age 24 in 1987, Born 03/09/63

			HOW MUCH HE PITCHED						WHAT HE GAVE UP												THE RESULTS					
Year	Team	League	G	GS	CG	GF	IP	BFP	H	R	ER	HR	SH	SF	HB	TBB	IBB	SO	WP	Bk	W	L	Pct	ShO	Sv	ERA
1986	San Francisco	N	15	10	0	1	54.2	245	51	33	30	3	5	1	1	35	2	27	6	0	1	7	.125	0	0	4.94

RANCE MULLINIKS

Bats Left-handed, Throws Right-handed — Turns Age 31 in 1987, Born 01/15/56

									BATTING										BASERUNNING				PERCENTAGES		
Year	Team	League	G	AB	H	2B	3B	HR	(Hm	Rd)	TB	R	RBI	TBB	IBB	SO	HBP	SH	SF	SB	CS	SB%	GIDP	AVE	OBP	SLG
1977	California	A	78	271	73	13	2	3	(2	1)	99	36	21	23	2	36	1	8	0	1	1	.50	2	.269	.329	.365
1978	California	A	50	119	22	3	1	1	(1	0)	30	6	6	8	0	23	1	0	2	2	0	1.00	3	.185	.238	.252
1979	California	A	22	68	10	0	0	1	(0	1)	13	7	8	4	0	14	1	0	5	0	0	.00	2	.147	.192	.191
1980	Kansas City	A	36	54	14	3	0	0	(0	0)	17	8	6	7	0	10	0	0	1	0	0	.00	2	.259	.339	.315
1981	Kansas City	A	24	44	10	3	0	0	(0	0)	13	6	5	2	0	7	0	0	0	0	1	.00	2	.227	.261	.295
1982	Toronto	A	112	311	76	25	0	4	(2	2)	113	32	35	37	1	49	1	3	1	3	2	.60	10	.244	.326	.363
1983	Toronto	A	129	364	100	34	3	10	(4	6)	170	54	49	57	5	43	1	3	2	0	2	.00	14	.275	.373	.467
1984	Toronto	A	125	343	111	21	5	3	(1	2)	151	41	42	33	3	44	1	0	2	2	3	.40	5	.324	.383	.440
1985	Toronto	A	129	366	108	26	1	10	(4	6)	166	55	57	55	2	54	0	1	5	2	0	1.00	10	.295	.383	.454
1986	Toronto	A	117	348	90	22	0	11	(5	6)	145	50	45	43	1	60	1	1	2	1	1	.50	12	.259	.340	.417
10 YEARS			822	2288	614	150	12	43	(19	24)	917	295	274	269	14	340	7	16	20	11	10	.52	62	.268	.344	.401

JERRY MUMPHREY

Bats both Right and Left-handed, Throws Right-handed — Turns Age 35 in 1987, Born 09/09/52

									BATTING										BASERUNNING				PERCENTAGES		
Year	Team	League	G	AB	H	2B	3B	HR	(Hm	Rd)	TB	R	RBI	TBB	IBB	SO	HBP	SH	SF	SB	CS	SB%	GIDP	AVE	OBP	SLG
1974	St Louis	N	5	2	0	0	0	0	(0	0)	0	2	0	0	0	0	0	0	0	0	0	.00	0	.000	.000	.000
1975	St Louis	N	11	16	6	2	0	0	(0	0)	8	2	1	4	0	3	0	0	0	0	0	.00	0	.375	.500	.500
1976	St Louis	N	112	384	99	15	5	1	(0	1)	127	51	26	37	0	53	1	2	3	22	6	.79	2	.258	.322	.331
1977	St Louis	N	145	463	133	20	10	2	(0	2)	179	73	38	47	6	70	1	1	0	22	15	.59	4	.287	.354	.387
1978	St Louis	N	125	367	96	13	4	2	(1	1)	123	41	37	30	0	40	1	2	3	14	10	.58	10	.262	.317	.335
1979	St Louis	N	124	339	100	10	3	3	(2	1)	125	53	32	26	2	39	0	6	4	8	11	.42	6	.295	.341	.369
1980	San Diego	N	160	564	168	24	3	4	(1	3)	210	61	59	49	4	90	0	5	4	52	5	.91	18	.298	.352	.372
1981	New York	A	80	319	98	11	5	6	(3	3)	137	44	32	24	1	27	0	5	2	14	9	.61	7	.307	.354	.429
1982	New York	A	123	477	143	24	10	9	(6	3)	214	76	68	50	4	66	0	3	3	11	3	.79	17	.300	.364	.449
1983	2 Teams		127	410	118	21	6	8	(2	6)	175	58	53	50	6	56	1	2	6	7	3	.70	12	.288	.362	.427
1984	Houston	N	151	524	152	20	3	9	(1	8)	205	66	83	56	7	79	0	1	6	15	7	.68	12	.290	.355	.391
1985	Houston	N	130	444	123	25	2	5	(4	1)	176	52	61	37	8	57	0	1	6	6	7	.46	9	.277	.329	.396
1986	Chicago	N	111	309	94	11	2	5	(4	1)	124	37	32	26	4	45	0	1	3	2	3	.40	3	.304	.355	.401
13 YEARS			1404	4618	1330	196	53	57	(24	33)	1803	616	522	436	42	625	4	28	40	173	79	.69	100	.288	.347	.390
1983	New York	A	83	267	70	11	4	7	(1	6)	110	41	36	28	3	33	0	2	5	2	3	.40	11	.262	.327	.412
1983	Houston	N	44	143	48	10	2	1	(1	0)	65	17	17	22	3	23	1	0	1	5	0	1.00	1	.336	.425	.455

DALE MURPHY

Bats Right-handed, Throws Right-handed — Turns Age 31 in 1987, Born 03/12/56

									BATTING										BASERUNNING				PERCENTAGES		
Year	Team	League	G	AB	H	2B	3B	HR	(Hm	Rd)	TB	R	RBI	TBB	IBB	SO	HBP	SH	SF	SB	CS	SB%	GIDP	AVE	OBP	SLG
1976	Atlanta	N	19	65	17	6	0	0	(0	0)	23	3	9	7	0	9	0	0	0	0	0	.00	0	.262	.333	.354
1977	Atlanta	N	18	76	24	8	1	2	(0	2)	40	5	14	0	0	8	0	0	0	0	1	.00	1	.316	.316	.526
1978	Atlanta	N	151	530	120	14	3	23	(17	6)	209	66	79	42	3	145	3	3	5	11	7	.61	15	.226	.284	.394
1979	Atlanta	N	104	384	106	7	2	21	(12	9)	180	53	57	38	5	67	2	0	5	6	1	.86	12	.276	.340	.469
1980	Atlanta	N	156	569	160	27	2	33	(17	16)	290	98	89	59	9	133	1	2	2	9	6	.60	8	.281	.349	.510
1981	Atlanta	N	104	369	91	12	1	13	(8	5)	144	43	50	44	8	72	0	1	2	14	5	.74	10	.247	.325	.390
1982	Atlanta	N	162	598	168	23	2	36	(24	12)	303	113	109	93	9	134	3	0	4	23	11	.68	10	.281	.378	.507
1983	Atlanta	N	162	589	178	24	4	36	(17	19)	318	131	121	90	12	110	2	0	6	30	4	.88	15	.302	.393	.540
1984	Atlanta	N	162	607	176	32	8	36	(18	18)	332	94	100	79	20	134	2	0	3	19	7	.73	13	.290	.372	.547
1985	Atlanta	N	162	616	185	32	2	37	(19	18)	332	118	111	90	15	141	1	0	5	10	3	.77	14	.300	.388	.539
1986	Atlanta	N	160	614	163	29	7	29	(17	12)	293	89	83	75	5	141	2	0	1	7	7	.50	10	.265	.347	.477
11 YEARS			1360	5017	1388	214	32	266	(149	117)	2464	813	822	617	86	1094	16	6	33	129	52	.71	110	.277	.356	.491

DWAYNE MURPHY

Bats Left-handed, Throws Right-handed — Turns Age 32 in 1987, Born 03/18/55

									BATTING										BASERUNNING				PERCENTAGES		
Year	Team	League	G	AB	H	2B	3B	HR	(Hm	Rd)	TB	R	RBI	TBB	IBB	SO	HBP	SH	SF	SB	CS	SB%	GIDP	AVE	OBP	SLG
1978	Oakland	A	60	52	10	2	0	0	(0	0)	12	15	5	7	0	14	0	1	2	0	1	.00	0	.192	.279	.231
1979	Oakland	A	121	388	99	10	4	11	(4	7)	150	57	40	84	6	80	1	13	3	15	11	.58	10	.255	.387	.387
1980	Oakland	A	159	573	157	18	2	13	(5	8)	218	86	68	102	7	96	2	22	3	26	15	.63	12	.274	.384	.380
1981	Oakland	A	107	390	98	10	3	15	(7	8)	159	58	60	73	6	91	2	8	4	10	4	.71	6	.251	.369	.408
1982	Oakland	A	151	543	129	15	1	27	(15	12)	227	84	94	94	2	122	3	12	8	26	8	.76	8	.238	.349	.418
1983	Oakland	A	130	471	107	17	2	17	(12	5)	179	55	75	62	4	105	0	7	6	7	5	.58	16	.227	.314	.380
1984	Oakland	A	153	559	143	18	2	33	(12	21)	264	93	88	74	1	111	3	4	7	4	5	.44	15	.256	.342	.472
1985	Oakland	A	152	523	122	21	3	20	(5	15)	209	77	59	84	3	123	3	5	4	4	5	.44	14	.233	.340	.400
1986	Oakland	A	98	329	83	11	3	9	(5	4)	127	50	39	56	4	80	4	7	4	3	1	.75	4	.252	.364	.386
9 YEARS			1131	3828	948	122	20	145	(65	80)	1545	575	528	636	33	822	18	79	41	95	55	.63	85	.248	.354	.404

ROB MURPHY

Pitches Left-handed, Bats Left-handed   Turns Age 27 in 1987, Born 05/26/60

			HOW MUCH HE PITCHED						WHAT HE GAVE UP												THE RESULTS					
Year	Team	League	G	GS	CG	GF	IP	BFP	H	R	ER	HR	SH	SF	HB	TBB	IBB	SO	WP	Bk	W	L	Pct	ShO	Sv	ERA
1985	Cincinnati	N	2	0	0	2	3	12	2	2	2	1	0	0	0	2	0	1	0	0	0	0	.000	0	0	6.00
1986	Cincinnati	N	34	0	0	12	50.1	195	26	4	4	0	3	3	0	21	2	36	5	0	6	0	1.000	0	1	0.72
2 YEARS			36	0	0	14	53.1	207	28	6	6	1	3	3	0	23	2	37	5	0	6	0	1.000	0	1	1.01

EDDIE MURRAY

Bats both Right and Left-handed, Throws Right-handed   Turns Age 31 in 1987, Born 02/24/56

						BATTING															BASERUNNING				PERCENTAGES		
Year	Team	League	G	AB	H	2B	3B	HR	(Hm	Rd)	TB	R	RBI	TBB	IBB	SO	HBP	SH	SF	SB	CS	SB%	GIDP	AVE	OBP	SLG
1977	Baltimore	A	160	611	173	29	2	27	(14	13)	287	81	88	48	6	104	1	0	6	0	1	.00	22	.283	.333	.470
1978	Baltimore	A	161	610	174	32	3	27	(10	17)	293	85	95	70	7	97	1	.1	8	6	5	.55	15	.285	.356	.480
1979	Baltimore	A	159	606	179	30	2	25	(10	15)	288	90	99	72	9	78	2	1	6	10	2	.83	16	.295	.369	.475
1980	Baltimore	A	158	621	186	36	2	32	(10	22)	322	100	116	54	10	71	2	0	6	7	2	.78	18	.300	.354	.519
1981	Baltimore	A	99	378	111	21	2	22	(12	10)	202	57	78	40	10	43	1	0	3	2	3	.40	10	.294	.360	.534
1982	Baltimore	A	151	550	174	30	1	32	(18	14)	302	87	110	70	18	82	1	0	9	7	2	.78	17	.316	.391	.549
1983	Baltimore	A	156	582	178	30	3	33	(16	17)	313	115	111	86	13	90	3	0	9	5	1	.83	13	.306	.393	.538
1984	Baltimore	A	162	588	180	26	3	29	(18	11)	299	97	110	107	25	87	2	0	8	10	2	.83	9	.306	.410	.509
1985	Baltimore	A	156	583	173	37	1	31	(15	16)	305	111	124	84	12	68	2	0	8	5	2	.71	8	.297	.383	.523
1986	Baltimore	A	137	495	151	25	1	17	(9	8)	229	61	84	78	7	49	0	0	5	3	0	1.00	17	.305	.396	.463
10 YEARS			1499	5624	1679	296	20	275	(132	143)	2840	884	1015	709	117	769	15	2	65	55	20	.73	145	.299	.375	.505

GENE NELSON

Pitches Right-handed, Bats Right-handed   Turns Age 27 in 1987, Born 12/03/60

					HOW MUCH HE PITCHED					WHAT HE GAVE UP										THE RESULTS					
Year	Team	League	G	GS	CG	GF	IP	BFP	H	R	ER	HR	SH	SF	HB	TBB	IBB	SO	WP	Bk	W	L	Pct	ShO	Sv	ERA
1981	New York	A	8	7	0	0	39	179	40	24	21	5	0	2	1	23	1	16	2	0	3	1	.750	0	0	4.85
1982	Seattle	A	22	19	2	2	122.2	545	133	70	63	16	4	2	2	60	1	71	4	2	6	9	.400	1	0	4.62
1983	Seattle	A	10	5	1	2	32	153	38	29	28	6	2	0	1	21	2	11	1	0	0	3	.000	0	0	7.87
1984	Chicago	A	20	9	2	4	74.2	304	72	38	37	9	1	2	1	17	0	36	4	1	3	5	.375	0	1	4.46
1985	Chicago	A	46	18	1	11	145.2	643	144	74	69	23	9	2	7	67	4	101	11	1	10	10	.500	0	2	4.26
1986	Chicago	A	54	1	0	26	114.2	488	118	52	49	7	7	1	3	41	5	70	3	0	6	6	.500	0	6	3.85
6 YEARS			160	59	6	45	528.2	2312	545	287	267	66	23	9	15	229	13	305	25	4	28	34	.452	1	9	4.55

GRAIG NETTLES

Bats Left-handed, Throws Right-handed   Turns Age 43 in 1987, Born 08/20/44

						BATTING															BASERUNNING				PERCENTAGES		
Year	Team	League	G	AB	H	2B	3B	HR	(Hm	Rd)	TB	R	RBI	TBB	IBB	SO	HBP	SH	SF	SB	CS	SB%	GIDP	AVE	OBP	SLG
1967	Minnesota	A	3	3	1	1	0	0	(0	0)	2	0	0	0	0	0	0	0	0	0	0	.00	0	.333	.333	.667
1968	Minnesota	A	22	76	17	2	1	5	(1	4)	36	13	8	7	1	20	1	0	0	0	0	.00	2	.224	.298	.474
1969	Minnesota	A	96	225	50	9	2	7	(2	5)	84	27	26	32	1	47	1	1	2	1	2	.33	6	.222	.319	.373
1970	Cleveland	A	157	549	129	13	1	26	(13	13)	222	81	62	81	3	77	3	0	0	3	1	.75	12	.235	.336	.404
1971	Cleveland	A	158	598	156	18	1	28	(15	13)	260	78	86	82	6	56	3	1	6	7	4	.64	15	.261	.350	.435
1972	Cleveland	A	150	557	141	28	0	17	(11	6)	220	65	70	57	4	50	4	2	3	2	3	.40	9	.253	.325	.395
1973	New York	A	160	552	129	18	0	22	(12	10)	213	65	81	78	3	76	7	0	4	0	0	.00	15	.234	.334	.386
1974	New York	A	155	566	139	21	1	22	(9	13)	228	74	75	59	8	75	3	1	9	1	0	1.00	9	.246	.316	.403
1975	New York	A	157	581	155	24	4	21	(14	7)	250	71	91	51	3	88	2	2	11	1	3	.25	8	.267	.322	.430
1976	New York	A	158	583	148	29	2	32	(18	14)	277	88	93	62	6	94	4	2	5	11	6	.65	8	.254	.327	.475
1977	New York	A	158	589	150	23	4	37	(18	19)	292	99	107	68	6	79	3	0	4	2	5	.29	8	.255	.333	.496
1978	New York	A	159	587	162	23	2	27	(16	11)	270	81	93	59	6	69	6	1	9	1	1	.50	20	.276	.343	.460
1979	New York	A	145	521	132	15	1	20	(11	9)	209	71	73	59	6	53	0	0	8	1	2	.33	14	.253	.325	.401
1980	New York	A	89	324	79	14	0	16	(11	5)	141	52	45	42	5	42	1	0	2	0	0	.00	8	.244	.331	.435
1981	New York	A	103	349	85	7	1	15	(11	4)	139	46	46	47	4	49	1	2	3	0	2	.00	5	.244	.333	.398
1982	New York	A	122	405	94	11	2	18	(10	8)	163	47	55	51	4	49	1	0	4	1	5	.17	11	.232	.317	.402
1983	New York	A	129	462	123	17	3	20	(11	9)	206	56	75	51	2	65	3	0	3	0	1	.00	9	.266	.341	.446
1984	San Diego	N	124	395	90	11	1	20	(11	9)	163	56	65	58	4	55	5	0	7	0	0	.00	12	.228	.329	.413
1985	San Diego	N	137	440	115	23	1	15	(6	9)	185	66	61	72	5	59	0	0	3	0	0	.00	10	.261	.363	.420
1986	San Diego	N	126	354	77	9	0	16	(13	3)	134	36	55	41	8	62	2	0	3	0	1	.00	6	.218	.300	.379
20 YEARS			2508	8716	2172	316	27	384	(213	171)	3694	1172	1267	1057	88	1165	50	12	86	31	36	.46	187	.249	.331	.424

AL NEWMAN

Bats both Right and Left-handed, Throws Right-handed   Turns Age 27 in 1987, Born 06/30/60

						BATTING															BASERUNNING				PERCENTAGES		
Year	Team	League	G	AB	H	2B	3B	HR	(Hm	Rd)	TB	R	RBI	TBB	IBB	SO	HBP	SH	SF	SB	CS	SB%	GIDP	AVE	OBP	SLG
1985	Montreal	N	25	29	5	1	0	0	(0	0)	6	7	1	3	0	4	0	0	0	2	1	.67	0	.172	.250	.207
1986	Montreal	N	95	185	37	3	0	1	(0	1)	43	23	8	21	2	20	0	4	2	11	11	.50	4	.200	.279	.232
2 YEARS			120	214	42	4	0	1	(0	1)	49	30	9	24	2	24	0	4	2	13	12	.52	4	.196	.275	.229

REID NICHOLS

Bats Right-handed, Throws Right-handed   Turns Age 29 in 1987, Born 08/05/58

											BATTING									BASERUNNING				PERCENTAGES		
Year	Team	League	G	AB	H	2B	3B	HR	(Hm	Rd)	TB	R	RBI	TBB	IBB	SO	HBP	SH	SF	SB	CS	SB%	GIDP	AVE	OBP	SLG
1980	Boston	A	12	36	8	0	1	0	(0	0)	10	5	3	3	0	8	0	0	0	0	1	.00	0	.222	.282	.278
1981	Boston	A	39	48	9	0	1	0	(0	0)	11	13	3	2	0	6	0	4	1	0	1	.00	0	.188	.216	.229
1982	Boston	A	92	245	74	16	1	7	(1	6)	113	35	33	14	1	28	1	4	1	5	3	.63	3	.302	.341	.461
1983	Boston	A	100	274	78	22	1	6	(3	3)	120	35	22	26	2	36	3	3	1	7	5	.58	5	.285	.352	.438
1984	Boston	A	74	124	28	5	1	1	(1	0)	38	14	14	12	1	18	3	1	1	2	1	.67	0	.226	.307	.306
1985	2 Teams		72	150	41	8	1	2	(1	1)	57	23	18	17	1	17	1	3	2	6	5	.55	2	.273	.347	.380
1986	Chicago	A	74	136	31	4	0	2	(2	0)	41	9	18	11	0	23	0	1	2	5	4	.56	2	.228	.282	.301
7 YEARS			463	1013	269	55	6	18	(8	10)	390	134	111	85	5	136	8	16	8	25	20	.56	12	.266	.325	.385
1985	Boston	A	21	32	6	1	0	1	(1	0)	10	3	3	2	0	4	1	1	1	1	0	1.00	1	.188	.250	.313
1985	Chicago	A	51	118	35	7	1	1	(0	1)	47	20	15	15	1	13	0	2	1	5	5	.50	1	.297	.373	.398

TOM NIEDENFUER

Pitches Right-handed, Bats Right-handed   Turns Age 28 in 1987, Born 08/13/59

			HOW MUCH HE PITCHED						WHAT HE GAVE UP										THE RESULTS					
Year	Team	League	G	GS	CG	GF	IP	BFP	H	R	ER	HR	SH	SF	HB	TBB	IBB	SO	WP	Bk	W	L	Pct	ShO	Sv	ERA
1981	Los Angeles	N	17	0	0	8	26	107	25	11	11	1	2	1	1	6	2	12	0	0	3	1	.750	0	2	3.81
1982	Los Angeles	N	55	0	0	24	69.2	299	71	22	21	3	5	3	2	25	8	60	1	0	3	4	.429	0	9	2.71
1983	Los Angeles	N	66	0	0	38	94.2	366	55	22	20	6	7	5	1	29	11	66	1	0	8	3	.727	0	11	1.90
1984	Los Angeles	N	33	0	0	21	47.1	203	39	14	13	3	6	0	2	23	7	45	1	1	2	5	.286	0	11	2.47
1985	Los Angeles	N	64	0	0	43	106.1	415	86	32	32	6	1	3	1	24	5	102	0	0	7	9	.438	0	19	2.71
1986	Los Angeles	N	60	0	0	27	80	345	86	35	33	11	5	3	1	29	15	55	2	0	6	6	.500	0	11	3.71
6 YEARS			295	0	0	161	424	1735	362	136	130	30	26	15	8	136	48	340	5	1	29	28	.509	0	63	2.76

JOE NIEKRO

Pitches Right-handed, Bats Right-handed   Turns Age 43 in 1987, Born 11/07/44

			HOW MUCH HE PITCHED						WHAT HE GAVE UP										THE RESULTS					
Year	Team	League	G	GS	CG	GF	IP	BFP	H	R	ER	HR	SH	SF	HB	TBB	IBB	SO	WP	Bk	W	L	Pct	ShO	Sv	ERA
1967	Chicago	N	36	22	7	9	170	706	171	68	63	15	2	5	2	32	7	77	1	0	10	7	.588	2	0	3.34
1968	Chicago	N	34	29	2	4	177	769	204	93	85	18	6	6	3	59	8	65	3	0	14	10	.583	0	2	4.32
1969	2 Teams		41	34	8	6	221.1	928	237	100	91	18	12	5	0	51	9	62	4	0	8	18	.308	3	0	3.70
1970	Detroit	A	38	34	6	2	213	842	221	107	96	28	4	5	3	72	4	101	1	0	12	13	.480	2	0	4.06
1971	Detroit	A	31	15	0	5	122	491	136	62	61	13	6	3	2	49	3	43	2	0	6	7	.462	0	1	4.50
1972	Detroit	A	18	7	1	4	47	191	62	20	20	3	2	0	1	8	1	24	2	0	3	2	.600	0	1	3.83
1973	Atlanta	N	20	0	0	11	24	99	23	11	11	2	2	3	0	11	1	12	3	0	2	4	.333	0	3	4.12
1974	Atlanta	N	27	2	0	9	43	178	36	19	17	5	4	2	2	18	2	31	3	0	3	2	.600	0	0	3.56
1975	Houston	N	40	4	1	21	88	378	79	32	30	3	3	5	2	39	4	54	2	0	6	4	.600	1	4	3.07
1976	Houston	N	36	13	0	5	118	515	107	60	44	8	6	3	1	56	1	77	8	0	4	8	.333	0	0	3.36
1977	Houston	N	44	14	9	12	181	737	155	66	61	14	13	6	1	64	3	101	5	1	13	8	.619	2	5	3.03
1978	Houston	N	35	29	10	2	203	861	190	97	87	13	5	8	8	73	1	97	9	0	14	14	.500	1	0	3.86
1979	Houston	N	38	38	11	0	264	1095	221	102	88	17	6	5	7	107	1	119	19	0	21	11	.656	5	0	3.00
1980	Houston	N	37	36	11	1	256	1096	268	100	101	12	9	11	4	79	3	127	12	0	20	12	.625	2	0	3.55
1981	Houston	N	24	24	5	0	166	676	150	60	52	8	6	6	0	47	4	77	7	0	9	9	.500	2	0	2.82
1982	Houston	N	35	35	16	0	270	1067	224	79	74	12	13	5	5	64	1	130	19	0	17	12	.586	5	0	2.47
1983	Houston	N	38	38	9	0	263.2	1113	238	115	102	15	13	9	3	101	5	152	14	1	15	14	.517	1	0	3.48
1984	Houston	N	38	38	6	0	248.1	1027	223	104	84	16	1	8	4	89	4	127	12	1	16	12	.571	1	0	3.04
1985	2 Teams		35	35	4	0	225.1	983	211	108	96	24	10	12	5	107	6	121	21	1	11	13	.458	1	0	3.83
1986	New York	A	25	25	0	0	125.2	571	139	84	68	15	1	0	1	63	3	59	10	1	9	10	.474	0	0	4.87
20 YEARS			670	472	106	91	3426.1	14323	3295	1506	1331	259	124	107	55	1189	71	1656	157	5	213	190	.529	29	16	3.50
1969	Chicago	N	4	3	0	0	19.1	86	24	9	8	3	0	1	0	6	0	7	0	0	0	1	.000	0	0	3.72
1969	San Diego	N	37	31	8	6	202	842	213	91	83	15	12	4	0	45	9	55	4	0	8	17	.320	3	0	3.70
1985	New York	A	3	3	0	0	12.1	58	14	8	8	0	0	0	0	8	0	4	0	0	2	1	.667	0	0	5.84
1985	Houston	N	32	32	4	0	213	925	197	100	88	21	10	12	5	99	6	117	21	1	9	12	.429	1	0	3.72

PHIL NIEKRO

Pitches Right-handed, Bats Right-handed   Turns Age 48 in 1987, Born 04/01/39

Year	Team	League	G	GS	CG	GF	IP	BFP	H	R	ER	HR	SH	SF	HB	TBB	IBB	SO	WP	Bk	W	L	Pct	ShO	Sv	ERA
1964	Milwaukee	N	10	0	0	2	15	66	15	10	8	1	3	0	1	7	0	8	1	0	0	0	.000	0	0	4.80
1965	Milwaukee	N	41	1	0	21	75	324	73	32	24	5	8	4	3	26	3	49	9	0	2	3	.400	0	6	2.88
1966	Atlanta	N	28	0	0	10	50	224	48	32	23	4	6	0	2	23	5	17	3	0	4	3	.571	0	2	4.14
1967	Atlanta	N	46	20	10	20	207	827	164	64	43	9	6	6	7	55	3	129	19	1	11	9	.550	1	9	1.87
1968	Atlanta	N	37	34	15	3	257	1019	228	83	74	16	10	5	5	45	13	140	16	3	14	12	.538	5	2	2.59
1969	Atlanta	N	40	35	21	4	284	1143	235	93	81	21	19	0	5	57	7	193	15	0	23	13	.639	4	1	2.57
1970	Atlanta	N	34	32	10	1	230	980	222	124	109	40	6	5	6	68	2	168	6	2	12	18	.400	3	0	4.27
1971	Atlanta	N	42	36	18	4	269	1101	248	112	89	27	11	4	3	70	6	173	8	1	15	14	.517	4	2	2.98
1972	Atlanta	N	38	36	17	1	282	1150	254	112	96	22	13	3	5	53	3	164	10	3	16	12	.571	1	0	3.06
1973	Atlanta	N	42	30	9	7	245	1023	214	103	90	21	13	2	5	89	4	131	11	0	13	10	.565	1	4	3.31
1974	Atlanta	N	41	39	18	1	302	1219	249	91	80	19	10	8	6	88	3	195	6	4	20	13	.606	6	1	2.38
1975	Atlanta	N	39	37	13	2	276	1160	285	115	98	29	14	3	11	72	3	144	15	2	15	15	.500	1	1	3.20
1976	Atlanta	N	38	37	10	1	271	1157	249	116	99	18	14	5	8	101	7	173	14	4	17	11	.607	2	0	3.29
1977	Atlanta	N	44	43	20	1	330	1428	315	166	148	26	11	8	8	164	12	262	17	3	16	20	.444	2	0	4.04
1978	Atlanta	N	44	42	22	1	334	1389	295	129	107	16	13	6	13	102	5	248	11	3	19	18	.514	4	1	2.88
1979	Atlanta	N	44	44	23	0	342	1436	311	160	129	41	14	7	11	113	8	208	18	4	21	20	.512	1	0	3.39
1980	Atlanta	N	40	38	11	2	275	1137	256	119	111	30	14	5	3	85	3	176	9	1	15	18	.455	3	1	3.63
1981	Atlanta	N	22	22	3	0	139	578	120	56	48	6	5	2	1	56	2	62	2	0	7	7	.500	3	0	3.11
1982	Atlanta	N	35	35	4	0	234.1	969	225	106	94	23	7	3	3	73	1	144	4	1	17	4	.810	2	0	3.61
1983	Atlanta	N	34	33	2	0	201.2	888	212	94	89	18	7	5	2	105	3	128	6	3	11	10	.524	0	0	3.97
1984	New York	A	32	31	5	1	215.2	916	219	85	74	15	5	11	3	76	0	136	2	0	16	8	.667	1	0	3.09
1985	New York	A	33	33	7	0	220	955	203	110	100	29	1	3	2	120	1	149	5	2	16	12	.571	1	0	4.09
1986	Cleveland	A	34	32	5	1	210.1	951	241	126	101	24	7	2	6	95	1	81	9	2	11	11	.500	0	0	4.32
23 YEARS			838	690	243	83	5265	22040	4881	2238	1915	460	217	97	119	1743	85	3278	216	39	311	261	.544	45	30	3.27

RANDY NIEMANN

Pitches Left-handed, Bats Right-handed   Turns Age 32 in 1987, Born 11/15/55

Year	Team	League	G	GS	CG	GF	IP	BFP	H	R	ER	HR	SH	SF	HB	TBB	IBB	SO	WP	Bk	W	L	Pct	ShO	Sv	ERA
1979	Houston	N	26	7	3	4	67	287	68	32	28	1	8	6	1	22	3	24	0	2	3	2	.600	2	1	3.76
1980	Houston	N	22	1	0	3	33	147	40	21	20	2	0	1	0	12	1	18	0	1	0	1	.000	0	1	5.45
1982	Pittsburgh	N	20	0	0	8	35.1	157	34	22	20	1	3	1	2	17	4	26	4	1	1	1	.500	0	1	5.09
1983	Pittsburgh	N	8	1	0	4	13.2	66	20	14	14	2	1	1	1	7	1	8	3	0	0	0	.000	0	0	9.22
1984	Chicago	A	5	0	0	3	5.1	24	5	1	1	0	0	0	0	5	1	5	1	0	0	0	.000	0	0	1.69
1985	New York	N	4	0	0	0	4.2	18	5	0	0	0	0	0	0	0	0	2	0	0	0	0	.000	0	0	0.00
1986	New York	N	31	1	0	11	35.2	158	44	17	15	2	2	1	0	12	2	18	2	0	2	3	.400	0	0	3.79
7 YEARS			116	10	3	33	194.2	857	216	107	98	8	14	10	4	75	12	101	10	4	6	8	.429	2	3	4.53

JUAN NIEVES

Pitches Left-handed, Bats Left-handed   Turns Age 22 in 1987, Born 01/05/65

Year	Team	League	G	GS	CG	GF	IP	BFP	H	R	ER	HR	SH	SF	HB	TBB	IBB	SO	WP	Bk	W	L	Pct	ShO	Sv	ERA
1986	Milwaukee	A	35	33	4	0	184.2	834	224	124	101	17	3	5	1	77	0	116	3	1	11	12	.478	3	0	4.92

AL NIPPER

Pitches Right-handed, Bats Right-handed   Turns Age 28 in 1987, Born 04/02/59

Year	Team	League	G	GS	CG	GF	IP	BFP	H	R	ER	HR	SH	SF	HB	TBB	IBB	SO	WP	Bk	W	L	Pct	ShO	Sv	ERA
1983	Boston	A	3	2	1	1	16	67	17	4	4	0	0	1	1	7	0	5	0	0	1	1	.500	0	0	2.25
1984	Boston	A	29	24	6	3	182.2	777	183	86	79	18	3	2	7	52	1	84	7	1	11	6	.647	0	0	3.89
1985	Boston	A	25	25	5	0	162	713	157	83	73	14	4	4	9	82	3	85	3	1	9	12	.429	0	0	4.06
1986	Boston	A	26	26	3	0	159	702	186	108	95	24	4	5	4	47	2	79	1	1	10	12	.455	0	0	5.38
4 YEARS			83	77	15	4	519.2	2259	543	281	251	56	11	12	21	188	6	253	11	3	31	31	.500	0	0	4.35

DICKIE NOLES

Pitches Right-handed, Bats Right-handed   Turns Age 31 in 1987, Born 11/19/56

Year	Team	League	G	GS	CG	GF	IP	BFP	H	R	ER	HR	SH	SF	HB	TBB	IBB	SO	WP	Bk	W	L	Pct	ShO	Sv	ERA
1979	Philadelphia	N	14	14	0	0	90	377	80	40	38	6	8	4	2	38	2	42	1	2	3	4	.429	0	0	3.80
1980	Philadelphia	N	48	3	0	20	81	367	80	42	35	5	7	2	1	42	11	57	2	0	1	4	.200	0	6	3.89
1981	Philadelphia	N	13	8	0	1	58	249	57	30	27	2	2	2	3	23	2	34	3	3	2	2	.500	0	0	4.19
1982	Chicago	N	31	30	2	1	171	744	180	99	84	11	11	10	5	61	2	85	4	6	10	13	.435	2	0	4.42
1983	Chicago	N	24	18	1	2	116.1	506	133	69	61	9	2	2	1	37	3	59	3	1	5	10	.333	1	0	4.72
1984	2 Teams		39	7	0	12	108.1	480	120	67	62	10	0	2	6	46	1	53	4	1	4	5	.444	0	0	5.15
1985	Texas	A	28	13	0	3	110.1	488	129	67	62	11	2	0	6	33	1	59	1	0	4	8	.333	0	1	5.06
1986	Cleveland	A	32	0	0	9	54.2	251	56	33	31	9	3	5	5	30	4	32	1	1	3	2	.600	0	0	5.10
8 YEARS			229	93	3	48	789.2	3462	835	447	400	63	35	27	29	310	26	421	19	14	32	48	.400	3	7	4.56
1984	Texas	A	18	6	0	6	57.2	264	60	38	33	6	0	0	5	30	0	39	3	1	2	3	.400	0	0	5.15
1984	Chicago	N	21	1	0	6	50.2	216	60	29	29	4	0	2	1	16	1	14	1	0	2	2	.500	0	0	5.15

PETE O'BRIEN

Bats Left-handed, Throws Left-handed   **Turns Age 29 in 1987, Born 02/09/58**

Year	Team	League	G	AB	H	2B	3B	HR	(Hm	Rd)	TB	R	RBI	TBB	IBB	SO	HBP	SH	SF	SB	CS	SB%	GIDP	AVE	OBP	SLG
1982	Texas	A	20	67	16	4	1	4	(2	2)	34	13	13	6	0	8	0	0	1	1	0	1.00	0	.239	.297	.507
1983	Texas	A	154	524	124	24	5	8	(4	4)	182	53	53	58	2	62	1	3	2	5	4	.56	11	.237	.313	.347
1984	Texas	A	142	520	149	26	2	18	(7	11)	233	57	80	53	8	50	0	1	7	3	5	.38	11	.287	.348	.448
1985	Texas	A	159	573	153	34	3	22	(12	10)	259	69	92	69	4	53	1	3	9	5	10	.33	18	.267	.342	.452
1986	Texas	A	156	551	160	23	3	23	(11	12)	258	86	90	87	11	66	0	0	3	4	4	.50	19	.290	.385	.468
5 YEARS			631	2235	602	111	14	75	(36	39)	966	278	328	273	25	239	2	7	22	18	23	.44	59	.269	.346	.432

TOM O'MALLEY

Bats Left-handed, Throws Right-handed   **Turns Age 27 in 1987, Born 12/25/60**

Year	Team	League	G	AB	H	2B	3B	HR	(Hm	Rd)	TB	R	RBI	TBB	IBB	SO	HBP	SH	SF	SB	CS	SB%	GIDP	AVE	OBP	SLG
1982	San Francisco	N	92	291	80	12	4	2	(0	2)	106	26	27	33	9	39	1	1	1	0	3	.00	11	.275	.350	.364
1983	San Francisco	N	135	410	106	16	1	5	(3	2)	139	40	45	52	4	47	4	4	3	2	4	.33	12	.259	.345	.339
1984	2 Teams		25	41	5	0	0	0	(0	0)	5	2	3	2	0	7	0	0	0	0	0	.00	1	.122	.163	.122
1985	Baltimore	A	8	14	1	0	0	1	(0	1)	4	1	2	0	0	2	0	0	0	0	0	.00	1	.071	.071	.286
1986	Baltimore	A	56	181	46	9	0	1	(1	0)	58	19	18	17	1	21	0	1	1	0	1	.00	4	.254	.317	.320
5 YEARS			316	937	238	37	5	9	(4	5)	312	88	95	104	14	116	5	6	5	2	8	.20	29	.254	.330	.333
1984	Chicago	A	12	16	2	0	0	0	(0	0)	2	0	3	0	0	5	0	0	0	0	0	.00	1	.125	.125	.125
1984	San Francisco	N	13	25	3	0	0	0	(0	0)	3	2	0	2	0	2	0	0	0	0	0	.00	0	.120	.185	.120

RANDY O'NEAL

Pitches Right-handed, Bats Right-handed   **Turns Age 27 in 1987, Born 08/30/60**

Year	Team	League	G	GS	CG	GF	IP	BFP	H	R	ER	HR	SH	SF	HB	TBB	IBB	SO	WP	Bk	W	L	Pct	ShO	Sv	ERA
1984	Detroit	A	4	3	0	0	18.2	78	16	7	7	0	0	0	0	6	0	12	1	0	2	1	.667	0	0	3.37
1985	Detroit	A	28	12	1	8	94.1	388	82	42	34	8	1	7	2	36	1	52	5	0	5	5	.500	0	1	3.24
1986	Detroit	A	37	11	1	9	122.2	522	121	69	59	13	3	6	3	44	9	68	8	0	3	7	.300	0	2	4.33
3 YEARS			69	26	2	17	235.2	988	219	118	100	21	4	13	5	86	12	132	14	0	10	13	.435	0	3	3.82

KEN OBERKFELL

Bats Left-handed, Throws Right-handed   **Turns Age 31 in 1987, Born 05/04/56**

Year	Team	League	G	AB	H	2B	3B	HR	(Hm	Rd)	TB	R	RBI	TBB	IBB	SO	HBP	SH	SF	SB	CS	SB%	GIDP	AVE	OBP	SLG
1977	St Louis	N	9	9	1	0	0	0	(0	0)	1	0	1	0	0	3	0	0	0	0	0	.00	0	.111	.111	.111
1978	St Louis	N	24	50	6	1	0	0	(0	0)	7	7	0	3	0	1	0	1	0	0	0	.00	1	.120	.170	.140
1979	St Louis	N	135	369	111	19	5	1	(1	0)	143	53	35	57	9	35	4	1	4	4	1	.80	9	.301	.396	.388
1980	St Louis	N	116	422	128	27	6	3	(0	3)	176	58	46	51	8	23	1	9	3	4	4	.50	11	.303	.377	.417
1981	St Louis	N	102	376	110	12	6	2	(0	2)	140	43	45	37	6	28	0	3	4	13	5	.72	18	.293	.353	.372
1982	St Louis	N	137	470	136	22	5	2	(1	1)	174	55	34	40	6	31	1	3	2	11	9	.55	11	.289	.345	.370
1983	St Louis	N	151	488	143	26	5	3	(0	3)	188	62	38	61	5	27	1	4	3	12	6	.67	12	.293	.371	.385
1984	2 Teams		100	324	87	19	2	1	(1	0)	113	38	21	31	3	27	1	3	3	2	5	.29	7	.269	.331	.349
1985	Atlanta	N	134	412	112	19	4	3	(2	1)	148	30	35	51	6	38	6	1	2	1	2	.33	10	.272	.359	.359
1986	Atlanta	N	151	503	136	24	3	5	(2	3)	181	62	48	83	6	40	2	4	4	7	4	.64	11	.270	.373	.360
10 YEARS			1059	3423	970	169	36	20	(7	13)	1271	408	303	414	49	253	16	29	25	54	36	.60	83	.283	.361	.371
1984	Atlanta	N	50	172	40	8	1	1	(1	0)	53	21	10	15	1	17	0	3	3	1	3	.25	4	.233	.289	.308
1984	St Louis	N	50	152	47	11	1	0	(0	0)	60	17	11	16	2	10	1	0	0	1	2	.33	5	.309	.379	.395

BRYAN OELKERS

Pitches Left-handed, Bats Left-handed   **Turns Age 26 in 1987, Born 03/11/61**

Year	Team	League	G	GS	CG	GF	IP	BFP	H	R	ER	HR	SH	SF	HB	TBB	IBB	SO	WP	Bk	W	L	Pct	ShO	Sv	ERA
1983	Minnesota	A	10	8	0	1	34.1	167	56	34	33	7	0	1	0	17	0	13	0	0	0	5	.000	0	0	8.65
1986	Cleveland	A	35	4	0	8	69	318	70	38	36	13	3	2	6	40	2	33	4	0	3	3	.500	0	1	4.70
2 YEARS			45	12	0	9	103.1	485	126	72	69	20	3	3	6	57	2	46	4	0	3	8	.273	0	1	6.01

RON OESTER

Bats both Right and Left-handed, Throws Right-handed   Turns Age 31 in 1987, Born 05/05/56

							BATTING													BASERUNNING				PERCENTAGES		
Year	Team	League	G	AB	H	2B	3B	HR	(Hm	Rd)	TB	R	RBI	TBB	IBB	SO	HBP	SH	SF	SB	CS	SB%	GIDP	AVE	OBP	SLG
1978	Cincinnati	N	6	8	3	0	0	0	(0	0)	3	1	1	0	0	2	0	1	0	0	0	.00	0	.375	.375	.375
1979	Cincinnati	N	6	3	0	0	0	0	(0	0)	0	0	0	0	0	1	0	0	0	0	0	.00	0	.000	.000	.000
1980	Cincinnati	N	100	303	84	16	2	2	(0	2)	110	40	20	26	7	44	1	5	0	6	2	.75	7	.277	.336	.363
1981	Cincinnati	N	105	354	96	16	7	5	(3	2)	141	45	42	42	8	49	0	5	7	2	5	.29	8	.271	.342	.398
1982	Cincinnati	N	151	549	143	19	4	9	(4	5)	197	63	47	35	8	82	0	8	3	5	6	.45	16	.260	.303	.359
1983	Cincinnati	N	157	549	145	23	5	11	(6	5)	211	63	58	49	14	106	1	7	6	2	2	.50	17	.264	.322	.384
1984	Cincinnati	N	150	553	134	26	3	3	(2	1)	175	54	38	41	7	97	1	5	1	7	2	.78	16	.242	.295	.316
1985	Cincinnati	N	152	526	155	26	3	1	(0	1)	190	59	34	51	17	65	0	2	5	5	0	1.00	13	.295	.354	.361
1986	Cincinnati	N	153	523	135	23	2	8	(6	2)	186	52	44	52	16	84	1	7	3	9	2	.82	18	.258	.325	.356
9 YEARS			980	3368	895	149	26	39	(21	18)	1213	377	284	296	77	530	4	40	25	36	19	.65	95	.266	.324	.360

BEN OGLIVIE

Bats Left-handed, Throws Left-handed   Turns Age 38 in 1987, Born 02/11/49

							BATTING													BASERUNNING				PERCENTAGES		
Year	Team	League	G	AB	H	2B	3B	HR	(Hm	Rd)	TB	R	RBI	TBB	IBB	SO	HBP	SH	SF	SB	CS	SB%	GIDP	AVE	OBP	SLG
1971	Boston	A	14	38	10	3	0	0	(0	0)	13	2	4	0	0	5	0	0	0	0	0	.00	0	.263	.263	.342
1972	Boston	A	94	253	61	10	2	8	(4	4)	99	27	30	18	2	61	1	0	1	1	1	.50	4	.241	.293	.391
1973	Boston	A	58	147	32	9	1	2	(1	1)	49	16	9	9	2	32	2	1	2	1	1	.50	4	.218	.269	.333
1974	Detroit	A	92	252	68	11	3	4	(2	2)	97	28	29	34	6	38	0	0	3	12	3	.80	5	.270	.353	.385
1975	Detroit	A	100	332	95	14	1	9	(2	7)	138	45	36	16	0	62	2	3	4	11	8	.58	10	.286	.319	.416
1976	Detroit	A	115	305	87	12	3	15	(8	7)	150	36	47	11	3	44	3	2	4	9	4	.69	11	.285	.313	.492
1977	Detroit	A	132	450	118	24	2	21	(9	12)	209	63	61	40	2	80	3	1	3	9	9	.50	11	.262	.325	.464
1978	Milwaukee	A	128	469	142	29	4	18	(6	12)	233	71	72	52	10	69	0	3	3	11	7	.61	10	.303	.370	.497
1979	Milwaukee	A	139	514	145	30	4	29	(16	13)	270	88	81	48	12	56	2	4	4	12	5	.71	11	.282	.343	.525
1980	Milwaukee	A	156	592	180	26	2	41	(15	26)	333	94	118	54	19	71	5	0	9	11	9	.55	5	.304	.362	.563
1981	Milwaukee	A	107	400	97	15	2	14	(3	11)	158	53	72	37	10	49	6	1	8	2	2	.50	9	.243	.310	.395
1982	Milwaukee	A	159	602	147	22	1	34	(16	18)	273	92	102	70	13	81	4	0	1	3	5	.38	9	.244	.326	.453
1983	Milwaukee	A	125	411	115	19	3	13	(8	5)	179	49	66	60	12	64	4	0	8	4	6	.40	9	.280	.371	.436
1984	Milwaukee	A	131	461	121	16	2	12	(7	5)	177	49	60	44	5	56	1	1	2	0	6	.00	12	.262	.327	.384
1985	Milwaukee	A	101	341	99	17	2	10	(4	6)	150	40	61	37	3	51	2	4	10	0	2	.00	13	.290	.354	.440
1986	Milwaukee	A	103	346	98	20	1	5	(2	3)	135	31	53	30	6	33	0	1	7	1	2	.33	7	.283	.334	.390
16 YEARS			1754	5913	1615	277	33	235	(103	132)	2663	784	901	560	105	852	35	21	69	87	70	.55	122	.273	.336	.450

BOB OJEDA

Pitches Left-handed, Bats Left-handed   Turns Age 30 in 1987, Born 12/17/57

			HOW MUCH HE PITCHED						WHAT HE GAVE UP										THE RESULTS					
Year	Team	League	G	GS	CG	GF	IP	BFP	H	R	ER	HR	SH	SF	HB	TBB	IBB	SO	WP	Bk	W	L	Pct	ShO	Sv	ERA
1980	Boston	A	7	7	0	0	26	122	39	20	20	2	0	0	0	14	1	12	1	0	1	1	.500	0	0	6.92
1981	Boston	A	10	10	2	0	66	267	50	25	23	6	3	1	2	25	2	28	0	0	6	2	.750	0	0	3.14
1982	Boston	A	22	14	0	6	78.1	352	95	53	49	13	0	1	1	29	0	52	5	0	4	6	.400	0	0	5.63
1983	Boston	A	29	28	5	0	173.2	746	173	85	78	15	6	11	3	73	2	94	2	0	12	7	.632	0	0	4.04
1984	Boston	A	33	32	8	0	216.2	928	211	106	96	17	8	6	2	96	2	137	0	1	12	12	.500	5	0	3.99
1985	Boston	A	39	22	5	10	157.2	671	166	74	70	11	10	3	2	48	9	102	3	3	9	11	.450	0	1	4.00
1986	New York	N	32	30	7	1	217.1	871	185	72	62	15	10	3	2	52	3	148	2	1	18	5	.783	2	0	2.57
7 YEARS			172	143	27	17	935.2	3957	919	435	398	79	37	25	12	337	19	573	13	5	62	44	.585	7	1	3.83

ED OLWINE

Pitches Left-handed, Bats Right-handed   Turns Age 29 in 1987, Born 05/28/58

			HOW MUCH HE PITCHED						WHAT HE GAVE UP										THE RESULTS					
Year	Team	League	G	GS	CG	GF	IP	BFP	H	R	ER	HR	SH	SF	HB	TBB	IBB	SO	WP	Bk	W	L	Pct	ShO	Sv	ERA
1986	Atlanta	N	37	0	0	12	47.2	189	35	20	18	5	1	1	1	17	7	37	5	2	0	0	.000	0	1	3.40

STEVE ONTIVEROS

Pitches Right-handed, Bats Right-handed   Turns Age 26 in 1987, Born 03/05/61

			HOW MUCH HE PITCHED						WHAT HE GAVE UP										THE RESULTS					
Year	Team	League	G	GS	CG	GF	IP	BFP	H	R	ER	HR	SH	SF	HB	TBB	IBB	SO	WP	Bk	W	L	Pct	ShO	Sv	ERA
1985	Oakland	A	39	0	0	18	74.2	284	45	17	16	4	2	2	2	19	2	36	1	0	1	3	.250	0	8	1.93
1986	Oakland	A	46	0	0	27	72.2	305	72	40	38	10	1	6	1	25	3	54	4	0	2	2	.500	0	10	4.71
2 YEARS			85	0	0	45	147.1	589	117	57	54	14	3	8	3	44	5	90	5	0	3	5	.375	0	18	3.30

JOSE OQUENDO

Bats both Right and Left-handed, Throws Right-handed   Turns Age 24 in 1987, Born 07/04/63

							BATTING													BASERUNNING				PERCENTAGES		
Year	Team	League	G	AB	H	2B	3B	HR	(Hm	Rd)	TB	R	RBI	TBB	IBB	SO	HBP	SH	SF	SB	CS	SB%	GIDP	AVE	OBP	SLG
1983	New York	N	120	328	70	7	0	1	(0	1)	80	29	17	19	2	60	2	3	1	8	9	.47	10	.213	.260	.244
1984	New York	N	81	189	42	5	0	0	(0	0)	47	23	10	15	2	26	2	3	2	10	1	.91	2	.222	.284	.249
1986	St Louis	N	76	138	41	4	1	0	(0	0)	47	20	13	15	4	20	0	2	3	2	3	.40	3	.297	.359	.341
3 YEARS			277	655	153	16	1	1	(0	1)	174	72	40	49	8	106	4	8	6	20	13	.61	15	.234	.289	.266

JESSE OROSCO

Pitches Left-handed, Bats Right-handed   Turns Age 30 in 1987, Born 04/21/57

			HOW MUCH HE PITCHED						WHAT HE GAVE UP										THE RESULTS					
Year	Team	League	G	GS	CG	GF	IP	BFP	H	R	ER	HR	SH	SF	HB	TBB	IBB	SO	WP	Bk	W	L	Pct	ShO	Sv	ERA
1979	New York	N	18	2	0	6	35	154	33	20	19	4	3	0	2	22	0	22	0	0	1	2	.333	0	0	4.89
1981	New York	N	8	0	0	4	17	69	13	4	3	2	2	0	0	6	2	18	0	1	0	1	.000	0	1	1.59
1982	New York	N	54	2	0	22	109.1	451	92	37	33	7	5	4	2	40	2	89	3	2	4	10	.286	0	4	2.72
1983	New York	N	62	0	0	42	110	432	76	27	18	3	4	3	1	38	7	84	1	2	13	7	.650	0	17	1.47
1984	New York	N	60	0	0	52	87	355	58	29	25	7	3	3	2	34	6	85	1	1	10	6	.625	0	31	2.59
1985	New York	N	54	0	0	39	79	331	66	26	24	6	1	1	0	34	7	68	4	0	8	6	.571	0	17	2.73
1986	New York	N	58	0	0	40	81	338	64	23	21	6	2	3	3	35	3	62	2	0	8	6	.571	0	21	2.33
7 YEARS			314	4	0	205	518.1	2130	402	166	143	35	20	14	10	209	27	428	11	6	44	38	.537	0	91	2.48

JORGE ORTA

Bats Left-handed, Throws Right-handed   Turns Age 37 in 1987, Born 11/26/50

						BATTING														BASERUNNING				PERCENTAGES		
Year	Team	League	G	AB	H	2B	3B	HR	(Hm	Rd)	TB	R	RBI	TBB	IBB	SO	HBP	SH	SF	SB	CS	SB%	GIDP	AVE	OBP	SLG
1972	Chicago	A	51	124	25	3	1	3	(0	3)	39	20	11	6	0	37	1	2	0	3	3	.50	2	.202	.244	.315
1973	Chicago	A	128	425	113	9	10	6	(2	4)	160	46	40	37	3	87	1	1	5	8	8	.50	7	.266	.323	.376
1974	Chicago	A	139	525	166	31	2	10	(1	9)	231	73	67	40	1	88	3	6	4	9	5	.64	8	.316	.365	.440
1975	Chicago	A	140	542	165	26	10	11	(6	5)	244	64	83	48	7	67	4	4	4	16	9	.64	17	.304	.363	.450
1976	Chicago	A	158	636	174	29	8	14	(8	6)	261	74	72	38	2	77	5	1	8	24	8	.75	15	.274	.316	.410
1977	Chicago	A	144	564	159	27	8	11	(7	4)	235	71	84	46	3	49	2	2	7	4	4	.50	12	.282	.334	.417
1978	Chicago	A	117	420	115	19	2	13	(9	4)	177	45	53	42	3	39	4	4	7	1	2	.33	9	.274	.340	.421
1979	Chicago	A	113	325	85	18	3	11	(5	6)	142	49	46	44	2	33	1	3	4	1	5	.17	6	.262	.348	.437
1980	Cleveland	A	129	481	140	18	3	10	(6	4)	194	78	64	71	2	44	2	2	8	6	5	.55	8	.291	.379	.403
1981	Cleveland	A	88	338	92	14	3	5	(2	3)	127	50	34	21	3	43	1	5	5	4	3	.57	11	.272	.312	.376
1982	Los Angeles	N	86	115	25	5	0	2	(1	1)	36	13	8	12	3	13	1	0	1	0	1	.00	1	.217	.295	.313
1983	Toronto	A	103	245	58	6	3	10	(7	3)	100	30	38	19	0	29	0	0	4	1	2	.33	6	.237	.287	.408
1984	Kansas City	A	122	403	120	23	7	9	(3	6)	184	50	50	28	8	39	2	1	4	0	1	.00	6	.298	.343	.457
1985	Kansas City	A	110	300	80	21	1	4	(1	3)	115	32	45	22	5	28	2	2	4	2	1	.67	6	.267	.317	.383
1986	Kansas City	A	106	336	93	14	2	9	(5	4)	138	35	46	23	3	34	0	0	2	0	3	.00	9	.277	.321	.411
15 YEARS			1734	5779	1610	263	63	128	(63	65)	2383	730	741	497	45	707	29	33	67	79	60	.57	125	.279	.335	.412

JUNIOR ORTIZ

Bats Right-handed, Throws Right-handed   Turns Age 28 in 1987, Born 10/24/59

						BATTING														BASERUNNING				PERCENTAGES		
Year	Team	League	G	AB	H	2B	3B	HR	(Hm	Rd)	TB	R	RBI	TBB	IBB	SO	HBP	SH	SF	SB	CS	SB%	GIDP	AVE	OBP	SLG
1982	Pittsburgh	N	7	15	3	1	0	0	(0	0)	4	1	0	1	0	3	0	0	0	0	0	.00	1	.200	.250	.267
1983	2 Teams		73	193	48	5	0	0	(0	0)	53	11	12	4	0	34	1	2	0	1	0	1.00	1	.249	.268	.275
1984	New York	N	40	91	18	3	0	0	(0	0)	21	6	11	5	0	15	0	1	2	1	0	1.00	2	.198	.235	.231
1985	Pittsburgh	N	23	72	21	2	0	1	(0	1)	26	4	5	3	1	17	0	1	0	1	0	1.00	1	.292	.320	.361
1986	Pittsburgh	N	49	110	37	6	0	0	(0	0)	43	11	14	9	0	13	0	1	2	0	1	.00	4	.336	.380	.391
5 YEARS			192	481	127	17	0	1	(0	1)	147	33	42	22	1	82	1	4	4	3	1	.75	9	.264	.295	.306
1983	New York	N	68	185	47	5	0	0	(0	0)	52	10	12	3	0	34	1	1	0	1	0	1.00	1	.254	.270	.281
1983	Pittsburgh	N	5	8	1	0	0	0	(0	0)	1	1	0	1	0	0	0	1	0	0	0	.00	0	.125	.222	.125

SPIKE OWEN

Bats both Right and Left-handed, Throws Right-handed   Turns Age 26 in 1987, Born 04/19/61

						BATTING														BASERUNNING				PERCENTAGES		
Year	Team	League	G	AB	H	2B	3B	HR	(Hm	Rd)	TB	R	RBI	TBB	IBB	SO	HBP	SH	SF	SB	CS	SB%	GIDP	AVE	OBP	SLG
1983	Seattle	A	80	306	60	11	3	2	(1	1)	83	36	21	24	0	44	2	5	3	10	6	.63	2	.196	.257	.271
1984	Seattle	A	152	530	130	18	8	3	(2	1)	173	67	43	46	0	63	3	9	2	16	8	.67	5	.245	.308	.326
1985	Seattle	A	118	352	91	10	6	6	(3	3)	131	41	37	34	0	27	0	5	2	11	5	.69	5	.259	.322	.372
1986	2 Teams		154	528	122	24	7	1	(0	1)	163	67	45	51	1	51	2	9	3	4	4	.50	13	.231	.300	.309
4 YEARS			504	1716	403	63	24	12	(6	6)	550	211	146	155	1	185	7	28	10	41	23	.64	25	.235	.299	.321
1986	Boston	A	42	126	23	2	1	1	(0	1)	30	21	10	17	0	9	1	2	1	3	1	.75	2	.183	.283	.238
1986	Seattle	A	112	402	99	22	6	0	(0	0)	133	46	35	34	1	42	1	7	2	1	3	.25	11	.246	.305	.331

RICK OWNBEY

Pitches Right-handed, Bats Right-handed   Turns Age 30 in 1987, Born 10/20/57

			HOW MUCH HE PITCHED						WHAT HE GAVE UP										THE RESULTS					
Year	Team	League	G	GS	CG	GF	IP	BFP	H	R	ER	HR	SH	SF	HB	TBB	IBB	SO	WP	Bk	W	L	Pct	ShO	Sv	ERA
1982	New York	N	8	8	2	0	50.1	232	44	23	21	3	4	3	0	43	1	28	0	3	1	3	.333	0	0	3.75
1983	New York	N	10	4	0	3	34.2	152	31	19	18	4	1	0	1	21	0	19	1	2	1	3	.250	0	0	4.67
1984	St Louis	N	4	4	0	0	19	88	23	13	10	1	0	2	0	8	0	11	0	0	0	3	.000	0	0	4.74
1986	St Louis	N	17	3	0	4	42.2	185	47	20	18	4	2	2	2	19	0	25	2	0	1	3	.250	0	0	3.80
4 YEARS			39	19	2	7	146.2	657	145	75	67	12	9	7	3	91	1	83	3	5	3	11	.214	0	0	4.11

TOM PACIOREK

Bats Right-handed, Throws Right-handed

Turns Age 41 in 1987, Born 11/02/46

							BATTING														BASERUNNING				PERCENTAGES		
Year	Team	League	G	AB	H	2B	3B	HR	(Hm	Rd)	TB	R	RBI	TBB	IBB	SO	HBP	SH	SF	SB	CS	SB%	GIDP	AVE	OBP	SLG
1970	Los Angeles	N	8	9	2	1	0	0	(0	0)	3	2	0	0	0	3	0	0	0	0	0	.00	0	.222	.222	.333
1971	Los Angeles	N	2	2	1	0	0	0	(0	0)	1	0	1	0	0	0	0	0	0	0	0	.00	0	.500	.500	.500
1972	Los Angeles	N	11	47	12	4	0	1	(0	1)	19	4	6	1	0	7	0	0	0	1	0	1.00	1	.255	.271	.404
1973	Los Angeles	N	96	195	51	8	0	5	(2	3)	74	26	18	11	2	35	1	3	0	3	3	.50	8	.262	.304	.379
1974	Los Angeles	N	85	175	42	8	6	1	(1	0)	65	23	24	10	1	32	1	1	0	1	3	.25	3	.240	.282	.371
1975	Los Angeles	N	62	145	28	8	0	1	(0	1)	39	14	5	11	1	29	0	1	0	4	3	.57	3	.193	.250	.269
1976	Atlanta	N	111	324	94	10	4	4	(2	2)	124	39	36	19	2	57	3	2	2	2	3	.40	8	.290	.333	.383
1977	Atlanta	N	72	155	37	8	0	3	(0	3)	54	20	15	6	2	46	0	0	3	1	0	1.00	1	.239	.262	.348
1978	2 Teams		75	260	78	20	3	4	(3	1)	116	34	30	15	0	40	0	0	2	2	2	.50	6	.300	.336	.446
1979	Seattle	A	103	310	89	23	4	6	(6	0)	138	38	42	28	1	62	5	3	3	6	4	.60	6	.287	.353	.445
1980	Seattle	A	126	418	114	19	1	15	(11	4)	180	44	59	17	1	67	1	3	2	3	2	.60	13	.273	.301	.431
1981	Seattle	A	104	405	132	28	2	14	(7	7)	206	50	66	35	3	50	4	1	7	13	10	.57	10	.326	.379	.509
1982	Chicago	A	104	382	119	27	4	11	(0	11)	187	49	55	24	3	53	9	1	6	3	3	.50	6	.312	.361	.490
1983	Chicago	A	115	420	129	32	3	9	(4	5)	194	65	63	25	4	58	3	4	4	6	1	.86	9	.307	.347	.462
1984	Chicago	A	111	363	93	21	2	4	(2	2)	130	35	29	25	4	69	4	1	4	6	0	1.00	5	.256	.308	.358
1985	2 Teams		92	238	63	5	1	1	(1	0)	73	28	20	14	1	36	2	1	2	3	0	1.00	5	.265	.309	.307
1986	Texas	A	88	213	61	7	0	4	(0	4)	80	17	22	3	0	41	3	0	1	1	3	.25	5	.286	.305	.376
17 YEARS			1365	4061	1145	229	30	83	(39	44)	1683	488	491	244	25	685	36	21	38	55	37	.60	89	.282	.325	.414
1978	Seattle	A	70	251	75	20	3	4	(3	1)	113	32	30	15	0	39	0	0	2	2	2	.50	6	.299	.336	.450
1978	Atlanta	N	5	9	3	0	0	0	(0	0)	3	2	0	0	0	1	0	0	0	0	0	.00	0	.333	.333	.333
1985	Chicago	A	46	122	30	2	0	0	(0	0)	32	14	9	8	0	22	1	0	2	2	0	1.00	3	.246	.293	.262
1985	New York	N	46	116	33	3	1	1	(1	0)	41	14	11	6	1	14	1	1	0	1	0	1.00	2	.284	.325	.353

MIKE PAGLIARULO

Bats Left-handed, Throws Right-handed

Turns Age 27 in 1987, Born 03/15/60

							BATTING														BASERUNNING				PERCENTAGES		
Year	Team	League	G	AB	H	2B	3B	HR	(Hm	Rd)	TB	R	RBI	TBB	IBB	SO	HBP	SH	SF	SB	CS	SB%	GIDP	AVE	OBP	SLG
1984	New York	A	67	201	48	15	3	7	(4	3)	90	24	34	15	0	46	0	0	3	0	0	.00	5	.239	.288	.448
1985	New York	A	138	380	91	16	2	19	(8	11)	168	55	62	45	4	86	4	3	3	0	0	.00	6	.239	.324	.442
1986	New York	A	149	504	120	24	3	28	(14	14)	234	71	71	54	10	120	4	1	2	4	1	.80	10	.238	.316	.464
3 YEARS			354	1085	259	55	8	54	(26	28)	492	150	167	114	14	252	8	4	8	4	1	.80	21	.239	.314	.453

DAVID PALMER

Pitches Right-handed, Bats Right-handed

Turns Age 30 in 1987, Born 10/19/57

			HOW MUCH HE PITCHED						WHAT HE GAVE UP											THE RESULTS					
Year	Team	League	G	GS	CG	GF	IP	BFP	H	R	ER	HR	SH	SF	HB	TBB	IBB	SO	WP	Bk	W	L	Pct	ShO	Sv	ERA
1978	Montreal	N	5	1	0	1	10	39	9	4	3	1	0	0	0	2	0	7	0	0	0	1	.000	0	0	2.70
1979	Montreal	N	36	11	2	13	123	502	110	41	36	10	4	2	2	30	7	72	2	0	10	2	.833	1	2	2.63
1980	Montreal	N	24	19	3	0	130	529	124	53	43	11	8	2	2	30	1	73	1	2	8	6	.571	1	0	2.98
1982	Montreal	N	13	13	1	0	73.2	312	60	34	26	3	1	5	2	36	2	46	6	1	6	4	.600	0	0	3.18
1984	Montreal	N	20	19	1	0	105.1	444	101	45	45	5	5	1	0	44	4	66	0	2	7	3	.700	1	0	3.84
1985	Montreal	N	24	23	0	0	135.2	588	128	60	56	5	5	2	3	67	5	106	9	0	7	10	.412	0	0	3.71
1986	Atlanta	N	35	35	2	0	209.2	889	181	98	85	17	4	5	5	102	8	170	9	0	11	10	.524	0	0	3.65
7 YEARS			157	121	9	14	787.1	3303	713	335	294	52	27	17	14	311	27	540	27	5	49	36	.576	3	2	3.36

JIM PANKOVITS

Bats Right-handed, Throws Right-handed

Turns Age 32 in 1987, Born 08/06/55

							BATTING														BASERUNNING				PERCENTAGES		
Year	Team	League	G	AB	H	2B	3B	HR	(Hm	Rd)	TB	R	RBI	TBB	IBB	SO	HBP	SH	SF	SB	CS	SB%	GIDP	AVE	OBP	SLG
1984	Pittsburgh	N	53	81	23	7	0	1	(0	1)	33	6	14	2	0	20	0	1	1	2	1	.67	1	.284	.298	.407
1985	Houston	N	75	172	42	3	0	4	(2	2)	57	24	14	17	1	29	1	1	0	1	0	1.00	3	.244	.316	.331
1986	Houston	N	70	113	32	6	1	1	(0	1)	43	12	7	11	1	25	0	0	0	1	1	.50	4	.283	.347	.381
3 YEARS			198	366	97	16	1	6	(2	4)	133	42	35	30	2	74	1	2	1	4	2	.67	8	.265	.322	.363

DAVE PARKER

Bats Left-handed, Throws Right-handed   Turns Age 36 in 1987, Born 06/09/51

Year	Team	League	G	AB	H	2B	3B	HR	(Hm	Rd)	TB	R	RBI	TBB	IBB	SO	HBP	SH	SF	SB	CS	SB%	GIDP	AVE	OBP	SLG
1973	Pittsburgh	N	54	139	40	9	1	4	(2	2)	63	17	14	2	1	27	2	1	0	1	1	.50	2	.288	.308	.453
1974	Pittsburgh	N	73	220	62	10	3	4	(3	1)	90	27	29	10	1	53	3	0	0	3	3	.50	3	.282	.322	.409
1975	Pittsburgh	N	148	558	172	35	10	25	(10	15)	302	75	101	38	4	89	5	0	1	8	6	.57	18	.308	.357	.541
1976	Pittsburgh	N	138	537	168	28	10	13	(5	8)	255	82	90	30	6	80	2	0	4	19	7	.73	16	.313	.349	.475
1977	Pittsburgh	N	159	637	215	44	8	21	(10	11)	338	107	88	58	13	107	7	0	4	17	19	.47	7	.338	.397	.531
1978	Pittsburgh	N	148	581	194	32	12	30	(14	16)	340	102	117	57	23	92	2	0	2	20	7	.74	8	.334	.394	.585
1979	Pittsburgh	N	158	622	193	45	7	25	(14	11)	327	109	94	67	14	101	9	0	9	20	4	.83	7	.310	.380	.526
1980	Pittsburgh	N	139	518	153	31	1	17	(10	7)	237	71	79	25	5	69	2	0	5	10	7	.59	8	.295	.327	.458
1981	Pittsburgh	N	67	240	62	14	3	9	(4	5)	109	29	48	9	3	25	2	0	3	6	2	.75	5	.258	.287	.454
1982	Pittsburgh	N	73	244	66	19	3	6	(4	2)	109	41	29	22	2	45	1	0	3	7	5	.58	7	.270	.330	.447
1983	Pittsburgh	N	144	552	154	29	4	12	(6	6)	227	68	69	28	6	89	0	0	6	12	9	.57	11	.279	.311	.411
1984	Cincinnati	N	156	607	173	28	0	16	(10	6)	249	73	94	41	10	89	1	0	6	11	10	.52	8	.285	.328	.410
1985	Cincinnati	N	160	635	198	42	4	34	(16	18)	350	88	125	52	24	80	3	0	4	5	13	.28	26	.312	.365	.551
1986	Cincinnati	N	162	637	174	31	3	31	(17	14)	304	89	116	56	16	126	1	0	6	1	6	.14	18	.273	.330	.477
14 YEARS			1779	6727	2024	397	69	247	(125	122)	3300	978	1093	495	128	1072	40	1	53	140	99	.59	144	.301	.350	.491

LANCE PARRISH

Bats Right-handed, Throws Right-handed   Turns Age 31 in 1987, Born 06/15/56

Year	Team	League	G	AB	H	2B	3B	HR	(Hm	Rd)	TB	R	RBI	TBB	IBB	SO	HBP	SH	SF	SB	CS	SB%	GIDP	AVE	OBP	SLG
1977	Detroit	A	12	46	9	2	0	3	(2	1)	20	10	7	5	0	12	0	0	0	0	0	.00	2	.196	.275	.435
1978	Detroit	A	85	288	63	11	3	14	(7	7)	122	37	41	11	0	71	3	1	1	0	0	.00	8	.219	.254	.424
1979	Detroit	A	143	493	136	26	3	19	(8	11)	225	65	65	49	2	105	2	3	1	6	7	.46	15	.276	.343	.456
1980	Detroit	A	144	553	158	34	6	24	(7	17)	276	79	82	31	3	109	3	2	3	6	4	.60	24	.286	.325	.499
1981	Detroit	A	96	348	85	18	2	10	(8	2)	137	39	46	34	6	52	0	1	1	2	3	.40	16	.244	.311	.394
1982	Detroit	A	133	486	138	19	2	32	(22	10)	257	75	87	40	5	99	1	0	2	3	4	.43	5	.284	.338	.529
1983	Detroit	A	155	605	163	42	3	27	(12	15)	292	80	114	44	7	106	1	0	13	1	3	.25	21	.269	.314	.483
1984	Detroit	A	147	578	137	16	2	33	(13	20)	256	75	98	41	6	120	2	2	6	2	3	.40	12	.237	.287	.443
1985	Detroit	A	140	549	150	27	1	28	(11	17)	263	64	98	41	5	90	2	3	5	2	6	.25	10	.273	.323	.479
1986	Detroit	A	91	327	84	6	1	22	(8	14)	158	53	62	38	3	83	5	1	3	0	0	.00	8	.257	.340	.483
10 YEARS			1146	4273	1123	201	23	212	(98	114)	2006	577	700	334	37	847	19	13	35	22	30	.42	116	.263	.317	.469

LARRY PARRISH

Bats Right-handed, Throws Right-handed   Turns Age 34 in 1987, Born 11/10/53

Year	Team	League	G	AB	H	2B	3B	HR	(Hm	Rd)	TB	R	RBI	TBB	IBB	SO	HBP	SH	SF	SB	CS	SB%	GIDP	AVE	OBP	SLG
1974	Montreal	N	25	69	14	5	0	0	(0	0)	19	9	4	6	2	19	2	2	0	0	0	.00	1	.203	.286	.275
1975	Montreal	N	145	532	146	32	5	10	(5	5)	218	50	65	28	5	74	4	7	2	4	5	.44	14	.274	.314	.410
1976	Montreal	N	154	543	126	28	5	11	(4	7)	197	65	61	41	2	91	2	1	6	2	6	.25	13	.232	.285	.363
1977	Montreal	N	123	402	99	19	2	11	(4	7)	155	50	46	37	9	71	4	3	3	2	4	.33	11	.246	.314	.386
1978	Montreal	N	144	520	144	39	4	15	(4	11)	236	68	70	32	9	103	2	5	1	2	3	.40	19	.277	.321	.454
1979	Montreal	N	153	544	167	39	2	30	(14	16)	300	83	82	41	11	101	2	7	1	5	1	.83	12	.307	.357	.551
1980	Montreal	N	126	452	115	27	3	15	(6	9)	193	55	72	36	6	80	4	1	8	2	6	.25	12	.254	.310	.427
1981	Montreal	N	97	349	85	19	3	8	(3	5)	134	41	44	28	2	73	0	5	3	0	0	.00	10	.244	.297	.384
1982	Texas	A	128	440	116	15	0	17	(6	11)	182	59	62	30	0	84	4	0	4	5	2	.71	20	.264	.314	.414
1983	Texas	A	145	555	151	26	4	26	(10	16)	263	76	88	46	8	91	3	0	9	0	0	.00	20	.272	.326	.474
1984	Texas	A	156	613	145	42	1	22	(11	11)	285	72	101	42	7	116	6	0	3	2	4	.33	20	.285	.336	.465
1985	Texas	A	94	346	86	11	1	17	(8	9)	150	44	51	33	2	77	1	0	2	0	2	.00	16	.249	.314	.434
1986	Texas	A	129	464	128	22	1	28	(14	14)	236	67	94	52	7	114	2	0	6	3	1	.75	16	.276	.347	.509
13 YEARS			1619	5829	1552	324	31	210	(89	121)	2568	739	840	452	70	1094	36	31	48	27	34	.44	169	.266	.321	.441

DAN PASQUA

Bats Left-handed, Throws Left-handed   Turns Age 26 in 1987, Born 10/17/61

Year	Team	League	G	AB	H	2B	3B	HR	(Hm	Rd)	TB	R	RBI	TBB	IBB	SO	HBP	SH	SF	SB	CS	SB%	GIDP	AVE	OBP	SLG
1985	New York	A	60	148	31	3	1	9	(7	2)	63	17	25	16	4	38	1	0	1	0	0	.00	1	.209	.289	.426
1986	New York	A	102	280	82	17	0	16	(9	7)	147	44	45	47	3	78	3	1	1	2	0	1.00	4	.293	.399	.525
2 YEARS			162	428	113	20	1	25	(16	9)	210	61	70	63	7	116	4	1	2	2	0	1.00	5	.264	.362	.491

FRANK PASTORE

Pitches Right-handed, Bats Right-handed   Turns Age 30 in 1987, Born 08/21/57

Year	Team	League	G	GS	CG	GF	IP	BFP	H	R	ER	HR	SH	SF	HB	TBB	IBB	SO	WP	Bk	W	L	Pct	ShO	Sv	ERA
1979	Cincinnati	N	30	9	2	10	95	407	102	47	45	8	5	2	1	23	5	63	2	0	6	7	.462	1	4	4.26
1980	Cincinnati	N	27	27	9	0	185	744	161	72	67	13	6	5	0	42	3	110	0	1	13	7	.650	2	0	3.26
1981	Cincinnati	N	22	22	2	0	132	556	125	73	59	11	7	5	3	35	1	81	3	2	4	9	.308	1	0	4.02
1982	Cincinnati	N	31	29	3	0	188.1	81	210	86	83	13	10	8	4	57	8	94	4	0	8	13	.381	2	0	3.97
1983	Cincinnati	N	36	29	4	2	184.1	791	207	104	100	20	6	6	1	64	9	93	6	3	9	12	.429	1	0	4.88
1984	Cincinnati	N	24	16	1	2	98.1	437	110	74	71	10	3	5	4	40	3	53	4	2	3	8	.273	0	0	6.50
1985	Cincinnati	N	17	6	1	3	54	232	60	23	23	1	3	3	1	16	1	29	2	0	2	1	.667	0	0	3.83
1986	Minnesota	A	33	1	0	15	49.1	223	54	28	22	4	4	4	0	24	6	18	1	0	3	1	.750	0	2	4.01
8 YEARS			220	139	22	32	986.1	3471	1029	507	470	80	44	38	13	301	30	541	22	8	48	58	.453	7	6	4.29

ALEJANDRO PENA

Pitches Right-handed, Bats Right-handed   Turns Age 28 in 1987, Born 06/25/59

			HOW MUCH HE PITCHED					WHAT HE GAVE UP											THE RESULTS					
Year	Team	League	G	GS	CG	GF	IP	BFP	H	R	ER	HR	SH	SF	HB	TBB	IBB	SO	WP	Bk	W	L	Pct	ShO	Sv	ERA
1981	Los Angeles	N	14	0	0	7	25	104	18	8	8	2	0	0	0	11	1	14	0	0	1	1	.500	0	2	2.88
1982	Los Angeles	N	29	0	0	11	35.2	160	37	24	19	2	2	0	1	21	7	20	1	1	0	2	.000	0	0	4.79
1983	Los Angeles	N	34	26	4	4	177	730	152	67	54	7	8	5	1	51	7	120	2	1	12	9	.571	3	1	2.75
1984	Los Angeles	N	28	28	8	0	199.1	813	186	67	55	7	6	2	3	46	7	135	5	1	12	6	.667	4	0	2.48
1985	Los Angeles	N	2	1	0	0	4.1	23	7	5	4	1	0	0	0	3	1	2	0	0	0	1	.000	0	0	8.31
1986	Los Angeles	N	24	10	0	6	70	309	74	40	38	6	3	1	1	30	5	46	1	1	1	2	.333	0	1	4.89
6 YEARS			131	65	12	28	511.1	2139	474	211	178	25	19	8	6	162	28	337	9	4	26	21	.553	7	4	3.13

TONY PENA

Bats Right-handed, Throws Right-handed   Turns Age 30 in 1987, Born 06/04/57

						BATTING												BASERUNNING				PERCENTAGES		
Year	Team	League	G	AB	H	2B	3B	HR	(Hm | Rd)	TB	R	RBI	TBB	IBB	SO	HBP	SH	SF	SB	CS	SB%	GIDP	AVE	OBP	SLG
1980	Pittsburgh	N	8	21	9	1	1	0	(0 | 0)	12	1	1	0	0	4	0	0	0	0	1	.00	1	.429	.429	.571
1981	Pittsburgh	N	66	210	63	9	1	2	(0 | 2)	80	16	17	8	2	23	1	2	2	1	2	.33	4	.300	.326	.381
1982	Pittsburgh	N	138	497	147	28	4	11	(5 | 6)	216	53	63	17	3	57	4	3	2	2	5	.29	17	.296	.323	.435
1983	Pittsburgh	N	151	542	163	22	3	15	(8 | 7)	236	51	70	31	8	73	0	6	1	6	7	.46	13	.301	.338	.435
1984	Pittsburgh	N	147	546	156	27	2	15	(7 | 8)	232	77	78	36	5	79	4	4	2	12	8	.60	14	.286	.333	.425
1985	Pittsburgh	N	147	546	136	27	2	10	(2 | 8)	197	53	59	29	4	67	0	7	5	12	8	.60	19	.249	.284	.361
1986	Pittsburgh	N	144	510	147	26	2	10	(5 | 5)	207	56	52	53	6	69	1	0	1	9	10	.47	21	.288	.356	.406
7 YEARS			801	2872	821	140	15	63	(27 | 36)	1180	307	340	174	28	372	10	22	13	42	41	.51	89	.286	.327	.411

TERRY PENDLETON

Bats both Right and Left-handed, Throws Right-handed   Turns Age 27 in 1987, Born 07/16/60

						BATTING												BASERUNNING				PERCENTAGES		
Year	Team	League	G	AB	H	2B	3B	HR	(Hm | Rd)	TB	R	RBI	TBB	IBB	SO	HBP	SH	SF	SB	CS	SB%	GIDP	AVE	OBP	SLG
1984	St Louis	N	67	262	85	16	3	1	(0 | 1)	110	37	33	16	3	32	0	0	5	20	5	.80	7	.324	.357	.420
1985	St Louis	N	149	559	134	16	3	5	(3 | 2)	171	56	69	37	4	75	0	3	3	17	12	.59	18	.240	.285	.306
1986	St Louis	N	159	578	138	26	5	1	(0 | 1)	177	56	59	34	10	59	1	6	7	24	6	.80	12	.239	.279	.306
3 YEARS			375	1399	357	58	11	7	(3 | 4)	458	149	161	87	17	166	1	9	15	61	23	.73	37	.255	.296	.327

TONY PEREZ

Bats Right-handed, Throws Right-handed   Turns Age 45 in 1987, Born 05/14/42

						BATTING												BASERUNNING				PERCENTAGES		
Year	Team	League	G	AB	H	2B	3B	HR	(Hm | Rd)	TB	R	RBI	TBB	IBB	SO	HBP	SH	SF	SB	CS	SB%	GIDP	AVE	OBP	SLG
1964	Cincinnati	N	12	25	2	1	0	0	(0 | 0)	3	1	1	3	0	9	0	0	0	0	0	.00	0	.080	.179	.120
1965	Cincinnati	N	104	281	73	14	4	12	(7 | 5)	131	40	47	21	5	67	2	2	1	0	2	.00	10	.260	.315	.466
1966	Cincinnati	N	99	257	68	10	4	4	(4 | 0)	98	25	39	14	2	44	2	2	3	1	0	1.00	12	.265	.304	.381
1967	Cincinnati	N	156	600	174	28	7	26	(11 | 15)	294	78	102	33	10	102	4	0	7	0	3	.00	15	.290	.328	.490
1968	Cincinnati	N	160	625	176	25	7	18	(5 | 13)	269	93	92	51	13	92	6	1	7	3	2	.60	19	.282	.338	.430
1969	Cincinnati	N	160	629	185	31	2	37	(15 | 22)	331	103	122	63	7	131	2	3	7	4	2	.67	20	.294	.357	.526
1970	Cincinnati	N	158	587	186	28	6	40	(19 | 21)	346	107	129	83	13	134	4	0	7	8	3	.73	15	.317	.401	.589
1971	Cincinnati	N	158	609	164	22	3	25	(11 | 14)	267	72	91	51	5	120	1	0	3	4	1	.80	13	.269	.325	.438
1972	Cincinnati	N	136	515	146	33	7	21	(11 | 10)	256	64	90	55	15	121	1	0	6	4	2	.67	9	.283	.349	.497
1973	Cincinnati	N	151	564	177	33	3	27	(9 | 18)	297	73	101	74	10	117	3	0	6	3	1	.75	13	.314	.393	.527
1974	Cincinnati	N	158	596	158	28	2	28	(17 | 11)	274	81	101	61	7	112	2	0	6	1	3	.25	17	.265	.331	.460
1975	Cincinnati	N	137	511	144	28	4	20	(12 | 8)	238	74	109	54	6	101	3	0	6	1	2	.33	12	.282	.350	.466
1976	Cincinnati	N	139	527	137	32	6	19	(9 | 10)	238	77	91	50	9	88	5	0	4	10	5	.67	10	.260	.328	.452
1977	Montreal	N	154	559	158	32	6	19	(8 | 11)	259	71	91	63	15	111	2	0	9	4	3	.57	14	.283	.352	.463
1978	Montreal	N	148	544	158	38	3	14	(5 | 9)	244	63	78	38	9	104	2	1	5	2	0	1.00	14	.290	.336	.449
1979	Montreal	N	132	489	132	29	4	13	(7 | 6)	208	58	73	38	4	82	3	0	7	2	1	.67	14	.270	.322	.425
1980	Boston	A	151	585	161	31	3	25	(9 | 16)	273	73	105	41	11	93	1	0	8	1	0	1.00	25	.275	.320	.467
1981	Boston	A	84	306	77	11	3	9	(7 | 2)	121	35	39	27	0	66	0	0	3	0	0	.00	9	.252	.310	.395
1982	Boston	A	69	196	51	14	2	6	(5 | 1)	87	18	31	19	3	48	0	0	0	0	1	.00	6	.260	.326	.444
1983	Philadelphia	N	91	253	61	11	2	6	(3 | 3)	94	18	43	28	1	57	1	0	1	1	0	1.00	9	.241	.316	.372
1984	Cincinnati	N	71	137	33	6	1	2	(2 | 0)	47	9	15	11	2	21	0	0	1	0	0	.00	8	.241	.295	.343
1985	Cincinnati	N	72	183	60	8	0	6	(4 | 2)	86	25	33	22	1	22	0	0	2	0	0	.00	2	.328	.396	.470
1986	Cincinnati	N	77	200	51	12	1	2	(2 | 0)	71	14	29	25	2	25	0	0	0	0	0	.00	6	.255	.333	.355
23 YEARS			2777	9778	2732	505	79	379	(182 | 197)	4532	1272	1652	925	150	1867	43	9	106	49	33	.60	268	.279	.341	.463

PAT PERRY

Pitches Left-handed, Bats Left-handed   Turns Age 28 in 1987, Born 02/04/59

			HOW MUCH HE PITCHED					WHAT HE GAVE UP											THE RESULTS					
Year	Team	League	G	GS	CG	GF	IP	BFP	H	R	ER	HR	SH	SF	HB	TBB	IBB	SO	WP	Bk	W	L	Pct	ShO	Sv	ERA
1985	St Louis	N	6	0	0	1	12.1	42	3	0	0	0	0	0	0	3	1	6	1	0	1	0	1.000	0	0	0.00
1986	St Louis	N	46	0	0	20	68.2	288	59	31	29	5	0	7	0	34	9	29	5	0	2	3	.400	0	2	3.80
2 YEARS			52	0	0	21	81	330	62	31	29	5	0	7	0	37	10	35	6	0	3	3	.500	0	2	3.22

GENO PETRALLI

Bats both Right and Left-handed, Throws Right-handed   Turns Age 28 in 1987, Born 09/25/59

								BATTING												BASERUNNING				PERCENTAGES		
Year	Team	League	G	AB	H	2B	3B	HR	(Hm	Rd)	TB	R	RBI	TBB	IBB	SO	HBP	SH	SF	SB	CS	SB%	GIDP	AVE	OBP	SLG
1982	Toronto	A	16	44	16	2	0	0	(0	0)	18	3	1	4	0	6	0	1	0	0	0	.00	1	.364	.417	.409
1983	Toronto	A	6	4	0	0	0	0	(0	0)	0	0	0	1	0	1	0	0	0	0	0	.00	0	.000	.200	.000
1984	Toronto	A	3	3	0	0	0	0	(0	0)	0	0	0	0	0	0	0	0	0	0	0	.00	0	.000	.000	.000
1985	Texas	A	42	100	27	2	0	0	(0	0)	29	7	11	8	0	12	1	3	4	1	0	1.00	4	.270	.319	.290
1986	Texas	A	69	137	35	9	3	2	(1	1)	56	17	18	5	0	14	0	0	0	3	0	1.00	7	.255	.282	.409
5 YEARS			136	288	78	13	3	2	(1	1)	103	27	30	18	0	33	1	4	4	4	0	1.00	12	.271	.312	.358

DAN PETRY

Pitches Right-handed, Bats Right-handed   Turns Age 29 in 1987, Born 11/13/58

			HOW MUCH HE PITCHED						WHAT HE GAVE UP										THE RESULTS					
Year	Team	League	G	GS	CG	GF	IP	BFP	H	R	ER	HR	SH	SF	HB	TBB	IBB	SO	WP	Bk	W	L	Pct	ShO	Sv	ERA
1979	Detroit	A	15	15	2	0	98	401	90	46	43	11	5	5	4	33	5	43	3	1	6	5	.545	0	0	3.95
1980	Detroit	A	27	25	4	1	165	716	156	82	72	9	10	5	1	83	14	88	5	2	10	9	.526	3	0	3.93
1981	Detroit	A	23	22	7	1	141	583	115	53	47	10	9	2	1	57	4	79	3	1	10	9	.526	2	0	3.00
1982	Detroit	A	35	35	8	0	246	1031	220	98	88	15	8	8	4	100	5	132	9	0	15	9	.625	1	0	3.22
1983	Detroit	A	38	38	9	0	266.1	1115	256	126	116	37	5	5	6	99	7	122	12	0	19	11	.633	2	0	3.92
1984	Detroit	A	35	35	7	0	233.1	968	231	94	84	21	5	2	3	66	4	144	7	0	18	8	.692	2	0	3.24
1985	Detroit	A	34	34	8	0	238.2	962	190	98	89	24	0	2	3	81	9	109	6	0	15	13	.536	0	0	3.36
1986	Detroit	A	20	20	2	0	116	520	122	78	60	15	3	3	5	53	3	56	5	0	5	10	.333	0	0	4.66
8 YEARS			227	224	47	2	1504.1	6296	1380	675	599	142	45	32	27	572	51	773	50	4	98	74	.570	10	0	3.58

GARY PETTIS

Bats both Right and Left-handed, Throws Right-handed   Turns Age 29 in 1987, Born 04/03/58

								BATTING												BASERUNNING				PERCENTAGES		
Year	Team	League	G	AB	H	2B	3B	HR	(Hm	Rd)	TB	R	RBI	TBB	IBB	SO	HBP	SH	SF	SB	CS	SB%	GIDP	AVE	OBP	SLG
1982	California	A	10	5	1	0	0	1	(1	0)	4	5	1	0	0	2	0	0	0	0	0	.00	0	.200	.200	.800
1983	California	A	22	85	25	2	3	3	(3	0)	42	19	6	7	0	15	0	1	0	8	3	.73	1	.294	.348	.494
1984	California	A	140	397	90	11	6	2	(1	1)	119	63	29	60	1	115	3	5	1	48	17	.74	4	.227	.332	.300
1985	California	A	125	443	114	10	8	1	(0	1)	143	67	32	62	0	125	0	9	2	56	9	.86	5	.257	.347	.323
1986	California	A	154	539	139	23	4	5	(1	4)	185	93	58	69	2	132	0	15	5	50	13	.79	7	.258	.339	.343
5 YEARS			451	1469	369	46	21	12	(6	6)	493	247	126	198	3	389	3	30	8	162	42	.79	17	.251	.340	.336

KEN PHELPS

Bats Left-handed, Throws Left-handed   Turns Age 33 in 1987, Born 08/06/54

								BATTING												BASERUNNING				PERCENTAGES		
Year	Team	League	G	AB	H	2B	3B	HR	(Hm	Rd)	TB	R	RBI	TBB	IBB	SO	HBP	SH	SF	SB	CS	SB%	GIDP	AVE	OBP	SLG
1980	Kansas City	A	3	4	0	0	0	0	(0	0)	0	0	0	0	0	2	0	0	0	0	0	.00	0	.000	.000	.000
1981	Kansas City	A	21	22	3	0	1	0	(0	0)	5	1	1	1	0	13	0	0	0	0	0	.00	0	.136	.174	.227
1982	Montreal	N	10	8	2	0	0	0	(0	0)	2	0	0	0	0	3	1	0	0	0	0	.00	0	.250	.333	.250
1983	Seattle	A	50	127	30	4	1	7	(6	1)	57	10	16	13	0	25	0	1	3	0	0	.00	0	.236	.301	.449
1984	Seattle	A	101	290	70	9	0	24	(13	11)	151	52	51	61	5	73	5	0	4	3	3	.50	1	.241	.378	.521
1985	Seattle	A	61	116	24	3	0	9	(5	4)	54	18	24	24	2	33	0	0	0	2	0	1.00	1	.207	.343	.466
1986	Seattle	A	125	344	85	16	4	24	(15	9)	181	69	64	88	6	96	6	0	3	2	3	.40	4	.247	.406	.526
7 YEARS			371	911	214	32	6	64	(39	25)	450	150	156	187	13	245	12	1	10	7	6	.54	6	.235	.369	.494

TONY PHILLIPS

Bats both Right and Left-handed, Throws Right-handed   Turns Age 28 in 1987, Born 04/25/59

								BATTING												BASERUNNING				PERCENTAGES		
Year	Team	League	G	AB	H	2B	3B	HR	(Hm	Rd)	TB	R	RBI	TBB	IBB	SO	HBP	SH	SF	SB	CS	SB%	GIDP	AVE	OBP	SLG
1982	Oakland	A	40	81	17	2	2	0	(0	0)	23	11	8	12	0	26	2	5	0	2	3	.40	0	.210	.326	.284
1983	Oakland	A	148	412	102	12	3	4	(1	3)	132	54	35	48	1	70	2	11	3	16	5	.76	5	.248	.327	.320
1984	Oakland	A	154	451	120	24	3	4	(2	2)	162	62	37	42	1	86	0	7	5	10	6	.63	5	.266	.325	.359
1985	Oakland	A	42	161	45	12	2	4	(2	2)	73	23	17	13	0	34	0	3	1	3	2	.60	1	.280	.331	.453
1986	Oakland	A	118	441	113	14	5	5	(3	2)	152	76	52	76	0	82	3	9	3	15	10	.60	2	.256	.367	.345
5 YEARS			502	1546	397	64	15	17	(8	9)	542	226	149	191	2	298	7	35	12	46	26	.64	13	.257	.339	.351

DAN PLESAC

Pitches Left-handed, Bats Left-handed   Turns Age 25 in 1987, Born 02/04/62

			HOW MUCH HE PITCHED						WHAT HE GAVE UP										THE RESULTS					
Year	Team	League	G	GS	CG	GF	IP	BFP	H	R	ER	HR	SH	SF	HB	TBB	IBB	SO	WP	Bk	W	L	Pct	ShO	Sv	ERA
1986	Milwaukee	A	51	0	0	33	91	377	81	34	30	5	6	5	0	29	1	75	4	0	10	7	.588	0	14	2.97

ERIC PLUNK

Pitches Right-handed, Bats Right-handed

Turns Age 24 in 1987, Born 09/03/63

			HOW MUCH HE PITCHED					WHAT HE GAVE UP										THE RESULTS					
Year	Team	League	G	GS	CG	GF	IP	BFP	H	R	ER	HR	SH	SF	HB	TBB	IBB	SO	WP	Bk	W	L	Pct	ShO	Sv	ERA
1986	Oakland	A	26	15	0	2	120.1	537	91	75	71	14	2	3	5	102	2	98	9	6	4	7	.364	0	0	5.31

DARRELL PORTER

Bats Left-handed, Throws Right-handed

Turns Age 35 in 1987, Born 01/17/52

									BATTING												BASERUNNING				PERCENTAGES		
Year	Team	League	G	AB	H	2B	3B	HR	(Hm	Rd)	TB	R	RBI	TBB	IBB	SO	HBP	SH	SF	SB	CS	SB%	GIDP	AVE	OBP	SLG
1971	Milwaukee	A	22	70	15	2	0	2	(2	0)	23	4	9	9	0	20	0	0	1	2	2	.50	0	.214	.300	.329
1972	Milwaukee	A	18	56	7	1	0	1	(1	0)	11	2	2	5	0	21	1	1	0	0	0	.00	1	.125	.210	.196
1973	Milwaukee	A	117	350	89	19	2	16	(7	9)	160	50	67	57	6	85	4	3	2	5	2	.71	6	.254	.363	.457
1974	Milwaukee	A	131	432	104	15	4	12	(7	5)	163	59	56	50	7	88	5	2	1	8	7	.53	6	.241	.326	.377
1975	Milwaukee	A	130	409	95	12	5	18	(9	9)	171	66	60	89	10	77	5	1	7	2	5	.29	8	.232	.371	.418
1976	Milwaukee	A	119	389	81	14	1	5	(3	2)	112	43	32	51	3	61	1	3	5	2	0	1.00	4	.208	.298	.288
1977	Kansas City	A	130	425	117	21	3	16	(4	12)	192	61	60	53	6	70	1	1	6	1	0	1.00	6	.275	.353	.452
1978	Kansas City	A	150	520	138	27	6	18	(7	11)	231	77	78	75	14	75	2	1	4	0	5	.00	13	.265	.358	.444
1979	Kansas City	A	157	533	155	23	10	20	(8	12)	258	101	112	121	8	65	8	4	13	3	4	.43	11	.291	.421	.484
1980	Kansas City	A	118	418	104	14	2	7	(1	6)	143	51	51	69	5	50	2	0	6	1	1	.50	6	.249	.354	.342
1981	St Louis	N	61	174	39	10	2	6	(2	4)	71	22	31	39	7	32	1	0	3	1	2	.33	3	.224	.364	.408
1982	St Louis	N	120	373	86	18	5	12	(3	9)	150	46	48	66	6	66	2	1	3	1	1	.50	8	.231	.347	.402
1983	St Louis	N	145	443	116	24	3	15	(5	10)	191	57	66	68	12	94	4	1	3	1	3	.25	3	.262	.363	.431
1984	St Louis	N	127	422	98	16	3	11	(4	7)	153	56	68	60	12	79	5	0	6	5	3	.63	10	.232	.331	.363
1985	St Louis	N	84	240	53	12	2	10	(4	6)	99	30	36	41	6	48	1	0	2	6	1	.86	3	.221	.335	.413
1986	Texas	A	68	155	41	6	0	12	(6	6)	83	21	29	22	0	51	1	0	0	1	1	.50	3	.265	.360	.535
16 YEARS			1697	5409	1338	234	48	181	(73	108)	2211	746	805	875	102	982	43	18	62	39	37	.51	100	.247	.353	.409

MARK PORTUGAL

Pitches Right-handed, Bats Right-handed

Turns Age 25 in 1987, Born 10/30/62

			HOW MUCH HE PITCHED					WHAT HE GAVE UP										THE RESULTS					
Year	Team	League	G	GS	CG	GF	IP	BFP	H	R	ER	HR	SH	SF	HB	TBB	IBB	SO	WP	Bk	W	L	Pct	ShO	Sv	ERA
1985	Minnesota	A	6	4	0	0	24.1	105	24	16	15	3	0	2	0	14	0	12	1	1	1	3	.250	0	0	5.55
1986	Minnesota	A	27	15	3	7	112.2	481	112	56	54	10	5	3	1	50	1	67	5	0	6	10	.375	0	1	4.31
2 YEARS			33	19	3	7	137	586	136	72	69	13	5	5	1	64	1	79	6	1	7	13	.350	0	1	4.53

DENNIS POWELL

Pitches Left-handed, Bats Right-handed

Turns Age 24 in 1987, Born 08/13/63

			HOW MUCH HE PITCHED					WHAT HE GAVE UP										THE RESULTS					
Year	Team	League	G	GS	CG	GF	IP	BFP	H	R	ER	HR	SH	SF	HB	TBB	IBB	SO	WP	Bk	W	L	Pct	ShO	Sv	ERA
1985	Los Angeles	N	16	2	0	6	29.1	133	30	19	17	7	4	1	1	13	3	19	3	0	1	1	.500	0	1	5.22
1986	Los Angeles	N	27	6	0	5	65.1	272	65	32	31	5	5	2	1	25	7	31	7	2	2	7	.222	0	0	4.27
2 YEARS			43	8	0	11	94.2	405	95	51	48	12	9	3	2	38	10	50	10	2	3	8	.273	0	1	4.56

TED POWER

Pitches Right-handed, Bats Right-handed

Turns Age 32 in 1987, Born 01/31/55

			HOW MUCH HE PITCHED					WHAT HE GAVE UP										THE RESULTS					
Year	Team	League	G	GS	CG	GF	IP	BFP	H	R	ER	HR	SH	SF	HB	TBB	IBB	SO	WP	Bk	W	L	Pct	ShO	Sv	ERA
1981	Los Angeles	N	5	2	0	1	14	66	16	6	5	0	0	2	1	7	2	7	0	0	1	3	.250	0	0	3.21
1982	Los Angeles	N	12	4	0	4	33.2	160	38	27	25	4	4	1	0	23	1	15	3	3	1	1	.500	0	0	6.68
1983	Cincinnati	N	49	6	1	14	111	480	120	62	56	10	4	6	1	49	4	57	1	0	5	6	.455	0	2	4.54
1984	Cincinnati	N	78	0	0	42	108.2	456	93	37	34	4	9	8	0	46	8	81	3	0	9	7	.563	0	11	2.82
1985	Cincinnati	N	64	0	0	50	80	342	65	27	24	2	6	4	1	45	8	42	1	0	8	6	.571	0	27	2.70
1986	Cincinnati	N	56	10	0	30	129	537	115	59	53	13	9	6	1	52	10	95	5	1	10	6	.625	0	1	3.70
6 YEARS			264	22	1	141	476.1	2041	447	218	197	33	32	27	4	222	33	297	13	4	34	29	.540	0	41	3.72

JIM PRESLEY

Bats Right-handed, Throws Right-handed

Turns Age 26 in 1987, Born 10/23/61

									BATTING												BASERUNNING				PERCENTAGES		
Year	Team	League	G	AB	H	2B	3B	HR	(Hm	Rd)	TB	R	RBI	TBB	IBB	SO	HBP	SH	SF	SB	CS	SB%	GIDP	AVE	OBP	SLG
1984	Seattle	A	70	251	57	12	1	10	(5	5)	101	27	36	6	1	63	1	0	1	1	1	.50	4	.227	.247	.402
1985	Seattle	A	155	570	157	33	1	28	(12	16)	276	71	84	44	9	100	1	1	9	2	2	.50	29	.275	.324	.484
1986	Seattle	A	155	616	163	33	4	27	(16	11)	285	83	107	32	3	172	4	3	5	0	4	.00	18	.265	.303	.463
3 YEARS			380	1437	377	78	6	65	(33	32)	662	181	227	82	13	335	6	4	15	3	7	.30	51	.262	.302	.461

JOE PRICE

Pitches Left-handed, Bats Right-handed — Turns Age 31 in 1987, Born 11/29/56

Year	Team	League	G	GS	CG	GF	IP	BFP	H	R	ER	HR	SH	SF	HB	TBB	IBB	SO	WP	Bk	W	L	Pct	ShO	Sv	ERA
1980	Cincinnati	N	24	13	2	3	111	448	95	45	44	10	8	0	1	37	0	44	1	1	7	3	.700	0	0	3.57
1981	Cincinnati	N	41	0	0	13	54	216	42	19	15	3	6	3	0	18	2	41	2	0	6	1	.857	0	4	2.50
1982	Cincinnati	N	59	1	0	17	72.2	318	73	26	23	7	3	1	4	32	8	71	1	0	3	4	.429	0	3	2.85
1983	Cincinnati	N	21	21	5	0	144	581	118	46	46	12	6	4	0	46	2	83	0	0	10	6	.625	0	0	2.87
1984	Cincinnati	N	30	30	3	0	171.2	748	176	91	80	19	5	5	2	61	5	129	3	0	7	13	.350	1	0	4.19
1985	Cincinnati	N	26	8	0	5	64.2	274	59	35	28	10	2	5	0	23	7	52	2	0	2	2	.500	0	1	3.90
1986	Cincinnati	N	25	2	0	4	41.2	194	49	30	25	5	0	5	0	22	2	30	1	0	1	2	.333	0	0	5.40
7 YEARS			226	75	10	40	659.2	2779	612	292	261	66	30	23	7	239	26	450	10	1	36	31	.537	1	8	3.56

GREG PRYOR

Bats Right-handed, Throws Right-handed — Turns Age 38 in 1987, Born 10/02/49

Year	Team	League	G	AB	H	2B	3B	HR	(Hm	Rd)	TB	R	RBI	TBB	IBB	SO	HBP	SH	SF	SB	CS	SB%	GIDP	AVE	OBP	SLG
1976	Texas	A	5	8	3	0	0	0	(0	0)	3	2	1	0	0	1	0	1	0	0	0	.00	0	.375	.375	.375
1978	Chicago	A	82	222	58	11	0	2	(2	0)	75	27	15	11	0	18	1	4	1	3	1	.75	4	.261	.298	.338
1979	Chicago	A	143	476	131	23	3	3	(1	2)	169	60	34	35	1	41	2	7	5	3	4	.43	16	.275	.324	.355
1980	Chicago	A	122	338	81	18	4	1	(1	0)	110	32	29	12	0	35	2	9	6	2	2	.50	10	.240	.265	.325
1981	Chicago	A	47	76	17	1	0	0	(0	0)	18	4	6	6	0	8	2	4	0	0	0	.00	5	.224	.298	.237
1982	Kansas City	A	73	152	41	10	1	2	(0	2)	59	23	12	10	0	20	0	4	0	2	0	1.00	5	.270	.315	.388
1983	Kansas City	A	68	115	25	4	0	1	(0	1)	32	9	14	7	0	8	0	2	1	0	0	.00	3	.217	.260	.278
1984	Kansas City	A	123	270	71	11	1	4	(4	0)	96	32	25	12	0	28	3	2	1	0	3	.00	9	.263	.301	.356
1985	Kansas City	A	63	114	25	3	0	1	(0	1)	31	8	3	8	0	12	0	3	0	0	1	.00	6	.219	.270	.272
1986	Kansas City	A	63	112	19	4	0	0	(0	0)	23	7	7	3	0	14	0	2	0	1	1	.50	5	.170	.191	.205
10 YEARS			789	1883	471	85	9	14	(8	6)	616	204	146	104	1	185	10	38	14	11	12	.48	60	.250	.291	.327

KIRBY PUCKETT

Bats Right-handed, Throws Right-handed — Turns Age 26 in 1987, Born 03/14/61

Year	Team	League	G	AB	H	2B	3B	HR	(Hm	Rd)	TB	R	RBI	TBB	IBB	SO	HBP	SH	SF	SB	CS	SB%	GIDP	AVE	OBP	SLG
1984	Minnesota	A	128	557	165	12	5	0	(0	0)	187	63	31	16	1	69	4	4	2	14	7	.67	11	.296	.320	.336
1985	Minnesota	A	161	691	199	29	13	4	(2	2)	266	80	74	41	0	87	4	5	3	21	12	.64	9	.288	.330	.385
1986	Minnesota	A	161	680	223	37	6	31	(14	17)	365	119	96	34	4	99	7	2	0	20	12	.63	14	.328	.366	.537
3 YEARS			450	1928	587	78	24	35	(16	19)	818	262	201	91	5	255	15	11	5	55	31	.64	34	.304	.340	.424

TERRY PUHL

Bats Left-handed, Throws Right-handed — Turns Age 31 in 1987, Born 07/08/56

Year	Team	League	G	AB	H	2B	3B	HR	(Hm	Rd)	TB	R	RBI	TBB	IBB	SO	HBP	SH	SF	SB	CS	SB%	GIDP	AVE	OBP	SLG
1977	Houston	N	60	229	69	13	5	0	(0	0)	92	40	10	30	0	31	1	5	0	10	1	.91	3	.301	.385	.402
1978	Houston	N	149	585	169	25	6	3	(1	2)	215	87	35	48	5	46	4	3	7	32	14	.70	11	.289	.343	.368
1979	Houston	N	157	600	172	22	4	8	(2	6)	226	87	49	58	8	46	4	8	2	30	22	.58	7	.287	.352	.377
1980	Houston	N	141	535	151	24	5	13	(4	9)	224	75	55	60	3	52	4	6	3	27	11	.71	3	.282	.357	.419
1981	Houston	N	96	350	88	19	4	3	(1	2)	124	43	28	31	5	49	4	4	5	22	4	.85	3	.251	.315	.354
1982	Houston	N	145	507	133	17	9	8	(5	3)	192	64	50	51	2	49	2	5	2	17	9	.65	6	.262	.331	.379
1983	Houston	N	137	465	136	25	7	8	(1	7)	199	66	44	36	2	48	2	5	4	24	11	.69	4	.292	.343	.428
1984	Houston	N	132	449	135	19	7	9	(2	7)	195	66	55	59	12	45	1	6	4	13	8	.62	5	.301	.380	.434
1985	Houston	N	57	194	55	14	3	2	(1	1)	81	34	23	18	4	23	1	4	3	6	2	.75	0	.284	.343	.418
1986	Houston	N	81	172	42	10	0	3	(1	2)	61	17	14	15	1	24	0	4	2	3	2	.60	6	.244	.302	.355
10 YEARS			1155	4086	1150	188	50	57	(18	39)	1609	579	363	406	42	413	23	50	32	184	84	.69	48	.281	.347	.394

LUIS QUINONES

Bats both Right and Left-handed, Throws Right-handed — Turns Age 25 in 1987, Born 04/28/62

Year	Team	League	G	AB	H	2B	3B	HR	(Hm	Rd)	TB	R	RBI	TBB	IBB	SO	HBP	SH	SF	SB	CS	SB%	GIDP	AVE	OBP	SLG
1983	Oakland	A	19	42	8	2	1	0	(0	0)	12	5	4	1	0	4	0	1	1	1	1	.50	0	.190	.205	.286
1986	San Francisco	N	71	106	19	1	3	0	(0	0)	26	13	11	3	1	17	1	4	1	3	1	.75	1	.179	.207	.245
2 YEARS			90	148	27	3	4	0	(0	0)	38	18	15	4	1	21	1	5	2	4	2	.67	1	.182	.206	.257

REY QUINONES

Bats Right-handed, Throws Right-handed — Turns Age 24 in 1987, Born 11/11/63

Year	Team	League	G	AB	H	2B	3B	HR	(Hm	Rd)	TB	R	RBI	TBB	IBB	SO	HBP	SH	SF	SB	CS	SB%	GIDP	AVE	OBP	SLG
1986	2 Teams		98	312	68	16	1	2	(0	0)	92	32	22	24	0	57	3	5	2	4	3	.57	7	.218	.279	.295
1986	Boston	A	62	190	45	12	1	2	(0	0)	65	26	15	19	0	26	3	2	1	3	2	.60	7	.237	.315	.342
1986	Seattle	A	36	122	23	4	0	0	(0	0)	27	6	7	5	0	31	0	3	1	1	1	.50	0	.189	.219	.221

JAMIE QUIRK

Bats Left-handed, Throws Right-handed   Turns Age 33 in 1987, Born 10/28/54

Year	Team	League	G	AB	H	2B	3B	HR	(Hm	Rd)	TB	R	RBI	TBB	IBB	SO	HBP	SH	SF	SB	CS	SB%	GIDP	AVE	OBP	SLG
1975	Kansas City	A	14	39	10	0	0	1	(1	0)	13	2	5	2	1	7	0	0	0	0	0	.00	1	.256	.293	.333
1976	Kansas City	A	64	114	28	6	0	1	(1	0)	37	11	15	2	0	22	0	0	3	0	0	.00	5	.246	.252	.325
1977	Milwaukee	A	93	221	48	14	1	3	(2	1)	73	16	13	8	2	47	2	2	0	0	1	.00	4	.217	.251	.330
1978	Kansas City	A	17	29	6	2	0	0	(0	0)	8	3	2	5	0	4	0	0	0	0	0	.00	0	.207	.324	.276
1979	Kansas City	A	51	79	24	6	1	1	(1	0)	35	8	11	5	0	13	1	0	0	0	0	.00	2	.304	.353	.443
1980	Kansas City	A	62	163	45	5	0	5	(3	2)	65	13	21	7	2	24	1	3	3	3	2	.60	7	.276	.305	.399
1981	Kansas City	A	46	100	25	7	0	0	(0	0)	32	8	10	6	1	17	1	0	0	0	2	.00	5	.250	.299	.320
1982	Kansas City	A	36	78	18	3	0	1	(1	0)	24	8	5	3	0	15	0	0	1	0	0	.00	2	.231	.256	.308
1983	St Louis	N	48	86	18	2	1	2	(0	2)	28	3	11	6	0	27	1	0	0	0	0	.00	2	.209	.269	.326
1984	2 Teams		4	3	1	0	0	1	(0	0)	4	1	2	0	0	2	0	0	1	0	0	.00	0	.333	.250	1.333
1985	Kansas City	A	19	57	16	3	1	0	(0	0)	21	3	4	2	0	9	0	0	0	0	0	.00	4	.281	.305	.368
1986	Kansas City	A	80	219	47	10	0	8	(5	3)	81	24	26	17	3	41	1	0	1	0	1	.00	4	.215	.273	.370
12 YEARS			534	1188	286	58	4	23	(14	8)	421	100	125	63	9	228	7	5	9	3	6	.33	31	.241	.281	.354
1984	Chicago	A	3	2	0	0	0	0	(0	0)	0	0	1	0	0	2	0	0	1	0	0	.00	0	.000	.000	.000
1984	Cleveland	A	1	1	1	0	0	1	(0	0)	4	1	1	0	0	0	0	0	0	0	0	.00	0	1.000	1.000	4.000

DAN QUISENBERRY

Pitches Right-handed, Bats Right-handed   Turns Age 34 in 1987, Born 02/07/53

			HOW MUCH HE PITCHED						WHAT HE GAVE UP												THE RESULTS					
Year	Team	League	G	GS	CG	GF	IP	BFP	H	R	ER	HR	SH	SF	HB	TBB	IBB	SO	WP	Bk	W	L	Pct	ShO	Sv	ERA
1979	Kansas City	A	32	0	0	21	40	163	42	16	14	5	3	2	0	7	5	13	1	0	3	2	.600	0	5	3.15
1980	Kansas City	A	75	0	0	68	128	528	129	47	44	5	8	5	1	27	15	37	1	0	12	7	.632	0	33	3.09
1981	Kansas City	A	40	0	0	35	62	254	59	16	12	1	5	4	1	15	8	20	0	0	1	4	.200	0	18	1.74
1982	Kansas City	A	72	0	0	68	136.2	529	126	43	39	12	10	7	0	12	2	46	1	0	9	7	.563	0	35	2.57
1983	Kansas City	A	69	0	0	62	139	536	118	35	30	6	4	0	1	11	2	48	0	0	5	3	.625	0	45	1.94
1984	Kansas City	A	72	0	0	67	129.1	506	121	39	38	10	2	3	0	12	4	41	0	0	6	3	.667	0	44	2.64
1985	Kansas City	A	84	0	0	76	129	532	142	41	34	8	4	3	1	16	5	54	0	0	8	9	.471	0	37	2.37
1986	Kansas City	A	62	0	0	54	81.1	352	92	30	25	2	4	5	3	24	12	36	0	0	3	7	.300	0	12	2.77
8 YEARS			506	0	0	451	845.1	3400	829	267	236	49	42	33	6	124	53	295	3	0	47	42	.528	0	229	2.51

TIM RAINES

Bats both Right and Left-handed, Throws Right-handed   Turns Age 28 in 1987, Born 09/16/59

Year	Team	League	G	AB	H	2B	3B	HR	(Hm	Rd)	TB	R	RBI	TBB	IBB	SO	HBP	SH	SF	SB	CS	SB%	GIDP	AVE	OBP	SLG
1979	Montreal	N	6	0	0	0	0	0	(0	0)	0	3	0	0	0	0	0	0	0	2	0	1.00	0	.000	.000	.000
1980	Montreal	N	15	20	1	0	0	0	(0	0)	1	5	0	6	0	3	0	1	0	5	1	1.00	0	.050	.269	.050
1981	Montreal	N	88	313	95	13	7	5	(3	2)	137	61	37	45	5	31	2	0	3	71	11	.87	7	.304	.391	.438
1982	Montreal	N	156	647	179	32	8	4	(1	3)	239	90	43	75	9	83	2	6	1	78	16	.83	6	.277	.353	.369
1983	Montreal	N	156	615	183	32	8	11	(5	6)	264	133	71	97	9	70	2	2	4	90	14	.87	12	.298	.393	.429
1984	Montreal	N	160	622	192	38	9	8	(2	6)	272	106	60	87	7	69	2	3	4	75	10	.88	7	.309	.393	.437
1985	Montreal	N	150	575	184	30	13	11	(4	7)	273	115	41	81	13	60	3	3	3	70	9	.89	9	.320	.405	.475
1986	Montreal	N	151	580	194	35	10	9	(4	5)	276	91	62	78	9	60	2	1	3	70	9	.89	6	.334	.413	.476
8 YEARS			882	3372	1028	180	55	48	(19	29)	1462	604	314	469	52	376	13	16	18	461	69	.87	47	.305	.390	.434

RAFAEL RAMIREZ

Bats Right-handed, Throws Right-handed   Turns Age 28 in 1987, Born 02/18/59

Year	Team	League	G	AB	H	2B	3B	HR	(Hm	Rd)	TB	R	RBI	TBB	IBB	SO	HBP	SH	SF	SB	CS	SB%	GIDP	AVE	OBP	SLG
1980	Atlanta	N	50	165	44	6	1	2	(2	0)	58	17	11	2	0	33	4	3	0	2	1	.67	2	.267	.292	.352
1981	Atlanta	N	95	307	67	16	2	2	(1	1)	93	30	20	24	3	47	1	9	1	7	3	.70	3	.218	.276	.303
1982	Atlanta	N	157	609	169	24	4	10	(7	3)	231	74	52	36	7	49	3	16	5	27	14	.66	10	.278	.319	.379
1983	Atlanta	N	152	622	185	13	5	7	(2	5)	229	82	58	36	4	48	2	6	2	16	12	.57	8	.297	.337	.368
1984	Atlanta	N	145	591	157	22	4	2	(1	1)	193	51	48	26	1	70	1	5	6	14	17	.45	9	.266	.295	.327
1985	Atlanta	N	138	568	141	25	4	5	(4	1)	189	54	58	20	1	63	0	2	5	2	6	.25	21	.248	.272	.333
1986	Atlanta	N	134	496	119	21	1	8	(1	7)	166	57	33	21	1	60	3	7	3	19	8	.70	16	.240	.273	.335
7 YEARS			871	3358	882	127	21	36	(18	18)	1159	365	280	165	17	370	14	48	22	87	61	.59	69	.263	.298	.345

WILLIE RANDOLPH

Bats Right-handed, Throws Right-handed

Turns Age 33 in 1987, Born 07/06/54

Year	Team	League	G	AB	H	2B	3B	HR	(Hm	Rd)	TB	R	RBI	TBB	IBB	SO	HBP	SH	SF	SB	CS	SB%	GIDP	AVE	OBP	SLG
1975	Pittsburgh	N	30	61	10	1	0	0	(0	0)	11	9	3	7	1	6	0	1	1	1	0	1.00	3	.164	.246	.180
1976	New York	A	125	430	115	15	4	1	(0	1)	141	59	40	58	5	39	3	6	3	37	12	.76	10	.267	.356	.328
1977	New York	A	147	551	151	28	11	4	(2	2)	213	91	40	64	1	53	1	2	6	13	6	.68	11	.274	.347	.387
1978	New York	A	134	499	139	18	6	3	(2	1)	178	87	42	82	1	51	4	6	5	36	7	.84	12	.279	.381	.357
1979	New York	A	153	574	155	15	13	5	(2	3)	211	98	61	95	5	39	3	5	5	33	12	.73	23	.270	.374	.368
1980	New York	A	138	513	151	23	7	7	(2	5)	209	99	46	119	4	45	2	5	3	30	5	.86	6	.294	.427	.407
1981	New York	A	93	357	83	14	3	2	(1	1)	109	59	24	57	0	24	0	5	3	14	5	.74	10	.232	.336	.305
1982	New York	A	144	553	155	21	4	3	(1	2)	193	85	36	75	3	35	3	10	2	16	9	.64	13	.280	.368	.349
1983	New York	A	104	420	117	21	1	2	(1	1)	146	73	38	53	0	32	1	3	0	12	4	.75	11	.279	.361	.348
1984	New York	A	142	564	162	24	2	2	(1	1)	196	86	31	86	4	42	0	7	7	10	6	.63	15	.287	.377	.348
1985	New York	A	143	497	137	21	2	5	(3	2)	177	75	40	85	3	39	4	5	6	16	9	.64	24	.276	.382	.356
1986	New York	A	141	492	136	15	2	5	(2	3)	170	76	50	94	0	49	3	8	4	15	2	.88	11	.276	.393	.346
12 YEARS			1494	5511	1511	216	55	39	(17	22)	1954	897	451	875	27	454	24	63	45	233	77	.75	149	.274	.373	.355

DENNIS RASMUSSEN

Pitches Left-handed, Bats Left-handed

Turns Age 28 in 1987, Born 04/18/59

Year	Team	League	G	GS	CG	GF	IP	BFP	H	R	ER	HR	SH	SF	HB	TBB	IBB	SO	WP	Bk	W	L	Pct	ShO	Sv	ERA
1983	San Diego	N	4	1	0	1	13.2	58	10	5	3	1	0	0	0	8	0	13	1	0	0	0	.000	0	0	1.98
1984	New York	A	24	24	1	0	147.2	616	127	79	75	16	3	7	4	60	0	110	8	2	9	6	.600	0	0	4.57
1985	New York	A	22	16	2	1	101.2	429	97	56	45	10	1	5	1	42	1	63	3	1	3	5	.375	0	0	3.98
1986	New York	A	31	31	3	0	202	819	160	91	87	28	1	5	2	74	0	131	5	0	18	6	.750	1	0	3.88
4 YEARS			81	72	6	2	465	1922	394	231	210	55	5	17	7	184	1	317	17	3	30	17	.638	1	0	4.06

SHANE RAWLEY

Pitches Left-handed, Bats Left-handed

Turns Age 32 in 1987, Born 07/27/55

Year	Team	League	G	GS	CG	GF	IP	BFP	H	R	ER	HR	SH	SF	HB	TBB	IBB	SO	WP	Bk	W	L	Pct	ShO	Sv	ERA
1978	Seattle	A	52	2	0	23	111	483	114	57	51	7	5	8	5	51	3	66	4	0	4	9	.308	0	4	4.14
1979	Seattle	A	48	3	0	30	84	364	88	40	36	2	3	4	1	40	5	48	5	0	5	9	.357	0	11	3.86
1980	Seattle	A	59	0	0	39	114	484	103	44	42	3	15	3	3	63	16	68	2	1	7	7	.500	0	13	3.32
1981	Seattle	A	46	0	0	28	68	295	64	31	30	1	4	3	1	38	6	35	8	0	4	6	.400	0	8	3.97
1982	New York	A	47	17	3	15	164	699	165	79	74	10	16	9	2	54	5	111	2	1	11	10	.524	0	3	4.06
1983	New York	A	34	33	13	1	238.1	1010	246	111	100	19	7	6	3	79	1	124	5	1	14	14	.500	2	1	3.78
1984	2 Teams		29	28	3	1	162.1	689	163	88	80	13	7	2	1	54	2	82	9	0	12	9	.571	0	0	4.44
1985	Philadelphia	N	36	31	6	1	198.2	849	188	82	73	16	6	5	2	81	6	106	7	0	13	8	.619	2	0	3.31
1986	Philadelphia	N	23	23	7	0	157.2	673	166	67	62	13	5	2	1	50	4	73	1	1	11	7	.611	1	0	3.54
9 YEARS			374	137	32	138	1298	5546	1297	599	548	84	68	42	19	510	48	713	43	4	81	79	.506	5	40	3.80
1984	New York	A	11	10	0	1	42	198	46	33	29	0	2	0	0	27	0	24	5	0	2	3	.400	0	0	6.21
1984	Philadelphia	N	18	18	3	0	120.1	491	117	55	51	13	5	2	1	27	2	58	4	0	10	6	.625	0	0	3.81

JOHNNY RAY

Bats both Right and Left-handed, Throws Right-handed

Turns Age 30 in 1987, Born 03/01/57

Year	Team	League	G	AB	H	2B	3B	HR	(Hm	Rd)	TB	R	RBI	TBB	IBB	SO	HBP	SH	SF	SB	CS	SB%	GIDP	AVE	OBP	SLG
1981	Pittsburgh	N	31	102	25	11	0	0	(0	0)	36	10	6	6	2	9	0	0	1	0	0	.00	3	.245	.284	.353
1982	Pittsburgh	N	162	647	182	30	7	7	(6	1)	247	79	63	36	1	34	1	13	5	16	7	.70	8	.281	.318	.382
1983	Pittsburgh	N	151	576	163	38	7	5	(3	2)	230	68	53	35	3	26	0	10	2	18	9	.67	11	.283	.323	.399
1984	Pittsburgh	N	155	555	173	38	6	6	(3	3)	241	75	67	37	2	31	3	2	6	11	6	.65	16	.312	.354	.434
1985	Pittsburgh	N	154	594	163	33	3	7	(3	4)	223	67	70	46	10	24	1	5	6	13	9	.59	11	.274	.325	.375
1986	Pittsburgh	N	155	579	174	33	0	7	(2	5)	228	67	78	58	10	47	3	1	7	6	9	.40	21	.301	.363	.394
6 YEARS			808	3053	880	183	23	32	(17	15)	1205	366	337	218	28	171	8	31	27	64	40	.62	70	.288	.335	.395

FLOYD RAYFORD

Bats Right-handed, Throws Right-handed

Turns Age 30 in 1987, Born 07/27/57

Year	Team	League	G	AB	H	2B	3B	HR	(Hm	Rd)	TB	R	RBI	TBB	IBB	SO	HBP	SH	SF	SB	CS	SB%	GIDP	AVE	OBP	SLG
1980	Baltimore	A	8	18	4	0	0	0	(0	0)	4	1	1	0	0	5	0	0	0	0	0	.00	1	.222	.222	.222
1982	Baltimore	A	34	53	7	0	0	3	(1	2)	16	7	5	6	0	14	0	0	0	0	1	.00	0	.132	.220	.302
1983	St Louis	N	56	104	22	4	0	3	(1	2)	35	5	14	10	1	27	0	2	1	1	0	1.00	3	.212	.278	.337
1984	Baltimore	A	86	250	64	14	0	4	(4	0)	90	24	27	12	0	51	3	2	2	0	3	.00	5	.256	.296	.360
1985	Baltimore	A	105	359	110	21	1	18	(6	12)	187	55	48	10	0	69	0	2	1	0	3	.00	10	.306	.324	.521
1986	Baltimore	A	81	210	37	4	0	8	(5	3)	65	15	19	15	0	50	0	3	0	0	0	.00	7	.176	.231	.310
6 YEARS			370	994	244	43	1	36	(17	19)	397	107	114	53	1	216	3	9	4	4	5	.44	26	.245	.285	.399

JEFF REARDON

Pitches Right-handed, Bats Right-handed

Turns Age 32 in 1987, Born 10/01/55

Year	Team	League	G	GS	CG	GF	IP	BFP	H	R	ER	HR	SH	SF	HB	TBB	IBB	SO	WP	Bk	W	L	Pct	ShO	Sv	ERA
1979	New York	N	18	0	0	10	21	81	12	7	4	2	1	0	0	9	3	10	2	0	1	2	.333	0	2	1.71
1980	New York	N	61	0	0	35	110	475	96	36	32	10	8	5	0	47	15	101	2	0	8	7	.533	0	6	2.62
1981	2 Teams		43	0	0	33	71	279	48	17	17	5	3	1	2	21	4	49	1	0	3	0	1.000	0	8	2.15
1982	Montreal	N	75	0	0	53	109	444	87	28	25	6	8	4	2	36	4	86	2	0	7	4	.636	0	26	2.06
1983	Montreal	N	66	0	0	53	92	403	87	34	31	7	8	2	1	44	9	78	2	0	7	9	.438	0	21	3.03
1984	Montreal	N	68	0	0	58	87	363	70	31	28	5	3	2	3	37	7	79	4	0	7	7	.500	0	23	2.90
1985	Montreal	N	63	0	0	50	87.2	356	68	31	31	7	3	1	1	26	4	67	2	0	2	8	.200	0	41	3.18
1986	Montreal	N	62	0	0	48	89	368	83	42	39	12	9	1	1	26	2	67	0	0	7	9	.438	0	35	3.94
8 YEARS			456	0	0	340	666.2	2769	551	226	207	54	44	17	10	246	48	537	15	0	42	46	.477	0	162	2.79
1981	Montreal	N	25	0	0	19	42	155	21	6	6	3	3	0	1	9	0	21	1	0	2	0	1.000	0	6	1.29
1981	New York	N	18	0	0	14	29	124	27	11	11	2	0	1	1	12	4	28	0	0	1	0	1.000	0	2	3.41

GARY REDUS

Bats Right-handed, Throws Right-handed

Turns Age 31 in 1987, Born 11/01/56

Year	Team	League	G	AB	H	2B	3B	HR	(Hm	Rd)	TB	R	RBI	TBB	IBB	SO	HBP	SH	SF	SB	CS	SB%	GIDP	AVE	OBP	SLG
1982	Cincinnati	N	20	83	18	3	2	1	(1	0)	28	12	7	5	0	21	0	0	1	11	2	.85	0	.217	.258	.337
1983	Cincinnati	N	125	453	112	20	9	17	(6	11)	201	90	51	71	4	111	3	2	2	39	14	.74	6	.247	.352	.444
1984	Cincinnati	N	123	394	100	21	3	7	(4	3)	148	69	22	52	3	71	1	3	5	48	11	.81	0	.254	.338	.376
1985	Cincinnati	N	101	246	62	14	4	6	(4	2)	102	51	28	44	2	52	1	2	1	48	12	.80	0	.252	.366	.415
1986	Philadelphia	N	90	340	84	22	4	11	(8	3)	147	62	33	47	4	78	3	1	1	25	7	.78	2	.247	.343	.432
5 YEARS			459	1516	376	80	22	42	(23	19)	626	284	141	219	13	333	8	8	10	171	46	.79	12	.248	.344	.413

JEFF REED

Bats Left-handed, Throws Right-handed

Turns Age 25 in 1987, Born 11/12/62

Year	Team	League	G	AB	H	2B	3B	HR	(Hm	Rd)	TB	R	RBI	TBB	IBB	SO	HBP	SH	SF	SB	CS	SB%	GIDP	AVE	OBP	SLG
1984	Minnesota	A	18	21	3	0	3	0	(0	0)	15	3	1	2	0	6	0	1	0	0	0	.00	0	.143	.217	.714
1985	Minnesota	A	7	10	2	0	0	0	(0	0)	2	2	0	0	0	3	0	0	0	0	0	.00	0	.200	.200	.200
1986	Minnesota	A	68	165	39	6	1	2	(1	1)	53	13	9	16	0	19	1	3	0	1	0	1.00	2	.236	.308	.321
3 YEARS			93	196	44	12	4	2	(1	1)	70	18	10	18	0	28	1	4	0	1	0	1.00	2	.224	.293	.357

RICK REUSCHEL

Pitches Right-handed, Bats Right-handed

Turns Age 38 in 1987, Born 05/16/49

Year	Team	League	G	GS	CG	GF	IP	BFP	H	R	ER	HR	SH	SF	HB	TBB	IBB	SO	WP	Bk	W	L	Pct	ShO	Sv	ERA
1972	Chicago	N	21	18	5	1	129	527	127	46	42	3	4	2	2	29	6	87	1	2	10	8	.556	4	0	2.93
1973	Chicago	N	36	36	7	0	237	1003	244	95	79	15	5	2	5	62	6	168	10	1	14	15	.483	3	0	3.00
1974	Chicago	N	41	38	8	2	241	1061	262	130	115	18	14	8	6	83	12	160	7	1	13	12	.520	2	0	4.29
1975	Chicago	N	38	37	6	1	234	1007	244	116	97	17	20	4	7	67	8	155	4	1	11	17	.393	0	1	3.73
1976	Chicago	N	38	37	9	1	260	1078	260	117	100	17	11	13	8	64	5	146	7	1	14	12	.538	2	1	3.46
1977	Chicago	N	39	37	8	2	252	1030	233	84	78	13	3	4	5	74	11	166	9	1	20	10	.667	4	1	2.79
1978	Chicago	N	35	35	9	0	243	1007	235	98	92	16	16	8	5	54	8	125	5	0	14	15	.483	1	0	3.41
1979	Chicago	N	36	36	5	0	239	1021	251	104	96	16	13	6	10	75	8	125	5	0	18	12	.600	1	0	3.62
1980	Chicago	N	38	38	6	0	257	1094	281	111	97	13	19	14	4	76	10	140	3	1	11	13	.458	0	0	3.40
1981	2 Teams		25	24	4	1	157	640	162	64	54	8	6	2	5	33	4	75	5	0	8	11	.421	0	0	3.10
1983	Chicago	N	4	4	0	0	20.2	88	18	9	9	1	0	1	0	10	2	9	0	0	1	1	.500	0	0	3.92
1984	Chicago	N	19	14	1	2	92.1	405	123	57	53	7	7	9	3	23	0	43	2	0	5	5	.500	0	0	5.17
1985	Pittsburgh	N	31	26	9	4	194	773	153	58	49	7	5	3	3	52	10	138	6	1	14	8	.636	1	1	2.27
1986	Pittsburgh	N	35	34	4	2	215.2	930	232	106	95	20	9	10	8	57	2	125	6	1	9	16	.360	2	0	3.96
14 YEARS			436	414	81	14	2771.2	11664	2825	1195	1056	171	132	86	71	759	92	1652	76	10	162	155	.511	20	4	3.43
1981	New York	A	12	11	3	1	71	282	75	24	21	4	1	2	1	10	0	22	0	0	4	4	.500	0	0	2.66
1981	Chicago	N	13	13	1	0	86	358	87	40	33	4	5	0	4	23	4	53	5	0	4	7	.364	0	0	3.45

JERRY REUSS

Pitches Left-handed, Bats Left-handed

Turns Age 38 in 1987, Born 06/19/49

| | | | HOW MUCH HE PITCHED | | | | | | WHAT HE GAVE UP | | | | | | | | | | | | THE RESULTS | | | | | |
Year	Team	League	G	GS	CG	GF	IP	BFP	H	R	ER	HR	SH	SF	HB	TBB	IBB	SO	WP	Bk	W	L	Pct	ShO	Sv	ERA
1969	St Louis	N	1	1	0	0	7	27	2	0	0	0	0	0	2	3	0	3	0	1	1	0	1.000	0	0	0.00
1970	St Louis	N	20	20	5	0	127	548	132	62	58	9	8	3	1	49	2	74	8	1	7	8	.467	2	0	4.11
1971	St Louis	N	36	35	7	0	211	952	228	125	112	15	13	5	7	109	11	131	9	2	14	14	.500	2	0	4.78
1972	Houston	N	33	30	4	1	192	832	177	101	89	14	12	7	10	83	3	174	7	2	9	13	.409	1	1	4.17
1973	Houston	N	41	40	12	1	279	1198	271	123	116	17	13	8	3	117	6	177	10	1	16	13	.552	3	0	3.74
1974	Pittsburgh	N	35	35	14	0	260	1125	259	115	101	20	20	9	1	101	16	105	7	1	16	11	.593	1	0	3.50
1975	Pittsburgh	N	32	32	15	0	237	984	224	73	67	10	18	3	0	78	8	131	4	1	18	11	.621	6	0	2.54
1976	Pittsburgh	N	31	29	11	2	209	880	209	98	82	16	9	2	2	51	10	108	7	0	14	9	.609	3	2	3.53
1977	Pittsburgh	N	33	33	8	0	208	894	225	109	95	11	10	5	4	71	2	116	11	1	10	13	.435	2	0	4.11
1978	Pittsburgh	N	23	12	3	0	83	361	97	48	45	5	5	3	3	23	1	42	3	1	3	2	.600	0	0	4.88
1979	Los Angeles	N	39	21	4	11	160	712	178	88	63	4	17	0	3	60	7	83	7	0	7	14	.333	1	3	3.54
1980	Los Angeles	N	37	29	10	7	229	907	193	74	64	12	10	5	0	40	9	111	3	1	18	6	.750	6	3	2.52
1981	Los Angeles	N	22	22	8	0	153	608	138	44	39	6	9	0	4	27	3	51	1	0	10	4	.714	2	0	2.29
1982	Los Angeles	N	39	37	8	2	254.2	1036	232	98	88	11	12	4	2	50	10	138	7	3	18	11	.621	4	0	3.11
1983	Los Angeles	N	32	31	7	0	223.1	935	233	94	73	12	18	6	2	50	5	143	3	2	12	11	.522	0	0	2.94
1984	Los Angeles	N	30	15	2	9	99	428	102	51	42	4	11	3	0	31	7	44	4	1	5	7	.417	0	1	3.82
1985	Los Angeles	N	34	33	5	0	212.2	883	210	78	69	13	8	6	3	58	7	84	5	0	14	10	.583	3	0	2.92
1986	Los Angeles	N	19	13	0	3	74	331	96	57	48	13	5	0	2	17	4	29	2	0	2	6	.250	0	1	5.84
18 YEARS			537	468	123	36	3218.2	13641	3206	1438	1251	192	198	69	49	1018	111	1744	98	18	194	163	.543	36	11	3.50

CRAIG REYNOLDS

Bats Left-handed, Throws Right-handed

Turns Age 35 in 1987, Born 12/27/52

| | | | BATTING | | | | | | | | | | | | | | | BASERUNNING | | | | PERCENTAGES | | |
Year	Team	League	G	AB	H	2B	3B	HR	(Hm	Rd)	TB	R	RBI	TBB	IBB	SO	HBP	SH	SF	SB	CS	SB%	GIDP	AVE	OBP	SLG
1975	Pittsburgh	N	31	76	17	3	0	0	(0	0)	20	8	4	3	1	5	0	0	0	0	1	.00	1	.224	.253	.263
1976	Pittsburgh	N	7	4	1	0	0	1	(0	1)	4	1	1	0	0	0	0	0	0	0	0	.00	0	.250	.250	1.000
1977	Seattle	A	135	420	104	12	3	4	(2	2)	134	41	28	15	1	23	3	15	2	6	6	.50	8	.248	.277	.319
1978	Seattle	A	148	548	160	16	7	5	(2	3)	205	57	44	36	1	41	3	11	6	9	6	.60	4	.292	.336	.374
1979	Houston	N	146	555	147	20	9	0	(0	0)	185	63	39	21	0	49	2	34	4	12	6	.67	2	.265	.292	.333
1980	Houston	N	137	381	86	9	6	3	(2	1)	116	34	28	20	1	39	0	13	4	2	1	.67	4	.226	.262	.304
1981	Houston	N	87	323	84	10	12	4	(0	4)	130	43	31	12	2	31	0	18	1	3	3	.50	1	.260	.286	.402
1982	Houston	N	54	118	30	2	3	1	(0	1)	41	16	7	11	3	9	1	3	1	3	1	.75	1	.254	.321	.347
1983	Houston	N	65	98	21	3	0	1	(1	0)	27	10	6	6	1	10	0	0	0	0	1	.00	4	.214	.260	.276
1984	Houston	N	146	527	137	15	11	6	(0	6)	192	61	60	22	2	53	0	16	6	7	1	.88	4	.260	.286	.364
1985	Houston	N	107	379	103	18	8	4	(1	3)	149	43	32	12	2	30	0	3	2	4	4	.50	4	.272	.293	.393
1986	Houston	N	114	313	78	7	3	6	(4	2)	109	32	41	12	5	31	0	1	3	3	1	.75	8	.249	.274	.348
12 YEARS			1177	3742	968	115	62	35	(12	23)	1312	409	321	170	19	321	9	114	29	49	31	.61	42	.259	.290	.351

HAROLD REYNOLDS

Bats both Right and Left-handed, Throws Right-handed

Turns Age 27 in 1987, Born 11/26/60

| | | | BATTING | | | | | | | | | | | | | | | BASERUNNING | | | | PERCENTAGES | | |
Year	Team	League	G	AB	H	2B	3B	HR	(Hm	Rd)	TB	R	RBI	TBB	IBB	SO	HBP	SH	SF	SB	CS	SB%	GIDP	AVE	OBP	SLG
1983	Seattle	A	20	59	12	4	1	0	(0	0)	18	8	1	2	0	9	0	1	1	0	2	.00	1	.203	.226	.305
1984	Seattle	A	10	10	3	0	0	0	(0	0)	3	3	0	0	0	1	1	1	0	1	1	.50	0	.300	.364	.300
1985	Seattle	A	67	104	15	3	1	0	(0	0)	20	15	6	17	0	14	0	1	0	3	2	.60	0	.144	.264	.192
1986	Seattle	A	126	445	99	19	4	1	(1	0)	129	46	24	29	0	42	3	9	0	30	12	.71	6	.222	.275	.290
4 YEARS			223	618	129	26	6	1	(1	0)	170	72	31	48	0	66	4	12	1	34	17	.67	7	.209	.270	.275

R.J. REYNOLDS

Bats both Right and Left-handed, Throws Right-handed

Turns Age 28 in 1987, Born 04/19/59

| | | | BATTING | | | | | | | | | | | | | | | BASERUNNING | | | | PERCENTAGES | | |
Year	Team	League	G	AB	H	2B	3B	HR	(Hm	Rd)	TB	R	RBI	TBB	IBB	SO	HBP	SH	SF	SB	CS	SB%	GIDP	AVE	OBP	SLG
1983	Los Angeles	N	24	55	13	0	0	2	(1	1)	19	5	11	3	1	11	0	1	2	5	0	1.00	5	.236	.267	.345
1984	Los Angeles	N	73	240	62	12	2	2	(1	1)	84	24	24	14	0	38	1	4	2	7	5	.58	6	.258	.300	.350
1985	2 Teams	N	104	337	95	15	7	3	(1	2)	133	44	42	22	1	49	2	7	3	18	5	.78	6	.282	.327	.395
1986	Pittsburgh	N	118	402	108	30	2	9	(6	3)	169	63	48	40	4	78	1	3	2	16	9	.64	10	.269	.335	.420
4 YEARS			319	1034	278	57	11	16	(9	7)	405	136	125	79	6	176	4	15	9	46	19	.71	23	.269	.321	.392
1985	Los Angeles	N	73	207	55	10	4	0	(0	0)	73	22	25	13	0	31	1	5	3	6	3	.67	3	.266	.308	.353
1985	Pittsburgh	N	31	130	40	5	3	3	(1	2)	60	22	17	9	1	18	1	2	0	12	2	.86	3	.308	.357	.462

RONN REYNOLDS

Bats Right-handed, Throws Right-handed

Turns Age 29 in 1987, Born 09/28/58

| | | | BATTING | | | | | | | | | | | | | | | BASERUNNING | | | | PERCENTAGES | | |
Year	Team	League	G	AB	H	2B	3B	HR	(Hm	Rd)	TB	R	RBI	TBB	IBB	SO	HBP	SH	SF	SB	CS	SB%	GIDP	AVE	OBP	SLG
1982	New York	N	2	4	0	0	0	0	(0	0)	0	0	0	1	0	1	0	0	0	0	0	.00	0	.000	.200	.000
1983	New York	N	24	66	13	1	0	0	(0	0)	14	4	2	8	1	12	0	0	1	0	0	.00	2	.197	.280	.212
1985	New York	N	28	43	9	2	0	0	(0	0)	11	4	1	4	0	18	1	2	0	0	0	.00	1	.209	.227	.256
1986	Philadelphia	N	43	126	27	4	0	3	(1	2)	40	8	10	5	0	30	0	0	1	0	0	.00	4	.214	.242	.317
4 YEARS			97	239	49	7	0	3	(1	2)	65	16	13	14	1	61	1	2	2	0	0	.00	7	.205	.250	.272

RICK RHODEN

Pitches Right-handed, Bats Right-handed

Turns Age 34 in 1987, Born 05/16/53

Year	Team	League	HOW MUCH HE PITCHED						WHAT HE GAVE UP											THE RESULTS				
			G	GS	CG	GF	IP	BFP	H	R	ER	HR	SH	SF	HB	TBB	IBB	SO	WP	Bk	W	L	Pct	ShO	Sv	ERA
1974	Los Angeles	N	4	0	0	1	9	35	5	2	2	1	0	0	0	4	1	7	0	0	1	0	1.000	0	0	2.00
1975	Los Angeles	N	26	11	1	5	99	415	94	40	34	8	5	5	1	32	1	40	2	2	3	3	.500	0	0	3.09
1976	Los Angeles	N	27	26	10	0	181	744	165	66	60	17	5	4	1	53	2	77	3	0	12	3	.800	3	0	2.98
1977	Los Angeles	N	31	31	4	0	216	906	223	98	90	20	10	4	2	63	1	122	5	0	16	10	.615	1	0	3.75
1978	Los Angeles	N	30	23	6	4	165	697	160	77	67	13	8	7	3	51	0	79	7	0	10	8	.556	3	0	3.65
1979	Pittsburgh	N	1	1	0	0	5	21	5	4	4	0	0	0	0	2	0	2	0	0	0	1	.000	0	0	7.20
1980	Pittsburgh	N	20	19	2	0	127	536	133	58	54	9	3	3	3	40	4	70	6	0	7	5	.583	0	0	3.83
1981	Pittsburgh	N	21	21	4	0	136	588	147	66	59	6	7	7	2	53	2	76	6	1	9	4	.692	2	0	3.90
1982	Pittsburgh	N	35	35	6	0	230.1	983	239	115	106	14	12	3	2	70	8	128	9	3	11	14	.440	1	0	4.14
1983	Pittsburgh	N	36	35	7	1	244.1	1012	256	95	84	13	8	6	2	68	15	153	6	5	13	13	.500	2	1	3.09
1984	Pittsburgh	N	33	33	6	0	238.1	961	216	81	72	13	6	4	1	62	0	136	10	4	14	9	.609	3	0	2.72
1985	Pittsburgh	N	35	35	2	0	213.1	944	254	119	106	18	10	0	6	69	3	128	8	3	10	15	.400	0	0	4.47
1986	Pittsburgh	N	34	34	12	0	253.2	1015	211	82	80	17	6	5	2	76	8	159	6	4	15	12	.556	1	0	2.84
13 YEARS			333	304	60	11	2118	8857	2108	903	818	149	80	48	25	643	45	1177	68	22	121	97	.555	16	1	3.48

JIM RICE

Bats Right-handed, Throws Right-handed

Turns Age 34 in 1987, Born 03/08/53

Year	Team	League	BATTING																BASERUNNING				PERCENTAGES		
			G	AB	H	2B	3B	HR	(Hm | Rd)	TB	R	RBI	TBB	IBB	SO	HBP	SH	SF	SB	CS	SB%	GIDP	AVE	OBP	SLG
1974	Boston	A	24	67	18	2	1	1	(1 | 0)	25	6	13	4	0	12	1	0	3	0	0	.00	2	.269	.307	.373
1975	Boston	A	144	564	174	29	4	22	(12 | 10)	277	92	102	36	7	122	4	1	8	10	5	.67	19	.309	.350	.491
1976	Boston	A	153	581	164	25	8	25	(12 | 13)	280	75	85	28	2	123	4	2	9	8	5	.62	18	.282	.315	.482
1977	Boston	A	160	644	206	29	15	39	(27 | 12)	382	104	114	53	10	120	8	0	5	5	4	.56	21	.320	.376	.593
1978	Boston	A	163	677	213	25	15	46	(28 | 18)	406	121	139	58	7	126	5	1	5	7	5	.58	15	.315	.370	.600
1979	Boston	A	158	619	201	39	6	39	(27 | 12)	369	117	130	57	4	97	4	0	8	9	4	.69	16	.325	.381	.596
1980	Boston	A	124	504	148	22	6	24	(11 | 13)	254	81	86	30	5	87	4	1	3	8	3	.73	16	.294	.336	.504
1981	Boston	A	108	451	128	18	1	17	(10 | 7)	199	51	62	34	3	76	3	0	7	2	2	.50	14	.284	.333	.441
1982	Boston	A	145	573	177	24	5	24	(9 | 15)	283	86	97	55	6	98	7	0	3	0	1	.00	29	.309	.375	.494
1983	Boston	A	155	626	191	34	1	39	(16 | 23)	344	90	126	52	10	102	6	0	5	0	2	.00	31	.305	.361	.550
1984	Boston	A	159	657	184	25	7	28	(17 | 11)	307	98	122	44	8	102	1	0	6	4	0	1.00	36	.280	.323	.467
1985	Boston	A	140	546	159	20	3	27	(17 | 10)	266	85	103	51	5	75	2	0	9	2	0	1.00	35	.291	.349	.487
1986	Boston	A	157	618	200	39	2	20	(10 | 10)	303	98	110	62	5	78	4	0	9	0	1	.00	19	.324	.384	.490
13 YEARS			1790	7127	2163	331	74	351	(190 | 161)	3695	1104	1289	564	72	1218	53	5	80	55	32	.63	271	.303	.355	.518

DAVE RIGHETTI

Pitches Left-handed, Bats Left-handed

Turns Age 29 in 1987, Born 11/28/58

Year	Team	League	HOW MUCH HE PITCHED						WHAT HE GAVE UP											THE RESULTS				
			G	GS	CG	GF	IP	BFP	H	R	ER	HR	SH	SF	HB	TBB	IBB	SO	WP	Bk	W	L	Pct	ShO	Sv	ERA
1979	New York	A	3	3	0	0	17	67	10	7	7	2	1	1	0	10	0	13	0	0	0	1	.000	0	0	3.71
1981	New York	A	15	15	2	0	105	422	75	25	24	1	0	2	0	38	0	89	1	1	8	4	.667	0	0	2.06
1982	New York	A	33	27	4	3	183	804	155	88	77	11	8	5	6	108	4	163	9	5	11	10	.524	0	1	3.79
1983	New York	A	31	31	7	0	217	900	194	96	83	12	10	4	2	67	2	169	10	1	14	8	.636	2	0	3.44
1984	New York	A	64	0	0	53	96.1	400	79	29	25	5	4	4	0	37	7	90	0	2	5	6	.455	0	31	2.34
1985	New York	A	74	0	0	60	107	452	96	36	33	6	6	3	0	45	3	92	7	0	12	7	.632	0	29	2.78
1986	New York	A	74	0	0	68	106.2	435	88	31	29	4	5	4	2	35	7	83	1	0	8	8	.500	0	46	2.45
7 YEARS			294	76	13	184	832	3480	697	312	278	40	34	23	10	340	23	699	28	9	58	44	.569	2	107	3.01

JOSE RIJO

Pitches Right-handed, Bats Right-handed

Turns Age 22 in 1987, Born 05/13/65

Year	Team	League	HOW MUCH HE PITCHED						WHAT HE GAVE UP											THE RESULTS				
			G	GS	CG	GF	IP	BFP	H	R	ER	HR	SH	SF	HB	TBB	IBB	SO	WP	Bk	W	L	Pct	ShO	Sv	ERA
1984	New York	A	24	5	0	8	62.1	289	74	40	33	5	6	1	1	33	1	47	2	1	2	8	.200	0	2	4.76
1985	Oakland	A	12	9	0	1	63.2	272	57	26	25	6	5	0	1	28	2	65	0	0	6	4	.600	0	0	3.53
1986	Oakland	A	39	26	4	9	193.2	856	172	116	100	24	10	9	4	108	7	176	6	4	9	11	.450	0	1	4.65
3 YEARS			75	40	4	18	319.2	1417	303	182	158	35	21	10	6	169	10	288	8	5	17	23	.425	0	3	4.45

EARNEST RILES

Bats Left-handed, Throws Right-handed

Turns Age 27 in 1987, Born 10/02/60

Year	Team	League	BATTING																BASERUNNING				PERCENTAGES		
			G	AB	H	2B	3B	HR	(Hm | Rd)	TB	R	RBI	TBB	IBB	SO	HBP	SH	SF	SB	CS	SB%	GIDP	AVE	OBP	SLG
1985	Milwaukee	A	116	448	128	12	7	5	(2 | 3)	169	54	45	36	0	54	0	6	3	2	2	.50	16	.286	.339	.377
1986	Milwaukee	A	145	524	132	24	2	9	(2 | 7)	187	69	47	54	0	80	1	6	3	7	7	.50	14	.252	.321	.357
2 YEARS			261	972	260	36	9	14	(4 | 10)	356	123	92	90	0	134	3	12	6	9	9	.50	30	.267	.330	.366

CAL RIPKEN

Bats Right-handed, Throws Right-handed   Turns Age 27 in 1987, Born 08/24/60

										BATTING													BASERUNNING				PERCENTAGES		
Year	Team	League	G	AB	H	2B	3B	HR	(Hm	Rd)	TB		R	RBI	TBB	IBB	SO	HBP	SH	SF		SB	CS	SB%	GIDP	AVE	OBP	SLG
1981	Baltimore	A	23	39	5	0	0	0	(0	0)	5		1	0	1	0	8	0	0	0		0	0	.00	4	.128	.150	.128
1982	Baltimore	A	160	598	158	32	5	28	(11	17)	284		90	93	46	3	95	3	2	6		3	3	.50	16	.264	.317	.475
1983	Baltimore	A	162	663	211	47	2	27	(12	15)	343		121	102	58	0	97	0	0	5		0	4	.00	24	.318	.371	.517
1984	Baltimore	A	162	641	195	37	7	27	(16	11)	327		103	86	71	1	89	2	0	2		2	1	.67	16	.304	.374	.510
1985	Baltimore	A	161	642	181	32	5	26	(15	11)	301		116	110	67	1	68	1	0	8		2	3	.40	32	.282	.347	.469
1986	Baltimore	A	162	627	177	35	1	25	(10	15)	289		98	81	70	5	60	4	0	6		4	2	.67	19	.282	.355	.461
6 YEARS			830	3210	927	183	20	133	(64	69)	1549		529	472	313	10	417	10	2	27		11	13	.46	111	.289	.351	.483

LUIS RIVERA

Bats Right-handed, Throws Right-handed   Turns Age 23 in 1987, Born 01/03/64

										BATTING													BASERUNNING				PERCENTAGES		
Year	Team	League	G	AB	H	2B	3B	HR	(Hm	Rd)	TB		R	RBI	TBB	IBB	SO	HBP	SH	SF		SB	CS	SB%	GIDP	AVE	OBP	SLG
1986	Montreal	N	55	166	34	11	1	0	(0	0)	47		20	13	17	0	33	2	1	1		1	1	.50	1	.205	.285	.283

BIP ROBERTS

Bats both Right and Left-handed, Throws Right-handed   Turns Age 24 in 1987, Born 10/27/63

										BATTING													BASERUNNING				PERCENTAGES		
Year	Team	League	G	AB	H	2B	3B	HR	(Hm	Rd)	TB		R	RBI	TBB	IBB	SO	HBP	SH	SF		SB	CS	SB%	GIDP	AVE	OBP	SLG
1986	San Diego	N	101	241	61	5	2	1	(0	1)	73		34	12	14	1	29	0	2	1		14	12	.54	2	.253	.293	.303

BILLY JOE ROBIDOUX

Bats Left-handed, Throws Right-handed   Turns Age 23 in 1987, Born 01/13/64

										BATTING													BASERUNNING				PERCENTAGES		
Year	Team	League	G	AB	H	2B	3B	HR	(Hm	Rd)	TB		R	RBI	TBB	IBB	SO	HBP	SH	SF		SB	CS	SB%	GIDP	AVE	OBP	SLG
1985	Milwaukee	A	18	51	9	2	0	3	(0	3)	20		5	8	12	0	16	0	0	0		0	0	.00	1	.176	.333	.392
1986	Milwaukee	A	56	181	41	8	0	1	(0	1)	52		15	21	33	1	36	0	0	1		0	0	.00	8	.227	.344	.287
2 YEARS			74	232	50	10	0	4	(0	4)	72		20	29	45	1	52	0	0	1		0	0	.00	9	.216	.342	.310

DON ROBINSON

Pitches Right-handed, Bats Right-handed   Turns Age 30 in 1987, Born 06/08/57

			HOW MUCH HE PITCHED						WHAT HE GAVE UP											THE RESULTS					
Year	Team	League	G	GS	CG	GF	IP	BFP	H	R	ER	HR	SH	SF	HB	TBB	IBB	SO	WP	Bk	W	L	Pct	ShO	Sv	ERA
1978	Pittsburgh	N	35	32	9	1	228	937	203	98	88	20	8	8	3	57	4	135	9	4	14	6	.700	0	1	3.47
1979	Pittsburgh	N	29	25	4	1	161	684	171	74	69	12	6	5	4	52	5	96	6	1	8	8	.500	0	0	3.86
1980	Pittsburgh	N	29	24	3	1	160	671	157	74	71	14	8	3	5	45	5	103	7	2	7	10	.412	2	1	3.99
1981	Pittsburgh	N	16	2	0	4	38	182	47	27	25	4	7	2	0	23	4	17	3	0	0	3	.000	0	2	5.92
1982	Pittsburgh	N	38	30	6	3	227	977	213	123	108	26	12	8	3	103	11	165	17	0	15	13	.536	0	0	4.28
1983	Pittsburgh	N	9	6	0	2	36.1	168	43	21	18	5	2	0	0	21	3	28	2	0	2	2	.500	0	0	4.46
1984	Pittsburgh	N	51	1	0	28	122	500	99	45	41	6	4	9	0	49	4	110	5	0	5	6	.455	0	10	3.02
1985	Pittsburgh	N	44	6	0	22	95.1	418	95	49	41	6	2	0	2	42	11	65	2	0	5	11	.313	0	3	3.87
1986	Pittsburgh	N	50	0	0	41	69.1	295	61	27	26	5	5	4	2	27	3	53	4	1	3	4	.429	0	14	3.38
9 YEARS			301	126	22	103	1137	4832	1089	538	487	98	54	39	19	419	50	772	55	8	59	63	.484	3	31	3.85

JEFF ROBINSON

Pitches Right-handed, Bats Right-handed   Turns Age 27 in 1987, Born 12/13/60

			HOW MUCH HE PITCHED						WHAT HE GAVE UP											THE RESULTS					
Year	Team	League	G	GS	CG	GF	IP	BFP	H	R	ER	HR	SH	SF	HB	TBB	IBB	SO	WP	Bk	W	L	Pct	ShO	Sv	ERA
1984	San Francisco	N	34	33	1	0	171.2	749	195	99	87	12	5	8	7	52	4	102	7	2	7	15	.318	1	0	4.56
1985	San Francisco	N	8	0	0	0	12.1	59	16	11	7	2	0	1	0	10	1	8	1	0	0	0	.000	0	0	5.11
1986	San Francisco	N	64	1	0	22	104.1	431	92	46	39	8	1	3	1	32	7	90	11	0	6	3	.667	0	8	3.36
3 YEARS			106	34	1	22	288.1	1239	303	156	133	22	6	12	8	94	12	200	19	2	13	18	.419	1	8	4.15

RON ROBINSON

Pitches Right-handed, Bats Right-handed   Turns Age 27 in 1987, Born 12/13/60

			HOW MUCH HE PITCHED						WHAT HE GAVE UP											THE RESULTS					
Year	Team	League	G	GS	CG	GF	IP	BFP	H	R	ER	HR	SH	SF	HB	TBB	IBB	SO	WP	Bk	W	L	Pct	ShO	Sv	ERA
1984	Cincinnati	N	12	5	0	2	39.2	166	35	18	12	3	1	1	0	13	3	24	0	2	1	2	.333	0	0	2.72
1985	Cincinnati	N	33	12	0	9	108.1	453	107	53	48	11	3	4	1	32	3	76	3	0	7	7	.500	0	1	3.99
1986	Cincinnati	N	70	0	0	32	116.2	487	110	44	42	10	4	3	2	43	8	117	3	0	10	3	.769	0	14	3.24
3 YEARS			115	17	1	43	264.2	1106	252	115	102	24	8	8	3	88	14	217	6	2	18	12	.600	0	15	3.47

GARY ROENICKE

Bats Right-handed, Throws Right-handed

Turns Age 33 in 1987, Born 12/05/54

Year	Team	League		BATTING																		BASERUNNING				PERCENTAGES		
Year	Team	League	G	AB	H	2B	3B	HR	(Hm	Rd)	TB	R	RBI	TBB	IBB	SO	HBP	SH	SF		SB	CS	SB%	GIDP		AVE	OBP	SLG
1976	Montreal	N	29	90	20	3	1	2	(0	2)	31	9	5	4	0	18	1	0	1		0	0	.00	1		.222	.260	.344
1978	Baltimore	A	27	58	15	3	0	3	(1	2)	27	5	15	8	0	3	1	1	2		0	1	.00	3		.259	.348	.466
1979	Baltimore	A	133	376	98	16	1	25	(9	16)	191	60	64	61	4	74	12	1	3		1	3	.25	11		.261	.378	.508
1980	Baltimore	A	118	297	71	13	0	10	(4	6)	114	40	28	41	5	49	6	2	3		2	0	1.00	10		.239	.340	.384
1981	Baltimore	A	85	219	59	16	0	3	(0	3)	84	31	20	23	1	29	2	5	3		1	2	.33	12		.269	.340	.384
1982	Baltimore	A	137	393	106	25	1	21	(6	15)	196	58	74	70	2	73	9	5	0		6	7	.46	7		.270	.392	.499
1983	Baltimore	A	115	323	84	13	0	19	(10	9)	154	45	64	30	2	35	4	4	5		2	2	.50	9		.260	.326	.477
1984	Baltimore	A	121	326	73	19	1	10	(7	3)	124	36	44	58	1	43	4	3	2		1	2	.33	10		.224	.346	.380
1985	Baltimore	A	114	225	49	9	0	15	(9	6)	103	36	43	44	1	36	0	2	3		2	2	.50	5		.218	.342	.458
1986	New York	A	69	136	36	5	0	3	(3	0)	50	11	18	27	0	30	1	0	1		1	1	.50	1		.265	.388	.368
10 YEARS			948	2443	611	122	4	111	(49	62)	1074	331	375	366	16	390	40	23	23		16	20	.44	69		.250	.354	.440

RON ROENICKE

Bats both Right and Left-handed, Throws Left-handed

Turns Age 31 in 1987, Born 08/19/56

Year	Team	League		BATTING																		BASERUNNING				PERCENTAGES		
Year	Team	League	G	AB	H	2B	3B	HR	(Hm	Rd)	TB	R	RBI	TBB	IBB	SO	HBP	SH	SF		SB	CS	SB%	GIDP		AVE	OBP	SLG
1981	Los Angeles	N	22	47	11	0	0	0	(0	0)	11	6	0	6	0	8	0	1	0		1	1	.50	0		.234	.321	.234
1982	Los Angeles	N	109	143	37	8	0	1	(0	1)	48	18	12	21	3	32	2	3	1		5	0	1.00	5		.259	.359	.336
1983	2 Teams		140	343	82	16	0	6	(4	2)	116	35	35	47	2	48	2	6	3		9	4	.69	7		.239	.332	.338
1984	San Diego	N	12	20	6	1	0	1	(0	1)	10	4	2	2	1	5	0	0	0		0	0	.00	0		.300	.364	.500
1985	San Francisco	N	65	133	34	9	1	3	(1	2)	54	23	13	35	3	27	0	1	1		6	2	.75	1		.256	.408	.406
1986	Philadelphia	N	102	275	68	13	1	5	(4	1)	98	42	42	61	4	52	0	4	3		2	2	.50	4		.247	.381	.356
6 YEARS			450	961	238	47	2	16	(9	7)	337	128	104	172	13	172	4	15	8		23	9	.72	14		.248	.362	.351
1983	Seattle	A	59	198	50	12	0	4	(2	2)	74	23	23	33	1	22	2	2	2		6	2	.75	2		.253	.362	.374
1983	Los Angeles	N	81	145	32	4	0	2	(2	0)	42	12	12	14	1	26	0	4	1		3	2	.60	5		.221	.288	.290

RON ROMANICK

Pitches Right-handed, Bats Right-handed

Turns Age 27 in 1987, Born 11/06/60

Year	Team	League		HOW MUCH HE PITCHED						WHAT HE GAVE UP													THE RESULTS					
Year	Team	League	G	GS	CG	GF	IP	BFP	H	R	ER	HR	SH	SF	HB	TBB	IBB	SO	WP	Bk		W	L	Pct	ShO	Sv	ERA
1984	California	A	33	33	8	0	229.2	973	240	107	96	23	8	12	4	61	3	87	3	0		12	12	.500	2	0	3.76
1985	California	A	31	31	6	0	195	831	210	101	89	29	4	10	4	62	1	64	2	3		14	9	.609	1	0	4.11
1986	California	A	18	18	1	0	106.1	470	124	68	65	13	3	5	0	44	0	38	4	0		5	8	.385	1	0	5.50
3 YEARS			82	82	15	0	531	2274	574	276	250	65	15	27	8	167	4	189	9	3		31	29	.517	4	0	4.24

ED ROMERO

Bats Right-handed, Throws Right-handed

Turns Age 30 in 1987, Born 12/09/57

Year	Team	League		BATTING																		BASERUNNING				PERCENTAGES		
Year	Team	League	G	AB	H	2B	3B	HR	(Hm	Rd)	TB	R	RBI	TBB	IBB	SO	HBP	SH	SF		SB	CS	SB%	GIDP		AVE	OBP	SLG
1977	Milwaukee	A	10	25	7	1	0	0	(0	0)	8	4	2	4	0	3	0	1	0		0	0	.00	1		.280	.379	.320
1980	Milwaukee	A	42	104	27	7	0	1	(0	1)	37	20	10	9	0	11	0	2	0		2	0	1.00	3		.260	.319	.356
1981	Milwaukee	A	44	91	18	3	0	1	(0	1)	24	6	10	4	0	9	0	1	2		0	2	.00	4		.198	.227	.264
1982	Milwaukee	A	52	144	36	8	0	1	(1	0)	47	18	7	8	0	16	0	3	0		0	0	.00	2		.250	.289	.326
1983	Milwaukee	A	59	145	46	7	0	1	(1	0)	56	17	18	8	0	8	0	3	2		1	0	1.00	2		.317	.348	.386
1984	Milwaukee	A	116	357	90	12	0	1	(1	0)	105	36	31	29	2	25	1	6	4		3	3	.50	12		.252	.307	.294
1985	Milwaukee	A	88	251	63	11	1	0	(0	0)	76	24	21	26	0	20	0	5	0		1	1	.50	3		.251	.321	.303
1986	Boston	A	100	233	49	11	0	2	(2	0)	66	41	23	18	0	16	2	7	3		2	0	1.00	5		.210	.270	.283
8 YEARS			511	1350	336	60	1	7	(5	2)	419	166	122	106	2	108	3	28	11		9	6	.60	34		.249	.303	.310

PETE ROSE

Bats both Right and Left-handed, Throws Right-handed   Turns Age 46 in 1987, Born 04/14/41

Year	Team	League	G	AB	H	2B	3B	HR	(Hm	Rd)	TB	R	RBI	TBB	IBB	SO	HBP	SH	SF	SB	CS	SB%	GIDP	AVE	OBP	SLG
1963	Cincinnati	N	157	623	170	25	9	6	(2	4)	231	101	41	55	0	72	5	6	6	13	15	.46	8	.273	.334	.371
1964	Cincinnati	N	136	516	139	13	2	4	(3	1)	168	64	34	36	0	51	2	3	1	4	10	.29	6	.269	.319	.326
1965	Cincinnati	N	162	670	209	35	11	11	(7	4)	299	117	81	69	2	76	8	8	2	8	3	.73	10	.312	.382	.446
1966	Cincinnati	N	156	654	205	38	5	16	(11	5)	301	97	70	37	3	61	1	7	1	4	9	.31	12	.313	.351	.460
1967	Cincinnati	N	148	585	176	32	8	12	(7	5)	260	86	76	56	9	66	3	1	2	11	6	.65	9	.301	.364	.444
1968	Cincinnati	N	149	626	210	42	6	10	(6	4)	294	94	49	56	15	76	4	2	4	3	7	.30	11	.335	.391	.470
1969	Cincinnati	N	156	627	218	33	11	16	(10	6)	321	120	82	88	18	65	5	2	6	7	10	.41	13	.348	.428	.512
1970	Cincinnati	N	159	649	205	37	9	15	(7	8)	305	120	52	73	10	64	2	0	4	12	7	.63	7	.316	.385	.470
1971	Cincinnati	N	160	632	192	27	4	13	(8	5)	266	86	44	68	15	50	3	1	3	13	9	.59	9	.304	.373	.421
1972	Cincinnati	N	154	645	198	31	11	6	(1	5)	269	107	57	73	4	46	7	2	2	10	3	.77	7	.307	.382	.417
1973	Cincinnati	N	160	680	230	36	8	5	(3	2)	297	115	64	65	6	42	6	1	0	10	7	.59	14	.338	.401	.437
1974	Cincinnati	N	163	652	185	45	7	3	(2	1)	253	110	51	106	14	54	5	1	6	2	4	.33	9	.284	.385	.388
1975	Cincinnati	N	162	662	210	47	4	7	(3	4)	286	112	74	89	8	50	11	1	1	0	1	.00	13	.317	.406	.432
1976	Cincinnati	N	162	665	215	42	6	10	(7	3)	299	130	63	86	7	54	6	0	2	9	5	.64	17	.323	.404	.450
1977	Cincinnati	N	162	655	204	38	7	9	(3	6)	283	95	64	66	7	42	5	1	4	16	4	.80	9	.311	.377	.432
1978	Cincinnati	N	159	655	198	51	3	7	(2	5)	276	103	52	62	6	30	3	2	7	13	9	.59	8	.302	.362	.421
1979	Philadelphia	N	163	628	208	40	5	4	(1	3)	270	90	59	95	10	32	2	0	5	20	11	.65	18	.331	.418	.430
1980	Philadelphia	N	162	655	185	42	1	1	(0	1)	232	95	64	66	5	33	6	4	4	12	8	.60	13	.282	.352	.354
1981	Philadelphia	N	107	431	140	18	5	0	(0	0)	168	73	33	46	5	26	3	1	3	4	4	.50	8	.325	.391	.390
1982	Philadelphia	N	162	634	172	25	4	3	(2	1)	214	80	54	66	9	32	7	8	3	8	8	.50	12	.271	.345	.338
1983	Philadelphia	N	151	493	121	14	3	0	(0	0)	141	52	45	52	5	28	2	1	7	7	7	.50	11	.245	.316	.286
1984	2 Teams		121	374	107	15	2	0	(0	0)	126	43	34	40	4	27	3	3	1	1	1	.50	11	.286	.359	.337
1985	Cincinnati	N	119	405	107	12	2	2	(0	2)	129	60	46	86	5	35	4	1	4	8	1	.89	10	.264	.395	.319
1986	Cincinnati	N	72	237	52	8	2	0	(0	0)	64	15	25	30	0	31	4	0	1	3	0	1.00	2	.219	.316	.270
24 YEARS			3562	14053	4256	746	135	160	(85	75)	5752	2165	1314	1566	167	1143	107	56	79	198	149	.57	247	.303	.375	.409
1984	Cincinnati	N	26	96	35	9	0	0	(0	0)	44	9	11	9	1	7	2	0	0	0	0	.00	1	.365	.430	.458
1984	Montreal	N	95	278	72	6	2	0	(0	0)	82	34	23	31	3	20	1	3	1	1	1	.50	10	.259	.334	.295

JERRY ROYSTER

Bats Right-handed, Throws Right-handed   Turns Age 35 in 1987, Born 10/18/52

Year	Team	League	G	AB	H	2B	3B	HR	(Hm	Rd)	TB	R	RBI	TBB	IBB	SO	HBP	SH	SF	SB	CS	SB%	GIDP	AVE	OBP	SLG
1973	Los Angeles	N	10	19	4	0	0	0	(0	0)	4	1	2	0	0	5	0	0	0	1	0	1.00	0	.211	.211	.211
1974	Los Angeles	N	6	0	0	0	0	0	(0	0)	0	2	0	0	0	0	0	0	0	0	0	.00	0	.000	.000	.000
1975	Los Angeles	N	13	36	9	2	1	0	(0	0)	13	2	1	1	0	3	0	0	0	1	0	1.00	1	.250	.270	.361
1976	Atlanta	N	149	533	132	13	1	5	(2	3)	162	65	45	52	4	53	1	14	5	24	13	.65	11	.248	.313	.304
1977	Atlanta	N	140	445	96	10	2	6	(5	1)	128	64	28	38	3	67	1	6	1	28	10	.74	11	.216	.278	.288
1978	Atlanta	N	140	529	137	17	8	2	(2	0)	176	67	35	56	2	49	3	8	4	27	17	.61	9	.259	.331	.333
1979	Atlanta	N	154	601	164	25	6	3	(2	1)	210	103	51	62	0	59	0	6	7	35	8	.81	8	.273	.337	.349
1980	Atlanta	N	123	392	95	17	5	1	(0	1)	125	42	20	37	1	48	1	4	1	22	13	.63	6	.242	.309	.319
1981	Atlanta	N	64	93	19	4	1	0	(0	0)	25	13	9	7	0	14	0	4	1	7	5	.58	2	.204	.257	.269
1982	Atlanta	N	108	261	77	13	2	2	(1	1)	100	43	25	22	1	36	2	5	3	14	6	.70	3	.295	.351	.383
1983	Atlanta	N	91	268	63	10	3	3	(2	1)	88	32	30	28	2	35	0	5	2	11	7	.61	12	.235	.305	.328
1984	Atlanta	N	81	227	47	13	2	1	(0	1)	67	22	21	15	1	41	1	2	2	6	4	.60	8	.207	.257	.295
1985	San Diego	N	90	249	70	13	2	5	(4	1)	102	31	31	32	1	31	1	3	1	6	5	.55	6	.281	.363	.410
1986	San Diego	N	118	257	66	12	0	5	(2	3)	93	31	26	32	3	45	0	6	3	3	5	.38	6	.257	.336	.362
14 YEARS			1287	3910	979	149	33	33	(20	13)	1293	518	324	382	18	486	10	63	31	185	93	.67	83	.250	.316	.331

BRUCE RUFFIN

Pitches Left-handed, Bats Left-handed

Year	Team	League	G	GS	CG	GF	IP	BFP	H	R	ER	HR	SH	SF	HB	TBB	IBB	SO	WP	Bk	W	L	Pct	ShO	Sv	ERA
1986	Philadelphia	N	21	21	6	0	146.1	600	138	53	40	6	2	4	1	44	6	70	0	1	9	4	.692	0	0	2.46

VERN RUHLE

Pitches Right-handed, Bats Right-handed   Turns Age 36 in 1987, Born 01/25/51

Year	Team	League	G	GS	CG	GF	IP	BFP	H	R	ER	HR	SH	SF	HB	TBB	IBB	SO	WP	Bk	W	L	Pct	ShO	Sv	ERA
1974	Detroit	A	5	3	1	1	33	138	35	13	10	1	1	2	1	6	0	10	0	0	2	0	1.000	0	0	2.73
1975	Detroit	A	32	31	8	1	190	830	199	104	85	17	4	5	7	65	6	67	2	1	11	12	.478	3	0	4.03
1976	Detroit	A	32	32	5	0	200	865	227	99	87	19	10	3	4	59	4	88	0	0	9	12	.429	1	0	3.92
1977	Detroit	A	14	10	0	1	66	294	83	44	42	9	2	2	3	15	0	27	4	0	3	5	.375	0	0	5.73
1978	Houston	N	13	10	2	1	68	279	57	17	16	0	2	1	1	20	1	27	1	1	3	3	.500	2	0	2.12
1979	Houston	N	13	10	2	0	66	269	64	33	30	9	2	0	2	8	0	33	2	0	2	6	.250	2	0	4.09
1980	Houston	N	28	22	6	1	159	638	148	51	42	7	11	5	3	29	1	55	0	2	12	4	.750	2	0	2.38
1981	Houston	N	20	15	1	3	102	412	97	36	33	6	2	1	1	20	1	39	0	0	4	6	.400	0	1	2.91
1982	Houston	N	31	21	3	3	149	625	169	81	65	12	8	4	4	24	4	56	0	1	9	13	.409	2	1	3.93
1983	Houston	N	41	9	0	11	114.2	480	107	49	47	13	6	6	3	36	7	43	1	0	8	5	.615	0	3	3.69
1984	Houston	N	40	6	0	11	90.1	405	112	58	46	5	8	2	3	29	7	60	2	0	1	9	.100	0	4	4.58
1985	Cleveland	A	42	16	1	7	125	532	139	65	60	16	4	4	2	30	6	54	2	0	2	10	.167	0	3	4.32
1986	California	A	16	3	0	5	47.2	197	46	25	22	5	1	2	1	7	0	23	1	0	1	3	.250	0	1	4.15
13 YEARS			327	188	29	45	1410.2	5964	1483	675	585	119	61	37	35	348	37	582	15	5	67	88	.432	12	11	3.73

BILL RUSSELL

Bats Right-handed, Throws Right-handed

Turns Age 39 in 1987, Born 10/21/48

Year	Team	League	G	AB	H	2B	3B	HR	(Hm	Rd)	TB	R	RBI	TBB	IBB	SO	HBP	SH	SF	SB	CS	SB%	GIDP	AVE	OBP	SLG
1969	Los Angeles	N	98	212	48	6	2	5	(1	4)	73	35	15	22	1	45	1	2	1	4	1	.80	3	.226	.301	.344
1970	Los Angeles	N	81	278	72	11	9	0	(0	0)	101	30	28	16	1	28	3	4	3	9	1	.90	5	.259	.303	.363
1971	Los Angeles	N	91	211	48	7	4	2	(1	1)	69	29	15	11	2	39	0	0	1	6	3	.67	2	.227	.265	.327
1972	Los Angeles	N	129	434	118	19	5	4	(3	1)	159	47	34	34	9	64	2	5	2	14	7	.67	4	.272	.326	.366
1973	Los Angeles	N	162	615	163	26	3	4	(2	2)	207	55	56	34	20	63	1	9	7	15	7	.68	9	.265	.301	.337
1974	Los Angeles	N	160	553	149	18	6	5	(3	2)	194	61	65	53	25	53	4	11	4	14	5	.74	18	.269	.336	.351
1975	Los Angeles	N	84	252	52	9	2	0	(0	0)	65	24	14	23	6	28	2	4	1	5	0	1.00	6	.206	.277	.258
1976	Los Angeles	N	149	554	152	17	3	5	(1	4)	190	53	65	21	9	46	3	6	6	15	5	.75	14	.274	.301	.343
1977	Los Angeles	N	153	634	176	28	6	4	(2	2)	228	84	51	24	1	43	2	9	4	16	7	.70	23	.278	.304	.360
1978	Los Angeles	N	155	625	179	32	4	3	(0	3)	228	72	46	30	8	34	2	12	3	10	6	.63	17	.286	.320	.365
1979	Los Angeles	N	153	627	170	26	4	7	(4	3)	225	72	56	24	2	43	1	14	4	6	9	.40	20	.271	.297	.359
1980	Los Angeles	N	130	466	123	23	2	3	(2	1)	159	38	34	18	0	44	3	12	1	13	2	.87	6	.264	.295	.341
1981	Los Angeles	N	82	262	61	9	2	0	(0	0)	74	20	22	19	3	20	1	5	3	2	1	.67	13	.233	.284	.282
1982	Los Angeles	N	153	497	136	20	2	3	(2	1)	169	64	46	63	11	30	4	8	4	10	2	.83	14	.274	.357	.340
1983	Los Angeles	N	131	451	111	13	1	1	(0	1)	129	47	30	33	4	31	4	12	2	13	9	.59	5	.246	.302	.286
1984	Los Angeles	N	89	262	70	12	1	0	(0	0)	84	25	19	25	1	24	0	9	2	4	4	.50	7	.267	.329	.321
1985	Los Angeles	N	76	169	44	6	1	0	(0	0)	52	19	18	18	1	9	1	3	1	4	0	1.00	2	.260	.333	.308
1986	Los Angeles	N	105	216	54	11	0	0	(0	0)	65	21	18	15	2	23	2	7	2	7	0	1.00	6	.250	.302	.301
18 YEARS			2181	7318	1926	293	57	46	(21	25)	2471	796	627	483	106	667	36	132	51	167	69	.71	174	.263	.310	.338

JEFF RUSSELL

Pitches Right-handed, Bats Right-handed

Turns Age 26 in 1987, Born 09/02/61

Year	Team	League	G	GS	CG	GF	IP	BFP	H	R	ER	HR	SH	SF	HB	TBB	IBB	SO	WP	Bk	W	L	Pct	ShO	Sv	ERA
1983	Cincinnati	N	10	10	2	0	68.1	282	58	30	23	7	6	5	0	22	3	40	1	1	4	5	.444	0	0	3.03
1984	Cincinnati	N	33	30	4	1	181.2	787	186	97	86	15	8	3	4	65	8	101	3	3	6	18	.250	2	0	4.26
1985	Texas	A	13	13	0	0	62	295	85	55	52	10	1	3	2	27	1	44	2	0	3	6	.333	0	0	7.55
1986	Texas	A	37	0	0	9	82	338	74	40	31	11	1	2	1	31	2	54	5	0	5	2	.714	0	2	3.40
4 YEARS			93	53	6	10	394	1702	403	222	192	43	16	13	7	145	14	239	11	4	18	31	.367	2	2	4.39

JOHN RUSSELL

Bats Right-handed, Throws Right-handed

Turns Age 26 in 1987, Born 01/05/61

Year	Team	League	G	AB	H	2B	3B	HR	(Hm	Rd)	TB	R	RBI	TBB	IBB	SO	HBP	SH	SF	SB	CS	SB%	GIDP	AVE	OBP	SLG
1984	Philadelphia	N	39	99	28	8	1	2	(1	1)	44	11	11	12	0	33	0	0	0	0	0	.00	0	.283	.360	.444
1985	Philadelphia	N	81	216	47	12	0	9	(6	3)	86	22	23	18	0	72	0	0	0	2	0	1.00	5	.218	.278	.398
1986	Philadelphia	N	93	315	76	21	2	13	(8	5)	140	35	60	25	2	103	3	1	4	0	1	.00	6	.241	.300	.444
3 YEARS			213	630	151	41	3	24	(15	9)	270	68	94	55	2	208	3	1	4	2	1	.67	11	.240	.302	.429

NOLAN RYAN

Pitches Right-handed, Bats Right-handed

Turns Age 40 in 1987, Born 01/31/47

Year	Team	League	G	GS	CG	GF	IP	BFP	H	R	ER	HR	SH	SF	HB	TBB	IBB	SO	WP	Bk	W	L	Pct	ShO	Sv	ERA
1966	New York	N	2	1	0	0	3	17	5	5	5	1	0	0	0	3	1	6	1	0	0	1	.000	0	0	15.00
1968	New York	N	21	18	3	1	134	559	93	50	46	12	12	4	4	75	4	133	7	0	6	9	.400	0	0	3.09
1969	New York	N	25	10	2	4	89	375	60	38	35	3	2	2	1	53	3	92	1	3	6	3	.667	0	1	3.54
1970	New York	N	27	19	5	4	132	570	86	59	50	10	8	4	4	97	2	125	8	0	7	11	.389	2	1	3.41
1971	New York	N	30	26	3	1	152	705	125	78	67	8	3	0	137	116	4	137	6	1	10	14	.417	0	0	3.97
1972	California	A	39	39	20	0	284	997	166	80	72	14	11	3	10	157	18	329	18	0	19	16	.543	9	0	2.28
1973	California	A	41	39	26	2	326	1193	238	113	104	18	7	7	7	162	2	383	15	0	21	16	.568	4	1	2.87
1974	California	A	42	41	26	1	333	1392	221	127	107	18	12	4	9	202	3	367	9	0	22	16	.579	3	0	2.89
1975	California	A	28	28	10	0	198	864	152	90	76	13	6	7	7	132	0	186	12	0	14	12	.538	5	0	3.45
1976	California	A	39	39	21	0	284	1196	193	117	106	13	13	4	5	183	2	327	5	2	17	18	.486	7	0	3.36
1977	California	A	37	37	22	0	299	1272	198	110	92	12	22	10	9	204	7	341	21	3	19	16	.543	4	0	2.77
1978	California	A	31	31	14	0	235	1008	183	106	97	12	11	14	3	148	7	260	13	2	10	13	.435	3	0	3.71
1979	California	A	34	34	17	0	223	937	169	104	89	15	8	10	6	114	9	223	9	0	16	14	.533	5	0	3.59
1980	Houston	N	35	35	4	0	234	982	205	100	87	10	7	7	3	98	1	200	10	1	11	10	.524	2	0	3.35
1981	Houston	N	21	21	5	0	149	605	99	34	28	2	5	3	1	68	1	140	16	2	11	5	.688	3	0	1.69
1982	Houston	N	35	35	10	0	250.1	1050	196	100	88	20	9	3	8	109	3	245	18	2	16	12	.571	3	0	3.16
1983	Houston	N	29	29	5	0	196.1	804	134	74	65	9	7	5	4	101	3	183	5	1	14	9	.609	2	0	2.98
1984	Houston	N	30	30	5	0	183.2	760	143	78	62	12	4	6	4	69	2	197	6	2	12	11	.522	2	0	3.04
1985	Houston	N	35	35	4	0	232	983	205	108	98	12	11	12	9	95	8	209	14	2	10	12	.455	0	0	3.80
1986	Houston	N	30	30	1	0	178	729	119	72	66	14	5	4	4	82	5	194	15	0	12	8	.600	0	0	3.34
20 YEARS			611	577	203	13	4115.1	16998	2990	1643	1440	228	163	109	235	2268	65	4277	209	22	253	226	.528	54	3	3.15

BRET SABERHAGEN

Pitches Right-handed, Bats Right-handed   Turns Age 23 in 1987, Born 04/13/64

Year	Team	League		HOW MUCH HE PITCHED						WHAT HE GAVE UP													THE RESULTS				
			G	GS	CG	GF	IP	BFP	H	R	ER	HR	SH	SF	HB	TBB	IBB	SO	WP	Bk	W	L	Pct	ShO	Sv	ERA
1984	Kansas City	A	38	18	2	9	157.2	634	138	71	61	13	8	5	2	36	4	73	7	1	10	11	.476	1	1	3.48
1985	Kansas City	A	32	32	10	0	235.1	931	211	79	75	19	9	7	1	38	1	158	1	3	20	6	.769	1	0	2.87
1986	Kansas City	A	30	25	4	4	156	652	165	77	72	15	3	3	2	29	1	112	1	1	7	12	.368	2	0	4.15
3 YEARS			100	75	16	13	549	2217	514	227	208	47	20	15	5	103	6	343	9	5	37	29	.561	4	1	3.41

MARK SALAS

Bats Left-handed, Throws Right-handed   Turns Age 26 in 1987, Born 03/08/61

Year	Team	League	G	AB	H	2B	3B	HR	(Hm	Rd)	TB	R	RBI	TBB	IBB	SO	HBP	SH	SF	SB	CS	SB%	GIDP	AVE	OBP	SLG
1984	St Louis	N	14	20	2	1	0	0	(0	0)	3	1	1	0	0	3	0	1	0	0	0	.00	0	.100	.100	.150
1985	Minnesota	A	120	360	108	20	5	9	(6	3)	165	51	41	18	5	37	1	0	3	0	1	.00	7	.300	.332	.458
1986	Minnesota	A	91	258	60	7	4	8	(5	3)	99	28	33	18	2	32	1	5	3	3	1	.75	8	.233	.282	.384
3 YEARS			225	638	170	28	9	17	(11	6)	267	80	75	36	7	72	2	6	6	3	2	.60	15	.266	.305	.418

ANGEL SALAZAR

Bats Right-handed, Throws Right-handed   Turns Age 26 in 1987, Born 11/04/61

Year	Team	League	G	AB	H	2B	3B	HR	(Hm	Rd)	TB	R	RBI	TBB	IBB	SO	HBP	SH	SF	SB	CS	SB%	GIDP	AVE	OBP	SLG
1983	Montreal	N	36	37	8	1	1	0	(0	0)	11	5	1	1	0	8	0	1	1	0	0	.00	1	.216	.231	.297
1984	Montreal	N	80	174	27	4	2	0	(0	0)	35	12	12	4	0	38	1	4	1	1	1	.50	2	.155	.178	.201
1986	Kansas City	A	117	298	73	20	2	0	(0	0)	97	24	24	7	0	47	2	5	1	1	1	.50	3	.245	.266	.326
3 YEARS			233	509	108	25	5	0	(0	0)	143	41	37	12	0	93	3	10	3	2	2	.50	6	.212	.233	.281

JOE SAMBITO

Pitches Left-handed, Bats Left-handed   Turns Age 35 in 1987, Born 06/28/52

Year	Team	League		HOW MUCH HE PITCHED						WHAT HE GAVE UP													THE RESULTS				
			G	GS	CG	GF	IP	BFP	H	R	ER	HR	SH	SF	HB	TBB	IBB	SO	WP	Bk	W	L	Pct	ShO	Sv	ERA
1976	Houston	N	20	4	1	8	53	207	45	21	21	4	1	2	0	14	1	26	2	0	3	2	.600	1	1	3.57
1977	Houston	N	54	1	0	32	89	357	77	34	23	6	4	1	0	24	2	67	2	1	5	5	.500	0	7	2.33
1978	Houston	N	62	0	0	45	88	371	85	32	30	5	8	4	0	32	7	96	1	0	4	9	.308	0	11	3.07
1979	Houston	N	63	0	0	51	91	375	80	20	18	8	6	2	4	23	4	83	0	0	8	7	.533	0	22	1.78
1980	Houston	N	64	0	0	40	90	354	65	26	22	3	4	1	2	22	3	75	3	0	8	4	.667	0	17	2.20
1981	Houston	N	49	0	0	32	64	255	43	17	13	4	6	1	2	22	5	41	0	0	5	5	.500	0	10	1.83
1982	Houston	N	9	0	0	7	12.2	47	7	2	1	0	1	0	0	2	2	7	0	0	0	0	.000	0	4	0.71
1984	Houston	N	32	0	0	14	47.2	191	39	16	16	5	1	3	0	16	2	26	3	0	0	0	.000	0	0	3.02
1985	New York	N	8	0	0	2	10.2	60	21	18	15	1	1	1	0	8	0	3	0	0	0	0	.000	0	0	12.66
1986	Boston	A	53	0	0	27	44.2	200	54	26	24	4	1	0	2	16	3	30	4	0	2	0	1.000	0	12	4.84
10 YEARS			414	5	1	258	590.2	2417	516	212	183	40	33	15	10	179	29	454	15	1	35	32	.522	1	84	2.79

BILLY SAMPLE

Bats Right-handed, Throws Right-handed   Turns Age 32 in 1987, Born 04/02/55

Year	Team	League	G	AB	H	2B	3B	HR	(Hm	Rd)	TB	R	RBI	TBB	IBB	SO	HBP	SH	SF	SB	CS	SB%	GIDP	AVE	OBP	SLG
1978	Texas	A	8	15	7	2	0	0	(0	0)	9	2	3	0	0	3	0	0	0	0	0	.00	0	.467	.467	.600
1979	Texas	A	128	325	95	21	2	5	(4	1)	135	60	35	37	1	28	2	10	3	8	6	.57	6	.292	.365	.415
1980	Texas	A	99	204	53	10	0	4	(2	2)	75	29	19	18	2	15	6	4	2	8	5	.62	4	.260	.335	.368
1981	Texas	A	66	230	65	16	0	3	(2	1)	90	36	29	17	1	21	7	3	3	4	1	.80	3	.283	.346	.391
1982	Texas	A	97	360	94	14	2	10	(7	3)	142	56	29	27	0	35	3	8	0	10	2	.83	4	.261	.318	.394
1983	Texas	A	147	554	152	28	3	12	(6	6)	222	80	57	44	2	46	5	4	4	44	8	.85	8	.274	.331	.401
1984	Texas	A	130	489	121	20	2	5	(2	3)	160	67	33	29	1	46	0	4	6	18	6	.75	9	.247	.286	.327
1985	New York	A	59	139	40	5	0	1	(1	0)	48	18	15	9	0	10	2	2	2	2	1	.67	2	.288	.336	.345
1986	Atlanta	N	92	200	57	11	0	6	(1	5)	86	23	14	14	1	26	3	2	2	4	2	.67	0	.285	.338	.430
9 YEARS			826	2516	684	127	9	46	(25	21)	967	371	230	195	8	230	28	37	22	98	31	.76	36	.272	.329	.384

JUAN SAMUEL

Bats Right-handed, Throws Right-handed   Turns Age 27 in 1987, Born 12/09/60

Year	Team	League	G	AB	H	2B	3B	HR	(Hm	Rd)	TB	R	RBI	TBB	IBB	SO	HBP	SH	SF	SB	CS	SB%	GIDP	AVE	OBP	SLG
1983	Philadelphia	N	18	65	18	1	2	2	(1	1)	29	14	5	4	1	16	1	0	1	3	2	.60	1	.277	.324	.446
1984	Philadelphia	N	160	701	191	36	19	15	(8	7)	310	105	69	28	2	168	7	0	1	72	15	.83	6	.272	.307	.442
1985	Philadelphia	N	161	663	175	31	13	19	(8	11)	289	101	74	33	2	141	6	2	5	53	19	.74	8	.264	.303	.436
1986	Philadelphia	N	145	591	157	36	12	16	(10	6)	265	90	78	26	3	142	8	1	7	42	14	.75	8	.266	.302	.448
4 YEARS			484	2020	541	104	46	52	(27	25)	893	310	226	91	8	467	22	3	14	170	50	.77	23	.268	.305	.442

RYNE SANDBERG

Bats Right-handed, Throws Right-handed
Turns Age 28 in 1987, Born 09/18/59

Year	Team	League	G	AB	H	2B	3B	HR	(Hm	Rd)	TB	R	RBI	TBB	IBB	SO	HBP	SH	SF	SB	CS	SB%	GIDP	AVE	OBP	SLG
1981	Philadelphia	N	13	6	1	0	0	0	(0	0)	1	2	0	0	1	0	0	0	0	0	0	.00	0	.167	.167	.167
1982	Chicago	N	156	635	172	33	5	7	(5	2)	236	103	54	36	3	90	4	7	5	32	12	.73	7	.271	.312	.372
1983	Chicago	N	158	633	165	25	4	8	(4	4)	222	94	48	51	3	79	3	7	5	37	11	.77	8	.261	.316	.351
1984	Chicago	N	156	636	200	36	19	19	(11	8)	331	114	84	52	3	101	3	5	4	32	7	.82	7	.314	.367	.520
1985	Chicago	N	153	609	186	31	6	26	(17	9)	307	113	83	57	5	97	1	2	4	51	11	.82	10	.305	.364	.504
1986	Chicago	N	154	627	178	28	5	14	(8	6)	258	68	76	46	6	79	0	3	6	34	11	.76	11	.284	.330	.411
6 YEARS			790	3146	902	153	39	74	(45	29)	1355	494	345	242	20	447	11	24	24	186	52	.78	43	.287	.337	.431

SCOTT SANDERSON

Pitches Right-handed, Bats Right-handed
Turns Age 31 in 1987, Born 07/22/56

Year	Team	League	G	GS	CG	GF	IP	BFP	H	R	ER	HR	SH	SF	HB	TBB	IBB	SO	WP	Bk	W	L	Pct	ShO	Sv	ERA
1978	Montreal	N	10	9	1	1	61	251	52	20	17	3	3	2	1	21	0	50	2	0	4	2	.667	1	0	2.51
1979	Montreal	N	34	24	5	3	168	696	148	69	64	16	5	7	3	54	4	138	2	3	9	8	.529	3	1	3.43
1980	Montreal	N	33	33	7	0	211	875	206	76	73	18	11	5	3	56	3	125	6	0	16	11	.593	3	0	3.11
1981	Montreal	N	22	22	4	0	137	560	122	50	45	10	7	4	1	31	2	77	2	0	9	7	.563	1	0	2.96
1982	Montreal	N	32	32	7	0	224	922	212	98	86	24	9	6	3	58	5	158	2	1	12	12	.500	0	0	3.46
1983	Montreal	N	18	16	0	1	81.1	346	98	50	42	12	2	1	0	20	0	55	0	0	6	7	.462	0	1	4.65
1984	Chicago	N	24	24	3	0	140.2	571	140	54	49	5	6	8	2	24	3	76	3	2	8	5	.615	0	0	3.14
1985	Chicago	N	19	19	2	0	121	480	100	49	42	13	7	7	0	27	4	80	1	0	5	6	.455	0	0	3.12
1986	Chicago	N	37	28	1	2	169.2	697	165	85	79	21	6	5	2	37	2	124	3	1	9	11	.450	1	1	4.19
9 YEARS			229	207	30	7	1313.2	5398	1243	551	497	122	56	45	15	328	23	883	21	7	78	69	.531	9	3	3.40

RAFAEL SANTANA

Bats Right-handed, Throws Right-handed
Turns Age 29 in 1987, Born 01/31/58

Year	Team	League	G	AB	H	2B	3B	HR	(Hm	Rd)	TB	R	RBI	TBB	IBB	SO	HBP	SH	SF	SB	CS	SB%	GIDP	AVE	OBP	SLG
1983	St Louis	N	30	14	3	0	0	0	(0	0)	3	1	2	2	0	2	1	0	0	0	1	.00	0	.214	.353	.214
1984	New York	N	51	152	42	11	1	1	(1	0)	58	14	12	9	0	17	0	1	0	0	3	.00	3	.276	.317	.382
1985	New York	N	154	529	136	19	1	1	(0	1)	160	41	29	29	12	54	0	4	2	1	0	1.00	14	.257	.295	.302
1986	New York	N	139	394	86	11	0	1	(0	1)	100	38	28	36	12	43	2	1	3	0	0	.00	15	.218	.285	.254
4 YEARS			374	1089	267	41	2	3	(1	2)	321	94	71	76	24	116	3	6	5	1	4	.20	32	.245	.295	.295

STEVE SAX

Bats Right-handed, Throws Right-handed
Turns Age 27 in 1987, Born 01/29/60

Year	Team	League	G	AB	H	2B	3B	HR	(Hm	Rd)	TB	R	RBI	TBB	IBB	SO	HBP	SH	SF	SB	CS	SB%	GIDP	AVE	OBP	SLG
1981	Los Angeles	N	31	119	33	2	0	2	(0	2)	41	15	9	7	1	14	0	1	0	5	7	.42	0	.277	.317	.345
1982	Los Angeles	N	150	638	180	23	7	4	(2	2)	229	88	47	49	1	53	2	10	0	49	19	.72	10	.282	.335	.359
1983	Los Angeles	N	155	623	175	18	5	5	(3	2)	218	94	41	58	3	73	1	8	2	56	30	.65	8	.281	.342	.350
1984	Los Angeles	N	145	569	138	24	4	1	(1	0)	173	70	35	47	3	53	1	2	3	34	19	.64	12	.243	.300	.304
1985	Los Angeles	N	136	488	136	8	4	1	(1	0)	155	62	42	54	12	43	3	3	3	27	11	.71	15	.279	.352	.318
1986	Los Angeles	N	157	633	210	43	4	6	(1	5)	279	91	56	59	5	58	3	6	3	40	17	.70	12	.332	.390	.441
6 YEARS			774	3070	872	118	24	19	(8	11)	1095	420	230	274	25	294	10	30	11	211	103	.67	57	.284	.344	.357

DAN SCHATZEDER

Pitches Left-handed, Bats Left-handed
Turns Age 33 in 1987, Born 12/01/54

Year	Team	League	G	GS	CG	GF	IP	BFP	H	R	ER	HR	SH	SF	HB	TBB	IBB	SO	WP	Bk	W	L	Pct	ShO	Sv	ERA
1977	Montreal	N	6	3	1	0	22	93	16	6	6	0	0	1	0	13	0	14	1	0	2	1	.667	1	0	2.45
1978	Montreal	N	29	18	2	1	144	586	108	54	49	10	5	4	2	68	5	69	4	3	7	7	.500	0	0	3.06
1979	Montreal	N	32	21	3	4	162	677	136	57	51	10	3	1	1	59	2	106	6	0	10	5	.667	0	1	2.83
1980	Detroit	A	32	26	9	2	193	794	178	88	86	23	6	3	3	58	1	94	6	0	11	13	.458	2	0	4.01
1981	Detroit	A	17	14	1	1	71	318	74	49	48	13	4	4	2	29	1	20	3	0	6	8	.429	0	0	6.08
1982	Montreal	N	39	4	0	11	69.1	307	84	46	41	4	3	3	2	24	9	33	4	0	1	6	.143	0	0	5.32
1983	Montreal	N	58	2	0	23	87	369	88	34	31	3	5	2	5	25	6	48	5	0	5	2	.714	0	2	3.21
1984	Montreal	N	36	14	1	6	136	547	112	44	41	13	4	4	2	36	1	89	3	1	7	7	.500	1	1	2.71
1985	Montreal	N	24	15	1	2	104.1	431	101	52	44	13	7	3	0	31	0	64	4	0	3	5	.375	0	0	3.80
1986	2 Teams		55	1	0	19	88.1	375	81	43	32	9	5	3	0	35	9	47	1	0	6	5	.545	0	2	3.26
10 YEARS			328	118	18	69	1077	4497	978	473	429	105	49	30	17	378	42	584	39	4	58	59	.496	4	6	3.58
1986	Montreal	N	30	1	0	9	59	244	53	29	21	6	2	2	0	19	2	33	1	0	3	2	.600	0	1	3.20
1986	Philadelphia	N	25	0	0	10	29.1	131	28	14	11	3	3	1	0	16	7	14	0	0	3	3	.500	0	1	3.38

CALVIN SCHIRALDI

Pitches Right-handed, Bats Right-handed

Turns Age 25 in 1987, Born 06/16/62

			HOW MUCH HE PITCHED							WHAT HE GAVE UP										THE RESULTS				
Year	Team	League	G	GS	CG	GF	IP	BFP	H	R	ER	HR	SH	SF	HB	TBB	IBB	SO	WP	Bk	W	L	Pct	ShO	Sv	ERA
1984	New York	N	5	3	0	0	17.1	80	20	13	11	3	0	0	0	10	0	16	0	0	0	2	.000	0	0	5.71
1985	New York	N	10	4	0	2	26.1	131	43	27	26	4	0	0	3	11	0	21	2	1	2	1	.667	0	0	8.89
1986	Boston	A	25	0	0	21	51	198	36	8	8	5	2	1	1	15	2	55	1	0	4	2	.667	0	9	1.41
3 YEARS			40	7	0	23	94.2	409	99	48	45	12	2	1	4	36	2	92	3	1	6	5	.545	0	9	4.28

DAVE SCHMIDT

Pitches Right-handed, Bats Right-handed

Turns Age 30 in 1987, Born 04/22/57

			HOW MUCH HE PITCHED							WHAT HE GAVE UP										THE RESULTS				
Year	Team	League	G	GS	CG	GF	IP	BFP	H	R	ER	HR	SH	SF	HB	TBB	IBB	SO	WP	Bk	W	L	Pct	ShO	Sv	ERA
1981	Texas	A	14	1	0	8	32	132	31	11	11	1	0	0	1	11	3	13	3	1	0	1	.000	0	1	3.09
1982	Texas	A	33	8	0	14	109.2	462	118	45	39	5	6	3	5	25	5	69	2	0	4	6	.400	0	6	3.20
1983	Texas	A	31	0	0	20	46.1	191	42	20	20	3	1	1	1	14	1	29	2	0	3	3	.500	0	2	3.88
1984	Texas	A	43	0	0	37	70.1	293	69	30	20	3	7	3	0	20	9	46	4	0	6	6	.500	0	12	2.56
1985	Texas	A	51	4	1	35	85.2	356	81	36	30	6	3	2	0	22	8	46	2	1	7	6	.538	1	5	3.15
1986	Chicago	A	49	1	0	21	92.1	394	94	37	34	10	3	3	5	27	7	67	5	0	3	6	.333	0	8	3.31
6 YEARS			221	14	1	135	436.1	1828	435	179	154	28	20	12	12	119	33	270	18	2	23	28	.451	1	34	3.18

MIKE SCHMIDT

Bats Right-handed, Throws Right-handed

Turns Age 38 in 1987, Born 09/27/49

			BATTING																	BASERUNNING				PERCENTAGES		
Year	Team	League	G	AB	H	2B	3B	HR	(Hm	Rd)	TB	R	RBI	TBB	IBB	SO	HBP	SH	SF	SB	CS	SB%	GIDP	AVE	OBP	SLG
1972	Philadelphia	N	13	34	7	0	0	1	(1	0)	10	2	3	5	0	15	1	0	0	0	0	.00	0	.206	.325	.294
1973	Philadelphia	N	132	367	72	11	0	18	(9	9)	137	43	52	62	3	136	9	1	4	8	2	.80	8	.196	.324	.373
1974	Philadelphia	N	162	568	160	28	7	36	(19	17)	310	108	116	106	14	138	4	3	5	23	12	.66	4	.282	.395	.546
1975	Philadelphia	N	158	562	140	34	3	38	(22	16)	294	93	95	101	10	180	4	6	1	29	12	.71	7	.249	.367	.523
1976	Philadelphia	N	160	584	153	31	4	38	(17	21)	306	112	107	100	8	149	11	3	7	14	9	.61	7	.262	.376	.524
1977	Philadelphia	N	154	544	149	27	11	38	(17	21)	312	114	101	104	4	122	9	1	9	15	8	.65	10	.274	.393	.574
1978	Philadelphia	N	145	513	129	27	2	21	(13	8)	223	93	78	91	12	103	4	0	8	19	6	.76	4	.251	.364	.435
1979	Philadelphia	N	160	541	137	25	4	45	(16	29)	305	109	114	120	12	115	3	2	9	9	5	.64	13	.253	.386	.564
1980	Philadelphia	N	150	548	157	25	8	48	(25	23)	342	104	121	89	10	119	2	0	13	12	5	.71	6	.286	.380	.624
1981	Philadelphia	N	102	354	112	19	2	31	(17	14)	228	78	91	73	18	71	4	0	3	12	4	.75	9	.316	.435	.644
1982	Philadelphia	N	148	514	144	26	3	35	(17	18)	281	108	87	107	17	131	3	0	7	14	7	.67	11	.280	.403	.547
1983	Philadelphia	N	154	534	136	16	4	40	(19	21)	280	104	109	128	17	148	3	0	4	7	8	.47	10	.255	.399	.524
1984	Philadelphia	N	151	528	146	23	3	36	(16	20)	283	93	106	92	14	116	4	0	8	5	7	.42	15	.277	.383	.536
1985	Philadelphia	N	158	549	152	31	5	33	(14	19)	292	89	93	87	8	117	3	0	6	1	3	.25	10	.277	.375	.532
1986	Philadelphia	N	160	552	160	29	1	37	(20	17)	302	97	119	89	25	84	7	0	9	1	2	.33	8	.290	.390	.547
15 YEARS			2107	7292	1954	352	57	495	(242	253)	3905	1347	1392	1354	172	1744	71	16	93	169	90	.65	122	.268	.384	.536

DICK SCHOFIELD

Bats Right-handed, Throws Right-handed

Turns Age 25 in 1987, Born 11/21/62

			BATTING																	BASERUNNING				PERCENTAGES		
Year	Team	League	G	AB	H	2B	3B	HR	(Hm	Rd)	TB	R	RBI	TBB	IBB	SO	HBP	SH	SF	SB	CS	SB%	GIDP	AVE	OBP	SLG
1983	California	A	21	54	11	2	0	3	(2	1)	22	4	4	6	0	8	1	1	0	0	0	.00	2	.204	.295	.407
1984	California	A	140	400	77	10	3	4	(0	4)	105	39	21	33	0	79	6	13	0	5	2	.71	7	.193	.264	.263
1985	California	A	147	438	96	19	3	8	(5	3)	145	50	41	35	0	70	8	12	3	11	4	.73	8	.219	.287	.331
1986	California	A	139	458	114	17	6	13	(7	6)	182	67	57	48	2	55	5	9	9	23	5	.82	8	.249	.321	.397
4 YEARS			447	1350	298	48	12	28	(14	14)	454	160	123	122	2	212	20	35	12	39	11	.78	25	.221	.293	.336

BILL SCHROEDER

Bats Right-handed, Throws Right-handed

Turns Age 29 in 1987, Born 09/07/58

			BATTING																	BASERUNNING				PERCENTAGES		
Year	Team	League	G	AB	H	2B	3B	HR	(Hm	Rd)	TB	R	RBI	TBB	IBB	SO	HBP	SH	SF	SB	CS	SB%	GIDP	AVE	OBP	SLG
1983	Milwaukee	A	23	73	13	2	1	3	(2	1)	26	7	7	3	0	23	1	2	0	0	1	.00	0	.178	.221	.356
1984	Milwaukee	A	61	210	54	6	0	14	(7	7)	102	29	25	8	2	54	2	4	2	0	1	.00	6	.257	.288	.486
1985	Milwaukee	A	53	194	47	8	0	8	(2	6)	79	18	25	12	1	61	2	0	2	0	1	.00	5	.242	.290	.407
1986	Milwaukee	A	64	217	46	14	0	7	(2	5)	81	32	19	9	0	59	6	4	1	1	0	1.00	3	.212	.262	.373
4 YEARS			201	694	160	30	1	32	(13	19)	288	86	76	32	3	197	11	10	5	1	3	.25	14	.231	.274	.415

KEN SCHROM

Pitches Right-handed, Bats Right-handed   Turns Age 33 in 1987, Born 11/23/54

			HOW MUCH HE PITCHED						WHAT HE GAVE UP												THE RESULTS					
Year	Team	League	G	GS	CG	GF	IP	BFP	H	R	ER	HR	SH	SF	HB	TBB	IBB	SO	WP	Bk	W	L	Pct	ShO	Sv	ERA
1980	Toronto	A	17	0	0	6	31	140	32	18	18	2	3	1	0	19	3	13	0	0	1	0	1.000	0	1	5.23
1982	Toronto	A	6	0	0	1	15.1	71	13	11	10	3	0	0	0	15	3	8	1	0	1	0	1.000	0	0	5.87
1983	Minnesota	A	33	28	6	2	196.1	843	196	92	81	14	7	9	9	80	3	80	2	1	15	8	.652	1	0	3.71
1984	Minnesota	A	25	21	3	1	137	596	156	75	68	15	2	4	1	41	2	49	2	0	5	11	.313	0	0	4.47
1985	Minnesota	A	29	26	6	1	160.2	679	164	95	89	28	9	8	0	59	2	74	2	0	9	12	.429	0	0	4.99
1986	Cleveland	A	34	33	3	1	206	883	217	118	104	34	8	12	12	49	3	87	2	1	14	7	.667	1	0	4.54
6 YEARS			144	108	18	12	746.1	3212	778	409	370	96	29	34	22	263	16	311	9	2	45	38	.542	2	1	4.46

RICK SCHU

Bats Right-handed, Throws Right-handed   Turns Age 25 in 1987, Born 01/26/62

			BATTING																		BASERUNNING				PERCENTAGES		
Year	Team	League	G	AB	H	2B	3B	HR	(Hm	Rd)	TB	R	RBI	TBB	IBB	SO	HBP	SH	SF	SB	CS	SB%	GIDP	AVE	OBP	SLG
1984	Philadelphia	N	17	29	8	2	1	2	(1	1)	18	12	5	6	0	6	0	0	1	0	0	.00	0	.276	.389	.621
1985	Philadelphia	N	112	416	105	21	4	7	(2	5)	155	54	24	38	3	78	2	1	0	8	6	.57	7	.252	.318	.373
1986	Philadelphia	N	92	208	57	10	1	8	(1	7)	93	32	25	18	1	44	2	3	2	2	2	.50	1	.274	.335	.447
3 YEARS			221	653	170	33	6	17	(4	13)	266	98	54	62	4	128	4	4	3	10	8	.56	8	.260	.327	.407

DON SCHULZE

Pitches Right-handed, Bats Right-handed   Turns Age 25 in 1987, Born 09/27/62

			HOW MUCH HE PITCHED						WHAT HE GAVE UP												THE RESULTS					
Year	Team	League	G	GS	CG	GF	IP	BFP	H	R	ER	HR	SH	SF	HB	TBB	IBB	SO	WP	Bk	W	L	Pct	ShO	Sv	ERA
1983	Chicago	N	4	3	0	0	14	67	19	11	11	1	0	0	1	7	0	8	1	0	0	1	.000	0	0	7.07
1984	2 Teams		20	15	2	2	88.2	396	113	57	50	9	2	4	0	28	0	41	5	2	3	6	.333	0	0	5.08
1985	Cleveland	A	19	18	1	0	94.1	429	128	75	63	10	6	3	4	19	2	37	3	0	4	10	.286	0	0	6.01
1986	Cleveland	A	19	13	1	1	84.2	371	88	48	47	9	0	1	5	34	0	33	6	0	4	4	.500	0	0	5.00
4 YEARS			62	49	4	3	281.2	1263	348	191	171	29	8	8	10	88	2	119	15	2	11	21	.344	0	0	5.46
1984	Cleveland	A	19	14	2	2	85.2	380	105	53	46	9	2	3	0	27	0	39	5	2	3	6	.333	0	0	4.83
1984	Chicago	N	1	1	0	0	3	16	8	4	4	0	0	1	0	1	0	2	0	0	0	0	.000	0	0	12.00

MIKE SCIOSCIA

Bats Left-handed, Throws Right-handed   Turns Age 29 in 1987, Born 11/27/58

			BATTING																		BASERUNNING				PERCENTAGES		
Year	Team	League	G	AB	H	2B	3B	HR	(Hm	Rd)	TB	R	RBI	TBB	IBB	SO	HBP	SH	SF	SB	CS	SB%	GIDP	AVE	OBP	SLG
1980	Los Angeles	N	54	134	34	5	1	1	(1	0)	44	8	8	12	2	9	0	5	1	1	0	1.00	2	.254	.313	.328
1981	Los Angeles	N	93	290	80	10	0	2	(0	2)	96	27	29	36	8	18	1	4	4	0	2	.00	8	.276	.353	.331
1982	Los Angeles	N	129	365	80	11	1	5	(2	3)	108	31	38	44	11	31	1	5	4	2	0	1.00	8	.219	.302	.296
1983	Los Angeles	N	12	35	11	3	0	1	(0	1)	17	3	7	5	1	2	0	0	0	0	0	.00	1	.314	.400	.486
1984	Los Angeles	N	114	341	93	18	0	5	(0	5)	126	29	38	52	10	26	1	1	4	2	1	.67	10	.273	.367	.370
1985	Los Angeles	N	141	429	127	26	3	7	(1	6)	180	47	53	77	9	21	5	11	3	3	3	.50	10	.296	.407	.420
1986	Los Angeles	N	122	374	94	18	1	5	(2	3)	129	36	26	62	4	23	3	6	4	3	3	.50	11	.251	.359	.345
7 YEARS			665	1968	519	91	6	26	(6	20)	700	181	199	288	45	130	11	32	20	11	9	.55	50	.264	.358	.356

MIKE SCOTT

Pitches Right-handed, Bats Right-handed   Turns Age 32 in 1987, Born 04/26/55

			HOW MUCH HE PITCHED						WHAT HE GAVE UP												THE RESULTS					
Year	Team	League	G	GS	CG	GF	IP	BFP	H	R	ER	HR	SH	SF	HB	TBB	IBB	SO	WP	Bk	W	L	Pct	ShO	Sv	ERA
1979	New York	N	18	9	0	0	52	229	59	35	31	4	4	1	0	20	3	21	1	0	1	3	.250	0	0	5.37
1980	New York	N	6	6	1	0	29	132	40	14	14	1	2	1	0	8	1	13	1	0	1	1	.500	1	0	4.34
1981	New York	N	23	23	1	0	136	551	130	65	59	11	12	5	1	34	1	54	1	2	5	10	.333	0	0	3.90
1982	New York	N	37	22	1	10	147	670	185	100	84	13	21	11	2	60	3	63	1	2	7	13	.350	0	3	5.14
1983	Houston	N	24	24	2	0	145	612	143	67	60	8	1	5	5	46	0	73	4	0	10	6	.625	2	0	3.72
1984	Houston	N	31	29	0	1	154	675	179	96	80	7	8	11	3	43	4	83	2	2	5	11	.313	0	0	4.68
1985	Houston	N	36	35	4	1	221.2	922	194	91	81	20	6	6	3	80	4	137	7	2	18	8	.692	2	0	3.29
1986	Houston	N	37	37	7	0	275.1	1065	182	73	68	17	8	6	2	72	6	306	3	0	18	10	.643	5	0	2.22
8 YEARS			212	185	16	12	1160	4856	1112	541	477	81	62	46	16	363	22	750	20	13	65	62	.512	10	3	3.70

ROD SCURRY

Pitches Left-handed, Bats Left-handed Turns Age 31 in 1987, Born 03/17/56

			HOW MUCH HE PITCHED						WHAT HE GAVE UP											THE RESULTS					
Year	Team	League	G	GS	CG	GF	IP	BFP	H	R	ER	HR	SH	SF	HB	TBB	IBB	SO	WP	Bk	W	L	Pct	ShO	Sv	ERA
1980	Pittsburgh	N	20	0	0	4	38	153	23	12	9	2	3	0	2	17	3	28	2	1	0	2	.000	0	0	2.13
1981	Pittsburgh	N	27	7	0	10	74	329	74	33	31	6	1	1	3	40	2	65	4	1	4	5	.444	0	7	3.77
1982	Pittsburgh	N	76	0	0	38	103.2	448	79	26	20	3	4	4	4	64	7	94	12	1	4	5	.444	0	14	1.74
1983	Pittsburgh	N	61	0	0	25	68	317	63	45	42	6	3	4	4	53	7	67	6	0	4	9	.308	0	7	5.56
1984	Pittsburgh	N	43	0	0	25	46.1	186	28	14	13	1	4	0	0	22	3	48	7	0	5	6	.455	0	4	2.53
1985	2 Teams		35	0	0	15	60.1	261	47	26	21	6	3	2	0	38	2	60	3	0	1	1	.500	0	3	3.13
1986	New York	A	31	0	0	10	39.1	177	38	18	16	1	2	0	2	22	1	36	5	0	1	2	.333	0	2	3.66
7 YEARS			293	7	0	127	429.2	1871	352	174	152	25	20	11	15	256	25	398	39	3	19	30	.388	0	37	3.18
1985	New York	A	5	0	0	2	12.2	51	5	4	4	2	1	0	0	10	1	17	0	0	1	0	1.000	0	1	2.84
1985	Pittsburgh	N	30	0	0	13	47.2	210	42	22	17	4	2	2	0	28	1	43	3	0	0	1	.000	0	2	3.21

RAY SEARAGE

Pitches Left-handed, Bats Left-handed Turns Age 32 in 1987, Born 05/01/55

			HOW MUCH HE PITCHED						WHAT HE GAVE UP											THE RESULTS					
Year	Team	League	G	GS	CG	GF	IP	BFP	H	R	ER	HR	SH	SF	HB	TBB	IBB	SO	WP	Bk	W	L	Pct	ShO	Sv	ERA
1981	New York	N	26	0	0	7	37	156	34	16	15	2	2	2	0	17	3	16	3	0	1	0	1.000	0	1	3.65
1984	Milwaukee	A	21	0	0	16	38.1	149	20	3	3	0	3	0	1	16	3	29	1	0	2	1	.667	0	6	0.70
1985	Milwaukee	A	33	0	0	18	38	189	54	27	25	2	4	1	0	24	4	36	0	0	1	4	.200	0	1	5.92
1986	2 Teams		46	0	0	17	51	220	44	20	19	7	1	2	1	28	4	36	1	1	1	1	.500	0	1	3.35
4 YEARS			126	0	0	58	164.1	714	152	66	62	11	10	5	2	85	14	117	5	1	5	6	.455	0	9	3.40
1986	Chicago	A	29	0	0	9	29	117	15	3	2	1	0	2	0	19	3	26	0	0	1	0	1.000	0	0	0.62
1986	Milwaukee	A	17	0	0	8	22	103	29	17	17	6	1	0	1	9	1	10	1	1	0	1	.000	0	1	6.95

TOM SEAVER

Pitches Right-handed, Bats Right-handed Turns Age 43 in 1987, Born 11/17/44

			HOW MUCH HE PITCHED						WHAT HE GAVE UP											THE RESULTS					
Year	Team	League	G	GS	CG	GF	IP	BFP	H	R	ER	HR	SH	SF	HB	TBB	IBB	SO	WP	Bk	W	L	Pct	ShO	Sv	ERA
1967	New York	N	35	34	18	1	251	1029	224	85	77	19	10	5	5	78	6	170	5	0	16	13	.552	2	0	2.76
1968	New York	N	36	35	14	1	278	1088	224	73	68	15	16	5	8	48	5	205	8	1	16	12	.571	5	1	2.20
1969	New York	N	36	35	18	1	273	1089	202	75	67	24	20	5	7	82	9	208	8	1	25	7	.781	5	0	2.21
1970	New York	N	37	36	19	1	291	1173	230	103	91	21	9	4	4	83	8	283	6	0	18	12	.600	2	0	2.81
1971	New York	N	36	35	21	1	286	1103	210	61	56	18	11	6	4	61	2	289	5	1	20	10	.667	4	0	1.76
1972	New York	N	35	35	13	0	262	1060	215	92	85	23	13	5	5	77	2	249	8	0	21	12	.636	3	0	2.92
1973	New York	N	36	36	18	0	290	1147	219	74	67	23	10	5	4	64	5	251	5	0	19	10	.655	3	0	2.08
1974	New York	N	32	32	12	0	236	956	199	89	84	19	10	2	3	75	10	201	4	2	11	11	.500	0	0	3.20
1975	New York	N	36	36	15	0	280	1115	217	81	74	11	9	2	4	88	6	243	7	1	22	9	.710	5	0	2.38
1976	New York	N	35	34	13	0	271	1079	211	83	78	14	7	2	4	77	9	235	12	0	14	11	.560	5	0	2.59
1977	2 Teams		33	33	19	0	261	1031	199	78	75	19	5	6	0	66	6	196	7	1	21	6	.778	7	0	2.59
1978	Cincinnati	N	36	36	8	0	260	1075	218	97	83	26	13	12	0	89	11	226	6	1	16	14	.533	1	0	2.87
1979	Cincinnati	N	32	32	9	0	215	868	187	85	75	16	10	6	0	61	6	131	4	0	16	6	.727	5	0	3.14
1980	Cincinnati	N	26	26	5	0	168	692	140	74	68	24	2	8	1	59	3	101	4	0	10	8	.556	1	0	3.64
1981	Cincinnati	N	23	23	6	0	166	671	120	51	47	10	9	8	3	66	8	87	5	0	14	2	.875	1	0	2.55
1982	Cincinnati	N	21	21	0	0	111.1	501	136	75	68	14	2	2	3	44	4	62	3	0	5	13	.278	0	0	5.50
1983	New York	N	34	34	5	0	231	962	201	104	91	19	9	7	4	86	5	135	10	0	9	14	.391	2	0	3.55
1984	Chicago	A	34	33	10	1	236.2	978	216	108	104	27	8	7	2	61	3	131	5	0	15	11	.577	4	0	3.95
1985	Chicago	A	35	33	6	0	238.2	993	223	103	84	22	9	7	8	69	6	134	10	0	16	11	.593	1	0	3.17
1986	2 Teams		28	28	2	0	176.1	759	180	83	79	17	7	6	7	56	2	103	4	0	7	13	.350	0	0	4.03
20 YEARS			656	647	231	6	4782	19369	3971	1674	1521	380	187	111	76	1390	116	3640	126	8	311	205	.603	61	1	2.86
1977	Cincinnati	N	20	20	14	0	165	641	120	45	43	12	4	3	0	38	3	124	4	0	14	3	.824	4	0	2.35
1977	New York	N	13	13	5	0	96	390	79	33	32	7	1	3	0	28	3	72	3	1	7	3	.700	3	0	3.00
1986	Boston	A	16	16	1	0	104.1	450	114	46	44	8	5	4	2	29	1	72	3	0	5	7	.417	0	0	3.80
1986	Chicago	A	12	12	1	0	72	309	66	37	35	9	2	2	5	27	1	31	1	0	2	6	.250	0	0	4.38

BOB SEBRA

Pitches Right-handed, Bats Right-handed Turns Age 26 in 1987, Born 12/11/61

			HOW MUCH HE PITCHED						WHAT HE GAVE UP											THE RESULTS					
Year	Team	League	G	GS	CG	GF	IP	BFP	H	R	ER	HR	SH	SF	HB	TBB	IBB	SO	WP	Bk	W	L	Pct	ShO	Sv	ERA
1985	Texas	A	7	4	0	0	20.1	102	26	17	17	4	0	2	1	14	2	13	0	0	0	2	.000	0	0	7.52
1986	Montreal	N	17	13	3	4	91.1	377	82	39	36	9	3	3	3	25	2	66	2	3	5	5	.500	1	0	3.55
2 YEARS			24	17	3	4	111.2	479	108	56	53	13	3	5	4	39	4	79	2	3	5	7	.417	1	0	4.27

LARRY SHEETS

Bats Left-handed, Throws Right-handed Turns Age 28 in 1987, Born 12/06/59

			BATTING																BASERUNNING				PERCENTAGES		
Year	Team	League	G	AB	H	2B	3B	HR	(Hm	Rd)	TB	R	RBI	TBB	IBB	SO	HBP	SH	SF	SB	CS	SB%	GIDP	AVE	OBP	SLG
1984	Baltimore	A	8	16	7	1	0	1	(0	1)	11	3	2	1	0	3	0	0	0	0	0	.00	0	.438	.471	.688
1985	Baltimore	A	113	328	86	8	0	17	(5	12)	145	43	50	28	2	52	1	1	1	0	1	.00	15	.262	.323	.442
1986	Baltimore	A	112	338	92	17	1	18	(10	8)	165	42	60	21	3	56	1	1	2	2	0	1.00	16	.272	.317	.488
3 YEARS			233	682	185	26	1	36	(15	21)	321	88	112	50	5	111	4	2	3	2	1	.67	31	.271	.323	.471

JOHN SHELBY

Bats both Right and Left-handed, Throws Right-handed   Turns Age 29 in 1987, Born 02/23/58

						BATTING													BASERUNNING				PERCENTAGES		
Year	Team	League	G	AB	H	2B	3B	HR	(Hm	Rd)	TB	R	RBI	TBB	IBB	SO	HBP	SH	SF	SB	CS	SB%	GIDP	AVE	OBP	SLG
1981	Baltimore	A	7	2	0	0	0	0	(0	0)	0	2	0	0	0	1	0	0	0	2	0	1.00	0	.000	.000	.000
1982	Baltimore	A	26	35	11	3	0	1	(1	0)	17	8	2	0	0	5	0	0	0	0	1	.00	0	.314	.314	.486
1983	Baltimore	A	126	325	84	15	2	5	(0	5)	118	52	27	18	2	64	0	6	0	15	2	.88	1	.258	.297	.363
1984	Baltimore	A	128	383	80	12	5	6	(2	4)	120	44	30	20	0	71	0	12	0	12	4	.75	4	.209	.248	.313
1985	Baltimore	A	69	205	58	6	2	7	(4	3)	89	28	27	7	0	44	0	2	0	5	1	.83	4	.283	.307	.434
1986	Baltimore	A	135	404	92	14	4	11	(5	6)	147	54	49	18	0	75	2	2	2	18	6	.75	3	.228	.263	.364
6 YEARS			491	1354	325	50	13	30	(12	18)	491	188	135	63	2	260	2	22	2	52	14	.79	13	.240	.274	.363

PAT SHERIDAN

Bats Left-handed, Throws Right-handed   Turns Age 30 in 1987, Born 12/04/57

						BATTING													BASERUNNING				PERCENTAGES		
Year	Team	League	G	AB	H	2B	3B	HR	(Hm	Rd)	TB	R	RBI	TBB	IBB	SO	HBP	SH	SF	SB	CS	SB%	GIDP	AVE	OBP	SLG
1981	Kansas City	A	3	1	0	0	0	0	(0	0)	0	0	0	0	0	1	0	0	0	0	0	.00	0	.000	.000	.000
1983	Kansas City	A	109	333	90	12	2	7	(4	3)	127	43	36	20	0	64	0	4	0	12	3	.80	3	.270	.312	.381
1984	Kansas City	A	138	481	136	24	4	8	(3	5)	192	64	53	41	3	91	1	5	3	19	6	.76	6	.283	.338	.399
1985	Kansas City	A	78	206	47	9	2	3	(2	1)	69	18	17	23	2	38	1	3	1	11	3	.79	4	.228	.307	.335
1986	Detroit	A	98	236	56	9	1	6	(3	3)	85	41	19	21	4	57	1	2	2	9	2	.82	3	.237	.300	.360
5 YEARS			426	1257	329	54	9	24	(12	12)	473	166	125	105	9	251	3	14	6	51	14	.78	16	.262	.319	.376

BOB SHIRLEY

Pitches Left-handed, Bats Right-handed   Turns Age 33 in 1987, Born 06/25/54

			HOW MUCH HE PITCHED						WHAT HE GAVE UP												THE RESULTS					
Year	Team	League	G	GS	CG	GF	IP	BFP	H	R	ER	HR	SH	SF	HB	TBB	IBB	SO	WP	Bk	W	L	Pct	ShO	Sv	ERA
1977	San Diego	N	39	35	1	0	214	948	215	107	88	22	8	5	4	100	14	146	5	6	12	18	.400	0	0	3.70
1978	San Diego	N	50	20	2	10	166	708	164	75	68	10	12	5	3	61	11	102	3	1	8	11	.421	0	5	3.69
1979	San Diego	N	49	25	4	13	205	843	196	89	77	15	9	7	6	59	8	117	0	0	8	16	.333	1	0	3.38
1980	San Diego	N	59	12	3	32	137	585	143	58	54	12	8	4	0	54	15	67	1	2	11	12	.478	0	7	3.55
1981	St Louis	N	28	11	1	5	79	342	78	42	36	6	5	2	1	34	3	36	1	0	6	4	.600	0	1	4.10
1982	Cincinnati	N	41	20	1	6	152.2	647	138	74	61	17	9	5	3	73	13	89	1	1	8	13	.381	0	0	3.60
1983	New York	A	25	17	1	3	108	467	122	71	61	10	9	6	0	36	3	53	1	1	5	8	.385	1	0	5.08
1984	New York	A	41	7	1	11	114.1	477	119	47	43	8	3	2	0	38	2	48	0	0	3	3	.500	0	0	3.38
1985	New York	A	48	8	2	9	109	446	103	34	32	5	5	4	0	26	2	55	1	0	5	5	.500	0	2	2.64
1986	New York	A	39	6	0	9	105.1	454	108	60	59	13	5	8	3	40	1	64	1	0	0	4	.000	0	3	5.04
10 YEARS			419	161	16	98	1390.1	5917	1386	657	579	118	73	48	20	521	72	777	14	11	66	94	.412	2	18	3.75

ERIC SHOW

Pitches Right-handed, Bats Right-handed   Turns Age 31 in 1987, Born 05/19/56

			HOW MUCH HE PITCHED						WHAT HE GAVE UP												THE RESULTS					
Year	Team	League	G	GS	CG	GF	IP	BFP	H	R	ER	HR	SH	SF	HB	TBB	IBB	SO	WP	Bk	W	L	Pct	ShO	Sv	ERA
1981	San Diego	N	15	0	0	4	23	92	17	9	8	2	2	0	1	9	3	22	0	0	1	3	.250	0	3	3.13
1982	San Diego	N	47	14	2	12	150	611	117	49	44	10	13	6	5	48	3	88	2	0	10	6	.625	2	3	2.64
1983	San Diego	N	35	33	4	0	200.2	857	201	97	93	25	9	4	6	74	3	120	4	2	15	12	.556	2	0	4.17
1984	San Diego	N	32	32	3	0	206.2	862	183	88	78	18	17	4	4	88	4	104	6	2	15	9	.625	1	0	3.40
1985	San Diego	N	35	35	5	0	233	977	212	95	80	27	9	5	5	87	7	141	4	0	12	11	.522	2	0	3.09
1986	San Diego	N	24	22	2	1	136.1	569	109	47	45	11	10	1	4	69	4	94	3	2	9	5	.643	0	0	2.97
6 YEARS			188	136	16	17	949.2	3968	831	385	348	93	60	20	25	375	24	569	19	6	62	46	.574	7	6	3.30

RUBEN SIERRA

Bats both Right and Left-handed, Throws Right-handed   Turns Age 22 in 1987, Born 10/06/65

						BATTING													BASERUNNING				PERCENTAGES		
Year	Team	League	G	AB	H	2B	3B	HR	(Hm	Rd)	TB	R	RBI	TBB	IBB	SO	HBP	SH	SF	SB	CS	SB%	GIDP	AVE	OBP	SLG
1986	Texas	A	113	382	101	13	10	16	(8	8)	182	50	55	22	3	65	1	1	5	7	8	.47	8	.264	.302	.476

TED SIMMONS

Bats both Right and Left-handed, Throws Right-handed Turns Age 38 in 1987, Born 08/09/49

													BATTING									BASERUNNING				PERCENTAGES		
Year	Team	League	G	AB	H	2B	3B	HR	(Hm	Rd)	TB	R	RBI	TBB	IBB	SO	HBP	SH	SF	SB	CS	SB%	GIDP	AVE	OBP	SLG
1968	St Louis	N	2	3	1	0	0	0	(0	0)	1	0	0	1	0	1	0	0	0	0	0	.00	0	.333	.500	.333
1969	St Louis	N	5	14	3	0	1	0	(0	0)	5	0	3	1	0	1	0	0	1	0	0	.00	1	.214	.250	.357
1970	St Louis	N	82	284	69	8	2	3	(2	1)	90	29	24	37	5	37	2	0	1	2	2	.50	5	.243	.333	.317
1971	St Louis	N	133	510	155	32	4	7	(2	5)	216	64	77	36	3	50	3	4	10	1	3	.25	20	.304	.347	.424
1972	St Louis	N	152	594	180	36	6	16	(6	10)	276	70	96	29	8	57	2	1	3	1	3	.25	18	.303	.336	.465
1973	St Louis	N	161	619	192	36	2	13	(4	9)	271	62	91	61	15	47	2	1	7	2	2	.50	29	.310	.370	.438
1974	St Louis	N	152	599	163	33	6	20	(13	7)	268	66	103	47	8	35	6	1	9	0	0	.00	22	.272	.327	.447
1975	St Louis	N	157	581	193	32	3	18	(10	8)	285	80	100	63	16	35	1	0	4	1	3	.25	23	.332	.396	.491
1976	St Louis	N	150	546	159	35	3	5	(1	4)	215	60	75	73	19	35	0	0	6	0	7	.00	9	.291	.371	.394
1977	St Louis	N	150	516	164	25	3	21	(9	12)	258	82	95	79	25	37	2	0	4	2	6	.25	20	.318	.408	.500
1978	St Louis	N	152	516	148	40	5	22	(9	13)	264	71	80	77	17	39	3	0	8	1	1	.50	19	.287	.377	.512
1979	St Louis	N	123	448	127	22	0	26	(17	9)	227	68	87	61	22	34	4	0	8	0	1	.00	10	.283	.369	.507
1980	St Louis	N	145	495	150	33	2	21	(8	13)	250	84	98	59	13	45	2	0	6	1	0	1.00	13	.303	.375	.505
1981	Milwaukee	A	100	380	82	13	3	14	(8	6)	143	45	61	23	2	32	3	1	6	0	1	.00	10	.216	.262	.376
1982	Milwaukee	A	137	539	145	29	2	23	(7	16)	243	73	97	32	5	40	2	1	7	0	0	.00	20	.269	.309	.451
1983	Milwaukee	A	153	600	185	39	3	13	(8	5)	269	76	108	41	6	51	2	0	7	4	2	.67	23	.308	.351	.448
1984	Milwaukee	A	132	497	110	23	2	4	(0	4)	149	44	52	30	3	40	3	1	1	1	0	1.00	23	.221	.269	.300
1985	Milwaukee	A	143	528	144	28	2	12	(8	4)	212	60	76	57	9	32	1	1	5	1	1	.50	17	.273	.342	.402
1986	Atlanta	N	76	127	32	5	0	4	(3	1)	49	14	25	12	5	14	1	0	4	1	0	1.00	1	.252	.313	.386
19 YEARS			2305	8396	2402	469	47	242	(115	127)	3691	1048	1348	819	181	662	39	11	97	20	32	.38	279	.286	.349	.440

DOUG SISK

Pitches Right-handed, Bats Right-handed Turns Age 30 in 1987, Born 09/26/57

			HOW MUCH HE PITCHED						WHAT HE GAVE UP												THE RESULTS					
Year	Team	League	G	GS	CG	GF	IP	BFP	H	R	ER	HR	SH	SF	HB	TBB	IBB	SO	WP	Bk	W	L	Pct	ShO	Sv	ERA
1982	New York	N	8	0	0	4	8.2	34	5	1	1	0	1	0	1	4	2	4	0	0	0	1	.000	0	1	1.04
1983	New York	N	67	0	0	39	104.1	447	88	38	26	1	6	4	4	59	7	33	5	1	5	4	.556	0	11	2.24
1984	New York	N	50	0	0	31	77.2	329	57	24	18	1	7	0	3	54	5	32	1	0	1	3	.250	0	15	2.09
1985	New York	N	42	0	0	22	73	341	86	48	43	3	3	0	2	40	2	26	1	1	4	5	.444	0	2	5.30
1986	New York	N	41	0	0	15	70.2	312	77	31	24	0	3	0	5	31	5	31	2	1	4	2	.667	0	1	3.06
5 YEARS			208	0	0	111	334.1	1463	313	142	112	6	19	4	15	188	21	126	9	3	14	15	.483	0	30	3.01

JOEL SKINNER

Bats Right-handed, Throws Right-handed Turns Age 26 in 1987, Born 02/21/61

													BATTING									BASERUNNING				PERCENTAGES		
Year	Team	League	G	AB	H	2B	3B	HR	(Hm	Rd)	TB	R	RBI	TBB	IBB	SO	HBP	SH	SF	SB	CS	SB%	GIDP	AVE	OBP	SLG
1983	Chicago	A	6	11	3	0	0	0	(0	0)	3	2	1	0	0	1	0	0	0	0	0	.00	2	.273	.273	.273
1984	Chicago	A	43	80	17	2	0	0	(0	0)	19	4	3	7	0	19	0	0	1	1	0	1.00	2	.213	.273	.238
1985	Chicago	A	22	44	15	4	1	1	(1	0)	24	9	5	5	0	13	0	1	0	0	0	.00	2	.341	.408	.545
1986	2 Teams	A	114	315	73	9	1	5	(0	0)	99	23	37	16	0	83	1	2	2	1	4	.20	6	.232	.269	.314
4 YEARS			185	450	108	15	2	6	(1	0)	145	38	46	28	0	116	1	3	3	2	4	.33	12	.240	.284	.322
1986	Chicago	A	60	149	30	5	1	4	(0	0)	49	17	20	9	0	43	1	2	1	1	0	1.00	2	.201	.250	.329
1986	New York	A	54	166	43	4	0	1	(0	0)	50	6	17	7	0	40	0	0	1	0	4	.00	4	.259	.287	.301

JIM SLATON

Pitches Right-handed, Bats Right-handed Turns Age 37 in 1987, Born 06/19/50

			HOW MUCH HE PITCHED						WHAT HE GAVE UP												THE RESULTS					
Year	Team	League	G	GS	CG	GF	IP	BFP	H	R	ER	HR	SH	SF	HB	TBB	IBB	SO	WP	Bk	W	L	Pct	ShO	Sv	ERA
1971	Milwaukee	A	26	23	5	0	148	0	140	67	62	16	4	2	1	71	9	63	5	2	10	8	.556	4	0	3.77
1972	Milwaukee	A	9	8	0	0	44	0	50	31	27	3	3	3	1	21	1	17	1	0	1	6	.143	0	0	5.52
1973	Milwaukee	A	38	38	13	0	276	0	266	127	114	30	4	8	1	99	4	134	11	0	13	15	.464	3	0	3.72
1974	Milwaukee	A	40	35	10	2	250	1072	255	117	109	22	10	7	3	102	6	126	14	0	13	16	.448	3	0	3.92
1975	Milwaukee	A	37	33	10	1	217	970	238	129	109	28	9	7	2	90	6	119	12	0	11	18	.379	3	0	4.52
1976	Milwaukee	A	38	38	12	0	293	1235	287	126	112	14	15	12	6	94	12	138	11	1	14	15	.483	2	0	3.44
1977	Milwaukee	A	32	31	7	1	221	942	223	104	88	25	8	9	11	77	5	104	1	1	10	14	.417	1	0	3.58
1978	Detroit	A	35	34	11	0	234	1003	235	117	107	27	7	9	8	85	1	92	10	1	17	11	.607	2	0	4.12
1979	Milwaukee	A	32	31	12	0	213	894	229	95	86	15	5	8	2	54	1	80	5	0	15	9	.625	3	0	3.63
1980	Milwaukee	A	3	3	0	0	16	68	17	10	8	3	0	0	0	5	0	4	1	0	1	1	.500	0	0	4.50
1981	Milwaukee	A	24	21	0	2	117	500	120	60	57	10	3	6	2	50	2	47	5	0	5	7	.417	0	0	4.38
1982	Milwaukee	A	39	7	0	21	117.2	494	117	48	43	14	6	2	1	41	3	59	2	1	10	6	.625	0	6	3.29
1983	Milwaukee	A	46	0	0	26	112.1	490	112	57	54	12	9	10	3	56	5	38	3	0	14	6	.700	0	5	4.33
1984	California	A	32	22	5	1	163	722	192	95	90	22	7	6	2	56	5	67	6	0	7	10	.412	1	0	4.97
1985	California	A	29	24	1	3	148.1	645	162	82	72	22	5	5	2	63	1	60	8	0	6	10	.375	0	1	4.37
1986	2 Teams	A	36	12	0	13	113.1	497	130	70	64	14	1	8	3	40	4	43	2	0	4	6	.400	0	2	5.08
16 YEARS			496	360	86	70	2683.2	9532	2773	1335	1202	277	96	102	48	1004	65	1191	97	6	151	158	.489	22	14	4.03
1986	California	A	14	12	0	0	73.1	323	84	52	46	9	1	6	2	29	1	31	1	0	4	6	.400	0	0	5.65
1986	Detroit	A	22	0	0	12	40	174	46	18	18	5	0	2	1	11	3	12	1	0	0	0	.000	0	2	4.05

DON SLAUGHT

Bats Right-handed, Throws Right-handed   Turns Age 28 in 1987, Born 09/11/59

						BATTING															BASERUNNING				PERCENTAGES		
Year	Team	League	G	AB	H	2B	3B	HR	(Hm	Rd)	TB	R	RBI	TBB	IBB	SO	HBP	SH	SF	SB	CS	SB%	GIDP	AVE	OBP	SLG
1982	Kansas City	A	43	115	32	6	0	3	(0	3)	47	14	8	9	0	12	0	2	0	0	0	.00	3	.278	.331	.409
1983	Kansas City	A	83	276	86	13	4	0	(0	0)	107	21	28	11	0	27	0	1	2	3	1	.75	8	.312	.336	.388
1984	Kansas City	A	124	409	108	27	4	4	(1	3)	155	48	42	20	4	55	2	8	7	0	0	.00	8	.264	.297	.379
1985	Texas	A	102	343	96	17	4	8	(4	4)	145	34	35	20	1	41	6	1	0	5	4	.56	8	.280	.331	.423
1986	Texas	A	95	314	83	17	1	13	(5	8)	141	39	46	16	0	59	5	3	3	3	1	.75	8	.264	.308	.449
5 YEARS			447	1457	405	80	13	28	(10	18)	595	156	159	76	5	194	13	15	12	11	6	.65	35	.278	.317	.408

ROY SMALLEY

Bats both Right and Left-handed, Throws Right-handed   Turns Age 35 in 1987, Born 10/25/52

						BATTING															BASERUNNING				PERCENTAGES		
Year	Team	League	G	AB	H	2B	3B	HR	(Hm	Rd)	TB	R	RBI	TBB	IBB	SO	HBP	SH	SF	SB	CS	SB%	GIDP	AVE	OBP	SLG
1975	Texas	A	78	250	57	8	0	3	(2	1)	74	22	33	30	1	42	0	4	2	4	0	1.00	6	.228	.309	.296
1976	2 Teams		144	513	133	18	3	3	(2	1)	166	61	44	76	4	106	2	25	2	2	4	.33	11	.259	.356	.324
1977	Minnesota	A	150	584	135	21	5	6	(2	4)	184	93	56	74	1	89	1	15	6	5	5	.50	12	.231	.316	.315
1978	Minnesota	A	158	586	160	31	3	19	(8	11)	254	80	77	85	3	70	1	23	7	2	8	.20	16	.273	.362	.433
1979	Minnesota	A	162	621	168	28	3	24	(19	5)	274	94	95	80	8	80	4	15	9	2	3	.40	7	.271	.353	.441
1980	Minnesota	A	133	486	135	24	1	12	(5	7)	197	64	63	65	4	63	2	2	9	3	3	.50	15	.278	.359	.405
1981	Minnesota	A	56	167	44	7	1	7	(2	5)	74	24	22	31	5	24	0	2	0	0	0	.00	8	.263	.375	.443
1982	2 Teams		146	499	127	15	2	20	(8	12)	206	57	67	71	8	104	0	7	4	0	1	.00	6	.255	.345	.413
1983	New York	A	130	451	124	24	1	18	(7	11)	204	70	62	58	2	68	2	5	4	3	3	.50	9	.275	.357	.452
1984	2 Teams		114	344	73	12	1	11	(8	3)	120	32	39	37	3	65	0	0	4	3	2	.60	6	.212	.286	.349
1985	Minnesota	A	129	388	100	20	0	12	(7	5)	156	57	45	60	3	65	1	1	2	0	0	.00	8	.258	.357	.402
1986	Minnesota	A	143	459	113	20	4	20	(9	11)	201	59	57	68	4	80	0	1	2	1	3	.25	10	.246	.342	.438
12 YEARS			1543	5348	1369	228	24	155	(79	76)	2110	713	660	735	46	856	13	98	53	25	34	.42	114	.256	.344	.395
1976	Minnesota	A	103	384	104	16	3	2	(1	1)	132	46	36	47	1	79	2	22	0	0	4	.00	7	.271	.353	.344
1976	Minnesota	A	41	129	29	2	0	1	(1	0)	34	15	8	29	3	27	0	3	2	2	0	1.00	4	.225	.363	.264
1982	Minnesota	A	4	13	2	1	0	0	(0	0)	3	2	0	3	1	4	0	0	0	0	0	.00	0	.154	.313	.231
1982	New York	A	142	486	125	14	2	20	(8	12)	203	55	67	68	7	100	0	7	4	0	1	.00	4	.257	.346	.418
1984	Chicago	A	47	135	23	4	0	4	(4	0)	39	15	13	22	1	30	0	0	1	1	1	.50	1	.170	.285	.289
1984	New York	A	67	209	50	8	1	7	(4	3)	81	17	26	15	2	35	0	0	3	2	1	.67	5	.239	.286	.388

BRYN SMITH

Pitches Right-handed, Bats Right-handed   Turns Age 32 in 1987, Born 08/11/55

			HOW MUCH HE PITCHED						WHAT HE GAVE UP											THE RESULTS					
Year	Team	League	G	GS	CG	GF	IP	BFP	H	R	ER	HR	SH	SF	HB	TBB	IBB	SO	WP	Bk	W	L	Pct	ShO	Sv	ERA
1981	Montreal	N	7	0	0	1	13	53	14	4	4	1	0	0	0	3	0	9	2	0	1	0	1.000	0	0	2.77
1982	Montreal	N	47	1	0	16	79.1	335	81	43	37	5	1	4	0	23	5	50	5	1	2	4	.333	0	0	4.20
1983	Montreal	N	49	12	5	17	155.1	636	142	51	43	13	14	2	5	43	6	101	5	3	6	11	.353	3	3	2.49
1984	Montreal	N	28	28	4	0	179	751	178	72	66	15	7	2	3	51	7	101	2	2	12	13	.480	2	0	3.32
1985	Montreal	N	32	32	4	0	222.1	890	193	85	72	12	13	4	1	41	3	127	1	1	18	5	.783	2	0	2.91
1986	Montreal	N	30	30	1	0	187.1	807	182	101	82	15	10	3	6	63	6	105	4	2	10	8	.556	0	0	3.94
6 YEARS			193	103	14	34	836.1	3472	790	356	304	61	45	15	15	224	27	493	19	9	49	41	.544	7	6	3.27

DAVE SMITH

Pitches Right-handed, Bats Right-handed   Turns Age 32 in 1987, Born 01/21/55

			HOW MUCH HE PITCHED						WHAT HE GAVE UP											THE RESULTS					
Year	Team	League	G	GS	CG	GF	IP	BFP	H	R	ER	HR	SH	SF	HB	TBB	IBB	SO	WP	Bk	W	L	Pct	ShO	Sv	ERA
1980	Houston	N	57	0	0	35	103	422	90	24	22	4	6	1	4	32	7	85	3	1	7	5	.583	0	10	1.92
1981	Houston	N	42	0	0	22	75	305	74	26	23	2	6	1	2	23	4	52	4	0	5	3	.625	0	8	2.76
1982	Houston	N	49	1	0	29	63.1	286	69	30	27	4	9	4	0	31	4	28	2	4	5	4	.556	0	11	3.84
1983	Houston	N	42	0	0	24	72.2	323	72	32	25	2	3	5	0	36	4	41	1	1	3	1	.750	0	6	3.10
1984	Houston	N	53	0	0	24	77.1	304	60	22	19	5	2	1	1	20	3	45	1	1	5	4	.556	0	5	2.21
1985	Houston	N	64	0	0	46	79.1	315	69	26	20	3	3	1	1	17	5	40	4	1	9	5	.643	0	27	2.27
1986	Houston	N	54	0	0	51	56	223	39	17	17	5	4	1	1	22	3	46	2	0	4	7	.364	0	33	2.73
7 YEARS			361	1	0	231	526.2	2178	473	177	153	22	33	14	9	181	30	337	17	8	38	29	.567	0	100	2.61

LEE SMITH

Pitches Right-handed, Bats Right-handed   Turns Age 30 in 1987, Born 12/04/57

			HOW MUCH HE PITCHED						WHAT HE GAVE UP											THE RESULTS					
Year	Team	League	G	GS	CG	GF	IP	BFP	H	R	ER	HR	SH	SF	HB	TBB	IBB	SO	WP	Bk	W	L	Pct	ShO	Sv	ERA
1980	Chicago	N	18	0	0	6	22	97	21	9	7	0	1	1	0	14	5	17	0	0	2	0	1.000	0	0	2.86
1981	Chicago	N	40	1	0	12	67	280	57	31	26	2	8	2	1	31	8	50	7	1	3	6	.333	0	1	3.49
1982	Chicago	N	72	5	0	38	117	480	105	38	35	5	6	5	3	37	5	99	6	1	2	5	.286	0	17	2.69
1983	Chicago	N	66	0	0	56	103.1	413	70	23	19	5	9	2	1	41	14	91	5	2	4	10	.286	0	29	1.65
1984	Chicago	N	69	0	0	59	101	428	98	44	41	6	4	5	0	35	7	86	6	0	9	7	.563	0	33	3.65
1985	Chicago	N	65	0	0	57	97.2	397	87	35	33	9	3	1	1	32	6	112	4	0	7	4	.636	0	33	3.04
1986	Chicago	N	66	0	0	59	90.1	372	69	32	31	7	6	3	0	42	11	93	2	0	9	9	.500	0	31	3.09
7 YEARS			396	6	0	287	598.1	2467	507	210	192	34	37	19	6	232	56	548	30	4	36	41	.468	0	144	2.89

LONNIE SMITH

Bats Right-handed, Throws Right-handed

Turns Age 32 in 1987, Born 12/22/55

Year	Team	League	G	AB	H	2B	3B	HR	(Hm	Rd)	TB	R	RBI	TBB	IBB	SO	HBP	SH	SF	SB	CS	SB%	GIDP	AVE	OBP	SLG
																							BATTING		BASERUNNING	PERCENTAGES
1978	Philadelphia	N	17	4	0	0	0	0	(0	0)	0	6	0	4	0	3	0	0	0	4	0	1.00	0	.000	.500	.000
1979	Philadelphia	N	17	30	5	2	0	0	(0	0)	7	4	3	1	0	7	0	0	0	2	1	.67	0	.167	.194	.233
1980	Philadelphia	N	100	298	101	14	4	3	(2	1)	132	69	20	26	2	48	4	1	2	33	13	.72	5	.339	.397	.443
1981	Philadelphia	N	62	176	57	14	3	2	(1	1)	83	40	11	18	1	14	5	3	0	21	10	.68	1	.324	.402	.472
1982	St Louis	N	156	592	182	35	8	8	(3	5)	257	120	69	64	2	74	9	3	4	68	26	.72	11	.307	.381	.434
1983	St Louis	N	130	492	158	31	5	8	(4	4)	223	83	45	41	2	55	9	1	4	43	18	.70	11	.321	.381	.453
1984	St Louis	N	145	504	126	20	4	6	(3	3)	172	77	49	70	0	90	9	3	4	50	13	.79	7	.250	.349	.341
1985	2 Teams		148	544	140	25	6	6	(2	4)	195	92	48	56	0	89	7	1	5	52	13	.80	4	.257	.332	.358
1986	Kansas City	A	134	508	146	25	7	8	(2	6)	209	80	44	46	0	78	10	2	2	26	9	.74	10	.287	.357	.411
9 YEARS			909	3148	915	166	37	41	(17	24)	1278	571	289	326	7	458	53	14	21	299	103	.74	49	.291	.365	.406
1985	Kansas City	A	120	448	115	23	4	6	(2	4)	164	77	41	41	0	69	4	0	5	40	6	.85	2	.257	.321	.366
1985	St Louis	N	28	96	25	2	2	0	(0	0)	31	15	7	15	0	20	3	1	0	12	6	.67	2	.260	.377	.323

OZZIE SMITH

Bats both Right and Left-handed, Throws Right-handed

Turns Age 33 in 1987, Born 12/26/54

Year	Team	League	G	AB	H	2B	3B	HR	(Hm	Rd)	TB	R	RBI	TBB	IBB	SO	HBP	SH	SF	SB	CS	SB%	GIDP	AVE	OBP	SLG
																							BATTING		BASERUNNING	PERCENTAGES
1978	San Diego	N	159	590	152	17	6	1	(0	1)	184	69	46	47	0	43	0	28	3	40	12	.77	11	.258	.311	.312
1979	San Diego	N	156	587	124	18	6	0	(0	0)	154	77	27	37	5	37	2	22	1	28	7	.80	11	.211	.260	.262
1980	San Diego	N	158	609	140	18	5	0	(0	0)	168	67	35	71	1	49	5	23	4	57	15	.79	9	.230	.313	.276
1981	San Diego	N	110	450	100	11	2	0	(0	0)	115	53	21	41	1	37	5	10	1	22	12	.65	2	.222	.294	.256
1982	St Louis	N	140	488	121	24	1	2	(0	2)	153	58	43	68	12	32	2	4	5	25	5	.83	10	.248	.339	.314
1983	St Louis	N	159	552	134	30	6	3	(1	2)	185	69	50	64	9	36	1	7	2	34	7	.83	10	.243	.321	.335
1984	St Louis	N	124	412	106	20	5	1	(1	0)	139	53	44	56	5	17	2	11	3	35	7	.83	8	.257	.347	.337
1985	St Louis	N	158	537	148	22	3	6	(2	4)	194	70	54	65	11	27	2	9	2	31	8	.79	13	.276	.355	.361
1986	St Louis	N	153	514	144	19	4	0	(0	0)	171	67	54	79	13	27	2	11	3	31	7	.82	15	.280	.376	.333
9 YEARS			1317	4739	1169	179	38	13	(4	9)	1463	583	374	528	57	305	21	125	24	303	80	.79	89	.247	.323	.309

ZANE SMITH

Pitches Left-handed, Bats Left-handed

Turns Age 27 in 1987, Born 12/28/60

Year	Team	League	G	GS	CG	GF	IP	BFP	H	R	ER	HR	SH	SF	HB	TBB	IBB	SO	WP	Bk	W	L	Pct	ShO	Sv	ERA
				HOW MUCH HE PITCHED						WHAT HE GAVE UP											THE RESULTS					
1984	Atlanta	N	3	3	0	0	20	87	16	7	5	1	1	0	0	13	2	16	0	0	1	0	1.000	0	0	2.25
1985	Atlanta	N	42	18	2	3	147	631	135	70	62	4	16	1	3	80	5	85	2	0	9	10	.474	2	0	3.80
1986	Atlanta	N	38	32	3	2	204.2	889	209	109	92	8	13	6	5	105	6	139	8	0	8	16	.333	1	1	4.05
3 YEARS			83	53	5	5	371.2	1607	360	186	159	13	30	7	8	198	13	240	10	0	18	26	.409	3	1	3.85

MIKE SMITHSON

Pitches Right-handed, Bats Left-handed

Turns Age 32 in 1987, Born 01/21/55

Year	Team	League	G	GS	CG	GF	IP	BFP	H	R	ER	HR	SH	SF	HB	TBB	IBB	SO	WP	Bk	W	L	Pct	ShO	Sv	ERA
				HOW MUCH HE PITCHED						WHAT HE GAVE UP											THE RESULTS					
1982	Texas	A	8	8	3	0	46.2	199	51	26	26	5	1	1	3	13	2	24	1	0	3	4	.429	0	0	5.01
1983	Texas	A	33	33	10	0	223.1	960	233	102	97	14	6	8	8	71	2	135	8	2	10	14	.417	0	0	3.91
1984	Minnesota	A	36	36	10	0	252	1047	246	113	103	35	5	3	8	54	7	144	7	2	15	13	.536	1	0	3.68
1985	Minnesota	A	37	37	8	0	257	1088	264	134	124	25	10	7	15	78	1	127	6	1	15	14	.517	3	0	4.34
1986	Minnesota	A	34	33	8	1	198	880	234	123	105	26	5	8	14	57	4	114	15	1	13	14	.481	1	0	4.77
5 YEARS			148	147	39	1	977	4174	1028	498	455	105	27	27	48	273	16	544	37	6	56	59	.487	5	0	4.19

NATE SNELL

Pitches Right-handed, Bats Right-handed

Turns Age 35 in 1987, Born 09/02/52

Year	Team	League	G	GS	CG	GF	IP	BFP	H	R	ER	HR	SH	SF	HB	TBB	IBB	SO	WP	Bk	W	L	Pct	ShO	Sv	ERA
				HOW MUCH HE PITCHED						WHAT HE GAVE UP											THE RESULTS					
1984	Baltimore	A	5	0	0	3	7.2	33	8	2	2	1	0	1	0	1	0	7	0	0	1	1	.500	0	0	2.35
1985	Baltimore	A	43	0	0	15	100.1	421	100	44	30	4	4	1	1	30	5	41	1	0	3	2	.600	0	5	2.69
1986	Baltimore	A	34	0	0	18	72.1	297	69	36	31	9	3	3	1	22	4	29	2	0	2	1	.667	0	0	3.86
3 YEARS			82	0	0	36	180.1	751	177	82	63	14	7	5	2	53	9	77	3	0	6	4	.600	0	5	3.14

CORY SNYDER

Bats Right-handed, Throws Right-handed

Turns Age 25 in 1987, Born 11/11/62

Year	Team	League	G	AB	H	2B	3B	HR	(Hm	Rd)	TB	R	RBI	TBB	IBB	SO	HBP	SH	SF	SB	CS	SB%	GIDP	AVE	OBP	SLG
																							BATTING		BASERUNNING	PERCENTAGES
1986	Cleveland	A	103	416	113	21	1	24	(12	12)	208	58	69	16	0	123	0	1	0	2	3	.40	8	.272	.299	.500

RAY SOFF

Pitches Right-handed, Bats Right-handed   Turns Age 29 in 1987, Born 10/31/58

			HOW MUCH HE PITCHED						WHAT HE GAVE UP												THE RESULTS					
Year	Team	League	G	GS	CG	GF	IP	BFP	H	R	ER	HR	SH	SF	HB	TBB	IBB	SO	WP	Bk	W	L	Pct	ShO	Sv	ERA
1986	St Louis	N	30	0	0	9	38.1	162	37	17	14	4	2	2	0	13	1	22	2	1	4	2	.667	0	0	3.29

JULIO SOLANO

Pitches Right-handed, Bats Right-handed   Turns Age 27 in 1987, Born 01/08/60

			HOW MUCH HE PITCHED						WHAT HE GAVE UP												THE RESULTS					
Year	Team	League	G	GS	CG	GF	IP	BFP	H	R	ER	HR	SH	SF	HB	TBB	IBB	SO	WP	Bk	W	L	Pct	ShO	Sv	ERA
1983	Houston	N	4	0	0	0	6	27	5	5	4	1	0	0	0	4	1	3	1	0	0	2	.000	0	0	6.00
1984	Houston	N	31	0	0	7	50.2	197	31	13	11	3	3	3	0	18	1	33	0	1	1	3	.250	0	0	1.95
1985	Houston	N	20	0	0	9	33.2	144	34	13	13	5	1	0	0	13	2	17	2	0	2	2	.500	0	0	3.48
1986	Houston	N	16	1	0	3	32	155	39	28	27	5	3	1	3	22	2	21	3	1	3	1	.750	0	0	7.59
4 YEARS			71	1	0	19	122.1	523	109	59	55	14	7	4	3	57	6	74	6	2	6	8	.429	0	0	4.05

MARIO SOTO

Pitches Right-handed, Bats Right-handed   Turns Age 31 in 1987, Born 07/12/56

			HOW MUCH HE PITCHED						WHAT HE GAVE UP												THE RESULTS					
Year	Team	League	G	GS	CG	GF	IP	BFP	H	R	ER	HR	SH	SF	HB	TBB	IBB	SO	WP	Bk	W	L	Pct	ShO	Sv	ERA
1977	Cincinnati	N	12	10	2	1	61	266	60	38	36	12	2	2	3	26	4	44	4	0	2	6	.250	1	0	5.31
1978	Cincinnati	N	5	1	0	1	18	79	13	5	5	1	0	0	0	13	3	13	0	0	1	0	1.000	0	0	2.50
1979	Cincinnati	N	25	0	0	7	37	169	33	25	22	2	1	1	1	30	2	32	0	0	3	2	.600	0	0	5.35
1980	Cincinnati	N	53	12	3	10	190	777	126	72	65	11	10	8	2	84	10	182	6	4	10	8	.556	1	4	3.08
1981	Cincinnati	N	25	25	10	0	175	717	142	69	64	13	3	4	3	61	3	151	4	3	12	9	.571	3	0	3.29
1982	Cincinnati	N	35	34	13	1	257.2	1033	202	88	80	19	12	8	4	71	3	274	6	1	14	13	.519	2	0	2.79
1983	Cincinnati	N	34	34	18	0	273.2	1114	207	96	82	28	8	9	5	95	6	242	2	2	17	13	.567	3	0	2.70
1984	Cincinnati	N	33	33	13	0	237.1	971	181	102	93	26	9	6	5	87	6	185	3	0	18	7	.720	0	0	3.53
1985	Cincinnati	N	36	36	9	0	256.2	1055	196	109	102	30	13	9	2	104	3	214	8	2	12	15	.444	1	0	3.58
1986	Cincinnati	N	19	19	1	0	105	461	113	61	55	15	6	4	1	46	6	67	3	0	5	10	.333	1	0	4.71
10 YEARS			277	204	69	20	1611.1	6642	1273	665	604	157	64	51	26	617	46	1404	36	12	94	83	.531	12	4	3.37

CHRIS SPEIER

Bats Right-handed, Throws Right-handed   Turns Age 37 in 1987, Born 06/28/50

									BATTING												BASERUNNING				PERCENTAGES		
Year	Team	League	G	AB	H	2B	3B	HR	(Hm	Rd)	TB	R	RBI	TBB	IBB	SO	HBP	SH	SF	SB	CS	SB%	GIDP	AVE	OBP	SLG
1971	San Francisco	N	157	601	141	17	6	8	(4	4)	194	74	46	56	6	90	7	5	1	4	7	.36	15	.235	.307	.323
1972	San Francisco	N	150	562	151	17	2	15	(11	4)	225	74	71	82	2	92	3	4	7	9	4	.69	8	.269	.361	.400
1973	San Francisco	N	153	542	135	17	4	11	(3	8)	193	58	71	66	4	69	2	5	2	4	5	.44	18	.249	.332	.356
1974	San Francisco	N	141	501	125	19	5	9	(3	6)	181	55	53	62	8	64	4	8	2	3	2	.60	7	.250	.336	.361
1975	San Francisco	N	141	487	132	30	5	10	(4	6)	202	60	69	70	7	50	1	3	3	4	5	.44	13	.271	.362	.415
1976	San Francisco	N	145	495	112	18	4	3	(0	3)	147	51	40	60	1	52	4	6	7	2	2	.50	16	.226	.311	.297
1977	2 Teams		145	548	128	31	6	5	(4	1)	186	59	38	67	3	81	1	3	2	1	2	.33	14	.234	.317	.339
1978	Montreal	N	150	501	126	18	3	5	(2	3)	165	47	51	60	10	75	1	2	6	1		1.00	14	.251	.329	.329
1979	Montreal	N	113	344	78	13	1	7	(1	6)	114	31	26	43	10	45	3	0	1	0	0	.00	13	.227	.317	.331
1980	Montreal	N	128	388	103	14	4	1	(0	1)	128	35	32	52	18	38	0	6	1	0	3	.00	10	.265	.351	.330
1981	Montreal	N	96	307	69	10	2	2	(1	1)	89	33	25	38	10	29	0	6	0	1	2	.33	9	.225	.310	.290
1982	Montreal	N	156	530	136	26	4	7	(2	5)	191	41	60	47	12	67	1	3	4	1	6	.14	13	.257	.316	.360
1983	Montreal	N	88	261	67	12	2	2	(1	1)	89	31	22	29	4	37	2	3	3	2	1	.67	4	.257	.332	.341
1984	3 Teams		75	191	34	7	1	3	(2	1)	52	12	10	13	1	34	1	4	0	0	0	.00	6	.178	.234	.272
1985	Chicago	N	106	218	53	11	0	4	(1	3)	76	16	24	17	0	34	0	3	2	1	3	.25	7	.243	.295	.349
1986	Chicago	N	95	155	44	8	0	6	(2	4)	70	21	23	15	3	32	1	4	1	2	2	.50	4	.284	.349	.452
16 YEARS			2039	6631	1634	276	49	98	(41	57)	2302	698	661	777	99	889	31	65	42	35	44	.44	171	.246	.326	.347
1977	Montreal	N	139	531	125	30	6	5	(4	1)	182	58	38	67	3	78	1	3	2	1	2	.33	14	.235	.321	.343
1977	San Francisco	N	6	17	3	1	0	0	(0	0)	4	1	0	0	0	3	0	0	0	0	0	.00	0	.176	.176	.235
1984	Minnesota	A	12	33	7	0	0	0	(0	0)	7	2	1	3	0	7	0	1	0	0	0	.00	1	.212	.278	.212
1984	Montreal	N	25	40	6	0	0	0	(0	0)	6	1	1	1	0	8	0	2	0	0	0	.00	0	.150	.171	.150
1984	St Louis	N	38	118	21	7	1	3	(2	1)	39	9	8	9	1	19	1	1	0	0	0	.00	1	.178	.242	.331

BOB STANLEY

Pitches Right-handed, Bats Right-handed   Turns Age 33 in 1987, Born 11/10/54

			HOW MUCH HE PITCHED						WHAT HE GAVE UP												THE RESULTS					
Year	Team	League	G	GS	CG	GF	IP	BFP	H	R	ER	HR	SH	SF	HB	TBB	IBB	SO	WP	Bk	W	L	Pct	ShO	Sv	ERA
1977	Boston	A	41	13	3	13	151	651	176	74	67	10	3	3	3	43	5	44	2	1	8	7	.533	1	3	3.99
1978	Boston	A	52	3	0	35	142	578	142	50	41	5	4	6	1	34	5	38	0	0	15	2	.882	0	10	2.60
1979	Boston	A	40	30	9	7	217	914	250	110	96	14	11	6	4	44	4	56	0	0	16	12	.571	4	1	3.98
1980	Boston	A	52	17	5	25	175	737	186	75	66	11	5	5	7	52	8	71	1	0	10	8	.556	1	14	3.39
1981	Boston	A	35	1	0	14	99	430	110	46	42	3	8	4	6	38	4	28	1	0	10	8	.556	0	0	3.82
1982	Boston	A	48	0	0	33	168.1	700	161	60	58	11	4	4	4	50	6	83	2	0	12	7	.632	0	14	3.10
1983	Boston	A	64	0	0	53	145.1	602	145	56	46	7	11	4	3	38	12	65	4	0	8	10	.444	0	33	2.85
1984	Boston	A	57	0	0	47	106.2	455	113	57	42	9	6	1	2	23	9	52	1	0	9	10	.474	0	22	3.54
1985	Boston	A	48	0	0	41	87.2	360	76	30	28	7	3	4	2	30	10	46	1	0	6	6	.500	0	10	2.87
1986	Boston	A	66	1	0	50	82.1	366	109	48	40	9	2	4	0	22	8	54	1	0	6	6	.500	0	16	4.37
10 YEARS			503	65	17	318	1374.1	5793	1468	606	526	86	57	41	32	374	71	537	13	1	100	76	.568	6	123	3.44

JOHN STEFERO

Bats Left-handed, Throws Right-handed

Turns Age 28 in 1987, Born 09/22/59

					BATTING													BASERUNNING				PERCENTAGES		
Year	Team	League	G	AB	H	2B	3B	HR	(Hm | Rd)	TB	R	RBI	TBB	IBB	SO	HBP	SH	SF	SB	CS	SB%	GIDP	AVE	OBP	SLG
1983	Baltimore	A	9	11	5	1	0	0	(0 | 0)	6	2	4	3	0	2	0	0	0	0	0	.00	0	.455	.571	.545
1986	Baltimore	A	52	120	28	2	0	2	(2 | 0)	36	14	13	16	0	25	0	0	1	0	1	.00	1	.233	.321	.300
2 YEARS			61	131	33	3	0	2	(2 | 0)	42	16	17	19	0	27	0	0	1	0	1	.00	1	.252	.344	.321

DAVE STEWART

Pitches Right-handed, Bats Right-handed

Turns Age 30 in 1987, Born 02/19/57

			HOW MUCH HE PITCHED						WHAT HE GAVE UP											THE RESULTS					
Year	Team	League	G	GS	CG	GF	IP	BFP	H	R	ER	HR	SH	SF	HB	TBB	IBB	SO	WP	Bk	W	L	Pct	ShO	Sv	ERA
1978	Los Angeles	N	1	0	0	1	2	6	1	0	0	0	0	0	0	0	0	1	0	0	0	0	.000	0	0	0.00
1981	Los Angeles	N	32	0	0	14	43	184	40	13	12	3	7	3	0	14	5	29	4	0	4	3	.571	0	6	2.51
1982	Los Angeles	N	45	14	0	9	146.1	616	137	72	62	14	10	5	2	49	11	80	3	0	9	8	.529	0	1	3.81
1983	2 Teams		54	9	2	25	135	565	117	43	39	6	9	4	4	50	7	78	3	0	10	4	.714	0	8	2.60
1984	Texas	A	32	27	3	2	192.1	847	193	106	101	26	4	5	4	87	3	119	12	0	7	14	.333	0	4	4.73
1985	2 Teams		46	5	0	32	85.2	383	91	57	52	13	5	2	2	41	5	66	7	1	0	6	.000	0	4	5.46
1986	2 Teams		37	17	4	4	161.2	700	152	76	71	16	4	7	3	69	0	111	10	3	9	5	.643	1	0	3.95
7 YEARS			247	72	9	87	766	3301	731	367	337	78	39	26	15	310	31	484	39	4	39	40	.494	1	19	3.96
1983	Texas	A	8	8	2	0	59	237	50	15	14	2	2	1	2	17	0	24	1	0	5	2	.714	0	0	2.14
1983	Los Angeles	N	46	1	0	25	76	328	67	28	25	4	7	3	2	33	7	54	2	0	5	2	.714	0	8	2.96
1985	Texas	A	42	5	0	29	81.1	361	86	53	49	13	5	2	2	37	5	64	5	1	0	6	.000	0	4	5.42
1985	Philadelphia	N	4	0	0	3	4.1	22	5	4	3	0	0	0	0	4	0	2	2	0	0	0	.000	0	0	6.23
1986	Oakland	A	29	17	4	2	149.1	644	137	67	62	15	4	4	3	65	0	102	9	0	9	5	.643	1	0	3.74
1986	Philadelphia	N	8	0	0	2	12.1	56	15	9	9	1	0	3	0	4	0	9	1	3	0	0	.000	0	0	6.57

SAMMY STEWART

Pitches Right-handed, Bats Right-handed

Turns Age 33 in 1987, Born 10/28/54

			HOW MUCH HE PITCHED						WHAT HE GAVE UP											THE RESULTS					
Year	Team	League	G	GS	CG	GF	IP	BFP	H	R	ER	HR	SH	SF	HB	TBB	IBB	SO	WP	Bk	W	L	Pct	ShO	Sv	ERA
1978	Baltimore	A	2	2	0	0	11	46	10	5	4	0	1	0	0	3	0	11	1	0	1	1	.500	0	0	3.27
1979	Baltimore	A	31	3	1	10	118	498	96	47	46	11	5	3	5	71	4	71	5	1	8	5	.615	0	1	3.51
1980	Baltimore	A	33	3	2	20	119	507	103	51	47	9	4	3	2	60	8	78	5	0	7	7	.500	0	3	3.55
1981	Baltimore	A	29	3	0	18	112	463	89	33	29	8	4	3	3	57	4	57	1	2	4	8	.333	0	4	2.33
1982	Baltimore	A	38	12	1	16	139	607	140	68	64	15	5	6	2	62	3	69	3	1	10	9	.526	1	5	4.14
1983	Baltimore	A	58	1	0	21	144.1	624	138	60	58	7	6	3	1	67	4	95	9	0	9	4	.692	0	7	3.62
1984	Baltimore	A	60	0	0	39	93	395	81	42	34	7	6	5	1	47	7	56	5	1	7	4	.636	0	13	3.29
1985	Baltimore	A	56	1	0	36	129.2	557	117	60	52	15	9	5	1	66	10	77	5	1	5	7	.417	0	9	3.61
1986	Boston	A	27	0	0	5	63.2	295	64	33	31	7	1	5	0	48	2	47	5	1	4	1	.800	0	0	4.38
9 YEARS			334	25	4	165	929.2	3992	838	399	365	73	41	33	15	481	42	561	39	7	55	46	.545	1	42	3.53

DAVE STIEB

Pitches Right-handed, Bats Right-handed

Turns Age 30 in 1987, Born 07/22/57

			HOW MUCH HE PITCHED						WHAT HE GAVE UP											THE RESULTS					
Year	Team	League	G	GS	CG	GF	IP	BFP	H	R	ER	HR	SH	SF	HB	TBB	IBB	SO	WP	Bk	W	L	Pct	ShO	Sv	ERA
1979	Toronto	A	18	18	7	0	129	563	139	70	62	11	4	4	4	48	3	52	3	1	8	8	.500	1	0	4.33
1980	Toronto	A	34	32	14	0	243	1004	232	108	100	12	12	9	6	83	6	108	6	2	12	15	.444	4	0	3.70
1981	Toronto	A	25	25	11	0	184	748	148	70	65	10	5	7	11	61	2	89	1	2	11	10	.524	2	0	3.18
1982	Toronto	A	38	38	19	0	288.1	1187	271	116	104	27	3	5	3	75	4	141	3	1	17	14	.548	5	0	3.25
1983	Toronto	A	36	36	14	0	278	1141	223	105	94	21	6	9	14	93	6	187	5	1	17	12	.586	4	0	3.04
1984	Toronto	A	35	35	11	0	267	1085	215	87	84	19	8	6	11	88	1	198	2	0	16	8	.667	2	0	2.83
1985	Toronto	A	36	36	8	0	265	1087	206	89	73	22	14	2	9	96	3	167	4	1	14	13	.519	2	0	2.48
1986	Toronto	A	37	34	1	2	205	919	239	128	108	29	6	6	15	87	1	127	7	0	7	12	.368	1	1	4.74
8 YEARS			259	254	85	6	1859.1	7734	1673	773	690	151	65	46	75	631	26	1069	31	8	102	92	.526	21	1	3.34

KURT STILLWELL

Bats both Right and Left-handed, Throws Right-handed

Turns Age 22 in 1987, Born 06/04/65

					BATTING													BASERUNNING				PERCENTAGES		
Year	Team	League	G	AB	H	2B	3B	HR	(Hm | Rd)	TB	R	RBI	TBB	IBB	SO	HBP	SH	SF	SB	CS	SB%	GIDP	AVE	OBP	SLG
1986	Cincinnati	N	104	279	64	6	1	0	(0 | 0)	72	31	26	30	1	47	2	4	0	6	2	.75	5	.229	.309	.258

TIM STODDARD

Pitches Right-handed, Bats Right-handed   Turns Age 34 in 1987, Born 01/24/53

			HOW MUCH HE PITCHED				WHAT HE GAVE UP													THE RESULTS					
Year Team League	G	GS	CG	GF	IP	BFP	H	R	ER	HR	SH	SF	HB	TBB	IBB	SO	WP	Bk	W	L	Pct	ShO	Sv	ERA
1975 Chicago A	1	0	0	0	1	5	2	1	1	1	0	0	0	0	0	0	0	0	0	0	.000	0	0	9.00
1978 Baltimore A	8	0	0	3	18	84	22	17	12	3	1	0	2	8	1	14	2	0	0	1	.000	0	0	6.00
1979 Baltimore A	29	0	0	15	58	228	44	12	11	3	1	0	0	19	2	47	3	0	3	1	.750	0	3	1.71
1980 Baltimore A	64	0	0	52	86	352	72	27	24	2	2	2	1	38	1	64	3	0	5	3	.625	0	26	2.51
1981 Baltimore A	31	0	0	20	37	162	38	16	16	6	0	0	2	18	0	32	2	0	4	2	.667	0	7	3.89
1982 Baltimore A	50	0	0	38	56	249	53	26	25	4	3	3	1	29	6	42	2	0	3	4	.429	0	12	4.02
1983 Baltimore A	47	0	0	34	57.2	261	65	39	39	10	4	4	1	29	4	50	2	1	4	3	.571	0	9	6.09
1984 Chicago N	58	0	0	26	92	398	77	41	39	9	8	6	1	57	11	87	3	1	10	6	.625	0	7	3.82
1985 San Diego N	44	0	0	20	60	279	63	35	31	3	6	2	0	37	7	42	5	0	1	6	.143	0	1	4.65
1986 2 Teams	54	0	0	15	94.2	411	74	43	40	12	10	2	0	57	9	81	5	0	5	4	.556	0	3	3.80
10 YEARS	386	0	0	223	560.1	2429	510	257	238	53	35	19	8	292	41	459	27	2	35	30	.538	0	65	3.82
1986 New York A	24	0	0	6	49.1	208	41	23	21	6	6	2	0	23	3	34	3	0	4	1	.800	0	0	3.83
1986 San Diego N	30	0	0	9	45.1	203	33	20	19	6	4	0	0	34	6	47	2	0	1	3	.250	0	0	3.77

JEFF STONE

Bats Left-handed, Throws Right-handed   Turns Age 27 in 1987, Born 12/26/60

				BATTING														BASERUNNING				PERCENTAGES		
Year Team League	G	AB	H	2B	3B	HR	(Hm Rd)	TB	R	RBI	TBB	IBB	SO	HBP	SH	SF	SB	CS	SB%	GIDP	AVE	OBP	SLG
1983 Philadelphia N	9	4	3	0	2	0	(0 0)	7	2	3	0	0	1	0	0	0	4	0	1.00	1	.750	.750	.750
1984 Philadelphia N	51	185	67	4	6	1	(1 0)	86	27	15	9	0	26	2	1	2	27	5	.84	2	.362	.394	.465
1985 Philadelphia N	88	264	70	4	3	3	(2 1)	89	36	11	15	0	50	1	2	0	15	5	.75	3	.265	.307	.337
1986 Philadelphia N	82	249	69	6	4	6	(4 2)	101	32	19	20	0	52	4	2	0	19	6	.76	3	.277	.341	.406
4 YEARS	230	702	209	14	15	10	(7 3)	283	97	48	44	0	129	7	5	2	65	16	.80	8	.298	.344	.403

DARRYL STRAWBERRY

Bats Left-handed, Throws Left-handed   Turns Age 25 in 1987, Born 03/12/62

				BATTING														BASERUNNING				PERCENTAGES		
Year Team League	G	AB	H	2B	3B	HR	(Hm Rd)	TB	R	RBI	TBB	IBB	SO	HBP	SH	SF	SB	CS	SB%	GIDP	AVE	OBP	SLG
1983 New York N	122	420	108	15	7	26	(10 16)	215	63	74	47	9	128	4	0	2	19	6	.76	5	.257	.336	.512
1984 New York N	147	522	131	27	4	26	(8 18)	244	75	97	75	15	131	0	1	4	27	8	.77	8	.251	.343	.467
1985 New York N	111	393	109	15	4	29	(14 15)	219	78	79	73	13	96	1	0	3	26	11	.70	9	.277	.389	.557
1986 New York N	136	475	123	27	5	27	(11 16)	241	76	93	72	9	141	6	0	9	28	12	.70	4	.259	.358	.507
4 YEARS	516	1810	471	84	20	108	(43 65)	919	292	343	267	46	496	11	1	18	100	37	.73	26	.260	.356	.508

FRANKLIN STUBBS

Bats Left-handed, Throws Left-handed   Turns Age 27 in 1987, Born 10/21/60

				BATTING														BASERUNNING				PERCENTAGES		
Year Team League	G	AB	H	2B	3B	HR	(Hm Rd)	TB	R	RBI	TBB	IBB	SO	HBP	SH	SF	SB	CS	SB%	GIDP	AVE	OBP	SLG
1984 Los Angeles N	87	217	42	2	3	8	(4 4)	74	22	17	24	3	63	0	3	1	2	2	.50	0	.194	.273	.341
1985 Los Angeles N	10	9	2	0	0	0	(0 0)	2	0	2	0	0	3	0	0	0	0	0	.00	0	.222	.222	.222
1986 Los Angeles N	132	420	95	11	1	23	(12 11)	177	55	58	37	11	107	2	4	2	7	1	.88	9	.226	.291	.421
3 YEARS	229	646	139	13	4	31	(16 15)	253	77	77	61	14	173	2	7	3	9	3	.75	9	.215	.284	.392

MARC SULLIVAN

Bats Right-handed, Throws Right-handed   Turns Age 29 in 1987, Born 07/25/58

				BATTING														BASERUNNING				PERCENTAGES		
Year Team League	G	AB	H	2B	3B	HR	(Hm Rd)	TB	R	RBI	TBB	IBB	SO	HBP	SH	SF	SB	CS	SB%	GIDP	AVE	OBP	SLG
1982 Boston A	2	6	2	0	0	0	(0 0)	2	0	0	0	0	2	0	0	0	0	0	.00	0	.333	.333	.333
1984 Boston A	2	6	3	0	0	0	(0 0)	3	1	1	1	0	0	0	0	0	0	0	.00	0	.500	.571	.500
1985 Boston A	32	69	12	2	0	2	(2 0)	20	10	3	6	0	15	0	2	0	0	0	.00	0	.174	.240	.290
1986 Boston A	41	119	23	4	0	1	(1 0)	30	15	14	7	0	32	4	3	1	0	0	.00	1	.193	.260	.252
4 YEARS	77	200	40	6	0	3	(3 0)	55	26	18	14	0	49	4	5	1	0	0	.00	1	.200	.265	.275

JIM SUNDBERG

Bats Right-handed, Throws Right-handed   Turns Age 36 in 1987, Born 05/18/51

														BATTING									BASERUNNING				PERCENTAGES		
Year	Team	League	G	AB	H	2B	3B	HR	(Hm	Rd)	TB	R	RBI	TBB	IBB	SO	HBP	SH	SF	SB	CS	SB%	GIDP	AVE	OBP	SLG
1974	Texas	A	132	368	91	13	3	3	(1	2)	119	45	36	62	0	61	0	17	2	2	4	.33	16	.247	.354	.323
1975	Texas	A	155	472	94	9	0	6	(1	5)	121	45	36	51	0	77	4	13	0	3	1	.75	16	.199	.283	.256
1976	Texas	A	140	448	102	24	2	3	(2	1)	139	33	34	37	0	61	0	9	2	0	0	.00	15	.228	.285	.310
1977	Texas	A	149	453	132	20	3	6	(3	3)	176	61	65	53	0	77	2	20	5	2	3	.40	8	.291	.365	.389
1978	Texas	A	149	518	144	23	6	6	(0	6)	197	54	58	64	6	70	3	3	4	2	5	.29	18	.278	.358	.380
1979	Texas	A	150	495	136	23	4	5	(3	2)	182	50	64	51	5	51	5	5	5	3	3	.50	17	.275	.345	.368
1980	Texas	A	151	505	138	24	1	10	(5	5)	194	59	63	64	3	67	1	6	5	2	2	.50	15	.273	.353	.384
1981	Texas	A	102	339	94	17	2	3	(1	2)	124	42	28	50	6	48	1	3	3	2	5	.29	5	.277	.369	.366
1982	Texas	A	139	470	118	22	5	10	(3	7)	180	37	47	49	2	57	1	9	1	2	6	.25	11	.251	.322	.383
1983	Texas	A	131	378	76	14	0	2	(0	2)	96	30	28	35	0	64	2	7	1	0	0	.00	8	.201	.272	.254
1984	Milwaukee	A	110	348	91	19	4	7	(4	3)	139	43	43	38	2	63	0	6	3	1	1	.50	5	.261	.332	.399
1985	Kansas City	A	115	367	90	12	4	10	(2	8)	140	38	35	33	3	67	1	4	2	0	2	.00	9	.245	.308	.381
1986	Kansas City	A	140	429	91	9	1	12	(5	7)	138	41	42	57	1	91	0	2	3	1	1	.50	7	.212	.303	.322
13 YEARS			1763	5590	1397	229	35	83	(30	53)	1945	578	579	644	28	854	20	104	36	20	37	.35	150	.250	.328	.348

RICK SUTCLIFFE

Pitches Right-handed, Bats Left-handed   Turns Age 31 in 1987, Born 06/21/56

			HOW MUCH HE PITCHED						WHAT HE GAVE UP												THE RESULTS					
Year	Team	League	G	GS	CG	GF	IP	BFP	H	R	ER	HR	SH	SF	HB	TBB	IBB	SO	WP	Bk	W	L	Pct	ShO	Sv	ERA
1976	Los Angeles	N	1	1	0	0	5	17	2	0	0	0	0	0	0	1	0	3	0	0	0	0	.000	0	0	0.00
1978	Los Angeles	N	2	0	0	0	2	9	2	0	0	0	0	0	1	1	0	0	0	0	0	0	.000	0	0	0.00
1979	Los Angeles	N	39	30	5	2	242	1016	217	104	93	16	16	9	2	97	6	117	8	6	17	10	.630	1	0	3.46
1980	Los Angeles	N	42	10	1	19	110	491	122	73	68	10	4	3	1	55	2	59	4	5	3	9	.250	1	5	5.56
1981	Los Angeles	N	14	6	0	5	47	197	41	24	21	5	1	2	2	20	2	16	0	0	2	2	.500	0	0	4.02
1982	Cleveland	A	34	27	6	3	216	887	174	81	71	16	7	8	4	98	2	142	6	1	14	8	.636	1	1	2.96
1983	Cleveland	A	36	35	10	0	243.1	1061	251	131	116	23	8	9	6	102	5	160	7	3	17	11	.607	2	0	4.29
1984	2 Teams		35	35	9	0	244.2	1030	234	113	99	16	5	4	3	85	3	213	6	3	20	6	.769	3	0	3.64
1985	Chicago	N	20	20	6	0	130	549	119	51	46	12	3	4	3	44	3	102	6	0	8	8	.500	0	0	3.18
1986	Chicago	N	28	27	4	0	176.2	764	166	92	91	18	6	2	1	96	8	122	13	1	5	14	.263	1	0	4.64
10 YEARS			251	191	41	29	1416.2	6021	1328	669	605	116	50	41	23	599	31	934	50	19	86	68	.558	12	6	3.84
1984	Cleveland	A	15	15	2	0	94.1	428	111	60	54	7	4	3	2	46	3	58	3	1	4	5	.444	0	0	5.15
1984	Chicago	N	20	20	7	0	150.1	602	123	53	45	9	1	1	1	39	0	155	3	2	16	1	.941	3	0	2.69

DON SUTTON

Pitches Right-handed, Bats Right-handed   Turns Age 42 in 1987, Born 04/02/45

			HOW MUCH HE PITCHED						WHAT HE GAVE UP												THE RESULTS					
Year	Team	League	G	GS	CG	GF	IP	BFP	H	R	ER	HR	SH	SF	HB	TBB	IBB	SO	WP	Bk	W	L	Pct	ShO	Sv	ERA
1966	Los Angeles	N	37	35	6	0	226	916	192	82	75	19	14	6	3	52	6	209	5	0	12	12	.500	2	0	2.99
1967	Los Angeles	N	37	34	11	2	233	962	223	106	102	18	5	3	6	57	9	169	3	0	11	15	.423	3	1	3.94
1968	Los Angeles	N	35	27	7	6	208	847	179	64	60	6	10	3	2	59	14	162	4	3	11	15	.423	2	1	2.60
1969	Los Angeles	N	41	41	11	0	293	1226	269	123	113	25	11	10	3	91	6	217	9	1	17	18	.486	4	0	3.47
1970	Los Angeles	N	38	38	10	0	260	1109	251	127	118	38	7	7	10	78	7	201	9	2	15	13	.536	4	0	4.08
1971	Los Angeles	N	38	37	12	1	265	1059	231	85	75	10	18	9	5	55	5	194	5	0	17	12	.586	4	1	2.55
1972	Los Angeles	N	33	33	18	0	273	1061	186	78	63	18	5	4	4	63	1	207	9	1	19	9	.679	9	0	2.08
1973	Los Angeles	N	33	33	14	0	256	1006	196	78	69	18	5	3	5	56	4	200	10	1	18	10	.643	3	0	2.43
1974	Los Angeles	N	40	40	10	0	276	1148	241	111	99	22	9	2	6	80	2	179	4	2	19	9	.679	5	0	3.23
1975	Los Angeles	N	35	35	11	0	254	1031	202	87	81	17	14	4	3	62	5	175	7	0	16	13	.552	4	0	2.87
1976	Los Angeles	N	35	34	15	1	268	1093	231	98	91	22	15	6	3	82	6	161	4	1	21	10	.677	3	0	3.06
1977	Los Angeles	N	33	33	9	0	240	979	207	93	85	23	12	7	3	69	2	150	5	1	14	8	.636	3	0	3.19
1978	Los Angeles	N	34	34	12	0	238	990	228	109	94	29	14	4	5	54	7	154	6	0	15	11	.577	2	0	3.55
1979	Los Angeles	N	33	32	6	1	226	927	201	109	96	21	15	9	1	61	6	146	4	1	12	15	.444	1	1	3.82
1980	Los Angeles	N	32	31	4	1	212	833	163	56	52	20	8	3	2	47	5	128	0	1	13	5	.722	2	1	2.21
1981	Houston	N	23	23	6	0	159	624	132	51	46	6	13	6	1	29	3	104	0	1	11	9	.550	3	0	2.60
1982	2 Teams		34	34	6	0	249.2	1012	224	96	85	18	5	5	1	64	2	175	3	1	17	9	.654	1	0	3.06
1983	Milwaukee	A	31	31	4	0	220.1	925	209	100	100	21	8	7	5	54	2	134	2	0	8	13	.381	0	0	4.08
1984	Milwaukee	A	33	33	1	0	212.2	912	224	103	89	24	4	11	3	51	2	143	6	1	14	12	.538	0	0	3.77
1985	2 Teams		34	34	1	0	226	943	221	101	97	25	4	5	0	59	0	107	6	0	15	10	.600	1	0	3.86
1986	California	A	34	34	3	0	207	853	192	93	86	31	3	3	3	49	2	116	4	1	15	11	.577	1	0	3.74
21 YEARS			723	706	177	12	5002.2	20456	4402	1959	1776	427	199	117	74	1272	96	3431	103	17	310	239	.565	58	5	3.20
1982	Milwaukee	A	7	7	2	0	54.2	228	55	21	20	8	1	0	0	18	0	36	0	0	4	1	.800	1	0	3.29
1982	Houston	N	27	27	4	0	195	784	169	75	65	10	4	5	1	46	2	139	3	1	13	8	.619	0	0	3.00
1985	California	A	5	5	0	0	31.2	124	27	13	13	6	0	0	0	8	0	16	0	0	2	2	.500	0	0	3.69
1985	Oakland	A	29	29	1	0	194.1	819	194	88	84	19	4	5	0	51	0	91	6	0	13	8	.619	1	0	3.89

DALE SVEUM

Bats both Right and Left-handed, Throws Right-handed   Turns Age 24 in 1987, Born 11/23/63

														BATTING									BASERUNNING				PERCENTAGES		
Year	Team	League	G	AB	H	2B	3B	HR	(Hm	Rd)	TB	R	RBI	TBB	IBB	SO	HBP	SH	SF	SB	CS	SB%	GIDP	AVE	OBP	SLG
1986	Milwaukee	A	91	317	78	13	2	7	(4	3)	116	35	35	32	0	63	1	5	1	4	3	.57	7	.246	.316	.366

BILL SWIFT

Pitches Right-handed, Bats Right-handed   Turns Age 26 in 1987, Born 12/27/61

			HOW MUCH HE PITCHED								WHAT HE GAVE UP									THE RESULTS					
Year	Team	League	G	GS	CG	GF	IP	BFP	H	R	ER	HR	SH	SF	HB	TBB	IBB	SO	WP	Bk	W	L	Pct	ShO	Sv	ERA
1985	Seattle	A	23	21	0	0	120.2	532	131	71	64	8	6	3	5	48	5	55	5	3	6	10	.375	0	0	4.77
1986	Seattle	A	29	17	1	3	115.1	534	148	85	70	5	5	3	7	55	2	55	2	1	2	9	.182	0	0	5.46
2 YEARS			52	38	1	3	236	1066	279	156	134	13	11	6	12	103	7	110	7	4	8	19	.296	0	0	5.11

PAT TABLER

Bats Right-handed, Throws Right-handed   Turns Age 29 in 1987, Born 02/02/58

						BATTING														BASERUNNING				PERCENTAGES		
Year	Team	League	G	AB	H	2B	3B	HR	(Hm	Rd)	TB	R	RBI	TBB	IBB	SO	HBP	SH	SF	SB	CS	SB%	GIDP	AVE	OBP	SLG
1981	Chicago	N	35	101	19	3	1	1	(1	0)	27	11	5	13	0	26	0	3	0	0	1	.00	4	.188	.281	.267
1982	Chicago	N	25	85	20	4	2	1	(0	1)	31	9	7	6	0	20	1	0	2	0	0	.00	3	.235	.287	.365
1983	Cleveland	A	124	430	125	23	5	6	(3	3)	176	56	65	56	1	63	1	0	5	2	4	.33	18	.291	.370	.409
1984	Cleveland	A	144	473	137	21	3	10	(5	5)	194	66	68	47	2	62	3	0	5	3	1	.75	16	.290	.354	.410
1985	Cleveland	A	117	404	111	18	3	5	(5	0)	150	47	59	27	2	55	2	2	3	0	6	.00	15	.275	.321	.371
1986	Cleveland	A	130	473	154	29	2	6	(5	1)	205	61	48	29	3	75	3	2	1	3	1	.75	11	.326	.368	.433
6 YEARS			575	1966	566	98	16	29	(19	10)	783	250	252	178	8	301	10	7	16	8	13	.38	67	.288	.347	.398

FRANK TANANA

Pitches Left-handed, Bats Left-handed   Turns Age 34 in 1987, Born 07/03/53

			HOW MUCH HE PITCHED								WHAT HE GAVE UP									THE RESULTS					
Year	Team	League	G	GS	CG	GF	IP	BFP	H	R	ER	HR	SH	SF	HB	TBB	IBB	SO	WP	Bk	W	L	Pct	ShO	Sv	ERA
1973	California	A	4	4	2	0	26	0	20	11	9	2	0	0	0	8	0	22	2	0	2	2	.500	1	0	3.12
1974	California	A	39	35	12	2	269	1127	262	104	93	27	10	4	8	77	4	180	4	2	14	19	.424	4	0	3.11
1975	California	A	34	33	16	1	257	1029	211	80	75	21	13	4	7	73	6	269	8	1	16	9	.640	5	0	2.63
1976	California	A	34	34	23	0	288	1142	212	88	78	24	14	3	9	73	5	261	5	0	19	10	.655	2	0	2.44
1977	California	A	31	31	20	0	241	973	201	72	68	19	8	7	12	61	2	205	8	1	15	9	.625	7	0	2.54
1978	California	A	33	33	10	0	239	1014	239	108	97	26	8	10	9	60	7	137	5	8	18	12	.600	4	0	3.65
1979	California	A	18	17	2	0	90	382	93	44	39	9	1	2	2	25	0	46	6	1	7	5	.583	1	0	3.90
1980	California	A	32	31	7	1	204	870	223	107	94	18	8	4	8	45	0	113	3	1	11	12	.478	0	0	4.15
1981	Boston	A	24	23	5	0	141	596	142	70	63	17	9	4	4	43	4	78	2	0	4	10	.286	2	0	4.02
1982	Texas	A	30	30	7	0	194.1	832	199	102	91	16	13	4	7	55	10	87	0	1	7	18	.280	0	0	4.21
1983	Texas	A	29	22	3	1	159.1	667	144	70	56	14	7	3	7	49	5	108	6	1	7	9	.438	0	0	3.16
1984	Texas	A	35	35	9	0	246.1	1055	234	117	89	30	7	5	6	81	3	141	12	4	15	15	.500	1	0	3.25
1985	2 Teams		33	33	4	0	215	907	220	112	102	28	5	8	3	57	8	159	5	1	12	14	.462	0	0	4.27
1986	Detroit	A	32	31	3	1	188.1	812	196	95	87	23	8	5	3	65	9	119	7	1	12	9	.571	1	0	4.16
14 YEARS			408	392	123	6	2758.1	11406	2596	1180	1041	274	111	63	85	772	63	1925	73	22	159	153	.510	28	0	3.40
1985	Detroit	A	20	20	4	0	137.1	567	131	59	51	13	3	4	2	34	6	107	2	1	10	7	.588	0	0	3.34
1985	Texas	A	13	13	0	0	77.2	340	89	53	51	15	2	4	1	23	2	52	3	0	2	7	.222	0	0	5.91

DANNY TARTABULL

Bats Right-handed, Throws Right-handed   Turns Age 25 in 1987, Born 10/30/62

						BATTING														BASERUNNING				PERCENTAGES		
Year	Team	League	G	AB	H	2B	3B	HR	(Hm	Rd)	TB	R	RBI	TBB	IBB	SO	HBP	SH	SF	SB	CS	SB%	GIDP	AVE	OBP	SLG
1984	Seattle	A	10	20	6	1	0	2	(1	1)	13	3	7	2	0	3	1	0	1	0	0	.00	0	.300	.375	.650
1985	Seattle	A	19	61	20	7	1	1	(0	1)	32	8	7	8	0	14	0	0	0	1	0	1.00	1	.328	.406	.525
1986	Seattle	A	137	511	138	25	6	25	(13	12)	250	76	96	61	2	157	1	2	3	4	8	.33	10	.270	.347	.489
3 YEARS			166	592	164	33	7	28	(14	14)	295	87	110	71	2	174	2	2	4	5	8	.38	11	.277	.354	.498

KENT TEKULVE

Pitches Right-handed, Bats Right-handed   Turns Age 40 in 1987, Born 03/05/47

			HOW MUCH HE PITCHED								WHAT HE GAVE UP									THE RESULTS					
Year	Team	League	G	GS	CG	GF	IP	BFP	H	R	ER	HR	SH	SF	HB	TBB	IBB	SO	WP	Bk	W	L	Pct	ShO	Sv	ERA
1974	Pittsburgh	N	8	0	0	5	9	44	12	6	6	1	1	2	1	5	2	6	0	0	1	1	.500	0	0	6.00
1975	Pittsburgh	N	34	0	0	9	56	232	43	20	14	2	6	2	1	23	6	28	3	0	1	2	.333	0	5	2.25
1976	Pittsburgh	N	64	0	0	33	103	409	91	30	28	3	5	1	0	25	7	68	0	0	5	3	.625	0	9	2.45
1977	Pittsburgh	N	72	0	0	35	103	422	89	41	35	5	6	5	1	33	6	59	2	1	10	1	.909	0	7	3.06
1978	Pittsburgh	N	91	0	0	65	135	573	115	44	35	5	7	4	2	55	18	77	5	0	8	7	.533	0	31	2.33
1979	Pittsburgh	N	94	0	0	67	134	550	109	46	41	5	7	2	2	49	20	75	4	0	10	8	.556	0	31	2.75
1980	Pittsburgh	N	78	0	0	57	93	407	96	39	35	6	6	0	1	40	16	47	0	0	8	12	.400	0	21	3.39
1981	Pittsburgh	N	45	0	0	27	65	268	61	19	18	1	4	2	1	17	5	34	1	0	5	5	.500	0	3	2.49
1982	Pittsburgh	N	85	0	0	64	128.2	541	113	47	41	7	10	6	3	46	23	66	1	0	12	8	.600	0	20	2.87
1983	Pittsburgh	N	76	0	0	56	99	398	78	27	18	1	9	4	0	36	12	52	1	0	7	5	.583	0	18	1.64
1984	Pittsburgh	N	72	0	0	51	88	370	86	30	26	4	6	2	1	33	12	36	0	0	3	9	.250	0	13	2.66
1985	2 Teams		61	0	0	42	75.2	327	74	35	30	5	6	2	2	30	10	40	0	0	4	10	.286	0	14	3.57
1986	Philadelphia	N	73	0	0	34	110	446	99	35	31	2	4	4	0	25	10	57	3	1	11	5	.688	0	2	2.54
13 YEARS			853	0	0	545	1199.1	4987	1066	419	358	47	77	36	15	417	147	645	20	2	85	76	.528	0	176	2.69
1985	Philadelphia	N	58	0	0	41	72.1	306	67	28	24	4	5	2	2	25	9	36	0	0	4	10	.286	0	14	2.99
1985	Pittsburgh	N	3	0	0	1	3.1	21	7	7	6	1	1	0	0	5	1	4	0	0	0	0	.000	0	0	16.20

GARRY TEMPLETON

Bats both Right and Left-handed, Throws Right-handed   Turns Age 31 in 1987, Born 03/24/56

							BATTING													BASERUNNING				PERCENTAGES		
Year	Team	League	G	AB	H	2B	3B	HR	(Hm	Rd)	TB	R	RBI	TBB	IBB	SO	HBP	SH	SF	SB	CS	SB%	GIDP	AVE	OBP	SLG
1976	St Louis	N	53	213	62	8	2	1	(1	0)	77	32	17	7	0	33	1	2	2	11	7	.61	1	.291	.314	.362
1977	St Louis	N	153	621	200	19	18	8	(2	6)	279	94	79	15	3	70	1	2	5	28	24	.54	9	.322	.336	.449
1978	St Louis	N	155	647	181	31	13	2	(1	1)	244	82	47	22	3	87	1	2	3	34	11	.76	7	.280	.303	.377
1979	St Louis	N	154	672	211	32	19	9	(2	7)	308	105	62	18	4	91	1	2	3	26	10	.72	8	.314	.331	.458
1980	St Louis	N	118	504	161	19	9	4	(1	3)	210	83	43	18	6	43	0	1	1	31	15	.67	13	.319	.342	.417
1981	St Louis	N	80	333	96	16	8	1	(1	0)	131	47	33	14	3	55	0	1	2	8	12	.40	4	.288	.315	.393
1982	San Diego	N	141	563	139	25	8	6	(2	4)	198	76	64	26	7	82	1	6	5	27	16	.63	19	.247	.279	.352
1983	San Diego	N	126	460	121	20	2	3	(1	2)	154	39	40	21	7	57	0	7	2	16	6	.73	16	.263	.294	.335
1984	San Diego	N	148	493	127	19	3	2	(2	0)	158	40	35	39	23	81	1	0	2	8	3	.73	10	.258	.312	.320
1985	San Diego	N	148	546	154	30	2	6	(0	6)	206	63	55	41	24	88	1	5	3	16	6	.73	5	.282	.332	.377
1986	San Diego	N	147	510	126	21	2	2	(1	1)	157	42	44	35	21	86	1	1	2	10	5	.67	12	.247	.296	.308
11 YEARS			1423	5562	1578	240	86	44	(14	30)	2122	703	519	256	101	773	8	29	30	215	115	.65	104	.284	.315	.382

WALT TERRELL

Pitches Right-handed, Bats Left-handed   Turns Age 29 in 1987, Born 05/11/58

			HOW MUCH HE PITCHED						WHAT HE GAVE UP											THE RESULTS					
Year	Team	League	G	GS	CG	GF	IP	BFP	H	R	ER	HR	SH	SF	HB	TBB	IBB	SO	WP	Bk	W	L	Pct	ShO	Sv	ERA
1982	New York	N	3	3	0	0	21	97	22	12	8	2	1	0	0	14	2	8	1	1	0	3	.000	0	0	3.43
1983	New York	N	21	20	4	1	133.2	561	123	57	53	7	9	5	2	55	2	59	5	1	8	8	.500	2	0	3.57
1984	New York	N	33	33	3	0	215	926	232	99	84	16	11	8	4	80	1	114	6	0	11	12	.478	1	0	3.52
1985	Detroit	A	34	34	5	0	229	983	221	107	98	9	11	7	4	95	5	130	5	0	15	10	.600	3	0	3.85
1986	Detroit	A	34	33	9	1	217.1	918	199	116	110	30	2	3	3	98	5	93	5	0	15	12	.556	2	0	4.56
5 YEARS			125	123	21	2	816	3485	797	391	353	64	34	23	13	342	15	404	22	2	49	45	.521	8	0	3.89

SCOTT TERRY

Pitches Right-handed, Bats Right-handed   Turns Age 28 in 1987, Born 11/11/59

			HOW MUCH HE PITCHED						WHAT HE GAVE UP											THE RESULTS					
Year	Team	League	G	GS	CG	GF	IP	BFP	H	R	ER	HR	SH	SF	HB	TBB	IBB	SO	WP	Bk	W	L	Pct	ShO	Sv	ERA
1986	Cincinnati	N	28	3	0	7	55.2	258	66	40	38	8	5	1	0	32	3	32	2	0	1	2	.333	0	0	6.14

MICKEY TETTLETON

Bats both Right and Left-handed, Throws Right-handed   Turns Age 27 in 1987, Born 09/16/60

							BATTING													BASERUNNING				PERCENTAGES		
Year	Team	League	G	AB	H	2B	3B	HR	(Hm	Rd)	TB	R	RBI	TBB	IBB	SO	HBP	SH	SF	SB	CS	SB%	GIDP	AVE	OBP	SLG
1984	Oakland	A	33	76	20	2	1	1	(1	0)	27	10	5	11	0	21	0	0	1	0	0	.00	3	.263	.352	.355
1985	Oakland	A	78	211	53	12	0	3	(1	2)	74	23	15	28	0	59	2	5	0	2	2	.50	6	.251	.344	.351
1986	Oakland	A	90	211	43	9	0	10	(4	6)	82	26	35	39	0	51	1	7	4	7	1	.88	3	.204	.325	.389
3 YEARS			201	498	116	23	1	14	(6	8)	183	59	55	78	0	131	3	12	5	9	3	.75	12	.233	.337	.367

TIM TEUFEL

Bats Right-handed, Throws Right-handed   Turns Age 29 in 1987, Born 07/07/58

							BATTING													BASERUNNING				PERCENTAGES		
Year	Team	League	G	AB	H	2B	3B	HR	(Hm	Rd)	TB	R	RBI	TBB	IBB	SO	HBP	SH	SF	SB	CS	SB%	GIDP	AVE	OBP	SLG
1983	Minnesota	A	21	78	24	7	1	3	(3	0)	42	11	6	2	0	8	2	0	0	0	0	.00	1	.308	.325	.538
1984	Minnesota	A	157	568	149	30	3	14	(9	5)	227	76	61	76	8	73	2	2	4	1	3	.25	18	.262	.349	.400
1985	Minnesota	A	138	434	113	24	3	10	(6	4)	173	58	50	48	2	70	3	7	4	4	2	.67	14	.260	.335	.399
1986	New York	N	93	279	69	20	1	4	(2	2)	103	35	31	32	1	42	1	3	3	1	2	.33	6	.247	.324	.369
4 YEARS			409	1359	355	81	8	31	(20	11)	545	180	148	158	11	193	6	14	11	6	7	.46	39	.261	.338	.401

BOB TEWKSBURY

Pitches Right-handed, Bats Right-handed   Turns Age 27 in 1987, Born 11/30/60

			HOW MUCH HE PITCHED						WHAT HE GAVE UP											THE RESULTS					
Year	Team	League	G	GS	CG	GF	IP	BFP	H	R	ER	HR	SH	SF	HB	TBB	IBB	SO	WP	Bk	W	L	Pct	ShO	Sv	ERA
1986	New York	A	23	20	2	0	130.1	558	144	58	48	8	4	7	5	31	0	49	3	2	9	5	.643	0	0	3.31

BOB THIGPEN

Pitches Right-handed, Bats Right-handed   Turns Age 24 in 1987, Born 07/17/63

			HOW MUCH HE PITCHED						WHAT HE GAVE UP											THE RESULTS					
Year	Team	League	G	GS	CG	GF	IP	BFP	H	R	ER	HR	SH	SF	HB	TBB	IBB	SO	WP	Bk	W	L	Pct	ShO	Sv	ERA
1986	Chicago	A	20	0	0	14	35.2	142	26	7	7	1	1	1	1	12	0	20	0	0	2	0	1.000	0	7	1.77

ANDRES THOMAS

Bats Right-handed, Throws Right-handed   Turns Age 24 in 1987, Born 11/10/63

Year	Team	League	G	AB	H	2B	3B	HR	(Hm	Rd)	TB	R	RBI	TBB	IBB	SO	HBP	SH	SF	SB	CS	SB%	GIDP	AVE	OBP	SLG
1985	Atlanta	N	15	18	5	0	0	0	(0	0)	5	6	2	0	0	2	0	1	0	0	0	.00	1	.278	.278	.278
1986	Atlanta	N	102	323	81	17	2	6	(1	5)	120	26	32	8	2	49	0	2	2	4	6	.40	14	.251	.267	.372
2 YEARS			117	341	86	17	2	6	(1	5)	125	32	34	8	2	51	0	3	2	4	6	.40	15	.252	.268	.367

GORMAN THOMAS

Bats Right-handed, Throws Right-handed   Turns Age 37 in 1987, Born 12/12/50

Year	Team	League	G	AB	H	2B	3B	HR	(Hm	Rd)	TB	R	RBI	TBB	IBB	SO	HBP	SH	SF	SB	CS	SB%	GIDP	AVE	OBP	SLG
1973	Milwaukee	A	59	155	29	7	1	2	(2	0)	44	16	11	14	1	61	0	3	0	5	5	.50	2	.187	.254	.284
1974	Milwaukee	A	17	46	12	4	0	2	(1	1)	22	10	11	8	0	15	0	1	2	4	0	1.00	2	.261	.357	.478
1975	Milwaukee	A	121	240	43	12	2	10	(5	5)	89	34	28	31	0	84	0	4	5	4	2	.67	4	.179	.268	.371
1976	Milwaukee	A	99	227	45	9	2	8	(4	4)	82	27	36	31	1	67	1	5	3	2	3	.40	7	.198	.294	.361
1978	Milwaukee	A	137	452	111	24	1	32	(19	13)	233	70	86	73	4	133	2	6	3	3	4	.43	6	.246	.351	.515
1979	Milwaukee	A	156	557	136	29	0	45	(22	23)	300	97	123	98	6	175	2	5	6	1	5	.17	8	.244	.356	.539
1980	Milwaukee	A	162	628	150	26	3	38	(18	20)	296	78	105	58	6	170	2	3	6	8	5	.62	7	.239	.303	.471
1981	Milwaukee	A	103	363	94	22	0	21	(8	13)	179	54	65	50	8	85	2	0	5	4	5	.44	6	.259	.348	.493
1982	Milwaukee	A	158	567	139	29	1	39	(19	20)	287	96	112	84	5	143	4	5	6	3	7	.30	10	.245	.343	.506
1983	2 Teams		152	535	112	23	1	22	(10	12)	203	72	69	80	2	148	2	4	8	10	4	.71	13	.209	.310	.379
1984	Seattle	A	35	108	17	3	0	1	(0	1)	23	6	13	28	0	27	1	0	6	0	3	.00	3	.157	.322	.213
1985	Seattle	A	135	484	104	16	1	32	(16	16)	218	76	87	84	6	126	1	2	3	3	2	.60	11	.215	.330	.450
1986	2 Teams		101	315	59	8	1	16	(7	9)	117	45	36	58	4	105	1	3	0	3	4	.43	5	.187	.316	.371
13 YEARS			1435	4677	1051	212	13	268	(131	137)	2093	681	782	697	41	1339	18	41	53	50	49	.51	84	.225	.324	.448
1983	Cleveland	A	106	371	82	17	0	17	(8	9)	150	51	51	57	2	98	1	2	6	8	3	.73	7	.221	.322	.404
1983	Milwaukee	A	46	164	30	6	1	5	(2	3)	53	21	18	23	0	50	1	2	2	2	1	.67	6	.183	.284	.323
1986	Milwaukee	A	44	145	26	4	1	6	(2	4)	50	21	10	31	1	50	0	2	0	2	2	.50	3	.179	.324	.345
1986	Seattle	A	57	170	33	4	0	10	(5	5)	67	24	26	27	3	55	1	1	0	1	2	.33	2	.194	.308	.394

MILT THOMPSON

Bats Left-handed, Throws Right-handed   Turns Age 28 in 1987, Born 01/05/59

Year	Team	League	G	AB	H	2B	3B	HR	(Hm	Rd)	TB	R	RBI	TBB	IBB	SO	HBP	SH	SF	SB	CS	SB%	GIDP	AVE	OBP	SLG
1984	Atlanta	N	25	99	30	1	0	2	(0	2)	37	16	4	11	1	11	0	1	0	14	2	.88	1	.303	.373	.374
1985	Atlanta	N	73	182	55	7	2	0	(0	0)	66	17	6	7	0	36	3	1	0	9	4	.69	1	.302	.339	.363
1986	Philadelphia	N	96	299	75	7	1	6	(4	2)	102	38	23	26	1	62	1	4	2	19	4	.83	4	.251	.311	.341
3 YEARS			194	580	160	15	3	8	(4	4)	205	71	33	44	2	109	4	6	2	42	10	.81	6	.276	.330	.353

ROB THOMPSON

Bats Right-handed, Throws Right-handed   Turns Age 25 in 1987, Born 05/10/62

Year	Team	League	G	AB	H	2B	3B	HR	(Hm	Rd)	TB	R	RBI	TBB	IBB	SO	HBP	SH	SF	SB	CS	SB%	GIDP	AVE	OBP	SLG
1986	San Francisco	N	149	549	149	27	3	7	(0	7)	203	73	47	42	0	112	5	18	1	12	15	.44	11	.271	.328	.370

DICKIE THON

Bats Right-handed, Throws Right-handed   Turns Age 29 in 1987, Born 06/20/58

Year	Team	League	G	AB	H	2B	3B	HR	(Hm	Rd)	TB	R	RBI	TBB	IBB	SO	HBP	SH	SF	SB	CS	SB%	GIDP	AVE	OBP	SLG
1979	California	A	35	56	19	3	0	0	(0	0)	22	6	8	5	0	10	0	1	0	0	0	.00	2	.339	.393	.393
1980	California	A	80	267	68	12	2	0	(0	0)	84	32	15	10	0	28	1	5	2	7	5	.58	5	.255	.282	.315
1981	Houston	N	49	95	26	6	0	0	(0	0)	32	13	3	9	1	13	0	1	0	6	1	.86	3	.274	.337	.337
1982	Houston	N	136	496	137	31	10	3	(1	2)	197	73	36	37	2	48	1	5	1	37	8	.82	4	.276	.327	.397
1983	Houston	N	154	619	177	28	9	20	(4	16)	283	81	79	54	10	73	2	3	8	34	16	.68	12	.286	.341	.457
1984	Houston	N	5	17	6	0	1	0	(0	0)	8	3	1	0	0	4	1	0	0	0	1	.00	1	.353	.389	.471
1985	Houston	N	84	251	63	6	1	6	(3	3)	89	26	29	18	4	50	0	1	2	8	3	.73	2	.251	.299	.355
1986	Houston	N	106	278	69	13	1	3	(0	3)	93	24	21	29	5	49	0	1	1	6	5	.55	4	.248	.318	.335
8 YEARS			649	2079	565	99	24	32	(8	24)	808	258	192	162	22	275	5	17	14	98	39	.72	37	.272	.324	.389

ANDRE THORNTON

Bats Right-handed, Throws Right-handed   Turns Age 38 in 1987, Born 08/13/49

Year	Team	League	G	AB	H	2B	3B	HR	(Hm	Rd)	TB	R	RBI	TBB	IBB	SO	HBP	SH	SF	SB	CS	SB%	GIDP	AVE	OBP	SLG
1973	Chicago	N	17	35	7	3	0	0	(0	0)	10	3	2	7	0	9	0	0	0	0	0	.00	1	.200	.333	.286
1974	Chicago	N	107	303	79	16	4	10	(6	4)	133	41	46	48	4	50	4	1	1	2	1	.67	6	.261	.368	.439
1975	Chicago	N	120	372	109	21	4	18	(8	10)	192	70	60	88	12	63	4	3	6	3	2	.60	6	.293	.428	.516
1976	2 Teams	A	96	268	52	11	2	11	(5	6)	100	28	38	48	1	46	5	1	5	4	1	.80	1	.194	.322	.373
1977	Cleveland	A	131	433	114	20	5	28	(19	9)	228	77	70	70	1	82	11	1	2	3	4	.43	9	.263	.378	.527
1978	Cleveland	A	145	508	133	22	4	33	(16	17)	262	97	105	93	4	72	6	2	8	4	7	.36	17	.262	.377	.516
1979	Cleveland	A	143	515	120	31	1	26	(17	9)	231	89	93	90	2	93	4	1	7	5	4	.56	8	.233	.347	.449
1981	Cleveland	A	69	226	54	12	0	6	(2	4)	84	22	30	23	1	37	0	2	5	3	1	.75	15	.239	.303	.372
1982	Cleveland	A	161	589	161	26	1	32	(16	16)	285	90	116	109	18	81	2	3	5	6	7	.46	21	.273	.386	.484
1983	Cleveland	A	141	508	143	27	1	17	(6	11)	223	78	77	87	14	72	2	0	8	4	2	.67	10	.281	.383	.439
1984	Cleveland	A	155	587	159	26	0	33	(19	14)	284	91	99	91	11	79	2	0	9	6	5	.55	9	.271	.366	.484
1985	Cleveland	A	124	461	109	13	0	22	(12	10)	188	49	88	47	1	75	0	0	6	3	2	.60	14	.236	.304	.408
1986	Cleveland	A	120	401	92	14	0	17	(12	5)	157	49	66	65	0	67	1	0	8	4	1	.80	11	.229	.333	.392
13 YEARS			1529	5206	1332	242	22	253	(138	115)	2377	784	890	866	69	826	41	14	70	47	37	.56	128	.256	.362	.457
1976	Chicago	N	27	85	17	6	0	2	(1	1)	29	8	2	20	1	14	2	0	2	2	0	1.00	0	.200	.358	.341
1976	Montreal	N	69	183	35	5	2	9	(4	5)	71	20	36	28	0	32	3	1	3	2	1	.67	1	.191	.304	.388

MARK THURMOND

Pitches Left-handed, Bats Left-handed   Turns Age 31 in 1987, Born 09/12/56

			HOW MUCH HE PITCHED						WHAT HE GAVE UP												THE RESULTS					
Year	Team	League	G	GS	CG	GF	IP	BFP	H	R	ER	HR	SH	SF	HB	TBB	IBB	SO	WP	Bk	W	L	Pct	ShO	Sv	ERA
1983	San Diego	N	21	18	2	2	115.1	466	104	40	34	7	9	3	2	33	2	49	0	1	7	3	.700	1	0	2.65
1984	San Diego	N	32	29	1	1	178.2	750	174	70	59	12	11	3	0	55	3	57	2	2	14	8	.636	1	0	2.97
1985	San Diego	N	36	23	1	4	138.1	592	154	70	61	9	12	4	3	44	5	57	0	0	7	11	.389	1	2	3.97
1986	2 Teams		42	19	2	5	122.1	537	140	71	62	14	7	3	0	44	7	49	1	1	7	8	.467	1	3	4.56
4 YEARS			131	89	6	12	554.2	2345	572	251	216	42	39	13	5	176	17	212	3	4	35	30	.538	3	5	3.50
1986	Detroit	A	25	4	0	5	51.2	209	44	13	11	7	3	1	0	17	2	17	1	0	4	1	.800	0	3	1.92
1986	San Diego	N	17	15	2	0	70.2	328	96	58	51	7	4	2	0	27	5	32	0	1	3	7	.300	1	0	6.50

JAY TIBBS

Pitches Right-handed, Bats Right-handed   Turns Age 25 in 1987, Born 01/04/62

			HOW MUCH HE PITCHED						WHAT HE GAVE UP												THE RESULTS					
Year	Team	League	G	GS	CG	GF	IP	BFP	H	R	ER	HR	SH	SF	HB	TBB	IBB	SO	WP	Bk	W	L	Pct	ShO	Sv	ERA
1984	Cincinnati	N	14	14	3	0	100.2	403	87	34	32	4	5	0	0	33	1	40	2	0	6	2	.750	1	0	2.86
1985	Cincinnati	N	35	34	5	0	218	918	216	111	95	14	11	8	0	83	10	98	12	1	10	16	.385	2	0	3.92
1986	Montreal	N	35	31	3	2	190.1	797	181	96	84	12	13	4	3	70	3	117	7	2	7	9	.438	2	0	3.97
3 YEARS			84	79	11	2	509	2118	484	241	211	30	29	12	3	186	14	255	21	3	23	27	.460	5	0	3.73

WAYNE TOLLESON

Bats both Right and Left-handed, Throws Right-handed   Turns Age 32 in 1987, Born 11/22/55

Year	Team	League	G	AB	H	2B	3B	HR	(Hm	Rd)	TB	R	RBI	TBB	IBB	SO	HBP	SH	SF	SB	CS	SB%	GIDP	AVE	OBP	SLG
1981	Texas	A	14	24	4	0	0	0	(0	0)	4	6	1	1	0	5	0	0	0	2	0	1.00	0	.167	.200	.167
1982	Texas	A	38	70	8	1	0	0	(0	0)	9	6	2	5	0	14	0	3	0	1	1	.50	1	.114	.173	.129
1983	Texas	A	134	470	122	13	2	3	(2	1)	148	64	20	40	0	68	2	7	2	33	9	.79	8	.260	.319	.315
1984	Texas	A	118	338	72	9	2	0	(0	0)	85	35	9	27	0	47	3	9	1	22	4	.85	12	.213	.276	.251
1985	Texas	A	123	323	101	9	5	1	(0	1)	123	45	18	21	0	46	0	9	2	21	12	.64	6	.313	.353	.381
1986	2 Teams	A	141	475	126	16	5	3	(0	0)	161	61	43	52	0	76	2	13	4	17	10	.63	6	.265	.338	.339
6 YEARS			568	1700	433	48	14	7	(2	2)	530	217	93	146	0	256	7	41	9	96	36	.73	33	.255	.315	.312
1986	Chicago	A	81	260	65	7	3	3	(0	0)	87	39	29	38	0	43	0	9	3	13	6	.68	3	.250	.342	.335
1986	New York	A	60	215	61	9	2	0	(0	0)	74	22	14	14	0	33	2	4	1	4	4	.50	3	.284	.332	.344

JIM TRABER

Bats Left-handed, Throws Left-handed   Turns Age 26 in 1987, Born 12/26/61

Year	Team	League	G	AB	H	2B	3B	HR	(Hm	Rd)	TB	R	RBI	TBB	IBB	SO	HBP	SH	SF	SB	CS	SB%	GIDP	AVE	OBP	SLG
1984	Baltimore	A	10	21	5	0	0	0	(0	0)	5	3	2	2	0	4	0	0	1	0	0	.00	1	.238	.292	.238
1986	Baltimore	A	65	212	54	7	0	13	(9	4)	100	28	44	18	2	31	5	0	5	0	0	.00	6	.255	.321	.472
2 YEARS			75	233	59	7	0	13	(9	4)	105	31	46	20	2	35	5	0	6	0	0	.00	7	.253	.318	.451

ALAN TRAMMELL

Bats Right-handed, Throws Right-handed   Turns Age 29 in 1987, Born 02/21/58

								BATTING												BASERUNNING				PERCENTAGES		
Year	Team	League	G	AB	H	2B	3B	HR	(Hm	Rd)	TB	R	RBI	TBB	IBB	SO	HBP	SH	SF	SB	CS	SB%	GIDP	AVE	OBP	SLG
1977	Detroit	A	19	43	8	0	0	0	(0	0)	8	6	0	4	0	12	0	1	0	0	0	.00	1	.186	.255	.186
1978	Detroit	A	139	448	120	14	6	2	(0	2)	152	49	34	45	0	56	2	6	3	3	1	.75	12	.268	.335	.339
1979	Detroit	A	142	460	127	11	4	6	(4	2)	164	68	50	43	0	55	0	12	5	17	14	.55	6	.276	.335	.357
1980	Detroit	A	146	560	168	21	5	9	(5	4)	226	107	65	69	2	63	3	13	7	12	12	.50	10	.300	.376	.404
1981	Detroit	A	105	392	101	15	3	2	(2	0)	128	52	31	49	2	31	3	16	3	10	3	.77	10	.258	.342	.327
1982	Detroit	A	157	489	126	34	3	9	(5	4)	193	66	57	52	0	47	0	9	6	19	8	.70	5	.258	.325	.395
1983	Detroit	A	142	505	161	31	2	14	(8	6)	238	83	66	57	2	64	0	15	4	30	10	.75	7	.319	.385	.471
1984	Detroit	A	139	555	174	34	5	14	(7	7)	260	85	69	60	2	63	3	6	2	19	13	.59	8	.314	.382	.468
1985	Detroit	A	149	605	156	21	7	13	(7	6)	230	79	57	50	4	71	2	11	9	14	5	.74	6	.258	.312	.380
1986	Detroit	A	151	574	159	33	7	21	(8	13)	269	107	75	59	4	57	5	11	4	25	12	.68	7	.277	.347	.469
10 YEARS			1289	4631	1300	214	42	90	(46	44)	1868	702	504	488	16	519	18	100	43	149	78	.66	72	.281	.349	.403

ALEX TREVINO

Bats Right-handed, Throws Right-handed   Turns Age 30 in 1987, Born 08/26/57

								BATTING												BASERUNNING				PERCENTAGES		
Year	Team	League	G	AB	H	2B	3B	HR	(Hm	Rd)	TB	R	RBI	TBB	IBB	SO	HBP	SH	SF	SB	CS	SB%	GIDP	AVE	OBP	SLG
1978	New York	N	6	12	3	0	0	0	(0	0)	3	3	0	1	0	2	0	0	0	0	0	.00	1	.250	.308	.250
1979	New York	N	79	207	56	11	1	0	(0	0)	69	24	20	20	2	27	1	4	0	2	2	.50	8	.271	.338	.333
1980	New York	N	106	355	91	11	2	0	(0	0)	106	26	37	13	1	41	1	2	5	0	3	.00	11	.256	.281	.299
1981	New York	N	56	149	39	2	0	0	(0	0)	41	17	10	13	0	19	1	1	1	3	0	1.00	4	.262	.323	.275
1982	Cincinnati	N	120	355	89	10	3	1	(0	1)	108	24	33	34	11	34	3	5	4	3	1	.75	16	.251	.318	.304
1983	Cincinnati	N	74	167	36	8	1	1	(0	1)	49	14	13	17	6	20	1	1	2	0	0	.00	3	.216	.285	.293
1984	2 Teams		85	272	66	16	0	3	(1	2)	91	36	28	16	1	29	1	5	1	5	2	.71	4	.243	.286	.335
1985	San Francisco	N	57	157	34	10	1	6	(3	3)	64	17	19	20	0	24	0	1	1	0	0	.00	5	.217	.303	.408
1986	Los Angeles	N	89	202	53	13	0	4	(2	2)	78	31	26	27	2	35	1	2	1	0	0	.00	6	.262	.351	.386
9 YEARS			672	1876	467	81	8	15	(6	9)	609	192	186	161	23	231	8	21	15	13	8	.62	58	.249	.309	.325
1984	Atlanta	N	79	266	65	16	0	3	(1	2)	90	36	28	16	1	27	1	5	1	5	2	.71	4	.244	.289	.338
1984	Cincinnati	N	6	6	1	0	0	0	(0	0)	1	0	0	0	0	2	0	0	0	0	0	.00	0	.167	.167	.167

MANNY TRILLO

Bats Right-handed, Throws Right-handed   Turns Age 37 in 1987, Born 12/25/50

								BATTING												BASERUNNING				PERCENTAGES		
Year	Team	League	G	AB	H	2B	3B	HR	(Hm	Rd)	TB	R	RBI	TBB	IBB	SO	HBP	SH	SF	SB	CS	SB%	GIDP	AVE	OBP	SLG
1973	Oakland	A	17	12	3	2	0	0	(0	0)	5	0	3	0	0	4	0	0	0	0	0	.00	1	.250	.250	.417
1974	Oakland	A	21	33	5	0	0	0	(0	0)	5	3	2	2	0	8	1	1	0	0	0	.00	0	.152	.222	.152
1975	Chicago	N	154	545	135	12	2	7	(3	4)	172	55	70	45	3	78	3	15	5	1	7	.13	10	.248	.306	.316
1976	Chicago	N	158	582	139	24	3	4	(2	2)	181	42	59	53	4	70	3	7	4	17	6	.74	17	.239	.304	.311
1977	Chicago	N	152	504	141	18	5	7	(6	1)	190	51	57	44	6	58	5	4	8	3	5	.38	17	.280	.339	.377
1978	Chicago	N	152	552	144	17	5	4	(0	0)	183	53	55	50	3	67	2	3	8	0	7	.00	10	.261	.320	.332
1979	Philadelphia	N	118	431	112	22	1	6	(5	1)	154	40	42	20	3	59	4	8	4	4	7	.36	13	.260	.296	.357
1980	Philadelphia	N	141	531	155	25	9	7	(4	3)	219	68	43	32	8	46	3	4	3	8	3	.73	16	.292	.334	.412
1981	Philadelphia	N	94	349	100	14	3	6	(5	1)	138	37	36	26	3	37	3	5	4	10	4	.71	6	.287	.338	.395
1982	Philadelphia	N	149	549	149	24	1	0	(0	0)	175	52	39	33	3	53	3	9	1	8	10	.44	14	.271	.316	.319
1983	2 Teams		119	441	119	21	1	3	(3	0)	151	49	45	31	2	64	2	7	2	1	3	.25	15	.270	.319	.342
1984	San Francisco	N	98	401	102	21	1	4	(3	1)	137	45	36	25	0	55	3	4	4	0	0	.00	8	.254	.300	.342
1985	San Francisco	N	125	451	101	16	2	3	(1	2)	130	36	25	40	0	44	1	11	2	2	0	1.00	6	.224	.287	.288
1986	Chicago	N	81	152	45	10	0	1	(1	0)	58	22	19	16	0	21	0	2	2	0	2	.00	2	.296	.359	.382
14 YEARS			1579	5533	1450	226	33	52	(37	15)	1898	553	531	417	35	664	33	80	47	54	54	.50	135	.262	.315	.343
1983	Cleveland	A	88	320	87	13	1	1	(1	0)	105	33	29	21	2	46	0	4	2	1	3	.25	13	.272	.315	.328
1983	Montreal	N	31	121	32	8	0	2	(2	0)	46	16	16	10	0	18	2	3	0	0	0	.00	2	.264	.331	.380

STEVE TROUT

Pitches Left-handed, Bats Left-handed   Turns Age 30 in 1987, Born 07/30/57

			HOW MUCH HE PITCHED						WHAT HE GAVE UP											THE RESULTS					
Year	Team	League	G	GS	CG	GF	IP	BFP	H	R	ER	HR	SH	SF	HB	TBB	IBB	SO	WP	Bk	W	L	Pct	ShO	Sv	ERA
1978	Chicago	A	4	3	1	1	22	97	19	10	10	0	1	2	0	11	0	11	0	0	3	0	1.000	0	0	4.09
1979	Chicago	A	34	18	6	12	155	677	165	77	67	10	6	3	5	59	1	76	1	0	11	8	.579	2	4	3.89
1980	Chicago	A	32	30	7	1	200	866	229	102	82	14	14	3	9	49	5	89	5	2	9	16	.360	2	0	3.69
1981	Chicago	A	20	18	3	0	125	517	122	53	48	7	4	4	4	38	0	54	2	0	8	7	.533	0	0	3.46
1982	Chicago	A	25	19	2	3	120.1	536	130	76	57	9	5	3	2	50	2	62	3	1	6	9	.400	1	0	4.26
1983	Chicago	N	34	32	1	0	180	789	217	105	93	13	11	6	2	59	5	80	7	2	10	14	.417	0	0	4.65
1984	Chicago	N	32	31	6	1	190	797	205	80	72	7	13	4	2	59	7	81	7	2	13	7	.650	2	0	3.41
1985	Chicago	N	24	24	3	0	140.2	601	142	57	53	8	7	5	1	63	7	44	2	1	9	7	.563	1	0	3.39
1986	Chicago	N	37	25	0	3	161	711	184	88	85	6	9	6	1	78	13	69	6	1	5	7	.417	0	0	4.75
9 YEARS			242	200	29	21	1294	5591	1413	648	567	74	70	36	26	466	44	566	33	9	74	75	.497	7	4	3.94

JOHN TUDOR

Pitches Left-handed, Bats Left-handed　　　　　　　　　　　Turns Age 33 in 1987, Born 02/02/54

			HOW MUCH HE PITCHED						WHAT HE GAVE UP												THE RESULTS					
Year	Team	League	G	GS	CG	GF	IP	BFP	H	R	ER	HR	SH	SF	HB	TBB	IBB	SO	WP	Bk	W	L	Pct	ShO	Sv	ERA
1979	Boston	A	6	6	1	0	28	128	39	23	20	2	3	3	0	9	1	11	0	0	1	2	.333	0	0	6.43
1980	Boston	A	16	13	5	0	92	382	81	35	31	4	4	3	3	31	1	45	1	0	8	5	.615	0	0	3.03
1981	Boston	A	18	11	2	3	79	331	74	44	40	11	2	4	3	28	1	44	1	1	4	3	.571	0	1	4.56
1982	Boston	A	32	30	6	1	195.2	847	215	90	79	20	8	5	8	59	3	146	0	2	13	10	.565	1	0	3.63
1983	Boston	A	34	34	7	0	242	1022	236	122	110	32	5	5	4	81	3	136	8	2	13	12	.520	2	0	4.09
1984	Pittsburgh	N	32	32	6	0	212	881	200	81	77	19	10	6	1	56	2	117	1	1	12	11	.522	1	0	3.27
1985	St Louis	N	36	36	14	0	275	1062	209	68	59	14	4	3	5	49	4	169	4	0	21	8	.724	10	0	1.93
1986	St Louis	N	30	30	3	0	219	879	197	81	71	22	9	8	1	53	5	107	2	1	13	7	.650	0	0	2.92
8 YEARS			204	192	44	4	1342.2	5532	1251	544	487	124	45	37	25	366	20	775	17	7	85	58	.594	14	1	3.26

WILLIE UPSHAW

Bats Left-handed, Throws Left-handed　　　　　　　　　　　Turns Age 30 in 1987, Born 04/27/57

									BATTING											BASERUNNING				PERCENTAGES		
Year	Team	League	G	AB	H	2B	3B	HR	(Hm	Rd)	TB	R	RBI	TBB	IBB	SO	HBP	SH	SF	SB	CS	SB%	GIDP	AVE	OBP	SLG
1978	Toronto	A	95	224	53	8	2	1	(0	1)	68	26	17	21	0	35	0	2	3	4	6	.40	4	.237	.298	.304
1980	Toronto	A	34	61	13	3	1	1	(0	1)	21	10	5	6	1	14	0	1	0	1	0	1.00	0	.213	.284	.344
1981	Toronto	A	61	111	19	3	1	4	(1	3)	36	15	10	11	0	16	1	0	0	2	1	.67	1	.171	.252	.324
1982	Toronto	A	160	580	155	25	7	21	(11	10)	257	77	75	52	8	90	1	10	3	8	8	.50	11	.267	.327	.443
1983	Toronto	A	160	579	177	26	7	27	(16	11)	298	99	104	61	8	98	5	3	7	10	7	.59	8	.306	.373	.515
1984	Toronto	A	152	569	158	31	9	19	(6	13)	264	79	84	55	14	86	5	3	3	10	4	.71	8	.278	.345	.464
1985	Toronto	A	148	501	138	31	5	15	(6	9)	224	79	65	48	7	71	4	1	3	8	8	.50	6	.275	.342	.447
1986	Toronto	A	155	573	144	28	6	9	(3	6)	211	85	60	78	4	87	2	4	4	23	5	.82	5	.251	.341	.368
8 YEARS			965	3198	857	155	38	97	(43	54)	1379	470	420	332	42	497	18	24	23	66	39	.63	43	.268	.338	.431

JOSE URIBE

Bats both Right and Left-handed, Throws Right-handed　　　　　　　　　Turns Age 28 in 1987, Born 01/21/59

									BATTING											BASERUNNING				PERCENTAGES		
Year	Team	League	G	AB	H	2B	3B	HR	(Hm	Rd)	TB	R	RBI	TBB	IBB	SO	HBP	SH	SF	SB	CS	SB%	GIDP	AVE	OBP	SLG
1984	St Louis	N	8	19	4	0	0	0	(0	0)	4	4	3	0	0	2	0	1	0	1	0	1.00	1	.211	.211	.211
1985	San Francisco	N	147	476	113	20	4	3	(0	3)	150	46	26	30	8	57	2	5	0	8	2	.80	5	.237	.285	.315
1986	San Francisco	N	157	453	101	15	1	3	(1	2)	127	46	43	61	19	76	0	3	0	22	11	.67	2	.223	.315	.280
3 YEARS			312	948	218	35	5	6	(1	5)	281	96	72	91	27	135	2	9	0	31	13	.70	8	.230	.299	.296

FERNANDO VALENZUELA

Pitches Left-handed, Bats Left-handed　　　　　　　　　　　Turns Age 27 in 1987, Born 11/01/60

			HOW MUCH HE PITCHED						WHAT HE GAVE UP												THE RESULTS					
Year	Team	League	G	GS	CG	GF	IP	BFP	H	R	ER	HR	SH	SF	HB	TBB	IBB	SO	WP	Bk	W	L	Pct	ShO	Sv	ERA
1980	Los Angeles	N	10	0	0	4	18	66	8	2	0	0	1	0	1	5	0	16	0	1	2	0	1.000	0	1	0.00
1981	Los Angeles	N	25	25	11	0	192	758	140	55	53	11	9	3	1	61	4	180	4	0	13	7	.650	8	0	2.48
1982	Los Angeles	N	37	37	18	0	285	1156	247	105	91	13	19	6	2	83	12	199	4	0	19	13	.594	4	0	2.87
1983	Los Angeles	N	35	35	9	0	257	1094	245	122	107	16	27	5	3	99	10	189	12	1	15	10	.600	4	0	3.75
1984	Los Angeles	N	34	34	12	0	261	1078	218	109	88	14	11	7	2	106	4	240	11	1	12	17	.414	2	0	3.03
1985	Los Angeles	N	35	35	14	0	272.1	1109	211	92	74	14	13	8	1	101	5	208	10	1	17	10	.630	5	0	2.45
1986	Los Angeles	N	34	34	20	0	269.1	1102	226	104	94	18	15	3	1	85	5	242	13	0	21	11	.656	3	0	3.14
7 YEARS			210	200	84	4	1554.2	6363	1295	589	507	86	95	33	10	540	40	1274	54	4	99	68	.593	26	1	2.94

ANDY VAN SLYKE

Bats Left-handed, Throws Right-handed　　　　　　　　　　　Turns Age 27 in 1987, Born 12/21/60

									BATTING											BASERUNNING				PERCENTAGES		
Year	Team	League	G	AB	H	2B	3B	HR	(Hm	Rd)	TB	R	RBI	TBB	IBB	SO	HBP	SH	SF	SB	CS	SB%	GIDP	AVE	OBP	SLG
1983	St Louis	N	101	309	81	15	5	8	(3	5)	130	51	38	46	5	64	1	2	3	21	7	.75	4	.262	.357	.421
1984	St Louis	N	137	361	88	16	4	7	(3	4)	133	45	50	63	9	71	0	0	2	28	5	.85	5	.244	.354	.368
1985	St Louis	N	146	424	110	25	6	13	(5	8)	186	61	55	47	6	54	2	1	1	34	6	.85	7	.259	.335	.439
1986	St Louis	N	137	418	113	23	7	13	(6	7)	189	48	61	47	5	85	1	1	3	21	8	.72	2	.270	.343	.452
4 YEARS			521	1512	392	79	22	41	(17	24)	638	205	204	203	25	274	4	4	9	104	26	.80	18	.259	.347	.422

ED VANDE BERG

Pitches Left-handed, Bats Right-handed　　　　　　　　　　　Turns Age 29 in 1987, Born 10/26/58

			HOW MUCH HE PITCHED						WHAT HE GAVE UP												THE RESULTS					
Year	Team	League	G	GS	CG	GF	IP	BFP	H	R	ER	HR	SH	SF	HB	TBB	IBB	SO	WP	Bk	W	L	Pct	ShO	Sv	ERA
1982	Seattle	A	78	0	0	27	76	303	54	21	20	5	6	2	2	32	7	60	3	2	9	4	.692	0	5	2.37
1983	Seattle	A	68	0	0	30	64.1	270	59	32	24	6	4	3	1	22	6	49	4	1	2	4	.333	0	3	3.36
1984	Seattle	A	50	17	2	13	130.1	588	165	76	69	18	3	4	0	50	4	71	5	2	8	12	.400	0	7	4.76
1985	Seattle	A	76	0	0	22	67.2	296	71	30	28	4	2	3	1	31	5	34	4	0	2	1	.667	0	3	3.72
1986	Los Angeles	N	60	0	0	29	71.1	325	83	32	27	8	4	1	1	33	7	42	1	0	1	5	.167	0	0	3.41
5 YEARS			332	17	2	121	409.2	1782	432	191	168	41	19	17	5	168	29	256	17	5	22	26	.458	0	20	3.69

MAX VENABLE

Bats Left-handed, Throws Right-handed

Turns Age 30 in 1987, Born 06/06/57

Year	Team	League	G	AB	H	2B	3B	HR	(Hm	Rd)	TB	R	RBI	TBB	IBB	SO	HBP	SH	SF	SB	CS	SB%	GIDP	AVE	OBP	SLG
1979	San Francisco	N	55	85	14	1	1	0	(0	0)	17	12	3	10	1	18	1	1	0	3	3	.50	0	.165	.260	.200
1980	San Francisco	N	64	138	37	5	0	0	(0	0)	42	13	10	15	0	22	0	1	3	8	2	.80	3	.268	.333	.304
1981	San Francisco	N	18	32	6	0	2	0	(0	0)	10	2	1	4	0	3	0	0	0	3	1	.75	0	.188	.278	.313
1982	San Francisco	N	71	125	28	2	1	1	(1	0)	35	17	7	7	0	16	0	0	0	9	3	.75	2	.224	.265	.280
1983	San Francisco	N	94	228	50	7	4	6	(3	3)	83	28	27	22	1	34	3	2	1	15	2	.88	3	.219	.295	.364
1984	Montreal	N	38	71	17	2	0	2	(0	2)	25	7	7	3	1	7	1	0	1	1	0	1.00	2	.239	.276	.352
1985	Cincinnati	N	77	135	39	12	3	0	(0	0)	57	21	10	6	0	17	0	3	2	11	3	.79	2	.289	.315	.422
1986	Cincinnati	N	108	147	31	7	1	2	(1	1)	46	17	15	17	2	24	0	2	2	7	2	.78	0	.211	.289	.313
8 YEARS			525	961	222	36	12	11	(5	6)	315	117	80	84	5	141	5	9	9	57	16	.78	10	.231	.294	.328

FRANK VIOLA

Pitches Left-handed, Bats Left-handed

Turns Age 27 in 1987, Born 04/19/60

Year	Team	League	G	GS	CG	GF	IP	BFP	H	R	ER	HR	SH	SF	HB	TBB	IBB	SO	WP	Bk	W	L	Pct	ShO	Sv	ERA
1982	Minnesota	A	22	22	3	0	126	543	152	77	73	22	2	0	0	38	2	84	4	1	4	10	.286	1	0	5.21
1983	Minnesota	A	35	34	4	0	210	949	242	141	128	34	5	2	8	92	7	127	6	2	7	15	.318	0	0	5.49
1984	Minnesota	A	35	35	10	0	257.2	1047	225	101	92	28	1	5	4	73	1	149	6	1	18	12	.600	4	0	3.21
1985	Minnesota	A	36	36	9	0	250.2	1059	262	136	114	26	5	5	2	68	3	135	6	2	18	14	.563	0	0	4.09
1986	Minnesota	A	37	37	7	0	245.2	1053	257	136	123	37	4	5	3	83	0	191	12	0	16	13	.552	1	0	4.51
5 YEARS			165	164	33	0	1090	4651	1138	591	530	147	17	17	17	354	13	686	34	6	63	64	.496	6	0	4.38

OZZIE VIRGIL

Bats Right-handed, Throws Right-handed

Turns Age 31 in 1987, Born 12/07/56

Year	Team	League	G	AB	H	2B	3B	HR	(Hm	Rd)	TB	R	RBI	TBB	IBB	SO	HBP	SH	SF	SB	CS	SB%	GIDP	AVE	OBP	SLG
1980	Philadelphia	N	1	5	1	1	0	0	(0	0)	2	1	0	0	0	1	0	0	0	0	0	.00	0	.200	.200	.400
1981	Philadelphia	N	6	6	0	0	0	0	(0	0)	0	0	0	0	0	2	0	0	0	0	0	.00	0	.000	.000	.000
1982	Philadelphia	N	49	101	24	6	0	3	(1	2)	39	11	8	10	0	26	0	0	0	0	1	.00	3	.238	.306	.386
1983	Philadelphia	N	55	140	30	7	0	6	(2	4)	55	11	23	8	0	34	3	0	0	0	2	.00	8	.214	.272	.393
1984	Philadelphia	N	141	456	119	21	2	18	(10	8)	198	61	68	45	5	91	5	1	5	1	1	.50	19	.261	.331	.434
1985	Philadelphia	N	131	426	105	16	3	19	(7	12)	184	47	55	49	6	85	5	1	2	0	0	.00	14	.246	.330	.432
1986	Atlanta	N	114	359	80	9	0	15	(6	9)	134	45	48	63	5	73	4	2	3	1	0	1.00	9	.223	.343	.373
7 YEARS			497	1493	359	60	5	61	(26	35)	612	176	202	175	16	312	17	4	10	2	4	.33	53	.240	.325	.410

BOB WALK

Pitches Right-handed, Bats Right-handed

Turns Age 31 in 1987, Born 11/26/56

Year	Team	League	G	GS	CG	GF	IP	BFP	H	R	ER	HR	SH	SF	HB	TBB	IBB	SO	WP	Bk	W	L	Pct	ShO	Sv	ERA
1980	Philadelphia	N	27	27	2	0	152	673	163	82	77	11	8	5	2	71	2	94	6	3	11	7	.611	0	0	4.56
1981	Atlanta	N	12	8	0	1	43	189	41	25	22	6	2	0	0	23	0	16	1	0	1	4	.200	0	0	4.60
1982	Atlanta	N	32	27	3	1	164.1	717	179	101	89	19	8	5	6	59	2	84	7	0	11	9	.550	1	0	4.87
1983	Atlanta	N	1	1	0	0	3.2	20	7	3	3	1	0	1	0	2	0	4	0	0	0	0	.000	0	0	7.36
1984	Pittsburgh	N	2	2	0	0	10.1	44	8	5	3	1	0	0	0	4	1	10	0	0	1	1	.500	0	0	2.61
1985	Pittsburgh	N	9	9	1	0	58.2	248	60	27	24	3	3	1	0	18	2	40	2	3	2	3	.400	1	0	3.68
1986	Pittsburgh	N	44	15	1	7	141.2	592	129	66	59	14	6	5	3	64	7	78	12	1	7	8	.467	1	2	3.75
7 YEARS			127	89	7	9	573.2	2483	587	309	277	51	25	16	11	241	14	326	28	7	33	32	.508	3	2	4.35

CHICO WALKER

Bats both Right and Left-handed, Throws Right-handed

Turns Age 30 in 1987, Born 11/25/57

Year	Team	League	G	AB	H	2B	3B	HR	(Hm	Rd)	TB	R	RBI	TBB	IBB	SO	HBP	SH	SF	SB	CS	SB%	GIDP	AVE	OBP	SLG
1980	Boston	A	19	57	12	0	0	1	(1	0)	15	3	5	6	1	10	1	1	1	3	2	.60	1	.211	.292	.263
1981	Boston	A	6	17	6	0	0	0	(0	0)	6	3	2	1	0	2	0	0	0	0	2	.00	0	.353	.389	.353
1983	Boston	A	4	5	2	0	2	0	(0	0)	6	2	1	0	0	0	0	0	0	0	0	.00	0	.400	.400	1.200
1984	Boston	A	3	2	0	0	0	0	(0	0)	0	0	0	0	0	1	0	0	0	0	0	.00	0	.000	.000	.000
1985	Chicago	N	21	12	1	0	0	0	(0	0)	1	1	3	0	0	5	0	0	0	1	0	1.00	0	.083	.083	.083
1986	Chicago	N	28	101	28	3	2	1	(0	1)	38	21	7	10	0	20	0	0	1	15	4	.79	3	.277	.339	.376
6 YEARS			81	194	49	3	4	2	(1	1)	66	32	16	17	1	38	1	1	3	19	8	.70	4	.253	.312	.340

GREG WALKER

Bats Left-handed, Throws Right-handed   Turns Age 28 in 1987, Born 10/06/59

Year	Team	League	G	AB	H	2B	3B	HR	(Hm	Rd)	TB	R	RBI	TBB	IBB	SO	HBP	SH	SF	SB	CS	SB%	GIDP	AVE	OBP	SLG
1982	Chicago	A	11	17	7	2	1	2	(1	1)	17	3	7	2	0	3	0	0	0	0	0	.00	0	.412	.474	.000
1983	Chicago	A	118	307	83	16	3	10	(4	6)	135	32	55	28	3	57	2	0	3	2	1	.67	3	.270	.332	.440
1984	Chicago	A	136	442	130	29	2	24	(16	8)	235	62	75	35	3	66	2	0	3	8	5	.62	9	.294	.346	.532
1985	Chicago	A	163	601	155	38	4	24	(11	13)	273	77	92	44	6	100	2	0	3	5	2	.71	16	.258	.309	.454
1986	Chicago	A	78	282	78	10	6	13	(6	7)	139	37	51	29	4	44	2	0	3	1	2	.33	4	.277	.345	.493
5 YEARS			506	1649	453	95	16	73	(38	35)	799	211	280	138	16	270	8	0	12	16	10	.62	32	.275	.331	.485

TIM WALLACH

Bats Right-handed, Throws Right-handed   Turns Age 30 in 1987, Born 09/14/57

Year	Team	League	G	AB	H	2B	3B	HR	(Hm	Rd)	TB	R	RBI	TBB	IBB	SO	HBP	SH	SF	SB	CS	SB%	GIDP	AVE	OBP	SLG
1980	Montreal	N	5	11	2	0	0	1	(0	1)	5	1	2	1	0	5	0	0	0	0	0	.00	0	.182	.250	.455
1981	Montreal	N	71	212	50	9	1	4	(1	3)	73	19	13	15	2	37	4	0	0	0	1	.00	3	.236	.299	.344
1982	Montreal	N	158	596	160	31	3	28	(11	17)	281	89	97	36	4	81	4	5	4	6	4	.60	15	.268	.313	.471
1983	Montreal	N	156	581	156	33	3	19	(9	10)	252	54	70	55	8	97	6	0	5	0	3	.00	9	.269	.335	.434
1984	Montreal	N	160	582	143	25	4	18	(4	14)	230	55	72	50	6	101	7	0	5	3	7	.30	12	.246	.311	.395
1985	Montreal	N	155	569	148	36	3	22	(9	13)	256	70	81	38	8	79	5	0	5	9	9	.50	17	.260	.310	.450
1986	Montreal	N	134	480	112	22	1	18	(6	12)	190	50	71	44	8	72	10	0	5	8	4	.67	16	.233	.308	.396
7 YEARS			839	3031	771	156	15	110	(40	70)	1287	338	406	239	36	472	36	5	23	26	28	.48	72	.254	.314	.425

DENNY WALLING

Bats Left-handed, Throws Right-handed   Turns Age 33 in 1987, Born 04/17/54

Year	Team	League	G	AB	H	2B	3B	HR	(Hm	Rd)	TB	R	RBI	TBB	IBB	SO	HBP	SH	SF	SB	CS	SB%	GIDP	AVE	OBP	SLG
1975	Oakland	A	6	8	1	1	0	0	(0	0)	2	0	2	0	0	4	0	0	0	0	0	.00	0	.125	.125	.250
1976	Oakland	A	3	11	3	0	0	0	(0	0)	3	1	0	0	0	3	0	0	0	0	0	.00	0	.273	.273	.273
1977	Houston	N	6	21	6	0	1	0	(0	0)	8	1	6	2	0	4	0	0	0	0	1	.00	0	.286	.348	.381
1978	Houston	N	120	247	62	11	3	3	(2	1)	88	30	36	30	3	24	1	0	2	9	2	.82	2	.251	.332	.356
1979	Houston	N	82	147	48	8	4	3	(3	0)	73	21	31	17	2	21	0	0	1	3	2	.60	2	.327	.394	.497
1980	Houston	N	100	284	85	6	5	3	(1	2)	110	30	29	35	4	26	0	0	2	4	3	.57	2	.299	.374	.387
1981	Houston	N	65	158	37	6	0	5	(2	3)	58	23	23	28	1	17	0	1	2	2	1	.67	3	.234	.346	.367
1982	Houston	N	85	146	30	4	1	1	(1	0)	39	22	14	23	3	19	0	0	1	4	2	.67	6	.205	.312	.267
1983	Houston	N	100	135	40	5	3	3	(1	2)	60	24	19	15	1	16	0	1	1	2	2	.50	1	.296	.364	.444
1984	Houston	N	87	249	70	11	5	3	(0	3)	100	37	31	16	2	28	1	0	2	7	1	.88	4	.281	.325	.402
1985	Houston	N	119	345	93	20	1	7	(2	5)	136	44	45	25	2	26	0	0	4	5	2	.71	8	.270	.316	.394
1986	Houston	N	130	382	119	23	1	13	(5	8)	183	54	58	36	5	31	0	0	4	1	1	.50	8	.312	.367	.479
12 YEARS			903	2133	594	95	24	41	(17	24)	860	287	294	227	23	219	2	2	19	37	17	.69	36	.278	.346	.403

GENE WALTER

Pitches Left-handed, Bats Left-handed   Turns Age 27 in 1987, Born 11/22/60

Year	Team	League	G	GS	CG	GF	IP	BFP	H	R	ER	HR	SH	SF	HB	TBB	IBB	SO	WP	Bk	W	L	Pct	ShO	Sv	ERA
1985	San Diego	N	15	0	0	7	22	86	12	6	5	0	1	1	0	8	1	18	0	0	0	2	.000	0	3	2.05
1986	San Diego	N	57	0	0	19	98	422	89	47	42	7	5	3	4	49	7	84	6	0	2	2	.500	0	1	3.86
2 YEARS			72	0	0	26	120	508	101	53	47	7	6	4	4	57	8	102	6	0	2	4	.333	0	4	3.52

GARY WARD

Bats Right-handed, Throws Right-handed   Turns Age 34 in 1987, Born 12/06/53

Year	Team	League	G	AB	H	2B	3B	HR	(Hm	Rd)	TB	R	RBI	TBB	IBB	SO	HBP	SH	SF	SB	CS	SB%	GIDP	AVE	OBP	SLG
1979	Minnesota	A	10	14	4	0	0	0	(0	0)	4	2	1	3	0	3	0	0	0	0	1	.00	0	.286	.412	.286
1980	Minnesota	A	13	41	19	6	2	1	(0	1)	32	11	10	3	1	6	0	1	1	0	0	.00	0	.463	.489	.780
1981	Minnesota	A	85	295	78	7	6	3	(2	1)	106	42	29	28	4	48	0	0	3	5	2	.71	10	.264	.325	.359
1982	Minnesota	A	152	570	165	33	7	28	(16	12)	296	85	91	37	4	105	1	1	7	13	1	.93	16	.289	.330	.519
1983	Minnesota	A	157	623	173	34	5	19	(7	12)	274	76	88	44	2	98	3	1	5	8	1	.89	24	.278	.326	.440
1984	Texas	A	155	602	171	21	7	21	(7	14)	269	97	79	55	3	95	0	1	1	7	5	.58	22	.284	.343	.447
1985	Texas	A	154	593	170	28	7	15	(10	5)	257	77	70	39	3	97	1	0	5	26	7	.79	19	.287	.329	.433
1986	Texas	A	105	380	120	15	2	5	(3	2)	154	54	51	31	3	72	4	1	2	12	8	.60	10	.316	.372	.405
8 YEARS			831	3118	900	144	36	92	(45	47)	1392	444	419	240	20	524	9	5	24	71	25	.74	101	.289	.339	.446

CLAUDELL WASHINGTON

Turns Age 33 in 1987, Born 08/31/54

Bats Left-handed, Throws Left-handed

								BATTING													BASERUNNING				PERCENTAGES		
Year	Team	League	G	AB	H	2B	3B	HR	(Hm	Rd)	TB	R	RBI	TBB	IBB	SO	HBP	SH	SF	SB	CS	SB%	GIDP	AVE	OBP	SLG
1974	Oakland	A	73	221	63	10	5	0	(0	0)	83	16	19	13	1	44	1	1	1	6	8	.43	6	.285	.326	.376
1975	Oakland	A	148	590	182	24	7	10	(7	3)	250	86	77	32	9	80	5	1	7	40	15	.73	12	.308	.345	.424
1976	Oakland	A	134	490	126	20	6	5	(1	4)	173	65	53	30	1	90	3	3	4	37	20	.65	13	.257	.302	.353
1977	Texas	A	129	521	148	31	2	12	(6	6)	219	63	68	25	9	112	3	1	4	21	8	.72	10	.284	.318	.420
1978	2 Teams		98	356	90	16	5	6	(3	3)	134	34	33	13	2	69	1	2	4	5	6	.45	8	.253	.278	.376
1979	Chicago	A	131	471	132	33	5	13	(10	3)	214	79	66	28	7	93	3	2	4	19	11	.63	10	.280	.322	.454
1980	2 Teams		111	374	104	20	6	11	(5	6)	169	53	54	25	5	82	2	1	1	21	7	.75	10	.278	.326	.452
1981	Atlanta	N	85	320	93	22	3	5	(3	2)	136	37	37	15	1	47	4	4	8	12	6	.67	6	.291	.328	.425
1982	Atlanta	N	150	563	150	24	6	16	(8	8)	234	94	80	50	9	107	6	1	6	33	10	.77	9	.266	.330	.416
1983	Atlanta	N	134	496	138	24	8	9	(4	5)	205	75	44	35	6	103	0	1	6	31	9	.78	9	.278	.322	.413
1984	Atlanta	N	120	416	119	21	2	17	(12	5)	195	62	61	59	8	77	1	0	3	21	9	.70	11	.286	.374	.469
1985	Atlanta	N	122	398	110	14	6	15	(4	11)	181	62	43	40	11	66	1	0	2	14	4	.78	11	.276	.342	.455
1986	2 Teams		94	272	69	16	0	11	(7	4)	118	36	30	21	0	59	2	1	1	10	8	.56	7	.254	.311	.434
13 YEARS			1529	5488	1524	275	61	130	(70	60)	2311	762	665	386	69	1029	32	22	45	270	121	.69	122	.278	.326	.421
1978	Chicago	A	86	314	83	16	5	6	(3	3)	127	33	31	12	2	57	1	2	4	5	5	.50	7	.264	.290	.404
1978	Texas	A	12	42	7	0	0	0	(0	0)	7	1	2	1	0	12	0	0	0	0	1	.00	1	.167	.186	.167
1980	Chicago	A	32	90	26	4	2	1	(0	1)	37	15	12	5	0	19	1	1	0	4	2	.67	5	.289	.333	.411
1980	New York	N	79	284	78	16	4	10	(5	5)	132	38	42	20	5	63	1	0	1	17	5	.77	5	.275	.324	.465
1986	New York	A	54	135	32	5	0	6	(4	2)	55	19	16	7	0	33	2	0	0	6	1	.86	3	.237	.285	.407
1986	Atlanta	N	40	137	37	11	0	5	(3	2)	63	17	14	14	0	26	0	1	1	4	7	.36	4	.270	.336	.460

U.L. WASHINGTON

Turns Age 34 in 1987, Born 10/27/53

Bats both Right and Left-handed, Throws Right-handed

								BATTING													BASERUNNING				PERCENTAGES		
Year	Team	League	G	AB	H	2B	3B	HR	(Hm	Rd)	TB	R	RBI	TBB	IBB	SO	HBP	SH	SF	SB	CS	SB%	GIDP	AVE	OBP	SLG
1977	Kansas City	A	10	20	4	1	1	0	(0	0)	7	0	1	5	0	4	0	1	0	1	0	1.00	0	.200	.360	.350
1978	Kansas City	A	69	129	34	2	1	0	(0	0)	38	10	9	10	0	20	0	2	1	12	6	.67	2	.264	.314	.295
1979	Kansas City	A	101	268	68	12	5	2	(0	2)	96	32	25	20	1	44	0	6	6	10	7	.59	1	.254	.299	.358
1980	Kansas City	A	153	549	150	16	11	6	(3	3)	206	79	53	53	0	78	0	10	2	20	7	.74	13	.273	.336	.375
1981	Kansas City	A	98	339	77	19	1	2	(0	2)	104	40	29	41	1	43	0	3	1	10	10	.50	6	.227	.310	.307
1982	Kansas City	A	119	437	125	19	3	10	(2	8)	180	64	60	38	0	48	0	5	7	23	7	.77	4	.286	.338	.412
1983	Kansas City	A	144	547	129	19	6	5	(1	4)	175	76	41	48	0	78	1	1	1	40	7	.85	1	.236	.298	.320
1984	Kansas City	A	63	170	38	6	0	1	(0	1)	47	18	10	14	0	31	0	4	1	4	6	.40	1	.224	.281	.276
1985	Montreal	N	68	193	48	9	4	1	(1	0)	68	24	17	15	1	33	0	0	1	6	3	.67	2	.249	.301	.352
1986	Pittsburgh	N	72	135	27	0	4	0	(0	0)	35	14	10	15	2	27	0	4	1	6	0	1.00	1	.200	.278	.259
10 YEARS			897	2787	700	103	36	27	(7	20)	956	357	255	259	5	406	1	42	21	132	53	.71	33	.251	.313	.343

MITCH WEBSTER

Turns Age 28 in 1987, Born 05/16/59

Bats both Right and Left-handed, Throws Left-handed

								BATTING													BASERUNNING				PERCENTAGES		
Year	Team	League	G	AB	H	2B	3B	HR	(Hm	Rd)	TB	R	RBI	TBB	IBB	SO	HBP	SH	SF	SB	CS	SB%	GIDP	AVE	OBP	SLG
1983	Toronto	A	11	11	2	0	0	0	(0	0)	2	2	0	1	0	1	0	0	0	0	1	.00	0	.182	.250	.182
1984	Toronto	A	26	22	5	2	1	0	(0	0)	9	9	4	1	0	7	0	0	0	0	0	.00	1	.227	.261	.409
1985	2 Teams		78	213	58	8	2	11	(3	8)	103	32	30	20	3	33	0	1	1	15	10	.60	3	.272	.333	.484
1986	Montreal	N	151	576	167	31	13	8	(2	6)	248	89	49	57	4	78	4	3	5	36	15	.71	9	.290	.355	.431
4 YEARS			266	822	232	41	16	19	(5	14)	362	132	83	79	7	119	4	4	6	51	25	.67	13	.282	.346	.440
1985	Toronto	A	4	1	0	0	0	0	(0	0)	0	0	0	0	0	0	0	0	0	0	1	.00	0	.000	.000	.000
1985	Montreal	N	74	212	58	8	2	11	(3	8)	103	32	30	20	3	33	0	1	1	15	9	.63	3	.274	.335	.486

BILL WEGMAN

Turns Age 25 in 1987, Born 12/19/62

Pitches Right-handed, Bats Right-handed

			HOW MUCH HE PITCHED						WHAT HE GAVE UP											THE RESULTS					
Year	Team	League	G	GS	CG	GF	IP	BFP	H	R	ER	HR	SH	SF	HB	TBB	IBB	SO	WP	Bk	W	L	Pct	ShO	Sv	ERA
1985	Milwaukee	A	3	3	0	0	17.2	73	17	8	7	3	0	1	0	3	0	6	0	1	2	0	1.000	0	0	3.57
1986	Milwaukee	A	35	32	2	1	198.1	836	217	120	113	32	4	5	7	43	2	82	5	2	5	12	.294	0	0	5.13
2 YEARS			38	35	2	1	216	909	234	128	120	35	4	6	7	46	2	88	5	3	7	12	.368	0	0	5.00

BOB WELCH

Turns Age 31 in 1987, Born 11/03/56

Pitches Right-handed, Bats Right-handed

			HOW MUCH HE PITCHED						WHAT HE GAVE UP											THE RESULTS					
Year	Team	League	G	GS	CG	GF	IP	BFP	H	R	ER	HR	SH	SF	HB	TBB	IBB	SO	WP	Bk	W	L	Pct	ShO	Sv	ERA
1978	Los Angeles	N	23	13	4	6	111	439	92	28	25	6	4	6	1	26	2	66	2	2	7	4	.636	3	3	2.03
1979	Los Angeles	N	25	12	1	10	81	349	82	42	36	7	4	1	3	32	4	64	0	0	5	6	.455	0	5	4.00
1980	Los Angeles	N	32	32	3	0	214	889	190	85	78	15	12	10	3	79	6	141	7	5	14	9	.609	2	0	3.28
1981	Los Angeles	N	23	23	2	0	141	601	141	56	54	11	4	4	3	41	0	88	2	0	9	5	.643	1	0	3.45
1982	Los Angeles	N	36	36	9	0	235.2	965	199	94	88	19	7	4	5	81	5	176	5	1	16	11	.593	3	0	3.36
1983	Los Angeles	N	31	31	4	0	204	828	164	73	60	13	8	7	3	72	4	156	4	0	15	12	.556	3	0	2.65
1984	Los Angeles	N	31	29	3	0	178.2	771	191	86	75	11	10	2	2	58	7	126	4	2	13	13	.500	1	0	3.78
1985	Los Angeles	N	23	23	8	0	167.1	675	141	49	43	16	6	2	6	35	2	96	7	4	14	4	.778	3	0	2.31
1986	Los Angeles	N	33	33	7	0	235.2	981	227	95	86	14	7	8	7	55	6	183	2	1	7	13	.350	3	0	3.28
9 YEARS			257	232	41	16	1568.1	6498	1427	608	545	112	67	44	33	479	36	1096	33	21	100	77	.565	19	8	3.13

CHRIS WELSH

Pitches Left-handed, Bats Left-handed
Turns Age 32 in 1987, Born 04/14/55

| Year Team | League | HOW MUCH HE PITCHED | | | | | | WHAT HE GAVE UP | | | | | | | | | | | | | THE RESULTS | | | | | |

Year	Team	League	G	GS	CG	GF	IP	BFP	H	R	ER	HR	SH	SF	HB	TBB	IBB	SO	WP	Bk	W	L	Pct	ShO	Sv	ERA
1981	San Diego	N	22	19	4	2	124	512	122	55	52	9	5	3	1	41	4	51	1	2	6	7	.462	2	0	3.77
1982	San Diego	N	28	20	3	7	139.1	618	146	88	76	16	5	2	3	63	2	48	2	0	8	8	.500	1	0	4.91
1983	2 Teams		23	6	0	6	59	254	59	35	29	7	2	1	1	20	4	22	5	0	0	2	.000	0	0	4.42
1985	Texas	A	25	6	0	4	76.1	351	101	40	35	11	1	1	4	25	3	31	5	0	2	5	.286	0	0	4.13
1986	Cincinnati	N	24	24	1	0	139.1	598	163	79	74	9	10	4	3	40	4	40	5	0	6	9	.400	0	0	4.78
5 YEARS			122	75	8	19	538	2333	591	297	266	52	23	11	12	189	17	192	18	2	22	31	.415	3	0	4.45
1983	Montreal	N	16	5	0	3	45	195	46	30	25	5	0	1	1	18	4	17	2	0	0	1	.000	0	0	5.00
1983	San Diego	N	7	1	0	3	14	59	13	5	4	2	2	0	0	2	0	5	3	0	0	1	.000	0	0	2.57

LOU WHITAKER

Bats Left-handed, Throws Right-handed
Turns Age 30 in 1987, Born 05/12/57

Year	Team	League	G	AB	H	2B	3B	HR	(Hm	Rd)	TB	R	RBI	TBB	IBB	SO	HBP	SH	SF	SB	CS	SB%	GIDP	AVE	OBP	SLG
1977	Detroit	A	11	32	8	1	0	0	(0	0)	9	5	2	4	0	6	0	1	0	2	2	.50	0	.250	.333	.281
1978	Detroit	A	139	484	138	12	7	3	(2	1)	173	71	58	61	0	65	1	13	8	7	7	.50	9	.285	.361	.357
1979	Detroit	A	127	423	121	14	8	3	(3	0)	160	75	42	78	2	66	1	14	4	20	10	.67	10	.286	.395	.378
1980	Detroit	A	145	477	111	19	1	1	(1	0)	135	68	45	73	0	79	0	12	6	8	4	.67	9	.233	.331	.283
1981	Detroit	A	109	335	88	14	4	5	(4	1)	125	48	36	40	3	42	1	3	3	5	3	.63	5	.263	.340	.373
1982	Detroit	A	152	560	160	22	8	15	(9	6)	243	76	65	48	4	58	1	6	4	11	3	.79	8	.286	.341	.434
1983	Detroit	A	161	643	206	40	6	12	(7	5)	294	94	72	67	8	70	0	2	8	17	10	.63	9	.320	.380	.457
1984	Detroit	A	143	558	161	25	4	13	(8	5)	227	90	56	62	5	63	0	4	5	6	5	.55	9	.289	.357	.407
1985	Detroit	A	152	609	170	29	8	21	(11	10)	278	102	73	80	9	56	2	5	5	6	4	.60	3	.279	.362	.456
1986	Detroit	A	144	584	157	26	6	20	(8	12)	255	95	73	63	5	70	0	0	4	13	8	.62	20	.269	.338	.437
10 YEARS			1283	4705	1320	202	49	93	(53	40)	1899	724	522	576	36	575	6	60	47	95	56	.63	82	.281	.357	.404

FRANK WHITE

Bats Right-handed, Throws Right-handed
Turns Age 37 in 1987, Born 09/04/50

Year	Team	League	G	AB	H	2B	3B	HR	(Hm	Rd)	TB	R	RBI	TBB	IBB	SO	HBP	SH	SF	SB	CS	SB%	GIDP	AVE	OBP	SLG
1973	Kansas City	A	51	139	31	6	1	0	(0	0)	39	20	5	8	0	23	0	2	2	3	1	.75	1	.223	.262	.281
1974	Kansas City	A	99	204	45	6	3	1	(1	0)	59	19	18	5	0	33	0	5	0	3	4	.43	4	.221	.239	.294
1975	Kansas City	A	111	304	76	10	2	7	(4	3)	111	43	36	20	0	39	1	2	2	11	3	.79	4	.250	.297	.365
1976	Kansas City	A	152	446	102	17	6	2	(0	2)	137	39	46	19	0	42	3	18	3	20	11	.65	4	.229	.263	.307
1977	Kansas City	A	152	474	116	21	5	5	(3	2)	162	59	50	25	0	67	2	11	2	23	5	.82	4	.245	.284	.342
1978	Kansas City	A	143	461	127	24	6	7	(3	4)	184	66	50	26	1	59	3	9	2	13	10	.57	2	.275	.317	.399
1979	Kansas City	A	127	467	124	26	4	10	(5	5)	188	73	48	25	3	54	1	3	7	28	8	.78	11	.266	.300	.403
1980	Kansas City	A	154	560	148	23	4	7	(1	6)	200	70	60	19	0	69	2	9	4	19	6	.76	11	.264	.289	.357
1981	Kansas City	A	94	364	91	17	1	9	(4	5)	137	35	38	19	0	50	0	4	3	4	2	.67	10	.250	.285	.376
1982	Kansas City	A	145	524	156	45	6	11	(7	4)	246	71	56	16	1	65	2	7	5	10	7	.59	12	.298	.318	.469
1983	Kansas City	A	146	549	143	35	6	11	(8	3)	223	52	77	20	4	51	0	4	6	13	5	.72	18	.260	.283	.406
1984	Kansas City	A	129	479	130	22	5	17	(6	11)	213	58	56	27	3	72	2	4	3	5	5	.50	11	.271	.311	.445
1985	Kansas City	A	149	563	140	25	1	22	(9	13)	233	62	69	28	2	86	1	5	3	10	4	.71	8	.249	.284	.414
1986	Kansas City	A	151	566	154	37	3	22	(12	10)	263	76	84	43	5	88	2	2	7	4	4	.50	10	.272	.322	.465
14 YEARS			1803	6100	1583	314	53	131	(63	68)	2396	743	693	300	19	798	19	85	49	166	75	.69	110	.260	.294	.393

ED WHITSON

Pitches Right-handed, Bats Right-handed
Turns Age 32 in 1987, Born 05/19/55

Year	Team	League	G	GS	CG	GF	IP	BFP	H	R	ER	HR	SH	SF	HB	TBB	IBB	SO	WP	Bk	W	L	Pct	ShO	Sv	ERA
1977	Pittsburgh	N	5	2	0	1	16	66	11	6	6	0	1	2	0	9	1	10	0	0	1	0	1.000	0	0	3.37
1978	Pittsburgh	N	43	0	0	14	74	318	66	31	27	5	3	4	2	37	5	64	1	0	5	6	.455	0	4	3.28
1979	2 Teams		37	24	2	5	158	702	151	83	72	11	10	3	5	75	9	93	5	2	7	11	.389	0	1	4.10
1980	San Francisco	N	34	34	6	0	212	898	222	88	73	7	10	9	4	56	7	90	1	1	11	13	.458	2	0	3.10
1981	San Francisco	N	22	22	2	0	123	534	130	61	55	10	6	2	4	47	5	65	3	2	6	9	.400	1	0	4.02
1982	Cleveland	A	40	9	1	18	107.2	467	91	43	39	6	7	8	0	58	3	61	4	1	4	2	.667	1	2	3.26
1983	San Diego	N	31	21	2	4	144.1	617	143	73	69	23	3	4	1	50	1	81	2	0	5	7	.417	0	1	4.30
1984	San Diego	N	31	31	1	0	189	773	181	72	68	16	10	7	3	42	1	103	3	1	14	8	.636	0	0	3.24
1985	New York	A	30	30	2	0	158.2	705	201	100	86	19	3	7	2	43	0	89	1	0	10	8	.556	0	0	4.88
1986	2 Teams		31	16	0	6	112.2	526	139	85	78	13	4	5	5	60	1	73	3	0	6	9	.400	0	0	6.23
10 YEARS			304	189	16	48	1295.1	5606	1335	642	573	110	57	51	19	477	33	729	23	7	69	73	.486	6	8	3.98
1979	Pittsburgh	N	19	7	0	4	58	263	53	36	28	6	3	0	1	36	3	31	2	1	2	3	.400	0	1	4.34
1979	San Francisco	N	18	17	2	1	100	439	98	47	44	5	7	3	4	39	6	62	3	1	5	8	.385	0	0	3.96
1986	New York	A	14	4	0	6	37	189	54	37	31	5	2	1	0	23	1	27	2	0	5	2	.714	0	0	7.54
1986	San Diego	N	17	12	0	0	75.2	337	85	48	47	8	2	2	0	37	0	46	1	0	1	7	.125	0	0	5.59

ERNIE WHITT

Bats Left-handed, Throws Right-handed   Turns Age 35 in 1987, Born 06/13/52

Year	Team	League	G	AB	H	2B	3B	HR	(Hm	Rd)	TB	R	RBI	TBB	IBB	SO	HBP	SH	SF	SB	CS	SB%	GIDP	AVE	OBP	SLG
1976	Boston	A	8	18	4	2	0	1	(1	0)	9	4	3	2	0	2	0	0	0	0	0	.00	0	.222	.300	.500
1977	Toronto	A	23	41	7	3	0	0	(0	0)	10	4	6	2	0	12	0	0	2	0	0	.00	1	.171	.200	.244
1978	Toronto	A	2	4	0	0	0	0	(0	0)	0	0	0	1	0	1	0	0	0	0	0	.00	0	.000	.200	.000
1980	Toronto	A	106	295	70	12	2	6	(2	4)	104	23	34	22	0	30	0	5	3	1	3	.25	11	.237	.288	.353
1981	Toronto	A	74	195	46	9	0	1	(0	1)	58	16	16	20	3	30	0	7	0	5	2	.71	2	.236	.307	.297
1982	Toronto	A	105	284	74	14	2	11	(8	3)	125	28	42	26	5	35	0	1	5	3	1	.75	5	.261	.317	.440
1983	Toronto	A	123	344	88	15	2	17	(11	6)	158	53	56	50	5	55	0	1	5	1	1	.50	9	.256	.346	.459
1984	Toronto	A	124	315	75	12	1	15	(5	10)	134	35	46	43	7	49	1	0	5	0	3	.00	7	.238	.327	.425
1985	Toronto	A	139	412	101	21	2	19	(7	12)	183	55	64	47	9	59	1	3	2	3	6	.33	7	.245	.323	.444
1986	Toronto	A	131	395	106	19	2	16	(7	9)	177	48	56	35	3	39	0	0	3	0	1	.00	11	.268	.326	.448
10 YEARS			835	2303	571	107	11	86	(41	45)	958	266	323	248	32	312	2	17	25	13	17	.43	53	.248	.318	.416

ALAN WIGGINS

Bats both Right and Left-handed, Throws Right-handed   Turns Age 29 in 1987, Born 02/17/58

Year	Team	League	G	AB	H	2B	3B	HR	(Hm	Rd)	TB	R	RBI	TBB	IBB	SO	HBP	SH	SF	SB	CS	SB%	GIDP	AVE	OBP	SLG
1981	San Diego	N	15	14	5	0	0	0	(0	0)	5	4	0	1	0	0	0	0	0	2	0	1.00	0	.357	.400	.357
1982	San Diego	N	72	254	65	3	3	1	(1	0)	77	40	15	13	0	19	1	6	0	33	6	.85	4	.256	.295	.303
1983	San Diego	N	144	503	139	20	2	0	(0	0)	163	83	22	65	3	43	1	16	0	66	13	.84	3	.276	.360	.324
1984	San Diego	N	158	596	154	19	7	3	(3	0)	196	106	34	75	1	57	3	14	4	70	21	.77	2	.258	.342	.329
1985	2 Teams		86	335	87	12	4	0	(0	0)	107	46	21	31	0	20	2	7	0	30	14	.68	3	.260	.326	.319
1986	Baltimore	A	71	239	60	3	1	0	(0	0)	65	30	11	22	0	20	0	5	4	21	7	.75	0	.251	.309	.272
6 YEARS			546	1941	510	57	17	4	(4	0)	613	309	103	207	4	159	7	48	8	222	61	.78	12	.263	.335	.316
1985	Baltimore	A	76	298	85	11	4	0	(0	0)	104	43	21	29	0	16	2	6	0	30	13	.70	2	.285	.353	.349
1985	San Diego	N	10	37	2	1	0	0	(0	0)	3	3	0	2	0	4	0	1	0	0	1	.00	1	.054	.103	.081

ROB WILFONG

Bats Left-handed, Throws Right-handed   Turns Age 34 in 1987, Born 09/01/53

Year	Team	League	G	AB	H	2B	3B	HR	(Hm	Rd)	TB	R	RBI	TBB	IBB	SO	HBP	SH	SF	SB	CS	SB%	GIDP	AVE	OBP	SLG
1977	Minnesota	A	73	171	42	1	1	1	(1	0)	48	22	13	17	0	26	2	3	0	10	4	.71	1	.246	.321	.281
1978	Minnesota	A	92	199	53	8	0	1	(1	0)	64	23	11	19	1	27	2	15	0	8	4	.67	1	.266	.336	.322
1979	Minnesota	A	140	419	131	22	6	9	(4	5)	192	71	59	29	3	54	2	25	10	11	4	.73	2	.313	.352	.458
1980	Minnesota	A	131	416	103	16	5	8	(3	5)	153	55	45	34	3	61	3	11	2	10	6	.63	8	.248	.308	.368
1981	Minnesota	A	93	305	75	11	3	3	(3	0)	101	32	19	29	1	43	0	5	0	2	4	.33	1	.246	.311	.331
1982	2 Teams		80	183	38	5	2	1	(0	1)	50	24	16	14	1	30	1	3	0	4	2	.67	5	.208	.268	.273
1983	California	A	65	177	45	7	1	2	(1	1)	60	17	17	10	1	25	0	2	1	3	2	.60	2	.254	.293	.339
1984	California	A	108	307	76	13	2	6	(3	3)	111	31	33	20	0	53	2	6	2	3	2	.60	2	.248	.296	.362
1985	California	A	83	217	41	3	0	4	(2	2)	56	16	16	16	1	32	0	8	2	4	1	.80	5	.189	.243	.258
1986	California	A	92	288	63	11	3	3	(3	0)	89	25	33	16	2	34	2	8	2	1	4	.20	4	.219	.263	.309
10 YEARS			957	2682	667	97	23	38	(21	17)	924	316	259	204	13	385	14	86	19	53	33	.62	26	.249	.303	.345
1982	California	A	55	102	25	4	2	1	(0	1)	36	17	11	7	1	17	0	2	0	4	0	1.00	1	.245	.294	.353
1982	Minnesota	A	25	81	13	1	0	0	(0	0)	14	7	5	7	0	13	1	1	0	0	2	.00	4	.160	.236	.173

CURTIS WILKERSON

Bats both Right and Left-handed, Throws Right-handed   Turns Age 26 in 1987, Born 04/26/61

Year	Team	League	G	AB	H	2B	3B	HR	(Hm	Rd)	TB	R	RBI	TBB	IBB	SO	HBP	SH	SF	SB	CS	SB%	GIDP	AVE	OBP	SLG
1983	Texas	A	16	35	6	0	1	0	(0	0)	8	7	1	2	0	5	0	0	0	3	0	1.00	0	.171	.216	.229
1984	Texas	A	153	484	120	12	0	1	(0	1)	135	47	26	22	0	72	2	12	2	12	10	.55	7	.248	.279	.279
1985	Texas	A	129	360	88	10	6	0	(0	0)	111	35	22	22	0	63	4	6	3	14	7	.67	5	.244	.293	.308
1986	Texas	A	110	236	56	10	3	0	(0	0)	72	27	15	11	0	42	1	0	1	9	7	.56	2	.237	.273	.305
4 YEARS			408	1115	270	33	10	1	(0	1)	326	116	64	57	0	182	7	18	6	38	24	.61	16	.242	.282	.292

JERRY WILLARD

Bats Left-handed, Throws Right-handed   Turns Age 27 in 1987, Born 03/14/60

Year	Team	League	G	AB	H	2B	3B	HR	(Hm	Rd)	TB	R	RBI	TBB	IBB	SO	HBP	SH	SF	SB	CS	SB%	GIDP	AVE	OBP	SLG
1984	Cleveland	A	87	246	55	8	1	10	(5	5)	95	21	37	26	0	55	0	0	3	1	0	1.00	6	.224	.295	.386
1985	Cleveland	A	104	300	81	13	0	7	(4	3)	115	39	36	28	1	59	1	4	1	0	0	.00	3	.270	.333	.383
1986	Oakland	A	75	161	43	7	0	4	(2	2)	62	17	26	22	0	28	2	4	4	0	1	.00	4	.267	.354	.385
3 YEARS			266	707	179	28	1	21	(11	10)	272	77	99	76	1	142	3	8	8	1	1	.50	13	.253	.325	.385

FRANK WILLIAMS

Pitches Right-handed, Bats Right-handed

Turns Age 29 in 1987, Born 02/13/58

Year	Team	League	G	GS	CG	GF	IP	BFP	H	R	ER	HR	SH	SF	HB	TBB	IBB	SO	WP	Bk	W	L	Pct	ShO	Sv	ERA
1984	San Francisco	N	61	1	1	15	106.1	454	88	49	42	7	9	2	3	51	6	91	8	5	9	4	.692	1	3	3.55
1985	San Francisco	N	49	0	0	15	73	318	65	39	34	5	4	4	6	35	7	54	1	1	2	4	.333	0	0	4.19
1986	San Francisco	N	36	0	0	12	52.1	194	35	8	7	0	3	1	4	21	4	33	1	0	3	1	.750	0	1	1.20
3 YEARS			146	1	1	42	231.2	966	188	96	83	7	16	7	13	107	17	178	12	6	14	9	.609	1	4	3.22

MITCH WILLIAMS

Pitches Left-handed, Bats Left-handed

Turns Age 23 in 1987, Born 11/17/64

Year	Team	League	G	GS	CG	GF	IP	BFP	H	R	ER	HR	SH	SF	HB	TBB	IBB	SO	WP	Bk	W	L	Pct	ShO	Sv	ERA
1986	Texas	A	80	0	0	38	98	435	69	39	39	8	1	3	11	79	8	90	5	5	8	6	.571	0	8	3.58

REGGIE WILLIAMS

Bats Right-handed, Throws Right-handed

Turns Age 27 in 1987, Born 08/29/60

Year	Team	League	G	AB	H	2B	3B	HR	(Hm	Rd)	TB	R	RBI	TBB	IBB	SO	HBP	SH	SF	SB	CS	SB%	GIDP	AVE	OBP	SLG
1985	Los Angeles	N	22	9	3	0	0	0	(0	0)	3	4	0	0	0	4	0	0	0	1	0	1.00	0	.333	.333	.333
1986	Los Angeles	N	128	303	84	14	2	4	(1	3)	114	35	32	23	9	57	2	9	1	9	3	.75	8	.277	.331	.376
2 YEARS			150	312	87	14	2	4	(1	3)	117	39	32	23	9	61	2	9	1	10	3	.77	8	.279	.331	.375

CARL WILLIS

Pitches Right-handed, Bats Left-handed

Turns Age 27 in 1987, Born 12/28/60

Year	Team	League	G	GS	CG	GF	IP	BFP	H	R	ER	HR	SH	SF	HB	TBB	IBB	SO	WP	Bk	W	L	Pct	ShO	Sv	ERA
1984	2 Teams		17	2	0	5	25.2	113	33	17	17	2	1	0	0	7	2	7	0	0	0	3	.000	0	1	5.96
1985	Cincinnati	N	11	0	0	6	13.2	69	21	18	14	3	1	2	0	5	0	6	1	0	1	0	1.000	0	1	9.22
1986	Cincinnati	N	29	0	0	7	52.1	233	54	29	26	4	5	1	1	32	9	24	3	1	1	3	.250	0	0	4.47
3 YEARS			57	2	0	18	91.2	415	108	64	57	9	7	3	1	44	11	37	4	1	2	6	.250	0	2	5.60
1984	Detroit	A	10	2	0	4	16	74	25	13	13	1	0	0	0	5	2	4	0	0	0	2	.000	0	0	7.31
1984	Cincinnati	N	7	0	0	1	9.2	39	8	4	4	1	1	0	0	2	0	3	0	0	0	1	.000	0	1	3.72

FRANK WILLS

Pitches Right-handed, Bats Right-handed

Turns Age 29 in 1987, Born 10/26/58

Year	Team	League	G	GS	CG	GF	IP	BFP	H	R	ER	HR	SH	SF	HB	TBB	IBB	SO	WP	Bk	W	L	Pct	ShO	Sv	ERA
1983	Kansas City	A	6	4	0	1	34.2	152	35	17	16	2	0	2	0	15	0	23	3	0	2	1	.667	0	0	4.15
1984	Kansas City	A	10	5	0	2	37	161	39	21	21	3	0	4	0	13	0	21	2	0	2	3	.400	0	0	5.11
1985	Seattle	A	24	18	1	2	123	541	122	85	82	18	4	8	3	68	3	67	9	1	5	11	.313	0	1	6.00
1986	Cleveland	A	26	0	0	16	40.1	182	43	23	22	6	6	2	0	16	4	32	2	0	4	4	.500	0	4	4.91
4 YEARS			66	27	1	21	235	1036	239	146	141	29	10	16	3	112	7	143	16	1	13	19	.406	0	5	5.40

GLENN WILSON

Bats Right-handed, Throws Right-handed

Turns Age 29 in 1987, Born 12/22/58

Year	Team	League	G	AB	H	2B	3B	HR	(Hm	Rd)	TB	R	RBI	TBB	IBB	SO	HBP	SH	SF	SB	CS	SB%	GIDP	AVE	OBP	SLG
1982	Detroit	A	84	322	94	15	1	12	(9	3)	147	39	34	15	0	51	0	3	2	2	3	.40	8	.292	.322	.457
1983	Detroit	A	144	503	135	25	6	11	(9	2)	205	55	65	25	1	79	3	0	2	1	1	.50	9	.268	.306	.408
1984	Philadelphia	N	132	341	82	21	3	6	(5	1)	127	28	31	17	1	56	1	1	3	7	1	.88	12	.240	.276	.372
1985	Philadelphia	N	161	608	167	39	5	14	(7	7)	258	73	102	35	1	117	0	0	7	7	4	.64	24	.275	.311	.424
1986	Philadelphia	N	155	584	158	30	4	15	(7	8)	241	70	84	42	1	91	4	0	9	5	1	.83	15	.271	.319	.413
5 YEARS			676	2358	636	130	19	58	(37	21)	978	265	316	134	4	394	8	4	23	22	10	.69	68	.270	.308	.415

MOOKIE WILSON

Bats both Right and Left-handed, Throws Right-handed

Turns Age 31 in 1987, Born 02/09/56

Year	Team	League	G	AB	H	2B	3B	HR	(Hm	Rd)	TB	R	RBI	TBB	IBB	SO	HBP	SH	SF	SB	CS	SB%	GIDP	AVE	OBP	SLG
1980	New York	N	27	105	26	5	3	0	(0	0)	37	16	4	12	0	19	0	2	0	7	7	.50	0	.248	.325	.352
1981	New York	N	92	328	89	8	8	3	(2	1)	122	49	14	20	3	59	2	0	0	24	12	.67	3	.271	.317	.372
1982	New York	N	159	639	178	25	9	5	(2	3)	236	90	55	32	4	102	2	1	3	58	16	.78	6	.279	.314	.369
1983	New York	N	152	638	176	25	6	7	(4	3)	234	91	51	18	3	103	4	2	1	54	16	.77	6	.276	.300	.367
1984	New York	N	154	587	162	28	10	10	(7	3)	240	88	54	26	2	90	2	2	2	46	9	.84	5	.276	.308	.409
1985	New York	N	93	337	93	16	8	6	(2	4)	143	56	26	28	6	52	0	1	1	24	9	.73	9	.276	.331	.424
1986	New York	N	123	381	110	17	5	9	(4	5)	164	61	45	32	5	72	1	0	1	25	7	.78	5	.289	.345	.430
7 YEARS			800	3015	834	124	49	40	(21	19)	1176	451	249	168	23	497	11	8	8	238	76	.76	33	.277	.316	.390

134

WILLIE WILSON

Bats both Right and Left-handed, Throws Right-handed

Turns Age 32 in 1987, Born 07/09/55

Year	Team	League		BATTING																		BASERUNNING				PERCENTAGES		
			G	AB	H	2B	3B	HR	(Hm	Rd)	TB	R	RBI	TBB	IBB	SO	HBP	SH	SF		SB	CS	SB%	GIDP		AVE	OBP	SLG
1976	Kansas City	A	12	6	1	0	0	0	(0	0)	1	0	0	0	0	2	0	0	0		2	1	.67	0		.167	.167	.167
1977	Kansas City	A	13	34	11	2	0	0	(0	0)	13	10	1	1	0	8	0	2	0		6	3	.67	1		.324	.343	.382
1978	Kansas City	A	127	198	43	8	2	0	(0	0)	55	43	16	16	0	33	2	5	2		46	12	.79	2		.217	.280	.278
1979	Kansas City	A	154	588	185	18	13	6	(3	3)	247	113	49	28	3	92	7	13	4		83	12	.87	1		.315	.351	.420
1980	Kansas City	A	161	705	230	28	15	3	(2	1)	297	133	49	28	3	81	6	5	1		79	10	.89	4		.326	.357	.421
1981	Kansas City	A	102	439	133	10	7	1	(0	1)	160	54	32	18	3	42	4	3	1		34	8	.81	5		.303	.335	.364
1982	Kansas City	A	136	585	194	19	15	3	(2	1)	252	87	46	26	2	81	6	2	2		37	11	.77	4		.332	.365	.431
1983	Kansas City	A	137	576	159	22	8	2	(2	0)	203	90	33	33	2	75	1	1	0		59	8	.88	4		.276	.316	.352
1984	Kansas City	A	128	541	163	24	9	2	(1	1)	211	81	44	39	2	56	3	2	3		47	5	.90	7		.301	.350	.390
1985	Kansas City	A	141	605	168	25	21	4	(1	3)	247	87	43	29	3	94	5	2	1		43	11	.80	6		.278	.316	.408
1986	Kansas City	A	156	631	170	20	7	9	(5	4)	231	77	44	31	1	97	9	3	1		34	8	.81	9		.269	.313	.366
11 YEARS			1267	4908	1457	176	97	30	(16	14)	1917	775	357	249	19	661	43	38	15		470	89	.84	40		.297	.335	.391

DAVE WINFIELD

Bats Right-handed, Throws Right-handed

Turns Age 36 in 1987, Born 10/03/51

Year	Team	League		BATTING																		BASERUNNING				PERCENTAGES		
			G	AB	H	2B	3B	HR	(Hm	Rd)	TB	R	RBI	TBB	IBB	SO	HBP	SH	SF		SB	CS	SB%	GIDP		AVE	OBP	SLG
1973	San Diego	N	56	141	39	4	1	3	(2	1)	54	9	12	12	1	19	0	0	1		0	0	.00	5		.277	.331	.383
1974	San Diego	N	145	498	132	18	4	20	(12	8)	218	57	75	40	2	96	1	0	5		9	7	.56	14		.265	.318	.438
1975	San Diego	N	143	509	136	20	2	15	(7	8)	205	74	76	69	14	82	3	3	7		23	4	.85	11		.267	.354	.403
1976	San Diego	N	137	492	139	26	4	13	(4	9)	212	81	69	65	8	78	3	2	5		26	7	.79	14		.283	.366	.431
1977	San Diego	N	157	615	169	29	7	25	(12	13)	287	104	92	58	10	75	0	0	5		16	7	.70	12		.275	.335	.467
1978	San Diego	N	158	587	181	30	5	24	(11	13)	293	88	97	55	20	81	2	0	5		21	9	.70	13		.308	.367	.499
1979	San Diego	N	159	597	184	27	10	34	(16	18)	333	97	118	85	24	71	2	0	2		15	9	.63	9		.308	.395	.558
1980	San Diego	N	162	558	154	25	6	20	(7	13)	251	89	87	79	14	83	2	0	4		23	7	.77	13		.276	.365	.450
1981	New York	A	105	388	114	25	1	13	(4	9)	180	52	68	43	3	41	1	1	7		11	1	.92	13		.294	.360	.464
1982	New York	A	140	539	151	24	8	37	(14	23)	302	84	106	45	7	64	0	5	8		5	3	.63	20		.280	.331	.560
1983	New York	A	152	598	169	26	8	32	(13	19)	307	99	116	58	2	77	2	0	6		15	6	.71	14		.283	.345	.513
1984	New York	A	141	567	193	34	4	19	(9	10)	292	106	100	53	9	71	0	0	6		6	4	.60	14		.340	.393	.515
1985	New York	A	155	633	174	34	6	26	(15	11)	298	105	114	52	8	96	0	0	4		19	7	.73	17		.275	.328	.471
1986	New York	A	154	565	148	31	5	24	(12	12)	261	90	104	77	9	106	2	2	6		6	5	.55	20		.262	.349	.462
14 YEARS			1964	7287	2083	353	71	305	(138	167)	3493	1135	1234	791	131	1040	18	13	71		195	76	.72	205		.286	.354	.479

JIM WINN

Pitches Right-handed, Bats Right-handed

Turns Age 28 in 1987, Born 09/23/59

Year	Team	League		HOW MUCH HE PITCHED						WHAT HE GAVE UP												THE RESULTS					
			G	GS	CG	GF	IP	BFP		H	R	ER	HR	SH	SF	HB	TBB	IBB	SO	WP	Bk		W	L	Pct	ShO	Sv	ERA
1983	Pittsburgh	N	7	0	0	3	11	51		12	9	9	2	0	0	0	6	0	3	1	0		0	0	.000	0	0	7.36
1984	Pittsburgh	N	9	0	0	2	18.2	81		19	8	8	2	0	0	0	9	1	11	2	1		1	0	1.000	0	1	3.86
1985	Pittsburgh	N	30	7	0	10	75.2	326		77	45	44	4	2	1	2	31	2	22	5	2		3	6	.333	0	0	5.23
1986	Pittsburgh	N	50	3	0	18	88	377		85	44	35	9	4	3	2	38	7	70	9	1		3	5	.375	0	3	3.58
4 YEARS			96	10	0	33	193.1	835		193	106	96	17	6	4	4	84	10	106	17	4		7	11	.389	0	4	4.47

HERM WINNINGHAM

Bats Left-handed, Throws Right-handed

Turns Age 26 in 1987, Born 12/01/61

Year	Team	League		BATTING																		BASERUNNING				PERCENTAGES		
			G	AB	H	2B	3B	HR	(Hm	Rd)	TB	R	RBI	TBB	IBB	SO	HBP	SH	SF		SB	CS	SB%	GIDP		AVE	OBP	SLG
1984	New York	N	14	27	11	1	1	0	(0	0)	14	5	5	1	0	7	0	0	0		2	1	.67	0		.407	.429	.519
1985	Montreal	N	125	312	74	6	5	3	(0	3)	99	30	21	28	3	72	0	1	4		20	9	.69	1		.237	.297	.317
1986	Montreal	N	90	185	40	6	3	4	(1	3)	64	23	11	18	3	51	0	1	0		12	7	.63	4		.216	.286	.346
3 YEARS			229	524	125	13	9	7	(1	6)	177	58	37	47	6	130	0	2	4		34	17	.67	5		.239	.299	.338

BOBBY WITT

Pitches Right-handed, Bats Right-handed

Turns Age 23 in 1987, Born 05/11/64

Year	Team	League		HOW MUCH HE PITCHED						WHAT HE GAVE UP												THE RESULTS					
			G	GS	CG	GF	IP	BFP		H	R	ER	HR	SH	SF	HB	TBB	IBB	SO	WP	Bk		W	L	Pct	ShO	Sv	ERA
1986	Texas	A	31	31	0	0	157.2	741		130	104	96	18	3	9	3	143	2	174	22	3		11	9	.550	0	0	5.48

MIKE WITT

Pitches Right-handed, Bats Right-handed

Turns Age 27 in 1987, Born 07/20/60

			HOW MUCH HE PITCHED					WHAT HE GAVE UP												THE RESULTS					
Year	Team	League	G	GS	CG	GF	IP	BFP	H	R	ER	HR	SH	SF	HB	TBB	IBB	SO	WP	Bk	W	L	Pct	ShO	Sv	ERA
1981	California	A	22	21	7	1	129	555	123	60	47	9	3	4	11	47	4	75	2	0	8	9	.471	1	0	3.28
1982	California	A	33	26	5	2	179.2	748	177	77	70	8	8	5	7	47	2	85	8	1	8	6	.571	1	0	3.51
1983	California	A	43	19	2	15	154	683	173	90	84	14	5	7	6	75	7	77	8	0	7	14	.333	0	5	4.91
1984	California	A	34	34	9	0	246.2	1032	227	103	95	17	7	7	5	84	3	196	7	1	15	11	.577	2	0	3.47
1985	California	A	35	35	6	0	250	1049	228	115	99	22	4	5	4	98	6	180	11	1	15	9	.625	1	0	3.56
1986	California	A	34	34	14	0	269	1071	218	95	85	22	3	5	3	73	2	208	6	0	18	10	.643	3	0	2.84
6 YEARS			201	169	43	18	1228.1	5138	1146	540	480	92	30	33	36	424	24	821	42	3	71	59	.546	8	5	3.52

TODD WORRELL

Pitches Right-handed, Bats Right-handed

Turns Age 28 in 1987, Born 09/28/59

			HOW MUCH HE PITCHED					WHAT HE GAVE UP												THE RESULTS					
Year	Team	League	G	GS	CG	GF	IP	BFP	H	R	ER	HR	SH	SF	HB	TBB	IBB	SO	WP	Bk	W	L	Pct	ShO	Sv	ERA
1985	St Louis	N	17	0	0	11	21.2	88	17	7	7	2	0	2	0	7	2	17	2	0	3	0	1.000	0	5	2.91
1986	St Louis	N	74	0	0	60	103.2	430	86	29	24	9	7	6	1	41	16	73	1	0	9	10	.474	0	36	2.08
2 YEARS			91	0	0	71	125.1	518	103	36	31	11	7	8	1	48	18	90	3	0	12	10	.545	0	41	2.23

GEORGE WRIGHT

Bats both Right and Left-handed, Throws Right-handed

Turns Age 29 in 1987, Born 12/22/58

					BATTING															BASERUNNING				PERCENTAGES		
Year	Team	League	G	AB	H	2B	3B	HR	(Hm	Rd)	TB	R	RBI	TBB	IBB	SO	HBP	SH	SF	SB	CS	SB%	GIDP	AVE	OBP	SLG
1982	Texas	A	150	557	147	20	5	11	(3	8)	210	69	50	30	4	78	3	8	1	3	7	.30	11	.264	.305	.377
1983	Texas	A	162	634	175	28	6	18	(7	11)	269	79	80	41	9	82	2	1	3	8	7	.53	9	.276	.321	.424
1984	Texas	A	101	383	93	19	4	9	(6	3)	147	40	48	15	2	54	2	1	3	0	2	.00	6	.243	.273	.384
1985	Texas	A	109	363	69	13	0	2	(2	0)	88	21	18	25	5	49	0	3	2	4	7	.36	9	.190	.241	.242
1986	2 Teams		105	223	45	8	3	2	(1	1)	65	22	12	15	1	51	2	1	4	4	6	.40	9	.202	.254	.291
5 YEARS			627	2160	529	88	18	42	(19	23)	779	231	208	126	21	314	9	14	13	19	29	.40	40	.245	.288	.361
1986	Texas	A	49	106	23	3	1	2	(1	1)	34	10	7	4	1	23	1	0	1	3	5	.38	2	.217	.250	.321
1986	Montreal	N	56	117	22	5	2	0	(0	0)	31	12	5	11	0	28	1	1	3	1	1	.50	3	.188	.258	.265

RICKY WRIGHT

Pitches Left-handed, Bats Left-handed

Turns Age 29 in 1987, Born 11/22/58

			HOW MUCH HE PITCHED					WHAT HE GAVE UP												THE RESULTS					
Year	Team	League	G	GS	CG	GF	IP	BFP	H	R	ER	HR	SH	SF	HB	TBB	IBB	SO	WP	Bk	W	L	Pct	ShO	Sv	ERA
1982	Los Angeles	N	14	5	0	3	32.2	145	28	12	11	1	4	1	0	20	6	24	1	0	2	1	.667	0	0	3.03
1983	2 Teams		7	0	0	3	8.1	34	5	2	2	0	3	1	0	3	1	7	1	0	0	0	.000	0	0	2.16
1984	Texas	A	8	1	0	3	14.2	69	20	10	10	3	2	0	0	11	0	6	0	0	0	2	.000	0	0	6.14
1985	Texas	A	5	0	0	1	7.2	32	5	4	4	0	0	0	0	5	1	7	0	0	0	0	.000	0	0	4.70
1986	Texas	A	21	1	0	2	39.1	177	44	22	22	1	1	0	0	21	0	23	2	0	1	0	1.000	0	0	5.03
5 YEARS			55	7	0	12	102.2	457	102	50	49	5	10	2	0	60	8	67	4	0	3	3	.500	0	0	4.30
1983	Texas	A	1	0	0	0	2	8	0	0	0	0	2	0	0	1	0	2	0	0	0	0	.000	0	0	0.00
1983	Los Angeles	N	6	0	0	3	6.1	26	5	2	2	0	1	1	0	2	1	5	1	0	0	0	.000	0	0	2.84

BUTCH WYNEGAR

Bats both Right and Left-handed, Throws Right-handed

Turns Age 31 in 1987, Born 03/14/56

					BATTING															BASERUNNING				PERCENTAGES		
Year	Team	League	G	AB	H	2B	3B	HR	(Hm	Rd)	TB	R	RBI	TBB	IBB	SO	HBP	SH	SF	SB	CS	SB%	GIDP	AVE	OBP	SLG
1976	Minnesota	A	149	534	139	21	2	10	(4	6)	194	58	69	79	7	63	2	4	3	0	0	.00	14	.260	.356	.363
1977	Minnesota	A	144	532	139	22	3	10	(4	6)	197	76	79	68	5	61	2	10	5	2	3	.40	11	.261	.344	.370
1978	Minnesota	A	135	454	104	22	1	4	(4	0)	140	36	45	47	2	42	6	11	4	1	0	1.00	7	.229	.307	.308
1979	Minnesota	A	149	504	136	20	0	7	(3	4)	177	74	57	74	5	36	4	11	4	2	2	.50	13	.270	.363	.351
1980	Minnesota	A	146	486	124	18	3	5	(3	2)	163	61	57	63	6	36	2	7	6	3	1	.75	9	.255	.339	.335
1981	Minnesota	A	47	150	37	5	0	0	(0	0)	42	11	10	17	2	9	1	1	3	0	1	.00	7	.247	.322	.280
1982	2 Teams		87	277	74	12	1	4	(2	2)	100	36	28	50	2	33	1	7	3	0	1	.00	9	.267	.378	.361
1983	New York	A	94	301	80	18	2	6	(4	2)	120	40	42	52	1	29	1	1	2	1	1	.50	7	.267	.378	.361
1984	New York	A	129	442	118	13	1	6	(3	3)	151	48	45	65	6	35	0	4	1	1	4	.20	18	.267	.360	.342
1985	New York	A	102	309	69	15	0	5	(2	3)	99	27	32	64	2	43	0	1	1	0	0	.00	11	.223	.356	.320
1986	New York	A	61	194	40	4	1	7	(3	4)	67	19	29	30	2	21	0	0	2	0	0	.00	9	.206	.310	.345
11 YEARS			1243	4183	1069	170	14	64	(32	32)	1459	486	493	609	40	408	17	57	34	10	13	.43	115	.256	.350	.349
1982	Minnesota	A	24	86	18	4	0	1	(1	0)	25	9	8	10	1	12	0	0	0	0	0	.00	2	.209	.292	.291
1982	New York	A	63	191	56	8	1	3	(1	2)	75	27	20	40	1	21	1	7	3	0	1	.00	7	.293	.413	.393

MARVELL WYNNE

Bats Left-handed, Throws Left-handed

Turns Age 28 in 1987, Born 12/17/59

Year	Team	League	G	AB	H	2B	3B	HR	(Hm	Rd)	TB	R	RBI	TBB	IBB	SO	HBP	SH	SF	SB	CS	SB%	GIDP	AVE	OBP	SLG
1983	Pittsburgh	N	103	366	89	16	2	7	(3	4)	130	66	26	38	0	52	3	7	1	12	10	.55	3	.243	.319	.355
1984	Pittsburgh	N	154	653	174	24	11	0	(0	0)	220	77	39	42	0	81	0	5	2	24	19	.56	8	.266	.310	.337
1985	Pittsburgh	N	103	337	69	6	3	2	(1	1)	87	21	18	18	2	48	1	7	0	10	5	.67	8	.205	.247	.258
1986	San Diego	N	137	288	76	19	2	7	(5	2)	120	34	37	15	2	45	1	1	3	11	11	.50	5	.264	.300	.417
4 YEARS			497	1644	408	65	18	16	(9	7)	557	198	120	113	4	226	5	20	6	57	45	.56	24	.248	.298	.339

STEVE YEAGER

Bats Right-handed, Throws Right-handed

Turns Age 39 in 1987, Born 11/24/48

Year	Team	League	G	AB	H	2B	3B	HR	(Hm	Rd)	TB	R	RBI	TBB	IBB	SO	HBP	SH	SF	SB	CS	SB%	GIDP	AVE	OBP	SLG
1972	Los Angeles	N	35	106	29	0	1	4	(2	2)	43	18	15	16	2	26	1	1	0	0	0	.00	3	.274	.374	.406
1973	Los Angeles	N	54	134	34	5	0	2	(0	2)	45	18	10	15	1	33	3	1	1	1	0	1.00	4	.254	.340	.336
1974	Los Angeles	N	94	316	84	16	1	12	(6	6)	138	41	41	32	5	77	2	1	3	2	2	.50	7	.266	.334	.437
1975	Los Angeles	N	135	452	103	16	1	12	(6	6)	157	34	54	40	7	75	8	9	6	2	5	.29	15	.228	.298	.347
1976	Los Angeles	N	117	359	77	11	3	11	(5	6)	127	42	35	30	3	84	7	1	2	3	1	.75	5	.214	.286	.354
1977	Los Angeles	N	125	387	99	21	2	16	(10	6)	172	53	55	43	11	84	4	1	3	0	0	.00	3	.256	.334	.444
1978	Los Angeles	N	94	228	44	7	0	4	(2	2)	63	19	23	36	11	41	0	0	2	1	0	1.00	12	.193	.301	.276
1979	Los Angeles	N	105	310	67	9	2	13	(6	7)	119	33	41	29	8	68	0	5	2	2	3	.40	7	.216	.282	.384
1980	Los Angeles	N	96	227	48	8	0	2	(0	2)	62	20	20	20	6	54	0	0	0	0	0	.00	3	.211	.274	.273
1981	Los Angeles	N	42	86	18	2	0	3	(1	2)	29	5	7	6	0	14	0	0	0	0	0	.00	3	.209	.261	.337
1982	Los Angeles	N	82	196	48	5	2	2	(2	0)	63	13	18	13	3	28	1	4	1	0	0	.00	3	.245	.294	.321
1983	Los Angeles	N	113	335	68	8	3	15	(7	8)	127	31	41	23	4	57	1	6	1	1	2	.33	15	.203	.256	.379
1984	Los Angeles	N	74	197	45	4	0	4	(1	3)	61	16	29	20	1	38	0	1	3	1	2	.33	3	.228	.295	.310
1985	Los Angeles	N	53	121	25	4	1	0	(0	0)	31	4	9	7	2	24	0	1	2	1	0	.00	3	.207	.246	.256
1986	Seattle	A	50	130	27	2	0	2	(1	1)	35	10	12	12	0	23	0	2	1	0	0	.00	5	.208	.273	.269
15 YEARS			1269	3584	816	118	16	102	(49	53)	1272	357	410	342	64	726	27	33	28	14	18	.44	93	.228	.298	.355

RICH YETT

Pitches Right-handed, Bats Right-handed

Turns Age 25 in 1987, Born 10/06/62

Year	Team	League	G	GS	CG	GF	IP	BFP	H	R	ER	HR	SH	SF	HB	TBB	IBB	SO	WP	Bk	W	L	Pct	ShO	Sv	ERA
1985	Minnesota	A	1	1	0	0	0.1	5	1	1	1	0	0	0	0	2	0	0	1	0	0	0	.000	0	0	27.00
1986	Cleveland	A	39	3	1	17	78.2	350	84	48	45	10	2	4	1	37	4	50	8	0	5	3	.625	1	1	5.15
2 YEARS			40	4	1	17	79	355	85	49	46	10	2	4	1	39	4	50	9	0	5	3	.625	1	1	5.24

FLOYD YOUMANS

Pitches Right-handed, Bats Right-handed

Turns Age 23 in 1987, Born 05/11/64

Year	Team	League	G	GS	CG	GF	IP	BFP	H	R	ER	HR	SH	SF	HB	TBB	IBB	SO	WP	Bk	W	L	Pct	ShO	Sv	ERA
1985	Montreal	N	14	12	0	2	77	331	57	27	21	3	2	2	1	49	1	54	5	0	4	3	.571	0	0	2.45
1986	Montreal	N	33	32	6	1	219	905	145	93	86	14	6	7	4	118	4	202	10	1	13	12	.520	2	0	3.53
2 YEARS			47	44	6	3	296	1236	202	120	107	17	8	9	5	167	5	256	15	1	17	15	.531	2	0	3.25

CURT YOUNG

Pitches Left-handed, Bats Right-handed

Turns Age 27 in 1987, Born 04/16/60

Year	Team	League	G	GS	CG	GF	IP	BFP	H	R	ER	HR	SH	SF	HB	TBB	IBB	SO	WP	Bk	W	L	Pct	ShO	Sv	ERA
1983	Oakland	A	8	2	0	0	9	50	17	17	16	1	0	0	1	5	0	5	1	0	0	1	.000	0	0	16.00
1984	Oakland	A	20	17	2	0	108.2	475	118	53	49	9	1	4	8	31	0	41	3	0	9	4	.692	1	0	4.06
1985	Oakland	A	19	7	0	5	46	214	57	38	37	15	0	1	1	22	0	19	1	0	0	4	.000	0	0	7.24
1986	Oakland	A	29	27	5	0	198	826	176	88	76	19	8	9	7	57	1	116	7	2	13	9	.591	2	0	3.45
4 YEARS			76	53	7	5	361.2	1565	368	196	178	44	9	14	17	115	1	181	12	2	22	18	.550	3	0	4.43

MATT YOUNG

Pitches Left-handed, Bats Left-handed

Turns Age 29 in 1987, Born 08/09/58

Year	Team	League	G	GS	CG	GF	IP	BFP	H	R	ER	HR	SH	SF	HB	TBB	IBB	SO	WP	Bk	W	L	Pct	ShO	Sv	ERA
1983	Seattle	A	33	32	5	0	203.2	851	178	86	74	17	4	8	7	79	2	130	4	2	11	15	.423	2	0	3.27
1984	Seattle	A	22	22	1	0	113.1	524	141	81	72	11	1	5	1	57	3	73	3	1	6	8	.429	0	0	5.72
1985	Seattle	A	37	35	5	2	218.1	950	242	135	119	23	7	4	7	76	3	136	6	2	12	19	.387	2	1	4.91
1986	Seattle	A	65	5	0	32	103.2	458	108	60	44	9	4	3	8	46	2	82	7	1	8	6	.571	0	13	3.82
4 YEARS			157	94	12	34	639	2783	669	352	309	60	16	19	23	258	10	421	20	6	37	48	.435	4	14	4.35

MIKE YOUNG

Bats both Right and Left-handed, Throws Right-handed

Turns Age 27 in 1987, Born 03/20/60

Year	Team	League	G	AB	H	2B	3B	HR	(Hm	Rd)	TB	R	RBI	TBB	IBB	SO	HBP	SH	SF	SB	CS	SB%	GIDP	AVE	OBP	SLG
1982	Baltimore	A	6	2	0	0	0	0	(0	0)	0	2	0	0	0	1	0	0	0	0	0	.00	0	.000	.000	.000
1983	Baltimore	A	25	36	6	2	1	0	(0	0)	10	5	2	2	0	8	1	4	0	1	0	1.00	1	.167	.231	.278
1984	Baltimore	A	123	401	101	17	2	17	(9	8)	173	59	52	58	2	110	7	2	2	6	2	.75	5	.252	.355	.431
1985	Baltimore	A	139	450	123	22	1	28	(15	13)	231	72	81	48	5	104	4	1	1	1	5	.17	9	.273	.348	.513
1986	Baltimore	A	117	369	93	15	1	9	(5	4)	137	43	42	49	2	90	3	2	3	3	1	.75	13	.252	.342	.371
5 YEARS			410	1258	323	56	5	54	(29	25)	551	181	177	157	9	313	15	9	6	11	8	.58	28	.257	.345	.438

JOEL YOUNGBLOOD

Bats Right-handed, Throws Right-handed

Turns Age 36 in 1987, Born 08/28/51

Year	Team	League	G	AB	H	2B	3B	HR	(Hm	Rd)	TB	R	RBI	TBB	IBB	SO	HBP	SH	SF	SB	CS	SB%	GIDP	AVE	OBP	SLG
1976	Cincinnati	N	55	57	11	1	1	0	(0	0)	14	8	1	2	0	8	1	0	0	1	0	1.00	1	.193	.233	.246
1977	2 Teams		95	209	51	13	1	0	(0	0)	66	17	12	16	1	45	0	1	1	1	5	.17	1	.244	.296	.316
1978	New York	N	113	266	67	12	8	7	(3	4)	116	40	30	16	1	39	1	1	3	4	0	1.00	4	.252	.294	.436
1979	New York	N	158	590	162	37	5	16	(8	8)	257	90	60	60	7	84	7	4	4	18	13	.58	4	.275	.346	.436
1980	New York	N	146	514	142	26	2	8	(6	2)	196	58	69	52	10	69	2	0	9	14	11	.56	10	.276	.340	.381
1981	New York	N	43	143	50	10	2	4	(2	2)	76	16	25	12	1	19	2	0	4	2	5	.29	4	.350	.398	.531
1982	2 Teams		120	292	70	14	0	3	(0	0)	93	37	29	17	2	58	8	2	1	2	5	.29	6	.240	.299	.318
1983	San Francisco	N	124	373	109	20	3	17	(6	11)	186	59	53	33	4	59	5	2	2	7	4	.64	11	.292	.356	.499
1984	San Francisco	N	134	469	119	17	1	10	(6	4)	168	50	51	48	1	86	4	3	0	5	6	.45	8	.254	.328	.358
1985	San Francisco	N	95	230	62	6	0	4	(1	3)	80	24	24	30	1	37	1	1	0	3	2	.60	6	.270	.355	.348
1986	San Francisco	N	97	184	47	12	0	5	(0	5)	74	20	28	18	0	34	1	2	3	1	1	.50	2	.255	.320	.402
11 YEARS			1180	3327	890	168	23	74	(32	39)	1326	419	382	304	28	538	32	16	28	58	52	.53	66	.268	.332	.399
1977	New York	N	70	182	46	11	1	0	(0	0)	59	16	11	13	1	40	0	1	1	1	3	.25	6	.253	.301	.324
1977	St Louis	N	25	27	5	2	0	0	(0	0)	7	1	1	3	0	5	0	0	0	0	2	.00	1	.185	.267	.259
1982	Montreal	N	40	90	18	2	0	0	(0	0)	20	16	8	9	1	21	3	1	1	2	1	.67	2	.200	.291	.222
1982	New York	N	80	202	52	12	0	3	(0	0)	73	21	21	8	1	37	5	1	0	0	4	.00	4	.257	.302	.361

ROBIN YOUNT

Bats Right-handed, Throws Right-handed

Turns Age 32 in 1987, Born 09/16/55

Year	Team	League	G	AB	H	2B	3B	HR	(Hm	Rd)	TB	R	RBI	TBB	IBB	SO	HBP	SH	SF	SB	CS	SB%	GIDP	AVE	OBP	SLG
1974	Milwaukee	A	107	344	86	14	5	3	(3	0)	119	48	26	12	0	46	1	5	2	7	7	.50	4	.250	.276	.346
1975	Milwaukee	A	147	558	149	28	2	8	(4	4)	205	67	52	33	3	69	1	10	5	12	4	.75	7	.267	.307	.367
1976	Milwaukee	A	161	638	161	19	3	2	(1	1)	192	59	54	38	3	69	0	8	6	16	11	.59	13	.252	.292	.301
1977	Milwaukee	A	154	605	174	34	4	4	(2	2)	228	66	49	41	1	80	2	11	4	16	7	.70	11	.288	.333	.377
1978	Milwaukee	A	127	502	147	23	9	9	(5	4)	215	66	71	24	1	43	1	13	5	16	5	.76	5	.293	.323	.428
1979	Milwaukee	A	149	577	154	26	5	8	(4	4)	214	72	51	35	3	52	1	10	3	11	8	.58	15	.267	.323	.371
1980	Milwaukee	A	143	611	179	49	10	23	(13	10)	317	121	87	26	1	67	1	6	3	20	5	.80	8	.293	.321	.519
1981	Milwaukee	A	96	377	103	15	5	10	(1	9)	158	50	49	22	1	37	2	4	6	4	1	.80	8	.273	.312	.419
1982	Milwaukee	A	156	635	210	46	12	29	(9	20)	367	129	114	54	2	63	1	4	10	14	3	.82	19	.331	.379	.578
1983	Milwaukee	A	149	578	178	42	10	17	(6	11)	291	102	80	72	6	58	3	1	8	12	5	.71	11	.308	.379	.503
1984	Milwaukee	A	160	624	186	27	7	16	(8	8)	275	105	80	67	7	67	1	1	9	14	4	.78	22	.298	.362	.441
1985	Milwaukee	A	122	466	129	26	3	15	(11	4)	206	76	68	49	3	56	2	1	9	10	4	.71	9	.277	.342	.442
1986	Milwaukee	A	140	522	163	31	7	9	(4	5)	235	82	46	62	7	73	4	5	2	14	5	.74	9	.312	.388	.450
13 YEARS			1811	7037	2019	380	82	153	(71	82)	3022	1043	827	535	38	780	20	79	72	166	69	.71	137	.287	.336	.429

III

PLAYER COMMENTARIES AND STATISTICAL BREAKDOWNS

INTRODUCTION TO PLAYER COMMENTARIES AND BREAKDOWNS

The next 260 pages of this book contain some of the most fascinating capsule commentaries regarding major league players you'll ever read. These commentaries were written by individuals who are not only baseball fans, but who follow their teams and players game by game, play by play. Nearly all of our writers are devoted scorers for Project Scoresheet. In fact, many of them score well over one hundred games per year. I think you will agree with me that their insight regarding major league players is truly extraordinary.

When we put out the word to Project Scoresheet members that we were putting this book together, we received an avalanche of responses from people who wanted to help. This book is the culmination of a tremendous amount of effort by literally hundreds of people. These people did everything imaginable. They compiled statistics. They checked calculations. They proofread boxscores. They scanned column after column of data. They wrote essays. They edited commentaries. They reviewed player breakdowns. There has never be a more devoted group of baseball enthusiasts.

There are two people who are primarily responsible for the statistical breakdowns on the following pages. One is my wife, Sue. I could never ask for a more supportive person than she has been. But support isn't all she provides. It is her computer skills that have brought each and every statistical breakdown in this book to fruition. The other is Mark Podrazik. He didn't know what he was getting into when I asked him to help with Project Scoresheet a couple of years ago. Mark has, like Sue and I, done nothing but eat, breathe, and dream about The Great American Baseball Stat Book for the last five months. And that doesn't even take into account his Project Scoresheet effort over the last two years.

In designing the player stat breakdowns we tried to include only relevant statistics. Let me give you an example. We thought about including stolen bases and caught stealings for offensive players. But we then wondered how important it is to know how players steal on ground-ball pitch-

ers as opposed to finesse pitchers. It might have some interest, but would probably not be very meaningful. (By the way, don't forget that SBs and CSs are in the Player Register section.)

When it got down to it, we felt that the most important thing we could include were breakdowns over a three year period. As most table game players know, an individual player can vary quite dramatically from year to year, especially when stats are broken into finer categories. Harold Baines of the White Sox is a good example here. In 1985, Harold hit .341 against left-handed pitching and .293 vs. RHP. In 1986, he reversed the pattern— .262 vs. LHP and .315 vs. RHP. Now it is possible that Baines simply forgot how to hit left-handers in 1986, but it is much more likely that his stats were simply a statistical fluctuation between the two years. Wouldn't it be nice to go back another year to get a better evaluation? Over the three-year period, Baines wound up hitting .295 vs. LHP and .308 vs. RHP. This is a very normal pattern for a good left-handed hitter like Baines. (Incidentally, as you'll see from the breakdowns, Baines loses a lot of power against lefties.)

There are commentaries and breakdowns for 260 players included in this section. It is followed by three-year breakdowns for another 390 players. Again, we felt that the three-year breakdowns were more relevant than only the most recent year.

Most of the column and row headings for the stat breakdowns are self-explanatory. (See Player Register for a legend of abbreviations.) However, we have included several categories that are probably a bit unfamiliar to you. Let me take you through some of these categories.

Take a look at a sample stat breakdown for a batter. Along the left side are the row headings. "Totals," "Left-Right," and "Home-Road" are self explanatory. But you probably have never seen stats based on "Groundball-Flyball" or "Power-Finesse" before. Here's how we got them. For each season and for each league as a whole, we determined the average ratio of Groundouts to Airouts. The Ground to Air ratio for every pitcher in the league was compared to the league average and the pitcher was then defined as either a groundball or flyball pitcher for a particular year. Then batting statistics were compiled based on performance against these groupings of pitchers. To put it more simply, the "Groundball" line shows the batting stats of a player when batting against pitchers who were above the league average in Ground to Air ratio.

We basically did the same thing for "Power-Finesse." Our working definition was that a power pitcher was a pitcher who was above the league average in walks PLUS strikeouts per inning pitched. With the league average generally being around 1.00, a pitcher like Don Aase with 28 walks and 67 strikeouts in 81.2 innings (a 1.16 ratio) gets categorized as a Power pitcher. Once again, we then compiled batting stats against each of these two groupings of pitchers. Simply said, the "Power" line shows the batting stats of a player when batting against pitchers who were above the league average in strikeouts plus walks per inning pitched.

The next three categories, "Grass-Turf", "Day-Night", and "By Month", are all pretty much self explanatory. But take note of the section labeled "Situational." The stats are first broken down by "Bases Empty" and "Runners On." Then within each of these, the stats are further divided, "Leadoff - Not Leadoff" and "Scoring Position - First Base Only". The category "Late Innings, Close" shows batting stats during the crucial part of games. By "Late Innings," we simply mean any time after the 6th inning. Our definition of "Close" is very similar to one aspect of the definition of a save for a relief pitcher. A game is close if the tying or go ahead run is on base, at bat, or in the on-deck circle for the team currently on the short end of the score. In addition, we also call the game close if the score is tied or a team leads by only one run. Note that the status of "Close" can change from one at-bat to the next.

The bottom section of the batter's breakdown is "RBI / Opportunities." This section focuses in on RBI abilities of batters. 'Scoring Position" identifies the actual number of runs driven in during all situations where there are men in scoring position. This is compared to their total opportunities in that situation. If there are men on both second and third, this counts as two opportunities. "Scoring Position, 2 Out" is the same except it only counts these situations when there are two outs. "On Third, Less than 2 Out" only counts the man on third as one opportunity with, of course, less than two outs. The last row, "RBI in close games / RBI Total," is a little different. It uses our definition of "close" as described above to determine the number of RBI while the game is close. This definition does not limit the situation to the late innings.

There are two things to point out regarding the stat breakdown for pitchers. The first thing you'll notice is that the line above the chart shows the type of pitcher in terms of "Groundball-Flyball" and "Power-Finesse" for each year. The definitions of catgories here are the same as those mentioned above for batters.

Secondly, there are two different charts for pitchers. The top chart breaks down performance using mostly traditional pitching statistics. One thing we've added here are opposition stolen base records. The bottom chart shows batting lines for opposing batters.

Now, if you've actually gotten this far into this introduction, I won't delay you any longer in getting to the most interesting part of this book. Dig in!

—John Dewan

Don Aase
Baltimore Orioles

Don Aase had a great year—unfortunately, he didn't have it all in the same season. Baltimore signed him in 1985, hoping that his surgically repaired elbow could give them some quality innings. He tore through the last three months of 1985 and started 1986 like he was never going to allow another earned run again. But his workload caught up with him by August—he had a tender arm, missed some time and didn't pitch effectively when he was healthy. Given that, you've got to wonder how he'll do next year—if I had to guess, I'd call him 1987's answer to Jay Howell.

I was surprised by how hard Aase threw this year, but maybe that's just me. I never really paid much attention to Aase's fastball in the past because I never had to—it never crossed the plate very often, so who cared how quickly it did? The bright side about Don's last two months is that he kept his control—if he gets even 80% of his movement back in 1987, he'll be impossible to hit.

The most interesting things about Aase's 1986 are where he was at his best and worst. Virtually every power pitcher does well at night—batters can't see as well, so they strike out more often, walk less and get fewer hits than they will in the day. But not in this case. Since Aase has never had that sort of split before (in 1984 and 1985, his day ERA was 3.45 and his night ERA was 2.92), I'd assume that he pitched most of his innings during the day very early in the season and wouldn't expect it to happen again in 1987.

It's stunning to see that Aase's worst pitching came with men in scoring position—that's very odd for a top reliever. But, luckily, I happened to see something about how he was used this year. In April and May, Weaver brought him in early—either with one man on or to start innings. As the season progressed, Aase began to tire and give up more hits; Weaver tried to "rest" him by not bringing him in until the game situation absolutely required it—like with men on base late in the game. I thought it was somewhat bizarre to use someone you couldn't count on when you had no room for error—but then I thought there were a lot of bizarre things about the 1986 Orioles.

—Geoff Beckman

1986: Power, Flyball   **1985: Power, Flyball**   **1984: Power, Flyball**

| | 1986 SEASON | | | | | | | | | | | | THREE YEARS (84 – 86) | | | | | | | | | | |
	G	IP	H	BB	SO	SB	CS	W	L	S	ERA		G	IP	H	BB	SO	SB	CS	W	L	S	ERA
Totals	66	81.2	71	28	67	3	0	6	7	34	2.98		143	208.2	184	82	162	7	4	20	14	56	3.06
At Home and on the Road																							
Home	33	46.1	37	12	36	2	0	5	3	15	2.91		74	119.2	103	42	92	4	4	14	6	27	3.08
Road	33	35.1	34	16	31	1	0	1	4	19	3.06		69	89.0	81	40	70	3	0	6	8	29	3.03
During the Day and at Night																							
Day	18	22.2	15	4	15	1	0	0	0	12	1.19		36	49.1	39	17	35	2	1	3	0	15	2.55
Night	48	59.0	56	24	52	2	0	6	7	22	3.66		107	159.1	145	65	127	5	3	17	14	41	3.22
On Grass and on Turf																							
Grass	56	71.0	61	25	59	3	0	6	7	27	2.92		121	178.2	159	73	140	5	4	18	14	46	3.07
Turf	10	10.2	10	3	8	0	0	0	0	7	3.37		22	30.0	25	9	22	2	0	2	0	10	3.00
By Month																							
April	10	11.0	6	6	7	0	0	1	2	4	1.64		16	18.2	16	11	10	0	1	3	2	4	4.34
May	12	13.0	10	5	12	0	0	1	0	9	0.69		20	26.1	24	9	22	1	0	3	2	10	2.05
June	12	15.2	13	4	18	1	0	1	1	7	2.87		25	34.0	39	9	32	1	1	1	2	8	4.24
July	11	16.1	16	5	14	0	0	1	0	7	2.76		28	43.0	38	18	32	1	1	3	3	12	3.14
August	10	12.2	14	4	7	2	0	1	3	4	4.26		25	42.0	39	18	30	2	1	5	3	11	2.14
Sept/Oct	11	13.0	12	4	9	0	0	1	1	3	5.54		29	44.2	28	17	36	2	0	5	2	11	3.02

vs. Opponent Batters

| | 1986 SEASON | | | | | | | | | | | | THREE YEARS (84 – 86) | | | | | | | | | | |
	Ave.	OBP	SLG	AB	H	2B	3B	HR	RBI	BB	SO		Ave.	OBP	SLG	AB	H	2B	3B	HR	RBI	BB	SO
Totals	.234	.296	.352	304	71	12	3	6	45	28	67		.241	.313	.350	762	184	34	5	13	111	82	162
Pitching vs. Left and Right-handed Batters																							
Left	.231	.290	.359	156	36	7	2	3	23	13	33		.229	.300	.340	397	91	14	3	8	59	41	77
Right	.236	.303	.345	148	35	5	1	3	22	15	34		.255	.328	.362	365	93	20	2	5	52	41	85
Situational																							
Bases Empty	.203	.242	.248	153	31	5	1	0	0	8	31		.205	.264	.269	376	77	17	2	1	1	30	75
Leadoff	.175	.203	.246	57	10	2	1	0	0	2	11		.209	.282	.311	148	31	8	2	1	1	15	23
Not Leadoff	.219	.265	.250	96	21	3	0	0	0	6	20		.202	.251	.241	228	46	9	0	0	0	15	52
Runners On	.265	.347	.457	151	40	7	2	6	45	20	36		.277	.359	.430	386	107	17	3	12	110	52	87
First Base Only	.210	.279	.435	62	13	2	0	4	8	6	18		.229	.293	.361	144	33	4	0	5	11	13	29
Scoring Position	.303	.390	.472	89	27	5	2	2	37	14	18		.306	.394	.471	242	74	13	3	7	99	39	58
Late Innings, Close	.247	.320	.377	223	55	11	3	4	37	25	55		.235	.314	.337	528	124	22	4	8	72	64	114

RBI/Opportunities

Scoring Position	30 / 128	(23%)		83 / 355	(23%)
Scoring Position, 2 Out	20 / 76	(26%)		45 / 169	(27%)
On Third, Less than 2 Out	9 / 16	(56%)		28 / 75	(37%)
RBI in close games / RBI Total	37 / 45	(82%)		72 / 111	(65%)

Doyle Alexander
Atlanta Braves

The Braves acquired Doyle Alexander in early July, when it still appeared that they were in the pennant race. He didn't really fit in with the pitching staff as far as control goes, with 1.3 walks/9 IP versus 3.6 walks/9 IP for the staff as a whole. Unfortunately, his control was too good; he gave up almost as many hits per inning as Mahler (a dubious achievement). His ERA should stabilize at around 4.25 with the Braves.

—John Stryker

Alexander has been a much more effective pitcher at home than on the road for the last three years, but the change in ballparks from Toronto's rug to Atlanta's grass may change that. His statistics at home show an excellent 28–12 won-lost record (vs. 15–14 on the road) and an excellent 3.02 ERA (vs. 4.33 while traveling). His grass/turf stats, of course, closely match his home/road stats because of the few AL turf venues outside of Toronto.

Doyle's previous stay in Atlanta for the 1980 season produced numbers very close to his road and grass records of the last three years (14–11, 4.19 ERA), thus confirming his more recent totals. So why did the Braves want him? Was GM Bobby Cox unable to understand that the Doyle Alexander who won 34 games for him and the Blue Jays in 1984–85 was more a creature of where he pitched than for whom he pitched? Did Cox think that Alexander (1987 seasonal age of 36) and Jim Acker (1987 S.A. of 28) would be worth more than Joe Johnson (S.A. 25) and Duane Ward (S.A. 23)?

Even though the 1986 Braves were desperate for pitching, and Acker and Alexander gave them two major-leaguers in return for one plus a minor-leaguer, these two deals seem to be classic examples of seriously hurting a club's future chances in return for a marginal increase in current playoff chances. It's reasonable to assume that Joe Johnson will be as good as Jim Acker over the next few years. That leaves one to compare the future of Alexander to that of Ward—not a comparison that is favorable to the Braves.

Atlanta's minor-league system was rated #22 of 26 by *Baseball America* in April 1986; Duane Ward was rated as the #5 right-handed pitching prospect *in the majors* in the same issue. The Braves were 3.5 games out of first place in the NL West on July 7; on July 28, they were 9 games out and in last place (where they ended the season).

—Gary Gillette

1986: Finesse, Flyball   **1985: Finesse, Flyball**   **1984: Finesse, Flyball**

	G	IP	H	BB	SO	SB	CS	W	L	S	ERA		G	IP	H	BB	SO	SB	CS	W	L	S	ERA
			1986 SEASON													**THREE YEARS (84 – 86)**								
Totals	34	228.1	255	37	139	18	3	11	10	0	4.14		106	750.2	761	163	420	37	17	45	26	0	3.55
At Home and on the Road																							
Home	17	123.1	127	22	88	9	1	6	4	0	3.87		58	449.1	414	96	265	20	7	29	12	0	3.02
Road	17	105.0	128	15	51	9	2	5	6	0	4.46		48	301.1	347	67	155	17	10	16	14	0	4.33
During the Day and at Night																							
Day	12	90.0	94	10	61	9	3	4	6	0	3.60		40	294.2	285	61	161	18	9	17	13	0	3.24
Night	22	138.1	161	27	78	9	0	7	4	0	4.49		66	456.0	476	102	259	19	8	28	13	0	3.75
On Grass and on Turf																							
Grass	20	129.1	155	21	76	12	1	8	5	0	4.18		44	279.0	325	65	160	19	6	14	12	0	4.39
Turf	14	99.0	100	16	63	6	2	3	5	0	4.09		62	471.2	436	98	260	18	11	31	14	0	3.05
By Month																							
April	5	40.2	35	4	24	2	1	3	1	0	2.21		15	101.2	91	22	63	3	4	7	1	0	2.83
May	6	34.2	44	7	19	3	0	0	1	0	7.01		17	108.1	131	26	54	5	6	6	4	0	5.15
June	5	33.0	33	7	21	2	0	2	1	0	3.00		17	120.0	132	26	66	3	2	5	6	0	3.60
July	6	38.1	40	7	24	3	1	1	4	0	4.46		18	123.0	135	30	75	9	1	7	7	0	4.02
August	6	41.0	53	5	27	4	1	3	2	0	5.05		19	138.0	139	22	78	9	2	9	4	0	3.65
Sept/Oct	6	40.2	50	7	24	4	0	2	1	0	3.32		20	159.2	133	37	84	8	2	11	4	0	2.42

vs. Opponent Batters

	Ave.	OBP	SLG	AB	H	2B	3B	HR	RBI	BB	SO		Ave.	OBP	SLG	AB	H	2B	3B	HR	RBI	BB	SO
			1986 SEASON												**THREE YEARS (84 – 86)**								
Totals	.280	.310	.437	910	255	54	4	27	102	37	139		.262	.303	.404	2901	761	148	18	76	279	163	420
Pitching vs. Left and Right-handed Batters																							
Left	.277	.318	.415	451	125	25	2	11	43	27	69		.266	.318	.417	1471	392	81	4	44	140	108	197
Right	.283	.301	.460	459	130	29	2	16	59	10	70		.258	.286	.392	1430	369	67	14	32	139	55	223
Situational																							
Bases Empty	.276	.308	.430	547	151	30	3	16	16	23	78		.265	.306	.409	1762	467	87	13	47	47	97	235
Leadoff	.244	.259	.389	234	57	12	2	6	6	4	35		.253	.286	.402	751	190	35	7	21	21	31	95
Not Leadoff	.300	.342	.460	313	94	18	1	10	10	19	43		.274	.320	.414	1011	277	52	6	26	26	66	140
Runners On	.287	.313	.449	363	104	24	1	11	86	14	61		.258	.298	.397	1139	294	61	5	29	232	66	185
First Base Only	.317	.333	.555	164	52	15	0	8	21	4	25		.269	.302	.443	551	148	35	2	19	51	24	78
Scoring Position	.261	.298	.362	199	52	9	1	3	65	10	36		.248	.294	.354	588	146	26	3	10	181	42	107
Late Innings, Close	.258	.283	.472	89	23	7	0	4	13	3	9		.281	.315	.472	335	94	15	2	15	42	17	37

RBI/Opportunities

Scoring Position	59 / 254	(23%)	159 / 752	(21%)
Scoring Position, 2 Out	25 / 127	(20%)	56 / 340	(16%)
On Third, Less than 2 Out	20 / 38	(53%)	67 / 131	(51%)
RBI in close games / RBI Total	80 / 102	(78%)	213 / 279	(76%)

Joaquin Andujar
Oakland A's

Over the last three seasons, pitching for one outstanding team and two teams which were around .500, Joaquin Andujar is twenty games over .500. That there should still be any doubts about the value of a pitcher with such an outstanding record is a measure of the man's idiosyncrasies.

Although reputed to have a good move to first base (*The Scouting Report: 1985* says that "He is one of the quickest fielding pitchers in baseball and his move to first may be the best"), Andujar is in fact easy to run on. Over the last three years opponents have stolen 70 bases against him, with only 18 runners caught stealing.

Andujar's record has dramatic splits in it. Most remarkably, over the last three years he is just 25–24 in his home parks, but 28–9 on the road. This came about because he did not pitch well in Busch Stadium; he did better in the Oakland Coliseum. Over the three years Andujar is just 28–25 on turf, but 25–8 on grass fields. Over the three years he is just 16–14 with a 3.88 ERA in day games, but 37–19, 3.24 at night. Andujar has a reputation for not pitching as well late in the season, and his three-year record reflects this; he is 21–7 over the first two months, 16–10 in the middle two and 16–16 the last two. However, he has had at least three seasons in his career when he closed strong, including 1986.

Batters facing Andujar have a larger-than-normal platoon differential. Right-handed hitters facing Andujar over three years have hit just .223, while left-handed hitters have hit 41 points higher and with more power. This is not unexpected in view of his overhand style and a fastball that rides in on right-handed hitters.

Andujar is remarkably strong, and this shows in his record. In the late innings of close games, he has held opponents to a .220 batting average and has allowed only 3 home runs in three years. Despite his reputation as a hothead who doesn't always think, he is a pitcher who adjusts to the hitters and adjusts to the game situation. He doesn't walk leadoff men. He doesn't give up the single with two men out and a man in scoring position. The charts below will demonstrate this.

—Bill James

| | | | | 1986: Finesse, Groundball | | | | | | | | | | 1985: Finesse, Flyball | | | | | | | 1984: Finesse, Flyball | | |

| | **1986 SEASON** | | | | | | | | | | | **THREE YEARS (84 – 86)** | | | | | | | | | | |
	G	IP	H	BB	SO	SB	CS	W	L	S	ERA		G	IP	H	BB	SO	SB	CS	W	L	S	ERA
Totals	28	155.1	139	56	72	12	2	12	7	1	3.82		102	686.1	622	208	331	70	18	53	33	1	3.47
										At Home and on the Road													
Home	15	88.1	76	33	47	7	1	8	4	1	3.87		53	371.1	329	111	191	39	11	25	24	1	3.49
Road	13	67.0	63	23	25	5	1	4	3	0	3.76		49	315.0	293	97	140	31	7	28	9	0	3.46
										During the Day and at Night													
Day	12	72.2	58	22	40	7	1	5	2	1	3.34		38	252.2	215	84	134	33	5	16	14	1	3.88
Night	16	82.2	81	34	32	5	1	7	5	0	4.25		64	433.2	407	124	197	37	13	37	19	0	3.24
										On Grass and on Turf													
Grass	24	137.2	117	48	64	10	1	11	6	1	3.46		45	272.0	243	92	128	27	3	25	8	1	3.41
Turf	4	17.2	22	8	8	2	1	1	1	0	6.62		57	414.1	379	116	203	43	15	28	25	0	3.52
										By Month													
April	4	22.1	16	9	12	3	0	2	1	0	4.43		14	98.0	80	29	51	11	2	9	3	0	3.21
May	5	22.0	17	6	9	2	0	2	1	0	3.27		18	115.2	110	25	51	4	3	12	4	0	3.19
June	1	0.1	0	1	0	0	0	0	0	0	0.00		14	99.0	78	25	61	13	0	9	4	0	2.27
July	4	19.1	19	7	9	1	0	2	1	1	3.72		16	106.1	97	33	45	12	3	7	6	1	3.05
August	8	44.1	47	21	17	4	1	2	3	0	4.26		20	132.2	124	60	60	11	6	8	7	0	4.07
Sept/Oct	6	47.0	40	12	25	2	1	4	1	0	3.45		20	134.2	133	36	63	19	4	8	9	0	4.54

| | | | | | | | | *vs. Opponent Batters* | | | | | | | | | | | |

| | **1986 SEASON** | | | | | | | | | | | **THREE YEARS (84 – 86)** | | | | | | | | | |
	Ave.	OBP	SLG	AB	H	2B	3B	HR	RBI	BB	SO		Ave.	OBP	SLG	AB	H	2B	3B	HR	RBI	BB	SO
Totals	.239	.308	.399	582	139	16	4	23	61	56	72		.243	.304	.364	2555	622	102	16	58	252	208	331
								Pitching vs. Left and Right-handed Batters														
Left	.254	.318	.453	307	78	10	3	15	36	29	28		.264	.327	.393	1267	335	56	7	31	130	120	128
Right	.222	.297	.338	275	61	6	1	8	25	27	44		.223	.281	.335	1288	287	46	9	27	122	88	203
								Situational														
Bases Empty	.239	.292	.404	376	90	10	2	16	16	25	47		.238	.294	.349	1561	372	56	9	33	33	110	215
Leadoff	.250	.333	.493	144	36	3	1	10	10	15	19		.244	.300	.370	652	159	26	4	16	16	45	84
Not Leadoff	.233	.264	.349	232	54	7	1	6	6	10	28		.234	.290	.334	909	213	30	5	17	17	65	131
Runners On	.238	.335	.388	206	49	6	2	7	45	31	25		.252	.319	.387	994	250	46	7	25	219	98	116
First Base Only	.294	.400	.494	85	25	3	1	4	10	15	14		.261	.314	.374	444	116	16	5	8	30	30	47
Scoring Position	.198	.289	.314	121	24	3	1	3	35	16	11		.244	.323	.398	550	134	30	2	17	189	68	69
Late Innings, Close	.211	.313	.254	71	15	0	0	1	4	11	10		.220	.336	.310	277	61	14	1	3	21	46	37
								RBI/Opportunities														
Scoring Position				30 / 164		(18%)								160 / 742		(22%)							
Scoring Position, 2 Out				9 / 76		(12%)								59 / 340		(17%)							
On Third, Less than 2 Out				12 / 24		(50%)								61 / 130		(47%)							
RBI in close games / RBI Total				50 / 61		(82%)								180 / 252		(71%)							

Alan Ashby
Houston Astros

Alan regained his job as the starting catcher for the Astros last season after several years on layoff. When Mark Bailey got off to a terrible start, he was farmed out to Tucson, Ashby was resurrected, and John Mizerock was brought up to serve as the backup. Ashby responded to his default selection with, well, a typical Alan Ashby year.

What is a typical Alan Ashby year? Alan hit well enough to retain the job, but not well enough for anyone to get excited about. His batting average dropped 23 points below his 1985 mark, his on-base average dropped 30 points, and his slugging average dropped 79 points. Mediocre as his stats were, they were substantially better than Bailey's .176 BA, .302 OBA, and .288 SA. Mizerock checked in with a .185 BA, .374 OBA (24 walks and only 81 at-bats), and .259 SA. Three wild and crazy guys, right?

Ashby's career has been distinguished by its relentless mediocrity. In 14 years in the bigs, he has never played in more than 124 games, and in only five years did he play in 100. His career high in at-bats is 396, and in only five years did he top 300 ABs. His career high in runs is 40; has never hit the century mark in base hits; never hit 20 doubles nor more than 3 triples; and has hit double-digit dingers only once. He was on the disabled list for parts of 1983, 1984 and 1985. While Alan was once a good defensive catcher, that part of his game has slipped, too. Last year, he had only 43 assists in 103 games (one of the worst logs for NL regular catchers) and made 10 errors to boot. What else can you say about such an impact player?

What can be said is that the Astros should get on with the business of finding a decent major-league catcher. They should work some more with Mark Bailey. Sure, the kid stunk last year, but he has potential. He still will be only 25 years old next season, he knows how to draw a walk (148 BBs and only 829 ABs, career), has shown some home run power, and can play better defense than Ashby at this stage in his career. Would Bailey have come out of his slump last year if Lanier had shown some more patience with him? Maybe not, but wouldn't it have been beneficial to him and to the Astros future catching?

—Gary Gillette

	1986 SEASON											THREE YEARS (84 – 86)									
	Ave.	OBP	SLG	AB	H	2B	3B	HR	RBI	BB	SO	Ave.	OBP	SLG	AB	H	2B	3B	HR	RBI	BB	SO
Totals	.257	.333	.371	315	81	15	0	7	38	39	56	.265	.341	.390	695	184	30	0	19	90	83	105
Batting vs. Left and Right-handed Pitchers																						
Left	.276	.315	.388	116	32	7	0	2	13	8	16	.256	.313	.370	262	67	12	0	6	32	23	33
Right	.246	.343	.362	199	49	8	0	5	25	31	40	.270	.357	.402	433	117	18	0	13	58	60	72
At Home and on the Road																						
Home	.252	.326	.316	155	39	7	0	1	18	18	25	.255	.333	.345	325	83	17	0	4	39	38	47
Road	.263	.341	.425	160	42	8	0	6	20	21	31	.273	.347	.430	370	101	13	0	15	51	45	58
Facing Groundball Pitchers and Flyball Pitchers																						
Groundball	.201	.296	.248	149	30	4	0	1	9	20	30	.230	.306	.322	335	77	10	0	7	32	37	57
Flyball	.307	.366	.482	166	51	11	0	6	29	19	26	.297	.372	.453	360	107	20	0	12	58	46	48
Facing Finesse Pitchers and Power Pitchers																						
Finesse	.281	.356	.401	167	47	8	0	4	20	22	29	.290	.350	.432	366	106	16	0	12	45	36	58
Power	.230	.307	.338	148	34	7	0	3	18	17	27	.237	.331	.343	329	78	14	0	7	45	47	47
On Grass and on Turf																						
Grass	.245	.330	.372	94	23	3	0	3	9	13	25	.265	.342	.406	234	62	6	0	9	31	29	42
Turf	.262	.335	.371	221	58	12	0	4	29	26	31	.265	.340	.382	461	122	24	0	10	59	54	63
During the Day and at Night																						
Day	.240	.333	.323	96	23	2	0	2	9	14	19	.266	.369	.422	173	46	3	0	8	25	29	27
Night	.265	.333	.393	219	58	13	0	5	29	25	37	.264	.330	.379	522	138	27	0	11	65	54	78
By Month																						
April	.275	.396	.550	40	11	2	0	3	6	8	3	.237	.329	.388	139	33	9	0	4	13	19	18
May	.087	.222	.087	23	2	0	0	0	1	4	7	.213	.329	.295	61	13	2	0	1	7	11	12
June	.267	.333	.300	30	8	1	0	0	2	3	7	.283	.357	.374	99	28	3	0	2	11	12	18
July	.298	.394	.386	57	17	2	0	1	11	9	10	.316	.397	.421	114	36	3	0	3	17	15	16
August	.262	.301	.321	84	22	5	0	0	7	6	14	.279	.320	.342	111	31	7	0	0	11	7	20
Sept/Oct	.259	.323	.432	81	21	5	0	3	11	9	15	.251	.320	.444	171	43	6	0	9	31	19	21
Situational																						
Bases Empty	.248	.316	.379	161	40	6	0	5	5	16	32	.271	.338	.418	373	101	13	0	14	14	38	63
Leadoff	.258	.292	.532	62	16	2	0	5	5	3	12	.252	.304	.403	159	40	3	0	7	7	12	27
Not Leadoff	.242	.330	.283	99	24	4	0	0	0	13	20	.285	.362	.430	214	61	10	0	7	7	26	36
Runners On	.266	.350	.364	154	41	9	0	2	33	23	24	.258	.343	.357	322	83	17	0	5	76	45	42
First Base Only	.297	.375	.422	64	19	5	0	1	4	8	13	.240	.319	.329	146	35	7	0	2	7	15	19
Scoring Position	.244	.333	.322	90	22	4	0	1	29	15	11	.273	.361	.381	176	48	10	0	3	69	30	23
Late Innings, Close	.222	.300	.315	54	12	2	0	1	7	6	13	.229	.304	.364	140	32	4	0	5	21	16	24
RBI/Opportunities																						
Scoring Position				28 / 130		(22%)									63 / 253		(25%)					
Scoring Position, 2 Out				7 / 66		(11%)									21 / 119		(18%)					
On Third, Less than 2 Out				16 / 28		(57%)									29 / 53		(55%)					
RBI in close games / RBI Total				27 / 38		(71%)									63 / 90		(70%)					

Wally Backman
New York Mets

Wally Backman makes believers! Throughout his career Wally has had to make people believe in him—not just the Met front office (with the exception of Davey Johnson), but even the editors of this book, who had to be convinced that Backman deserved an essay. Time after time in '84, '85 and '86, Wally Backman did what needed to be done and made believers of us all. Backman's season and career were encapsulated in that instant when he avoided the Glenn Davis tag, diving headfirst to clutch first base in the third game of the LCS. Did he run out of the basepath? Maybe. Did Wally do what was necessary for his team? Yes! It is Wally's drive, determination and dedication that have made him one of the better second basemen in the league.

Over the last five years Wally has turned his career around. He has learned to turn the double play not just adequately, but well. He has become a capable fielder through long, hard hours of practice. (Naturally having Hernandez on your left helps.) He has made the same kind of progress as a batsman. From the left side, he is one of the tougher outs in the league. As a switch hitter, he still needs improvement—to say the least—but he was close to 100 points better from the right side in '86 than in '85.

Wally continues to improve his bunting skills. His eye at the plate is exceptional—36 walks with only 32 Ks. Once on base he is both a threat to steal and to take the extra base. Despite his platoon role he was fifth on the Mets in runs scored with 67.

It is Wally's scrappy determination and willingness to do what is necessary that, when brought to bear in a team context, makes him important to the Mets. His presence in the lineup, in tandem with Lenny Dykstra (let's call them Lanny Back-stra; it sounds better than Wenny Dyke-man) gives the Met attack the flexibility to be either a big-hit or sequential offense. With Back-stra's abilities to get on base the Mets can either wait for a three-run homer from Carter or Strawberry or they can create a run. The Back-stra flexibility took a good team and made it great.

Backman has the ability to hit behind the runner, walk and generally unnerve opponents. All this contributes to Met wins. In fact, when Wally started the Mets were 63–29 for a .685 percentage. Without him they were 45–25 (.643).

—J. Randolph Burnham

	1986 SEASON											THREE YEARS (84 – 86)										
	Ave.	OBP	SLG	AB	H	2B	3B	HR	RBI	BB	SO	Ave.	OBP	SLG	AB	H	2B	3B	HR	RBI	BB	SO
Totals	.320	.376	.385	387	124	18	2	1	27	36	32	.289	.349	.354	1343	388	61	9	3	91	128	167
	Batting vs. Left and Right-handed Pitchers																					
Left	.192	.259	.250	52	10	1	1	0	6	5	10	.149	.247	.190	221	33	7	1	0	16	28	42
Right	.340	.394	.406	335	114	17	1	1	21	31	22	.316	.370	.387	1122	355	54	8	3	75	100	125
	At Home and on the Road																					
Home	.311	.377	.372	180	56	6	1	1	9	19	12	.289	.359	.350	634	183	26	5	1	43	71	76
Road	.329	.374	.396	207	68	12	1	0	18	17	20	.289	.340	.358	709	205	35	4	2	48	57	91
	Facing Groundball Pitchers and Flyball Pitchers																					
Groundball	.325	.380	.367	166	54	7	0	0	13	16	16	.279	.345	.344	619	173	27	5	1	43	63	83
Flyball	.317	.372	.398	221	70	11	2	1	14	20	16	.297	.353	.363	724	215	34	4	2	48	65	84
	Facing Finesse Pitchers and Power Pitchers																					
Finesse	.305	.360	.386	220	67	11	2	1	12	20	13	.272	.324	.341	757	206	33	8	1	38	59	81
Power	.341	.397	.383	167	57	7	0	0	15	16	19	.311	.381	.372	586	182	28	1	2	53	69	86
	On Grass and on Turf																					
Grass	.308	.367	.365	260	80	10	1	1	16	26	20	.288	.348	.353	937	270	40	6	3	67	88	113
Turf	.346	.394	.425	127	44	8	1	0	11	10	12	.291	.353	.357	406	118	21	3	0	24	40	54
	During the Day and at Night																					
Day	.338	.391	.414	157	53	10	1	0	12	15	17	.281	.334	.346	526	148	26	4	0	34	43	78
Night	.309	.365	.365	230	71	8	1	1	15	21	15	.294	.359	.360	817	240	35	5	3	57	85	89
	By Month																					
April	.371	.425	.457	35	13	1	1	0	2	4	2	.310	.385	.387	142	44	5	3	0	7	18	15
May	.333	.360	.458	48	16	6	0	0	4	2	3	.253	.307	.310	174	44	10	0	0	6	14	26
June	.333	.398	.357	84	28	2	0	0	9	6	6	.300	.370	.333	243	73	8	0	0	12	27	23
July	.316	.342	.355	76	24	3	0	0	8	3	7	.335	.382	.416	257	86	12	3	1	27	21	30
August	.320	.384	.373	75	24	4	0	0	7	9	8	.287	.333	.362	279	80	16	1	1	25	21	33
Sept/Oct	.275	.359	.377	69	19	2	1	1	2	9	6	.246	.321	.315	248	61	10	2	1	14	27	40
	Situational																					
Bases Empty	.332	.384	.412	238	79	12	2	1	1	20	17	.288	.346	.360	851	245	44	7	1	1	74	106
Leadoff	.353	.397	.456	68	24	4	0	1	1	5	6	.292	.340	.378	400	117	25	3	1	1	29	55
Not Leadoff	.324	.378	.394	170	55	8	2	0	0	15	11	.284	.350	.344	451	128	19	4	0	0	45	51
Runners On	.302	.363	.342	149	45	6	0	0	26	16	15	.291	.356	.346	492	143	17	2	2	90	54	61
First Base Only	.406	.465	.438	64	26	2	0	0	1	7	1	.304	.360	.355	217	66	6	1	1	7	19	18
Scoring Position	.224	.289	.271	85	19	4	0	0	25	9	14	.280	.352	.338	275	77	11	1	1	83	35	43
Late Innings, Close	.368	.427	.412	68	25	1	1	0	4	7	6	.304	.368	.359	217	66	7	1	0	20	23	29
	RBI/Opportunities																					

Scoring Position	23 / 120	(19%)	80 / 386	(21%)
Scoring Position, 2 Out	12 / 45	(27%)	34 / 176	(19%)
On Third, Less than 2 Out	8 / 18	(44%)	30 / 63	(48%)
RBI in close games / RBI Total	14 / 27	(52%)	58 / 91	(64%)

Harold Baines
Chicago White Sox

Harold Baines is the Charlie Gehringer of the nineteen eighties, a seemingly mechanical man who racks up great numbers every year without changing the expression on his face. Over the past five seasons Baines has averaged 23 homers, 100 RBIs and .292 average, with not a lot of year-to-year variation. Consistency? Look at his doubles totals from '82 to '86: 29, 33, 28, 29, 29. Or the homers: 25, 20, 29, 22, 21. In addition, Baines has generally hit well in the clutch, been a pillar of strength with men in scoring position, played right field in exemplory fashion and exhibited a strong, accurate throwing arm. His teammates look up to him, and it's easy to see why; he's the kind of person you'd like your son to be.

Baines is a firm disciple of the Charlie Lau school of hitting. While other Lau pupils, notably George Brett, have learned to pull the ball to increase their homer totals, Baines continues to use the whole ballpark: Of his outfield hits in '86, 25 percent were to left field, 29 percent to center, 46 percent to right. This tendency probably keeps him from becoming a consistent 30-home run man. It's hard to criticize

him for not tampering with success in this area . . . but one could fault him for not drawing enough walks. After getting his walk total up to 54 in 1984—not coincidentally, his best season to date—Baines went the other way, drawing only 42 and 38 bases on balls the last two seasons. My pitch-by-pitch data showed him swinging at the first pitch 44 percent of the time in '86, which is on a par with Ozzie Guillen. To be fair, Baines performed very well in these plate appearances, hitting over .320 with excellent power, but it's hard to believe that such a tendency could help in the long run; it goes against the grain of almost all the data I've seen on the subject, and Baines' numbers in '84 as well. Even Harold has criticized himself for lacking patience.

Until '86 Baines had always finished his seasons with a strong second half. A late-August knee injury which required arthroscopic surgery probably hindered him last season, but for his career Harold has hit .282 with 55 homers and 282 ribbies during the first half, .292–85–307 in the second half. His low walk totals notwithstanding, Baines is an outstanding player in every sense of the word.

—Don Zminda

	1986 SEASON											THREE YEARS (84 – 86)										
	Ave.	OBP	SLG	AB	H	2B	3B	HR	RBI	BB	SO	Ave.	OBP	SLG	AB	H	2B	3B	HR	RBI	BB	SO
Totals	.296	.338	.465	570	169	29	2	21	88	38	89	.304	.349	.490	1779	540	86	15	72	295	133	253
Batting vs. Left and Right-handed Pitchers																						
Left	.262	.297	.354	206	54	8	1	3	18	10	38	.295	.328	.444	621	183	22	7	19	82	33	98
Right	.316	.361	.527	364	115	21	1	18	70	28	51	.308	.359	.515	1158	357	64	8	53	213	100	155
At Home and on the Road																						
Home	.331	.372	.491	275	91	16	2	8	51	21	35	.313	.358	.509	851	266	42	7	37	160	66	108
Road	.264	.306	.441	295	78	13	0	13	37	17	54	.295	.340	.473	928	274	44	8	35	135	67	145
Facing Groundball Pitchers and Flyball Pitchers																						
Groundball	.333	.368	.536	222	74	10	1	11	40	13	22	.318	.360	.501	806	256	37	6	33	133	56	95
Flyball	.273	.319	.420	348	95	19	1	10	48	25	67	.292	.340	.481	973	284	49	9	39	162	77	158
Facing Finesse Pitchers and Power Pitchers																						
Finesse	.291	.322	.487	337	98	19	1	15	61	17	46	.315	.353	.535	1021	322	56	9	50	191	67	117
Power	.305	.361	.433	233	71	10	1	6	27	21	43	.288	.343	.430	758	218	30	6	22	104	66	136
On Grass and on Turf																						
Grass	.302	.347	.473	486	147	22	2	19	81	35	78	.308	.356	.486	1501	462	75	11	57	250	118	215
Turf	.262	.287	.417	84	22	7	0	2	7	3	11	.281	.311	.511	278	78	11	4	15	45	15	38
During the Day and at Night																						
Day	.295	.345	.468	173	51	9	0	7	27	16	33	.299	.348	.477	511	153	26	4	19	84	42	81
Night	.297	.335	.463	397	118	20	2	14	61	22	56	.305	.349	.495	1268	387	60	11	53	211	91	172
By Month																						
April	.253	.282	.467	75	19	1	0	5	14	3	15	.249	.297	.412	221	55	6	0	10	34	15	33
May	.330	.370	.462	106	35	5	0	3	15	8	12	.267	.312	.395	296	79	15	1	7	35	22	31
June	.324	.383	.467	105	34	7	1	2	19	12	12	.325	.375	.500	314	102	16	3	11	58	30	45
July	.278	.340	.474	97	27	8	1	3	11	9	18	.317	.377	.505	303	96	20	2	11	52	28	49
August	.293	.311	.515	99	29	1	0	7	16	2	16	.336	.365	.592	333	112	14	7	19	62	16	45
Sept/Oct	.284	.315	.398	88	25	7	0	1	13	4	16	.308	.349	.503	312	96	15	2	14	54	22	50
Situational																						
Bases Empty	.277	.321	.457	328	91	18	1	13	13	19	51	.284	.329	.455	972	276	47	7	35	35	64	142
Leadoff	.260	.295	.360	100	26	7	0	1	1	5	15	.278	.321	.421	299	83	14	4	7	7	19	40
Not Leadoff	.285	.332	.500	228	65	11	1	12	12	14	36	.287	.333	.470	673	193	33	3	28	28	45	102
Runners On	.322	.361	.475	242	78	11	1	8	75	19	38	.327	.371	.533	807	264	39	8	37	260	69	111
First Base Only	.370	.394	.500	100	37	4	0	3	8	4	16	.345	.373	.553	351	121	17	4	16	42	16	39
Scoring Position	.289	.339	.458	142	41	7	1	5	67	15	22	.314	.370	.518	456	143	22	4	21	218	53	72
Late Innings, Close	.311	.380	.567	90	28	2	0	7	17	10	16	.294	.369	.524	252	74	13	0	15	45	30	33
RBI/Opportunities																						

Scoring Position	57 / 194	(29%)		177 / 603	(29%)
Scoring Position, 2 Out	15 / 75	(20%)		61 / 248	(25%)
On Third, Less than 2 Out	28 / 52	(54%)		77 / 138	(56%)
RBI in close games / RBI Total	63 / 88	(72%)		195 / 295	(66%)

Steve Balboni
Kansas City Royals

Likable, bald, modest and even a little bit talented, Steve Balboni in 1986 was on target for his first 100 RBI season until stopped in early September by a back injury of indeterminant origin and seriousness.

Balboni has never exactly been in the right place at the right time. He fought his way up through the Yankee system at a time when a) they weren't bringing up any young players and b) the left field fence was seven miles away. He went up and down on George's yo-yo several times, and by the time this all sorted itself out his career was several years late getting started and he was playing in Royals Stadium in Kansas City, perhaps the worst park for him as a hitter except for Yankee Stadium. Since joining the Royals, he has hit 93 homers—37 in Kansas City, and 56 on the road, with a batting average also 25 points higher away from his "home" park. Healthy, Balboni could comfortably clear 30 homers a year in Kansas City—but in another park, he'd hit over 40.

One thing that puzzles me has been the Royals' reluctance to let Balboni hit cleanup. With Brett hitting third and Jorge Orta cleanup, Brett has been walked any time there's a man on second for three years, while Balboni has hit sixth or seventh most of the time. Even hitting way down in the order, even hitting behind people who don't get on base much, even hitting in a park that kills him, Balboni's RBI counts for the last three years is about one RBI per six at bats, which is pretty darn good, better than a lot of middle of the order guys like Brunansky, Cooper and Buckner. I'd have to figure that, particularly in road games, if there was a runner on second and you walked Brett with Balboni hitting fourth, you'd be looking down the barrel of a three-run homer, which is going to fire on you about one time in fifteen at bats (on the road). I don't think that managers would be too anxious to do that three or four times a series, when with Orta batting fourth it's just a question of "who do we want to give a chance to drive in the one run?" and obviously you'd rather give Orta that chance than Brett. Balboni over the last three years has hit a lot like Kingman only somewhat better (slugging .474 as opposed to Kingman's .448) and nobody's ever been reluctant to use Kingman as a cleanup hitter. Maybe it's a personality trait, but if it is I think they've misread his personality. "Shy" doesn't mean "scared."

—Bill James

	1986 SEASON											THREE YEARS (84 – 86)										
	Ave.	OBP	SLG	AB	H	2B	3B	HR	RBI	BB	SO	Ave.	OBP	SLG	AB	H	2B	3B	HR	RBI	BB	SO
Totals	.229	.286	.451	512	117	25	1	29	88	43	146	.239	.304	.474	1551	370	76	5	93	252	140	451
Batting vs. Left and Right-handed Pitchers																						
Left	.276	.370	.590	134	37	6	0	12	30	20	37	.253	.348	.500	450	114	21	0	30	69	65	138
Right	.212	.255	.402	378	80	19	1	17	58	23	109	.233	.285	.463	1101	256	55	5	63	183	75	313
At Home and on the Road																						
Home	.203	.264	.386	251	51	14	1	10	37	23	75	.226	.286	.442	773	175	48	4	37	120	63	213
Road	.253	.309	.513	261	66	11	0	19	51	20	71	.251	.321	.505	778	195	28	1	56	132	77	238
Facing Groundball Pitchers and Flyball Pitchers																						
Groundball	.250	.304	.457	232	58	9	0	13	44	18	59	.242	.300	.484	707	171	32	2	45	131	55	168
Flyball	.211	.272	.446	280	59	16	1	16	44	25	87	.236	.307	.466	844	199	44	3	48	121	85	283
Facing Finesse Pitchers and Power Pitchers																						
Finesse	.245	.283	.448	310	76	16	1	15	50	18	73	.251	.302	.475	887	223	45	3	49	133	62	214
Power	.203	.291	.455	202	41	9	0	14	38	25	73	.221	.306	.473	664	147	31	2	44	119	78	237
On Grass and on Turf																						
Grass	.256	.316	.549	215	55	9	0	18	46	18	53	.255	.332	.535	615	157	23	1	49	109	66	180
Turf	.209	.265	.380	297	62	16	1	11	42	25	93	.228	.285	.434	936	213	53	4	44	143	74	271
During the Day and at Night																						
Day	.291	.344	.567	141	41	4	1	11	33	12	42	.253	.314	.464	392	99	18	1	21	61	35	119
Night	.205	.265	.407	371	76	21	0	18	55	31	104	.234	.300	.477	1159	271	58	4	72	191	105	332
By Month																						
April	.247	.295	.411	73	18	3	0	3	5	5	16	.253	.302	.447	217	55	9	0	11	29	14	50
May	.179	.284	.337	95	17	3	0	4	12	13	30	.215	.296	.355	279	60	12	0	9	30	30	83
June	.219	.271	.524	105	23	8	0	8	25	9	35	.232	.289	.502	259	60	16	0	18	49	23	86
July	.268	.321	.485	97	26	6	0	5	17	8	19	.265	.338	.554	298	79	19	2	21	59	29	75
August	.264	.289	.527	110	29	3	1	8	24	4	33	.221	.271	.466	262	58	7	3	17	43	18	80
Sept/Oct	.125	.216	.281	32	4	2	0	1	5	4	13	.246	.321	.517	236	58	13	0	17	42	26	77
Situational																						
Bases Empty	.229	.300	.473	279	64	12	1	18	18	27	84	.228	.297	.476	863	197	40	3	56	56	77	256
Leadoff	.283	.353	.625	120	34	6	1	11	11	12	30	.274	.339	.589	350	96	21	1	29	29	32	97
Not Leadoff	.189	.259	.358	159	30	6	0	7	7	15	54	.197	.268	.400	513	101	19	2	27	27	45	159
Runners On	.227	.271	.425	233	53	13	0	11	70	16	62	.251	.312	.471	688	173	36	2	37	196	63	195
First Base Only	.236	.261	.461	89	21	8	0	4	14	3	22	.260	.303	.483	292	76	20	0	15	41	17	75
Scoring Position	.222	.276	.403	144	32	5	0	7	56	13	40	.245	.319	.462	396	97	16	2	22	155	46	120
Late Innings, Close	.198	.218	.365	96	19	4	0	4	16	3	22	.252	.313	.496	262	66	14	1	16	44	22	66
RBI/Opportunities																						
Scoring Position				44 / 190		(23%)									117 / 518		(23%)					
Scoring Position, 2 Out				14 / 76		(18%)									46 / 228		(20%)					
On Third, Less than 2 Out				18 / 34		(53%)									39 / 81		(48%)					
RBI in close games / RBI Total				51 / 88		(58%)									158 / 252		(63%)					

Floyd Bannister
Chicago White Sox

In White Sox circles late last season, there was talk of a "new" Floyd Bannister. The statistical evidence seemed impressive: Bannister's ERA for the season, 3.54, was his lowest since 1983, and from August 1 until season's end it was even better, 3.04. More interesting was the way he was pitching. In '85, on his way to a 4.87 ERA, Bannister averaged 8.5 strikeouts a game and 4.3 walks. In '86 his strikeouts were down to 5 a game, but the walks declined also, down to 2.6. The word around town was that Jim Fregosi and pitching coach Dick Bosman had shortened Bannister's stride, convinced him to pitch within himself, and turned his career around.

That's an interesting theory, but a closer look leaves one with a lot less reason to be optimistic. In the first place, the turnaround, if there was one, seemed to have little to do with Fregosi and Bosman. Under Tony LaRussa and Dave Duncan last year, Floyd fashioned a 2.96 ERA; with Fregosi/Bosman, it was 3.88. And in the second place, we've heard this kind of talk before . . . many times, in fact. With a pitcher like Bannister, it's easy to get lost in the way he looks, which is like someone who should never lose a game,

and to forget about the way he performs, which is revealed in his 101–117 career record and 4.03 ERA. Looking at Bannister's career, one sees two distinctly different kinds of seasons. In his bad years he has control trouble and his ERA soars above the 4.00 mark; in his better years his control improves (he "shortens his stride") and he gets the ERA down to around 3.50. It's two completely different pitchers: for the six lousy seasons he's turned in a 4.53 ERA (ranging from 4.03 to 4.87) and averaged 3.8 walks per nine innings; for the four "good" seasons—his record for them is 54–67—the ERA is 3.44 (ranging from 3.35 to 3.54) and the walks are down to 2.8 per nine innings. Bannister's '86 season (10–14, 3.54, 2.6 W/9 inn.) is almost a dead ringer for his 1980 campaign at Seattle (9–13, 3.47, 2.7); I guess people thought he'd turned it around then, also. It's a bewildering career: bad followed by good—sometimes in the same season, like in '83, when he was 3–9 first half, 13–1 second half—followed by bad again. So when someone tells me Floyd has it all together at last, you'll forgive me if I withhold judgment.

—Don Zminda

1986: Finesse, Flyball **1985: Power, Flyball** **1984: Power, Flyball**

	1986 SEASON											THREE YEARS (84 – 86)										
	G	IP	H	BB	SO	SB	CS	W	L	S	ERA	G	IP	H	BB	SO	SB	CS	W	L	S	ERA
Totals	28	165.1	162	48	92	11	8	10	14	0	3.54	96	594.0	584	228	442	39	22	34	39	0	4.48
At Home and on the Road																						
Home	14	98.1	78	27	61	6	4	5	6	0	2.84	44	297.2	254	111	235	20	11	16	16	0	3.66
Road	14	67.0	84	21	31	5	4	5	8	0	4.57	52	296.1	330	117	207	19	11	18	23	0	5.31
During the Day and at Night																						
Day	7	39.1	31	12	17	2	1	3	3	0	2.06	24	140.0	138	63	94	11	6	6	12	0	4.76
Night	21	126.0	131	36	75	9	7	7	11	0	4.00	72	454.0	446	165	348	28	16	28	27	0	4.40
On Grass and on Turf																						
Grass	24	145.1	142	42	80	11	6	7	13	0	3.59	79	496.1	480	191	372	31	20	25	35	0	4.42
Turf	4	20.0	20	6	12	0	2	3	1	0	3.15	17	97.2	104	37	70	8	2	9	4	0	4.79
By Month																						
April	4	24.0	21	9	6	0	1	1	2	0	3.00	13	79.1	84	33	39	1	4	3	7	0	4.76
May	4	23.1	22	11	19	2	1	1	2	0	2.70	16	95.2	80	46	81	8	3	5	6	0	3.76
June	1	1.1	1	0	0	0	0	1	0	0	6.75	11	59.0	69	24	50	5	5	4	3	0	5.34
July	6	33.2	38	7	17	4	2	2	4	0	5.61	18	119.1	108	48	79	11	3	6	7	0	4.30
August	6	36.2	39	9	26	3	1	3	2	0	3.68	18	117.0	113	35	102	5	3	8	7	0	4.38
Sept/Oct	7	46.1	41	12	24	2	3	2	4	0	2.53	20	123.2	130	42	91	9	4	8	9	0	4.73

vs. Opponent Batters

	1986 SEASON											THREE YEARS (84 – 86)									
	Ave.	OBP	SLG	AB	H	2B	3B	HR	RBI	BB	SO	Ave.	OBP	SLG	AB	H	2B	3B	HR	RBI	BB	SO
Totals	.259	.311	.398	626	162	26	5	17	67	48	92	.258	.326	.423	2267	584	115	15	77	285	228	442
Pitching vs. Left and Right-handed Batters																						
Left	.204	.255	.316	98	20	5	0	2	9	6	16	.261	.325	.439	394	103	24	2	14	56	37	70
Right	.269	.322	.413	528	142	21	5	15	58	42	76	.257	.326	.420	1873	481	91	13	63	229	191	372
Situational																						
Bases Empty	.263	.301	.419	391	103	20	4	11	11	20	59	.253	.315	.409	1367	346	69	9	42	42	118	268
Leadoff	.274	.299	.381	168	46	7	1	3	3	6	26	.269	.323	.433	584	157	31	4	19	19	45	108
Not Leadoff	.256	.303	.448	223	57	13	3	8	8	14	33	.241	.309	.391	783	189	38	5	23	23	73	160
Runners On	.251	.327	.362	235	59	6	1	6	56	28	33	.264	.341	.446	900	238	46	6	35	243	110	174
First Base Only	.298	.376	.413	104	31	3	0	3	6	13	12	.311	.378	.503	392	122	26	2	15	41	41	61
Scoring Position	.214	.289	.321	131	28	3	1	3	50	15	21	.228	.314	.402	508	116	20	4	20	202	69	113
Late Innings, Close	.229	.302	.271	48	11	2	0	0	4	5	9	.311	.391	.473	148	46	7	1	5	26	20	27

RBI/Opportunities

Scoring Position	42 / 170	(25%)		161 / 699	(23%)	
Scoring Position, 2 Out	10 / 77	(13%)		50 / 302	(17%)	
On Third, Less than 2 Out	21 / 28	(75%)		71 / 121	(59%)	
RBI in close games / RBI Total	51 / 67	(76%)		222 / 285	(78%)	

Jesse Barfield
Toronto Blue Jays

Jesse Barfield is the best right fielder in baseball—none of his peers had more putouts (368), no outfielder had more assists (20) or double plays (8) and he made only three errors, too. After only two years as a regular, he's posted 42 assists and 16 DPs—nobody is even close to those numbers—and collected the first of many Gold Gloves. He has 62 assists in his career and Bill James's Favorite Toy says that he has a 9% chance of breaking Tris Speaker's record for career assists (450). Barfield can hit, too—he led the majors in homers, finished second in Slugging Average, tied for seventh in RBIs and his On-Base average continues to climb. He was the best righty hitter in the AL in 1986; not bad for a guy who the scouts said couldn't hit righties.

Well, maybe that isn't totally fair. The hallmark of Barfield's career is that he's been able to turn weaknesses into strengths. Look at his progress against righties since 1982: .223, .247, .244, .280 and .290. Or his road batting averages since 1982: .244, .193, .279, .292 and .299. The only thing that hasn't changed is what he does to a fastball. Looking at his stats, you have to wonder why anyone challenges him. Yes, you do have a 25% chance of getting him fanning the breeze—you've also got a 13% chance that he'll rattle it off (or rocket it over) the fences. Pitchers seem to be catching onto that, though. He hit hit 8 of his 14 homers (57.1%) with the bases empty in 1984, 16 of 27 in '85 (59.2%) and 27 of 40 (67.5%) this year. If the pattern holds out, he'll hit 53 homers in 1987 and 41 will come with the bases empty.

That probably won't happen, but you never know. If anyone playing now is a 50-homer man, Barfield is it. He's the AL's only 30-homer man who also hit 30 doubles and drew 60 walks—if you won't let him pull you, he beats you some other way. The only month that he doesn't hit homers is April; he's pretty consistent overall. The only reason that he might not is if Toronto insists on keeping that Brillo pad that he plays on.

It's interesting—Toronto has three super outfielders, they all have good wheels and they all complain about the field. The only one who hits better at home is Bell, all three go bonkers when they hit on other turf surfaces (Barfield, for example, hit .301 and slugged .714) and all three of them have habitual September slumps. It may not be the carpet, but something is affecting Barfield and it's definitely causing his partner's physical problems.

—Marco Bresba and Geoff Beckman

	1986 SEASON											THREE YEARS (84 – 86)										
	Ave.	OBP	SLG	AB	H	2B	3B	HR	RBI	BB	SO	Ave.	OBP	SLG	AB	H	2B	3B	HR	RBI	BB	SO
Totals	.289	.368	.559	589	170	35	2	40	108	69	146	.288	.366	.530	1448	417	83	12	81	241	170	370
Batting vs. Left and Right-handed Pitchers																						
Left	.284	.397	.527	148	42	9	0	9	26	27	41	.303	.385	.509	542	164	34	3	24	85	75	138
Right	.290	.358	.569	441	128	26	2	31	82	42	105	.279	.354	.542	906	253	49	9	57	156	95	232
At Home and on the Road																						
Home	.278	.371	.526	291	81	22	1	16	51	42	70	.284	.364	.542	712	202	47	7	41	134	89	184
Road	.299	.365	.591	298	89	13	1	24	57	27	76	.292	.368	.518	736	215	36	5	40	107	81	186
Facing Groundball Pitchers and Flyball Pitchers																						
Groundball	.293	.381	.522	249	73	13	1	14	43	32	60	.301	.379	.520	652	196	35	6	32	109	78	164
Flyball	.285	.359	.585	340	97	22	1	26	65	37	86	.278	.356	.538	796	221	48	6	49	132	92	206
Facing Finesse Pitchers and Power Pitchers																						
Finesse	.280	.353	.551	343	96	16	1	25	67	37	82	.275	.347	.517	812	223	40	8	47	132	86	187
Power	.301	.389	.569	246	74	19	1	15	41	32	64	.305	.390	.546	636	194	43	4	34	109	84	183
On Grass and on Turf																						
Grass	.298	.370	.557	235	70	11	1	16	43	24	59	.294	.379	.519	541	159	24	4	30	84	69	129
Turf	.282	.367	.559	354	100	24	1	24	65	45	87	.284	.358	.536	907	258	59	8	51	157	101	241
During the Day and at Night																						
Day	.258	.358	.459	209	54	15	0	9	30	30	52	.263	.350	.464	498	131	32	4	20	77	60	127
Night	.305	.374	.613	380	116	20	2	31	78	39	94	.301	.375	.564	950	286	51	8	61	164	110	243
By Month																						
April	.253	.300	.413	75	19	6	0	2	6	4	25	.231	.282	.396	212	49	11	0	8	24	12	60
May	.276	.358	.571	105	29	4	0	9	23	12	16	.305	.381	.586	239	73	14	1	17	47	29	53
June	.318	.379	.618	110	35	7	1	8	27	10	20	.277	.351	.479	238	66	9	3	11	46	26	56
July	.341	.455	.670	91	31	7	1	7	17	17	23	.316	.410	.641	234	74	16	3	18	42	33	57
August	.323	.418	.527	93	30	7	0	4	20	16	26	.339	.426	.556	248	84	22	4	8	42	38	61
Sept/Oct	.226	.288	.522	115	26	4	0	10	15	10	36	.256	.333	.509	277	71	11	1	19	40	32	83
Situational																						
Bases Empty	.287	.358	.588	335	96	16	2	27	27	31	85	.286	.357	.549	818	234	43	8	52	52	80	208
Leadoff	.281	.353	.570	135	38	6	0	11	11	14	36	.279	.345	.531	337	94	17	1	22	22	31	79
Not Leadoff	.290	.360	.600	200	58	10	2	16	16	17	49	.291	.365	.561	481	140	26	7	30	30	49	129
Runners On	.291	.381	.520	254	74	19	0	13	81	38	61	.290	.377	.505	630	183	40	4	29	189	90	162
First Base Only	.316	.368	.602	98	31	10	0	6	18	6	25	.315	.370	.539	254	80	21	3	10	32	19	65
Scoring Position	.276	.389	.468	156	43	9	0	7	63	32	36	.274	.382	.481	376	103	19	1	19	157	71	97
Late Innings, Close	.308	.377	.542	107	33	7	0	6	22	11	29	.277	.347	.482	253	70	12	2	12	40	26	61

RBI/Opportunities			
Scoring Position	47 / 224 (21%)	124 / 527 (24%)
Scoring Position, 2 Out	15 / 94 (16%)	46 / 222 (21%)
On Third, Less than 2 Out	21 / 49 (43%)	48 / 115 (42%)
RBI in close games / RBI Total	74 / 108 (69%)	151 / 241 (63%)

Marty Barrett
Boston Red Sox

Marty Barrett is the most overrated underrated player in baseball. Not since Joe Rudi played in Oakland have so many announcers felt compelled to tell us how unfairly overlooked a player is. Is he really that good? Is he rated lower than he deserves?

If you evaluate every regular in the AL by Bill James's Offensive Won/Lost Percentage, Barrett finishes sixth among second basemen, a hair behind Willie Randolph. Barrett has more power; Randolph gets on base more often and makes fewer outs. Barrett does not have the power that Tony Bernazard, Frank White and Lou Whitaker do—if you call him the fourth or fifth-best hitting second baseman in the league, you'd do him justice.

Defensively, it's a judgement call. Barrett has soft hands, but he isn't fast; on appearances, he's mediocre. The statistics, though, say that he's good—Marty consistently has one of the best range factors in the league and, Chuck Waseleski reports, since 1984 he has exactly the same number of chances accepted as Frank White. I am amazed by that—I've seen many balls that speedier men have no trouble getting to go through—but you can't argue with the evidence. Possibly, like Glenn Hubbard, Marty's positioning makes up for his footspeed. He does have a strong arm, plays with confidence and (since Jackie Gutierrez has been dispatched) turns the double play well. It's fair to call him one of the top five glove men and in the top five as an overall player.

Is he underrated? I don't think so. Barrett's best two months of 1986 were May (when Boston grabbed the lead in the AL East) and August (when they padded the lead until it was insurmountable) and he got quite a lot of credit for it. He hits well in the clutch; I heard a lot about that, too. He's the sort of player that the media loves (a short, white guy who gives good interview). Finally, he was the MVP of the Championship Series, even though Rich Gedman outhit him and shut California's running game down (one steal in five tries) and Dave Henderson had as dramatic a series as you can have and nobody ever says that he doesn't deserve to bat higher than Dwight Evans. Marty is a good player—no, let's make that a HECKuva player—but I don't see how anyone could possibly get the notion that he's underrated.

—David Pinto

	1986 SEASON											THREE YEARS (84 – 86)										
	Ave.	OBP	SLG	AB	H	2B	3B	HR	RBI	BB	SO	Ave.	OBP	SLG	AB	H	2B	3B	HR	RBI	BB	SO
Totals	.286	.353	.381	625	179	39	4	4	60	65	31	.285	.349	.368	1634	465	87	7	12	161	163	106
Batting vs. Left and Right-handed Pitchers																						
Left	.322	.418	.485	171	55	12	2	4	23	29	7	.306	.375	.407	496	152	31	2	5	55	58	21
Right	.273	.326	.341	454	124	27	2	0	37	36	24	.275	.337	.351	1138	313	56	5	7	106	105	85
At Home and on the Road																						
Home	.278	.350	.377	302	84	18	0	4	32	33	19	.287	.356	.383	792	227	48	2	8	85	86	67
Road	.294	.355	.384	323	95	21	4	0	28	32	12	.283	.342	.355	842	238	39	5	4	76	77	39
Facing Groundball Pitchers and Flyball Pitchers																						
Groundball	.273	.325	.360	286	78	15	2	2	28	23	8	.271	.336	.344	793	215	37	3	5	75	79	40
Flyball	.298	.375	.398	339	101	24	2	2	32	42	23	.297	.361	.391	841	250	50	4	7	86	84	66
Facing Finesse Pitchers and Power Pitchers																						
Finesse	.308	.364	.416	377	116	23	3	4	36	33	15	.302	.359	.389	940	284	56	4	6	86	86	48
Power	.254	.336	.327	248	63	16	1	0	24	32	16	.261	.335	.340	694	181	31	3	6	75	77	58
On Grass and on Turf																						
Grass	.287	.353	.378	529	152	30	3	4	47	54	28	.285	.352	.367	1369	390	71	6	10	136	144	94
Turf	.281	.352	.396	96	27	9	1	0	13	11	3	.283	.330	.374	265	75	16	1	2	25	19	12
During the Day and at Night																						
Day	.303	.362	.381	218	66	14	0	1	17	21	12	.284	.345	.356	531	151	25	2	3	48	51	42
Night	.278	.347	.381	407	113	25	4	3	43	44	19	.285	.350	.374	1103	314	62	5	9	113	112	64
By Month																						
April	.302	.380	.444	63	19	4	1	1	6	8	1	.292	.376	.394	137	40	6	1	2	14	19	8
May	.278	.331	.383	115	32	8	2	0	11	10	6	.289	.343	.371	256	74	14	2	1	22	23	14
June	.286	.339	.357	112	32	8	0	0	5	9	5	.279	.335	.340	297	83	15	0	1	21	25	18
July	.274	.325	.340	106	29	4	0	1	6	8	6	.299	.373	.370	281	84	11	0	3	29	34	17
August	.313	.382	.435	115	36	11	0	1	16	14	7	.293	.357	.405	331	97	25	0	4	33	33	28
Sept/Oct	.272	.366	.351	114	31	4	1	1	16	16	6	.262	.323	.343	332	87	16	4	1	42	29	21
Situational																						
Bases Empty	.285	.337	.366	383	109	24	2	1	1	29	19	.291	.347	.366	966	281	49	3	6	6	81	64
Leadoff	.301	.343	.403	186	56	14	1	1	1	11	7	.320	.368	.415	434	139	28	2	3	3	31	22
Not Leadoff	.269	.330	.330	197	53	10	1	0	0	18	12	.267	.330	.327	532	142	21	1	3	3	50	42
Runners On	.289	.376	.405	242	70	15	2	3	59	36	12	.275	.351	.371	668	184	38	4	6	155	82	42
First Base Only	.264	.361	.358	106	28	4	0	2	5	16	1	.253	.333	.317	281	71	12	0	2	7	33	10
Scoring Position	.309	.388	.441	136	42	11	2	1	54	20	11	.292	.363	.411	387	113	26	4	4	148	49	32
Late Innings, Close	.317	.398	.439	82	26	8	1	0	14	11	4	.283	.361	.376	237	67	14	1	2	31	29	19
RBI/Opportunities																						
Scoring Position			49 / 195		(25%)									132 / 550		(24%)						
Scoring Position, 2 Out			27 / 92		(29%)									70 / 265		(26%)						
On Third, Less than 2 Out			14 / 32		(44%)									42 / 96		(44%)						
RBI in close games / RBI Total			30 / 60		(50%)									83 / 161		(52%)						

Kevin Bass
Houston Astros

Baseball announcers and sportswriters love to call players "underrated." Some of those so labeled are actually underrated, although it is a good bet that by the time the announcers and writers figure out that a player is better than they thought, that player probably isn't that good anymore and probably isn't underrated anymore.

Kevin Bass has as good a claim to being underrated as any active player. Take a glance at his road stats for 1986: .308 BA, .353 OBA, .546 SA, 22 2B + 3B, 15 HR. Double those numbers and get a rough idea of what he would produce if he played in an average NL park rather than the pitchers haven that he calls home now. Nevertheless, how many fans do you think know about Kevin Bass? Sure, for every 100 articles written about Glenn Davis, his star teammate, there might have been a couple of references *en passant* to the Astros rightfielder. Would it help get him recognition if he told lurid stories about his past or considered committing suicide?

Bass finished seventh in the NL MVP balloting last year with 73 points, receiving no votes for first-, second-, or third-place, and only one vote for fourth place. Glenn Davis finished second in the voting with 231 points, 6 first-place votes, and only one vote *lower* than fourth-place. Kevin created 99.38 runs (6.23 per 25.5-out game) while playing a solid rightfield; Glenn created 95.92 runs, (5.80 per game) while playing the least important defensive position. Was Kevin Bass underrated? You bet.

A switch-hitter, Bass hits for a better average versus left-handers, has a better on-base versus right-handers, but slugs much better versus lefties. He does hit well in the Astrodome, but his power shows up much more clearly on the road, where he slugged 120 points higher last year. He started the season a little slowly, but finished very strongly. His isolated power has improved from .100 in 1984 to .158 in '85 to .175 last year. He is a good rightfielder with a decent arm (12 assists in '86, 10 assists in '85 as a centerfielder) and can play a credible centerfield if needed. Bass is fast enough to steal 41 bases the past two years, but his 21 caught stealings negate their value.

Bass will turn 28 during 1987, meaning that he should be at the peak of his game. If he turns in a couple more seasons like 1986, he should be ready to be called "underrated" by about 1989.

—Gary Gillette

	1986 SEASON											THREE YEARS (84 – 86)										
	Ave.	OBP	SLG	AB	H	2B	3B	HR	RBI	BB	SO	Ave.	OBP	SLG	AB	H	2B	3B	HR	RBI	BB	SO
Totals	.311	.357	.486	591	184	33	5	20	79	38	72	.284	.324	.435	1461	415	77	15	38	176	76	193
Batting vs. Left and Right-handed Pitchers																						
Left	.323	.345	.540	248	80	18	0	12	42	7	31	.294	.329	.491	625	184	41	5	24	85	25	94
Right	.303	.365	.446	343	104	15	5	8	37	31	41	.276	.321	.394	836	231	36	10	14	91	51	99
At Home and on the Road																						
Home	.314	.361	.426	296	93	14	2	5	36	18	37	.286	.332	.412	721	206	32	7	15	81	43	95
Road	.308	.353	.546	295	91	19	3	15	43	20	35	.282	.317	.458	740	209	45	8	23	95	33	98
Facing Groundball Pitchers and Flyball Pitchers																						
Groundball	.287	.334	.430	272	78	13	1	8	35	18	31	.257	.296	.373	670	172	32	5	12	74	33	98
Flyball	.332	.376	.533	319	106	20	4	12	44	20	41	.307	.348	.488	791	243	45	10	26	102	43	95
Facing Finesse Pitchers and Power Pitchers																						
Finesse	.319	.355	.494	332	106	17	4	11	45	17	34	.290	.320	.429	787	228	45	7	17	90	32	87
Power	.301	.359	.475	259	78	16	1	9	34	21	38	.277	.329	.442	674	187	32	8	21	86	44	106
On Grass and on Turf																						
Grass	.300	.333	.576	170	51	11	3	10	26	9	20	.282	.310	.470	457	129	31	5	15	58	17	61
Turf	.316	.366	.449	421	133	22	2	10	53	29	52	.285	.331	.419	1004	286	46	10	23	118	59	132
During the Day and at Night																						
Day	.289	.319	.475	204	59	12	1	8	24	8	34	.272	.313	.427	382	104	21	4	10	38	20	55
Night	.323	.376	.491	387	125	21	4	12	55	30	38	.288	.328	.438	1079	311	56	11	28	138	56	138
By Month																						
April	.260	.316	.397	73	19	2	1	2	5	6	9	.276	.320	.422	185	51	6	3	5	19	12	25
May	.287	.308	.426	101	29	8	0	2	9	3	12	.243	.262	.351	222	54	9	0	5	23	6	26
June	.378	.460	.663	98	37	5	1	7	15	12	10	.288	.337	.462	260	75	16	1	9	27	15	28
July	.298	.333	.423	104	31	4	0	3	14	5	17	.285	.331	.417	242	69	10	2	6	29	13	40
August	.290	.349	.500	100	29	3	3	4	14	7	13	.264	.308	.429	212	56	9	4	6	30	11	33
Sept/Oct	.339	.358	.487	115	39	11	0	2	22	5	11	.324	.362	.494	340	110	27	5	7	48	19	41
Situational																						
Bases Empty	.325	.354	.531	335	109	18	3	15	15	12	39	.284	.313	.444	859	244	42	10	25	25	30	108
Leadoff	.315	.329	.566	143	45	12	3	6	6	3	16	.267	.285	.458	356	95	21	7	11	11	9	45
Not Leadoff	.333	.373	.505	192	64	6	0	9	9	9	23	.296	.332	.433	503	149	21	3	14	14	21	63
Runners On	.293	.360	.426	256	75	15	2	5	64	26	33	.284	.340	.424	602	171	35	5	13	151	46	85
First Base Only	.269	.325	.398	108	29	6	1	2	9	7	11	.266	.322	.410	244	65	15	1	6	22	16	26
Scoring Position	.311	.384	.446	148	46	9	1	3	55	19	22	.296	.352	.433	358	106	20	4	7	129	30	59
Late Innings, Close	.324	.395	.451	102	33	2	1	3	13	11	14	.313	.364	.452	259	81	11	2	7	35	19	39

RBI/Opportunities					
Scoring Position	49 / 210	(23%)	117 / 468	(25%)
Scoring Position, 2 Out	25 / 119	(21%)	55 / 227	(24%)
On Third, Less than 2 Out	12 / 28	(43%)	32 / 72	(44%)
RBI in close games / RBI Total	46 / 79	(58%)	103 / 176	(59%)

Don Baylor
Boston Red Sox

Pitching coaches tell their pitchers to pitch inside often—that they must control both edges of the plate if they hope to succeed. Don Baylor agrees—his offensive strategy is based on denying pitchers that control. He leans forward, dangling his beefy arms over the plate and moving the strike zone several inches laterally. Balls that are merely inside to most hitters are free passes for Baylor—he simply turns his broad back into the ball to ensure that it won't miss him, and considers the plate appearance well-spent. A normally hittable delivery meets the Sox DH on the hands, and is hacked foul down the left field line. Pitches on the outside corner are fat city for Don; he makes his living off them. The ball must be well wide of the plate to be beyond his reach; in that case, he cheerfully draws the walk. On occasion, a rookie will experiment with a brushback—it's always fun to see how far the ball caroms.

His stance forces Baylor to start his swing early, to let him get around on inside deliveries—he's always out in front of the pitch as a result. He may be the most extreme pull hitter in the league; he rarely hits the ball to the right of second base. When Don played for California, Gene Mauch offered him a bounty for each opposite-field homer—as far as I know, Mauch never paid a cent.

Baylor's style is the mirror image of Wade Boggs's—he is incapable of adjusting at the plate. Pitchers who change speeds well keep him off stride constantly; he destroys power pitchers. Don thrives wherever and whenever fastball pitchers are used most. He hits very well in cavernous Yankee Stadium; he has difficulty in cozy Fenway Park. Many managers use their strongest arms at night; Baylor is at his best under the lights. The high, hard season is from May to July; Baylor has his best months then. Turf teams, who collect those pesky finesse pitchers, give him fits. Late in the game, facing a flamethrowing reliever, he rises to the occasion—with men in scoring position and the pitcher nibbling at the corners, he is helpless.

Baylor joined Boston in 1986 because the Yankees wanted to rest him against right-handed pitching and Don wanted a larger role. The Red Sox, who platoon nobody, were happy to make him a full-time employee. Don hit well in 1986, no matter which side the pitches originated from.

—Fred Percival

	1986 SEASON											THREE YEARS (84 – 86)										
	Ave.	OBP	SLG	AB	H	2B	3B	HR	RBI	BB	SO	Ave.	OBP	SLG	AB	H	2B	3B	HR	RBI	BB	SO
Totals	.238	.344	.439	585	139	23	1	31	94	62	111	.243	.339	.452	1555	378	76	3	81	274	152	269
Batting vs. Left and Right-handed Pitchers																						
Left	.230	.359	.388	152	35	7	1	5	18	24	27	.257	.368	.456	533	137	29	1	25	93	74	84
Right	.240	.338	.457	433	104	16	0	26	76	38	84	.236	.323	.450	1022	241	47	2	56	181	78	185
At Home and on the Road																						
Home	.233	.370	.376	279	65	13	0	9	44	40	46	.232	.340	.411	733	170	38	0	31	136	80	128
Road	.242	.317	.497	306	74	10	1	22	50	22	65	.253	.338	.489	822	208	38	3	50	138	72	141
Facing Groundball Pitchers and Flyball Pitchers																						
Groundball	.249	.351	.415	265	66	14	0	10	35	22	51	.238	.331	.409	755	180	39	0	30	132	65	125
Flyball	.228	.338	.459	320	73	9	1	21	59	40	60	.247	.345	.492	800	198	37	3	51	142	87	144
Facing Finesse Pitchers and Power Pitchers																						
Finesse	.224	.326	.392	339	76	12	0	15	50	32	54	.239	.328	.450	871	208	41	1	47	152	76	127
Power	.256	.368	.504	246	63	11	1	16	44	30	57	.249	.352	.455	684	170	35	2	34	122	76	142
On Grass and on Turf																						
Grass	.240	.357	.444	491	118	20	1	26	83	59	89	.241	.340	.442	1313	317	69	1	64	235	136	224
Turf	.223	.267	.415	94	21	3	0	5	11	3	22	.252	.333	.508	242	61	7	2	17	39	16	45
During the Day and at Night																						
Day	.216	.322	.417	204	44	3	1	12	35	20	37	.227	.318	.418	524	119	21	2	25	87	45	91
Night	.249	.355	.451	381	95	20	0	19	59	42	74	.251	.349	.469	1031	259	55	1	56	187	107	178
By Month																						
April	.239	.333	.408	71	17	0	0	4	11	10	9	.238	.315	.419	210	50	11	0	9	27	19	29
May	.257	.360	.495	105	27	7	0	6	24	10	19	.262	.368	.535	271	71	15	1	19	62	30	47
June	.253	.379	.484	95	24	5	1	5	16	9	20	.231	.339	.446	260	60	9	1	15	50	29	45
July	.229	.299	.385	96	22	3	0	4	13	7	20	.259	.331	.459	255	66	12	0	13	45	21	44
August	.206	.325	.421	107	22	2	0	7	14	14	20	.218	.329	.411	280	61	13	1	13	45	30	51
Sept/Oct	.243	.356	.432	111	27	6	0	5	16	12	23	.251	.343	.437	279	70	16	0	12	45	23	55
Situational																						
Bases Empty	.253	.342	.456	296	75	10	1	16	16	28	64	.237	.325	.444	779	185	29	3	42	42	70	138
Leadoff	.241	.343	.491	116	28	2	0	9	9	11	28	.227	.317	.437	348	79	8	1	21	21	31	67
Not Leadoff	.261	.342	.433	180	47	8	1	7	7	17	36	.246	.331	.450	431	106	21	2	21	21	39	71
Runners On	.221	.345	.422	289	64	13	0	15	78	34	47	.249	.352	.460	776	193	47	0	39	232	82	131
First Base Only	.235	.326	.471	119	28	4	0	8	16	6	18	.254	.341	.508	327	83	17	0	22	51	19	57
Scoring Position	.212	.356	.388	170	36	9	0	7	62	28	29	.245	.359	.425	449	110	30	0	17	181	63	74
Late Innings, Close	.253	.352	.494	79	20	4	0	5	20	5	14	.263	.322	.527	262	69	13	1	18	56	15	40
RBI/Opportunities																						
Scoring Position				51 / 258		(20%)									154 / 654		(24%)					
Scoring Position, 2 Out				13 / 119		(11%)									47 / 300		(16%)					
On Third, Less than 2 Out				23 / 53		(43%)									65 / 120		(54%)					
RBI in close games / RBI Total				63 / 94		(67%)									177 / 274		(65%)					

Steve Bedrosian
Philadelphia Phillies

After being used as a starter by the '85 Braves, Steve Bedrosian was traded to Philadelphia and given the late-inning relief job last year. Bedrock responded with 29 saves, by far the most of his career, and turned in some other impressive stats: a .163 opponents' batting average with men in scoring position, a .209 OBA in the late innings of close games, an imposing strikeout ratio, and the fewest walks-per-nine-innings of his major league career. His ERA was a little bit higher than you'd want from your top bullpen man and as usual he was easy to steal on, but Bedrosian's season certainly filled all of Philadelphia's expectations. Since he'll only be 29 when the '87 season begins, the Phils seem set in short relief for the next few years.

Or do they? I have to point out a lingering problem with Bedrosian, and it's not a good one for a bullpen ace: he's never shown much durability. In each of the last four seasons Steve has either broken down or pitched very poorly late in the year. Look at the record. In '83 he hurled in 70 games for Atlanta, but after posting 18 saves and a 2.99 ERA through August, Bedrock managed only one save

and a 6.53 ERA thereafter. In '84 he was sailing along with a 2.37 ERA for 40 games when he developed arm trouble; he went on the disabled list August 20 and didn't pitch for the rest of the year. The Braves were alarmed enough to switch Bedrosian to a starter's role for the '85 campaign. Bedrock hurled 206 innings and finished the year intact, but the experiment was hardly a success: his record was 7–15 and he set a new major league record for most starts in a season without a complete game (37). His September record was 2–4 with a 6.06 ERA. One couldn't blame the Phillies for returning him to the pen last season. Bedrosian's work was outstanding, as noted, but once again he wore down at the finish, with a 5.02 September ERA. That isn't going to cut it if the Phils are fighting for a division title late in '87.

One possible solution might be for the Phillies to lighten Bedrosian's workload a little. Houston has had a lot of success with Dave Smith the last few years by working him in fewer games and then usually for one inning only. Perhaps the same kind of schedule could help Bedrock; I'd say it's worth a try.

—Don Zminda

1986: Power, Flyball   **1985: Power, Flyball**   **1984: Power, Flyball**

	1986 SEASON											THREE YEARS (84 – 86)										
	G	IP	H	BB	SO	SB	CS	W	L	S	ERA	G	IP	H	BB	SO	SB	CS	W	L	S	ERA
Totals	68	90.1	79	34	82	14	0	8	6	29	3.39	145	380.2	342	178	297	58	16	24	27	40	3.40
At Home and on the Road																						
Home	29	39.0	28	7	31	3	0	2	3	14	3.00	64	181.1	165	63	135	16	10	9	11	18	3.23
Road	39	51.1	51	27	51	11	0	6	3	15	3.68	81	199.1	177	115	162	42	6	15	16	22	3.57
During the Day and at Night																						
Day	21	26.0	21	9	23	2	0	4	2	9	2.77	51	132.2	112	74	109	21	7	10	12	14	3.12
Night	47	64.1	58	25	59	12	0	4	4	20	3.64	94	248.0	230	104	188	37	9	14	15	26	3.56
On Grass and on Turf																						
Grass	20	24.1	25	12	25	3	0	2	2	9	4.44	77	238.2	224	106	181	28	14	13	17	15	3.70
Turf	48	66.0	54	22	57	11	0	6	4	20	3.00	68	142.0	118	72	116	30	2	11	10	25	2.92
By Month																						
April	8	8.2	13	5	5	1	0	1	1	3	7.27	20	47.0	46	21	30	4	2	2	3	6	3.45
May	11	12.2	7	3	11	0	0	1	1	3	2.13	25	65.0	57	25	55	7	5	5	3	5	1.94
June	12	17.0	14	10	15	5	0	3	1	3	3.18	32	79.0	71	44	68	19	3	8	8	6	3.19
July	11	16.0	11	8	14	1	0	2	0	4	1.12	26	64.2	50	35	51	10	2	4	5	6	3.90
August	15	21.1	17	4	23	2	0	1	0	9	2.53	24	74.2	64	27	54	6	3	3	1	10	2.65
Sept/Oct	11	14.2	17	4	14	5	0	0	3	7	6.14	18	50.1	54	26	39	12	1	2	7	7	6.08

	vs. Opponent Batters																					
	1986 SEASON											THREE YEARS (84 – 86)										
	Ave.	OBP	SLG	AB	H	2B	3B	HR	RBI	BB	SO	Ave.	OBP	SLG	AB	H	2B	3B	HR	RBI	BB	SO
Totals	.232	.299	.364	341	79	9	0	12	47	34	82	.239	.324	.360	1429	342	60	5	34	156	178	297
Pitching vs. Left and Right-handed Batters																						
Left	.213	.300	.410	178	38	5	0	10	30	23	43	.255	.355	.420	740	189	35	3	27	92	115	126
Right	.252	.297	.313	163	41	4	0	2	17	11	39	.222	.289	.295	689	153	25	2	7	64	63	171
Situational																						
Bases Empty	.231	.289	.382	173	40	2	0	8	8	14	42	.236	.310	.360	806	190	37	3	19	19	86	176
Leadoff	.286	.333	.514	70	20	1	0	5	5	5	17	.255	.324	.411	341	87	19	2	10	10	35	71
Not Leadoff	.194	.259	.291	103	20	1	0	3	3	9	25	.222	.300	.323	465	103	18	1	9	9	51	105
Runners On	.232	.309	.345	168	39	7	0	4	39	20	40	.244	.341	.360	623	152	23	2	15	137	92	121
First Base Only	.344	.373	.563	64	22	5	0	3	7	3	11	.303	.364	.461	241	73	14	0	8	19	22	36
Scoring Position	.163	.274	.212	104	17	2	0	1	32	17	29	.207	.328	.296	382	79	9	2	7	118	70	85
Late Innings, Close	.209	.281	.350	263	55	7	0	10	34	27	66	.221	.292	.355	411	91	16	1	13	48	42	106

RBI/Opportunities						
Scoring Position	29 / 167	(17%)		106 / 584	(18%)	
Scoring Position, 2 Out	15 / 78	(19%)		45 / 268	(17%)	
On Third, Less than 2 Out	9 / 30	(30%)		36 / 96	(38%)	
RBI in close games / RBI Total	34 / 47	(72%)		116 / 156	(74%)	

Buddy Bell
Cincinnati Reds

Buddy Bell salvaged his career last year, and it now looks like he might turn in Hall-of-Fame credentials before he retires. After a very successful 1984 with Texas where he hit .315, slugged .458, and won his sixth consecutive Gold Glove, Bell was traded to his hometown of Cincinnati in 1985 in the midst of a terrible year. The change of scenery didn't help, as he hit only .219 in the NL and his excellence afield seemed to desert him.

Buddy opened 1986 in the same miserable slump. He did manage to improve a little bit in May and June, but the prognosis was still poor. Buddy finally solved his problems in the second half of last year, hitting over .300 from July onward, including tearing up the league in August with a .431 on-base, .623 slugging performance (10 HRs and 24 BBs). His 20 homers on the season was a career high.

Bell did very well in 1986 at home, on turf and at night; his normal pattern of being better against southpaws was reversed. He really teed off in late-inning, close situations.

In his 15-year major-league career, Buddy has been disabled only twice, so he has the durability to run his career totals up a lot more. He has 2273 hits now; with only three more years as a regular, he should have 2700–2800 hits.

Then, if he can still play at least part-time, he should be able to top the select 3000-hit mark. A big boost to his chances would be the Reds winning one or more pennants in the next few years, for that is one important factor that his career lacks to date. His five AL All-Star selections will help his chances, too.

If Bell finishes with around 2800 hits and plays over 2500 total games played at third, short and second (current game totals of 1998), the *1986 Baseball Abstract*'s Hall-of-Fame prediction system would award him 82 points, plus any points that he would get in the NL for additional Gold Gloves, All-Star selections, single-season offensive performances, and playing on championship teams. This total would make him a possible, but unlikely Hall-of-Famer. However, if he exceeds the 3000 career-hit level, he would have amassed 107 points or more, making him a likely inductee.

Buddy Bell has been a steady, good-to-excellent player who has shown occasional brilliance. Buddy is an intelligent, durable player, and is a good bet to eventually be inducted into Cooperstown.

—Gary Gillette

	1986 SEASON											THREE YEARS (84 – 86)										
	Ave.	OBP	SLG	AB	H	2B	3B	HR	RBI	BB	SO	Ave.	OBP	SLG	AB	H	2B	3B	HR	RBI	BB	SO
Totals	.278	.362	.445	568	158	29	3	20	75	73	49	.274	.351	.418	1681	460	93	13	41	226	202	151
Batting vs. Left and Right-handed Pitchers																						
Left	.270	.348	.471	174	47	9	1	8	25	22	16	.291	.366	.454	474	138	24	7	13	67	61	33
Right	.282	.368	.434	394	111	20	2	12	50	51	33	.267	.345	.403	1207	322	69	6	28	159	141	118
At Home and on the Road																						
Home	.308	.387	.525	276	85	12	3	14	45	34	19	.284	.359	.454	820	233	43	9	26	129	96	69
Road	.250	.339	.370	292	73	17	0	6	30	39	30	.264	.343	.383	861	227	50	4	15	97	106	82
Facing Groundball Pitchers and Flyball Pitchers																						
Groundball	.271	.357	.414	280	76	14	1	8	37	38	30	.275	.355	.403	796	219	42	6	16	100	102	77
Flyball	.285	.367	.476	288	82	15	2	12	38	35	19	.272	.347	.431	885	241	51	7	25	126	100	74
Facing Finesse Pitchers and Power Pitchers																						
Finesse	.269	.332	.449	294	79	13	2	12	34	27	24	.271	.333	.419	945	256	53	9	23	120	91	70
Power	.288	.391	.442	274	79	16	1	8	41	46	25	.277	.372	.416	736	204	40	4	18	106	111	81
On Grass and on Turf																						
Grass	.250	.338	.381	176	44	11	0	4	21	23	20	.269	.343	.393	988	266	52	8	18	124	115	99
Turf	.291	.373	.474	392	114	18	3	16	54	50	29	.280	.362	.453	693	194	41	5	23	102	87	52
During the Day and at Night																						
Day	.223	.330	.321	184	41	7	1	3	14	27	15	.255	.326	.386	458	117	24	6	8	51	46	37
Night	.305	.378	.505	384	117	22	2	17	61	46	34	.280	.360	.429	1223	343	69	7	33	175	156	114
By Month																						
April	.157	.228	.235	51	8	4	0	0	1	3	4	.254	.322	.349	209	53	13	2	1	19	19	13
May	.273	.354	.375	88	24	4	1	1	9	10	10	.298	.371	.448	248	74	15	2	6	28	27	18
June	.240	.325	.375	96	23	4	0	3	14	14	7	.241	.314	.337	315	76	11	2	5	32	36	26
July	.319	.379	.479	94	30	6	0	3	10	8	7	.270	.356	.403	278	75	18	2	5	33	38	32
August	.302	.431	.623	106	32	4	0	10	22	24	9	.269	.363	.452	305	82	17	0	13	53	46	30
Sept/Oct	.308	.376	.459	133	41	7	2	3	19	14	12	.307	.374	.497	326	100	19	5	11	61	36	32
Situational																						
Bases Empty	.274	.356	.414	321	88	16	1	9	9	40	28	.256	.335	.391	905	232	43	5	23	23	106	90
Leadoff	.284	.376	.422	109	31	6	0	3	3	15	10	.270	.345	.420	307	83	17	1	9	9	34	35
Not Leadoff	.269	.346	.410	212	57	10	1	6	6	25	18	.249	.330	.376	598	149	26	4	14	14	72	55
Runners On	.283	.369	.486	247	70	13	2	11	66	33	21	.294	.368	.448	776	228	50	8	18	203	96	61
First Base Only	.347	.407	.520	98	34	6	1	3	9	9	6	.315	.364	.452	352	111	22	4	6	24	24	24
Scoring Position	.242	.346	.463	149	36	7	1	8	57	24	15	.276	.372	.446	424	117	28	4	12	179	72	37
Late Innings, Close	.320	.417	.454	97	31	7	0	2	14	17	12	.277	.353	.394	282	78	14	2	5	37	36	37
RBI/Opportunities																						

	1986 SEASON			THREE YEARS (84 – 86)		
Scoring Position	43 / 207	(21%)		149 / 601	(25%)	
Scoring Position, 2 Out	15 / 99	(15%)		45 / 268	(17%)	
On Third, Less than 2 Out	16 / 34	(47%)		64 / 119	(54%)	
RBI in close games / RBI Total	55 / 75	(73%)		163 / 226	(72%)	

George Bell
Toronto Blue Jays

Since 1984, George Bell has been one of the best hitters in the American League. Only four men (Kingman, Balboni, Mattingly and Evans) have more homers. Only five men (Mattingly, Rice, Murray, Winfield and Kong) have more RBIs. Bell is third in slugging percentage (minimum 1500 at-bats) behind only Mattingly and Gibson. The best measure of offensive performance is Bill James's Runs Created; Bell is one of only four AL players who created 95+ runs each year (Boggs, Henderson and Mattingly). Bell's total of 307 runs created is exceeded by only six men—Mattingly, Boggs, Henderson, Dwight Evans, Murray and Ripken.

The frightening thing about Bell is that his batting eye is improving. In 1984, he fanned 86 times and walked 24, giving him a poor 3.6–1 K/W ratio. He cut it in half in 1985 (90–43 or 2.1–1) and got it even further down in 1986 (1.5–1)—he was the eighteenth most difficult man in the AL to strike out this year.

Bell hits well despite consistent September slumps. In the last three years, his batting (.248), on-base (.279) and slugging (.415) have been well below his normal levels (.292, .335 and .504, respectively). It can't be that he minds cold weather (he hits .346 in April), so his knee problems may be the reason. George stole only seven bases in 1986 (down from 32 in 1985), and should probably be moved to first or DH to keep him healthy.

Getting Bell out is a difficult task. He had no platoon differential until 1986. It helps to catch him away from home, but not if you have a turf park. Your best bet is to avoid challenging him (he murders power pitchers) and keep the ball down (he's human against groundball pitchers) and try to have someone on first (he led Toronto in grounding into DPs and it's his worst situational breakdown).

But Bell has his flaws. He'll probably never walk often, because he can and does hit whatever he's thrown. His knee problems make him only an average outfielder (range factor is ordinary; he made 10 errors in 1986), despite his arm (his 17 assists were second only to Barfield in the AL). He has a foul temper—he was overwhelmingly voted the AL's dirtiest player in the *Toronto Globe and Mail*'s player poll this summer; given his outbursts in the 1985 playoffs, it probably isn't just envy. If George expects the acclaim that his talent deserves, he'll either have to change his approach, or be traded to the Mets.

—Andrew Berman, Marco Bresba and Dave Easby

	1986 SEASON											THREE YEARS (84 – 86)										
	Ave.	OBP	SLG	AB	H	2B	3B	HR	RBI	BB	SO	Ave.	OBP	SLG	AB	H	2B	3B	HR	RBI	BB	SO
Totals	.309	.349	.532	641	198	38	6	31	108	41	62	.292	.335	.504	1854	542	105	16	85	290	108	238
Batting vs. Left and Right-handed Pitchers																						
Left	.330	.363	.553	179	59	10	0	10	27	10	18	.295	.340	.522	603	178	33	4	32	96	39	74
Right	.301	.344	.524	462	139	28	6	21	81	31	44	.291	.332	.495	1251	364	72	12	53	194	69	164
At Home and on the Road																						
Home	.327	.375	.567	300	98	17	5	15	57	24	22	.301	.350	.511	880	265	56	9	37	154	64	109
Road	.293	.326	.501	341	100	21	1	16	51	17	40	.284	.320	.497	974	277	49	7	48	136	44	129
Facing Groundball Pitchers and Flyball Pitchers																						
Groundball	.305	.337	.482	282	86	16	2	10	45	14	32	.282	.317	.459	870	245	43	6	33	119	39	115
Flyball	.312	.359	.571	359	112	22	4	21	63	27	30	.302	.350	.544	984	297	62	10	52	171	69	123
Facing Finesse Pitchers and Power Pitchers																						
Finesse	.298	.326	.503	366	109	23	5	14	51	16	31	.279	.309	.465	1055	294	57	10	40	132	45	107
Power	.324	.379	.571	275	89	15	1	17	57	25	31	.310	.366	.554	799	248	48	6	45	158	63	131
On Grass and on Turf																						
Grass	.294	.327	.472	265	78	14	0	11	39	13	34	.289	.324	.486	751	217	37	3	35	103	35	97
Turf	.319	.364	.574	376	120	24	6	20	69	28	28	.295	.342	.516	1103	325	68	13	50	187	73	141
During the Day and at Night																						
Day	.311	.342	.542	225	70	13	3	11	43	10	23	.282	.331	.484	634	179	36	7	26	108	40	89
Night	.308	.353	.526	416	128	25	3	20	65	31	39	.298	.336	.514	1220	363	69	9	59	182	68	149
By Month																						
April	.361	.390	.597	72	26	5	0	4	18	4	7	.346	.385	.573	234	81	15	1	12	42	15	35
May	.310	.363	.487	113	35	5	3	3	16	10	11	.280	.327	.457	300	84	17	6	8	44	20	41
June	.299	.325	.547	117	35	6	1	7	21	6	6	.299	.327	.506	338	101	13	3	17	54	14	42
July	.317	.374	.654	104	33	6	1	9	23	10	13	.274	.327	.518	299	82	15	2	18	57	23	40
August	.342	.398	.530	117	40	10	0	4	17	10	6	.321	.375	.574	336	108	25	0	20	57	22	37
Sept/Oct	.246	.258	.415	118	29	6	1	4	13	1	19	.248	.279	.415	347	86	20	4	10	36	14	43
Situational																						
Bases Empty	.301	.343	.555	335	101	19	3	20	20	19	38	.292	.340	.528	981	286	54	8	54	54	58	144
Leadoff	.304	.329	.522	161	49	9	1	8	8	5	22	.297	.344	.514	418	124	24	2	21	21	24	61
Not Leadoff	.299	.354	.586	174	52	10	2	12	12	14	16	.288	.337	.538	563	162	30	6	33	33	34	83
Runners On	.317	.356	.507	306	97	19	3	11	88	22	24	.293	.328	.477	873	256	51	8	31	236	50	94
First Base Only	.318	.333	.462	132	42	6	2	3	13	3	9	.298	.318	.450	369	110	21	4	9	34	10	32
Scoring Position	.316	.372	.540	174	55	13	1	8	75	19	15	.290	.335	.496	504	146	30	4	22	202	40	62
Late Innings, Close	.263	.290	.466	118	31	5	2	5	22	5	10	.310	.355	.527	313	97	17	3	15	52	20	37
RBI/Opportunities																						
Scoring Position		59 / 226	(26%)										162 / 640	(25%)								
Scoring Position, 2 Out		28 / 101	(28%)										68 / 299	(23%)								
On Third, Less than 2 Out		16 / 40	(40%)										48 / 107	(45%)								
RBI in close games / RBI Total		84 / 108	(78%)										198 / 290	(68%)								

Tony Bernazard
Cleveland Indians

Tony Bernazard's 1986 both vindicated and stunned me. I've always said that he could be a super player; given his past (inconsistent, sometimes just lousy), I didn't think he ever would be. At 29, he's a bit old to be hitting his prime, but he's had two good years in a row, he played as well as any second baseman did in 1986 and he still could have a fine career.

Tony isn't Cleveland's best hitter in any area, but he's their best overall one. In 1986, he was second on the team in batting, on-base and slugging averages, first in sacrifice flies and GWRBIs and hit into the fewest double plays. He's an intelligent hitter who adapts to what the game situation dictates. His batting eye and bat control (he's easily Cleveland's best hit and run man) make him devastating with runners on first. His individual stats could have been better had he been more selfish—he refuses to take a big swing with two outs, or with the heart of the order following. If he can't walk, he tries only to meet the ball. If he hadn't, he could have had 90+ RBIs—but Joe Carter would never have had 121 RBIs and it would have cost the team runs.

He did passably when he got the leadoff job in June, but his views of what leadoff men do don't make him a good choice for the job. With nobody on, he goes for the long ball—he hit five homers in the first at-bat of a game in 1986, but his average suffers.

The most striking thing about Bernazard's fielding is his intensity. He's never forgotten that Chicago traded him because of his defense and he tries hard to erase that blot on his record. He insists on fielding any pop fly he can reach and eats "Texas leaguers" up. He's always turned the double play well, but he's never regained the range he lost after a 1982 injury.

Thornton's role has shrunk and Carter leads by example, so Tony is the team leader. He's the regular who usually visits the mound; if he wants the pitcher to bear down more, it's obvious from the way he acts. If a teammate takes his griping to the papers, Tony will answer him—often bluntly. He can be abrasive, but his teammates seem to admire his frankness more than they resent it. Given his recent determination to excel, it's easy to understand why.

—Geoff Beckman

	1986 SEASON												THREE YEARS (84 – 86)										
	Ave.	OBP	SLG	AB	H	2B	3B	HR	RBI	BB	SO		Ave.	OBP	SLG	AB	H	2B	3B	HR	RBI	BB	SO
Totals	.301	.362	.456	562	169	28	4	17	73	53	77		.268	.341	.389	1501	403	69	11	30	170	165	219
Batting vs. Left and Right-handed Pitchers																							
Left	.338	.419	.510	151	51	11	0	5	21	19	17		.280	.370	.394	414	116	24	1	7	45	59	49
Right	.287	.341	.436	411	118	17	4	12	52	34	60		.264	.329	.387	1087	287	45	10	23	125	106	170
At Home and on the Road																							
Home	.329	.384	.486	286	94	12	3	9	40	26	37		.296	.367	.428	739	219	37	9	14	89	85	102
Road	.272	.341	.424	276	75	16	1	8	33	27	40		.241	.315	.352	762	184	32	2	16	81	80	117
Facing Groundball Pitchers and Flyball Pitchers																							
Groundball	.321	.373	.460	265	85	9	2	8	34	21	34		.269	.339	.380	737	198	28	6	14	93	77	98
Flyball	.283	.353	.451	297	84	19	2	9	39	32	43		.268	.342	.398	764	205	41	5	16	77	88	121
Facing Finesse Pitchers and Power Pitchers																							
Finesse	.314	.366	.473	328	103	17	1	11	49	25	35		.286	.342	.424	868	248	44	5	22	108	74	106
Power	.282	.358	.432	234	66	11	3	6	24	28	42		.245	.339	.341	633	155	25	6	8	62	91	113
On Grass and on Turf																							
Grass	.305	.363	.459	486	148	25	4	14	62	44	65		.273	.347	.400	1266	345	63	10	26	146	145	185
Turf	.276	.356	.434	76	21	3	0	3	11	9	12		.247	.307	.332	235	58	6	1	4	24	20	34
During the Day and at Night																							
Day	.286	.373	.429	175	50	11	1	4	20	23	26		.255	.347	.367	471	120	18	4	9	44	68	70
Night	.307	.358	.468	387	119	17	3	13	53	30	51		.275	.338	.399	1030	283	51	7	21	126	97	149
By Month																							
April	.277	.333	.369	65	18	1	1	1	6	5	9		.299	.394	.431	174	52	5	3	4	22	29	29
May	.315	.382	.438	89	28	6	1	1	8	10	13		.244	.324	.345	258	63	15	1	3	22	30	43
June	.333	.388	.495	93	31	6	0	3	14	9	12		.281	.334	.383	274	77	11	1	5	34	23	44
July	.300	.376	.473	110	33	4	0	5	16	13	10		.275	.354	.387	284	78	11	0	7	31	33	28
August	.308	.374	.462	117	36	7	1	3	17	11	20		.256	.314	.397	305	78	17	4	6	35	26	44
Sept/Oct	.261	.302	.466	88	23	4	1	4	12	5	13		.267	.343	.408	206	55	10	2	5	26	24	31
Situational																							
Bases Empty	.293	.356	.464	338	99	14	4	12	12	30	52		.263	.334	.400	870	229	39	7	22	22	89	135
Leadoff	.300	.354	.505	190	57	12	3	7	7	15	25		.262	.330	.416	401	105	22	5	10	10	40	59
Not Leadoff	.284	.358	.412	148	42	2	1	5	5	15	27		.264	.337	.386	469	124	17	2	12	12	49	76
Runners On	.313	.372	.442	224	70	14	0	5	61	23	25		.276	.350	.374	631	174	30	4	8	148	76	84
First Base Only	.363	.389	.505	91	33	7	0	2	7	3	10		.318	.351	.438	258	82	15	2	4	19	11	29
Scoring Position	.278	.362	.398	133	37	7	0	3	54	20	15		.247	.350	.330	373	92	15	2	4	129	65	55
Late Innings, Close	.250	.330	.362	80	20	9	0	0	7	9	14		.231	.320	.329	225	52	16	0	2	20	30	34
RBI/Opportunities																							
Scoring Position				50 / 188		(27%)										121 / 543		(22%)					
Scoring Position, 2 Out				13 / 89		(15%)										40 / 243		(16%)					
On Third, Less than 2 Out				19 / 30		(63%)										46 / 85		(54%)					
RBI in close games / RBI Total				45 / 73		(62%)										103 / 170		(61%)					

Bud Black
Kansas City Royals

The Kansas City Royals have long since got their money's worth out of Bud Black. Harry Ralston Black, who had won just eight games in the Seattle farm system, was acquired by KC on March 2, 1982 in exchange for an infielder named Manny Castillo. From mid-1983 through 1984 he was the Royals best starting pitcher. He had a poor year in 1985 but pitched a 3-hit shutout over the Angels on October 2 that was perhaps the biggest game of the regular season. In April, 1986, he was again floundering as a starter and was moved to the bullpen, where he pitched very well.

Black lacks an outstanding fastball or the crackling curve that speed can create; he must get by changing speeds and spotting the ball in the strike zone. In the period when he was not effective, in 1985 and early 1986, he was working behind hitters a great deal, nibbling for corners and getting into trouble. I note that in the last couple of years he has struck out more batters (per inning) than he did when pitching his best ball. In 1983, when he established himself as a major league player, he struck out only 58 men in 161 innings. In 1984, his best season, he struck out less than five per nine innings. But in 1985, when his ERA shot up, his strikeouts increased to about 5.4 per nine innings, with a more-than-proportional increase in walks, and in 1986 his K rate remained over five. In the early part of 1986, when he was not effective, his strikeouts were high (in May he struck out 17 men in 18 and two-thirds innings), but as the season progressed and he got more effective, his strikeouts declined. He just missed a perfect straight in his ERA column in 1986, with his ERAs by months reading 6.14, 4.34, 2.79, 2.82, 2.55 and 1.69. Had he gotten just one more man out in July, he would have had a better ERA in each month than in the month before.

Black is an excellent athlete. On the mound he would remind you of an oversized Ron Guidry, standing perfectly balanced with his feet together, looking almost like a ballet dancer waiting for the music to start. He cuts off the running game and is an excellent fielder. He has pitched much more effectively on artificial turf than on grass.

—Bill James

1986: Finesse, Flyball   **1985: Finesse, Groundball**   **1984: Finesse, Groundball**

	G	IP	H	BB	SO	SB	CS	W	L	S	ERA		G	IP	H	BB	SO	SB	CS	W	L	S	ERA
			1986 SEASON													**THREE YEARS (84 – 86)**								
Totals	56	121.0	100	43	68	6	5	5	10	9	3.20		124	583.2	542	166	330	30	23	32	37	9	3.56
												At Home and on the Road											
Home	28	61.2	45	18	35	2	2	3	2	5	2.63		65	316.1	288	87	170	19	14	19	16	5	3.24
Road	28	59.1	55	25	33	4	3	2	8	4	3.79		59	267.1	254	79	160	11	9	13	21	4	3.94
												During the Day and at Night											
Day	16	38.2	36	12	24	2	1	1	4	3	3.49		37	179.2	167	54	119	10	11	11	12	3	3.61
Night	40	82.1	64	31	44	4	4	4	6	6	3.06		87	404.0	375	112	211	20	12	21	25	6	3.54
												On Grass and on Turf											
Grass	20	45.1	37	16	22	4	2	2	6	4	3.97		45	209.2	194	61	123	9	5	11	17	4	4.12
Turf	36	75.2	63	27	46	2	3	3	4	5	2.74		79	374.0	348	105	207	21	18	21	20	5	3.25
												By Month											
April	4	14.2	21	4	7	2	0	1	2	0	6.14		14	87.2	87	24	36	7	7	6	4	0	3.49
May	10	18.2	15	7	17	0	0	2	1	2	4.34		22	105.1	91	26	61	1	1	7	6	2	3.25
June	11	19.1	15	9	9	3	3	1	1	0	2.79		22	93.0	82	34	53	7	6	5	7	0	3.68
July	10	22.1	20	4	14	0	1	0	1	1	2.82		21	91.0	97	29	61	4	2	3	8	1	4.75
August	13	24.2	15	11	12	0	0	0	2	3	2.55		25	106.1	106	28	62	6	3	5	6	3	3.39
Sept/Oct	8	21.1	14	8	9	1	1	1	3	3	1.69		20	100.1	79	25	57	5	4	6	6	3	2.96

vs. Opponent Batters

	Ave.	OBP	SLG	AB	H	2B	3B	HR	RBI	BB	SO		Ave.	OBP	SLG	AB	H	2B	3B	HR	RBI	BB	SO
			1986 SEASON													**THREE YEARS (84 – 86)**								
Totals	.225	.301	.373	445	100	18	3	14	54	43	68		.244	.301	.370	2219	542	93	14	53	228	166	330
												Pitching vs. Left and Right-handed Batters											
Left	.219	.285	.336	137	30	3	2	3	14	11	27		.230	.283	.330	518	119	15	5	9	48	35	80
Right	.227	.307	.390	308	70	15	1	11	40	32	41		.249	.307	.383	1701	423	78	9	44	180	131	250
												Situational											
Bases Empty	.240	.300	.378	246	59	15	2	5	5	19	37		.242	.293	.366	1318	319	62	9	28	28	87	182
Leadoff	.262	.321	.369	103	27	3	1	2	2	8	11		.232	.278	.382	557	129	23	5	17	17	29	70
Not Leadoff	.224	.284	.385	143	32	12	1	3	3	11	26		.250	.305	.355	761	190	39	4	11	11	58	112
Runners On	.206	.302	.367	199	41	3	1	9	49	24	31		.248	.312	.376	901	223	31	5	25	200	79	148
First Base Only	.172	.226	.333	87	15	0	1	4	9	4	13		.222	.270	.361	427	95	8	3	15	35	24	64
Scoring Position	.232	.353	.393	112	26	3	0	5	40	20	18		.270	.347	.390	474	128	23	2	10	165	55	84
Late Innings, Close	.190	.293	.336	137	26	2	0	6	16	17	20		.249	.319	.410	334	83	13	1	13	39	32	46

RBI/Opportunities

Scoring Position	31 / 168	(18%)		141 / 644	(22%)
Scoring Position, 2 Out	17 / 79	(22%)		53 / 266	(20%)
On Third, Less than 2 Out	10 / 35	(29%)		50 / 134	(37%)
RBI in close games / RBI Total	31 / 54	(57%)		171 / 228	(75%)

Bert Blyleven
Minnesota Twins

Bert's first tour with the Twins ended following one of the crazier nights at now demolished Metropolitan Stadium in May of 1976. The crowd was one of those intimate gatherings common to mid-seventies Twins baseball. With Blyleven facing the Angels and Frank Tanana, the fans, familiar with Bert's recent contract requests and his impending trade to the Rangers, were in a festively hostile mood. Antagonizing Blyleven by song and shouts, the fans received the anticipated obscene salute from the right-hander as he departed the mound following the top of the ninth with the Twins trailing 3–1 despite a well-pitched 6-hitter. In the bottom of the inning, Craig Kusick, who had not threatened the ball in three previous at bats, received a standing O for fouling a pitch into the seats. He deposited the next ball over the left field fence and after completing the circuit, saluted the crowd in the Dutchman's manner and disappeared into the dugout bringing to a close another pleasant spring evening at the park.

Symbolic gestures, but more good natured fan support, have characterized Blyleven's recent stint with the Twins. The beard that he shaved after his return to the team in '85 was regrown in order to regain his effectiveness. That worked for July and August, but he was still unable to prevent accruing his highest career ERA. Earlier, Bert had ripped up a huge sombrero that the Twins staff, fun-loving guys that they are, awarded to a pitcher giving up three or more home runs in a game. He was to accomplish that feat seven times last year. The home run pace he set would have tired a mere mortal, but Blyleven hung tough for 271 innings and delivered shots to Ron's, Don's, Lonnie's, and John's; Joe's, Jay's, Donnie's, and Dave's; plus Reggie's, Reuben's, Rickey's, and Rick's, until he had given up a shot for every state, a record-breaking 50. The record blast was delivered by Cleveland's Jay Bell, one of the players for whom Bert was traded.

Blyleven is one of two players left from the Twins 1970 division champs, with Rick Dempsey (five games in 1970) the other. Bert's curveball, after 17 years, still causes right-handers to duck-and-cover (although, oddly, he is more effective against left-handers), and now he has begun to throw a pitch that acts suspiciously like a knuckler. If an arm that has launched thousands of curves can master a knuckler, he might just pitch long enough to see the Twins win again.

—Bill Jensen

1986: Finesse, Flyball **1985: Power, Flyball** **1984: Power, Flyball**

| | 1986 SEASON | | | | | | | | | | | THREE YEARS (84 – 86) | | | | | | | | | | |
	G	IP	H	BB	SO	SB	CS	W	L	S	ERA	G	IP	H	BB	SO	SB	CS	W	L	S	ERA
Totals	36	271.2	262	58	215	26	7	17	14	0	4.01	106	810.1	730	207	591	77	24	53	37	0	3.35
At Home and on the Road																						
Home	20	155.0	159	29	133	17	6	12	5	0	4.12	58	447.2	430	97	345	47	15	33	16	0	3.42
Road	16	116.2	103	29	82	9	1	5	9	0	3.86	48	362.2	300	110	246	30	9	20	21	0	3.28
During the Day and at Night																						
Day	10	80.1	64	21	59	8	2	4	4	0	4.15	35	262.2	241	83	179	22	8	14	12	0	3.56
Night	26	191.1	198	37	156	18	5	13	10	0	3.95	71	547.2	489	124	412	55	16	39	25	0	3.25
On Grass and on Turf																						
Grass	12	85.0	71	23	58	7	1	4	7	0	4.34	64	478.1	415	134	331	43	14	29	24	0	3.33
Turf	24	186.2	191	35	157	19	6	13	7	0	3.86	42	332.0	315	73	260	34	10	24	13	0	3.39
By Month																						
April	5	40.1	38	14	28	2	3	2	1	0	3.57	15	106.2	111	36	75	11	5	5	4	0	3.97
May	6	43.2	51	5	35	8	0	2	3	0	6.39	16	114.1	121	25	91	16	3	6	7	0	4.41
June	6	35.1	45	9	21	6	1	2	3	0	6.37	17	117.0	106	34	74	14	4	8	6	0	3.62
July	6	47.1	38	11	33	4	2	3	3	0	2.85	18	146.0	115	43	102	11	4	9	8	0	3.21
August	6	49.2	32	7	46	2	0	5	0	0	1.45	19	156.0	118	32	110	7	4	14	3	0	2.13
Sept/Oct	7	55.1	58	12	52	4	1	3	4	0	4.23	21	170.1	159	37	139	18	4	11	9	0	3.33

vs. Opponent Batters

| | 1986 SEASON | | | | | | | | | | | THREE YEARS (84 – 86) | | | | | | | | | |
	Ave.	OBP	SLG	AB	H	2B	3B	HR	RBI	BB	SO	Ave.	OBP	SLG	AB	H	2B	3B	HR	RBI	BB	SO
Totals	.250	.294	.448	1049	262	42	8	50	124	58	215	.238	.290	.378	3065	730	108	23	92	307	207	591
Pitching vs. Left and Right-handed Batters																						
Left	.238	.279	.415	638	152	25	5	26	65	35	138	.235	.288	.360	1757	413	61	13	44	163	124	343
Right	.268	.318	.499	411	110	17	3	24	59	23	77	.242	.293	.404	1308	317	47	10	48	144	83	248
Situational																						
Bases Empty	.252	.292	.436	663	167	29	6	27	27	35	134	.237	.285	.372	1897	450	66	15	53	53	114	376
Leadoff	.259	.296	.425	266	69	13	2	9	9	12	60	.251	.289	.386	792	199	28	8	21	21	38	155
Not Leadoff	.247	.290	.443	397	98	16	4	18	18	23	74	.227	.283	.361	1105	251	38	7	32	32	76	221
Runners On	.246	.298	.469	386	95	13	2	23	97	23	81	.240	.297	.390	1168	280	42	8	39	254	93	215
First Base Only	.267	.302	.517	180	48	6	0	13	27	8	26	.244	.288	.391	542	132	19	2	19	48	32	76
Scoring Position	.228	.294	.427	206	47	7	2	10	70	15	55	.236	.304	.388	626	148	23	6	20	206	61	139
Late Innings, Close	.310	.340	.560	100	31	3	2	6	21	5	19	.241	.304	.388	299	72	10	2	10	34	26	60

RBI/Opportunities

	1986		THREE YEARS	
Scoring Position	53 / 284	(19%)	169 / 847	(20%)
Scoring Position, 2 Out	28 / 132	(21%)	80 / 397	(20%)
On Third, Less than 2 Out	16 / 49	(33%)	62 / 150	(41%)
RBI in close games / RBI Total	88 / 124	(71%)	216 / 307	(70%)

Bruce Bochte
Oakland A's

Bruce Bochte was released by the Oakland A's in November and decided to retire to Oregon. He retired once before, in 1982, but it will take this time. Since he un-retired in 1984 and chose to play for Oakland, Bruce was known for his consistent bat and dependable glove. Over his three years in Oakland, he hit .312 with men on base, as opposed to .242 with the bases empty.

Bochte may not be appreciated now because of the abundance of first base candidates for 1987. At times, he provided stability at a position where in the past even during the World Championship years first base was always a problem.

It is a possibility that Carney Lansford may move to first and rookie Mark McGwire may start at third. Bochte was steady all season, with a .257 average. His only fault may have been his lack of power and the hope that McGwire can provide power at third, while Lansford moves to first. Lansford played 60 games at first in 1986. Dusty Baker, Dave Kingman and Bob Nelson also played a little bit

at first. Bochte came up with the Angels in 1974, and was regarded by some as an exciting young player. The expectations for him were not completely realistic, and the pressure put on him might have poisoned the attitude of many men. Bochte was a line-driver hitter without speed or power; to have developed into a star he would have had to be Wade Boggs. He wasn't Wade Boggs, but he did hit .301 for California and Cleveland in 1977, .316 for Seattle in 1979, .300 for Seattle in 1980, .297 for Seattle in 1982 and .295 for Oakland in 1985. He hit a hundred home runs in his career (exactly a hundred), and drove in a hundred runs for Seattle in 1979 (also exactly a hundred).

Bochte is remembered fondly by baseball fans as one of the few people on either side of the line who tried to rise above the endemic greed which dominated baseball news in the early 1980s. The A's should be able to replace his bat and his glove and certainly won't miss his speed on the basepaths, but they certainly will not replace him with a classier individual.

—Bill James and Chris Chew

	1986 SEASON											THREE YEARS (84 – 86)										
	Ave.	OBP	SLG	AB	H	2B	3B	HR	RBI	BB	SO	Ave.	OBP	SLG	AB	H	2B	3B	HR	RBI	BB	SO
Totals	.256	.357	.337	407	104	13	1	6	43	65	68	.272	.352	.373	1300	353	53	2	25	155	166	185
Batting vs. Left and Right-handed Pitchers																						
Left	.204	.278	.204	49	10	0	0	0	4	5	9	.256	.321	.335	215	55	5	0	4	28	21	35
Right	.263	.368	.355	358	94	13	1	6	39	60	59	.275	.358	.381	1085	298	48	2	21	127	145	150
At Home and on the Road																						
Home	.247	.362	.328	198	49	5	1	3	24	36	32	.277	.365	.373	625	173	28	1	10	76	90	85
Road	.263	.353	.344	209	55	8	0	3	19	29	36	.267	.339	.373	675	180	25	1	15	79	76	100
Facing Groundball Pitchers and Flyball Pitchers																						
Groundball	.256	.339	.340	215	55	6	0	4	20	27	33	.273	.342	.361	660	180	22	0	12	71	71	89
Flyball	.255	.377	.333	192	49	7	1	2	23	38	35	.270	.361	.386	640	173	31	2	13	84	95	96
Facing Finesse Pitchers and Power Pitchers																						
Finesse	.267	.370	.370	243	65	7	0	6	26	40	29	.281	.359	.403	740	208	28	1	20	90	92	82
Power	.238	.339	.287	164	39	6	1	0	17	25	39	.259	.342	.334	560	145	25	1	5	65	74	103
On Grass and on Turf																						
Grass	.259	.361	.337	347	90	10	1	5	37	56	55	.279	.359	.385	1102	307	50	2	21	134	142	152
Turf	.233	.333	.333	60	14	3	0	1	6	9	13	.232	.313	.308	198	46	3	0	4	21	24	33
During the Day and at Night																						
Day	.268	.378	.363	157	42	6	0	3	16	28	24	.287	.363	.389	471	135	22	1	8	52	60	63
Night	.248	.344	.320	250	62	7	1	3	27	37	44	.263	.345	.364	829	218	31	1	17	103	106	122
By Month																						
April	.241	.349	.333	54	13	2	0	1	7	9	8	.264	.347	.316	174	46	6	0	1	19	23	20
May	.222	.333	.397	63	14	2	0	3	5	11	10	.272	.369	.382	191	52	9	0	4	20	30	29
June	.264	.360	.333	87	23	3	0	1	10	13	16	.267	.344	.387	243	65	11	0	6	26	29	33
July	.370	.469	.426	54	20	3	0	0	4	10	10	.312	.398	.399	218	68	7	0	4	23	31	33
August	.250	.349	.333	72	18	1	1	1	8	11	9	.275	.348	.396	240	66	12	1	5	36	28	34
Sept/Oct	.208	.307	.234	77	16	2	0	0	9	11	15	.239	.308	.346	234	56	8	1	5	31	25	36
Situational																						
Bases Empty	.243	.338	.349	235	57	10	0	5	5	34	38	.241	.330	.325	750	181	33	0	10	10	99	113
Leadoff	.276	.370	.356	87	24	4	0	1	1	13	14	.255	.339	.335	275	70	19	0	1	1	35	40
Not Leadoff	.223	.320	.345	148	33	6	0	4	4	21	24	.234	.325	.320	475	111	14	0	9	9	64	73
Runners On	.273	.382	.320	172	47	3	1	1	38	31	30	.313	.381	.438	550	172	20	2	15	145	67	72
First Base Only	.304	.351	.391	69	21	1	1	1	3	5	9	.342	.375	.519	243	83	14	1	9	26	13	26
Scoring Position	.252	.400	.272	103	26	2	0	0	35	26	21	.290	.385	.375	307	89	6	1	6	119	54	46
Late Innings, Close	.258	.387	.290	62	16	2	0	0	3	13	13	.285	.378	.350	200	57	7	0	2	15	30	36
RBI/Opportunities																						
Scoring Position				35 / 149		(23%)									109 / 431		(25%)					
Scoring Position, 2 Out				17 / 84		(20%)									39 / 204		(19%)					
On Third, Less than 2 Out				11 / 20		(55%)									38 / 69		(55%)					
RBI in close games / RBI Total				28 / 43		(65%)									100 / 155		(65%)					

Mike Boddicker
Baltimore Orioles

Every pitcher has some margin of error—for Mike Boddicker, the gap has become a very narrow one. From 1983 to May of 1985, (when he was 6–1), Boddicker was one of the best pitchers in baseball. Since that point, he has been thoroughly mediocre—other than a 10–1 start in 1986, he has not pitched effectively at all.

There have been many reasons offered. Boddicker was reportedly tipping his changeups off in 1985. He has battled tendinitis in his left knee, making it difficult for him to use his natural motion. A general decline in team defense may have played a role. But the reality is simply this—batters are now all too familiar with Boddicker's repertoire and have begun showing their contempt. Boddicker has never dominated hitters—even in his 20-win year, his control (1.58–1 K/W ratio) was poor and he was vulnerable to the extra-base hit (he allowed 30 doubles, six triples and 30 homers in 916 at-bats). He won by forcing batters to put the ball in play—he hasn't done so since then and he's losing because of it.

A winning pitcher retires opposing hitters on as few pitches as he can. Unless he has overpowering speed, the more pitches he throws to a hitter, the more likely that hitter is to judge one of them correctly and hit safely—if he is forced to throw more than 15 pitches in an inning, he'll tire sooner and be easier to hit as the game progresses. The simplest way to see how quickly a pitcher gets batters out is the percentage of walks and strikeouts he has. In 1984, Boddicker walked or struck out only 20% of the batters; that figure rose to 25% in 1985 and 27% in 1986. Leadoff hitters are being more patient, working the count—Boddicker strikes them out more often, but he also allows more hits and walks. With men on first, teams have continued to try to force Boddicker to throw the ball. In '84–85, Mike struck out 12.6% of the men he faced with men on first—in 1986, that figure rose to 24.7%. The effect of throwing that many pitches shows up in his statistics with men in scoring position—batters now hit him more easily than they have done before and they do so with power.

Nothing has happened to Mike Boddicker—he is still the same pitcher that he was in 1983. It is his own personal tragedy that American League hitters have progressed.

—Geoff Beckman and Tim Mulligan

1986: Power, Groundball   1985: Power, Groundball   1984: Finesse, Groundball

	G	IP	H	BB	SO	SB	CS	W	L	S	ERA		G	IP	H	BB	SO	SB	CS	W	L	S	ERA
1986 SEASON												**THREE YEARS (84 – 86)**											
Totals	33	218.1	214	74	175	32	7	14	12	0	4.70		99	683.0	659	244	438	92	23	46	40	0	3.78
At Home and on the Road																							
Home	16	102.1	96	44	87	13	4	7	4	0	4.66		47	326.0	297	130	212	42	12	20	19	0	3.34
Road	17	116.0	118	30	88	19	3	7	8	0	4.73		52	357.0	362	114	226	50	11	26	21	0	4.18
During the Day and at Night																							
Day	10	70.0	58	20	43	12	0	6	3	0	3.73		30	213.1	196	62	125	24	3	18	10	0	3.12
Night	23	148.1	156	54	132	20	7	8	9	0	5.16		69	469.2	463	182	313	68	20	28	30	0	4.08
On Grass and on Turf																							
Grass	27	169.2	171	67	138	24	6	10	10	0	5.15		84	578.0	561	219	361	78	21	37	36	0	3.83
Turf	6	48.2	43	7	37	8	1	4	2	0	3.14		15	105.0	98	25	77	14	2	9	4	0	3.51
By Month																							
April	3	21.1	19	8	21	5	2	2	0	0	3.38		13	81.0	75	44	62	13	4	5	4	0	3.56
May	4	32.1	27	15	29	3	0	3	1	0	3.34		16	124.0	104	51	75	12	3	12	4	0	2.69
June	7	49.2	44	16	32	7	1	5	2	0	5.07		19	129.1	120	47	65	17	3	10	8	0	4.59
July	6	43.1	40	6	31	7	1	3	2	0	3.74		18	132.2	125	32	88	26	3	8	8	0	3.66
August	7	42.1	47	16	33	6	1	1	4	0	5.31		17	114.0	111	33	77	15	3	7	7	0	4.03
Sept/Oct	6	29.1	37	13	29	4	2	0	3	0	7.06		16	102.0	124	37	71	9	7	4	9	0	4.15

	Ave.	OBP	SLG	AB	H	2B	3B	HR	RBI	BB	SO		Ave.	OBP	SLG	AB	H	2B	3B	HR	RBI	BB	SO
vs. Opponent Batters																							
1986 SEASON												**THREE YEARS (84 – 86)**											
Totals	.255	.321	.410	840	214	32	4	30	114	74	175		.254	.322	.378	2590	659	98	12	66	284	244	438
Pitching vs. Left and Right-handed Batters																							
Left	.266	.329	.404	428	114	19	2	12	51	37	72		.266	.333	.382	1404	373	62	4	31	146	133	189
Right	.243	.313	.415	412	100	13	2	18	63	37	103		.241	.308	.374	1186	286	36	8	35	138	111	249
Situational																							
Bases Empty	.240	.324	.374	484	116	19	2	14	14	53	88		.254	.325	.379	1498	380	62	7	37	37	146	234
Leadoff	.309	.378	.469	207	64	10	1	7	7	20	33		.293	.356	.436	652	191	35	2	18	18	56	100
Not Leadoff	.188	.283	.303	277	52	9	1	7	7	33	55		.223	.302	.335	846	189	27	5	19	19	90	134
Runners On	.275	.318	.458	356	98	13	2	16	100	21	87		.255	.317	.377	1092	279	36	5	29	247	98	204
First Base Only	.247	.293	.347	170	42	6	1	3	9	9	42		.280	.327	.384	479	134	17	3	9	27	28	81
Scoring Position	.301	.340	.559	186	56	7	1	13	91	12	45		.237	.310	.372	613	145	19	2	20	220	70	123
Late Innings, Close	.246	.319	.369	65	16	2	0	2	6	6	13		.194	.295	.320	253	49	5	0	9	24	33	41

RBI/Opportunities					
Scoring Position	70 / 237	(30%)		186 / 798	(23%)
Scoring Position, 2 Out	30 / 111	(27%)		71 / 358	(20%)
On Third, Less than 2 Out	19 / 34	(56%)		66 / 129	(51%)
RBI in close games / RBI Total	75 / 114	(66%)		208 / 284	(73%)

Wade Boggs
Boston Red Sox

Wade Boggs had a difficult season both emotionally and physically. He battled injuries and personal tragedy. His average dropped 11 points, he sat out the last series with New York to keep his batting crown and he actually had a batting slump. But, despite everything, he was a more effective leadoff man in 1986 than in '85. Both his on-base and slugging averages improved; he hit fewer singles but more doubles. He was the fourth player (Ruth, Williams, Yastrzemski) to lead the AL in both hitting and walks in the same year. He struck out less and scored the same number of runs while making many fewer outs (373, down from 439).

Boggs also drove in more runs. In plate appearances where he didn't walk, there were 152 men in scoring position—Wade drove 59 of them (39%) home. Scoring Boston basecrawlers from second with a single is no easy trick—especially given the amount of walks he had. When people talk about pitching around third basemen, George Brett is always mentioned—but Wade actually had more walks than hits with men in scoring position.

Boggs's batting tactics are similar to Ted Williams's—wait for the pitch . . . then hit it. Boggs commits on a pitch very late so, unlike Williams, he rarely pulls the ball. But that does mean that he can foul off strikes that he doesn't want to put into play and that he can handle any type of moving baseball. He was the only Boston player who had over 125 at-bats who wasn't hit by a pitch.

In 1986 (credit Chuck Waseleski), he took the first pitch 15 out of every 16 tries. If the first pitch was a ball (about 51% of the time, it was), he wound up with an on-base average of .524 and slugged .581. It doesn't help to make the first pitch a good one, to try to get ahead of him—if Wade hit the first pitch, he batted .560. Your best bet is to get him to foul a few off. Wade's OBA with less than two strikes was .547; when he had to protect the plate, it was 'only' .359.

There is one potentially terrifying footnote. 1986 was the first year that Boggs didn't do most of his hitting in Boston (his home/road splits were .352/.296 in 1984 and .418/.322 in 1985). It may mean nothing . . . he may return to normal in 1987. But his road averages ARE clearly rising. If 1986 means that Boggs has learned to hit .350 in every park, I shudder to think what he might do in 1987.

—Fred Percival

	1986 SEASON											THREE YEARS (84 – 86)									
	Ave.	OBP	SLG	AB	H	2B	3B	HR	RBI	BB	SO	Ave.	OBP	SLG	AB	H	2B	3B	HR	RBI	BB	SO
Totals	.357	.453	.486	580	207	47	2	8	71	105	44	.350	.437	.460	1858	650	120	9	22	204	290	149
Batting vs. Left and Right-handed Pitchers																						
Left	.352	.420	.489	182	64	12	2	3	27	22	18	.317	.394	.414	561	178	27	3	7	67	70	53
Right	.359	.467	.485	398	143	35	0	5	44	83	26	.364	.454	.480	1297	472	93	6	15	137	220	96
At Home and on the Road																						
Home	.357	.456	.495	277	99	29	0	3	36	51	24	.376	.465	.511	906	341	70	5	14	102	150	84
Road	.356	.450	.479	303	108	18	2	5	35	54	20	.325	.409	.411	952	309	50	4	8	102	140	65
Facing Groundball Pitchers and Flyball Pitchers																						
Groundball	.336	.458	.456	250	84	18	0	4	36	59	11	.351	.442	.465	893	313	55	4	13	100	148	64
Flyball	.373	.448	.509	330	123	29	2	4	35	46	33	.349	.432	.455	965	337	65	5	9	104	142	85
Facing Finesse Pitchers and Power Pitchers																						
Finesse	.376	.456	.520	348	131	28	2	6	41	51	21	.357	.433	.478	1080	386	70	6	16	113	144	72
Power	.328	.448	.435	232	76	19	0	2	30	54	23	.339	.441	.434	778	264	50	3	6	91	146	77
On Grass and on Turf																						
Grass	.352	.449	.488	488	172	42	0	8	63	89	40	.351	.437	.464	1578	554	103	6	21	174	244	131
Turf	.380	.472	.478	92	35	5	2	0	8	16	4	.343	.433	.436	280	96	17	3	1	30	46	18
During the Day and at Night																						
Day	.325	.421	.472	197	64	17	0	4	30	34	15	.343	.432	.464	578	198	43	3	7	63	92	37
Night	.373	.469	.493	383	143	30	2	4	41	71	29	.353	.439	.458	1280	452	77	6	15	141	198	112
By Month																						
April	.306	.438	.486	72	22	7	0	2	13	17	5	.301	.424	.411	219	66	13	1	3	23	49	23
May	.471	.567	.647	102	48	9	0	3	20	24	5	.367	.465	.473	300	110	16	2	4	41	56	19
June	.338	.414	.403	77	26	5	0	0	5	10	13	.326	.407	.416	298	97	22	1	1	20	39	28
July	.247	.357	.309	97	24	6	0	0	7	17	13	.321	.413	.421	299	96	19	1	3	37	48	28
August	.353	.436	.504	119	42	8	2	2	15	19	4	.358	.426	.501	371	133	25	2	8	45	45	27
Sept/Oct	.398	.481	.531	113	45	12	0	1	11	18	4	.399	.474	.501	371	148	25	2	3	38	53	24
Situational																						
Bases Empty	.343	.417	.462	353	121	26	2	4	4	45	23	.345	.422	.453	1110	383	68	5	14	14	144	87
Leadoff	.362	.433	.480	152	55	11	2	1	1	19	6	.366	.439	.472	511	187	35	2	5	5	67	35
Not Leadoff	.328	.405	.448	201	66	15	0	3	3	26	17	.327	.406	.437	599	196	33	3	9	9	77	52
Runners On	.379	.502	.524	227	86	21	0	4	67	60	21	.357	.457	.469	748	267	52	4	8	190	146	62
First Base Only	.407	.488	.602	108	44	12	0	3	10	17	8	.352	.430	.473	332	117	26	1	4	44	44	27
Scoring Position	.353	.512	.454	119	42	9	0	1	57	43	13	.361	.477	.466	416	150	26	3	4	176	102	35
Late Innings, Close	.405	.477	.500	74	30	7	0	0	16	12	8	.369	.467	.421	252	93	13	0	0	32	48	21
RBI/Opportunities																						

	1986 SEASON			THREE YEARS (84 – 86)		
Scoring Position	54 / 204	(26%)		168 / 629	(27%)	
Scoring Position, 2 Out	27 / 108	(25%)		69 / 306	(23%)	
On Third, Less than 2 Out	17 / 32	(53%)		57 / 102	(56%)	
RBI in close games / RBI Total	48 / 71	(68%)		122 / 204	(60%)	

Barry Bonds
Pittsburgh Pirates

The urge to compare is irresistable when the son of a major leaguer makes it to the bigs himself. With Barry Bonds, the urge is even greater because he and his father, Bobby, seem like such similar players.

Let's put their rookie years side by side, Barry first, Bobby second: Games, 113 to 81; Batting average, .223 to .254; Home Runs per 100 at-bats, 3.87 to 2.93; Strikeouts per 100 at-bats, 24.7 to 27.4; Stolen Bases, 36 to 16; On-Base Percentage .330 to .336; Slugging Average, .416 to .407.

Here are a couple more less obvious ones: Secondary Average (Barry first), .439 to .329; Power-Speed Number, 22.15 to 11.52. Ultimately, such comparisons are unfair because of the differences of time and space. Yet the similarities are striking. They certainly are the same type of player. It will be interesting to see how Bonds the Younger turns out.

One area where it is hoped they will differ is in longevity with one team. Bobby Bonds' travels late in his career—seven teams in seven years— tarnished his reputation as one of the great players of his time. What is often overlooked is that he did spend seven full and productive years with the Giants.

Other tidbits: Barry hit substantially better in Three Rivers Stadium than he did on the road, .242 to .203. Turf seems to agree with him. . . . He scored 45.3 percent of the time he got on base, second best in the National League. . . . For a rookie who played in only 113 games to lead his team in stolen bases and walks (65), and rank second in runs (72) and home runs (16) says more about the Pirates than about Barry Bonds. . . . Recorded nine assists from the outfield in 110 games and his range factor (2.67) is one of the best in the league. . . . Had his best month in August (.250 BA, 6 homers) then slumped badly in September and October (.205 BA, 2 homers). . . . Hit better at night, with 13 of his homers coming under the lights. . . . He's a left-hander at the plate; his dad was a righty. Barry hit .225 against right-handed pitching and .219 against lefties, but had a better on-base average against lefties.

—Michael O'Donnell

	1986 SEASON											THREE YEARS (84 – 86)										
	Ave.	OBP	SLG	AB	H	2B	3B	HR	RBI	BB	SO	Ave.	OBP	SLG	AB	H	2B	3B	HR	RBI	BB	SO
Totals	.223	.330	.416	413	92	26	3	16	48	65	102	.223	.330	.416	413	92	26	3	16	48	65	102
Batting vs. Left and Right-handed Pitchers																						
Left	.219	.348	.371	151	33	10	2	3	14	29	39	.219	.348	.371	151	33	10	2	3	14	29	39
Right	.225	.319	.443	262	59	16	1	13	34	36	63	.225	.319	.443	262	59	16	1	13	34	36	63
At Home and on the Road																						
Home	.242	.355	.469	211	51	17	2	9	26	36	56	.242	.355	.469	211	51	17	2	9	26	36	56
Road	.203	.303	.361	202	41	9	1	7	22	29	46	.203	.303	.361	202	41	9	1	7	22	29	46
Facing Groundball Pitchers and Flyball Pitchers																						
Groundball	.230	.313	.380	200	46	11	2	5	26	23	49	.230	.313	.380	200	46	11	2	5	26	23	49
Flyball	.216	.345	.451	213	46	15	1	11	22	42	53	.216	.345	.451	213	46	15	1	11	22	42	53
Facing Finesse Pitchers and Power Pitchers																						
Finesse	.202	.292	.380	242	49	13	0	10	29	30	50	.202	.292	.380	242	49	13	0	10	29	30	50
Power	.251	.380	.468	171	43	13	3	6	19	35	52	.251	.380	.468	171	43	13	3	6	19	35	52
On Grass and on Turf																						
Grass	.234	.327	.415	94	22	5	0	4	11	13	29	.234	.327	.415	94	22	5	0	4	11	13	29
Turf	.219	.331	.417	319	70	21	3	12	37	52	73	.219	.331	.417	319	70	21	3	12	37	52	73
During the Day and at Night																						
Day	.196	.283	.355	107	21	8	0	3	10	13	29	.196	.283	.355	107	21	8	0	3	10	13	29
Night	.232	.345	.438	306	71	18	3	13	38	52	73	.232	.345	.438	306	71	18	3	13	38	52	73
By Month																						
April	1.000	1.000	1.000	1	1	0	0	0	1	0	0	1.000	1.000	1.000	1	1	0	0	0	1	0	0
May	.125	.300	.250	8	1	1	0	0	0	2	3	.125	.300	.250	8	1	1	0	0	0	2	3
June	.243	.364	.505	111	27	9	1	6	14	20	33	.243	.364	.505	111	27	9	1	6	14	20	33
July	.178	.274	.342	73	13	4	1	2	6	10	24	.178	.274	.342	73	13	4	1	2	6	10	24
August	.250	.354	.509	108	27	8	1	6	19	18	20	.250	.354	.509	108	27	8	1	6	19	18	20
Sept/Oct	.205	.305	.295	112	23	4	0	2	8	15	22	.205	.305	.295	112	23	4	0	2	8	15	22
Situational																						
Bases Empty	.205	.320	.414	273	56	17	2	12	12	45	64	.205	.320	.414	273	56	17	2	12	12	45	64
Leadoff	.235	.343	.451	153	36	10	1	7	7	24	35	.235	.343	.451	153	36	10	1	7	7	24	35
Not Leadoff	.167	.291	.367	120	20	7	1	5	5	21	29	.167	.291	.367	120	20	7	1	5	5	21	29
Runners On	.257	.350	.421	140	36	9	1	4	36	20	38	.257	.350	.421	140	36	9	1	4	36	20	38
First Base Only	.364	.440	.636	44	16	6	0	2	6	5	11	.364	.440	.636	44	16	6	0	2	6	5	11
Scoring Position	.208	.310	.323	96	20	3	1	2	30	15	27	.208	.310	.323	96	20	3	1	2	30	15	27
Late Innings, Close	.200	.325	.329	70	14	4	1	1	6	13	23	.200	.325	.329	70	14	4	1	1	6	13	23

RBI/Opportunities						
Scoring Position	27 / 132	(20%)		27 / 132	(20%)
Scoring Position, 2 Out	8 / 65	(12%)		8 / 65	(12%)
On Third, Less than 2 Out	11 / 26	(42%)		11 / 26	(42%)
RBI in close games / RBI Total	29 / 48	(60%)		29 / 48	(60%)

Bob Boone
California Angels

Bob Boone represents the dilemma of the Angels. Overall, despite batting marks that were weak in virtually every situation, he had a good, solid year in 1986. But the Angels asked him to catch 144 games at age 38. Only one man in history, Al Lopez, has caught more games than Boone. So here's the situation: Boone played well in '86, and his performance late in the year indicates he can continue to handle a big workload, but the Angels know he can't last forever. The problem for California is that the same thing is happening at second base, third base, left field and right field. If the Angels bring along youth, or make intelligent trades to get replacements at these positions, then I'll believe that they have learned their lesson from those silly free agent days. But if they make panic trades like the Al Holland/George Hendrick deal of 1985, then we'll know that we won't see the Angels in the World Series any time soon.

Bob Boone was the one everyday player the Angels couldn't have done without in 1986. His defense and handling of the pitching staff were indispensable. Boone won a Gold Glove, and had the lowest opposition stolen base rate in the American League. But at age 39 for the 1987 season, the Angels should at least have a prospect on the horizon. They don't have a replacement for Boone in the minor leagues, at least not at AA or AAA. A December trade brought Butch Wynegar to Anaheim, but that can't be seen as a long-term solution. Either catchers are extremely hard to develop in the minor leagues, or the Angel front office simply hasn't responded to the needs of the organization.

Need a trivia question to amaze your friends? Ask them to name a player in 1986 who scored from second base on a sacrifice fly. Give them 300 guesses. And then tell them it was Bob Boone on September 15 in the seventh inning. Rupe Jones lofted a flyball to the track that was bobbled by John Cangelosi of the White Sox. Cangelosi then threw a rainbow in the general direction of the infield that allowed Dick Schofield to tag up from third, and Boone to fly home from second base. He made it, in fact, without much trouble.

—Dennis Bretz

	1986 SEASON											THREE YEARS (84 – 86)										
	Ave.	OBP	SLG	AB	H	2B	3B	HR	RBI	BB	SO	Ave.	OBP	SLG	AB	H	2B	3B	HR	RBI	BB	SO
Totals	.222	.287	.305	442	98	12	2	7	49	43	30	.224	.279	.295	1352	303	45	3	15	136	105	109
Batting vs. Left and Right-handed Pitchers																						
Left	.217	.292	.276	152	33	3	0	2	17	17	9	.215	.280	.269	446	96	15	0	3	41	41	27
Right	.224	.284	.321	290	65	9	2	5	32	26	21	.228	.278	.308	906	207	30	3	12	95	64	82
At Home and on the Road																						
Home	.189	.264	.250	212	40	6	2	1	18	23	17	.208	.273	.253	653	136	19	2	2	62	59	58
Road	.252	.310	.357	230	58	6	0	6	31	20	13	.239	.284	.335	699	167	26	1	13	74	46	51
Facing Groundball Pitchers and Flyball Pitchers																						
Groundball	.239	.302	.343	201	48	9	0	4	23	19	15	.231	.278	.304	662	153	28	1	6	68	41	53
Flyball	.207	.275	.274	241	50	3	2	3	26	24	15	.217	.279	.287	690	150	17	2	9	68	64	56
Facing Finesse Pitchers and Power Pitchers																						
Finesse	.234	.288	.316	269	63	8	1	4	26	21	18	.211	.263	.279	797	168	26	2	8	70	56	65
Power	.202	.286	.289	173	35	4	1	3	23	22	12	.243	.300	.319	555	135	19	1	7	66	49	44
On Grass and on Turf																						
Grass	.225	.294	.314	373	84	11	2	6	42	39	27	.228	.283	.304	1147	262	39	3	14	116	90	95
Turf	.203	.247	.261	69	14	1	0	1	7	4	3	.200	.257	.244	205	41	6	0	1	20	15	14
During the Day and at Night																						
Day	.233	.287	.336	116	27	3	0	3	16	10	8	.235	.277	.329	362	85	13	0	7	44	24	32
Night	.218	.287	.294	326	71	9	2	4	33	33	22	.220	.279	.283	990	218	32	3	8	92	81	77
By Month																						
April	.226	.273	.323	62	14	0	0	2	4	4	5	.217	.257	.300	207	45	11	0	2	14	12	17
May	.208	.289	.208	72	15	0	0	0	8	9	3	.237	.305	.253	198	47	1	1	0	21	21	17
June	.183	.239	.280	82	15	3	1	1	4	6	6	.207	.260	.306	232	48	9	1	4	24	15	16
July	.224	.273	.328	67	15	4	0	1	11	6	2	.209	.260	.284	225	47	8	0	3	21	17	15
August	.259	.333	.407	81	21	3	0	3	14	9	7	.222	.290	.309	230	51	5	0	5	27	22	18
Sept/Oct	.231	.310	.282	78	18	2	1	0	8	9	7	.250	.298	.312	260	65	11	1	1	29	18	26
Situational																						
Bases Empty	.209	.283	.304	230	48	6	2	4	4	24	15	.230	.289	.317	735	169	25	3	11	11	58	59
Leadoff	.255	.333	.394	94	24	4	0	3	3	11	5	.238	.303	.351	302	72	10	0	8	8	25	21
Not Leadoff	.176	.248	.243	136	24	2	2	1	1	13	10	.224	.279	.293	433	97	15	3	3	3	33	38
Runners On	.236	.291	.307	212	50	6	0	3	45	19	15	.217	.267	.269	617	134	20	0	4	125	47	50
First Base Only	.253	.291	.320	75	19	5	0	0	2	4	4	.221	.250	.277	235	52	10	0	1	8	9	18
Scoring Position	.226	.291	.299	137	31	1	0	3	43	15	11	.215	.276	.264	382	82	10	0	3	117	38	32
Late Innings, Close	.208	.256	.325	77	16	0	0	3	10	5	3	.234	.289	.329	222	52	6	0	5	28	18	18
RBI/Opportunities																						
Scoring Position	38 / 183	(21%)										111 / 515	(22%)									
Scoring Position, 2 Out	10 / 65	(15%)										42 / 244	(17%)									
On Third, Less than 2 Out	19 / 41	(46%)										45 / 88	(51%)									
RBI in close games / RBI Total	24 / 49	(49%)										79 / 136	(58%)									

Dennis Boyd
Boston Red Sox

It's staggering to think that one of the best pitchers in baseball has no confidence in himself at all, but that is the problem that Dennis Ray Boyd has. Boyd is a textbook case of a sheep in wolf's clothing. In public, he puts forth the impression of being very cocky; privately, he worries about anything and everything. If Boyd were as confident as he pretends, he'd be a tremendous pitcher; since he isn't, he consistently beats himself.

Boyd's problems stem from two things—that he has very little natural talent and that he knows it. Boyd throws hard, but his pitches have very little movement. He hasn't been able to develop an off-speed pitch to let him win by changing speeds and has trouble making hitters beat the ball into the ground consistently. He relies solely on location and control—if he can put the ball precisely where he wants to, he's unstoppable; if not, he's defenseless.

Boyd's understanding of his problems makes it difficult for him to stay calm. Each good pitch builds confidence; each bad one tears it down. If he hit the spot he wanted and allows a hit, he shrugs. If he hangs a slider—even if he retires the hitter on it—he begins worrying. Boyd has been told to forget what happened to his last pitch and worry about the next countless times, but he simply isn't capable of doing that. Once he loses confidence in his ability to throw strikes, he is a beaten man.

Not surprisingly, Boyd works quickly—the less time he has to think, the better—and likes to start as often as possible. He can treat teammates who make mental or physical errors in his starts shamefully. An umpire with an inconsistent strike zone can ruin him; he demands that they call a consistent game. And, as everyone knows, he desperately craves the stature and respect that winning 20 games and making the All-Star team bring; when he feels he has failed, his disappointment and panic make him capable of explosive, self-destructive behavior.

Despite his problems, Boyd is a good starter. He has his control often enough to win regularly—if he develops skills that let him survive when he isn't in top form, he'll win consistently. Failing that, he has to accept failure—to understand that there will be days when he simply isn't fated to win and learn to cope with it better than he has done so far.

—Geoff Beckman

1986: Finesse, Groundball   **1985: Finesse, Flyball**   **1984: Power, Flyball**

	1986 SEASON											THREE YEARS (84 – 86)										
	G	IP	H	BB	SO	SB	CS	W	L	S	ERA	G	IP	H	BB	SO	SB	CS	W	L	S	ERA
Totals	30	214.1	222	45	129	14	10	16	10	0	3.78	94	684.1	702	165	417	39	40	43	35	0	3.92
At Home and on the Road																						
Home	17	120.1	139	24	75	10	8	9	6	0	3.66	53	394.0	429	93	240	24	26	26	22	0	3.88
Road	13	94.0	83	21	54	4	2	7	4	0	3.93	41	290.1	273	72	177	15	14	17	13	0	3.97
During the Day and at Night																						
Day	12	88.0	86	16	52	4	6	6	3	0	3.48	34	238.2	232	52	153	13	12	14	13	0	3.73
Night	18	126.1	136	29	77	10	4	10	7	0	3.99	60	445.2	470	113	264	26	28	29	22	0	4.02
On Grass and on Turf																						
Grass	29	208.1	216	43	126	13	10	16	9	0	3.67	85	625.0	639	149	387	34	37	40	33	0	3.86
Turf	1	6.0	6	2	3	1	0	0	1	0	7.50	9	59.1	63	16	30	5	3	3	2	0	4.55
By Month																						
April	4	29.0	26	8	15	2	0	1	2	0	4.66	12	85.2	83	29	51	6	2	3	5	0	4.31
May	6	47.1	37	5	24	1	0	5	1	0	2.66	14	103.1	93	26	59	8	5	8	5	0	3.05
June	6	41.2	50	14	21	5	3	4	2	0	3.46	19	137.2	145	37	83	8	9	10	7	0	3.60
July	2	10.2	14	3	10	1	1	1	1	0	6.75	13	91.0	92	18	59	3	7	6	6	0	5.04
August	6	43.0	51	6	28	4	3	2	3	0	3.98	18	136.2	148	27	79	9	13	6	6	0	3.82
Sept/Oct	6	42.2	44	9	31	1	3	3	1	0	3.80	18	130.0	141	28	86	5	4	10	6	0	4.02

vs. Opponent Batters

	1986 SEASON												THREE YEARS (84 – 86)									
	Ave.	OBP	SLG	AB	H	2B	3B	HR	RBI	BB	SO		Ave.	OBP	SLG	AB	H	2B	3B	HR	RBI	BB	SO
Totals	.265	.302	.430	837	222	30	6	32	88	45	129		.265	.307	.412	2651	702	127	18	76	288	165	417
Pitching vs. Left and Right-handed Batters																							
Left	.280	.307	.456	439	123	17	3	18	53	18	58		.252	.291	.375	1471	371	64	9	33	153	79	231
Right	.249	.298	.402	398	99	13	3	14	35	27	71		.281	.327	.458	1180	331	63	9	43	135	86	186
Situational																							
Bases Empty	.272	.308	.433	529	144	18	5	19	19	26	85		.260	.308	.400	1613	420	73	12	43	43	107	264
Leadoff	.278	.314	.406	212	59	9	0	6	6	10	30		.251	.302	.368	665	167	30	3	14	14	45	96
Not Leadoff	.268	.303	.451	317	85	9	5	13	13	16	55		.267	.313	.423	948	253	43	9	29	29	62	168
Runners On	.253	.293	.425	308	78	12	1	13	69	19	44		.272	.306	.431	1038	282	54	6	33	245	58	153
First Base Only	.264	.302	.411	163	43	7	1	5	12	9	22		.280	.312	.415	496	139	23	4	12	34	21	73
Scoring Position	.241	.284	.441	145	35	5	0	8	57	10	22		.264	.301	.445	542	143	31	2	21	211	37	80
Late Innings, Close	.296	.324	.366	71	21	2	0	1	4	3	6		.312	.350	.435	292	91	12	0	8	30	16	35

RBI/Opportunities

Scoring Position	47 / 189	(25%)		179 / 696	(26%)
Scoring Position, 2 Out	16 / 91	(18%)		68 / 317	(21%)
On Third, Less than 2 Out	18 / 33	(55%)		69 / 124	(56%)
RBI in close games / RBI Total	62 / 88	(70%)		205 / 288	(71%)

Phil Bradley
Seattle Mariners

With the exception of 23 games late in 1983, Phil Bradley has never hit below .300 for any professional team. While his power was off a little in 1986 from his unexpected 26 homers in 1985, his .310 average was a career high, and another marker in Bradley's strong march toward recognition as one of the game's best hitters.

Bradley is a slow starter who, despite the gloom that gathers over the Seattle team, grows stronger as the season progresses. Over the three years of his career he has hit .274 in April, .286 in May, .287 in June, but .316 or better in each of the last three months. Despite his famous hot power start in 1985, he has hit more homers (10) and driven in more runs (40) in September than in any other month.

Bradley has a lot of positives besides the steady .300 average. With 77 walks in 1986, he had a .405 on base percentage, second best among American League regulars (502 plate appearances). Only Boggs was on base more often. That, combined with good to excellent speed, make Bradley one of the league's best #1 or #2 place hitters, a position for which his medium range power is just another asset.

While Bradley is a fine outfielder, his defensive skills would be stretched to cover either center field or right field. He could do it, but the Mariners so far haven't had to ask, and that's just as well. Bradley is a graceful athlete who makes few mistakes. You may remember that when John Elway was trying to play baseball the word about him was that as a baseball player he really didn't throw exceptionally well. Bradley is like that, too, a college quarterback who tends to make the throwing motion with his elbow more than with his shoulder, which is appropriate in football but not in baseball. Well, you throw in any sport with the shoulder, elbow and wrist, but you use the latter two more for football than for baseball.

Bradley's even balance of skills, intelligence and pattern of getting stronger over the course of the year bespeak a player who may surprise us again, getting even better. If the Mariners emerge as a contender in 1987, and there's a good chance they will, Phil Bradley will be one of the big reasons why.

—Bill James

	1986 SEASON											THREE YEARS (84 – 86)										
	Ave.	OBP	SLG	AB	H	2B	3B	HR	RBI	BB	SO	Ave.	OBP	SLG	AB	H	2B	3B	HR	RBI	BB	SO
Totals	.310	.405	.445	526	163	27	4	12	50	77	134	.304	.381	.450	1489	452	72	16	38	162	166	324
Batting vs. Left and Right-handed Pitchers																						
Left	.325	.418	.421	126	41	4	1	2	9	19	25	.268	.345	.408	414	111	15	5	11	41	46	83
Right	.305	.400	.453	400	122	23	3	10	41	58	109	.317	.395	.466	1075	341	57	11	27	121	120	241
At Home and on the Road																						
Home	.324	.417	.467	287	93	20	3	5	30	43	64	.318	.397	.481	771	245	46	10	20	89	91	147
Road	.293	.390	.418	239	70	7	1	7	20	34	70	.288	.363	.416	718	207	26	6	18	73	75	177
Facing Groundball Pitchers and Flyball Pitchers																						
Groundball	.293	.378	.432	259	76	13	1	7	23	32	56	.297	.371	.466	708	210	32	8	24	85	75	127
Flyball	.326	.429	.457	267	87	14	3	5	27	45	78	.310	.390	.435	781	242	40	8	14	77	91	197
Facing Finesse Pitchers and Power Pitchers																						
Finesse	.338	.408	.486	325	110	18	3	8	30	35	54	.343	.405	.511	901	309	53	10	26	97	80	135
Power	.264	.399	.378	201	53	9	1	4	20	42	80	.243	.346	.357	588	143	19	6	12	65	86	189
On Grass and on Turf																						
Grass	.264	.382	.393	178	47	3	1	6	15	30	55	.292	.367	.423	541	158	16	5	15	59	58	136
Turf	.333	.416	.471	348	116	24	3	6	35	47	79	.310	.389	.465	948	294	56	11	23	103	108	188
During the Day and at Night																						
Day	.295	.382	.443	149	44	13	0	3	13	20	39	.310	.394	.424	384	119	24	4	4	32	51	87
Night	.316	.413	.446	377	119	14	4	9	37	57	95	.301	.377	.459	1105	333	48	12	34	130	115	237
By Month																						
April	.215	.303	.278	79	17	5	0	0	3	10	28	.274	.345	.420	212	58	12	2	5	23	21	39
May	.278	.400	.430	79	22	4	1	2	4	15	17	.286	.394	.414	210	60	9	3	4	13	32	42
June	.286	.367	.514	70	20	2	1	4	12	9	19	.287	.346	.457	247	71	12	3	8	34	21	53
July	.355	.445	.419	93	33	3	0	1	12	14	21	.329	.403	.401	222	73	5	1	3	20	25	47
August	.349	.444	.528	106	37	8	1	3	11	15	24	.320	.387	.491	291	93	18	4	8	32	27	71
Sept/Oct	.343	.431	.475	99	34	5	1	2	8	14	25	.316	.402	.485	307	97	16	3	10	40	40	72
Situational																						
Bases Empty	.311	.401	.473	334	104	17	2	11	11	47	88	.295	.369	.453	879	259	37	9	28	28	92	190
Leadoff	.340	.426	.510	100	34	8	0	3	3	14	31	.295	.362	.425	285	84	16	3	5	5	27	62
Not Leadoff	.299	.390	.457	234	70	9	2	8	8	33	57	.295	.372	.466	594	175	21	6	23	23	65	128
Runners On	.307	.410	.396	192	59	10	2	1	39	30	46	.316	.399	.446	610	193	35	7	10	134	74	134
First Base Only	.370	.474	.407	81	30	3	0	0	3	12	18	.348	.419	.463	270	94	17	1	4	15	27	52
Scoring Position	.261	.364	.387	111	29	7	2	1	36	18	28	.291	.383	.432	340	99	18	6	6	119	47	82
Late Innings, Close	.313	.412	.422	83	26	5	2	0	11	11	24	.319	.390	.491	226	72	8	5	7	40	24	49

RBI/Opportunities	1986		THREE YEARS	
Scoring Position	31 / 146	(21%)	103 / 473	(22%)
Scoring Position, 2 Out	12 / 57	(21%)	41 / 192	(21%)
On Third, Less than 2 Out	12 / 26	(46%)	36 / 87	(41%)
RBI in close games / RBI Total	34 / 50	(68%)	108 / 162	(67%)

Sid Bream
Pittsburgh Pirates

After being buried in the Dodger farm system for several years, Sid Bream finally got a chance to play regularly when he was traded to Pittsburgh in late 1985. The results were very encouraging: Bream batted .284 for his one month with the Bucs that year, then hit .268 with good power in 1986. Bream's stroke proved ideal for the fast turf at Three Rivers Stadium, as he hit 37 doubles last season, 23 of them at home; his total was the third highest in the National League. In addition, Sid swatted 16 homers, drew 60 walks, and even stole 13 bases in 20 attempts, which wasn't bad for a guy who stands 6'4" and weighs 215.

All in all, it was a really solid campaign, exactly the sort of hitting the Dodgers could have used last year. In L.A., though, Bream never had a chance. It wasn't just that the Dodgers had two other left-handed hitting first baseman in Greg Brock and Franklin Stubbs; it was timing. Bream came knocking on the major-league door at the exact moment when everyone from The Sporting News to the little old lady in Pasadena was talking about how overrated the young Dodger prospects were—the old bit about how "everybody" hit .350 at Albuquerque, so you couldn't trust what anyone did down there. After a while the Dodgers came to believe this themselves, and give only half-hearted shots to Bream and Candy Maldonado and R.J. Reynolds before getting whatever they could for them. They even played I-don't-want-him, you-can-have-him, he's-too-fat-for-me with their brightest pitching prospect, Sid Fernandez, as though they had to get rid of El Sid quickly (and for next to nothing), before folks found out he was overrated, too. Was this really the Dodgers, the Tiffany of franchises, showing such desperation?

In Bream's case, it should have been obvious that the guy had talent: Sid played for seven teams in five minor league seasons, and never hit less than .307. He's no slouch with the glove, either, as he showed when he set a new league record for assists by a first sacker last year. Sid has his offensive weaknesses, especially against lefthanded pitching, and probably won't be a 30-home run guy or a high-average hitter, but he'll only be 26 when the '87 season starts, and has a chance to improve some of his shortcomings. I'd have to say I like his future better than I like Bill Madlock's.

—Don Zminda

	1986 SEASON											THREE YEARS (84 – 86)										
	Ave.	OBP	SLG	AB	H	2B	3B	HR	RBI	BB	SO	Ave.	OBP	SLG	AB	H	2B	3B	HR	RBI	BB	SO
Totals	.268	.341	.450	522	140	37	5	16	77	60	73	.255	.329	.426	719	183	47	5	22	104	84	106
Batting vs. Left and Right-handed Pitchers																						
Left	.224	.268	.349	152	34	11	1	2	21	11	23	.210	.260	.323	195	41	11	1	3	26	15	33
Right	.286	.370	.492	370	106	26	4	14	56	49	50	.271	.353	.464	524	142	36	4	19	78	69	73
At Home and on the Road																						
Home	.282	.348	.450	262	74	23	3	5	33	27	34	.262	.331	.417	343	90	26	3	7	45	37	46
Road	.254	.333	.450	260	66	14	2	11	44	33	39	.247	.327	.434	376	93	21	2	15	59	47	60
Facing Groundball Pitchers and Flyball Pitchers																						
Groundball	.283	.348	.446	240	68	20	5	3	29	26	32	.272	.341	.424	323	88	24	5	5	41	36	44
Flyball	.255	.334	.454	282	72	17	0	13	48	34	41	.240	.319	.427	396	95	23	0	17	63	48	62
Facing Finesse Pitchers and Power Pitchers																						
Finesse	.257	.326	.411	292	75	15	3	8	34	32	32	.250	.323	.405	412	103	22	3	12	54	48	50
Power	.283	.359	.500	230	65	22	2	8	43	28	41	.261	.336	.453	307	80	25	2	10	50	36	56
On Grass and on Turf																						
Grass	.235	.303	.412	136	32	7	1	5	21	14	23	.221	.294	.387	235	52	10	1	9	35	26	40
Turf	.280	.354	.464	386	108	30	4	11	56	46	50	.271	.346	.444	484	131	37	4	13	69	58	66
During the Day and at Night																						
Day	.184	.274	.323	158	29	9	2	3	17	20	26	.190	.277	.323	232	44	12	2	5	24	29	44
Night	.305	.370	.505	364	111	28	3	13	60	40	47	.285	.354	.474	487	139	35	3	17	80	55	62
By Month																						
April	.241	.364	.537	54	13	4	0	4	7	11	8	.184	.305	.439	98	18	4	0	7	13	18	17
May	.295	.382	.516	95	28	8	2	3	14	14	10	.293	.377	.505	99	29	8	2	3	14	14	10
June	.244	.340	.430	86	21	5	1	3	13	12	19	.244	.337	.422	90	22	5	1	3	13	12	20
July	.310	.359	.437	71	22	4	1	1	12	6	7	.278	.316	.400	90	25	6	1	1	15	6	9
August	.295	.333	.474	95	28	6	1	3	14	6	11	.295	.333	.474	95	28	6	1	3	14	6	11
Sept/Oct	.231	.291	.364	121	28	10	0	2	17	11	18	.247	.319	.381	247	61	18	0	5	35	28	39
Situational																						
Bases Empty	.242	.306	.416	281	68	19	3	8	8	26	39	.233	.292	.409	386	90	23	3	13	13	32	54
Leadoff	.246	.322	.478	134	33	9	2	6	6	15	12	.223	.294	.469	179	40	10	2	10	10	18	17
Not Leadoff	.238	.291	.361	147	35	10	1	2	2	11	27	.242	.290	.357	207	50	13	1	3	3	14	37
Runners On	.299	.378	.490	241	72	18	2	8	69	34	34	.279	.368	.444	333	93	24	2	9	91	52	52
First Base Only	.306	.354	.512	121	37	10	0	5	14	9	16	.280	.322	.466	161	45	12	0	6	17	10	25
Scoring Position	.292	.399	.467	120	35	8	2	3	55	25	18	.279	.403	.424	172	48	12	2	3	74	42	27
Late Innings, Close	.232	.322	.384	99	23	7	1	2	16	15	19	.213	.315	.360	136	29	9	1	3	22	23	27

RBI/Opportunities					
Scoring Position	47 / 175	(27%)		65 / 262	(25%)
Scoring Position, 2 Out	13 / 70	(19%)		21 / 108	(19%)
On Third, Less than 2 Out	21 / 28	(75%)		27 / 47	(57%)
RBI in close games / RBI Total	51 / 77	(66%)		72 / 104	(69%)

Bob Brenly
San Francisco Giants

In the *1986 Baseball Abstract*, Bill James states: "[I]t is generally true that between 1958 and 1975 the Giants tried to make a third baseman out of every outfielder in their system except Willie Mays."

The outfield-to-third shuttle is an example of a broader problem with the franchise: what I call the "theory of maybe," involving drawing conclusions based upon blind faith, absent any consideration of the facts. This logic has applied to their attempts at positional transformation. There has been no plan, no foresight—only crisis management.

Enter Bob Brenly, 1986. On September 1, the Giants were 9 games behind Houston; not great, but certainly not time to throw in the towel. That same day, Chris Brown was scratched from the line-up with a bum shoulder, out for the season. In September, Brenly moved to third base, with Bob Melvin playing catcher. This made little sense, for the following reasons:

1) Essentially, the Giants traded Brown's production for Melvin's (.224 BA, .262 OBA, .347 SA). Brown created 63 runs, one every 6.6 at-bats; Melvin created 24, one every 11 at-bats.

2) Randy Johnson was producing respectable numbers at Phoenix, hitting .332 with 62 runs and 67 RBIs. While Atlanta's third baseman in 1984, Johnson hit .279 with a .329 OBA. His range factor of 2.65 was well above average.

3) Brenly had already proved inadequate at third, failing there in the minors. That position change paid off; although no defensive gem, he was better catching than playing a rock at third base. He proved it in 1986—in 45 games at third, he committed 10 errors.

None of these facts justified the move—particularly since rosters expanded on September 1. I can just hear the Giants' management saying, "Well, *maybe* Bob can hold his own at third; after all, he's been there before; and *maybe* Melvin can become a major-league hitter."

I'd like to believe that the Giants have learned something from past meddling—that analysis of the facts merits more than wishful thinking. September's events do not bode well. The latest word is that the heir to Brenly at catcher is Micky Sasser—a converted third baseman.

Brenly is a player whose batting average does not aptly describe his offensive abilities. Brenly had a great year in 1984: .291 average, .464 slugging average, 79 runs created. Although his average has slipped since, his production has not declined as much. His secondary average has increased over the span: in 1984, 1985 and 1986, his secondary averages were .281, .302, and .335, respectively; his runs created were 79, 55, and 66, respectively.

— David Walsh

	1986 SEASON											THREE YEARS (84 – 86)										
	Ave.	OBP	SLG	AB	H	2B	3B	HR	RBI	BB	SO	Ave.	OBP	SLG	AB	H	2B	3B	HR	RBI	BB	SO
Totals	.246	.350	.403	472	116	26	0	16	62	74	97	.254	.338	.421	1418	360	70	1	55	198	179	211
Batting vs. Left and Right-handed Pitchers																						
Left	.268	.378	.484	157	42	16	0	6	24	29	31	.250	.347	.424	396	99	24	0	15	54	60	49
Right	.235	.335	.362	315	74	10	0	10	38	45	66	.255	.335	.420	1022	261	46	1	40	144	119	162
At Home and on the Road																						
Home	.234	.331	.379	235	55	10	0	8	31	34	53	.245	.328	.396	709	174	36	1	23	93	85	103
Road	.257	.368	.426	237	61	16	0	8	31	40	44	.262	.349	.446	709	186	34	0	32	105	94	108
Facing Groundball Pitchers and Flyball Pitchers																						
Groundball	.279	.390	.450	229	64	18	0	7	31	39	38	.279	.374	.459	660	184	44	0	25	88	95	79
Flyball	.214	.311	.358	243	52	8	0	9	31	35	59	.232	.307	.388	758	176	26	1	30	110	84	132
Facing Finesse Pitchers and Power Pitchers																						
Finesse	.250	.355	.418	256	64	13	0	10	33	40	45	.265	.342	.440	822	218	43	1	33	105	93	102
Power	.241	.343	.384	216	52	13	0	6	29	34	52	.238	.334	.394	596	142	27	0	22	93	86	109
On Grass and on Turf																						
Grass	.243	.348	.395	354	86	18	0	12	43	57	72	.258	.344	.431	1054	272	54	1	42	150	135	152
Turf	.254	.355	.424	118	30	8	0	4	19	17	25	.242	.324	.393	364	88	16	0	13	48	44	59
During the Day and at Night																						
Day	.216	.323	.349	218	47	8	0	7	25	35	41	.241	.324	.387	664	160	34	0	21	84	80	90
Night	.272	.372	.449	254	69	18	0	9	37	39	56	.265	.351	.451	754	200	36	1	34	114	99	121
By Month																						
April	.254	.421	.441	59	15	2	0	3	8	17	13	.230	.352	.364	165	38	5	1	5	12	30	27
May	.219	.359	.274	73	16	4	0	0	7	17	19	.268	.373	.416	190	51	10	0	6	22	32	33
June	.265	.383	.324	68	18	1	0	1	6	12	12	.272	.375	.431	246	67	9	0	10	41	39	31
July	.233	.291	.438	73	17	6	0	3	12	6	10	.257	.308	.457	245	63	19	0	10	39	19	31
August	.259	.330	.412	85	22	7	0	2	10	8	16	.271	.337	.480	273	74	15	0	14	46	27	43
Sept/Oct	.246	.331	.482	114	28	6	0	7	19	14	27	.224	.300	.365	299	67	12	0	10	38	32	46
Situational																						
Bases Empty	.255	.361	.410	271	69	15	0	9	9	43	65	.256	.345	.407	801	205	38	1	27	27	104	132
Leadoff	.276	.366	.459	98	27	6	0	4	4	13	23	.248	.325	.396	323	80	15	0	11	11	35	46
Not Leadoff	.243	.358	.382	173	42	9	0	5	5	30	42	.262	.358	.414	478	125	23	1	16	16	69	86
Runners On	.234	.335	.393	201	47	11	0	7	53	31	32	.251	.330	.439	617	155	32	0	28	171	75	79
First Base Only	.182	.241	.208	77	14	2	0	0	1	6	10	.259	.301	.406	251	65	13	0	8	24	14	24
Scoring Position	.266	.386	.508	124	33	9	0	7	52	25	22	.246	.348	.462	366	90	19	0	20	147	61	55
Late Innings, Close	.206	.283	.304	102	21	7	0	1	9	10	26	.222	.294	.359	315	70	13	0	10	33	31	50
RBI/Opportunities																						

	1986 SEASON			THREE YEARS (84 – 86)		
Scoring Position	38 / 183	(21%)		113 / 526	(21%)	
Scoring Position, 2 Out	12 / 75	(16%)		41 / 247	(17%)	
On Third, Less than 2 Out	14 / 32	(44%)		39 / 81	(48%)	
RBI in close games / RBI Total	42 / 62	(68%)		128 / 198	(65%)	

George Brett
Kansas City Royals

A few random notes about a player who needs no introduction:

1) George is a very pronounced hot weather hitter. This tendency has been noted and talked about in Kansas City since the late seventies, and is quite visible in the 1984–86 breakdowns, which show him hitting just .262 in April and .251 in September. His career batting average in April is probably in that range, while in July and August it must be about .340. The summer of 1980, when Brett hit .390, was the hottest summer in Kansas City in my lifetime.

2) It is generally felt in Kansas City that the acquisition of Tartabull will "help" Brett. Brett is now such a disciplined hitter that he doesn't need the protection of anybody behind him. What Tartabull certainly will do, if he is effective, is cut down on Brett's walks with runners in scoring position, of which there were 113 over the last three years. This will give him an extra 25–30 at bats with men in scoring position, hence an extra 10–12 RBI. Over the last three years, Brett's on-base percentage with runners in scoring position is .460, because they just walk him.

3) Brett was playing very well on defense last year until he hurt himself diving after a ball in the Kingdome, July 3. The play on which he injured himself was a spectacular feet-in-the-air dive to his left, heck of a play but not worth the cost. Brett had surgery after the season and is reported doing well.

4) As he has throughout almost all of his career, Brett in 1986 hit much better against right-handers than lefties, and better at home than on the road. However, in recent years, he has hit better against finesse pitchers than power pitchers—something that surely wouldn't have been true early in his career.

5) Brett now has 2,095 career hits. At the same age Kaline had 2,320, Clemente had 2,284, Yastrzemski had 2,114 and Brock had 2,001.

6) 1987 will be the fifteenth season that Brett and White have been teammates with the Royals. I wonder how many infielders have played as many games together? And from the way they're playing, they might make it to twenty.

7) Brett in 1986 hit just .237 when leading off an inning.

8) Brett's .401 on-base percentage in 1986 was third best in the America League.

—Bill James

	1986 SEASON										THREE YEARS (84 – 86)										
	Ave.	OBP	SLG	AB	H	2B	3B	HR	RBI	BB	SO	Ave.	OBP	SLG	AB	H	2B	3B	HR	RBI	BB	SO
Totals	.290	.401	.481	441	128	28	4	16	73	80	45	.306	.400	.517	1368	419	87	12	59	254	220	131
Batting vs. Left and Right-handed Pitchers																						
Left	.243	.329	.385	148	36	4	1	5	19	19	24	.286	.355	.483	476	136	21	2	23	86	54	54
Right	.314	.435	.529	293	92	24	3	11	54	61	21	.317	.423	.535	892	283	66	10	36	168	166	77
At Home and on the Road																						
Home	.322	.418	.556	205	66	16	4	8	41	36	15	.340	.432	.574	662	225	48	10	29	138	116	55
Road	.263	.386	.415	236	62	12	0	8	32	44	30	.275	.369	.463	706	194	39	2	30	116	104	76
Facing Groundball Pitchers and Flyball Pitchers																						
Groundball	.286	.395	.447	199	57	13	2	5	25	37	23	.322	.413	.516	639	206	46	6	22	118	102	60
Flyball	.293	.405	.508	242	71	15	2	11	48	43	22	.292	.389	.517	729	213	41	6	37	136	118	71
Facing Finesse Pitchers and Power Pitchers																						
Finesse	.285	.393	.482	249	71	18	2	9	41	42	23	.314	.396	.516	777	244	54	8	29	134	107	65
Power	.297	.411	.479	192	57	10	2	7	32	38	22	.296	.405	.518	591	175	33	4	30	120	113	66
On Grass and on Turf																						
Grass	.265	.383	.429	196	52	11	0	7	27	36	25	.274	.369	.469	563	154	28	2	26	94	85	64
Turf	.310	.415	.522	245	76	17	4	9	46	44	20	.329	.422	.550	805	265	59	10	33	160	135	67
During the Day and at Night																						
Day	.319	.464	.543	116	37	12	1	4	20	30	11	.287	.379	.494	348	100	25	4	13	62	52	35
Night	.280	.376	.458	325	91	16	3	12	53	50	34	.313	.407	.525	1020	319	62	8	46	192	168	96
By Month																						
April	.241	.451	.552	58	14	4	1	4	9	21	6	.262	.440	.500	126	33	8	2	6	19	39	9
May	.242	.377	.374	99	24	7	0	2	13	22	11	.303	.397	.502	251	76	19	2	9	44	41	26
June	.355	.448	.458	107	38	5	0	2	17	16	7	.315	.410	.453	267	84	12	2	7	40	42	18
July	.217	.321	.457	46	10	3	1	2	6	7	5	.332	.421	.545	253	84	17	2	11	46	40	25
August	.364	.425	.636	99	36	8	2	5	22	12	13	.338	.399	.614	272	92	22	4	15	61	32	34
Sept/Oct	.188	.235	.313	32	6	1	0	1	6	2	3	.251	.336	.462	199	50	9	0	11	44	26	19
Situational																						
Bases Empty	.277	.380	.485	235	65	18	2	9	9	36	25	.293	.371	.504	764	224	52	8	31	31	89	67
Leadoff	.237	.355	.462	93	22	3	0	6	6	16	11	.280	.359	.535	275	77	16	3	16	16	32	22
Not Leadoff	.303	.396	.500	142	43	15	2	3	3	20	14	.301	.377	.487	489	147	36	5	15	15	57	45
Runners On	.306	.424	.476	206	63	10	2	7	64	44	20	.323	.433	.533	604	195	35	4	28	223	131	64
First Base Only	.295	.368	.537	95	28	4	2	5	14	11	8	.337	.383	.589	246	83	13	2	15	41	18	17
Scoring Position	.315	.463	.423	111	35	6	0	2	50	33	12	.313	.460	.494	358	112	22	2	13	182	113	47
Late Innings, Close	.273	.400	.439	66	18	2	0	3	10	13	7	.303	.429	.520	198	60	14	1	9	43	44	19
RBI/Opportunities																						

	1986 SEASON		THREE YEARS (84 – 86)	
Scoring Position	46 / 168	(27%)	152 / 554	(27%)
Scoring Position, 2 Out	17 / 61	(28%)	59 / 214	(28%)
On Third, Less than 2 Out	17 / 35	(49%)	58 / 108	(54%)
RBI in close games / RBI Total	54 / 73	(74%)	184 / 254	(72%)

Hubie Brooks
Montreal Expos

I remember it as plainly as game six of the '86 World Series. It was August 31, 1984, and my dad and I were on our annual doubleheader visit to Shea Stadium. The Padres were in town, and Sid Fernandez and Ed Whitson were pitching zeroes for the first six innings. The 3–4–5 hitters were up in the home seventh. Keith Hernandez led off with a single and George Foster singled also, putting runners on first and second. "Batting for the Mets, the shortstop, number seven, Hubie Brooks." Most the fans wanted to see Hubie bunt, but I yelled, "Let him rip, Davey!" The large, drunk gentleman next to me explained that your shortstop's job is to bunt the runners over, especially in a scoreless game. I told him Hubie couldn't bunt. Davey listened to the large man and Hubie missed bunting the first pitch by a foot. He bunted the second pitch OVER THE SCREEN behind the plate. He swung away at the third pitch, though, and the result was a rope to left center to score Hernandez. It turned out to be the only run the Mets scored, but that wasn't Hubie's fault.

When Brooks came to the Mets in 1980 he was expected to give them something they always lacked, a big-hitting third baseman. He turned out to be a decent glove man, certainly not a liability, and he hit .307 in 1981—but he also hit only four homers that year. In fact, in the equivalent of four seasons he hit only 28 homers. Not so good for your hard-hitting third baseman. But very good for your shortstop.

He may not be as good a shortstop as I or his managers think he is, but he isn't as bad as some writers (including Bill James) think he is, either. If you can make most of the plays and hit .289, slug .447 and hit 43 homers with 230 RBIs in two and a half seasons, I'd play you at shortstop. Davey Johnson was a good enough judge of talent to see that Hubie could do the job, and ended up with the best catcher in baseball when he traded him.

Brooks will never be great in the field, but a team can win with an average defensive shortstop who hits like Hubie does. Don't ask Hubie Brooks to be Ozzie Smith. Don't ask him to bunt, either. But if you ask him to do what he CAN do, Hubie will do it very well.

—Joe Nunziata III

| | 1986 SEASON | | | | | | | | | | THREE YEARS (84 – 86) | | | | | | | | | |
	Ave.	OBP	SLG	AB	H	2B	3B	HR	RBI	BB	SO	Ave.	OBP	SLG	AB	H	2B	3B	HR	RBI	BB	SO
Totals	.340	.388	.569	306	104	18	5	14	58	25	60	.289	.338	.447	1472	426	75	14	43	231	107	217
Batting vs. Left and Right-handed Pitchers																						
Left	.365	.450	.682	85	31	6	3	5	17	13	13	.312	.379	.508	455	142	31	5	16	72	46	59
Right	.330	.361	.525	221	73	12	2	9	41	12	47	.279	.319	.420	1017	284	44	9	27	159	61	158
At Home and on the Road																						
Home	.350	.409	.504	137	48	8	2	3	26	14	24	.311	.360	.478	692	215	45	7	19	118	51	105
Road	.331	.370	.621	169	56	10	3	11	32	11	36	.271	.318	.419	780	211	30	7	24	113	56	112
Facing Groundball Pitchers and Flyball Pitchers																						
Groundball	.407	.455	.660	150	61	13	2	7	35	14	21	.326	.378	.499	714	233	47	5	22	135	59	92
Flyball	.276	.322	.481	156	43	5	3	7	23	11	39	.255	.300	.398	758	193	28	9	21	96	48	125
Facing Finesse Pitchers and Power Pitchers																						
Finesse	.337	.388	.534	163	55	10	2	6	29	13	30	.305	.351	.460	826	252	45	4	25	138	57	99
Power	.343	.388	.608	143	49	8	3	8	29	12	30	.269	.322	.430	646	174	30	10	18	93	50	118
On Grass and on Turf																						
Grass	.330	.366	.641	103	34	8	0	8	21	6	24	.303	.352	.478	676	205	30	5	26	94	50	99
Turf	.345	.398	.532	203	70	10	5	6	37	19	36	.278	.326	.421	796	221	45	9	17	137	57	118
During the Day and at Night																						
Day	.326	.383	.630	135	44	11	3	8	32	12	28	.280	.334	.448	558	156	25	9	17	90	46	77
Night	.351	.392	.520	171	60	7	2	6	26	13	32	.295	.341	.446	914	270	50	5	26	141	61	140
By Month																						
April	.312	.384	.584	77	24	6	0	5	16	8	11	.275	.336	.441	222	61	11	1	8	37	20	30
May	.341	.379	.706	85	29	4	3	7	24	6	27	.318	.365	.535	258	82	10	5	12	43	18	44
June	.354	.420	.532	79	28	4	2	2	8	9	15	.318	.378	.487	267	85	17	2	8	37	24	53
July	.349	.348	.397	63	22	3	0	0	10	1	6	.272	.301	.348	287	78	13	0	3	36	14	33
August	.500	.667	1.000	2	1	1	0	0	0	1	1	.284	.336	.479	215	61	11	5	7	44	16	23
Sept/Oct	.000	.000	.000	0	0	0	0	0	0	0	0	.265	.310	.399	223	59	13	1	5	34	15	34
Situational																						
Bases Empty	.361	.402	.639	158	57	9	4	9	9	10	24	.288	.327	.467	808	233	38	8	30	30	43	105
Leadoff	.329	.370	.500	76	25	4	3	1	1	5	12	.317	.346	.476	357	113	23	5	8	8	16	44
Not Leadoff	.390	.432	.768	82	32	5	1	8	8	5	12	.266	.313	.459	451	120	15	3	22	22	27	61
Runners On	.318	.373	.493	148	47	9	1	5	49	15	36	.291	.350	.423	664	193	37	6	13	201	64	112
First Base Only	.389	.431	.537	54	21	3	1	1	4	4	5	.287	.323	.377	265	76	11	2	3	13	11	30
Scoring Position	.277	.342	.468	94	26	6	0	4	45	11	31	.293	.367	.454	399	117	26	4	10	188	53	82
Late Innings, Close	.385	.437	.662	65	25	5	2	3	12	4	14	.302	.356	.457	265	80	11	3	8	44	21	50
RBI/Opportunities																						

	1986 SEASON		THREE YEARS (84 – 86)	
Scoring Position	38 / 133	(29%)	162 / 555	(29%)
Scoring Position, 2 Out	12 / 57	(21%)	65 / 259	(25%)
On Third, Less than 2 Out	17 / 32	(53%)	64 / 117	(55%)
RBI in close games / RBI Total	42 / 58	(72%)	165 / 231	(71%)

Chris Brown
San Francisco Giants

Chris Brown ended 1986 recuperating from arthroscopic shoulder surgery. Giants' President Al Rosen believes that certain body types, such as Brown's, are so heavily-muscled compared to their skeletal size that they are very prone to muscle injuries. Brown's career has been one of short seasons, supporting Rosen's theory. Some things are certain, though: Brown played extremely well until August 1, playing hurt while the Giants were in the pennant race. Brown dove into the LA dugout early in the season—hardly the act of a man "afraid of pain or injury," as suggested.

On June 26, Brown led the National League in hitting, as well as fielding average for third basemen, completing a streak of six multiple-hit games. He led the Giants in BA and OBA, hitting .374 with RISP, raising his career average to .355 with RISP. In 1985, he hit 83 points higher vs. RHP; in 1986 he cut that to 38 points, hitting .292 vs. LHP. Brown hit poorly when leading off an inning, but hit very well with runners on and in late-inning, close situations. He was one of the resurgent Giants' three All-Stars.

Brown has remarkable reflexes for a big man, along with a good arm. He bare-hands bunts as well as anyone in the league. The Giants feel he will anchor a solid infield for many years to come.

—J. Michael Duca

Doesn't anyone remember J.R. Richard? It wasn't long ago that he was the NL's best pitcher, an outstanding athlete in his prime. He had never shown any inclination toward hypochondria, nor did he have a reputation as a malcontent, a drunk or a druggie. Nevertheless, when Richard repeatedly complained about his arm, no one would listen to him. After all, the doctors examined him and pronounced him healthy, right? Wrong—almost *dead* wrong.

There are obvious parallels between J.R. Richard and Chris Brown. Both players are black; almost all baseball executives are white. (Try to name any black baseball executive other than Henry Aaron.) Now, which players come to mind as having "bad attitudes" —the surly, hostile guys who are "malcontents" or "lazy" or "ungrateful" or whatever code words you choose. George Hendrick? George Foster? Chris Brown? Bill Madlock? Dave Parker (in Pittsburgh)? Reggie? Joaquin Andujar? Oil Can Boyd? Alan Wiggins? Rickey Henderson? Claudell Washington? Dave Kingman? Does this tell you something?

Chris Brown was finally diagnosed by one of the top sports doctors in the country as having a serious but nearly undetectable shoulder problem. The problem was not Chris Brown's attitude; the problem was and is baseball's attitude towards minority athletes, especially rich and famous ones.

—Gary Gillette

	1986 SEASON											THREE YEARS (84 – 86)									
	Ave.	OBP	SLG	AB	H	2B	3B	HR	RBI	BB	SO	Ave.	OBP	SLG	AB	H	2B	3B	HR	RBI	BB	SO
Totals	.317	.376	.421	416	132	16	3	7	49	33	43	.293	.360	.429	932	273	43	6	24	121	80	140
Batting vs. Left and Right-handed Pitchers																						
Left	.292	.331	.431	137	40	8	1	3	10	6	14	.258	.325	.415	260	67	15	1	8	21	21	38
Right	.330	.396	.416	279	92	8	2	4	39	27	29	.307	.373	.435	672	206	28	5	16	100	59	102
At Home and on the Road																						
Home	.333	.400	.421	228	76	7	2	3	30	23	25	.297	.367	.412	478	142	25	3	8	67	46	72
Road	.298	.345	.420	188	56	9	1	4	19	10	18	.289	.352	.447	454	131	18	3	16	54	34	68
Facing Groundball Pitchers and Flyball Pitchers																						
Groundball	.333	.388	.433	201	67	10	2	2	22	17	14	.316	.377	.491	411	130	24	3	14	58	33	49
Flyball	.302	.364	.409	215	65	6	1	5	27	16	29	.274	.346	.380	521	143	19	3	10	63	47	91
Facing Finesse Pitchers and Power Pitchers																						
Finesse	.335	.376	.441	245	82	13	2	3	28	12	20	.315	.374	.478	542	171	32	4	16	71	37	71
Power	.292	.375	.392	171	50	3	1	4	21	21	23	.262	.342	.362	390	102	11	2	8	50	43	69
On Grass and on Turf																						
Grass	.325	.387	.412	311	101	9	3	4	38	27	30	.302	.370	.426	705	213	34	4	15	96	62	107
Turf	.295	.339	.448	105	31	7	0	3	11	6	13	.264	.327	.441	227	60	9	2	9	25	18	33
During the Day and at Night																						
Day	.333	.406	.428	201	67	8	1	3	27	24	27	.292	.367	.402	483	141	22	2	9	60	50	82
Night	.302	.345	.414	215	65	8	2	4	22	9	16	.294	.352	.459	449	132	21	4	15	61	30	58
By Month																						
April	.349	.408	.460	63	22	2	1	1	10	5	5	.308	.385	.411	107	33	4	2	1	14	11	13
May	.319	.375	.472	72	23	3	1	2	10	7	8	.268	.318	.401	157	42	5	2	4	19	10	27
June	.337	.413	.478	92	31	4	0	3	10	12	8	.315	.389	.497	165	52	10	1	6	20	18	21
July	.330	.381	.436	94	31	5	1	1	11	6	10	.326	.385	.495	184	60	11	1	6	27	14	25
August	.278	.327	.300	90	25	2	0	0	8	3	10	.289	.345	.365	159	46	3	0	3	17	8	22
Sept/Oct	.000	.000	.000	5	0	0	0	0	0	0	2	.250	.339	.388	160	40	10	0	4	24	19	32
Situational																						
Bases Empty	.275	.327	.385	244	67	8	2	5	5	16	28	.259	.324	.397	549	142	20	4	16	16	43	82
Leadoff	.222	.278	.311	90	20	3	1	1	1	5	12	.238	.307	.414	210	50	7	3	8	8	17	38
Not Leadoff	.305	.355	.429	154	47	5	1	4	4	11	16	.271	.334	.386	339	92	13	1	8	8	26	44
Runners On	.378	.440	.471	172	65	8	1	2	44	17	15	.342	.410	.475	383	131	23	2	8	105	37	58
First Base Only	.383	.425	.506	81	31	4	0	2	4	4	11	.325	.377	.450	169	55	13	1	2	10	11	21
Scoring Position	.374	.451	.440	91	34	4	1	0	40	13	4	.355	.433	.495	214	76	10	1	6	95	26	37
Late Innings, Close	.333	.404	.427	75	25	2	1	1	9	10	8	.333	.403	.460	189	63	6	3	4	25	23	32
RBI/Opportunities																						
Scoring Position				40 / 131		(31%)									83 / 291		(29%)					
Scoring Position, 2 Out				16 / 55		(29%)									37 / 130		(28%)					
On Third, Less than 2 Out				17 / 31		(55%)									27 / 56		(48%)					
RBI in close games / RBI Total				36 / 49		(73%)									92 / 121		(76%)					

Tom Browning
Cincinnati Reds

Overshadowed by Dwight Gooden, Tom Browning quietly won 20 games as a rookie in 1985 for a strong Cincinnati team which surprised many of its own fans. The attention of the baseball world was focused on the Big Apple and the young Doctor K, thus relieving Browning of outside pressure. The question Reds fans were asking in the spring of 1986 was, "Will the sophomore jinx get him?" Browning did lead a charmed life in 1985, posting nearly identical stats to those of Mario Soto, who went 12–15 despite giving up two less runs in five fewer innings. Those of you who still believe all pitchers on a team get the same offensive support are sentenced to explaining your position to Mario, who received an average of 1.1 run less per start in '85 than Tom, for records of 20–9 (Browning) vs. 12–15 (Soto). One run per game that you can't control.

If you cling to the assumption that W-L is the only valid indicator of pitching performance, you probably thought Browning was a bust in 1986. His record slipped to "only" 14–13, and his ERA increased from 3.55 to 3.81. But there are Reds fans out there encouraged by the way this guy is developing. He turned in another 240 innings, and discarding his 0–3 start in April, he was 14–10 with a 3.56 ERA. Runs scored in NL play increased in 1986, making his performance look even better.

Not convinced? Opponents' on-base average and slugging average actually declined against Browning in 1986. His strikeout and walk data were nearly identical from 1985 to 1986, and he cut back on extra-base hits yielded (65 vs. 78). His performance against left-handed batters slipped, but he improved against the righties. Tom does need to cut down on gopher balls, especially against right-handed batters, who hit 50 of the 55 home runs that he allowed in 1985–86. However, Tom doesn't complicate matters by issuing too many walks.

Yes, Browning is a man of balance. He is the counterweight of the Cincinnati staff. The Reds play better on turf; he pitches well on grass. He is effective in day games and on the road; the Reds had been weak in those breakdowns. He and Gullickson threw over 240 innings each; no one else surpassed 180. Browning's hobbies probably include tightrope walking, mountain climbing, and juggling.

The "jinx" may have tossed him some bad luck, but quality pitchers don't tend to get hung up about jinxes. In two short years, Browning, at 26, has established himself as one of the top southpaws in the NL.

—A. S. Nakamura

1986: Finesse, Flyball   **1985: Finesse, Flyball**   **1984: Finesse, Flyball**

	G	IP	H	BB	SO	SB	CS	W	L	S	ERA	G	IP	H	BB	SO	SB	CS	W	L	S	ERA
		1986 SEASON												**THREE YEARS (84 – 86)**									
Totals	39	243.1	225	70	147	18	6	14	13	0	3.81	80	528.0	494	148	316	35	17	35	22	0	3.58
											At Home and on the Road											
Home	17	106.2	93	38	59	7	1	7	6	0	3.80	37	246.0	237	76	132	13	6	17	12	0	3.91
Road	22	136.2	132	32	88	11	5	7	7	0	3.82	43	282.0	257	72	184	22	11	18	10	0	3.29
											During the Day and at Night											
Day	16	92.1	92	24	54	5	1	7	5	0	4.00	35	219.2	212	62	133	17	6	16	8	0	3.85
Night	23	151.0	133	46	93	13	5	7	8	0	3.70	45	308.1	282	86	183	18	11	19	14	0	3.39
											On Grass and on Turf											
Grass	13	90.0	82	14	57	5	2	5	3	0	3.50	26	179.0	161	42	114	14	5	10	5	0	3.27
Turf	26	153.1	143	56	90	13	4	9	10	0	3.99	54	349.0	333	106	202	21	12	25	17	0	3.74
											By Month											
April	5	23.2	25	9	11	1	0	0	3	0	6.08	8	47.2	39	12	25	2	2	2	3	0	3.21
May	7	39.2	45	14	27	1	1	2	2	0	4.54	13	81.2	88	27	49	6	2	4	6	0	4.30
June	6	40.1	34	12	23	4	2	3	2	0	3.35	12	74.2	68	31	49	7	4	6	3	0	4.22
July	6	39.0	34	7	31	1	2	4	1	0	3.00	13	87.2	78	17	52	1	3	6	4	0	3.70
August	8	48.0	45	17	26	6	1	2	3	0	4.31	15	98.2	92	28	54	6	3	7	4	0	3.37
Sept/Oct	7	52.2	42	11	29	5	0	3	2	0	2.73	19	137.2	129	33	87	13	3	10	2	0	3.01

vs. Opponent Batters

	Ave.	OBP	SLG	AB	H	2B	3B	HR	RBI	BB	SO	Ave.	OBP	SLG	AB	H	2B	3B	HR	RBI	BB	SO
		1986 SEASON												**THREE YEARS (84 – 86)**								
Totals	.245	.296	.375	918	225	37	2	26	104	70	147	.248	.298	.378	1994	494	89	3	55	207	148	316
						Pitching vs. Left and Right-handed Batters																
Left	.235	.318	.346	136	32	3	0	4	13	17	24	.240	.309	.318	296	71	8	0	5	27	29	57
Right	.247	.292	.380	782	193	34	2	22	91	53	123	.249	.296	.389	1698	423	81	3	50	180	119	259
							Situational															
Bases Empty	.231	.281	.365	589	136	20	1	19	19	40	105	.246	.293	.369	1252	308	44	1	36	36	80	215
Leadoff	.218	.277	.338	234	51	8	1	6	6	18	50	.230	.279	.353	513	118	16	1	15	15	34	91
Not Leadoff	.239	.284	.383	355	85	12	0	13	13	22	55	.257	.303	.380	739	190	28	0	21	21	46	124
Runners On	.271	.321	.392	329	89	17	1	7	85	30	42	.251	.306	.394	742	186	45	2	19	171	68	101
First Base Only	.269	.303	.425	167	45	8	0	6	16	8	18	.238	.273	.362	387	92	22	1	8	26	19	52
Scoring Position	.272	.337	.358	162	44	9	1	1	69	22	24	.265	.338	.428	355	94	23	1	11	145	49	49
Late Innings, Close	.190	.235	.266	79	15	3	0	1	8	5	16	.211	.269	.306	147	31	5	0	3	16	12	23

RBI/Opportunities

Scoring Position	62 / 228	(27%)	121 / 497	(24%)
Scoring Position, 2 Out	24 / 117	(21%)	50 / 239	(21%)
On Third, Less than 2 Out	27 / 40	(68%)	48 / 84	(57%)
RBI in close games / RBI Total	72 / 104	(69%)	150 / 207	(72%)

Tom Brunansky
Minnesota Twins

The Twins' home run caravan went on the road in 1986 and left Tom Brunansky behind. Bruno fell to a four-year low of 23 homers while three teammates passed him on the power parade. Whatever influence provided the Twins with their extra muscle seemed to pass Brunansky by, and that's bad news for a man who makes his living on the long ball. It was a very unusual season from Brunansky. In previous years, Bruno has had significant trouble with left-handers. In 1985, for instance, he batted .214 and slugged a measly .379 against lefties. But last year, he ripped southpaws to shreds, batting .311, with 11 homers and a whopping .575 slugging percentage. Unfortunately, while he solved that problem in 1986, right-handers plagued him like never before, as his .364 slugging percentage against them attests.

Likewise, Brunansky finally figured out how to hit home runs in the Metrodome. He hit 15 round-trippers in Minneapolis, and for the first time in his career hit more homers in the Dome than on the road. But his road homer production dropped drastically to eight (after seasons of 20, 17, and 15), and his slugging percentage was a mere .367 away from his home turf.

The problems all started in July. Brunansky sizzled through the first three months of the season with a .294 batting average and 18 homers, contending for the league home run lead, along with four other Twins. But the lion turned into a pussycat when July rolled around, and Bruno hobbled home with a .220 average and only six homers in the last three months of the season. Worse yet, Brunansky, who had established a reputation as a clutch performer, fell apart in pressure situations in 1986. In the late innings of close games, he batted only .180. It was a bad season by Bruno's high standards.

Still, Brunansky can point to many positives. He's young (he'll be 27 in August), and has proven that he can deliver 20 to 30 home runs consistently. He's a decent fielder with a good arm, and he's a good baserunner. Perhaps his skills are miscast in Minnesota. The fairly long left-field wall there offers no advantages to a pull hitter like Brunansky, and the bouncy turf makes playing in the field a chore for even the fastest of American League outfielders.

In 1987, Brunansky will have to solve the problems that plagued him in the second half of 1986. The Twins used Bruno as trade bait last winter, and it's quite likely that by the end of the season he'll be playing somewhere else, which just might not be such a bad thing for him.

—Scott Johnson

	1986 SEASON											THREE YEARS (84 – 86)										
	Ave.	OBP	SLG	AB	H	2B	3B	HR	RBI	BB	SO	Ave.	OBP	SLG	AB	H	2B	3B	HR	RBI	BB	SO
Totals	.256	.315	.423	593	152	28	1	23	75	53	98	.251	.318	.444	1727	433	77	5	82	250	181	278
Batting vs. Left and Right-handed Pitchers																						
Left	.311	.354	.575	167	52	9	1	11	27	12	22	.254	.331	.496	512	130	25	3	31	84	64	62
Right	.235	.300	.364	426	100	19	0	12	48	41	76	.249	.313	.421	1215	303	52	2	51	166	117	216
At Home and on the Road																						
Home	.267	.324	.480	296	79	16	1	15	45	26	43	.252	.320	.449	856	216	39	3	41	135	92	133
Road	.246	.306	.367	297	73	12	0	8	30	27	55	.249	.316	.439	871	217	38	2	41	115	89	145
Facing Groundball Pitchers and Flyball Pitchers																						
Groundball	.272	.330	.421	261	71	9	0	10	38	24	35	.255	.332	.466	832	212	38	3	44	132	101	131
Flyball	.244	.303	.425	332	81	19	1	13	37	29	63	.247	.305	.422	895	221	39	2	38	118	80	147
Facing Finesse Pitchers and Power Pitchers																						
Finesse	.279	.322	.402	326	91	10	0	10	38	20	41	.254	.309	.418	942	239	35	0	40	126	79	128
Power	.228	.307	.449	267	61	18	1	13	37	33	57	.247	.329	.474	785	194	42	5	42	124	102	150
On Grass and on Turf																						
Grass	.238	.306	.341	223	53	8	0	5	16	22	42	.230	.305	.419	647	149	27	1	31	78	71	100
Turf	.268	.320	.473	370	99	20	1	18	59	31	56	.263	.326	.458	1080	284	50	4	51	172	110	178
During the Day and at Night																						
Day	.231	.276	.319	182	42	10	0	2	14	12	36	.246	.313	.395	512	126	25	0	17	58	53	88
Night	.268	.332	.470	411	110	18	1	21	61	41	62	.253	.320	.464	1215	307	52	5	65	192	128	190
By Month																						
April	.280	.310	.451	82	23	2	0	4	13	4	14	.275	.361	.475	240	66	9	0	13	38	35	38
May	.312	.361	.587	109	34	7	1	7	18	8	19	.304	.364	.530	296	90	13	3	16	49	30	44
June	.279	.333	.505	111	31	7	0	6	16	10	20	.237	.313	.460	291	69	14	0	17	46	33	54
July	.218	.255	.267	101	22	2	0	1	8	5	11	.215	.264	.352	284	61	11	2	8	31	20	54
August	.230	.325	.350	100	23	6	0	2	8	15	14	.254	.321	.444	311	79	14	0	15	38	32	42
Sept/Oct	.211	.294	.356	90	19	4	0	3	12	11	20	.223	.289	.403	305	68	16	0	13	48	31	57
Situational																						
Bases Empty	.273	.327	.453	311	85	18	1	12	12	25	45	.257	.323	.476	910	234	44	4	49	49	89	127
Leadoff	.285	.313	.410	144	41	3	0	5	5	6	17	.253	.307	.436	411	104	14	2	19	19	32	50
Not Leadoff	.263	.339	.491	167	44	15	1	7	7	19	28	.261	.336	.509	499	130	30	2	30	30	57	77
Runners On	.238	.302	.390	282	67	10	0	11	63	28	53	.244	.313	.408	817	199	33	1	33	201	92	151
First Base Only	.237	.290	.474	135	32	8	0	8	19	9	23	.259	.322	.492	370	96	15	1	23	51	33	61
Scoring Position	.238	.312	.313	147	35	2	0	3	44	19	30	.230	.306	.338	447	103	18	0	10	150	59	90
Late Innings, Close	.180	.232	.315	89	16	6	0	2	11	7	22	.259	.327	.466	266	69	11	1	14	45	29	48

RBI/Opportunities

	1986 SEASON		THREE YEARS (84 – 86)	
Scoring Position	40 / 195	(21%)	127 / 608	(21%)
Scoring Position, 2 Out	13 / 84	(15%)	40 / 274	(15%)
On Third, Less than 2 Out	14 / 33	(42%)	52 / 112	(46%)
RBI in close games / RBI Total	40 / 75	(53%)	164 / 250	(66%)

Bill Buckner
Boston Red Sox

If you're a Bill Buckner fan, skip this page; I'm not and I'll only raise your blood pressure. Buckner has always been a much worse player than people think. He's done nothing but hit for average—he had to play in the two best hitters' parks in baseball before he could manage that. In his prime, he was a mediocre player—25% better than Pat Tabler is now. At 37 and in consistently poor health, he's a wretched excuse for a regular.

The bright side of Buckner's 1986 is short and sweet. He had 102 RBIs, hit 18 homers (a career best), 39 doubles, hit well in the clutch and finished strongly. He may not have been Boston's MVP in September (see Boggs, Clemens, Hurst and Rice), but he came close. He led AL first basemen in assists and homered almost as often as he struck out.

Buckner's list of drawbacks is a bit longer. His on-base average is terrible; he's helpless against lefties. Given the fact that he batted with 268 men in scoring position, 102 RBIs are not a lot. He hit badly for the first five months of the year (nowhere near what a #3 hitter or a first baseman should do) and he made 499 outs. The simplest way to show how badly Buckner hurt Boston is to look at the number of times that the first four men in the order led off innings in 1986. Boggs, as you'd expect, led off 153 innings. Barrett, the #2 man, led off 107. Buckner was the first hitter 102 times. Rice led off innings 158, repeat, "one hundred and fifty-eight" times. Could Boston have had somebody more likely to kill rallies batting third? Other than their shortstops, no. According to Bill James's formulas for rating offense, Buckner had 76 runs created, created 4.08 runs per 27 outs and his offensive winning percentage (which tells you how well Boston would have done if everyone in their lineup hit like Buckner) was .438.

The thing that amazes me is that Boston can't see what a miserable player Buckner is. They're convinced that he's a key player—they're worrying about the day that they have to replace him. How on earth could they have won a pennant if they're that desperately stupid? If Boston wants to play Buckner, the least they could do is bat him eighth and platoon him—that would be halfway intelligent. But if they'd ever like to win another pennant, they should give serious consideration to finding a first baseman who can outhit Brooke Shields.

—Geoff Beckman

	1986 SEASON										THREE YEARS (84 – 86)										
	Ave.	OBP	SLG	AB	H	2B	3B	HR	RBI	BB	SO	Ave.	OBP	SLG	AB	H	2B	3B	HR	RBI	BB	SO
Totals	.267	.311	.421	629	168	39	2	18	102	40	25	.280	.317	.423	1784	500	106	7	45	281	95	100
Batting vs. Left and Right-handed Pitchers																						
Left	.218	.257	.322	202	44	7	1	4	30	8	10	.262	.298	.375	581	152	21	3	13	90	26	36
Right	.290	.336	.468	427	124	32	1	14	72	32	15	.289	.326	.446	1203	348	85	4	32	191	69	64
At Home and on the Road																						
Home	.258	.303	.411	299	77	18	2	8	45	19	13	.273	.312	.414	879	240	52	6	20	137	50	59
Road	.276	.318	.430	330	91	21	0	10	57	21	12	.287	.322	.432	905	260	54	1	25	144	45	41
Facing Groundball Pitchers and Flyball Pitchers																						
Groundball	.302	.341	.496	278	84	19	1	11	52	18	11	.299	.335	.432	870	260	52	2	20	144	48	45
Flyball	.239	.288	.362	351	84	20	1	7	50	22	14	.263	.300	.415	914	240	54	5	25	137	47	55
Facing Finesse Pitchers and Power Pitchers																						
Finesse	.275	.313	.448	364	100	22	1	13	62	20	10	.288	.320	.442	999	288	61	3	29	164	47	51
Power	.257	.309	.385	265	68	17	1	5	40	20	15	.270	.314	.399	785	212	45	4	16	117	48	49
On Grass and on Turf																						
Grass	.264	.308	.426	538	142	35	2	16	89	35	19	.278	.315	.424	1522	423	95	7	38	240	83	85
Turf	.286	.333	.396	91	26	4	0	2	13	5	6	.294	.329	.416	262	77	11	0	7	41	12	15
During the Day and at Night																						
Day	.228	.262	.362	224	51	16	1	4	24	10	7	.254	.292	.379	591	150	35	3	11	85	33	33
Night	.289	.338	.454	405	117	23	1	14	78	30	18	.293	.330	.445	1193	350	71	4	34	196	62	67
By Month																						
April	.215	.259	.380	79	17	8	1	1	7	4	6	.255	.296	.391	184	47	14	1	3	21	10	9
May	.264	.325	.400	110	29	6	0	3	20	10	3	.288	.336	.436	243	70	15	0	7	36	18	9
June	.230	.254	.381	113	26	3	1	4	13	4	2	.250	.284	.378	312	78	15	2	7	41	14	20
July	.276	.294	.419	105	29	9	0	2	16	3	8	.267	.301	.419	315	84	25	1	7	49	13	21
August	.289	.352	.368	114	33	9	0	0	24	10	2	.292	.333	.439	360	105	22	2	9	67	22	16
Sept/Oct	.315	.364	.574	108	34	4	0	8	22	9	4	.314	.340	.457	370	116	15	1	12	67	18	25
Situational																						
Bases Empty	.257	.284	.438	288	74	15	2	11	11	10	10	.254	.282	.398	893	227	48	7	22	22	32	47
Leadoff	.245	.267	.402	102	25	5	1	3	3	3	2	.239	.275	.382	322	77	15	5	7	7	15	15
Not Leadoff	.263	.294	.457	186	49	10	1	8	8	7	8	.263	.285	.406	571	150	33	2	15	15	17	32
Runners On	.276	.332	.408	341	94	24	0	7	91	30	15	.306	.351	.449	891	273	58	0	23	259	63	53
First Base Only	.320	.371	.497	147	47	11	0	5	13	11	6	.325	.366	.447	409	133	23	0	9	26	23	24
Scoring Position	.242	.305	.340	194	47	13	0	2	78	19	9	.290	.339	.450	482	140	35	0	14	233	40	29
Late Innings, Close	.311	.409	.432	74	23	6	0	1	10	10	1	.359	.419	.488	248	89	17	0	5	39	21	12
RBI/Opportunities																						

Scoring Position	69 / 268	(26%)
Scoring Position, 2 Out	26 / 108	(24%)
On Third, Less than 2 Out	25 / 41	(61%)
RBI in close games / RBI Total	69 / 102	(68%)

	200 / 668	(30%)
	70 / 274	(26%)
	82 / 135	(61%)
	179 / 281	(64%)

Tim Burke
Montreal Expos

A member of the "Traded for Lee Mazilli All Stars" (along with Ron Darling, Walt Terrell and Bucky Dent), Tim Burke first pitched on opening day of 1985 and, for most of the next two seasons, averaged close on one appearance for every two games the Expos played. His '85 rookie season was superb in almost every respect. Tim's 78 appearances not only led the league, but set a National League record for games pitched by a rookie; and though he had only eight saves, he was outstanding as the set-up man for Jeff Reardon, finishing with a lowly 2.39 ERA. His work early in the year was especially good, as he won his first eight decisions (an Expo record for wins starting a season) and recorded an 0.87 ERA from April 21 to July 21. He did tail off late in the season, however; his September/October ERA was 4.35, and for the year his ERA was 1.59 first half, 2.99 second half.

For the most part, Burke's '86 campaign repeated the same patterns. Again he was a workhorse, recording the 100th appearance of his career in his 203rd game in an Expo uniform for another club record. And again he pitched magnificently in the first half of the season, posting a 6–2 record with four saves and and a 1.84 ERA. But once more he tired in the second half, turning in a 3–5 mark, 0 saves, and a 4.78 ERA. After the September roster increase Burke was used sparingly; in the Expos' last 22 games, he made only one appearance. His 6.23 September ERA indicated a tired arm. Nonetheless he led the Expos with 68 appearances, and his 2.93 ERA was second on the club among pitchers hurling more than 20 innings.

Because of injuries and the 24-man roster, Buck Rodgers had Burke start two games in '86. In both games he pitched very well: on August 15 he threw five shutout innings against the Cubs, striking out five and getting the win, and on August 27 he gave up only one run in seven innings at San Francisco, striking out six and allowing only five hits but getting no decision. Burke could probably adapt to a starter's role with little difficulty, as he started, and for the most part pitched effectively, throughout his minor-league career.

If Burke is ever put on the trading block, the Chicago Cubs might be interested: in each of his two seasons, he has pitched much better on grass fields than on turf, and has been more effective in day games than at night.

—Martin Lacoste

1986: Power, Groundball **1985: Power, Groundball** **1984: Did not play**

	G	IP	H	BB	SO	SB	CS	W	L	S	ERA		G	IP	H	BB	SO	SB	CS	W	L	S	ERA
1986 SEASON												**THREE YEARS (84 – 86)**											
Totals	68	101.1	102	46	82	14	3	9	7	4	2.93		146	221.2	188	90	169	31	11	18	11	12	2.64
At Home and on the Road																							
Home	29	46.2	40	24	36	5	0	4	2	2	1.74		64	96.2	80	41	78	12	2	8	5	4	2.33
Road	39	54.2	62	22	46	9	3	5	5	2	3.95		82	125.0	108	49	91	19	9	10	6	8	2.88
During the Day and at Night																							
Day	26	44.0	53	24	30	5	2	2	2	1	2.66		57	97.2	84	44	68	14	5	3	2	6	2.30
Night	42	57.1	49	22	52	9	1	7	5	3	3.14		89	124.0	104	46	101	17	6	15	9	6	2.90
On Grass and on Turf																							
Grass	19	31.0	26	8	26	1	1	4	2	1	1.74		41	73.2	53	22	54	5	4	6	2	6	1.83
Turf	49	70.1	76	38	56	13	2	5	5	3	3.45		105	148.0	135	68	115	26	7	12	9	6	3.04
By Month																							
April	11	18.2	10	6	19	2	0	1	0	2	0.96		19	30.2	21	13	28	7	1	1	0	3	1.76
May	13	21.2	19	8	10	1	0	1	1	1	2.08		21	36.1	29	11	23	2	3	2	1	1	1.98
June	16	20.0	17	10	18	2	1	3	1	1	2.70		31	38.2	30	15	31	3	2	6	1	2	1.86
July	11	14.0	19	16	10	6	0	2	2	0	5.79		24	36.1	29	28	21	9	1	3	2	2	2.97
August	10	18.1	21	5	17	1	1	1	2	0	2.45		26	40.0	34	10	35	2	2	4	4	1	2.25
Sept/Oct	7	8.2	16	1	8	2	1	1	1	0	6.23		25	39.2	45	13	31	8	2	2	3	3	4.76

vs. Opponent Batters

	Ave.	OBP	SLG	AB	H	2B	3B	HR	RBI	BB	SO		Ave.	OBP	SLG	AB	H	2B	3B	HR	RBI	BB	SO
1986 SEASON												**THREE YEARS (84 – 86)**											
Totals	.260	.342	.367	392	102	19	1	7	41	46	82		.231	.314	.337	813	188	36	1	16	83	90	169
Pitching vs. Left and Right-handed Batters																							
Left	.298	.387	.410	205	61	8	0	5	29	31	37		.275	.370	.384	393	108	19	0	8	50	61	67
Right	.219	.291	.321	187	41	11	1	2	12	15	45		.190	.260	.293	420	80	17	1	8	33	29	102
Situational																							
Bases Empty	.249	.305	.378	209	52	10	1	5	5	15	47		.233	.299	.356	438	102	19	1	11	11	36	95
Leadoff	.278	.330	.422	90	25	5	1	2	2	7	22		.286	.356	.449	185	53	10	1	6	6	19	38
Not Leadoff	.227	.287	.345	119	27	5	0	3	3	8	25		.194	.255	.289	253	49	9	0	5	5	17	57
Runners On	.273	.381	.355	183	50	9	0	2	36	31	35		.229	.332	.315	375	86	17	0	5	72	54	74
First Base Only	.357	.400	.500	56	20	5	0	1	5	3	7		.327	.372	.442	113	37	7	0	2	9	6	15
Scoring Position	.236	.373	.291	127	30	4	0	1	31	28	28		.187	.317	.260	262	49	10	0	3	63	48	59
Late Innings, Close	.263	.347	.358	232	61	10	0	4	28	29	50		.235	.323	.329	422	99	16	0	8	42	51	84

RBI/Opportunities

Scoring Position	28 / 196	(14%)	55 / 396	(14%)
Scoring Position, 2 Out	8 / 77	(10%)	18 / 175	(10%)
On Third, Less than 2 Out	13 / 32	(41%)	24 / 63	(38%)
RBI in close games / RBI Total	33 / 41	(80%)	56 / 83	(67%)

Brett Butler
Cleveland Indians

Brett Butler is one of those players who was too small to play as a kid and had to make himself into one by learning to do what he was physically able to do. He's done a good job—if the GMs were choosing up sides, he wouldn't be the last one chosen anymore.

There are five things that a hitter with very little natural talent can do—Brett does them all. He has good strike zone judgement—his worst on-base average in any performance split is .324. He makes good contact—he walks more often than he strikes out. He sprays the ball around and gets extra base hits by "hitting them where they ain't"—he has fair power for a good leadoff man. He hits to the opposite field well—he's a good hit and run man who can advance a runner from first if that's what the team needs. Finally, he bunts well. He is possibly the best bunter in the league and he makes sure that he does it often enough to keep the infield in close. No, he doesn't get as many bunt hits as he used to (he had 16 this year, down from 30 in 1985), but he slaps the ball by fielders more than he used to, too.

Brett's baserunning needs work. He's very fast and very aggressive, but the word "smart" isn't in his vocabulary. He's rarely thrown out on a steal attempt, but he gets picked off more often than anyone I've ever seen. He has a nasty habit of stealing a base at a key moment and turning a "must pitch" situation into a setup for an intentional walk; he gets thrown out at home about half a dozen times a year.

Brett is a fine centerfielder—not as good as he thinks (he feels that he has deserved a Gold Glove for the last two years), but he has very high range factors and his arm is (though not strong) accurate. He plays very shallow, which allows him to do two things—take away bloop singles and make the over the shoulder catches that he lives to make.

Butler's only problem is his attitude. He complains about not being appreciated so often that the people who used to appreciate him no longer do. His periodic tantrums affect his play—he blasted management in April, the fans in May and his teammates (who had told him to stop griping) in June. He had to be dropped to the #7 spot in the order before he quit sulking and started working—when he did, he played very well. If Brett drives opposing pitchers half as crazy as he does me, he must be one hell of a distraction in a game.

—Geoff Beckman

	1986 SEASON											THREE YEARS (84 – 86)									
	Ave.	OBP	SLG	AB	H	2B	3B	HR	RBI	BB	SO	Ave.	OBP	SLG	AB	H	2B	3B	HR	RBI	BB	SO
Totals	.278	.356	.375	587	163	17	14	4	51	70	65	.286	.365	.387	1780	509	70	37	12	150	220	169
Batting vs. Left and Right-handed Pitchers																						
Left	.306	.390	.412	160	49	6	4	1	18	21	29	.311	.390	.401	543	169	21	11	2	47	69	68
Right	.267	.342	.361	427	114	11	10	3	33	49	36	.275	.354	.381	1237	340	49	26	10	103	151	101
At Home and on the Road																						
Home	.272	.360	.351	276	75	4	9	0	14	39	34	.294	.368	.381	862	253	27	21	2	59	103	75
Road	.283	.352	.395	311	88	13	5	4	37	31	31	.279	.362	.393	918	256	43	16	10	91	117	94
Facing Groundball Pitchers and Flyball Pitchers																						
Groundball	.285	.373	.370	270	77	9	4	2	26	37	22	.272	.358	.362	854	232	27	16	6	70	113	67
Flyball	.271	.341	.379	317	86	8	10	2	25	33	43	.299	.371	.410	926	277	43	21	6	80	107	102
Facing Finesse Pitchers and Power Pitchers																						
Finesse	.309	.380	.430	337	104	9	10	4	25	37	29	.305	.365	.420	1015	310	39	22	11	81	95	74
Power	.236	.324	.300	250	59	8	4	0	26	33	36	.260	.364	.344	765	199	31	15	1	69	125	95
On Grass and on Turf																						
Grass	.273	.349	.364	494	135	13	13	2	38	59	54	.284	.360	.383	1502	426	57	33	9	125	182	141
Turf	.301	.389	.430	93	28	4	1	2	13	11	11	.299	.388	.406	278	83	13	4	3	25	38	28
During the Day and at Night																						
Day	.249	.349	.348	181	45	5	5	1	17	27	28	.265	.349	.365	586	155	18	13	5	49	77	60
Night	.291	.359	.387	406	118	12	9	3	34	43	37	.296	.373	.398	1194	354	52	24	7	101	143	109
By Month																						
April	.242	.351	.394	66	16	5	1	1	4	11	4	.269	.361	.368	212	57	10	4	1	13	31	16
May	.235	.342	.286	98	23	3	1	0	10	17	10	.251	.336	.331	311	78	16	3	1	26	41	33
June	.236	.296	.321	106	25	3	3	0	7	9	11	.287	.360	.389	321	92	17	5	2	30	38	26
July	.318	.408	.459	85	27	3	3	1	9	13	12	.284	.354	.361	299	85	8	6	1	19	32	31
August	.226	.278	.274	106	24	0	1	1	6	7	16	.276	.351	.392	301	83	7	8	4	28	34	37
Sept/Oct	.381	.444	.508	126	48	3	5	1	15	13	12	.339	.419	.467	336	114	12	11	3	34	44	26
Situational																						
Bases Empty	.279	.346	.401	359	100	10	11	4	4	35	42	.278	.352	.389	1175	327	50	28	8	8	128	118
Leadoff	.280	.360	.440	168	47	9	6	2	2	21	22	.267	.337	.377	656	175	29	17	3	3	69	70
Not Leadoff	.277	.333	.366	191	53	1	5	2	2	14	20	.293	.370	.405	519	152	21	11	5	5	59	48
Runners On	.276	.370	.333	228	63	7	3	0	47	35	23	.301	.389	.383	605	182	20	9	4	142	92	51
First Base Only	.282	.358	.282	85	24	0	0	0	0	9	9	.276	.360	.333	246	68	3	4	1	7	29	19
Scoring Position	.273	.377	.364	143	39	7	3	0	47	26	14	.318	.407	.418	359	114	17	5	3	135	63	32
Late Innings, Close	.356	.396	.414	87	31	2	0	1	14	7	6	.266	.343	.310	274	73	7	1	1	25	33	25
RBI/Opportunities																						
Scoring Position				43 / 208	(21%)										125 / 537	(23%)						
Scoring Position, 2 Out				20 / 99	(20%)										46 / 219	(21%)						
On Third, Less than 2 Out				17 / 35	(49%)										54 / 97	(56%)						
RBI in close games / RBI Total				29 / 51	(57%)										95 / 150	(63%)						

Tom Candiotti
Cleveland Indians

In 1985, Tom Candiotti was on a treadmill to oblivion. Given two shots with Milwaukee in '83 and '84, he posted a 6–6 record wih a 3.99 ERA in 18 starts. Then, in spring training of 1985, he started experimenting with the knuckleball. Like many pitchers, he had thrown one when he was young—when he was warming up on the sidelines one day, he began throwing it as a joke. As he finished, he discovered that George Bamberger was staring at him in amazement. Bamberger told Tom to work on the pitch if he wanted to make the majors; down in Vancouver, he did just that. The only problem was that Milwaukee had too many young arms and too few roster spots—at the end of 1985, they released Candiotti.

Enter the Cleveland Indians, a team with no such problems. Desperate to find a pitcher worthy of the name, the Indians signed 37 castoffs in the spring of 1986. One was Candiotti, who had improved his knuckleball enough to win a job in the starting rotation. With help from Phil Niekro and the offense, Tom won 16 games. He was often the one who stopped a Cleveland losing streak and, by hurling a league-leading 17 complete games, gave the bullpen a much-needed rest.

Candiotti is hard to classify—he is in the majors because of the knuckler, but he doesn't always use it exclusively. At times, he mixes it in with a fastball and a curve; at others he throws it constantly, changing speeds on it to keep batters off balance. Tom throws harder than most knuckleball pitchers (some people call his pitch the "power knuckler")—the ball comes in looking like a straight fastball and then suddenly veers off—to devastating effect. Like all knuckleball pitchers, Candiotti is subject to bouts of periodic wildness but, because he has other pitches to fall back on, he can pitch out of trouble more easily and is more likely to stay in the game.

For some reason, many fans have labelled Candiotti's 1986 as a fluke. If you are one, bear this in mind: at 28, Tom became a regular starter sooner than either Phil (29) or Joe Niekro (31) or Charlie Hough (34) did. Had he pitched enough innings to qualify, he would have led the PCL in ERA in 1983 and been third in 1984. He is younger than Leibrandt, Thurmond or Show and has had as many good years—there is no reason to suspect that he won't continue to win in 1987.

—Jim Shaarda

1986: Finesse, Groundball **1985: Did not play** **1984: Finesse, Groundball**

| | 1986 SEASON | | | | | | | | | | | THREE YEARS (84 – 86) | | | | | | | | | | |
	G	IP	H	BB	SO	SB	CS	W	L	S	ERA	G	IP	H	BB	SO	SB	CS	W	L	S	ERA
Totals	36	252.1	234	106	167	28	10	16	12	0	3.57	44	284.2	272	116	190	31	11	18	14	0	3.76
At Home and on the Road
Home	19	137.0	129	56	96	14	7	10	6	0	3.35	23	153.2	144	56	108	14	7	12	6	0	3.22
Road	17	115.1	105	50	71	14	3	6	6	0	3.82	21	131.0	128	60	82	17	4	6	8	0	4.40
During the Day and at Night
Day	9	64.0	64	23	40	6	5	3	4	0	3.94	11	68.1	70	24	43	6	5	3	4	0	3.95
Night	27	188.1	170	83	127	22	5	13	8	0	3.44	33	216.1	202	92	147	25	6	15	10	0	3.70
On Grass and on Turf
Grass	30	208.1	185	91	130	21	10	15	9	0	3.15	37	238.0	219	97	152	24	10	17	10	0	3.25
Turf	6	44.0	49	15	37	7	0	1	3	0	5.52	7	46.2	53	19	38	7	1	1	4	0	6.36
By Month
April	5	27.2	16	21	24	3	0	1	2	0	2.28	5	27.2	16	21	24	3	0	1	2	0	2.28
May	5	32.2	33	17	24	5	2	2	3	0	4.68	5	32.2	33	17	24	5	2	2	3	0	4.68
June	8	45.0	55	18	39	6	5	3	1	0	4.60	8	45.0	55	18	39	6	5	3	1	0	4.60
July	5	40.1	38	11	21	4	0	4	1	0	2.90	8	53.0	54	16	27	4	1	5	2	0	3.74
August	6	50.0	41	21	21	4	2	3	2	0	3.42	6	50.0	41	21	21	4	2	3	2	0	3.42
Sept/Oct	7	56.2	51	18	38	6	1	3	3	0	3.34	12	76.1	73	23	55	9	1	4	4	0	3.66

vs. Opponent Batters

| | 1986 SEASON | | | | | | | | | | | THREE YEARS (84 – 86) | | | | | | | | | |
	Ave.	OBP	SLG	AB	H	2B	3B	HR	RBI	BB	SO	Ave.	OBP	SLG	AB	H	2B	3B	HR	RBI	BB	SO
Totals	.246	.324	.357	952	234	44	4	18	93	106	167	.250	.324	.367	1089	272	47	6	23	114	116	190
Pitching vs. Left and Right-handed Batters
Left	.237	.311	.334	497	118	19	4	7	45	56	74	.254	.321	.365	587	149	22	5	11	61	61	88
Right	.255	.337	.382	455	116	25	0	11	48	50	93	.245	.327	.371	502	123	25	1	12	53	55	102
Situational
Bases Empty	.264	.328	.400	537	142	27	2	14	14	48	103	.258	.322	.389	619	160	29	2	16	16	55	119
Leadoff	.285	.345	.418	239	68	15	1	5	5	20	45	.273	.337	.406	271	74	16	1	6	6	24	54
Not Leadoff	.248	.315	.386	298	74	12	1	9	9	28	58	.247	.311	.376	348	86	13	1	10	10	31	65
Runners On	.222	.318	.301	415	92	17	2	4	79	58	64	.238	.327	.338	470	112	18	4	7	98	61	71
First Base Only	.215	.284	.274	186	40	6	1	1	5	15	27	.229	.292	.294	214	49	6	1	2	7	16	29
Scoring Position	.227	.343	.323	229	52	11	1	3	74	43	37	.246	.353	.375	256	63	12	3	5	91	45	42
Late Innings, Close	.257	.345	.378	74	19	1	1	2	9	9	8	.291	.371	.430	86	25	1	1	3	10	10	9

RBI/Opportunities

Scoring Position	65 / 326 (20%)	79 / 363 (22%)
Scoring Position, 2 Out	23 / 148 (16%)	28 / 165 (17%)
On Third, Less than 2 Out	28 / 60 (47%)	34 / 71 (48%)
RBI in close games / RBI Total	61 / 93 (66%)	76 / 114 (67%)

Jose Canseco
Oakland A's

In 1986, the American League rookie crop was so strong that Pete Incaviglia hit 30 home runs and was not listed on any Rookie-of-the-Year ballot. Jose Canseco was the Rookie of the Year.

Canseco led the A's in RBI, runs, Game-Winning RBI, doubles and slugging percentage. In road games he slugged .528, which is in the Mattingly-Schmidt class. With the bases empty he hit just .182 with a .331 slugging percentage, while with men on base he hit .310 and slugged .609. He hit 22 of his 33 home runs with men on and hit .345 with men in scoring position. He hit well in the late innings of close games. He missed leading the league in RBI only because of a hand injury that took him out of the last week of the season.

Canseco runs relatively well, and could develop into a good outfielder. Canseco and Kirby Puckett were the only major leaguers to hit 30 homers and steal 15 bases, but he committed 14 errors, as many as any major league outfielder. His range factor (2.08) was average, and although he has a strong arm, he had only four assists, probably because most of his throws are wild. The A's may hire Joe Rudi to work with him on his defense.

Jose tinkers with his stance constantly, and has trouble with outside pitches because of his extreme open crouch. At the start of the season he was driving the ball to the opposite field as far as Reggie Jackson used to pull it, but in August he went through a terrible slump when (depending on who you believe) he started putting on a show in batting practice and picked up bad habits, or, upon the advice of coaches, he started pulling everything. He hit for average in the minor leagues, and has enough natural talent to hit .300 with power. The addition of Jim Lefebvre as hitting coach could help.

Canseco hit markedly better at night, which is unusual in the Coliseum. The A's will have more night games in 1987, which may help Jose although it will hurt most of the other hitters.

Jose handled the pressure of stardom well for a 21-year-old. He is even-tempered and doesn't get excited about much, at least in public. Even the 0 for 40 slump was taken in stride, which gives an indication of how he will handle himself over what must be expected to be a long career.

—Susan Nelson and Bill Weydig

| | 1986 SEASON | | | | | | | | | | | | THREE YEARS (84 – 86) | | | | | | | | | |
	Ave.	OBP	SLG	AB	H	2B	3B	HR	RBI	BB	SO		Ave.	OBP	SLG	AB	H	2B	3B	HR	RBI	BB	SO
Totals	.240	.318	.457	600	144	29	1	33	117	65	175		.249	.320	.461	696	173	32	1	38	130	69	206
Batting vs. Left and Right-handed Pitchers																							
Left	.281	.323	.470	185	52	11	0	8	35	13	44		.277	.317	.460	213	59	12	0	9	39	14	52
Right	.222	.316	.451	415	92	18	1	25	82	52	131		.236	.321	.462	483	114	20	1	29	91	55	154
At Home and on the Road																							
Home	.213	.296	.385	301	64	10	0	14	54	34	82		.228	.306	.416	346	79	11	0	18	62	37	98
Road	.268	.340	.528	299	80	19	1	19	63	31	93		.269	.333	.506	350	94	21	1	20	68	32	108
Facing Groundball Pitchers and Flyball Pitchers																							
Groundball	.242	.331	.447	273	66	12	1	14	48	34	62		.252	.333	.457	322	81	13	1	17	54	37	78
Flyball	.239	.307	.465	327	78	17	0	19	69	31	113		.246	.308	.465	374	92	19	0	21	76	32	128
Facing Finesse Pitchers and Power Pitchers																							
Finesse	.258	.322	.468	361	93	14	1	20	64	33	84		.269	.325	.466	412	111	16	1	21	69	33	96
Power	.213	.313	.439	239	51	15	0	13	53	32	91		.218	.312	.454	284	62	16	0	17	61	36	110
On Grass and on Turf																							
Grass	.228	.312	.440	496	113	19	1	28	95	57	143		.241	.316	.453	581	140	22	1	33	107	60	171
Turf	.298	.348	.538	104	31	10	0	5	22	8	32		.287	.339	.504	115	33	10	0	5	23	9	35
During the Day and at Night																							
Day	.207	.307	.394	241	50	9	0	12	47	30	72		.210	.304	.399	271	57	9	0	14	50	32	85
Night	.262	.326	.499	359	94	20	1	21	70	35	103		.273	.330	.501	425	116	23	1	24	80	37	121
By Month																							
April	.267	.396	.493	75	20	2	0	5	19	16	26		.267	.396	.493	75	20	2	0	5	19	16	26
May	.275	.355	.596	109	30	5	0	10	27	13	36		.275	.355	.596	109	30	5	0	10	27	13	36
June	.241	.331	.444	108	26	10	0	4	20	15	30		.241	.331	.444	108	26	10	0	4	20	15	30
July	.267	.309	.396	101	27	1	0	4	17	7	30		.267	.309	.396	101	27	1	0	4	17	7	30
August	.168	.211	.366	101	17	6	1	4	16	4	31		.168	.211	.366	101	17	6	1	4	16	4	31
Sept/Oct	.226	.314	.443	106	24	5	0	6	18	10	22		.262	.321	.465	202	53	8	0	11	31	14	53
Situational																							
Bases Empty	.182	.277	.331	329	60	14	1	11	11	39	113		.198	.283	.366	383	76	17	1	15	15	41	132
Leadoff	.197	.279	.311	132	26	6	0	3	3	14	45		.224	.301	.385	156	35	7	0	6	6	16	53
Not Leadoff	.173	.276	.345	197	34	8	1	8	8	25	68		.181	.271	.352	227	41	10	1	9	9	25	79
Runners On	.310	.368	.609	271	84	15	0	22	106	26	62		.310	.364	.578	313	97	15	0	23	115	28	74
First Base Only	.268	.313	.610	123	33	6	0	12	29	7	28		.260	.303	.568	146	38	6	0	13	31	8	36
Scoring Position	.345	.408	.608	148	51	9	0	10	77	19	34		.353	.412	.587	167	59	9	0	10	84	20	38
Late Innings, Close	.289	.349	.557	97	28	8	0	6	29	9	28		.300	.358	.536	110	33	8	0	6	31	10	31
RBI/Opportunities																							
Scoring Position				61 / 204		(30%)										68 / 226		(30%)					
Scoring Position, 2 Out				23 / 85		(27%)										25 / 95		(26%)					
On Third, Less than 2 Out				21 / 37		(57%)										23 / 40		(57%)					
RBI in close games / RBI Total				87 / 117		(74%)										94 / 130		(72%)					

Don Carman
Philadelphia Phillies

After a six-year apprenticeship and two brief trials with the Phillies, Don Carman established himself as a major leaguer in 1985. His work as a lefthanded set-up man was outstanding: 71 appearances, a 9–4 record with 7 saves, a 2.08 ERA, 87 strikeouts in 86 innings. Carman resumed the same role when the '86 campaign began, but this time he struggled, carrying an ERA of around 5.00 into July. Out of desperation as much as anything, the Phils decided to try him as a starter. The result was a complete turnaround: Carman was 7–4 over the last three months, with an ERA well below 3.00, and came within an eyelash of a no-hitter against the Giants. A strong finish (3–0, 1.73 in September) underscored how well Don had adapted to the change.

As the '87 season approaches, the Phillies would obviously like to keep Carman as a starter, where they need him most. But there's concern about whether his shoulder, which was bothering him at the end of the year, is strong enough to handle the strain of a starting job. It's a little confusing. First there was medical advice given that Carman's shoulder muscles were "too loose," or something (was his arm falling out of its socket?), and better suited for bullpen

work. So the Phils announced that Carman was going back to the pen. Then another opinion was given, to the effect that starting was no big deal, that Don's shoulder could handle it. Now everyone seems a little confused. The Phillies would much prefer to use Carman as a starter . . . they're just not sure it's a good idea. No doubt we'll unravel this mystery—hopefully without unraveling Carman's shoulder—in the spring.

While Carman has pitched well in each of his two full major league seasons, his work thus far has shown no consistent pattern. In '85 he was unhittable at home (6–0, 1.05), good but not spectacular on the road (3–4, 3.09); in '86 it was 6–2, 3.90 at home, 5–3, 2.54 road. In '85 his daytime ERA was 2.49; in '86 it was 5.11. He showed little grass/turf variation in '85, but was much better on grass in '86. He was dynamite in late inning clutch situations in '85, struggled in the same role in '86. In each year he showed a good, live fastball, though, and did his strongest work late in the season. If his shoulder is okay, there's every reason to think he'll be effective in '87.

—Don Zminda

1986: Power, Flyball   **1985: Power, Flyball**   **1984: Power, Flyball**

	1986 SEASON											THREE YEARS (84 – 86)										
	G	IP	H	BB	SO	SB	CS	W	L	S	ERA	G	IP	H	BB	SO	SB	CS	W	L	S	ERA
Totals	50	134.1	113	52	98	22	11	10	5	1	3.22	132	234.0	179	96	201	32	17	19	10	8	2.92
At Home and on the Road																						
Home	23	67.0	60	29	57	7	8	6	2	1	3.90	63	118.2	88	48	106	13	10	12	2	5	2.96
Road	27	67.1	53	23	41	15	3	4	3	0	2.54	69	115.1	91	48	95	19	7	7	8	3	2.89
During the Day and at Night																						
Day	11	24.2	21	11	25	4	1	1	0	0	5.11	34	50.1	38	22	54	4	4	3	2	1	3.75
Night	39	109.2	92	41	73	18	10	9	5	1	2.79	98	183.2	141	74	147	28	13	16	8	7	2.70
On Grass and on Turf																						
Grass	14	35.2	26	11	23	2	2	2	1	0	2.52	34	56.2	40	19	50	4	4	4	3	1	2.70
Turf	36	98.2	87	41	75	20	9	8	4	1	3.47	98	177.1	139	77	151	28	13	15	7	7	2.99
By Month																						
April	6	9.0	9	3	10	0	0	0	0	0	5.00	15	15.0	15	5	12	2	0	0	0	0	3.00
May	11	13.0	13	7	8	0	1	2	0	0	5.54	24	25.2	18	12	19	3	1	2	0	1	3.51
June	16	14.2	17	9	16	9	1	1	1	1	4.30	29	33.0	26	16	36	10	2	3	2	2	3.55
July	6	22.0	19	6	13	3	3	2	1	0	2.05	23	45.1	40	18	35	5	6	3	4	1	3.18
August	7	49.2	35	20	36	7	3	2	3	0	3.26	18	64.1	41	28	47	8	3	5	4	2	2.80
Sept/Oct	4	26.0	20	7	15	3	3	3	0	0	1.73	23	50.2	39	17	52	4	5	6	0	2	2.13

	vs. Opponent Batters																				
	1986 SEASON										THREE YEARS (84 – 86)									
	Ave.	OBP	SLG	AB	H	2B	3B	HR	RBI	BB	SO	Ave.	OBP	SLG	AB	H	2B	3B	HR	RBI	BB	SO
Totals	.234	.311	.359	482	113	23	2	11	42	52	98	.216	.299	.334	829	179	31	5	19	86	96	201
Pitching vs. Left and Right-handed Batters																						
Left	.233	.289	.389	90	21	5	0	3	10	5	18	.222	.278	.340	194	43	7	2	4	24	12	44
Right	.235	.316	.352	392	92	18	2	8	32	47	80	.214	.305	.332	635	136	24	3	15	62	84	157
Situational																						
Bases Empty	.247	.308	.398	299	74	13	1	10	10	25	55	.218	.288	.341	496	108	15	2	14	14	47	123
Leadoff	.279	.343	.385	122	34	7	0	2	2	12	14	.251	.321	.365	203	51	8	0	5	5	21	40
Not Leadoff	.226	.283	.407	177	40	6	1	8	8	13	41	.195	.265	.324	293	57	7	2	9	9	26	83
Runners On	.213	.316	.295	183	39	10	1	1	32	27	43	.213	.313	.324	333	71	16	3	5	72	49	78
First Base Only	.191	.226	.247	89	17	2	0	1	4	4	21	.187	.233	.267	150	28	3	0	3	8	9	36
Scoring Position	.234	.385	.340	94	22	8	1	0	28	23	22	.235	.368	.372	183	43	13	3	2	64	40	42
Late Innings, Close	.288	.367	.371	132	38	9	1	0	16	17	28	.215	.305	.294	340	73	12	3	3	34	45	88

	RBI/Opportunities					
Scoring Position	26 / 144	(18%)		56 / 291	(19%)
Scoring Position, 2 Out	12 / 67	(18%)		30 / 143	(21%)
On Third, Less than 2 Out	8 / 28	(29%)		17 / 51	(33%)
RBI in close games / RBI Total	32 / 42	(76%)		51 / 86	(59%)

Gary Carter
New York Mets

In many ways 1986 was Gary Carter's worst season as a regular, yet he finished third in the MVP voting. Carter's RBI and runs scored totals were excellent, but those figures were partly the result of playing for a high-scoring team; in other respects his numbers were way off. Carter's .255 batting average was his lowest in five seasons, his home run total of 24 his lowest in three and his 14 doubles the fewest he'd hit since 1976, when he played in only 91 games. How many players are good enough to have an off-season, yet still be considered the third most valuable player in the league? Not many.

The fact of the matter is that Gary Carter is a very special player, and if his knees can hold up for a few more seasons, he'll be remembered as one of the greatest catchers in baseball history. No catcher in the game today can be called his peer—Lance Parrish lacks the ability to get on base, Tony Pena lacks both power and on-base ability, Rich Gedman still needs to improve defensively, and Jody Davis is a notch below the rest. Compare the five offesively, with career stats based on 162 games:

	AB	H	D	T	HR	R	BI	BB	BA	OBA	SA
Carter	582	158	28	2	26	81	96	65	.271	.345	.460
Pena	588	168	29	3	13	63	70	36	.286	.327	.412
Parrish	604	159	28	3	30	82	99	47	.263	.316	.469
J. Davis	551	140	29	2	20	57	80	41	.254	.313	.423
Gedman	526	144	33	3	17	60	71	37	.274	.321	.445

Offensively, Carter would have to rate the best all-around, despite the fact that's he played for teams with poor hitters' parks throughout his career; the others have benefitted from their home parks. Defensively it would be a toss-up between Carter, Parrish and Pena; Gedman and Davis (despite his strong throwing arm) lag behind the others in this category.

Carter has a reputation for being extremely tough in the clutch, and his clutch figures for '86, plus his post-season performance, did nothing to dispel the notion. Carter also did well with runners in scoring position. He may not win any popularity contests, but Gary Carter is one great ballplayer.

—Kent Kirchstein

	1986 SEASON											THREE YEARS (84 – 86)										
	Ave.	OBP	SLG	AB	H	2B	3B	HR	RBI	BB	SO	Ave.	OBP	SLG	AB	H	2B	3B	HR	RBI	BB	SO
Totals	.255	.337	.439	490	125	14	2	24	105	62	63	.278	.357	.473	1641	456	63	4	83	311	195	167
Batting vs. Left and Right-handed Pitchers																						
Left	.275	.397	.480	171	47	5	0	10	33	37	16	.315	.412	.535	546	172	28	1	30	101	95	36
Right	.245	.301	.417	319	78	9	2	14	72	25	47	.259	.327	.442	1095	284	35	3	53	210	100	131
At Home and on the Road																						
Home	.268	.352	.478	228	61	5	2	13	51	33	28	.279	.369	.470	777	217	27	2	39	143	108	77
Road	.244	.323	.405	262	64	9	0	11	54	29	35	.277	.345	.476	864	239	36	2	44	168	87	90
Facing Groundball Pitchers and Flyball Pitchers																						
Groundball	.265	.356	.447	219	58	4	0	12	49	32	25	.287	.366	.443	783	225	22	2	32	135	91	68
Flyball	.247	.321	.432	271	67	10	2	12	56	30	38	.269	.348	.500	858	231	41	2	51	176	104	99
Facing Finesse Pitchers and Power Pitchers																						
Finesse	.255	.315	.433	275	70	9	2	12	55	26	28	.270	.334	.478	929	251	35	4	50	170	84	78
Power	.256	.363	.447	215	55	5	0	12	50	36	35	.288	.385	.466	712	205	28	0	33	141	111	89
On Grass and on Turf																						
Grass	.263	.342	.481	312	82	7	2	19	73	41	41	.279	.356	.490	857	239	22	3	51	181	105	100
Turf	.242	.327	.365	178	43	7	0	5	32	21	22	.277	.358	.454	784	217	41	1	32	130	90	67
During the Day and at Night																						
Day	.294	.382	.497	163	48	6	0	9	34	23	18	.274	.354	.479	583	160	27	1	30	112	67	64
Night	.235	.314	.410	327	77	8	2	15	71	39	45	.280	.358	.470	1058	296	36	3	53	199	128	103
By Month																						
April	.281	.364	.469	64	18	3	0	3	19	10	6	.280	.371	.473	207	58	13	0	9	46	29	24
May	.200	.300	.412	85	17	3	0	5	13	12	16	.239	.333	.436	264	63	13	0	13	50	36	40
June	.279	.362	.465	86	24	1	0	5	22	13	9	.303	.371	.502	287	87	7	1	16	44	30	21
July	.228	.324	.380	92	21	2	0	4	19	12	13	.261	.330	.434	295	77	10	1	13	59	29	25
August	.232	.323	.411	56	13	2	1	2	14	6	10	.276	.361	.449	254	70	9	1	11	47	33	29
Sept/Oct	.299	.347	.486	107	32	3	1	5	18	9	9	.302	.374	.530	334	101	11	1	21	65	38	28
Situational																						
Bases Empty	.250	.324	.425	228	57	8	1	10	10	24	27	.268	.332	.463	833	223	28	3	43	43	74	84
Leadoff	.270	.331	.432	111	30	6	0	4	4	9	15	.299	.345	.499	411	123	16	0	22	22	26	40
Not Leadoff	.231	.318	.419	117	27	2	1	6	6	15	12	.237	.319	.429	422	100	12	3	21	21	48	44
Runners On	.260	.347	.450	262	68	6	1	14	95	38	36	.288	.380	.483	808	233	35	1	40	268	121	83
First Base Only	.224	.296	.439	98	22	3	0	6	14	9	13	.251	.311	.476	307	77	15	0	18	41	22	27
Scoring Position	.280	.373	.457	164	46	3	1	8	81	29	23	.311	.417	.487	501	156	20	1	22	227	99	56
Late Innings, Close	.318	.406	.443	88	28	2	0	3	13	10	15	.282	.357	.430	298	84	11	0	11	42	31	40
RBI/Opportunities																						
Scoring Position				66 / 240		(28%)									185 / 717		(26%)					
Scoring Position, 2 Out				19 / 104		(18%)									68 / 348		(20%)					
On Third, Less than 2 Out				31 / 52		(60%)									72 / 128		(56%)					
RBI in close games / RBI Total				70 / 105		(67%)									208 / 311		(67%)					

Joe Carter
Cleveland Indians

It's difficult for me to talk about Joe Carter without lapsing into superlatives. There doesn't seem to be anything he can't do or couldn't learn. 1986 won't be his best season; he's easily capable of more. If Carter's health holds out and he keeps maturing, he'll be one of the ten best players in baseball.

Carter has great strength, quickness and flexibility, and his stance allows him to use it all. He stands well back in the box, digging in with his back foot and bringing his arms up and away from his body. When he swings, he pushes off hard (exactly like the track star he once was) with his back leg and whips his arms around. He can hit any pitch to any spot, which leads to a problem.

The fact that Joe can hit anything means that he isn't picky. He won't look for any pitch (even if a pitcher is relying on it almost exclusively in the game) and he never bothers to work the count to his advantage unless there are two outs—the pitchers he hits best are the ones who throw the most strikes. It is a tribute to Joe's natural ability that he led the league in RBIs, despite the fact that he swings at

anything (see his walk totals with men on first), but he'd do even better if pitchers knew that they had to throw strikes to get him out.

In the field, Carter is an adventure. He has the tools to be a fine fielder and the desire to excel, but he dislikes not being involved in every play and often has lapses of concentration in the outfield. It would be a shame to waste his agility, speed and arm at first base, so Cleveland is hoping that he can learn to keep his mind in the game.

The only question mark about Joe are his knees. He depends heavily on them to hit—when they are bothering him, he has problems. He had surgery in the winter of '84 and didn't get his stroke back until August of 1985; he admits to having trouble in cold weather. Cleveland may need to shift him to first to keep him out of trouble in the future.

Joe is an exuberant player, but a serious young man, which bodes well for his future. He has expressed a desire to learn the fine points of the game and is beginning to do just that. I expect him to win an MVP award someday and appreciate the fact that he allows me to watch him play.

—Geoff Beckman

	1986 SEASON											THREE YEARS (84 – 86)										
	Ave.	OBP	SLG	AB	H	2B	3B	HR	RBI	BB	SO	Ave.	OBP	SLG	AB	H	2B	3B	HR	RBI	BB	SO
Totals	.302	.335	.514	663	200	36	9	29	121	32	95	.283	.317	.469	1396	395	69	10	57	221	68	217
Batting vs. Left and Right-handed Pitchers																						
Left	.315	.354	.530	181	57	10	4	7	34	12	36	.293	.334	.504	427	125	20	5	20	69	27	83
Right	.297	.327	.508	482	143	26	5	22	87	20	59	.279	.310	.454	969	270	49	5	37	152	41	134
At Home and on the Road																						
Home	.312	.350	.522	324	101	16	5	14	51	19	46	.296	.338	.483	696	206	34	6	28	101	43	115
Road	.292	.320	.507	339	99	20	4	15	70	13	49	.270	.296	.456	700	189	35	4	29	120	25	102
Facing Groundball Pitchers and Flyball Pitchers																						
Groundball	.309	.334	.521	311	96	19	1	15	54	11	36	.283	.309	.453	644	182	36	1	24	93	24	88
Flyball	.295	.335	.509	352	104	17	8	14	67	21	59	.283	.324	.483	752	213	33	9	33	128	44	129
Facing Finesse Pitchers and Power Pitchers																						
Finesse	.313	.335	.544	384	120	23	6	18	68	11	36	.291	.316	.492	805	234	43	7	35	127	29	90
Power	.287	.334	.473	279	80	13	3	11	53	21	59	.272	.318	.438	591	161	26	3	22	94	39	127
On Grass and on Turf																						
Grass	.297	.331	.504	556	165	29	7	24	96	27	81	.287	.322	.480	1163	334	58	8	50	186	58	184
Turf	.327	.357	.570	107	35	7	2	5	25	5	14	.262	.293	.416	233	61	11	2	7	35	10	33
During the Day and at Night																						
Day	.310	.349	.551	216	67	9	5	11	45	14	41	.291	.327	.500	474	138	24	6	21	84	27	84
Night	.298	.328	.497	447	133	27	4	18	76	18	54	.279	.312	.453	922	257	45	4	36	137	41	133
By Month																						
April	.250	.299	.431	72	18	1	0	4	10	5	14	.221	.265	.377	122	27	4	0	5	18	8	31
May	.294	.324	.441	102	30	4	1	3	19	6	17	.270	.296	.382	178	48	6	1	4	28	8	27
June	.349	.383	.578	109	38	8	1	5	23	4	13	.315	.363	.540	200	63	13	1	10	33	13	25
July	.330	.367	.518	112	37	7	1	4	16	6	11	.265	.294	.368	234	62	10	1	4	23	9	33
August	.256	.281	.511	133	34	6	2	8	22	4	16	.266	.300	.503	286	76	14	3	16	47	13	39
Sept/Oct	.319	.349	.563	135	43	10	4	5	31	7	24	.316	.347	.540	376	119	22	4	18	72	17	62
Situational																						
Bases Empty	.311	.347	.532	344	107	21	5	15	15	17	42	.273	.309	.468	750	205	32	6	34	34	35	113
Leadoff	.292	.325	.483	120	35	5	0	6	6	5	14	.279	.310	.482	272	76	7	0	16	16	9	42
Not Leadoff	.321	.359	.558	224	72	16	5	9	9	12	28	.270	.309	.460	478	129	25	6	18	18	26	71
Runners On	.292	.322	.495	319	93	15	4	14	106	15	53	.294	.326	.471	646	190	37	4	23	187	33	104
First Base Only	.291	.291	.575	127	37	6	3	8	23	0	17	.318	.338	.540	261	83	16	3	12	36	7	35
Scoring Position	.292	.339	.443	192	56	9	1	6	83	15	36	.278	.319	.423	385	107	21	1	11	151	26	69
Late Innings, Close	.315	.343	.511	92	29	3	3	3	21	4	19	.322	.348	.483	211	68	4	3	8	39	9	37
RBI/Opportunities																						
Scoring Position				68 / 244		(28%)									130 / 482		(27%)					
Scoring Position, 2 Out				24 / 94		(26%)									42 / 193		(22%)					
On Third, Less than 2 Out				31 / 63		(49%)									61 / 112		(54%)					
RBI in close games / RBI Total				85 / 121		(70%)									145 / 221		(66%)					

Jim Clancy
Toronto Blue Jays

Jim Clancy is an enigma in blue stirrups. He began experimenting with a slow curve in spring training, after discarding a terrible changeup. It worked wonders for a time, but his performance didn't improve as much as it should have and he finished the season at 14–14, much the same as he has in the past.

Clancy's problem had been a lack of diversity. He has a good fastball, but never had it under control (a typical example of a power pitcher with very low strikeout totals). His slider, though a wicked one, is the pitch that batters have waited for. With the curveball added to his arsenal, he now had a weapon to keep hitters off-stride; he used it with devastating results.

If you check the records below, you'll see that lefties have hit .264 against "Diamond Jim" in the past, while righties have recorded a .256 average. In 1986, southpaw hitters fell to .228, thanks largely to the curve and its underlying effects. The curve helped set up the slider (his out pitch)—if a hitter didn't expect the slider, he couldn't hit it. In the month of July, Clancy pitched as well as any starter in baseball and, at 12–5, seemed poised to be the first Blue Jay ever to win 20 games. But, sadly, he fell victim to a problem that has dogged many pitchers in the past.

It is difficult to throw both a slider and curve for strikes; the two pitches break differently and must be thrown to different spots. A slider (which breaks down and in) should be thrown high and outside; a curve must be thrown lower, to allow for its sail. Men who try to feature both pitches equally in a game often begin confusing the locations and having control problems. Few successful starters throw both; those that do will pick whichever one is working best that day, using the other only in spots.

When Clancy began relying on his curve more heavily, control problems ensued. By September, he couldn't get anything over the plate and paid the price for falling behind in the count. He lost all seven of his Sepetember starts and was a key reason for Toronto's collapse down the stretch.

Clancy's long term future is bleak. He feels that he is a top starter and has expressed the desire to be paid like one. But, unless he makes the necessary adjustments quickly, he's only a third or fourth starter. Given the presence of the pitching prospects in the system, expect Toronto to inject some new blood into the rotation within the next two years.

—David Driscoll

	1986: Finesse, Flyball											1985: Finesse, Flyball										1984: Power, Flyball
	1986 SEASON											**THREE YEARS (84 – 86)**									
	G	IP	H	BB	SO	SB	CS	W	L	S	ERA	G	IP	H	BB	SO	SB	CS	W	L	S	ERA
Totals	34	219.1	202	63	126	10	2	14	14	0	3.94	93	567.2	568	188	310	36	14	36	35	0	4.36
At Home and on the Road																						
Home	15	87.1	94	26	57	7	1	5	6	0	5.26	38	219.2	233	72	129	17	4	15	16	0	4.92
Road	19	132.0	108	37	69	3	1	9	8	0	3.07	55	348.0	335	116	181	19	10	21	19	0	4.01
During the Day and at Night																						
Day	13	81.1	65	29	43	4	1	6	4	0	3.21	35	197.1	197	77	92	14	4	12	13	0	4.38
Night	21	138.0	137	34	83	6	1	8	10	0	4.37	58	370.1	371	111	218	22	10	24	22	0	4.35
On Grass and on Turf																						
Grass	14	95.1	76	29	53	3	1	5	7	0	2.93	43	265.1	265	94	136	15	8	15	17	0	4.21
Turf	20	124.0	126	34	73	7	1	9	7	0	4.72	50	302.1	303	94	174	21	6	21	18	0	4.50
By Month																						
April	4	27.0	26	8	11	2	0	2	1	0	3.00	10	67.1	62	27	33	7	0	3	3	0	2.81
May	6	41.0	45	13	29	1	0	3	2	0	4.17	17	105.1	122	35	63	6	4	7	6	0	4.96
June	6	27.2	30	12	19	0	1	2	2	0	5.86	18	91.2	107	38	49	3	3	7	8	0	5.89
July	5	41.0	20	12	23	3	0	5	0	0	1.54	16	106.1	78	31	46	8	1	9	3	0	3.13
August	6	36.2	37	7	17	2	0	2	2	0	4.42	13	85.2	85	28	49	5	1	5	4	0	3.89
Sept/Oct	7	46.0	44	11	27	2	1	0	7	0	4.89	19	111.1	114	29	70	7	5	5	11	0	5.01

	vs. Opponent Batters																				
	1986 SEASON											**THREE YEARS (84 – 86)**									
	Ave.	OBP	SLG	AB	H	2B	3B	HR	RBI	BB	SO	Ave.	OBP	SLG	AB	H	2B	3B	HR	RBI	BB	SO
Totals	.243	.296	.373	832	202	28	4	24	90	63	126	.260	.318	.403	2184	568	90	15	64	246	188	310
Pitching vs. Left and Right-handed Batters																						
Left	.229	.287	.333	441	101	15	2	9	43	36	66	.264	.331	.385	1124	297	51	8	23	106	114	151
Right	.258	.307	.417	391	101	13	2	15	47	27	60	.256	.304	.422	1060	271	39	7	41	140	74	159
Situational																						
Bases Empty	.219	.281	.350	517	113	19	2	15	15	43	86	.246	.312	.380	1303	321	60	6	34	34	123	201
Leadoff	.250	.298	.386	220	55	9	0	7	7	15	28	.271	.326	.410	561	152	34	1	14	14	46	70
Not Leadoff	.195	.269	.323	297	58	10	2	8	8	28	58	.228	.302	.357	742	169	26	5	20	20	77	131
Runners On	.283	.321	.410	315	89	9	2	9	75	20	40	.280	.327	.437	881	247	30	9	30	212	65	109
First Base Only	.268	.325	.380	142	38	2	1	4	9	11	12	.288	.340	.421	420	121	11	6	11	29	30	39
Scoring Position	.295	.318	.434	173	51	7	1	5	66	9	28	.273	.316	.451	461	126	19	3	19	183	35	70
Late Innings, Close	.355	.414	.500	62	22	3	0	2	7	9	9	.357	.420	.470	168	60	7	0	4	19	18	19

RBI/Opportunities						
Scoring Position		57 / 218	(26%)		150 / 585	(26%)
Scoring Position, 2 Out		27 / 105	(26%)		70 / 280	(25%)
On Third, Less than 2 Out		16 / 33	(48%)		45 / 97	(46%)
RBI in close games / RBI Total		71 / 90	(79%)		185 / 246	(75%)

Jack Clark
St. Louis Cardinals

If "ifs" and "buts" were candied nuts, Jack Clark might have more than one heck of a Christmas. He might have an MVP trophy, and possibly a plaque in Cooperstown some day. IF Clark could stay healthy for an entire season, and IF Clark could play in a home park conducive to his style of hitting, and IF Clark were surrounded in the lineup by another power hitter or two, and IF . . . the list goes on. And these things have a merit of sorts, too. Clark has had more than his share of serious injuries in recent seasons. He'd probably be a household name if he played in Wrigley Field or Atlanta-Fulton County Stadium. And certainly he would be pitched around less if the Cardinals could come up with a good number five hitter. For five seasons (1981–85) Clark outhit Dale Murphy on the road, .294–.270, hit more home runs per 100 at bats (5.6–5.2), and drove in more runs per 100 at bats (19.7–16.5). To make a truly accurate comparison you'd need to exclude Clark's games in Atlanta and Murphy's in St. Louis, but these numbers do indicate that Clark is in Murphy's class as a hitter. Murphy will be in Cooperstown some day; Clark probably will not.

Clark has put up some impressive numbers, though, even if he hasn't gotten the notoriety he might have under different circumstances. And Busch Stadium is a good hitter's park. It may not be perfect for Clark, but he showed that he could do just fine there in the first half of '85, when only an injury (that word again) kept him from becoming Busch Stadium's first 30-home run man since Dick Allen in 1970.

After an amazing season on grass in 1985 (.392 average, .683 slugging, 35 RBIs in 34 games), Clark hit just .164 in 55 at bats on grass in '86, with only one extra-base hit. This is especially strange since all three West Coast teams play on grass and Clark hit .333 with with a .489 slugging percentage against these teams in '86. He simply did most of the damage on Busch Stadium's carpet.

Clark was having a decent year when he was injured in '86 despite the low average and RBI totals. He and Ozzie were the only Cardinals producing for most of early '86, and Clark was being pitched around ever more than usual; he was leading the league in walks with 45 when he was hurt. His secondary average was .384, while his offensive winning percentage was over .600.

—Russ Eagle

	1986 SEASON											THREE YEARS (84 – 86)										
	Ave.	OBP	SLG	AB	H	2B	3B	HR	RBI	BB	SO	Ave.	OBP	SLG	AB	H	2B	3B	HR	RBI	BB	SO
Totals	.237	.362	.422	232	55	12	2	9	23	45	61	.278	.394	.489	877	244	47	6	42	154	171	178
Batting vs. Left and Right-handed Pitchers																						
Left	.303	.415	.596	89	27	6	1	6	13	16	20	.310	.454	.584	281	87	16	2	19	55	75	46
Right	.196	.329	.315	143	28	6	1	3	10	29	41	.263	.364	.445	596	157	31	4	23	99	96	132
At Home and on the Road																						
Home	.274	.393	.453	117	32	7	1	4	12	23	32	.253	.368	.428	439	111	23	3	16	68	82	90
Road	.200	.331	.391	115	23	5	1	5	11	22	29	.304	.421	.550	438	133	24	3	26	86	89	88
Facing Groundball Pitchers and Flyball Pitchers																						
Groundball	.208	.320	.331	130	27	7	0	3	9	21	30	.289	.408	.476	429	124	25	2	17	71	87	76
Flyball	.275	.413	.539	102	28	5	2	6	14	24	31	.268	.381	.502	448	120	22	4	25	83	84	102
Facing Finesse Pitchers and Power Pitchers																						
Finesse	.288	.380	.505	111	32	9	0	5	10	16	18	.298	.395	.502	484	144	26	2	23	80	81	65
Power	.190	.347	.347	121	23	3	2	4	13	29	43	.254	.393	.473	393	100	21	4	19	74	90	113
On Grass and on Turf																						
Grass	.164	.281	.182	55	9	1	0	0	1	9	13	.313	.437	.528	335	105	12	3	18	73	74	54
Turf	.260	.386	.497	177	46	11	2	9	22	36	48	.256	.367	.465	542	139	35	3	24	81	97	124
During the Day and at Night																						
Day	.208	.339	.337	101	21	3	2	2	9	19	24	.268	.397	.459	388	104	17	3	17	68	82	76
Night	.260	.380	.489	131	34	9	0	7	14	26	37	.286	.392	.513	489	140	30	3	25	86	89	102
By Month																						
April	.231	.342	.446	65	15	3	1	3	5	11	18	.266	.389	.467	214	57	12	2	9	30	43	40
May	.276	.400	.391	87	24	4	0	2	8	18	22	.320	.422	.556	250	80	12	1	15	54	46	44
June	.200	.337	.438	80	16	5	1	4	10	16	21	.252	.368	.466	234	59	13	2	11	39	43	54
July	.000	.000	.000	0	0	0	0	0	0	0	0	.297	.414	.527	91	27	6	0	5	20	19	20
August	.000	.000	.000	0	0	0	0	0	0	0	0	.226	.372	.371	62	14	4	1	1	8	15	15
Sept/Oct	.000	.000	.000	0	0	0	0	0	0	0	0	.269	.387	.385	26	7	0	0	1	3	5	5
Situational																						
Bases Empty	.262	.347	.500	130	34	6	2	7	7	17	33	.291	.402	.518	444	129	23	3	24	24	81	90
Leadoff	.254	.342	.493	67	17	3	2	3	3	9	23	.292	.402	.561	212	62	12	3	13	13	38	43
Not Leadoff	.270	.352	.508	63	17	3	0	4	4	8	10	.289	.402	.478	232	67	11	0	11	11	43	47
Runners On	.206	.379	.324	102	21	6	0	2	16	28	28	.266	.386	.460	433	115	24	3	18	130	90	88
First Base Only	.256	.373	.419	43	11	1	0	2	4	8	10	.254	.328	.462	173	44	6	0	10	22	19	30
Scoring Position	.169	.383	.254	59	10	5	0	0	12	20	18	.273	.419	.458	260	71	18	3	8	108	71	58
Late Innings, Close	.245	.365	.396	53	13	3	1	1	3	10	15	.325	.452	.525	160	52	10	2	6	26	37	37
RBI/Opportunities																						
Scoring Position				11 / 90		(12%)									91 / 393		(23%)					
Scoring Position, 2 Out				4 / 48		(8%)									28 / 174		(16%)					
On Third, Less than 2 Out				4 / 11		(36%)									45 / 91		(49%)					
RBI in close games / RBI Total				17 / 23		(74%)									92 / 154		(60%)					

Will Clark
San Francisco Giants

Will missed 47 games after hyperextending his elbow, possibly costing him a Rookie-of-the-Year award. Nevertheless, the former Olympian won many fans around the league with his easygoing personality. He won the hearts of Giants fans early on, when he became the 53rd ML player (3rd SF Giant) to homer in his first at-bat, making his first go the distance off Nolan Ryan in the Astrodome. He electrified an opening-day Candlestick crowd with another home run. Most unusual of all, he homered in his first pro swing last year in Class-A ball.

The Giants improved 21 games over 1985—one of the half-dozen best season-to-season improvements in major-league baseball this century. They had the 4th highest scoring offense, improved defensively, and stole more bases than any Giants team in 67 years. They dropped from 121 GIDP in 1985 to 83 last year, best in the NL. Uribe was the toughest major-leaguer to double up, with only 2 GIDPs all season; Clark had only 3. Will says he frequently uses the first at-bat to try to learn a pitcher. His late inning stats seem to bear this out.

—J. Michael Duca

In the *1985 Abstract*, Bill James gave four players the tag of "Young McCoveys:" Alvin Davis, Kent Hrbek, Don Mattingly and Greg Walker. Of them, Mattingly has moved to the forefront by showing unexpected power, yet he is physically the smallest and didn't pull the ball often in the minors. Since James was comparing them to McCovey, a notorious pull hitter, I looked for some constant to get some sense of where they and Will Clark might be headed. Looking at the percentage of extra-base hits, both in the majors and the minors, Clark can be compared to these four and some other Giants power-hitters:

McCovey 41.6% (major-league XBH%), 41.1% (minor-league XBH%); Mattingly 35.8%, 26.9%; Walker 40.6%, 33.7%; Hrbek 35.3%, 31.8%; A. Davis 33.5%, 35.6%; W. Clark 34.2%, 35.8%; Mays 40.3%, 34.1%; Cepeda 35.0%, 34.7%; Hart 32.9%, 34.1%; Bonds 37.1%, 35.6%.

Clark's frequency rate is comparable to the other Giants stars in Candlestick. Clark's college XBH% is higher, but he has undergone a weight training program this winter.

Will Clark's home stats are excellent; what is holding him back is his road performance, especially on turf. Clark's stats also reflect the Giants' lack of success in turf parks.

Clark was very consistent in average with the bases empty, but he concentrated more in getting on base with runners on, the exception being late-inning situations.

—Victor Hester

	1986 SEASON											THREE YEARS (84 – 86)										
	Ave.	OBP	SLG	AB	H	2B	3B	HR	RBI	BB	SO	Ave.	OBP	SLG	AB	H	2B	3B	HR	RBI	BB	SO
Totals	.287	.343	.444	408	117	27	2	11	41	34	76	.287	.343	.444	408	117	27	2	11	41	34	76
Batting vs. Left and Right-handed Pitchers																						
Left	.308	.348	.415	130	40	8	0	2	14	8	27	.308	.348	.415	130	40	8	0	2	14	8	27
Right	.277	.341	.457	278	77	19	2	9	27	26	49	.277	.341	.457	278	77	19	2	9	27	26	49
At Home and on the Road																						
Home	.336	.388	.509	220	74	15	1	7	26	19	35	.336	.388	.509	220	74	15	1	7	26	19	35
Road	.229	.290	.367	188	43	12	1	4	15	15	41	.229	.290	.367	188	43	12	1	4	15	15	41
Facing Groundball Pitchers and Flyball Pitchers																						
Groundball	.292	.333	.386	202	59	10	0	3	21	13	35	.292	.333	.386	202	59	10	0	3	21	13	35
Flyball	.282	.352	.500	206	58	17	2	8	20	21	41	.282	.352	.500	206	58	17	2	8	20	21	41
Facing Finesse Pitchers and Power Pitchers																						
Finesse	.273	.335	.376	205	56	11	2	2	20	19	30	.273	.335	.376	205	56	11	2	2	20	19	30
Power	.300	.352	.512	203	61	16	0	9	21	15	46	.300	.352	.512	203	61	16	0	9	21	15	46
On Grass and on Turf																						
Grass	.315	.378	.482	311	98	21	2	9	33	31	61	.315	.378	.482	311	98	21	2	9	33	31	61
Turf	.196	.225	.320	97	19	6	0	2	8	3	15	.196	.225	.320	97	19	6	0	2	8	3	15
During the Day and at Night																						
Day	.273	.329	.412	194	53	11	2	4	17	16	37	.273	.329	.412	194	53	11	2	4	17	16	37
Night	.299	.356	.472	214	64	16	0	7	24	18	39	.299	.356	.472	214	64	16	0	7	24	18	39
By Month																						
April	.317	.374	.500	82	26	6	0	3	7	8	25	.317	.374	.500	82	26	6	0	3	7	8	25
May	.221	.283	.394	104	23	5	2	3	10	8	23	.221	.283	.394	104	23	5	2	3	10	8	23
June	.167	.286	.167	6	1	0	0	0	1	1	0	.167	.286	.167	6	1	0	0	0	1	1	0
July	.600	.667	1.000	5	3	2	0	0	0	1	1	.600	.667	1.000	5	3	2	0	0	0	1	1
August	.327	.370	.500	98	32	5	0	4	13	8	6	.327	.370	.500	98	32	5	0	4	13	8	6
Sept/Oct	.283	.339	.389	113	32	9	0	1	10	8	21	.283	.339	.389	113	32	9	0	1	10	8	21
Situational																						
Bases Empty	.316	.347	.480	250	79	16	2	7	7	11	44	.316	.347	.480	250	79	16	2	7	7	11	44
Leadoff	.313	.374	.422	83	26	4	1	1	1	7	10	.313	.374	.422	83	26	4	1	1	1	7	10
Not Leadoff	.317	.333	.509	167	53	12	1	6	6	4	34	.317	.333	.509	167	53	12	1	6	6	4	34
Runners On	.241	.337	.386	158	38	11	0	4	34	23	32	.241	.337	.386	158	38	11	0	4	34	23	32
First Base Only	.297	.338	.516	64	19	5	0	3	8	4	12	.297	.338	.516	64	19	5	0	3	8	4	12
Scoring Position	.202	.336	.298	94	19	6	0	1	26	19	20	.202	.336	.298	94	19	6	0	1	26	19	20
Late Innings, Close	.402	.457	.659	82	33	6	0	5	13	9	10	.402	.457	.659	82	33	6	0	5	13	9	10
RBI/Opportunities																						
Scoring Position				25 / 145		(17%)									25 / 145		(17%)					
Scoring Position, 2 Out				7 / 50		(14%)									7 / 50		(14%)					
On Third, Less than 2 Out				11 / 31		(35%)									11 / 31		(35%)					
RBI in close games / RBI Total				30 / 41		(73%)									30 / 41		(73%)					

Mark Clear
Milwaukee Brewers

Mark Clear is a manager's nightmare—an extremely talented "role pitcher." Clear has the ability to get any hitter out, but he must be used in a very particular way to do so, which makes it hard for him to contribute to many major league teams.

The problem with Clear has always been control. Mark throws a hard curve, which breaks down and in on a lefty hitter; if it stays in the strike zone, it is a fine "out pitch." The problem is that it rarely does—hitters can usually ignore it and wait for his fastball. A good pitcher strikes out about twice as many batters as he walks; 1986 is the only year that Mark has managed this feat.

Clear thrives on frequent work. He has an elaborate motion that falls apart if he doesn't work every two or three days—the more time he has between outings, the worse his control is. Clear has appeared in over 50 games three times in his career—those three years are easily his best. But Clear also tires easily. He can pitch to about five hitters effectively before he weakens—when he does, the curve flattens out and becomes easy to hit. The two problems combine to make him difficult to use effectively, which keeps him from being successful.

The manager who wishes to get the best from Clear must be willing to bring him into the game every few days, regardless of the score. The ideal situation is to let him work the ninth inning, but this poses two problems. Since Clear isn't capable of pitching many innings, the team must have another ace in the bullpen. And, if Clear gets into trouble in a close game, the other ace must replace him. This risks burning the other man out; few managers are willing to run that risk in exchange for the one good inning of work that Clear can provide. One of the few managers who will take that risk is George Bamberger. The teams he has worked for always have two or three men who have many appearances, but pitch very few innings—he has consistently been able to find these men (in 1986 he had Clear, Dan Plesac and John Henry Johnson) and use them effectively. Clear's 1986 is neither a surprise nor a fluke but, with Bamberger gone, he is highly unlikely to repeat it. If his new manager tries to change his role, he will immediately revert back to his past, journeyman form.

—Geoff Beckman

| 1986: Power, Groundball | | 1985: Power, Flyball | 1984: Power, Flyball |

	1986 SEASON											THREE YEARS (84 – 86)											
	G	IP	H	BB	SO	SB	CS	W	L	S	ERA		G	IP	H	BB	SO	SB	CS	W	L	S	ERA
Totals	59	73.2	53	36	85	4	4	5	5	16	2.20		147	196.1	145	156	216	38	5	14	11	27	3.25
At Home and on the Road																							
Home	31	42.0	25	17	48	2	4	5	2	6	0.86		70	97.0	65	61	113	19	4	9	3	12	2.51
Road	28	31.2	28	19	37	2	0	0	3	10	3.98		77	99.1	80	95	103	19	1	5	8	15	3.99
During the Day and at Night																							
Day	20	23.2	11	16	30	2	1	3	3	5	1.14		53	64.1	49	54	79	12	1	5	5	7	4.20
Night	39	50.0	42	20	55	2	3	2	2	11	2.70		94	132.0	96	102	137	26	4	9	6	20	2.80
On Grass and on Turf																							
Grass	51	64.2	41	31	74	4	4	5	4	13	1.53		125	168.0	123	130	188	32	5	14	8	21	3.16
Turf	8	9.0	12	5	11	0	0	0	1	3	7.00		22	28.1	22	26	28	6	0	0	3	6	3.81
By Month																							
April	6	6.1	6	4	9	0	1	0	1	1	1.42		20	23.0	23	22	25	2	1	2	1	1	4.70
May	9	12.1	8	6	20	3	0	2	1	2	0.73		25	32.1	20	24	37	9	0	3	2	2	1.95
June	7	8.2	7	12	9	0	2	0	1	2	4.15		20	30.0	22	39	29	11	3	3	2	3	3.00
July	10	13.1	6	5	14	0	0	0	1	2	2.03		28	44.2	28	21	50	9	0	1	2	6	2.42
August	14	20.0	11	5	19	1	1	3	0	5	0.00		31	38.2	27	34	43	6	1	4	2	10	2.79
Sept/Oct	13	13.0	15	4	14	0	0	0	1	4	6.23		23	27.2	25	16	32	1	0	1	2	5	5.86

| | vs. Opponent Batters | | | | | | | | | | | | | | | | | | | | | |

	1986 SEASON											THREE YEARS (84 – 86)									
	Ave.	OBP	SLG	AB	H	2B	3B	HR	RBI	BB	SO		Ave.	OBP	SLG	AB	H	2B	3B	HR	RBI	BB	SO
Totals	.201	.295	.280	264	53	5	2	4	31	36	85		.207	.352	.274	701	145	22	2	7	100	156	216
Pitching vs. Left and Right-handed Batters																						
Left	.189	.346	.226	106	20	1	0	1	11	25	35		.188	.374	.216	319	60	6	0	1	42	94	106
Right	.209	.256	.316	158	33	4	2	3	20	11	50		.223	.333	.322	382	85	16	2	6	58	62	110
Situational																						
Bases Empty	.218	.288	.293	133	29	4	0	2	2	13	43		.223	.370	.299	274	61	12	0	3	3	62	82
Leadoff	.185	.279	.222	54	10	2	0	0	0	7	20		.222	.388	.262	126	28	5	0	0	0	34	35
Not Leadoff	.241	.294	.342	79	19	2	0	2	2	6	23		.223	.354	.331	148	33	7	0	3	3	28	47
Runners On	.183	.302	.267	131	24	1	2	2	29	23	42		.197	.341	.258	427	84	10	2	4	97	94	134
First Base Only	.229	.351	.333	48	11	0	1	1	3	9	13		.204	.314	.248	137	28	1	1	1	3	21	39
Scoring Position	.157	.275	.229	83	13	1	1	1	26	14	29		.193	.353	.262	290	56	9	1	3	94	73	95
Late Innings, Close	.147	.253	.186	156	23	2	2	0	16	22	53		.204	.348	.269	324	66	11	2	2	51	73	109
RBI/Opportunities																						
Scoring Position			23 / 124		(19%)										86 / 492		(17%)					
Scoring Position, 2 Out			8 / 57		(14%)										31 / 228		(14%)					
On Third, Less than 2 Out			11 / 21		(52%)										37 / 92		(40%)					
RBI in close games / RBI Total			16 / 31		(52%)										54 / 100		(54%)					

Roger Clemens
Boston Red Sox

Roger Clemens's ERA in Fenway park was, for the first time in his career, only slightly higher than his road ERAs. Why did this happen? The answer is in his platoon splits.

A normal pitcher faces righty hitters twice as often as lefties—in 1985, American League pitchers faced a righty hitter 68.6% of the time. Since righthanders are supposedly the most able to take advantage of the "Green Monster," we can assume that they'll do the most damage in Fenway Park and that this is the reason that opposing batters hit well against Clemens in Fenway in the past.

Clemens, however, destroyed righty hitters in 1986—so much so that opposing managers were using as many lefties as they could fit into the lineup. Of the 997 men who faced Clemens in 1986, only 421 (42.2%) batted righty, which means two things: that Clemens didn't have to face as many batters who were capable of pulling him (assuming that anyone tried) and that he was facing some players who weren't normally in the lineup. By doing that, the opposition won the battle (lefty hitters hit Clemens more often), but Clemens (reports Chuck Waseleski) allowed only eight hits off the left field wall in 1986 and probably won the war.

The fascinating point about Clemens's 1986 is that the most universally accepted statement—that he was the dominant strikeout pitcher in the AL in 1986—isn't true. Mark Langston (245) won the strikeout title from Clemens (238). Of pitchers with over 155 innings pitched, Bret Saberhagen (3.86), Bert Blyleven (3.71), Mark Eichhorn (3.69) and Ron Guidry (3.68) had better strikeout to walk ratios than Clemens's 3.55. Clemens struck out 8.43 men per nine innings pitched, but that wasn't even best on his team—Bobby Witt (9.93), Eichhorn (9.52), Langston (9.21) and Bruce Hurst (8.62) finished above him. Clemens had a superb year and he struck out a lot of people, but he was arguably not the best strikeout pitcher in the league and certainly not in a class by himself.

The only thing that Clemens didn't do in 1986 was pitch a no-hitter—what were his chances of doing that? According to Waseleski, opposing hitters hit .204 with none out, .198 with one out and .184 with two out, so he had a 52% chance of pitching a hitless inning and a .28% chance (or 1 in 354) of a no-hitter.

—Patrick J. Hoye and Michael O'Donnell

1986: Power, Flyball   **1985: Power, Flyball**   **1984: Power, Groundball**

	1986 SEASON											THREE YEARS (84 – 86)										
	G	IP	H	BB	SO	SB	CS	W	L	S	ERA	G	IP	H	BB	SO	SB	CS	W	L	S	ERA
Totals	33	254.0	179	67	238	8	15	24	4	0	2.48	69	485.2	408	133	438	43	19	40	13	0	3.15
At Home and on the Road																						
Home	16	119.1	89	24	121	6	8	11	3	0	2.56	35	248.0	216	58	242	24	11	20	7	0	3.34
Road	17	134.2	90	43	117	2	7	13	1	0	2.41	34	237.2	192	75	196	19	8	20	6	0	2.95
During the Day and at Night																						
Day	9	72.0	46	21	70	2	3	8	0	0	2.00	23	156.1	123	46	146	14	7	14	4	0	2.88
Night	24	182.0	133	46	168	6	12	16	4	0	2.67	46	329.1	285	87	292	29	12	26	9	0	3.28
On Grass and on Turf																						
Grass	28	213.0	153	56	204	8	13	19	4	0	2.54	57	402.1	347	107	370	35	17	32	10	0	3.13
Turf	5	41.0	26	11	34	0	2	5	0	0	2.20	12	83.1	61	26	68	8	2	8	3	0	3.24
By Month																						
April	4	33.1	22	10	39	1	3	4	0	0	1.62	8	62.1	41	21	64	8	4	6	2	0	2.31
May	5	40.1	28	11	42	0	0	4	0	0	3.57	14	104.0	95	31	97	14	3	9	2	0	4.07
June	6	50.0	32	9	44	0	2	6	0	0	1.44	14	96.1	88	17	77	6	2	8	2	0	2.90
July	6	43.0	31	10	37	4	4	3	3	0	3.56	13	81.0	82	19	65	9	4	5	5	0	4.11
August	6	46.2	31	17	45	2	4	3	1	0	2.70	14	101.1	67	35	104	5	4	8	2	0	2.66
Sept/Oct	6	40.2	35	10	31	1	2	4	0	0	1.99	6	40.2	35	10	31	1	2	4	0	0	1.99

	1986 SEASON											THREE YEARS (84 – 86)									
	Ave.	OBP	SLG	AB	H	2B	3B	HR	RBI	BB	SO	Ave.	OBP	SLG	AB	H	2B	3B	HR	RBI	BB	SO
Totals	.195	.252	.306	916	179	34	2	21	67	67	238	.224	.279	.332	1818	408	67	6	39	158	133	438
Pitching vs. Left and Right-handed Batters																						
Left	.210	.274	.317	520	109	28	2	8	39	45	115	.230	.288	.322	1009	232	47	5	12	81	80	216
Right	.177	.221	.290	396	70	6	0	13	28	22	123	.218	.268	.345	809	176	20	1	27	77	53	222
Situational																						
Bases Empty	.192	.248	.302	599	115	23	2	13	13	42	160	.217	.270	.323	1140	247	46	3	23	23	77	280
Leadoff	.203	.262	.315	241	49	8	2	5	5	19	63	.222	.270	.333	472	105	13	3	11	11	29	113
Not Leadoff	.184	.240	.293	358	66	15	0	8	8	23	97	.213	.270	.316	668	142	33	0	12	12	48	167
Runners On	.202	.258	.312	317	64	11	0	8	54	25	78	.237	.293	.348	678	161	21	3	16	135	56	158
First Base Only	.215	.277	.368	163	35	4	0	7	17	13	42	.252	.304	.409	313	79	7	3	12	30	22	70
Scoring Position	.188	.238	.253	154	29	7	0	1	37	12	36	.225	.285	.296	365	82	14	0	4	105	34	88
Late Innings, Close	.212	.266	.314	118	25	3	0	3	9	9	27	.263	.306	.386	171	45	6	0	5	16	11	33

RBI/Opportunities					
Scoring Position	36 / 198	(18%)	97 / 469	(21%)
Scoring Position, 2 Out	15 / 103	(15%)	43 / 231	(19%)
On Third, Less than 2 Out	14 / 21	(67%)	34 / 65	(52%)
RBI in close games / RBI Total	36 / 67	(54%)	105 / 158	(66%)

Vince Coleman
St. Louis Cardinals

The famous trivia question "Who was Harry Steinfeldt?" can now be amended to read, "Who was Harry Steinfeldt, and what record does he share with Vince Coleman?" A stolen base record, right? Well, Harry was a decent base stealer, swiping 194 during his career. He played, of course, in an era when the stolen base flourished. But Harry never set any stolen base records. He was a good RBI man too, however, and in 1909 he set a major league record with three sacrifice flies in one game, a record that still stands. It has been tied a number of times, the last player to do so being Russ Nixon in 1965. That is, the last until Coleman delivered three on May 1, 1986 against San Diego. Going into the game, Vince had only one career sacrifice fly in 714 at bats. So to all the critics who claim Vince is a one-dimensional player . . . .

Of course Coleman isn't paid to drive in runs; his job is to get on base and score runs. He hasn't mastered the former, but as to the latter he has shown an amazing ability to score once he reaches. For his career Coleman is averaging .480 runs scored per time reached base (by hit or walk), which exceeds the career marks of both Rickey Henderson (.455) and Tim Raines (.403). Contributing to this success

has been Coleman's ability to force opposing pitchers to commit balks, something he did twenty times in 1986. More than eleven per cent of all balks committed in the National League last season came with Coleman on base.

Of course the stolen bases kept coming, too. Coleman's 88% success rate was the second highest ever for a player with 100 or more steals, only a percentage point behind Maury Wills. He established a club record with a string of 28 consecutive steals, and moved up to second on the all-time Cardinal list with 217, trailing only Brock (888). He'll continue to set records if he can learn to get on base. Coleman did show improvement in this area early in 1986, compiling a .294 average and an OBP of .361 through June 8. He then went into an 0-for-38 skid, however, and never seemed to recover.

Vince hit .415 and slugged .488 against Cincinnati in 1986, easily his best performance against one team. The only other team he hit .300 against was Pittsburgh, and that was an even .300. Coleman stole 20 bases against Philadelphia despite a .176 average. He had 26 multiple-steal games in 1986.

—Russ Eagle

	1986 SEASON											THREE YEARS (84 – 86)										
	Ave.	OBP	SLG	AB	H	2B	3B	HR	RBI	BB	SO	Ave.	OBP	SLG	AB	H	2B	3B	HR	RBI	BB	SO
Totals	.232	.301	.280	600	139	13	8	0	29	60	98	.250	.311	.308	1236	309	33	18	1	69	110	213
Batting vs. Left and Right-handed Pitchers																						
Left	.238	.327	.278	227	54	5	2	0	11	31	31	.237	.307	.308	438	104	15	8	0	24	45	70
Right	.228	.285	.282	373	85	8	6	0	18	29	67	.257	.313	.308	798	205	18	10	1	45	65	143
At Home and on the Road																						
Home	.269	.345	.316	320	86	5	5	0	13	36	56	.287	.351	.351	635	182	16	11	1	35	61	96
Road	.189	.250	.239	280	53	8	3	0	16	24	42	.211	.269	.263	601	127	17	7	0	34	49	117
Facing Groundball Pitchers and Flyball Pitchers																						
Groundball	.234	.306	.275	316	74	7	3	0	9	31	37	.276	.335	.337	602	166	18	8	1	26	52	83
Flyball	.229	.297	.285	284	65	6	5	0	20	29	61	.226	.288	.281	634	143	15	10	0	43	58	130
Facing Finesse Pitchers and Power Pitchers																						
Finesse	.219	.287	.255	333	73	8	2	0	11	31	43	.259	.311	.316	702	182	20	10	0	34	53	103
Power	.247	.319	.311	267	66	5	6	0	18	29	55	.238	.310	.298	534	127	13	8	1	35	57	110
On Grass and on Turf																						
Grass	.158	.231	.187	139	22	2	1	0	8	14	21	.214	.263	.268	313	67	7	5	0	20	22	63
Turf	.254	.323	.308	461	117	11	7	0	21	46	77	.262	.327	.322	923	242	26	13	1	49	88	150
During the Day and at Night																						
Day	.249	.314	.343	213	53	8	6	0	16	22	38	.240	.301	.323	458	110	14	12	0	28	42	82
Night	.222	.294	.245	387	86	5	2	0	13	38	60	.256	.317	.299	778	199	19	6	1	41	68	131
By Month																						
April	.231	.302	.321	78	18	3	2	0	4	8	14	.258	.326	.352	128	33	6	3	0	9	13	20
May	.319	.380	.394	94	30	1	3	0	10	11	15	.288	.348	.369	198	57	5	4	1	15	20	36
June	.216	.303	.268	97	21	1	2	0	3	11	16	.232	.312	.280	207	48	2	4	0	9	23	32
July	.210	.292	.250	100	21	4	0	0	5	11	13	.250	.312	.315	200	50	7	3	0	8	18	35
August	.267	.320	.284	116	31	2	0	0	5	9	17	.268	.306	.318	239	64	6	3	0	11	13	47
Sept/Oct	.157	.222	.191	115	18	2	1	0	2	10	23	.216	.278	.250	264	57	7	1	0	17	23	43
Situational																						
Bases Empty	.241	.316	.287	407	98	11	4	0	0	44	67	.258	.323	.316	849	219	24	11	1	1	80	154
Leadoff	.250	.317	.303	264	66	8	3	0	0	25	46	.268	.334	.331	541	145	18	8	0	0	53	102
Not Leadoff	.224	.315	.259	143	32	3	1	0	0	19	21	.240	.301	.289	308	74	6	3	1	1	27	52
Runners On	.212	.270	.264	193	41	2	4	0	29	16	31	.233	.285	.292	387	90	9	7	0	68	30	59
First Base Only	.235	.257	.250	68	16	1	0	0	1	2	7	.215	.248	.267	135	29	5	1	0	2	6	16
Scoring Position	.200	.276	.272	125	25	1	4	0	28	14	24	.242	.304	.306	252	61	4	6	0	66	24	43
Late Innings, Close	.235	.313	.287	115	27	4	1	0	12	14	17	.230	.295	.296	196	45	9	2	0	23	19	32
RBI/Opportunities																						
Scoring Position				28 / 178		(16%)									66 / 335		(20%)					
Scoring Position, 2 Out				8 / 92		(9%)									28 / 170		(16%)					
On Third, Less than 2 Out				13 / 26		(50%)									24 / 47		(51%)					
RBI in close games / RBI Total				21 / 29		(72%)									47 / 69		(68%)					

Darnell Coles
Detroit Tigers

Does "somebody up there" like Darnell Coles? It sure seems that way. In late 1985, Coles's career was in trouble. He was only 23 and a proven minor league hitter, but he'd washed out in three trials in Seattle and, with Jim Presley around, seemed destined to be trapped there for the rest of his career. Despite the fact that many teams needed a third baseman, there was no interest in Coles—when Detroit came calling, they swindled him away for the price of a journeyman prospect. Coles had to win the starting job in spring training, but it wasn't much of a contest. Coles started slowly, caught on fire in May and, despite a wretched July, held the job for the rest of the year—possibly for many to come.

Detroit was the perfect team for Coles. Over the last three years, Darnell has hit only .229 on turf; in the AL East, he'll have to play only 24 games on turf. Detroit plays mostly at night; Coles does consistently well under the lights. He seems to be a dead pull hitter (if he had any homers to right, I don't remember them); Detroit's left field porch is most inviting. Finally, the state of the Tigers' farm system (identical to Old Mother Hubbard's) leaves no doubt that Detroit will stand behind him as he matures.

Currently, Coles has four problems. He has great range and a strong arm (he is a converted shortstop), but his arm is erratic. That may be due to the fact that he was a rookie in 1986, but he's always had trouble with errors in his career. Despite the fact that he bats righthanded, he has trouble with lefthanders. That may change in time, but he has had this problem consistently. He draws very few walks and is prone to slumps. He does work hard to improve himself, so he'll probably master both in time.

Coles's most serious problem, though, is out of his hands. Late in the season, Detroit began trying him in right, to allow Kirk Gibson to play left and hide his weak arm. Coles certainly didn't suffer by this (after May, September was his best month), but the Tigers ought to leave him alone. If the switch works, they'll be using an outstanding player at a spot that he is overqualified for and reopening a hole at third. If it doesn't . . . they could be ruining their best young third baseman since George Kell.

—Steve Lysogorski and Geoff Beckman

	1986 SEASON											THREE YEARS (84 – 86)									
	Ave.	OBP	SLG	AB	H	2B	3B	HR	RBI	BB	SO	Ave.	OBP	SLG	AB	H	2B	3B	HR	RBI	BB	SO
Totals	.273	.333	.453	521	142	30	2	20	86	45	84	.248	.319	.394	723	179	37	3	21	97	71	127
Batting vs. Left and Right-handed Pitchers																						
Left	.282	.346	.400	170	48	11	0	3	28	18	20	.238	.315	.335	239	57	11	0	4	29	28	32
Right	.268	.326	.479	351	94	19	2	17	58	27	64	.252	.320	.424	484	122	26	3	17	68	43	95
At Home and on the Road																						
Home	.286	.346	.468	252	72	10	0	12	48	25	47	.263	.332	.406	342	90	13	0	12	53	36	67
Road	.260	.320	.439	269	70	20	2	8	38	20	37	.234	.306	.383	381	89	24	3	9	44	35	60
Facing Groundball Pitchers and Flyball Pitchers																						
Groundball	.251	.323	.379	203	51	9	1	5	26	18	36	.225	.308	.331	311	70	14	2	5	33	32	56
Flyball	.286	.339	.500	318	91	21	1	15	60	27	48	.265	.327	.442	412	109	23	1	16	64	39	71
Facing Finesse Pitchers and Power Pitchers																						
Finesse	.282	.333	.463	309	87	15	1	13	47	22	42	.251	.315	.389	419	105	17	1	13	50	35	61
Power	.259	.332	.439	212	55	15	1	7	39	23	42	.243	.323	.401	304	74	20	2	8	47	36	66
On Grass and on Turf																						
Grass	.274	.332	.455	435	119	26	1	17	71	38	71	.254	.319	.418	531	135	29	2	18	75	49	91
Turf	.267	.337	.442	86	23	4	1	3	15	7	13	.229	.318	.328	192	44	8	1	3	22	22	36
During the Day and at Night																						
Day	.217	.291	.376	157	34	7	0	6	15	15	29	.204	.276	.332	196	40	7	0	6	16	18	37
Night	.297	.352	.486	364	108	23	2	14	71	30	55	.264	.334	.417	527	139	30	3	15	81	53	90
By Month																						
April	.271	.292	.414	70	19	4	0	2	9	2	8	.233	.274	.344	90	21	4	0	2	10	3	12
May	.326	.398	.621	95	31	8	1	6	20	9	15	.293	.364	.479	188	55	13	2	6	24	20	34
June	.259	.317	.370	54	14	3	0	1	9	5	10	.216	.319	.294	102	22	5	0	1	12	16	20
July	.194	.267	.323	93	18	3	0	3	13	8	25	.187	.264	.327	107	20	3	0	4	14	9	29
August	.283	.325	.462	106	30	7	0	4	16	6	13	.283	.325	.462	106	30	7	0	4	16	6	13
Sept/Oct	.291	.372	.476	103	30	5	1	4	19	15	13	.238	.320	.385	130	31	5	1	4	21	17	19
Situational																						
Bases Empty	.261	.340	.441	299	78	14	2	12	12	32	57	.242	.327	.397	418	101	20	3	13	13	47	84
Leadoff	.226	.284	.371	124	28	7	1	3	3	8	20	.202	.289	.324	173	35	10	1	3	3	17	30
Not Leadoff	.286	.378	.491	175	50	7	1	9	9	24	37	.269	.354	.449	245	66	10	2	10	10	30	54
Runners On	.288	.322	.468	222	64	16	0	8	74	13	27	.256	.307	.390	305	78	17	0	8	84	24	43
First Base Only	.287	.321	.535	101	29	7	0	6	15	4	12	.263	.300	.459	133	35	8	0	6	15	6	15
Scoring Position	.289	.324	.413	121	35	9	0	2	59	9	15	.250	.312	.337	172	43	9	0	2	69	18	28
Late Innings, Close	.227	.294	.320	75	17	1	0	2	10	8	18	.186	.269	.265	113	21	3	0	2	13	13	28

RBI/Opportunities		
Scoring Position	52 / 186 (28%)	62 / 263 (24%)
Scoring Position, 2 Out	22 / 86 (26%)	25 / 115 (22%)
On Third, Less than 2 Out	20 / 38 (53%)	26 / 51 (51%)
RBI in close games / RBI Total	55 / 86 (64%)	61 / 97 (63%)

Cecil Cooper
Milwaukee Brewers

One of the most puzzling things in Dan Okrent's *Nine Innings* is the section on Cecil Cooper. Okrent portrays Cooper as a man with a meticulous, painstakingly analytical man who practiced long and hard and became a star despite limited natural ability. That made no sense to me when I read it. Cooper has never had any of the traits that characterize those men—he didn't walk, was a poor baserunner and fielder, and refused to do much winter training—and there was nothing in his past to suggest that he'd ever had to think very deeply or very much about playing baseball.

From the moment that Cooper turned professional, he always hit for average and with power. Boston forced him to fight for playing time with Bernie Carbo and Carl Yastrzemski; in his limited role, he'd done well. He was traded to Milwaukee, got a chance to play regularly and continued to hit well. As we all prefer to be respected for our minds (which we can develop) rather than our bodies (which we have little control over), I thought it far more likely that Cooper was simply a man with tremendous natural ability who had convinced himself that he had succeeded due to his intelligence and been able to induce a sympathetic writer into believing it, too.

I guess I was right—since 1984, Cooper has declined markedly. His high averages and most of his power have vanished. Cooper has taken no steps to compensate—his performance splits are exactly the same (albeit at a much lower level) as they've always been. He has done exactly what a purely natural talent with no deep understanding of the game does when age begins eroding his skills—not a blessed thing.

Cooper could still be a good role player. He has always hit worse in Milwaukee than he has on the road and he is an outstanding player on turf. Except for 1985, he has always hit much better against righties and could do well in a platoon role. He hits well enough with men on base to be a good #6 hitter—if he walked more, he'd be a good #2 hitter. But Cooper, like so many other aging stars have done, has fought every attempt that Milwaukee has made to redefine his role. Cooper needs to recognize that his fine career is winding down; it may take the humbling experience of being released and having to talk a team into signing him before he does.

—Geoff Beckman

	1986 SEASON											THREE YEARS (84 – 86)										
	Ave.	OBP	SLG	AB	H	2B	3B	HR	RBI	BB	SO	Ave.	OBP	SLG	AB	H	2B	3B	HR	RBI	BB	SO
Totals	.258	.310	.373	542	140	24	1	12	75	41	87	.276	.313	.407	1776	491	91	12	39	241	98	223
Batting vs. Left and Right-handed Pitchers																						
Left	.285	.342	.358	137	39	1	0	3	23	11	28	.303	.347	.421	561	170	26	5	10	94	36	82
Right	.249	.298	.378	405	101	23	1	9	52	30	59	.264	.298	.401	1215	321	65	7	29	147	62	141
At Home and on the Road																						
Home	.235	.294	.349	255	60	9	1	6	32	21	46	.268	.308	.384	836	224	40	6	15	107	50	117
Road	.279	.324	.394	287	80	15	0	6	43	20	41	.284	.318	.428	940	267	51	6	24	134	48	106
Facing Groundball Pitchers and Flyball Pitchers																						
Groundball	.275	.335	.373	244	67	12	0	4	34	21	33	.277	.321	.398	876	243	42	8	16	119	54	94
Flyball	.245	.289	.372	298	73	12	1	8	41	20	54	.276	.306	.416	900	248	49	4	23	122	44	129
Facing Finesse Pitchers and Power Pitchers																						
Finesse	.260	.303	.335	319	83	9	0	5	38	20	49	.275	.307	.387	1011	278	45	4	20	124	47	106
Power	.256	.319	.426	223	57	15	1	7	37	21	38	.278	.322	.434	765	213	46	8	19	117	51	117
On Grass and on Turf																						
Grass	.250	.299	.372	460	115	21	1	11	67	33	76	.273	.308	.403	1485	405	74	10	33	203	77	193
Turf	.305	.367	.378	82	25	3	0	1	8	8	11	.296	.341	.430	291	86	17	2	6	38	21	30
During the Day and at Night																						
Day	.253	.317	.329	146	37	5	0	2	14	14	28	.266	.301	.370	519	138	26	2	8	56	26	80
Night	.260	.307	.389	396	103	19	1	10	61	27	59	.281	.318	.422	1257	353	65	10	31	185	72	143
By Month																						
April	.184	.289	.342	38	7	3	0	1	8	6	13	.289	.347	.364	173	50	10	0	1	18	15	28
May	.293	.349	.448	116	34	4	1	4	24	9	20	.294	.325	.444	293	86	12	7	6	52	13	39
June	.236	.261	.337	89	21	3	0	2	10	3	15	.266	.291	.421	316	84	19	3	8	42	12	34
July	.263	.337	.338	80	21	6	0	0	11	9	13	.249	.291	.333	309	77	17	0	3	37	19	36
August	.274	.319	.434	106	29	5	0	4	14	8	14	.316	.346	.483	329	104	17	1	12	54	16	38
Sept/Oct	.248	.283	.301	113	28	3	0	1	8	6	12	.253	.296	.379	356	90	16	1	9	38	23	48
Situational																						
Bases Empty	.223	.275	.320	278	62	10	1	5	5	20	60	.258	.294	.374	914	236	39	5	19	19	43	141
Leadoff	.236	.277	.340	106	25	3	1	2	2	6	22	.259	.302	.352	352	91	14	2	5	5	19	48
Not Leadoff	.215	.274	.308	172	37	7	0	3	3	14	38	.258	.288	.388	562	145	25	3	14	14	24	93
Runners On	.295	.345	.428	264	78	14	0	7	70	21	27	.296	.333	.442	862	255	52	7	20	222	55	82
First Base Only	.252	.283	.365	115	29	7	0	2	8	5	8	.292	.313	.432	400	117	26	3	8	30	12	29
Scoring Position	.329	.388	.477	149	49	7	0	5	62	16	19	.299	.349	.450	462	138	26	4	12	192	43	53
Late Innings, Close	.316	.384	.408	76	24	2	1	1	11	9	16	.306	.348	.381	268	82	10	2	2	34	19	40

RBI/Opportunities

	1986 SEASON			THREE YEARS (84 – 86)		
Scoring Position	52 / 191	(27%)		164 / 594	(28%)	
Scoring Position, 2 Out	19 / 74	(26%)		53 / 240	(22%)	
On Third, Less than 2 Out	19 / 36	(53%)		72 / 118	(61%)	
RBI in close games / RBI Total	49 / 75	(65%)		155 / 241	(64%)	

Ed Correa
Texas Rangers

It is appropriate that the baby-faced Rangers had the youngest player in the majors in 1986. He was 15 days shy of his twentieth birthday when he won his first game in a Ranger uniform. Actually, Kid Correa is a remarkably mature player both physically and emotionally. The native Puerto Rican has made a splendid adjustment to life in the States. His command of English as his second language is astounding, and he handles himself like a veteran on the post-game shows. Physically he is a bull of a young man. José Guzman is three years older but looks far younger than Correa. The rookie ended up with 189 strikeouts to lead the team. That also was a club record for a rookie, as were his 12 wins. He led all 1986 rookie pitchers in innings (202 1/3) as well as in strikeouts. With Bobby Witt striking out 174, the Rangers became the first team in history to have two rookie pitchers over 150 strikeouts in the same season. Ed-

win's 7.43 hit average was good enough to rank sixth in the league. His only real weakness was his control, a common problem with young pitchers. In a game in May he walked eight batters. He finished with a 5.60 walk average and even managed to throw more wild pitches than Charlie Hough. Between the minors, majors, and winter ball, Correa threw almost 250 innings in 1985. He started to drag a little in the middle of the 1986 season but bounced back strong after being given a little more rest. In his last four starts he had a 0.55 ERA and struck out 38 in 32 2/3 innings (10.47 per 9 IP). There may be another benefit to the Rangers' super trade with the White Sox. Ed has a younger brother back in Puerto Rico who all the scouts are drooling over. Puerto Rican ballplayers are not part of the amateur draft. They sign with who they choose, and it looks like Kid Correa II would like to team up with his brother as a Texas Ranger.

—Craig Wright

1986: Power, Groundball												1985: Power, Flyball											1984: Did not play
	1986 SEASON												THREE YEARS (84 – 86)										
	G	IP	H	BB	SO	SB	CS	W	L	S	ERA		G	IP	H	BB	SO	SB	CS	W	L	S	ERA
Totals	32	202.1	167	126	189	35	9	12	14	0	4.23		37	212.2	178	137	199	35	9	13	14	0	4.36
At Home and on the Road																							
Home	13	83.2	64	41	89	13	4	6	6	0	3.98		16	91.0	71	48	97	13	4	7	6	0	3.96
Road	19	118.2	103	85	100	22	5	6	8	0	4.40		21	121.2	107	89	102	22	5	6	8	0	4.66
During the Day and at Night																							
Day	5	35.0	25	28	34	9	3	2	2	0	3.09		6	40.0	29	34	40	9	3	3	2	0	3.15
Night	27	167.1	142	98	155	26	6	10	12	0	4.46		31	172.2	149	103	159	26	6	10	12	0	4.64
On Grass and on Turf																							
Grass	26	164.0	129	103	153	24	8	11	10	0	4.06		30	173.1	139	114	163	24	8	12	10	0	4.26
Turf	6	38.1	38	23	36	11	1	1	4	0	4.93		7	39.1	39	23	36	11	1	1	4	0	4.81
By Month																							
April	4	25.1	22	13	21	4	0	1	2	0	4.62		4	25.1	22	13	21	4	0	1	2	0	4.62
May	5	37.2	23	26	37	6	3	2	1	0	1.67		5	37.2	23	26	37	6	3	2	1	0	1.67
June	6	38.2	35	20	35	5	2	2	3	0	5.59		6	38.2	35	20	35	5	2	2	3	0	5.59
July	5	25.2	27	18	29	5	1	1	3	0	6.66		5	25.2	27	18	29	5	1	1	3	0	6.66
August	5	27.0	30	23	18	6	1	2	2	0	6.67		5	27.0	30	23	18	6	1	2	2	0	6.67
Sept/Oct	7	48.0	30	26	49	9	2	4	3	0	2.25		12	58.1	41	37	59	9	2	5	3	0	3.09

vs. Opponent Batters																							
	1986 SEASON												THREE YEARS (84 – 86)										
	Ave.	OBP	SLG	AB	H	2B	3B	HR	RBI	BB	SO		Ave.	OBP	SLG	AB	H	2B	3B	HR	RBI	BB	SO
Totals	.223	.336	.324	750	167	29	1	15	84	126	189		.225	.341	.333	790	178	32	1	17	89	137	199
Pitching vs. Left and Right-handed Batters																							
Left	.224	.327	.290	397	89	15	1	3	35	61	88		.226	.330	.299	411	93	16	1	4	36	64	91
Right	.221	.345	.363	353	78	14	0	12	49	65	101		.224	.352	.369	379	85	16	0	13	53	73	108
Situational																							
Bases Empty	.202	.326	.290	410	83	13	1	7	7	75	103		.204	.332	.300	427	87	15	1	8	8	82	107
Leadoff	.230	.354	.303	178	41	7	0	2	2	34	39		.227	.359	.303	185	42	8	0	2	2	38	40
Not Leadoff	.181	.304	.280	232	42	6	1	5	5	41	64		.186	.311	.298	242	45	7	1	6	6	44	67
Runners On	.247	.348	.365	340	84	16	0	8	77	51	86		.251	.351	.372	363	91	17	0	9	81	55	92
First Base Only	.317	.396	.488	123	39	6	0	5	12	14	26		.313	.391	.493	134	42	6	0	6	14	15	30
Scoring Position	.207	.322	.295	217	45	10	0	3	65	37	60		.214	.330	.301	229	49	11	0	3	67	40	62
Late Innings, Close	.154	.267	.231	52	8	1	0	1	3	6	12		.154	.267	.231	52	8	1	0	1	3	6	12

RBI/Opportunities					
Scoring Position	54 / 305	(18%)		56 / 328	(17%)
Scoring Position, 2 Out	27 / 140	(19%)		27 / 149	(18%)
On Third, Less than 2 Out	17 / 45	(38%)		18 / 50	(36%)
RBI in close games / RBI Total	65 / 84	(77%)		66 / 89	(74%)

Joe Cowley

Chicago White Sox

Joe Cowley's no hitter against the Angels on September 19 was certainly one of the most bizarre ever pitched. Cowley staggered through the game, giving up seven bases on balls, and was nearly removed after walking the bases loaded with none out in the sixth. It was, during 1986 at least, a typical Cowley performance. Often he was unhittable, as is reflected in his .223 opponents' batting average and his average of 7.3 strikeouts per nine innings. Just as often he was his own worst enemy, as shown by his total of 83 walks given up in only 162 innings. And often he was both brilliant and pathetic in the same performance: the no-hitter, for example, or the night in Texas when he fanned the first seven batters to face him—an American League record—only to be kayoed in the fifth inning.

Cowley's control lapses could spring up anytime, but most often they surfaced in the first inning. In 27 starts he gave up 27 first-inning walks—nearly a third of his season total—and hit two batters in addition. Only nine times could he make it through the first without either walking or hitting someone, and five of those starts came in succession, during an effective September streak which included the no-hitter. Lest the Sox start to think he was over his troubles, though, Cowley quickly returned to his old ways in his final two starts.

Can he improve? Though he's pitched in organized ball since 1976, Cowley won't be 29 until late in the '87 season, and it's not unprecedented for a pitcher to mature late; it's also true that for all his erratic tendencies, Cowley's major league record is an impressive 33–21. He has major league stuff, without doubt; the question is whether he can get the ball over the plate consistently enough to be more than an 11 or 12-game winner. Looking over his career, it's apparent that Cowley has never been able to avoid wildness for more than short stretches at a time. As a youngster he led two minor leagues in hit batsmen and one in walks. Joe's control improved enough to earn a shot with the Braves in '82, but soon he was back in the minors. Ultimately he hooked on with the Yankees and pitched effectively in '84 and '85, turning in a 21–8 record. But his walk ratio in '85 was virtually the same as his '86 Sox season. There's no evidence yet that he's over the hump.

—Don Zminda

1986: Power, Flyball | 1985: Power, Flyball | 1984: Power, Flyball

	1986 SEASON											THREE YEARS (84 – 86)										
	G	IP	H	BB	SO	SB	CS	W	L	S	ERA	G	IP	H	BB	SO	SB	CS	W	L	S	ERA
Totals	27	162.1	133	83	132	17	5	11	11	0	3.88	73	405.1	340	199	300	33	12	32	19	0	3.84
At Home and on the Road																						
Home	12	79.2	56	36	67	3	3	6	5	0	2.37	35	211.0	152	91	167	12	8	17	8	0	2.64
Road	15	82.2	77	47	65	14	2	5	6	0	5.33	38	194.1	188	108	133	21	4	15	11	0	5.14
During the Day and at Night																						
Day	8	48.0	37	28	37	8	1	3	4	0	3.75	24	134.0	100	86	93	15	2	11	7	0	3.22
Night	19	114.1	96	55	95	9	4	8	7	0	3.94	49	271.1	240	113	207	18	10	21	12	0	4.15
On Grass and on Turf																						
Grass	21	122.1	99	65	105	12	4	9	9	0	3.97	62	341.0	281	170	265	25	11	28	14	0	3.64
Turf	6	40.0	34	18	27	5	1	2	2	0	3.60	11	64.1	59	29	35	8	1	4	5	0	4.90
By Month																						
April	1	2.1	3	3	2	1	0	0	1	0	19.29	6	21.2	17	15	13	2	0	0	2	0	5.82
May	2	12.0	9	5	11	1	0	1	1	0	4.50	7	43.2	34	19	34	2	3	5	2	0	3.71
June	6	41.0	28	17	36	5	2	3	1	0	3.07	9	58.1	39	26	51	7	3	5	2	0	3.24
July	5	26.2	27	10	17	2	0	2	3	0	5.40	15	65.2	58	27	36	6	1	6	5	0	4.52
August	6	26.1	36	21	21	3	2	2	3	0	5.81	16	89.2	95	45	68	6	4	7	4	0	4.42
Sept/Oct	7	54.0	30	27	45	5	1	3	2	0	2.00	20	126.1	97	67	98	10	1	9	4	0	3.06

vs. Opponent Batters

	1986 SEASON											THREE YEARS (84 – 86)										
	Ave.	OBP	SLG	AB	H	2B	3B	HR	RBI	BB	SO	Ave.	OBP	SLG	AB	H	2B	3B	HR	RBI	BB	SO
Totals	.223	.319	.369	596	133	25	1	20	71	83	132	.226	.319	.392	1505	340	51	8	61	164	199	300
Pitching vs. Left and Right-handed Batters																						
Left	.244	.342	.388	320	78	16	0	10	43	48	57	.237	.341	.400	839	199	30	4	33	92	129	132
Right	.199	.292	.348	276	55	9	1	10	28	35	75	.212	.290	.381	666	141	21	4	28	72	70	168
Situational																						
Bases Empty	.215	.304	.381	362	78	13	1	15	15	44	83	.233	.314	.412	932	217	29	6	42	42	102	182
Leadoff	.191	.285	.309	152	29	4	1	4	4	20	38	.224	.302	.389	388	87	10	3	16	16	39	78
Not Leadoff	.233	.318	.433	210	49	9	0	11	11	24	45	.239	.324	.428	544	130	19	3	26	26	63	104
Runners On	.235	.342	.350	234	55	12	0	5	56	39	49	.215	.326	.360	573	123	22	2	19	122	97	118
First Base Only	.224	.309	.327	98	22	4	0	2	6	11	13	.250	.340	.407	248	62	7	1	10	25	32	38
Scoring Position	.243	.363	.368	136	33	8	0	3	50	28	36	.188	.315	.323	325	61	15	1	9	97	65	80
Late Innings, Close	.236	.288	.327	55	13	2	0	1	4	4	11	.213	.293	.360	150	32	4	0	6	15	16	34

RBI/Opportunities

	1986 SEASON	THREE YEARS (84 – 86)
Scoring Position	45 / 204 (22%)	83 / 468 (18%)
Scoring Position, 2 Out	21 / 94 (22%)	36 / 222 (16%)
On Third, Less than 2 Out	16 / 34 (47%)	33 / 72 (46%)
RBI in close games / RBI Total	43 / 71 (61%)	106 / 164 (65%)

Danny Cox
St. Louis Cardinals

Danny Cox got off to an excellent start in '85, so it's probably safe to assume that his slow start in '86 was due to his ankle injury. It's at least as good an assumption that Whitey Herzog won't give Cox any time off to go fishing in spring training this season. Danny actually had two seasons in one in 1986. During the Cardinals' first 81 games he was 2–7 with an ERA of 4.00. In the final 80 games, however, he was 10–6 with seven complete games and an ERA of only 2.15. The Cardinals were 2–10 in Cox's first twelve starts of the year and 13–7 for the final 20 starts.

The Cardinal offense did not provide much support for any of their pitchers in '86, and none had more reason to complain than Cox. His run support was 3.44 runs per game, the lowest of any Cardinal pitcher with ten or more starts. In nineteen of Cox's 32 starts he received three runs or less from the offense. The Cards were 4–15 in these games. On the other hand, in the thirteen games in which Cox was given four or more runs to work with, the Redbirds were 11–2.

Cox's problems didn't end with the offense, though. He also received the worst defensive support of any starter, at least in terms of errors. The Cards made 37 errors in his 32 games, an average of 1.16 per start. No other pitcher had an average of over one error per start, and Tudor (.73), Forsch (.48) and Mathews (.54) each received much better support.

Despite the nonsupport and the losing record, 1986 was an impressive year for Cox. For the second straight year he finished among the top eight in the NL in terms of ERA— the only other top ten repeaters were Tudor, Gooden and Darling. He had an ERA under 3.00 when pitching on three, four or five days' rest, but was bombed (6.55 ERA) in his two off-rotation starts. Danny's always seemed to have first-inning troubles, and 1986 was no exception. He surrendered 22 first-inning runs, twice as many as his second worst inning, the fifth. In 1985 he gave up 25 first-inning runs in 35 starts. He had 21 starts in '86 in which he surrendered three earned runs or less. Cox had the NL's best ERA in day games in '85 (1.87, 5–2 record) but fell to 2–7 with a 3.99 ERA in day games during '86.

—Russ Eagle

1986: Finesse, Groundball   **1985: Finesse, Groundball**   **1984: Finesse, Groundball**

	1986 SEASON											THREE YEARS (84 – 86)										
	G	IP	H	BB	SO	SB	CS	W	L	S	ERA	G	IP	H	BB	SO	SB	CS	W	L	S	ERA
Totals	32	220.0	189	60	108	17	9	12	13	0	2.90	96	617.1	586	178	309	36	25	39	33	0	3.18
At Home and on the Road																						
Home	17	124.1	97	31	52	3	4	6	6	0	2.90	49	330.0	299	84	157	11	10	21	16	0	2.92
Road	15	95.2	92	29	56	14	5	6	7	0	2.92	47	287.1	287	94	152	25	15	18	17	0	3.48
During the Day and at Night																						
Day	10	58.2	56	18	27	5	1	2	7	0	3.99	33	203.1	196	70	96	16	10	11	14	0	3.28
Night	22	161.1	133	42	81	12	8	10	6	0	2.51	63	414.0	390	108	213	20	15	28	19	0	3.13
On Grass and on Turf																						
Grass	7	46.2	43	16	30	4	1	2	5	0	2.51	23	132.0	138	49	65	11	4	7	12	0	4.16
Turf	25	173.1	146	44	78	13	8	10	8	0	3.01	73	485.1	448	129	244	25	21	32	21	0	2.91
By Month																						
April	1	3.0	7	0	0	0	0	0	1	0	12.00	10	53.0	55	17	22	2	2	3	4	0	4.08
May	6	41.0	35	17	20	3	1	0	3	0	3.51	19	123.2	108	45	62	8	6	5	7	0	3.13
June	6	32.0	34	9	16	3	3	2	1	0	4.22	16	95.2	100	30	51	5	7	6	5	0	3.39
July	6	46.1	33	3	21	1	1	3	3	0	2.53	14	103.2	96	16	50	2	3	8	6	0	2.86
August	6	43.0	32	15	24	5	1	3	3	0	2.09	18	104.0	109	34	54	10	4	6	7	0	4.07
Sept/Oct	7	54.2	48	16	27	5	3	4	2	0	2.14	19	137.1	118	36	70	9	3	11	4	0	2.29

vs. Opponent Batters

	1986 SEASON											THREE YEARS (84 – 86)										
	Ave.	OBP	SLG	AB	H	2B	3B	HR	RBI	BB	SO	Ave.	OBP	SLG	AB	H	2B	3B	HR	RBI	BB	SO
Totals	.234	.288	.347	808	189	43	3	14	69	60	108	.255	.309	.375	2301	586	118	16	42	214	178	309
Pitching vs. Left and Right-handed Batters																						
Left	.227	.279	.346	431	98	20	2	9	40	32	59	.263	.319	.389	1134	298	56	9	23	103	95	124
Right	.241	.297	.347	377	91	23	1	5	29	28	59	.247	.300	.361	1167	288	62	7	19	111	83	185
Situational																						
Bases Empty	.223	.281	.344	503	112	24	2	11	11	40	69	.252	.313	.374	1379	348	74	8	26	26	112	190
Leadoff	.248	.294	.364	214	53	8	1	5	5	14	33	.277	.334	.420	595	165	34	6	13	13	47	81
Not Leadoff	.204	.272	.329	289	59	16	1	6	6	26	36	.233	.296	.339	784	183	40	2	13	13	65	109
Runners On	.252	.298	.351	305	77	19	1	3	58	20	39	.258	.305	.375	922	238	44	8	16	188	66	119
First Base Only	.254	.287	.354	130	33	5	1	2	6	6	18	.270	.302	.399	411	111	18	4	9	29	19	45
Scoring Position	.251	.306	.349	175	44	14	0	1	52	14	21	.249	.306	.356	511	127	26	4	7	159	47	74
Late Innings, Close	.232	.296	.273	99	23	4	0	0	11	9	7	.251	.298	.333	219	55	8	2	2	20	15	21

RBI/Opportunities

	1986 SEASON		THREE YEARS (84 – 86)	
Scoring Position	49 / 215	(23%)	145 / 658	(22%)
Scoring Position, 2 Out	15 / 97	(15%)	59 / 305	(19%)
On Third, Less than 2 Out	18 / 39	(46%)	55 / 119	(46%)
RBI in close games / RBI Total	55 / 69	(80%)	177 / 214	(83%)

Jose Cruz
Houston Astros

Jose CRUUUUUUZ may be the most popular Houston Astros player ever. Overlooked for nearly a decade, Cruz in the last two years has received some of the respect due him. Baseball professionals and fans have finally recognized (with some prodding from sabermetricians) what excellent batting stats Cruz has produced, especially considering the Astrodome's deleterious effect. If Jose's subpar 1986 is subtracted from the stats shown below, the resulting road stats (1984–85) show 109 RBIs, a .318 average, a .372 OBA and a .501 SA!

Cruz has been remarkably consistent. He has maintained his skills by playing winter ball in his native Puerto Rico. Jose's 1986 dropoff raises concern that he finally has entered the twilight of his career. Cruz no longer is a base-stealing threat, having experienced a smooth descent from 30 steals in 1983 to 3 in 1986. A decrease in triples (he had 13 in 1984) also indicates that his legs (knees?) are aging. The last two years he has suffered from injuries, playing in 141 games each year (after playing 160 each in 1983 and '84). On the other hand, a strong showing from August '86 on suggests that Cruz still may have all his hitting skills, albeit with a loss of some speed and durability.

Cruz is a tough hitter with runners in scoring position. In the past his hitting approach at home (foregoing the home-run swing in favor of making more contact) was different from that on the road. From 1975 to 1985, Jose hit 80 homers on the road, only 35 at home. With the Astrodome fences now moved in somewhat, Cruz appears willing to try occasional home-run cuts at home, too. He is a good outfielder, though his range has dropped from good to mediocre in the last few years. His arm seems to be below average but fairly accurate— sufficient for a left fielder.

Jose is a rare example of a star ballplayer who changed major-league teams before the twilight of his career in a straight cash deal: he was sold by St. Louis to Houston after the 1974 season. At age 39, Cruz has played in more major-league games without a World Series appearance than any other active player. I doubt that I'll ever forget the image of a heartbroken Jose Cruz in the Astro dugout following the final game of the 1980 League Championship Series against the Phillies. That Cruz has virtually no chance for induction into the Hall of Fame is unfortunate.

—Steven Copley

	1986 SEASON											THREE YEARS (84 – 86)										
	Ave.	OBP	SLG	AB	H	2B	3B	HR	RBI	BB	SO	Ave.	OBP	SLG	AB	H	2B	3B	HR	RBI	BB	SO
Totals	.278	.351	.403	479	133	22	4	10	72	55	86	.298	.362	.433	1623	483	84	21	31	246	171	227
Batting vs. Left and Right-handed Pitchers																						
Left	.284	.325	.392	194	55	7	4	2	28	12	41	.286	.330	.408	637	182	23	11	11	108	45	102
Right	.274	.367	.411	285	78	15	0	8	44	43	45	.305	.381	.448	986	301	61	10	20	138	126	125
At Home and on the Road																						
Home	.298	.378	.416	245	73	10	2	5	44	32	46	.294	.367	.393	786	231	38	11	6	109	95	106
Road	.256	.322	.389	234	60	12	2	5	28	23	40	.301	.357	.470	837	252	46	10	25	137	76	121
Facing Groundball Pitchers and Flyball Pitchers																						
Groundball	.241	.320	.371	224	54	6	4	5	31	26	39	.289	.349	.420	795	230	35	12	15	118	76	101
Flyball	.310	.378	.431	255	79	16	0	5	41	29	47	.306	.373	.444	828	253	49	9	16	128	95	126
Facing Finesse Pitchers and Power Pitchers																						
Finesse	.285	.358	.423	284	81	17	2	6	42	33	40	.306	.365	.438	893	273	52	9	16	131	89	94
Power	.267	.339	.374	195	52	5	2	4	30	22	46	.288	.357	.426	730	210	32	12	15	115	82	133
On Grass and on Turf																						
Grass	.220	.288	.305	141	31	6	0	2	14	14	28	.282	.336	.455	503	142	26	5	17	92	44	75
Turf	.302	.376	.444	338	102	16	4	8	58	41	58	.304	.373	.422	1120	341	58	16	14	154	127	152
During the Day and at Night																						
Day	.273	.371	.370	154	42	9	0	2	20	24	32	.269	.351	.417	391	105	25	3	9	65	50	61
Night	.280	.341	.418	325	91	13	4	8	52	31	54	.307	.365	.438	1232	378	59	18	22	181	121	166
By Month																						
April	.121	.194	.152	33	4	1	0	0	3	3	8	.274	.346	.353	190	52	6	3	1	21	22	26
May	.293	.348	.354	82	24	3	1	0	9	7	11	.274	.332	.405	259	71	13	3	5	30	23	34
June	.287	.364	.351	94	27	4	1	0	14	12	17	.285	.329	.378	288	82	9	6	2	49	21	51
July	.250	.312	.369	84	21	2	1	2	8	8	22	.319	.390	.458	295	94	19	2	6	37	36	43
August	.327	.377	.490	98	32	5	1	3	18	8	14	.338	.392	.495	305	103	20	5	6	55	30	38
Sept/Oct	.284	.400	.534	88	25	7	0	5	20	17	14	.283	.367	.472	286	81	17	2	11	54	39	35
Situational																						
Bases Empty	.220	.292	.311	273	60	11	1	4	4	28	52	.275	.335	.394	893	246	40	9	16	16	80	138
Leadoff	.190	.261	.276	105	20	4	1	1	1	10	19	.277	.329	.374	404	112	16	4	5	5	31	65
Not Leadoff	.238	.312	.333	168	40	7	0	3	3	18	33	.274	.340	.411	489	134	24	5	11	11	49	73
Runners On	.354	.426	.524	206	73	11	3	6	68	27	34	.325	.392	.479	730	237	44	12	15	230	91	89
First Base Only	.300	.356	.450	80	24	4	1	2	7	7	11	.294	.341	.421	299	88	19	2	5	18	21	29
Scoring Position	.389	.466	.571	126	49	7	2	4	61	20	23	.346	.424	.520	431	149	25	10	10	212	70	60
Late Innings, Close	.244	.354	.341	82	20	0	1	2	11	14	18	.272	.373	.366	268	73	7	3	4	33	43	44

RBI/Opportunities				
Scoring Position	52 / 173	(30%)	183 / 585	(31%)
Scoring Position, 2 Out	19 / 62	(31%)	58 / 234	(25%)
On Third, Less than 2 Out	19 / 38	(50%)	75 / 127	(59%)
RBI in close games / RBI Total	45 / 72	(63%)	163 / 246	(66%)

Ron Darling
New York Mets

Ron Darling is one of the new breed of pitchers who relies heavily on the split-fingered fastball. During the 1986 season Darling went away from his big-breaking curveball, which was often erratic, and began using the split-finger instead. By combining it with his fastball he greatly increased his effectiveness, becoming one of the best starters in the National League.

Over the course of his career, Darling's frequent companion has been the No Decision. Although the Mets win the lion's share of his starts, Ron often fails to share in the wealth. In 1986 Darling started 34 games and had a 15–6 record, for an impressive .727 winning percentage. But in his 13 no-decisions the Mets went 11–2, an even-better .846 percentage. Is Darling just the mandatory hard-luck pitcher on the staff? Well, sometimes, but usually the problem is that he pitches according to how well the Met offense is doing. Give him a four-run lead and he's apt to give it right back, while if you don't score for him, he'll pitch his heart out. There are certain pitchers who always seem to pitch just well enough to lose. Darling, it seems, pitches well enough to get a No Decision. The Mets won't complain,

though, if keep posting records like the 26–8 mark they compiled in games Darling started last year; the record even included two 1–0 losses. That 26–8 mark was the best one they compiled for any of the starters on their elite staff. In the early going, when the Mets were piling up their insurmountable lead, they won the first nine times Darling took the hill, not tasting defeat until June 1. Once New York reached post-season play they must have figured it was dangerous to change the pattern, because in the playoffs and Series they won three of Darling's four starts; his own record, typically, was 1–1.

Because of his trouble controlling his curveball, Darling has had a tendency to get very wild. He gave up the most bases on balls of any pitcher in the majors in 1984–85, walking over 100 in each season. In '86 the walk total was down to 86, however, probably because of the change to the split-fingered pitch. He's getting better in every way: from '84 to '86 his hits plus walks per nine innings have gone down every year while his strikeout ratio has gone up. He could be entering Cy Young territory soon if he can pick up some more wins.

—Sunil Agarwal

1986: Power, Flyball											1985: Power, Flyball										1984: Power, Flyball	
1986 SEASON											**THREE YEARS (84 – 86)**											
	G	IP	H	BB	SO	SB	CS	W	L	S	ERA	G	IP	H	BB	SO	SB	CS	W	L	S	ERA
Totals	34	237.0	203	81	184	24	15	15	6	0	2.81	103	690.2	596	299	487	60	42	43	21	0	3.14
At Home and on the Road																						
Home	16	118.1	95	30	95	11	4	10	2	0	2.36	52	368.1	316	132	280	27	19	26	9	0	2.83
Road	18	118.2	108	51	89	13	11	5	4	0	3.26	51	322.1	280	167	207	33	23	17	12	0	3.49
During the Day and at Night																						
Day	12	83.0	73	31	60	13	3	6	3	0	2.82	35	222.0	212	104	147	28	9	12	11	0	3.97
Night	22	154.0	130	50	124	11	12	9	3	0	2.81	68	468.2	384	195	340	32	33	31	10	0	2.75
On Grass and on Turf																						
Grass	23	162.2	138	51	127	18	5	12	3	0	2.77	73	491.1	428	204	365	39	25	32	13	0	3.15
Turf	11	74.1	65	30	57	6	10	3	3	0	2.91	30	199.1	168	95	122	21	17	11	8	0	3.12
By Month																						
April	4	20.0	23	9	14	3	1	1	0	0	6.75	13	76.0	72	37	48	9	4	3	2	0	4.50
May	5	38.2	23	17	28	1	1	5	0	0	1.63	16	112.2	91	41	84	3	4	10	2	0	2.64
June	6	40.0	34	13	31	6	4	2	2	0	2.92	17	118.0	98	49	86	10	10	9	3	0	2.59
July	6	49.0	36	11	41	3	4	3	1	0	1.47	19	131.0	111	61	87	6	11	9	3	0	2.61
August	6	39.1	45	13	28	2	2	1	2	0	4.81	18	120.1	113	60	87	8	8	5	5	0	3.74
Sept/Oct	7	50.0	42	18	42	9	3	3	1	0	1.80	20	132.2	111	51	95	24	5	7	6	0	3.26

vs. Opponent Batters																				
1986 SEASON										**THREE YEARS (84 – 86)**									
	Ave.	OBP	SLG	AB	H	2B	3B	HR	RBI	BB	SO	Ave.	OBP	SLG	AB	H	2B	3B	HR	RBI	BB	SO
Totals	.234	.300	.354	867	203	35	3	21	77	81	184	.235	.316	.357	2537	596	109	12	59	239	299	487
Pitching vs. Left and Right-handed Batters																						
Left	.226	.287	.343	505	114	21	1	12	41	44	106	.237	.314	.349	1328	315	63	7	24	118	150	241
Right	.246	.318	.370	362	89	14	2	9	36	37	78	.232	.319	.366	1209	281	46	5	35	121	149	246
Situational																						
Bases Empty	.251	.312	.396	538	135	23	2	17	17	47	114	.248	.326	.380	1506	374	65	7	40	40	167	285
Leadoff	.289	.333	.439	228	66	10	0	8	8	15	45	.254	.324	.377	645	164	24	2	17	17	63	123
Not Leadoff	.223	.297	.365	310	69	13	2	9	9	32	69	.244	.327	.383	861	210	41	5	23	23	104	162
Runners On	.207	.280	.286	329	68	12	1	4	60	34	70	.215	.303	.323	1031	222	44	5	19	199	132	202
First Base Only	.217	.291	.329	143	31	7	0	3	9	14	24	.234	.304	.361	457	107	22	3	10	31	43	79
Scoring Position	.199	.272	.253	186	37	5	1	1	51	20	46	.200	.302	.293	574	115	22	2	9	168	89	123
Late Innings, Close	.198	.267	.281	96	19	5	0	1	6	8	15	.228	.330	.317	259	59	14	0	3	20	38	37

RBI/Opportunities					
Scoring Position	50 / 241	(21%)	152 / 782	(19%)
Scoring Position, 2 Out	11 / 104	(11%)	55 / 370	(15%)
On Third, Less than 2 Out	26 / 42	(62%)	60 / 123	(49%)
RBI in close games / RBI Total	53 / 77	(69%)	176 / 239	(74%)

Alvin Davis
Seattle Mariners

Since winning the American League's Rookie of the Year Award in 1984, Alvin Davis has not been able to move forward. Moving forward, to begin with, is not Alvin Davis' category. Alvin has three speeds: slow, slower and GIDP. He is a fine hitter and a contributing player, but to this point he is regarded in Seattle as a disappointment, and looks to the 1987 season to get his career moving in the right direction.

The three strong parts of Davis' game are power, hitting for average and strike zone judgment. The two outstanding weaknesses are speed and defense. He hit 27 home runs as a rookie in 1984, but as was true with Wally Joyner last year, you could pretty much tell that was above his norm. He hadn't hit more than eighteen homers in the minors and his HR production slowed down throughout the 1984 season. Since then he has dropped to eighteen a year. It was hoped, however, that he could compensate in batting average for the homers he didn't hit, and that hasn't happened. No one is complaining about a .281 batting average. Though he hasn't done it yet, he's a guy who is going to walk a hundred times a year.

But Davis is awfully slow, and apart from being slow is not a good defensive first baseman. This is not perceived as being from a lack of interest or a lack of effort. Davis, who has a B.S. in finance and obviously is in the right profession to take advantage of it, is well regarded by teammates and fans. Still, he doesn't make the plays, and it is possible that Williams may flip-flop him with Phelps, making Phelps the first baseman and Davis the DH.

Davis, a lefty, has a good-sized platoon differential (.359 slugging percentage against lefties, .499 against right-handers), hits much better in Seattle than on the road and much better in day games than at night. He has not hit well in the late innings of close games, .247 over three years. Still, their remains a perception that Davis is capable of exploding for an MVP type of offensive season. If he does, he could carry the Mariners into the pennant race. If he doesn't, hitting .280 with twenty homers and a hundred walks is good enough that nobody's going to complain.

—Bill James

	Ave.	OBP	SLG	AB	H	2B	3B	HR	RBI	BB	SO		Ave.	OBP	SLG	AB	H	2B	3B	HR	RBI	BB	SO
	1986 SEASON												**THREE YEARS (84 – 86)**										
Totals	.271	.373	.426	479	130	18	1	18	72	76	68		.281	.382	.456	1624	457	85	5	63	266	263	217
Batting vs. Left and Right-handed Pitchers																							
Left	.246	.376	.270	122	30	3	0	0	16	25	24		.260	.369	.361	504	131	22	1	9	74	85	80
Right	.280	.372	.479	357	100	15	1	18	56	51	44		.291	.388	.499	1120	326	63	4	54	192	178	137
At Home and on the Road																							
Home	.281	.385	.494	249	70	9	1	14	48	40	29		.290	.396	.503	823	239	45	5	40	147	139	95
Road	.261	.361	.352	230	60	9	0	4	24	36	39		.272	.368	.408	801	218	40	0	23	119	124	122
Facing Groundball Pitchers and Flyball Pitchers																							
Groundball	.290	.406	.434	221	64	5	0	9	33	41	26		.302	.404	.445	752	227	38	2	22	106	128	95
Flyball	.256	.344	.419	258	66	13	1	9	39	35	42		.264	.363	.466	872	230	47	3	41	160	135	122
Facing Finesse Pitchers and Power Pitchers																							
Finesse	.288	.373	.417	288	83	10	0	9	40	37	37		.291	.378	.450	961	280	47	3	33	149	134	112
Power	.246	.373	.440	191	47	8	1	9	32	39	31		.267	.388	.466	663	177	38	2	30	117	129	105
On Grass and on Turf																							
Grass	.225	.320	.320	178	40	5	0	4	16	25	32		.262	.354	.412	614	161	29	0	21	92	88	98
Turf	.299	.404	.488	301	90	13	1	14	56	51	36		.293	.399	.483	1010	296	56	5	42	174	175	119
During the Day and at Night																							
Day	.262	.359	.361	122	32	3	0	3	13	19	17		.270	.382	.388	392	106	17	1	9	50	71	58
Night	.275	.378	.448	357	98	15	1	15	59	57	51		.285	.382	.478	1232	351	68	4	54	216	192	159
By Month																							
April	.207	.303	.517	58	12	1	1	5	9	8	12		.294	.393	.556	187	55	8	1	13	30	30	24
May	.350	.472	.530	100	35	6	0	4	22	23	14		.306	.434	.504	258	79	16	1	11	48	59	40
June	.253	.381	.405	79	20	6	0	2	13	17	7		.246	.345	.391	297	73	13	0	10	54	45	31
July	.341	.438	.415	41	14	0	0	1	4	6	4		.300	.395	.405	247	74	8	0	6	36	38	24
August	.296	.355	.480	98	29	3	0	5	15	8	15		.313	.396	.510	304	95	21	0	13	47	40	42
Sept/Oct	.194	.294	.243	103	20	2	0	1	9	14	16		.245	.345	.411	331	81	19	3	10	51	51	56
Situational																							
Bases Empty	.265	.360	.454	249	66	8	0	13	13	35	34		.281	.373	.453	879	247	45	2	34	34	122	113
Leadoff	.280	.362	.355	93	26	4	0	1	1	11	11		.288	.368	.442	319	92	18	2	9	9	36	31
Not Leadoff	.256	.359	.513	156	40	4	0	12	12	24	23		.277	.376	.459	560	155	27	0	25	25	86	82
Runners On	.278	.387	.396	230	64	10	1	5	59	41	34		.282	.393	.460	745	210	40	3	29	232	141	104
First Base Only	.253	.302	.404	99	25	4	1	3	10	7	16		.283	.357	.446	307	87	19	2	9	31	34	40
Scoring Position	.298	.440	.389	131	39	6	0	2	49	34	18		.281	.414	.470	438	123	21	1	20	201	107	64
Late Innings, Close	.230	.367	.365	74	17	1	0	3	5	16	10		.247	.385	.410	239	59	10	1	9	32	53	30

RBI/Opportunities					
Scoring Position	44 / 195	(23%)		157 / 662	(24%)
Scoring Position, 2 Out	10 / 68	(15%)		55 / 271	(20%)
On Third, Less than 2 Out	21 / 41	(51%)		66 / 129	(51%)
RBI in close games / RBI Total	49 / 72	(68%)		170 / 266	(64%)

Chili Davis
San Francisco Giants

Chili was born in Jamaica, and his tropical beginnings must have prepared him for the constant trade winds that swirl around him. It was widely assumed in the Bay Area that Chili would be dealt away in the '86 Winter Meetings. However, as 1987 came along, Chili continues to be a Giant.

Chili hit one of the worst mid-season slumps in my memory in 1986. During this slump, Chili's strikeout ratio went from 1 per 6.7 at-bats to 1 per 4.5 at-bats. Note the unbelievable fall-off in power—dropping from 1 extra base hit every 9.6 at-bats to a deplorable 1 every 24.6 (approximately 1 per week), worse even than Jose Uribe. Further, half of Chili's games against the Mets came during the slump—and he hit .400 (14-for-35) with 11 RBIs against them in 1986. Chili's mastery of Dwight Gooden is reminiscent of when Willie McCovey owned Don Drysdale. Chili was 5 for 9 against Dr. K this year, and has a lifetime BA of .522 and OBA of .577 against Gooden. Davis reversed his previous trend and hit 65 points better on grass than turf; he reversed another trend and hit 26 points better at home than away.

Chili continues to switch hit, although I'm damned if I can figure out why. His differential worsened this year: his OBA as a left-handed hitter was .420, while right-handed it was .267. Chili did finish the year with 84 walks (3rd in the NL), 23 intentional walks (2nd to Mike Schmidt's 26), and his .375 on-base average placed 8th among all NL hitters, just behind Chris Brown's .376.

—J. Michael Duca

Davis's major-league numbers are very comparable to his minor-league record. Chili is now an excellent left-handed hitter, hitting for average and power with a high OBA. What hides his accomplishments are his right-handed numbers. In his rookie year, he actually hit for a higher average from the right side; his sophomore year, his power increased on the right side but his average dropped. It may be time for him to try another approach against southpaws. Even if Davis remains productive only from the left side, though, this helps give the Giants balance in their lineup.

Davis is very dangerous with runners on base. In the late innings, pitchers seem to prefer to walk him rather than give him a hittable pitch.

A sore shoulder affected Chili's throwing last year, but when he is healthy he is one of the best defensive outfielders in the NL.

—Victor Hester

	1986 SEASON											THREE YEARS (84 – 86)										
	Ave.	OBP	SLG	AB	H	2B	3B	HR	RBI	BB	SO	Ave.	OBP	SLG	AB	H	2B	3B	HR	RBI	BB	SO
Totals	.278	.375	.416	526	146	28	3	13	70	84	96	.288	.364	.445	1506	433	74	11	47	207	188	244
Batting vs. Left and Right-handed Pitchers																						
Left	.226	.267	.345	168	38	3	1	5	24	10	24	.242	.284	.348	385	93	15	1	8	44	25	58
Right	.302	.420	.450	358	108	25	2	8	46	74	72	.303	.390	.478	1121	340	59	10	39	163	163	186
At Home and on the Road																						
Home	.291	.389	.426	258	75	14	0	7	37	43	52	.287	.360	.433	721	207	36	3	21	99	87	120
Road	.265	.361	.407	268	71	14	3	6	33	41	44	.288	.368	.456	785	226	38	8	26	108	101	124
Facing Groundball Pitchers and Flyball Pitchers																						
Groundball	.301	.369	.443	246	74	12	1	7	38	29	31	.292	.361	.448	686	200	29	6	22	96	79	86
Flyball	.257	.380	.393	280	72	16	2	6	32	55	65	.284	.367	.443	820	233	45	5	25	111	109	158
Facing Finesse Pitchers and Power Pitchers																						
Finesse	.293	.366	.451	297	87	19	2	8	40	35	46	.295	.347	.479	879	259	40	7	36	130	74	117
Power	.258	.386	.371	229	59	9	1	5	30	49	50	.278	.387	.397	627	174	34	4	11	77	114	127
On Grass and on Turf																						
Grass	.294	.392	.428	395	116	21	1	10	53	66	77	.287	.365	.432	1115	320	51	6	33	149	143	184
Turf	.229	.322	.382	131	30	7	2	3	17	18	19	.289	.361	.481	391	113	23	5	14	58	45	60
During the Day and at Night																						
Day	.309	.403	.466	236	73	12	2	7	33	39	47	.288	.360	.448	728	210	34	5	24	97	88	124
Night	.252	.352	.376	290	73	16	1	6	37	45	49	.287	.368	.442	778	223	40	6	23	110	100	120
By Month																						
April	.264	.321	.431	72	19	3	0	3	14	7	12	.269	.307	.420	212	57	14	0	6	31	14	40
May	.309	.374	.457	81	25	4	1	2	20	9	7	.305	.382	.510	249	76	15	3	10	38	31	28
June	.302	.419	.500	96	29	9	2	2	17	20	14	.273	.340	.438	304	83	13	5	9	44	33	40
July	.273	.337	.364	88	24	2	0	2	7	9	20	.282	.348	.377	252	71	7	1	5	24	26	45
August	.238	.354	.274	84	20	3	0	0	4	15	22	.287	.392	.451	268	77	13	2	9	38	47	51
Sept/Oct	.276	.415	.457	105	29	7	0	4	8	24	21	.312	.412	.475	221	69	12	0	8	32	37	40
Situational																						
Bases Empty	.237	.313	.364	308	73	16	1	7	7	33	57	.275	.339	.429	879	242	42	6	27	27	83	142
Leadoff	.253	.323	.384	146	37	8	1	3	3	15	28	.274	.333	.426	376	103	18	3	11	11	33	59
Not Leadoff	.222	.304	.346	162	36	8	0	4	4	18	29	.276	.344	.431	503	139	24	3	16	16	50	83
Runners On	.335	.453	.491	218	73	12	2	6	63	51	39	.305	.397	.467	627	191	32	5	20	180	105	102
First Base Only	.377	.435	.558	77	29	6	1	2	7	8	9	.315	.360	.485	260	82	16	2	8	24	18	37
Scoring Position	.312	.460	.454	141	44	6	1	4	56	43	30	.297	.419	.455	367	109	16	3	12	156	87	65
Late Innings, Close	.245	.379	.394	94	23	6	1	2	14	20	15	.249	.369	.433	277	69	12	3	11	44	52	51

RBI/Opportunities	1986		THREE YEARS	
Scoring Position	48 / 211	(23%)	131 / 524	(25%)
Scoring Position, 2 Out	16 / 102	(16%)	42 / 232	(18%)
On Third, Less than 2 Out	24 / 43	(56%)	57 / 104	(55%)
RBI in close games / RBI Total	47 / 70	(67%)	169 / 207	(82%)

Eric Davis
Cincinnati Reds

It has been obvious for some time that Davis had the all the necessary baseball skills; it just wasn't obvious when he would put everything together. After two fairly unsuccessful trials in the majors, he finally has surpassed everyone's expectations. He can hit for average, and his ability to hit for power and his speed are exceptional. He is still young enough to improve, so much that he could make this year look like an off-season. He is lucky that he doesn't play in New York, where he might never fulfill people's expectations. His situation is quite comparable to Darryl Strawberry's.

It's interesting to note that he hit with incredible power in turf parks on the road, hitting ten homers in just 88 at bats. I don't know if this is meaningful or not, but it's even more interesting when you note that the two toughest home run parks in the National League, Busch Stadium and the Astrodome, fall into this category.

—by Bill Weydig

I developed conversion factors to project Eric Davis for an entire season (590 at-bats), and see how he might have done the last 3 years. His actual stats are below; these are his projections:

YEAR	AB	R	H	2B	3B	HR	RBI	BB	SB	BA	OBA	SA
1984	590	112	132	34	3	34	102	81	34	.224	.320	.466
1985	590	126	145	15	15	39	87	34	87	.246	.287	.516
1986	590	138	163	21	4	38	101	97	114	.277	.378	.523

These projections make you wonder what took the Reds so long to make him a regular. He could lead the league in runs, homers, stolen bases, and RBIs. His '86 stats project that, given 590 ABs, he would put himself into scoring position under his own power (extra base hits plus stolen bases) 177 times! The biggest decision to make about him is whether to bat him leadoff or cleanup. He'll win an MVP during his career.

People say that Davis seems pretty lackadaisical in the field. Why do people concentrate on the negative? Good centerfielders make about 3 putouts a game. Here's a player who's creating about a sixth of the runs the Reds score when he's in the lineup—and people don't think he hustles! I guess they're upset because he's never hurt himself by running into a wall. Even if he were lackadaisical (and he's not) his speed would give him adequate range in the outfield.

It's time for the Reds to stop bringing in players in the twilight of their careers and give their own young men, like Davis, a chance to play.

—by Thomas Locker

	1986 SEASON											THREE YEARS (84 – 86)										
	Ave.	OBP	SLG	AB	H	2B	3B	HR	RBI	BB	SO	Ave.	OBP	SLG	AB	H	2B	3B	HR	RBI	BB	SO
Totals	.277	.378	.523	415	115	15	3	27	71	68	100	.259	.349	.508	711	184	28	7	45	119	99	187
Batting vs. Left and Right-handed Pitchers																						
Left	.319	.422	.590	144	46	4	1	11	28	27	25	.270	.363	.543	278	75	7	3	21	47	42	69
Right	.255	.354	.487	271	69	11	2	16	43	41	75	.252	.340	.485	433	109	21	4	24	72	57	118
At Home and on the Road																						
Home	.264	.368	.497	197	52	6	2	12	33	32	42	.263	.366	.486	323	85	16	4	16	52	52	82
Road	.289	.387	.546	218	63	9	1	15	38	36	58	.255	.335	.526	388	99	12	3	29	67	47	105
Facing Groundball Pitchers and Flyball Pitchers																						
Groundball	.300	.398	.488	217	65	11	3	8	24	35	37	.287	.372	.518	380	109	19	6	19	55	52	86
Flyball	.253	.356	.561	198	50	4	0	19	47	33	63	.227	.323	.495	331	75	9	1	26	64	47	101
Facing Finesse Pitchers and Power Pitchers																						
Finesse	.292	.372	.569	216	63	11	2	15	36	28	45	.278	.344	.567	381	106	19	5	27	62	38	84
Power	.261	.383	.472	199	52	4	1	12	35	40	55	.236	.355	.439	330	78	9	2	18	57	61	103
On Grass and on Turf																						
Grass	.277	.356	.438	130	36	4	1	5	13	16	29	.261	.332	.513	238	62	5	2	17	36	25	51
Turf	.277	.387	.561	285	79	11	2	22	58	52	71	.258	.358	.505	473	122	23	5	28	83	74	136
During the Day and at Night																						
Day	.295	.413	.576	139	41	4	1	11	29	28	32	.281	.377	.590	249	70	9	4	20	50	39	62
Night	.268	.359	.496	276	74	11	2	16	42	40	68	.247	.334	.463	462	114	19	3	25	69	60	125
By Month																						
April	.185	.290	.370	54	10	1	0	3	6	8	10	.167	.237	.367	120	20	2	2	6	10	11	35
May	.222	.310	.361	36	8	0	1	1	6	5	11	.220	.270	.402	82	18	2	2	3	13	6	25
June	.361	.458	.656	61	22	1	1	5	12	11	12	.391	.475	.696	69	27	4	1	5	14	11	14
July	.381	.465	.702	84	32	9	0	6	16	14	23	.277	.368	.532	141	39	12	0	8	22	20	40
August	.256	.384	.537	82	21	2	0	7	18	17	16	.265	.403	.487	117	31	2	0	8	23	27	27
Sept/Oct	.224	.319	.418	98	22	2	1	5	13	13	28	.269	.354	.571	182	49	6	2	15	37	24	46
Situational																						
Bases Empty	.267	.362	.504	240	64	11	2	14	14	36	50	.242	.333	.482	417	101	16	6	24	24	56	98
Leadoff	.254	.345	.515	130	33	5	1	9	9	18	24	.237	.318	.502	211	50	8	3	14	14	24	43
Not Leadoff	.282	.383	.491	110	31	6	1	5	5	18	26	.248	.349	.461	206	51	8	3	10	10	32	55
Runners On	.291	.398	.549	175	51	4	1	13	57	32	50	.282	.371	.544	294	83	12	1	21	95	43	89
First Base Only	.288	.350	.534	73	21	3	0	5	11	7	19	.276	.333	.526	116	32	8	0	7	15	10	35
Scoring Position	.294	.427	.559	102	30	1	1	8	46	25	31	.287	.394	.556	178	51	4	1	14	80	33	54
Late Innings, Close	.316	.398	.566	76	24	1	0	6	19	11	17	.271	.362	.488	129	35	1	0	9	32	19	33
RBI/Opportunities																						
Scoring Position				33 / 156	(21%)										57 / 260	(22%)						
Scoring Position, 2 Out				16 / 73	(22%)										30 / 124	(24%)						
On Third, Less than 2 Out				10 / 32	(31%)										15 / 49	(31%)						
RBI in close games / RBI Total				48 / 71	(68%)										82 / 119	(69%)						

Glenn Davis
Houston Astros

Glenn Davis was second in the National League MVP voting last year, and he certainly deserved that kind of consideration. He was one of the two power sources on a team with little other power, he accounted for 24.8% of his team's home runs and drove in 15.4% of all of Houston's runs. He did all this in a park which is designed to not give up home runs. Glenn Davis's 31 HRs while playing for Houston are equivalent to 35–40 while playing for almost anyone else.

Glenn did all this by compiling a great home record. In the dome, he hit 17 home runs and batted nearly .300. It is incredible for a player whose strengths are counteracted by the characteristics of his park to have such an outstanding record playing there. To put Davis's performance into perspective, in 1985 the Astros and their opponents hit 240 home runs, yet only 94 of those 240 home runs were hit in the dome. So Davis's 17 HRs in the dome are the equivalent of 26 HRs on the road. Davis, however, hit only 14 homers on the road, and that is less than we could expect based on his performance at home. Not that 14 road home runs is a bad record, but for some reason it is not up to his level of performance in the Astrodome.

Some scattered observations: Davis leans all over the plate, leading to his being hit by the pitcher 9 times, 3rd highest in the league . . . In addition to driving in 100 runs, he was 5th in the league for percentage of runs scored per times on base with 40% . . . His home record is consistent throughout his short career—he hit .317 with 8 HRs in 164 at-bats at home in 1985 . . . His great turf statistics are not entirely a function of his home record—although his average is only .234 on road turf, he has 25 extra-base hits in 192 at-bats, yielding a .516 slugging average.

—Scott M. Daniel

To put Glenn's power into perspective as an Astros first baseman and power-hitter, his 31 home runs were the most for an Astros hitter since Jimmy Wynn's 33 in 1969; they were 2 more than Lee May's record set in 1972 for an Astros first basemen; they represented 63% of the Astros *team* total of 49 in 1979.

So far in his short major-league career, Davis has had notably more success against finesse pitchers than power pitchers.

—Gary Gillette

	1986 SEASON											THREE YEARS (84 – 86)										
	Ave.	OBP	SLG	AB	H	2B	3B	HR	RBI	BB	SO	Ave.	OBP	SLG	AB	H	2B	3B	HR	RBI	BB	SO
Totals	.265	.344	.493	574	152	32	3	31	101	64	72	.264	.335	.479	985	260	47	3	53	173	95	152
Batting vs. Left and Right-handed Pitchers																						
Left	.270	.359	.512	211	57	13	1	12	43	28	23	.271	.348	.518	388	105	22	1	24	78	44	52
Right	.262	.335	.482	363	95	19	2	19	58	36	49	.260	.326	.454	597	155	25	2	29	95	51	100
At Home and on the Road																						
Home	.298	.372	.547	285	85	16	2	17	58	32	30	.299	.361	.513	489	146	23	2	26	96	45	71
Road	.232	.316	.439	289	67	16	1	14	43	32	42	.230	.309	.446	496	114	24	1	27	77	50	81
Facing Groundball Pitchers and Flyball Pitchers																						
Groundball	.257	.336	.498	265	68	11	1	17	38	26	41	.261	.331	.482	463	121	16	1	28	69	39	79
Flyball	.272	.351	.489	309	84	21	2	14	63	38	31	.266	.338	.477	522	139	31	2	25	104	56	73
Facing Finesse Pitchers and Power Pitchers																						
Finesse	.273	.352	.514	319	87	19	2	18	60	33	33	.286	.348	.523	549	157	27	2	33	105	45	63
Power	.255	.333	.467	255	65	13	1	13	41	31	39	.236	.319	.424	436	103	20	1	20	68	50	89
On Grass and on Turf																						
Grass	.231	.299	.391	169	39	9	0	6	18	15	26	.227	.294	.401	304	69	14	0	13	38	27	46
Turf	.279	.362	.536	405	113	23	3	25	83	49	46	.280	.353	.514	681	191	33	3	40	135	68	106
During the Day and at Night																						
Day	.250	.324	.447	188	47	11	1	8	27	18	26	.251	.323	.436	303	76	15	1	13	46	29	45
Night	.272	.354	.516	386	105	21	2	23	74	46	46	.270	.340	.499	682	184	32	2	40	127	66	107
By Month																						
April	.227	.268	.467	75	17	4	1	4	14	5	10	.227	.268	.467	75	17	4	1	4	14	5	10
May	.301	.377	.484	93	28	5	0	4	14	10	13	.301	.377	.484	93	28	5	0	4	14	10	13
June	.278	.336	.574	108	30	6	1	8	20	8	10	.265	.315	.490	155	41	6	1	9	23	10	18
July	.269	.339	.529	104	28	6	0	7	24	10	17	.269	.346	.544	182	49	8	0	14	45	17	38
August	.191	.313	.330	94	18	4	0	3	8	15	12	.225	.318	.374	187	42	10	0	6	23	23	25
Sept/Oct	.310	.410	.550	100	31	7	1	5	21	16	10	.283	.352	.502	293	83	14	1	16	54	30	48
Situational																						
Bases Empty	.272	.336	.498	309	84	18	2	16	16	24	36	.257	.317	.482	541	139	25	2	31	31	38	85
Leadoff	.250	.317	.454	152	38	5	1	8	8	10	16	.264	.328	.516	250	66	10	1	17	17	17	35
Not Leadoff	.293	.355	.541	157	46	13	1	8	8	14	20	.251	.308	.454	291	73	15	1	14	14	21	50
Runners On	.257	.352	.487	265	68	14	1	15	85	40	36	.273	.355	.475	444	121	22	1	22	142	57	67
First Base Only	.243	.328	.534	103	25	6	0	8	21	11	13	.256	.339	.506	168	43	9	0	11	29	18	22
Scoring Position	.265	.367	.457	162	43	8	1	7	64	29	23	.283	.364	.457	276	78	13	1	11	113	39	45
Late Innings, Close	.294	.368	.520	102	30	5	0	6	17	10	19	.242	.305	.422	161	39	8	0	7	25	13	36

RBI/Opportunities				
Scoring Position	51 / 230	(22%)	93 / 386	(24%)
Scoring Position, 2 Out	20 / 111	(18%)	35 / 189	(19%)
On Third, Less than 2 Out	21 / 43	(49%)	35 / 67	(52%)
RBI in close games / RBI Total	70 / 101	(69%)	119 / 173	(69%)

Jody Davis
Chicago Cubs

Jody Davis is a man who works hard and does the best with what he has. As the Cubs starting—and seemingly only—catcher, Davis has averaged 147 games per season over the last four years, but has not really distinguished himself as a master of any particular aspect of his game. Despite this, the fans of Chicago have always held him as a favorite. Must be the red hair . . . .

The fact that Davis plays virtually every day has had a predictable effect on his offensive output during the season. A glance at his By Month breakdown shows a definite falling off in late summer (July and August) followed by a resurgence at the close of the season. For some reason, Cub backup catchers, with the exception of Keith Moreland, keep getting injured or stricken with illness. In recent memory, two Steves—Lake and Christmas—have assumed that role, and have suffered from a variety of injuries. This usually forces Keith Moreland to the backup spot, where he is unlikely to see a great deal of action because of the added wear and tear at the catching position (Moreland did catch 90 innings in 1986, second to Davis' 1257).

Let us assume then that given sufficient rest, Davis could sustain the offensive level represented by his figures for the first three months of the last three seasons. It is reasonable to assume that about 73 games comprise the first three months of a season. We can extrapolate Davis' totals for these months to a full season, if we allow him to play, say, 130 games (11% less, or an extra game off every nine). This adds up to a different Jody Davis: 113 H in 420 AB for a .269 AVE; 24 2B and 17 HR give him a projected SLG of .452. The net difference from the real Davis is a gain of 22 points in average and 35 points in slugging.

Granted, this is a numerical exercise with an unproven tie to reality. Nevertheless, Davis' swoon in July and August is too real to ignore and the Cubs might do well to get him the needed rest early in the year (or whatever else it is he might need) to protract his useful offensive production through the entire season.

Not regarded as much of a thrower for several seasons, Davis had a tremendous year in '86 defensing the stolen base. With Davis behind the plate, opponent baserunners stole at just a 48% success rate, far below the 62% success rate in '85.

—Mark Podrazik

	1986 SEASON											THREE YEARS (84 – 86)									
	Ave.	OBP	SLG	AB	H	2B	3B	HR	RBI	BB	SO	Ave.	OBP	SLG	AB	H	2B	3B	HR	RBI	BB	SO
Totals	.250	.300	.428	528	132	27	2	21	74	41	110	.247	.305	.417	1533	378	82	4	57	226	136	292
Batting vs. Left and Right-handed Pitchers																						
Left	.233	.286	.353	133	31	7	0	3	12	11	15	.247	.313	.439	392	97	29	2	14	50	40	54
Right	.256	.305	.453	395	101	20	2	18	62	30	95	.246	.302	.409	1141	281	53	2	43	176	96	238
At Home and on the Road																						
Home	.267	.315	.481	262	70	12	1	14	49	20	57	.268	.332	.468	769	206	41	1	37	141	79	142
Road	.233	.285	.376	266	62	15	1	7	25	21	53	.225	.277	.365	764	172	41	3	20	85	57	150
Facing Groundball Pitchers and Flyball Pitchers																						
Groundball	.248	.304	.425	254	63	16	1	9	43	22	55	.266	.329	.437	743	198	46	3	25	128	74	145
Flyball	.252	.296	.431	274	69	11	1	12	31	19	55	.228	.282	.397	790	180	36	1	32	98	62	147
Facing Finesse Pitchers and Power Pitchers																						
Finesse	.261	.297	.436	307	80	17	2	11	44	18	47	.249	.300	.408	863	215	43	2	30	123	69	137
Power	.235	.304	.416	221	52	10	0	10	30	23	63	.243	.311	.428	670	163	39	2	27	103	67	155
On Grass and on Turf																						
Grass	.239	.295	.419	377	90	18	1	16	56	32	80	.251	.312	.429	1106	278	60	2	44	171	104	210
Turf	.278	.313	.450	151	42	9	1	5	18	9	30	.234	.285	.386	427	100	22	2	13	55	32	82
During the Day and at Night																						
Day	.250	.306	.426	352	88	15	1	15	53	30	72	.261	.324	.444	1009	263	55	2	42	169	101	175
Night	.250	.288	.432	176	44	12	1	6	21	11	38	.219	.266	.365	524	115	27	2	15	57	35	117
By Month																						
April	.254	.280	.380	71	18	3	0	2	9	3	20	.279	.333	.416	190	53	11	0	5	28	16	38
May	.240	.308	.531	96	23	5	1	7	17	10	25	.253	.319	.480	269	68	14	1	15	47	27	58
June	.275	.313	.385	91	25	5	1	1	9	5	15	.281	.344	.470	249	70	16	2	9	49	25	41
July	.207	.240	.348	92	19	4	0	3	9	4	18	.208	.238	.339	289	60	12	1	8	27	12	50
August	.212	.248	.364	99	21	6	0	3	11	6	20	.199	.258	.356	267	53	15	0	9	34	24	48
Sept/Oct	.329	.415	.570	79	26	4	0	5	19	13	12	.275	.349	.450	269	74	14	0	11	41	32	57
Situational																						
Bases Empty	.237	.307	.406	278	66	15	1	10	10	28	65	.244	.300	.400	807	197	40	1	28	28	64	168
Leadoff	.274	.349	.469	113	31	10	0	4	4	13	22	.249	.298	.407	329	82	19	0	11	11	23	63
Not Leadoff	.212	.278	.364	165	35	5	1	6	6	15	43	.241	.301	.395	478	115	21	1	17	17	41	105
Runners On	.264	.292	.452	250	66	12	1	11	64	13	45	.249	.311	.435	726	181	42	3	29	198	72	124
First Base Only	.283	.308	.460	113	32	6	1	4	11	4	21	.270	.316	.469	318	86	19	1	14	34	21	50
Scoring Position	.248	.279	.445	137	34	6	0	7	53	9	24	.233	.307	.409	408	95	23	2	15	164	51	74
Late Innings, Close	.232	.275	.404	99	23	2	0	5	12	7	29	.211	.285	.317	265	56	7	0	7	33	30	63
RBI/Opportunities																						
Scoring Position				42 / 179		(23%)									136 / 571		(24%)					
Scoring Position, 2 Out				14 / 83		(17%)									48 / 267		(18%)					
On Third, Less than 2 Out				16 / 33		(48%)									53 / 99		(54%)					
RBI in close games / RBI Total				42 / 74		(57%)									129 / 226		(57%)					

Mike Davis
Oakland A's

Oakland has been waiting a long time for Mike Davis to develop, and now that he is here it is hard to know what to do with him. Davis, now 27, is regarded as one of the best athletes in baseball. From 1980 through 1984 he struggled to find consistency as a hitter. After an outstanding season in 1985, he consolidated some of his gains in 1986, and there is no longer any question about his ability to hold a job in the majors.

Davis has some power and excellent speed. He hit 24 homers in 1985, but almost all of them in two streaks, so there was some question about his ability to sustain his power production in 1986. He answered that by hitting 19 homers, and producing fairly consistently throughout the year. He hits doubles as well—34 in 1985, 28 last year.

Davis steals bases in a way that helps his team. In 1986 he was caught stealing only four times while stealing 27 bases. This was the best stolen base percentage in the American League among players with 20 or more steals. Davis uses his speed well in the outfield, and has a strong if somewhat erratic arm.

Now the bad news: What do you do with him? Davis has hit best when leading off an inning, hitting .356 in the leadoff role in 1986 and consistently showing power when leading off. Over a three-year period he has hit 18 homers in 326 at bats as a leadoff man, perhaps because pitchers don't want a man with his speed on base to lead off an inning. He has the speed of a lead-off hitter, but he doesn't get on base enough to do the job well (.314 on base percentage in 1986, .319 over the last three years.) With his power he tends to wind up in the middle of the lineup, but in 1986 he drove in only 8 of 70 runners who were in scoring position with two out, an abysmal 11%. He his just .238 with runners in scoring position, and just .171 in the late innings of close games. All of those figures are poor, although not as poor, over a three-year period. He may yet develop into a valuable player, but at this point his lack of bat control and lack of plate discipline make it difficult to find an offensive role for him.

—Bill James

	1986 SEASON											THREE YEARS (84 – 86)										
	Ave.	OBP	SLG	AB	H	2B	3B	HR	RBI	BB	SO	Ave.	OBP	SLG	AB	H	2B	3B	HR	RBI	BB	SO
Totals	.268	.314	.454	489	131	28	3	19	55	34	91	.265	.319	.441	1418	376	80	7	52	183	115	256
Batting vs. Left and Right-handed Pitchers																						
Left	.299	.339	.479	117	35	5	2	4	17	6	30	.267	.320	.455	345	92	20	3	13	52	25	84
Right	.258	.306	.446	372	96	23	1	15	38	28	61	.265	.319	.437	1073	284	60	4	39	131	90	172
At Home and on the Road																						
Home	.266	.338	.475	244	65	14	2	11	29	28	40	.262	.330	.454	667	175	37	5	27	88	70	113
Road	.269	.287	.433	245	66	14	1	8	26	6	51	.268	.309	.430	751	201	43	2	25	95	45	143
Facing Groundball Pitchers and Flyball Pitchers																						
Groundball	.301	.339	.525	236	71	18	1	11	30	14	38	.299	.347	.510	700	209	50	4	30	104	53	116
Flyball	.237	.291	.387	253	60	10	2	8	25	20	53	.233	.292	.375	718	167	30	3	22	79	62	140
Facing Finesse Pitchers and Power Pitchers																						
Finesse	.287	.325	.461	293	84	19	1	10	31	17	45	.260	.309	.420	823	214	45	3	27	89	57	132
Power	.240	.298	.444	196	47	9	2	9	24	17	46	.272	.333	.471	595	162	35	4	25	94	58	124
On Grass and on Turf																						
Grass	.251	.302	.419	418	105	21	2	15	41	32	79	.261	.319	.432	1197	313	63	6	43	152	105	216
Turf	.366	.387	.662	71	26	7	1	4	14	2	12	.285	.321	.493	221	63	17	1	9	31	10	40
During the Day and at Night																						
Day	.249	.310	.431	209	52	11	3	7	26	19	38	.257	.326	.460	533	137	32	5	22	83	55	97
Night	.282	.316	.471	280	79	17	0	12	29	15	53	.270	.315	.431	885	239	48	2	30	100	60	159
By Month																						
April	.234	.260	.298	47	11	3	0	0	4	2	6	.282	.323	.511	174	49	13	0	9	28	11	26
May	.250	.309	.477	88	22	8	0	4	11	8	22	.247	.324	.446	231	57	15	2	9	29	27	41
June	.261	.320	.489	92	24	6	0	5	13	9	17	.252	.308	.408	282	71	20	0	8	34	24	54
July	.265	.307	.373	83	22	1	1	2	7	4	12	.242	.286	.398	256	62	11	1	9	31	15	35
August	.286	.329	.584	77	22	5	0	6	8	5	18	.281	.344	.478	224	63	12	1	10	27	22	48
Sept/Oct	.294	.330	.441	102	30	5	2	2	12	6	16	.295	.336	.438	251	74	9	3	7	34	16	52
Situational																						
Bases Empty	.270	.312	.491	293	79	18	1	15	15	18	54	.265	.318	.460	818	217	48	3	35	35	61	139
Leadoff	.356	.385	.654	104	37	8	1	7	7	5	15	.288	.337	.521	326	94	20	1	18	18	23	46
Not Leadoff	.222	.272	.402	189	42	10	0	8	8	13	39	.250	.305	.419	492	123	28	2	17	17	38	93
Runners On	.265	.317	.398	196	52	10	2	4	40	16	37	.265	.321	.417	600	159	32	4	17	148	54	117
First Base Only	.297	.347	.462	91	27	4	1	3	9	7	16	.287	.334	.448	268	77	14	1	9	23	19	48
Scoring Position	.238	.292	.343	105	25	6	1	1	31	9	21	.247	.311	.392	332	82	18	3	8	125	35	69
Late Innings, Close	.171	.198	.366	82	14	2	1	4	9	3	18	.243	.290	.434	235	57	10	1	11	30	17	51
RBI/Opportunities																						
Scoring Position				27 / 147		(18%)									108 / 461		(23%)					
Scoring Position, 2 Out				8 / 70		(11%)									36 / 220		(16%)					
On Third, Less than 2 Out				11 / 24		(46%)									40 / 77		(52%)					
RBI in close games / RBI Total				37 / 55		(67%)									106 / 183		(58%)					

Storm Davis
Baltimore Orioles

Storm Davis has had the terrible luck to suffer through a series of unflattering comparisons to other Oriole starters. He arrived in 1982 as the "next Jim Palmer;" he left in 1986 as the "new Dennis Martinez." For the sake of fairness, I shall try to compare him only to himself.

After pitching only 26.2 innings in Rochester, the 20 year old Davis was promoted to Baltimore, to serve as the long relief/spot starter. He did well enough to win a spot in the 1983 rotation and be hailed as the Orioles' "designated power pitcher." It was a sadly limiting and misleading description; Davis was already trying to become a more complete pitcher. Despite his success, Davis felt that his best chance to pitch effectively was to rely less on his velocity and more on location—until 1985, he appeared to be making the transition well. In 1984, he set career bests in wins (14) and ERA. He had some control problems, but he allowed only 8.20 hits per game and the trade was one that the Orioles were willing to live with.

1985, however, saw Davis take giant strides backwards in every way. His ERA rose to 4.53, he barely avoided allowing a hit per inning, walked 3.6 men a game and had the worst K/W ratio of his career. Rather than take it as a discouraging but not unusual off year (many talented 23 year olds have done far worse), management decided that it was positive proof that Davis's new approach was failing and ordered him to be "more aggressive" in 1986. Davis tried hard to oblige. He improved his control, struck more hitters out and had the lowest ERA of any Baltimore starter, despite missing nearly a month with strained muscles and going down with an ankle injury in September. He pitched well enough to win, but he got no help from his team. Supported by only 3.96 runs a game, his record fell to 9–13 and his career in Baltimore ended.

Davis has never lived up to his team's expectations, but he can hardly be blamed for this. He is 25, has had only one losing season in the majors and has pitched as effectively (given his support) as anyone. Had Baltimore shown a bit more patience with him and allowed him to grow at his own pace—to be, in short, Storm Davis instead of Jim Palmer—he might be well on his way to a successful career. As it is, he must now begin picking up the pieces with a new team and in a new league.

—Tim Mulligan

1986: Finesse, Groundball   1985: Finesse, Flyball   1984: Finesse, Groundball

	G	IP	H	BB	SO	SB	CS	W	L	S	ERA		G	IP	H	BB	SO	SB	CS	W	L	S	ERA
	1986 SEASON												**THREE YEARS (84 – 86)**										
Totals	25	154.0	166	49	96	10	11	9	12	0	3.62		91	554.0	543	190	294	44	23	33	29	1	3.70
At Home and on the Road																							
Home	14	83.1	99	23	58	4	7	5	7	0	3.35		47	292.0	295	97	172	19	11	18	18	1	3.64
Road	11	70.2	67	26	38	6	4	4	5	0	3.95		44	262.0	248	93	122	25	12	15	11	0	3.78
During the Day and at Night																							
Day	6	32.1	41	4	20	3	1	3	3	0	3.90		28	147.2	148	39	68	12	8	8	9	0	3.96
Night	19	121.2	125	45	76	7	10	6	9	0	3.55		63	406.1	395	151	226	32	15	25	20	1	3.61
On Grass and on Turf																							
Grass	23	141.1	150	46	88	7	10	8	11	0	3.31		79	488.1	478	165	270	35	22	30	25	1	3.61
Turf	2	12.2	16	3	8	3	1	1	1	0	7.11		12	65.2	65	25	24	9	1	3	4	0	4.39
By Month																							
April	4	26.1	17	11	17	0	1	1	1	0	2.73		16	88.1	65	34	38	5	3	3	1	1	3.46
May	6	35.1	45	11	26	5	5	3	3	0	4.33		18	116.0	107	38	68	11	5	9	5	0	3.10
June	6	38.1	41	9	20	1	3	2	4	0	2.82		19	110.0	128	37	57	11	10	4	10	0	4.09
July	2	11.1	13	4	9	2	1	1	0	0	5.56		10	68.1	57	25	34	5	2	6	2	0	3.56
August	6	39.2	48	12	22	2	1	2	4	0	3.63		18	113.0	125	35	68	11	1	7	8	0	3.98
Sept/Oct	1	3.0	2	2	2	0	0	0	0	0	6.00		10	58.1	61	21	29	1	2	4	3	0	4.17

vs. Opponent Batters

	Ave.	OBP	SLG	AB	H	2B	3B	HR	RBI	BB	SO		Ave.	OBP	SLG	AB	H	2B	3B	HR	RBI	BB	SO
	1986 SEASON												**THREE YEARS (84 – 86)**										
Totals	.275	.329	.400	603	166	21	3	16	63	49	96		.258	.319	.361	2107	543	91	12	34	216	190	294
Pitching vs. Left and Right-handed Batters																							
Left	.293	.358	.453	300	88	9	3	11	32	31	42		.267	.343	.387	1065	284	54	7	20	118	129	169
Right	.257	.298	.347	303	78	12	0	5	31	18	54		.249	.293	.334	1042	259	37	5	14	98	61	125
Situational																							
Bases Empty	.256	.320	.400	355	91	11	2	12	12	33	58		.234	.299	.334	1229	287	44	8	21	21	111	169
Leadoff	.314	.364	.516	153	48	5	1	8	8	12	21		.250	.302	.354	537	134	18	1	12	12	39	58
Not Leadoff	.213	.287	.312	202	43	6	1	4	4	21	37		.221	.296	.318	692	153	26	7	9	9	72	111
Runners On	.302	.342	.399	248	75	10	1	4	51	16	38		.292	.347	.399	878	256	47	4	13	195	79	125
First Base Only	.321	.368	.413	109	35	4	0	2	4	8	19		.289	.340	.390	395	114	21	2	5	15	29	58
Scoring Position	.288	.322	.388	139	40	6	1	2	47	8	19		.294	.352	.406	483	142	26	2	8	180	50	67
Late Innings, Close	.255	.305	.436	55	14	1	0	3	5	4	4		.266	.327	.415	188	50	10	0	6	19	18	19

RBI/Opportunities

Scoring Position	44 / 175	(25%)	162 / 650	(25%)
Scoring Position, 2 Out	14 / 64	(22%)	62 / 286	(22%)
On Third, Less than 2 Out	20 / 38	(53%)	69 / 125	(55%)
RBI in close games / RBI Total	48 / 63	(76%)	163 / 216	(75%)

Andre Dawson
Montreal Expos

Chronic knee problems have seriously reduced Andre Dawson's talents the past three seasons. During this span he has averaged 20 home runs, 85 RBIs, 13 stolen bases and a .262 average. From '81 to '83 the Hawk's average had been 26 HR, 87 RBI, 30 SB and a .301 average; those figures include the '81 strike year, but Dawson actually had more at bats in this period than in '84-'86.

Clearly Andre's abilities to play every day, run and hit for average have been seriously affected. He's not the Gold Glove center fielder any more; he's just a good right fielder. However, Dawson has made the necessary adjustments to remain a vital bat in the Expo attack. He has continued to produce homers and RBIs at a consistent rate, a rate not too far from his premium numbers. He has accepted the limitations imposed on him by his ailments. He carefully avoids trying too hard or overreaching, knowing that this will only result in more pain and curtailed productiveness. These days, an Andre Dawson season is a compromise between staying healthy and producing decent statistics. The numbers have been so consistent the past three seasons that he seems to be saying, "Listen, I can't play as hard as before, it's just too painful, but I'll still give you 20 homers, 80 RBIs and a decent batting average."

When one thinks about it, this sort of compromise makes sense. Many other players don't face up to chronic injuries; they try too hard, physically and mentally burning out under the strain of pain and pressure. Dawson's former teammate Larry Parrish played about three seasons with an injured wrist in Montreal and Texas, and was almost released in 1984 before he went on a second half binge. Unlike Parrish, who of course also has the luxury of the designated hitter rule, Dawson has carefully adjusted his approach to the game and his consistent play has been no coincidence. Both at bat and in the field, he doesn't stride toward the ball as strongly and swiftly as in the past, and he takes a day off when he has to. His game lacks its former beauty, but it doesn't lack in productivity. Last year was only the second time in Dawson's career that he has hit better at home. He continues to play better on grass—grass fields are of course easier on his aching knees—and in day games. No wonder he'd like to play for the Cubs.

—Marco Bresba

	1986 SEASON											THREE YEARS (84 – 86)										
	Ave.	OBP	SLG	AB	H	2B	3B	HR	RBI	BB	SO	Ave.	OBP	SLG	AB	H	2B	3B	HR	RBI	BB	SO
Totals	.284	.338	.478	496	141	32	2	20	78	37	79	.262	.310	.443	1558	408	82	10	60	255	106	252
Batting vs. Left and Right-handed Pitchers																						
Left	.331	.384	.625	160	53	12	1	11	25	14	20	.296	.347	.541	473	140	26	3	28	80	37	68
Right	.262	.315	.408	336	88	20	1	9	53	23	59	.247	.294	.400	1085	268	56	7	32	175	69	184
At Home and on the Road																						
Home	.296	.356	.477	243	72	11	0	11	32	19	39	.251	.306	.413	748	188	27	5	28	112	55	116
Road	.273	.320	.478	253	69	21	2	9	46	18	40	.272	.315	.470	810	220	55	5	32	143	51	136
Facing Groundball Pitchers and Flyball Pitchers																						
Groundball	.294	.351	.462	238	70	13	0	9	35	18	34	.275	.328	.451	728	200	36	4	28	115	57	110
Flyball	.275	.325	.492	258	71	19	2	11	43	18	45	.251	.294	.436	830	208	46	6	32	140	49	142
Facing Finesse Pitchers and Power Pitchers																						
Finesse	.266	.314	.472	290	77	17	2	13	43	19	32	.260	.306	.439	917	238	39	6	38	137	61	115
Power	.311	.370	.485	206	64	15	0	7	35	18	47	.265	.317	.448	641	170	43	4	22	118	45	137
On Grass and on Turf																						
Grass	.294	.340	.462	143	42	10	1	4	23	10	25	.279	.314	.487	452	126	28	3	20	84	24	81
Turf	.280	.337	.484	353	99	22	1	16	55	27	54	.255	.309	.425	1106	282	54	7	40	171	82	171
During the Day and at Night																						
Day	.293	.375	.515	167	49	8	1	9	23	21	30	.297	.351	.539	558	166	28	4	33	114	46	87
Night	.280	.317	.459	329	92	24	1	11	55	16	49	.242	.287	.389	1000	242	54	6	27	141	60	165
By Month																						
April	.333	.395	.697	66	22	4	1	6	8	8	6	.313	.377	.564	211	66	9	4	12	36	22	26
May	.263	.320	.432	95	25	5	1	3	12	7	21	.230	.287	.369	274	63	18	1	6	36	22	48
June	.286	.286	.929	14	4	0	0	3	5	0	1	.204	.228	.357	157	32	6	0	6	22	4	27
July	.222	.287	.344	90	20	5	0	2	15	8	20	.257	.311	.377	268	69	11	0	7	41	20	47
August	.272	.313	.447	103	28	9	0	3	18	4	15	.278	.311	.469	309	86	19	2	12	55	13	53
Sept/Oct	.328	.381	.469	128	42	9	0	3	20	10	16	.271	.322	.496	339	92	19	3	17	65	25	51
Situational																						
Bases Empty	.291	.326	.535	254	74	16	2	14	14	9	34	.244	.275	.419	807	197	40	7	29	29	29	130
Leadoff	.255	.286	.457	94	24	7	0	4	4	2	9	.230	.260	.403	318	73	20	1	11	11	10	44
Not Leadoff	.313	.349	.581	160	50	9	2	10	10	7	25	.254	.284	.429	489	124	20	6	18	18	19	86
Runners On	.277	.349	.417	242	67	16	0	6	64	28	45	.281	.345	.469	751	211	42	3	31	226	77	122
First Base Only	.309	.356	.420	81	25	6	0	1	5	4	13	.267	.311	.445	281	75	13	2	11	29	14	45
Scoring Position	.261	.346	.416	161	42	10	0	5	59	24	32	.289	.364	.483	470	136	29	1	20	197	63	77
Late Innings, Close	.290	.364	.430	107	31	4	1	3	11	11	15	.247	.308	.401	299	74	12	2	10	49	26	59

RBI/Opportunities					
Scoring Position	51 / 218	(23%)	166 / 645	(26%)
Scoring Position, 2 Out	19 / 87	(22%)	61 / 239	(26%)
On Third, Less than 2 Out	20 / 49	(41%)	60 / 136	(44%)
RBI in close games / RBI Total	56 / 78	(72%)	194 / 255	(76%)

Doug DeCinces
California Angels

If Wally Joyner carried the Angels the first half of 1986, then Doug DeCinces carried them the second half. The day before the All-Star break, Joyner had 71 RBI's, and DeCinces had 45. By September 21, DeCinces had caught him. He was the American League Player of the Month for August, in which his slugging percentage was .684. August was essentially the month that won the Angels a division, and DeCinces was the key to the Angel offense during that period. Joyner's last homerun of 1986 came on August 5th, and at that point, Doug took over the offense. Does that sound like a team destined to win a division?

For 1987, the Angels are a team waiting to disintegrate into the mediocrity of the American League West. As DeCinces and other veterans begin their natural decline, the Angels can expect to see their place in the standings decline. DeCinces' back may carry him through another good year, but his back won't last much longer. The vultures are starting to circle around Boone, Hendrick, Downing, and DeCinces. For each of these players, a natural move might be to move them to first base to finish their careers. Unfortunately, one of the products of the Angel youth movement is a 24 year old first baseman, thus clogging up the natural progression of an aging team.

Unlike some other positions, the Angels have a replacement ready for DeCinces. His name is Jack Howell, and he's proven that he's too big for the Pacific Coast League, and it's time he got at least 400 at-bats in a major league season. Then Angels seem undecided whether he will eventually take over at third base, or in left field. Personally, I'd move DeCinces to DH, and give third base to Jack Howell for the next ten years.

Only two teams in the American League had three players with at least 95 RBI's. The Red Sox had Jim Rice (110), Bill Buckner (102), and Dwight Evans (97). The Angels had Wally Joyner (100), Doug DeCinces (96), and Brian Downing (95). For the Angels to seriously contend in 1987, all three of those players are going to have to reach their 1986 levels.

—Dennis Bretz

	1986 SEASON											THREE YEARS (84 – 86)										
	Ave.	OBP	SLG	AB	H	2B	3B	HR	RBI	BB	SO	Ave.	OBP	SLG	AB	H	2B	3B	HR	RBI	BB	SO
Totals	.256	.325	.459	512	131	20	3	26	96	52	74	.257	.323	.443	1486	382	65	7	66	256	152	225
Batting vs. Left and Right-handed Pitchers																						
Left	.272	.345	.486	173	47	8	1	9	35	21	24	.278	.359	.486	475	132	21	3	24	91	64	60
Right	.248	.314	.445	339	84	12	2	17	61	31	50	.247	.306	.423	1011	250	44	4	42	165	88	165
At Home and on the Road																						
Home	.263	.328	.456	259	68	8	0	14	49	25	39	.261	.332	.452	733	191	26	3	36	124	81	107
Road	.249	.322	.462	253	63	12	3	12	47	27	35	.254	.314	.436	753	191	39	4	30	132	71	118
Facing Groundball Pitchers and Flyball Pitchers																						
Groundball	.284	.353	.491	222	63	8	1	12	44	23	29	.291	.356	.480	721	210	34	3	32	131	75	102
Flyball	.234	.302	.434	290	68	12	2	14	52	29	45	.225	.292	.409	765	172	31	4	34	125	77	123
Facing Finesse Pitchers and Power Pitchers																						
Finesse	.270	.330	.497	300	81	10	2	18	60	26	37	.258	.312	.446	834	215	35	4	38	147	69	105
Power	.236	.317	.406	212	50	10	1	8	36	26	37	.256	.336	.440	652	167	30	3	28	109	83	120
On Grass and on Turf																						
Grass	.262	.327	.466	451	118	17	3	23	88	43	66	.260	.328	.452	1240	322	50	7	58	217	131	174
Turf	.213	.306	.410	61	13	3	0	3	8	9	8	.244	.298	.402	246	60	15	0	8	39	21	51
During the Day and at Night																						
Day	.266	.331	.487	154	41	5	1	9	33	15	23	.265	.335	.447	412	109	17	2	18	69	46	64
Night	.251	.322	.447	358	90	15	2	17	63	37	51	.254	.319	.442	1074	273	48	5	48	187	106	161
By Month																						
April	.237	.303	.412	80	19	3	1	3	13	7	7	.264	.325	.453	258	68	14	1	11	50	24	29
May	.211	.292	.305	95	20	3	0	2	11	11	11	.220	.291	.356	205	45	7	0	7	22	22	28
June	.288	.361	.548	73	21	4	0	5	17	9	14	.254	.329	.421	252	64	13	1	9	37	30	39
July	.264	.299	.417	72	19	5	0	2	15	4	13	.274	.318	.433	252	69	14	1	8	42	18	39
August	.337	.407	.684	95	32	4	1	9	25	12	7	.292	.365	.545	253	74	12	2	16	62	31	36
Sept/Oct	.206	.280	.392	97	20	1	1	5	15	9	22	.233	.305	.436	266	62	5	2	15	43	27	54
Situational																						
Bases Empty	.238	.321	.467	244	58	12	1	14	14	29	35	.254	.325	.443	741	188	38	3	32	32	77	99
Leadoff	.277	.388	.542	83	23	2	1	6	6	14	7	.266	.332	.447	320	85	14	1	14	14	31	36
Not Leadoff	.217	.284	.429	161	35	10	0	8	8	15	28	.245	.319	.439	421	103	24	2	18	18	46	63
Runners On	.272	.328	.451	268	73	8	2	12	82	23	39	.260	.322	.444	745	194	27	4	34	224	75	126
First Base Only	.269	.290	.519	104	28	2	0	8	17	3	13	.258	.301	.452	310	80	13	1	15	37	18	52
Scoring Position	.274	.349	.409	164	45	6	2	4	65	20	26	.262	.335	.439	435	114	14	3	19	187	57	74
Late Innings, Close	.311	.347	.533	90	28	3	1	5	16	5	13	.273	.327	.419	253	69	8	1	9	41	21	41

RBI/Opportunities

Scoring Position	58 / 226	(26%)		153 / 609	(25%)	
Scoring Position, 2 Out	25 / 102	(25%)		51 / 264	(19%)	
On Third, Less than 2 Out	22 / 41	(54%)		69 / 125	(55%)	
RBI in close games / RBI Total	66 / 96	(69%)		176 / 256	(69%)	

Rob Deer
Milwaukee Brewers

In 1986, Rob Deer came to Milwaukee and blossomed into a major league outfielder. The critical factor in his development was merely the chance to play regularly. Deer's ability to hit for power has been evident throughout his career—he has led three minor leagues in homers in the past. In 1985, Deer had the NL's second highest home run percentage against lefties, but his overall stats drew very little acclaim—the Giants were deep in outfielders and were unwilling to allow him to play more often in 1986.

George Bamberger was willing, which is no surprise. He has always stressed the importance of letting the defense do the work for a pitcher and growled that "the only two things you can't defense are the homer and the walk." As such, it is only natural that he would be attracted to men who can do those two things—Deer, like Gorman Thomas before him, does them both very well. Milwaukee obtained him cheaply, for two borderline pitching prospects, hoping that his ability to walk and homer would boost his on-base and slugging averages up to major league levels despite his always-low batting averages. Deer did exactly that. It is worth noting that Deer is not as undisciplined a player as

his 179 strikeouts imply. He did extremely well with men on first base. If a pitcher threw him a ball, he let it pass by—if he got a strike, he crushed it. If he were somewhat more selective with the bases empty, he could get his average up to respectable levels in the future. Rob has a strong throwing arm and above-average speed—his defensive skills were a pleasant surprise to the Milwaukee faithful, who expected someone far clumsier afield.

But Deer may be caught in a trap in 1987. Milwaukee is trying to rebuild themselves around speed, pitching and defense—despite his power, he may have trouble playing a major role in the team's future. It is safe to assume that he won't have his job taken away—one of the noted rookies will have to beat him out of a job—and he may be able to hang on as one of the few reliable power sources in the order. But it does not augur well for him and a sudden trade would not be out of the question.

There have been 11 times when a major league hitter has struck out 170 or more times in a year; four men (Deer, Canseco, Presley and Incaviglia) did so in the AL in 1986.

—Steven Copley and Scott Segrin

	1986 SEASON											THREE YEARS (84 – 86)										
	Ave.	OBP	SLG	AB	H	2B	3B	HR	RBI	BB	SO	Ave.	OBP	SLG	AB	H	2B	3B	HR	RBI	BB	SO
Totals	.232	.336	.494	466	108	17	3	33	86	72	179	.218	.325	.466	652	142	22	4	44	109	102	260
	Batting vs. Left and Right-handed Pitchers																					
Left	.279	.416	.605	129	36	5	2	11	27	31	40	.256	.375	.588	199	51	8	2	18	40	39	65
Right	.214	.303	.451	337	72	12	1	22	59	41	139	.201	.302	.413	453	91	14	2	26	69	63	195
	At Home and on the Road																					
Home	.227	.329	.504	238	54	7	1	19	49	37	91	.207	.320	.476	334	69	8	2	26	62	56	128
Road	.237	.345	.482	228	54	10	2	14	37	35	88	.230	.331	.456	318	73	14	2	18	47	46	132
	Facing Groundball Pitchers and Flyball Pitchers																					
Groundball	.222	.328	.502	207	46	7	0	17	44	34	81	.234	.348	.517	286	67	12	0	23	56	52	114
Flyball	.239	.343	.486	259	62	10	3	16	42	38	98	.205	.306	.426	366	75	10	4	21	53	50	146
	Facing Finesse Pitchers and Power Pitchers																					
Finesse	.249	.342	.509	281	70	11	1	20	49	37	98	.239	.332	.489	393	94	15	1	27	65	53	136
Power	.205	.329	.470	185	38	6	2	13	37	35	81	.185	.315	.432	259	48	7	3	17	44	49	124
	On Grass and on Turf																					
Grass	.226	.333	.470	411	93	15	2	27	73	64	158	.212	.325	.455	552	117	17	3	37	91	90	216
Turf	.273	.365	.673	55	15	2	1	6	13	8	21	.250	.327	.530	100	25	5	1	7	18	12	44
	During the Day and at Night																					
Day	.208	.320	.423	130	27	5	1	7	19	20	56	.197	.306	.443	228	45	7	2	15	35	35	99
Night	.241	.343	.521	336	81	12	2	26	67	52	123	.229	.335	.479	424	97	15	2	29	74	67	161
	By Month																					
April	.208	.309	.479	48	10	1	0	4	8	6	18	.216	.310	.529	51	11	1	0	5	10	6	18
May	.257	.389	.527	74	19	3	1	5	15	15	28	.267	.380	.500	90	24	4	1	5	18	16	32
June	.192	.247	.384	73	14	0	1	4	12	6	33	.183	.250	.357	115	21	0	1	6	16	11	48
July	.257	.356	.554	74	19	4	0	6	17	11	23	.238	.350	.512	84	20	5	0	6	18	14	29
August	.248	.347	.600	105	26	4	0	11	29	16	36	.243	.339	.604	111	27	4	0	12	30	16	40
Sept/Oct	.217	.345	.391	92	20	5	1	3	5	18	41	.194	.326	.403	201	39	8	2	10	17	39	93
	Situational																					
Bases Empty	.214	.322	.445	238	51	6	2	15	15	36	90	.224	.330	.471	340	76	9	3	23	23	51	129
Leadoff	.226	.339	.425	106	24	3	0	6	6	18	32	.237	.358	.482	139	33	4	0	10	10	26	44
Not Leadoff	.205	.309	.462	132	27	3	2	9	9	18	58	.214	.310	.463	201	43	5	3	13	13	25	85
Runners On	.250	.351	.544	228	57	11	1	18	71	36	89	.212	.320	.462	312	66	13	1	21	86	51	131
First Base Only	.260	.347	.615	104	27	7	0	10	21	14	47	.213	.306	.507	150	32	8	0	12	25	20	68
Scoring Position	.242	.353	.484	124	30	4	1	8	50	22	42	.210	.332	.420	162	34	5	1	9	61	31	63
Late Innings, Close	.209	.293	.418	67	14	1	2	3	9	7	27	.179	.281	.368	106	19	1	2	5	14	14	48

RBI/Opportunities					
Scoring Position	36 / 170	(21%)		44 / 229	(19%)
Scoring Position, 2 Out	10 / 78	(13%)		12 / 108	(11%)
On Third, Less than 2 Out	17 / 38	(45%)		21 / 49	(43%)
RBI in close games / RBI Total	53 / 86	(62%)		67 / 109	(61%)

Rick Dempsey
Baltimore Orioles

Rick Dempsey has been a walking embodiment of everything that the Orioles have stood for in the past decade. His successes and failures have coincided precisely with the Orioles' own. He came to them from the Yankees in one of the best deals in Baltimore history, at a time when Baltimore was struggling to bridge the gap between powerhouse teams—he leaves with the team about to enter one of the darkest periods in their illustrious history. A perennial fan favorite, Rick captured the spirit of a time when "Oriole Magic" wasn't merely an airy marketing catch phrase. Whether performing his Babe Ruth pantomime and pratfalling around the bases on a rain-slick tarp during a delay, or exhorting the crowd by waving a towel from the dugout steps during a rally, Rick represented a lot of what was right with the Orioles in their heyday. Tom Boswell, the *Washington Post*'s baseball savant, described Dempsey not as a throwback, but as " . . . a recurrent baseball incarnation. Each generation has its tiny allotment of this precious type: the life lover, the joyous competitor, the happy warrior with plenty of sand in his craw." An example of Dempsey's incomparable approach can be seen by comparison to one of his predecessors—the malingering, malcontented Earl Williams. Williams despised blocking the plate—he felt it was

a distasteful duty that was beneath a player with his skills. Dempsey always felt that it was one of his job's most rewarding perks.

Rick got caught up in his '83 World Series MVP award and its accompanying hoopla and decided that he could contribute with the long ball. He developed an uppercut that saw his homeruns increase from a total of 9 in '82 and '83 to 23 in the following two seasons. After hearing that Carlton Fisk's 37 dingers in 1985 were the direct result of a rigorous weight training program, Dempsey hired his own strength coach and reported to Miami in '86 with 15 new pounds of muscle. But he typically couldn't resist the temptation to get some humorous mileage out of it. During the opening day ceremonies, Dempsey raced to home plate and then struck a classic body-builder pose to the delighted roars of the crowd.

The Orioles refused to pick up his option following a disastrous '86 season and Dempsey's infectious spirit will be missed. Dempsey came up for a cup of coffee in '69 with Minnesota so, if he can find work somewhere until 1990, he will become only the second catcher in history to have his career span four decades (Tim McCarver 1959–1980).

—Greg Pryor

	1986 SEASON											THREE YEARS (84 – 86)										
	Ave.	OBP	SLG	AB	H	2B	3B	HR	RBI	BB	SO	Ave.	OBP	SLG	AB	H	2B	3B	HR	RBI	BB	SO
Totals	.208	.309	.379	327	68	15	1	13	29	45	78	.231	.322	.383	1020	236	45	1	36	115	135	223
Batting vs. Left and Right-handed Pitchers																						
Left	.254	.356	.457	138	35	8	1	6	15	22	21	.289	.384	.500	380	110	24	1	18	61	59	73
Right	.175	.274	.323	189	33	7	0	7	14	23	57	.197	.285	.314	640	126	21	0	18	54	76	150
At Home and on the Road																						
Home	.215	.326	.380	158	34	5	0	7	15	25	35	.226	.330	.371	482	109	19	0	17	57	73	113
Road	.201	.293	.379	169	34	10	1	6	14	20	43	.236	.315	.394	538	127	26	1	19	58	62	110
Facing Groundball Pitchers and Flyball Pitchers																						
Groundball	.194	.291	.324	139	27	6	0	4	11	18	35	.264	.356	.403	462	122	25	0	13	57	68	101
Flyball	.218	.323	.420	188	41	9	1	9	18	27	43	.204	.294	.367	558	114	20	1	23	58	67	122
Facing Finesse Pitchers and Power Pitchers																						
Finesse	.226	.297	.402	199	45	12	1	7	19	18	35	.231	.302	.380	579	134	30	1	18	57	58	108
Power	.180	.327	.344	128	23	3	0	6	10	27	43	.231	.347	.388	441	102	15	0	18	58	77	115
On Grass and on Turf																						
Grass	.199	.308	.372	261	52	10	1	11	24	38	60	.231	.324	.386	849	196	34	1	32	102	115	188
Turf	.242	.315	.409	66	16	5	0	2	5	7	18	.234	.314	.368	171	40	11	0	4	13	20	35
During the Day and at Night																						
Day	.232	.318	.368	95	22	7	0	2	9	11	28	.238	.329	.383	290	69	18	0	8	34	40	72
Night	.198	.306	.384	232	46	8	1	11	20	34	50	.229	.320	.384	730	167	27	1	28	81	95	151
By Month																						
April	.222	.300	.463	54	12	4	0	3	5	6	11	.265	.343	.471	155	41	8	0	8	26	19	28
May	.213	.294	.377	61	13	1	0	3	8	6	13	.202	.312	.283	173	35	2	0	4	15	27	43
June	.182	.308	.327	55	10	2	0	2	5	9	16	.186	.279	.293	167	31	9	0	3	16	21	37
July	.279	.395	.515	68	19	5	1	3	6	12	16	.281	.373	.455	178	50	14	1	5	17	24	42
August	.082	.196	.122	49	4	2	0	0	2	7	14	.197	.273	.350	183	36	4	0	8	18	19	43
Sept/Oct	.250	.333	.425	40	10	1	0	2	3	5	8	.262	.358	.457	164	43	8	0	8	23	25	30
Situational																						
Bases Empty	.278	.375	.517	180	50	11	1	10	10	27	42	.250	.351	.414	548	137	25	1	21	21	82	115
Leadoff	.318	.400	.652	66	21	4	0	6	6	9	14	.270	.355	.491	222	60	13	0	12	12	28	42
Not Leadoff	.254	.361	.439	114	29	7	1	4	4	18	28	.236	.348	.362	326	77	12	1	9	9	54	73
Runners On	.122	.228	.211	147	18	4	0	3	19	18	36	.210	.289	.347	472	99	20	0	15	94	53	108
First Base Only	.109	.222	.127	55	6	1	0	0	0	8	17	.228	.297	.396	202	46	7	0	9	20	20	49
Scoring Position	.130	.231	.261	92	12	3	0	3	19	10	19	.196	.283	.311	270	53	13	0	6	74	33	59
Late Innings, Close	.160	.250	.220	50	8	0	0	1	3	6	13	.226	.307	.349	146	33	3	0	5	13	18	35

RBI/Opportunities				
Scoring Position	14 / 137	(10%)	64 / 392	(16%)
Scoring Position, 2 Out	4 / 68	(6%)	19 / 179	(11%)
On Third, Less than 2 Out	5 / 16	(31%)	27 / 60	(45%)
RBI in close games / RBI Total	18 / 29	(62%)	72 / 115	(63%)

Bo Diaz
Cincinnati Reds

In 1986, Bo Diaz provided the Reds with their first productive season from a catcher since 1980. In 1984–85, Dave Van Gorder, Dann Bilardello, Brad Gulden, and Alan Knicely combined for a batting average below .230, an on-base average below .300, and a slugging average around .305. In his 185 games with the Reds, Diaz has hit .269 and slugged .376. Cincinnati's record slipped 3 1/2 games in 1986, but no one is blaming Bo.

When acquired from Philadelphia in mid-season 1985, Diaz was expected to provide stability and offense. The rap against Diaz was his durability, having played only two full seasons in nine years. That, coupled with a surplus of catchers, made Diaz available at a modest price. However, for a 33-year-old catcher, Bo is a low-mileage model, who has caught only 697 games in his career, including his 134 games in 1986. Barring further injury, Bo could have several productive years remaining.

Ex-Phillies teammate Pete Rose brought Diaz to the Reds, and his history probably didn't escape either of them. In 1982, when Bo arrived in Philadelphia, he immediately stepped in and contributed to a veteran team which ultimately went to a World Series in 1983. In 1985, it was hoped he would be party to a repeat performance. Though it has yet to occur, with their blend of young talent and proven veterans, the Reds certainly should contend for several years.

In 1986, Diaz returned to his 1982–83 form, his other full seasons. His offensive statistics were in the same range, and his defense remained solid. Only Jody Davis (145 games) and Tony Pena (139) among NL receivers caught more games than Diaz last year. Having a full-time catcher may have aided the Reds staff, but Bo's primary contribution was on offense.

Especially impressive was Diaz's improvement throughout the season. He picked up steam throughout the summer and closed with a rush, hitting .318 in the final month; his hitting in the late innings of close games was remarkable. Diaz continues to show no left/right differential. With age, he appears to be developing into a tough hitter on grass; however, his performance on turf hasn't suffered (especially at Riverfront Stadium).

Bo Diaz is yet another vindication of Pete Rose's short-term strategy of bringing in experience to fill gaps. If Pete can now judiciously select a couple of young stars from the Reds talent pool, the Reds may have problems losing pennant races for the next five years.

—A. S. Nakamura

| | 1986 SEASON | | | | | | | | | | | THREE YEARS (84 – 86) | | | | | | | | | | |
	Ave.	OBP	SLG	AB	H	2B	3B	HR	RBI	BB	SO	Ave.	OBP	SLG	AB	H	2B	3B	HR	RBI	BB	SO
Totals	.272	.327	.380	474	129	21	0	10	56	40	52	.258	.314	.370	786	203	38	1	16	96	66	90
Batting vs. Left and Right-handed Pitchers																						
Left	.271	.333	.398	133	36	8	0	3	18	13	11	.254	.326	.376	213	54	15	1	3	28	24	18
Right	.273	.324	.372	341	93	13	0	7	38	27	41	.260	.309	.368	573	149	23	0	13	68	42	72
At Home and on the Road																						
Home	.286	.338	.450	220	63	12	0	8	30	17	27	.279	.332	.445	348	97	19	0	13	51	27	42
Road	.260	.318	.319	254	66	9	0	2	26	23	25	.242	.300	.311	438	106	19	1	3	45	39	48
Facing Groundball Pitchers and Flyball Pitchers																						
Groundball	.282	.333	.368	234	66	14	0	2	31	19	31	.273	.336	.375	384	105	25	1	4	51	38	47
Flyball	.263	.321	.392	240	63	7	0	8	25	21	21	.244	.293	.366	402	98	13	0	12	45	28	43
Facing Finesse Pitchers and Power Pitchers																						
Finesse	.288	.342	.390	236	68	9	0	5	30	20	21	.274	.320	.391	427	117	18	1	10	55	30	36
Power	.256	.312	.370	238	61	12	0	5	26	20	31	.240	.307	.345	359	86	20	0	6	41	36	54
On Grass and on Turf																						
Grass	.310	.352	.381	168	52	6	0	2	20	12	13	.294	.340	.375	248	73	11	0	3	28	18	21
Turf	.252	.313	.379	306	77	15	0	8	36	28	39	.242	.302	.368	538	130	27	1	13	68	48	69
During the Day and at Night																						
Day	.303	.354	.423	142	43	8	0	3	16	13	13	.282	.345	.408	238	67	13	1	5	31	24	23
Night	.259	.315	.361	332	86	13	0	7	40	27	39	.248	.300	.354	548	136	25	0	11	65	42	67
By Month																						
April	.250	.311	.393	56	14	2	0	2	5	5	5	.257	.311	.389	113	29	6	0	3	15	9	11
May	.258	.354	.364	66	17	4	0	1	7	11	10	.258	.354	.364	66	17	4	0	1	7	11	10
June	.250	.289	.293	92	23	4	0	0	11	5	13	.218	.262	.271	133	29	7	0	0	17	8	18
July	.284	.324	.418	67	19	3	0	2	9	4	7	.265	.315	.451	102	27	5	1	4	17	8	11
August	.267	.328	.400	105	28	5	0	3	12	10	9	.238	.297	.326	193	46	8	0	3	17	17	25
Sept/Oct	.318	.355	.420	88	28	3	0	2	12	5	8	.307	.354	.436	179	55	8	0	5	23	13	15
Situational																						
Bases Empty	.265	.305	.401	279	74	14	0	8	8	16	33	.245	.294	.371	461	113	20	1	12	12	32	59
Leadoff	.264	.288	.413	121	32	3	0	5	5	4	12	.233	.262	.364	206	48	6	0	7	7	8	21
Not Leadoff	.266	.318	.392	158	42	11	0	3	3	12	21	.255	.319	.376	255	65	14	1	5	5	24	38
Runners On	.282	.356	.349	195	55	7	0	2	48	24	19	.277	.341	.369	325	90	18	0	4	84	34	31
First Base Only	.271	.311	.343	70	19	2	0	1	4	4	5	.248	.299	.352	125	31	7	0	2	9	9	9
Scoring Position	.288	.378	.352	125	36	5	0	1	44	20	14	.295	.365	.380	200	59	11	0	2	75	25	22
Late Innings, Close	.330	.361	.495	91	30	3	0	4	14	5	15	.284	.327	.439	148	42	6	1	5	19	10	22
RBI/Opportunities																						
Scoring Position				41 / 176		(23%)									71 / 275		(26%)					
Scoring Position, 2 Out				17 / 83		(20%)									27 / 128		(21%)					
On Third, Less than 2 Out				17 / 35		(49%)									29 / 50		(58%)					
RBI in close games / RBI Total				40 / 56		(71%)									57 / 96		(59%)					

Ken Dixon
Baltimore Orioles

When Ken Dixon arrived in the majors in 1985, it was the second time in recent history that Baltimore had given a spot to a man with less than a year's experience in AAA ball. Like Storm Davis before him, Dixon's promotion appeared justified by his past performance and promise; like Davis, the decision now appears to reflect the Orioles' recent trend toward making decisions based on wishful thinking rather than analysis.

Relying on overpowering fastballs and sharp curves, Dixon opened 1985 impressively, with a 3–0 record and a 1.52 ERA in his first four starts. Hitters adjusted quickly, though—by June, Dixon was in the bullpen after allowing 28 earned runs in as many innings. Working in long relief and spot starts, Ken gradually regained his mastery; his 4–1 record and 2.85 ERA over the last three months of 1985 boded well for the future.

1986 proved to be crushingly disappointing. Another fast start (2–0, 0.84 ERA) disappeared in a barrage of homers. After 54 games, Dixon's record was a solid 6–3; his ERA was a bloated 4.84 and he had allowed 63 hits (20 of them homers) in 67 innings. Over the next seven weeks, Dixon worked on changing speeds on his two key pitches with good results. In an 11-game stretch, he allowed only five homers and 51 hits in 74 innings, fanning 62 and posting a 3.04 ERA. The anemic Oriole offense produced only a 4–5 record, but he appeared to have blossomed again.

But, again, the hitters adjusted with painful results. Over the last seven weeks, Dixon allowed only eight homers in 61.3 innings, but gave up 80 hits, went 1–5 and had a 6.16 ERA. In his second year, Ken allowed hits, homers and walks more often than he had in his first and his ERA rose almost a run (3.67 to 4.58).

Dixon's progress has been clearly slowed by his team. He's an extreme power pitcher, who has a very low ground/air ratio (.73–1 through 1985) and is very vulnerable to the walk, stolen base and extra-base hit. His home/road, day/night and grass/turf splits are extremely large; were he playing for a team that had good outfield defense and in a park that made it difficult to hit for power, he would probably be an effective starter already. The Orioles, however, lack team speed, play in a park that favors the power hitter and (with the release of Rick Dempsey) don't contain the running game. Dixon is unable to take advantage of the double play support that his defense provides—while he is a talented pitcher, he'll need to make drastic adjustments in order to prosper in Baltimore.

—Tim Mulligan

1986: Power, Flyball   **1985: Power, Flyball**   **1984: Finesse, Groundball**

	1986 SEASON											THREE YEARS (84 – 86)										
	G	IP	H	BB	SO	SB	CS	W	L	S	ERA	G	IP	H	BB	SO	SB	CS	W	L	S	ERA
Totals	35	202.1	194	83	170	22	6	11	13	0	4.58	71	377.1	352	151	286	36	9	19	18	1	4.17
At Home and on the Road																						
Home	19	101.1	104	54	87	10	5	4	10	0	5.24	41	210.1	207	99	151	23	8	9	14	1	4.75
Road	16	101.0	90	29	83	12	1	7	3	0	3.92	30	167.0	145	52	135	13	1	10	4	0	3.45
During the Day and at Night																						
Day	12	55.0	56	28	50	11	1	2	3	0	5.40	22	99.0	104	43	84	15	2	3	6	1	5.18
Night	23	147.1	138	55	120	11	5	9	10	0	4.28	49	278.1	248	108	202	21	7	16	12	0	3.82
On Grass and on Turf																						
Grass	29	159.2	167	71	140	17	6	7	12	0	5.13	60	308.0	307	129	235	31	9	13	17	1	4.56
Turf	6	42.2	27	12	30	5	0	4	1	0	2.53	11	69.1	45	22	51	5	0	6	1	0	2.47
By Month																						
April	4	24.0	20	7	20	4	0	2	1	0	2.62	6	39.2	28	12	33	4	0	3	1	0	2.04
May	5	31.0	27	11	25	5	1	3	1	0	5.23	11	58.2	57	21	45	7	2	6	3	0	5.37
June	7	32.2	34	23	23	5	1	1	4	0	6.89	15	54.1	65	29	38	7	1	1	5	0	6.79
July	6	46.0	25	15	41	4	2	3	2	0	1.57	12	73.2	48	26	58	5	2	4	2	0	2.44
August	6	29.1	37	10	25	2	0	1	2	0	6.44	11	62.0	58	24	46	5	2	3	2	0	4.21
Sept/Oct	7	39.1	51	17	36	2	2	1	3	0	5.49	16	89.0	96	39	66	8	2	3	5	1	4.15

	vs. Opponent Batters																			
	1986 SEASON										THREE YEARS (84 – 86)									
	Ave.	OBP	SLG	AB	H	2B	3B	HR	RBI	BB	SO	Ave.	OBP	SLG	AB	H	2B	3B	HR	RBI	BB	SO
Totals	.249	.320	.438	779	194	30	9	33	97	83	170	.245	.316	.418	1437	352	60	13	54	172	151	285
Pitching vs. Left and Right-handed Batters																					
Left	.242	.320	.418	385	93	13	5	15	38	46	70	.238	.319	.401	744	177	33	8	24	74	90	127
Right	.256	.320	.457	394	101	17	4	18	59	37	100	.253	.314	.436	693	175	27	5	30	98	61	158
Situational																					
Bases Empty	.243	.311	.457	470	114	19	5	24	24	47	92	.237	.303	.421	876	208	36	7	37	37	80	164
Leadoff	.233	.286	.450	202	47	7	2	11	11	15	40	.236	.286	.428	369	87	13	2	18	18	25	70
Not Leadoff	.250	.330	.463	268	67	12	3	13	13	32	52	.239	.314	.416	507	121	23	5	19	19	55	94
Runners On	.259	.332	.408	309	80	11	4	9	73	36	78	.257	.337	.412	561	144	24	6	17	135	71	121
First Base Only	.291	.336	.425	134	39	5	2	3	10	8	33	.275	.326	.421	240	66	13	2	6	19	17	48
Scoring Position	.234	.330	.394	175	41	6	2	6	63	28	45	.243	.345	.405	321	78	11	4	11	116	54	73
Late Innings, Close	.210	.289	.370	81	17	2	1	3	6	9	13	.260	.336	.405	131	34	6	2	3	13	15	17

	RBI/Opportunities		
Scoring Position	51 / 242	(21%)	95 / 456	(21%)
Scoring Position, 2 Out	24 / 114	(21%)	38 / 209	(18%)
On Third, Less than 2 Out	21 / 51	(41%)	42 / 89	(47%)
RBI in close games / RBI Total	73 / 97	(75%)	114 / 172	(66%)

Bill Doran
Houston Astros

It's interesting how playing for a good team increases the recognition of a player in the media, and, therefore, the eyes of the public. A classic example of this is Bill Doran. In 1985, he hit .287 with a .362 on-base average and 14 home runs. In 1986, he hit .276 with a .368 OBA and only 6 HRs. He did steal 20 more bases last year, but the power drop was not compensated for by the extra stolen bases. Using Pete Palmer's values from *The Hidden Game of Baseball*, the 20 SBs and 6 extra CSs were worth approximately 3 runs while the 8 lost HRs cost the team approximately 11 runs.

In 1985, when Sandberg and Herr were having spectacular years, Doran was lost in the shuffle while playing for an also-ran. In 1986, with Sandberg and Herr having worse years and the Astros winning the division, Doran garnered some MVP support while having a worse year, too. However, his defensive skills suddenly became noticed, and this was certainly deserved. Doran is great on the pivot and has very good range. His numbers are a little low, but he plays behind Mike Scott, Jim Deshaies and Nolan Ryan, so there aren't a lot of balls put into play.

Still, Doran did have a good year. He was 10th in the NL in on-base average, 6th in stolen bases, 9th in times reaching base (H + BB + HBP), and he was 9th in percentage of times scored per times on base with 39%. These abilities led to his being 7th in runs. His skills are perfect for a leadoff man: he gets on base and he runs the bases well. His stolen base percentage of 69% is not that good, but it is above the break-even point.

Somebody, please let this man out of Houston. He hit better on the road for the past three years, better on grass in 1984 and 1985, and better on road turf in 1984 and 1986. He is one of the top second basemen in baseball with his park working against his strengths. If he played anywhere else, he would have a shot at hitting .300 with 50+ extra-base hits. Those statistics might have gotten him even more MVP support as well as some recognition for the post-season All-Star teams. Doran is one of those switch-hitters who collects each type of extra-base hit from a different side. Batting left-handed, he hits three times as many triples per plate appearance; batting right-handed, he hits 50% more doubles and his BA rises 40 points.

—Scott M. Daniel

	1986 SEASON											THREE YEARS (84 – 86)										
	Ave.	OBP	SLG	AB	H	2B	3B	HR	RBI	BB	SO	Ave.	OBP	SLG	AB	H	2B	3B	HR	RBI	BB	SO
Totals	.276	.368	.373	550	152	29	3	6	37	81	57	.275	.357	.388	1676	461	78	20	24	137	218	195
Batting vs. Left and Right-handed Pitchers																						
Left	.304	.371	.407	214	65	13	0	3	19	25	18	.300	.377	.414	607	182	33	3	10	54	77	63
Right	.259	.366	.351	336	87	16	3	3	18	56	39	.261	.346	.374	1069	279	45	17	14	83	141	132
At Home and on the Road																						
Home	.274	.379	.374	270	74	18	0	3	20	44	24	.263	.355	.386	806	212	43	13	10	67	114	87
Road	.279	.358	.371	280	78	11	3	3	17	37	33	.286	.360	.391	870	249	35	7	14	70	104	108
Facing Groundball Pitchers and Flyball Pitchers																						
Groundball	.281	.358	.365	249	70	12	0	3	16	31	21	.273	.351	.377	794	217	33	8	11	70	97	85
Flyball	.272	.376	.379	301	82	17	3	3	21	50	36	.277	.363	.399	882	244	45	12	13	67	121	110
Facing Finesse Pitchers and Power Pitchers																						
Finesse	.266	.349	.370	305	81	16	2	4	16	39	29	.272	.345	.393	914	249	39	10	17	68	101	85
Power	.290	.391	.376	245	71	13	1	2	21	42	28	.278	.372	.383	762	212	39	10	7	69	117	110
On Grass and on Turf																						
Grass	.246	.325	.368	171	42	8	2	3	10	21	23	.293	.364	.414	522	153	23	5	10	49	60	68
Turf	.290	.387	.375	379	110	21	1	3	27	60	34	.267	.354	.377	1154	308	55	15	14	88	158	127
During the Day and at Night																						
Day	.294	.385	.356	177	52	9	1	0	10	26	16	.273	.362	.380	400	109	16	3	7	34	56	42
Night	.268	.360	.381	373	100	20	2	6	27	55	41	.276	.356	.391	1276	352	62	17	17	103	162	153
By Month																						
April	.306	.425	.361	72	22	4	0	0	3	15	8	.237	.329	.303	211	50	12	1	0	8	29	26
May	.239	.327	.307	88	21	3	0	1	6	12	9	.272	.359	.391	235	64	7	3	5	17	33	24
June	.282	.370	.455	110	31	3	2	4	9	16	8	.284	.369	.416	327	93	11	4	8	36	45	30
July	.282	.360	.336	110	31	6	0	0	7	13	10	.292	.355	.379	319	93	19	3	1	23	32	37
August	.261	.373	.333	69	18	5	0	0	3	12	10	.314	.404	.482	280	88	16	5	7	30	42	39
Sept/Oct	.287	.365	.416	101	29	8	1	1	9	13	12	.240	.322	.339	304	73	13	4	3	23	37	39
Situational																						
Bases Empty	.280	.365	.389	393	110	21	2	6	6	53	36	.277	.354	.405	1138	315	57	16	19	19	134	129
Leadoff	.300	.371	.418	220	66	8	0	6	6	25	14	.285	.353	.407	671	191	28	9	12	12	70	70
Not Leadoff	.254	.358	.353	173	44	13	2	0	0	28	22	.266	.355	.403	467	124	29	7	7	7	64	59
Runners On	.268	.375	.331	157	42	8	1	0	31	28	21	.271	.364	.353	538	146	21	4	5	118	84	66
First Base Only	.308	.366	.415	65	20	7	0	0	2	6	5	.313	.366	.411	224	70	13	0	3	10	19	19
Scoring Position	.239	.380	.272	92	22	1	1	0	29	22	16	.242	.363	.312	314	76	8	4	2	108	65	47
Late Innings, Close	.217	.309	.325	83	18	4	1	1	7	11	10	.259	.337	.368	266	69	10	2	5	25	31	36
RBI/Opportunities																						

Scoring Position	29 / 146	(20%)	102 / 473	(22%)
Scoring Position, 2 Out	13 / 83	(16%)	47 / 264	(18%)
On Third, Less than 2 Out	11 / 17	(65%)	40 / 72	(56%)
RBI in close games / RBI Total	24 / 37	(65%)	92 / 137	(67%)

Brian Downing
California Angels

Probably no other player of our generation has undergone such a remarkable evolution as Brian Downing. Compared to the player who came to the majors thirteen years ago, Downing's build is different, his batting stance is different, his position is different, his batting output is completely different and even his face is different. If he didn't use the same name and birth date, no fan would recognize in this player the chubby, bespectacled Chicago catcher of so many years ago.

I hope you won't think I'm fawning over him, but Brian Downing is my favorite player. Gene Mauch has said about him that if you lead him off, he scores runs, and if you hit him in the middle of the lineup he drives in runs. Why wouldn't he? Being hit by seventeen pitches and drawing 90 walks, Downing had an on base percentage of .389 last year, one of the best in the league. He runs fairly well and gets on base, so if he leads off he'll score runs. On the other hand he has power, twenty-homer a year power, and has hit .290 with runners in scoring position over the last three years, so if he hits third or fourth, he'll drive in runs.

Yet the fact that he can play either major offensive role so well tends to hurt him in the public's eyes. If Downing led off all the time he would score 100–120 runs a year, and the idea that he was an effective leadoff man would eventually soak through to the public even though he doesn't look a thing like Vince Coleman. If he batted third consistently he would drive in 95–110 runs a year, and get the recognition he deserves that way. The fact that he does both things causes him to wind up with a kind of a "hedged" record, too subtle for the All-Star voters.

Downing is a fine outfielder, a player who hardly ever makes a mistake and, as you saw in the playoffs, will make a brilliant play on occasion (he made three during the seven-game Boston series). His speed isn't terrific but he's never short of hustle. I've seen him make several catches in foul territory just because he didn't give up on a ball that was slicing away from him. Tie up the package with a .563 slugging percentage in the late innings of close games, and you've got Brian Downing.

—Bill James

	1986 SEASON											THREE YEARS (84 – 86)										
	Ave.	OBP	SLG	AB	H	2B	3B	HR	RBI	BB	SO	Ave.	OBP	SLG	AB	H	2B	3B	HR	RBI	BB	SO
Totals	.267	.389	.452	513	137	27	4	20	95	90	84	.268	.373	.447	1572	422	78	7	63	271	237	211
Batting vs. Left and Right-handed Pitchers																						
Left	.240	.385	.443	183	44	14	1	7	31	42	34	.265	.374	.465	529	140	36	2	22	93	92	76
Right	.282	.390	.458	330	93	13	3	13	64	48	50	.270	.372	.438	1043	282	42	5	41	178	145	135
At Home and on the Road																						
Home	.277	.392	.488	260	72	10	3	13	53	47	37	.258	.366	.433	772	199	31	4	32	131	124	95
Road	.257	.385	.415	253	65	17	1	7	42	43	47	.279	.379	.461	800	223	47	3	31	140	113	116
Facing Groundball Pitchers and Flyball Pitchers																						
Groundball	.309	.428	.477	220	68	7	3	8	41	37	31	.274	.374	.441	753	206	30	6	28	133	103	91
Flyball	.235	.359	.433	293	69	20	1	12	54	53	53	.264	.371	.453	819	216	48	1	35	138	134	120
Facing Finesse Pitchers and Power Pitchers																						
Finesse	.297	.405	.494	310	92	18	2	13	53	49	44	.283	.376	.451	895	253	51	5	30	130	117	100
Power	.222	.365	.389	203	45	9	2	7	42	41	40	.250	.368	.442	677	169	27	2	33	141	120	111
On Grass and on Turf																						
Grass	.276	.397	.460	435	120	20	3	18	80	79	73	.267	.375	.446	1306	349	62	5	54	224	208	176
Turf	.218	.340	.410	78	17	7	1	2	15	11	11	.274	.362	.451	266	73	16	2	9	47	29	35
During the Day and at Night																						
Day	.233	.340	.423	163	38	9	2	6	23	23	23	.261	.360	.441	467	122	27	3	17	84	64	57
Night	.283	.410	.466	350	99	18	2	14	72	67	61	.271	.378	.450	1105	300	51	4	46	187	173	154
By Month																						
April	.280	.385	.573	75	21	5	1	5	18	11	14	.268	.390	.473	239	64	11	1	12	52	41	35
May	.311	.441	.422	90	28	8	1	0	7	18	15	.236	.361	.356	250	59	13	1	5	24	45	32
June	.306	.416	.518	85	26	4	1	4	18	14	10	.246	.348	.384	232	57	13	2	5	37	33	26
July	.202	.336	.326	89	18	0	1	3	13	16	13	.258	.349	.444	252	65	9	1	12	43	32	41
August	.212	.343	.329	85	18	4	0	2	15	15	16	.313	.402	.524	294	92	15	1	15	59	39	34
Sept/Oct	.292	.409	.562	89	26	6	0	6	24	16	16	.279	.379	.479	305	85	17	1	14	56	47	43
Situational																						
Bases Empty	.259	.375	.404	270	70	14	2	7	7	37	47	.254	.356	.401	875	222	42	3	27	27	115	106
Leadoff	.286	.395	.476	105	30	6	1	4	4	12	16	.263	.353	.438	361	95	20	2	13	13	41	40
Not Leadoff	.242	.362	.358	165	40	8	1	3	3	25	31	.247	.358	.375	514	127	22	1	14	14	74	66
Runners On	.276	.403	.506	243	67	13	2	13	88	53	37	.287	.393	.505	697	200	36	4	36	244	122	105
First Base Only	.284	.414	.516	95	27	4	0	6	14	20	14	.282	.385	.471	280	79	14	0	13	34	41	41
Scoring Position	.270	.396	.500	148	40	9	2	7	74	33	23	.290	.397	.528	417	121	22	4	23	210	81	64
Late Innings, Close	.296	.451	.563	71	21	5	1	4	16	16	11	.283	.402	.485	233	66	13	2	10	45	41	27
RBI/Opportunities																						

RBI/Opportunities				
Scoring Position	60 / 227	(26%)	168 / 612	(27%)
Scoring Position, 2 Out	23 / 104	(22%)	66 / 291	(23%)
On Third, Less than 2 Out	25 / 44	(57%)	65 / 116	(56%)
RBI in close games / RBI Total	61 / 95	(64%)	167 / 271	(62%)

Dave Dravecky
San Diego Padres

One of the stupidest beliefs in baseball is the idea that a starting pitcher "wins" or "loses" a game. A pitcher may be the only reason that his team won (a 1–0 win) or lost (seven runs in 2.2 innings), but it's usually a team win. A pitcher who plays for a good hitting team may win even if he pitches ineffectively; a pitcher who plays for a bad team may lose no matter how well he does. Dave Dravecky is an example. Dravecky has been a fine pitcher for several years—had he played for a good hitting club, he'd be known as one of the best starters in baseball. As he hasn't, the thing that he's most noted for is his membership in the John Birch Society.

The simplest method for seeing whether a pitcher gets good support is to compare the number of runs that his team scores in his starts to the number that they score when his teammates start. If you do that, it becomes easy to see why Dravecky has never been a consistent winner. In 1982, he had 3.60 runs a game to work with; well below the 4.20 other Padre starters had. He went 4–2 in 10 starts only because he had a fine 2.57 ERA. In 1983, his ERA rose to 3.58, but the support that he got also improved. Dravecky had 3.96 runs scored for him (his teammates got 4.04) and he finished 14–10 in 28 starts. 1984 was the one year that Dave had outstanding support and didn't capitalize on it—despite getting 4.93 runs a game to work with (other Padre starters had 4.16) and having a 2.93 ERA, he was only 5–4 in 14 starts. Perhaps his teammates were annoyed that he didn't put their offense to better use—it was the last time that they scored for him.

In 1985, Dave made 31 starts and finished 13–10. It wasn't a bad record, but it could have been much better. Other Padre starters had 4.12 runs to work with—Dave had 3.55. Only seven regular (20+ starts) starters in baseball had worse support—here were their records: 7–17, 8–11, 5–12, 2–19, 5–16, 7–10 and 15–13. In such circumstances, winning three more games than you lose is impressive.

But in 1986, the Padre offense finally bested Dravecky. Other San Diego starters got 4.16 runs per game; Dave got 3.46. I don't know where he'll wind up in the league; obviously it won't be good. If 1985 is any guide, 9–11 isn't bad at all.

Dravecky's arm injury makes it unlikely that he'll ever regain his past effectiveness. It would have been nice if his teammates had helped him have a better career to look back on.

—Geoff Beckman

1986: Finesse, Groundball **1985: Finesse, Flyball** **1984: Finesse, Flyball**

| | 1986 SEASON | | | | | | | | | | | THREE YEARS (84 – 86) | | | | | | | | | | |
	G	IP	H	BB	SO	SB	CS	W	L	S	ERA	G	IP	H	BB	SO	SB	CS	W	L	S	ERA
Totals	26	161.1	149	54	87	10	10	9	11	0	3.07	110	532.2	474	162	263	37	23	31	30	8	2.97
At Home and on the Road																						
Home	14	86.0	77	27	55	8	4	3	6	0	3.45	55	261.2	229	75	146	26	10	14	13	6	3.20
Road	12	75.1	72	27	32	2	6	6	5	0	2.63	55	271.0	245	87	117	11	13	17	17	2	2.76
During the Day and at Night																						
Day	11	63.2	59	26	36	4	6	4	5	0	2.69	41	182.0	159	70	90	11	10	12	10	2	3.02
Night	15	97.2	90	28	51	6	4	5	6	0	3.32	69	350.2	315	92	173	26	13	19	20	6	2.95
On Grass and on Turf																						
Grass	18	111.2	98	35	64	10	7	5	7	0	2.82	81	377.2	337	112	186	33	16	19	21	7	3.00
Turf	8	49.2	51	19	23	0	3	4	4	0	3.62	29	155.0	137	50	77	4	7	12	9	1	2.90
By Month																						
April	5	36.0	21	8	20	1	2	2	1	0	0.75	19	69.2	53	21	32	3	3	3	4	2	2.20
May	6	43.0	39	10	30	1	2	3	3	0	3.14	22	100.1	85	30	56	6	4	8	5	1	2.96
June	6	35.1	40	16	12	3	2	2	3	0	3.82	23	111.2	88	41	61	8	6	8	6	4	1.93
July	4	23.0	21	10	12	5	2	0	1	0	3.52	18	107.1	92	33	54	8	6	4	4	0	2.43
August	5	24.0	28	10	13	0	2	2	3	0	4.87	15	86.1	89	22	39	5	4	5	7	0	3.75
Sept/Oct	0	0.0	0	0	0	0	0	0	0	0	0.00	13	57.1	67	15	21	7	0	3	4	1	5.81

vs. Opponent Batters

| | 1986 SEASON | | | | | | | | | | | THREE YEARS (84 – 86) | | | | | | | | | |
	Ave.	OBP	SLG	AB	H	2B	3B	HR	RBI	BB	SO	Ave.	OBP	SLG	AB	H	2B	3B	HR	RBI	BB	SO
Totals	.246	.307	.387	605	149	28	3	17	54	54	87	.241	.299	.357	1970	474	79	5	47	169	162	263
Pitching vs. Left and Right-handed Batters																						
Left	.222	.258	.321	81	18	3	1	1	7	5	19	.228	.290	.298	272	62	8	1	3	23	24	56
Right	.250	.314	.397	524	131	25	2	16	47	49	68	.243	.300	.367	1698	412	71	4	44	146	138	207
Situational																						
Bases Empty	.257	.308	.392	385	99	20	1	10	10	28	62	.251	.304	.363	1216	305	57	1	26	26	92	155
Leadoff	.245	.294	.403	159	39	10	0	5	5	11	25	.232	.284	.343	513	119	24	0	11	11	36	60
Not Leadoff	.265	.317	.385	226	60	10	1	5	5	17	37	.265	.319	.378	703	186	33	1	15	15	56	95
Runners On	.227	.306	.377	220	50	8	2	7	44	26	25	.224	.290	.347	754	169	22	4	21	143	70	108
First Base Only	.277	.355	.422	83	23	4	1	2	6	10	4	.236	.277	.371	348	82	12	1	11	28	18	39
Scoring Position	.197	.277	.350	137	27	4	1	5	38	16	21	.214	.300	.328	406	87	10	3	10	115	52	69
Late Innings, Close	.300	.339	.440	50	15	4	0	1	5	4	3	.265	.328	.450	260	69	12	0	12	33	24	33

RBI/Opportunities

Scoring Position	29 / 180	(16%)		96 / 556	(17%)
Scoring Position, 2 Out	17 / 87	(20%)		49 / 259	(19%)
On Third, Less than 2 Out	10 / 29	(34%)		29 / 91	(32%)
RBI in close games / RBI Total	40 / 54	(74%)		126 / 169	(75%)

Shawon Dunston
Chicago Cubs

In a controversial move by then manager Jim Frey, Shawon Dunston was boldly, recklessly thrust into the role of starting Cub shortstop on opening day, 1985. The error in judgement was unmistakable. Dunston managed a not-so-robust .194 average in his first six weeks, with a handful of errors thrown in. His arm reminded some in Chicago of the legendary Bear quarterback Bobby Douglass, who would rifle screen passes and managed to overthrow receivers 70 yards downfield.

After a few months in the minors to repair the damage, Dunston returned to the Cubs with some style, hitting .328 and scoring 28 runs in the final 35 games of the '85 season. Despite the strong offensive finish, he still won the punt, throw, and boot competition among Cub shortstops. Nonetheless fans and critics alike recognized that he was an exciting player with substantial talent.

To have expected Shawon to continue in '86 season as he finished in '85 would have been naive, but Shawon started the new year doing just that. Through May, his .298 AVE was just a point behind Sandberg for the club lead, and on the strength of 20 extra-base hits out of his total of 53, his .483 SLG was tops on the team. He gradually faded, though, on offense, and finished 6 points below the team's .256 AVE.

Two things must be remembered. Dunston is inexperienced and will have to develop a certain amount of "mental stamina"—if you will—to carry him through a full season. He is also impressionable, and is likely to be easily affected by the ups and downs of the team in general; his offensive slide in '86 came about in June when Frey was fired and it was clear that the Cubs were not going to be in the race. In this regard, nothing would help Dunston come along quite as well as a winning year for his ballclub. Getting caught up in the excitement would keep him from thinking about his game instead of playing it instinctively.

Dunston's 3YR totals are somewhat meager, given his eight-plus months in the majors, but a few points can be noted. Obviously, Shawon is a free swinger. This probably accounts for his lower AVE against Flyball and Power pitchers. It likely also accounts for the fact that his power does not vary appreciably across these same categories.

Like a newborn babe, you can, for a while, expect Dunston to look a little different each season.

—Mark Podrazik

	1986 SEASON											THREE YEARS (84 – 86)										
	Ave.	OBP	SLG	AB	H	2B	3B	HR	RBI	BB	SO	Ave.	OBP	SLG	AB	H	2B	3B	HR	RBI	BB	SO
Totals	.250	.278	.411	581	145	37	3	17	68	21	114	.253	.288	.404	831	210	49	7	21	86	40	156
Batting vs. Left and Right-handed Pitchers																						
Left	.231	.247	.423	156	36	10	1	6	25	4	27	.229	.249	.408	201	46	13	1	7	29	6	32
Right	.256	.290	.407	425	109	27	2	11	43	17	87	.260	.300	.403	630	164	36	6	14	57	34	124
At Home and on the Road																						
Home	.262	.287	.443	305	80	23	1	10	38	9	61	.274	.313	.445	452	124	30	4	13	46	24	86
Road	.236	.269	.377	276	65	14	2	7	30	12	53	.227	.259	.356	379	86	19	3	8	40	16	70
Facing Groundball Pitchers and Flyball Pitchers																						
Groundball	.267	.301	.408	262	70	17	1	6	27	11	43	.289	.328	.440	384	111	23	4	9	38	21	53
Flyball	.235	.260	.414	319	75	20	2	11	41	10	71	.221	.254	.374	447	99	26	3	12	48	19	103
Facing Finesse Pitchers and Power Pitchers																						
Finesse	.258	.290	.409	337	87	19	1	10	31	12	52	.275	.308	.421	480	132	29	4	11	41	21	69
Power	.238	.263	.414	244	58	18	2	7	37	9	62	.222	.261	.382	351	78	20	3	10	45	19	87
On Grass and on Turf																						
Grass	.260	.284	.433	427	111	29	3	13	53	13	78	.264	.298	.427	592	156	37	6	16	61	28	108
Turf	.221	.264	.351	154	34	8	0	4	15	8	36	.226	.265	.347	239	54	12	1	5	25	12	48
During the Day and at Night																						
Day	.251	.279	.422	403	101	28	1	13	51	14	73	.261	.300	.426	578	151	36	4	17	64	31	101
Night	.247	.278	.388	178	44	9	2	4	17	7	41	.233	.260	.356	253	59	13	3	4	22	9	55
By Month																						
April	.262	.304	.477	65	17	5	0	3	7	4	10	.248	.286	.416	113	28	8	1	3	9	6	13
May	.313	.342	.478	115	36	8	1	3	11	4	16	.281	.329	.446	139	39	9	1	4	13	9	26
June	.245	.292	.377	106	26	8	0	2	13	6	24	.245	.292	.377	106	26	8	0	2	13	6	24
July	.240	.260	.438	96	23	6	2	3	14	3	19	.240	.260	.438	96	23	6	2	3	14	3	19
August	.198	.212	.323	96	19	3	0	3	12	1	25	.196	.205	.301	143	28	4	1	3	15	1	31
Sept/Oct	.233	.255	.388	103	24	7	0	3	11	3	20	.282	.323	.436	234	66	14	2	6	22	15	43
Situational																						
Bases Empty	.231	.250	.382	351	81	16	2	11	11	8	73	.238	.263	.395	504	120	25	6	14	14	16	99
Leadoff	.237	.254	.396	169	40	9	0	6	6	4	29	.254	.277	.417	228	58	12	2	7	7	7	39
Not Leadoff	.225	.246	.368	182	41	7	2	5	5	4	44	.225	.252	.377	276	62	13	4	7	7	9	60
Runners On	.278	.320	.457	230	64	21	1	6	57	13	41	.275	.325	.419	327	90	24	1	7	72	24	57
First Base Only	.281	.324	.469	96	27	9	0	3	7	4	19	.291	.331	.444	151	44	11	0	4	9	7	26
Scoring Position	.276	.317	.448	134	37	12	1	3	50	9	22	.261	.320	.398	176	46	13	1	3	63	17	31
Late Innings, Close	.182	.204	.336	110	20	3	1	4	12	3	22	.195	.217	.331	133	26	4	1	4	13	4	26
RBI/Opportunities																						
Scoring Position				42 / 175		(24%)									55 / 241		(23%)					
Scoring Position, 2 Out				14 / 75		(19%)									17 / 99		(17%)					
On Third, Less than 2 Out				16 / 32		(50%)									23 / 44		(52%)					
RBI in close games / RBI Total				47 / 68		(69%)									61 / 86		(71%)					

Leon Durham
Chicago Cubs

The '87 season ought be a year of reckoning for Leon Durham. Durham was used more selectively during the '86 season (he played about 100 less innings than in 1985), and he undid some of the progress he made toward dispelling the image of himself as a platoon or conditional player.

At issue here primarily is Durham's adaptability on offense. For example, manager Jim Frey gave Leon the opportunity to play regularly against left-handed pitching during the 1985 season. Durham responded with a respectable .276 AVE vs. LHP (.284 vs.RHP, similar for OBP and SLG), but struggled early in the '86 season against left-handers. Mired in a slump for the first two months of the season, Durham began to see more selective action against left-handed pitching and eventually pulled his average here up to .262, which was still 50 points below his AVE vs RHP.

This type of disparity in Durham's offensive production carries over into other A/B type statistical breakdowns. Since all Durham's Home games are also Day, Grass games, we can break Durham's report down a little:

Condition	1984	1985	1986
Day/Home	.326 (80/245)	.331 (85/257)	.283 (79/279)
Day/Road	.221 (19/86)	.157 (14/89)	.292 (21/72)
Night (Road)	.232 (33/142)	.276 (54/196)	.203 (27/133)
Grass/Home	.326 (80/245)	.331 (85/257)	.283 (79/279)
Grass/Road	.280 (21/75)	.256 (31/121)	.271 (19/70)
Turf (Road)	.203 (31/153)	.226 (37/164)	.215 (29/135)

Recognizing the limitations of the above statistical presentation, e.g., no Night/Home data is available, we may (cautiously) draw the following conclusions: 1) Durham shows strong offensive preference for Home conditions over Road, and 2) he also indicates an offensive preference for Grass over Turf. Keep in mind that a Grass/Turf difference goes well beyond considerations of photosynthesis; the game on Turf usually implies defenses designed for range and speed, pitchers chosen for the ability to get outs in the air rather than on the ground.

—Mark Podrazik

	1986 SEASON											THREE YEARS (84 – 86)										
	Ave.	OBP	SLG	AB	H	2B	3B	HR	RBI	BB	SO	Ave.	OBP	SLG	AB	H	2B	3B	HR	RBI	BB	SO
Totals	.262	.350	.452	484	127	18	7	20	65	67	98	.275	.359	.474	1499	412	80	13	64	236	200	283
Batting vs. Left and Right-handed Pitchers																						
Left	.227	.275	.367	128	29	3	3	3	15	9	28	.250	.325	.393	364	91	17	4	9	52	40	93
Right	.275	.375	.483	356	98	15	4	17	50	58	70	.283	.369	.500	1135	321	63	9	55	184	160	190
At Home and on the Road																						
Home	.283	.360	.505	279	79	13	5	13	43	35	48	.312	.396	.579	781	244	49	9	47	154	111	126
Road	.234	.338	.380	205	48	5	2	7	22	32	50	.234	.318	.359	718	168	31	4	17	82	89	157
Facing Groundball Pitchers and Flyball Pitchers																						
Groundball	.316	.402	.563	215	68	9	4	12	30	32	43	.294	.379	.493	691	203	42	6	28	114	96	125
Flyball	.219	.307	.364	269	59	9	3	8	35	35	55	.259	.341	.457	808	209	38	7	36	122	104	158
Facing Finesse Pitchers and Power Pitchers																						
Finesse	.297	.376	.486	276	82	15	5	9	31	35	45	.304	.376	.512	871	265	49	6	40	134	101	135
Power	.216	.317	.409	208	45	3	2	11	34	32	53	.234	.336	.420	628	147	31	7	24	102	99	148
On Grass and on Turf																						
Grass	.281	.351	.484	349	98	14	6	15	52	40	61	.299	.378	.524	1036	310	58	11	51	182	136	170
Turf	.215	.348	.370	135	29	4	1	5	13	27	37	.220	.315	.361	463	102	22	2	13	54	64	113
During the Day and at Night																						
Day	.285	.370	.516	351	100	16	7	17	53	50	64	.290	.376	.529	1028	298	60	12	54	182	146	182
Night	.203	.296	.286	133	27	2	0	3	12	17	34	.242	.319	.352	471	114	20	1	10	54	54	101
By Month																						
April	.226	.324	.371	62	14	0	0	3	9	10	12	.253	.330	.414	174	44	5	1	7	21	21	38
May	.277	.341	.410	83	23	3	1	2	9	8	14	.291	.382	.515	268	78	11	2	15	57	40	48
June	.221	.324	.379	95	21	2	2	3	15	15	20	.276	.349	.416	279	77	17	2	6	40	33	58
July	.275	.359	.464	69	19	2	1	3	12	9	10	.269	.362	.444	234	63	13	2	8	32	34	30
August	.250	.319	.464	84	21	6	3	2	5	9	25	.286	.370	.539	241	69	17	4	12	34	33	55
Sept/Oct	.319	.422	.604	91	29	5	0	7	15	16	17	.267	.352	.495	303	81	17	2	16	52	39	54
Situational																						
Bases Empty	.249	.322	.438	281	70	13	5	10	10	29	60	.266	.331	.452	819	218	48	7	30	30	78	156
Leadoff	.267	.318	.500	120	32	4	3	6	6	8	23	.249	.314	.455	341	85	22	3	14	14	31	65
Not Leadoff	.236	.324	.391	161	38	9	2	4	4	21	37	.278	.343	.450	478	133	26	4	16	16	47	91
Runners On	.281	.386	.473	203	57	5	2	10	55	38	38	.285	.389	.500	680	194	32	6	34	206	122	127
First Base Only	.311	.360	.566	106	33	2	2	7	17	8	19	.294	.337	.505	303	89	11	4	15	40	20	52
Scoring Position	.247	.409	.371	97	24	3	0	3	38	30	19	.279	.424	.496	377	105	21	2	19	166	102	75
Late Innings, Close	.286	.434	.560	84	24	2	0	7	16	22	18	.259	.375	.461	243	63	16	0	11	38	45	52

	RBI/Opportunities						
Scoring Position		33 / 151	(22%)		133 / 555	(24%)	
Scoring Position, 2 Out		12 / 72	(17%)		47 / 248	(19%)	
On Third, Less than 2 Out		12 / 23	(52%)		50 / 107	(47%)	
RBI in close games / RBI Total		51 / 65	(78%)		171 / 236	(72%)	

213

Lenny Dykstra
New York Mets

In Lenny Dykstra's first at bat of 1986 he took five pitches, walked, and then scored from first on a double by Keith Hernandez. This became a familiar sight throughout the season: Dykstra getting on whatever way he could, then coming around to score in spectacular fashion, usually with a headfirst slide. For most of the year Dykstra batted leadoff against righthanded pitching, with Wally Backman in the number two slot, and the pair was so effective that they were labeled "The Busboys" by Tim McCarver—no one set the table better. Early on, when the Mets were putting the division away, the Busboys led the juggernaut. The New Yorkers won the first ten games the duo started together and were 22–6 with The Busboys in the lineup through July 4th. By then winning the East was a foregone conclusion, but Dykstra and Backman cooled off only a little after that. For the full year the Mets posted a 54–24 record with The Busboys setting the table.

As a leadoff man, Dykstra's greatest assets are his great eye and his speed. His .377 on-base average attests to his walk-drawing ability, but Dykstra can get on in other ways as well; he'll even sacrifice his body to reach on base. He's an accomplished bunter and handles the bat very well, going to the opposite field when he wants to but pulling the ball occasionally with surprising power, as he showed in the post-season last year. He also has the ability to bear down in a pressure situation and come through; he demonstrated this ability throughout the '86 campaign.

Dykstra played brilliantly throughout the first half of the '86 season and was leading the league with a .349 average at the All Star break. It seemed for a time that he could do just about whatever he wanted to at the plate. But soon afterward he hit a major slump and was down to .295 by season's end. Perhaps because of his fascination with the home run ball, Dykstra hasn't shown much consistency at bat thus far. In '86 he hit well over .320 during April, June and July, but was in the .220s during May and August. He needs some work in this area.

As a fielder, Dykstra is fearless, with a willingness to collide with either a wall or a teammate to make a catch. He has a good arm and gets an excellent jump, but tends to play too deep.

—Sunil Agarwal

	1986 SEASON											THREE YEARS (84 – 86)										
	Ave.	OBP	SLG	AB	H	2B	3B	HR	RBI	BB	SO	Ave.	OBP	SLG	AB	H	2B	3B	HR	RBI	BB	SO
Totals	.295	.377	.445	431	127	27	7	8	45	58	55	.280	.363	.405	667	187	36	10	9	64	88	79
Batting vs. Left and Right-handed Pitchers																						
Left	.233	.336	.291	103	24	6	0	0	9	16	20	.245	.341	.302	159	39	9	0	0	14	22	27
Right	.314	.390	.494	328	103	21	7	8	36	42	35	.291	.370	.437	508	148	27	10	9	50	66	52
At Home and on the Road																						
Home	.322	.397	.493	211	68	16	4	4	24	27	25	.294	.372	.425	320	94	20	5	4	32	41	37
Road	.268	.357	.400	220	59	11	3	4	21	31	30	.268	.355	.386	347	93	16	5	5	32	47	42
Facing Groundball Pitchers and Flyball Pitchers																						
Groundball	.265	.356	.381	189	50	10	3	2	15	28	23	.254	.341	.350	303	77	15	4	2	26	42	35
Flyball	.318	.393	.496	242	77	17	4	6	30	30	32	.302	.382	.451	364	110	21	6	7	38	46	44
Facing Finesse Pitchers and Power Pitchers																						
Finesse	.326	.383	.483	242	79	15	4	5	26	23	26	.319	.377	.445	364	116	21	5	5	36	35	38
Power	.254	.369	.397	189	48	12	3	3	19	35	29	.234	.347	.356	303	71	15	5	4	28	53	41
On Grass and on Turf																						
Grass	.309	.383	.455	301	93	22	5	4	29	37	38	.285	.364	.404	470	134	28	8	4	42	60	55
Turf	.262	.362	.423	130	34	5	2	4	16	21	17	.269	.361	.406	197	53	8	2	5	22	28	24
During the Day and at Night																						
Day	.309	.378	.497	175	54	13	4	4	17	20	20	.290	.360	.430	272	79	16	5	4	24	30	26
Night	.285	.376	.410	256	73	14	3	4	28	38	35	.273	.365	.387	395	108	20	5	5	40	58	53
By Month																						
April	.327	.413	.436	55	18	1	1	1	5	8	7	.327	.413	.436	55	18	1	1	1	5	8	7
May	.221	.293	.279	68	15	2	1	0	1	7	6	.247	.307	.333	81	20	2	1	1	4	7	7
June	.397	.470	.638	58	23	7	2	1	11	8	9	.347	.417	.560	75	26	7	3	1	12	9	15
July	.357	.415	.619	84	30	9	2	3	15	9	10	.289	.361	.426	190	55	13	2	3	26	22	20
August	.225	.307	.360	89	20	4	1	2	9	11	14	.248	.335	.352	165	41	7	2	2	12	22	20
Sept/Oct	.273	.391	.364	77	21	4	0	1	4	15	9	.267	.388	.376	101	27	6	1	1	5	20	10
Situational																						
Bases Empty	.293	.373	.450	307	90	22	4	6	6	39	42	.286	.371	.410	451	129	28	5	6	6	60	60
Leadoff	.306	.392	.481	183	56	13	2	5	5	26	26	.286	.373	.421	266	76	17	2	5	5	37	37
Not Leadoff	.274	.343	.403	124	34	9	2	1	1	13	16	.286	.368	.395	185	53	11	3	1	1	23	23
Runners On	.298	.386	.435	124	37	5	3	2	39	19	13	.269	.347	.394	216	58	8	5	3	58	28	19
First Base Only	.205	.314	.250	44	9	0	1	0	1	7	3	.231	.318	.333	78	18	1	2	1	4	10	6
Scoring Position	.350	.426	.537	80	28	5	2	2	38	12	10	.290	.362	.428	138	40	7	3	2	54	18	13
Late Innings, Close	.324	.412	.459	74	24	5	1	1	8	11	11	.290	.369	.402	107	31	7	1	1	11	14	15
RBI/Opportunities																						
Scoring Position				34 / 118		(29%)									50 / 197		(25%)					
Scoring Position, 2 Out				19 / 63		(30%)									27 / 109		(25%)					
On Third, Less than 2 Out				5 / 13		(38%)									11 / 23		(48%)					
RBI in close games / RBI Total				26 / 45		(58%)									38 / 64		(59%)					

Mike Easler
New York Yankees

Mike Easler has been unwittingly participating in a study of park effect for the last two years. His move from a great hitters' park (Fenway) to a pitchers'park (Yankee Stadium) lets us compare the same man in different environments. Although he hit for a higher average with the Yankees than he did in his two seasons with Boston (.303 with New York; .288 for Boston), the real measure comes from looking at his home and road stats. While playing for Boston in '84–85, Easler hit .315 at home and .263 on the road with almost identical power; when he came to New York, those numbers were reversed. He hit .289 in Yankee Stadium in 1986 and .315 (with slightly better power) on the road. While three seasons of data on one player don't prove anything, they do give an indication of how much Fenway helps a lefty hitter. It also demonstrates that Yankee Stadium is not nearly as kind to lefties as many people believe.

A word of warning to the Pittsburgh Pirates: The next time you play the Phillies, avoid pitching to Mike Easler. Mike evidently felt that he had something to prove to the Red Sox this year, because he played like a man posessed. He played in 11 games against Boston this year, had at least one hit in every game and hit .468 overall. He and Don Baylor seemed to be having a contest to see who could hurt his old team most; Baylor hit .311 against the Yankees and drove in nine runs in only 45 at-bats. It's sort of a shame that they won't be going head to head again; make it a point to pay attention to what Mike does when he faces John Tudor in 1987.

The answer to the question "Who won the Easler/Baylor deal?" is a tossup. Mike had a higher batting, on-base and slugging average and he did so despite playing in a park that damaged his stats. Some people may feel that Baylor's leadership capabilities made the deal a steal for Boston; I am not one of them. The point that makes the deal a close call is the way they hit lefties. Easler hit .257 against lefties with one homer and 10 RBIs in 105 at-bats; Baylor hit .254 with 11 homers and 39 RBIs in 193 AB in 1985. Baylor's output certainly wasn't spectacular, but it was some sort of a threat. Removing that threat from a lineup that already had problems against southpaws and adding yet another lefty gave opposing managers too much incentive to throw lefties against New York; the Yankees paid for it.

—Craig Christmann

	1986 SEASON											THREE YEARS (84 – 86)										
	Ave.	OBP	SLG	AB	H	2B	3B	HR	RBI	BB	SO	Ave.	OBP	SLG	AB	H	2B	3B	HR	RBI	BB	SO
Totals	.302	.362	.449	490	148	26	2	14	78	49	87	.292	.354	.461	1659	485	86	11	57	243	160	350
Batting vs. Left and Right-handed Pitchers																						
Left	.226	.252	.302	106	24	3	1	1	8	4	31	.251	.303	.373	458	115	20	3	10	47	33	137
Right	.323	.390	.490	384	124	23	1	13	70	45	56	.308	.373	.494	1201	370	66	8	47	196	127	213
At Home and on the Road																						
Home	.288	.349	.442	233	67	16	1	6	37	24	42	.307	.368	.483	805	247	50	7	26	125	80	183
Road	.315	.375	.455	257	81	10	1	8	41	25	45	.279	.341	.439	854	238	36	4	31	118	80	167
Facing Groundball Pitchers and Flyball Pitchers																						
Groundball	.316	.375	.508	250	79	11	2	11	41	24	37	.297	.362	.459	826	245	38	6	28	115	82	166
Flyball	.287	.349	.388	240	69	15	0	3	37	25	50	.288	.346	.462	833	240	48	5	29	128	78	184
Facing Finesse Pitchers and Power Pitchers																						
Finesse	.314	.374	.466	277	87	15	0	9	41	29	44	.290	.344	.441	947	275	52	5	27	128	78	188
Power	.286	.346	.427	213	61	11	2	5	37	20	43	.295	.368	.486	712	210	34	6	30	115	82	162
On Grass and on Turf																						
Grass	.297	.351	.450	404	120	24	1	12	63	36	63	.291	.351	.460	1400	407	76	10	47	207	133	297
Turf	.326	.414	.442	86	28	2	1	2	15	13	24	.301	.372	.463	259	78	10	1	10	36	27	53
During the Day and at Night																						
Day	.272	.327	.408	184	50	11	1	4	26	16	33	.266	.330	.423	534	142	30	3	16	77	50	121
Night	.320	.383	.474	306	98	15	1	10	52	33	54	.305	.366	.478	1125	343	56	8	41	166	110	229
By Month																						
April	.254	.299	.365	63	16	4	0	1	10	4	6	.266	.329	.440	218	58	12	1	8	30	22	53
May	.347	.412	.547	75	26	4	1	3	14	9	14	.283	.361	.438	258	73	9	2	9	29	31	50
June	.374	.410	.505	107	40	8	0	2	17	8	15	.332	.379	.512	322	107	24	2	10	56	25	77
July	.290	.389	.398	93	27	4	0	2	8	15	21	.295	.366	.470	302	89	13	2	12	40	32	58
August	.195	.253	.378	82	16	4	1	3	15	7	19	.256	.305	.383	277	71	13	2	6	41	20	62
Sept/Oct	.329	.382	.486	70	23	2	0	3	14	6	12	.309	.376	.504	282	87	15	2	12	47	30	50
Situational																						
Bases Empty	.293	.343	.462	249	73	13	1	9	9	19	46	.290	.344	.456	933	271	41	4	35	35	73	205
Leadoff	.340	.386	.594	106	36	6	0	7	7	8	13	.279	.332	.448	402	112	18	1	16	16	30	79
Not Leadoff	.259	.312	.364	143	37	7	1	2	2	11	33	.299	.353	.461	531	159	23	3	19	19	43	126
Runners On	.311	.380	.436	241	75	13	1	5	69	30	41	.295	.367	.467	726	214	45	7	22	208	87	145
First Base Only	.321	.356	.473	112	36	6	1	3	11	6	17	.315	.371	.505	289	91	16	3	11	31	24	53
Scoring Position	.302	.399	.403	129	39	7	0	2	58	24	24	.281	.364	.442	437	123	29	4	11	177	63	92
Late Innings, Close	.268	.381	.380	71	19	5	0	1	12	13	15	.279	.345	.438	265	74	14	2	8	30	26	64

RBI/Opportunities	1986 SEASON		THREE YEARS (84 – 86)	
Scoring Position	53 / 191	(28%)	153 / 619	(25%)
Scoring Position, 2 Out	17 / 87	(20%)	59 / 312	(19%)
On Third, Less than 2 Out	21 / 39	(54%)	52 / 102	(51%)
RBI in close games / RBI Total	51 / 78	(65%)	150 / 243	(62%)

Mark Eichhorn
Toronto Blue Jays

Since most fans know nothing about him, I'll begin with some background on Mark Eichhorn. When an arm injury threatened to end Mark's career in 1983, Toronto came to him with a unique request: if Eichhorn would become the Quisenberry-style reliever that Toronto was looking for, they'd stand by him while he learned the submarine delivery. Eichhorn accepted the proposal and spent the 1984 campaign at Syracuse (AAA), where he compiled a 5–9 record, allowed 147 hits and 51 walks in 117.7 innings and posted a 5.97 ERA. Obviously he needed work on his control, but Toronto kept their promise and delayed any decision on Mark's career for another year.

Eichhorn began 1985 at Knoxville (AA), where he was 5–1 with a 3.02 ERA. That was exactly what Toronto was hoping for—he had adapted to the unique style and had learned to keep his pitches in the strike zone. Toronto invited him to the major league camp in 1986; the rest is recent history.

Eichhorn was an almost immediate success. The first batter to face him (Texas's Larry Parrish) unloaded a three-run, game-winning homer on opening day—they were the only runs he allowed in April. He consistently managed to

either keep Toronto in the game or preserve leads until it was Henke time. Eichhorn had it easy in his first trip around the AL—only one other pitcher out of the 140 in the league had a similar delivery, so he gave hitters fits.

July marked his second go-round—naturally, word of how to hit Mark had preceded him. He went through a mild slump (3.69 ERA for that month), but he finished the season on a high note, because he continued to throw strikes and get ahead of the hitters. Once he did that, he threw tantalizing breaking balls—batters would try to protect the corner of the plate they felt it would cross and wave feebly as it slid by them.

1987, however, is not likely to be quite so kind to Mark. When he hit the majors, batters saw the ball floating up to the plate at 70 MPH, tried to hit it to kingdom come and went down waving. By September, hitters (particularly lefties) were resisting the temptation to swing from the heels and trying only to meet the ball. Eichhorn allowed many singles in September and (since he was a short reliever by then) those singles hurt. Mark won't be a dominating closer in 1987, but he can probably post an ERA of 2.35–3.30 and be a capable middle reliever.

—David Driscoll

1986: Power, Groundball **1985: Did not play** **1984: Did not play**

		1986 SEASON											THREE YEARS (84 – 86)									
	G	IP	H	BB	SO	SB	CS	W	L	S	ERA		G	IP	H	BB	SO	SB	CS	W	L	S	ERA
Totals	69	157.0	105	45	166	15	5	14	6	10	1.72		69	157.0	105	45	166	15	5	14	6	10	1.72
At Home and on the Road																							
Home	34	79.0	56	23	90	5	2	7	5	4	1.94		34	79.0	56	23	90	5	2	7	5	4	1.94
Road	35	78.0	49	22	76	10	3	7	1	6	1.50		35	78.0	49	22	76	10	3	7	1	6	1.50
During the Day and at Night																							
Day	22	44.1	26	11	50	4	1	2	1	4	1.02		22	44.1	26	11	50	4	1	2	1	4	1.02
Night	47	112.2	79	34	116	11	4	12	5	6	2.00		47	112.2	79	34	116	11	4	12	5	6	2.00
On Grass and on Turf																							
Grass	27	60.1	37	18	55	9	3	7	1	4	1.49		27	60.1	37	18	55	9	3	7	1	4	1.49
Turf	42	96.2	68	27	111	6	2	7	5	6	1.86		42	96.2	68	27	111	6	2	7	5	6	1.86
By Month																							
April	8	18.2	5	3	20	1	0	2	1	0	0.48		8	18.2	5	3	20	1	0	2	1	0	0.48
May	12	26.1	15	9	26	3	1	2	1	4	1.37		12	26.1	15	9	26	3	1	2	1	4	1.37
June	4	13.2	7	6	18	0	0	2	1	0	1.32		4	13.2	7	6	18	0	0	2	1	0	1.32
July	13	31.2	36	9	34	3	1	1	0	1	3.69		13	31.2	36	9	34	3	1	1	0	1	3.69
August	17	39.2	21	7	36	1	2	5	1	3	1.13		17	39.2	21	7	36	1	2	5	1	3	1.13
Sept/Oct	15	27.0	21	11	32	7	1	2	2	2	1.67		15	27.0	21	11	32	7	1	2	2	2	1.67

vs. Opponent Batters

			1986 SEASON												THREE YEARS (84 – 86)								
	Ave.	OBP	SLG	AB	H	2B	3B	HR	RBI	BB	SO		Ave.	OBP	SLG	AB	H	2B	3B	HR	RBI	BB	SO
Totals	.192	.261	.288	548	105	23	3	8	49	45	166		.192	.261	.288	548	105	23	3	8	49	45	166
Pitching vs. Left and Right-handed Batters																							
Left	.259	.345	.434	251	65	17	3	7	34	29	54		.259	.345	.434	251	65	17	3	7	34	29	54
Right	.135	.186	.165	297	40	6	0	1	15	16	112		.135	.186	.165	297	40	6	0	1	15	16	112
Situational																							
Bases Empty	.198	.231	.318	324	64	15	3	6	6	11	99		.198	.231	.318	324	64	15	3	6	6	11	99
Leadoff	.214	.250	.317	126	27	5	1	2	2	4	30		.214	.250	.317	126	27	5	1	2	2	4	30
Not Leadoff	.187	.218	.318	198	37	10	2	4	4	7	69		.187	.218	.318	198	37	10	2	4	4	7	69
Runners On	.183	.299	.246	224	41	8	0	2	43	34	67		.183	.299	.246	224	41	8	0	2	43	34	67
First Base Only	.159	.227	.217	69	11	1	0	1	2	6	26		.159	.227	.217	69	11	1	0	1	2	6	26
Scoring Position	.194	.328	.258	155	30	7	0	1	41	28	41		.194	.328	.258	155	30	7	0	1	41	28	41
Late Innings, Close	.193	.267	.246	285	55	9	0	2	21	28	79		.193	.267	.246	285	55	9	0	2	21	28	79

RBI/Opportunities

Scoring Position	39 / 243	(16%)		39 / 243	(16%)
Scoring Position, 2 Out	13 / 119	(11%)		13 / 119	(11%)
On Third, Less than 2 Out	17 / 40	(42%)		17 / 40	(42%)
RBI in close games / RBI Total	32 / 49	(65%)		32 / 49	(65%)

Nick Esasky
Cincinnati Reds

Once upon a time there was a young slugger who came to the majors with an incredible ability to hit the long ball, and an even more incredible ability to swing and miss. In his first three seasons, he struck out more than one-third of the time, but when he made contact . . .

The team had several openings in their lineup, so they tried him at third, at first, and in the outfield. He inspired little confidence anywhere, but he still hit those long drives when he made contact.

Management decided to wait and see if the kid could cut down on his strikeouts and learn to play defense. They waited four years before they traded him for $150,000 and some peace of mind. That slugger grew up to be Dave Kingman.

The parallels between Kingman and Esasky are distressing. Just when we thought we were almost rid of the baseball underachiever of the decade, along comes his clone. The biggest differences between the two so far is that Esasky doesn't display any of Kingman's unpleasant habits, but he also doesn't hit as many home runs.

The Reds keep hoping Nick will blossom, but I can't see what they plan to do with him if he does. While Nick fiddled, the Reds traded for or promoted another player at every position at which they've tried him. Maybe they could try him at pitcher, or maybe he could be exchanged for a pitcher. Detroit might be able to spare Walt Terrell, and Sparky Anderson seems to have a soft spot in his head or heart for former Reds. I think the Reds should do Esasky a favor and get him out of Cincinnati.

There is a chance, however, that Esasky is just conditioned to fail in Cincinnati. He was brought up in 1983, probably before he was ready, by the Dick Wagner regime. Desperate bunch that they were, they touted Esasky, Redus and Milner (as well as others who turned out even less notable), trying to make the fans forget the complete reversal of the club's fortunes over which it had presided—if not precipitated—by its rebuilding efforts. They started yanking young hot shots out of the minors, sending them out to fail, and trying to balance the books between what they saved in salaries and lost in revenue. The whole program was bad for the players and for the team.

Look at the numbers and think about it. Esasky either needs a change of scenery or a change of jobs. He seems like a nice guy; I hope he likes it wherever he's traded.

—Tim McKenzie

	1986 SEASON											THREE YEARS (84 – 86)										
	Ave.	OBP	SLG	AB	H	2B	3B	HR	RBI	BB	SO	Ave.	OBP	SLG	AB	H	2B	3B	HR	RBI	BB	SO
Totals	.230	.325	.403	330	76	17	2	12	41	47	97	.231	.320	.410	1065	246	48	7	43	152	140	302
Batting vs. Left and Right-handed Pitchers																						
Left	.237	.331	.458	118	28	9	1	5	11	17	30	.254	.349	.473	402	102	22	6	18	52	60	108
Right	.226	.321	.373	212	48	8	1	7	30	30	67	.217	.302	.373	663	144	26	1	25	100	80	194
At Home and on the Road																						
Home	.226	.306	.459	159	36	10	0	9	23	19	55	.222	.301	.411	523	116	30	3	21	78	61	149
Road	.234	.342	.351	171	40	7	2	3	18	28	42	.240	.338	.410	542	130	18	4	22	74	79	153
Facing Groundball Pitchers and Flyball Pitchers																						
Groundball	.230	.332	.348	161	37	9	2	2	10	25	49	.248	.339	.404	532	132	24	4	17	63	74	151
Flyball	.231	.318	.456	169	39	8	0	10	31	22	48	.214	.301	.417	533	114	24	3	26	89	66	151
Facing Finesse Pitchers and Power Pitchers																						
Finesse	.209	.286	.350	163	34	9	1	4	17	18	43	.228	.305	.426	580	132	29	4	26	87	65	142
Power	.251	.360	.455	167	42	8	1	8	24	29	54	.235	.337	.392	485	114	19	3	17	65	75	160
On Grass and on Turf																						
Grass	.247	.373	.351	97	24	5	1	1	12	19	26	.243	.354	.403	325	79	12	2	12	47	54	95
Turf	.223	.303	.425	233	52	12	1	11	29	28	71	.226	.304	.414	740	167	36	5	31	105	86	207
During the Day and at Night																						
Day	.216	.372	.314	102	22	7	0	1	10	25	33	.215	.323	.358	344	74	19	0	10	44	54	111
Night	.237	.300	.443	228	54	10	2	11	31	22	64	.239	.318	.436	721	172	29	7	33	108	86	191
By Month																						
April	.196	.317	.451	51	10	2	1	3	5	8	16	.211	.306	.428	180	38	11	2	8	30	24	59
May	.222	.355	.333	63	14	4	0	1	5	13	12	.209	.313	.320	153	32	8	0	3	16	24	36
June	.276	.333	.552	29	8	2	0	2	6	3	9	.252	.377	.445	119	30	8	0	5	19	23	31
July	.282	.349	.410	39	11	2	0	1	3	4	13	.255	.319	.441	145	37	5	2	6	19	14	43
August	.229	.287	.386	83	19	5	1	2	12	8	23	.237	.306	.424	257	61	9	3	11	36	26	67
Sept/Oct	.215	.329	.385	65	14	2	0	3	10	11	24	.227	.321	.403	211	48	7	0	10	32	29	66
Situational																						
Bases Empty	.235	.313	.385	187	44	12	2	4	4	21	52	.227	.315	.381	598	136	26	3	20	20	74	177
Leadoff	.305	.367	.512	82	25	6	1	3	3	8	19	.230	.299	.365	274	63	11	1	8	8	26	73
Not Leadoff	.181	.271	.286	105	19	6	1	1	1	13	33	.225	.327	.395	324	73	15	2	12	12	48	104
Runners On	.224	.339	.427	143	32	5	0	8	37	26	45	.236	.327	.448	467	110	22	4	23	132	66	125
First Base Only	.300	.373	.600	60	18	0	0	6	12	7	16	.223	.285	.416	197	44	3	1	11	24	16	45
Scoring Position	.169	.318	.301	83	14	5	0	2	25	19	29	.244	.353	.470	270	66	19	3	12	108	50	80
Late Innings, Close	.185	.297	.352	54	10	0	0	3	10	9	15	.213	.304	.391	197	42	3	1	10	32	28	62
RBI/Opportunities																						

	1986 SEASON			THREE YEARS (84 – 86)		
Scoring Position	21 / 122	(17%)		87 / 386	(23%)	
Scoring Position, 2 Out	6 / 61	(10%)		27 / 177	(15%)	
On Third, Less than 2 Out	11 / 24	(46%)		36 / 74	(49%)	
RBI in close games / RBI Total	24 / 41	(59%)		93 / 152	(61%)	

Darrell Evans
Detroit Tigers

When Darrell Evans came to Detroit as a free-agent, everyone had high hopes for him. After all, he had just hit 30 home runs for San Francisco, and he was moving to a park that is very kind to left-handed pull hitters. Darrell suffered through a poor season (.232 BA, 16 HR), though, ending up being platooned at first and DH. However, because of his nice personality, not many people in Detroit worried too much about his off-year when the Tigers were tearing up the league.

When Darrell's slump continued in April of 1985, no one was willing to overlook his performance. Evans hit only .188 with one dinger that month; by the start of May, the Tigers were desperately trying to unload him. There weren't any takers, though, and the management was preparing to eat the $1.5 million left on his contract by releasing him outright. The sage opinion of the major-league scouts was that his career was over because he couldn't get around on the fastball anymore. At the eleventh hour, of course, Darrell suddenly got hot, and he went on to hit 39 home runs the rest of the year. Keep this example in mind the next time you read the pontifications of the oft-quoted scouts.

At the age of 39, Darrell Evans had another good year for Detroit in 1986. The most dramatic improvement in his season was his return to effectiveness against left-handed pitchers. In 1985, Evans hit only .208 with a .275 on-base average and a .467 slugging average against southpaws; last year, he increased his average against them by 68 points, his on-base by 103 points, and his slugging by 23 points. On the other hand, Darrell was weaker against right-handers last year, dropping 33 points in average, 32 points in on-base, and 112 in slugging. His home and road stats were roughly comparable last year; for the past three years, they are almost identical. In the past three years, he has shown a marked preference for day games. In August 1986, he tatooed AL pitchers for 10 home runs and a .584 slugging average, but he tailed off badly in September and October with a meager .180 BA and .290 SA. Evans has been weakest at the bat with the bases empty for the last three years, improving significantly with runners on. His late-and-close stats for 1986 were tremendous—.338 BA, .433 OBA, .688 SA.

Darrell improved significantly in the field last year, cutting his errors from 15 to 2 while still getting 108 assists at first base in only 105 games.

—Gary Gillette

	1986 SEASON											THREE YEARS (84 – 86)										
	Ave.	OBP	SLG	AB	H	2B	3B	HR	RBI	BB	SO	Ave.	OBP	SLG	AB	H	2B	3B	HR	RBI	BB	SO
Totals	.241	.357	.442	507	122	15	0	29	85	92	105	.241	.355	.453	1413	340	43	1	85	242	254	260
Batting vs. Left and Right-handed Pitchers																						
Left	.272	.378	.483	147	40	4	0	9	32	24	39	.249	.351	.443	357	89	12	0	19	61	55	84
Right	.228	.349	.425	360	82	11	0	20	53	68	66	.238	.357	.456	1056	251	31	1	66	181	199	176
At Home and on the Road																						
Home	.236	.353	.451	246	58	8	0	15	47	44	48	.240	.356	.454	676	162	19	0	42	123	122	126
Road	.245	.361	.433	261	64	7	0	14	38	48	57	.242	.355	.452	737	178	24	1	43	119	132	134
Facing Groundball Pitchers and Flyball Pitchers																						
Groundball	.223	.336	.427	206	46	9	0	11	31	35	44	.226	.335	.420	669	151	23	1	35	98	111	119
Flyball	.252	.371	.452	301	76	6	0	18	54	57	61	.254	.373	.483	744	189	20	0	50	144	143	141
Facing Finesse Pitchers and Power Pitchers																						
Finesse	.244	.358	.457	291	71	8	0	18	49	51	52	.242	.352	.461	796	193	22	1	50	131	136	130
Power	.236	.357	.421	216	51	7	0	11	36	41	53	.238	.360	.442	617	147	21	0	35	111	118	130
On Grass and on Turf																						
Grass	.241	.355	.452	431	104	13	0	26	75	76	89	.237	.351	.441	1187	281	36	0	69	203	212	215
Turf	.237	.370	.382	76	18	2	0	3	10	16	16	.261	.377	.513	226	59	7	1	16	39	42	45
During the Day and at Night																						
Day	.293	.403	.524	164	48	5	0	11	34	31	40	.283	.385	.522	441	125	19	1	28	92	76	80
Night	.216	.335	.402	343	74	10	0	18	51	61	65	.221	.342	.422	972	215	24	0	57	150	178	180
By Month																						
April	.237	.328	.508	59	14	1	0	5	8	8	11	.238	.314	.423	168	40	7	0	8	25	19	25
May	.213	.315	.383	94	20	4	0	4	12	14	16	.259	.360	.445	247	64	7	0	13	38	39	34
June	.299	.415	.478	67	20	3	0	3	18	14	11	.254	.399	.437	213	54	9	0	10	40	54	36
July	.267	.394	.442	86	23	3	0	4	14	17	14	.215	.348	.446	251	54	7	0	17	47	49	44
August	.267	.378	.584	101	27	2	0	10	22	18	25	.246	.359	.512	260	64	7	1	20	52	46	59
Sept/Oct	.180	.320	.290	100	18	2	0	3	11	21	28	.234	.343	.442	274	64	6	0	17	40	47	62
Situational																						
Bases Empty	.230	.329	.457	278	64	6	0	19	19	40	51	.226	.320	.444	811	183	21	0	52	52	112	150
Leadoff	.206	.320	.346	107	22	0	0	5	5	17	21	.228	.324	.453	333	76	3	0	24	24	46	58
Not Leadoff	.246	.335	.526	171	42	6	0	14	14	23	30	.224	.318	.437	478	107	18	0	28	28	66	92
Runners On	.253	.389	.424	229	58	9	0	10	66	52	54	.261	.398	.465	602	157	22	1	33	190	142	110
First Base Only	.250	.377	.386	88	22	3	0	3	8	18	21	.264	.390	.459	242	64	8	0	13	29	49	42
Scoring Position	.255	.395	.447	141	36	6	0	7	58	34	33	.258	.403	.469	360	93	14	1	20	161	93	68
Late Innings, Close	.338	.433	.688	77	26	3	0	8	28	13	15	.259	.365	.514	216	56	7	0	16	45	36	34
RBI/Opportunities																						
Scoring Position				47 / 213		(22%)									125 / 550		(23%)					
Scoring Position, 2 Out				24 / 112		(21%)									52 / 280		(19%)					
On Third, Less than 2 Out				14 / 35		(40%)									43 / 98		(44%)					
RBI in close games / RBI Total				58 / 85		(68%)									148 / 242		(61%)					

Dwight Evans
Boston Red Sox

Fenway Park's most famous feature is its short left field, which makes peculiar demands of defenders. Less celebrated, but just as demanding, is the opposite field. Fenway boasts the most spacious right field in the AL; a sizable pasture for the defender to cover. The foul line vanishes into the stands well before the corner—the seats are effectively in fair territory. In other parks, a rightfielder fighting for a ball in the seats is pursuing a foul . . . if he doesn't make a play here, it's a home run. Fenway's rightfield wall is like a hockey rink's—the corner is rounded and the ball will scoot over to center quickly. Line drives down the line that keep clear of the seats are do-or-die plays—if a player tries to cut the ball off and fails, it will be the last he sees of it.

This is the setting where Dwight Evans has made his reputation as one of the best outfielders in the game. He begins by using his encyclopediac knowledge of hitters to position himself. He moves quickly to the ball, be it fly, line or ground. His years of experience let him make complex caroms look easy and prevent short hops from getting by him. He held runners in check with a strong arm for years (he does it more on the strength of his reputation now, though).

Dwight covers the most difficult territory in the league and looks great doing it.

In 1986, Evans was second in the AL (and the team) in total walks, but walked just as often as Boggs (who had more at-bats) did. His on-base average was 117 points higher than his batting average—a phenomenal amount for most players (best on his team) but normal for Dwight. Evans also led the team in strikeouts—when you combine this and his walks, it means that he didn't put the ball in play in over 33% of his plate apperances. He waits until he sees his pitch—when he gets it, he crushes it.

Evans's 1986 provided several surprises. It was the first time he had ever hit better against righties and on the road (especially on turf), but those figures probably do not mean anything in particular. His performance at night, though, does signify a problem. 1986 is the third straight year that his output has fallen; the drops are not large, but the fact that they keep happening is bothersome. As he's having no trouble in other areas, perhaps the problem is vision-related; Evans might benefit by making a trip to his opthamologist this year.

—Fred Percival

	1986 SEASON												THREE YEARS (84 – 86)										
	Ave.	OBP	SLG	AB	H	2B	3B	HR	RBI	BB	SO		Ave.	OBP	SLG	AB	H	2B	3B	HR	RBI	BB	SO
Totals	.259	.376	.476	529	137	33	2	26	97	97	117		.273	.381	.488	1776	485	99	11	87	279	307	337
Batting vs. Left and Right-handed Pitchers																							
Left	.228	.363	.397	136	31	5	0	6	23	29	25		.277	.415	.502	448	124	20	3	25	73	108	72
Right	.270	.381	.504	393	106	28	2	20	74	68	92		.272	.369	.483	1328	361	79	8	62	206	199	265
At Home and on the Road																							
Home	.253	.384	.436	241	61	18	1	8	41	51	42		.290	.394	.508	848	246	58	8	37	131	146	139
Road	.264	.370	.510	288	76	15	1	18	56	46	75		.258	.369	.470	928	239	41	3	50	148	161	198
Facing Groundball Pitchers and Flyball Pitchers																							
Groundball	.277	.401	.455	231	64	12	1	9	39	45	42		.276	.387	.451	851	235	43	5	32	112	150	129
Flyball	.245	.357	.493	298	73	21	1	17	58	52	75		.270	.375	.522	925	250	56	6	55	167	157	208
Facing Finesse Pitchers and Power Pitchers																							
Finesse	.268	.371	.473	317	85	23	0	14	55	50	60		.290	.387	.492	1032	299	71	6	42	145	163	167
Power	.245	.383	.481	212	52	10	2	12	42	47	57		.250	.373	.483	744	186	28	5	45	134	144	170
On Grass and on Turf																							
Grass	.247	.369	.459	438	108	26	2	21	80	83	94		.274	.383	.488	1485	407	86	11	70	231	261	277
Turf	.319	.411	.560	91	29	7	0	5	17	14	23		.268	.368	.488	291	78	13	0	17	48	46	60
During the Day and at Night																							
Day	.294	.389	.500	194	57	14	1	8	34	30	42		.298	.406	.509	574	171	39	2	26	81	102	101
Night	.239	.369	.463	335	80	19	1	18	63	67	75		.261	.369	.478	1202	314	60	9	61	198	205	236
By Month																							
April	.260	.382	.425	73	19	4	1	2	9	14	8		.221	.374	.358	226	50	14	1	5	21	55	37
May	.196	.327	.348	92	18	11	0	1	7	18	22		.213	.345	.395	286	61	19	0	11	32	56	62
June	.274	.366	.505	95	26	2	1	6	26	15	20		.311	.409	.529	293	91	11	4	15	54	52	56
July	.289	.385	.511	90	26	5	0	5	22	13	24		.302	.384	.503	308	93	15	1	15	54	40	62
August	.292	.413	.528	89	26	6	0	5	18	18	19		.288	.378	.551	323	93	23	4	18	57	46	57
Sept/Oct	.244	.386	.533	90	22	5	0	7	15	19	24		.285	.393	.544	340	97	17	1	23	61	58	63
Situational																							
Bases Empty	.241	.366	.442	294	71	15	1	14	14	53	66		.266	.378	.485	959	255	48	9	48	48	165	176
Leadoff	.246	.359	.437	142	35	12	0	5	5	23	36		.264	.354	.485	439	116	28	3	21	21	57	80
Not Leadoff	.237	.373	.447	152	36	3	1	9	9	30	30		.267	.397	.485	520	139	20	6	27	27	108	96
Runners On	.281	.388	.519	235	66	18	1	12	83	44	51		.282	.384	.492	817	230	51	2	39	231	142	161
First Base Only	.290	.360	.640	100	29	11	0	8	21	11	23		.306	.394	.545	396	121	32	0	21	50	55	73
Scoring Position	.274	.406	.430	135	37	7	1	4	62	33	28		.259	.376	.442	421	109	19	2	18	181	87	88
Late Innings, Close	.284	.429	.567	67	19	4	0	5	13	16	9		.294	.396	.565	269	79	11	1	20	62	45	49
RBI/Opportunities																							
Scoring Position				52 / 217		(24%)										149 / 635		(23%)					
Scoring Position, 2 Out				29 / 102		(28%)										70 / 289		(24%)					
On Third, Less than 2 Out				18 / 32		(56%)										55 / 110		(50%)					
RBI in close games / RBI Total				58 / 97		(60%)										192 / 279		(69%)					

Sid Fernandez
New York Mets

Around Shea Stadium Sid Fernandez is affectionately known as El Sid. The historical El Cid (from the Arabic word meaning Lord) was one Rodrigo Diaz de Bivar, a Spanish soldier and epic hero from the eleventh century. The similarity between the two lies in more than just a name; when they were good they were invincible, and when they were bad they were horrible. The original El Cid fought for BOTH sides in the Crusades—and there were moments last year when Met fans had the same feeling about Fernandez. That's a peculiar thing to say about a 16–6 pitcher with unbelievable stuff, but Sid is a very peculiar pitcher.

When the Mets got Fernandez from Los Angeles for Bob Bailor and Carlos (not Rodrigo) Diaz, he came with the reputation of being an immature, overweight kid with an attitude problem. The Dodgers were wrong on most counts. Sid has matured and his "attitude problem" appears to stem from shyness and is not a reason for concern. His weight, though, is another matter. Although he arrived for spring training in '86 much slimmer than ever before, he was unable to maintain that weight. It is here that El Sid's

seasons turns, because although he was 16–6 for the season, he was 12–2 before the All-Star break and only 4–4 after, with a jump in ERA. The problem was that he started putting on some extra pounds. While Fernandez claimed that the weight didn't affect his stamina, it clearly affected his pitching. During the second half he seemed to be having difficulty getting his curveball over. Without command of the curve, Sid's sneaky 89-m.p.h. fastball ceased to be sneaky and became not just hittable, but bangable.

So now we come to his peculiarities. It is true that El Sid struck out 8.81 batters per nine innings—third best in the league. He was also fourth in the league in fewest hits allowed at 7.09 per nine innings. But unlike many pitchers who are on for a game or an inning, El Sid seems to change from pitch to pitch. He is a timing/movement pitcher. When he can control his pitches they can't hit him. When he can't keep the batters off balance he gets dinged. Unlike others who tire, Sid loses and regains his movement again and again. He relies on mechanics, and that's just what the weight gain affected. Hopefully the problem will diminish as Sid continues to mature.

—J. Randolph Burnham

1986: Power, Flyball												1985: Power, Flyball											1984: Power, Flyball	
	1986 SEASON											**THREE YEARS (84 – 86)**												
	G	IP	H	BB	SO	SB	CS	W	L	S	ERA	G	IP	H	BB	SO	SB	CS	W	L	S	ERA		
Totals	32	204.1	161	91	200	22	4	16	6	1	3.52	73	464.2	343	205	442	69	16	31	21	1	3.25		
At Home and on the Road																								
Home	16	107.2	67	45	109	12	2	8	3	1	2.17	34	218.2	143	94	229	35	7	16	10	1	2.59		
Road	16	96.2	94	46	91	10	2	8	3	0	5.03	39	246.0	200	111	213	34	9	15	11	0	3.84		
During the Day and at Night																								
Day	15	93.0	67	47	92	12	3	7	2	1	3.58	31	183.1	125	103	173	34	9	13	4	1	3.29		
Night	17	111.1	94	44	108	10	1	9	4	0	3.48	42	281.1	218	102	269	35	7	18	17	0	3.23		
On Grass and on Turf																								
Grass	22	143.1	110	61	139	16	3	10	5	1	3.39	50	316.1	228	144	306	48	12	21	15	1	3.19		
Turf	10	61.0	51	30	61	6	1	6	1	0	3.84	23	148.1	115	61	136	21	4	10	6	0	3.40		
By Month																								
April	3	20.1	6	12	20	3	1	2	0	0	2.66	3	20.1	6	12	20	3	1	2	0	0	2.66		
May	6	40.2	30	18	35	3	1	3	1	0	3.10	10	65.1	42	34	60	9	1	4	2	0	2.62		
June	5	34.1	21	18	29	3	0	4	1	0	3.41	10	65.1	48	31	63	9	6	5	4	0	3.44		
July	6	37.2	35	14	41	8	2	3	2	0	3.35	15	97.0	80	36	98	19	1	7	4	0	2.88		
August	5	31.1	34	12	30	4	0	3	0	0	5.46	16	103.0	82	38	93	17	3	6	5	0	3.58		
Sept/Oct	7	40.0	35	17	45	1	2	1	2	1	3.15	19	113.2	85	54	108	12	4	7	6	1	3.64		

	vs. Opponent Batters																				
	1986 SEASON											**THREE YEARS (84 – 86)**									
	Ave.	OBP	SLG	AB	H	2B	3B	HR	RBI	BB	SO	Ave.	OBP	SLG	AB	H	2B	3B	HR	RBI	BB	SO
Totals	.216	.300	.324	746	161	34	4	13	75	91	200	.206	.292	.325	1669	343	79	8	35	155	205	442
Pitching vs. Left and Right-handed Batters																					
Left	.227	.350	.289	97	22	3	0	1	5	18	32	.195	.279	.293	256	50	13	0	4	16	29	88
Right	.214	.292	.330	649	139	31	4	12	70	73	168	.207	.294	.331	1413	293	66	8	31	139	176	354
Situational																					
Bases Empty	.218	.303	.307	436	95	17	2	6	6	53	116	.205	.287	.333	1026	210	45	6	25	25	117	271
Leadoff	.209	.299	.294	187	39	7	0	3	3	24	48	.196	.290	.318	424	83	16	3	10	10	55	124
Not Leadoff	.225	.306	.317	249	56	10	2	3	3	29	68	.211	.286	.344	602	127	29	3	15	15	62	147
Runners On	.213	.297	.348	310	66	17	2	7	69	38	84	.207	.298	.313	643	133	34	2	10	130	88	171
First Base Only	.226	.298	.349	146	33	10	1	2	13	13	33	.218	.303	.328	271	59	16	1	4	21	31	63
Scoring Position	.201	.296	.348	164	33	7	1	5	56	25	51	.199	.295	.301	372	74	18	1	6	.109	57	108
Late Innings, Close	.298	.375	.447	47	14	4	0	1	7	7	8	.242	.317	.452	124	30	7	2	5	18	15	23

	RBI/Opportunities					
Scoring Position		45 / 222	(20%)	94 / 494	(19%)	
Scoring Position, 2 Out		16 / 98	(16%)	32 / 229	(14%)	
On Third, Less than 2 Out		17 / 31	(55%)	35 / 71	(49%)	
RBI in close games / RBI Total		65 / 75	(87%)	132 / 155	(85%)	

Tony Fernandez
Toronto Blue Jays

Tony Fernandez improved again in 1986. He hit .300 with 200 hits, (which was expected) and got even better defensively (which wasn't). He's not perfect. But he's close.

Despite boosting his average 20 points, Tony's on-base average fell. Like many young players, he exchanged hits for walks (they fell from 43 to 27), despite having more plate appearances. He should change that in time. His strikeouts, however, didn't move at all; if he draws 50 walks, he'll be one of the few men who walks more often than he fans. He wasn't a bad leadoff man, but he isn't a good one; given his power and his stats with men on base, he's probably a better #2 hitter.

He seems to be able to do anything; his stats against lefties are proof of that. In '84 and the first half of '85, he had a lot of trouble hitting them—he's beating up on them now. He raised his slugging average 30 points by hitting more singles (led the league in singles) and setting career highs in doubles and homers. He had almost identical numbers of triples and homers, which is odd. It seems likely that one will drop and the other will climb—if you're a gambler, bet on five triples and 15 homers in 1987.

Defensively, he was spectacular. His range factor fell a bit from 1985 (4.76 to 4.53), but he compensated by cutting his errors from 31 to 13 and winning his first Gold Glove. The problem he'd had was mental—in 1985, he'd scramble to get to the ball and throw it immediately, no matter what awkward position he was in at the time. This year he realized what a strong arm he had—that, 90% of the time, he could straighten up, make an accurate throw and still get hitters out. His 1986 stats are very comparable to Ozzie Smith's superb 1985. Their fielding percentages were identical (.983), they had similar DP totals (108–103, Ozzie) and Fernandez had 30 more putouts (294–264). The Wizard had 104 more assists (549–445), but that will change when Tony learns to position himself—after all, he's only in his second year as a regular.

Toronto's front office feels that Tony must be rested more (see his September stats) and promises to do so in 1987. It's a good idea, but don't expect it. The Jays don't have the bench to rest him often; unless they win the division in a walk or finish out of it in 1987, Fernandez will play 160+ games for his third straight year.

—Marco Bresba

	1986 SEASON											THREE YEARS (84 – 86)										
	Ave.	OBP	SLG	AB	H	2B	3B	HR	RBI	BB	SO	Ave.	OBP	SLG	AB	H	2B	3B	HR	RBI	BB	SO
Totals	.310	.338	.428	687	213	33	9	10	65	27	52	.296	.335	.402	1485	439	69	22	15	135	87	108
Batting vs. Left and Right-handed Pitchers																						
Left	.317	.347	.468	205	65	12	2	5	30	9	21	.296	.349	.418	476	141	27	8	5	51	38	42
Right	.307	.334	.411	482	148	21	7	5	35	18	31	.295	.329	.394	1009	298	42	14	10	84	49	66
At Home and on the Road																						
Home	.320	.345	.427	337	108	14	5	4	24	11	21	.302	.344	.418	699	211	39	12	6	55	42	44
Road	.300	.332	.429	350	105	19	4	6	41	16	31	.290	.328	.388	786	228	30	10	9	80	45	64
Facing Groundball Pitchers and Flyball Pitchers																						
Groundball	.285	.311	.383	298	85	14	3	3	27	9	23	.294	.338	.392	687	202	33	8	6	69	43	39
Flyball	.329	.358	.463	389	128	19	6	7	38	18	29	.297	.333	.411	798	237	36	14	9	66	44	69
Facing Finesse Pitchers and Power Pitchers																						
Finesse	.331	.357	.475	396	131	20	8	7	41	15	29	.306	.340	.426	827	253	42	15	9	72	40	57
Power	.282	.312	.364	291	82	13	1	3	24	12	23	.283	.330	.372	658	186	27	7	6	63	47	51
On Grass and on Turf																						
Grass	.294	.328	.415	272	80	14	2	5	30	13	26	.287	.320	.372	610	175	21	5	7	56	30	54
Turf	.320	.345	.436	415	133	19	7	5	35	14	26	.302	.346	.423	875	264	48	17	8	79	57	54
During the Day and at Night																						
Day	.292	.317	.396	250	73	12	1	4	23	8	18	.294	.329	.392	528	155	27	5	5	47	27	30
Night	.320	.350	.446	437	140	21	8	6	42	19	34	.297	.339	.408	957	284	42	17	10	88	60	78
By Month																						
April	.265	.307	.313	83	22	2	1	0	4	5	8	.265	.302	.325	151	40	5	2	0	9	7	13
May	.275	.319	.367	109	30	5	1	1	7	8	9	.267	.312	.361	202	54	9	2	2	18	15	14
June	.385	.414	.566	122	47	7	3	3	16	6	4	.345	.387	.502	249	86	15	6	4	31	16	11
July	.317	.331	.458	120	38	10	2	1	15	2	7	.263	.301	.359	270	71	14	3	2	25	15	19
August	.312	.348	.456	125	39	7	1	3	16	4	11	.333	.375	.478	297	99	16	6	5	37	17	23
Sept/Oct	.289	.298	.367	128	37	2	1	2	7	2	13	.282	.317	.351	316	89	10	3	2	15	17	28
Situational																						
Bases Empty	.301	.333	.396	455	137	18	5	5	5	19	39	.299	.339	.401	920	275	45	14	7	7	52	70
Leadoff	.305	.336	.415	236	72	12	1	4	4	8	18	.303	.339	.428	442	134	28	6	5	5	20	31
Not Leadoff	.297	.330	.374	219	65	6	4	1	1	11	21	.295	.339	.377	478	141	17	8	2	2	32	39
Runners On	.328	.347	.491	232	76	15	4	5	60	8	13	.290	.330	.404	565	164	24	8	8	128	35	38
First Base Only	.310	.328	.509	116	36	4	2	5	12	2	5	.290	.314	.427	255	74	6	4	7	19	8	11
Scoring Position	.345	.365	.474	116	40	11	2	0	48	6	8	.290	.341	.384	310	90	18	4	1	109	27	27
Late Innings, Close	.360	.372	.532	111	40	7	3	2	16	2	4	.315	.354	.458	260	82	12	8	3	36	16	22
RBI/Opportunities																						
Scoring Position				45 / 148		(30%)									104 / 421		(25%)					
Scoring Position, 2 Out				19 / 58		(33%)									48 / 190		(25%)					
On Third, Less than 2 Out				18 / 29		(62%)									35 / 79		(44%)					
RBI in close games / RBI Total				36 / 65		(55%)									84 / 135		(62%)					

Carlton Fisk
Chicago White Sox

Carlton Fisk's 1986 batting average of .221 was his lowest in the majors since he went 0 for 5 in a late-season call-up way back in 1969. The 1986 season was also his first at any level that he did not have more stolen bases than caught stealings. His career steal record stands at 115–49, a remarkable 70% success rate.

Fisk is the only player in the lively ball era (since 1920) to steal 100 bases as a catcher. That many not sound like a lot, but no other catcher is even in the nineties. Going further back in history, you find only four catchers ahead of him—Johnny Kling, Red Dooin, Roger Bresnehan and Ray Schalk, the leader with 176 steals as a catcher. Of course, the style of play in the deadball era was drastically different. The hit-and-run play was at its peak and EVERY-BODY was expected to run. The success rates of these catchers were hardly electrifying. In the eleven seasons that we have caught stealing data for Schalk, his success rate was 63%. In 1915 he stole fifteen bases but was caught eighteen times.

Fisk also holds the obscure record of being the only catcher in American League history to lead the circuit in triples (1972). Considering the frequency and success rate of his steal attempts relative to his era, a strong case can be made for Carlton Fisk as the best base-running catcher in the game's history.

I wonder what games the Yankees were watching when they pegged Joel Skinner as a standout defensive catcher. In his seven starts against New York, Skinner caught five losses and allowed 5.61 runs per nine innings. Ironically, Fisk caught some of his best games against the Yanks: four wins in four tries, and they never scored more than two runs in any of them.

It's hard to figure the whispers that the White Sox were unhappy with Fisk's game calling. In 1986 the Sox allowed 4.13 runs per nine innings in games in which Fisk was the primary catcher, 4.51 when he was not. The difference in winning percentage was .484 to .418, and Fisk faced a slightly tougher opponent on average than the other Sox catchers. It was the third season in a row that the White Sox staff had a better ERA with Fisk starting behind the plate.

—Craig Wright

| | 1986 SEASON | | | | | | | | | | | THREE YEARS (84 – 86) | | | | | | | | | | |
	Ave.	OBP	SLG	AB	H	2B	3B	HR	RBI	BB	SO	Ave.	OBP	SLG	AB	H	2B	3B	HR	RBI	BB	SO
Totals	.221	.263	.337	457	101	11	0	14	63	22	92	.230	.293	.432	1359	313	54	2	72	213	100	233
Batting vs. Left and Right-handed Pitchers																						
Left	.223	.253	.350	157	35	5	0	5	22	7	35	.239	.294	.430	481	115	23	0	23	71	35	80
Right	.220	.268	.330	300	66	6	0	9	41	15	57	.226	.293	.433	878	198	31	2	49	142	65	153
At Home and on the Road																						
Home	.207	.236	.289	232	48	4	0	5	27	8	43	.212	.274	.410	698	148	26	2	36	102	53	121
Road	.236	.290	.387	225	53	7	0	9	36	14	49	.250	.314	.455	661	165	28	0	36	111	47	112
Facing Groundball Pitchers and Flyball Pitchers																						
Groundball	.265	.301	.357	196	52	3	0	5	34	7	33	.236	.304	.407	639	151	23	1	28	104	51	110
Flyball	.188	.234	.322	261	49	8	0	9	29	15	59	.225	.284	.454	720	162	31	1	44	109	49	123
Facing Finesse Pitchers and Power Pitchers																						
Finesse	.243	.283	.381	268	65	7	0	10	41	11	45	.243	.302	.467	790	192	28	1	49	138	54	115
Power	.190	.234	.275	189	36	4	0	4	22	11	47	.213	.282	.383	569	121	26	1	23	75	46	118
On Grass and on Turf																						
Grass	.214	.250	.304	388	83	8	0	9	42	17	74	.221	.285	.421	1149	254	43	2	61	176	87	202
Turf	.261	.329	.522	69	18	3	0	5	21	5	18	.281	.339	.490	210	59	11	0	11	37	13	31
During the Day and at Night																						
Day	.230	.290	.393	122	28	2	0	6	26	9	25	.221	.308	.424	344	76	13	0	19	60	38	52
Night	.218	.252	.316	335	73	9	0	8	37	13	67	.233	.288	.434	1015	237	41	2	53	153	62	181
By Month																						
April	.194	.241	.333	72	14	4	0	2	6	3	18	.233	.301	.443	176	41	10	0	9	26	14	32
May	.232	.325	.303	99	23	1	0	2	16	12	23	.229	.304	.410	249	57	7	1	12	44	24	47
June	.247	.296	.371	97	24	3	0	3	23	6	23	.212	.282	.377	212	45	5	0	10	34	15	43
July	.082	.100	.082	49	4	0	0	0	0	1	8	.198	.274	.459	207	41	7	1	15	30	17	35
August	.250	.250	.440	84	21	1	0	5	11	0	14	.247	.285	.470	304	75	14	0	18	46	14	50
Sept/Oct	.268	.268	.411	56	15	2	0	2	7	0	6	.256	.318	.422	211	54	11	0	8	33	16	26
Situational																						
Bases Empty	.198	.233	.312	247	49	7	0	7	7	8	52	.217	.273	.425	757	164	27	1	43	43	42	139
Leadoff	.184	.245	.367	98	18	3	0	5	5	6	18	.206	.270	.426	296	61	9	1	18	18	17	57
Not Leadoff	.208	.224	.275	149	31	4	0	2	2	2	34	.223	.275	.425	461	103	18	0	25	25	25	82
Runners On	.248	.296	.367	210	52	4	0	7	56	14	40	.248	.317	.440	602	149	27	1	29	170	58	94
First Base Only	.256	.295	.344	90	23	2	0	2	4	4	17	.234	.287	.421	273	64	9	0	14	32	16	39
Scoring Position	.242	.297	.383	120	29	2	0	5	52	10	23	.258	.340	.456	329	85	18	1	15	138	42	55
Late Innings, Close	.230	.274	.356	87	20	2	0	3	19	5	22	.265	.324	.469	226	60	9	2	11	41	16	42

RBI/Opportunities					
Scoring Position	41 / 166	(25%)	106 / 465	(23%)
Scoring Position, 2 Out	14 / 73	(19%)	39 / 198	(20%)
On Third, Less than 2 Out	19 / 37	(51%)	42 / 104	(40%)
RBI in close games / RBI Total	42 / 63	(67%)	150 / 213	(70%)

Scott Fletcher
Texas Rangers

All teams have their "problem" positions. The Rangers have had several revolving door positions, notably at shortstop, second base, (lately) catcher, and (until lately) manager. The 1986 season will be remembered as the year Curtis (Leave 'Em on First) Wilkerson played his way out of the shortstop post and Scott Fletcher played his way in.

Toby Harrah may have been the best all-around shortstop in Ranger history, but this team has never had a better defensive shortstop than "Scooter" Fletcher. Good range, good hands, a strong, accurate arm, and his play is so steady you tend to forget how good his glove is until he is out of the lineup for a day or two.

Fletcher hit .394 in July to be named AL Player of the Month. He also hit .429 in July of 1983. Over the last four seasons he has a .321 average for the month of July compared to .254 for the other months. A scrappy hitter, Fletcher practically willed himself to hit .300 at the end of the season. On October 2nd, with his average down to .294, he tied a club record with five hits to get back to the .300 mark. And maybe that .300 average isn't such a fluke after all. Fletcher hit over .300 the second half of 1985 while still with the White Sox. That means he has maintained a .300 average for over 650 at bats now.

Fletcher was never meant to be a back-up. He hits lefties and righties about the same. In the last four years he has identical .266 average against both. He has also been a consistently tough out with men in scoring position— batting averages of .297, .360, .306 and .283 over the last four years. In the same span his situational numbers have gone:

	AB	H	AVE
Bases Empty	969	246	.254
Men on Base	580	166	.286
Men in Scoring Position	328	102	.311

Over the last three years Fletcher has driven in 27% of the runners who were in scoring position for him, an excellent figure.

—Craig Wright and Wes Osborn

	1986 SEASON											THREE YEARS (84 – 86)										
	Ave.	OBP	SLG	AB	H	2B	3B	HR	RBI	BB	SO	Ave.	OBP	SLG	AB	H	2B	3B	HR	RBI	BB	SO
Totals	.300	.360	.400	530	159	34	5	3	50	47	59	.272	.342	.347	1287	350	55	9	8	116	128	152
Batting vs. Left and Right-handed Pitchers																						
Left	.291	.347	.423	175	51	13	2	2	19	15	17	.274	.352	.358	508	139	22	3	5	41	62	54
Right	.304	.365	.389	355	108	21	3	1	31	32	42	.271	.335	.340	779	211	33	6	3	75	66	98
At Home and on the Road																						
Home	.308	.360	.415	253	78	15	3	2	25	19	27	.280	.353	.357	622	174	24	6	4	66	65	67
Road	.292	.359	.386	277	81	19	2	1	25	28	32	.265	.332	.338	665	176	31	3	4	50	63	85
Facing Groundball Pitchers and Flyball Pitchers																						
Groundball	.300	.364	.371	237	71	13	2	0	15	20	30	.262	.327	.317	561	147	22	3	1	40	45	69
Flyball	.300	.356	.423	293	88	21	3	3	35	27	29	.280	.353	.371	726	203	33	6	7	76	83	83
Facing Finesse Pitchers and Power Pitchers																						
Finesse	.313	.357	.410	339	106	22	4	1	32	23	33	.279	.335	.351	757	211	31	6	4	63	57	75
Power	.277	.364	.382	191	53	12	1	2	18	24	26	.262	.352	.342	530	139	24	3	4	53	71	77
On Grass and on Turf																						
Grass	.312	.365	.411	443	138	27	4	3	40	37	48	.273	.338	.347	1064	290	45	8	6	100	99	130
Turf	.241	.333	.345	87	21	7	1	0	10	10	11	.269	.361	.350	223	60	10	1	2	16	29	22
During the Day and at Night																						
Day	.294	.339	.471	102	30	8	2	2	10	6	13	.270	.345	.351	319	86	16	2	2	23	32	43
Night	.301	.364	.383	428	129	26	3	1	40	41	46	.273	.341	.346	968	264	39	7	6	93	96	109
By Month																						
April	.275	.362	.353	51	14	2	1	0	3	6	6	.260	.360	.325	154	40	3	2	1	16	22	24
May	.308	.379	.410	78	24	4	2	0	7	8	10	.239	.327	.301	226	54	8	3	0	22	28	28
June	.286	.340	.385	91	26	5	2	0	7	8	12	.286	.357	.352	196	56	7	3	0	16	19	24
July	.394	.430	.577	104	41	13	0	2	12	7	3	.306	.346	.412	245	75	17	0	3	20	14	18
August	.280	.336	.327	107	30	5	0	0	16	9	13	.268	.321	.335	224	60	6	0	3	23	18	29
Sept/Oct	.242	.312	.323	99	24	5	0	1	5	9	15	.269	.347	.347	242	65	14	1	1	19	27	29
Situational																						
Bases Empty	.296	.357	.397	335	99	20	4	2	2	31	38	.261	.329	.343	817	213	35	7	6	6	77	92
Leadoff	.310	.360	.397	116	36	7	0	1	1	9	13	.249	.324	.341	305	76	14	1	4	4	30	31
Not Leadoff	.288	.355	.397	219	63	13	4	1	1	22	25	.268	.332	.344	512	137	21	6	2	2	47	61
Runners On	.308	.364	.405	195	60	14	1	1	48	16	21	.291	.364	.355	470	137	20	2	2	110	51	60
First Base Only	.341	.393	.476	82	28	6	1	1	5	6	8	.261	.320	.324	207	54	8	1	1	5	16	24
Scoring Position	.283	.344	.354	113	32	8	0	0	43	10	13	.316	.396	.380	263	83	12	1	1	105	35	36
Late Innings, Close	.212	.264	.263	80	17	4	0	0	10	5	15	.240	.287	.269	175	42	5	0	1	19	11	31

RBI/Opportunities						
Scoring Position	41 / 148	(28%)		101 / 375	(27%)	
Scoring Position, 2 Out	12 / 58	(21%)		34 / 154	(22%)	
On Third, Less than 2 Out	20 / 31	(65%)		43 / 78	(55%)	
RBI in close games / RBI Total	35 / 50	(70%)		84 / 116	(72%)	

Bob Forsch
St. Louis Cardinals

Every time you think Bob Forsch's about had it, he turns in a performance like 1986. If he'd pitched game five of the '85 World Series like he did last season, Cardinal fans might not even know who Don Denkinger was. Bob ended the season fifth on the all-time Cardinal list in wins (143), games pitched (392) and strikeouts (950). Forsch's 230 innings in '86 were his most since '81. In 24 of his 33 starts Forsch went six or more innings and surrendered three earned runs or less—he had 24 "quality starts," if you insist. In nineteen of those games he gave up two or fewer earned runs. And at 4.30 runs per start, he was the best supported of all Cardinal starting pitchers. So why were the Cardinals only 16–17 in the games Forsch started? Because the 4.30 runs per start figure is misleading. In seven of Forsch's starts the Cardinals scored eight or more runs, with St. Louis winning all seven. These seven games were responsible for the high support number. But in seventeen of Forsch's remaining starts, the Cardinals scored three runs or less. They won only three of these.

Some other Forsch facts in '86: Also received the best defensive support of Cardinal starting pitcher. There were only 16 errors committed in his 33 starts . . . . The Cardinals turned five consecutive double plays behind Forsch on July 12 . . . . Hit Cardinals' only grand slam of the season on August 10, his ninth career homer . . . . Was 4–0 vs. Phillies despite 4.11 ERA . . . Had 2.91 ERA in 21 starts on four days' rest, 4.11 ERA in five starts on five days' rest, and an ERA of 3.69 when pitching off-rotation, which he did seven times . . . . Worst inning was the first, where he surrendered seventeen runs. Allowed twelve runs in both the second and third innings . . . . Is generally, as in '86, most successful at Busch Stadium, where it's hard to hit home runs. Record since 1981 is 31–17 at Busch and 19–25 on the road . . . . Has now been in double figures in wins nine times . . . . Forsch was seeking a multi-year contract at the end of 1986 worth well over a million bucks. It's hard to believe that just ten years ago he and John Denny were both threatening to hold out for $100,000 a year . . . . Is due for his third no-hitter any season now. Perhaps he's waiting for brother Ken to throw number two first.

—Russ Eagle

1986: Finesse, Flyball · **1985: Finesse, Flyball** · **1984: Finesse, Groundball**

| | 1986 SEASON | | | | | | | | | | | THREE YEARS (84 – 86) | | | | | | | | | | |
	G	IP	H	BB	SO	SB	CS	W	L	S	ERA	G	IP	H	BB	SO	SB	CS	W	L	S	ERA
Totals	33	230.0	211	68	104	13	7	14	10	0	3.25	83	418.1	407	134	173	25	12	25	21	2	3.81
At Home and on the Road																						
Home	17	125.0	107	28	49	7	6	8	4	0	2.66	42	219.1	205	57	77	11	8	14	10	0	3.36
Road	16	105.0	104	40	55	6	1	6	6	0	3.94	41	199.0	202	77	96	14	4	11	11	2	4.30
During the Day and at Night																						
Day	10	68.0	53	24	32	3	1	5	1	0	3.97	33	145.1	147	57	58	11	4	8	8	2	4.64
Night	23	162.0	158	44	72	10	6	9	9	0	2.94	50	273.0	260	77	115	14	8	17	13	0	3.36
On Grass and on Turf																						
Grass	9	58.0	61	25	34	3	1	2	5	0	3.57	22	110.1	106	44	53	8	2	6	7	2	3.75
Turf	24	172.0	150	43	70	10	6	12	5	0	3.14	61	308.0	301	90	120	17	10	19	14	0	3.83
By Month																						
April	4	27.2	25	9	19	3	1	1	1	0	2.60	13	78.1	75	22	34	4	2	3	4	0	3.45
May	6	39.2	36	19	18	4	0	3	2	0	2.95	15	71.1	78	31	26	5	1	6	5	0	4.29
June	5	40.1	27	14	22	2	1	2	1	0	1.79	10	56.0	41	26	30	5	2	2	3	1	2.89
July	6	38.1	45	7	10	1	0	4	2	0	2.82	11	44.1	55	10	14	2	0	4	2	1	2.84
August	6	47.1	38	9	20	1	4	3	2	0	3.23	15	75.2	62	15	29	3	5	5	3	0	3.57
Sept/Oct	6	36.2	40	10	15	2	1	1	2	0	6.14	19	92.2	96	30	40	6	2	5	4	0	4.95

vs. Opponent Batters

| | 1986 SEASON | | | | | | | | | | | THREE YEARS (84 – 86) | | | | | | | | | |
	Ave.	OBP	SLG	AB	H	2B	3B	HR	RBI	BB	SO	Ave.	OBP	SLG	AB	H	2B	3B	HR	RBI	BB	SO
Totals	.247	.301	.374	855	211	38	7	19	75	68	104	.258	.315	.388	1578	407	70	14	36	154	134	173
Pitching vs. Left and Right-handed Batters																						
Left	.265	.333	.399	419	111	22	2	10	31	44	49	.261	.329	.376	728	190	34	7	12	59	76	71
Right	.229	.269	.351	436	100	16	5	9	44	24	55	.255	.303	.399	850	217	36	7	24	95	58	102
Situational																						
Bases Empty	.242	.280	.398	561	136	29	5	16	16	29	71	.252	.296	.402	1009	254	48	10	28	28	63	115
Leadoff	.242	.271	.429	231	56	10	3	9	9	9	24	.240	.276	.413	421	101	19	6	14	14	20	44
Not Leadoff	.242	.286	.376	330	80	19	2	7	7	20	47	.260	.311	.395	588	153	29	4	14	14	43	71
Runners On	.255	.337	.330	294	75	9	2	3	59	39	33	.269	.347	.364	569	153	22	4	8	126	71	58
First Base Only	.221	.279	.235	136	30	2	0	0	1	11	14	.229	.302	.291	258	59	6	2	2	11	26	27
Scoring Position	.285	.381	.411	158	45	7	2	3	58	28	19	.302	.381	.424	311	94	16	2	6	115	45	31
Late Innings, Close	.240	.326	.440	75	18	3	0	4	7	10	4	.274	.348	.453	117	32	3	0	6	11	13	8

RBI/Opportunities

	1986 SEASON		THREE YEARS (84 – 86)	
Scoring Position	51 / 231	(22%)	103 / 434	(24%)
Scoring Position, 2 Out	15 / 96	(16%)	31 / 179	(17%)
On Third, Less than 2 Out	23 / 50	(46%)	40 / 87	(46%)
RBI in close games / RBI Total	60 / 75	(80%)	109 / 154	(71%)

John Franco
Cincinnati Reds

In 1986, Franco reversed several of his previous patterns. He was more effective on grass, at home and during the day. John's three-year stats give some evidence that his heavy workload is affecting him late in the year. His 1984–86 totals for September/October show a 4.28 ERA; in 1986, he suffered through a poor August (4.38 ERA) and a miserable September/October (5.09 ERA). His 74 appearances were his career high. Manager Pete Rose should seriously consider cutting Franco's games down somewhat, else he risk damaging such a valuable property.

It may simply be coincidence, but Franco's predecessor as the Reds' closer, Ted Power, burned out after his third season in relief. After his three seasons in the pen (1983–85), Power had appeared in 191 games, throwing 299.2 innings and recording 40 saves—all of these numbers being close to Franco's totals after his first three years. By the end of 1986, Ted had been converted to a starter in an attempt to save his career. Of course, Power and Franco are not the same type of pitcher, and their differences are substantial.

Nevertheless, if you were the Cincinnati manager, would you be taking chances with Franco's future? John is only 26 years old and he kills left-handed batters while still being effective against righties. Good left-handed short relievers are tough enough to find in baseball.

—Gary Gillette

There seems to be an lot of young relief pitchers around the majors lately. In my mind they're all jumbled together—I can't think about one without associating him with the others. Among these pitchers are John Franco, Don Carman, Todd Worrell, and Scott Garrelts.

There is one other pitcher whom I associate with this group who has not yet established himself: Randy Myers. Within this group is a subgroup that consists of Franco, Carman and Myers. They're all lefties, they're all young, and they're all good. Sometimes I think that they are all the same pitcher; at least, Carman's and Franco's stats in 1985 were similar enough to belong to the same pitcher. Franco was 12–3 with a 2.18 ERA and 61 strikeouts in 99 innings-pitched; Carmen was 9–4 with a 2.08 ERA and 87 strikeouts in 86.1 innings-pitched. I expect Myers statistics will be quite similar to those of Franco and Carman in 1985 once he makes it full-time with the Mets. Garrelts and Carman have tried their luck as starters and have done well, but they are both first-rate relievers.

—Bill Weydig

1986: Power, Groundball												1985: Power, Groundball												1984: Power, Groundball			
1986 SEASON												**THREE YEARS (84 – 86)**											
	G	IP	H	BB	SO	SB	CS	W	L	S	ERA		G	IP	H	BB	SO	SB	CS	W	L	S	ERA
Totals	74	101.0	90	44	84	4	5	6	6	29	2.94		195	279.1	247	120	200	15	19	24	11	45	2.58
At Home and on the Road																							
Home	40	53.2	51	20	37	2	2	2	2	16	3.02		105	159.1	131	58	102	10	9	13	4	24	2.15
Road	34	47.1	39	24	47	2	3	4	4	13	2.85		90	120.0	116	62	98	5	10	11	7	21	3.15
During the Day and at Night																							
Day	21	25.2	18	6	20	2	2	0	0	8	2.45		60	76.1	71	30	49	3	7	6	4	15	3.42
Night	53	75.1	72	38	64	2	3	6	6	21	3.11		135	203.0	176	90	151	12	12	18	7	30	2.26
On Grass and on Turf																							
Grass	22	30.0	23	14	30	1	2	2	3	9	2.70		54	67.1	63	30	57	3	6	7	5	13	3.48
Turf	52	71.0	67	30	54	3	3	4	3	20	3.04		141	212.0	184	90	143	12	13	17	6	32	2.29
By Month																							
April	9	13.0	12	6	10	1	1	0	0	2	3.46		16	22.2	21	15	15	1	1	0	1	3	2.78
May	12	22.0	15	11	22	0	1	0	1	6	1.64		32	49.1	47	29	43	3	3	4	1	8	3.10
June	16	20.1	16	8	10	0	2	1	3	4	2.66		38	53.1	45	19	31	1	3	4	3	7	2.36
July	10	15.2	12	7	16	1	0	2	0	4	1.15		32	49.1	33	17	37	2	5	7	0	5	1.46
August	12	12.1	12	5	8	1	1	2	0	6	4.38		36	56.1	48	20	35	5	5	5	0	10	1.76
Sept/Oct	15	17.2	23	7	18	1	1	1	2	7	5.09		41	48.1	53	20	39	3	5	4	6	12	4.28

vs. Opponent Batters																					
1986 SEASON												**THREE YEARS (84 – 86)**								
	Ave.	OBP	SLG	AB	H	2B	3B	HR	RBI	BB	SO		Ave.	OBP	SLG	AB	H	2B	3B	HR	RBI	BB	SO
Totals	.243	.324	.332	371	90	10	1	7	50	44	84		.244	.324	.327	1014	247	30	5	15	118	120	200
Pitching vs. Left and Right-handed Batters																					
Left	.211	.250	.250	76	16	1	1	0	11	3	13		.207	.264	.253	237	49	3	1	2	28	17	42
Right	.251	.341	.353	295	74	9	0	7	39	41	71		.255	.342	.350	777	198	27	4	13	90	103	158
Situational																					
Bases Empty	.247	.315	.313	182	45	3	0	3	3	16	36		.242	.317	.325	541	131	16	4	7	7	57	102
Leadoff	.208	.256	.247	77	16	0	0	1	1	4	14		.245	.310	.335	233	57	5	2	4	4	21	28
Not Leadoff	.276	.356	.362	105	29	3	0	2	2	12	22		.240	.322	.318	308	74	11	2	3	3	36	74
Runners On	.238	.332	.349	189	45	7	1	4	47	28	48		.245	.333	.330	473	116	14	1	8	111	63	98
First Base Only	.250	.296	.382	76	19	1	0	3	7	5	17		.258	.296	.355	186	48	3	0	5	12	10	34
Scoring Position	.230	.353	.327	113	26	6	1	1	40	23	31		.237	.353	.314	287	68	11	1	3	99	53	64
Late Innings, Close	.243	.335	.339	280	68	7	1	6	40	38	63		.237	.314	.323	691	164	18	4	11	81	76	146

RBI/Opportunities						
Scoring Position		36 / 180	(20%)		90 / 443	(20%)
Scoring Position, 2 Out		18 / 93	(19%)		39 / 219	(18%)
On Third, Less than 2 Out		14 / 27	(52%)		37 / 81	(46%)
RBI in close games / RBI Total		40 / 50	(80%)		86 / 118	(73%)

Julio Franco
Cleveland Indians

Having natural ability is a great thing, but it can sometimes keep you from learning how to play. Julio Franco is one of the best hitting shortstops in baseball, runs well, covers a lot of ground in the field and has a gun for an arm; he's also a wild streak hitter with a poor batting eye, a mediocre baserunner and an erratic fielder. Julio is a good player who could be a lot better. It's taken him a lot of time to see where and how he has to improve, but he's beginning to make progress fast.

Despite his batting average, Julio isn't much of a hitter yet. The only goal he has is hitting .300; he doesn't worry much about power or drawing walks as long as he does that. Like most latin players, he's a free swinger. When he's hot, he's impossible to get out; when he's not, he hits as empty a .240 as you can imagine. If you remember where he hits (second or third), the number of outs he makes (he gets about 700 at-bats a year and led the AL in grounding into double plays this year) and the players around him, his Runs and RBI totals aren't that impressive. Unless he's on one of his tears or until he broadens his skills, he shouldn't bat higher than sixth; you could almost say that his bat is overrated.

But that's only fair—Julio is nowhere near as bad a fielder as he's made out to be. For some reason, nobody in Cleveland remembers the cliche "he has errors that nobody else can reach" anymore; the way fans talk about him, you'd think they wanted Tom Veryzer back. Of course, if Julio concentrated as hard on the easy plays (he'll nonchalant them and boot the ball) as he does on the stories people write about his errors, he wouldn't have these problems.

The amazing thing about Julio is how effortlessly he seems to improve. He lost his arbitration case this year because he supposedly didn't hit well enough to make up for the errors, vowed that he wasn't going to lose in 1987 and set career highs in homers, batting average and fielding percentage. He spent most of April and May working on his fielding; when he had that under control, he decided to start hitting. It's easy to envision him hitting .320 with 15 homers; if he keeps working on his fielding and ever decides that he wants to walk 65 times and stop stealing 59% of his bases, it's going to be awfully hard to decide who the best shortstop in baseball is.

—Geoff Beckman

	1986 SEASON											THREE YEARS (84 – 86)										
---	Ave.	OBP	SLG	AB	H	2B	3B	HR	RBI	BB	SO	Ave.	OBP	SLG	AB	H	2B	3B	HR	RBI	BB	SO
Totals	.306	.338	.422	599	183	30	5	10	74	32	66	.293	.337	.382	1893	554	84	14	19	243	129	207
Batting vs. Left and Right-handed Pitchers																						
Left	.341	.370	.537	164	56	12	1	6	22	8	10	.318	.363	.460	548	174	33	3	13	75	41	56
Right	.292	.326	.379	435	127	18	4	4	52	24	56	.283	.327	.350	1345	380	51	11	6	168	88	151
At Home and on the Road																						
Home	.291	.318	.401	302	88	15	3	4	37	13	29	.300	.344	.384	927	278	42	6	8	126	63	85
Road	.320	.358	.444	297	95	15	2	6	37	19	37	.286	.331	.380	966	276	42	8	11	117	66	122
Facing Groundball Pitchers and Flyball Pitchers																						
Groundball	.317	.353	.421	278	88	15	1	4	34	18	32	.295	.339	.373	918	271	35	6	8	102	59	104
Flyball	.296	.324	.424	321	95	15	4	6	40	14	34	.290	.336	.391	975	283	49	8	11	141	70	103
Facing Finesse Pitchers and Power Pitchers																						
Finesse	.313	.337	.445	355	111	18	4	7	42	15	29	.308	.344	.395	1087	335	49	6	11	128	58	101
Power	.295	.340	.389	244	72	12	1	3	32	17	37	.272	.328	.365	806	219	35	8	8	115	71	106
On Grass and on Turf																						
Grass	.309	.341	.434	525	162	29	5	9	66	27	53	.299	.345	.395	1614	482	76	13	18	214	116	168
Turf	.284	.321	.338	74	21	1	0	1	8	5	13	.258	.289	.305	279	72	8	1	1	29	13	39
During the Day and at Night																						
Day	.306	.336	.422	206	63	6	0	6	24	10	31	.300	.352	.394	637	191	27	3	9	86	50	88
Night	.305	.339	.422	393	120	24	5	4	50	22	35	.289	.330	.376	1256	363	57	11	10	157	79	119
By Month																						
April	.234	.298	.390	77	18	6	0	2	10	7	11	.299	.379	.425	214	64	16	1	3	38	27	27
May	.263	.292	.351	114	30	2	1	2	9	5	18	.238	.274	.311	328	78	9	3	3	28	18	50
June	.308	.354	.385	91	28	5	1	0	8	7	12	.284	.339	.344	299	85	13	1	1	29	22	35
July	.317	.349	.386	101	32	5	1	0	11	5	9	.308	.343	.372	328	101	13	1	2	41	19	22
August	.313	.331	.496	115	36	9	0	4	20	3	13	.320	.350	.429	378	121	18	1	7	55	17	40
Sept/Oct	.386	.404	.515	101	39	3	2	2	16	5	3	.303	.348	.413	346	105	15	7	3	52	26	33
Situational																						
Bases Empty	.312	.344	.436	321	100	18	2	6	6	16	41	.287	.334	.375	1037	298	50	7	9	9	66	125
Leadoff	.374	.389	.472	123	46	7	1	1	1	3	12	.301	.342	.375	336	101	15	2	2	2	18	40
Not Leadoff	.273	.318	.414	198	54	11	1	5	5	13	29	.281	.331	.375	701	197	35	5	7	7	48	85
Runners On	.299	.331	.406	278	83	12	3	4	68	16	25	.299	.341	.390	856	256	34	7	10	234	63	82
First Base Only	.295	.317	.393	122	36	3	0	3	9	4	10	.284	.318	.370	335	95	11	0	6	19	16	29
Scoring Position	.301	.341	.417	156	47	9	3	1	59	12	15	.309	.354	.403	521	161	23	7	4	215	47	53
Late Innings, Close	.274	.329	.384	73	20	3	1	1	10	6	12	.242	.290	.330	273	66	7	4	3	41	19	23
RBI/Opportunities																						
Scoring Position	53 / 195	(27%)										199 / 699	(28%)									
Scoring Position, 2 Out	15 / 87	(17%)										65 / 290	(22%)									
On Third, Less than 2 Out	26 / 44	(59%)										98 / 163	(60%)									
RBI in close games / RBI Total	44 / 74	(59%)										156 / 243	(64%)									

Gary Gaetti
Minnesota Twins

Winner of the 1986 Gold Glove at third base, the funny thing is that Gaetti has been slow to convince the Twins of his defensive abilities. Until this season, there was usually talk of moving him to left field. As strange as it may seem, there were at least three reasons why the organization wanted to relocate a player with his talents.

1. The hole opened in left field after the Gary Ward trade in 1983 provided an available location for Gaetti's power. Ward had 47 HR's and 179 RBI in '82 and '83, while his replacement, Mickey Hatcher, totaled 8 HR's and 118 RBI in two years for much better Twins teams. Putting Gaetti in left would have helped close an obvious gap. Oddly, Gaetti's home run and RBI totals in '84 were about the same as Hatcher's.

2. The anticipated return of John Castino to third base following the elevation of Tim Teufel to second, in 1984, would have forced Gaetti into left or even to short. Neither Castino nor Teufel remained with the Twins, and the episode now serves to point out the interrelationships that can make the correct solution difficult for some teams to see.

3. This leaves the third reason—errors. Errors at third base occur frequently enough for most fans to remember and are among the most annoying in the sport. The high and wide throw to first that sails down the line or the misplayed between the legs double are some of the baseball's most obvious miscues. Gaetti is no exception, and the Twins front office has a memory. Over the last two years he has been credited with 39 errors, although I have only identified 38. These errors are evenly split between throwing (21) and fielding (17) with the majority of the throwing errors occurring on throws to first. Including his 20 errors in 1984, 40 of Gaetti's 58 errors have been committed with right handers at the plate, and most of them in the middle of the game. A breakdown of innings shows a curious pattern.

Inning	1	2	3	4	5	6	7	8	9	10
Errors	4	8	2	5	8	9	12	9	0	1

Innings 5 through 8 produced almost 2/3 of the errors. These are the innings when the starters tire and the Twins turn to a troubled bullpen, although the numbers are too small to indicate a definite pattern. Over the last three years his monthly error totals are April-11, May-8, June-14, Aug.-8, Sept./Oct.-10 with 66% of them occuring in losses.

—Bill Jensen

	1986 SEASON											THREE YEARS (84 – 86)										
	Ave.	OBP	SLG	AB	H	2B	3B	HR	RBI	BB	SO	Ave.	OBP	SLG	AB	H	2B	3B	HR	RBI	BB	SO
Totals	.287	.347	.518	596	171	34	1	34	108	52	108	.265	.321	.426	1745	463	94	5	59	237	133	278
Batting vs. Left and Right-handed Pitchers																						
Left	.344	.409	.603	151	52	6	0	11	32	18	22	.259	.322	.420	505	131	22	1	19	61	46	76
Right	.267	.325	.490	445	119	28	1	23	76	34	86	.268	.321	.429	1240	332	72	4	40	176	87	202
At Home and on the Road																						
Home	.250	.311	.473	296	74	16	1	16	57	25	56	.264	.317	.429	870	230	51	4	28	124	63	151
Road	.323	.383	.563	300	97	18	0	18	51	27	52	.266	.326	.424	875	233	43	1	31	113	70	127
Facing Groundball Pitchers and Flyball Pitchers																						
Groundball	.250	.320	.431	260	65	9	1	12	48	27	45	.254	.311	.379	842	214	37	1	22	108	66	128
Flyball	.315	.369	.586	336	106	25	0	22	60	25	63	.276	.331	.471	903	249	57	4	37	129	67	150
Facing Finesse Pitchers and Power Pitchers																						
Finesse	.304	.362	.585	335	102	20	1	24	67	29	54	.283	.337	.458	956	271	58	2	35	136	73	131
Power	.264	.328	.433	261	69	14	0	10	41	29	54	.243	.302	.388	789	192	36	3	24	101	60	147
On Grass and on Turf																						
Grass	.364	.421	.645	228	83	16	0	16	39	22	40	.287	.347	.460	672	193	35	0	27	92	56	92
Turf	.239	.300	.440	368	88	18	1	18	69	30	68	.252	.305	.405	1073	270	59	5	32	145	77	186
During the Day and at Night																						
Day	.264	.338	.414	174	46	8	0	6	26	17	32	.262	.329	.370	522	137	29	0	9	57	46	84
Night	.296	.351	.562	422	125	26	1	28	82	35	76	.267	.318	.451	1223	326	65	5	50	180	87	194
By Month																						
April	.282	.317	.449	78	22	4	0	3	7	4	11	.292	.358	.446	240	70	19	0	6	33	25	37
May	.293	.377	.626	99	29	6	0	9	19	13	15	.271	.353	.493	284	77	14	2	15	49	33	51
June	.230	.304	.460	100	23	8	0	5	19	11	22	.220	.279	.374	273	60	19	1	7	32	22	48
July	.257	.312	.446	101	26	5	1	4	15	8	19	.269	.302	.410	305	82	15	2	8	40	13	46
August	.321	.376	.545	112	36	7	0	6	27	10	20	.268	.324	.413	310	83	15	0	10	45	23	49
Sept/Oct	.330	.383	.566	106	35	4	0	7	21	6	21	.273	.315	.426	333	91	12	0	13	38	17	47
Situational																						
Bases Empty	.289	.343	.520	329	95	20	1	18	18	24	58	.266	.322	.422	995	265	57	4	30	30	73	151
Leadoff	.279	.316	.512	129	36	6	0	8	8	6	19	.249	.296	.410	393	98	21	3	12	12	22	55
Not Leadoff	.295	.359	.525	200	59	14	1	10	10	18	39	.277	.339	.430	602	167	36	1	18	18	51	96
Runners On	.285	.352	.517	267	76	14	0	16	90	28	50	.264	.320	.432	750	198	37	1	29	207	60	127
First Base Only	.306	.364	.550	111	34	6	0	7	17	9	20	.269	.314	.437	323	87	13	1	13	32	19	52
Scoring Position	.269	.344	.494	156	42	8	0	9	73	19	30	.260	.325	.429	427	111	24	0	16	175	41	75
Late Innings, Close	.253	.343	.448	87	22	5	0	4	10	12	19	.238	.325	.367	256	61	15	0	6	25	32	37
RBI/Opportunities																						
Scoring Position				56 / 212	(26%)										140 / 577	(24%)						
Scoring Position, 2 Out				20 / 88	(23%)										51 / 260	(20%)						
On Third, Less than 2 Out				23 / 42	(55%)										53 / 101	(52%)						
RBI in close games / RBI Total				69 / 108	(64%)										146 / 237	(62%)						

Greg Gagne
Minnesota Twins

The battle for the Twins shortstop position has had all of the excitement of watching Super-Turf fade. Oh, there were your personality clashes—Lenny Faedo vs. Billy Gardner. There was the excitement of the smallest player in the majors, named after a large Texas town, Houston Jimenez, hitting doubles to the glass in left center. And who would want to forget the satisfaction of seeing a regular guy like Ron Washington stay on a major league roster. But, generally, barring an infrequent appearance by Roy Smalley, Twins fans have tended to look past the difficulties at short and other unproductive positions and have preferred instead to place the blame for the teams difficulties on more obvious targets such as Hrbek, Brunansky, or, until late last season, Ron Davis.

This was all very kind and splendid fun, but unfortunately, it does matter that left field has been the domain of a terrible offensive player, Mickey Hatcher. It does matter that the shortstop position has been the home of the "tough hop" misplay. And it certainly matters that the bench has held more deadwood than the bat rack. The front office has simply been unable to provide its good players with any help. So, why Greg Gagne? He represents the Twins attempt to find that often elusive creature called an "average major leaguer" to fill one of the gaps. In this case, "average" means a player who is supposed to help the club with his offense and not hurt it with his defense.

Defensively, Gagne has always been suspect. He spent three years in the Yankee organization without ever getting close to joining the legion of players who have had a chance next to Willie. And now his error totals don't show much improvement from his minor league days. Last season his range was better than Ernest Riles, but so was nearly everyone else's.

Has he countered his defensive problems with a hot bat? Not quite. At times, his offense was only sufficient to allow him to remain in the lineup, although he closed the season with a mini-flourish that gave hope to those who think he has the potential to produce a third baseman's offensive numbers. Last year was the first of the Project Scoresheet seasons in which Gagne was able to stay off the disabled list. Why Jay Bell was traded without ever playing a major league game for the Twins is a question the Twins front office hopes never needs to be answered.

—Bill Jensen

	1986 SEASON										THREE YEARS (84 – 86)									
	Ave.	OBP	SLG	AB	H	2B	3B	HR	RBI	BB	SO	Ave.	OBP	SLG	AB	H	2B	3B	HR	RBI	BB	SO
Totals	.250	.301	.398	472	118	22	6	12	54	30	108	.241	.293	.367	765	184	37	9	14	77	50	165
Batting vs. Left and Right-handed Pitchers																						
Left	.230	.277	.452	126	29	8	1	6	20	9	36	.237	.271	.403	253	60	15	3	7	29	13	60
Right	.257	.310	.379	346	89	14	5	6	34	21	72	.242	.303	.350	512	124	22	6	7	48	37	105
At Home and on the Road																						
Home	.239	.295	.441	238	57	10	4	10	31	17	52	.237	.296	.400	380	90	20	6	10	44	29	74
Road	.261	.308	.355	234	61	12	2	2	23	13	56	.244	.290	.335	385	94	17	3	4	33	21	91
Facing Groundball Pitchers and Flyball Pitchers																						
Groundball	.204	.280	.281	196	40	8	2	1	16	16	36	.206	.270	.287	349	72	11	4	3	30	25	64
Flyball	.283	.317	.482	276	78	14	4	11	38	14	72	.269	.312	.435	416	112	26	5	11	47	25	101
Facing Finesse Pitchers and Power Pitchers																						
Finesse	.251	.307	.461	267	67	18	4	10	36	16	51	.236	.288	.400	440	104	27	6	11	51	25	77
Power	.249	.294	.317	205	51	4	2	2	18	14	57	.246	.299	.323	325	80	10	3	3	26	25	88
On Grass and on Turf																						
Grass	.255	.302	.364	184	47	10	2	2	15	10	45	.243	.292	.354	288	70	14	3	4	22	17	69
Turf	.247	.301	.420	288	71	12	4	10	39	20	63	.239	.293	.375	477	114	23	6	10	55	33	96
During the Day and at Night																						
Day	.258	.304	.391	151	39	5	3	3	17	8	35	.231	.285	.329	234	54	8	3	3	21	14	50
Night	.246	.300	.402	321	79	17	3	9	37	22	73	.245	.296	.384	531	130	29	6	11	56	36	115
By Month																						
April	.224	.246	.328	67	15	2	1	1	5	2	18	.262	.314	.377	130	34	8	2	1	11	9	25
May	.302	.354	.477	86	26	5	2	2	8	8	18	.297	.351	.441	118	35	7	2	2	9	11	24
June	.205	.258	.229	83	17	2	0	0	7	5	19	.210	.260	.294	143	30	4	1	2	14	8	33
July	.229	.308	.371	70	16	5	1	1	8	5	13	.207	.267	.326	135	28	9	2	1	12	8	26
August	.256	.311	.463	82	21	6	1	3	17	6	21	.244	.298	.442	86	21	6	1	3	17	6	24
Sept/Oct	.274	.315	.500	84	23	2	1	5	9	4	19	.235	.279	.366	153	36	3	1	5	14	8	33
Situational																						
Bases Empty	.242	.295	.399	281	68	12	4	8	8	17	63	.232	.293	.375	440	102	21	6	10	10	31	96
Leadoff	.231	.291	.407	108	25	6	2	3	3	8	23	.217	.279	.366	175	38	10	2	4	4	14	32
Not Leadoff	.249	.297	.393	173	43	6	2	5	5	9	40	.242	.302	.381	265	64	11	4	6	6	17	64
Runners On	.262	.311	.398	191	50	10	2	4	46	13	45	.252	.293	.357	325	82	16	3	4	67	19	69
First Base Only	.256	.289	.326	86	22	3	0	1	4	2	18	.215	.252	.264	144	31	4	0	1	5	5	28
Scoring Position	.267	.328	.457	105	28	7	2	3	42	11	27	.282	.323	.431	181	51	12	3	3	62	14	41
Late Innings, Close	.242	.324	.306	62	15	4	0	0	7	6	17	.244	.349	.311	90	22	6	0	0	11	12	24
RBI/Opportunities																						
Scoring Position				34 / 143		(24%)									54 / 241		(22%)					
Scoring Position, 2 Out				15 / 73		(21%)									21 / 113		(19%)					
On Third, Less than 2 Out				11 / 25		(44%)									16 / 40		(40%)					
RBI in close games / RBI Total				27 / 54		(50%)									43 / 77		(56%)					

Jim Gantner
Milwaukee Brewers

Jim Gantner is, at 32, now the second-oldest second baseman in the majors, behind only Frank White. The fact that he is a hometown boy and a Paul Molitor-type player has helped him stay popular with his team and his fans despite mediocre performances for the last several years. His .274 batting average this year tells you the whole story—no power, run production or ability to get on base to go along with it. Given that, the fact that he had a humungous platoon differential in 1986 and Milwaukee's present spot in the standings, the Brewers should start looking for a good replacement.

When Gantner first became a regular, he overwhelmed everyone with his defense—people expected him to be good, but he was better than great. If he's hit well enough to call attention to himself, he might have picked up a few Gold Gloves by now. He's still a pretty good fielder, but the signs of age are beginning to show.

One thing that surprises me a bit about Gantner's stats is how well he does against pitchers with good heat. Looking at his overall stats, you'd figure that a good power pitcher would knock the bat out of his hands; given the amount of playing time he gets against them, you've got to think that Milwaukee believed that, too. But he hangs in there pretty well—he has some pop and, if they aren't throwing strikes, he won't swing. He's not Jesse Barfield, but it's something. I suppose this is because he has a compact swing and players like that have less trouble getting around on a 98-MPH pitch—Earl Weaver always likes to talk about how well Mark Belanger used to hit Nolan Ryan. I don't think this means he should play more—but if he does play, maybe he should play against the people he's been rested against.

Given his problems, there are two things that Gantner could do—demand a trade to a National League team so that he can get fat on all the power pitchers there or start shagging fly balls in his spare time. I'm utterly amazed at what a good utility player Davey Lopes has turned himself into and I think Gantner could probably get himself up to that level, too. I admire players who accept the fact that their skills are declining and make changes that let them be more useful to their teams; it would be nice if Jim could make that transition and stick around as a role player.

—Scott Segrin

	1986 SEASON											THREE YEARS (84 – 86)										
	Ave.	OBP	SLG	AB	H	2B	3B	HR	RBI	BB	SO	Ave.	OBP	SLG	AB	H	2B	3B	HR	RBI	BB	SO
Totals	.274	.313	.370	497	136	25	1	7	38	26	50	.271	.309	.347	1633	442	67	6	15	138	89	143
Batting vs. Left and Right-handed Pitchers																						
Left	.219	.268	.250	128	28	4	0	0	7	6	12	.276	.320	.310	496	137	15	1	0	39	28	42
Right	.293	.329	.412	369	108	21	1	7	31	20	38	.268	.305	.362	1137	305	52	5	15	99	61	101
At Home and on the Road																						
Home	.259	.301	.372	247	64	14	1	4	25	15	24	.264	.301	.341	804	212	32	3	8	77	46	68
Road	.288	.326	.368	250	72	11	0	3	13	11	26	.277	.317	.352	829	230	35	3	7	61	43	75
Facing Groundball Pitchers and Flyball Pitchers																						
Groundball	.267	.313	.347	225	60	12	0	2	22	13	16	.256	.297	.317	785	201	28	1	6	81	44	53
Flyball	.279	.314	.390	272	76	13	1	5	16	13	34	.284	.321	.374	848	241	39	5	9	57	45	90
Facing Finesse Pitchers and Power Pitchers																						
Finesse	.240	.278	.341	296	71	12	0	6	27	14	30	.272	.303	.351	950	258	35	2	12	87	42	74
Power	.323	.365	.413	201	65	13	1	1	11	12	20	.269	.319	.341	683	184	32	4	3	51	47	69
On Grass and on Turf																						
Grass	.270	.311	.366	423	114	21	1	6	34	25	42	.262	.301	.336	1365	357	53	5	13	119	79	118
Turf	.297	.329	.392	74	22	4	0	1	4	1	8	.317	.353	.399	268	85	14	1	2	19	10	25
During the Day and at Night																						
Day	.279	.308	.361	147	41	9	0	1	17	6	15	.268	.306	.339	478	128	20	1	4	48	27	41
Night	.271	.316	.374	350	95	16	1	6	21	20	35	.272	.311	.350	1155	314	47	5	11	90	62	102
By Month																						
April	.316	.371	.456	57	18	3	1	1	5	4	4	.263	.314	.347	190	50	7	3	1	19	13	17
May	.265	.347	.373	83	22	6	0	1	5	9	7	.275	.314	.363	262	72	12	1	3	21	13	21
June	.232	.263	.295	95	22	3	0	1	5	3	7	.279	.314	.353	312	87	11	0	4	34	16	22
July	.333	.375	.469	81	27	5	0	2	9	4	10	.281	.329	.342	295	83	12	0	2	22	20	23
August	.286	.310	.374	91	26	5	0	1	7	5	12	.285	.311	.381	270	77	17	0	3	19	12	25
Sept/Oct	.233	.239	.300	90	21	3	0	1	7	1	10	.240	.277	.299	304	73	8	2	2	23	15	35
Situational																						
Bases Empty	.303	.333	.421	304	92	16	1	6	6	11	26	.278	.314	.362	964	268	45	3	10	10	45	75
Leadoff	.299	.319	.423	137	41	8	0	3	3	3	8	.273	.307	.347	366	100	16	1	3	3	15	23
Not Leadoff	.305	.345	.419	167	51	8	1	3	3	8	18	.281	.317	.371	598	168	29	2	7	7	30	52
Runners On	.228	.284	.290	193	44	9	0	1	32	15	24	.260	.304	.324	669	174	22	3	5	128	44	68
First Base Only	.268	.286	.329	82	22	5	0	0	1	2	13	.286	.317	.370	311	89	13	2	3	13	11	25
Scoring Position	.198	.284	.261	111	22	4	0	1	31	13	11	.237	.293	.285	358	85	9	1	2	115	33	43
Late Innings, Close	.341	.388	.440	91	31	3	0	2	9	7	9	.286	.339	.348	287	82	7	1	3	20	24	29
RBI/Opportunities																						
Scoring Position				29 / 162		(18%)									111 / 493		(23%)					
Scoring Position, 2 Out				10 / 79		(13%)									34 / 230		(15%)					
On Third, Less than 2 Out				15 / 28		(54%)									57 / 97		(59%)					
RBI in close games / RBI Total				21 / 38		(55%)									89 / 138		(64%)					

Gene Garber
Atlanta Braves

As 1986 began, Gene Garber's role with the Braves was in doubt. Bruce Sutter was the right-handed relief ace, and Garber was to be a set-up man. However, Sutter's season was over by late April and Garber was unexpectedly made the closer, and he thrived, having his best season in several years. Along with fellow committee members Paul Assenmacher, Jeff Dedmon, and Ed Olwine, Garber headed the finest bullpen this side of .500 baseball. On the rare occasion that relief pitching was a factor, the Braves did well; their 9–5 record in extra innings was the best in the National League.

Garber's delivery is unique. He turns around as he kicks his leg, showing the batter the name on his back before spinning around and releasing. One would think that his control would suffer with such a motion, yet he has always had fine strikeout to walk ratios with the Braves. I suspect that his neutrality with respect to left- and right-handed batting might be attributed to his delivery, as left-handed hitters don't get the edge that they would with a normal motion.

The Braves will continue to rely on Garber for some time. The earliest estimates for the return of Sutter are mid-1987, if he can return at all. The only decent right-handed prospect the system produced lately was Duane Ward, and he went to Toronto for Jim Acker. Although Garber is getting on in years (he turned 39 during the off-season), the Braves will need him for at least another few years.

—John Stryker

Garber won back his job as the closer with a torrid May and June record, going 4–0 with 7 saves and an ERA of 0.82. He remained steady throughout the summer. In the fall, however, he was torched in his eight September and October appearances, allowing almost 2 hits per inning. One of the most remarkable aspects of Garber's season was his exceptionally low total of home runs allowed—only three while pitching in Atlanta's friendly confines.

With his 24 saves last year, Gene now has a career total of 194, which places him seventh on the all-time list. Garber, Hoyt Wilhelm and Tug McGraw are the only pitchers in the top ten in career saves to never have led the league in saves. Although he has been a good pitcher during most of his career, and although he has had some excellent seasons (check out 1976, 1977, 1978 and 1982), he seems to be relatively unknown to most fans today.

—Gary Gillette

1986: Finesse, Groundball **1985: Finesse, Groundball** **1984: Finesse, Groundball**

	1986 SEASON											THREE YEARS (84 – 86)										
	G	IP	H	BB	SO	SB	CS	W	L	S	ERA	G	IP	H	BB	SO	SB	CS	W	L	S	ERA
Totals	61	78.0	76	20	56	9	3	5	5	24	2.54	182	281.1	277	69	177	30	11	14	17	36	3.10
At Home and on the Road																						
Home	29	35.1	35	7	24	5	1	3	3	9	2.55	98	148.2	167	32	94	17	5	9	10	13	3.63
Road	32	42.2	41	13	32	4	2	2	2	15	2.53	84	132.2	110	37	83	13	6	5	7	23	2.51
During the Day and at Night																						
Day	19	28.0	27	6	27	1	1	1	1	7	2.25	59	98.0	104	18	67	9	2	2	5	13	3.49
Night	42	50.0	49	14	29	8	2	4	4	17	2.70	123	183.1	173	51	110	21	9	12	12	23	2.90
On Grass and on Turf																						
Grass	45	57.1	58	17	40	6	2	4	5	17	2.83	139	216.0	227	51	141	23	7	10	14	25	3.21
Turf	16	20.2	18	3	16	3	1	1	0	7	1.74	43	65.1	50	18	36	7	4	4	3	11	2.76
By Month																						
April	7	8.0	10	4	4	1	0	0	1	1	3.37	18	23.2	25	8	14	6	0	2	1	2	4.18
May	12	18.2	15	2	14	3	2	1	0	2	0.48	32	52.1	58	6	32	6	3	1	1	3	3.44
June	10	14.1	10	4	10	3	1	3	0	5	1.26	22	38.0	44	14	24	5	5	3	3	6	3.32
July	11	12.2	8	3	7	1	0	0	1	5	1.42	29	45.2	32	11	29	5	1	0	1	6	1.38
August	13	16.1	18	5	13	0	0	1	1	8	2.76	45	66.2	62	16	41	4	1	6	6	10	3.37
Sept/Oct	8	8.0	15	2	8	1	0	0	2	3	10.12	36	55.0	56	14	37	4	1	2	5	9	3.27

vs. Opponent Batters

	1986 SEASON											THREE YEARS (84 – 86)										
	Ave.	OBP	SLG	AB	H	2B	3B	HR	RBI	BB	SO	Ave.	OBP	SLG	AB	H	2B	3B	HR	RBI	BB	SO
Totals	.260	.309	.332	292	76	12	0	3	35	20	56	.258	.304	.353	1068	276	45	1	18	128	69	177
Pitching vs. Left and Right-handed Batters																						
Left	.254	.322	.312	138	35	8	0	0	15	14	26	.249	.299	.344	526	131	24	1	8	57	36	84
Right	.266	.296	.351	154	41	4	0	3	20	6	30	.268	.309	.362	542	145	21	0	10	71	33	93
Situational																						
Bases Empty	.267	.296	.370	146	39	6	0	3	3	5	27	.258	.286	.349	598	154	20	1	11	11	20	95
Leadoff	.259	.306	.345	58	15	2	0	1	1	4	12	.237	.258	.298	245	58	9	0	2	2	6	40
Not Leadoff	.273	.289	.386	88	24	4	0	2	2	1	15	.272	.305	.385	353	96	11	1	9	9	14	55
Runners On	.253	.321	.295	146	37	6	0	0	32	15	29	.260	.325	.357	470	122	25	0	7	117	49	82
First Base Only	.208	.255	.229	48	10	1	0	0	0	3	13	.243	.284	.353	173	42	10	0	3	11	10	30
Scoring Position	.276	.351	.327	98	27	5	0	0	32	12	16	.269	.347	.360	297	80	15	0	4	106	39	52
Late Innings, Close	.253	.309	.326	190	48	8	0	2	27	15	35	.261	.313	.355	501	131	18	1	9	67	38	70

RBI/Opportunities

	1986 SEASON		THREE YEARS (84 – 86)	
Scoring Position	31 / 131	(24%)	98 / 412	(24%)
Scoring Position, 2 Out	15 / 61	(25%)	43 / 204	(21%)
On Third, Less than 2 Out	10 / 25	(40%)	32 / 70	(46%)
RBI in close games / RBI Total	27 / 35	(77%)	69 / 128	(54%)

Damaso Garcia
Toronto Blue Jays

The 1986 season was one that I'm sure that Damaso Garcia would prefer to forget. Beset by injuries, Damo finished the campaign with a .280 batting average (very much in line with his career mark of .283), but tendinitis developed in his shoulder very early on and never left him. It weakened Garcia's throwing arm considerably and explained, to some extent, why Toronto turned fewer double plays than they had expected. When healthy, Damo plays defense with the best of them. He displays a lot of range, laterally and backwards. With his ability to go back on shallow popups to right, Jesse Barfield's job is definitely easier—and you never see him drop a popup.

Offensively, 1986 was frustrating. Demoted from the leadoff position in spring training, Garcia never adapted to playing at the very end of the order. The move was necessary—Garcia's .299 On-Base Average over the last three seasons make him a poor choice for the job—but Damaso felt comfortable there. When relieved of his role, he felt betrayed and became sullen and moody—the injuries only added to his distemper.

Garcia's future with the Blue Jays remains clouded. Toronto has capable replacements (Manny Lee and Mike Sharperson), so they wouldn't miss him, but working out a trade will be difficult. Garcia has two years left on his contract—when it expires, he has decided to retire from the game. Damaso is a very proud individual who reasons that, if he can't perform up to his standards (meaning 100% healthy), he'd prefer not playing at all.

Needless to say, this makes GM Pat Gillick's job tricky. He'd need to find a club that currently has a hole at second base, but has a prospect only a few years away—a team looking for only a temporary answer to a problem. There are very few clubs who fit that description and the talks have been brief. Gillick is understandably reluctant to part with a 29 year old player who has been productive in the past and one who might (if he could make a Dennis Leonard-type comeback) continue playing for the next seven years without getting a good return on his investment—nobody is willing to trade very much for a second baseman who has trouble throwing, does not hit well enough to play anywhere else and is talking about retiring. Unless Garcia's shoulder heals to the point where other teams are willing to gamble on him, it is very likely that Toronto may simply be forced to eat the rest of his contract.

—David Driscoll

	1986 SEASON											THREE YEARS (84 – 86)										
	Ave.	OBP	SLG	AB	H	2B	3B	HR	RBI	BB	SO	Ave.	OBP	SLG	AB	H	2B	3B	HR	RBI	BB	SO
Totals	.281	.306	.375	424	119	22	0	6	46	13	32	.282	.306	.375	1657	468	79	9	19	158	44	119
Batting vs. Left and Right-handed Pitchers																						
Left	.324	.336	.432	139	45	9	0	2	15	2	14	.304	.328	.404	560	170	31	2	7	45	18	48
Right	.260	.292	.347	285	74	13	0	4	31	11	18	.272	.295	.361	1097	298	48	7	12	113	26	71
At Home and on the Road																						
Home	.282	.300	.391	174	49	10	0	3	27	3	17	.285	.314	.388	787	224	42	6	9	91	25	62
Road	.280	.311	.364	250	70	12	0	3	19	10	15	.280	.299	.364	870	244	37	3	10	67	19	57
Facing Groundball Pitchers and Flyball Pitchers																						
Groundball	.290	.311	.349	186	54	8	0	1	23	6	14	.267	.289	.357	793	212	41	3	8	73	20	49
Flyball	.273	.303	.395	238	65	14	0	5	23	7	18	.296	.322	.392	864	256	38	6	11	85	24	70
Facing Finesse Pitchers and Power Pitchers																						
Finesse	.276	.296	.388	250	69	16	0	4	27	6	18	.279	.293	.371	951	265	45	5	11	84	13	51
Power	.287	.321	.356	174	50	6	0	2	19	7	14	.288	.323	.381	706	203	34	4	8	74	31	68
On Grass and on Turf																						
Grass	.306	.339	.400	180	55	11	0	2	11	7	11	.289	.307	.374	653	189	25	3	8	47	13	45
Turf	.262	.282	.357	244	64	11	0	4	35	6	21	.278	.306	.376	1004	279	54	6	11	111	31	74
During the Day and at Night																						
Day	.260	.280	.355	169	44	10	0	2	20	3	9	.276	.304	.379	580	160	33	3	7	47	13	37
Night	.294	.323	.388	255	75	12	0	4	26	10	23	.286	.307	.373	1077	308	46	6	12	111	31	82
By Month																						
April	.209	.261	.233	43	9	1	0	0	2	2	3	.287	.322	.372	223	64	12	2	1	16	10	13
May	.267	.319	.343	105	28	5	0	1	15	7	7	.297	.329	.356	320	95	14	1	1	37	13	22
June	.346	.346	.494	81	28	9	0	1	9	0	7	.287	.304	.393	328	94	21	4	2	28	5	26
July	.286	.305	.396	91	26	4	0	2	11	3	7	.290	.307	.423	307	89	17	0	8	39	6	18
August	.273	.284	.394	66	18	2	0	2	9	1	3	.275	.291	.348	276	76	9	1	3	21	4	17
Sept/Oct	.263	.282	.289	38	10	1	0	0	0	0	5	.246	.274	.345	203	50	6	1	4	17	6	23
Situational																						
Bases Empty	.273	.300	.352	253	69	11	0	3	3	8	20	.285	.308	.379	1068	304	52	5	13	13	27	83
Leadoff	.224	.250	.302	116	26	3	0	2	2	3	9	.274	.300	.370	621	170	31	4	7	7	17	53
Not Leadoff	.314	.343	.394	137	43	8	0	1	1	5	11	.300	.320	.391	447	134	21	1	6	6	10	30
Runners On	.292	.315	.409	171	50	11	0	3	43	5	12	.278	.303	.368	589	164	27	4	6	145	17	36
First Base Only	.308	.325	.449	78	24	5	0	2	4	2	5	.265	.276	.354	257	68	9	1	4	11	4	12
Scoring Position	.280	.307	.376	93	26	6	0	1	39	3	7	.289	.322	.380	332	96	18	3	2	134	13	24
Late Innings, Close	.263	.282	.303	76	20	3	0	0	2	1	7	.262	.288	.335	263	69	11	1	2	27	8	16
RBI/Opportunities																						

Scoring Position	37 / 126	(29%)		126 / 441	(29%)	
Scoring Position, 2 Out	16 / 67	(24%)		57 / 225	(25%)	
On Third, Less than 2 Out	14 / 24	(58%)		46 / 80	(57%)	
RBI in close games / RBI Total	20 / 46	(43%)		92 / 158	(58%)	

Scott Garrelts
San Francisco Giants

Scott Garrelts is one of the few players that the Giants have signed and developed who has made an impact recently. He has a great arm, an excellent fastball, slider, and a split-finger fastball which can make hitters look silly. He does throw a curveball, but it's not quite as good. What characterizes Garrelts' professional career is his high strike-out per innings-pitched ratio, and almost equally high walks per innings-pitched ratio, and an excellent hits per innings-pitched ratio.

Garrelts' leaped forward in 1985 when he was used exclusively in the bullpen. By pitching out of the stretch, he improved his mechanics, which helped his control, while still allowing him to maintain his velocity.

Garrelts has been very tough at Candlestick. As a relief pitcher, not many of the hits he's given up have gone for extra bases. The wind and visibility at Candlestick are a factor, but pitchers have to know how to use it to their advantage to be successful. On the road, Garrelts has found less success. This is symptomatic of the Giants as a team. Most of their regulars have less than four years experience in the bigs, and experience helps to downplay these factors. Of course, the bottom line is that good teams win anywhere. It doesn't matter if the grass isn't real, the sun isn't shining, or it's a month named June.

—Victor Hester

At the beginning of 1986, Roger Craig decided to move Scott Garrelts out of the bullpen and into the starting rotation. He pitched as a starter until late July when he was returned to the bullpen, and he had a 1.79 ERA from August on.

Obviously this experiment failed. Looking over Garrelts' statistics, it can be seen that in the bullpen he struck out more, walked more, and gave up fewer hits. His baserunners allowed per 9 innings-pitched were 11.4 starting and 11.1 in relief, so there is little difference there.

Garrelts' ERA is a full 1.51 higher on the road for the last three years. Although he appears to be more effective on grass, this is actually tainted by his great home record. His road grass ERA is 4.21, his road turf ERA is 3.67. Scott has problems with the home run, so since Garrelts' home park and most of the NL turf parks don't have many home runs hit there, Garrelts thrives in those conditions. Garrelts also has problems with basestealers. It seems that he comes from the Gossage school of relief pitching: "Strike 'em out and who cares what the runners are doing."

—Scott M. Daniel

1986: Power, Groundball   **1985: Power, Groundball**   **1984: Power, Flyball**

	G	IP	H	BB	SO	SB	CS	W	L	S	ERA		G	IP	H	BB	SO	SB	CS	W	L	S	ERA
				1986 SEASON												**THREE YEARS (84 – 86)**							
Totals	53	173.2	144	74	125	28	6	13	9	10	3.11		148	322.1	265	166	263	53	12	24	18	23	3.18
At Home and on the Road																						
Home	28	97.0	66	33	66	14	4	8	4	7	2.23		76	176.1	129	80	140	27	7	17	9	11	2.50
Road	25	76.2	78	41	59	14	2	5	5	3	4.23		72	146.0	136	86	123	26	5	7	9	12	4.01
During the Day and at Night																						
Day	28	86.2	70	28	60	18	1	6	2	5	2.49		82	180.1	139	89	145	36	6	17	8	9	2.70
Night	25	87.0	74	46	65	10	5	7	7	5	3.72		66	142.0	126	77	118	17	6	7	10	14	3.80
On Grass and on Turf																						
Grass	43	144.1	114	55	99	22	4	11	6	9	2.81		119	268.1	214	133	209	43	9	22	14	17	3.09
Turf	10	29.1	30	19	26	6	2	2	3	1	4.60		29	54.0	51	33	54	10	3	2	4	6	3.67
By Month																						
April	6	37.1	33	13	20	7	2	3	2	0	2.65		16	51.2	40	18	28	7	2	3	2	1	2.61
May	7	41.2	38	19	24	8	1	2	3	0	4.32		25	74.1	62	45	62	17	5	5	6	3	3.51
June	5	33.0	26	8	19	3	1	1	1	0	1.91		27	70.1	58	29	49	8	1	1	2	1	2.82
July	10	16.1	17	8	16	1	0	3	1	1	7.16		23	36.2	29	16	37	2	1	6	1	4	4.66
August	12	20.1	15	15	21	3	1	2	2	5	2.21		23	35.2	30	25	34	3	2	5	2	9	2.27
Sept/Oct	13	25.0	15	11	25	6	1	2	0	4	1.44		34	53.2	46	33	53	16	1	4	5	5	3.35

vs. Opponent Batters

	Ave.	OBP	SLG	AB	H	2B	3B	HR	RBI	BB	SO		Ave.	OBP	SLG	AB	H	2B	3B	HR	RBI	BB	SO
				1986 SEASON												**THREE YEARS (84 – 86)**							
Totals	.231	.311	.351	624	144	20	2	17	68	74	125		.226	.323	.325	1171	265	32	4	25	134	166	263
Pitching vs. Left and Right-handed Batters																						
Left	.241	.326	.325	332	80	8	1	6	35	43	54		.248	.346	.323	576	143	13	3	8	65	86	98
Right	.219	.294	.380	292	64	12	1	11	33	31	71		.205	.299	.326	595	122	19	1	17	69	80	165
Situational																						
Bases Empty	.238	.307	.357	370	88	13	2	9	9	36	64		.220	.301	.319	665	146	21	3	13	13	74	138
Leadoff	.253	.314	.380	158	40	6	1	4	4	14	24		.246	.322	.344	285	70	11	1	5	5	31	49
Not Leadoff	.226	.302	.340	212	48	7	1	5	5	22	40		.200	.285	.300	380	76	10	2	8	8	43	89
Runners On	.220	.317	.343	254	56	7	0	8	59	38	61		.235	.349	.332	506	119	11	1	12	121	92	125
First Base Only	.234	.301	.351	94	22	2	0	3	6	9	18		.246	.313	.317	183	45	4	0	3	7	18	40
Scoring Position	.212	.325	.338	160	34	5	0	5	53	29	43		.229	.367	.341	323	74	7	1	9	114	74	85
Late Innings, Close	.239	.336	.330	188	45	5	0	4	19	27	45		.218	.325	.274	445	97	11	1	4	46	72	117

RBI/Opportunities

Scoring Position	44 / 241	(18%)	97 / 522	(19%)
Scoring Position, 2 Out	13 / 110	(12%)	32 / 236	(14%)
On Third, Less than 2 Out	21 / 44	(48%)	43 / 94	(46%)
RBI in close games / RBI Total	48 / 68	(71%)	94 / 134	(70%)

Steve Garvey
San Diego Padres

Steve Garvey is a terrible baseball player. That is a simple enough statement, but because he is a household name, because he has been a star in the past, because he makes approximately one million dollars per year, because he was a key part of multiple World Series teams, because the few things he does well are exactly those things that the fans appreciate, and because the many things he does poorly are exactly those things that the fans ignore, most people do not understand or believe that simple statement.

So why is he so bad? Let me count the ways: his BA is merely acceptable, his OBA is terrible, his SA is poor for a power-hitter, he strikes out a lot, he plays the least demanding defensive position, he plays that poorly, and he doesn't steal bases. Did I miss any negatives?

While Garvey is clearly hurting the team by playing every day, his 1984–86 statistics indicate that there is a more limited, but potentially valuable, role for him to play. His numbers versus right-handed pitchers are clearly unacceptable for a player with no defensive value, but his numbers versus left-handers are good enough to justify using him in a platoon role. In 1986, he hit 12 of his 21 homers, as well as slugging .527, vs. southpaws (in about half as many at-bats as against righties).

Garvey is one of a short, but still impressive, list of ball players who have come out of Michigan State University. In addition to Steve, the list includes Robin Roberts, Dick Radatz, and Kirk Gibson. Of course, the reason that this is notable is that, with the possible exception of the University of Michigan, no northern colleges or universities have baseball programs on the level of the Sunbelt schools in Florida, Texas, Arizona and California.

—Gary Gillette

Long one of the most feared power-hitters in baseball, Steve Garvey is on a downhill slide. It's no big deal, it's happened to the best of them, but Garvey is no longer feared to the degree he once was. Sure, he ripped 21 taters in 1986, but 12 of them came with the bases empty and five of them came as a leadoff hitter. Further expounding on his leadoff capabilities, approximately one-fourth of his 557 at-bats came in that capacity, and he hit .308 vs. .257 overall. Finally, his 1986 RBI production vs. potential production was noticeably down from prior years. His strikeout ratio is creeping upward and he's showing a marked weakness against right-handed pitching.

—Bill Thomas

	1986 SEASON											THREE YEARS (84 – 86)										
	Ave.	OBP	SLG	AB	H	2B	3B	HR	RBI	BB	SO	Ave.	OBP	SLG	AB	H	2B	3B	HR	RBI	BB	SO
Totals	.255	.284	.408	557	142	22	0	21	81	23	72	.274	.304	.404	1828	501	83	8	46	248	82	203
Batting vs. Left and Right-handed Pitchers																						
Left	.283	.311	.527	184	52	9	0	12	34	8	19	.291	.329	.473	588	171	33	1	24	83	36	57
Right	.241	.271	.349	373	90	13	0	9	47	15	53	.266	.292	.371	1240	330	50	7	22	165	46	146
At Home and on the Road																						
Home	.244	.282	.398	279	68	10	0	11	39	15	37	.270	.306	.412	894	241	41	4	26	126	50	106
Road	.266	.287	.417	278	74	12	0	10	42	8	35	.278	.302	.396	934	260	42	4	20	122	32	97
Facing Groundball Pitchers and Flyball Pitchers																						
Groundball	.228	.270	.316	285	65	13	0	4	31	16	36	.264	.296	.374	943	249	43	5	17	124	45	95
Flyball	.283	.300	.504	272	77	9	0	17	50	7	36	.285	.313	.435	885	252	40	3	29	124	37	108
Facing Finesse Pitchers and Power Pitchers																						
Finesse	.261	.287	.413	310	81	14	0	11	44	11	32	.272	.298	.415	1013	276	44	5	30	138	37	87
Power	.247	.281	.401	247	61	8	0	10	37	12	40	.276	.312	.390	815	225	39	3	16	110	45	116
On Grass and on Turf																						
Grass	.244	.271	.381	409	100	17	0	13	53	15	51	.275	.305	.411	1342	369	63	6	36	180	60	152
Turf	.284	.321	.480	148	42	5	0	8	28	8	21	.272	.301	.383	486	132	20	2	10	68	22	51
During the Day and at Night																						
Day	.247	.280	.408	174	43	7	0	7	26	8	19	.255	.280	.390	585	149	26	4	15	72	23	67
Night	.258	.286	.407	383	99	15	0	14	55	15	53	.283	.315	.410	1243	352	57	4	31	176	59	136
By Month																						
April	.215	.241	.380	79	17	4	0	3	7	3	10	.245	.262	.384	245	60	10	0	8	37	7	31
May	.297	.330	.564	101	30	3	0	8	17	5	7	.293	.316	.480	304	89	12	3	13	40	11	26
June	.204	.212	.291	103	21	3	0	2	10	1	11	.251	.279	.359	343	86	13	0	8	40	15	37
July	.244	.287	.302	86	21	2	0	1	12	6	10	.254	.281	.357	311	79	16	2	4	38	11	31
August	.319	.352	.534	116	37	7	0	6	26	5	18	.302	.335	.455	334	101	16	1	11	55	17	38
Sept/Oct	.222	.253	.306	72	16	3	0	1	9	3	16	.296	.344	.385	291	86	16	2	2	38	21	40
Situational																						
Bases Empty	.266	.284	.424	278	74	8	0	12	12	6	38	.271	.296	.421	940	255	46	4	29	29	32	120
Leadoff	.308	.323	.469	130	40	6	0	5	5	3	14	.287	.306	.443	366	105	18	3	11	11	10	38
Not Leadoff	.230	.250	.385	148	34	2	0	7	7	3	24	.261	.290	.408	574	150	28	1	18	18	22	82
Runners On	.244	.284	.391	279	68	14	0	9	69	17	34	.277	.312	.385	888	246	37	4	17	219	50	83
First Base Only	.234	.274	.360	111	26	8	0	2	8	6	11	.263	.296	.344	384	101	16	3	3	17	15	29
Scoring Position	.250	.291	.411	168	42	6	0	7	61	11	23	.288	.324	.417	504	145	21	1	14	202	35	54
Late Innings, Close	.239	.287	.301	113	27	4	0	1	13	8	19	.262	.300	.325	332	87	10	1	3	38	18	47

RBI/Opportunities

	1986		THREE YEARS (84 – 86)	
Scoring Position	50 / 208	(24%)	176 / 641	(27%)
Scoring Position, 2 Out	21 / 95	(22%)	59 / 246	(24%)
On Third, Less than 2 Out	18 / 44	(41%)	79 / 151	(52%)
RBI in close games / RBI Total	56 / 81	(69%)	178 / 248	(72%)

Rich Gedman
Boston Red Sox

The *Boston Globe* recently noted that Rich Gedman had become a better hitter on the road and, thus a better hitter. The credit for this miraculous change went to Walt Hriniak, the Boston batting coach. It was kind of him to accept credit for it, considering that he took a player who was about to become the best hitting catcher in baseball, raised his road average 42 points, cut his home average 121 points and took off a healthy chunk of both his slugging and on-base averages. You did great, Walt—thanks a lot.

My feeling about Gedman is that you don't tinker with a player's form unless either he's got a serious problem already or you know that he'll have one unless you do something right away—I don't see how either one applies here. Gedman had a brilliant 1985; he didn't need to be fixed and I don't feel that hitting .335 in Fenway Park and .256 on the road is a big problem. Any number of Boston players have turned in successful careers with those kinds of splits in their records. The only thing that Hriniak did was make Rich more likely to succeed if he becomes a free agent—is that really what he's being paid to do?

But who knows—maybe Hriniak was just trying to iron out the kinks in Rich's month-by-month totals. If so, he did a great job; Gedman's batting and on-base average stats since 1984 now look like they were produced by a xerox machine. They've still got his slugging to deal with, but there's always next year.

Fate certainly has a strange sense of humor. Both Gedman and Oil Can Boyd would have been good choices for the All-Star team. Boyd didn't make it, Gedman did and they both fell apart as a result. Gedman had been having some minor problems with his defense, for reasons that nobody could explain, before the break. Having to catch Charlie Hough turned a molehill into a mountain, which also began affecting his hitting. But, after film study, Rich realized that he had been setting up further behind home plate than he had in 1985; when he made the adjustment, his defense returned to its normal level of excellence. He cuts down the running game very well (only 56 steals in 116 tries) and the team ERA in games that he started was lower than the overall team ERA. Despite Hriniak he is, if not the best catcher in the league, within spitting distance.

—David Pinto and Dan Feinstein

	1986 SEASON										THREE YEARS (84 – 86)									
	Ave.	OBP	SLG	AB	H	2B	3B	HR	RBI	BB	SO	Ave.	OBP	SLG	AB	H	2B	3B	HR	RBI	BB	SO
Totals	.258	.315	.424	462	119	29	0	16	65	37	61	.275	.331	.471	1409	387	85	9	58	217	116	212
Batting vs. Left and Right-handed Pitchers																						
Left	.186	.210	.347	118	22	4	0	5	14	3	18	.224	.271	.354	308	69	12	2	8	50	18	60
Right	.282	.349	.451	344	97	25	0	11	51	34	43	.289	.347	.504	1101	318	73	7	50	167	98	152
At Home and on the Road																						
Home	.214	.284	.299	224	48	13	0	2	26	21	34	.291	.343	.491	700	204	47	6	27	120	56	106
Road	.298	.345	.542	238	71	16	0	14	39	16	27	.258	.318	.451	709	183	38	3	31	97	60	106
Facing Groundball Pitchers and Flyball Pitchers																						
Groundball	.285	.358	.430	214	61	13	0	6	26	23	23	.292	.351	.483	712	208	37	6	29	113	62	95
Flyball	.234	.276	.419	248	58	16	0	10	39	14	38	.257	.310	.459	697	179	48	3	29	104	54	117
Facing Finesse Pitchers and Power Pitchers																						
Finesse	.257	.317	.389	257	66	13	0	7	30	21	22	.276	.326	.449	780	215	44	5	27	101	57	93
Power	.259	.313	.468	205	53	16	0	9	35	16	39	.273	.336	.499	629	172	41	4	31	116	59	119
On Grass and on Turf																						
Grass	.245	.306	.394	388	95	22	0	12	55	32	48	.279	.334	.471	1209	337	70	8	49	190	100	178
Turf	.324	.362	.581	74	24	7	0	4	10	5	13	.250	.311	.470	200	50	15	1	9	27	16	34
During the Day and at Night																						
Day	.266	.335	.430	158	42	8	0	6	23	16	18	.274	.339	.461	460	126	24	4	18	69	44	66
Night	.253	.304	.421	304	77	21	0	10	42	21	43	.275	.327	.476	949	261	61	5	40	148	72	146
By Month																						
April	.303	.333	.455	66	20	4	0	2	7	3	3	.289	.333	.458	190	55	11	0	7	23	13	26
May	.241	.310	.342	79	19	5	0	1	6	8	11	.276	.335	.469	239	66	14	4	8	31	21	40
June	.264	.321	.361	72	19	4	0	1	10	7	12	.278	.325	.395	223	62	15	1	3	30	17	35
July	.241	.279	.456	79	19	5	0	4	16	2	13	.270	.328	.473	226	61	14	1	10	38	16	30
August	.224	.320	.424	85	19	5	0	4	12	11	10	.268	.338	.531	254	68	16	0	17	46	27	36
Sept/Oct	.284	.330	.506	81	23	6	0	4	14	6	12	.271	.326	.487	277	75	15	3	13	49	22	45
Situational																						
Bases Empty	.253	.291	.415	241	61	9	0	10	10	10	37	.268	.310	.475	779	209	33	4	40	40	42	121
Leadoff	.235	.272	.408	98	23	5	0	4	4	4	14	.244	.290	.418	311	76	15	0	13	13	19	47
Not Leadoff	.266	.305	.420	143	38	4	0	6	6	6	23	.284	.323	.513	468	133	18	4	27	27	23	74
Runners On	.262	.339	.434	221	58	20	0	6	55	27	24	.283	.355	.467	630	178	52	5	18	177	74	91
First Base Only	.267	.319	.381	105	28	9	0	1	5	7	10	.298	.347	.471	289	86	28	2	6	26	19	39
Scoring Position	.259	.355	.483	116	30	11	0	5	50	20	14	.270	.360	.463	341	92	24	3	12	151	55	52
Late Innings, Close	.289	.357	.500	76	22	4	0	4	13	8	9	.273	.340	.459	231	63	11	1	10	37	24	34
RBI/Opportunities																						
Scoring Position	40 / 178		(22%)									124 / 501		(25%)								
Scoring Position, 2 Out	20 / 95		(21%)									59 / 260		(23%)								
On Third, Less than 2 Out	10 / 27		(37%)									38 / 83		(46%)								
RBI in close games / RBI Total	37 / 65		(57%)									114 / 217		(53%)								

Kirk Gibson
Detroit Tigers

When Kirk Gibson hit the majors, people kept comparing him to Mickey Mantle. Since, at this point in his career, the only thing he's done as well as Mantle is get hurt, it's time to adopt another yardstick—the late-70's Reggie Jackson. Both men play right field; both less well than they have the tools to. They hit for pretty good averages, draw some walks and have power. They've each got speed, but they lack good judgement. And, finally, they've both had trouble dealing with their teams and the fans.

Kirk hasn't become what everyone expected him to be, but he's a pretty fair player in his own right. Despite the fact that he's missed about a half season over the last three years, he's averaged .280 with 28 homers. 1986, in many ways, may have been his best year—despite missing six weeks with an injury, he had career highs in On-Base Average and homers and just missed career bests in RBIs and walks. He's starting to hit lefties much better than he has in the past (.224 in 1984, .256 in 1985, .262 in 1986) and he hit well on turf for the first time in his career. Words can't describe his fielding (execrable comes close, though), but that problem may be dealt with in 1987. If Detroit can find

a solid rightfielder, they will shift Kirk to left (maybe even if they can't—see the comment on Darnell Coles) to reduce the demands on his popgun arm.

The only thing that Gibson isn't doing that he should be is bunting. A power hitter who drops down a bunt every so often forces the defense to play him closer, increasing his chances to slap a hit by the right side. Joe Carter can do this (he gives Detroit fits this way) and Kirk is probably faster than he is. He should also stop asking to bat fourth. When he gets into the cleanup spot, he puts pressure on himself to drive in runs and his hitting suffers. It would be nice if he were a consistent 100-RBI man, but he isn't that type and he should stop hurting himself by trying to be.

Another similarity between Gibson and Reggie is that they are the straws that stir the drink. When the Tigers were breathing down Boston's neck in June and July, Gibby was their MVP. When he collapsed in August, so did the team. In one week in July, he had the game-winning RBI in five consecutive games—if Detroit hopes to contend in 1987, Gibson will have to lead them.

—Steve Lysogorski and Geoff Beckman

	1986 SEASON											THREE YEARS (84 – 86)										
	Ave.	OBP	SLG	AB	H	2B	3B	HR	RBI	BB	SO	Ave.	OBP	SLG	AB	H	2B	3B	HR	RBI	BB	SO
Totals	.268	.371	.492	441	118	11	2	28	86	68	107	.280	.366	.510	1553	435	71	17	84	274	202	347
Batting vs. Left and Right-handed Pitchers																						
Left	.262	.360	.421	164	43	5	0	7	29	20	44	.247	.330	.436	502	124	20	3	23	80	54	143
Right	.271	.378	.534	277	75	6	2	21	57	48	63	.296	.383	.545	1051	311	51	14	61	194	148	204
At Home and on the Road																						
Home	.278	.378	.505	216	60	2	1	15	48	32	50	.289	.370	.534	764	221	37	9	44	146	97	166
Road	.258	.365	.480	225	58	9	1	13	38	36	57	.271	.362	.487	789	214	34	8	40	128	105	181
Facing Groundball Pitchers and Flyball Pitchers																						
Groundball	.294	.386	.485	163	48	3	2	8	29	22	37	.304	.387	.531	697	212	25	11	37	131	91	142
Flyball	.252	.363	.496	278	70	8	0	20	57	46	70	.261	.349	.493	856	223	46	6	47	143	111	205
Facing Finesse Pitchers and Power Pitchers																						
Finesse	.236	.330	.421	254	60	6	1	13	38	32	55	.285	.363	.530	877	250	40	11	51	151	99	171
Power	.310	.425	.588	187	58	5	1	15	48	36	52	.274	.370	.484	676	185	31	6	33	123	103	176
On Grass and on Turf																						
Grass	.266	.372	.486	391	104	9	1	25	77	60	99	.292	.381	.521	1320	386	61	14	71	231	180	292
Turf	.280	.367	.540	50	14	2	1	3	9	8	8	.210	.277	.446	233	49	10	3	13	43	22	55
During the Day and at Night																						
Day	.289	.382	.526	135	39	3	1	9	24	17	32	.287	.355	.520	487	140	26	6	25	90	48	99
Night	.258	.366	.477	306	79	8	1	19	62	51	75	.277	.371	.506	1066	295	45	11	59	184	154	248
By Month																						
April	.359	.479	.615	39	14	2	1	2	7	9	7	.279	.370	.486	179	50	7	3	8	30	27	39
May	.000	.000	.000	0	0	0	0	0	0	0	0	.295	.362	.536	166	49	10	3	8	27	15	35
June	.257	.400	.525	101	26	1	1	8	21	21	25	.281	.366	.554	303	85	12	4	21	65	39	66
July	.269	.359	.500	108	29	4	0	7	23	16	31	.282	.374	.491	287	81	13	1	15	53	43	74
August	.210	.325	.305	105	22	1	0	3	12	16	26	.273	.372	.466	337	92	13	5	14	41	48	72
Sept/Oct	.307	.354	.614	88	27	3	0	8	23	6	18	.278	.349	.534	281	78	16	1	18	58	30	61
Situational																						
Bases Empty	.263	.358	.419	236	62	6	2	9	9	32	57	.268	.355	.494	838	225	33	9	46	46	104	192
Leadoff	.268	.341	.402	82	22	2	0	3	3	9	13	.282	.373	.486	255	72	9	5	11	11	34	50
Not Leadoff	.260	.367	.429	154	40	4	2	6	6	23	44	.262	.347	.497	583	153	24	4	35	35	70	142
Runners On	.273	.386	.576	205	56	5	0	19	77	36	50	.294	.379	.529	715	210	38	8	38	228	98	155
First Base Only	.289	.392	.614	83	24	0	0	9	18	13	18	.301	.376	.497	316	95	16	2	14	37	33	59
Scoring Position	.262	.382	.549	122	32	5	0	10	59	23	32	.288	.381	.554	399	115	22	6	24	191	65	96
Late Innings, Close	.281	.410	.438	64	18	1	0	3	15	11	19	.251	.356	.463	231	58	6	2	13	38	34	61

RBI/Opportunities						
Scoring Position	44 / 180	(24%)		146 / 573	(25%)	
Scoring Position, 2 Out	12 / 72	(17%)		45 / 229	(20%)	
On Third, Less than 2 Out	16 / 40	(40%)		59 / 126	(47%)	
RBI in close games / RBI Total	59 / 86	(69%)		168 / 274	(61%)	

Dan Gladden
San Francisco Giants

1986 was a comeback year for Danny Gladden. His .243 BA in 1985 was not just disappointing after his .351 in 1984—it was the lowest average of his pro career. Dan missed 44 games due to torn thumb ligaments, but he hit .274 and led the Giants in stolen bases for the third straight year (27/37, 73%).

Over his career, Dan has hit best with a runner on first, while hitting only .281 as a leadoff hitter. 1986 was no different—Dan hit .378, slugged .405, and had an OBA of .410 with a runner on first only, while hitting .273, slugging .331 and having an OBA of .377 as a leadoff hitter. This is one area where Dan is inconsistent—he hit .276 vs. both RHP and LHP; .272 at home and .280 on the road. Dan's speed serves him well on turf, where he hit .324 and slugged .451, against .257 and .325 on grass. All of these closely match his career averages.

Gladden got his chance as a 26-year-old rookie after a mid-season injury to Jack Clark. History repeated itself this year when Dan went on the DL, 26-year old rookie Randy Kutcher came up. Kutcher has more power and less speed than Gladden. Otherwise, they're very similar: both are hard-nosed, line-drive hitters with similar batting averages, slugging averages around .375, decent speed, and hustling defense. *Deja vu*.

—J. Michael Duca

The Giants have a history of promoting young outfielders. The ones that made an impact were 20–24 years old when called up, including the Alou brothers, Bobby Bonds, Garry Maddox, Gary Matthews, Chili Davis, Jack Clark, and #24. Those called up at ages 25–28 include such notables as Dave Marshall, Jimmy Rosario, and Jimmy Howarth.

Gladden was an early favorite, making off-balance catches and crashing into fences. Fair weather fans (Chili Davis can give you a count) could easily identify with Gladden's grit and determination to overcome his limited talent. What these fans couldn't see is that a Davis or Leonard would just glide over and make the catch look easy, but Gladden couldn't do that.

A consistent .300 grass hitter in the minors, Gladden has seen less success in the majors on grass. His turf stats do coincide with his background. Many of the NL turf stadiums enhance a line-drive type of hitter. If he were to raise his OBA 15–20 points while improving his basestealing success rate he would become an excellent leadoff hitter. However, at his recent pace, he could become a utility player very quickly.

—Victor Hester

	1986 SEASON												THREE YEARS (84 – 86)										
	Ave.	OBP	SLG	AB	H	2B	3B	HR	RBI	BB	SO		Ave.	OBP	SLG	AB	H	2B	3B	HR	RBI	BB	SO
Totals	.276	.357	.362	351	97	16	1	4	29	39	59		.284	.351	.380	1195	339	48	11	15	101	112	174
Batting vs. Left and Right-handed Pitchers																							
Left	.276	.373	.325	123	34	6	0	0	7	17	24		.291	.375	.369	350	102	14	2	3	19	44	54
Right	.276	.348	.382	228	63	10	1	4	22	22	35		.280	.341	.385	845	237	34	9	12	82	68	120
At Home and on the Road																							
Home	.272	.376	.321	162	44	5	0	1	10	26	30		.283	.362	.386	586	166	19	4	11	52	65	90
Road	.280	.340	.397	189	53	11	1	3	19	13	29		.284	.340	.374	609	173	29	7	4	49	47	84
Facing Groundball Pitchers and Flyball Pitchers																							
Groundball	.306	.395	.365	170	52	10	0	0	10	24	29		.305	.381	.394	558	170	26	6	4	39	64	70
Flyball	.249	.320	.359	181	45	6	1	4	19	15	30		.265	.324	.367	637	169	22	5	11	62	48	104
Facing Finesse Pitchers and Power Pitchers																							
Finesse	.302	.387	.352	179	54	9	0	0	11	24	21		.291	.359	.386	678	197	32	6	7	50	67	83
Power	.250	.325	.372	172	43	7	1	4	18	15	38		.275	.341	.371	517	142	16	5	8	51	45	91
On Grass and on Turf																							
Grass	.257	.349	.325	249	64	8	0	3	17	31	42		.276	.351	.367	861	238	31	4	13	74	87	131
Turf	.324	.378	.451	102	33	8	1	1	12	8	17		.302	.353	.413	334	101	17	7	2	27	25	43
During the Day and at Night																							
Day	.273	.371	.354	161	44	7	0	2	12	23	36		.285	.368	.383	582	166	20	5	9	51	68	101
Night	.279	.344	.368	190	53	9	1	2	17	16	23		.282	.334	.377	613	173	28	6	6	50	44	73
By Month																							
April	.287	.361	.322	87	25	3	0	0	4	7	13		.294	.356	.350	160	47	6	0	1	12	12	28
May	.247	.316	.371	89	22	5	0	2	7	8	14		.222	.292	.328	189	42	6	4	2	11	17	32
June	.556	.556	.667	9	5	1	0	0	2	0	0		.244	.297	.378	119	29	5	1	3	10	8	10
July	.250	.379	.375	24	6	3	0	0	4	5	2		.308	.363	.379	214	66	10	1	1	24	15	24
August	.315	.419	.382	89	28	4	1	0	6	16	15		.298	.374	.370	262	78	11	4	0	18	30	35
Sept/Oct	.208	.263	.321	53	11	0	0	2	6	3	15		.307	.383	.450	251	77	10	4	8	26	30	45
Situational																							
Bases Empty	.268	.366	.347	239	64	11	1	2	2	33	41		.279	.353	.380	820	229	32	9	11	11	85	125
Leadoff	.273	.377	.331	139	38	3	1	1	1	21	21		.281	.355	.379	480	135	15	4	8	8	50	73
Not Leadoff	.260	.351	.370	100	26	8	0	1	1	12	20		.276	.349	.382	340	94	17	5	3	3	35	52
Runners On	.295	.336	.393	112	33	5	0	2	27	6	18		.293	.348	.379	375	110	16	2	4	90	27	49
First Base Only	.378	.410	.405	37	14	1	0	0	0	2	4		.353	.392	.439	139	49	7	1	1	6	7	16
Scoring Position	.253	.300	.387	75	19	4	0	2	27	4	14		.258	.323	.343	236	61	9	1	3	84	20	33
Late Innings, Close	.211	.325	.296	71	15	3	0	1	4	12	16		.252	.326	.350	234	59	9	4	2	19	23	46

RBI/Opportunities					
Scoring Position	23 / 102	(23%)		77 / 328	(23%)
Scoring Position, 2 Out	9 / 50	(18%)		37 / 177	(21%)
On Third, Less than 2 Out	9 / 14	(64%)		29 / 46	(63%)
RBI in close games / RBI Total	14 / 29	(48%)		68 / 101	(67%)

Dwight Gooden
New York Mets

Let me say this at the start: Dwight Gooden is still the pitcher he was in 1984 and 1985, and in fact may be even better. But given the events in Dwight's life both on and off the field in 1986, we must explain what happened to him both as a pitcher and as a person. His on-field problems, which were mostly the result of trying to learn to throw an offspeed curve, are correctable, as long as the off-field issues are addressed. I'm a clinical psychologist, and in my opinion the personality difficulties Dwight faced in 1986 are the psychological problems of being a prodigy. Basically, Dwight overidentified with being Dr. K and underidentified with being 21-year old Dwight Gooden.

No, Doc's not a head case in the usual sense, but he is showing all the signs of important psychological disorientation that prodigies experience. Dwight's success and fame have finally overwhelmed his considerable ability to know who and where he is. He has lost touch with the fact that when not playing baseball, he is just an ordinary human being. There are fully understandable reasons for this.

Four years ago Dwight Gooden was only a senior in high school. Most seventeen year olds go to college, and if they get drunk or in a scrape with the police or impregnate a young woman, family and friends find out and just deal with it. Gooden's indiscretions have not been treated so kindly.

Until he won the Cy Young Award and obtained a huge increase in salary, Dwight seemed to be taking his success in stride. But at that point he developed a sense that he was special in other ways than on the field. He came, understandably, to the disoriented belief that he should command the same treatment off the field that his talent gives him on the field. This man/child has been through a lot in four years. These drastic changes have led to important psychological disorientation which has manifested itself in diminished performance, poor judgment and poor behavior.

Dwight's success caused him to lose his sense of himself as an ordinary person, and it was this strong, centered sense of who he was that distiguished him from other young, talented players. In 1986 he tried to take Dr. K off the field, and in the process he lost not only a part of Dr. K, but also the best of Dwight Gooden. With supportive assistance he has the ability to reorient himself both personally and professionally and to re-emerge in 1987 as the dominant pitcher and personality in baseball.

—J. Randolph Burnham

1986: Power, Groundball   **1985: Power, Flyball**   **1984: Power, Flyball**

| | 1986 SEASON | | | | | | | | | | | THREE YEARS (84 – 86) | | | | | | | | | | |
	G	IP	H	BB	SO	SB	CS	W	L	S	ERA	G	IP	H	BB	SO	SB	CS	W	L	S	ERA
Totals	33	250.0	197	80	200	33	5	17	6	0	2.84	99	744.2	556	222	744	102	23	58	19	0	2.28
At Home and on the Road																						
Home	16	123.0	79	42	103	14	5	9	3	0	2.20	50	385.1	258	114	401	42	13	34	7	0	1.85
Road	17	127.0	118	38	97	19	0	8	3	0	3.47	49	359.1	298	108	343	60	10	24	12	0	2.76
During the Day and at Night																						
Day	10	74.0	65	25	51	11	1	4	3	0	3.41	34	233.2	208	72	209	35	10	15	11	0	3.39
Night	23	176.0	132	55	149	22	4	13	3	0	2.61	65	511.0	348	150	535	67	13	43	8	0	1.78
On Grass and on Turf																						
Grass	24	183.2	139	60	152	21	5	12	4	0	2.60	73	554.1	404	165	575	60	15	45	13	0	2.14
Turf	9	66.1	58	20	48	12	0	5	2	0	3.53	26	190.1	152	57	169	42	8	13	6	0	2.70
By Month																						
April	5	43.0	28	6	32	4	0	4	0	0	1.26	14	102.1	66	26	92	14	4	8	2	0	1.67
May	5	35.0	31	8	30	2	0	2	2	0	2.83	16	112.1	91	33	132	7	3	9	6	0	2.88
June	6	45.1	35	23	32	10	1	3	1	0	3.97	18	141.2	106	53	117	35	5	9	3	0	2.41
July	4	25.0	25	10	13	3	1	1	1	0	4.32	15	106.2	82	39	101	11	1	9	2	0	2.62
August	6	46.2	41	14	42	6	1	3	0	0	2.89	18	131.2	117	29	140	14	2	11	3	0	2.87
Sept/Oct	7	55.0	37	19	51	8	2	4	2	0	2.45	18	150.0	94	42	162	21	8	12	3	0	1.38

vs. Opponent Batters

| | 1986 SEASON | | | | | | | | | | | THREE YEARS (84 – 86) | | | | | | | | | | |
	Ave.	OBP	SLG	AB	H	2B	3B	HR	RBI	BB	SO	Ave.	OBP	SLG	AB	H	2B	3B	HR	RBI	BB	SO
Totals	.215	.278	.321	917	197	36	5	17	83	80	200	.206	.267	.289	2702	556	83	15	37	191	222	744
Pitching vs. Left and Right-handed Batters																						
Left	.209	.280	.303	532	111	21	4	7	36	50	115	.212	.275	.284	1531	324	47	11	14	97	130	364
Right	.223	.276	.345	385	86	15	1	10	47	30	85	.198	.257	.295	1171	232	36	4	23	94	92	380
Situational																						
Bases Empty	.223	.289	.338	533	119	26	4	9	9	45	111	.210	.273	.303	1642	344	59	11	24	24	139	436
Leadoff	.249	.332	.378	225	56	10	2	5	5	25	40	.208	.278	.321	688	143	19	7	15	15	64	176
Not Leadoff	.205	.255	.308	308	63	16	2	4	4	20	71	.211	.269	.289	954	201	40	4	9	9	75	260
Runners On	.203	.265	.297	384	78	10	1	8	74	35	89	.200	.258	.267	1060	212	24	4	13	167	83	308
First Base Only	.247	.290	.337	166	41	4	1	3	9	10	32	.223	.261	.290	480	107	13	2	5	17	24	118
Scoring Position	.170	.247	.266	218	37	6	0	5	65	25	57	.181	.255	.248	580	105	11	2	8	150	59	190
Late Innings, Close	.169	.252	.250	124	21	4	0	2	7	13	35	.215	.273	.274	413	89	9	0	5	21	33	127

RBI/Opportunities

	1986		THREE YEARS	
Scoring Position	56 / 301	(19%)	138 / 780	(18%)
Scoring Position, 2 Out	19 / 125	(15%)	46 / 338	(14%)
On Third, Less than 2 Out	26 / 58	(45%)	64 / 155	(41%)
RBI in close games / RBI Total	61 / 83	(73%)	142 / 191	(74%)

Rich Gossage
San Diego Padres

The "Goose" finally got cooked in 1986. After years of being frustrated by Gossage's mastery of them, enemy batters got some measure of revenge. Rich's ERA of 4.45 was the second highest of his career after his 7.38 ERA in 50 innings with the White Sox in 1973. Since 1977 when he was traded to Pittsburgh after an abortive experiment as a starting pitcher with the Sox, he had never had an ERA of greater than 2.90.

There is no question that Gossage is one of the greatest relief pitchers in the history of baseball. His 278 career saves places him 3rd on the all-time list, behind Rollie Fingers and Bruce Sutter. He has pitched in the big time for 16 years now, and, at age 35, is still a power pitcher. Last year, he struck out 63 batters in 64.2 innings and had a strikeout-to-walk ratio of greater than 3 to 1.

In Gossage's first season with the Padres, he was instrumental in their first-ever trip to the World Series. The Goose's role in Game 5 of that Series is a classic. San Diego was behind 5–4 in the bottom of the eighth and Gossage was on the mound, visibly agitated that Manager Dick Williams wanted him to intentionally walk Tigers slugger Kirk Gibson with two runners on base. He succeeded in persuading Williams not to walk Kirk, who had homered earlier in the game. Gibson proceeded to crush one of the Goose's fastballs deep into the upper deck at Tiger Stadium, bringing down the house and giving the Tigers an insurmountable four-run lead and the World Championship. The tableau of Gossage standing defeated on the mound while Gibson triumphantly danced around the bases symbolized everything in that magical year for Detroit.

Nevertheless, just as he had rebounded from watching another of his fastballs that had been crushed by George Brett to vanquish the hated Yankees in the 1980 ALCS, the Goose excelled again in 1985. In fact, his 1984–85 seasons were so good that his poor '86 numbers could not ruin his three-year averages: .230 BA, .287 OBA, .321 SA and 24 saves per year. Most relief pitchers would kill for those numbers for one year alone. His only serious weakness throughout his career has been the ease with which runners steal on him.

Rich Gossage may be finished as a dominant pitcher, but I wouldn't bet on it. If he is, he certainly deserves a bronze plaque in Cooperstown after he retires.

—Gary Gillette

1986: Power, Flyball   **1985: Finesse, Flyball**   **1984: Power, Flyball**

	1986 SEASON											THREE YEARS (84 – 86)										
	G	IP	H	BB	SO	SB	CS	W	L	S	ERA	G	IP	H	BB	SO	SB	CS	W	L	S	ERA
Totals	45	64.2	69	20	63	6	2	5	7	21	4.45	157	246.0	208	73	199	22	6	20	16	72	2.96
At Home and on the Road																						
Home	26	38.0	44	11	39	5	1	5	5	9	3.79	81	124.1	104	29	96	11	3	14	7	37	2.53
Road	19	26.2	25	9	24	1	1	0	2	12	5.40	76	121.2	104	44	103	11	3	6	9	35	3.40
During the Day and at Night																						
Day	15	21.2	22	4	18	3	1	1	1	8	2.49	51	79.2	76	22	64	10	2	4	4	25	2.94
Night	30	43.0	47	16	45	3	1	4	6	13	5.44	106	166.1	132	51	135	12	4	16	12	47	2.98
On Grass and on Turf																						
Grass	36	55.2	58	19	56	6	2	5	6	16	4.37	121	194.2	159	56	155	19	5	16	10	57	2.87
Turf	9	9.0	11	1	7	0	0	0	1	5	5.00	36	51.1	49	17	44	3	1	4	6	15	3.33
By Month																						
April	8	12.0	14	3	14	1	1	2	1	3	3.00	27	41.1	29	10	32	1	2	3	1	15	2.40
May	9	13.0	13	6	11	1	1	1	2	5	4.15	29	46.1	48	12	37	5	1	2	4	17	3.88
June	7	12.0	8	7	10	1	0	0	0	5	5.25	28	47.1	32	20	33	3	0	2	1	11	2.66
July	8	11.0	12	2	14	1	0	2	1	4	3.27	30	49.2	38	12	42	7	2	5	3	15	2.17
August	11	14.2	19	2	13	2	0	0	3	4	5.52	21	24.1	25	5	23	3	0	3	4	9	4.81
Sept/Oct	2	2.0	3	0	1	0	0	0	0	0	9.00	22	37.0	36	14	32	3	1	5	3	5	2.68

vs. Opponent Batters

	1986 SEASON											THREE YEARS (84 – 86)									
	Ave.	OBP	SLG	AB	H	2B	3B	HR	RBI	BB	SO	Ave.	OBP	SLG	AB	H	2B	3B	HR	RBI	BB	SO
Totals	.273	.326	.419	253	69	9	2	8	47	20	63	.230	.287	.321	904	208	25	6	15	112	73	199
Pitching vs. Left and Right-handed Batters																						
Left	.281	.347	.445	128	36	5	2	4	24	14	26	.249	.315	.362	445	111	13	5	9	61	45	85
Right	.264	.304	.392	125	33	4	0	4	23	6	37	.211	.260	.281	459	97	12	1	6	51	28	114
Situational																						
Bases Empty	.274	.336	.419	117	32	6	1	3	3	10	31	.204	.264	.269	490	100	11	3	5	5	38	121
Leadoff	.250	.321	.417	48	12	0	1	2	2	5	12	.190	.262	.256	195	37	2	1	3	3	18	54
Not Leadoff	.290	.347	.420	69	20	6	0	1	1	5	19	.214	.266	.278	295	63	9	2	2	2	20	67
Runners On	.272	.318	.419	136	37	3	1	5	44	10	32	.261	.314	.382	414	108	14	3	10	107	35	78
First Base Only	.320	.370	.380	50	16	0	0	1	2	3	8	.276	.318	.398	181	50	7	0	5	11	10	23
Scoring Position	.244	.289	.442	86	21	3	1	4	42	7	24	.249	.311	.369	233	58	7	3	5	96	25	55
Late Innings, Close	.288	.340	.434	212	61	8	1	7	41	17	50	.229	.286	.318	741	170	21	3	13	96	60	164

RBI/Opportunities

Scoring Position	34 / 120	(28%)	84 / 341	(25%)
Scoring Position, 2 Out	12 / 51	(24%)	43 / 168	(26%)
On Third, Less than 2 Out	15 / 26	(58%)	28 / 63	(44%)
RBI in close games / RBI Total	41 / 47	(87%)	96 / 112	(86%)

Alfredo Griffin
Oakland A's

Alfredo Griffin's career appears to have matured and stabilized with Oakland. His hitting, although not nearly as productive as the top shortstops, contributed to the A's offense. His on base percentage, once a miserable .290, was up to to .324 in 1986, with 35 walks, more than the last two years combined. He even walked twice in a game last year, the first time he has done this since 1983. He can be a clutch hitter, as shown by his slugging percentage in the late innings of close games, and by his eight game winning runs-batted-in. Alfredo reversed his previous tendency of having higher batting statistics on natural grass in 1986. He likes to bunt over the pitcher toward second or short, and will even try to do so with two strikes. He also has been trying to chop down on the ball more, which might explain the increase in production on artificial turf.

His thirty-three stolen bases (67% success rate) were the highest total of his career. Alfredo does, however, occasionally get thrown out on the bases trying to stretch hits or advance more than he should. It sometimes seems that he is trying to win games all by himself, rather than letting others drive him in.

As a defensive player, Alfredo can be either awful or spectacular. He was second to Greg Gagne in shortstop errors (25), but second to Fernandez in putouts. His range factor (4.34) was average for American League regulars at the position. Compared to other shortstops the A's have had recently, he is Ozzie Smith. He has made some incredible plays, mostly diving stops and off-balance throws. He does, however, do things like throwing the ball into the third base dugout trying to force a runner at third or letting grounders go between his legs. To say that he could be more consistent defensively would be an understatement.

It's hard, however, to resist someone who has an absolute joy in playing baseball and Alfredo Griffin expresses this joy. Because he is such a pleasure to watch, he often gives the impression of being a better player than he shows on paper. When Alfredo was traded by the Blue Jays and the Toronto fans were upset, the baseball experts couldn't understand why. Didn't those Canadians realize that Fernandez was twice the player Alfredo is, for heavens sake? The Toronto fans' reaction is actually easy to understand, and has to do with something that is becoming rare in professional sports—genuine affection. Alfredo has inspired that affection in Oakland, too.

—Susan Nelson

	1986 SEASON												THREE YEARS (84 – 86)										
	Ave.	OBP	SLG	AB	H	2B	3B	HR	RBI	BB	SO		Ave.	OBP	SLG	AB	H	2B	3B	HR	RBI	BB	SO
Totals	.285	.323	.364	594	169	23	6	4	51	35	52		.268	.292	.335	1626	436	49	15	10	145	59	135
Batting vs. Left and Right-handed Pitchers																							
Left	.254	.282	.298	205	52	7	1	0	6	8	24		.274	.291	.330	522	143	13	5	2	40	13	40
Right	.301	.344	.398	389	117	16	5	4	45	27	28		.265	.293	.338	1104	293	36	10	8	105	46	95
At Home and on the Road																							
Home	.281	.319	.331	302	85	10	1	1	26	17	26		.254	.277	.300	796	202	19	6	2	70	28	69
Road	.288	.328	.397	292	84	13	5	3	25	18	26		.282	.307	.369	830	234	30	9	8	75	31	66
Facing Groundball Pitchers and Flyball Pitchers																							
Groundball	.292	.332	.352	264	77	9	2	1	31	18	17		.272	.300	.337	772	210	22	5	6	74	34	55
Flyball	.279	.316	.373	330	92	14	4	3	20	17	35		.265	.285	.334	854	226	27	10	4	71	25	80
Facing Finesse Pitchers and Power Pitchers																							
Finesse	.274	.307	.339	351	96	11	3	2	26	17	26		.250	.269	.303	936	234	24	7	4	70	27	65
Power	.300	.347	.399	243	73	12	3	2	25	18	26		.293	.323	.378	690	202	25	8	6	75	32	70
On Grass and on Turf																							
Grass	.282	.323	.358	497	140	19	5	3	45	30	44		.277	.305	.347	1182	327	39	10	8	118	51	102
Turf	.299	.327	.392	97	29	4	1	1	6	5	8		.245	.257	.304	444	109	10	5	2	27	8	33
During the Day and at Night																							
Day	.266	.296	.328	256	68	7	3	1	24	13	22		.266	.284	.337	605	161	16	9	3	68	20	48
Night	.299	.344	.391	338	101	16	3	3	27	22	30		.269	.297	.334	1021	275	33	6	7	77	39	87
By Month																							
April	.280	.341	.320	75	21	3	0	0	4	7	6		.259	.301	.308	224	58	8	0	1	16	14	16
May	.320	.346	.381	97	31	6	0	0	9	4	6		.283	.300	.357	258	73	9	2	2	38	8	23
June	.273	.330	.384	99	27	4	2	1	10	9	7		.293	.327	.382	280	82	8	4	3	28	14	22
July	.260	.308	.323	96	25	3	0	1	10	7	9		.229	.252	.298	262	60	6	3	2	24	9	20
August	.277	.296	.348	112	31	3	1	1	8	3	9		.255	.273	.302	298	76	7	2	1	19	8	25
Sept/Oct	.296	.325	.409	115	34	4	3	1	10	5	15		.286	.299	.359	304	87	11	4	1	20	6	29
Situational																							
Bases Empty	.284	.331	.376	348	99	17	3	3	3	22	34		.264	.297	.328	955	252	35	4	6	6	43	82
Leadoff	.321	.365	.423	156	50	8	1	2	2	11	11		.250	.289	.311	440	110	16	1	3	3	24	35
Not Leadoff	.255	.302	.339	192	49	9	2	1	1	11	18		.276	.304	.342	515	142	19	3	3	3	19	47
Runners On	.285	.313	.346	246	70	6	3	1	48	13	18		.274	.285	.346	671	184	14	11	4	139	16	53
First Base Only	.359	.377	.437	103	37	4	2	0	3	3	8		.295	.302	.372	285	84	8	4	2	9	3	25
Scoring Position	.231	.270	.280	143	33	2	1	1	45	10	10		.259	.273	.326	386	100	6	7	2	130	13	28
Late Innings, Close	.289	.327	.454	97	28	4	3	2	13	6	9		.230	.252	.302	265	61	5	4	2	26	9	25
RBI/Opportunities																							

	1986 SEASON			THREE YEARS (84 – 86)	
Scoring Position	43 / 193	(22%)		123 / 511	(24%)
Scoring Position, 2 Out	16 / 86	(19%)		44 / 229	(19%)
On Third, Less than 2 Out	22 / 41	(54%)		58 / 105	(55%)
RBI in close games / RBI Total	34 / 51	(67%)		94 / 145	(65%)

Kevin Gross
Philadelphia Phillies

Who led the Philadelphia Phillies in earned run average in 1986? Gross did. Who went through the season undefeated? It was Gross, again. Who had a 2-to-1 strikeout to walk ratio, the infallible sign of the true power pitcher? None other than Gross, of course. Who came into a game when the Phils were getting shellacked and calmly finished the contest without yielding a run, teaching those young hurlers a thing a two and bringing tears of joy to his manager's eyes? If you said Gross, you're beginning to get my drift. Yessir, Gross was a tower of strength on the Phillie mound staff last year.

The Gross I'm talking about, of course, is Greg Gross, the erstwhile pinch hitter, who came in at the end of a hopeless contest last year and showed his teammates that pitching really isn't so complicated after all. The other Gross, Kevin, didn't fare quite as well—his ERA was 4.02, while Greg's was a dazzling 0.00—but Kevin did some pretty fair work himself last year. Throughout the season, the Phillies struggled with their starting mound corps. They began the year hoping that Lefty Carlton had some decent work left in him (he didn't), that Charles Hudson could turn his career around (he couldn't) and that the staff could avoid injuries (it couldn't; Shane Rawley was lost for the year in midseason). Eventually the starting staff had to be reworked, with Bruce Ruffin recalled from the minors and Don Carman shifted from the bullpen. In the midst of all that chaos, Kevin Gross was a steadying force, hurling 241 innings and never missing a turn all season. While his work was hardly brilliant (12–12 for the year), it was consistent throughout the year, and gave the starting corps a little stability, at least.

One tendency Kevin has shown in his three full seasons with the Phils has been a large grass-turf differential. In '84 his ERA was 3.91 on turf, 4.97 on grass, in '85 it was 2.71 turf, 5.66 grass, and last year 3.59 turf-5.11 grass. It would figure that he'd be more effective in Veterans' Stadium than on the road, and he is, but Kevin has actually pitched much better on road turf (3.09 ERA for '84-'86) than at the Vet (3.55). I'm not exactly sure why this is; of course not all turf surfaces are alike, and perhaps he's better on some fields than on others. In '86 Gross was very effective against Houston (2.00 ERA) and Pittsburgh (1.95), for whatever that's worth.

—Don Zminda

1986: Finesse, Flyball **1985: Power, Flyball** **1984: Power, Groundball**

	G	IP	H	BB	SO	SB	CS	W	L	S	ERA		G	IP	H	BB	SO	SB	CS	W	L	S	ERA
	1986 SEASON												**THREE YEARS (84 – 86)**											
Totals	37	241.2	240	94	154	30	13	12	12	0	4.02		119	576.1	574	219	389	72	26	35	30	1	3.83
At Home and on the Road																							
Home	20	134.0	128	47	99	11	8	7	7	0	3.56		62	301.2	293	103	227	32	13	20	15	0	3.55
Road	17	107.2	112	47	55	19	5	5	5	0	4.60		57	274.2	281	116	162	40	13	15	15	1	4.13
During the Day and at Night																							
Day	14	92.1	82	40	64	14	8	4	5	0	4.00		46	217.1	210	86	156	27	13	13	13	1	4.18
Night	23	149.1	158	54	90	16	5	8	7	0	4.04		73	359.0	364	133	233	45	13	22	17	0	3.61
On Grass and on Turf																							
Grass	10	68.2	73	30	36	10	3	3	3	0	5.11		30	143.1	169	63	95	17	7	8	10	0	5.27
Turf	27	173.0	167	64	118	20	10	9	9	0	3.59		89	433.0	405	156	294	55	19	27	20	1	3.35
By Month																							
April	5	29.1	33	14	12	2	2	1	3	0	4.30		18	57.2	52	21	37	5	3	3	5	0	3.28
May	6	41.2	42	14	19	5	2	3	2	0	4.32		22	85.1	93	28	53	9	4	5	6	0	4.01
June	6	41.0	40	19	29	8	4	2	0	0	4.39		18	115.1	114	37	79	17	5	8	3	0	3.36
July	6	36.2	34	9	17	3	3	0	3	0	3.44		19	109.1	108	41	54	12	6	6	7	0	4.12
August	7	52.1	50	21	45	10	1	3	2	0	3.27		20	102.0	105	45	79	13	6	8	3	0	3.71
Sept/Oct	7	40.2	41	17	32	2	1	3	2	0	4.65		22	106.2	102	47	87	16	2	5	6	1	4.30

vs. Opponent Batters

	Ave.	OBP	SLG	AB	H	2B	3B	HR	RBI	BB	SO		Ave.	OBP	SLG	AB	H	2B	3B	HR	RBI	BB	SO
	1986 SEASON												**THREE YEARS (84 – 86)**											
Totals	.260	.332	.417	923	240	41	10	28	102	94	154		.261	.332	.390	2200	574	89	27	47	238	219	389
Pitching vs. Left and Right-handed Batters																							
Left	.274	.364	.450	525	144	26	9	16	59	70	82		.263	.349	.405	1204	317	55	19	26	123	148	215
Right	.241	.288	.374	398	96	15	1	12	43	24	72		.258	.309	.371	996	257	34	8	21	115	71	174
Situational																							
Bases Empty	.257	.328	.445	533	137	27	5	21	21	52	85		.258	.326	.406	1262	326	53	14	35	35	115	227
Leadoff	.259	.335	.478	228	59	11	0	13	13	24	34		.248	.316	.416	548	136	23	6	19	19	48	91
Not Leadoff	.256	.322	.420	305	78	16	5	8	8	28	51		.266	.334	.398	714	190	30	8	16	16	67	136
Runners On	.264	.339	.379	390	103	14	5	7	81	42	69		.264	.339	.369	938	248	36	13	12	203	104	162
First Base Only	.258	.341	.390	159	41	6	3	3	9	18	22		.251	.319	.359	382	96	16	5	5	20	35	54
Scoring Position	.268	.337	.372	231	62	8	2	4	72	24	47		.273	.352	.376	556	152	20	8	7	183	69	108
Late Innings, Close	.264	.333	.377	106	28	4	1	2	11	9	18		.309	.387	.410	249	77	11	4	2	27	29	40

RBI/Opportunities

Scoring Position	63 / 298	(21%)		165 / 753	(22%)
Scoring Position, 2 Out	32 / 156	(21%)		65 / 366	(18%)
On Third, Less than 2 Out	18 / 39	(46%)		65 / 124	(52%)
RBI in close games / RBI Total	79 / 102	(77%)		170 / 238	(71%)

Ron Guidry
New York Yankees

People who write Ron Guidry off based on his 1986 may be making a serious mistake. He may well be on the downside of an excellent career, but his 1986 record doesn't give a true picture of how he pitched. Guidry had two problems in 1986—he got very little support from the Yankee offense and he just couldn't put away opponents late in the game. Toss in the fact that he was hurt by the new dimensions of his park and you wind up with a disastrous year.

In 1985, the Yankees scored 5.24 runs per nine innings; when Guidry pitched, that figure jumped to 5.94. He was the best supported regular starter on the best offense in baseball; not surprisingly, he posted a 22–6 record. In 1986, New York scored 4.97 runs per nine innings—when the Gid pitched, they scored only 3.79. When any pitcher gets over two runs less a game to work with than he did the year before, you expect him to win less often; if his ERA goes up 71 points at the same time, it's easy to see that he won't win at all.

Another way to look at it is to consider the number of runs that New York scored in Guidry's 30 starts: 7 runs once, 5 runs four times, 4 runs three times, 3 runs nine times, 2 runs four times, 1 seven times and none twice—he had less than four runs scored for him 73% of the time. Given that, 9–12 looks almost impressive.

Guidry's other problem (which he had some control over) was getting the key hitters out late in the game. In five of his 12 losses, he allowed the winning run in the last three innings; he allowed four homers in the late innings of close games (compared to only one in 1985). But that isn't surprising, I suppose—virtually every game he started was a close game.

It would have helped if Guidry had been able to benefit from Dave Righetti's record year, but it usually wasn't possible. Continual injuries to the rotation starters meant that some people with questionable talent were starting games and getting bombed by the fifth inning—the bullpen was always exhausted by the time it was Guidry's turn to start. Lou Piniella stayed with Ron as long as possible, hoping that his workhorse could gut his way through the tight squeezes and give the bullpen a day off without taking a loss. Unfortunately for them both, it rarely worked out that way.

—Craig Christmann

1986: Finesse, Flyball **1985: Finesse, Flyball** **1984: Finesse, Flyball**

	G	IP	H	BB	SO	SB	CS	W	L	S	ERA		G	IP	H	BB	SO	SB	CS	W	L	S	ERA
		1986 SEASON												**THREE YEARS (84 – 86)**									
Totals	30	192.1	202	38	140	18	6	9	12	0	3.98		93	647.0	668	124	410	37	26	41	29	0	3.85
At Home and on the Road																							
Home	19	121.0	137	22	84	8	4	6	8	0	4.39		50	359.2	367	56	235	18	19	27	12	0	3.38
Road	11	71.1	65	16	56	10	2	3	4	0	3.28		43	287.1	301	68	175	19	7	14	17	0	4.45
During the Day and at Night																							
Day	12	79.0	69	18	61	5	4	5	3	0	3.19		31	216.1	200	49	142	13	9	17	8	0	3.33
Night	18	113.1	133	20	79	13	2	4	9	0	4.53		62	430.2	468	75	268	24	17	24	21	0	4.12
On Grass and on Turf																							
Grass	26	169.2	179	34	127	18	5	8	11	0	3.93		82	578.1	599	110	375	36	25	37	25	0	3.72
Turf	4	22.2	23	4	13	0	1	1	1	0	4.37		11	68.2	69	14	35	1	1	4	4	0	4.98
By Month																							
April	5	33.0	35	5	21	3	1	3	0	0	2.45		15	106.0	103	24	65	7	5	5	5	0	3.48
May	6	42.1	40	9	40	7	1	1	4	0	4.25		18	128.0	119	23	80	11	6	7	6	0	3.59
June	5	24.1	36	9	12	6	0	0	3	0	5.92		17	114.2	131	20	68	8	2	7	5	0	4.00
July	2	12.0	13	1	12	0	0	1	1	0	3.00		13	95.0	94	20	51	4	4	8	4	0	3.79
August	6	37.1	40	7	32	0	2	1	2	0	5.06		14	97.1	104	15	76	4	3	5	4	0	3.70
Sept/Oct	6	43.1	38	7	23	2	2	3	2	0	3.12		16	106.0	117	22	70	3	6	9	5	0	4.58

	Ave.	OBP	SLG	AB	H	2B	3B	HR	RBI	BB	SO		Ave.	OBP	SLG	AB	H	2B	3B	HR	RBI	BB	SO
			vs. Opponent Batters																				
		1986 SEASON												**THREE YEARS (84 – 86)**									
Totals	.265	.300	.424	761	202	27	5	28	84	38	140		.265	.298	.421	2518	668	112	20	80	268	124	410
Pitching vs. Left and Right-handed Batters																							
Left	.248	.290	.394	137	34	4	2	4	15	8	32		.250	.276	.383	452	113	12	3	14	44	18	81
Right	.269	.302	.431	624	168	23	3	24	69	30	108		.269	.303	.429	2066	555	100	17	66	224	106	329
Situational																							
Bases Empty	.259	.292	.423	471	122	14	3	19	19	21	93		.265	.301	.417	1519	402	56	14	49	49	76	254
Leadoff	.276	.294	.423	196	54	6	1	7	7	5	33		.286	.319	.443	639	183	25	6	21	21	30	98
Not Leadoff	.247	.291	.422	275	68	8	2	12	12	16	60		.249	.287	.398	880	219	31	8	28	28	46	156
Runners On	.276	.312	.428	290	80	13	2	9	65	17	47		.266	.294	.427	999	266	56	6	31	219	48	156
First Base Only	.305	.331	.473	131	40	6	2	4	12	5	27		.287	.310	.450	478	137	30	3	14	38	15	70
Scoring Position	.252	.297	.390	159	40	7	0	5	53	12	20		.248	.281	.407	521	129	26	3	17	181	33	86
Late Innings, Close	.263	.317	.487	76	20	3	1	4	8	6	10		.307	.335	.452	261	80	13	2	7	30	12	39

	RBI/Opportunities				
Scoring Position	47 / 199	(24%)		155 / 658	(24%)
Scoring Position, 2 Out	22 / 101	(22%)		62 / 292	(21%)
On Third, Less than 2 Out	14 / 25	(56%)		57 / 106	(54%)
RBI in close games / RBI Total	66 / 84	(79%)		199 / 268	(74%)

Ozzie Guillen
Chicago White Sox

A year ago Ozzie Guillen was the toast of Chicago's South Side. After a season in which he batted .273 and committed only twelve errors, Guillen was named the American League's Rookie of the Year. Convinced that this was only the beginning, the White Sox traded Guillen's alternate, Scott Fletcher. Then they immodestly put Ozzie's portrait on the cover of their media guide, along with Hall of Famers Luke Appling and Luis Aparicio. The message was clear: unless Ozzie broke both his legs, it would be next stop, Cooperstown.

But, as they say, what a difference a year makes. To his credit, Ozzie greatly improved his hitting against left-handers in '86 (from .200 to .262) and continued to hit well with men in scoring position (.299 in '85, .315 in '86). For the most part, though, Guillen's 1986 campaign was one of regression. Ozzie's batting average declined, from .273 to .250, and his extra-base hit total fell from 31 to 25. In the clutch, Guillen's batting average of .229 was about half what it was in '85 (.388). And Guillen remained a leading practitioner of the Will Rogers School of Hitting: he never met a pitch he didn't like. In that area, at least, Oz was con-

sistent, drawing 12 walks in '85, 12 again in '86. At that rate he can break Babe Ruth's career walk record in only 170 more seasons.

All that would have been forgiven if Guillen had continued his steady work in the field. But here, too, he regressed. Ozzie doesn't have the strongest arm in the world, and despite what you may have heard, his range isn't the greatest, either. In '85 his game was based more on consistency than brilliance, and last year that consistency disappeared. The jump in errors, from 12 to 22, was well-noted, but it was more than that: there were way too many instances of throwing to the wrong base and lobbing the ball to first with a fast runner motoring down the line. And, of course, while all this was going on Scott Fletcher was hitting .300, fielding well and helping keep Texas in the pennant race.

I do want to be clear about this: I think Ozzie Guillen is a fine ballplayer, even if he continues playing like he did in '86. But let's not any ask artists to start working on his Hall of Fame plaque just yet.

—Don Zminda

	1986 SEASON											THREE YEARS (84 – 86)										
	Ave.	OBP	SLG	AB	H	2B	3B	HR	RBI	BB	SO	Ave.	OBP	SLG	AB	H	2B	3B	HR	RBI	BB	SO
Totals	.250	.265	.311	547	137	19	4	2	47	12	52	.261	.278	.333	1038	271	40	13	3	80	24	88
Batting vs. Left and Right-handed Pitchers																						
Left	.257	.283	.299	167	43	4	0	1	9	6	20	.241	.264	.280	257	62	5	1	1	19	7	30
Right	.247	.258	.316	380	94	15	4	1	38	6	32	.268	.282	.351	781	209	35	12	2	61	17	58
At Home and on the Road																						
Home	.254	.264	.305	272	69	9	1	1	23	5	23	.266	.280	.339	516	137	16	8	2	43	12	40
Road	.247	.267	.316	275	68	10	3	1	24	7	29	.257	.275	.328	522	134	24	5	1	37	12	48
Facing Groundball Pitchers and Flyball Pitchers																						
Groundball	.281	.299	.317	224	63	5	0	1	18	6	18	.265	.285	.322	479	127	12	6	1	36	13	34
Flyball	.229	.243	.307	323	74	14	4	1	29	6	34	.258	.271	.343	559	144	28	7	2	44	11	54
Facing Finesse Pitchers and Power Pitchers																						
Finesse	.244	.261	.316	320	78	13	2	2	23	7	27	.258	.273	.337	617	159	26	7	3	39	13	44
Power	.260	.272	.304	227	59	6	2	0	24	5	25	.266	.284	.328	421	112	14	6	0	41	11	44
On Grass and on Turf																						
Grass	.240	.258	.297	455	109	15	4	1	37	12	47	.263	.282	.339	880	231	35	13	2	68	24	77
Turf	.304	.301	.380	92	28	4	0	1	10	0	5	.253	.252	.304	158	40	5	0	1	12	0	11
During the Day and at Night																						
Day	.238	.247	.305	164	39	7	2	0	13	3	14	.257	.278	.329	292	75	13	4	0	23	9	23
Night	.256	.273	.313	383	98	12	2	2	34	9	38	.263	.277	.335	746	196	27	9	3	57	15	65
By Month																						
April	.245	.275	.327	49	12	2	1	0	6	2	1	.262	.292	.318	107	28	4	1	0	10	5	5
May	.219	.232	.292	96	21	2	1	1	7	2	9	.214	.230	.266	173	37	2	2	1	10	4	13
June	.271	.287	.376	85	23	4	1	1	15	2	9	.241	.259	.309	162	39	6	1	1	16	4	16
July	.272	.284	.320	103	28	5	0	0	6	3	8	.301	.319	.403	176	53	14	2	0	18	5	13
August	.235	.250	.255	98	23	2	0	0	5	1	11	.284	.298	.340	194	55	6	1	1	12	3	17
Sept/Oct	.259	.269	.310	116	30	4	1	0	8	2	14	.261	.270	.350	226	59	8	6	0	14	3	24
Situational																						
Bases Empty	.211	.232	.258	318	67	7	1	2	2	8	37	.239	.259	.309	615	147	20	7	3	3	16	62
Leadoff	.234	.246	.273	128	30	3	1	0	0	2	18	.240	.260	.287	258	62	8	2	0	0	7	32
Not Leadoff	.195	.223	.247	190	37	4	0	2	2	6	19	.238	.259	.325	357	85	12	5	3	3	9	30
Runners On	.306	.311	.384	229	70	12	3	0	45	4	15	.293	.304	.369	423	124	20	6	0	77	8	26
First Base Only	.293	.307	.354	99	29	6	0	0	0	2	8	.274	.282	.339	186	51	12	0	0	1	2	13
Scoring Position	.315	.314	.408	130	41	6	3	0	45	2	7	.308	.320	.392	237	73	8	6	0	76	6	13
Late Innings, Close	.236	.237	.292	89	21	0	1	1	11	1	10	.305	.323	.362	177	54	3	2	1	15	6	14
RBI/Opportunities																						
Scoring Position				43 / 165		(26%)									72 / 303		(24%)					
Scoring Position, 2 Out				21 / 75		(28%)									33 / 149		(22%)					
On Third, Less than 2 Out				16 / 34		(47%)									23 / 51		(45%)					
RBI in close games / RBI Total				36 / 47		(77%)									48 / 80		(60%)					

Bill Gullickson
Cincinnati Reds

During spring training last year, new arrivals John Denny and Bill Gullickson garnered much attention. Though recent performance dictated otherwise, many felt Denny was the better acquisition and would adapt well to Riverfront. These fans cited Gullickson's poor career road record (26–41, .388, versus .697 at home). Others regarded Denny and Gullickson as just more of Pete Rose's "veteran names."

When the Reds started slowly and Gullickson lost two of his first three starts, "wasted trade" was being muttered by the media. However, when the Reds became hot, Bill led the way, winning seven of nine in July and August, with a 1.51 ERA in 101 innings. He did slump in the stretch drive, but this should have been expected from past performance. Nevertheless, Gullickson left a distinctly positive impression on Cincinnati fans, as he combined with Browning to give the Reds two solid starters when the team was dependent on the bullpen.

It shouldn't have surprised people that Gullickson was capable of a smooth transition to Cincinnati—he's full of surprises. Gullickson has successfully made the transition from a power to a control pitcher, with modest strikeout totals and a strikeout-to-walk ratio normally at 2:1 or better.

In 1986, Bill reversed several of his career statistics. From 1983–85, his record on turf away from Montreal had been 6–13, but not only was he 9–6 at Riverfront Stadium in 1986, he also went 4–1 with a 1.68 ERA on enemy turf. His excellent 1985 day record (9–2, 2.00 ERA) proved to be an aberration.

It was Gullickson, not Denny or Soto, who gave the Reds 240 innings and 15 wins. The symmetry of Gullickson and Jay Tibbs was ironic. Bill went 14–12 with a 3.52 ERA in '85, and 15–12 with a 3.38 ERA in '86. Tibbs was 10–16, 3.92, for Cincinnati in '85, and 7–9, 3.97, for Montreal in '86. Gullickson is only 28 and should surpass 100 career wins in 1987. Some teams, such as the Pirates, seem to invite disaster by acquiring veteran players. Cincinnati continues to pick out key contributors Parker, Diaz, Bell, Gullickson with little loss to the organization.

—A. S. Nakamura

Gullickson has always seemed to be hot in August, and 1986 was no exception as he started seven games, won five, struck out 36 while walking only nine, and turned in an 0.79 ERA. His three-year stats confirm (12–4, 2.00) that this was not a fluke.

—Gary Gillette

1986: Finesse, Flyball · 1985: Finesse, Flyball · 1984: Finesse, Flyball

	1986 SEASON											THREE YEARS (84 – 86)										
	G	IP	H	BB	SO	SB	CS	W	L	S	ERA	G	IP	H	BB	SO	SB	CS	W	L	S	ERA
Totals	37	244.2	245	60	121	26	12	15	12	0	3.38	98	652.2	662	144	289	64	27	41	33	0	3.50
At Home and on the Road																						
Home	19	124.0	131	31	74	11	5	9	6	0	3.70	49	345.1	324	70	167	25	11	26	11	0	2.92
Road	18	120.2	114	29	47	15	7	6	6	0	3.06	49	307.1	338	74	122	39	16	15	22	0	4.16
During the Day and at Night																						
Day	12	67.0	83	16	35	11	4	5	6	0	5.24	33	207.1	218	48	82	26	9	16	8	0	3.69
Night	25	177.2	162	44	86	15	8	10	6	0	2.68	65	445.1	444	96	207	38	18	25	25	0	3.42
On Grass and on Turf																						
Grass	12	72.1	74	19	29	6	4	2	5	0	3.98	29	174.2	201	40	73	19	8	7	13	0	4.43
Turf	25	172.1	171	41	92	20	8	13	7	0	3.13	69	478.0	461	104	216	45	19	34	20	0	3.16
By Month																						
April	3	20.1	16	9	3	2	2	0	2	0	3.10	12	67.2	76	23	23	9	7	3	6	0	4.79
May	7	44.2	48	16	15	9	3	4	2	0	4.03	18	114.2	118	26	48	18	6	8	8	0	3.85
June	6	37.0	41	7	17	5	1	1	2	0	4.86	12	85.0	83	15	33	5	2	5	2	0	2.86
July	6	44.0	37	10	26	3	2	2	0	0	2.45	17	120.0	115	28	57	8	4	7	4	0	3.08
August	7	57.0	46	9	36	3	2	5	2	0	0.79	19	143.2	123	19	76	9	4	12	4	0	2.00
Sept/Oct	8	41.2	57	9	24	4	2	3	4	0	6.05	20	121.2	147	33	52	15	4	6	9	0	5.10

vs. Opponent Batters

	1986 SEASON											THREE YEARS (84 – 86)									
	Ave.	OBP	SLG	AB	H	2B	3B	HR	RBI	BB	SO	Ave.	OBP	SLG	AB	H	2B	3B	HR	RBI	BB	SO
Totals	.264	.306	.392	927	245	42	2	24	93	60	121	.266	.305	.399	2487	662	120	17	59	257	144	289
Pitching vs. Left and Right-handed Batters																						
Left	.274	.328	.398	485	133	26	2	10	32	40	56	.271	.317	.397	1296	351	62	12	26	114	93	129
Right	.253	.282	.385	442	112	16	0	14	61	20	65	.261	.290	.401	1191	311	58	5	33	143	51	160
Situational																						
Bases Empty	.262	.314	.409	562	147	28	2	17	17	42	75	.262	.299	.402	1541	403	76	9	41	41	79	190
Leadoff	.236	.296	.335	233	55	9	1	4	4	19	30	.274	.316	.413	639	175	30	4	17	17	37	67
Not Leadoff	.280	.327	.462	329	92	19	1	13	13	23	45	.253	.287	.395	902	228	46	5	24	24	42	123
Runners On	.268	.295	.364	365	98	14	0	7	76	18	46	.274	.313	.394	946	259	44	8	18	216	65	99
First Base Only	.301	.309	.434	173	52	8	0	5	14	2	21	.305	.329	.432	403	123	18	3	9	29	14	42
Scoring Position	.240	.284	.302	192	46	6	0	2	62	16	25	.250	.303	.366	543	136	26	5	9	187	51	57
Late Innings, Close	.192	.236	.232	99	19	4	0	0	2	6	10	.232	.284	.299	271	63	10	1	2	13	20	26

RBI/Opportunities

	1986 SEASON		THREE YEARS (84 – 86)	
Scoring Position	57 / 255	(22%)	164 / 707	(23%)
Scoring Position, 2 Out	18 / 117	(15%)	59 / 322	(18%)
On Third, Less than 2 Out	31 / 48	(65%)	76 / 129	(59%)
RBI in close games / RBI Total	67 / 93	(72%)	189 / 257	(74%)

Tony Gwynn
San Diego Padres

The San Diego State graduate had possibly his best year ever. His 211 hits were only two below his 1984 team record. His overall line was among the NL's leaders in these categories: Hits, 211 (ranking #1); runs, 107 (Tied for #1); BA, .329 (3); OBA, .381 (5); triples, 7 (T-5); doubles, 33 (T-9); stolen bases, 37 (T-9). His 107 runs broke Alan Wiggins 1984 team record of 106. His 37 stolen bases were a career best; on Sept. 20, against the Astros, Tony became only the 5th player in modern major-league history to steal five bases in a game. A model of consistency, Tony never went more than two games without a hit, while playing in 160 games. After a SB% of only .560 in 1985 (14 of 25, 2nd worst in the NL), he improved to .803 (37 of 46) this year, placing him among baseball's best. Oddly, he is a better grass than turf hitter, even though he is a career 2-to-1 ground-ball hitter. Tony has the third-highest career average on grass among active players with .329. Tony finished second to Glenn Wilson in outfield assists and tied a team record with three assists in a single game on August 27 in New York.

—J. Michael Duca

When Tony Gwynn was a rookie, he was compared to Rod Carew: a singles hitter who could steal a few bases but was of dubious defensive value. The word was that, if you could afford to keep him in the lineup, he might win a batting title some day.

1986 was a very interesting year for Tony. Remember the guy who looked so uncomfortable in right field as a rookie? He led all NL outfielders (yes, even the center fielders) in putouts last season with 337. Remember the rookie rightfielder with the worst arm this side of Mickey Rivers? He had 19 assists last year. Remember the Punch-and-Judy hitter? Tony fashioned a .467 slugging average, his isolated power increasing to .138 (from .063 in 1983).

It is ironic that an examination of Tony's past three years shows that his range numbers have remained consistent (and good) and he has made only four errors each year. Although his assists totals have increased, he was awarded a Gold Glove this year for essentially the same fielding stats as he was criticized for early in his career.

It's been a pleasure watching Tony Gwynn develop into such an excellent all-around ballplayer. With any luck, Gwynn will not suffer from Dave Winfield's affliction, where his talents go unnoticed in a media backwater.

—Jeff Held

	1986 SEASON											THREE YEARS (84 – 86)										
	Ave.	OBP	SLG	AB	H	2B	3B	HR	RBI	BB	SO	Ave.	OBP	SLG	AB	H	2B	3B	HR	RBI	BB	SO
Totals	.329	.381	.467	642	211	33	7	14	59	52	35	.332	.385	.440	1870	621	83	22	25	176	156	91
Batting vs. Left and Right-handed Pitchers																						
Left	.328	.384	.523	235	77	13	6	7	30	21	12	.310	.369	.416	642	199	22	8	10	62	57	38
Right	.329	.379	.435	407	134	20	1	7	29	31	23	.344	.393	.453	1228	422	61	14	15	114	99	53
At Home and on the Road																						
Home	.341	.392	.486	317	108	14	4	8	26	27	20	.347	.394	.467	936	325	42	14	14	86	70	49
Road	.317	.369	.449	325	103	19	3	6	33	25	15	.317	.376	.413	934	296	41	8	11	90	86	42
Facing Groundball Pitchers and Flyball Pitchers																						
Groundball	.282	.331	.422	341	96	19	4	7	28	24	10	.325	.375	.425	971	316	42	11	11	85	75	34
Flyball	.382	.435	.518	301	115	14	3	7	31	28	25	.339	.395	.456	899	305	41	11	14	91	81	57
Facing Finesse Pitchers and Power Pitchers																						
Finesse	.320	.361	.462	359	115	18	3	9	29	21	15	.334	.379	.445	1039	347	53	10	14	91	70	32
Power	.339	.404	.473	283	96	15	4	5	30	31	20	.330	.392	.434	831	274	30	12	11	85	86	59
On Grass and on Turf																						
Grass	.333	.381	.473	474	158	24	6	10	40	36	29	.335	.384	.444	1386	464	62	18	18	125	108	71
Turf	.315	.380	.452	168	53	9	1	4	19	16	6	.324	.386	.428	484	157	21	4	7	51	48	20
During the Day and at Night																						
Day	.315	.383	.453	203	64	12	2	4	23	23	12	.315	.379	.417	588	185	25	4	9	66	62	28
Night	.335	.379	.474	439	147	21	5	10	36	29	23	.340	.387	.451	1282	436	58	18	16	110	94	63
By Month																						
April	.322	.372	.506	87	28	7	0	3	7	7	12	.352	.406	.516	244	86	17	4	5	19	21	16
May	.361	.432	.454	97	35	1	1	2	6	12	5	.303	.385	.408	287	87	9	6	3	24	37	16
June	.349	.410	.523	109	38	7	3	2	14	11	2	.349	.398	.489	350	122	19	6	6	42	29	14
July	.307	.346	.495	101	31	5	1	4	17	6	5	.337	.366	.430	323	109	13	1	5	37	13	18
August	.341	.372	.439	123	42	6	0	2	10	6	4	.331	.376	.404	332	110	13	1	3	23	24	11
Sept/Oct	.296	.353	.408	125	37	7	2	1	5	10	7	.320	.380	.407	334	107	12	4	3	31	32	16
Situational																						
Bases Empty	.338	.377	.488	402	136	26	5	8	8	23	22	.320	.363	.434	1142	366	60	14	14	14	72	56
Leadoff	.373	.403	.486	142	53	11	1	1	1	7	3	.363	.395	.480	358	130	21	6	3	3	19	14
Not Leadoff	.319	.363	.488	260	83	15	4	7	7	16	19	.301	.348	.413	784	236	39	8	11	11	53	42
Runners On	.313	.386	.433	240	75	7	2	6	51	29	13	.350	.417	.449	728	255	23	8	11	162	84	35
First Base Only	.305	.355	.398	128	39	3	0	3	8	9	6	.360	.406	.457	361	130	11	3	6	21	25	13
Scoring Position	.321	.418	.473	112	36	4	2	3	43	20	7	.341	.427	.441	367	125	12	5	5	141	59	22
Late Innings, Close	.350	.411	.496	117	41	4	2	3	12	12	8	.340	.418	.459	318	108	12	4	6	40	43	20
RBI/Opportunities																						

RBI/Opportunities

	1986		THREE YEARS
Scoring Position	35 / 154	(23%)	128 / 495	(26%)
Scoring Position, 2 Out	13 / 72	(18%)	51 / 217	(24%)
On Third, Less than 2 Out	10 / 20	(50%)	41 / 77	(53%)
RBI in close games / RBI Total	35 / 59	(59%)	114 / 176	(65%)

Mel Hall
Cleveland Indians

Mel Hall's career suffered a severe blow in May of 1985, when a car that he was riding in was struck by another car. Mel suffered a fractured clavicle, broken pelvis and ruptured spleen, missed the rest of 1985 and many observers wondered whether he'd ever be able to fulfill his promise again. Mel silenced them by having his best year yet in 1986; at age 26, he still may become a topnotch player. He seems to put out best when he feels wanted and he knows that he is wanted in Cleveland.

The Chicago Cubs, in contrast, seemed only too glad to be rid of Mel. He tore apart AA and AAA ball in 1981–82, showing both power and speed and seeming destined for stardom, but didn't progress as quickly as he had hoped and made the mistake of saying so. He broke in well with the Cubs in 1983, finishing second in the Rookie of the Year voting, but acquired the dreaded "can't hit the lefties" label in the process. In 1984, Chicago traded for Bob Dernier and Gary Matthews—Mel became a platoon player with Keith Moreland. He again offered his opinion about management's acumen and was swiftly dispatched to Cleveland.

At home in Cleveland, Hall has steadily improved. He cut his strikeouts and flashed more power than he had shown before. He was on his way to an outstanding 1986 until the strain of recovering from the injuries began telling on him—his power tailed off until very late in the year.

Hall's defense is questionable. He has managed to embarrass himself in the field regularly and his arm is weak, so he plays mostly in left—he does, however, have the speed to be able to play anywhere in a pinch. As his fielding miscues do seem to affect his hitting, it is not unlikely that the Indians will move him to DH when Andre Thornton's career is over.

The only real question about Mel is his ability to hit left-handers; until that is resolved, nobody can say whether he will be a star or just a good platoon player. The evidence of his progress suggests that he could learn in time, but the Indians are not likely to allow him to do so unless they disperse some of their surplus outfield talent. It is evidence of Mel's growing maturity that, despite his distaste for platooning, he has managed to hold his tongue on the subject.

—William E. McMahon and Geoff Beckman

| | 1986 SEASON | | | | | | | | | | | THREE YEARS (84 – 86) | | | | | | | | | | |
	Ave.	OBP	SLG	AB	H	2B	3B	HR	RBI	BB	SO	Ave.	OBP	SLG	AB	H	2B	3B	HR	RBI	BB	SO
Totals	.296	.346	.493	442	131	29	2	18	77	33	65	.284	.346	.457	915	260	59	6	29	141	89	155
Batting vs. Left and Right-handed Pitchers																						
Left	.154	.241	.231	26	4	2	0	0	3	3	5	.138	.287	.185	65	9	3	0	0	4	14	18
Right	.305	.353	.510	416	127	27	2	18	74	30	60	.295	.351	.478	850	251	56	6	29	137	75	137
At Home and on the Road																						
Home	.277	.318	.466	206	57	13	1	8	33	12	25	.285	.340	.457	442	126	27	2	15	67	38	65
Road	.314	.369	.517	236	74	16	1	10	44	21	40	.283	.352	.457	473	134	32	4	14	74	51	90
Facing Groundball Pitchers and Flyball Pitchers																						
Groundball	.306	.350	.483	242	74	15	2	8	35	16	39	.290	.349	.433	455	132	28	2	11	57	43	84
Flyball	.285	.341	.505	200	57	14	0	10	42	17	26	.278	.344	.480	460	128	31	4	18	84	46	71
Facing Finesse Pitchers and Power Pitchers																						
Finesse	.295	.342	.498	261	77	20	1	11	43	18	31	.293	.341	.460	546	160	37	3	16	74	41	80
Power	.298	.352	.486	181	54	9	2	7	34	15	34	.271	.354	.453	369	100	22	3	13	67	48	75
On Grass and on Turf																						
Grass	.288	.329	.470	379	109	22	1	15	64	23	55	.282	.338	.451	751	212	46	3	25	115	65	126
Turf	.349	.438	.635	63	22	7	1	3	13	10	10	.293	.384	.482	164	48	13	3	4	26	24	29
During the Day and at Night																						
Day	.328	.397	.590	134	44	12	1	7	24	15	21	.334	.391	.557	341	114	33	2	13	57	33	49
Night	.282	.322	.451	308	87	17	1	11	53	18	44	.254	.320	.397	574	146	26	4	16	84	56	106
By Month																						
April	.171	.239	.390	41	7	3	0	2	8	4	10	.262	.316	.397	141	37	10	0	3	24	12	25
May	.286	.357	.571	63	18	7	1	3	8	6	9	.280	.342	.524	143	40	14	3	5	19	13	24
June	.378	.423	.667	90	34	5	0	7	23	7	12	.348	.422	.604	164	57	10	1	10	36	21	25
July	.253	.326	.458	83	21	2	0	5	21	9	15	.245	.315	.405	163	40	6	1	6	27	17	36
August	.318	.330	.388	85	27	4	1	0	9	2	10	.289	.346	.390	159	46	8	1	2	19	15	24
Sept/Oct	.300	.345	.438	80	24	8	0	1	8	5	9	.276	.327	.414	145	40	11	0	3	16	11	21
Situational																						
Bases Empty	.335	.378	.511	233	78	12	1	9	9	15	35	.287	.345	.450	491	141	26	3	16	16	41	89
Leadoff	.344	.371	.516	93	32	7	0	3	3	4	14	.309	.343	.479	194	60	17	2	4	4	10	33
Not Leadoff	.329	.382	.507	140	46	5	1	6	6	11	21	.273	.345	.431	297	81	9	1	12	12	31	56
Runners On	.254	.312	.474	209	53	17	1	9	68	18	30	.281	.348	.465	424	119	33	3	13	125	48	66
First Base Only	.222	.276	.444	81	18	6	0	4	10	5	13	.269	.330	.457	175	47	10	1	7	19	14	36
Scoring Position	.273	.333	.492	128	35	11	1	5	58	13	17	.289	.361	.470	249	72	23	2	6	106	34	30
Late Innings, Close	.317	.417	.517	60	19	6	0	2	12	11	5	.305	.372	.519	131	40	10	0	6	28	15	16
RBI/Opportunities																						
Scoring Position				47 / 157		(30%)									90 / 333		(27%)					
Scoring Position, 2 Out				24 / 79		(30%)									39 / 147		(27%)					
On Third, Less than 2 Out				13 / 24		(54%)									28 / 59		(47%)					
RBI in close games / RBI Total				45 / 77		(58%)									90 / 141		(64%)					

Greg Harris
Texas Rangers

Over the last three years Harris has allowed less than 7 hits per 9 innings and averaged 8.11 strikeouts. Those sound like the marks of a pitcher with an unhittable fastball. The truth is his fastball isn't even average, generally under 85 MPH. The pitch that made him a major league reliever is an outstanding curveball. When his curve is breaking practically straight down, he ties even left-handed batters in knots. Over the last three years lefty hitters have actually hit slightly lower against Harris than right-handed batters (.213 versus .217).

Harris set a new club record with 63 games finished and was third in the league with 73 appearances. What makes it odd is that he had an off-year. His ERA and hit average were not up to the standard of the past two seasons, and he allowed 12 homers compared to a combined total of 10 in 1983 and 1984. He also allowed 31% of his inherited runners to score compared to 27% for Dale Mohorcic and 24% for Mitch Williams.

Greg was the Rangers' closer in the first half because the team's other top relievers were both rookies. When Harris started off the second half by blowing his first five save situations, Valentine started giving the ball to the rookies in the tight situations. Harris went from 15 saves in the first half to 5 in the second. Williams' and Mohorcic's combined total went from 2 to 13.

Harris' appearance rate was a result of pitching coach Tom House's belief that with proper handling and preparation a reliever needs less rest. The whole Ranger bullpen was used a lot, they were the only AL team to top 300 appearances and they cleared it with plenty to spare (328). The truth is that Harris was only the third most frequently used Ranger reliever.

RELIEF APPEARANCES PER GAME ON 1985 TEXAS ROSTER

MOHORCIC	58 FOR 117	49.6%
WILLIAMS	80 FOR 162	49.4%
HARRIS	73 FOR 162	45.1%

—Craig Wright

1986: Power, Flyball   **1985: Power, Groundball**   **1984: Power, Flyball**

	1986 SEASON											THREE YEARS (84–86)										
	G	IP	H	BB	SO	SB	CS	W	L	S	ERA	G	IP	H	BB	SO	SB	CS	W	L	S	ERA
Totals	73	111.1	103	42	95	5	2	10	8	20	2.83	165	278.2	215	110	251	21	10	17	14	34	2.62
At Home and on the Road																						
Home	40	64.2	60	12	50	3	2	9	4	13	2.64	79	138.0	110	38	116	10	4	13	7	16	2.67
Road	33	46.2	43	30	45	2	0	1	4	7	3.09	86	140.2	105	72	135	11	6	4	7	18	2.56
During the Day and at Night																						
Day	17	34.0	28	20	32	0	0	1	1	6	2.65	43	76.2	59	42	73	3	3	2	2	9	2.82
Night	56	77.1	75	22	63	5	2	9	7	14	2.91	122	202.0	156	68	178	18	7	15	12	25	2.54
On Grass and on Turf																						
Grass	63	97.2	90	37	82	5	2	10	7	18	2.86	133	231.2	167	88	215	17	9	15	10	30	2.45
Turf	10	13.2	13	5	13	0	0	0	1	2	2.63	32	47.0	48	22	36	4	1	2	4	4	3.45
By Month																						
April	10	16.1	23	7	12	0	0	2	3	2	6.06	24	35.2	33	16	28	0	1	2	4	3	4.04
May	12	22.1	19	9	17	1	0	1	3	5	1.61	26	51.2	34	19	46	3	5	1	4	9	1.74
June	13	15.1	14	5	14	1	0	0	1	7	2.35	26	40.2	33	11	32	3	0	2	1	10	2.43
July	11	18.2	20	10	19	2	0	2	1	1	2.41	25	38.2	31	20	33	5	0	3	3	2	2.33
August	14	22.0	15	7	13	0	1	3	0	0	2.05	37	63.0	45	26	64	7	2	5	1	2	2.29
Sept/Oct	13	16.2	12	4	20	1	1	2	0	5	3.24	27	49.0	39	18	48	3	2	4	1	8	3.31

vs. Opponent Batters

	1986 SEASON											THREE YEARS (84–86)										
	Ave.	OBP	SLG	AB	H	2B	3B	HR	RBI	BB	SO	Ave.	OBP	SLG	AB	H	2B	3B	HR	RBI	BB	SO
Totals	.252	.319	.403	409	103	22	2	12	58	42	95	.215	.297	.339	998	215	43	7	22	111	110	251
Pitching vs. Left and Right-handed Batters																						
Left	.253	.337	.399	178	45	7	2	5	30	24	30	.212	.299	.338	471	100	14	6	11	54	56	107
Right	.251	.304	.407	231	58	15	0	7	28	18	65	.218	.295	.340	527	115	29	1	11	57	54	144
Situational																						
Bases Empty	.265	.330	.413	196	52	10	2	5	5	19	45	.210	.293	.313	544	114	22	5	8	8	57	146
Leadoff	.256	.322	.427	82	21	5	0	3	3	8	15	.167	.252	.240	221	37	7	0	3	3	23	52
Not Leadoff	.272	.336	.404	114	31	5	2	2	2	11	30	.238	.320	.362	323	77	15	5	5	5	34	94
Runners On	.239	.309	.394	213	51	12	0	7	53	23	50	.222	.301	.370	454	101	21	2	14	103	53	105
First Base Only	.265	.307	.422	83	22	4	0	3	11	4	18	.236	.287	.401	182	43	8	2	6	20	11	40
Scoring Position	.223	.310	.377	130	29	8	0	4	42	19	32	.213	.310	.349	272	58	13	0	8	83	42	65
Late Innings, Close	.227	.297	.384	242	55	12	1	8	41	25	61	.212	.291	.351	439	93	16	3	13	61	48	109

RBI/Opportunities

	1986 SEASON		THREE YEARS (84–86)	
Scoring Position	32 / 199	(16%)	68 / 409	(17%)
Scoring Position, 2 Out	16 / 104	(15%)	26 / 206	(13%)
On Third, Less than 2 Out	8 / 29	(28%)	23 / 62	(37%)
RBI in close games / RBI Total	42 / 58	(72%)	69 / 111	(62%)

Ron Hassey
Chicago White Sox

Since mid-season 1984, Ron Hassey has gone from the Indians to the Cubs to the Yankees to the White Sox to the Yankees to the White Sox again. My diagram of where he's headed next is a little muddled—is it the Yankees, the Mets or back to Cleveland again?—but one would understand if the Sox decided to let him stay put for awhile. Hassey was the star of the Chicago offense late last year, and a godsend after Greg Walker was injured. He hit .425 in Comiskey Park—I'll bet that hasn't happened since Shoeless Joe sold out.

Hassey looks like a lefthanded pull hitter, but in fact he's a line drive hitter who sprays the ball around: in his Sox at-bats last year, he hit the ball to the left side of the diamond 37% of the time. For much of his career he had decent offensive stats but was hampered by the Cleveland ballpark, turning in home/road differentials like .205/.288 (1982) and .296/.338 (1980). Hassey's stats improved once he left Cleveland. As a Yankee he couldn't take advantage of the short fence in right field—only three of his 13 homers in '85 came at home—but he loved the Stadium's wide-open spaces, hitting .330 there in 1985. For a hitter of his style, the new dimensions in Comiskey Park (home plate was moved back eight feet before the '86 season) were made to order. He probably won't approach .425 again (who will?), but he should definitely continue to hit well.

Of course, the Sox obtained Hassey as a catcher, and there's the rub: he reported to Chicago saying his knees were so sore that he couldn't squat down, which seemed to be news to both the Sox and Yankees. Eventually he did catch a handful of games, and didn't do badly—he even threw out three of six basestealers—but how much catching he can do in the future is an open question. Throughout his career Hassey has had the rep of being a decent receiver and handler of pitchers with an above-average arm: not great, but not a liability either. He caught Len Barker's perfect game back in '81. With the Sox apparently committed to giving Ron Karkovice a shot at the regular catching job, and with Pudge Fisk still around, Hassey may not be asked to catch very often, anyway. But if he continues to hit as he did in '86, he's sure to see plenty of action.

—Don Zminda

| | 1986 SEASON | | | | | | | | | | | THREE YEARS (84 – 86) | | | | | | | | | | |
	Ave.	OBP	SLG	AB	H	2B	3B	HR	RBI	BB	SO	Ave.	OBP	SLG	AB	H	2B	3B	HR	RBI	BB	SO
Totals	.323	.406	.481	341	110	25	1	9	49	46	27	.301	.378	.458	790	238	46	3	24	115	93	80
Batting vs. Left and Right-handed Pitchers																						
Left	.297	.361	.359	64	19	4	0	0	8	6	6	.237	.297	.272	169	40	6	0	0	13	14	23
Right	.329	.416	.509	277	91	21	1	9	41	40	21	.319	.399	.509	621	198	40	3	24	102	79	57
At Home and on the Road																						
Home	.329	.421	.509	167	55	13	1	5	26	26	13	.313	.404	.455	367	115	23	1	9	52	53	39
Road	.316	.390	.454	174	55	12	0	4	23	20	14	.291	.354	.461	423	123	23	2	15	63	40	41
Facing Groundball Pitchers and Flyball Pitchers																						
Groundball	.298	.383	.441	161	48	11	0	4	23	21	11	.283	.350	.406	399	113	22	0	9	52	40	46
Flyball	.344	.426	.517	180	62	14	1	5	26	25	16	.320	.405	.512	391	125	24	3	15	63	53	34
Facing Finesse Pitchers and Power Pitchers																						
Finesse	.315	.385	.477	197	62	14	0	6	29	20	11	.296	.361	.446	442	131	28	1	12	59	41	33
Power	.333	.433	.486	144	48	11	1	3	20	26	16	.307	.398	.474	348	107	18	2	12	56	52	47
On Grass and on Turf																						
Grass	.343	.424	.525	280	96	25	1	8	42	38	20	.317	.391	.489	660	209	44	2	22	103	77	66
Turf	.230	.319	.279	61	14	0	0	1	7	8	7	.223	.313	.300	130	29	2	1	2	12	16	14
During the Day and at Night																						
Day	.320	.408	.515	103	33	8	0	4	17	16	6	.303	.397	.470	264	80	17	0	9	41	41	21
Night	.324	.404	.466	238	77	17	1	5	32	30	21	.300	.368	.452	526	158	29	3	15	74	52	59
By Month																						
April	.214	.340	.357	42	9	3	0	1	7	7	5	.261	.344	.333	111	29	5	0	1	16	13	15
May	.194	.310	.278	36	7	0	0	1	4	6	6	.250	.322	.338	136	34	4	1	2	20	15	18
June	.462	.514	.754	65	30	10	0	3	13	7	4	.350	.419	.608	143	50	17	1	6	19	17	18
July	.216	.293	.294	51	11	1	0	1	5	5	1	.219	.303	.305	128	28	5	0	2	11	12	7
August	.356	.424	.559	59	21	6	0	2	10	7	7	.350	.404	.630	100	35	7	0	7	22	9	13
Sept/Oct	.364	.452	.477	88	32	5	1	1	10	14	4	.360	.448	.523	172	62	8	1	6	27	27	9
Situational																						
Bases Empty	.331	.428	.506	172	57	13	1	5	5	27	11	.308	.384	.496	413	127	27	3	15	15	47	37
Leadoff	.394	.500	.697	66	26	8	0	4	4	14	6	.341	.412	.629	167	57	13	1	11	11	20	16
Not Leadoff	.292	.380	.387	106	31	5	1	1	1	13	5	.285	.365	.407	246	70	14	2	4	4	27	21
Runners On	.314	.382	.456	169	53	12	0	4	44	19	16	.294	.371	.416	377	111	19	0	9	100	46	43
First Base Only	.329	.372	.479	73	24	2	0	3	7	5	6	.292	.352	.398	161	47	5	0	4	9	15	18
Scoring Position	.302	.389	.438	96	29	10	0	1	37	14	10	.296	.385	.431	216	64	14	0	5	91	31	25
Late Innings, Close	.404	.466	.538	52	21	4	0	1	10	6	4	.304	.377	.422	135	41	7	0	3	21	16	16
RBI/Opportunities																						

	1986 SEASON		THREE YEARS (84 – 86)	
Scoring Position	33 / 127	(26%)	80 / 288	(28%)
Scoring Position, 2 Out	16 / 71	(23%)	32 / 142	(23%)
On Third, Less than 2 Out	11 / 16	(69%)	26 / 45	(58%)
RBI in close games / RBI Total	26 / 49	(53%)	65 / 115	(57%)

Billy Hatcher
Houston Astros

It is still too early to tell whether the acquisition of Billy Hatcher by the Astros was a steal, or whether he is just another journeyman outfielder. The Cubs obviously thought the latter, for they traded Hatcher (plus pitcher Steve Engel) to the Astros for Jerry Mumphrey. True, Mumphrey has had far better credentials, but he is on the down side of his career. The evidence indicates that Hatcher would not have been an impact player in Wrigley Field, especially given his sub-.300 OBA. Hatcher's speed needs to be complemented by something else, e.g., more walks, or else he is not a good offensive player.

Where the Cubs evidently did make a mistake was in underestimating Hatcher's defensive abilities. I think that he could have done about as well as Bobby Dernier for them in this respect. The Cubs seem to have been convinced that he couldn't player center, for when Dernier went down, they tried several others (including a Double-A player) before turning to Hatcher. However, with Hatcher in center, the club's performance improved. In 1986, the division-champion Astros used Hatcher in center for most of the season, including the playoffs.

Hatcher proved to be well-suited for the Astros' running attack, hence he made a strong contribution to their success. In late July he took over center field, covering a lot of ground and making a number of outstanding catches. Initially, the Astros didn't do well, but with Hatcher in the leadoff sport from late August on, their record was 23–10, and they did well both at home and on the road, as well as against both left- and right-handed pitchers.

The stats suggest that Billy Hatcher is a mediocre ballplayer who may not last long in the majors. In this case, however, I think Hatcher is better than what it says on paper. He had just a few game-winning hits, but one was a home run to win an 18-inning game, another was a hit in the 9th, and he tied Game 6 of the NLCS with a home run in the 14th, as well as batting in a run in the abortive 16th-inning rally. All of this indicates that he is a competitor.

Hatcher is just getting started at age 26, so he probably won't show much more than what he already has. Thus, he seems destined to be a useful role-player, and his is fortunately in the right place for that.

—William E. McMahon

	1986 SEASON											THREE YEARS (84 – 86)									
	Ave.	OBP	SLG	AB	H	2B	3B	HR	RBI	BB	SO	Ave.	OBP	SLG	AB	H	2B	3B	HR	RBI	BB	SO
Totals	.258	.302	.356	419	108	15	4	6	36	22	52	.252	.297	.355	591	149	27	5	8	46	31	64
Batting vs. Left and Right-handed Pitchers																						
Left	.286	.326	.390	210	60	5	4	3	21	13	23	.275	.315	.367	251	69	6	4	3	22	15	24
Right	.230	.278	.321	209	48	10	0	3	15	9	29	.235	.284	.347	340	80	21	1	5	24	16	40
At Home and on the Road																						
Home	.257	.300	.339	218	56	8	2	2	16	10	23	.245	.285	.335	331	81	12	3	4	26	14	31
Road	.259	.304	.373	201	52	7	2	4	20	12	29	.262	.312	.381	260	68	15	2	4	20	17	33
Facing Groundball Pitchers and Flyball Pitchers																						
Groundball	.255	.305	.372	196	50	5	3	4	21	12	28	.246	.299	.356	289	71	11	3	5	25	18	34
Flyball	.260	.300	.341	223	58	10	1	2	15	10	24	.258	.295	.354	302	78	16	2	3	21	13	30
Facing Finesse Pitchers and Power Pitchers																						
Finesse	.262	.313	.352	244	64	8	1	4	18	14	25	.249	.299	.343	338	84	15	1	5	25	19	31
Power	.251	.286	.360	175	44	7	3	2	18	8	27	.257	.294	.372	253	65	12	4	3	21	12	33
On Grass and on Turf																						
Grass	.250	.311	.379	124	31	3	2	3	15	10	18	.237	.287	.357	241	57	8	3	5	25	15	26
Turf	.261	.298	.346	295	77	12	2	3	21	12	34	.263	.304	.354	350	92	19	2	3	21	16	38
During the Day and at Night																						
Day	.279	.319	.441	136	38	9	2	3	10	6	16	.265	.304	.410	268	71	18	3	5	20	11	24
Night	.247	.294	.314	283	70	6	2	3	26	16	36	.241	.291	.310	323	78	9	2	3	26	20	40
By Month																						
April	.222	.250	.222	27	6	0	0	0	0	1	8	.222	.250	.222	27	6	0	0	0	0	1	8
May	.310	.341	.381	42	13	3	0	0	3	2	4	.310	.341	.381	42	13	3	0	0	3	2	4
June	.239	.255	.326	92	22	3	1	1	7	2	14	.256	.280	.380	121	31	7	1	2	9	4	15
July	.231	.268	.308	52	12	4	0	0	3	1	6	.250	.288	.336	116	29	10	0	0	7	4	12
August	.322	.366	.460	87	28	4	1	2	11	6	8	.322	.371	.456	90	29	4	1	2	11	7	8
Sept/Oct	.227	.303	.345	119	27	1	2	3	12	10	12	.210	.276	.318	195	41	3	3	4	16	13	17
Situational																						
Bases Empty	.269	.317	.377	260	70	10	3	4	4	16	33	.270	.312	.393	374	101	20	4	6	6	21	43
Leadoff	.275	.331	.321	109	30	1	2	0	0	7	13	.267	.320	.352	165	44	7	2	1	1	11	22
Not Leadoff	.265	.306	.417	151	40	9	1	4	4	9	20	.273	.306	.426	209	57	13	2	5	5	10	21
Runners On	.239	.278	.321	159	38	5	1	2	32	6	19	.221	.271	.290	217	48	7	1	2	40	10	21
First Base Only	.261	.271	.333	69	18	2	0	1	2	1	9	.228	.260	.283	92	21	2	0	1	2	3	10
Scoring Position	.222	.283	.311	90	20	3	1	1	30	5	10	.216	.279	.296	125	27	5	1	1	38	7	11
Late Innings, Close	.254	.286	.388	67	17	3	0	2	12	3	10	.267	.308	.384	86	23	4	0	2	13	5	12

RBI/Opportunities

Scoring Position	27 / 126	(21%)		35 / 182	(19%)
Scoring Position, 2 Out	10 / 50	(20%)		14 / 75	(19%)
On Third, Less than 2 Out	10 / 21	(48%)		14 / 32	(44%)
RBI in close games / RBI Total	22 / 36	(61%)		27 / 46	(59%)

Andy Hawkins
San Diego Padres

One of baseball's least-understood truths is that differences in levels of physical ability are very slight at the major league level. Almost any player has the talent to star or they wouldn't be in the majors; the ability to develop that talent, learn the fine points of the game and continually adapt to the adjustments that your opponents make is what separates a great player from a mediocre one.

Is that too general? Let's be blunt: Anyone can get hot for a week. Anyone but Omar Moreno can get hot for a month. Some people even get hot for a year—but that doesn't make you a star. Jack Morris and Rich Dotson each won 20 games in 1983 because they were great physical talents. Morris worked diligently to improve himself and became a star. Dotson did nothing and became a trivia question. The only test of a player's star quality is "Does he always play well?"; if the answer is no, he's no star. He may be having a good year, but, until he has another one, take it with a grain of salt. If he can't repeat it, the theme of his career isn't "greatness is a fleeting thing" but "even a blind pig finds an acorn sometimes." But few people do, so they wonder why a jounreyman who has a fluke year does not repeat.

Case in point: Andy Hawkins. Hawkins has four seasons of major league experience. He has pitched 777.1 innings, allowed 772 hits, struck out 347 hitters, walked 287, his lifetime ERA is 3.75 and he is 43–37. That's a #4–5 starter—a .500 pitcher who fills a minor role on a team in a capable but undistinguished way. Had he not won his first 11 decisions in 1985, nobody would know anything about him.

Hawkins's 11–0 start, moreover, was totally unimpressive. He pitched 84 innings, allowed 83 hits, struck out 27 and walked 17. He had pitched like that before and he has done so since—the question isn't "Why has he gone 17–16 in the year and a half since his 11–0 start?" but "How did he get to 11–0 in the first place?" The most obvious answer is that he had help from his teammates and that, without it, he's a .500 pitcher (either that or he was pitching to a lot of right-handed hitters in night games in San Diego). Hawkins is a useful pitcher—saying anything more is hopelessly unrealistic.

—Geoff Beckman

1986: Finesse, Flyball											1985: Finesse, Flyball										1984: Power, Flyball

	1986 SEASON											**THREE YEARS (84 – 86)**									
	G	IP	H	BB	SO	SB	CS	W	L	S	ERA	G	IP	H	BB	SO	SB	CS	W	L	S	ERA
Totals	37	209.1	218	75	117	29	9	10	8	0	4.30	106	584.0	590	212	263	49	20	36	25	0	3.95
At Home and on the Road																						
Home	18	108.1	109	32	54	13	3	6	2	0	3.07	56	326.0	323	104	133	24	9	21	13	0	3.37
Road	19	101.0	109	43	63	16	6	4	6	0	5.61	50	258.0	267	108	130	25	11	15	12	0	4.67
During the Day and at Night																						
Day	16	97.1	97	38	59	10	5	6	3	0	4.81	36	207.2	217	85	98	17	7	13	8	0	4.64
Night	21	112.0	121	37	58	19	4	4	5	0	3.86	70	376.1	373	127	165	32	13	23	17	0	3.56
On Grass and on Turf																						
Grass	28	165.0	165	46	91	16	7	8	4	0	3.44	81	456.0	452	145	201	31	17	28	19	0	3.61
Turf	9	44.1	53	29	26	13	2	2	4	0	7.51	25	128.0	138	67	62	18	3	8	6	0	5.13
By Month																						
April	5	27.2	24	10	19	2	0	1	2	0	4.55	14	80.1	71	26	44	4	0	8	2	0	4.03
May	5	33.0	34	5	16	6	3	2	1	0	3.55	15	102.0	107	20	49	11	6	8	2	0	3.26
June	7	34.1	36	15	19	5	3	2	1	0	4.72	20	103.2	110	49	39	9	8	4	5	0	4.77
July	6	36.2	46	15	18	7	1	2	3	0	4.91	15	83.1	89	36	35	9	3	5	5	0	3.56
August	7	38.0	39	12	24	5	2	2	1	0	4.03	19	103.1	107	34	51	8	2	7	5	0	3.92
Sept/Oct	7	39.2	39	18	21	4	0	1	0	0	4.08	23	111.1	106	47	45	8	1	4	6	0	4.04

			vs. Opponent Batters																	
	1986 SEASON											**THREE YEARS (84 – 86)**									
	Ave.	OBP	SLG	AB	H	2B	3B	HR	RBI	BB	SO	Ave.	OBP	SLG	AB	H	2B	3B	HR	RBI	BB	SO
Totals	.268	.332	.411	812	218	38	3	24	101	75	117	.264	.328	.397	2232	590	104	13	55	253	212	263
Pitching vs. Left and Right-handed Batters																						
Left	.324	.385	.463	404	131	21	1	11	49	42	58	.292	.362	.438	1086	317	57	6	30	128	124	121
Right	.213	.278	.360	408	87	17	2	13	52	33	59	.238	.296	.357	1146	273	47	7	25	125	88	142
Situational																						
Bases Empty	.265	.319	.387	476	126	23	1	11	11	37	71	.266	.317	.403	1321	352	67	9	32	32	94	167
Leadoff	.280	.348	.395	200	56	6	1	5	5	21	31	.276	.327	.425	569	157	27	5	16	16	41	70
Not Leadoff	.254	.297	.380	276	70	17	0	6	6	16	40	.259	.310	.387	752	195	40	4	16	16	53	97
Runners On	.274	.349	.446	336	92	15	2	13	90	38	46	.261	.343	.386	911	238	37	4	23	221	118	96
First Base Only	.262	.305	.396	164	43	6	2	4	12	9	21	.267	.332	.395	390	104	18	4	8	28	36	35
Scoring Position	.285	.386	.494	172	49	9	0	9	78	29	25	.257	.351	.380	521	134	19	0	15	193	82	61
Late Innings, Close	.348	.412	.565	46	16	4	0	2	3	4	8	.283	.365	.487	191	54	8	2	9	19	25	17

RBI/Opportunities					
Scoring Position	62 / 247	(25%)	168 / 745	(23%)
Scoring Position, 2 Out	21 / 111	(19%)	62 / 319	(19%)
On Third, Less than 2 Out	27 / 43	(63%)	71 / 130	(55%)
RBI in close games / RBI Total	80 / 101	(79%)	194 / 253	(77%)

Von Hayes
Philadelphia Phillies

After a terribly disappointing season in 1985, Von Hayes really put it together last year, leading the National League in doubles with 46, tying for the league lead in runs scored with 107, and ranking among the top six in batting average, on-base percentage, hits, total bases and the late, lamented game-winning RBIs. Dick Cramer also notes that Von led the NL in runs produced with 186, adding the word "yecch!" in parentheses . . . I think he's referring to the stat, not Von's performance. Any way you look at it, Hayes had a great year, the kind of season the Phillies had in mind when they traded five players for him back in '82. I'd say that probably only Mike Schmidt had a better all-around season in the National League last year.

Curiously, Hayes turned in those big numbers while continuing to struggle against left-handed pitching. He's a guy you'd consider platooning if you had him in a table game league, since he's consistently hit for neither power nor average against southpaws. What's strange about this is that, early in his career, Hayes showed hardly any weakness at all against left-handers—in fact in '83, he hit lefties better, .304 to .259. Since then he's been consistently bad against lefties every year (.234, .229, .231) while his work against righties has ranged from decent to great (.307, .276, .340). If Hayes is developing as a hitter, it's because he seems to be learning to murder right-handers; he's showing no progress at all against lefties, though at least he's not getting any worse.

I don't know whether Von went on a weightlifting program after poor year in '85, but he seemed noticeably stronger last year. He had career highs in doubles and home runs, and also avoided the late-season fadeout which had plagued him in the past. In '84 he hit only .214 in September-October, in '85 .238, but last season he was a terror in September, hitting .317 with eight homers and a mighty .603 slugging average; that suggests he had more stamina than before. On the other hand, he got off to a very slow start, hitting only .183 in April; that reversed his '84-'85 pattern of starting out fast—he'd hit .314 in April of '84, .366 in '85. Maybe he just had to get used to swinging with all those new muscles.

—Don Zminda

	1986 SEASON											THREE YEARS (84 – 86)										
	Ave.	OBP	SLG	AB	H	2B	3B	HR	RBI	BB	SO	Ave.	OBP	SLG	AB	H	2B	3B	HR	RBI	BB	SO
Totals	.305	.379	.480	610	186	46	2	19	98	74	77	.287	.357	.443	1741	500	103	12	48	235	194	260
Batting vs. Left and Right-handed Pitchers																						
Left	.231	.301	.328	195	45	10	0	3	33	19	27	.231	.290	.333	463	107	18	1	9	62	38	87
Right	.340	.414	.552	415	141	36	2	16	65	55	50	.308	.381	.483	1278	393	85	11	39	173	156	173
At Home and on the Road																						
Home	.314	.393	.503	296	93	19	2	11	53	38	36	.298	.372	.490	838	250	44	9	33	132	99	117
Road	.296	.365	.459	314	93	27	0	8	45	36	41	.277	.343	.399	903	250	59	3	15	103	95	143
Facing Groundball Pitchers and Flyball Pitchers																						
Groundball	.293	.381	.427	300	88	20	1	6	50	42	41	.272	.343	.401	835	227	44	5	18	110	91	135
Flyball	.316	.377	.532	310	98	26	1	13	48	32	36	.301	.370	.481	906	273	59	7	30	125	103	125
Facing Finesse Pitchers and Power Pitchers																						
Finesse	.303	.387	.445	310	94	16	2	8	52	43	35	.286	.349	.432	937	268	49	8	24	129	93	130
Power	.307	.370	.517	300	92	30	0	11	46	31	42	.289	.366	.455	804	232	54	4	24	106	101	130
On Grass and on Turf																						
Grass	.347	.392	.541	170	59	15	0	6	27	14	23	.289	.348	.423	485	140	33	1	10	53	46	74
Turf	.289	.374	.457	440	127	31	2	13	71	60	54	.287	.361	.451	1256	360	70	11	38	182	148	186
During the Day and at Night																						
Day	.277	.363	.390	195	54	13	0	3	24	28	29	.275	.348	.430	561	154	33	3	16	74	66	92
Night	.318	.387	.523	415	132	33	2	16	74	46	48	.293	.362	.449	1180	346	70	9	32	161	128	168
By Month																						
April	.183	.275	.300	60	11	4	0	1	8	8	5	.293	.369	.431	188	55	11	3	3	28	24	23
May	.347	.434	.520	98	34	11	0	2	13	15	20	.304	.387	.449	263	80	20	0	6	32	36	51
June	.324	.405	.435	108	35	9	0	1	17	15	17	.273	.365	.398	264	72	15	0	6	41	39	45
July	.291	.365	.476	103	30	4	0	5	20	12	10	.271	.341	.488	299	81	15	4	14	49	33	44
August	.313	.365	.452	115	36	6	2	2	18	10	14	.327	.377	.486	358	117	24	3	9	47	30	54
Sept/Oct	.317	.386	.603	126	40	12	0	8	22	14	11	.257	.317	.398	369	95	18	2	10	38	32	43
Situational																						
Bases Empty	.282	.361	.475	337	95	30	1	11	11	42	51	.281	.344	.462	980	275	69	8	31	31	95	168
Leadoff	.368	.444	.669	133	49	14	1	8	8	18	13	.314	.374	.545	347	109	26	6	14	14	33	40
Not Leadoff	.225	.307	.348	204	46	16	0	3	3	24	38	.262	.328	.417	633	166	43	2	17	17	62	128
Runners On	.333	.400	.487	273	91	16	1	8	87	32	26	.296	.373	.418	761	225	34	4	17	204	99	92
First Base Only	.327	.358	.505	101	33	3	0	5	11	5	8	.299	.340	.430	291	87	11	0	9	24	18	33
Scoring Position	.337	.422	.477	172	58	13	1	3	76	27	18	.294	.391	.411	470	138	23	4	8	180	81	59
Late Innings, Close	.259	.311	.384	112	29	5	0	3	16	9	17	.268	.327	.397	310	83	13	0	9	38	29	51
RBI/Opportunities																						

	1986 SEASON		THREE YEARS (84 – 86)	
Scoring Position	68 / 233	(29%)	161 / 639	(25%)
Scoring Position, 2 Out	30 / 109	(28%)	58 / 272	(21%)
On Third, Less than 2 Out	22 / 40	(55%)	64 / 112	(57%)
RBI in close games / RBI Total	63 / 98	(64%)	155 / 235	(66%)

Rickey Henderson
New York Yankees

How good is Rickey Henderson? His 1986 batting and on-base averages are career lows and his slugging average dropped 50 points from 1985—despite all that, he was still one of the best hitters in baseball. He led the AL in Secondary Average (.495) again, set career highs in homers, RBIs and doubles (despite hitting .214 during July and August), stole 87 bases in 105 tries and led the league in that category for the seventh straight year.

Despite playing in New York and for a contender, many fans still have misconceptions about Rickey. First, they underestimate his power. The best way to measure a player's power is by subtracting his batting average from his slugging average (Bill James's Isolated Power). In 1986, Henderson's isolated power was .206—higher than Brett, Ripken, Winfield, Rice, Jackson, Murray or DeCinces. That isn't due to his speed, either. Given Rickey's wheels, he hasn't hit that many doubles and triples at any point in his career. It isn't the parks, either—his totals on the road are almost the same.

In fact, changing teams has actually hurt Rickey. In his two years with New York, he's hit worse at home than he did in Oakland. With Oakland, he hit .291 at home and .292 on the road, with almost identical power; with the Yankees, he has hit .267 at home and .306 on the road. His power isn't helped by playing in the Bronx, either. In 1985-6, he hit a total of 21 homers in 544 AB at home and 31 in 611 AB on the road. He's crushed the ball since he came to New York, but his home park isn't the reason why.

One reason why Rickey doesn't excel in New York is his poor rapport with the fans and media. Both feel that Rickey is arrogant and surly—much of that is silly, but not returning to the team after the strike ended didn't help. He gripes about not getting a Gold Glove, forgetting that, while his range is outstanding, his arm isn't. Finally, he took heat for New York's poor performance against lefties, which is only partly fair. He hit .234 against lefties in 1986 and his power was down, but he drew more walks and he's always hit them well in the past.

1986 was the second time in Rickey's career that his BA has dropped 50 points. The last time (when he fell from .314 in 1981 to .263 in 1982), he rebounded to hit .292—it is very likely that 1987 will be another highlight in a brilliant career.

—Marco Bresba, Craig Christmann and Darren Peterson

	1986 SEASON											THREE YEARS (84 – 86)										
	Ave.	OBP	SLG	AB	H	2B	3B	HR	RBI	BB	SO	Ave.	OBP	SLG	AB	H	2B	3B	HR	RBI	BB	SO
Totals	.263	.358	.469	608	160	31	5	28	74	89	81	.289	.391	.481	1657	479	86	14	68	204	274	227
Batting vs. Left and Right-handed Pitchers																						
Left	.234	.370	.443	192	45	10	3	8	18	42	27	.293	.412	.519	557	163	35	5	27	61	115	80
Right	.276	.352	.481	416	115	21	2	20	56	47	54	.287	.380	.462	1100	316	51	9	41	143	159	147
At Home and on the Road																						
Home	.235	.332	.440	298	70	16	3	13	33	43	38	.272	.382	.448	772	210	40	6	28	85	135	107
Road	.290	.383	.497	310	90	15	2	15	41	46	43	.304	.399	.510	885	269	46	8	40	119	139	120
Facing Groundball Pitchers and Flyball Pitchers																						
Groundball	.285	.373	.472	284	81	17	3	10	33	38	33	.299	.395	.487	835	250	41	7	34	112	127	114
Flyball	.244	.345	.466	324	79	14	2	18	41	51	48	.279	.387	.474	822	229	45	7	34	92	147	113
Facing Finesse Pitchers and Power Pitchers																						
Finesse	.255	.340	.434	364	93	21	1	14	39	46	38	.281	.369	.448	977	275	52	3	35	103	132	117
Power	.275	.384	.520	244	67	10	4	14	35	43	43	.300	.421	.528	680	204	34	11	33	101	142	110
On Grass and on Turf																						
Grass	.253	.344	.433	510	129	24	4	20	59	70	68	.284	.388	.467	1399	398	72	11	54	170	232	190
Turf	.316	.427	.653	98	31	7	1	8	15	19	13	.314	.411	.554	258	81	14	3	14	34	42	37
During the Day and at Night																						
Day	.237	.347	.426	190	45	9	0	9	24	31	34	.274	.392	.441	503	138	26	2	18	56	97	75
Night	.275	.363	.488	418	115	22	5	19	50	58	47	.295	.390	.498	1154	341	60	12	50	148	177	152
By Month																						
April	.263	.379	.412	80	21	4	1	2	11	15	14	.249	.345	.383	201	50	7	1	6	26	28	31
May	.267	.331	.517	116	31	6	1	7	16	11	18	.294	.397	.486	282	83	16	4	10	34	45	43
June	.328	.414	.569	116	38	10	0	6	17	16	15	.364	.437	.595	341	124	22	3	17	50	45	43
July	.233	.380	.430	86	20	6	1	3	12	21	10	.295	.417	.515	241	71	18	1	11	34	51	25
August	.200	.276	.409	110	22	3	1	6	12	11	13	.248	.334	.431	290	72	10	2	13	34	38	41
Sept/Oct	.280	.374	.440	100	28	2	1	4	6	15	11	.262	.396	.434	302	79	13	3	11	26	67	44
Situational																						
Bases Empty	.272	.369	.482	394	107	17	3	20	20	59	58	.283	.389	.483	1080	306	62	11	44	44	177	158
Leadoff	.271	.365	.512	258	70	13	2	15	15	36	33	.275	.383	.488	690	190	39	9	30	30	115	98
Not Leadoff	.272	.377	.426	136	37	4	1	5	5	23	25	.297	.400	.474	390	116	23	2	14	14	62	60
Runners On	.248	.337	.444	214	53	14	2	8	54	30	23	.300	.395	.477	577	173	24	3	24	160	97	69
First Base Only	.309	.371	.556	81	25	7	2	3	11	8	9	.371	.451	.594	224	83	13	2	11	32	33	19
Scoring Position	.211	.318	.376	133	28	7	0	5	43	22	14	.255	.361	.402	353	90	11	1	13	128	64	50
Late Innings, Close	.352	.442	.705	88	31	8	1	7	22	14	7	.327	.421	.546	251	82	13	3	12	39	42	29
RBI/Opportunities																						
Scoring Position				36 / 188		(19%)									109 / 509		(21%)					
Scoring Position, 2 Out				12 / 85		(14%)									42 / 243		(17%)					
On Third, Less than 2 Out				12 / 31		(39%)									39 / 83		(47%)					
RBI in close games / RBI Total				47 / 74		(64%)									124 / 204		(61%)					

Tom Henke
Toronto Blue Jays

Toronto owes Texas a great deal for allowing them to spirit Tom Henke away in the 1984 Free Agent Draft. Henke had always been a power pitcher, but never had effective enough control to pitch in short relief. When Toronto got Tom, they ironed out some mechanical flaws in his delivery and he began throwing strikes, strikes and more strikes. After blistering AAA for three months in 1985, Henke was called to Toronto and has been the answer to a prayer ever since.

Henke's success hinges on his ability to throw nothing but strikes. In 1985, he threw 546 pitches—384 (70.3%) were strikes. How impressive is that number? Put it this way—according to Chuck Waseleski, Roger Clemens threw only 65.8% of his pitches for strikes in 1986. Prorated to 546 pitches, that is 25 fewer strikes. Being ahead in the count 25 times more than a Cy Young Award winner is a tremendous advantage—it makes a pitcher virtually unhittable. How much of an advantage? In 1986, Henke threw only 66.7% of his pitches for strikes—his ERA rose from 2.03 to 3.35.

How hard does Henke throw? The best way to measure it is to compare the number of pitches that opposing batters swung at to the number of times that they missed. In 1985, opposing hitters swung at 308 Henke deliveries and missed 92 times—29.9% of the time. In 1986, they swung 791 times at Tom's combination plate of good ol' country fastball and nasty little forkball and missed 286 times—36.2%. Is that Cy Young-level pitching? It's 10% better. In 1986, AL hitters swung at 1,939 Roger Clemens specials and missed 489 times—only 26.6% of the time. Clemens is a great pitcher; Henke is better than great.

Tom is particularly tough on right-handed hitters (.156 BA in 1986; .195 over the past three years). That's especially impressive if you remember that he had a tender elbow this year and shied away from using his sidearm delivery when he had two strikes on the batter. His one drawback is that he's a big man with the typical inability to field his position and a poor move to first (runners stole 10 bases in 11 tries in 1986). But it's a small price to pay, and he does compensate for it by being especially tough with men in scoring position—opposing hitters slugged .271 in those situations. As long as Henke's heat is on, Blue Jay starters and fans need never worry about being left out in the cold.

—David Driscoll

1986: Power, Flyball												1985: Power, Flyball											1984: Power, Flyball	
	1986 SEASON											**THREE YEARS (84 – 86)**												
	G	IP	H	BB	SO	SB	CS	W	L	S	ERA		G	IP	H	BB	SO	SB	CS	W	L	S	ERA
Totals	63	91.1	63	32	118	10	1	9	5	27	3.35		116	159.2	128	60	185	12	4	13	9	42	3.55
At Home and on the Road																							
Home	33	42.2	28	12	46	8	0	5	2	12	3.16		61	77.2	64	26	75	9	2	6	4	19	3.36
Road	30	48.2	35	20	72	2	1	4	3	15	3.51		55	82.0	64	34	110	3	2	7	5	23	3.73
During the Day and at Night																							
Day	22	30.0	28	12	32	7	0	6	2	5	5.10		36	50.0	47	21	52	8	2	7	4	6	4.14
Night	41	61.1	35	20	86	3	1	3	3	22	2.49		80	109.2	81	39	133	4	2	6	5	36	3.28
On Grass and on Turf																							
Grass	25	37.0	27	11	54	2	0	3	1	14	3.16		57	76.1	63	31	90	4	2	6	2	20	3.42
Turf	38	54.1	36	21	64	8	1	6	4	13	3.48		59	83.1	65	29	95	8	2	7	7	22	3.67
By Month																							
April	6	7.0	8	4	13	1	0	2	1	3	11.57		11	11.2	10	12	14	1	1	2	1	3	10.03
May	11	17.1	12	9	27	2	0	2	2	1	4.15		11	17.1	12	9	27	2	0	2	2	1	4.15
June	11	15.2	12	5	14	1	0	2	0	6	1.15		13	19.0	16	8	19	1	0	2	0	6	2.37
July	11	14.2	6	8	19	4	1	1	0	5	2.45		14	20.2	9	10	23	4	1	3	0	5	2.18
August	10	17.1	13	2	20	0	0	1	0	4	2.08		28	43.1	34	8	48	0	1	3	1	12	2.08
Sept/Oct	14	19.1	12	4	25	2	0	1	2	8	3.26		39	47.2	47	13	54	4	1	1	5	15	4.15

vs. Opponent Batters																					
	1986 SEASON											**THREE YEARS (84 – 86)**									
	Ave.	OBP	SLG	AB	H	2B	3B	HR	RBI	BB	SO		Ave.	OBP	SLG	AB	H	2B	3B	HR	RBI	BB	SO
Totals	.191	.261	.286	329	63	13	0	6	42	32	118		.219	.288	.313	585	128	23	1	10	76	60	185
Pitching vs. Left and Right-handed Batters																							
Left	.220	.299	.322	177	39	6	0	4	23	20	62		.238	.319	.346	315	75	10	0	8	41	38	100
Right	.158	.216	.243	152	24	7	0	2	19	12	56		.196	.252	.274	270	53	13	1	2	35	22	85
Situational																							
Bases Empty	.164	.231	.251	171	28	6	0	3	3	14	67		.195	.257	.272	302	59	11	0	4	4	23	102
Leadoff	.123	.208	.185	65	8	1	0	1	1	6	24		.203	.277	.254	118	24	3	0	1	1	11	35
Not Leadoff	.189	.246	.292	106	20	5	0	2	2	8	43		.190	.244	.283	184	35	8	0	3	3	12	67
Runners On	.222	.291	.323	158	35	7	0	3	39	18	51		.244	.319	.357	283	69	12	1	6	72	37	83
First Base Only	.226	.262	.403	62	14	5	0	2	6	3	15		.250	.298	.422	116	29	8	0	4	11	8	29
Scoring Position	.219	.308	.271	96	21	2	0	1	33	15	36		.240	.332	.311	167	40	4	1	2	61	29	54
Late Innings, Close	.188	.272	.309	223	42	9	0	6	35	26	86		.215	.284	.323	368	79	13	0	9	53	38	127

RBI/Opportunities						
Scoring Position		30 / 145	(21%)		56 / 260	(22%)
Scoring Position, 2 Out		14 / 69	(20%)		26 / 125	(21%)
On Third, Less than 2 Out		15 / 32	(47%)		25 / 56	(45%)
RBI in close games / RBI Total		35 / 42	(83%)		55 / 76	(72%)

Keith Hernandez
New York Mets

Keith Hernandez has had some problems the past few years, but that doesn't seem to have affected his play. Talk about consistent: since 1984 Keith has batted .311, .309 and .310. He's hit 15, 10 and 13 home runs. He's knocked in 94, 91 and 83 runs. He's drawn 97, 77 and 94 walks. His runs created totals have been 108, 100 and 101. And he's won the Gold Glove each year, which is automatic by now: Keith has been a Gold Glover for nine straight seasons.

Despite his difficulty with drugs, Hernandez earns the respect of almost everyone around him. He's not a natural talent. He was a low draft pick, going in the 42nd round, and probably wasn't given much chance to make the majors after batting no higher than .260 for his first three minor league teams. Keith made it because he's intelligent, and because he worked hard. He learned when to pull, when to go the other way, when to lay off a borderline pitch. The defensive skills came more easily—his father was a great defensive first baseman in the minors—but polishing them required a lot of effort, effort that Hernandez was always willing to make. Eventually he became such an outstanding fielder that watching him changes one's expectations of a first baseman. It is a pleasant and smug feeling for a Met fan to visit another park and hear the home fans singing the praises of their first sacker for a play that Keith makes routinely. (No wonder we're arrogant.)

Along the way he developed great leadership skills. There's such an aura of professionalism about him that it seems to rub off on his teammates. It's no exaggeration to say that Keith's been the heart of every team he's played on; certainly his coming to New York heralded the turning point in Met fortunes. Before Gary Carter arrived in '85, Keith would often go to the mound to settle down a shaky young pitcher. Even now his leadership skills in that area are essential, as in the sixth game of the LCS against Houston. The pennant was at stake with the Astros threatening to come from behind with two outs in the sixteenth and Kevin Bass at bat. There was a conference on the mound and Keith reportedly told Carter, "If you call another fast ball, I'll punch you out." End of conference; Bass struck out on breaking balls to end the game. The Met turnaround was complete.

—J. Randolph Burnham and Bill Weydig

	1986 SEASON												THREE YEARS (84 – 86)									
	Ave.	OBP	SLG	AB	H	2B	3B	HR	RBI	BB	SO		Ave.	OBP	SLG	AB	H	2B	3B	HR	RBI	BB	SO
Totals	.310	.413	.446	551	171	34	1	13	83	94	69		.310	.402	.442	1694	525	99	5	38	268	268	217
Batting vs. Left and Right-handed Pitchers
Left	.312	.409	.422	218	68	12	0	4	26	32	31		.307	.379	.402	674	207	32	1	10	86	77	83
Right	.309	.415	.462	333	103	22	1	9	57	62	38		.312	.416	.468	1020	318	67	4	28	182	191	134
At Home and on the Road
Home	.310	.422	.431	239	74	9	1	6	36	46	31		.319	.415	.447	792	253	37	2	20	134	135	101
Road	.311	.405	.458	312	97	25	0	7	47	48	38		.302	.390	.437	902	272	62	3	18	134	133	116
Facing Groundball Pitchers and Flyball Pitchers
Groundball	.320	.412	.470	266	85	17	1	7	47	40	35		.321	.408	.442	822	264	45	3	16	132	121	99
Flyball	.302	.413	.425	285	86	17	0	6	36	54	34		.299	.397	.442	872	261	54	2	22	136	147	118
Facing Finesse Pitchers and Power Pitchers
Finesse	.346	.438	.516	318	110	22	1	10	53	52	33		.320	.401	.439	952	305	55	2	18	140	133	96
Power	.262	.379	.352	233	61	12	0	3	30	42	36		.296	.403	.445	742	220	44	3	20	128	135	121
On Grass and on Turf
Grass	.320	.422	.465	372	119	19	1	11	62	66	49		.315	.407	.449	1167	368	60	3	30	197	189	154
Turf	.291	.392	.408	179	52	15	0	2	21	28	20		.298	.390	.425	527	157	39	2	8	71	79	63
During the Day and at Night
Day	.354	.430	.517	209	74	11	1	7	38	25	25		.316	.396	.452	621	196	38	1	15	101	83	73
Night	.284	.402	.404	342	97	23	0	6	45	69	44		.307	.405	.435	1073	329	61	4	23	167	185	144
By Month
April	.303	.403	.394	66	20	6	0	0	7	9	4		.300	.387	.376	213	64	13	0	1	24	27	17
May	.363	.436	.520	102	37	7	0	3	17	14	11		.309	.394	.445	265	82	12	0	8	42	41	29
June	.227	.318	.309	97	22	2	0	2	9	13	15		.264	.351	.382	296	78	15	1	6	34	41	43
July	.250	.394	.420	88	22	4	1	3	9	20	10		.311	.436	.497	286	89	19	2	10	61	66	39
August	.368	.464	.544	114	42	11	0	3	26	22	16		.318	.407	.442	330	105	23	0	6	59	52	53
Sept/Oct	.333	.446	.452	84	28	4	0	2	15	16	13		.352	.428	.490	304	107	17	2	7	48	41	36
Situational
Bases Empty	.284	.379	.411	275	78	14	0	7	7	40	42		.294	.380	.398	921	271	44	2	16	16	124	133
Leadoff	.260	.330	.354	96	25	3	0	2	2	9	16		.314	.374	.409	318	100	16	1	4	4	29	38
Not Leadoff	.296	.403	.441	179	53	11	0	5	5	31	26		.284	.383	.393	603	171	28	1	12	12	95	95
Runners On	.337	.445	.482	276	93	20	1	6	76	54	27		.329	.426	.493	773	254	55	3	22	252	144	84
First Base Only	.393	.469	.518	112	44	11	0	1	8	15	11		.357	.411	.524	294	105	22	0	9	34	25	23
Scoring Position	.299	.430	.457	164	49	9	1	5	68	39	16		.311	.434	.474	479	149	33	3	13	218	119	61
Late Innings, Close	.283	.395	.424	99	28	5	0	3	16	18	11		.303	.409	.401	297	90	15	1	4	42	56	41
RBI/Opportunities
Scoring Position		59 / 234	(25%)											191 / 700	(27%)								
Scoring Position, 2 Out		14 / 85	(16%)											53 / 250	(21%)								
On Third, Less than 2 Out		24 / 48	(50%)											87 / 149	(58%)								
RBI in close games / RBI Total		64 / 83	(77%)											207 / 268	(77%)								

Willie Hernandez
Detroit Tigers

Before he was acquired in 1984, Willie Hernandez had pitched seven years in the NL, but never as the ace of the bullpen. Further, while he had had several good years, there was nothing in his background to indicate what he would do in 1984.

1985 was an up and down year for Hernandez. He saved only one less game than in '84, but he allowed 14 homers in 106.2 innings, an exceptionally high ratio. Nevertheless, combined with his very low runners-to-innings-pitched numbers, his gopher-ball tendencies could be lived with. When Hernandez got lit up for a 7.13 ERA in August, blowing several leads, the fans started to boo and hiss.

Everything got worse last year. Willie's hit and walk ratios deteriorated, his ERA went up, and his gopher ball problem got much worse. Sure, he still racked up the saves, but he was blowing too many leads. The jeering got worse, and Willie stopped being defiantly proud and started acting hurt and confused. After another terrible August, Sparky decided to demote Willie. The crowning insult was on August 29th in California, when he allowed a ninth-inning grand-slam home run by Dickie Schofield, capping an 8-run rally and giving the Angels a 13–12 win! Rookie Eric King had been turning in spectacular numbers, and the management started thinking about next year, so a bullpen-by-committee was established to save face for Hernandez. According to Anderson's typically fractured logic, Willie was still "numero uno", but he was now just "first among equals." Fat chance.

The truth of the matter is that the Tigers have lost confidence in their erstwhile ace. They project Eric King as the right-handed closer next year, and unless he flops, he will be the ace and Willie will be the left-handed gun and #2 man in the pen. Not a bad role: in fact, just what he was in the NL. However, when you are being paid $1,000,000-plus per year and you were sitting on top of the baseball world recently, you tend to view the slide downhill from a different perspective.

Willie Hernandez is still a good pitcher, but he is too proud to admit that he's not the best. Nevertheless, if he gets hot next year and King is struggling, he knows and expects that Sparky will make him the ace again. In the meantime, the Tigers would like to move Gibson to left and get a rightfielder with some power and a good arm. Does Philadelphia want Willie and Dave Bergman for Glenn Wilson?

—Gary Gillette

1986: Power, Flyball | **1985: Finesse, Flyball** | **1984: Power, Flyball**

	1986 SEASON											THREE YEARS (84 – 86)										
	G	IP	H	BB	SO	SB	CS	W	L	S	ERA	G	IP	H	BB	SO	SB	CS	W	L	S	ERA
Totals	64	88.2	87	21	77	7	3	8	7	24	3.55	218	335.2	265	71	265	16	8	25	20	87	2.60
At Home and on the Road																						
Home	29	43.0	42	12	39	6	1	6	3	9	3.77	109	167.1	129	37	141	13	4	15	9	40	2.58
Road	35	45.2	45	9	38	1	2	2	4	15	3.35	109	168.1	136	34	124	3	4	10	11	47	2.62
During the Day and at Night																						
Day	21	28.0	23	8	24	3	0	3	1	8	2.57	74	115.2	78	25	88	8	0	10	3	29	2.02
Night	43	60.2	64	13	53	4	3	5	6	16	4.01	144	220.0	187	46	177	8	8	15	17	58	2.90
On Grass and on Turf																						
Grass	55	78.0	76	19	65	6	3	7	5	22	3.35	187	288.2	237	65	234	15	6	19	18	78	2.74
Turf	9	10.2	11	2	12	1	0	1	2	2	5.06	31	47.0	28	6	31	1	2	6	2	9	1.72
By Month																						
April	9	11.1	16	1	12	0	0	1	1	5	5.56	29	41.0	42	10	36	1	0	4	1	11	4.17
May	11	15.2	15	5	18	2	1	1	1	2	2.30	37	61.0	40	11	51	3	2	3	2	14	1.48
June	15	22.1	24	4	17	1	1	1	1	8	2.82	42	73.1	59	16	57	3	2	4	3	20	2.09
July	12	17.1	13	3	10	0	0	4	2	4	2.08	36	58.0	42	11	43	1	1	7	3	16	1.86
August	9	13.1	12	5	12	2	1	0	1	2	6.75	40	58.1	55	14	45	4	2	4	8	14	4.78
Sept/Oct	8	8.2	7	3	8	2	0	1	1	3	3.12	34	44.0	27	9	33	4	1	3	3	12	1.64

vs. Opponent Batters

	1986 SEASON											THREE YEARS (84 – 86)									
	Ave.	OBP	SLG	AB	H	2B	3B	HR	RBI	BB	SO	Ave.	OBP	SLG	AB	H	2B	3B	HR	RBI	BB	SO
Totals	.251	.301	.413	346	87	17	0	13	49	21	77	.215	.261	.330	1233	265	40	3	32	134	71	265
Pitching vs. Left and Right-handed Batters																						
Left	.206	.238	.268	97	20	3	0	1	11	3	20	.181	.213	.225	342	62	9	0	2	27	11	72
Right	.269	.325	.470	249	67	14	0	12	38	18	57	.228	.279	.370	891	203	31	3	30	107	60	193
Situational																						
Bases Empty	.247	.300	.414	186	46	10	0	7	7	12	43	.211	.253	.342	705	149	22	2	22	22	35	152
Leadoff	.200	.233	.329	70	14	3	0	2	2	2	13	.209	.253	.330	273	57	10	1	7	7	15	54
Not Leadoff	.276	.339	.466	116	32	7	0	5	5	10	30	.213	.253	.350	432	92	12	1	15	15	20	98
Runners On	.256	.303	.412	160	41	7	0	6	42	9	34	.220	.272	.314	528	116	18	1	10	112	36	113
First Base Only	.261	.301	.449	69	18	4	0	3	7	3	11	.197	.230	.287	254	50	8	0	5	14	8	53
Scoring Position	.253	.304	.385	91	23	3	0	3	35	6	23	.241	.307	.339	274	66	10	1	5	98	28	60
Late Innings, Close	.265	.309	.447	219	58	10	0	10	39	14	49	.211	.255	.332	777	164	21	2	23	98	45	176

RBI/Opportunities

Scoring Position	30 / 130	(23%)	88 / 381	(23%)
Scoring Position, 2 Out	17 / 79	(22%)	41 / 206	(20%)
On Third, Less than 2 Out	10 / 16	(63%)	33 / 56	(59%)
RBI in close games / RBI Total	39 / 49	(80%)	98 / 134	(73%)

Tommy Herr
St. Louis Cardinals

Before Tom Herr had even completed his outstanding 1985 season, it seemed that radio and TV announcers were calling it a fluke and saying he would never have another one like it. It was almost like they didn't believe it was actually happening. But Herr's numbers in 1985 were not really out of context with his abilities. And despite what a quick glance at the stats might indicate, neither were his figures for 1986. There was one major difference between the Herr of '85 and the Herr of '86, and that was the first 40 games of each season. In April and May of '85 Herr hit .372, slugged .470 and drove in 39 runs, a remarkable start. For the same two months of '86 he went to the other extreme, hitting .166, slugging .219 and driving in only eleven runs, numbers as bad as the first were impressive. For the remainders of the two seasons Herr was basically the same player, hitting with a little more power in '85 and for a little better average in '86. His batting averages were almost the same (.275, .284), as were his slugging percentages (.396, .373), RBIs (62, 50), doubles (27, 25), triples (2, 4) walks (57, 53) and hits (119, 116; in all cases the 1985 figure is listed first). And these figures are probably the most representative of

Tommy Herr's abilities. He's certainly not as good as he was in early 1985, but it's just as certain that he's not as bad as he was in early 1986.

Herr hit 103 points higher against lefthanded pitching in 1986 than off righthanded hurlers. In 1982 he had a 93 point advantage against righthanders (.294–.201). In fact, '86 was the first poor season he's ever had agianst righthanded pitching. It was also his first time hitting .300 off southpaws, though he's come close a couple of times.

Herr batted .349 and slugged at a .512 clip against Houston in 1986. He led the Cardinals with 12 game-winning RBIs, with five of those coming in the first or second inning, five more in the sixth or seventh. Tommy's 75 strikeouts in '86 were a career high. He committed only nine errors in 150 starts at second base. He'd hit two homers in '83, four in '84, and eight in '85, but didn't quite make it to sixteen in '86—he went down to two again. A final note: in the first eight games following the birth of his second child in June, Herr was 16 for 31 with two game-winning RBIs.

—Russ Eagle

	1986 SEASON											THREE YEARS (84 – 86)										
	Ave.	OBP	SLG	AB	H	2B	3B	HR	RBI	BB	SO	Ave.	OBP	SLG	AB	H	2B	3B	HR	RBI	BB	SO
Totals	.252	.342	.331	559	141	30	4	2	61	73	75	.277	.353	.365	1713	475	91	9	14	220	202	186
Batting vs. Left and Right-handed Pitchers																						
Left	.315	.407	.402	219	69	14	1	1	22	31	24	.296	.361	.386	609	180	31	3	6	70	60	49
Right	.212	.299	.285	340	72	16	3	1	39	42	51	.267	.348	.354	1104	295	60	6	8	150	142	137
At Home and on the Road																						
Home	.260	.367	.322	273	71	10	2	1	38	44	36	.278	.356	.361	826	230	40	5	6	119	100	79
Road	.245	.315	.339	286	70	20	2	1	23	29	39	.276	.350	.370	887	245	51	4	8	101	102	107
Facing Groundball Pitchers and Flyball Pitchers																						
Groundball	.292	.373	.395	281	82	20	3	1	33	36	29	.306	.376	.389	839	257	50	5	3	116	93	72
Flyball	.212	.309	.266	278	59	10	1	1	28	37	46	.249	.331	.343	874	218	41	4	11	104	109	114
Facing Finesse Pitchers and Power Pitchers																						
Finesse	.270	.340	.362	318	86	17	3	2	28	30	33	.292	.354	.385	957	279	58	5	7	119	90	77
Power	.228	.344	.290	241	55	13	1	0	33	43	42	.259	.352	.341	756	196	33	4	7	101	112	109
On Grass and on Turf																						
Grass	.205	.255	.301	146	30	9	1	1	8	10	21	.268	.335	.376	471	126	27	3	6	51	50	61
Turf	.269	.370	.341	413	111	21	3	1	53	63	54	.281	.359	.362	1242	349	64	6	8	169	152	125
During the Day and at Night																						
Day	.233	.303	.305	210	49	12	0	1	18	19	28	.269	.348	.354	605	163	32	2	5	67	72	76
Night	.264	.364	.347	349	92	18	4	1	43	54	47	.282	.355	.372	1108	312	59	7	9	153	130	110
By Month																						
April	.147	.244	.191	68	10	3	0	0	5	9	7	.279	.382	.341	208	58	8	1	1	22	35	23
May	.181	.277	.241	83	15	2	0	1	6	11	16	.262	.320	.340	294	77	11	0	4	41	27	50
June	.307	.397	.396	101	31	4	1	1	11	13	16	.307	.374	.417	309	95	21	2	3	38	32	38
July	.304	.396	.367	79	24	5	0	0	9	9	7	.249	.325	.292	281	70	12	0	0	29	29	25
August	.218	.315	.327	110	24	8	2	0	18	17	15	.270	.342	.367	319	86	18	5	1	43	38	26
Sept/Oct	.314	.386	.398	118	37	8	1	0	12	14	14	.295	.379	.421	302	89	21	1	5	47	41	24
Situational																						
Bases Empty	.235	.329	.308	328	77	21	0	1	1	44	46	.256	.340	.340	964	247	50	2	9	9	117	111
Leadoff	.202	.297	.279	104	21	8	0	0	0	14	16	.224	.325	.294	313	70	16	0	2	2	46	39
Not Leadoff	.250	.344	.321	224	56	13	0	1	1	30	30	.272	.347	.363	651	177	34	2	7	7	71	72
Runners On	.277	.360	.364	231	64	9	4	1	60	29	29	.304	.369	.398	749	228	41	7	5	211	85	75
First Base Only	.347	.410	.480	75	26	6	2	0	8	8	5	.340	.386	.465	282	96	23	3	2	21	21	20
Scoring Position	.244	.337	.308	156	38	3	2	1	52	21	24	.283	.360	.358	467	132	18	4	3	190	64	55
Late Innings, Close	.222	.289	.265	117	26	2	0	1	8	10	17	.245	.316	.314	290	71	8	0	4	37	29	31
RBI/Opportunities																						
Scoring Position				50 / 214		(23%)									180 / 652		(28%)					
Scoring Position, 2 Out				12 / 85		(14%)									55 / 249		(22%)					
On Third, Less than 2 Out				23 / 55		(42%)									83 / 155		(54%)					
RBI in close games / RBI Total				43 / 61		(70%)									140 / 220		(64%)					

255

Orel Hershiser
Los Angeles Dodgers

Every pitcher has idiosyncracies. Orel Hershiser's is that he loves to pitch in Dodger Stadium. After three years in the bigs, there is no doubt that Orel Hershiser is a much different pitcher in Chavez Ravine than on the road.

Hershiser strikes out nearly 5 batters per game, will make 30–35 starts and still will relieve if asked. More than anything, though, Orel excels at home.

In 1985, while he was posting a 19–3 record, Orel was 11–0 at home, "only" 8–3 on the road. While his ERA was an excellent 2.03, it was 1.08 at home and 3.22 on the road, and he completed twice as many games and threw 50% more shutouts at home.

Last season had to be a letdown for Orel. Dwight Gooden was 17–6, had a 2.84 ERA with 200 strikeouts, and every other story stated it was an off-season. (Ten or fifteen more "off-seasons" and Dwight will be in the Hall of Fame.) In fact, Orel did let down, but he still had a good year. His road numbers were subpar—4–9 with a 4.96 ERA. However, he compensated when he came home with a fine 10–5 record and a 3.07 ERA.

Even in the pitcher's parks on the road, Orel has a tough time. St. Louis and New York are pitcher's parks, yet, over the past two seasons, Hershiser has a 6.75 ERA in Busch Stadium and a 5.06 ERA in Shea Stadium. Against the same two teams at home, his ERA drops to 2.57 and 2.61, respectively.

It may be far-fetched to consider using Orel as a part-time starter and part-time reliever, but a case can be made for it. Before World War II, the number one starters were often used in relief. Today, relievers may spot start, but the best starters do not get used in relief. Orel should certainly start as many games as possible in Dodger Stadium, but on the road, maybe he should come out of the pen. Perhaps, he can be of more value to the team in relief on the road than as a starter with an ERA over 4.00.

No matter how Orel Hershiser is used, if he stays healthy, he will have a fine career. He is smart, trains hard, and has all the tools. He has a good fastball, excellent control, and a sharp-breaking curve ball. Still, I can't help picturing Orel Hershiser sitting next to the campfire, guitar in hand, wearing a cowboy hat, singing, "I wanna go home."

—Carmen J. Corica

1986: Finesse, Groundball   **1985: Finesse, Groundball**   **1984: Power, Groundball**

| | 1986 SEASON | | | | | | | | | | | THREE YEARS (84 – 86) | | | | | | | | | | |
	G	IP	H	BB	SO	SB	CS	W	L	S	ERA	G	IP	H	BB	SO	SB	CS	W	L	S	ERA
Totals	35	231.1	213	86	153	25	8	14	14	0	3.85	116	660.2	552	204	460	64	23	44	25	2	2.85
At Home and on the Road																						
Home	18	129.0	112	41	85	16	5	10	5	0	3.07	61	363.0	282	109	259	37	12	26	10	0	2.43
Road	17	102.1	101	45	68	9	3	4	9	0	4.84	55	297.2	270	95	201	27	11	18	15	2	3.36
During the Day and at Night																						
Day	11	80.0	72	27	40	8	3	4	5	0	3.83	47	248.2	217	74	161	30	8	11	9	1	3.04
Night	24	151.1	141	59	113	17	5	10	9	0	3.87	69	412.0	335	130	299	34	15	33	16	1	2.73
On Grass and on Turf																						
Grass	25	173.0	157	53	102	16	5	12	9	0	3.38	84	494.1	398	143	344	45	14	35	16	1	2.68
Turf	10	58.1	56	33	51	9	3	2	5	0	5.25	32	166.1	154	61	116	19	9	9	9	1	3.35
By Month																						
April	5	35.0	34	14	24	2	2	3	2	0	2.06	19	74.0	63	29	51	5	4	7	2	0	2.43
May	6	42.1	30	19	36	5	1	2	1	0	2.55	20	101.0	87	37	96	13	4	5	2	0	2.58
June	6	41.0	42	18	25	7	2	2	2	0	5.27	21	104.1	101	32	66	13	5	5	6	2	4.40
July	5	28.0	30	11	24	4	0	3	2	0	5.46	17	115.2	82	35	98	15	1	11	4	0	2.41
August	6	39.0	36	12	23	3	1	2	3	0	4.62	18	117.1	104	35	69	11	5	6	6	0	2.91
Sept/Oct	7	46.0	41	12	21	4	2	2	4	0	3.52	21	148.1	115	36	80	7	4	11	5	0	2.43

vs. Opponent Batters

| | 1986 SEASON | | | | | | | | | | | | THREE YEARS (84 – 86) | | | | | | | | | |
	Ave.	OBP	SLG	AB	H	2B	3B	HR	RBI	BB	SO		Ave.	OBP	SLG	AB	H	2B	3B	HR	RBI	BB	SO
Totals	.243	.312	.339	877	213	33	6	13	92	86	153		.224	.287	.303	2459	552	81	11	30	218	204	460
Pitching vs. Left and Right-handed Batters																							
Left	.253	.320	.356	463	117	21	3	7	50	48	72		.239	.298	.316	1286	307	51	6	12	118	110	204
Right	.232	.303	.319	414	96	12	3	6	42	38	81		.209	.274	.289	1173	245	30	5	18	100	94	256
Situational																							
Bases Empty	.240	.290	.356	525	126	24	5	9	9	35	90		.221	.271	.300	1504	333	50	7	18	18	93	282
Leadoff	.253	.294	.364	225	57	10	0	5	5	13	37		.233	.282	.323	634	148	22	1	11	11	40	111
Not Leadoff	.230	.287	.350	300	69	14	5	4	4	22	53		.213	.263	.283	870	185	28	6	7	7	53	171
Runners On	.247	.342	.313	352	87	9	1	4	83	51	63		.229	.309	.308	955	219	31	4	12	200	111	178
First Base Only	.288	.347	.356	132	38	4	1	1	6	10	17		.240	.292	.318	409	98	15	1	5	16	26	59
Scoring Position	.223	.340	.286	220	49	5	0	3	77	41	46		.222	.321	.300	546	121	16	3	7	184	85	119
Late Innings, Close	.237	.327	.366	93	22	2	2	2	19	12	16		.212	.298	.314	274	58	6	2	6	29	31	56

RBI/Opportunities

Scoring Position	71 / 323	(22%)		169 / 776	(22%)
Scoring Position, 2 Out	37 / 157	(24%)		73 / 363	(20%)
On Third, Less than 2 Out	24 / 54	(44%)		62 / 135	(46%)
RBI in close games / RBI Total	74 / 92	(80%)		153 / 218	(70%)

Ted Higuera
Milwaukee Brewers

The Mexican League draws a little less then 2,000 fans a game, so it's run on a shoestring—one thing teams skimp on is the parks. They're major-league size but the infields are sandlot all the way—a man who hits a lot of grounders can be reasonably sure that a lot of them will take a bad bounce over a glove. League average usually ranges from .270 to .295—it's a tremendous hitters' league. How good? In 1984, Mario Mendoza (yes, THE Mario Mendoza) hit .325 there.

That fact begs a question: If it's so easy to hit south of the border, isn't it also terribly difficult to pitch there? Baseball men don't see it that way. If you ask Joe GM why he won't sign the .375 hitter, he tells you that he probably got 60 extra hits because of the playing conditions and that he'd bomb out in the majors, where he wouldn't have that advantage. Ask him why he won't sign the pitcher who pitched 200 innings and allowed 180 hits and he says "sure he did well—he didn't face good hitters." It's great reasoning—hitters get helped by the parks but pitchers aren't hurt by them. It's reasoning like that that got John Tudor traded even up for Mike Easler.

The funny thing about Teddy Higuera is that he made the majors on a fluke. He had a 2.54 ERA in the ML's strike season of 1980—the next year his manager tried to make him a reliever. He had an off year in 1982 and that normally would have finished any chances that he had of playing in America. But the 1983 season was a year like the American League had in 1968—everyone hit 40–50 points less. Every competent pitcher had sub-2.40 ERAs (48 year old George Brunet's was 1.94); it was the one time when you could have said that the pitchers weren't as good as they looked and been right. But all Milwaukee saw was that he'd allowed 7.17 hits per nine innings, so they signed him (they must have been mesmerized by stats back then; they also signed the Japanese League's ERA leader that year). Higuera is a super pitcher—always has been—but, had the ball behaved like it normally does in 1983, no gringo would ever have known it.

—Geoff Beckman

1986: Power, Flyball		1985: Finesse, Flyball		1984: Did not play

1986 SEASON

	G	IP	H	BB	SO	SB	CS	W	L	S	ERA
Totals	34	248.1	226	74	207	10	9	20	11	0	2.79
At Home and on the Road											
Home	16	131.0	106	36	108	6	3	10	3	0	1.79
Road	18	117.1	120	38	99	4	6	10	8	0	3.91
During the Day and at Night											
Day	13	99.2	79	39	84	4	5	7	4	0	2.26
Night	21	148.2	147	35	123	6	4	13	7	0	3.15
On Grass and on Turf											
Grass	28	213.1	185	68	171	8	8	17	8	0	2.40
Turf	6	35.0	41	6	36	2	1	3	3	0	5.14
By Month											
April	5	40.1	30	12	34	2	1	3	1	0	2.23
May	6	45.0	39	14	40	2	2	3	3	0	2.60
June	6	44.0	39	13	36	1	3	4	2	0	2.25
July	5	30.2	30	11	26	1	1	3	1	0	3.52
August	6	44.2	47	9	37	2	0	4	1	0	3.02
Sept/Oct	6	43.2	41	15	34	2	2	3	3	0	3.30

THREE YEARS (84 – 86)

	G	IP	H	BB	SO	SB	CS	W	L	S	ERA
Totals	66	460.2	412	137	334	23	18	35	19	0	3.30
Home	31	220.1	192	68	161	13	8	17	7	0	3.27
Road	35	240.1	220	69	173	10	10	18	12	0	3.33
Day	22	144.1	122	55	101	5	5	10	7	0	3.37
Night	44	316.1	290	82	233	18	13	25	12	0	3.27
Grass	54	379.2	338	117	273	19	15	28	15	0	3.25
Turf	12	81.0	74	20	61	4	3	7	4	0	3.56
April	7	53.2	42	17	42	2	1	3	2	0	3.19
May	12	80.1	64	29	65	3	2	6	5	0	3.02
June	12	70.0	67	19	51	3	4	5	4	0	4.11
July	11	74.2	67	21	55	2	3	7	2	0	3.74
August	12	87.2	94	21	57	9	3	8	1	0	3.08
Sept/Oct	12	94.1	78	30	64	4	5	6	5	0	2.86

vs. Opponent Batters

1986 SEASON

	Ave.	OBP	SLG	AB	H	2B	3B	HR	RBI	BB	SO
Totals	.241	.296	.379	936	226	43	4	26	76	74	207
Pitching vs. Left and Right-handed Batters											
Left	.243	.275	.382	152	37	7	1	4	15	7	37
Right	.241	.300	.379	784	189	36	3	22	61	67	170
Situational											
Bases Empty	.243	.306	.397	567	138	26	2	19	19	49	117
Leadoff	.232	.289	.392	237	55	6	1	10	10	18	46
Not Leadoff	.252	.318	.400	330	83	20	1	9	9	31	71
Runners On	.238	.281	.352	369	88	17	2	7	57	25	90
First Base Only	.267	.296	.318	195	52	8	1	0	2	7	38
Scoring Position	.207	.266	.391	174	36	9	1	7	55	18	52
Late Innings, Close	.236	.294	.285	123	29	2	2	0	7	11	29

THREE YEARS (84 – 86)

	Ave.	OBP	SLG	AB	H	2B	3B	HR	RBI	BB	SO
Totals	.238	.293	.377	1729	412	75	10	48	160	137	334
Left	.240	.283	.380	279	67	14	2	7	26	17	64
Right	.238	.295	.376	1450	345	61	8	41	134	120	270
Bases Empty	.241	.301	.393	1070	258	45	8	34	34	88	200
Leadoff	.234	.290	.398	445	104	17	4	16	16	34	78
Not Leadoff	.246	.308	.390	625	154	28	4	18	18	54	122
Runners On	.234	.281	.349	659	154	30	2	14	126	49	134
First Base Only	.234	.270	.303	346	81	13	1	3	11	15	58
Scoring Position	.233	.293	.399	313	73	17	1	11	115	34	76
Late Innings, Close	.253	.304	.315	257	65	3	2	3	17	20	50

RBI/Opportunities

	1986 SEASON		THREE YEARS (84 – 86)	
Scoring Position	45 / 237	(19%)	97 / 426	(23%)
Scoring Position, 2 Out	13 / 112	(12%)	31 / 194	(16%)
On Third, Less than 2 Out	19 / 36	(53%)	44 / 75	(59%)
RBI in close games / RBI Total	53 / 76	(70%)	113 / 160	(71%)

Bob Horner
Atlanta Braves

Bob Horner has been one of the most injury-prone players of this era. The move to first base in mid-1985 was made to alleviate this, and it has succeeded. Most of the games Horner missed in 1986 were due to his brother's fight with leukemia.

Horner got off to his usual slow start, then came around in May. He is a streak player, and he lived up to his reputation. His high point was July 6th, with four home runs as the Braves lost to Montreal, 11–8.

Defensively, Horner plays a decent first base. The dives that characterized his play at third (and which figured in his wrist problems) are less necessary now.

Bob Horner is not over the hill yet. He is still very capable of having outstanding seasons. The career totals that he might have recorded appear to be a fantasy now, with all the time he has lost to injury the last several seasons. It is sad to wonder what he could have done if he had remained healthy.

Given the great similarity of Horner and Murphy (both hit for average against lefties, power against righties), look for Ken Griffey to bat between them if Horner remains with the Braves.

—John Stryker

Horner's powerful swing has little wasted motion—"compact" is the word announcers use to describe it. He waits and then explodes on the ball. Dale Murphy pulls back and sweeps powerfully through the strike zone, often missing. Bob Horner generates his power by waiting, then lashing out suddenly. He does not strike out often for a power-hitter: Murphy, Juan Samuel, and Darryl Strawberry all just missed matching Horner's three-year K total in 1986 alone. In the AL, seven players each exceeded Horners three-year total in 1986 alone.

Apparently, the "experiment" at third is finally over. Eleven errors in only forty games at third in 1985 must have convinced the management. The adjustment to first has been smoother than expected: no errors in 87 games in 1985, and fourth in the league among first basemen in assists in 1986.

Horner was helped by Atlanta-Fulton County Stadium in 1986, especially in power. He homered in 7.3% of his at-bats in daylight, but only 4.2% of the time at night.

If the Braves lose Horner, they would also lose some of their personality. Horner and Murphy still represent the high-powered slugging which has characterized the club since its move to the South.

—Robert Jones

	1986 SEASON											THREE YEARS (84 – 86)									
	Ave.	OBP	SLG	AB	H	2B	3B	HR	RBI	BB	SO	Ave.	OBP	SLG	AB	H	2B	3B	HR	RBI	BB	SO
Totals	.273	.336	.472	517	141	22	0	27	87	52	72	.270	.336	.479	1113	301	55	3	57	195	116	145
Batting vs. Left and Right-handed Pitchers																						
Left	.313	.385	.500	166	52	10	0	7	26	20	19	.297	.365	.503	354	105	22	0	17	61	40	36
Right	.254	.312	.459	351	89	12	0	20	61	32	53	.258	.322	.468	759	196	33	3	40	134	76	109
At Home and on the Road																						
Home	.306	.360	.571	268	82	11	0	20	59	26	29	.283	.344	.531	554	157	34	2	33	119	58	66
Road	.237	.309	.365	249	59	11	0	7	28	26	43	.258	.327	.428	559	144	21	1	24	76	58	79
Facing Groundball Pitchers and Flyball Pitchers																						
Groundball	.257	.331	.452	241	62	8	0	13	37	27	33	.290	.358	.479	535	155	24	1	25	91	59	67
Flyball	.286	.340	.489	276	79	14	0	14	50	25	39	.253	.315	.479	578	146	31	2	32	104	57	78
Facing Finesse Pitchers and Power Pitchers																						
Finesse	.293	.349	.493	294	86	17	0	14	45	27	33	.280	.338	.475	640	179	38	0	29	99	58	67
Power	.247	.319	.444	223	55	5	0	13	42	25	39	.258	.334	.484	473	122	17	3	28	96	58	78
On Grass and on Turf																						
Grass	.279	.335	.491	405	113	17	0	23	71	37	57	.273	.335	.485	840	229	45	2	43	149	85	112
Turf	.250	.338	.402	112	28	5	0	4	16	15	15	.264	.338	.462	273	72	10	1	14	46	31	33
During the Day and at Night																						
Day	.311	.362	.567	164	51	6	0	12	31	15	15	.304	.361	.550	369	112	17	1	24	67	35	39
Night	.255	.323	.428	353	90	16	0	15	56	37	57	.254	.324	.444	744	189	38	2	33	128	81	106
By Month																						
April	.194	.278	.306	62	12	1	0	2	9	7	12	.192	.261	.322	177	34	8	0	5	22	17	28
May	.287	.361	.525	101	29	6	0	6	23	13	16	.303	.376	.505	218	66	14	0	10	42	27	25
June	.323	.380	.525	99	32	5	0	5	15	9	9	.308	.361	.561	198	61	12	1	12	37	18	18
July	.250	.270	.467	60	15	1	0	4	9	2	9	.324	.372	.662	142	46	7	1	13	36	11	22
August	.291	.345	.405	79	23	3	0	2	11	7	9	.280	.346	.405	168	47	6	0	5	26	18	21
Sept/Oct	.259	.333	.517	116	30	6	0	8	20	14	17	.224	.303	.443	210	47	8	1	12	32	25	31
Situational																						
Bases Empty	.291	.337	.516	275	80	11	0	17	17	18	41	.279	.329	.477	577	161	25	1	29	29	41	77
Leadoff	.285	.333	.496	137	39	5	0	8	8	9	12	.286	.336	.502	269	77	13	0	15	15	19	27
Not Leadoff	.297	.340	.536	138	41	6	0	9	9	9	29	.273	.323	.455	308	84	12	1	14	14	22	50
Runners On	.252	.334	.421	242	61	11	0	10	70	34	31	.261	.343	.481	536	140	30	2	28	166	75	68
First Base Only	.207	.258	.328	116	24	2	0	4	9	8	16	.249	.304	.470	253	63	12	1	14	36	20	27
Scoring Position	.294	.393	.508	126	37	9	0	6	61	26	15	.272	.373	.491	283	77	18	1	14	130	55	41
Late Innings, Close	.217	.313	.325	83	18	3	0	2	14	12	15	.272	.347	.497	191	52	8	1	11	39	23	26

RBI/Opportunities					
Scoring Position	49 / 180	(27%)	103 / 399	(26%)
Scoring Position, 2 Out	12 / 88	(14%)	32 / 190	(17%)
On Third, Less than 2 Out	24 / 36	(67%)	49 / 81	(60%)
RBI in close games / RBI Total	57 / 87	(66%)	138 / 195	(71%)

Charlie Hough
Texas Rangers

When the ACE of your pitching staff is a 38-year-old knuckleballer, you KNOW you're in trouble, Now, please don't take this wrongly. I like Charlie Hough. He is fun as all getout to watch. His knuckleball is probably the very best of the handful of pitchers currently practicing this black art. He is undoubtedly the best pitcher on the team. Charlie just dumbfounds us that he always gets the job done.

Out of uniform, Charlie is lunching with teammate Tom Paciorek at manager Bobby Valentine's Sports Gallery in Arlington, Texas, a noisy, very busy sports bar. Valentine flits from table to table like a nervous moth, gladhanding customers, trading bon mots. He looks the part of an ex-athlete entrepreneur. Paciorek, too, looks like a ballplayer in the twilight of a modestly successful career. Hough; well, Charlie looks like a high school history teacher. This writer had to look twice before he realized he was sharing the same air space with an All Star pitcher.

So what's the point of this shameless attack? Spread before me are Charlie's 1986 and career statistics. I'm trying to find, among the team-leading and league-challenging numbers, some chink in this guy's armor. Finding few, I've had to create flaws; to make this guy, who will probably still be pitching when Halley's Comet comes around again, human.

How's this for defamation of character? Not counting

Charlie, the Rangers have probably the youngest pitching staff in the majors. They are also the wildest staff in the major leagues, Bobby Witt being the King of Fling. But who is their role model? Charlie Hough. Hough was third in the AL in wild pitches per base runner. Hell, Charlie doesn't even know where his pitches are heading. If Hough (the seasoned pro) doesn't know, how can you expect raw rookies, who were still making in their diapers when Hough was breaking into the bigs, to know? Shucks.

Want more? Charlie gave up more home runs per inning and per hit than any other Ranger pitcher in 1986. Hah! Unmasked at last, you charlatan. Only the fact that you were sixth in the wins in the AL, first in complete games on the Rangers, and were a reliable stopper, saves your cookies, pal.

But wait, there's more. Charlie is no lightning bolt off the mound, either. He was late covering home at least once in 1986, which cost the Rangers a key win against California. Never mind that he had pitched a one-hitter. Never mind it was another player's error that set up the winning run. Never mind the strain in facing all of this in front of a hostile, screaming Angel crowd. Never mind all that stuff. Such mental lapses shall not be tolerated. The prosecution rests.

I feel so much better.

—Wes Osborn

| 1986: Finesse, Flyball | 1985: Finesse, Groundball | 1984: Finesse, Groundball |

	1986 SEASON											THREE YEARS (84 – 86)										
	G	IP	H	BB	SO	SB	CS	W	L	S	ERA	G	IP	H	BB	SO	SB	CS	W	L	S	ERA
Totals	33	230.1	188	89	146	22	5	17	10	0	3.79	103	746.2	646	266	451	55	19	47	40	0	3.62
											At Home and on the Road											
Home	15	106.0	93	39	69	6	3	8	5	0	3.99	47	349.2	307	116	214	26	8	24	16	0	3.45
Road	18	124.1	95	50	77	16	2	9	5	0	3.62	56	397.0	339	150	237	29	11	23	24	0	3.76
											During the Day and at Night											
Day	6	41.2	36	18	17	2	1	3	3	0	5.62	21	158.0	132	62	82	9	6	8	8	0	3.53
Night	27	188.2	152	71	129	20	4	14	7	0	3.39	82	588.2	514	204	369	46	13	39	32	0	3.64
											On Grass and on Turf											
Grass	27	186.1	148	72	121	18	4	14	8	0	3.67	83	598.2	515	209	373	48	15	38	32	0	3.64
Turf	6	44.0	40	17	25	4	1	3	2	0	4.30	20	148.0	131	57	78	7	4	9	8	0	3.53
											By Month											
April	0	0.0	0	0	0	0	0	0	0	0	0.00	11	69.2	62	33	44	6	1	2	3	0	4.26
May	5	31.0	29	7	16	2	0	3	2	0	5.23	18	120.0	114	38	67	8	0	9	9	0	4.28
June	6	53.2	25	15	34	3	1	4	1	0	1.51	19	158.1	113	52	97	7	7	9	7	0	2.22
July	6	43.0	39	24	28	3	3	2	3	0	4.40	16	124.2	97	49	82	5	4	9	6	0	3.47
August	7	40.0	42	22	24	5	0	3	2	0	5.40	20	139.0	135	55	80	13	3	11	7	0	4.34
Sept/Oct	9	62.2	53	21	44	9	1	5	2	0	3.59	19	135.0	125	39	81	16	4	7	8	0	3.73

| | | | | | vs. Opponent Batters | | | | | | | | | | | | | | | | | |

	1986 SEASON											THREE YEARS (84 – 86)									
	Ave.	OBP	SLG	AB	H	2B	3B	HR	RBI	BB	SO	Ave.	OBP	SLG	AB	H	2B	3B	HR	RBI	BB	SO
Totals	.221	.301	.379	850	188	32	3	32	103	89	146	.232	.303	.374	2786	646	118	17	81	306	266	451
						Pitching vs. Left and Right-handed Batters																
Left	.204	.282	.335	436	89	16	1	13	40	43	78	.237	.307	.369	1472	349	54	13	38	170	137	234
Right	.239	.322	.425	414	99	16	2	19	63	46	68	.226	.299	.379	1314	297	64	4	43	136	129	217
							Situational														
Bases Empty	.205	.283	.366	555	114	19	2	22	22	54	102	.225	.287	.371	1756	395	75	11	53	53	135	287
Leadoff	.181	.239	.341	226	41	7	1	9	9	15	47	.222	.269	.373	726	161	31	5	23	23	41	115
Not Leadoff	.222	.312	.383	329	73	12	1	13	13	39	55	.227	.299	.369	1030	234	44	6	30	30	94	172
Runners On	.251	.335	.403	295	74	13	1	10	81	35	44	.244	.329	.379	1030	251	43	6	28	253	131	164
First Base Only	.218	.273	.361	119	26	5	0	4	12	8	13	.235	.310	.361	421	99	20	3	9	27	44	51
Scoring Position	.273	.374	.432	176	48	8	1	6	69	27	31	.250	.342	.391	609	152	23	3	19	226	87	113
Late Innings, Close	.195	.252	.263	118	23	3	1	1	4	8	25	.216	.277	.292	384	83	13	2	4	31	31	68
							RBI/Opportunities														
Scoring Position			58 / 238	(24%)										195 / 827	(24%)							
Scoring Position, 2 Out			20 / 99	(20%)										72 / 368	(20%)							
On Third, Less than 2 Out			22 / 50	(44%)										74 / 145	(51%)							
RBI in close games / RBI Total			58 / 103	(56%)										204 / 306	(67%)							

Jay Howell
Oakland A's

One could argue that no player in the majors had more impact on his team in 1986 than Jay Howell. Howell's inability to pitch effectively in the first half of the season, due first to a heel injury and later to tendinitis, was the pebble on the track that threw the A's bullpen skidding out of control, and was perhaps the critical factor in the early-season degeneration of the team. When Howell couldn't pitch, Steve Ontiveros was tried as the bullpen stopper, and was unsuccessful. Keith Atherton was tried, and was traded to Minnesota. Jose Rijo was taken out of the rotation to be the bullpen stopper, and was awful. As in the novel *Ragtime* a trivial harrassment incident snowballed into tragedy, so with the A's the loss of Howell snowballed into a team-wide calamity.

Howell was able to pitch well late in the year, posting a 0.51 ERA in 12 outings in August (7 saves, 2 wins). This was a great help to Tony LaRussa in getting the team moving, and he is counted on heavily in 1987. The 1986 problems had been foreshadowed by the second half of 1985, when Howell had posted a 1–5 record with a 4.23 ERA, after being perhaps the best reliever in the league the first half. After two straight years of half-season performance, the A's must be worried about Howell's ability to pitch a full year, and should have a backup plan.

Howell pitches much more effectively in Oakland, where he has a 2.43 ERA and 17–8 record over the last three seasons, than he does on the road (4–10, 3.46 ERA). He also has, over a three-year period, a 2.18 ERA in day games, as opposed to 3.29 at night.

One worrisome note about Howell in the breakdowns below is that (over three years) batters have hit .273 against him with runners in scoring position, as opposed to .241 with the bases empty and .246 overall. In 1986, the batting average of opponents with runners in scoring position was .333. However, over the three years he has limited leadoff men to a .200 batting average and a miserable .247 on-base percentage. That might suggest that in a marginal case it would be good to bring him in to start the inning, rather than waiting for the starter to get in trouble.

—Bill James

1986: Power, Groundball   1985: Power, Flyball   1984: Power, Groundball

	G	IP	H	BB	SO	SB	CS	W	L	S	ERA		G	IP	H	BB	SO	SB	CS	W	L	S	ERA
1986 SEASON												**THREE YEARS (84 – 86)**											
Totals	38	53.1	53	23	42	1	1	3	6	16	3.38		162	255.0	237	88	219	13	6	21	18	52	2.89
At Home and on the Road																							
Home	19	29.0	32	8	25	1	0	1	3	9	3.72		84	140.2	132	41	117	9	1	17	8	27	2.43
Road	19	24.1	21	15	17	0	1	2	3	7	2.96		78	114.1	105	47	102	4	5	4	10	25	3.46
During the Day and at Night																							
Day	20	28.1	27	11	25	1	0	1	3	7	3.18		56	90.2	76	29	80	4	4	8	4	21	2.18
Night	18	25.0	26	12	17	0	1	2	3	9	3.60		106	164.1	161	59	139	9	2	13	14	31	3.29
On Grass and on Turf																							
Grass	31	42.1	50	20	33	1	1	2	6	12	4.04		140	217.0	202	81	180	13	5	20	16	44	2.94
Turf	7	11.0	3	3	9	0	0	1	0	4	0.82		22	38.0	35	7	39	0	1	1	2	8	2.61
By Month																							
April	10	14.2	17	2	15	0	0	0	2	4	4.91		26	35.2	36	8	34	0	2	1	4	10	3.53
May	4	3.2	7	5	3	0	0	0	2	1	9.82		25	41.1	42	27	36	5	2	3	4	6	3.27
June	0	0.0	0	0	0	0	0	0	0	0	0.00		23	45.2	42	13	43	2	0	6	3	7	2.17
July	3	4.0	2	0	1	0	0	0	0	1	0.00		26	35.0	36	11	26	1	0	3	1	7	1.80
August	12	17.2	11	7	11	0	0	2	0	7	0.51		31	45.0	29	11	33	2	0	4	1	12	2.40
Sept/Oct	9	13.1	16	9	12	1	1	1	2	3	4.73		31	52.1	52	18	47	3	2	4	5	10	3.96

vs. Opponent Batters

	Ave.	OBP	SLG	AB	H	2B	3B	HR	RBI	BB	SO		Ave.	OBP	SLG	AB	H	2B	3B	HR	RBI	BB	SO
1986 SEASON												**THREE YEARS (84 – 86)**											
Totals	.262	.339	.351	202	53	9	0	3	25	23	42		.246	.308	.327	963	237	35	2	13	104	88	219
Pitching vs. Left and Right-handed Batters																							
Left	.330	.420	.464	97	32	7	0	2	16	15	16		.257	.331	.336	479	123	21	1	5	48	54	101
Right	.200	.261	.248	105	21	2	0	1	9	8	26		.236	.285	.318	484	114	14	1	8	56	34	118
Situational																							
Bases Empty	.238	.313	.307	101	24	4	0	1	1	11	24		.241	.295	.330	503	121	21	0	8	8	39	119
Leadoff	.262	.295	.310	42	11	2	0	0	0	2	6		.200	.247	.271	210	42	6	0	3	3	13	47
Not Leadoff	.220	.324	.305	59	13	2	0	1	1	9	18		.270	.329	.372	293	79	15	0	5	5	26	72
Runners On	.287	.365	.396	101	29	5	0	2	24	12	18		.252	.322	.324	460	116	14	2	5	96	49	100
First Base Only	.234	.308	.340	47	11	2	0	1	2	4	9		.224	.276	.316	196	44	9	0	3	12	13	41
Scoring Position	.333	.413	.444	54	18	3	0	1	22	8	9		.273	.353	.330	264	72	5	2	2	84	36	59
Late Innings, Close	.279	.356	.377	154	43	9	0	2	20	18	33		.250	.307	.327	675	169	26	1	8	81	56	142

RBI/Opportunities

Scoring Position	20 / 82	(24%)		79 / 377	(21%)
Scoring Position, 2 Out	4 / 33	(12%)		23 / 166	(14%)
On Third, Less than 2 Out	9 / 17	(53%)		41 / 82	(50%)
RBI in close games / RBI Total	20 / 25	(80%)		89 / 104	(86%)

Kent Hrbek
Minnestota Twins

Kent Hrbek is a genuine Minnesota folk hero, every bit as important to the popular culture as Bud Grant or Garrison Keillor. A hometown boy who grew up in the shadow of Metropolitan Stadium (the last "real ballpark" in Minnesota), he's a guy who looks comfortable in flannel shirts, baits a mean hook, and eats a lot of boiled potatoes. Unlike other major league stars from Minnesota (Winfield, Morris, Molitor), Hrbek has been forced to toil for the Twins, and that in itself makes him a candidate for sainthood. He's probably stuck with the Twins for good, too; like Ernie Banks with the Cubs, he's simply too popular to let go. When Hrbek rtires, he'll be eligible for a uniquely Minnesotan form of immortality: the giant statue. And like Paul Bunyan, Babe, the Blue Ox, and the Jolly Green Giant before him, Kent will gaze out over the frozen prairie for eternity, a 280-inch Louisville Slugger resting on his shoulder.

Hrbek only played a handful of games in Bloomington before the Twins moved to the Metrodome, but he should shed no tears for the old park. No one has owned the Hump like Hrbek. In the last three years he batted .315 and slugged .536 at home with 183 RBI. The Dome's short right-field wall was raised after the first year and no longer beckons, so most of Hrbek's added power came in the form of doubles and triples. In 1986, Hrbek's batting average at home fell to .273, but his slugging percentage remained high.

In the late innings of close games, the statistics show that Hrbek has struggled. Last year he hit only .212 with four extra-base hits in these situations, and over the last three years Hrbek's batting average was better but his slugging percentage was still very low at .341. In general RBI situations, Hrbek has done about average, driving in 29% of runners in scoring position in the last three seasons.

If only every month could be June! Hrbek's .341 batting average and .549 slugging percentage in June during the past three years stands head and shoulders over the rest of the season. Perhaps not coincidentally, that's the month when the Twins see a lot of Western Division teams for the first time.

Hrbek will be 27 this year, just entering his prime years. He's a good fielder, a consistent hitter for average and power, and a team leader. If he stays in a favorable ballpark, his career numbers could be very impressive in ten or fifteen years; if he's wise, Hrbek will consider taking up permanent residence under the Teflon-coated roof.

—Scott Johnson

	1986 SEASON											THREE YEARS (84 – 86)										
	Ave.	OBP	SLG	AB	H	2B	3B	HR	RBI	BB	SO	Ave.	OBP	SLG	AB	H	2B	3B	HR	RBI	BB	SO
Totals	.267	.353	.478	550	147	27	1	29	91	71	81	.286	.362	.481	1702	486	89	6	77	291	203	255
Batting vs. Left and Right-handed Pitchers																						
Left	.270	.333	.382	152	41	5	0	4	28	14	33	.274	.342	.428	537	147	21	1	20	86	53	102
Right	.266	.361	.515	398	106	22	1	25	63	57	48	.291	.371	.505	1165	339	68	5	57	205	150	153
At Home and on the Road																						
Home	.273	.359	.529	278	76	15	1	18	57	36	43	.315	.388	.536	877	276	53	6	43	183	105	134
Road	.261	.347	.426	272	71	12	0	11	34	35	38	.255	.335	.422	825	210	36	0	34	108	98	121
Facing Groundball Pitchers and Flyball Pitchers																						
Groundball	.285	.368	.528	246	70	15	0	15	41	29	31	.289	.369	.483	836	242	44	2	38	145	101	123
Flyball	.253	.342	.438	304	77	12	1	14	50	42	50	.282	.356	.478	866	244	45	4	39	146	102	132
Facing Finesse Pitchers and Power Pitchers																						
Finesse	.282	.360	.513	316	89	16	0	19	52	39	43	.297	.368	.493	949	282	56	2	42	146	106	120
Power	.248	.344	.432	234	58	11	1	10	39	32	38	.271	.356	.465	753	204	33	4	35	145	97	135
On Grass and on Turf																						
Grass	.264	.352	.457	197	52	11	0	9	27	26	26	.250	.323	.424	609	152	28	0	26	81	65	90
Turf	.269	.354	.490	353	95	16	1	20	64	45	55	.306	.384	.512	1093	334	61	6	51	210	138	165
During the Day and at Night																						
Day	.278	.361	.527	169	47	9	0	11	28	19	23	.285	.354	.495	523	149	31	2	25	94	57	70
Night	.262	.350	.457	381	100	18	1	18	63	52	58	.286	.366	.474	1179	337	58	4	52	197	146	185
By Month																						
April	.316	.424	.447	76	24	7	0	1	9	15	8	.276	.388	.436	243	67	13	1	8	34	42	29
May	.261	.352	.565	92	24	4	0	8	19	13	14	.277	.340	.479	267	74	15	0	13	52	27	36
June	.400	.482	.726	95	38	5	1	8	27	13	12	.343	.413	.551	274	94	17	2	12	49	31	41
July	.180	.255	.427	89	16	4	0	6	15	8	12	.257	.331	.514	276	71	11	0	20	63	29	41
August	.227	.315	.351	97	22	0	0	4	9	13	16	.287	.355	.442	317	91	10	0	13	43	35	52
Sept/Oct	.228	.295	.356	101	23	7	0	2	12	9	19	.274	.351	.465	325	89	23	3	11	50	39	56
Situational																						
Bases Empty	.245	.344	.472	290	71	15	0	17	17	41	49	.277	.347	.467	915	253	53	2	39	39	92	144
Leadoff	.302	.400	.558	86	26	4	0	6	6	13	10	.290	.353	.532	331	96	21	1	19	19	29	41
Not Leadoff	.221	.321	.436	204	45	11	0	11	11	28	39	.269	.344	.430	584	157	32	1	20	20	63	103
Runners On	.292	.363	.485	260	76	12	1	12	74	30	32	.296	.379	.497	787	233	36	4	38	252	111	111
First Base Only	.336	.390	.632	125	42	5	1	10	24	9	13	.301	.364	.521	355	107	11	2	21	53	33	50
Scoring Position	.252	.341	.348	135	34	7	0	2	50	21	19	.292	.391	.477	432	126	25	2	17	199	78	61
Late Innings, Close	.212	.302	.329	85	18	1	0	3	11	11	16	.260	.365	.341	246	64	8	0	4	30	40	41
RBI/Opportunities																						
Scoring Position				47 / 178		(26%)									169 / 587		(29%)					
Scoring Position, 2 Out				10 / 63		(16%)									47 / 224		(21%)					
On Third, Less than 2 Out				24 / 37		(65%)									74 / 128		(58%)					
RBI in close games / RBI Total				59 / 91		(65%)									189 / 291		(65%)					

Glenn Hubbard
Atlanta Braves

What is it about Glenn Hubbard? I read his stats, quite below average, yet I still like him. I find myself having to defend liking him. Maybe it's the consecutive game error-less streaks of recent years. Maybe it's one of the "hundreds" of perfectly-placed sacrifice bunts. Has the management made an error over the last few years in allowing him to keep his job? I think not. You just have to dig deeper to determine his value. It is there; it is simply not obvious to a superficial glance.

This guy is steady. That's it! Steady. Maybe he's lost a little on defense (19 errors in 1986 compared to 18 total for 1984–85). Batting average gives a falsely low impression of Hubbard (.232 over three years), because he has an excellent eye: he reaches base about one-third of the time (.330 OBA over three years), considerably more often than Rafael Ramirez, who is generally considered the better offensive performer because of his higher batting average. He is terrific at turning the double play (127 in 1985 and 120 in 1986). His range at second base is always good, although that is influenced by the Atlanta staffs' heavy groundball tendencies. Yes, we must measure Glenn Hubbard in other ways.

Hubbard is a better home, grass, and night hitter, the perfect combination for Atlanta-Fulton County Stadium.

Hub has hit better when leading off in the past, but his 1986 numbers when leading off were miserable. He has hit even worse in late-inning, close situations the past three years. Except for August swoons, Glenn has been consistent on a month-to-month basis when the 1984–86 seasons are averaged.

However, in 1986, inconsistency was the word for Hubbard. On a monthly basis, he was down, up, down, up, down, and up. Average, on-base and slugging were all affected in this schizophrenic season. Which is the real Glenn Hubbard at this point in his career? Can he improve as a hitter, possibly to his level of performance in 1982–83, or are those low months the barometer of his failing abilities? For example, the 8 doubles in May were a surprise, but he hit only 8 more in the other five combined. Hubbard did hit well above his average with runners in scoring position, though.

Sure, I'd be happier (along with Ted Turner and Chuck Tanner) if Hub hit for a higher average and some more power, but Glenn's got grit. He makes plays in the field that most second basemen cannot; he fouls off pitches to draw a substantial number of walks. The change to another player had better be obvious, otherwise, Hubbard should keep his job.

—Robert L. Jones

	1986 SEASON											THREE YEARS (84 – 86)										
	Ave.	OBP	SLG	AB	H	2B	3B	HR	RBI	BB	SO	Ave.	OBP	SLG	AB	H	2B	3B	HR	RBI	BB	SO
Totals	.230	.340	.304	408	94	16	1	4	36	66	74	.232	.330	.332	1244	289	64	3	18	118	176	189
Batting vs. Left and Right-handed Pitchers																						
Left	.220	.365	.291	127	28	6	0	1	12	29	23	.225	.336	.309	391	88	19	1	4	33	67	59
Right	.235	.328	.310	281	66	10	1	3	24	37	51	.236	.327	.342	853	201	45	2	14	85	109	130
At Home and on the Road																						
Home	.246	.370	.355	203	50	8	1	4	21	39	31	.250	.351	.357	624	156	31	3	10	67	96	89
Road	.215	.309	.254	205	44	8	0	0	15	27	43	.215	.309	.306	620	133	33	0	8	51	80	100
Facing Groundball Pitchers and Flyball Pitchers																						
Groundball	.230	.356	.295	183	42	9	0	1	14	35	35	.242	.339	.322	603	146	28	1	6	55	87	86
Flyball	.231	.327	.311	225	52	7	1	3	22	31	39	.223	.322	.342	641	143	36	2	12	63	89	103
Facing Finesse Pitchers and Power Pitchers																						
Finesse	.237	.328	.309	236	56	9	1	2	16	31	40	.244	.328	.348	709	173	37	2	11	60	86	87
Power	.221	.355	.297	172	38	7	0	2	20	35	34	.217	.333	.310	535	116	27	1	7	58	90	102
On Grass and on Turf																						
Grass	.243	.361	.326	304	74	11	1	4	26	53	52	.242	.340	.343	925	224	45	3	14	92	132	139
Turf	.192	.277	.240	104	20	5	0	0	10	13	22	.204	.302	.301	319	65	19	0	4	26	44	50
During the Day and at Night																						
Day	.200	.278	.303	145	29	7	1	2	13	14	24	.197	.285	.305	442	87	23	2	7	45	52	62
Night	.247	.372	.304	263	65	9	0	2	23	52	50	.252	.354	.347	802	202	41	1	11	73	124	127
By Month																						
April	.222	.338	.315	54	12	2	0	1	5	10	11	.256	.378	.365	156	40	8	0	3	13	30	20
May	.273	.350	.398	88	24	8	0	1	11	10	16	.244	.314	.380	250	61	19	0	5	33	24	35
June	.208	.394	.283	53	11	1	0	1	7	16	9	.224	.362	.323	223	50	10	0	4	25	48	31
July	.277	.407	.340	47	13	3	0	0	8	10	9	.236	.340	.365	203	48	15	1	3	26	32	31
August	.170	.263	.182	88	15	1	0	0	2	10	14	.197	.278	.243	218	43	5	1	1	13	24	39
Sept/Oct	.244	.330	.321	78	19	1	1	1	3	10	15	.242	.316	.320	194	47	7	1	2	8	18	33
Situational																						
Bases Empty	.218	.295	.282	248	54	8	1	2	2	24	43	.239	.321	.341	725	173	38	3	10	10	83	100
Leadoff	.184	.273	.224	98	18	2	1	0	0	10	20	.258	.348	.373	295	76	17	1	5	5	39	34
Not Leadoff	.240	.309	.320	150	36	6	0	2	2	14	23	.226	.302	.319	430	97	21	2	5	5	44	66
Runners On	.250	.401	.338	160	40	8	0	2	34	42	31	.224	.342	.320	519	116	26	0	8	108	93	89
First Base Only	.229	.289	.277	83	19	1	0	1	2	7	12	.216	.297	.306	232	50	9	0	4	11	24	39
Scoring Position	.273	.487	.403	77	21	7	0	1	32	35	19	.230	.373	.331	287	66	17	0	4	97	69	50
Late Innings, Close	.153	.275	.203	59	9	3	0	0	0	8	11	.193	.312	.278	187	36	10	0	2	11	29	28

RBI/Opportunities						
Scoring Position	28 / 141	(20%)		84 / 442	(19%)	
Scoring Position, 2 Out	9 / 69	(13%)		28 / 200	(14%)	
On Third, Less than 2 Out	12 / 30	(40%)		34 / 88	(39%)	
RBI in close games / RBI Total	24 / 36	(67%)		61 / 118	(52%)	

Tim Hulett
Chicago White Sox

Tim Hulett was something of a surprise last year, hitting seventeen homers after belting only five as a rookie. To be honest, however, Hulett's 1986 campaign was basically home-run-or-nothing. He didn't hit for average (.231), he didn't draw walks (only 21 in over 550 plate appearances), he didn't hit with runners in scoring position (.175), he didn't hit in the clutch (.160). That he hit some home runs wasn't a great shock; in the minor leagues Hulett homered in double figures five straight years, with two seasons over twenty. But last year, after a hot streak that saw him hit eleven four-baggers in a 37-day period, Tim seemed to become homer-happy, like he was trying to make up for the loss of Ron Kittle and Greg Walker (to trade and injury, respectively) all by himself. Eventually Hulett got so messed up that he hit only .184 during the last two months. The home runs stopped as well: only two after August 16.

Except for the big increase in homers, Hulett's first two seasons have shown a consistent pattern. In each year he's hit better against lefties than righties, better during the day than at night, and not at all in the clutch. This isn't what you like to see in a young player. Looking at his pitch-by-pitch data for '86, I see other strong tendencies. He took the first pitch over 80% of the time, about on a par with noted walkers John Cangelosi and Jerry Hairston. Hulett, however, hardly walks at all—his philosophy seems to be to wait for the pitch he wants, then try to drive it. He let the count go to 0–2 more than any regular on the club, but even then was still looking for his pitch to whack: last year he hit four doubles, two triples and five homers on counts which started off 0-and-2, a record that no Sox hitter could come close to matching. When the count started 2–0, Hulett didn't do nearly as well, hitting less than .200 with only one homer. Probably he just got anxious and started ripping at everything. I don't know, but maybe the same thing happens to him in pressure situations. It's certainly something he can work on.

Defensively, Hulett played well at both second and third last year; according to the range statistics we keep at the *Chicago Baseball Report*, he was the best Sox fielder at each position. His work at third was a big improvement over '85.

— Don Zminda

	1986 SEASON											THREE YEARS (84 – 86)										
	Ave.	OBP	SLG	AB	H	2B	3B	HR	RBI	BB	SO	Ave.	OBP	SLG	AB	H	2B	3B	HR	RBI	BB	SO
Totals	.231	.260	.379	520	120	16	5	17	44	21	91	.245	.287	.374	922	226	35	9	22	81	52	176
Batting vs. Left and Right-handed Pitchers																						
Left	.253	.297	.443	194	49	6	2	9	16	13	34	.270	.321	.434	355	96	13	6	11	32	28	64
Right	.218	.237	.340	326	71	10	3	8	28	8	57	.229	.265	.337	567	130	22	3	11	49	24	112
At Home and on the Road																						
Home	.247	.286	.380	263	65	8	3	7	20	14	48	.248	.297	.372	460	114	16	7	9	35	31	90
Road	.214	.233	.377	257	55	8	2	10	24	7	43	.242	.277	.377	462	112	19	2	13	46	21	86
Facing Groundball Pitchers and Flyball Pitchers																						
Groundball	.221	.245	.271	199	44	2	1	2	11	6	41	.239	.285	.302	397	95	9	2	4	25	22	80
Flyball	.237	.269	.445	321	76	14	4	15	33	15	50	.250	.289	.429	525	131	26	7	18	56	30	96
Facing Finesse Pitchers and Power Pitchers																						
Finesse	.226	.252	.384	305	69	8	2	12	25	10	43	.252	.281	.403	544	137	19	6	17	52	22	83
Power	.237	.272	.372	215	51	8	3	5	19	11	48	.235	.296	.333	378	89	16	3	5	29	30	93
On Grass and on Turf																						
Grass	.235	.265	.397	438	103	10	5	17	40	18	76	.244	.288	.388	779	190	28	9	22	71	46	150
Turf	.207	.233	.280	82	17	6	0	0	4	3	15	.252	.280	.301	143	36	7	0	0	10	6	26
During the Day and at Night																						
Day	.295	.323	.470	149	44	6	1	6	18	6	19	.300	.335	.442	240	72	12	2	6	27	13	38
Night	.205	.235	.342	371	76	10	4	11	26	15	72	.226	.270	.350	682	154	23	7	16	54	39	138
By Month																						
April	.222	.317	.250	36	8	1	0	0	2	5	8	.224	.297	.259	58	13	2	0	0	4	6	15
May	.289	.304	.489	90	26	6	3	2	9	2	13	.327	.349	.524	147	48	7	5	4	19	3	19
June	.244	.300	.415	82	20	4	2	2	7	7	13	.227	.281	.352	176	40	10	3	2	12	14	34
July	.291	.293	.519	79	23	0	0	6	12	1	11	.277	.328	.440	166	46	4	1	7	21	12	34
August	.198	.225	.345	116	23	2	0	5	7	4	18	.180	.234	.287	178	32	4	0	5	9	13	35
Sept/Oct	.171	.190	.248	117	20	3	0	2	7	2	28	.239	.256	.340	197	47	8	0	4	16	4	39
Situational																						
Bases Empty	.250	.285	.441	288	72	12	5	11	11	13	46	.259	.302	.418	533	138	24	8	15	15	29	93
Leadoff	.203	.248	.347	118	24	4	2	3	3	7	19	.231	.266	.363	212	49	10	3	4	4	9	38
Not Leadoff	.282	.311	.506	170	48	8	3	8	8	6	27	.277	.326	.455	321	89	14	5	11	11	20	55
Runners On	.207	.230	.302	232	48	4	0	6	33	8	45	.226	.267	.314	389	88	11	1	7	66	23	83
First Base Only	.241	.274	.375	112	27	3	0	4	8	5	14	.247	.283	.352	182	45	5	1	4	11	8	26
Scoring Position	.175	.189	.233	120	21	1	0	2	25	3	31	.208	.253	.280	207	43	6	0	3	55	15	57
Late Innings, Close	.160	.198	.210	81	13	1	0	1	10	3	21	.176	.201	.230	148	26	2	0	2	11	4	39

RBI/Opportunities			
Scoring Position	21 / 156	(13%)	48 / 279 (17%)
Scoring Position, 2 Out	9 / 76	(12%)	24 / 145 (17%)
On Third, Less than 2 Out	7 / 25	(28%)	16 / 43 (37%)
RBI in close games / RBI Total	31 / 44	(70%)	51 / 81 (63%)

Bruce Hurst
Boston Red Sox

Injuries, any manager will tell you, are a curse—they can and do blame anything that goes wrong in a season on them. But, in 1986, an injury may actually have helped Boston win a pennant. Bruce Hurst had started strong and helped Boston into first place; on Memorial Day, he suffered a groin injury and was lost until late July. During this time, the offense held the fort; when Hurst returned, he had the luxury of being able to take as long as he needed to regain his form. He was hammered in his first two starts, but that was all he needed. Hurst was good in August, spectacular in September and the star of the playoffs—it may well have been because he was fresh. As the season progressed and Boston's pitching staff wore down, Hurst was just getting into a groove. In September, Boston buried the rest of the AL East; Hurst was the point man for the staff. It could have been a different story had he been as worn down as everyone else.

Despite starting only 25 games, Hurst led the team in complete games (11; sixth in the AL) and finished second in the league with four shutouts. When he started a game and Boston scored more than two runs (Chuck Waseleski reports), they won EVERY game. What turned him from a .500 pitcher into a monster? A new pitch (repeat after me)—the split-fingered fastball. In the 12/8/86 New Yorker, Hurst revealed that he had gone to Roger Craig in 1984 and learned the basics. He introduced it in 1985 and featured it extensively in 1986. The pitch breaks down and toward the fists on a right-handed batter, which allows him to save his wicked curve exclusively for lefties. In 1986, Bruce was as dominating against righties as he was against his own kind; the splitter is the reason why.

The beautiful part about Hurst is that, while he is a power pitcher, he is always able to keep the double play in hand. Only 58 men reached first base with none out; only 18 advanced and he got 9 double plays. Hurst cuts down the running game exceptionally well—he picked four men off first base (best on Boston) and only four of the 14 men who tried to steal actually did so (again, the best on the team). With the bases empty, he'll challenge a hitter (16 of the 18 homers he allowed came with the bases empty)—otherwise it's nibble, nibble, nibble. Hurst has made good on every bit of his promise and should continue to excel in 1987.

—Fred Percival

1986: Power, Flyball | **1985: Power, Groundball** | **1984: Power, Flyball**

1986 SEASON	G	IP	H	BB	SO	SB	CS	W	L	S	ERA	THREE YEARS (84–86)	G	IP	H	BB	SO	SB	CS	W	L	S	ERA
Totals	25	174.1	169	50	167	4	10	13	8	0	2.99		93	621.2	644	208	492	25	33	36	33	0	3.88
At Home and on the Road																							
Home	14	102.1	89	26	106	2	8	8	3	0	2.37		47	316.2	330	101	256	12	15	20	17	0	3.92
Road	11	72.0	80	24	61	2	2	5	5	0	3.87		46	305.0	314	107	236	13	18	16	16	0	3.84
During the Day and at Night																							
Day	7	47.2	51	10	43	1	1	4	1	0	3.21		31	196.2	215	56	135	11	5	11	11	0	4.35
Night	18	126.2	118	40	124	3	9	9	7	0	2.91		62	425.0	429	152	357	14	28	25	22	0	3.66
On Grass and on Turf																							
Grass	23	161.1	160	44	159	4	10	12	7	0	2.96		82	550.2	579	180	439	21	27	34	29	0	3.87
Turf	2	13.0	9	6	8	0	0	1	1	0	3.46		11	71.0	65	28	53	4	6	2	4	0	3.93
By Month																							
April	5	33.1	29	13	41	1	5	1	2	0	3.78		15	98.1	100	35	78	3	7	5	5	0	3.57
May	6	44.0	42	7	48	2	2	4	1	0	2.05		16	109.0	110	33	92	7	9	7	6	0	3.22
June	0	0.0	0	0	0	0	0	0	0	0	0.00		12	68.0	76	21	44	6	1	4	4	0	4.63
July	2	9.0	12	5	5	0	0	0	2	0	8.00		13	92.0	85	27	70	3	2	6	4	0	3.62
August	6	41.0	40	16	26	1	1	3	2	0	3.73		18	125.0	133	47	96	4	4	6	6	0	4.46
Sept/Oct	6	47.0	46	9	47	0	2	5	1	0	1.72		19	129.1	140	45	112	2	10	8	8	0	3.90

vs. Opponent Batters

1986 SEASON	Ave.	OBP	SLG	AB	H	2B	3B	HR	RBI	BB	SO	THREE YEARS (84–86)	Ave.	OBP	SLG	AB	H	2B	3B	HR	RBI	BB	SO
Totals	.256	.310	.392	660	169	28	4	18	59	50	167		.268	.328	.423	2407	644	133	10	74	251	208	492
Pitching vs. Left and Right-handed Batters																							
Left	.256	.312	.442	86	22	4	0	4	10	7	20		.263	.318	.398	392	103	23	0	10	40	30	81
Right	.256	.310	.385	574	147	24	4	14	49	43	147		.268	.329	.428	2015	541	110	10	64	211	178	411
Situational																							
Bases Empty	.274	.335	.449	383	105	13	3	16	16	33	92		.271	.338	.439	1381	374	68	7	50	50	132	263
Leadoff	.309	.374	.497	165	51	5	1	8	8	16	30		.278	.348	.451	590	164	30	3	22	22	57	99
Not Leadoff	.248	.305	.413	218	54	8	2	8	8	17	62		.265	.331	.430	791	210	38	4	28	28	75	164
Runners On	.231	.275	.314	277	64	15	1	2	43	17	75		.263	.313	.403	1026	270	65	3	24	201	76	229
First Base Only	.243	.273	.333	144	35	8	1	1	6	6	39		.294	.340	.437	506	149	33	3	11	34	35	96
Scoring Position	.218	.277	.293	133	29	7	0	1	37	11	36		.233	.287	.369	520	121	32	0	13	167	41	133
Late Innings, Close	.259	.306	.328	58	15	4	0	0	1	4	13		.284	.336	.441	236	67	18	2	5	20	18	37

RBI/Opportunities

	1986		THREE YEARS	
Scoring Position	32 / 172	(19%)	144 / 682	(21%)
Scoring Position, 2 Out	12 / 79	(15%)	67 / 319	(21%)
On Third, Less than 2 Out	10 / 30	(33%)	48 / 119	(40%)
RBI in close games / RBI Total	50 / 59	(85%)	188 / 251	(75%)

Pete Incaviglia
Texas Rangers

Still searching for the right nickname . . . Ink-man, Inky, Mongo, and Re-Pete all got some play in 1986. The last came from his usual line-up position being behind Pete O'Brien. Because Incaviglia was a starter from day one, it is easy to forget the magnitude of his accomplishment coming directly to the majors without any prior professional experience. He joins Dave Winfield and Bob Horner as the only active players to make that jump. Incaviglia is the only one of the three to put in a full season his rookie year. In fact, his power numbers and runs and RBI's surpass the COMBINED rookie records of Winfield and Horner:

ROOKIE SEASON	2B/3B/HR	RUNS & RBI's
INCAVIGLIA	21/ 2/ 30	82 + 88 = 170
HORNER & WINFIELD	21/ 2/ 26	89 + 75 = 164

Inky's 30 homers were a record for a Texas Ranger and a remarkable accomplishment for a rookie. Pete lost points with the Rookie-of-the-Year voters with his glove and lack of speed. But let the trivia buffs know that the very first steal of his career was a steal of home, the Rangers' first since 1981.

Of course, some of the purists were offended by his setting a new AL record with 185 strikeouts. I was surprised to see him strike out so much. This is not a Dave Kingman type hitter. He has a lot of motion as he waits on the pitch—possibly a timing mechanism—and I suspect this makes him more vulnerable to pitchers who constantly change speeds on him. But other than that he has a sweet swing, decent plate discipline, and he does a little thinking up there. He'll adjust. He's a lot better than the .250 average of his rookie year. In the off-season they also discovered some visual problems that may have affected him. Next year he'll test the theory of whether contacts can make you a better contact hitter.

Too bad Pete isn't a lefty hitter picking up an extra 200 at-bats of platoon advantage. The early indications are of a large broad platoon difference. Against LHP he hit .306, slugged .600, and had a .374 on-base average.

The big rookie was also a positive personality in the dugout and in the clubhouse. He showed a tremendous enthusiasm for the game and, from what I saw, must have led the team in early arrivals at the park.

—Craig Wright

		1986 SEASON											THREE YEARS (84 – 86)									
	Ave.	OBP	SLG	AB	H	2B	3B	HR	RBI	BB	SO	Ave.	OBP	SLG	AB	H	2B	3B	HR	RBI	BB	SO
Totals	.250	.320	.463	540	135	21	2	30	88	55	185	.250	.320	.463	540	135	21	2	30	88	55	185
Batting vs. Left and Right-handed Pitchers																						
Left	.306	.374	.600	160	49	7	2	12	31	18	55	.306	.374	.600	160	49	7	2	12	31	18	55
Right	.226	.297	.405	380	86	14	0	18	57	37	130	.211	.297	.405	380	86	14	0	18	57	37	130
At Home and on the Road																						
Home	.287	.353	.527	275	79	13	1	17	49	27	94	.287	.353	.527	275	79	13	1	17	49	27	94
Road	.211	.286	.396	265	56	8	1	13	39	28	91	.211	.286	.396	265	56	8	1	13	39	28	91
Facing Groundball Pitchers and Flyball Pitchers																						
Groundball	.240	.314	.468	233	56	12	1	13	44	25	76	.240	.314	.468	233	56	12	1	13	44	25	76
Flyball	.257	.325	.459	307	79	9	1	17	44	30	109	.257	.325	.459	307	79	9	1	17	44	30	109
Facing Finesse Pitchers and Power Pitchers																						
Finesse	.246	.311	.465	329	81	14	2	18	45	32	93	.246	.311	.465	329	81	14	2	18	45	32	93
Power	.256	.333	.460	211	54	7	0	12	43	23	92	.256	.333	.460	211	54	7	0	12	43	23	92
On Grass and on Turf																						
Grass	.258	.329	.484	461	119	19	2	27	81	48	154	.258	.329	.484	461	119	19	2	27	81	48	154
Turf	.203	.264	.342	79	16	2	0	3	7	7	31	.203	.264	.342	79	16	2	0	3	7	7	31
During the Day and at Night																						
Day	.232	.275	.429	112	26	5	1	5	15	7	39	.232	.275	.429	112	26	5	1	5	15	7	39
Night	.255	.331	.472	428	109	16	1	25	73	48	146	.255	.331	.472	428	109	16	1	25	73	48	146
By Month																						
April	.159	.239	.349	63	10	3	0	3	8	6	21	.159	.239	.349	63	10	3	0	3	8	6	21
May	.356	.404	.678	87	31	6	2	6	19	7	31	.356	.404	.678	87	31	6	2	6	19	7	31
June	.255	.330	.415	94	24	3	0	4	16	12	34	.255	.330	.415	94	24	3	0	4	16	12	34
July	.250	.305	.406	96	24	3	0	4	15	7	31	.250	.305	.406	96	24	3	0	4	15	7	31
August	.222	.313	.343	99	22	3	0	3	9	12	33	.222	.313	.343	99	22	3	0	3	9	12	33
Sept/Oct	.238	.313	.564	101	24	3	0	10	21	11	35	.238	.313	.564	101	24	3	0	10	21	11	35
Situational																						
Bases Empty	.268	.329	.504	276	74	14	0	17	17	23	94	.268	.329	.504	276	74	14	0	17	17	23	94
Leadoff	.259	.306	.457	116	30	8	0	5	5	7	38	.259	.306	.457	116	30	8	0	5	5	7	38
Not Leadoff	.275	.345	.537	160	44	6	0	12	12	16	56	.275	.345	.537	160	44	6	0	12	12	16	56
Runners On	.231	.311	.420	264	61	7	2	13	71	32	91	.231	.311	.420	264	61	7	2	13	71	32	91
First Base Only	.225	.306	.358	120	27	2	1	4	11	13	38	.225	.306	.358	120	27	2	1	4	11	13	38
Scoring Position	.236	.316	.472	144	34	5	1	9	60	19	53	.236	.316	.472	144	34	5	1	9	60	19	53
Late Innings, Close	.284	.379	.486	74	21	3	0	4	16	11	25	.284	.379	.486	74	21	3	0	4	16	11	25

RBI/Opportunities	1986 SEASON		THREE YEARS (84–86)	
Scoring Position	45 / 206	(22%)	45 / 206	(22%)
Scoring Position, 2 Out	19 / 102	(19%)	19 / 102	(19%)
On Third, Less than 2 Out	18 / 41	(44%)	18 / 41	(44%)
RBI in close games / RBI Total	64 / 88	(73%)	64 / 88	(73%)

Danny Jackson
Kansas City Royals

Over the last three years, Danny Jackson has a won-lost record of 27–30, and he's got to be the best 27–30 pitcher in the majors. I wrote a year ago that if Danny Jackson were consistent and had a strikeout pitch, he would be the best pitcher in the American League. In 1986 he was markedly more consistent than in previous years, and also began to learn to change speeds with two strikes on the hitter, thus converting a lot of situations that had bogged down into repeated foul balls into quick Ks. He wasn't quite the best pitcher in the league, but he was certainly one of the best.

Jackson's won-lost record was only 11–12, but you can throw that out the window. In the 27 games that Danny started, the Royals scored only 79 runs, an average of 2.93 runs per game. This was the worst offensive support received by any major league pitcher, and that was the sole reason that Jackson did not post a favorable won-lost log. To post almost a .500 record with that abysmal level of offensive support is an impressive accomplishment. Jackson's ERA, 3.20 was the fifth best in the American League.

In the early part of the year Jackson was not able to pitch because of a twisted ankle, and once he got over that it took him a time to find his rhythm. But he made eight starts after September 1, pitched 57 innings and had a 1.88 ERA.

Jackson's bread and butter pitch is a nasty slider that breaks in on a right-handed hitter and down. This causes him to be actually more effective against right-handed hitters than left-handers, as the breakdown will attest (left-handers hit .292 against him, right-handers .247). One area in which he showed particular improvement in 1986 was his ability to pitch into the late innings. In the previous two years opponents had hit over .300 against him in the late innings of close games. Last year, it was .237.

Statistically, Jackson has the defining characteristics of Tommy John: He is impossible to run against, gets lots of ground balls and gives up very few home runs (less than one per 80 bats.) That means that he can win if opponents hit .280 against him, as long as he doesn't walk people. In that area, he does need to improve—but he throws hard, much harder than John ever did. Danny Jackson is one of the finest pitchers in the American League.

—Bill James

	1986: Power, Groundball											1985: Finesse, Groundball											1984: Power, Groundball
	1986 SEASON												**THREE YEARS (84 – 86)**										
	G	IP	H	BB	SO	SB	CS	W	L	S	ERA		G	IP	H	BB	SO	SB	CS	W	L	S	ERA
Totals	32	185.2	177	79	115	9	12	11	12	1	3.20		79	469.2	470	190	269	17	22	27	30	1	3.47
At Home and on the Road																							
Home	15	79.2	73	36	45	4	4	6	4	1	2.15		37	215.1	215	83	111	5	6	14	11	1	3.05
Road	17	106.0	104	43	70	5	8	5	8	0	3.99		42	254.1	255	107	158	12	16	13	19	0	3.82
During the Day and at Night																							
Day	5	22.1	20	12	19	0	3	2	0	1	3.63		22	116.0	121	52	80	1	9	5	7	1	4.34
Night	27	163.1	157	67	96	9	9	9	12	0	3.14		57	353.2	349	138	189	16	13	22	23	0	3.18
On Grass and on Turf																							
Grass	14	87.0	86	34	59	4	6	5	5	0	3.93		33	200.0	206	87	125	11	13	11	12	0	3.65
Turf	18	98.2	91	45	56	5	6	6	7	1	2.55		46	269.2	264	103	144	6	9	16	18	1	3.34
By Month																							
April	3	6.2	6	7	3	1	1	0	0	0	4.05		10	51.2	47	30	23	2	4	1	2	0	2.44
May	4	24.2	25	10	20	1	1	2	1	0	3.28		16	83.2	103	38	46	4	2	5	6	0	4.73
June	6	36.1	44	14	23	0	5	2	4	0	4.21		11	70.1	71	29	40	0	5	5	6	0	3.58
July	5	24.1	19	11	14	3	0	2	1	1	3.33		11	67.0	58	23	43	3	2	6	3	1	2.96
August	6	36.1	37	13	23	1	4	3	3	0	3.96		11	69.1	73	21	53	2	4	5	5	0	3.76
Sept/Oct	8	57.1	46	24	32	3	1	2	3	0	1.88		20	127.2	118	49	64	6	5	5	8	0	3.10

	vs. Opponent Batters																					
	1986 SEASON											**THREE YEARS (84 – 86)**									
	Ave.	OBP	SLG	AB	H	2B	3B	HR	RBI	BB	SO		Ave.	OBP	SLG	AB	H	2B	3B	HR	RBI	BB	SO
Totals	.256	.334	.364	692	177	24	6	13	76	79	115		.263	.337	.365	1788	470	75	18	24	185	190	269
Pitching vs. Left and Right-handed Batters																						
Left	.292	.362	.409	137	40	6	2	2	13	15	25		.270	.349	.380	355	96	15	6	4	34	41	70
Right	.247	.327	.353	555	137	18	4	11	63	64	90		.261	.334	.361	1433	374	60	12	20	151	149	199
Situational																						
Bases Empty	.251	.333	.364	387	97	14	3	8	8	47	69		.256	.338	.358	993	254	37	11	14	14	115	161
Leadoff	.235	.335	.325	166	39	4	1	3	3	25	29		.240	.331	.343	434	104	15	6	6	6	55	65
Not Leadoff	.262	.332	.394	221	58	10	2	5	5	22	40		.268	.345	.369	559	150	22	5	8	8	60	96
Runners On	.262	.334	.364	305	80	10	3	5	68	32	46		.272	.336	.375	795	216	38	7	10	171	75	108
First Base Only	.263	.324	.353	133	35	4	1	2	7	12	18		.290	.342	.398	352	102	14	3	6	19	28	41
Scoring Position	.262	.342	.372	172	45	6	2	3	61	20	28		.257	.331	.357	443	114	24	4	4	152	47	67
Late Innings, Close	.237	.333	.289	97	23	2	0	1	7	13	14		.284	.361	.404	218	62	11	3	3	23	24	28

RBI/Opportunities					
Scoring Position	52 / 231	(23%)		139 / 591	(24%)
Scoring Position, 2 Out	20 / 105	(19%)		51 / 251	(20%)
On Third, Less than 2 Out	17 / 35	(49%)		50 / 111	(45%)
RBI in close games / RBI Total	56 / 76	(74%)		137 / 185	(74%)

Reggie Jackson
California Angels

There are two players of the current era that very much irritate me. They are Reggie Jackson and Steve Garvey. They don't irritate me because of what they've done on the field, but because of the casual fan's reaction to them. One day, I was reading box scores at work during my lunch break, and one of my co-workers was looking over my shoulder. He said, "Hmm, Garvey made an error. Must be a misprint." It wasn't a misprint, and no amount of evidence would prove to him that Garvey isn't the best ballplayer in baseball. And hasn't been. And won't be.

If you turned to this page of the book because you figured you might as well start with Reggie Jackson, the best and most exciting player in baseball, I have some advice for you. I'm sure there are some excellent books on arts and crafts in this bookstore. Go find the National Enquirer. Go on. You're dying to read it anyway. You have an inquiring mind, and want to know. But please stay out of the baseball section of the bookstore, because you are woefully misinformed. Please don't sit behind me at the ballpark and holler "Reggie, Reggie" while ignoring the great stars of this game. If you insist on staying in this section of the bookstore, at least look up Don Mattingly, Rickey Henderson, or Kevin Bass, and bring yourself up to the correct decade.

Now that we've sent that crowd off to the astrology books and the "Where's the Beef?" bumper stickers, we can talk about Reggie in a calmer tone. I've never been much of a Reggie Jackson fan, but mostly because he has played for teams I don't care for. When he came to the Angels, I just knew he was going to be arrogant and selfish, and hurt the ballclub. But I'll have to grudgingly admit that I now appreciate Reggie Jackson. His years with the Angels weren't the best of his career, but I found myself impressed with his contributions to the club.

The thing that surprises me the most about Reggie is his hustle. He doesn't just hustle in games on national TV, or games against the Yankees. He hustles all the time, every groundball. He works hard at his craft. During spring training, Reggie was doing 1,200 situps a day. Even if you could, do you think you would do 1,200 situps? And now pretend that you're 39 and have already made your millions, and have 500 homeruns and have the Hall of Fame made. And you're fighting for a spot as a role player on the ballclub. Now let's see your 1,200 situps. Every day.

—Dennis Bretz

	1986 SEASON											THREE YEARS (84 – 86)										
	Ave.	OBP	SLG	AB	H	2B	3B	HR	RBI	BB	SO	Ave.	OBP	SLG	AB	H	2B	3B	HR	RBI	BB	SO
Totals	.241	.379	.408	419	101	12	2	18	58	92	115	.238	.345	.433	1404	334	56	4	70	224	225	393
Batting vs. Left and Right-handed Pitchers																						
Left	.239	.349	.282	71	17	3	0	0	4	11	24	.224	.316	.388	330	74	12	0	14	53	42	110
Right	.241	.385	.434	348	84	9	2	18	54	81	91	.242	.353	.447	1074	260	44	4	56	171	183	283
At Home and on the Road																						
Home	.277	.426	.497	195	54	6	2	11	32	51	54	.233	.345	.455	666	155	21	2	41	124	114	187
Road	.210	.336	.330	224	47	6	0	7	26	41	61	.243	.345	.413	738	179	35	2	29	100	111	206
Facing Groundball Pitchers and Flyball Pitchers																						
Groundball	.266	.394	.431	188	50	6	2	7	27	40	49	.253	.358	.446	668	169	28	4	31	107	109	179
Flyball	.221	.367	.390	231	51	6	0	11	31	52	66	.224	.333	.421	736	165	28	0	39	117	116	214
Facing Finesse Pitchers and Power Pitchers																						
Finesse	.251	.369	.442	267	67	7	1	14	38	49	63	.253	.345	.449	831	210	38	1	41	130	115	200
Power	.224	.396	.349	152	34	5	1	4	20	43	52	.216	.345	.410	573	124	18	3	29	94	110	193
On Grass and on Turf																						
Grass	.247	.390	.408	360	89	9	2	15	48	83	98	.237	.344	.436	1187	281	45	3	62	195	190	331
Turf	.203	.309	.407	59	12	3	0	3	10	9	17	.244	.349	.415	217	53	11	1	8	29	35	62
During the Day and at Night																						
Day	.215	.368	.380	121	26	6	1	4	15	29	38	.239	.349	.455	380	91	21	2	19	63	62	99
Night	.252	.384	.419	298	75	6	1	14	43	63	77	.237	.343	.425	1024	243	35	2	51	161	163	294
By Month																						
April	.407	.500	.741	54	22	3	0	5	13	10	15	.289	.357	.539	204	59	10	1	13	41	21	53
May	.235	.342	.338	68	16	1	0	2	5	11	23	.218	.333	.406	202	44	8	0	10	25	34	64
June	.290	.468	.319	69	20	2	0	0	9	22	16	.280	.411	.422	232	65	12	0	7	35	50	66
July	.190	.354	.354	79	15	3	2	2	8	20	26	.243	.354	.453	243	59	11	2	12	34	41	69
August	.158	.297	.263	76	12	2	0	2	5	15	19	.195	.298	.328	256	50	8	1	8	35	37	67
Sept/Oct	.219	.341	.521	73	16	1	0	7	18	14	16	.213	.321	.464	267	57	7	0	20	54	42	74
Situational																						
Bases Empty	.232	.358	.394	203	47	4	1	9	9	38	53	.216	.322	.382	727	157	29	1	30	30	108	212
Leadoff	.217	.368	.359	92	20	1	0	4	4	21	19	.211	.325	.353	303	64	7	0	12	12	49	79
Not Leadoff	.243	.349	.423	111	27	3	1	5	5	17	34	.219	.320	.403	424	93	22	1	18	18	59	133
Runners On	.250	.398	.421	216	54	8	1	9	49	54	62	.261	.369	.487	677	177	27	3	40	194	117	181
First Base Only	.282	.388	.505	103	29	5	0	6	13	18	31	.284	.355	.528	320	91	13	1	21	48	35	92
Scoring Position	.221	.405	.345	113	25	3	1	3	36	36	31	.241	.380	.451	357	86	14	2	19	146	82	89
Late Innings, Close	.188	.342	.250	64	12	1	0	1	5	15	21	.190	.313	.253	221	42	5	0	3	17	40	75
RBI/Opportunities																						

			RBI/Opportunities		
Scoring Position	29 / 180	(16%)	107 / 525	(20%)
Scoring Position, 2 Out	11 / 88	(13%)	43 / 256	(17%)
On Third, Less than 2 Out	9 / 29	(31%)	29 / 93	(31%)
RBI in close games / RBI Total	41 / 58	(71%)	151 / 224	(67%)

Brook Jacoby
Cleveland Indians

Brook Jacoby is a rarity—a player who is universally liked and respected. I've never heard an opposing player or manager knock him, his teammates like him a lot, the media is fond of him (while they pointed out that Howser made some bad choices for the 1986 All-Star team, they didn't mention that Brook was one) and even Cleveland fans who'd like to trade him for pitching admit that he can play. Brook is a strong, silent type who plays hard, gets his uniform dirty, never complains (he hit eighth for much of 1986; how many men with his stats would have accepted that?) and is a little bit better than the average third baseman in every area.

Jacoby has played well in Cleveland, but many people think that he could do better. They have a point—Brook is a stocky, right-handed hitter who has problems with off-speed pitches, but you'd never know it from his stats. He doesn't hit nearly as well against lefties as he might and it's hard to see why. He kills finesse pitchers but has trouble with power pitchers; nobody knows why, either. Finally, while Cleveland Stadium is a slight hitter's park and Brook is popular with the fans, he just doesn't hit well here. When a man doesn't hit well here, it usually means that he has a vision problem and it affects his day/night splits, but Brook hits better at night.

The reason, I feel, stems from his 1984. He had a huge buildup when he arrived—people expected him to hit 25 homers and have 100 RBIs every year. He started trying to jerk everything out of the park and died—he hit .224 for April and May. After that, he began trying to spray the ball around and his average started to climb; he's kept doing that ever since. At times, I think that Cleveland should point out to him that, since he knows the pitchers now and has the ability to crank balls, he might want to try doing it when he gets ahead in the count. If he did that, he might be capable of 27 homers, 95 RBIs and 75 walks. Other times, I don't—he tries to crank the ball when there's nobody on and look where it gets him.

To be honest, I'd prefer to see Brook traded, so that Cory Snyder can play his natural position. But I won't complain about Jacoby if he's still on the team in 1987.

—Geoff Beckman

	1986 SEASON											THREE YEARS (84 – 86)										
	Ave.	OBP	SLG	AB	H	2B	3B	HR	RBI	BB	SO	Ave.	OBP	SLG	AB	H	2B	3B	HR	RBI	BB	SO
Totals	.288	.350	.441	583	168	30	4	17	80	56	137	.276	.331	.416	1628	450	75	10	44	207	136	331
Batting vs. Left and Right-handed Pitchers																						
Left	.261	.339	.404	161	42	6	1	5	23	19	34	.282	.349	.437	485	137	18	3	17	63	51	85
Right	.299	.354	.455	422	126	24	3	12	57	37	103	.274	.323	.407	1143	313	57	7	27	144	85	246
At Home and on the Road																						
Home	.266	.338	.431	274	73	11	2	10	45	30	68	.267	.327	.404	799	213	37	5	21	107	73	162
Road	.307	.361	.450	309	95	19	2	7	35	26	69	.286	.334	.427	829	237	38	5	23	100	63	169
Facing Groundball Pitchers and Flyball Pitchers																						
Groundball	.283	.349	.404	272	77	17	2	4	33	28	52	.269	.322	.401	798	215	40	4	19	98	65	153
Flyball	.293	.351	.473	311	91	13	2	13	47	28	85	.283	.338	.430	830	235	35	6	25	109	71	178
Facing Finesse Pitchers and Power Pitchers																						
Finesse	.317	.378	.515	328	104	18	4	13	44	32	57	.305	.353	.466	909	277	46	7	29	116	70	141
Power	.251	.314	.345	255	64	12	0	4	36	24	80	.241	.303	.352	719	173	29	3	15	91	66	190
On Grass and on Turf																						
Grass	.289	.352	.450	491	142	22	3	17	74	48	117	.271	.327	.410	1387	376	61	9	38	184	119	283
Turf	.283	.340	.391	92	26	8	1	0	6	8	20	.307	.351	.448	241	74	14	1	6	23	17	48
During the Day and at Night																						
Day	.277	.332	.467	195	54	7	0	10	34	16	54	.270	.318	.428	551	149	23	2	20	76	41	123
Night	.294	.359	.428	388	114	23	4	7	46	40	83	.279	.337	.409	1077	301	52	8	24	131	95	208
By Month																						
April	.329	.388	.507	73	24	5	1	2	11	7	20	.254	.326	.383	209	53	10	1	5	24	22	39
May	.235	.310	.353	102	24	3	0	3	15	11	24	.270	.324	.399	296	80	11	0	9	39	25	64
June	.260	.308	.450	100	26	5	1	4	16	7	23	.272	.318	.421	309	84	11	1	10	41	22	60
July	.261	.333	.386	88	23	5	0	2	14	10	22	.259	.322	.369	282	73	14	1	5	36	29	60
August	.279	.359	.394	104	29	4	1	2	9	13	28	.305	.364	.433	282	86	10	4	6	32	25	57
Sept/Oct	.362	.403	.552	116	42	8	1	4	15	8	20	.296	.330	.492	250	74	16	3	9	35	13	51
Situational																						
Bases Empty	.259	.326	.399	313	81	15	1	9	9	31	73	.263	.313	.396	883	232	36	5	24	24	64	185
Leadoff	.299	.364	.474	137	41	4	1	6	6	14	28	.291	.334	.448	357	104	13	2	13	13	22	64
Not Leadoff	.227	.295	.341	176	40	11	0	3	3	17	45	.243	.299	.361	526	128	23	3	11	11	42	121
Runners On	.322	.378	.489	270	87	15	3	8	71	25	64	.293	.350	.439	745	218	39	5	20	183	72	146
First Base Only	.341	.372	.447	123	42	7	0	2	8	6	22	.321	.359	.447	349	112	16	2	8	23	20	58
Scoring Position	.306	.383	.524	147	45	8	3	6	63	19	42	.268	.343	.432	396	106	23	3	12	160	52	88
Late Innings, Close	.370	.433	.556	81	30	4	1	3	12	9	21	.286	.321	.396	255	73	6	2	6	25	15	49

RBI/Opportunities					
Scoring Position	52 / 190	(27%)	136 / 543	(25%)
Scoring Position, 2 Out	23 / 93	(25%)	51 / 250	(20%)
On Third, Less than 2 Out	12 / 34	(35%)	53 / 104	(51%)
RBI in close games / RBI Total	51 / 80	(64%)	122 / 207	(59%)

Bob James
Chicago White Sox

Will the real Bob James please stand up? In 1985, after coming over from the Expos, James turned in perhaps the best season ever for a White Sox relief pitcher: a 2.13 ERA, a club-record 32 saves, 88 strikeouts and only 23 walks in 110 innings, a .303 opponents' slugging average. This was the James whose talent had prompted Montreal to make him the ninth player selected in the 1976 draft, ahead of such first-rounders as Leon Durham, Pat Tabler, Mike Scioscia and Bruce Hurst. With a 95-mile-per-hour fastball and a wicked curve, James finally appeared to have everything together at the age of 27.

But then came 1986, and it was back to the James who had struggled for years in the minors. The ERA soared to 5.25, the saves fell to 14, the strikeouts were down to an average of only 4.7 per nine innings. White Sox fans would have been forgiven for suspecting that it was actually BILL James out there on the mound, trying to sneak his fast one past American League hitters. There were extenuating circumstances, of course. James (Bob, not Bill) had control problems all season, walking batters at a rate nearly twice that of 1985. The curve was the main culprit: unless he could control it, James was apt to get hammered. To make the disaster complete, Bob suffered an injury as well, a torn triceps muscle in his throwing arm which forced him to the disabled list. The injury isn't believed to be serious, but it added to the doubts in peoples' minds. Some wondered if Bob wasn't another one-year wonder, following the footsteps of former Sox closers like Lerrin LaGrow, Ed Farmer and Salome Barojas.

One question I asked when looking at James' pitch-by-pitch data for '86 was whether he was continually falling behind in the count; after all, this is a fellow who had yielded nearly a walk an inning for a number of seasons in the minors. Somewhat surprisingly, the answer was no: James threw the first pitch for a strike about 57% of the time (counting all pitches swung at as strikes), which was better than the team average. But there was a catch. In order to get the first pitch in there, James seemed to be taking something off it. Hence the decline in strikeouts, and hence the .649 slugging average the opponents racked up against James when they put the first pitch in play. That's a heavy price to pay for getting a ball over.

—Don Zminda

1986: Finesse, Flyball   **1985: Power, Flyball**   **1984: Power, Flyball**

	1986 SEASON											THREE YEARS (84 – 86)										
	G	IP	H	BB	SO	SB	CS	W	L	S	ERA	G	IP	H	BB	SO	SB	CS	W	L	S	ERA
Totals	49	58.1	61	23	32	5	0	5	4	14	5.25	180	264.1	243	91	211	29	3	19	17	56	3.37
At Home and on the Road																						
Home	24	30.0	38	13	18	2	0	3	2	6	6.30	91	139.1	130	52	114	14	3	11	8	30	3.49
Road	25	28.1	23	10	14	3	0	2	2	8	4.13	89	125.0	113	39	97	15	0	8	9	26	3.24
During the Day and at Night																						
Day	15	23.1	21	8	13	3	0	3	2	4	4.24	55	85.1	76	27	66	6	1	6	5	16	3.48
Night	34	35.0	40	15	19	2	0	2	2	10	5.91	125	179.0	167	64	145	23	2	13	12	40	3.32
On Grass and on Turf																						
Grass	41	51.1	50	18	30	4	0	5	3	13	4.91	118	167.1	149	47	132	14	3	15	8	41	3.23
Turf	8	7.0	11	5	2	1	0	0	1	1	7.71	62	97.0	94	44	79	15	0	4	9	15	3.62
By Month																						
April	11	10.2	12	1	9	0	0	1	1	4	5.06	25	31.1	45	12	26	3	1	2	2	6	6.32
May	12	17.2	21	8	6	2	0	1	3	3	7.13	31	40.2	45	19	32	5	0	2	7	10	4.65
June	15	15.2	17	9	9	2	0	1	0	4	4.02	39	63.0	48	18	50	8	1	4	0	13	1.57
July	8	10.0	10	3	6	0	0	1	0	3	6.30	26	38.2	36	11	28	4	0	4	2	9	4.42
August	2	3.1	0	1	1	1	0	0	0	0	0.00	28	41.2	31	14	31	6	0	4	2	5	2.16
Sept/Oct	1	1.0	1	1	1	0	0	1	0	0	0.00	31	49.0	38	17	44	3	1	3	4	13	2.94

vs. Opponent Batters																						
	1986 SEASON											THREE YEARS (84 – 86)										
	Ave.	OBP	SLG	AB	H	2B	3B	HR	RBI	BB	SO	Ave.	OBP	SLG	AB	H	2B	3B	HR	RBI	BB	SO
Totals	.268	.340	.478	228	61	18	3	8	47	23	32	.244	.309	.364	994	243	52	5	19	144	91	211
Pitching vs. Left and Right-handed Batters																						
Left	.239	.344	.469	113	27	7	2	5	20	16	18	.249	.328	.362	494	123	23	3	9	66	56	109
Right	.296	.336	.487	115	34	11	1	3	27	7	14	.240	.290	.366	500	120	29	2	10	78	35	102
Situational																						
Bases Empty	.263	.358	.495	95	25	7	0	5	5	12	11	.228	.306	.346	457	104	25	1	9	9	47	93
Leadoff	.220	.319	.439	41	9	3	0	2	2	5	3	.216	.307	.342	190	41	10	1	4	4	23	35
Not Leadoff	.296	.387	.537	54	16	4	0	3	3	7	8	.236	.306	.348	267	63	15	0	5	5	24	58
Runners On	.271	.327	.466	133	36	11	3	3	42	11	21	.259	.312	.380	537	139	27	4	10	135	44	118
First Base Only	.306	.333	.510	49	15	5	1	1	6	2	8	.303	.345	.410	188	57	12	1	2	9	11	43
Scoring Position	.250	.323	.440	84	21	6	2	2	36	9	13	.235	.295	.364	349	82	15	3	8	126	33	75
Late Innings, Close	.245	.318	.432	155	38	11	3	4	36	16	24	.235	.293	.348	600	141	29	3	11	90	51	127

RBI/Opportunities				
Scoring Position	29 / 123	(24%)	106 / 508	(21%)
Scoring Position, 2 Out	9 / 53	(17%)	30 / 223	(13%)
On Third, Less than 2 Out	12 / 24	(50%)	53 / 98	(54%)
RBI in close games / RBI Total	36 / 47	(77%)	98 / 144	(68%)

Wally Joyner
California Angels

When the California Angels decided a year ago to let Rod Carew walk away, it was widely perceived as an economic decision. The Angels figured to save the better part of a million dollars. While Wally Joyner was in place to inherit the job, the feeling was not that he'd be terrific, but that he might be OK and if he wasn't they had the position backed up with guys like Hendrick, Grich, DeCinces and even Reggie who could probably play first in a pinch.

After about the 20th of April, no other options were being considered. For economic reasons or not, the Angels chose well: Joyner was terrific. He drove in 100 runs, matching Carew's career high. He was the first rookie to be voted to the All-Star team. His defense was a plus, he hit .320 with men on base and he hit .314 in the late innings of close games. He walked as often as he struck out. There were some gaps in his production. He didn't hit left-handers (.234 against left-handers, .317 against right-handers) and he faded badly the second half of the season (.232 with one homer in August, .239 with none in September). Still, the Angels fans had reason to believe that the infection which laid Wally low during the playoffs had denied his team a chance to go further.

It is doubtful that Joyner will be able to produce the home runs in 1987 that he did in 1986, and that may create some problems. There is an element of any team's fans which tends to focus on a single player as a symbol for the team. For the last five years. Reggie Jackson has been that symbol for the Angels. With Reggie gone, those fans may swing to Joyner and expect him to produce the power. Since Joyner didn't hit for power in the minors, didn't hit for power the second half of 1986 and hit a lot of home runs early in the season that just skimmed the walls, he may not develop as a power hitter. It is important to remember that, like Mickey Vernon, Pete O'Brien or Keith Hernandez, Wally is not a slugger but a multi-faceted talent who happens to be a first baseman. He is too young to be expected to carry the team.

—Bill James and Diana Barnum

	1986 SEASON											THREE YEARS (84 – 86)										
	Ave.	OBP	SLG	AB	H	2B	3B	HR	RBI	BB	SO	Ave.	OBP	SLG	AB	H	2B	3B	HR	RBI	BB	SO
Totals	.290	.348	.457	593	172	27	3	22	100	57	58	.290	.348	.457	593	172	27	3	22	100	57	58
Batting vs. Left and Right-handed Pitchers																						
Left	.234	.289	.354	192	45	3	1	6	24	14	24	.234	.289	.354	192	45	3	1	6	24	14	24
Right	.317	.375	.506	401	127	24	2	16	76	43	34	.317	.375	.506	401	127	24	2	16	76	43	34
At Home and on the Road																						
Home	.279	.347	.432	294	82	10	1	11	40	33	27	.279	.347	.432	294	82	10	1	11	40	33	27
Road	.301	.348	.482	299	90	17	2	11	60	24	31	.301	.348	.482	299	90	17	2	11	60	24	31
Facing Groundball Pitchers and Flyball Pitchers																						
Groundball	.302	.360	.455	268	81	12	1	9	45	27	26	.302	.360	.455	268	81	12	1	9	45	27	26
Flyball	.280	.338	.458	325	91	15	2	13	55	30	32	.280	.338	.458	325	91	15	2	13	55	30	32
Facing Finesse Pitchers and Power Pitchers																						
Finesse	.299	.350	.460	354	106	19	1	12	58	32	26	.299	.350	.460	354	106	19	1	12	58	32	26
Power	.276	.345	.452	239	66	8	2	10	42	25	32	.276	.345	.452	239	66	8	2	10	42	25	32
On Grass and on Turf																						
Grass	.292	.349	.450	520	152	22	3	18	84	48	47	.292	.349	.450	520	152	22	3	18	84	48	47
Turf	.274	.341	.507	73	20	5	0	4	16	9	11	.274	.341	.507	73	20	5	0	4	16	9	11
During the Day and at Night																						
Day	.328	.379	.517	174	57	12	0	7	28	13	18	.328	.379	.517	174	57	12	0	7	28	13	18
Night	.274	.335	.432	419	115	15	3	15	72	44	40	.274	.335	.432	419	115	15	3	15	72	44	40
By Month																						
April	.333	.379	.598	87	29	5	0	6	16	6	8	.333	.379	.598	87	29	5	0	6	16	6	8
May	.282	.325	.564	110	31	1	0	10	25	8	15	.282	.325	.564	110	31	1	0	10	25	8	15
June	.297	.336	.455	101	30	5	1	3	17	7	9	.297	.336	.455	101	30	5	1	3	17	7	9
July	.352	.410	.491	108	38	5	2	2	16	11	11	.352	.410	.491	108	38	5	2	2	16	11	11
August	.232	.307	.323	99	23	6	0	1	15	12	9	.232	.307	.323	99	23	6	0	1	15	12	9
Sept/Oct	.239	.330	.295	88	21	5	0	0	11	13	6	.239	.330	.295	88	21	5	0	0	11	13	6
Situational																						
Bases Empty	.264	.316	.440	318	84	15	1	13	13	22	33	.264	.316	.440	318	84	15	1	13	13	22	33
Leadoff	.255	.303	.422	102	26	2	0	5	5	7	13	.255	.303	.422	102	26	2	0	5	5	7	13
Not Leadoff	.269	.322	.449	216	58	13	1	8	8	15	20	.269	.322	.449	216	58	13	1	8	8	15	20
Runners On	.320	.382	.476	275	88	12	2	9	87	35	25	.320	.382	.476	275	88	12	2	9	87	35	25
First Base Only	.357	.417	.609	115	41	6	1	7	18	12	6	.357	.417	.609	115	41	6	1	7	18	12	6
Scoring Position	.294	.359	.381	160	47	6	1	2	69	23	19	.294	.359	.381	160	47	6	1	2	69	23	19
Late Innings, Close	.314	.398	.488	86	27	5	2	2	12	12	10	.314	.398	.488	86	27	5	2	2	12	12	10

RBI/Opportunities					
Scoring Position	64 / 229	(28%)	64 / 229	(28%)
Scoring Position, 2 Out	29 / 102	(28%)	29 / 102	(28%)
On Third, Less than 2 Out	23 / 40	(57%)	23 / 40	(57%)
RBI in close games / RBI Total	61 / 100	(61%)	61 / 100	(61%)

Terry Kennedy
San Diego Padres

The suggestion could be made that the Padres' braintrust had to wait a year to trade Terry Kennedy; after all, his 1985 season was quite poor compared to 1984, wasn't it? (In fact, didn't everyone on the Padres slip in 1985?) Well, Terry Kennedy didn't slip between '84 and '85, and, in fact, 1986 was the best of the three seasons. His BA climbed from .240 to .261 to .264; his strikeouts were down from 102 to 74, and his Ks/AB went from 1/5.3 to 1/5.85. Doubles, HRs, walks, slugging, on-base and GWRBIs all increased in 1986. Why did it seem like 1986 was such a poor season for Kennedy?

Terry's lifetime batting average is a respectable .276, but a look at a "standardized" season shows that his productivity this year was reasonably close to his career averages:

The worst dropoff was in RBI, but RBI/AB, 2B/AB, and runs/AB were very close to his career averages. Apparently, the Padres simply decided that an "average" Terry Kennedy, after three years of improvement, was no longer acceptable. Larry Bowa has some rebuilding to do here, but he does have some fine young players; the key will be whether the Padres' pitching improves from its team ERA of 3.99 last year.

—J. Michael Duca

Kennedy has had lots of trouble with left-handed pitchers in the past, hitting only .229 with a .288 OBA in 1986. His three-year totals are even worse (.223 BA, .254 OBA). So, where is Terry headed for in 1987? The American League, of course, where good left-handed pitching is much more common than in the NL.

—Gary Gillette

	G	AB	R	H	2B	3B	HR	TB	RBI	BB	SO	SB	CS	BA	SA
Norm	162	567	58	15	30	2	14	229	80	40	95	1	1	.276	.405
1986	141	432	46	11	22	1	12	174	57	37	74	0	3	.264	.403

	1986 SEASON										THREE YEARS (84 – 86)									
	Ave.	OBP	SLG	AB	H	2B	3B	HR	RBI	BB	SO	Ave.	OBP	SLG	AB	H	2B	3B	HR	RBI	BB	SO
Totals	.264	.324	.403	432	114	22	1	12	57	37	74	.254	.302	.374	1494	380	65	3	36	188	101	275
Batting vs. Left and Right-handed Pitchers																						
Left	.229	.288	.396	96	22	7	0	3	10	7	23	.223	.254	.345	403	90	17	1	10	53	15	107
Right	.274	.334	.405	336	92	15	1	9	47	30	51	.266	.319	.385	1091	290	48	2	26	135	86	168
At Home and on the Road																						
Home	.280	.346	.421	214	60	9	0	7	26	20	39	.247	.295	.380	765	189	32	2	22	102	51	145
Road	.248	.302	.385	218	54	13	1	5	31	17	35	.262	.309	.368	729	191	33	1	14	86	50	130
Facing Groundball Pitchers and Flyball Pitchers																						
Groundball	.295	.364	.441	227	67	13	1	6	30	24	29	.273	.326	.391	774	211	36	1	18	94	60	122
Flyball	.229	.279	.361	205	47	9	0	6	27	13	45	.235	.275	.356	720	169	29	2	18	94	41	153
Facing Finesse Pitchers and Power Pitchers																						
Finesse	.293	.342	.458	249	73	18	1	7	31	19	31	.277	.316	.409	847	235	46	1	21	105	48	121
Power	.224	.300	.328	183	41	4	0	5	26	18	43	.224	.284	.329	647	145	19	2	15	83	53	154
On Grass and on Turf																						
Grass	.272	.335	.403	320	87	12	0	10	38	29	55	.251	.300	.375	1116	280	45	2	30	141	77	210
Turf	.241	.292	.402	112	27	10	1	2	19	8	19	.265	.308	.370	378	100	20	1	6	47	24	65
During the Day and at Night																						
Day	.225	.286	.333	129	29	3	1	3	16	10	22	.230	.273	.331	453	104	17	1	9	62	27	85
Night	.281	.340	.432	303	85	19	0	9	41	27	52	.265	.314	.393	1041	276	48	2	27	126	74	190
By Month																						
April	.224	.307	.373	67	15	2	1	2	10	8	11	.205	.267	.340	215	44	6	1	7	28	19	33
May	.244	.308	.366	82	20	4	0	2	15	8	11	.286	.332	.423	248	71	13	0	7	51	18	39
June	.316	.381	.447	76	24	4	0	2	7	7	12	.275	.330	.407	280	77	15	2	6	32	21	55
July	.269	.329	.410	78	21	5	0	2	4	6	14	.254	.295	.375	264	67	14	0	6	25	15	51
August	.225	.271	.325	80	18	2	0	2	6	5	16	.207	.245	.272	261	54	8	0	3	20	13	52
Sept/Oct	.327	.365	.551	49	16	5	0	2	15	3	10	.296	.339	.429	226	67	9	0	7	32	15	45
Situational																						
Bases Empty	.259	.301	.398	266	69	14	1	7	7	15	38	.247	.284	.370	835	206	33	2	22	22	42	144
Leadoff	.234	.287	.336	107	25	3	1	2	2	8	16	.219	.257	.316	351	77	8	1	8	8	18	58
Not Leadoff	.277	.311	.440	159	44	11	0	5	5	7	22	.267	.304	.409	484	129	25	1	14	14	24	86
Runners On	.271	.358	.410	166	45	8	0	5	50	22	36	.264	.323	.379	659	174	32	1	14	166	59	131
First Base Only	.224	.297	.328	67	15	1	0	2	5	6	15	.264	.301	.351	265	70	11	0	4	13	13	49
Scoring Position	.303	.397	.465	99	30	7	0	3	45	16	21	.264	.336	.398	394	104	21	1	10	153	46	82
Late Innings, Close	.289	.379	.422	90	26	6	0	2	12	13	17	.269	.339	.353	283	76	12	0	4	27	29	54

RBI/Opportunities

Scoring Position	38 / 131	(29%)		133 / 524	(25%)
Scoring Position, 2 Out	24 / 72	(33%)		49 / 248	(20%)
On Third, Less than 2 Out	6 / 16	(38%)		47 / 103	(46%)
RBI in close games / RBI Total	44 / 57	(77%)		133 / 188	(71%)

Jimmy Key
Toronto Blue Jays

Jimmy Key has progressed so rapidly that very few people realize that he is already one of the top pitchers in the American League. In 1984, he served the Blue Jays mainly from the bullpen, compiling a 4–5 record with a 4.65 ERA. He became the first Toronto lefty to win a start in years in 1985 and went 14–6 with a 3.00 ERA. The only negative to his year was that he was largely ineffective in the playoffs; that should have been expected. A young starter often has a tendency to tail off late in the year. They have usually never had to pitch more than 200 innings in any one year and the workload in a major league environment catches up to them. Key was one such case; Kirk McCaskill was another.

In '86, Jimmy had a terrible start. He was unable to locate the strike zone and, accordingly, gave up a lot of runs early in the game. As a matter of fact, he never pitched into the sixth inning until his seventh start (on 5/11)—it was no coincidence that that was also his first victory. Eventually, Key found the plate, began getting ahead of hitters and began winning some ballgames. From May 11th to July 17th, Jimmy started 14 games and went 9–3 (one no-decision was a one-run, ten-inning performance) with a fine 2.61 ERA.

One part of his game that improved over the course of the season was his ability to hold runners. Most intriguing was the fact that, during Key's early struggles, men actually took liberties on him—an appalling event for groundballing southpaw. Baserunners of any kind make life more difficult for pitchers. Infielders must play closer to their bases (to allow themselves a chance at the double play), rather than where the batter is most likely to hit the ball; hitters tend to hit for a higher average with runners on base than they will with the bases empty. The closer a pitcher can hold them, the more naturally the defense can position themselves and the lower his ERA is likely to be. With help from pitching coach Al Widmar, Jimmy redesigned his move to first. And, predictably, potential basestealers found themselves picked off before they could make any attempt toward second.

Despite his fine year, Key is unsatisfied. He is working on a forkball to add to his good curve, excellent change and average fastball. If he is successful, the AL had best watch out in 1987.

—David Driscoll

	1986: Finesse, Groundball											1985: Finesse, Groundball										1984: Power, Groundball
	1986 SEASON											**THREE YEARS (84 – 86)**										
	G	IP	H	BB	SO	SB	CS	W	L	S	ERA	G	IP	H	BB	SO	SB	CS	W	L	S	ERA
Totals	36	232.0	222	74	141	8	7	14	11	0	3.57	134	506.2	480	156	270	22	13	32	22	10	3.46
At Home and on the Road																						
Home	18	114.0	121	40	69	8	4	7	9	0	4.50	67	269.0	268	80	138	12	7	18	14	3	3.68
Road	18	118.0	101	34	72	0	3	7	2	0	2.67	67	237.2	212	76	132	10	6	14	8	7	3.22
During the Day and at Night																						
Day	15	104.0	95	29	57	5	1	6	6	0	3.46	42	179.0	166	50	97	8	3	12	9	1	3.52
Night	21	128.0	127	45	84	3	6	8	5	0	3.66	92	327.2	314	106	173	14	10	20	13	9	3.43
On Grass and on Turf																						
Grass	15	101.2	78	30	65	0	3	6	2	0	2.04	54	205.1	176	66	119	9	6	13	8	5	2.85
Turf	21	130.1	144	44	76	8	4	8	9	0	4.76	80	301.1	304	90	151	13	7	19	14	5	3.88
By Month																						
April	4	13.2	20	7	7	1	0	0	1	0	11.85	15	44.0	47	16	24	1	2	2	4	1	5.93
May	7	34.2	34	17	19	2	0	3	2	0	5.19	26	74.1	64	32	38	6	1	6	3	3	4.12
June	6	47.1	40	11	38	3	2	3	2	0	2.09	24	100.2	88	28	63	5	2	6	4	0	2.24
July	6	41.2	46	14	25	0	3	3	1	0	3.24	22	93.1	103	26	46	0	4	6	3	0	3.95
August	6	41.0	40	9	22	1	1	2	3	0	3.51	23	89.2	93	22	45	6	2	6	6	3	3.61
Sept/Oct	7	53.2	42	16	30	1	1	3	2	0	2.01	24	104.2	85	32	54	4	2	6	2	3	2.58

	vs. Opponent Batters																			
	1986 SEASON										**THREE YEARS (84 – 86)**									
	Ave.	OBP	SLG	AB	H	2B	3B	HR	RBI	BB	SO	Ave.	OBP	SLG	AB	H	2B	3B	HR	RBI	BB	SO
Totals	.256	.315	.403	866	222	47	4	24	83	74	141	.252	.309	.401	1905	480	101	10	54	200	156	270
Pitching vs. Left and Right-handed Batters																						
Left	.268	.319	.321	190	51	5	1	1	8	12	45	.247	.305	.342	442	109	15	3	7	42	36	96
Right	.253	.314	.426	676	171	42	3	23	75	62	96	.254	.310	.418	1463	371	86	7	47	158	120	174
Situational																						
Bases Empty	.274	.337	.401	526	144	31	3	10	10	49	92	.257	.307	.394	1156	297	61	8	27	27	82	168
Leadoff	.299	.341	.455	231	69	14	2	6	6	15	40	.267	.306	.442	491	131	27	4	17	17	28	65
Not Leadoff	.254	.333	.359	295	75	17	1	4	4	34	52	.250	.307	.358	665	166	34	4	10	10	54	103
Runners On	.229	.282	.406	340	78	16	1	14	73	25	49	.244	.312	.411	749	183	40	2	27	173	74	102
First Base Only	.243	.276	.452	177	43	7	0	10	23	8	23	.251	.293	.455	347	87	20	0	17	43	20	45
Scoring Position	.215	.287	.356	163	35	9	1	4	50	17	26	.239	.326	.373	402	96	20	2	10	130	54	57
Late Innings, Close	.280	.325	.393	107	30	3	0	3	8	7	12	.277	.343	.396	328	91	13	1	8	47	32	45

	RBI/Opportunities				
Scoring Position	41 / 214	(19%)	111 / 538	(21%)
Scoring Position, 2 Out	12 / 79	(15%)	47 / 235	(20%)
On Third, Less than 2 Out	16 / 38	(42%)	40 / 93	(43%)
RBI in close games / RBI Total	59 / 83	(71%)	143 / 200	(71%)

Dave Kingman
Oakland A's

Dave Kingman will never win a popularity contest, especially if the voters are sportswriters. Dumping icewater on and sending dead rats to them will not win friends and influence people. His misanthropic behavior may be fodder for psychologists, but looking at his performance on the field, the interesting question is whether he should be regarded as Hall of Fame material.

The main argument for Kingman's candidacy is the home run total of 442, which is now 19th on the All-Time list. He has 1210 RBI, which is fairly good, and a decent Secondary Average of .346. His home run percentage of 6.6 is one of the highest. Negatives include a low batting average of .236, poor strike zone judgment, and lousy defensive work. His total of Runs Produced/500 AB is only 125.0, which is rather poor for a slugger. Considering that he's played about 15 1/3 years, we get the following profile of his career:

AB	R	H	B	3B	HR	RBI	SB	Pct.	SO	BB	SLG
436	59	103	6	2	29	79	6	.236	119	40	.482

The intangibles are not in his favor. He has changed uniforms seven times. He has played in two All-Star games but never in the World Series; in his rookie year he made the playoffs with the Giants. He had one outstanding year, 1979, but finished 11th in the MVP voting, receiving no first place votes. He is never mentioned when "insiders" give their views on the best candidates for the Hall.

My conclusion about Kingman is that he is not a great player, but merely a good one. Using James' Approximate Value concept, I calculate that Kingman has 128 career AV points. The average of his best five years is 10.2, of the best 10 is 9.1, and average AV Pts./500 AB is 9.6. All these criteria place Kingman in the "good" range among ballplayers, in a class with someone like Willie Horton. The insight that his talent lies within one dimension (hitting home runs) of one dimension (hitting) is essentially correct. Now he will be only 36 in 1987 and theoretically could hit another 100 home runs, which would make it difficult to exclude him from the Hall. However, the A's don't seem inclined to re-sign him, and I doubt that anyone else wants him, so that may be it for Dave.

—Bill McMahon

	Ave.	OBP	SLG	AB	H	2B	3B	HR	RBI	BB	SO		Ave.	OBP	SLG	AB	H	2B	3B	HR	RBI	BB	SO
	1986 SEASON												**THREE YEARS (84 – 86)**										
Totals	.210	.255	.431	561	118	19	0	35	94	33	126		.239	.296	.450	1702	406	58	1	100	303	139	359
Batting vs. Left and Right-handed Pitchers																							
Left	.220	.277	.509	173	38	8	0	14	31	13	44		.245	.317	.488	527	129	18	1	36	102	58	119
Right	.206	.245	.397	388	80	11	0	21	63	20	82		.236	.286	.433	1175	277	40	0	64	201	81	240
At Home and on the Road																							
Home	.212	.244	.391	297	63	8	0	15	45	14	68		.235	.295	.436	854	201	27	0	48	153	71	184
Road	.208	.266	.477	264	55	11	0	20	49	19	58		.242	.296	.465	848	205	31	1	52	150	68	175
Facing Groundball Pitchers and Flyball Pitchers																							
Groundball	.217	.260	.386	254	55	4	0	13	43	14	51		.256	.315	.470	813	208	28	1	48	162	70	164
Flyball	.205	.251	.469	307	63	15	0	22	51	19	75		.223	.278	.432	889	198	30	0	52	141	69	195
Facing Finesse Pitchers and Power Pitchers																							
Finesse	.220	.259	.418	328	72	11	0	18	56	18	61		.231	.276	.404	982	227	30	1	46	150	62	184
Power	.197	.249	.451	233	46	8	0	17	38	15	65		.249	.321	.512	720	179	28	0	54	153	77	175
On Grass and on Turf																							
Grass	.199	.244	.384	477	95	16	0	24	68	28	113		.232	.292	.431	1412	327	49	1	77	246	122	301
Turf	.274	.315	.702	84	23	3	0	11	26	5	13		.272	.311	.541	290	79	9	0	23	57	17	58
During the Day and at Night																							
Day	.212	.250	.385	226	48	6	0	11	30	12	49		.270	.312	.498	637	172	22	0	41	121	42	127
Night	.209	.258	.463	335	70	13	0	24	64	21	77		.220	.286	.422	1065	234	36	1	59	182	97	232
By Month																							
April	.158	.197	.263	57	9	0	0	2	10	3	15		.214	.284	.467	210	45	5	0	16	47	19	46
May	.238	.277	.505	105	25	1	0	9	20	3	30		.253	.304	.486	296	75	7	1	20	56	20	73
June	.189	.248	.406	106	20	5	0	6	22	9	21		.232	.294	.471	280	65	7	0	20	60	25	58
July	.198	.238	.385	96	19	3	0	5	12	5	18		.252	.289	.441	313	79	11	0	16	47	18	62
August	.286	.330	.592	98	28	6	0	8	18	7	19		.269	.335	.481	308	83	17	0	16	56	31	56
Sept/Oct	.172	.215	.364	99	17	4	0	5	12	6	23		.200	.263	.359	295	59	11	0	12	37	26	64
Situational																							
Bases Empty	.200	.254	.479	305	61	10	0	25	25	20	70		.227	.291	.438	906	206	27	1	54	54	76	195
Leadoff	.164	.219	.297	128	21	5	0	4	4	7	30		.214	.267	.378	415	89	12	1	18	18	26	94
Not Leadoff	.226	.279	.610	177	40	5	0	21	21	13	40		.238	.310	.489	491	117	15	0	36	36	50	101
Runners On	.223	.256	.375	256	57	9	0	10	69	13	56		.251	.301	.464	796	200	31	0	46	249	63	164
First Base Only	.187	.202	.290	107	20	2	0	3	7	2	23		.244	.280	.467	360	88	11	0	23	53	17	76
Scoring Position	.248	.292	.436	149	37	7	0	7	62	11	33		.257	.316	.461	436	112	20	0	23	196	46	88
Late Innings, Close	.200	.250	.412	85	17	0	0	6	15	6	16		.230	.299	.456	248	57	2	0	18	44	25	56
RBI/Opportunities																							
Scoring Position				48 / 200		(24%)								155 / 598		(26%)							
Scoring Position, 2 Out				18 / 94		(19%)								60 / 282		(21%)							
On Third, Less than 2 Out				18 / 46		(39%)								64 / 132		(48%)							
RBI in close games / RBI Total				66 / 94		(70%)								190 / 303		(63%)							

Bob Knepper
Houston Astros

Bob Knepper won his tenth game of the season last year on June 10th; he slumped to a 7–9 record the rest of the way. He rallied to end the season with a 5-inning, no-hit outing against the Braves, then became the victim of two Mets rallies during Games 3 and 6 of the NL Championship Series. The last two games seem to sum up Knepper's career: a mechanically sound, good control pitcher who doesn't have the killer instinct to win the close games. Knepper is thought to be one of the game's top pitchers and is paid over a million dollars annually, yet last year he tied his season-high win total with only 17, and has a career losing record of 114–118.

Knepper's control is better inside the dome. He strikes out 5.20 batters per nine innings-pitched at home while walking a stingy 1.64, but on alien ground he whiffs 4.70 and his walk total increases to 2.71. Over the last three seasons, Knepper's years have come in two-month chapters. He's a fast starter, going 25–18 during April and May. He fades quickly during the heat of June and July to a 12–17 record, but he recovers to save face during the last two months with a 17–12 mark.

—Bill Young

Bob Knepper was acquired from the San Francisco Giants on December 8th, 1980, for the price of Enos Cabell and Chris Bourjous. Bourjous's major-league career consisted of 13 games with the Giants; Cabell played regularly for the Giants in 1981, hitting .255 with a .326 slugging average. Cabell was then traded with cash to Detroit for the immortal Champ Summers. Since the trade, Knepper has pitched in 202 games for Houston, throwing 1272.2 innings.

Sure, Bob Knepper is not a great pitcher. Yes, after his very successful 1977 and 1978 seasons, he was a disappointment to the Giants in 1979–80. Does this excuse, however, the sheer stupidity of the Giants in this case? I think not. Knepper was dumped because he wasn't as good as he was supposed to be, not because he wasn't valuable as he was. It is too easy to dismiss a player who doesn't meet expectations, whether unrealistic or not. The Giants should have had more patience with Knepper. About the only good thing that can be said of this deal is that the Giants made another terrible trade involving a left-handed pitcher, but at least they sent the poor lefty packing, rather than giving up the farm to get him.

—Gary Gillette

1986: Finesse, Groundball   **1985: Finesse, Groundball**   **1984: Finesse, Groundball**

	G	IP	H	BB	SO	SB	CS	W	L	S	ERA		G	IP	H	BB	SO	SB	CS	W	L	S	ERA
	1986 SEASON												**THREE YEARS (84 – 86)**										
Totals	40	258.0	232	62	143	16	9	17	12	0	3.14		112	732.2	708	171	414	35	34	47	35	0	3.29
At Home and on the Road																							
Home	20	131.2	123	24	77	9	3	9	6	0	3.62		58	393.1	379	72	223	21	20	24	18	0	3.23
Road	20	126.1	109	38	66	7	6	8	6	0	2.64		54	339.1	329	99	191	14	14	23	17	0	3.37
During the Day and at Night																							
Day	18	100.2	104	28	56	8	1	8	5	0	3.75		33	198.1	198	51	120	10	3	15	9	0	3.49
Night	22	157.1	128	34	87	8	8	9	7	0	2.75		79	534.1	510	120	294	25	31	32	26	0	3.22
On Grass and on Turf																							
Grass	13	82.2	70	21	44	6	3	4	4	0	2.72		31	202.0	185	50	108	10	6	13	9	0	3.07
Turf	27	175.1	162	41	99	10	6	13	8	0	3.34		81	530.2	523	121	306	25	28	34	26	0	3.37
By Month																							
April	5	35.1	28	9	19	1	1	4	0	0	1.27		14	97.1	77	23	58	4	5	7	3	0	2.13
May	7	49.1	41	15	29	0	3	4	2	0	2.74		19	129.1	118	40	73	2	8	11	4	0	2.78
June	7	50.0	48	8	26	6	2	2	4	0	3.78		20	133.1	141	29	68	8	9	7	11	0	3.92
July	7	46.1	30	5	27	2	1	3	1	0	2.33		19	121.0	113	20	75	4	3	5	5	0	2.98
August	7	45.0	45	10	24	2	1	2	3	0	3.40		19	130.1	123	28	71	5	4	9	6	0	3.25
Sept/Oct	7	32.0	40	15	18	5	1	2	2	0	5.63		21	121.1	136	31	69	12	5	8	6	0	4.45

vs. Opponent Batters

	Ave.	OBP	SLG	AB	H	2B	3B	HR	RBI	BB	SO		Ave.	OBP	SLG	AB	H	2B	3B	HR	RBI	BB	SO
	1986 SEASON												**THREE YEARS (84 – 86)**										
Totals	.242	.289	.367	960	232	47	8	19	86	62	143		.254	.298	.387	2782	708	132	20	66	269	171	414
Pitching vs. Left and Right-handed Batters																							
Left	.231	.258	.385	156	36	8	2	4	10	6	37		.249	.274	.387	377	94	19	3	9	32	14	92
Right	.244	.295	.363	804	196	39	6	15	76	56	106		.255	.301	.388	2405	614	113	17	57	237	157	322
Situational																							
Bases Empty	.240	.273	.363	612	147	27	6	12	12	28	97		.255	.288	.384	1720	439	79	10	41	41	77	268
Leadoff	.251	.288	.355	251	63	8	3	4	4	13	38		.270	.308	.383	715	193	31	4	14	14	38	101
Not Leadoff	.233	.263	.368	361	84	19	3	8	8	15	59		.245	.274	.385	1005	246	48	6	27	27	39	167
Runners On	.244	.315	.374	348	85	20	2	7	74	34	46		.253	.313	.393	1062	269	53	10	25	228	94	146
First Base Only	.266	.314	.364	143	38	6	1	2	6	8	14		.263	.293	.403	491	129	23	5	12	36	19	62
Scoring Position	.229	.315	.380	205	47	14	1	5	68	26	32		.245	.328	.384	571	140	30	5	13	192	75	84
Late Innings, Close	.237	.303	.362	80	19	5	1	1	9	8	9		.250	.304	.349	212	53	8	2	3	13	17	27

RBI/Opportunities

Scoring Position	57 / 297	(19%)		165 / 794	(21%)
Scoring Position, 2 Out	19 / 131	(15%)		64 / 370	(17%)
On Third, Less than 2 Out	25 / 65	(38%)		61 / 146	(42%)
RBI in close games / RBI Total	62 / 86	(72%)		187 / 269	(70%)

Ray Knight
New York Mets

Ray Knight isn't just a player, he's an example, a lesson to ballplayers everywhere who Ask Too Much. His 1986 season was solid in almost every respect: he was a key member of a World Championship ballclub, batted close to .300, hit well in the clutch and with runners in scoring position, and wound up as a World Series hero with a well-deserved MVP award. A few years ago that would have been enough to induce a grateful ballclub into giving him a multi-year, multi-million dollar contract. When you add that Ray is good-looking, clean-cut and married to Nancy Lopez, the Mets would have been considered ingrates if they hadn't given him whatever he wanted. Fans would have muttered about boycotts and accused management of tampering with the chemistry of a champion.

How times have changed! When Ray asked the Mets for a million a year, perhaps pointing out that he was at least half as good as George Foster, he was treated like Oliver Twist asking for more gruel. The club cut him loose without a thought, and no one seemed to mind that Howard Johnson had previously been found wanting and that Dave Magadan was a singles-hitting minor leaguer. Enough was

enough already. Ray was worth what the Mets said he was worth; did he think the franchise was worth ninety million or something? There was no boycott; there wasn't even a whimper.

I bring all this up not really to criticize the Met management, just to point out how the worm has turned in baseball. Looking at it objectively, Ray Knight is a player of obvious limitations. Even in his outstanding season of 1986, he showed his normal problem areas: he struggles against righthanders, has so-so power, doesn't have much strike zone judgment and isn't exactly Mike Schmidt in the field. He hit .298 in '86, but in 1985 it was .218, in 1984 .237. The Mets couldn't be blamed for asking Ray to show some more consistency, at least, before they started shelling out the really big bucks. Ray Knight made only one mistake: he thought it was still 1982. "Worth" is always a relative term; you may have justice and rightness on your side, but you've still got to convince somebody to pay it out. And in an era when even George Steinbrenner thinks of the bottom line before winning, Ray got caught in the middle.

—Don Zminda

	1986 SEASON											THREE YEARS (84 – 86)										
	Ave.	OBP	SLG	AB	H	2B	3B	HR	RBI	BB	SO	Ave.	OBP	SLG	AB	H	2B	3B	HR	RBI	BB	SO
Totals	.298	.351	.424	486	145	24	2	11	76	40	63	.259	.304	.360	1128	292	50	2	20	147	74	138
Batting vs. Left and Right-handed Pitchers																						
Left	.381	.410	.604	197	75	15	1	9	35	11	17	.304	.331	.469	503	153	30	1	17	78	22	55
Right	.242	.314	.301	289	70	9	1	2	41	29	46	.222	.283	.272	625	139	20	1	3	69	52	83
At Home and on the Road																						
Home	.289	.353	.452	228	66	12	2	7	35	22	34	.250	.302	.381	544	136	28	2	13	82	41	77
Road	.306	.350	.399	258	79	12	0	4	41	18	29	.267	.306	.341	584	156	22	0	7	65	33	61
Facing Groundball Pitchers and Flyball Pitchers																						
Groundball	.274	.338	.371	237	65	15	1	2	28	23	26	.245	.296	.342	556	136	31	1	7	67	39	63
Flyball	.321	.364	.474	249	80	9	1	9	48	17	37	.273	.312	.378	572	156	19	1	13	80	35	75
Facing Finesse Pitchers and Power Pitchers																						
Finesse	.280	.331	.410	271	76	15	1	6	33	20	30	.253	.295	.353	645	163	30	1	11	66	37	65
Power	.321	.377	.442	215	69	9	1	5	43	20	33	.267	.316	.369	483	129	20	1	9	81	37	73
On Grass and on Turf																						
Grass	.301	.363	.433	326	98	18	2	7	50	32	47	.261	.310	.372	683	178	30	2	14	91	48	83
Turf	.294	.326	.406	160	47	6	0	4	26	8	16	.256	.295	.342	445	114	20	0	6	56	26	55
During the Day and at Night																						
Day	.286	.328	.405	185	53	7	0	5	28	11	21	.263	.301	.366	350	92	15	0	7	44	19	33
Night	.306	.365	.435	301	92	17	2	6	48	29	42	.257	.306	.357	778	200	35	2	13	103	55	105
By Month																						
April	.306	.364	.714	49	15	2	0	6	12	5	4	.262	.304	.434	145	38	7	0	6	22	9	13
May	.348	.396	.461	89	31	10	0	0	11	8	13	.273	.325	.404	183	50	15	0	3	22	15	24
June	.286	.327	.378	98	28	1	1	2	14	6	16	.234	.271	.316	256	60	7	1	4	28	13	37
July	.186	.306	.271	70	13	1	1	1	8	11	15	.214	.285	.307	140	30	5	1	2	22	13	25
August	.330	.359	.381	97	32	5	0	0	17	5	6	.281	.314	.326	178	50	5	0	1	27	10	14
Sept/Oct	.313	.356	.446	83	26	5	0	2	14	5	9	.283	.329	.385	226	64	11	0	4	26	14	25
Situational																						
Bases Empty	.275	.331	.417	276	76	14	2	7	7	21	44	.241	.288	.339	638	154	28	2	10	10	39	87
Leadoff	.288	.342	.405	111	32	5	1	2	2	9	12	.242	.283	.346	240	58	11	1	4	4	13	23
Not Leadoff	.267	.324	.424	165	44	9	1	5	5	12	32	.241	.291	.334	398	96	17	1	6	6	26	64
Runners On	.329	.377	.433	210	69	10	0	4	69	19	19	.282	.324	.388	490	138	22	0	10	137	35	51
First Base Only	.296	.324	.459	98	29	7	0	3	11	3	9	.245	.281	.364	220	54	11	0	5	16	9	17
Scoring Position	.357	.416	.411	112	40	3	0	1	58	16	10	.311	.356	.407	270	84	11	0	5	121	26	34
Late Innings, Close	.325	.345	.494	83	27	6	1	2	14	3	10	.239	.269	.354	209	50	10	1	4	20	8	29
RBI/Opportunities																						

	1986 SEASON		THREE YEARS (84 – 86)	
Scoring Position	56 / 162	(35%)	107 / 369	(29%)
Scoring Position, 2 Out	23 / 70	(33%)	37 / 148	(25%)
On Third, Less than 2 Out	21 / 37	(57%)	48 / 89	(54%)
RBI in close games / RBI Total	39 / 76	(51%)	75 / 147	(51%)

Mike Krukow
San Francisco Giants

The big question Giants fans are asking this off-season is: Did Mike Krukow have a career season in 1986, or has Roger Craig done it again? Throughout his career, Krukow was a good #3 or #4 starter. Last year, at age 34, he became one of the league's premier pitchers.

The Giants first 20-game winner in 13 years, Mike Krukow set career bests in wins, 20 (2nd in National League), 3.05 ERA (7th in the league), complete games, 10 (4th in NL), innings pitched, 245, (6th in NL), and strikeouts, 178, (9th in NL). He posted the third best walks per 9 IP ratio in the league 2.02. He won his 100th game August 15 in LA, a 5–1 complete game with a career-high 12 strikeouts.

Mike was 12–4 at home, with a 2.47 ERA and 8 CGs in 16 starts. He was NL Pitcher-of-the-Month in September, going 6–0, 1.37 ERA in 6 starts. He was the only pitcher to beat the Mets four times. Mike closed the season very strong—after coming off the DL, he had a two-month ERA of 2.36 with 79 strikeouts in 95.1 innings.

Twelve of Krukow's 20 victories stopped losing streaks. The Giants were 23–11 in his starts, 60–68 in all other games. Another success for the split-fingered fastball.

—J. Michael Duca

Mike Krukow had his finest season last year. He shook off the label of a .500 pitcher and put together a 20–9 record. In thirteen of his fourteen professional seasons, Krukow has fanned more than 100 batters. In his first season, he led the Gulf Coast League with 80 Ks. He has a good fastball, a slider, a changeup, a split-finger and an outstanding curveball. His command of these pitches along with good location and changing speeds made for his impressive season. Krukow's strong finish was helped by a forced mid-season rest after a rib injury suffered in a fracas in St. Louis.

Krukow has for quite some time pitched much better on grass. Last year, he did better on turf than he has in the past, though. His ability to use the elements at Candlestick to his advantage gives him a big edge. The wind helps his breaking ball, while the high grass helps his fielders. The infield of Brown, Thompson, Uribe and Clark also helped reduce the number of hits he allowed, and Krukow himself is an excellent fielder.

Krukow is 35–17 at Candlestick (lifetime), with and ERA under 3.00, including a 4–1 record there before being traded to the Giants.

—Victor Hester

1986: Finesse, Flyball   **1985: Power, Flyball**   **1984: Power, Flyball**

	G	IP	H	BB	SO	SB	CS	W	L	S	ERA		G	IP	H	BB	SO	SB	CS	W	L	S	ERA
			1986 SEASON												**THREE YEARS (84 – 86)**									
Totals	34	245.0	204	55	178	23	7	20	9	0	3.05		97	639.0	614	182	469	74	17	39	32	1	3.62
										At Home and on the Road													
Home	16	127.1	95	17	92	7	4	12	4	0	2.47		48	347.0	308	86	259	28	12	24	13	0	2.75
Road	18	117.2	109	38	86	16	3	8	5	0	3.67		49	292.0	306	96	210	46	5	15	19	1	4.65
										During the Day and at Night													
Day	18	136.1	114	24	90	8	3	11	6	0	3.17		46	327.2	308	77	228	30	12	21	13	0	3.32
Night	16	108.2	90	31	88	15	4	9	3	0	2.90		51	311.1	306	105	241	44	5	18	19	1	3.93
										On Grass and on Turf													
Grass	26	191.2	161	32	138	12	5	17	6	0	3.15		73	501.1	468	134	366	48	14	33	20	0	3.43
Turf	8	53.1	43	23	40	11	2	3	3	0	2.70		24	137.2	146	48	103	26	3	6	12	1	4.31
										By Month													
April	5	31.0	22	9	23	4	1	3	1	0	3.77		15	97.0	92	31	75	12	2	6	5	0	3.53
May	6	43.2	36	9	31	4	0	3	2	0	3.50		15	109.0	85	28	80	11	3	7	6	0	2.97
June	6	44.0	40	9	27	7	3	3	1	0	3.07		17	96.2	110	28	61	14	5	4	5	0	5.31
July	4	31.0	27	5	18	3	2	2	2	0	3.77		16	118.2	120	27	77	14	4	8	6	0	3.41
August	5	37.0	34	7	30	1	1	2	2	0	2.68		18	117.1	115	38	94	14	1	6	6	1	3.38
Sept/Oct	8	58.1	45	16	49	4	0	7	1	0	2.16		16	100.1	92	30	82	9	2	8	4	0	3.32

vs. Opponent Batters

	Ave.	OBP	SLG	AB	H	2B	3B	HR	RBI	BB	SO		Ave.	OBP	SLG	AB	H	2B	3B	HR	RBI	BB	SO
			1986 SEASON												**THREE YEARS (84 – 86)**									
Totals	.223	.269	.355	913	204	36	6	24	82	55	178		.250	.303	.388	2460	614	110	18	65	253	182	469
							Pitching vs. Left and Right-handed Batters																	
Left	.226	.284	.350	517	117	23	4	11	46	41	95		.269	.327	.420	1313	353	66	11	37	149	115	235
Right	.220	.249	.361	396	87	13	2	13	36	14	83		.228	.274	.351	1147	261	44	7	28	104	67	234
								Situational															
Bases Empty	.221	.258	.348	587	130	23	6	13	13	27	117		.250	.295	.385	1488	372	68	14	35	35	88	281
Leadoff	.235	.272	.370	238	56	9	4	5	5	11	39		.256	.297	.417	624	160	29	7	19	19	33	114
Not Leadoff	.212	.249	.332	349	74	14	2	8	8	16	78		.245	.294	.362	864	212	39	7	16	16	55	167
Runners On	.227	.288	.368	326	74	13	0	11	69	28	61		.249	.314	.393	972	242	42	4	30	218	94	188
First Base Only	.271	.306	.464	140	38	9	0	6	16	7	22		.289	.327	.448	391	113	22	2	12	34	21	54
Scoring Position	.194	.276	.296	186	36	4	0	5	53	21	39		.222	.306	.356	581	129	20	2	18	184	73	134
Late Innings, Close	.223	.248	.268	112	25	2	0	1	5	4	21		.208	.260	.295	288	60	11	1	4	20	21	53

RBI/Opportunities

Scoring Position	45 / 244	(18%)		155 / 768	(20%)		
Scoring Position, 2 Out	11 / 109	(10%)		57 / 354	(16%)		
On Third, Less than 2 Out	24 / 46	(52%)		61 / 145	(42%)		
RBI in close games / RBI Total	61 / 82	(74%)		189 / 253	(75%)		

Lee Lacy
Baltimore Orioles

I can sum up every problem that Baltimore has in two words: Lee Lacy. Lacy hasn't been a bad player for most of his career—he's never been a good one. He can hit, he has middling power and he gets on base more often than an average player will. But he can't field well, he's a mediocre baserunner (some people aren't even that kind) and it's always been obvious what the ceiling on his production is. Lacy would never have hit .330, hit 25 homers or had 95 RBIs if given 600 at-bats. It is very likely that he might have hit 10–12 homers, get 65–80 RBIs and hit .280–.300—but so what?

Building a championship team is like belling the cat—easy to plan and difficult to do. Teams talk about their "blueprint for a championship" like it's a state secret; anyone with a grain of sense can see what you need. First, you need 2–3 players who are one of the very best in the game at their positions (men like Carter, Gooden and Hernandez). To support them, you need 4–5 other men who are very good at what they do, but not the best in the game (Darling, Ojeda, Strawberry, Dykstra, Orosco and McDo-

well). You get them and make sure that the rest of your team is collectively average—a few (Backman, Fernandez) who are above average, a few (Knight, Aguilera) who are average and a few who aren't terrible (Mitchell, Santana)—and you'll win 100 games. Finding those players is hard—very few teams get them all at once—but a team shouldn't have trouble identifying their needs and finding people to fill them.

The problem with Lacy is that he isn't the sort of player Baltimore needs. They've got Ripken and Murray, so they don't have to have any more superstars. But what stars do they have? If Aase and Lynn were reliable, they'd have two—but they'd still be missing three others. At his best, Lacy is a supporting player—the man ain't gonna win you no pennants. Players like Ken Gerhart, Jim Traber, Larry Sheets and Mike Young might—but with Lacy eating up 500 at-bats that could be going to them, how can you tell? If Lee Lacy were a title deed in a Monopoly game, he'd be a railroad—you can't win by collecting a lot of them.

—Geoff Beckman

	1986 SEASON											THREE YEARS (84 – 86)									
	Ave.	OBP	SLG	AB	H	2B	3B	HR	RBI	BB	SO	Ave.	OBP	SLG	AB	H	2B	3B	HR	RBI	BB	SO
Totals	.287	.334	.391	491	141	18	0	11	47	37	71	.300	.346	.421	1457	437	66	7	32	165	108	227
Batting vs. Left and Right-handed Pitchers																						
Left	.280	.333	.408	157	44	5	0	5	14	13	14	.314	.369	.477	491	154	23	3	17	54	42	56
Right	.290	.334	.383	334	97	13	0	6	33	24	57	.293	.335	.392	966	283	43	4	15	111	66	171
At Home and on the Road																						
Home	.304	.353	.404	230	70	8	0	5	19	18	34	.315	.363	.430	718	226	37	2	14	79	56	124
Road	.272	.317	.379	261	71	10	0	6	28	19	37	.286	.330	.411	739	211	29	5	18	86	52	103
Facing Groundball Pitchers and Flyball Pitchers																						
Groundball	.282	.333	.356	216	61	4	0	4	16	17	35	.291	.341	.380	705	205	29	2	10	66	55	108
Flyball	.291	.334	.418	275	80	14	0	7	31	20	36	.309	.351	.459	752	232	37	5	22	99	53	119
Facing Finesse Pitchers and Power Pitchers																						
Finesse	.282	.319	.349	301	85	11	0	3	26	18	34	.292	.324	.388	837	244	41	5	10	80	45	114
Power	.295	.357	.458	190	56	7	0	8	21	19	37	.311	.374	.465	620	193	25	2	22	85	63	113
On Grass and on Turf																						
Grass	.293	.337	.401	399	117	13	0	10	38	29	55	.297	.346	.407	936	278	36	2	21	92	74	160
Turf	.261	.320	.348	92	24	5	0	1	9	8	16	.305	.346	.445	521	159	30	5	11	73	34	67
During the Day and at Night																						
Day	.277	.316	.412	148	41	5	0	5	15	9	23	.306	.348	.449	412	126	18	1	13	45	28	64
Night	.292	.341	.382	343	100	13	0	6	32	28	48	.298	.345	.410	1045	311	48	6	19	120	80	163
By Month																						
April	.333	.347	.391	69	23	4	0	0	7	2	9	.355	.375	.430	107	38	6	1	0	13	4	15
May	.239	.278	.352	88	21	4	0	2	12	6	13	.239	.279	.336	226	54	7	0	5	27	14	33
June	.270	.311	.420	100	27	3	0	4	10	6	18	.306	.345	.458	288	88	12	1	10	33	19	51
July	.293	.360	.404	99	29	2	0	3	11	11	13	.324	.377	.433	284	92	12	2	5	36	25	42
August	.308	.363	.394	104	32	3	0	2	6	9	14	.293	.347	.433	314	92	13	2	9	37	26	49
Sept/Oct	.290	.353	.355	31	9	2	0	0	1	3	4	.307	.360	.420	238	73	16	1	3	19	20	37
Situational																						
Bases Empty	.306	.358	.422	294	90	13	0	7	7	24	42	.293	.340	.418	868	254	38	4	21	21	61	136
Leadoff	.370	.388	.550	100	37	6	0	4	4	3	11	.302	.331	.425	301	91	15	2	6	6	13	36
Not Leadoff	.273	.344	.356	194	53	7	0	3	3	21	31	.287	.344	.414	567	163	23	2	15	15	48	100
Runners On	.259	.298	.345	197	51	5	0	4	40	13	29	.311	.355	.424	589	183	28	3	11	144	47	91
First Base Only	.326	.347	.391	92	30	3	0	1	4	3	12	.337	.357	.453	258	87	16	1	4	15	8	31
Scoring Position	.200	.258	.305	105	21	2	0	3	36	10	17	.290	.354	.402	331	96	12	2	7	129	39	60
Late Innings, Close	.300	.341	.388	80	24	4	0	1	9	5	12	.295	.354	.419	234	69	9	1	6	28	21	40
RBI/Opportunities																						
Scoring Position				31 / 145		(21%)									114 / 455		(25%)					
Scoring Position, 2 Out				9 / 59		(15%)									38 / 192		(20%)					
On Third, Less than 2 Out				15 / 30		(50%)									52 / 88		(59%)					
RBI in close games / RBI Total				25 / 47		(53%)									92 / 165		(56%)					

Ken Landreaux
Los Angeles Dodgers

Ken Landreaux is a "wait 'til next year" Dodger. In 1979, his second full season, Ken had his career year. He was 25 years old then, and great things were expected of him, as he batted .305 that year. He had career highs in runs (81), RBIs (83), hits (172), doubles (27), extra-base hits (47) and at-bats (564). He also hit 15 home runs, a total that he has surpassed only once in his career.

Stardom was expected for Ken, but the Twins, never having been bastions of patience and nuturing, gave him only one more season to produce. They traded Landreaux to the Dodgers the following year, after his average dropped to .281. In return, they received Mickey Hatcher, Kelly Snider and Matt Reeves.

In Los Angeles, Landreaux has never quite lived up to what was expected of him. He is not a liability on defense, but NL runners have been known to take liberties on his arm. Offensively, Ken has been a .267 hitter in his six years with the Dodgers; in 1982 and 1983 he showed good speed by stealing 31 and 30 bases, respectively. He hasn't stolen more than 15 bases since.

Though they haven't had a major effect on Landreaux's career, each year he misses 15 or more games due to injuries. 1986 was his worst year, injury-wise—he was sidelined for 59 games. Except for the strike-shortened season, Kenny had never played in less than 129 games.

Over the past three seasons, Ken's hitting pattern has been the same. He is notoriously slow starting: his combined April batting average is .229. By the end of June, he is loosened up and ready for the summer game, peaking in July with a .305 average. After July, it is all down hill; by September, his average drops back to .241.

Landreaux will have to work hard in 1987 to come back from his injuries. He has only one year left on his contract, and, with the way free-agents are being treated now, he could have trouble signing with a new team. One more bad season could leave Landreaux in the unemployment line.

Ken Landreaux has had many high points. At one time he hit in 31 straight games; he has played for three division winners, one World Championship team and in one All-Star game. If Landreaux comes back in 1987 and plays up to his potential, it could finally be the long-awaited "next year" for Kenny.

—Carmen J. Corica

	1986 SEASON											THREE YEARS (84 – 86)										
	Ave.	OBP	SLG	AB	H	2B	3B	HR	RBI	BB	SO	Ave.	OBP	SLG	AB	H	2B	3B	HR	RBI	BB	SO
Totals	.261	.313	.364	283	74	13	2	4	29	22	39	.260	.306	.384	1203	313	50	9	27	126	84	111
Batting vs. Left and Right-handed Pitchers																						
Left	.267	.313	.333	45	12	3	0	0	8	2	5	.242	.311	.348	161	39	8	0	3	23	15	24
Right	.261	.313	.370	238	62	10	2	4	21	20	34	.263	.305	.390	1042	274	42	9	24	103	69	87
At Home and on the Road																						
Home	.236	.308	.291	127	30	4	0	1	14	14	14	.246	.303	.329	581	143	22	1	8	55	51	53
Road	.282	.317	.423	156	44	9	2	3	15	8	25	.273	.308	.436	622	170	28	8	19	71	33	58
Facing Groundball Pitchers and Flyball Pitchers																						
Groundball	.281	.344	.397	146	41	9	1	2	21	14	16	.287	.336	.416	543	156	27	2	13	73	43	39
Flyball	.241	.279	.328	137	33	4	1	2	8	8	23	.238	.280	.358	660	157	23	7	14	53	41	72
Facing Finesse Pitchers and Power Pitchers																						
Finesse	.250	.306	.375	144	36	10	1	2	21	12	12	.249	.291	.375	688	171	36	3	15	73	45	50
Power	.273	.320	.353	139	38	3	1	2	8	10	27	.276	.325	.396	515	142	14	6	12	53	39	61
On Grass and on Turf																						
Grass	.244	.303	.346	205	50	10	1	3	18	18	28	.260	.306	.373	881	229	37	6	17	78	63	78
Turf	.308	.341	.410	78	24	3	1	1	11	4	11	.261	.305	.413	322	84	13	3	10	48	21	33
During the Day and at Night																						
Day	.337	.387	.477	86	29	7	1	1	8	7	13	.285	.328	.435	379	108	22	4	9	37	26	37
Night	.228	.281	.315	197	45	6	1	3	21	15	26	.249	.296	.360	824	205	28	5	18	89	58	74
By Month																						
April	.247	.287	.397	73	18	5	0	2	9	5	5	.229	.276	.380	192	44	11	0	6	21	13	14
May	.254	.333	.365	63	16	2	1	1	8	8	14	.257	.298	.351	191	49	8	2	2	19	12	22
June	.264	.298	.340	53	14	2	1	0	3	3	9	.278	.337	.378	230	64	9	1	4	24	22	18
July	.301	.354	.397	73	22	4	0	1	9	5	8	.305	.347	.443	203	62	9	2	5	25	14	23
August	.000	.000	.000	0	0	0	0	0	0	0	0	.246	.275	.401	167	41	6	1	6	15	7	5
Sept/Oct	.190	.227	.190	21	4	0	0	0	0	1	3	.241	.290	.355	220	53	7	3	4	22	16	29
Situational																						
Bases Empty	.262	.298	.366	172	45	7	1	3	3	8	28	.258	.298	.399	722	186	26	5	22	22	40	74
Leadoff	.333	.358	.471	51	17	4	0	1	1	2	8	.267	.296	.442	217	58	10	2	8	8	9	17
Not Leadoff	.231	.273	.322	121	28	3	1	2	2	6	20	.253	.299	.380	505	128	16	3	14	14	31	57
Runners On	.261	.333	.360	111	29	6	1	1	26	14	11	.264	.316	.362	481	127	24	4	5	104	44	37
First Base Only	.304	.333	.413	46	14	2	0	1	3	2	2	.324	.361	.430	207	67	11	1	3	10	12	11
Scoring Position	.231	.333	.323	65	15	4	1	0	23	12	9	.219	.286	.310	274	60	13	3	2	94	32	26
Late Innings, Close	.213	.258	.328	61	13	2	1	1	7	4	4	.250	.287	.407	216	54	9	2	7	22	12	17
RBI/Opportunities																						
Scoring Position			22 / 100	(22%)										90 / 376	(24%)							
Scoring Position, 2 Out			6 / 39	(15%)										31 / 151	(21%)							
On Third, Less than 2 Out			10 / 15	(67%)										40 / 66	(61%)							
RBI in close games / RBI Total			21 / 29	(72%)										96 / 126	(76%)							

Mark Langston
Seattle Mariners

Mark Langston won 17 games as a rookie in 1984 and led the league with 204 strikeouts. Bothered by an injury, he was not effective in 1985 or early 1986, but regained his stuff and put on a late surge to pass Roger Clemens, once again leading the American League in strikeouts with 245. However, inconsistency kept his record to 12–14 with a 4.85 ERA—the second-highest ERA ever for a pitcher with 200 strikeouts (Bobo Newsome was at 5.08 in 1938).

Langston relies primarily on an excellent fastball and an exceptional slider. He also throws a slow curve ball which can be devastating if he throws it for strikes. Throwing strikes, however, is Langston's biggest problem. In his three year career he has averaged 5.06 walks per nine innings and has yet to pitch a walkless complete game. The major league average over the same three year period is 3.30 walks per nine innings. The walks keep him constantly in trouble and result in him throwing a great number of pitches. In 1986 Langston threw 4,123 pitches (60.7% strikes) or an average of 155.2 pitches per nine innings. He has a tendency to lose his poise when in trouble or when he makes a mistake. The result is big innings which have kept him from becoming the consistent winner a pitcher of his talents should be.

Langston's greatest strength is his ability to get out left-handed batters. In his three seasons, lefties have a combined .194 average against him. His dominance is so great that opposing managers stack their lineups with right-handed batters. Only 17.1% of the at bats against Langston in his three seasons have been by lefties; an average of only 5.77 at bats per nine innings.

Langston is averaging 7.93 strikeouts per nine innings for his career, but 8.71 for his two completely healthy seasons. He has fanned ten or more batters twelve times—four times in 1984 and eight times in 1986, including four games in a row in September. His career high is fifteen strikeouts against Cleveland in 1986.

Langston has the arm, the ability, and seemingly the desire to become the top left-handed pitcher in baseball. If he can learn to control his pitches and his composure without losing any of his stuff, the results could be comparable with Koufax or Carlton.

—Dennis Orr

1986: Power, Flyball **1985: Power, Groundball** **1984: Power, Flyball**

	G	IP	H	BB	SO	SB	CS	W	L	S	ERA	G	IP	H	BB	SO	SB	CS	W	L	S	ERA
	1986 SEASON											**THREE YEARS (84 – 86)**										
Totals	37	239.1	234	123	245	14	8	12	14	0	4.85	96	591.0	544	332	521	38	22	36	38	0	4.43
At Home and on the Road																						
Home	19	120.1	115	65	142	10	5	5	7	0	5.39	46	298.1	256	156	295	23	11	19	15	0	4.22
Road	18	119.0	119	58	103	4	3	7	7	0	4.31	50	292.2	288	176	226	15	11	17	23	0	4.64
During the Day and at Night																						
Day	11	72.1	78	38	75	5	1	3	6	0	5.10	28	167.0	168	95	148	13	6	10	12	0	4.58
Night	26	167.0	156	85	170	9	7	9	8	0	4.74	68	424.0	376	237	373	25	16	26	26	0	4.37
On Grass and on Turf																						
Grass	16	101.0	107	54	88	2	3	5	7	0	4.72	39	224.1	232	141	178	9	8	13	19	0	4.73
Turf	21	138.1	127	69	157	12	5	7	7	0	4.94	57	366.2	312	191	343	29	14	23	19	0	4.25
By Month																						
April	5	24.2	30	18	19	1	1	1	2	0	6.20	14	84.1	81	54	48	5	3	5	6	0	4.48
May	6	45.0	49	23	35	2	2	3	2	0	4.60	17	104.2	108	58	70	4	3	6	7	0	4.56
June	6	40.1	31	19	45	4	1	5	1	0	3.35	14	82.1	69	36	86	6	4	8	4	0	3.28
July	5	31.1	27	17	34	2	1	0	2	0	5.74	13	80.0	62	40	87	3	5	4	5	0	4.05
August	7	44.0	43	25	47	2	2	2	3	0	6.14	19	122.2	106	77	107	6	4	8	8	0	4.55
Sept/Oct	8	54.0	54	21	65	3	1	1	4	0	4.00	19	117.0	118	67	123	14	3	5	8	0	5.23

vs. Opponent Batters

	Ave.	OBP	SLG	AB	H	2B	3B	HR	RBI	BB	SO	Ave.	OBP	SLG	AB	H	2B	3B	HR	RBI	BB	SO
	1986 SEASON											**THREE YEARS (84 – 86)**										
Totals	.255	.343	.425	917	234	52	7	30	119	123	245	.246	.345	.404	2215	544	109	19	68	277	332	521
Pitching vs. Left and Right-handed Batters																						
Left	.184	.260	.294	163	30	6	0	4	15	16	50	.194	.293	.317	382	74	16	2	9	39	51	111
Right	.271	.361	.454	754	204	46	7	26	104	107	195	.256	.356	.422	1833	470	93	17	59	238	281	410
Situational																						
Bases Empty	.240	.336	.408	512	123	30	4	16	16	72	156	.232	.343	.402	1246	289	59	12	43	43	204	322
Leadoff	.259	.351	.441	220	57	14	1	8	8	30	64	.212	.326	.354	537	114	23	4	15	15	89	128
Not Leadoff	.226	.325	.384	292	66	16	3	8	8	42	92	.247	.356	.439	709	175	36	8	28	28	115	194
Runners On	.274	.352	.447	405	111	22	3	14	103	51	89	.263	.348	.407	969	255	50	7	25	234	128	199
First Base Only	.277	.382	.426	148	41	8	1	4	12	23	34	.259	.341	.381	409	106	18	1	10	25	48	86
Scoring Position	.272	.334	.459	257	70	14	2	10	91	28	55	.266	.352	.425	560	149	32	6	15	209	80	113
Late Innings, Close	.355	.412	.486	107	38	6	1	2	13	11	16	.272	.377	.401	217	59	14	1	4	22	38	42

RBI/Opportunities

Scoring Position	73 / 332	(22%)	176 / 767	(23%)
Scoring Position, 2 Out	17 / 135	(13%)	66 / 338	(20%)
On Third, Less than 2 Out	33 / 60	(55%)	69 / 140	(49%)
RBI in close games / RBI Total	76 / 119	(64%)	200 / 277	(72%)

Carney Lansford
Oakland A's

Carney Lansford is Buddy Bell without the Gold Glove. As an offensive player, Lansford is as similar to Buddy Bell as a hitter can be—a right-handed line drive hitter, a .290 hitter with 12-to-20 home run power and adequate speed, but not base stealing speed. As a defensive third baseman, he was good but never golden, and at 30 he may now be moving to first base, to allow the rookie Mark McGwire to play third base and hit home runs.

The season isn't long enough for Lansford. Over a three-year period, he has hit just .260 in April, but increased that average steadily to .317 in August and .324 after the first of September. This would probably testify to good work habits during the season, or maybe (who knows?) poor work habits in the off-season.

Over the three-year period Lansford has hit .346 with runners on first base only, but just .280 with the bases empty and .269 with men in scoring position. This would be not unusual for a left-handed hitter but is somewhat unusual for a right-hander, and no doubt occurs because Lansford hits to the opposite field, and thus benefits from the runner being held on. Since the A's lead-off man (Phillips) doesn't steal bases anyway, this might make Lansford a number two hitter. However, he doesn't walk a lot and does dribble into quite a few double plays.

Lansford's career has been hampered by injuries and serious family health problems which have reduced his playing time, but he has been a full-time player in two of the last three seasons, so it's probably time to quit talking about that.

Unlike several of the Oakland players, Lansford hits much better in the Coliseum than on the road. Over a three-year period he has hit .318 in Oakland, but just .260 on the road. It is still a poor hitter's park. He's consistent in that breakdown, having hit .329, .302, and .319 at home, but .274, .250 and .249 on the road.

Lansford hits much better in day baseball than at night, hitting (over three years) .310 in day games, .276 at night, and with more power in day games. Our stats show that he hits finesse pitchers much better than power pitchers.

Lansford has not hit well in the late innings of close games.

—Bill James

	1986 SEASON												THREE YEARS (84 – 86)										
	Ave.	OBP	SLG	AB	H	2B	3B	HR	RBI	BB	SO		Ave.	OBP	SLG	AB	H	2B	3B	HR	RBI	BB	SO
Totals	.284	.332	.421	591	168	16	4	19	72	39	51		.288	.330	.430	1589	458	65	11	46	192	97	140
Batting vs. Left and Right-handed Pitchers																							
Left	.305	.363	.460	187	57	7	2	6	15	15	14		.302	.343	.437	520	157	21	5	13	41	33	42
Right	.275	.317	.403	404	111	9	2	13	57	24	37		.282	.324	.427	1069	301	44	6	33	151	64	98
At Home and on the Road																							
Home	.319	.368	.477	298	95	11	3	10	48	24	20		.318	.353	.475	783	249	41	5	24	113	45	57
Road	.249	.294	.365	293	73	5	1	9	24	15	31		.259	.309	.386	806	209	24	6	22	79	52	83
Facing Groundball Pitchers and Flyball Pitchers																							
Groundball	.297	.333	.418	273	81	5	2	8	36	14	18		.289	.330	.429	779	225	31	6	22	99	48	59
Flyball	.274	.330	.425	318	87	11	2	11	36	25	33		.288	.331	.431	810	233	34	5	24	93	49	81
Facing Finesse Pitchers and Power Pitchers																							
Finesse	.295	.321	.418	359	106	9	1	11	41	13	19		.309	.331	.458	955	295	40	6	30	115	33	55
Power	.267	.347	.427	232	62	7	3	8	31	26	32		.257	.329	.388	634	163	25	5	16	77	64	85
On Grass and on Turf																							
Grass	.291	.337	.430	495	144	15	3	16	63	33	41		.296	.335	.445	1336	395	57	8	42	169	78	113
Turf	.250	.305	.375	96	24	1	1	3	9	6	10		.249	.306	.352	253	63	8	3	4	23	19	27
During the Day and at Night																							
Day	.305	.349	.465	256	78	7	2	10	37	18	20		.307	.353	.478	613	188	23	5	24	83	44	47
Night	.269	.319	.388	335	90	9	2	9	35	21	31		.277	.316	.400	976	270	42	6	22	109	53	93
By Month																							
April	.300	.341	.362	80	24	3	1	0	10	5	5		.260	.309	.329	258	67	6	3	2	30	18	23
May	.276	.311	.449	98	27	2	0	5	12	5	8		.287	.339	.498	279	80	12	1	15	37	22	29
June	.280	.345	.360	100	28	2	0	2	6	8	8		.274	.322	.388	317	87	12	0	8	32	20	26
July	.283	.321	.434	99	28	2	2	3	14	5	11		.284	.313	.404	282	80	13	3	5	32	11	25
August	.275	.306	.490	102	28	2	1	6	18	4	10		.316	.345	.516	225	71	9	3	10	31	10	22
Sept/Oct	.295	.363	.420	112	33	5	0	3	12	12	9		.320	.364	.465	228	73	13	1	6	30	16	15
Situational																							
Bases Empty	.274	.317	.423	350	96	12	2	12	12	19	31		.278	.316	.419	936	260	37	7	27	27	48	81
Leadoff	.309	.338	.511	139	43	5	1	7	7	6	11		.271	.298	.410	339	92	12	1	11	11	13	27
Not Leadoff	.251	.304	.365	211	53	7	1	5	5	13	20		.281	.327	.424	597	168	25	6	16	16	35	54
Runners On	.299	.352	.419	241	72	4	2	7	60	20	20		.303	.349	.446	653	198	28	4	19	165	49	59
First Base Only	.317	.343	.396	101	32	2	0	2	4	4	12		.346	.369	.496	280	97	16	1	8	19	9	25
Scoring Position	.286	.358	.436	140	40	2	2	5	56	16	8		.271	.336	.408	373	101	12	3	11	146	40	34
Late Innings, Close	.233	.310	.467	90	21	2	2	5	15	10	14		.253	.311	.418	249	63	6	4	9	43	20	36
RBI/Opportunities																							
Scoring Position				47 / 192		(24%)										127 / 507		(25%)					
Scoring Position, 2 Out				20 / 104		(19%)										52 / 236		(22%)					
On Third, Less than 2 Out				19 / 31		(61%)										51 / 98		(52%)					
RBI in close games / RBI Total				52 / 72		(72%)										127 / 192		(66%)					

Tim Leary
Milwaukee Brewers

It's hard for me to put my faith in a player whose stats for any particular year read "(did not play)" and Tim Leary's had two such seasons in the minors. I haven't had much faith in George Bamberger's ability to judge talent lately, either. Bambi thought that Leary had the ability to be Milwaukee's best starter; I couldn't tell you why. Maybe he was still seeing that 23-year-old that teams drooled over when they both were with the Mets. If so, it explains a lot about why Tim didn't miss a start all year despite giving up 10.32 hits per nine innings and giving up extra base hits like free tickets to the circus.

When most pitchers have a .500 record and a 4.21 ERA, you can see why—there's some split in the breakdowns that explains it. Leary's 1986 doesn't have anything like it—he was mediocre anywhere he went. His best performances came out of Milwaukee and on grass fields—he was 5–2 with a 3.85 ERA—but he gave up 72 hits in 53.2 innings, walked 23 and struck out 30, so you can't exactly say that he pitched well.

Leary's problems were pretty clear—he put the first man on 37% of the time. If he put the runner on first, there was a 41% chance that he'd put somebody else on, too. After that, he'd rise to the occasion, but it was a little late. He gave up a lot of cheap hits with men in scoring position—mostly flares to the opposite field—so you could argue that he had bad luck if you wanted to. I don't—when you put people on base that often, you deserve whatever you get.

Leary had some bright spots to his '86. His strikeout to walk ratio was very good; first time in his career since 1980 that that's happened. He did a good job of holding runners on base. He threw two shutouts and two four-hitters. Like just about every Brewer, he finished 1986 strongly (5–2 with a 3.26 ERA in the last two months). But the man is 28, he exemplified the words "journeyman starter" this year and, even though he's supposed to be 100%, I don't trust anyone with his history of injuries—you don't rebuild a ballclub with men like him. If Leary were 25, I'd be higher on him and sorry to see him go. Since he isn't, I don't see how or why we'll miss him.

—Scott Segrin and Geoff Beckman

| 1986: Finesse, Groundball | | 1985: Power, Groundball | | 1984: Finesse, Groundball |

	1986 SEASON											THREE YEARS (84 – 86)										
	G	IP	H	BB	SO	SB	CS	W	L	S	ERA	G	IP	H	BB	SO	SB	CS	W	L	S	ERA
Totals	33	188.1	216	53	110	17	13	12	12	0	4.21	58	275.1	317	79	168	27	14	16	19	0	4.15
At Home and on the Road																						
Home	17	96.1	103	24	57	9	7	5	8	0	4.30	29	140.1	158	38	78	15	8	8	11	0	4.30
Road	16	92.0	113	29	53	8	6	7	4	0	4.11	29	135.0	159	41	90	12	6	8	8	0	4.00
During the Day and at Night																						
Day	14	80.2	88	28	45	8	7	5	6	0	4.24	20	100.2	108	34	52	9	8	7	8	0	3.67
Night	19	107.2	128	25	65	9	6	7	6	0	4.18	38	174.2	209	45	116	18	6	9	11	0	4.43
On Grass and on Turf																						
Grass	27	150.0	175	47	87	13	11	10	10	0	4.14	45	216.2	254	69	128	21	12	13	16	0	4.28
Turf	6	38.1	41	6	23	4	2	2	2	0	4.46	13	58.2	63	10	40	6	2	3	3	0	3.68
By Month																						
April	4	24.0	30	9	19	5	4	2	1	0	4.50	8	45.0	50	16	31	7	4	3	2	0	3.40
May	7	38.0	50	12	25	5	3	1	3	0	6.39	14	53.0	69	20	31	9	3	2	4	0	6.45
June	6	44.2	43	9	26	0	1	3	3	0	3.02	13	55.0	55	11	35	1	1	3	4	0	3.11
July	4	20.2	24	6	9	3	0	1	3	0	5.23	6	28.0	34	7	11	3	1	2	3	0	5.14
August	6	27.1	36	10	16	2	4	2	1	0	3.62	6	27.1	36	10	16	2	4	2	1	0	3.62
Sept/Oct	6	33.2	33	7	15	2	1	3	1	0	2.94	11	67.0	73	15	44	5	1	4	5	0	3.49

vs. Opponent Batters

	1986 SEASON											THREE YEARS (84 – 86)										
	Ave.	OBP	SLG	AB	H	2B	3B	HR	RBI	BB	SO	Ave.	OBP	SLG	AB	H	2B	3B	HR	RBI	BB	SO
Totals	.289	.339	.422	747	216	31	4	20	82	53	110	.289	.340	.417	1096	317	45	7	27	120	79	168
Pitching vs. Left and Right-handed Batters																						
Left	.282	.354	.423	369	104	17	1	11	34	42	47	.296	.362	.429	548	162	23	1	16	58	56	69
Right	.296	.324	.421	378	112	14	3	9	48	11	63	.283	.317	.405	548	155	22	6	11	62	23	99
Situational																						
Bases Empty	.284	.337	.426	423	120	18	3	12	12	29	56	.280	.329	.430	625	175	28	6	18	18	40	88
Leadoff	.319	.370	.530	185	59	11	2	8	8	13	16	.316	.359	.533	272	86	13	5	12	12	16	26
Not Leadoff	.256	.311	.345	238	61	7	1	4	4	16	40	.252	.307	.351	353	89	15	1	6	6	24	62
Runners On	.296	.343	.417	324	96	13	1	8	70	24	54	.301	.354	.399	471	142	17	1	9	102	39	80
First Base Only	.368	.409	.521	144	53	5	1	5	13	8	19	.366	.410	.500	202	74	7	1	6	16	13	27
Scoring Position	.239	.292	.333	180	43	8	0	3	57	16	35	.253	.315	.323	269	68	10	0	3	86	26	53
Late Innings, Close	.313	.353	.396	48	15	1	0	1	2	3	6	.355	.400	.473	93	33	5	0	2	6	7	16

RBI/Opportunities

Scoring Position	51 / 228	(22%)	80 / 350	(23%)
Scoring Position, 2 Out	16 / 95	(17%)	28 / 155	(18%)
On Third, Less than 2 Out	23 / 42	(55%)	36 / 66	(55%)
RBI in close games / RBI Total	54 / 82	(66%)	80 / 120	(67%)

Craig Lefferts
San Diego Padres

If you study the question "When are games most often won and lost?", you find that the answer tends to be "In the fifth, sixth and seventh innings." It is common for a pitcher to stagger through a game, leading 5–3 and put two men on with two out in the sixth. What can his manager do? If he leaves his starter in, he risks losing the lead; it's too early for the ace. Unless he has a way to get the team into the late innings without losing the lead, that game is probably lost— and my studies show that those situations happen about 40 times a year. Craig Lefferts is that way.

A setup man must have three skills. First, he must be consistent—his team must be able to rely on him day in and day out. Lefferts is—in his four seasons in the majors, his ERAs range between 2.13 and 3.35. He has pitched in 18 months since 1984—his ERA for that month has been 3.50 or less 13 times. He has been consistently healthy and can pitch in 55–60 games every year.

Next, he must be able to pitch effectively in some situations. Lefferts's pitches have a lot of movement—hitters swing at what appear to be fat pitches only to find that the ball hopped, slid or broke more than they expected. Lefferts gets a lot of strikeouts and fly outs; the two things that beat him are extra base hits and walks. Pitching in a park where the ball doesn't carry well (i.e., at home) or during the day (when players walk less), he's very tough. Lefferts destroys lefties—he's so overwhelming that very few lefties ever face him. When a setup man can almost force managers to pinch-hit, he becomes immeasurably valuable—when the closer comes in, the opposition has one option less.

Finally, he must be able to keep the leadoff hitter off base. The reason that a setup man isn't a closer is that he has trouble with men in scoring position; he must keep the bases clear as a result. Lefferts keeps men off base very effectively; when they get on, he cuts down the running game.

Craig's 1986 would have been much better had Steve Boros had asked less of him. Lefferts had 21 more appearances than he'd ever had before and was very close to his career high in innings pitched—he fell apart in the last two months. If new manager Larry Bowa reduces his workload in 1987, Lefferts should have an outstanding year.

—Geoff Beckman

1986: Power, Flyball   **1985: Finesse, Flyball**   **1984: Finesse, Flyball**

	1986 SEASON											THREE YEARS (84 – 86)										
	G	IP	H	BB	SO	SB	CS	W	L	S	ERA	G	IP	H	BB	SO	SB	CS	W	L	S	ERA
Totals	83	107.2	98	44	72	11	9	9	8	4	3.09	205	296.2	261	98	176	27	14	19	18	16	2.82
At Home and on the Road																						
Home	40	58.0	48	18	45	5	6	7	5	2	2.48	102	154.1	122	42	105	17	8	14	8	7	2.33
Road	43	49.2	50	26	27	6	3	2	3	2	3.81	103	142.1	139	56	71	10	6	5	10	9	3.35
During the Day and at Night																						
Day	34	48.0	39	22	35	7	3	4	5	2	3.19	71	105.1	82	31	76	14	3	7	10	6	2.22
Night	49	59.2	59	22	37	4	6	5	3	2	3.02	134	191.1	179	67	100	13	11	12	8	10	3.15
On Grass and on Turf																						
Grass	64	85.1	73	29	61	8	8	9	6	2	2.74	159	228.2	183	68	147	20	11	18	10	11	2.36
Turf	19	22.1	25	15	11	3	1	0	2	2	4.43	46	68.0	78	30	29	7	3	1	8	5	4.37
By Month																						
April	11	12.1	9	3	10	1	2	3	0	0	2.92	26	30.0	18	7	19	1	3	4	0	0	1.80
May	15	19.0	12	8	13	6	2	0	2	1	1.89	33	47.1	37	19	26	11	2	0	6	4	2.66
June	16	22.2	19	12	16	0	1	2	0	0	1.99	37	62.2	53	24	40	5	4	6	1	1	2.59
July	13	20.2	10	7	17	1	2	2	2	2	1.74	37	60.0	45	14	34	2	2	4	4	4	1.95
August	14	19.0	25	7	9	0	0	0	1	0	3.79	38	57.2	65	20	34	4	0	2	5	2	3.75
Sept/Oct	14	14.0	23	7	7	3	2	2	3	1	7.71	34	39.0	43	14	23	4	3	3	5	2	4.15

vs. Opponent Batters

	1986 SEASON												THREE YEARS (84 – 86)										
	Ave.	OBP	SLG	AB	H	2B	3B	HR	RBI	BB	SO		Ave.	OBP	SLG	AB	H	2B	3B	HR	RBI	BB	SO
Totals	.253	.327	.370	387	98	16	4	7	42	44	72		.242	.303	.348	1079	261	50	5	18	112	98	176
Pitching vs. Left and Right-handed Batters																							
Left	.220	.268	.286	91	20	3	0	1	10	6	25		.204	.262	.257	265	54	8	0	2	23	22	59
Right	.264	.344	.395	296	78	13	4	6	32	38	47		.254	.316	.377	814	207	42	5	16	89	76	117
Situational																							
Bases Empty	.243	.305	.383	214	52	10	1	6	6	19	40		.249	.303	.378	587	146	32	1	14	14	45	86
Leadoff	.225	.289	.348	89	20	2	0	3	3	8	13		.253	.303	.395	253	64	9	0	9	9	18	32
Not Leadoff	.256	.316	.408	125	32	8	1	3	3	11	27		.246	.304	.365	334	82	23	1	5	5	27	54
Runners On	.266	.353	.353	173	46	6	3	1	36	25	32		.234	.303	.311	492	115	18	4	4	98	53	90
First Base Only	.278	.307	.347	72	20	3	1	0	2	3	13		.234	.284	.284	197	46	6	2	0	14	14	40
Scoring Position	.257	.380	.356	101	26	3	2	1	34	22	19		.234	.314	.329	295	69	12	2	4	93	39	50
Late Innings, Close	.269	.339	.394	216	58	10	1	5	26	23	43		.249	.309	.347	522	130	22	1	9	54	47	90

RBI/Opportunities

	1986 SEASON			THREE YEARS (84 – 86)		
Scoring Position	32 / 169	(19%)		84 / 419	(20%)	
Scoring Position, 2 Out	8 / 65	(12%)		29 / 184	(16%)	
On Third, Less than 2 Out	17 / 37	(46%)		37 / 81	(46%)	
RBI in close games / RBI Total	32 / 42	(76%)		67 / 112	(60%)	

Charlie Leibrandt
Kansas City Royals

Over the last three seasons, Charlie Leibrandt has won 42 games and lost only 27, an excellent .609 winning percentage, with an equally good 3.44 ERA in a league where the norms are over 4.00. He was not quite as sharp in 1986 as in the two previous seasons, or perhaps he wasn't sharp quite as often, but he remains a quality pitcher.

Leibrandt has two defining characteristics as a pitcher. One is that although he doesn't have an outstanding fastball—he is what they call "sneaky fast"—Leibrandt loves to work inside to right-handed hitters. His normal fast ball has good movement on it, but his game is to get the hitter leaning with off-speed pitches and an occasional fast ball away, and then bust a fastball inside, straight as a string and right at the hitter's knuckles. It's not a great fastball, but it is very hard to generate any power with three inches of leverage, so if he gets the pitch where he wants it he'll get a lot of little popups and weak dribbles.

Of course, the downside is that the pitch is effective within a five-inch diameter. If you get it out over the plate it's a fat pitch, and the basic reason that Leibrandt was less effective last year was just that he got a few more pitches out over the plate at the wrong times. Although the batting average of left-handers against him is higher than the average of right-handers (watching him pitch, I would have expected that), right-handers hit for much more power against him, because of those occasional mistakes. He was stung for 53 doubles in 1986, 45 of them by right-handed hitters.

The other characteristic thing about Leibrandt is the inclination to save his best stuff for when he really needs it. Over a three-year period, batters have hit just .241 against him with runners in scoring position, and the opposition has been able to score only 16% of runners who were on second base with two out, an exceptional percentage (Roger Clemens has allowed 19% of those runners to score and Nolan Ryan 18%).

Leibrandt is the smartest of the Royals' pitchers, and has worked hard to refine his skills. Once vulnerable to the running game, he allowed opponents only three stolen bases (!) in 1986, while ten opponents were caught trying.

—Bill James

1986: Finesse, Flyball   **1985: Finesse, Groundball**   **1984: Finesse, Groundball**

	G	IP	H	BB	SO	SB	CS	W	L	S	ERA		G	IP	H	BB	SO	SB	CS	W	L	S	ERA
				1986 SEASON												**THREE YEARS (84 – 86)**							
Totals	35	231.1	238	63	108	3	10	14	11	0	4.09		91	612.2	619	169	269	26	21	42	27	0	3.44
												At Home and on the Road											
Home	17	108.0	125	21	45	2	8	7	7	0	4.25		42	275.0	298	65	110	11	16	19	12	0	3.44
Road	18	123.1	113	42	63	1	2	7	4	0	3.94		49	337.2	321	104	159	15	5	23	15	0	3.44
												During the Day and at Night											
Day	9	69.2	64	18	32	0	5	7	2	0	3.49		22	160.1	154	37	62	12	7	13	6	0	2.75
Night	26	161.2	174	45	76	3	5	7	9	0	4.34		69	452.1	465	132	207	14	14	29	21	0	3.68
												On Grass and on Turf											
Grass	15	100.1	89	36	44	1	1	5	4	0	4.04		36	238.1	235	77	106	11	3	15	12	0	3.74
Turf	20	131.0	149	27	64	2	9	9	7	0	4.12		55	374.1	384	92	163	15	18	27	15	0	3.25
												By Month											
April	5	34.2	26	16	12	0	1	4	0	0	3.37		9	66.2	54	21	28	0	3	7	0	0	2.56
May	5	31.1	32	12	14	0	1	0	3	0	4.31		11	77.0	72	26	22	8	4	2	6	0	3.74
June	6	42.0	48	7	20	1	2	4	2	0	3.86		17	114.0	120	33	55	3	5	7	7	0	3.63
July	6	37.0	42	12	11	0	2	1	2	0	5.11		18	112.2	125	31	38	4	3	8	4	0	3.83
August	6	38.0	36	6	22	1	0	2	3	0	3.55		18	121.0	120	31	63	5	0	8	6	0	3.42
Sept/Oct	7	48.1	54	10	29	1	4	3	1	0	4.28		18	121.1	128	27	63	6	6	10	4	0	3.19

vs. Opponent Batters

	Ave.	OBP	SLG	AB	H	2B	3B	HR	RBI	BB	SO		Ave.	OBP	SLG	AB	H	2B	3B	HR	RBI	BB	SO
				1986 SEASON												**THREE YEARS (84 – 86)**							
Totals	.268	.317	.398	889	238	54	4	18	96	63	108		.263	.312	.380	2358	619	112	13	46	232	169	269
												Pitching vs. Left and Right-handed Batters											
Left	.281	.342	.388	178	50	8	1	3	23	13	27		.271	.321	.367	490	133	16	2	9	53	32	67
Right	.264	.311	.401	711	188	46	3	15	73	50	81		.260	.310	.383	1868	486	96	11	37	179	137	202
												Situational											
Bases Empty	.262	.300	.393	534	140	33	2	11	11	27	61		.270	.312	.387	1402	378	69	6	28	28	84	155
Leadoff	.261	.292	.387	230	60	15	1	4	4	9	14		.264	.303	.370	605	160	28	3	10	10	32	46
Not Leadoff	.263	.307	.398	304	80	18	1	7	7	18	47		.274	.320	.400	797	218	41	3	18	18	52	109
Runners On	.276	.342	.406	355	98	21	2	7	85	36	47		.252	.312	.368	956	241	43	7	18	204	85	114
First Base Only	.301	.348	.438	153	46	9	0	4	10	10	20		.265	.315	.399	434	115	23	1	11	29	30	57
Scoring Position	.257	.338	.381	202	52	12	2	3	75	26	27		.241	.309	.343	522	126	20	6	7	175	55	57
Late Innings, Close	.274	.338	.397	73	20	4	1	1	6	7	10		.265	.327	.397	204	54	9	3	4	19	18	28

RBI/Opportunities

Scoring Position	67 / 280	(24%)	161 / 716	(22%)
Scoring Position, 2 Out	19 / 126	(15%)	55 / 345	(16%)
On Third, Less than 2 Out	27 / 49	(55%)	70 / 127	(55%)
RBI in close games / RBI Total	75 / 96	(78%)	173 / 232	(75%)

Chet Lemon
Detroit Tigers

In 1986, Chet Lemon batted .262 with 12 homers and 54 RBIs and made $800,000. His salary will increase every year until the final year of his contract and the final year is 1992. At that point, he will be paid 1.3 million dollars. Chet Lemon represents all that is good and bad about free agency and is a perfect metaphor for fiscal irresponsibility shown by baseball teams in the last ten years.

The Tigers paid heavily when they traded for Lemon in 1982 and, at the time, it seemed well worth it. Lemon hit .300 in '78, '79 and '81 and he was a superior defensive outfielder. After signing a 10-year deal with Detroit in 1983, Lemon has yet to reach .300 again. That would be fine if he were doing other things in exchange—he isn't. Lemon drew 54 walks in 1982 and slugged .464 and seemed set for much better things. He has surpassed the walks figure once (59) and his slugging averages have been .495, .434 and .407 since then.

The opposite end of the scale is Kirk Gibson. He didn't get a lengthy contract in 1986 and he responded with one of his best years. By refusing to commit themselves to Gibson, Detroit did two things. In the short term, they headed off the spiralling inflation in salaries that has become common since 1976. But, more importantly, they sent players a message—you get only what you deserve. If your statistics don't progress, neither will your salary.

Am I saying that Lemon is a lazy player? No—I'm saying that he is human. When he had an uncertain future—when his career depended entirely on how well he played—he pushed himself as hard as he could to improve himself, so that he could earn a better living. He no longer has that incentive; he no longer plays that well. Would you work as hard at your job if you knew that you couldn't get a raise and were already financially independent? No. You'd do your best to do an honest day's work, but the frantic, driving urgency to succeed would be lost.

Free agency does not work. Research shows that even the best free agents have won only 3–4 games for their new teams and that the money is better spent on developing young talent. It hurts the players (what has Willie Wilson done since getting a lifetime contract?), which hurts the intensity of the game, which hurts the fan (who pays to see good, hard play). It is devoutly to be wished that, by the time Lemon's contract expires, so will the free agent system.

—Mark Unger

	1986 SEASON											THREE YEARS (84 – 86)										
	Ave.	OBP	SLG	AB	H	2B	3B	HR	RBI	BB	SO	Ave.	OBP	SLG	AB	H	2B	3B	HR	RBI	BB	SO
Totals	.251	.326	.407	403	101	21	3	12	53	39	53	.269	.340	.450	1429	384	83	13	50	197	135	229
Batting vs. Left and Right-handed Pitchers																						
Left	.284	.346	.500	162	46	10	2	7	21	15	17	.334	.393	.572	509	170	39	5	24	84	50	79
Right	.228	.313	.344	241	55	11	1	5	32	24	36	.233	.311	.383	920	214	44	8	26	113	85	150
At Home and on the Road																						
Home	.237	.318	.416	190	45	9	2	7	25	19	21	.269	.340	.454	689	185	34	5	28	96	64	102
Road	.263	.333	.399	213	56	12	1	5	28	20	32	.269	.340	.446	740	199	49	8	22	101	71	127
Facing Groundball Pitchers and Flyball Pitchers																						
Groundball	.265	.357	.404	136	36	7	0	4	19	17	21	.290	.362	.477	656	190	38	8	23	95	62	107
Flyball	.243	.310	.408	267	65	14	3	8	34	22	32	.251	.322	.427	773	194	45	5	27	102	73	122
Facing Finesse Pitchers and Power Pitchers																						
Finesse	.256	.337	.410	227	58	12	1	7	26	23	28	.285	.348	.470	824	235	55	8	27	109	65	114
Power	.244	.311	.403	176	43	9	2	5	27	16	25	.246	.329	.423	605	149	28	5	23	88	70	115
On Grass and on Turf																						
Grass	.245	.313	.411	355	87	17	3	12	48	30	47	.267	.334	.448	1222	326	66	10	45	167	106	189
Turf	.292	.414	.375	48	14	4	0	0	5	9	6	.280	.372	.464	207	58	17	3	5	30	29	40
During the Day and at Night																						
Day	.202	.291	.347	124	25	2	2	4	15	12	14	.258	.322	.451	472	122	23	4	20	73	37	80
Night	.272	.342	.434	279	76	19	1	8	38	27	39	.274	.348	.449	957	262	60	9	30	124	98	149
By Month																						
April	.222	.290	.365	63	14	3	0	2	7	6	12	.282	.345	.471	206	58	17	2	6	29	16	26
May	.429	.459	.607	56	24	5	1	1	9	3	5	.314	.388	.480	229	72	11	3	7	37	26	39
June	.105	.190	.158	57	6	3	0	0	2	5	5	.244	.298	.424	217	53	17	2	6	25	15	28
July	.239	.312	.299	67	16	4	0	0	7	5	11	.271	.336	.373	255	69	16	2	2	18	22	46
August	.273	.325	.468	77	21	3	0	4	14	5	9	.231	.295	.414	251	58	7	0	13	41	19	44
Sept/Oct	.241	.366	.506	83	20	3	2	5	14	15	11	.273	.371	.535	271	74	15	4	16	47	37	46
Situational																						
Bases Empty	.222	.297	.384	216	48	13	2	6	6	19	28	.266	.338	.461	773	206	53	8	27	27	67	121
Leadoff	.260	.319	.442	104	27	10	0	3	3	8	15	.290	.347	.502	321	93	27	1	13	13	24	47
Not Leadoff	.188	.278	.330	112	21	3	2	3	3	11	13	.250	.331	.431	452	113	26	7	14	14	43	74
Runners On	.283	.358	.433	187	53	8	1	6	47	20	25	.271	.343	.438	656	178	30	5	23	170	68	108
First Base Only	.297	.360	.462	91	27	6	0	3	8	7	13	.278	.325	.425	313	87	15	2	9	27	19	46
Scoring Position	.271	.357	.406	96	26	2	1	3	39	13	12	.265	.357	.449	343	91	15	3	14	143	49	62
Late Innings, Close	.240	.313	.307	75	18	2	0	1	7	8	10	.263	.349	.394	236	62	11	1	6	29	29	35

RBI/Opportunities

Scoring Position	33 / 137	(24%)	115 / 493	(23%)
Scoring Position, 2 Out	13 / 66	(20%)	55 / 252	(22%)
On Third, Less than 2 Out	14 / 27	(52%)	38 / 80	(47%)
RBI in close games / RBI Total	24 / 53	(45%)	109 / 197	(55%)

Jeff Leonard
San Francisco Giants

Jeffrey Leonard had a fine half-season for the Giants last year. Leonard is one of the team leaders, and his positive relationship with Roger Craig last year keyed a major attitude change in the Giants.

Jeffrey Leonard had 11 GWRBIs out of his 42 total RBIs in his abbreviated season—putting him among the leaders. His season ended with surgery on his right wrist in August; in September, he underwent surgery on his left shoulder.

Over his career, Jeffrey has been a slow starter, with an April average of .201 in 1984–85 combined (with only 10 extra-base hits) and an average of only .261 with 13 extra-base hits in May. He completely reversed that pattern in 1986. Since, in those years, he hit .301 from June on, it was reasonable for Craig to expect a rewarding summer. It was not to be, though. Playing hurt, Leonard slumped badly in June and July.

Over the past few years, Leonard has been pretty consistent, home vs. road and grass vs. turf, but he has worn out left-handed pitching at a .324 clip, with a .549 slugging average (compared to his .250 and .369 vs. right-handers). He also prefers sunlight to arc lights, hitting .331 with a .501 SA in daylight, while hitting .252 with a .397 SA after

dark. In 1986, however, he had clear preferences in all areas—he hit lefthanders at a .328 pace, he hit .315 at home, .305 on grass, .342 during day games—all marks 70 to 100 points above their counterpart stats. Other major improvements in 1986 include his performance in late-inning close situations and with runners in scoring position.

—J. Michael Duca

After winning *The Sporting News* NL Rookie Player of the Year Award in 1979 with the Astros, Leonard languished in Houston. When the Astros acquired Joe Morgan, they moved incumbent second basemen Art Howe to first base, returned Cesar Cedeno to center field and moved Terry Puhl to right, pushing Leonard to the bench. After slumping in 1980, he was traded to San Francisco (along with Dave Bergman) during the 1981 season for the immortal Mike Ivie. After a mediocre 1982, Jeff finally hit his stride in 1983, proving that his rookie year was no fluke.

Given what the Astros got out of playing Howe, Ivie, and Tony Scott in lieu of Leonard, trading him to the Giants has to be one of their worst decisions. While Leonard is not a great ballplayer, Houston looked in vain for a right-handed power hitter until Glenn Davis developed.

—Gary Gillette

	1986 SEASON											THREE YEARS (84–86)										
	Ave.	OBP	SLG	AB	H	2B	3B	HR	RBI	BB	SO	Ave.	OBP	SLG	AB	H	2B	3B	HR	RBI	BB	SO
Totals	.279	.322	.384	341	95	12	3	6	42	20	62	.273	.317	.425	1362	372	59	8	44	190	88	292
Batting vs. Left and Right-handed Pitchers																						
Left	.328	.350	.437	119	39	4	0	3	20	4	9	.324	.351	.549	426	138	21	3	23	69	18	49
Right	.252	.307	.356	222	56	8	3	3	22	16	53	.250	.303	.369	936	234	38	5	21	121	70	243
At Home and on the Road																						
Home	.315	.350	.423	168	53	6	3	2	20	8	30	.282	.325	.435	666	188	23	5	23	86	42	154
Road	.243	.294	.347	173	42	6	0	4	22	12	32	.264	.309	.415	696	184	36	3	21	104	46	138
Facing Groundball Pitchers and Flyball Pitchers																						
Groundball	.331	.370	.404	151	50	2	0	3	19	8	16	.310	.348	.436	617	191	30	3	14	90	36	95
Flyball	.237	.283	.368	190	45	10	3	3	23	12	46	.243	.291	.416	745	181	29	5	30	100	52	197
Facing Finesse Pitchers and Power Pitchers																						
Finesse	.306	.333	.448	183	56	10	2	4	28	7	28	.283	.320	.451	780	221	33	4	30	112	41	142
Power	.247	.309	.310	158	39	2	1	2	14	13	34	.259	.314	.390	582	151	26	4	14	78	47	150
On Grass and on Turf																						
Grass	.305	.347	.430	256	78	11	3	5	34	16	48	.279	.322	.442	1029	287	39	6	39	157	65	230
Turf	.200	.244	.247	85	17	1	0	1	8	4	14	.255	.304	.372	333	85	20	2	5	33	23	62
During the Day and at Night																						
Day	.348	.391	.465	155	54	8	2	2	20	11	25	.289	.329	.459	664	192	30	4	25	95	40	152
Night	.220	.263	.317	186	41	4	1	4	22	9	37	.258	.306	.393	698	180	29	4	19	95	48	140
By Month																						
April	.329	.370	.565	85	28	4	2	4	17	6	9	.249	.304	.415	229	57	10	2	8	32	19	54
May	.315	.360	.402	92	29	2	0	2	14	5	17	.281	.336	.390	249	70	10	1	5	30	19	55
June	.227	.262	.289	97	22	4	1	0	7	4	25	.271	.315	.440	332	90	12	4	12	44	22	74
July	.239	.292	.269	67	16	2	0	0	4	5	11	.286	.325	.439	262	75	13	0	9	34	15	48
August	.000	.000	.000	0	0	0	0	0	0	0	0	.317	.351	.549	164	52	9	1	9	34	9	34
Sept/Oct	.000	.000	.000	0	0	0	0	0	0	0	0	.222	.250	.286	126	28	5	0	1	16	4	27
Situational																						
Bases Empty	.271	.313	.380	166	45	8	2	2	2	8	31	.274	.311	.428	691	189	33	4	22	22	36	141
Leadoff	.309	.319	.471	68	21	4	2	1	1	1	10	.286	.307	.466	294	84	14	3	11	11	9	56
Not Leadoff	.245	.308	.316	98	24	4	0	1	1	7	21	.264	.315	.401	397	105	19	1	11	11	27	85
Runners On	.286	.330	.389	175	50	4	1	4	40	12	31	.273	.323	.422	671	183	26	4	22	168	52	151
First Base Only	.260	.299	.274	73	19	1	0	0	0	4	12	.309	.347	.449	272	84	12	1	8	23	16	44
Scoring Position	.304	.351	.471	102	31	3	1	4	40	8	19	.248	.307	.404	399	99	14	3	14	145	36	107
Late Innings, Close	.276	.328	.448	58	16	2	1	2	6	4	12	.243	.301	.382	251	61	10	2	7	27	21	65
RBI/Opportunities																						
Scoring Position				31 / 127		(24%)									117 / 511		(23%)					
Scoring Position, 2 Out				12 / 56		(21%)									43 / 229		(19%)					
On Third, Less than 2 Out				14 / 27		(52%)									44 / 91		(48%)					
RBI in close games / RBI Total				30 / 42		(71%)									139 / 190		(73%)					

Fred Lynn
Baltimore Orioles

Fred Lynn has never been able to live up to his 1975. That year, Lynn hit the Rookie of the Year/MVP exacta (the only player ever to do so) and it has been downhill ever since. Unrealistic expectations and injuries have been Lynn's nemeses. He is a solid, well-rounded player, but that has never satisfied his detractors. He has also had constant problems with injuries. The list of body parts that Lynn has damaged reads like an introductory text in anatomy: ankle, knee, wrist, back, groin, foot, toe and rib. The injuries have cut his playing time to about 130 games a year and earned him the cruel (but not inaccurate) nickname of "Fragile Fred."

Anyone who ever watches Lynn play for an extended period of time can tell you why he is so often hurt. The man is a fence-crashing belly-flopper, who never differentiates between close games and blowouts. Lynn never calculates the potential reward vs. risk and acts accordingly. He simply charges and lets the bone chips fall where they may. He is a reckless, headstrong baserunner—his knee injuries in 1981 resulted from trying to break up double plays and his wrist injury last year came on a slide into third. The most remarkable thing about Lynn is his stubbornness—it is incredible that a man with his record of ice packs, ace bandages and arthroscopic surgery still has his throttle stuck on "full speed ahead."

Another enigma is his behavior at the plate. The transformation that Clark Kent makes in phone booths is nothing compared to what happens to Lynn in the batter's box. About 90% of the time, he is an extremely patient hitter, willing to do whatever his team needs him to. He doesn't enjoy drawing walks or shortening his swing to spank the ball by a drawn-in infield, but he can and will do it if he has to. The only time he reverts to form is when he leads off an inning; he is as undisciplined there as he is in the field.

Lynn turned 35 in February and the dangers of relying on him grow larger every day. In the past, he could be counted on to have 450 at-bats a year and provide 23 homers and 70 RBIs; given his age, even that amount may be asking too much. Given his injury history, it is very unlikely that his production will decline slowly and gradually—the only question is when he will fall completely apart and whether Baltimore will have a replacement ready when he does.

—Greg Pryor

	1986 SEASON											THREE YEARS (84 – 86)										
	Ave.	OBP	SLG	AB	H	2B	3B	HR	RBI	BB	SO	Ave.	OBP	SLG	AB	H	2B	3B	HR	RBI	BB	SO
Totals	.287	.371	.499	397	114	13	1	23	67	53	59	.273	.359	.473	1362	372	53	6	69	214	183	257
Batting vs. Left and Right-handed Pitchers																						
Left	.271	.333	.521	96	26	3	0	7	21	7	24	.242	.330	.432	384	93	18	2	17	65	48	97
Right	.292	.382	.492	301	88	10	1	16	46	46	35	.285	.369	.489	978	279	35	4	52	149	135	160
At Home and on the Road																						
Home	.284	.371	.513	197	56	6	0	13	38	28	28	.264	.351	.502	656	173	25	1	43	119	88	133
Road	.290	.370	.485	200	58	7	1	10	29	25	31	.282	.366	.446	706	199	28	5	26	95	95	124
Facing Groundball Pitchers and Flyball Pitchers																						
Groundball	.359	.445	.602	181	65	9	1	11	30	28	19	.306	.396	.532	709	217	34	3	40	115	105	119
Flyball	.227	.306	.412	216	49	4	0	12	37	25	40	.237	.317	.409	653	155	19	3	29	99	78	138
Facing Finesse Pitchers and Power Pitchers																						
Finesse	.297	.375	.494	239	71	9	1	12	30	30	23	.289	.361	.492	783	226	29	5	40	118	91	107
Power	.272	.364	.506	158	43	4	0	11	37	23	36	.252	.355	.447	579	146	24	1	29	96	92	150
On Grass and on Turf																						
Grass	.266	.356	.447	304	81	10	0	15	48	42	46	.273	.360	.471	1105	302	41	3	57	175	150	210
Turf	.355	.419	.667	93	33	3	1	8	19	11	13	.272	.353	.482	257	70	12	3	12	39	33	47
During the Day and at Night																						
Day	.325	.427	.624	117	38	5	0	10	27	23	20	.283	.376	.524	353	100	14	1	23	61	54	74
Night	.271	.345	.446	280	76	8	1	13	40	30	39	.270	.352	.455	1009	272	39	5	46	153	129	183
By Month																						
April	.324	.377	.412	68	22	3	0	1	9	7	7	.303	.379	.444	234	71	10	1	7	24	31	35
May	.326	.410	.535	86	28	1	1	5	16	13	11	.283	.364	.478	247	70	7	1	13	42	32	42
June	.231	.333	.462	26	6	0	0	2	5	4	7	.222	.292	.402	194	43	3	1	10	29	20	41
July	.287	.351	.614	101	29	6	0	9	22	9	17	.285	.345	.533	270	77	15	2	16	47	22	60
August	.274	.407	.452	73	20	1	0	4	12	16	12	.265	.399	.441	238	63	10	1	10	37	53	47
Sept/Oct	.209	.277	.395	43	9	2	0	2	3	4	5	.268	.356	.531	179	48	8	0	13	35	25	32
Situational																						
Bases Empty	.278	.362	.481	212	59	8	1	11	11	28	33	.271	.351	.466	746	202	34	5	34	34	89	151
Leadoff	.221	.338	.412	68	15	1	0	4	4	12	7	.233	.321	.381	257	60	9	1	9	9	31	44
Not Leadoff	.306	.375	.514	144	44	7	1	7	7	16	26	.290	.367	.511	489	142	25	4	25	25	58	107
Runners On	.297	.380	.519	185	55	5	0	12	56	25	26	.276	.367	.481	616	170	19	1	35	180	94	106
First Base Only	.313	.404	.485	99	31	2	0	5	10	14	12	.294	.376	.465	303	89	11	1	13	31	39	49
Scoring Position	.279	.353	.558	86	24	3	0	7	46	11	14	.259	.360	.495	313	81	8	0	22	149	55	57
Late Innings, Close	.295	.377	.525	61	18	3	1	3	10	7	16	.262	.378	.460	202	53	8	1	10	29	37	46
RBI/Opportunities																						
Scoring Position				33 / 115		(29%)									110 / 439		(25%)					
Scoring Position, 2 Out				7 / 37		(19%)									30 / 182		(16%)					
On Third, Less than 2 Out				19 / 25		(76%)									56 / 92		(61%)					
RBI in close games / RBI Total				43 / 67		(64%)									130 / 214		(61%)					

Bill Madlock
Los Angeles Dodgers

Talk about coming to the right place at the right time! Prior to his arrival in Pittsburgh during the summer of 1979, Bill Madlock earned his reputation as a terrific hitter with the Rangers, Cubs and Giants. That was it, though, just hitting. Nothing about defense, hustle, team play, or attitude. *Mon Dieu!* This guy's a hitter! Who cares about that other stuff?

So Madlock arrived to play third base for the Bucs, and was adopted by the "Fam-A-Lee." He was everything he was cracked up to be, winning batting titles in 1981 and 1983. His defense was adequate, he played hard, seemed to fit in, and did his share of community work. Any potential problems with Madlock's play were lost in the groundswell demanding the head of Dave Parker, the "man Pittsburgh loved to hate."

Pittsburgh baseball fortunes have deteriorated markedly since the magic World Championship year of 1979. Stargell retired, Parker opted for free agency (the fans still boo him when the Reds come to town), Blyleven, Easler, Tekulve and others have been traded, often for little or nothing. With Stargell's retirement, then-Manager Chuck Tanner named Madlock team captain during spring training 1983. Bill seemed a little unnerved at the prospect, but soon settled in with the team captaincy of a club that was going down in flames.

In 1984, battling various injuries and the general apathy enveloping the team, Bill had a very uncharacteristic year, finishing with a .253 BA. Suddenly, Bill Madlock had all kinds of flaws, foremost of which was: "The guy can't even hit anymore!" Then came 1985. Saddled with an expensive and truly bad team, and with rumor, speculation, and indictments coming out of Pittsburgh concerning baseball's cocaine problem, the Pirates' management seemed powerless to reverse the public's hostility or the media's relentless coverage of the whole goddamn mess. Captain Bill "Mad Dog" Madlock? He proved he was a dog, all right. Kids like Joe Orsulak and Jim Winn were faced not only with trying to stick in the bigs, but doing so in this kind of atmosphere. Inspiration or support from Madlock? Not that I saw—he was too busy lobbying for a change of scenery which, mercifully, he was granted.

Bill, you did Pittsburgh and the Pirates a favor, for in Sid Bream and R.J. Reynolds, we see something you would never deliver: enthusiasm. You're a terrific hitter, but as an all-around ballplayer, you were barely adequate. As a team leader, well, the taste of ashes will take some time to dissipate.

—Bill Thomas

		1986 SEASON										THREE YEARS (84 – 86)										
	Ave.	OBP	SLG	AB	H	2B	3B	HR	RBI	BB	SO	Ave.	OBP	SLG	AB	H	2B	3B	HR	RBI	BB	SO
Totals	.280	.336	.404	379	106	17	0	10	60	30	43	.269	.328	.378	1295	349	60	1	26	160	107	125
Batting vs. Left and Right-handed Pitchers																						
Left	.312	.364	.482	141	44	6	0	6	23	11	11	.287	.354	.428	414	119	22	0	12	58	44	36
Right	.261	.320	.357	238	62	11	0	4	37	19	32	.261	.316	.354	881	230	38	1	14	102	63	89
At Home and on the Road																						
Home	.263	.336	.360	186	49	6	0	4	29	19	22	.277	.346	.375	632	175	29	0	11	83	64	65
Road	.295	.335	.446	193	57	11	0	6	31	11	21	.262	.310	.380	663	174	31	1	15	77	43	60
Facing Groundball Pitchers and Flyball Pitchers																						
Groundball	.278	.340	.385	169	47	3	0	5	21	15	21	.280	.339	.367	608	170	21	1	10	65	49	62
Flyball	.281	.332	.419	210	59	14	0	5	39	15	22	.261	.318	.387	687	179	39	0	16	95	58	63
Facing Finesse Pitchers and Power Pitchers																						
Finesse	.278	.313	.377	212	59	9	0	4	29	10	21	.276	.315	.374	779	215	35	1	13	91	43	70
Power	.281	.363	.437	167	47	8	0	6	31	20	22	.260	.346	.384	516	134	25	0	13	69	64	55
On Grass and on Turf																						
Grass	.282	.345	.393	262	74	11	0	6	37	23	26	.279	.336	.386	594	166	21	0	14	65	47	47
Turf	.274	.315	.427	117	32	6	0	4	23	7	17	.261	.321	.371	701	183	39	1	12	95	60	78
During the Day and at Night																						
Day	.315	.350	.378	111	35	4	0	1	16	6	12	.297	.336	.404	408	121	14	0	10	51	24	41
Night	.265	.330	.414	268	71	13	0	9	44	24	31	.257	.325	.365	887	228	46	1	16	109	83	84
By Month																						
April	.237	.275	.342	38	9	1	0	1	2	1	3	.194	.235	.259	170	33	8	0	1	15	9	14
May	.239	.267	.254	71	17	1	0	0	11	3	12	.272	.327	.336	250	68	10	0	2	21	20	31
June	.215	.292	.400	65	14	3	0	3	9	7	8	.257	.318	.393	272	70	14	1	7	28	23	23
July	.341	.400	.463	41	14	2	0	1	6	4	2	.267	.322	.386	236	63	13	0	5	34	19	21
August	.340	.405	.485	97	33	5	0	3	19	8	10	.299	.375	.444	187	56	6	0	7	34	19	17
Sept/Oct	.284	.338	.448	67	19	5	0	2	13	7	8	.328	.387	.444	180	59	9	0	4	28	17	19
Situational																						
Bases Empty	.271	.315	.371	221	60	13	0	3	3	12	28	.261	.307	.367	728	190	33	1	14	14	44	73
Leadoff	.250	.305	.342	76	19	4	0	1	1	6	8	.282	.329	.409	259	73	12	0	7	7	18	23
Not Leadoff	.283	.320	.386	145	41	9	0	2	2	6	20	.249	.295	.343	469	117	21	1	7	7	26	50
Runners On	.291	.362	.449	158	46	4	0	7	57	18	15	.280	.354	.392	567	159	27	0	12	146	63	52
First Base Only	.246	.300	.492	65	16	1	0	5	11	4	7	.265	.324	.433	238	63	13	0	9	23	19	22
Scoring Position	.323	.400	.419	93	30	3	0	2	46	14	8	.292	.373	.362	329	96	14	0	3	123	44	30
Late Innings, Close	.209	.280	.299	67	14	3	0	1	11	6	9	.234	.300	.307	244	57	9	0	3	29	22	22
RBI/Opportunities																						

Scoring Position	43 / 137	(31%)	118 / 453	(26%)
Scoring Position, 2 Out	10 / 51	(20%)	29 / 178	(16%)
On Third, Less than 2 Out	22 / 31	(71%)	58 / 96	(60%)
RBI in close games / RBI Total	43 / 60	(72%)	119 / 160	(74%)

Rick Mahler
Atlanta Braves

Rick Mahler was the workhorse of the Braves staff the last three years. In 1986, his performance did not merit such activity—at least, not for a major-league franchise.

The numbers below are not misprints: Mahler allowed 283 hits and 95 walks in 237.2 innings. There is no way to make those numbers look good; he started every turn without fail, when fail was all he did. In his best month (June) he was 6–0, yet he still gave up a hit per inning and 3.6 walks/9 IP. In his worst month (July) he allowed nearly 10 baserunners per start.

Mahler was treated poorly by Joe Torre. With Bob Gibson as pitching guru, it was a sin to throw junk instead of heat. Perhaps it was in compensation that Tanner stuck with him far too long in 1986.

The Braves are now actively shopping for starting pitching. It is hard to say if Mahler will have a job next year, but you cannot win giving so many innings to a pitcher performing at this level.

—John Stryker

If Timex ever went looking for someone who exemplified their advertising slogan, "It takes a licking and keeps on ticking," they would not have to look any further than Atlanta. Over the past couple of seasons, the Braves have

had one of the most dependable and durable pitchers in NL. In that same period, they have had one of the most abused pitchers in the league. Those pitchers are one and the same: Rick Mahler.

Examining the "takes a licking" aspect of Mahler's 1986 and 1985 campaigns, he has led the NL in the following categories: losses (18 and 15, respectively), runs allowed and hits allowed. His 4.85 ERA was the highest of any #1 starter in the NL.

Then, there is the "keeps on ticking" side of Mahler's past two seasons. He has led the NL in games started both years and has pitched 237.2 and 266.2 innings. He ranks third in innings-pitched over the past two seasons behind Valenzuela and Gooden.

When looking at some of Mahler's less-than-proud accomplishments, one must take into account that he has not been blessed with the best offensive support, since Atlanta's offense was 11th in runs in 1986 and 12th in 1985. During the past three years, Mahler has a definite winning trend in the months of April, May and June. He has posted a 27–14 record with ERAs of 2.95, 3.81, and 3.20 in that time. Over the last four months of the season, his record is 17–29 and his ERA never dips below 3.63.

Mahler took a licking, but kept on pitching.

—Stuart Hall

1986: Finesse, Groundball   **1985: Finesse, Groundball**   **1984: Finesse, Groundball**

	1986 SEASON											THREE YEARS (84 – 86)										
	G	IP	H	BB	SO	SB	CS	W	L	S	ERA	G	IP	H	BB	SO	SB	CS	W	L	S	ERA
Totals	39	237.2	283	95	137	15	17	14	18	0	4.88	116	726.1	764	236	350	51	29	44	43	0	3.83
At Home and on the Road																						
Home	18	118.1	130	44	56	8	7	8	6	0	4.56	54	346.1	365	110	156	23	12	21	17	0	3.92
Road	21	119.1	153	51	81	7	10	6	12	0	5.20	62	380.0	399	126	194	28	17	23	26	0	3.74
During the Day and at Night																						
Day	9	45.0	66	23	35	5	3	3	5	0	6.80	38	230.1	257	75	102	19	10	14	15	0	4.10
Night	30	192.2	217	72	102	10	14	11	13	0	4.44	78	496.0	507	161	248	32	19	30	28	0	3.70
On Grass and on Turf																						
Grass	28	178.2	198	69	92	11	13	11	11	0	4.23	83	531.1	548	176	245	36	23	31	30	0	3.54
Turf	11	59.0	85	26	45	4	4	3	7	0	6.86	33	195.0	216	60	105	15	6	13	13	0	4.62
By Month																						
April	6	32.0	41	12	12	1	3	1	4	0	5.34	18	82.1	80	22	29	3	4	6	4	0	2.95
May	7	43.2	49	24	32	3	2	3	1	0	4.33	21	125.1	129	48	60	14	4	9	6	0	3.73
June	7	51.2	52	20	25	5	2	6	0	0	3.31	19	137.2	138	45	64	8	5	12	4	0	3.27
July	6	25.0	44	12	16	3	1	0	5	0	10.44	19	117.0	136	44	64	9	3	5	10	0	4.62
August	6	37.1	49	16	21	2	6	1	4	0	5.54	20	125.0	143	42	54	12	7	5	10	0	4.61
Sept/Oct	7	48.0	48	11	31	1	3	3	4	0	3.37	19	139.0	138	35	79	5	6	7	9	0	3.63

vs. Opponent Batters

	1986 SEASON											THREE YEARS (84 – 86)									
	Ave.	OBP	SLG	AB	H	2B	3B	HR	RBI	BB	SO	Ave.	OBP	SLG	AB	H	2B	3B	HR	RBI	BB	SO
Totals	.301	.364	.439	940	283	41	7	25	123	95	137	.274	.330	.396	2786	764	114	20	62	306	236	350
Pitching vs. Left and Right-handed Batters																						
Left	.335	.399	.499	519	174	29	7	14	83	57	71	.290	.345	.422	1524	442	70	16	33	178	132	172
Right	.259	.320	.366	421	109	12	0	11	40	38	66	.255	.313	.365	1262	322	44	4	29	128	104	178
Situational																						
Bases Empty	.288	.337	.415	559	161	20	3	15	15	38	88	.269	.314	.397	1687	453	73	12	40	40	106	213
Leadoff	.272	.310	.381	239	65	7	2	5	5	13	38	.256	.303	.393	704	180	24	8	19	19	46	85
Not Leadoff	.300	.356	.441	320	96	13	1	10	10	25	50	.278	.321	.400	983	273	49	4	21	21	60	128
Runners On	.320	.401	.475	381	122	21	4	10	108	57	49	.283	.354	.395	1099	311	41	8	22	266	130	137
First Base Only	.341	.401	.435	170	58	10	0	2	7	17	13	.310	.363	.412	468	145	22	1	8	28	37	36
Scoring Position	.303	.402	.507	211	64	11	4	8	101	40	36	.263	.349	.382	631	166	19	7	14	238	93	101
Late Innings, Close	.333	.419	.397	63	21	1	0	1	6	10	4	.292	.371	.391	243	71	6	0	6	22	31	25

RBI/Opportunities

Scoring Position	81 / 313	(26%)	
Scoring Position, 2 Out	31 / 156	(20%)	
On Third, Less than 2 Out	29 / 53	(55%)	
RBI in close games / RBI Total	83 / 123	(67%)	

	204 / 880	(23%)	
	80 / 427	(19%)	
	81 / 151	(54%)	
	214 / 306	(70%)	

Candy Maldonado
San Francisco Giants

Candy Maldonado was acquired from LA in a December 1985 trade for Alex Trevino. San Francisco's primary reason for the deal was to rid themselves of Trevino's expensive contract. Batting coach Jose Morales worked extensively with Candy in spring training, changing Maldonado's batting stance so that it became more open, with less of a crouch.

Maldonado's profile is unusual in that his slugging has been quite high while his on-base is very poor for an outfielder. His .477 slugging average in 1986 was comparable to those of Von Hayes (.480), Andre Dawson (.478), Dave Parker (.477) and Dale Murphy (.477), all of whom were in the NL's top ten. These players combined for an on-base average of .349, with Parker's .330 being the lowest.

Maldonado's BB/K ratio has dropped off rapidly since 1984. His platoon differential was so large prior to 1986 (.254 BA vs. LHP, .179 vs. RHP) that Lasorda would rarely use him against righthanders. Last year, though, he reversed that pattern with a higher BA and OBA vs. RHP. Candy has always hit poorly in Candlestick, and 1986 was no exception. Still, with his low on-base, Maldonado must continue to slug as he did in 1986 to play regularly.

Along with Roger Craig, Mike Krukow and Robby Thompson, Candy was strongly associated with the competitive turnaround of the Giants. He did not get much playing time until the second half, which caused substantial friction between Maldonado and Manager Roger Craig.

Skoal named Maldonado 1986's "Pinch Hitter of the Year." Candy's combined pinch-hitting stats for 1984–86 are 102 ABs, 33 hits, 7 HRs, 27 RBIs and a .324 batting average. In 1986, Maldonado tied for 4th in the NL in game-winning hits with 14, and was 10th in RBIs although he had only 432 plate appearances. His high success rate in crucial situations added much to his popularity with Giants fans. Maldonado's career average with runners on base is .284, while his average is only .222 with the bases empty. (A player typically hits about 10 points higher with runners on base.) It appears that Maldonado's batting approach is inappropriate when he's at the plate with the bases clear.

Maldonado has a very strong throwing arm, though he sometimes has accuracy or judgement lapses which prevent him from being a top-rated defensive outfielder. He is a below-average baserunner and not a threat to steal.

—Steven Copley

	1986 SEASON											THREE YEARS (84 – 86)									
	Ave.	OBP	SLG	AB	H	2B	3B	HR	RBI	BB	SO	Ave.	OBP	SLG	AB	H	2B	3B	HR	RBI	BB	SO
Totals	.252	.289	.477	405	102	31	3	18	85	20	77	.250	.297	.415	872	218	52	4	28	132	58	146
Batting vs. Left and Right-handed Pitchers																						
Left	.235	.252	.477	132	31	10	2	6	31	3	20	.263	.306	.423	499	131	29	3	15	73	33	75
Right	.260	.307	.476	273	71	21	1	12	54	17	57	.233	.285	.405	373	87	23	1	13	59	25	71
At Home and on the Road																						
Home	.228	.258	.411	197	45	16	1	6	42	8	39	.230	.273	.357	417	96	24	1	9	61	24	78
Road	.274	.318	.538	208	57	15	2	12	43	12	38	.268	.319	.468	455	122	28	3	19	71	34	68
Facing Groundball Pitchers and Flyball Pitchers																						
Groundball	.277	.310	.550	202	56	18	2	11	47	9	40	.272	.313	.448	415	113	24	2	15	68	25	67
Flyball	.227	.269	.404	203	46	13	1	7	38	11	37	.230	.283	.385	457	105	28	2	13	64	33	79
Facing Finesse Pitchers and Power Pitchers																						
Finesse	.256	.287	.498	223	57	17	2	11	54	9	36	.263	.298	.444	486	128	31	3	17	80	24	65
Power	.247	.292	.451	182	45	14	1	7	31	11	41	.233	.296	.378	386	90	21	1	11	52	34	81
On Grass and on Turf																						
Grass	.259	.289	.493	282	73	23	2	13	63	11	55	.258	.299	.427	620	160	38	2	21	101	36	110
Turf	.236	.291	.439	123	29	8	1	5	22	9	22	.230	.292	.385	252	58	14	2	7	31	22	36
During the Day and at Night																						
Day	.215	.271	.414	186	40	11	1	8	39	13	36	.247	.297	.408	365	90	19	2	12	61	25	65
Night	.283	.306	.530	219	62	20	2	10	46	7	41	.252	.297	.420	507	128	33	2	16	71	33	81
By Month																						
April	.320	.346	.680	25	8	1	1	2	6	0	6	.309	.345	.473	110	34	4	1	4	13	4	18
May	.235	.257	.441	68	16	5	0	3	12	2	9	.199	.249	.340	156	31	10	0	4	18	11	22
June	.238	.284	.397	63	15	8	1	0	7	4	14	.261	.314	.414	111	29	9	1	2	15	9	16
July	.303	.342	.394	33	10	0	0	1	13	3	6	.256	.321	.368	117	30	4	0	3	19	12	21
August	.253	.326	.518	83	21	4	0	6	22	8	12	.212	.276	.423	156	33	6	0	9	28	13	23
Sept/Oct	.241	.259	.489	133	32	13	1	6	25	3	30	.275	.302	.459	222	61	19	2	6	39	9	46
Situational																						
Bases Empty	.203	.234	.365	222	45	15	0	7	7	8	45	.222	.259	.376	481	107	23	0	17	17	23	82
Leadoff	.172	.193	.328	116	20	6	0	4	4	2	30	.201	.223	.349	209	42	7	0	8	8	5	43
Not Leadoff	.236	.277	.406	106	25	9	0	3	3	6	15	.239	.286	.397	272	65	16	0	9	9	18	39
Runners On	.311	.353	.612	183	57	16	3	11	78	12	32	.284	.341	.463	391	111	29	4	11	115	35	64
First Base Only	.323	.333	.613	62	20	4	1	4	10	0	12	.278	.308	.426	162	45	8	2	4	13	6	28
Scoring Position	.306	.362	.612	121	37	12	2	7	68	12	20	.288	.362	.489	229	66	21	2	7	102	29	36
Late Innings, Close	.313	.350	.625	96	30	10	1	6	30	6	17	.272	.309	.508	191	52	10	1	11	37	11	35
RBI/Opportunities																						
Scoring Position				52 / 171	(30%)										83 / 326	(25%)						
Scoring Position, 2 Out				22 / 76	(29%)										32 / 154	(21%)						
On Third, Less than 2 Out				20 / 36	(56%)										30 / 60	(50%)						
RBI in close games / RBI Total				61 / 85	(72%)										90 / 132	(68%)						

Mike Marshall
Los Angeles Dodgers

As long as there are athletes like Mike Marshall, sports medicine will thrive. 1986 was Mike's fourth full year in the majors; injuries have sidelined him each year.

Minor-league player *extraordinaire*, Mike feasted on minor-league pitching. In 1981, he won the first Triple Crown in the Pacific Coast League in 25 years with a .373 BA, 34 HRs and 137 RBIs. He was on close to the same pace in 1982 when the Dodgers called him up.

There have been two major differences between the minor-league Mike Marshall and the major-league one. In the minors, he drew almost 1 walk per strikeout; in the majors, he has drawn only 1 BB per 3 Ks. Also, he has hit for a .268 average in the bigs, compared to his minor-league career BA of .351. If nothing else, his .450 slugging average will assure him of a spot in the lineup.

Because Pedro Guerrero has overshadowed Mike, the numbers he has posted have gone relatively unnoticed. He has excellent power; over the last three years his secondary average is .281, and he has averaged one HR per 19.75 at-bats.

It is the injuries that have slowed Marshall's career down. 1986 was his worst year—a back injury limited him to 63 at-bats after June. Though not diagnosed as serious, he made his last appearance of the year on August 20th, hitting a three-run homer in that game against the Mets.

An appendectomy and other assorted injuries kept Mike out of 27 games in 1985; foot surgery kept him out of action for a month in 1984. In 1987, the team physician will likely be Mike's roommate.

Over the past three years, Marshall's best month has been September, when he has posted a .320 BA and a .581 SA. He seems to come alive for the pennant drive.

Affectionately called big-foot by his teammates because of his size-14 feet, Mike is a quiet giant who lets his bat do the talking for him. He is already tied for seventh on the all-time Dodgers list in career grand slams with Steve Garvey. His power has been compared to that of Mike Schmidt and Dale Murphy. If he stays healthy, Marshall will be one of the best power-hitters in the league.

Mike is one of the young players that the Dodgers are resting their future pennant hopes on. If he stays away from those nagging injuries he will be able to get the job done. With his health, he can be a superstar.

—Carmen J. Corica

	1986 SEASON											THREE YEARS (84 – 86)										
	Ave.	OBP	SLG	AB	H	2B	3B	HR	RBI	BB	SO	Ave.	OBP	SLG	AB	H	2B	3B	HR	RBI	BB	SO
Totals	.233	.298	.439	330	77	11	0	19	53	27	90	.265	.321	.468	1343	356	65	2	68	213	104	320
Batting vs. Left and Right-handed Pitchers																						
Left	.248	.329	.512	129	32	7	0	9	21	16	34	.273	.354	.500	444	121	26	0	25	76	57	109
Right	.224	.278	.393	201	45	4	0	10	32	11	56	.261	.304	.453	899	235	39	2	43	137	47	211
At Home and on the Road																						
Home	.240	.305	.497	179	43	7	0	13	34	16	40	.271	.319	.490	694	188	33	1	39	119	48	160
Road	.225	.291	.371	151	34	4	0	6	19	11	50	.259	.323	.445	649	168	32	1	29	94	56	160
Facing Groundball Pitchers and Flyball Pitchers																						
Groundball	.266	.325	.474	154	41	5	0	9	27	13	42	.278	.342	.457	589	164	28	1	25	92	53	140
Flyball	.205	.275	.409	176	36	6	0	10	26	14	48	.255	.305	.477	754	192	37	1	43	121	51	180
Facing Finesse Pitchers and Power Pitchers																						
Finesse	.247	.303	.465	170	42	7	0	10	29	12	49	.274	.320	.466	766	210	40	1	35	111	48	159
Power	.219	.294	.412	160	35	4	0	9	24	15	41	.253	.322	.471	577	146	25	1	33	102	56	161
On Grass and on Turf																						
Grass	.257	.323	.498	261	67	9	0	18	48	22	63	.272	.322	.476	1026	279	42	1	55	169	70	235
Turf	.145	.203	.217	69	10	2	0	1	5	5	27	.243	.317	.445	317	77	23	1	13	44	34	85
During the Day and at Night																						
Day	.223	.305	.383	94	21	3	0	4	16	9	25	.267	.317	.476	420	112	13	0	25	73	28	83
Night	.237	.296	.462	236	56	8	0	15	37	18	65	.264	.323	.465	923	244	52	2	43	140	76	237
By Month																						
April	.225	.266	.449	89	20	2	0	6	17	3	25	.264	.318	.494	265	70	10	0	17	47	18	65
May	.297	.379	.593	91	27	6	0	7	20	10	22	.271	.353	.502	207	56	12	0	12	39	25	48
June	.276	.347	.448	87	24	3	0	4	9	10	22	.277	.345	.454	238	66	9	0	11	29	25	63
July	.120	.120	.240	25	3	0	0	1	2	0	7	.242	.287	.451	182	44	11	0	9	27	11	39
August	.079	.167	.158	38	3	0	0	1	5	4	14	.222	.271	.347	248	55	10	0	7	27	16	59
Sept/Oct	.000	.000	.000	0	0	0	0	0	0	0	0	.320	.353	.581	203	65	13	2	12	44	9	46
Situational																						
Bases Empty	.213	.279	.437	174	37	3	0	12	12	14	52	.255	.302	.463	730	186	33	1	39	39	44	180
Leadoff	.226	.286	.488	84	19	1	0	7	7	7	25	.258	.307	.462	314	81	10	0	18	18	20	67
Not Leadoff	.200	.273	.389	90	18	2	0	5	5	7	27	.252	.298	.464	416	105	23	1	21	21	24	113
Runners On	.256	.320	.442	156	40	8	0	7	41	13	38	.277	.343	.475	613	170	32	1	29	174	60	140
First Base Only	.270	.299	.541	74	20	5	0	5	13	1	19	.291	.333	.483	265	77	15	0	12	30	14	63
Scoring Position	.244	.337	.354	82	20	3	0	2	28	12	19	.267	.350	.468	348	93	17	1	17	144	46	77
Late Innings, Close	.271	.343	.458	59	16	2	0	3	8	5	12	.250	.297	.392	232	58	6	0	9	32	14	47
RBI/Opportunities																						
Scoring Position				24 / 113		(21%)									115 / 465		(25%)					
Scoring Position, 2 Out				8 / 43		(19%)									47 / 211		(22%)					
On Third, Less than 2 Out				12 / 30		(40%)									44 / 90		(49%)					
RBI in close games / RBI Total				43 / 53		(81%)									157 / 213		(74%)					

Gary Matthews
Chicago Cubs

Instrumental in the Cubs' 1984 pennant drive, Gary Matthews rebounded from a poor, injury-ridden '85 campaign to tally some solid numbers in 1986. Even so, at the age of 36, Matthews is almost certainly reduced now to a fill-in role.

Matthews' 21 homers led the Cubs and placed him twelfth among National League hitters—in just 370 at-bats! His totals in SLG and OBP put him behind another veteran, Ron Cey (.384 OBP, .508 SLG) for the club lead among players with 100 or more AB. Matthews also had the dubious honor of leading the Cubs in grounding into double plays with 15, no doubt indicative of diminished hitting and baserunning skills; infielders are well aware that they have more time to execute the clean double-play with Matthews running to first.

One of Matthews' assets has always been drawing the base-on-balls. This still holds true, and his three year totals show a BB/SO ratio slightly greater than one. Matthews shows no apparent preference with respect to LHP and RHP, drawing about 15 BB per 100 plate appearances against either side. This figure holds across other breakdowns, such as Grass/Turf and Day/Night as well.

To a Chicago fan, Gary's greatest liability is likely his fielding. It is an awesome sight to see this relatively large man lumbering after a fly to left, and some of his routine plays are downright frightening; his nine errors last year (in 779 innings) are triple his '85 total (in 652 innings). Most of his spectacular plays need not have been so.

With the '86 season history, Matthews finds himself on a team trying to regroup. The Cubs are, at the moment, in the uncomfortable position of carrying a roster filled with older, high-salaried players, and it would seem that a few of them must be gleaned soon if the young players are to make it to the Cub roster before they reach retirement themselves. What is to be gained by keeping a Gary Matthews on the roster? If it is true that Matthews' leadership abilities were essential in winning the 1984 pennant—and they were highly touted by the Chicago management—then it became equally clear one year later that his mere presence on the bench was insufficient to inspire a high level of play on the field. Matthews' highly touted role as "The Sarge" can only be realized on the field, if at all, and part-time play would certainly diminish that contribution.

—Mark Podrazik

	1986 SEASON											THREE YEARS (84 – 86)										
	Ave.	OBP	SLG	AB	H	2B	3B	HR	RBI	BB	SO	Ave.	OBP	SLG	AB	H	2B	3B	HR	RBI	BB	SO
Totals	.259	.361	.478	370	96	16	1	21	46	60	59	.267	.383	.438	1159	309	49	3	48	168	222	220
Batting vs. Left and Right-handed Pitchers																						
Left	.352	.465	.600	105	37	6	1	6	15	23	9	.311	.404	.492	331	103	13	1	15	50	54	41
Right	.223	.317	.430	265	59	10	0	15	31	37	50	.249	.375	.417	828	206	36	2	33	118	168	179
At Home and on the Road																						
Home	.286	.382	.514	185	53	7	1	11	28	30	31	.275	.390	.471	550	151	21	3	27	92	105	114
Road	.232	.340	.443	185	43	9	0	10	18	30	28	.259	.376	.409	609	158	28	0	21	76	117	106
Facing Groundball Pitchers and Flyball Pitchers																						
Groundball	.257	.354	.459	183	47	8	1	9	24	28	24	.263	.375	.438	544	143	23	3	22	73	99	92
Flyball	.262	.368	.497	187	49	8	0	12	22	32	35	.270	.389	.439	615	166	26	0	26	95	123	128
Facing Finesse Pitchers and Power Pitchers																						
Finesse	.247	.337	.455	235	58	10	0	13	28	33	29	.265	.357	.429	697	185	31	1	27	91	100	96
Power	.281	.401	.519	135	38	6	1	8	18	27	30	.268	.417	.452	462	124	18	2	21	77	122	124
On Grass and on Turf																						
Grass	.274	.370	.518	274	75	11	1	18	40	43	43	.279	.401	.480	806	225	30	3	42	128	167	159
Turf	.219	.336	.365	96	21	5	0	3	6	17	16	.238	.338	.343	353	84	19	0	6	40	55	61
During the Day and at Night																						
Day	.246	.338	.448	252	62	10	1	13	30	36	40	.266	.379	.453	753	200	30	3	35	118	138	149
Night	.288	.408	.542	118	34	6	0	8	16	24	19	.268	.389	.411	406	109	19	0	13	50	84	71
By Month																						
April	.161	.316	.194	31	5	1	0	0	2	7	3	.264	.406	.385	148	39	6	0	4	21	36	23
May	.227	.346	.455	66	15	3	0	4	9	12	12	.230	.351	.385	187	43	8	0	7	22	36	40
June	.241	.406	.389	54	13	3	1	1	4	15	8	.256	.394	.362	160	41	7	2	2	22	38	35
July	.313	.389	.637	80	25	5	0	7	14	10	11	.302	.403	.548	199	60	10	0	13	38	35	32
August	.258	.317	.452	93	24	3	0	5	11	9	14	.261	.344	.400	280	73	13	1	8	26	37	50
Sept/Oct	.304	.396	.587	46	14	1	0	4	6	7	11	.286	.417	.541	185	53	5	0	14	39	40	40
Situational																						
Bases Empty	.285	.378	.538	221	63	11	0	15	15	33	34	.251	.372	.432	658	165	28	2	29	29	127	126
Leadoff	.286	.375	.468	77	22	2	0	4	4	11	10	.245	.354	.415	229	56	7	1	10	10	39	39
Not Leadoff	.285	.380	.576	144	41	9	0	11	11	22	24	.254	.381	.441	429	109	21	1	19	19	88	87
Runners On	.221	.337	.389	149	33	5	1	6	31	27	25	.287	.396	.447	501	144	21	1	19	139	95	94
First Base Only	.237	.357	.390	59	14	3	0	2	6	11	7	.350	.458	.503	177	62	9	0	6	18	32	27
Scoring Position	.211	.324	.389	90	19	2	1	4	25	16	18	.253	.364	.417	324	82	12	1	13	121	63	67
Late Innings, Close	.234	.338	.391	64	15	1	0	3	5	10	9	.244	.357	.384	164	40	8	0	5	25	31	27
RBI/Opportunities																						
Scoring Position	19 / 121			(16%)								101 / 460			(22%)							
Scoring Position, 2 Out	7 / 46			(15%)								28 / 162			(17%)							
On Third, Less than 2 Out	9 / 23			(39%)								44 / 93			(47%)							
RBI in close games / RBI Total	30 / 46			(65%)								113 / 168			(67%)							

Don Mattingly
New York Yankees

When you're consistently cited by your peers as the best player in baseball, you must be doing something right—for Don Mattingly, that something is just about everything. Save for speed, he's a complete player—he doesn't walk much, but with a career on-base average of about .380 and only 35 strikeouts a year, you can live with that. He has led the major leagues in doubles and had 200+ hits for three consecutive years.

Much is made of the fact that Mattingly plays in Yankee Stadium and thus benefits from the short right field fence. It's true that he gets about five homers a year from his park; it doesn't help him get any other sort of hits. Since 1984, he has hit 18 points higher on the road (.348/.330) and had 24 more doubles and triples on the road. It seems fair to assume that Yankee Stadium's short porch reduces doubles totals (especially with his lack of speed). He'd probably have hit 60 doubles in a neutral park with longer foul lines; there's no telling what he'd have done in Boston.

It's sometimes difficult to understand how good Don is—1986 provided a frame of reference. He broke two Yankee team records this year—hits (set by Earl Combs in 1927) and doubles (set by Lou Gehrig that same year). His career stats also give us a clue—here are his totals compared with past stars at the same age:

AVERAGE: Mattingly's career mark is .332; the following players had similar marks at his age: Arky Vaughan (.336), George Sisler (.331), Earl Averill (.329), Goose Goslin (.324), Bill Terry (.313), Charlie Gehringer (.315), Tony Oliva (.311), Pie Traynor (.309) and George Brett (.308).

DOUBLES: Mattingly's 160 tops Averill (159), Jim Bottomley (157), Traynor and Joe DiMaggio (143), Brett (124), Gehringer (122) and Terry (118). His most impressive feat is that he tops the two men who hit the most doubles in their careers (Tris Speaker had 135; Pete Rose 111) and is within shouting distance of Lou Gehrig (174).

RUNS AND RBIS: Mattingly has scored 349 runs and driven in 401 to date; better than Sisler (336/281), Terry (329/359) and Brett (334/291) and above the following in one area or another—Gehringer (416/290), Traynor (403/374), Oliva (394/366), Hank Aaron (387/399), Goslin (354/400) and Willie Mays (319/412).

Finally . . . Don now has a 42% chance to get 3000 hits, a 14% chance to get 4000 and a 1% chance at 5000.

—Craig Christmann and Bud Podrazik

	1986 SEASON											THREE YEARS (84 – 86)										
	Ave.	OBP	SLG	AB	H	2B	3B	HR	RBI	BB	SO	Ave.	OBP	SLG	AB	H	2B	3B	HR	RBI	BB	SO
Totals	.352	.394	.573	677	238	53	2	31	113	53	35	.340	.382	.560	1932	656	145	7	89	368	150	109
Batting vs. Left and Right-handed Pitchers																						
Left	.358	.398	.523	243	87	23	1	5	41	17	13	.323	.364	.534	691	223	58	2	28	139	50	41
Right	.348	.392	.601	434	151	30	1	26	72	36	22	.349	.392	.575	1241	433	87	5	61	229	100	68
At Home and on the Road																						
Home	.334	.383	.566	320	107	23	0	17	60	28	16	.330	.372	.567	920	304	63	1	51	196	71	50
Road	.367	.404	.580	357	131	30	2	14	53	25	19	.348	.391	.553	1012	352	82	6	38	172	79	59
Facing Groundball Pitchers and Flyball Pitchers																						
Groundball	.366	.398	.588	320	117	25	2	14	55	20	12	.343	.379	.566	955	328	68	5	45	174	61	46
Flyball	.339	.390	.560	357	121	28	0	17	58	33	23	.336	.385	.554	977	328	77	2	44	194	89	63
Facing Finesse Pitchers and Power Pitchers																						
Finesse	.357	.394	.570	381	136	27	0	18	58	25	18	.331	.368	.535	1072	355	75	3	46	171	70	51
Power	.345	.394	.578	296	102	26	2	13	55	28	17	.350	.400	.591	860	301	70	4	43	197	80	58
On Grass and on Turf																						
Grass	.335	.381	.543	565	189	38	1	26	94	46	30	.337	.381	.552	1624	547	117	4	75	314	131	91
Turf	.438	.463	.723	112	49	15	1	5	19	7	5	.354	.386	.601	308	109	28	3	14	54	19	18
During the Day and at Night																						
Day	.333	.388	.532	231	77	14	1	10	40	24	12	.339	.385	.562	626	212	49	2	29	106	52	31
Night	.361	.397	.594	446	161	39	1	21	73	29	23	.340	.381	.559	1306	444	96	5	60	262	98	78
By Month																						
April	.268	.341	.354	82	22	4	0	1	19	9	2	.297	.352	.423	222	66	20	1	2	39	19	9
May	.376	.412	.632	117	44	12	0	6	20	10	8	.348	.390	.583	319	111	22	1	17	65	27	20
June	.350	.379	.553	123	43	7	0	6	17	7	5	.324	.359	.496	339	110	20	1	12	53	23	20
July	.336	.368	.627	110	37	12	1	6	16	6	8	.333	.373	.568	324	108	30	2	14	59	24	21
August	.325	.375	.538	117	38	7	0	6	18	9	5	.365	.418	.620	342	125	22	1	21	65	29	15
Sept/Oct	.422	.465	.664	128	54	11	1	6	23	12	7	.352	.389	.617	386	136	31	1	23	87	28	24
Situational																						
Bases Empty	.372	.410	.619	360	134	28	2	19	19	22	18	.344	.379	.578	1024	352	76	7	50	50	54	69
Leadoff	.397	.421	.647	116	46	9	1	6	6	5	8	.356	.378	.629	337	120	28	2	20	20	11	19
Not Leadoff	.361	.405	.607	244	88	19	1	13	13	17	10	.338	.379	.553	687	232	48	5	30	30	43	50
Runners On	.328	.377	.521	317	104	25	0	12	94	31	17	.335	.385	.540	908	304	69	0	39	318	96	40
First Base Only	.349	.381	.467	152	53	9	0	3	7	8	5	.330	.364	.543	418	138	32	0	19	52	22	15
Scoring Position	.309	.374	.570	165	51	16	0	9	87	23	12	.339	.401	.537	490	166	37	0	20	266	74	25
Late Innings, Close	.351	.421	.521	94	33	4	0	4	23	12	2	.352	.409	.546	304	107	15	1	14	64	31	8

RBI/Opportunities					
Scoring Position	71 / 234	(30%)	225 / 706	(32%)
Scoring Position, 2 Out	19 / 87	(22%)	69 / 266	(26%)
On Third, Less than 2 Out	31 / 50	(62%)	102 / 156	(65%)
RBI in close games / RBI Total	81 / 113	(72%)	260 / 368	(71%)

Kirk McCaskill
California Angels

If you want a good time at the ballpark, when the Angels come to play in your hometown go see the game that Kirk McCaskill pitches. I can guarantee that you'll enjoy it. Chances are, the Homeville Nine will score a couple runs in the first, and come close to scoring even more. You'll wonder how long Kirk McCaskill will last in the game. You'll see the offensive prowess of your team. You'll see doubles up the alley, possibly a booming homerun. You'll feel great about yourself and your team. In the second inning, Homeville will load the bases quickly. You'll be amazed that the Angels are leaving McCaskill in the game. When you think about the good stats Kirk has, you'll be even more impressed with how well your team is hitting. "Hey, our guys are starting to hit even the good pitchers! We're starting our pennant drive now!" Go have a beer as Homeville finishes the second inning with a run or two. Enjoy a hotdog. Talk to that girl in the row in front of you. How can they leave this guy in the game? You can't beat fun at the ol' ballpark.

Same game, seventh inning. As the Angels score the go-ahead run, you start to wonder. "Hey, our guys don't have a hit since the second inning. We looked so great early in the game. Now all our hitters look so confused. This guy was such a bum before, and now he's killing us." Chances are, you'll get a scratch hit in the eighth, maybe a walk in the ninth, and the game will be over quickly. So much for the pennant drive.

But think back on all the good times you had. You felt so good about your offense. And weren't the hotdogs good? Too bad about the girl in the row in front of you. Maybe she does have to be to work early tomorrow. And while we're at it, why are you living in a city like "Homeville" anyway? At any rate, you will have a great time at the game. Promise.

Kirk McCaskill is the definition of a streak pitcher. I'll predict a no-hitter in 1987. He consistently has streaks of retiring 15 out of 16, 17 out of 19, and the like. His habit of giving up runs in the first two or three innings improved in 1986 from his 1985 performance, by a change in his pre-game schedule. Some night in 1987 he's going to get them out 1-2-3 in the first three innings, and then look out.

Keep in mind that as late as 1984, Kirk was playing minor league hockey in the Winnipeg Jets system. He hasn't been pitching all that long. Don't be surprised if he's an honest Cy Young candidate in the next two years. He's already in the top ten in the American League among starters in the ratio of hits to innings pitched and the ratio of hits plus walks to innings pitched. He was one of only twelve starters (with more than 150 innings pitched) in the American League to have both fewer hits than innings pitched, and also a better than 2:1 ratio of strikeouts to walks (the Angels have three of the twelve; the other two are Mike Witt and Don Sutton).

—Dennis Bretz

1986: Power, Flyball **1985: Finesse, Groundball** **1984: Did not play**

	1986 SEASON											THREE YEARS (84 – 86)										
---	G	IP	H	BB	SO	SB	CS	W	L	S	ERA	G	IP	H	BB	SO	SB	CS	W	L	S	ERA
Totals	34	246.1	207	92	202	7	10	17	10	0	3.36	64	436.0	396	156	304	13	13	29	22	0	3.94
At Home and on the Road																						
Home	15	113.2	88	40	86	3	6	6	5	0	2.93	30	210.0	181	63	138	6	7	13	9	0	3.69
Road	19	132.2	119	52	116	4	4	11	5	0	3.73	34	226.0	215	93	166	7	6	16	13	0	4.18
During the Day and at Night																						
Day	7	49.1	49	23	50	1	2	4	2	0	4.93	16	105.2	113	37	85	2	2	7	6	0	5.11
Night	27	197.0	158	69	152	6	8	13	8	0	2.97	48	330.1	283	119	219	11	11	22	16	0	3.57
On Grass and on Turf																						
Grass	29	218.2	174	84	183	6	10	15	9	0	3.17	56	387.1	346	142	275	12	13	26	20	0	3.93
Turf	5	27.2	33	8	19	1	0	2	1	0	4.88	8	48.2	50	14	29	1	0	3	2	0	4.07
By Month																						
April	4	31.2	26	13	24	1	3	2	1	0	3.13	4	31.2	26	13	24	1	3	2	1	0	3.13
May	6	37.2	36	17	39	0	1	2	2	0	4.54	12	67.2	69	31	56	0	1	2	5	0	5.32
June	6	45.1	37	15	40	1	2	4	2	0	3.38	11	80.1	71	26	63	5	2	6	4	0	3.47
July	5	44.0	33	15	37	0	0	4	1	0	1.64	11	83.0	79	28	50	0	1	8	3	0	2.93
August	6	39.0	41	18	22	2	2	2	1	0	5.08	12	85.0	74	30	47	3	3	5	3	0	4.24
Sept/Oct	7	48.2	34	14	40	3	2	3	3	0	2.77	14	88.1	77	28	64	4	3	6	6	0	4.28

	vs. Opponent Batters																					
	1986 SEASON											THREE YEARS (84 – 86)										
	Ave.	OBP	SLG	AB	H	2B	3B	HR	RBI	BB	SO	Ave.	OBP	SLG	AB	H	2B	3B	HR	RBI	BB	SO
Totals	.229	.302	.341	905	207	33	6	19	91	92	202	.242	.310	.371	1637	396	64	11	42	180	156	304
Pitching vs. Left and Right-handed Batters																						
Left	.234	.311	.355	504	118	18	5	11	55	55	98	.254	.323	.385	910	231	39	7	22	96	94	144
Right	.222	.291	.324	401	89	15	1	8	36	37	104	.227	.292	.355	727	165	25	4	20	84	62	160
Situational																						
Bases Empty	.207	.292	.302	547	113	20	4	8	8	62	121	.217	.293	.323	989	215	38	6	18	18	99	186
Leadoff	.234	.311	.329	231	54	14	1	2	2	26	46	.248	.317	.345	415	103	21	2	5	5	41	65
Not Leadoff	.187	.278	.282	316	59	6	3	6	6	36	75	.195	.275	.307	574	112	17	4	13	13	58	121
Runners On	.263	.317	.402	358	94	13	2	11	83	30	81	.279	.336	.446	648	181	26	5	24	162	57	118
First Base Only	.240	.303	.358	179	43	9	0	4	13	15	39	.289	.352	.472	305	88	16	2	12	36	28	49
Scoring Position	.285	.332	.447	179	51	4	2	7	70	15	42	.271	.321	.423	343	93	10	3	12	126	29	69
Late Innings, Close	.191	.264	.382	110	21	4	1	5	11	10	30	.238	.294	.421	164	39	7	1	7	18	11	34

RBI/Opportunities					
Scoring Position	55 / 221	(25%)	102 / 430	(24%)
Scoring Position, 2 Out	23 / 102	(23%)	39 / 179	(22%)
On Third, Less than 2 Out	18 / 45	(40%)	34 / 87	(39%)
RBI in close games / RBI Total	76 / 91	(84%)	128 / 180	(71%)

Lance McCullers
San Diego Padres

Managing Lance McCullers is like buying uncut diamonds—you know you have something valuable but you don't know how much. Lance has already shown that he is a fine setup man, a great #2 man and a good closer. He could be a brilliant relief ace; he might be only fair—we'll find out in time.

Lance changes speeds well—if your idea of changing speeds is hard, harder and "get the snowball through the blast furnace without melting it." He depends mostly on stuff to get hitters out and his stuff can be unhittable. But there are two potential holes in his game.

The first is his location. A righty hitter gets the ball in on the fists, where it's impossible to hit very often or very far. To a lefty, the ball is up and over the plate—right where the batting practice pitcher throws them. Lance has a big platoon differential and, to make matters worse, other teams know it. In 1985, Lance faced about as many lefties (42%) as a typical righty; in 1986 it was up to 52%.

A second problem is his stamina. Lance tires very easily; he doesn't have the strength to pitch more than two innings and he works best with a day between relief outings.

Lance would like to start, the Padres would like to use him there and they did try him there in 1986 (the last week of June through the first week in August), but anyone who looks at his July can see that he simply wasn't effective there. McCullers pitched a heavy number of innings in 1986 and it began wearing on him as the year progressed; much as he dislikes being in the bullpen, Lance benefits by it.

It is impossible to predict what kind of a career McCullers will have just yet. A big, strong righthander can only overpower major league hitters for a short period of time before they catch up to him; the trick is to stay one step ahead of them. Rich Gossage had precisely the same strengths and weaknesses that Lance has and he made the adjustments—he learned to change speeds just enough to let him get lefties out and began to insist that his managers not overwork him—that let him become a great reliever. Tim Stoddard was equally talented, but he didn't adjust and turned into a mopup man. Whether Lance cuts his platoon differential and begins conserving his arm will determine whether he becomes the new Goose or just another turkey.

—Geoff Beckman

1986: Power, Flyball   **1985: Power, Flyball**   **1984: Did not play**

	1986 SEASON											THREE YEARS (84 – 86)										
	G	IP	H	BB	SO	SB	CS	W	L	S	ERA	G	IP	H	BB	SO	SB	CS	W	L	S	ERA
Totals	70	136.0	103	58	92	16	8	10	10	5	2.78	91	171.0	126	74	119	17	11	10	12	10	2.68
At Home and on the Road																						
Home	32	61.0	46	21	46	9	5	5	3	1	2.66	43	83.2	64	31	63	10	6	5	3	5	2.58
Road	38	75.0	57	37	46	7	3	5	7	4	2.88	48	87.1	62	43	56	7	5	5	9	5	2.78
During the Day and at Night																						
Day	17	28.1	25	20	20	2	4	3	4	1	3.49	23	40.2	33	26	31	2	6	3	5	3	3.10
Night	53	107.2	78	38	72	14	4	7	6	4	2.59	68	130.1	93	48	88	15	5	7	7	7	2.55
On Grass and on Turf																						
Grass	53	98.1	79	48	74	14	7	8	8	2	2.84	68	125.2	99	61	94	15	9	8	9	7	2.79
Turf	17	37.2	24	10	18	2	1	2	2	3	2.63	23	45.1	27	13	25	2	2	2	3	3	2.38
By Month																						
April	7	8.0	7	2	7	2	1	1	1	0	2.25	7	8.0	7	2	7	2	1	1	1	0	2.25
May	15	16.1	6	9	10	2	0	0	0	1	0.55	15	16.1	6	9	10	2	0	0	0	1	0.55
June	15	26.1	21	9	19	2	2	3	1	0	2.39	15	26.1	21	9	19	2	2	3	1	0	2.39
July	5	31.0	26	15	20	5	1	1	3	0	3.48	5	31.0	26	15	20	5	1	1	3	0	3.48
August	13	32.1	24	8	19	1	3	2	1	1	2.78	20	46.1	33	16	30	1	4	2	2	5	2.53
Sept/Oct	15	22.0	19	15	17	4	1	3	4	3	4.09	29	43.0	33	23	33	5	3	3	5	4	3.35

vs. Opponent Batters																						
	1986 SEASON											THREE YEARS (84 – 86)										
	Ave.	OBP	SLG	AB	H	2B	3B	HR	RBI	BB	SO	Ave.	OBP	SLG	AB	H	2B	3B	HR	RBI	BB	SO
Totals	.216	.304	.331	477	103	17	1	12	49	58	92	.212	.303	.329	595	126	23	1	15	69	74	119
Pitching vs. Left and Right-handed Batters																						
Left	.280	.372	.390	236	66	9	1	5	29	35	30	.273	.377	.397	282	77	12	1	7	36	46	35
Right	.154	.235	.274	241	37	8	0	7	20	23	62	.157	.232	.268	313	49	11	0	8	33	28	84
Situational																						
Bases Empty	.234	.303	.340	291	68	11	1	6	6	26	55	.227	.305	.339	348	79	13	1	8	8	35	65
Leadoff	.229	.300	.297	118	27	5	0	1	1	10	19	.220	.308	.284	141	31	6	0	1	1	15	23
Not Leadoff	.237	.305	.370	173	41	6	1	5	5	16	36	.232	.303	.377	207	48	7	1	7	7	20	42
Runners On	.188	.306	.317	186	35	6	0	6	43	32	37	.190	.300	.316	247	47	10	0	7	61	39	54
First Base Only	.188	.243	.319	69	13	3	0	2	6	5	13	.161	.212	.290	93	15	3	0	3	8	6	22
Scoring Position	.188	.338	.316	117	22	3	0	4	37	27	24	.208	.346	.331	154	32	7	0	4	53	33	32
Late Innings, Close	.225	.338	.332	187	42	5	0	5	22	31	37	.222	.337	.330	261	58	10	0	6	34	43	56

RBI/Opportunities					
Scoring Position	30 / 187	(16%)	43 / 244	(18%)
Scoring Position, 2 Out	10 / 86	(12%)	20 / 118	(17%)
On Third, Less than 2 Out	15 / 33	(45%)	17 / 38	(45%)
RBI in close games / RBI Total	32 / 49	(65%)	45 / 69	(65%)

Oddibe McDowell, Jr.
Texas Rangers

Yes, Oddibe is his real name, and, yes, there is an Oddibe McDowell, Sr. Little Mac set a club record with 105 runs scored in 1986. I credit that to his improved discipline at the plate. Raising his batting average from .239 to .266 and jumping his walk average over 25% gave him a .341 on-base average to go with his power and speed. And it is reasonable to expect him to continue to improve. He plays in such a professional, polished manner that folks sometimes forget how young he is and the extent of his professional experience. He is only 24 and has played less than 300 games as a pro. That sounds like a lot by the standard of other sports, but it is nothing in baseball. Pete O'Brien entered baseball at age 21 and played nearly 600 pro games before he hit higher than .239 in the majors. Gary Ward had nearly 1000 games of experience before he became a major league regular. McDowell had 31.

There are other reasons to believe in McDowell's continued improvement. He's competitive with a real fire to succeed, but a lot players are like that—particularly when they are starting out. There is more to Oddibe. He's a student; he looks upon baseball as his craft and believes he can improve his skills. And then there is an aspect of his personality which has held him back in the early going but will help stabilize his career in the long run.

McDowell is a quiet man, much more introverted than your average professional athlete. He is less brash, exceedingly modest, and his type of personality generally takes more time to ground itself comfortably into a new lifestyle. With time I expect him to become more at peace with the bright lights and the nomadic lifestyle of a major leaguer. In his first two seasons he has hit much better at home than on the road. Overall he has hit .274 at home versus .235 on the road.

You can't help but be reminded of Joe Morgan when you watch McDowell play. Oddibe is unusually short (5–9) but powerful, a left-handed hitter, a fast base stealer, he walks more than normal, and, like Morgan was, Mac is a good defensive player despite a sub-par throwing arm.

—Craig Wright

	1986 SEASON											THREE YEARS (84 – 86)										
	Ave.	OBP	SLG	AB	H	2B	3B	HR	RBI	BB	SO	Ave.	OBP	SLG	AB	H	2B	3B	HR	RBI	BB	SO
Totals	.266	.341	.427	572	152	24	7	18	49	65	112	.255	.326	.428	978	249	38	12	36	91	101	197
Batting vs. Left and Right-handed Pitchers																						
Left	.219	.296	.336	128	28	4	1	3	11	14	32	.231	.303	.382	251	58	10	5	6	19	24	66
Right	.279	.353	.453	444	124	20	6	15	38	51	80	.263	.333	.444	727	191	28	7	30	72	77	131
At Home and on the Road																						
Home	.279	.340	.441	290	81	13	5	8	28	27	62	.274	.333	.450	493	135	17	8	18	51	42	97
Road	.252	.342	.411	282	71	11	2	10	21	38	50	.235	.319	.406	485	114	21	4	18	40	59	100
Facing Groundball Pitchers and Flyball Pitchers																						
Groundball	.268	.334	.415	284	76	15	3	7	23	29	48	.265	.328	.436	498	132	24	5	17	45	46	85
Flyball	.264	.347	.438	288	76	9	4	11	26	36	64	.244	.323	.421	480	117	14	7	19	46	55	112
Facing Finesse Pitchers and Power Pitchers																						
Finesse	.290	.344	.507	355	103	17	6	16	34	30	51	.281	.334	.501	573	161	25	10	27	54	45	81
Power	.226	.336	.295	217	49	7	1	2	15	35	61	.217	.315	.326	405	88	13	2	9	37	56	116
On Grass and on Turf																						
Grass	.258	.336	.404	480	124	18	5	14	42	56	93	.249	.323	.410	826	206	28	9	29	77	87	163
Turf	.304	.366	.543	92	28	6	2	4	7	9	19	.283	.339	.526	152	43	10	3	7	14	14	34
During the Day and at Night																						
Day	.290	.367	.519	131	38	8	2	6	13	16	17	.266	.349	.473	188	50	11	2	8	16	24	32
Night	.259	.333	.399	441	114	16	5	12	36	49	95	.252	.320	.418	790	199	27	10	28	75	77	165
By Month																						
April	.271	.386	.486	70	19	6	0	3	7	13	12	.271	.386	.486	70	19	6	0	3	7	13	12
May	.243	.310	.369	103	25	4	0	3	9	10	21	.219	.273	.331	151	33	6	1	3	18	11	30
June	.310	.373	.570	100	31	3	4	5	10	10	18	.278	.333	.483	205	57	8	5	8	19	17	38
July	.242	.303	.354	99	24	3	1	2	8	9	21	.251	.307	.454	207	52	6	3	10	21	16	52
August	.293	.364	.465	99	29	6	1	3	7	10	23	.265	.347	.423	189	50	10	1	6	11	23	40
Sept/Oct	.238	.322	.337	101	24	2	1	2	8	13	17	.244	.335	.397	156	38	2	2	6	15	21	25
Situational																						
Bases Empty	.246	.323	.436	390	96	17	6	15	15	44	78	.254	.325	.457	650	165	27	9	29	29	66	130
Leadoff	.260	.323	.485	235	61	10	5	11	11	22	48	.254	.323	.469	390	99	17	8	17	17	39	80
Not Leadoff	.226	.322	.361	155	35	7	1	4	4	22	30	.254	.329	.438	260	66	10	1	12	12	27	50
Runners On	.308	.379	.407	182	56	7	1	3	34	21	34	.256	.326	.372	328	84	11	3	7	62	35	67
First Base Only	.337	.396	.398	83	28	2	0	1	4	7	9	.265	.321	.361	147	39	5	0	3	10	11	17
Scoring Position	.283	.365	.414	99	28	5	1	2	30	14	25	.249	.330	.381	181	45	6	3	4	52	24	50
Late Innings, Close	.287	.386	.414	87	25	3	1	2	9	14	21	.248	.349	.430	149	37	4	1	7	18	22	32

RBI/Opportunities	1986 SEASON			THREE YEARS (84 – 86)		
Scoring Position	26 / 129	(20%)		45 / 245	(18%)	
Scoring Position, 2 Out	11 / 62	(18%)		18 / 117	(15%)	
On Third, Less than 2 Out	8 / 25	(32%)		14 / 43	(33%)	
RBI in close games / RBI Total	26 / 49	(53%)		53 / 91	(58%)	

Willie McGee
St. Louis Cardinals

At the beginning of each season Willie McGee's father, who is a minister, annoints the Cardinal outfielder's feet. In 1986 it appeared that he must have forgotten to carry out the ritual, or perhaps he mumbled the wrong words during the ceremony. Maybe he just got hold of some bad holy water. Whatever the case, the "annointed one" of 1985, the National League MVP, more resembled the "afflicted one" in 1986. For just as everything went right for Willie in 1985, he couldn't seem to get a break in '86. His slump even extended to his baserunning, where he was thrown out in 16 of his 35 stolen base attempts. Even when McGee did play well, things didn't go right. He hit .299 for the month of July, with a .522 slugging percentage. In a four-game stretch from July 19 to July 22 Willie had a double, two triples, and three home runs, and seemed to be back in form. The next day he was injured, however, and played in only two of the next 33 games. Then after a strong finish McGee was injured again on the final weekend of the season, this time requiring surgery. To top it all off, Willie was involved in a number of off-season trade rumors.

Except for injuries, the second half of the season was a good one for McGee. In the final 80 games McGee hit .292, slugged .476 and had an OBA of .350. For the first 81 games the same numbers read .237, .316 and .284. Problem was, Willie played in 80 games during the first half but only 44 in the second half.

Amazingly, all seven McGee home runs in 1986 came in Busch Stadium. The entire rest of the team hit only 20 there. Willie also became the first Cardinal since David Green in 1984 to hit two home runs in one game; it was McGee's first two-homer game since his memorable performance in the third game of the '82 World Series. McGee batted leadoff seven times in 1986, hitting only .172, and hit cleanup seven times also, at a .161 clip. He hit well in day games in '86, which seems to be habit for McGee; his slugging percentage was up for day games also. Willie will move into third on the alltime Cardinal stolen base list with his 23rd steal in 1987; only Brock and Coleman are ahead of him. The last two Cardinal MVPs, Torre and Hernandez, were traded to the Mets three seasons later, so you can look for Willie in the Big Apple by 1989.

—Russ Eagle

	1986 SEASON											THREE YEARS (84 – 86)										
	Ave.	OBP	SLG	AB	H	2B	3B	HR	RBI	BB	SO	Ave.	OBP	SLG	AB	H	2B	3B	HR	RBI	BB	SO
Totals	.256	.306	.370	497	127	22	7	7	48	37	82	.303	.341	.427	1680	509	67	36	23	180	100	248
Batting vs. Left and Right-handed Pitchers																						
Left	.246	.301	.387	199	49	7	3	5	21	15	40	.290	.326	.468	573	166	23	14	17	74	32	122
Right	.262	.310	.359	298	78	15	4	2	27	22	42	.310	.348	.406	1107	343	44	22	6	106	68	126
At Home and on the Road																						
Home	.280	.325	.462	264	74	15	6	7	29	17	47	.314	.345	.443	810	254	31	19	12	74	41	122
Road	.227	.285	.266	233	53	7	1	0	19	20	35	.293	.337	.411	870	255	36	17	11	106	59	126
Facing Groundball Pitchers and Flyball Pitchers																						
Groundball	.251	.307	.345	267	67	11	4	2	22	22	37	.293	.333	.400	843	247	36	21	4	82	53	112
Flyball	.261	.305	.400	230	60	11	3	5	26	15	45	.313	.348	.454	837	262	31	15	19	98	47	136
Facing Finesse Pitchers and Power Pitchers																						
Finesse	.272	.323	.369	268	73	14	3	2	22	21	35	.303	.341	.429	944	286	46	23	9	90	58	116
Power	.236	.286	.371	229	54	8	4	5	26	16	47	.303	.340	.424	736	223	21	13	14	90	42	132
On Grass and on Turf																						
Grass	.205	.244	.228	127	26	3	0	0	6	7	13	.292	.333	.406	456	133	25	6	5	55	28	58
Turf	.273	.327	.419	370	101	19	7	7	42	30	69	.307	.344	.435	1224	376	42	30	18	125	72	190
During the Day and at Night																						
Day	.271	.317	.417	192	52	6	5	4	22	13	37	.322	.357	.477	612	197	23	18	12	71	34	83
Night	.246	.299	.341	305	75	16	2	3	26	24	45	.292	.331	.398	1068	312	44	18	11	109	66	165
By Month																						
April	.222	.247	.296	81	18	0	0	2	9	3	18	.264	.304	.358	201	53	0	5	3	21	11	37
May	.266	.308	.358	109	29	2	4	0	11	6	19	.283	.332	.395	311	88	11	9	2	35	23	47
June	.230	.299	.319	113	26	5	1	1	10	12	19	.287	.323	.388	317	91	12	7	2	35	19	47
July	.299	.347	.522	67	20	2	2	3	10	5	8	.326	.351	.522	230	75	15	6	6	23	10	30
August	.300	.440	.400	20	6	2	0	0	3	5	1	.360	.396	.502	239	86	9	5	5	33	15	34
Sept/Oct	.262	.301	.393	107	28	11	0	1	5	6	17	.304	.341	.416	382	116	20	4	5	33	22	53
Situational																						
Bases Empty	.269	.309	.381	294	79	12	3	5	5	16	47	.311	.340	.432	999	311	40	21	13	13	41	149
Leadoff	.291	.328	.418	110	32	4	2	2	2	6	15	.310	.336	.427	384	119	16	10	3	3	15	56
Not Leadoff	.255	.297	.359	184	47	8	1	3	3	10	32	.312	.342	.436	615	192	24	11	10	10	26	93
Runners On	.236	.303	.355	203	48	10	4	2	43	21	35	.291	.342	.419	681	198	27	15	10	167	59	99
First Base Only	.205	.256	.342	73	15	3	2	1	5	5	10	.253	.303	.345	249	63	6	4	3	11	18	34
Scoring Position	.254	.327	.362	130	33	7	2	1	38	16	25	.313	.363	.461	432	135	21	11	7	156	41	65
Late Innings, Close	.214	.275	.255	98	21	2	1	0	9	9	19	.257	.304	.370	265	68	8	5	4	40	20	49

RBI/Opportunities						
Scoring Position	36 / 168	(21%)		143 / 555	(26%)	
Scoring Position, 2 Out	12 / 72	(17%)		53 / 240	(22%)	
On Third, Less than 2 Out	15 / 34	(44%)		55 / 108	(51%)	
RBI in close games / RBI Total	34 / 48	(71%)		114 / 180	(63%)	

Scott McGregor
Baltimore Orioles

Like teammate Mike Boddicker, Scott McGregor is coming off his second straight poor year. Unlike Boddicker, though, the reason why is simple. McGregor was 32 in 1986 and he no longer has the ability to get major league hitters out.

In the past, McGregor has been a consistently winning pitcher. From 1978 to 1981 and again in 1983, the Oriole lefty had ERAs that ranged from 3.18 to 3.34 and an average record of 16–8. When he was winning, Scott was doing so by avoiding the components of that Baltimore standby, the three-run homer. In that stretch, he allowed 8.95 hits per nine innings, but only 1.77 walks and an impressive .76 homers. This point can be underscored by looking at his two off-seasons in that span (1982 and 1984). In those years, Scott was 54–53 with a 4.48 ERA. He allowed almost one extra hit (9.72), and allowed walks (2.34) and homers (1.28) about half again as often.

The most fascinating thing about these figures is that the conclusion that you'd be likely to draw—that Scott won by consistently getting good groundball support—is completely wrong. The *1986 Elias Baseball Analyst* lists the men who have gotten the highest percentage of flyouts in their careers—Scott is eighth on the list. That fact brings his career into clearer focus—a man who throws hard, changes speeds very well and depends on location and movement to get hitters out. It would have been reasonable to expect that, the instant that Scott lost velocity on his fastball, he would begin losing; this is exactly what has happened.

Scott's disastrous 1985 was written off in Baltimore—people said that he had been injured in 1984, had not been able to lift weights that winter and said that, when healthy, the zip on his pitches would return. It was very logical; it proved not to be true. McGregor made small steps forward last year (he cut his hits per game from 9.97 to 9.58 and walks from 2.87 to 2.53), but he has made no progress at all in his homers (1.50 in 1985; 1.55 in 1986), his other figures are nowhere near the level that they were in the past and there is no reason to expect them to improve in 1987.

The Scott McGregor of the past is gone—the best that anyone can hope for is that he has temporarily checked the slide. He can no longer help any team win and Baltimore must find a replacement if they hope to win in 1987.

—Geoff Beckman and Tim Mulligan

1986: Finesse, Flyball   **1985: Finesse, Flyball**   **1984: Finesse, Flyball**

	1986 SEASON												THREE YEARS (84 – 86)											
	G	IP	H	BB	SO	SB	CS	W	L	S	ERA		G	IP	H	BB	SO	SB	CS	W	L	S	ERA
Totals	34	203.0	216	57	95	16	5	11	15	0	4.52		99	603.1	658	176	248	40	19	40	41	0	4.43
At Home and on the Road																							
Home	15	87.1	96	25	43	7	4	5	8	0	4.53		49	311.1	328	82	134	18	7	24	18	0	3.76
Road	19	115.2	120	32	52	9	1	6	7	0	4.51		50	292.0	330	94	114	22	12	16	23	0	5.15
During the Day and at Night																							
Day	13	74.2	89	24	40	7	1	6	4	0	4.58		30	183.1	195	66	75	13	9	13	10	0	4.37
Night	21	128.1	127	33	55	9	4	5	11	0	4.49		69	420.0	463	110	173	27	10	27	31	0	4.46
On Grass and on Turf																							
Grass	30	181.1	193	49	85	15	4	10	14	0	4.42		85	523.1	548	150	214	33	13	37	33	0	4.11
Turf	4	21.2	23	8	10	1	1	1	1	0	5.40		14	80.0	110	26	34	7	6	3	8	0	6.53
By Month																							
April	4	25.0	24	1	12	1	0	2	2	0	4.32		14	85.2	91	26	36	4	5	6	7	0	4.41
May	5	32.1	40	9	16	0	1	2	1	0	4.73		16	101.2	97	30	34	3	2	7	3	0	4.51
June	7	49.1	43	18	22	6	1	2	4	0	3.83		19	128.0	132	39	51	12	2	8	9	0	3.52
July	6	22.1	31	8	8	2	0	1	3	0	7.66		19	107.1	127	27	41	6	4	7	8	0	5.28
August	5	25.0	26	12	13	0	1	1	1	0	4.32		17	83.0	110	32	40	6	4	5	8	0	5.42
Sept/Oct	7	49.0	52	9	24	7	2	3	4	0	3.86		14	97.2	101	22	46	9	2	7	6	0	3.78

vs. Opponent Batters																					
	1986 SEASON											THREE YEARS (84 – 86)									
	Ave.	OBP	SLG	AB	H	2B	3B	HR	RBI	BB	SO	Ave.	OBP	SLG	AB	H	2B	3B	HR	RBI	BB	SO
Totals	.270	.319	.457	799	216	34	5	35	95	57	95	.278	.327	.442	2371	658	102	14	87	280	176	248
Pitching vs. Left and Right-handed Batters																						
Left	.223	.260	.452	166	37	8	0	10	20	8	26	.243	.282	.454	502	122	21	2	27	68	23	61
Right	.283	.334	.458	633	179	26	5	25	75	49	69	.287	.339	.439	1869	536	81	12	60	212	153	187
Situational																						
Bases Empty	.274	.325	.466	489	134	22	3	22	22	37	57	.277	.324	.437	1426	395	60	6	52	52	95	142
Leadoff	.298	.336	.512	205	61	7	2	11	11	12	20	.278	.315	.438	608	169	23	4	22	22	33	56
Not Leadoff	.257	.317	.433	284	73	15	1	11	11	25	37	.276	.330	.436	818	226	37	2	30	30	62	86
Runners On	.265	.310	.442	310	82	12	2	13	73	20	38	.278	.332	.451	945	263	42	8	35	228	81	106
First Base Only	.274	.316	.459	146	40	6	0	7	16	6	19	.287	.333	.476	471	135	23	3	20	55	30	55
Scoring Position	.256	.304	.427	164	42	6	2	6	57	14	19	.270	.332	.426	474	128	19	5	15	173	51	51
Late Innings, Close	.348	.386	.576	66	23	6	0	3	8	4	7	.289	.338	.408	218	63	12	1	4	18	16	22

RBI/Opportunities						
Scoring Position	48 / 200	(24%)		146 / 615	(24%)	
Scoring Position, 2 Out	19 / 96	(20%)		50 / 267	(19%)	
On Third, Less than 2 Out	14 / 32	(44%)		52 / 100	(52%)	
RBI in close games / RBI Total	71 / 95	(75%)		211 / 280	(75%)	

Kevin McReynolds
San Diego Padres

There are a number of misconceptions in New York about McReynolds and the Mets. He's been described as a "Strawberry-type" player: they've both shown a tendency to sulk, that's true. But Strawberry has hit 40% more homers in only 20 more games, walked 30% more and stolen six times as many bases. The result is a career secondary average of .450 for Strawberry, .271 for McReynolds.

Another interesting comment about the McReynolds deal is the praise for the Mets not standing pat after winning a World Series. The common wisdom is that Series-winning organizations freeze up and are scared to change. The Mets have shed Ray Knight. Second, they added McReynolds as a regular left fielder without losing Mookie Wilson, who will still see plenty of time in center. That's a total of two changes in the lineup. Have the Mets done something unusual?

Not really. While Knight and McReynolds are probably the two players with the biggest numbers to change places for a Series winner recently, the ten Series winners previous to the Mets all made at least one, sometimes two, changes in the off-season. The last team that made no changes in its everyday eight was the 1975–76 Reds. Cincinnati unloaded Tony Perez before the '77 season and didn't repeat. The '77 Yankees, '79 Pirates, '82 Cardinals and '83

Orioles all made two changes, just like the Mets.

The Mets, however, are keeping their pitching staff together. Their predecessors either couldn't, didn't or got poor performances the second year. Pitching changes, and possible injuries, will make more difference to the Mets chances than the McReynolds trade.

—Chris Smith

McReynolds will probably not hit as well at Shea as he will on the road. His record on road grass over the past three years is unimpressive (.239 BA, .298 OBA, .413 SA in 414 at-bats). Last year, he only hit .224 with a .373 SA on road grass. Unless he continues to be a terror in his home park, his production is going to fall off drastically. On the other hand, he will help protect Dykstra, Backman, and Strawberry against left-handed pitching, which he tears apart, and he will help the Mets in their division because of the way he hits on turf.

It is interesting how similar the slugging and on-base averages of Strawberry and McReynolds were. Both had an OBA of .358, with slugging averages of .507 and .504, respectively. He improved his strike-zone judgment dramatically last year (one walk per 9.8 plate appearances compared to one per 15.1 PA for the previous two years).

—Scott Daniel

	1986 SEASON											THREE YEARS (84 – 86)										
	Ave.	OBP	SLG	AB	H	2B	3B	HR	RBI	BB	SO	Ave.	OBP	SLG	AB	H	2B	3B	HR	RBI	BB	SO
Totals	.287	.358	.504	560	161	31	6	26	96	66	83	.266	.322	.446	1649	439	81	16	61	246	143	233
Batting vs. Left and Right-handed Pitchers																						
Left	.339	.395	.589	192	65	12	3	10	34	22	21	.291	.358	.492	526	153	26	7	22	87	59	60
Right	.261	.339	.459	368	96	19	3	16	62	44	62	.255	.305	.424	1123	286	55	9	39	159	84	173
At Home and on the Road																						
Home	.293	.368	.514	276	81	13	3	14	45	35	46	.276	.334	.458	804	222	36	10	30	116	75	127
Road	.282	.349	.493	284	80	18	3	12	51	31	37	.257	.311	.434	845	217	45	6	31	130	68	106
Facing Groundball Pitchers and Flyball Pitchers																						
Groundball	.312	.393	.563	295	92	15	4	17	56	41	32	.284	.340	.489	859	244	39	7	41	146	76	98
Flyball	.260	.319	.438	265	69	16	2	9	40	25	51	.247	.303	.399	790	195	42	9	20	100	67	135
Facing Finesse Pitchers and Power Pitchers																						
Finesse	.321	.379	.522	312	100	18	3	13	48	32	37	.306	.350	.495	903	276	45	9	36	142	66	85
Power	.246	.333	.480	248	61	13	3	13	48	34	46	.218	.290	.386	746	163	36	7	25	104	77	148
On Grass and on Turf																						
Grass	.271	.344	.468	410	111	19	4	18	64	49	63	.264	.321	.443	1218	321	54	13	46	177	110	189
Turf	.333	.399	.600	150	50	12	2	8	32	17	20	.274	.325	.455	431	118	27	3	15	69	33	44
During the Day and at Night																						
Day	.281	.357	.514	185	52	11	1	10	32	24	29	.251	.309	.440	546	137	22	6	23	86	48	87
Night	.291	.359	.499	375	109	20	5	16	64	42	54	.274	.329	.449	1103	302	59	10	38	160	95	146
By Month																						
April	.250	.321	.395	76	19	2	0	3	8	8	11	.270	.325	.455	222	60	10	2	9	34	20	36
May	.330	.414	.628	94	31	8	1	6	21	15	16	.290	.344	.513	279	81	13	2	15	55	23	40
June	.242	.294	.434	99	24	6	2	3	13	8	16	.253	.302	.411	297	75	14	6	7	35	22	38
July	.272	.384	.407	81	22	5	0	2	7	16	11	.226	.306	.387	261	59	16	1	8	34	30	36
August	.307	.364	.557	88	27	4	0	6	22	9	9	.282	.328	.469	262	74	11	1	12	44	21	33
Sept/Oct	.311	.366	.557	122	38	6	3	6	25	10	20	.274	.329	.442	328	90	17	4	10	44	27	50
Situational																						
Bases Empty	.286	.358	.485	297	85	15	4	12	12	33	41	.248	.297	.433	913	226	39	11	36	36	63	128
Leadoff	.318	.359	.545	110	35	6	2	5	5	7	12	.262	.303	.466	367	96	14	8	15	15	22	43
Not Leadoff	.267	.357	.449	187	50	9	2	7	7	26	29	.238	.293	.410	546	130	25	3	21	21	41	85
Runners On	.289	.359	.525	263	76	16	2	14	84	33	42	.289	.352	.462	736	213	42	5	25	210	80	105
First Base Only	.314	.351	.590	105	33	7	2	6	17	6	11	.285	.324	.443	309	88	19	3	8	26	18	35
Scoring Position	.272	.364	.481	158	43	9	0	8	67	27	31	.293	.370	.475	427	125	23	2	17	184	62	70
Late Innings, Close	.252	.325	.423	111	28	4	0	5	22	13	32	.238	.287	.395	324	77	14	2	11	48	24	63

RBI/Opportunities			
Scoring Position	54 / 228	(24%)	153 / 608	(25%)
Scoring Position, 2 Out	20 / 82	(24%)	60 / 258	(23%)
On Third, Less than 2 Out	22 / 47	(47%)	62 / 112	(55%)
RBI in close games / RBI Total	67 / 96	(70%)	175 / 246	(71%)

Paul Molitor
Milwaukee Brewers

I can't talk about Paul Molitor's 1986 stats, because the stats aren't accurate. The guy walking around Milwaukee with the number 4 on his back isn't Paul Molitor—he's a golem, created by the Frankensteins who ran Milwaukee for the last nine years. Let's walk through Paul's career together—if you can make any sense out of it, I wish you'd write and tell me why.

In the spring of 1978, Robin Yount was pondering a career as a pro golfer and chose not to report to Milwaukee until May. Molitor (the third player chosen in the 1977 Free Agent Draft) was so impressive in spring training that, despite having played only 77 games of class A ball the year before, he won Yount's starting job. But Robin returned, so Molitor moved over to second for him. He played well for the next three years, but missed the last six weeks of 1980 with a rib injury. His replacement, Jim Gantner, so impressed the Brewers that they decided to move Molitor to centerfield in 1981. Unfortunately, the incumbent centerfielder (Gorman Thomas) didn't want to move. He kicked, screamed and held his breath until Milwaukee put him back in center and moved Molitor to right.

In 1982, Milwaukee had an excellent team, but they were missing a third baseman; you KNOW who was shifted there, don't you? Paul did well there—well enough to keep his job for two whole years. Even when he missed 149 games in 1984 (diving for a ball, of course), the job was waiting for him when he returned.

Molitor pulled a hamstring in '86, so Milwaukee called up Dale Sveum. Sveum was hitting .350 in 50 at-bats when Paul was ready again—guess which one was moved to left field. In Molitor's first night back, he reinjured the hamstring going all out for a drive in the gap; Sveum went 0 for the duration of his second stay on the DL and began making an error per game. When Paul returned, he went back to third.

Six times. Six times when somebody burst into tears or a rookie got a few infield hits, Paul Molitor lost his job. Didn't anyone think that he might get hurt by always playing out of position? Didn't anyone think that the Route 66 impression might affect his hitting? Molitor is one of the four best players that the Brewers have ever had, he could be turning in a near-Hall of Fame career at second and I think it's a damned shame that he didn't get to play for a team that would have let him do it.

—Scott Segrin

	1986 SEASON											THREE YEARS (84 – 86)										
	Ave.	OBP	SLG	AB	H	2B	3B	HR	RBI	BB	SO	Ave.	OBP	SLG	AB	H	2B	3B	HR	RBI	BB	SO
Totals	.281	.340	.426	437	123	24	6	9	55	40	81	.287	.345	.408	1059	304	53	9	19	109	96	169
Batting vs. Left and Right-handed Pitchers																						
Left	.270	.318	.400	100	27	6	2	1	8	7	23	.300	.355	.426	303	91	14	3	6	30	25	43
Right	.285	.346	.433	337	96	18	4	8	47	33	58	.282	.341	.401	756	213	39	6	13	79	71	126
At Home and on the Road																						
Home	.300	.345	.451	213	64	9	4	5	34	16	34	.310	.362	.452	491	152	25	6	11	66	42	68
Road	.263	.335	.402	224	59	15	2	4	21	24	47	.268	.330	.370	568	152	28	3	8	43	54	101
Facing Groundball Pitchers and Flyball Pitchers																						
Groundball	.299	.348	.444	187	56	14	2	3	22	14	28	.293	.347	.404	505	148	27	4	7	43	41	73
Flyball	.268	.333	.412	250	67	10	4	6	33	26	53	.282	.342	.412	554	156	26	5	12	66	55	96
Facing Finesse Pitchers and Power Pitchers																						
Finesse	.291	.335	.429	261	76	14	5	4	27	17	48	.294	.340	.420	612	180	29	6	12	55	43	88
Power	.267	.347	.420	176	47	10	1	5	28	23	33	.277	.350	.391	447	124	24	3	7	54	53	81
On Grass and on Turf																						
Grass	.295	.355	.451	390	115	22	6	9	55	38	69	.299	.357	.424	893	267	48	8	16	101	83	133
Turf	.170	.204	.213	47	8	2	0	0	0	2	12	.223	.278	.319	166	37	5	1	3	8	13	36
During the Day and at Night																						
Day	.209	.270	.309	139	29	6	1	2	16	12	34	.260	.323	.348	339	88	16	1	4	29	33	62
Night	.315	.372	.480	298	94	18	5	7	39	28	47	.300	.355	.436	720	216	37	8	15	80	63	107
By Month																						
April	.261	.378	.406	69	18	8	1	0	9	13	17	.280	.364	.368	182	51	11	1	1	21	25	37
May	.342	.422	.632	38	13	0	1	3	9	6	5	.288	.360	.447	132	38	5	2	4	17	16	16
June	.231	.231	.231	13	3	0	0	0	0	0	3	.333	.396	.542	120	40	8	1	5	15	13	21
July	.284	.321	.405	74	21	6	0	1	6	4	14	.273	.321	.361	194	53	11	0	2	13	13	21
August	.270	.326	.421	126	34	5	1	4	20	11	20	.269	.319	.386	171	46	6	1	4	24	13	32
Sept/Oct	.291	.323	.410	117	34	5	3	1	11	6	22	.292	.332	.404	260	76	12	4	3	19	16	42
Situational																						
Bases Empty	.266	.312	.411	282	75	15	4	6	6	19	56	.277	.325	.411	705	195	38	6	15	15	49	118
Leadoff	.272	.313	.438	169	46	7	3	5	5	10	38	.294	.340	.438	418	123	20	5	10	10	29	66
Not Leadoff	.257	.311	.372	113	29	8	1	1	1	9	18	.251	.302	.373	287	72	18	1	5	5	20	52
Runners On	.310	.385	.452	155	48	9	2	3	49	21	25	.308	.381	.401	354	109	15	3	4	94	47	51
First Base Only	.246	.324	.361	61	15	5	1	0	4	7	6	.288	.344	.374	139	40	7	1	1	8	12	12
Scoring Position	.351	.423	.511	94	33	4	1	3	45	14	19	.321	.403	.419	215	69	8	2	3	86	35	39
Late Innings, Close	.324	.342	.541	74	24	7	0	3	14	3	12	.333	.369	.503	171	57	12	1	5	23	12	26
RBI/Opportunities																						
Scoring Position				41 / 128	(32%)										79 / 302	(26%)						
Scoring Position, 2 Out				22 / 65	(34%)										40 / 151	(26%)						
On Third, Less than 2 Out				10 / 20	(50%)										23 / 47	(49%)						
RBI in close games / RBI Total				37 / 55	(67%)										63 / 109	(58%)						

Donnie Moore
California Angels

The next time somebody tells you that you can't win a championship without a strong bullpen, ask him about the American League in 1986. Both champions, the Angels and Red Sox, stumbled into the pennant race with malfunctioning bullpens, and got them straightened out just in time for the race.

The Angels acquired Donnie Moore, I am told, because they liked his work habits. Besides his work habits, there were other things to like about him—his strikeout to walk ratios, his 2.94 ERA in the Launching Pad in 1984. Moore is now 33 years old and has a chronic injury, so he fits right in with the Angels. When healthy, he has fair stuff and knows how to use it.

An interesting thing about Moore is that, although a right-handed pitcher, he is much, much more effective against left-handers than he is against his own kind. In 1986 he gave up two homers in 146 at bats against left-handers, but 8 in 117 at bats against right-handers—a home run rate five times as great. Over the three-year period right-handers have hit .266 with 18 homers in 418 at bats against him, but left-handers have been held to .218 with four homers in 472 at bats—the same ratio of right-handers homering five times as often against him. Of course, the big blow of the playoff, Dave Henderson's home run, was hit by a right-hander as well. It would be interesting to study the box scores and see how many times managers have pinch-hit left-handers against him. I'd bet that there are some managers in the league who do it all the time.

Like most successful pitchers, Moore almost never walks a leadoff man—twelve times in three years. Only fourteen per cent of the runners on second or third base with two out against him have been able to score, an excellent figure.

Like all of the Angel pitchers, Moore is tough to run against. In a three-year period, he has pitched 32 times in the month of July—a great hitter's month—and has a 1.09 ERA to show for it. It was in July of 1986 that he got straightened out.

—Bill James

1986: Power, Flyball		1985: Finesse, Flyball	1984: Power, Flyball

	1986 SEASON											THREE YEARS (84 – 86)											
	G	IP	H	BB	SO	SB	CS	W	L	S	ERA	G	IP	H	BB	SO	SB	CS	W	L	S	ERA
Totals	49	72.2	60	22	53	3	2	4	5	21	2.97	161	240.0	214	61	172	8	4	16	18	68	2.51
At Home and on the Road																						
Home	21	31.1	22	5	21	1	2	4	0	8	2.30	86	123.2	103	30	80	3	3	13	6	36	2.11
Road	28	41.1	38	17	32	2	0	0	5	13	3.48	75	116.1	111	31	92	5	1	3	12	32	2.94
During the Day and at Night																						
Day	18	25.0	20	11	20	0	1	3	2	8	2.88	57	83.2	75	28	61	2	1	5	5	25	2.80
Night	31	47.2	40	11	33	3	1	1	3	13	3.02	104	156.1	139	33	111	6	3	11	13	43	2.36
On Grass and on Turf																						
Grass	40	60.1	49	17	45	3	2	4	3	16	2.83	138	207.0	181	51	146	8	4	15	14	56	2.43
Turf	9	12.1	11	5	8	0	0	0	2	5	3.65	23	33.0	33	10	26	0	0	1	4	12	3.00
By Month																						
April	9	11.2	7	3	12	0	0	1	1	5	4.63	23	32.2	30	9	22	0	0	2	2	9	3.31
May	5	7.1	9	6	3	0	1	0	2	2	6.14	17	29.2	25	10	19	0	1	2	2	11	1.82
June	1	1.0	0	1	1	0	0	0	0	0	0.00	24	36.0	26	10	27	2	0	1	2	9	2.50
July	9	14.0	11	5	9	2	0	0	0	5	1.29	32	41.1	36	10	30	2	2	4	3	15	1.09
August	13	19.2	15	5	17	1	0	2	2	6	2.29	33	44.2	45	15	37	1	0	4	6	13	3.22
Sept/Oct	12	19.0	18	2	11	0	1	1	0	3	2.84	32	55.2	52	7	37	3	1	3	3	11	2.91

	vs. Opponent Batters																				

	1986 SEASON											THREE YEARS (84 – 86)									
	Ave.	OBP	SLG	AB	H	2B	3B	HR	RBI	BB	SO	Ave.	OBP	SLG	AB	H	2B	3B	HR	RBI	BB	SO
Totals	.228	.285	.373	263	60	6	1	10	36	22	53	.240	.288	.346	890	214	22	3	22	104	61	171
Pitching vs. Left and Right-handed Batters																						
Left	.212	.275	.295	146	31	4	1	2	14	13	25	.218	.275	.286	472	103	14	3	4	44	37	88
Right	.248	.297	.470	117	29	2	0	8	22	9	28	.266	.303	.414	418	111	8	0	18	60	24	83
Situational																						
Bases Empty	.194	.252	.299	144	28	3	0	4	4	11	33	.241	.283	.338	473	114	13	0	11	11	27	88
Leadoff	.264	.316	.340	53	14	1	0	1	1	4	13	.240	.291	.328	183	44	4	0	4	4	12	40
Not Leadoff	.154	.214	.275	91	14	2	0	3	3	7	20	.241	.279	.345	290	70	9	0	7	7	15	48
Runners On	.269	.323	.462	119	32	3	1	6	32	11	20	.240	.293	.355	417	100	9	3	11	93	34	83
First Base Only	.300	.314	.480	50	15	0	0	3	6	1	7	.239	.267	.300	180	43	2	0	3	8	7	34
Scoring Position	.246	.329	.449	69	17	3	1	3	26	10	13	.241	.310	.397	237	57	7	3	8	85	27	49
Late Innings, Close	.219	.288	.372	183	40	4	0	8	30	19	40	.233	.280	.350	618	144	14	2	18	83	43	125

	RBI/Opportunities					
Scoring Position	20 / 102	(20%)		68 / 344	(20%)
Scoring Position, 2 Out	6 / 34	(18%)		20 / 144	(14%)
On Third, Less than 2 Out	8 / 19	(42%)		32 / 65	(49%)
RBI in close games / RBI Total	30 / 36	(83%)		85 / 104	(82%)

Mike Moore
Seattle Mariners

Mike Moore, Bret Saberhagen and Dave Steib have a lot in common. All three are extremely talented and all three had bad years following good years. In 1985, Moore became the ace of the Seattle pitching staff. A very respectable 17 wins in a very respectable 247 innings, completing a very respectable 14 games. So respectable in fact, that maybe too much was expected from Mike Moore in 1986.

1986 was not so respectable. Moore, early on, was plagued with first inning runs. As the opening night pitcher, the first pitch found its way into the Kingdome stands. So did the tenth pitch. As it turned out, opening night would be an indication of how Mike's season would go. First inning runs, coupled with the apparent inability to hold a lead, would eventually haunt Moore for nearly the entire season. As if Mike wasn't haunted enough by his pitching problems, the Seattle press took it upon themselves to badger the mild mannered pitcher to the point that he finally quit talking. The Mariners had their very own Steve Carlton.

It wasn't so much the silly questions, but the insinuations that the future of the Mariners was in the hands of Mike Moore. By the All Star break, one reporter indicated that only Mike Moore could "lead" the Mariners into contention in the second half. A big responsibility for someone that only plays every five days. Finally Dick Williams interceded stating that maybe everyone was expecting too much from Moore. The insistent badgering eventually subsided.

Before the All Star break, Mike allowed 18 first inning runs, after the break, he allowed 3 first inning runs. Before the break he was 5–9, after the break he was 6–4. Before the break, he was hounded by the press, after the break he wasn't.

Opponents have had a higher batting average against Moore with men on base than with the bases empty in each of his five seasons. The four late inning pressure homeruns he allowed in 1986 were the first of his career in such situations.

Moore's left/right breakdown over the last three seasons reveals something very interesting. Lefties have hit only .004 higher than righties, yet they have a .027 higher on base percentage. For some inexplicable reason Moore has walked almost twice as many lefties as righties.

—Merrianna McCully and Dennis Orr

1986: Finesse, Groundball   **1985: Finesse, Groundball**   **1984: Power, Groundball**

	1986 SEASON											THREE YEARS (84 – 86)										
	G	IP	H	BB	SO	SB	CS	W	L	S	ERA	G	IP	H	BB	SO	SB	CS	W	L	S	ERA
Totals	38	266.0	279	94	146	11	14	11	13	1	4.30	107	725.0	745	249	459	38	29	35	40	1	4.21
At Home and on the Road																						
Home	19	127.0	135	47	75	5	5	7	4	1	4.18	55	380.2	400	139	256	19	13	21	17	1	3.95
Road	19	139.0	144	47	71	6	9	4	9	0	4.40	52	344.1	345	110	203	19	16	14	23	0	4.50
During the Day and at Night																						
Day	10	69.2	82	15	38	3	3	3	6	0	5.17	33	227.1	232	63	153	9	6	11	15	0	3.84
Night	28	196.1	197	79	108	8	11	8	7	1	3.99	74	497.2	513	186	306	29	23	24	25	1	4.38
On Grass and on Turf																						
Grass	14	104.1	110	37	57	4	8	3	6	0	4.31	38	248.0	251	80	154	12	14	10	16	0	4.46
Turf	24	161.2	169	57	89	7	6	8	7	1	4.29	69	477.0	494	169	305	26	15	25	24	1	4.08
By Month																						
April	5	42.0	38	15	23	1	4	1	2	0	2.36	16	111.0	116	47	66	6	6	4	5	0	3.81
May	6	38.0	45	19	16	4	1	1	4	0	6.87	15	95.1	88	38	65	7	2	4	8	0	4.25
June	6	44.2	49	10	27	1	2	2	1	0	5.04	16	97.1	107	35	55	4	4	5	3	0	5.09
July	6	43.1	50	12	22	0	3	2	3	0	4.98	19	130.2	138	33	68	1	7	7	9	0	4.34
August	8	48.1	45	18	28	4	2	3	1	1	2.98	20	137.2	134	46	93	9	5	6	7	1	3.66
Sept/Oct	7	49.2	52	20	30	1	2	2	2	0	3.99	21	153.0	162	50	112	11	5	9	8	0	4.29

	vs. Opponent Batters																				
	1986 SEASON										THREE YEARS (84 – 86)									
	Ave.	OBP	SLG	AB	H	2B	3B	HR	RBI	BB	SO	Ave.	OBP	SLG	AB	H	2B	3B	HR	RBI	BB	SO
Totals	.273	.339	.408	1023	279	42	6	28	121	94	146	.267	.329	.393	2792	745	131	18	62	313	249	459
Pitching vs. Left and Right-handed Batters																						
Left	.282	.362	.405	529	149	26	3	11	57	65	58	.267	.340	.384	1520	406	67	12	29	157	167	217
Right	.263	.314	.411	494	130	16	3	17	64	29	88	.267	.316	.404	1272	339	64	6	33	156	82	242
Situational																						
Bases Empty	.271	.335	.394	597	162	24	5	13	13	52	93	.252	.318	.372	1646	415	78	12	32	32	147	289
Leadoff	.297	.362	.434	256	76	10	2	7	7	23	24	.255	.312	.382	706	180	30	6	16	16	54	111
Not Leadoff	.252	.315	.364	341	86	14	3	6	6	29	69	.250	.322	.365	940	235	48	6	16	16	93	178
Runners On	.275	.345	.427	426	117	18	1	15	108	42	53	.288	.346	.423	1146	330	53	6	30	281	102	170
First Base Only	.332	.392	.553	190	63	12	0	10	20	16	19	.316	.357	.483	516	163	24	4	18	43	28	74
Scoring Position	.229	.309	.326	236	54	6	1	5	88	26	34	.265	.338	.375	630	167	29	2	12	238	74	96
Late Innings, Close	.354	.447	.531	113	40	8	0	4	21	16	15	.279	.349	.391	297	83	15	3	4	33	29	47

RBI/Opportunities					
Scoring Position	79 / 339	(23%)		214 / 871	(25%)
Scoring Position, 2 Out	30 / 149	(20%)		85 / 386	(22%)
On Third, Less than 2 Out	34 / 69	(49%)		90 / 177	(51%)
RBI in close games / RBI Total	96 / 121	(79%)		229 / 313	(73%)

Keith Moreland
Chicago Cubs

One of the better types of stories is the one about a self-made ballplayer. Brian Downing was an ordinary catcher for the White Sox and Angels who suddenly became a power-hitting outfielder in 1982. Ozzie Smith was always a great shortstop, but over the past few years he has become a more accomplished hitter. Keith Moreland was always a good hitter, but when he first came to the Cubs in 1982 he was not a good catcher. Since the Cubs at the time did not have an outfield to speak of, Moreland ended up in right field.

At first, Moreland had a good deal of trouble in the outfield. He had some trouble judging fly balls, and since he lacked speed, when he was out of position a ball hit in the gap meant real trouble. Complicating matters was his lack of enthusiasm for playing for a losing ballclub. In time, he became a better outfielder and he even grew to like being a Cub. But more impressive is his growth as an all-around, versatile ballplayer. Case in point: no one ever accused Moreland of being fast, and his five career stolen bases through 1984 attest to his lack of speed, but in the past two years he has stolen 15 bases. Not bad for a player who in 1982–83 was compared to Ron Cey and Greg Luzinski. In the past few seasons, he has also played a few games at both first and third base—in part because of injuries or batting slumps to the regulars at those positions.

It wasn't that long ago when Moreland's best position was nowhere. His fielding at first and third base was forgettable (and, thankfully, temporary), but at least he could play there. Besides, the Cubs are used to having immobile third basemen. Ex-manager Jim Frey even considered moving Moreland to third semi-permanently before the 1986 season began.

Another case in point: in 1982, Moreland got off to a great start in April and May at the plate, only to slip to .261. Since then he has hit between .271 and .307 every year, and the .271 was in 1986, obviously an "off year." He has hit .300 twice. And, for a player who only hits about 14 home runs per season, he has done an effective job as the Cubs' cleanup hitter. He is also, if you listen to Cub broadcaster Harry Caray long enough, an outstanding two-out hitter. Not a bad story at all, the development of Keith Moreland.

—Andrew Berman

	1986 SEASON											THREE YEARS (84 – 86)										
	Ave.	OBP	SLG	AB	H	2B	3B	HR	RBI	BB	SO	Ave.	OBP	SLG	AB	H	2B	3B	HR	RBI	BB	SO
Totals	.271	.326	.384	586	159	30	0	12	79	53	48	.286	.343	.415	1668	477	77	6	42	265	155	177
Batting vs. Left and Right-handed Pitchers																						
Left	.311	.399	.459	148	46	7	0	5	17	23	7	.307	.390	.473	433	133	21	3	15	60	62	40
Right	.258	.300	.358	438	113	23	0	7	62	30	41	.279	.326	.394	1235	344	56	3	27	205	93	137
At Home and on the Road																						
Home	.293	.339	.438	297	87	19	0	8	45	22	24	.301	.360	.473	841	253	43	3	32	158	79	85
Road	.249	.314	.329	289	72	11	0	4	34	31	24	.271	.327	.356	827	224	34	3	10	107	76	92
Facing Groundball Pitchers and Flyball Pitchers																						
Groundball	.234	.308	.288	278	65	12	0	1	26	31	22	.286	.348	.395	774	221	29	4	16	120	78	72
Flyball	.305	.343	.471	308	94	18	0	11	53	22	26	.286	.339	.432	894	256	48	2	26	145	77	105
Facing Finesse Pitchers and Power Pitchers																						
Finesse	.276	.321	.373	359	99	17	0	6	50	26	23	.297	.344	.415	956	284	41	3	22	155	73	90
Power	.264	.335	.401	227	60	13	0	6	29	27	25	.271	.342	.414	712	193	36	3	20	110	82	87
On Grass and on Turf																						
Grass	.288	.344	.417	417	120	24	0	10	58	38	38	.294	.356	.441	1181	347	55	4	37	195	118	136
Turf	.231	.283	.302	169	39	6	0	2	21	15	10	.267	.312	.351	487	130	22	2	5	70	37	41
During the Day and at Night																						
Day	.288	.345	.432	396	114	24	0	11	62	37	32	.294	.353	.452	1122	330	58	4	37	200	104	112
Night	.237	.288	.284	190	45	6	0	1	17	16	16	.269	.324	.339	546	147	19	2	5	65	51	65
By Month																						
April	.320	.376	.400	75	24	3	0	1	10	8	6	.280	.338	.371	186	52	8	0	3	27	19	20
May	.250	.324	.390	100	25	2	0	4	12	11	9	.282	.365	.392	227	64	7	0	6	33	31	20
June	.272	.316	.398	103	28	7	0	2	16	9	9	.287	.353	.453	300	86	16	2	10	49	33	35
July	.322	.398	.400	90	29	7	0	0	16	12	7	.273	.330	.395	286	78	15	1	6	45	27	41
August	.211	.248	.284	109	23	5	0	1	10	6	10	.303	.340	.435	333	101	18	1	8	54	18	33
Sept/Oct	.275	.316	.440	109	30	6	0	4	15	7	7	.286	.337	.417	336	96	13	2	9	57	27	28
Situational																						
Bases Empty	.294	.351	.406	320	94	15	0	7	7	28	23	.285	.342	.412	860	245	38	1	23	23	73	92
Leadoff	.302	.351	.420	162	49	10	0	3	3	12	10	.296	.346	.441	406	120	20	0	13	13	30	36
Not Leadoff	.285	.351	.392	158	45	5	0	4	4	16	13	.275	.339	.385	454	125	18	1	10	10	43	56
Runners On	.244	.298	.357	266	65	15	0	5	72	25	25	.287	.345	.418	808	232	39	5	19	242	82	85
First Base Only	.236	.264	.340	106	25	5	0	2	7	4	8	.275	.326	.399	291	80	11	2	7	22	22	30
Scoring Position	.250	.318	.369	160	40	10	0	3	65	21	17	.294	.354	.429	517	152	28	3	12	220	60	55
Late Innings, Close	.311	.380	.509	106	33	6	0	5	19	13	5	.303	.373	.458	284	86	17	0	9	57	34	31
RBI/Opportunities																						

	1986 SEASON		THREE YEARS (84 – 86)	
Scoring Position	59 / 218	(27%)	194 / 702	(28%)
Scoring Position, 2 Out	24 / 114	(21%)	77 / 347	(22%)
On Third, Less than 2 Out	25 / 43	(58%)	73 / 127	(57%)
RBI in close games / RBI Total	60 / 79	(76%)	197 / 265	(74%)

Mike Morgan
Seattle Mariners

Mike Morgan is very different than any other pitcher. He ices his leg, as well as his arm, after every game. During Morgan's second start in 1985, he leaped high in the air after a line drive. He missed the ball and ended his season abruptly as his teammates carried him off the field. He tore a groin muscle so bad that it nearly required surgery. The next day, Morgan was black and blue from his calf to his chest as the severity of his injury finally was realized. The next six months were filled with agonizing rehabilitation as he continued to re-injure himself.

Mike's career has been less than sparkling. Morgan was one of the few high school players that went directly to the majors. He was picked by Charlie Finley to be a star, but it didn't happen. Pushed too hard too fast, he wound up playing for New York and Toronto before finding himself in the Mariner system.

During winter ball, Mike made up his mind that it was time. Time to get back in the rotation and earn that spot that would be his for as long as he kept producing. A good attitude and an immense amount of determination paid off.

The Mariner pitching coach set a goal of ten wins. Not what you would deem aggressive, but realistic considering Morgan's past. 1982 was his last season in the majors of any significance, and his record for the Yankees was a dismal 7-11 in 150 innings.

Mike exceeded his goal by one game, and before the season was half over with, had worked himself into the number three spot behind Moore and Langston. This threesome proved to be real workhorses as they were one of only two teams in baseball whose starting three pitchers pitched over 50% of the innings for their clubs.

Mike started 33 games, completing 9 of them, four more than in his entire major league career. Two of his CG were pitched without walks. On September 16, he threw his first shutout. I considered that game one of the best pitching performances by a Mariner in 1986. Mike had some brilliant outings as well as some disasters (17 losses, 4.53 ERA), but he has proven that he can pitch in the big leagues, and you can bet your socks that Dick Williams' win goal for him will be much more aggressive than ten.

—Merrianna McCully

1986: Finesse, Groundball **1985: Power, Groundball** **1984: Did not play**

	1986 SEASON											THREE YEARS (84 – 86)										
	G	IP	H	BB	SO	SB	CS	W	L	S	ERA	G	IP	H	BB	SO	SB	CS	W	L	S	ERA
Totals	37	216.1	243	86	116	17	10	11	17	1	4.53	39	222.1	254	91	118	17	10	12	18	1	4.74
At Home and on the Road																						
Home	18	100.1	116	42	64	12	4	4	10	0	5.11	19	105.1	125	46	66	12	4	5	10	0	5.38
Road	19	116.0	127	44	52	5	6	7	7	1	4.03	20	117.0	129	45	52	5	6	7	8	1	4.15
During the Day and at Night																						
Day	9	51.2	55	28	33	3	1	3	6	0	4.70	9	51.2	55	28	33	3	1	3	6	0	4.70
Night	28	164.2	188	58	83	14	9	8	11	1	4.48	30	170.2	199	63	85	14	9	9	12	1	4.75
On Grass and on Turf																						
Grass	13	77.1	79	27	40	2	3	3	6	1	3.96	14	78.1	81	28	40	2	3	3	7	1	4.14
Turf	24	139.0	164	59	76	15	7	8	11	0	4.86	25	144.0	173	63	78	15	7	9	11	0	5.06
By Month																						
April	6	27.0	21	13	10	1	1	1	2	1	2.00	8	33.0	32	18	12	1	1	2	3	1	3.82
May	6	29.2	42	20	20	1	1	2	4	0	6.67	6	29.2	42	20	20	1	1	2	4	0	6.67
June	6	36.0	42	10	19	4	4	2	1	0	3.50	6	36.0	42	10	19	4	4	2	1	0	3.50
July	6	36.2	50	14	10	4	1	3	3	0	5.65	6	36.2	50	14	10	4	1	3	3	0	5.65
August	6	41.2	40	15	32	4	2	1	4	0	4.32	6	41.2	40	15	32	4	2	1	4	0	4.32
Sept/Oct	7	45.1	48	14	25	3	1	2	3	0	4.76	7	45.1	48	14	25	3	1	2	3	0	4.76

vs. Opponent Batters

	1986 SEASON											THREE YEARS (84 – 86)									
	Ave.	OBP	SLG	AB	H	2B	3B	HR	RBI	BB	SO	Ave.	OBP	SLG	AB	H	2B	3B	HR	RBI	BB	SO
Totals	.286	.353	.427	851	243	44	2	24	95	86	116	.289	.357	.432	879	254	44	2	26	101	91	118
Pitching vs. Left and Right-handed Batters																						
Left	.274	.347	.390	441	121	19	1	10	48	48	56	.281	.354	.399	459	129	19	1	11	52	51	57
Right	.298	.359	.466	410	122	25	1	14	47	38	60	.298	.361	.469	420	125	25	1	15	49	40	61
Situational																						
Bases Empty	.300	.369	.474	464	139	28	1	17	17	47	62	.299	.369	.474	481	144	28	1	18	18	49	64
Leadoff	.267	.354	.441	202	54	6	1	9	9	26	28	.260	.347	.428	208	54	6	1	9	9	27	30
Not Leadoff	.324	.381	.500	262	85	22	0	8	8	21	34	.330	.386	.509	273	90	22	0	9	9	22	34
Runners On	.269	.333	.370	387	104	16	1	7	78	39	54	.276	.343	.382	398	110	16	1	8	83	42	54
First Base Only	.282	.341	.400	170	48	6	1	4	13	15	18	.291	.354	.406	175	51	6	1	4	13	17	18
Scoring Position	.258	.328	.346	217	56	10	0	3	65	24	36	.265	.335	.363	223	59	10	0	4	70	25	36
Late Innings, Close	.434	.483	.528	53	23	2	0	1	6	5	7	.434	.483	.528	53	23	2	0	1	6	5	7

RBI/Opportunities

Scoring Position	60 / 280	(21%)	63 / 288	(22%)
Scoring Position, 2 Out	24 / 137	(18%)	27 / 144	(19%)
On Third, Less than 2 Out	19 / 34	(56%)	19 / 34	(56%)
RBI in close games / RBI Total	66 / 95	(69%)	66 / 101	(65%)

Jack Morris
Detroit Tigers

At the start of the 1986 season, Jack Morris was in trouble. In the season opener versus Boston, he allowed a home run on his first pitch of the year, and watched three more pitches sail out of the park that day. In the month of April, he checked in with a 5.60 ERA, allowing 50 runners in only 35 innings. By the end of May, Morris had a 4–4 record and a 4.39 ERA; June brought 3 wins and only 1 loss, but the ERA of 4.34 was not vintage Morris.

The combination of Morris's poor performance and Dan Petry's ineffectiveness had the Tigers' management and fans wondering what had happened. The two aces of the Tigers' staff had combined for 189 wins from 1980 to 1985, and everyone was worried about the future.

Well, the future is here, and the news is both good and bad. The bad news is that Dan Petry required elbow surgery and was out for much of the year, finishing with a 5–10 record and a 4.66 ERA. While there was some indication that Dan might recover fully, the prognosis is far from certain. The good news is that nothing was wrong with Jack Morris—at least, nothing that Jack himself couldn't fix.

Jack Morris has been a classic streak pitcher for the last few years; the only difference between 1986 and previous years was that the bad streak that he normally has to endure came right at the start of the season. For example, in June 1985, Jack had a 5.31 ERA, and enemy batters hit .270 and slugged .472 against him. That slugging average was a full 137 points greater than he allowed in any other month that year. In 1984, Jack went 10–1 in April and May with a sub-2.00 ERA; he also went 3–6 in June and July with an ERA well over 5.00. Whatever happens during these cold streaks, Morris survives and ends up the year with quite good numbers overall.

So, Jack did some adjusting and went on a tear. In July, he was 5–1 with an incredible 0.54 ERA, allowing only 41 runners in 50 innings. True to form, in August he got shelled, then finished the season 6–0, allowing only 61 runners in 63.2 innings.

Jack Morris is an excellent pitcher. If he could truncate or moderate these cold streaks a little bit, he could be a superstar pitcher in the mold of a Tom Seaver. Still, any other major-league team would greatly benefit from Jack's performance as it is now. Collusion, anyone?

—Gary Gillette

1986: Power, Flyball   **1985: Power, Flyball**   **1984: Power, Groundball**

	G	IP	H	BB	SO	SB	CS	W	L	S	ERA	G	IP	H	BB	SO	SB	CS	W	L	S	ERA
	1986 SEASON											**THREE YEARS (84 – 86)**										
Totals	35	267.0	229	82	223	21	8	21	8	0	3.27	105	764.1	662	279	562	59	24	56	30	0	3.39
At Home and on the Road																						
Home	15	111.0	91	32	88	8	4	10	3	0	2.76	51	356.2	322	132	241	28	14	26	15	0	3.68
Road	20	156.0	138	50	135	13	4	11	5	0	3.63	54	407.2	340	147	321	31	10	30	15	0	3.13
During the Day and at Night																						
Day	11	91.2	82	25	77	5	1	8	2	0	3.24	32	241.0	202	82	167	15	6	18	8	0	3.44
Night	24	175.1	147	57	146	16	7	13	6	0	3.29	73	523.1	460	197	395	44	18	38	22	0	3.37
On Grass and on Turf																						
Grass	28	209.1	185	66	165	15	7	17	8	0	3.40	86	615.0	546	238	433	46	21	46	26	0	3.59
Turf	7	57.2	44	16	58	6	1	4	0	0	2.81	19	149.1	116	41	129	13	3	10	4	0	2.59
By Month																						
April	5	35.1	40	10	31	2	0	3	2	0	5.60	16	127.0	101	41	92	8	3	11	4	0	3.05
May	5	32.1	23	14	37	3	3	1	2	0	3.06	18	132.2	95	59	116	11	9	9	6	0	2.31
June	6	47.2	52	15	36	3	1	3	1	0	4.34	17	119.2	129	39	75	9	4	8	4	0	4.89
July	6	50.0	33	8	47	4	3	5	1	0	0.54	16	119.1	109	37	94	7	6	9	5	0	2.49
August	6	38.0	38	17	24	4	0	3	2	0	5.21	19	122.0	116	52	81	10	1	9	6	0	4.72
Sept/Oct	7	63.2	43	18	48	5	1	6	0	0	2.26	19	143.2	112	51	104	14	1	10	5	0	3.07

vs. Opponent Batters

	Ave.	OBP	SLG	AB	H	2B	3B	HR	RBI	BB	SO	Ave.	OBP	SLG	AB	H	2B	3B	HR	RBI	BB	SO
	1986 SEASON											**THREE YEARS (84 – 86)**										
Totals	.229	.287	.403	1000	229	38	8	40	95	82	223	.231	.300	.366	2862	662	101	21	81	278	279	562
Pitching vs. Left and Right-handed Batters																						
Left	.224	.283	.347	522	117	17	4	13	44	43	114	.230	.301	.355	1537	353	52	15	37	154	158	302
Right	.234	.291	.464	478	112	21	4	27	51	39	109	.233	.299	.379	1325	309	49	6	44	124	121	260
Situational																						
Bases Empty	.240	.298	.445	629	151	30	3	31	31	52	141	.230	.303	.380	1723	397	72	12	54	54	176	347
Leadoff	.241	.277	.456	261	63	9	1	15	15	13	47	.234	.288	.405	731	171	27	7	28	28	55	129
Not Leadoff	.239	.312	.438	368	88	21	2	16	16	39	94	.228	.314	.362	992	226	45	5	26	26	121	218
Runners On	.210	.267	.332	371	78	8	5	9	64	30	82	.233	.295	.345	1139	265	29	9	27	224	103	215
First Base Only	.226	.254	.360	186	42	3	2	6	15	7	30	.244	.284	.341	546	133	13	2	12	30	29	91
Scoring Position	.195	.280	.303	185	36	5	3	3	49	23	52	.223	.305	.349	593	132	16	7	15	194	74	124
Late Innings, Close	.248	.315	.444	133	33	5	0	7	14	13	26	.249	.318	.398	337	84	12	1	12	36	35	59

RBI/Opportunities

Scoring Position	43 / 236	(18%)	163 / 790	(21%)
Scoring Position, 2 Out	16 / 119	(13%)	51 / 361	(14%)
On Third, Less than 2 Out	17 / 40	(42%)	71 / 142	(50%)
RBI in close games / RBI Total	72 / 95	(76%)	214 / 278	(77%)

Jim Morrison
Pittsburgh Pirates

I'm a slow-pitch softball player. Good field, sporadic hit. Nobody really expects much of me offensively and anything above that is gravy.

Then came October 24, 1979. I was living in Columbia, South Carolina at the time and playing for Columbia Exterminating—Murder, Inc.—at Pinehurst, a quasi-bandbox field with a short left field but a sixty-foot fence in the power alley. Top of the fifth, we're down 3–2 and our first five hitters take the pitcher downtown, which brings me to the plate. Mr. Ump says, "I've never seen anything like this," to which I reply, "Don't worry, there ain't no homer gonna happen here." (I had about two homers in 295 at bats at that point.) So, on a 2–0 pitch—with the right fielder screaming "Throw strikes!"—I drilled a line drive homer about five feet to the right of the elevated screen. I fairly danced around the bases.

So it must have been for Jim Morrison in 1986.

I've followed this guy for years, ever since he was hitting in the low-to-mid .300s at Oklahoma City in the Phillies' chain. He never really got an opportunity in Philadelphia and was traded to the White Sox, where he was a semi-starter until dealt again, to the Pirates, in the summer of '82. With Bill Madlock around until midway through the 1985 season, Morrison sort of snoozed on the Pirates' bench; he should have been used to that, given his experiences in Philadelphia and Chicago. Then, with the transfer of Madlock to the Dodgers, Morrison looked like a lock for the Pirates' third base job. No such luck!

Denio Gonzalez was designated to be the starter at third for 1986, but he struggled through spring training with a recuperative knee. The knee wasn't working, so it was to Hawaii with Gonzalez (tough assignment). The job is Morrison's. But, no, "Let's try Mike Brown (an outfielder) at third," says Jim Leyland. That experiment doesn't work, either, and—by default—Jim Morrison becomes the Pirate third baseman for 1986. At least for now.

Naturally Jim gets off to a horrific start. The fans are on him for that and because he had the audacity to make one disparaging remark—even though it was true and justly deserved—during the nightmarish 1985 season. Something about Pirate fans and how much they truly stink.

But Jim Morrison came back with a vengeance. And, like me, Jim had his day in the sun: it was the 1986 season.

—Bill Thomas

	1986 SEASON											THREE YEARS (84 – 86)										
	Ave.	OBP	SLG	AB	H	2B	3B	HR	RBI	BB	SO	Ave.	OBP	SLG	AB	H	2B	3B	HR	RBI	BB	SO
Totals	.274	.334	.482	537	147	35	4	23	88	47	88	.273	.320	.444	1085	296	60	6	38	155	75	184
Batting vs. Left and Right-handed Pitchers																						
Left	.266	.329	.438	192	51	13	1	6	26	20	24	.278	.325	.421	418	116	23	2	11	50	32	57
Right	.278	.337	.507	345	96	22	3	17	62	27	64	.270	.317	.459	667	180	37	4	27	105	43	127
At Home and on the Road																						
Home	.297	.374	.506	269	80	15	4	11	49	30	46	.284	.338	.458	546	155	30	4	19	75	42	86
Road	.250	.292	.459	268	67	20	0	12	39	17	42	.262	.302	.430	539	141	30	2	19	80	33	98
Facing Groundball Pitchers and Flyball Pitchers																						
Groundball	.272	.360	.439	228	62	13	2	7	30	29	46	.277	.336	.424	488	135	27	3	13	67	44	91
Flyball	.275	.313	.515	309	85	22	2	16	58	18	42	.270	.307	.461	597	161	33	3	25	88	31	93
Facing Finesse Pitchers and Power Pitchers																						
Finesse	.269	.319	.466	305	82	21	3	11	36	23	41	.270	.308	.437	623	168	33	4	21	77	36	91
Power	.280	.352	.504	232	65	14	1	12	52	24	47	.277	.335	.455	462	128	27	2	17	78	39	93
On Grass and on Turf																						
Grass	.296	.338	.528	142	42	9	0	8	21	9	25	.285	.322	.485	260	74	15	2	11	40	15	48
Turf	.266	.333	.466	395	105	26	4	15	67	38	63	.269	.319	.432	825	222	45	4	27	115	60	136
During the Day and at Night																						
Day	.321	.363	.554	168	54	13	1	8	29	9	24	.314	.353	.521	363	114	23	2	16	64	20	50
Night	.252	.321	.450	369	93	22	3	15	59	38	64	.252	.304	.406	722	182	37	4	22	91	55	134
By Month																						
April	.208	.269	.333	48	10	0	0	2	4	3	11	.244	.314	.333	78	19	1	0	2	4	7	19
May	.253	.352	.462	91	23	2	1	5	16	14	21	.251	.319	.383	167	42	3	2	5	20	17	38
June	.223	.282	.383	94	21	7	1	2	16	8	18	.214	.246	.363	182	39	11	2	4	27	9	35
July	.298	.362	.476	84	25	6	0	3	13	9	11	.295	.351	.475	183	54	12	0	7	30	16	22
August	.270	.311	.468	111	30	8	1	4	18	5	10	.255	.296	.427	192	49	13	1	6	26	9	23
Sept/Oct	.349	.392	.670	109	38	12	1	7	21	8	17	.329	.365	.555	283	93	20	1	14	48	17	47
Situational																						
Bases Empty	.259	.318	.469	286	74	22	1	12	12	25	48	.261	.310	.444	594	155	38	1	23	23	42	107
Leadoff	.301	.358	.551	136	41	11	1	7	7	12	17	.296	.336	.528	250	74	17	1	13	13	15	37
Not Leadoff	.220	.282	.393	150	33	11	0	5	5	13	31	.235	.291	.384	344	81	21	0	10	10	27	70
Runners On	.291	.351	.498	251	73	13	3	11	76	22	40	.287	.332	.444	491	141	22	5	15	132	33	77
First Base Only	.282	.319	.509	110	31	5	1	6	15	4	14	.287	.322	.449	216	62	10	2	7	21	9	28
Scoring Position	.298	.373	.489	141	42	8	2	5	61	18	26	.287	.340	.440	275	79	12	3	8	111	24	49
Late Innings, Close	.240	.313	.423	104	25	5	1	4	14	10	23	.244	.296	.406	217	53	8	3	7	28	15	44

RBI/Opportunities					
Scoring Position	51 / 195	(26%)		96 / 373	(26%)
Scoring Position, 2 Out	18 / 83	(22%)		39 / 168	(23%)
On Third, Less than 2 Out	22 / 46	(48%)		38 / 81	(47%)
RBI in close games / RBI Total	46 / 88	(52%)		94 / 155	(61%)

Lloyd Moseby
Toronto Blue Jays

Some statistics can be deceiving. Undoubtedly, Lloyd Moseby had a disappointing 1986 season. Since he hit .315 in 1983, his batting average has fallen every year—his .253 is his worst since age 22. Is Moseby's career declining? Not exactly. Can something be done about it? I'm glad you asked.

A centerfielder is one of the most vital spokes on the team wheel. I very strongly believe in the adage "you win pennants up the middle"; if you don't protect these key players by keeping them fresh, you risk watching your pennant hopes fly right out the window.

Moseby's 1986 is an example. He came out of the gate quickly, batting .302 in April and .319 in May. By May 30, he had played in 48 of Toronto's first 49 games—a hefty workload for a centerfielder with exceptional range. He played the first 14 games in June, but then succumbed to the flu on June 16 and was forced out of the lineup.

Lloyd returned to the lineup the next day, but struggled for a week against both the virus and opposing pitchers, going 5–25. He never missed a start in that time.

Moseby caught a second wind at the All-Star break and blazed through August hitting a lusty .309. But, by September, his back gave out (love that astroturf) and Lloyd staggered through the rest of the year, hitting .149. What could have been—what should have been—a promising season was ruined. But he did play in 152 games.

What did Jimy Williams do about this? Not much. None of the men on the bench were hitting when the season began; quality replacements were hard to find. When the pitching floundered in April, Toronto fell well behind Boston— so far back that they were forced to play their regulars as often as possible in order to try to catch up. It had to be done, but the players paid the price down the stretch. There's nothing wrong with Moseby that a day off wouldn't cure; Toronto should (literally and figuratively) give the kid a break.

Moseby's situational breakdowns vividly explain why he usually batted second or third—he is an exceptional hitter with men on first. When the first baseman moves over to hold the runner, Lloyd's ability to hit to all fields lets him guide the ball into the opened hole. Given his statistics when leading off innings, some readers may wonder why he led off in 1986. The answer is simple—a .329 on-base average isn't outstanding, but it is better than Garcia's .299.

—David Driscoll

| | 1986 SEASON | | | | | | | | | | | THREE YEARS (84 – 86) | | | | | | | | | |
	Ave.	OBP	SLG	AB	H	2B	3B	HR	RBI	BB	SO	Ave.	OBP	SLG	AB	H	2B	3B	HR	RBI	BB	SO
Totals	.253	.329	.418	589	149	24	5	21	86	64	122	.264	.348	.438	1765	466	82	27	57	248	218	335
Batting vs. Left and Right-handed Pitchers																						
Left	.229	.277	.378	188	43	6	2	6	25	10	37	.247	.315	.381	632	156	26	7	15	74	55	133
Right	.264	.352	.436	401	106	18	3	15	61	54	85	.274	.365	.470	1133	310	56	20	42	174	163	202
At Home and on the Road																						
Home	.248	.337	.410	290	72	14	0	11	43	38	67	.267	.356	.469	850	227	42	17	32	140	113	163
Road	.258	.320	.425	299	77	10	5	10	43	26	55	.261	.339	.409	915	239	40	10	25	108	105	172
Facing Groundball Pitchers and Flyball Pitchers																						
Groundball	.281	.362	.451	253	71	10	3	9	36	31	43	.270	.351	.451	821	222	33	14	29	117	101	139
Flyball	.232	.303	.393	336	78	14	2	12	50	33	79	.258	.344	.427	944	244	49	13	28	131	117	196
Facing Finesse Pitchers and Power Pitchers																						
Finesse	.291	.364	.493	337	98	15	4	15	54	38	58	.283	.361	.468	1014	287	49	17	35	132	119	152
Power	.202	.282	.317	252	51	9	1	6	32	26	64	.238	.330	.397	751	179	33	10	22	116	99	183
On Grass and on Turf																						
Grass	.261	.328	.419	222	58	9	4	6	31	21	43	.255	.342	.399	687	175	28	7	19	77	88	128
Turf	.248	.329	.417	367	91	15	1	15	55	43	79	.270	.351	.463	1078	291	54	20	38	171	130	207
During the Day and at Night																						
Day	.271	.349	.457	221	60	9	1	10	38	25	39	.274	.361	.450	627	172	23	9	23	86	79	111
Night	.242	.317	.394	368	89	15	4	11	48	39	83	.258	.340	.431	1138	294	59	18	34	162	139	224
By Month																						
April	.302	.341	.453	86	26	2	1	3	9	5	17	.281	.359	.471	242	68	10	3	10	35	30	42
May	.319	.417	.496	113	36	6	1	4	19	16	20	.282	.369	.472	309	87	18	7	9	41	38	54
June	.263	.370	.485	99	26	5	1	5	16	17	27	.268	.362	.455	321	86	16	7	10	42	48	67
July	.170	.239	.260	100	17	1	1	2	10	9	20	.228	.305	.364	294	67	12	5	6	39	30	60
August	.309	.389	.588	97	30	7	1	6	20	14	17	.286	.363	.466	311	89	14	3	12	49	38	52
Sept/Oct	.149	.186	.213	94	14	3	0	1	12	3	21	.240	.324	.399	288	69	12	2	10	42	34	60
Situational																						
Bases Empty	.229	.321	.381	354	81	12	3	12	12	44	82	.248	.336	.403	1031	256	43	13	30	30	126	204
Leadoff	.248	.329	.389	149	37	4	1	5	5	17	33	.255	.333	.414	372	95	13	5	12	12	42	73
Not Leadoff	.215	.315	.376	205	44	8	2	7	7	27	49	.244	.338	.396	659	161	30	8	18	18	84	131
Runners On	.289	.341	.472	235	68	12	2	9	74	20	40	.286	.363	.488	734	210	39	14	27	218	92	131
First Base Only	.337	.375	.582	98	33	7	1	5	13	6	13	.322	.374	.545	314	101	20	4	14	40	25	44
Scoring Position	.255	.319	.394	137	35	5	1	4	61	14	27	.260	.357	.445	420	109	19	10	13	178	67	87
Late Innings, Close	.237	.327	.392	97	23	3	0	4	14	11	23	.259	.349	.406	278	72	12	4	7	39	35	56

RBI/Opportunities

	1986			THREE YEARS
Scoring Position	53 / 192	(28%)	157 / 593	(26%)
Scoring Position, 2 Out	11 / 70	(16%)	37 / 214	(17%)
On Third, Less than 2 Out	26 / 39	(67%)	74 / 131	(56%)
RBI in close games / RBI Total	60 / 86	(70%)	157 / 248	(63%)

Jerry Mumphrey
Chicago Cubs

Jerry Mumphrey has now finished his 13th season in the majors. He has about 89 Approximate Value points and should get at least 100, which is a decent career. He reminds me of old-timer Ethan Allen, inventor of the Cadaco baseball game, a journeyman outfielder who temporarily filled a need in one city and then moved on to the next client. Like Allen, Mumphrey rarely gets 500 AB in a season; although Jerry is a switch hitter, he is essentially a platoon and role player. As can be seen, he hits much better lefthanded, and there are sizable differences in his performances under different conditions. Jerry has been in a World Series (1981 with the Yankees) and an All-Star Game (1984). Of the five teams for whom he has played he is a "lifetime member" (my description for one having 1500 AB for a team) only of the Cardinals.

As a young player, Mumphrey had a reputation as a speedster, stealing 52 bases for San Diego in 1980. He also played a respectable center field. Hence I was somewhat surprised when in a game witnessed by SABR members last summer a drive was hit to right center; catching it would have been difficult, but Jerry hardly made an effort. Perhaps the key factor is that his playing weight used to be 185, and he is now listed at 200. His statistics peg him as a slap hitter, but I thought he might show more power in Wrigley Field. He did show a little there, but his overall secondary average was only .188.

The conclusion from this is that Mumphrey is really over the hill; he can still hit for average but no longer has the tools to play regularly. The Cubs appear to have recognized this, for he played little in the latter part of the season. After August 1 he started only five games in center on the road, none in September, and he played even less in left or right. One wonders, then, why the Cubs acquired him—presumably to add bench strength for their pennant drive. Billy Hatcher was much more valuable to the Astros than Mumphrey was to the Cubs. With Mumphrey as a starter the last two months of the season the Cubs' record was only 4–12. Mumphrey's main value now is as a lefthanded bat off the bench, and he is quite likely to play for a few more teams before he is through.

—Bill McMahon

	1986 SEASON											THREE YEARS (84 – 86)										
	Ave.	OBP	SLG	AB	H	2B	3B	HR	RBI	BB	SO	Ave.	OBP	SLG	AB	H	2B	3B	HR	RBI	BB	SO
Totals	.304	.355	.401	309	94	11	2	5	32	26	45	.289	.346	.395	1277	369	56	7	22	176	119	181
Batting vs. Left and Right-handed Pitchers																						
Left	.197	.279	.213	61	12	1	0	0	2	7	9	.236	.309	.274	369	87	14	0	0	40	42	55
Right	.331	.374	.448	248	82	10	2	5	30	19	36	.311	.361	.445	908	282	42	7	22	136	77	126
At Home and on the Road																						
Home	.361	.417	.517	147	53	7	2	4	22	15	19	.317	.382	.433	605	192	31	6	9	88	65	83
Road	.253	.297	.296	162	41	4	0	1	10	11	26	.263	.313	.362	672	177	25	1	13	88	54	98
Facing Groundball Pitchers and Flyball Pitchers																						
Groundball	.302	.347	.405	116	35	3	0	3	12	8	18	.303	.354	.421	594	180	30	5	10	96	51	71
Flyball	.306	.360	.399	193	59	8	2	2	20	18	27	.277	.339	.373	683	189	26	2	12	80	68	110
Facing Finesse Pitchers and Power Pitchers																						
Finesse	.326	.363	.453	172	56	7	0	5	18	10	16	.299	.353	.424	696	208	28	4	17	94	61	71
Power	.277	.346	.336	137	38	4	2	0	14	16	29	.277	.337	.361	581	161	28	3	5	82	58	110
On Grass and on Turf																						
Grass	.328	.386	.447	235	77	9	2	5	25	23	36	.307	.358	.430	528	162	17	3	14	73	45	79
Turf	.230	.253	.257	74	17	2	0	0	7	3	9	.276	.337	.371	749	207	39	4	8	103	74	102
During the Day and at Night																						
Day	.317	.376	.432	199	63	7	2	4	26	20	28	.302	.365	.428	397	120	16	2	10	62	43	55
Night	.282	.316	.345	110	31	4	0	1	6	6	17	.283	.337	.381	880	249	40	5	12	114	76	126
By Month																						
April	.290	.303	.419	31	9	1	0	1	3	1	7	.283	.347	.367	180	51	6	3	1	23	18	24
May	.302	.403	.358	53	16	3	0	0	2	9	9	.276	.350	.378	225	62	9	1	4	29	28	23
June	.243	.338	.271	70	17	2	0	0	6	10	7	.273	.323	.366	216	59	8	0	4	29	17	34
July	.378	.418	.486	74	28	3	1	1	4	5	9	.318	.376	.417	242	77	11	2	3	28	25	40
August	.306	.313	.468	62	19	2	1	2	12	1	10	.288	.339	.424	257	74	15	1	6	41	21	42
Sept/Oct	.263	.250	.421	19	5	0	0	1	5	0	3	.293	.331	.414	157	46	7	0	4	26	10	18
Situational																						
Bases Empty	.326	.370	.430	172	56	10	1	2	2	12	21	.279	.323	.374	682	190	35	3	8	8	45	96
Leadoff	.373	.427	.467	75	28	4	0	1	1	7	8	.304	.343	.386	303	92	14	1	3	3	18	33
Not Leadoff	.289	.324	.402	97	28	6	1	1	1	5	13	.259	.308	.364	379	98	21	2	5	5	27	63
Runners On	.277	.338	.365	137	38	1	1	3	30	14	24	.301	.370	.420	595	179	21	4	14	168	74	85
First Base Only	.274	.338	.371	62	17	0	0	2	4	6	6	.309	.364	.442	233	72	8	1	7	18	20	26
Scoring Position	.280	.337	.360	75	21	1	1	1	26	8	18	.296	.374	.406	362	107	13	3	7	150	54	59
Late Innings, Close	.208	.281	.286	77	16	0	0	2	12	9	15	.274	.342	.327	248	68	7	0	2	37	28	45

	RBI/Opportunities						
Scoring Position	24 / 99	(24%)		136 / 495	(27%)	
Scoring Position, 2 Out	9 / 42	(21%)		48 / 217	(22%)	
On Third, Less than 2 Out	9 / 18	(50%)		62 / 102	(61%)	
RBI in close games / RBI Total	22 / 32	(69%)		115 / 176	(65%)	

Dale Murphy
Atlanta Braves

Take a look at the season totals below and forget that they belong to Dale Murphy. For almost any other player, this would have been an outstanding season, yet baseball fans are wondering, "What is wrong with Dale Murphy?" We have been spoiled by consistency.

Normally there is considerable year-to-year variation in a player's statistics. Batting average can vary by +/− 15 points, home runs by 20%, etc., without attracting much attention. When a player doesn't show such variance, that is consistency. In the years 1982–1985, Dale Murphy was one of the most consistent players in baseball, comparable to Steve Garvey in the late 1970's. The "off-season" that he did experience in 1986 looks worse because of our expectations.

Murphy is showing signs of age in the field. He has always relied more on a quick start rather than on pure speed, and this year he appeared to get more poor starts from which he could not recover. He also misplayed several balls, a rarity in the past. There has been much talk in the front office of moving Murphy to right field for the remainder of his career. The time may have come. The Gold Gloves that he was awarded the past two years were based on reputation alone. In both 1985 and 1986, his range was at the bottom of the list of regular NL centerfielders, substantially below the average.

Can Murphy recover his past form? Sure. I would have to see another year at 1986 levels before accepting that he has lost anything offensively. Even at that level of performance he is still valuable, still an All-Star— just not the MVP-caliber player he was for the last four seasons.

—John Stryker

Home/road breakdowns are not significantly different for Murphy, except for walks (many more at home). His biggest differential is in the day/night stats for homers and RBIs. Months which start with the letter *A* are Dale's "Grade-A" efforts. Months which start with the letter *J* prove him to be merely mortal. He consistently performs above his personal averages when runners are on base.

If I could build a team from square one, I'd start with Dale Murphy. He hits, fields, runs, throws, hustles, and never complains. Normally you would have to settle for about three or four of those qualities in one player.

Was 1986 a disappointment? In a relative sense, "Yes." In an absolute sense, "No." It was a very good season by most standards. Dale earns every penny of every paycheck, and there are few players for whom that can be unequivocally said.

—Robert Jones

	1986 SEASON											THREE YEARS (84 – 86)										
	Ave.	OBP	SLG	AB	H	2B	3B	HR	RBI	BB	SO	Ave.	OBP	SLG	AB	H	2B	3B	HR	RBI	BB	SO
Totals	.265	.347	.477	614	163	29	7	29	83	75	141	.285	.369	.521	1837	524	93	17	102	294	245	416
Batting vs. Left and Right-handed Pitchers																						
Left	.280	.382	.508	193	54	7	5	9	23	32	37	.308	.412	.567	545	168	25	7	34	89	97	116
Right	.259	.330	.463	421	109	22	2	20	60	43	104	.276	.350	.502	1292	356	68	10	68	205	148	300
At Home and on the Road																						
Home	.268	.366	.503	298	80	11	4	17	40	44	66	.288	.382	.529	906	261	44	6	54	145	135	188
Road	.263	.328	.453	316	83	18	3	12	43	31	75	.282	.356	.513	931	263	49	11	48	149	110	228
Facing Groundball Pitchers and Flyball Pitchers																						
Groundball	.260	.359	.430	265	69	10	1	11	39	39	62	.281	.371	.477	851	239	39	4	40	135	120	192
Flyball	.269	.337	.513	349	94	19	6	18	44	36	79	.289	.368	.559	986	285	54	13	62	159	125	224
Facing Finesse Pitchers and Power Pitchers																						
Finesse	.264	.328	.444	349	92	19	4	12	43	33	71	.297	.363	.535	1066	317	59	13	56	174	112	202
Power	.268	.370	.521	265	71	10	3	17	40	42	70	.268	.377	.502	771	207	34	4	46	120	133	214
On Grass and on Turf																						
Grass	.274	.362	.499	453	124	18	6	24	61	61	98	.289	.377	.526	1358	393	63	12	78	212	188	284
Turf	.242	.301	.416	161	39	11	1	5	22	14	43	.273	.348	.507	479	131	30	5	24	82	57	132
During the Day and at Night																						
Day	.276	.341	.422	192	53	8	1	6	25	19	41	.293	.382	.519	590	173	28	3	33	88	83	128
Night	.261	.349	.502	422	110	21	6	23	58	56	100	.281	.363	.522	1247	351	65	14	69	206	162	288
By Month																						
April	.344	.440	.688	64	22	5	1	5	10	11	16	.313	.403	.668	214	67	15	2	19	51	33	46
May	.287	.379	.444	108	31	5	0	4	15	16	26	.282	.362	.480	319	90	13	1	16	42	40	68
June	.243	.339	.402	107	26	3	1	4	8	16	27	.260	.365	.439	319	83	14	2	13	39	54	82
July	.220	.284	.340	100	22	6	0	2	7	9	23	.267	.358	.534	296	79	16	3	19	49	42	79
August	.337	.430	.750	104	35	9	2	10	30	16	23	.313	.387	.579	323	101	20	3	20	57	39	69
Sept/Oct	.206	.252	.351	131	27	1	3	4	13	7	26	.284	.352	.481	366	104	15	6	15	56	37	72
Situational																						
Bases Empty	.256	.327	.453	351	90	18	6	13	13	36	80	.282	.358	.505	1024	289	55	13	49	49	119	226
Leadoff	.276	.345	.514	105	29	6	2	5	5	11	22	.309	.382	.552	388	120	22	6	20	20	45	81
Not Leadoff	.248	.320	.427	246	61	12	4	8	8	25	58	.266	.343	.476	636	169	33	7	29	29	74	145
Runners On	.278	.372	.510	263	73	11	1	16	70	39	61	.289	.383	.541	813	235	38	4	53	245	126	190
First Base Only	.250	.320	.431	116	29	3	0	6	12	12	23	.288	.350	.524	368	106	16	1	23	54	34	70
Scoring Position	.299	.409	.571	147	44	8	1	10	58	27	38	.290	.407	.555	445	129	22	3	30	191	92	120
Late Innings, Close	.288	.422	.606	104	30	5	2	8	22	23	29	.298	.413	.567	312	93	18	3	20	62	60	77
RBI/Opportunities																						

	RBI/Opportunities (1986)		THREE YEARS	
Scoring Position	41 / 183	(22%)	143 / 613	(23%)
Scoring Position, 2 Out	20 / 74	(27%)	63 / 264	(24%)
On Third, Less than 2 Out	12 / 34	(35%)	48 / 120	(40%)
RBI in close games / RBI Total	54 / 83	(65%)	213 / 294	(72%)

Eddie Murray
Baltimore Orioles

No, that was no misprint in the final stats—the Baltimore Orioles really did finish last in the AL East in 1986. And that ordinary-looking fellow at first for them was really Eddie Murray. How bad of a season was it for Murray and his fellow Birds? Well, the Orioles finished below .500 for the first time since 1967 and in last for the first time since they came to Baltimore. Murray did just as dismally, setting career lows in games (137), runs (61), hits (151), doubles (25), homers (17) and RBIs (84) (strike season stats not included). The man who defines the words "clutch player" hit only .250 with 11 RBIs in late innings of close games. The three time Gold Glover's .989 fielding percentage was seventh among the 11 first basemen who played over 100 games in 1986. It wouldn't be a bad season for many players—but Eddie Murray isn't just any player.

Throughout the season, everyone speculated on the reason for Murray's dramatic decline. His slow offensive start was written off to history (it is his worst month every year). Later, people wondered if he was having vision trouble. When he started to make defensive lapses, people said that he wasn't trying. Then a wrist injury struck, keeping him out of the lineup for most of July. When his replacement (Jim Traber) got off to a hot start, people began wondering if maybe it wasn't time for a change. When Murray heard that, he exploded and demanded to be traded—that set off a backlash among the fans. One thing kept running into another—fate must have decided that 1986 wasn't Eddie's year.

The tumult eventually began to die down, though, and Eddie's bat began showing signs of life. He hit .320 over the last three months—10 points higher than he has done in the past. The Orioles didn't play many close games at the end of the year, so Eddie didn't get much chance to work on his average there—he did hit 60 points better than he had in the past. And, with a .513 slugging average for the month of September, he closed out the year with a bang.

Some people are writing Eddie Murray off for 1987; some people pay no attention to history. In 1967, Boog Powell, Baltimore's star first baseman, staggered through the worst year of his career (to that point) and Baltimore finished under .500 and sixth in the AL. Powell came back in '68 and so did the Orioles. Murray will come back in 1987, and so, I expect, will his team.

—Stuart Hall

	1986 SEASON											THREE YEARS (84 – 86)										
	Ave.	OBP	SLG	AB	H	2B	3B	HR	RBI	BB	SO	Ave.	OBP	SLG	AB	H	2B	3B	HR	RBI	BB	SO
Totals	.305	.396	.463	495	151	25	1	17	84	78	49	.303	.396	.500	1666	504	88	5	77	318	269	204
Batting vs. Left and Right-handed Pitchers																						
Left	.301	.360	.493	136	41	8	0	6	23	13	13	.284	.380	.472	489	139	27	1	21	82	74	61
Right	.306	.409	.451	359	110	17	1	11	61	65	36	.310	.403	.511	1177	365	61	4	56	236	195	143
At Home and on the Road																						
Home	.310	.387	.471	242	75	10	1	9	47	31	24	.311	.408	.522	816	254	40	3	42	167	135	84
Road	.300	.405	.455	253	76	15	0	8	37	47	25	.294	.385	.479	850	250	48	2	35	151	134	120
Facing Groundball Pitchers and Flyball Pitchers																						
Groundball	.274	.362	.391	230	63	10	1	5	32	33	25	.299	.389	.482	792	237	42	2	33	147	120	99
Flyball	.332	.425	.525	265	88	15	0	12	52	45	24	.305	.403	.516	874	267	46	3	44	171	149	105
Facing Finesse Pitchers and Power Pitchers																						
Finesse	.269	.354	.374	305	82	12	1	6	47	42	30	.290	.371	.463	921	267	47	2	36	164	123	104
Power	.363	.461	.605	190	69	13	0	11	37	36	19	.318	.426	.546	745	237	41	3	41	154	146	100
On Grass and on Turf																						
Grass	.308	.404	.472	422	130	22	1	15	76	71	42	.305	.400	.510	1428	435	77	3	70	278	234	174
Turf	.288	.350	.411	73	21	3	0	2	8	7	7	.290	.378	.441	238	69	11	2	7	40	35	30
During the Day and at Night																						
Day	.316	.406	.503	155	49	6	1	7	31	24	19	.296	.393	.491	507	150	23	2	24	95	83	68
Night	.300	.392	.444	340	102	19	0	10	53	54	30	.305	.398	.504	1159	354	65	3	53	223	186	136
By Month																						
April	.267	.360	.453	75	20	2	0	4	13	11	12	.274	.371	.466	208	57	4	0	12	48	32	31
May	.337	.427	.483	89	30	4	0	3	24	17	10	.335	.430	.527	281	94	17	2	11	66	53	32
June	.265	.361	.431	102	27	5	0	4	15	16	10	.278	.363	.460	302	84	16	0	13	49	43	37
July	.348	.423	.348	23	8	0	0	0	0	3	1	.296	.382	.535	230	68	13	0	14	47	34	30
August	.333	.408	.448	87	29	4	0	2	11	11	6	.349	.435	.534	292	102	14	2	12	59	46	30
Sept/Oct	.311	.410	.513	119	37	10	1	4	21	20	10	.280	.389	.482	353	99	24	1	15	49	61	44
Situational																						
Bases Empty	.288	.399	.416	250	72	12	1	6	6	46	27	.272	.372	.432	870	237	35	1	34	34	136	111
Leadoff	.270	.378	.389	126	34	6	0	3	3	22	11	.274	.377	.428	430	118	18	0	16	16	69	53
Not Leadoff	.306	.419	.444	124	38	6	1	3	3	24	16	.270	.367	.436	440	119	17	1	18	18	67	58
Runners On	.322	.394	.510	245	79	13	0	11	78	32	22	.335	.422	.574	796	267	53	4	43	284	133	93
First Base Only	.281	.341	.413	121	34	4	0	4	10	11	10	.324	.391	.515	392	127	25	1	16	43	43	38
Scoring Position	.363	.440	.605	124	45	9	0	7	68	21	12	.347	.449	.631	404	140	28	3	27	241	90	55
Late Innings, Close	.250	.349	.458	72	18	3	0	4	11	12	9	.339	.433	.657	242	82	15	1	20	72	44	29
RBI/Opportunities																						
Scoring Position				54 / 171		(32%)									188 / 613		(31%)					
Scoring Position, 2 Out				22 / 66		(33%)									65 / 269		(24%)					
On Third, Less than 2 Out				21 / 36		(58%)									76 / 125		(61%)					
RBI in close games / RBI Total				51 / 84		(61%)									227 / 318		(71%)					

Tom Niedenfuer
Los Angeles Dodgers

Much has been written about Tom Niedenfuer's nightmarish 1985 NL Championship Series. He surrendered home runs in the ninth innings of both Games 5 and 6 to put the Cardinals in the World Series. That was how the nightmares began. They still may not be over.

Tom Niedenfuer came up to stay in 1982, and was impressive from the start. In 1983, he followed with what has been his career year. He appeared in 66 games, won 8, had a 1.90 ERA and allowed a miserly 0.86 runners per inning (all career highs).

1984 brought various injuries to Niedenfuer. He appeared in only 33 games, but was very effective. He looked to 1985 to return to top form, and for five months, he was one of the best in the league. It was on September 2nd that the real nightmares began.

Going into September, Niedenfuer was 6–4 with 14 saves and a 1.86 ERA. Then, perhaps from overuse, he became a liability. In his last 17 appearances, his ERA was 5.70, he allowed 38 runners to reach base in 23 innings, and he had a 1–5 record. Before Game 6 of the NLCS, he had surrendered game-winning homers during the final at-bat in two of his last three appearances. *If* Tom Lasorda had known these numbers, and *if* he had walked Clark, or *if* he

had . . . if, if, if. If cats could fly there would be no birds left in the sky.

The bad dreams continued into 1986. It is hard to imagine what it must be like to absorb so much blame for a team's playoff loss. Let it be remembered that Tom Niedenfuer never tried to deny any of the responsibility. Baseball is a better game because of him.

Nevertheless, 1986 was not a good year. Before the All-Star break, his 3.29 ERA, 5–4 record and 4 saves hid the fact that Dodgers fans thought Bobo Holloman had been reincarnated. He allowed 17 of 39 inherited runners to score, blowing numerous save opportunities. During a five-day catastrophe in May he allowed two grand slams.

By the end of August, Niedenfuer had settled down somewhat, but then he ended up on the DL. When he came back in September, he made seven more appearances, going 0–2 with 1 save and a 10.80 ERA—not encouraging numbers.

Tom Niedenfuer can be the Dodgers stopper, but he won't last if he is the only pitcher that they have to go to. He is not a Sutter or Quisenberry, but he is young and resilient. With good coaching, the nightmares could end. Pleasant dreams, Tom.

—Carmen J. Corica

	1986: Power, Flyball											1985: Power, Flyball									1984: Power, Flyball	
	1986 SEASON											**THREE YEARS (84 – 86)**										
	G	IP	H	BB	SO	SB	CS	W	L	S	ERA	G	IP	H	BB	SO	SB	CS	W	L	S	ERA
Totals	60	80.0	86	29	55	5	5	6	6	11	3.71	157	233.2	211	76	202	18	14	15	20	41	3.00
											At Home and on the Road										
Home	30	46.0	43	7	31	4	3	4	4	5	3.33	83	130.2	121	23	112	12	8	7	9	24	2.82
Road	30	34.0	43	22	24	1	2	2	2	6	4.24	74	103.0	90	53	90	6	6	8	11	17	3.23
											During the Day and at Night										
Day	21	26.0	24	11	18	2	2	3	3	4	3.81	57	81.1	69	28	66	5	7	7	11	16	3.54
Night	39	54.0	62	18	37	3	3	3	3	7	3.67	100	152.1	142	48	136	13	7	8	9	25	2.72
											On Grass and on Turf										
Grass	46	62.1	65	17	43	5	4	5	6	8	3.47	120	179.2	168	45	151	15	10	11	16	32	2.91
Turf	14	17.2	21	12	12	0	1	1	0	3	4.58	37	54.0	43	31	51	3	4	4	4	9	3.33
											By Month										
April	8	12.2	17	4	12	0	1	0	1	2	4.26	23	38.1	37	12	32	1	3	1	2	6	3.29
May	15	19.0	15	9	17	1	2	3	1	1	2.37	37	55.2	39	26	59	3	4	4	6	8	2.10
June	11	13.1	15	3	10	1	1	2	1	1	4.05	24	34.1	30	7	34	4	2	3	1	5	2.36
July	12	18.1	16	8	10	2	1	0	1	2	2.95	24	40.1	35	11	26	3	3	3	3	5	2.90
August	7	10.0	11	1	3	0	0	1	0	4	1.80	20	28.2	23	7	25	4	0	2	1	10	1.57
Sept/Oct	7	6.2	12	4	3	1	0	0	2	1	10.80	29	36.1	47	13	26	3	1	2	7	7	5.94

	vs. Opponent Batters																			
	1986 SEASON										**THREE YEARS (84 – 86)**									
	Ave.	OBP	SLG	AB	H	2B	3B	HR	RBI	BB	SO	Ave.	OBP	SLG	AB	H	2B	3B	HR	RBI	BB	SO
Totals	.280	.341	.453	307	86	16	2	11	50	29	55	.244	.306	.365	866	211	39	3	20	105	76	202
							Pitching vs. Left and Right-handed Batters													
Left	.282	.369	.474	156	44	8	2	6	22	22	29	.258	.341	.408	453	117	25	2	13	56	54	100
Right	.278	.311	.430	151	42	8	0	5	28	7	26	.228	.265	.317	413	94	14	1	7	49	22	102
								Situational											
Bases Empty	.297	.335	.477	155	46	8	1	6	6	8	25	.248	.304	.377	467	116	25	1	11	11	35	99
Leadoff	.284	.314	.433	67	19	4	0	2	2	3	14	.208	.261	.340	197	41	11	0	5	5	13	51
Not Leadoff	.307	.351	.511	88	27	4	1	4	4	5	11	.278	.334	.404	270	75	14	1	6	6	22	48
Runners On	.263	.347	.428	152	40	8	1	5	44	21	30	.238	.308	.351	399	95	14	2	9	94	41	103
First Base Only	.233	.246	.367	60	14	2	0	2	5	1	12	.227	.256	.318	154	35	2	0	4	9	6	36
Scoring Position	.283	.400	.467	92	26	6	1	3	39	20	18	.245	.337	.371	245	60	12	2	5	85	35	67
Late Innings, Close	.284	.347	.456	204	58	10	2	7	29	20	36	.253	.319	.371	598	151	28	2	13	71	57	144

	RBI/Opportunities						
Scoring Position		33 / 143	(23%)		76 / 350	(22%)	
Scoring Position, 2 Out		17 / 73	(23%)		38 / 185	(21%)	
On Third, Less than 2 Out		10 / 23	(43%)		23 / 53	(43%)	
RBI in close games / RBI Total		31 / 50	(62%)		78 / 105	(74%)	

Phil Niekro
Cleveland Indians

I'm asked many questions about the 1986 Indians; the one I've grown to hate answering is "What's wrong with Phil Niekro?" People don't want to accept the fact that he's declining—but he is. Niekro has been falling apart; were it not for two things, it would be very easy to see:

SUPPORT: The 1982 Braves led their league in runs scored. The 1983 Braves led their league in runs scored. The 1985 Yankees led their league in runs scored. The 1986 Indians led their league in runs scored. Niekro has been one of the 10 best-supported pitchers in his league twice in the last five years and in the top 20 the other three times.

CIRCUMSTANCE: 1983 was unquestionably Niekro's worst year in Atlanta; it made sense to conclude that he was nearly finished. Had New York not signed him, he would have been. But he joined a good offensive team with a strong bullpen that played in a pitchers' park in a league where only one knuckleballer pitched and nobody had ever seen Niekro before. Is it any wonder that he was 10–5 with a 2.07 ERA in his first three months? Is it fair to suggest that the reason that he went 6–4 with a 4.66 ERA after July

1 was that hitters caught onto him? Does the fact that his winning percentage and ERA have steadily declined since then suggest anything? Or what about this:

The only major league team that Niekro had never faced was the Yankees. He made five appearances against them in 1986. In his first three, he was 2–0 with a 2.12 ERA; after that he was 0–1, 7.20.

The last time that Niekro had a higher ERA than he did in 1986, Lyndon Johnson was president. His ERA was bad enough—he also allowed 25 unearned runs. Do I blame him for them? Yes—when you give up three hits and two walks in an inning, I don't think you should be charged with no runs at all.

Niekro is one of the ten greatest pitchers in baseball history. Had the Braves brought him to the majors sooner or been a better team during his career, he would have won 400 and lost 200, own the career strikeout mark and have a sub-3.00 ERA. I admire the man; it hurts to write this. But if he doesn't retire soon, nobody will remember that he could pitch—that would hurt even more.

—Geoff Beckman

1986: Finesse, Flyball **1985: Finesse, Flyball** **1984: Finesse, Flyball**

	1986 SEASON											THREE YEARS (84 – 86)											
	G	IP	H	BB	SO	SB	CS	W	L	S	ERA	G	IP	H	BB	SO	SB	CS	W	L	S	ERA
Totals	34	210.1	241	95	81	13	6	11	11	0	4.32	99	646.0	663	291	366	44	23	43	31	0	3.83
At Home and on the Road																						
Home	17	95.2	105	44	41	3	3	6	5	0	4.05	50	311.1	313	146	172	19	13	22	14	0	3.79
Road	17	114.2	136	51	40	10	3	5	6	0	4.55	49	334.2	350	145	194	25	10	21	17	0	3.87
During the Day and at Night																						
Day	12	82.2	83	36	38	6	0	5	3	0	4.25	35	227.2	223	98	131	11	7	17	8	0	3.64
Night	22	127.2	158	59	43	7	6	6	8	0	4.37	64	418.1	440	193	235	33	16	26	23	0	3.94
On Grass and on Turf																						
Grass	29	174.2	200	86	69	9	4	8	10	0	4.59	82	521.2	545	249	298	31	20	33	27	0	4.09
Turf	5	35.2	41	9	12	4	2	3	1	0	3.03	17	124.1	118	42	68	13	3	10	4	0	2.75
By Month																						
April	4	28.0	26	16	12	3	0	1	2	0	2.57	14	96.0	91	41	66	6	7	8	4	0	2.81
May	7	36.2	51	17	12	4	4	2	2	0	5.40	18	114.2	131	53	56	10	6	8	6	0	3.37
June	5	29.1	35	13	15	1	1	1	2	0	5.52	16	101.1	114	49	68	8	5	5	7	0	4.80
July	6	43.2	45	14	16	3	1	3	1	0	3.50	16	113.1	116	41	62	7	2	8	3	0	3.49
August	7	39.1	44	23	16	1	0	3	3	0	4.81	20	118.0	112	54	62	7	0	10	6	0	3.97
Sept/Oct	5	33.1	40	12	10	1	0	1	1	0	4.05	15	102.2	113	53	52	6	3	4	5	0	4.56

vs. Opponent Batters

	1986 SEASON											THREE YEARS (84 – 86)									
	Ave.	OBP	SLG	AB	H	2B	3B	HR	RBI	BB	SO	Ave.	OBP	SLG	AB	H	2B	3B	HR	RBI	BB	SO
Totals	.287	.362	.429	841	241	40	4	24	105	95	81	.266	.344	.405	2491	663	112	15	68	279	291	366
Pitching vs. Left and Right-handed Batters																						
Left	.284	.360	.404	455	129	22	3	9	59	52	37	.268	.351	.407	1339	359	51	12	37	164	169	158
Right	.290	.365	.459	386	112	18	1	15	46	43	44	.264	.334	.403	1152	304	61	3	31	115	122	208
Situational																						
Bases Empty	.296	.370	.449	452	134	23	2	14	14	49	44	.271	.346	.425	1401	379	74	8	42	42	157	196
Leadoff	.264	.339	.383	201	53	10	1	4	4	21	21	.256	.323	.360	620	159	26	4	10	10	58	78
Not Leadoff	.323	.395	.502	251	81	13	1	10	10	28	23	.282	.364	.476	781	220	48	4	32	32	99	118
Runners On	.275	.353	.406	389	107	17	2	10	91	46	37	.261	.340	.380	1090	284	38	7	26	237	134	170
First Base Only	.247	.285	.384	190	47	6	1	6	14	10	15	.265	.315	.383	499	132	19	2	12	33	36	57
Scoring Position	.302	.410	.427	199	60	11	1	4	77	36	22	.257	.359	.377	591	152	19	5	14	204	98	113
Late Innings, Close	.303	.403	.561	66	20	2	0	5	8	11	8	.271	.365	.452	199	54	7	1	9	20	29	32

RBI/Opportunities

Scoring Position	65 / 279	(23%)	172 / 822	(21%)
Scoring Position, 2 Out	35 / 149	(23%)	76 / 402	(19%)
On Third, Less than 2 Out	21 / 43	(49%)	60 / 134	(45%)
RBI in close games / RBI Total	75 / 105	(71%)	197 / 279	(71%)

Ken Oberkfell
Atlanta Braves

When Ken Oberkfell was traded from the Cardinals to the Braves, the most important reasons were his lack of power and his low RBI counts. His replacement, Terry Pendleton, has not done any better at home run production, and his batting average is also lower. Pendleton has, however, provided better defense and more RBIs. While Oberkfell is a fine fielder, Pendleton has more range at this stage of their careers. Oberkfell does, of course, have much more range at third base than Bob Horner did, but he is not as good a second basemen as Glenn Hubbard is.

What Oberkfell does best is hit right-handed pitching. Throughout his career, there has been a wide gap in his on-base average facing right- and left-handed pitching. He hits for a good average versus right-handers, but more importantly, he receives numerous walks as well as not striking out often. The Braves might be advised to bat Oberkfell second when facing a right-hander.

Since the trade, Oberkfell's batting average on turf has dropped dramatically while his grass stats have improved. Part of this improvement is because Atlanta is a better hitter's park than St. Louis. In any case, Oberkfell has made the adjustment to grass. If Oberkfell were to hit in the #2

slot, the main problem would be where his hits usually go. Most of his hits are towards centerfield, so he doesn't pull the ball often enough to utilize the gap in the infield if there were a runner being held on first. Hit-and-run plays could end up as double plays if he didn't hit the ball toward the hole. Run-and-hit plays might be more successful in this case. Certainly his talents would be wasted in the bottom third of the lineup if he continues to reach base as he did in 1986.

—Victor Hester

Oberkfell shows a clear trend of wearing down as the season wears on: his combined September/October stats for the past three years are truly execrable, including a slugging(?) average of .255 with an isolated power of .048!

While Oberkfell's career is certainly distinguished by a low RBI rate, it seems unfair to focus on that. Ken has never been and likely will not ever be the type of hitter that drives in runs; he is the type of hitter that gets on base so that others can drive him in. With his relatively-high OBA and his good fielding, he can be a valuable ballplayer if he is used appropriately.

—Gary Gillette

| | 1986 SEASON | | | | | | | | | | | THREE YEARS (84 – 86) | | | | | | | | | | |
	Ave.	OBP	SLG	AB	H	2B	3B	HR	RBI	BB	SO	Ave.	OBP	SLG	AB	H	2B	3B	HR	RBI	BB	SO
Totals	.270	.373	.360	503	136	24	3	5	48	83	40	.270	.358	.357	1239	335	62	9	9	104	165	105
Batting vs. Left and Right-handed Pitchers																						
Left	.238	.338	.315	130	31	4	0	2	20	19	17	.243	.320	.308	305	74	10	2	2	34	33	39
Right	.282	.386	.375	373	105	20	3	3	28	64	23	.279	.370	.373	934	261	52	7	7	70	132	66
At Home and on the Road																						
Home	.284	.382	.362	268	76	11	2	2	25	43	18	.277	.365	.365	639	177	29	6	5	60	87	44
Road	.255	.363	.357	235	60	13	1	3	23	40	22	.263	.350	.348	600	158	33	3	4	44	78	61
Facing Groundball Pitchers and Flyball Pitchers																						
Groundball	.272	.346	.360	228	62	10	2	2	24	27	16	.258	.326	.327	600	155	25	5	2	47	60	41
Flyball	.269	.395	.360	275	74	14	1	3	24	56	24	.282	.386	.385	639	180	37	4	7	57	105	64
Facing Finesse Pitchers and Power Pitchers																						
Finesse	.288	.379	.403	295	85	16	3	4	25	43	17	.284	.359	.382	714	203	41	7	5	55	83	48
Power	.245	.365	.298	208	51	8	0	1	23	40	23	.251	.356	.322	525	132	21	2	4	49	82	57
On Grass and on Turf																						
Grass	.279	.381	.362	384	107	19	2	3	31	64	28	.280	.369	.371	857	240	43	7	7	71	119	67
Turf	.244	.350	.353	119	29	5	1	2	17	19	12	.249	.333	.325	382	95	19	2	2	33	46	38
During the Day and at Night																						
Day	.331	.425	.422	154	51	9	1	1	16	26	13	.272	.357	.349	401	109	21	2	2	32	54	37
Night	.244	.350	.332	349	85	15	2	4	32	57	27	.270	.358	.360	838	226	41	7	7	72	111	68
By Month																						
April	.323	.389	.387	62	20	4	0	0	8	8	6	.281	.346	.353	139	39	8	1	0	14	15	9
May	.316	.416	.368	76	24	1	0	1	6	12	3	.313	.391	.374	198	62	7	1	1	12	24	15
June	.281	.369	.472	89	25	5	0	4	13	13	7	.297	.358	.429	273	81	17	2	5	29	27	16
July	.279	.374	.326	86	24	4	0	0	9	12	9	.256	.351	.338	234	60	12	2	1	23	32	29
August	.241	.396	.361	83	20	6	2	0	7	22	6	.261	.380	.362	207	54	11	2	2	16	39	20
Sept/Oct	.215	.317	.271	107	23	4	1	0	5	16	9	.207	.317	.255	188	39	7	1	0	10	28	16
Situational																						
Bases Empty	.258	.364	.344	302	78	15	1	3	3	48	30	.269	.354	.348	728	196	39	3	4	4	88	66
Leadoff	.183	.254	.261	115	21	6	0	1	1	11	7	.239	.315	.304	280	67	15	0	1	1	28	17
Not Leadoff	.305	.425	.396	187	57	9	1	2	2	37	23	.288	.377	.375	448	129	24	3	3	3	60	49
Runners On	.289	.388	.383	201	58	9	2	2	45	35	10	.272	.364	.370	511	139	23	6	5	100	77	39
First Base Only	.277	.326	.325	83	23	4	0	0	0	6	1	.298	.343	.361	238	71	12	0	1	3	16	16
Scoring Position	.297	.424	.424	118	35	5	2	2	45	29	9	.249	.380	.377	273	68	11	6	4	97	61	23
Late Innings, Close	.261	.394	.330	88	23	3	0	1	8	20	5	.232	.341	.282	220	51	8	1	0	15	36	16
RBI/Opportunities																						
Scoring Position			41 / 175	(23%)										87 / 410	(21%)							
Scoring Position, 2 Out			19 / 89	(21%)										40 / 201	(20%)							
On Third, Less than 2 Out			13 / 23	(57%)										26 / 55	(47%)							
RBI in close games / RBI Total			33 / 48	(69%)										68 / 104	(65%)							

Pete O'Brien
Texas Rangers

Pete O'Brien had his finest season in 1986, setting career highs in batting average and home runs and hitting an outstanding .346 with runners in scoring position. Traditionally one of the Rangers' most patient hitters, Pete was ninth in the American League with 87 walks (another career high), which contributed to his fine .385 on-base average, also ninth in the league.

The big story of Pete's season was a successful change in his hitting style against left-handed pitching. Prior to 1986 he really struggled against LHP, hitting about 30 points less than against righties and with little power—a .318 slugging average, versus .473 against RHP. His old strategy seemed to revolve around simply waiting for the right pitch from a lefty. He didn't get it very often, and the only thing he did well against LHP was walk a lot.

In 1986 Pete began to take charge in the battle against LHP. He anticipated the pitches more and began dumping the lefty breaking balls into left field. He actually hit over .300 against lefties, and even though he still has far better power against RHP, he increased his power against lefties by about 70%.

This is the kind of adjustment which has made Pete's career a delight to watch. He was a fairly low draft pick, going in the fifteenth round in June of 1979. He wasn't a raw talent that the scouts might underestimate. He was 21; he had played Legion ball, semi-pro, and put in three years of college ball. He was strictly a long shot at making the majors. And when he did and hit .237 in his first 591 at bats, you wondered if he would last. Pete kept working, adjusting, doing everything he could to improve as a player. In my eyes, O'Brien's approach to his profession, not his talents, is responsible for his jump from back-up talent to front-line first baseman.

Pete is also an exceptional defensive first baseman with good range and excels at starting the double play. There is no question in my mind that if he threw right-handed he could be a very good third baseman. Who knows, maybe someday Don Mattingly will have some competition as a lefty third baseman.

—Craig Wright

	1986 SEASON											THREE YEARS (84 – 86)										
	Ave.	OBP	SLG	AB	H	2B	3B	HR	RBI	BB	SO	Ave.	OBP	SLG	AB	H	2B	3B	HR	RBI	BB	SO
Totals	.290	.385	.468	551	160	23	3	23	90	87	66	.281	.359	.456	1644	462	83	8	63	262	209	170
Batting vs. Left and Right-handed Pitchers																						
Left	.309	.380	.448	165	51	11	0	4	25	19	28	.250	.322	.347	484	121	23	0	8	65	53	74
Right	.282	.387	.477	386	109	12	3	19	65	68	38	.294	.374	.502	1160	341	60	8	55	197	156	96
At Home and on the Road																						
Home	.268	.356	.442	265	71	13	0	11	41	37	34	.292	.367	.464	804	235	48	0	30	142	100	83
Road	.311	.411	.493	286	89	10	3	12	49	50	32	.270	.351	.449	840	227	35	8	33	120	109	87
Facing Groundball Pitchers and Flyball Pitchers																						
Groundball	.293	.380	.446	249	73	11	3	7	33	36	21	.286	.360	.449	816	233	37	6	28	115	100	75
Flyball	.288	.390	.487	302	87	12	0	16	57	51	45	.277	.357	.464	828	229	46	2	35	147	109	95
Facing Finesse Pitchers and Power Pitchers																						
Finesse	.271	.348	.447	347	94	12	2	15	53	42	33	.279	.341	.472	975	272	48	4	44	161	98	80
Power	.324	.444	.505	204	66	11	1	8	37	45	33	.284	.383	.433	669	190	35	4	19	101	111	90
On Grass and on Turf																						
Grass	.289	.387	.468	453	131	20	2	19	77	74	56	.285	.363	.455	1371	391	71	3	52	223	176	142
Turf	.296	.378	.469	98	29	3	1	4	13	13	10	.260	.335	.462	273	71	12	5	11	39	33	28
During the Day and at Night																						
Day	.336	.424	.480	125	42	7	1	3	16	19	13	.274	.354	.399	343	94	13	3	8	46	44	35
Night	.277	.374	.465	426	118	16	2	20	74	68	53	.283	.360	.471	1301	368	70	5	55	216	165	135
By Month																						
April	.394	.467	.758	66	26	7	1	5	16	9	8	.278	.360	.510	194	54	11	2	10	36	26	19
May	.255	.330	.337	98	25	5	0	1	9	11	13	.259	.308	.369	290	75	18	1	4	31	22	27
June	.262	.360	.381	84	22	2	1	2	13	14	9	.299	.389	.470	281	84	16	1	10	45	44	31
July	.263	.342	.414	99	26	1	1	4	15	12	9	.272	.336	.460	309	84	11	1	15	55	31	36
August	.315	.385	.583	108	34	5	0	8	27	13	14	.303	.364	.513	314	95	18	3	14	56	32	32
Sept/Oct	.281	.444	.406	96	27	3	0	3	10	28	13	.273	.396	.426	256	70	9	0	10	39	54	25
Situational																						
Bases Empty	.281	.365	.434	302	85	11	1	11	11	40	40	.278	.349	.457	891	248	41	2	38	38	96	100
Leadoff	.292	.330	.491	106	31	4	1	5	5	6	10	.257	.316	.420	300	77	14	1	11	11	26	33
Not Leadoff	.276	.383	.403	196	54	7	0	6	6	34	30	.289	.365	.475	591	171	27	1	27	27	70	67
Runners On	.301	.408	.510	249	75	12	2	12	79	47	26	.284	.370	.456	753	214	42	6	25	224	113	70
First Base Only	.252	.310	.479	119	30	4	1	7	17	10	10	.267	.333	.435	352	94	17	3	12	35	34	25
Scoring Position	.346	.482	.538	130	45	8	1	5	62	37	16	.299	.399	.474	401	120	25	3	13	189	79	45
Late Innings, Close	.291	.396	.430	86	25	3	0	3	10	15	12	.269	.358	.391	271	73	12	0	7	28	39	32

RBI/Opportunities						
Scoring Position		48 / 189	(25%)		152 / 572	(27%)
Scoring Position, 2 Out		15 / 65	(23%)		45 / 234	(19%)
On Third, Less than 2 Out		17 / 34	(50%)		60 / 105	(57%)
RBI in close games / RBI Total		58 / 90	(64%)		169 / 262	(65%)

Ron Oester
Cincinnati Reds

Ron Oester is like tofu. He's good for the team—a solid defensive second baseman who has a knack for getting key hits in late innings. He's just not very exciting to watch, and you really have to think about it to appreciate him.

Oester's defensive play has been remarkable. His partners on the right side of the Cincinnati infield in the last two years have been Pete Rose, Tony Perez, Nick Esasky and Cesar Cedeno. Rose and Perez have the lateral mobility of a backhoe, ground balls in Esasky's direction are an adventure, and Cedeno wasn't exactly a Gold Glove. Oester had to cover a lot of extra ground.

In 1985, he did that with so few errors as to be almost unbelievable. It caught up with him in 1986 to some extent, but he was still far more than adequate in the field. He was tied for second in the NL in errors with 19, but had far and away the highest rate of chances per game among second basemen in more than 120 games. In 1985, he had the second fewest errors and the third most chances per game.

If I might belabor a point, the lack of speed in the Reds' infield was so alarming that it had to be a contributing factor in the team's not winning the West the last two years.

In games with Buddy Bell, Dave Concepcion, Oester and Petony Perose out there, the average age was just under 37—and these guys are playing on a fast artificial surface! Four out of five might wind up in the Hall of Fame, but they conspired to turn a helluva lot of groundouts into base hits.

Offensively, Oester is, well, a really good defensive second baseman. He doesn't hit with enough power or for a high enough average to walk as seldom as he does. Batting eighth might dampen his selectivity (runners on and the pitcher coming up); it also makes him more likely to be walked intentionally than a career .260 hitter with no power. Rose tried moving Oester to different spots in the order, including second. This presumably was to take advantage of his ability to make contact. The move flopped, at least in part because there was so rarely a leadoff man on base to move along.

Once on base, Oester has average speed and little inclination to be daring. He doesn't steal much or go for the extra base, but then he doesn't make a lot of pointless baserunning outs.

Tofu.

—Tim McKenzie

	1986 SEASON											THREE YEARS (84 – 86)										
	Ave.	OBP	SLG	AB	H	2B	3B	HR	RBI	BB	SO	Ave.	OBP	SLG	AB	H	2B	3B	HR	RBI	BB	SO
Totals	.258	.325	.356	523	135	23	2	8	44	52	84	.265	.324	.344	1602	424	75	8	12	116	144	246
Batting vs. Left and Right-handed Pitchers																						
Left	.184	.263	.243	136	25	5	0	1	9	15	22	.232	.282	.290	448	104	18	1	2	26	32	77
Right	.284	.347	.395	387	110	18	2	7	35	37	62	.277	.340	.365	1154	320	57	7	10	90	112	169
At Home and on the Road																						
Home	.280	.349	.410	261	73	14	1	6	22	27	43	.276	.336	.370	819	226	43	5	8	65	74	121
Road	.237	.300	.302	262	62	9	1	2	22	25	41	.253	.312	.317	783	198	32	3	4	51	70	125
Facing Groundball Pitchers and Flyball Pitchers																						
Groundball	.230	.315	.318	261	60	10	2	3	21	33	41	.259	.331	.339	790	205	36	6	5	56	87	122
Flyball	.286	.335	.393	262	75	13	0	5	23	19	43	.270	.317	.349	812	219	39	2	7	60	57	124
Facing Finesse Pitchers and Power Pitchers																						
Finesse	.273	.319	.383	264	72	13	2	4	23	18	33	.266	.311	.348	896	238	41	6	7	62	60	115
Power	.243	.330	.328	259	63	10	0	4	21	34	51	.263	.340	.339	706	186	34	2	5	54	84	131
On Grass and on Turf																						
Grass	.245	.301	.318	151	37	6	1	1	9	13	26	.232	.292	.290	465	108	16	1	3	32	41	80
Turf	.263	.334	.371	372	98	17	1	7	35	39	58	.278	.338	.366	1137	316	59	7	9	84	103	166
During the Day and at Night																						
Day	.217	.302	.323	161	35	5	0	4	12	20	28	.239	.306	.318	507	121	15	2	7	33	51	90
Night	.276	.335	.370	362	100	18	2	4	32	32	56	.277	.333	.356	1095	303	60	6	5	83	93	156
By Month																						
April	.200	.238	.233	60	12	2	0	0	2	3	14	.203	.256	.267	187	38	8	2	0	14	13	39
May	.269	.359	.500	78	21	3	0	5	15	12	16	.278	.351	.409	230	64	11	2	5	21	27	32
June	.228	.278	.277	101	23	5	0	0	5	7	14	.240	.288	.297	296	71	15	1	0	20	21	39
July	.309	.374	.381	97	30	5	1	0	11	9	13	.307	.360	.363	267	82	13	1	0	18	21	34
August	.265	.314	.327	98	26	3	0	1	6	7	13	.293	.343	.385	304	89	17	1	3	26	24	41
Sept/Oct	.258	.356	.404	89	23	5	1	2	5	14	14	.252	.330	.330	318	80	11	1	4	17	38	61
Situational																						
Bases Empty	.255	.303	.371	278	71	15	1	5	5	18	49	.265	.307	.348	907	240	44	4	8	8	54	140
Leadoff	.261	.315	.391	115	30	7	1	2	2	9	22	.265	.299	.358	358	95	18	3	3	3	16	49
Not Leadoff	.252	.295	.356	163	41	8	0	3	3	9	27	.264	.313	.342	549	145	26	1	5	5	38	91
Runners On	.261	.348	.339	245	64	8	1	3	39	34	35	.265	.345	.338	695	184	31	4	4	108	90	106
First Base Only	.256	.291	.339	121	31	4	0	2	6	6	15	.296	.333	.389	324	96	19	1	3	16	18	38
Scoring Position	.266	.394	.339	124	33	4	1	1	33	28	20	.237	.354	.294	371	88	12	3	1	92	72	68
Late Innings, Close	.320	.383	.447	103	33	4	0	3	13	11	15	.305	.364	.397	305	93	14	1	4	19	29	44

RBI/Opportunities						
Scoring Position	31 / 177	(18%)		86 / 519	(17%)	
Scoring Position, 2 Out	11 / 73	(15%)		31 / 226	(14%)	
On Third, Less than 2 Out	15 / 31	(48%)		39 / 75	(52%)	
RBI in close games / RBI Total	31 / 44	(70%)		80 / 116	(69%)	

Bob Ojeda
New York Mets

If I were a National League general manager and heard that the Boston Red Sox were shopping Bruce Hurst around, I'd mail myself Federal Express to Boston so I could be among the first to talk to them. Given the recent performances of two ex-Boston lefthanded starters, John Tudor and Bob Ojeda, there is a strong tendency to believe that Bruce Hurst would be found money for an NL club.

But the subject of this treatise isn't Bruce Hurst, it's Bob Ojeda. In my opinion Bob Ojeda is the reason the Mets won the World Championship in 1986. Frank Cashen's acquisition of Ojeda allowed Davey Johnson to get the consistently inconsistent Rick Aguilera out of his starting rotation and into a middle reliever-spot starter role, for which he's better suited at this stage of his career. At first blush, obtaining Ojeda appeared to be a sound move, strengthening the pitching staff to complement the considerable offensive firepower of the Mets. As the 1986 season progressed, the acquisition transcended into a godsend.

While the supposedly-unhittable Dwight Gooden struggled through a (for him) sub-par season, Sid Fernandez went South after a strong start, and Ron Darling short-circuited his efforts on too many occasions by being cute, Ojeda was terrific all season and became the staff stopper. With the exception of a temporary lapse in August, he handled the role very well. Check the consistency of his performance month-to-month. If the Mets needed a quality seven or eight-inning start, Ojeda was usually up to it.

Pitching in bases-empty situation, Ojeda is consistent but not spectacular. It's with runners on base that this guy really shines. Armed with a bewildering assortment of off-speed stuff, he'll battle hitters with the best of them. I'm impressed with the fact that only four of the fifteen homers he allowed in 1986 came with runners on base; that's gutty pitching. However, one area of his game that suffered in 1986 was holding runners on. After a 21 out of 48 (44%) stolen base rate by opponents in 1984–5, 27 out of 35 (77%) runners were successful against him in 1986.

All things considered, Bobby Ojeda surely delivered more than the Mets were expecting. Instead of a day-in, day-out fourth starter, they got a guy who held their staff together.

—Bill Thomas

1986: Finesse, Flyball **1985: Power, Flyball** **1984: Power, Flyball**

	1986 SEASON										THREE YEARS (84 – 86)									
	G	IP	H	BB	SO	SB	CS	W	L	S	ERA	G	IP	H	BB	SO	SB	CS	W	L	S	ERA
Totals	32	217.1	185	52	148	27	8	18	5	0	2.57	104	591.2	562	196	387	45	35	39	28	1	3.47
At Home and on the Road																						
Home	15	107.0	89	23	81	7	6	9	2	0	2.86	51	296.2	289	92	212	16	16	17	14	0	3.70
Road	17	110.1	96	29	67	20	2	9	3	0	2.28	53	295.0	273	104	175	29	19	22	14	1	3.23
During the Day and at Night																						
Day	12	84.1	66	17	53	10	2	6	0	0	1.92	30	163.1	137	48	105	11	9	11	2	1	2.53
Night	20	133.0	119	35	95	17	6	12	5	0	2.98	74	428.1	425	148	282	34	26	28	26	0	3.82
On Grass and on Turf																						
Grass	19	136.0	113	32	101	11	6	12	2	0	2.78	80	460.0	432	153	317	22	24	31	21	1	3.54
Turf	13	81.1	72	20	47	16	2	6	3	0	2.21	24	131.2	130	43	70	23	11	8	7	0	3.21
By Month																						
April	4	21.1	17	2	8	3	1	3	0	0	2.11	19	61.2	59	34	32	5	8	6	3	0	3.50
May	6	40.1	40	12	32	10	1	3	2	0	2.90	20	88.1	88	33	70	12	8	7	4	1	2.85
June	5	37.2	35	13	20	8	1	3	0	0	2.39	17	122.1	126	43	73	11	6	6	4	0	3.97
July	5	35.0	28	7	26	1	2	3	0	0	1.54	16	98.2	80	22	70	7	3	7	4	0	2.83
August	6	41.1	39	13	34	4	3	3	2	0	3.92	14	85.1	103	27	55	8	5	4	7	0	5.38
Sept/Oct	6	41.2	26	5	28	1	0	3	1	0	2.16	18	135.1	106	37	87	2	5	9	6	0	2.66

vs. Opponent Batters

	1986 SEASON											THREE YEARS (84 – 86)									
	Ave.	OBP	SLG	AB	H	2B	3B	HR	RBI	BB	SO	Ave.	OBP	SLG	AB	H	2B	3B	HR	RBI	BB	SO
Totals	.230	.278	.330	804	185	27	4	15	65	52	148	.252	.313	.365	2228	562	91	16	43	211	196	387
Pitching vs. Left and Right-handed Batters																						
Left	.145	.202	.200	110	16	1	1	1	7	8	26	.241	.291	.327	394	95	15	2	5	30	29	88
Right	.244	.290	.350	694	169	26	3	14	58	44	122	.255	.317	.374	1834	467	76	14	38	181	167	299
Situational																						
Bases Empty	.248	.295	.356	480	119	17	1	11	11	31	85	.267	.322	.376	1294	345	59	4	25	25	102	202
Leadoff	.248	.295	.354	206	51	8	1	4	4	13	33	.271	.326	.369	561	152	25	3	8	8	44	81
Not Leadoff	.248	.295	.358	274	68	9	0	7	7	18	52	.263	.318	.382	733	193	34	1	17	17	58	121
Runners On	.204	.252	.290	324	66	10	3	4	54	21	63	.232	.301	.350	934	217	32	12	18	186	94	185
First Base Only	.200	.248	.264	140	28	2	2	1	6	9	25	.216	.279	.315	435	94	13	3	8	25	38	81
Scoring Position	.207	.255	.310	184	38	8	1	3	48	12	38	.246	.319	.381	499	123	19	9	10	161	56	104
Late Innings, Close	.274	.319	.340	106	29	1	0	2	10	8	19	.271	.351	.361	266	72	10	1	4	26	34	41

RBI/Opportunities

Scoring Position	44 / 221	(20%)		144 / 681	(21%)
Scoring Position, 2 Out	15 / 105	(14%)		57 / 304	(19%)
On Third, Less than 2 Out	18 / 36	(50%)		50 / 120	(42%)
RBI in close games / RBI Total	41 / 65	(63%)		146 / 211	(69%)

Jesse Orosco
New York Mets

I find myself continually ruminating about Davey Johnson's hair. Has he just not started to gray or is he a secretive big-time Graecian Formula user? If it's the latter, I'm sure a significant contributor to the condition must be Jesse Orosco.

If you've ever watched Jesse pitch over any length of time, you know what I mean. A typical Jesse Orosco scenario: the Astros are in town and, in the eighth, Bob Ojeda starts to falter and is pulled in favor of Orosco, who inherits a one-run lead with two outs and Billy Doran on second. Jose Cruz is the batter. Big, sweeping curveball at the knees: called strike. Fastball, chest-high, nibbling inside: ball one. Same pitch: ball two. Curve outside at the knees missed: ball three. Fastball down the pipe, fouled back: strike two. Curve at the knees, grounded foul. Johnson's down the runway, sneaking a smoke or chugging Maalox or something, so he misses the fastball inside that sends Cruz on to first. He's hardly settled into his perch on the bench when Glenn Davis whistles a 1–0 single over a leaping Rafael Santana at short, scoring Doran and sending Cruz to second. Kevin Bass swings and misses on a curve at the knees and watches two pitches for balls, one high and tight and the other low and away, before popping out to Hernandez. Orosco strides off the mound with a tie ball game and a hyperventilating manager.

I half-expected Orosco to go in the Kevin McReynolds deal, for if there has ever been a pitcher working in the wrong ballpark, it is Jesse Orosco. Keep in mind that Shea is a natural grass field where most games are played at night, then consider Mr. Orosco's 1986 ERA in the following situations: road vs. home, 0.97—4.15; day vs. night, 0.74—3.02; turf vs. grass, 0.30—3.55. Do we detect a pattern here? Given Orosco's maddening pitching style, his penchant for giving up big runs in close games and Randy Myers' potential as a lefty stopper, I strongly suspect that Jesse will be changing uniforms shortly. Coupled with Frank Cashen's philosophy of trading strength to fill other needs while promoting promising young ballplayers at the same time, and considering Orosco's ineptness at Shea vs. his performance overall, his departure from New York is practically a foregone conclusion.

—Bill Thomas

	1986: Power, Flyball										1985: Power, Flyball									1984: Power, Flyball	

	1986 SEASON											**THREE YEARS (84 – 86)**									
	G	IP	H	BB	SO	SB	CS	W	L	S	ERA	G	IP	H	BB	SO	SB	CS	W	L	S	ERA
Totals	58	81.0	64	35	62	11	0	8	6	21	2.33	172	247.0	188	103	215	21	1	26	18	69	2.55
At Home and on the Road																						
Home	23	34.2	38	15	25	3	0	4	4	7	4.15	77	114.2	109	46	102	6	0	12	11	29	3.37
Road	35	46.1	26	20	37	8	0	4	2	14	0.97	95	132.1	79	57	113	15	1	14	7	40	1.84
During the Day and at Night																						
Day	17	24.1	14	14	17	3	0	2	1	7	0.74	56	83.1	61	36	68	7	0	11	5	21	1.73
Night	41	56.2	50	21	45	8	0	6	5	14	3.02	116	163.2	127	67	147	14	1	15	13	48	2.97
On Grass and on Turf																						
Grass	36	50.2	49	22	36	5	0	6	6	11	3.55	113	160.1	144	71	138	10	0	19	15	42	3.42
Turf	22	30.1	15	13	26	6	0	2	0	10	0.30	59	86.2	44	32	77	11	1	7	3	27	0.93
By Month																						
April	7	9.2	4	6	9	1	0	0	0	3	0.00	21	33.2	18	16	36	3	0	3	1	9	0.80
May	11	15.0	9	8	15	4	0	2	2	5	3.00	25	37.1	30	17	36	5	0	4	4	12	3.13
June	10	10.0	9	9	8	0	0	1	2	3	5.40	31	38.1	40	24	27	0	0	2	5	9	3.52
July	8	11.2	12	2	7	4	0	1	0	2	3.09	30	44.1	31	12	39	7	1	5	1	15	3.05
August	12	17.1	15	6	11	0	0	1	1	4	1.04	32	45.0	33	9	34	0	0	4	3	13	1.60
Sept/Oct	10	17.1	15	4	12	2	0	3	1	4	2.08	33	48.1	36	25	43	6	0	8	4	11	2.98

	vs. Opponent Batters																			

	1986 SEASON											**THREE YEARS (84 – 86)**								
	Ave.	OBP	SLG	AB	H	2B	3B	HR	RBI	BB	SO	Ave.	OBP	SLG	AB	H	2B	3B	HR	RBI	BB	SO
Totals	.217	.304	.305	295	64	8	0	6	29	35	62	.208	.291	.306	903	188	29	1	19	95	103	215
Pitching vs. Left and Right-handed Batters																						
Left	.187	.235	.253	75	14	2	0	1	9	5	24	.188	.237	.213	202	38	2	0	1	18	14	57
Right	.227	.325	.323	220	50	6	0	5	20	30	38	.214	.305	.332	701	150	27	1	18	77	89	158
Situational																						
Bases Empty	.254	.333	.352	142	36	8	0	2	2	17	27	.231	.311	.345	429	99	22	0	9	9	49	101
Leadoff	.228	.323	.351	57	13	1	0	2	2	8	13	.226	.318	.367	177	40	10	0	5	5	23	41
Not Leadoff	.271	.340	.353	85	23	7	0	0	0	9	14	.234	.306	.329	252	59	12	0	4	4	26	60
Runners On	.183	.277	.261	153	28	0	0	4	27	18	35	.188	.273	.270	474	89	7	1	10	86	54	114
First Base Only	.200	.294	.350	60	12	0	0	3	6	7	7	.207	.257	.316	193	40	3	0	6	12	12	41
Scoring Position	.172	.266	.204	93	16	0	0	1	21	11	28	.174	.282	.238	281	49	4	1	4	74	42	73
Late Innings, Close	.239	.330	.352	230	55	8	0	6	28	29	46	.219	.305	.325	723	158	27	1	16	88	87	167

	RBI/Opportunities					
Scoring Position	19 / 134	(14%)		66 / 429	(15%)
Scoring Position, 2 Out	9 / 67	(13%)		25 / 195	(13%)
On Third, Less than 2 Out	10 / 24	(42%)		30 / 83	(36%)
RBI in close games / RBI Total	28 / 29	(97%)		88 / 95	(93%)

Spike Owen
Boston Red Sox

Spike Owen is, beyond any possible doubt, the best defensive shortstop in the American League. He is as overwhelmingly good at the art of catching batted balls and turning them into outs as Don Mattingly is at hitting pitched balls. Like Mattingly, nobody in his league is even close to challenging him.

A shortstop has two jobs—to get to as many balls as he can and to turn them into as many outs as possible. The standards we use to measure these skills are range factor (the number of successful chances he handles per games played) and double plays per 162 games played. In 1985, Spike tied for the lead in range factor with Tony Fernandez with 4.76 and was fifth in the league with 105 DPs per 162 games (Cal Ripken, Fernandez, Schofield and Meacham).

Why, you may wonder, do I claim that Owen was better than Fernandez? Very simple—Frenandez played complete games; Owen didn't. Seattle had two other shortstop prospects that they were trying out; Owen was used 22 times as a defensive replacement. If we recompute things, substituting nine innings played for games (Tim Marcou's Adjusted Range Factor), Owen's range factor jumps to 5.27—38 points better than the #2 man (Glenn Hoffman)

—and he turned 116 DPs per 162 games (fourth behind Ripken, Schofield and Hoffman).

In 1986, three things happened to Owen. He was traded. He battled a series of injuries, which destroyed his ability to hit for either average or power (he batted .262 and slugged .363 for the first four months of the season; .174 and .217 after August 1) and probably cut into his range, too. Third, he led the AL in range factor with a 4.84 figure (16 points ahead of Alan Trammell) and turned an amazing 140 DPs per 162 games. According to Pete Palmer's Linear Weights System, he was the best defensive player in the AL in 1986. Fernandez and Ripken are fine fielders—no denying that. But the statistical evidence is beyond dispute—Owen is the best fielder in the league.

If Spike had stayed healthy, 1986 would have been his best offensive season. He showed signs of being able to hit .270, slug .400 and have a .340 on-base average in Seattle; Fenway appears to help him (he hit .231 in Boston and .131 on the road after the trade), so he may be capable of more now. If so, he'd be a good hitting shortstop; coupled with his defense, he'd be one of the ten best shortstops in baseball.

—Geoff Beckman

	1986 SEASON											THREE YEARS (84 – 86)									
	Ave.	OBP	SLG	AB	H	2B	3B	HR	RBI	BB	SO	Ave.	OBP	SLG	AB	H	2B	3B	HR	RBI	BB	SO
Totals	.231	.300	.309	528	122	24	7	1	45	51	51	.243	.308	.331	1410	343	52	21	10	125	130	141
Batting vs. Left and Right-handed Pitchers																						
Left	.273	.341	.364	121	33	6	1	1	16	12	15	.252	.313	.352	369	93	18	5	3	37	30	42
Right	.219	.287	.292	407	89	18	6	0	29	39	36	.240	.307	.324	1041	250	34	16	7	88	100	99
At Home and on the Road																						
Home	.246	.328	.354	268	66	17	6	0	27	31	28	.247	.316	.344	730	180	30	13	5	65	71	82
Road	.215	.270	.262	260	56	7	1	1	18	20	23	.240	.301	.318	680	163	22	8	5	60	59	59
Facing Groundball Pitchers and Flyball Pitchers																						
Groundball	.194	.252	.273	253	49	10	5	0	22	19	22	.227	.289	.314	643	146	20	12	4	60	54	60
Flyball	.265	.342	.342	275	73	14	2	1	23	32	29	.257	.324	.346	767	197	32	9	6	65	76	81
Facing Finesse Pitchers and Power Pitchers																						
Finesse	.218	.267	.282	308	67	10	5	0	29	22	26	.235	.279	.313	814	191	27	14	3	74	52	69
Power	.250	.343	.345	220	55	14	2	1	16	29	25	.255	.346	.356	596	152	25	7	7	51	78	72
On Grass and on Turf																						
Grass	.217	.297	.262	267	58	7	1	1	19	30	25	.236	.311	.313	581	137	19	7	4	51	63	54
Turf	.245	.303	.356	261	64	17	6	0	26	21	26	.248	.306	.344	829	206	33	14	6	74	67	87
During the Day and at Night																						
Day	.248	.310	.299	157	39	6	1	0	12	15	14	.274	.333	.355	372	102	15	3	3	31	34	37
Night	.224	.295	.313	371	83	18	6	1	33	36	37	.232	.300	.323	1038	241	37	18	7	94	96	104
By Month																						
April	.242	.296	.318	66	16	3	1	0	1	5	7	.226	.291	.282	195	44	7	2	0	7	17	18
May	.230	.323	.391	87	20	8	3	0	5	11	11	.253	.335	.403	233	59	11	9	2	22	28	31
June	.291	.308	.379	103	30	5	2	0	14	3	10	.295	.351	.421	278	82	14	6	3	34	22	22
July	.273	.330	.330	88	24	5	0	0	13	8	9	.280	.331	.352	236	66	12	1	1	23	19	23
August	.163	.241	.214	98	16	2	0	1	5	10	5	.176	.245	.204	250	44	4	0	1	20	23	25
Sept/Oct	.186	.304	.221	86	16	1	1	0	7	14	9	.220	.290	.307	218	48	4	3	3	19	21	22
Situational																						
Bases Empty	.212	.280	.283	307	65	13	3	1	1	28	29	.234	.299	.312	826	193	31	8	6	6	75	89
Leadoff	.185	.257	.250	124	23	4	2	0	0	12	16	.231	.300	.306	337	78	13	3	2	2	33	34
Not Leadoff	.230	.295	.306	183	42	9	1	1	1	16	13	.235	.298	.317	489	115	18	5	4	4	42	55
Runners On	.258	.327	.344	221	57	11	4	0	44	23	22	.257	.322	.358	584	150	21	13	4	119	55	52
First Base Only	.323	.391	.485	99	32	10	3	0	8	11	8	.263	.318	.382	259	68	14	7	1	17	21	16
Scoring Position	.205	.275	.230	122	25	1	1	0	36	12	14	.252	.324	.338	325	82	7	6	3	102	34	36
Late Innings, Close	.160	.232	.200	75	12	3	0	0	3	6	12	.200	.285	.250	220	44	7	2	0	13	25	29
RBI/Opportunities																						
Scoring Position				35 / 182		(19%)									95 / 455		(21%)					
Scoring Position, 2 Out				12 / 86		(14%)									37 / 220		(17%)					
On Third, Less than 2 Out				19 / 39		(49%)									42 / 81		(52%)					
RBI in close games / RBI Total				32 / 45		(71%)									79 / 125		(63%)					

Mike Pagliarulo
New York Yankees

In June, Mike Pagliarulo raised his average into the .280's after getting off to a brutal (.222 for April and May) start. He then went through a lengthy period of illnesses and injuries that cut his average almost 50 points in the final two months of the year. The falling average was bad enough—it was also coupled with a complete loss of power. Pags didn't hit a single homer over the last six weeks of the year and only three doubles. He drew some walks, but it wasn't much compensation overall.

The good news, though, is that the problem is obvious and that it's easy to correct. Mike doesn't have to do anything if he wants to finish stronger in 1987—literally. When Mike made the majors in 1984, he designed a demanding set of daily practice workouts for himself. It helped him without taking away from his play when he was a part-time player (although he's also fallen off at the end of '84 and '85), but it isn't the sort of thing that you keep doing when you become a regular. Doing it even when you have the flu is just lunacy. Former Yankee broadcaster Jim Kaat was of the opinion that Mike hasn't learned to pace himself yet—given the evidence of 1986, I have to agree.

New York has had a lot of trouble with left-handed pitching over the past few seasons and Pagliarulo is very much part of that problem. In 1986, he hit only .198 against lefties. That can't be due to his physical troubles for the simple reason that he hits .193 against them lifetime. Horrifying as it sounds, Pags's 1986 mark against lefties is a career best.

The problem is exacerbated by his lack of power. Mike hit only two homers off lefties in 1986 and has only four in his career. Projected to 600 at-bats, the 1986 figure is seven and the career total is 10. I think that the fact that his 1986 figure is lower than his career stats indicates what effect his workouts had, but that's beside the point—that sort of power production coupled with a .200 average isn't good enough.

The fact that his performance against righties (36 homers per 600 AB over his career; 46 for 1986 alone) accounts for so much of his total offense is threatening Mike's career. New York would prefer to play him every day but, if he doesn't begin hitting lefties before the Yankees find a partner for him, he's liable to be a platoon player for the rest of his career.

—Craig Christmann

	1986 SEASON												THREE YEARS (84 – 86)									
	Ave.	OBP	SLG	AB	H	2B	3B	HR	RBI	BB	SO		Ave.	OBP	SLG	AB	H	2B	3B	HR	RBI	BB	SO
Totals	.238	.316	.464	504	120	24	3	28	71	54	120		.239	.314	.453	1085	259	55	8	54	167	114	252
Batting vs. Left and Right-handed Pitchers																							
Left	.196	.254	.288	163	32	9	0	2	11	11	54		.193	.271	.295	244	47	11	1	4	26	23	80
Right	.258	.344	.548	341	88	15	3	26	60	43	66		.252	.326	.499	841	212	44	7	50	141	91	172
At Home and on the Road																							
Home	.230	.325	.453	243	56	8	2	14	31	31	64		.240	.321	.441	526	126	18	5	26	78	60	130
Road	.245	.307	.475	261	64	16	1	14	40	23	56		.238	.307	.465	559	133	37	3	28	89	54	122
Facing Groundball Pitchers and Flyball Pitchers																							
Groundball	.211	.289	.392	237	50	10	0	11	30	26	53		.230	.306	.413	540	124	21	3	24	79	60	119
Flyball	.262	.339	.528	267	70	14	3	17	41	28	67		.248	.321	.494	545	135	34	5	30	88	54	133
Facing Finesse Pitchers and Power Pitchers																							
Finesse	.239	.309	.478	276	66	12	0	18	42	27	62		.262	.316	.498	614	161	32	4	35	98	48	137
Power	.237	.323	.447	228	54	12	3	10	29	27	58		.208	.310	.395	471	98	23	4	19	69	66	115
On Grass and on Turf																							
Grass	.235	.322	.464	422	99	21	2	24	56	51	101		.239	.316	.455	920	220	47	7	46	139	98	211
Turf	.256	.279	.463	82	21	3	1	4	15	3	19		.236	.302	.442	165	39	8	1	8	28	16	41
During the Day and at Night																							
Day	.212	.300	.429	184	39	3	2	11	25	22	45		.211	.293	.408	370	78	9	2	20	55	41	91
Night	.253	.325	.484	320	81	21	1	17	46	32	75		.253	.324	.477	715	181	46	6	34	112	73	161
By Month																							
April	.213	.319	.426	61	13	4	0	3	7	10	17		.228	.351	.435	92	21	7	0	4	12	18	23
May	.229	.312	.494	83	19	4	0	6	13	9	20		.195	.295	.398	128	25	5	0	7	24	16	31
June	.280	.333	.561	107	30	9	0	7	17	9	25		.266	.332	.508	177	47	13	0	10	24	18	37
July	.325	.371	.602	83	27	2	0	7	19	5	11		.300	.339	.557	210	63	11	2	13	39	11	38
August	.211	.310	.513	76	16	2	3	5	12	10	18		.246	.325	.522	224	55	8	6	14	39	26	52
Sept/Oct	.160	.255	.191	94	15	3	0	0	3	11	29		.189	.265	.303	254	48	11	0	6	29	25	71
Situational																							
Bases Empty	.238	.304	.502	273	65	14	2	18	18	24	65		.230	.299	.440	586	135	27	6	28	28	52	136
Leadoff	.225	.301	.568	111	25	3	1	11	11	12	30		.218	.294	.452	239	52	7	2	15	15	25	55
Not Leadoff	.247	.307	.457	162	40	11	1	7	7	12	35		.239	.302	.432	347	83	20	4	13	13	27	81
Runners On	.238	.328	.420	231	55	10	1	10	53	30	55		.248	.330	.469	499	124	28	2	26	139	62	116
First Base Only	.243	.308	.364	107	26	4	0	3	7	9	25		.245	.296	.466	249	61	14	1	13	32	17	54
Scoring Position	.234	.345	.468	124	29	6	1	7	46	21	30		.252	.361	.472	250	63	14	1	13	107	45	62
Late Innings, Close	.256	.333	.449	78	20	3	0	4	9	8	24		.237	.324	.419	160	38	5	0	8	25	20	46

RBI/Opportunities						
Scoring Position	35 / 172	(20%)		86 / 365	(24%)	
Scoring Position, 2 Out	9 / 68	(13%)		28 / 158	(18%)	
On Third, Less than 2 Out	15 / 33	(45%)		33 / 72	(46%)	
RBI in close games / RBI Total	37 / 71	(52%)		100 / 167	(60%)	

Dave Parker
Cincinnati Reds

Dave Parker is a study in modern controversy. From King Cobra of the Pirates Fam-A-Lee in 1979 to the constant target of abuse from Pirates fans in the early '80s. However, despite subpar performance and physical problems, Parker could rarely be accused of less than full effort.

As the "hometown boy made good" in Cincinnati, Parker was erasing the memories of 1981–83; then, the drug trials of 1985 brought his private life into family rooms across America. That he could play effectively in 1985 was amazing; that he hit .312 with 34 homers and 125 RBIs was incredible.

However, there was more controversy to come. When Dave was not selected as the NL MVP in 1985, his fans cited his Triple Crown stats and claimed persecution. His detractors presented his supposedly subpar outfield play, his poor strikeout/walk numbers, his stolen base percentage, and his GIDP totals.

In 1986, the new Pirate management wanted to renege on Parker's deferred salary payments, and Pirates fans applauded, while Cincinnati fans felt that the Pittsburghers deserved to suffer with the Pirates. After all this, the question is: who is Dave Parker now?

The simple answer is, Dave Parker is still one heck of a ballplayer, though cracks have appeared in his armor. At 35, his speed is gone, his arm is not what it was, and his one-handed "snags" have cost the Reds on occasion. His troubles with balls hit at his legs continue, and the Reds must consider moving him to first base to free an outfield slot for Tracy Jones, Kal Daniels, Paul O'Neill, or Nick Esasky. At the plate, however, he is still the feared Dave Parker.

In 1986, Parker slipped noticeably after a hot start, but his contribution to the Red offense was unquestioned. As usual, Parker hit better with men on than with the bases empty. However, he also hit over .300 with 6 homers when leading off an inning (20 homers in 339 AB in 1984–86). He led the Reds' futile pennant drive with a late season charge.

Parker passed 1000 RBI and 2000 hits in 1986, and should reach 250 homers and 1000 runs scored in 1987. To remain a valuable player, he must become a more patient hitter. Then, if his outfield defense deteriorates further and he fails at first base, he can still DH in the American League.

Just don't count Dave Parker out. The Cobra played in all 162 games last season. They say that work is the best therapy.

—A. S. Nakamura

	1986 SEASON											THREE YEARS (84 – 86)										
	Ave.	OBP	SLG	AB	H	2B	3B	HR	RBI	BB	SO	Ave.	OBP	SLG	AB	H	2B	3B	HR	RBI	BB	SO
Totals	.273	.330	.477	637	174	31	3	31	116	56	126	.290	.341	.481	1879	545	101	7	81	336	149	295
Batting vs. Left and Right-handed Pitchers																						
Left	.302	.325	.513	232	70	13	3	10	49	9	48	.289	.312	.452	640	185	30	4	22	125	21	119
Right	.257	.333	.457	405	104	18	0	21	67	47	78	.291	.355	.496	1239	360	71	3	59	211	128	176
At Home and on the Road																						
Home	.268	.325	.505	313	84	19	2	17	57	28	59	.294	.346	.500	924	272	55	3	43	175	79	139
Road	.278	.335	.451	324	90	12	1	14	59	28	67	.286	.336	.462	955	273	46	4	38	161	70	156
Facing Groundball Pitchers and Flyball Pitchers																						
Groundball	.278	.328	.480	327	91	16	1	16	67	25	59	.282	.329	.446	944	266	47	3	34	178	69	137
Flyball	.268	.332	.474	310	83	15	2	15	49	31	67	.298	.354	.516	935	279	54	4	47	158	80	158
Facing Finesse Pitchers and Power Pitchers																						
Finesse	.287	.335	.484	314	90	14	0	16	63	24	53	.288	.333	.481	1048	302	56	1	48	182	72	135
Power	.260	.325	.471	323	84	17	3	15	53	32	73	.292	.351	.480	831	243	45	6	33	154	77	160
On Grass and on Turf																						
Grass	.284	.352	.463	190	54	5	1	9	34	19	40	.294	.347	.478	565	166	24	1	26	91	43	94
Turf	.268	.320	.483	447	120	26	2	22	82	37	86	.288	.338	.482	1314	379	77	6	55	245	106	201
During the Day and at Night																						
Day	.255	.316	.471	204	52	8	0	12	36	19	42	.285	.347	.494	603	172	35	2	29	122	60	98
Night	.282	.337	.480	433	122	23	3	19	80	37	84	.292	.338	.474	1276	373	66	5	52	214	89	197
By Month																						
April	.286	.315	.557	70	20	4	0	5	14	3	16	.278	.313	.400	230	64	13	0	5	28	12	32
May	.330	.400	.547	106	35	5	0	6	18	13	21	.329	.374	.546	313	103	21	1	15	64	24	40
June	.248	.323	.407	113	28	6	0	4	17	13	22	.275	.345	.459	327	90	15	0	15	56	36	48
July	.293	.352	.596	99	29	6	0	8	25	9	17	.303	.381	.485	303	81	14	2	16	56	23	51
August	.215	.269	.355	121	26	4	2	3	21	9	23	.257	.309	.426	343	88	16	3	12	52	27	64
Sept/Oct	.281	.326	.461	128	36	6	1	6	21	9	27	.328	.374	.543	363	119	22	1	18	80	27	60
Situational																						
Bases Empty	.225	.272	.357	342	77	16	1	9	9	22	67	.256	.298	.423	965	247	56	3	33	33	56	165
Leadoff	.305	.327	.600	95	29	8	1	6	6	3	13	.322	.345	.590	339	109	27	2	20	20	12	46
Not Leadoff	.194	.252	.263	247	48	8	0	3	3	19	54	.220	.274	.332	626	138	29	1	13	13	44	119
Runners On	.329	.393	.617	295	97	15	2	22	107	34	59	.326	.384	.542	914	298	45	4	48	303	93	130
First Base Only	.308	.331	.510	143	44	8	0	7	17	5	28	.322	.350	.521	413	133	23	1	19	48	17	53
Scoring Position	.349	.441	.717	152	53	7	2	15	90	29	31	.329	.408	.559	501	165	22	3	29	255	76	77
Late Innings, Close	.255	.331	.491	110	28	8	0	6	23	13	27	.281	.354	.487	335	94	23	2	14	58	39	63
RBI/Opportunities																						
Scoring Position				65 / 211	(31%)										206 / 678	(30%)						
Scoring Position, 2 Out				28 / 82	(34%)										78 / 285	(27%)						
On Third, Less than 2 Out				25 / 53	(47%)										79 / 144	(55%)						
RBI in close games / RBI Total				84 / 116	(72%)										238 / 336	(71%)						

Larry Parrish
Texas Rangers

Larry Parrish led the major leagues in RBIs per plate appearance in 1986, with 94 RBI in only 524 trips to the plate. It's hard to believe this is the same guy who once hit .307 with 30 homers and a .551 slugging percentage, but knocked in only 82 runs (1979).

Larry's slugging percentage of .509 set a new Ranger record. His 52 walks were also a career high, and his walk average of .101 was a 46% increase over his career average going into 1986. I would peg Parrish's improved plate discipline and his success in avoiding his annual deep slump as the keys to a very successful season.

Parrish's recovery from his serious knee surgery was quite successful. He lost enough speed that he is not likely to ever return to the outfield, but it didn't hurt his bat or his durability. The injury that caused him to miss 27 games was a painful muscle pull around the rib cage.

This Florida boy loves the hot weather. In the last six seasons he has hit 35 points higher in June, July and August compared to the other months (.286 versus .251).

When Larry broke his wrist way back in 1980, it set off an odd pattern where he hit right-handed pitching better than lefties. He has returned to a more normal platoon difference in recent years:

1981-83	BA	SP	1984-86	BA	SP
Lefties	.244	.422	Lefties	.276	.537
Righties	.268	.434	Righties	.272	.446

He also transformed into a very successful situational hitter. Combined with his power, it has made him an ideal RBI man for the middle of the order:

1981-1983	AB	BA	1984-86	AB	BA
Bases empty	748	.259	Bases empty	753	.259
Men on Base	596	.265	Men on base	670	.290
Scoring Pos.	320	.272	Scoring Pos.	375	.312

—Craig Wright

	1986 SEASON											THREE YEARS (84 – 86)										
	Ave.	OBP	SLG	AB	H	2B	3B	HR	RBI	BB	SO	Ave.	OBP	SLG	AB	H	2B	3B	HR	RBI	BB	SO
Totals	.276	.347	.509	464	128	22	1	28	94	52	114	.273	.334	.472	1423	389	75	3	67	246	127	307
Batting vs. Left and Right-handed Pitchers																						
Left	.254	.351	.569	130	33	6	1	11	29	20	33	.276	.350	.537	402	111	22	1	27	79	47	84
Right	.284	.346	.485	334	95	16	0	17	65	32	81	.272	.328	.446	1021	278	53	2	40	167	80	223
At Home and on the Road																						
Home	.289	.354	.533	225	65	11	1	14	45	25	53	.279	.342	.479	723	202	41	2	33	133	67	154
Road	.264	.341	.485	239	63	11	0	14	49	27	61	.267	.327	.464	700	187	34	1	34	113	60	153
Facing Groundball Pitchers and Flyball Pitchers																						
Groundball	.324	.387	.556	207	67	16	1	10	44	23	45	.296	.348	.482	693	205	41	2	28	117	56	129
Flyball	.237	.315	.471	257	61	6	0	18	50	29	69	.252	.322	.462	730	184	34	1	39	129	71	178
Facing Finesse Pitchers and Power Pitchers																						
Finesse	.304	.368	.567	270	82	18	1	17	57	28	50	.275	.329	.487	817	225	46	2	41	151	65	141
Power	.237	.318	.428	194	46	4	0	11	37	24	64	.271	.342	.450	606	164	29	1	26	95	62	166
On Grass and on Turf																						
Grass	.280	.353	.515	396	111	19	1	24	77	46	96	.271	.334	.473	1206	327	65	2	58	209	110	255
Turf	.250	.311	.471	68	17	3	0	4	17	6	18	.286	.336	.465	217	62	10	1	9	37	17	52
During the Day and at Night																						
Day	.320	.378	.650	100	32	6	0	9	28	10	19	.270	.319	.467	304	82	15	0	15	51	23	51
Night	.264	.339	.470	364	96	16	1	19	66	42	95	.274	.338	.473	1119	307	60	3	52	195	104	256
By Month																						
April	.258	.320	.470	66	17	3	1	3	17	7	19	.288	.336	.468	222	64	8	1	10	40	17	44
May	.262	.348	.557	61	16	3	0	5	15	8	17	.229	.300	.394	236	54	12	0	9	36	24	56
June	.182	.200	.386	44	8	0	0	3	5	1	14	.276	.347	.528	254	70	13	0	17	53	25	56
July	.344	.430	.567	90	31	8	0	4	21	14	15	.290	.347	.521	217	63	16	2	10	36	19	40
August	.314	.342	.552	105	33	7	0	6	19	4	25	.306	.345	.500	216	66	15	0	9	39	12	45
Sept/Oct	.235	.350	.459	98	23	1	0	7	17	18	24	.259	.332	.428	278	72	11	0	12	42	30	66
Situational																						
Bases Empty	.252	.325	.512	258	65	13	0	18	18	27	68	.259	.313	.467	753	195	36	2	39	39	56	170
Leadoff	.245	.328	.500	106	26	6	0	7	7	12	24	.246	.302	.448	362	89	20	1	17	17	27	81
Not Leadoff	.257	.323	.520	152	39	7	0	11	11	15	44	.271	.323	.486	391	106	16	1	22	22	29	89
Runners On	.306	.374	.505	206	63	9	1	10	76	25	46	.290	.358	.476	670	194	39	1	28	207	71	137
First Base Only	.210	.262	.380	100	21	2	0	5	12	7	22	.259	.319	.431	297	77	15	0	12	31	25	56
Scoring Position	.396	.466	.623	106	42	7	1	5	64	18	24	.314	.386	.512	373	117	24	1	16	176	46	81
Late Innings, Close	.224	.338	.373	67	15	4	0	2	11	12	20	.252	.340	.459	222	56	13	0	11	40	27	65
RBI/Opportunities																						
Scoring Position				53 / 158		(34%)									146 / 502		(29%)					
Scoring Position, 2 Out				22 / 71		(31%)									48 / 198		(24%)					
On Third, Less than 2 Out				17 / 29		(59%)									60 / 113		(53%)					
RBI in close games / RBI Total				60 / 94		(64%)									159 / 246		(65%)					

Lance Parrish
Detroit Tigers

Lance Parrish was off to another fine season in 1986 when he was disabled in late July by a back injury. While the injury did not require surgery, Parrish was out of the lineup for the rest of the year. Parrish and his doctors claim that his injury is not catching-induced nor baseball related. It is, however, difficult to see how Lance can continue to be a regular catcher if he has chronic back problems, especially since he suffered from the same problems in 1985. He has been put on a exercise regimen to strengthen his back muscles and control the pain, but the acid test will come next summer when his employer expects him to catch 120 games in return for their million dollars.

With 1039 career games at catcher now, Parrish is approaching the point where any serious injuries could end his career behind the plate. While he hits like an All-Star as a catcher, the only other positions he could play would be first base or designated hitter, and his offensive production at either of those positions would be merely acceptable. Lance can't run well anymore, totaling only 7 doubles and triples last year in 327 at-bats. He did notably improve his patience at the plate last year, drawing 38 walks, only a half-dozen less than he would normally draw in 500–600 at-bats.

In the past, Lance has hit lefties much better than righties, but he reversed that pattern in 1986, perhaps due to the problems with his back. Some years ago, after encountering serious back problems, Bobby Grich changed his batting stance and also reversed his career pattern for lefty/righty differentials.

Parrish fits the stereotype of a clean-up hitter (big, strong, tremendous power) so well that Tigers Manager Sparky Anderson bats him religiously in the #4 spot. This would seem to be a mistake, as he must then bat Darrell Evans #5; frequently, Sparky has batted [DA] even lower in the line-up. Given Darrell's power and ability to draw walks, and the fact that Evans's slugging average is comparable to Parrish's, but Lance's on-base is normally much lower and his batting average is only a little higher, a more sensible order would be to bat Evans clean-up and Parrish behind him.

—Gary Gillette

	1986 SEASON											THREE YEARS (84 – 86)										
	Ave.	OBP	SLG	AB	H	2B	3B	HR	RBI	BB	SO	Ave.	OBP	SLG	AB	H	2B	3B	HR	RBI	BB	SO
Totals	.257	.340	.483	327	84	6	1	22	62	38	83	.255	.313	.466	1454	371	49	4	83	258	120	293
Batting vs. Left and Right-handed Pitchers																						
Left	.262	.328	.410	122	32	1	1	5	20	13	23	.276	.347	.498	482	133	17	3	28	83	55	79
Right	.254	.347	.527	205	52	5	0	17	42	25	60	.245	.296	.450	972	238	32	1	55	175	65	214
At Home and on the Road																						
Home	.247	.341	.411	158	39	2	0	8	27	20	29	.268	.332	.451	697	187	25	3	32	115	64	129
Road	.266	.340	.550	169	45	4	1	14	35	18	54	.243	.295	.480	757	184	24	1	51	143	56	164
Facing Groundball Pitchers and Flyball Pitchers																						
Groundball	.250	.333	.461	128	32	1	1	8	24	15	35	.265	.316	.455	664	176	23	2	33	117	48	135
Flyball	.261	.345	.497	199	52	5	0	14	38	23	48	.247	.311	.475	790	195	26	2	50	141	72	158
Facing Finesse Pitchers and Power Pitchers																						
Finesse	.273	.353	.545	198	54	3	0	17	39	20	46	.269	.324	.491	823	221	28	1	51	158	66	141
Power	.233	.322	.388	129	30	3	1	5	23	18	37	.238	.298	.433	631	150	21	3	32	100	54	152
On Grass and on Turf																						
Grass	.253	.343	.460	265	67	5	1	16	49	33	55	.265	.325	.485	1206	320	41	4	72	223	104	220
Turf	.274	.329	.581	62	17	1	0	6	13	5	28	.206	.255	.371	248	51	8	0	11	35	16	73
During the Day and at Night																						
Day	.188	.288	.375	96	18	0	0	6	14	12	31	.228	.284	.378	460	105	18	0	17	65	35	106
Night	.286	.363	.528	231	66	6	1	16	48	26	52	.268	.326	.506	994	266	31	4	66	193	85	187
By Month																						
April	.155	.241	.254	71	11	1	0	2	9	8	21	.217	.268	.368	212	46	5	0	9	38	15	41
May	.315	.411	.620	92	29	2	1	8	22	13	27	.308	.357	.527	279	86	9	2	16	49	21	63
June	.263	.339	.516	95	25	3	0	7	21	11	20	.274	.327	.477	321	88	14	0	17	57	25	58
July	.275	.346	.493	69	19	0	0	5	10	6	15	.201	.279	.402	229	46	4	0	14	34	22	44
August	.000	.000	.000	0	0	0	0	0	0	0	0	.260	.333	.581	215	56	11	2	18	51	25	46
Sept/Oct	.000	.000	.000	0	0	0	0	0	0	0	0	.247	.294	.414	198	49	6	0	9	29	12	41
Situational																						
Bases Empty	.266	.351	.538	169	45	2	1	14	14	21	43	.253	.309	.483	739	187	28	2	46	46	57	151
Leadoff	.244	.337	.500	78	19	2	0	6	6	11	19	.216	.275	.410	356	77	16	1	17	17	27	75
Not Leadoff	.286	.363	.571	91	26	0	1	8	8	10	24	.287	.341	.551	383	110	12	1	29	29	30	76
Runners On	.247	.330	.424	158	39	4	0	8	48	17	40	.257	.317	.448	715	184	21	2	37	212	63	142
First Base Only	.232	.306	.464	56	13	1	0	4	9	6	12	.272	.316	.519	283	77	8	1	20	49	16	46
Scoring Position	.255	.342	.402	102	26	3	0	4	39	11	28	.248	.318	.400	432	107	13	1	17	163	47	96
Late Innings, Close	.180	.344	.180	50	9	0	0	0	4	13	17	.243	.317	.412	226	55	5	0	11	37	24	50

RBI/Opportunities					
Scoring Position	32 / 134	(24%)		132 / 589	(22%)
Scoring Position, 2 Out	13 / 69	(19%)		53 / 259	(20%)
On Third, Less than 2 Out	10 / 23	(43%)		49 / 112	(44%)
RBI in close games / RBI Total	33 / 62	(53%)		170 / 258	(66%)

Tony Pena
Pittsburgh Pirates

The Pirates have come to a crossroad in dealing with Tony Pena. On the one hand, management fully realizes his value, both on the playing field and as a drawing card for a team that needs all the help it can get in attracting fans. Ever since his debut in the strike-shortened 1981 season (he did appear briefly in 1980), Tony's popularity has steadily increased. Though not all that powerful, he is one of the Pirates' most potent bats, year-in and year-out. His enthusiasm and love for the game are readily apparent, and he's like a cat coming from behind the plate on a steal attempt. How he does that from his otherwise indescribable banana-split receiving position is beyond me.

If there is a paradox about Tony, it's his performance at bat. Every year he has two seasons, separated roughly by the All-Star break. If an uninformed observer were to see him just about any time during the first half of the season, he would be justified in thinking that a late-inning pinch hitter is forthcoming, and an option to Hawaii is not out of the question. Then comes June or July and one could easily make the mistaken assumption that this guy has got to be in contention for the batting title. My opinion is that the Jekyll-Hyde tendencies can be explained by Tony's need for bat control: early in the year, he wants to hit anything, while he's a more patient and controlled hitter in the latter half of the season.

So he's good and he's immensely popular. Thus the Pirate management's quandary: 1987 is Tony Pena's option year. And to keep him, the Pirates are going to have to shell out some big bucks, given the number of teams that are literally drooling over the prospect of adding him to their roster. And there's the rub. For the baseball gods have not been kind to Pittsburgh; since the tightly-knit, hugely popular World Championship team of 1979, the club has been beset by overpaid, undermotivated, petulant players, dwindling and increasing antagonistic attendance, Chuck Tanner's insufferable optimism, severe drug allegations, a concerted effort to transfer the franchise elsewhere, and changes in ownership and field management. The Pirates, it is clear, will not be able to realistically compete for Pena's services.

That, coupled with Pena's desire to play for a competing team, dictates that Pittsburgh trade him now rather than lose him and receive nothing in return. Bye, Tony! I'll miss ya!

—Bill Thomas

	1986 SEASON											THREE YEARS (84 – 86)										
---	Ave.	OBP	SLG	AB	H	2B	3B	HR	RBI	BB	SO	Ave.	OBP	SLG	AB	H	2B	3B	HR	RBI	BB	SO
Totals	.288	.356	.406	510	147	26	2	10	52	53	69	.274	.324	.397	1602	439	80	6	35	189	118	215
Batting vs. Left and Right-handed Pitchers																						
Left	.333	.405	.471	174	58	8	2	4	15	20	18	.305	.358	.446	475	145	24	2	13	51	38	52
Right	.265	.330	.372	336	89	18	0	6	37	33	51	.261	.310	.376	1127	294	56	4	22	138	80	163
At Home and on the Road																						
Home	.298	.384	.404	255	76	12	0	5	25	35	29	.274	.333	.384	799	219	38	4	14	92	69	87
Road	.278	.326	.408	255	71	14	2	5	27	18	40	.274	.316	.410	803	220	42	2	21	97	49	128
Facing Groundball Pitchers and Flyball Pitchers																						
Groundball	.278	.331	.388	227	63	11	1	4	21	17	30	.295	.346	.417	756	223	39	4	15	92	57	89
Flyball	.297	.375	.420	283	84	15	1	6	31	36	39	.255	.305	.379	846	216	41	2	20	97	61	126
Facing Finesse Pitchers and Power Pitchers																						
Finesse	.299	.335	.436	298	89	19	2	6	29	17	34	.266	.307	.383	954	254	46	4	19	98	55	106
Power	.274	.382	.363	212	58	7	0	4	23	36	35	.285	.349	.418	648	185	34	2	16	91	63	109
On Grass and on Turf																						
Grass	.255	.315	.336	137	35	5	0	2	14	12	21	.250	.298	.367	420	105	19	0	10	45	28	70
Turf	.300	.370	.432	373	112	21	2	8	38	41	48	.283	.334	.408	1182	334	61	6	25	144	90	145
During the Day and at Night																						
Day	.312	.406	.413	138	43	6	1	2	13	22	19	.278	.340	.378	474	132	21	1	8	56	44	62
Night	.280	.336	.403	372	104	20	1	8	39	31	50	.272	.317	.405	1128	307	59	5	27	133	74	153
By Month																						
April	.246	.333	.361	61	15	4	0	1	4	8	11	.267	.336	.410	195	52	10	0	6	16	20	28
May	.215	.295	.354	79	17	3	1	2	9	8	15	.242	.280	.365	260	63	10	2	6	35	12	42
June	.255	.324	.398	98	25	8	0	2	13	10	14	.276	.323	.402	301	83	18	1	6	34	21	47
July	.284	.352	.383	81	23	2	0	2	7	9	10	.298	.352	.404	282	84	12	0	6	26	24	30
August	.356	.420	.489	90	32	4	1	2	12	10	10	.283	.332	.394	279	79	12	2	5	41	20	40
Sept/Oct	.347	.394	.426	101	35	5	0	1	7	8	9	.274	.321	.407	285	78	18	1	6	37	21	28
Situational																						
Bases Empty	.312	.382	.479	263	82	15	1	9	9	30	40	.276	.330	.414	877	242	47	4	22	22	70	120
Leadoff	.339	.383	.446	112	38	6	0	2	2	8	16	.293	.338	.438	365	107	22	2	9	9	25	51
Not Leadoff	.291	.382	.503	151	44	9	1	7	7	22	24	.264	.324	.396	512	135	25	2	13	13	45	69
Runners On	.263	.327	.328	247	65	11	1	1	43	23	29	.272	.317	.377	725	197	33	2	13	167	48	95
First Base Only	.333	.381	.422	90	30	3	1	1	5	6	8	.282	.318	.387	287	81	13	1	5	18	12	32
Scoring Position	.223	.297	.274	157	35	8	0	0	38	17	21	.265	.317	.370	438	116	20	1	8	149	36	63
Late Innings, Close	.281	.328	.316	114	32	4	0	0	10	8	17	.256	.307	.338	328	84	15	0	4	36	25	42

RBI/Opportunities				
Scoring Position	38 / 205	(19%)	131 / 579	(23%)
Scoring Position, 2 Out	13 / 88	(15%)	47 / 254	(19%)
On Third, Less than 2 Out	12 / 35	(34%)	44 / 97	(45%)
RBI in close games / RBI Total	33 / 52	(63%)	132 / 189	(70%)

Terry Pendleton
St. Louis Cardinals

It's going to be a shame if Terry Pendleton doesn't develop into some sort of offensive threat, because he is quickly becoming one of the most exciting defensive players in the game. Offensively, however, he appears to be on the path toward becoming the black Ken Reitz. After a promising rookie season in 1984 Pendleton has turned in nearly two identical offensive seasons—identically unimpressive, that is. He hasn't hit for average (.240 in '85, .239 in '86), hasn't gotten on base (OBPs of .285 and .279), and he hasn't hit with any power (.306 slugging for both seasons; even Reitz topped that). About the only thing he has done on offense is steal bases, which he has gotten pretty good at. That does put him one up on Reitz, at least; if Reitz had ever been on base ahead of Coleman, he would have had cleat marks up his back. But 24 stolen bases do not make an offensive player, and Pendleton has got to contribute something with the bat in '87 if he's going to be in the lineup every day.

Despite the similarity between Pendleton's last two seasons, he completely reversed his splits over the period. In '85 he hit better on the road (.251–.228) while in 1986 he hit for a higher average at home (.255–.223). In '85 Pendleton was a better hitter on grass than turf (.255–.234), but

last season he was more productive on the carpet (.255–.185). In '85 he preferred righthanded pitching (.245–.228), so of course he hit lefthanders better in '86 (.278–.217). Pendleton may put it all together yet and develop into a productive offensive player, but the highest batting average among the above splits is .278, and a player with a .168 secondary average needs to hit higher than .278 to be an offensive asset.

Pendleton had six game-winning RBIs in '86, with three of them coming in the eighth inning or later. He's always seemed to get his share of big hits, even when he's not producing—Charlie Leibrandt can attest to that. Two of Pendleton's seven career homers are grand slams, both coming in 1985.

Pendleton batted .333 and slugged .417 against the Braves in 1986; that was the the only team against which he hit over .300. He did drive in fourteen runs against the Phillies on eighteen base hits, including six doubles and a triple. He hit only .223 against West Division opponents in '86, including a combined .179 mark against the three West Coast teams.

—Russ Eagle

	1986 SEASON											THREE YEARS (84 – 86)										
	Ave.	OBP	SLG	AB	H	2B	3B	HR	RBI	BB	SO	Ave.	OBP	SLG	AB	H	2B	3B	HR	RBI	BB	SO
Totals	.239	.279	.306	578	138	26	5	1	59	34	59	.255	.296	.327	1399	357	58	11	7	161	87	166
Batting vs. Left and Right-handed Pitchers																						
Left	.278	.325	.364	209	58	12	3	0	27	16	16	.256	.292	.338	468	120	24	4	2	55	26	45
Right	.217	.253	.274	369	80	14	2	1	32	18	43	.255	.298	.322	931	237	34	7	5	106	61	121
At Home and on the Road																						
Home	.255	.294	.336	286	73	15	4	0	28	17	26	.265	.306	.351	699	185	33	9	3	81	45	74
Road	.223	.264	.277	292	65	11	1	1	31	17	33	.246	.286	.304	700	172	25	2	4	80	42	92
Facing Groundball Pitchers and Flyball Pitchers																						
Groundball	.263	.298	.333	300	79	17	2	0	32	16	29	.277	.312	.344	692	192	32	4	2	84	37	74
Flyball	.212	.259	.277	278	59	9	3	1	27	18	30	.233	.282	.311	707	165	26	7	5	77	50	92
Facing Finesse Pitchers and Power Pitchers																						
Finesse	.244	.270	.315	324	79	17	3	0	37	12	25	.246	.272	.303	783	193	28	5	2	79	30	73
Power	.232	.290	.295	254	59	9	2	1	22	22	34	.266	.325	.359	616	164	30	6	5	82	57	93
On Grass and on Turf																						
Grass	.185	.245	.230	135	25	3	0	1	8	11	16	.230	.281	.270	322	74	7	0	2	34	24	43
Turf	.255	.290	.330	443	113	23	5	0	51	23	43	.263	.301	.344	1077	283	51	11	5	127	63	123
During the Day and at Night																						
Day	.243	.288	.297	202	49	9	1	0	14	12	25	.272	.317	.333	493	134	19	1	3	53	32	64
Night	.237	.274	.311	376	89	17	4	1	45	22	34	.246	.285	.325	906	223	39	10	4	108	55	102
By Month																						
April	.194	.280	.224	67	13	2	0	0	1	8	13	.214	.286	.271	140	30	5	0	1	10	14	31
May	.230	.289	.310	87	20	7	0	0	9	8	9	.255	.298	.318	192	49	12	0	0	28	13	20
June	.216	.256	.270	111	24	6	0	0	9	5	15	.185	.224	.241	162	30	6	0	1	14	7	20
July	.250	.280	.298	84	21	4	0	0	13	5	9	.289	.316	.336	232	67	8	0	1	24	12	25
August	.252	.289	.357	115	29	3	3	1	15	6	7	.238	.286	.335	319	76	11	4	4	43	22	37
Sept/Oct	.272	.282	.342	114	31	4	2	0	12	2	6	.297	.329	.381	354	105	16	7	0	42	19	33
Situational																						
Bases Empty	.240	.269	.312	321	77	14	3	1	1	12	35	.255	.291	.328	737	188	34	4	4	4	36	90
Leadoff	.262	.290	.333	126	33	5	2	0	0	5	15	.279	.301	.355	287	80	13	3	1	1	9	37
Not Leadoff	.226	.256	.297	195	44	9	1	1	1	7	20	.240	.285	.311	450	108	21	1	3	3	27	53
Runners On	.237	.290	.300	257	61	12	2	0	58	22	24	.255	.302	.326	662	169	24	7	3	157	51	76
First Base Only	.259	.292	.306	85	22	4	0	0	2	4	3	.246	.282	.288	236	58	7	0	1	6	12	21
Scoring Position	.227	.289	.297	172	39	8	2	0	56	18	21	.261	.313	.347	426	111	17	7	2	151	39	55
Late Innings, Close	.215	.280	.273	121	26	7	0	0	9	11	14	.257	.312	.342	257	66	15	2	1	21	21	39

RBI/Opportunities						
Scoring Position	53 / 224	(24%)		139 / 564	(25%)	
Scoring Position, 2 Out	18 / 100	(18%)		50 / 232	(22%)	
On Third, Less than 2 Out	24 / 34	(71%)		57 / 102	(56%)	
RBI in close games / RBI Total	38 / 59	(64%)		98 / 161	(61%)	

Gary Pettis
California Angels

Gary Pettis is, and with good reason, generally regarded as the finest defensive outfielder in baseball today. In 1986 he ran down 462 fly balls, the most of any major league outfielder. To this point, his offensive skills have not matched his defensive ones, but his overall value is such that he isn't in any danger of losing the opportunity to hit better.

Whenever Pettis' offensive game is discussed, the first thing that is mentioned is the strikeouts. A slightly built man with speed to burn, Pettis looks like a man who should choke up and swat at the ball like a ping pong player, but that's not his style. He has, however, made excellent progress insofar as the strikeouts are concerned, cutting them down from 29% of his at bats in 1984 to 23% in 1986, and raising his batting average 31 points to .258. While people like to talk about Matty Alou and one or two other odd cases, the reality is that you probably could not name a case in which a player started out striking out in 30% of his at bats, then suddenly stopped doing that and became a .300 hitter. The skills required to hit .300 in the major leagues cannot be created out of thin air; a 29-year old player, like Pettis, has spent years refining the skills that he has. It is almost impossible to radically re-define a player's skills after the age of 24 or 25. The progress that Pettis has made is as much as can be realistically hoped for.

Somewhat saving Pettis as an offensive player is that the strikeouts are accompanied by enough walks to give him a decent on-base percentage. In 1986 he walked 69 times for an OBP of .339, which is pretty fair for a player who is no threat in the batter's box and a big threat on the bases. Pettis scored 93 runs and pilfered 50 bases.

Figures compiled by Dennis Bretz show that in 1986 Pettis hit much better when at the bottom of the order than when at the top. When batting eighth he hit .296 (16 for 54) and when batting ninth he hit .280 (40/153), but when hitting leadoff he hit just .248 (59/238) and when hitting second hit just .243 (18/74). This data is surprising in that one would presume that Mauch bats him leadoff against pitchers that he should be able to hit.

—Bill James and Dennis Bretz

	1986 SEASON											THREE YEARS (84 – 86)										
	Ave.	OBP	SLG	AB	H	2B	3B	HR	RBI	BB	SO	Ave.	OBP	SLG	AB	H	2B	3B	HR	RBI	BB	SO
Totals	.258	.339	.343	539	139	23	4	5	58	69	132	.249	.340	.324	1379	343	44	18	8	119	193	372
Batting vs. Left and Right-handed Pitchers																						
Left	.278	.328	.369	176	49	6	2	2	22	14	35	.269	.342	.336	449	121	14	5	2	41	50	95
Right	.248	.344	.331	363	90	17	2	3	36	55	97	.239	.340	.318	930	222	30	13	6	78	143	277
At Home and on the Road																						
Home	.235	.320	.283	251	59	7	1	1	19	32	63	.236	.330	.296	615	145	15	8	2	52	88	164
Road	.278	.356	.396	288	80	16	3	4	39	37	69	.259	.349	.347	764	198	29	10	6	67	105	208
Facing Groundball Pitchers and Flyball Pitchers																						
Groundball	.283	.357	.412	240	68	12	2	5	28	28	56	.247	.336	.343	659	163	22	10	7	59	88	172
Flyball	.237	.326	.288	299	71	11	2	0	30	41	76	.250	.345	.307	720	180	22	8	1	60	105	200
Facing Finesse Pitchers and Power Pitchers																						
Finesse	.265	.333	.359	343	91	19	2	3	27	35	74	.257	.337	.333	787	202	29	8	5	55	95	194
Power	.245	.349	.316	196	48	4	2	2	31	34	58	.238	.345	.313	592	141	15	10	3	64	98	178
On Grass and on Turf																						
Grass	.249	.331	.330	458	114	18	2	5	48	59	113	.248	.339	.322	1135	282	32	14	8	103	158	299
Turf	.309	.385	.420	81	25	5	2	0	10	10	19	.250	.346	.332	244	61	12	4	0	16	35	73
During the Day and at Night																						
Day	.274	.335	.348	164	45	9	0	1	17	17	35	.282	.367	.379	390	110	15	7	3	44	55	96
Night	.251	.341	.341	375	94	14	4	4	41	52	97	.236	.330	.302	989	233	29	11	5	75	138	276
By Month																						
April	.208	.262	.247	77	16	3	0	0	4	6	17	.245	.342	.333	237	58	8	5	1	17	36	63
May	.260	.272	.364	77	20	2	0	2	13	2	18	.210	.288	.276	210	44	4	2	2	19	24	59
June	.268	.377	.330	97	26	4	1	0	5	17	26	.267	.352	.330	270	72	7	2	2	18	36	81
July	.261	.349	.359	92	24	4	1	1	13	13	25	.260	.355	.324	173	45	6	1	1	19	24	44
August	.268	.366	.309	97	26	4	0	0	7	15	21	.231	.336	.279	247	57	8	2	0	16	38	63
Sept/Oct	.273	.371	.434	99	27	6	2	2	16	16	25	.277	.366	.397	242	67	11	6	2	30	35	62
Situational																						
Bases Empty	.237	.306	.307	342	81	12	3	2	2	34	86	.240	.331	.306	895	215	30	10	3	3	119	245
Leadoff	.255	.322	.321	184	47	5	2	1	1	18	45	.240	.342	.305	492	118	14	6	2	2	75	136
Not Leadoff	.215	.287	.291	158	34	7	1	1	1	16	41	.241	.317	.308	403	97	16	4	1	1	44	109
Runners On	.294	.392	.406	197	58	11	1	3	56	35	46	.264	.358	.357	484	128	14	8	5	116	74	127
First Base Only	.247	.351	.272	81	20	2	0	0	0	13	15	.221	.323	.266	199	44	3	3	0	4	30	45
Scoring Position	.328	.420	.500	116	38	9	1	3	56	22	31	.295	.382	.421	285	84	11	5	5	112	44	82
Late Innings, Close	.217	.291	.290	69	15	3	1	0	5	8	18	.226	.322	.288	177	40	5	3	0	14	25	50
RBI/Opportunities																						

	1986 SEASON		THREE YEARS (84 – 86)	
Scoring Position	51 / 179	(28%)	99 / 411	(24%)
Scoring Position, 2 Out	18 / 90	(20%)	48 / 209	(23%)
On Third, Less than 2 Out	24 / 36	(67%)	38 / 73	(52%)
RBI in close games / RBI Total	35 / 58	(60%)	74 / 119	(62%)

Ken Phelps
Seattle Mariners

Ken Phelps' career in Seattle could be summed up in two chapters. Before DW. After DW. The arrival of Dick Williams as the new Mariner manager had a big impact on the 32-year old first baseman who had never really had much chance to play on an everyday basis for the Mariners or any other club. At the start of the 1986 season, Kenny's major league service totaled a mere three years, 144 days.

After Williams arrived, he waited just one game before inserting the lefty Phelps into the lineup as the DH. It seemed only logical since righthander Doyle Alexander was pitching. It was a lineup move that was never changed, and a common sense decision that a lot of Mariner fans had been waiting a very long time for. Chuck Cottier, the former manager, had used righty hitter Gorman Thomas as the permanent DH against all pitchers.

After several excellent outings, the normally quiet bench warmer spoke out. It was that often-heard "Play me or trade me" statement. The Mariners chose to play Phelps and eventually released Gorman Thomas, eating a big contract in the process. With a chance to play on a regular basis, "Digger" was able to finally amass some numbers that were quite impressive and indicative of the power and discipline he possesses. In 344 AB he hit 24 homers, second only to Presley (27 in 616 AB) and Tartabull (25 in 511 AB). Stop and figure out those ratios and then decide who's the big gun on the Mariner team. Phelps averaged one home run for every 14.3 AB, one of the best HR ratios in the majors. Among Mariners with 60 or more at bats, he led the club in on base percentage (.405) and slugging percentage (.526).

Phelps' low average (.247) but high OBP is explained by his ability to draw the BB. His stance is close to the plate and, on any inside pitch, he throws his arms in the air and draws his body into a question mark, making the pitch appear to nearly hit him. That, coupled with an excellent knowledge of the strike zone, put him among the league leaders in BB even though he had fewer plate appearances. His ratio of walks to AB was far the highest among the league leaders.

If the Mariners had a secret weapon in their arsenal, it was Ken Phelps. Too bad it took so long to find a commanding officer who issued orders to take this high powered artillery out of mothballs.

—Merrianna McCully

	1986 SEASON											THREE YEARS (84 – 86)										
	Ave.	OBP	SLG	AB	H	2B	3B	HR	RBI	BB	SO	Ave.	OBP	SLG	AB	H	2B	3B	HR	RBI	BB	SO
Totals	.247	.406	.526	344	85	16	4	24	64	88	96	.239	.386	.515	749	179	28	4	57	139	173	202
Batting vs. Left and Right-handed Pitchers																						
Left	.237	.373	.390	59	14	4	1	1	13	10	18	.211	.343	.339	109	23	6	1	2	20	17	31
Right	.249	.413	.554	285	71	12	3	23	51	78	78	.244	.393	.545	640	156	22	3	55	119	156	171
At Home and on the Road																						
Home	.287	.445	.626	174	50	8	3	15	40	47	42	.261	.397	.568	391	102	15	3	33	82	84	102
Road	.206	.364	.424	170	35	8	1	9	24	41	54	.215	.374	.458	358	77	13	1	24	57	89	100
Facing Groundball Pitchers and Flyball Pitchers																						
Groundball	.231	.397	.503	169	39	5	1	13	30	46	39	.239	.383	.514	356	85	9	1	29	69	82	83
Flyball	.263	.414	.549	175	46	11	3	11	34	42	57	.239	.389	.517	393	94	19	3	28	70	91	119
Facing Finesse Pitchers and Power Pitchers																						
Finesse	.262	.402	.545	191	50	10	1	14	37	44	41	.269	.393	.598	435	117	18	1	41	95	87	93
Power	.229	.411	.503	153	35	6	3	10	27	44	55	.197	.377	.401	314	62	10	3	16	44	86	109
On Grass and on Turf																						
Grass	.178	.339	.333	135	24	3	0	6	12	31	43	.194	.359	.408	289	56	5	0	19	35	72	83
Turf	.292	.447	.651	209	61	13	4	18	52	57	53	.267	.403	.583	460	123	23	4	38	104	101	119
During the Day and at Night																						
Day	.184	.336	.368	87	16	4	0	4	12	19	24	.225	.362	.503	187	42	7	0	15	31	38	46
Night	.268	.428	.580	257	69	12	4	20	52	69	72	.244	.394	.520	562	137	21	4	42	108	135	156
By Month																						
April	.150	.346	.450	20	3	0	0	2	3	6	9	.214	.377	.595	42	9	1	0	5	8	10	15
May	.303	.477	.818	33	10	0	1	5	10	11	9	.224	.369	.612	98	22	0	1	12	24	23	30
June	.250	.400	.500	68	17	5	0	4	11	16	15	.237	.378	.513	152	36	9	0	11	28	34	37
July	.257	.448	.543	70	18	5	0	5	13	23	21	.268	.439	.570	149	40	9	0	12	31	42	35
August	.221	.346	.384	86	19	3	1	3	13	15	25	.229	.352	.419	179	41	5	1	9	24	32	48
Sept/Oct	.269	.419	.597	67	18	3	2	5	14	17	17	.240	.393	.488	129	31	4	2	8	24	32	37
Situational																						
Bases Empty	.240	.362	.500	192	46	9	1	13	13	33	47	.243	.360	.511	411	100	15	1	31	31	66	102
Leadoff	.253	.374	.530	83	21	5	0	6	6	15	22	.222	.348	.438	176	39	8	0	10	10	31	51
Not Leadoff	.229	.354	.477	109	25	4	1	7	7	18	25	.260	.370	.566	235	61	7	1	21	21	35	51
Runners On	.257	.453	.559	152	39	7	3	11	51	55	49	.234	.414	.521	338	79	13	3	26	108	107	100
First Base Only	.243	.418	.457	70	17	1	1	4	10	19	23	.240	.409	.500	150	36	4	1	11	24	41	39
Scoring Position	.268	.479	.646	82	22	6	2	7	41	36	26	.229	.418	.537	188	43	9	2	15	84	66	61
Late Innings, Close	.208	.408	.509	53	11	1	0	5	9	16	17	.211	.390	.488	123	26	1	0	11	21	34	35
RBI/Opportunities																						

	1986 SEASON			THREE YEARS (84 – 86)		
Scoring Position	29 / 140	(21%)		58 / 307	(19%)	
Scoring Position, 2 Out	9 / 66	(14%)		15 / 142	(11%)	
On Third, Less than 2 Out	10 / 27	(37%)		24 / 57	(42%)	
RBI in close games / RBI Total	43 / 64	(67%)		96 / 139	(69%)	

Tony Phillips
Oakland A's

After an incredible start in 1986, during which he hit for the cycle, was named American League player of the week, and had one of the highest on-base percentages in baseball, Tony Phillips fell to earth with a thud. However, using Tony in the lead-off spot was an experiment which didn't turn out too badly, in spite of his terrible June. Although he did not hit at all for a period of about six weeks, Tony continued to draw bases on balls at an impressive rate. Tony's 76 walks (in only 118 games) was fifteenth highest in the American League. His 76 runs score would project to 104 runs in 162 games. Tony actually had a higher on-base-percentage in 1986 than Rickey Henderson (.367 to .358). Since Tony did not walk much at all in previous years, with only 55 in 1984–5 combined, it is apparent that he worked on his lead-off skills in winter ball. He has transformed himself from a free swinger to a disciplined hitter in less than a year.

Tony has had a lot of trouble with injuries, mostly leg and ankle problems, averaging only 350 at bats in the last three years. Possibly due to these injuries, Tony is a tentative baserunner, in spite of his speed. He stole 15 bases in twenty-five attempts, for a 60% average. He has not learned to read a pitcher's move or to get a good jump off of first base.

Defensively, only Tony Bernazard and Hal Reynolds of Seattle had higher range factors among regular second basemen in the League. Tony turns the double play well, and is not intimidated by runners barreling in. He has an accurate arm, and can play shortstop and third base in a pinch. He tied the American League record for assists by a second baseman with 12 on July 6 versus Milwaukee (Rijo's slider was working that day).

Tony's main competition for the last couple of years had been Donnie Hill, who was traded to the White Sox in the winter of 1986, so this is the first year he will go to spring training with a guaranteed position. If Tony can deal with his inconsistent hitting as well as he dealt with his inability to get on base, he could be one of the best lead-off men in baseball. On the other hand, the trade of Hill puts the pressure on Phillips to come through. The A's have not had a dependable second baseman since they traded Phil Garner ten years ago, and no second basemen are charging through the system. For the A's to contend, Phillips almost needs to have the best season of his career.

—Susan Nelson

	1986 SEASON											THREE YEARS (84 – 86)										
	Ave.	OBP	SLG	AB	H	2B	3B	HR	RBI	BB	SO	Ave.	OBP	SLG	AB	H	2B	3B	HR	RBI	BB	SO
Totals	.256	.367	.345	441	113	14	5	5	52	76	82	.264	.344	.368	1053	278	50	10	13	106	131	202
Batting vs. Left and Right-handed Pitchers																						
Left	.321	.443	.455	134	43	5	2	3	18	29	22	.322	.394	.443	345	111	18	3	6	42	42	41
Right	.228	.331	.296	307	70	9	3	2	34	47	60	.236	.320	.331	708	167	32	7	7	64	89	161
At Home and on the Road																						
Home	.234	.362	.322	214	50	8	1	3	32	42	39	.238	.324	.339	513	122	25	3	7	59	66	101
Road	.278	.373	.366	227	63	6	4	2	20	34	43	.289	.364	.394	540	156	25	7	6	47	65	101
Facing Groundball Pitchers and Flyball Pitchers																						
Groundball	.266	.373	.335	203	54	7	2	1	27	34	35	.255	.333	.345	498	127	23	5	4	48	58	94
Flyball	.248	.362	.353	238	59	7	3	4	25	42	47	.272	.355	.387	555	151	27	5	9	58	73	108
Facing Finesse Pitchers and Power Pitchers																						
Finesse	.256	.351	.333	258	66	7	2	3	25	39	39	.267	.335	.368	589	157	31	4	7	50	63	92
Power	.257	.388	.361	183	47	7	3	2	27	37	43	.261	.356	.366	464	121	19	6	6	56	68	110
On Grass and on Turf																						
Grass	.248	.358	.332	355	88	12	3	4	44	60	63	.261	.341	.362	900	235	43	6	12	94	111	170
Turf	.291	.404	.395	86	25	2	2	1	8	16	19	.281	.366	.399	153	43	7	4	1	12	20	32
During the Day and at Night																						
Day	.268	.397	.369	179	48	6	3	2	24	37	36	.254	.339	.366	382	97	16	6	5	46	50	79
Night	.248	.345	.328	262	65	8	2	3	28	39	46	.270	.348	.368	671	181	34	4	8	60	81	123
By Month																						
April	.315	.457	.356	73	23	3	0	0	5	17	16	.303	.415	.354	99	30	5	0	0	5	17	21
May	.288	.359	.407	118	34	4	2	2	17	12	17	.297	.362	.396	192	57	6	2	3	21	19	28
June	.188	.300	.232	112	21	1	2	0	11	18	21	.194	.282	.235	196	38	4	2	0	13	24	38
July	.253	.367	.394	99	25	5	0	3	14	19	17	.281	.377	.413	196	55	15	1	3	25	32	32
August	.256	.400	.333	39	10	1	1	0	5	10	11	.228	.321	.323	167	38	7	3	1	13	24	36
Sept/Oct	.000	.000	.000	0	0	0	0	0	0	0	0	.296	.339	.468	203	60	13	2	6	29	15	47
Situational																						
Bases Empty	.223	.338	.307	287	64	5	2	5	5	49	56	.251	.331	.355	674	169	28	6	10	10	80	129
Leadoff	.236	.355	.326	178	42	5	1	3	3	32	33	.253	.344	.355	332	84	14	1	6	6	45	61
Not Leadoff	.202	.310	.275	109	22	0	1	2	2	17	23	.249	.318	.354	342	85	14	5	4	4	35	68
Runners On	.318	.419	.416	154	49	9	3	0	47	27	26	.288	.367	.391	379	109	22	4	3	96	51	73
First Base Only	.250	.354	.286	56	14	2	0	0	1	7	11	.276	.352	.345	145	40	8	1	0	4	15	23
Scoring Position	.357	.455	.490	98	35	7	3	0	46	20	15	.295	.376	.419	234	69	14	3	3	92	36	50
Late Innings, Close	.308	.432	.385	65	20	3	1	0	9	15	8	.296	.402	.414	162	48	12	2	1	17	30	32

RBI/Opportunities				
Scoring Position	43 / 145	(30%)	81 / 329	(25%)
Scoring Position, 2 Out	17 / 62	(27%)	30 / 145	(21%)
On Third, Less than 2 Out	12 / 24	(50%)	26 / 54	(48%)
RBI in close games / RBI Total	26 / 52	(50%)	59 / 106	(56%)

Ted Power
Cincinnati Reds

Ted Power was on his way to becoming an ex-major-leaguer last August. The right-handed stopper of 1984–85 had been rocked repeatedly throughout 1986, and the Reds' fans were calling for his scalp. A quick glance at his "Late Innings, Close" stat line clearly shows that he needed to be used differently. With the development of Rob Murphy and Ron Robinson as complements to ace southpaw John Franco, Power was seeing almost no action in tight games.

Power's role had been stripped from him, much as he had replaced Tom Hume in 1983 upon his arrival from the Dodgers. In 1984–85, Power was 17–13 (38 saves). Combined with Franco's 18–5 (16 saves), they gave the Reds arguably the best relief tandem in the NL. Yet, Power had never been afforded his fair share of the credit, as his critics pointed to his negative statistics, such as a subpar strikeout-to-walk ratio. He had worse won-lost records and higher ERAs than Franco, who, coincidentally, had followed Power over from the Dodgers organization. Overlooked was Power's deadliness against right-handed hitters, as well as his strong overall performance.

As September began, the Reds still had faint hopes of catching the Astros, but their makeshift starting rotation was one man short. Power, at the time, was 4–6 with one save in 48 appearances, so Pete Rose made a critical decision to start Power and was rewarded with vintage Power pitching. Ted won his last six decisions, striking out 43 and walking 16 in 56 innings, turning in an ERA of 2.43. He had always pitched well late in the season, so his resurgence might have been predicted. Power was rewarded with the promise of the opportunity to retain a starting role in 1987.

Power is 31; this will be his final chance to remain an established big-league pitcher, so motivation won't be a problem. However, the pressure on him to produce immediately will be considerable, and like most power pitchers, April is not his best month.

Nevertheless, if he can make the transition from 70 games per year to 220 innings per year, the Reds will have a place for Power. His home/road statistics are nearly identical, and he appears to do very well on road turf, at least in the spacious parks where his fly-ball tendencies are favored. Finally, an experienced relief pitcher is a valuable commodity. Despite any arguments to the contrary, Ted Power has been an effective pitcher.

—A. S. Nakamura

1986: Power, Flyball   **1985: Power, Flyball**   **1984: Power, Flyball**

	1986 SEASON											THREE YEARS (84 – 86)										
	G	IP	H	BB	SO	SB	CS	W	L	S	ERA	G	IP	H	BB	SO	SB	CS	W	L	S	ERA
Totals	56	129.0	115	52	95	9	10	10	6	1	3.70	198	317.2	273	143	218	23	13	27	19	39	3.14
At Home and on the Road																						
Home	32	69.1	67	25	52	5	5	6	2	0	3.38	109	171.2	161	71	114	13	8	14	10	20	3.15
Road	24	59.2	48	27	43	4	5	4	4	1	4.07	89	146.0	112	72	104	10	5	13	9	19	3.14
During the Day and at Night																						
Day	20	45.2	40	24	33	0	5	2	2	1	4.53	67	103.0	91	57	69	4	6	8	4	14	3.67
Night	36	83.1	75	28	62	9	5	8	4	0	3.24	131	214.2	182	86	149	19	7	19	15	25	2.89
On Grass and on Turf																						
Grass	14	39.0	34	22	27	0	4	2	3	1	4.85	50	87.0	74	47	57	3	4	8	6	11	3.72
Turf	42	90.0	81	30	68	9	6	8	3	0	3.20	148	230.2	199	96	161	20	9	19	13	28	2.93
By Month																						
April	7	6.0	13	5	6	1	0	0	2	0	6.00	27	32.2	40	19	23	2	1	1	3	3	4.68
May	12	16.0	13	7	14	2	3	2	1	0	3.94	34	49.2	29	20	39	6	3	3	1	7	2.17
June	10	11.2	19	9	6	1	0	1	2	1	7.71	34	48.0	47	28	31	2	0	4	7	7	4.12
July	10	18.1	12	5	9	0	0	1	0	0	3.44	32	47.0	35	20	25	2	0	3	1	6	2.49
August	9	21.1	19	10	17	4	1	0	1	0	4.22	33	45.2	49	24	35	9	3	5	3	2	4.53
Sept/Oct	8	55.2	39	16	43	1	6	6	0	0	2.43	38	94.2	73	32	65	2	6	11	4	14	2.28

vs. Opponent Batters

	1986 SEASON												THREE YEARS (84 – 86)									
	Ave.	OBP	SLG	AB	H	2B	3B	HR	RBI	BB	SO		Ave.	OBP	SLG	AB	H	2B	3B	HR	RBI	BB	SO
Totals	.245	.318	.371	469	115	16	2	13	65	52	95		.238	.319	.334	1148	273	43	5	19	146	143	218
Pitching vs. Left and Right-handed Batters																							
Left	.263	.344	.404	228	60	10	2	6	38	29	41		.255	.351	.376	529	135	24	5	10	71	81	91
Right	.228	.293	.340	241	55	6	0	7	27	23	54		.223	.290	.297	619	138	19	0	9	75	62	127
Situational																							
Bases Empty	.249	.311	.342	269	67	10	0	5	5	24	46		.233	.305	.313	588	137	21	1	8	8	61	104
Leadoff	.288	.333	.398	118	34	7	0	2	2	8	19		.271	.334	.359	262	71	14	0	3	3	25	41
Not Leadoff	.219	.293	.298	151	33	3	0	3	3	16	27		.202	.282	.276	326	66	7	1	5	5	36	63
Runners On	.240	.328	.410	200	48	6	2	8	60	28	49		.243	.332	.355	560	136	22	4	11	138	82	114
First Base Only	.244	.306	.449	78	19	1	0	5	10	6	18		.258	.329	.388	209	54	7	1	6	14	20	38
Scoring Position	.238	.340	.385	122	29	5	2	3	50	22	31		.234	.334	.336	351	82	15	3	5	124	62	76
Late Innings, Close	.353	.424	.529	85	30	3	0	4	19	12	11		.266	.349	.373	485	129	19	3	9	74	68	77

RBI/Opportunities

Scoring Position	44 / 197	(22%)	111 / 561	(20%)
Scoring Position, 2 Out	19 / 87	(22%)	45 / 243	(19%)
On Third, Less than 2 Out	14 / 37	(38%)	44 / 113	(39%)
RBI in close games / RBI Total	33 / 65	(51%)	88 / 146	(60%)

Jim Presley
Seattle Mariners

Jim Presley in 1986 substantially repeated and perhaps improved upon his fine 1985 season, thus establishing himself as one of the top half-dozen third baseman in the major leagues. In 1985 Presley hit .275 with 33 doubles and 28 homers. In 1986 he essentially matched those figures, but hit much better with runners in scoring position to improve his RBI count to 107, up by 27. His improvements were but subtle, even debatable, but he clearly established that his fine previous season represented a true level of ability.

It is generally agreed that a de facto redefinition of the strike zone before the 1986 season, intended to help the hitters, made the strike zone smaller. Presley didn't seem to appreciate the effort: he hit just .205 in April and struck out 30 times, leading the Mariners on the well-publicized hunt for the strikeout record. (His career batting average in April is just .207, so maybe he's just not an April person.) When Dick Williams arrived he made a direct effort to get the Mariners to shorten their strokes in certain situations. While Presley continued to strike out with impressive frequency, ending the year with 172 strikeouts (he struck out only a hundred times in 1985) his performance as a situation hitter did improve dramatically. With runners in scoring position he improved from .273 to .299, while his average in the late innings of close games improved by over a hundred points. In addition to the increase in RBI, he cut his double play balls from 29 to 18.

Presley has been described as a young Mike Schmidt, which is not strictly accurate. Schmidt when he came up was fast, while Presley is quite slow. Schmidt one time struck out 180 times in a season, but with 101 walks. Presley struck out 172 times and walked 32 times. It is enough to say that Presley is an impressive young power-hitting third baseman who strikes out a lot.

However, despite the lack of speed, Presley is a fine third baseman with an excellent arm. In 1986 he was second to Gold Glove Gary Gaetti in assists, total chances and double plays, and committed just fifteen errors in 155 games.

Presley entered baseball at 17, and is just 25 now. If he can control the strikeouts just a little, he might well be one of the top RBI men of the next decade.

—Bill James

	1986 SEASON												THREE YEARS (84 – 86)										
	Ave.	OBP	SLG	AB	H	2B	3B	HR	RBI	BB	SO		Ave.	OBP	SLG	AB	H	2B	3B	HR	RBI	BB	SO
Totals	.265	.303	.463	616	163	33	4	27	107	32	172		.262	.302	.460	1438	377	78	6	65	227	82	335
Batting vs. Left and Right-handed Pitchers																							
Left	.323	.367	.506	158	51	9	1	6	23	11	49		.298	.342	.496	399	119	21	2	18	62	27	91
Right	.245	.281	.448	458	112	24	3	21	84	21	123		.248	.286	.447	1039	258	57	4	47	165	55	244
At Home and on the Road																							
Home	.307	.348	.549	319	98	25	2	16	60	18	84		.274	.318	.480	741	203	48	3	33	116	46	165
Road	.219	.254	.370	297	65	8	2	11	47	14	88		.250	.284	.439	697	174	30	3	32	111	36	170
Facing Groundball Pitchers and Flyball Pitchers																							
Groundball	.247	.295	.415	275	68	18	2	8	41	15	75		.258	.305	.417	648	167	36	2	21	98	42	149
Flyball	.279	.309	.501	341	95	15	2	19	66	17	97		.266	.299	.496	790	210	42	4	44	129	40	186
Facing Finesse Pitchers and Power Pitchers																							
Finesse	.250	.284	.420	352	88	21	3	11	49	16	87		.255	.290	.440	819	209	49	3	32	115	41	157
Power	.284	.327	.519	264	75	12	1	16	58	16	85		.271	.317	.488	619	168	29	3	33	112	41	178
On Grass and on Turf																							
Grass	.214	.258	.395	220	47	5	1	11	37	13	60		.237	.273	.427	539	128	20	2	26	85	28	129
Turf	.293	.328	.500	396	116	28	3	16	70	19	112		.277	.319	.481	899	249	58	4	39	142	54	206
During the Day and at Night																							
Day	.278	.331	.530	151	42	7	2	9	31	9	40		.281	.324	.526	342	96	18	3	20	67	20	76
Night	.260	.294	.441	465	121	26	2	18	76	23	132		.256	.295	.440	1096	281	60	3	45	160	62	259
By Month																							
April	.205	.244	.308	78	16	2	0	2	9	3	30		.207	.268	.400	150	31	5	0	8	22	12	42
May	.306	.318	.500	108	33	9	0	4	19	2	29		.300	.324	.498	203	61	16	0	8	30	7	45
June	.318	.392	.692	107	34	8	1	10	29	10	23		.316	.375	.632	228	72	17	2	17	49	19	51
July	.211	.216	.385	109	23	6	2	3	12	1	31		.254	.289	.424	295	75	13	2	11	34	14	75
August	.283	.336	.404	99	28	4	1	2	15	9	22		.242	.274	.385	252	61	14	2	6	37	12	52
Sept/Oct	.252	.290	.443	115	29	4	0	6	23	7	37		.248	.284	.435	310	77	13	0	15	55	18	70
Situational																							
Bases Empty	.254	.291	.452	323	82	18	2	14	14	15	89		.263	.294	.462	780	205	41	3	36	36	32	181
Leadoff	.269	.301	.500	130	35	10	1	6	6	4	24		.271	.290	.474	329	89	18	2	15	15	7	59
Not Leadoff	.244	.284	.420	193	47	8	1	8	8	11	65		.257	.298	.452	451	116	23	1	21	21	25	122
Runners On	.276	.315	.474	293	81	15	2	13	93	17	83		.261	.310	.459	658	172	37	3	29	191	50	154
First Base Only	.252	.299	.430	135	34	6	0	6	17	7	34		.237	.277	.420	312	74	12	0	15	36	15	64
Scoring Position	.297	.329	.513	158	47	9	2	7	76	10	49		.283	.338	.494	346	98	25	3	14	155	35	90
Late Innings, Close	.303	.347	.596	89	27	5	0	7	24	6	22		.242	.299	.427	211	51	9	0	10	33	17	55

RBI/Opportunities					
Scoring Position	63 / 203	(31%)	129 / 473	(27%)
Scoring Position, 2 Out	29 / 98	(30%)	55 / 223	(25%)
On Third, Less than 2 Out	18 / 37	(49%)	41 / 88	(47%)
RBI in close games / RBI Total	72 / 107	(67%)	134 / 227	(59%)

Kirby Puckett
Minnesota Twins

A few notes about Kirby . . .

1) The controversy about Puckett concerns whether or not he should hit leadoff. As a leadoff man, Kirby has two drawbacks—his on-base percentage is not exceptionally good, inasmuch as he rarely walks, and his newfound power is wasted in the leadoff spot. So he has both the wrong weakness and the wrong strength for the spot. On the other hand, he runs reasonable well and hits .300.

2) Kirby's walk frequency, despite the increase in power, actually went down last year.

3) Over the entire period of his career, Kirby has done an excellent job of delivering runners from scoring position. His record of driving in 30% of runners from scoring position with two out is exceptional and contrasts with 21% for Kent Hrbek, 15% for Brunansky and 20% for Gaetti. This might be another reason not to hit him leadoff—but somebody's got to, and the Twins simply don't have a leadoff hitter.

4) Kirby hits very well with runners on first base, which is common for a left-handed hitter but not common for a right-hander. That he continued to do this is an indication that he continued to go to right field when there was an advantage to be gained by it.

5) In the last few years there have been a number of players with what we might call "bowling ball bodies," of whom Puckett and Tony Gwynn are the most notable. One thing that is good about this is that, watching Kirby, you can understand how Hack Wilson could have been a good ballplayer and could have run well. Just looking at the photos of Wilson, I could never quite believe that he actually ran well. Having seen Kirby, I can visualize Wilson in motion so much better.

6) Puckett hit 17 of his 31 homers last year on the road, but his average was 80 points higher at home and his career average is 72 points higher in Minnesota than it is on the road.

7) Kirby has a career slugging percentage of .474 with men on base, as opposed to .398 with the bases empty. Although he has hit 19 of his 35 homers with no one on, as a leadoff man he has almost two-thirds of his at-bats in that condition.

—Bill James

	1986 SEASON											THREE YEARS (84 – 86)										
	Ave.	OBP	SLG	AB	H	2B	3B	HR	RBI	BB	SO	Ave.	OBP	SLG	AB	H	2B	3B	HR	RBI	BB	SO
Totals	.328	.366	.537	680	223	37	6	31	96	34	99	.304	.340	.424	1928	587	78	24	35	200	91	255
Batting vs. Left and Right-handed Pitchers																						
Left	.325	.364	.524	166	54	11	2	6	19	9	26	.333	.362	.472	564	188	28	10	10	61	24	68
Right	.329	.367	.541	514	169	26	4	25	77	25	73	.293	.331	.405	1364	399	50	14	25	139	67	187
At Home and on the Road																						
Home	.367	.405	.584	346	127	21	6	14	51	16	53	.340	.378	.468	974	331	47	15	16	107	49	129
Road	.287	.326	.488	334	96	16	0	17	45	18	46	.268	.301	.379	954	256	31	9	19	93	42	126
Facing Groundball Pitchers and Flyball Pitchers																						
Groundball	.317	.369	.514	290	92	14	5	11	42	20	32	.298	.339	.415	920	274	33	15	15	90	51	107
Flyball	.336	.364	.554	390	131	23	1	20	54	14	67	.311	.341	.433	1008	313	45	9	20	110	40	148
Facing Finesse Pitchers and Power Pitchers																						
Finesse	.312	.357	.539	388	121	21	5	19	48	21	46	.297	.331	.425	1081	321	46	16	20	100	45	113
Power	.349	.379	.534	292	102	16	1	12	48	13	53	.314	.351	.424	847	266	32	8	15	100	46	142
On Grass and on Turf																						
Grass	.287	.322	.496	254	73	14	0	13	39	13	38	.281	.311	.393	722	203	27	6	14	74	31	100
Turf	.352	.392	.561	426	150	23	6	18	57	21	61	.318	.357	.443	1206	384	51	18	21	126	60	155
During the Day and at Night																						
Day	.318	.366	.507	201	64	15	1	7	24	9	32	.292	.336	.385	558	163	25	3	7	55	29	76
Night	.332	.366	.549	479	159	22	5	24	72	25	67	.309	.342	.440	1370	424	53	21	28	145	62	179
By Month																						
April	.396	.433	.747	91	36	6	1	8	16	4	10	.363	.389	.593	182	66	9	3	9	33	6	19
May	.345	.392	.569	116	40	5	0	7	22	8	12	.324	.365	.451	306	99	10	4	7	39	17	37
June	.301	.333	.366	123	37	6	1	0	6	4	16	.291	.317	.360	350	102	13	4	1	21	10	31
July	.324	.354	.602	108	35	8	2	6	17	5	18	.280	.319	.413	339	95	16	4	7	34	19	53
August	.357	.408	.574	115	41	8	1	5	15	9	21	.310	.357	.415	352	109	12	5	5	32	23	55
Sept/Oct	.268	.295	.433	127	34	4	1	5	20	4	22	.291	.321	.401	399	116	18	4	6	41	16	60
Situational																						
Bases Empty	.325	.366	.518	446	145	28	2	18	18	23	66	.293	.327	.398	1263	370	54	11	19	19	56	167
Leadoff	.344	.385	.526	253	87	12	2	10	10	13	29	.300	.337	.393	761	228	26	6	11	11	37	87
Not Leadoff	.301	.341	.508	193	58	16	0	8	8	10	37	.283	.312	.406	502	142	28	5	8	8	19	80
Runners On	.333	.366	.573	234	78	9	4	13	78	11	33	.326	.364	.474	665	217	24	13	16	181	35	88
First Base Only	.354	.379	.616	99	35	2	3	6	16	3	9	.347	.388	.466	268	93	6	4	6	17	13	24
Scoring Position	.319	.357	.541	135	43	7	1	7	62	8	24	.312	.347	.479	397	124	18	9	10	164	22	64
Late Innings, Close	.308	.364	.484	91	28	1	0	5	14	6	10	.297	.343	.406	256	76	2	4	6	35	14	41

RBI/Opportunities					
Scoring Position	49 / 169	(29%)	140 / 498	(28%)
Scoring Position, 2 Out	25 / 73	(34%)	66 / 217	(30%)
On Third, Less than 2 Out	12 / 28	(43%)	43 / 87	(49%)
RBI in close games / RBI Total	61 / 96	(64%)	124 / 200	(62%)

Dan Quisenberry
Kansas City Royals

Dan Quisenberry in 1986 endured the most disappointing season of his major league career. After leading the American League in saves for four straight seasons, Quisenberry was able to save only twelve games. Some of the decline was his fault, some wasn't. During one 40-day stretch, Quisenberry saved every game that he had a chance to save—two. The Royals weren't ahead often enough to provide regular work for one relief ace, and at times were impatiently trying to feed two of them, Quisenberry and Farr. Yet, for whatever reason, Quisenberry was not as sharp as he had been in other years.

Quisenberry pitched seven times in April, with an ERA of 0.00. He hit a rough patch in May, but no rougher than he has hit many times before, yet this time the Royals seemed to lose confidence in him. They seemed to be afraid to let him face a left-handed hitter. Quisenberry does have an unusual platoon effect. Over a three year period left-handers have hit .295 against him, right-handers only .243.

I trace a good portion of Quisenberry's loss in effectiveness over the last two seasons to an inexplicable decision to stop using the knuckleball. Quisenberry did get beat with the knuckler once or twice, and apparently decided that he didn't want to get beat with a pitch that wasn't his best. But the idea is not to get beat, at all, and Quiz's knuckler was throwing the lefties off-stride enough to damage their timing—a critical piece of the puzzle in his case. Another possibility is that Sundberg doesn't like to call the knuckleball.

Despite Quisenberry's off season, the Royals did not lose an inordinate number of games in which they were ahead late. If they had won every game in which they had a lead through six, they still wouldn't have been anywhere near Texas, let alone California.

Quisenberry has never been tried as a starter, but if they're afraid to let him face a lefty with a game on the line, maybe it's time to consider this. It's my belief that Quisenberry would be an effective starter. With few walks, few homers and many double play balls, he'd beat you even if you hit .300 against him. In any role, his ERA would be below 3.00—and there's got to be some way that a pitcher like that can help you.

—Bill James

1986: Finesse, Groundball **1985: Finesse, Groundball** **1984: Finesse, Groundball**

	G	IP	H	BB	SO	SB	CS	W	L	S	ERA		G	IP	H	BB	SO	SB	CS	W	L	S	ERA
					1986 SEASON										**THREE YEARS (84 – 86)**								
Totals	62	81.1	92	24	36	5	5	3	7	12	2.77		218	339.2	355	52	131	16	10	17	19	93	2.57
												At Home and on the Road											
Home	27	36.2	36	11	15	1	2	2	3	2	2.45		111	170.1	174	25	65	4	7	11	7	46	2.38
Road	35	44.2	56	13	21	4	3	1	4	10	3.02		107	169.1	181	27	66	12	3	6	12	47	2.76
												During the Day and at Night											
Day	15	21.2	24	7	13	0	3	0	1	5	1.25		58	87.0	95	18	33	3	5	5	5	22	2.90
Night	47	59.2	68	17	23	5	2	3	6	7	3.32		160	252.2	260	34	98	13	5	12	14	71	2.46
												On Grass and on Turf											
Grass	26	32.2	45	10	17	3	2	0	3	7	3.03		86	137.1	152	23	56	11	2	4	11	37	2.69
Turf	36	48.2	47	14	19	2	3	3	4	5	2.59		132	202.1	203	29	75	5	8	13	8	56	2.49
												By Month											
April	7	9.2	9	0	6	1	1	0	0	3	0.00		26	41.1	42	5	18	2	1	3	3	12	1.96
May	10	12.2	20	5	5	1	3	0	1	0	4.97		36	57.2	51	9	23	1	3	2	3	13	2.81
June	10	14.2	13	4	7	0	1	0	0	5	0.61		36	55.2	58	9	17	2	2	2	1	17	1.94
July	11	13.2	20	7	4	2	0	0	3	1	5.27		40	58.1	77	10	21	4	2	1	5	18	3.55
August	11	15.0	10	5	8	0	0	1	1	2	1.20		38	60.2	55	11	25	3	2	3	4	17	2.23
Sept/Oct	13	15.2	20	3	6	1	0	2	2	1	4.02		42	66.0	72	8	27	4	0	3	3	16	2.73

vs. Opponent Batters

	Ave.	OBP	SLG	AB	H	2B	3B	HR	RBI	BB	SO		Ave.	OBP	SLG	AB	H	2B	3B	HR	RBI	BB	SO
					1986 SEASON											**THREE YEARS (84 – 86)**							
Totals	.291	.342	.348	316	92	8	2	2	42	24	36		.270	.298	.357	1313	355	42	6	20	151	52	131
												Pitching vs. Left and Right-handed Batters											
Left	.310	.380	.379	145	45	3	2	1	19	18	14		.295	.332	.394	691	204	30	4	10	72	40	48
Right	.275	.308	.322	171	47	5	0	1	23	6	22		.243	.259	.317	622	151	12	2	10	79	12	83
												Situational											
Bases Empty	.283	.314	.342	152	43	4	1	1	1	6	13		.266	.281	.357	703	187	20	4	12	12	14	62
Leadoff	.309	.338	.353	68	21	1	1	0	0	3	4		.250	.263	.368	288	72	10	3	6	6	5	20
Not Leadoff	.262	.295	.333	84	22	3	0	1	1	3	9		.277	.294	.349	415	115	10	1	6	6	9	42
Runners On	.299	.365	.354	164	49	4	1	1	41	18	23		.275	.316	.357	610	168	22	2	8	139	38	69
First Base Only	.246	.281	.295	61	15	1	1	0	1	2	8		.285	.294	.376	242	69	9	2	3	11	2	18
Scoring Position	.330	.408	.388	103	34	3	0	1	40	16	15		.269	.329	.345	368	99	13	0	5	128	36	51
Late Innings, Close	.317	.383	.359	142	45	4	1	0	28	15	22		.270	.301	.347	836	226	26	4	10	116	37	97

RBI/Opportunities

Scoring Position	39 / 162	(24%)		118 / 522	(23%)
Scoring Position, 2 Out	19 / 78	(24%)		58 / 249	(23%)
On Third, Less than 2 Out	15 / 32	(47%)		40 / 90	(44%)
RBI in close games / RBI Total	28 / 42	(67%)		116 / 151	(77%)

Tim Raines
Montreal Expos

Tim Raines enjoyed his greatest season in 1986, winning the batting championship, leading the NL in on-base percentage with .413 and placing 10th in slugging percentage (.476). Raines' batting average has consistently moved up since 1982, the year he had the drug problem: .279 in '82, then .298, .309, .320 and .334. Even back in '82, he was the National League's best leadoff man, and he's improved every year since then. Raines and Rickey Henderson are probably the greatest leadoff men in the history of the game; but unlike Rickey, Tim's skills are being wasted, as the Expos continually fail to exploit his enormous leadoff skills. Last year, for example, he scored only 91 runs while his stats projected that he should have scored 124. If he had been in the Yankee lineup instead, Raines would have scored the same number of runs (130) as Henderson; Rickey was also projected to score 124. Thus, despite having his best year, Raines failed to surpass 100 runs for the first time since 1982.

Raines' leadoff skills are enhanced by the fact that he's the greatest percentage base-stealer in the game, maybe the best ever. His 1986 stolen base data was an exact copy of '85—70 steals in 79 attempts for an amazing 89% success

race. Lifetime he's stolen 454 bases and been successful 87% of the time. Montreal fans understandably want him to run more, arguing that he has the opportunity to steal 100 or more bases. Raines admits that this is true, but prefers not to steal so often, fearing that the physical pain associated with stealing would detract from the rest of his game. Anyone who's seen Raines—or Henderson or Vince Coleman—is tempted to agree. Whether consciously or not, Raines appears to have picked 70 steals as a compromise between a one-dimensional achievement and staying healthy enough to excel in other areas. This type of concern for delivering a complete performance speaks well for him. (After all, this isn't football.)

Defensively, Raines is better than many people think. That includes the Expos' brass, who decided he was a horrible centerfielder and that they needed Herm Winningham instead. Tim's stats reveal that he's good in both center and left. His arm is poor, but that aspect of his game has been overrated, since he has the strong-armed Hubie Brooks to help him. Raines had 13 assists last year, the second highest total for NL outfielders.

—Marco Bresba

	1986 SEASON										THREE YEARS (84 – 86)										
	Ave.	OBP	SLG	AB	H	2B	3B	HR	RBI	BB	SO	Ave.	OBP	SLG	AB	H	2B	3B	HR	RBI	BB	SO
Totals	.334	.413	.476	580	194	35	10	9	62	78	60	.321	.403	.462	1777	570	103	32	28	163	246	189
Batting vs. Left and Right-handed Pitchers																						
Left	.315	.382	.453	181	57	9	2	4	28	20	17	.299	.366	.446	552	165	26	8	13	64	60	57
Right	.343	.427	.486	399	137	26	8	5	34	58	43	.331	.420	.469	1225	405	77	24	15	99	186	132
At Home and on the Road																						
Home	.326	.409	.450	282	92	17	3	4	36	39	28	.317	.406	.450	865	274	47	19	10	78	127	90
Road	.342	.417	.500	298	102	18	7	5	26	39	32	.325	.401	.474	912	296	56	13	18	85	119	99
Facing Groundball Pitchers and Flyball Pitchers																						
Groundball	.348	.418	.518	276	96	20	6	5	34	34	28	.325	.402	.471	849	276	51	17	13	83	110	80
Flyball	.322	.409	.438	304	98	15	4	4	28	44	32	.317	.405	.454	928	294	52	15	15	80	136	109
Facing Finesse Pitchers and Power Pitchers																						
Finesse	.326	.396	.435	340	111	16	3	5	40	38	27	.315	.391	.443	1032	325	49	13	19	106	127	95
Power	.346	.436	.533	240	83	19	7	4	22	40	33	.329	.420	.489	745	245	54	19	9	57	119	94
On Grass and on Turf																						
Grass	.335	.425	.445	155	52	9	1	2	13	25	16	.332	.418	.482	479	159	30	3	12	55	73	56
Turf	.334	.409	.487	425	142	26	9	7	49	53	44	.317	.398	.455	1298	411	73	29	16	108	173	133
During the Day and at Night																						
Day	.351	.444	.525	202	71	14	6	3	21	35	21	.341	.429	.490	637	217	33	16	10	63	101	68
Night	.325	.396	.450	378	123	21	4	6	41	43	39	.310	.389	.446	1140	353	70	16	18	100	145	121
By Month																						
April	.270	.382	.473	74	20	7	1	2	4	14	5	.300	.382	.443	237	71	16	3	4	20	33	23
May	.347	.443	.520	98	34	5	3	2	8	17	13	.287	.393	.445	272	78	10	6	7	31	45	36
June	.358	.402	.526	95	34	8	1	2	16	7	13	.333	.392	.470	300	100	20	3	5	33	31	34
July	.360	.398	.530	100	36	3	4	2	13	7	10	.316	.393	.446	316	100	15	7	4	21	39	32
August	.307	.412	.396	101	31	7	1	0	13	17	7	.343	.437	.469	318	109	23	4	3	30	52	23
Sept/Oct	.348	.431	.420	112	39	5	0	1	8	16	12	.335	.415	.491	334	112	19	9	5	28	46	41
Situational																						
Bases Empty	.334	.413	.491	371	124	28	6	6	6	49	38	.326	.402	.480	1170	382	81	24	17	17	144	117
Leadoff	.347	.404	.511	190	66	13	3	4	4	17	21	.318	.388	.466	635	202	40	15	8	8	69	67
Not Leadoff	.320	.423	.470	181	58	15	3	2	2	32	17	.336	.419	.497	535	180	41	9	9	9	75	50
Runners On	.335	.413	.450	209	70	7	4	3	56	29	22	.310	.406	.427	607	188	22	8	11	146	102	72
First Base Only	.333	.371	.488	84	28	4	3	1	6	4	6	.355	.394	.500	262	93	12	4	6	20	16	27
Scoring Position	.336	.438	.424	125	42	3	1	2	50	25	16	.275	.413	.371	345	95	10	4	5	126	86	45
Late Innings, Close	.339	.441	.452	115	39	5	1	2	10	20	15	.335	.425	.447	322	108	18	3	4	29	49	36
RBI/Opportunities																						
Scoring Position				45 / 174		(26%)									117 / 515		(23%)					
Scoring Position, 2 Out				15 / 77		(19%)									43 / 230		(19%)					
On Third, Less than 2 Out				18 / 31		(58%)									44 / 90		(49%)					
RBI in close games / RBI Total				41 / 62		(66%)									105 / 163		(64%)					

Rafael Ramirez
Atlanta Braves

1986 was a transition year for Rafael Ramirez. He went from a full-time shortstop to a utility player, splitting time at shortstop and third base, and appearing sporadically in the outfield.

Much has been made in sabermetric publications in the past of Ramirez's inadequacies. Year after year his secondary average is at the bottom of the league; his errors are always at the top. He should not be a regular major-league shortstop.

Ramirez may have a future as a "supersub" along the lines of a Joel Youngblood or Jerry Royster. At shortstop he has always been something of an enigma, showing great range and making the spectacular play, yet having great difficulty with the routine plays. This year at third base, he showed a good arm and decent range, but still booted more than his share of chances. Perhaps he would have less to lose in timing and positioning than most players if he was moved around. There is no doubt that the athletic ability is there.

Regardless of what Ramirez does, it appears that Andres Thomas is the shortstop of the future in Atlanta. He had a great first half, then seemed to pick up on all of Rafael's bad habits (mental lapses in the field, batting average sole indicator of offensive value) and tailed off. He shows the same promise that Ramirez showed a few years ago, a promise that Ramirez left unfulfilled.

—John Stryker

In 1986, July was Rafael's doom—only nine singles in 67 at-bats! If that were the only problem, though, it might still have been a good year for him. However, July and September/October were poor as well. The question is why Tanner was continuing to play him. Ramirez was backwards statistically for an Atlanta player, hitting better on the road, on artificial turf and in the daytime. He was a terrible hitter in 1986 with runners on base.

If he'd played his usual 130 or more games at shortstop, he'd also have led the league in errors for the sixth straight year. Coupled with Thomas's 19 errors, Atlanta shortstops did lead the league.

Ramirez has served his purpose; he may now be trade bait for a desperate team. They've got a Ramirez clone ready to step in and continue the tradition of low on-base, low power, high errors, but "look-good-while-doing-it" shortstop play in Atlanta. Tanner still has a huge problem at the position. What Atlanta needs is a Trammell, Franco, Ripken, Brooks or Dunston at shortstop, instead.

—Robert Jones

	1986 SEASON											THREE YEARS (84 – 86)										
	Ave.	OBP	SLG	AB	H	2B	3B	HR	RBI	BB	SO	Ave.	OBP	SLG	AB	H	2B	3B	HR	RBI	BB	SO
Totals	.240	.273	.335	496	119	21	1	8	33	21	60	.252	.280	.331	1655	417	67	9	15	139	67	194
Batting vs. Left and Right-handed Pitchers																						
Left	.207	.247	.263	179	37	4	0	2	5	9	20	.236	.268	.305	538	127	20	4	3	44	24	61
Right	.259	.288	.375	317	82	17	1	6	28	12	40	.260	.286	.343	1117	290	47	5	12	95	43	133
At Home and on the Road																						
Home	.235	.287	.311	238	56	13	1	1	18	15	31	.263	.301	.341	777	204	33	5	6	70	43	84
Road	.244	.260	.357	258	63	8	0	7	15	6	29	.243	.262	.321	878	213	34	4	9	69	24	110
Facing Groundball Pitchers and Flyball Pitchers																						
Groundball	.225	.266	.275	236	53	6	0	2	12	12	20	.268	.292	.336	809	217	31	6	4	67	28	84
Flyball	.254	.280	.388	260	66	15	1	6	21	9	40	.236	.270	.325	846	200	36	3	11	72	39	110
Facing Finesse Pitchers and Power Pitchers																						
Finesse	.270	.284	.369	282	76	13	0	5	18	6	26	.263	.279	.339	963	253	40	6	7	77	24	91
Power	.201	.260	.290	214	43	8	1	3	15	15	34	.237	.282	.319	692	164	27	3	8	62	43	103
On Grass and on Turf																						
Grass	.233	.273	.333	369	86	17	1	6	28	18	48	.258	.290	.341	1200	310	48	6	13	101	53	138
Turf	.260	.275	.339	127	33	4	0	2	5	3	12	.235	.256	.303	455	107	19	3	2	38	14	56
During the Day and at Night																						
Day	.248	.261	.362	149	37	5	0	4	11	3	25	.254	.278	.359	527	134	27	2	8	51	18	70
Night	.236	.278	.323	347	82	16	1	4	22	18	35	.251	.282	.317	1128	283	40	7	7	88	49	124
By Month																						
April	.293	.312	.427	75	22	4	0	2	9	2	9	.270	.303	.344	241	65	7	1	3	16	12	23
May	.245	.250	.353	102	25	8	0	1	6	1	9	.271	.291	.365	288	78	20	2	1	28	9	30
June	.208	.236	.287	101	21	5	0	1	3	3	12	.279	.296	.362	326	91	16	1	3	29	8	35
July	.134	.224	.134	67	9	0	0	0	3	7	10	.208	.251	.238	269	56	3	1	1	15	15	34
August	.341	.349	.463	82	28	2	1	2	6	1	8	.272	.288	.348	290	79	14	1	2	28	6	34
Sept/Oct	.203	.286	.319	69	14	2	0	2	6	7	12	.199	.251	.315	241	48	7	3	5	23	17	38
Situational																						
Bases Empty	.282	.314	.396	298	84	14	1	6	6	12	36	.255	.281	.332	1011	258	35	5	11	11	34	135
Leadoff	.303	.330	.424	99	30	7	1	1	1	4	12	.287	.314	.356	362	104	15	2	2	2	13	46
Not Leadoff	.271	.306	.382	199	54	7	0	5	5	8	24	.237	.263	.319	649	154	20	3	9	9	21	89
Runners On	.177	.213	.242	198	35	7	0	2	27	9	24	.247	.279	.328	644	159	32	4	4	128	33	59
First Base Only	.227	.261	.307	88	20	4	0	1	3	3	11	.288	.316	.380	274	79	17	1	2	12	10	22
Scoring Position	.136	.176	.191	110	15	3	0	1	24	6	13	.216	.253	.289	370	80	15	3	2	116	23	37
Late Innings, Close	.250	.284	.375	88	22	5	0	2	10	3	14	.277	.311	.358	282	78	12	3	3	38	14	35

RBI/Opportunities					
Scoring Position	22 / 146	(15%)	109 / 486	(22%)
Scoring Position, 2 Out	6 / 73	(8%)	46 / 242	(19%)
On Third, Less than 2 Out	11 / 24	(46%)	43 / 80	(54%)
RBI in close games / RBI Total	22 / 33	(67%)	95 / 139	(68%)

Willie Randolph
New York Yankees

Stanley, Mason, Dent, Smalley, Robertson, Meacham, Tolleson. Each has two things in common. They have all been Yankee regular shortstops in the past 11 years and they have all played beside Willie Randolph. Willie was a three-year veteran when the Yankees won their last World Series in 1978. At that time, Lou Piniella was a DH-outfielder and Don Mattingly, Dan Pasqua, Mike Pagliarulo, Joel Skinner, Bobby Meacham, and Wayne Tolleson were in high school. Willie has had an impressive career; the fact that he still plays in New York is perhaps his most amazing feat.

The 1986 season was typical for Willie Randolph. He hit .280, slugged .350 and reached base 39% of the time. He stole 15 bases in 17 attempts. He scored over 70 runs for the ninth time in 11 years. He walked twice for every time he struck out. Willie could lead off for about twenty teams. His lack of power and decline in fielding are cause for concern, yet many teams would gladly free the Yankees of Randolph.

His other tendencies on offense are consistent, if prone to brief aberrations. He continues to hit about 60 points higher facing southpaws. In 1986, he began hitting better in Yankee Stadium after a two-year slide. His performance on artificial turf also fell back to normal after a peak in 1985.

His biggest weakness on offense continues to be his hitting with men in scoring position. In the past three years, he has hit only .243 in that situation as compared to .280 overall. He loses none of his ability to reach base, but what little power he has vanishes. The problem is reportedly that Willie is so intent on driving men in that he becomes over-anxious and swings more often than he normally does. He thus loses his skill of working the count in his favor—as well as hitting pitches that he normally would not touch. The Yankees take this problem seriously, because they have spoken to him about being more patient with men on base; it has had no effect so far.

Randolph committed a career-high 20 errors in 1986. He never appeared as comfortable or confident as he had in the past; possibly due to the fact that he played beside six different shortstops. Players also complained bitterly about the infield dirt; some called it the worst in the league. The Yankees have responded to the problem by tearing out the old surface and replacing it with an expensive, new one. If that factor explains Randolph's defensive lapses, expect his glove to rebound in 1987.

—A. S. Nakamura and Craig Christmann

	1986 SEASON											THREE YEARS (84 – 86)										
	Ave.	OBP	SLG	AB	H	2B	3B	HR	RBI	BB	SO	Ave.	OBP	SLG	AB	H	2B	3B	HR	RBI	BB	SO
Totals	.276	.393	.346	492	136	15	2	5	50	94	49	.280	.384	.350	1553	435	60	6	12	121	265	130
Batting vs. Left and Right-handed Pitchers																						
Left	.311	.392	.426	183	57	7	1	4	13	25	14	.320	.411	.423	553	177	28	4	7	34	87	32
Right	.256	.393	.298	309	79	8	1	1	37	69	35	.258	.369	.309	1000	258	32	2	5	87	178	98
At Home and on the Road																						
Home	.311	.451	.390	241	75	9	2	2	24	61	20	.282	.403	.358	740	209	28	5	6	61	151	57
Road	.243	.332	.303	251	61	6	0	3	26	33	29	.278	.366	.342	813	226	32	1	6	60	114	73
Facing Groundball Pitchers and Flyball Pitchers																						
Groundball	.251	.387	.318	211	53	6	1	2	20	46	21	.281	.391	.333	741	208	28	1	3	50	135	59
Flyball	.295	.398	.367	281	83	9	1	3	30	48	28	.280	.377	.365	812	227	32	5	9	71	130	71
Facing Finesse Pitchers and Power Pitchers																						
Finesse	.262	.367	.362	279	73	11	1	5	32	44	21	.274	.361	.351	878	241	31	3	10	69	118	56
Power	.296	.425	.324	213	63	4	1	0	18	50	28	.287	.411	.348	675	194	29	3	2	52	147	74
On Grass and on Turf																						
Grass	.289	.410	.361	418	121	14	2	4	43	85	40	.285	.392	.357	1310	374	51	5	11	103	232	110
Turf	.203	.291	.257	74	15	1	0	1	7	9	9	.251	.339	.309	243	61	9	1	1	18	33	20
During the Day and at Night																						
Day	.295	.436	.391	156	46	5	2	2	15	38	20	.275	.391	.351	462	127	17	3	4	34	87	41
Night	.268	.372	.324	336	90	10	0	3	35	56	29	.282	.381	.349	1091	308	43	3	8	87	178	89
By Month																						
April	.319	.437	.361	72	23	3	0	0	7	15	8	.288	.399	.346	205	59	9	0	1	12	38	21
May	.302	.460	.365	96	29	4	1	0	13	28	10	.307	.427	.369	290	89	9	3	1	24	61	23
June	.212	.316	.283	99	21	4	0	1	10	15	15	.244	.338	.310	303	74	14	0	2	25	44	33
July	.218	.337	.253	87	19	1	1	0	7	15	6	.297	.376	.360	286	85	10	1	2	29	38	12
August	.293	.391	.387	75	22	1	0	2	3	12	7	.254	.352	.324	272	69	9	2	2	16	42	22
Sept/Oct	.349	.432	.476	63	22	2	0	2	10	9	3	.299	.424	.406	197	59	9	0	4	15	42	19
Situational																						
Bases Empty	.276	.391	.372	293	81	9	2	5	5	54	33	.289	.397	.371	964	279	40	6	9	9	170	80
Leadoff	.323	.438	.441	93	30	3	1	2	2	18	5	.317	.425	.399	436	138	16	4	4	4	81	26
Not Leadoff	.255	.369	.340	200	51	6	1	3	3	36	28	.267	.374	.348	528	141	24	2	5	5	89	54
Runners On	.276	.396	.307	199	55	6	0	0	45	40	16	.265	.363	.314	589	156	20	0	3	112	95	50
First Base Only	.303	.418	.348	66	20	3	0	0	1	11	6	.301	.375	.360	236	71	8	0	2	8	26	17
Scoring Position	.263	.386	.286	133	35	3	0	0	44	29	10	.241	.355	.283	353	85	12	0	1	104	69	33
Late Innings, Close	.299	.395	.343	67	20	1	1	0	13	11	9	.286	.374	.340	262	75	9	1	1	23	37	25

RBI/Opportunities					
Scoring Position	43 / 197	(22%)	101 / 523	(19%)
Scoring Position, 2 Out	19 / 91	(21%)	31 / 231	(13%)
On Third, Less than 2 Out	16 / 43	(37%)	47 / 102	(46%)
RBI in close games / RBI Total	32 / 50	(64%)	71 / 121	(59%)

Dennis Rasmussen
New York Yankees

When the Yankees went into spring training in 1986, they weren't counting on Dennis Rasmussen—I'm not even sure that they felt that he'd make the team. He not only made the team—he became the most pleasant surprise of the season. He pitched with the confidence that he had been lacking in previous years and became the ace of the staff. He tore up the league until he got hit on his pitching elbow by a line drive in July. He missed five starts on the DL and went 6–4 with a 4.94 ERA when he returned; it's not hard to imagine him winning 20 if it hadn't been for that.

One of the keys to Rasmussen's success was his ability to cut down on his walks. Dennis has never allowed many hits—opposing hitters had only a .243 average against him in 1984 and '85—so you have to walk in order to beat him. Until 1986, hitters had—he allowed 3.66 walks per nine innings in '84 and 3.72 in '85. This year he challenged everyone from day one and he cut that number to 3.30 as a result. Naturally he gave up more homers (he allowed 16 per 600 at-bats in 1985 and 23 in '86), but it was worth it. Oddly, keeping more men off the bases didn't mean that he allowed more homers with the bases empty—his 57% figure was the same as for '84–5 combined.

Rasmussen may be the only lefty who doesn't benefit from Yankee Stadium. For the past three years, his ERA is 4.43 at home and 3.89 on the road. The reason why may be that he doesn't handle lefties that well. In that same period, lefties actually hit better against him than righties; with the short right field fences in Yankee Stadium you have got to get lefties out if you expect to win here.

Finally, if I were Lou Piniella, I'd move heaven and earth to keep Rasmussen from starting day games. He's pitched so much better at night over the last three years that you have to believe it's a pattern—his ERAs are 5.02 with natural light and 3.79 with Con Ed's version. He's given up over a hit an inning and that's extremely unusual for Dennis. The odd thing is that he strikes more batters out during the day and he doesn't walk them any more often at night. Perhaps Piniella could work out some kind of platoon arrangement so that he only starts road games at night.

—Craig Christmann

1986: Finesse, Flyball **1985: Power, Flyball** **1984: Power, Flyball**

		1986 SEASON											THREE YEARS (84 – 86)									
	G	IP	H	BB	SO	SB	CS	W	L	S	ERA		G	IP	H	BB	SO	SB	CS	W	L	S	ERA
Totals	31	202.0	160	74	131	10	8	18	6	0	3.88		77	451.1	384	176	304	19	22	30	17	0	4.13
At Home and on the Road																							
Home	12	75.0	55	33	54	3	2	8	2	0	4.32		34	197.0	165	89	138	6	10	15	7	0	4.43
Road	19	127.0	105	41	77	7	6	10	4	0	3.61		43	254.1	219	87	166	13	12	15	10	0	3.89
During the Day and at Night																							
Day	9	51.2	53	16	38	2	0	6	3	0	5.05		24	123.2	130	48	89	4	7	8	8	0	5.02
Night	22	150.1	107	58	93	8	8	12	3	0	3.47		53	327.2	254	128	215	15	15	22	9	0	3.79
On Grass and on Turf																							
Grass	24	153.2	121	63	96	10	5	13	5	0	3.92		60	350.2	307	148	230	15	18	21	13	0	4.11
Turf	7	48.1	39	11	35	0	3	5	1	0	3.72		17	100.2	77	28	74	4	4	9	4	0	4.20
By Month																							
April	3	18.2	12	6	13	0	0	2	0	0	2.41		6	37.2	33	12	25	1	2	2	1	0	2.63
May	6	38.1	27	17	33	5	4	3	1	0	4.70		13	86.0	57	34	67	6	6	6	3	0	3.98
June	6	43.0	33	17	21	2	2	3	1	0	3.56		17	99.0	99	45	58	4	6	3	5	0	4.91
July	4	31.0	16	14	26	1	0	4	0	0	1.74		14	86.0	55	38	60	1	4	9	1	0	3.03
August	5	28.2	26	8	20	0	0	2	2	0	4.71		11	68.0	50	19	52	2	0	5	3	0	3.84
Sept/Oct	7	42.1	46	12	18	2	2	4	2	0	5.10		16	74.2	90	28	42	5	4	5	4	0	5.54

vs. Opponent Batters

		1986 SEASON										THREE YEARS (84 – 86)									
	Ave.	OBP	SLG	AB	H	2B	3B	HR	RBI	BB	SO	Ave.	OBP	SLG	AB	H	2B	3B	HR	RBI	BB	SO
Totals	.217	.289	.366	737	160	24	1	28	76	74	131	.231	.305	.385	1659	384	67	13	54	192	176	304
Pitching vs. Left and Right-handed Batters																						
Left	.184	.247	.250	136	25	3	0	2	8	12	23	.231	.293	.347	320	74	11	1	8	32	28	51
Right	.225	.298	.393	601	135	21	1	26	68	62	108	.232	.308	.394	1339	310	56	12	46	160	148	253
Situational																						
Bases Empty	.194	.271	.327	490	95	15	1	16	16	51	83	.208	.292	.352	1053	219	43	8	31	31	123	190
Leadoff	.193	.267	.294	197	38	5	0	5	5	20	34	.232	.312	.369	431	100	19	2	12	12	49	72
Not Leadoff	.195	.274	.348	293	57	10	1	11	11	31	49	.191	.278	.341	622	119	24	6	19	19	74	118
Runners On	.263	.322	.445	247	65	9	0	12	60	23	48	.272	.327	.442	606	165	24	5	23	161	53	114
First Base Only	.233	.282	.336	146	34	3	0	4	9	10	31	.262	.313	.387	313	82	10	1	9	23	21	60
Scoring Position	.307	.375	.604	101	31	6	0	8	51	13	17	.283	.342	.502	293	83	14	4	14	138	32	54
Late Innings, Close	.237	.303	.356	59	14	1	0	2	5	6	7	.288	.338	.408	125	36	6	0	3	14	10	14

RBI/Opportunities

Scoring Position	37 / 144	(26%)		108 / 407	(27%)
Scoring Position, 2 Out	13 / 63	(21%)		35 / 161	(22%)
On Third, Less than 2 Out	15 / 26	(58%)		46 / 77	(60%)
RBI in close games / RBI Total	58 / 76	(76%)		139 / 192	(72%)

Shane Rawley
Philadelphia Phillies

Shane Rawley is something of an enigma. He doesn't look like the kind of pitcher who would be a consistent winner, because nothing in his makeup stands out. He's never struck out more than 124 batters in a season, so you couldn't classify him as a power pitcher; he doesn't have great control; he gets only a slightly higher-than-average number of groundball outs; he doesn't cut off the running game particularly well; he's not especially tough on left-handed hitters; and he's always been cuffed around in day games, when the batters get a better look at his stuff. Yet Rawley has won in double figures for five straight seasons, posting records of 11–10, 14–14, 12–9, 13–8 and 11–7, and has gone 34–21 since coming over to Philadelphia in mid-1984. Nothing exciting about that, but he's the kind of guy you'd like having as your third or fourth starter, someone you can count on for 12 wins or so. It's the same role that Milt Wilcox played for a number of years with the Tigers, and one that helps give stability to a pitching staff.

Rawley seemed certain to break out of the pattern in 1986 when he posted 10 wins by the end of June. But as though his body were reminding him what his niche in life was, he suffered an injury, a fracture of a small bone in his left shoulder, and couldn't pitch after late July. The injury isn't believed to be serious, and Shane is expected to be ready by spring training. The Phils certainly hope so; even though he missed more than two months of the season, Rawley was second on the club in innings pitched, and tied for second in wins.

One characteristic Rawley has shown with Philadelphia has been toughness under pressure. He's consistently pitched well with runners in scoring position, and generally been good in the clutch . . . especially in '86. He's also done well against clubs with winning records, going 18–12 in '84-'86. If he's developed a tough hide over the years, perhaps his background has something to do with it. He pitched for two different organizations in the minors, then finally made the big leagues with a third, the Mariners. Working as a reliever in the small Seattle ballpark must have honed his survival skills, and two and a half years in the Bronx Zoo didn't hurt either. He's a pro, and should help the Phils again in '87 if he's healthy.

—Don Zminda

1986: Finesse, Flyball   **1985: Finesse, Groundball**   **1984: Finesse, Groundball**

	G	IP	H	BB	SO	SB	CS	W	L	S	ERA		G	IP	H	BB	SO	SB	CS	W	L	S	ERA
			1986 SEASON												**THREE YEARS (84 – 86)**								
Totals	23	157.2	166	50	73	21	11	11	7	0	3.54		88	518.2	517	185	261	51	21	36	24	0	3.73
											At Home and on the Road												
Home	11	69.0	76	29	31	13	7	7	3	0	3.91		48	270.1	269	114	142	31	15	19	15	0	3.76
Road	12	88.2	90	21	42	8	4	4	4	0	3.25		40	248.1	248	71	119	20	6	17	9	0	3.70
											During the Day and at Night												
Day	7	39.2	61	6	16	0	3	1	5	0	6.58		28	146.2	184	50	76	16	7	5	13	0	5.28
Night	16	118.0	105	44	57	21	8	10	2	0	2.52		60	372.0	333	135	185	35	14	31	11	0	3.12
											On Grass and on Turf												
Grass	4	27.2	36	3	15	2	1	1	2	0	5.20		26	140.1	141	51	78	9	5	6	6	0	4.43
Turf	19	130.0	130	47	58	19	10	10	5	0	3.18		62	378.1	376	134	183	42	16	30	18	0	3.47
											By Month												
April	5	41.0	37	12	14	1	2	3	1	0	2.41		12	76.0	67	28	30	4	3	6	3	0	2.96
May	6	36.0	43	5	21	7	1	3	3	0	4.25		15	77.2	88	33	43	12	4	5	7	0	4.64
June	6	51.0	40	16	23	6	2	4	0	0	1.76		19	87.0	82	33	46	8	3	6	3	0	3.21
July	6	29.2	46	17	15	7	6	1	3	0	7.28		18	112.1	119	42	70	14	6	6	6	0	4.01
August	0	0.0	0	0	0	0	0	0	0	0	0.00		12	89.0	71	27	42	2	2	8	0	0	2.53
Sept/Oct	0	0.0	0	0	0	0	0	0	0	0	0.00		12	76.2	90	22	30	11	3	5	5	0	5.17

vs. Opponent Batters

	Ave.	OBP	SLG	AB	H	2B	3B	HR	RBI	BB	SO		Ave.	OBP	SLG	AB	H	2B	3B	HR	RBI	BB	SO
				1986 SEASON											**THREE YEARS (84 – 86)**								
Totals	.270	.325	.405	615	166	38	3	13	57	50	73		.259	.322	.379	1995	517	100	7	42	196	185	261
												Pitching vs. Left and Right-handed Batters												
Left	.287	.313	.425	80	23	6	1	1	10	3	15		.254	.321	.367	264	67	13	1	5	31	25	42
Right	.267	.326	.402	535	143	32	2	12	47	47	58		.260	.322	.381	1731	450	87	6	37	165	160	219
												Situational												
Bases Empty	.270	.319	.430	363	98	19	3	11	11	26	41		.258	.314	.381	1193	308	50	6	28	28	96	154
Leadoff	.288	.327	.526	156	45	8	1	9	9	9	17		.254	.305	.393	507	129	15	2	17	17	35	71
Not Leadoff	.256	.313	.357	207	53	11	2	2	2	17	24		.261	.321	.372	686	179	35	4	11	11	61	83
Runners On	.270	.333	.369	252	68	19	0	2	46	24	32		.261	.333	.378	802	209	50	1	14	168	89	107
First Base Only	.303	.345	.431	109	33	8	0	2	6	6	11		.290	.332	.426	359	104	26	1	7	26	22	41
Scoring Position	.245	.325	.322	143	35	11	0	0	40	18	21		.237	.333	.339	443	105	24	0	7	142	67	66
Late Innings, Close	.195	.235	.312	77	15	3	0	2	4	4	11		.220	.269	.329	173	38	7	0	4	8	12	26

RBI/Opportunities

Scoring Position	37 / 195	(19%)		124 / 606	(20%)
Scoring Position, 2 Out	12 / 101	(12%)		45 / 294	(15%)
On Third, Less than 2 Out	14 / 26	(54%)		47 / 91	(52%)
RBI in close games / RBI Total	37 / 57	(65%)		137 / 196	(70%)

Johnny Ray
Pittsburgh Pirates

Johnny Ray is Pittsburgh's candidate for doing the next American Express commercial. Sandberg, Sax, Doran, Samuel have had the opportunity of playing for winning teams. But Johnny Ray is no loser, either.

Ray is currently the best all-around player on the Pirates. Barry Bonds should eventually be an All-Star, but he needs time to develop. Tony Pena is brilliant in flashes, but is not consistent. Jim Morrison and Sid Bream are strong on offense but can't match Ray on defense. Ray plays hurt, which affects his statistics adversely, but the Pirates need both his bat and glove in the lineup. Last season, Johnny bounced back from a subpar 1985 season, hitting .301, banging out over 30 doubles for the fifth consecutive year, and driving in a career-high 79 runs. His strikeout/walk totals were 47/58, also both career highs. On the minus side, he stole only 6 bases in 15 attempts (previously 58/90, 64%), and continues to hit into too many double plays. In the field, Ray turned in a strong season, fielding .993 (5 errors), second only to Sandberg in fielding percentage. His positioning is superb, which covers his lack of great speed. Thus, most of his plays appear routine. Actually, rangewise, he's behind Oester, Sandberg, and Sax, and about equal to the other full-time regulars.

Ray is 29, and in his prime as a hitter. His overall tendencies are consistent. He is a better, more powerful hitter from the right side. He generally hits better on the road, both on grass and turf, and is tough in day games. Jim Leyland's main problem in structuring his offense is setting the top of the batting order. Last year, with Bonds leading off and Ray hitting third, two spots were solid, but the Number 2 hole was a black hole, with Joe Orsulak, Bobby Bonilla, and occasionally even Rafael Belliard failing in the role. Ray has generally resisted hitting leadoff, but he may need to reevaluate his position in the context of team needs. His stats leading off innings are outstanding, and Bonds' power would be of more use behind Johnny. Then Leyland could shift Sid Bream and Jim Morrison up one spot each in the order to concentrate the power potential up front.

Ray can hit anywhere in the lineup if need be. The Pirates need 4 of him in the batting order and 3 in the infield. But, for now, he settles for being the calm spot at the eye of the hurricane. Do You Know Him?

—A.S. Nakamura

	1986 SEASON											THREE YEARS (84 – 86)										
	Ave.	OBP	SLG	AB	H	2B	3B	HR	RBI	BB	SO	Ave.	OBP	SLG	AB	H	2B	3B	HR	RBI	BB	SO
Totals	.301	.363	.394	579	174	33	0	7	78	58	47	.295	.347	.400	1728	510	104	9	20	215	141	102
Batting vs. Left and Right-handed Pitchers																						
Left	.261	.318	.311	222	58	8	0	1	26	19	18	.270	.318	.339	493	133	26	1	2	51	35	40
Right	.325	.390	.445	357	116	25	0	6	52	39	29	.305	.359	.425	1235	377	78	8	18	164	106	62
At Home and on the Road																						
Home	.285	.356	.366	298	85	18	0	2	37	33	28	.276	.338	.373	850	235	52	3	8	98	78	57
Road	.317	.371	.423	281	89	15	0	5	41	25	19	.313	.357	.427	878	275	52	6	12	117	63	45
Facing Groundball Pitchers and Flyball Pitchers																						
Groundball	.300	.348	.392	263	79	15	0	3	38	20	17	.305	.352	.398	822	251	47	4	7	105	62	39
Flyball	.301	.375	.396	316	95	18	0	4	40	38	30	.286	.343	.403	906	259	57	5	13	110	79	63
Facing Finesse Pitchers and Power Pitchers																						
Finesse	.301	.364	.388	312	94	15	0	4	38	30	21	.303	.347	.400	971	294	54	5	10	114	68	42
Power	.300	.362	.401	267	80	18	0	3	40	28	26	.285	.347	.402	757	216	50	4	10	101	73	60
On Grass and on Turf																						
Grass	.308	.372	.397	146	45	7	0	2	22	14	12	.313	.361	.414	444	139	24	3	5	61	34	27
Turf	.298	.360	.393	433	129	26	0	5	56	44	35	.289	.343	.396	1284	371	80	6	15	154	107	75
During the Day and at Night																						
Day	.346	.416	.523	153	53	15	0	4	34	19	12	.317	.377	.439	526	167	38	4	6	83	53	32
Night	.284	.343	.347	426	121	18	0	3	44	39	35	.285	.334	.384	1202	343	66	5	14	132	88	70
By Month																						
April	.384	.432	.493	73	28	5	0	1	18	7	4	.332	.370	.423	220	73	15	1	1	32	15	8
May	.344	.413	.469	96	33	9	0	1	11	12	9	.313	.375	.418	275	86	19	2	2	26	27	24
June	.184	.265	.241	87	16	5	0	0	12	10	12	.231	.275	.317	303	70	16	2	2	36	19	24
July	.275	.359	.352	91	25	4	0	1	8	10	9	.289	.345	.379	256	74	12	1	3	18	20	19
August	.353	.386	.454	119	42	6	0	2	16	7	6	.312	.358	.420	317	99	20	1	4	42	22	12
Sept/Oct	.265	.333	.354	113	30	4	0	2	13	12	7	.303	.364	.443	357	108	22	2	8	61	38	15
Situational																						
Bases Empty	.300	.371	.397	320	96	16	0	5	5	34	21	.294	.343	.399	996	293	55	5	13	13	72	50
Leadoff	.340	.394	.470	100	34	7	0	2	2	8	3	.303	.342	.413	356	108	17	2	6	6	20	12
Not Leadoff	.282	.360	.364	220	62	9	0	3	3	26	18	.289	.343	.391	640	185	38	3	7	7	52	38
Runners On	.301	.354	.390	259	78	17	0	2	73	24	26	.296	.353	.403	732	217	49	4	7	202	69	52
First Base Only	.327	.358	.423	104	34	7	0	1	8	5	10	.286	.328	.366	276	79	15	2	1	14	16	18
Scoring Position	.284	.352	.368	155	44	10	0	1	65	19	16	.303	.367	.425	456	138	34	2	6	188	53	34
Late Innings, Close	.264	.341	.364	110	29	5	0	2	10	13	11	.259	.328	.369	336	87	19	3	4	39	36	27
RBI/Opportunities																						

	1986 SEASON		THREE YEARS (84 – 86)	
Scoring Position	59 / 208	(28%)	170 / 601	(28%)
Scoring Position, 2 Out	15 / 76	(20%)	58 / 224	(26%)
On Third, Less than 2 Out	26 / 48	(54%)	68 / 122	(56%)
RBI in close games / RBI Total	54 / 78	(69%)	156 / 215	(73%)

Jeff Reardon
Montreal Expos

Let's imagine a player, say, Jody Davis of the Cubs. In 1986, he hit .250 with a .428 slugging average, .300 on-base average and 3.98 home runs per 100 at-bats.

Now, let's imagine that a pitcher—a right-handed relief pitcher—had to face Jody Davis every time he entered a game; that is, over the long run, he would allow totals similar to those of Jody Davis.

In 1986, that pitcher was Jeff Reardon.

This little mental exercise is useful because it gives us a way of imagining just how far Reardon, the ace of the Montreal Expos' bullpen, slipped during the past season. If we look at Reardon's three-season totals against left-handed hitters and compare them to his 1986 totals, we see little difference other than a rise in slugging average. The typical left-handed hitter against Reardon would have been Terry Kennedy (.264 BA, .403 Slg., .324 OBA and 2.78 HR percentage in 1986). Of course, as a right-handed thrower, Reardon should be expected to have more trouble with left-handed hitters.

Now, look at his three-season totals against right-handed hitters. Those numbers define a hitter such as Dann Bilardello (.194 BA, .283 Slg., .249 OBA and 2.09 HR percentage in 1986).

The difference between the Reardon of 1986 and the Reardon of old is the difference between Terry Kennedy and Dann Bilardello. Such a thought must be disturbing to the Expos because most of his slippage came against right-handed hitters, the bread and butter for a righty reliever. In the 1984 and '85 seasons combined, Reardon allowed only four home runs to right-handed batters; in 1986, he gave up seven.

A few other points of interest: Reardon's innings were split almost exactly between home and away games, but he did far worse in the Oly Almost-a-Dome than on the road (4.73 earned run average at home, 3.12 away). This was in keeping with his three-season history (3.66 ERA at home, 2.77 away). Maybe it's the turf or maybe it's that curious malaise known as Expos Disease. . . . He had his best month in May, when he lived up to his nickname, The Terminator (1.25 ERA). He also put in his busiest month in May. The roof caved in during June (4.12 ERA) and the Expos began to use him less. He was horrible the rest of the season.

—Michael O'Donnell

1986: Finesse, Flyball   **1985: Power, Flyball**   **1984: Power, Flyball**

1986 SEASON

	G	IP	H	BB	SO	SB	CS	W	L	S	ERA
Totals	62	89.0	83	26	67	11	2	7	9	35	3.94
At Home and on the Road											
Home	30	45.2	50	17	42	5	1	5	6	14	4.73
Road	32	43.1	33	9	25	6	1	2	3	21	3.12
During the Day and at Night											
Day	23	35.0	29	12	27	3	1	5	5	10	3.86
Night	39	54.0	54	14	40	8	1	2	4	25	4.00
On Grass and on Turf											
Grass	14	19.1	13	4	10	1	0	1	1	10	3.26
Turf	48	69.2	70	22	57	10	2	6	8	25	4.13
By Month											
April	8	14.0	13	4	10	2	1	2	2		3.86
May	13	21.2	16	5	17	4	0	3	0	10	1.25
June	11	19.2	15	7	17	2	0	1	2	6	4.12
July	9	10.2	18	4	6	3	1	0	2	5	6.75
August	9	11.1	6	4	5	0	0	0	2	5	4.76
Sept/Oct	12	11.2	15	2	12	0	0	1	1	7	5.40

THREE YEARS (84 – 86)

	G	IP	H	BB	SO	SB	CS	W	L	S	ERA
Totals	193	263.2	221	89	213	26	6	16	24	99	3.35
At Home and on the Road											
Home	93	127.1	121	49	105	15	4	11	16	45	3.96
Road	100	136.1	100	40	108	11	2	5	8	54	2.77
During the Day and at Night											
Day	72	97.0	84	36	73	6	4	8	9	32	3.43
Night	121	166.2	137	53	140	20	2	8	15	67	3.29
On Grass and on Turf											
Grass	49	68.1	54	19	48	3	1	3	4	26	3.16
Turf	144	195.1	167	70	165	23	5	13	20	73	3.41
By Month											
April	25	42.1	31	17	31	5	1	3	3	11	2.34
May	39	57.1	35	12	51	7	1	6	1	22	0.78
June	33	46.0	40	15	41	4	0	2	5	18	3.91
July	27	28.2	42	11	19	5	3	0	5	11	6.91
August	34	44.1	33	25	31	3	1	2	7	19	4.67
Sept/Oct	35	45.0	40	9	40	2	0	3	3	18	3.40

vs. Opponent Batters

1986 SEASON

	Ave.	OBP	SLG	AB	H	2B	3B	HR	RBI	BB	SO
Totals	.251	.306	.417	331	83	13	3	12	42	26	67
Pitching vs. Left and Right-handed Batters											
Left	.250	.330	.390	172	43	5	2	5	29	20	31
Right	.252	.279	.447	159	40	8	1	7	13	6	36
Situational											
Bases Empty	.278	.323	.506	180	50	9	1	10	10	11	32
Leadoff	.274	.338	.507	73	20	3	1	4	4	7	16
Not Leadoff	.280	.313	.505	107	30	6	0	6	6	4	16
Runners On	.219	.287	.311	151	33	4	2	2	32	15	35
First Base Only	.244	.292	.356	45	11	0	1	1	3	3	9
Scoring Position	.208	.286	.292	106	22	4	1	1	29	12	26
Late Innings, Close	.252	.304	.406	298	75	10	3	10	37	22	64

THREE YEARS (84 – 86)

	Ave.	OBP	SLG	AB	H	2B	3B	HR	RBI	BB	SO
Totals	.227	.294	.340	974	221	30	4	24	110	89	213
Pitching vs. Left and Right-handed Batters											
Left	.245	.325	.354	511	125	13	2	13	68	59	91
Right	.207	.258	.324	463	96	17	2	11	42	30	122
Situational											
Bases Empty	.230	.281	.353	535	123	16	1	16	16	36	106
Leadoff	.199	.254	.315	216	43	5	1	6	6	15	42
Not Leadoff	.251	.299	.379	319	80	11	0	10	10	21	64
Runners On	.223	.309	.323	439	98	14	3	8	94	53	107
First Base Only	.239	.302	.374	155	37	4	1	5	14	13	35
Scoring Position	.215	.312	.296	284	61	10	2	3	80	40	72
Late Innings, Close	.230	.299	.341	769	177	20	4	19	95	73	171

RBI/Opportunities

	1986		THREE YEARS	
Scoring Position	25 / 145	(17%)	71 / 402	(18%)
Scoring Position, 2 Out	6 / 54	(11%)	24 / 200	(12%)
On Third, Less than 2 Out	11 / 27	(41%)	24 / 58	(41%)
RBI in close games / RBI Total	37 / 42	(88%)	95 / 110	(86%)

Rick Reuschel
Pittsburgh Pirates

When Rick Reuschel first reached the majors in the middle of 1972, he was an immediate sucess. The big sinker-slider thrower was virtually a paradigmatic Wrigley Field pitcher. For the 1973–80 period, he was the rubber-armed staff leader for second division teams, averaging 14 wins, 245 innings pitched and a 3.46 ERA.

But then he was traded to the Yankees, and in 1982 Reuschel developed arm trouble at age 33. He worked his way back and served as a mop-up man for the 1984 Cub division champions, but was cut from the playoff roster and released after the season. Although he has never complained, one has to think he was treated shabbily by the Green organization, as inadequate ex-Phillies such as Ruthven and Brusstar were kept instead of Reuschel. The Pirates took a chance on Rick in 1985, and we saw a slimmer Reuschel pitching better than ever for a team that lost 104 games. He hardly pitched a bad game in '85 and was named NL Comeback Player of the Year. 1986 didn't go so well, but aside from W-L and ERA, his stats were close to what they've always been, and although he will be 38 next year, one has to believe he can still pitch into his 40's. One surprise in the recent data is how well he has adapted to pitching on turf;

because of his reliance on the double play, one would have thought him especially suited for grass.

Cub fans will note a comparison between Reuschel and another favorite with a similar name, Bob Rush. Their Cub career records:

	G	Sh.O	W	L	IP	H	SO	BB	ERA
Reuschel	358	17	135	127	2291	2365	1367	640	3.50
Rush	339	13	110	140	2132	2043	1076	725	3.71

Other interesting comparisons are Wins vs. Team (Reuschel +14.1, Rush +4.7), ERA/250 IP vs. Team (Rush +4.29, Reuschel +4.25), and Approximate Value/250 IP (both 10.0). Rick has been easier to hit than Rush but has better control, and hence slightly more successful. Besides Fergie Jenkins, these are the only Cub 100-game winners of the postwar period.

Rick Reuschel is a throwback to an earlier era in that he speaks through performance rather than words. He will never make the Hall of Fame, but one would like to see him win another 38 games so as to end up with 200 victories.

—William E. McMahon

1986: Finesse, Groundball   **1985: Finesse, Groundball**   **1984: Finesse, Groundball**

	1986 SEASON											THREE YEARS (84 – 86)										
	G	IP	H	BB	SO	SB	CS	W	L	S	ERA	G	IP	H	BB	SO	SB	CS	W	L	S	ERA
Totals	35	215.2	232	57	125	17	7	9	16	0	3.96	85	502.0	508	132	306	28	22	28	29	1	3.53
At Home and on the Road																						
Home	17	104.1	105	32	60	10	3	5	8	0	3.28	45	271.2	266	73	164	18	11	22	12	0	3.28
Road	18	111.1	127	25	65	7	4	4	8	0	4.61	40	230.1	242	59	142	10	11	6	17	1	3.83
During the Day and at Night																						
Day	12	77.0	86	13	39	4	1	4	4	0	3.51	35	210.2	222	50	115	8	7	10	10	0	3.67
Night	23	138.2	146	44	86	13	6	5	12	0	4.22	50	291.1	286	82	191	20	15	18	19	1	3.43
On Grass and on Turf																						
Grass	9	51.1	63	17	29	1	0	2	3	0	5.96	32	171.0	199	49	101	5	5	7	8	0	4.63
Turf	26	164.1	169	40	96	16	7	7	13	0	3.34	53	331.0	309	83	205	23	17	21	21	1	2.96
By Month																						
April	5	27.2	34	11	12	0	0	2	2	0	4.23	6	33.0	41	12	13	0	0	2	2	0	4.36
May	5	37.0	34	9	19	1	1	1	2	0	2.43	11	78.0	73	17	34	1	2	4	3	0	2.88
June	6	36.1	37	17	16	5	1	1	4	0	4.21	19	111.2	127	34	66	8	7	7	7	0	4.51
July	7	34.0	45	10	24	6	1	2	4	0	6.88	17	86.2	100	29	58	9	2	5	8	0	4.67
August	6	40.2	47	3	30	3	2	2	3	0	3.54	16	97.1	95	25	65	6	8	5	7	0	2.77
Sept/Oct	6	40.0	35	7	24	2	2	1	1	0	2.92	16	95.1	72	15	70	4	3	5	2	1	2.36

vs. Opponent Batters																		
	1986 SEASON									THREE YEARS (84 – 86)								
	Ave.	OBP	SLG	AB	H	2B	3B	HR	RBI	BB	SO	Ave.	OBP	SLG	AB	H	2B	3B	HR	RBI	BB	SO
Totals	.274	.322	.406	844	231	44	4	20	95	57	125	.264	.313	.379	1917	507	96	11	34	205	132	306
Pitching vs. Left and Right-handed Batters																		
Left	.305	.360	.442	462	141	30	3	9	56	38	50	.281	.333	.392	968	272	54	7	13	99	78	104
Right	.236	.276	.364	382	90	14	1	11	39	19	75	.248	.293	.367	949	235	42	4	21	106	54	202
Situational																		
Bases Empty	.283	.327	.430	477	135	27	2	13	13	29	74	.257	.298	.376	1138	293	56	8	21	21	61	185
Leadoff	.327	.370	.512	205	67	13	2	7	7	13	23	.277	.316	.413	484	134	28	4	10	10	26	60
Not Leadoff	.250	.294	.368	272	68	14	0	6	6	16	51	.243	.284	.349	654	159	28	4	11	11	35	125
Runners On	.262	.316	.376	367	96	17	2	7	82	28	51	.275	.334	.384	779	214	40	3	13	184	71	121
First Base Only	.298	.329	.437	151	45	5	2	4	13	7	19	.297	.331	.440	327	97	16	2	9	28	16	49
Scoring Position	.236	.308	.333	216	51	12	0	3	69	21	32	.259	.336	.343	452	117	24	1	4	156	55	72
Late Innings, Close	.356	.400	.559	59	21	6	0	2	9	4	8	.297	.355	.434	182	54	13	0	4	22	16	24

RBI/Opportunities					
Scoring Position	62 / 296	(21%)	147 / 634	(23%)
Scoring Position, 2 Out	19 / 122	(16%)	52 / 269	(19%)
On Third, Less than 2 Out	29 / 64	(45%)	64 / 121	(53%)
RBI in close games / RBI Total	70 / 95	(74%)	148 / 205	(72%)

Craig Reynolds
Houston Astros

Craig Reynolds was the Astros regular shortstop from 1979 to 1981. He lost his starting job in 1982 to the young but very promising Dickie Thon, and rode the pines during the 1982 and 1983 seasons. However, an errant fastball to the face cost Dickie his season and almost his career early in 1984, and Reynolds was returned to the starting lineup.

Over the last three years, Craig has performed adequately. After the 1984 season, Thon attempted to come back with limited success, so Houston has ended up platooning Reynolds and Thon to try to make the best of the situation.

Reynolds' situational statistics last year showed very large differentials in almost every category. In very limited usage (35 at-bats), he hit only .143 with no walks versus left-handers; his road statistics were atrocious (.189 BA, .219 OBA, .272 SA); he was terrible against flyball pitchers and power pitchers; and couldn't hit a lick on grass. He started the year hitting .379 with a .419 on-base and a .621 slugging average; he finished it hitting .179 with a .230 on-base and a .232 slugging average. With the bases empty, he hit .189 with no on-base and no power; with runners on base he hit

.326 with a .356 on-base and .116 points of isolated power. His range, which was above-average in 1985, slipped to below-average in 1986, and he turned a low number of double plays.

The real crime in all of this is that the baseball world will never get to discover just how good a shortstop Dickie Thon might have been. Thon's 1983 season was spectacularly good, yet few recognized it then and almost no one remembers that now. Dickie was 25 years old at that time, and he hit .286 with a .457 slugging average, cracking 37 doubles and triples along with 20 home runs while stealing 34 bases. He led all NL shortstops with 533 assists and showed better range than Ozzie Smith did that year. Playing for a fifth-place team and playing in the Astrodome combined to cheat him of the recognition he deserved. He could hit for average, hit for power, run and field, and it looked like he would get even better, but it was not to be.

The Astros were lucky to have a valuable role-player like Craig Reynolds available to step in for Thon in 1984. It is too bad they had to call upon him in such circumstances.

—Gary Gillette

	1986 SEASON											THREE YEARS (84 – 86)										
	Ave.	OBP	SLG	AB	H	2B	3B	HR	RBI	BB	SO	Ave.	OBP	SLG	AB	H	2B	3B	HR	RBI	BB	SO
Totals	.249	.274	.348	313	78	7	3	6	41	12	31	.261	.285	.369	1219	318	40	22	16	133	46	114
Batting vs. Left and Right-handed Pitchers																						
Left	.143	.143	.171	35	5	1	0	0	1	0	7	.232	.256	.301	246	57	7	2	2	12	8	45
Right	.263	.290	.371	278	73	6	3	6	40	12	24	.268	.293	.386	973	261	33	20	14	121	38	69
At Home and on the Road																						
Home	.319	.340	.438	144	46	3	1	4	21	5	14	.266	.294	.363	586	156	18	12	5	61	26	57
Road	.189	.219	.272	169	32	4	2	2	20	7	17	.256	.277	.374	633	162	22	10	11	72	20	57
Facing Groundball Pitchers and Flyball Pitchers																						
Groundball	.293	.305	.388	147	43	3	1	3	27	3	14	.277	.300	.401	559	155	17	14	8	74	21	51
Flyball	.211	.249	.313	166	35	4	2	3	14	9	17	.247	.272	.342	660	163	23	8	8	59	25	63
Facing Finesse Pitchers and Power Pitchers																						
Finesse	.266	.283	.384	177	47	4	1	5	25	5	12	.270	.296	.386	648	175	19	13	10	73	27	48
Power	.228	.264	.301	136	31	3	2	1	16	7	19	.250	.273	.350	571	143	21	9	6	60	19	66
On Grass and on Turf																						
Grass	.200	.226	.264	110	22	4	0	1	15	4	14	.260	.283	.376	362	94	15	3	7	54	13	31
Turf	.276	.300	.394	203	56	3	3	5	26	8	17	.261	.286	.366	857	224	25	19	9	79	33	83
During the Day and at Night																						
Day	.241	.274	.336	116	28	1	2	2	15	6	12	.293	.318	.429	280	82	11	3	7	38	12	22
Night	.254	.275	.355	197	50	6	1	4	26	6	19	.251	.276	.351	939	236	29	19	9	95	34	92
By Month																						
April	.379	.419	.621	29	11	1	0	2	10	2	1	.321	.352	.536	112	36	6	0	6	23	7	7
May	.205	.255	.295	44	9	0	2	0	4	3	6	.272	.294	.360	228	62	8	6	0	19	8	26
June	.296	.286	.370	54	16	1	0	1	8	0	4	.266	.286	.385	218	58	4	5	4	25	7	27
July	.206	.242	.317	63	13	1	0	2	4	3	9	.232	.268	.320	241	56	6	3	3	20	12	22
August	.284	.284	.373	67	19	3	0	1	7	0	4	.287	.301	.386	223	64	12	2	2	21	5	15
Sept/Oct	.179	.230	.232	56	10	1	1	0	8	4	7	.213	.238	.310	197	42	4	6	1	25	7	17
Situational																						
Bases Empty	.189	.207	.274	175	33	3	0	4	4	4	23	.236	.259	.334	692	163	20	9	10	10	22	67
Leadoff	.159	.159	.203	69	11	0	0	1	1	0	13	.253	.265	.356	253	64	8	3	4	4	4	27
Not Leadoff	.208	.236	.321	106	22	3	0	3	3	4	10	.226	.256	.321	439	99	12	6	6	6	18	40
Runners On	.326	.356	.442	138	45	4	3	2	37	8	8	.294	.319	.416	527	155	20	13	6	123	24	47
First Base Only	.290	.302	.403	62	18	2	1	1	3	1	3	.301	.317	.423	246	74	7	7	3	17	6	21
Scoring Position	.355	.395	.474	76	27	2	2	1	34	7	5	.288	.319	.409	281	81	13	6	3	106	18	26
Late Innings, Close	.259	.295	.414	58	15	1	1	2	9	3	3	.246	.278	.332	211	52	7	1	3	20	10	16
RBI/Opportunities																						

	1986			THREE YEARS (84 – 86)		
Scoring Position	31 / 100	(31%)		96 / 368	(26%)	
Scoring Position, 2 Out	12 / 36	(33%)		39 / 167	(23%)	
On Third, Less than 2 Out	11 / 22	(50%)		35 / 67	(52%)	
RBI in close games / RBI Total	31 / 41	(76%)		95 / 133	(71%)	

R. J. Reynolds
Pittsburgh Pirates

By the middle of last year, R.J. Reynolds looked like an emerging star. A sizzling (.360) July had lifted his average to .304, and it wasn't a soft .304, either: Reynolds was showing some power (26 doubles, 9 homers through July), driving in his share of runs (40 for his first 312 at bats) and even drawing a few walks for the first time in his major league career. People weren't saying the Pirates got robbed in the Bill Madlock deal any more; heck, the way Reynolds and Sid Bream were playing, it seemed to be the other way around.

But right at that point, as July faded into August, R.J.'s season went—dare I say it?—up in smoke. For the rest of the campaign he batted an anemic .144 (13 for 90) with no homers and only eight RBIs. In September and October there were no Reynolds raps at all; R.J. spent the last five weeks nailed to the bench and didn't get a single hit after September 1. By season's end his average was down to .269; coupled with his terrible clutch performance (.182), it didn't look like a good season at all.

The horrendous slump was bewildering both to the Bucs and to Reynolds. Nothing in R.J.'s past indicated this could happen. He'd hit solidly at every stop of his minor league career, in fact doing better as he rose through the Dodger farm system: .277 at Vero Beach, .313 at Lodi, .337 at San Antonio, .347 at Albuquerque. He'd had some trouble adjusting to a part-time role when he finally made the big club, but once he was traded to Pittsburgh and put in the lineup, he started hitting right away. He kept it up, until last August.

Was it just a slump, or did the pitchers find a weakness? My own feeling, both from observation and from looking at Reynolds' record, is that the guy can play; he has line-drive power, speed, a decent throwing arm, and could probably hit .280–.300. But I wonder if the Pirates feel the same way. For the past couple of years they've been trading marketable veterans for young prospects, which isn't a bad idea . . . except that some of the prospects—Mike Brown, Bobby Bonilla, Joe Orsulak and Trench Davis from their own system, and possibly Reynolds—seem to have gone out of style pretty quickly. When you're losing 98 games, why not stick with a guy who's hit everywhere he's been given a chance to play? It's just a question.

—Don Zminda

	1986 SEASON											THREE YEARS (84 – 86)										
	Ave.	OBP	SLG	AB	H	2B	3B	HR	RBI	BB	SO	Ave.	OBP	SLG	AB	H	2B	3B	HR	RBI	BB	SO
Totals	.269	.335	.420	402	108	30	2	9	48	40	78	.271	.324	.394	979	265	57	11	14	114	76	165
Batting vs. Left and Right-handed Pitchers																						
Left	.219	.278	.286	105	23	5	1	0	11	9	21	.256	.292	.346	289	74	15	4	1	33	15	39
Right	.286	.355	.468	297	85	25	1	9	37	31	57	.277	.336	.414	690	191	42	7	13	81	61	126
At Home and on the Road																						
Home	.283	.357	.485	198	56	18	2	6	29	24	34	.276	.337	.423	468	129	33	6	8	59	43	81
Road	.255	.312	.358	204	52	12	0	3	19	16	44	.266	.311	.368	511	136	24	5	6	55	33	84
Facing Groundball Pitchers and Flyball Pitchers																						
Groundball	.315	.392	.491	165	52	16	2	3	23	22	23	.311	.359	.438	425	132	25	7	5	55	33	53
Flyball	.236	.293	.371	237	56	14	0	6	25	18	55	.240	.297	.361	554	133	32	4	9	59	43	112
Facing Finesse Pitchers and Power Pitchers																						
Finesse	.267	.320	.440	225	60	17	2	6	27	17	33	.265	.306	.379	554	147	24	6	9	71	31	67
Power	.271	.353	.395	177	48	13	0	3	21	23	45	.278	.346	.414	425	118	33	5	5	43	45	98
On Grass and on Turf																						
Grass	.307	.368	.430	114	35	5	0	3	12	11	26	.279	.327	.371	426	119	20	2	5	51	30	81
Turf	.253	.322	.417	288	73	25	2	6	36	29	52	.264	.321	.412	553	146	37	9	9	63	46	84
During the Day and at Night																						
Day	.246	.308	.364	118	29	8	0	2	16	11	26	.248	.283	.329	310	77	13	3	2	37	16	58
Night	.278	.346	.444	284	79	22	2	7	32	29	52	.281	.342	.425	669	188	44	8	12	77	60	107
By Month																						
April	.296	.351	.493	71	21	8	0	2	9	6	16	.289	.337	.470	83	24	9	0	2	9	6	17
May	.268	.348	.415	82	22	6	0	2	7	10	17	.289	.337	.404	228	66	16	2	2	23	18	36
June	.298	.372	.488	84	25	8	1	2	11	10	18	.271	.339	.399	218	59	12	2	4	27	21	39
July	.360	.422	.533	75	27	4	0	3	13	8	9	.287	.342	.426	136	39	8	1	3	21	12	20
August	.165	.209	.241	79	13	4	1	0	8	5	17	.193	.237	.266	109	21	4	2	0	10	7	21
Sept/Oct	.000	.154	.000	11	0	0	0	0	0	1	1	.273	.320	.395	205	56	8	4	3	24	12	32
Situational																						
Bases Empty	.275	.350	.419	236	65	19	0	5	5	26	46	.268	.325	.394	579	155	37	6	8	8	47	89
Leadoff	.311	.398	.515	103	32	9	0	4	4	14	13	.280	.345	.435	232	65	15	3	5	5	22	30
Not Leadoff	.248	.310	.346	133	33	10	0	1	1	12	33	.259	.311	.366	347	90	22	3	3	3	25	59
Runners On	.259	.313	.422	166	43	11	2	4	43	14	32	.275	.322	.395	400	110	20	5	6	106	29	76
First Base Only	.279	.313	.459	61	17	3	1	2	7	3	11	.286	.318	.415	147	42	6	2	3	12	7	26
Scoring Position	.248	.314	.400	105	26	8	1	2	36	11	21	.269	.324	.383	253	68	14	3	3	94	22	50
Late Innings, Close	.182	.250	.250	88	16	6	0	0	6	8	21	.243	.288	.354	206	50	14	3	1	20	13	48

RBI/Opportunities				
Scoring Position	29 / 136	(21%)	85 / 334	(25%)
Scoring Position, 2 Out	12 / 54	(22%)	35 / 148	(24%)
On Third, Less than 2 Out	12 / 21	(57%)	33 / 61	(54%)
RBI in close games / RBI Total	29 / 48	(60%)	75 / 114	(66%)

Rick Rhoden
Pittsburgh Pirates

This is getting to be a routine matter here in Pirateland. Even before the season starts, a Bucco starting pitcher issues a demand to be traded. In 1985 (and 1984 for that matter), it was John Candelaria. In 1986, it was Rick Rhoden.

Whereas Candelaria conducted himself with all the charm and diplomacy of a Shiite terrorist, Rhoden and his agent, Tony Attanasio, handled themselves with (mostly) class throughout their negotiations with Pirate GM Syd "Mr. Molasses" Thrift. And while Candelaria closed out his Pirate career with a spotty, indifferent performance, Rhoden faced the possibility of a 20-win season with a last-place ballclub until it all blew up in September. Sailing into the final month of the season, Rhoden was 15–7 with a 2.45 ERA and had gone 5–1 during August. So what happened? In six September starts, he generated five decisions, not one of which was in his favor. If he didn't just flat out get rocked, he got nailed by some inane baserunning gaffe or a defensive misplay by one of the New Bucs ("We Play Hardball!"). This guy only gave up three gopher balls with men on base all year and I swear they all came in September. So what promised to be a milestone year in Rhoden's career died in the debacle of the Pirates' finish and—even

worse—a subpar Steeler start. A man of pride and dignity soon to be departing the Pittsburgh sporting scene was relegated to the back pages; people were too busy asking, "What's wrong with the Steelers?" Rick Rhoden's gone now, recently shipped to the Yankees (personally, I find it almost incomprehensible that Syd Thrift actually completed a trade). The Pirates received three young pitchers—Drabek, Fisher and Easley—in return. The trade was forced by Rhoden, as everyone knows; I don't think he'd be gone if he hadn't done this, considering Mr. Thrift's reluctance to deal. I don't know the clinical definition of a man's competitive nature, but as a softball player, I've played on some bad teams, and losing game after game gets old real fast—and the Pirates have been getting old real fast since 1984. This is the Marquis de Sade's vision of a professional baseball franchise.

To wrap this up, I wish I could say, "Good luck, Rick, to you and your new team." But I can't. You see, I despise the Yankees. So, good luck, Rick, and I hope you can find the inner strength you'll need to play for another cellar dweller.

—Bill Thomas

1986: Finesse, Groundball **1985: Finesse, Groundball** **1984: Finesse, Groundball**

	1986 SEASON											THREE YEARS (84 – 86)											
	G	IP	H	BB	SO	SB	CS	W	L	S	ERA	G	IP	H	BB	SO	SB	CS	W	L	S	ERA
Totals	34	253.2	211	76	159	20	15	15	12	0	2.84	102	705.1	681	207	423	48	40	39	36	0	3.29
At Home and on the Road																							
Home	19	140.0	111	42	93	10	9	9	6	0	2.76	55	387.1	369	112	229	26	24	24	18	0	2.97
Road	15	113.2	100	34	66	10	6	6	6	0	2.93	47	318.0	312	95	194	22	16	15	18	0	3.68
During the Day and at Night																							
Day	9	65.2	59	19	37	5	3	5	2	0	2.47	31	214.2	202	64	124	16	13	13	9	0	2.98
Night	25	188.0	152	57	122	15	12	10	10	0	2.97	71	490.2	479	143	299	32	27	26	27	0	3.43
On Grass and on Turf																							
Grass	8	56.2	53	19	31	4	4	2	3	0	2.86	26	173.1	168	55	110	9	8	7	12	0	3.79
Turf	26	197.0	158	57	128	16	11	13	9	0	2.83	76	532.0	513	152	313	39	32	32	24	0	3.13
By Month																							
April	4	27.2	22	9	19	2	4	2	1	0	2.28	14	88.1	100	27	48	5	8	5	6	0	3.77
May	5	36.2	32	13	21	2	2	1	2	0	3.19	16	111.2	110	37	49	5	4	6	5	0	2.82
June	6	45.1	33	13	35	1	0	5	1	0	1.99	17	119.2	111	27	82	7	5	8	5	0	3.01
July	6	43.1	37	17	27	4	5	2	2	0	1.87	18	124.0	118	42	79	6	11	5	10	0	3.05
August	7	56.0	45	11	30	7	1	5	1	0	2.73	17	129.0	114	35	90	11	6	10	3	0	3.00
Sept/Oct	6	44.2	42	13	27	4	3	0	5	0	4.84	20	132.2	128	39	75	14	6	5	7	0	4.14

vs. Opponent Batters

	1986 SEASON											THREE YEARS (84 – 86)									
	Ave.	OBP	SLG	AB	H	2B	3B	HR	RBI	BB	SO	Ave.	OBP	SLG	AB	H	2B	3B	HR	RBI	BB	SO
Totals	.228	.286	.347	926	211	45	7	17	78	76	159	.255	.310	.370	2673	681	129	17	48	247	207	423
Pitching vs. Left and Right-handed Batters																						
Left	.228	.292	.300	513	117	21	2	4	40	46	72	.260	.317	.345	1425	371	58	10	14	116	117	183
Right	.228	.280	.404	413	94	24	5	13	38	30	87	.248	.301	.398	1248	310	71	7	34	131	90	240
Situational																						
Bases Empty	.229	.281	.357	594	136	30	2	14	14	41	91	.259	.302	.383	1639	425	82	8	35	35	99	242
Leadoff	.220	.260	.359	245	54	10	0	8	8	12	35	.275	.308	.435	697	192	37	4	22	22	32	89
Not Leadoff	.235	.296	.355	349	82	20	2	6	6	29	56	.247	.298	.345	942	233	45	4	13	13	67	153
Runners On	.226	.296	.328	332	75	15	5	3	64	35	68	.248	.320	.348	1034	256	47	9	13	212	108	181
First Base Only	.217	.253	.273	143	31	4	2	0	2	7	32	.247	.296	.320	438	108	12	4	4	16	30	59
Scoring Position	.233	.324	.370	189	44	11	3	3	62	28	36	.248	.337	.369	596	148	35	5	9	196	78	122
Late Innings, Close	.210	.282	.310	100	21	4	0	2	6	10	19	.285	.346	.376	274	78	12	2	3	19	26	48

RBI/Opportunities

Scoring Position		54 / 252	(21%)		173 / 790	(22%)
Scoring Position, 2 Out		27 / 136	(20%)		76 / 394	(19%)
On Third, Less than 2 Out		14 / 30	(47%)		51 / 114	(45%)
RBI in close games / RBI Total		59 / 78	(76%)		180 / 247	(73%)

Jim Rice
Boston Red Sox

In 1986, Jim Rice decided that his homers were coming too dearly. In 1984–85, he had hit 55 and grounded into 71 double plays; if a DP ball can be considered as the defensive equivelant of a 'tater, Rice's balance sheet was well into the red.

In 1986, he made himself less a swinger and more a hitter. He choked up on the bat and stopped trying to jerk everything. As a result, Jim was the only Red Sock (?) to substantially increase his offensive output last year. For the first time in three years, he had more HRs than GIDPs. Every offensive category save triples and homers was up. He doubled his doubles. After years of marginal offense on turf, he was second only to Boggs; his road BA went up 78 points overall. Since he tried only to meet the ball, he began doing better against power pitchers and hitting well at night. The cost of all this was only seven homers; the jumps in singles and doubles offset this. The most exciting statistic is his month-by-month data; Rice was, in every way, a more consistent hitter.

Where Rice hit the ball seemed to hinge on how hard he hit it. Many of his homers were to center, most of the doubles went to right-center and the singles went all over the place; that raises interesting questions about the time-honored Fenway cliches. In the past, Jim was a classic righthanded slugger who tried to put everything over the "Green Monster;" just the sort of player that Boston has always tried to build its offense around. Now, he's begun to hit the ball the other way—into that huge right field—and his team won the pennant and he was in the running for MVP. Is this what the successful Boston hitter does? Will Rice continue to be successful by doing this? Time will tell—we'll see what happens in 1987 first.

A line drive off the monster is always an exciting play—Jim's forte is the slick way that he gets the rebound. He looks amazingly like a jai alai player as he grabs, turns and throws in one motion. Rice's arm isn't strong but it is very accurate—he turns many doubles into singles and makes most of the doubles entertainingly close. Away from Fenway, his range is a problem; he mitigates this by excellant defensive positioning. Overall, he probably saves Boston as many runs at home as he costs them on the road.

—Fred Percival

	1986 SEASON											THREE YEARS (84 – 86)										
	Ave.	OBP	SLG	AB	H	2B	3B	HR	RBI	BB	SO	Ave.	OBP	SLG	AB	H	2B	3B	HR	RBI	BB	SO
Totals	.324	.384	.490	618	200	39	2	20	110	62	78	.298	.352	.481	1821	543	84	12	75	335	157	255
Batting vs. Left and Right-handed Pitchers																						
Left	.351	.413	.560	168	59	14	0	7	39	19	14	.314	.390	.521	472	148	28	2	22	88	62	51
Right	.313	.373	.464	450	141	25	2	13	71	43	64	.293	.338	.467	1349	395	56	10	53	247	95	204
At Home and on the Road																						
Home	.337	.387	.526	312	105	25	2	10	48	28	35	.323	.369	.523	916	296	53	8	38	183	71	128
Road	.310	.381	.454	306	95	14	0	10	62	34	43	.273	.335	.439	905	247	31	4	37	152	86	127
Facing Groundball Pitchers and Flyball Pitchers																						
Groundball	.321	.372	.446	287	92	17	2	5	35	24	34	.301	.352	.452	883	266	35	7	28	146	72	108
Flyball	.326	.394	.529	331	108	22	0	15	75	38	44	.295	.352	.509	938	277	49	5	47	189	85	147
Facing Finesse Pitchers and Power Pitchers																						
Finesse	.313	.369	.510	355	111	24	2	14	62	32	33	.291	.340	.478	1046	304	45	5	47	181	80	110
Power	.338	.404	.464	263	89	15	0	6	48	30	45	.308	.368	.485	775	239	39	7	28	154	77	145
On Grass and on Turf																						
Grass	.317	.378	.484	523	166	32	2	17	95	53	65	.302	.354	.495	1542	465	71	12	68	301	130	211
Turf	.358	.419	.526	95	34	7	0	3	15	9	13	.280	.343	.401	279	78	13	0	7	34	27	44
During the Day and at Night																						
Day	.293	.355	.476	208	61	12	1	8	29	20	21	.293	.345	.491	580	170	25	3	28	106	47	77
Night	.339	.398	.498	410	139	27	1	12	81	42	57	.301	.355	.476	1241	373	59	9	47	229	110	178
By Month																						
April	.260	.313	.442	77	20	5	0	3	14	6	4	.246	.310	.394	236	58	9	1	8	41	22	27
May	.368	.430	.491	114	42	8	0	2	23	13	15	.300	.343	.467	323	97	13	1	13	57	22	50
June	.340	.385	.500	106	36	11	0	2	16	9	19	.341	.387	.565	331	113	26	3	14	65	27	49
July	.330	.379	.500	88	29	5	2	2	9	7	8	.265	.310	.395	309	82	7	3	9	45	21	41
August	.308	.378	.453	117	36	5	0	4	21	13	21	.268	.340	.431	332	89	13	1	13	55	37	54
Sept/Oct	.319	.393	.543	116	37	5	0	7	27	14	11	.359	.411	.621	290	104	16	3	18	72	28	34
Situational																						
Bases Empty	.309	.364	.469	311	96	19	2	9	9	25	39	.282	.334	.459	856	241	39	4	35	35	63	117
Leadoff	.266	.326	.399	158	42	9	0	4	4	13	18	.279	.335	.456	366	102	20	0	15	15	28	44
Not Leadoff	.353	.404	.542	153	54	10	2	5	5	12	21	.284	.333	.461	490	139	19	4	20	20	35	73
Runners On	.339	.403	.511	307	104	20	0	11	101	37	39	.313	.367	.501	965	302	45	8	40	300	94	138
First Base Only	.333	.386	.467	105	35	8	0	2	4	8	8	.288	.323	.466	410	118	19	3	16	38	20	51
Scoring Position	.342	.411	.535	202	69	12	0	9	97	29	31	.332	.397	.526	555	184	26	5	24	262	74	87
Late Innings, Close	.337	.427	.506	83	28	8	0	2	12	12	12	.255	.323	.456	263	67	12	1	13	50	27	43
RBI/Opportunities																						
Scoring Position				85 / 285	(30%)										224 / 777	(29%)						
Scoring Position, 2 Out				29 / 113	(26%)										69 / 288	(24%)						
On Third, Less than 2 Out				39 / 66	(59%)										95 / 177	(54%)						
RBI in close games / RBI Total				83 / 110	(75%)										229 / 335	(68%)						

Dave Righetti
New York Yankees

When a pitcher records a record-shattering 46 saves, people wonder what happened—it's easy to see what it was by comparing Dave Righetti's '86 stats to 1985. In 1985, he was the worst of the Yankees' regular relievers at stranding inherited runners, allowing 26 of 68 (38%) to score. In 1986, he didn't allow an inherited runner to score until June 9 and only allowed nine of 48 (19%) overall. He went from being about average in the most important area of his job to just about the best.

A key reason why was his new manager. It's obvious that Billy Martin brought Righetti into games more often with men on base than Lou Piniella did. Righetti had almost identical numbers of appearances and innings pitched in '85 and '86, but he inherited 20 more runners in 1985. He started an inning 51 times in 1985—that figure rose to 83 in 1986. Lou didn't use Dave any less than Billy had, but he made sure that he was in there before trouble started—apparently Dave liked being handled that way.

There are other comparisons that show how well Righetti pitched. In 1985, he allowed 69% of opposing runners to score from third with less than two outs—in 1986, only 35% crossed the plate. Hitters batted .241 against Dave and slugged .327 in 1985. He held them to .226 and .296 in 1986. With men in scoring position, opposing batters hit .258 in 1985; it fell to .218 this year. Righetti walked ten less men in 1986 and he even cut down the running game. In 1985, seven of nine steal attempts succeeded—in 1986, only four of seven made it.

It's interesting to note how much Yankee Stadium means to Dave. In the last three seasons, his ERA at home is nearly a full run lower, he's won twice as many games and lost half as many. His record in June is also impressive, but in a different way. Absolutely everything goes wrong—he allows more hits, walks and steals, loses most often, saves the least and has the highest ERA. Righetti has spent part of the year on the disabled list in four separate years—three of those times he missed part of the month of June. It's enough to make you believe in astrology.

Finally, the debate about where Righetti belongs is temporarily over. Piniella says that Dave will be the stopper for as long as he manages (how long that will be is anyone's guess). If Billy returns, though, Rags won't stay in the pen for long. Martin's policy is to put the best arms into the rotation—right now, Righetti is the best on the Yankee staff.

—Craig Christmann

1986: Power, Groundball											1985: Power, Flyball										1984: Power, Groundball

	1986 SEASON											**THREE YEARS (84 – 86)**									
	G	IP	H	BB	SO	SB	CS	W	L	S	ERA	G	IP	H	BB	SO	SB	CS	W	L	S	ERA
Totals	74	106.2	88	35	83	4	3	8	8	46	2.45	212	310.0	263	117	265	19	9	25	21	**	2.50
At Home and on the Road																						
Home	32	49.2	37	12	48	0	1	5	5	18	1.99	101	156.0	124	49	149	12	4	17	7	51	2.02
Road	42	57.0	51	23	35	4	2	3	3	28	2.84	111	154.0	139	68	116	7	5	8	14	55	2.98
During the Day and at Night																						
Day	25	36.0	33	11	32	2	2	5	4	11	3.25	68	99.1	86	44	88	6	4	12	7	30	2.17
Night	49	70.2	55	24	51	2	1	3	4	35	2.04	144	210.2	177	73	177	13	5	13	14	76	2.65
On Grass and on Turf																						
Grass	59	88.0	71	29	72	4	3	7	7	34	2.35	179	267.0	221	104	232	16	9	23	18	87	2.53
Turf	15	18.2	17	6	11	0	0	1	1	12	2.89	33	43.0	42	13	33	3	0	2	3	19	2.30
By Month																						
April	9	13.2	15	9	11	1	2	2	1	5	4.61	27	43.0	42	22	31	2	4	4	2	12	2.93
May	13	16.0	10	3	16	0	1	2	1	7	1.69	35	51.0	34	14	45	3	1	4	4	16	1.41
June	13	13.1	17	9	7	2	0	1	2	5	6.08	34	41.2	42	28	37	6	1	4	5	11	4.97
July	10	18.0	12	3	16	0	0	2	0	6	1.00	34	53.2	41	15	46	1	1	4	3	19	1.84
August	13	22.0	15	6	17	0	0	0	3	10	1.23	40	60.2	43	21	50	3	1	6	4	20	1.34
Sept/Oct	16	23.2	19	5	16	1	0	1	1	13	1.90	42	60.0	61	17	56	4	1	3	3	28	3.15

	vs. Opponent Batters																		

	1986 SEASON										**THREE YEARS (84 – 86)**								
	Ave.	OBP	SLG	AB	H	2B	3B	HR	RBI	BB	SO	Ave.	OBP	SLG	AB	H	2B	3B	HR	RBI	BB	SO
Totals	.226	.291	.296	389	88	15	0	4	39	35	83	.230	.300	.306	1142	263	40	2	14	133	117	265
Pitching vs. Left and Right-handed Batters																						
Left	.304	.388	.391	69	21	3	0	1	12	8	16	.219	.326	.297	256	56	11	0	3	35	39	69
Right	.209	.269	.275	320	67	12	0	3	27	27	67	.234	.293	.308	886	207	29	2	11	98	78	196
Situational																						
Bases Empty	.226	.279	.289	190	43	9	0	1	1	14	46	.216	.278	.286	556	120	18	0	7	7	48	137
Leadoff	.253	.295	.325	83	21	3	0	1	1	5	18	.225	.285	.326	227	51	8	0	5	5	19	55
Not Leadoff	.206	.267	.262	107	22	6	0	0	0	9	28	.210	.274	.258	329	69	10	0	2	2	29	82
Runners On	.226	.301	.302	199	45	6	0	3	38	21	37	.244	.320	.324	586	143	22	2	7	126	69	128
First Base Only	.237	.299	.325	80	19	1	0	2	4	6	13	.245	.313	.314	229	56	7	0	3	8	22	51
Scoring Position	.218	.302	.286	119	26	5	0	1	34	15	24	.244	.325	.331	357	87	15	2	4	118	47	77
Late Innings, Close	.237	.306	.322	295	70	13	0	4	36	29	63	.237	.308	.312	894	212	32	1	11	117	95	205

RBI/Opportunities						
Scoring Position	31 / 174	(18%)		104 / 515	(20%)	
Scoring Position, 2 Out	13 / 77	(17%)		44 / 246	(18%)	
On Third, Less than 2 Out	8 / 23	(35%)		37 / 87	(43%)	
RBI in close games / RBI Total	36 / 39	(92%)		125 / 133	(94%)	

Earnest Riles
Milwaukee Brewers

I try never to use intangibles to evaluate players, so I'll have trouble discussing Earnie Riles. I can't, on principle, say that he had a bad year because he decided that he'd locked up a job and goofed off. But I'd like to.

There was nothing bad you could say about Riles's 1985. He hit .286, slugged .377 and had a .339 on-base average, each of which was fair. His defense was marginal—4.29 range factor, 86 double plays per 162 games—but he had super defensive stats in the minors, and I felt that he'd improve. I knew he wouldn't hit .286 again (he had hit .332 at home; nobody has ever been able to do that consistently), but I felt that he'd develop power, walk more, field better and become a pretty fair player.

What happened in 1986? You got me. Earnie increased his power and walked more, but his average dropped so much that they were actually worse than 1985. I can see two explanations; neither makes Earnie look very good. First, the rest of the league caught up with him. In 1985, Riles hit flyball pitchers for a .290 average; he hit .233 this year. He'd hit .251 against power pitchers in 1985—he hit .208 in 1986. The most obvious explanation for that drop is that pitchers

stopped playing patty-cake, began challenging him and he just couldn't handle it. That happens more often than people realize (Mark Salas or Vince Coleman are clear examples from 1986), but it is very hard for me to accept that. Riles's stints in AA and AAA suggested that he would be a .260–.275 hitter who have 25 doubles, 8 homers and 70 walks; it would be very unusual for them to be that far off.

Besides, even if he wasn't the hitter I thought, there is no excuse for his fielding. Earnie had the worst range factor of any regular shortstop in baseball (3.80) and turned an abysmal 87 DPs per 162 games. Did the hitters catch up to him and start challenging him? I think not. All summer, my friends in Milwaukee told me that Earnie was dogging it; given the evidence, I've got to agree with them.

The 1985 Riles was a good player; the 1986 one isn't a major leaguer. He hit far less than expected, played awful defense and fought with the media a lot. I don't know which year represents the true Riles, but, for his own career's sake, it had better be the earlier model—if he isn't going full throttle now, he'd better start doing it fast.

—Geoff Beckman

| | 1986 SEASON | | | | | | | | | | | THREE YEARS (84 – 86) | | | | | | | | | | |
	Ave.	OBP	SLG	AB	H	2B	3B	HR	RBI	BB	SO	Ave.	OBP	SLG	AB	H	2B	3B	HR	RBI	BB	SO
Totals	.252	.321	.357	524	132	24	2	9	47	54	80	.267	.330	.366	972	260	36	9	14	92	90	134
Batting vs. Left and Right-handed Pitchers																						
Left	.209	.272	.322	115	24	2	1	3	13	9	22	.227	.293	.309	256	58	4	4	3	24	22	46
Right	.264	.335	.367	409	108	22	1	6	34	45	58	.282	.343	.387	716	202	32	5	11	68	68	88
At Home and on the Road																						
Home	.260	.337	.337	246	64	9	2	2	18	29	31	.294	.358	.379	472	139	18	5	4	42	47	60
Road	.245	.307	.374	278	68	15	0	7	29	25	49	.242	.303	.354	500	121	18	4	10	50	43	74
Facing Groundball Pitchers and Flyball Pitchers																						
Groundball	.273	.345	.357	249	68	12	0	3	23	28	32	.276	.343	.361	474	131	17	4	5	44	47	63
Flyball	.233	.299	.356	275	64	12	2	6	24	26	48	.259	.317	.371	498	129	19	5	9	48	43	71
Facing Finesse Pitchers and Power Pitchers																						
Finesse	.289	.344	.408	284	82	17	1	5	25	25	31	.300	.347	.410	537	161	26	6	7	54	41	63
Power	.208	.295	.296	240	50	7	1	4	22	29	49	.228	.309	.313	435	99	10	3	7	38	49	71
On Grass and on Turf																						
Grass	.244	.318	.352	446	109	20	2	8	40	48	68	.268	.331	.369	813	218	30	8	12	77	76	117
Turf	.295	.341	.385	78	23	4	0	1	7	6	12	.264	.322	.352	159	42	6	1	2	15	14	17
During the Day and at Night																						
Day	.247	.320	.354	178	44	7	0	4	14	19	27	.254	.321	.352	315	80	9	2	6	29	31	39
Night	.254	.322	.358	346	88	17	2	5	33	35	53	.274	.334	.373	657	180	27	7	8	63	59	95
By Month																						
April	.214	.257	.329	70	15	0	1	2	8	4	16	.214	.257	.329	70	15	0	1	2	8	4	16
May	.287	.342	.389	108	31	5	0	2	13	10	12	.305	.344	.411	141	43	6	0	3	18	10	16
June	.278	.381	.367	90	25	5	0	1	4	14	11	.254	.335	.357	185	47	7	3	2	17	22	23
July	.221	.295	.316	95	21	4	1	1	8	10	17	.267	.338	.364	176	47	7	2	2	13	19	24
August	.247	.322	.358	81	20	3	0	2	5	9	12	.299	.353	.401	187	56	4	3	3	21	14	24
Sept/Oct	.250	.307	.375	80	20	7	0	1	9	7	12	.244	.311	.329	213	52	12	0	2	15	21	31
Situational																						
Bases Empty	.251	.318	.329	307	77	17	2	1	1	30	53	.263	.322	.351	552	145	25	6	4	4	47	85
Leadoff	.266	.331	.347	124	33	10	0	0	0	12	17	.284	.335	.364	225	64	14	2	0	0	17	27
Not Leadoff	.240	.308	.317	183	44	7	2	1	1	18	36	.248	.313	.343	327	81	11	4	4	4	30	58
Runners On	.253	.327	.396	217	55	7	0	8	46	24	27	.274	.340	.386	420	115	11	3	10	88	43	49
First Base Only	.341	.394	.538	91	31	6	0	4	10	7	7	.319	.385	.447	188	60	10	1	4	13	19	16
Scoring Position	.190	.281	.294	126	24	1	0	4	36	17	20	.237	.304	.336	232	55	1	2	6	75	24	33
Late Innings, Close	.270	.333	.360	89	24	2	0	2	12	8	13	.255	.324	.317	161	41	4	0	2	17	15	21
RBI/Opportunities																						

	1986 SEASON			THREE YEARS (84 – 86)		
Scoring Position	29 / 178	(16%)		63 / 311	(20%)	
Scoring Position, 2 Out	10 / 79	(13%)		29 / 145	(20%)	
On Third, Less than 2 Out	12 / 32	(38%)		22 / 51	(43%)	
RBI in close games / RBI Total	35 / 47	(74%)		61 / 92	(66%)	

Cal Ripken
Baltimore Orioles

It says something good about Cal Ripken that the biggest controversies surrounding him are "should he move to third base?" and "should he sit out an inning?"; let's answer both here.

The only question in the debate about where to play Ripken is "Does he do the job defensively?" If he does, he stays; you can find a third baseman who can outhit Jackie Gutierrez on a sandlot. Since we obviously can't compare their defensive stats at shortstop for 1986, we'll use 1985 data. If we project their stats out to 162 games, Ripken has 12 more putouts, 17 more assists, 18 less errors and turns 33 more double plays. The fact that he turns so many DPs means that he actually has fewer total chances, but that's not important. Your job is to make outs—Ripken made 760 outs, Gutierrez made 731 and Ripken made fewer errors. End of dispute.

The answer to the second question is less clear. The question here is "Has there been a progressive drop in Ripken's performance as the streak has progressed?"; to measure that, we'll use Bill James's Runs Created Per 27 Outs (for offense) and Tim Marcou's Adjusted Range Factor (defense) covering the last three years. In 1984, Ripken created 7.08 runs per 27 outs and had an ARF of 5.45. In 1985, he had 5.17 RC/27 and his ARF was 4.79. In 1986, he had 6.04 RC/27 and an ARF of 4.52. Ripken's offense isn't hurt, but his defense has gotten progressively worse. The streak should be broken.

Ripken seems determined to make his breakdowns as odd as possible—in the last three years he has had no consistency at all. He has hit equally well against both righties and lefties ('84), better against righties ('85) and murdered lefties ('86); he has similar "patterns" in his other splits, too. Suffice it to say that he can hit anyone well, but you never know who that anyone will be. His only consistent splits are for leading off innings, which suggests where he should hit in the order. Davis Jackson's research on the number of times that each spot in the order leads off innings in a year gives these rankings for the AL (in order): 1, 4, 5, 8, 6, 7, 9, 2 and 3. Ripken should bat either fourth or fifth—certainly anywhere but third.

—Scott M. Daniel, Geoff Beckman and Tony Sabatino

	1986 SEASON											THREE YEARS (84 – 86)										
	Ave.	OBP	SLG	AB	H	2B	3B	HR	RBI	BB	SO	Ave.	OBP	SLG	AB	H	2B	3B	HR	RBI	BB	SO
Totals	.282	.355	.461	627	177	35	1	25	81	70	60	.290	.359	.480	1910	553	104	13	78	277	208	217
Batting vs. Left and Right-handed Pitchers																						
Left	.360	.428	.683	164	59	17	0	12	25	20	12	.310	.384	.547	525	163	41	4	25	75	63	41
Right	.255	.329	.382	463	118	18	1	13	56	50	48	.282	.349	.455	1385	390	63	9	53	202	145	176
At Home and on the Road																						
Home	.265	.344	.430	291	77	18	0	10	37	36	35	.281	.361	.474	909	255	45	4	41	134	114	113
Road	.298	.365	.488	336	100	17	1	15	44	34	25	.298	.357	.486	1001	298	59	9	37	143	94	104
Facing Groundball Pitchers and Flyball Pitchers																						
Groundball	.287	.365	.430	279	80	13	0	9	34	34	25	.297	.363	.482	892	265	40	7	37	139	95	93
Flyball	.279	.347	.486	348	97	22	1	16	47	36	35	.283	.355	.478	1018	288	64	6	41	138	113	124
Facing Finesse Pitchers and Power Pitchers																						
Finesse	.288	.369	.481	372	107	19	1	17	45	47	35	.290	.358	.486	1054	306	55	8	45	148	111	99
Power	.275	.335	.431	255	70	16	0	8	36	23	25	.289	.359	.473	856	247	49	5	33	129	97	118
On Grass and on Turf																						
Grass	.265	.341	.424	524	139	27	1	18	60	60	51	.283	.356	.466	1607	454	85	12	62	225	186	187
Turf	.369	.426	.650	103	38	8	0	7	21	10	9	.327	.372	.554	303	99	19	1	16	52	22	30
During the Day and at Night																						
Day	.307	.374	.479	192	59	12	0	7	29	20	16	.294	.362	.485	581	171	29	5	24	94	64	76
Night	.271	.347	.453	435	118	23	1	18	52	50	44	.287	.357	.478	1329	382	75	8	54	183	144	141
By Month																						
April	.247	.330	.416	77	19	4	0	3	14	10	11	.289	.375	.523	235	68	12	2	13	45	33	30
May	.253	.367	.451	91	23	6	0	4	14	15	11	.272	.347	.502	305	83	20	4	14	46	34	49
June	.311	.381	.462	106	33	8	1	2	7	12	8	.281	.350	.394	317	89	16	1	6	32	35	32
July	.379	.459	.660	103	39	8	0	7	21	16	10	.338	.404	.579	328	111	19	3	18	60	37	32
August	.250	.320	.405	116	29	3	0	5	13	12	10	.283	.353	.438	336	95	18	2	10	44	36	33
Sept/Oct	.254	.282	.388	134	34	6	0	4	12	5	10	.275	.330	.460	389	107	19	1	17	50	33	41
Situational																						
Bases Empty	.302	.370	.509	324	98	17	1	16	16	33	30	.291	.357	.490	1029	299	54	5	47	47	103	121
Leadoff	.361	.402	.622	119	43	7	0	8	8	8	10	.348	.387	.588	362	126	25	1	20	20	22	39
Not Leadoff	.268	.353	.444	205	55	10	1	8	8	25	20	.259	.342	.436	667	173	29	4	27	27	81	82
Runners On	.261	.339	.409	303	79	18	0	9	65	37	30	.288	.360	.469	881	254	50	8	31	230	105	96
First Base Only	.263	.320	.442	156	41	10	0	6	14	12	17	.276	.330	.474	416	115	27	5	15	41	32	43
Scoring Position	.259	.358	.374	147	38	8	0	3	51	25	13	.299	.385	.465	465	139	23	3	16	189	73	53
Late Innings, Close	.284	.337	.558	95	27	8	0	6	24	8	9	.333	.391	.553	291	97	17	1	15	55	29	37

RBI/Opportunities						
Scoring Position	44 / 202	(22%)		162 / 639	(25%)	
Scoring Position, 2 Out	5 / 82	(6%)		40 / 253	(16%)	
On Third, Less than 2 Out	22 / 35	(63%)		71 / 124	(57%)	
RBI in close games / RBI Total	59 / 81	(73%)		185 / 277	(67%)	

Don Robinson
Pittsburgh Pirates

If one word could describe Don Robinson, it would be "guts." Then again, "knees," "shoulder," and "misery" could also apply to the big 29-year-old pitcher from the West Virginia—Kentucky oil/coal area. Leg and arm injuries have plagued his career, but Don keeps pitching. Robinson's good-natured determination have made him a respected favorite of many Pirate fans. To them, he personifies the hard-working, blue-collar ideal that has faded both in baseball and on the streets of Pittsburgh. He is also the only Pirate remaining from the 1979 World Champions.

Robinson had a terrific rookie campaign as a starter in 1978 (14–6,3.47). Then injuries began to slow him down; nevertheless, he had a fine season in 1982, winning 15 games. Shoulder surgery in 1983 put his career in jeopardy, but he returned after a long rehabilitation period.

In his first six seasons, Robinson had pitched in 156 games, starting 119. Upon returning in 1984, he was shifted to the bullpen. That year, all he did was appear in a career-high 51 games, become the Pirates' top reliever, and win the Hutch award for courage. Despite suffering from minor injuries since, Don has appeared in 145 games in the past three seasons.

In 1986, with the Pirates totally lacking a stopper, Robby was suddenly thrust into prime time. His ERA of 3.38 won't win him any awards, but his 14 saves were the most by any Buc since 1983. Don looked comfortable and may have been pitching without pain, although you can't always believe what he says.

Despite his injuries, Robinson has remained a power pitcher. He struck out 101 men in relief in 1984, the only reliever to reach 100 that year. He maintains a strikeout/walk ratio of almost 2 to 1. Overall batting statistics against him have been generally poor, with batting, on-base, and slugging average all below league norms. Curiously, right-handed hitters give Don more trouble than lefties, who have hit for neither average nor power against him.

The addition of Brian Fisher to the Pirate bullpen may be ominous for Robinson. If Fisher pans out, then Don will either try starting, which has always been hard on his body, or switch to middle relief. Knowing Robinson's drive, he won't like the latter, and his courage hasn't been defeated yet. Expect to see Don in at least an occasional starting role this season.

—A.S.Nakamura

1986: Power, Flyball													1985: Power, Flyball													1984: Power, Flyball	

	1986 SEASON												THREE YEARS (84 – 86)											
	G	IP	H	BB	SO	SB	CS	W	L	S	ERA		G	IP	H	BB	SO	SB	CS	W	L	S	ERA
Totals	50	69.1	61	27	53	6	2	3	4	14	3.38		145	286.2	255	118	228	23	12	13	21	27	3.39
At Home and on the Road																							
Home	25	36.2	33	13	36	3	1	3	3	6	3.19		67	136.2	127	46	123	11	5	9	7	11	3.16
Road	25	32.2	28	14	17	3	1	0	1	8	3.58		78	150.0	128	72	105	12	7	4	14	16	3.60
During the Day and at Night																							
Day	19	23.2	22	8	19	1	1	0	1	6	3.42		51	89.0	77	38	67	7	1	3	5	11	3.54
Night	31	45.2	39	19	34	5	1	3	3	8	3.35		94	197.2	178	80	161	16	11	10	16	16	3.32
On Grass and on Turf																							
Grass	14	18.2	19	9	9	1	1	0	1	3	4.34		40	66.0	57	33	45	4	2	1	6	6	4.50
Turf	36	50.2	42	18	44	5	1	3	3	11	3.02		105	220.2	198	85	183	19	10	12	15	21	3.06
By Month																							
April	3	3.1	7	2	5	0	0	0	0	0	16.20		17	30.0	27	16	29	2	2	1	0	3	4.80
May	0	0.0	0	0	0	0	0	0	0	0	0.00		14	33.1	22	18	23	2	3	1	1	1	3.51
June	9	15.0	14	6	12	1	1	2	0	1	2.40		28	63.0	72	22	49	5	2	2	5	3	4.00
July	11	17.1	14	3	13	0	0	0	0	4	0.52		27	51.0	43	15	45	1	0	0	3	7	2.82
August	13	15.0	15	8	8	1	1	0	3	5	6.60		32	61.1	62	25	47	5	3	5	9	6	4.11
Sept/Oct	14	18.2	11	8	15	4	0	1	1	4	1.93		27	48.0	29	22	35	8	2	4	3	7	1.31

vs. Opponent Batters

	1986 SEASON											THREE YEARS (84 – 86)									
	Ave.	OBP	SLG	AB	H	2B	3B	HR	RBI	BB	SO	Ave.	OBP	SLG	AB	H	2B	3B	HR	RBI	BB	SO
Totals	.237	.310	.342	257	61	10	1	5	25	27	53	.239	.314	.342	1067	255	53	3	17	119	118	228
Pitching vs. Left and Right-handed Batters																					
Left	.193	.291	.220	109	21	3	0	0	5	15	25	.221	.320	.288	458	101	20	1	3	36	68	99
Right	.270	.325	.432	148	40	7	1	5	20	12	28	.253	.309	.383	609	154	33	2	14	83	50	129
Situational																					
Bases Empty	.235	.318	.326	132	31	6	0	2	2	16	27	.230	.301	.323	579	133	32	2	6	6	57	130
Leadoff	.273	.375	.309	55	15	2	0	0	0	9	12	.219	.301	.291	247	54	15	0	1	1	28	49
Not Leadoff	.208	.274	.338	77	16	4	0	2	2	7	15	.238	.301	.346	332	79	17	2	5	5	29	81
Runners On	.240	.303	.360	125	30	4	1	3	23	11	26	.250	.328	.365	488	122	21	1	11	113	61	98
First Base Only	.314	.352	.490	51	16	1	1	2	5	3	8	.295	.330	.405	190	56	7	1	4	13	10	34
Scoring Position	.189	.273	.270	74	14	3	0	1	18	8	18	.221	.327	.339	298	66	14	0	7	100	51	64
Late Innings, Close	.226	.300	.314	159	36	5	0	3	14	16	35	.214	.296	.304	514	110	22	0	8	53	60	125

RBI/Opportunities

Scoring Position	16 / 107	(15%)	84 / 440	(19%)
Scoring Position, 2 Out	5 / 51	(10%)	29 / 194	(15%)
On Third, Less than 2 Out	8 / 20	(40%)	35 / 81	(43%)
RBI in close games / RBI Total	14 / 25	(56%)	78 / 119	(66%)

Nolan Ryan
Houston Astros

Over the last three years, Nolan Ryan has been one of the great hot-and-cold pitchers in the game. Consider these facts: Ryan had a 7–2 start in 1984, a spectacular finish for 1986 (9–2, 5 or less hits allowed in 16 of 18 starts), and a contrasting three-year drought in July (4–10, 4.28 ERA) along with sluggish beginnings (4.22 three-year ERA in April). Now it appears to some that Ryan's age (40) has caught up with his phenomenal hits-allowed and strikeout artist. Dr. Frank Jobe, famous for his surgery on Tommy John, has said that a tendon transplant is the only solution to the Astros' fastballer's sore arm. Nolan, fearful of missing the '87 season, has decided to skip surgery to pitch, possibly in pain, for more abbreviated outings the remainder of his career.

This led me to curiosity about what the Ryan express would have accomplished over the last three years if he had been held to five-inning stints. I realize this extravagently assumes that the relief pitching holds the lead the rest of the way, but the won-lost records still make for interesting observation. If pulled after five innings, Ryan's record of the last three years would be 46–35; his actual record has been 34–31.

Ryan still also does what any good pitcher will do when behind, i.e., keep you in the game. Again, under the five-inning example, the Astros would have been down by more than two runs when Ryan left only 16 times out of 95 starts for 1984–86—a meager 16.8%.

The statistics below show plenty beneath the surface of Nolan Ryan's 34–31 record. How can you not love a pitcher who allows opposing batters no more than a .237 BA or a .338 OBA in any given situation? The overall opponents' batting average of .216 against Ryan is pretty impressive, too. In 1986, enemy batters hit only .187 against the Express, fourth best in the NL. Further, Ryan was the stingiest in the league for wild pitches and balks, although he is poor at holding baserunners—a pitcher from the old school who concentrates on the "out" standing at the plate.

The Ryan Express has not been shut down, just rerouted. Maybe the five-inning project would suit him well all year, or maybe he should be pampered for five innings in April and May only. Ryan always seems to wind up on the disabled list around June, maybe from overuse. Whatever, the Astros fine bullpen should complement the experiment well.

—Bud Podrazik

1986: Power, Flyball												1985: Power, Groundball											1984: Power, Flyball		
1986 SEASON												**THREE YEARS (84 – 86)**												
	G	IP	H	BB	SO	SB	CS	W	L	S	ERA		G	IP	H	BB	SO	SB	CS	W	L	S	ERA
Totals	30	178.0	119	82	194	26	9	12	8	0	3.34		95	593.2	467	246	600	94	26	34	31	0	3.43
At Home and on the Road																							
Home	17	109.0	56	49	122	16	5	9	4	0	2.56		49	322.2	220	124	320	53	9	21	12	0	2.71
Road	13	69.0	63	33	72	10	4	3	4	0	4.57		46	271.0	247	122	280	41	17	13	19	0	4.28
During the Day and at Night																							
Day	9	52.2	38	26	58	9	3	3	0	0	2.73		23	136.2	104	62	154	19	7	10	2	0	2.90
Night	21	125.1	81	56	136	17	6	9	8	0	3.59		72	457.0	363	184	446	75	19	24	29	0	3.58
On Grass and on Turf																							
Grass	7	39.2	34	15	38	3	2	1	2	0	3.86		25	150.2	144	51	140	17	7	8	9	0	4.18
Turf	23	138.1	85	67	156	23	7	11	6	0	3.19		70	443.0	323	195	460	77	19	26	22	0	3.17
By Month																							
April	6	34.0	32	15	31	6	4	3	3	0	5.56		16	100.1	83	32	90	15	7	6	6	0	4.22
May	6	31.2	31	15	28	5	3	0	3	0	4.83		18	122.2	86	50	126	18	8	8	4	0	2.27
June	2	11.0	5	8	12	0	0	1	0	0	1.64		10	63.1	58	26	58	13	4	5	3	0	3.27
July	6	39.0	19	18	55	6	0	3	1	0	2.31		18	109.1	83	52	125	21	0	4	10	0	4.28
August	4	22.1	14	12	22	3	1	2	1	0	2.82		17	109.1	91	49	112	17	6	6	5	0	3.87
Sept/Oct	6	40.0	18	14	46	6	1	3	0	0	2.02		16	88.2	66	37	89	10	1	5	3	0	2.64

vs. Opponent Batters																					
1986 SEASON												**THREE YEARS (84 – 86)**								
	Ave.	OBP	SLG	AB	H	2B	3B	HR	RBI	BB	SO		Ave.	OBP	SLG	AB	H	2B	3B	HR	RBI	BB	SO
Totals	.187	.283	.313	635	119	30	4	14	61	82	194		.216	.298	.321	2167	467	82	16	38	228	246	600
Pitching vs. Left and Right-handed Batters																							
Left	.185	.297	.281	313	58	14	2	4	24	50	90		.211	.298	.295	1063	224	35	8	13	100	133	289
Right	.189	.269	.345	322	61	16	2	10	37	32	104		.220	.297	.345	1104	243	47	8	25	128	113	311
Situational																							
Bases Empty	.173	.257	.274	405	70	20	3	5	5	45	124		.202	.279	.287	1294	262	42	11	15	15	133	366
Leadoff	.193	.272	.319	166	32	8	2	3	3	18	46		.228	.312	.334	545	124	22	6	8	8	67	139
Not Leadoff	.159	.247	.243	239	38	12	1	2	2	27	78		.184	.255	.252	749	138	20	5	7	7	66	227
Runners On	.213	.325	.383	230	49	10	1	9	56	37	70		.235	.324	.371	873	205	40	5	23	213	113	234
First Base Only	.167	.239	.274	84	14	3	0	2	7	7	23		.238	.300	.394	340	81	20	3	9	33	25	73
Scoring Position	.240	.368	.445	146	35	7	1	7	49	30	47		.233	.337	.356	533	124	20	2	14	180	88	161
Late Innings, Close	.232	.348	.393	56	13	3	0	2	9	10	10		.223	.280	.357	224	50	7	1	7	29	16	53

RBI/Opportunities						
Scoring Position		38 / 201	(19%)		153 / 760	(20%)
Scoring Position, 2 Out		16 / 96	(17%)		56 / 319	(18%)
On Third, Less than 2 Out		13 / 32	(41%)		66 / 157	(42%)
RBI in close games / RBI Total		49 / 61	(80%)		185 / 228	(81%)

Bret Saberhagen
Kansas City Royals

After a Cy Young season as a 21-year-old in 1985, Bret Saberhagen underwent a crisis of confidence in 1986, and struggled from the beginning to the end of the season. Though he didn't pitch badly—his ERA was just better than the league average, and his strikeout to walk ratio was terrific—Saberhagen also didn't pitch well.

Around the country, you probably don't know about the car commercial, and it may not strike you as sensible that a car commercial could play a major role in messing up a young player. Perhaps it was just a symbol of the problem and not a cause of it. Bret did a car commercial a year ago, a really disgusting locally produced effort in which he wiggled around and chanted about the "Saberhagen Shuffle." The damn thing ran constantly, and everybody in the region just hated it. People talked to one another frequently about how much they hated it. It was a pretty nauseating little film, sort of an "Ain't I sexy? Ain't I cute?" angle. With Saberhagen not pitching well, the commercial seemed to symbolize Bret's loss of innocence—and, in fact, that may have been exactly what was happening. Estranged from the fans, Saberhagen's preternatural self-confidence wavered. Saberhagen's task in 1987 will be to replace the confidence of a kid who doesn't know he can lose, with the mature confidence of a man who knows that he can win.

At the end of the year Saberhagen was pitching better, but then he usually does. There was some talk of a sore shoulder—and that is scary, because all of the young pitchers who have carried the workload that Bret did in 1985, certainly most have been destroyed by it. The loss of innocence is inevitable; it happened to Gooden right on schedule just like Saberhagen. But we can hope that the shoulder will hold up.

The most amazing thing about Saberhagen in 1985 was his command of the tricks of the trade. He was very careful, usually, to establish the fastball before trying to work in the breaking pitches. In his entire career he has only walked the leadoff hitter 27 times in over 500 innings. He took a fiendish delight in dropping down sidearm on a right-handed hitter. In the late innings of a close game, he became more aggressive, challenging hitters with rising fastballs that they couldn't lay off. In 1986, he seemed to forget about doing a lot of those things.

—Bill James

1986: Finesse, Groundball   **1985: Finesse, Flyball**   **1984: Finesse, Groundball**

	1986 SEASON											THREE YEARS (84 – 86)										
	G	IP	H	BB	SO	SB	CS	W	L	S	ERA	G	IP	H	BB	SO	SB	CS	W	L	S	ERA
Totals	30	156.0	165	29	112	10	5	7	12	0	4.15	100	549.0	514	103	343	35	21	37	29	1	3.41
At Home and on the Road																						
Home	13	76.0	88	12	55	6	2	2	5	0	3.67	46	282.1	251	48	167	17	10	16	13	1	2.87
Road	17	80.0	77	17	57	4	3	5	7	0	4.61	54	266.2	263	55	176	18	11	21	16	0	3.98
During the Day and at Night																						
Day	13	57.0	57	13	37	2	3	3	6	0	5.37	26	117.2	100	31	68	11	4	7	10	0	4.05
Night	17	99.0	108	16	75	8	2	4	6	0	3.45	74	431.1	414	72	275	24	17	30	19	1	3.23
On Grass and on Turf																						
Grass	14	70.0	59	14	50	4	0	4	5	0	3.86	45	237.1	219	47	160	15	6	19	12	0	3.56
Turf	16	86.0	106	15	62	6	5	3	7	0	4.40	55	311.2	295	56	183	20	15	18	17	1	3.29
By Month																						
April	4	23.2	23	5	12	2	0	1	2	0	4.56	14	74.1	72	14	30	8	2	4	5	0	3.39
May	6	42.0	47	10	31	1	0	1	3	0	3.21	16	106.0	107	23	59	3	1	5	7	0	3.74
June	6	36.2	39	6	23	4	1	2	4	0	4.91	18	104.0	98	24	61	6	4	4	8	0	3.55
July	6	28.2	25	3	23	1	1	2	1	0	4.71	19	106.0	88	12	76	6	2	9	3	1	2.89
August	2	3.0	3	2	3	1	0	0	0	0	6.00	14	56.2	54	12	40	4	3	7	1	0	4.29
Sept/Oct	6	22.0	28	3	20	1	3	1	2	0	3.27	19	102.0	95	18	77	8	9	8	5	0	3.00

vs. Opponent Batters

	1986 SEASON											THREE YEARS (84 – 86)									
	Ave.	OBP	SLG	AB	H	2B	3B	HR	RBI	BB	SO	Ave.	OBP	SLG	AB	H	2B	3B	HR	RBI	BB	SO
Totals	.268	.302	.402	615	165	21	8	15	70	29	112	.248	.283	.372	2074	514	77	20	47	204	103	343
Pitching vs. Left and Right-handed Batters																						
Left	.253	.288	.394	368	93	16	6	8	46	18	76	.249	.288	.389	1158	288	37	15	32	125	65	206
Right	.291	.323	.413	247	72	5	2	7	24	11	36	.247	.277	.350	916	226	40	5	15	79	38	137
Situational																						
Bases Empty	.263	.296	.387	372	98	7	3	11	11	15	72	.249	.284	.361	1295	322	39	10	29	29	58	222
Leadoff	.287	.335	.360	150	43	3	1	2	2	9	36	.255	.294	.358	533	136	15	5	10	10	27	91
Not Leadoff	.248	.268	.405	222	55	4	2	9	9	6	36	.244	.276	.364	762	186	24	5	19	19	31	131
Runners On	.276	.312	.424	243	67	14	5	4	59	14	40	.246	.282	.390	779	192	38	10	18	175	45	121
First Base Only	.244	.261	.374	131	32	1	5	2	10	3	23	.227	.250	.365	384	87	11	6	10	31	12	59
Scoring Position	.313	.365	.482	112	35	13	0	2	49	11	17	.266	.312	.415	395	105	27	4	8	144	33	62
Late Innings, Close	.216	.245	.314	51	11	0	1	1	2	2	7	.204	.247	.323	226	46	1	1	8	14	13	34

RBI/Opportunities

	1986 SEASON		THREE YEARS (84 – 86)	
Scoring Position	43 / 141	(30%)	128 / 504	(25%)
Scoring Position, 2 Out	17 / 65	(26%)	43 / 220	(20%)
On Third, Less than 2 Out	18 / 26	(69%)	57 / 92	(62%)
RBI in close games / RBI Total	51 / 70	(73%)	146 / 204	(72%)

Juan Samuel
Philadelphia Phillies

Juan Samuel, who burst upon the scene in 1984 with his exciting blend of power and speed, is not developing as a hitter. Since his rookie year he's neither progressed nor regressed in any major offensive category. Just look at his 1986 stats: his BA, SA and OBP are virtually identical to his career totals, even with respect to right and lefthanded pitching. He's produced double totals of 36, 31, 36, triple totals of 19, 13, 12, homer totals of 15, 19, 16 and RBI counts of 69, 74 and 78. This lack of movement is uncommon for a "raw" player like Juan, and usually indicates that future progress is unlikely.

The Phillies, of course, are delighted with Samuel's consistently high extra-base hit totals, as they should be; Juan's 64 EBH in '86 were sixth in the league behind Schmidt, Hayes, Glenn Davis, Parker and Murphy. But just as Samuel repeatedly displays these good numbers, he also repeats his major negative, an on-base percentage barely over the "Moreno line" of .300. Not coincidentally, his strikeout-walk ratio remains in the 5 to 1 neighborhood, which is no place you'd want to settle down. Usually a good young hitter with that kind of ratio will improve by his third year;

Samuel, obviously a good hitter, needs to improve if he's going to develop. To do this he'll have to learn to lay off the low outside pitch, which is the major cause of his high strikeout total. He's simply a sucker for it, swinging at this pitch no matter how bad it is, particularly when he's behind on the count. His trouble with this pitch might be the reason his stats are consistently worse against lefthanders than against righties. Having watched Samuel bat frequently during his three major league seasons, I marvel over the fact that he can maintain a .260 average with such poor judgment. He makes up for it with short but intense hitting binges. Every month or so he'll have a week of multiple hit games where he collects a lot of extra base hits. If he wises up he could be a truly great hitter.

Samuel's stolen base output slipped to 42 in '86 (he'd stolen 72 and 53 in '84-'85) as he was shuffled in and out of the leadoff spot; that's one area where he's not remaining constant. On defense he'd shown a lot of improvement in '85, but let both leagues in errors again in 1986. He remains brutal on the double play.

—Marco Bresba

	1986 SEASON											THREE YEARS (84 – 86)										
	Ave.	OBP	SLG	AB	H	2B	3B	HR	RBI	BB	SO	Ave.	OBP	SLG	AB	H	2B	3B	HR	RBI	BB	SO
Totals	.266	.302	.448	591	157	36	12	16	78	26	142	.268	.304	.442	1955	523	103	44	50	221	87	450
Batting vs. Left and Right-handed Pitchers																						
Left	.256	.283	.456	180	46	13	4	5	27	5	46	.257	.278	.406	569	146	32	10	11	59	16	131
Right	.270	.310	.445	411	111	23	8	11	51	21	96	.272	.314	.457	1386	377	71	34	39	162	71	319
At Home and on the Road																						
Home	.266	.313	.486	286	76	19	7	10	45	18	71	.254	.299	.432	944	240	46	22	26	104	51	226
Road	.266	.292	.413	305	81	17	5	6	33	8	71	.280	.309	.451	1011	283	57	22	24	117	36	224
Facing Groundball Pitchers and Flyball Pitchers																						
Groundball	.266	.311	.434	274	73	17	7	5	29	13	66	.270	.311	.427	903	244	46	21	18	88	42	203
Flyball	.265	.295	.461	317	84	19	5	11	49	13	76	.265	.298	.454	1052	279	57	23	32	133	45	247
Facing Finesse Pitchers and Power Pitchers																						
Finesse	.279	.311	.472	326	91	22	10	7	44	10	61	.275	.305	.451	1115	307	61	27	27	126	37	214
Power	.249	.291	.419	265	66	14	2	9	34	16	81	.257	.303	.430	840	216	42	17	23	95	50	236
On Grass and on Turf																						
Grass	.293	.329	.414	157	46	7	0	4	15	5	39	.292	.323	.477	518	151	25	10	17	65	19	123
Turf	.256	.292	.461	434	111	29	12	12	63	21	103	.259	.297	.429	1437	372	78	34	33	156	68	327
During the Day and at Night																						
Day	.298	.337	.564	181	54	11	5	9	32	9	39	.278	.317	.513	622	173	36	16	26	87	32	132
Night	.251	.287	.398	410	103	25	7	7	46	17	103	.263	.298	.409	1333	350	67	28	24	134	55	318
By Month																						
April	.286	.375	.357	14	4	1	0	0	1	2	2	.289	.338	.406	180	52	7	4	2	13	11	41
May	.253	.290	.313	99	25	3	0	1	8	4	25	.266	.302	.412	323	86	15	7	6	31	14	77
June	.250	.288	.500	124	31	10	3	5	26	4	35	.284	.320	.472	373	106	24	8	10	50	15	83
July	.283	.322	.504	113	32	6	5	3	13	6	24	.270	.308	.479	330	89	17	11	10	44	16	80
August	.254	.280	.483	118	30	8	2	5	20	4	27	.259	.282	.455	367	95	21	6	13	53	11	83
Sept/Oct	.285	.321	.431	123	35	8	2	2	10	6	29	.249	.291	.411	382	95	19	8	9	30	20	86
Situational																						
Bases Empty	.262	.292	.402	328	86	17	4	7	7	13	79	.268	.306	.426	1182	317	65	23	25	25	57	282
Leadoff	.277	.305	.396	101	28	7	1	1	1	4	22	.255	.303	.402	557	142	30	11	10	10	33	126
Not Leadoff	.256	.287	.405	227	58	10	3	6	6	9	57	.280	.309	.446	625	175	35	12	15	15	24	156
Runners On	.270	.314	.506	263	71	19	8	9	71	13	63	.266	.301	.467	773	206	38	21	25	196	30	168
First Base Only	.279	.322	.477	111	31	7	3	3	11	5	26	.278	.303	.464	306	85	17	8	8	27	8	66
Scoring Position	.263	.308	.526	152	40	12	5	6	60	8	37	.259	.300	.469	467	121	21	13	17	169	22	102
Late Innings, Close	.283	.333	.485	99	28	3	1	5	14	6	21	.251	.300	.410	315	79	12	4	10	39	18	86
RBI/Opportunities																						
Scoring Position				49 / 196		(25%)									141 / 594		(24%)					
Scoring Position, 2 Out				20 / 87		(23%)									62 / 281		(22%)					
On Third, Less than 2 Out				17 / 34		(50%)									42 / 87		(48%)					
RBI in close games / RBI Total				51 / 78		(65%)									141 / 221		(64%)					

Ryne Sandberg
Chicago Cubs

When Detroit's Al Kaline was but a pup of twenty, he made the mistake of leading the American League in hitting with .340. He also hit 27 homers and drove in 102, played a mean right field, and dared baserunners to, just once, try to take an extra base on his arm. The future was his. And he never did it again.

Oh, he was good—3,000 hits, Hall-of-Fame and all that. Even got to a World Series in 1968 as a part-timer, playing the role of distinguished elder statesman on a club dominated by the likes of Denny McLain and Mickey Lolich. He just never did what he was annointed to do following his remarkable 1955 season. Had he waited until he was 27 or 28 to have his biggest year, the true sparkle of his career would have been more evident. Instead, he induced visions of .400 batting averages, 40 home runs and oodles of RBIs, and then never made those dreams come true.

So, too, Ryne Sandberg. Not that he burst onto the scene in his rookie year posting all sorts of ridiculously good numbers, but rather that he put it all together in 1984 when the Cubs won something for the first time since V-J Day.

The whole baseball world was watching.

A batting average of .314, with 19 homers and 84 RBI. He had 36 doubles, 19 triples, stole 32 bases and played second base like he invented it. Like Robin Yount two years earlier, he heard chants of "MVP, MVP" every time he set foot on Wrigley Field's grass. He was young, talented, good-looking and All-American.

It hasn't been quite the same since. The Kaline Curse is alive and well. Some expectations can never be reached.

Of course, he still qualifies as the best in the business at his position. It's just that he's supposed to be better than that. He made just five errors again last season and, don't forget, the Cubs play most of their games on real grass, not ping-pong tables. He hit .284 with some power. He can still run. Unfortunately, most of his offensive numbers nose-dived from the previous two seasons.

Sandberg still strikes out too much and walks too little. He's dangerous, but he's not George Brett or Don Mattingly. He's not the 1955 Al Kaline, either, but he's still plenty good.

—Tom Henry

| | 1986 SEASON | | | | | | | | | | | THREE YEARS (84 – 86) | | | | | | | | | | |
	Ave.	OBP	SLG	AB	H	2B	3B	HR	RBI	BB	SO	Ave.	OBP	SLG	AB	H	2B	3B	HR	RBI	BB	SO
Totals	.284	.330	.411	627	178	28	5	14	76	46	79	.301	.354	.479	1872	564	95	30	59	243	155	277
Batting vs. Left and Right-handed Pitchers																						
Left	.264	.314	.377	159	42	4	1	4	21	12	15	.300	.351	.459	473	142	23	8	12	48	38	58
Right	.291	.335	.423	468	136	24	4	10	55	34	64	.302	.354	.485	1399	422	72	22	47	195	117	219
At Home and on the Road																						
Home	.302	.344	.445	321	97	18	2	8	41	23	42	.313	.371	.525	927	290	51	19	36	132	89	143
Road	.265	.315	.376	306	81	10	3	6	35	23	37	.290	.336	.433	945	274	44	11	23	111	66	134
Facing Groundball Pitchers and Flyball Pitchers																						
Groundball	.287	.340	.419	296	85	13	4	6	36	24	31	.310	.366	.490	865	268	48	15	26	113	78	119
Flyball	.281	.321	.405	331	93	15	1	8	40	22	48	.294	.343	.469	1007	296	47	15	33	130	77	158
Facing Finesse Pitchers and Power Pitchers																						
Finesse	.290	.327	.409	369	107	11	3	9	48	21	36	.305	.349	.481	1076	328	47	16	37	148	75	140
Power	.275	.334	.415	258	71	17	2	5	28	25	43	.296	.359	.475	796	236	48	14	22	95	80	137
On Grass and on Turf																						
Grass	.281	.330	.413	445	125	22	2	11	51	35	59	.308	.362	.509	1325	408	68	24	50	181	118	198
Turf	.291	.330	.407	182	53	6	3	3	25	11	20	.285	.332	.406	547	156	27	6	9	62	37	79
During the Day and at Night																						
Day	.293	.340	.442	430	126	22	3	12	56	33	51	.303	.359	.493	1248	378	68	23	41	163	112	180
Night	.264	.308	.345	197	52	6	2	2	20	13	28	.298	.342	.450	624	186	27	7	18	80	43	97
By Month																						
April	.247	.295	.395	81	20	4	1	2	9	6	12	.234	.289	.391	235	55	13	3	6	26	18	33
May	.337	.395	.510	104	35	7	1	3	17	12	12	.340	.390	.511	321	109	19	6	8	41	29	50
June	.259	.283	.388	116	30	4	1	3	17	4	10	.316	.355	.534	326	103	15	7	14	45	18	41
July	.266	.300	.394	94	25	3	0	3	8	5	13	.306	.356	.500	314	96	13	6	12	41	26	49
August	.291	.339	.382	110	32	4	0	2	8	8	15	.302	.352	.453	338	102	16	1	11	37	26	49
Sept/Oct	.295	.351	.402	122	36	6	2	1	17	11	17	.293	.361	.462	338	99	19	7	8	53	38	55
Situational																						
Bases Empty	.267	.313	.400	360	96	16	4	8	8	24	44	.303	.349	.489	1087	329	60	16	37	37	76	160
Leadoff	.215	.257	.393	107	23	5	1	4	4	6	13	.314	.352	.588	328	103	24	6	18	18	19	53
Not Leadoff	.289	.336	.403	253	73	11	3	4	4	18	31	.298	.348	.447	759	226	36	10	19	19	57	107
Runners On	.307	.353	.427	267	82	12	1	6	68	22	35	.299	.360	.464	785	235	35	14	22	206	79	117
First Base Only	.311	.330	.456	103	32	6	0	3	8	3	10	.307	.348	.490	335	103	17	4	12	35	21	41
Scoring Position	.305	.365	.409	164	50	6	1	3	60	19	25	.293	.368	.444	450	132	18	10	10	171	58	76
Late Innings, Close	.257	.297	.330	109	28	2	3	0	10	7	18	.302	.352	.495	285	86	10	9	9	46	23	45
RBI/Opportunities																						
Scoring Position				55 / 211		(26%)									153 / 602		(25%)					
Scoring Position, 2 Out				23 / 91		(25%)									53 / 254		(21%)					
On Third, Less than 2 Out				19 / 35		(54%)									54 / 94		(57%)					
RBI in close games / RBI Total				44 / 76		(58%)									158 / 243		(65%)					

Steve Sax
Los Angeles Dodgers

Magic fascinates almost everyone. It's not because we believe the magician really pulled a rabbit from nowhere. It is the act of illusion— knowing that the magician is fooling us but not knowing how. Sometimes ballplayers are the same. They have seasons that seem magical. In 1986, Steve Sax had that kind of year.

A .307 hitter in the minors, Steve got his major-league career off to a fine start. He came up in 1982 and became the fourth consecutive Dodger to win the Rookie-of-the-Year award. He led the Dodgers in five offensive catagories including runs, hits and stolen bases.

Steve's 1983 season was marred by errors. In the first half, he found himself having trouble throwing to first base. By the All-Star break, he had committed 24 errors. He worked hard, and he turned his fielding around in the second half, committing nary an error in his last 38 ballgames. Of course, his season was remembered for his defensive liabilities. Offensively, Steve had another banner year. Again he led the Dodgers in hits and runs, raising his two-year stolen base total to 105. Steve was developing into a fine hitter.

1984 was a year Sax would rather consign to oblivion. He batted more than 40 points below his career average, and 1985 started the same way. Steve's batting average at the end of June was .230. Steve was injured in spring training and missed the first month of the season. Lasorda moved him to the bottom of the order while he tried to break out of his slump. Good hitters eventually come around, and Sax did, hitting .307 from July on.

Coming into 1986, Sax had had one bad year; he was ready for a career year. He was 26 when the season began, he finished very strongly the year before, and he was starting to show some patience at the plate. In fact, 1986 was Sax's career year. He batted 48 points higher than his .284 lifetime batting average; he was second in the league in BA, doubles, and hits; third in OBA; seventh in stolen bases and eighth in runs. It was a fabulous year for a man who the year before was a #8 hitter.

Magic is fun to watch. It is fun to think that a rabbit really did appear from nowhere. Steve Sax is also fun to watch. Some people think that he came from nowhere. Those fans probably believe in magic, too.

—Carmen J. Corica

	1986 SEASON											THREE YEARS (84 – 86)									
	Ave.	OBP	SLG	AB	H	2B	3B	HR	RBI	BB	SO	Ave.	OBP	SLG	AB	H	2B	3B	HR	RBI	BB	SO
Totals	.332	.390	.441	633	210	43	4	6	56	59	58	.286	.349	.359	1690	484	74	12	8	133	160	154
Batting vs. Left and Right-handed Pitchers																						
Left	.329	.374	.467	225	74	20	1	3	21	18	17	.281	.343	.375	576	162	36	3	4	45	57	43
Right	.333	.398	.426	408	136	23	3	3	35	41	41	.289	.352	.350	1114	322	38	9	4	88	103	111
At Home and on the Road																						
Home	.310	.377	.389	306	95	19	1	1	21	33	27	.265	.333	.322	814	216	31	3	3	53	82	72
Road	.352	.402	.489	327	115	24	3	5	35	26	31	.306	.363	.393	876	268	43	9	5	80	78	82
Facing Groundball Pitchers and Flyball Pitchers																						
Groundball	.295	.364	.367	281	83	12	1	2	20	29	24	.271	.338	.327	734	199	29	3	2	56	70	65
Flyball	.361	.410	.500	352	127	31	3	4	36	30	34	.298	.357	.383	956	285	45	9	6	77	90	89
Facing Finesse Pitchers and Power Pitchers																						
Finesse	.343	.385	.427	347	119	20	3	1	24	23	29	.295	.343	.353	969	286	38	6	2	64	69	70
Power	.318	.395	.458	286	91	23	1	5	32	36	29	.275	.356	.366	721	198	36	6	6	69	91	84
On Grass and on Turf																						
Grass	.309	.380	.414	447	138	27	4	4	36	51	43	.269	.339	.333	1209	325	43	8	6	86	126	112
Turf	.387	.413	.505	186	72	16	0	2	20	8	15	.331	.376	.424	481	159	31	4	2	47	34	42
During the Day and at Night																						
Day	.321	.387	.440	193	62	12	1	3	23	21	15	.289	.359	.361	526	152	23	3	3	50	58	37
Night	.336	.391	.441	440	148	31	3	3	33	38	43	.285	.344	.357	1164	332	51	9	5	83	102	117
By Month																						
April	.333	.397	.409	66	22	2	0	1	3	7	8	.325	.390	.408	157	51	7	0	2	13	18	11
May	.315	.345	.472	108	34	8	0	3	15	6	13	.270	.328	.370	281	76	15	2	3	23	25	32
June	.319	.403	.425	113	36	8	2	0	9	16	11	.247	.320	.301	296	73	8	4	0	19	32	29
July	.348	.412	.446	92	32	6	0	1	4	9	7	.294	.351	.360	286	84	11	1	2	25	24	28
August	.273	.315	.339	121	33	8	0	0	9	7	10	.255	.300	.308	321	82	17	0	0	20	19	35
Sept/Oct	.398	.459	.534	133	53	11	2	1	16	14	9	.338	.411	.421	349	118	16	5	1	33	42	19
Situational																						
Bases Empty	.329	.377	.436	459	151	31	3	4	4	32	39	.286	.340	.358	1141	326	54	7	5	5	90	98
Leadoff	.321	.365	.426	249	80	16	2	2	2	15	25	.280	.335	.351	653	183	34	3	2	2	51	54
Not Leadoff	.338	.390	.448	210	71	15	1	2	2	17	14	.293	.347	.369	488	143	20	4	3	3	39	44
Runners On	.339	.422	.454	174	59	12	1	2	52	27	19	.288	.366	.359	549	158	20	5	3	128	70	56
First Base Only	.333	.385	.433	60	20	3	0	1	3	5	6	.264	.319	.318	220	58	6	0	2	5	16	21
Scoring Position	.342	.439	.465	114	39	9	1	1	49	22	13	.304	.394	.386	329	100	14	5	1	123	54	35
Late Innings, Close	.370	.433	.500	108	40	8	0	2	13	12	10	.322	.376	.413	276	89	12	2	3	24	25	25

RBI/Opportunities				
Scoring Position	46 / 166	(28%)	117 / 480	(24%)
Scoring Position, 2 Out	19 / 86	(22%)	50 / 241	(21%)
On Third, Less than 2 Out	12 / 23	(52%)	35 / 73	(48%)
RBI in close games / RBI Total	40 / 56	(71%)	89 / 133	(67%)

Mike Schmidt
Philadelphia Phillies

There is no doubt that Mike Schmidt has been THE premier third baseman in the major leagues for the last twelve years. Schmidt is what I always liked to call a "multiple." A multiple is simply a player who does it all—run, score, drive runs in, hit home runs, hit for average and/or get on base with high percentages, field his position well, and maybe steal ten bases a year. Willie Mays, Mickey Mantle, Hank Aaron, Frank Robinson, Al Kaline and Joe Morgan come quickly to mind from my 1960s-70s memory bank. What amazes me, however is what Schmidt has done at his present age (37) compared to the others at that point. Let's go down the line:

1.POWER. Sometimes, when a player regresses, his seasonal home-road home run toals become lopsided; certain parks become a crutch for him. Not Mike. For his career, Schmidt has hit 243 homers in Philly, 253 on the road. His last three years it's been 50 home, 56 road; in '86, 20—17. Consistently balanced. He's still averaging his 26 doubles per year, too.

2.ON-BASE PERCENTAGE. This stat is more indicative of Schmidt's holding power than his batting average. Mike's hit over .300 only once, in the strike-shortened 1981 season, and his season averages read like a hospital electrocardiogram—.249, .251, .253 along with some .270–.290s. But in OBP Schmidt has been below .370 just once in the last thirteen years. His career OBP after 1984 was .383. After 1986 it was still .383, and he was third in the NL in 1986 with .390.

3.RUN PRODUCTION. Mike has consistently scored 90 runs and driven in 100. He shows no sign of stopping. His '84-'86 RS/RBI totals were 93/106, 89/93, 97/119.

4.DEFENSE. The ten Gold Gloves speak eloquently, but many, including Mike, feel he had his best year in the field in '86. He only committed six errors—his previous low was thirteen—and appears to have lost little, if any range. Is this guy human?

5.STOLEN BASES. Yeah, he's human. He can't steal bases any more—only two (total) in '85-'86.

In '86 Schmidt was among the top four NL players in at least ten categories (HR, R, RBI, RP, TB, EBH, SA, BB, OBP, FA). The only bad thing is that he's talking about retirement after the '87 season. Why? Seems like he's just getting started.

—Bud Podrazik

| | 1986 SEASON | | | | | | | | | | | THREE YEARS (84 – 86) | | | | | | | | | | |
	Ave.	OBP	SLG	AB	H	2B	3B	HR	RBI	BB	SO	Ave.	OBP	SLG	AB	H	2B	3B	HR	RBI	BB	SO
Totals	.290	.390	.547	552	160	29	1	37	119	89	84	.281	.383	.538	1629	458	83	9	106	318	268	317
Batting vs. Left and Right-handed Pitchers																						
Left	.357	.474	.707	157	56	10	0	15	42	33	11	.299	.417	.557	442	132	25	1	29	77	89	84
Right	.263	.354	.484	395	104	19	1	22	77	56	73	.275	.369	.532	1187	326	58	8	77	241	179	233
At Home and on the Road																						
Home	.298	.406	.597	258	77	17	0	20	63	46	43	.282	.387	.545	758	214	43	3	50	157	130	141
Road	.282	.374	.503	294	83	12	1	17	56	43	41	.280	.379	.533	871	244	40	6	56	161	138	176
Facing Groundball Pitchers and Flyball Pitchers																						
Groundball	.299	.388	.579	271	81	14	1	20	68	39	40	.281	.381	.513	741	208	38	1	44	146	119	139
Flyball	.281	.391	.516	281	79	15	0	17	51	50	44	.282	.384	.560	888	250	45	8	62	172	149	178
Facing Finesse Pitchers and Power Pitchers																						
Finesse	.284	.349	.518	299	85	13	0	19	64	29	30	.284	.364	.534	933	265	41	6	60	177	114	146
Power	.296	.433	.581	253	75	16	1	18	55	60	54	.277	.406	.545	696	193	42	3	46	141	154	171
On Grass and on Turf																						
Grass	.287	.378	.453	150	43	4	0	7	28	21	22	.280	.380	.517	443	124	18	3	27	80	71	93
Turf	.291	.394	.582	402	117	25	1	30	91	68	62	.282	.384	.546	1186	334	65	6	79	238	197	224
During the Day and at Night																						
Day	.291	.386	.519	189	55	10	0	11	37	29	30	.303	.394	.577	551	167	30	2	39	115	83	113
Night	.289	.391	.562	363	105	19	1	26	82	60	54	.270	.377	.519	1078	291	53	7	67	203	185	204
By Month																						
April	.328	.385	.582	67	22	2	0	5	19	8	11	.279	.355	.474	215	60	9	0	11	44	29	42
May	.276	.382	.460	87	24	7	0	3	15	13	17	.254	.368	.480	256	65	13	0	15	46	46	57
June	.308	.365	.558	104	32	6	1	6	18	9	13	.300	.385	.519	293	88	19	3	13	48	38	48
July	.244	.381	.522	90	22	1	0	8	24	18	13	.250	.352	.489	280	70	8	1	19	52	43	55
August	.299	.410	.598	97	29	8	0	7	19	18	12	.303	.411	.624	287	87	22	2	22	64	52	48
Sept/Oct	.290	.409	.561	107	31	5	0	8	24	23	18	.295	.413	.617	298	88	12	3	26	64	60	67
Situational																						
Bases Empty	.276	.361	.510	286	79	17	1	16	16	33	36	.281	.372	.570	855	240	49	3	64	64	117	163
Leadoff	.275	.340	.556	142	39	8	1	10	10	12	16	.288	.362	.615	379	109	23	1	33	33	41	71
Not Leadoff	.278	.381	.465	144	40	9	0	6	6	21	20	.275	.381	.534	476	131	26	2	31	31	76	92
Runners On	.305	.417	.586	266	81	12	0	21	103	56	48	.282	.393	.504	774	218	34	6	42	254	151	154
First Base Only	.294	.345	.618	102	30	6	0	9	21	7	10	.272	.340	.477	298	81	15	2	14	38	28	47
Scoring Position	.311	.453	.567	164	51	6	0	12	82	49	38	.288	.421	.521	476	137	19	4	28	216	123	107
Late Innings, Close	.290	.411	.516	93	27	3	0	6	12	19	16	.306	.424	.565	271	83	11	4	17	52	54	59

RBI/Opportunities					
Scoring Position	62 / 253	(25%)		169 / 700	(24%)
Scoring Position, 2 Out	30 / 133	(23%)		64 / 319	(20%)
On Third, Less than 2 Out	20 / 41	(49%)		64 / 139	(46%)
RBI in close games / RBI Total	82 / 119	(69%)		222 / 318	(70%)

Dick Schofield
California Angels

August 29, 1986. As we go to the bottom of the ninth, Detroit leads California, 12–5. Most fans have left the ballpark, preferring to see the parking lot than watch a lost cause. They'd do this even if the game was close—Los Angeles must have the world's most appealing parking lots—but tonight more fans than usual have left. In the stadium, kids are popping cups, and generally killing time.

Dick Schofield leads off the inning by beating out an infield single. Mock applause and cheers, as the local heroes have obviously disappointed their fans tonight. Designated hitter Rick Burleson lines out, and the end is coming near. The remaining fans begin to gather their belongings. The scoreboard tells everyone to yell "Charge!" Angel fans oblige obediently. Joyner walks, and there are runners on first and second. As Brian Downing singles to center, loading the bases, the general attitude of the crowd is that this ninth inning is going to take longer than we planned. They've long since stopped selling beer, so there's not much choice but to watch the ballgame. It's Friday night, and most people don't have to work tomorrow anyway.

Jack Howell doubles to right center. Two runs score,

bringing relief ace Willie Hernandez into the game. Hernandez isn't impressive tonight. George Hendrick sneaks a single through the hole at short, scoring a run, cutting Detroit's lead to four runs, with runners on fist and third. Quickly, Bobby Grich lines a single to left, scoring another run and putting runners on first and second. Detroit's lead is down to 12–9. Hopes start to rise as the tying run comes to the plate. They sink again when Gary Pettis grounds to Whitaker, who forces Grich for the second out. But when Ruppert Jones walks, the bases are loaded and Schofield comes to the plate for the second time, representing the winning run.

Earlier in his career, Schofield wouldn't have been allowed to hit in this situation. Gene Mauch would have taken volunteers from the crowd before sending Ducky to the plate. But no pinch hitter is used, a tribute to the progress Schofield has made. He takes the first pitch for a strike. He swings weakly at the second pitch and misses. The next pitch is also the last pitch of the game. Angel fans dance in the aisles, even without prompting from the scoreboard. Dick Schofield has arrived as a major leaguer.

—Dennis Bretz

	1986 SEASON												THREE YEARS (84 – 86)									
	Ave.	OBP	SLG	AB	H	2B	3B	HR	RBI	BB	SO		Ave.	OBP	SLG	AB	H	2B	3B	HR	RBI	BB	SO
Totals	.249	.321	.397	458	114	17	6	13	57	48	55		.221	.292	.333	1296	287	46	12	25	119	116	204
Batting vs. Left and Right-handed Pitchers																							
Left	.294	.397	.454	163	48	8	3	4	18	28	20		.251	.332	.364	451	113	18	6	7	32	50	69
Right	.224	.276	.366	295	66	9	3	9	39	20	35		.206	.271	.317	845	174	28	6	18	87	66	135
At Home and on the Road																							
Home	.230	.322	.363	226	52	5	2	7	28	30	32		.203	.278	.304	626	127	17	5	12	57	57	109
Road	.267	.321	.431	232	62	12	4	6	29	18	23		.239	.306	.361	670	160	29	7	13	62	59	95
Facing Groundball Pitchers and Flyball Pitchers																							
Groundball	.229	.289	.356	205	47	9	1	5	22	15	24		.231	.295	.326	616	142	21	4	10	51	47	80
Flyball	.265	.346	.431	253	67	8	5	8	35	33	31		.213	.290	.340	680	145	25	8	15	68	69	124
Facing Finesse Pitchers and Power Pitchers																							
Finesse	.255	.321	.398	274	70	10	4	7	29	25	32		.226	.287	.340	749	169	27	10	13	63	55	102
Power	.239	.321	.397	184	44	7	2	6	28	23	23		.216	.300	.324	547	118	19	2	12	56	61	102
On Grass and on Turf																							
Grass	.246	.322	.387	403	99	12	6	11	50	45	52		.221	.293	.331	1100	243	36	11	21	102	100	174
Turf	.273	.311	.473	55	15	5	0	2	7	3	3		.224	.290	.347	196	44	10	1	4	17	16	30
During the Day and at Night																							
Day	.308	.347	.474	133	41	4	3	4	18	9	19		.247	.313	.368	364	90	15	7	5	36	33	58
Night	.225	.311	.366	325	73	13	3	9	39	39	36		.211	.284	.320	932	197	31	5	20	83	83	146
By Month																							
April	.226	.250	.581	31	7	2	0	3	5	1	4		.233	.293	.429	189	44	8	1	9	25	14	28
May	.276	.347	.391	87	24	4	0	2	13	9	13		.209	.282	.313	211	44	9	2	3	19	16	45
June	.188	.298	.287	80	15	3	1	1	6	12	8		.186	.269	.260	231	43	7	2	2	15	24	38
July	.257	.341	.392	74	19	2	1	2	7	9	4		.208	.301	.325	154	32	4	1	4	13	20	18
August	.275	.320	.473	91	25	2	2	4	19	6	13		.238	.297	.359	248	59	9	3	5	30	18	39
Sept/Oct	.253	.324	.368	95	24	4	2	1	7	11	13		.247	.313	.327	263	65	9	3	2	17	24	36
Situational																							
Bases Empty	.268	.338	.444	257	69	10	4	9	9	24	27		.239	.294	.348	758	181	26	6	15	15	52	110
Leadoff	.323	.380	.596	99	32	5	2	6	6	9	10		.233	.297	.350	300	70	10	2	7	7	25	44
Not Leadoff	.234	.313	.348	158	37	5	2	3	3	15	17		.242	.292	.347	458	111	16	4	8	8	27	66
Runners On	.224	.301	.338	201	45	7	2	4	48	24	28		.197	.291	.312	538	106	20	6	10	104	64	94
First Base Only	.205	.271	.261	88	18	3	1	0	2	7	9		.192	.272	.297	239	46	9	2	4	12	20	35
Scoring Position	.239	.321	.398	113	27	4	1	4	46	17	19		.201	.305	.324	299	60	11	4	6	92	44	59
Late Innings, Close	.200	.270	.325	80	16	2	1	2	10	8	9		.218	.276	.353	170	37	6	1	5	19	14	25
RBI/Opportunities																							
Scoring Position				37 / 174	(21%)											76 / 436	(17%)						
Scoring Position, 2 Out				11 / 65	(17%)											29 / 203	(14%)						
On Third, Less than 2 Out				15 / 34	(44%)											26 / 65	(40%)						
RBI in close games / RBI Total				34 / 57	(60%)											67 / 119	(56%)						

Mike Scioscia
Los Angeles Dodgers

According to the rules, Mike Scioscia is a cheater, and he is one of the best. The rules clearly state that a defensive player is not allowed to block a base, home plate included, without having the baseball. A catcher is not allowed to block runners from home plate while he awaits a throw from the field. Scioscia blocks the plate better than anyone in baseball today. It has only been in the past twenty years that catchers have been blocking the plate in this way. The rule in now uniformly ignored to the point that a catcher is *expected* to block the plate on close plays before he has the ball. Twenty years ago this was not common; fifty years ago it was unheard of.

Each season Mike adds new episodes to his heartwarming tales of "Home Plate Can Wait." He doesn't just pick on the small players, either—he has been in collisions with big guys like Jack Clark as well as the little guys like Bryan Little.

The price Scioscia and the Dodgers have paid for his plate blocking is great. In 1984, he missed two weeks with a strained ligament, and it took him over a month to fully recover. He suffered a concussion when Clark ran into him in 1985. On June 9th of last season, Mike blocked the plate against Tom Browning; that collision kept Mike out of action for the next four weeks. If you want to dance, you have to pay the band.

Mike Scioscia has other value to the Dodgers, though. He does a good job of throwing out stealers, and he handles the pitching staff well. Mike also makes a big contribution to the team on offense. Over the last three seasons, Scioscia has averaged 2.7 walks per strikeout as well as better than 17 plate appearances per K. More importantly, he has a .380 OBA over the past three years.

Scioscia still has problems with southpaws. Since 1984, he has a .394 OBA with a .402 SA against righties. Lefties, however, cut his power dramatically: his slugging drops to only .297. With his bat control, the Dodgers play hit-and-run often and with confidence with Mike at bat. They need to put more runs on the board if they are going to make a run for the division title in 1987, and he can help a lot.

Mike Scioscia is a quiet leader who leads by example. No one plays the game of baseball harder than he does, and no one cheats any better!

—Carmen J. Corica

	1986 SEASON												THREE YEARS (84 – 86)										
	Ave.	OBP	SLG	AB	H	2B	3B	HR	RBI	BB	SO		Ave.	OBP	SLG	AB	H	2B	3B	HR	RBI	BB	SO
Totals	.251	.359	.345	374	94	18	1	5	26	62	23		.274	.379	.380	1144	314	62	4	17	117	191	70
Batting vs. Left and Right-handed Pitchers																							
Left	.234	.341	.308	107	25	2	0	2	6	18	7		.223	.321	.296	233	52	8	0	3	16	34	16
Right	.258	.366	.360	267	69	16	1	3	20	44	16		.288	.394	.402	911	262	54	4	14	101	157	54
At Home and on the Road																							
Home	.249	.350	.325	169	42	7	0	2	9	25	12		.277	.389	.341	516	143	24	0	3	51	95	33
Road	.254	.366	.361	205	52	11	1	3	17	37	11		.272	.371	.412	628	171	38	4	14	66	96	37
Facing Groundball Pitchers and Flyball Pitchers																							
Groundball	.280	.378	.363	168	47	8	0	2	15	26	7		.286	.389	.374	500	143	24	1	6	50	82	24
Flyball	.228	.344	.330	206	47	10	1	3	11	36	16		.266	.372	.385	644	171	38	3	11	67	109	46
Facing Finesse Pitchers and Power Pitchers																							
Finesse	.243	.370	.349	189	46	11	0	3	15	38	8		.295	.400	.404	634	187	41	2	8	77	111	25
Power	.259	.347	.341	185	48	7	1	2	11	24	15		.249	.353	.351	510	127	21	2	9	40	80	45
On Grass and on Turf																							
Grass	.253	.365	.357	277	70	14	0	5	18	47	21		.290	.398	.405	828	240	46	2	15	84	147	53
Turf	.247	.342	.309	97	24	4	1	0	8	15	2		.234	.330	.316	316	74	16	2	2	33	44	17
During the Day and at Night																							
Day	.220	.331	.291	127	28	4	1	1	6	21	8		.272	.380	.365	375	102	20	3	3	28	64	24
Night	.267	.373	.372	247	66	14	0	4	20	41	15		.276	.379	.388	769	212	42	1	14	89	127	46
By Month																							
April	.281	.418	.438	64	18	4	0	2	6	13	10		.290	.412	.381	155	45	6	1	2	19	32	16
May	.261	.400	.304	69	18	3	0	0	2	15	3		.240	.325	.344	183	44	8	1	3	13	22	11
June	.280	.400	.360	25	7	2	0	0	2	5	0		.292	.421	.364	154	45	8	0	1	22	33	6
July	.385	.409	.436	39	15	2	0	0	6	3	1		.333	.419	.420	150	50	10	0	1	22	25	8
August	.222	.347	.333	81	18	4	1	1	6	16	5		.266	.392	.411	214	57	14	1	5	19	44	15
Sept/Oct	.188	.262	.281	96	18	3	0	2	4	10	4		.253	.337	.368	288	73	16	1	5	22	35	14
Situational																							
Bases Empty	.258	.358	.373	225	58	12	1	4	4	32	12		.255	.361	.377	671	171	35	4	13	13	103	45
Leadoff	.250	.337	.381	84	21	5	0	2	2	11	4		.242	.362	.410	256	62	11	1	10	10	46	18
Not Leadoff	.262	.370	.369	141	37	7	1	2	2	21	8		.263	.360	.357	415	109	24	3	3	3	57	27
Runners On	.242	.361	.302	149	36	6	0	1	22	30	11		.302	.405	.385	473	143	27	0	4	104	88	25
First Base Only	.347	.453	.444	72	25	4	0	1	4	14	3		.347	.428	.438	219	76	14	0	2	8	31	9
Scoring Position	.143	.278	.169	77	11	2	0	0	18	16	8		.264	.387	.339	254	67	13	0	2	96	57	16
Late Innings, Close	.250	.364	.292	72	18	3	0	0	7	14	5		.228	.340	.296	206	47	9	1	1	14	35	17
RBI/Opportunities																							
Scoring Position				17 / 113		(15%)										88 / 388		(23%)					
Scoring Position, 2 Out				3 / 45		(7%)										39 / 178		(22%)					
On Third, Less than 2 Out				10 / 22		(45%)										31 / 70		(44%)					
RBI in close games / RBI Total				14 / 26		(54%)										77 / 117		(66%)					

Mike Scott
Houston Astros

Houston retires the Mets in the ninth inning of Game 6 of the NLCS, winning 3–0 and setting the stage for Game 7. The odds are overwhelmingly in favor of the Astros because of two previous playoff starts by Mike Scott, coupled with his September no-hitter that clinched the NL West title. How did Mike Scott come to dominate baseball during the last month of Roger Clemens's dream season?

The amazing fact about Scott's 1986 season are that he won only 18 games and, somehow, lost 10. Never had a National League Cy Young Award winner (considering starters only, and excluding strike-shortened '81) won as few as 18 games or had as low a winning percentage except for Randy Jones, who was 22–14 for the fifth-place Padres in 1976.

These negative facets were far outweighed by the positive ones. Scott's '86 season rivaled Sandy Koufax's 1965 season (26–8) and Bob Gibson's 1968 season (1.12 ERA). Only these two Hall-of-Famers allowed fewer hits per nine innings, and only Koufax had more strikeouts per nine innings in their Cy Young years than Scott had in '86. Additionally, his 4.26 strikeout-to-walk ratio is the highest of any Cy Young pitcher since Ferguson Jenkins in 1971.

Scott's season looks good even when measured against Dwight Gooden's '85 season (24–4). Scott allowed 0.50 fewer hits, 0.10 fewer walks and struck out 1.25 more batters per 9 IP than Gooden. Compared to Rick Sutcliffe's '84 season (16–1), the differences are almost twice as great.

While Mike's record at home was only 10–8, his other statistics were better than when traveling (the Astros home record was 52–29). Nine of his ten losses came on turf. He lost two 1–0 games at home, twice allowed only 2 runs and four times allowed only 3 runs among his ten defeats. Three times he struck out 10 or more batters in losing efforts. Like many right-handed power pitchers, Scott was very easy to run on in 1986 (41 SB, 11 CS). His splits between day and night games are exactly the reverse of normal power pitchers; this presumably indicates their irrelevance when pitching in the dome.

Despite averaging almost 7.5 innings per start, Scott completed only 7 games. Being able to finish a half-dozen or so more games would probably have resulted in the 20 wins one would expect from a pitcher with his phenomenal statistics.

—Bill Young

	1986: Power, Flyball											1985: Finesse, Flyball											1984: Finesse, Groundball
	1986 SEASON											**THREE YEARS (84 – 86)**										
	G	IP	H	BB	SO	SB	CS	W	L	S	ERA	G	IP	H	BB	SO	SB	CS	W	L	S	ERA
Totals	37	275.1	182	72	306	41	11	18	10	0	2.22	104	651.0	555	195	526	84	29	41	29	0	3.17
										At Home and on the Road												
Home	20	151.1	96	28	155	23	5	10	8	0	2.20	51	350.0	266	79	278	39	15	25	15	0	2.57
Road	17	124.0	86	44	151	18	6	8	2	0	2.25	53	301.0	289	116	248	45	14	16	14	0	3.86
										During the Day and at Night												
Day	9	67.0	50	19	80	12	6	4	2	0	2.82	23	129.1	131	49	121	25	8	8	6	0	4.66
Night	28	208.1	132	53	226	29	5	14	8	0	2.03	81	521.2	424	146	405	59	21	33	23	0	2.79
										On Grass and on Turf												
Grass	8	59.0	40	18	77	5	4	3	1	0	1.98	31	173.0	164	62	139	21	10	7	10	0	3.80
Turf	29	216.1	142	54	229	36	7	15	9	0	2.29	73	478.0	391	133	387	63	19	34	19	0	2.94
										By Month												
April	6	39.2	35	11	34	5	1	3	2	0	3.18	16	90.0	85	32	64	11	3	5	4	0	3.60
May	7	49.0	40	16	64	8	3	1	2	0	2.57	18	105.0	101	38	102	16	7	3	5	0	3.86
June	6	49.1	26	9	50	11	4	3	1	0	1.46	18	127.0	98	27	87	17	7	9	5	0	2.34
July	6	46.1	26	12	49	3	1	3	2	0	2.14	18	113.1	92	29	91	9	4	7	7	0	2.94
August	6	44.2	32	17	44	6	1	4	2	0	2.01	15	100.1	81	34	73	16	3	9	6	0	2.69
Sept/Oct	6	46.1	23	7	65	8	1	4	1	0	2.14	19	115.1	98	35	109	15	5	8	2	0	3.75

	vs. Opponent Batters																				
	1986 SEASON										**THREE YEARS (84 – 86)**									
	Ave.	OBP	SLG	AB	H	2B	3B	HR	RBI	BB	SO	Ave.	OBP	SLG	AB	H	2B	3B	HR	RBI	BB	SO
Totals	.186	.242	.291	976	182	41	5	17	65	72	306	.230	.287	.341	2412	555	98	19	44	225	195	526
					Pitching vs. Left and Right-handed Batters																	
Left	.211	.280	.304	507	107	23	3	6	32	49	114	.234	.299	.322	1235	289	50	13	11	95	114	205
Right	.160	.201	.277	469	75	18	2	11	33	23	192	.226	.275	.361	1177	266	48	6	33	130	81	321
					Situational																	
Bases Empty	.189	.242	.293	645	122	30	2	11	11	44	180	.218	.271	.331	1517	331	63	12	28	28	107	301
Leadoff	.208	.261	.356	264	55	13	1	8	8	18	78	.220	.278	.351	626	138	21	5	17	17	48	124
Not Leadoff	.176	.229	.249	381	67	17	1	3	3	26	102	.217	.266	.316	891	193	42	7	11	11	59	177
Runners On	.181	.243	.287	331	60	11	3	6	54	28	126	.250	.314	.359	895	224	35	7	16	197	88	225
First Base Only	.218	.254	.347	124	27	5	1	3	11	6	32	.275	.325	.390	364	100	16	4	6	23	27	69
Scoring Position	.159	.237	.251	207	33	6	2	3	43	22	94	.234	.306	.337	531	124	19	3	10	174	61	156
Late Innings, Close	.218	.301	.364	110	24	5	1	3	10	13	30	.193	.278	.307	202	39	9	1	4	13	24	41

	RBI/Opportunities					
Scoring Position	39 / 255	(15%)		156 / 702	(22%)	
Scoring Position, 2 Out	12 / 121	(10%)		49 / 308	(16%)	
On Third, Less than 2 Out	17 / 33	(52%)		77 / 135	(57%)	
RBI in close games / RBI Total	51 / 65	(78%)		164 / 225	(73%)	

Tom Seaver
Boston Red Sox

You hope it won't end like this. You think of Ted Williams crashing a homer in his last at-bat, Babe Ruth hitting three in a game and taking his final curtain call or Sandy Koufax winning 27 in his last year and sigh. That's the way it ought to be—one last, long, lingering wonder to remember the aging superstar by. One more good season, a tight pennant race—maybe even a World Championship. But it never works out that way . . . Johnny Bench hopelessly miscast at third . . . Carl Yastrzemski battling Reid Nichols for playing time and losing . . . Pete Rose having to cut himself . . . It isn't fair to the athlete or the fans who admired them.

Barring a miracle, Tom Seaver finished his career on the disabled list, limping gingerly on a knee that needed surgery, urging teammates he had known for barely three months on in pursuit of a World Series victory and 'fashioning' a 7–13 record.

It isn't right—it is a sin. Would it have been so terrible for Seaver to have been pitching in the fourth game of the World Series, coming off a 15–10 season and trying to put the penultimate nail in his old team's coffin? Who wouldn't have smiled at the irony of the man who carried one team to a world title and brought another—one of the worst pennant winners ever, facing one of the most dominant powerhouses in history—close to another tossing one last six-hit shutout? Are the baseball fates so jealous that they begrudge an aging star one more day of 95-MPH glory?

Apparently so. When Boston needed him most, Seaver was helpless. They now refuse to take him back at his asking price; Seaver will go nowhere else. GM Lou Gorman reminds us that "we're talking about a 42-year-old pitcher coming off knee surgery" and, of course, he's right. But what is reality where legends are concerned?

Boston got what they desparately needed from Seaver. Stability. Leadership. Innings. Time. When Seaver arrived, Bruce Hurst was on the disabled list. Al Nipper was coming off of it; hopelessly out of shape. Oil Can Boyd was less than two weeks away from another suspension. Calvin Schiraldi was still in the minors. Tom Terrific nailed down the #2 spot—even as late as August, he still had one of the ten best ERAs in his league. But some post-injury thrashings took even that away.

—Tom Henry and Geoff Beckman

1986: Finesse, Groundball												1985: Finesse, Groundball											1984: Finesse, Groundball
1986 SEASON												**THREE YEARS (84 – 86)**											
	G	IP	H	BB	SO	SB	CS	W	L	S	ERA		G	IP	H	BB	SO	SB	CS	W	L	S	ERA
Totals	28	176.1	180	56	103	22	6	7	13	0	4.03		97	651.2	619	186	368	73	20	38	35	0	3.69
At Home and on the Road																							
Home	14	81.1	87	21	40	10	3	3	7	0	4.65		47	310.2	295	93	162	41	11	17	17	0	4.14
Road	14	95.0	93	35	63	12	3	4	6	0	3.51		50	341.0	324	93	206	32	9	21	18	0	3.27
During the Day and at Night																							
Day	8	43.1	52	13	29	7	2	1	5	0	4.98		30	194.2	205	56	120	22	4	9	13	0	4.30
Night	20	133.0	128	43	74	15	4	6	8	0	3.72		67	457.0	414	130	248	51	16	29	22	0	3.43
On Grass and on Turf																							
Grass	23	143.0	147	43	81	16	5	5	11	0	4.15		83	547.1	525	156	310	60	18	34	27	0	3.83
Turf	5	33.1	33	13	22	6	1	2	2	0	3.51		14	104.1	94	30	58	13	2	4	8	0	2.93
By Month																							
April	4	29.0	22	7	14	3	0	2	2	0	2.79		13	77.2	76	25	43	11	0	4	4	0	4.17
May	3	12.2	15	10	4	1	1	0	0	0	5.68		16	95.1	85	33	38	8	5	7	5	0	3.40
June	5	30.1	29	10	13	4	1	0	4	0	5.34		17	114.1	105	37	64	15	5	4	9	0	4.01
July	6	39.1	46	13	21	6	1	2	3	0	3.43		18	135.0	123	29	84	15	3	10	5	0	2.93
August	6	41.0	41	9	38	3	2	3	2	0	3.51		17	117.1	117	28	77	13	5	6	6	0	4.14
Sept/Oct	4	24.0	27	7	13	5	1	0	2	0	4.87		16	112.0	113	34	62	11	2	7	6	0	3.70

	vs. Opponent Batters																					
	1986 SEASON											**THREE YEARS (84 – 86)**										
	Ave.	OBP	SLG	AB	H	2B	3B	HR	RBI	BB	SO	Ave.	OBP	SLG	AB	H	2B	3B	HR	RBI	BB	SO
Totals	.264	.323	.401	683	180	31	6	17	74	56	103	.249	.304	.385	2484	619	110	15	66	249	186	368
Pitching vs. Left and Right-handed Batters																						
Left	.277	.339	.436	346	96	21	5	8	41	32	52	.246	.307	.385	1283	316	59	10	33	129	112	216
Right	.249	.307	.365	337	84	10	1	9	33	24	51	.252	.300	.386	1201	303	51	5	33	120	74	152
Situational																						
Bases Empty	.265	.314	.403	412	109	19	4	10	10	26	62	.243	.292	.385	1539	374	73	7	44	44	97	222
Leadoff	.236	.269	.382	178	42	6	1	6	6	7	24	.231	.279	.364	640	148	31	3	16	16	39	90
Not Leadoff	.286	.348	.419	234	67	13	3	4	4	19	38	.251	.301	.400	899	226	42	4	28	28	58	132
Runners On	.262	.335	.399	271	71	12	2	7	64	30	41	.259	.322	.385	945	245	37	8	22	205	89	146
First Base Only	.270	.336	.396	111	30	4	2	2	7	9	15	.294	.337	.427	391	115	18	5	8	28	21	43
Scoring Position	.256	.335	.400	160	41	8	0	5	57	21	26	.235	.312	.356	554	130	19	3	14	177	68	103
Late Innings, Close	.351	.397	.491	57	20	4	2	0	4	4	4	.262	.325	.385	301	79	16	3	5	30	26	39

	RBI/Opportunities				
Scoring Position	52 / 222	(23%)		157 / 758	(21%)
Scoring Position, 2 Out	21 / 98	(21%)		69 / 348	(20%)
On Third, Less than 2 Out	20 / 39	(51%)		54 / 129	(42%)
RBI in close games / RBI Total	55 / 74	(74%)		177 / 249	(71%)

Roy Smalley
Minnesota Twins

It speaks volumes about the Minnesota organization that for two years they have used Roy Smalley as a designated hitter/shortstop. Designated hitters in baseball are usually big, slow veterans who don't move or throw well but carry a big bat. Shortstops are usually acrobatic kids who scamper around the infield and can throw hard even off-balance, but who don't hit well. The requirements of the two positions don't mix, and any team which would ask one player to do both jobs has obviously got some problems with the configuration of its talent. It's sort of like asking Robert Redford to double as Quasimodo.

Smalley was once a fine shortstop, in the manner of Cal Ripken and Robin Yount—a power hitter with a powerful arm that enabled him to make the plays from the hole, thus setting up deep and compensating for his lack of movement by gaining a half-second before the ball got to him. This has been several years ago. He is not a shortstop anymore, and might have been a good DH except for a shortage of meaningful hits. Smalley hit just .176 in the late innings of close

games (over the last three years, he has hit only .182 in that situation) and also drove in only 19% of the runners in scoring position for him. He got home only 5 of 17 runners on third base with less than two out. Over a three-year period he has driven in only 16% of his runners in scoring position with two out, and (perhaps most damaging of all) has hit 34 of his 43 home runs with the bases empty. Batting left-handed most of the time, he does hit well with men on first base.

At one time, Smalley was an effective switch hitter. He is still somewhat effective against right-handed pitchers, but is now pretty helpless when he turns around.

Billy Goodman's famous line about Smalley was that "I wish Sid had never made that trade," referring to a famous Minnesota sportswriter whose pernicious influence over the Twins' front office goes back many years. But I liked Smalley, too, and I think acquiring Smalley was a reasonable gamble which might have helped the team. It just didn't work out.

—Bill James

	1986 SEASON											THREE YEARS (84 – 86)										
	Ave.	OBP	SLG	AB	H	2B	3B	HR	RBI	BB	SO	Ave.	OBP	SLG	AB	H	2B	3B	HR	RBI	BB	SO
Totals	.246	.342	.438	459	113	20	4	20	57	68	80	.240	.331	.401	1191	286	52	5	43	141	165	210
Batting vs. Left and Right-handed Pitchers																						
Left	.138	.250	.310	58	8	4	0	2	7	9	12	.174	.273	.286	213	37	12	0	4	21	30	41
Right	.262	.356	.456	401	105	16	4	18	50	59	68	.255	.344	.425	978	249	40	5	39	120	135	169
At Home and on the Road																						
Home	.266	.368	.464	222	59	11	3	9	28	36	40	.247	.342	.421	596	147	26	3	24	80	87	106
Road	.228	.317	.414	237	54	9	1	11	29	32	40	.234	.320	.380	595	139	26	2	19	61	78	104
Facing Groundball Pitchers and Flyball Pitchers																						
Groundball	.283	.377	.507	219	62	14	1	11	32	33	35	.267	.352	.427	585	156	30	2	20	78	79	93
Flyball	.212	.310	.375	240	51	6	3	9	25	35	45	.215	.311	.375	606	130	22	3	23	63	86	117
Facing Finesse Pitchers and Power Pitchers																						
Finesse	.259	.349	.446	251	65	15	1	10	28	36	38	.259	.346	.426	659	171	37	2	23	70	88	101
Power	.231	.333	.428	208	48	5	3	10	29	32	42	.216	.313	.368	532	115	15	3	20	71	77	109
On Grass and on Turf																						
Grass	.222	.314	.389	180	40	7	1	7	21	25	31	.233	.318	.378	614	143	22	2	21	69	80	112
Turf	.262	.360	.470	279	73	13	3	13	36	43	49	.248	.345	.425	577	143	30	3	22	72	85	98
During the Day and at Night																						
Day	.262	.345	.455	145	38	5	1	7	21	19	27	.228	.324	.348	356	81	14	1	9	35	52	71
Night	.239	.341	.430	314	75	15	3	13	36	49	53	.246	.334	.423	835	205	38	4	34	106	113	139
By Month																						
April	.284	.369	.500	74	21	5	1	3	11	10	9	.281	.368	.433	178	50	13	1	4	22	25	26
May	.250	.351	.547	64	16	4	0	5	9	10	12	.284	.368	.488	211	60	10	0	11	27	28	34
June	.253	.303	.554	83	21	3	2	6	12	6	14	.236	.297	.444	216	51	9	3	10	29	20	40
July	.250	.374	.400	80	20	6	0	2	9	17	17	.223	.342	.361	202	45	10	0	6	24	38	38
August	.206	.283	.353	102	21	1	1	4	11	11	16	.191	.276	.348	204	39	3	1	9	19	23	41
Sept/Oct	.250	.400	.268	56	14	1	0	0	5	14	12	.228	.340	.317	180	41	7	0	3	20	31	31
Situational																						
Bases Empty	.236	.314	.468	263	62	10	3	15	15	30	43	.232	.315	.427	682	158	25	3	34	34	82	112
Leadoff	.230	.304	.398	113	26	4	0	5	5	12	15	.255	.328	.455	286	73	12	0	15	15	31	38
Not Leadoff	.240	.321	.520	150	36	6	3	10	10	18	28	.215	.306	.407	396	85	13	3	19	19	51	74
Runners On	.260	.377	.398	196	51	10	1	5	42	38	37	.251	.352	.365	509	128	27	2	9	107	83	98
First Base Only	.274	.361	.421	95	26	5	0	3	9	13	12	.270	.324	.414	237	64	14	1	6	21	19	31
Scoring Position	.248	.391	.376	101	25	5	1	2	33	25	25	.235	.372	.324	272	64	13	1	3	86	64	67
Late Innings, Close	.176	.300	.265	68	12	4	1	0	7	12	14	.182	.282	.273	209	38	8	1	3	28	30	46
RBI/Opportunities																						
Scoring Position				28 / 144		(19%)									76 / 394		(19%)					
Scoring Position, 2 Out				16 / 78		(21%)									31 / 192		(16%)					
On Third, Less than 2 Out				5 / 17		(29%)									28 / 60		(47%)					
RBI in close games / RBI Total				37 / 57		(65%)									87 / 141		(62%)					

Bryn Smith
Montreal Expos

After winning 18 games in 1985, Bryn Smith had a difficult time last year, going only 10–8 while his ERA climbed by more than a run to 3.94. Smith needs pinpoint control to be effective, and in '86 that sort of control was missing, as he walked over three batters per nine innings, nearly double his '85 rate. An arm injury was almost certainly the reason for Smith's decline; X-rays taken in mid-September revealed a fractured bone spur in his right elbow, and surgery had to be performed. It's a serious injury, one that is expected to sideline Smith for the entire 1987 season. Since he doesn't even have a contract at this point, Bryn's career appears to be in jeopardy.

It would be a shame if Smith doesn't pitch any more for the Expos, for he has served the club well since 1981. At first Montreal used him in the bullpen, with so-so results: in his only full season as a reliever, 1982, Bryn went 2–4 with only three saves and 4.20 ERA. When he was finally shifted to a starter's role in the middle of '83, Smith immediately showed he'd been miscast, posting a brilliant 2.26 ERA for 12 starts during the remainder of that season, with five complete games and three shutouts. In 1984 he pitched decently, with a 3.32 ERA; his 12–13 record was deceptive, as the Expos averaged only 1.9 runs per game in the 13 losses.

In 1985 Smith not only pitched better, but had more support from his teammates; in fact his batting support of 5.4 runs per start was the highest in the league. But Bryn's superb 18–5 record—his .783 winning percentage was fourth in the NL and set an Expo record—was the result of strong pitching as well. Bryn was tenth in the league in ERA with 2.91 and allowed only 12 homers in 222 innings. Relying heavily on the palmball, an offspeed pitch popularized by Paul Richards in the fifties, Smith also exhibited the best control of his career—an average of only 1.7 walks per nine innings. His pitching was vital to the Expos; the club was 23–9 in his 32 starts (they were 84–77 overall) and never lost more than two of his starts in a row.

Then came the trying season of 1986, and finally the surgery. Hopefully Smith will be healthy and pitching well again in 1988.

—Martin Lacoste and Don Zminda

1986: Finesse, Groundball   **1985: Finesse, Groundball**   **1984: Finesse, Groundball**

	G	IP	H	BB	SO	SB	CS	W	L	S	ERA		G	IP	H	BB	SO	SB	CS	W	L	S	ERA
	1986 SEASON												**THREE YEARS (84 – 86)**										
Totals	30	187.1	182	63	105	22	8	10	8	0	3.94		90	588.2	553	155	333	58	25	40	26	0	3.38
At Home and on the Road																							
Home	13	86.1	81	28	52	9	2	5	3	0	3.75		43	292.2	257	81	181	22	13	20	13	0	3.01
Road	17	101.0	101	35	53	13	6	5	5	0	4.10		47	296.0	296	74	152	36	12	20	13	0	3.74
During the Day and at Night																							
Day	11	67.1	66	22	31	4	3	3	2	0	3.61		33	208.0	196	62	100	13	10	14	8	0	3.16
Night	19	120.0	116	41	74	18	5	7	6	0	4.12		57	380.2	357	93	233	45	15	26	18	0	3.50
On Grass and on Turf																							
Grass	11	64.1	69	27	26	7	5	2	5	0	4.76		30	189.2	191	52	89	17	9	12	11	0	3.75
Turf	19	123.0	113	36	79	15	3	8	3	0	3.51		60	399.0	362	103	244	41	16	28	15	0	3.20
By Month																							
April	5	32.2	28	13	19	4	2	2	2	0	3.58		14	94.2	84	27	53	8	3	9	3	0	3.14
May	6	34.2	39	14	19	5	4	2	2	0	4.15		16	105.2	113	28	58	8	11	5	6	0	3.32
June	6	34.0	31	11	21	6	0	1	1	0	3.97		16	100.2	96	26	52	14	1	6	5	0	3.67
July	5	31.2	36	9	19	3	0	2	1	0	3.98		16	113.0	99	23	73	9	4	8	4	0	2.55
August	6	42.2	36	14	19	3	2	2	2	0	3.80		15	98.1	91	29	53	8	2	5	5	0	3.84
Sept/Oct	2	11.2	12	2	8	1	0	1	0	0	4.63		13	76.1	70	22	44	11	4	7	3	0	4.01

vs. Opponent Batters

	Ave.	OBP	SLG	AB	H	2B	3B	HR	RBI	BB	SO		Ave.	OBP	SLG	AB	H	2B	3B	HR	RBI	BB	SO
	1986 SEASON												**THREE YEARS (84 – 86)**										
Totals	.252	.316	.380	723	182	32	8	15	88	63	105		.247	.297	.363	2242	553	99	18	42	224	155	333
Pitching vs. Left and Right-handed Batters																							
Left	.286	.354	.421	409	117	19	6	8	47	40	56		.264	.316	.373	1190	314	55	12	17	117	90	158
Right	.207	.265	.328	314	65	13	2	7	41	23	49		.227	.275	.352	1052	239	44	6	25	107	65	175
Situational																							
Bases Empty	.246	.309	.373	410	101	19	6	7	7	34	55		.248	.298	.363	1324	328	64	13	21	21	90	193
Leadoff	.268	.325	.413	179	48	6	4	4	4	13	19		.284	.330	.419	570	162	28	8	11	11	36	74
Not Leadoff	.229	.296	.342	231	53	13	2	3	3	21	36		.220	.273	.321	754	166	36	5	10	10	54	119
Runners On	.259	.325	.390	313	81	13	2	8	81	29	50		.245	.297	.363	918	225	35	5	21	203	65	140
First Base Only	.254	.288	.413	126	32	6	1	4	13	6	17		.261	.297	.379	375	98	15	1	9	27	17	45
Scoring Position	.262	.347	.374	187	49	7	1	4	68	23	33		.234	.296	.352	543	127	20	4	12	176	48	95
Late Innings, Close	.394	.429	.576	33	13	2	2	0	4	2	3		.260	.313	.435	154	40	9	3	4	14	12	21

RBI/Opportunities

Scoring Position	60 / 255	(24%)		155 / 685	(23%)
Scoring Position, 2 Out	24 / 122	(20%)		57 / 312	(18%)
On Third, Less than 2 Out	26 / 50	(52%)		71 / 135	(53%)
RBI in close games / RBI Total	61 / 88	(69%)		178 / 224	(79%)

Dave Smith
Houston Astros

Dave Smith will be remembered by Astros fans for his arsonist's display in a fireman's role during the 1986 NLCS. Nevertheless, he remains one of the key reasons the club made it that far. Smith finished the season with a 4–7 record and a 2.37 ERA to go with his 33 saves, yet most of the attention on the bullpen was focused on the wonderfully candid Charles Kerfeld.

Smith inherited the job as closer by attrition rather than design, outlasting such comrades as Joe Sambito, Frank LaCorte, Bill Dawley and Frank DiPino. While he is likely to have the effervescent Kerfeld breathing down his neck next year, he put together better stats than the round Nevadan in 1986.

Smith held the opposition to a miserly .200 BA last year while he was appearing exclusively in late-inning save situations. He was especially tough with runners in scoring position, allowing the opposition only a .175 average, .232 on-base and a .286 slugging average. The one drawback was his home runs allowed: 5 in 56 innings-pitched, a large total given the time he is in the game while pitching for the low-scoring Astros.

More than likely, Smith will open next season as the stopper for Houston. While righties hit a paltry .221 against him, lefties hit an anemic .180, making him especially valuable during late-game pinch-hitting situations. However, if he is to remain the ace, he will have to become grittier than he was in NLCS Games 3 and 6.

—Bill Young

In the last two years, the Astros have used Smith frequently, but for very short stints only: in 118 games he has pitched only 135.1 innings, but has recorded 60 saves. Dave has been with Houston since he came up in 1980, but has rarely been the #1 pitcher out of the pen, even though he has pitched effectively most of that time.

Last year, Smith started the season with a rush, racking up 12 saves with an ERA of 2.00 in 17 games in April and May. He suffered from a mid-season slump in June and July, though, logging only 7 saves in 18 games as his ERA ballooned to 4.34. He recovered nicely for the stretch drive, saving 14 games after the end of July, allowing only 10 hits and 7 walks with an ERA of less than 2.00 in 19.1 innings. In particular, his August was remarkable—in 9 outings he allowed only 2 hits and 2 walks while striking out 12 in 10.1 innings, saving or winning every game he got into.

—Gary Gillette

1986: Power, Flyball   **1985: Finesse, Flyball**   **1984: Finesse, Groundball**

	1986 SEASON											THREE YEARS (84 – 86)										
	G	IP	H	BB	SO	SB	CS	W	L	S	ERA	G	IP	H	BB	SO	SB	CS	W	L	S	ERA
Totals	54	56.0	39	22	46	5	1	4	7	33	2.73	171	212.2	168	59	131	18	4	18	16	65	2.37
At Home and on the Road																						
Home	24	24.2	18	7	24	2	1	3	1	14	2.92	91	112.2	94	26	73	7	2	15	7	32	2.40
Road	30	31.1	21	15	22	3	0	1	6	19	2.59	80	100.0	74	33	58	11	2	3	9	33	2.34
During the Day and at Night																						
Day	23	27.0	19	14	19	4	0	0	5	11	3.33	40	44.2	31	19	24	5	1	2	6	17	2.62
Night	31	29.0	20	8	27	1	1	4	2	22	2.17	131	168.0	137	40	107	13	3	16	10	48	2.30
On Grass and on Turf																						
Grass	20	22.2	14	11	16	3	0	0	4	13	2.38	48	61.0	48	24	35	8	2	2	7	21	2.95
Turf	34	33.1	25	11	30	2	1	4	3	20	2.97	123	151.2	120	35	96	10	2	16	9	44	2.14
By Month																						
April	7	8.0	8	1	5	0	0	0	0	7	2.25	26	33.1	26	3	24	2	1	3	1	10	1.08
May	10	10.0	7	5	8	0	0	1	2	5	1.80	29	33.2	29	11	17	3	0	2	4	9	2.94
June	9	7.2	7	4	7	1	1	0	2	4	3.52	28	35.2	17	15	30	2	2	0	4	13	2.02
July	9	11.0	7	5	9	2	0	2	2	3	4.91	24	33.2	30	11	14	5	1	4	2	6	3.48
August	9	10.1	2	2	12	0	0	1	0	8	0.00	29	36.0	30	10	27	2	0	5	2	13	2.50
Sept/Oct	10	9.0	8	5	5	2	0	0	1	6	4.00	35	40.1	36	9	19	4	0	4	3	14	2.23

vs. Opponent Batters

	1986 SEASON											THREE YEARS (84 – 86)										
	Ave.	OBP	SLG	AB	H	2B	3B	HR	RBI	BB	SO	Ave.	OBP	SLG	AB	H	2B	3B	HR	RBI	BB	SO
Totals	.200	.283	.292	195	39	3	0	5	22	22	46	.219	.276	.302	768	168	17	4	13	74	59	131
Pitching vs. Left and Right-handed Batters																						
Left	.173	.243	.245	98	17	1	0	2	12	9	18	.187	.250	.253	348	65	7	2	4	31	29	50
Right	.227	.321	.340	97	22	2	0	3	10	13	28	.245	.298	.343	420	103	10	2	9	43	30	81
Situational																						
Bases Empty	.204	.304	.286	98	20	2	0	2	2	14	23	.220	.285	.293	396	87	7	2	6	6	34	74
Leadoff	.139	.311	.250	36	5	1	0	1	1	9	6	.226	.317	.333	159	36	3	1	4	4	20	22
Not Leadoff	.242	.299	.306	62	15	1	0	1	1	5	17	.215	.262	.266	237	51	4	1	2	2	14	52
Runners On	.196	.262	.299	97	19	1	0	3	20	8	23	.218	.267	.312	372	81	10	2	7	68	25	57
First Base Only	.235	.316	.324	34	8	0	0	1	2	3	7	.266	.291	.343	143	38	4	2	1	6	4	23
Scoring Position	.175	.232	.286	63	11	1	0	2	18	5	16	.188	.253	.293	229	43	6	0	6	62	21	34
Late Innings, Close	.215	.291	.325	163	35	3	0	5	22	17	35	.233	.291	.331	528	123	13	3	11	61	41	80

RBI/Opportunities

	1986		THREE YEARS	
Scoring Position	15 / 85	(18%)	52 / 301	(17%)
Scoring Position, 2 Out	3 / 38	(8%)	18 / 144	(13%)
On Third, Less than 2 Out	7 / 14	(50%)	22 / 49	(45%)
RBI in close games / RBI Total	22 / 22	(100%)	62 / 74	(84%)

Lee Smith
Chicago Cubs

The Cubs lead 4–1 in the ninth inning as Lee Smith comes in with a runner on first and no outs. A walk follows, then a single on a 3–1 pitch that scores the runner from second. Two long flyouts and a wild pitch later, another run is in and the tying run is on second. After a foul home run and a called strike the batter swings at a bad pitch and misses, ending the contest.

To many people I know, the above is an example of a typical Lee Smith save. In other words, cheap. Of course, the logic goes, when not getting cheap saves Lee blows them and gets cheap wins. He has good ERAs because he lets other pitchers' runs score, but not his own. His stats are deceiving; he is worthless, say these fans.

Sorry, folks, but you are dead wrong. Lee Smith is a fine relief pitcher. Using every Smith appearance from 1984–85, plus twenty 1986 outings (a biased group; although they represent 30% of his '86 appearances, he gave up 50% of his runs in them, so note that this part of the sample is slanted AGAINST him), I kept track of six items: the lead when Smith came in, runners on, number of those runners that scored, runs charged to Smith, whether it was a save situation or not, and the resulting decision if any.

The results were quite impressive. Lee Smith allowed no runs, his own or other pitchers', in 58 of 75 saves covered in the analysis (77.3%). Of the seventeen saves in which he did allow runs, only four times did he give up more than one run. He also didn't give up a lot of other pitchers' runs; of 93 runners inherited by Smith in the study, only 22 (23.6%) scored. Cheap saves, indeed.

Big Lee doesn't convert of lot of blown saves into wins, either. Of 100 save situations in the study he collected 75 saves. He does get some cheap wins, however; out of seventeen wins he let at least one run score in eleven (two or more runs in six of those eleven). He seems to get out of other pitchers' jams, then create his own. Nevertheless, when Smith comes in for the save, the odds are 3–1 that he will save it; if he gets the save chances are better than 3–1 that no runs will cross the plate while he is on the mound.

Baseball fans, give Lee Smith credit. He has done an excellent job.

—Pat McCormick

1986: Power, Flyball   **1985: Power, Flyball**   **1984: Power, Flyball**

	1986 SEASON											THREE YEARS (84 – 86)										
	G	IP	H	BB	SO	SB	CS	W	L	S	ERA	G	IP	H	BB	SO	SB	CS	W	L	S	ERA
Totals	66	90.1	69	42	93	15	6	9	9	31	3.09	200	289.0	254	109	291	37	13	25	20	97	3.27
At Home and on the Road																						
Home	39	55.2	43	25	52	10	3	6	3	20	2.75	110	164.0	149	54	170	24	8	14	9	51	3.62
Road	27	34.2	26	17	41	5	3	3	6	11	3.63	90	125.0	105	55	121	13	5	11	11	46	2.81
During the Day and at Night																						
Day	51	70.2	55	37	73	15	5	9	7	23	3.31	144	210.0	191	77	214	30	11	21	14	64	3.73
Night	15	19.2	14	5	20	0	1	0	2	8	2.29	56	79.0	63	32	77	7	2	4	6	33	2.05
On Grass and on Turf																						
Grass	49	70.0	50	30	72	11	4	7	5	25	2.70	151	220.0	196	76	217	26	10	20	14	72	3.44
Turf	17	20.1	19	12	21	4	2	2	4	6	4.43	49	69.0	58	33	74	11	3	5	6	25	2.74
By Month																						
April	5	6.1	6	6	7	0	0	1	2	1	7.11	21	30.2	27	14	37	1	2	2	3	11	2.93
May	10	17.1	10	7	15	3	0	1	2	6	2.60	34	54.2	49	21	52	8	2	6	3	17	3.46
June	13	18.1	9	9	19	2	3	2	2	4	1.96	38	54.0	38	30	52	7	5	3	6	14	3.17
July	15	21.1	13	10	26	3	1	2	1	8	3.38	39	60.0	46	22	69	5	1	5	3	22	3.00
August	11	15.0	14	2	14	4	2	2	2	6	1.80	34	47.0	46	7	38	8	2	7	3	15	2.68
Sept/Oct	12	12.0	17	8	12	3	0	1	0	6	4.50	34	42.2	48	15	43	8	1	2	2	18	4.43

vs. Opponent Batters

	1986 SEASON											THREE YEARS (84 – 86)										
	Ave.	OBP	SLG	AB	H	2B	3B	HR	RBI	BB	SO	Ave.	OBP	SLG	AB	H	2B	3B	HR	RBI	BB	SO
Totals	.215	.303	.318	321	69	12	0	7	43	42	93	.239	.308	.354	1064	254	41	8	22	130	109	291
Pitching vs. Left and Right-handed Batters																						
Left	.221	.343	.349	172	38	7	0	5	27	33	53	.254	.338	.364	582	148	26	4	10	76	77	148
Right	.208	.252	.282	149	31	5	0	2	16	9	40	.220	.269	.342	482	106	15	4	12	54	32	143
Situational																						
Bases Empty	.237	.299	.337	169	40	5	0	4	4	15	45	.257	.316	.378	537	138	22	2	13	13	45	153
Leadoff	.254	.329	.465	71	18	3	0	4	4	8	18	.273	.327	.441	227	62	10	2	8	8	17	57
Not Leadoff	.224	.276	.245	98	22	2	0	0	0	7	27	.245	.308	.332	310	76	12	0	5	5	28	96
Runners On	.191	.308	.296	152	29	7	0	3	39	27	48	.220	.300	.330	527	116	19	6	9	117	64	138
First Base Only	.111	.245	.156	45	5	2	0	0	2	8	14	.266	.325	.402	184	49	9	2	4	16	16	36
Scoring Position	.224	.333	.355	107	24	5	0	3	37	19	34	.195	.287	.292	343	67	10	4	5	101	48	102
Late Innings, Close	.217	.297	.329	277	60	10	0	7	41	33	81	.235	.305	.357	842	198	34	6	19	115	87	232

RBI/Opportunities

	1986 SEASON		THREE YEARS (84 – 86)	
Scoring Position	29 / 150	(19%)	86 / 485	(18%)
Scoring Position, 2 Out	12 / 69	(17%)	29 / 208	(14%)
On Third, Less than 2 Out	10 / 24	(42%)	35 / 86	(41%)
RBI in close games / RBI Total	41 / 43	(95%)	115 / 130	(88%)

Lonnie Smith
Kansas City Royals

Unlike some players who are described as "the next Willie Mays," I've long felt that Lonnie Smith had the potential to become the next Fred Merkle. Surely you remember your first impression of Lonnie: fourth game of the 1980 NLCS, when, after gloving a sacrifice fly, his throw was cut off by—himself. He whiffed on it . . . a major league ballplayer . . . have you ever seen anything like it? Unfortunately for his chances of becoming a great bonehead, his rebound toss to third was true, cutting down an advancing Astro. It was almost the same story in the '85 ALCS: with Blue Jays on first and second, Lonnie muffed the easiest of fly balls, only to recover instantaneously and get a fortuitous force at third. On both occasions it was as if Merkle, halfway to the clubhouse without touching second, had suddenly realized the enormity of his oversight, fought his way through the surging throng back to the diamond, and slid in safely an eyelash ahead of Evers' belated force.

But if thus far, with the eyes of the baseball world upon him, Lonnie has botched every opportunity to enter the pantheon of boneheads, he has demonstrated repeatedly, in less significant games, that the potential is still there. Remember the network TV game, where Sutton first went for number 300? With Lonnie at third, Brett nubs a grounder down the first base line. Lonnie trots amiably toward home, watching the ball roll, seemingly confident the only play is at first. Which it is, assuming he runs. Instead, Joyner throws him out easily. In a pennant race or post-season game, this is a boner of Merklesque proportions, but with the Royals in the doldrums everyone has forgotten, and I for one am glad, because easy as it is to belittle Lonnie, I do not think harshly of him as a ballplayer—or a man. He trotted down the line, not because he's different, but because every now and then, without warning, his mind goes blank. It just does, and there's nothing he or anyone else can do about it; it's part of his make-up. He showed courage in admitting his drug problem and battling back from it, and he has after all helped three teams win the World Series. As I write, the Royals have cut him loose, so he may never live up to the Merklean ideal after all, but that's an honor no one really deserves, no matter how splendidly qualified.

—Mike Kopf

	1986 SEASON											THREE YEARS (84 – 86)										
	Ave.	OBP	SLG	AB	H	2B	3B	HR	RBI	BB	SO	Ave.	OBP	SLG	AB	H	2B	3B	HR	RBI	BB	SO
Totals	.287	.357	.411	508	146	25	7	8	44	46	78	.265	.346	.370	1556	412	70	17	20	141	173	257
Batting vs. Left and Right-handed Pitchers																						
Left	.309	.360	.443	149	46	6	4	2	14	12	19	.280	.355	.396	482	135	26	6	6	40	57	73
Right	.279	.356	.398	359	100	19	3	6	30	34	59	.258	.342	.358	1074	277	44	11	14	101	116	184
At Home and on the Road																						
Home	.317	.390	.432	243	77	14	4	2	20	24	30	.267	.359	.375	749	200	36	12	7	71	96	116
Road	.260	.327	.392	265	69	11	3	6	24	22	48	.263	.334	.366	807	212	34	5	13	70	77	141
Facing Groundball Pitchers and Flyball Pitchers																						
Groundball	.307	.373	.436	225	69	16	2	3	15	19	32	.289	.359	.404	797	230	41	9	11	70	75	110
Flyball	.272	.344	.392	283	77	9	5	5	29	27	46	.240	.332	.335	759	182	29	8	9	71	98	147
Facing Finesse Pitchers and Power Pitchers																						
Finesse	.271	.316	.390	310	84	16	3	5	25	17	36	.272	.328	.376	915	249	40	8	13	82	68	114
Power	.313	.415	.444	198	62	9	4	3	19	29	42	.254	.370	.362	641	163	30	9	7	59	105	143
On Grass and on Turf																						
Grass	.259	.329	.390	205	53	8	2	5	18	17	38	.263	.333	.370	551	145	25	2	10	48	51	97
Turf	.307	.376	.426	303	93	17	5	3	26	29	40	.266	.353	.370	1005	267	45	15	10	93	122	160
During the Day and at Night																						
Day	.258	.294	.367	128	33	5	3	1	10	5	31	.263	.331	.362	445	117	20	6	4	35	41	87
Night	.297	.377	.426	380	113	20	4	7	34	41	47	.266	.352	.374	1111	295	50	11	16	106	132	170
By Month																						
April	.200	.273	.200	20	4	0	0	0	0	1	5	.278	.376	.395	162	45	7	3	2	17	22	33
May	.193	.292	.228	57	11	0	1	0	4	7	9	.238	.352	.300	223	53	4	2	2	14	34	41
June	.292	.394	.491	106	31	6	3	3	19	16	18	.242	.336	.384	302	73	14	7	5	39	41	47
July	.286	.364	.429	105	30	6	0	3	7	11	14	.281	.375	.392	263	74	17	0	4	14	34	40
August	.291	.336	.325	117	34	4	0	0	3	6	21	.267	.330	.332	277	74	7	1	3	22	23	50
Sept/Oct	.350	.385	.553	103	36	9	3	2	11	5	11	.283	.324	.407	329	93	21	4	4	35	19	46
Situational																						
Bases Empty	.277	.346	.399	321	89	17	2	6	6	29	46	.263	.339	.355	982	258	43	3	14	14	99	149
Leadoff	.291	.335	.358	148	43	7	0	1	1	9	23	.270	.331	.355	445	120	21	1	5	5	39	69
Not Leadoff	.266	.355	.434	173	46	10	2	5	5	20	23	.257	.345	.356	537	138	22	2	9	9	60	80
Runners On	.305	.374	.433	187	57	8	5	2	38	17	32	.268	.358	.395	574	154	27	14	6	127	74	108
First Base Only	.330	.379	.489	88	29	7	2	1	8	4	12	.313	.373	.479	240	75	16	6	4	22	17	34
Scoring Position	.283	.371	.384	99	28	1	3	1	30	13	20	.237	.348	.335	334	79	11	8	2	105	57	74
Late Innings, Close	.277	.326	.349	83	23	1	1	1	8	3	8	.238	.355	.307	231	55	7	3	1	21	36	42

RBI/Opportunities

	1986		THREE YEARS	
Scoring Position	28 / 136	(21%)	96 / 478	(20%)
Scoring Position, 2 Out	13 / 61	(21%)	36 / 219	(16%)
On Third, Less than 2 Out	10 / 25	(40%)	42 / 104	(40%)
RBI in close games / RBI Total	30 / 44	(68%)	100 / 141	(71%)

Ozzie Smith
St. Louis Cardinals

Ozzie denied it and the Cardinals denied it, but it's still hard to believe that Smith's arm wasn't giving him trouble in '86, at least early in the season. His throwing errors were up noticeably, but Ozzie claimed this was due to poor play rather than a sore arm. That may be true, but his throws into the hole kept coming up short early in the season. Ozzie's never had a terribly strong arm to begin with, but he's always been able to arch his throws so that they hit their mark. This, along with his quick release, make up for any lack of arm strength. In early 1986, however, those throws seemed to be coming up a few feet short. Most were on plays that no other shortstop would make, so it wasn't a case of him hurting the team. But if you watched a number of St. Louis games in April or May you could see that Smith's arm wasn't one hundred per cent. In the second half of the season, however, he seemed to have regained strength and/or confidence in his arm, and at one stretch he went 44 consecutive games without an error. The injury seemed to be cured, and both the Cardinals and their fans could breathe a little more easily.

Though he continues to be known for his defensive skills, Ozzie had another good year with the bat in '86, arguably his best ever. He didn't hit with as much power as the previous year, but his average and on-base percentage were both career highs, as were his 79 walks. He also managed to equal his 54 RBIs of the previous season, and for a while was threatening to lead the team. Smith also stole the 300th base of his career in September; for the year he stole 31 bases while being caught only seven times. He did fail to hit a home run for the first time since joining the Cardinals, but he probably saves those for playoff games now.

The starting shortstop for the NL in the All-Star game, Smith was also named to the Sporting News National League All-Star team at season's end. He hit .370 against the Cubs in '86, and also had good seasons against Houston and San Francisco, hitting .351 against each team. His worst performance was against the Mets (.193). Ozzie struck out only once per 22.6 plate appearances in '86. He hit only .243 for the 70 games he batted in the number two spot, but was over .300 batting seventh or eighth.

—Russ Eagle

| | 1986 SEASON | | | | | | | | | | | THREE YEARS (84 – 86) | | | | | | | | | | |
	Ave.	OBP	SLG	AB	H	2B	3B	HR	RBI	BB	SO	Ave.	OBP	SLG	AB	H	2B	3B	HR	RBI	BB	SO
Totals	.280	.376	.333	514	144	19	4	0	54	79	27	.272	.360	.344	1463	398	61	12	7	152	200	71
Batting vs. Left and Right-handed Pitchers																						
Left	.276	.370	.315	203	56	8	0	0	14	31	9	.290	.396	.396	482	140	28	1	7	45	86	27
Right	.283	.380	.344	311	88	11	4	0	40	48	18	.263	.341	.319	981	258	33	11	0	107	114	44
At Home and on the Road																						
Home	.287	.400	.346	254	73	13	1	0	31	47	16	.281	.373	.353	688	193	33	4	3	73	98	35
Road	.273	.352	.319	260	71	6	3	0	23	32	11	.265	.349	.337	775	205	28	8	4	79	102	36
Facing Groundball Pitchers and Flyball Pitchers																						
Groundball	.304	.377	.355	276	84	10	2	0	29	31	10	.296	.373	.364	726	215	36	5	1	80	88	29
Flyball	.252	.375	.307	238	60	9	2	0	25	48	17	.248	.358	.326	737	183	25	7	6	72	112	42
Facing Finesse Pitchers and Power Pitchers																						
Finesse	.266	.347	.315	286	76	10	2	0	27	35	13	.281	.356	.363	822	231	38	7	5	80	93	35
Power	.298	.412	.355	228	68	9	2	0	27	44	14	.261	.365	.321	641	167	23	5	2	72	107	36
On Grass and on Turf																						
Grass	.222	.298	.278	126	28	3	2	0	10	14	6	.268	.344	.339	407	109	18	4	1	42	48	17
Turf	.299	.400	.351	388	116	16	2	0	44	65	21	.274	.366	.347	1056	289	43	8	6	110	152	54
During the Day and at Night																						
Day	.312	.401	.371	170	53	8	1	0	20	26	8	.296	.376	.380	527	156	27	4	3	59	68	23
Night	.265	.364	.314	344	91	11	3	0	34	53	19	.259	.352	.325	936	242	34	8	4	93	132	48
By Month																						
April	.310	.394	.362	58	18	3	0	0	6	8	5	.237	.339	.320	194	46	6	2	2	19	30	10
May	.291	.404	.405	79	23	7	1	0	7	14	3	.270	.355	.357	263	71	18	1	1	26	34	10
June	.300	.397	.330	100	30	1	1	0	12	16	4	.289	.366	.339	280	81	9	1	1	25	34	15
July	.256	.337	.314	86	22	3	1	0	10	11	2	.277	.341	.374	206	57	11	3	1	22	18	5
August	.194	.299	.226	93	18	3	0	0	7	14	8	.229	.320	.274	223	51	8	1	0	18	29	14
Sept/Oct	.337	.427	.378	98	33	2	1	0	12	16	5	.310	.413	.387	297	92	9	4	2	42	55	17
Situational																						
Bases Empty	.271	.352	.315	321	87	12	1	0	0	40	20	.264	.343	.338	857	226	42	5	4	4	102	47
Leadoff	.336	.440	.407	113	38	6	1	0	0	21	5	.298	.394	.385	309	92	20	2	1	1	49	13
Not Leadoff	.236	.300	.264	208	49	6	0	0	0	19	15	.245	.313	.312	548	134	22	3	3	3	53	34
Runners On	.295	.414	.363	193	57	7	3	0	54	39	7	.284	.383	.353	606	172	19	7	3	148	98	24
First Base Only	.277	.329	.385	65	18	3	2	0	3	5	1	.306	.351	.389	229	70	11	4	0	10	15	6
Scoring Position	.305	.449	.352	128	39	4	1	0	51	34	6	.271	.399	.332	377	102	8	3	3	138	83	18
Late Innings, Close	.279	.400	.375	104	29	4	3	0	11	21	3	.273	.367	.367	264	72	9	5	2	28	40	15
RBI/Opportunities																						

	RBI/Opportunities				RBI/Opportunities	
Scoring Position	50 / 198	(25%)		131 / 575	(23%)
Scoring Position, 2 Out	17 / 93	(18%)		38 / 243	(16%)
On Third, Less than 2 Out	22 / 36	(61%)		64 / 117	(55%)
RBI in close games / RBI Total	38 / 54	(70%)		100 / 152	(66%)

Mike Smithson
Minnesota Twins

Mike Smithson, making his first relief appearance in the majors on September 17th, entered the game in the top of the seventh inning with the Indians and the Twins deadlocked at 2. Three outs and three runs later, he was on his way to his first relief lost. After having averaged 244 IP in his three previous seasons, he failed to reach 200 innings in '86. These items are, of course, related. A series of bad outings during a season in which he established his second highest ERA made people think of moving the righthander to a relief role. Unfortunately, there are at least two good reasons as to why this may not work. First, Smithson possesses one of the slowest windups in baseball. To bring him out of the bullpen with runners on base (even when pitching from the stretch) would be an invitation to base running madness. Second, left handers may be close to knocking him out of the league. Managers have noticed this, therefore 61% of the batters sent up to face Smithson last season were lefties and over the last three years the figure is over 58%. His numbers against lefthanders just will not do for a good late inning ace.

Smithson arrived in Minnesota in 1984 preaching the

benefits of pitching inside. We hear the same refrain from someone each season, but something that year caused the Twins staff to produce its lowest ERA of the last eight years. Whatever the reasons were, the Tennessee native proceeded to hit batters with increasing frequency (8 in '84, 15 in '85, and 14 in '86). 27 of the batters were righthanders, and the totals are distributed fairly evenly by month: April-5, May-9, June-6, July-6, Aug.-7, and Sept./Oct.-4. That he was attempting to establish control of the inside part of the plate is inferred by three items. First, 15 of the HBP's took place in the first two innings (10 in the first and 5 in the second). Second, 26 of the HBP's occurred when the score was either tied or with one run separating the teams. Third, the ten first inning efforts never occurred with the Twins trailing. The low number of walks he allows and the situations in which his HBP's occur, suggest that it is not necessarily a lack of control, but simply a desire to back hitters off of the plate that is keeping his totals so high. If this is true, it doesn't seem to be working with lefthanders and unless he finds something that does, his reign as the major league's tallest player may end prematurely.

—Bill Jensen

1986: Finesse, Groundball   **1985: Finesse, Groundball**   **1984: Finesse, Flyball**

	G	IP	H	BB	SO	SB	CS	W	L	S	ERA	G	IP	H	BB	SO	SB	CS	W	L	S	ERA
1986 SEASON												**THREE YEARS (84 – 86)**										
Totals	34	198.0	234	57	114	20	4	13	14	0	4.77	107	707.0	744	189	386	68	21	43	41	0	4.24
At Home and on the Road																						
Home	18	110.0	135	26	73	12	4	9	6	0	4.34	52	346.1	368	86	208	34	11	24	17	0	4.21
Road	16	88.0	99	31	41	8	0	4	8	0	5.32	55	360.2	376	103	178	34	10	19	24	0	4.27
During the Day and at Night																						
Day	9	52.0	58	13	25	0	1	3	5	0	5.19	32	208.1	211	52	109	16	7	12	14	0	3.76
Night	25	146.0	176	44	89	20	3	10	9	0	4.62	75	498.2	533	137	277	52	14	31	27	0	4.44
On Grass and on Turf																						
Grass	11	60.1	68	24	23	3	0	3	5	0	4.77	39	257.2	265	77	113	18	10	15	15	0	3.81
Turf	23	137.2	166	33	91	17	4	10	9	0	4.77	68	449.1	479	112	273	50	11	28	26	0	4.49
By Month																						
April	5	33.2	33	7	22	1	0	2	2	0	4.01	16	117.1	109	29	64	6	3	8	6	0	3.30
May	7	47.2	56	12	23	1	2	3	2	0	3.40	19	129.2	146	36	66	16	5	7	7	0	4.79
June	5	20.2	34	4	11	5	1	2	2	0	6.10	16	90.1	116	21	46	16	3	6	7	0	4.98
July	5	21.0	32	9	12	6	1	1	3	0	9.86	17	109.0	107	32	65	12	3	9	4	0	4.13
August	6	36.1	36	18	17	4	0	1	3	0	4.71	18	118.1	124	41	69	7	5	4	9	0	4.64
Sept/Oct	6	38.2	43	7	29	3	0	4	2	0	3.72	21	142.1	142	30	76	11	2	9	8	0	3.79

vs. Opponent Batters

	Ave.	OBP	SLG	AB	H	2B	3B	HR	RBI	BB	SO	Ave.	OBP	SLG	AB	H	2B	3B	HR	RBI	BB	SO
1986 SEASON												**THREE YEARS (84 – 86)**										
Totals	.294	.349	.462	796	234	50	3	26	105	57	114	.270	.324	.428	2751	744	138	19	86	314	189	386
Pitching vs. Left and Right-handed Batters																						
Left	.315	.368	.495	483	152	30	3	17	66	41	48	.287	.335	.468	1635	470	92	13	59	211	114	188
Right	.262	.319	.412	313	82	20	0	9	39	16	66	.246	.307	.370	1116	274	46	6	27	103	75	198
Situational																						
Bases Empty	.287	.353	.484	442	127	30	3	17	17	35	70	.269	.325	.426	1652	445	88	12	49	49	113	243
Leadoff	.296	.352	.505	196	58	13	2	8	8	12	32	.265	.320	.418	698	185	40	5	19	19	45	105
Not Leadoff	.280	.354	.467	246	69	17	1	9	9	23	38	.273	.329	.432	954	260	48	7	30	30	68	138
Runners On	.302	.343	.435	354	107	20	0	9	88	22	44	.272	.322	.431	1099	299	50	7	37	265	76	143
First Base Only	.318	.340	.483	151	48	10	0	5	12	3	12	.278	.312	.429	497	138	27	3	14	42	20	57
Scoring Position	.291	.345	.399	203	59	10	0	4	76	19	32	.267	.329	.434	602	161	23	4	23	223	56	86
Late Innings, Close	.345	.393	.455	55	19	1	1	1	6	4	8	.294	.352	.466	221	65	8	3	8	26	18	26

RBI/Opportunities

Scoring Position	67 / 273 (25%)	184 / 791 (23%)
Scoring Position, 2 Out	29 / 122 (24%)	68 / 355 (19%)
On Third, Less than 2 Out	23 / 49 (47%)	69 / 140 (49%)
RBI in close games / RBI Total	69 / 105 (66%)	216 / 314 (69%)

Cory Snyder
Cleveland Indians

Every losing team has a designated savior; Cory Snyder is Cleveland's. He has already established himself as a force in the majors—the question is how great that force will be. In his first season, Snyder showed an ability to hit for average with outstanding power, displayed impressive fielding skills at several spots and displayed an Achilles' heel that he simply must deal with.

Snyder's power is overwhelming. Balls fly off his bat like they have been shot out of a cannon. His singles sizzle over the infield dirt; his doubles are the homers that he didn't quite uppercut enough. He is a dead pull hitter who takes a huge swing at everything; his few opposite field hits come when he swings late. Pitching to Snyder can be humiliating; if he makes contact, no matter how good the pitch is, he can crush you.

The problem is that he doesn't make contact nearly enough. Snyder is a pure guess hitter, who depends on his ability to think with a pitcher and do damage when he connects to survive. He seems to decide to swing at a pitch before the catcher has flashed the sign; it may become an automatic fine to throw him a strike shortly. As other teams began seeing that Cory swung at anything, they stopped throwing him good pitches; he began drawing a few walks, but the jump in strikeouts offset this. Cleveland refused to do any work with Snyder at all in 1986, arguing that you don't fix something that isn't broken. True, Snyder never had a slump in 1986—but unless American League pitchers are blind to reality or he makes adjustments in his game, he will in 1987.

Snyder's fielding is also a problem, but a much happier one. He had to move to rightfield to make the majors; he played so well that some people want to keep him there. His range factor and his assists totals don't support the claims his admirers make for him, but he is an exciting player with an incredible arm. Snyder professes to be most comfortable at third base; if 11 games played is any evidence, he'd be an easy Gold Glove winner there. Pat Corrales, relishing the thought of his own Cal Ripken, prefers Snyder at short; Cory's glove would have to improve markedly to play there. The Indians plan to keep him moving around in 1987; where he starts will depend on which one of his teammates feels tired that day.

—Geoff Beckman

	1986 SEASON											THREE YEARS (84 – 86)										
	Ave.	OBP	SLG	AB	H	2B	3B	HR	RBI	BB	SO	Ave.	OBP	SLG	AB	H	2B	3B	HR	RBI	BB	SO
Totals	.272	.299	.500	416	113	21	1	24	69	16	123	.272	.299	.500	416	113	21	1	24	69	16	123
Batting vs. Left and Right-handed Pitchers																						
Left	.322	.333	.585	118	38	7	0	8	23	2	31	.322	.333	.585	118	38	7	0	8	23	2	31
Right	.252	.285	.466	298	75	14	1	16	46	14	92	.252	.285	.466	298	75	14	1	16	46	14	92
At Home and on the Road																						
Home	.280	.309	.532	186	52	9	1	12	32	8	60	.280	.309	.532	186	52	9	1	12	32	8	60
Road	.265	.290	.474	230	61	12	0	12	37	8	63	.265	.290	.474	230	61	12	0	12	37	8	63
Facing Groundball Pitchers and Flyball Pitchers																						
Groundball	.313	.337	.526	192	60	11	0	10	34	7	50	.313	.337	.526	192	60	11	0	10	34	7	50
Flyball	.237	.266	.478	224	53	10	1	14	35	9	73	.237	.266	.478	224	53	10	1	14	35	9	73
Facing Finesse Pitchers and Power Pitchers																						
Finesse	.283	.304	.561	230	65	14	1	16	41	7	57	.283	.304	.561	230	65	14	1	16	41	7	57
Power	.258	.292	.425	186	48	7	0	8	28	9	66	.258	.292	.425	186	48	7	0	8	28	9	66
On Grass and on Turf																						
Grass	.282	.315	.529	333	94	14	1	22	57	16	98	.282	.315	.529	333	94	14	1	22	57	16	98
Turf	.229	.229	.386	83	19	7	0	2	12	0	25	.229	.229	.386	83	19	7	0	2	12	0	25
During the Day and at Night																						
Day	.265	.292	.500	132	35	4	0	9	21	5	50	.265	.292	.500	132	35	4	0	9	21	5	50
Night	.275	.302	.500	284	78	17	1	15	48	11	73	.275	.302	.500	284	78	17	1	15	48	11	73
By Month																						
April	.000	.000	.000	0	0	0	0	0	0	0	0	.000	.000	.000	0	0	0	0	0	0	0	0
May	.000	.000	.000	0	0	0	0	0	0	0	0	.000	.000	.000	0	0	0	0	0	0	0	0
June	.274	.286	.629	62	17	5	1	5	11	1	20	.274	.286	.629	62	17	5	1	5	11	1	20
July	.281	.312	.449	89	25	3	0	4	12	4	23	.281	.312	.449	89	25	3	0	4	12	4	23
August	.265	.292	.477	132	35	4	0	8	19	5	35	.265	.292	.477	132	35	4	0	8	19	5	35
Sept/Oct	.271	.302	.496	133	36	9	0	7	27	6	45	.271	.302	.496	133	36	9	0	7	27	6	45
Situational																						
Bases Empty	.270	.301	.500	226	61	11	1	13	13	10	61	.270	.301	.500	226	61	11	1	13	13	10	61
Leadoff	.273	.314	.414	99	27	3	1	3	3	6	22	.273	.314	.414	99	27	3	1	3	3	6	22
Not Leadoff	.268	.290	.567	127	34	8	0	10	10	4	39	.268	.290	.567	127	34	8	0	10	10	4	39
Runners On	.274	.296	.500	190	52	10	0	11	56	6	62	.274	.296	.500	190	52	10	0	11	56	6	62
First Base Only	.295	.304	.590	78	23	5	0	6	12	1	23	.295	.304	.590	78	23	5	0	6	12	1	23
Scoring Position	.259	.291	.438	112	29	5	0	5	44	5	39	.259	.291	.438	112	29	5	0	5	44	5	39
Late Innings, Close	.262	.297	.426	61	16	4	0	2	9	3	16	.262	.297	.426	61	16	4	0	2	9	3	16
RBI/Opportunities																						
Scoring Position				37 / 132	(28%)										37 / 132	(28%)						
Scoring Position, 2 Out				15 / 59	(25%)										15 / 59	(25%)						
On Third, Less than 2 Out				13 / 25	(52%)										13 / 25	(52%)						
RBI in close games / RBI Total				41 / 69	(59%)										41 / 69	(59%)						

Dave Stieb
Toronto Blue Jays

"I have never gotten off to a poorer start than I did this season but, to be honest, my mechanics were mainly at fault . . . With my arm coming up too high, pitching coach Al Widmar pointed out . . . I had lost the precision on my release point and stopped following through. Trying to correct the habit while working against major league hitters was not easy . . . "

Tomorrow I'll Be Perfect Kevin Boland (Doubleday, Toronto 1986).

That last sentence is an understatement. In 1986, Dave Stieb did something that nobody in Toronto believed he could do—look completely inept on the mound. It wasn't until the middle of August that the real Stieb began making occasional appearances. By September 1, Dave was back to normal on a regular basis; he finished the season with a 3–2 mark and a very respectable 2.45 ERA. The Toronto management plans to keep a keen eye on Dave's progress and with good reason—there's no way that they can expect to win anything if Stieb gets off to another 2–8 start in 1987.

Obviously Stieb's 1986 was not representative of him; there is little point to analyzing it in depth. But it should be noted that the way that he was used in 1986 did exacerbate an already-bad situation. Stieb, being a power pitcher, was much more effective at night in 1984–85 (2.47 to 3.17) and he started 70% of his games under the lights; in 1986, he started only 57% of his games at night. Stieb has been more successful on the road than he has at home (2.49/2.83 in '84–5) and started 58% of his games on the road; he had only 43% of his starts on the road in 1986. These are the details that a veteran manager knows and a rookie must learn; as Jimy Williams becomes more adept at handling pitchers, he should be able to avoid these mistakes. Finally—while Stieb pitched atrociously on grass in 1986, he was not hurt by it in the past (2.72/2.58).

The one area that Stieb continued to excel at in 1986 was controlling the running game. Of the 25 runners who tried to steal, only 13 (52%) were successful—the lowest percentage of any Toronto pitcher. Stieb is one of the few Blue Jays who understands the value of keeping the potential tying or winning run on first and works at mastering it; it's the little things that keep you in the upper echelon of American League starters.

—David Driscoll and Dave Easby

1986: Power, Groundball   **1985: Power, Groundball**   **1984: Power, Flyball**

| | 1986 SEASON | | | | | | | | | | | THREE YEARS (84 – 86) | | | | | | | | | | |
	G	IP	H	BB	SO	SB	CS	W	L	S	ERA	G	IP	H	BB	SO	SB	CS	W	L	S	ERA
Totals	37	205.0	239	87	127	13	12	7	12	1	4.74	108	737.0	660	271	492	33	28	37	33	1	3.24
At Home and on the Road																						
Home	21	130.2	147	53	77	6	8	5	5	0	3.93	51	359.1	345	125	228	19	18	22	15	0	3.23
Road	16	74.1	92	34	50	7	4	2	7	1	6.17	57	377.2	315	146	264	14	10	15	18	1	3.24
During the Day and at Night																						
Day	15	69.2	95	27	42	5	4	0	5	1	5.94	37	238.0	242	82	155	9	10	10	13	1	3.89
Night	22	135.1	144	60	85	8	8	7	7	0	4.12	71	499.0	418	189	337	24	18	27	20	0	2.92
On Grass and on Turf																						
Grass	11	50.2	68	25	35	7	2	1	5	0	6.57	42	278.2	239	120	189	13	7	10	13	0	3.49
Turf	26	154.1	171	62	92	6	10	6	7	1	4.14	66	458.1	421	151	303	20	21	27	20	1	3.08
By Month																						
April	5	26.2	36	11	12	1	1	0	3	0	6.75	15	95.2	89	38	56	2	3	5	5	0	3.57
May	6	40.1	43	20	28	1	4	1	3	0	5.36	18	130.2	102	52	98	4	9	8	5	0	3.03
June	6	38.0	47	15	25	4	0	1	2	0	4.97	18	130.1	116	44	79	6	2	5	6	0	3.04
July	7	23.1	28	13	12	4	3	1	2	1	5.01	18	112.0	97	39	61	8	7	7	4	1	2.73
August	6	32.2	38	13	20	1	1	1	0	0	4.96	19	129.2	111	41	95	3	3	5	4	0	3.47
Sept/Oct	7	44.0	47	15	30	2	3	3	2	0	2.45	20	138.2	145	57	103	10	4	7	9	0	3.57

vs. Opponent Batters

| | 1986 SEASON | | | | | | | | | | | THREE YEARS (84 – 86) | | | | | | | | | |
	Ave.	OBP	SLG	AB	H	2B	3B	HR	RBI	BB	SO	Ave.	OBP	SLG	AB	H	2B	3B	HR	RBI	BB	SO
Totals	.297	.373	.476	805	239	43	7	29	112	87	127	.241	.315	.370	2743	660	112	16	70	265	271	492
Pitching vs. Left and Right-handed Batters																						
Left	.329	.410	.546	416	137	25	7	17	65	52	48	.244	.321	.376	1486	363	59	11	38	149	161	219
Right	.262	.333	.401	389	102	18	0	12	47	35	79	.236	.308	.363	1257	297	53	5	32	116	110	273
Situational																						
Bases Empty	.281	.364	.461	449	126	23	5	16	16	52	75	.236	.318	.379	1598	377	64	12	47	47	169	275
Leadoff	.268	.335	.455	198	53	9	2	8	8	18	29	.247	.328	.401	684	169	29	5	22	22	72	119
Not Leadoff	.291	.386	.466	251	73	14	3	8	8	34	46	.228	.311	.363	914	208	35	7	25	25	97	156
Runners On	.317	.385	.494	356	113	20	2	13	96	35	52	.247	.312	.356	1145	283	48	4	23	218	102	217
First Base Only	.329	.393	.555	173	57	10	1	9	22	16	23	.266	.326	.392	553	147	26	1	14	38	46	93
Scoring Position	.306	.379	.437	183	56	10	1	4	74	19	29	.230	.300	.323	592	136	22	3	9	180	56	124
Late Innings, Close	.450	.511	.875	40	18	5	0	4	10	4	6	.300	.365	.474	327	98	19	1	12	44	33	53

RBI/Opportunities

	1986 SEASON		THREE YEARS (84 – 86)	
Scoring Position	63 / 254	(25%)	155 / 781	(20%)
Scoring Position, 2 Out	26 / 116	(22%)	61 / 359	(17%)
On Third, Less than 2 Out	20 / 48	(42%)	55 / 131	(42%)
RBI in close games / RBI Total	87 / 112	(78%)	218 / 265	(82%)

Darryl Strawberry
New York Mets

There are two sets of issues in evaluating Darryl Strawberry. The first set lies with the fan and media perception of Strawberry; the second lies with Darryl himself. Let's deal with the first set of issues. Darryl is still saddled with the media and fan perception that he is not living up to his promise. To the extent that Strawberry has failed to bat .325, hit 40 home runs, knock in 120 RBIs and steal 40 bases, he has indeed failed to live up to his potential. But I wish I knew who projected those kind of numbers for Darryl . . . maybe it was the same guys who booed Mickey Mantle early in his career. It doesn't matter; I'd venture to say that there isn't a GM in either league who would not be very happy to add an "underachiever" like Darryl to his everyday lineup. Will Strawberry ever produce those kind of numbers? Who knows? When we get beyond that sort of thinking and evaluate the numbers the Strawman HAS put up, they speak very loudly. At age 25 he ranks seventh on the alltime home run list for his age with 108; Willie Mays had 112 at the same point. People forget that due to injuries and his late call-up in '83, Darryl has averaged only 129 games a year; per 162 games he's averaged 34 homers, 108

RBIs, 31 steals, 84 walks and a .259 BA. Even if we just divide his career stats by four years, he still averages 27 HRs, 86 RBIs, 67 BB and 25 SBs. So let us be clear and understand that regardless of potential, Darryl does produce consistently good, if not great, numbers—good enough to carry a team for a month or more.

In evaluating his actual performance rather than performance compared to "potential," there are three major areas where Darryl needs improvement. First of all, the man can't hit lefties—while he's batted .259 overall, he's hit southpaws at a wimpy .209 rate. Secondly, Strawberry struck out 142 times in '86. Thirdly, Darryl still can't go back on a flyball. He plays so deep he needs to make diving catches, resulting in thumb injuries.

All these deficiencies are a function of Darryl's difficulty in disciplining his talent. Without guidance and discipline (the kind Jim Frey provided in '83) Strawberry will continue to be a good to great player. With it Darryl will be the superstar much of New York thinks he should already be.

—J. Randolph Burnham

	1986 SEASON											THREE YEARS (84 – 86)									
	Ave.	OBP	SLG	AB	H	2B	3B	HR	RBI	BB	SO	Ave.	OBP	SLG	AB	H	2B	3B	HR	RBI	BB	SO
Totals	.259	.358	.507	475	123	27	5	27	93	72	142	.261	.362	.506	1390	363	69	13	82	269	220	369
Batting vs. Left and Right-handed Pitchers																						
Left	.209	.296	.353	187	39	8	2	5	27	21	65	.227	.307	.402	510	116	15	4	22	78	56	156
Right	.292	.397	.608	288	84	19	3	22	66	51	77	.281	.391	.567	880	247	54	9	60	191	164	213
At Home and on the Road																						
Home	.227	.325	.445	211	48	11	1	11	33	30	69	.243	.341	.466	641	156	34	5	33	121	97	173
Road	.284	.385	.557	264	75	16	4	16	60	42	73	.276	.379	.541	749	207	35	8	49	148	123	196
Facing Groundball Pitchers and Flyball Pitchers																						
Groundball	.286	.381	.487	224	64	14	2	9	40	32	63	.262	.364	.461	675	177	34	8	28	110	107	165
Flyball	.235	.338	.526	251	59	13	3	18	53	40	79	.260	.359	.550	715	186	35	5	54	159	113	204
Facing Finesse Pitchers and Power Pitchers																						
Finesse	.268	.352	.475	265	71	17	1	12	39	33	68	.283	.378	.523	746	211	48	7	39	135	115	153
Power	.248	.365	.548	210	52	10	4	15	54	39	74	.236	.343	.488	644	152	21	6	43	134	105	216
On Grass and on Turf																						
Grass	.265	.363	.505	309	82	18	1	18	60	46	94	.260	.358	.480	939	244	49	7	48	179	143	255
Turf	.247	.350	.512	166	41	9	4	9	33	26	48	.264	.369	.561	451	119	20	6	34	90	77	114
During the Day and at Night																						
Day	.240	.332	.434	175	42	9	2	7	31	21	53	.264	.353	.510	522	138	24	4	32	109	69	128
Night	.270	.373	.550	300	81	18	3	20	62	51	89	.259	.367	.505	868	225	45	9	50	160	151	241
By Month																						
April	.313	.400	.547	64	20	6	0	3	14	10	15	.291	.369	.553	206	60	12	0	14	38	26	47
May	.208	.319	.403	77	16	4	1	3	13	12	24	.222	.316	.346	185	41	10	2	3	19	25	47
June	.352	.471	.648	71	25	7	1	4	12	16	16	.276	.403	.506	156	43	10	1	8	26	34	38
July	.276	.363	.586	87	24	7	1	6	18	12	31	.276	.366	.563	293	81	16	4	20	69	42	83
August	.176	.276	.308	91	16	1	1	3	16	11	29	.226	.348	.410	266	60	9	2	12	45	49	75
Sept/Oct	.259	.347	.588	85	22	2	1	8	20	11	27	.275	.370	.609	284	78	12	4	25	72	44	79
Situational																						
Bases Empty	.226	.331	.472	235	53	15	2	13	13	34	65	.232	.327	.480	723	168	38	6	43	43	99	197
Leadoff	.219	.344	.495	105	23	4	2	7	7	20	21	.222	.319	.503	316	70	14	6	21	21	45	74
Not Leadoff	.231	.320	.454	130	30	11	0	6	6	14	44	.241	.334	.462	407	98	24	0	22	22	54	123
Runners On	.292	.384	.542	240	70	12	3	14	80	38	77	.292	.397	.535	667	195	31	7	39	226	121	172
First Base Only	.330	.377	.660	106	35	7	2	8	20	8	29	.309	.364	.570	298	92	19	4	17	45	25	61
Scoring Position	.261	.389	.448	134	35	5	1	6	60	30	48	.279	.418	.507	369	103	12	3	22	181	96	111
Late Innings, Close	.255	.333	.447	94	24	4	1	4	19	11	31	.249	.355	.457	245	61	10	1	13	44	41	78
RBI/Opportunities																						

Scoring Position	50 / 211	(24%)		144 / 572	(25%)
Scoring Position, 2 Out	18 / 109	(17%)		58 / 296	(20%)
On Third, Less than 2 Out	20 / 40	(50%)		53 / 105	(50%)
RBI in close games / RBI Total	60 / 93	(65%)		174 / 269	(65%)

Jim Sundberg
Kansas City Royals

How do you evaluate a trade? When after the '84 season I heard that Don Slaught had been traded for Sunny Jim, my reaction was "John Schuerholz has gone off his nut." The justifications given for swapping a promising young catcher for an aging veteran were: Sunny will take away the opposition's running game (in '85 Slaught yielded .57 SBs per game started, Sundberg .56), and he'll stabilize the young pitching staff (he may have done that; the Royals' ERA was a remarkable 3.49 in '85, down from 3.92 the previous year). No one in Kansas City seemed interested in discussing the offensive implications of the deal, and no wonder.

In '85 Slaught had the edge over Sunny in BA, SA and OBP; homers were about equal, as was their deplorable tendency to strike out twice as often as they walked. In '86, however, there was not a ghost of parity—Sundberg's offense simply collapsed: BA down 34 points, SA down 59, OBP down 22 (although surprisingly he held steady in RBIs and increased his walks considerably, the latter not necessarily a good sign at age 35). It didn't help that, with Sundberg healthy and the Royals lacking an adequate back-up, he caught more games than in '85. The future is bleak; at this writing, having failed to entice Ed Hearn from the Mets, the Royals face the prospect of catching Sunny at least 120 times in '87—that is a game plan for disaster. Meanwhile, Slaught could well become an All-Star. Some fiasco of a trade, right?

Well, maybe. But, remember, in '85 the Royals were not looking down the road; like the Cubs in '84 trading Carter and Hall for Sutcliffe, they wanted a quick fix. But while Dallas Green's fix didn't bring a league championship, no one in KC has forgotten that it was Sundberg's bases-loaded triple that clinched the AL title, and that his perfect head-first slide into home culminated the immortal "Iorgy of Recrimination," the greatest single moment in KC baseball history. I guess that's why, when he went into the tank last year, never was heard a discouraging word; not from teammates, fans, media or management.

His career is shot, and Slaught may catch for ten more years, but for one brief shining moment, when all the money was on the line, Sunny was equal to the task. How many such moments does it take to balance an otherwise hideous trade?

—Mike Kopf

	1986 SEASON											THREE YEARS (84 – 86)										
	Ave.	OBP	SLG	AB	H	2B	3B	HR	RBI	BB	SO	Ave.	OBP	SLG	AB	H	2B	3B	HR	RBI	BB	SO
Totals	.212	.303	.322	429	91	9	1	12	42	57	91	.238	.313	.365	1144	272	40	9	29	120	128	221
Batting vs. Left and Right-handed Pitchers																						
Left	.191	.272	.348	141	27	2	1	6	15	16	36	.233	.309	.414	377	88	15	4	15	45	42	72
Right	.222	.317	.309	288	64	7	0	6	27	41	55	.240	.315	.340	767	184	25	5	14	75	86	149
At Home and on the Road																						
Home	.196	.278	.287	209	41	4	0	5	24	25	47	.226	.290	.327	571	129	19	3	11	57	53	115
Road	.227	.325	.355	220	50	5	1	7	18	32	44	.250	.335	.401	573	143	21	6	18	63	75	106
Facing Groundball Pitchers and Flyball Pitchers																						
Groundball	.208	.276	.266	173	36	4	0	2	15	17	31	.233	.300	.340	497	116	18	4	9	44	48	93
Flyball	.215	.320	.359	256	55	5	1	10	27	40	60	.241	.323	.383	647	156	22	5	20	76	80	128
Facing Finesse Pitchers and Power Pitchers																						
Finesse	.215	.286	.327	260	56	3	1	8	32	27	51	.241	.300	.350	668	161	18	5	15	66	58	113
Power	.207	.327	.314	169	35	6	0	4	10	30	40	.233	.331	.384	476	111	22	4	14	54	70	108
On Grass and on Turf																						
Grass	.205	.306	.322	171	35	5	0	5	14	25	34	.245	.323	.386	621	152	29	4	17	72	74	114
Turf	.217	.300	.322	258	56	4	1	7	28	32	57	.229	.301	.338	523	120	11	5	12	48	54	107
During the Day and at Night																						
Day	.194	.333	.340	103	20	3	0	4	12	22	24	.195	.302	.299	231	45	9	0	5	25	36	40
Night	.218	.292	.316	326	71	6	1	8	30	35	67	.249	.316	.381	913	227	31	9	24	95	92	181
By Month																						
April	.161	.200	.161	62	10	0	0	0	5	3	12	.222	.277	.307	176	39	5	2	2	19	14	29
May	.277	.367	.422	83	23	6	0	2	10	13	14	.269	.320	.416	245	66	13	1	7	31	20	36
June	.191	.257	.206	68	13	1	0	0	2	6	14	.254	.322	.380	213	54	7	4	4	17	22	42
July	.182	.313	.318	66	12	0	0	3	9	13	13	.230	.331	.333	213	49	4	0	6	28	33	43
August	.192	.352	.329	73	14	1	0	3	6	18	16	.212	.340	.356	118	25	5	0	4	7	22	25
Sept/Oct	.247	.284	.442	77	19	1	1	4	10	4	22	.218	.286	.374	179	39	6	2	6	18	17	46
Situational																						
Bases Empty	.200	.287	.310	245	49	7	1	6	6	30	45	.220	.295	.340	682	150	21	5	17	17	72	117
Leadoff	.233	.310	.444	90	21	5	1	4	4	10	17	.271	.329	.431	269	73	15	2	8	8	23	45
Not Leadoff	.181	.274	.232	155	28	2	0	2	2	20	28	.186	.274	.281	413	77	6	3	9	9	49	72
Runners On	.228	.322	.337	184	42	2	0	6	36	27	46	.264	.338	.400	462	122	19	4	12	103	56	104
First Base Only	.237	.315	.287	80	19	1	0	1	3	9	22	.260	.338	.352	196	51	6	0	4	10	23	46
Scoring Position	.221	.328	.375	104	23	1	0	5	33	18	24	.267	.339	.436	266	71	13	4	8	93	33	58
Late Innings, Close	.260	.337	.351	77	20	2	1	1	8	10	17	.294	.350	.406	197	58	6	2	4	27	19	42

RBI/Opportunities

	1986 SEASON		THREE YEARS (84 – 86)	
Scoring Position	25 / 144	(17%)	77 / 366	(21%)
Scoring Position, 2 Out	9 / 68	(13%)	29 / 159	(18%)
On Third, Less than 2 Out	9 / 17	(53%)	28 / 58	(48%)
RBI in close games / RBI Total	31 / 42	(74%)	86 / 120	(72%)

Rick Sutcliffe
Chicago Cubs

For one glorious Chicago summer, Rick Sutcliffe was at the top of the game. Acquired from Cleveland partway through the '84 season, Sutcliffe led a remarkably deep Cub pitching staff to an NL East title. A less than mediocre 4–5, 5.15 start with the Indians was totally eclipsed by a 16–1, 2.69 season with Chicago, and appropriately rewarded with the NL Cy Young Award.

Since then, Sutcliffe has been riddled with injuries which have diminished his effectiveness and limited his time on the mound. In '84, Sutcliffe started 20 games and completed 7, throwing 150 innings. A year later, he again started 20, completed 6 for 130 IP, but finished only 8–8 (3.18); a shoulder injury, which would end his season in early September, limited him to just 7.1 IP after July.

Injuries to a pitcher place him under greater scrutiny than a position player when he comes back. He cannot hide on the mound, and the '86 season began with all eyes on Sutcliffe. He started poorly (1–3, 4.41 for April), then contracted food poisoning in May after several Cub players ordered extra (bad) mayonnaise from room service, losing fourteen pounds during a brief hospital stay. To Rick Sutcliffe watchers, his pitching motion had clearly changed; he was more "open" to the batter at the point of delivery, and his lessened control was reflected in his escalating SO/BB ratio. In 1984, Sutcliffe had a fine 3.97 (155/39) which dropped the following year to 2.31 (102/44). In April '86, that ratio bombed to 1.12 (28/25), and would only rise to 1.27 (122/96) by season's end.

Another injury would sideline Sutcliffe for the entire month of July: a pulled hamstring on a run down to first base which hindered his pitching motion and put him on the disabled list. After a too-hasty return, he averaged a mere 5.5 innings pitched per start (contrast with 7.5 IP/GS in 1984, 7.3 before the hamstring pull in 1986.) The rest of the figures were just as bleak: 11 GS, 60.1 IP, 67 H, 34 BB, 40 SO, 5.52 ERA.

For Sutcliffe to come back in '87, he must regain his control. His increased BB/IP was the single most important factor for his woes in '86. Batters' averages against him remained reasonably low last season, so a more accurate Sutcliffe may achieve something near his previous level of dominance. We should learn quickly if the long winter has ridden him of the bad habits which effected his delivery last season.

—Mark Podrazik

1986: Power, Flyball												1985: Power, Flyball											1984: Power, Flyball
1986 SEASON												**THREE YEARS (84 – 86)**											
	G	IP	H	BB	SO	SB	CS	W	L	S	ERA		G	IP	H	BB	SO	SB	CS	W	L	S	ERA
Totals	28	176.2	166	96	122	22	13	5	14	0	4.64		83	551.1	519	225	437	57	25	33	28	0	3.85
At Home and on the Road																							
Home	16	99.1	98	58	73	14	8	3	6	0	4.35		39	263.1	248	117	205	23	16	17	10	0	3.76
Road	12	77.1	68	38	49	8	5	2	8	0	5.00		44	288.0	271	108	232	34	9	16	18	0	3.94
During the Day and at Night																							
Day	22	137.0	134	77	98	18	10	3	11	0	4.47		54	352.1	331	139	288	33	17	20	17	0	3.83
Night	6	39.2	32	19	24	4	3	2	3	0	5.22		29	199.0	188	86	149	24	8	13	11	0	3.89
On Grass and on Turf																							
Grass	20	130.1	122	71	93	15	11	3	9	0	4.21		61	406.0	382	172	303	37	21	25	18	0	3.70
Turf	8	46.1	44	25	29	7	2	2	5	0	5.83		22	145.1	137	53	134	20	4	8	10	0	4.27
By Month																							
April	6	34.2	30	25	28	4	2	1	3	0	4.41		17	121.0	109	50	82	11	7	7	6	0	2.90
May	5	39.2	30	16	29	3	4	2	3	0	3.40		15	94.2	99	39	71	12	4	4	8	0	5.04
June	6	42.0	39	21	25	5	1	1	4	0	4.71		17	121.0	105	54	95	15	4	6	8	0	3.42
July	0	0.0	0	0	0	0	0	0	0	0	0.00		10	61.2	60	28	48	5	0	6	1	0	3.79
August	6	32.0	33	19	17	5	2	0	2	0	4.78		12	78.0	77	33	65	8	3	6	2	0	4.04
Sept/Oct	5	28.1	34	15	23	5	4	1	2	0	6.35		12	75.0	69	21	76	6	7	4	3	0	4.44

vs. Opponent Batters																						
1986 SEASON												**THREE YEARS (84 – 86)**									
	Ave.	OBP	SLG	AB	H	2B	3B	HR	RBI	BB	SO		Ave.	OBP	SLG	AB	H	2B	3B	HR	RBI	BB	SO
Totals	.252	.347	.393	659	166	25	7	18	78	96	122		.249	.322	.379	2087	519	89	22	46	220	225	437
Pitching vs. Left and Right-handed Batters																						
Left	.243	.336	.365	375	91	12	5	8	35	52	78		.252	.322	.377	1134	286	55	13	20	107	116	247
Right	.264	.361	.430	284	75	13	2	10	43	44	44		.244	.323	.381	953	233	34	9	26	113	109	190
Situational																						
Bases Empty	.242	.322	.367	392	95	13	6	8	8	45	74		.240	.303	.359	1247	299	50	15	23	23	107	266
Leadoff	.274	.337	.411	168	46	6	4	3	3	16	29		.269	.321	.400	535	144	26	10	8	8	40	113
Not Leadoff	.219	.311	.335	224	49	7	2	5	5	29	45		.218	.290	.329	712	155	24	5	15	15	67	153
Runners On	.266	.381	.431	267	71	12	1	10	70	51	48		.262	.350	.407	840	220	39	7	23	197	118	171
First Base Only	.259	.314	.411	112	29	5	0	4	10	9	15		.269	.310	.395	372	100	17	3	8	24	22	60
Scoring Position	.271	.422	.445	155	42	7	1	6	60	42	33		.256	.377	.417	468	120	22	4	15	173	96	111
Late Innings, Close	.262	.370	.393	61	16	1	2	1	7	11	12		.261	.320	.394	203	53	9	3	4	20	18	38

RBI/Opportunities						
Scoring Position		48 / 225	(21%)		144 / 672	(21%)
Scoring Position, 2 Out		23 / 122	(19%)		58 / 332	(17%)
On Third, Less than 2 Out		13 / 37	(35%)		48 / 108	(44%)
RBI in close games / RBI Total		58 / 78	(74%)		159 / 220	(72%)

Don Sutton
California Angels

You've just been named the general manager of your favorite team. Mysteriously, you gain some marvelous, secret knowledge. Acquire a certain pitcher, and you'll be guaranteed of all of the following: He will pitch for at least 21 years, and never spend a day on the disabled list. He will win 300 games, something only 18 other pitchers in history have done. He will get at least 100 strikeouts for at least 21 straight years. He will average 240 innings a season. He will pitch over 5,000 innings—only Cy Young will start more games. Over those 21 years, he will average 15 wins a season— year in and year out. He will pitch in four All-Star games, and never be scored upon. He will average 61 walks and 163 strikeouts a year over his career. Even at age 41, he will win 15 games, and pitch 207 innings. Would a general manager be interested in such a player? Such a player exists, and his name is Don Sutton. And he's not done yet.

But there are some negatives. He's won 20 games only once. He gives up lots of homeruns. He doesn't induce the doubleplay ball. At 41, his stats are starting to erode. The ERA is going up, innings pitched are going down. For the most part, he was limited to 100 pitches per game in his 1986 starts. In April and May of 1986, he was 2–5 with an ERA of 7.05. In April and May of 1985, he was 3–5 with an ERA of 6.41. But after June 1 in 1986, Don was 13–6 and had a 2.83 ERA. Age 42 at the start of the 1987 season, a similar pattern in April and May might land him in the "Transactions" column of the sports page. And some astute general manager will pick him up for the stretch drive, not unlike Milwaukee in 1982 and California in 1985. After all, in his last nine starts in 1986, he pitched 54 1/3 innings, gave up 41 hits, and had an ERA of 2.15.

Should Don Sutton be in the Hall of Fame? David Letterman has a saying: "We lose money on every sale, but we make it up in volume." While Don Sutton doesn't have a Cy Young award, or an MVP award, and only one 20 win season, he has sure made up for it in volume. If you needed one great year out of a pitcher, you wouldn't pick Don Sutton. But if you were starting a baseball franchise, you'd like to have Don Sutton as your pitcher every five days for twenty years.

—Dennis Bretz

1986: Finesse, Flyball   **1985: Finesse, Flyball**   **1984: Finesse, Flyball**

	1986 SEASON											THREE YEARS (84 – 86)										
	G	IP	H	BB	SO	SB	CS	W	L	S	ERA	G	IP	H	BB	SO	SB	CS	W	L	S	ERA
Totals	34	207.0	192	49	116	13	6	15	11	0	3.74	101	645.2	637	159	366	51	16	44	33	0	3.79
At Home and on the Road																						
Home	20	128.1	111	30	69	7	4	10	6	0	3.23	56	368.2	350	86	204	19	11	25	18	0	3.52
Road	14	78.2	81	19	47	6	2	5	5	0	4.58	45	277.0	287	73	162	32	5	19	15	0	4.16
During the Day and at Night																						
Day	10	65.0	60	19	37	3	3	5	3	0	3.60	31	211.0	204	53	111	16	5	15	7	0	3.37
Night	24	142.0	132	30	79	10	3	10	8	0	3.80	70	434.2	433	106	255	35	11	29	26	0	4.00
On Grass and on Turf																						
Grass	28	174.1	156	39	91	9	5	13	9	0	3.56	81	527.1	500	127	292	32	14	36	25	0	3.53
Turf	6	32.2	36	10	25	4	1	2	2	0	4.68	20	118.1	137	32	74	19	2	8	8	0	4.94
By Month																						
April	4	18.1	27	7	12	1	1	0	2	0	10.31	13	73.0	86	34	42	5	1	4	6	0	6.04
May	5	26.1	34	2	14	2	1	2	3	0	4.78	16	97.0	114	19	59	8	2	4	7	0	5.01
June	6	44.1	31	7	30	2	1	4	0	0	2.84	18	129.0	100	23	78	7	6	10	4	0	2.79
July	5	33.2	29	8	21	0	1	3	2	0	2.94	17	111.0	115	23	62	10	2	10	4	0	3.24
August	6	37.1	34	10	21	4	2	3	2	0	3.38	18	121.0	112	24	69	10	2	9	5	0	3.27
Sept/Oct	8	47.0	37	15	18	4	0	3	2	0	2.30	19	114.2	110	36	56	11	3	7	7	0	3.53

vs. Opponent Batters

	1986 SEASON											THREE YEARS (84 – 86)								
	Ave.	OBP	SLG	AB	H	2B	3B	HR	RBI	BB	SO	Ave.	OBP	SLG	AB	H	2B	3B	HR	RBI	BB	SO
Totals	.242	.287	.411	795	192	36	3	31	84	49	116	.253	.297	.398	2514	637	107	8	80	271	159	366
Pitching vs. Left and Right-handed Batters																						
Left	.224	.282	.346	407	91	17	0	11	39	34	53	.251	.303	.381	1290	324	51	4	36	142	100	201
Right	.260	.293	.479	388	101	19	3	20	45	15	63	.256	.292	.416	1224	313	56	4	44	129	59	165
Situational																						
Bases Empty	.227	.271	.400	528	120	23	1	22	22	30	79	.244	.286	.389	1576	384	69	5	50	50	90	235
Leadoff	.201	.234	.354	209	42	5	0	9	9	8	31	.241	.276	.384	644	155	25	2	21	21	30	95
Not Leadoff	.245	.295	.429	319	78	18	1	13	13	22	48	.246	.293	.393	932	229	44	3	29	29	60	140
Runners On	.270	.317	.434	267	72	13	2	9	62	19	37	.270	.315	.413	938	253	38	3	30	221	69	131
First Base Only	.276	.302	.381	134	37	6	1	2	6	4	17	.297	.331	.438	461	137	21	1	14	42	21	63
Scoring Position	.263	.331	.489	133	35	7	1	7	56	15	20	.243	.302	.388	477	116	17	2	16	179	48	68
Late Innings, Close	.238	.304	.476	42	10	1	0	3	4	3	6	.309	.340	.513	152	47	5	1	8	17	6	14

RBI/Opportunities

Scoring Position	41 / 168	(24%)	148 / 604	(25%)
Scoring Position, 2 Out	23 / 102	(23%)	62 / 317	(20%)
On Third, Less than 2 Out	11 / 22	(50%)	52 / 86	(60%)
RBI in close games / RBI Total	61 / 84	(73%)	183 / 271	(68%)

Pat Tabler
Cleveland Indians

Pat Tabler is a fair ballplayer. He plays four positions, hits decently, has some good batting splits and does anything his manager asks. The problem is that he can't hit well enough to play first, third or DH and he can't field well enough to play anywhere else. Tabler is good enough to deserve getting 300 at-bats a year; he isn't a quality regular.

Tabler has never hit less than .275 in a year and he's only had one month since 1984 when he had 60+ at-bats and didn't hit .250. Pat could probably hit .290 in his sleep, but his .290 is very soft—he has next to no power, he doesn't walk very much and he can't run. Secondary Average is a way to see how much a player can do for you besides hit singles—the figures mean about the same thing as batting averages do. Tabler's figures since 1984 are (in order) .226, .163 and .180. They'd be bad for a shortstop; they're about 150 points less than what a typical 1B-DH will do.

Another problem is when Pat hits .290. He's hit .337 in Cleveland, .281 on road grass and .203 on road turf in the last three years. He hits flyball pitchers well, tears up

the league at the beginning and end of the year (.324 in April, August and September; .263 otherwise) and you can't help him with platooning. There are two ways to use him—as an Earl Weaver platoon player (where he'd hit .340 in 60 games) or (like Cleveland does) as a spare part—a way to rest a starter or give someone who can't handle a particular pitcher a day off.

If Pat fielded superbly, you might be able to use him at third or in the outfield and live with his bat. He can't. When he filled in for Toby Harrah at third in 1983, his range factor was a fair 2.72. He made 12 errors in 131 games in the outfield—Willie Mays he ain't. If he plays, it must be first or DH; you can't live with his bat there.

Tabler is a poor man's Bill Buckner; Mickey Hatcher's twin brother. If you use him sparingly, he'll do OK for you—if he's one of your regulars, you're flushing 2–3 games a year down the toilet. Given the problems with a 24-man roster, he's valuable—but you can't win a pennant with him in the lineup every day.

—Geoff Beckman and William E. McMahon

	1986 SEASON											THREE YEARS (84 – 86)										
	Ave.	OBP	SLG	AB	H	2B	3B	HR	RBI	BB	SO	Ave.	OBP	SLG	AB	H	2B	3B	HR	RBI	BB	SO
Totals	.326	.368	.433	473	154	29	2	6	48	29	75	.298	.349	.407	1350	402	68	8	21	175	103	193
Batting vs. Left and Right-handed Pitchers																						
Left	.333	.387	.447	150	50	11	0	2	15	13	18	.309	.370	.421	463	143	24	2	8	59	47	53
Right	.322	.359	.427	323	104	18	2	4	33	16	57	.292	.338	.399	887	259	44	6	13	116	56	140
At Home and on the Road																						
Home	.348	.389	.467	227	79	12	0	5	30	15	34	.337	.387	.460	668	225	33	2	15	109	54	82
Road	.305	.347	.402	246	75	17	2	1	18	14	41	.260	.311	.355	682	177	35	6	6	66	49	111
Facing Groundball Pitchers and Flyball Pitchers																						
Groundball	.313	.357	.384	211	66	9	0	2	15	12	35	.287	.334	.366	644	185	24	3	7	65	43	94
Flyball	.336	.376	.473	262	88	20	2	4	33	17	40	.307	.363	.443	706	217	44	5	14	110	60	99
Facing Finesse Pitchers and Power Pitchers																						
Finesse	.356	.380	.472	284	101	22	1	3	28	10	37	.311	.347	.422	785	244	46	4	11	100	44	100
Power	.280	.349	.376	189	53	7	1	3	20	19	38	.280	.351	.386	565	158	22	4	10	75	59	93
On Grass and on Turf																						
Grass	.346	.388	.455	396	137	25	0	6	44	26	65	.313	.364	.422	1163	364	60	5	19	159	93	161
Turf	.221	.259	.325	77	17	4	2	0	4	3	10	.203	.251	.310	187	38	8	3	2	16	10	32
During the Day and at Night																						
Day	.333	.376	.457	162	54	12	1	2	12	9	30	.302	.354	.399	454	137	24	4	4	49	35	70
Night	.322	.363	.421	311	100	17	1	4	36	20	45	.296	.347	.411	896	265	44	4	17	126	68	123
By Month																						
April	.371	.429	.586	70	26	9	0	2	7	7	8	.335	.396	.471	206	69	17	1	3	25	21	23
May	.259	.296	.361	108	28	6	1	1	11	4	22	.263	.322	.336	259	68	10	3	1	30	21	42
June	.150	.190	.150	20	3	0	0	0	1	1	6	.269	.312	.326	175	47	2	1	2	24	10	25
July	.233	.258	.317	60	14	2	0	1	4	2	10	.275	.309	.406	207	57	9	0	6	29	9	32
August	.463	.513	.546	108	50	6	0	1	12	11	15	.327	.382	.438	297	97	16	1	5	37	29	48
Sept/Oct	.308	.339	.411	107	33	6	1	1	13	4	14	.311	.357	.456	206	64	14	2	4	30	13	23
Situational																						
Bases Empty	.327	.358	.435	269	88	18	1	3	3	13	43	.287	.338	.385	732	210	39	3	9	9	53	113
Leadoff	.385	.391	.451	91	35	6	0	0	0	1	12	.313	.350	.384	281	88	15	1	1	1	15	40
Not Leadoff	.298	.342	.427	178	53	12	1	3	3	12	31	.271	.330	.386	451	122	24	2	8	8	38	73
Runners On	.324	.379	.431	204	66	11	1	3	45	16	32	.311	.362	.432	618	192	29	5	12	166	50	80
First Base Only	.358	.429	.469	81	29	4	1	1	4	8	11	.298	.352	.408	262	78	13	2	4	13	19	30
Scoring Position	.301	.346	.407	123	37	7	0	2	41	8	21	.320	.369	.449	356	114	16	3	8	153	31	50
Late Innings, Close	.284	.354	.419	74	21	1	0	3	12	6	16	.276	.349	.424	203	56	6	3	6	34	21	33
RBI/Opportunities																						

	1986			THREE YEARS		
Scoring Position	38 / 157	(24%)		138 / 470	(29%)	
Scoring Position, 2 Out	11 / 63	(17%)		42 / 210	(20%)	
On Third, Less than 2 Out	14 / 28	(50%)		57 / 88	(65%)	
RBI in close games / RBI Total	29 / 48	(60%)		115 / 175	(66%)	

Frank Tanana
Detroit Tigers

Frank Tanana came to the Tigers in June, 1985, for the price of one Duane James, an undistinguished AA-pitching prospect at best. Tanana, however, had been suffering through a miserable year with the Rangers, could declare free-agency at the end of the season, and didn't fit into the Rangers' plans.

With Texas in 1985, Tanana had started 13 games, allowing 89 hits (including 15 HRs) and 23 walks in 77.2 innings for a 2–7 record and a 5.91 ERA. Tanana had successfully completed the transition from power pitcher to control pitcher several years earlier after a serious arm injury, and he had had a very good '84, going 15–15 with a 3.25 ERA in 246.1 innings for a last-place club. There was nothing wrong with him physically, he was just having a bad streak, the kind that intelligent, experienced pitchers can usually work out of. With Detroit, he started 20 games, allowing 131 hits (including 13 HRs) and 34 walks in 137.1 innings for a 10–7 record and a 3.34 ERA. What was the reason for the big difference? Nothing, probably.

The Tigers signed Tanana after the season, and, in 1986, he turned in a decent year. Frank was more effective on the road during 1984–85, but he apparently adjusted well to Tiger Stadium last year. He has had poor results in limited usage on turf the past three years, and has pitched much better under the lights. In both 1984 and 1986, left-handed batters did better against Tanana, which is unusual since his various curveballs are his primary pitches.

The Tigers' acquisition of Tanana was not one of the most important deals of the year, but it does serve to illustrate several points. The first is that it is often possible to get a veteran player who is in a serious slump at a bargain-basement price. The key is determining whether there is some reason the player is doing so poorly, or whether it is something that the player can turn around. Absent physical problems, it is a good choice to bet on those players who have shown in their careers that they can adjust to changing circumstances. Second, it is often possible to pick up a veteran player with a large salary for a small price in talent. Essentially, you are trading money for talent by absorbing the contract of the veteran; there is little difference between this type of deal and purchasing a player outright. Thirdly, it is often possible to pick up a player at little cost when his current team has a surfeit of talent at that position. The Rangers had lots of pitching talent on the way, and it made Frank Tanana expendable.

—Gary Gillette

1986: Finesse, Flyball **1985: Power, Groundball** **1984: Finesse, Groundball**

	G	IP	H	BB	SO	SB	CS	W	L	S	ERA	G	IP	H	BB	SO	SB	CS	W	L	S	ERA
	1986 SEASON											**THREE YEARS (84 – 86)**										
Totals	32	188.1	196	65	119	11	5	12	9	0	4.16	100	649.2	650	203	420	39	15	39	38	0	3.85
At Home and on the Road																						
Home	18	111.2	112	28	84	3	2	8	6	0	3.87	53	334.0	342	100	210	16	9	22	22	0	4.15
Road	14	76.2	84	37	35	8	3	4	3	0	4.58	47	315.2	308	103	210	23	6	17	16	0	3.54
During the Day and at Night																						
Day	11	52.2	63	20	33	6	1	3	4	0	5.13	28	157.2	172	57	107	17	4	10	12	0	4.62
Night	21	135.2	133	45	86	5	4	9	5	0	3.78	72	492.0	478	146	313	22	11	29	26	0	3.60
On Grass and on Turf																						
Grass	28	169.2	168	58	108	8	3	12	7	0	3.71	88	579.1	564	179	372	33	10	37	31	0	3.65
Turf	4	18.2	28	7	11	3	2	0	2	0	8.20	12	70.1	86	24	48	6	5	2	7	0	5.50
By Month																						
April	5	31.2	28	12	16	0	0	3	1	0	3.13	14	81.2	92	32	49	4	2	5	6	0	4.74
May	5	24.1	34	10	15	2	1	1	2	0	8.14	16	100.1	94	28	66	8	1	5	7	0	4.04
June	6	41.0	34	16	23	3	3	3	1	0	2.41	17	118.1	110	44	66	10	6	8	5	0	3.50
July	4	22.2	30	11	10	4	0	1	0	0	5.96	16	105.0	107	37	80	6	2	5	6	0	3.60
August	6	31.1	39	7	19	1	0	2	2	0	4.31	18	119.2	123	25	68	3	1	8	6	0	3.76
Sept/Oct	6	37.1	31	9	36	1	1	2	3	0	3.13	19	124.2	124	37	91	8	3	8	8	0	3.75

vs. Opponent Batters

	Ave.	OBP	SLG	AB	H	2B	3B	HR	RBI	BB	SO	Ave.	OBP	SLG	AB	H	2B	3B	HR	RBI	BB	SO
	1986 SEASON											**THREE YEARS (84 – 86)**										
Totals	.268	.328	.431	731	196	34	8	23	86	65	119	.258	.314	.418	2521	650	114	23	81	286	203	420
Pitching vs. Left and Right-handed Batters																						
Left	.317	.354	.447	123	39	8	1	2	9	7	12	.267	.313	.428	446	119	26	5	12	48	29	87
Right	.258	.323	.428	608	157	26	7	21	77	58	107	.256	.314	.415	2075	531	88	18	69	238	174	333
Situational																						
Bases Empty	.281	.327	.449	441	124	23	6	13	13	27	70	.254	.300	.416	1552	394	72	13	51	51	95	258
Leadoff	.263	.301	.419	186	49	9	1	6	6	9	34	.247	.280	.386	645	159	30	3	18	18	26	104
Not Leadoff	.294	.345	.471	255	75	14	5	7	7	18	36	.259	.314	.437	907	235	42	10	33	33	69	154
Runners On	.248	.330	.403	290	72	11	2	10	73	38	49	.264	.335	.421	969	256	42	10	30	235	108	162
First Base Only	.254	.291	.418	134	34	7	0	5	12	7	24	.288	.330	.465	434	125	22	5	15	41	24	60
Scoring Position	.244	.359	.391	156	38	4	2	5	61	31	25	.245	.339	.385	535	131	20	5	15	194	84	102
Late Innings, Close	.250	.333	.313	64	16	2	1	0	7	8	5	.286	.359	.472	161	46	7	1	7	23	19	20

RBI/Opportunities

Scoring Position		50 / 230	(22%)		161 / 753	(21%)
Scoring Position, 2 Out		23 / 100	(23%)		61 / 359	(17%)
On Third, Less than 2 Out		20 / 49	(41%)		74 / 146	(51%)
RBI in close games / RBI Total		60 / 86	(70%)		191 / 286	(67%)

Danny Tartabull
Seattle Mariners

I credit the best line of the 1986 season to Jose Tartabull, who hit only two home runs in 749 major league games. Son Danny equalled this total in 20 at bats as a September callup in 1984 and shows no signs of stopping. Asked about it, Jose allowed as how Danny got his power from his mother.

Wherever he gets it, he's definitely got it. Tartabull is one of those players who seems to draw ink. A record of his 1986 season could focus on his production, his mysterious illness and weight loss, the controversy about what position he should play, the questions about his attitude and work habits or the arguments about his trade. Let's start with the performance. Five points:

1) Tartabull hit 16 of his 25 homers with men on base and also hit singles, doubles, triples and home runs more frequently with men on base than with the bases empty. Per 1000 at bats with no one on, he hit 159 singles, 43 doubles, 7 triples and 32 homers. Per 1000 at bats with men on, he upped it to 162 singles, 55 doubles, 17 triples and 68 homers. He also walked more often when there were men on.

2) He was even more effective with men in scoring position than with men on first. His slugging percentage with the bases empty was .399, with men on first .557, with men in scoring position .628.

3) Tartabull was much more effective against "finesse" pitchers (or "placement" pitchers, we might have called them) than against power pitchers.

4) Despite comments to the contrary, Tartabull showed remarkable improvement in his strikeout frequency as the season wore on. He struck out in 42% of his at bats in April and 36% in May, but cut it to 26% in July and 28% in September. His performance by months was quite steady, and he had no month in which his slugging percentage was less than .421.

5) Despite the strikeouts he drove home 50% of the runners he found on third base with less than two out, a decent percentage. League RBI leader Joe Carter drove in only 49% in that situation.

Darn, almost used up all our space without getting to the gossip. As to the position he plays, I don't see how anyone can expect a man to be a good defensive player after having played five positions in the last three years. As to the trade and the attitude, as a Royals' fan I'll take the whole package.

—Bill James

	1986 SEASON											THREE YEARS (84 – 86)										
	Ave.	OBP	SLG	AB	H	2B	3B	HR	RBI	BB	SO	Ave.	OBP	SLG	AB	H	2B	3B	HR	RBI	BB	SO
Totals	.270	.347	.489	511	138	25	6	25	96	61	157	.277	.354	.498	592	164	33	7	28	110	71	174
Batting vs. Left and Right-handed Pitchers																						
Left	.304	.385	.464	125	38	9	1	3	16	17	37	.314	.398	.490	153	48	13	1	4	22	22	41
Right	.259	.335	.497	386	100	16	5	22	80	44	120	.264	.339	.501	439	116	20	6	24	88	49	133
At Home and on the Road																						
Home	.272	.338	.500	268	73	14	4	13	47	26	83	.279	.349	.503	298	83	17	4	14	52	31	89
Road	.267	.357	.477	243	65	11	2	12	49	35	74	.276	.359	.493	294	81	16	3	14	58	40	85
Facing Groundball Pitchers and Flyball Pitchers																						
Groundball	.266	.333	.459	244	65	16	2	9	36	25	70	.280	.342	.498	289	81	21	3	12	46	27	81
Flyball	.273	.359	.517	267	73	9	4	16	60	36	87	.274	.366	.498	303	83	12	4	16	64	44	93
Facing Finesse Pitchers and Power Pitchers																						
Finesse	.293	.361	.523	300	88	14	5	15	60	32	71	.307	.379	.560	339	104	20	6	18	71	39	75
Power	.237	.328	.441	211	50	11	1	10	36	29	86	.237	.322	.415	253	60	13	1	10	39	32	99
On Grass and on Turf																						
Grass	.274	.366	.486	175	48	6	2	9	39	26	56	.278	.365	.495	216	60	11	3	10	46	31	66
Turf	.268	.337	.491	336	90	19	4	16	57	35	101	.277	.348	.500	376	104	22	4	18	64	40	108
During the Day and at Night																						
Day	.244	.326	.546	119	29	7	1	9	25	15	40	.250	.344	.559	136	34	8	2	10	29	19	45
Night	.278	.354	.472	392	109	18	5	16	71	46	117	.285	.357	.480	456	130	25	5	18	81	52	129
By Month																						
April	.235	.350	.471	68	16	4	0	4	16	12	28	.235	.350	.471	68	16	4	0	4	16	12	28
May	.268	.333	.571	56	15	2	3	3	9	6	20	.268	.333	.571	56	15	2	3	3	9	6	20
June	.311	.376	.500	90	28	5	0	4	13	10	20	.311	.376	.500	90	28	5	0	4	13	10	20
July	.293	.330	.495	99	29	3	1	5	25	6	26	.293	.330	.495	99	29	3	1	5	25	6	26
August	.231	.307	.516	91	21	5	0	7	19	10	33	.231	.307	.516	91	21	5	0	7	19	10	33
Sept/Oct	.271	.376	.421	107	29	6	2	2	14	17	30	.293	.385	.479	188	55	14	3	5	28	27	47
Situational																						
Bases Empty	.243	.315	.399	276	67	12	2	9	9	29	82	.254	.333	.420	319	81	17	3	10	10	37	88
Leadoff	.232	.309	.408	125	29	6	2	4	4	14	36	.243	.325	.429	140	34	7	2	5	5	17	38
Not Leadoff	.252	.319	.391	151	38	6	0	5	5	15	46	.263	.340	.413	179	47	10	1	5	5	20	50
Runners On	.302	.384	.596	235	71	13	4	16	87	32	75	.304	.378	.590	273	83	16	4	18	100	34	86
First Base Only	.283	.382	.557	106	30	6	1	7	18	17	35	.301	.386	.577	123	37	8	1	8	22	17	39
Scoring Position	.318	.385	.628	129	41	7	3	9	69	15	40	.307	.372	.600	150	46	8	3	10	78	17	47
Late Innings, Close	.287	.347	.448	87	25	4	2	2	15	8	32	.297	.360	.446	101	30	5	2	2	17	10	39
RBI/Opportunities																						

	RBI/Opportunities (1986)		THREE YEARS	
Scoring Position	49 / 180	(27%)	56 / 210	(27%)
Scoring Position, 2 Out	21 / 91	(23%)	24 / 108	(22%)
On Third, Less than 2 Out	16 / 32	(50%)	18 / 36	(50%)
RBI in close games / RBI Total	64 / 96	(67%)	76 / 110	(69%)

Kent Tekulve
Pittsburgh Pirates.

He sure doesn't look a like tough guy, but that's exactly what Kent Tekulve is. Two years ago, Tekulve seemed ready for the scrap heap. After a decade with Pittsburgh his performance had slipped, and finally the Bucs traded him to Philadelphia for a large box of doughnuts (Al Holland). It seemed like a one-way ticket to palookaville, considering how much money Kent was making, and how badly he was pitching. But Kent Tekulve is a survivor. He finished well in '85, made the Phillie ballclub last spring, and last year was one of the bright spots on a mediocre pitching staff. In a year of major comebacks, it wasn't a big story, but it was one my favorites.

Tekulve first came to prominence back in 1977, when he worked as a set-up man for the young Goose Gossage. After nearly a decade as a closer, Tekulve returned to the set-up role last year, this time for Steve Bedrosian. His performance in the two seasons was remarkably similar:

Year	G	W	L	S	IP	H	SO	BB	ERA
1977	72	10	1	7	103	89	59	33	3.06
1986	73	10	5	4	110	99	57	25	2.54

If anything, Tekulve pitched better last year than he had a decade ago. As usual, he displayed good control, got a lot of groundball outs and yielded very few homeruns. He also displayed his Achilles' heel, weakness against left-handed hitting. It was that weakness which caused him to lose his closer's role in Pittsburgh. Dan Quisenberry, a pitcher with a very similar throwing motion, has shown the same vulnerabilty, and lost his late-inning job for the same reason: opposing teams began to save their lefty swingers for him, which is what Earl Weaver did to Tekulve in the fourth game of the '79 Series. In middle relief Kent is apt to face more of a right/left balance, so perhaps the change has given him a new lease on life.

If he can stay effective for a while longer, Tekulve is in sight of some major records. He needs 46 appearances to tie Sparky Lyle's record for most games without a start (899), 53 to move into third place in games pitched. One thousand games, a plateau reached only by Hoyt Wilhelm, is still a slight possibility. I'll be rooting for him.

—Don Zminda

1986: Finesse, Groundball												1985: Finesse, Groundball										1984: Finesse, Groundball			
	1986 SEASON												**THREE YEARS (84 – 86)**										
	G	IP	H	BB	SO	SB	CS	W	L	S	ERA		G	IP	H	BB	SO	SB	CS	W	L	S	ERA
Totals	73	110.0	99	25	57	18	5	11	5	4	2.54		206	273.2	259	88	133	34	10	18	24	31	2.83
											At Home and on the Road												
Home	34	53.2	50	9	30	8	2	6	2	2	2.35		101	144.0	138	44	65	13	4	10	11	13	3.00
Road	39	56.1	49	16	27	10	3	5	3	2	2.72		105	129.2	121	44	68	21	6	8	13	18	2.64
											During the Day and at Night												
Day	27	37.1	36	12	22	6	3	5	3	1	2.65		70	88.0	90	33	48	10	4	9	10	7	3.37
Night	46	72.2	63	13	35	12	2	6	2	3	2.48		136	185.2	169	55	85	24	6	9	14	24	2.57
											On Grass and on Turf												
Grass	23	33.2	32	11	17	8	1	4	3	1	3.21		56	69.1	67	25	37	13	4	5	9	5	3.25
Turf	50	76.1	67	14	40	10	4	7	2	3	2.24		150	204.1	192	63	96	21	6	13	15	26	2.69
											By Month												
April	5	4.2	6	1	4	0	0	0	0	0	1.93		18	21.0	21	14	10	1	0	1	1	2	3.86
May	12	16.0	14	4	13	7	0	0	1	1	2.81		33	41.0	43	15	21	9	1	3	6	5	3.73
June	16	27.1	26	4	11	5	0	2	0	0	2.96		43	63.0	57	13	29	5	0	4	2	6	2.43
July	14	19.1	23	4	11	2	2	1	0	1	3.26		40	48.2	62	18	24	6	1	6	9	9	3.70
August	14	20.2	14	7	6	1	0	5	2	1	1.74		32	43.1	39	17	14	7	2	5	6	4	2.70
Sept/Oct	12	22.0	16	5	12	3	3	3	2	1	2.05		40	56.2	37	11	35	6	3	4	3	5	1.59

			vs. Opponent Batters																		
	1986 SEASON											**THREE YEARS (84 – 86)**									
	Ave.	OBP	SLG	AB	H	2B	3B	HR	RBI	BB	SO	Ave.	OBP	SLG	AB	H	2B	3B	HR	RBI	BB	SO
Totals	.240	.281	.300	413	99	13	3	2	36	25	57	.251	.310	.334	1027	258	34	9	11	109	88	133
					Pitching vs. Left and Right-handed Batters																
Left	.251	.301	.293	191	48	5	0	1	11	14	11	.274	.346	.349	435	119	13	4	4	42	46	30
Right	.230	.263	.306	222	51	8	3	1	25	11	46	.235	.283	.323	592	139	21	5	7	67	42	103
						Situational															
Bases Empty	.248	.267	.330	230	57	7	3	2	2	6	31	.256	.287	.342	544	139	18	7	5	5	23	68
Leadoff	.224	.255	.306	98	22	1	2	1	1	4	14	.258	.286	.381	236	61	8	6	3	3	8	24
Not Leadoff	.265	.276	.348	132	35	6	1	1	1	2	17	.253	.288	.312	308	78	10	1	2	2	15	44
Runners On	.230	.296	.262	183	42	6	0	0	34	19	26	.246	.333	.325	483	119	16	2	6	104	65	65
First Base Only	.313	.323	.328	64	20	1	0	0	0	1	7	.292	.324	.339	171	50	3	1	1	3	7	22
Scoring Position	.185	.284	.227	119	22	5	0	0	34	18	19	.221	.338	.317	312	69	13	1	5	101	58	43
Late Innings, Close	.274	.329	.368	190	52	10	1	2	19	16	19	.279	.349	.394	587	164	25	6	10	74	62	62

	RBI/Opportunities					
Scoring Position		32 / 173	(18%)		89 / 487	(18%)
Scoring Position, 2 Out		16 / 91	(18%)		41 / 245	(17%)
On Third, Less than 2 Out		13 / 25	(52%)		36 / 82	(44%)
RBI in close games / RBI Total		23 / 36	(64%)		78 / 109	(72%)

Garry Templeton
San Diego Padres

Garry Templeton was once in the top echelon of National League players. Alas, time and tide wait for no man, and age sure seems to be catching up with Garry. His performance is now uniformly worse than it used to be. Of course, the drop-off in at-bats is due to Garry's drop from the lead-off spot to the 8th hole in the order. The drop in runs is undoubtedly due to the same factor; however, his power is now only producing doubles. His batting average has really suffered—1986 was a full 42 points below his pre-1986 lifetime BA. That is a significant drop, and, a quick glance at his on-base shows why Manager Steve Boros didn't try to get Garry another 100 at bats near the top of the order.

In 713 games with the Cardinals (1976–81), Garry hit 69 triples, and was the only player in National League history to lead the league for three straight years in three-base hits. In 710 games with the Padres, he has 17 triples—only 7 in the last three years, 6 of those on grass.

Garry's clutch hitting has fallen off, too. In 1985, he drove in 65% of all runners on 3rd with less than 2 out, 33% of all runners in scoring position, and 29% of runners in scoring position with 2 outs. In 1986, these percentages all fell, to 44%, 24%, and 19%, respectively. Worse, he had more opportunities in each situation in 1986.

—J. Michael Duca

In addition to his deterioration at the plate, Templeton's baserunning and defense appear to have gone south. Problems with both of his knees have cut his stolen base totals as well as his defensive range. Garry stole only 10 bases in 1986, a far cry from the 30 SB he averaged from 1977–1981.

Defensively, Templeton was once a premier shortstop with tremendous range: he led NL shortstops in put outs, total chances and double plays in both 1978 and 1979, although he also led the league in errors for the years 1978, 1979, and 1980. Templeton's range, measured by his total of put outs and assists per 9 defensive innings, was the lowest in the league among regular shortstops last year. Further, he participated in only 60 double plays, 8th in the league.

Templeton is an example of a player who survives on his reputation and not on his abilities. He can no longer hit, run or field adequately. Although he is certainly not old (1987 seasonal age of 31), it seems highly unlikely that he will recover enough of his skills to make him worth playing.

—Gary Gillette

	1986 SEASON											THREE YEARS (84 – 86)										
	Ave.	OBP	SLG	AB	H	2B	3B	HR	RBI	BB	SO	Ave.	OBP	SLG	AB	H	2B	3B	HR	RBI	BB	SO
Totals	.247	.296	.308	510	126	21	2	2	44	35	86	.263	.314	.336	1549	407	70	7	10	134	115	255
Batting vs. Left and Right-handed Pitchers																						
Left	.257	.323	.343	175	45	7	1	2	14	17	28	.254	.301	.325	496	126	22	2	3	38	33	82
Right	.242	.281	.290	335	81	14	1	0	30	18	58	.267	.320	.342	1053	281	48	5	7	96	82	173
At Home and on the Road																						
Home	.230	.284	.294	269	62	10	2	1	24	20	54	.251	.300	.332	790	198	33	5	7	68	55	137
Road	.266	.309	.324	241	64	11	0	1	20	15	32	.275	.328	.341	759	209	37	2	3	66	60	118
Facing Groundball Pitchers and Flyball Pitchers																						
Groundball	.239	.307	.320	272	65	14	1	2	24	27	39	.274	.330	.352	807	221	42	3	5	59	70	114
Flyball	.256	.282	.294	238	61	7	1	0	20	8	47	.251	.295	.319	742	186	28	4	5	75	45	141
Facing Finesse Pitchers and Power Pitchers																						
Finesse	.253	.294	.322	292	74	15	1	1	22	16	36	.258	.304	.322	857	221	39	2	4	60	57	107
Power	.239	.298	.289	218	52	6	1	1	22	19	50	.269	.326	.354	692	186	31	5	6	74	58	148
On Grass and on Turf																						
Grass	.242	.298	.297	380	92	14	2	1	32	30	71	.261	.314	.336	1158	302	48	6	9	101	89	201
Turf	.262	.289	.338	130	34	7	0	1	12	5	15	.269	.313	.338	391	105	22	1	1	33	26	54
During the Day and at Night																						
Day	.236	.287	.276	174	41	5	1	0	13	12	25	.270	.320	.356	477	129	22	2	5	46	35	84
Night	.253	.300	.324	336	85	16	1	2	31	23	61	.259	.311	.327	1072	278	48	5	5	88	80	171
By Month																						
April	.213	.280	.213	75	16	0	0	0	2	7	17	.250	.312	.307	212	53	9	0	1	15	19	35
May	.183	.208	.204	93	17	2	0	0	3	3	12	.224	.249	.306	268	60	11	1	3	21	10	50
June	.299	.365	.414	87	26	2	1	2	17	9	14	.314	.364	.390	290	91	10	3	2	32	22	40
July	.198	.227	.253	91	18	5	0	0	8	4	21	.262	.330	.344	256	67	16	1	1	26	27	46
August	.276	.317	.367	98	27	7	1	0	10	5	12	.236	.294	.308	276	65	10	2	2	17	22	47
Sept/Oct	.333	.397	.409	66	22	5	0	0	4	7	10	.287	.328	.356	247	71	14	0	1	23	15	37
Situational																						
Bases Empty	.251	.270	.301	299	75	12	0	1	1	8	45	.257	.281	.326	938	241	42	4	5	5	31	144
Leadoff	.252	.264	.291	127	32	5	0	0	0	2	18	.244	.268	.305	393	96	17	2	1	1	12	54
Not Leadoff	.250	.275	.308	172	43	7	0	1	1	6	27	.266	.291	.341	545	145	25	2	4	4	19	90
Runners On	.242	.328	.318	211	51	9	2	1	43	27	41	.272	.358	.352	611	166	28	3	5	129	84	111
First Base Only	.220	.245	.253	91	20	1	1	0	1	2	19	.271	.287	.331	266	72	9	2	1	9	5	52
Scoring Position	.258	.381	.367	120	31	8	1	1	42	25	22	.272	.403	.368	345	94	19	1	4	120	79	59
Late Innings, Close	.336	.397	.395	119	40	7	0	0	16	12	25	.285	.353	.338	302	86	13	0	1	26	30	60

RBI/Opportunities	1986 SEASON		THREE YEARS	
Scoring Position	39 / 166	(23%)	110 / 497	(22%)
Scoring Position, 2 Out	16 / 84	(19%)	44 / 250	(18%)
On Third, Less than 2 Out	12 / 27	(44%)	38 / 85	(45%)
RBI in close games / RBI Total	34 / 44	(77%)	86 / 134	(64%)

Walt Terrell
Detroit Tigers

Walt Terrell is a tank—the kind of pitcher that just clanks forward, turning in an acceptable performance and pitching a large number of innings. In the last three years, Walt has averaged about 33 games started and over 220 innings-pitched per year, winning about 14 games and losing about 11 each season. If he is the number one starter on your team, you're in trouble. As number two, you are probably mediocre. With Terrell as your number three starter, you're most likely a contender. As your number four guy in the rotation, you'll probably win. As the fifth starter in your stable, you're the World Champion Mets.

With his primary pitch being a sinking fastball, Walt is a heavy ground-ball pitcher. Traditional wisdom tells us that such pitchers are very effective on grass but not so good on turf, where the ball can get by the infielders quicker. Terrell was much more effective on turf in 1984 with the Mets; in the AL, he has had an ERA of over 6.00 on turf the last two years. One thing is certain: the elephant grass in the infield in Tiger Stadium slows down the grounders that Walt is so proficient at inducing. His record in Motown the last two years is much better than when he is living out of a suitcase. He was very effective in late-and-close situations in 1986; of course, given the way he pitched, he didn't get into too many of those situations.

Walt started last year as the Tigers #3 starter; with his 6–2 record in April and May, he was the staff ace while Morris and Petry struggled. He finished the season as Avis to Morris's Hertz, indicative of the Tigers' mediocrity. He has been extremely tough to run on the last three years, but part of this is undoubtedly due to pitching to Gary Carter and Lance Parrish. Terrell's strikeout-to-walk ratio is poor: in fact, he walked more batters than he whiffed last year, a very unusual statistic for a starter who hurled 200 innings.

Terrell is on the trading block this off-season. If the Tigers' braintrust thinks Dan Petry is healthy, they will attempt to trade a starter for a third baseman, outfielder or reliever. Walt Terrell is the most likely one to go, for most teams can use a tank in their rotation.

—Gary Gillette

1986: Finesse, Groundball **1985: Power, Groundball** **1984: Finesse, Groundball**

	G	IP	H	BB	SO	SB	CS	W	L	S	ERA		G	IP	H	BB	SO	SB	CS	W	L	S	ERA
	1986 SEASON												**THREE YEARS (84 – 86)**										
Totals	34	217.1	199	98	93	2	6	15	12	0	4.56		101	661.1	652	273	337	17	27	41	34	0	3.97
	At Home and on the Road																						
Home	16	115.2	89	42	53	1	2	10	3	0	3.35		50	337.1	303	127	174	8	12	22	12	0	3.42
Road	18	101.2	110	56	40	1	4	5	9	0	5.93		51	324.0	349	146	163	9	15	19	22	0	4.56
	During the Day and at Night																						
Day	9	64.2	50	29	25	1	3	4	1	0	3.62		32	204.1	210	82	116	8	12	8	11	0	4.40
Night	25	152.2	149	69	68	1	3	11	11	0	4.95		69	457.0	442	191	221	9	15	33	23	0	3.78
	On Grass and on Turf																						
Grass	28	188.2	163	78	80	2	3	15	9	0	4.20		79	523.1	503	211	257	13	18	33	25	0	3.87
Turf	6	28.2	36	20	13	0	3	0	3	0	6.91		22	138.0	149	62	80	4	9	8	9	0	4.37
	By Month																						
April	4	23.2	29	10	7	1	0	2	1	0	6.08		14	86.1	94	33	35	2	3	7	2	0	4.38
May	7	46.2	41	19	18	0	4	4	1	0	3.47		18	117.0	117	43	68	2	6	8	6	0	3.69
June	6	36.0	32	20	12	0	2	1	4	0	4.75		16	106.0	102	53	42	1	6	6	8	0	3.74
July	5	36.1	26	15	29	1	0	2	2	0	3.22		17	119.2	90	49	76	4	4	6	6	0	3.53
August	6	40.0	33	23	14	0	0	2	3	0	5.85		18	127.2	128	54	66	4	6	7	6	0	4.16
Sept/Oct	6	34.2	38	11	13	0	0	4	1	0	4.67		18	104.2	121	41	50	4	2	7	6	0	4.47

vs. Opponent Batters

	Ave.	OBP	SLG	AB	H	2B	3B	HR	RBI	BB	SO		Ave.	OBP	SLG	AB	H	2B	3B	HR	RBI	BB	SO
	1986 SEASON												**THREE YEARS (84 – 86)**										
Totals	.245	.328	.415	812	199	38	5	30	101	98	93		.261	.334	.384	2500	652	110	16	55	276	273	337
	Pitching vs. Left and Right-handed Batters																						
Left	.243	.326	.390	420	102	27	1	11	41	52	38		.253	.324	.353	1316	333	64	8	17	122	141	142
Right	.247	.330	.441	392	97	11	4	19	60	46	55		.269	.346	.418	1184	319	46	8	38	154	132	195
	Situational																						
Bases Empty	.224	.315	.395	474	106	17	2	20	20	62	63		.249	.330	.376	1408	350	58	7	36	36	168	218
Leadoff	.234	.330	.358	201	47	5	1	6	6	29	28		.250	.331	.355	620	155	24	4	11	11	74	87
Not Leadoff	.216	.303	.421	273	59	12	1	14	14	33	35		.247	.329	.393	788	195	34	3	25	25	94	131
Runners On	.275	.346	.444	338	93	21	3	10	81	36	30		.277	.339	.393	1092	302	52	9	19	240	105	119
First Base Only	.287	.352	.472	178	51	14	2	5	18	16	12		.293	.347	.426	549	161	30	5	11	40	40	42
Scoring Position	.263	.339	.412	160	42	7	1	5	63	20	18		.260	.332	.359	543	141	22	4	8	200	65	77
Late Innings, Close	.198	.278	.346	81	16	3	0	3	9	8	7		.272	.348	.424	224	61	7	3	7	26	23	23

RBI/Opportunities

Scoring Position	52 / 216	(24%)		177 / 732	(24%)
Scoring Position, 2 Out	21 / 101	(21%)		63 / 326	(19%)
On Third, Less than 2 Out	19 / 35	(54%)		69 / 131	(53%)
RBI in close games / RBI Total	68 / 101	(67%)		202 / 276	(73%)

Rob Thompson
San Francisco Giants

The NL Rookie-of-the-Year Award generated less debate about a pitcher beating out an everyday player than the AL MVP balloting, but the same arguments are applicable. The BBWAA was nearly unanimous in its acclaim for Todd Worrell. *The Sporting News* picked Thompson as Rookie of the Year, selecting Worrell as Rookie Pitcher of the Year.

Worrell led the league in saves, had an ERA of 2.08 and pitched in 74 games with a losing record. Thompson played in 149 games, led the majors in sacrifice hits, and led the Giants in several other offensive categories such as runs, hits, strikeouts and caught stealings. (Yes, the last two were offensive.) If this were a political election, Thompson would have won the popular vote but lost the election. Worrell gave an impressive performance on national television in the 1985 World Series, and, since he retained his rookie status in 1986, he was the dark-horse candidate once the usual New York and Los Angeles promotions had run their course. He led the league in saves, breaking the record for a rookie in doing so. There you have it—good TV presence, leadership, coolness under fire—the guy you want out there when the game is on the line. The BBWAA ate it up. Worrell had an excellent season, to be sure, but was he more valuable to the Cardinals as they slumped from 101 wins in 1985 to 79 in 1986, or was Thompson more valuable to the Giants as they improved from 62 wins in '85 to 83 last year?

The Giants promoted Thompson at second base because of his character and savvy in the field. They also saw that he had led the AA Texas League in total chances and double plays. Thompson's background (along with Jose Uribe's) forecast the better middle-infield defense that the Giants were looking for. This combination, along with the very high grass and a resurfaced dirt part of the infield, produced fewer "rocky horror" shows at the 'Stick.

Thompson did well when leading off, but his bunting ability makes him more suited for the traditional #2 position in the lineup. His on-base average, though, is more like that of a #7 hitter.

Thompson and Uribe have something in common other than their defensive play. This is the allergic reaction their batting eyes have in stadiums with plastic rugs. Their eyes must really water, since they certainly don't see much of the ball when up at the plate. It must have something to do with the freshly vacuumed and zippered grass. If a horse can't eat it . . .

—Victor Hester

	1986 SEASON											THREE YEARS (84 – 86)										
	Ave.	OBP	SLG	AB	H	2B	3B	HR	RBI	BB	SO	Ave.	OBP	SLG	AB	H	2B	3B	HR	RBI	BB	SO
Totals	.271	.328	.370	549	149	27	3	7	47	42	112	.271	.328	.370	549	149	27	3	7	47	42	112
Batting vs. Left and Right-handed Pitchers																						
Left	.286	.344	.411	168	48	10	1	3	15	14	33	.286	.344	.411	168	48	10	1	3	15	14	33
Right	.265	.321	.352	381	101	17	2	4	32	28	79	.265	.321	.352	381	101	17	2	4	32	28	79
At Home and on the Road																						
Home	.294	.364	.424	255	75	17	2	4	28	26	43	.294	.364	.424	255	75	17	2	4	28	26	43
Road	.252	.296	.323	294	74	10	1	3	19	16	69	.252	.296	.323	294	74	10	1	3	19	16	69
Facing Groundball Pitchers and Flyball Pitchers																						
Groundball	.272	.339	.369	268	73	13	2	3	23	24	56	.272	.339	.369	268	73	13	2	3	23	24	56
Flyball	.270	.318	.370	281	76	14	1	4	24	18	56	.270	.318	.370	281	76	14	1	4	24	18	56
Facing Finesse Pitchers and Power Pitchers																						
Finesse	.321	.362	.439	312	100	18	2	5	30	20	52	.321	.362	.439	312	100	18	2	5	30	20	52
Power	.207	.285	.278	237	49	9	1	2	17	22	60	.207	.285	.278	237	49	9	1	2	17	22	60
On Grass and on Turf																						
Grass	.294	.362	.418	395	116	22	3	7	39	38	75	.294	.362	.418	395	116	22	3	7	39	38	75
Turf	.214	.237	.247	154	33	5	0	0	8	4	37	.214	.237	.247	154	33	5	0	0	8	4	37
During the Day and at Night																						
Day	.285	.350	.405	242	69	14	3	3	25	21	45	.285	.350	.405	242	69	14	3	3	25	21	45
Night	.261	.311	.342	307	80	13	0	4	22	21	67	.261	.311	.342	307	80	13	0	4	22	21	67
By Month																						
April	.244	.337	.308	78	19	5	0	0	8	10	17	.244	.337	.308	78	19	5	0	0	8	10	17
May	.305	.352	.439	82	25	5	0	2	8	6	15	.305	.352	.439	82	25	5	0	2	8	6	15
June	.245	.292	.306	98	24	3	0	1	9	7	15	.245	.292	.306	98	24	3	0	1	9	7	15
July	.280	.350	.409	93	26	5	2	1	7	7	27	.280	.350	.409	93	26	5	2	1	7	7	27
August	.270	.300	.365	115	31	5	0	2	8	5	20	.270	.300	.365	115	31	5	0	2	8	5	20
Sept/Oct	.289	.352	.398	83	24	4	1	1	7	7	18	.289	.352	.398	83	24	4	1	1	7	7	18
Situational																						
Bases Empty	.282	.328	.389	337	95	19	1	5	5	19	77	.282	.328	.389	337	95	19	1	5	5	19	77
Leadoff	.300	.364	.445	110	33	7	0	3	3	10	21	.300	.364	.445	110	33	7	0	3	3	10	21
Not Leadoff	.273	.310	.361	227	62	12	1	2	2	9	56	.273	.310	.361	227	62	12	1	2	2	9	56
Runners On	.255	.329	.340	212	54	8	2	2	42	23	35	.255	.329	.340	212	54	8	2	2	42	23	35
First Base Only	.261	.301	.375	88	23	5	1	1	5	5	10	.261	.301	.375	88	23	5	1	1	5	5	10
Scoring Position	.250	.347	.315	124	31	3	1	1	37	18	25	.250	.347	.315	124	31	3	1	1	37	18	25
Late Innings, Close	.295	.337	.358	95	28	3	0	1	8	6	19	.295	.337	.358	95	28	3	0	1	8	6	19
RBI/Opportunities																						
Scoring Position				34 / 180		(19%)									34 / 180		(19%)					
Scoring Position, 2 Out				11 / 71		(15%)									11 / 71		(15%)					
On Third, Less than 2 Out				17 / 36		(47%)									17 / 36		(47%)					
RBI in close games / RBI Total				34 / 47		(72%)									34 / 47		(72%)					

Alan Trammell
Detroit Tigers

At mid-season last year, Alan Trammell was at the nadir of his career. He was batting only .245 with 14 doubles, 2 triples, 5 home runs, and 18 walks at the end of June. Coming off of his sub-par 1985 (.258 BA, .312 OBA, .380 SA), he was at a complete loss to explain the erosion of his talents.

Alan Trammell made it to the big leagues at the tender age of 19, he was a regular shortstop at the age of 20, and he was an All-Star at the age of 22. He had reached his peak during the 1983–84 seasons, when he hit .319 and .314 with totals of 65 doubles, 7 triples, and 28 home runs. He won his third and fourth Gold Gloves in those years, and he capped all of this off by winning the 1984 World Series Most Valuable Player Award. Even nagging knee and arm injuries didn't tarnish the glow of success.

1985 was a different story, though. As the Tigers struggled, so did Trammell. While he was pronounced healthy by the doctors after operations on his knee and shoulder, and while he insisted that he was the same, dependable star that Tigers fans adored, something was clearly wrong. His offensive production skidded, and it was obvious to those who bothered to look that his defensive play was being affected by his supposedly-healed injuries.

For the first half of 1986, Trammell looked healthy again but still couldn't find his batting eye. While there was lots of finger-pointing going on in Detroit as to who was to blame for the Tigers second straight disappointing year, no one seemed to blame Alan. After all, they said, he was trying as hard as he could. Well, something must have worked, because he was ungodly good in the second half of the year. From July onward, Alan hit .304 with 19 doubles, 5 triples, 16 homers and 41 walks. His defense seemed to recover, too. From distinctly below-average range in '85, he improved to above-average in '86 as well as increasing his DP total from 89 to 99.

As 1987 dawns, the Tigers seem confident that the Trammell of old is back. I do not expect him to repeat his second-half streak next year, but he should settle in comfortably above his 1985 level.

—Gary Gillette

	1986 SEASON											THREE YEARS (84 – 86)										
	Ave.	OBP	SLG	AB	H	2B	3B	HR	RBI	BB	SO	Ave.	OBP	SLG	AB	H	2B	3B	HR	RBI	BB	SO
Totals	.277	.347	.469	574	159	33	7	21	75	59	57	.282	.346	.438	1734	489	88	19	48	201	169	191
Batting vs. Left and Right-handed Pitchers																						
Left	.279	.344	.505	204	57	16	3	8	24	19	19	.283	.363	.473	586	166	34	7	21	62	71	53
Right	.276	.349	.449	370	102	17	4	13	51	40	38	.281	.338	.420	1148	323	54	12	27	139	98	138
At Home and on the Road																						
Home	.262	.335	.415	282	74	13	3	8	35	28	35	.284	.357	.424	838	238	37	7	22	99	92	93
Road	.291	.359	.521	292	85	20	4	13	40	31	22	.280	.336	.451	896	251	51	12	26	102	77	98
Facing Groundball Pitchers and Flyball Pitchers																						
Groundball	.343	.404	.563	213	73	17	3	8	37	21	20	.304	.364	.464	782	238	46	11	19	101	73	83
Flyball	.238	.313	.413	361	86	16	4	13	38	38	37	.264	.332	.416	952	251	42	8	29	100	96	108
Facing Finesse Pitchers and Power Pitchers																						
Finesse	.294	.351	.518	330	97	17	6	15	44	25	26	.283	.335	.461	988	280	45	14	34	119	75	93
Power	.254	.343	.402	244	62	16	1	6	31	34	31	.280	.361	.408	746	209	43	5	14	82	94	98
On Grass and on Turf																						
Grass	.266	.340	.454	482	128	26	7	17	59	52	52	.274	.344	.424	1447	396	68	16	39	160	152	158
Turf	.337	.386	.543	92	31	7	0	4	16	7	5	.324	.360	.509	287	93	20	3	9	41	17	33
During the Day and at Night																						
Day	.241	.304	.425	174	42	9	1	7	20	14	21	.272	.337	.436	559	152	33	7	15	66	52	61
Night	.292	.366	.487	400	117	24	6	14	55	45	36	.287	.351	.438	1175	337	55	12	33	135	117	130
By Month																						
April	.242	.286	.530	66	16	6	2	3	10	4	8	.320	.390	.562	219	70	14	6	9	34	25	21
May	.256	.315	.293	82	21	3	0	0	6	7	8	.270	.325	.392	296	80	16	1	6	27	25	31
June	.239	.281	.336	113	27	5	0	2	13	7	11	.264	.308	.365	345	91	14	3	5	36	23	34
July	.297	.415	.495	101	30	6	1	4	10	18	10	.254	.351	.392	232	59	13	2	5	21	32	29
August	.305	.362	.559	118	36	6	3	6	21	10	11	.296	.353	.479	365	108	15	5	14	50	32	48
Sept/Oct	.309	.394	.596	94	29	7	1	6	15	13	9	.292	.367	.462	277	81	16	2	9	33	32	28
Situational																						
Bases Empty	.297	.350	.532	333	99	21	6	15	15	25	34	.283	.339	.452	1004	284	49	14	31	31	83	108
Leadoff	.300	.333	.630	100	30	5	2	8	8	5	9	.297	.334	.520	306	91	16	5	14	14	17	25
Not Leadoff	.296	.357	.489	233	69	16	4	7	7	20	25	.277	.342	.423	698	193	33	9	17	17	66	83
Runners On	.249	.344	.382	241	60	12	1	6	60	34	23	.281	.356	.418	730	205	39	5	17	170	86	83
First Base Only	.196	.268	.324	102	20	5	1	2	7	8	11	.293	.354	.448	335	98	21	2	9	27	28	37
Scoring Position	.288	.394	.424	139	40	7	0	4	53	26	12	.271	.357	.392	395	107	18	3	8	143	58	46
Late Innings, Close	.268	.375	.366	82	22	5	0	1	15	12	10	.265	.346	.335	260	69	9	0	3	35	31	27
RBI/Opportunities																						
Scoring Position				48 / 201		(24%)									131 / 557		(24%)					
Scoring Position, 2 Out				24 / 94		(26%)									70 / 268		(26%)					
On Third, Less than 2 Out				13 / 30		(43%)									43 / 88		(49%)					
RBI in close games / RBI Total				46 / 75		(61%)									123 / 201		(61%)					

John Tudor
St. Louis Cardinals

John Tudor's 13–7 record and 2.92 ERA in 1986 may pale beside his '85 marks of 21–8 and 1.93, but he still had an excellent season. It's true that, per nine innings, his hits (from 6.8 to 8.1), walks (1.6–2.2) and home runs (0.5–0.9) all rose along with the ERA, and that he failed to record a shutout after throwing ten—the most by a lefty since Sandy Koufax—in '85, but the big dropoff in wins was due in large measure to lack of support. For the season the Cardinals scored four or more runs in only eleven of Tudor's 30 starts. They were 10–1 in those games. In the nineteen Tudor starts in which they scored three runs or less, the Redbirds were a very-respectable 8–11. Based on runs scored and allowed, the Cardinal record with Tudor pitching projected to only 16–14. Their actual mark was 18–12, the best record they posted with any starting pitcher.

In many ways Tudor's '86 campaign was similar to the season he had with the Pirates in 1984, when he went 12–11 with a 3.27 ERA; the hits, walks and strikeouts per inning were pretty close in the two years, also. Since the '84 Bucs went 75–87 and the '86 Cardinals were 79–82, while the 1985 Redbirds had a 101–61 mark, one might suspect that

Tudor belongs to the group of lefthanded sinkerballers (Tommy John, Steve Trout, Bill Lee, Mike Caldwell are other examples) described by Bill James in the *1984 Baseball Abstract*. These hurlers share certain traits: they are control-type pitchers who cut off the running game and keep the ball down, getting lots of groundouts and double plays while giving up very few homers. More importantly, these pitchers are extremely "team-dependent"—that is, their won-lost record goes way up with a good team, way down with a bad or mediocre team. Tudor, though, doesn't really fit the mold. He does have superior control and he has an outstanding record against base stealers (especially in '86), but the similarity ends there. In actuality he's not a sinkerballer at all. His groundball ratio has always been below average, he usually gives up a good number of home runs, he has struck out as many as 169 batters in a season, and his ERA and hits-per-nine-innings are much lower than the Tommy John type usually turns in. He's much more likely than that group to have a good record with a bad club, and that's just what happened in 1986.

—Russ Eagle and Don Zminda

1986: Finesse, Flyball **1985: Finesse, Flyball** **1984: Finesse, Flyball**

	G	IP	H	BB	SO	SB	CS	W	L	S	ERA	G	IP	H	BB	SO	SB	CS	W	L	S	ERA
	1986 SEASON											**THREE YEARS (84 – 86)**										
Totals	30	219.0	197	53	107	7	14	13	7	0	2.92	98	706.0	606	158	393	32	32	46	26	0	2.64
At Home and on the Road																						
Home	17	127.0	110	27	60	1	9	9	2	0	2.48	50	380.2	309	73	202	11	19	29	9	0	2.15
Road	13	92.0	87	26	47	6	5	4	5	0	3.52	48	325.1	297	85	191	21	13	17	17	0	3.21
During the Day and at Night																						
Day	12	93.2	76	28	46	4	7	5	3	0	2.88	36	269.2	209	64	143	12	15	19	8	0	2.47
Night	18	125.1	121	25	61	3	7	8	4	0	2.94	62	436.1	397	94	250	20	17	27	18	0	2.74
On Grass and on Turf																						
Grass	8	56.0	56	20	27	5	2	1	4	0	3.70	26	181.0	157	47	111	13	5	9	11	0	2.83
Turf	22	163.0	141	33	80	2	12	12	3	0	2.65	72	525.0	449	111	282	19	27	37	15	0	2.57
By Month																						
April	5	39.0	30	8	18	1	3	3	1	0	2.08	14	99.1	80	30	47	9	4	4	5	0	2.63
May	6	45.0	36	13	17	4	2	1	2	0	3.40	17	120.1	109	31	51	8	5	4	7	0	3.52
June	6	50.1	30	10	27	0	0	2	1	0	1.79	18	133.1	97	26	72	1	2	9	5	0	2.23
July	5	36.1	40	8	19	1	3	3	1	0	3.47	16	118.2	113	17	64	3	6	10	4	0	2.73
August	6	38.2	47	13	24	1	6	4	1	0	3.96	17	121.0	116	33	82	5	11	9	2	0	2.75
Sept/Oct	2	9.2	14	1	2	0	0	0	1	0	3.72	16	113.1	91	21	77	6	4	10	3	0	1.99

vs. Opponent Batters

	Ave.	OBP	SLG	AB	H	2B	3B	HR	RBI	BB	SO	Ave.	OBP	SLG	AB	H	2B	3B	HR	RBI	BB	SO
	1986 SEASON											**THREE YEARS (84 – 86)**										
Totals	.244	.289	.388	807	197	40	5	22	72	53	107	.232	.276	.343	2616	606	103	12	55	198	158	393
Pitching vs. Left and Right-handed Batters																						
Left	.194	.225	.285	144	28	8	1	1	5	6	37	.210	.249	.295	404	85	14	1	6	26	21	110
Right	.255	.302	.410	663	169	32	4	21	67	47	70	.236	.280	.352	2212	521	89	11	49	172	137	283
Situational																						
Bases Empty	.225	.268	.362	538	121	25	5	13	13	31	61	.224	.262	.339	1720	385	69	9	37	37	83	250
Leadoff	.252	.301	.393	214	54	13	1	5	5	14	22	.233	.271	.368	696	162	35	4	17	17	34	91
Not Leadoff	.207	.246	.343	324	67	12	4	8	8	17	39	.218	.255	.319	1024	223	34	5	20	20	49	159
Runners On	.283	.328	.439	269	76	15	0	9	59	22	46	.247	.301	.352	896	221	34	3	18	161	75	143
First Base Only	.295	.306	.475	122	36	7	0	5	11	2	15	.273	.310	.378	407	111	20	1	7	18	21	57
Scoring Position	.272	.343	.408	147	40	8	0	4	48	20	31	.225	.294	.329	489	110	14	2	11	143	54	86
Late Innings, Close	.245	.296	.374	147	36	5	1	4	15	10	13	.269	.316	.375	320	86	11	1	7	30	22	34

RBI/Opportunities

Scoring Position	43 / 207	(21%)		124 / 649	(19%)	
Scoring Position, 2 Out	15 / 94	(16%)		43 / 303	(14%)	
On Third, Less than 2 Out	22 / 42	(52%)		53 / 114	(46%)	
RBI in close games / RBI Total	61 / 72	(85%)		160 / 198	(81%)	

Willie Upshaw
Toronto Blue Jays

From the penthouse to the outhouse in two seasons . . . Willie Upshaw's career has left the Blue Jays' organization completely baffled. Thrust into the cleanup spot in 1983, Upshaw responded with 27 homers and 104 RBIs—since then his power output has fallen with frustrating consistency—19 in 1984, 15 in 1985 and now only nine.

What is the explanation? In my opinion, Upshaw is a line drive hitter, at his best driving the ball up the power alleys in left and right center. He hit homers because he was content to meet the ball wherever it was pitched. If a pitcher threw him an outside pitch, he drove it to left; if the ball came inside, he went deep. As pitchers began respecting his power, they began choosing the lesser of two evils—the outside corner and a single to left—which is when the problem began.

In 1984, Upshaw grew impatient because he wasn't getting many chances to hit homers. He began trying to pull the outside pitch, which resulted in weak groundouts to the right side of the infield. In time, his swing became totally messed up—he couldn't handle either the inside or outside pitch—and the diminished power production is the result.

But there is hope for Willie yet. He is a very dedicated worker, both on the field and off. If he worked on both his swing and his mental approach in the off-season, he should be able to rebound and achieve respectable results in 1987.

Upshaw has other phases to his game that consistently go unnoticed. He is the best baserunner that the Blue Jays have—he was third on the team in steals and had the best success ratio (82%, or 23 of 28). He takes delight in using his speed—not only to take the extra base, but to beat out potential double play grounders and break up the pivot at second.

In this respect, he is a joy to watch. He seems to eclipse world record speeds when he sees a chance to break up a potential double play. He gives no consideration to the idea that he might get scrapes or bruises with a reckless slide—to him, it's satisfaction enough if he hurts as much as the shortstop is about to.

It's this same intensity which some others on the team could use. On the field, he garners a lot of respect for the way he plays. If he were more vocal in the clubhouse, Toronto would have the team leader that they so desperately need.

—David Driscoll

	1986 SEASON												THREE YEARS (84 – 86)									
	Ave.	OBP	SLG	AB	H	2B	3B	HR	RBI	BB	SO		Ave.	OBP	SLG	AB	H	2B	3B	HR	RBI	BB	SO
Totals	.251	.341	.368	573	144	28	6	9	60	78	87		.268	.343	.425	1643	440	90	20	43	208	181	244
Batting vs. Left and Right-handed Pitchers																							
Left	.223	.291	.341	179	40	7	1	4	19	17	38		.255	.305	.412	549	140	25	11	13	79	36	101
Right	.264	.362	.381	394	104	21	5	5	41	61	49		.274	.361	.432	1094	300	65	9	30	129	145	143
At Home and on the Road																							
Home	.247	.350	.363	267	66	16	3	3	32	43	46		.275	.354	.437	774	213	56	12	15	106	96	127
Road	.255	.332	.373	306	78	12	3	6	28	35	41		.261	.332	.415	869	227	34	8	28	102	85	117
Facing Groundball Pitchers and Flyball Pitchers																							
Groundball	.259	.356	.368	247	64	14	5	1	25	38	27		.277	.353	.421	779	216	43	12	15	95	87	96
Flyball	.245	.329	.368	326	80	14	1	8	35	40	60		.259	.333	.429	864	224	47	8	28	113	94	148
Facing Finesse Pitchers and Power Pitchers																							
Finesse	.242	.304	.363	331	80	18	5	4	32	29	42		.269	.324	.408	938	252	57	10	18	111	73	114
Power	.264	.386	.376	242	64	10	1	5	28	49	45		.267	.366	.448	705	188	33	10	25	97	108	130
On Grass and on Turf																							
Grass	.248	.336	.361	238	59	8	2	5	21	31	31		.256	.331	.407	673	172	24	3	24	81	69	91
Turf	.254	.345	.373	335	85	20	4	4	39	47	56		.276	.351	.438	970	268	66	17	19	127	112	153
During the Day and at Night																							
Day	.227	.328	.300	207	47	10	1	1	20	30	31		.242	.325	.383	587	142	35	6	12	60	72	101
Night	.265	.349	.407	366	97	18	5	8	40	48	56		.282	.353	.449	1056	298	55	14	31	148	109	143
By Month																							
April	.300	.419	.414	70	21	3	1	1	12	15	12		.315	.402	.577	213	67	17	3	11	39	31	30
May	.273	.363	.343	99	27	5	1	0	10	13	11		.254	.332	.359	287	73	11	5	3	35	31	42
June	.231	.346	.341	91	21	5	1	1	9	16	20		.249	.345	.403	305	76	14	3	9	43	43	56
July	.252	.316	.398	103	26	6	3	1	8	9	12		.290	.349	.469	303	88	19	7	7	41	27	40
August	.226	.299	.374	115	26	8	0	3	9	12	20		.260	.320	.414	292	76	19	1	8	28	24	41
Sept/Oct	.242	.327	.347	95	23	1	0	3	12	13	12		.247	.315	.358	243	60	10	1	5	22	25	35
Situational																							
Bases Empty	.254	.350	.372	323	82	19	2	5	5	47	47		.268	.342	.431	880	236	47	6	28	28	92	127
Leadoff	.262	.340	.381	126	33	6	0	3	3	14	18		.272	.331	.423	364	99	18	2	11	11	30	50
Not Leadoff	.249	.357	.365	197	49	13	2	2	2	33	29		.266	.349	.436	516	137	29	4	17	17	62	77
Runners On	.248	.329	.364	250	62	9	4	4	55	31	40		.267	.344	.419	763	204	43	14	15	180	89	117
First Base Only	.270	.341	.432	111	30	6	3	2	9	11	16		.299	.349	.483	298	89	21	5	8	26	20	44
Scoring Position	.230	.319	.309	139	32	3	1	2	46	20	24		.247	.341	.378	465	115	22	9	7	154	69	73
Late Innings, Close	.230	.322	.380	100	23	1	1	4	13	14	18		.244	.330	.396	275	67	10	4	8	31	36	50
RBI/Opportunities																							
Scoring Position				41 / 184		(22%)										139 / 613		(23%)					
Scoring Position, 2 Out				15 / 86		(17%)										56 / 298		(19%)					
On Third, Less than 2 Out				19 / 35		(54%)										54 / 106		(51%)					
RBI in close games / RBI Total				49 / 60		(82%)										139 / 208		(67%)					

Jose Uribe
San Francisco Giants

Jose Uribe provides the Giants with consistent play in the field. This doesn't mean that he is a fixture for the future, though. Uribe is the only player left from the ill-fated Jack Clark trade. David Green, Gary Rajsich and Dave LaPoint are all now gone. In addition, Clark's replacement, Dan Gladden, was not as effective as in 1984. A further evolution of this trade occurred when LaPoint was traded to Detroit with Eric King and Matt Nokes for Juan Berenguer, Bob Melvin and Scott Medvin. The trade-off in value is more muddled considering Clark's short 1986 campaign, but it still ranks as a very lopsided trade against the Giants.

The Giants obtained Uribe to provide better defense and more consistent play at shortstop. The Giants saw in Uribe's background that he led the AAA American Association twice in total chances and double plays and led the AA Texas League once in double plays. Uribe had to handle the pressure of being a rookie, being part of the Clark trade, and of replacing the fan's SF Dream Team shortstop, Johnny LeMaster. His 1985 stats were slightly better than LeMaster's 1984 ones. It was in the early part of 1986 that Uribe showed confidence both at the plate and in the field.

He made ten fewer errors for the season while keeping nearly the same range. He combined with Rob Thompson and the high infield grass at Candlestick (a sheep's dream) to give the Giants solid middle-infield play. Routine double-play balls became just that. Uribe, Chris Brown and the wind at the 'Stick helped the Giants to pitch inside on right-handed batters with more effectiveness. This, in turn, helped make the Giants' pitchers very effective at home.

It was the June swoon for Uribe as a hitter which casts doubt as to how long he can be a starter. The swoon never really ended, although pitchers gave him respect for his hitting prowess by walking him nearly twice as often as Will Clark. Of course, one-third of Uribe's walks were intentional to get to the pitcher, usually meaning that Candy Maldonado would bat. Coach Jose Morales has helped Uribe's walking eye, but the batting eye still can't find the big "E" on the eye chart.

Uribe did well in one particular situation: getting on base with runners in scoring position. He hit .292 with a .429 OBA in these situations. If Jose can raise his average 10 to 15 points, he will continue to be a starter. Otherwise, in a year or two, he'll become a utility player.

—Victor Hester

	Ave.	OBP	SLG	AB	H	2B	3B	HR	RBI	BB	SO		Ave.	OBP	SLG	AB	H	2B	3B	HR	RBI	BB	SO
	1986 SEASON												**THREE YEARS (84 – 86)**										
Totals	.223	.315	.280	453	101	15	1	3	43	61	76		.230	.299	.296	948	218	35	5	6	72	91	135
Batting vs. Left and Right-handed Pitchers																							
Left	.214	.287	.324	145	31	7	0	3	17	15	33		.214	.274	.308	276	59	14	0	4	29	22	53
Right	.227	.328	.260	308	70	8	1	0	26	46	43		.237	.309	.292	672	159	21	5	2	43	69	82
At Home and on the Road																							
Home	.219	.332	.265	219	48	7	0	1	18	37	35		.218	.301	.287	477	104	20	2	3	30	56	59
Road	.226	.298	.295	234	53	8	1	2	25	24	41		.242	.296	.306	471	114	15	3	3	42	35	76
Facing Groundball Pitchers and Flyball Pitchers																							
Groundball	.231	.312	.308	221	51	8	0	3	27	26	38		.239	.306	.315	426	102	18	1	4	41	41	61
Flyball	.216	.318	.254	232	50	7	1	0	16	35	38		.222	.293	.282	522	116	17	4	2	31	50	74
Facing Finesse Pitchers and Power Pitchers																							
Finesse	.224	.298	.278	255	57	9	1	1	22	27	36		.233	.280	.303	557	130	22	4	3	40	35	63
Power	.222	.336	.283	198	44	6	0	2	21	34	40		.225	.324	.286	391	88	13	1	3	32	56	72
On Grass and on Turf																							
Grass	.234	.333	.282	337	79	10	0	2	34	50	53		.234	.308	.299	708	166	28	3	4	54	74	93
Turf	.190	.260	.276	116	22	5	1	1	9	11	23		.217	.271	.287	240	52	7	2	2	18	17	42
During the Day and at Night																							
Day	.218	.301	.256	211	46	6	1	0	18	25	34		.229	.295	.285	498	114	21	2	1	37	46	64
Night	.227	.327	.302	242	55	9	0	3	25	36	42		.231	.302	.309	450	104	14	3	5	35	45	71
By Month																							
April	.258	.324	.290	62	16	2	0	0	6	6	11		.250	.291	.298	104	26	5	0	0	6	6	14
May	.262	.340	.321	84	22	5	0	0	14	10	15		.231	.293	.306	173	40	8	1	1	17	14	27
June	.202	.272	.234	94	19	0	0	1	4	9	7		.201	.260	.280	189	38	6	3	1	11	15	18
July	.192	.298	.301	73	14	2	0	2	6	11	9		.240	.324	.312	154	37	5	0	2	12	18	19
August	.191	.267	.279	68	13	4	1	0	7	7	20		.225	.287	.278	151	34	6	1	0	10	13	29
Sept/Oct	.236	.389	.264	72	17	2	0	0	6	18	14		.243	.337	.305	177	43	5	0	2	16	25	28
Situational																							
Bases Empty	.202	.293	.245	257	52	5	0	2	2	33	43		.212	.276	.278	557	118	16	3	5	5	49	85
Leadoff	.250	.339	.304	112	28	3	0	1	1	15	14		.197	.278	.253	233	46	5	1	2	2	26	30
Not Leadoff	.166	.258	.200	145	24	2	0	1	1	18	29		.222	.274	.296	324	72	11	2	3	3	23	55
Runners On	.250	.344	.327	196	49	10	1	1	41	28	33		.256	.331	.322	391	100	19	2	1	67	42	50
First Base Only	.193	.202	.253	83	16	2	0	1	3	1	10		.221	.230	.273	172	38	4	1	1	5	1	16
Scoring Position	.292	.429	.381	113	33	8	1	0	38	27	23		.283	.398	.361	219	62	15	1	0	62	41	34
Late Innings, Close	.185	.362	.259	54	10	1	0	1	4	15	8		.215	.311	.285	158	34	6	1	1	9	21	18

RBI/Opportunities								
Scoring Position			35 / 168	(21%)		59 / 317	(19%)	
Scoring Position, 2 Out			15 / 81	(19%)		27 / 159	(17%)	
On Third, Less than 2 Out			9 / 28	(32%)		16 / 52	(31%)	
RBI in close games / RBI Total			23 / 43	(53%)		44 / 72	(61%)	

Fernando Valenzuela
Los Angeles Dodgers

You know the old slogan about the mailman, "Neither rain, nor snow, nor gloom of night . . . " He is always there. To most, his steady, efficient service causes them to take him for granted.

The same can be said of Freddie "The Mailman" Valenzuela. To Dodgers fans, Fernando has been their mailman. Every fifth day you know that the Mailman will be making his deliveries.

How consistent has the Mailman been? In his six seasons of delivering pitches for the Dodgers, he has started more than 21% of all Dodgers games and has thrown better than 17% of all Dodgers innings. Fernando doesn't miss his turn. In the last six years, he has averaged 7.2 innings per start, and along with quantity comes quality. Fernando's lifetime ERA is 2.94. INCLUDING the strike-shortened 1981 season, he has averaged over 16 wins and 4 shutouts per year, along with 7 strikeouts per game and a .590 winning percentage. The Dodgers winning percentage is only .517 when Fernando is on the bench.

1986 was Valenzuela's best season. Though he won the Cy Young Award as a rookie (and finished second last year), his winning percentage, walks per game, wins and complete games were not as good in 1981 as they were in 1986. In 1986, he won 21 games, averaging over 8 strikeouts per 9 innings-pitched.

Fernando was magnificently consistent. He was 11–6 in the first half and 10–5 in the second half. He struck out 7.9 per 9 IP in the first half, and 8.3 in the second. His ERA was 2.95 in the first half, 3.31 in the second. Valenzuela did his best work at home where he was 11–3; in his first six starts at home he was 5–0 with a 0.51 ERA. By the year's end, he had a 2.20 ERA at home, compared to 3.96 on the road. His control was also better at home than on the road—he walked 3.6 batters per 9 IP on the road, while at home he cut that nearly in half to 2.1. Valenzuela finished what he started, leading the majors with 20 complete games.

Six more seasons like the ones Fernando has had will make him a serious candidate for the Hall of Fame. He is one of the premier pitchers of his day. When the Dodgers need a good game delivered, they can count on the Mailman to make it first-class. He always has.

—Carmen J. Corica

1986: Power, Groundball   **1985: Power, Groundball**   **1984: Power, Groundball**

	G	IP	H	BB	SO	SB	CS	W	L	S	ERA		G	IP	H	BB	SO	SB	CS	W	L	S	ERA

	\multicolumn{11}{c}{1986 SEASON}												\multicolumn{12}{c}{THREE YEARS (84 – 86)}											
	G	IP	H	BB	SO	SB	CS	W	L	S	ERA		G	IP	H	BB	SO	SB	CS	W	L	S	ERA
Totals	34	269.1	226	85	242	15	11	21	11	0	3.14		103	802.2	655	292	690	60	39	50	38	0	2.87
\multicolumn{24}{c}{At Home and on the Road}																							
Home	16	130.2	104	30	121	5	6	11	3	0	2.27		50	399.0	316	122	344	22	21	24	16	0	2.44
Road	18	138.2	122	55	121	10	5	10	8	0	3.96		53	403.2	339	170	346	38	18	26	22	0	3.30
\multicolumn{24}{c}{During the Day and at Night}																							
Day	10	78.0	78	23	77	9	4	5	5	0	3.92		33	249.2	213	86	225	26	11	14	15	0	3.50
Night	24	191.1	148	62	165	6	7	16	6	0	2.82		70	553.0	442	206	465	34	28	36	23	0	2.59
\multicolumn{24}{c}{On Grass and on Turf}																							
Grass	24	190.1	165	57	168	9	8	15	7	0	3.07		75	584.0	474	204	507	39	30	36	28	0	2.73
Turf	10	79.0	61	28	74	6	3	6	4	0	3.30		28	218.2	181	88	183	21	9	14	10	0	3.25
\multicolumn{24}{c}{By Month}																							
April	5	41.0	39	12	32	2	4	3	1	0	2.41		16	126.0	97	34	105	4	10	8	6	0	1.86
May	6	50.0	31	17	44	3	1	4	2	0	2.88		17	136.2	105	57	123	12	7	9	7	0	2.63
June	6	44.1	43	15	42	2	2	3	2	0	3.25		17	125.2	125	55	113	11	6	8	8	0	3.87
July	5	40.0	26	11	40	1	0	4	1	0	2.70		17	132.1	94	42	112	10	3	10	5	0	2.45
August	6	47.0	46	15	40	3	3	3	3	0	3.83		17	136.1	115	50	120	9	8	8	7	0	3.37
Sept/Oct	6	47.0	41	15	44	4	1	4	2	0	3.64		19	145.2	119	54	117	14	5	7	5	0	3.03

	\multicolumn{10}{c}{vs. Opponent Batters}																				
	\multicolumn{10}{c}{1986 SEASON}											\multicolumn{10}{c}{THREE YEARS (84 – 86)}									
	Ave.	OBP	SLG	AB	H	2B	3B	HR	RBI	BB	SO		Ave.	OBP	SLG	AB	H	2B	3B	HR	RBI	BB	SO
Totals	.226	.287	.325	998	226	40	2	18	94	85	242		.223	.293	.314	2936	655	111	9	46	260	292	690
\multicolumn{24}{c}{Pitching vs. Left and Right-handed Batters}																							
Left	.246	.286	.321	187	46	14	0	0	11	11	42		.243	.295	.341	563	137	27	2	8	50	43	126
Right	.222	.287	.326	811	180	26	2	18	83	74	200		.218	.292	.308	2373	518	84	7	38	210	249	564
\multicolumn{24}{c}{Situational}																							
Bases Empty	.207	.271	.304	598	124	24	2	10	10	51	163		.203	.273	.288	1784	362	71	3	25	25	171	466
Leadoff	.193	.246	.272	254	49	12	1	2	2	18	70		.201	.259	.276	756	152	32	2	7	7	59	193
Not Leadoff	.218	.288	.328	344	75	12	1	8	8	33	93		.204	.284	.297	1028	210	39	1	18	18	112	273
Runners On	.255	.311	.355	400	102	16	0	8	84	34	79		.254	.322	.354	1152	293	40	6	21	235	121	224
First Base Only	.255	.285	.388	165	42	7	0	5	14	7	27		.271	.307	.394	498	135	23	4	10	33	26	84
Scoring Position	.255	.328	.332	235	60	9	0	3	70	27	52		.242	.332	.324	654	158	17	2	11	202	95	140
Late Innings, Close	.291	.331	.351	148	43	6	0	1	18	9	36		.221	.291	.281	452	100	15	0	4	46	46	95
\multicolumn{24}{c}{RBI/Opportunities}																							
Scoring Position				65 / 305	(21%)											182 / 898	(20%)						
Scoring Position, 2 Out				26 / 145	(18%)											68 / 422	(16%)						
On Third, Less than 2 Out				24 / 53	(45%)											76 / 154	(49%)						
RBI in close games / RBI Total				70 / 94	(74%)											197 / 260	(76%)						

Andy Van Slyke
St. Louis Cardinals

In the context of the Cardinals' offensive collapse last season, Andy Van Slyke was Babe Ruth. He hit 22 per cent of the Redbird homers, and his club-leading total was 44 per cent higher than the number two man's . . . pretty heady stuff until you add that the whole team hit only 58, the number two guy had nine, and Andy had a grand total of 13. If it's any comfort to Andy, I could point out that those 13 homers would have led the National League if it had only been 1916—as the Cardinals apparently thought—instead of 1986.

I don't mean to lampoon Andy Van Slyke; he's had enough of that in his short career. It's hardly his fault that he entered baseball as the sixth player chosen in the bizarre '79 draft: other first rounders included the immortal Al Chambers, Tim Leary, Brad Komminsk, Steve Buechele, Jay Schroeder (yes, THAT Jay Schroeder; he was the third player chosen, by the Blue Jays, who apparently wanted to enter him in The Superstars with Danny Ainge), Rick Leach (was there a pattern here?), Jerry Don Gleaton, Ricky Seilheimer, Steve Howe (figures) and Atlee Hammaker—probably the bad karma draft of all time, at least

where baseball was concerned. Andy was certainly the least eccentric of that group, and when he blew into St. Louis in 1983, toting a AAA average of .368, the expectations in St. Louis were sky-high. He'd only been converted to third base that very year, but the Cards quickly traded their regular third sacker, Ken Oberkfell, to open up the spot for him. Van Slyke lost that job pretty quickly to Terry Pendleton, who, naturally, played like Pie Traynor for the rest of the season. Not to worry, Andy, the Cardinals said; how about replacing Keith Hernandez? When that didn't work out, either, there was grumbling about what a "disappointment" Van Slyke was. Well, maybe so, if he was supposed to play six positions, hit .330, and keep Whitey from looking like a bad trader. But taking that viewpoint, people lost sight of Van Slyke's considerable attributes, like his speed, his extra-base power, his ability to draw walks, his extraordinary throwing arm, his versatility. He'll probably never hit left-handers very well or do a number of other things the Cardinals once expected, but he's a good one. And at age 26, he has lots of productive years ahead of him.

—Don Zminda

	1986 SEASON											THREE YEARS (84 – 86)										
	Ave.	OBP	SLG	AB	H	2B	3B	HR	RBI	BB	SO	Ave.	OBP	SLG	AB	H	2B	3B	HR	RBI	BB	SO
Totals	.270	.343	.452	418	113	23	7	13	61	47	85	.259	.344	.422	1203	311	64	17	33	166	157	209
Batting vs. Left and Right-handed Pitchers																						
Left	.207	.290	.353	116	24	6	4	1	13	14	26	.193	.268	.311	212	41	10	6	1	26	22	50
Right	.295	.364	.490	302	89	17	3	12	48	33	59	.272	.360	.446	991	270	54	11	32	140	135	159
At Home and on the Road																						
Home	.280	.365	.474	211	59	11	6	6	39	30	39	.272	.366	.442	581	158	33	12	14	89	87	98
Road	.261	.320	.430	207	54	12	1	7	22	17	46	.246	.323	.404	622	153	31	5	19	77	70	111
Facing Groundball Pitchers and Flyball Pitchers																						
Groundball	.268	.326	.427	213	57	13	3	5	29	19	40	.257	.344	.394	564	145	31	5	12	73	73	87
Flyball	.273	.360	.478	205	56	10	4	8	32	28	45	.260	.344	.448	639	166	33	12	21	93	84	122
Facing Finesse Pitchers and Power Pitchers																						
Finesse	.319	.385	.555	229	73	17	5	9	34	25	31	.274	.352	.466	650	178	43	11	20	82	79	86
Power	.212	.292	.328	189	40	6	2	4	27	22	54	.241	.334	.371	553	133	21	6	13	84	78	123
On Grass and on Turf																						
Grass	.259	.320	.402	112	29	5	1	3	8	10	25	.258	.332	.408	333	86	16	2	10	37	37	63
Turf	.275	.352	.471	306	84	18	6	10	53	37	60	.259	.349	.428	870	225	48	15	23	129	120	146
During the Day and at Night																						
Day	.235	.316	.386	153	36	9	1	4	23	19	26	.249	.338	.399	454	113	26	3	12	62	63	67
Night	.291	.359	.491	265	77	14	6	9	38	28	59	.264	.347	.437	749	198	38	14	21	104	94	142
By Month																						
April	.225	.326	.250	40	9	1	0	0	6	6	11	.268	.377	.359	142	38	8	1	1	14	24	26
May	.242	.315	.379	66	16	3	0	2	10	7	9	.270	.361	.478	178	48	9	2	8	34	25	23
June	.213	.298	.387	75	16	1	3	2	8	9	15	.236	.325	.369	225	53	13	4	3	23	30	46
July	.333	.414	.533	60	20	2	2	2	10	9	13	.220	.319	.374	182	40	5	4	5	23	27	35
August	.354	.419	.631	65	23	10	1	2	11	7	10	.275	.345	.475	200	55	15	2	7	31	21	30
Sept/Oct	.259	.311	.464	112	29	6	1	5	16	9	27	.279	.346	.457	276	77	14	4	9	41	30	49
Situational																						
Bases Empty	.257	.314	.442	226	58	13	4	7	7	19	46	.248	.320	.405	644	160	32	9	17	17	67	110
Leadoff	.301	.351	.621	103	31	8	2	7	7	8	18	.275	.328	.511	280	77	19	4	13	13	22	42
Not Leadoff	.220	.284	.293	123	27	5	2	0	0	11	28	.228	.315	.324	364	83	13	5	4	4	45	68
Runners On	.286	.375	.464	192	55	10	3	6	54	28	39	.270	.370	.442	559	151	32	8	16	149	90	99
First Base Only	.296	.387	.481	81	24	4	1	3	10	12	11	.278	.342	.460	237	66	16	3	7	22	22	32
Scoring Position	.279	.366	.450	111	31	6	2	3	44	16	28	.264	.388	.429	322	85	16	5	9	127	68	67
Late Innings, Close	.264	.368	.385	91	24	5	0	2	5	15	25	.240	.353	.359	217	52	10	2	4	24	38	49

RBI/Opportunities				
Scoring Position	39 / 154	(25%)	113 / 477	(24%)
Scoring Position, 2 Out	14 / 67	(21%)	38 / 215	(18%)
On Third, Less than 2 Out	13 / 29	(45%)	50 / 96	(52%)
RBI in close games / RBI Total	43 / 61	(70%)	100 / 166	(60%)

Frank Viola
Minnesota Twins

Before Blyleven's record setting home run numbers last season, there were some who believed that Frank Viola would eventually be the Twins' starter to establish a new mark. It wasn't to be last year, but Frank made a strong effort and finished with 37 by giving up one home run for about every 26 at bats. During the three years of Project Scoresheet, Viola has allowed a home run every 32 ABs compared to Blyleven's one per 33 ABs mark. Counting Smithson, the top three Twins starters combine for 113 four-baggers, 66 of which came with the bases empty. Bert's record may not be safe.

Viola has been effective in cutting off the running game. Stolen base totals against him were 12 in '86 and 6 in both '84 and '85. During this time, 31 runners have been caught stealing. In addition to the advantages a lefthander has in holding men on first, he has also developed an excellent snap throw to Hrbek. This ability is reflected in the number of pickoffs (13) and caught stealings initiated by pickoffs (8) that he has engineered in the last three years. There were 6 in '86, 10 in '85 and 5 in 84. Possibly because Ray Miller may have been calling the throws to first, there was an increase in activity on the base paths last season. Miller did this with some Twins pitchers, but I am not certain that he called them for Viola. Frank has picked off some speedsters, including Gary Pettis (twice), Willie Wilson and Lloyd Moseby (twice) and also some non-threats including Jim Rice and Jeff Burroughs. His pick-off attempts have been accompanied by three errors on throws to first.

Whether it's an increase in runs allowed, throws to first or managers urging him to take more time between pitches, games that Viola has started have shown a remarkable time increase. In 1984, he had two three hour games (one of which went extra innings) and twenty-one games finished in less than 2 hours and 30 minutes. In 1986, fifteen of his starts lasted in excess of 3 hours while only 3 were completed under 2 hours and 30 minutes. This increase was typical in Twins games under Ray Miller, a former pitching coach, who, compared to Billy Gardner, seemed to have his staff in slow motion. Gardner just liked his pitchers to get the ball over the plate. Under Tom Kelly, the game times are likely to decrease because he doesn't like to have fielders just standing around. Perhaps, given the number of balls put in play against the Twins, they need the rest.

—Bill Jensen

1986: Power, Flyball **1985: Finesse, Flyball** **1984: Finesse, Flyball**

	1986 SEASON											THREE YEARS (84 – 86)											
	G	IP	H	BB	SO	SB	CS	W	L	S	ERA	G	IP	H	BB	SO	SB	CS	W	L	S	ERA
Totals	37	245.2	257	83	191	12	15	16	13	0	4.51	108	754.0	744	224	475	25	33	52	39	0	3.93
At Home and on the Road																						
Home	18	123.2	142	38	100	5	7	6	6	0	4.58	48	353.1	350	94	237	10	17	23	14	0	3.62
Road	19	122.0	115	45	91	7	8	10	7	0	4.43	60	400.2	394	130	238	15	16	29	25	0	4.20
During the Day and at Night																						
Day	10	64.2	70	18	56	4	4	4	3	0	4.59	34	239.1	235	67	149	7	8	13	15	0	4.02
Night	27	181.0	187	65	135	8	11	12	10	0	4.48	74	514.2	509	157	326	18	25	39	24	0	3.88
On Grass and on Turf																						
Grass	16	101.2	92	35	74	7	6	8	6	0	4.16	48	322.0	305	104	188	13	11	25	18	0	3.94
Turf	21	144.0	165	48	117	5	9	8	7	0	4.75	60	432.0	439	120	287	12	22	27	21	0	3.92
By Month																						
April	5	39.1	32	15	29	3	4	3	1	0	2.97	16	119.0	108	37	70	3	5	7	6	0	3.48
May	7	36.1	56	13	24	1	1	1	4	0	7.93	18	114.2	127	40	69	4	5	7	8	0	4.71
June	6	44.0	42	17	40	3	4	4	1	0	3.48	16	111.2	111	33	79	9	7	10	5	0	3.87
July	6	39.2	35	10	28	2	0	3	2	0	4.76	18	129.1	121	42	70	4	5	8	7	0	3.97
August	6	40.1	41	15	25	1	2	2	2	0	4.46	18	126.1	132	34	65	1	5	8	6	0	3.70
Sept/Oct	7	46.0	51	13	45	2	4	3	3	0	3.91	22	153.0	145	38	122	4	6	12	7	0	3.88

vs. Opponent Batters

	1986 SEASON											THREE YEARS (84 – 86)									
	Ave.	OBP	SLG	AB	H	2B	3B	HR	RBI	BB	SO	Ave.	OBP	SLG	AB	H	2B	3B	HR	RBI	BB	SO
Totals	.268	.327	.442	958	257	45	5	37	118	83	191	.256	.310	.408	2901	744	133	17	91	321	224	475
Pitching vs. Left and Right-handed Batters																					
Left	.273	.311	.409	154	42	6	0	5	21	8	21	.275	.322	.419	530	146	25	3	15	63	33	79
Right	.267	.330	.448	804	215	39	5	32	97	75	170	.252	.308	.406	2371	598	108	14	76	258	191	396
Situational																					
Bases Empty	.283	.341	.457	565	160	28	2	22	22	49	108	.248	.305	.395	1759	437	78	12	52	52	140	305
Leadoff	.283	.333	.487	240	68	11	1	12	12	17	51	.253	.304	.413	736	186	29	4	27	27	52	129
Not Leadoff	.283	.347	.434	325	92	17	1	10	10	32	57	.245	.306	.382	1023	251	49	8	25	25	88	176
Runners On	.247	.306	.420	393	97	17	3	15	96	34	83	.269	.318	.428	1142	307	55	5	39	269	84	170
First Base Only	.208	.274	.372	207	43	10	0	8	20	17	35	.252	.298	.401	588	148	32	1	18	50	36	80
Scoring Position	.290	.341	.473	186	54	7	3	7	76	17	48	.287	.338	.457	554	159	23	4	21	219	48	90
Late Innings, Close	.347	.390	.558	95	33	5	3	3	21	7	17	.264	.314	.417	242	64	10	3	7	34	18	35

RBI/Opportunities

	1986			THREE YEARS		
Scoring Position	64 / 243	(26%)		182 / 710	(26%)	
Scoring Position, 2 Out	24 / 108	(22%)		80 / 322	(25%)	
On Third, Less than 2 Out	25 / 42	(60%)		60 / 115	(52%)	
RBI in close games / RBI Total	88 / 118	(75%)		215 / 321	(67%)	

Ozzie Virgil
Atlanta Braves

The Braves obtained Ozzie Virgil before the 1986 season with hopes of a 30-homer, 100-RBI season. They received about half of that, along with a low batting average, a poor arm, and mediocre handling of the pitching staff. Even with all of this, Virgil was not a total disappointment.

Virgil matched his poor batting average with a fine on-base average and slugging average, giving him a secondary average well over .300. His ratio of walks to strikeouts was .863, not bad for a power hitter and third (to Mike Scioscia and Gary Carter) among National League catchers with 325 or more at-bats.

From June 1st onward, Virgil batted .245; from August 1st, .262. At the first he is effective, and at the second valuable, due to his other offensive assets. He will have to perform at that level for an entire season before the Braves catching problems can be considered solved, but past performance indicates that it is possible. Already they are better off than they were with Cerone, although that could also be said with Simmons behind the plate.

It was not a good year early on for the Virgil family; Ozzie's dad became a major issue in the San Diego Civil War (Smith vs. Williams), and Junior had the poor April and May. Ozzie became a better hitter around the time Pop was re-employed in Seattle. Any connection there?

—John Stryker

When Ozzie Virgil was traded from Philadelphia to Atlanta, many felt that his home field stats would significantly improve with the change of parks. The numbers below show that, in fact, his home stats were worse in 1986 for on-base and slugging, implying that Oz had difficulties adjusting to the Atlanta launching pad. Although he increased his walks total to 63 from his '85 total of 49, the ratio between walks at home and walks on the road was reversed—only natural when a power-hitter changes to a hitters park like Atlanta. The problem, though, was that Ozzie suffered through two gruesome, month-long slumps, never being able to completely hit his stride.

Virgil reversed his pattern of the previous year, hitting left-handers better than righties (although 13 of his 15 HR were hit off RHP, similar to his 15 of 19 HR vs. RHP in 1985).

It would be foolish for the Atlanta brain trust to give him any less than another full year to demonstrate his worth to the team. Even at his present level of performance, Virgil is much better than any of the current alternatives.

—Jeff Held

| | 1986 SEASON | | | | | | | | | | | | THREE YEARS (84 – 86) | | | | | | | | | | |
	Ave.	OBP	SLG	AB	H	2B	3B	HR	RBI	BB	SO		Ave.	OBP	SLG	AB	H	2B	3B	HR	RBI	BB	SO
Totals	.223	.343	.373	359	80	9	0	15	48	63	73		.245	.334	.416	1241	304	46	5	52	171	157	249
Batting vs. Left and Right-handed Pitchers																							
Left	.262	.396	.355	107	28	4	0	2	12	25	10		.250	.344	.399	348	87	12	2	12	44	52	47
Right	.206	.319	.381	252	52	5	0	13	36	38	63		.243	.330	.422	893	217	34	3	40	127	105	202
At Home and on the Road																							
Home	.265	.344	.406	170	45	6	0	6	25	20	37		.270	.352	.447	611	165	29	5	23	85	73	133
Road	.185	.342	.344	189	35	3	0	9	23	43	36		.221	.317	.386	630	139	17	0	29	86	84	116
Facing Groundball Pitchers and Flyball Pitchers																							
Groundball	.217	.335	.329	152	33	2	0	5	20	26	32		.225	.318	.399	543	122	13	5	17	65	71	107
Flyball	.227	.348	.406	207	47	7	0	10	28	37	41		.261	.346	.458	698	182	33	0	35	106	86	142
Facing Finesse Pitchers and Power Pitchers																							
Finesse	.230	.339	.440	191	44	4	0	12	33	29	30		.249	.326	.463	700	174	33	0	39	111	74	105
Power	.214	.346	.298	168	36	5	0	3	15	34	43		.240	.344	.355	541	130	13	5	13	60	83	144
On Grass and on Turf																							
Grass	.234	.358	.381	265	62	6	0	11	34	49	59		.222	.323	.394	513	114	13	0	25	75	71	107
Turf	.191	.297	.351	94	18	3	0	4	14	14	14		.261	.342	.431	728	190	33	5	27	96	86	142
During the Day and at Night																							
Day	.241	.333	.454	108	26	5	0	6	13	13	24		.254	.324	.463	389	99	17	2	20	62	35	76
Night	.215	.346	.339	251	54	4	0	9	35	50	49		.241	.338	.394	852	205	29	3	32	109	122	173
By Month																							
April	.086	.220	.171	35	3	0	0	1	5	6	8		.269	.331	.462	119	32	5	0	6	22	10	20
May	.217	.320	.458	83	18	2	0	6	14	12	15		.253	.347	.454	249	63	9	1	13	34	32	53
June	.311	.476	.541	61	19	2	0	4	11	18	7		.278	.358	.489	223	62	8	0	13	34	27	42
July	.138	.250	.172	58	8	2	0	0	3	9	14		.229	.320	.367	218	50	11	2	5	25	28	38
August	.257	.350	.414	70	18	2	0	3	9	10	16		.241	.356	.448	212	51	9	1	11	32	36	45
Sept/Oct	.269	.377	.346	52	14	1	0	1	6	8	13		.209	.287	.291	220	46	4	1	4	24	24	51
Situational																							
Bases Empty	.206	.311	.373	204	42	7	0	9	9	27	40		.250	.329	.422	677	169	27	3	28	28	69	137
Leadoff	.184	.303	.395	76	14	4	0	4	4	11	9		.262	.341	.462	275	72	15	2	12	12	27	38
Not Leadoff	.219	.315	.359	128	28	3	0	5	5	16	31		.241	.321	.396	402	97	12	1	16	16	42	99
Runners On	.245	.381	.374	155	38	2	0	6	39	36	33		.239	.340	.408	564	135	19	2	24	143	88	112
First Base Only	.266	.373	.469	64	17	1	0	4	8	11	10		.242	.303	.471	240	58	8	1	15	32	19	45
Scoring Position	.231	.387	.308	91	21	1	0	2	31	25	23		.238	.364	.361	324	77	11	1	9	111	69	67
Late Innings, Close	.254	.378	.299	67	17	0	0	1	8	13	15		.238	.342	.316	231	55	4	1	4	31	36	62
RBI/Opportunities																							
Scoring Position				28 / 137		(20%)										96 / 479		(20%)					
Scoring Position, 2 Out				13 / 60		(22%)										39 / 219		(18%)					
On Third, Less than 2 Out				12 / 31		(39%)										38 / 84		(45%)					
RBI in close games / RBI Total				36 / 48		(75%)										113 / 171		(66%)					

Greg Walker
Chicago White Sox

Greg Walker's 1986 season was spoiled by two separate injuries, a broken right wrist suffered in April and a broken right hand which put him out for the season in early August. That's a shame, because Walker's stats, projected out to the 160 game pace he was on, would be pretty impressive:

AB	R	H	D	T	HR	RBI	BB	SO
578	76	160	21	12	27	105	59	90

"What might have been" is becoming a familiar theme with Walker. Like some other young players, notably Darryl Strawberry and Kevin McReynolds, whatever Greg does always seems to fall short of what is expected of him. In Walker's case, it's easy to understand why people fall in love with him: he has one of the best-looking swings you'd ever want to see. It's not much of an exaggeration to say that Greg Walker swings the bat the way Ozzie Smith goes into the hole. Just three years ago Bill James wrote this about Greg: "Terrific offensive potential. Just 25 and a proven power hitter, he might hit 35–40 homers this year."

Bill wasn't alone; that sentiment was shared by Sox players, management and fans. It seemed like the kid couldn't miss becoming not only a star, but a big star.

If it hasn't happened, it's hard to blame Walker, because he works about as hard on his game as any player I've seen. Back in '83, he was such an inept first baseman that the Sox felt compelled to keep Mike Squires around as his caddy. Hour after hour of practice turned Walker into a competent fielder. Similarly Walker has learned more patience at the plate (his walk ratio last year was a career-best), improved his work against lefties and even adjusted to the more spacious dimensions at Comiskey Park last year, belting five triples in about 40 games. He's a laborer, a lunch-bucket kind of ballplayer.

I suspect that, more than anything, it's been his problems with southpaws that have kept Greg from becoming a big star. Despite all the hard work he's hit only 8 homers in his career off lefties, vs. 65 against righties. I'm sure he'll continue to plug away, though, and even if he can't raise his game beyond its current level, that's still plenty good.

—Don Zminda

		1986 SEASON										THREE YEARS (84 – 86)									
	Ave.	OBP	SLG	AB	H	2B	3B	HR	RBI	BB	SO	Ave.	OBP	SLG	AB	H	2B	3B	HR	RBI	BB	SO
Totals	.277	.345	.493	282	78	10	6	13	51	29	44	.274	.330	.488	1325	363	77	12	61	218	109	210
Batting vs. Left and Right-handed Pitchers
Left	.236	.324	.360	89	21	3	1	2	12	11	17	.222	.282	.360	356	79	23	1	8	45	29	72
Right	.295	.355	.554	193	57	7	5	11	39	18	27	.293	.347	.536	969	284	54	11	53	173	80	138
At Home and on the Road
Home	.278	.366	.517	151	42	8	5	6	27	21	22	.286	.351	.534	661	189	43	11	33	115	64	118
Road	.275	.319	.466	131	36	2	1	7	24	8	22	.262	.309	.443	664	174	34	1	28	103	45	92
Facing Groundball Pitchers and Flyball Pitchers
Groundball	.318	.409	.626	107	34	3	3	8	27	17	16	.287	.350	.528	606	174	38	6	32	102	58	86
Flyball	.251	.302	.411	175	44	7	3	5	24	12	28	.263	.312	.455	719	189	39	6	29	116	51	124
Facing Finesse Pitchers and Power Pitchers
Finesse	.276	.349	.572	152	42	5	2	12	36	16	17	.281	.332	.543	770	216	43	6	49	143	57	105
Power	.277	.340	.400	130	36	5	4	1	15	13	27	.265	.327	.413	555	147	34	6	12	75	52	105
On Grass and on Turf
Grass	.272	.346	.489	235	64	8	5	11	43	26	36	.272	.331	.487	1118	304	65	11	51	190	98	185
Turf	.298	.340	.511	47	14	2	1	2	8	3	8	.285	.321	.498	207	59	12	1	10	28	11	25
During the Day and at Night
Day	.330	.406	.580	88	29	5	4	3	15	11	12	.277	.328	.500	376	104	21	6	17	52	29	56
Night	.253	.316	.454	194	49	5	2	10	36	18	32	.273	.330	.484	949	259	56	6	44	166	80	154
By Month
April	.364	.462	.818	22	8	2	1	2	2	4	3	.296	.342	.548	135	40	10	3	6	20	10	22
May	.323	.408	.516	62	20	4	1	2	8	8	14	.300	.360	.493	203	61	11	2	8	26	17	40
June	.194	.273	.398	98	19	3	1	5	23	10	17	.240	.301	.483	271	65	16	1	16	60	22	40
July	.312	.347	.484	93	29	1	3	3	16	6	7	.259	.314	.420	293	76	15	4	8	41	25	39
August	.286	.375	.714	7	2	0	0	1	2	1	3	.262	.319	.492	195	51	13	1	10	33	16	34
Sept/Oct	.000	.000	.000	0	0	0	0	0	0	0	0	.307	.360	.539	228	70	12	1	13	38	19	35
Situational
Bases Empty	.278	.345	.481	158	44	4	5	6	6	14	27	.268	.316	.460	721	193	41	7	28	28	45	125
Leadoff	.287	.337	.525	80	23	2	4	3	3	6	17	.281	.322	.500	334	94	24	5	13	13	20	65
Not Leadoff	.269	.352	.436	78	21	2	1	3	3	8	10	.256	.311	.426	387	99	17	2	15	15	25	60
Runners On	.274	.345	.508	124	34	6	1	7	45	15	17	.281	.346	.522	604	170	36	5	33	190	64	85
First Base Only	.275	.315	.451	51	14	4	1	1	4	3	8	.275	.322	.473	273	75	17	2	11	29	19	41
Scoring Position	.274	.364	.548	73	20	2	0	6	41	12	9	.287	.364	.562	331	95	19	3	22	161	45	44
Late Innings, Close	.268	.279	.366	41	11	2	1	0	6	1	11	.259	.295	.452	197	51	9	1	9	38	11	38
RBI/Opportunities
Scoring Position				32 / 106		(30%)									121 / 448		(27%)
Scoring Position, 2 Out				10 / 45		(22%)									44 / 216		(20%)
On Third, Less than 2 Out				12 / 22		(55%)									37 / 72		(51%)
RBI in close games / RBI Total				34 / 51		(67%)									166 / 218		(76%)

Tim Wallach
Montreal Expos

Tim Wallach had a rough year in 1986, hitting only .233 with 18 homers and 71 RBIs; it was easily his worst season since his rookie year of 1981. Big things have been expected of Wallach ever since 1982, when he hit 28 homers and drove in 97 runs, but he hasn't come near those totals since then. Though he shows lots of ability with the bat at times—the first half of '86 is a good example—he is just as apt to go into the deep freeze. And for Tim that means a Montreal, midwinter deep freeze. There was September-October of '83, for example, when he hit .165 with one homer; or September of '84, when he closed out what could have been a good season by hitting .133 with no homers; or the last two months of '86, when he batted a mighty .163 until an injury mercifully ended his year. It isn't always just a bad finish; Wallach's also had nine- and ten-homer Septembers. But then he falls off at another time.

Yet as he approaches his thirtieth birthday in 1987, Tim Wallach remains a valued commodity, with such sharp baseball men as Whitey Herzog openly vying for his services. His fielding ability is part of the reason, of course; the Gold Glove he won in 1985 was several years past due, and only a rough beginning (five errors in the first ten games) and Mike Schmidt's sensational play kept him from winning another one last year. But baseball people like Wallach for his bat as well as his glove, despite his mediocre batting and on-base averages. Many of them know how much he's been penalized by the Montreal ballpark. Playing in the Big O doesn't seem to have affected Wallach's batting average adversely—despite the '86 figures Wallach's hit .260 at home over the last five years, .252 on the road—but it drastically curtails his home run power. Over the same period (1982–86) Wallach has hit 105 homers, a respectable average of 21 per year. But only 39 of those have been hit in the Big O. If he'd hit 66 homers in his home ball park, as he did on the road, the total would have been 132, and the average would jump to 26 a year; doing that, he'd be a valuable commodity even hitting .233. For his sake, let's hope he doesn't get traded to St. Louis; let's hope he finds a nice, fair ballpark to hit home runs in.

—Don Zminda and Martin Lacoste

	1986 SEASON											THREE YEARS (84 – 86)										
	Ave.	OBP	SLG	AB	H	2B	3B	HR	RBI	BB	SO	Ave.	OBP	SLG	AB	H	2B	3B	HR	RBI	BB	SO
Totals	.233	.308	.396	480	112	22	1	18	71	44	72	.247	.310	.414	1631	403	83	8	58	224	132	252
Batting vs. Left and Right-handed Pitchers																						
Left	.215	.305	.356	135	29	10	0	3	16	17	19	.247	.311	.419	458	113	30	2	15	64	43	57
Right	.241	.309	.412	345	83	12	1	15	55	27	53	.247	.309	.413	1173	290	53	6	43	160	89	195
At Home and on the Road																						
Home	.226	.309	.348	230	52	8	1	6	34	21	34	.246	.317	.379	781	192	37	5	19	102	74	122
Road	.240	.307	.440	250	60	14	0	12	37	23	38	.248	.302	.447	850	211	46	3	39	122	58	130
Facing Groundball Pitchers and Flyball Pitchers																						
Groundball	.216	.290	.383	227	49	11	0	9	35	20	33	.246	.316	.408	775	191	31	2	30	113	71	117
Flyball	.249	.324	.407	253	63	11	1	9	36	24	39	.248	.304	.421	856	212	52	6	28	111	61	135
Facing Finesse Pitchers and Power Pitchers																						
Finesse	.255	.315	.398	274	70	13	1	8	41	18	36	.264	.311	.428	956	252	52	6	31	127	57	136
Power	.204	.300	.393	206	42	9	0	10	30	26	36	.224	.307	.396	675	151	31	2	27	97	75	116
On Grass and on Turf																						
Grass	.204	.284	.394	137	28	8	0	6	19	15	27	.242	.301	.464	459	111	23	2	25	66	35	79
Turf	.245	.318	.397	343	84	14	1	12	52	29	45	.249	.313	.395	1172	292	60	6	33	158	97	173
During the Day and at Night																						
Day	.238	.328	.419	172	41	10	0	7	26	18	26	.258	.318	.450	600	155	31	3	26	88	46	97
Night	.231	.296	.383	308	71	12	1	11	45	26	46	.241	.305	.394	1031	248	52	5	32	136	86	155
By Month																						
April	.297	.384	.547	64	19	4	0	4	13	8	10	.314	.369	.525	223	70	15	1	10	44	18	28
May	.265	.313	.480	102	27	8	1	4	16	4	13	.259	.312	.432	294	76	20	2	9	33	17	40
June	.273	.374	.455	88	24	4	0	4	17	13	12	.269	.350	.443	264	71	15	2	9	37	30	42
July	.216	.290	.371	97	21	3	0	4	12	10	17	.220	.278	.389	296	65	12	1	12	45	23	56
August	.175	.238	.258	97	17	2	0	2	11	6	15	.234	.294	.360	303	71	10	2	8	39	21	45
Sept/Oct	.125	.200	.156	32	4	1	0	0	2	3	5	.199	.267	.363	251	50	11	0	10	26	23	41
Situational																						
Bases Empty	.219	.296	.383	256	56	7	1	11	11	23	41	.238	.287	.398	923	220	43	7	30	30	58	153
Leadoff	.255	.347	.453	106	27	3	0	6	6	11	17	.282	.333	.492	372	105	24	3	16	16	24	52
Not Leadoff	.193	.258	.333	150	29	4	1	5	5	12	24	.209	.256	.334	551	115	19	4	14	14	34	101
Runners On	.250	.322	.411	224	56	15	0	7	60	21	31	.258	.337	.436	708	183	40	1	28	194	74	99
First Base Only	.291	.325	.481	79	23	6	0	3	8	4	12	.274	.311	.441	281	77	14	0	11	30	10	40
Scoring Position	.228	.320	.372	145	33	9	0	4	52	17	19	.248	.352	.433	427	106	26	1	17	164	64	59
Late Innings, Close	.242	.345	.374	99	24	4	0	3	12	14	14	.231	.316	.369	295	68	11	0	10	35	33	48
RBI/Opportunities																						
Scoring Position				44 / 191	(23%)										133 / 590	(23%)						
Scoring Position, 2 Out				18 / 82	(22%)										53 / 272	(19%)						
On Third, Less than 2 Out				18 / 37	(49%)										46 / 103	(45%)						
RBI in close games / RBI Total				55 / 71	(77%)										167 / 224	(75%)						

Gary Ward
Texas Rangers

Gary hit .366 in his last 49 games to finish '86 with a batting average of .316, his first .300 season at any level. However, that figure is deceptive in detailing Ward's offensive efficiency. 1986 was also his worst year for power-hitting, just 22 extra-base hits with only five homers, and one of those was an inside-the-park homer. Even when you consider that he had only 380 at bats, a normal projection from his past career would have produced 35 power hits, twelve of them for homers. From watching Ward play, it seemed to be a conscious choice in hitting strategy. In '86 he rarely pulled the ball, and against right-handed pitching he seemed to intentionally shoot for the opposite field.

Ward had a reputation with Ranger fans of being a great hitter only after the team had fallen out of the race. He laid that theory to rest in 1986 when Texas remained in contention to the end while Ward had his familiar hot finish. His August/ September performance with Texas has been rather remarkable:

Gary Ward 1984-86	AB	BA	R	HR Frequency
Start of season to July 31	1050	.269	9	1 every 55.3 AB
August 1 to end of season	525	.341	2	1 every 23.9 AB

When future historians are looking over Ward's record, there is one number that will make them do a double take: 24 outfield assists with the Twins in 1983. That remains the most by an AL outfielder since World War II. What makes it all the odder is that he never had another season remotely close. That 24 matches his two next best seasons combined.

Probably the best explanation is simply a freakish fluctuation, but there were contributing factors. The Twins' pitching in '83 was second in all of baseball in runners allowed (H + W + HBP—HR). The runners were a bit wilder: the league totaled 517 outfield assists compared to an average of 455 the next three years. Oddly enough, among outfielders with ten assists or more, Ward was only third in assists per game, behind Ron Roenicke and Jesse Barfield. And, of course, that brings up the theory of runners and coaches misjudging the faster, more accurate one-hop throws on turf. Roenicke, Barfield and Ward all had turf home fields in 1983.

—Craig Wright

	1986 SEASON											THREE YEARS (84 – 86)										
	Ave.	OBP	SLG	AB	H	2B	3B	HR	RBI	BB	SO	Ave.	OBP	SLG	AB	H	2B	3B	HR	RBI	BB	SO
Totals	.316	.372	.405	380	120	15	2	5	51	31	72	.293	.345	.432	1575	461	64	16	41	200	125	264
Batting vs. Left and Right-handed Pitchers																						
Left	.317	.388	.467	120	38	7	1	3	20	14	23	.293	.354	.468	481	141	25	7	15	73	46	72
Right	.315	.364	.377	260	82	8	1	2	31	17	49	.293	.341	.416	1094	320	39	9	26	127	79	192
At Home and on the Road																						
Home	.321	.370	.420	193	62	8	1	3	24	13	34	.316	.367	.465	763	241	36	9	20	110	61	123
Road	.310	.373	.390	187	58	7	1	2	27	18	38	.271	.324	.400	812	220	28	7	21	90	64	141
Facing Groundball Pitchers and Flyball Pitchers																						
Groundball	.319	.379	.373	166	53	9	0	0	22	13	24	.321	.367	.460	757	243	39	6	18	106	53	100
Flyball	.313	.366	.430	214	67	6	2	5	29	18	48	.267	.325	.406	818	218	25	10	23	94	72	164
Facing Finesse Pitchers and Power Pitchers																						
Finesse	.354	.406	.436	243	86	11	0	3	35	19	31	.313	.359	.450	935	293	38	9	24	120	66	124
Power	.248	.311	.350	137	34	4	2	2	16	12	41	.263	.324	.405	640	168	26	7	17	80	59	140
On Grass and on Turf																						
Grass	.311	.370	.393	331	103	13	1	4	36	28	65	.288	.340	.421	1329	383	54	12	33	166	103	233
Turf	.347	.382	.490	49	17	2	1	1	15	3	7	.317	.373	.488	246	78	10	4	8	34	22	31
During the Day and at Night																						
Day	.246	.324	.311	61	15	1	0	1	6	7	13	.236	.302	.309	314	74	8	0	5	23	30	55
Night	.329	.381	.423	319	105	14	2	4	45	24	59	.307	.356	.462	1261	387	56	16	36	177	95	209
By Month																						
April	.286	.357	.365	63	18	2	0	1	10	7	13	.256	.322	.348	207	53	5	1	4	23	20	35
May	.259	.355	.346	81	21	4	0	1	9	11	15	.247	.318	.361	291	72	13	1	6	32	29	43
June	.333	.368	.481	81	27	5	2	1	16	3	14	.289	.331	.401	304	88	14	4	4	39	18	47
July	.357	.408	.429	70	25	2	0	1	4	5	10	.278	.325	.399	248	69	9	3	5	24	17	48
August	.324	.354	.392	74	24	2	0	1	11	4	17	.338	.380	.556	284	96	13	5	13	49	20	48
Sept/Oct	.455	.500	.455	11	5	0	0	0	1	1	3	.344	.395	.515	241	83	10	2	9	33	21	43
Situational																						
Bases Empty	.301	.357	.358	229	69	7	0	2	2	18	43	.285	.335	.409	934	266	32	9	22	22	67	158
Leadoff	.340	.394	.410	100	34	4	0	1	1	9	17	.329	.369	.476	380	125	20	6	8	8	24	50
Not Leadoff	.271	.329	.318	129	35	3	0	1	1	9	26	.255	.312	.363	554	141	12	3	14	14	43	108
Runners On	.338	.393	.477	151	51	8	2	3	49	13	29	.304	.360	.465	641	195	32	7	19	178	58	106
First Base Only	.294	.351	.397	68	20	1	0	2	5	5	8	.296	.325	.446	280	83	9	3	9	28	11	32
Scoring Position	.373	.426	.542	83	31	7	2	1	44	8	21	.310	.384	.479	361	112	23	4	10	150	47	74
Late Innings, Close	.323	.362	.415	65	21	2	2	0	8	4	15	.279	.336	.395	258	72	9	3	5	28	23	47
RBI/Opportunities																						
Scoring Position				39 / 111		(35%)									125 / 479		(26%)					
Scoring Position, 2 Out				18 / 55		(33%)									52 / 211		(25%)					
On Third, Less than 2 Out				9 / 18		(50%)									33 / 78		(42%)					
RBI in close games / RBI Total				37 / 51		(73%)									144 / 200		(72%)					

387

Mitch Webster
Montreal Expos

By June of 1985, Mitch Webster's career was at a standstill. Though only 26, he was in his ninth minor league season and his fourth at Syracuse, his only taste of the big time being 34 scattered at bats with the Blue Jays. He seemed like the quintessential career minor leaguer—good glove and decent bat (four .300 seasons), but no power. In eight years of trying he'd homered in double figures only once (with 13) and had never driven in more that 68 runs. At this point, one wouldn't have blamed him for thinking about packing it in.

But then Mitch got lucky: the Blue Jays sold him to Montreal, and the Expos put him in their lineup. He hasn't been out of it since. He hit a solid .274 for 212 at bats during the remainder of '85, but the revelation was the power he showed in hitting eleven homers. It seemed like such a fluke that even the astute Bill James wrote that "the odds are that pitchers are going to catch up to him pretty quickly in '86." In a way they did—Mitch's home runs came down to a more normal eight in 576 at bats. But in more ways they didn't—Webster batted .290, slugged .431 with 52 extra base hits (including 13 triples), showed on-base ability with 57 walks, and stole 15 bases as well. It was a solid season in every respect, and Webster enters 1987 as an established major league performer.

It's an inspirational story, and the remarkable part of it is that Mitch is succeeding in a ballpark that's ill-suited for him. I'm sure a lot of Expos would say they're playing in the wrong ballpark, and maybe the wrong country, too, but it's especially true in Webster's case. He's a flyball hitter, and as noted in the Tim Wallach essay, the Big O is a groundball hitter's park; and he's a grass field hitter to an extreme (just look at the figures), playing in an artificial turf stadium. His home/road breakdowns favor foreign ballyards in every category except triples; even his surprising home run power has been hurt, as he's only hit five of his nineteen National League homers in Montreal. Study his numbers and imagine what he could do for a grass field team in the American League.

One odd thing about Webster is that even though he's a lefthanded thrower, he hits much, much better as a righty. He seems to battle the odds that way, too.

—Don Zminda

	1986 SEASON											THREE YEARS (84 – 86)										
	Ave.	OBP	SLG	AB	H	2B	3B	HR	RBI	BB	SO	Ave.	OBP	SLG	AB	H	2B	3B	HR	RBI	BB	SO
Totals	.290	.355	.431	576	167	31	13	8	49	57	78	.286	.350	.445	788	225	39	15	19	79	77	111
Batting vs. Left and Right-handed Pitchers																						
Left	.337	.376	.513	199	67	16	2	5	20	11	23	.332	.371	.533	289	96	19	3	11	39	17	38
Right	.265	.345	.387	377	100	15	11	3	29	46	55	.259	.338	.395	499	129	20	12	8	40	60	73
At Home and on the Road																						
Home	.265	.329	.396	283	75	15	8	2	24	28	34	.261	.320	.407	364	95	18	10	5	36	33	44
Road	.314	.380	.464	293	92	16	5	6	25	29	44	.307	.375	.479	424	130	21	5	14	43	44	67
Facing Groundball Pitchers and Flyball Pitchers																						
Groundball	.322	.382	.461	267	86	18	5	3	23	28	25	.324	.380	.492	364	118	22	6	9	35	35	37
Flyball	.262	.331	.405	309	81	13	8	5	26	29	53	.252	.323	.406	424	107	17	9	10	44	42	74
Facing Finesse Pitchers and Power Pitchers																						
Finesse	.296	.353	.421	335	99	14	8	4	25	29	37	.297	.356	.441	458	136	17	8	11	43	42	50
Power	.282	.358	.444	241	68	17	5	4	24	28	41	.270	.341	.452	330	89	22	7	8	36	35	61
On Grass and on Turf																						
Grass	.351	.411	.480	148	52	10	0	3	12	13	21	.344	.401	.500	212	73	12	0	7	23	18	35
Turf	.269	.336	.414	428	115	21	13	5	37	44	57	.264	.331	.425	576	152	27	15	12	56	59	76
During the Day and at Night																						
Day	.270	.339	.402	204	55	11	5	2	21	21	27	.292	.357	.482	274	80	15	5	9	39	28	39
Night	.301	.364	.446	372	112	20	8	6	28	36	51	.282	.346	.426	514	145	24	10	10	40	49	72
By Month																						
April	.246	.297	.377	69	17	6	0	1	7	5	13	.246	.297	.377	69	17	6	0	1	7	5	13
May	.300	.396	.438	80	24	5	0	2	9	13	6	.300	.396	.438	80	24	5	0	2	9	13	6
June	.240	.347	.356	104	25	5	2	1	6	17	12	.250	.345	.403	124	31	7	3	2	8	18	14
July	.353	.402	.494	85	30	5	2	1	9	7	15	.288	.325	.451	153	44	7	3	4	15	9	25
August	.330	.364	.470	115	38	6	5	0	9	5	9	.293	.346	.420	150	44	6	5	1	14	11	15
Sept/Oct	.268	.326	.439	123	33	4	4	3	9	10	23	.307	.370	.509	212	65	8	4	9	26	21	38
Situational																						
Bases Empty	.290	.344	.459	338	98	21	9	6	6	28	50	.289	.345	.479	463	134	26	10	14	14	39	68
Leadoff	.331	.368	.517	118	39	11	1	3	3	7	14	.335	.381	.530	164	55	12	1	6	6	12	20
Not Leadoff	.268	.332	.427	220	59	10	8	3	3	21	36	.264	.325	.452	299	79	14	9	8	8	27	48
Runners On	.290	.370	.391	238	69	10	4	2	43	29	28	.280	.357	.397	325	91	13	5	5	65	38	43
First Base Only	.333	.379	.426	108	36	6	2	0	4	7	14	.309	.352	.416	149	46	7	3	1	8	9	20
Scoring Position	.254	.362	.362	130	33	4	2	2	39	22	14	.256	.360	.381	176	45	6	2	4	57	29	23
Late Innings, Close	.231	.309	.322	121	28	3	1	2	15	13	12	.219	.296	.338	160	35	5	1	4	20	17	18
RBI/Opportunities																						

	1986 SEASON		THREE YEARS (84 – 86)	
Scoring Position	36 / 180	(20%)	52 / 244	(21%)
Scoring Position, 2 Out	14 / 81	(17%)	22 / 110	(20%)
On Third, Less than 2 Out	13 / 27	(48%)	19 / 37	(51%)
RBI in close games / RBI Total	33 / 49	(67%)	53 / 79	(67%)

Bob Welch
Los Angeles Dodgers

If it is opening night on Broadway and you get laryngitis, that's hard luck. If your car breaks down on the way to see your first World Series game, that's hard luck. If you pitched for the Dodgers in 1986 and your name is Bob Welch, that's hard luck.

What else can you say about a starter whose bullpen gave up grand slams in consecutive starts, allowed over half of the inherited runners to score, and only saved two games for him the whole season? That's right, hard luck.

In two words, "hard luck" describes Bob Welch's season. He might have done better in 1986 as a craps shooter in Vegas; he certainly couldn't have done worse.

Bob Welch was 7–13 last year. He was 2–7 on the road and 0–5 on turf. At the risk of never being taken seriously about baseball again, I'm going to say that Bob Welch had a good year. You had to see it to believe it.

Welch's 1986 ERA was 3.28, yet he only averaged one win per month. This sounds even better when you hear that the Dodgers averaged only 3.27 runs per start for Welch. That powerhouse Dodgers offense supported the rest of the staff to the tune of 4.11 runs per game. The Dodgers only scored 77 runs in the 26 games (2.77 per start) that Bob either lost or got no decision. That's hard luck.

Between August 1st and October 1st, Bob made 10 starts. In that period, he threw 75 innings with a 2.04 ERA, 52 Ks, only 18 walks—he even picked up a save. The Dodgers translated that into a 3–7 record, but, unfortunately, Bob only got credited with two wins (along with four losses).

Of the eight times last year that Welch held the opposition to one run or less, he received credit for only 3 wins. Somehow, he even managed to lose twice; the other three decisions went to the arson squad (good-naturedly referred to as the bullpen by the Dodgers brass).

In retrospect, Bob Welch's season was a good one, but don't look for the statistics to prove that. He had minimal offensive support, even less help from the bullpen, and mediocre defense. Bob Welch has made an excellent recovery from alcoholism to become one of baseball's top pitchers. This season Welch was tempted by the devil himself. There's only one way to summarize the kind of year that Bob Welch had in 1986—that's right, hard luck.

—Carmen J. Corica

1986: Finesse, Flyball **1985: Finesse, Flyball** **1984: Power, Flyball**

	G	IP	H	BB	SO	SB	CS	W	L	S	ERA	G	IP	H	BB	SO	SB	CS	W	L	S	ERA
	1986 SEASON											**THREE YEARS (84 – 86)**										
Totals	33	235.2	227	55	183	22	9	7	13	0	3.28	87	581.2	559	148	405	49	24	34	30	0	3.16
At Home and on the Road																						
Home	18	132.0	124	30	93	11	6	5	6	0	2.66	45	317.0	312	74	222	28	15	20	15	0	2.95
Road	15	103.2	103	25	90	11	3	2	7	0	4.08	42	264.2	247	74	183	21	9	14	15	0	3.40
During the Day and at Night																						
Day	13	90.2	98	27	71	9	3	2	6	0	4.07	30	192.1	195	54	134	18	7	10	11	0	3.79
Night	20	145.0	129	28	112	13	6	5	7	0	2.79	57	389.1	364	94	271	31	17	24	19	0	2.84
On Grass and on Turf																						
Grass	27	198.2	186	46	151	18	7	7	8	0	2.94	66	456.0	439	112	323	39	18	28	19	0	3.00
Turf	6	37.0	41	9	32	4	2	0	5	0	5.11	21	125.2	120	36	82	10	6	6	11	0	3.72
By Month																						
April	5	43.2	33	12	37	2	2	3	1	0	1.44	11	82.2	72	25	57	4	4	5	4	0	1.63
May	5	29.1	42	7	32	4	0	0	3	0	6.44	10	56.1	71	15	44	6	0	2	5	0	5.91
June	6	38.1	44	10	24	7	1	0	2	0	5.17	17	100.2	119	30	61	12	3	3	6	0	4.47
July	6	44.0	39	6	34	2	2	2	3	0	2.45	16	108.2	88	22	78	5	6	8	6	0	2.48
August	5	36.1	35	10	29	2	1	1	1	0	2.72	17	118.2	103	32	89	9	4	8	5	0	2.88
Sept/Oct	6	44.0	34	10	27	5	3	1	3	0	2.66	16	114.2	106	24	76	13	7	8	4	0	2.67

vs. Opponent Batters

	Ave.	OBP	SLG	AB	H	2B	3B	HR	RBI	BB	SO	Ave.	OBP	SLG	AB	H	2B	3B	HR	RBI	BB	SO
	1986 SEASON											**THREE YEARS (84 – 86)**										
Totals	.251	.297	.357	904	227	46	4	14	78	55	183	.251	.300	.368	2229	559	96	21	41	196	148	405
Pitching vs. Left and Right-handed Batters																						
Left	.262	.305	.367	485	127	24	3	7	37	30	82	.243	.292	.340	1130	275	47	13	12	84	76	175
Right	.239	.287	.346	419	100	22	1	7	41	25	101	.258	.309	.397	1099	284	49	8	29	112	72	230
Situational																						
Bases Empty	.256	.287	.381	543	139	31	2	11	11	23	101	.259	.290	.392	1338	346	59	13	31	31	59	229
Leadoff	.277	.313	.416	231	64	13	2	5	5	12	34	.270	.312	.400	563	152	23	4	14	14	34	83
Not Leadoff	.240	.269	.356	312	75	18	0	6	6	11	67	.250	.275	.386	775	194	36	9	17	17	25	146
Runners On	.244	.310	.321	361	88	15	2	3	67	32	82	.239	.314	.332	891	213	37	8	10	165	89	176
First Base Only	.252	.302	.374	139	35	8	0	3	10	8	31	.259	.327	.369	347	90	16	2	6	22	27	62
Scoring Position	.239	.314	.288	222	53	7	2	0	57	24	51	.226	.306	.309	544	123	21	6	4	143	62	114
Late Innings, Close	.235	.272	.445	119	28	4	0	7	14	6	21	.245	.279	.406	229	56	9	2	8	25	11	33

RBI/Opportunities

Scoring Position	55 / 295	(19%)	132 / 708	(19%)
Scoring Position, 2 Out	20 / 124	(16%)	55 / 323	(17%)
On Third, Less than 2 Out	24 / 57	(42%)	52 / 117	(44%)
RBI in close games / RBI Total	65 / 78	(83%)	157 / 196	(80%)

Lou Whitaker
Detroit Tigers

Lou Whitaker is, in my opinion, the best second baseman in baseball. In 1986 he hit 20 homers and had 73 RBIs—impressive numbers for anyone and simply amazing when you realize that he did it with no help from his home park. I have no idea why Whitaker would not hit well in Tiger Stadium—you'd think that a player who makes good contact and sprays the ball to all fields would benefit from the short power alleys here. But he doesn't. Since 1981, he's hit better on the road four years out of six ('82 and '84 excepted) and he hits about 60% of his homers on the road. For this reason, he gets my nod over Chicago's Ryne Sandberg (whose stats would be less impressive if he played in another park). Lou gets his numbers the old fashioned way—he earns them.

Defensively? I don't see the Ryno often, but it's difficult to believe that anyone is better than Lou. He has a cannon for an arm and invariably makes the throws he needs to make to get the runner at first. He may not turn the double play quite as well as White, but that may be due to Trammell's arm woes. Anyway, if he isn't the best fielder, he's close enough to let his bat put him out in front.

For some incomprehensible reason, local writers sometimes talk about Lou's alleged lack of intensity—they say that he just goes through the motions at times. For my part, I think that the only problem Lou has is that he's so talented that he doesn't look like he's playing as hard as he really is—he'll do things that some players have to break their necks to do without breaking a sweat—and I don't know why people want to hassle him because he makes everything look easy. Even if he WERE going through the motions, he bears down like . . . well, a Tiger when the game is on the line. Since 1984, he's delivered 54% of the time with men on third and less than two out.

Two problems Lou has are both related to the fact that he leads off. His on-base average is only average because he's not that good at leading off innings. Since half of his homers came with the bases empty and he does a lot better with a runner on first, it would help if Detroit finds somebody who gets on base more often and let Lou concentrate on pounding him home in 1987.

—Steve Lysogorski

	1986 SEASON											THREE YEARS (84 – 86)										
	Ave.	OBP	SLG	AB	H	2B	3B	HR	RBI	BB	SO	Ave.	OBP	SLG	AB	H	2B	3B	HR	RBI	BB	SO
Totals	.269	.338	.437	584	157	26	6	20	73	63	70	.279	.352	.434	1751	488	80	15	54	202	205	189
Batting vs. Left and Right-handed Pitchers																						
Left	.221	.283	.325	163	36	4	2	3	20	15	33	.226	.299	.317	482	109	15	4	7	52	51	88
Right	.287	.359	.480	421	121	22	4	17	53	48	37	.299	.373	.478	1269	379	65	11	47	150	154	101
At Home and on the Road																						
Home	.248	.334	.406	286	71	11	5	8	38	37	37	.271	.349	.427	862	234	37	8	27	108	107	95
Road	.289	.341	.466	298	86	15	1	12	35	26	33	.286	.355	.441	889	254	43	7	27	94	98	94
Facing Groundball Pitchers and Flyball Pitchers																						
Groundball	.282	.359	.500	252	71	17	4	10	38	31	35	.281	.351	.460	832	234	51	7	28	98	90	86
Flyball	.259	.322	.389	332	86	9	2	10	35	32	35	.276	.354	.410	919	254	29	8	26	104	115	103
Facing Finesse Pitchers and Power Pitchers																						
Finesse	.265	.321	.444	347	92	14	3	14	49	29	30	.277	.339	.430	1009	279	46	8	31	109	97	89
Power	.274	.361	.426	237	65	12	3	6	24	34	40	.282	.370	.439	742	209	34	7	23	93	108	100
On Grass and on Turf																						
Grass	.273	.341	.425	499	136	22	6	14	62	54	59	.275	.348	.423	1474	405	62	12	44	170	171	156
Turf	.247	.319	.506	85	21	4	0	6	11	9	11	.300	.377	.495	277	83	18	3	10	32	34	33
During the Day and at Night																						
Day	.250	.318	.430	172	43	8	1	7	21	19	24	.259	.342	.400	532	138	20	2	17	64	70	61
Night	.277	.346	.439	412	114	18	5	13	52	44	46	.287	.357	.449	1219	350	60	13	37	138	135	128
By Month																						
April	.277	.304	.369	65	18	4	1	0	5	3	8	.316	.373	.459	209	66	11	2	5	20	21	21
May	.291	.354	.524	103	30	7	1	5	15	10	10	.296	.373	.439	301	89	14	1	9	33	36	27
June	.246	.313	.424	118	29	5	2	4	14	12	17	.280	.353	.447	329	92	13	3	12	40	40	37
July	.263	.324	.394	99	26	2	1	3	5	9	11	.300	.361	.471	310	93	18	4	9	28	30	36
August	.273	.369	.473	110	30	5	1	5	26	18	13	.255	.347	.422	322	82	15	3	11	48	46	34
Sept/Oct	.270	.350	.404	89	24	3	0	3	8	11	11	.236	.312	.368	280	66	9	2	8	33	32	34
Situational																						
Bases Empty	.251	.317	.404	359	90	17	4	10	10	35	40	.268	.338	.409	1126	302	56	9	28	28	117	122
Leadoff	.256	.324	.457	199	51	10	3	8	8	20	23	.273	.347	.425	673	184	30	6	20	20	74	65
Not Leadoff	.244	.309	.338	160	39	7	1	2	2	15	17	.260	.325	.384	453	118	26	3	8	8	43	57
Runners On	.298	.370	.489	225	67	9	2	10	63	28	30	.298	.377	.480	625	186	24	6	26	174	88	67
First Base Only	.362	.417	.648	105	38	6	0	8	17	10	12	.351	.399	.586	285	100	15	2	16	37	23	23
Scoring Position	.242	.331	.350	120	29	3	2	2	46	18	18	.253	.360	.391	340	86	9	4	10	137	65	44
Late Innings, Close	.289	.359	.400	90	26	4	0	2	11	11	17	.300	.397	.436	257	77	11	0	8	39	44	37
RBI/Opportunities																						
Scoring Position				41 / 169		(24%)									120 / 499		(24%)					
Scoring Position, 2 Out				19 / 79		(24%)									58 / 249		(23%)					
On Third, Less than 2 Out				14 / 30		(47%)									44 / 84		(52%)					
RBI in close games / RBI Total				44 / 73		(60%)									130 / 202		(64%)					

Frank White
Kansas City Royals

The veteran second baseman of the Kansas City Royals had his best season in 1986. He established career highs in runs scored (76), runs batted in (84) ans walks (43) and matched his career high in homers (22). When White turned 30 in 1980, his career high in homers was 10 and his career home run total was 39. In the last three years he has hit 61 homers, more than any other major league second baseman (Sandberg has hit 59, Whitaker 54) despite playing in a tough home run park (White has hit 34 homers on the road, as opposed to 27 in Kansas City). In addition, White played his usual sterling defense at second base (good enough for a Gold Glove), hit a big home run in the All Star game and went through the season without a major slump. He was the man who got the Royals' big hits, hitting 8 home runs in the late innings of close games— as many as Don Mattingly and Eddie Murray combined. He was, by acclamation, the team's best player.

White's sustained, broad-based development as a hitter has been remarkable. A player who for years would draw less than 20 walks a year, White in 1986 drew 26 walks after the All Star break. A player who once lived off of left-handed pitchers, White in 1986 hit 21 of his 22 homers off of right-handers, and for the last three years has had no platoon differential. The only black mark against his game was that he did drive in only 14% of his runners in scoring position with two out, a very poor figure, and left 91 men in scoring position. This contributed heavily to the Royals scoring 29 runs fewer than expected in view of their other totals.

Royals fans are beginning to think of White as a Hall of Fame candidate, which certainly is not unreasonable and will become more reasonable if he has two or three more good seasons. For Frank, there is an excellent guidepost to his eventual success: Bill Mazeroski. In addition to the fact that both are regarded as superior second basemen, their career batting averages are the same (.260) and their home run totals close (Mazeroski 138, White 131). Both players have poor strikeout and walks totals, but have contributed to several championships. White has more speed and will likely wind up with quite a few more homers.

—Bill James

	1986 SEASON											THREE YEARS (84 – 86)									
	Ave.	OBP	SLG	AB	H	2B	3B	HR	RBI	BB	SO	Ave.	OBP	SLG	AB	H	2B	3B	HR	RBI	BB	SO
Totals	.272	.322	.465	566	154	37	3	22	84	43	88	.264	.306	.441	1608	424	84	9	61	209	98	246
Batting vs. Left and Right-handed Pitchers																						
Left	.267	.335	.347	150	40	7	1	1	12	17	21	.269	.314	.433	443	119	18	2	17	55	31	53
Right	.274	.317	.507	416	114	30	2	21	72	26	67	.262	.302	.444	1165	305	66	7	44	154	67	193
At Home and on the Road																						
Home	.282	.329	.491	277	78	18	2	12	54	21	38	.260	.304	.426	814	212	44	5	27	118	50	107
Road	.263	.315	.439	289	76	19	1	10	30	22	50	.267	.308	.456	794	212	40	4	34	91	48	139
Facing Groundball Pitchers and Flyball Pitchers																						
Groundball	.316	.360	.572	250	79	21	2	13	45	18	36	.279	.316	.447	739	206	44	4	24	86	39	105
Flyball	.237	.292	.380	316	75	16	1	9	39	25	52	.251	.297	.436	869	218	40	5	37	123	59	141
Facing Finesse Pitchers and Power Pitchers																						
Finesse	.271	.322	.476	336	91	24	0	15	44	25	49	.270	.308	.459	909	245	47	4	39	108	48	124
Power	.274	.323	.448	230	63	13	3	7	40	25	49	.256	.303	.418	699	179	37	5	22	101	50	122
On Grass and on Turf																						
Grass	.215	.280	.372	223	48	11	0	8	21	20	45	.249	.288	.441	622	155	26	3	29	75	35	116
Turf	.309	.349	.525	343	106	26	3	14	63	23	43	.273	.316	.441	986	269	58	6	32	134	63	130
During the Day and at Night																						
Day	.273	.316	.478	161	44	11	2	6	22	11	28	.267	.311	.454	416	111	28	4	14	48	28	78
Night	.272	.324	.459	405	110	26	1	16	62	32	60	.263	.304	.436	1192	313	56	5	47	161	70	168
By Month																						
April	.286	.300	.429	77	22	6	1	1	10	2	13	.256	.287	.442	199	51	12	2	7	25	8	34
May	.269	.304	.472	108	29	7	0	5	18	6	19	.268	.314	.455	299	80	18	1	12	41	20	42
June	.289	.340	.423	97	28	5	1	2	12	7	11	.252	.289	.349	258	65	6	2	5	25	13	32
July	.225	.314	.438	89	20	4	0	5	16	13	14	.238	.296	.472	231	55	9	0	15	41	20	36
August	.270	.342	.500	100	27	8	0	5	20	11	18	.277	.317	.452	310	86	19	1	11	45	19	51
Sept/Oct	.295	.327	.516	95	28	7	1	4	8	4	13	.280	.319	.469	311	87	20	3	11	32	18	51
Situational																						
Bases Empty	.269	.318	.489	305	82	21	2	14	14	20	48	.251	.292	.454	922	231	48	4	44	44	51	139
Leadoff	.261	.320	.464	138	36	8	1	6	6	10	24	.263	.301	.432	396	104	20	1	15	15	20	62
Not Leadoff	.275	.316	.509	167	46	13	1	8	8	10	24	.241	.285	.471	526	127	28	3	29	29	31	77
Runners On	.276	.326	.437	261	72	16	1	8	70	23	40	.281	.324	.423	686	193	36	5	17	165	47	107
First Base Only	.313	.352	.495	99	31	6	0	4	9	6	17	.303	.333	.439	287	87	13	1	8	19	12	48
Scoring Position	.253	.312	.401	162	41	10	1	4	61	17	23	.266	.317	.411	399	106	23	4	9	146	35	59
Late Innings, Close	.284	.327	.559	102	29	4	0	8	23	7	19	.268	.309	.452	272	73	11	0	13	44	17	40
RBI/Opportunities																						
Scoring Position				51 / 210		(24%)									124 / 521		(24%)					
Scoring Position, 2 Out				15 / 106		(14%)									49 / 251		(20%)					
On Third, Less than 2 Out				21 / 35		(60%)									44 / 81		(54%)					
RBI in close games / RBI Total				57 / 84		(68%)									140 / 209		(67%)					

Ernie Whitt
Toronto Blue Jays

Many scouts feel that Ernie Whitt has the worst mechanics of any hitter in the American League. How, they say, can anyone hit well if he drags the knee of his back leg on the ground? They point out that, if the back leg drops down during the stride, the bat will also drop—hitters who do that will either make contact under the ball or make no contact at all. So what keeps Ernie Whitt in baseball?

The answer is twofold. First, Ernie switched to an open stance back in 1985. This allowed him to see the ball better, which let him start his swing sooner, make more consistent contact and compensate for his flaws. The second reason is that Ernie is a catcher and a good one—the better a catcher is at calling a game, the better a "guess hitter" he is. I chart every pitch thrown in Toronto games, which allows me to check the counts when a batter gets a hit. In 1985, Whitt batted .357 when he was ahead in the count (ie, 1–0, 2–0, 2–1, 3–0 or 3–1). Of his 41 hits in 115 at bats, 21 were for extra bases (10 were homers) and he slugged .722. In 1986, he hit .315 in those same circumstances (34–108) with 14 extra-base hits and 10 homers.

Ernie knows what to expect at the plate and what to do. When he can afford the luxury of taking a strike, he'll wait for his pitch. When he gets it, he takes advantage of it. If he didn't do that, he certainly wouldn't be in the majors.

If you glance at the stats below, you may note that Ernie has hit .253 against lefties in the last three years, but hit .370 with three homers in 46 at-bats in 1986. Why? Credit an injury.

In 1985, Buck Martinez suffered a season-ending injury in July. Ernie, who had been a platoon player, suddenly became a full-time player and, for the first time in his career with Toronto, saw a steady diet of lefty pitching. It wasn't pretty—he hit .213 against lefties in 1985—but the experience began paying dividends this year.

As with anything in everyday life, you can't be good at something until you do it over and over again. In Whitt's case, the repetition paid off—he paid a price in 1985, but he put the lessons that he had learned to good use in 1986. Buck will hardly appreciate this fact, but he is responsible for making Ernie into a productive regular.

—David Driscoll

	1986 SEASON											THREE YEARS (84 – 86)										
	Ave.	OBP	SLG	AB	H	2B	3B	HR	RBI	BB	SO	Ave.	OBP	SLG	AB	H	2B	3B	HR	RBI	BB	SO
Totals	.268	.326	.448	395	106	19	2	16	56	35	39	.251	.325	.440	1122	282	52	5	50	166	125	147
Batting vs. Left and Right-handed Pitchers																						
Left	.370	.396	.565	46	17	0	0	3	7	2	8	.252	.323	.395	147	37	4	1	5	15	15	40
Right	.255	.317	.433	349	89	19	2	13	49	33	31	.251	.325	.447	975	245	48	4	45	151	110	107
At Home and on the Road																						
Home	.265	.341	.460	189	50	12	2	7	27	22	21	.242	.333	.425	530	128	32	4	19	75	74	73
Road	.272	.311	.437	206	56	7	0	9	29	13	18	.260	.317	.454	592	154	20	1	31	91	51	74
Facing Groundball Pitchers and Flyball Pitchers																						
Groundball	.295	.366	.446	193	57	8	0	7	27	22	14	.270	.339	.436	571	154	25	2	22	89	61	59
Flyball	.243	.286	.450	202	49	11	2	9	29	13	25	.232	.310	.445	551	128	27	3	28	77	64	88
Facing Finesse Pitchers and Power Pitchers																						
Finesse	.274	.327	.465	226	62	13	0	10	35	19	16	.261	.326	.459	641	167	37	3	28	91	65	67
Power	.260	.324	.426	169	44	6	2	6	21	16	23	.239	.323	.416	481	115	15	2	22	75	60	80
On Grass and on Turf																						
Grass	.259	.307	.432	162	42	4	0	8	22	12	12	.264	.320	.472	470	124	14	0	28	75	41	59
Turf	.275	.339	.459	233	64	15	2	8	34	23	27	.242	.328	.417	652	158	38	5	22	91	84	88
During the Day and at Night																						
Day	.281	.341	.455	121	34	7	1	4	16	11	10	.262	.333	.429	366	96	19	3	12	59	40	50
Night	.263	.319	.445	274	72	12	1	12	40	24	29	.246	.321	.446	756	186	33	2	38	107	85	97
By Month																						
April	.000	.000	.000	12	0	0	0	0	0	0	1	.204	.301	.352	108	22	7	0	3	11	14	13
May	.207	.298	.390	82	17	3	0	4	15	11	7	.253	.314	.446	186	47	9	0	9	35	18	19
June	.294	.360	.529	68	20	4	0	4	11	7	1	.293	.364	.529	174	51	12	1	9	30	20	12
July	.241	.294	.380	79	19	3	1	2	8	6	8	.255	.333	.428	208	53	6	3	8	28	24	27
August	.317	.337	.524	82	26	6	1	3	15	3	14	.265	.321	.478	226	60	13	1	11	36	20	40
Sept/Oct	.333	.395	.500	72	24	3	0	3	7	8	8	.223	.311	.382	220	49	5	0	10	26	29	36
Situational																						
Bases Empty	.243	.298	.450	202	49	10	1	10	10	16	18	.241	.300	.446	607	146	34	2	29	29	51	80
Leadoff	.244	.295	.500	82	20	4	1	5	5	6	8	.239	.296	.433	238	57	14	1	10	10	19	26
Not Leadoff	.242	.300	.417	120	29	6	0	5	5	10	10	.241	.303	.455	369	89	20	1	19	19	32	54
Runners On	.295	.353	.446	193	57	9	1	6	46	19	21	.264	.352	.433	515	136	18	3	21	137	74	67
First Base Only	.372	.413	.570	86	32	3	1	4	10	6	8	.319	.374	.532	216	69	7	3	11	30	18	27
Scoring Position	.234	.309	.346	107	25	6	0	2	36	13	13	.224	.337	.361	299	67	11	0	10	107	56	40
Late Innings, Close	.324	.355	.437	71	23	2	0	2	9	4	5	.277	.345	.416	202	56	8	1	6	29	21	21
RBI/Opportunities																						
Scoring Position				32 / 143		(22%)									87 / 420		(21%)					
Scoring Position, 2 Out				8 / 62		(13%)									20 / 181		(11%)					
On Third, Less than 2 Out				14 / 31		(45%)									42 / 81		(52%)					
RBI in close games / RBI Total				36 / 56		(64%)									110 / 166		(66%)					

Glenn Wilson
Philadelphia Phillies

Glenn Wilson is the type of player who is highly regarded by a lot of "baseball people" but considered overrated by most sabermetricians. Wilson is sort of a junior-grade Bill Buckner: he has some power, hits for a respectable average, and drives in an impressive number of runs, but walks infrequently and uses up an enormous number of outs for the success he achieves. Not being a baseball person (I don't even own a checkered sportcoat), I was more than a little surprised to see Wilson labeled an untouchable by Bill Giles last fall. It isn't that Glenn doesn't have some attributes; he's an excellent defensive outfielder with a strong throwing arm, an aggressive player both on the bases and in the field (Clem Conly notes that Wilson frequently throws behind baserunners to catch them napping), and everyone appreciates a hitter who drives in runs. A lot of clubs could use a guy like that. But an untouchable, the kind of guy who you'd want as one of the foundations of your franchise? I don't think so.

To be fair to Wilson, he did show some signs of development last season. He increased his walk total (from 35 to 42) while cutting down on his strikeouts (from 117 to 91). And after a terrible start in which he hit only .181 through May 31, Wilson turned it on and finished with a bang, hitting over .320 during the last two months of the season. Perhaps that's the Wilson Giles was thinking of; if so, I have to point out that Glenn has never shown much consistency. In '83, while still with the Tigers, Wilson hit .281 with 44 RBI during the first half of the season, .255 with 21 during the second. In 1984 it was the same story—a fair first half, then a no homer, six RBI finish. Wilson's '85 season was up-and-down all the way through . . . so can anyone say with conviction that the last two months of 1986 represent the real Glenn Wilson? If anything, 1986 was a season in which Wilson treaded water; he came into the campaign with a lifetime batting average of .269 and a lifetime slugging mark of .415, then proceeded to hit .271 and slug .413. That's progress?

One final note about Glenn: throughout his career, even during his years with the Tigers, he's always hit much better at night than during day games. In '86 he closed the gap a little, but the difference was still pretty great. If he ever leaves the Eliot Ness ranks, I don't think the Cubs should make a bid.

—Don Zminda

| | 1986 SEASON | | | | | | | | | | | THREE YEARS (84 – 86) | | | | | | | | | | |
	Ave.	OBP	SLG	AB	H	2B	3B	HR	RBI	BB	SO	Ave.	OBP	SLG	AB	H	2B	3B	HR	RBI	BB	SO
Totals	.271	.319	.413	584	158	30	4	15	84	42	91	.265	.306	.408	1533	407	90	12	35	217	94	264
Batting vs. Left and Right-handed Pitchers																						
Left	.222	.271	.335	185	41	9	0	4	21	12	25	.256	.298	.407	481	123	34	0	13	65	30	69
Right	.293	.341	.449	399	117	21	4	11	63	30	66	.270	.310	.409	1052	284	56	12	22	152	64	195
At Home and on the Road																						
Home	.302	.357	.467	285	86	22	2	7	40	24	41	.286	.330	.445	746	213	48	7	19	120	51	118
Road	.241	.283	.361	299	72	8	2	8	44	18	50	.247	.284	.374	787	194	42	5	16	97	43	146
Facing Groundball Pitchers and Flyball Pitchers																						
Groundball	.275	.321	.368	280	77	15	1	3	39	20	47	.278	.314	.386	712	198	37	5	10	97	39	104
Flyball	.266	.317	.454	304	81	15	3	12	45	22	44	.255	.300	.428	821	209	53	7	25	120	55	160
Facing Finesse Pitchers and Power Pitchers																						
Finesse	.248	.273	.386	303	75	12	3	8	45	13	36	.266	.298	.412	832	221	42	10	20	124	42	124
Power	.295	.366	.441	281	83	18	1	7	39	29	55	.265	.316	.404	701	186	48	2	15	93	52	140
On Grass and on Turf																						
Grass	.221	.251	.313	163	36	5	2	2	20	5	25	.235	.268	.353	408	96	19	4	7	44	17	77
Turf	.290	.344	.451	421	122	25	2	13	64	37	66	.276	.320	.428	1125	311	71	8	28	173	77	187
During the Day and at Night																						
Day	.247	.286	.404	178	44	9	2	5	26	11	25	.246	.290	.402	492	121	26	3	15	66	33	85
Night	.281	.333	.416	406	114	21	2	10	58	31	66	.275	.314	.411	1041	286	64	9	20	151	61	179
By Month																						
April	.161	.260	.177	62	10	1	0	0	4	8	9	.228	.283	.371	202	46	9	4	4	30	16	34
May	.194	.260	.323	93	18	3	0	3	15	8	15	.240	.276	.357	263	63	14	1	5	34	13	53
June	.308	.341	.470	117	36	10	0	3	17	6	21	.279	.317	.476	269	75	22	2	9	48	15	51
July	.247	.316	.424	85	21	3	0	4	12	10	10	.244	.298	.370	270	66	11	1	7	31	22	36
August	.316	.344	.513	117	37	7	2	4	20	4	14	.284	.328	.436	264	75	15	2	7	37	17	43
Sept/Oct	.327	.362	.445	110	36	6	2	1	16	6	22	.309	.332	.430	265	82	19	2	3	37	11	47
Situational																						
Bases Empty	.260	.315	.405	311	81	20	2	7	7	25	45	.267	.315	.396	820	219	54	5	14	14	57	141
Leadoff	.246	.308	.402	122	30	8	1	3	3	11	19	.286	.337	.419	339	97	24	3	5	5	26	57
Not Leadoff	.270	.320	.407	189	51	12	1	4	4	14	26	.254	.299	.380	481	122	30	2	9	9	31	84
Runners On	.282	.323	.421	273	77	10	2	8	77	17	46	.264	.297	.422	713	188	36	7	21	203	37	123
First Base Only	.263	.294	.368	114	30	4	1	2	7	4	17	.244	.273	.376	303	74	15	2	7	22	11	49
Scoring Position	.296	.342	.459	159	47	6	1	6	70	13	29	.278	.314	.456	410	114	21	5	14	181	26	74
Late Innings, Close	.320	.379	.408	103	33	6	0	1	11	9	17	.283	.331	.412	272	77	17	0	6	32	19	57

RBI/Opportunities				
Scoring Position	58 / 209	(28%)	145 / 551	(26%)
Scoring Position, 2 Out	19 / 95	(20%)	49 / 252	(19%)
On Third, Less than 2 Out	21 / 34	(62%)	57 / 100	(57%)
RBI in close games / RBI Total	60 / 84	(71%)	155 / 217	(71%)

Mookie Wilson
New York Mets

If there is a player on the Mets who best exemplifies the transition from the old to the new, it is Mookie Wilson. During bad times and good Wilson was amazingly consistent, hitting in the .270s for five straight seasons, including .276 three years in succession (1983–85). Eventually a shoulder problem forced Mookie to undergo surgery during the '85 season, and during Wilson's two-month absense the now-fabled Lenny Dykstra got his first taste of major league ball. Dykstra, who worked for walks in the leadoff role, highlighted Mookie's shortcomings in that area. But the Mook is a good student and seemed to learn something from watching Lenny while he recuperated. When he returned to action he began drawing more walks than ever before, and as he showed in his crucial tenth inning at-bat in the sixth game of the '86 Series, learned to foul off borderline pitches as well. Though forced into a platoon role during most of '86, Mookie played some of the best ball of his career; he batted a personal-best .289 and had a career-high in slugging as well with .430.

A dangerous low-ball hitter, Wilson has usually hit better for average and power from the left side. In recent seasons his stats have been more even, however, and in '85-'86 he hit seven of his fifteen homers from the right side. He's a good bad-ball hitter, possibly because of the slapping thrust of his swing, but has problems with the good slider; don't we all? On the bases Wilson is very dangerous, with the capability of rattling the opposition with his speed. In '86 he was typically excellent, with 25 steals in 32 attempts, but the stolen bases came in streaks. Early on he stole 11 bases in the space of 69 at bats and later, in early August, had 6 steals in 46 at bats. For the rest of the year, however, he stole only 8 in 266 ABs.

Defensively, Mookie is only adequate. While his speed allows him to get to a lot of balls, he has trouble going back on long flies and his arm, which was never better than average, has been very suspect ever since his shoulder injury. Still, he's a decent enough center fielder to platoon with Dykstra, and can fill in well in left. Unless he's traded, he figures to be the fourth outfielder behind McReynolds, Dykstra and Strawberry. If he plays as he has in the past, he'll do well in that role.

—David Gordon and Jay Gregory

	1986 SEASON											THREE YEARS (84 – 86)										
	Ave.	OBP	SLG	AB	H	2B	3B	HR	RBI	BB	SO	Ave.	OBP	SLG	AB	H	2B	3B	HR	RBI	BB	SO
Totals	.289	.345	.430	381	110	17	5	9	45	32	72	.280	.325	.419	1305	365	61	23	25	125	86	214
Batting vs. Left and Right-handed Pitchers																						
Left	.291	.341	.418	196	57	6	5	3	23	15	37	.287	.334	.445	544	156	27	13	11	56	40	89
Right	.286	.348	.443	185	53	11	0	6	22	17	35	.275	.318	.401	761	209	34	10	14	69	46	125
At Home and on the Road																						
Home	.289	.351	.422	173	50	9	1	4	17	17	32	.293	.342	.435	634	186	35	8	13	64	47	101
Road	.288	.339	.438	208	60	8	4	5	28	15	40	.267	.309	.404	671	179	26	15	12	61	39	113
Facing Groundball Pitchers and Flyball Pitchers																						
Groundball	.283	.332	.450	191	54	7	2	7	27	13	32	.287	.331	.422	642	184	30	9	13	61	41	90
Flyball	.295	.357	.411	190	56	10	3	2	18	19	40	.273	.318	.416	663	181	31	14	12	64	45	124
Facing Finesse Pitchers and Power Pitchers																						
Finesse	.274	.307	.402	219	60	10	3	4	16	10	38	.288	.328	.422	742	214	33	15	12	69	43	101
Power	.309	.391	.469	162	50	7	2	5	29	22	34	.268	.321	.416	563	151	28	8	13	56	43	113
On Grass and on Turf																						
Grass	.313	.367	.454	262	82	11	4	6	35	23	43	.292	.340	.427	903	264	44	12	18	96	65	138
Turf	.235	.295	.378	119	28	6	1	3	10	9	29	.251	.291	.400	402	101	17	11	7	29	21	76
During the Day and at Night																						
Day	.278	.336	.383	133	37	4	2	2	18	12	22	.273	.322	.395	484	132	22	8	7	37	35	82
Night	.294	.349	.456	248	73	13	3	7	27	20	50	.284	.326	.434	821	233	39	15	18	88	51	132
By Month																						
April	.000	.000	.000	0	0	0	0	0	0	0	0	.271	.302	.361	133	36	6	3	0	10	6	18
May	.273	.365	.436	55	15	2	2	1	5	8	8	.301	.350	.419	229	69	10	4	3	15	17	29
June	.298	.322	.476	84	25	6	0	3	7	3	19	.257	.280	.393	280	72	11	0	9	26	8	50
July	.298	.355	.421	57	17	1	0	2	7	5	11	.266	.319	.403	154	41	6	3	3	16	11	28
August	.330	.400	.489	94	31	5	2	2	17	10	14	.305	.354	.469	213	65	15	4	4	27	15	35
Sept/Oct	.242	.286	.330	91	22	3	1	1	9	6	20	.277	.337	.443	296	82	13	9	6	31	29	54
Situational																						
Bases Empty	.270	.316	.385	252	68	10	2	5	5	16	58	.280	.326	.422	820	230	40	14	16	16	53	144
Leadoff	.262	.316	.440	141	37	6	2	5	5	10	31	.272	.329	.442	389	106	19	7	11	11	31	65
Not Leadoff	.279	.316	.315	111	31	4	0	0	0	6	27	.288	.322	.404	431	124	21	7	5	5	22	79
Runners On	.326	.397	.519	129	42	7	3	4	40	16	14	.278	.323	.414	485	135	21	9	9	109	33	70
First Base Only	.264	.291	.528	53	14	3	1	3	8	2	7	.276	.298	.437	199	55	8	3	6	17	6	26
Scoring Position	.368	.462	.513	76	28	4	2	1	32	14	7	.280	.340	.399	286	80	13	6	3	92	27	44
Late Innings, Close	.268	.318	.378	82	22	4	1	1	14	6	22	.269	.335	.420	238	64	10	4	6	28	24	47

RBI/Opportunities				
Scoring Position	30 / 108	(28%)	83 / 372	(22%)
Scoring Position, 2 Out	9 / 46	(20%)	34 / 175	(19%)
On Third, Less than 2 Out	12 / 20	(60%)	28 / 58	(48%)
RBI in close games / RBI Total	30 / 45	(67%)	76 / 125	(61%)

Willie Wilson
Kansas City Royals

I remember when I first thought that Willie Wilson was going to be a ball player. It was the fourth game of the 1978 ALCS, when he stood in against Ron Guidry and promptly fell behind 0–2. You did not fall behind Guidry in those days and survive, but damn if Willie didn't line the next pitch up the middle for a hit. In baseball parlance, he showed me something.

Prior to that moment, there was some reason to think that Willie was just another designated rabbit, á la Herb Washington. Used sparingly by Herzog during the '78 season, he banjo hit for a robust .217. But then came that at bat in the playoffs, and in '79 he raised plenty of eyebrows by hitting .315, leading the league in steals, and circling the bases for in-house four baggers with at least some frequency. When in '80 he raised the average to .326 and led the league in runs scored, it seemed as though another superstar had arrived.

But all the while there was a time bomb ticking in Willie's future. It was ticking as he wore the goat horns for the '80 Series. It was still ticking when he won the '82 batting title, and it began to detonate in '83, and no, I'm not talking about the drug scandal: the real time bomb was Willie's strikeout to walk ratio. It started out bad (in his first two years as a regular 173 strikeouts, 56 walks), and has never gotten appreciably better. By 1983, opposing pitchers were beginning to master the art of getting Willie out without throwing strikes. In contrast, Rickey Henderson and Tim Raines had K/W ratios of 148/233 and 153/172, respectively, in their first two seasons. As recently as 1984, Wilson, Henderson and Raines were considered players of approximately equal ability. Now the latter two are legitimate stars, while Wilson . . . well, he continues to strike out and neglects to walk, and a speed-burner with little power simply cannot perform that way and expect to excel over the long haul. Omar Moreno and Marvell Wynne have already discovered this, and chances are Willie McGee is in the process. So Wilson's average continues to stagnate. He shows occasional power and is still terrific defensively: he's a good, useful player. But Henderson and Raines are on a collision course with the Hall of Fame, and there are days when you have to ask yourself why isn't, why couldn't, Wilson be on the same course?

—Mike Kopf

	1986 SEASON											THREE YEARS (84 – 86)										
	Ave.	OBP	SLG	AB	H	2B	3B	HR	RBI	BB	SO	Ave.	OBP	SLG	AB	H	2B	3B	HR	RBI	BB	SO
Totals	.269	.313	.366	631	170	20	7	9	44	31	97	.282	.325	.388	1777	501	69	37	15	131	98	247
Batting vs. Left and Right-handed Pitchers																						
Left	.309	.328	.429	175	54	5	2	4	11	4	33	.314	.344	.429	506	159	24	8	6	37	23	75
Right	.254	.307	.342	456	116	15	5	5	33	27	64	.269	.317	.371	1271	342	45	29	9	94	75	172
At Home and on the Road																						
Home	.265	.322	.379	309	82	8	6	5	19	20	40	.280	.330	.393	871	244	27	25	7	66	54	110
Road	.273	.303	.354	322	88	12	1	4	25	11	57	.284	.320	.383	906	257	42	12	8	65	44	137
Facing Groundball Pitchers and Flyball Pitchers																						
Groundball	.272	.309	.354	302	82	10	3	3	23	12	45	.294	.336	.394	831	244	34	17	5	61	47	103
Flyball	.267	.315	.377	329	88	10	4	6	21	19	52	.272	.315	.383	946	257	35	20	10	70	51	144
Facing Finesse Pitchers and Power Pitchers																						
Finesse	.286	.321	.389	391	112	16	6	4	22	16	50	.288	.328	.400	1028	296	42	23	9	72	56	111
Power	.242	.299	.329	240	58	4	1	5	22	15	47	.274	.320	.371	749	205	27	14	6	59	42	136
On Grass and on Turf																						
Grass	.272	.310	.343	239	65	9	1	2	17	11	48	.287	.324	.390	682	196	33	11	5	45	34	105
Turf	.268	.314	.380	392	105	11	6	7	27	20	49	.279	.325	.386	1095	305	36	26	10	86	64	142
During the Day and at Night																						
Day	.280	.311	.439	157	44	5	1	6	15	6	24	.282	.321	.412	422	119	15	8	8	38	22	61
Night	.266	.313	.342	474	126	15	6	3	29	25	73	.282	.326	.380	1355	382	54	29	7	93	76	186
By Month																						
April	.211	.247	.263	76	16	1	0	1	8	2	12	.272	.318	.373	158	43	3	5	1	14	7	27
May	.280	.336	.381	118	33	3	0	3	10	8	17	.262	.310	.381	294	77	12	4	5	19	18	40
June	.274	.339	.372	113	31	3	4	0	5	10	19	.283	.338	.383	329	93	12	9	1	22	26	46
July	.238	.292	.352	105	25	5	2	1	7	6	16	.294	.339	.398	357	105	13	6	4	28	21	40
August	.294	.319	.358	109	32	4	0	1	6	2	15	.294	.329	.389	347	102	10	10	1	30	15	50
Sept/Oct	.300	.319	.436	110	33	4	1	3	8	3	18	.277	.305	.394	292	81	19	3	3	18	11	44
Situational																						
Bases Empty	.270	.315	.379	396	107	12	5	7	7	18	68	.274	.316	.382	1151	315	43	26	10	10	61	169
Leadoff	.230	.269	.342	187	43	5	2	4	4	8	31	.262	.310	.380	621	163	23	16	6	6	38	91
Not Leadoff	.306	.356	.411	209	64	7	3	3	3	10	37	.287	.324	.385	530	152	20	10	4	4	23	78
Runners On	.268	.308	.345	235	63	8	2	2	37	13	29	.297	.340	.398	626	186	26	11	5	121	37	78
First Base Only	.255	.298	.367	98	25	6	1	1	3	6	11	.304	.336	.407	273	83	12	5	2	10	11	34
Scoring Position	.277	.315	.328	137	38	2	1	1	34	7	18	.292	.343	.391	353	103	14	6	3	111	26	44
Late Innings, Close	.303	.337	.354	99	30	1	2	0	12	5	18	.289	.326	.352	273	79	7	5	0	28	14	39

RBI/Opportunities			
Scoring Position	32 / 163	(20%)	101 / 430	(23%)
Scoring Position, 2 Out	10 / 80	(13%)	33 / 206	(16%)
On Third, Less than 2 Out	13 / 24	(54%)	48 / 77	(62%)
RBI in close games / RBI Total	29 / 44	(66%)	90 / 131	(69%)

Dave Winfield
New York Yankees

Dave Winfield hit .299 over the second half of the season to bring his average up to a respectable .262. It was a surprising achievement, since he had hit better in the second half only once before in his career with the Yankees—in those five years, he'd hit .303 before the break and .285 after it. It shows something about Winfield's desire, too. He had gotten off to a terrible start and taken a lot of heat from all sides. Fans quietly wondered if his career was nearing its end—the owner did so publicly—but Dave silenced them all. The amazing thing about Winfield's 1986 is that, despite all the garbage he had to put up with, he still wants to play in New York. He became the first Yankee since DiMaggio to get 100 RBIs in five straight years in 1986; you'd never have known it by listening to the team or the media.

One of the persistent complaints about Winfield was that he was a key reason why the Yankees couldn't beat a left-hander in 1986. It's true in a way, but it really isn't fair. Winfield hits lefties very well—it's just that he doesn't hit them as well as most righties do. A typical player hits about 35 points better with the platoon edge and slugs 70 points higher; Winfield isn't a typical player. In six seasons with New York, he has hit .283 against southpaws and .292 against normal people, though he hits with much more power (24 homers per 600 at-bats against righties and 34 against lefties). Winfield carries his share of the load, but he doesn't pick up enough slack to make up for the batters who get tied in knots. People shouldn't blame Dave, but it's hard to behave rationally if you've just been two-hit by a lefty fresh from the Yonkers Slo-Pitch Softball Association.

Winfield's range is starting to slip, but he's still a master at taking homers away from opposing hitters. There aren't many 6'6" rightfielders in the league; Dave uses every inch. He unquestionably wins games with his glove, by making catches that would either have been hard or impossible for a normal player. On June 12, in Baltimore, he took homers away from Lee Lacy and Mike Young, saving Alfonso Pulido three runs—New York won by two. Winfield does receive credit for this in New York; it's too bad that the compliments usually run something like "Sure he's a great fielder, but . . . ."

—Craig Christmann

	1986 SEASON												THREE YEARS (84 – 86)										
	Ave.	OBP	SLG	AB	H	2B	3B	HR	RBI	BB	SO		Ave.	OBP	SLG	AB	H	2B	3B	HR	RBI	BB	SO
Totals	.262	.349	.462	565	148	31	5	24	104	77	106		.292	.356	.482	1765	515	99	15	69	318	182	273
Batting vs. Left and Right-handed Pitchers																							
Left	.259	.373	.523	197	51	10	3	12	41	37	29		.275	.368	.490	582	160	28	8	27	106	90	74
Right	.264	.336	.429	368	97	21	2	12	63	40	77		.300	.349	.478	1183	355	71	7	42	212	92	199
At Home and on the Road																							
Home	.272	.362	.477	279	76	15	3	12	56	40	46		.295	.367	.496	837	247	46	7	36	168	98	115
Road	.252	.336	.448	286	72	16	2	12	48	37	60		.289	.345	.470	928	268	53	8	33	150	84	158
Facing Groundball Pitchers and Flyball Pitchers																							
Groundball	.276	.370	.455	268	74	14	2	10	44	40	51		.287	.356	.443	867	249	47	8	24	141	94	143
Flyball	.249	.330	.468	297	74	17	3	14	60	37	55		.296	.356	.520	898	266	52	7	45	177	88	130
Facing Finesse Pitchers and Power Pitchers																							
Finesse	.265	.347	.440	302	80	13	2	12	54	38	53		.297	.351	.460	974	289	52	7	31	158	83	128
Power	.259	.352	.487	263	68	18	3	12	50	39	53		.286	.362	.509	791	226	47	8	38	160	99	145
On Grass and on Turf																							
Grass	.265	.355	.483	476	126	28	5	22	97	68	87		.294	.360	.493	1496	440	85	13	62	283	160	223
Turf	.247	.316	.348	89	22	3	0	2	7	9	19		.279	.333	.424	269	75	14	2	7	35	22	50
During the Day and at Night																							
Day	.300	.403	.583	180	54	11	2	12	40	30	33		.309	.372	.520	563	174	26	6	27	108	58	83
Night	.244	.323	.405	385	94	20	3	12	64	47	73		.284	.348	.464	1202	341	73	9	42	210	124	190
By Month																							
April	.274	.411	.425	73	20	6	1	1	10	17	15		.272	.362	.428	180	49	9	2	5	19	26	30
May	.211	.316	.474	95	20	5	1	6	21	16	18		.255	.313	.461	310	79	19	3	13	55	28	45
June	.212	.322	.414	99	21	3	1	5	16	16	22		.345	.392	.518	307	106	16	2	11	57	25	47
July	.338	.400	.597	77	26	6	1	4	19	7	12		.307	.373	.525	280	86	18	2	13	57	29	37
August	.288	.357	.423	104	30	5	0	3	13	11	16		.298	.378	.491	326	97	15	3	14	61	42	52
Sept/Oct	.265	.320	.462	117	31	6	1	5	25	10	23		.271	.325	.456	362	98	22	3	13	69	32	62
Situational																							
Bases Empty	.254	.343	.430	272	69	18	0	10	10	36	58		.286	.345	.465	860	246	57	2	31	31	76	147
Leadoff	.265	.368	.436	117	31	8	0	4	4	18	23		.319	.380	.487	357	114	27	0	11	11	34	60
Not Leadoff	.245	.324	.426	155	38	10	0	6	6	18	35		.262	.319	.449	503	132	30	2	20	20	42	87
Runners On	.270	.355	.491	293	79	13	5	14	94	41	48		.297	.366	.498	905	269	42	13	38	287	106	126
First Base Only	.236	.319	.520	123	29	5	3	8	20	14	13		.272	.330	.469	390	106	17	6	16	42	33	42
Scoring Position	.294	.379	.471	170	50	8	2	6	74	27	35		.317	.391	.520	515	163	25	7	22	245	73	84
Late Innings, Close	.238	.305	.345	84	20	3	0	2	11	9	20		.271	.327	.426	277	75	11	1	10	42	24	53

RBI/Opportunities					
Scoring Position	64 / 237	(27%)		209 / 702	(30%)
Scoring Position, 2 Out	25 / 116	(22%)		69 / 298	(23%)
On Third, Less than 2 Out	28 / 46	(61%)		89 / 151	(59%)
RBI in close games / RBI Total	53 / 104	(51%)		201 / 318	(63%)

Mike Witt
California Angels

A fine pitcher for several years, Mike Witt in 1986 developed the consistency to be listed as one of the three or four top starters in the American League—and arguably the best.

It would require more space than we have here to detail all of the things that Witt does well:

1) He throws strikes.

2) He strikes people out.

3) Despite his large, rather ungainly frame, he is extremely tough to run against, with only five runners stealing bases against him and ten men caught stealing in 1986.

4) He dominates the first hitter up against him in an inning, holding leadoff hitters to a .183 batting average and .246 on base percentage (1986 data).

5) He remains very strong in the late innings, with opponents hitting just .217 against him in the late innings of close games over the last three years.

Having taken a few shots about not pitching up to his "potential" in recent years, Witt in 1986 responded by stonewalling the press to get even. One must hope that he will outgrow that attitude, and we should remember that although he's been around for years he is very young, two years younger than Teddy Higuera or Orel Hershiser.

Witt usually starts slowly, with a 10–14 record in the first two months (April and May, 1984–86), but then pours it on with a 30–10 record in the hot-weather months of June, July and August. He followed this pattern in 1986, going 12–3 those three months, 6–7 the other three. Like most power pitchers, he is much more effective at night than in day games, with a 2.92 ERA in night games over the last three years, as opposed to 4.15 in day games.

Witt has 71 career wins, an impressive total at his age (26 at the end of last season).

With one of the best breaking pitches in the league, Witt is tough on right-handed hitters, holding them to a .224 average over the last three years, but a hardly a pushover for lefties, either. Under Boone's direction, he works the inside and the outside part of the plate, up and down with curve balls and fastballs, and he changes speeds. His fastball isn't overpowering; it's just hard to catch up with in the middle of the pattern. And if he gets the hitters 0–2 or 1–2 and can throw the curve ball over, he's got a K.

—Bill James, Kent Kirchstien and Kenneth Houghton

1986: Power, Groundball   **1985: Power, Groundball**   **1984: Power, Groundball**

	1986 SEASON											THREE YEARS (84 – 86)										
	G	IP	H	BB	SO	SB	CS	W	L	S	ERA	G	IP	H	BB	SO	SB	CS	W	L	S	ERA
Totals	34	269.0	218	73	208	5	10	18	10	0	2.84	103	765.2	673	255	584	40	34	48	30	0	3.28
At Home and on the Road																						
Home	17	141.0	106	37	114	1	4	11	5	0	2.62	50	384.0	316	123	294	12	19	27	15	0	2.88
Road	17	128.0	112	36	94	4	6	7	5	0	3.09	53	381.2	357	132	290	28	15	21	15	0	3.68
During the Day and at Night																						
Day	12	90.0	82	31	71	1	4	6	5	0	4.40	31	223.1	195	85	175	9	10	15	10	0	4.15
Night	22	179.0	136	42	137	4	6	12	5	0	2.06	72	542.1	478	170	409	31	24	33	20	0	2.92
On Grass and on Turf																						
Grass	30	238.2	196	69	177	3	7	17	9	0	2.83	88	657.1	568	232	495	33	28	43	27	0	3.20
Turf	4	30.1	22	4	31	2	3	1	1	0	2.97	15	108.1	105	23	89	7	6	5	3	0	3.74
By Month																						
April	5	34.0	31	9	31	3	1	2	1	0	2.91	16	115.0	95	46	84	6	4	6	5	0	3.37
May	5	42.0	37	18	30	1	1	2	3	0	3.43	15	106.0	109	49	75	6	5	4	9	0	4.16
June	6	50.0	47	13	40	0	3	4	2	0	3.42	18	140.2	127	42	117	8	6	11	5	0	2.88
July	6	48.2	39	11	39	1	3	3	1	0	2.59	17	138.2	115	44	109	5	8	9	2	0	2.79
August	5	43.0	17	8	28	0	0	5	0	0	0.21	16	122.0	100	35	87	5	5	10	3	0	2.36
Sept/Oct	7	51.1	47	14	40	0	2	2	3	0	4.21	21	143.1	127	39	112	10	6	8	6	0	4.21

vs. Opponent Batters

	1986 SEASON											THREE YEARS (84 – 86)										
	Ave.	OBP	SLG	AB	H	2B	3B	HR	RBI	BB	SO	Ave.	OBP	SLG	AB	H	2B	3B	HR	RBI	BB	SO
Totals	.221	.275	.335	987	218	39	4	22	89	73	208	.236	.300	.350	2854	673	112	16	61	272	255	584
Pitching vs. Left and Right-handed Batters																						
Left	.215	.270	.339	578	124	23	2	15	49	43	104	.245	.307	.360	1640	401	64	10	35	154	141	292
Right	.230	.282	.330	409	94	16	2	7	40	30	104	.224	.290	.338	1214	272	48	6	26	118	114	292
Situational																						
Bases Empty	.210	.263	.305	623	131	23	3	10	10	43	141	.231	.293	.335	1742	402	62	9	34	34	144	386
Leadoff	.183	.242	.265	257	47	7	1	4	4	20	59	.225	.288	.325	733	165	19	3	16	16	63	158
Not Leadoff	.230	.279	.333	366	84	16	2	6	6	23	82	.235	.296	.343	1009	237	43	6	18	18	81	228
Runners On	.239	.295	.387	364	87	16	1	12	79	30	67	.244	.310	.374	1112	271	50	7	27	238	111	198
First Base Only	.217	.267	.333	189	41	10	0	4	13	12	36	.241	.296	.370	543	131	29	4	11	40	39	90
Scoring Position	.263	.323	.446	175	46	6	1	8	66	18	31	.246	.323	.378	569	140	21	3	16	198	72	108
Late Innings, Close	.223	.281	.331	157	35	5	0	4	20	11	28	.217	.300	.337	374	81	10	1	11	37	42	69

RBI/Opportunities

	1986 SEASON		THREE YEARS (84 – 86)	
Scoring Position	49 / 233	(21%)	167 / 776	(22%)
Scoring Position, 2 Out	24 / 106	(23%)	69 / 347	(20%)
On Third, Less than 2 Out	16 / 40	(40%)	63 / 137	(46%)
RBI in close games / RBI Total	62 / 89	(70%)	189 / 272	(69%)

Todd Worrell
St. Louis Cardinals

It seems that when a pitcher compiles a high save total, he usually does it with a mediocre team. Todd Worrell's 36 saves in 1986 and Bruce Sutter's 45 in 1984 are two such examples. Of course this isn't always the case; Sutter in '82 and Dan Quisenberry in '85 had 36 and 37 saves, respectively, and both pitched for World Champions. But on the whole, high save totals have not meant successful team records. There have been eleven occasions in the eighties in which a pitcher has recorded 35 or more saves. The eleven teams won an average of 84.6 games, for a .522 winning percentage. Each time it happens, as with Worrell in '86, you hear or read some sportswriter or sportscaster asking the same question: how many saves could he have had playing with a contender? And each year the answer is the same: probably no more than he had with a noncontender. What these people fail to understand is that in order to record a high number of saves you have to be involved in a high number of relatively close games. And the better the team is, the less likely that is to happen. The Mets with 108 wins and the Cardinals with 79 each had team totals of 46 saves

in 1986. The Mets did have better starting pitching, but even if you subtract complete games the Mets had saves in 57% of their wins, the Cardinals in 74% of theirs (not all complete games are wins, but most are in the NL).

Of course, playing on a bad team would also make it difficult to accumulate a high save total. The worst record of the eleven teams mentioned was that of the 1984 Oakland A's (77–85), whose Bill Caudill recorded 36 saves. The best type of team for a pitcher looking for a high number of saves, then, is one that wins but doesn't dominate. The Kansas City Royals have been a good example of such a team, and it's probably no coincidence that Quisenberry owns four of the eleven 35-plus save totals. While you have to give him most of the credit, it's also true that Quiz has usually been in the ideal situation to post high save totals.

A final note on Worrell: he wasn't the first rookie to play in a World Series the season before he was named Rookie of the Year. Steve Sax also did it, getting into one game of the '81 Series before being named the NL's top rookie of 1982.

—Russ Eagle

1986: Power, Flyball   **1985: Power, Flyball**   **1984: Did not play**

	1986 SEASON												THREE YEARS (84 – 86)											
	G	IP	H	BB	SO	SB	CS	W	L	S	ERA		G	IP	H	BB	SO	SB	CS	W	L	S	ERA
Totals	74	103.2	86	41	73	9	6	9	10	36	2.08		91	125.1	103	48	90	10	6	12	10	41	2.23
At Home and on the Road
Home	37	54.2	43	17	32	4	4	6	5	17	1.65		48	67.0	52	21	43	5	4	8	5	20	2.15
Road	37	49.0	43	24	41	5	2	3	5	19	2.57		43	58.1	51	27	47	5	2	4	5	21	2.31
During the Day and at Night
Day	28	38.2	31	25	27	3	1	3	5	13	2.09		35	47.1	40	30	35	3	1	4	5	16	2.47
Night	46	65.0	55	16	46	6	5	6	5	23	2.08		56	78.0	63	18	55	7	5	8	5	25	2.08
On Grass and on Turf
Grass	21	26.1	25	9	19	3	1	2	3	9	3.08		23	30.2	28	11	24	3	1	2	3	10	2.93
Turf	53	77.1	61	32	54	6	5	7	7	27	1.75		68	94.2	75	37	66	7	5	10	7	31	2.00
By Month
April	9	16.2	11	15	7	3	0	1	1	3	1.08		9	16.2	11	15	7	3	0	1	1	3	1.08
May	11	17.0	15	3	9	1	2	2	2	3	1.59		11	17.0	15	3	9	1	2	2	2	3	1.59
June	17	22.0	19	13	24	2	2	2	5	7	2.05		17	22.0	19	13	24	2	2	2	5	7	2.05
July	12	15.1	7	4	10	1	0	1	0	8	1.17		12	15.1	7	4	10	1	0	1	0	8	1.17
August	13	14.2	18	3	7	0	1	2	1	8	3.68		14	16.1	19	3	7	0	1	2	1	8	3.31
Sept/Oct	12	18.0	16	3	16	2	1	1	1	7	3.00		28	38.0	32	10	33	3	1	4	1	12	3.08

	1986 SEASON										THREE YEARS (84 – 86)									
	Ave.	OBP	SLG	AB	H	2B	3B	HR	RBI	BB	SO	Ave.	OBP	SLG	AB	H	2B	3B	HR	RBI	BB	SO

vs. Opponent Batters

	Ave.	OBP	SLG	AB	H	2B	3B	HR	RBI	BB	SO		Ave.	OBP	SLG	AB	H	2B	3B	HR	RBI	BB	SO
Totals	.229	.303	.352	375	86	17	1	9	39	41	73		.227	.297	.361	454	103	22	3	11	51	48	90
Pitching vs. Left and Right-handed Batters
Left	.265	.352	.425	181	48	6	1	7	22	26	36		.255	.335	.425	212	54	8	2	8	26	27	43
Right	.196	.254	.284	194	38	11	0	2	17	15	37		.202	.264	.306	242	49	14	1	3	25	21	47
Situational
Bases Empty	.280	.337	.434	175	49	15	0	4	4	14	34		.272	.328	.447	217	59	18	1	6	6	17	39
Leadoff	.329	.388	.534	73	24	6	0	3	3	7	8		.319	.374	.538	91	29	8	0	4	4	8	10
Not Leadoff	.245	.300	.363	102	25	9	0	1	1	7	26		.238	.294	.381	126	30	10	1	2	2	9	29
Runners On	.185	.275	.280	200	37	2	1	5	35	27	39		.186	.272	.283	237	44	4	2	5	45	31	51
First Base Only	.194	.217	.284	67	13	0	0	2	4	2	9		.197	.228	.276	76	15	0	0	2	4	3	12
Scoring Position	.180	.299	.278	133	24	2	1	3	31	25	30		.180	.289	.286	161	29	4	2	3	41	28	39
Late Innings, Close	.226	.297	.335	319	72	12	1	7	37	35	62		.226	.292	.343	359	81	14	2	8	45	37	71

RBI/Opportunities

Scoring Position	25 / 191	(13%)		34 / 236	(14%)
Scoring Position, 2 Out	9 / 91	(10%)		10 / 110	(9%)
On Third, Less than 2 Out	9 / 30	(30%)		15 / 42	(36%)
RBI in close games / RBI Total	37 / 39	(95%)		47 / 51	(92%)

Floyd Youmans
Montreal Expos

Floyd Youmans has the stuff to be a big winner, just like his boyhood buddy Dwight Gooden. In 1986 Youmans displayed enormous potential, striking out 202 batters in 219 innings and holding his opponents to a meager .189 batting average. I see only three things standing between him and stardom: the Expos' sinking fortunes, Floyd's problems with opposing base-stealers and his penchant for giving up walks. Youmans can't do much about the first problem, but he can certainly help the other two. Fastball pitchers with high leg kicks generally have difficulty keeping runners on first, but hardly anybody has as much trouble as Youmans—any way you look at it, 56 steals in 63 attempts is much too much. Even worse, the problem affected his pitching, as Floyd was much less effective with a runner on first base only than in any other situation. Youmans might do well to emulate Gooden and devote some time to working on his move; even a small improvement, such as that shown by Gooden, would be a big help to him.

As for the walks, Youmans has already shown some progress. I saw him pitch against the Cubs early last year and he was simply pathetic, going 2–0 on six of the first seven batters and eventually getting knocked out after three innings. That was fairly typical of his work at the time, but as the season wore on his control got better: he averaged 4.8 walks per nine innings for the year, but only 4.2 after June and 4.0 in September-October. It's not easy to win while giving up a lot of walks, but it's possible. Bob Feller, for example, gave up over 100 walks nine times, Early Wynn eight, Wes Ferrell and Hal Newhouser seven, Bob Lemon six, and the alltime king, Nolan Ryan, eleven. And it wasn't just a case of them being wild early in their careers and then settling down. Wynn gave up over a hundred walks four years in a row starting at age 37, including 119 in 1959, when he went 22–10 and won the Cy Young award. In general, most of these guys were at their best when they got their walk levels down to around four a game . . . and that's the direction Youmans seems headed.

If Floyd needs any further inspiration, I could point that his 1986 season was extremely similar to another young hurler's back in 1961. Floyd was 13–12, 3.53, with 118 walks in 219 IP, the other guy 13–12, 3.24, with 119 walks in 211. The other guy's name was Bob Gibson.

—Don Zminda

1986: Power, Flyball   **1985: Power, Flyball**   **1984: Did not play**

	G	IP	H	BB	SO	SB	CS	W	L	S	ERA		G	IP	H	BB	SO	SB	CS	W	L	S	ERA
				1986 SEASON												**THREE YEARS (84 – 86)**							
Totals	33	219.0	145	118	202	56	7	13	12	0	3.53		47	296.0	202	167	256	77	8	17	15	0	3.25
												At Home and on the Road											
Home	17	112.2	72	66	109	30	2	6	9	0	4.15		22	146.2	93	87	133	40	3	6	11	0	3.74
Road	16	106.1	73	52	93	26	5	7	3	0	2.88		25	149.1	109	80	123	37	5	11	4	0	2.77
												During the Day and at Night											
Day	11	67.1	42	37	59	17	1	5	3	0	3.21		18	107.0	75	61	83	26	1	7	4	0	2.94
Night	22	151.2	103	81	143	39	6	8	9	0	3.68		29	189.0	127	106	173	51	7	10	11	0	3.43
												On Grass and on Turf											
Grass	8	54.2	38	31	39	12	4	4	1	0	2.96		12	75.2	60	44	50	14	4	6	2	0	2.85
Turf	25	164.1	107	87	163	44	3	9	11	0	3.72		35	220.1	142	123	206	63	4	11	13	0	3.39
												By Month											
April	4	15.2	15	15	15	9	0	0	2	0	6.89		4	15.2	15	15	15	9	0	0	2	0	6.89
May	6	34.2	28	19	25	10	1	4	2	0	5.19		6	34.2	28	19	25	10	1	4	2	0	5.19
June	6	39.1	29	23	35	9	1	3	1	0	2.97		6	39.1	29	23	35	9	1	3	1	0	2.97
July	5	39.0	18	19	40	13	1	3	1	0	2.08		8	50.2	27	27	52	16	1	4	1	0	2.13
August	5	36.0	30	18	26	6	3	1	3	0	3.50		9	62.1	49	30	44	15	4	1	4	0	2.60
Sept/Oct	7	54.1	25	24	61	9	1	2	3	0	2.98		14	93.1	54	53	85	18	1	5	5	0	3.09

vs. Opponent Batters

	Ave.	OBP	SLG	AB	H	2B	3B	HR	RBI	BB	SO		Ave.	OBP	SLG	AB	H	2B	3B	HR	RBI	BB	SO
				1986 SEASON												**THREE YEARS (84 – 86)**							
Totals	.189	.297	.295	769	145	30	5	14	82	118	202		.193	.305	.293	1046	202	37	8	17	107	167	256
												Pitching vs. Left and Right-handed Batters											
Left	.187	.311	.296	423	79	16	3	8	45	77	108		.196	.315	.288	598	117	18	5	9	58	106	142
Right	.191	.280	.295	346	66	14	2	6	37	41	94		.190	.290	.299	448	85	19	3	8	49	61	114
												Situational											
Bases Empty	.166	.297	.243	453	75	16	2	5	5	82	120		.177	.304	.251	610	108	20	5	5	5	107	153
Leadoff	.158	.298	.263	190	30	9	1	3	3	37	51		.166	.296	.247	259	43	10	1	3	3	47	67
Not Leadoff	.171	.297	.228	263	45	7	1	2	2	45	69		.185	.309	.254	351	65	10	4	2	2	60	86
Runners On	.222	.297	.370	316	70	14	3	9	77	36	82		.216	.306	.351	436	94	17	3	12	102	60	103
First Base Only	.246	.308	.418	122	30	5	2	4	12	11	27		.253	.322	.410	166	42	7	2	5	16	17	33
Scoring Position	.206	.291	.340	194	40	9	1	5	65	25	55		.193	.297	.315	270	52	10	1	7	86	43	70
Late Innings, Close	.205	.340	.352	88	18	3	2	2	14	18	22		.213	.346	.370	108	23	4	2	3	17	22	26

RBI/Opportunities

Scoring Position	53 / 254	(21%)	70 / 374	(19%)
Scoring Position, 2 Out	23 / 121	(19%)	32 / 181	(18%)
On Third, Less than 2 Out	20 / 37	(54%)	28 / 57	(49%)
RBI in close games / RBI Total	58 / 82	(71%)	78 / 107	(73%)

Curt Young
Oakland A's

Despite pitching part of 1986 in the minor leagues, Curt Young had the best season of any left-handed A's starter since Vida Blue went 18–13 back in 1976. Young led Oakland starters in innings pitched, shutouts, K/W ratio, wins, earned run average and innings per game started (7.33). In 27 starts, he gave up more than four earned runs only six times, and 17 of them (63%) met the definition of "quality start." As a starter he allowed only twelve stolen bases in 24 attempts. For the year, his statistics were similar to those of another lefty, Bruce Hurst—Young was 13–9, 3.45, Hurst 13–8, 2.99.

Young was very successful in 1986 against top opponents. His record against the Yankees was 3–0, and 9–2 against all Eastern Division opponents. The A's played two games that lasted less than two hours last year; Young started and completed both of them. The second of these games was the brilliant near-perfect game on the last day of the season against the Royals, in which the only man to reach base was via a high chopper to third off home plate. Both of his shutouts were pitched against Bret Saberhagen, and he beat Guidry and Righetti separately by 2–1 scores in Yankee Stadium.

Curt was very tough on lefty swingers in '86, giving up only one of his nineteen home runs to a left handed hitter, Darrell Evans. As a rule, only real sluggers took him deep; those who hit homers off Young averaged 20 four-baggers each for the year. No one homered more than once against him.

Young took full advantage of the Oakland Coliseum's inherent advantage to pitchers by giving up few walks and home runs. His poor record on artificial turf is partly explained by the A's infield defense and partly his own tendency to be more of a ground ball pitcher than other A's starters.

Curt has had arm trouble in the past, but avoided injury after he was called up in May. On a staff of healthy, experienced veterans (Andujar, Stewart, Haas), Young should not have the pressure of being the ace of the staff, and that should help him solidify a position as one of the top starters in the American League. Curt did not enter the rotation in 1986 until May 14. If the A's use him from the beginning of the year, he has a chance to win twenty games.

—Susan Nelson

1986: Finesse, Flyball   **1985: Finesse, Flyball**   **1984: Finesse, Flyball**

	G	IP	H	BB	SO	SB	CS	W	L	S	ERA		G	IP	H	BB	SO	SB	CS	W	L	S	ERA
	1986 SEASON												**THREE YEARS (84 – 86)**										
Totals	29	198.0	176	57	116	13	11	13	9	0	3.45		68	352.2	351	110	176	18	14	22	17	0	4.13
	At Home and on the Road																						
Home	16	121.2	88	31	69	8	6	9	2	0	2.37		35	201.1	177	62	96	11	8	12	7	0	3.58
Road	13	76.1	88	26	47	5	5	4	7	0	5.19		33	151.1	174	48	80	7	6	10	10	0	4.88
	During the Day and at Night																						
Day	12	78.0	66	25	47	6	1	6	3	0	3.35		27	134.2	128	49	71	6	2	8	8	0	4.01
Night	17	120.0	110	32	69	7	10	7	6	0	3.52		41	218.0	223	61	105	12	12	14	9	0	4.21
	On Grass and on Turf																						
Grass	25	179.1	153	46	103	11	11	11	7	0	3.11		56	307.0	302	88	150	15	14	18	14	0	3.90
Turf	4	18.2	23	11	13	2	0	2	2	0	6.75		12	45.2	49	22	26	3	0	4	3	0	5.72
	By Month																						
April	0	0.0	0	0	0	0	0	0	0	0	0.00		4	18.1	26	10	9	1	1	0	2	0	10.31
May	5	34.2	31	6	18	2	1	3	1	0	2.60		5	34.2	31	6	18	2	1	3	1	0	2.60
June	6	41.1	37	16	24	5	1	2	4	0	4.35		7	48.0	39	17	27	5	1	3	4	0	3.75
July	5	31.2	30	12	16	2	3	2	1	0	3.41		17	79.1	78	29	38	4	4	4	2	0	3.18
August	6	40.2	41	12	30	2	2	3	2	0	3.32		15	72.0	79	20	40	2	2	6	4	0	4.12
Sept/Oct	7	49.2	37	11	28	2	4	3	1	0	3.44		20	100.1	98	28	44	4	5	6	4	0	4.49

vs. Opponent Batters

	Ave.	OBP	SLG	AB	H	2B	3B	HR	RBI	BB	SO		Ave.	OBP	SLG	AB	H	2B	3B	HR	RBI	BB	SO
	1986 SEASON												**THREE YEARS (84 – 86)**										
Totals	.236	.293	.365	745	176	33	3	19	79	57	116		.257	.317	.412	1366	351	71	6	43	163	110	176
	Pitching vs. Left and Right-handed Batters																						
Left	.219	.286	.260	146	32	3	0	1	14	10	30		.229	.290	.296	284	65	7	0	4	30	17	43
Right	.240	.295	.391	599	144	30	3	18	65	47	86		.264	.324	.443	1082	286	64	6	39	133	93	133
	Situational																						
Bases Empty	.223	.282	.341	452	101	20	3	9	9	33	68		.249	.306	.399	812	202	42	4	24	24	57	104
Leadoff	.250	.304	.422	192	48	11	2	6	6	11	25		.274	.319	.470	347	95	22	2	14	14	17	36
Not Leadoff	.204	.266	.281	260	53	9	1	3	3	22	43		.230	.297	.346	465	107	20	2	10	10	40	68
Runners On	.256	.310	.403	293	75	13	0	10	70	24	48		.269	.332	.431	554	149	29	2	19	139	53	72
First Base Only	.269	.317	.415	130	35	7	0	4	14	9	15		.286	.351	.420	238	68	12	1	6	22	23	27
Scoring Position	.245	.305	.393	163	40	6	0	6	56	15	33		.256	.318	.440	316	81	17	1	13	117	30	45
Late Innings, Close	.185	.254	.292	65	12	4	0	1	3	3	9		.191	.255	.277	94	18	5	0	1	5	5	10

RBI/Opportunities

Scoring Position	48 / 221	(22%)		97 / 430	(23%)
Scoring Position, 2 Out	15 / 99	(15%)		36 / 193	(19%)
On Third, Less than 2 Out	25 / 43	(58%)		41 / 74	(55%)
RBI in close games / RBI Total	60 / 79	(76%)		115 / 163	(71%)

Matt Young
Seattle Mariners

If I had to make a comparison, I would venture to say that Matt Young's career as a starter was somewhat like a trip to the dentist. You know, we've all had the same experience. About four days before the appointment, you start to think. As the visit draws nearer, the anxiety deepens. By the time the dentist picks up the drill, you're a bundle of nerves ready to explode. The emergency trips are much easier. There's no time to think about it. You just go and get it over with.

Nearly every trip to the mound for Matt was similar to a trip to the dentist. By the time game started, Matt was so hyped that losing his control and concentration was his biggest enemy. He would be overpowering at times, but usually he was awful.

After struggling through spring training learning to land on his toe and not his heel, Matt's first start was a thing of beauty! A complete game against California. One run on six hits with less than 100 pitches. The next outing against the same team was a struggle, but he got the win simply because his teammates staked him to a 8 run lead and Cottier could afford to leave him in for five innings. His third start lasted 3.2 innings, his fourth lasted 2/3 of an inning. Eigh-

teen games and one manager later, Matt got his fifth start. He lasted 1.2 innings. It was his last performance in a starting role.

After several slow outings in the pen, Matt found his niche in life as the Mariner closer. For the most part he was extremely effective in his new role, although he ended the season poorly with no saves after August 30th. During one stretch of 17 appearances, he pitched 29.2 innings, gave up 22 hits and 3 runs, walked four and struck out 30, for an ERA of 0.91. When asked later if he would eventually like to return to the role of a starter, his answer was a flat "NO." No more trips to the dentist for Matt Young, no starts to think about. One minute you're on the bench flicking sunflower seeds and the next minute you're asked to stop a Boston rally in the bottom of the ninth. No time to think about it, just go get the job done.

Dick Williams said that he had a similar situation happen to one of his very high strung starters in Oakland. His name was Rollie Fingers. Young will continue his career with the Dodgers this season, as he was traded for starter Dennis Powell.

—Merrianna McCully

1986: Power, Groundball | **1985: Power, Groundball** | **1984: Power, Groundball**

	G	IP	H	BB	SO	SB	CS	W	L	S	ERA		G	IP	H	BB	SO	SB	CS	W	L	S	ERA
	1986 SEASON												THREE YEARS (84 – 86)										
Totals	65	103.2	108	46	82	4	3	8	6	13	3.82		124	435.1	491	179	291	23	24	26	33	14	4.90
At Home and on the Road																							
Home	34	64.0	57	23	50	1	1	6	2	8	3.52		67	261.1	261	99	190	11	10	19	14	8	3.96
Road	31	39.2	51	23	32	3	2	2	4	5	4.31		57	174.0	230	80	101	12	14	7	19	6	6.31
During the Day and at Night																							
Day	14	25.1	30	13	20	0	0	1	2	3	3.91		23	75.0	92	31	46	5	5	4	8	3	4.92
Night	51	78.1	78	33	62	4	3	7	4	10	3.79		101	360.1	399	148	245	18	19	22	25	11	4.90
On Grass and on Turf																							
Grass	22	31.0	42	18	22	3	2	2	4	3	4.94		41	123.0	166	63	71	11	8	6	14	4	7.02
Turf	43	72.2	66	28	60	1	1	6	2	10	3.34		83	312.1	325	116	220	12	16	20	19	10	4.06
By Month																							
April	6	20.0	26	12	10	0	0	2	2	0	6.30		15	68.2	80	39	44	5	3	5	7	0	6.03
May	14	23.0	25	14	17	1	1	2	1	2	3.13		24	81.2	89	33	47	3	3	7	4	2	3.75
June	11	14.2	7	3	15	0	1	3	1	3	1.84		24	74.1	89	32	47	6	5	6	7	4	6.17
July	12	19.2	21	5	18	0	0	0	0	5	1.83		19	61.1	77	23	49	2	4	0	3	5	5.28
August	12	12.0	9	5	10	3	0	0	1	3	5.25		18	41.2	39	13	35	4	4	2	4	3	4.54
Sept/Oct	10	14.1	20	7	12	0	1	1	1	0	5.02		24	107.2	117	39	69	3	5	6	8	0	4.10

vs. Opponent Batters

	Ave.	OBP	SLG	AB	H	2B	3B	HR	RBI	BB	SO		Ave.	OBP	SLG	AB	H	2B	3B	HR	RBI	BB	SO
	1986 SEASON												THREE YEARS (84 – 86)										
Totals	.272	.357	.403	397	108	19	3	9	65	46	82		.286	.357	.419	1715	491	75	12	43	236	179	291
Pitching vs. Left and Right-handed Batters																							
Left	.209	.306	.310	129	27	5	1	2	13	13	35		.245	.328	.318	355	87	10	2	4	36	37	88
Right	.302	.381	.448	268	81	14	2	7	52	33	47		.297	.365	.446	1360	404	65	10	39	200	142	203
Situational																							
Bases Empty	.298	.392	.460	161	48	8	0	6	6	23	27		.276	.344	.419	914	252	42	7	25	25	90	144
Leadoff	.257	.345	.324	74	19	5	0	0	0	10	12		.289	.348	.402	405	117	19	3	7	7	36	51
Not Leadoff	.333	.431	.575	87	29	3	0	6	6	13	15		.265	.340	.432	509	135	23	4	18	18	54	93
Runners On	.254	.332	.364	236	60	11	3	3	59	23	55		.298	.372	.419	801	239	33	5	18	211	89	147
First Base Only	.258	.327	.315	89	23	3	1	0	1	8	18		.281	.339	.368	345	97	13	1	5	11	27	60
Scoring Position	.252	.335	.395	147	37	8	2	3	58	15	37		.311	.395	.458	456	142	20	4	13	200	62	87
Late Innings, Close	.291	.357	.413	189	55	10	2	3	32	15	39		.288	.357	.387	302	87	14	2	4	39	26	54

RBI/Opportunities

Scoring Position	49 / 218	(22%)		171 / 653	(26%)
Scoring Position, 2 Out	24 / 111	(22%)		71 / 314	(23%)
On Third, Less than 2 Out	16 / 34	(47%)		63 / 119	(53%)
RBI in close games / RBI Total	41 / 65	(63%)		153 / 236	(65%)

Robin Yount
Milwaukee Brewers

Robin Yount's career is at the crossroads. The next few years will tell us if he'll play until he's 42 and be a cinch for the Hall of Fame or be already eligible at age 42 and the subject of the same debates that Pete Reiser is. There is, surprisingly, a lot of talk of Robin retiring coming from normally-intelligent sources. I'm hoping it's just delayed frustration at being injured so often lately—if Yount stays reasonably whole, he has a chance to post some amazing career totals.

The bright side of Robin's 1986 was that he brought his batting average, doubles and triples up to their normal, respectable levels. The dark side was that he saw his homers total decline for the fourth year in a row, his strikeout/walk ratio slide for the third straight year and his RBI per at-bat drop to his worst figure since 1977. He has also become a much less consistent hitter, too. In 1986, he hit five of his nine homers in September; in '85, he hit all 15 in May, July and August. I think that all of that is attributable to his injuries. He's missed some games, he's had to play with all kinds of nagging hurts and (most importantly of all), he's been unable to keep doing his fitness program in the off-season for the last two years. Robin's intensive weight training program during the winter of '79–80 was the reason that his power jumped so dramatically all of a sudden; he's had to spend the last two winters recuperating from surgeries. He didn't have that problem this year, so I expect better things from him in 1987.

Even though I'm still not used to seeing Yount play center, I don't expect that he'll ever play short again. He hasn't played there in two full seasons; if he did return, he'd either be a defensive liability or the other parts of his game would sag while he struggled to readjust. More likely the latter—Robin Yount would never allow himself to look foolish no matter where he played.

This isn't exactly related to Robin, but I wanted to mention it. Why has every broadcaster on earth suddenly begun mispronouncing his name? He's been "Robin Yownt" for 13 years; now he's "Robin Yunt." The way I see it, either this is what they call a "baptism of fire" or the media forgot his name when he was on the DL. I don't know why they started, I wish to high heaven that they'd stop and I shudder to think what will happen if John Montefusco ever recovers from HIS arm troubles.

—Scott Segrin

	1986 SEASON											THREE YEARS (84 – 86)										
	Ave.	OBP	SLG	AB	H	2B	3B	HR	RBI	BB	SO	Ave.	OBP	SLG	AB	H	2B	3B	HR	RBI	BB	SO
Totals	.312	.388	.450	522	163	31	7	9	46	62	73	.297	.365	.444	1612	478	84	17	40	194	178	195
Batting vs. Left and Right-handed Pitchers																						
Left	.248	.343	.355	121	30	2	1	3	11	18	18	.289	.367	.431	478	138	20	6	12	60	63	62
Right	.332	.402	.479	401	133	29	6	6	35	44	55	.300	.364	.450	1134	340	64	11	28	134	115	133
At Home and on the Road																						
Home	.297	.370	.436	259	77	12	6	4	22	28	37	.306	.370	.475	805	246	45	11	23	110	83	95
Road	.327	.406	.464	263	86	19	1	5	24	34	36	.287	.360	.414	807	232	39	6	17	84	95	100
Facing Groundball Pitchers and Flyball Pitchers																						
Groundball	.351	.434	.489	231	81	13	2	5	26	33	28	.320	.402	.473	746	239	44	5	20	95	103	81
Flyball	.282	.351	.419	291	82	18	5	4	20	29	45	.276	.332	.419	866	239	40	12	20	99	75	114
Facing Finesse Pitchers and Power Pitchers																						
Finesse	.345	.414	.503	290	100	18	5	6	33	33	22	.304	.366	.462	920	280	53	13	22	118	91	82
Power	.272	.356	.384	232	63	13	2	3	13	29	51	.286	.364	.421	692	198	31	4	18	76	87	113
On Grass and on Turf																						
Grass	.308	.382	.425	452	139	20	6	7	41	52	64	.299	.367	.443	1395	417	65	14	36	168	152	168
Turf	.343	.425	.614	70	24	11	1	2	5	10	9	.281	.352	.452	217	61	19	3	4	26	26	27
During the Day and at Night																						
Day	.327	.399	.512	168	55	14	1	5	16	20	25	.285	.354	.456	515	147	30	5	16	59	55	58
Night	.305	.383	.421	354	108	17	6	4	30	42	48	.302	.370	.438	1097	331	54	12	24	135	123	137
By Month																						
April	.408	.462	.535	71	29	4	1	1	7	6	9	.300	.374	.395	223	67	9	3	2	19	26	24
May	.333	.403	.449	69	23	5	0	1	6	8	10	.345	.391	.512	252	87	11	2	9	38	21	29
June	.318	.416	.471	85	27	8	1	1	5	15	12	.286	.365	.412	301	86	24	1	4	32	39	39
July	.247	.343	.344	93	23	3	3	0	7	13	17	.281	.355	.430	302	85	17	5	6	38	36	36
August	.311	.398	.408	103	32	7	0	1	9	14	11	.276	.361	.422	315	87	15	2	9	38	43	35
Sept/Oct	.287	.333	.515	101	29	4	2	5	12	6	14	.301	.343	.511	219	66	8	4	10	29	13	32
Situational																						
Bases Empty	.316	.379	.479	326	103	24	4	7	7	31	42	.285	.350	.429	929	265	49	11	21	21	89	114
Leadoff	.317	.379	.533	120	38	10	2	4	4	11	16	.269	.328	.405	368	99	20	6	6	6	31	41
Not Leadoff	.316	.379	.447	206	65	14	2	3	3	20	26	.296	.364	.446	561	166	29	5	15	15	58	73
Runners On	.306	.403	.403	196	60	7	3	2	39	31	31	.312	.384	.464	683	213	35	6	19	173	89	81
First Base Only	.330	.388	.468	94	31	3	2	2	6	7	12	.332	.389	.557	325	108	17	4	16	40	27	28
Scoring Position	.284	.414	.343	102	29	4	1	0	33	24	19	.293	.381	.380	358	105	18	2	3	133	62	53
Late Innings, Close	.346	.422	.487	78	27	8	0	1	8	11	8	.314	.394	.456	239	75	13	0	7	30	34	26

RBI/Opportunities					
Scoring Position	31 / 149	(21%)	123 / 507	(24%)
Scoring Position, 2 Out	13 / 66	(20%)	36 / 204	(18%)
On Third, Less than 2 Out	11 / 24	(46%)	58 / 106	(55%)
RBI in close games / RBI Total	30 / 46	(65%)	130 / 194	(67%)

Jim Acker
Atlanta Braves

1986: Finesse, Groundball 1985: Power, Groundball 1984: Finesse, Groundball

THREE YEARS (84 – 86)

	G	IP	H	BB	SO	SB	CS	W	L	S	ERA
Totals	137	313.1	328	116	144	25	15	15	19	11	3.88
At Home and on the Road											
Home	63	156.0	145	52	73	16	8	6	7	5	3.58
Road	74	157.1	183	64	71	9	7	9	12	6	4.18
During the Day and and at Night											
Day	52	118.0	115	41	62	9	7	4	6	6	3.28
Night	85	195.1	213	75	82	16	8	11	13	5	4.24
On Grass and on Turf											
Grass	60	157.0	164	59	61	9	4	9	12	3	3.90
Turf	77	156.1	164	57	83	16	11	6	7	8	3.86
By Month											
April	19	45.1	46	14	21	4	1	1	2	3	2.38
May	29	49.0	48	14	26	2	3	1	3	5	4.59
June	28	52.2	63	28	27	5	1	5	5	2	5.13
July	29	52.0	59	21	22	7	3	4	2	1	3.12
August	13	47.1	50	16	16	3	4	3	2	0	3.04
Sept/Oct	19	67.0	62	23	32	4	3	1	5	0	4.57

vs. Opponent Batters
THREE YEARS (84 – 86)

	Ave.	OBP	SLG	AB	H	2B	3B	HR	RBI	BB	SO
Totals	.277	.344	.389	1186	328	48	8	23	154	116	144
Pitching vs. Left and Right-handed Batters											
Left	.297	.364	.407	607	180	22	6	11	85	67	56
Right	.256	.323	.370	579	148	26	2	12	69	49	88
Situational											
Bases Empty	.271	.341	.375	634	172	27	3	11	11	61	72
Leadoff	.301	.367	.428	269	81	12	2	6	6	25	30
Not Leadoff	.249	.322	.337	365	91	15	1	5	5	36	42
Runners On	.283	.347	.404	552	156	21	5	12	143	55	72
First Base Only	.298	.349	.427	218	65	6	2	6	17	14	25
Scoring Position	.272	.346	.389	334	91	15	3	6	126	41	47
Late Innings, Close	.308	.381	.392	237	73	9	1	3	33	25	17

RBI/Opportunities

Scoring Position	116 / 471	(25%)
Scoring Position, 2 Out	44 / 212	(21%)
On Third, Less than 2 Out	48 / 82	(59%)
RBI in close games / RBI Total	83 / 154	(54%)

Luis Aguayo
Philadelphia Phillies

THREE YEARS (84 – 86)

	Ave.	OBP	SLG	AB	H	2B	3B	HR	RBI	BB	SO
Totals	.254	.334	.427	370	94	17	4	13	45	38	68
Batting vs. Left and Right-handed Pitchers											
Left	.206	.309	.303	165	34	5	1	3	12	21	26
Right	.293	.355	.527	205	60	12	3	10	33	17	42
At Home and on the Road											
Home	.267	.360	.471	191	51	11	2	8	27	22	40
Road	.240	.305	.380	179	43	6	2	5	18	16	28
Facing Groundball Pitchers and Flyball Pitchers											
Groundball	.271	.333	.431	188	51	11	2	5	24	15	31
Flyball	.236	.335	.423	182	43	6	2	8	21	23	37
Facing Finesse Pitchers and Power Pitchers											
Finesse	.272	.333	.440	184	50	9	2	6	22	16	27
Power	.237	.335	.414	186	44	8	2	7	23	22	41
On Grass and on Turf											
Grass	.242	.307	.451	91	22	4	0	5	13	9	17
Turf	.258	.343	.419	279	72	13	4	8	32	29	51
During the Day and at Night											
Day	.232	.308	.464	138	32	7	2	7	19	11	21
Night	.267	.350	.405	232	62	10	2	6	26	27	47
By Month											
April	.143	.214	.254	63	9	2	1	1	4	4	10
May	.214	.313	.386	70	15	1	1	3	10	9	20
June	.343	.455	.486	35	12	3	1	0	4	6	5
July	.278	.297	.361	36	10	0	0	1	1	1	5
August	.311	.406	.478	90	28	7	1	2	14	13	16
Sept/Oct	.263	.317	.553	76	20	4	0	6	12	5	12
Situational											
Bases Empty	.233	.308	.399	223	52	6	2	9	9	18	41
Leadoff	.253	.340	.451	91	23	2	2	4	4	11	15
Not Leadoff	.220	.285	.364	132	29	4	0	5	5	7	26
Runners On	.286	.371	.469	147	42	11	2	4	36	20	27
First Base Only	.215	.292	.446	65	14	3	0	4	8	7	11
Scoring Position	.341	.427	.488	82	28	8	2	0	28	13	16
Late Innings, Close	.329	.412	.471	70	23	4	0	2	8	9	14

RBI/Opportunities

Scoring Position	26 / 133	(20%)
Scoring Position, 2 Out	7 / 57	(12%)
On Third, Less than 2 Out	14 / 25	(56%)
RBI in close games / RBI Total	25 / 45	(56%)

Rick Aguilera
New York Mets

1986: Finesse, Groundball 1985: Finesse, Flyball 1984: Did not play

THREE YEARS (84 – 86)

	G	IP	H	BB	SO	SB	CS	W	L	S	ERA
Totals	49	264.0	263	73	178	18	14	20	14	0	3.58
At Home and on the Road											
Home	22	114.0	106	29	87	6	4	8	4	0	3.08
Road	27	150.0	157	44	91	12	10	12	10	0	3.96
During the Day and and at Night											
Day	22	107.0	103	31	70	9	7	8	7	0	3.79
Night	27	157.0	160	42	108	9	7	12	7	0	3.44
On Grass and on Turf											
Grass	32	174.0	165	38	123	11	10	12	7	0	3.10
Turf	17	90.0	98	35	55	7	4	8	7	0	4.50
By Month											
April	2	12.0	13	2	12	0	0	0	1	0	6.00
May	5	13.2	14	7	14	1	2	2	0	0	7.24
June	9	30.1	32	20	20	7	1	2	2	0	4.75
July	10	74.2	65	15	44	2	4	6	1	0	1.69
August	11	67.0	70	13	48	5	5	5	0	0	4.57
Sept/Oct	12	66.1	69	16	40	3	2	7	3	0	2.98

vs. Opponent Batters
THREE YEARS (84 – 86)

	Ave.	OBP	SLG	AB	H	2B	3B	HR	RBI	BB	SO
Totals	.261	.314	.401	1008	263	56	8	23	108	73	178
Pitching vs. Left and Right-handed Batters											
Left	.268	.327	.394	493	132	33	4	7	49	41	72
Right	.254	.301	.408	515	131	23	4	16	59	32	106
Situational											
Bases Empty	.253	.308	.389	601	152	33	5	13	13	43	105
Leadoff	.242	.295	.381	252	61	15	1	6	6	16	47
Not Leadoff	.261	.317	.395	349	91	18	4	7	7	27	58
Runners On	.273	.322	.418	407	111	23	3	10	95	30	73
First Base Only	.292	.339	.491	171	50	13	0	7	20	11	31
Scoring Position	.258	.311	.364	236	61	10	3	3	75	19	42
Late Innings, Close	.254	.318	.322	59	15	1	0	1	5	6	9

RBI/Opportunities

Scoring Position	69 / 306	(23%)
Scoring Position, 2 Out	31 / 147	(21%)
On Third, Less than 2 Out	24 / 48	(50%)
RBI in close games / RBI Total	71 / 108	(66%)

Mike Aldrete
San Francisco Giants

THREE YEARS (84 – 86)

	Ave.	OBP	SLG	AB	H	2B	3B	HR	RBI	BB	SO
Totals	.250	.353	.389	216	54	18	3	2	25	33	34
Batting vs. Left and Right-handed Pitchers											
Left	.192	.222	.231	26	5	1	0	0	1	1	6
Right	.258	.369	.411	190	49	17	3	2	24	32	28
At Home and on the Road											
Home	.299	.401	.436	117	35	9	2	1	15	20	16
Road	.192	.296	.333	99	19	9	1	1	10	13	18
Facing Groundball Pitchers and Flyball Pitchers											
Groundball	.210	.297	.352	105	22	7	1	2	9	12	18
Flyball	.288	.403	.423	111	32	11	2	0	16	21	16
Facing Finesse Pitchers and Power Pitchers											
Finesse	.230	.317	.373	126	29	10	1	2	14	14	15
Power	.278	.400	.411	90	25	8	2	0	11	19	19
On Grass and on Turf											
Grass	.267	.370	.412	165	44	12	3	2	20	26	24
Turf	.196	.300	.314	51	10	6	0	0	5	7	10
During the Day and at Night											
Day	.240	.387	.390	100	24	10	1	1	13	23	20
Night	.259	.320	.388	116	30	8	2	1	12	10	14
By Month											
April	.000	.000	.000	0	0	0	0	0	0	0	0
May	.100	.250	.100	10	1	0	0	0	0	1	1
June	.216	.322	.338	74	16	6	0	1	8	12	12
July	.133	.350	.267	15	2	2	0	0	0	5	5
August	.354	.404	.583	48	17	4	2	1	9	3	8
Sept/Oct	.261	.370	.377	69	18	6	1	0	8	12	8
Situational											
Bases Empty	.261	.336	.409	115	30	9	1	2	2	12	17
Leadoff	.250	.333	.400	40	10	3	0	1	1	4	6
Not Leadoff	.267	.337	.413	75	20	6	1	1	1	8	11
Runners On	.238	.371	.366	101	24	9	2	0	23	21	17
First Base Only	.235	.297	.324	34	8	3	0	0	2	3	6
Scoring Position	.239	.402	.388	67	16	6	2	0	21	18	11
Late Innings, Close	.326	.423	.535	43	14	4	1	1	8	8	4

RBI/Opportunities

Scoring Position	20 / 112	(18%)
Scoring Position, 2 Out	9 / 63	(14%)
On Third, Less than 2 Out	7 / 12	(58%)
RBI in close games / RBI Total	22 / 25	(88%)

Andy Allanson
Cleveland Indians

THREE YEARS (84 – 86)

	Ave.	OBP	SLG	AB	H	2B	3B	HR	RBI	BB	SO
Totals	.225	.260	.280	293	66	7	3	1	29	14	36
Batting vs. Left and Right-handed Pitchers											
Left	.274	.307	.333	84	23	3	1	0	7	4	12
Right	.206	.241	.258	209	43	4	2	1	22	10	24
At Home and on the Road											
Home	.238	.268	.286	147	35	3	2	0	16	6	13
Road	.212	.252	.274	146	31	4	1	1	13	8	23
Facing Groundball Pitchers and Flyball Pitchers											
Groundball	.239	.268	.291	117	28	1	1		13	5	14
Flyball	.216	.254	.273	176	38	6	2	0	16	9	22
Facing Finesse Pitchers and Power Pitchers											
Finesse	.244	.280	.311	180	44	5	2	1	19	9	17
Power	.195	.227	.230	113	22	2	1	0	10	5	19
On Grass and on Turf											
Grass	.221	.255	.263	262	58	5	3	0	26	12	31
Turf	.258	.294	.419	31	8	2	0	1	3	2	5
During the Day and at Night											
Day	.241	.283	.286	112	27	3	1	0	10	7	12
Night	.215	.245	.276	181	39	4	2	1	19	7	24
By Month											
April	.388	.392	.429	49	19	0	1	0	6	1	2
May	.203	.250	.281	64	13	3	1	0	4	3	7
June	.208	.241	.340	53	11	2	1	1	9	3	11
July	.214	.292	.214	42	9	0	0	0	6	5	2
August	.128	.146	.149	47	6	1	0	0	0	1	10
Sept/Oct	.211	.231	.237	38	8	1	0	0	4	1	4
Situational											
Bases Empty	.188	.244	.208	149	28	3	0	0	0	10	16
Leadoff	.286	.318	.302	63	18	1	0	0	0	2	3
Not Leadoff	.116	.191	.140	86	10	2	0	0	0	8	13
Runners On	.264	.276	.354	144	38	4	3	1	29	4	20
First Base Only	.276	.300	.345	58	16	4	0	0	1	2	11
Scoring Position	.256	.261	.360	86	22	0	3	1	28	2	9
Late Innings, Close	.341	.357	.439	41	14	2	1	0	3	1	5

RBI/Opportunities

Scoring Position	25 / 105	(24%)
Scoring Position, 2 Out	12 / 55	(22%)
On Third, Less than 2 Out	8 / 16	(50%)
RBI in close games / RBI Total	9 / 29	(31%)

Neil Allen
Chicago White Sox

1986: Finesse, Groundball   1985: Power, Flyball   1984: Finesse, Groundball

THREE YEARS (84 – 86)

	G	IP	H	BB	SO	SB	CS	W	L	S	ERA
Totals	119	290.1	264	117	149	9	16	18	12	6	3.78
At Home and on the Road											
Home	53	129.2	101	46	74	3	5	10	1	4	3.40
Road	66	160.2	163	71	75	6	11	8	11	2	4.09
During the Day and and at Night											
Day	45	109.2	109	50	52	3	11	6	5	0	4.27
Night	74	180.2	155	67	97	6	5	12	7	6	3.49
On Grass and on Turf											
Grass	56	166.2	159	67	91	6	10	13	9	0	4.05
Turf	63	123.2	105	50	58	3	6	5	3	6	3.42
By Month											
April	19	29.0	35	17	16	0	1	1	1	2	7.45
May	26	67.2	60	34	33	5	3	3	3	2	3.33
June	19	60.2	66	24	39	1	8	4	1	1	5.79
July	24	70.0	46	21	27	2	2	6	6	0	1.80
August	16	29.0	28	14	20	0	1	2	0	1	3.41
Sept/Oct	15	34.0	29	7	14	1	1	2	1	0	2.38

vs. Opponent Batters
THREE YEARS (84 – 86)

	Ave.	OBP	SLG	AB	H	2B	3B	HR	RBI	BB	SO
Totals	.245	.317	.348	1078	264	47	5	18	130	117	149
Pitching vs. Left and Right-handed Batters											
Left	.233	.310	.336	494	115	21	3	8	51	57	72
Right	.255	.324	.358	584	149	26	2	10	79	60	77
Situational											
Bases Empty	.217	.277	.323	654	142	31	4	10	10	53	92
Leadoff	.215	.283	.265	265	57	16	2	4	4	24	36
Not Leadoff	.219	.273	.314	389	85	15	2	6	6	29	56
Runners On	.288	.375	.387	424	122	16	1	8	120	64	57
First Base Only	.273	.344	.375	176	48	6	0	4	8	19	30
Scoring Position	.298	.394	.395	248	74	10	1	4	112	45	27
Late Innings, Close	.214	.324	.277	220	47	5	0	3	27	36	26

RBI/Opportunities

Scoring Position	103 / 395	(26%)
Scoring Position, 2 Out	32 / 163	(20%)
On Third, Less than 2 Out	44 / 91	(48%)
RBI in close games / RBI Total	72 / 130	(55%)

Bill Almon
Pittsburgh Pirates

THREE YEARS (84 – 86)

	Ave.	OBP	SLG	AB	H	2B	3B	HR	RBI	BB	SO
Totals	.240	.303	.392	651	156	35	2	20	71	63	141
Batting vs. Left and Right-handed Pitchers											
Left	.247	.316	.404	389	96	21	2	12	29	40	78
Right	.229	.284	.374	262	60	14	0	8	42	23	63
At Home and on the Road											
Home	.260	.332	.430	342	89	22	0	12	43	39	68
Road	.217	.270	.350	309	67	13	2	8	28	24	73
Facing Groundball Pitchers and Flyball Pitchers											
Groundball	.273	.333	.405	311	85	18	1	7	34	30	67
Flyball	.209	.276	.379	340	71	17	1	13	37	33	74
Facing Finesse Pitchers and Power Pitchers											
Finesse	.259	.313	.368	348	90	19	2	5	33	30	68
Power	.218	.293	.419	303	66	16	0	15	38	33	73
On Grass and on Turf											
Grass	.199	.244	.359	301	60	13	1	11	32	20	61
Turf	.274	.353	.420	350	96	22	1	9	39	43	80
During the Day and at Night											
Day	.245	.288	.456	241	59	13	1	12	30	15	38
Night	.237	.312	.354	410	97	22	1	8	41	48	103
By Month											
April	.265	.330	.458	83	22	7	0	3	13	8	16
May	.243	.327	.358	148	36	5	0	4	19	20	42
June	.237	.308	.390	118	28	4	1	4	14	13	22
July	.227	.293	.387	119	27	8	1	3	8	12	27
August	.200	.240	.311	90	18	4	0	2	5	5	21
Sept/Oct	.269	.307	.473	93	25	7	0	4	12	5	13
Situational											
Bases Empty	.240	.303	.383	405	97	23	1	11	11	36	85
Leadoff	.258	.304	.412	194	50	15	0	5	5	12	37
Not Leadoff	.223	.302	.355	211	47	8	1	6	6	24	48
Runners On	.240	.304	.407	246	59	12	1	9	60	27	56
First Base Only	.272	.341	.439	114	31	5	1	4	10	12	19
Scoring Position	.212	.274	.379	132	28	7	0	5	50	15	37
Late Innings, Close	.236	.314	.393	140	33	7	0	5	12	17	28

RBI/Opportunities

Scoring Position	42 / 211	(20%)
Scoring Position, 2 Out	15 / 96	(16%)
On Third, Less than 2 Out	20 / 43	(47%)
RBI in close games / RBI Total	40 / 71	(56%)

Larry Andersen
Houston Astros

1986: Finesse, Groundball   1985: Power, Groundball   1984: Finesse, Groundball

THREE YEARS (84 – 86)

	G	IP	H	BB	SO	SB	CS	W	L	S	ERA
Totals	169	241.0	246	77	146	32	16	8	11	8	3.17
At Home and on the Road											
Home	81	116.1	106	33	67	14	8	6	2	4	2.71
Road	88	124.2	140	44	79	18	8	2	9	4	3.61
During the Day and and at Night											
Day	63	91.0	83	24	56	11	7	2	2	4	2.18
Night	106	150.0	163	53	90	21	9	6	9	4	3.78
On Grass and on Turf											
Grass	48	63.0	82	16	39	6	2	0	5	1	3.57
Turf	121	178.0	164	61	107	26	14	8	6	7	3.03
By Month											
April	19	22.1	29	7	19	1	3	1	2	2	4.43
May	27	41.1	42	12	26	4	3	1	1	1	3.27
June	37	57.2	58	16	27	11	4	2	0	1	2.65
July	24	37.0	36	12	22	3	2	1	1	1	2.43
August	32	42.2	49	15	27	4	2	2	3	2	4.22
Sept/Oct	30	40.0	32	15	25	9	2	1	4	1	2.70

vs. Opponent Batters
THREE YEARS (84 – 86)

	Ave.	OBP	SLG	AB	H	2B	3B	HR	RBI	BB	SO
Totals	.271	.327	.370	909	246	38	8	12	126	77	146
Pitching vs. Left and Right-handed Batters											
Left	.291	.365	.390	413	120	15	4	6	58	48	59
Right	.254	.294	.353	496	126	23	4	6	68	29	87
Situational											
Bases Empty	.272	.314	.361	460	125	20	3	5	5	27	68
Leadoff	.302	.344	.396	202	61	10	0	3	3	12	23
Not Leadoff	.248	.289	.333	258	64	10	3	2	2	15	45
Runners On	.269	.340	.379	449	121	18	5	7	121	50	78
First Base Only	.245	.283	.377	151	37	4	2	4	11	6	34
Scoring Position	.282	.365	.379	298	84	14	3	3	110	44	44
Late Innings, Close	.273	.332	.369	344	94	11	2	6	50	32	54

RBI/Opportunities

Scoring Position	102 / 449	(23%)
Scoring Position, 2 Out	36 / 199	(18%)
On Third, Less than 2 Out	46 / 79	(58%)
RBI in close games / RBI Total	68 / 126	(54%)

Allan Anderson
Minnesota Twins

1986: Finesse, Flyball   1985: Did not play   1984: Did not play

THREE YEARS (84 – 86)

	G	IP	H	BB	SO	SB	CS	W	L	S	ERA
Totals	21	84.1	106	30	51	5	4	3	6	0	5.55
At Home and on the Road											
Home	11	48.1	66	18	27	4	2	1	4	0	6.52
Road	10	36.0	40	12	24	1	2	2	2	0	4.25
During the Day and and at Night											
Day	12	42.0	62	13	29	3	1	2	4	0	7.07
Night	9	42.1	44	17	22	2	3	1	2	0	4.04
On Grass and on Turf											
Grass	8	32.2	37	10	21	1	2	2	1	0	4.41
Turf	13	51.2	69	20	30	4	2	1	5	0	6.27
By Month											
April	0	0.0	0	0	0	0	0	0	0	0	0.00
May	0	0.0	0	0	0	0	0	0	0	0	0.00
June	4	31.2	28	10	20	1	2	2	1	0	3.69
July	6	22.1	37	6	12	2	0	1	2	0	8.46
August	6	12.2	16	8	8	0	0	0	2	0	4.97
Sept/Oct	5	17.2	25	6	11	2	2	0	1	0	5.60

vs. Opponent Batters

THREE YEARS (84 – 86)

	Ave.	OBP	SLG	AB	H	2B	3B	HR	RBI	BB	SO
Totals	.316	.371	.501	335	106	27	1	11	45	30	51
Pitching vs. Left and Right-handed Batters											
Left	.337	.392	.551	89	30	10	0	3	12	8	12
Right	.309	.364	.484	246	76	17	1	8	33	22	39
Situational											
Bases Empty	.303	.358	.511	188	57	15	0	8	8	16	35
Leadoff	.333	.379	.543	81	27	8	0	3	3	6	12
Not Leadoff	.280	.342	.486	107	30	7	0	5	5	10	23
Runners On	.333	.388	.490	147	49	12	1	3	37	14	16
First Base Only	.309	.356	.500	68	21	5	1	2	8	4	4
Scoring Position	.354	.413	.481	79	28	7	0	1	29	10	12
Late Innings, Close	.200	.310	.200	25	5	0	0	0	0	4	6

RBI/Opportunities

Scoring Position	27 / 111	(24%)
Scoring Position, 2 Out	10 / 42	(24%)
On Third, Less than 2 Out	11 / 26	(42%)
RBI in close games / RBI Total	25 / 45	(56%)

Dave Anderson
Los Angeles Dodgers

THREE YEARS (84 – 86)

	Ave.	OBP	SLG	AB	H	2B	3B	HR	RBI	BB	SO
Totals	.236	.321	.308	811	191	31	2	8	67	102	137
Batting vs. Left and Right-handed Pitchers											
Left	.252	.356	.344	262	66	10	1	4	25	42	46
Right	.228	.303	.291	549	125	21	1	4	42	60	91
At Home and on the Road											
Home	.255	.336	.304	381	97	10	0	3	28	46	60
Road	.219	.307	.312	430	94	21	2	5	39	56	77
Facing Groundball Pitchers and Flyball Pitchers											
Groundball	.247	.330	.321	361	89	11	2	4	36	46	50
Flyball	.227	.313	.298	450	102	20	0	4	31	56	87
Facing Finesse Pitchers and Power Pitchers											
Finesse	.239	.316	.315	476	114	17	2	5	39	52	70
Power	.230	.327	.299	335	77	14	0	3	28	50	67
On Grass and on Turf											
Grass	.231	.320	.295	603	139	18	0	7	41	79	94
Turf	.250	.322	.346	208	52	13	2	1	26	23	43
During the Day and at Night											
Day	.234	.326	.324	299	70	18	0	3	23	40	48
Night	.236	.318	.299	512	121	13	2	5	44	62	89
By Month											
April	.201	.279	.242	149	30	0	0	2	7	16	24
May	.273	.329	.364	77	21	5	1	0	6	7	9
June	.257	.347	.309	152	39	5	0	1	9	20	29
July	.241	.338	.358	137	33	10	0	2	13	21	29
August	.238	.333	.341	126	30	7	0	2	13	17	18
Sept/Oct	.224	.306	.276	170	38	4	1	1	19	21	28
Situational											
Bases Empty	.240	.338	.323	470	113	21	0	6	6	66	95
Leadoff	.212	.316	.295	217	46	12	0	2	2	32	52
Not Leadoff	.265	.356	.348	253	67	9	0	4	4	34	43
Runners On	.229	.297	.287	341	78	10	2	2	61	36	42
First Base Only	.243	.298	.321	140	34	5	0	2	8	11	13
Scoring Position	.219	.296	.264	201	44	5	2	0	53	25	29
Late Innings, Close	.231	.320	.301	156	36	8	0	1	14	20	21

RBI/Opportunities

Scoring Position	53 / 291	(18%)
Scoring Position, 2 Out	16 / 128	(13%)
On Third, Less than 2 Out	27 / 63	(43%)
RBI in close games / RBI Total	42 / 67	(63%)

Rick Anderson
New York Mets

1986: Finesse, Flyball   1985: Did not play   1984: Did not play

THREE YEARS (84 – 86)

	G	IP	H	BB	SO	SB	CS	W	L	S	ERA
Totals	15	49.2	45	11	21	7	1	2	1	1	2.72
At Home and on the Road											
Home	6	29.0	28	5	13	3	1	1	1	0	2.79
Road	9	20.2	17	6	8	4	0	1	0	1	2.61
During the Day and and at Night											
Day	5	16.2	10	6	5	2	0	1	0	1	2.70
Night	10	33.0	35	5	16	5	1	1	1	0	2.73
On Grass and on Turf											
Grass	9	37.1	38	8	18	5	1	2	1	0	3.13
Turf	6	12.1	7	3	3	2	0	0	0	1	1.46
By Month											
April	0	0.0	0	0	0	0	0	0	0	0	0.00
May	0	0.0	0	0	0	0	0	0	0	0	0.00
June	1	7.0	4	2	5	1	0	0	0	0	0.00
July	4	12.1	12	5	4	4	0	0	0	0	1.46
August	5	19.0	15	3	7	1	1	1	1	1	3.79
Sept/Oct	5	11.1	14	1	5	1	0	1	0	0	3.97

vs. Opponent Batters

THREE YEARS (84 – 86)

	Ave.	OBP	SLG	AB	H	2B	3B	HR	RBI	BB	SO
Totals	.245	.283	.326	184	45	2	2	3	16	11	21
Pitching vs. Left and Right-handed Batters											
Left	.215	.267	.323	93	20	0	2	2	9	7	8
Right	.275	.299	.330	91	25	2	0	1	7	4	13
Situational											
Bases Empty	.235	.261	.296	115	27	2	1	1	1	4	14
Leadoff	.292	.320	.375	48	14	2	1	0	0	2	3
Not Leadoff	.194	.217	.239	67	13	0	0	1	1	2	11
Runners On	.261	.316	.377	69	18	0	1	2	15	7	7
First Base Only	.313	.333	.406	32	10	0	0	1	2	1	3
Scoring Position	.216	.304	.351	37	8	0	1	1	13	6	4
Late Innings, Close	.235	.350	.235	17	4	0	0	0	0	3	2

RBI/Opportunities

Scoring Position	12 / 52	(23%)
Scoring Position, 2 Out	4 / 24	(17%)
On Third, Less than 2 Out	6 / 10	(60%)
RBI in close games / RBI Total	6 / 16	(38%)

Tony Armas
Boston Red Sox

THREE YEARS (84 – 86)

	Ave.	OBP	SLG	AB	H	2B	3B	HR	RBI	BB	SO
Totals	.266	.301	.491	1449	385	67	14	77	245	74	323
Batting vs. Left and Right-handed Pitchers											
Left	.289	.331	.480	419	121	25	5	15	57	29	71
Right	.256	.288	.495	1030	264	42	9	62	188	45	252
At Home and on the Road											
Home	.284	.328	.516	698	198	37	7	37	137	46	127
Road	.249	.275	.467	751	187	30	7	40	108	28	196
Facing Groundball Pitchers and Flyball Pitchers											
Groundball	.247	.293	.462	692	171	33	7	34	115	43	149
Flyball	.283	.308	.517	757	214	34	7	43	130	31	174
Facing Finesse Pitchers and Power Pitchers											
Finesse	.256	.286	.483	812	208	38	4	46	134	35	158
Power	.278	.320	.501	637	177	29	10	31	111	39	165
On Grass and on Turf											
Grass	.268	.307	.502	1230	330	59	12	68	214	69	276
Turf	.251	.263	.429	219	55	8	2	9	31	5	47
During the Day and at Night											
Day	.279	.315	.569	466	130	24	6	33	77	24	110
Night	.259	.294	.454	983	255	43	8	44	168	50	213
By Month											
April	.251	.290	.481	231	58	10	2	13	32	11	49
May	.234	.258	.410	244	57	8	1	11	28	8	60
June	.335	.369	.617	188	63	13	2	12	39	15	49
July	.253	.279	.513	158	40	6	1	11	24	6	42
August	.258	.291	.497	310	80	15	4	17	65	14	62
Sept/Oct	.274	.314	.469	318	87	15	4	13	57	20	61
Situational											
Bases Empty	.266	.299	.510	762	203	34	7	46	46	32	164
Leadoff	.288	.320	.586	326	94	13	6	24	24	14	57
Not Leadoff	.250	.283	.454	436	109	21	1	22	22	18	107
Runners On	.265	.303	.469	687	182	33	7	31	199	42	159
First Base Only	.248	.269	.481	318	79	14	3	18	44	7	79
Scoring Position	.279	.330	.458	369	103	19	4	13	155	35	80
Late Innings, Close	.200	.225	.353	215	43	5	2	8	22	7	58

RBI/Opportunities

Scoring Position	131 / 502	(26%)
Scoring Position, 2 Out	46 / 203	(23%)
On Third, Less than 2 Out	54 / 115	(47%)
RBI in close games / RBI Total	146 / 245	(60%)

Paul Assenmacher
Atlanta Braves

1986: Power, Groundball   1985: Did not play   1984: Did not play

	G	IP	H	BB	SO	SB	CS	W	L	S	ERA
THREE YEARS (84 – 86)											
Totals	61	68.1	61	26	56	4	3	7	3	7	2.50
At Home and on the Road											
Home	31	39.0	24	11	35	3	2	4	1	5	1.15
Road	30	29.1	37	15	21	1	1	3	2	2	4.30
During the Day and and at Night											
Day	15	17.2	13	7	13	1	0	1	2	3	3.06
Night	46	50.2	48	19	43	3	3	6	1	4	2.31
On Grass and on Turf											
Grass	45	52.0	45	21	47	3	3	5	3	6	2.77
Turf	16	16.1	16	5	9	1	0	2	0	1	1.65
By Month											
April	9	7.1	7	4	7	0	1	0	0	0	2.45
May	11	15.2	6	5	10	1	0	2	1	4	1.15
June	12	14.1	17	5	11	2	1	1	1	3	3.14
July	8	8.2	10	5	5	0	1	1	0	0	6.23
August	10	9.0	7	5	8	1	0	1	0	0	2.00
Sept/Oct	11	13.1	14	2	15	1	0	2	1	0	1.35

	Ave.	OBP	SLG	AB	H	2B	3B	HR	RBI	BB	SO
vs. Opponent Batters											
THREE YEARS (84 – 86)											
Totals	.241	.311	.332	253	61	4	2	5	27	26	56
Pitching vs. Left and Right-handed Batters											
Left	.272	.352	.358	81	22	2	1	1	9	10	19
Right	.227	.291	.320	172	39	2	1	4	18	16	37
Situational											
Bases Empty	.234	.295	.380	137	32	3	1	5	5	12	31
Leadoff	.241	.313	.431	58	14	3	1	2	2	6	13
Not Leadoff	.228	.282	.342	79	18	0	0	3	3	6	18
Runners On	.250	.328	.276	116	29	1	1	0	22	14	25
First Base Only	.256	.289	.279	43	11	1	0	0	0	2	9
Scoring Position	.247	.349	.274	73	18	0	1	0	22	12	16
Late Innings, Close	.252	.315	.348	135	34	2	1	3	16	13	34

RBI/Opportunities

Scoring Position	21 / 112	(19%)
Scoring Position, 2 Out	7 / 47	(15%)
On Third, Less than 2 Out	10 / 23	(43%)
RBI in close games / RBI Total	16 / 27	(59%)

Keith Atherton
Minnesota Twins

1986: Power, Flyball   1985: Power, Flyball   1984: Power, Flyball

	G	IP	H	BB	SO	SB	CS	W	L	S	ERA
THREE YEARS (84 – 86)											
Totals	173	305.2	299	127	202	22	14	17	23	15	4.24
At Home and on the Road											
Home	90	160.1	141	70	115	11	6	10	7	9	3.76
Road	83	145.1	158	57	87	11	8	7	16	6	4.77
During the Day and and at Night											
Day	58	101.2	94	38	73	3	4	3	9	2	4.60
Night	115	204.0	205	89	129	19	10	14	14	13	4.06
On Grass and on Turf											
Grass	116	206.2	198	94	141	14	10	11	11	9	4.22
Turf	57	99.0	101	33	61	8	4	6	12	6	4.27
By Month											
April	24	46.0	35	20	27	1	1	2	4	0	3.52
May	32	54.1	54	25	34	3	4	4	2	0	3.98
June	34	71.0	54	27	44	8	2	6	5	6	2.66
July	25	38.0	62	21	30	5	3	2	1	6	7.82
August	31	55.2	61	26	39	0	3	2	9	1	5.01
Sept/Oct	27	40.2	33	8	28	5	1	1	2	2	3.76

	Ave.	OBP	SLG	AB	H	2B	3B	HR	RBI	BB	SO
vs. Opponent Batters											
THREE YEARS (84 – 86)											
Totals	.258	.328	.427	1160	299	57	8	41	169	127	202
Pitching vs. Left and Right-handed Batters											
Left	.286	.372	.467	514	147	24	3	21	71	75	76
Right	.235	.292	.395	646	152	33	5	20	98	52	126
Situational											
Bases Empty	.258	.321	.426	585	151	23	6	21	21	52	104
Leadoff	.261	.318	.477	241	63	10	3	12	12	18	44
Not Leadoff	.256	.323	.390	344	88	13	3	9	9	34	60
Runners On	.257	.336	.428	575	148	34	2	20	148	75	98
First Base Only	.258	.314	.418	244	63	15	0	8	23	20	37
Scoring Position	.257	.350	.435	331	85	19	2	12	125	55	61
Late Innings, Close	.255	.330	.430	435	111	19	3	17	60	49	84

RBI/Opportunities

Scoring Position	102 / 530	(19%)
Scoring Position, 2 Out	26 / 231	(11%)
On Third, Less than 2 Out	45 / 102	(44%)
RBI in close games / RBI Total	78 / 169	(46%)

Scott Bailes
Cleveland Indians

1986: Finesse, Groundball   1985: Did not play   1984: Did not play

	G	IP	H	BB	SO	SB	CS	W	L	S	ERA
THREE YEARS (84 – 86)											
Totals	62	112.2	123	43	60	7	1	10	10	7	4.95
At Home and on the Road											
Home	31	63.0	58	22	27	4	1	5	5	4	4.29
Road	31	49.2	65	21	33	3	0	5	5	3	5.80
During the Day and and at Night											
Day	23	42.2	43	16	27	3	0	7	2	3	3.37
Night	39	70.0	80	27	33	4	1	3	8	4	5.91
On Grass and on Turf											
Grass	51	103.1	111	38	51	6	1	10	9	6	4.88
Turf	11	9.1	12	5	9	1	0	0	1	1	5.79
By Month											
April	10	16.0	17	8	14	0	0	3	1	2	5.06
May	15	13.1	17	5	7	2	0	2	3	2	4.73
June	12	15.2	17	7	8	1	0	2	0	2	4.60
July	10	11.0	10	4	5	1	0	1	2	1	2.45
August	10	34.1	33	13	15	1	1	1	2	0	4.46
Sept/Oct	5	22.1	29	6	11	2	0	1	2	0	7.25

	Ave.	OBP	SLG	AB	H	2B	3B	HR	RBI	BB	SO
vs. Opponent Batters											
THREE YEARS (84 – 86)											
Totals	.276	.339	.411	445	123	22	1	12	75	43	60
Pitching vs. Left and Right-handed Batters											
Left	.299	.354	.427	117	35	6	0	3	30	11	17
Right	.268	.333	.405	328	88	16	1	9	45	32	43
Situational											
Bases Empty	.283	.343	.402	219	62	9	1	5	5	19	33
Leadoff	.292	.327	.406	96	28	2	0	3	3	5	14
Not Leadoff	.276	.355	.398	123	34	7	1	2	2	14	19
Runners On	.270	.331	.420	226	61	13	0	7	70	24	27
First Base Only	.185	.248	.269	108	20	3	0	2	5	9	16
Scoring Position	.347	.409	.559	118	41	10	0	5	65	15	11
Late Innings, Close	.283	.354	.372	145	41	10	0	1	27	16	25

RBI/Opportunities

Scoring Position	51 / 178	(29%)
Scoring Position, 2 Out	21 / 74	(28%)
On Third, Less than 2 Out	19 / 39	(49%)
RBI in close games / RBI Total	44 / 75	(59%)

Mark Bailey
Houston Astros

	Ave.	OBP	SLG	AB	H	2B	3B	HR	RBI	BB	SO
THREE YEARS (84 – 86)											
Totals	.227	.344	.355	829	188	35	1	23	94	148	186
Batting vs. Left and Right-handed Pitchers											
Left	.241	.354	.356	303	73	14	0	7	34	52	56
Right	.219	.339	.354	526	115	21	1	16	60	96	130
At Home and on the Road											
Home	.248	.360	.386	415	103	21	0	12	51	73	93
Road	.205	.329	.324	414	85	14	1	11	43	75	93
Facing Groundball Pitchers and Flyball Pitchers											
Groundball	.217	.337	.333	414	90	15	0	11	45	76	91
Flyball	.236	.376	.367	415	98	20	1	12	49	72	95
Facing Finesse Pitchers and Power Pitchers											
Finesse	.225	.325	.344	453	102	18	0	12	47	67	87
Power	.229	.366	.367	376	86	17	1	11	47	81	99
On Grass and on Turf											
Grass	.221	.351	.342	231	51	11	1	5	27	46	58
Turf	.229	.341	.360	598	137	24	0	18	67	102	128
During the Day and at Night											
Day	.241	.363	.364	195	47	10	1	4	23	37	53
Night	.222	.338	.352	634	141	25	0	19	71	111	133
By Month											
April	.179	.266	.214	56	10	2	0	0	4	7	17
May	.220	.321	.322	205	45	6	0	5	27	30	41
June	.226	.354	.407	177	40	8	0	8	22	35	44
July	.234	.338	.387	137	32	9	0	4	14	22	30
August	.268	.398	.403	149	40	6	1	4	20	32	28
Sept/Oct	.200	.344	.295	105	21	4	0	2	7	22	26
Situational											
Bases Empty	.202	.307	.348	445	90	21	1	14	14	66	101
Leadoff	.222	.310	.409	203	45	12	1	8	8	26	47
Not Leadoff	.186	.304	.298	242	45	9	0	6	6	40	54
Runners On	.255	.385	.362	384	98	14	0	9	80	82	85
First Base Only	.310	.372	.450	171	53	6	0	6	15	16	29
Scoring Position	.211	.393	.291	213	45	8	0	3	65	66	56
Late Innings, Close	.237	.352	.368	152	36	8	0	4	20	26	35

RBI/Opportunities

Scoring Position	58 / 329	(18%)
Scoring Position, 2 Out	25 / 147	(17%)
On Third, Less than 2 Out	19 / 60	(32%)
RBI in close games / RBI Total	57 / 94	(61%)

Doug Bair
Oakland A's

1986: Power, Flyball   1985: Power, Flyball   1984: Power, Groundball

THREE YEARS (84 – 86)

	G	IP	H	BB	SO	SB	CS	W	L	S	ERA
Totals	101	189.2	174	81	127	12	4	9	6	8	4.18
At Home and on the Road											
Home	48	89.1	76	48	53	6	3	3	3	5	4.03
Road	53	100.1	98	33	74	6	1	6	3	3	4.31
During the Day and and at Night											
Day	36	69.1	53	32	51	5	3	4	2	3	3.12
Night	65	120.1	121	49	76	7	1	5	4	5	4.79
On Grass and on Turf											
Grass	79	147.2	138	70	95	11	4	7	6	7	4.57
Turf	22	42.0	36	11	32	1	0	2	0	1	2.79
By Month											
April	7	18.0	17	7	13	0	0	2	0	1	3.50
May	13	28.0	24	7	19	2	0	0	0	1	2.89
June	23	49.1	44	20	37	2	0	4	2	2	4.56
July	24	37.1	34	17	24	4	2	1	2	3	4.58
August	18	37.0	39	16	20	1	1	1	2	1	5.84
Sept/Oct	16	20.0	16	14	14	3	1	1	0	0	1.80

vs. Opponent Batters
THREE YEARS (84 – 86)

	Ave.	OBP	SLG	AB	H	2B	3B	HR	RBI	BB	SO
Totals	.246	.320	.390	708	174	30	9	18	115	81	127
Pitching vs. Left and Right-handed Batters											
Left	.255	.332	.386	345	88	12	6	7	50	43	47
Right	.237	.308	.394	363	86	18	3	11	65	38	80
Situational											
Bases Empty	.243	.312	.379	367	89	15	4	9	9	36	61
Leadoff	.235	.313	.369	149	35	8	3	2	2	17	23
Not Leadoff	.248	.311	.385	218	54	7	1	7	7	19	38
Runners On	.249	.327	.402	341	85	15	5	9	106	45	66
First Base Only	.228	.291	.407	145	33	5	3	5	17	13	31
Scoring Position	.265	.351	.398	196	52	10	2	4	89	32	35
Late Innings, Close	.112	.209	.175	143	16	1	1	2	15	18	32

RBI/Opportunities

Scoring Position	78 / 304	(26%)
Scoring Position, 2 Out	32 / 148	(22%)
On Third, Less than 2 Out	36 / 58	(62%)
RBI in close games / RBI Total	48 / 115	(42%)

Dusty Baker
Oakland A's

THREE YEARS (84 – 86)

	Ave.	OBP	SLG	AB	H	2B	3B	HR	RBI	BB	SO
Totals	.267	.354	.386	828	221	30	3	21	103	117	111
Batting vs. Left and Right-handed Pitchers											
Left	.250	.349	.348	336	84	12	0	7	35	53	46
Right	.278	.358	.413	492	137	18	3	14	68	64	65
At Home and on the Road											
Home	.260	.362	.358	385	100	10	2	8	40	63	53
Road	.273	.347	.411	443	121	20	1	13	63	54	58
Facing Groundball Pitchers and Flyball Pitchers											
Groundball	.288	.370	.386	396	114	12	0	9	54	54	53
Flyball	.248	.337	.432	432	107	18	3	12	49	63	58
Facing Finesse Pitchers and Power Pitchers											
Finesse	.265	.332	.373	490	130	16	2	11	56	51	64
Power	.269	.384	.405	338	91	14	1	10	47	66	47
On Grass and on Turf											
Grass	.267	.359	.387	641	171	22	2	17	75	94	89
Turf	.267	.340	.385	187	50	8	1	4	28	23	22
During the Day and at Night											
Day	.268	.361	.350	306	82	9	2	4	43	48	34
Night	.266	.350	.408	522	139	21	1	17	60	69	77
By Month											
April	.306	.397	.469	98	30	1	0	5	24	16	11
May	.231	.308	.350	117	27	3	1	3	12	14	15
June	.297	.387	.407	145	43	2	1	4	16	22	23
July	.287	.369	.448	174	50	7	0	7	21	23	21
August	.240	.328	.304	171	41	8	0	1	16	24	29
Sept/Oct	.244	.340	.358	123	30	9	1	1	14	18	12
Situational											
Bases Empty	.267	.338	.380	460	123	17	1	11	11	49	63
Leadoff	.257	.333	.330	191	49	8	0	2	2	22	35
Not Leadoff	.275	.341	.416	269	74	9	1	9	9	27	28
Runners On	.266	.373	.394	368	98	13	2	10	92	68	48
First Base Only	.269	.353	.353	156	42	5	1	2	7	25	26
Scoring Position	.264	.375	.425	212	56	8	1	8	85	43	22
Late Innings, Close	.296	.384	.478	159	47	6	1	7	33	24	23

RBI/Opportunities

Scoring Position	70 / 303	(23%)
Scoring Position, 2 Out	34 / 143	(24%)
On Third, Less than 2 Out	27 / 60	(45%)
RBI in close games / RBI Total	73 / 103	(71%)

Jay Baller
Chicago Cubs

1986: Power, Flyball   1985: Finesse, Flyball   1984: Did not play

THREE YEARS (84 – 86)

	G	IP	H	BB	SO	SB	CS	W	L	S	ERA
Totals	56	105.2	110	45	73	9	6	4	7	6	4.43
At Home and on the Road											
Home	25	42.2	53	16	38	3	2	3	3	2	5.48
Road	31	63.0	57	29	35	6	4	1	4	4	3.71
During the Day and and at Night											
Day	37	65.2	75	28	47	6	2	3	4	3	4.52
Night	19	40.0	35	17	26	3	4	1	3	3	4.28
On Grass and on Turf											
Grass	35	53.2	64	22	47	5	2	3	3	5	5.53
Turf	21	52.0	46	23	26	4	4	1	4	1	3.29
By Month											
April	10	15.2	14	10	12	4	0	1	0	3	2.87
May	15	17.0	22	5	14	0	0	0	2	2	5.82
June	11	21.0	22	13	16	3	4	1	2	0	6.86
July	0	0.0	0	0	0	0	0	0	0	0	0.00
August	3	18.2	21	8	7	1	0	0	2	0	3.37
Sept/Oct	17	33.1	31	9	24	1	2	2	1	1	3.51

vs. Opponent Batters
THREE YEARS (84 – 86)

	Ave.	OBP	SLG	AB	H	2B	3B	HR	RBI	BB	SO
Totals	.268	.341	.482	411	110	31	6	15	58	45	73
Pitching vs. Left and Right-handed Batters											
Left	.263	.341	.404	228	60	15	4	3	20	28	34
Right	.273	.341	.579	183	50	16	2	12	38	17	39
Situational											
Bases Empty	.256	.312	.508	246	63	21	4	11	11	18	47
Leadoff	.295	.343	.684	95	28	10	3	7	7	7	12
Not Leadoff	.232	.293	.397	151	35	11	1	4	4	11	35
Runners On	.285	.381	.442	165	47	10	2	4	47	27	26
First Base Only	.327	.339	.491	55	18	4	1	1	4	1	8
Scoring Position	.264	.397	.418	110	29	6	1	3	43	26	18
Late Innings, Close	.235	.328	.435	170	40	10	3	6	27	22	37

RBI/Opportunities

Scoring Position	37 / 169	(22%)
Scoring Position, 2 Out	13 / 87	(15%)
On Third, Less than 2 Out	14 / 24	(58%)
RBI in close games / RBI Total	42 / 58	(72%)

Chris Bando
Cleveland Indians

THREE YEARS (84 – 86)

	Ave.	OBP	SLG	AB	H	2B	3B	HR	RBI	BB	SO
Totals	.241	.319	.346	647	156	24	1	14	80	77	105
Batting vs. Left and Right-handed Pitchers											
Left	.260	.299	.362	254	66	9	1	5	31	15	31
Right	.229	.330	.336	393	90	15	0	9	49	62	74
At Home and on the Road											
Home	.255	.325	.361	310	79	13	1	6	43	35	47
Road	.228	.313	.332	337	77	11	0	8	37	42	58
Facing Groundball Pitchers and Flyball Pitchers											
Groundball	.239	.317	.306	310	74	9	0	4	30	36	43
Flyball	.243	.320	.383	337	82	15	1	10	50	41	62
Facing Finesse Pitchers and Power Pitchers											
Finesse	.258	.319	.335	349	90	13	1	4	36	32	39
Power	.221	.319	.359	298	66	11	0	10	44	45	66
On Grass and on Turf											
Grass	.231	.319	.338	527	122	21	1	11	65	70	79
Turf	.283	.318	.383	120	34	3	0	3	15	7	26
During the Day and at Night											
Day	.196	.282	.296	189	37	4	0	5	26	23	28
Night	.260	.334	.367	458	119	20	1	9	54	54	77
By Month											
April	.209	.292	.233	43	9	1	0	0	4	5	3
May	.197	.282	.295	61	12	1	1	1	9	8	15
June	.211	.277	.303	76	16	1	0	2	7	7	12
July	.267	.337	.393	150	40	7	0	4	23	17	20
August	.261	.323	.322	180	47	8	0	1	15	17	29
Sept/Oct	.234	.340	.409	137	32	6	0	6	22	23	26
Situational											
Bases Empty	.246	.309	.355	338	83	11	1	8	8	30	58
Leadoff	.256	.319	.388	129	33	3	1	4	4	12	29
Not Leadoff	.239	.303	.335	209	50	8	0	4	4	18	29
Runners On	.236	.329	.337	309	73	13	0	6	72	47	47
First Base Only	.208	.285	.323	130	27	6	0	3	9	14	18
Scoring Position	.257	.357	.346	179	46	7	0	3	63	33	29
Late Innings, Close	.230	.302	.336	122	28	4	0	3	18	14	23

RBI/Opportunities

Scoring Position	56 / 256	(22%)
Scoring Position, 2 Out	18 / 102	(18%)
On Third, Less than 2 Out	24 / 44	(55%)
RBI in close games / RBI Total	47 / 80	(59%)

Scott Bankhead
Kansas City Royals

1986: Power, Flyball   1985: Did not play   1984: Did not play

THREE YEARS (84 – 86)										
	G	IP	H	BB	SO	SB	CS	W	L	S	ERA
Totals	24	121.0	121	37	94	9	4	8	9	0	4.61
At Home and on the Road											
Home	14	63.2	67	19	47	6	2	4	6	0	5.80
Road	10	57.1	54	18	47	3	2	4	3	0	3.30
During the Day and and at Night											
Day	6	32.0	26	11	27	2	0	4	1	0	3.09
Night	18	89.0	95	26	67	7	4	4	8	0	5.16
On Grass and on Turf											
Grass	6	36.2	34	11	26	2	1	3	1	0	2.45
Turf	18	84.1	87	26	68	7	3	5	8	0	5.55
By Month											
April	0	0.0	0	0	0	0	0	0	0	0	0.00
May	2	6.0	2	1	7	0	0	1	0	0	0.00
June	6	33.2	30	10	29	6	1	2	1	0	3.74
July	6	34.0	35	11	21	3	2	1	4	0	5.03
August	6	37.1	41	8	28	0	1	4	2	0	4.34
Sept/Oct	4	10.0	13	7	9	0	0	0	2	0	9.90

vs. Opponent Batters										
THREE YEARS (84 – 86)										
	Ave.	OBP	SLG	AB	H	2B	3B	HR	RBI	BB	SO
Totals	.259	.314	.418	467	121	24	4	14	56	37	94
Pitching vs. Left and Right-handed Batters											
Left	.242	.296	.414	273	66	8	3	11	39	21	54
Right	.284	.340	.423	194	55	16	1	3	17	16	40
Situational											
Bases Empty	.261	.306	.456	283	74	18	2	11	11	16	61
Leadoff	.289	.317	.463	121	35	4	1	5	5	4	23
Not Leadoff	.241	.297	.451	162	39	14	1	6	6	12	38
Runners On	.255	.327	.359	184	47	6	2	3	45	21	33
First Base Only	.296	.384	.380	71	21	1	1	1	4	3	8
Scoring Position	.230	.328	.345	113	26	5	1	2	41	18	25
Late Innings, Close	.152	.250	.304	46	7	1	0	2	2	6	10

RBI/Opportunities		
Scoring Position	35 / 163	(21%)
Scoring Position, 2 Out	9 / 71	(13%)
On Third, Less than 2 Out	17 / 36	(47%)
RBI in close games / RBI Total	35 / 56	(63%)

Bill Bathe
Oakland A's

THREE YEARS (84 – 86)										
	Ave.	OBP	SLG	AB	H	2B	3B	HR	RBI	BB	SO
Totals	.184	.208	.359	103	19	3	0	5	11	2	20
Batting vs. Left and Right-handed Pitchers											
Left	.204	.204	.408	49	10	1	0	3	5	0	10
Right	.167	.211	.315	54	9	2	0	2	6	2	10
At Home and on the Road											
Home	.239	.239	.522	46	11	1	0	4	7	0	9
Road	.140	.183	.228	57	8	2	0	1	4	2	11
Facing Groundball Pitchers and Flyball Pitchers											
Groundball	.154	.195	.256	39	6	1	0	1	1	1	5
Flyball	.203	.215	.422	64	13	2	0	4	10	1	15
Facing Finesse Pitchers and Power Pitchers											
Finesse	.184	.205	.421	76	14	3	0	5	8	1	11
Power	.185	.214	.185	27	5	0	0	0	3	1	9
On Grass and on Turf											
Grass	.176	.202	.352	91	16	1	0	5	9	2	16
Turf	.250	.250	.417	12	3	2	0	0	2	0	4
During the Day and at Night											
Day	.188	.212	.281	32	6	0	0	1	3	1	5
Night	.183	.205	.394	71	13	3	0	4	8	1	15
By Month											
April	.190	.190	.238	21	4	1	0	0	2	0	5
May	.155	.169	.379	58	9	1	0	4	7	1	12
June	.250	.308	.417	24	6	1	0	1	2	1	3
July	.000	.000	.000	0	0	0	0	0	0	0	0
August	.000	.000	.000	0	0	0	0	0	0	0	0
Sept/Oct	.000	.000	.000	0	0	0	0	0	0	0	0
Situational											
Bases Empty	.233	.270	.467	60	14	2	0	4	4	2	11
Leadoff	.222	.250	.370	27	6	1	0	1	1	1	4
Not Leadoff	.242	.286	.545	33	8	1	0	3	3	1	7
Runners On	.116	.116	.209	43	5	1	0	1	7	0	9
First Base Only	.100	.100	.200	10	1	1	0	0	1	0	1
Scoring Position	.121	.121	.212	33	4	0	0	1	6	0	8
Late Innings, Close	.111	.111	.111	9	1	0	0	0	0	0	0

RBI/Opportunities		
Scoring Position	5 / 38	(13%)
Scoring Position, 2 Out	3 / 17	(18%)
On Third, Less than 2 Out	2 / 6	(33%)
RBI in close games / RBI Total	9 / 11	(82%)

Billy Beane
Minnesota Twins

THREE YEARS (84 – 86)										
	Ave.	OBP	SLG	AB	H	2B	3B	HR	RBI	BB	SO
Totals	.209	.250	.289	201	42	7	0	3	16	11	59
Batting vs. Left and Right-handed Pitchers											
Left	.257	.286	.317	101	26	3	0	1	7	4	25
Right	.160	.215	.260	100	16	4	0	2	9	7	34
At Home and on the Road											
Home	.196	.253	.217	92	18	2	0	0	4	7	27
Road	.220	.248	.349	109	24	5	0	3	12	4	32
Facing Groundball Pitchers and Flyball Pitchers											
Groundball	.205	.247	.346	78	16	5	0	2	8	6	22
Flyball	.211	.242	.252	123	26	2	0	1	8	5	37
Facing Finesse Pitchers and Power Pitchers											
Finesse	.243	.291	.350	103	25	5	0	2	10	7	25
Power	.173	.206	.224	98	17	2	0	1	6	4	34
On Grass and on Turf											
Grass	.213	.229	.340	94	20	3	0	3	10	2	28
Turf	.206	.267	.243	107	22	4	0	0	6	9	31
During the Day and at Night											
Day	.148	.161	.180	61	9	2	0	0	3	1	19
Night	.236	.287	.336	140	33	5	0	3	13	10	40
By Month											
April	.417	.500	.667	12	5	0	0	1	4	2	3
May	.114	.162	.143	35	4	1	0	0	1	2	10
June	.059	.111	.059	17	1	0	0	0	0	1	3
July	.000	.000	.000	0	0	0	0	0	0	0	0
August	.216	.259	.255	51	11	2	0	0	4	3	15
Sept/Oct	.244	.270	.360	86	21	4	0	2	7	3	28
Situational											
Bases Empty	.212	.252	.274	113	24	4	0	1	1	6	33
Leadoff	.154	.200	.212	52	8	0	0	1	1	3	12
Not Leadoff	.262	.297	.328	61	16	4	0	0	0	3	21
Runners On	.205	.247	.307	88	18	3	0	2	15	5	26
First Base Only	.167	.189	.222	36	6	2	0	0	0	1	9
Scoring Position	.231	.286	.365	52	12	1	0	2	15	4	17
Late Innings, Close	.200	.226	.233	30	6	1	0	0	2	1	10

RBI/Opportunities		
Scoring Position	13 / 70	(19%)
Scoring Position, 2 Out	3 / 29	(10%)
On Third, Less than 2 Out	4 / 11	(36%)
RBI in close games / RBI Total	9 / 16	(56%)

Rafael Belliard
Pittsburgh Pirates

THREE YEARS (84 – 86)										
	Ave.	OBP	SLG	AB	H	2B	3B	HR	RBI	BB	SO
Totals	.231	.289	.256	351	81	5	2	0	32	26	60
Batting vs. Left and Right-handed Pitchers											
Left	.234	.285	.234	128	30	0	0	0	11	9	18
Right	.229	.291	.269	223	51	5	2	0	21	17	42
At Home and on the Road											
Home	.205	.265	.228	171	35	2	1	0	17	12	22
Road	.256	.311	.283	180	46	3	1	0	15	14	38
Facing Groundball Pitchers and Flyball Pitchers											
Groundball	.241	.295	.241	158	38	0	0	0	14	17	30
Flyball	.223	.265	.269	193	43	5	2	0	18	9	30
Facing Finesse Pitchers and Power Pitchers											
Finesse	.242	.288	.263	198	48	2	1	0	18	13	30
Power	.216	.290	.248	153	33	3	1	0	14	13	30
On Grass and on Turf											
Grass	.307	.352	.347	101	31	2	1	0	10	6	24
Turf	.200	.264	.220	250	50	3	1	0	22	20	36
During the Day and at Night											
Day	.257	.302	.266	109	28	1	0	0	9	6	19
Night	.219	.283	.252	242	53	4	2	0	23	20	41
By Month											
April	.229	.245	.250	48	11	1	0	0	5	1	13
May	.103	.133	.103	29	3	0	0	0	1	1	6
June	.271	.340	.294	85	23	0	1	0	12	7	14
July	.240	.321	.300	50	12	1	1	0	6	5	5
August	.224	.262	.241	58	13	1	0	0	4	3	9
Sept/Oct	.235	.308	.259	81	19	2	0	0	4	9	13
Situational											
Bases Empty	.237	.299	.253	194	46	3	0	0	0	16	37
Leadoff	.282	.325	.282	78	22	0	0	0	0	5	12
Not Leadoff	.207	.281	.233	116	24	3	0	0	0	11	25
Runners On	.223	.276	.261	157	35	2	2	0	32	10	23
First Base Only	.179	.220	.214	56	10	0	1	0	1	3	7
Scoring Position	.248	.306	.287	101	25	2	1	0	31	7	16
Late Innings, Close	.189	.318	.216	37	7	1	0	0	2	6	10

RBI/Opportunities		
Scoring Position	30 / 142	(21%)
Scoring Position, 2 Out	15 / 62	(24%)
On Third, Less than 2 Out	11 / 28	(39%)
RBI in close games / RBI Total	23 / 32	(72%)

Bruce Benedict
Atlanta Braves

	Ave.	OBP	SLG	AB	H	2B	3B	HR	RBI	BB	SO
THREE YEARS (84 – 86)											
Totals	.217	.293	.277	668	145	24	2	4	58	71	47
Batting vs. Left and Right-handed Pitchers											
Left	.237	.323	.340	194	46	10	2	2	19	23	5
Right	.209	.281	.251	474	99	14	0	2	39	48	42
At Home and on the Road											
Home	.241	.317	.307	352	85	17	0	2	32	37	21
Road	.190	.267	.244	316	60	7	2	2	26	34	26
Facing Groundball Pitchers and Flyball Pitchers											
Groundball	.241	.313	.282	323	78	10	0	1	27	33	17
Flyball	.194	.276	.272	345	67	14	2	3	31	38	30
Facing Finesse Pitchers and Power Pitchers											
Finesse	.210	.274	.276	395	83	18	1	2	33	34	25
Power	.227	.320	.278	273	62	6	1	2	25	37	22
On Grass and on Turf											
Grass	.227	.299	.285	512	116	19	1	3	46	52	36
Turf	.186	.274	.250	156	29	5	1	1	12	19	11
During the Day and at Night											
Day	.235	.303	.287	251	59	10	0	1	21	24	20
Night	.206	.288	.271	417	86	14	2	3	37	47	27
By Month											
April	.224	.298	.282	85	19	2	0	1	3	8	5
May	.214	.309	.262	84	18	4	0	0	5	12	6
June	.258	.355	.376	93	24	9	1	0	17	15	12
July	.224	.313	.259	116	26	1	0	1	8	13	2
August	.252	.312	.330	115	29	4	1	1	13	9	7
Sept/Oct	.166	.223	.206	175	29	4	0	1	12	14	15
Situational											
Bases Empty	.219	.284	.285	393	86	10	2	4	4	35	31
Leadoff	.232	.279	.303	185	43	3	2	2	2	12	13
Not Leadoff	.207	.289	.269	208	43	7	0	2	2	23	18
Runners On	.215	.305	.265	275	59	14	0	0	54	36	16
First Base Only	.205	.268	.248	117	24	5	0	0	2	7	5
Scoring Position	.222	.330	.278	158	35	9	0	0	52	29	11
Late Innings, Close	.198	.264	.228	101	20	3	0	0	3	9	8

RBI/Opportunities		
Scoring Position	48 / 231	(21%)
Scoring Position, 2 Out	24 / 104	(23%)
On Third, Less than 2 Out	17 / 35	(49%)
RBI in close games / RBI Total	35 / 58	(60%)

Juan Beniquez
Baltimore Orioles

	Ave.	OBP	SLG	AB	H	2B	3B	HR	RBI	BB	SO
THREE YEARS (84 – 86)											
Totals	.313	.369	.422	1108	347	45	5	22	117	92	138
Batting vs. Left and Right-handed Pitchers											
Left	.355	.404	.492	465	165	20	4	12	51	37	36
Right	.283	.343	.372	643	182	25	1	10	66	55	102
At Home and on the Road											
Home	.338	.391	.461	571	193	19	3	15	69	49	66
Road	.287	.345	.382	537	154	26	2	7	48	43	72
Facing Groundball Pitchers and Flyball Pitchers											
Groundball	.308	.369	.391	471	145	19	1	6	48	40	62
Flyball	.317	.369	.446	637	202	26	4	16	69	52	76
Facing Finesse Pitchers and Power Pitchers											
Finesse	.308	.358	.417	607	187	23	2	13	59	41	66
Power	.319	.381	.429	501	160	22	3	9	58	51	72
On Grass and on Turf											
Grass	.325	.379	.444	951	309	40	5	21	106	77	121
Turf	.242	.309	.293	157	38	5	0	1	11	15	17
During the Day and at Night											
Day	.356	.425	.488	303	108	10	3	8	31	32	39
Night	.297	.347	.398	805	239	35	2	14	86	60	99
By Month											
April	.286	.350	.429	105	30	3	0	4	14	10	15
May	.317	.360	.407	199	63	6	0	4	19	13	22
June	.335	.389	.473	203	68	7	3	5	25	18	19
July	.284	.344	.370	208	59	6	0	4	17	15	27
August	.320	.385	.446	175	56	8	1	4	23	18	18
Sept/Oct	.326	.376	.417	218	71	15	1	1	19	18	37
Situational											
Bases Empty	.318	.372	.425	633	201	32	3	10	10	49	79
Leadoff	.322	.386	.424	258	83	19	1	2	2	25	38
Not Leadoff	.315	.362	.424	375	118	13	2	8	8	24	41
Runners On	.307	.364	.419	475	146	13	2	12	107	43	59
First Base Only	.315	.376	.417	216	68	5	1	5	13	19	24
Scoring Position	.301	.355	.421	259	78	8	1	7	94	24	35
Late Innings, Close	.314	.358	.386	207	65	6	0	3	22	15	31

RBI/Opportunities		
Scoring Position	82 / 355	(23%)
Scoring Position, 2 Out	26 / 125	(21%)
On Third, Less than 2 Out	32 / 72	(44%)
RBI in close games / RBI Total	75 / 117	(64%)

Juan Berenguer
San Francisco Giants

1986: Power, Flyball **1985: Power, Flyball** **1984: Power, Flyball**

	G	IP	H	BB	SO	SB	CS	W	L	S	ERA
THREE YEARS (84 – 86)											
Totals	108	336.2	306	171	272	27	20	18	19	4	3.90
At Home and on the Road											
Home	54	179.1	169	90	150	15	10	10	11	3	4.42
Road	54	157.1	137	81	122	12	10	8	8	1	3.32
During the Day and and at Night											
Day	40	105.0	110	66	86	14	10	7	12	2	4.97
Night	68	231.2	196	105	186	13	10	11	7	2	3.42
On Grass and on Turf											
Grass	85	278.2	249	137	221	21	16	16	16	4	3.94
Turf	23	58.0	57	34	51	6	4	2	3	0	3.72
By Month											
April	7	26.1	27	11	20	2	2	1	1	0	3.76
May	20	64.1	68	34	52	3	5	3	5	0	4.48
June	20	59.2	44	31	47	5	5	3	2	3	3.02
July	21	37.1	35	15	28	3	2	1	4	0	5.06
August	22	74.2	67	35	69	6	3	4	1	1	3.37
Sept/Oct	18	74.1	65	45	56	8	3	6	6	0	4.12

	Ave.	OBP	SLG	AB	H	2B	3B	HR	RBI	BB	SO
vs. Opponent Batters											
THREE YEARS (84 – 86)											
Totals	.242	.334	.365	1262	306	51	7	30	149	171	272
Pitching vs. Left and Right-handed Batters											
Left	.257	.354	.387	680	175	26	4	18	66	101	140
Right	.225	.311	.340	582	131	25	3	12	83	70	132
Situational											
Bases Empty	.225	.314	.332	739	166	26	4	15	15	92	172
Leadoff	.190	.275	.294	310	59	13	2	5	5	35	72
Not Leadoff	.249	.342	.359	429	107	13	2	10	10	57	100
Runners On	.268	.361	.413	523	140	25	3	15	134	79	100
First Base Only	.259	.323	.396	255	66	12	1	7	20	24	45
Scoring Position	.276	.393	.429	268	74	13	2	8	114	55	55
Late Innings, Close	.230	.384	.310	126	29	1	0	3	14	32	34

RBI/Opportunities		
Scoring Position	99 / 406	(24%)
Scoring Position, 2 Out	44 / 206	(21%)
On Third, Less than 2 Out	36 / 77	(47%)
RBI in close games / RBI Total	93 / 149	(62%)

Dave Bergman
Detroit Tigers

	Ave.	OBP	SLG	AB	H	2B	3B	HR	RBI	BB	SO
THREE YEARS (84 – 86)											
Totals	.238	.321	.351	541	129	16	6	11	60	67	71
Batting vs. Left and Right-handed Pitchers											
Left	.222	.317	.306	36	8	1	1	0	2	5	3
Right	.240	.322	.354	505	121	15	5	11	58	62	68
At Home and on the Road											
Home	.217	.311	.342	272	59	6	5	6	37	39	32
Road	.260	.332	.361	269	70	10	1	5	23	28	39
Facing Groundball Pitchers and Flyball Pitchers											
Groundball	.236	.336	.322	258	61	8	1	4	26	38	27
Flyball	.240	.308	.378	283	68	8	5	7	34	29	44
Facing Finesse Pitchers and Power Pitchers											
Finesse	.246	.323	.340	297	73	9	2	5	27	35	30
Power	.230	.319	.365	244	56	7	4	6	33	32	41
On Grass and on Turf											
Grass	.227	.313	.333	463	105	12	5	9	52	58	59
Turf	.308	.375	.462	78	24	4	1	2	8	9	12
During the Day and at Night											
Day	.240	.326	.338	154	37	7	1	2	15	20	20
Night	.238	.320	.357	387	92	9	5	9	45	47	51
By Month											
April	.244	.320	.267	45	14	1	0	0	7	5	6
May	.333	.416	.449	78	26	3	3	0	8	9	7
June	.235	.344	.382	102	24	3	0	4	12	18	14
July	.190	.283	.317	126	24	4	0	4	15	17	13
August	.237	.304	.371	97	23	3	2	2	13	10	12
Sept/Oct	.226	.287	.301	93	21	2	1	1	5	8	19
Situational											
Bases Empty	.240	.327	.359	304	73	11	2	7	7	36	37
Leadoff	.252	.299	.444	135	34	6	1	6	6	9	15
Not Leadoff	.231	.347	.290	169	39	5	1	1	1	27	22
Runners On	.236	.315	.342	237	56	5	4	4	53	31	34
First Base Only	.283	.345	.368	106	30	4	1	1	4	10	10
Scoring Position	.198	.294	.321	131	26	1	3	3	49	21	24
Late Innings, Close	.264	.317	.455	110	29	4	1	5	17	10	21

RBI/Opportunities		
Scoring Position	43 / 201	(21%)
Scoring Position, 2 Out	13 / 86	(15%)
On Third, Less than 2 Out	22 / 39	(56%)
RBI in close games / RBI Total	33 / 60	(55%)

Dale Berra
New York Yankees

THREE YEARS (84 – 86)	Ave.	OBP	SLG	AB	H	2B	3B	HR	RBI	BB	SO
Totals	.225	.277	.324	667	150	28	1	12	73	50	112
Batting vs. Left and Right-handed Pitchers											
Left	.257	.315	.406	276	71	15	1	8	29	23	38
Right	.202	.251	.266	391	79	13	0	4	44	27	74
At Home and on the Road											
Home	.249	.298	.385	317	79	11	1	10	39	23	47
Road	.203	.258	.269	350	71	17	0	2	34	27	65
Facing Groundball Pitchers and Flyball Pitchers											
Groundball	.234	.268	.353	320	75	17	0	7	39	16	49
Flyball	.216	.285	.297	347	75	11	1	5	34	34	63
Facing Finesse Pitchers and Power Pitchers											
Finesse	.228	.275	.335	373	85	19	0	7	49	26	54
Power	.221	.280	.310	294	65	9	1	5	24	24	58
On Grass and on Turf											
Grass	.247	.301	.349	312	77	18	1	4	33	24	47
Turf	.206	.256	.301	355	73	10	0	8	40	26	65
During the Day and at Night											
Day	.215	.265	.305	233	50	7	1	4	26	16	43
Night	.230	.284	.334	434	100	21	0	8	47	34	69
By Month											
April	.234	.274	.280	107	25	3	1	0	5	6	14
May	.213	.263	.333	141	30	8	0	3	23	10	26
June	.230	.287	.304	161	37	6	0	2	15	13	28
July	.271	.329	.431	144	39	8	0	5	18	13	22
August	.190	.261	.304	79	15	3	0	2	9	8	15
Sept/Oct	.114	.111	.114	35	4	0	0	0	3	0	7
Situational											
Bases Empty	.215	.261	.344	390	84	18	1	10	10	23	71
Leadoff	.267	.321	.400	150	40	9	1	3	3	11	43
Not Leadoff	.183	.222	.308	240	44	9	0	7	7	12	48
Runners On	.238	.298	.296	277	66	10	0	2	63	27	41
First Base Only	.218	.262	.269	119	26	3	0	1	3	7	18
Scoring Position	.253	.323	.316	158	40	7	0	1	60	20	23
Late Innings, Close	.202	.234	.310	129	26	2	0	4	13	6	26

RBI/Opportunities		
Scoring Position	54 / 233	(23%)
Scoring Position, 2 Out	20 / 110	(18%)
On Third, Less than 2 Out	24 / 42	(57%)
RBI in close games / RBI Total	46 / 73	(63%)

Karl Best
Seattle Mariners

1986: Power, Flyball   1985: Power, Flyball   1984: Power, Flyball

THREE YEARS (84 – 86)	G	IP	H	BB	SO	SB	CS	W	L	S	ERA
Totals	46	74.0	67	27	61	6	0	5	5	5	3.04
At Home and on the Road											
Home	28	50.1	45	13	40	3	0	4	3	2	2.68
Road	18	23.2	22	14	21	3	0	1	2	3	3.80
During the Day and and at Night											
Day	14	20.1	15	7	17	1	0	2	0	2	3.54
Night	32	53.2	52	20	44	5	0	3	5	3	2.85
On Grass and on Turf											
Grass	14	20.2	19	13	18	2	0	1	1	3	3.48
Turf	32	53.1	48	14	43	4	0	4	4	2	2.87
By Month											
April	10	15.1	17	8	15	0	0	1	0	1	4.11
May	13	19.2	16	6	21	3	0	1	1	2	3.20
June	6	10.0	6	2	7	0	0	1	1	2	0.90
July	6	10.0	9	2	2	0	0	0	1	0	2.70
August	6	13.0	12	9	10	2	0	1	1	0	3.46
Sept/Oct	5	6.0	7	0	6	1	0	1	1	0	3.00

vs. Opponent Batters THREE YEARS (84 – 86)	Ave.	OBP	SLG	AB	H	2B	3B	HR	RBI	BB	SO
Totals	.238	.306	.337	282	67	12	2	4	36	27	61
Pitching vs. Left and Right-handed Batters											
Left	.254	.343	.357	126	32	5	1	2	14	16	27
Right	.224	.275	.321	156	35	7	1	2	22	11	34
Situational											
Bases Empty	.223	.281	.318	148	33	6	1	2	2	11	32
Leadoff	.200	.250	.333	60	12	2	0	2	2	3	11
Not Leadoff	.239	.302	.307	88	21	4	1	0	0	8	21
Runners On	.254	.331	.358	134	34	6	1	2	34	16	29
First Base Only	.292	.404	.396	48	14	2	0	1	2	8	11
Scoring Position	.233	.289	.337	86	20	4	1	1	32	8	18
Late Innings, Close	.247	.310	.390	77	19	3	1	2	12	6	18

RBI/Opportunities		
Scoring Position	31 / 126	(25%)
Scoring Position, 2 Out	17 / 72	(24%)
On Third, Less than 2 Out	10 / 19	(53%)
RBI in close games / RBI Total	18 / 36	(50%)

Buddy Biancalana
Kansas City Royals

THREE YEARS (84 – 86)	Ave.	OBP	SLG	AB	H	2B	3B	HR	RBI	BB	SO
Totals	.212	.272	.303	462	98	15	6	5	23	38	128
Batting vs. Left and Right-handed Pitchers											
Left	.233	.289	.278	90	21	2	1	0	4	7	17
Right	.207	.268	.309	372	77	13	5	5	19	31	111
At Home and on the Road											
Home	.227	.307	.322	242	55	10	5	1	14	28	62
Road	.195	.230	.282	220	43	5	1	4	9	10	66
Facing Groundball Pitchers and Flyball Pitchers											
Groundball	.214	.261	.300	220	47	9	2	2	12	14	52
Flyball	.211	.282	.306	242	51	6	4	3	11	24	76
Facing Finesse Pitchers and Power Pitchers											
Finesse	.228	.280	.333	267	61	11	4	3	13	19	65
Power	.190	.262	.262	195	37	4	2	2	10	19	63
On Grass and on Turf											
Grass	.185	.216	.281	178	33	3	1	4	9	7	58
Turf	.229	.305	.317	284	65	12	5	1	14	31	70
During the Day and at Night											
Day	.213	.241	.315	108	23	3	1	2	3	4	30
Night	.212	.281	.299	354	75	12	5	3	20	34	98
By Month											
April	.154	.233	.231	39	6	0	0	1	5	4	13
May	.231	.231	.231	13	3	0	0	0	1	0	4
June	.256	.315	.415	82	21	3	2	2	5	7	24
July	.159	.198	.159	82	13	0	0	0	0	4	23
August	.248	.336	.352	105	26	6	1	1	4	14	30
Sept/Oct	.206	.253	.312	141	29	6	3	1	8	9	34
Situational											
Bases Empty	.226	.283	.303	297	67	11	3	2	2	24	86
Leadoff	.246	.301	.325	126	31	5	1	1	1	10	31
Not Leadoff	.211	.270	.287	171	36	6	2	1	1	14	55
Runners On	.188	.251	.303	165	31	4	3	3	21	14	42
First Base Only	.177	.226	.304	79	14	3	2	1	5	5	19
Scoring Position	.198	.274	.302	86	17	1	1	2	16	9	23
Late Innings, Close	.140	.245	.163	43	6	1	0	0	0	6	16

RBI/Opportunities		
Scoring Position	12 / 130	(9%)
Scoring Position, 2 Out	3 / 62	(5%)
On Third, Less than 2 Out	6 / 18	(33%)
RBI in close games / RBI Total	9 / 23	(39%)

Mike Bielecki
Pittsburgh Pirates

1986: Power, Groundball   1985: Power, Flyball   1984: Finesse, Groundball

THREE YEARS (84 – 86)	G	IP	H	BB	SO	SB	CS	W	L	S	ERA
Totals	47	198.2	198	114	106	18	12	8	14	0	4.53
At Home and on the Road											
Home	21	101.2	103	62	57	9	6	3	8	0	5.05
Road	26	97.0	95	52	49	9	6	5	6	0	3.99
During the Day and and at Night											
Day	19	59.1	59	36	23	7	7	1	5	0	5.92
Night	28	139.1	139	78	83	11	5	7	9	0	3.94
On Grass and on Turf											
Grass	16	57.2	49	28	27	1	5	4	2	0	3.75
Turf	31	141.0	149	86	79	17	7	4	12	0	4.85
By Month											
April	6	27.2	37	19	14	2	1	2	1	0	6.51
May	10	47.0	44	29	25	3	2	2	5	0	4.98
June	6	36.0	36	17	22	4	4	1	2	0	3.75
July	5	23.0	19	15	16	2	1	2	1	0	4.70
August	6	32.0	30	16	18	5	1	0	3	0	3.94
Sept/Oct	14	33.0	32	18	11	2	3	1	2	0	3.55

vs. Opponent Batters THREE YEARS (84 – 86)	Ave.	OBP	SLG	AB	H	2B	3B	HR	RBI	BB	SO
Totals	.261	.357	.392	760	198	35	10	15	91	114	106
Pitching vs. Left and Right-handed Batters											
Left	.256	.331	.402	425	109	20	6	10	54	49	42
Right	.266	.388	.379	335	89	15	4	5	37	65	64
Situational											
Bases Empty	.251	.349	.394	411	103	20	6	9	9	59	44
Leadoff	.246	.348	.363	179	44	8	2	3	3	26	17
Not Leadoff	.254	.348	.418	232	59	12	4	6	6	33	27
Runners On	.272	.366	.390	349	95	15	4	6	82	55	62
First Base Only	.305	.372	.443	131	40	11	2	1	10	14	20
Scoring Position	.252	.362	.358	218	55	4	2	5	72	41	42
Late Innings, Close	.250	.438	.292	24	6	1	0	0	4	8	4

RBI/Opportunities		
Scoring Position	59 / 298	(20%)
Scoring Position, 2 Out	28 / 157	(18%)
On Third, Less than 2 Out	24 / 52	(46%)
RBI in close games / RBI Total	67 / 91	(74%)

Dann Bilardello
Montreal Expos

	Ave.	OBP	SLG	AB	H	2B	3B	HR	RBI	BB	SO
THREE YEARS (84 – 86)											
Totals	.194	.255	.263	475	92	12	0	7	36	37	81
Batting vs. Left and Right-handed Pitchers											
Left	.212	.280	.253	170	36	4	0	1	12	16	33
Right	.184	.241	.269	305	56	8	0	6	24	21	48
At Home and on the Road											
Home	.213	.267	.300	230	49	8	0	4	21	17	44
Road	.176	.243	.229	245	43	4	0	3	15	20	37
Facing Groundball Pitchers and Flyball Pitchers											
Groundball	.192	.231	.251	239	46	5	0	3	14	11	39
Flyball	.195	.278	.275	236	46	7	0	4	22	26	42
Facing Finesse Pitchers and Power Pitchers											
Finesse	.201	.237	.285	274	55	8	0	5	20	13	38
Power	.184	.278	.234	201	37	4	0	2	16	24	43
On Grass and on Turf											
Grass	.178	.254	.225	129	23	0	0	2	6	11	22
Turf	.199	.255	.277	346	69	12	0	5	30	26	59
During the Day and at Night											
Day	.204	.271	.289	152	31	4	0	3	14	14	22
Night	.189	.247	.251	323	61	8	0	4	22	23	59
By Month											
April	.219	.310	.307	114	25	4	0	2	12	13	15
May	.185	.264	.262	65	12	2	0	1	5	7	19
June	.173	.225	.240	75	13	2	0	1	2	5	12
July	.183	.224	.226	93	17	1	0	1	5	5	15
August	.195	.235	.195	77	15	0	0	0	6	4	11
Sept/Oct	.196	.241	.373	51	10	3	0	2	6	3	9
Situational											
Bases Empty	.204	.254	.245	265	54	5	0	2	2	16	46
Leadoff	.171	.239	.187	123	21	2	0	0	0	10	26
Not Leadoff	.232	.268	.296	142	33	3	0	2	2	6	20
Runners On	.181	.255	.286	210	38	7	0	5	34	21	35
First Base Only	.170	.240	.318	88	15	4	0	3	8	8	8
Scoring Position	.189	.267	.262	122	23	3	0	2	26	13	27
Late Innings, Close	.163	.234	.198	86	14	3	0	0	4	8	19

RBI/Opportunities		
Scoring Position	24 / 152	(16%)
Scoring Position, 2 Out	4 / 61	(7%)
On Third, Less than 2 Out	8 / 25	(32%)
RBI in close games / RBI Total	28 / 36	(78%)

Vida Blue
San Francisco Giants

1986: Power, Flyball   **1985: Power, Flyball**   **1984: Did not play**

	G	IP	H	BB	SO	SB	CS	W	L	S	ERA
THREE YEARS (84 – 86)											
Totals	61	287.2	252	157	203	19	17	18	18	0	3.82
At Home and on the Road											
Home	35	174.2	140	91	113	9	8	12	8	0	3.66
Road	26	113.0	112	66	90	10	9	6	10	0	4.06
During the Day and and at Night											
Day	32	159.0	130	77	113	9	11	10	8	0	3.57
Night	29	128.2	122	80	90	10	6	8	10	0	4.13
On Grass and on Turf											
Grass	48	229.2	196	124	159	15	11	15	12	0	3.72
Turf	13	58.0	56	33	44	4	6	3	6	0	4.19
By Month											
April	7	16.2	18	7	12	1	2	3	2	0	3.78
May	5	10.1	14	7	9	1	0	0	2	0	9.58
June	12	63.1	39	33	48	4	2	6	2	0	1.99
July	11	44.2	48	27	28	6	6	3	4	0	5.24
August	12	78.0	68	40	60	2	3	2	5	0	3.46
Sept/Oct	14	74.2	65	43	46	5	4	4	3	0	4.10

	Ave.	OBP	SLG	AB	H	2B	3B	HR	RBI	BB	SO
vs. Opponent Batters											
THREE YEARS (84 – 86)											
Totals	.240	.336	.401	1052	252	52	5	36	120	157	203
Pitching vs. Left and Right-handed Batters											
Left	.210	.293	.346	162	34	5	1	5	17	18	38
Right	.245	.344	.411	890	218	47	4	31	103	139	165
Situational											
Bases Empty	.251	.365	.449	593	149	35	5	24	24	105	115
Leadoff	.254	.351	.450	260	66	15	3	10	10	38	46
Not Leadoff	.249	.375	.447	333	83	20	2	14	14	67	69
Runners On	.224	.298	.340	459	103	17	0	12	96	52	88
First Base Only	.201	.272	.299	224	45	10	0	4	11	22	51
Scoring Position	.247	.321	.379	235	58	7	0	8	85	30	37
Late Innings, Close	.239	.297	.552	67	16	4	1	5	11	6	13

RBI/Opportunities		
Scoring Position	73 / 317	(23%)
Scoring Position, 2 Out	30 / 155	(19%)
On Third, Less than 2 Out	27 / 42	(64%)
RBI in close games / RBI Total	98 / 120	(82%)

Bruce Bochy
San Diego Padres

	Ave.	OBP	SLG	AB	H	2B	3B	HR	RBI	BB	SO
THREE YEARS (84 – 86)											
Totals	.251	.299	.468	331	83	16	1	18	50	23	74
Batting vs. Left and Right-handed Pitchers											
Left	.248	.293	.505	210	52	10	1	14	35	14	41
Right	.256	.308	.405	121	31	6	0	4	15	9	33
At Home and on the Road											
Home	.237	.296	.511	131	31	6	0	10	22	11	33
Road	.260	.300	.440	200	52	10	1	8	28	12	41
Facing Groundball Pitchers and Flyball Pitchers											
Groundball	.250	.301	.442	172	43	7	1	8	25	13	36
Flyball	.252	.296	.497	159	40	9	0	10	25	10	38
Facing Finesse Pitchers and Power Pitchers											
Finesse	.265	.306	.497	151	40	8	0	9	23	9	25
Power	.239	.292	.444	180	43	8	1	9	27	14	49
On Grass and on Turf											
Grass	.229	.273	.458	227	52	10	0	14	36	14	54
Turf	.298	.354	.490	104	31	6	1	4	14	9	20
During the Day and at Night											
Day	.250	.274	.429	140	35	10	0	5	21	5	36
Night	.251	.316	.497	191	48	6	1	13	29	18	38
By Month											
April	.176	.222	.412	17	3	1	0	1	1	1	3
May	.256	.319	.512	43	11	2	0	3	6	4	13
June	.190	.262	.328	58	11	2	0	2	4	6	12
July	.360	.385	.640	50	18	3	1	3	10	2	7
August	.296	.359	.592	71	21	6	0	5	19	7	17
Sept/Oct	.207	.232	.359	92	19	2	0	4	10	3	22
Situational											
Bases Empty	.251	.286	.497	183	46	7	1	12	12	9	40
Leadoff	.313	.337	.639	83	26	6	0	7	7	3	14
Not Leadoff	.200	.245	.380	100	20	1	1	5	5	6	26
Runners On	.250	.313	.432	148	37	9	0	6	38	14	34
First Base Only	.246	.292	.508	61	15	4	0	4	10	4	14
Scoring Position	.253	.327	.379	87	22	5	0	2	28	10	20
Late Innings, Close	.273	.313	.468	77	21	3	0	4	11	5	20

RBI/Opportunities		
Scoring Position	25 / 114	(22%)
Scoring Position, 2 Out	9 / 54	(17%)
On Third, Less than 2 Out	11 / 21	(52%)
RBI in close games / RBI Total	30 / 50	(60%)

Bobby Bonilla
Pittsburgh Pirates

	Ave.	OBP	SLG	AB	H	2B	3B	HR	RBI	BB	SO
THREE YEARS (84 – 86)											
Totals	.256	.352	.333	426	109	16	4	3	43	62	88
Batting vs. Left and Right-handed Pitchers											
Left	.269	.353	.330	182	49	9	1	0	19	23	25
Right	.246	.352	.336	244	60	7	3	3	24	39	63
At Home and on the Road											
Home	.270	.366	.365	200	54	7	3	2	31	29	37
Road	.243	.340	.305	226	55	9	1	1	12	33	51
Facing Groundball Pitchers and Flyball Pitchers											
Groundball	.249	.342	.290	169	42	7	0	0	17	23	27
Flyball	.261	.359	.362	257	67	9	4	3	26	39	61
Facing Finesse Pitchers and Power Pitchers											
Finesse	.286	.379	.400	245	70	15	2	3	27	35	39
Power	.215	.316	.243	181	39	1	2	0	16	27	49
On Grass and on Turf											
Grass	.294	.385	.382	238	70	8	3	2	27	35	43
Turf	.207	.310	.271	188	39	8	2	0	16	27	45
During the Day and at Night											
Day	.279	.359	.360	136	38	8	0	1	19	16	23
Night	.245	.349	.321	290	71	8	4	2	24	46	65
By Month											
April	.298	.370	.383	47	14	2	1	0	4	6	8
May	.221	.316	.291	86	19	3	0	1	7	11	14
June	.294	.422	.426	68	20	4	1	1	13	15	19
July	.289	.347	.311	45	13	1	0	0	2	4	10
August	.256	.354	.349	86	22	6	1	0	14	12	15
Sept/Oct	.223	.324	.277	94	21	0	1	1	3	14	22
Situational											
Bases Empty	.223	.330	.262	256	57	5	1	1	1	39	56
Leadoff	.258	.365	.281	89	23	2	0	0	0	13	17
Not Leadoff	.204	.311	.251	167	34	3	1	1	1	26	39
Runners On	.306	.387	.441	170	52	11	3	2	42	23	32
First Base Only	.388	.438	.537	67	26	3	2	1	4	6	10
Scoring Position	.252	.355	.379	103	26	8	1	1	38	17	22
Late Innings, Close	.218	.315	.295	78	17	3	0	1	6	11	19

RBI/Opportunities		
Scoring Position	33 / 142	(23%)
Scoring Position, 2 Out	8 / 51	(16%)
On Third, Less than 2 Out	13 / 29	(45%)
RBI in close games / RBI Total	28 / 43	(65%)

Juan Bonilla
Baltimore Orioles

	Ave.	OBP	SLG	AB	H	2B	3B	HR	RBI	BB	SO
THREE YEARS (84 – 86)											
Totals	.237	.302	.290	300	71	11	1	1	20	25	24
Batting vs. Left and Right-handed Pitchers											
Left	.226	.282	.296	115	26	5	0	1	9	9	10
Right	.243	.314	.286	185	45	6	1	0	11	16	14
At Home and on the Road											
Home	.187	.264	.216	134	25	4	0	0	7	12	12
Road	.277	.333	.349	166	46	7	1	1	13	13	12
Facing Groundball Pitchers and Flyball Pitchers											
Groundball	.178	.254	.212	118	21	4	0	0	9	11	9
Flyball	.275	.333	.341	182	50	7	1	1	11	14	15
Facing Finesse Pitchers and Power Pitchers											
Finesse	.238	.291	.297	185	44	9	1	0	14	12	11
Power	.235	.318	.278	115	27	2	0	1	6	13	13
On Grass and on Turf											
Grass	.225	.285	.267	236	53	8	1	0	13	18	21
Turf	.281	.361	.375	64	18	3	0	1	7	7	3
During the Day and at Night											
Day	.269	.333	.308	104	28	4	0	0	9	10	12
Night	.219	.285	.281	196	43	7	1	1	11	15	12
By Month											
April	.250	.333	.333	48	12	4	0	0	5	6	5
May	.200	.294	.400	15	3	0	0	1	2	2	1
June	.273	.319	.295	44	12	1	0	0	1	3	2
July	.278	.316	.333	90	25	3	1	0	6	3	8
August	.169	.270	.185	65	11	1	0	0	3	9	4
Sept/Oct	.211	.268	.263	38	8	2	0	0	3	2	4
Situational											
Bases Empty	.210	.287	.267	176	37	7	0	1	1	18	14
Leadoff	.202	.306	.266	94	19	3	0	1	1	13	7
Not Leadoff	.220	.264	.268	82	18	4	0	0	0	5	7
Runners On	.274	.323	.323	124	34	4	1	0	19	7	10
First Base Only	.255	.281	.309	55	14	3	0	0	0	1	2
Scoring Position	.290	.355	.333	69	20	1	1	0	19	6	8
Late Innings, Close	.186	.239	.233	43	8	2	0	0	3	3	4

RBI/Opportunities

Scoring Position	18 / 95	(19%)
Scoring Position, 2 Out	7 / 40	(17%)
On Third, Less than 2 Out	6 / 14	(43%)
RBI in close games / RBI Total	9 / 20	(45%)

Rich Bordi
Baltimore Orioles

1986: Power, Flyball   1985: Finesse, Flyball   1984: Finesse, Groundball

	G	IP	H	BB	SO	SB	CS	W	L	S	ERA
THREE YEARS (84 – 86)											
Totals	134	288.1	278	90	188	32	8	17	14	9	3.75
At Home and on the Road											
Home	75	182.1	164	48	106	16	6	11	8	7	2.96
Road	59	106.0	114	42	82	16	2	6	6	2	5.09
During the Day and and at Night											
Day	62	143.2	134	41	84	15	5	10	4	6	3.45
Night	72	144.2	144	49	104	17	3	7	10	3	4.04
On Grass and on Turf											
Grass	114	254.0	241	68	163	23	8	16	11	9	3.51
Turf	20	34.1	37	22	25	9	0	1	3	0	5.50
By Month											
April	18	30.2	26	13	18	3	2	1	0	1	2.35
May	18	47.0	43	10	30	5	2	4	0	3	2.49
June	27	63.0	62	23	35	7	2	2	2	1	3.71
July	26	64.2	50	19	51	6	0	3	3	2	3.06
August	21	33.0	32	6	20	4	1	3	3	2	5.18
Sept/Oct	24	50.0	65	19	34	7	1	4	6	0	5.76

vs. Opponent Batters

	Ave.	OBP	SLG	AB	H	2B	3B	HR	RBI	BB	SO
THREE YEARS (84 – 86)											
Totals	.250	.307	.377	1112	278	38	8	29	142	90	188
Pitching vs. Left and Right-handed Batters											
Left	.287	.350	.435	494	142	18	5	15	69	49	68
Right	.220	.271	.330	618	136	20	3	14	73	41	120
Situational											
Bases Empty	.244	.301	.386	598	146	19	3	20	20	44	97
Leadoff	.281	.332	.470	249	70	10	2	11	11	18	41
Not Leadoff	.218	.280	.327	349	76	9	1	9	9	26	56
Runners On	.257	.313	.366	514	132	19	5	9	122	46	91
First Base Only	.255	.298	.354	212	54	5	2	4	12	13	30
Scoring Position	.258	.323	.374	302	78	14	3	5	110	33	61
Late Innings, Close	.294	.374	.403	248	73	9	0	6	27	30	43

RBI/Opportunities

Scoring Position	99 / 407	(24%)
Scoring Position, 2 Out	37 / 181	(20%)
On Third, Less than 2 Out	35 / 73	(48%)
RBI in close games / RBI Total	70 / 142	(49%)

Thad Bosley
Chicago Cubs

	Ave.	OBP	SLG	AB	H	2B	3B	HR	RBI	BB	SO
THREE YEARS (84 – 86)											
Totals	.304	.381	.440	398	121	12	6	10	50	51	75
Batting vs. Left and Right-handed Pitchers											
Left	.400	.500	.467	15	6	1	0	0	4	3	6
Right	.300	.376	.439	383	115	11	6	10	46	48	69
At Home and on the Road											
Home	.351	.435	.469	211	74	9	2	4	34	34	33
Road	.251	.314	.406	187	47	3	4	6	16	17	42
Facing Groundball Pitchers and Flyball Pitchers											
Groundball	.310	.391	.443	203	63	5	5	4	28	28	31
Flyball	.297	.370	.436	195	58	7	1	6	22	23	44
Facing Finesse Pitchers and Power Pitchers											
Finesse	.330	.385	.532	203	67	7	5	8	31	20	29
Power	.277	.376	.344	195	54	5	1	2	19	31	46
On Grass and on Turf											
Grass	.306	.389	.429	294	90	10	4	6	39	42	52
Turf	.298	.354	.471	104	31	2	2	4	11	9	23
During the Day and at Night											
Day	.325	.407	.445	274	89	10	4	5	42	40	45
Night	.258	.319	.427	124	32	2	2	5	8	11	30
By Month											
April	.185	.281	.370	27	5	1	2	0	3	4	3
May	.200	.347	.250	40	8	2	0	0	3	9	9
June	.306	.375	.361	72	22	1	0	1	3	8	15
July	.338	.392	.485	68	23	3	2	1	9	6	12
August	.364	.429	.606	99	36	3	0	7	20	12	17
Sept/Oct	.293	.371	.391	92	27	2	2	1	12	12	19
Situational											
Bases Empty	.298	.358	.421	242	72	7	4	5	5	23	48
Leadoff	.327	.357	.455	110	36	2	3	2	2	5	19
Not Leadoff	.273	.360	.394	132	36	5	1	3	3	18	29
Runners On	.314	.412	.468	156	49	5	2	5	45	28	27
First Base Only	.313	.380	.531	64	20	3	1	3	10	7	14
Scoring Position	.315	.431	.424	92	29	2	1	2	35	21	13
Late Innings, Close	.367	.456	.516	128	47	4	0	5	18	21	31

RBI/Opportunities

Scoring Position	31 / 133	(23%)
Scoring Position, 2 Out	6 / 52	(12%)
On Third, Less than 2 Out	16 / 27	(59%)
RBI in close games / RBI Total	31 / 50	(62%)

Daryl Boston
Chicago White Sox

	Ave.	OBP	SLG	AB	H	2B	3B	HR	RBI	BB	SO
THREE YEARS (84 – 86)											
Totals	.233	.286	.352	514	120	27	5	8	40	39	97
Batting vs. Left and Right-handed Pitchers											
Left	.183	.264	.280	82	15	3	1	1	5	9	19
Right	.243	.291	.366	432	105	24	4	7	35	30	78
At Home and on the Road											
Home	.228	.291	.329	237	54	12	3	2	14	22	42
Road	.238	.282	.372	277	66	15	2	6	26	17	55
Facing Groundball Pitchers and Flyball Pitchers											
Groundball	.259	.308	.386	259	67	19	1	4	19	19	42
Flyball	.208	.264	.318	255	53	8	4	4	21	20	55
Facing Finesse Pitchers and Power Pitchers											
Finesse	.249	.286	.396	313	78	17	4	7	27	16	49
Power	.209	.288	.284	201	42	10	1	1	13	23	48
On Grass and on Turf											
Grass	.234	.291	.338	402	94	22	4	4	31	33	70
Turf	.232	.271	.402	112	26	5	1	4	9	6	27
During the Day and at Night											
Day	.220	.267	.319	141	31	7	2	1	10	9	29
Night	.239	.294	.365	373	89	20	3	7	30	30	68
By Month											
April	.292	.320	.417	48	14	4	1	0	4	2	5
May	.189	.259	.284	74	14	2	1	1	3	7	18
June	.200	.235	.338	65	13	3	0	2	6	3	18
July	.000	.000	.000	1	0	0	0	0	0	0	0
August	.333	.389	.520	102	34	6	2	3	15	10	13
Sept/Oct	.201	.256	.290	224	45	12	1	2	12	17	43
Situational											
Bases Empty	.236	.284	.356	326	77	20	2	5	5	22	64
Leadoff	.270	.312	.399	148	40	11	1	2	2	9	33
Not Leadoff	.208	.262	.320	178	37	9	1	3	3	13	31
Runners On	.229	.290	.346	188	43	7	3	3	35	17	33
First Base Only	.256	.291	.329	82	21	3	0	1	4	4	14
Scoring Position	.208	.289	.358	106	22	4	3	2	31	13	19
Late Innings, Close	.138	.207	.188	80	11	1	0	1	4	7	26

RBI/Opportunities

Scoring Position	27 / 150	(18%)
Scoring Position, 2 Out	12 / 74	(16%)
On Third, Less than 2 Out	6 / 17	(35%)
RBI in close games / RBI Total	16 / 40	(40%)

Scott Bradley
Seattle Mariners

	Ave.	OBP	SLG	AB	H	2B	3B	HR	RBI	BB	SO
THREE YEARS (84 – 86)											
Totals	.276	.321	.393	290	80	11	4	5	31	15	13
Batting vs. Left and Right-handed Pitchers											
Left	.154	.185	.269	26	4	1	1	0	0	0	3
Right	.288	.333	.405	264	76	10	3	5	31	15	10
At Home and on the Road											
Home	.324	.381	.486	142	46	7	2	4	18	11	6
Road	.230	.261	.304	148	34	4	2	1	13	4	7
Facing Groundball Pitchers and Flyball Pitchers											
Groundball	.243	.299	.349	152	37	3	2	3	12	8	8
Flyball	.312	.345	.442	138	43	8	2	2	19	7	5
Facing Finesse Pitchers and Power Pitchers											
Finesse	.248	.288	.379	153	38	7	2	3	14	6	7
Power	.307	.356	.409	137	42	4	2	2	17	9	6
On Grass and on Turf											
Grass	.237	.275	.281	139	33	1	1	1	13	7	6
Turf	.311	.362	.497	151	47	10	3	4	18	8	7
During the Day and at Night											
Day	.203	.250	.311	74	15	2	0	2	12	4	4
Night	.301	.345	.421	216	65	9	4	3	19	11	9
By Month											
April	.000	.000	.000	5	0	0	0	0	0	0	0
May	.250	.308	.250	12	3	0	0	0	0	0	0
June	.262	.326	.310	42	11	2	0	0	3	2	2
July	.263	.284	.447	76	20	2	3	2	13	3	3
August	.328	.368	.500	64	21	3	1	2	6	4	2
Sept/Oct	.275	.333	.352	91	25	4	0	1	9	6	6
Situational											
Bases Empty	.290	.324	.414	162	47	8	3	2	2	5	8
Leadoff	.282	.292	.324	71	20	1	1	0	0	0	2
Not Leadoff	.297	.347	.484	91	27	7	2	2	2	5	6
Runners On	.258	.317	.367	128	33	3	1	3	29	10	5
First Base Only	.259	.295	.414	58	15	1	1	2	5	2	2
Scoring Position	.257	.333	.329	70	18	2	0	1	24	8	3
Late Innings, Close	.356	.420	.444	45	16	2	1	0	4	4	3
RBI/Opportunities											
Scoring Position				21 / 97	(22%)						
Scoring Position, 2 Out				7 / 36	(19%)						
On Third, Less than 2 Out				6 / 17	(35%)						
RBI in close games / RBI Total				16 / 31	(52%)						

Glenn Braggs
Milwaukee Brewers

	Ave.	OBP	SLG	AB	H	2B	3B	HR	RBI	BB	SO
THREE YEARS (84 – 86)											
Totals	.237	.274	.349	215	51	8	2	4	18	11	47
Batting vs. Left and Right-handed Pitchers											
Left	.293	.313	.517	58	17	4	0	3	10	2	13
Right	.217	.259	.287	157	34	4	2	1	8	9	34
At Home and on the Road											
Home	.314	.368	.453	86	27	4	1	2	8	7	13
Road	.186	.207	.279	129	24	4	1	2	10	4	34
Facing Groundball Pitchers and Flyball Pitchers											
Groundball	.304	.345	.456	79	24	1	1	3	8	6	16
Flyball	.199	.231	.287	136	27	7	1	1	10	5	31
Facing Finesse Pitchers and Power Pitchers											
Finesse	.230	.258	.310	113	26	3	0	2	10	4	22
Power	.245	.291	.392	102	25	5	2	2	8	7	25
On Grass and on Turf											
Grass	.239	.281	.359	184	44	6	2	4	16	11	39
Turf	.226	.226	.290	31	7	2	0	0	2	0	8
During the Day and at Night											
Day	.186	.265	.233	43	8	2	0	0	5	5	15
Night	.250	.276	.378	172	43	6	2	4	13	6	32
By Month											
April	.000	.000	.000	0	0	0	0	0	0	0	0
May	.000	.000	.000	0	0	0	0	0	0	0	0
June	.000	.000	.000	0	0	0	0	0	0	0	0
July	.279	.295	.372	43	12	4	0	0	4	1	8
August	.231	.265	.352	91	21	2	0	3	7	5	18
Sept/Oct	.222	.273	.333	81	18	2	2	1	7	5	21
Situational											
Bases Empty	.264	.296	.411	129	34	6	2	3	3	5	28
Leadoff	.311	.311	.556	45	14	1	2	2	2	0	7
Not Leadoff	.238	.289	.333	84	20	5	0	1	1	5	21
Runners On	.198	.242	.256	86	17	2	0	1	15	6	19
First Base Only	.289	.325	.368	38	11	0	0	1	2	2	9
Scoring Position	.125	.182	.167	48	6	2	0	0	13	4	10
Late Innings, Close	.216	.293	.243	37	8	1	0	0	2	4	9
RBI/Opportunities											
Scoring Position				12 / 68	(18%)						
Scoring Position, 2 Out				5 / 32	(16%)						
On Third, Less than 2 Out				5 / 12	(42%)						
RBI in close games / RBI Total				10 / 18	(56%)						

Mickey Brantley
Seattle Mariners

	Ave.	OBP	SLG	AB	H	2B	3B	HR	RBI	BB	SO
THREE YEARS (84 – 86)											
Totals	.196	.268	.353	102	20	3	2	3	7	10	21
Batting vs. Left and Right-handed Pitchers											
Left	.182	.206	.333	33	6	0	1	1	2	1	7
Right	.203	.295	.362	69	14	3	1	2	5	9	14
At Home and on the Road											
Home	.171	.244	.366	41	7	2	0	2	6	4	7
Road	.213	.284	.344	61	13	1	2	1	1	6	14
Facing Groundball Pitchers and Flyball Pitchers											
Groundball	.205	.262	.462	39	8	2	1	2	2	3	7
Flyball	.190	.271	.286	63	12	1	1	1	5	7	14
Facing Finesse Pitchers and Power Pitchers											
Finesse	.239	.286	.478	46	11	2	0	3	4	3	7
Power	.161	.254	.250	56	9	1	2	0	3	7	14
On Grass and on Turf											
Grass	.236	.311	.382	55	13	1	2	1	1	6	13
Turf	.149	.216	.319	47	7	2	0	2	6	4	8
During the Day and at Night											
Day	.136	.269	.273	22	3	0	0	1	1	4	3
Night	.212	.267	.375	80	17	3	2	2	6	6	18
By Month											
April	.000	.000	.000	0	0	0	0	0	0	0	0
May	.000	.000	.000	0	0	0	0	0	0	0	0
June	.000	.000	.000	0	0	0	0	0	0	0	0
July	.000	.000	.000	0	0	0	0	0	0	0	0
August	.185	.264	.323	65	12	1	1	2	6	7	13
Sept/Oct	.216	.275	.405	37	8	2	1	1	1	3	8
Situational											
Bases Empty	.231	.324	.415	65	15	2	2	2	2	9	14
Leadoff	.250	.341	.528	36	9	0	2	2	2	5	4
Not Leadoff	.207	.303	.276	29	6	2	0	0	0	4	10
Runners On	.135	.158	.243	37	5	1	0	1	5	1	7
First Base Only	.118	.167	.176	17	2	0	0	0	0	1	1
Scoring Position	.150	.150	.350	20	3	1	0	1	5	0	6
Late Innings, Close	.133	.235	.400	15	2	1	0	1	1	2	4
RBI/Opportunities											
Scoring Position				3 / 24	(13%)						
Scoring Position, 2 Out				2 / 13	(15%)						
On Third, Less than 2 Out				0 / 4	(0%)						
RBI in close games / RBI Total				7 / 7	(100%)						

Greg Brock
Los Angeles Dodgers

	Ave.	OBP	SLG	AB	H	2B	3B	HR	RBI	BB	SO
THREE YEARS (84 – 86)											
Totals	.239	.322	.424	1034	247	38	0	51	152	131	169
Batting vs. Left and Right-handed Pitchers											
Left	.168	.232	.298	238	40	7	0	8	26	20	56
Right	.260	.348	.461	796	207	31	0	43	126	111	113
At Home and on the Road											
Home	.246	.322	.395	504	124	15	0	20	77	58	79
Road	.232	.322	.451	530	123	23	0	31	75	73	90
Facing Groundball Pitchers and Flyball Pitchers											
Groundball	.258	.342	.445	449	116	18	0	22	78	59	70
Flyball	.224	.306	.407	585	131	20	0	29	74	72	99
Facing Finesse Pitchers and Power Pitchers											
Finesse	.258	.334	.450	573	148	20	0	30	81	68	68
Power	.215	.307	.390	461	99	18	0	21	71	63	101
On Grass and on Turf											
Grass	.240	.323	.415	792	190	25	0	38	123	101	126
Turf	.236	.318	.450	242	57	13	0	13	29	30	43
During the Day and at Night											
Day	.269	.340	.492	331	89	11	0	21	61	38	50
Night	.225	.313	.391	703	158	27	0	30	91	93	119
By Month											
April	.196	.281	.361	158	31	2	0	8	16	19	25
May	.217	.304	.399	143	31	2	0	8	23	18	25
June	.253	.344	.495	182	46	8	0	12	27	27	29
July	.308	.361	.492	120	37	4	0	6	30	11	24
August	.243	.316	.396	235	57	12	0	8	27	26	34
Sept/Oct	.230	.330	.418	196	45	10	0	9	29	30	32
Situational											
Bases Empty	.225	.294	.410	561	126	23	0	27	27	55	85
Leadoff	.201	.257	.388	224	45	6	0	12	12	17	38
Not Leadoff	.240	.317	.424	337	81	17	0	15	15	38	47
Runners On	.256	.353	.440	473	121	15	0	24	125	76	84
First Base Only	.277	.373	.450	202	56	8	0	9	18	31	38
Scoring Position	.240	.338	.432	271	65	7	0	15	107	45	46
Late Innings, Close	.167	.254	.233	180	30	3	0	3	12	21	36
RBI/Opportunities											
Scoring Position				81 / 380	(21%)						
Scoring Position, 2 Out				29 / 191	(15%)						
On Third, Less than 2 Out				30 / 64	(47%)						
RBI in close games / RBI Total				91 / 152	(60%)						

Tom Brookens
Detroit Tigers

THREE YEARS (84 – 86)

	Ave.	OBP	SLG	AB	H	2B	3B	HR	RBI	BB	SO
Totals	.248	.296	.375	990	246	56	12	15	98	67	153
Batting vs. Left and Right-handed Pitchers											
Left	.285	.336	.435	471	134	28	8	9	45	37	60
Right	.216	.260	.320	519	112	28	4	6	53	30	93
At Home and on the Road											
Home	.243	.294	.383	486	118	29	6	9	48	35	83
Road	.254	.299	.367	504	128	27	6	6	50	32	70
Facing Groundball Pitchers and Flyball Pitchers											
Groundball	.257	.298	.378	452	116	28	6	5	45	26	66
Flyball	.242	.295	.372	538	130	28	6	10	53	41	87
Facing Finesse Pitchers and Power Pitchers											
Finesse	.254	.283	.363	575	146	33	6	6	50	24	64
Power	.241	.314	.390	415	100	23	6	9	48	43	89
On Grass and on Turf											
Grass	.246	.296	.374	835	205	46	8	15	89	60	131
Turf	.265	.296	.381	155	41	10	4	0	9	7	22
During the Day and at Night											
Day	.258	.314	.385	291	75	18	5	3	36	25	38
Night	.245	.289	.371	699	171	38	7	12	62	42	115
By Month											
April	.280	.322	.415	82	23	5	3	0	14	5	8
May	.238	.287	.311	151	36	7	2	0	10	11	17
June	.285	.344	.460	200	57	16	2	5	29	18	25
July	.187	.252	.275	193	36	10	2	1	8	16	38
August	.257	.296	.397	179	46	8	1	5	21	10	32
Sept/Oct	.259	.286	.400	185	48	10	2	4	16	7	33
Situational											
Bases Empty	.250	.298	.392	572	143	34	7	11	11	38	88
Leadoff	.236	.293	.352	250	59	11	3	4	4	19	39
Not Leadoff	.261	.302	.422	322	84	23	4	7	7	19	49
Runners On	.246	.294	.352	418	103	22	5	4	87	29	65
First Base Only	.221	.284	.309	181	40	8	1	2	5	16	32
Scoring Position	.266	.302	.384	237	63	14	4	2	82	13	33
Late Innings, Close	.295	.352	.417	132	39	8	1	2	15	12	22

RBI/Opportunities

Scoring Position	75 / 308	(24%)
Scoring Position, 2 Out	36 / 149	(24%)
On Third, Less than 2 Out	22 / 42	(52%)
RBI in close games / RBI Total	46 / 98	(47%)

Mike C. Brown
Pittsburgh Pirates

THREE YEARS (84 – 86)

	Ave.	OBP	SLG	AB	H	2B	3B	HR	RBI	BB	SO
Totals	.272	.332	.425	749	204	42	6	20	101	69	103
Batting vs. Left and Right-handed Pitchers											
Left	.281	.349	.435	331	93	15	3	10	48	36	43
Right	.266	.319	.416	418	111	27	3	10	53	33	60
At Home and on the Road											
Home	.247	.309	.368	356	88	19	0	8	48	33	48
Road	.295	.353	.476	393	116	23	6	12	53	36	55
Facing Groundball Pitchers and Flyball Pitchers											
Groundball	.301	.335	.445	326	98	20	3	7	40	18	44
Flyball	.251	.330	.409	423	106	22	3	13	61	51	59
Facing Finesse Pitchers and Power Pitchers											
Finesse	.294	.330	.450	398	117	28	5	8	47	23	41
Power	.248	.334	.396	351	87	14	1	12	54	46	62
On Grass and on Turf											
Grass	.270	.338	.451	355	96	17	4	13	49	36	48
Turf	.274	.326	.401	394	108	25	2	7	52	33	55
During the Day and at Night											
Day	.302	.356	.554	258	78	16	2	15	45	23	29
Night	.257	.320	.356	491	126	26	4	5	56	46	74
By Month											
April	.242	.314	.337	95	23	3	0	2	9	10	12
May	.273	.320	.410	139	38	10	0	3	22	9	24
June	.232	.280	.355	138	32	4	2	3	18	10	15
July	.257	.324	.495	101	26	4	1	6	14	10	16
August	.304	.333	.393	112	34	10	0	0	12	6	16
Sept/Oct	.311	.397	.524	164	51	11	3	6	26	24	20
Situational											
Bases Empty	.294	.348	.451	388	114	25	3	10	10	31	54
Leadoff	.312	.357	.522	157	49	16	1	5	5	11	16
Not Leadoff	.281	.341	.403	231	65	9	2	5	5	20	38
Runners On	.249	.316	.396	361	90	17	3	10	91	38	49
First Base Only	.255	.316	.414	145	37	9	1	4	14	13	16
Scoring Position	.245	.316	.384	216	53	8	2	6	77	25	33
Late Innings, Close	.198	.252	.298	131	26	3	2	2	13	10	18

RBI/Opportunities

Scoring Position	62 / 294	(21%)
Scoring Position, 2 Out	25 / 113	(22%)
On Third, Less than 2 Out	32 / 64	(50%)
RBI in close games / RBI Total	73 / 101	(72%)

Mike G. Brown
Seattle Mariners

1986: Power, Groundball   1985: Power, Groundball   1984: Finesse, Groundball

THREE YEARS (84 – 86)

	G	IP	H	BB	SO	SB	CS	W	L	S	ERA
Totals	38	143.1	204	58	76	20	7	5	14	0	6.66
At Home and on the Road											
Home	22	85.1	120	35	43	13	5	2	6	0	5.80
Road	16	58.0	84	23	33	7	2	3	8	0	7.91
During the Day and at Night											
Day	12	44.1	62	14	20	4	2	1	5	0	6.90
Night	26	99.0	142	44	56	16	5	4	9	0	6.55
On Grass and on Turf											
Grass	29	109.2	170	44	56	16	4	4	11	0	7.22
Turf	9	33.2	34	14	20	4	3	1	3	0	4.81
By Month											
April	8	29.2	40	9	16	6	2	1	2	0	6.37
May	11	57.0	70	18	24	4	3	3	4	0	5.37
June	5	21.0	30	9	11	3	1	1	3	0	5.14
July	4	4.1	11	5	5	1	0	0	0	0	16.62
August	3	13.2	19	10	7	4	1	0	3	0	9.88
Sept/Oct	7	17.2	34	7	13	2	0	0	2	0	8.15

vs. Opponent Batters

THREE YEARS (84 – 86)

	Ave.	OBP	SLG	AB	H	2B	3B	HR	RBI	BB	SO
Totals	.335	.392	.539	609	204	43	6	23	107	58	76
Pitching vs. Left and Right-handed Batters											
Left	.380	.435	.584	303	115	22	5	10	59	32	25
Right	.291	.349	.493	306	89	21	1	13	48	26	51
Situational											
Bases Empty	.344	.399	.546	317	109	20	4	12	12	29	31
Leadoff	.365	.420	.591	137	50	13	3	4	4	13	7
Not Leadoff	.328	.383	.511	180	59	7	1	8	8	16	24
Runners On	.325	.386	.531	292	95	23	2	11	95	29	45
First Base Only	.345	.395	.647	119	41	10	1	8	21	10	11
Scoring Position	.312	.379	.451	173	54	13	1	3	74	19	34
Late Innings, Close	.316	.480	.421	19	6	0	1	0	5	5	2

RBI/Opportunities

Scoring Position	68 / 240	(28%)
Scoring Position, 2 Out	23 / 98	(23%)
On Third, Less than 2 Out	27 / 52	(52%)
RBI in close games / RBI Total	62 / 107	(58%)

T.R. Bryden
California Angels

1986: Power, Flyball   1985: Did not play   1984: Did not play

THREE YEARS (84 – 86)

	G	IP	H	BB	SO	SB	CS	W	L	S	ERA
Totals	16	34.1	38	21	25	4	0	2	1	0	6.55
At Home and on the Road											
Home	9	15.1	22	10	12	0	0	0	1	0	7.63
Road	7	19.0	16	11	13	4	0	2	0	0	5.68
During the Day and at Night											
Day	3	10.1	13	7	6	2	0	1	0	0	7.84
Night	13	24.0	25	14	19	2	0	1	1	0	6.00
On Grass and on Turf											
Grass	13	24.1	32	18	18	4	0	0	1	0	7.77
Turf	3	10.0	6	3	7	0	0	2	0	0	3.60
By Month											
April	6	14.2	13	10	11	1	0	2	0	0	4.30
May	7	12.2	12	7	11	2	0	0	1	0	5.68
June	3	7.0	13	4	3	1	0	0	0	0	12.86
July	0	0.0	0	0	0	0	0	0	0	0	0.00
August	0	0.0	0	0	0	0	0	0	0	0	0.00
Sept/Oct	0	0.0	0	0	0	0	0	0	0	0	0.00

vs. Opponent Batters

THREE YEARS (84 – 86)

	Ave.	OBP	SLG	AB	H	2B	3B	HR	RBI	BB	SO
Totals	.290	.386	.450	131	38	5	2	4	25	21	25
Pitching vs. Left and Right-handed Batters											
Left	.283	.403	.550	60	17	2	1	4	12	11	10
Right	.296	.372	.366	71	21	3	1	0	13	10	15
Situational											
Bases Empty	.230	.373	.344	61	14	1	0	2	2	13	12
Leadoff	.261	.414	.565	23	6	1	0	2	2	6	5
Not Leadoff	.211	.348	.211	38	8	0	0	0	0	7	7
Runners On	.343	.398	.543	70	24	4	2	2	23	8	13
First Base Only	.429	.448	.786	28	12	2	1	2	5	1	3
Scoring Position	.286	.370	.381	42	12	2	1	0	18	7	10
Late Innings, Close	.500	.529	.857	14	7	2	0	1	5	2	1

RBI/Opportunities

Scoring Position	18 / 65	(28%)
Scoring Position, 2 Out	2 / 21	(10%)
On Third, Less than 2 Out	12 / 20	(60%)
RBI in close games / RBI Total	7 / 25	(28%)

Steve Buechele
Texas Rangers

	Ave.	OBP	SLG	AB	H	2B	3B	HR	RBI	BB	SO
THREE YEARS (84 – 86)											
Totals	.235	.292	.393	680	160	25	5	24	75	49	136
Batting vs. Left and Right-handed Pitchers											
Left	.271	.332	.439	214	58	8	2	8	24	20	48
Right	.219	.273	.371	466	102	17	3	16	51	29	88
At Home and on the Road											
Home	.231	.281	.371	334	77	12	1	11	32	20	65
Road	.240	.303	.413	346	83	13	4	13	43	29	71
Facing Groundball Pitchers and Flyball Pitchers											
Groundball	.258	.306	.394	310	80	9	3	9	44	20	57
Flyball	.216	.280	.392	370	80	16	2	15	31	29	79
Facing Finesse Pitchers and Power Pitchers											
Finesse	.225	.289	.366	383	86	17	2	11	44	30	68
Power	.249	.296	.428	297	74	8	3	13	31	19	68
On Grass and on Turf											
Grass	.234	.292	.383	564	132	16	4	20	64	41	113
Turf	.241	.290	.440	116	28	9	1	4	11	8	23
During the Day and at Night											
Day	.216	.252	.352	125	27	5	0	4	11	6	34
Night	.240	.300	.402	555	133	20	5	20	64	43	102
By Month											
April	.263	.323	.509	57	15	2	0	4	6	5	10
May	.234	.272	.429	77	18	3	0	4	9	4	14
June	.293	.350	.478	92	27	5	0	4	10	7	22
July	.193	.264	.237	114	22	2	0	1	7	9	24
August	.237	.326	.375	152	36	6	3	3	20	17	30
Sept/Oct	.223	.249	.410	188	42	7	2	8	23	7	36
Situational											
Bases Empty	.233	.290	.423	421	98	18	4	18	18	29	84
Leadoff	.268	.302	.486	183	49	8	1	10	10	7	32
Not Leadoff	.206	.281	.374	238	49	10	3	8	8	22	52
Runners On	.239	.295	.344	259	62	7	1	6	57	20	52
First Base Only	.243	.283	.383	107	26	4	1	3	10	5	22
Scoring Position	.237	.302	.316	152	36	3	0	3	47	15	30
Late Innings, Close	.272	.309	.437	103	28	5	0	4	11	4	15

RBI/Opportunities

Scoring Position	42 / 202	(21%)
Scoring Position, 2 Out	15 / 89	(17%)
On Third, Less than 2 Out	18 / 31	(58%)
RBI in close games / RBI Total	39 / 75	(52%)

Rick Burleson
California Angels

	Ave.	OBP	SLG	AB	H	2B	3B	HR	RBI	BB	SO
THREE YEARS (84 – 86)											
Totals	.280	.360	.385	275	77	14	0	5	29	34	34
Batting vs. Left and Right-handed Pitchers											
Left	.247	.328	.364	154	38	6	0	4	17	19	21
Right	.322	.401	.413	121	39	8	0	1	12	15	13
At Home and on the Road											
Home	.254	.343	.369	122	31	8	0	2	11	17	17
Road	.301	.374	.399	153	46	6	0	3	18	17	17
Facing Groundball Pitchers and Flyball Pitchers											
Groundball	.283	.354	.336	113	32	3	0	1	15	12	15
Flyball	.278	.364	.420	162	45	11	0	4	14	22	19
Facing Finesse Pitchers and Power Pitchers											
Finesse	.290	.360	.419	155	45	8	0	4	11	17	14
Power	.267	.360	.342	120	32	6	0	1	18	17	20
On Grass and on Turf											
Grass	.261	.335	.351	211	55	10	0	3	21	24	30
Turf	.344	.440	.500	64	22	4	0	2	8	10	4
During the Day and at Night											
Day	.264	.326	.299	87	23	3	0	0	10	8	10
Night	.287	.375	.426	188	54	11	0	5	19	26	24
By Month											
April	.358	.460	.528	53	19	6	0	1	7	9	6
May	.212	.268	.250	52	11	2	0	0	3	4	10
June	.321	.375	.393	28	9	2	0	0	2	3	3
July	.385	.442	.615	39	15	0	0	3	7	4	5
August	.244	.306	.333	45	11	1	0	1	2	4	3
Sept/Oct	.207	.324	.259	58	12	3	0	0	8	10	7
Situational											
Bases Empty	.259	.322	.414	162	42	10	0	5	5	15	21
Leadoff	.256	.330	.415	82	21	4	0	3	3	9	14
Not Leadoff	.263	.314	.412	80	21	6	0	2	2	6	7
Runners On	.310	.410	.345	113	35	4	0	0	24	19	13
First Base Only	.311	.404	.333	45	14	1	0	0	0	6	4
Scoring Position	.309	.415	.353	68	21	3	0	0	24	13	9
Late Innings, Close	.200	.297	.255	55	11	0	0	1	6	7	9

RBI/Opportunities

Scoring Position	24 / 100	(24%)
Scoring Position, 2 Out	13 / 52	(25%)
On Third, Less than 2 Out	4 / 13	(31%)
RBI in close games / RBI Total	19 / 29	(66%)

Ray Burris
St. Louis Cardinals

1986: Finesse, Flyball   1985: Finesse, Flyball   1984: Finesse, Flyball

	G	IP	H	BB	SO	SB	CS	W	L	S	ERA
THREE YEARS (84 – 86)											
Totals	86	464.0	467	175	208	22	20	26	28	0	4.19
At Home and on the Road											
Home	47	275.0	254	84	124	13	9	19	12	0	3.50
Road	39	189.0	213	91	84	9	11	7	16	0	5.19
During the Day and at Night											
Day	24	129.1	137	45	68	9	5	6	7	0	4.87
Night	62	334.2	330	130	140	13	15	20	21	0	3.93
On Grass and on Turf											
Grass	60	352.2	349	123	163	15	15	22	18	0	3.90
Turf	26	111.1	118	52	45	7	5	4	10	0	5.09
By Month											
April	11	52.1	41	17	25	0	1	3	3	0	1.38
May	14	82.0	77	26	37	4	3	6	4	0	3.40
June	17	106.1	98	41	46	6	6	6	5	0	3.55
July	16	65.2	81	30	31	2	3	3	6	0	6.72
August	17	99.2	101	35	40	4	5	6	3	0	3.70
Sept/Oct	11	58.0	69	26	29	6	2	2	7	0	6.98

vs. Opponent Batters

	Ave.	OBP	SLG	AB	H	2B	3B	HR	RBI	BB	SO
THREE YEARS (84 – 86)											
Totals	.262	.331	.424	1783	467	90	20	53	211	175	208
Pitching vs. Left and Right-handed Batters											
Left	.251	.319	.411	924	232	46	12	26	107	90	103
Right	.274	.343	.438	859	235	44	8	27	104	85	105
Situational											
Bases Empty	.258	.316	.437	1078	278	55	12	38	38	81	126
Leadoff	.223	.273	.403	452	101	20	8	15	15	28	51
Not Leadoff	.283	.345	.462	626	177	35	4	23	23	53	75
Runners On	.268	.353	.404	705	189	35	8	15	173	94	82
First Base Only	.286	.340	.390	315	90	14	2	5	18	24	34
Scoring Position	.254	.362	.415	390	99	21	6	10	155	70	48
Late Innings, Close	.236	.316	.369	157	37	5	2	4	16	19	26

RBI/Opportunities

Scoring Position	129 / 562	(23%)
Scoring Position, 2 Out	58 / 282	(21%)
On Third, Less than 2 Out	49 / 96	(51%)
RBI in close games / RBI Total	141 / 211	(67%)

Randy Bush
Minnesota Twins

	Ave.	OBP	SLG	AB	H	2B	3B	HR	RBI	BB	SO
THREE YEARS (84 – 86)											
Totals	.245	.321	.417	902	221	49	11	28	123	94	153
Batting vs. Left and Right-handed Pitchers											
Left	.111	.226	.185	27	3	2	0	0	1	4	4
Right	.249	.324	.424	875	218	47	11	28	122	90	149
At Home and on the Road											
Home	.263	.343	.482	471	124	30	8	19	78	50	76
Road	.225	.297	.346	431	97	19	3	9	45	44	77
Facing Groundball Pitchers and Flyball Pitchers											
Groundball	.235	.297	.404	443	104	27	6	12	58	36	72
Flyball	.255	.343	.429	459	117	22	5	16	65	58	81
Facing Finesse Pitchers and Power Pitchers											
Finesse	.257	.321	.449	499	128	36	6	16	77	45	64
Power	.231	.321	.377	403	93	13	5	12	46	49	89
On Grass and on Turf											
Grass	.229	.305	.363	336	77	15	3	8	34	38	62
Turf	.254	.330	.449	566	144	34	8	20	89	56	91
During the Day and at Night											
Day	.243	.328	.451	288	70	20	5	10	43	33	49
Night	.246	.317	.401	614	151	29	6	18	80	61	104
By Month											
April	.264	.346	.484	91	24	6	1	4	13	11	15
May	.234	.309	.473	167	39	10	3	8	30	17	25
June	.208	.278	.396	149	31	9	2	5	26	14	23
July	.277	.342	.446	177	49	8	2	6	19	17	32
August	.243	.338	.373	177	43	13	2	2	17	23	34
Sept/Oct	.248	.316	.348	141	35	3	1	3	18	12	24
Situational											
Bases Empty	.225	.303	.390	497	112	29	4	15	15	46	87
Leadoff	.229	.285	.401	192	44	10	1	7	7	12	28
Not Leadoff	.223	.313	.384	305	68	19	3	8	8	34	59
Runners On	.269	.343	.449	405	109	20	7	13	108	48	66
First Base Only	.326	.378	.503	181	59	9	4	5	17	15	23
Scoring Position	.223	.318	.406	224	50	11	3	8	91	33	43
Late Innings, Close	.260	.341	.407	150	39	8	1	4	20	18	23

RBI/Opportunities

Scoring Position	74 / 314	(24%)
Scoring Position, 2 Out	21 / 140	(15%)
On Third, Less than 2 Out	34 / 56	(61%)
RBI in close games / RBI Total	87 / 123	(71%)

John Butcher
Cleveland Indians

1986: Finesse, Groundball 1985: Finesse, Groundball 1984: Finesse, Groundball

THREE YEARS (84 – 86)

	G	IP	H	BB	SO	SB	CS	W	L	S	ERA
Totals	97	553.1	649	133	220	31	19	25	33	0	4.70
At Home and on the Road											
Home	49	274.2	343	62	115	12	10	14	16	0	4.95
Road	48	278.2	306	71	105	19	9	11	17	0	4.46
During the Day and and at Night											
Day	28	158.0	174	33	57	8	6	7	13	0	5.01
Night	69	395.1	475	100	163	23	13	18	20	0	4.58
On Grass and on Turf											
Grass	43	245.1	288	63	89	15	8	9	17	0	4.81
Turf	54	308.0	361	70	131	16	11	16	16	0	4.62
By Month											
April	15	108.1	94	25	47	3	4	5	4	0	3.16
May	15	88.2	111	24	35	3	3	2	5	0	4.77
June	19	84.2	107	14	27	10	5	3	8	0	5.95
July	19	119.0	148	31	48	6	3	7	6	0	4.61
August	13	78.1	98	24	34	5	2	3	5	0	4.94
Sept/Oct	16	74.1	91	15	29	4	2	5	5	0	5.33

vs. Opponent Batters
THREE YEARS (84 – 86)

	Ave.	OBP	SLG	AB	H	2B	3B	HR	RBI	BB	SO
Totals	.294	.334	.444	2208	649	124	15	59	273	133	220
Pitching vs. Left and Right-handed Batters											
Left	.300	.339	.464	1255	377	69	11	38	165	76	126
Right	.285	.329	.418	953	272	55	4	21	108	57	94
Situational											
Bases Empty	.281	.320	.428	1307	367	68	13	33	33	69	154
Leadoff	.296	.332	.451	557	165	30	10	12	12	27	53
Not Leadoff	.269	.311	.412	750	202	38	3	21	21	42	101
Runners On	.313	.355	.466	901	282	56	2	26	240	64	66
First Base Only	.334	.369	.482	380	127	18	1	12	31	17	21
Scoring Position	.298	.345	.455	521	155	38	1	14	209	47	45
Late Innings, Close	.289	.332	.444	180	52	7	0	7	17	11	19

RBI/Opportunities

Scoring Position	183 / 691	(26%)
Scoring Position, 2 Out	67 / 292	(23%)
On Third, Less than 2 Out	79 / 141	(56%)
RBI in close games / RBI Total	190 / 273	(70%)

Sal Butera
Cincinnati Reds

THREE YEARS (84 – 86)

	Ave.	OBP	SLG	AB	H	2B	3B	HR	RBI	BB	SO
Totals	.216	.318	.318	236	51	7	1	5	28	35	22
Batting vs. Left and Right-handed Pitchers											
Left	.275	.363	.412	80	22	3	1	2	8	11	3
Right	.186	.295	.269	156	29	4	0	3	20	24	19
At Home and on the Road											
Home	.178	.258	.229	118	21	4	1	0	11	13	12
Road	.254	.373	.407	118	30	3	0	5	17	22	10
Facing Groundball Pitchers and Flyball Pitchers											
Groundball	.224	.319	.353	116	26	6	0	3	13	16	11
Flyball	.208	.317	.283	120	25	1	1	2	15	19	11
Facing Finesse Pitchers and Power Pitchers											
Finesse	.199	.272	.287	136	27	3	0	3	13	14	15
Power	.240	.374	.360	100	24	4	1	2	15	21	7
On Grass and on Turf											
Grass	.246	.329	.435	69	17	1	0	4	15	8	6
Turf	.204	.313	.269	167	34	6	1	1	13	27	16
During the Day and at Night											
Day	.235	.331	.378	119	28	3	1	4	21	17	7
Night	.197	.304	.256	117	23	4	0	1	7	18	15
By Month											
April	.222	.222	.556	9	2	0	0	1	1	0	1
May	.231	.348	.282	39	9	2	0	0	4	7	2
June	.147	.275	.176	34	5	1	0	0	4	6	5
July	.204	.310	.327	49	10	3	0	1	5	8	5
August	.310	.394	.517	29	9	0	0	2	4	4	1
Sept/Oct	.211	.307	.289	76	16	1	1	1	10	10	8
Situational											
Bases Empty	.208	.299	.292	130	27	5	0	2	2	17	15
Leadoff	.193	.292	.263	57	11	1	0	1	1	8	9
Not Leadoff	.219	.305	.315	73	16	4	0	1	1	9	6
Runners On	.226	.339	.349	106	24	2	1	3	26	18	7
First Base Only	.204	.259	.370	54	11	1	1	2	5	4	4
Scoring Position	.250	.406	.327	52	13	1	0	1	21	14	3
Late Innings, Close	.154	.241	.269	26	4	0	0	1	1	3	2

RBI/Opportunities

Scoring Position	19 / 83	(23%)
Scoring Position, 2 Out	6 / 31	(19%)
On Third, Less than 2 Out	10 / 20	(50%)
RBI in close games / RBI Total	10 / 28	(36%)

Enos Cabell
Los Angeles Dodgers

THREE YEARS (84 – 86)

	Ave.	OBP	SLG	AB	H	2B	3B	HR	RBI	BB	SO
Totals	.283	.325	.370	1048	297	47	4	12	109	65	109
Batting vs. Left and Right-handed Pitchers											
Left	.304	.354	.400	562	171	29	2	7	53	42	50
Right	.259	.292	.335	486	126	18	2	5	56	23	59
At Home and on the Road											
Home	.270	.314	.362	538	145	29	3	5	62	34	55
Road	.298	.338	.378	510	152	18	1	7	47	31	54
Facing Groundball Pitchers and Flyball Pitchers											
Groundball	.282	.331	.367	518	146	17	3	7	62	39	57
Flyball	.285	.320	.374	530	151	30	1	5	47	26	52
Facing Finesse Pitchers and Power Pitchers											
Finesse	.291	.327	.375	546	159	22	3	6	49	30	45
Power	.275	.323	.365	502	138	25	1	6	60	35	64
On Grass and on Turf											
Grass	.300	.340	.377	530	159	21	1	6	60	32	61
Turf	.266	.310	.363	518	138	26	3	6	49	33	48
During the Day and at Night											
Day	.292	.321	.397	277	81	12	1	5	31	12	22
Night	.280	.327	.361	771	216	35	3	7	78	53	87
By Month											
April	.222	.252	.296	108	24	5	0	1	7	4	9
May	.321	.356	.435	168	54	6	2	3	18	10	19
June	.289	.348	.364	187	54	9	1	1	22	17	19
July	.227	.273	.289	194	44	6	0	2	20	13	21
August	.315	.339	.455	222	70	14	1	5	25	7	22
Sept/Oct	.302	.359	.343	169	51	7	0	0	17	14	19
Situational											
Bases Empty	.287	.321	.377	600	172	28	1	8	8	29	66
Leadoff	.313	.338	.387	217	68	13	0	1	1	8	23
Not Leadoff	.272	.311	.371	383	104	15	1	7	7	21	43
Runners On	.279	.331	.362	448	125	19	3	4	101	36	43
First Base Only	.316	.346	.407	177	56	8	1	2	8	6	19
Scoring Position	.255	.322	.332	271	69	11	2	2	93	30	24
Late Innings, Close	.271	.318	.338	207	56	8	0	2	25	14	28

RBI/Opportunities

Scoring Position	86 / 366	(23%)
Scoring Position, 2 Out	21 / 153	(14%)
On Third, Less than 2 Out	44 / 72	(61%)
RBI in close games / RBI Total	75 / 109	(69%)

Ivan Calderon
Chicago White Sox

THREE YEARS (84 – 86)

	Ave.	OBP	SLG	AB	H	2B	3B	HR	RBI	BB	SO
Totals	.266	.322	.435	398	106	24	5	11	44	30	89
Batting vs. Left and Right-handed Pitchers											
Left	.269	.338	.463	134	36	10	2	4	17	13	32
Right	.265	.313	.420	264	70	14	3	7	27	17	57
At Home and on the Road											
Home	.253	.314	.425	186	47	9	1	7	21	15	38
Road	.278	.329	.443	212	59	15	4	4	23	15	51
Facing Groundball Pitchers and Flyball Pitchers											
Groundball	.261	.309	.394	180	47	11	2	3	17	11	34
Flyball	.271	.332	.468	218	59	13	3	8	27	19	55
Facing Finesse Pitchers and Power Pitchers											
Finesse	.276	.324	.418	232	64	15	3	4	23	15	32
Power	.253	.319	.458	166	42	9	2	7	21	15	57
On Grass and on Turf											
Grass	.281	.330	.425	167	47	9	3	3	16	12	41
Turf	.255	.316	.442	231	59	15	2	8	28	18	48
During the Day and at Night											
Day	.267	.302	.405	131	35	10	1	2	19	5	28
Night	.266	.331	.449	267	71	14	4	9	25	25	61
By Month											
April	.235	.293	.318	85	20	4	0	1	6	6	21
May	.250	.308	.472	108	27	4	1	6	19	7	22
June	.276	.333	.466	58	16	6	1	1	5	5	10
July	.303	.364	.494	89	27	7	2	2	10	9	22
August	.220	.256	.317	41	9	1	0	1	2	2	10
Sept/Oct	.412	.444	.647	17	7	2	1	0	2	1	4
Situational											
Bases Empty	.276	.329	.469	228	63	12	4	8	8	16	53
Leadoff	.295	.319	.466	88	26	3	3	2	2	2	14
Not Leadoff	.264	.335	.471	140	37	9	1	6	6	14	39
Runners On	.253	.312	.388	170	43	12	1	3	36	14	36
First Base Only	.243	.282	.338	74	18	5	1	0	3	4	15
Scoring Position	.260	.333	.427	96	25	7	0	3	33	10	21
Late Innings, Close	.271	.329	.443	70	19	3	0	3	6	6	19

RBI/Opportunities

Scoring Position	28 / 127	(22%)
Scoring Position, 2 Out	4 / 42	(10%)
On Third, Less than 2 Out	14 / 27	(52%)
RBI in close games / RBI Total	30 / 44	(68%)

Ernie Camacho
Cleveland Indians

1986: Power, Groundball   1985: Power, Flyball   1984: Finesse, Groundball

THREE YEARS (84 – 86)

	G	IP	H	BB	SO	SB	CS	W	L	S	ERA
Totals	122	160.2	147	69	86	16	1	7	14	43	3.14
At Home and on the Road											
Home	62	81.0	83	36	44	10	1	3	5	20	3.89
Road	60	79.2	64	33	42	6	0	4	9	23	2.37
During the Day and and at Night											
Day	50	64.0	54	28	33	7	1	3	6	18	3.23
Night	72	96.2	93	41	53	9	0	4	8	25	3.07
On Grass and on Turf											
Grass	106	142.1	124	59	76	16	1	7	10	36	2.85
Turf	16	18.1	23	10	10	0	0	0	4	7	5.40
By Month											
April	18	22.2	23	8	16	3	0	0	2	9	3.97
May	15	24.2	21	13	8	3	1	2	3	3	2.92
June	23	27.2	22	13	15	3	0	2	4	9	2.60
July	18	22.1	18	12	11	1	0	1	1	4	1.21
August	26	36.2	39	11	16	3	0	1	2	11	3.68
Sept/Oct	22	26.2	24	12	20	3	0	1	2	7	4.05

vs. Opponent Batters — THREE YEARS (84 – 86)

	Ave.	OBP	SLG	AB	H	2B	3B	HR	RBI	BB	SO
Totals	.247	.322	.314	596	147	17	1	7	81	69	86
Pitching vs. Left and Right-handed Batters											
Left	.284	.357	.377	292	83	10	1	5	42	38	39
Right	.211	.287	.253	304	64	7	0	2	39	31	47
Situational											
Bases Empty	.273	.349	.357	249	68	6	0	5	5	26	34
Leadoff	.296	.387	.361	108	32	4	0	1	1	15	12
Not Leadoff	.255	.318	.355	141	36	2	0	4	4	11	22
Runners On	.228	.303	.282	347	79	11	1	2	76	43	52
First Base Only	.237	.303	.309	139	33	5	1	1	7	13	19
Scoring Position	.221	.304	.264	208	46	6	0	1	69	30	33
Late Innings, Close	.253	.322	.326	451	114	13	1	6	70	49	62

RBI/Opportunities

Scoring Position	65 / 314	(21%)
Scoring Position, 2 Out	18 / 140	(13%)
On Third, Less than 2 Out	32 / 54	(59%)
RBI in close games / RBI Total	70 / 81	(86%)

Bill Campbell
Detroit Tigers

1986: Power, Flyball   1985: Finesse, Groundball   1984: Power, Flyball

THREE YEARS (84 – 86)

	G	IP	H	BB	SO	SB	CS	W	L	S	ERA
Totals	141	201.1	169	77	130	29	2	14	14	8	3.62
At Home and on the Road											
Home	71	109.2	84	33	73	12	0	5	4	2	3.12
Road	70	91.2	85	44	57	17	2	9	10	6	4.22
During the Day and and at Night											
Day	53	69.1	64	33	51	12	1	6	4	3	4.15
Night	88	132.0	105	44	79	17	1	8	10	5	3.34
On Grass and on Turf											
Grass	55	87.2	66	26	56	9	1	6	8	7	2.87
Turf	86	113.2	103	51	74	20	1	8	6	1	4.20
By Month											
April	19	31.0	25	7	23	4	0	2	2	0	2.90
May	19	30.2	25	8	12	3	0	2	0	2	2.64
June	26	35.0	34	23	23	10	1	3	4	1	5.91
July	26	42.2	37	14	28	5	0	0	2	2	2.95
August	29	36.0	23	8	27	3	1	5	4	3	3.50
Sept/Oct	22	26.0	25	17	17	4	0	2	2	0	3.81

vs. Opponent Batters — THREE YEARS (84 – 86)

	Ave.	OBP	SLG	AB	H	2B	3B	HR	RBI	BB	SO
Totals	.226	.298	.327	744	168	27	6	12	89	77	130
Pitching vs. Left and Right-handed Batters											
Left	.235	.316	.341	323	76	14	4	4	42	40	44
Right	.219	.284	.316	421	92	13	2	8	47	37	86
Situational											
Bases Empty	.200	.249	.295	430	86	17	3	6	6	27	72
Leadoff	.212	.269	.318	179	38	9	2	2	2	14	25
Not Leadoff	.191	.234	.279	251	48	8	1	4	4	13	47
Runners On	.261	.359	.369	314	82	10	3	6	83	50	58
First Base Only	.329	.391	.405	79	26	3	0	1	3	7	14
Scoring Position	.238	.350	.357	235	56	7	3	5	80	43	44
Late Innings, Close	.264	.355	.347	239	63	6	4	2	32	35	41

RBI/Opportunities

Scoring Position	70 / 356	(20%)
Scoring Position, 2 Out	28 / 143	(20%)
On Third, Less than 2 Out	27 / 74	(36%)
RBI in close games / RBI Total	37 / 89	(42%)

Casey Candaele
Montreal Expos

THREE YEARS (84 – 86)

	Ave.	OBP	SLG	AB	H	2B	3B	HR	RBI	BB	SO
Totals	.231	.264	.288	104	24	4	1	0	6	5	15
Batting vs. Left and Right-handed Pitchers											
Left	.268	.286	.366	41	11	4	0	0	5	1	7
Right	.206	.250	.238	63	13	0	1	0	1	4	8
At Home and on the Road											
Home	.274	.308	.355	62	17	3	1	0	5	3	12
Road	.167	.200	.190	42	7	1	0	0	1	2	3
Facing Groundball Pitchers and Flyball Pitchers											
Groundball	.302	.327	.340	53	16	2	0	0	3	2	5
Flyball	.157	.200	.235	51	8	2	1	0	3	3	10
Facing Finesse Pitchers and Power Pitchers											
Finesse	.271	.307	.329	70	19	2	1	0	4	4	5
Power	.147	.171	.206	34	5	2	0	0	2	1	10
On Grass and on Turf											
Grass	.222	.200	.222	9	2	0	0	0	1	0	0
Turf	.232	.270	.295	95	22	4	1	0	5	5	15
During the Day and at Night											
Day	.229	.263	.343	35	8	2	1	0	3	2	5
Night	.232	.264	.261	69	16	2	0	0	3	3	10
By Month											
April	.000	.000	.000	0	0	0	0	0	0	0	0
May	.000	.000	.000	0	0	0	0	0	0	0	0
June	.250	.400	.500	4	1	1	0	0	2	1	2
July	.000	.000	.000	0	0	0	0	0	0	0	0
August	.000	.000	.000	0	0	0	0	0	0	0	0
Sept/Oct	.230	.257	.280	100	23	3	1	0	4	4	13
Situational											
Bases Empty	.260	.308	.329	73	19	3	1	0	0	5	11
Leadoff	.222	.271	.222	45	10	0	0	0	0	3	6
Not Leadoff	.321	.367	.500	28	9	3	1	0	0	2	5
Runners On	.161	.156	.194	31	5	1	0	0	6	0	4
First Base Only	.154	.154	.154	13	2	0	0	0	0	0	3
Scoring Position	.167	.158	.222	18	3	1	0	0	6	0	1
Late Innings, Close	.200	.304	.200	20	4	0	0	0	1	3	2

RBI/Opportunities

Scoring Position	5 / 25	(20%)
Scoring Position, 2 Out	2 / 12	(17%)
On Third, Less than 2 Out	3 / 5	(60%)
RBI in close games / RBI Total	3 / 6	(50%)

John Candelaria
California Angels

1986: Power, Flyball   1985: Power, Flyball   1984: Finesse, Flyball

THREE YEARS (84 – 86)

	G	IP	H	BB	SO	SB	CS	W	L	S	ERA
Totals	99	402.1	374	98	314	11	13	31	20	11	3.00
At Home and on the Road											
Home	50	204.0	198	52	172	4	7	14	11	7	3.66
Road	49	198.1	176	46	142	7	6	17	9	4	2.31
During the Day and and at Night											
Day	30	110.2	104	28	81	3	6	8	7	4	3.50
Night	69	291.2	270	70	233	8	7	23	13	7	2.81
On Grass and on Turf											
Grass	44	204.0	161	57	165	3	5	19	7	4	2.65
Turf	55	198.1	213	41	149	8	8	12	13	7	3.36
By Month											
April	14	46.1	50	8	41	2	1	4	4	4	2.53
May	17	47.1	48	15	38	1	4	2	3	3	3.80
June	12	26.1	33	5	21	1	0	0	2	0	4.10
July	20	91.2	74	20	61	1	2	9	3	2	2.16
August	18	102.2	98	32	81	5	3	9	5	0	3.59
Sept/Oct	18	88.0	71	18	72	1	3	7	3	2	2.66

vs. Opponent Batters — THREE YEARS (84 – 86)

	Ave.	OBP	SLG	AB	H	2B	3B	HR	RBI	BB	SO
Totals	.249	.295	.394	1504	374	73	17	37	158	98	314
Pitching vs. Left and Right-handed Batters											
Left	.188	.217	.250	240	45	10	1	1	15	9	81
Right	.260	.309	.421	1264	329	63	16	36	143	89	233
Situational											
Bases Empty	.248	.297	.390	910	226	42	12	21	21	57	188
Leadoff	.255	.297	.394	381	97	17	6	8	8	22	78
Not Leadoff	.244	.297	.388	529	129	25	6	13	13	35	110
Runners On	.249	.291	.399	594	148	31	5	16	137	41	126
First Base Only	.258	.301	.400	275	71	15	3	6	21	17	56
Scoring Position	.241	.283	.398	319	77	16	2	10	116	24	70
Late Innings, Close	.231	.285	.385	234	54	10	4	6	36	21	50

RBI/Opportunities

Scoring Position	99 / 414	(24%)
Scoring Position, 2 Out	29 / 180	(16%)
On Third, Less than 2 Out	44 / 83	(53%)
RBI in close games / RBI Total	126 / 158	(80%)

John Cangelosi
Chicago White Sox

THREE YEARS (84 – 86)	Ave.	OBP	SLG	AB	H	2B	3B	HR	RBI	BB	SO
Totals	.234	.349	.298	440	103	16	3	2	32	71	62
Batting vs. Left and Right-handed Pitchers											
Left	.216	.354	.343	134	29	9	1	2	11	26	21
Right	.242	.346	.278	306	74	7	2	0	21	45	41
At Home and on the Road											
Home	.235	.381	.314	204	48	7	3	1	15	42	28
Road	.233	.319	.284	236	55	9	0	1	17	29	34
Facing Groundball Pitchers and Flyball Pitchers											
Groundball	.250	.343	.319	188	47	6	2	1	15	23	22
Flyball	.222	.353	.282	252	56	10	1	1	17	48	40
Facing Finesse Pitchers and Power Pitchers											
Finesse	.274	.365	.346	266	73	12	2	1	23	34	28
Power	.172	.326	.224	174	30	4	1	1	9	37	34
On Grass and on Turf											
Grass	.220	.346	.285	368	81	13	3	2	24	65	54
Turf	.306	.362	.361	72	22	4	0	0	8	6	8
During the Day and at Night											
Day	.227	.351	.312	141	32	7	1	1	8	24	15
Night	.237	.348	.291	299	71	9	2	1	24	47	47
By Month											
April	.241	.416	.328	58	14	2	0	1	2	17	8
May	.232	.315	.244	82	19	1	0	0	4	10	7
June	.261	.430	.337	92	24	7	0	0	10	24	14
July	.271	.346	.385	96	26	4	2	1	7	8	19
August	.174	.240	.217	69	12	1	1	0	4	6	10
Sept/Oct	.186	.280	.209	43	8	1	0	0	5	6	4
Situational											
Bases Empty	.227	.314	.293	300	68	11	3	1	1	34	47
Leadoff	.241	.316	.293	191	46	6	2	0	0	19	29
Not Leadoff	.202	.310	.294	109	22	5	1	1	1	15	18
Runners On	.250	.413	.307	140	35	5	0	1	31	37	15
First Base Only	.271	.427	.356	59	16	2	0	1	3	15	3
Scoring Position	.235	.404	.272	81	19	3	0	0	28	22	12
Late Innings, Close	.262	.338	.415	65	17	3	2	1	5	8	7

RBI/Opportunities		
Scoring Position	28 / 143	(20%)
Scoring Position, 2 Out	10 / 58	(17%)
On Third, Less than 2 Out	12 / 32	(38%)
RBI in close games / RBI Total	22 / 32	(69%)

Steve Carlton
Chicago White Sox

1986: Power, Flyball   1985: Power, Flyball   1984: Power, Flyball

THREE YEARS (84 – 86)	G	IP	H	BB	SO	SB	CS	W	L	S	ERA
Totals	81	497.1	494	218	331	23	23	29	0		4.07
At Home and on the Road											
Home	38	242.0	227	104	164	26	6	10	12	0	3.90
Road	43	255.1	267	114	167	24	17	13	17	0	4.23
During the Day and and at Night											
Day	26	147.2	174	68	85	14	7	6	9	0	5.06
Night	55	349.2	320	150	246	36	16	17	20	0	3.65
On Grass and on Turf											
Grass	32	184.2	183	88	125	20	11	7	13	0	4.09
Turf	49	312.2	311	130	206	30	12	16	16	0	4.06
By Month											
April	15	92.0	91	51	64	7	2	2	6	0	4.01
May	16	101.1	89	30	69	10	7	4	7	0	2.13
June	15	86.2	103	45	54	12	6	5	6	0	5.61
July	10	63.1	57	23	37	7	3	4	3	0	3.27
August	12	72.2	71	36	51	12	2	4	4	0	5.20
Sept/Oct	13	81.1	83	33	56	2	3	4	4	0	4.54

vs. Opponent Batters										
THREE YEARS (84 – 86)	Ave.	OBP	SLG	AB	H	2B	3B	HR	RBI	BB	SO
Totals	.260	.334	.393	1900	494	93	12	45	231	218	331
Pitching vs. Left and Right-handed Batters											
Left	.240	.301	.336	250	60	9	3	3	33	22	52
Right	.263	.339	.401	1650	434	84	9	42	198	196	279
Situational											
Bases Empty	.258	.326	.393	1090	281	54	6	27	27	109	196
Leadoff	.266	.346	.418	459	122	21	2	15	15	55	79
Not Leadoff	.252	.311	.374	631	159	33	4	12	12	54	117
Runners On	.263	.345	.393	810	213	39	6	18	204	109	135
First Base Only	.270	.323	.388	345	93	17	3	6	20	27	57
Scoring Position	.258	.361	.396	465	120	22	3	12	184	82	78
Late Innings, Close	.288	.361	.398	118	34	6	2	1	10	14	19

RBI/Opportunities		
Scoring Position	164 / 669	(25%)
Scoring Position, 2 Out	85 / 315	(27%)
On Third, Less than 2 Out	51 / 118	(43%)
RBI in close games / RBI Total	163 / 231	(71%)

Chuck Cary
Detroit Tigers

1986: Power, Flyball   1985: Power, Flyball   1984: Did not play

THREE YEARS (84 – 86)	G	IP	H	BB	SO	SB	CS	W	L	S	ERA
Totals	38	55.1	49	23	43	3	1	1	3	2	3.42
At Home and on the Road											
Home	17	25.0	20	9	18	0	1	0	1	1	2.52
Road	21	30.1	29	14	25	3	0	1	2	1	4.15
During the Day and and at Night											
Day	13	20.0	22	4	17	0	1	0	1	0	3.15
Night	25	35.1	27	19	26	3	0	1	2	2	3.57
On Grass and on Turf											
Grass	30	45.2	30	16	39	2	1	1	1	2	1.97
Turf	8	9.2	19	7	4	1	0	0	2	0	10.24
By Month											
April	7	10.0	11	4	3	0	0	0	0	0	1.80
May	6	7.2	7	7	5	3	0	0	1	0	4.70
June	6	12.0	13	2	12	0	0	0	1	0	4.50
July	0	0.0	0	0	0	0	0	0	0	0	0.00
August	6	6.1	2	3	6	0	0	0	0	1	2.84
Sept/Oct	13	19.1	16	7	17	0	1	1	1	1	3.26

vs. Opponent Batters										
THREE YEARS (84 – 86)	Ave.	OBP	SLG	AB	H	2B	3B	HR	RBI	BB	SO
Totals	.239	.318	.371	205	49	10	1	5	33	23	43
Pitching vs. Left and Right-handed Batters											
Left	.212	.254	.273	66	14	1	0	1	11	3	18
Right	.252	.346	.417	139	35	9	1	4	22	20	25
Situational											
Bases Empty	.197	.254	.308	117	23	8	1	1	1	8	23
Leadoff	.149	.184	.234	47	7	4	0	0	0	2	9
Not Leadoff	.229	.299	.357	70	16	4	1	1	1	6	14
Runners On	.295	.393	.455	88	26	2	0	4	32	15	20
First Base Only	.300	.364	.400	30	9	0	0	1	2	3	7
Scoring Position	.293	.405	.483	58	17	2	0	3	30	12	13
Late Innings, Close	.250	.388	.325	40	10	3	0	0	5	8	9

RBI/Opportunities		
Scoring Position	24 / 95	(25%)
Scoring Position, 2 Out	8 / 37	(22%)
On Third, Less than 2 Out	11 / 23	(48%)
RBI in close games / RBI Total	14 / 33	(42%)

Carmen Castillo
Cleveland Indians

THREE YEARS (84 – 86)	Ave.	OBP	SLG	AB	H	2B	3B	HR	RBI	BB	SO
Totals	.262	.313	.455	600	157	23	3	29	93	41	120
Batting vs. Left and Right-handed Pitchers											
Left	.260	.312	.480	377	98	14	3	21	58	27	77
Right	.265	.316	.413	223	59	9	0	8	35	14	43
At Home and on the Road											
Home	.291	.334	.516	289	84	14	3	15	54	19	54
Road	.235	.294	.399	311	73	9	0	14	39	22	66
Facing Groundball Pitchers and Flyball Pitchers											
Groundball	.268	.304	.484	246	66	10	2	13	33	11	55
Flyball	.257	.320	.435	354	91	13	1	16	60	30	65
Facing Finesse Pitchers and Power Pitchers											
Finesse	.252	.293	.449	321	81	12	3	15	46	17	53
Power	.272	.335	.462	279	76	11	0	14	47	24	67
On Grass and on Turf											
Grass	.260	.310	.435	508	132	20	3	21	77	34	97
Turf	.272	.330	.565	92	25	3	0	8	16	7	23
During the Day and at Night											
Day	.244	.288	.427	164	40	9	0	7	25	10	37
Night	.268	.323	.466	436	117	14	3	22	68	31	83
By Month											
April	.167	.203	.233	60	10	1	0	1	7	3	14
May	.185	.250	.309	81	15	4	0	2	8	6	15
June	.339	.407	.661	109	37	6	1	9	22	11	22
July	.285	.313	.460	137	39	4	1	6	20	4	30
August	.209	.250	.364	110	23	3	1	4	16	6	18
Sept/Oct	.320	.388	.573	103	33	5	0	7	20	11	21
Situational											
Bases Empty	.277	.333	.474	321	89	16	1	15	15	24	62
Leadoff	.307	.367	.526	137	42	9	0	7	7	11	27
Not Leadoff	.255	.308	.435	184	47	7	1	8	8	13	35
Runners On	.244	.290	.434	279	68	7	2	14	78	17	58
First Base Only	.250	.306	.449	136	34	1	1	8	18	8	27
Scoring Position	.238	.276	.420	143	34	6	1	6	60	9	31
Late Innings, Close	.190	.274	.298	84	16	4	1	1	15	10	21

RBI/Opportunities		
Scoring Position	51 / 193	(26%)
Scoring Position, 2 Out	20 / 84	(24%)
On Third, Less than 2 Out	16 / 34	(47%)
RBI in close games / RBI Total	51 / 93	(55%)

Bill Caudill
Toronto Blue Jays

1986: Power, Flyball 1985: Power, Flyball 1984: Power, Flyball

THREE YEARS (84 – 86)										
	G	IP	H	BB	SO	SB	CS	W	L	S	ERA
Totals	175	202.0	166	83	167	19	6	15	17	52	3.43

At Home and on the Road										
Home	93	115.2	93	48	97	7	5	12	7	28	3.11
Road	82	86.1	73	35	70	12	1	3	10	24	3.86

During the Day and at Night										
Day	66	70.1	60	31	61	6	2	5	5	16	4.09
Night	109	131.2	106	52	106	13	4	10	12	36	3.08

On Grass and on Turf										
Grass	103	122.1	103	49	106	15	6	9	12	38	3.38
Turf	72	79.2	63	34	61	4	0	6	5	14	3.50

By Month										
April	22	29.0	28	6	22	2	3	6	2	10	4.03
May	31	32.0	30	18	23	3	0	2	9	9	4.78
June	34	36.0	19	13	36	3	0	3	0	8	1.00
July	32	39.1	38	15	28	1	1	2	7	9	4.35
August	31	36.1	29	15	35	5	2	1	6	7	3.96
Sept/Oct	25	29.1	22	16	23	5	0	0	0	9	2.45

vs. Opponent Batters										
THREE YEARS (84 – 86)										
	Ave.	OBP	SLG	AB	H	2B	3B	HR	RBI	BB	SO
Totals	.222	.300	.368	748	166	27	5	24	109	83	167

Pitching vs. Left and Right-handed Batters										
Left	.251	.366	.435	363	91	14	4	15	67	66	76
Right	.195	.231	.304	385	75	13	1	9	42	17	91

Situational										
Bases Empty	.226	.304	.375	363	82	16	1	12	12	38	82
Leadoff	.183	.270	.331	142	26	3	0	6	6	15	27
Not Leadoff	.253	.327	.403	221	56	13	1	6	6	23	55
Runners On	.218	.295	.361	385	84	11	4	12	97	45	85
First Base Only	.210	.266	.325	157	33	4	1	4	10	12	34
Scoring Position	.224	.314	.386	228	51	7	3	8	87	33	51
Late Innings, Close	.240	.320	.406	421	101	15	2	17	77	51	100

RBI/Opportunities		
Scoring Position	67 / 333	(20%)
Scoring Position, 2 Out	24 / 173	(14%)
On Third, Less than 2 Out	28 / 57	(49%)
RBI in close games / RBI Total	77 / 109	(71%)

John Cerutti
Toronto Blue Jays

1986: Finesse, Flyball 1985: Power, Flyball 1984: Did not play

THREE YEARS (84 – 86)										
	G	IP	H	BB	SO	SB	CS	W	L	S	ERA
Totals	38	152.0	160	51	94	6	8	9	6	1	4.20

At Home and on the Road										
Home	17	63.1	71	18	46	2	4	2	3	0	4.97
Road	21	88.2	89	33	48	4	4	7	3	1	3.65

During the Day and and at Night										
Day	10	41.1	29	14	27	2	3	3	2	0	3.70
Night	28	110.2	131	37	67	4	5	6	4	1	4.39

On Grass and on Turf										
Grass	17	69.2	71	28	39	4	4	5	3	1	3.62
Turf	21	82.1	89	23	55	2	4	4	3	0	4.70

By Month										
April	0	0.0	0	0	0	0	0	0	0	0	0.00
May	3	17.0	11	7	12	0	2	1	1	0	2.65
June	8	30.2	40	10	16	1	1	2	0	0	4.40
July	7	30.2	31	12	14	3	2	2	2	1	4.11
August	10	34.1	39	8	26	0	1	3	0	0	5.24
Sept/Oct	10	39.1	39	14	26	2	2	1	3	0	3.89

vs. Opponent Batters										
THREE YEARS (84 – 86)										
	Ave.	OBP	SLG	AB	H	2B	3B	HR	RBI	BB	SO
Totals	.271	.329	.458	590	160	26	3	26	80	51	94

Pitching vs. Left and Right-handed Batters										
Left	.271	.311	.457	140	38	4	2	6	19	8	26
Right	.271	.334	.458	450	122	22	1	20	61	43	68

Situational										
Bases Empty	.276	.336	.506	344	95	15	2	20	20	31	50
Leadoff	.275	.340	.486	142	39	7	1	7	7	14	16
Not Leadoff	.277	.332	.520	202	56	8	1	13	13	17	34
Runners On	.264	.319	.390	246	65	11	1	6	60	20	44
First Base Only	.265	.301	.402	117	31	7	0	3	8	6	18
Scoring Position	.264	.333	.380	129	34	4	1	3	52	14	26
Late Innings, Close	.306	.333	.653	49	15	2	0	5	7	1	9

RBI/Opportunities		
Scoring Position	45 / 179	(25%)
Scoring Position, 2 Out	19 / 84	(23%)
On Third, Less than 2 Out	19 / 38	(50%)
RBI in close games / RBI Total	52 / 80	(65%)

Rick Cerone
Milwaukee Brewers

THREE YEARS (84 – 86)									
	Ave.	OBP	SLG	AB	H	2B	3B	HR	RBI	BB	SO
Totals	.230	.290	.316	618	142	26	0	9	56	53	68

Batting vs. Left and Right-handed Pitchers									
Left	.211	.257	.294	228	48	10	0	3	20	15	22
Right	.241	.308	.328	390	94	16	0	6	36	38	46

At Home and on the Road									
Home	.230	.279	.335	322	74	16	0	6	33	24	26
Road	.230	.301	.294	296	68	10	0	3	23	29	42

Facing Groundball Pitchers and Flyball Pitchers									
Groundball	.187	.239	.251	283	53	9	0	3	26	18	37
Flyball	.266	.332	.370	335	89	17	0	6	30	35	31

Facing Finesse Pitchers and Power Pitchers									
Finesse	.237	.287	.326	384	91	16	0	6	32	29	43
Power	.218	.294	.299	234	51	10	0	3	24	24	25

On Grass and on Turf									
Grass	.239	.301	.326	497	119	22	0	7	47	45	51
Turf	.190	.240	.273	121	23	4	0	2	9	8	17

During the Day and at Night									
Day	.212	.276	.251	179	38	4	0	1	13	15	24
Night	.237	.295	.342	439	104	22	0	8	43	38	44

By Month									
April	.216	.272	.302	116	25	1	0	3	12	8	13
May	.223	.272	.319	94	21	3	0	2	10	7	14
June	.259	.281	.352	54	14	5	0	0	4	2	6
July	.209	.252	.270	115	24	7	0	0	6	7	9
August	.252	.321	.343	143	36	4	0	3	15	15	19
Sept/Oct	.229	.330	.323	96	22	6	0	1	9	14	7

Situational									
Bases Empty	.230	.279	.313	339	78	13	0	5	5	22	41
Leadoff	.234	.285	.359	128	30	10	0	2	2	9	15
Not Leadoff	.227	.276	.284	211	48	3	0	3	3	13	26
Runners On	.229	.302	.319	279	64	13	0	4	51	31	27
First Base Only	.237	.290	.333	135	32	10	0	1	5	10	13
Scoring Position	.222	.313	.306	144	32	3	0	3	46	21	14
Late Innings, Close	.255	.322	.292	106	27	4	0	0	9	10	10

RBI/Opportunities		
Scoring Position	40 / 208	(19%)
Scoring Position, 2 Out	15 / 96	(16%)
On Third, Less than 2 Out	18 / 38	(47%)
RBI in close games / RBI Total	36 / 56	(64%)

Ron Cey
Chicago Cubs

THREE YEARS (84 – 86)									
	Ave.	OBP	SLG	AB	H	2B	3B	HR	RBI	BB	SO
Totals	.243	.333	.442	1261	307	66	2	60	196	163	280

Batting vs. Left and Right-handed Pitchers									
Left	.257	.371	.518	334	86	21	0	22	61	57	73
Right	.238	.319	.414	927	221	45	2	38	135	106	207

At Home and on the Road									
Home	.247	.344	.452	624	154	33	1	31	110	90	150
Road	.240	.323	.432	637	153	33	1	29	86	73	130

Facing Groundball Pitchers and Flyball Pitchers									
Groundball	.242	.337	.431	582	141	24	1	28	89	78	125
Flyball	.244	.330	.451	679	166	42	1	32	107	85	155

Facing Finesse Pitchers and Power Pitchers									
Finesse	.258	.337	.481	697	180	35	0	40	118	81	119
Power	.225	.329	.394	564	127	31	2	20	78	82	161

On Grass and on Turf									
Grass	.240	.333	.439	911	219	47	1	44	142	121	208
Turf	.251	.335	.449	350	88	19	1	16	54	42	72

During the Day and at Night									
Day	.246	.339	.456	821	202	44	1	42	139	113	185
Night	.239	.322	.416	440	105	22	1	18	57	50	95

By Month									
April	.192	.275	.358	151	29	7	0	6	21	17	37
May	.258	.355	.508	240	62	16	1	14	42	35	55
June	.237	.326	.384	211	50	7	0	8	26	27	53
July	.228	.319	.393	206	47	13	0	7	23	26	48
August	.309	.401	.581	265	82	16	1	18	53	38	44
Sept/Oct	.197	.276	.346	188	37	7	0	7	31	20	43

Situational									
Bases Empty	.243	.314	.437	695	169	36	0	33	33	65	152
Leadoff	.263	.324	.492	297	78	10	0	17	17	25	49
Not Leadoff	.229	.307	.397	398	91	19	0	16	16	40	103
Runners On	.244	.355	.447	566	138	30	2	27	163	98	128
First Base Only	.203	.296	.331	251	51	8	0	8	18	30	53
Scoring Position	.276	.397	.540	315	87	22	2	19	145	68	75
Late Innings, Close	.235	.333	.394	221	52	11	0	8	25	32	48

RBI/Opportunities		
Scoring Position	109 / 469	(23%)
Scoring Position, 2 Out	45 / 213	(21%)
On Third, Less than 2 Out	39 / 100	(39%)
RBI in close games / RBI Total	121 / 196	(62%)

Chris Chambliss
Atlanta Braves

	THREE YEARS (84 – 86)										
	Ave.	OBP	SLG	AB	H	2B	3B	HR	RBI	BB	SO
Totals	.261	.345	.366	681	178	29	0	14	79	90	99
Batting vs. Left and Right-handed Pitchers											
Left	.192	.255	.231	130	25	5	0	0	13	11	21
Right	.278	.365	.397	551	153	24	0	14	66	79	78
At Home and on the Road											
Home	.270	.338	.402	333	90	17	0	9	39	35	38
Road	.253	.351	.330	348	88	12	0	5	40	55	61
Facing Groundball Pitchers and Flyball Pitchers											
Groundball	.256	.351	.355	301	77	12	0	6	39	46	47
Flyball	.266	.340	.374	380	101	17	0	8	40	44	52
Facing Finesse Pitchers and Power Pitchers											
Finesse	.242	.331	.332	368	89	18	0	5	34	50	53
Power	.284	.361	.406	313	89	11	0	9	45	40	46
On Grass and on Turf											
Grass	.239	.322	.358	481	115	21	0	12	58	60	64
Turf	.315	.399	.385	200	63	8	0	2	21	30	35
During the Day and at Night											
Day	.300	.395	.436	243	73	9	0	8	28	39	32
Night	.240	.316	.326	438	105	20	0	6	51	51	67
By Month											
April	.245	.312	.367	139	34	5	0	4	13	14	14
May	.296	.385	.352	125	37	4	0	1	15	19	20
June	.244	.327	.336	131	32	6	0	2	16	17	18
July	.291	.362	.433	127	37	6	0	4	16	14	16
August	.242	.356	.354	99	24	5	0	2	9	18	23
Sept/Oct	.233	.319	.333	60	14	3	0	1	10	8	8
Situational											
Bases Empty	.262	.331	.376	362	95	14	0	9	9	37	50
Leadoff	.274	.325	.452	146	40	8	0	6	6	11	22
Not Leadoff	.255	.335	.324	216	55	6	0	3	3	26	28
Runners On	.260	.360	.354	319	83	15	0	5	70	53	49
First Base Only	.282	.311	.387	142	40	6	0	3	8	5	25
Scoring Position	.243	.391	.328	177	43	9	0	2	62	48	24
Late Innings, Close	.223	.284	.301	193	43	6	0	3	23	18	34

RBI/Opportunities		
Scoring Position	58 / 278	(21%)
Scoring Position, 2 Out	23 / 131	(18%)
On Third, Less than 2 Out	23 / 49	(47%)
RBI in close games / RBI Total	49 / 79	(62%)

Pat Clements
Pittsburgh Pirates

1986: Finesse, Groundball 1985: Finesse, Groundball 1984: Did not play

	THREE YEARS (84 – 86)										
	G	IP	H	BB	SO	SB	CS	W	L	S	ERA
Totals	133	157.1	139	72	67	9	4	5	6	5	3.20
At Home and on the Road											
Home	67	87.1	64	39	36	4	2	4	2	3	2.27
Road	66	70.0	75	33	31	5	2	1	4	2	4.37
During the Day and and at Night											
Day	38	46.1	41	19	18	3	0	1	1	2	2.53
Night	95	111.0	98	53	49	6	4	4	5	3	3.49
On Grass and on Turf											
Grass	57	75.0	63	28	31	0	0	5	2	3	3.36
Turf	76	82.1	76	44	36	9	4	0	4	2	3.06
By Month											
April	16	21.0	14	7	9	0	0	1	1	0	3.86
May	26	28.2	25	16	11	1	1	3	0	2	2.83
June	25	25.0	20	14	12	1	0	0	3	0	2.88
July	20	30.2	28	16	10	2	1	1	0	1	4.11
August	24	29.0	28	11	15	3	2	0	1	1	2.17
Sept/Oct	22	23.0	24	8	10	2	0	0	1	1	3.52

	vs. Opponent Batters THREE YEARS (84 – 86)										
	Ave.	OBP	SLG	AB	H	2B	3B	HR	RBI	BB	SO
Totals	.249	.335	.334	563	140	25	1	7	64	72	67
Pitching vs. Left and Right-handed Batters											
Left	.267	.375	.374	195	52	9	0	4	33	31	28
Right	.239	.313	.313	368	88	16	1	3	31	41	39
Situational											
Bases Empty	.236	.310	.306	297	70	13	1	2	2	30	37
Leadoff	.242	.336	.305	128	31	6	1	0	0	18	19
Not Leadoff	.231	.290	.308	169	39	7	0	2	2	12	18
Runners On	.263	.362	.365	266	70	12	0	5	62	42	30
First Base Only	.213	.289	.328	122	26	8	0	2	7	13	13
Scoring Position	.306	.417	.396	144	44	4	0	3	55	29	17
Late Innings, Close	.328	.432	.396	192	63	13	0	0	28	38	23

RBI/Opportunities		
Scoring Position	47 / 218	(22%)
Scoring Position, 2 Out	19 / 93	(20%)
On Third, Less than 2 Out	15 / 31	(48%)
RBI in close games / RBI Total	40 / 64	(63%)

Bryan Clutterbuck
Milwaukee Brewers

1986: Finesse, Flyball 1985: Did not play 1984: Did not play

	THREE YEARS (84 – 86)										
	G	IP	H	BB	SO	SB	CS	W	L	S	ERA
Totals	20	56.2	68	16	38	8	4	0	1	0	4.29
At Home and on the Road											
Home	8	28.0	32	7	19	5	1	0	0	0	4.18
Road	12	28.2	36	9	19	3	3	0	1	0	4.40
During the Day and and at Night											
Day	2	4.0	7	1	1	2	0	0	1	0	9.00
Night	18	52.2	61	15	37	6	4	0	0	0	3.93
On Grass and on Turf											
Grass	18	48.2	57	14	28	7	4	0	1	0	3.88
Turf	2	8.0	11	2	10	1	0	0	0	0	6.75
By Month											
April	0	0.0	0	0	0	0	0	0	0	0	0.00
May	0	0.0	0	0	0	0	0	0	0	0	0.00
June	0	0.0	0	0	0	0	0	0	0	0	0.00
July	2	7.0	6	3	3	0	2	0	0	0	0.00
August	10	27.0	40	5	17	5	2	0	1	0	5.00
Sept/Oct	8	22.2	22	8	18	3	0	0	0	0	4.76

	vs. Opponent Batters THREE YEARS (84 – 86)										
	Ave.	OBP	SLG	AB	H	2B	3B	HR	RBI	BB	SO
Totals	.296	.345	.448	230	68	11	0	8	35	16	38
Pitching vs. Left and Right-handed Batters											
Left	.379	.440	.592	103	39	4	0	6	23	10	14
Right	.228	.263	.331	127	29	7	0	2	12	6	24
Situational											
Bases Empty	.315	.368	.491	108	34	7	0	4	4	7	18
Leadoff	.391	.429	.609	46	18	4	0	2	2	3	6
Not Leadoff	.258	.324	.403	62	16	3	0	2	2	4	12
Runners On	.279	.326	.410	122	34	4	0	4	31	9	20
First Base Only	.318	.348	.432	44	14	2	0	1	3	2	4
Scoring Position	.256	.314	.397	78	20	2	0	3	28	7	16
Late Innings, Close	.400	.455	.400	10	4	0	0	0	1	1	2

RBI/Opportunities		
Scoring Position	22 / 100	(22%)
Scoring Position, 2 Out	8 / 47	(17%)
On Third, Less than 2 Out	7 / 19	(37%)
RBI in close games / RBI Total	3 / 35	(9%)

Jaime Cocanower
Milwaukee Brewers

1986: Power, Groundball 1985: Power, Groundball 1984: Finesse, Groundball

	THREE YEARS (84 – 86)										
	G	IP	H	BB	SO	SB	CS	W	L	S	ERA
Totals	74	335.2	350	189	131	29	20	14	25	0	4.24
At Home and on the Road											
Home	32	163.1	168	94	67	9	12	9	13	0	3.64
Road	42	172.1	182	95	64	20	8	5	12	0	4.80
During the Day and and at Night											
Day	21	98.1	114	53	34	8	4	3	7	0	5.03
Night	53	237.1	236	136	97	21	16	11	18	0	3.91
On Grass and on Turf											
Grass	60	277.1	287	154	111	21	17	14	19	0	3.93
Turf	14	58.1	63	35	20	8	3	0	6	0	5.71
By Month											
April	7	36.1	33	24	13	5	4	0	4	0	3.47
May	12	54.2	52	23	25	6	6	4	2	0	2.47
June	20	84.0	74	48	45	6	2	3	2	0	3.21
July	11	50.1	62	29	14	1	3	2	4	0	6.26
August	10	53.0	63	32	18	6	4	3	6	0	5.94
Sept/Oct	14	57.1	66	33	16	5	1	2	7	0	4.55

	vs. Opponent Batters THREE YEARS (84 – 86)										
	Ave.	OBP	SLG	AB	H	2B	3B	HR	RBI	BB	SO
Totals	.274	.372	.367	1279	350	51	4	20	158	189	131
Pitching vs. Left and Right-handed Batters											
Left	.285	.391	.384	643	183	32	4	8	84	112	57
Right	.263	.353	.349	636	167	19	0	12	74	77	74
Situational											
Bases Empty	.273	.382	.374	660	180	25	3	12	12	103	69
Leadoff	.251	.369	.312	295	74	10	1	2	2	51	35
Not Leadoff	.290	.393	.425	365	106	15	2	10	10	52	34
Runners On	.275	.362	.359	619	170	26	1	8	146	86	62
First Base Only	.292	.366	.371	267	78	13	1	2	10	27	24
Scoring Position	.261	.359	.349	352	92	13	0	6	136	59	38
Late Innings, Close	.211	.324	.325	114	24	4	0	3	14	19	13

RBI/Opportunities		
Scoring Position	124 / 522	(24%)
Scoring Position, 2 Out	46 / 219	(21%)
On Third, Less than 2 Out	53 / 108	(49%)
RBI in close games / RBI Total	100 / 158	(63%)

Chris Codiroli
Oakland A's

1986: Finesse, Flyball 1985: Finesse, Groundball 1984: Finesse, Groundball

THREE YEARS (84 – 86)	G	IP	H	BB	SO	SB	CS	W	L	S	ERA
Totals	81	407.0	430	150	198	26	13	25	26	1	4.60
At Home and on the Road											
Home	41	197.1	191	81	85	10	5	16	9	0	3.97
Road	40	209.2	239	69	113	16	8	9	17	1	5.19
During the Day and and at Night											
Day	29	139.0	145	50	65	4	2	14	5	0	4.66
Night	52	268.0	285	100	133	22	11	11	21	1	4.57
On Grass and on Turf											
Grass	70	343.2	367	135	161	22	13	21	22	0	4.61
Turf	11	63.1	63	15	37	4	0	4	4	1	4.55
By Month											
April	18	73.2	69	34	37	7	0	5	3	1	3.91
May	18	94.0	100	38	43	2	5	5	7	0	5.46
June	15	73.0	86	27	35	4	3	4	4	0	5.42
July	10	52.0	54	17	21	3	3	0	5	0	3.98
August	6	38.1	36	16	21	2	1	2	2	0	4.46
Sept/Oct	14	76.0	85	18	41	8	1	9	5	0	3.91

vs. Opponent Batters THREE YEARS (84 – 86)	Ave.	OBP	SLG	AB	H	2B	3B	HR	RBI	BB	SO
Totals	.267	.331	.426	1610	430	74	10	54	218	150	198
Pitching vs. Left and Right-handed Batters											
Left	.259	.321	.413	833	216	42	4	26	102	75	100
Right	.275	.341	.440	777	214	32	6	28	116	75	98
Situational											
Bases Empty	.261	.323	.430	941	246	48	6	33	33	82	120
Leadoff	.252	.322	.445	389	98	20	2	17	17	38	49
Not Leadoff	.268	.323	.420	552	148	28	4	16	16	44	71
Runners On	.275	.341	.420	669	184	26	4	21	185	68	78
First Base Only	.252	.306	.409	301	76	12	1	11	26	20	30
Scoring Position	.293	.368	.429	368	108	14	3	10	159	48	48
Late Innings, Close	.277	.354	.393	112	31	4	0	3	11	14	13

RBI/Opportunities		
Scoring Position	135 / 486	(28%)
Scoring Position, 2 Out	53 / 234	(23%)
On Third, Less than 2 Out	57 / 91	(63%)
RBI in close games / RBI Total	144 / 218	(66%)

Dave Collins
Detroit Tigers

THREE YEARS (84 – 86)	Ave.	OBP	SLG	AB	H	2B	3B	HR	RBI	BB	SO
Totals	.278	.338	.375	1239	344	58	21	7	99	106	127
Batting vs. Left and Right-handed Pitchers											
Left	.256	.293	.357	258	66	14	3	2	31	12	23
Right	.283	.350	.380	981	278	44	18	5	68	94	104
At Home and on the Road											
Home	.265	.332	.374	596	158	28	14	3	42	56	64
Road	.289	.344	.376	643	186	30	7	4	57	50	63
Facing Groundball Pitchers and Flyball Pitchers											
Groundball	.286	.343	.387	569	163	26	11	3	51	46	56
Flyball	.270	.334	.366	670	181	32	10	4	48	60	71
Facing Finesse Pitchers and Power Pitchers											
Finesse	.267	.320	.370	711	190	38	10	5	51	51	56
Power	.292	.362	.383	528	154	20	11	2	48	55	71
On Grass and on Turf											
Grass	.262	.323	.332	858	225	37	7	3	59	74	89
Turf	.312	.372	.472	381	119	21	14	4	40	32	38
During the Day and at Night											
Day	.249	.330	.357	409	102	20	9	2	38	48	51
Night	.292	.342	.384	830	242	38	12	5	61	58	76
By Month											
April	.311	.376	.378	196	61	6	2	1	21	20	18
May	.272	.310	.415	246	67	15	7	2	17	14	31
June	.261	.319	.361	238	62	15	3	1	12	16	25
July	.283	.356	.390	187	53	8	3	2	11	20	15
August	.268	.325	.344	224	60	8	3	1	26	20	19
Sept/Oct	.277	.359	.358	148	41	6	3	0	12	16	19
Situational											
Bases Empty	.275	.337	.373	766	211	39	12	4	4	63	76
Leadoff	.248	.326	.331	314	78	12	4	2	2	33	31
Not Leadoff	.294	.345	.403	452	133	27	8	2	2	30	45
Runners On	.281	.340	.378	473	133	19	9	3	95	43	51
First Base Only	.248	.282	.333	210	52	11	2	1	7	8	20
Scoring Position	.308	.382	.414	263	81	8	7	2	88	35	31
Late Innings, Close	.293	.361	.356	225	66	9	1	1	23	21	32

RBI/Opportunities		
Scoring Position	83 / 357	(23%)
Scoring Position, 2 Out	30 / 165	(18%)
On Third, Less than 2 Out	33 / 59	(56%)
RBI in close games / RBI Total	62 / 99	(63%)

Dave Concepcion
Cincinnati Reds

THREE YEARS (84 – 86)	Ave.	OBP	SLG	AB	H	2B	3B	HR	RBI	BB	SO
Totals	.251	.312	.330	1402	352	58	5	14	136	128	182
Batting vs. Left and Right-handed Pitchers											
Left	.283	.349	.397	448	127	27	0	8	37	47	48
Right	.236	.294	.298	954	225	31	5	6	99	81	134
At Home and on the Road											
Home	.250	.318	.326	691	173	32	4	4	72	70	88
Road	.252	.305	.333	711	179	26	1	10	64	58	94
Facing Groundball Pitchers and Flyball Pitchers											
Groundball	.266	.334	.353	689	183	38	2	6	64	72	88
Flyball	.237	.290	.307	713	169	20	3	8	72	56	94
Facing Finesse Pitchers and Power Pitchers											
Finesse	.256	.313	.340	788	202	41	2	7	69	67	73
Power	.244	.310	.316	614	150	17	3	7	67	61	109
On Grass and on Turf											
Grass	.267	.307	.351	419	112	12	1	7	36	25	57
Turf	.244	.313	.320	983	240	46	4	7	100	103	125
During the Day and at Night											
Day	.266	.333	.343	443	118	16	3	4	41	47	53
Night	.244	.302	.323	959	234	42	2	10	95	81	129
By Month											
April	.233	.283	.372	215	50	9	0	7	28	16	37
May	.271	.340	.357	266	72	15	1	2	23	29	31
June	.253	.295	.323	288	73	11	3	1	26	18	31
July	.267	.343	.316	187	50	6	0	1	14	22	29
August	.205	.288	.267	195	40	6	0	2	14	22	22
Sept/Oct	.267	.318	.331	251	67	11	1	1	31	21	32
Situational											
Bases Empty	.260	.315	.351	830	216	39	3	10	10	66	109
Leadoff	.280	.323	.376	311	87	15	0	5	5	20	41
Not Leadoff	.249	.311	.335	519	129	24	3	5	5	46	68
Runners On	.238	.306	.299	572	136	19	2	4	126	62	73
First Base Only	.244	.278	.329	234	57	13	2	1	12	11	21
Scoring Position	.234	.324	.278	338	79	6	0	3	114	51	52
Late Innings, Close	.221	.277	.321	280	62	11	1	5	29	22	45

RBI/Opportunities		
Scoring Position	106 / 489	(22%)
Scoring Position, 2 Out	38 / 252	(15%)
On Third, Less than 2 Out	43 / 75	(57%)
RBI in close games / RBI Total	103 / 136	(76%)

Tim Conroy
St. Louis Cardinals

1986: Power, Flyball 1985: Finesse, Flyball 1984: Power, Flyball

THREE YEARS (84 – 86)	G	IP	H	BB	SO	SB	CS	W	L	S	ERA
Totals	79	233.2	226	134	156	25	8	6	18	0	5.12
At Home and on the Road											
Home	43	135.2	130	73	80	15	6	3	11	0	4.84
Road	36	98.0	96	61	76	10	2	3	7	0	5.51
During the Day and and at Night											
Day	29	93.0	86	45	69	9	6	4	8	0	4.16
Night	50	140.2	140	89	87	16	2	2	10	0	5.76
On Grass and on Turf											
Grass	49	132.1	116	77	89	8	5	2	8	0	4.96
Turf	30	101.1	110	57	67	17	3	4	10	0	5.33
By Month											
April	19	40.1	24	26	19	6	0	1	2	0	3.79
May	14	34.1	42	15	18	3	0	1	3	0	5.77
June	5	14.0	6	12	14	2	1	1	1	0	5.79
July	11	30.0	36	15	30	4	0	1	3	0	6.30
August	13	56.0	52	23	35	5	2	1	2	0	3.37
Sept/Oct	17	59.0	66	43	40	5	5	1	7	0	6.56

vs. Opponent Batters THREE YEARS (84 – 86)	Ave.	OBP	SLG	AB	H	2B	3B	HR	RBI	BB	SO
Totals	.255	.352	.424	885	226	46	8	29	123	134	156
Pitching vs. Left and Right-handed Batters											
Left	.218	.332	.351	211	46	6	5	4	21	35	42
Right	.267	.358	.447	674	180	40	3	25	102	99	114
Situational											
Bases Empty	.245	.347	.369	502	123	23	3	11	11	74	98
Leadoff	.224	.329	.410	210	47	14	2	7	7	30	43
Not Leadoff	.260	.359	.339	292	76	9	1	4	4	44	55
Runners On	.269	.359	.496	383	103	23	5	18	112	60	58
First Base Only	.282	.355	.559	177	50	10	0	13	30	19	24
Scoring Position	.257	.361	.442	206	53	13	5	5	82	41	34
Late Innings, Close	.279	.367	.515	68	19	5	1	3	13	10	10

RBI/Opportunities		
Scoring Position	70 / 309	(23%)
Scoring Position, 2 Out	19 / 123	(15%)
On Third, Less than 2 Out	39 / 75	(52%)
RBI in close games / RBI Total	87 / 123	(71%)

Doug Corbett
California Angels

1986: Finesse, Groundball 1985: Power, Groundball 1984: Finesse, Groundball

THREE YEARS (84 – 86)

	G	IP	H	BB	SO	SB	CS	W	L	S	ERA
Totals	121	209.2	191	72	108	6	7	12	6	14	3.31
At Home and on the Road											
Home	59	110.2	93	32	57	6	4	9	2	7	2.77
Road	62	99.0	98	40	51	0	3	3	4	7	3.91
During the Day and and at Night											
Day	39	71.0	75	23	35	2	4	4	3	5	5.07
Night	82	138.2	116	49	73	4	3	8	3	9	2.40
On Grass and on Turf											
Grass	107	188.2	169	64	98	6	6	10	5	14	3.48
Turf	14	21.0	22	8	10	0	1	2	1	0	1.71
By Month											
April	14	28.2	22	10	16	2	1	2	0	1	2.51
May	22	36.0	41	13	16	3	1	1	1	4	5.50
June	26	43.0	31	13	22	1	2	3	2	5	2.09
July	17	27.0	25	7	15	0	0	1	1	2	3.00
August	21	39.2	48	15	24	0	1	2	1	1	4.31
Sept/Oct	21	35.1	24	14	15	0	2	3	1	1	2.29

vs. Opponent Batters
THREE YEARS (84 – 86)

	Ave.	OBP	SLG	AB	H	2B	3B	HR	RBI	BB	SO
Totals	.246	.310	.364	777	191	26	3	20	105	72	108
Pitching vs. Left and Right-handed Batters											
Left	.275	.338	.397	345	95	15	0	9	50	33	29
Right	.222	.289	.338	432	96	11	3	11	55	39	79
Situational											
Bases Empty	.219	.275	.338	411	90	10	3	11	11	29	53
Leadoff	.226	.266	.335	164	37	4	1	4	4	8	18
Not Leadoff	.215	.281	.340	247	53	6	2	7	7	21	35
Runners On	.276	.348	.393	366	101	16	0	9	94	43	55
First Base Only	.279	.311	.377	154	43	9	0	2	8	7	23
Scoring Position	.274	.371	.406	212	58	7	0	7	86	36	32
Late Innings, Close	.224	.295	.328	241	54	8	1	5	38	25	34

RBI/Opportunities

Scoring Position	70 / 321	(22%)
Scoring Position, 2 Out	25 / 135	(19%)
On Third, Less than 2 Out	31 / 67	(46%)
RBI in close games / RBI Total	50 / 105	(48%)

Steve Crawford
Boston Red Sox

1986: Finesse, Flyball 1985: Finesse, Groundball 1984: Finesse, Groundball

THREE YEARS (84 – 86)

	G	IP	H	BB	SO	SB	CS	W	L	S	ERA
Totals	119	210.1	241	68	111	7	7	11	7	17	3.68
At Home and on the Road											
Home	66	102.2	126	37	62	4	6	6	2	10	4.38
Road	53	107.2	115	31	49	3	1	5	5	7	3.01
During the Day and and at Night											
Day	37	62.1	71	19	32	3	4	5	2	5	3.90
Night	82	148.0	170	49	79	4	3	6	5	12	3.59
On Grass and on Turf											
Grass	101	172.0	207	57	94	7	6	10	6	14	3.92
Turf	18	38.1	34	11	17	0	1	1	1	3	2.58
By Month											
April	10	24.0	29	5	11	1	1	2	2	0	3.75
May	16	31.0	29	8	18	1	1	2	0	2	4.65
June	24	43.2	47	10	27	2	3	2	0	1	2.06
July	20	26.1	27	13	14	1	1	1	0	3	4.44
August	19	43.2	49	16	21	0	0	3	2	4	3.09
Sept/Oct	30	41.2	60	16	20	2	1	1	3	7	4.75

vs. Opponent Batters
THREE YEARS (84 – 86)

	Ave.	OBP	SLG	AB	H	2B	3B	HR	RBI	BB	SO
Totals	.293	.344	.414	822	241	43	4	16	129	68	111
Pitching vs. Left and Right-handed Batters											
Left	.314	.380	.439	392	123	26	1	7	67	46	43
Right	.274	.310	.391	430	118	17	3	9	62	22	68
Situational											
Bases Empty	.292	.326	.424	394	115	19	0	11	11	20	55
Leadoff	.272	.296	.347	173	47	10	0	1	1	6	21
Not Leadoff	.308	.349	.484	221	68	9	0	10	10	14	34
Runners On	.294	.360	.404	428	126	24	4	5	118	48	56
First Base Only	.285	.340	.389	144	41	7	1	2	8	12	14
Scoring Position	.299	.370	.412	284	85	17	3	3	110	36	42
Late Innings, Close	.277	.349	.344	256	71	12	1	1	42	30	42

RBI/Opportunities

Scoring Position	102 / 425	(24%)
Scoring Position, 2 Out	41 / 188	(22%)
On Third, Less than 2 Out	38 / 80	(47%)
RBI in close games / RBI Total	55 / 129	(43%)

Julio Cruz
Chicago White Sox

THREE YEARS (84 – 86)

	Ave.	OBP	SLG	AB	H	2B	3B	HR	RBI	BB	SO
Totals	.213	.308	.267	858	183	17	7	5	77	119	126
Batting vs. Left and Right-handed Pitchers											
Left	.243	.331	.313	345	84	10	4	2	35	47	50
Right	.193	.292	.236	513	99	7	3	3	42	72	76
At Home and on the Road											
Home	.218	.328	.261	399	87	6	4	1	40	68	52
Road	.209	.289	.272	459	96	11	3	4	37	51	74
Facing Groundball Pitchers and Flyball Pitchers											
Groundball	.213	.295	.269	375	80	10	4	1	28	44	52
Flyball	.213	.317	.265	483	103	7	3	4	49	75	74
Facing Finesse Pitchers and Power Pitchers											
Finesse	.197	.272	.250	513	101	11	5	2	32	55	67
Power	.238	.357	.293	345	82	6	2	3	45	64	59
On Grass and on Turf											
Grass	.201	.302	.245	706	142	13	6	2	61	105	105
Turf	.270	.337	.368	152	41	4	1	3	16	14	21
During the Day and at Night											
Day	.210	.294	.266	248	52	3	1	3	23	31	42
Night	.215	.313	.267	610	131	14	6	2	54	88	84
By Month											
April	.214	.308	.262	126	27	3	0	1	12	18	21
May	.165	.244	.243	115	19	1	1	2	11	12	18
June	.232	.347	.251	207	48	4	0	0	14	35	31
July	.176	.270	.239	142	25	2	2	1	15	19	19
August	.224	.297	.311	161	36	7	2	1	18	18	21
Sept/Oct	.262	.360	.299	107	28	0	2	0	7	17	16
Situational											
Bases Empty	.200	.295	.244	504	101	11	4	1	1	66	81
Leadoff	.182	.277	.220	214	39	4	2	0	0	28	31
Not Leadoff	.214	.309	.262	290	62	7	2	1	1	38	50
Runners On	.232	.325	.299	354	82	6	3	4	76	53	45
First Base Only	.179	.264	.256	156	28	1	1	3	8	18	17
Scoring Position	.273	.368	.333	198	54	5	2	1	68	35	28
Late Innings, Close	.221	.323	.265	136	30	3	0	1	16	21	20

RBI/Opportunities

Scoring Position	64 / 292	(22%)
Scoring Position, 2 Out	30 / 143	(21%)
On Third, Less than 2 Out	26 / 53	(49%)
RBI in close games / RBI Total	39 / 77	(51%)

Kal Daniels
Cincinnati Reds

THREE YEARS (84 – 86)

	Ave.	OBP	SLG	AB	H	2B	3B	HR	RBI	BB	SO
Totals	.320	.398	.519	181	58	10	4	6	23	22	30
Batting vs. Left and Right-handed Pitchers											
Left	.188	.278	.219	32	6	1	0	0	0	3	7
Right	.349	.424	.584	149	52	9	4	6	23	19	23
At Home and on the Road											
Home	.309	.369	.482	110	34	4	3	3	15	10	22
Road	.338	.440	.577	71	24	6	1	3	8	12	8
Facing Groundball Pitchers and Flyball Pitchers											
Groundball	.353	.421	.506	85	30	4	3	1	10	8	18
Flyball	.292	.378	.531	96	28	6	1	5	13	14	12
Facing Finesse Pitchers and Power Pitchers											
Finesse	.329	.409	.500	82	27	2	3	2	11	10	14
Power	.313	.389	.535	99	31	8	1	4	12	12	16
On Grass and on Turf											
Grass	.351	.489	.622	37	13	4	0	2	5	9	5
Turf	.313	.371	.493	144	45	6	4	4	18	13	25
During the Day and at Night											
Day	.328	.438	.525	61	20	4	1	2	10	12	7
Night	.317	.376	.517	120	38	6	3	4	13	10	23
By Month											
April	.353	.405	.647	34	12	2	1	2	5	3	8
May	.083	.267	.083	12	1	0	0	0	0	3	3
June	.429	.500	.429	7	3	0	0	0	1	1	3
July	.371	.465	.514	35	13	3	1	0	5	5	4
August	.309	.356	.494	81	25	4	1	3	6	6	10
Sept/Oct	.333	.500	.833	12	4	1	1	1	5	4	2
Situational											
Bases Empty	.330	.403	.539	115	38	8	2	4	4	13	21
Leadoff	.375	.429	.656	64	24	7	1	3	3	5	13
Not Leadoff	.275	.373	.392	51	14	1	1	1	1	8	8
Runners On	.303	.390	.485	66	20	2	2	2	19	9	9
First Base Only	.355	.375	.645	31	11	1	1	2	6	1	3
Scoring Position	.257	.400	.343	35	9	1	1	0	13	8	6
Late Innings, Close	.333	.439	.636	33	11	4	0	2	8	7	5

RBI/Opportunities

Scoring Position	13 / 55	(24%)
Scoring Position, 2 Out	6 / 25	(24%)
On Third, Less than 2 Out	4 / 9	(44%)
RBI in close games / RBI Total	16 / 23	(70%)

Danny Darwin
Houston Astros

1986: Finesse, Flyball   1985: Finesse, Flyball   1984: Finesse, Flyball

THREE YEARS (84 – 86)	G	IP	H	BB	SO	SB	CS	W	L	S	ERA
Totals	113	626.0	631	163	368	55	19	27	40	2	3.67
At Home and on the Road											
Home	52	289.2	300	87	173	25	9	8	24	1	3.57
Road	61	336.1	331	76	195	30	10	19	16	1	3.75
During the Day and and at Night											
Day	38	178.2	190	54	125	26	6	9	16	1	4.08
Night	75	447.1	441	109	243	29	13	18	24	1	3.50
On Grass and on Turf											
Grass	92	513.2	510	142	302	43	16	21	33	2	3.64
Turf	21	112.1	121	21	66	12	3	6	7	0	3.77
By Month											
April	15	76.0	65	18	36	12	0	5	2	0	2.96
May	19	108.1	114	27	51	9	2	5	5	0	3.82
June	17	117.0	129	27	73	10	6	5	8	0	4.23
July	19	122.1	116	42	68	10	5	3	9	0	3.31
August	16	96.0	97	24	68	4	4	3	9	0	3.94
Sept/Oct	27	106.1	110	25	72	10	2	6	7	2	3.55

vs. Opponent Batters THREE YEARS (84 – 86)	Ave.	OBP	SLG	AB	H	2B	3B	HR	RBI	BB	SO
Totals	.261	.308	.401	2421	631	105	14	69	289	163	368
Pitching vs. Left and Right-handed Batters											
Left	.288	.349	.459	1230	354	70	7	42	163	116	161
Right	.233	.263	.342	1191	277	35	7	27	126	47	207
Situational											
Bases Empty	.243	.289	.386	1450	353	68	6	42	42	87	229
Leadoff	.248	.287	.404	601	149	31	3	19	19	33	87
Not Leadoff	.240	.290	.372	849	204	37	3	23	23	54	142
Runners On	.286	.335	.424	971	278	37	8	27	247	76	139
First Base Only	.293	.345	.457	409	120	15	2	16	43	28	54
Scoring Position	.281	.329	.400	562	158	22	6	11	204	48	85
Late Innings, Close	.274	.319	.437	332	91	12	3	12	43	24	48

RBI/Opportunities		
Scoring Position	182 / 724	(25%)
Scoring Position, 2 Out	84 / 340	(25%)
On Third, Less than 2 Out	60 / 123	(49%)
RBI in close games / RBI Total	209 / 289	(72%)

Darren Daulton
Philadelphia Phillies

THREE YEARS (84 – 86)	Ave.	OBP	SLG	AB	H	2B	3B	HR	RBI	BB	SO
Totals	.216	.360	.402	241	52	7	1	12	32	54	78
Batting vs. Left and Right-handed Pitchers											
Left	.172	.314	.207	29	5	1	0	0	0	6	15
Right	.222	.366	.429	212	47	6	1	12	32	48	63
At Home and on the Road											
Home	.214	.389	.375	112	24	4	1	4	13	31	32
Road	.217	.333	.426	129	28	3	0	8	19	23	46
Facing Groundball Pitchers and Flyball Pitchers											
Groundball	.297	.414	.577	111	33	5	1	8	18	22	30
Flyball	.146	.317	.254	130	19	2	0	4	14	32	48
Facing Finesse Pitchers and Power Pitchers											
Finesse	.276	.408	.490	98	27	3	0	6	19	22	27
Power	.175	.328	.343	143	25	4	1	6	13	32	51
On Grass and on Turf											
Grass	.195	.272	.439	82	16	2	0	6	12	9	32
Turf	.226	.400	.384	159	36	5	1	6	20	45	46
During the Day and at Night											
Day	.225	.337	.539	89	20	4	0	8	14	15	33
Night	.211	.373	.322	152	32	3	1	4	18	39	45
By Month											
April	.283	.441	.565	46	13	1	0	4	9	13	11
May	.132	.310	.250	68	9	2	0	2	5	17	22
June	.267	.441	.444	45	12	2	0	2	9	14	14
July	.000	.000	.000	0	0	0	0	0	0	0	0
August	.250	.325	.556	36	9	2	0	3	5	4	13
Sept/Oct	.196	.288	.304	46	9	0	1	1	4	6	18
Situational											
Bases Empty	.211	.327	.429	133	28	6	1	7	7	23	36
Leadoff	.218	.259	.327	55	12	3	0	1	1	3	11
Not Leadoff	.205	.367	.500	78	16	3	1	6	6	20	25
Runners On	.222	.397	.370	108	24	1	0	5	25	31	42
First Base Only	.306	.457	.500	36	11	1	0	2	4	9	11
Scoring Position	.181	.368	.306	72	13	0	0	3	21	22	31
Late Innings, Close	.143	.265	.167	42	6	1	0	0	0	7	15

RBI/Opportunities		
Scoring Position	15 / 102	(15%)
Scoring Position, 2 Out	5 / 54	(9%)
On Third, Less than 2 Out	7 / 16	(44%)
RBI in close games / RBI Total	13 / 32	(41%)

Joel Davis
Chicago White Sox

1986: Finesse, Groundball 1985: Finesse, Groundball   1984: Did not play

THREE YEARS (84 – 86)	G	IP	H	BB	SO	SB	CS	W	L	S	ERA
Totals	31	176.2	186	77	91	15	6	7	8	0	4.48
At Home and on the Road											
Home	15	86.1	88	39	47	2	5	4	3	0	4.07
Road	16	90.1	98	38	44	13	1	3	5	0	4.88
During the Day and and at Night											
Day	10	56.2	53	21	40	5	4	2	2	0	4.61
Night	21	120.0	133	56	51	10	2	5	6	0	4.42
On Grass and on Turf											
Grass	24	139.2	144	62	75	8	5	7	5	0	4.00
Turf	7	37.0	42	15	16	7	1	0	3	0	6.32
By Month											
April	4	27.1	22	11	15	1	1	1	1	0	3.29
May	6	40.2	41	22	27	6	2	1	1	0	3.76
June	6	26.2	37	16	9	4	1	2	2	0	7.09
July	3	10.2	15	2	3	0	0	0	1	0	5.91
August	5	32.1	30	15	19	1	1	1	2	0	4.73
Sept/Oct	7	39.0	41	11	18	3	1	2	1	0	3.69

vs. Opponent Batters THREE YEARS (84 – 86)	Ave.	OBP	SLG	AB	H	2B	3B	HR	RBI	BB	SO
Totals	.270	.344	.410	688	186	29	11	15	78	77	91
Pitching vs. Left and Right-handed Batters											
Left	.291	.364	.442	371	108	17	6	9	43	44	45
Right	.246	.319	.372	317	78	12	5	6	35	33	46
Situational											
Bases Empty	.243	.319	.387	408	99	19	8	8	8	44	61
Leadoff	.213	.279	.368	174	37	4	4	5	5	15	26
Not Leadoff	.265	.348	.402	234	62	15	4	3	3	29	35
Runners On	.311	.379	.443	280	87	10	3	7	70	33	30
First Base Only	.320	.370	.464	125	40	6	0	4	11	10	14
Scoring Position	.303	.385	.426	155	47	4	3	3	59	23	16
Late Innings, Close	.338	.407	.519	77	26	6	1	2	11	9	16

RBI/Opportunities		
Scoring Position	52 / 205	(25%)
Scoring Position, 2 Out	23 / 98	(23%)
On Third, Less than 2 Out	18 / 39	(46%)
RBI in close games / RBI Total	58 / 78	(74%)

Mark Davis
San Francisco Giants

1986: Power, Flyball   1985: Power, Flyball   1984: Power, Flyball

THREE YEARS (84 – 86)	G	IP	H	BB	SO	SB	CS	W	L	S	ERA
Totals	190	373.1	353	129	345	30	16	15	36	11	4.27
At Home and on the Road											
Home	86	185.1	179	61	170	12	11	10	19	5	4.08
Road	104	188.0	174	68	175	18	5	5	17	6	4.45
During the Day and and at Night											
Day	101	196.2	201	69	177	16	7	9	21	6	4.90
Night	89	176.2	152	60	168	14	9	6	15	5	3.57
On Grass and on Turf											
Grass	139	282.0	274	95	259	21	13	13	30	7	4.37
Turf	51	91.1	79	34	86	9	3	2	6	4	3.94
By Month											
April	27	54.0	46	21	53	5	5	2	5	1	2.83
May	33	58.0	60	19	52	5	1	3	6	2	4.19
June	31	74.2	66	30	65	3	5	3	4	4	3.13
July	30	63.0	76	16	47	6	2	0	7	2	6.14
August	33	61.1	50	29	68	5	1	4	5	1	4.40
Sept/Oct	36	62.1	55	14	60	6	2	3	9	1	4.91

vs. Opponent Batters THREE YEARS (84 – 86)	Ave.	OBP	SLG	AB	H	2B	3B	HR	RBI	BB	SO
Totals	.254	.318	.401	1390	353	60	6	44	189	129	345
Pitching vs. Left and Right-handed Batters											
Left	.185	.238	.284	341	63	9	2	7	38	24	109
Right	.276	.343	.439	1049	290	51	4	37	151	105	236
Situational											
Bases Empty	.234	.294	.369	805	188	34	3	23	23	63	217
Leadoff	.251	.314	.382	327	82	12	2	9	9	28	83
Not Leadoff	.222	.280	.360	478	106	22	1	14	14	35	134
Runners On	.282	.349	.444	585	165	26	3	21	166	66	128
First Base Only	.290	.341	.484	248	72	10	1	12	28	17	40
Scoring Position	.276	.355	.415	337	93	16	2	9	138	49	88
Late Innings, Close	.211	.294	.349	375	79	11	1	13	55	42	114

RBI/Opportunities		
Scoring Position	118 / 493	(24%)
Scoring Position, 2 Out	45 / 220	(20%)
On Third, Less than 2 Out	42 / 87	(48%)
RBI in close games / RBI Total	131 / 189	(69%)

Ron Davis
Chicago Cubs

1986: Power, Flyball   1985: Power, Groundball   1984: Power, Flyball

THREE YEARS (84 – 86)

	G	IP	H	BB	SO	SB	CS	W	L	S	ERA
Totals	174	206.1	220	108	186	23	2	11	25	56	5.37
At Home and on the Road											
Home	85	104.2	110	53	104	12	1	9	5	28	4.39
Road	89	101.2	110	55	82	11	1	2	20	28	6.37
During the Day and and at Night											
Day	57	73.0	76	33	73	7	1	6	3	19	4.32
Night	117	133.1	144	75	113	16	1	5	22	37	5.94
On Grass and on Turf											
Grass	73	81.0	90	42	66	6	1	2	16	25	6.78
Turf	101	125.1	130	66	120	17	1	9	9	31	4.45
By Month											
April	23	25.1	27	14	24	3	0	4	5	8	8.53
May	33	37.2	47	25	42	5	0	0	8	8	6.93
June	28	39.2	30	14	27	2	1	2	3	10	3.40
July	27	31.2	39	16	30	3	0	2	1	10	5.12
August	32	34.0	33	18	32	9	1	2	5	9	4.50
Sept/Oct	31	38.0	44	21	31	1	0	1	3	11	4.74

vs. Opponent Batters
THREE YEARS (84 – 86)

	Ave.	OBP	SLG	AB	H	2B	3B	HR	RBI	BB	SO
Totals	.275	.363	.445	800	220	34	9	28	162	108	186
Pitching vs. Left and Right-handed Batters											
Left	.278	.381	.467	392	109	14	6	16	86	65	86
Right	.272	.346	.424	408	111	20	3	12	76	43	100
Situational											
Bases Empty	.266	.337	.455	319	85	11	5	13	13	29	66
Leadoff	.293	.352	.414	133	39	3	2	3	3	10	24
Not Leadoff	.247	.327	.484	186	46	8	3	10	10	19	42
Runners On	.281	.380	.439	481	135	23	4	15	149	79	120
First Base Only	.317	.400	.483	145	46	9	0	5	14	18	32
Scoring Position	.265	.371	.420	336	89	14	4	10	135	61	88
Late Innings, Close	.271	.367	.462	468	127	18	4	21	103	67	122

RBI/Opportunities

Scoring Position	113 / 520	(22%)
Scoring Position, 2 Out	46 / 257	(18%)
On Third, Less than 2 Out	41 / 97	(42%)
RBI in close games / RBI Total	104 / 162	(64%)

Bill Dawley
Chicago White Sox

1986: Finesse, Flyball   1985: Power, Flyball   1984: Finesse, Flyball

THREE YEARS (84 – 86)

	G	IP	H	BB	SO	SB	CS	W	L	S	ERA
Totals	155	276.2	249	100	161	14	8	16	14	9	2.90
At Home and on the Road											
Home	78	141.0	117	48	90	10	2	5	6	5	2.87
Road	77	135.2	132	52	71	4	6	11	8	4	2.92
During the Day and and at Night											
Day	35	61.2	67	27	39	4	0	3	4	3	4.52
Night	120	215.0	182	73	122	10	8	13	10	6	2.43
On Grass and on Turf											
Grass	71	139.0	128	48	83	7	4	5	6	3	2.85
Turf	84	137.2	121	52	78	7	4	11	8	6	2.94
By Month											
April	17	25.0	31	21	13	0	2	1	2	0	3.96
May	30	49.2	39	20	18	3	3	3	6	2	2.72
June	30	52.0	52	13	35	1	0	2	2	1	3.12
July	19	39.0	40	12	22	0	1	0	0	2	3.69
August	26	45.1	37	16	30	2	0	4	1	1	2.58
Sept/Oct	33	65.2	50	18	43	8	2	6	3	3	2.19

vs. Opponent Batters
THREE YEARS (84 – 86)

	Ave.	OBP	SLG	AB	H	2B	3B	HR	RBI	BB	SO
Totals	.246	.311	.359	1012	249	38	5	22	129	100	161
Pitching vs. Left and Right-handed Batters											
Left	.269	.339	.402	435	117	20	4	10	62	48	52
Right	.229	.290	.326	577	132	18	1	12	67	52	109
Situational											
Bases Empty	.245	.295	.352	551	135	24	4	9	9	38	95
Leadoff	.275	.327	.356	236	65	11	1	2	2	18	34
Not Leadoff	.222	.271	.349	315	70	13	3	7	7	20	61
Runners On	.247	.328	.367	461	114	14	1	13	120	62	66
First Base Only	.237	.275	.321	173	41	3	1	2	7	9	30
Scoring Position	.253	.356	.406	288	73	11	0	11	113	53	36
Late Innings, Close	.229	.313	.314	420	96	12	0	8	42	53	65

RBI/Opportunities

Scoring Position	95 / 449	(21%)
Scoring Position, 2 Out	36 / 203	(18%)
On Third, Less than 2 Out	43 / 86	(50%)
RBI in close games / RBI Total	62 / 129	(48%)

Ken Dayley
St. Louis Cardinals

1986: Power, Groundball   1985: Power, Groundball   1984: Finesse, Flyball

THREE YEARS (84 – 86)

	G	IP	H	BB	SO	SB	CS	W	L	S	ERA
Totals	95	127.2	151	40	105	7	1	4	12	16	3.88
At Home and on the Road											
Home	50	72.2	83	18	56	3	0	3	7	9	3.22
Road	45	55.0	68	22	49	4	1	1	5	7	4.75
During the Day and and at Night											
Day	34	43.2	45	19	37	3	0	3	3	3	3.71
Night	61	84.0	106	21	68	4	1	1	9	13	3.96
On Grass and on Turf											
Grass	29	53.1	66	19	43	2	1	1	6	3	4.56
Turf	66	74.1	85	21	62	5	0	3	6	13	3.39
By Month											
April	17	36.2	47	11	24	3	0	0	3	0	4.66
May	16	21.2	24	4	17	1	0	0	3	6	2.91
June	24	29.2	44	13	22	1	0	2	2	4	5.76
July	13	15.0	8	3	16	1	1	1	0	2	0.60
August	13	13.1	16	7	12	0	0	0	1	3	1.35
Sept/Oct	12	11.1	12	2	14	1	0	1	3	1	5.56

vs. Opponent Batters
THREE YEARS (84 – 86)

	Ave.	OBP	SLG	AB	H	2B	3B	HR	RBI	BB	SO
Totals	.297	.349	.421	508	151	28	4	9	80	40	105
Pitching vs. Left and Right-handed Batters											
Left	.319	.362	.404	141	45	7	1	1	23	10	31
Right	.289	.344	.428	367	106	21	3	8	57	30	74
Situational											
Bases Empty	.263	.315	.378	251	66	10	2	5	5	18	57
Leadoff	.278	.339	.417	108	30	5	2	2	2	10	26
Not Leadoff	.252	.296	.350	143	36	5	0	3	3	8	31
Runners On	.331	.382	.463	257	85	18	2	4	75	22	48
First Base Only	.366	.392	.559	93	34	9	0	3	8	4	16
Scoring Position	.311	.376	.409	164	51	9	2	1	67	18	32
Late Innings, Close	.288	.340	.375	264	76	13	2	2	34	20	71

RBI/Opportunities

Scoring Position	63 / 233	(27%)
Scoring Position, 2 Out	22 / 100	(22%)
On Third, Less than 2 Out	29 / 51	(57%)
RBI in close games / RBI Total	50 / 80	(63%)

Jose DeLeon
Chicago White Sox

1986: Power, Flyball   1985: Power, Flyball   1984: Power, Flyball

THREE YEARS (84 – 86)

	G	IP	H	BB	SO	SB	CS	W	L	S	ERA
Totals	83	450.1	351	240	381	76	29	14	40	4	4.12
At Home and on the Road											
Home	43	252.2	186	118	234	43	15	10	23	2	3.81
Road	40	197.2	165	122	147	33	14	4	17	2	4.51
During the Day and and at Night											
Day	28	145.1	123	86	114	30	9	5	9	0	3.90
Night	55	305.0	228	154	267	46	20	9	31	4	4.22
On Grass and on Turf											
Grass	25	133.1	103	76	114	17	8	6	10	1	4.12
Turf	58	317.0	248	164	267	59	21	8	30	3	4.12
By Month											
April	7	34.2	35	22	41	6	4	1	3	0	5.19
May	19	82.0	64	50	66	17	4	3	8	1	4.50
June	13	84.0	65	40	70	12	4	4	6	0	3.43
July	11	72.1	55	35	62	13	3	2	7	0	4.23
August	15	89.2	68	51	72	13	8	2	10	0	4.32
Sept/Oct	18	87.2	64	42	70	15	6	2	6	3	3.70

vs. Opponent Batters
THREE YEARS (84 – 86)

	Ave.	OBP	SLG	AB	H	2B	3B	HR	RBI	BB	SO
Totals	.217	.320	.330	1621	351	56	13	34	179	240	381
Pitching vs. Left and Right-handed Batters											
Left	.256	.370	.388	809	207	35	9	18	106	147	127
Right	.177	.267	.272	812	144	21	4	16	73	93	254
Situational											
Bases Empty	.208	.321	.303	931	194	33	5	15	15	150	227
Leadoff	.230	.340	.325	400	92	15	4	5	5	64	91
Not Leadoff	.192	.307	.286	531	102	18	1	10	10	86	136
Runners On	.228	.317	.367	690	157	23	8	19	164	90	154
First Base Only	.216	.272	.321	287	62	5	2	7	18	22	61
Scoring Position	.236	.346	.400	403	95	18	6	12	146	68	93
Late Innings, Close	.245	.342	.428	159	39	3	4	6	24	23	28

RBI/Opportunities

Scoring Position	120 / 560	(21%)
Scoring Position, 2 Out	44 / 237	(19%)
On Third, Less than 2 Out	54 / 113	(48%)
RBI in close games / RBI Total	137 / 179	(77%)

Jeff Dedmon
Atlanta Braves

1986: Finesse, Groundball 1985: Power, Groundball 1984: Power, Groundball

	THREE YEARS (84 – 86)										
	G	IP	H	BB	SO	SB	CS	W	L	S	ERA
Totals	171	266.2	260	123	150	32	7	16	12	7	3.58
At Home and on the Road											
Home	92	145.0	149	51	86	14	5	7	5	3	3.29
Road	79	121.2	111	72	64	18	2	9	7	4	3.92
During the Day and and at Night											
Day	56	87.0	74	52	43	10	3	7	3	2	3.72
Night	115	179.2	186	71	107	22	4	9	9	5	3.51
On Grass and on Turf											
Grass	136	215.0	205	102	123	26	5	13	9	6	3.35
Turf	35	51.2	55	21	27	6	2	3	3	1	4.53
By Month											
April	15	25.2	24	13	23	7	0	0	1	2	3.16
May	29	49.2	51	23	29	6	0	6	0	3	4.17
June	28	42.2	31	18	23	4	1	3	2	1	1.90
July	34	51.2	57	25	29	8	4	1	4	0	3.66
August	29	42.2	43	18	24	2	1	3	3	0	3.80
Sept/Oct	36	54.1	54	26	22	5	1	3	2	1	4.31

	vs. Opponent Batters THREE YEARS (84 – 86)										
	Ave.	OBP	SLG	AB	H	2B	3B	HR	RBI	BB	SO
Totals	.260	.344	.357	999	260	35	4	18	131	123	150
Pitching vs. Left and Right-handed Batters											
Left	.259	.363	.373	467	121	15	4	10	62	76	70
Right	.261	.327	.344	532	139	20	0	8	69	47	80
Situational											
Bases Empty	.275	.336	.381	501	138	21	1	10	10	44	78
Leadoff	.272	.344	.382	217	59	10	1	4	4	23	28
Not Leadoff	.278	.330	.380	284	79	11	0	6	6	21	50
Runners On	.245	.351	.333	498	122	14	3	8	121	79	72
First Base Only	.246	.293	.341	179	44	5	0	4	10	11	29
Scoring Position	.245	.379	.329	319	78	9	3	4	111	68	43
Late Innings, Close	.261	.355	.347	329	86	13	0	5	34	46	59

RBI/Opportunities		
Scoring Position	102 / 503	(20%)
Scoring Position, 2 Out	39 / 234	(17%)
On Third, Less than 2 Out	41 / 90	(46%)
RBI in close games / RBI Total	56 / 131	(43%)

Bob Dernier
Chicago Cubs

	THREE YEARS (84 – 86)										
	Ave.	OBP	SLG	AB	H	2B	3B	HR	RBI	BB	SO
Totals	.257	.322	.333	1329	341	60	9	8	71	125	145
Batting vs. Left and Right-handed Pitchers											
Left	.283	.355	.370	346	98	18	3	2	28	38	26
Right	.247	.311	.320	983	243	42	6	6	43	87	119
At Home and on the Road											
Home	.282	.341	.371	641	181	32	5	5	36	55	58
Road	.233	.305	.298	688	160	28	4	3	35	70	87
Facing Groundball Pitchers and Flyball Pitchers											
Groundball	.271	.339	.340	624	169	26	4	3	43	62	57
Flyball	.244	.307	.328	705	172	34	5	5	28	63	88
Facing Finesse Pitchers and Power Pitchers											
Finesse	.256	.322	.328	755	193	34	6	3	33	71	59
Power	.258	.323	.340	574	148	26	3	5	38	54	86
On Grass and on Turf											
Grass	.268	.331	.356	924	248	47	5	8	57	84	98
Turf	.230	.302	.281	405	93	13	4	0	14	41	47
During the Day and at Night											
Day	.259	.320	.337	881	228	42	6	5	46	77	83
Night	.252	.327	.326	448	113	18	3	3	25	48	62
By Month											
April	.223	.302	.279	179	40	7	0	1	9	20	19
May	.277	.349	.326	264	73	9	2	0	17	29	38
June	.282	.352	.374	174	49	8	1	2	12	19	23
July	.283	.338	.367	180	51	11	2	0	10	15	20
August	.223	.263	.314	283	63	10	2	4	11	15	21
Sept/Oct	.261	.341	.349	249	65	15	2	1	12	27	24
Situational											
Bases Empty	.265	.327	.347	948	251	46	7	6	6	85	103
Leadoff	.280	.347	.367	540	151	29	3	4	4	55	52
Not Leadoff	.245	.300	.321	408	100	17	4	2	2	30	51
Runners On	.236	.311	.299	381	90	14	2	2	65	40	42
First Base Only	.231	.257	.279	147	34	4	0	1	2	5	10
Scoring Position	.239	.341	.312	234	56	10	2	1	63	35	32
Late Innings, Close	.233	.313	.312	189	44	10	1	1	14	21	21

RBI/Opportunities		
Scoring Position	59 / 331	(18%)
Scoring Position, 2 Out	25 / 172	(15%)
On Third, Less than 2 Out	20 / 46	(43%)
RBI in close games / RBI Total	37 / 71	(52%)

John Denny
Cincinnati Reds

1986: Finesse, Groundball 1985: Finesse, Groundball 1984: Finesse, Groundball

	THREE YEARS (84 – 86)										
	G	IP	H	BB	SO	SB	CS	W	L	S	ERA
Totals	82	556.1	553	168	332	48	21	29	31	0	3.56
At Home and on the Road											
Home	44	300.1	309	84	165	25	12	13	20	0	3.69
Road	38	256.0	244	84	167	23	9	16	11	0	3.41
During the Day and and at Night											
Day	30	197.2	187	57	112	17	6	15	10	0	3.73
Night	52	358.2	366	111	220	31	15	14	21	0	3.46
On Grass and on Turf											
Grass	24	166.1	146	49	108	9	4	11	5	0	2.92
Turf	58	390.0	407	119	224	39	17	18	26	0	3.83
By Month											
April	13	81.0	86	21	46	6	3	4	5	0	3.22
May	18	115.0	131	36	60	6	3	5	8	0	4.30
June	11	78.2	83	25	57	9	5	5	2	0	2.86
July	12	79.2	73	32	48	9	3	2	6	0	4.18
August	16	120.0	101	23	69	11	4	9	5	0	2.85
Sept/Oct	12	82.0	79	31	52	7	3	4	5	0	3.95

	vs. Opponent Batters THREE YEARS (84 – 86)										
	Ave.	OBP	SLG	AB	H	2B	3B	HR	RBI	BB	SO
Totals	.261	.316	.380	2121	553	94	18	41	215	168	332
Pitching vs. Left and Right-handed Batters											
Left	.275	.336	.398	1110	305	55	11	20	115	99	146
Right	.245	.294	.360	1011	248	39	7	21	100	69	186
Situational											
Bases Empty	.259	.311	.379	1250	324	54	12	24	24	87	199
Leadoff	.276	.328	.383	533	147	23	5	8	8	39	86
Not Leadoff	.247	.299	.377	717	177	31	7	16	16	48	113
Runners On	.263	.323	.381	871	229	40	6	17	191	81	133
First Base Only	.304	.332	.421	382	116	23	2	6	20	16	43
Scoring Position	.231	.318	.350	489	113	17	4	11	171	65	90
Late Innings, Close	.266	.330	.424	184	49	10	2	5	24	17	31

RBI/Opportunities		
Scoring Position	149 / 669	(22%)
Scoring Position, 2 Out	53 / 301	(18%)
On Third, Less than 2 Out	63 / 119	(53%)
RBI in close games / RBI Total	166 / 215	(77%)

Jim Deshaies
Houston Astros

1986: Power, Flyball 1985: Finesse, Flyball 1984: Power, Flyball

	THREE YEARS (84 – 86)										
	G	IP	H	BB	SO	SB	CS	W	L	S	ERA
Totals	30	154.0	139	66	135	13	9	12	6	0	3.56
At Home and on the Road											
Home	17	90.1	80	33	75	10	5	6	4	0	3.59
Road	13	63.2	59	33	60	3	4	6	2	0	3.53
During the Day and and at Night											
Day	6	24.1	24	14	17	3	2	3	0	0	2.22
Night	24	129.2	115	52	118	10	7	9	6	0	3.82
On Grass and on Turf											
Grass	7	34.0	41	15	34	0	2	2	2	0	5.29
Turf	23	120.0	98	51	101	13	7	10	4	0	3.08
By Month											
April	2	8.2	8	2	6	2	2	0	0	0	4.15
May	3	13.1	12	5	17	0	2	1	1	0	5.40
June	6	38.0	32	15	27	5	0	4	1	0	3.08
July	4	22.1	18	12	28	0	2	1	1	0	3.63
August	8	41.0	44	25	30	5	1	3	2	0	4.61
Sept/Oct	7	30.2	25	7	27	1	2	3	1	0	1.76

	vs. Opponent Batters THREE YEARS (84 – 86)										
	Ave.	OBP	SLG	AB	H	2B	3B	HR	RBI	BB	SO
Totals	.243	.321	.389	573	139	29	2	17	57	66	135
Pitching vs. Left and Right-handed Batters											
Left	.267	.345	.475	101	27	5	2	4	10	12	22
Right	.237	.316	.371	472	112	24	0	13	47	54	113
Situational											
Bases Empty	.269	.343	.424	349	94	22	1	10	10	38	84
Leadoff	.272	.344	.435	147	40	10	1	4	4	16	35
Not Leadoff	.267	.342	.416	202	54	12	0	6	6	22	49
Runners On	.201	.288	.335	224	45	7	1	7	47	28	51
First Base Only	.240	.303	.490	100	24	2	1	7	17	9	23
Scoring Position	.169	.277	.210	124	21	5	0	0	30	19	28
Late Innings, Close	.222	.222	.222	27	6	0	0	0	2	0	3

RBI/Opportunities		
Scoring Position	29 / 172	(17%)
Scoring Position, 2 Out	11 / 76	(14%)
On Third, Less than 2 Out	13 / 29	(45%)
RBI in close games / RBI Total	45 / 57	(79%)

Frank DiPino
Chicago Cubs

1986: Power, Groundball   1985: Power, Flyball   1984: Power, Groundball

THREE YEARS (84 – 86)

	G	IP	H	BB	SO	SB	CS	W	L	S	ERA
Totals	172	231.2	217	109	184	18	9	10	23	23	3.92
At Home and on the Road										
Home	86	112.1	107	50	82	14	1	7	12	9	4.09
Road	86	119.1	110	59	102	4	8	3	11	14	3.77
During the Day and and at Night										
Day	54	69.1	73	35	53	4	3	2	8	3	5.19
Night	118	162.1	144	74	131	14	6	8	15	20	3.38
On Grass and on Turf										
Grass	57	79.2	80	40	61	1	3	2	7	6	4.29
Turf	115	152.0	137	69	123	17	6	8	16	17	3.73
By Month										
April	26	33.1	24	13	24	6	0	2	4	5	3.24
May	33	38.1	32	26	30	4	2	1	6	8	2.82
June	23	31.2	29	19	21	1	0	0	2	3	5.12
July	29	43.0	41	11	35	3	3	3	5	0	3.98
August	30	42.0	47	22	37	2	3	1	3	5	3.86
Sept/Oct	31	43.1	44	18	37	2	1	3	3	2	4.57

vs. Opponent Batters
THREE YEARS (84 – 86)

	Ave.	OBP	SLG	AB	H	2B	3B	HR	RBI	BB	SO
Totals	.251	.336	.372	864	217	37	2	21	127	109	184
Pitching vs. Left and Right-handed Batters										
Left	.230	.306	.326	230	53	7	0	5	36	25	48
Right	.259	.346	.388	634	164	30	2	16	91	84	136
Situational										
Bases Empty	.240	.320	.363	441	106	16	1	12	12	50	97
Leadoff	.259	.343	.376	189	49	11	1	3	3	22	37
Not Leadoff	.226	.304	.353	252	57	5	0	9	9	28	60
Runners On	.262	.351	.382	423	111	21	1	9	115	59	87
First Base Only	.291	.345	.468	158	46	11	1	5	17	12	24
Scoring Position	.245	.354	.328	265	65	10	0	4	98	47	63
Late Innings, Close	.266	.351	.381	459	122	18	1	11	78	58	104

RBI/Opportunities

Scoring Position	88 / 405	(22%)
Scoring Position, 2 Out	43 / 175	(25%)
On Third, Less than 2 Out	30 / 85	(35%)
RBI in close games / RBI Total	82 / 127	(65%)

Mike Diaz
Pittsburgh Pirates

THREE YEARS (84 – 86)

	Ave.	OBP	SLG	AB	H	2B	3B	HR	RBI	BB	SO
Totals	.268	.330	.483	209	56	9	0	12	36	19	43
Batting vs. Left and Right-handed Pitchers										
Left	.267	.326	.511	131	35	5	0	9	19	11	32
Right	.269	.337	.436	78	21	4	0	3	17	8	11
At Home and on the Road										
Home	.253	.301	.474	95	24	3	0	6	18	6	21
Road	.281	.354	.491	114	32	6	0	6	18	13	22
Facing Groundball Pitchers and Flyball Pitchers										
Groundball	.277	.317	.457	94	26	5	0	4	16	7	20
Flyball	.261	.341	.504	115	30	4	0	8	20	12	23
Facing Finesse Pitchers and Power Pitchers										
Finesse	.282	.342	.515	103	29	3	0	7	19	11	10
Power	.255	.319	.453	106	27	6	0	5	17	8	33
On Grass and on Turf										
Grass	.224	.313	.466	58	13	2	0	4	11	7	15
Turf	.285	.337	.490	151	43	7	0	8	25	12	28
During the Day and at Night										
Day	.209	.267	.418	67	14	2	0	4	13	6	15
Night	.296	.361	.514	142	42	7	0	8	23	13	28
By Month										
April	.250	.333	.250	16	4	0	0	0	2	1	5
May	.154	.267	.231	13	2	1	0	0	1	2	4
June	.296	.367	.481	27	8	2	0	1	4	2	7
July	.269	.296	.692	26	7	2	0	3	5	1	8
August	.368	.444	.868	38	14	1	0	6	12	6	6
Sept/Oct	.236	.286	.337	89	21	3	0	2	12	7	13
Situational										
Bases Empty	.262	.303	.544	103	27	5	0	8	8	6	18
Leadoff	.205	.244	.385	39	8	1	0	2	2	2	6
Not Leadoff	.297	.338	.641	64	19	4	0	6	6	4	12
Runners On	.274	.355	.425	106	29	4	0	4	28	13	25
First Base Only	.326	.380	.522	46	15	3	0	2	6	3	11
Scoring Position	.233	.338	.350	60	14	1	0	2	22	10	14
Late Innings, Close	.370	.452	.500	54	20	4	0	1	11	6	9

RBI/Opportunities

Scoring Position	19 / 92	(21%)
Scoring Position, 2 Out	5 / 43	(12%)
On Third, Less than 2 Out	9 / 16	(56%)
RBI in close games / RBI Total	28 / 36	(78%)

Richard Dotson
Chicago White Sox

1986: Finesse, Groundball   1985: Power, Groundball   1984: Finesse, Groundball

THREE YEARS (84 – 86)

	G	IP	H	BB	SO	SB	CS	W	L	S	ERA
Totals	75	495.0	495	189	263	46	17	27	36	0	4.44
At Home and on the Road										
Home	41	278.2	259	108	153	25	11	16	19	0	4.10
Road	34	216.1	236	81	110	21	6	11	17	0	4.87
During the Day and and at Night										
Day	27	185.2	185	61	97	19	6	12	9	0	3.64
Night	48	309.1	310	128	166	27	11	15	27	0	4.92
On Grass and on Turf										
Grass	64	423.1	413	165	228	39	14	24	30	0	4.27
Turf	11	71.2	82	24	35	7	3	3	6	0	5.40
By Month										
April	12	82.2	74	38	37	3	5	4	4	0	4.25
May	15	98.1	86	41	62	11	6	7	6	0	3.57
June	14	96.2	93	30	49	10	1	8	5	0	4.19
July	10	48.0	69	19	13	2	1	2	8	0	8.81
August	13	90.0	98	31	47	11	2	4	5	0	3.70
Sept/Oct	11	79.1	75	30	55	9	2	2	8	0	4.20

vs. Opponent Batters
THREE YEARS (84 – 86)

	Ave.	OBP	SLG	AB	H	2B	3B	HR	RBI	BB	SO
Totals	.262	.330	.403	1892	495	71	19	53	232	189	263
Pitching vs. Left and Right-handed Batters										
Left	.255	.332	.409	990	252	30	9	35	122	112	147
Right	.269	.328	.397	902	243	41	10	18	110	77	116
Situational										
Bases Empty	.256	.322	.405	1132	290	38	14	34	34	105	158
Leadoff	.261	.309	.402	490	128	18	6	13	13	32	55
Not Leadoff	.252	.331	.407	642	162	20	8	21	21	73	103
Runners On	.270	.342	.401	760	205	33	5	19	198	84	105
First Base Only	.292	.348	.435	336	98	15	3	9	29	27	41
Scoring Position	.252	.338	.375	424	107	18	2	10	169	57	64
Late Innings, Close	.280	.332	.453	214	60	7	3	8	25	18	19

RBI/Opportunities

Scoring Position	147 / 587	(25%)
Scoring Position, 2 Out	45 / 251	(18%)
On Third, Less than 2 Out	66 / 117	(56%)
RBI in close games / RBI Total	176 / 232	(76%)

Doug Drabek
New York Yankees

1986: Finesse, Flyball   1985: Did not play   1984: Did not play

THREE YEARS (84 – 86)

	G	IP	H	BB	SO	SB	CS	W	L	S	ERA
Totals	27	131.2	126	50	76	3	4	7	8	0	4.10
At Home and on the Road										
Home	12	62.1	63	18	39	1	2	2	3	0	3.75
Road	15	69.1	63	32	37	2	2	5	5	0	4.41
During the Day and at Night										
Day	8	31.1	38	13	18	1	2	0	3	0	5.46
Night	19	100.1	88	37	58	2	2	7	5	0	3.68
On Grass and on Turf										
Grass	22	97.0	94	38	57	2	3	4	7	0	4.45
Turf	5	34.2	32	12	19	1	1	3	1	0	3.12
By Month										
April	0	0.0	0	0	0	0	0	0	0	0	0.00
May	1	4.1	1	3	4	0	1	0	0	0	2.08
June	7	18.1	18	10	9	0	0	0	1	0	7.85
July	7	34.0	35	10	14	0	0	2	3	0	4.76
August	6	39.1	42	15	30	2	1	1	3	0	3.66
Sept/Oct	6	35.2	30	12	19	1	2	4	1	0	2.27

vs. Opponent Batters
THREE YEARS (84 – 86)

	Ave.	OBP	SLG	AB	H	2B	3B	HR	RBI	BB	SO
Totals	.251	.322	.397	501	126	26	4	13	56	50	76
Pitching vs. Left and Right-handed Batters										
Left	.278	.356	.456	259	72	13	3	9	34	32	31
Right	.223	.284	.335	242	54	13	1	4	22	18	45
Situational										
Bases Empty	.251	.320	.419	303	76	14	2	11	11	29	50
Leadoff	.250	.329	.398	128	32	7	0	4	4	13	20
Not Leadoff	.251	.314	.434	175	44	7	2	7	7	16	30
Runners On	.253	.324	.364	198	50	12	2	2	45	21	26
First Base Only	.213	.282	.362	94	20	6	1	2	8	8	11
Scoring Position	.288	.361	.365	104	30	6	1	0	37	13	15
Late Innings, Close	.200	.375	.440	25	5	0	2	3	2	7	3

RBI/Opportunities

Scoring Position	36 / 146	(25%)
Scoring Position, 2 Out	13 / 63	(21%)
On Third, Less than 2 Out	13 / 33	(39%)
RBI in close games / RBI Total	30 / 56	(54%)

Mariano Duncan
Los Angeles Dodgers

THREE YEARS (84 – 86)

	Ave.	OBP	SLG	AB	H	2B	3B	HR	RBI	BB	SO
Totals	.237	.289	.325	969	230	31	6	14	69	68	191
Batting vs. Left and Right-handed Pitchers											
Left	.273	.314	.389	355	97	13	2	8	31	20	63
Right	.217	.275	.288	614	133	18	4	6	38	48	128
At Home and on the Road											
Home	.231	.281	.290	480	111	15	2	3	24	31	97
Road	.243	.297	.360	489	119	16	4	11	45	37	94
Facing Groundball Pitchers and Flyball Pitchers											
Groundball	.238	.297	.297	424	101	11	4	2	27	33	72
Flyball	.237	.283	.347	545	129	20	2	12	42	35	119
Facing Finesse Pitchers and Power Pitchers											
Finesse	.235	.284	.316	548	129	16	2	8	39	36	92
Power	.240	.297	.337	421	101	15	4	6	30	32	99
On Grass and on Turf											
Grass	.232	.284	.313	751	174	23	4	10	52	51	148
Turf	.257	.309	.367	218	56	8	2	4	17	17	43
During the Day and at Night											
Day	.272	.316	.361	305	83	12	0	5	16	19	63
Night	.221	.277	.309	664	147	19	6	9	53	49	128
By Month											
April	.216	.281	.314	153	33	6	0	3	6	14	24
May	.227	.297	.293	150	34	4	0	2	8	14	42
June	.250	.280	.331	172	43	5	0	3	14	8	24
July	.240	.289	.344	154	37	6	2	2	12	9	31
August	.287	.313	.400	160	46	5	2	3	10	6	32
Sept/Oct	.206	.279	.272	180	37	5	2	1	19	17	38
Situational											
Bases Empty	.233	.290	.319	627	146	21	3	9	9	47	127
Leadoff	.203	.268	.253	340	69	6	1	3	3	28	69
Not Leadoff	.268	.316	.397	287	77	15	2	6	6	19	58
Runners On	.246	.289	.336	342	84	10	3	5	60	21	64
First Base Only	.284	.314	.366	134	38	6	1	1	4	5	26
Scoring Position	.221	.274	.317	208	46	4	2	4	56	16	38
Late Innings, Close	.254	.307	.370	138	35	2	1	4	13	10	27

RBI/Opportunities

Scoring Position	47 / 284	(17%)
Scoring Position, 2 Out	21 / 140	(15%)
On Third, Less than 2 Out	18 / 50	(36%)
RBI in close games / RBI Total	44 / 69	(64%)

Jim Dwyer
Baltimore Orioles

THREE YEARS (84 – 86)

	Ave.	OBP	SLG	AB	H	2B	3B	HR	RBI	BB	SO
Totals	.249	.344	.413	554	138	30	5	17	88	83	86
Batting vs. Left and Right-handed Pitchers											
Left	.167	.167	.250	12	2	1	0	0	0	0	3
Right	.251	.347	.417	542	136	29	5	17	88	83	83
At Home and on the Road											
Home	.221	.333	.355	276	61	12	2	7	47	47	42
Road	.277	.355	.471	278	77	18	3	10	41	36	44
Facing Groundball Pitchers and Flyball Pitchers											
Groundball	.247	.324	.390	251	62	12	3	6	42	31	38
Flyball	.251	.362	.432	303	76	18	2	11	46	52	48
Facing Finesse Pitchers and Power Pitchers											
Finesse	.230	.313	.390	318	73	15	3	10	43	40	43
Power	.275	.384	.445	236	65	15	2	7	45	43	43
On Grass and on Turf											
Grass	.233	.336	.372	476	111	22	4	12	72	75	76
Turf	.346	.398	.667	78	27	8	1	5	16	8	10
During the Day and at Night											
Day	.239	.333	.400	180	43	7	2	6	30	26	28
Night	.254	.349	.420	374	95	23	3	11	58	57	58
By Month											
April	.218	.255	.356	87	19	4	1	2	10	5	12
May	.299	.392	.478	134	40	4	1	6	22	21	17
June	.252	.335	.370	135	34	4	0	4	21	18	18
July	.264	.341	.458	72	19	8	0	2	12	9	10
August	.196	.333	.490	51	10	5	2	2	17	10	14
Sept/Oct	.213	.375	.347	75	16	5	1	1	6	20	19
Situational											
Bases Empty	.236	.346	.403	305	72	19	1	10	10	50	47
Leadoff	.284	.364	.470	134	38	11	1	4	4	17	16
Not Leadoff	.199	.332	.351	171	34	8	0	6	6	33	31
Runners On	.265	.342	.426	249	66	11	4	7	78	33	39
First Base Only	.225	.295	.288	111	25	4	0	1	3	11	13
Scoring Position	.297	.376	.536	138	41	7	4	6	75	22	26
Late Innings, Close	.270	.382	.540	100	27	8	2	5	22	20	22

RBI/Opportunities

Scoring Position	59 / 219	(27%)
Scoring Position, 2 Out	26 / 95	(27%)
On Third, Less than 2 Out	23 / 39	(59%)
RBI in close games / RBI Total	59 / 88	(67%)

Dennis Eckersley
Chicago Cubs

1986: Finesse, Flyball   1985: Finesse, Flyball   1984: Finesse, Flyball

THREE YEARS (84 – 86)

	G	IP	H	BB	SO	SB	CS	W	L	S	ERA
Totals	91	595.1	594	111	368	63	23	31	30	0	3.78
At Home and on the Road											
Home	40	264.1	275	51	190	28	14	18	14	0	4.19
Road	51	331.0	319	60	178	35	9	13	16	0	3.45
During the Day and and at Night											
Day	53	348.1	334	65	240	34	16	22	14	0	3.64
Night	38	247.0	260	46	128	29	7	9	16	0	3.97
On Grass and on Turf											
Grass	60	394.2	402	71	270	37	19	23	19	0	3.92
Turf	31	200.2	192	40	98	26	4	8	11	0	3.50
By Month											
April	14	105.1	101	16	73	7	4	5	5	0	4.10
May	17	113.0	125	18	64	12	7	7	6	0	4.78
June	16	96.2	90	23	50	10	1	2	7	0	4.75
July	15	101.1	82	17	75	8	5	7	3	0	2.31
August	12	80.0	91	19	40	11	3	5	3	0	2.81
Sept/Oct	17	99.0	105	18	66	15	3	5	6	0	3.64

vs. Opponent Batters

THREE YEARS (84 – 86)

	Ave.	OBP	SLG	AB	H	2B	3B	HR	RBI	BB	SO
Totals	.260	.295	.404	2285	594	131	14	57	247	111	368
Pitching vs. Left and Right-handed Batters											
Left	.277	.318	.436	1204	334	76	11	31	145	73	131
Right	.241	.269	.369	1081	260	55	3	26	102	38	237
Situational											
Bases Empty	.266	.293	.403	1426	379	82	7	33	33	50	243
Leadoff	.278	.299	.421	594	165	39	2	14	14	16	86
Not Leadoff	.257	.289	.389	832	214	43	5	19	19	34	157
Runners On	.250	.298	.407	859	215	49	7	24	214	61	125
First Base Only	.257	.288	.431	343	88	18	3	12	30	13	42
Scoring Position	.246	.304	.391	516	127	31	4	12	184	48	83
Late Innings, Close	.230	.269	.379	174	40	10	2	4	19	9	22

RBI/Opportunities

Scoring Position	164 / 681	(24%)
Scoring Position, 2 Out	59 / 307	(19%)
On Third, Less than 2 Out	72 / 128	(56%)
RBI in close games / RBI Total	193 / 247	(78%)

Steve Farr
Kansas City Royals

1986: Power, Flyball   1985: Power, Flyball   1984: Power, Groundball

THREE YEARS (84 – 86)

	G	IP	H	BB	SO	SB	CS	W	L	S	ERA
Totals	103	263.0	230	105	202	13	16	13	16	10	3.76
At Home and on the Road											
Home	56	151.0	134	61	121	10	10	10	6	5	3.52
Road	47	112.0	96	44	81	3	6	3	10	5	4.10
During the Day and and at Night											
Day	24	54.0	50	21	46	3	4	2	4	2	5.17
Night	79	209.0	180	84	156	10	12	11	12	8	3.40
On Grass and on Turf											
Grass	52	154.0	135	61	105	6	7	4	13	4	4.50
Turf	51	109.0	95	44	97	7	9	9	3	6	2.72
By Month											
April	5	12.1	7	5	7	2	1	1	0	1	2.19
May	16	49.1	38	14	37	0	3	2	4	2	3.10
June	14	38.1	26	17	27	3	3	2	1	2	3.05
July	20	51.1	47	20	42	3	3	3	4	1	2.98
August	25	63.0	68	24	45	4	4	2	5	2	5.57
Sept/Oct	23	48.2	44	25	44	1	2	3	2	2	3.88

vs. Opponent Batters

THREE YEARS (84 – 86)

	Ave.	OBP	SLG	AB	H	2B	3B	HR	RBI	BB	SO
Totals	.238	.318	.367	966	230	35	6	26	116	105	202
Pitching vs. Left and Right-handed Batters											
Left	.228	.320	.354	491	112	16	5	12	58	66	83
Right	.248	.315	.381	475	118	19	1	14	58	39	119
Situational											
Bases Empty	.240	.318	.371	550	132	20	2	16	16	55	116
Leadoff	.247	.329	.423	227	56	8	1	10	10	26	37
Not Leadoff	.235	.310	.334	323	76	12	1	6	6	29	79
Runners On	.236	.317	.363	416	98	15	4	10	100	50	86
First Base Only	.231	.275	.405	195	45	12	2	6	20	10	36
Scoring Position	.240	.349	.326	221	53	3	2	4	80	40	50
Late Innings, Close	.238	.319	.292	185	44	2	1	2	15	20	41

RBI/Opportunities

Scoring Position	71 / 343	(21%)
Scoring Position, 2 Out	33 / 172	(19%)
On Third, Less than 2 Out	24 / 63	(38%)
RBI in close games / RBI Total	59 / 116	(51%)

Mike Felder
Milwaukee Brewers

	Ave.	OBP	SLG	AB	H	2B	3B	HR	RBI	BB	SO
THREE YEARS (84 – 86)											
Totals	.227	.282	.294	211	48	3	4	1	13	18	22
Batting vs. Left and Right-handed Pitchers											
Left	.303	.329	.364	66	20	0	2	0	3	3	4
Right	.193	.262	.262	145	28	3	2	1	10	15	18
At Home and on the Road											
Home	.258	.328	.350	120	31	2	3	1	8	13	9
Road	.187	.220	.220	91	17	1	1	0	5	5	13
Facing Groundball Pitchers and Flyball Pitchers											
Groundball	.233	.280	.267	90	21	1	1	0	5	7	7
Flyball	.223	.284	.314	121	27	2	3	1	8	11	15
Facing Finesse Pitchers and Power Pitchers											
Finesse	.275	.328	.367	109	30	1	3	1	6	10	9
Power	.176	.232	.216	102	18	2	1	0	7	8	13
On Grass and on Turf											
Grass	.239	.290	.314	188	45	3	4	1	12	15	21
Turf	.130	.222	.130	23	3	0	0	0	1	3	1
During the Day and at Night											
Day	.235	.300	.309	81	19	1	1	1	4	8	12
Night	.223	.271	.285	130	29	2	3	0	9	10	10
By Month											
April	.250	.328	.354	48	12	1	2	0	6	7	6
May	.000	.000	.000	4	0	0	0	0	0	0	0
June	.281	.333	.406	64	18	1	2	1	6	6	6
July	.179	.179	.179	39	7	0	0	0	1	0	4
August	.000	.000	.000	0	0	0	0	0	0	0	0
Sept/Oct	.196	.262	.214	56	11	1	0	0	0	5	6
Situational											
Bases Empty	.234	.295	.299	137	32	3	3	0	0	12	11
Leadoff	.215	.295	.241	79	17	0	1	0	0	9	7
Not Leadoff	.259	.295	.379	58	15	3	2	0	0	3	4
Runners On	.216	.259	.284	74	16	0	1	1	13	6	11
First Base Only	.206	.250	.294	34	7	0	0	1	2	2	6
Scoring Position	.225	.265	.275	40	9	0	1	0	11	4	5
Late Innings, Close	.233	.244	.326	43	10	0	2	0	4	1	2
RBI/Opportunities											
Scoring Position				10 / 59	(17%)						
Scoring Position, 2 Out				2 / 28	(7%)						
On Third, Less than 2 Out				6 / 11	(55%)						
RBI in close games / RBI Total				10 / 13	(77%)						

Chuck Finley
California Angels

1986: Power, Groundball   1985: Did not play   1984: Did not play

	G	IP	H	BB	SO	SB	CS	W	L	S	ERA
THREE YEARS (84 – 86)											
Totals	25	46.1	40	23	37	4	3	3	1	0	3.30
At Home and on the Road											
Home	14	26.0	22	16	18	2	2	1	0	0	4.50
Road	11	20.1	18	7	19	2	1	2	1	0	1.77
During the Day and and at Night											
Day	4	5.1	4	3	8	0	0	0	0	0	0.00
Night	21	41.0	36	20	29	4	3	3	1	0	3.73
On Grass and on Turf											
Grass	23	39.2	38	22	32	4	3	2	1	0	3.86
Turf	2	6.2	2	1	5	0	0	1	0	0	0.00
By Month											
April	0	0.0	0	0	0	0	0	0	0	0	0.00
May	1	1.0	2	3	1	0	0	0	0	0	18.00
June	5	9.1	12	3	4	0	1	1	0	0	3.86
July	7	10.0	8	6	12	2	2	0	0	0	0.90
August	5	14.0	10	7	10	2	0	0	0	0	3.86
Sept/Oct	7	12.0	8	4	10	0	0	2	1	0	3.00

	Ave.	OBP	SLG	AB	H	2B	3B	HR	RBI	BB	SO
vs. Opponent Batters											
THREE YEARS (84 – 86)											
Totals	.235	.330	.306	170	40	6	0	2	23	23	37
Pitching vs. Left and Right-handed Batters											
Left	.269	.360	.308	78	21	3	0	0	11	10	10
Right	.207	.305	.304	92	19	3	0	2	12	13	27
Situational											
Bases Empty	.207	.330	.305	82	17	2	0	2	2	14	17
Leadoff	.229	.372	.257	35	8	1	0	0	0	7	7
Not Leadoff	.191	.296	.340	47	9	1	0	2	2	7	10
Runners On	.261	.330	.307	88	23	4	0	0	21	9	20
First Base Only	.231	.286	.282	39	9	2	0	0	2	3	11
Scoring Position	.286	.364	.327	49	14	2	0	0	19	6	9
Late Innings, Close	.214	.353	.286	14	3	1	0	0	2	3	4
RBI/Opportunities											
Scoring Position				17 / 68	(25%)						
Scoring Position, 2 Out				11 / 39	(28%)						
On Third, Less than 2 Out				3 / 7	(43%)						
RBI in close games / RBI Total				3 / 23	(13%)						

Mike Fischlin
New York Yankees

	Ave.	OBP	SLG	AB	H	2B	3B	HR	RBI	BB	SO
THREE YEARS (84 – 86)											
Totals	.214	.274	.278	295	63	10	3	1	19	25	56
Batting vs. Left and Right-handed Pitchers											
Left	.271	.345	.430	107	29	10	2	1	8	12	18
Right	.181	.233	.191	188	34	0	1	0	11	13	38
At Home and on the Road											
Home	.263	.329	.350	137	36	6	3	0	13	14	21
Road	.171	.225	.215	158	27	4	0	1	6	11	35
Facing Groundball Pitchers and Flyball Pitchers											
Groundball	.195	.267	.244	123	24	4	1	0	9	12	29
Flyball	.227	.280	.302	172	39	6	2	1	10	13	27
Facing Finesse Pitchers and Power Pitchers											
Finesse	.174	.204	.226	155	27	6	1	0	10	6	23
Power	.257	.346	.336	140	36	4	2	1	9	19	33
On Grass and on Turf											
Grass	.220	.285	.292	250	55	9	3	1	18	23	43
Turf	.178	.213	.200	45	8	1	0	0	1	2	13
During the Day and at Night											
Day	.210	.270	.248	105	22	2	1	0	8	9	16
Night	.216	.277	.295	190	41	8	2	1	11	16	40
By Month											
April	.105	.150	.158	19	2	1	0	0	1	1	2
May	.238	.360	.286	21	5	1	0	0	0	4	4
June	.192	.289	.205	73	14	1	0	0	3	10	15
July	.286	.278	.600	35	10	2	3	1	6	0	5
August	.200	.263	.229	70	14	2	0	0	3	6	18
Sept/Oct	.234	.272	.273	77	18	3	0	0	6	4	12
Situational											
Bases Empty	.246	.302	.326	175	43	7	2	1	1	14	33
Leadoff	.200	.284	.217	60	12	1	0	0	0	7	10
Not Leadoff	.270	.311	.383	115	31	6	2	1	1	7	23
Runners On	.167	.235	.208	120	20	3	1	0	18	11	23
First Base Only	.143	.192	.163	49	7	1	0	0	1	3	9
Scoring Position	.183	.263	.239	71	13	2	1	0	17	8	14
Late Innings, Close	.286	.302	.333	42	12	2	0	0	0	1	5
RBI/Opportunities											
Scoring Position				15 / 121	(12%)						
Scoring Position, 2 Out				3 / 52	(6%)						
On Third, Less than 2 Out				8 / 22	(36%)						
RBI in close games / RBI Total				9 / 19	(47%)						

Brian Fisher
New York Yankees

1986: Power, Flyball   1985: Power, Flyball   1984: Did not play

	G	IP	H	BB	SO	SB	CS	W	L	S	ERA
THREE YEARS (84 – 86)											
Totals	117	195.0	182	66	152	24	5	13	9	20	3.65
At Home and on the Road											
Home	62	98.1	103	31	76	11	4	5	6	10	4.12
Road	55	96.2	79	35	76	13	1	8	3	10	3.17
During the Day and and at Night											
Day	43	71.2	74	27	55	3	2	1	4	8	4.14
Night	74	123.1	108	39	97	21	3	12	5	12	3.36
On Grass and on Turf											
Grass	98	164.2	150	62	127	19	5	11	9	16	3.61
Turf	19	30.1	32	4	25	5	0	2	0	4	3.86
By Month											
April	11	16.2	16	8	11	3	0	0	1	3	3.78
May	18	31.2	32	11	21	2	0	3	1	1	4.26
June	23	40.1	35	19	28	5	2	3	5	2	3.79
July	19	33.0	29	9	24	7	0	0	0	2	2.18
August	26	42.2	45	10	41	6	2	5	1	7	4.22
Sept/Oct	20	30.2	25	9	27	1	1	2	1	5	3.52

	Ave.	OBP	SLG	AB	H	2B	3B	HR	RBI	BB	SO
vs. Opponent Batters											
THREE YEARS (84 – 86)											
Totals	.247	.309	.360	736	182	21	4	18	109	66	152
Pitching vs. Left and Right-handed Batters											
Left	.269	.350	.386	324	87	10	2	8	44	41	66
Right	.231	.274	.340	412	95	11	2	10	65	25	86
Situational											
Bases Empty	.243	.299	.343	382	93	9	1	9	9	29	95
Leadoff	.248	.302	.350	157	39	1	0	5	5	12	35
Not Leadoff	.240	.296	.338	225	54	8	1	4	4	17	60
Runners On	.251	.319	.379	354	89	12	3	9	100	37	57
First Base Only	.239	.281	.312	138	33	7	0	1	6	8	22
Scoring Position	.259	.341	.421	216	56	5	3	8	94	29	35
Late Innings, Close	.243	.323	.374	313	76	11	3	8	54	38	69
RBI/Opportunities											
Scoring Position				75 / 310	(24%)						
Scoring Position, 2 Out				29 / 146	(20%)						
On Third, Less than 2 Out				28 / 51	(55%)						
RBI in close games / RBI Total				77 / 109	(71%)						

Mike Fitzgerald
Montreal Expos

THREE YEARS (84 – 86)

	Ave.	OBP	SLG	AB	H	2B	3B	HR	RBI	BB	SO
Totals	.240	.310	.332	864	207	35	3	13	104	89	160
Batting vs. Left and Right-handed Pitchers											
Left	.237	.319	.299	304	72	10	0	3	25	37	51
Right	.241	.305	.350	560	135	25	3	10	79	52	109
At Home and on the Road											
Home	.211	.275	.285	446	94	9	3	6	39	40	93
Road	.270	.347	.383	418	113	26	0	7	65	49	67
Facing Groundball Pitchers and Flyball Pitchers											
Groundball	.240	.318	.304	425	102	13	1	4	50	49	69
Flyball	.239	.302	.360	439	105	22	2	9	54	40	91
Facing Finesse Pitchers and Power Pitchers											
Finesse	.264	.319	.335	492	130	19	2	4	65	42	74
Power	.207	.299	.328	372	77	16	1	9	39	47	86
On Grass and on Turf											
Grass	.257	.310	.366	382	98	19	1	7	51	30	66
Turf	.226	.310	.305	482	109	16	2	6	53	59	94
During the Day and at Night											
Day	.256	.322	.357	277	71	15	2	3	33	27	47
Night	.232	.304	.320	587	136	20	1	10	71	62	113
By Month											
April	.253	.356	.373	75	19	3	0	2	10	12	12
May	.220	.305	.312	186	41	3	1	4	25	23	28
June	.245	.327	.347	196	48	6	1	4	22	25	41
July	.249	.306	.353	201	50	12	0	3	28	15	36
August	.226	.271	.286	133	30	6	1	0	14	9	30
Sept/Oct	.260	.304	.329	73	19	5	0	0	5	5	13
Situational											
Bases Empty	.225	.269	.322	506	114	15	2	10	10	28	109
Leadoff	.258	.303	.343	198	51	6	1	3	3	13	38
Not Leadoff	.205	.246	.308	308	63	9	1	7	7	15	71
Runners On	.260	.361	.346	358	93	20	1	3	94	61	51
First Base Only	.232	.272	.311	164	38	8	1	1	7	9	14
Scoring Position	.284	.421	.376	194	55	12	0	2	87	52	37
Late Innings, Close	.206	.279	.297	165	34	6	0	3	17	16	39

RBI/Opportunities

Scoring Position	81 / 310	(26%)
Scoring Position, 2 Out	29 / 130	(22%)
On Third, Less than 2 Out	39 / 71	(55%)
RBI in close games / RBI Total	68 / 104	(65%)

Mike Flanagan
Baltimore Orioles

1986: Finesse, Groundball 1985: Finesse, Groundball 1984: Finesse, Groundball

THREE YEARS (84 – 86)

	G	IP	H	BB	SO	SB	CS	W	L	S	ERA
Totals	78	484.2	493	175	253	24	13	24	29	0	4.07
At Home and on the Road											
Home	36	213.1	211	82	106	9	5	15	8	0	3.71
Road	42	271.1	282	93	147	15	8	9	21	0	4.35
During the Day and at Night											
Day	24	150.1	157	63	86	14	2	9	11	0	4.55
Night	54	334.1	336	112	167	10	11	15	18	0	3.85
On Grass and on Turf											
Grass	65	404.1	414	144	213	21	10	22	22	0	3.94
Turf	13	80.1	79	31	40	3	3	2	7	0	4.71
By Month											
April	10	57.1	61	26	30	4	2	3	4	0	4.24
May	12	63.1	71	30	31	7	1	1	4	0	4.55
June	8	59.1	47	20	31	1	1	5	2	0	2.73
July	15	105.2	88	32	56	1	5	6	7	0	3.32
August	18	105.2	121	30	53	5	2	5	6	0	4.68
Sept/Oct	15	93.1	105	37	52	6	2	4	6	0	4.63

vs. Opponent Batters
THREE YEARS (84 – 86)

	Ave.	OBP	SLG	AB	H	2B	3B	HR	RBI	BB	SO
Totals	.266	.328	.408	1855	493	86	9	53	218	175	253
Pitching vs. Left and Right-handed Batters											
Left	.237	.291	.327	342	81	15	2	4	40	25	65
Right	.272	.336	.426	1513	412	71	7	49	178	150	188
Situational											
Bases Empty	.256	.333	.369	1061	272	49	4	21	21	119	145
Leadoff	.253	.304	.385	478	121	20	2	13	13	35	54
Not Leadoff	.259	.355	.357	583	151	29	2	8	8	84	91
Runners On	.278	.321	.458	794	221	37	5	32	197	56	108
First Base Only	.299	.327	.522	402	120	15	3	23	53	17	46
Scoring Position	.258	.316	.393	392	101	22	2	9	144	39	62
Late Innings, Close	.242	.324	.349	149	36	6	2	2	14	19	16

RBI/Opportunities

Scoring Position	129 / 525	(25%)
Scoring Position, 2 Out	38 / 229	(17%)
On Third, Less than 2 Out	56 / 107	(52%)
RBI in close games / RBI Total	173 / 218	(79%)

Tim Flannery
San Diego Padres

THREE YEARS (84 – 86)

	Ave.	OBP	SLG	AB	H	2B	3B	HR	RBI	BB	SO
Totals	.280	.377	.350	880	246	28	8	6	78	124	117
Batting vs. Left and Right-handed Pitchers											
Left	.151	.217	.236	106	16	4	1	1	4	8	21
Right	.297	.397	.366	774	230	24	7	5	74	116	96
At Home and on the Road											
Home	.285	.393	.351	407	116	9	3	4	37	63	56
Road	.275	.363	.349	473	130	19	5	2	41	61	61
Facing Groundball Pitchers and Flyball Pitchers											
Groundball	.271	.377	.320	435	118	11	2	2	36	62	54
Flyball	.288	.384	.380	445	128	17	6	4	42	62	63
Facing Finesse Pitchers and Power Pitchers											
Finesse	.303	.382	.374	492	149	17	6	2	46	58	45
Power	.250	.371	.320	388	97	11	2	4	32	66	72
On Grass and on Turf											
Grass	.289	.385	.358	634	183	16	5	6	58	86	73
Turf	.256	.357	.329	246	63	12	3	0	20	38	44
During the Day and at Night											
Day	.274	.367	.377	310	85	13	5	3	27	40	38
Night	.282	.383	.335	570	161	15	3	3	51	84	79
By Month											
April	.276	.349	.357	98	27	6	1	0	5	10	9
May	.279	.377	.414	140	39	7	3	2	17	20	17
June	.283	.398	.420	138	39	2	4	3	20	21	12
July	.292	.398	.323	161	47	5	0	0	10	25	21
August	.306	.396	.350	180	55	5	0	1	14	23	31
Sept/Oct	.239	.344	.258	163	39	3	0	0	12	25	27
Situational											
Bases Empty	.264	.378	.325	579	153	17	3	4	4	93	76
Leadoff	.234	.360	.306	304	71	10	3	2	2	51	39
Not Leadoff	.298	.399	.345	275	82	7	0	2	2	42	37
Runners On	.309	.375	.399	301	93	11	5	2	74	31	41
First Base Only	.321	.392	.438	112	36	8	1	1	6	11	13
Scoring Position	.302	.366	.376	189	57	3	4	1	68	20	28
Late Innings, Close	.226	.306	.282	195	44	6	1	1	11	20	33

RBI/Opportunities

Scoring Position	64 / 265	(24%)
Scoring Position, 2 Out	34 / 148	(23%)
On Third, Less than 2 Out	23 / 43	(53%)
RBI in close games / RBI Total	51 / 78	(65%)

Tom Foley
Montreal Expos

THREE YEARS (84 – 86)

	Ave.	OBP	SLG	AB	H	2B	3B	HR	RBI	BB	SO
Totals	.253	.314	.351	790	200	36	7	9	73	73	107
Batting vs. Left and Right-handed Pitchers											
Left	.238	.291	.246	130	31	1	0	0	8	10	26
Right	.256	.319	.371	660	169	35	7	9	65	63	81
At Home and on the Road											
Home	.273	.346	.392	355	97	19	4	5	35	42	41
Road	.237	.287	.317	435	103	17	3	4	38	31	66
Facing Groundball Pitchers and Flyball Pitchers											
Groundball	.227	.297	.322	357	81	16	3	4	37	38	47
Flyball	.275	.329	.374	433	119	20	4	5	36	35	60
Facing Finesse Pitchers and Power Pitchers											
Finesse	.264	.317	.381	444	117	21	5	7	43	36	48
Power	.240	.310	.312	346	83	15	2	2	30	37	59
On Grass and on Turf											
Grass	.233	.278	.326	236	55	6	2	4	23	15	30
Turf	.262	.329	.361	554	145	30	5	5	50	58	77
During the Day and at Night											
Day	.246	.307	.349	284	70	12	4	3	29	26	41
Night	.257	.318	.352	506	130	24	3	6	44	47	66
By Month											
April	.194	.235	.419	31	6	0	2	1	5	2	7
May	.262	.329	.341	126	33	6	2	0	9	13	15
June	.239	.321	.338	71	17	2	1	1	10	9	14
July	.241	.307	.310	116	28	5	0	1	11	11	15
August	.259	.313	.370	243	63	14	2	3	21	20	32
Sept/Oct	.261	.320	.350	203	53	9	0	3	17	18	24
Situational											
Bases Empty	.256	.307	.338	468	120	20	3	4	4	34	60
Leadoff	.259	.296	.349	212	55	8	1	3	3	11	29
Not Leadoff	.254	.315	.328	256	65	12	2	1	1	23	31
Runners On	.248	.324	.370	322	80	16	4	5	69	39	47
First Base Only	.274	.313	.395	157	43	6	2	3	10	9	23
Scoring Position	.224	.333	.345	165	37	10	2	2	59	30	24
Late Innings, Close	.250	.326	.351	168	42	1	2	3	18	19	31

RBI/Opportunities

Scoring Position	53 / 235	(23%)
Scoring Position, 2 Out	21 / 127	(17%)
On Third, Less than 2 Out	25 / 41	(61%)
RBI in close games / RBI Total	45 / 73	(62%)

Ray Fontenot
Minnesota Twins

1986: Finesse, Groundball 1985: Finesse, Groundball 1984: Finesse, Groundball

THREE YEARS (84 – 86)

	G	IP	H	BB	SO	SB	CS	W	L	S	ERA
Totals	130	396.1	450	128	189	28	23	17	24	2	4.20
At Home and on the Road											
Home	68	212.1	247	67	96	16	13	8	14	1	4.28
Road	62	184.0	203	61	93	12	10	9	10	1	4.11
During the Day and and at Night											
Day	74	217.1	250	71	96	18	15	8	15	2	4.39
Night	56	179.0	200	57	93	10	8	9	9	0	3.97
On Grass and on Turf											
Grass	98	324.0	364	101	148	21	19	13	23	2	4.11
Turf	32	72.1	86	27	41	7	4	4	1	0	4.60
By Month											
April	11	31.2	35	11	10	1	3	1	4	0	3.69
May	26	62.2	65	25	27	7	3	1	2	1	4.16
June	29	70.1	71	24	36	5	5	5	5	0	3.84
July	19	73.2	82	22	41	5	2	4	5	1	3.30
August	25	86.1	90	25	30	4	5	3	5	0	3.86
Sept/Oct	20	71.2	107	21	45	6	5	3	3	0	6.15

vs. Opponent Batters
THREE YEARS (84 – 86)

	Ave.	OBP	SLG	AB	H	2B	3B	HR	RBI	BB	SO
Totals	.292	.347	.428	1542	450	57	18	39	196	128	189
Pitching vs. Left and Right-handed Batters											
Left	.241	.308	.357	294	71	7	3	7	42	27	66
Right	.304	.356	.445	1248	379	50	15	32	154	101	123
Situational											
Bases Empty	.285	.345	.410	859	245	37	8	18	18	74	106
Leadoff	.290	.344	.391	373	108	17	3	5	5	30	49
Not Leadoff	.282	.345	.424	486	137	20	5	13	13	44	57
Runners On	.300	.349	.451	683	205	20	10	21	178	54	83
First Base Only	.295	.329	.404	292	86	6	1	8	21	15	40
Scoring Position	.304	.364	.486	391	119	14	9	13	157	39	43
Late Innings, Close	.317	.378	.458	227	72	10	2	6	32	22	28

RBI/Opportunities

Scoring Position	129 / 497	(26%)
Scoring Position, 2 Out	56 / 235	(24%)
On Third, Less than 2 Out	37 / 76	(49%)
RBI in close games / RBI Total	129 / 196	(66%)

Curt Ford
St. Louis Cardinals

THREE YEARS (84 – 86)

	Ave.	OBP	SLG	AB	H	2B	3B	HR	RBI	BB	SO
Totals	.261	.337	.381	226	59	17	2	2	32	27	30
Batting vs. Left and Right-handed Pitchers											
Left	.207	.281	.276	29	6	2	0	0	4	3	7
Right	.269	.345	.396	197	53	15	2	2	28	24	23
At Home and on the Road											
Home	.294	.376	.431	102	30	12	1	0	20	14	13
Road	.234	.304	.339	124	29	5	1	2	12	13	17
Facing Groundball Pitchers and Flyball Pitchers											
Groundball	.214	.277	.291	103	22	8	0	0	11	9	16
Flyball	.301	.385	.455	123	37	9	2	2	21	18	14
Facing Finesse Pitchers and Power Pitchers											
Finesse	.288	.329	.397	146	42	11	1	0	20	10	14
Power	.212	.351	.350	80	17	6	1	1	12	17	16
On Grass and on Turf											
Grass	.137	.182	.157	51	7	1	0	0	3	3	9
Turf	.297	.380	.446	175	52	16	2	2	29	24	21
During the Day and at Night											
Day	.212	.308	.318	66	14	7	0	0	8	10	4
Night	.281	.350	.406	160	45	10	2	2	24	17	26
By Month											
April	.000	.000	.000	0	0	0	0	0	0	0	0
May	.000	.000	.000	0	0	0	0	0	0	0	0
June	.296	.367	.481	54	16	5	1	1	4	6	7
July	.281	.333	.359	64	18	5	0	0	11	5	8
August	.205	.264	.308	78	16	3	1	1	12	7	10
Sept/Oct	.300	.462	.433	30	9	4	0	0	5	9	5
Situational											
Bases Empty	.229	.317	.339	109	25	7	1	1	1	14	18
Leadoff	.241	.305	.352	54	13	3	0	1	1	5	9
Not Leadoff	.218	.328	.327	55	12	4	1	0	0	9	9
Runners On	.291	.356	.419	117	34	10	1	1	31	13	12
First Base Only	.289	.325	.447	38	11	1	1	1	3	2	1
Scoring Position	.291	.370	.405	79	23	9	0	0	28	11	11
Late Innings, Close	.370	.482	.522	46	17	5	1	0	6	10	5

RBI/Opportunities

Scoring Position	27 / 106	(25%)
Scoring Position, 2 Out	11 / 50	(22%)
On Third, Less than 2 Out	7 / 17	(41%)
RBI in close games / RBI Total	22 / 32	(69%)

Terry Forster
California Angels

1986: Power, Groundball 1985: Power, Groundball 1984: Finesse, Groundball

THREE YEARS (84 – 86)

	G	IP	H	BB	SO	SB	CS	W	L	S	ERA
Totals	112	127.0	126	52	75	12	3	8	4	11	2.76
At Home and on the Road											
Home	65	68.2	66	25	44	5	1	3	1	6	3.15
Road	47	58.1	60	27	31	7	2	5	3	5	2.31
During the Day and and at Night											
Day	40	37.0	42	21	21	3	1	4	1	4	2.68
Night	72	90.0	84	31	54	9	2	4	3	7	2.80
On Grass and on Turf											
Grass	91	103.2	101	40	57	7	3	6	2	9	2.95
Turf	21	23.1	25	12	18	5	0	2	2	2	1.93
By Month											
April	20	21.0	14	8	11	1	0	2	1	1	1.71
May	29	32.0	41	9	22	1	1	2	1	3	3.66
June	26	14.1	23	16	19	7	1	1	1	6	0.79
July	9	14.1	17	4	10	1	1	2	0	0	3.14
August	15	11.0	14	5	3	0	0	1	1	0	6.55
Sept/Oct	13	14.1	17	10	10	2	0	0	0	1	3.77

vs. Opponent Batters
THREE YEARS (84 – 86)

	Ave.	OBP	SLG	AB	H	2B	3B	HR	RBI	BB	SO
Totals	.264	.337	.391	481	127	25	3	10	70	52	75
Pitching vs. Left and Right-handed Batters											
Left	.264	.343	.352	159	42	8	0	2	22	18	26
Right	.264	.334	.410	322	85	17	3	8	48	34	49
Situational											
Bases Empty	.270	.351	.399	233	63	13	1	5	5	26	33
Leadoff	.196	.241	.294	102	20	7	0	1	1	5	15
Not Leadoff	.328	.429	.481	131	43	6	1	4	4	21	18
Runners On	.258	.324	.383	248	64	12	2	5	65	26	42
First Base Only	.243	.271	.379	103	25	6	1	2	8	4	12
Scoring Position	.269	.357	.386	145	39	6	1	3	57	22	30
Late Innings, Close	.273	.343	.417	216	59	5	1	8	30	20	32

RBI/Opportunities

Scoring Position	51 / 213	(24%)
Scoring Position, 2 Out	28 / 97	(29%)
On Third, Less than 2 Out	14 / 39	(36%)
RBI in close games / RBI Total	35 / 70	(50%)

George Foster
Chicago White Sox

THREE YEARS (84 – 86)

	Ave.	OBP	SLG	AB	H	2B	3B	HR	RBI	BB	SO
Totals	.258	.312	.443	1289	332	52	5	59	205	100	270
Batting vs. Left and Right-handed Pitchers											
Left	.262	.320	.461	508	133	21	1	26	82	44	99
Right	.255	.308	.431	781	199	31	4	33	123	56	171
At Home and on the Road											
Home	.247	.311	.434	620	153	22	2	30	105	54	123
Road	.268	.314	.451	669	179	30	3	29	100	46	147
Facing Groundball Pitchers and Flyball Pitchers											
Groundball	.252	.315	.415	620	156	30	1	23	104	53	116
Flyball	.263	.309	.469	669	176	22	4	36	101	47	154
Facing Finesse Pitchers and Power Pitchers											
Finesse	.266	.313	.488	726	193	27	4	42	119	48	136
Power	.247	.311	.385	563	139	25	1	17	86	52	134
On Grass and on Turf											
Grass	.243	.305	.430	882	214	29	2	44	144	78	183
Turf	.290	.328	.472	407	118	23	3	15	61	22	87
During the Day and at Night											
Day	.242	.287	.450	433	105	16	1	24	69	28	91
Night	.265	.325	.439	856	227	36	4	35	136	72	179
By Month											
April	.272	.321	.445	173	47	12	0	6	30	13	36
May	.202	.250	.452	228	46	6	0	17	37	16	45
June	.245	.291	.425	233	57	9	0	11	31	25	49
July	.274	.324	.435	223	61	13	1	7	48	16	53
August	.271	.311	.418	251	68	8	1	9	31	15	55
Sept/Oct	.293	.358	.497	181	53	4	3	9	28	15	32
Situational											
Bases Empty	.255	.303	.459	690	176	27	3	36	36	43	141
Leadoff	.241	.284	.371	286	69	7	0	10	10	15	55
Not Leadoff	.265	.316	.522	404	107	20	3	26	26	28	86
Runners On	.260	.323	.424	599	156	25	2	23	169	57	129
First Base Only	.273	.326	.459	242	66	13	1	10	26	17	39
Scoring Position	.252	.321	.401	357	90	12	1	13	143	40	90
Late Innings, Close	.203	.265	.264	227	46	3	1	3	32	21	57

RBI/Opportunities

Scoring Position	117 / 476	(25%)
Scoring Position, 2 Out	50 / 223	(22%)
On Third, Less than 2 Out	41 / 93	(44%)
RBI in close games / RBI Total	131 / 205	(64%)

Terry Francona
Chicago Cubs

THREE YEARS (84 – 86)	Ave.	OBP	SLG	AB	H	2B	3B	HR	RBI	BB	SO
Totals	.291	.317	.384	619	180	37	3	5	57	23	33
Batting vs. Left and Right-handed Pitchers											
Left	.351	.364	.392	74	26	3	0	0	11	2	10
Right	.283	.311	.383	545	154	34	3	5	46	21	23
At Home and on the Road											
Home	.285	.319	.386	267	76	18	3	1	20	13	18
Road	.295	.316	.384	352	104	19	0	4	37	10	15
Facing Groundball Pitchers and Flyball Pitchers											
Groundball	.280	.311	.351	279	78	16	2	0	23	12	12
Flyball	.300	.323	.412	340	102	21	1	5	34	11	21
Facing Finesse Pitchers and Power Pitchers											
Finesse	.280	.302	.401	347	97	23	2	5	26	11	17
Power	.305	.337	.364	272	83	14	1	0	31	12	16
On Grass and on Turf											
Grass	.265	.291	.350	223	59	13	0	2	25	8	11
Turf	.306	.333	.404	396	121	24	3	3	32	15	22
During the Day and at Night											
Day	.281	.313	.352	253	71	13	1	1	25	11	16
Night	.298	.320	.407	366	109	24	2	4	32	12	17
By Month											
April	.341	.398	.412	85	29	6	0	0	5	7	8
May	.321	.323	.420	162	52	10	3	0	16	1	6
June	.248	.283	.336	113	28	7	0	1	10	4	5
July	.259	.281	.352	54	14	2	0	1	7	2	3
August	.352	.378	.514	105	37	8	0	3	14	5	8
Sept/Oct	.200	.231	.240	100	20	4	0	0	5	4	3
Situational											
Bases Empty	.266	.280	.385	364	97	24	2	5	5	6	23
Leadoff	.271	.292	.421	140	38	10	1	3	3	4	13
Not Leadoff	.263	.273	.362	224	59	14	1	2	2	2	10
Runners On	.325	.367	.384	255	83	13	1	0	52	17	10
First Base Only	.365	.377	.442	104	38	8	0	0	4	2	4
Scoring Position	.298	.360	.344	151	45	5	1	0	48	15	6
Late Innings, Close	.296	.305	.400	135	40	11	0	1	23	3	6

RBI/Opportunities		
Scoring Position	46 / 201	(23%)
Scoring Position, 2 Out	21 / 104	(20%)
On Third, Less than 2 Out	16 / 34	(47%)
RBI in close games / RBI Total	40 / 57	(70%)

George Frazier
Minnesota Twins

1986: Power, Flyball   1985: Power, Groundball   1984: Power, Flyball

THREE YEARS (84 – 86)	G	IP	H	BB	SO	SB	CS	W	L	S	ERA
Totals	160	262.1	272	142	194	35	18	19	18	12	4.97
At Home and on the Road											
Home	85	140.2	138	64	109	17	8	11	7	7	4.80
Road	75	121.2	134	78	85	18	10	8	11	5	5.18
During the Day and at Night											
Day	96	150.2	161	75	113	17	11	15	13	5	5.44
Night	64	111.2	111	67	81	18	7	4	5	7	4.35
On Grass and on Turf											
Grass	115	184.2	185	96	142	23	14	13	13	8	4.92
Turf	45	77.2	87	46	52	12	4	6	5	4	5.10
By Month											
April	19	27.2	37	16	14	8	1	2	3	1	7.16
May	28	48.0	49	24	35	3	5	5	3	0	3.00
June	29	50.1	50	32	36	7	4	3	1	0	5.01
July	25	40.2	30	20	24	4	3	2	2	2	3.76
August	34	58.1	68	22	53	8	3	3	4	6	4.78
Sept/Oct	25	37.1	38	28	32	5	2	4	5	3	7.47

vs. Opponent Batters											
THREE YEARS (84 – 86)	Ave.	OBP	SLG	AB	H	2B	3B	HR	RBI	BB	SO
Totals	.269	.359	.406	1010	272	51	6	25	161	142	194
Pitching vs. Left and Right-handed Batters											
Left	.272	.366	.397	486	132	22	6	9	72	72	76
Right	.267	.352	.414	524	140	29	0	16	89	70	118
Situational											
Bases Empty	.250	.331	.379	541	135	20	4	14	14	64	116
Leadoff	.233	.319	.368	223	52	10	1	6	6	28	37
Not Leadoff	.261	.340	.387	318	83	10	3	8	8	36	79
Runners On	.292	.389	.437	469	137	31	2	11	147	78	78
First Base Only	.310	.341	.450	171	53	10	1	4	13	7	25
Scoring Position	.282	.412	.430	298	84	21	1	7	134	71	53
Late Innings, Close	.264	.352	.410	368	97	17	2	11	55	51	70

RBI/Opportunities		
Scoring Position	120 / 480	(25%)
Scoring Position, 2 Out	45 / 223	(20%)
On Third, Less than 2 Out	49 / 101	(49%)
RBI in close games / RBI Total	75 / 161	(47%)

Andres Galarraga
Montreal Expos

THREE YEARS (84 – 86)	Ave.	OBP	SLG	AB	H	2B	3B	HR	RBI	BB	SO
Totals	.255	.318	.384	396	101	14	0	12	46	33	97
Batting vs. Left and Right-handed Pitchers											
Left	.296	.360	.407	162	48	6	0	4	15	16	31
Right	.226	.289	.363	234	53	8	0	8	31	17	66
At Home and on the Road											
Home	.264	.324	.371	197	52	9	0	4	22	16	51
Road	.246	.312	.392	199	49	5	0	8	24	17	46
Facing Groundball Pitchers and Flyball Pitchers											
Groundball	.258	.324	.376	194	50	8	0	5	23	17	50
Flyball	.252	.312	.386	202	51	6	0	7	23	16	47
Facing Finesse Pitchers and Power Pitchers											
Finesse	.265	.329	.355	211	56	7	0	4	18	17	51
Power	.243	.305	.411	185	45	7	0	8	28	16	46
On Grass and on Turf											
Grass	.233	.299	.362	116	27	3	0	4	15	10	25
Turf	.264	.326	.389	280	74	11	0	8	31	23	72
During the Day and at Night											
Day	.272	.357	.426	162	44	4	0	7	18	19	39
Night	.244	.289	.350	234	57	10	0	5	28	14	58
By Month											
April	.415	.500	.683	41	17	2	0	3	8	8	9
May	.187	.256	.280	75	14	1	0	2	7	6	18
June	.253	.309	.402	87	22	4	0	3	11	6	19
July	.118	.167	.118	17	2	0	0	0	0	0	8
August	.125	.222	.125	16	2	0	0	0	0	2	2
Sept/Oct	.275	.326	.394	160	44	7	0	4	20	11	41
Situational											
Bases Empty	.247	.304	.402	219	54	10	0	8	8	18	58
Leadoff	.290	.365	.516	93	27	6	0	5	5	11	30
Not Leadoff	.214	.256	.317	126	27	4	0	3	3	7	28
Runners On	.266	.335	.356	177	47	4	0	4	38	15	39
First Base Only	.292	.301	.389	72	21	1	0	2	4	1	15
Scoring Position	.248	.355	.333	105	26	3	0	2	34	14	24
Late Innings, Close	.256	.333	.430	86	22	6	0	3	9	10	20

RBI/Opportunities		
Scoring Position	30 / 143	(21%)
Scoring Position, 2 Out	21 / 79	(27%)
On Third, Less than 2 Out	4 / 21	(19%)
RBI in close games / RBI Total	31 / 46	(67%)

Phil Garner
Houston Astros

THREE YEARS (84 – 86)	Ave.	OBP	SLG	AB	H	2B	3B	HR	RBI	BB	SO
Totals	.270	.333	.400	1150	311	54	19	19	137	107	180
Batting vs. Left and Right-handed Pitchers											
Left	.294	.355	.435	589	173	30	13	9	75	59	76
Right	.246	.310	.364	561	138	24	6	10	62	48	104
At Home and on the Road											
Home	.289	.351	.391	578	167	26	9	5	65	55	80
Road	.252	.315	.409	572	144	28	10	14	72	52	100
Facing Groundball Pitchers and Flyball Pitchers											
Groundball	.249	.313	.358	551	137	17	11	7	64	52	81
Flyball	.290	.351	.439	599	174	37	8	12	73	55	99
Facing Finesse Pitchers and Power Pitchers											
Finesse	.258	.308	.386	616	159	21	11	12	69	44	74
Power	.285	.361	.416	534	152	33	8	7	68	63	106
On Grass and on Turf											
Grass	.277	.335	.480	329	91	19	9	10	50	28	53
Turf	.268	.332	.368	821	220	35	10	9	87	79	127
During the Day and at Night											
Day	.276	.346	.455	297	82	13	8	8	40	33	37
Night	.268	.328	.381	853	229	41	11	11	97	74	143
By Month											
April	.267	.311	.424	165	44	9	1	5	20	11	29
May	.227	.294	.316	225	51	11	3	1	21	21	41
June	.246	.328	.386	207	51	6	4	5	30	26	24
July	.269	.335	.386	145	39	6	1	3	16	13	28
August	.311	.378	.409	164	51	6	2	2	20	18	24
Sept/Oct	.307	.356	.475	244	75	16	8	3	30	18	34
Situational											
Bases Empty	.272	.332	.403	632	172	32	6	13	13	55	105
Leadoff	.262	.314	.371	237	62	12	1	4	4	16	35
Not Leadoff	.278	.343	.423	395	110	20	5	9	9	39	70
Runners On	.268	.334	.396	518	139	22	13	6	124	52	75
First Base Only	.265	.325	.350	234	62	8	3	2	12	19	29
Scoring Position	.271	.340	.433	284	77	14	10	4	112	33	46
Late Innings, Close	.282	.351	.455	220	62	6	4	8	38	23	38

RBI/Opportunities		
Scoring Position	96 / 384	(25%)
Scoring Position, 2 Out	37 / 162	(23%)
On Third, Less than 2 Out	39 / 82	(48%)
RBI in close games / RBI Total	99 / 137	(72%)

Bobby Grich
California Angels

	Ave.	OBP	SLG	AB	H	2B	3B	HR	RBI	BB	SO
THREE YEARS (84 – 86)											
Totals	.254	.355	.408	1155	293	50	4	40	141	177	200
Batting vs. Left and Right-handed Pitchers											
Left	.270	.365	.444	455	123	21	2	18	57	68	71
Right	.243	.349	.384	700	170	29	2	22	84	109	129
At Home and on the Road											
Home	.266	.358	.419	580	154	22	2	21	78	80	90
Road	.242	.353	.397	575	139	28	2	19	63	97	110
Facing Groundball Pitchers and Flyball Pitchers											
Groundball	.236	.337	.382	550	130	23	3	17	76	81	98
Flyball	.269	.363	.419	605	163	27	1	23	65	96	102
Facing Finesse Pitchers and Power Pitchers											
Finesse	.256	.341	.418	653	167	37	3	21	74	80	95
Power	.251	.373	.394	502	126	13	1	19	67	97	105
On Grass and on Turf											
Grass	.261	.362	.412	971	253	42	3	33	119	151	160
Turf	.217	.318	.386	184	40	8	1	7	22	26	40
During the Day and at Night											
Day	.279	.403	.466	294	82	17	1	12	43	59	54
Night	.245	.338	.388	861	211	33	3	28	98	118	146
By Month											
April	.289	.402	.472	142	41	5	0	7	20	25	24
May	.233	.308	.313	176	41	6	1	2	10	18	26
June	.212	.297	.308	156	33	6	0	3	19	19	21
July	.265	.362	.441	211	56	8	1	9	28	31	35
August	.259	.342	.472	212	55	13	1	10	27	26	43
Sept/Oct	.260	.397	.419	258	67	12	1	9	37	58	51
Situational											
Bases Empty	.249	.344	.418	675	168	29	2	27	27	94	124
Leadoff	.258	.343	.410	310	80	12	1	11	11	39	54
Not Leadoff	.241	.345	.425	365	88	17	1	16	16	55	70
Runners On	.260	.371	.394	480	125	21	2	13	114	83	76
First Base Only	.290	.377	.458	214	62	10	1	8	21	28	29
Scoring Position	.237	.366	.342	266	63	11	1	5	93	55	47
Late Innings, Close	.260	.332	.370	192	50	15	0	2	23	21	33

RBI/Opportunities		
Scoring Position	83 / 392	(21%)
Scoring Position, 2 Out	37 / 189	(20%)
On Third, Less than 2 Out	27 / 61	(44%)
RBI in close games / RBI Total	85 / 141	(60%)

Ken Griffey
Atlanta Braves

	Ave.	OBP	SLG	AB	H	2B	3B	HR	RBI	BB	SO
THREE YEARS (84 – 86)											
Totals	.286	.335	.436	1327	379	70	8	38	182	105	150
Batting vs. Left and Right-handed Pitchers											
Left	.257	.289	.380	350	90	23	1	6	49	16	44
Right	.296	.351	.456	977	289	47	7	32	133	89	106
At Home and on the Road											
Home	.293	.348	.477	648	190	36	4	25	94	55	76
Road	.278	.322	.398	679	189	34	4	13	88	50	74
Facing Groundball Pitchers and Flyball Pitchers											
Groundball	.257	.310	.374	661	170	31	2	14	78	52	70
Flyball	.314	.359	.498	666	209	39	6	24	104	53	80
Facing Finesse Pitchers and Power Pitchers											
Finesse	.279	.326	.426	735	205	42	3	20	95	54	62
Power	.294	.346	.449	592	174	28	5	18	87	51	88
On Grass and on Turf											
Grass	.287	.339	.443	1096	315	58	5	34	155	91	124
Turf	.277	.315	.407	231	64	12	3	4	27	14	26
During the Day and at Night											
Day	.297	.359	.469	424	126	29	4	12	59	42	52
Night	.280	.323	.421	903	253	41	4	26	123	63	98
By Month											
April	.282	.338	.385	195	55	10	2	2	24	18	11
May	.240	.286	.369	179	43	8	0	5	24	13	27
June	.297	.349	.438	192	57	10	1	5	23	17	16
July	.293	.340	.454	249	73	11	1	9	37	18	33
August	.295	.325	.471	261	77	13	3	9	43	13	31
Sept/Oct	.295	.362	.470	251	74	18	1	8	31	26	32
Situational											
Bases Empty	.296	.340	.458	729	216	36	5	24	24	46	85
Leadoff	.324	.355	.477	287	93	11	3	9	9	14	26
Not Leadoff	.278	.330	.446	442	123	25	2	15	15	32	59
Runners On	.273	.329	.410	598	163	34	3	14	158	59	65
First Base Only	.287	.320	.418	244	70	20	0	4	11	12	21
Scoring Position	.263	.335	.404	354	93	14	3	10	147	47	44
Late Innings, Close	.306	.357	.427	248	76	9	0	7	36	21	26

RBI/Opportunities		
Scoring Position	124 / 493	(25%)
Scoring Position, 2 Out	39 / 213	(18%)
On Third, Less than 2 Out	50 / 82	(61%)
RBI in close games / RBI Total	99 / 182	(54%)

John Grubb
Detroit Tigers

	Ave.	OBP	SLG	AB	H	2B	3B	HR	RBI	BB	SO
THREE YEARS (84 – 86)											
Totals	.287	.384	.484	541	155	25	2	26	93	86	89
Batting vs. Left and Right-handed Pitchers											
Left	.238	.304	.333	21	5	2	0	0	2	2	6
Right	.288	.387	.490	520	150	23	2	26	91	84	83
At Home and on the Road											
Home	.286	.378	.461	297	85	9	2	13	50	43	43
Road	.287	.392	.512	244	70	16	0	13	43	43	46
Facing Groundball Pitchers and Flyball Pitchers											
Groundball	.285	.382	.430	235	67	8	1	8	45	38	44
Flyball	.288	.386	.526	306	88	17	1	18	48	48	45
Facing Finesse Pitchers and Power Pitchers											
Finesse	.277	.369	.489	282	78	14	2	14	51	42	36
Power	.297	.401	.479	259	77	11	0	12	42	44	53
On Grass and on Turf											
Grass	.280	.377	.456	471	132	19	2	20	78	72	70
Turf	.329	.435	.671	70	23	6	0	6	15	14	19
During the Day and at Night											
Day	.317	.429	.476	164	52	9	1	5	17	30	26
Night	.273	.365	.488	377	103	16	1	21	76	56	63
By Month											
April	.200	.305	.320	50	10	1	1	1	2	8	7
May	.322	.412	.492	59	19	2	1	2	12	9	13
June	.159	.297	.268	82	13	3	0	2	10	15	15
July	.382	.431	.719	89	34	3	0	9	28	9	17
August	.302	.397	.484	126	38	11	0	4	17	20	13
Sept/Oct	.304	.415	.519	135	41	5	0	8	24	25	24
Situational											
Bases Empty	.277	.383	.500	314	87	11	1	19	19	52	47
Leadoff	.315	.403	.600	130	41	5	1	10	10	18	18
Not Leadoff	.250	.370	.429	184	46	6	0	9	9	34	29
Runners On	.300	.386	.463	227	68	14	1	7	74	34	42
First Base Only	.316	.409	.484	95	30	8	1	2	9	15	15
Scoring Position	.288	.370	.447	132	38	6	0	5	65	19	27
Late Innings, Close	.212	.355	.341	85	18	2	0	3	13	19	20

RBI/Opportunities		
Scoring Position	52 / 200	(26%)
Scoring Position, 2 Out	27 / 105	(26%)
On Third, Less than 2 Out	18 / 34	(53%)
RBI in close games / RBI Total	58 / 93	(62%)

Kelly Gruber
Toronto Blue Jays

	Ave.	OBP	SLG	AB	H	2B	3B	HR	RBI	BB	SO
THREE YEARS (84 – 86)											
Totals	.186	.207	.326	172	32	4	1	6	18	5	35
Batting vs. Left and Right-handed Pitchers											
Left	.189	.197	.297	74	14	2	0	2	6	1	15
Right	.184	.214	.347	98	18	2	1	4	12	4	20
At Home and on the Road											
Home	.174	.215	.349	86	15	1	1	4	14	5	22
Road	.198	.198	.302	86	17	3	0	2	4	0	13
Facing Groundball Pitchers and Flyball Pitchers											
Groundball	.200	.205	.443	70	14	2	0	5	13	1	10
Flyball	.176	.208	.245	102	18	2	1	1	5	4	25
Facing Finesse Pitchers and Power Pitchers											
Finesse	.209	.225	.326	86	18	2	1	2	9	2	15
Power	.163	.189	.326	86	14	2	0	4	9	3	20
On Grass and on Turf											
Grass	.205	.205	.313	83	17	3	0	2	4	0	12
Turf	.169	.208	.337	89	15	1	1	4	14	5	23
During the Day and at Night											
Day	.141	.153	.254	71	10	2	0	2	6	1	17
Night	.218	.243	.376	101	22	2	1	4	12	4	18
By Month											
April	.294	.294	.647	17	5	0	0	2	3	0	7
May	.067	.125	.133	30	2	0	1	0	0	2	5
June	.143	.182	.333	21	3	1	0	1	3	1	4
July	.000	.000	.000	11	0	0	0	0	1	0	4
August	.269	.286	.385	26	7	0	0	1	2	1	2
Sept/Oct	.224	.235	.358	67	15	3	0	2	9	1	13
Situational											
Bases Empty	.146	.153	.270	89	13	3	1	2	2	4	20
Leadoff	.100	.156	.100	30	3	0	0	0	0	2	6
Not Leadoff	.169	.197	.356	59	10	3	1	2	2	2	14
Runners On	.229	.233	.386	83	19	1	0	4	16	1	15
First Base Only	.333	.355	.433	30	10	0	0	1	2	1	4
Scoring Position	.170	.164	.358	53	9	1	0	3	14	0	11
Late Innings, Close	.103	.133	.103	29	3	0	0	0	1	1	5

RBI/Opportunities		
Scoring Position	11 / 76	(14%)
Scoring Position, 2 Out	3 / 37	(8%)
On Third, Less than 2 Out	5 / 12	(42%)
RBI in close games / RBI Total	8 / 18	(44%)

Cecilio Guante
Pittsburgh Pirates

1986: Power, Flyball 1985: Power, Flyball 1984: Power, Flyball

THREE YEARS (84 – 86)	G	IP	H	BB	SO	SB	CS	W	L	S	ERA
Totals	142	228.1	181	85	185	18	15	11	11	11	2.92
At Home and on the Road											
Home	70	114.1	83	38	91	6	6	4	1	6	2.60
Road	72	114.0	98	47	94	12	9	7	10	5	3.24
During the Day and and at Night											
Day	50	73.2	59	37	67	5	8	2	6	5	3.30
Night	92	154.2	122	48	118	13	7	9	5	6	2.73
On Grass and on Turf											
Grass	42	65.2	62	25	61	5	5	3	6	4	3.56
Turf	100	162.2	119	60	124	13	10	8	5	7	2.66
By Month											
April	28	41.2	31	12	37	4	3	1	1	3	2.16
May	28	45.1	35	23	33	3	4	3	1	0	2.38
June	34	59.2	37	21	43	7	5	1	3	3	2.11
July	22	37.1	36	11	36	1	1	4	3	1	4.34
August	17	24.0	23	13	21	2	1	1	2	1	5.25
Sept/Oct	13	20.1	19	5	15	1	1	1	1	3	2.66

vs. Opponent Batters THREE YEARS (84 – 86)	Ave.	OBP	SLG	AB	H	2B	3B	HR	RBI	BB	SO
Totals	.219	.297	.359	825	181	40	9	19	91	85	185
Pitching vs. Left and Right-handed Batters											
Left	.250	.348	.398	332	83	16	6	7	33	46	58
Right	.199	.262	.333	493	98	24	3	12	58	39	127
Situational											
Bases Empty	.214	.291	.333	472	101	26	3	8	8	43	105
Leadoff	.219	.279	.333	192	42	11	1	3	3	14	34
Not Leadoff	.211	.298	.332	280	59	15	2	5	5	29	71
Runners On	.227	.306	.394	353	80	14	6	11	83	42	80
First Base Only	.248	.317	.426	129	32	4	2	5	12	12	25
Scoring Position	.214	.300	.375	224	48	10	4	6	71	30	55
Late Innings, Close	.214	.309	.339	387	83	18	3	8	38	51	83

RBI/Opportunities		
Scoring Position	58 / 314	(18%)
Scoring Position, 2 Out	24 / 167	(14%)
On Third, Less than 2 Out	21 / 46	(46%)
RBI in close games / RBI Total	58 / 91	(64%)

Mark Gubicza
Kansas City Royals

1986: Power, Groundball 1985: Power, Groundball 1984: Power, Groundball

THREE YEARS (84 – 86)	G	IP	H	BB	SO	SB	CS	W	L	S	ERA
Totals	93	547.0	487	236	328	52	22	36	30	0	3.92
At Home and on the Road											
Home	54	337.2	279	129	205	36	11	23	17	0	3.09
Road	39	209.1	208	107	123	16	11	13	13	0	5.25
During the Day and and at Night											
Day	23	133.0	114	65	84	11	8	8	8	0	3.92
Night	70	414.0	373	171	244	41	14	28	22	0	3.91
On Grass and on Turf											
Grass	27	145.2	140	75	88	11	10	11	8	0	4.82
Turf	66	401.1	347	161	240	41	12	25	22	0	3.59
By Month											
April	8	47.2	43	22	26	8	2	0	6	0	4.15
May	16	93.2	87	39	61	13	2	6	5	0	4.42
June	16	95.1	68	52	64	3	5	8	4	0	3.02
July	16	81.0	74	26	49	11	5	5	3	0	3.56
August	18	109.1	106	45	65	7	3	8	6	0	4.53
Sept/Oct	19	120.0	109	52	63	10	5	9	6	0	3.83

vs. Opponent Batters THREE YEARS (84 – 86)	Ave.	OBP	SLG	AB	H	2B	3B	HR	RBI	BB	SO
Totals	.238	.319	.351	2042	487	92	16	35	225	236	328
Pitching vs. Left and Right-handed Batters											
Left	.247	.333	.367	1094	270	46	10	22	114	138	170
Right	.229	.302	.331	948	217	46	6	13	111	98	158
Situational											
Bases Empty	.229	.315	.352	1170	268	61	7	23	23	139	180
Leadoff	.250	.328	.372	513	128	27	3	10	10	55	65
Not Leadoff	.213	.304	.336	657	140	34	4	13	13	84	115
Runners On	.251	.324	.349	872	219	31	9	12	202	97	148
First Base Only	.236	.300	.325	369	87	15	6	2	18	31	56
Scoring Position	.262	.340	.366	503	132	16	3	10	184	66	92
Late Innings, Close	.252	.362	.391	151	38	7	1	4	12	26	32

RBI/Opportunities		
Scoring Position	164 / 682	(24%)
Scoring Position, 2 Out	54 / 289	(19%)
On Third, Less than 2 Out	73 / 126	(58%)
RBI in close games / RBI Total	161 / 225	(72%)

Lee Guetterman
Seattle Mariners

1986: Finesse, Groundball 1985: Did not play 1984: Power, Groundball

THREE YEARS (84 – 86)	G	IP	H	BB	SO	SB	CS	W	L	S	ERA
Totals	44	80.1	117	32	40	4	3	0	4	0	7.17
At Home and on the Road											
Home	25	42.2	65	17	21	3	0	0	3	0	8.23
Road	19	37.2	52	15	19	1	3	0	1	0	5.97
During the Day and and at Night											
Day	14	23.2	31	10	9	1	1	0	0	0	6.08
Night	30	56.2	86	22	31	3	2	0	4	0	7.62
On Grass and on Turf											
Grass	14	30.2	41	12	17	1	3	0	1	0	6.16
Turf	30	49.2	76	20	23	3	0	0	3	0	7.79
By Month											
April	7	10.2	12	4	3	0	1	0	0	0	3.37
May	7	16.1	23	9	7	0	1	0	0	0	8.27
June	9	18.2	24	7	14	2	0	0	3	0	7.23
July	6	14.1	17	4	6	2	0	0	0	0	4.40
August	6	9.1	15	3	5	0	1	0	0	0	10.61
Sept/Oct	9	11.0	26	5	5	0	0	0	1	0	9.82

vs. Opponent Batters THREE YEARS (84 – 86)	Ave.	OBP	SLG	AB	H	2B	3B	HR	RBI	BB	SO
Totals	.355	.412	.488	330	117	17	3	7	61	32	40
Pitching vs. Left and Right-handed Batters											
Left	.336	.403	.467	107	36	4	2	2	20	10	12
Right	.363	.417	.498	223	81	13	1	5	41	22	28
Situational											
Bases Empty	.336	.395	.395	152	51	7	1	0	0	13	22
Leadoff	.405	.463	.500	74	30	5	1	0	0	7	11
Not Leadoff	.269	.329	.295	78	21	2	0	0	0	6	11
Runners On	.371	.426	.567	178	66	10	2	7	61	19	18
First Base Only	.380	.421	.620	71	27	4	2	3	9	3	4
Scoring Position	.364	.430	.533	107	39	6	0	4	52	16	14
Late Innings, Close	.452	.550	.581	31	14	1	0	1	9	5	4

RBI/Opportunities		
Scoring Position	45 / 146	(31%)
Scoring Position, 2 Out	11 / 52	(21%)
On Third, Less than 2 Out	19 / 36	(53%)
RBI in close games / RBI Total	21 / 61	(34%)

Dave Gumpert
Chicago Cubs

1986: Power, Groundball 1985: Power, Groundball 1984: Did not play

THREE YEARS (84 – 86)	G	IP	H	BB	SO	SB	CS	W	L	S	ERA
Totals	47	70.0	72	35	49	9	1	3	0	2	4.24
At Home and on the Road											
Home	29	47.0	49	24	35	7	1	2	0	1	4.02
Road	18	23.0	23	11	14	2	0	1	0	1	4.70
During the Day and and at Night											
Day	36	56.2	58	30	43	7	1	3	0	1	3.81
Night	11	13.1	14	5	6	2	0	0	0	1	6.08
On Grass and on Turf											
Grass	37	58.2	57	27	40	7	1	3	0	1	3.53
Turf	10	11.1	15	8	9	2	0	0	0	1	7.94
By Month											
April	1	0.2	1	0	0	0	0	0	0	0	0.00
May	0	0.0	0	0	0	0	0	0	0	0	0.00
June	2	4.2	5	2	1	1	0	0	0	0	1.93
July	12	19.2	18	11	16	1	1	2	0	1	2.75
August	19	31.0	30	13	21	7	0	1	0	0	4.06
Sept/Oct	13	14.0	18	9	11	0	0	0	0	1	7.71

vs. Opponent Batters THREE YEARS (84 – 86)	Ave.	OBP	SLG	AB	H	2B	3B	HR	RBI	BB	SO
Totals	.269	.352	.369	268	72	11	2	4	41	35	49
Pitching vs. Left and Right-handed Batters											
Left	.348	.400	.496	115	40	7	2	2	18	10	11
Right	.209	.319	.275	153	32	4	0	2	23	25	38
Situational											
Bases Empty	.248	.331	.372	129	32	5	1	3	3	16	20
Leadoff	.268	.339	.429	56	15	1	1	2	2	6	7
Not Leadoff	.233	.325	.329	73	17	4	0	1	1	10	13
Runners On	.288	.370	.367	139	40	6	1	1	38	19	29
First Base Only	.191	.255	.234	47	9	2	0	0	1	4	11
Scoring Position	.337	.423	.435	92	31	4	1	1	37	15	18
Late Innings, Close	.343	.396	.485	99	34	7	2	1	14	10	14

RBI/Opportunities		
Scoring Position	36 / 135	(27%)
Scoring Position, 2 Out	12 / 65	(18%)
On Third, Less than 2 Out	13 / 24	(54%)
RBI in close games / RBI Total	16 / 41	(39%)

Jackie Gutierrez
Baltimore Orioles

THREE YEARS (84 – 86)	Ave.	OBP	SLG	AB	H	2B	3B	HR	RBI	BB	SO
Totals	.236	.260	.284	869	205	20	5	4	54	30	113
Batting vs. Left and Right-handed Pitchers											
Left	.235	.255	.304	260	61	7	4	1	17	8	29
Right	.236	.263	.276	609	144	13	1	3	37	22	84
At Home and on the Road											
Home	.233	.260	.290	434	101	13	3	2	34	16	53
Road	.239	.261	.278	435	104	7	2	2	20	14	60
Facing Groundball Pitchers and Flyball Pitchers											
Groundball	.227	.249	.277	444	101	14	1	2	29	14	60
Flyball	.245	.272	.292	425	104	6	4	2	25	16	53
Facing Finesse Pitchers and Power Pitchers											
Finesse	.227	.240	.272	503	114	9	4	2	25	8	57
Power	.249	.288	.301	366	91	11	1	2	29	22	56
On Grass and on Turf											
Grass	.242	.267	.288	736	178	16	3	4	48	26	96
Turf	.203	.225	.263	133	27	4	2	0	6	4	17
During the Day and at Night											
Day	.231	.257	.296	247	57	6	2	2	13	8	26
Night	.238	.262	.280	622	148	14	3	2	41	22	87
By Month											
April	.196	.243	.320	97	19	2	2	2	10	6	6
May	.270	.287	.302	126	34	4	0	0	6	3	12
June	.242	.273	.305	95	23	2	2	0	6	4	16
July	.222	.241	.231	108	24	1	0	0	7	3	14
August	.270	.296	.332	244	66	7	1	2	17	9	27
Sept/Oct	.196	.214	.216	199	39	4	0	0	8	5	38
Situational											
Bases Empty	.265	.290	.325	465	123	13	3	3	3	16	62
Leadoff	.273	.297	.322	205	56	5	1	1	1	7	26
Not Leadoff	.258	.285	.327	260	67	8	2	2	2	9	36
Runners On	.203	.226	.238	404	82	7	2	1	51	14	51
First Base Only	.239	.268	.295	176	42	5	1	1	6	7	22
Scoring Position	.175	.195	.193	228	40	2	1	0	45	7	29
Late Innings, Close	.213	.261	.213	108	23	0	0	0	4	7	20

RBI/Opportunities		
Scoring Position	44 / 294	(15%)
Scoring Position, 2 Out	16 / 128	(13%)
On Third, Less than 2 Out	22 / 54	(41%)
RBI in close games / RBI Total	31 / 54	(57%)

Jose Guzman
Texas Rangers

1986: Finesse, Groundball **1985: Power, Flyball** **1984: Did not play**

THREE YEARS (84 – 86)	G	IP	H	BB	SO	SB	CS	W	L	S	ERA
Totals	34	205.0	226	74	111	21	5	12	17	0	4.26
At Home and on the Road											
Home	20	126.0	135	44	73	11	5	9	7	0	3.36
Road	14	79.0	91	30	38	10	0	3	10	0	5.70
During the Day and and at Night											
Day	7	37.1	46	15	28	9	0	1	5	0	5.79
Night	27	167.2	180	59	83	12	5	11	12	0	3.92
On Grass and on Turf											
Grass	30	182.0	200	69	99	20	5	11	15	0	4.10
Turf	4	23.0	26	5	12	1	0	1	2	0	5.48
By Month											
April	5	27.2	37	7	13	4	1	1	4	0	5.53
May	5	32.2	33	12	19	2	1	3	1	0	2.20
June	6	42.1	44	15	24	6	1	3	3	0	4.46
July	5	28.2	32	13	18	5	1	1	2	0	3.45
August	4	19.2	27	8	7	0	1	1	2	0	7.32
Sept/Oct	9	54.0	53	19	30	4	0	3	5	0	4.00

vs. Opponent Batters THREE YEARS (84 – 86)	Ave.	OBP	SLG	AB	H	2B	3B	HR	RBI	BB	SO
Totals	.280	.344	.427	806	226	40	0	26	89	74	111
Pitching vs. Left and Right-handed Batters											
Left	.297	.352	.461	445	132	28	0	15	52	38	56
Right	.260	.333	.385	361	94	12	0	11	37	36	55
Situational											
Bases Empty	.286	.334	.428	486	139	24	0	15	15	33	71
Leadoff	.251	.312	.404	203	51	10	0	7	7	18	32
Not Leadoff	.311	.350	.445	283	88	14	0	8	8	15	39
Runners On	.272	.358	.425	320	87	16	0	11	74	41	40
First Base Only	.333	.410	.536	138	46	10	0	6	16	16	14
Scoring Position	.225	.319	.341	182	41	6	0	5	58	25	26
Late Innings, Close	.309	.397	.418	55	17	3	0	1	5	8	5

RBI/Opportunities		
Scoring Position	49 / 251	(20%)
Scoring Position, 2 Out	15 / 106	(14%)
On Third, Less than 2 Out	22 / 49	(45%)
RBI in close games / RBI Total	63 / 89	(71%)

Jerry Hairston
Chicago White Sox

THREE YEARS (84 – 86)	Ave.	OBP	SLG	AB	H	2B	3B	HR	RBI	BB	SO
Totals	.260	.363	.389	592	154	36	2	12	65	96	73
Batting vs. Left and Right-handed Pitchers											
Left	.258	.349	.402	132	34	7	0	4	18	17	24
Right	.261	.367	.385	460	120	29	2	8	47	79	49
At Home and on the Road											
Home	.283	.397	.428	290	82	22	1	6	38	56	37
Road	.238	.330	.351	302	72	14	1	6	27	40	36
Facing Groundball Pitchers and Flyball Pitchers											
Groundball	.293	.389	.428	297	87	23	1	5	38	45	36
Flyball	.227	.338	.349	295	67	13	1	7	27	51	37
Facing Finesse Pitchers and Power Pitchers											
Finesse	.307	.399	.486	329	101	27	1	10	43	52	38
Power	.202	.319	.266	263	53	9	1	2	22	44	35
On Grass and on Turf											
Grass	.267	.373	.409	472	126	29	1	12	58	82	59
Turf	.233	.326	.308	120	28	7	1	0	7	14	14
During the Day and at Night											
Day	.268	.379	.353	153	41	10	0	1	11	28	15
Night	.257	.358	.401	439	113	26	2	11	54	68	58
By Month											
April	.295	.360	.455	44	13	1	0	2	8	5	4
May	.195	.315	.345	87	17	4	0	3	15	17	15
June	.263	.400	.368	76	20	5	0	1	9	16	6
July	.360	.471	.550	100	36	10	0	3	15	21	13
August	.220	.314	.309	123	27	6	1	1	4	16	15
Sept/Oct	.253	.341	.364	162	41	10	1	2	14	21	20
Situational											
Bases Empty	.227	.327	.369	344	78	25	0	8	8	49	42
Leadoff	.211	.333	.387	142	30	13	0	4	4	26	17
Not Leadoff	.238	.322	.356	202	48	12	0	4	4	23	25
Runners On	.306	.411	.415	248	76	11	2	4	57	47	31
First Base Only	.351	.435	.447	94	33	5	2	0	4	14	14
Scoring Position	.279	.398	.396	154	43	6	0	4	53	33	17
Late Innings, Close	.291	.385	.412	165	48	11	0	3	17	25	23

RBI/Opportunities		
Scoring Position	48 / 227	(21%)
Scoring Position, 2 Out	17 / 118	(14%)
On Third, Less than 2 Out	22 / 41	(54%)
RBI in close games / RBI Total	40 / 65	(62%)

Jeff Hamilton
Los Angeles Dodgers

THREE YEARS (84 – 86)	Ave.	OBP	SLG	AB	H	2B	3B	HR	RBI	BB	SO
Totals	.224	.232	.361	147	33	5	0	5	19	2	43
Batting vs. Left and Right-handed Pitchers											
Left	.273	.281	.382	55	15	3	0	1	8	1	11
Right	.196	.202	.348	92	18	2	0	4	11	1	32
At Home and on the Road											
Home	.282	.282	.437	71	20	5	0	2	11	0	22
Road	.171	.188	.289	76	13	0	0	3	8	2	21
Facing Groundball Pitchers and Flyball Pitchers											
Groundball	.213	.210	.279	61	13	1	0	1	9	0	16
Flyball	.233	.247	.419	86	20	4	0	4	10	2	27
Facing Finesse Pitchers and Power Pitchers											
Finesse	.253	.263	.413	75	19	3	0	3	10	1	21
Power	.194	.200	.306	72	14	2	0	2	9	1	22
On Grass and on Turf											
Grass	.239	.237	.389	113	27	5	0	4	17	0	36
Turf	.176	.216	.265	34	6	0	0	1	2	2	7
During the Day and at Night											
Day	.216	.231	.297	37	8	0	0	1	6	1	13
Night	.227	.232	.382	110	25	5	0	4	13	1	30
By Month											
April	.000	.000	.000	0	0	0	0	0	0	0	0
May	.000	.000	.000	0	0	0	0	0	0	0	0
June	.182	.231	.182	11	2	0	0	0	1	1	3
July	.241	.254	.414	58	14	4	0	2	11	1	16
August	.261	.261	.261	23	6	0	0	0	2	0	10
Sept/Oct	.200	.196	.382	55	11	1	0	3	5	0	14
Situational											
Bases Empty	.174	.184	.372	86	15	2	0	5	5	1	30
Leadoff	.118	.118	.206	34	4	0	0	1	1	0	16
Not Leadoff	.212	.226	.481	52	11	2	0	4	4	1	14
Runners On	.295	.297	.344	61	18	3	0	0	14	1	13
First Base Only	.286	.286	.357	28	8	2	0	0	6	0	8
Scoring Position	.303	.306	.333	33	10	1	0	0	13	1	5
Late Innings, Close	.233	.258	.467	30	7	1	0	2	5	1	6

RBI/Opportunities		
Scoring Position	12 / 50	(24%)
Scoring Position, 2 Out	2 / 15	(13%)
On Third, Less than 2 Out	7 / 14	(50%)
RBI in close games / RBI Total	14 / 19	(74%)

Terry Harper
Atlanta Braves

THREE YEARS (84 – 86)	Ave.	OBP	SLG	AB	H	2B	3B	HR	RBI	BB	SO
Totals	.249	.313	.378	859	214	30	3	25	110	77	136
Batting vs. Left and Right-handed Pitchers											
Left	.231	.285	.364	346	80	14	1	10	43	27	48
Right	.261	.332	.388	513	134	16	2	15	67	50	88
At Home and on the Road											
Home	.283	.349	.427	403	114	20	1	12	57	38	66
Road	.219	.281	.336	456	100	10	2	13	53	39	70
Facing Groundball Pitchers and Flyball Pitchers											
Groundball	.255	.329	.394	411	105	10	1	15	66	42	60
Flyball	.243	.298	.364	448	109	20	2	10	44	35	76
Facing Finesse Pitchers and Power Pitchers											
Finesse	.241	.303	.397	474	114	16	2	18	74	41	59
Power	.260	.325	.356	385	100	14	1	7	36	36	77
On Grass and on Turf											
Grass	.269	.331	.399	602	162	24	3	16	84	53	95
Turf	.202	.271	.331	257	52	6	0	9	26	24	41
During the Day and at Night											
Day	.227	.301	.376	295	67	8	0	12	42	30	45
Night	.261	.319	.379	564	147	22	3	13	68	47	91
By Month											
April	.214	.293	.291	103	22	3	1	1	13	10	21
May	.232	.302	.411	190	44	8	1	8	27	18	36
June	.218	.299	.286	147	32	4	0	2	17	17	23
July	.267	.308	.436	172	46	3	1	8	27	10	26
August	.205	.279	.333	117	24	3	0	4	11	12	12
Sept/Oct	.354	.400	.469	130	46	9	0	2	15	10	18
Situational											
Bases Empty	.262	.312	.394	470	123	19	2	13	13	32	59
Leadoff	.245	.298	.455	200	49	10	1	10	10	15	28
Not Leadoff	.274	.322	.348	270	74	9	1	3	3	17	31
Runners On	.234	.314	.360	389	91	11	1	12	97	45	77
First Base Only	.215	.304	.337	172	37	3	0	6	13	21	32
Scoring Position	.249	.323	.378	217	54	8	1	6	84	24	45
Late Innings, Close	.314	.388	.478	159	50	11	0	5	24	18	20

RBI/Opportunities		
Scoring Position	71 / 294	(24%)
Scoring Position, 2 Out	38 / 151	(25%)
On Third, Less than 2 Out	20 / 44	(45%)
RBI in close games / RBI Total	71 / 110	(65%)

Toby Harrah
Texas Rangers

THREE YEARS (84 – 86)	Ave.	OBP	SLG	AB	H	2B	3B	HR	RBI	BB	SO
Totals	.240	.374	.357	938	225	45	7	17	111	199	141
Batting vs. Left and Right-handed Pitchers											
Left	.262	.400	.392	385	101	21	4	7	49	90	52
Right	.224	.355	.333	553	124	24	3	10	62	109	89
At Home and on the Road											
Home	.246	.383	.355	448	110	19	3	8	53	99	63
Road	.235	.365	.359	490	115	26	4	9	58	100	78
Facing Groundball Pitchers and Flyball Pitchers											
Groundball	.267	.409	.381	420	112	24	3	6	55	101	49
Flyball	.218	.344	.338	518	113	21	4	11	56	98	92
Facing Finesse Pitchers and Power Pitchers											
Finesse	.253	.381	.374	513	130	26	6	8	62	107	61
Power	.224	.365	.336	425	95	19	1	9	49	92	80
On Grass and on Turf											
Grass	.242	.376	.349	794	192	35	4	14	92	169	119
Turf	.229	.362	.403	144	33	10	3	3	19	30	22
During the Day and at Night											
Day	.231	.359	.325	212	49	11	0	3	25	43	34
Night	.242	.378	.366	726	176	34	7	14	86	156	107
By Month											
April	.241	.384	.362	141	34	9	1	2	20	32	14
May	.215	.379	.311	219	47	9	3	2	15	57	39
June	.239	.356	.362	163	39	3	1	5	23	28	22
July	.265	.379	.359	117	31	8	0	1	9	21	19
August	.260	.386	.434	196	51	9	2	7	30	41	35
Sept/Oct	.225	.347	.294	102	23	7	0	0	14	20	12
Situational											
Bases Empty	.219	.354	.335	544	119	26	2	11	11	111	89
Leadoff	.241	.365	.336	232	56	13	0	3	3	45	44
Not Leadoff	.202	.346	.333	312	63	13	2	8	8	66	45
Runners On	.269	.400	.388	394	106	19	5	6	100	88	52
First Base Only	.244	.392	.341	164	40	4	3	2	8	38	18
Scoring Position	.287	.405	.422	230	66	15	2	4	92	50	34
Late Innings, Close	.250	.373	.355	172	43	6	0	4	27	33	24

RBI/Opportunities		
Scoring Position	84 / 349	(24%)
Scoring Position, 2 Out	27 / 155	(17%)
On Third, Less than 2 Out	36 / 62	(58%)
RBI in close games / RBI Total	72 / 111	(65%)

Mickey Hatcher
Minnesota Twins

THREE YEARS (84 – 86)	Ave.	OBP	SLG	AB	H	2B	3B	HR	RBI	BB	SO
Totals	.289	.324	.383	1337	387	76	8	11	150	72	83
Batting vs. Left and Right-handed Pitchers											
Left	.326	.363	.442	448	146	30	2	6	58	30	25
Right	.271	.304	.353	889	241	46	6	5	92	42	58
At Home and on the Road											
Home	.302	.334	.421	686	207	50	7	6	78	34	44
Road	.276	.314	.343	651	180	26	1	5	72	38	39
Facing Groundball Pitchers and Flyball Pitchers											
Groundball	.310	.338	.399	632	196	39	4	3	90	30	30
Flyball	.271	.312	.369	705	191	37	4	8	60	42	53
Facing Finesse Pitchers and Power Pitchers											
Finesse	.298	.331	.388	738	220	35	5	7	73	38	41
Power	.279	.317	.377	599	167	41	3	4	77	34	42
On Grass and on Turf											
Grass	.265	.309	.329	513	136	19	1	4	58	34	32
Turf	.305	.334	.416	824	251	57	7	7	92	38	51
During the Day and at Night											
Day	.319	.352	.420	429	137	22	3	5	49	21	29
Night	.275	.312	.366	908	250	54	5	6	101	51	54
By Month											
April	.250	.260	.347	216	54	11	2	2	24	4	11
May	.320	.353	.407	253	81	14	1	2	27	14	18
June	.278	.328	.339	248	69	13	1	0	21	18	17
July	.259	.310	.351	174	45	8	1	2	18	11	15
August	.305	.349	.421	233	71	19	1	2	35	16	13
Sept/Oct	.315	.333	.427	213	67	11	2	3	25	9	9
Situational											
Bases Empty	.272	.311	.358	749	204	42	5	4	4	39	48
Leadoff	.276	.308	.390	254	70	15	4	2	2	9	17
Not Leadoff	.271	.315	.341	495	134	27	1	2	2	30	31
Runners On	.311	.341	.415	588	183	34	3	7	146	33	35
First Base Only	.317	.335	.408	262	83	13	1	3	9	7	14
Scoring Position	.307	.346	.420	326	100	21	2	4	137	26	21
Late Innings, Close	.269	.316	.363	182	49	8	0	3	30	12	12

RBI/Opportunities		
Scoring Position	125 / 424	(29%)
Scoring Position, 2 Out	52 / 205	(25%)
On Third, Less than 2 Out	50 / 87	(57%)
RBI in close games / RBI Total	84 / 150	(56%)

Brad Havens
Baltimore Orioles

1986: Power, Flyball   1985: Power, Flyball   1984: Did not play

THREE YEARS (84 – 86)	G	IP	H	BB	SO	SB	CS	W	L	S	ERA
Totals	54	85.1	84	39	76	8	5	3	4	1	5.27
At Home and on the Road											
Home	31	47.1	51	22	46	4	2	1	2	0	5.32
Road	23	38.0	33	17	30	4	3	2	2	1	5.21
During the Day and and at Night											
Day	23	40.1	37	17	40	2	2	3	2	0	4.69
Night	31	45.0	47	22	36	6	3	0	2	1	5.80
On Grass and on Turf											
Grass	47	78.0	75	36	70	8	4	2	4	1	4.96
Turf	7	7.1	9	3	6	0	1	1	0	0	8.59
By Month											
April	6	11.0	13	6	8	1	1	1	1	0	7.36
May	7	13.1	12	3	12	1	1	1	0	0	4.73
June	10	15.1	14	9	9	3	0	0	0	0	3.52
July	7	7.2	7	2	6	1	1	1	0	1	3.52
August	11	15.0	11	4	11	0	1	0	1	0	4.80
Sept/Oct	13	23.0	27	15	30	2	1	0	2	0	6.65

vs. Opponent Batters

THREE YEARS (84 – 86)	Ave.	OBP	SLG	AB	H	2B	3B	HR	RBI	BB	SO
Totals	.264	.344	.447	318	84	19	3	11	56	39	76
Pitching vs. Left and Right-handed Batters											
Left	.221	.304	.352	122	27	5	1	3	17	15	30
Right	.291	.368	.505	196	57	14	2	8	39	24	46
Situational											
Bases Empty	.235	.306	.392	166	39	9	1	5	5	17	38
Leadoff	.194	.280	.343	67	13	4	0	2	2	8	17
Not Leadoff	.263	.324	.424	99	26	5	1	3	3	9	21
Runners On	.296	.383	.507	152	45	10	2	6	51	22	38
First Base Only	.245	.327	.347	49	12	0	1	1	3	6	12
Scoring Position	.320	.408	.583	103	33	10	1	5	48	16	26
Late Innings, Close	.349	.429	.442	43	15	1	0	1	6	6	10

RBI/Opportunities		
Scoring Position	41 / 153	(27%)
Scoring Position, 2 Out	15 / 73	(21%)
On Third, Less than 2 Out	13 / 28	(46%)
RBI in close games / RBI Total	14 / 56	(25%)

Ed Hearn
New York Mets

THREE YEARS (84 – 86)

	Ave.	OBP	SLG	AB	H	2B	3B	HR	RBI	BB	SO
Totals	.265	.322	.390	136	36	5	0	4	10	12	19
Batting vs. Left and Right-handed Pitchers											
Left	.234	.275	.328	64	15	0	0	2	5	4	10
Right	.292	.362	.444	72	21	5	0	2	5	8	9
At Home and on the Road											
Home	.250	.333	.453	64	16	1	0	4	7	8	8
Road	.278	.312	.333	72	20	4	0	0	3	4	11
Facing Groundball Pitchers and Flyball Pitchers											
Groundball	.278	.342	.347	72	20	2	0	1	3	7	11
Flyball	.250	.300	.438	64	16	3	0	3	7	5	8
Facing Finesse Pitchers and Power Pitchers											
Finesse	.273	.324	.303	66	18	2	0	0	1	5	4
Power	.257	.321	.471	70	18	3	0	4	9	7	15
On Grass and on Turf											
Grass	.257	.328	.385	109	28	2	0	4	9	12	14
Turf	.296	.296	.407	27	8	3	0	0	1	0	5
During the Day and at Night											
Day	.266	.333	.380	79	21	3	0	2	6	8	9
Night	.263	.306	.404	57	15	2	0	2	4	4	10
By Month											
April	.000	.000	.000	0	0	0	0	0	0	0	0
May	.429	.556	.571	7	3	1	0	0	0	2	1
June	.240	.296	.560	25	6	2	0	2	4	2	5
July	.333	.391	.524	21	7	1	0	1	2	2	3
August	.250	.292	.317	60	15	1	0	1	3	4	8
Sept/Oct	.217	.280	.217	23	5	0	0	0	1	2	2
Situational											
Bases Empty	.325	.365	.500	80	26	5	0	3	3	5	10
Leadoff	.324	.361	.382	34	11	2	0	0	0	2	4
Not Leadoff	.326	.367	.587	46	15	3	0	3	3	3	6
Runners On	.179	.266	.232	56	10	0	0	1	7	7	9
First Base Only	.269	.269	.269	26	7	0	0	0	0	0	3
Scoring Position	.100	.263	.200	30	3	0	0	1	7	7	6
Late Innings, Close	.320	.393	.360	25	8	1	0	1	0	3	2

RBI/Opportunities

Scoring Position	5 / 46	(11%)
Scoring Position, 2 Out	2 / 21	(10%)
On Third, Less than 2 Out	3 / 8	(38%)
RBI in close games / RBI Total	6 / 10	(60%)

Mike Heath
Detroit Tigers

THREE YEARS (84 – 86)

	Ave.	OBP	SLG	AB	H	2B	3B	HR	RBI	BB	SO
Totals	.244	.298	.390	1199	292	50	12	34	155	95	188
Batting vs. Left and Right-handed Pitchers											
Left	.279	.330	.457	499	139	29	6	16	75	41	77
Right	.219	.276	.343	700	153	21	6	18	80	54	111
At Home and on the Road											
Home	.247	.298	.408	578	143	21	6	20	75	42	84
Road	.240	.299	.374	621	149	29	6	14	80	53	104
Facing Groundball Pitchers and Flyball Pitchers											
Groundball	.234	.300	.371	563	132	26	3	15	79	53	79
Flyball	.252	.297	.407	636	160	24	9	19	76	42	109
Facing Finesse Pitchers and Power Pitchers											
Finesse	.242	.288	.388	637	154	21	9	18	86	40	71
Power	.246	.310	.393	562	138	29	3	16	69	55	117
On Grass and on Turf											
Grass	.252	.302	.405	869	219	33	8	28	115	63	142
Turf	.221	.290	.352	330	73	17	4	6	40	32	46
During the Day and at Night											
Day	.269	.323	.437	398	107	17	7	12	55	30	61
Night	.231	.287	.367	801	185	33	5	22	100	65	127
By Month											
April	.222	.294	.383	180	40	10	2	5	24	18	25
May	.255	.325	.373	220	56	7	2	5	29	23	33
June	.234	.270	.386	184	43	6	2	6	21	10	27
July	.265	.301	.417	204	54	9	2	4	24	12	37
August	.209	.280	.326	230	48	9	0	6	28	21	38
Sept/Oct	.282	.320	.475	181	51	9	4	6	29	11	28
Situational											
Bases Empty	.224	.271	.367	679	152	27	5	20	20	43	103
Leadoff	.252	.300	.398	274	69	13	3	7	7	19	38
Not Leadoff	.205	.251	.346	405	83	14	2	13	13	24	65
Runners On	.269	.332	.421	520	140	23	7	14	135	52	85
First Base Only	.247	.289	.391	235	58	8	4	6	18	13	36
Scoring Position	.288	.364	.446	285	82	15	3	8	117	39	49
Late Innings, Close	.214	.279	.329	210	45	8	2	4	17	19	38

RBI/Opportunities

Scoring Position	100 / 407	(25%)
Scoring Position, 2 Out	48 / 195	(25%)
On Third, Less than 2 Out	31 / 61	(51%)
RBI in close games / RBI Total	106 / 155	(68%)

Neal Heaton
Minnesota Twins

1986: Finesse, Flyball   1985: Finesse, Flyball   1984: Finesse, Flyball

THREE YEARS (84 – 86)

	G	IP	H	BB	SO	SB	CS	W	L	S	ERA
Totals	107	605.0	676	236	247	53	29	28	47	1	4.73
At Home and on the Road											
Home	52	324.1	346	111	138	23	18	17	20	1	3.86
Road	55	280.2	330	125	109	30	11	11	27	0	5.74
During the Day and at Night											
Day	36	205.1	223	80	75	20	7	11	13	0	4.16
Night	71	399.2	453	156	172	33	22	17	34	1	5.02
On Grass and on Turf											
Grass	84	465.0	532	181	183	36	24	23	37	0	4.84
Turf	23	140.0	144	55	64	17	5	5	10	1	4.37
By Month											
April	14	82.2	87	37	26	6	2	3	4	0	3.48
May	18	107.0	106	44	41	9	10	5	8	0	4.54
June	18	93.2	103	36	30	9	4	4	9	1	5.09
July	20	107.2	115	47	52	12	3	5	11	0	4.93
August	18	109.2	137	31	54	9	7	5	7	0	4.60
Sept/Oct	19	104.1	128	41	44	8	3	6	8	0	5.52

vs. Opponent Batters
THREE YEARS (84 – 86)

	Ave.	OBP	SLG	AB	H	2B	3B	HR	RBI	BB	SO
Totals	.286	.350	.437	2364	676	129	15	66	306	236	247
Pitching vs. Left and Right-handed Batters											
Left	.286	.343	.445	447	128	28	5	11	64	39	55
Right	.286	.352	.435	1917	548	101	10	55	242	197	192
Situational											
Bases Empty	.298	.358	.447	1333	397	65	10	38	38	121	145
Leadoff	.303	.362	.471	588	178	34	7	17	17	54	66
Not Leadoff	.294	.355	.428	745	219	31	3	21	21	67	79
Runners On	.271	.340	.424	1031	279	64	5	28	268	115	102
First Base Only	.262	.321	.389	493	129	31	1	10	39	41	50
Scoring Position	.279	.356	.455	538	150	33	4	18	229	74	52
Late Innings, Close	.299	.364	.490	147	44	11	1	5	16	15	16

RBI/Opportunities

Scoring Position	196 / 735	(27%)
Scoring Position, 2 Out	75 / 336	(22%)
On Third, Less than 2 Out	75 / 142	(53%)
RBI in close games / RBI Total	215 / 306	(70%)

Danny Heep
New York Mets

THREE YEARS (84 – 86)

	Ave.	OBP	SLG	AB	H	2B	3B	HR	RBI	BB	SO
Totals	.266	.345	.388	665	177	34	4	13	87	83	80
Batting vs. Left and Right-handed Pitchers											
Left	.241	.357	.291	79	19	4	0	0	14	14	15
Right	.270	.343	.401	586	158	30	4	13	73	69	65
At Home and on the Road											
Home	.284	.370	.396	313	89	13	2	6	38	42	35
Road	.250	.322	.381	352	88	21	2	7	49	41	45
Facing Groundball Pitchers and Flyball Pitchers											
Groundball	.269	.354	.382	275	74	12	2	5	41	38	29
Flyball	.264	.338	.392	390	103	22	2	8	46	45	51
Facing Finesse Pitchers and Power Pitchers											
Finesse	.275	.331	.412	345	95	16	2	9	47	30	34
Power	.256	.359	.362	320	82	18	2	4	40	53	46
On Grass and on Turf											
Grass	.266	.342	.381	467	124	23	2	9	55	55	56
Turf	.268	.351	.404	198	53	11	2	4	32	28	24
During the Day and at Night											
Day	.289	.378	.429	287	83	16	0	8	42	41	26
Night	.249	.319	.357	378	94	18	4	5	45	42	54
By Month											
April	.323	.354	.468	62	20	4	1	1	14	3	7
May	.250	.323	.398	108	27	8	1	2	12	13	15
June	.272	.366	.432	162	44	8	0	6	21	25	17
July	.260	.338	.328	131	34	4	1	1	11	17	16
August	.269	.327	.365	104	28	4	0	2	9	9	10
Sept/Oct	.245	.353	.357	98	24	6	1	1	20	16	15
Situational											
Bases Empty	.244	.325	.335	385	94	14	3	5	5	44	47
Leadoff	.244	.305	.319	160	39	5	2	1	1	13	19
Not Leadoff	.244	.339	.347	225	55	9	1	4	4	31	28
Runners On	.296	.370	.461	280	83	20	1	8	82	39	33
First Base Only	.320	.366	.496	125	40	10	0	4	9	9	12
Scoring Position	.277	.374	.432	155	43	10	1	4	73	30	21
Late Innings, Close	.283	.374	.406	138	39	6	1	3	19	22	21

RBI/Opportunities

Scoring Position	63 / 241	(26%)
Scoring Position, 2 Out	24 / 109	(22%)
On Third, Less than 2 Out	25 / 48	(52%)
RBI in close games / RBI Total	49 / 87	(56%)

Dave Henderson
Boston Red Sox

	Ave.	OBP	SLG	AB	H	2B	3B	HR	RBI	BB	SO
				THREE YEARS (84 – 86)							
Totals	.260	.321	.432	1240	322	73	6	43	158	106	270
			Batting vs. Left and Right-handed Pitchers								
Left	.281	.335	.469	367	103	23	2	14	54	27	57
Right	.251	.315	.417	873	219	50	4	29	104	79	213
			At Home and on the Road								
Home	.280	.342	.473	647	181	37	5	26	94	57	128
Road	.238	.297	.388	593	141	36	1	17	64	49	142
			Facing Groundball Pitchers and Flyball Pitchers								
Groundball	.259	.319	.422	583	151	31	2	20	73	50	130
Flyball	.260	.322	.441	657	171	42	4	23	85	56	140
			Facing Finesse Pitchers and Power Pitchers								
Finesse	.256	.319	.409	694	178	36	5	20	87	62	124
Power	.264	.322	.462	546	144	37	1	23	71	44	146
			On Grass and on Turf								
Grass	.218	.279	.353	499	109	28	0	13	48	41	122
Turf	.287	.348	.486	741	213	45	6	30	110	65	148
			During the Day and at Night								
Day	.273	.327	.457	304	83	17	0	13	45	24	58
Night	.255	.318	.424	936	239	56	6	30	113	82	212
			By Month								
April	.205	.293	.323	161	33	5	1	4	16	19	43
May	.271	.324	.457	221	60	9	1	10	29	17	44
June	.258	.321	.437	252	65	16	1	9	34	22	58
July	.272	.324	.474	228	62	12	2	10	32	18	46
August	.272	.339	.418	158	43	12	1	3	14	14	35
Sept/Oct	.268	.321	.450	220	59	19	0	7	33	16	44
			Situational								
Bases Empty	.257	.324	.460	692	178	42	4	30	30	64	151
Leadoff	.286	.340	.482	280	80	18	2	11	11	21	54
Not Leadoff	.238	.313	.444	412	98	24	2	19	19	43	97
Runners On	.263	.317	.398	548	144	31	2	13	128	42	119
First Base Only	.237	.272	.379	232	55	13	1	6	17	11	55
Scoring Position	.282	.347	.411	316	89	18	1	7	111	31	64
Late Innings, Close	.263	.311	.505	198	52	7	1	13	26	13	45

RBI/Opportunities		
Scoring Position	95 / 425	(22%)
Scoring Position, 2 Out	49 / 222	(22%)
On Third, Less than 2 Out	27 / 70	(39%)
RBI in close games / RBI Total	94 / 158	(59%)

George Hendrick
California Angels

	Ave.	OBP	SLG	AB	H	2B	3B	HR	RBI	BB	SO
				THREE YEARS (84 – 86)							
Totals	.258	.309	.397	1021	263	57	2	27	147	80	166
			Batting vs. Left and Right-handed Pitchers								
Left	.262	.318	.416	450	118	28	1	13	64	40	55
Right	.254	.303	.382	571	145	29	1	14	83	40	111
			At Home and on the Road								
Home	.254	.309	.372	524	133	32	0	10	77	43	82
Road	.262	.310	.423	497	130	25	2	17	70	37	84
			Facing Groundball Pitchers and Flyball Pitchers								
Groundball	.254	.312	.374	460	117	26	1	9	64	40	72
Flyball	.260	.307	.415	561	146	31	1	18	83	40	94
			Facing Finesse Pitchers and Power Pitchers								
Finesse	.237	.288	.348	561	133	33	1	9	65	41	90
Power	.283	.335	.457	460	130	24	1	18	82	39	76
			On Grass and on Turf								
Grass	.252	.312	.404	460	116	23	1	15	59	41	72
Turf	.262	.307	.390	561	147	34	1	12	88	39	94
			During the Day and at Night								
Day	.280	.325	.449	296	83	14	0	12	46	20	44
Night	.248	.303	.375	725	180	43	2	15	101	60	122
			By Month								
April	.264	.314	.415	159	42	6	0	6	19	12	20
May	.250	.298	.381	236	59	14	1	5	32	17	48
June	.244	.316	.343	201	49	11	0	3	29	21	41
July	.250	.298	.386	176	44	12	0	4	24	13	20
August	.278	.328	.402	169	47	10	1	3	25	13	28
Sept/Oct	.275	.302	.550	80	22	4	0	6	18	4	9
			Situational								
Bases Empty	.264	.310	.419	535	141	28	2	17	17	34	91
Leadoff	.280	.330	.412	243	68	14	0	6	6	18	37
Not Leadoff	.250	.294	.425	292	73	14	2	11	11	16	54
Runners On	.251	.309	.372	486	122	29	0	10	130	46	75
First Base Only	.222	.276	.376	189	42	14	0	5	13	14	23
Scoring Position	.269	.328	.370	297	80	15	0	5	117	32	52
Late Innings, Close	.193	.255	.295	176	34	9	0	3	15	15	40

RBI/Opportunities		
Scoring Position	106 / 403	(26%)
Scoring Position, 2 Out	43 / 198	(22%)
On Third, Less than 2 Out	44 / 80	(55%)
RBI in close games / RBI Total	96 / 147	(65%)

Larry Herndon
Detroit Tigers

	Ave.	OBP	SLG	AB	H	2B	3B	HR	RBI	BB	SO
				THREE YEARS (84 – 86)							
Totals	.258	.314	.390	1132	292	43	13	27	117	92	182
			Batting vs. Left and Right-handed Pitchers								
Left	.273	.337	.430	567	155	20	9	17	72	56	76
Right	.242	.290	.350	565	137	23	4	10	45	36	106
			At Home and on the Road								
Home	.272	.324	.411	552	150	19	8	14	55	43	82
Road	.245	.303	.371	580	142	24	5	13	62	49	100
			Facing Groundball Pitchers and Flyball Pitchers								
Groundball	.253	.305	.367	521	132	15	4	12	54	39	88
Flyball	.262	.311	.411	611	160	28	9	15	63	53	94
			Facing Finesse Pitchers and Power Pitchers								
Finesse	.269	.314	.402	650	175	23	9	15	62	41	80
Power	.243	.313	.376	482	117	20	4	12	55	51	102
			On Grass and on Turf								
Grass	.265	.324	.404	969	257	37	11	25	109	84	163
Turf	.215	.251	.313	163	35	6	2	2	8	8	19
			During the Day and at Night								
Day	.246	.334	.379	354	87	21	1	8	33	46	58
Night	.263	.304	.396	778	205	22	12	19	84	46	124
			By Month								
April	.245	.307	.350	200	49	12	3	1	12	17	29
May	.231	.291	.361	208	48	10	1	5	20	18	43
June	.251	.295	.359	223	56	6	3	4	20	14	36
July	.282	.310	.412	177	50	7	2	4	22	8	27
August	.264	.337	.429	163	43	6	3	5	19	17	26
Sept/Oct	.286	.354	.460	161	46	2	1	8	24	18	21
			Situational								
Bases Empty	.274	.324	.423	636	174	21	10	18	18	45	90
Leadoff	.287	.327	.461	254	73	6	7	8	8	14	28
Not Leadoff	.264	.321	.398	382	101	15	3	10	10	31	62
Runners On	.238	.301	.349	496	118	22	3	9	99	47	92
First Base Only	.268	.317	.397	224	60	12	1	5	14	15	41
Scoring Position	.213	.290	.309	272	58	10	2	4	85	32	51
Late Innings, Close	.258	.332	.365	178	46	6	2	3	21	19	34

RBI/Opportunities		
Scoring Position	75 / 379	(20%)
Scoring Position, 2 Out	33 / 173	(19%)
On Third, Less than 2 Out	28 / 66	(42%)
RBI in close games / RBI Total	64 / 117	(55%)

Joe Hesketh
Montreal Expos

1986: Power, Flyball   1985: Power, Flyball   1984: Power, Flyball

	G	IP	H	BB	SO	SB	CS	W	L	S	ERA
			THREE YEARS (84 – 86)								
Totals	51	283.0	255	91	212	28	11	18	12	1	3.12
			At Home and on the Road								
Home	26	145.0	142	41	122	12	3	10	6	0	3.23
Road	25	138.0	113	50	90	16	8	8	6	1	3.00
			During the Day and and at Night								
Day	19	102.1	107	32	71	14	5	6	8	0	3.69
Night	32	180.2	148	59	141	14	6	12	4	1	2.79
			On Grass and on Turf								
Grass	9	61.1	44	25	37	6	2	5	2	0	1.91
Turf	42	221.2	211	66	175	22	9	13	10	1	3.45
			By Month								
April	6	34.1	37	11	28	9	2	4	0	0	4.98
May	11	70.1	52	21	59	3	3	6	1	0	2.56
June	12	68.0	71	20	47	10	2	3	2	0	3.57
July	6	42.0	35	16	33	1	1	3	2	0	2.79
August	9	44.2	39	15	27	5	3	1	0	0	2.82
Sept/Oct	7	23.2	21	8	18	0	0	1	2	1	1.90

vs. Opponent Batters

	Ave.	OBP	SLG	AB	H	2B	3B	HR	RBI	BB	SO
				THREE YEARS (84 – 86)							
Totals	.243	.303	.374	1050	255	59	5	23	99	91	212
			Pitching vs. Left and Right-handed Batters								
Left	.212	.278	.261	165	35	3	1	1	14	14	37
Right	.249	.308	.395	885	220	56	4	22	85	77	175
			Situational								
Bases Empty	.231	.291	.344	655	151	29	3	13	13	55	131
Leadoff	.215	.271	.341	270	58	12	2	6	6	21	43
Not Leadoff	.242	.305	.345	385	93	17	1	7	7	34	88
Runners On	.263	.322	.425	395	104	30	2	10	86	36	81
First Base Only	.277	.326	.458	177	49	17	0	5	15	13	29
Scoring Position	.252	.319	.399	218	55	13	2	5	71	23	52
Late Innings, Close	.282	.345	.340	103	29	6	0	0	4	10	27

RBI/Opportunities		
Scoring Position	62 / 279	(22%)
Scoring Position, 2 Out	26 / 131	(20%)
On Third, Less than 2 Out	25 / 58	(43%)
RBI in close games / RBI Total	81 / 99	(82%)

Donnie Hill
Oakland A's

THREE YEARS (84 – 86)	Ave.	OBP	SLG	AB	H	2B	3B	HR	RBI	BB	SO
Totals	.274	.310	.351	906	248	35	4	9	93	51	84
Batting vs. Left and Right-handed Pitchers											
Left	.249	.294	.311	273	68	12	1	1	22	18	29
Right	.284	.318	.368	633	180	23	3	8	71	33	55
At Home and on the Road											
Home	.265	.303	.317	441	117	17	3	0	33	25	45
Road	.282	.318	.383	465	131	18	1	9	60	26	39
Facing Groundball Pitchers and Flyball Pitchers											
Groundball	.299	.330	.357	431	129	17	1	2	47	21	39
Flyball	.251	.293	.345	475	119	18	3	7	46	30	45
Facing Finesse Pitchers and Power Pitchers											
Finesse	.290	.313	.375	517	150	17	3	7	48	18	44
Power	.252	.308	.319	389	98	18	1	2	45	33	40
On Grass and on Turf											
Grass	.262	.300	.316	749	196	26	3	3	68	43	71
Turf	.331	.359	.516	157	52	9	1	6	25	8	13
During the Day and at Night											
Day	.313	.355	.388	348	109	13	2	3	40	24	27
Night	.249	.282	.328	558	139	22	2	6	53	27	57
By Month											
April	.234	.272	.351	154	36	4	1	4	17	8	9
May	.281	.308	.324	139	39	3	0	1	14	6	16
June	.255	.314	.305	141	36	5	1	0	10	12	14
July	.280	.294	.348	161	45	8	0	1	16	5	12
August	.311	.350	.403	206	64	14	1	1	24	13	18
Sept/Oct	.267	.313	.352	105	28	1	1	2	12	7	15
Situational											
Bases Empty	.258	.299	.330	503	130	20	2	4	4	29	52
Leadoff	.264	.317	.363	193	51	8	1	3	3	15	14
Not Leadoff	.255	.287	.310	310	79	12	1	1	1	14	38
Runners On	.293	.325	.377	403	118	15	2	5	89	22	32
First Base Only	.279	.304	.370	165	46	7	1	2	7	6	12
Scoring Position	.303	.338	.382	238	72	8	1	3	82	16	20
Late Innings, Close	.287	.338	.368	136	39	3	1	2	8	11	8

RBI/Opportunities		
Scoring Position	75 / 309	(24%)
Scoring Position, 2 Out	34 / 129	(26%)
On Third, Less than 2 Out	28 / 54	(52%)
RBI in close games / RBI Total	43 / 93	(46%)

Guy Hoffman
Chicago Cubs

1986: Finesse, Flyball — 1985: Did not play — 1984: Did not play

THREE YEARS (84 – 86)	G	IP	H	BB	SO	SB	CS	W	L	S	ERA
Totals	32	84.0	92	29	47	3	10	6	2	0	3.86
At Home and on the Road											
Home	14	48.2	50	11	32	1	5	4	0	0	3.33
Road	18	35.1	42	18	15	2	5	2	2	0	4.58
During the Day and and at Night											
Day	19	58.1	59	15	38	1	7	5	0	0	3.09
Night	13	25.2	33	14	9	2	3	1	2	0	5.61
On Grass and on Turf											
Grass	20	61.1	67	20	36	1	6	4	1	0	3.82
Turf	12	22.2	25	9	11	2	4	2	1	0	3.97
By Month											
April	1	7.0	6	1	5	0	1	0	0	0	2.57
May	6	22.1	29	8	11	1	3	1	1	0	6.04
June	9	25.1	29	8	15	2	3	2	1	0	3.20
July	4	9.1	11	5	4	0	1	1	0	0	5.79
August	0	0.0	0	0	0	0	0	0	0	0	0.00
Sept/Oct	12	20.0	17	7	12	0	2	2	0	0	1.80

vs. Opponent Batters — THREE YEARS (84 – 86)	Ave.	OBP	SLG	AB	H	2B	3B	HR	RBI	BB	SO
Totals	.288	.348	.411	319	92	21	0	6	42	29	47
Pitching vs. Left and Right-handed Batters											
Left	.246	.367	.308	65	16	4	0	0	9	12	11
Right	.299	.343	.437	254	76	17	0	6	33	17	36
Situational											
Bases Empty	.290	.339	.409	176	51	12	0	3	3	12	30
Leadoff	.333	.390	.427	75	25	7	0	0	0	6	12
Not Leadoff	.257	.299	.396	101	26	5	0	3	3	6	18
Runners On	.287	.360	.413	143	41	9	0	3	39	17	17
First Base Only	.262	.297	.361	61	16	3	0	1	4	2	4
Scoring Position	.305	.400	.451	82	25	6	0	2	35	15	13
Late Innings, Close	.308	.317	.333	39	12	1	0	0	2	1	5

RBI/Opportunities		
Scoring Position	31 / 119	(26%)
Scoring Position, 2 Out	14 / 57	(25%)
On Third, Less than 2 Out	8 / 20	(40%)
RBI in close games / RBI Total	19 / 42	(45%)

Al Holland
New York Yankees

1986: Power, Flyball — 1985: Power, Flyball — 1984: Finesse, Flyball

THREE YEARS (84 – 86)	G	IP	H	BB	SO	SB	CS	W	L	S	ERA
Totals	149	226.0	196	70	160	22	5	7	15	34	3.50
At Home and on the Road											
Home	76	121.1	101	42	98	12	3	4	6	13	3.34
Road	73	104.2	95	28	62	10	2	3	9	21	3.70
During the Day and and at Night											
Day	53	72.0	65	24	57	10	3	4	6	10	3.75
Night	96	154.0	131	46	103	12	2	3	9	24	3.39
On Grass and on Turf											
Grass	70	93.0	91	33	65	9	2	4	7	9	4.06
Turf	79	133.0	105	37	95	13	3	3	8	25	3.11
By Month											
April	18	27.1	16	10	17	5	0	0	3	6	2.63
May	29	45.1	30	12	26	3	0	5	1	7	1.99
June	32	48.1	50	18	43	6	2	1	4	9	4.47
July	34	52.1	40	10	43	3	3	1	1	5	2.41
August	25	43.0	47	16	28	5	0	0	4	6	5.65
Sept/Oct	11	9.2	13	4	3	0	0	0	2	1	4.66

vs. Opponent Batters — THREE YEARS (84 – 86)	Ave.	OBP	SLG	AB	H	2B	3B	HR	RBI	BB	SO
Totals	.233	.289	.392	842	196	40	5	28	117	70	160
Pitching vs. Left and Right-handed Batters											
Left	.230	.287	.396	222	51	6	2	9	39	19	61
Right	.234	.290	.390	620	145	34	3	19	78	51	99
Situational											
Bases Empty	.206	.258	.371	461	95	14	4	18	18	31	93
Leadoff	.234	.277	.359	184	43	7	2	4	4	11	33
Not Leadoff	.188	.245	.379	277	52	7	2	14	14	20	60
Runners On	.265	.325	.417	381	101	26	1	10	99	39	67
First Base Only	.257	.298	.421	152	39	8	1	5	12	9	21
Scoring Position	.271	.341	.415	229	62	18	0	5	87	30	46
Late Innings, Close	.256	.311	.410	407	104	23	2	12	58	35	74

RBI/Opportunities		
Scoring Position	77 / 332	(23%)
Scoring Position, 2 Out	36 / 159	(23%)
On Third, Less than 2 Out	26 / 60	(43%)
RBI in close games / RBI Total	69 / 117	(59%)

Rick Honeycutt
Los Angeles Dodgers

1986: Finesse, Groundball — 1985: Finesse, Groundball — 1984: Finesse, Groundball

THREE YEARS (84 – 86)	G	IP	H	BB	SO	SB	CS	W	L	S	ERA
Totals	92	496.2	485	145	242	34	25	29	30	1	3.17
At Home and on the Road											
Home	48	273.1	255	64	130	13	11	17	12	0	2.54
Road	44	223.1	230	81	112	21	14	12	18	1	3.95
During the Day and and at Night											
Day	24	131.1	130	46	70	13	5	10	5	0	3.29
Night	68	365.1	355	99	172	21	20	19	25	1	3.13
On Grass and on Turf											
Grass	70	384.0	360	102	190	18	17	22	21	0	2.74
Turf	22	112.2	125	43	52	16	8	7	9	1	4.63
By Month											
April	14	79.0	65	15	41	3	3	5	3	0	2.28
May	16	94.0	89	34	48	12	7	6	7	0	2.30
June	16	99.0	88	23	50	4	5	5	4	0	3.00
July	15	69.1	88	23	31	4	3	4	7	0	4.54
August	17	87.2	89	27	44	6	6	6	8	1	3.49
Sept/Oct	14	67.2	66	23	28	5	1	3	1	0	3.86

vs. Opponent Batters — THREE YEARS (84 – 86)	Ave.	OBP	SLG	AB	H	2B	3B	HR	RBI	BB	SO
Totals	.256	.309	.364	1897	485	96	11	29	170	145	242
Pitching vs. Left and Right-handed Batters											
Left	.208	.239	.297	317	66	13	3	3	38	12	61
Right	.265	.323	.377	1580	419	83	8	26	132	133	181
Situational											
Bases Empty	.242	.282	.339	1187	287	58	6	15	15	63	151
Leadoff	.240	.276	.345	495	119	24	2	8	8	22	57
Not Leadoff	.243	.287	.334	692	168	34	4	7	7	41	94
Runners On	.279	.351	.406	710	198	38	5	14	155	82	91
First Base Only	.272	.305	.403	335	91	20	3	6	21	16	45
Scoring Position	.285	.386	.408	375	107	18	2	8	134	66	46
Late Innings, Close	.209	.258	.248	153	32	3	0	1	7	9	19

RBI/Opportunities		
Scoring Position	118 / 542	(22%)
Scoring Position, 2 Out	50 / 269	(19%)
On Third, Less than 2 Out	37 / 83	(45%)
RBI in close games / RBI Total	134 / 170	(79%)

Ricky Horton
St. Louis Cardinals

1986: Finesse, Groundball   1985: Power, Groundball   1984: Finesse, Flyball

	G	IP	H	BB	SO	SB	CS	W	L	S	ERA
THREE YEARS (84 – 86)											
Totals	128	315.2	301	99	184	14	11	16	9	5	2.91
At Home and on the Road											
Home	60	142.2	136	43	82	5	6	7	2	3	2.71
Road	68	173.0	165	56	102	9	5	9	7	2	3.07
During the Day and and at Night											
Day	51	118.0	113	45	65	4	5	5	3	1	2.67
Night	77	197.2	188	54	119	10	6	11	6	4	3.05
On Grass and on Turf											
Grass	35	87.2	70	29	56	3	3	3	2	2	2.67
Turf	93	228.0	231	70	128	11	8	13	7	3	3.00
By Month											
April	18	43.2	37	14	28	1	0	0	3	0	3.30
May	22	35.1	25	12	24	2	0	1	1	1	1.02
June	17	42.0	35	17	30	3	4	4	1	0	2.36
July	24	55.2	64	17	34	4	4	1	1	2	3.23
August	22	59.0	66	17	34	2	0	6	2	2	4.58
Sept/Oct	25	80.0	74	22	34	2	3	4	1	0	2.36

	Ave.	OBP	SLG	AB	H	2B	3B	HR	RBI	BB	SO
vs. Opponent Batters											
THREE YEARS (84 – 86)											
Totals	.255	.313	.378	1179	301	55	6	26	116	99	184
Pitching vs. Left and Right-handed Batters											
Left	.225	.276	.274	307	69	6	0	3	32	20	60
Right	.266	.326	.415	872	232	49	6	23	84	79	124
Situational											
Bases Empty	.245	.294	.387	714	175	33	4	20	20	48	112
Leadoff	.254	.300	.388	291	74	12	3	7	7	19	41
Not Leadoff	.239	.289	.385	423	101	21	1	13	13	29	71
Runners On	.271	.342	.366	465	126	22	2	6	96	51	72
First Base Only	.267	.322	.374	195	52	9	0	4	11	14	30
Scoring Position	.274	.355	.359	270	74	13	2	2	85	37	42
Late Innings, Close	.219	.307	.281	210	46	6	1	1	13	25	37

RBI/Opportunities

Scoring Position	80 / 389	(21%)
Scoring Position, 2 Out	31 / 179	(17%)
On Third, Less than 2 Out	33 / 70	(47%)
RBI in close games / RBI Total	63 / 116	(54%)

Jack Howell
California Angels

	Ave.	OBP	SLG	AB	H	2B	3B	HR	RBI	BB	SO
THREE YEARS (84 – 86)											
Totals	.236	.316	.406	288	68	18	2	9	39	35	61
Batting vs. Left and Right-handed Pitchers											
Left	.188	.243	.344	64	12	3	2	1	10	5	14
Right	.250	.336	.424	224	56	15	0	8	29	30	47
At Home and on the Road											
Home	.199	.295	.338	136	27	8	1	3	17	19	31
Road	.270	.335	.467	152	41	10	1	6	22	16	30
Facing Groundball Pitchers and Flyball Pitchers											
Groundball	.311	.378	.528	106	33	9	1	4	16	12	17
Flyball	.192	.280	.335	182	35	9	1	5	23	23	44
Facing Finesse Pitchers and Power Pitchers											
Finesse	.193	.265	.337	166	32	10	1	4	19	17	31
Power	.295	.383	.500	122	36	8	1	5	20	18	30
On Grass and on Turf											
Grass	.212	.307	.358	240	51	13	2	6	29	33	53
Turf	.354	.365	.646	48	17	5	0	3	10	2	8
During the Day and at Night											
Day	.235	.306	.306	98	23	5	1	0	10	10	25
Night	.237	.321	.458	190	45	13	1	9	29	25	36
By Month											
April	.000	.000	.000	0	0	0	0	0	0	0	0
May	.088	.225	.176	34	3	0	0	1	2	6	12
June	.255	.294	.447	47	12	5	2	0	8	3	5
July	.255	.321	.392	51	13	1	0	2	5	5	12
August	.286	.350	.549	91	26	6	0	6	16	9	22
Sept/Oct	.215	.329	.308	65	14	6	0	0	8	12	10
Situational											
Bases Empty	.217	.288	.372	180	39	8	1	6	6	18	35
Leadoff	.258	.329	.515	66	17	3	1	4	4	7	12
Not Leadoff	.193	.264	.289	114	22	5	0	2	2	11	23
Runners On	.269	.359	.463	108	29	10	1	3	33	17	26
First Base Only	.250	.313	.455	44	11	4	1	1	3	4	10
Scoring Position	.281	.388	.469	64	18	6	0	2	30	13	16
Late Innings, Close	.157	.189	.294	51	8	1	0	2	3	2	16

RBI/Opportunities

Scoring Position	25 / 95	(26%)
Scoring Position, 2 Out	8 / 46	(17%)
On Third, Less than 2 Out	9 / 14	(64%)
RBI in close games / RBI Total	23 / 39	(59%)

Ken Howell
Los Angeles Dodgers

1986: Power, Flyball   1985: Power, Flyball   1984: Power, Flyball

	G	IP	H	BB	SO	SB	CS	W	L	S	ERA
THREE YEARS (84 – 86)											
Totals	150	235.0	203	107	243	21	14	15	24	30	3.71
At Home and on the Road											
Home	81	125.2	106	51	118	13	11	8	14	14	3.65
Road	69	109.1	97	56	125	8	3	7	10	16	3.79
During the Day and and at Night											
Day	48	76.1	57	37	90	8	5	6	6	11	3.30
Night	102	158.2	146	70	153	13	9	9	18	19	3.91
On Grass and on Turf											
Grass	111	175.2	153	79	179	16	11	12	18	18	3.84
Turf	39	59.1	50	28	64	5	3	3	6	12	3.34
By Month											
April	14	28.1	21	18	36	1	2	0	2	4	1.91
May	20	31.2	20	16	38	2	2	3	2	3	1.99
June	23	38.1	30	21	33	5	3	3	6	3	3.52
July	24	38.0	30	9	35	2	1	3	2	10	4.03
August	34	44.2	45	12	45	3	2	2	5	7	3.83
Sept/Oct	35	54.0	57	31	56	8	4	4	7	3	5.50

	Ave.	OBP	SLG	AB	H	2B	3B	HR	RBI	BB	SO
vs. Opponent Batters											
THREE YEARS (84 – 86)											
Totals	.234	.307	.329	868	203	29	3	16	108	107	243
Pitching vs. Left and Right-handed Batters											
Left	.239	.333	.315	435	104	15	3	4	44	62	103
Right	.229	.303	.344	433	99	14	0	12	64	45	140
Situational											
Bases Empty	.228	.302	.304	457	104	12	1	7	7	47	132
Leadoff	.252	.311	.381	202	51	8	0	6	6	16	53
Not Leadoff	.208	.296	.243	255	53	4	1	1	1	31	79
Runners On	.241	.335	.358	411	99	17	2	9	101	60	111
First Base Only	.203	.290	.314	172	35	5	1	4	10	20	48
Scoring Position	.268	.366	.389	239	64	12	1	5	91	40	63
Late Innings, Close	.241	.332	.350	609	147	24	3	12	89	82	178

RBI/Opportunities

Scoring Position	78 / 369	(21%)
Scoring Position, 2 Out	27 / 162	(17%)
On Third, Less than 2 Out	34 / 74	(46%)
RBI in close games / RBI Total	97 / 108	(90%)

LaMarr Hoyt
San Diego Padres

1986: Finesse, Flyball   1985: Finesse, Flyball   1984: Finesse, Groundball

	G	IP	H	BB	SO	SB	CS	W	L	S	ERA
THREE YEARS (84 – 86)											
Totals	100	605.0	624	131	294	54	20	37	37	0	4.30
At Home and on the Road											
Home	53	326.0	336	71	165	29	11	23	17	0	4.36
Road	47	279.0	288	60	129	25	9	14	20	0	4.23
During the Day and at Night											
Day	31	175.0	199	45	90	19	9	9	12	0	5.09
Night	69	430.0	425	86	204	35	11	28	25	0	3.98
On Grass and on Turf											
Grass	78	480.1	483	101	241	40	17	28	30	0	4.25
Turf	22	124.2	141	30	53	14	3	9	7	0	4.48
By Month											
April	13	79.0	68	11	40	4	2	4	4	0	3.53
May	17	104.0	108	22	44	8	1	7	6	0	4.07
June	17	111.0	117	31	54	9	7	8	5	0	4.14
July	17	114.0	116	21	61	12	4	7	7	0	4.11
August	16	100.0	125	23	42	10	4	4	10	0	5.85
Sept/Oct	20	97.0	90	23	53	11	2	7	5	0	3.99

	Ave.	OBP	SLG	AB	H	2B	3B	HR	RBI	BB	SO
vs. Opponent Batters											
THREE YEARS (84 – 86)											
Totals	.267	.307	.430	2338	624	111	18	78	273	131	294
Pitching vs. Left and Right-handed Batters											
Left	.279	.327	.445	1249	348	52	12	44	149	88	126
Right	.253	.284	.412	1089	276	59	6	34	124	43	168
Situational											
Bases Empty	.251	.284	.407	1493	374	64	10	50	50	63	189
Leadoff	.242	.277	.390	600	145	28	2	19	19	26	60
Not Leadoff	.256	.288	.419	893	229	36	8	31	31	37	129
Runners On	.296	.340	.470	845	250	47	8	28	223	68	105
First Base Only	.315	.340	.478	362	114	20	3	11	36	13	38
Scoring Position	.282	.351	.464	483	136	27	5	17	187	55	67
Late Innings, Close	.231	.277	.376	221	51	9	1	7	20	13	23

RBI/Opportunities

Scoring Position	156 / 621	(25%)
Scoring Position, 2 Out	49 / 275	(18%)
On Third, Less than 2 Out	54 / 106	(51%)
RBI in close games / RBI Total	189 / 273	(69%)

Charles Hudson
Philadelphia Phillies
1986: Finesse, Flyball   1985: Power, Flyball   1984: Finesse, Flyball

THREE YEARS (84 – 86)

	G	IP	H	BB	SO	SB	CS	W	L	S	ERA
Totals	101	510.2	534	184	298	67	12	24	34	0	4.19
At Home and on the Road											
Home	49	236.0	262	72	143	27	5	9	17	0	4.42
Road	52	274.2	272	112	155	40	7	15	17	0	4.00
During the Day and and at Night											
Day	33	182.0	166	61	87	23	1	14	5	0	3.71
Night	68	328.2	368	123	211	44	11	10	29	0	4.46
On Grass and on Turf											
Grass	25	128.0	141	51	68	15	3	6	8	0	4.50
Turf	76	382.2	393	133	230	52	9	18	26	0	4.09
By Month											
April	18	56.2	63	24	19	12	2	5	3	0	3.81
May	18	92.1	80	29	40	5	4	5	8	0	4.09
June	17	99.2	118	38	59	14	3	4	9	0	5.06
July	15	87.0	97	33	61	9	0	5	7	0	4.55
August	13	79.2	88	27	53	10	1	3	3	0	4.41
Sept/Oct	20	95.1	88	33	66	17	2	2	4	0	3.12

vs. Opponent Batters
THREE YEARS (84 – 86)

	Ave.	OBP	SLG	AB	H	2B	3B	HR	RBI	BB	SO
Totals	.268	.328	.411	1995	534	89	16	55	243	184	298
Pitching vs. Left and Right-handed Batters											
Left	.280	.347	.416	1058	296	49	10	25	130	112	134
Right	.254	.306	.406	937	238	40	6	30	113	72	164
Situational											
Bases Empty	.250	.314	.400	1167	292	48	8	37	37	107	168
Leadoff	.245	.293	.371	502	123	18	3	13	13	34	67
Not Leadoff	.254	.329	.423	665	169	30	5	24	24	73	101
Runners On	.292	.348	.426	828	242	41	8	18	206	77	130
First Base Only	.300	.336	.449	350	105	16	3	10	31	17	47
Scoring Position	.287	.356	.410	478	137	25	5	8	175	60	83
Late Innings, Close	.276	.324	.440	134	37	4	0	6	21	10	18

RBI/Opportunities

Scoring Position	154 / 627	(25%)
Scoring Position, 2 Out	60 / 285	(21%)
On Third, Less than 2 Out	58 / 107	(54%)
RBI in close games / RBI Total	174 / 243	(72%)

Mark Huismann
Seattle Mariners
1986: Finesse, Groundball 1985: Finesse, Groundball   1984: Power, Groundball

THREE YEARS (84 – 86)

	G	IP	H	BB	SO	SB	CS	W	L	S	ERA
Totals	93	191.0	196	49	135	14	5	7	7	8	3.77
At Home and on the Road											
Home	51	110.1	108	27	80	9	4	5	4	3	3.34
Road	42	80.2	88	22	55	5	1	2	3	5	4.35
During the Day and at Night											
Day	24	59.1	51	18	38	2	3	1	2	2	3.03
Night	69	131.2	145	31	97	12	2	6	5	6	4.10
On Grass and on Turf											
Grass	31	54.2	60	16	37	4	1	1	1	4	4.77
Turf	62	136.1	136	33	98	10	4	6	6	4	3.37
By Month											
April	10	23.2	25	10	18	4	2	0	1	0	5.32
May	18	31.0	38	9	22	2	0	1	3	1	4.94
June	12	17.2	20	6	9	2	0	0	0	2	5.09
July	13	33.2	44	9	25	0	0	2	2	2	5.08
August	17	40.2	32	6	26	3	1	2	0	2	1.99
Sept/Oct	23	44.1	37	9	35	3	2	2	1	1	2.23

vs. Opponent Batters
THREE YEARS (84 – 86)

	Ave.	OBP	SLG	AB	H	2B	3B	HR	RBI	BB	SO
Totals	.266	.309	.431	738	196	31	5	27	96	49	135
Pitching vs. Left and Right-handed Batters											
Left	.301	.344	.453	369	111	15	4	11	46	26	39
Right	.230	.274	.409	369	85	16	1	16	50	23	96
Situational											
Bases Empty	.294	.338	.488	385	113	20	2	17	17	25	68
Leadoff	.335	.378	.540	161	54	9	0	8	11	23
Not Leadoff	.263	.310	.451	224	59	11	2	9	9	14	45
Runners On	.235	.278	.368	353	83	11	3	10	79	24	67
First Base Only	.283	.327	.457	138	39	5	2	5	15	8	28
Scoring Position	.205	.249	.312	215	44	6	1	5	64	16	39
Late Innings, Close	.251	.321	.409	171	43	7	1	6	20	18	37

RBI/Opportunities

Scoring Position	56 / 287	(20%)
Scoring Position, 2 Out	18 / 126	(14%)
On Third, Less than 2 Out	24 / 52	(46%)
RBI in close games / RBI Total	31 / 96	(32%)

Tom Hume
Philadelphia Phillies
1986: Finesse, Groundball 1985: Power, Groundball 1984: Finesse, Groundball

THREE YEARS (84 – 86)

	G	IP	H	BB	SO	SB	CS	W	L	S	ERA
Totals	158	287.2	296	110	160	61	10	11	19	10	4.04
At Home and on the Road											
Home	74	142.1	143	56	78	30	7	5	5	2	3.79
Road	84	145.1	153	54	82	31	3	6	14	8	4.27
During the Day and at Night											
Day	58	105.1	98	44	53	31	5	5	9	4	3.67
Night	100	182.1	198	66	107	30	5	6	10	6	4.24
On Grass and on Turf											
Grass	46	79.2	97	23	39	13	3	3	9	2	4.63
Turf	112	208.0	199	87	121	48	7	8	10	8	3.81
By Month											
April	18	24.0	26	11	11	6	2	1	5	2	3.37
May	22	40.0	41	18	31	10	3	3	1	2	5.40
June	30	57.0	61	25	28	12	0	0	3	3	5.21
July	31	66.1	71	19	38	15	2	3	5	3	3.26
August	26	45.0	44	15	22	8	1	3	1	0	3.40
Sept/Oct	31	55.1	53	22	30	10	2	1	4	0	3.58

vs. Opponent Batters
THREE YEARS (84 – 86)

	Ave.	OBP	SLG	AB	H	2B	3B	HR	RBI	BB	SO
Totals	.269	.335	.404	1102	296	45	13	26	161	110	160
Pitching vs. Left and Right-handed Batters											
Left	.275	.370	.412	495	136	16	8	12	67	75	57
Right	.264	.304	.397	607	160	29	5	14	94	35	103
Situational											
Bases Empty	.262	.322	.390	603	158	26	6	13	13	50	80
Leadoff	.254	.305	.412	260	66	15	4	6	6	17	34
Not Leadoff	.268	.334	.373	343	92	11	2	7	7	33	46
Runners On	.277	.350	.421	499	138	19	7	13	148	60	80
First Base Only	.287	.332	.427	178	51	6	2	5	14	12	29
Scoring Position	.271	.359	.417	321	87	13	5	8	134	48	51
Late Innings, Close	.269	.352	.387	305	82	11	2	7	46	36	39

RBI/Opportunities

Scoring Position	116 / 477	(24%)
Scoring Position, 2 Out	55 / 217	(25%)
On Third, Less than 2 Out	43 / 91	(47%)
RBI in close games / RBI Total	72 / 161	(45%)

Clint Hurdle
St. Louis Cardinals

THREE YEARS (84 – 86)

	Ave.	OBP	SLG	AB	H	2B	3B	HR	RBI	BB	SO
Totals	.195	.312	.318	236	46	9	1	6	22	39	58
Batting vs. Left and Right-handed Pitchers											
Left	.208	.321	.292	24	5	2	0	0	3	4	8
Right	.193	.311	.321	212	41	7	1	6	19	35	50
At Home and on the Road											
Home	.170	.303	.270	100	17	4	0	2	8	19	20
Road	.213	.318	.353	136	29	5	1	4	14	20	38
Facing Groundball Pitchers and Flyball Pitchers											
Groundball	.190	.310	.295	105	20	2	0	3	8	18	24
Flyball	.198	.314	.336	131	26	7	1	3	14	21	34
Facing Finesse Pitchers and Power Pitchers											
Finesse	.207	.301	.356	135	28	5	0	5	13	19	24
Power	.178	.325	.267	101	18	4	1	1	9	20	34
On Grass and on Turf											
Grass	.204	.339	.378	98	20	3	1	4	13	18	26
Turf	.188	.292	.275	138	26	6	0	2	9	21	32
During the Day and at Night											
Day	.205	.314	.398	88	18	3	1	4	11	13	19
Night	.189	.311	.270	148	28	6	0	2	11	26	39
By Month											
April	.348	.348	.478	23	8	1	1	0	4	0	5
May	.065	.171	.065	31	2	0	0	0	0	4	10
June	.176	.323	.412	51	9	3	0	3	7	10	16
July	.150	.292	.300	40	6	0	0	2	4	8	13
August	.270	.391	.338	74	20	5	0	0	6	15	14
Sept/Oct	.059	.158	.235	17	1	0	1	0	1	2	3
Situational											
Bases Empty	.209	.312	.306	134	28	4	0	3	3	18	34
Leadoff	.250	.354	.357	56	14	3	0	1	1	8	13
Not Leadoff	.179	.281	.269	78	14	1	0	2	2	10	21
Runners On	.176	.312	.333	102	18	5	1	3	19	21	24
First Base Only	.186	.327	.209	43	8	1	0	0	0	9	9
Scoring Position	.169	.301	.424	59	10	4	1	3	19	12	15
Late Innings, Close	.212	.328	.365	52	11	0	1	2	8	8	13

RBI/Opportunities

Scoring Position	13 / 80	(16%)
Scoring Position, 2 Out	4 / 37	(11%)
On Third, Less than 2 Out	4 / 14	(29%)
RBI in close games / RBI Total	12 / 22	(55%)

Dane Iorg
San Diego Padres

THREE YEARS (84 – 86)

	Ave.	OBP	SLG	AB	H	2B	3B	HR	RBI	BB	SO
Totals	.234	.267	.357	499	117	29	4	8	65	25	59
Batting vs. Left and Right-handed Pitchers											
Left	.194	.219	.323	31	6	2	1	0	4	1	8
Right	.237	.271	.359	468	111	27	3	8	61	24	51
At Home and on the Road											
Home	.214	.255	.323	229	49	12	2	3	26	14	23
Road	.252	.278	.385	270	68	17	2	5	39	11	36
Facing Groundball Pitchers and Flyball Pitchers											
Groundball	.219	.243	.342	260	57	17	3	3	33	10	26
Flyball	.251	.294	.372	239	60	12	1	5	32	15	33
Facing Finesse Pitchers and Power Pitchers											
Finesse	.229	.253	.358	271	62	19	2	4	28	11	23
Power	.241	.284	.355	228	55	10	2	4	37	14	36
On Grass and on Turf											
Grass	.218	.233	.305	239	52	10	1	3	32	6	37
Turf	.250	.298	.404	260	65	19	3	5	33	19	22
During the Day and at Night											
Day	.248	.270	.372	145	36	10	1	2	19	5	22
Night	.229	.266	.350	354	81	19	3	6	46	20	37
By Month											
April	.188	.235	.271	48	9	2	1	0	6	3	11
May	.247	.261	.416	89	22	6	0	3	14	2	8
June	.156	.198	.200	90	14	4	0	0	5	5	8
July	.280	.286	.430	93	26	4	2	2	19	2	9
August	.258	.305	.383	120	31	10	1	1	13	9	14
Sept/Oct	.254	.302	.407	59	15	3	0	2	8	4	9
Situational											
Bases Empty	.238	.273	.383	269	64	18	3	5	5	13	25
Leadoff	.303	.327	.468	109	33	7	1	3	3	4	12
Not Leadoff	.194	.237	.325	160	31	11	2	2	2	9	13
Runners On	.230	.261	.326	230	53	11	1	3	60	12	34
First Base Only	.215	.240	.269	93	20	2	0	1	3	3	14
Scoring Position	.241	.275	.365	137	33	9	1	2	57	9	20
Late Innings, Close	.176	.222	.259	108	19	4	1	1	10	7	21

RBI/Opportunities

Scoring Position	49 / 179	(27%)
Scoring Position, 2 Out	11 / 73	(15%)
On Third, Less than 2 Out	22 / 38	(58%)
RBI in close games / RBI Total	48 / 65	(74%)

Garth Iorg
Toronto Blue Jays

THREE YEARS (84 – 86)

	Ave.	OBP	SLG	AB	H	2B	3B	HR	RBI	BB	SO
Totals	.268	.306	.377	862	231	51	5	11	106	47	89
Batting vs. Left and Right-handed Pitchers											
Left	.284	.324	.414	546	155	36	4	9	77	32	42
Right	.241	.275	.313	316	76	15	1	2	29	15	47
At Home and on the Road											
Home	.279	.312	.400	420	117	24	3	7	55	19	46
Road	.258	.300	.355	442	114	27	2	4	51	28	43
Facing Groundball Pitchers and Flyball Pitchers											
Groundball	.277	.328	.349	350	97	15	2	2	44	25	32
Flyball	.262	.291	.390	512	134	36	3	9	62	22	57
Facing Finesse Pitchers and Power Pitchers											
Finesse	.269	.303	.373	464	125	26	2	6	52	22	41
Power	.266	.310	.382	398	106	25	3	5	54	25	48
On Grass and on Turf											
Grass	.266	.305	.366	331	88	22	1	3	39	20	34
Turf	.269	.307	.384	531	143	29	4	8	67	27	55
During the Day and at Night											
Day	.250	.293	.373	308	77	18	1	6	35	19	37
Night	.278	.313	.379	554	154	33	4	5	71	28	52
By Month											
April	.231	.273	.298	104	24	2	1	1	12	6	12
May	.320	.361	.360	125	40	5	0	4	8	8	11
June	.263	.296	.391	133	35	8	0	3	22	5	15
July	.203	.271	.273	128	26	7	1	0	11	12	12
August	.257	.298	.371	202	52	11	3	2	34	12	19
Sept/Oct	.318	.331	.512	170	54	18	0	5	23	4	20
Situational											
Bases Empty	.247	.279	.347	450	111	26	2	5	5	18	50
Leadoff	.250	.277	.364	184	46	11	2	2	2	7	14
Not Leadoff	.244	.280	.335	266	65	15	0	3	3	11	36
Runners On	.291	.335	.410	412	120	25	3	6	101	29	39
First Base Only	.273	.307	.361	183	50	11	1	1	9	9	17
Scoring Position	.306	.356	.450	229	70	14	2	5	92	20	22
Late Innings, Close	.316	.362	.434	152	48	8	2	2	20	11	14

RBI/Opportunities

Scoring Position	79 / 314	(25%)
Scoring Position, 2 Out	39 / 147	(27%)
On Third, Less than 2 Out	20 / 45	(44%)
RBI in close games / RBI Total	72 / 106	(68%)

Roy Lee Jackson
Minnesota Twins

1986: Finesse, Flyball   1985: Power, Groundball   1984: Power, Flyball

THREE YEARS (84 – 86)

	G	IP	H	BB	SO	SB	CS	W	L	S	ERA
Totals	104	184.1	162	60	118	15	6	9	12	13	3.47
At Home and on the Road											
Home	55	101.0	85	30	74	9	2	5	6	7	3.30
Road	49	83.1	77	30	44	6	4	4	6	6	3.67
During the Day and and at Night											
Day	37	73.0	61	23	53	3	3	3	3	6	2.71
Night	67	111.1	101	37	65	12	3	6	9	7	3.96
On Grass and on Turf											
Grass	46	76.0	61	25	46	5	2	4	6	4	3.08
Turf	58	108.1	101	35	72	10	4	5	6	9	3.74
By Month											
April	9	11.0	7	7	10	1	0	0	1	2	2.45
May	12	20.2	17	7	15	1	0	6	0	0	1.74
June	15	32.0	27	10	22	2	0	0	1	1	3.66
July	23	40.1	45	11	24	6	4	0	3	7	4.24
August	24	47.0	41	12	22	4	0	3	4	1	3.64
Sept/Oct	21	33.1	25	13	25	1	2	0	3	2	3.51

vs. Opponent Batters

THREE YEARS (84 – 86)

	Ave.	OBP	SLG	AB	H	2B	3B	HR	RBI	BB	SO
Totals	.237	.299	.399	684	162	26	8	23	89	60	119
Pitching vs. Left and Right-handed Batters											
Left	.209	.272	.342	316	66	10	4	8	41	27	42
Right	.261	.323	.448	368	96	16	4	15	48	33	77
Situational											
Bases Empty	.242	.286	.438	388	94	17	4	17	17	22	58
Leadoff	.255	.299	.452	157	40	8	1	7	7	10	24
Not Leadoff	.234	.278	.429	231	54	9	3	10	10	12	34
Runners On	.230	.315	.348	296	68	9	4	6	72	38	61
First Base Only	.250	.289	.389	108	27	5	2	2	8	5	14
Scoring Position	.218	.328	.324	188	41	4	2	4	64	33	47
Late Innings, Close	.242	.330	.451	244	59	8	5	11	35	31	51

RBI/Opportunities

Scoring Position	54 / 284	(19%)
Scoring Position, 2 Out	22 / 136	(16%)
On Third, Less than 2 Out	21 / 49	(43%)
RBI in close games / RBI Total	44 / 89	(49%)

Stan Javier
Oakland A's

THREE YEARS (84 – 86)

	Ave.	OBP	SLG	AB	H	2B	3B	HR	RBI	BB	SO
Totals	.198	.297	.264	121	24	8	0	0	8	16	28
Batting vs. Left and Right-handed Pitchers											
Left	.145	.230	.218	55	8	4	0	0	4	5	10
Right	.242	.351	.303	66	16	4	0	0	4	11	18
At Home and on the Road											
Home	.194	.342	.242	62	12	3	0	0	5	13	15
Road	.203	.242	.288	59	12	5	0	0	3	3	13
Facing Groundball Pitchers and Flyball Pitchers											
Groundball	.182	.297	.255	55	10	4	0	0	3	8	14
Flyball	.212	.297	.273	66	14	4	0	0	5	8	14
Facing Finesse Pitchers and Power Pitchers											
Finesse	.202	.287	.274	84	17	6	0	0	4	10	17
Power	.189	.318	.243	37	7	2	0	0	4	6	11
On Grass and on Turf											
Grass	.178	.290	.234	107	19	6	0	0	8	16	26
Turf	.357	.357	.500	14	5	2	0	0	0	0	2
During the Day and at Night											
Day	.203	.347	.271	59	12	4	0	0	7	12	11
Night	.194	.242	.258	62	12	4	0	0	1	4	17
By Month											
April	.143	.143	.143	7	1	0	0	0	0	0	1
May	.147	.237	.235	34	5	3	0	0	3	4	6
June	.225	.380	.275	40	9	2	0	0	3	9	13
July	.143	.250	.143	7	1	0	0	0	0	1	3
August	.000	.000	.000	0	0	0	0	0	0	0	0
Sept/Oct	.242	.286	.333	33	8	3	0	0	2	2	5
Situational											
Bases Empty	.171	.241	.224	76	13	4	0	0	0	7	17
Leadoff	.138	.167	.172	29	4	1	0	0	0	1	6
Not Leadoff	.191	.283	.255	47	9	3	0	0	0	6	11
Runners On	.244	.382	.333	45	11	4	0	0	8	9	11
First Base Only	.190	.227	.238	21	4	1	0	0	0	1	5
Scoring Position	.292	.485	.417	24	7	3	0	0	8	8	6
Late Innings, Close	.158	.200	.211	19	3	1	0	0	4	0	4

RBI/Opportunities

Scoring Position	7 / 49	(14%)
Scoring Position, 2 Out	6 / 36	(17%)
On Third, Less than 2 Out	1 / 5	(20%)
RBI in close games / RBI Total	5 / 8	(63%)

Steve Jeltz
Philadelphia Phillies

	Ave.	OBP	SLG	AB	H	2B	3B	HR	RBI	BB	SO
THREE YEARS (84 – 86)											
Totals	.209	.305	.252	703	147	15	6	1	55	98	163
Batting vs. Left and Right-handed Pitchers											
Left	.213	.314	.258	221	47	5	1	1	18	33	54
Right	.207	.301	.249	482	100	10	5	0	37	65	109
At Home and on the Road											
Home	.208	.287	.269	361	75	12	5	0	34	42	85
Road	.211	.323	.234	342	72	3	1	1	21	56	78
Facing Groundball Pitchers and Flyball Pitchers											
Groundball	.208	.302	.243	342	71	6	3	0	25	46	80
Flyball	.211	.308	.260	361	76	9	3	1	30	52	83
Facing Finesse Pitchers and Power Pitchers											
Finesse	.204	.282	.243	378	77	8	2	1	21	41	65
Power	.215	.331	.262	325	70	7	4	0	34	57	98
On Grass and on Turf											
Grass	.190	.280	.202	168	32	2	0	0	11	20	32
Turf	.215	.313	.267	535	115	13	6	1	44	78	131
During the Day and at Night											
Day	.231	.337	.298	208	48	5	3	1	25	34	50
Night	.200	.291	.232	495	99	10	3	0	30	64	113
By Month											
April	.231	.328	.269	108	25	0	2	0	10	16	26
May	.193	.290	.229	109	21	4	0	0	7	15	28
June	.211	.338	.241	133	28	4	0	0	12	26	25
July	.218	.344	.264	110	24	3	1	0	7	20	32
August	.205	.263	.273	88	18	2	2	0	4	7	19
Sept/Oct	.200	.263	.245	155	31	2	1	1	15	14	33
Situational											
Bases Empty	.203	.290	.231	399	81	8	0	1	1	48	93
Leadoff	.218	.311	.250	156	34	2	0	1	1	21	31
Not Leadoff	.193	.277	.218	243	47	6	0	0	0	27	62
Runners On	.217	.324	.280	304	66	7	6	0	54	50	70
First Base Only	.208	.299	.238	130	27	2	1	0	3	17	30
Scoring Position	.224	.341	.310	174	39	5	5	0	51	33	40
Late Innings, Close	.206	.342	.237	97	20	1	1	0	8	20	18

RBI/Opportunities

Scoring Position	45 / 250	(18%)
Scoring Position, 2 Out	23 / 129	(18%)
On Third, Less than 2 Out	14 / 30	(47%)
RBI in close games / RBI Total	33 / 55	(60%)

Cliff Johnson
Toronto Blue Jays

	Ave.	OBP	SLG	AB	H	2B	3B	HR	RBI	BB	SO
THREE YEARS (84 – 86)											
Totals	.272	.360	.450	1064	289	52	3	44	182	142	178
Batting vs. Left and Right-handed Pitchers											
Left	.313	.417	.509	399	125	30	0	16	67	71	59
Right	.247	.324	.415	665	164	22	3	28	115	71	119
At Home and on the Road											
Home	.276	.369	.459	510	141	20	2	23	104	72	91
Road	.267	.352	.442	554	148	32	1	21	78	70	87
Facing Groundball Pitchers and Flyball Pitchers											
Groundball	.267	.362	.430	465	124	20	1	18	83	65	85
Flyball	.275	.358	.466	599	165	32	2	26	99	77	93
Facing Finesse Pitchers and Power Pitchers											
Finesse	.259	.342	.448	607	157	33	2	26	107	74	92
Power	.289	.383	.453	457	132	19	1	18	75	68	86
On Grass and on Turf											
Grass	.258	.346	.456	570	147	28	2	27	101	73	90
Turf	.287	.376	.443	494	142	24	1	17	81	69	88
During the Day and at Night											
Day	.319	.403	.533	345	110	17	0	19	62	44	46
Night	.249	.340	.410	719	179	35	3	25	120	98	132
By Month											
April	.279	.377	.491	165	46	11	0	8	32	25	28
May	.251	.352	.422	223	56	9	1	9	39	34	33
June	.303	.367	.528	178	54	12	2	8	32	17	29
July	.333	.415	.548	93	31	5	0	5	19	13	19
August	.239	.336	.393	234	56	9	0	9	36	32	37
Sept/Oct	.269	.351	.392	171	46	6	0	5	24	21	32
Situational											
Bases Empty	.245	.334	.428	580	142	30	2	24	24	72	104
Leadoff	.227	.315	.388	242	55	7	1	10	10	28	45
Not Leadoff	.257	.348	.456	338	87	23	1	14	14	44	59
Runners On	.304	.390	.477	484	147	22	1	20	158	70	74
First Base Only	.306	.383	.522	186	57	5	1	11	28	20	26
Scoring Position	.302	.394	.450	298	90	17	0	9	130	50	48
Late Innings, Close	.317	.392	.468	205	65	11	1	6	37	26	32

RBI/Opportunities

Scoring Position	112 / 413	(27%)
Scoring Position, 2 Out	53 / 215	(25%)
On Third, Less than 2 Out	34 / 66	(52%)
RBI in close games / RBI Total	110 / 182	(60%)

Howard Johnson
New York Mets

	Ave.	OBP	SLG	AB	H	2B	3B	HR	RBI	BB	SO
THREE YEARS (84 – 86)											
Totals	.245	.318	.406	964	236	46	5	33	135	104	209
Batting vs. Left and Right-handed Pitchers											
Left	.199	.272	.344	221	44	7	2	7	24	22	57
Right	.258	.331	.424	743	192	39	3	26	111	82	152
At Home and on the Road											
Home	.224	.314	.367	460	103	20	2	14	64	60	96
Road	.264	.321	.440	504	133	26	3	19	71	44	113
Facing Groundball Pitchers and Flyball Pitchers											
Groundball	.241	.307	.402	448	108	18	3	16	68	42	92
Flyball	.248	.327	.409	516	128	28	2	17	67	62	117
Facing Finesse Pitchers and Power Pitchers											
Finesse	.228	.293	.343	499	114	24	0	11	54	45	94
Power	.262	.344	.473	465	122	22	5	22	81	59	115
On Grass and on Turf											
Grass	.234	.317	.402	721	169	30	5	27	106	87	151
Turf	.276	.322	.416	243	67	16	0	6	29	17	58
During the Day and at Night											
Day	.235	.327	.377	345	81	15	2	10	45	49	73
Night	.250	.312	.422	619	155	31	3	23	90	55	136
By Month											
April	.231	.325	.324	108	25	4	0	2	12	15	25
May	.213	.310	.316	136	29	6	1	2	21	19	30
June	.277	.340	.459	148	41	6	0	7	19	14	38
July	.256	.303	.453	223	57	14	0	10	38	17	44
August	.222	.326	.376	189	42	7	2	6	15	28	41
Sept/Oct	.263	.310	.456	160	42	9	2	6	30	11	31
Situational											
Bases Empty	.247	.304	.401	531	131	25	3	17	17	43	104
Leadoff	.215	.275	.346	205	44	10	1	5	5	16	41
Not Leadoff	.267	.323	.436	326	87	15	2	12	12	27	63
Runners On	.242	.333	.411	433	105	21	2	16	118	61	105
First Base Only	.239	.291	.371	205	49	5	2	6	16	15	50
Scoring Position	.246	.367	.447	228	56	16	0	10	102	46	55
Late Innings, Close	.212	.280	.413	189	40	6	1	10	26	17	50

RBI/Opportunities

Scoring Position	82 / 354	(23%)
Scoring Position, 2 Out	39 / 174	(22%)
On Third, Less than 2 Out	29 / 58	(50%)
RBI in close games / RBI Total	90 / 135	(67%)

John Henry Johnson
Milwaukee Brewers

1986: Power, Flyball   1985: Did not play   1984: Power, Flyball

	G	IP	H	BB	SO	SB	CS	W	L	S	ERA
THREE YEARS (84 – 86)											
Totals	49	107.2	107	37	99	3	3	3	3	2	3.18
At Home and on the Road											
Home	22	55.1	54	16	46	1	1	1	1	0	3.42
Road	27	52.1	53	21	53	2	2	2	2	2	2.92
During the Day and and at Night											
Day	15	36.2	35	5	29	0	0	1	1	0	2.70
Night	34	71.0	72	32	70	3	3	2	2	2	3.42
On Grass and on Turf											
Grass	40	93.0	96	30	87	2	2	3	3	2	3.39
Turf	9	14.2	11	7	12	1	1	0	0	0	1.84
By Month											
April	4	6.2	6	2	4	0	0	0	0	0	5.40
May	6	8.1	5	6	7	1	0	0	1	0	3.24
June	4	4.0	5	1	1	0	0	0	0	0	6.75
July	6	12.1	14	5	17	0	1	0	0	0	2.19
August	13	39.0	36	8	42	1	1	1	2	2	3.46
Sept/Oct	16	37.1	41	15	28	1	1	2	0	0	2.41

vs. Opponent Batters

	Ave.	OBP	SLG	AB	H	2B	3B	HR	RBI	BB	SO
THREE YEARS (84 – 86)											
Totals	.257	.317	.374	417	107	18	2	9	49	37	99
Pitching vs. Left and Right-handed Batters											
Left	.238	.300	.376	101	24	5	0	3	18	9	23
Right	.263	.323	.373	316	83	13	2	6	31	28	76
Situational											
Bases Empty	.275	.332	.427	211	58	10	2	6	6	18	47
Leadoff	.370	.414	.598	92	34	8	2	3	3	7	17
Not Leadoff	.202	.269	.294	119	24	2	0	3	3	11	30
Runners On	.238	.302	.320	206	49	8	0	3	43	19	52
First Base Only	.254	.274	.268	71	18	1	0	0	0	2	15
Scoring Position	.230	.316	.348	135	31	7	0	3	43	17	37
Late Innings, Close	.333	.422	.538	39	13	2	0	2	11	6	6

RBI/Opportunities

Scoring Position	36 / 202	(18%)
Scoring Position, 2 Out	13 / 84	(15%)
On Third, Less than 2 Out	13 / 46	(28%)
RBI in close games / RBI Total	26 / 49	(53%)

Joe Johnson
Toronto Blue Jays

1986: Finesse, Flyball   1985: Finesse, Flyball   1984: Did not play

THREE YEARS (84 – 86)

	G	IP	H	BB	SO	SB	CS	W	L	S	ERA
Totals	48	260.2	290	81	122	16	9	17	13	0	4.32
At Home and on the Road											
Home	23	119.1	135	27	54	4	4	7	7	0	4.30
Road	25	141.1	155	54	68	12	5	10	6	0	4.33
During the Day and and at Night											
Day	17	94.1	101	25	44	6	2	7	3	0	3.63
Night	31	166.1	189	56	78	10	7	10	10	0	4.71
On Grass and on Turf											
Grass	33	173.2	211	61	81	13	7	9	10	0	4.72
Turf	15	87.0	79	20	41	3	2	8	3	0	3.52
By Month											
April	4	28.1	26	9	16	3	1	3	1	0	2.86
May	7	38.1	39	15	19	0	1	3	2	0	4.70
June	4	17.2	30	8	13	2	1	0	3	0	7.64
July	8	38.0	41	15	16	0	1	1	1	0	3.55
August	12	71.2	78	14	26	5	2	5	1	0	3.52
Sept/Oct	13	66.2	76	20	32	6	3	5	5	0	5.13

vs. Opponent Batters
THREE YEARS (84 – 86)

	Ave.	OBP	SLG	AB	H	2B	3B	HR	RBI	BB	SO
Totals	.285	.340	.402	1017	290	45	7	20	122	81	122
Pitching vs. Left and Right-handed Batters											
Left	.296	.352	.424	533	158	24	4	12	65	48	78
Right	.273	.327	.378	484	132	21	3	8	57	33	44
Situational											
Bases Empty	.264	.320	.372	594	157	28	6	8	8	46	68
Leadoff	.251	.295	.332	259	65	12	3	1	1	15	31
Not Leadoff	.275	.340	.403	335	92	16	3	7	7	31	37
Runners On	.314	.367	.444	423	133	17	1	12	114	35	54
First Base Only	.350	.388	.475	177	62	8	1	4	12	9	16
Scoring Position	.289	.353	.423	246	71	9	0	8	102	26	38
Late Innings, Close	.273	.347	.318	66	18	3	0	0	4	8	6

RBI/Opportunities

Scoring Position	84 / 326	(26%)
Scoring Position, 2 Out	28 / 138	(20%)
On Third, Less than 2 Out	42 / 73	(58%)
RBI in close games / RBI Total	80 / 122	(66%)

Wallace Johnson
Montreal Expos

THREE YEARS (84 – 86)

	Ave.	OBP	SLG	AB	H	2B	3B	HR	RBI	BB	SO
Totals	.272	.325	.325	151	41	3	1	1	14	12	13
Batting vs. Left and Right-handed Pitchers											
Left	.244	.320	.267	45	11	1	0	0	4	5	7
Right	.283	.327	.349	106	30	2	1	1	10	7	6
At Home and on the Road											
Home	.288	.350	.370	73	21	1	1	1	7	7	7
Road	.256	.301	.282	78	20	2	0	0	7	5	6
Facing Groundball Pitchers and Flyball Pitchers											
Groundball	.273	.326	.341	88	24	1	1	1	13	7	4
Flyball	.270	.324	.302	63	17	2	0	0	1	5	9
Facing Finesse Pitchers and Power Pitchers											
Finesse	.250	.266	.293	92	23	2	1	0	6	2	5
Power	.305	.406	.373	59	18	1	0	1	8	10	8
On Grass and on Turf											
Grass	.324	.378	.353	34	11	1	0	0	1	3	3
Turf	.256	.310	.316	117	30	2	1	1	13	9	10
During the Day and at Night											
Day	.292	.358	.292	48	14	0	0	0	1	5	2
Night	.262	.309	.340	103	27	3	1	1	13	7	11
By Month											
April	.000	.000	.000	0	0	0	0	0	0	0	0
May	.000	.000	.000	0	0	0	0	0	0	0	0
June	.000	.000	.000	0	0	0	0	0	0	0	0
July	.154	.154	.385	13	2	0	0	1	1	0	1
August	.273	.314	.333	66	18	2	1	0	6	4	5
Sept/Oct	.292	.362	.306	72	21	1	0	0	7	8	7
Situational											
Bases Empty	.275	.333	.341	91	25	3	0	1	1	8	5
Leadoff	.375	.434	.500	48	18	3	0	1	1	5	0
Not Leadoff	.163	.217	.163	43	7	0	0	0	0	3	5
Runners On	.267	.313	.300	60	16	0	1	0	13	4	8
First Base Only	.185	.241	.185	27	5	0	0	0	0	2	4
Scoring Position	.333	.371	.394	33	11	0	1	0	13	2	4
Late Innings, Close	.302	.375	.442	43	13	1	1	1	6	5	6

RBI/Opportunities

Scoring Position	13 / 42	(31%)
Scoring Position, 2 Out	10 / 23	(43%)
On Third, Less than 2 Out	3 / 5	(60%)
RBI in close games / RBI Total	9 / 14	(64%)

Barry Jones
Pittsburgh Pirates

1986: Power, Groundball   1985: Did not play   1984: Did not play

THREE YEARS (84 – 86)

	G	IP	H	BB	SO	SB	CS	W	L	S	ERA
Totals	26	37.1	29	21	29	5	0	3	4	3	2.89
At Home and on the Road											
Home	15	21.2	18	14	13	4	0	1	2	1	2.49
Road	11	15.2	11	7	16	1	0	2	2	2	3.45
During the Day and and at Night											
Day	5	7.2	5	4	11	0	0	1	1	1	4.70
Night	21	29.2	24	17	18	5	0	2	3	2	2.43
On Grass and on Turf											
Grass	4	6.2	3	4	10	0	0	1	0	1	2.70
Turf	22	30.2	26	17	19	5	0	2	4	2	2.93
By Month											
April	1	4.0	2	3	8	0	0	0	0	0	0.00
May	0	0.0	0	0	0	0	0	0	0	0	0.00
June	0	0.0	0	0	0	0	0	0	0	0	0.00
July	5	8.2	4	4	7	1	0	0	1	0	5.19
August	9	12.2	13	8	6	3	0	0	2	1	2.13
Sept/Oct	11	12.0	10	6	8	1	0	2	2	1	3.00

vs. Opponent Batters
THREE YEARS (84 – 86)

	Ave.	OBP	SLG	AB	H	2B	3B	HR	RBI	BB	SO
Totals	.215	.318	.348	135	29	5	2	3	18	21	29
Pitching vs. Left and Right-handed Batters											
Left	.250	.317	.411	56	14	1	1	2	10	6	9
Right	.190	.319	.304	79	15	4	1	1	8	15	20
Situational											
Bases Empty	.163	.256	.300	80	13	3	1	2	2	10	21
Leadoff	.176	.243	.353	34	6	3	0	1	1	3	8
Not Leadoff	.152	.264	.261	46	7	0	1	1	1	7	13
Runners On	.291	.403	.418	55	16	2	1	1	16	11	8
First Base Only	.400	.500	.400	15	6	0	0	0	0	3	2
Scoring Position	.250	.367	.425	40	10	2	1	1	16	8	6
Late Innings, Close	.289	.388	.458	83	24	4	2	2	14	14	16

RBI/Opportunities

Scoring Position	14 / 61	(23%)
Scoring Position, 2 Out	7 / 27	(26%)
On Third, Less than 2 Out	4 / 12	(33%)
RBI in close games / RBI Total	14 / 18	(78%)

Odell Jones
Baltimore Orioles

1986: Power, Flyball   1985: Did not play   1984: Finesse, Flyball

THREE YEARS (84 – 86)

	G	IP	H	BB	SO	SB	CS	W	L	S	ERA
Totals	54	108.2	120	46	60	17	7	4	6	2	3.73
At Home and on the Road											
Home	30	60.2	68	25	28	12	5	0	2	1	3.41
Road	24	48.0	52	21	32	5	2	4	4	1	4.12
During the Day and and at Night											
Day	11	17.0	18	8	14	2	0	2	1	0	4.76
Night	43	91.2	102	38	46	15	7	2	5	2	3.53
On Grass and on Turf											
Grass	48	99.0	113	43	53	16	7	3	5	2	3.82
Turf	6	9.2	7	3	7	1	0	1	1	0	2.79
By Month											
April	6	9.0	9	6	8	1	1	1	0	0	2.00
May	6	8.2	9	1	7	0	2	0	1	1	3.12
June	8	14.0	12	7	3	2	1	0	2	1	3.86
July	13	29.0	35	8	14	2	0	2	2	0	4.34
August	10	22.2	20	6	19	7	1	0	1	0	1.59
Sept/Oct	11	25.1	35	18	9	5	2	0	1	0	5.68

vs. Opponent Batters
THREE YEARS (84 – 86)

	Ave.	OBP	SLG	AB	H	2B	3B	HR	RBI	BB	SO
Totals	.293	.362	.434	410	120	19	3	11	64	46	60
Pitching vs. Left and Right-handed Batters											
Left	.302	.390	.484	192	58	8	3	7	31	29	29
Right	.284	.336	.390	218	62	11	0	4	33	17	31
Situational											
Bases Empty	.297	.355	.411	209	62	9	0	5	5	19	36
Leadoff	.366	.410	.484	93	34	5	0	2	2	7	9
Not Leadoff	.241	.313	.353	116	28	4	0	3	3	12	27
Runners On	.289	.369	.458	201	58	10	3	6	59	27	24
First Base Only	.250	.313	.342	76	19	1	0	2	5	5	9
Scoring Position	.312	.399	.528	125	39	9	3	4	54	22	15
Late Innings, Close	.333	.377	.511	135	45	9	0	5	27	9	17

RBI/Opportunities

Scoring Position	48 / 192	(25%)
Scoring Position, 2 Out	20 / 88	(23%)
On Third, Less than 2 Out	16 / 32	(50%)
RBI in close games / RBI Total	33 / 64	(52%)

Ruppert Jones
California Angels

THREE YEARS (84 – 86)

	Ave.	OBP	SLG	AB	H	2B	3B	HR	RBI	BB	SO
Totals	.242	.336	.454	997	241	50	6	50	153	142	216
Batting vs. Left and Right-handed Pitchers											
Left	.178	.270	.366	101	18	5	1	4	19	13	26
Right	.249	.344	.464	896	223	45	5	46	134	129	190
At Home and on the Road											
Home	.257	.366	.490	467	120	27	2	26	76	80	105
Road	.228	.309	.423	530	121	23	4	24	77	62	111
Facing Groundball Pitchers and Flyball Pitchers											
Groundball	.256	.341	.462	468	120	23	2	23	73	61	97
Flyball	.229	.332	.448	529	121	27	4	27	80	81	119
Facing Finesse Pitchers and Power Pitchers											
Finesse	.249	.329	.473	594	148	29	4	32	95	73	116
Power	.231	.346	.427	403	93	21	2	18	58	69	100
On Grass and on Turf											
Grass	.238	.339	.446	825	196	41	4	41	123	127	185
Turf	.262	.324	.494	172	45	9	2	9	30	15	31
During the Day and at Night											
Day	.278	.355	.582	299	83	18	2	23	59	35	70
Night	.226	.328	.400	698	158	32	4	27	94	107	146
By Month											
April	.247	.373	.461	89	22	7	0	4	17	19	21
May	.263	.409	.466	118	31	12	0	4	21	30	22
June	.244	.313	.556	180	44	5	3	15	34	18	47
July	.290	.377	.514	214	62	13	1	11	32	29	41
August	.227	.303	.432	229	52	9	1	12	32	24	46
Sept/Oct	.180	.274	.287	167	30	4	1	4	17	22	39
Situational											
Bases Empty	.213	.304	.406	572	122	25	2	27	27	74	115
Leadoff	.229	.313	.494	253	58	9	2	18	18	30	54
Not Leadoff	.201	.298	.335	319	64	16	0	9	9	44	61
Runners On	.280	.377	.520	425	119	25	4	23	126	68	101
First Base Only	.339	.422	.607	168	57	13	1	10	25	24	29
Scoring Position	.241	.350	.463	257	62	12	3	13	101	44	72
Late Innings, Close	.237	.374	.401	152	36	5	1	6	22	33	35

RBI/Opportunities

Scoring Position	79 / 357	(22%)
Scoring Position, 2 Out	36 / 170	(21%)
On Third, Less than 2 Out	31 / 65	(48%)
RBI in close games / RBI Total	90 / 153	(59%)

Bob Kearney
Seattle Mariners

THREE YEARS (84 – 86)

	Ave.	OBP	SLG	AB	H	2B	3B	HR	RBI	BB	SO
Totals	.234	.269	.349	940	220	47	2	19	95	41	166
Batting vs. Left and Right-handed Pitchers											
Left	.205	.239	.337	303	62	16	0	8	25	12	49
Right	.248	.283	.355	637	158	31	2	11	70	29	117
At Home and on the Road											
Home	.267	.305	.411	465	124	29	1	12	58	24	80
Road	.202	.233	.288	475	96	18	1	7	37	17	86
Facing Groundball Pitchers and Flyball Pitchers											
Groundball	.245	.284	.361	421	103	23	1	8	44	19	66
Flyball	.225	.256	.339	519	117	24	1	11	51	22	100
Facing Finesse Pitchers and Power Pitchers											
Finesse	.264	.292	.405	556	147	31	1	15	67	19	76
Power	.190	.235	.268	384	73	16	1	4	28	22	90
On Grass and on Turf											
Grass	.193	.224	.255	353	68	10	0	4	25	12	56
Turf	.259	.295	.405	587	152	37	2	15	70	29	110
During the Day and at Night											
Day	.242	.267	.329	219	53	13	0	2	19	7	31
Night	.232	.269	.355	721	167	34	2	17	76	34	135
By Month											
April	.162	.203	.206	136	22	6	0	0	8	7	26
May	.235	.272	.389	149	35	11	0	4	21	7	29
June	.258	.290	.419	217	56	9	1	8	31	8	33
July	.306	.345	.444	160	49	11	1	3	11	9	24
August	.240	.268	.337	175	42	8	0	3	19	7	32
Sept/Oct	.155	.187	.204	103	16	2	0	1	5	3	22
Situational											
Bases Empty	.226	.267	.335	532	120	29	1	9	9	27	103
Leadoff	.220	.238	.335	209	46	12	0	4	4	4	43
Not Leadoff	.229	.284	.334	323	74	17	1	5	5	23	60
Runners On	.245	.271	.368	408	100	18	1	10	86	14	63
First Base Only	.234	.260	.383	175	41	8	0	6	19	5	27
Scoring Position	.253	.280	.356	233	59	10	1	4	67	9	36
Late Innings, Close	.244	.265	.308	156	38	7	0	1	14	5	23

RBI/Opportunities

Scoring Position	59 / 305	(19%)
Scoring Position, 2 Out	32 / 151	(21%)
On Third, Less than 2 Out	17 / 54	(31%)
RBI in close games / RBI Total	51 / 95	(54%)

Matt Keough
Houston Astros

1986: Power, Flyball   1985: Power, Groundball   1984: Did not play

THREE YEARS (84 – 86)

	G	IP	H	BB	SO	SB	CS	W	L	S	ERA
Totals	33	74.0	68	34	54	4	6	5	5	0	4.01
At Home and on the Road											
Home	15	23.0	25	10	21	2	3	1	1	0	5.09
Road	18	51.0	43	24	33	2	3	5	4	0	3.53
During the Day and and at Night											
Day	14	28.0	24	19	19	1	4	0	2	0	3.86
Night	19	46.0	44	15	35	3	2	5	3	0	4.11
On Grass and on Turf											
Grass	22	40.0	36	23	32	2	5	4	3	0	4.50
Turf	11	34.0	32	11	22	2	1	1	2	0	3.44
By Month											
April	5	11.2	9	4	8	0	2	1	1	0	3.09
May	12	13.0	21	6	9	1	2	1	0	0	6.23
June	2	4.1	6	2	2	0	0	0	1	0	6.23
July	0	0.0	0	0	0	0	0	0	0	0	0.00
August	3	14.0	11	10	10	0	0	1	1	0	4.50
Sept/Oct	11	31.0	21	12	25	3	2	2	2	0	2.90

vs. Opponent Batters

THREE YEARS (84 – 86)

	Ave.	OBP	SLG	AB	H	2B	3B	HR	RBI	BB	SO
Totals	.249	.338	.403	273	68	13	1	9	29	34	54
Pitching vs. Left and Right-handed Batters											
Left	.242	.326	.339	124	30	6	0	2	9	14	19
Right	.255	.347	.456	149	38	7	1	7	20	20	35
Situational											
Bases Empty	.258	.320	.368	155	40	8	0	3	3	13	31
Leadoff	.338	.419	.508	65	22	5	0	2	2	9	11
Not Leadoff	.200	.242	.267	90	18	3	0	1	1	4	20
Runners On	.237	.359	.449	118	28	5	1	6	26	21	23
First Base Only	.340	.426	.660	47	16	1	1	4	9	6	7
Scoring Position	.169	.318	.310	71	12	4	0	2	17	15	16
Late Innings, Close	.188	.350	.406	32	6	1	0	2	2	7	7

RBI/Opportunities

Scoring Position	14 / 103	(14%)
Scoring Position, 2 Out	6 / 45	(13%)
On Third, Less than 2 Out	6 / 14	(43%)
RBI in close games / RBI Total	17 / 29	(59%)

Charlie Kerfeld
Houston Astros

1986: Power, Groundball   1985: Power, Groundball   1984: Did not play

THREE YEARS (84 – 86)

	G	IP	H	BB	SO	SB	CS	W	L	S	ERA
Totals	72	138.0	115	67	107	19	1	15	4	7	3.07
At Home and on the Road											
Home	34	70.0	56	28	53	9	1	8	1	4	2.57
Road	38	68.0	59	39	54	10	0	7	3	3	3.57
During the Day and at Night											
Day	28	57.0	40	31	47	8	0	6	2	2	2.37
Night	44	81.0	75	36	60	11	1	9	2	5	3.56
On Grass and on Turf											
Grass	24	47.2	45	30	38	7	0	5	2	1	4.34
Turf	48	90.1	70	37	69	12	1	10	2	6	2.39
By Month											
April	8	17.1	7	7	15	5	0	2	0	2	0.52
May	15	21.0	12	8	16	1	1	3	1	0	2.14
June	4	4.2	6	1	2	2	0	0	0	0	5.79
July	12	19.0	21	15	8	3	0	2	1	1	5.68
August	12	22.1	21	9	21	3	0	2	1	3	4.43
Sept/Oct	21	53.2	48	27	45	5	0	6	1	1	2.52

vs. Opponent Batters

THREE YEARS (84 – 86)

	Ave.	OBP	SLG	AB	H	2B	3B	HR	RBI	BB	SO
Totals	.231	.319	.304	497	115	11	2	7	56	67	107
Pitching vs. Left and Right-handed Batters											
Left	.267	.362	.391	225	60	9	2	5	27	36	38
Right	.202	.283	.232	272	55	2	0	2	29	31	69
Situational											
Bases Empty	.225	.306	.284	275	62	5	1	3	3	30	59
Leadoff	.271	.363	.322	118	32	3	0	1	1	16	25
Not Leadoff	.191	.262	.255	157	30	2	1	2	2	14	34
Runners On	.239	.335	.329	222	53	6	1	4	53	37	48
First Base Only	.303	.380	.416	89	27	4	0	2	5	11	19
Scoring Position	.195	.308	.271	133	26	2	1	2	48	26	29
Late Innings, Close	.214	.314	.271	192	41	3	1	2	19	28	35

RBI/Opportunities

Scoring Position	42 / 219	(19%)
Scoring Position, 2 Out	10 / 89	(11%)
On Third, Less than 2 Out	26 / 57	(46%)
RBI in close games / RBI Total	32 / 56	(57%)

Sammy Khalifa
Pittsburgh Pirates

	Ave.	OBP	SLG	AB	H	2B	3B	HR	RBI	BB	SO
THREE YEARS (84 – 86)											
Totals	.221	.296	.289	471	104	20	3	2	35	52	84
Batting vs. Left and Right-handed Pitchers											
Left	.265	.329	.344	151	40	8	2	0	9	15	13
Right	.200	.281	.263	320	64	12	1	2	26	37	71
At Home and on the Road											
Home	.231	.326	.306	242	56	15	0	1	17	35	44
Road	.210	.262	.271	229	48	5	3	1	18	17	40
Facing Groundball Pitchers and Flyball Pitchers											
Groundball	.230	.326	.296	196	45	6	2	1	16	29	31
Flyball	.215	.273	.284	275	59	14	1	1	19	23	53
Facing Finesse Pitchers and Power Pitchers											
Finesse	.225	.295	.277	289	65	12	0	1	23	30	40
Power	.214	.298	.308	182	39	8	3	1	12	22	44
On Grass and on Turf											
Grass	.168	.206	.224	125	21	4	0	1	11	6	21
Turf	.240	.326	.312	346	83	16	3	1	24	46	63
During the Day and at Night											
Day	.220	.298	.293	150	33	6	1	1	10	17	23
Night	.221	.295	.287	321	71	14	2	1	25	35	61
By Month											
April	.071	.133	.071	28	2	0	0	0	1	2	6
May	.246	.347	.292	65	16	3	0	0	3	10	16
June	.260	.339	.380	50	13	6	0	0	0	6	7
July	.215	.270	.280	93	20	3	0	1	8	7	7
August	.193	.254	.272	114	22	4	1	1	8	10	20
Sept/Oct	.256	.343	.322	121	31	4	2	0	15	17	28
Situational											
Bases Empty	.246	.290	.333	285	70	16	3	1	1	18	41
Leadoff	.252	.292	.383	107	27	7	2	1	1	6	17
Not Leadoff	.242	.289	.303	178	43	9	1	0	0	12	24
Runners On	.183	.304	.220	186	34	4	0	1	34	34	43
First Base Only	.208	.265	.234	77	16	2	0	0	0	6	19
Scoring Position	.165	.326	.211	109	18	2	0	1	34	28	24
Late Innings, Close	.244	.295	.305	82	20	3	1	0	2	6	16

RBI/Opportunities

Scoring Position	32 / 179	(18%)
Scoring Position, 2 Out	10 / 96	(10%)
On Third, Less than 2 Out	15 / 29	(52%)
RBI in close games / RBI Total	26 / 35	(74%)

Eric King
Detroit Tigers

1986: Finesse, Groundball   1985: Did not play   1984: Did not play

	G	IP	H	BB	SO	SB	CS	W	L	S	ERA
THREE YEARS (84 – 86)											
Totals	33	138.1	108	63	79	8	5	11	4	3	3.51
At Home and on the Road											
Home	14	67.2	36	25	33	3	4	6	0	1	2.00
Road	19	70.2	72	38	46	5	1	5	4	2	4.97
During the Day and and at Night											
Day	9	38.0	38	16	21	2	2	3	3	0	5.92
Night	24	100.1	70	47	58	6	3	8	1	3	2.60
On Grass and on Turf											
Grass	27	112.0	80	46	66	4	5	9	3	3	3.05
Turf	6	26.1	28	17	13	4	0	2	1	0	5.47
By Month											
April	0	0.0	0	0	0	0	0	0	0	0	0.00
May	5	15.0	6	4	9	0	1	1	0	1	1.20
June	7	44.1	30	20	28	3	1	3	0	0	2.64
July	6	36.1	33	18	22	2	2	4	2	0	3.96
August	4	24.0	24	14	8	2	1	1	2	0	6.37
Sept/Oct	11	18.2	15	7	12	1	0	2	0	2	2.89

vs. Opponent Batters

	Ave.	OBP	SLG	AB	H	2B	3B	HR	RBI	BB	SO
THREE YEARS (84 – 86)											
Totals	.216	.312	.329	501	108	24	0	11	50	63	79
Pitching vs. Left and Right-handed Batters											
Left	.240	.327	.390	246	59	13	0	8	29	28	35
Right	.192	.298	.271	255	49	11	0	3	21	35	44
Situational											
Bases Empty	.206	.316	.342	281	58	11	0	9	9	39	54
Leadoff	.222	.310	.341	126	28	3	0	4	4	15	20
Not Leadoff	.194	.321	.342	155	30	8	0	5	5	24	34
Runners On	.227	.308	.314	220	50	13	0	2	41	24	25
First Base Only	.235	.299	.357	98	23	6	0	2	7	8	13
Scoring Position	.221	.314	.279	122	27	7	0	0	34	16	12
Late Innings, Close	.191	.214	.294	68	13	1	0	2	4	2	14

RBI/Opportunities

Scoring Position	32 / 169	(19%)
Scoring Position, 2 Out	10 / 78	(13%)
On Third, Less than 2 Out	12 / 28	(43%)
RBI in close games / RBI Total	42 / 50	(84%)

Mike Kingery
Kansas City Royals

	Ave.	OBP	SLG	AB	H	2B	3B	HR	RBI	BB	SO
THREE YEARS (84 – 86)											
Totals	.258	.296	.388	209	54	8	5	3	14	12	30
Batting vs. Left and Right-handed Pitchers											
Left	.067	.121	.067	30	2	0	0	0	2	2	8
Right	.291	.326	.441	179	52	8	5	3	12	10	22
At Home and on the Road											
Home	.278	.309	.400	115	32	5	3	1	6	6	12
Road	.234	.280	.372	94	22	3	2	2	8	6	18
Facing Groundball Pitchers and Flyball Pitchers											
Groundball	.276	.327	.449	98	27	5	3	2	8	8	17
Flyball	.243	.267	.333	111	27	3	2	1	6	4	13
Facing Finesse Pitchers and Power Pitchers											
Finesse	.235	.281	.361	119	28	3	3	2	8	8	21
Power	.289	.316	.422	90	26	5	2	1	6	4	9
On Grass and on Turf											
Grass	.254	.306	.403	67	17	3	2	1	5	5	10
Turf	.261	.291	.380	142	37	5	3	2	9	7	20
During the Day and at Night											
Day	.326	.367	.435	46	15	1	2	0	4	3	6
Night	.239	.276	.374	163	39	7	3	3	10	9	24
By Month											
April	.000	.000	.000	0	0	0	0	0	0	0	0
May	.000	.000	.000	0	0	0	0	0	0	0	0
June	.000	.000	.000	0	0	0	0	0	0	0	0
July	.282	.325	.423	71	20	3	2	1	4	5	7
August	.208	.237	.312	77	16	3	1	1	2	3	15
Sept/Oct	.295	.333	.443	61	18	2	2	1	8	4	8
Situational											
Bases Empty	.258	.298	.435	124	32	6	5	2	2	7	20
Leadoff	.225	.295	.550	40	9	2	4	1	1	4	9
Not Leadoff	.274	.299	.381	84	23	4	1	1	1	3	11
Runners On	.259	.293	.318	85	22	2	0	1	12	5	10
First Base Only	.395	.425	.500	38	15	1	0	1	2	2	6
Scoring Position	.149	.192	.170	47	7	1	0	0	10	3	4
Late Innings, Close	.216	.237	.378	37	8	2	2	0	0	1	8

RBI/Opportunities

Scoring Position	10 / 54	(19%)
Scoring Position, 2 Out	2 / 24	(8%)
On Third, Less than 2 Out	6 / 9	(67%)
RBI in close games / RBI Total	9 / 14	(64%)

Bob Kipper
Pittsburgh Pirates

1986: Finesse, Flyball   1985: Finesse, Flyball   1984: Did not play

	G	IP	H	BB	SO	SB	CS	W	L	S	ERA
THREE YEARS (84 – 86)											
Totals	27	142.0	151	44	94	19	8	7	11	0	4.63
At Home and on the Road											
Home	12	68.0	78	22	46	10	5	2	7	0	5.43
Road	15	74.0	73	22	48	9	3	5	4	0	3.89
During the Day and and at Night											
Day	7	37.2	32	11	20	2	1	2	3	0	4.06
Night	20	104.1	119	33	74	17	7	5	8	0	4.83
On Grass and on Turf											
Grass	10	43.1	48	16	24	6	1	2	4	0	5.82
Turf	17	98.2	103	28	70	13	7	5	7	0	4.10
By Month											
April	5	13.1	19	9	6	5	1	0	3	0	9.45
May	6	39.2	46	14	27	4	4	1	2	0	4.31
June	4	22.0	25	5	19	1	2	2	2	0	4.50
July	0	0.0	0	0	0	0	0	0	0	0	0.00
August	0	0.0	0	0	0	0	0	0	0	0	0.00
Sept/Oct	12	67.0	61	16	42	9	1	4	4	0	3.90

vs. Opponent Batters

	Ave.	OBP	SLG	AB	H	2B	3B	HR	RBI	BB	SO
THREE YEARS (84 – 86)											
Totals	.268	.320	.455	563	151	31	4	22	74	44	94
Pitching vs. Left and Right-handed Batters											
Left	.282	.295	.365	85	24	5	1	0	10	2	15
Right	.266	.324	.471	478	127	26	3	22	64	42	79
Situational											
Bases Empty	.254	.311	.424	342	87	16	3	12	12	26	62
Leadoff	.270	.329	.467	137	37	7	1	6	6	12	25
Not Leadoff	.244	.299	.395	205	50	9	2	6	6	14	37
Runners On	.290	.335	.502	221	64	15	1	10	62	18	32
First Base Only	.344	.378	.559	93	32	6	1	4	10	5	10
Scoring Position	.250	.306	.461	128	32	9	0	6	52	13	22
Late Innings, Close	.324	.361	.441	34	11	1	0	1	2	1	6

RBI/Opportunities

Scoring Position	39 / 174	(22%)
Scoring Position, 2 Out	16 / 86	(19%)
On Third, Less than 2 Out	16 / 31	(52%)
RBI in close games / RBI Total	51 / 74	(69%)

Ron Kittle
New York Yankees

	Ave.	OBP	SLG	AB	H	2B	3B	HR	RBI	BB	SO
THREE YEARS (84 – 86)											
Totals	.220	.292	.447	1221	269	40	0	79	192	115	339
Batting vs. Left and Right-handed Pitchers											
Left	.217	.303	.423	506	110	17	0	29	76	60	136
Right	.222	.284	.464	715	159	23	0	50	116	55	203
At Home and on the Road											
Home	.215	.290	.426	608	131	23	0	35	89	63	164
Road	.225	.294	.468	613	138	17	0	44	103	52	175
Facing Groundball Pitchers and Flyball Pitchers											
Groundball	.222	.301	.443	499	111	14	0	32	82	50	126
Flyball	.219	.286	.450	722	158	26	0	47	110	65	213
Facing Finesse Pitchers and Power Pitchers											
Finesse	.234	.294	.472	708	166	24	0	48	109	54	159
Power	.201	.289	.413	513	103	16	0	31	83	61	180
On Grass and on Turf											
Grass	.215	.287	.428	1029	221	33	0	62	153	100	296
Turf	.250	.316	.552	192	48	7	0	17	39	15	43
During the Day and at Night											
Day	.205	.263	.418	361	74	8	0	23	54	29	103
Night	.227	.304	.459	860	195	32	0	56	138	86	236
By Month											
April	.237	.283	.526	152	36	5	0	13	32	11	48
May	.204	.278	.345	206	42	5	0	8	29	21	61
June	.212	.304	.481	241	51	11	0	18	36	29	64
July	.198	.283	.373	177	35	4	0	9	19	19	54
August	.222	.284	.409	198	44	7	0	10	24	15	56
Sept/Oct	.247	.309	.534	247	61	8	0	21	52	20	56
Situational											
Bases Empty	.217	.297	.436	674	146	22	0	42	42	65	180
Leadoff	.200	.295	.367	275	55	10	0	12	12	29	76
Not Leadoff	.228	.298	.484	399	91	12	0	30	30	36	104
Runners On	.225	.285	.461	547	123	18	0	37	150	50	159
First Base Only	.236	.305	.514	259	61	6	0	22	45	24	70
Scoring Position	.215	.268	.413	288	62	12	0	15	105	26	89
Late Innings, Close	.169	.249	.301	183	31	3	0	7	21	19	58

RBI/Opportunities		
Scoring Position	79 / 380	(21%)
Scoring Position, 2 Out	30 / 169	(18%)
On Third, Less than 2 Out	33 / 75	(44%)
RBI in close games / RBI Total	129 / 192	(67%)

Wayne Krenchicki
Montreal Expos

	Ave.	OBP	SLG	AB	H	2B	3B	HR	RBI	BB	SO
THREE YEARS (84 – 86)											
Totals	.268	.342	.386	575	154	24	4	12	70	69	75
Batting vs. Left and Right-handed Pitchers											
Left	.200	.237	.200	35	7	0	0	0	4	2	13
Right	.272	.349	.398	540	147	24	4	12	66	67	62
At Home and on the Road											
Home	.297	.391	.418	263	78	13	2	5	34	44	40
Road	.244	.297	.359	312	76	11	2	7	36	25	35
Facing Groundball Pitchers and Flyball Pitchers											
Groundball	.260	.343	.357	269	70	8	3	4	37	37	38
Flyball	.275	.341	.412	306	84	16	1	8	33	32	37
Facing Finesse Pitchers and Power Pitchers											
Finesse	.265	.331	.375	339	90	15	2	6	38	35	37
Power	.271	.358	.403	236	64	9	2	6	32	34	38
On Grass and on Turf											
Grass	.282	.351	.431	188	53	5	1	7	30	21	22
Turf	.261	.338	.364	387	101	19	3	5	40	48	53
During the Day and at Night											
Day	.308	.369	.421	195	60	9	2	3	26	22	21
Night	.247	.328	.368	380	94	15	2	9	44	47	54
By Month											
April	.200	.310	.320	25	5	0	0	1	2	4	6
May	.198	.272	.358	81	16	4	0	3	9	9	14
June	.308	.391	.485	130	40	6	1	5	19	19	21
July	.278	.346	.357	115	32	7	1	0	7	12	11
August	.245	.307	.284	102	25	2	1	0	13	10	11
Sept/Oct	.295	.367	.426	122	36	5	1	3	20	15	12
Situational											
Bases Empty	.284	.339	.435	324	92	16	3	9	9	27	38
Leadoff	.302	.343	.481	129	39	9	1	4	4	8	12
Not Leadoff	.272	.336	.405	195	53	7	2	5	5	19	26
Runners On	.247	.346	.323	251	62	8	1	3	61	42	37
First Base Only	.247	.351	.296	81	20	2	1	0	2	13	13
Scoring Position	.247	.343	.335	170	42	6	0	3	59	29	24
Late Innings, Close	.225	.302	.338	151	34	5	0	4	18	18	23

RBI/Opportunities		
Scoring Position	53 / 241	(22%)
Scoring Position, 2 Out	20 / 115	(17%)
On Third, Less than 2 Out	24 / 41	(59%)
RBI in close games / RBI Total	52 / 70	(74%)

John Kruk
San Diego Padres

	Ave.	OBP	SLG	AB	H	2B	3B	HR	RBI	BB	SO
THREE YEARS (84 – 86)											
Totals	.309	.403	.424	278	86	16	2	4	38	45	58
Batting vs. Left and Right-handed Pitchers											
Left	.304	.402	.342	79	24	3	0	0	12	13	20
Right	.312	.403	.457	199	62	13	2	4	26	32	38
At Home and on the Road											
Home	.311	.408	.447	103	32	11	0	1	12	17	25
Road	.309	.400	.411	175	54	5	2	3	26	28	33
Facing Groundball Pitchers and Flyball Pitchers											
Groundball	.250	.347	.318	148	37	7	0	1	17	23	35
Flyball	.377	.467	.546	130	49	9	2	3	21	22	23
Facing Finesse Pitchers and Power Pitchers											
Finesse	.321	.386	.423	168	54	11	0	2	20	19	28
Power	.291	.426	.427	110	32	5	2	2	18	26	30
On Grass and on Turf											
Grass	.294	.377	.406	187	55	12	0	3	24	26	44
Turf	.341	.455	.462	91	31	4	2	1	14	19	14
During the Day and at Night											
Day	.339	.410	.459	109	37	7	0	2	12	13	20
Night	.290	.399	.402	169	49	9	2	2	26	32	38
By Month											
April	.222	.250	.296	27	6	2	0	0	1	1	8
May	.391	.462	.565	23	9	1	0	1	4	3	4
June	.286	.444	.333	21	6	1	0	0	5	6	3
July	.343	.410	.429	35	12	3	0	0	3	4	7
August	.308	.427	.484	91	28	8	1	2	10	19	19
Sept/Oct	.309	.389	.383	81	25	1	1	1	15	12	17
Situational											
Bases Empty	.247	.356	.364	154	38	10	1	2	2	26	36
Leadoff	.259	.355	.296	54	14	2	0	0	0	8	10
Not Leadoff	.240	.356	.400	100	24	8	1	2	2	18	26
Runners On	.387	.462	.500	124	48	6	1	2	36	19	22
First Base Only	.490	.559	.686	51	25	4	0	2	5	8	3
Scoring Position	.315	.395	.370	73	23	2	1	0	31	11	19
Late Innings, Close	.308	.390	.327	52	16	1	0	0	8	7	13

RBI/Opportunities		
Scoring Position	29 / 101	(29%)
Scoring Position, 2 Out	18 / 44	(41%)
On Third, Less than 2 Out	8 / 17	(47%)
RBI in close games / RBI Total	28 / 38	(74%)

Randy Kutcher
San Francisco Giants

	Ave.	OBP	SLG	AB	H	2B	3B	HR	RBI	BB	SO
THREE YEARS (84 – 86)											
Totals	.237	.279	.409	186	44	9	1	7	16	11	41
Batting vs. Left and Right-handed Pitchers											
Left	.203	.257	.319	69	14	3	1	1	5	5	18
Right	.256	.293	.462	117	30	6	0	6	11	6	23
At Home and on the Road											
Home	.261	.313	.489	92	24	6	0	5	9	7	21
Road	.213	.245	.330	94	20	3	1	2	7	4	20
Facing Groundball Pitchers and Flyball Pitchers											
Groundball	.244	.284	.378	90	22	4	1	2	6	5	18
Flyball	.229	.275	.438	96	22	5	0	5	10	6	23
Facing Finesse Pitchers and Power Pitchers											
Finesse	.258	.305	.442	120	31	7	0	5	13	8	20
Power	.197	.232	.348	66	13	2	1	2	3	3	21
On Grass and on Turf											
Grass	.227	.270	.420	150	34	6	1	7	12	9	39
Turf	.278	.316	.361	36	10	3	0	0	4	2	2
During the Day and at Night											
Day	.264	.310	.481	106	28	5	0	6	9	7	23
Night	.200	.238	.313	80	16	4	1	1	7	4	18
By Month											
April	.000	.000	.000	0	0	0	0	0	0	0	0
May	.000	.000	.000	0	0	0	0	0	0	0	0
June	.259	.259	.426	54	14	3	0	2	4	0	14
July	.224	.280	.487	76	17	3	1	5	9	6	13
August	.192	.276	.231	26	5	1	0	0	1	3	5
Sept/Oct	.267	.313	.333	30	8	2	0	0	2	2	9
Situational											
Bases Empty	.258	.308	.492	124	32	8	0	7	7	9	23
Leadoff	.284	.329	.541	74	21	4	0	5	5	5	13
Not Leadoff	.220	.278	.420	50	11	4	0	2	2	4	10
Runners On	.194	.219	.242	62	12	1	1	0	9	2	18
First Base Only	.278	.278	.389	18	5	0	1	0	1	0	5
Scoring Position	.159	.196	.182	44	7	1	0	0	8	2	13
Late Innings, Close	.205	.262	.256	39	8	2	0	0	0	3	9

RBI/Opportunities		
Scoring Position	8 / 59	(14%)
Scoring Position, 2 Out	5 / 33	(15%)
On Third, Less than 2 Out	2 / 7	(29%)
RBI in close games / RBI Total	11 / 16	(69%)

Mike LaCoss
San Francisco Giants

1986: Finesse, Groundball 1985: Power, Groundball 1984: Power, Groundball

	THREE YEARS (84 – 86)										
	G	IP	H	BB	SO	SB	CS	W	L	S	ERA
Totals	97	377.0	360	154	198	46	25	18	19	4	3.89
At Home and on the Road											
Home	47	199.2	169	79	104	24	8	11	6	3	3.38
Road	50	177.1	191	75	94	22	17	7	13	1	4.47
During the Day and and at Night											
Day	34	133.0	133	64	62	13	11	6	10	0	5.08
Night	63	244.0	227	90	136	33	14	12	9	4	3.25
On Grass and on Turf											
Grass	53	205.1	195	79	102	22	12	10	12	0	4.16
Turf	44	171.2	165	75	96	24	13	8	7	4	3.57
By Month											
April	16	27.1	21	10	14	3	1	1	0	0	3.62
May	16	71.0	60	24	36	9	2	5	1	1	2.66
June	23	86.1	77	38	44	4	9	5	2	3	3.23
July	17	81.2	71	30	46	10	6	4	5	0	3.86
August	13	56.0	72	27	31	11	4	2	6	0	6.27
Sept/Oct	12	54.2	59	25	27	9	3	1	5	0	4.28

	vs. Opponent Batters THREE YEARS (84 – 86)										
	Ave.	OBP	SLG	AB	H	2B	3B	HR	RBI	BB	SO
Totals	.255	.330	.345	1412	360	48	11	19	172	154	198
Pitching vs. Left and Right-handed Batters											
Left	.237	.321	.311	739	175	19	9	6	80	92	99
Right	.275	.340	.382	673	185	29	2	13	92	62	99
Situational											
Bases Empty	.230	.291	.297	831	191	23	6	7	7	69	124
Leadoff	.262	.323	.321	355	93	8	2	3	3	32	47
Not Leadoff	.206	.267	.279	476	98	15	4	4	4	37	77
Runners On	.291	.381	.413	581	169	25	5	12	165	85	74
First Base Only	.258	.337	.360	225	58	6	1	5	16	25	27
Scoring Position	.312	.408	.447	356	111	19	4	7	149	60	47
Late Innings, Close	.200	.287	.265	155	31	8	1	0	11	19	23

RBI/Opportunities		
Scoring Position	131 / 510	(26%)
Scoring Position, 2 Out	55 / 214	(26%)
On Third, Less than 2 Out	45 / 99	(45%)
RBI in close games / RBI Total	100 / 172	(58%)

Dave LaPoint
San Diego Padres

1986: Finesse, Groundball 1985: Finesse, Groundball 1984: Power, Groundball

	THREE YEARS (84 – 86)										
	G	IP	H	BB	SO	SB	CS	W	L	S	ERA
Totals	104	528.2	572	207	329	47	24	23	37	0	4.07
At Home and on the Road											
Home	48	266.2	267	106	167	23	16	11	13	0	3.44
Road	56	262.0	305	101	162	24	8	12	24	0	4.71
During the Day and and at Night											
Day	35	189.2	202	70	110	22	6	8	16	0	3.46
Night	69	339.0	370	137	219	25	18	15	21	0	4.41
On Grass and on Turf											
Grass	61	286.1	307	116	174	28	11	8	22	0	4.05
Turf	43	242.1	265	91	155	19	13	15	15	0	4.09
By Month											
April	12	67.2	73	26	38	5	4	2	7	0	3.86
May	18	113.0	102	53	72	10	10	7	7	0	3.35
June	14	75.2	91	18	44	7	1	2	6	0	4.64
July	18	79.1	93	36	47	10	3	4	4	0	4.54
August	20	89.0	94	36	62	9	3	4	4	0	3.64
Sept/Oct	22	104.0	119	38	66	6	3	4	9	0	4.59

	vs. Opponent Batters THREE YEARS (84 – 86)										
	Ave.	OBP	SLG	AB	H	2B	3B	HR	RBI	BB	SO
Totals	.278	.343	.406	2058	572	79	23	46	241	207	329
Pitching vs. Left and Right-handed Batters											
Left	.270	.313	.369	355	96	8	3	7	29	22	41
Right	.280	.349	.413	1703	476	71	20	39	212	185	288
Situational											
Bases Empty	.270	.329	.399	1184	320	40	17	26	26	103	196
Leadoff	.290	.339	.412	517	150	17	11	8	8	38	80
Not Leadoff	.255	.321	.388	667	170	23	6	18	18	65	116
Runners On	.288	.362	.415	874	252	39	6	20	215	104	133
First Base Only	.286	.331	.405	385	110	17	1	9	27	26	55
Scoring Position	.290	.383	.423	489	142	22	5	11	188	78	78
Late Innings, Close	.283	.363	.408	152	43	4	0	5	15	19	29

RBI/Opportunities		
Scoring Position	166 / 699	(24%)
Scoring Position, 2 Out	64 / 318	(20%)
On Third, Less than 2 Out	63 / 124	(51%)
RBI in close games / RBI Total	153 / 241	(63%)

Pete Ladd
Seattle Mariners

1986: Finesse, Flyball 1985: Finesse, Flyball 1984: Power, Flyball

	THREE YEARS (84 – 86)										
	G	IP	H	BB	SO	SB	CS	W	L	S	ERA
Totals	135	207.1	221	66	150	17	11	12	15	10	4.60
At Home and on the Road											
Home	61	101.1	103	35	77	5	5	10	5	4	4.44
Road	74	106.0	118	31	73	12	6	2	10	6	4.75
During the Day and and at Night											
Day	43	68.2	86	27	46	7	3	1	5	5	5.77
Night	92	138.2	135	39	104	10	8	11	10	5	4.02
On Grass and on Turf											
Grass	86	127.0	132	44	88	8	7	5	12	7	4.89
Turf	49	80.1	89	22	62	9	4	7	3	3	4.15
By Month											
April	22	34.2	38	8	25	2	4	2	1	1	3.37
May	25	35.0	33	17	19	5	3	3	2	5	4.89
June	20	39.0	46	13	26	5	1	0	3	1	5.77
July	29	53.2	52	15	48	2	1	4	1	1	3.69
August	24	29.2	29	10	19	1	2	3	6	0	4.55
Sept/Oct	15	15.1	23	3	13	2	0	0	2	2	7.04

	vs. Opponent Batters THREE YEARS (84 – 86)										
	Ave.	OBP	SLG	AB	H	2B	3B	HR	RBI	BB	SO
Totals	.275	.328	.465	804	221	48	6	31	140	66	150
Pitching vs. Left and Right-handed Batters											
Left	.275	.346	.504	345	95	18	2	19	53	39	59
Right	.275	.315	.436	459	126	30	4	12	87	27	91
Situational											
Bases Empty	.273	.322	.458	400	109	28	2	14	14	27	73
Leadoff	.306	.351	.531	160	49	11	2	7	7	9	26
Not Leadoff	.250	.302	.408	240	60	17	0	7	7	18	47
Runners On	.277	.335	.473	404	112	20	4	17	126	39	77
First Base Only	.313	.357	.478	134	42	7	0	5	13	9	24
Scoring Position	.259	.325	.470	270	70	13	4	12	113	30	53
Late Innings, Close	.268	.323	.482	280	75	16	1	14	60	23	51

RBI/Opportunities		
Scoring Position	90 / 383	(23%)
Scoring Position, 2 Out	30 / 183	(16%)
On Third, Less than 2 Out	41 / 75	(55%)
RBI in close games / RBI Total	68 / 140	(49%)

Dennis Lamp
Toronto Blue Jays

1986: Finesse, Groundball 1985: Finesse, Groundball 1984: Power, Groundball

	THREE YEARS (84 – 86)										
	G	IP	H	BB	SO	SB	CS	W	L	S	ERA
Totals	149	263.2	286	88	143	26	2	21	14	13	4.20
At Home and on the Road											
Home	68	128.2	139	44	74	11	1	11	6	8	3.85
Road	81	135.0	147	44	69	15	1	10	8	5	4.53
During the Day and and at Night											
Day	54	90.1	97	30	50	14	1	8	5	6	4.18
Night	95	173.1	189	58	93	12	1	13	9	7	4.21
On Grass and on Turf											
Grass	62	99.1	112	32	53	9	1	9	6	4	4.80
Turf	87	164.1	174	56	90	17	1	12	8	9	3.83
By Month											
April	23	39.0	38	13	24	2	0	4	4	3	4.38
May	28	38.2	42	18	24	6	1	3	1	5	4.66
June	31	48.1	51	14	27	5	0	4	2	2	4.28
July	23	43.2	56	12	22	4	0	1	3	0	4.53
August	23	48.2	47	15	18	3	1	3	3	2	2.77
Sept/Oct	21	45.1	52	16	28	6	0	6	1	1	4.76

	vs. Opponent Batters THREE YEARS (84 – 86)										
	Ave.	OBP	SLG	AB	H	2B	3B	HR	RBI	BB	SO
Totals	.278	.333	.375	1028	286	26	5	21	146	88	142
Pitching vs. Left and Right-handed Batters											
Left	.291	.359	.360	444	129	9	2	6	59	50	46
Right	.269	.313	.385	584	157	17	3	15	87	38	96
Situational											
Bases Empty	.252	.309	.309	528	133	8	2	6	6	44	74
Leadoff	.239	.305	.307	218	52	4	1	3	3	21	42
Not Leadoff	.261	.312	.310	310	81	4	1	3	3	23	32
Runners On	.306	.358	.444	500	153	18	3	15	140	44	68
First Base Only	.287	.315	.374	195	56	5	0	4	10	8	23
Scoring Position	.318	.383	.489	305	97	13	3	11	130	36	45
Late Innings, Close	.308	.381	.409	286	88	6	1	7	58	34	47

RBI/Opportunities		
Scoring Position	109 / 430	(25%)
Scoring Position, 2 Out	46 / 187	(25%)
On Third, Less than 2 Out	42 / 92	(46%)
RBI in close games / RBI Total	85 / 146	(58%)

Tito Landrum
St. Louis Cardinals

THREE YEARS (84 – 86)

	Ave.	OBP	SLG	AB	H	2B	3B	HR	RBI	BB	SO
Totals	.250	.309	.360	539	135	24	4	9	64	47	98
Batting vs. Left and Right-handed Pitchers											
Left	.237	.305	.352	426	101	19	3	8	57	43	77
Right	.301	.325	.389	113	34	5	1	1	7	4	21
At Home and on the Road											
Home	.273	.335	.419	253	69	13	3	6	42	25	40
Road	.231	.285	.308	286	66	11	1	3	22	22	58
Facing Groundball Pitchers and Flyball Pitchers											
Groundball	.247	.303	.339	283	70	10	2	4	32	22	44
Flyball	.254	.315	.383	256	65	14	2	5	32	25	54
Facing Finesse Pitchers and Power Pitchers											
Finesse	.256	.292	.345	293	75	11	3	3	27	16	41
Power	.244	.327	.378	246	60	13	1	6	37	31	57
On Grass and on Turf											
Grass	.212	.270	.308	146	31	3	1	3	13	12	30
Turf	.265	.323	.379	393	104	21	3	6	51	35	68
During the Day and at Night											
Day	.249	.311	.338	201	50	11	2	1	19	19	32
Night	.251	.307	.373	338	85	13	2	8	45	28	66
By Month											
April	.192	.250	.269	52	10	1	0	1	2	3	4
May	.269	.315	.463	67	18	7	0	2	17	5	14
June	.239	.337	.296	71	17	2	1	0	6	11	10
July	.278	.323	.382	144	40	9	0	2	17	10	31
August	.284	.323	.379	116	33	4	2	1	10	7	20
Sept/Oct	.191	.275	.326	89	17	1	1	3	12	11	19
Situational											
Bases Empty	.231	.288	.343	277	64	16	3	3	3	21	52
Leadoff	.206	.280	.330	97	20	5	2	1	1	9	18
Not Leadoff	.244	.292	.350	180	44	11	1	2	2	12	34
Runners On	.271	.330	.378	262	71	8	1	6	61	26	46
First Base Only	.289	.319	.386	114	33	2	0	3	8	5	15
Scoring Position	.257	.337	.372	148	38	6	1	3	53	21	31
Late Innings, Close	.298	.349	.456	114	34	6	0	4	22	9	27

RBI/Opportunities

Scoring Position	48 / 203	(24%)
Scoring Position, 2 Out	12 / 79	(15%)
On Third, Less than 2 Out	20 / 43	(47%)
RBI in close games / RBI Total	46 / 64	(72%)

Rick Langford
Oakland A's

1986: Finesse, Flyball   1985: Finesse, Flyball   1984: Finesse, Flyball

THREE YEARS (84 – 86)

	G	IP	H	BB	SO	SB	CS	W	L	S	ERA
Totals	42	122.2	144	35	53	6	6	4	15	0	5.58
At Home and on the Road											
Home	16	56.0	45	14	27	1	2	4	3	0	4.34
Road	26	66.2	99	21	26	5	4	0	12	0	6.61
During the Day and and at Night											
Day	13	37.2	42	12	16	4	2	1	3	0	5.73
Night	29	85.0	102	23	37	2	4	3	12	0	5.51
On Grass and on Turf											
Grass	34	109.2	115	29	49	5	5	4	12	0	4.84
Turf	8	13.0	29	6	4	1	1	0	3	0	11.77
By Month											
April	3	16.2	11	6	12	0	2	1	2	0	4.32
May	3	9.0	18	8	2	1	0	0	2	0	12.00
June	9	35.2	42	3	19	0	1	0	5	0	5.55
July	10	22.0	27	10	13	1	1	0	5	0	6.55
August	7	16.0	16	2	11	0	2	2	1	0	2.81
Sept/Oct	10	23.1	30	6	6	4	0	1	0	0	5.01

vs. Opponent Batters
THREE YEARS (84 – 86)

	Ave.	OBP	SLG	AB	H	2B	3B	HR	RBI	BB	SO
Totals	.287	.334	.487	501	144	27	2	23	76	35	53
Pitching vs. Left and Right-handed Batters											
Left	.326	.381	.548	230	75	13	1	12	35	20	21
Right	.255	.293	.435	271	69	14	1	11	41	15	32
Situational											
Bases Empty	.270	.306	.444	311	84	13	1	13	13	15	37
Leadoff	.228	.264	.325	123	28	6	0	2	2	6	13
Not Leadoff	.298	.333	.521	188	56	7	1	11	11	9	24
Runners On	.316	.377	.558	190	60	14	1	10	63	20	16
First Base Only	.271	.326	.459	85	23	2	1	4	10	7	9
Scoring Position	.352	.417	.638	105	37	12	0	6	53	13	7
Late Innings, Close	.276	.300	.276	29	8	0	0	0	2	1	4

RBI/Opportunities

Scoring Position	45 / 140	(32%)
Scoring Position, 2 Out	24 / 77	(31%)
On Third, Less than 2 Out	11 / 18	(61%)
RBI in close games / RBI Total	49 / 76	(64%)

Barry Larkin
Cincinnati Reds

THREE YEARS (84 – 86)

	Ave.	OBP	SLG	AB	H	2B	3B	HR	RBI	BB	SO
Totals	.283	.320	.403	159	45	4	3	3	19	9	21
Batting vs. Left and Right-handed Pitchers											
Left	.340	.382	.480	50	17	1	0	2	8	4	0
Right	.257	.289	.367	109	28	3	3	1	11	5	21
At Home and on the Road											
Home	.280	.310	.463	82	23	2	2	3	11	4	8
Road	.286	.329	.338	77	22	2	1	0	8	5	13
Facing Groundball Pitchers and Flyball Pitchers											
Groundball	.316	.342	.395	76	24	1	1	1	7	3	7
Flyball	.253	.290	.410	83	21	3	2	2	12	6	14
Facing Finesse Pitchers and Power Pitchers											
Finesse	.263	.287	.368	76	20	2	0	2	5	3	10
Power	.301	.348	.434	83	25	2	3	1	14	6	11
On Grass and on Turf											
Grass	.348	.400	.391	46	16	2	0	0	7	4	7
Turf	.257	.286	.407	113	29	2	3	3	12	5	14
During the Day and at Night											
Day	.373	.418	.510	51	19	2	1	1	10	4	9
Night	.241	.272	.352	108	26	2	2	2	9	5	12
By Month											
April	.000	.000	.000	0	0	0	0	0	0	0	0
May	.000	.000	.000	0	0	0	0	0	0	0	0
June	.000	.000	.000	0	0	0	0	0	0	0	0
July	.000	.000	.000	0	0	0	0	0	0	0	0
August	.246	.277	.344	61	15	1	1	1	5	3	10
Sept/Oct	.306	.346	.439	98	30	3	2	2	14	6	11
Situational											
Bases Empty	.228	.257	.327	101	23	2	1	2	2	4	13
Leadoff	.241	.290	.310	58	14	1	0	1	1	4	5
Not Leadoff	.209	.209	.349	43	9	1	1	1	1	0	8
Runners On	.379	.422	.534	58	22	2	2	1	17	5	8
First Base Only	.444	.500	.556	18	8	0	1	0	1	2	3
Scoring Position	.350	.386	.525	40	14	2	1	1	16	3	5
Late Innings, Close	.458	.458	.500	24	11	1	0	0	3	0	0

RBI/Opportunities

Scoring Position	15 / 55	(27%)
Scoring Position, 2 Out	7 / 29	(24%)
On Third, Less than 2 Out	7 / 13	(54%)
RBI in close games / RBI Total	11 / 19	(58%)

Tim Laudner
Minnesota Twins

THREE YEARS (84 – 86)

	Ave.	OBP	SLG	AB	H	2B	3B	HR	RBI	BB	SO
Totals	.226	.291	.410	619	140	31	1	27	83	54	179
Batting vs. Left and Right-handed Pitchers											
Left	.268	.352	.502	321	86	19	1	18	45	38	77
Right	.181	.223	.312	298	54	12	0	9	38	16	102
At Home and on the Road											
Home	.248	.322	.504	270	67	18	0	17	47	26	79
Road	.209	.266	.338	349	73	13	1	10	36	28	100
Facing Groundball Pitchers and Flyball Pitchers											
Groundball	.243	.294	.442	292	71	14	1	14	38	19	83
Flyball	.211	.289	.382	327	69	17	0	13	45	35	96
Facing Finesse Pitchers and Power Pitchers											
Finesse	.239	.298	.415	352	84	17	0	15	47	28	89
Power	.210	.282	.404	267	56	14	1	12	36	26	90
On Grass and on Turf											
Grass	.204	.266	.325	265	54	11	0	7	28	23	76
Turf	.243	.310	.475	354	86	20	1	20	55	31	103
During the Day and at Night											
Day	.203	.259	.330	182	37	11	0	4	16	12	59
Night	.236	.305	.444	437	103	20	1	23	67	42	120
By Month											
April	.191	.242	.393	89	17	3	0	5	13	5	28
May	.247	.336	.464	97	24	6	0	5	16	13	28
June	.224	.325	.448	67	15	3	0	4	11	9	24
July	.232	.260	.400	95	22	4	0	4	13	3	27
August	.242	.301	.386	132	32	5	1	4	16	11	34
Sept/Oct	.216	.283	.396	139	30	10	0	5	14	13	39
Situational											
Bases Empty	.245	.322	.481	310	76	14	1	19	19	30	84
Leadoff	.250	.330	.420	100	25	3	1	4	4	9	24
Not Leadoff	.243	.318	.510	210	51	11	0	15	15	21	60
Runners On	.207	.260	.340	309	64	17	0	8	64	24	95
First Base Only	.214	.250	.381	126	27	6	0	5	14	6	34
Scoring Position	.202	.267	.311	183	37	11	0	3	50	18	59
Late Innings, Close	.159	.235	.284	88	14	5	0	2	8	9	31

RBI/Opportunities

Scoring Position	44 / 246	(18%)
Scoring Position, 2 Out	20 / 121	(17%)
On Third, Less than 2 Out	14 / 44	(32%)
RBI in close games / RBI Total	45 / 83	(54%)

Mike Lavalliere
St. Louis Cardinals

THREE YEARS (84 – 86)

	Ave.	OBP	SLG	AB	H	2B	3B	HR	RBI	BB	SO
Totals	.221	.310	.291	344	76	11	2	3	36	45	42
Batting vs. Left and Right-handed Pitchers											
Left	.203	.273	.322	59	12	4	0	1	10	6	13
Right	.225	.318	.284	285	64	7	2	2	26	39	29
At Home and on the Road											
Home	.208	.305	.260	173	36	4	1	1	18	25	20
Road	.234	.316	.322	171	40	7	1	2	18	20	22
Facing Groundball Pitchers and Flyball Pitchers											
Groundball	.215	.314	.260	181	39	3	1	1	16	25	21
Flyball	.227	.306	.325	163	37	8	1	2	20	20	21
Facing Finesse Pitchers and Power Pitchers											
Finesse	.243	.325	.301	206	50	6	0	2	26	25	21
Power	.188	.289	.275	138	26	5	2	1	10	20	21
On Grass and on Turf											
Grass	.239	.338	.313	67	16	3	1	0	8	10	9
Turf	.217	.304	.285	277	60	8	1	3	28	35	33
During the Day and at Night											
Day	.221	.302	.270	122	27	4	1	0	16	15	18
Night	.221	.315	.302	222	49	7	1	3	20	30	24
By Month											
April	.180	.279	.200	50	9	1	0	0	6	8	7
May	.250	.348	.250	20	5	0	0	0	2	3	2
June	.298	.385	.421	57	17	2	1	1	9	8	7
July	.180	.286	.213	61	11	2	0	0	6	9	6
August	.174	.260	.304	69	12	4	1	1	5	7	7
Sept/Oct	.253	.330	.310	87	22	2	0	1	8	10	13
Situational											
Bases Empty	.215	.289	.283	191	41	6	2	1	1	20	24
Leadoff	.261	.346	.391	69	18	2	2	1	1	9	6
Not Leadoff	.189	.256	.221	122	23	4	0	0	0	11	18
Runners On	.229	.335	.301	153	35	5	0	2	35	25	18
First Base Only	.193	.281	.246	57	11	0	0	1	2	7	6
Scoring Position	.250	.364	.333	96	24	5	0	1	33	18	12
Late Innings, Close	.227	.297	.364	66	15	4	1	1	8	7	11

RBI/Opportunities

Scoring Position	31 / 140	(22%)
Scoring Position, 2 Out	14 / 69	(20%)
On Third, Less than 2 Out	13 / 24	(54%)
RBI in close games / RBI Total	24 / 36	(67%)

Rudy Law
Kansas City Royals

THREE YEARS (84 – 86)

	Ave.	OBP	SLG	AB	H	2B	3B	HR	RBI	BB	SO
Totals	.256	.315	.366	1184	303	61	18	11	109	95	104
Batting vs. Left and Right-handed Pitchers											
Left	.211	.240	.257	171	36	4	2	0	14	7	12
Right	.264	.327	.384	1013	267	57	16	11	95	88	92
At Home and on the Road											
Home	.264	.330	.393	568	150	32	7	9	55	51	40
Road	.248	.301	.341	616	153	29	11	2	54	44	64
Facing Groundball Pitchers and Flyball Pitchers											
Groundball	.243	.291	.337	585	142	26	4	7	58	38	51
Flyball	.269	.337	.394	599	161	35	14	4	51	57	53
Facing Finesse Pitchers and Power Pitchers											
Finesse	.251	.297	.354	720	181	28	11	8	55	42	56
Power	.263	.341	.384	464	122	33	7	3	54	53	48
On Grass and on Turf											
Grass	.258	.318	.366	871	225	39	14	9	72	71	85
Turf	.249	.307	.364	313	78	22	4	2	37	24	19
During the Day and at Night											
Day	.288	.354	.403	313	90	15	6	3	28	31	27
Night	.245	.300	.352	871	213	46	12	8	81	64	77
By Month											
April	.271	.343	.401	177	48	12	4	1	15	19	15
May	.295	.342	.438	217	64	17	4	2	22	16	23
June	.257	.317	.341	249	64	12	3	1	26	19	18
July	.189	.268	.257	148	28	3	2	1	14	14	16
August	.256	.321	.364	176	45	6	2	3	12	16	14
Sept/Oct	.249	.287	.369	217	54	11	3	3	20	11	18
Situational											
Bases Empty	.244	.305	.343	767	187	35	10	7	7	62	71
Leadoff	.242	.304	.343	434	105	20	6	4	4	36	43
Not Leadoff	.246	.305	.342	333	82	15	4	3	3	26	28
Runners On	.278	.333	.408	417	116	26	8	4	102	33	33
First Base Only	.219	.253	.326	178	39	2	4	3	10	7	11
Scoring Position	.322	.389	.469	239	77	24	4	1	92	26	22
Late Innings, Close	.264	.313	.393	178	47	7	2	4	18	12	15

RBI/Opportunities

Scoring Position	88 / 321	(27%)
Scoring Position, 2 Out	34 / 123	(28%)
On Third, Less than 2 Out	34 / 62	(55%)
RBI in close games / RBI Total	72 / 109	(66%)

Vance Law
Montreal Expos

THREE YEARS (84 – 86)

	Ave.	OBP	SLG	AB	H	2B	3B	HR	RBI	BB	SO
Totals	.250	.330	.383	1360	340	65	10	32	155	164	237
Batting vs. Left and Right-handed Pitchers											
Left	.245	.324	.408	473	116	24	1	17	53	55	69
Right	.253	.333	.370	887	224	41	9	15	102	109	168
At Home and on the Road											
Home	.264	.352	.420	662	175	36	5	19	90	91	110
Road	.236	.308	.348	698	165	29	5	13	65	73	127
Facing Groundball Pitchers and Flyball Pitchers											
Groundball	.258	.329	.382	636	164	31	6	12	74	70	104
Flyball	.243	.331	.384	724	176	34	4	20	81	94	133
Facing Finesse Pitchers and Power Pitchers											
Finesse	.244	.304	.368	799	195	35	5	18	88	69	127
Power	.258	.364	.405	561	145	30	5	14	67	95	110
On Grass and on Turf											
Grass	.248	.301	.402	641	159	27	3	22	77	52	109
Turf	.252	.354	.366	719	181	38	7	10	78	112	128
During the Day and at Night											
Day	.248	.333	.400	467	116	26	3	13	60	62	88
Night	.251	.328	.374	893	224	39	7	19	95	102	149
By Month											
April	.227	.298	.324	185	42	9	0	3	15	19	39
May	.221	.338	.312	231	51	9	0	6	22	24	44
June	.245	.331	.414	278	68	12	4	9	36	37	60
July	.252	.340	.381	226	57	11	3	4	28	30	29
August	.266	.342	.381	244	65	10	3	4	25	22	31
Sept/Oct	.291	.385	.454	196	57	14	0	6	29	32	34
Situational											
Bases Empty	.239	.315	.373	794	190	36	5	20	20	85	137
Leadoff	.244	.300	.375	275	67	8	2	8	8	20	54
Not Leadoff	.237	.323	.372	519	123	28	3	12	12	65	83
Runners On	.265	.350	.398	566	150	29	5	12	135	79	100
First Base Only	.298	.363	.482	228	68	16	1	8	25	22	34
Scoring Position	.243	.342	.340	338	82	13	4	4	110	57	66
Late Innings, Close	.274	.348	.389	234	64	10	4	3	26	28	39

RBI/Opportunities

Scoring Position	101 / 479	(21%)
Scoring Position, 2 Out	40 / 195	(21%)
On Third, Less than 2 Out	37 / 87	(43%)
RBI in close games / RBI Total	107 / 155	(69%)

Rick Leach
Toronto Blue Jays

THREE YEARS (84 – 86)

	Ave.	OBP	SLG	AB	H	2B	3B	HR	RBI	BB	SO
Totals	.287	.324	.404	369	106	20	4	5	47	24	47
Batting vs. Left and Right-handed Pitchers											
Left	.194	.194	.194	31	6	0	0	0	2	0	4
Right	.296	.335	.423	338	100	20	4	5	45	24	43
At Home and on the Road											
Home	.276	.298	.402	199	55	9	2	4	24	7	24
Road	.300	.352	.406	170	51	11	2	1	23	17	23
Facing Groundball Pitchers and Flyball Pitchers											
Groundball	.296	.324	.384	159	47	9	1	1	18	8	25
Flyball	.281	.325	.419	210	59	11	3	4	29	16	22
Facing Finesse Pitchers and Power Pitchers											
Finesse	.311	.329	.402	209	65	14	1	1	20	8	21
Power	.256	.318	.406	160	41	6	3	4	27	16	26
On Grass and on Turf											
Grass	.270	.345	.336	122	33	8	0	0	13	16	19
Turf	.296	.313	.437	247	73	12	4	5	34	8	28
During the Day and at Night											
Day	.286	.340	.383	133	38	7	3	0	13	11	18
Night	.288	.315	.415	236	68	13	1	5	34	13	29
By Month											
April	.333	.364	.333	21	7	0	0	0	5	1	1
May	.296	.305	.463	54	16	4	1	1	8	2	6
June	.327	.364	.462	52	17	4	0	1	8	3	3
July	.269	.322	.410	78	21	7	2	0	6	7	9
August	.271	.318	.424	59	16	3	0	2	10	5	8
Sept/Oct	.276	.313	.343	105	29	2	1	1	10	6	20
Situational											
Bases Empty	.275	.317	.399	193	53	12	3	2	2	12	24
Leadoff	.183	.212	.293	82	15	3	0	2	2	3	9
Not Leadoff	.342	.392	.477	111	38	9	3	0	0	9	15
Runners On	.301	.332	.409	176	53	8	1	3	45	12	23
First Base Only	.314	.342	.414	70	22	4	0	1	3	3	8
Scoring Position	.292	.325	.406	106	31	4	1	2	42	9	15
Late Innings, Close	.325	.385	.450	80	26	3	2	1	13	9	11

RBI/Opportunities

Scoring Position	37 / 151	(25%)
Scoring Position, 2 Out	13 / 74	(18%)
On Third, Less than 2 Out	15 / 27	(56%)
RBI in close games / RBI Total	27 / 47	(57%)

David Leiper
Oakland A's

1986: Power, Flyball   1985: Did not play   1984: Power, Groundball

THREE YEARS (84 – 86)

	G	IP	H	BB	SO	SB	CS	W	L	S	ERA
Totals	41	38.2	40	23	18	2	3	3	2	1	5.59
At Home and on the Road											
Home	22	16.0	22	10	7	1	1	2	2	0	7.87
Road	19	22.2	18	13	11	1	2	1	0	1	3.97
During the Day and and at Night											
Day	16	17.0	18	11	7	1	2	1	1	1	5.82
Night	25	21.2	22	12	11	1	1	2	1	0	5.40
On Grass and on Turf											
Grass	34	28.1	34	20	13	1	2	3	2	0	6.35
Turf	7	10.1	6	3	5	1	1	0	0	1	3.48
By Month											
April	0	0.0	0	0	0	0	0	0	0	0	0.00
May	0	0.0	0	0	0	0	0	0	0	0	0.00
June	10	12.2	14	5	5	0	2	0	1	0	2.84
July	11	9.2	8	6	3	1	1	1	1	1	4.66
August	6	5.2	4	6	4	0	1	1	0	0	9.53
Sept/Oct	14	10.2	14	6	6	1	0	1	0	0	7.59

vs. Opponent Batters — THREE YEARS (84 – 86)

	Ave.	OBP	SLG	AB	H	2B	3B	HR	RBI	BB	SO
Totals	.276	.376	.462	145	40	8	2	5	31	23	18
Pitching vs. Left and Right-handed Batters											
Left	.226	.344	.377	53	12	2	0	2	17	10	11
Right	.304	.394	.511	92	28	6	2	3	14	13	7
Situational											
Bases Empty	.268	.350	.437	71	19	2	2	2	2	8	7
Leadoff	.143	.226	.357	28	4	1	1	1	1	2	1
Not Leadoff	.349	.429	.488	43	15	1	1	1	1	6	6
Runners On	.284	.398	.486	74	21	6	0	3	29	15	11
First Base Only	.261	.292	.435	23	6	1	0	1	3	1	4
Scoring Position	.294	.435	.510	51	15	5	0	2	26	14	7
Late Innings, Close	.227	.400	.409	22	5	1	0	1	6	6	5

RBI/Opportunities

Scoring Position	21 / 93	(23%)
Scoring Position, 2 Out	4 / 37	(11%)
On Third, Less than 2 Out	11 / 23	(48%)
RBI in close games / RBI Total	14 / 31	(45%)

Dennis Leonard
Kansas City Royals

1986: Finesse, Flyball   1985: Finesse, Groundball   1984: Did not play

THREE YEARS (84 – 86)

	G	IP	H	BB	SO	SB	CS	W	L	S	ERA
Totals	35	194.2	208	51	115	19	7	8	13	0	4.39
At Home and on the Road											
Home	21	116.0	116	23	58	13	4	6	5	0	3.57
Road	14	78.2	92	28	57	6	3	2	8	0	5.61
During the Day and and at Night											
Day	8	55.0	40	15	43	5	1	2	1	0	2.13
Night	27	139.2	168	36	72	14	6	6	12	0	5.28
On Grass and on Turf											
Grass	10	58.2	68	22	45	5	2	1	6	0	5.83
Turf	25	136.0	140	29	70	14	5	7	7	0	3.77
By Month											
April	4	30.0	23	4	14	1	1	2	2	0	0.90
May	6	46.0	36	9	29	2	1	3	2	0	2.54
June	6	32.2	44	9	24	4	2	1	3	0	6.61
July	5	27.2	39	9	14	3	1	0	3	0	7.16
August	6	26.2	33	6	16	4	0	0	1	0	4.39
Sept/Oct	8	31.2	33	14	16	5	2	2	2	0	5.68

vs. Opponent Batters — THREE YEARS (84 – 86)

	Ave.	OBP	SLG	AB	H	2B	3B	HR	RBI	BB	SO
Totals	.274	.319	.422	760	208	31	8	22	92	51	115
Pitching vs. Left and Right-handed Batters											
Left	.304	.353	.491	395	120	19	5	15	59	34	46
Right	.241	.281	.348	365	88	12	3	7	33	17	69
Situational											
Bases Empty	.276	.321	.424	450	124	16	6	13	13	27	58
Leadoff	.260	.304	.380	192	50	6	1	5	5	10	21
Not Leadoff	.287	.333	.457	258	74	10	5	8	8	17	37
Runners On	.271	.317	.419	310	84	15	2	9	79	24	57
First Base Only	.253	.291	.407	150	38	6	1	5	13	8	28
Scoring Position	.287	.339	.431	160	46	9	1	4	66	16	29
Late Innings, Close	.244	.289	.390	82	20	2	2	2	7	4	10

RBI/Opportunities

Scoring Position	57 / 213	(27%)
Scoring Position, 2 Out	18 / 90	(20%)
On Third, Less than 2 Out	22 / 40	(55%)
RBI in close games / RBI Total	61 / 92	(66%)

Tim Lollar
Boston Red Sox

1986: Power, Flyball   1985: Power, Flyball   1984: Power, Flyball

THREE YEARS (84 – 86)

	G	IP	H	BB	SO	SB	CS	W	L	S	ERA
Totals	97	388.2	359	237	264	34	17	21	23	1	4.52
At Home and on the Road											
Home	46	201.2	178	119	150	13	9	11	9	0	3.79
Road	51	187.0	181	118	114	21	8	10	14	1	5.29
During the Day and at Night											
Day	31	130.2	110	84	108	18	4	7	7	0	4.55
Night	66	258.0	249	153	156	16	13	14	16	1	4.50
On Grass and on Turf											
Grass	80	316.1	299	193	222	26	15	17	18	0	4.52
Turf	17	72.1	60	44	42	8	2	4	5	1	4.48
By Month											
April	12	57.2	52	41	30	10	1	4	3	0	4.68
May	16	57.0	44	40	51	6	2	1	3	0	3.79
June	21	81.0	71	57	65	5	5	5	4	0	3.78
July	18	65.2	68	26	40	4	5	4	5	0	5.21
August	12	63.2	61	37	35	4	2	3	5	0	4.95
Sept/Oct	18	63.2	63	36	43	5	2	4	3	1	4.81

vs. Opponent Batters — THREE YEARS (84 – 86)

	Ave.	OBP	SLG	AB	H	2B	3B	HR	RBI	BB	SO
Totals	.248	.354	.400	1446	359	55	11	44	191	237	264
Pitching vs. Left and Right-handed Batters											
Left	.234	.326	.348	325	76	10	3	7	43	42	69
Right	.252	.362	.415	1121	283	55	8	37	148	195	195
Situational											
Bases Empty	.241	.358	.373	788	190	33	7	19	19	141	154
Leadoff	.223	.328	.350	346	77	15	1	9	9	53	64
Not Leadoff	.256	.382	.391	442	113	18	6	10	10	88	90
Runners On	.257	.348	.432	658	169	32	4	25	172	96	110
First Base Only	.278	.363	.505	277	77	9	0	18	38	34	45
Scoring Position	.241	.338	.378	381	92	23	4	7	134	62	65
Late Innings, Close	.328	.452	.716	67	22	7	2	5	19	12	11

RBI/Opportunities

Scoring Position	111 / 532	(21%)
Scoring Position, 2 Out	38 / 243	(16%)
On Third, Less than 2 Out	41 / 86	(48%)
RBI in close games / RBI Total	112 / 191	(59%)

Steve Lombardozzi
Minnesota Twins

THREE YEARS (84 – 86)

	Ave.	OBP	SLG	AB	H	2B	3B	HR	RBI	BB	SO
Totals	.243	.321	.361	507	123	24	6	8	39	58	82
Batting vs. Left and Right-handed Pitchers											
Left	.227	.306	.355	141	32	9	0	3	17	16	19
Right	.249	.327	.363	366	91	15	6	5	22	42	63
At Home and on the Road											
Home	.269	.347	.424	264	71	17	3	6	27	31	40
Road	.214	.293	.292	243	52	7	3	2	12	27	42
Facing Groundball Pitchers and Flyball Pitchers											
Groundball	.265	.346	.389	234	62	11	3	4	13	28	31
Flyball	.223	.337		273	61	13	3	4	26	30	51
Facing Finesse Pitchers and Power Pitchers											
Finesse	.270	.342	.419	289	78	15	5	6	31	31	35
Power	.206	.294	.284	218	45	9	1	2	8	27	47
On Grass and on Turf											
Grass	.213	.294	.306	183	39	5	3	2	12	21	34
Turf	.259	.336	.392	324	84	19	3	6	27	37	48
During the Day and at Night											
Day	.216	.281	.320	153	33	8	1	2	11	14	25
Night	.254	.338	.379	354	90	16	5	6	28	44	57
By Month											
April	.224	.269	.347	49	11	3	0	1	4	3	10
May	.253		.544	79	20	4	2	5	16	14	14
June	.309	.385	.423	97	30	5	3	0	4	12	10
July	.183	.296		71	13	5	0	1	2	8	15
August	.165	.253	.188	85	14	2	0	0	3	10	15
Sept/Oct	.278	.333	.357	126	35	5	1	1	10	11	18
Situational											
Bases Empty	.249	.305	.374	313	78	16	4	5	5	24	44
Leadoff	.264	.309	.436	140	37	8	2	4	4	8	19
Not Leadoff	.237	.302	.324	173	41	8	2	1	1	16	25
Runners On	.232	.345	.340	194	45	8	2	3	34	34	38
First Base Only	.262	.319	.333	84	22	2	2	0	3	7	12
Scoring Position	.209	.362	.345	110	23	6	0	3	31	27	26
Late Innings, Close	.279	.323	.393	61	17	2	1	1	5	4	9

RBI/Opportunities

Scoring Position	24 / 160	(15%)
Scoring Position, 2 Out	15 / 85	(18%)
On Third, Less than 2 Out	3 / 20	(15%)
RBI in close games / RBI Total	23 / 39	(59%)

Davey Lopes
Houston Astros

THREE YEARS (84 – 86)	Ave.	OBP	SLG	AB	H	2B	3B	HR	RBI	BB	SO
Totals	.272	.372	.429	777	211	33	4	27	115	126	103
Batting vs. Left and Right-handed Pitchers											
Left	.259	.367	.456	305	79	16	1	14	50	54	38
Right	.280	.375	.411	472	132	17	3	13	65	72	65
At Home and on the Road											
Home	.283	.386	.471	361	102	16	2	16	59	63	48
Road	.262	.360	.392	416	109	17	2	11	56	63	55
Facing Groundball Pitchers and Flyball Pitchers											
Groundball	.288	.376	.438	379	109	16	4	11	55	56	44
Flyball	.256	.368	.420	398	102	17	0	16	60	70	59
Facing Finesse Pitchers and Power Pitchers											
Finesse	.275	.355	.445	461	127	21	3	17	79	60	54
Power	.266	.395	.405	316	84	12	1	10	36	66	49
On Grass and on Turf											
Grass	.269	.375	.445	521	140	22	2	22	82	90	70
Turf	.277	.365	.395	256	71	11	2	5	33	36	33
During the Day and at Night											
Day	.293	.404	.479	403	118	20	2	17	70	77	55
Night	.249	.336	.374	374	93	13	2	10	45	49	48
By Month											
April	.282	.366	.453	117	33	6	1	4	19	16	16
May	.285	.403	.438	144	41	4	0	6	28	32	20
June	.283	.396	.463	205	58	9	2	8	29	37	26
July	.274	.361	.444	117	32	6	1	4	17	15	13
August	.216	.285	.320	125	27	4	0	3	9	12	18
Sept/Oct	.290	.405	.435	69	20	4	0	2	13	14	10
Situational											
Bases Empty	.265	.362	.405	430	114	20	2	12	12	63	60
Leadoff	.281	.378	.417	192	54	8	0	6	6	28	26
Not Leadoff	.252	.348	.395	238	60	12	2	6	6	35	34
Runners On	.280	.384	.458	347	97	13	2	15	103	63	43
First Base Only	.313	.387	.522	134	42	6	2	6	15	16	14
Scoring Position	.258	.383	.418	213	55	7	0	9	88	47	29
Late Innings, Close	.253	.319	.433	150	38	9	0	6	28	14	20

RBI/Opportunities		
Scoring Position	73 / 318	(23%)
Scoring Position, 2 Out	29 / 133	(22%)
On Third, Less than 2 Out	28 / 64	(44%)
RBI in close games / RBI Total	79 / 115	(69%)

Aurelio Lopez
Houston Astros

1986: Finesse, Flyball   1985: Power, Flyball   1984: Power, Flyball

THREE YEARS (84 – 86)	G	IP	H	BB	SO	SB	CS	W	L	S	ERA
Totals	167	302.0	255	118	191	28	13	16	11	26	3.61
At Home and on the Road											
Home	88	164.0	147	55	93	16	8	7	5	11	4.01
Road	79	138.0	108	63	98	12	5	9	6	15	3.13
During the Day and at Night											
Day	55	96.2	85	28	58	9	2	3	3	9	3.44
Night	112	205.1	170	90	133	19	11	13	8	17	3.68
On Grass and on Turf											
Grass	121	217.0	187	86	138	19	9	14	6	15	3.44
Turf	46	85.0	68	32	53	9	4	2	5	11	4.02
By Month											
April	16	31.1	15	11	21	2	2	2	1	4	2.59
May	23	45.0	38	16	27	1	2	2	1	6	2.20
June	33	57.0	55	24	28	9	1	4	4	7	4.74
July	30	56.1	36	20	39	5	4	2	2	3	2.40
August	35	67.0	52	27	53	4	3	6	0	2	3.09
Sept/Oct	30	45.1	59	20	23	7	1	0	3	4	6.55

vs. Opponent Batters THREE YEARS (84 – 86)	Ave.	OBP	SLG	AB	H	2B	3B	HR	RBI	BB	SO
Totals	.230	.302	.376	1110	255	39	6	37	160	118	191
Pitching vs. Left and Right-handed Batters											
Left	.219	.303	.353	553	121	16	2	18	77	68	99
Right	.241	.300	.399	557	134	23	4	19	83	50	92
Situational											
Bases Empty	.219	.285	.381	640	140	18	4	26	26	56	114
Leadoff	.224	.282	.351	259	58	8	2	7	7	20	45
Not Leadoff	.215	.286	.402	381	82	10	2	19	19	36	69
Runners On	.245	.323	.368	470	115	21	2	11	134	62	77
First Base Only	.220	.313	.339	177	39	9	0	4	14	24	29
Scoring Position	.259	.329	.386	293	76	12	2	7	120	38	48
Late Innings, Close	.221	.305	.363	430	95	12	2	15	55	52	86

RBI/Opportunities		
Scoring Position	107 / 424	(25%)
Scoring Position, 2 Out	45 / 201	(22%)
On Third, Less than 2 Out	38 / 78	(49%)
RBI in close games / RBI Total	75 / 160	(47%)

Dwight Lowry
Detroit Tigers

THREE YEARS (84 – 86)	Ave.	OBP	SLG	AB	H	2B	3B	HR	RBI	BB	SO
Totals	.292	.370	.400	195	57	6	0	5	25	20	30
Batting vs. Left and Right-handed Pitchers											
Left	.375	.459	.500	32	12	1	0	1	5	3	4
Right	.276	.352	.380	163	45	5	0	4	20	17	26
At Home and on the Road											
Home	.269	.336	.352	108	29	3	0	2	14	10	17
Road	.322	.410	.460	87	28	3	0	3	11	10	13
Facing Groundball Pitchers and Flyball Pitchers											
Groundball	.310	.400	.460	87	27	4	0	3	10	10	15
Flyball	.278	.345	.352	108	30	2	0	2	15	10	15
Facing Finesse Pitchers and Power Pitchers											
Finesse	.339	.406	.391	115	39	3	0	1	15	13	16
Power	.225	.319	.412	80	18	3	0	4	10	7	14
On Grass and on Turf											
Grass	.285	.352	.412	165	47	6	0	5	22	15	26
Turf	.333	.459	.333	30	10	0	0	0	3	5	4
During the Day and at Night											
Day	.328	.403	.500	64	21	2	0	3	8	6	12
Night	.275	.354	.351	131	36	4	0	2	17	14	18
By Month											
April	.300	.364	.300	10	3	0	0	0	0	1	0
May	.200	.273	.450	20	4	2	0	1	2	1	5
June	.393	.414	.429	28	11	1	0	0	3	1	3
July	.351	.429	.541	37	13	1	0	2	5	3	8
August	.258	.361	.339	62	16	2	0	1	7	10	4
Sept/Oct	.263	.349	.342	38	10	0	0	1	8	4	10
Situational											
Bases Empty	.346	.435	.477	107	37	5	0	3	3	14	19
Leadoff	.244	.346	.267	45	11	1	0	0	0	6	10
Not Leadoff	.419	.500	.629	62	26	4	0	3	3	8	9
Runners On	.227	.284	.307	88	20	1	0	2	22	6	11
First Base Only	.182	.206	.212	33	6	1	0	0	1	1	3
Scoring Position	.255	.328	.364	55	14	0	0	2	21	5	8
Late Innings, Close	.364	.440	.364	22	8	0	0	0	2	2	3

RBI/Opportunities		
Scoring Position	19 / 71	(27%)
Scoring Position, 2 Out	5 / 25	(20%)
On Third, Less than 2 Out	6 / 12	(50%)
RBI in close games / RBI Total	13 / 25	(52%)

Gary Lucas
California Angels

1986: Finesse, Flyball   1985: Finesse, Flyball   1984: Power, Groundball

THREE YEARS (84 – 86)	G	IP	H	BB	SO	SB	CS	W	L	S	ERA
Totals	131	166.1	162	50	104	20	5	10	6	12	3.03
At Home and on the Road											
Home	65	97.0	81	24	59	9	4	6	1	6	2.13
Road	66	69.1	81	26	45	11	1	4	5	6	4.28
During the Day and and at Night											
Day	47	63.0	62	20	42	11	2	4	2	7	2.43
Night	84	103.1	100	30	62	9	3	6	4	5	3.40
On Grass and on Turf											
Grass	55	72.2	77	17	46	8	4	6	2	5	3.10
Turf	76	93.2	85	33	58	12	1	4	4	7	2.98
By Month											
April	13	12.1	12	5	9	2	0	0	0	3	2.92
May	16	15.1	14	5	10	4	0	0	0	1	2.93
June	20	25.2	27	8	14	3	0	2	2	2	2.81
July	23	33.1	33	11	20	4	2	1	3	1	2.43
August	28	40.0	38	9	31	2	1	3	0	3	3.60
Sept/Oct	31	39.2	38	12	20	5	2	4	1	2	3.18

vs. Opponent Batters THREE YEARS (84 – 86)	Ave.	OBP	SLG	AB	H	2B	3B	HR	RBI	BB	SO
Totals	.257	.309	.365	631	162	29	3	11	70	50	104
Pitching vs. Left and Right-handed Batters											
Left	.274	.317	.368	212	58	11	0	3	25	15	41
Right	.248	.305	.363	419	104	18	3	8	45	35	63
Situational											
Bases Empty	.251	.281	.387	359	90	18	2	9	9	15	61
Leadoff	.253	.278	.425	146	37	8	1	5	5	5	28
Not Leadoff	.249	.283	.362	213	53	10	1	4	4	10	33
Runners On	.265	.343	.335	272	72	11	1	2	61	35	43
First Base Only	.264	.310	.321	106	28	4	1	0	4	7	10
Scoring Position	.265	.362	.343	166	44	7	0	2	57	28	33
Late Innings, Close	.266	.318	.390	267	71	12	0	7	37	22	44

RBI/Opportunities		
Scoring Position	53 / 241	(22%)
Scoring Position, 2 Out	16 / 92	(17%)
On Third, Less than 2 Out	22 / 50	(44%)
RBI in close games / RBI Total	47 / 70	(67%)

Ed Lynch
Chicago Cubs

1986: Finesse, Flyball   1985: Finesse, Flyball   1984: Finesse, Flyball

THREE YEARS (84 – 86)

	G	IP	H	BB	SO	SB	CS	W	L	S	ERA
Totals	95	416.1	464	74	185	8	16	26	21	2	3.83
At Home and on the Road											
Home	48	225.1	254	33	98	3	10	16	12	2	3.71
Road	47	191.0	210	41	87	5	6	10	9	0	3.96
During the Day and and at Night											
Day	44	189.1	218	36	80	4	8	11	8	1	3.90
Night	51	227.0	246	38	105	4	8	15	13	1	3.77
On Grass and on Turf											
Grass	65	308.1	339	49	131	5	14	20	16	2	3.62
Turf	30	108.0	125	25	54	3	2	6	5	0	4.42
By Month											
April	13	37.1	33	9	19	2	3	2	1	0	3.13
May	12	68.1	66	6	28	2	2	5	3	0	3.03
June	12	73.0	76	10	20	0	2	4	5	0	3.33
July	16	78.0	89	19	29	2	1	7	3	2	3.69
August	17	93.1	113	14	43	1	5	4	6	0	3.86
Sept/Oct	25	66.1	87	16	46	1	3	4	3	0	5.70

vs. Opponent Batters
THREE YEARS (84 – 86)

	Ave.	OBP	SLG	AB	H	2B	3B	HR	RBI	BB	SO
Totals	.283	.314	.425	1640	464	82	11	43	194	74	185
Pitching vs. Left and Right-handed Batters											
Left	.305	.336	.465	863	263	44	8	26	99	40	75
Right	.259	.290	.381	777	201	38	3	17	95	34	110
Situational											
Bases Empty	.280	.314	.431	961	269	48	5	29	29	45	101
Leadoff	.271	.312	.426	399	108	18	1	14	14	21	42
Not Leadoff	.286	.316	.434	562	161	30	4	15	15	24	59
Runners On	.287	.314	.417	679	195	34	6	14	165	29	84
First Base Only	.292	.307	.417	319	93	14	1	8	24	7	38
Scoring Position	.283	.319	.417	360	102	20	5	6	141	22	46
Late Innings, Close	.235	.282	.348	132	31	4	1	3	8	9	16

RBI/Opportunities

Scoring Position	123 / 453	(27%)
Scoring Position, 2 Out	51 / 216	(24%)
On Third, Less than 2 Out	40 / 73	(55%)
RBI in close games / RBI Total	120 / 194	(62%)

Steve Lyons
Chicago White Sox

THREE YEARS (84 – 86)

	Ave.	OBP	SLG	AB	H	2B	3B	HR	RBI	BB	SO
Totals	.249	.305	.335	618	154	23	6	6	50	51	111
Batting vs. Left and Right-handed Pitchers											
Left	.260	.312	.360	100	26	1	3	1	10	8	25
Right	.247	.304	.330	518	128	22	3	5	40	43	86
At Home and on the Road											
Home	.259	.320	.366	317	82	11	4	5	32	29	51
Road	.239	.290	.302	301	72	12	2	1	18	22	60
Facing Groundball Pitchers and Flyball Pitchers											
Groundball	.247	.293	.328	320	79	9	4	3	33	23	53
Flyball	.252	.318	.342	298	75	14	2	3	17	28	58
Facing Finesse Pitchers and Power Pitchers											
Finesse	.269	.323	.367	346	93	14	4	4	26	27	48
Power	.224	.283	.294	272	61	9	2	2	24	24	63
On Grass and on Turf											
Grass	.255	.309	.334	518	132	16	5	5	44	42	91
Turf	.220	.286	.340	100	22	7	1	1	6	9	20
During the Day and at Night											
Day	.242	.303	.342	190	46	6	2	3	14	16	31
Night	.252	.306	.332	428	108	17	4	3	36	35	80
By Month											
April	.250	.333	.375	16	4	1	0	1	3	2	3
May	.263	.317	.432	95	25	5	1	3	15	8	14
June	.248	.288	.288	125	31	5	0	0	7	13	15
July	.267	.323	.333	150	40	7	0	1	10	13	35
August	.271	.308	.353	85	23	2	1	1	7	5	14
Sept/Oct	.211	.261	.299	147	31	4	3	1	8	10	30

Situational

	Ave.	OBP	SLG	AB	H	2B	3B	HR	RBI	BB	SO
Bases Empty	.253	.308	.347	352	89	18	3	3	3	26	56
Leadoff	.247	.299	.340	162	40	10	1	1	1	11	26
Not Leadoff	.258	.316	.353	190	49	8	2	2	2	15	30
Runners On	.244	.302	.320	266	65	5	3	3	47	25	55
First Base Only	.207	.264	.267	116	24	2	1	1	3	9	24
Scoring Position	.273	.329	.360	150	41	3	2	2	44	16	31
Late Innings, Close	.250	.342	.320	100	25	4	0	1	9	14	17

RBI/Opportunities

Scoring Position	40 / 227	(18%)
Scoring Position, 2 Out	14 / 96	(15%)
On Third, Less than 2 Out	18 / 43	(42%)
RBI in close games / RBI Total	25 / 50	(50%)

Mike Maddux
Philadelphia Phillies

1986: Finesse, Groundball   1985: Did not play   1984: Did not play

THREE YEARS (84 – 86)

	G	IP	H	BB	SO	SB	CS	W	L	S	ERA
Totals	16	78.0	88	34	44	18	5	3	7	0	5.42
At Home and on the Road											
Home	8	37.2	49	11	24	9	2	3	3	0	4.78
Road	8	40.1	39	23	20	9	3	0	4	0	6.02
During the Day and and at Night											
Day	6	28.0	27	16	16	7	2	0	4	0	7.39
Night	10	50.0	61	18	28	11	3	3	3	0	4.32
On Grass and on Turf											
Grass	4	19.0	18	12	10	5	1	0	2	0	7.11
Turf	12	59.0	70	22	34	13	4	3	5	0	4.88
By Month											
April	0	0.0	0	0	0	0	0	0	0	0	0.00
May	0	0.0	0	0	0	0	0	0	0	0	0.00
June	4	15.1	19	7	9	6	1	0	3	0	9.98
July	1	5.1	6	5	4	2	2	0	0	0	1.69
August	5	28.2	28	14	12	6	2	2	2	0	4.40
Sept/Oct	6	28.2	35	8	19	4	0	1	2	0	4.71

vs. Opponent Batters
THREE YEARS (84 – 86)

	Ave.	OBP	SLG	AB	H	2B	3B	HR	RBI	BB	SO
Totals	.286	.359	.396	308	88	16	0	6	42	34	44
Pitching vs. Left and Right-handed Batters											
Left	.255	.346	.346	188	48	8	0	3	19	24	27
Right	.333	.382	.475	120	40	8	0	3	23	10	17
Situational											
Bases Empty	.269	.351	.335	167	45	8	0	1	1	18	22
Leadoff	.324	.412	.446	74	24	6	0	1	1	8	10
Not Leadoff	.226	.301	.247	93	21	2	0	0	0	10	12
Runners On	.305	.369	.468	141	43	8	0	5	41	16	22
First Base Only	.254	.313	.322	59	15	1	0	1	5	9	5
Scoring Position	.341	.406	.573	82	28	7	0	4	38	11	13
Late Innings, Close	.333	.333	.389	18	6	1	0	0	2	0	0

RBI/Opportunities

Scoring Position	30 / 108	(28%)
Scoring Position, 2 Out	9 / 43	(21%)
On Third, Less than 2 Out	11 / 19	(58%)
RBI in close games / RBI Total	36 / 42	(86%)

Mickey Mahler
Texas Rangers

1986: Finesse, Flyball   1985: Power, Flyball   1984: Did not play

THREE YEARS (84 – 86)

	G	IP	H	BB	SO	SB	CS	W	L	S	ERA
Totals	43	133.0	131	57	74	6	2	2	8	4	3.52
At Home and on the Road											
Home	20	60.2	62	26	31	5	2	1	3	1	3.26
Road	23	72.1	69	31	43	1	0	1	5	3	3.73
During the Day and and at Night											
Day	12	38.2	35	11	21	3	1	1	3	1	2.33
Night	31	94.1	96	46	53	3	1	1	5	3	4.01
On Grass and on Turf											
Grass	33	92.1	87	42	54	3	1	2	4	2	3.02
Turf	10	40.2	44	15	20	3	1	0	4	2	4.65
By Month											
April	5	16.2	18	7	7	1	0	0	1	1	2.70
May	10	13.0	15	7	5	1	0	0	0	1	4.15
June	13	54.0	47	27	36	2	1	1	3	2	3.50
July	10	27.2	31	12	12	2	1	0	2	0	5.20
August	0	0.0	0	0	0	0	0	0	0	0	0.00
Sept/Oct	5	21.2	20	4	14	0	0	1	2	0	1.66

vs. Opponent Batters
THREE YEARS (84 – 86)

	Ave.	OBP	SLG	AB	H	2B	3B	HR	RBI	BB	SO
Totals	.262	.340	.378	500	131	28	3	8	52	57	74
Pitching vs. Left and Right-handed Batters											
Left	.311	.373	.379	103	32	2	1	1	15	9	12
Right	.249	.332	.378	397	99	26	2	7	37	48	62
Situational											
Bases Empty	.267	.342	.429	273	73	16	2	8	8	27	38
Leadoff	.268	.338	.423	123	33	7	0	4	4	12	11
Not Leadoff	.267	.345	.433	150	40	9	2	4	4	15	27
Runners On	.256	.338	.317	227	58	12	1	0	44	30	36
First Base Only	.234	.280	.277	94	22	2	1	0	1	6	14
Scoring Position	.271	.374	.346	133	36	10	0	0	43	24	22
Late Innings, Close	.265	.342	.382	34	9	1	0	1	3	4	7

RBI/Opportunities

Scoring Position	42 / 196	(21%)
Scoring Position, 2 Out	22 / 80	(28%)
On Third, Less than 2 Out	14 / 46	(30%)
RBI in close games / RBI Total	32 / 52	(62%)

Rick Manning
Milwaukee Brewers

	Ave.	OBP	SLG	AB	H	2B	3B	HR	RBI	BB	SO
THREE YEARS (84 – 86)											
Totals	.241	.301	.366	762	184	26	9	17	76	65	71
Batting vs. Left and Right-handed Pitchers											
Left	.208	.259	.322	149	31	3	1	4	23	11	21
Right	.250	.311	.377	613	153	23	8	13	53	54	50
At Home and on the Road											
Home	.234	.292	.349	338	79	11	5	6	30	28	30
Road	.248	.309	.380	424	105	15	4	11	46	37	41
Facing Groundball Pitchers and Flyball Pitchers											
Groundball	.246	.299	.372	395	97	12	4	10	53	30	33
Flyball	.237	.304	.360	367	87	14	5	7	23	35	38
Facing Finesse Pitchers and Power Pitchers											
Finesse	.237	.293	.362	426	101	12	7	9	42	34	32
Power	.247	.312	.372	336	83	14	2	8	34	31	39
On Grass and on Turf											
Grass	.238	.290	.357	610	145	19	9	12	56	44	54
Turf	.257	.343	.401	152	39	7	0	5	20	21	17
During the Day and at Night											
Day	.235	.300	.294	238	56	6	1	2	16	23	23
Night	.244	.302	.399	524	128	20	8	15	60	42	48
By Month											
April	.270	.316	.360	89	24	3	1	1	10	6	9
May	.279	.338	.411	129	36	8	3	1	8	11	10
June	.188	.233	.261	138	26	2	1	2	12	8	9
July	.244	.338	.356	135	33	2	2	3	12	18	16
August	.267	.312	.416	161	43	5	2	5	13	11	14
Sept/Oct	.200	.268	.391	110	22	6	0	5	21	11	13
Situational											
Bases Empty	.254	.309	.390	441	112	19	7	9	9	33	39
Leadoff	.225	.280	.349	209	47	7	5	3	3	16	15
Not Leadoff	.280	.335	.427	232	65	12	2	6	6	17	24
Runners On	.224	.291	.333	321	72	7	2	8	67	32	32
First Base Only	.243	.278	.319	144	35	5	0	2	6	7	11
Scoring Position	.209	.301	.345	177	37	2	2	6	61	25	21
Late Innings, Close	.237	.303	.405	131	31	3	2	5	17	13	13

RBI/Opportunities		
Scoring Position	50 / 255	(20%)
Scoring Position, 2 Out	17 / 128	(13%)
On Third, Less than 2 Out	20 / 39	(51%)
RBI in close games / RBI Total	43 / 76	(57%)

Buck Martinez
Toronto Blue Jays

	Ave.	OBP	SLG	AB	H	2B	3B	HR	RBI	BB	SO
THREE YEARS (84 – 86)											
Totals	.196	.279	.316	491	96	24	1	11	63	59	86
Batting vs. Left and Right-handed Pitchers											
Left	.190	.277	.310	348	66	18	0	8	41	43	51
Right	.210	.285	.329	143	30	6	1	3	22	16	35
At Home and on the Road											
Home	.212	.291	.345	226	48	13	1	5	31	26	33
Road	.181	.269	.291	265	48	11	0	6	32	33	53
Facing Groundball Pitchers and Flyball Pitchers											
Groundball	.155	.221	.235	200	31	8	1	2	22	18	38
Flyball	.223	.317	.371	291	65	16	0	9	41	41	48
Facing Finesse Pitchers and Power Pitchers											
Finesse	.182	.235	.276	275	50	12	1	4	32	21	44
Power	.213	.330	.366	216	46	12	0	7	31	38	42
On Grass and on Turf											
Grass	.165	.251	.273	194	32	6	0	5	24	23	44
Turf	.215	.297	.343	297	64	18	1	6	39	36	42
During the Day and at Night											
Day	.180	.255	.259	189	34	9	0	2	21	20	28
Night	.205	.294	.351	302	62	15	1	9	42	39	58
By Month											
April	.133	.176	.229	83	11	5	0	1	5	5	11
May	.195	.297	.287	87	17	5	0	1	11	12	8
June	.213	.292	.425	127	27	7	1	6	22	15	27
July	.206	.308	.286	63	13	2	0	1	9	10	17
August	.254	.307	.388	67	17	3	0	2	9	6	10
Sept/Oct	.172	.299	.203	64	11	2	0	0	7	11	13
Situational											
Bases Empty	.170	.277	.277	264	45	10	0	6	6	37	50
Leadoff	.140	.222	.228	114	16	4	0	2	2	11	21
Not Leadoff	.193	.316	.313	150	29	6	0	4	4	26	29
Runners On	.225	.281	.361	227	51	14	1	5	57	22	36
First Base Only	.224	.276	.367	98	22	8	0	2	10	6	14
Scoring Position	.225	.285	.357	129	29	6	1	3	47	16	22
Late Innings, Close	.247	.322	.351	77	19	2	0	2	9	8	10

RBI/Opportunities		
Scoring Position	43 / 194	(22%)
Scoring Position, 2 Out	20 / 85	(24%)
On Third, Less than 2 Out	18 / 41	(44%)
RBI in close games / RBI Total	39 / 63	(62%)

Carmelo Martinez
San Diego Padres

	Ave.	OBP	SLG	AB	H	2B	3B	HR	RBI	BB	SO
THREE YEARS (84 – 86)											
Totals	.249	.348	.410	1246	310	66	3	43	163	190	210
Batting vs. Left and Right-handed Pitchers											
Left	.263	.384	.453	437	115	30	1	17	60	88	68
Right	.241	.328	.387	809	195	36	2	26	103	102	142
At Home and on the Road											
Home	.246	.360	.429	609	150	26	2	27	93	109	108
Road	.251	.336	.392	637	160	40	1	16	70	81	102
Facing Groundball Pitchers and Flyball Pitchers											
Groundball	.249	.356	.403	647	161	38	1	20	82	107	107
Flyball	.249	.339	.417	599	149	28	2	23	81	83	103
Facing Finesse Pitchers and Power Pitchers											
Finesse	.252	.351	.411	643	162	33	3	21	91	95	102
Power	.245	.345	.410	603	148	33	0	22	72	95	108
On Grass and on Turf											
Grass	.259	.363	.434	918	238	46	3	36	133	152	155
Turf	.220	.303	.345	328	72	20	0	7	30	38	55
During the Day and at Night											
Day	.273	.376	.444	399	109	18	1	16	54	68	57
Night	.237	.334	.394	847	201	48	2	27	109	122	153
By Month											
April	.266	.361	.448	154	41	7	0	7	20	24	32
May	.255	.337	.435	216	55	13	1	8	27	27	43
June	.268	.363	.429	261	70	15	0	9	35	37	42
July	.200	.310	.350	200	40	10	1	6	24	33	31
August	.233	.328	.372	172	40	10	1	4	23	26	28
Sept/Oct	.263	.378	.420	243	64	11	0	9	34	43	34
Situational											
Bases Empty	.229	.342	.387	685	157	32	2	24	24	116	122
Leadoff	.218	.328	.385	275	60	12	2	10	10	45	48
Not Leadoff	.237	.352	.388	410	97	20	0	14	14	71	74
Runners On	.273	.355	.439	561	153	34	1	19	139	74	88
First Base Only	.322	.386	.512	242	78	19	0	9	24	23	24
Scoring Position	.235	.333	.382	319	75	15	1	10	115	51	64
Late Innings, Close	.245	.326	.364	261	64	13	0	6	37	34	48

RBI/Opportunities		
Scoring Position	97 / 453	(21%)
Scoring Position, 2 Out	29 / 200	(14%)
On Third, Less than 2 Out	43 / 95	(45%)
RBI in close games / RBI Total	104 / 163	(64%)

Dave Martinez
Chicago Cubs

	Ave.	OBP	SLG	AB	H	2B	3B	HR	RBI	BB	SO
THREE YEARS (84 – 86)											
Totals	.139	.190	.194	108	15	1	1	1	7	6	22
Batting vs. Left and Right-handed Pitchers											
Left	.200	.200	.200	10	2	0	0	0	0	0	4
Right	.133	.189	.194	98	13	1	1	1	7	6	18
At Home and on the Road											
Home	.136	.186	.212	66	9	0	1	1	3	3	15
Road	.143	.196	.167	42	6	1	0	0	4	3	7
Facing Groundball Pitchers and Flyball Pitchers											
Groundball	.118	.151	.157	51	6	0	1	0	1	1	8
Flyball	.158	.222	.228	57	9	1	0	1	6	5	14
Facing Finesse Pitchers and Power Pitchers											
Finesse	.145	.197	.242	62	9	1	1	1	4	3	12
Power	.130	.180	.130	46	6	0	0	0	3	3	10
On Grass and on Turf											
Grass	.113	.155	.175	80	9	0	1	1	3	3	19
Turf	.214	.281	.250	28	6	1	0	0	4	3	3
During the Day and at Night											
Day	.125	.170	.182	88	11	0	1	1	5	4	19
Night	.200	.273	.250	20	4	1	0	0	2	2	3
By Month											
April	.000	.000	.000	0	0	0	0	0	0	0	0
May	.000	.000	.000	0	0	0	0	0	0	0	0
June	.182	.250	.212	33	6	1	0	0	2	2	4
July	.063	.091	.156	32	2	0	0	1	3	1	11
August	.000	.000	.000	2	0	0	0	0	0	0	0
Sept/Oct	.171	.222	.220	41	7	0	1	0	2	3	7
Situational											
Bases Empty	.095	.149	.175	63	6	0	1	1	1	3	14
Leadoff	.129	.206	.129	31	4	0	0	0	0	2	6
Not Leadoff	.063	.091	.219	32	2	0	1	1	1	1	8
Runners On	.200	.245	.222	45	9	1	0	0	6	3	8
First Base Only	.227	.261	.227	22	5	0	0	0	0	1	2
Scoring Position	.174	.231	.217	23	4	1	0	0	6	2	6
Late Innings, Close	.167	.211	.278	18	3	0	1	0	0	1	2

RBI/Opportunities		
Scoring Position	5 / 34	(15%)
Scoring Position, 2 Out	1 / 10	(10%)
On Third, Less than 2 Out	4 / 9	(44%)
RBI in close games / RBI Total	4 / 7	(57%)

Dennis Martinez
Montreal Expos

1986: Finesse, Groundball 1985: Finesse, Flyball 1984: Finesse, Flyball

THREE YEARS (84 – 86)

	G	IP	H	BB	SO	SB	CS	W	L	S	ERA
Totals	90	426.1	462	130	210	49	9	22	26	0	5.00
At Home and on the Road											
Home	43	200.1	229	62	112	29	4	9	16	0	5.62
Road	47	226.0	233	68	98	20	5	13	10	0	4.46
During the Day and and at Night											
Day	29	140.1	154	40	69	22	3	6	10	0	4.49
Night	61	286.0	308	90	141	27	6	16	16	0	5.26
On Grass and on Turf											
Grass	66	292.0	321	94	133	35	3	14	19	0	5.30
Turf	24	134.1	141	36	77	14	6	8	7	0	4.35
By Month											
April	13	36.2	39	11	16	3	0	2	1	0	4.17
May	12	40.1	52	18	16	5	2	3	4	0	6.25
June	14	66.0	67	26	22	8	1	2	4	0	4.64
July	16	91.0	101	19	61	11	3	4	6	0	5.54
August	16	92.0	88	20	41	10	0	7	4	0	3.82
Sept/Oct	19	100.1	115	36	54	12	3	4	7	0	5.65

vs. Opponent Batters
THREE YEARS (84 – 86)

	Ave.	OBP	SLG	AB	H	2B	3B	HR	RBI	BB	SO
Totals	.278	.333	.459	1663	462	85	9	66	226	130	210
Pitching vs. Left and Right-handed Batters											
Left	.253	.315	.422	894	226	43	6	32	109	84	123
Right	.307	.355	.502	769	236	42	3	34	117	46	87
Situational											
Bases Empty	.270	.320	.442	1040	281	49	8	38	38	65	140
Leadoff	.264	.298	.437	428	113	26	3	14	14	17	61
Not Leadoff	.275	.334	.446	612	168	23	5	24	24	48	79
Runners On	.291	.354	.486	623	181	36	1	28	188	65	70
First Base Only	.280	.338	.460	261	73	17	0	10	27	20	20
Scoring Position	.298	.364	.506	362	108	19	1	18	161	45	50
Late Innings, Close	.275	.333	.427	131	36	7	2	3	15	11	13

RBI/Opportunities

Scoring Position	132 / 503	(26%)
Scoring Position, 2 Out	62 / 233	(27%)
On Third, Less than 2 Out	45 / 91	(49%)
RBI in close games / RBI Total	140 / 226	(62%)

Greg Mathews
St. Louis Cardinals

1986: Finesse, Flyball 1985: Did not play 1984: Did not play

THREE YEARS (84 – 86)

	G	IP	H	BB	SO	SB	CS	W	L	S	ERA
Totals	23	145.1	139	44	67	7	8	11	8	0	3.65
At Home and on the Road											
Home	8	53.2	45	13	24	2	1	5	2	0	3.19
Road	15	91.2	94	31	43	5	7	6	6	0	3.93
During the Day and and at Night											
Day	9	58.0	58	15	25	2	3	5	3	0	3.41
Night	14	87.1	81	29	42	5	5	6	5	0	3.81
On Grass and on Turf											
Grass	7	40.2	37	12	17	2	5	2	2	0	3.10
Turf	16	104.2	102	32	50	5	3	9	6	0	3.87
By Month											
April	0	0.0	0	0	0	0	0	0	0	0	0.00
May	0	0.0	0	0	0	0	0	0	0	0	0.00
June	6	46.2	37	15	23	2	2	4	1	0	2.89
July	5	24.0	27	6	9	2	4	2	1	0	4.12
August	6	42.0	37	10	16	2	1	4	2	0	3.00
Sept/Oct	6	32.2	38	13	19	1	1	1	4	0	5.23

vs. Opponent Batters
THREE YEARS (84 – 86)

	Ave.	OBP	SLG	AB	H	2B	3B	HR	RBI	BB	SO
Totals	.259	.317	.406	537	139	32	1	15	54	44	67
Pitching vs. Left and Right-handed Batters											
Left	.245	.297	.383	94	23	5	1	2	8	7	13
Right	.262	.321	.411	443	116	27	0	13	46	37	54
Situational											
Bases Empty	.252	.315	.412	325	82	19	0	11	11	28	44
Leadoff	.261	.340	.440	134	35	9	0	5	5	14	17
Not Leadoff	.246	.298	.393	191	47	10	0	6	6	14	27
Runners On	.269	.319	.396	212	57	13	1	4	43	16	23
First Base Only	.276	.300	.425	87	24	8	1	1	7	3	4
Scoring Position	.264	.331	.376	125	33	5	0	3	36	13	19
Late Innings, Close	.191	.240	.277	47	9	1	0	1	4	3	4

RBI/Opportunities

Scoring Position	31 / 164	(19%)
Scoring Position, 2 Out	12 / 74	(16%)
On Third, Less than 2 Out	9 / 19	(47%)
RBI in close games / RBI Total	40 / 54	(74%)

Mike Mason
Texas Rangers

1986: Power, Groundball 1985: Finesse, Flyball 1984: Finesse, Groundball

THREE YEARS (84 – 86)

	G	IP	H	BB	SO	SB	CS	W	L	S	ERA
Totals	101	498.1	506	180	290	39	14	24	31	0	4.24
At Home and on the Road											
Home	48	241.1	251	85	165	18	5	12	13	0	4.36
Road	53	257.0	255	95	125	21	9	12	18	0	4.13
During the Day and and at Night											
Day	22	113.0	123	49	59	4	4	7	9	0	4.62
Night	79	385.1	383	131	231	35	10	17	22	0	4.13
On Grass and on Turf											
Grass	85	399.0	412	144	235	34	8	18	26	0	4.29
Turf	16	99.1	94	36	55	5	6	6	5	0	4.08
By Month											
April	15	63.0	62	25	44	6	3	4	2	0	3.86
May	18	107.2	110	37	58	4	2	6	7	0	4.01
June	13	81.0	74	23	53	6	3	4	5	0	3.78
July	17	87.1	92	34	34	9	3	4	8	0	4.23
August	22	68.0	76	29	41	7	1	1	4	0	5.03
Sept/Oct	16	91.1	92	32	60	7	2	5	5	0	4.63

vs. Opponent Batters
THREE YEARS (84 – 86)

	Ave.	OBP	SLG	AB	H	2B	3B	HR	RBI	BB	SO
Totals	.264	.325	.400	1917	506	82	13	51	223	180	290
Pitching vs. Left and Right-handed Batters											
Left	.266	.334	.376	394	105	17	1	8	44	42	53
Right	.263	.323	.406	1523	401	65	12	43	179	138	237
Situational											
Bases Empty	.260	.326	.407	1102	286	51	12	29	29	105	158
Leadoff	.275	.345	.439	472	130	26	6	13	13	49	59
Not Leadoff	.248	.311	.383	630	156	25	6	16	16	56	99
Runners On	.270	.325	.391	815	220	31	1	22	194	75	132
First Base Only	.276	.322	.397	395	109	16	1	10	28	26	63
Scoring Position	.264	.327	.386	420	111	15	0	12	166	49	69
Late Innings, Close	.256	.357	.372	121	31	4	2	2	11	17	11

RBI/Opportunities

Scoring Position	142 / 570	(25%)
Scoring Position, 2 Out	44 / 232	(19%)
On Third, Less than 2 Out	66 / 121	(55%)
RBI in close games / RBI Total	163 / 223	(73%)

Len Matuszek
Los Angeles Dodgers

THREE YEARS (84 – 86)

	Ave.	OBP	SLG	AB	H	2B	3B	HR	RBI	BB	SO
Totals	.250	.338	.445	524	131	26	2	24	84	68	115
Batting vs. Left and Right-handed Pitchers											
Left	.164	.220	.200	55	9	2	0	0	3	3	17
Right	.260	.351	.473	469	122	24	2	24	81	65	98
At Home and on the Road											
Home	.264	.362	.444	239	63	7	0	12	43	36	45
Road	.239	.318	.446	285	68	19	2	12	41	32	70
Facing Groundball Pitchers and Flyball Pitchers											
Groundball	.278	.354	.486	216	60	15	0	10	38	26	41
Flyball	.231	.328	.416	308	71	11	2	14	46	42	74
Facing Finesse Pitchers and Power Pitchers											
Finesse	.242	.313	.405	289	70	11	0	12	39	29	48
Power	.260	.367	.494	235	61	15	2	12	45	39	67
On Grass and on Turf											
Grass	.292	.361	.545	264	77	15	2	16	55	28	50
Turf	.208	.316	.342	260	54	11	0	8	29	40	65
During the Day and at Night											
Day	.254	.314	.476	185	47	7	2	10	30	16	36
Night	.248	.351	.428	339	84	19	0	14	54	52	79
By Month											
April	.250	.342	.422	64	16	5	0	2	9	9	13
May	.260	.360	.534	73	19	5	0	5	16	10	14
June	.222	.314	.356	45	10	0	0	2	5	5	12
July	.272	.320	.565	92	25	5	2	6	14	7	18
August	.250	.362	.382	144	36	7	0	4	19	24	33
Sept/Oct	.236	.311	.415	106	25	4	0	5	21	13	25
Situational											
Bases Empty	.214	.291	.404	285	61	16	1	12	12	28	56
Leadoff	.186	.267	.356	118	22	5	0	5	5	11	24
Not Leadoff	.234	.308	.437	167	39	11	1	7	7	17	32
Runners On	.293	.390	.494	239	70	10	1	12	72	40	59
First Base Only	.402	.495	.678	87	35	4	1	6	14	15	18
Scoring Position	.230	.332	.388	152	35	6	0	6	58	25	41
Late Innings, Close	.255	.339	.510	102	26	4	2	6	23	14	23

RBI/Opportunities

Scoring Position	49 / 223	(22%)
Scoring Position, 2 Out	19 / 118	(16%)
On Third, Less than 2 Out	19 / 41	(46%)
RBI in close games / RBI Total	58 / 84	(69%)

Lee Mazzilli
New York Mets

	THREE YEARS (84 – 86)										
	Ave.	OBP	SLG	AB	H	2B	3B	HR	RBI	BB	SO
Totals	.249	.376	.346	534	133	24	2	8	45	107	95
Batting vs. Left and Right-handed Pitchers											
Left	.223	.324	.277	94	21	2	0	1	10	14	23
Right	.255	.387	.361	440	112	22	2	7	35	93	72
At Home and on the Road											
Home	.268	.391	.370	257	69	12	1	4	24	53	47
Road	.231	.362	.325	277	64	12	1	4	21	54	48
Facing Groundball Pitchers and Flyball Pitchers											
Groundball	.237	.362	.317	240	57	8	1	3	15	47	39
Flyball	.259	.387	.371	294	76	16	1	5	30	60	56
Facing Finesse Pitchers and Power Pitchers											
Finesse	.263	.357	.377	308	81	16	2	5	21	44	52
Power	.230	.399	.305	226	52	8	0	3	24	63	43
On Grass and on Turf											
Grass	.228	.332	.335	206	47	8	1	4	21	31	37
Turf	.262	.402	.354	328	86	16	1	4	24	76	58
During the Day and at Night											
Day	.260	.392	.398	181	47	10	0	5	22	38	26
Night	.244	.368	.320	353	86	14	2	3	23	69	69
By Month											
April	.184	.404	.211	38	7	1	0	0	5	14	11
May	.245	.398	.372	94	23	3	0	3	12	24	20
June	.241	.365	.316	158	38	7	1	1	10	32	20
July	.293	.375	.414	99	29	6	0	2	7	12	16
August	.225	.310	.348	89	20	3	1	2	4	11	19
Sept/Oct	.286	.444	.357	56	16	4	0	0	7	14	9
Situational											
Bases Empty	.253	.368	.370	292	74	12	2	6	6	53	56
Leadoff	.284	.419	.432	95	27	6	1	2	2	22	21
Not Leadoff	.239	.342	.340	197	47	6	1	4	4	31	35
Runners On	.244	.385	.318	242	59	12	0	2	39	54	39
First Base Only	.279	.348	.404	104	29	7	0	2	7	11	13
Scoring Position	.217	.409	.254	138	30	5	0	0	32	43	26
Late Innings, Close	.256	.369	.317	164	42	7	0	1	15	28	34

RBI/Opportunities		
Scoring Position	32 / 214	(15%)
Scoring Position, 2 Out	14 / 89	(16%)
On Third, Less than 2 Out	14 / 41	(34%)
RBI in close games / RBI Total	31 / 45	(69%)

Bob McClure
Montreal Expos

1986: Power, Groundball 1985: Power, Flyball 1984: Finesse, Flyball

	THREE YEARS (84 – 86)										
	G	IP	H	BB	SO	SB	CS	W	L	S	ERA
Totals	142	304.1	316	115	178	11	11	12	15	10	4.05
At Home and on the Road											
Home	66	153.1	165	53	89	8	8	9	6	3	3.93
Road	76	151.0	151	62	89	3	3	3	9	7	4.17
During the Day and and at Night											
Day	51	119.2	128	43	69	5	5	4	8	2	3.53
Night	91	184.2	188	72	109	6	6	8	7	8	4.39
On Grass and on Turf											
Grass	92	239.1	243	91	136	6	9	10	12	6	4.02
Turf	50	65.0	73	24	42	5	2	2	3	4	4.15
By Month											
April	19	26.1	18	15	12	0	1	2	1	1	1.71
May	14	32.1	35	12	22	0	1	1	0	0	6.12
June	25	59.0	61	22	36	4	2	3	3	4	3.81
July	30	54.2	63	22	42	3	6	1	4	0	4.28
August	25	60.2	65	19	29	0	0	2	3	2	4.15
Sept/Oct	29	71.1	74	25	37	4	1	3	4	3	3.91

	vs. Opponent Batters THREE YEARS (84 – 86)										
	Ave.	OBP	SLG	AB	H	2B	3B	HR	RBI	BB	SO
Totals	.271	.336	.397	1170	317	55	12	23	158	115	178
Pitching vs. Left and Right-handed Batters											
Left	.233	.298	.343	309	72	9	5	5	45	30	65
Right	.285	.350	.417	861	245	46	7	18	113	85	113
Situational											
Bases Empty	.265	.323	.372	645	171	27	6	10	10	50	87
Leadoff	.259	.306	.338	278	72	13	3	1	1	17	37
Not Leadoff	.270	.335	.398	367	99	14	3	9	9	33	50
Runners On	.278	.351	.429	525	146	28	6	13	148	65	91
First Base Only	.243	.289	.352	247	60	12	0	5	14	15	41
Scoring Position	.309	.399	.496	278	86	16	6	8	134	50	50
Late Innings, Close	.272	.354	.373	268	73	9	6	2	26	35	47

RBI/Opportunities		
Scoring Position	117 / 419	(28%)
Scoring Position, 2 Out	53 / 210	(25%)
On Third, Less than 2 Out	37 / 68	(54%)
RBI in close games / RBI Total	90 / 158	(57%)

Roger McDowell
New York Mets

1986: Finesse, Groundball 1985: Finesse, Groundball 1984: Did not play

	THREE YEARS (84 – 86)										
	G	IP	H	BB	SO	SB	CS	W	L	S	ERA
Totals	137	255.1	215	79	135	23	11	20	14	39	2.93
At Home and on the Road											
Home	65	130.2	98	40	66	8	5	12	6	19	1.93
Road	72	124.2	117	39	69	15	6	8	8	20	3.97
During the Day and and at Night											
Day	58	118.2	99	34	69	10	6	9	7	17	3.56
Night	79	136.2	116	45	66	13	5	11	7	22	2.37
On Grass and on Turf											
Grass	99	189.1	154	52	100	15	5	16	9	29	2.52
Turf	38	66.0	61	27	35	8	6	4	5	10	4.09
By Month											
April	15	26.0	25	9	22	4	2	4	0	1	3.46
May	22	50.2	39	14	28	2	2	4	1	6	2.66
June	18	41.1	32	19	23	2	2	4	2	3	1.96
July	23	41.2	37	11	23	3	1	1	6	8	2.81
August	29	45.2	33	8	18	5	2	5	3	12	3.15
Sept/Oct	30	50.0	49	18	21	7	2	2	2	9	3.60

	vs. Opponent Batters THREE YEARS (84 – 86)										
	Ave.	OBP	SLG	AB	H	2B	3B	HR	RBI	BB	SO
Totals	.229	.290	.314	939	215	33	4	13	88	79	135
Pitching vs. Left and Right-handed Batters											
Left	.241	.315	.342	453	109	20	4	6	51	48	49
Right	.218	.266	.288	486	106	13	0	7	37	31	86
Situational											
Bases Empty	.217	.274	.268	549	119	17	1	3	3	42	85
Leadoff	.217	.283	.261	230	50	7	0	1	1	21	28
Not Leadoff	.216	.267	.273	319	69	10	1	2	2	21	57
Runners On	.246	.313	.379	390	96	16	3	10	85	37	50
First Base Only	.239	.263	.337	184	44	6	0	4	12	6	18
Scoring Position	.252	.351	.417	206	52	10	3	6	73	31	32
Late Innings, Close	.236	.300	.328	573	135	18	4	9	60	53	78

RBI/Opportunities		
Scoring Position	61 / 297	(21%)
Scoring Position, 2 Out	18 / 129	(14%)
On Third, Less than 2 Out	29 / 56	(52%)
RBI in close games / RBI Total	70 / 88	(80%)

Andy McGaffigan
Montreal Expos

1986: Power, Groundball 1985: Power, Flyball 1984: Power, Groundball

	THREE YEARS (84 – 86)										
	G	IP	H	BB	SO	SB	CS	W	L	S	ERA
Totals	93	306.0	262	108	244	36	9	16	14	3	3.18
At Home and on the Road											
Home	46	154.2	126	50	118	22	4	7	7	2	3.03
Road	47	151.1	136	58	126	14	5	9	7	1	3.33
During the Day and and at Night											
Day	36	123.2	109	41	107	13	6	7	7	1	3.49
Night	57	182.1	153	67	137	23	3	9	7	2	2.96
On Grass and on Turf											
Grass	28	82.2	83	29	63	7	4	3	7	1	4.46
Turf	65	223.1	179	79	181	29	5	13	7	2	2.70
By Month											
April	9	29.0	22	15	23	2	1	2	0	0	3.72
May	15	43.0	34	20	26	3	0	4	4	1	2.30
June	11	35.1	32	11	28	4	2	2	3	0	3.82
July	10	36.1	35	8	32	3	1	0	1	0	2.72
August	23	83.2	74	30	66	9	4	4	5	1	3.76
Sept/Oct	25	78.2	65	24	69	15	1	4	1	1	2.75

	vs. Opponent Batters THREE YEARS (84 – 86)										
	Ave.	OBP	SLG	AB	H	2B	3B	HR	RBI	BB	SO
Totals	.233	.301	.339	1123	262	52	8	17	107	108	244
Pitching vs. Left and Right-handed Batters											
Left	.234	.315	.312	593	139	23	4	5	46	72	123
Right	.232	.285	.370	530	123	29	4	12	61	36	121
Situational											
Bases Empty	.235	.295	.343	665	156	32	5	10	10	56	139
Leadoff	.255	.318	.379	282	72	11	0	8	8	26	54
Not Leadoff	.219	.278	.316	383	84	21	5	2	2	30	85
Runners On	.231	.310	.334	458	106	20	3	7	97	52	105
First Base Only	.222	.276	.330	185	41	10	2	2	8	14	38
Scoring Position	.238	.331	.337	273	65	10	1	5	89	38	67
Late Innings, Close	.231	.309	.325	160	37	10	1	1	14	19	32

RBI/Opportunities		
Scoring Position	78 / 380	(21%)
Scoring Position, 2 Out	37 / 182	(20%)
On Third, Less than 2 Out	24 / 59	(41%)
RBI in close games / RBI Total	78 / 107	(73%)

Joel McKeon
Chicago White Sox

1986: Power, Groundball   1985: Did not play   1984: Did not play

THREE YEARS (84 – 86)

	G	IP	H	BB	SO	SB	CS	W	L	S	ERA
Totals	30	33.0	18	17	18	0	2	3	1	1	2.45
At Home and on the Road											
Home	11	15.1	3	8	6	0	0	1	0	1	0.59
Road	19	17.2	15	9	12	0	2	2	1	0	4.08
During the Day and and at Night											
Day	9	12.1	9	3	5	0	1	1	1	0	3.65
Night	21	20.2	9	14	13	0	1	2	0	1	1.74
On Grass and on Turf											
Grass	22	29.0	11	13	18	0	1	3	0	1	1.24
Turf	8	4.0	7	4	0	0	1	0	1	0	11.25
By Month											
April	0	0.0	0	0	0	0	0	0	0	0	0.00
May	11	10.1	5	7	4	0	1	2	0	0	0.87
June	13	10.2	8	8	6	0	0	1	1	1	6.75
July	6	12.0	5	2	8	0	1	0	0	0	0.00
August	0	0.0	0	0	0	0	0	0	0	0	0.00
Sept/Oct	0	0.0	0	0	0	0	0	0	0	0	0.00

vs. Opponent Batters — THREE YEARS (84 – 86)

	Ave.	OBP	SLG	AB	H	2B	3B	HR	RBI	BB	SO
Totals	.165	.273	.284	109	18	3	2	2	11	17	18
Pitching vs. Left and Right-handed Batters											
Left	.211	.281	.386	57	12	0	2	2	9	6	11
Right	.115	.266	.173	52	6	3	0	0	2	11	7
Situational											
Bases Empty	.164	.243	.239	67	11	1	2	0	0	7	12
Leadoff	.192	.276	.308	26	5	1	1	0	0	3	1
Not Leadoff	.146	.222	.195	41	6	0	1	0	0	4	11
Runners On	.167	.315	.357	42	7	2	0	2	11	10	6
First Base Only	.174	.296	.391	23	4	2	0	1	3	4	2
Scoring Position	.158	.333	.316	19	3	0	0	1	8	6	4
Late Innings, Close	.242	.390	.303	33	8	2	0	0	8	3	

RBI/Opportunities

Scoring Position	6 / 30	(20%)
Scoring Position, 2 Out	2 / 13	(15%)
On Third, Less than 2 Out	3 / 6	(50%)
RBI in close games / RBI Total	6 / 11	(55%)

Craig McMurtry
Atlanta Braves

1986: Power, Flyball   1985: Power, Groundball   1984: Power, Groundball

THREE YEARS (84 – 86)

	G	IP	H	BB	SO	SB	CS	W	L	S	ERA
Totals	91	308.0	322	172	177	40	15	10	26	1	4.76
At Home and on the Road											
Home	49	171.1	201	86	77	18	12	4	17	1	5.25
Road	42	136.2	121	86	100	22	3	6	9	0	4.15
During the Day and and at Night											
Day	33	108.1	101	66	73	19	6	3	12	0	4.57
Night	58	199.2	221	106	104	21	9	7	14	1	4.87
On Grass and on Turf											
Grass	68	249.1	273	130	135	28	14	7	22	1	4.91
Turf	23	58.2	49	42	42	12	1	3	4	0	4.14
By Month											
April	14	51.0	51	23	23	7	3	2	3	0	4.41
May	19	50.2	42	34	34	8	2	2	6	0	4.97
June	13	60.0	68	26	30	6	1	3	4	0	4.80
July	13	43.2	50	35	25	6	1	2	5	0	6.39
August	12	41.0	52	21	26	4	3	0	4	1	4.61
Sept/Oct	20	61.2	59	33	39	9	5	1	4	0	3.79

vs. Opponent Batters — THREE YEARS (84 – 86)

	Ave.	OBP	SLG	AB	H	2B	3B	HR	RBI	BB	SO
Totals	.273	.364	.408	1179	322	50	11	29	170	172	177
Pitching vs. Left and Right-handed Batters											
Left	.320	.427	.475	590	189	33	8	14	95	113	67
Right	.226	.296	.341	589	133	17	3	15	75	59	110
Situational											
Bases Empty	.294	.383	.432	623	183	26	6	16	16	88	81
Leadoff	.285	.372	.413	281	80	13	1	7	7	38	34
Not Leadoff	.301	.392	.447	342	103	13	5	9	9	50	47
Runners On	.250	.344	.381	556	139	24	5	13	154	84	96
First Base Only	.221	.314	.356	208	46	7	0	7	19	27	28
Scoring Position	.267	.360	.397	348	93	17	5	6	135	57	68
Late Innings, Close	.325	.429	.488	123	40	5	0	5	20	23	13

RBI/Opportunities

Scoring Position	122 / 507	(24%)
Scoring Position, 2 Out	49 / 224	(22%)
On Third, Less than 2 Out	40 / 91	(44%)
RBI in close games / RBI Total	97 / 170	(57%)

Hal McRae
Kansas City Royals

THREE YEARS (84 – 86)

	Ave.	OBP	SLG	AB	H	2B	3B	HR	RBI	BB	SO
Totals	.272	.339	.410	915	249	46	4	24	149	96	131
Batting vs. Left and Right-handed Pitchers											
Left	.278	.354	.452	460	128	28	2	16	78	58	60
Right	.266	.323	.367	455	121	18	2	8	71	38	71
At Home and on the Road											
Home	.285	.352	.421	463	132	27	3	10	84	50	62
Road	.259	.325	.398	452	117	19	1	14	65	46	69
Facing Groundball Pitchers and Flyball Pitchers											
Groundball	.301	.365	.429	399	120	22	1	9	73	43	53
Flyball	.250	.318	.395	516	129	24	3	15	76	53	78
Facing Finesse Pitchers and Power Pitchers											
Finesse	.287	.342	.447	477	137	26	1	16	91	41	47
Power	.256	.336	.370	438	112	20	3	8	58	55	84
On Grass and on Turf											
Grass	.251	.315	.381	362	91	12	1	11	48	35	52
Turf	.286	.354	.429	553	158	34	3	13	101	61	79
During the Day and at Night											
Day	.263	.327	.410	251	66	14	1	7	41	27	43
Night	.276	.343	.410	664	183	32	3	17	108	69	88
By Month											
April	.261	.322	.381	134	35	6	2	2	18	14	13
May	.223	.296	.309	175	39	9	0	2	21	19	26
June	.283	.359	.504	113	32	10	0	5	21	14	16
July	.320	.368	.451	175	56	5	0	6	40	14	21
August	.285	.348	.436	179	51	8	2	5	32	18	33
Sept/Oct	.259	.344	.403	139	36	8	0	4	17	17	22
Situational											
Bases Empty	.273	.336	.388	454	124	23	1	9	9	42	71
Leadoff	.327	.370	.493	205	67	16	0	6	6	13	26
Not Leadoff	.229	.309	.301	249	57	7	1	3	3	29	45
Runners On	.271	.342	.432	461	125	23	3	15	140	54	60
First Base Only	.261	.329	.482	199	52	9	1	11	30	19	28
Scoring Position	.279	.350	.393	262	73	14	2	4	110	35	32
Late Innings, Close	.300	.389	.431	160	48	6	0	5	24	25	25

RBI/Opportunities

Scoring Position	101 / 356	(28%)
Scoring Position, 2 Out	34 / 171	(20%)
On Third, Less than 2 Out	46 / 70	(66%)
RBI in close games / RBI Total	99 / 149	(66%)

Larry McWilliams
Pittsburgh Pirates

1986: Power, Groundball   1985: Finesse, Flyball   1984: Power, Groundball

THREE YEARS (84 – 86)

	G	IP	H	BB	SO	SB	CS	W	L	S	ERA
Totals	113	476.0	494	189	281	12	15	22	31	1	3.97
At Home and on the Road											
Home	54	228.0	248	84	133	8	7	11	17	1	4.18
Road	59	248.0	246	105	148	4	8	11	14	0	3.77
During the Day and at Night											
Day	32	124.2	135	49	70	2	5	6	9	0	4.40
Night	81	351.1	359	140	211	10	10	16	22	1	3.82
On Grass and on Turf											
Grass	31	138.0	154	61	88	1	3	5	10	0	4.70
Turf	82	338.0	340	128	193	11	12	17	21	1	3.67
By Month											
April	11	67.0	62	30	33	2	1	2	6	0	4.03
May	14	80.1	91	33	62	1	4	4	3	0	4.15
June	20	88.2	88	31	48	2	4	3	7	0	3.45
July	21	86.1	90	38	50	0	2	3	5	0	3.44
August	20	83.2	81	34	56	4	1	3	6	1	4.30
Sept/Oct	27	70.0	82	23	32	3	3	7	4	0	4.63

vs. Opponent Batters — THREE YEARS (84 – 86)

	Ave.	OBP	SLG	AB	H	2B	3B	HR	RBI	BB	SO
Totals	.270	.342	.413	1831	494	116	9	43	211	189	281
Pitching vs. Left and Right-handed Batters											
Left	.269	.338	.422	249	67	15	1	7	35	21	51
Right	.270	.342	.412	1582	427	101	8	36	176	168	230
Situational											
Bases Empty	.274	.337	.423	1033	283	64	6	26	26	90	161
Leadoff	.286	.342	.455	451	129	29	4	13	13	37	60
Not Leadoff	.265	.334	.399	582	154	35	2	13	13	53	101
Runners On	.264	.347	.401	798	211	52	3	17	185	99	120
First Base Only	.273	.333	.396	333	91	19	2	6	20	28	42
Scoring Position	.258	.356	.404	465	120	33	1	11	165	71	78
Late Innings, Close	.238	.323	.354	164	39	4	0	5	17	21	23

RBI/Opportunities

Scoring Position	139 / 654	(21%)
Scoring Position, 2 Out	65 / 311	(21%)
On Third, Less than 2 Out	42 / 101	(42%)
RBI in close games / RBI Total	146 / 211	(69%)

Bobby Meacham
New York Yankees

THREE YEARS (84 – 86)

	Ave.	OBP	SLG	AB	H	2B	3B	HR	RBI	BB	SO
Totals	.232	.307	.290	1002	232	36	7	3	82	103	211
Batting vs. Left and Right-handed Pitchers											
Left	.243	.316	.302	354	86	13	4	0	28	35	75
Right	.225	.302	.284	648	146	23	3	3	54	68	136
At Home and on the Road											
Home	.235	.306	.299	489	115	17	4	2	37	50	111
Road	.228	.307	.283	513	117	19	3	1	45	53	100
Facing Groundball Pitchers and Flyball Pitchers											
Groundball	.229	.294	.274	525	120	20	2	0	42	45	102
Flyball	.235	.320	.308	477	112	16	5	3	40	58	109
Facing Finesse Pitchers and Power Pitchers											
Finesse	.250	.305	.317	583	146	23	5	2	45	42	106
Power	.205	.310	.253	419	86	13	2	1	37	61	105
On Grass and on Turf											
Grass	.235	.312	.293	846	199	30	5	3	72	90	191
Turf	.212	.277	.276	156	33	6	2	0	10	13	20
During the Day and at Night											
Day	.220	.309	.271	328	72	12	1	1	28	40	62
Night	.237	.305	.300	674	160	24	6	2	54	63	149
By Month											
April	.277	.368	.311	119	33	4	0	0	13	17	28
May	.231	.342	.314	156	36	11	1	0	17	23	34
June	.180	.250	.223	139	25	6	0	0	8	13	35
July	.276	.323	.351	174	48	5	4	0	12	12	26
August	.237	.303	.308	211	50	4	1	3	21	20	42
Sept/Oct	.197	.271	.236	203	40	6	1	0	11	18	46
Situational											
Bases Empty	.226	.301	.292	554	125	19	6	2	2	54	118
Leadoff	.253	.322	.338	237	60	13	2	1	1	23	50
Not Leadoff	.205	.286	.259	317	65	6	4	1	1	31	68
Runners On	.239	.313	.288	448	107	17	1	1	80	49	93
First Base Only	.251	.317	.299	187	47	6	0	1	5	18	34
Scoring Position	.230	.311	.280	261	60	11	1	0	75	31	59
Late Innings, Close	.228	.304	.295	149	34	7	0	1	19	16	34

RBI/Opportunities

Scoring Position	73 / 389	(19%)
Scoring Position, 2 Out	26 / 179	(15%)
On Third, Less than 2 Out	33 / 72	(46%)
RBI in close games / RBI Total	55 / 82	(67%)

Bob Melvin
San Francisco Giants

THREE YEARS (84 – 86)

	Ave.	OBP	SLG	AB	H	2B	3B	HR	RBI	BB	SO
Totals	.223	.259	.334	350	78	18	3	5	29	18	90
Batting vs. Left and Right-handed Pitchers											
Left	.296	.340	.444	142	42	10	1	3	13	10	28
Right	.173	.202	.260	208	36	8	2	2	16	8	62
At Home and on the Road											
Home	.216	.236	.320	153	33	10	0	2	11	4	36
Road	.228	.276	.345	197	45	8	3	3	18	14	54
Facing Groundball Pitchers and Flyball Pitchers											
Groundball	.243	.287	.355	152	37	9	1	2	13	10	35
Flyball	.207	.237	.318	198	41	9	2	3	16	8	55
Facing Finesse Pitchers and Power Pitchers											
Finesse	.270	.298	.365	178	48	9	1	2	13	8	27
Power	.174	.219	.302	172	30	9	2	3	16	10	63
On Grass and on Turf											
Grass	.188	.220	.286	245	46	10	1	4	18	11	64
Turf	.305	.348	.448	105	32	8	2	1	11	7	26
During the Day and at Night											
Day	.190	.222	.307	137	26	7	0	3	11	6	37
Night	.244	.282	.352	213	52	11	3	2	18	12	53
By Month											
April	.154	.150	.205	39	6	2	0	0	4	0	10
May	.271	.271	.438	48	13	6	1	0	4	0	14
June	.339	.369	.435	62	21	3	0	1	3	3	15
July	.185	.214	.222	81	15	3	0	0	4	3	17
August	.143	.219	.321	28	4	0	1	1	5	3	7
Sept/Oct	.207	.275	.370	92	19	4	1	3	9	9	27
Situational											
Bases Empty	.204	.239	.311	196	40	8	2	3	3	9	47
Leadoff	.208	.237	.377	77	16	3	2	2	2	3	19
Not Leadoff	.202	.240	.269	119	24	5	0	1	1	6	28
Runners On	.247	.283	.364	154	38	10	1	2	26	9	43
First Base Only	.358	.370	.528	53	19	3	0	2	4	1	13
Scoring Position	.188	.241	.277	101	19	7	1	0	22	8	30
Late Innings, Close	.148	.206	.180	61	9	2	0	0	5	5	18

RBI/Opportunities

Scoring Position	20 / 131	(15%)
Scoring Position, 2 Out	5 / 60	(8%)
On Third, Less than 2 Out	9 / 29	(31%)
RBI in close games / RBI Total	16 / 29	(55%)

Orlando Mercado
Texas Rangers

THREE YEARS (84 – 86)

	Ave.	OBP	SLG	AB	H	2B	3B	HR	RBI	BB	SO
Totals	.228	.273	.289	180	41	4	2	1	12	10	25
Batting vs. Left and Right-handed Pitchers											
Left	.220	.298	.280	50	11	0	0	1	2	6	6
Right	.231	.263	.292	130	30	4	2	0	10	4	19
At Home and on the Road											
Home	.270	.313	.371	89	24	2	2	1	9	6	12
Road	.187	.235	.209	91	17	2	0	0	3	4	13
Facing Groundball Pitchers and Flyball Pitchers											
Groundball	.209	.247	.279	86	18	4	1	0	8	5	9
Flyball	.245	.297	.295	94	23	0	1	1	4	5	16
Facing Finesse Pitchers and Power Pitchers											
Finesse	.244	.287	.311	119	29	3	1	1	10	7	14
Power	.197	.246	.246	61	12	1	1	0	2	3	11
On Grass and on Turf											
Grass	.219	.278	.286	105	23	2	1	1	6	7	16
Turf	.240	.266	.293	75	18	2	1	0	6	3	9
During the Day and at Night											
Day	.300	.340	.360	50	15	3	0	0	3	3	3
Night	.200	.248	.262	130	26	1	2	1	9	7	22
By Month											
April	.000	.167	.000	5	0	0	0	0	0	1	1
May	.188	.257	.188	32	6	0	0	0	0	3	4
June	.235	.281	.275	51	12	0	1	0	4	3	7
July	.227	.244	.295	44	10	1	1	0	5	1	5
August	.207	.258	.207	29	6	0	0	0	0	2	7
Sept/Oct	.368	.400	.684	19	7	3	0	1	3	0	1
Situational											
Bases Empty	.273	.322	.327	110	30	3	0	1	1	7	18
Leadoff	.351	.368	.351	37	13	0	0	0	0	1	5
Not Leadoff	.233	.300	.315	73	17	3	0	1	1	6	13
Runners On	.157	.197	.229	70	11	1	2	0	11	3	7
First Base Only	.118	.167	.194	34	4	0	0	0	0	1	3
Scoring Position	.194	.225	.333	36	7	1	2	0	11	2	4
Late Innings, Close	.269	.296	.308	26	7	1	0	0	0	0	5

RBI/Opportunities

Scoring Position	11 / 47	(23%)
Scoring Position, 2 Out	5 / 22	(23%)
On Third, Less than 2 Out	5 / 12	(42%)
RBI in close games / RBI Total	6 / 12	(50%)

Eddie Milner
Cincinnati Reds

THREE YEARS (84 – 86)

	Ave.	OBP	SLG	AB	H	2B	3B	HR	RBI	BB	SO
Totals	.250	.331	.380	1213	303	49	17	25	109	148	137
Batting vs. Left and Right-handed Pitchers											
Left	.220	.309	.280	182	40	6	1	1	13	24	33
Right	.255	.335	.398	1031	263	43	16	24	96	124	104
At Home and on the Road											
Home	.266	.349	.411	579	154	26	8	14	57	76	64
Road	.235	.314	.352	634	149	23	9	11	52	72	73
Facing Groundball Pitchers and Flyball Pitchers											
Groundball	.281	.353	.370	576	162	30	4	7	44	64	60
Flyball	.221	.311	.370	637	141	19	11	18	65	84	77
Facing Finesse Pitchers and Power Pitchers											
Finesse	.250	.320	.377	673	168	30	7	14	52	72	51
Power	.250	.344	.383	540	135	19	10	11	57	76	86
On Grass and on Turf											
Grass	.235	.318	.358	358	84	10	5	8	27	43	37
Turf	.256	.336	.389	855	219	39	12	17	82	105	100
During the Day and at Night											
Day	.263	.341	.412	403	106	15	9	9	43	49	46
Night	.243	.326	.364	810	197	34	8	16	66	99	91
By Month											
April	.281	.344	.356	135	38	5	1	1	15	13	16
May	.231	.332	.328	238	55	6	4	3	16	36	25
June	.239	.329	.369	268	64	9	4	6	25	36	25
July	.256	.320	.445	164	42	12	2	5	11	16	19
August	.235	.313	.352	162	38	6	2	3	11	18	20
Sept/Oct	.268	.343	.431	246	66	11	4	7	31	29	32
Situational											
Bases Empty	.251	.327	.385	805	202	36	9	18	18	90	92
Leadoff	.240	.313	.369	442	106	19	4	10	10	46	55
Not Leadoff	.264	.344	.405	363	96	17	5	8	8	44	37
Runners On	.248	.338	.400	408	101	13	8	7	91	58	45
First Base Only	.281	.347	.412	160	45	6	3	3	11	15	12
Scoring Position	.226	.333	.343	248	56	7	5	4	80	43	33
Late Innings, Close	.245	.342	.380	200	49	3	3	6	23	29	29

RBI/Opportunities

Scoring Position	67 / 373	(18%)
Scoring Position, 2 Out	28 / 182	(15%)
On Third, Less than 2 Out	26 / 61	(43%)
RBI in close games / RBI Total	70 / 109	(64%)

Greg Minton
San Francisco Giants

1986: Finesse, Groundball 1985: Finesse, Groundball 1984: Finesse, Groundball

THREE YEARS (84 – 86)	G	IP	H	BB	SO	SB	CS	W	L	S	ERA
Totals	190	289.2	291	145	119	40	16	13	17	28	3.73
At Home and on the Road											
Home	85	128.1	125	50	50	16	6	6	7	13	3.58
Road	105	161.1	166	95	69	24	10	7	10	15	3.85
During the Day and and at Night											
Day	77	117.0	119	48	45	15	8	6	7	10	3.62
Night	113	172.2	172	97	74	25	8	7	10	18	3.81
On Grass and on Turf											
Grass	138	212.2	210	90	87	24	12	10	13	20	3.77
Turf	52	77.0	81	55	32	16	4	3	4	8	3.62
By Month											
April	25	42.1	43	22	16	5	3	3	3	4	4.04
May	30	48.1	57	21	22	8	1	1	5	1	4.28
June	37	57.1	50	25	25	10	1	1	2	6	3.30
July	31	49.0	39	18	25	6	2	1	3	7	2.39
August	33	46.2	57	31	15	3	6	2	2	6	4.24
Sept/Oct	34	46.0	45	28	16	8	3	5	2	4	4.30

vs. Opponent Batters THREE YEARS (84 – 86)	Ave.	OBP	SLG	AB	H	2B	3B	HR	RBI	BB	SO
Totals	.265	.348	.358	1097	291	38	8	16	160	145	119
Pitching vs. Left and Right-handed Batters											
Left	.293	.384	.389	481	141	20	4	6	78	77	37
Right	.244	.318	.334	616	150	18	4	10	82	68	82
Situational											
Bases Empty	.257	.329	.372	537	138	22	2	12	12	57	64
Leadoff	.270	.340	.367	237	64	5	0	6	6	24	28
Not Leadoff	.247	.321	.377	300	74	17	2	6	6	33	36
Runners On	.273	.365	.345	560	153	16	6	4	148	88	55
First Base Only	.278	.321	.324	176	49	3	1	1	4	11	15
Scoring Position	.271	.382	.354	384	104	13	5	3	144	77	40
Late Innings, Close	.267	.349	.355	622	166	18	3	11	89	83	69

RBI/Opportunities		
Scoring Position	129 / 602	(21%)
Scoring Position, 2 Out	54 / 282	(19%)
On Third, Less than 2 Out	48 / 110	(44%)
RBI in close games / RBI Total	93 / 160	(58%)

Kevin Mitchell
New York Mets

THREE YEARS (84 – 86)	Ave.	OBP	SLG	AB	H	2B	3B	HR	RBI	BB	SO
Totals	.275	.341	.456	342	94	22	2	12	44	34	64
Batting vs. Left and Right-handed Pitchers											
Left	.306	.356	.495	206	63	16	1	7	27	16	31
Right	.228	.321	.397	136	31	6	1	5	17	18	33
At Home and on the Road											
Home	.298	.364	.470	168	50	15	1	4	25	18	32
Road	.253	.319	.443	174	44	7	1	8	19	16	32
Facing Groundball Pitchers and Flyball Pitchers											
Groundball	.292	.353	.464	168	49	12	1	5	20	15	24
Flyball	.259	.330	.448	174	45	10	1	7	24	19	40
Facing Finesse Pitchers and Power Pitchers											
Finesse	.276	.325	.476	185	51	14	1	7	19	13	24
Power	.274	.360	.433	157	43	8	1	5	25	21	40
On Grass and on Turf											
Grass	.279	.346	.446	240	67	17	1	7	31	25	50
Turf	.265	.330	.480	102	27	5	1	5	13	9	14
During the Day and at Night											
Day	.272	.327	.478	136	37	10	0	6	20	11	24
Night	.277	.351	.442	206	57	12	2	6	24	23	40
By Month											
April	.391	.417	.652	23	9	3	0	1	4	1	3
May	.268	.302	.390	41	11	2	0	1	4	2	9
June	.426	.500	.689	61	26	10	0	2	12	9	8
July	.242	.315	.500	66	16	2	0	5	7	7	12
August	.200	.292	.365	85	17	4	2	2	8	10	23
Sept/Oct	.227	.278	.288	66	15	1	0	1	9	5	9
Situational											
Bases Empty	.263	.321	.444	198	52	11	2	7	7	16	29
Leadoff	.222	.273	.403	72	16	2	1	3	3	5	12
Not Leadoff	.286	.348	.468	126	36	9	1	4	4	11	17
Runners On	.292	.368	.472	144	42	11	0	5	37	18	35
First Base Only	.340	.415	.489	47	16	2	0	2	5	6	9
Scoring Position	.268	.345	.464	97	26	10	0	3	32	12	26
Late Innings, Close	.283	.317	.483	60	17	3	0	3	8	2	12

RBI/Opportunities		
Scoring Position	28 / 130	(22%)
Scoring Position, 2 Out	15 / 58	(26%)
On Third, Less than 2 Out	8 / 27	(30%)
RBI in close games / RBI Total	27 / 44	(61%)

Dale Mohorcic
Texas Rangers

1986: Finesse, Groundball   1985: Did not play   1984: Did not play

THREE YEARS (84 – 86)	G	IP	H	BB	SO	SB	CS	W	L	S	ERA
Totals	58	79.0	86	15	29	3	5	2	4	7	2.51
At Home and on the Road											
Home	27	40.1	39	7	15	2	3	2	0	2	1.56
Road	31	38.2	47	8	14	1	2	0	4	5	3.49
During the Day and and at Night											
Day	8	7.0	8	0	5	0	0	0	1	1	5.14
Night	50	72.0	78	15	24	3	5	2	3	6	2.25
On Grass and on Turf											
Grass	46	65.2	67	11	26	3	5	2	2	7	2.19
Turf	12	13.1	19	4	3	0	0	0	2	0	4.05
By Month											
April	0	0.0	0	0	0	0	0	0	0	0	0.00
May	1	0.2	1	1	0	0	0	0	0	0	0.00
June	11	17.0	20	5	3	0	0	1	0	0	1.59
July	12	16.1	15	1	4	1	3	0	0	1	2.20
August	19	22.1	23	2	11	1	1	1	1	4	2.42
Sept/Oct	15	22.2	27	6	11	1	1	0	3	2	3.57

vs. Opponent Batters THREE YEARS (84 – 86)	Ave.	OBP	SLG	AB	H	2B	3B	HR	RBI	BB	SO
Totals	.279	.315	.373	308	86	14	0	5	33	15	29
Pitching vs. Left and Right-handed Batters											
Left	.285	.343	.358	123	35	6	0	1	9	11	11
Right	.276	.295	.384	185	51	8	0	4	24	4	18
Situational											
Bases Empty	.290	.317	.394	155	45	4	0	4	4	5	16
Leadoff	.349	.369	.476	63	22	2	0	2	2	2	8
Not Leadoff	.250	.281	.337	92	23	2	0	2	2	3	8
Runners On	.268	.313	.353	153	41	10	0	1	29	10	13
First Base Only	.313	.323	.469	64	20	7	0	1	4	1	7
Scoring Position	.236	.306	.270	89	21	3	0	0	25	9	6
Late Innings, Close	.263	.300	.323	133	35	5	0	1	11	6	16

RBI/Opportunities		
Scoring Position	25 / 126	(20%)
Scoring Position, 2 Out	11 / 60	(18%)
On Third, Less than 2 Out	9 / 24	(38%)
RBI in close games / RBI Total	24 / 33	(73%)

Bill Mooneyham
Oakland A's

1986: Power, Groundball   1985: Did not play   1984: Did not play

THREE YEARS (84 – 86)	G	IP	H	BB	SO	SB	CS	W	L	S	ERA
Totals	45	99.2	103	67	75	9	3	4	5	2	4.52
At Home and on the Road											
Home	26	52.2	47	39	40	3	2	4	2	2	4.27
Road	19	47.0	56	28	35	6	1	0	3	0	4.79
During the Day and and at Night											
Day	19	40.2	42	31	34	1	3	1	3	1	5.53
Night	26	59.0	61	36	41	8	0	3	2	1	3.81
On Grass and on Turf											
Grass	40	90.2	88	62	70	9	3	4	3	2	4.27
Turf	5	9.0	15	5	5	0	0	0	2	0	7.00
By Month											
April	3	4.1	3	3	4	0	0	0	0	0	0.00
May	12	19.2	18	15	14	2	0	1	0	1	3.20
June	10	29.1	31	20	17	2	1	1	2	0	3.99
July	7	26.1	34	12	20	3	1	1	1	0	5.81
August	6	8.1	9	5	5	0	0	1	1	0	6.48
Sept/Oct	7	11.2	8	12	15	2	1	0	1	1	5.40

vs. Opponent Batters THREE YEARS (84 – 86)	Ave.	OBP	SLG	AB	H	2B	3B	HR	RBI	BB	SO
Totals	.270	.382	.352	381	103	17	1	4	48	67	75
Pitching vs. Left and Right-handed Batters											
Left	.270	.394	.323	189	51	5	1	1	21	38	28
Right	.271	.369	.380	192	52	12	0	3	27	29	47
Situational											
Bases Empty	.305	.426	.401	167	51	7	0	3	3	34	28
Leadoff	.269	.424	.359	78	21	4	0	1	1	21	14
Not Leadoff	.337	.427	.438	89	30	3	0	2	2	13	14
Runners On	.243	.347	.313	214	52	10	1	1	45	33	47
First Base Only	.291	.398	.354	79	23	3	1	0	2	13	20
Scoring Position	.215	.316	.289	135	29	7	0	1	43	16	27
Late Innings, Close	.282	.424	.372	78	22	4	0	1	12	20	14

RBI/Opportunities		
Scoring Position	40 / 199	(20%)
Scoring Position, 2 Out	14 / 90	(16%)
On Third, Less than 2 Out	17 / 36	(47%)
RBI in close games / RBI Total	29 / 48	(60%)

Charlie Moore
Milwaukee Brewers

THREE YEARS (84 – 86)

	Ave.	OBP	SLG	AB	H	2B	3B	HR	RBI	BB	SO
Totals	.241	.294	.323	772	186	32	8	5	87	58	117
Batting vs. Left and Right-handed Pitchers											
Left	.269	.322	.370	305	82	12	5	3	39	24	35
Right	.223	.275	.291	467	104	20	3	2	48	34	82
At Home and on the Road											
Home	.269	.312	.374	390	105	20	6	3	46	24	56
Road	.212	.276	.270	382	81	12	2	2	41	34	61
Facing Groundball Pitchers and Flyball Pitchers											
Groundball	.234	.292	.319	364	85	20	4	1	43	30	58
Flyball	.248	.295	.326	408	101	12	4	4	44	28	59
Facing Finesse Pitchers and Power Pitchers											
Finesse	.227	.277	.293	440	100	19	2	2	45	29	54
Power	.259	.316	.361	332	86	13	6	3	42	29	63
On Grass and on Turf											
Grass	.251	.299	.341	630	158	28	7	5	70	43	91
Turf	.197	.274	.239	142	28	4	1	0	17	15	26
During the Day and at Night											
Day	.269	.326	.367	264	71	12	4	2	32	24	46
Night	.226	.277	.299	508	115	20	4	3	55	34	71
By Month											
April	.240	.321	.370	100	24	6	2	1	14	12	17
May	.252	.319	.364	151	38	8	3	1	19	14	29
June	.248	.304	.317	145	36	5	1	1	14	11	19
July	.232	.276	.288	125	29	5	1	0	15	8	15
August	.226	.274	.274	124	28	3	0	1	10	9	18
Sept/Oct	.244	.265	.323	127	31	5	1	1	15	4	19
Situational											
Bases Empty	.237	.286	.313	418	99	18	1	4	4	28	72
Leadoff	.182	.212	.220	159	29	3	0	1	1	6	30
Not Leadoff	.270	.330	.371	259	70	15	1	3	3	22	42
Runners On	.246	.303	.333	354	87	14	7	1	83	30	45
First Base Only	.196	.232	.236	148	29	2	2	0	3	6	23
Scoring Position	.282	.349	.403	206	58	12	5	1	80	24	22
Late Innings, Close	.258	.309	.311	151	39	3	1	1	17	11	27

RBI/Opportunities

Scoring Position	73 / 290	(25%)
Scoring Position, 2 Out	28 / 134	(21%)
On Third, Less than 2 Out	29 / 56	(52%)
RBI in close games / RBI Total	59 / 87	(68%)

Omar Moreno
Atlanta Braves

THREE YEARS (84 – 86)

	Ave.	OBP	SLG	AB	H	2B	3B	HR	RBI	BB	SO
Totals	.242	.279	.360	850	206	35	16	11	81	43	149
Batting vs. Left and Right-handed Pitchers											
Left	.194	.244	.266	124	24	3	3	0	13	9	28
Right	.251	.285	.376	726	182	32	13	11	68	34	121
At Home and on the Road											
Home	.266	.304	.416	421	112	17	11	8	49	24	70
Road	.219	.254	.305	429	94	18	5	3	32	19	79
Facing Groundball Pitchers and Flyball Pitchers											
Groundball	.249	.292	.349	413	103	18	7	3	39	26	79
Flyball	.236	.266	.371	437	103	17	9	8	42	17	70
Facing Finesse Pitchers and Power Pitchers											
Finesse	.253	.280	.365	498	126	28	8	4	41	19	81
Power	.227	.278	.352	352	80	7	8	7	40	24	68
On Grass and on Turf											
Grass	.244	.282	.355	651	159	30	9	8	58	36	118
Turf	.236	.268	.377	199	47	5	7	3	23	7	31
During the Day and at Night											
Day	.227	.267	.311	299	68	15	5	0	17	16	48
Night	.250	.285	.387	551	138	20	11	11	64	27	101
By Month											
April	.186	.225	.268	97	18	1	2	1	4	5	15
May	.295	.333	.508	122	36	13	5	1	13	7	22
June	.202	.256	.250	124	25	3	0	1	8	9	29
July	.243	.264	.386	140	34	3	4	3	20	4	23
August	.275	.299	.399	178	49	11	1	3	17	7	31
Sept/Oct	.233	.278	.328	189	44	4	4	2	19	11	29
Situational											
Bases Empty	.258	.289	.364	530	137	25	8	5	5	21	92
Leadoff	.267	.290	.365	277	74	14	2	3	3	8	44
Not Leadoff	.249	.288	.364	253	63	11	6	2	2	13	48
Runners On	.216	.262	.353	320	69	10	8	6	76	22	57
First Base Only	.203	.266	.339	118	24	6	2	2	9	10	15
Scoring Position	.223	.260	.361	202	45	4	6	4	67	12	42
Late Innings, Close	.215	.257	.341	135	29	4	5	1	17	8	21

RBI/Opportunities

Scoring Position	57 / 275	(21%)
Scoring Position, 2 Out	27 / 140	(19%)
On Third, Less than 2 Out	18 / 41	(44%)
RBI in close games / RBI Total	43 / 81	(53%)

Russ Morman
Chicago White Sox

THREE YEARS (84 – 86)

	Ave.	OBP	SLG	AB	H	2B	3B	HR	RBI	BB	SO
Totals	.252	.324	.358	159	40	5	0	4	17	16	36
Batting vs. Left and Right-handed Pitchers											
Left	.242	.329	.371	62	15	2	0	2	7	6	17
Right	.258	.321	.351	97	25	3	0	2	10	10	19
At Home and on the Road											
Home	.281	.359	.368	57	16	2	0	1	4	5	14
Road	.235	.304	.353	102	24	3	0	3	13	11	22
Facing Groundball Pitchers and Flyball Pitchers											
Groundball	.321	.431	.509	53	17	1	0	3	7	10	11
Flyball	.217	.263	.283	106	23	4	0	1	10	6	25
Facing Finesse Pitchers and Power Pitchers											
Finesse	.280	.348	.354	82	23	3	0	1	7	9	16
Power	.221	.299	.364	77	17	2	0	3	10	7	20
On Grass and on Turf											
Grass	.227	.279	.297	128	29	3	0	2	13	8	27
Turf	.355	.487	.613	31	11	2	0	2	4	8	9
During the Day and at Night											
Day	.216	.293	.294	51	11	1	0	1	4	5	11
Night	.269	.339	.389	108	29	4	0	3	13	11	25
By Month											
April	.000	.000	.000	0	0	0	0	0	0	0	0
May	.000	.000	.000	0	0	0	0	0	0	0	0
June	.000	.000	.000	0	0	0	0	0	0	0	0
July	.000	.000	.000	0	0	0	0	0	0	0	0
August	.256	.308	.341	82	21	1	0	2	9	6	17
Sept/Oct	.247	.341	.377	77	19	4	0	2	8	10	19
Situational											
Bases Empty	.271	.320	.396	96	26	3	0	3	3	6	22
Leadoff	.333	.394	.567	30	10	1	0	2	2	3	5
Not Leadoff	.242	.286	.318	66	16	2	0	1	1	3	17
Runners On	.222	.329	.302	63	14	2	0	1	14	10	14
First Base Only	.167	.333	.292	24	4	0	0	1	2	6	6
Scoring Position	.256	.326	.308	39	10	2	0	0	12	4	8
Late Innings, Close	.250	.405	.357	28	7	0	0	1	4	6	4

RBI/Opportunities

Scoring Position	12 / 50	(24%)
Scoring Position, 2 Out	5 / 25	(20%)
On Third, Less than 2 Out	5 / 10	(50%)
RBI in close games / RBI Total	10 / 17	(59%)

John Morris
St. Louis Cardinals

THREE YEARS (84 – 86)

	Ave.	OBP	SLG	AB	H	2B	3B	HR	RBI	BB	SO
Totals	.240	.287	.290	100	24	0	1	1	14	7	15
Batting vs. Left and Right-handed Pitchers											
Left	.462	.500	.462	13	6	0	0	0	5	1	2
Right	.207	.255	.264	87	18	0	1	1	9	6	13
At Home and on the Road											
Home	.231	.302	.308	39	9	0	0	1	5	4	7
Road	.246	.277	.279	61	15	0	1	0	9	3	8
Facing Groundball Pitchers and Flyball Pitchers											
Groundball	.255	.288	.291	55	14	0	0	1	9	3	6
Flyball	.222	.286	.289	45	10	0	0	1	5	4	9
Facing Finesse Pitchers and Power Pitchers											
Finesse	.264	.308	.333	72	19	0	1	1	11	5	6
Power	.179	.233	.179	28	5	0	0	0	3	2	9
On Grass and on Turf											
Grass	.313	.333	.375	32	10	0	1	0	7	1	4
Turf	.206	.267	.250	68	14	0	0	1	7	6	11
During the Day and at Night											
Day	.214	.267	.286	28	6	0	1	0	5	2	3
Night	.250	.295	.292	72	18	0	0	1	9	5	12
By Month											
April	.000	.000	.000	0	0	0	0	0	0	0	0
May	.000	.000	.000	0	0	0	0	0	0	0	0
June	.000	.000	.000	0	0	0	0	0	0	0	0
July	.000	.000	.000	0	0	0	0	0	0	0	0
August	.283	.343	.317	60	17	0	1	0	11	6	9
Sept/Oct	.175	.195	.250	40	7	0	0	1	3	1	6
Situational											
Bases Empty	.184	.231	.245	49	9	0	0	1	1	3	7
Leadoff	.273	.333	.409	22	6	0	0	1	1	2	3
Not Leadoff	.111	.143	.111	27	3	0	0	0	0	1	4
Runners On	.294	.339	.333	51	15	0	1	0	13	4	8
First Base Only	.133	.133	.133	15	2	0	0	0	0	0	2
Scoring Position	.361	.415	.417	36	13	0	1	0	13	4	6
Late Innings, Close	.346	.346	.423	26	9	0	1	0	5	0	3

RBI/Opportunities

Scoring Position	13 / 47	(28%)
Scoring Position, 2 Out	4 / 20	(20%)
On Third, Less than 2 Out	5 / 9	(56%)
RBI in close games / RBI Total	11 / 14	(79%)

John Moses
Seattle Mariners

THREE YEARS (84 – 86)

	Ave.	OBP	SLG	AB	H	2B	3B	HR	RBI	BB	SO
Totals	.254	.306	.323	496	126	17	4	3	39	38	78
Batting vs. Left and Right-handed Pitchers											
Left	.275	.345	.382	131	36	6	1	2	8	14	17
Right	.247	.292	.301	365	90	11	3	1	31	24	61
At Home and on the Road											
Home	.234	.300	.322	261	61	9	4	2	20	24	38
Road	.277	.313	.323	235	65	8	0	1	19	14	40
Facing Groundball Pitchers and Flyball Pitchers											
Groundball	.242	.291	.304	240	58	8	2	1	21	18	37
Flyball	.266	.320	.340	256	68	9	2	2	18	20	41
Facing Finesse Pitchers and Power Pitchers											
Finesse	.261	.294	.336	307	80	13	2	2	26	16	31
Power	.243	.325	.302	189	46	4	2	1	13	22	47
On Grass and on Turf											
Grass	.250	.287	.287	160	40	3	0	1	11	9	23
Turf	.256	.315	.339	336	86	14	4	2	28	29	55
During the Day and at Night											
Day	.246	.275	.342	114	28	3	1	2	9	5	14
Night	.257	.315	.317	382	98	14	3	1	30	33	64
By Month											
April	.000	.000	.000	0	0	0	0	0	0	0	0
May	.158	.304	.263	19	3	0	1	0	1	4	3
June	.286	.341	.348	112	32	2	1	1	14	10	16
July	.277	.351	.356	101	28	6	1	0	12	12	19
August	.210	.238	.235	81	17	2	0	0	2	3	15
Sept/Oct	.251	.287	.333	183	46	7	1	2	10	9	25
Situational											
Bases Empty	.228	.285	.308	334	76	12	3	3	3	27	57
Leadoff	.244	.306	.310	168	41	7	2	0	0	15	24
Not Leadoff	.211	.264	.307	166	35	5	1	3	3	12	33
Runners On	.309	.348	.352	162	50	5	1	0	36	11	21
First Base Only	.262	.318	.279	61	16	1	0	0	0	5	7
Scoring Position	.337	.366	.396	101	34	4	1	0	36	6	14
Late Innings, Close	.273	.337	.299	77	21	2	0	0	8	8	15

RBI/Opportunities

Scoring Position	36 / 146	(25%)
Scoring Position, 2 Out	17 / 62	(27%)
On Third, Less than 2 Out	10 / 19	(53%)
RBI in close games / RBI Total	25 / 39	(64%)

Darryl Motley
Kansas City Royals

THREE YEARS (84 – 86)

	Ave.	OBP	SLG	AB	H	2B	3B	HR	RBI	BB	SO
Totals	.246	.283	.413	1132	279	55	8	39	139	59	162
Batting vs. Left and Right-handed Pitchers											
Left	.269	.307	.463	443	119	25	5	17	55	25	48
Right	.232	.268	.380	689	160	30	3	22	84	34	114
At Home and on the Road											
Home	.243	.280	.397	536	130	29	6	14	67	30	65
Road	.250	.286	.426	596	149	26	2	25	72	29	97
Facing Groundball Pitchers and Flyball Pitchers											
Groundball	.236	.282	.350	492	116	25	2	9	56	33	72
Flyball	.255	.285	.461	640	163	30	6	30	83	26	90
Facing Finesse Pitchers and Power Pitchers											
Finesse	.245	.274	.408	617	151	28	5	21	73	25	70
Power	.249	.295	.417	515	128	27	3	18	66	34	92
On Grass and on Turf											
Grass	.245	.284	.407	469	115	18	2	18	55	24	80
Turf	.247	.283	.416	663	164	37	6	21	84	35	82
During the Day and at Night											
Day	.260	.278	.445	319	83	17	3	12	39	7	50
Night	.241	.286	.400	813	196	38	5	27	100	52	112
By Month											
April	.239	.280	.398	176	42	9	2	5	14	9	20
May	.234	.271	.404	235	55	11	1	9	28	13	40
June	.317	.340	.483	145	46	4	1	6	20	6	15
July	.233	.264	.333	189	44	11	1	2	17	7	32
August	.234	.283	.473	184	43	7	2	11	32	12	31
Sept/Oct	.241	.280	.404	203	49	13	1	6	28	12	24
Situational											
Bases Empty	.238	.279	.410	648	154	31	6	23	23	36	86
Leadoff	.242	.278	.448	281	68	13	3	13	13	13	37
Not Leadoff	.234	.279	.381	367	86	18	3	10	10	23	49
Runners On	.258	.290	.415	484	125	24	2	16	116	23	76
First Base Only	.273	.298	.382	220	60	12	0	4	13	7	35
Scoring Position	.246	.283	.443	264	65	12	2	12	103	16	41
Late Innings, Close	.186	.222	.276	199	37	9	0	3	14	10	34

RBI/Opportunities

Scoring Position	81 / 338	(24%)
Scoring Position, 2 Out	31 / 142	(22%)
On Third, Less than 2 Out	29 / 62	(47%)
RBI in close games / RBI Total	81 / 139	(58%)

Jamie Moyer
Chicago Cubs

1986: Finesse, Groundball   1985: Did not play   1984: Did not play

THREE YEARS (84 – 86)

	G	IP	H	BB	SO	SB	CS	W	L	S	ERA
Totals	16	87.1	107	42	45	10	5	7	4	0	5.05
At Home and on the Road											
Home	10	59.0	74	33	28	5	3	4	1	0	4.88
Road	6	28.1	33	9	17	5	2	3	3	0	5.40
During the Day and at Night											
Day	10	59.0	74	33	28	5	3	4	1	0	4.88
Night	6	28.1	33	9	17	5	2	3	3	0	5.40
On Grass and on Turf											
Grass	12	67.1	84	37	33	6	3	5	2	0	4.81
Turf	4	20.0	23	5	12	4	2	2	2	0	5.85
By Month											
April	0	0.0	0	0	0	0	0	0	0	0	0.00
May	0	0.0	0	0	0	0	0	0	0	0	0.00
June	2	9.0	15	4	5	4	0	1	1	0	10.00
July	4	23.0	22	9	16	2	1	2	1	0	3.13
August	5	26.1	29	13	13	2	0	2	2	0	5.81
Sept/Oct	5	29.0	41	16	11	2	4	2	0	0	4.34

vs. Opponent Batters
THREE YEARS (84 – 86)

	Ave.	OBP	SLG	AB	H	2B	3B	HR	RBI	BB	SO
Totals	.311	.388	.451	344	107	18	0	10	43	42	45
Pitching vs. Left and Right-handed Batters											
Left	.293	.408	.561	41	12	5	0	2	7	8	6
Right	.314	.385	.436	303	95	13	0	8	36	34	39
Situational											
Bases Empty	.310	.394	.454	174	54	10	0	5	5	23	26
Leadoff	.349	.391	.523	86	30	3	0	4	4	5	13
Not Leadoff	.273	.396	.386	88	24	7	0	1	1	18	13
Runners On	.312	.381	.447	170	53	8	0	5	38	19	19
First Base Only	.412	.487	.544	68	28	6	0	1	3	9	7
Scoring Position	.245	.310	.382	102	25	2	0	4	35	10	12
Late Innings, Close	.214	.267	.321	28	6	0	0	1	5	2	5

RBI/Opportunities

Scoring Position	28 / 136	(21%)
Scoring Position, 2 Out	8 / 51	(16%)
On Third, Less than 2 Out	13 / 31	(42%)
RBI in close games / RBI Total	29 / 43	(67%)

Terry Mulholland
San Francisco Giants

1986: Power, Groundball   1985: Did not play   1984: Did not play

THREE YEARS (84 – 86)

	G	IP	H	BB	SO	SB	CS	W	L	S	ERA
Totals	15	54.2	51	35	27	6	2	1	7	0	4.94
At Home and on the Road											
Home	6	31.2	22	19	16	3	0	1	3	0	3.13
Road	9	23.0	29	16	11	3	2	0	4	0	7.43
During the Day and at Night											
Day	5	23.1	20	14	14	3	0	0	3	0	3.86
Night	10	31.1	31	21	13	3	2	1	4	0	5.74
On Grass and on Turf											
Grass	11	45.1	40	27	24	5	2	1	6	0	4.17
Turf	4	9.1	11	8	3	1	0	0	1	0	8.68
By Month											
April	0	0.0	0	0	0	0	0	0	0	0	0.00
May	0	0.0	0	0	0	0	0	0	0	0	0.00
June	6	21.0	19	10	12	2	0	0	3	0	4.29
July	2	7.0	7	2	5	1	1	0	1	0	3.86
August	2	12.0	7	8	4	1	0	0	1	0	3.75
Sept/Oct	5	14.2	18	15	6	2	1	1	2	0	7.36

vs. Opponent Batters
THREE YEARS (84 – 86)

	Ave.	OBP	SLG	AB	H	2B	3B	HR	RBI	BB	SO
Totals	.251	.362	.360	203	51	7	3	3	20	35	27
Pitching vs. Left and Right-handed Batters											
Left	.273	.407	.432	44	12	2	1	1	4	10	7
Right	.245	.349	.340	159	39	5	2	2	16	25	20
Situational											
Bases Empty	.235	.343	.330	115	27	6	1	1	1	18	14
Leadoff	.269	.387	.346	52	14	4	0	0	0	10	6
Not Leadoff	.206	.306	.317	63	13	2	1	1	1	8	8
Runners On	.273	.387	.398	88	24	1	2	2	19	17	13
First Base Only	.344	.424	.500	32	11	0	1	1	3	4	3
Scoring Position	.232	.371	.339	56	13	1	1	1	16	13	10
Late Innings, Close	.500	.526	.722	18	9	4	0	1	1	1	2

RBI/Opportunities

Scoring Position	13 / 79	(16%)
Scoring Position, 2 Out	4 / 38	(11%)
On Third, Less than 2 Out	8 / 15	(53%)
RBI in close games / RBI Total	16 / 20	(80%)

Rance Mulliniks
Toronto Blue Jays

	Ave.	OBP	SLG	AB	H	2B	3B	HR	RBI	BB	SO
THREE YEARS (84 – 86)											
Totals	.292	.368	.437	1057	309	69	6	24	144	130	158
Batting vs. Left and Right-handed Pitchers											
Left	.245	.351	.306	49	12	3	0	0	2	8	10
Right	.295	.369	.443	1008	297	66	6	24	142	122	148
At Home and on the Road											
Home	.299	.380	.450	509	152	41	3	10	71	67	79
Road	.286	.357	.425	548	157	28	3	14	73	63	79
Facing Groundball Pitchers and Flyball Pitchers											
Groundball	.278	.347	.404	554	154	36	2	10	66	60	81
Flyball	.308	.391	.473	503	155	33	4	14	78	70	77
Facing Finesse Pitchers and Power Pitchers											
Finesse	.312	.372	.462	628	196	40	3	17	92	62	90
Power	.263	.363	.394	429	113	29	3	7	52	68	68
On Grass and on Turf											
Grass	.275	.347	.418	440	121	23	2	12	62	51	62
Turf	.305	.383	.451	617	188	46	4	12	82	79	96
During the Day and at Night											
Day	.285	.356	.421	368	105	19	2	9	47	42	47
Night	.296	.375	.446	689	204	50	4	15	97	88	111
By Month											
April	.232	.322	.338	151	35	10	0	2	16	20	27
May	.320	.406	.465	172	55	11	1	4	33	27	29
June	.288	.378	.428	215	62	10	1	6	29	33	32
July	.352	.412	.573	199	70	19	2	7	34	20	27
August	.282	.326	.473	131	37	8	1	5	15	9	18
Sept/Oct	.265	.340	.333	189	50	11	1	0	17	21	25
Situational											
Bases Empty	.270	.348	.416	630	170	37	5	15	15	74	97
Leadoff	.273	.340	.426	216	59	12	3	5	5	21	35
Not Leadoff	.268	.353	.411	414	111	25	2	10	10	53	62
Runners On	.326	.396	.468	427	139	32	1	9	129	56	61
First Base Only	.282	.342	.408	174	49	10	0	4	12	16	24
Scoring Position	.356	.430	.510	253	90	22	1	5	117	40	37
Late Innings, Close	.264	.361	.410	144	38	8	2	3	23	23	19

RBI/Opportunities

Scoring Position	107 / 340	(31%)
Scoring Position, 2 Out	40 / 147	(27%)
On Third, Less than 2 Out	39 / 60	(65%)
RBI in close games / RBI Total	95 / 144	(66%)

Dwayne Murphy
Oakland A's

	Ave.	OBP	SLG	AB	H	2B	3B	HR	RBI	BB	SO
THREE YEARS (84 – 86)											
Totals	.247	.347	.425	1411	348	49	8	62	186	215	314
Batting vs. Left and Right-handed Pitchers											
Left	.223	.305	.369	452	101	10	4	16	54	54	113
Right	.258	.366	.450	959	247	39	4	46	132	161	201
At Home and on the Road											
Home	.232	.346	.373	681	158	22	4	22	73	118	147
Road	.260	.348	.473	730	190	27	4	40	113	97	167
Facing Groundball Pitchers and Flyball Pitchers											
Groundball	.250	.350	.397	696	174	20	5	24	79	105	137
Flyball	.243	.344	.452	715	174	29	3	38	107	110	177
Facing Finesse Pitchers and Power Pitchers											
Finesse	.274	.366	.482	789	216	30	4	42	121	115	146
Power	.212	.323	.352	622	132	19	4	20	65	100	168
On Grass and on Turf											
Grass	.243	.345	.419	1161	282	38	7	51	152	180	253
Turf	.264	.356	.448	250	66	11	1	11	34	35	61
During the Day and at Night											
Day	.277	.380	.484	537	149	24	6	25	68	88	118
Night	.228	.326	.388	874	199	25	2	37	118	127	196
By Month											
April	.249	.373	.373	225	56	7	0	7	27	45	48
May	.226	.332	.427	164	37	5	2	8	21	24	34
June	.244	.341	.503	193	47	8	0	14	28	28	42
July	.232	.338	.405	259	60	8	2	11	36	41	63
August	.249	.333	.382	309	77	12	1	9	40	39	73
Sept/Oct	.272	.363	.479	261	71	9	3	13	34	38	54
Situational											
Bases Empty	.257	.345	.455	798	205	28	2	42	42	101	171
Leadoff	.242	.337	.472	265	64	11	1	15	15	37	54
Not Leadoff	.265	.349	.447	533	141	14	1	27	27	64	117
Runners On	.233	.350	.385	613	143	21	6	20	144	114	143
First Base Only	.243	.362	.407	263	64	11	1	10	30	46	60
Scoring Position	.226	.341	.369	350	79	10	5	10	114	68	83
Late Innings, Close	.226	.341	.404	208	47	3	2	10	27	36	52

RBI/Opportunities

Scoring Position	96 / 507	(19%)
Scoring Position, 2 Out	32 / 211	(15%)
On Third, Less than 2 Out	39 / 90	(43%)
RBI in close games / RBI Total	126 / 186	(68%)

Rob Murphy
Cincinnati Reds

1986: Power, Groundball   **1985: Power, Flyball**   **1984: Did not play**

	G	IP	H	BB	SO	SB	CS	W	L	S	ERA
THREE YEARS (84 – 86)											
Totals	36	53.1	28	23	37	2	1	6	0	1	1.01
At Home and on the Road											
Home	19	28.2	15	14	18	1	0	2	0	1	1.26
Road	17	24.2	13	9	19	1	1	4	0	0	0.73
During the Day and and at Night											
Day	13	17.1	11	7	12	1	1	1	0	0	0.52
Night	23	36.0	17	16	25	1	0	5	0	1	1.25
On Grass and on Turf											
Grass	10	15.0	6	4	12	0	1	3	0	0	0.00
Turf	26	38.1	22	19	25	2	0	3	0	1	1.41
By Month											
April	0	0.0	0	0	0	0	0	0	0	0	0.00
May	0	0.0	0	0	0	0	0	0	0	0	0.00
June	0	0.0	0	0	0	0	0	0	0	0	0.00
July	9	11.1	4	4	8	0	1	0	0	0	0.79
August	13	21.2	18	10	18	1	0	1	0	1	1.25
Sept/Oct	14	20.1	6	9	11	1	0	4	0	0	0.89

	Ave.	OBP	SLG	AB	H	2B	3B	HR	RBI	BB	SO
vs. Opponent Batters											
THREE YEARS (84 – 86)											
Totals	.157	.250	.202	178	28	5	0	1	12	23	37
Pitching vs. Left and Right-handed Batters											
Left	.128	.192	.149	47	6	1	0	0	3	4	13
Right	.168	.270	.221	131	22	4	0	1	9	19	24
Situational											
Bases Empty	.179	.264	.242	95	17	3	0	1	1	11	18
Leadoff	.244	.340	.341	41	10	1	0	1	1	6	3
Not Leadoff	.130	.203	.167	54	7	2	0	0	0	5	15
Runners On	.133	.235	.157	83	11	2	0	0	11	12	19
First Base Only	.152	.222	.182	33	5	1	0	0	1	3	7
Scoring Position	.120	.242	.140	50	6	1	0	0	10	9	12
Late Innings, Close	.197	.286	.212	66	13	1	0	0	5	9	14

RBI/Opportunities

Scoring Position	10 / 72	(14%)
Scoring Position, 2 Out	1 / 34	(3%)
On Third, Less than 2 Out	7 / 16	(44%)
RBI in close games / RBI Total	6 / 12	(50%)

Gene Nelson
Chicago White Sox

1986: Finesse, Flyball   **1985: Power, Groundball**   **1984: Finesse, Groundball**

	G	IP	H	BB	SO	SB	CS	W	L	S	ERA
THREE YEARS (84 – 86)											
Totals	120	335.0	334	125	207	16	16	19	21	9	4.16
At Home and on the Road											
Home	59	160.2	156	65	104	6	8	11	10	2	3.87
Road	61	174.1	178	60	103	10	8	8	11	7	4.44
During the Day and and at Night											
Day	32	78.0	79	28	50	0	4	3	4	2	3.81
Night	88	257.0	255	97	157	16	12	16	17	7	4.27
On Grass and on Turf											
Grass	99	288.2	282	107	175	13	15	18	17	6	4.21
Turf	21	46.1	52	18	32	3	1	1	4	3	3.88
By Month											
April	14	27.0	30	18	17	0	1	2	2	0	4.67
May	22	45.2	27	16	28	3	2	5	1	2	1.38
June	21	34.1	37	21	29	3	2	1	4	1	4.98
July	17	80.0	81	19	53	2	4	4	6	2	3.71
August	21	79.2	91	22	30	7	4	3	5	3	5.99
Sept/Oct	25	68.1	68	29	50	1	3	4	3	1	3.82

	Ave.	OBP	SLG	AB	H	2B	3B	HR	RBI	BB	SO
vs. Opponent Batters											
THREE YEARS (84 – 86)											
Totals	.262	.332	.430	1276	334	68	15	39	160	125	207
Pitching vs. Left and Right-handed Batters											
Left	.257	.326	.413	618	159	36	6	16	68	61	95
Right	.266	.337	.447	658	175	32	9	23	92	64	112
Situational											
Bases Empty	.272	.339	.463	712	194	39	8	27	27	65	108
Leadoff	.295	.360	.536	302	89	21	5	14	14	26	47
Not Leadoff	.256	.324	.410	410	105	18	3	13	13	39	61
Runners On	.248	.322	.388	564	140	29	7	12	133	60	99
First Base Only	.290	.338	.491	224	65	15	3	8	28	16	32
Scoring Position	.221	.313	.321	340	75	14	4	4	105	44	67
Late Innings, Close	.216	.322	.337	255	55	8	4	5	31	38	48

RBI/Opportunities

Scoring Position	95 / 460	(21%)
Scoring Position, 2 Out	37 / 200	(18%)
On Third, Less than 2 Out	35 / 86	(41%)
RBI in close games / RBI Total	98 / 160	(61%)

Graig Nettles
San Diego Padres

THREE YEARS (84 – 86)

	Ave.	OBP	SLG	AB	H	2B	3B	HR	RBI	BB	SO
Totals	.237	.333	.405	1189	282	43	2	51	181	171	176
Batting vs. Left and Right-handed Pitchers											
Left	.176	.251	.330	227	40	11	0	8	30	19	40
Right	.252	.352	.423	962	242	32	2	43	151	152	136
At Home and on the Road											
Home	.244	.348	.434	578	141	20	0	30	109	92	92
Road	.231	.320	.378	611	141	23	2	21	72	79	84
Facing Groundball Pitchers and Flyball Pitchers											
Groundball	.270	.369	.449	599	162	24	1	27	99	93	81
Flyball	.203	.297	.361	590	120	19	1	24	82	78	95
Facing Finesse Pitchers and Power Pitchers											
Finesse	.260	.352	.431	647	168	22	1	29	104	91	68
Power	.210	.311	.375	542	114	21	1	22	77	80	108
On Grass and on Turf											
Grass	.237	.342	.418	847	201	27	0	42	140	134	130
Turf	.237	.310	.374	342	81	16	2	9	41	37	46
During the Day and at Night											
Day	.224	.339	.375	352	79	9	1	14	49	60	45
Night	.243	.331	.418	837	203	34	1	37	132	111	131
By Month											
April	.186	.314	.307	140	26	2	0	5	20	26	17
May	.249	.368	.438	217	54	5	0	12	30	39	29
June	.223	.323	.437	215	48	4	0	14	40	32	37
July	.261	.346	.408	211	55	11	1	6	30	29	31
August	.224	.303	.439	223	50	9	0	13	34	25	41
Sept/Oct	.268	.341	.361	183	49	12	1	1	27	20	21
Situational											
Bases Empty	.214	.318	.380	640	137	20	1	28	28	94	97
Leadoff	.217	.304	.350	286	62	9	1	9	9	35	41
Not Leadoff	.212	.328	.404	354	75	11	0	19	19	59	56
Runners On	.264	.351	.435	549	145	23	1	23	153	77	79
First Base Only	.280	.341	.462	225	63	9	1	10	26	19	21
Scoring Position	.253	.358	.417	324	82	14	0	13	127	58	58
Late Innings, Close	.234	.341	.445	209	49	6	1	12	33	35	37

RBI/Opportunities

Scoring Position	108 / 461	(23%)
Scoring Position, 2 Out	36 / 211	(17%)
On Third, Less than 2 Out	52 / 83	(63%)
RBI in close games / RBI Total	114 / 181	(63%)

Al Newman
Montreal Expos

THREE YEARS (84 – 86)

	Ave.	OBP	SLG	AB	H	2B	3B	HR	RBI	BB	SO
Totals	.196	.275	.229	214	42	4	0	1	9	24	24
Batting vs. Left and Right-handed Pitchers											
Left	.220	.322	.320	50	11	2	0	1	3	8	8
Right	.189	.260	.201	164	31	2	0	0	6	16	16
At Home and on the Road											
Home	.180	.270	.190	100	18	1	0	0	6	13	15
Road	.211	.280	.263	114	24	3	0	1	3	11	9
Facing Groundball Pitchers and Flyball Pitchers											
Groundball	.255	.346	.330	94	24	4	0	1	3	13	8
Flyball	.150	.218	.150	120	18	0	0	0	6	11	16
Facing Finesse Pitchers and Power Pitchers											
Finesse	.181	.289	.210	105	19	3	0	0	2	16	12
Power	.211	.261	.248	109	23	1	0	1	7	8	12
On Grass and on Turf											
Grass	.189	.286	.270	37	7	0	0	1	2	5	3
Turf	.198	.273	.220	177	35	4	0	0	7	19	21
During the Day and at Night											
Day	.236	.284	.281	89	21	1	0	1	5	6	11
Night	.168	.269	.192	125	21	3	0	0	4	18	13
By Month											
April	.286	.333	.286	14	4	0	0	0	0	1	1
May	.256	.318	.256	39	10	0	0	0	4	4	5
June	.204	.295	.241	54	11	2	0	0	1	7	1
July	.170	.259	.255	47	8	1	0	1	3	6	5
August	.143	.226	.143	28	4	0	0	0	0	3	5
Sept/Oct	.156	.229	.188	32	5	1	0	0	1	3	7
Situational											
Bases Empty	.174	.261	.188	144	25	2	0	0	0	17	19
Leadoff	.122	.198	.135	74	9	1	0	0	0	7	9
Not Leadoff	.229	.325	.243	70	16	1	0	0	0	10	10
Runners On	.243	.304	.314	70	17	2	0	1	9	7	5
First Base Only	.345	.387	.379	29	10	1	0	0	0	2	4
Scoring Position	.171	.250	.268	41	7	1	0	1	9	5	1
Late Innings, Close	.194	.203	.242	62	12	3	0	0	3	1	8

RBI/Opportunities

Scoring Position	8 / 60	(13%)
Scoring Position, 2 Out	1 / 29	(3%)
On Third, Less than 2 Out	6 / 10	(60%)
RBI in close games / RBI Total	9 / 9	(100%)

Reid Nichols
Chicago White Sox

THREE YEARS (84 – 86)

	Ave.	OBP	SLG	AB	H	2B	3B	HR	RBI	BB	SO
Totals	.244	.314	.332	410	100	17	2	5	50	40	58
Batting vs. Left and Right-handed Pitchers											
Left	.260	.321	.347	285	74	14	1	3	35	27	41
Right	.208	.298	.296	125	26	3	1	2	15	13	17
At Home and on the Road											
Home	.274	.343	.391	215	59	12	2	3	37	21	30
Road	.210	.281	.267	195	41	5	0	2	13	19	28
Facing Groundball Pitchers and Flyball Pitchers											
Groundball	.235	.326	.327	162	38	7	1	2	13	19	28
Flyball	.250	.305	.335	248	62	10	1	3	37	21	30
Facing Finesse Pitchers and Power Pitchers											
Finesse	.245	.311	.361	241	59	11	1	5	27	22	35
Power	.243	.318	.290	169	41	6	1	0	23	18	23
On Grass and on Turf											
Grass	.255	.329	.357	345	88	16	2	5	45	36	52
Turf	.185	.229	.200	65	12	1	0	0	5	4	6
During the Day and at Night											
Day	.267	.336	.314	105	28	5	0	0	5	10	14
Night	.236	.306	.338	305	72	12	2	5	45	30	44
By Month											
April	.286	.367	.386	70	20	5	1	0	9	7	9
May	.177	.188	.203	79	14	2	0	0	5	0	14
June	.174	.286	.348	23	4	1	0	1	7	3	5
July	.220	.373	.317	41	9	1	0	1	5	10	10
August	.239	.284	.272	92	22	3	0	0	10	7	15
Sept/Oct	.295	.370	.448	105	31	5	1	3	14	13	5
Situational											
Bases Empty	.206	.274	.287	247	51	9	1	3	3	22	35
Leadoff	.222	.294	.343	108	24	5	1	2	2	11	15
Not Leadoff	.194	.258	.245	139	27	4	0	1	1	11	20
Runners On	.301	.399	.399	163	49	8	1	2	47	18	23
First Base Only	.265	.342	.279	68	18	1	0	0	0	6	8
Scoring Position	.326	.389	.484	95	31	7	1	2	47	12	15
Late Innings, Close	.303	.357	.408	76	23	2	0	2	14	5	14

RBI/Opportunities

Scoring Position	42 / 157	(27%)
Scoring Position, 2 Out	22 / 70	(31%)
On Third, Less than 2 Out	13 / 41	(32%)
RBI in close games / RBI Total	35 / 50	(70%)

Joe Niekro
New York Yankees

1986: Finesse, Flyball   1985: Finesse, Flyball   1984: Finesse, Groundball

THREE YEARS (84 – 86)

	G	IP	H	BB	SO	SB	CS	W	L	S	ERA
Totals	98	599.1	573	259	307	104	24	36	35	0	3.72
At Home and on the Road											
Home	50	296.0	289	144	156	46	17	14	18	0	3.77
Road	48	303.1	284	115	151	58	7	22	17	0	3.68
During the Day and and at Night											
Day	20	120.1	123	48	53	28	1	6	7	0	4.56
Night	78	479.0	450	211	254	76	23	30	28	0	3.51
On Grass and on Turf											
Grass	45	263.1	258	105	127	38	3	23	13	0	3.93
Turf	53	336.0	315	154	180	66	21	13	22	0	3.56
By Month											
April	16	102.1	86	42	50	13	5	6	7	0	2.55
May	18	111.2	107	45	62	21	5	3	8	0	3.71
June	17	102.1	102	46	44	17	2	11	5	0	4.05
July	15	104.0	94	33	58	18	4	7	3	0	2.68
August	18	106.0	102	54	59	16	3	4	5	0	4.42
Sept/Oct	14	73.0	82	39	34	19	5	5	7	0	5.42

vs. Opponent Batters
THREE YEARS (84 – 86)

	Ave.	OBP	SLG	AB	H	2B	3B	HR	RBI	BB	SO
Totals	.251	.328	.370	2279	573	86	10	55	239	259	307
Pitching vs. Left and Right-handed Batters											
Left	.266	.357	.383	1111	296	42	5	26	100	157	121
Right	.237	.299	.358	1168	277	44	5	29	139	102	186
Situational											
Bases Empty	.246	.317	.372	1360	335	42	6	39	39	134	188
Leadoff	.221	.283	.348	578	128	15	2	18	18	47	83
Not Leadoff	.265	.341	.390	782	207	27	4	21	21	87	105
Runners On	.259	.344	.368	919	238	44	4	16	200	125	119
First Base Only	.276	.328	.430	370	102	23	2	10	32	29	32
Scoring Position	.248	.353	.326	549	136	21	2	6	168	96	87
Late Innings, Close	.293	.389	.507	140	41	5	2	7	19	21	21

RBI/Opportunities

Scoring Position	154 / 785	(20%)
Scoring Position, 2 Out	71 / 409	(17%)
On Third, Less than 2 Out	47 / 118	(40%)
RBI in close games / RBI Total	168 / 239	(70%)

Randy Niemann
New York Mets

1986: Finesse, Groundball 1985: Finesse, Groundball 1984: Power, Groundball

THREE YEARS (84 – 86)

	G	IP	H	BB	SO	SB	CS	W	L	S	ERA
Totals	40	45.2	54	17	25	3	3	2	3	0	3.15
At Home and on the Road											
Home	21	28.2	30	6	14	2	3	1	2	0	2.83
Road	19	17.0	24	11	11	1	0	1	1	0	3.71
During the Day and and at Night											
Day	19	27.1	33	8	11	1	1	2	2	0	2.96
Night	21	18.1	21	9	14	2	2	0	1	0	3.44
On Grass and on Turf											
Grass	29	36.1	38	10	19	2	3	2	2	0	2.72
Turf	11	9.1	16	7	6	1	0	0	1	0	4.82
By Month											
April	4	4.0	7	3	1	1	0	0	2	0	9.00
May	8	9.1	7	3	6	1	0	1	0	0	0.00
June	7	7.2	11	1	6	0	1	0	0	0	5.87
July	3	2.1	4	1	0	0	0	0	1	0	7.71
August	4	7.1	8	2	2	0	0	1	0	0	1.23
Sept/Oct	14	15.0	17	7	10	1	2	0	0	0	2.40

vs. Opponent Batters — THREE YEARS (84 – 86)

	Ave.	OBP	SLG	AB	H	2B	3B	HR	RBI	BB	SO
Totals	.300	.359	.383	180	54	7	1	2	23	17	25
Pitching vs. Left and Right-handed Batters											
Left	.263	.373	.404	57	15	5	0	1	14	10	12
Right	.317	.351	.374	123	39	2	1	1	9	7	13
Situational											
Bases Empty	.299	.324	.355	107	32	3	0	1	1	4	16
Leadoff	.273	.289	.386	44	12	2	0	1	1	1	8
Not Leadoff	.317	.348	.333	63	20	1	0	0	0	3	8
Runners On	.301	.402	.425	73	22	4	1	1	22	13	9
First Base Only	.267	.333	.433	30	8	0	1	1	3	3	2
Scoring Position	.326	.444	.419	43	14	4	0	0	19	10	7
Late Innings, Close	.417	.512	.528	36	15	1	0	1	7	7	3

RBI/Opportunities

Scoring Position	19 / 72	(26%)	
Scoring Position, 2 Out	7 / 38	(18%)	
On Third, Less than 2 Out	8 / 13	(62%)	
RBI in close games / RBI Total	11 / 23	(48%)	

Juan Nieves
Milwaukee Brewers

1986: Power, Flyball 1985: Did not play 1984: Did not play

THREE YEARS (84 – 86)

	G	IP	H	BB	SO	SB	CS	W	L	S	ERA
Totals	35	184.2	224	77	116	8	13	11	12	0	4.92
At Home and on the Road											
Home	17	78.0	105	38	49	5	6	4	6	0	6.35
Road	18	106.2	119	39	67	3	7	7	6	0	3.88
During the Day and and at Night											
Day	9	54.2	55	23	35	0	4	3	1	0	3.79
Night	26	130.0	169	54	81	8	9	8	11	0	5.40
On Grass and on Turf											
Grass	31	162.2	197	72	99	8	12	9	11	0	4.92
Turf	4	22.0	27	5	17	0	1	2	1	0	4.91
By Month											
April	4	23.1	23	13	19	0	4	0	1	0	4.63
May	7	42.0	49	20	20	0	1	5	0	0	4.71
June	5	31.2	34	8	15	4	2	1	1	0	3.41
July	6	37.0	35	21	30	2	4	4	2	0	3.16
August	5	19.0	39	5	11	0	0	0	3	0	10.42
Sept/Oct	8	31.2	44	10	21	2	2	1	5	0	5.68

vs. Opponent Batters — THREE YEARS (84 – 86)

	Ave.	OBP	SLG	AB	H	2B	3B	HR	RBI	BB	SO
Totals	.299	.363	.418	748	224	36	1	17	99	77	116
Pitching vs. Left and Right-handed Batters											
Left	.318	.384	.409	132	42	7	1	1	11	14	30
Right	.295	.359	.420	616	182	29	0	16	88	63	86
Situational											
Bases Empty	.280	.349	.401	404	113	20	1	9	9	43	69
Leadoff	.294	.378	.441	177	52	12	1	4	4	24	29
Not Leadoff	.269	.325	.370	227	61	8	0	5	5	19	40
Runners On	.323	.380	.439	344	111	16	0	8	90	34	47
First Base Only	.316	.376	.411	158	50	3	0	4	8	15	21
Scoring Position	.328	.384	.462	186	61	13	0	4	82	19	26
Late Innings, Close	.264	.321	.361	72	19	1	0	2	6	6	13

RBI/Opportunities

Scoring Position	73 / 242	(30%)	
Scoring Position, 2 Out	35 / 117	(30%)	
On Third, Less than 2 Out	19 / 32	(59%)	
RBI in close games / RBI Total	72 / 99	(73%)	

Al Nipper
Boston Red Sox

1986: Finesse, Groundball 1985: Power, Groundball 1984: Finesse, Groundball

THREE YEARS (84 – 86)

	G	IP	H	BB	SO	SB	CS	W	L	S	ERA
Totals	80	503.2	526	181	248	20	17	30	30	0	4.41
At Home and on the Road											
Home	39	265.2	269	80	132	12	10	13	13	0	3.83
Road	41	238.0	257	101	116	8	7	17	17	0	5.07
During the Day and and at Night											
Day	26	167.1	188	60	81	5	6	8	11	0	4.25
Night	54	336.1	338	121	167	15	11	22	19	0	4.50
On Grass and on Turf											
Grass	62	397.0	419	135	201	15	11	22	23	0	4.58
Turf	18	106.2	107	46	47	5	6	8	7	0	3.80
By Month											
April	11	65.1	59	22	25	2	1	2	4	0	3.72
May	12	69.1	72	34	36	2	2	2	6	0	5.19
June	12	75.1	81	26	39	4	3	5	2	0	4.54
July	14	93.2	98	31	41	4	4	6	5	0	3.84
August	15	98.0	103	26	49	2	1	7	7	0	4.59
Sept/Oct	16	102.0	113	42	58	6	6	8	6	0	4.59

vs. Opponent Batters — THREE YEARS (84 – 86)

	Ave.	OBP	SLG	AB	H	2B	3B	HR	RBI	BB	SO
Totals	.267	.333	.421	1969	526	110	12	56	245	181	248
Pitching vs. Left and Right-handed Batters											
Left	.278	.349	.410	1036	288	56	9	21	125	110	124
Right	.255	.316	.432	933	238	54	3	35	120	71	124
Situational											
Bases Empty	.266	.333	.408	1126	299	69	5	27	27	102	151
Leadoff	.291	.343	.447	488	142	37	3	11	11	34	66
Not Leadoff	.246	.324	.378	638	157	32	2	16	16	68	85
Runners On	.269	.334	.438	843	227	41	7	29	218	79	97
First Base Only	.272	.337	.431	371	101	20	3	11	31	32	36
Scoring Position	.267	.333	.443	472	126	21	4	18	187	47	61
Late Innings, Close	.293	.329	.419	198	58	10	0	5	18	10	21

RBI/Opportunities

Scoring Position	157 / 619	(25%)	
Scoring Position, 2 Out	61 / 265	(23%)	
On Third, Less than 2 Out	54 / 108	(50%)	
RBI in close games / RBI Total	179 / 245	(73%)	

Dickie Noles
Cleveland Indians

1986: Power, Groundball 1985: Finesse, Groundball 1984: Power, Flyball

THREE YEARS (84 – 86)

	G	IP	H	BB	SO	SB	CS	W	L	S	ERA
Totals	99	273.1	305	109	144	38	6	11	15	1	5.10
At Home and on the Road											
Home	48	134.1	163	58	59	20	5	5	6	0	5.43
Road	51	139.0	142	51	85	18	1	6	9	1	4.79
During the Day and and at Night											
Day	33	80.1	97	31	36	10	1	5	5	1	4.82
Night	66	193.0	208	78	108	28	5	6	10	0	5.22
On Grass and on Turf											
Grass	84	238.1	261	93	122	32	5	9	10	0	4.98
Turf	15	35.0	44	16	22	6	1	2	5	1	5.91
By Month											
April	13	36.0	25	12	11	2	0	2	2	1	3.25
May	14	57.2	66	18	29	12	4	2	6	0	4.68
June	15	34.2	51	11	18	4	1	2	1	0	6.23
July	19	54.1	59	25	30	8	0	3	2	0	5.47
August	26	65.0	70	30	39	9	1	1	2	0	4.98
Sept/Oct	12	25.2	34	13	17	3	0	1	2	0	6.66

vs. Opponent Batters — THREE YEARS (84 – 86)

	Ave.	OBP	SLG	AB	H	2B	3B	HR	RBI	BB	SO
Totals	.282	.355	.416	1081	305	45	5	30	163	109	144
Pitching vs. Left and Right-handed Batters											
Left	.317	.395	.467	568	180	25	3	18	100	68	67
Right	.244	.309	.361	513	125	20	2	12	63	41	77
Situational											
Bases Empty	.256	.332	.379	562	144	20	2	15	15	56	72
Leadoff	.247	.326	.377	239	59	11	1	6	6	23	29
Not Leadoff	.263	.337	.381	323	85	9	1	9	9	33	43
Runners On	.310	.384	.457	519	161	25	3	15	148	53	72
First Base Only	.307	.378	.447	199	61	9	2	5	14	17	28
Scoring Position	.313	.380	.463	320	100	16	1	10	134	36	44
Late Innings, Close	.283	.364	.404	166	47	5	0	5	18	20	28

RBI/Opportunities

Scoring Position	115 / 429	(27%)	
Scoring Position, 2 Out	50 / 199	(25%)	
On Third, Less than 2 Out	36 / 75	(48%)	
RBI in close games / RBI Total	78 / 163	(48%)	

Tom O'Malley
Baltimore Orioles

THREE YEARS (84 – 86)

	Ave.	OBP	SLG	AB	H	2B	3B	HR	RBI	BB	SO
Totals	.220	.277	.284	236	52	9	0	2	23	19	30
Batting vs. Left and Right-handed Pitchers											
Left	.208	.269	.250	24	5	1	0	0	3	2	3
Right	.222	.278	.288	212	47	8	0	2	20	17	27
At Home and on the Road											
Home	.197	.248	.248	117	23	3	0	1	7	8	16
Road	.244	.305	.319	119	29	6	0	1	16	11	14
Facing Groundball Pitchers and Flyball Pitchers											
Groundball	.225	.269	.270	111	25	5	0	0	9	7	7
Flyball	.216	.285	.296	125	27	4	0	2	14	12	23
Facing Finesse Pitchers and Power Pitchers											
Finesse	.240	.287	.295	146	35	5	0	1	15	10	14
Power	.189	.263	.267	90	17	4	0	1	8	9	16
On Grass and on Turf											
Grass	.218	.272	.287	202	44	8	0	2	20	15	22
Turf	.235	.308	.265	34	8	1	0	0	3	4	8
During the Day and at Night											
Day	.227	.274	.295	88	20	3	0	1	7	6	12
Night	.216	.280	.277	148	32	6	0	1	16	13	18
By Month											
April	.000	.000	.000	0	0	0	0	0	0	0	0
May	.105	.190	.105	19	2	0	0	0	0	2	2
June	.273	.317	.364	77	21	4	0	1	11	5	9
July	.254	.333	.310	71	18	4	0	0	5	9	6
August	.205	.262	.231	39	8	1	0	0	2	3	6
Sept/Oct	.100	.100	.200	30	3	0	0	1	5	0	7
Situational											
Bases Empty	.239	.275	.303	142	34	6	0	1	1	7	13
Leadoff	.203	.230	.288	59	12	2	0	1	1	2	4
Not Leadoff	.265	.307	.313	83	22	4	0	0	0	5	9
Runners On	.191	.280	.255	94	18	3	0	1	22	12	17
First Base Only	.188	.257	.188	32	6	0	0	0	0	3	5
Scoring Position	.194	.292	.290	62	12	3	0	1	22	9	12
Late Innings, Close	.195	.261	.268	41	8	0	0	1	3	4	10

RBI/Opportunities

Scoring Position	20 / 89	(22%)
Scoring Position, 2 Out	13 / 45	(29%)
On Third, Less than 2 Out	6 / 11	(55%)
RBI in close games / RBI Total	5 / 23	(22%)

Randy O'Neal
Detroit Tigers

1986: Finesse, Groundball 1985: Finesse, Groundball 1984: Power, Groundball

THREE YEARS (84 – 86)

	G	IP	H	BB	SO	SB	CS	W	L	S	ERA
Totals	69	235.2	219	86	132	8	9	10	13	3	3.82
At Home and on the Road											
Home	33	96.1	93	36	54	4	2	4	6	2	3.64
Road	36	139.1	126	50	78	4	7	6	7	1	3.94
During the Day and and at Night											
Day	21	64.1	73	29	34	6	5	1	6	0	4.34
Night	48	171.1	146	57	98	2	4	9	7	3	3.62
On Grass and on Turf											
Grass	59	206.0	193	73	112	8	9	9	11	3	3.71
Turf	10	29.2	26	13	20	0	0	1	2	0	4.55
By Month											
April	7	14.0	16	2	7	1	0	0	1	0	2.57
May	5	8.2	10	11	6	0	0	0	1	0	10.38
June	11	51.2	42	18	30	2	3	4	2	0	2.79
July	11	60.0	51	22	32	1	2	4	0	1	3.60
August	15	40.0	48	21	19	2	2	2	4	2	5.63
Sept/Oct	20	61.1	52	12	38	2	2	2	1	1	3.08

vs. Opponent Batters
THREE YEARS (84 – 86)

	Ave.	OBP	SLG	AB	H	2B	3B	HR	RBI	BB	SO
Totals	.249	.315	.383	880	219	47	4	21	102	86	132
Pitching vs. Left and Right-handed Batters											
Left	.228	.306	.362	448	102	19	1	13	50	52	55
Right	.271	.324	.405	432	117	28	3	8	52	34	77
Situational											
Bases Empty	.233	.294	.375	536	125	28	3	14	14	42	85
Leadoff	.242	.303	.384	219	53	10	0	7	7	16	40
Not Leadoff	.227	.288	.369	317	72	18	3	7	7	26	45
Runners On	.273	.346	.395	344	94	19	1	7	88	44	47
First Base Only	.307	.358	.489	137	42	8	1	5	17	10	17
Scoring Position	.251	.339	.333	207	52	11	0	2	71	34	30
Late Innings, Close	.345	.385	.483	87	30	3	0	3	17	7	10

RBI/Opportunities

Scoring Position	67 / 290	(23%)
Scoring Position, 2 Out	23 / 129	(18%)
On Third, Less than 2 Out	29 / 55	(53%)
RBI in close games / RBI Total	60 / 102	(59%)

Bryan Oelkers
Cleveland Indians

1986: Power, Flyball   1985: Did not play   1984: Did not play

THREE YEARS (84 – 86)

	G	IP	H	BB	SO	SB	CS	W	L	S	ERA
Totals	35	69.0	70	40	33			3	3	1	4.70
At Home and on the Road											
Home	17	43.1	41	28	18	3	0	2	2	1	4.36
Road	18	25.2	29	12	15	1	0	1	1	0	5.26
During the Day and and at Night											
Day	11	16.2	11	11	9	1	0	2	0	1	2.16
Night	24	52.1	59	29	24	3	0	1	3	0	5.50
On Grass and on Turf											
Grass	31	60.2	61	37	27	4	0	2	3	1	4.75
Turf	4	8.1	9	3	6	0	0	1	0	0	4.32
By Month											
April	0	0.0	0	0	0	0	0	0	0	0	0.00
May	0	0.0	0	0	0	0	0	0	0	0	0.00
June	7	21.2	20	15	10	1	0	0	0	0	2.91
July	8	16.2	11	11	12	0	0	1	2	0	3.78
August	13	25.1	34	9	8	3	0	1	1	1	6.75
Sept/Oct	7	5.1	5	5	3	0	0	1	0	0	5.06

vs. Opponent Batters
THREE YEARS (84 – 86)

	Ave.	OBP	SLG	AB	H	2B	3B	HR	RBI	BB	SO
Totals	.262	.368	.449	267	70	7	2	13	38	40	33
Pitching vs. Left and Right-handed Batters											
Left	.232	.339	.432	95	22	3	2	4	14	12	13
Right	.279	.384	.459	172	48	4	0	9	24	28	20
Situational											
Bases Empty	.286	.387	.529	140	40	5	1	9	9	20	18
Leadoff	.311	.391	.607	61	19	3	0	5	5	7	7
Not Leadoff	.266	.383	.468	79	21	2	1	4	4	13	11
Runners On	.236	.349	.362	127	30	2	1	4	29	20	15
First Base Only	.224	.308	.431	58	13	0	0	4	8	7	8
Scoring Position	.246	.379	.304	69	17	2	1	0	21	13	7
Late Innings, Close	.195	.340	.390	41	8	0	1	2	6	8	3

RBI/Opportunities

Scoring Position	20 / 102	(20%)
Scoring Position, 2 Out	11 / 56	(20%)
On Third, Less than 2 Out	5 / 11	(45%)
RBI in close games / RBI Total	15 / 38	(39%)

Ben Oglivie
Milwaukee Brewers

THREE YEARS (84 – 86)

	Ave.	OBP	SLG	AB	H	2B	3B	HR	RBI	BB	SO
Totals	.277	.337	.402	1148	318	53	5	27	174	111	139
Batting vs. Left and Right-handed Pitchers											
Left	.234	.285	.337	291	68	16	1	4	38	21	40
Right	.292	.354	.425	857	250	37	4	23	136	90	99
At Home and on the Road											
Home	.288	.341	.431	545	157	33	3	18	88	46	62
Road	.267	.334	.376	603	161	20	2	14	86	65	77
Facing Groundball Pitchers and Flyball Pitchers											
Groundball	.299	.359	.415	579	173	31	0	12	85	55	64
Flyball	.255	.330	.390	569	145	22	5	15	89	56	75
Facing Finesse Pitchers and Power Pitchers											
Finesse	.294	.358	.429	643	189	30	3	17	96	69	66
Power	.255	.311	.368	505	129	23	2	10	78	42	73
On Grass and on Turf											
Grass	.284	.345	.417	976	277	51	5	23	151	97	118
Turf	.238	.291	.320	172	41	2	0	4	23	14	21
During the Day and at Night											
Day	.314	.362	.460	376	118	26	1	9	59	31	48
Night	.259	.325	.374	772	200	27	4	18	115	80	91
By Month											
April	.248	.328	.333	117	29	5	1	1	10	13	21
May	.288	.344	.396	222	64	9	0	5	37	20	20
June	.278	.327	.377	273	76	13	1	4	42	21	29
July	.281	.349	.434	221	62	14	1	6	28	25	21
August	.273	.337	.436	220	60	8	2	8	38	25	32
Sept/Oct	.284	.333	.421	95	27	4	0	3	19	7	13
Situational											
Bases Empty	.265	.321	.366	648	172	27	1	12	12	51	73
Leadoff	.311	.356	.437	270	84	11	1	7	7	18	34
Not Leadoff	.233	.296	.315	378	88	16	0	5	5	33	39
Runners On	.292	.357	.450	500	146	26	4	15	162	60	66
First Base Only	.273	.332	.459	205	56	9	1	9	24	18	30
Scoring Position	.305	.373	.444	295	90	17	3	6	138	42	36
Late Innings, Close	.286	.387	.439	189	54	9	1	6	31	31	31

RBI/Opportunities

Scoring Position	121 / 408	(30%)
Scoring Position, 2 Out	44 / 183	(24%)
On Third, Less than 2 Out	48 / 81	(59%)
RBI in close games / RBI Total	118 / 174	(68%)

Ed Olwine
Atlanta Braves

1986: Power, Groundball   1985: Did not play   1984: Did not play

THREE YEARS (84 – 86)

	G	IP	H	BB	SO	SB	CS	W	L	S	ERA
Totals	37	47.2	35	17	37	6	1	0	0	1	3.40
At Home and on the Road											
Home	22	21.0	18	8	16	0	0	0	0	0	3.86
Road	15	26.2	17	9	21	6	1	0	0	1	3.04
During the Day and and at Night											
Day	12	11.1	8	4	6	0	0	0	0	0	3.18
Night	25	36.1	27	13	31	6	1	0	0	1	3.47
On Grass and on Turf											
Grass	29	33.0	23	11	22	0	0	0	0	1	2.73
Turf	8	14.2	12	6	15	6	1	0	0	0	4.91
By Month											
April	0	0.0	0	0	0	0	0	0	0	0	0.00
May	0	0.0	0	0	0	0	0	0	0	0	0.00
June	7	9.1	8	1	5	0	0	0	0	0	1.93
July	9	10.0	9	3	13	1	1	0	0	0	3.60
August	10	13.0	10	7	10	5	0	0	0	1	6.23
Sept/Oct	11	15.1	8	6	9	0	0	0	0	0	1.76

vs. Opponent Batters
THREE YEARS (84 – 86)

	Ave.	OBP	SLG	AB	H	2B	3B	HR	RBI	BB	SO
Totals	.207	.282	.343	169	35	6	1	5	17	17	37
Pitching vs. Left and Right-handed Batters											
Left	.174	.186	.304	69	12	3	0	2	7	1	18
Right	.230	.339	.370	100	23	3	1	3	10	16	19
Situational											
Bases Empty	.242	.272	.384	99	24	5	0	3	3	3	19
Leadoff	.279	.295	.395	43	12	2	0	1	1	1	12
Not Leadoff	.214	.254	.375	56	12	3	0	2	2	2	7
Runners On	.157	.294	.286	70	11	1	1	2	14	14	18
First Base Only	.100	.143	.100	20	2	0	0	0	0	1	2
Scoring Position	.180	.344	.360	50	9	1	1	2	14	13	16
Late Innings, Close	.059	.158	.235	17	1	0	0	1	1	2	3

RBI/Opportunities

Scoring Position	11 / 75	(15%)
Scoring Position, 2 Out	4 / 37	(11%)
On Third, Less than 2 Out	3 / 10	(30%)
RBI in close games / RBI Total	5 / 17	(29%)

Steve Ontiveros
Oakland A's

1986: Power, Flyball   1985: Finesse, Groundball   1984: Did not play

THREE YEARS (84 – 86)

	G	IP	H	BB	SO	SB	CS	W	L	S	ERA
Totals	85	147.1	117	44	90	8	2	3	5	18	3.30
At Home and on the Road											
Home	45	83.0	51	23	50	4	2	2	5	9	2.60
Road	40	64.1	66	21	40	4	0	1	0	9	4.20
During the Day and and at Night											
Day	33	53.2	37	15	29	2	0	2	2	9	3.19
Night	52	93.2	80	29	61	6	2	1	3	9	3.36
On Grass and on Turf											
Grass	70	124.2	99	38	82	8	2	2	5	13	3.25
Turf	15	22.2	18	6	8	0	0	1	0	5	3.57
By Month											
April	10	16.1	14	5	10	0	0	0	0	1	2.76
May	11	21.0	27	9	14	1	0	1	2	2	7.29
June	17	32.1	20	7	23	4	2	0	0	3	1.67
July	18	30.2	20	5	17	2	0	1	1	6	2.64
August	11	22.0	11	10	10	1	0	0	0	5	0.82
Sept/Oct	18	25.0	25	8	16	0	0	1	2	1	5.40

vs. Opponent Batters
THREE YEARS (84 – 86)

	Ave.	OBP	SLG	AB	H	2B	3B	HR	RBI	BB	SO
Totals	.220	.280	.347	531	117	21	2	14	60	44	90
Pitching vs. Left and Right-handed Batters											
Left	.259	.326	.372	266	69	13	1	5	36	28	37
Right	.181	.232	.321	265	48	8	1	9	24	16	53
Situational											
Bases Empty	.237	.297	.409	279	66	13	1	11	11	21	48
Leadoff	.273	.339	.527	110	30	7	0	7	7	11	16
Not Leadoff	.213	.269	.331	169	36	6	1	4	4	10	32
Runners On	.202	.261	.278	252	51	8	1	3	49	23	42
First Base Only	.188	.229	.268	112	21	4	1	1	5	6	15
Scoring Position	.214	.285	.286	140	30	4	0	2	44	17	27
Late Innings, Close	.196	.262	.304	276	54	10	1	6	30	25	47

RBI/Opportunities

Scoring Position	40 / 205	(20%)
Scoring Position, 2 Out	20 / 103	(19%)
On Third, Less than 2 Out	13 / 32	(41%)
RBI in close games / RBI Total	36 / 60	(60%)

Jose Oquendo
St. Louis Cardinals

THREE YEARS (84 – 86)

	Ave.	OBP	SLG	AB	H	2B	3B	HR	RBI	BB	SO
Totals	.254	.316	.287	327	83	9	1	0	23	30	46
Batting vs. Left and Right-handed Pitchers											
Left	.291	.348	.340	103	30	5	0	0	7	9	10
Right	.237	.301	.263	224	53	4	1	0	16	21	36
At Home and on the Road											
Home	.261	.311	.303	165	43	5	1	0	9	13	23
Road	.247	.321	.272	162	40	4	0	0	14	17	23
Facing Groundball Pitchers and Flyball Pitchers											
Groundball	.253	.301	.292	178	45	5	1	0	12	16	22
Flyball	.255	.323	.282	149	38	4	0	0	11	14	24
Facing Finesse Pitchers and Power Pitchers											
Finesse	.220	.273	.258	182	40	5	1	0	9	13	26
Power	.297	.367	.324	145	43	4	0	0	14	17	20
On Grass and on Turf											
Grass	.241	.301	.271	170	41	5	0	0	5	14	19
Turf	.268	.331	.306	157	42	4	1	0	18	16	27
During the Day and at Night											
Day	.270	.376	.310	100	27	4	0	0	6	16	13
Night	.247	.287	.278	227	56	5	1	0	17	14	33
By Month											
April	.157	.259	.157	51	8	0	0	0	1	5	6
May	.284	.372	.321	81	23	1	1	0	4	12	13
June	.269	.301	.327	104	28	6	0	0	13	6	14
July	.333	.333	.333	30	10	0	0	0	3	3	4
August	.139	.158	.167	36	5	1	0	0	2	1	5
Sept/Oct	.360	.429	.400	25	9	1	0	0	0	3	4
Situational											
Bases Empty	.220	.286	.247	182	40	3	1	0	0	15	27
Leadoff	.203	.250	.228	79	16	2	0	0	0	5	12
Not Leadoff	.233	.313	.262	103	24	1	1	0	0	10	15
Runners On	.297	.314	.338	145	43	6	0	0	23	15	19
First Base Only	.299	.333	.312	77	23	1	0	0	0	4	8
Scoring Position	.294	.369	.368	68	20	5	0	0	23	11	11
Late Innings, Close	.267	.361	.267	60	16	0	0	0	6	10	14

RBI/Opportunities

Scoring Position	22 / 109	(20%)
Scoring Position, 2 Out	6 / 47	(13%)
On Third, Less than 2 Out	13 / 24	(54%)
RBI in close games / RBI Total	13 / 23	(57%)

Jorge Orta
Kansas City Royals

THREE YEARS (84 – 86)

	Ave.	OBP	SLG	AB	H	2B	3B	HR	RBI	BB	SO
Totals	.282	.329	.421	1039	293	58	10	22	141	73	101
Batting vs. Left and Right-handed Pitchers											
Left	.235	.291	.235	51	12	0	0	0	3	4	11
Right	.284	.331	.430	988	281	58	10	22	138	69	90
At Home and on the Road											
Home	.279	.329	.418	526	147	36	5	9	70	39	48
Road	.285	.329	.423	513	146	22	5	13	71	34	53
Facing Groundball Pitchers and Flyball Pitchers											
Groundball	.301	.354	.441	492	148	29	5	10	72	40	55
Flyball	.265	.305	.402	547	145	29	5	12	69	33	46
Facing Finesse Pitchers and Power Pitchers											
Finesse	.291	.335	.448	632	184	42	6	15	82	43	43
Power	.268	.319	.378	407	109	16	4	7	59	30	58
On Grass and on Turf											
Grass	.301	.344	.424	375	113	14	4	8	56	25	33
Turf	.271	.320	.419	664	180	44	6	14	85	48	68
During the Day and at Night											
Day	.291	.331	.421	261	76	16	0	6	28	14	31
Night	.279	.328	.420	778	217	42	10	16	113	59	70
By Month											
April	.299	.321	.448	134	40	10	2	2	21	5	14
May	.263	.337	.400	175	46	10	1	4	23	19	16
June	.319	.348	.435	216	69	14	1	3	33	10	18
July	.251	.297	.392	171	43	9	3	3	18	11	14
August	.293	.347	.425	174	51	8	3	3	21	14	18
Sept/Oct	.260	.314	.426	169	44	7	0	7	25	14	21
Situational											
Bases Empty	.297	.344	.439	508	151	30	6	10	10	34	45
Leadoff	.301	.352	.447	226	68	17	2	4	4	16	15
Not Leadoff	.294	.337	.433	282	83	13	4	6	6	18	30
Runners On	.267	.314	.403	531	142	28	4	12	131	39	56
First Base Only	.290	.318	.402	224	65	9	2	4	13	8	22
Scoring Position	.251	.312	.404	307	77	19	2	8	118	31	34
Late Innings, Close	.319	.374	.487	160	51	6	3	5	27	16	24

RBI/Opportunities

Scoring Position	103 / 389	(26%)
Scoring Position, 2 Out	32 / 174	(18%)
On Third, Less than 2 Out	49 / 73	(67%)
RBI in close games / RBI Total	96 / 141	(68%)

Junior Ortiz
Pittsburgh Pirates

	Ave.	OBP	SLG	AB	H	2B	3B	HR	RBI	BB	SO
THREE YEARS (84 – 86)											
Totals	.278	.316	.330	273	76	11	0	1	30	17	45
Batting vs. Left and Right-handed Pitchers											
Left	.282	.333	.329	85	24	4	0	0	7	8	13
Right	.277	.308	.330	188	52	7	0	1	23	9	32
At Home and on the Road											
Home	.278	.303	.322	115	32	5	0	0	9	5	15
Road	.278	.326	.335	158	44	6	0	1	21	12	30
Facing Groundball Pitchers and Flyball Pitchers											
Groundball	.245	.281	.273	143	35	4	0	0	16	8	18
Flyball	.315	.355	.392	130	41	7	0	1	14	9	27
Facing Finesse Pitchers and Power Pitchers											
Finesse	.277	.313	.314	137	38	2	0	1	13	8	21
Power	.279	.320	.346	136	38	9	0	0	17	9	24
On Grass and on Turf											
Grass	.255	.308	.309	110	28	3	0	1	11	9	12
Turf	.294	.322	.344	163	48	8	0	0	19	8	33
During the Day and at Night											
Day	.248	.299	.289	121	30	2	0	1	10	10	18
Night	.303	.331	.362	152	46	9	0	0	20	7	27
By Month											
April	.167	.211	.167	36	6	0	0	0	3	2	5
May	.205	.256	.282	39	8	3	0	0	4	3	11
June	.342	.375	.447	38	13	4	0	0	4	2	5
July	.281	.323	.316	57	16	2	0	0	9	5	5
August	.326	.354	.348	46	15	1	0	0	3	2	10
Sept/Oct	.316	.350	.386	57	18	1	0	1	7	3	9
Situational											
Bases Empty	.219	.265	.274	146	32	5	0	1	1	9	24
Leadoff	.320	.382	.460	50	16	4	0	1	1	5	7
Not Leadoff	.167	.200	.177	96	16	1	0	0	0	4	17
Runners On	.346	.374	.394	127	44	6	0	0	29	8	21
First Base Only	.322	.322	.356	59	19	2	0	0	1	0	9
Scoring Position	.368	.412	.426	68	25	4	0	0	28	8	12
Late Innings, Close	.267	.298	.378	45	12	2	0	1	3	2	10

RBI/Opportunities

Scoring Position	27 / 89	(30%)
Scoring Position, 2 Out	9 / 37	(24%)
On Third, Less than 2 Out	10 / 17	(59%)
RBI in close games / RBI Total	18 / 30	(60%)

Rick Ownbey
St. Louis Cardinals

1986: Power, Flyball   1985: Did not play   1984: Power, Flyball

	G	IP	H	BB	SO	SB	CS	W	L	S	ERA
THREE YEARS (84 – 86)											
Totals	21	61.2	70	27	36	6	5	1	6	0	4.09
At Home and on the Road											
Home	13	32.1	39	18	16	3	3	1	3	0	4.73
Road	8	29.1	31	9	20	3	2	0	3	0	3.38
During the Day and and at Night											
Day	8	36.2	37	15	23	3	3	1	2	0	3.19
Night	13	25.0	33	12	13	3	2	0	4	0	5.40
On Grass and on Turf											
Grass	6	28.1	27	9	18	3	2	0	3	0	2.86
Turf	15	33.1	43	18	18	3	3	1	3	0	5.13
By Month											
April	3	17.2	18	9	10	1	3	1	1	0	3.57
May	4	9.0	9	3	7	1	1	0	0	0	2.00
June	8	12.2	17	6	7	0	1	0	1	0	5.68
July	4	11.2	16	6	5	3	0	0	3	0	5.40
August	0	0.0	0	0	0	0	0	0	0	0	0.00
Sept/Oct	2	10.2	10	3	7	1	0	0	1	0	3.37

vs. Opponent Batters

	Ave.	OBP	SLG	AB	H	2B	3B	HR	RBI	BB	SO
THREE YEARS (84 – 86)											
Totals	.297	.368	.415	236	70	11	1	5	27	27	36
Pitching vs. Left and Right-handed Batters											
Left	.345	.426	.466	58	20	2	1	1	6	9	6
Right	.281	.348	.399	178	50	9	0	4	21	18	30
Situational											
Bases Empty	.328	.401	.489	131	43	7	1	4	4	15	22
Leadoff	.316	.404	.404	57	18	2	0	1	1	8	9
Not Leadoff	.338	.402	.554	74	25	5	1	3	3	7	13
Runners On	.257	.328	.324	105	27	4	0	1	23	12	14
First Base Only	.240	.255	.320	50	12	1	0	1	3	1	6
Scoring Position	.273	.380	.327	55	15	3	0	0	20	11	8
Late Innings, Close	.346	.414	.500	26	9	1	0	1	3	2	5

RBI/Opportunities

Scoring Position	20 / 85	(24%)
Scoring Position, 2 Out	10 / 45	(22%)
On Third, Less than 2 Out	8 / 13	(62%)
RBI in close games / RBI Total	14 / 27	(52%)

Tom Paciorek
Texas Rangers

	Ave.	OBP	SLG	AB	H	2B	3B	HR	RBI	BB	SO
THREE YEARS (84 – 86)											
Totals	.267	.307	.348	814	217	33	3	9	71	42	146
Batting vs. Left and Right-handed Pitchers											
Left	.287	.323	.364	494	142	16	2	6	41	26	85
Right	.234	.284	.322	320	75	17	1	3	30	16	61
At Home and on the Road											
Home	.278	.324	.353	385	107	18	1	3	36	24	60
Road	.256	.293	.343	429	110	15	2	6	35	18	86
Facing Groundball Pitchers and Flyball Pitchers											
Groundball	.253	.294	.306	376	95	8	3	2	33	17	55
Flyball	.279	.318	.384	438	122	25	0	7	38	25	91
Facing Finesse Pitchers and Power Pitchers											
Finesse	.269	.312	.344	457	123	18	2	4	34	25	77
Power	.263	.301	.353	357	94	15	1	5	37	17	69
On Grass and on Turf											
Grass	.266	.310	.336	628	167	24	1	6	54	36	112
Turf	.269	.299	.387	186	50	9	2	3	17	6	34
During the Day and at Night											
Day	.264	.304	.351	231	61	11	0	3	19	13	44
Night	.268	.309	.346	583	156	22	3	6	52	29	102
By Month											
April	.279	.339	.356	104	29	8	0	0	5	8	25
May	.272	.304	.312	173	47	5	1	0	13	8	30
June	.284	.311	.411	141	40	6	0	4	18	4	24
July	.232	.289	.293	82	19	2	0	1	6	6	12
August	.244	.314	.314	156	38	6	1	1	14	13	25
Sept/Oct	.278	.288	.386	158	44	6	1	3	15	3	30
Situational											
Bases Empty	.278	.318	.370	479	133	21	1	7	7	24	76
Leadoff	.238	.281	.343	181	43	7	0	4	4	10	25
Not Leadoff	.302	.340	.386	298	90	14	1	3	3	14	51
Runners On	.251	.293	.316	335	84	12	2	2	64	18	70
First Base Only	.256	.303	.361	133	34	6	1	2	6	5	26
Scoring Position	.248	.287	.287	202	50	6	1	0	58	13	44
Late Innings, Close	.325	.374	.389	126	41	4	2	0	18	9	23

RBI/Opportunities

Scoring Position	57 / 264	(22%)
Scoring Position, 2 Out	23 / 125	(18%)
On Third, Less than 2 Out	24 / 46	(52%)
RBI in close games / RBI Total	47 / 71	(66%)

David Palmer
Atlanta Braves

1986: Power, Groundball   1985: Power, Groundball   1984: Power, Groundball

	G	IP	H	BB	SO	SB	CS	W	L	S	ERA
THREE YEARS (84 – 86)											
Totals	79	450.2	410	213	342	81	35	25	23	0	3.71
At Home and on the Road											
Home	39	230.0	207	101	168	38	13	11	12	0	3.33
Road	40	220.2	203	112	174	43	22	14	11	0	4.12
During the Day and at Night											
Day	22	127.2	103	67	93	23	10	8	5	0	3.45
Night	57	323.0	307	146	249	58	25	17	18	0	3.82
On Grass and on Turf											
Grass	33	198.2	177	99	150	33	18	9	6	0	3.49
Turf	46	252.0	233	114	192	48	17	16	17	0	3.89
By Month											
April	10	57.0	35	18	42	13	2	4	3	0	2.84
May	17	98.0	76	41	78	15	7	4	6	0	3.31
June	18	111.1	101	57	80	20	15	4	6	0	3.23
July	14	75.0	91	41	58	15	5	6	5	0	5.28
August	7	41.2	29	19	34	6	1	3	0	0	3.24
Sept/Oct	13	67.2	78	37	50	12	5	4	3	0	4.39

vs. Opponent Batters

	Ave.	OBP	SLG	AB	H	2B	3B	HR	RBI	BB	SO
THREE YEARS (84 – 86)											
Totals	.244	.331	.337	1678	410	53	11	27	173	213	342
Pitching vs. Left and Right-handed Batters											
Left	.246	.340	.324	883	217	31	7	8	70	125	193
Right	.243	.320	.352	795	193	22	4	19	103	88	149
Situational											
Bases Empty	.236	.318	.331	970	229	24	10	16	16	113	192
Leadoff	.241	.318	.307	424	102	11	4	3	3	48	76
Not Leadoff	.233	.318	.350	546	127	13	6	13	13	65	116
Runners On	.256	.348	.346	708	181	29	1	11	157	100	150
First Base Only	.268	.322	.375	291	78	11	1	6	17	22	60
Scoring Position	.247	.365	.326	417	103	18	0	5	140	78	90
Late Innings, Close	.382	.411	.480	123	47	7	1	1	12	5	18

RBI/Opportunities

Scoring Position	127 / 593	(21%)
Scoring Position, 2 Out	50 / 275	(18%)
On Third, Less than 2 Out	43 / 96	(45%)
RBI in close games / RBI Total	128 / 173	(74%)

Jim Pankovits
Houston Astros

	Ave.	OBP	SLG	AB	H	2B	3B	HR	RBI	BB	SO
THREE YEARS (84 – 86)											
Totals	.265	.322	.363	366	97	16	1	6	35	30	74
Batting vs. Left and Right-handed Pitchers											
Left	.240	.285	.338	225	54	8	1	4	20	14	45
Right	.305	.377	.404	141	43	8	0	2	15	16	29
At Home and on the Road											
Home	.241	.315	.331	166	40	7	1	2	12	18	35
Road	.285	.327	.390	200	57	9	0	4	23	12	39
Facing Groundball Pitchers and Flyball Pitchers											
Groundball	.283	.343	.386	184	52	7	0	4	17	16	33
Flyball	.247	.299	.341	182	45	9	1	2	18	14	41
Facing Finesse Pitchers and Power Pitchers											
Finesse	.264	.300	.335	212	56	12	0	1	15	11	27
Power	.266	.349	.403	154	41	4	1	5	20	19	47
On Grass and on Turf											
Grass	.336	.383	.475	122	41	8	0	3	13	9	26
Turf	.230	.291	.307	244	56	8	1	3	22	21	48
During the Day and at Night											
Day	.294	.343	.444	126	37	5	1	4	13	9	22
Night	.250	.310	.321	240	60	11	0	2	22	21	52
By Month											
April	.600	.714	.600	10	6	0	0	0	1	4	1
May	.231	.286	.365	52	12	1	0	2	6	3	10
June	.279	.340	.419	86	24	4	1	2	6	8	13
July	.147	.216	.176	34	5	1	0	0	2	3	8
August	.380	.418	.500	50	19	3	0	1	12	4	12
Sept/Oct	.231	.275	.306	134	31	7	0	1	8	8	30
Situational											
Bases Empty	.273	.327	.397	209	57	12	1	4	4	16	45
Leadoff	.253	.279	.422	83	21	3	1	3	3	3	17
Not Leadoff	.286	.357	.381	126	36	9	0	1	1	13	28
Runners On	.255	.314	.318	157	40	4	0	2	31	14	29
First Base Only	.250	.273	.297	64	16	3	0	0	0	2	16
Scoring Position	.258	.340	.333	93	24	1	0	2	31	12	13
Late Innings, Close	.282	.344	.400	85	24	1	0	3	14	7	18

RBI/Opportunities		
Scoring Position	27 / 126	(21%)
Scoring Position, 2 Out	13 / 62	(21%)
On Third, Less than 2 Out	6 / 12	(50%)
RBI in close games / RBI Total	23 / 35	(66%)

Dan Pasqua
New York Yankees

	Ave.	OBP	SLG	AB	H	2B	3B	HR	RBI	BB	SO
THREE YEARS (84 – 86)											
Totals	.264	.362	.491	428	113	20	1	25	70	63	116
Batting vs. Left and Right-handed Pitchers											
Left	.197	.293	.379	66	13	3	0	3	12	7	23
Right	.276	.374	.511	362	100	17	1	22	58	56	93
At Home and on the Road											
Home	.251	.356	.511	227	57	11	0	16	40	37	56
Road	.279	.369	.468	201	56	9	1	9	30	26	60
Facing Groundball Pitchers and Flyball Pitchers											
Groundball	.271	.365	.471	221	60	9	1	11	34	31	58
Flyball	.256	.360	.512	207	53	11	0	14	36	32	58
Facing Finesse Pitchers and Power Pitchers											
Finesse	.278	.349	.522	230	64	11	0	15	36	25	61
Power	.247	.377	.455	198	49	9	1	10	34	38	55
On Grass and on Turf											
Grass	.248	.355	.467	347	86	14	1	20	54	56	96
Turf	.333	.396	.593	81	27	6	0	5	16	7	20
During the Day and at Night											
Day	.276	.355	.500	174	48	12	0	9	25	21	43
Night	.256	.367	.484	254	65	8	1	16	45	42	73
By Month											
April	.000	.000	.000	0	0	0	0	0	0	0	0
May	.286	.444	.686	35	10	2	0	4	7	10	11
June	.225	.300	.296	71	16	2	0	1	5	8	18
July	.311	.393	.622	74	23	3	1	6	15	9	16
August	.276	.376	.488	127	35	6	0	7	19	20	33
Sept/Oct	.240	.338	.471	121	29	7	0	7	24	16	38
Situational											
Bases Empty	.261	.344	.509	230	60	9	0	16	16	25	54
Leadoff	.274	.343	.579	95	26	2	0	9	9	8	26
Not Leadoff	.252	.344	.459	135	34	7	0	7	7	17	28
Runners On	.268	.382	.470	198	53	11	1	9	54	38	62
First Base Only	.292	.417	.472	89	26	5	1	3	7	19	26
Scoring Position	.248	.354	.468	109	27	6	0	6	47	19	36
Late Innings, Close	.177	.369	.355	62	11	2	0	3	12	19	20

RBI/Opportunities		
Scoring Position	36 / 148	(24%)
Scoring Position, 2 Out	16 / 68	(24%)
On Third, Less than 2 Out	11 / 19	(58%)
RBI in close games / RBI Total	37 / 70	(53%)

Frank Pastore
Minnesota Twins

1986: Finesse, Groundball   1985: Finesse, Groundball   1984: Finesse, Flyball

	G	IP	H	BB	SO	SB	CS	W	L	S	ERA
THREE YEARS (84 – 86)											
Totals	74	201.2	224	80	100	21	2	8	10	2	5.18
At Home and on the Road											
Home	44	94.2	127	46	40	9	1	4	7	0	6.46
Road	30	107.0	97	34	60	12	1	4	3	2	4.04
During the Day and and at Night											
Day	25	93.0	99	39	41	13	0	2	5	2	5.13
Night	49	108.2	125	41	59	8	2	6	5	0	5.22
On Grass and on Turf											
Grass	20	64.2	71	25	34	7	1	2	3	1	5.15
Turf	54	137.0	153	55	66	14	1	6	7	1	5.19
By Month											
April	7	25.2	33	13	16	3	0	0	2	0	7.01
May	20	66.1	55	18	40	5	0	4	2	0	3.26
June	22	57.0	60	22	26	9	1	3	2	2	4.42
July	12	24.1	31	12	7	2	0	0	1	0	5.55
August	9	23.2	36	13	8	2	1	1	3	0	9.51
Sept/Oct	4	4.2	9	2	3	0	1	0	0	0	7.71

vs. Opponent Batters

	Ave.	OBP	SLG	AB	H	2B	3B	HR	RBI	BB	SO
THREE YEARS (84 – 86)											
Totals	.285	.308	.349	786	224	51	5	15	129	80	100
Pitching vs. Left and Right-handed Batters											
Left	.275	.345	.398	342	94	18	3	6	55	37	46
Right	.293	.353	.441	444	130	35	2	9	74	43	54
Situational											
Bases Empty	.280	.338	.420	421	118	31	2	8	8	36	56
Leadoff	.291	.345	.407	182	53	15	0	2	2	14	19
Not Leadoff	.272	.333	.431	239	65	16	2	6	6	22	37
Runners On	.290	.361	.425	365	106	22	3	7	121	44	44
First Base Only	.248	.292	.403	129	32	7	2	3	13	8	19
Scoring Position	.314	.394	.436	236	74	15	1	4	108	36	25
Late Innings, Close	.268	.306	.381	97	26	8	0	1	17	7	8

RBI/Opportunities		
Scoring Position	98 / 344	(28%)
Scoring Position, 2 Out	40 / 151	(26%)
On Third, Less than 2 Out	41 / 73	(56%)
RBI in close games / RBI Total	73 / 129	(57%)

Alejandro Pena
Los Angeles Dodgers

1986: Power, Flyball   1985: Power, Flyball   1984: Finesse, Groundball

	G	IP	H	BB	SO	SB	CS	W	L	S	ERA
THREE YEARS (84 – 86)											
Totals	54	273.2	267	79	183	26	18	13	9	1	3.19
At Home and on the Road											
Home	25	129.1	109	36	75	13	10	8	6	1	2.51
Road	29	144.1	158	43	108	13	8	5	3	0	3.80
During the Day and and at Night											
Day	15	84.2	87	19	54	6	5	5	2	0	3.40
Night	39	189.0	180	60	129	20	13	8	7	1	3.10
On Grass and on Turf											
Grass	36	186.1	176	50	116	17	14	11	7	1	2.90
Turf	18	87.1	91	29	67	9	4	2	2	0	3.81
By Month											
April	5	38.1	30	6	22	1	2	4	1	0	1.41
May	7	35.2	39	11	26	4	1	1	1	0	3.53
June	13	49.2	53	17	48	5	4	3	3	0	3.62
July	11	70.1	62	19	36	5	6	4	1	0	3.20
August	10	59.1	53	17	37	8	5	1	2	0	2.43
Sept/Oct	8	20.1	30	9	14	3	0	0	1	1	7.08

vs. Opponent Batters

	Ave.	OBP	SLG	AB	H	2B	3B	HR	RBI	BB	SO
THREE YEARS (84 – 86)											
Totals	.254	.308	.349	1050	267	49	4	14	93	79	183
Pitching vs. Left and Right-handed Batters											
Left	.264	.334	.370	527	139	24	4	8	39	53	83
Right	.245	.281	.327	523	128	25	0	6	54	26	100
Situational											
Bases Empty	.255	.310	.358	595	152	24	2	11	11	46	96
Leadoff	.263	.323	.382	259	68	11	1	6	6	23	49
Not Leadoff	.250	.300	.339	336	84	13	1	5	5	23	47
Runners On	.253	.306	.336	455	115	25	2	3	82	33	87
First Base Only	.274	.299	.371	197	54	12	2	1	11	5	33
Scoring Position	.236	.310	.310	258	61	13	0	2	71	28	54
Late Innings, Close	.250	.329	.313	128	32	6	1	0	12	14	25

RBI/Opportunities		
Scoring Position	65 / 323	(20%)
Scoring Position, 2 Out	32 / 156	(21%)
On Third, Less than 2 Out	19 / 48	(40%)
RBI in close games / RBI Total	77 / 93	(83%)

Tony Perez
Cincinnati Reds

THREE YEARS (84 – 86)	Ave.	OBP	SLG	AB	H	2B	3B	HR	RBI	BB	SO
Totals	.277	.346	.392	520	144	26	2	10	77	58	68
Batting vs. Left and Right-handed Pitchers											
Left	.280	.352	.396	318	89	13	0	8	44	37	37
Right	.272	.336	.386	202	55	13	2	2	33	21	31
At Home and on the Road											
Home	.302	.380	.461	258	78	15	1	8	54	34	21
Road	.252	.311	.324	262	66	11	1	2	23	24	47
Facing Groundball Pitchers and Flyball Pitchers											
Groundball	.328	.376	.455	299	98	19	2	5	55	25	38
Flyball	.208	.307	.308	221	46	7	0	5	22	33	30
Facing Finesse Pitchers and Power Pitchers											
Finesse	.310	.371	.422	277	86	15	2	4	43	29	22
Power	.239	.318	.358	243	58	11	0	6	34	29	46
On Grass and on Turf											
Grass	.256	.297	.349	172	44	8	1	2	17	11	34
Turf	.287	.368	.414	348	100	18	1	8	60	47	34
During the Day and at Night											
Day	.289	.355	.412	194	56	10	1	4	24	21	24
Night	.270	.341	.380	326	88	16	1	6	53	37	44
By Month											
April	.281	.339	.386	57	16	4	1	0	6	5	10
May	.224	.333	.418	67	15	1	0	4	16	11	14
June	.261	.333	.341	88	23	4	0	1	9	10	10
July	.281	.343	.348	89	25	6	0	0	12	9	13
August	.260	.322	.356	104	27	2	1	2	10	10	12
Sept/Oct	.330	.389	.487	115	38	16	0	3	24	13	9
Situational											
Bases Empty	.259	.322	.371	259	67	14	0	5	5	24	36
Leadoff	.269	.327	.317	104	28	5	0	0	0	9	11
Not Leadoff	.252	.318	.406	155	39	9	0	5	5	15	25
Runners On	.295	.369	.414	261	77	12	2	5	72	34	32
First Base Only	.320	.358	.456	103	33	5	0	3	9	6	9
Scoring Position	.278	.375	.386	158	44	7	2	2	63	28	23
Late Innings, Close	.339	.408	.444	124	42	8	1	1	26	16	21

RBI/Opportunities

Scoring Position	56 / 225	(25%)
Scoring Position, 2 Out	19 / 103	(18%)
On Third, Less than 2 Out	29 / 48	(60%)
RBI in close games / RBI Total	61 / 77	(79%)

Pat Perry
St. Louis Cardinals

1986: Finesse, Flyball 1985: Finesse, Flyball 1984: Did not play

THREE YEARS (84 – 86)	G	IP	H	BB	SO	SB	CS	W	L	S	ERA
Totals	52	81.0	63	37	35	2	2	3	3	2	3.22
At Home and on the Road											
Home	20	30.0	36	14	15	1	2	0	1	0	5.70
Road	32	51.0	27	23	20	1	0	3	2	2	1.76
During the Day and and at Night											
Day	23	36.1	25	15	17	0	1	2	1	2	2.97
Night	29	44.2	38	22	18	2	1	1	2	0	3.43
On Grass and on Turf											
Grass	15	19.1	11	9	12	0	0	2	1	2	2.33
Turf	37	61.2	52	28	23	2	2	1	2	0	3.50
By Month											
April	7	8.2	6	7	4	0	0	1	1	1	6.23
May	4	5.1	2	4	4	0	0	0	0	0	1.69
June	11	19.0	18	10	8	2	0	0	1	0	4.26
July	6	8.2	10	2	4	0	0	0	0	0	6.23
August	9	15.2	9	4	4	0	1	1	0	1	1.72
Sept/Oct	15	23.2	16	12	11	0	1	1	1	0	1.52

vs. Opponent Batters — THREE YEARS (84 – 86)	Ave.	OBP	SLG	AB	H	2B	3B	HR	RBI	BB	SO
Totals	.220	.302	.331	287	63	11	3	5	33	37	35
Pitching vs. Left and Right-handed Batters											
Left	.253	.289	.342	79	20	2	1	1	6	4	7
Right	.207	.306	.327	208	43	9	2	4	27	33	28
Situational											
Bases Empty	.156	.241	.274	179	28	8	2	3	3	20	28
Leadoff	.141	.239	.237	71	10	2	1	1	1	7	12
Not Leadoff	.167	.256	.296	108	18	6	1	2	2	13	16
Runners On	.324	.394	.426	108	35	3	1	2	30	17	7
First Base Only	.326	.340	.413	46	15	1	0	1	2	1	3
Scoring Position	.323	.424	.435	62	20	2	1	1	28	16	4
Late Innings, Close	.216	.348	.297	74	16	1	1	1	6	16	10

RBI/Opportunities

Scoring Position	25 / 107	(23%)
Scoring Position, 2 Out	4 / 44	(9%)
On Third, Less than 2 Out	16 / 29	(55%)
RBI in close games / RBI Total	6 / 33	(18%)

Geno Petralli
Texas Rangers

THREE YEARS (84 – 86)	Ave.	OBP	SLG	AB	H	2B	3B	HR	RBI	BB	SO
Totals	.258	.295	.354	240	62	11	3	2	29	13	26
Batting vs. Left and Right-handed Pitchers											
Left	.125	.125	.125	16	2	0	0	0	1	0	3
Right	.268	.306	.371	224	60	11	3	2	28	13	23
At Home and on the Road											
Home	.225	.293	.281	89	20	2	0	1	9	9	11
Road	.278	.296	.397	151	42	9	3	1	20	4	15
Facing Groundball Pitchers and Flyball Pitchers											
Groundball	.300	.345	.418	110	33	9	2	0	15	7	15
Flyball	.223	.252	.300	130	29	2	1	2	14	6	11
Facing Finesse Pitchers and Power Pitchers											
Finesse	.290	.318	.400	145	42	9	2	1	17	5	11
Power	.211	.262	.284	95	20	2	1	1	12	8	15
On Grass and on Turf											
Grass	.247	.290	.345	194	48	7	3	2	21	13	21
Turf	.304	.313	.391	46	14	4	0	0	8	0	5
During the Day and at Night											
Day	.324	.347	.479	71	23	4	2	1	9	3	6
Night	.231	.273	.302	169	39	7	1	1	20	10	20
By Month											
April	.100	.182	.100	10	1	0	0	0	0	1	0
May	.176	.176	.294	17	3	0	1	0	0	0	2
June	.318	.333	.432	44	14	5	0	0	8	1	2
July	.211	.281	.263	57	12	0	0	1	5	6	7
August	.265	.297	.353	68	18	3	0	1	9	4	5
Sept/Oct	.318	.340	.477	44	14	3	2	0	7	1	10
Situational											
Bases Empty	.213	.250	.298	141	30	5	2	1	1	6	20
Leadoff	.164	.220	.182	55	9	1	0	0	0	4	8
Not Leadoff	.244	.270	.372	86	21	4	2	1	1	2	12
Runners On	.323	.355	.434	99	32	6	1	1	28	7	6
First Base Only	.280	.280	.400	50	14	1	1	1	3	0	4
Scoring Position	.367	.417	.469	49	18	5	0	0	25	7	2
Late Innings, Close	.256	.293	.487	39	10	1	1	2	7	2	3

RBI/Opportunities

Scoring Position	24 / 73	(33%)
Scoring Position, 2 Out	11 / 35	(31%)
On Third, Less than 2 Out	8 / 12	(67%)
RBI in close games / RBI Total	20 / 29	(69%)

Dan Petry
Detroit Tigers

1986: Finesse, Groundball 1985: Finesse, Groundball 1984: Finesse, Groundball

THREE YEARS (84 – 86)	G	IP	H	BB	SO	SB	CS	W	L	S	ERA
Totals	89	588.0	543	200	309	40	29	38	31	0	3.57
At Home and on the Road											
Home	47	315.2	278	107	172	22	19	18	20	0	3.48
Road	42	272.1	265	93	137	18	10	20	11	0	3.67
During the Day and and at Night											
Day	30	215.0	188	67	118	9	14	15	13	0	2.93
Night	59	373.0	355	133	191	31	15	23	18	0	3.93
On Grass and on Turf											
Grass	77	509.0	462	174	268	32	27	34	26	0	3.62
Turf	12	79.0	81	26	41	8	2	4	5	0	3.19
By Month											
April	15	97.0	88	30	50	3	3	8	4	0	3.62
May	17	111.2	107	46	61	7	7	11	5	0	3.47
June	14	95.1	84	27	38	8	6	5	5	0	3.30
July	11	83.2	70	24	50	4	4	5	5	0	3.55
August	16	106.2	105	32	60	9	6	3	7	0	3.54
Sept/Oct	16	93.2	89	41	50	9	3	6	5	0	3.94

vs. Opponent Batters — THREE YEARS (84 – 86)	Ave.	OBP	SLG	AB	H	2B	3B	HR	RBI	BB	SO
Totals	.244	.309	.381	2222	543	102	11	60	234	200	309
Pitching vs. Left and Right-handed Batters											
Left	.236	.307	.377	1218	287	45	8	37	126	125	166
Right	.255	.311	.386	1004	256	57	3	23	108	75	143
Situational											
Bases Empty	.231	.295	.359	1355	313	56	5	36	36	115	191
Leadoff	.226	.285	.359	566	128	21	3	16	16	45	78
Not Leadoff	.234	.301	.360	789	185	35	2	20	20	70	113
Runners On	.265	.331	.415	867	230	46	6	24	198	85	118
First Base Only	.256	.317	.401	399	102	18	2	12	33	34	49
Scoring Position	.274	.343	.427	468	128	28	4	12	165	51	69
Late Innings, Close	.193	.267	.262	187	36	7	0	2	11	19	30

RBI/Opportunities

Scoring Position	142 / 601	(24%)
Scoring Position, 2 Out	69 / 290	(24%)
On Third, Less than 2 Out	39 / 86	(45%)
RBI in close games / RBI Total	166 / 234	(71%)

Dan Plesac
Milwaukee Brewers

1986: Power, Flyball   1985: Did not play   1984: Did not play

THREE YEARS (84 – 86)

	G	IP	H	BB	SO	SB	CS	W	L	S	ERA
Totals	51	91.0	81	29	75	6	4	10	7	14	2.97
At Home and on the Road											
Home	26	50.1	50	17	43	6	1	6	3	6	3.58
Road	25	40.2	31	12	32	0	3	4	4	8	2.21
During the Day and at Night											
Day	16	29.2	27	10	23	5	2	2	1	5	3.34
Night	35	61.1	54	19	52	1	2	8	6	9	2.79
On Grass and on Turf											
Grass	45	80.0	71	26	66	6	4	9	6	12	3.26
Turf	6	11.0	10	3	9	0	0	1	1	2	0.82
By Month											
April	5	9.2	6	3	8	1	1	1	1	0	4.66
May	7	17.1	17	5	13	0	1	2	2	3	3.12
June	10	12.0	10	5	9	0	0	1	2	4	2.25
July	7	12.2	13	5	8	5	0	1	1	2	3.55
August	11	20.1	16	6	20	0	0	4	0	1	1.77
Sept/Oct	11	19.0	19	5	17	0	2	1	1	4	3.32

vs. Opponent Batters
THREE YEARS (84 – 86)

	Ave.	OBP	SLG	AB	H	2B	3B	HR	RBI	BB	SO
Totals	.240	.296	.340	338	81	11	4	5	38	29	75
Pitching vs. Left and Right-handed Batters											
Left	.263	.330	.362	80	21	3	1	1	13	9	17
Right	.233	.285	.333	258	60	8	3	4	25	20	58
Situational											
Bases Empty	.251	.304	.351	171	43	7	2	2	2	13	40
Leadoff	.273	.300	.377	77	21	3	1	1	1	3	12
Not Leadoff	.234	.308	.330	94	22	4	1	1	1	10	28
Runners On	.228	.287	.329	167	38	4	2	3	36	16	35
First Base Only	.242	.296	.348	66	16	2	1	1	4	5	8
Scoring Position	.218	.282	.317	101	22	2	1	2	32	11	27
Late Innings, Close	.243	.300	.350	206	50	9	2	3	25	19	46

RBI/Opportunities

Scoring Position	29 / 148	(20%)
Scoring Position, 2 Out	8 / 75	(11%)
On Third, Less than 2 Out	13 / 28	(46%)
RBI in close games / RBI Total	26 / 38	(68%)

Eric Plunk
Oakland A's

1986: Power, Flyball   1985: Did not play   1984: Did not play

THREE YEARS (84 – 86)

	G	IP	H	BB	SO	SB	CS	W	L	S	ERA
Totals	26	120.1	91	102	98	17	7	4	7	0	5.31
At Home and on the Road											
Home	13	63.1	50	59	54	6	3	3	3	0	5.68
Road	13	57.0	41	43	44	11	4	1	4	0	4.89
During the Day and at Night											
Day	9	46.0	30	46	39	2	1	2	3	0	5.28
Night	17	74.1	61	56	59	15	6	2	4	0	5.33
On Grass and on Turf											
Grass	22	101.1	76	84	84	16	5	3	6	0	5.33
Turf	4	19.0	15	18	14	1	2	1	1	0	5.21
By Month											
April	0	0.0	0	0	0	0	0	0	0	0	0.00
May	5	22.2	15	17	17	5	1	0	1	0	4.76
June	6	34.2	25	31	32	3	2	2	2	0	5.45
July	5	30.1	26	26	18	0	0	1	4	0	5.34
August	4	18.1	12	12	15	2	1	1	0	0	4.91
Sept/Oct	6	14.1	13	16	16	7	3	0	0	0	6.28

vs. Opponent Batters
THREE YEARS (84 – 86)

	Ave.	OBP	SLG	AB	H	2B	3B	HR	RBI	BB	SO
Totals	.214	.370	.341	425	91	12	0	14	56	102	98
Pitching vs. Left and Right-handed Batters											
Left	.226	.377	.339	239	54	6	0	7	27	58	45
Right	.199	.362	.344	186	37	6	0	7	29	44	53
Situational											
Bases Empty	.191	.367	.296	230	44	6	0	6	6	63	57
Leadoff	.252	.346	.360	111	28	3	0	3	3	16	24
Not Leadoff	.134	.383	.235	119	16	3	0	3	3	47	33
Runners On	.241	.373	.395	195	47	6	0	8	50	39	41
First Base Only	.227	.352	.409	88	20	1	0	5	10	13	9
Scoring Position	.252	.390	.383	107	27	5	0	3	40	26	32
Late Innings, Close	.310	.429	.517	29	9	0	0	2	6	6	2

RBI/Opportunities

Scoring Position	34 / 165	(21%)
Scoring Position, 2 Out	14 / 70	(20%)
On Third, Less than 2 Out	11 / 29	(38%)
RBI in close games / RBI Total	36 / 56	(64%)

Darrell Porter
Texas Rangers

THREE YEARS (84 – 86)

	Ave.	OBP	SLG	AB	H	2B	3B	HR	RBI	BB	SO
Totals	.235	.337	.410	817	192	34	5	33	133	123	178
Batting vs. Left and Right-handed Pitchers											
Left	.246	.340	.448	134	33	5	2	6	36	20	31
Right	.233	.337	.403	683	159	29	3	27	97	103	147
At Home and on the Road											
Home	.250	.349	.427	372	93	18	3	14	68	55	87
Road	.222	.327	.396	445	99	16	2	19	65	68	91
Facing Groundball Pitchers and Flyball Pitchers											
Groundball	.207	.309	.329	377	78	8	1	12	52	54	92
Flyball	.259	.361	.480	440	114	26	4	21	81	69	86
Facing Finesse Pitchers and Power Pitchers											
Finesse	.253	.351	.440	439	111	19	0	21	73	67	90
Power	.214	.321	.376	378	81	15	5	12	60	56	88
On Grass and on Turf											
Grass	.230	.332	.427	330	76	10	2	17	51	48	75
Turf	.238	.341	.398	487	116	24	3	16	82	75	103
During the Day and at Night											
Day	.208	.303	.391	284	59	11	1	13	41	37	59
Night	.250	.355	.420	533	133	23	4	20	92	86	119
By Month											
April	.263	.336	.505	95	25	3	1	6	12	10	20
May	.225	.344	.411	151	34	5	1	7	23	27	29
June	.214	.361	.262	84	18	4	0	0	12	20	12
July	.228	.310	.455	101	23	6	1	5	23	12	16
August	.197	.308	.341	173	34	5	1	6	34	26	50
Sept/Oct	.272	.358	.460	213	58	11	1	9	29	28	51
Situational											
Bases Empty	.224	.314	.392	434	97	20	1	17	17	54	96
Leadoff	.262	.346	.412	187	49	10	0	6	6	23	31
Not Leadoff	.194	.289	.377	247	48	10	1	11	11	31	65
Runners On	.248	.362	.431	383	95	14	4	16	116	69	82
First Base Only	.267	.333	.433	150	40	5	1	6	15	15	26
Scoring Position	.236	.378	.429	233	55	9	3	10	101	54	56
Late Innings, Close	.215	.314	.356	149	32	4	1	5	26	21	38

RBI/Opportunities

Scoring Position	80 / 353	(23%)
Scoring Position, 2 Out	27 / 161	(17%)
On Third, Less than 2 Out	31 / 72	(43%)
RBI in close games / RBI Total	79 / 133	(59%)

Mark Portugal
Minnesota Twins

1986: Power, Groundball   1985: Power, Groundball   1984: Did not play

THREE YEARS (84 – 86)

	G	IP	H	BB	SO	SB	CS	W	L	S	ERA
Totals	33	137.0	136	64	79	4	4	7	13	1	4.53
At Home and on the Road											
Home	15	59.0	58	30	33	1	2	4	4	1	4.42
Road	18	78.0	78	34	46	3	2	3	9	0	4.62
During the Day and at Night											
Day	13	67.0	61	35	44	2	2	2	6	0	4.30
Night	20	70.0	75	29	35	2	2	5	7	1	4.76
On Grass and on Turf											
Grass	12	52.1	57	18	31	2	0	1	7	0	4.47
Turf	21	84.2	79	46	48	2	4	6	6	1	4.57
By Month											
April	3	2.1	6	3	0	0	0	0	2	0	23.14
May	4	21.0	23	9	8	0	0	1	3	0	4.71
June	4	26.0	28	14	22	1	0	1	2	0	5.19
July	3	10.1	9	5	5	0	1	0	1	0	4.35
August	6	35.2	35	18	17	0	1	3	1	0	3.79
Sept/Oct	13	41.2	35	15	27	3	2	2	4	1	3.67

vs. Opponent Batters
THREE YEARS (84 – 86)

	Ave.	OBP	SLG	AB	H	2B	3B	HR	RBI	BB	SO
Totals	.266	.346	.399	511	136	27	1	13	53	64	79
Pitching vs. Left and Right-handed Batters											
Left	.242	.337	.367	256	62	15	1	5	28	38	43
Right	.290	.356	.431	255	74	12	0	8	25	26	36
Situational											
Bases Empty	.285	.364	.406	281	80	17	1	5	5	35	39
Leadoff	.341	.432	.500	126	43	6	1	4	4	20	18
Not Leadoff	.239	.306	.329	155	37	11	0	1	1	15	21
Runners On	.243	.325	.391	230	56	10	0	8	48	29	40
First Base Only	.296	.377	.417	108	32	4	0	3	8	13	21
Scoring Position	.197	.280	.369	122	24	6	0	5	40	16	19
Late Innings, Close	.425	.489	.625	40	17	2	0	2	6	4	2

RBI/Opportunities

Scoring Position	32 / 164	(20%)
Scoring Position, 2 Out	10 / 63	(16%)
On Third, Less than 2 Out	14 / 30	(47%)
RBI in close games / RBI Total	39 / 53	(74%)

Dennis Powell
Los Angeles Dodgers

1986: Finesse, Groundball 1985: Power, Groundball 1984: Did not play

THREE YEARS (84 – 86)	G	IP	H	BB	SO	SB	CS	W	L	S	ERA
Totals	43	94.2	95	38	50	4	7	3	8	1	4.56
At Home and on the Road											
Home	16	26.2	35	10	14	0	0	0	3	0	6.41
Road	27	68.0	60	28	36	4	7	3	5	1	3.84
During the Day and and at Night											
Day	13	32.1	31	14	20	2	0	1	1	0	3.62
Night	30	62.1	64	24	30	2	7	2	7	1	5.05
On Grass and on Turf											
Grass	31	66.0	71	25	37	3	4	1	6	1	4.77
Turf	12	28.2	24	13	13	1	3	2	2	0	4.08
By Month											
April	4	12.1	9	6	8	1	1	0	3	0	5.84
May	0	0.0	0	0	0	0	0	0	0	0	0.00
June	0	0.0	0	0	0	0	0	0	0	0	0.00
July	10	25.1	25	11	11	0	2	1	1	0	5.33
August	10	25.1	26	8	17	3	2	1	2	0	3.55
Sept/Oct	19	31.2	35	13	14	0	2	1	2	1	4.26

vs. Opponent Batters

THREE YEARS (84 – 86)	Ave.	OBP	SLG	AB	H	2B	3B	HR	RBI	BB	SO
Totals	.269	.341	.411	353	95	14	0	12	47	38	50
Pitching vs. Left and Right-handed Batters											
Left	.165	.224	.209	91	15	1	0	1	8	7	16
Right	.305	.379	.481	262	80	13	0	11	39	31	34
Situational											
Bases Empty	.289	.361	.448	194	56	7	0	8	8	21	30
Leadoff	.329	.394	.529	85	28	5	0	4	4	9	11
Not Leadoff	.257	.336	.385	109	28	2	0	4	4	12	19
Runners On	.245	.317	.365	159	39	7	0	4	39	17	20
First Base Only	.217	.229	.304	69	15	3	0	1	3	1	10
Scoring Position	.267	.373	.411	90	24	4	0	3	36	16	10
Late Innings, Close	.327	.414	.429	49	16	2	0	1	6	8	3

RBI/Opportunities		
Scoring Position	30 / 129	(23%)
Scoring Position, 2 Out	11 / 54	(20%)
On Third, Less than 2 Out	10 / 25	(40%)
RBI in close games / RBI Total	25 / 47	(53%)

Joe Price
Cincinnati Reds

1986: Power, Flyball 1985: Power, Flyball 1984: Power, Flyball

THREE YEARS (84 – 86)	G	IP	H	BB	SO	SB	CS	W	L	S	ERA
Totals	81	278.0	284	106	211	15	10	10	17	1	4.31
At Home and on the Road											
Home	41	157.1	157	60	112	8	5	7	6	0	3.78
Road	40	120.2	127	46	99	7	5	3	11	1	5.00
During the Day and and at Night											
Day	28	86.1	90	32	63	7	3	2	4	1	4.17
Night	53	191.2	194	74	148	8	7	8	13	0	4.37
On Grass and on Turf											
Grass	20	55.0	60	23	46	2	4	2	5	1	4.09
Turf	61	223.0	224	83	165	13	6	8	12	0	4.36
By Month											
April	16	40.2	43	9	33	4	1	2	2	0	3.98
May	21	49.1	49	27	37	1	1	2	2	0	5.11
June	15	65.1	74	23	41	5	3	2	4	0	4.55
July	9	50.2	53	23	44	3	1	1	5	0	4.44
August	14	45.0	38	12	33	0	2	2	4	1	3.40
Sept/Oct	6	27.0	27	12	23	2	2	1	2	0	4.00

vs. Opponent Batters

THREE YEARS (84 – 86)	Ave.	OBP	SLG	AB	H	2B	3B	HR	RBI	BB	SO
Totals	.262	.324	.416	1086	284	52	7	34	146	106	211
Pitching vs. Left and Right-handed Batters											
Left	.258	.306	.423	213	55	8	3	7	26	16	37
Right	.262	.329	.415	873	229	44	4	27	120	90	174
Situational											
Bases Empty	.244	.298	.384	623	152	28	1	19	19	47	124
Leadoff	.264	.322	.421	261	69	16	1	8	8	22	46
Not Leadoff	.229	.281	.354	362	83	12	0	11	11	25	78
Runners On	.285	.357	.460	463	132	24	6	15	127	59	87
First Base Only	.310	.361	.514	210	65	13	3	8	25	17	35
Scoring Position	.265	.354	.415	253	67	11	3	7	102	42	52
Late Innings, Close	.207	.260	.356	87	18	4	0	3	9	7	18

RBI/Opportunities		
Scoring Position	88 / 378	(23%)
Scoring Position, 2 Out	31 / 174	(18%)
On Third, Less than 2 Out	36 / 69	(52%)
RBI in close games / RBI Total	101 / 146	(69%)

Greg Pryor
Kansas City Royals

THREE YEARS (84 – 86)	Ave.	OBP	SLG	AB	H	2B	3B	HR	RBI	BB	SO
Totals	.232	.271	.302	496	115	18	1	5	35	24	54
Batting vs. Left and Right-handed Pitchers											
Left	.261	.288	.382	157	41	10	0	3	16	6	13
Right	.218	.263	.265	339	74	8	1	2	19	18	41
At Home and on the Road											
Home	.266	.305	.347	248	66	8	0	4	23	12	26
Road	.198	.237	.258	248	49	10	1	1	12	12	28
Facing Groundball Pitchers and Flyball Pitchers											
Groundball	.207	.247	.269	227	47	8	0	2	14	10	23
Flyball	.253	.291	.331	269	68	10	1	3	21	14	31
Facing Finesse Pitchers and Power Pitchers											
Finesse	.207	.248	.254	299	62	8	0	2	12	14	26
Power	.269	.306	.376	197	53	10	1	3	23	10	28
On Grass and on Turf											
Grass	.219	.251	.273	183	40	8	1	0	8	7	16
Turf	.240	.282	.319	313	75	10	0	5	27	17	38
During the Day and at Night											
Day	.267	.299	.374	131	35	3	1	3	11	6	13
Night	.219	.261	.277	365	80	15	0	2	24	18	41
By Month											
April	.277	.318	.398	83	23	2	1	2	7	4	8
May	.185	.214	.241	54	10	3	0	0	4	2	6
June	.228	.247	.329	79	18	5	0	1	5	2	4
July	.226	.255	.255	106	24	3	0	0	6	3	13
August	.277	.338	.369	65	18	0	0	2	7	5	4
Sept/Oct	.202	.254	.248	109	22	5	0	0	6	8	19
Situational											
Bases Empty	.239	.279	.329	289	69	12	1	4	4	16	35
Leadoff	.242	.260	.336	128	31	4	1	2	2	3	18
Not Leadoff	.236	.293	.323	161	38	8	0	2	2	13	17
Runners On	.222	.260	.266	207	46	6	0	1	31	8	19
First Base Only	.203	.212	.241	79	16	3	0	0	2	1	10
Scoring Position	.234	.288	.281	128	30	3	0	1	29	7	9
Late Innings, Close	.233	.289	.333	90	21	3	0	2	9	7	7

RBI/Opportunities		
Scoring Position	26 / 159	(16%)
Scoring Position, 2 Out	11 / 79	(14%)
On Third, Less than 2 Out	7 / 23	(30%)
RBI in close games / RBI Total	21 / 35	(60%)

Terry Puhl
Houston Astros

THREE YEARS (84 – 86)	Ave.	OBP	SLG	AB	H	2B	3B	HR	RBI	BB	SO
Totals	.285	.355	.413	815	232	43	10	14	92	92	92
Batting vs. Left and Right-handed Pitchers											
Left	.274	.328	.348	230	63	10	2	1	29	19	36
Right	.289	.366	.439	585	169	33	8	13	63	73	56
At Home and on the Road											
Home	.292	.363	.426	414	121	19	6	4	46	47	38
Road	.277	.347	.431	401	111	24	4	10	46	45	54
Facing Groundball Pitchers and Flyball Pitchers											
Groundball	.285	.360	.409	389	111	17	5	7	44	47	32
Flyball	.284	.351	.418	426	121	26	5	7	48	45	60
Facing Finesse Pitchers and Power Pitchers											
Finesse	.305	.366	.447	463	141	26	5	10	51	46	32
Power	.259	.341	.369	352	91	17	5	4	41	46	60
On Grass and on Turf											
Grass	.278	.345	.426	209	58	15	2	4	24	23	25
Turf	.287	.359	.409	606	174	28	8	10	68	69	67
During the Day and at Night											
Day	.275	.346	.427	178	49	10	2	6	27	22	17
Night	.287	.358	.402	637	183	33	8	8	65	70	75
By Month											
April	.267	.375	.349	86	23	3	2	0	10	15	6
May	.262	.308	.381	210	55	14	1	3	21	15	28
June	.321	.367	.447	159	51	9	1	3	25	13	19
July	.270	.352	.387	111	30	3	2	2	6	14	10
August	.338	.428	.515	136	46	9	3	3	17	22	14
Sept/Oct	.239	.317	.381	113	27	5	1	3	13	13	15
Situational											
Bases Empty	.290	.355	.416	486	141	25	3	10	10	49	47
Leadoff	.277	.317	.383	188	52	9	1	3	3	11	13
Not Leadoff	.299	.378	.436	298	89	16	2	7	7	38	34
Runners On	.277	.355	.410	329	91	18	7	4	82	43	45
First Base Only	.259	.315	.407	135	35	7	5	1	9	11	17
Scoring Position	.289	.380	.412	194	56	11	2	3	73	32	28
Late Innings, Close	.300	.414	.371	140	42	3	2	1	14	28	24

RBI/Opportunities		
Scoring Position	66 / 278	(24%)
Scoring Position, 2 Out	17 / 127	(13%)
On Third, Less than 2 Out	28 / 50	(56%)
RBI in close games / RBI Total	62 / 92	(67%)

Luis Quinones
San Francisco Giants

	Ave.	OBP	SLG	AB	H	2B	3B	HR	RBI	BB	SO
THREE YEARS (84 – 86)											
Totals	.179	.207	.245	106	19	1	3	0	11	3	17
Batting vs. Left and Right-handed Pitchers											
Left	.111	.138	.111	27	3	0	0	0	3	1	8
Right	.203	.232	.291	79	16	1	3	0	8	2	9
At Home and on the Road											
Home	.196	.208	.217	46	9	1	0	0	5	1	10
Road	.167	.206	.267	60	10	0	3	0	6	2	7
Facing Groundball Pitchers and Flyball Pitchers											
Groundball	.203	.226	.288	59	12	1	2	0	5	1	7
Flyball	.149	.184	.191	47	7	0	1	0	6	2	10
Facing Finesse Pitchers and Power Pitchers											
Finesse	.164	.200	.224	67	11	0	2	0	6	2	11
Power	.205	.220	.282	39	8	1	1	0	5	1	6
On Grass and on Turf											
Grass	.167	.185	.179	78	13	1	0	0	5	2	15
Turf	.214	.267	.429	28	6	0	3	0	6	1	2
During the Day and at Night											
Day	.204	.200	.222	54	11	1	0	0	7	0	6
Night	.154	.214	.269	52	8	0	3	0	4	3	11
By Month											
April	.000	.000	.000	0	0	0	0	0	0	0	0
May	.313	.313	.375	16	5	1	0	0	2	0	2
June	.280	.308	.520	25	7	0	3	0	6	1	1
July	.111	.100	.111	9	1	0	0	0	1	0	2
August	.136	.174	.136	22	3	0	0	0	2	1	4
Sept/Oct	.088	.139	.088	34	3	0	0	0	0	1	8
Situational											
Bases Empty	.140	.140	.211	57	8	0	2	0	0	0	11
Leadoff	.217	.217	.391	23	5	0	2	0	0	0	3
Not Leadoff	.088	.088	.088	34	3	0	0	0	0	0	8
Runners On	.224	.278	.286	49	11	1	1	0	11	3	6
First Base Only	.217	.250	.217	23	5	0	0	0	0	1	4
Scoring Position	.231	.300	.346	26	6	1	1	0	11	2	2
Late Innings, Close	.194	.194	.323	31	6	0	2	0	6	0	8

RBI/Opportunities		
Scoring Position	10 / 48	(21%)
Scoring Position, 2 Out	7 / 25	(28%)
On Third, Less than 2 Out	2 / 7	(29%)
RBI in close games / RBI Total	10 / 11	(91%)

Rey Quinones
Seattle Mariners

	Ave.	OBP	SLG	AB	H	2B	3B	HR	RBI	BB	SO
THREE YEARS (84 – 86)											
Totals	.218	.279	.295	312	68	16	1	2	22	24	57
Batting vs. Left and Right-handed Pitchers											
Left	.214	.274	.272	103	22	6	0	0	7	8	22
Right	.220	.281	.306	209	46	10	1	2	15	16	35
At Home and on the Road											
Home	.234	.284	.348	158	37	12	0	2	12	11	25
Road	.201	.273	.240	154	31	4	1	0	10	13	32
Facing Groundball Pitchers and Flyball Pitchers											
Groundball	.229	.290	.300	140	32	7	0	1	9	11	24
Flyball	.209	.269	.291	172	36	9	1	1	13	13	33
Facing Finesse Pitchers and Power Pitchers											
Finesse	.208	.260	.313	192	40	14	0	2	16	13	31
Power	.233	.308	.267	120	28	2	1	0	6	11	26
On Grass and on Turf											
Grass	.250	.320	.343	204	51	11	1	2	20	19	37
Turf	.157	.195	.204	108	17	5	0	0	2	5	20
During the Day and at Night											
Day	.221	.309	.326	86	19	6	0	1	4	9	11
Night	.217	.266	.283	226	49	10	1	1	18	15	46
By Month											
April	.000	.000	.000	0	0	0	0	0	0	0	0
May	.216	.420	.270	37	8	2	0	0	4	11	7
June	.209	.229	.299	67	14	1	1	1	7	2	7
July	.286	.324	.429	70	20	7	0	1	4	4	10
August	.193	.254	.246	57	11	3	0	0	2	4	10
Sept/Oct	.185	.214	.222	81	15	3	0	0	5	3	23
Situational											
Bases Empty	.202	.281	.260	173	35	7	0	1	1	18	32
Leadoff	.224	.283	.259	85	19	3	0	0	0	7	17
Not Leadoff	.182	.280	.261	88	16	4	0	1	1	11	15
Runners On	.237	.275	.338	139	33	9	1	1	21	6	25
First Base Only	.233	.281	.333	60	14	3	0	1	4	3	13
Scoring Position	.241	.271	.342	79	19	6	1	0	17	3	12
Late Innings, Close	.093	.204	.116	43	4	1	0	0	0	4	13

RBI/Opportunities		
Scoring Position	17 / 104	(16%)
Scoring Position, 2 Out	6 / 55	(11%)
On Third, Less than 2 Out	8 / 18	(44%)
RBI in close games / RBI Total	11 / 22	(50%)

Jamie Quirk
Kansas City Royals

	Ave.	OBP	SLG	AB	H	2B	3B	HR	RBI	BB	SO
THREE YEARS (84 – 86)											
Totals	.229	.279	.380	279	64	13	1	9	32	19	52
Batting vs. Left and Right-handed Pitchers											
Left	.125	.125	.125	16	2	0	0	0	1	0	6
Right	.236	.288	.395	263	62	13	1	9	31	19	46
At Home and on the Road											
Home	.238	.299	.430	151	36	9	1	6	17	12	27
Road	.219	.255	.320	128	28	4	0	3	15	7	25
Facing Groundball Pitchers and Flyball Pitchers											
Groundball	.242	.289	.359	153	37	6	0	4	20	10	26
Flyball	.214	.267	.405	126	27	7	1	5	12	9	26
Facing Finesse Pitchers and Power Pitchers											
Finesse	.266	.304	.408	169	45	10	1	4	20	10	29
Power	.173	.242	.336	110	19	3	0	5	12	9	23
On Grass and on Turf											
Grass	.238	.286	.393	84	20	1	0	4	14	6	17
Turf	.226	.276	.374	195	44	12	1	5	18	13	35
During the Day and at Night											
Day	.250	.287	.338	80	20	4	0	1	8	4	12
Night	.221	.276	.397	199	44	9	1	8	24	15	40
By Month											
April	.222	.200	.556	9	2	0	0	1	2	0	1
May	.241	.353	.345	29	7	3	0	0	0	5	5
June	.179	.256	.282	39	7	1	0	1	1	3	9
July	.188	.229	.219	32	6	1	0	0	4	2	8
August	.176	.222	.294	34	6	1	0	1	7	2	9
Sept/Oct	.265	.301	.463	136	36	7	1	6	18	7	20
Situational											
Bases Empty	.215	.260	.344	163	35	9	0	4	4	9	31
Leadoff	.279	.310	.368	68	19	6	0	0	0	3	13
Not Leadoff	.168	.225	.326	95	16	3	0	4	4	6	18
Runners On	.250	.305	.431	116	29	4	1	5	28	10	21
First Base Only	.304	.328	.464	56	17	3	0	2	6	2	12
Scoring Position	.200	.286	.400	60	12	1	1	3	22	8	9
Late Innings, Close	.246	.293	.377	69	17	6	0	1	8	5	10

RBI/Opportunities		
Scoring Position	18 / 84	(21%)
Scoring Position, 2 Out	2 / 42	(5%)
On Third, Less than 2 Out	12 / 16	(75%)
RBI in close games / RBI Total	26 / 32	(81%)

Floyd Rayford
Baltimore Orioles

	Ave.	OBP	SLG	AB	H	2B	3B	HR	RBI	BB	SO
THREE YEARS (84 – 86)											
Totals	.258	.291	.418	819	211	39	1	30	94	37	170
Batting vs. Left and Right-handed Pitchers											
Left	.286	.319	.499	339	97	15	0	19	44	17	67
Right	.237	.271	.360	480	114	24	1	11	50	20	103
At Home and on the Road											
Home	.281	.319	.453	402	113	22	1	15	52	21	79
Road	.235	.264	.384	417	98	17	0	15	42	16	91
Facing Groundball Pitchers and Flyball Pitchers											
Groundball	.265	.294	.410	388	103	21	1	11	43	16	77
Flyball	.251	.289	.425	431	108	18	0	19	51	21	93
Facing Finesse Pitchers and Power Pitchers											
Finesse	.278	.306	.439	421	117	21	1	15	39	16	73
Power	.236	.276	.394	398	94	18	0	15	55	21	97
On Grass and on Turf											
Grass	.274	.310	.448	701	192	36	1	28	87	35	138
Turf	.161	.175	.237	118	19	3	0	2	7	2	32
During the Day and at Night											
Day	.230	.265	.387	235	54	7	0	10	26	11	52
Night	.269	.302	.430	584	157	32	1	20	68	26	118
By Month											
April	.200	.231	.300	50	10	2	0	1	5	2	13
May	.182	.234	.283	99	18	4	0	2	14	6	22
June	.330	.353	.455	112	37	8	0	2	11	4	24
July	.263	.301	.401	167	44	8	0	5	11	7	38
August	.274	.293	.429	168	46	6	1	6	19	5	26
Sept/Oct	.251	.291	.489	223	56	11	0	14	34	13	47
Situational											
Bases Empty	.254	.297	.410	481	122	24	0	17	17	30	95
Leadoff	.238	.291	.421	202	48	10	0	9	9	9	41
Not Leadoff	.265	.317	.401	279	74	14	0	8	8	21	54
Runners On	.263	.282	.429	338	89	15	1	13	77	7	75
First Base Only	.297	.307	.486	148	44	5	1	7	18	1	29
Scoring Position	.237	.264	.384	190	45	10	0	6	59	6	46
Late Innings, Close	.203	.247	.391	138	28	8	0	6	18	8	39

RBI/Opportunities		
Scoring Position	48 / 248	(19%)
Scoring Position, 2 Out	21 / 111	(19%)
On Third, Less than 2 Out	16 / 35	(46%)
RBI in close games / RBI Total	54 / 94	(57%)

Gary Redus
Philadelphia Phillies

	Ave.	OBP	SLG	AB	H	2B	3B	HR	RBI	BB	SO
THREE YEARS (84 – 86)											
Totals	.251	.347	.405	980	246	57	11	24	83	143	201
Batting vs. Left and Right-handed Pitchers											
Left	.256	.379	.379	406	104	22	5	6	30	80	82
Right	.247	.323	.423	574	142	35	6	18	53	63	119
At Home and on the Road											
Home	.278	.377	.468	511	142	35	7	16	52	80	104
Road	.222	.314	.337	469	104	22	4	8	31	63	97
Facing Groundball Pitchers and Flyball Pitchers											
Groundball	.251	.336	.388	498	125	22	5	12	34	61	83
Flyball	.251	.358	.423	482	121	35	6	12	49	82	118
Facing Finesse Pitchers and Power Pitchers											
Finesse	.267	.358	.444	550	147	35	7	16	49	75	80
Power	.230	.333	.356	430	99	22	4	8	34	68	121
On Grass and on Turf											
Grass	.220	.314	.344	250	55	15	2	4	23	35	53
Turf	.262	.358	.426	730	191	42	9	20	60	108	148
During the Day and at Night											
Day	.243	.338	.430	342	83	22	6	10	26	49	72
Night	.255	.352	.392	638	163	35	5	14	57	94	129
By Month											
April	.291	.400	.410	117	34	9	1	1	8	21	21
May	.328	.373	.489	131	43	7	1	4	9	9	32
June	.216	.349	.373	153	33	11	2	3	16	31	25
July	.236	.321	.404	208	49	15	1	6	17	26	41
August	.241	.336	.426	216	52	8	4	8	20	31	40
Sept/Oct	.226	.333	.335	155	35	7	2	2	13	25	42
Situational											
Bases Empty	.252	.347	.408	671	169	39	9	16	16	94	138
Leadoff	.232	.323	.379	393	91	22	3	10	10	52	73
Not Leadoff	.281	.381	.450	278	78	17	6	6	6	42	65
Runners On	.249	.347	.398	309	77	18	2	8	67	49	63
First Base Only	.267	.340	.371	116	31	6	0	2	5	21	16
Scoring Position	.238	.328	.415	193	46	12	2	6	62	28	47
Late Innings, Close	.206	.312	.309	175	36	7	1	3	17	28	46

RBI/Opportunities

Scoring Position	55 / 274	(20%)
Scoring Position, 2 Out	29 / 153	(19%)
On Third, Less than 2 Out	13 / 33	(39%)
RBI in close games / RBI Total	55 / 83	(66%)

Jeff Reed
Minnesota Twins

	Ave.	OBP	SLG	AB	H	2B	3B	HR	RBI	BB	SO
THREE YEARS (84 – 86)											
Totals	.224	.293	.311	196	44	9	1	2	10	18	28
Batting vs. Left and Right-handed Pitchers											
Left	.273	.333	.273	11	3	0	0	0	0	0	3
Right	.222	.291	.314	185	41	9	1	2	10	18	25
At Home and on the Road											
Home	.227	.303	.328	119	27	9	1	0	8	13	17
Road	.221	.277	.286	77	17	0	1	2	2	5	11
Facing Groundball Pitchers and Flyball Pitchers											
Groundball	.333	.393	.457	81	27	2	1	2	6	8	10
Flyball	.148	.222	.209	115	17	7	0	0	4	10	18
Facing Finesse Pitchers and Power Pitchers											
Finesse	.210	.242	.311	119	25	6	0	2	4	5	13
Power	.247	.363	.312	77	19	3	1	0	6	13	15
On Grass and on Turf											
Grass	.143	.192	.143	49	7	0	0	0	0	2	9
Turf	.252	.325	.367	147	37	9	1	2	10	16	19
During the Day and at Night											
Day	.207	.274	.253	87	18	2	1	0	1	7	12
Night	.239	.308	.358	109	26	7	0	2	9	11	16
By Month											
April	.158	.273	.316	19	3	3	0	0	0	3	5
May	.200	.250	.267	15	3	1	0	0	0	1	1
June	.244	.320	.400	45	11	1	0	2	4	4	6
July	.125	.222	.125	16	2	0	0	0	3	2	2
August	.286	.324	.400	35	10	2	1	0	0	2	4
Sept/Oct	.227	.292	.258	66	15	2	0	0	2	6	10
Situational											
Bases Empty	.268	.316	.378	127	34	9	1	1	1	9	18
Leadoff	.273	.322	.382	55	15	3	0	1	1	4	7
Not Leadoff	.264	.312	.375	72	19	6	1	0	0	5	11
Runners On	.145	.253	.188	69	10	0	0	1	9	9	10
First Base Only	.171	.216	.257	35	6	0	0	1	2	2	4
Scoring Position	.118	.286	.118	34	4	0	0	0	7	7	6
Late Innings, Close	.364	.417	.455	22	8	2	0	0	1	2	0

RBI/Opportunities

Scoring Position	7 / 53	(13%)
Scoring Position, 2 Out	4 / 30	(13%)
On Third, Less than 2 Out	3 / 5	(60%)
RBI in close games / RBI Total	5 / 10	(50%)

Jerry Reuss
Los Angeles Dodgers

1986: Finesse, Groundball 1985: Finesse, Groundball 1984: Finesse, Groundball

	G	IP	H	BB	SO	SB	CS	W	L	S	ERA
THREE YEARS (84 – 86)											
Totals	83	385.2	408	106	157	24	17	21	23	2	3.71
At Home and on the Road											
Home	39	198.0	206	46	74	16	9	11	10	0	3.32
Road	44	187.2	202	60	83	8	8	10	13	2	4.12
During the Day and and at Night											
Day	24	112.2	122	32	43	10	6	5	7	0	3.91
Night	59	273.0	286	74	114	14	11	16	16	2	3.63
On Grass and on Turf											
Grass	60	280.2	290	73	106	18	11	15	15	1	3.46
Turf	23	105.0	118	33	51	6	6	6	8	1	4.37
By Month											
April	12	56.1	73	18	24	6	2	3	4	0	4.79
May	15	79.0	75	13	35	2	2	4	7	1	3.87
June	11	66.1	70	10	25	3	3	3	4	0	4.48
July	14	41.2	46	16	15	4	1	2	2	0	5.18
August	16	52.1	48	21	23	3	5	4	3	1	1.38
Sept/Oct	15	90.0	96	28	35	6	4	5	3	0	3.00

vs. Opponent Batters

	Ave.	OBP	SLG	AB	H	2B	3B	HR	RBI	BB	SO
THREE YEARS (84 – 86)											
Totals	.272	.321	.385	1498	408	61	9	30	148	106	157
Pitching vs. Left and Right-handed Batters											
Left	.268	.310	.364	228	61	6	2	4	26	12	29
Right	.273	.323	.389	1270	347	55	7	26	122	94	128
Situational											
Bases Empty	.268	.308	.378	884	237	36	8	15	15	47	93
Leadoff	.274	.314	.375	379	104	17	3	5	5	20	42
Not Leadoff	.263	.303	.380	505	133	19	5	10	10	27	51
Runners On	.279	.338	.396	614	171	25	1	15	133	59	64
First Base Only	.292	.337	.401	267	78	8	0	7	18	18	25
Scoring Position	.268	.339	.392	347	93	17	1	8	115	41	39
Late Innings, Close	.283	.346	.383	120	34	3	0	3	13	12	11

RBI/Opportunities

Scoring Position	100 / 462	(22%)
Scoring Position, 2 Out	33 / 205	(16%)
On Third, Less than 2 Out	39 / 77	(51%)
RBI in close games / RBI Total	109 / 148	(74%)

Harold Reynolds
Seattle Mariners

	Ave.	OBP	SLG	AB	H	2B	3B	HR	RBI	BB	SO
THREE YEARS (84 – 86)											
Totals	.209	.274	.272	559	117	22	5	1	30	46	57
Batting vs. Left and Right-handed Pitchers											
Left	.199	.269	.256	156	31	6	0	1	9	13	18
Right	.213	.276	.278	403	86	16	5	0	21	33	39
At Home and on the Road											
Home	.214	.284	.309	285	61	14	5	1	16	26	28
Road	.204	.264	.234	274	56	8	0	0	14	20	29
Facing Groundball Pitchers and Flyball Pitchers											
Groundball	.246	.307	.314	264	65	14	2	0	14	21	27
Flyball	.176	.245	.234	295	52	8	3	1	16	25	30
Facing Finesse Pitchers and Power Pitchers											
Finesse	.213	.268	.283	343	73	15	3	1	21	24	34
Power	.204	.283	.255	216	44	7	2	0	9	22	23
On Grass and on Turf											
Grass	.177	.237	.200	215	38	5	0	0	6	16	26
Turf	.230	.297	.317	344	79	17	5	1	24	30	31
During the Day and at Night											
Day	.219	.313	.274	146	32	6	1	0	10	19	22
Night	.206	.260	.271	413	85	16	4	1	20	27	35
By Month											
April	.037	.212	.074	27	1	1	0	0	0	6	3
May	.234	.279	.328	64	15	6	0	0	5	4	8
June	.218	.271	.255	110	24	4	0	0	3	5	12
July	.212	.286	.274	146	31	5	2	0	13	15	11
August	.152	.222	.182	99	15	3	0	0	3	9	9
Sept/Oct	.274	.322	.381	113	31	3	3	1	6	7	14
Situational											
Bases Empty	.214	.287	.284	341	73	15	3	1	1	31	34
Leadoff	.223	.303	.301	166	37	7	3	1	1	16	21
Not Leadoff	.206	.272	.269	175	36	8	0	1	1	15	13
Runners On	.202	.253	.252	218	44	7	2	0	29	15	23
First Base Only	.208	.245	.238	101	21	3	0	0	1	5	13
Scoring Position	.197	.260	.265	117	23	4	2	0	28	10	10
Late Innings, Close	.159	.266	.217	69	11	2	1	0	1	9	9

RBI/Opportunities

Scoring Position	27 / 172	(16%)
Scoring Position, 2 Out	12 / 93	(13%)
On Third, Less than 2 Out	8 / 24	(33%)
RBI in close games / RBI Total	15 / 30	(50%)

Ronn Reynolds
Philadelphia Phillies

THREE YEARS (84 – 86)	Ave.	OBP	SLG	AB	H	2B	3B	HR	RBI	BB	SO
Totals	.213	.239	.302	169	36	6	0	3	11	5	48
Batting vs. Left and Right-handed Pitchers											
Left	.247	.276	.411	73	18	3	0	3	7	3	21
Right	.188	.210	.219	96	18	3	0	0	4	2	27
At Home and on the Road											
Home	.267	.282	.360	75	20	4	0	1	8	1	22
Road	.170	.204	.255	94	16	2	0	2	3	4	26
Facing Groundball Pitchers and Flyball Pitchers											
Groundball	.224	.250	.342	76	17	3	0	2	6	2	17
Flyball	.204	.229	.269	93	19	3	0	1	5	3	31
Facing Finesse Pitchers and Power Pitchers											
Finesse	.247	.283	.376	93	23	3	0	3	10	4	28
Power	.171	.182	.211	76	13	3	0	0	1	1	20
On Grass and on Turf											
Grass	.171	.200	.195	82	14	2	0	0	2	2	27
Turf	.253	.275	.402	87	22	4	0	3	9	3	21
During the Day and at Night											
Day	.188	.207	.250	80	15	5	0	0	1	2	30
Night	.236	.266	.348	89	21	1	0	3	10	3	18
By Month											
April	.000	.000	.000	0	0	0	0	0	0	0	0
May	.500	.500	.500	2	1	0	0	0	1	0	1
June	.353	.421	.765	17	6	1	0	2	3	2	5
July	.231	.250	.308	39	9	3	0	0	0	0	12
August	.193	.220	.193	57	11	0	0	0	1	2	16
Sept/Oct	.167	.179	.259	54	9	2	0	1	6	1	14
Situational											
Bases Empty	.255	.283	.353	102	26	4	0	2	2	3	23
Leadoff	.227	.261	.341	44	10	2	0	1	1	1	12
Not Leadoff	.276	.300	.362	58	16	2	0	1	1	2	11
Runners On	.149	.171	.224	67	10	2	0	1	9	2	25
First Base Only	.135	.158	.243	37	5	1	0	1	2	1	14
Scoring Position	.167	.188	.200	30	5	1	0	0	7	1	11
Late Innings, Close	.194	.242	.226	31	6	1	0	0	0	2	7

RBI/Opportunities		
Scoring Position	6 / 34	(18%)
Scoring Position, 2 Out	3 / 15	(20%)
On Third, Less than 2 Out	2 / 6	(33%)
RBI in close games / RBI Total	6 / 11	(55%)

Jose Rijo
Oakland A's

1986: Power, Flyball   1985: Power, Flyball   1984: Power, Flyball

THREE YEARS (84 – 86)	G	IP	H	BB	SO	SB	CS	W	L	S	ERA
Totals	75	319.2	303	169	288	38	13	17	23	3	4.45
At Home and on the Road											
Home	30	133.1	116	77	122	15	8	6	7	1	3.98
Road	45	186.1	187	92	166	23	5	11	16	2	4.78
During the Day and and at Night											
Day	23	91.1	87	56	83	11	5	6	6	0	4.53
Night	52	228.1	216	113	205	27	8	11	17	3	4.41
On Grass and on Turf											
Grass	59	250.2	224	138	218	30	10	14	18	3	4.16
Turf	16	69.0	79	31	70	8	3	3	5	0	5.48
By Month											
April	14	50.1	43	24	60	7	3	1	4	1	4.83
May	12	55.1	47	37	48	9	2	2	3	0	3.42
June	19	36.1	48	25	32	7	2	1	7	2	6.94
July	7	43.1	40	16	39	4	1	2	2	0	3.12
August	10	58.2	48	32	44	5	2	4	3	0	4.45
Sept/Oct	13	75.2	77	35	65	6	3	7	4	0	4.52

vs. Opponent Batters THREE YEARS (84 – 86)	Ave.	OBP	SLG	AB	H	2B	3B	HR	RBI	BB	SO
Totals	.250	.342	.401	1211	303	58	10	35	163	169	288
Pitching vs. Left and Right-handed Batters											
Left	.266	.374	.436	621	165	32	7	20	101	107	137
Right	.234	.307	.364	590	138	26	3	15	62	62	151
Situational											
Bases Empty	.241	.333	.399	676	163	37	5	20	20	91	156
Leadoff	.253	.349	.418	292	74	17	2	9	9	42	69
Not Leadoff	.232	.320	.385	384	89	20	3	11	11	49	87
Runners On	.262	.354	.404	535	140	21	5	15	143	78	132
First Base Only	.258	.352	.449	198	51	10	2	8	22	29	42
Scoring Position	.264	.355	.377	337	89	11	3	7	121	49	90
Late Innings, Close	.289	.383	.421	152	44	5	3	3	21	23	27

RBI/Opportunities		
Scoring Position	106 / 476	(22%)
Scoring Position, 2 Out	37 / 211	(18%)
On Third, Less than 2 Out	39 / 76	(51%)
RBI in close games / RBI Total	124 / 163	(76%)

Luis Rivera
Montreal Expos

THREE YEARS (84 – 86)	Ave.	OBP	SLG	AB	H	2B	3B	HR	RBI	BB	SO
Totals	.205	.285	.283	166	34	11	1	0	13	17	33
Batting vs. Left and Right-handed Pitchers											
Left	.246	.312	.333	69	17	4	1	0	3	7	11
Right	.175	.266	.247	97	17	7	0	0	10	10	22
At Home and on the Road											
Home	.207	.275	.293	92	19	6	1	0	9	9	15
Road	.203	.298	.270	74	15	5	0	0	4	8	18
Facing Groundball Pitchers and Flyball Pitchers											
Groundball	.203	.300	.266	79	16	3	1	0	4	10	15
Flyball	.207	.271	.299	87	18	8	0	0	9	7	18
Facing Finesse Pitchers and Power Pitchers											
Finesse	.250	.288	.357	112	28	10	1	0	12	6	23
Power	.111	.279	.130	54	6	1	0	0	1	11	10
On Grass and on Turf											
Grass	.190	.277	.238	42	8	2	0	0	2	4	9
Turf	.210	.288	.298	124	26	9	1	0	11	13	24
During the Day and at Night											
Day	.190	.255	.214	42	8	1	0	0	2	4	8
Night	.210	.295	.306	124	26	10	1	0	11	13	25
By Month											
April	.000	.000	.000	0	0	0	0	0	0	0	0
May	.000	.000	.000	0	0	0	0	0	0	0	0
June	.000	.000	.000	0	0	0	0	0	0	0	0
July	.000	.000	.000	0	0	0	0	0	0	0	0
August	.187	.282	.267	75	14	4	1	0	6	10	12
Sept/Oct	.220	.287	.297	91	20	7	0	0	7	7	21
Situational											
Bases Empty	.188	.284	.271	96	18	6	1	0	0	11	19
Leadoff	.214	.327	.333	42	9	3	1	0	0	6	7
Not Leadoff	.167	.250	.222	54	9	3	0	0	0	5	12
Runners On	.229	.286	.300	70	16	5	0	0	13	6	14
First Base Only	.300	.344	.333	30	9	1	0	0	1	2	5
Scoring Position	.175	.244	.275	40	7	4	0	0	12	4	9
Late Innings, Close	.323	.364	.355	31	10	1	0	0	3	2	4

RBI/Opportunities		
Scoring Position	11 / 54	(20%)
Scoring Position, 2 Out	6 / 28	(21%)
On Third, Less than 2 Out	3 / 8	(38%)
RBI in close games / RBI Total	9 / 13	(69%)

Bip Roberts
San Diego Padres

THREE YEARS (84 – 86)	Ave.	OBP	SLG	AB	H	2B	3B	HR	RBI	BB	SO
Totals	.253	.293	.303	241	61	5	2	1	12	14	29
Batting vs. Left and Right-handed Pitchers											
Left	.203	.247	.268	138	28	4	1	1	6	8	16
Right	.320	.355	.350	103	33	1	1	0	6	6	13
At Home and on the Road											
Home	.237	.283	.271	118	28	2	1	0	8	8	16
Road	.268	.302	.333	123	33	3	1	1	4	6	13
Facing Groundball Pitchers and Flyball Pitchers											
Groundball	.229	.258	.248	157	36	1	1	0	6	6	18
Flyball	.298	.355	.405	84	25	4	1	1	6	8	11
Facing Finesse Pitchers and Power Pitchers											
Finesse	.239	.286	.304	138	33	2	2	1	6	9	12
Power	.272	.303	.301	103	28	3	0	0	6	5	17
On Grass and on Turf											
Grass	.257	.296	.289	187	48	4	1	0	10	11	27
Turf	.241	.292	.352	54	13	1	1	1	2	3	2
During the Day and at Night											
Day	.308	.344	.363	91	28	3	1	0	6	5	10
Night	.220	.263	.267	150	33	2	1	1	6	9	19
By Month											
April	.000	.048	.000	20	0	0	0	0	0	1	8
May	.348	.388	.413	46	16	1	1	0	2	3	5
June	.200	.224	.277	65	13	3	1	0	5	2	6
July	.240	.310	.280	25	6	1	0	0	2	3	2
August	.250	.294	.313	48	12	0	0	1	2	3	2
Sept/Oct	.378	.410	.378	37	14	0	0	0	1	1	6
Situational											
Bases Empty	.244	.284	.287	160	39	2	1	1	1	9	23
Leadoff	.189	.207	.200	90	17	1	0	0	0	2	17
Not Leadoff	.314	.377	.400	70	22	1	1	1	1	7	6
Runners On	.272	.310	.333	81	22	3	1	0	11	5	6
First Base Only	.297	.333	.405	37	11	2	1	0	1	2	3
Scoring Position	.250	.292	.273	44	11	1	0	0	10	3	3
Late Innings, Close	.200	.294	.200	30	6	1	0	0	1	4	4

RBI/Opportunities		
Scoring Position	9 / 70	(13%)
Scoring Position, 2 Out	4 / 29	(14%)
On Third, Less than 2 Out	5 / 12	(42%)
RBI in close games / RBI Total	7 / 12	(58%)

Billy Joe Robidoux
Milwaukee Brewers

	THREE YEARS (84 – 86)										
	Ave.	OBP	SLG	AB	H	2B	3B	HR	RBI	BB	SO
Totals	.216	.342	.310	232	50	10	0	4	29	45	52
Batting vs. Left and Right-handed Pitchers											
Left	.302	.404	.535	43	13	1	0	3	11	8	15
Right	.196	.327	.259	189	37	9	0	1	18	37	37
At Home and on the Road											
Home	.180	.328	.230	100	18	5	0	0	4	22	18
Road	.242	.353	.371	132	32	5	0	4	25	23	34
Facing Groundball Pitchers and Flyball Pitchers											
Groundball	.272	.366	.404	114	31	6	0	3	17	17	21
Flyball	.161	.320	.220	118	19	4	0	1	12	28	31
Facing Finesse Pitchers and Power Pitchers											
Finesse	.186	.290	.230	113	21	5	0	0	12	17	19
Power	.244	.388	.387	119	29	5	0	4	17	28	33
On Grass and on Turf											
Grass	.231	.351	.337	208	48	10	0	4	29	39	44
Turf	.083	.267	.083	24	2	0	0	0	0	6	8
During the Day and at Night											
Day	.198	.333	.283	106	21	3	0	2	16	22	24
Night	.230	.349	.333	126	29	7	0	2	13	23	28
By Month											
April	.333	.456	.460	63	21	5	0	1	12	15	15
May	.227	.346	.295	44	10	3	0	0	6	8	5
June	.171	.277	.171	41	7	0	0	0	2	6	5
July	.000	.667	.000	1	0	0	0	0	0	2	0
August	.000	.000	.000	0	0	0	0	0	0	0	0
Sept/Oct	.145	.268	.277	83	12	2	0	3	9	14	27
Situational											
Bases Empty	.175	.314	.246	114	20	5	0	1	1	23	28
Leadoff	.178	.351	.222	45	8	2	0	0	0	12	8
Not Leadoff	.174	.287	.261	69	12	3	0	1	1	11	20
Runners On	.254	.369	.373	118	30	5	0	3	28	22	24
First Base Only	.280	.390	.340	50	14	0	0	1	2	9	11
Scoring Position	.235	.354	.397	68	16	5	0	2	26	13	13
Late Innings, Close	.297	.500	.378	37	11	3	0	0	4	15	5

RBI/Opportunities		
Scoring Position	22 / 91	(24%)
Scoring Position, 2 Out	7 / 44	(16%)
On Third, Less than 2 Out	10 / 16	(63%)
RBI in close games / RBI Total	20 / 29	(69%)

Ron Robinson
Cincinnati Reds

1986: Power, Flyball 1985: Power, Flyball 1984: Finesse, Groundball

	THREE YEARS (84 – 86)										
	G	IP	H	BB	SO	SB	CS	W	L	S	ERA
Totals	115	264.2	252	88	217	23	19	18	12	15	3.47
At Home and on the Road											
Home	60	144.2	142	45	110	11	12	8	7	8	3.79
Road	55	120.0	110	43	107	12	7	10	5	7	3.08
During the Day and and at Night											
Day	41	87.1	69	29	73	7	5	6	3	7	2.58
Night	74	177.1	183	59	144	16	14	12	9	8	3.91
On Grass and on Turf											
Grass	38	83.0	74	31	73	6	6	7	3	5	2.60
Turf	77	181.2	178	57	144	17	13	11	9	10	3.86
By Month											
April	7	19.2	12	4	14	0	1	2	0	1	1.37
May	13	25.2	18	10	26	2	1	1	0	2	2.10
June	23	35.0	28	17	20	6	3	6	0	2	1.80
July	17	48.2	61	13	40	6	5	4	4	3	5.36
August	25	38.1	35	12	31	2	3	1	3	3	3.29
Sept/Oct	30	97.1	98	32	86	7	6	4	5	4	3.98

	vs. Opponent Batters THREE YEARS (84 – 86)										
	Ave.	OBP	SLG	AB	H	2B	3B	HR	RBI	BB	SO
Totals	.252	.312	.386	999	252	46	8	24	114	88	217
Pitching vs. Left and Right-handed Batters											
Left	.288	.363	.409	479	138	19	6	9	58	57	73
Right	.219	.264	.365	520	114	27	2	15	56	31	144
Situational											
Bases Empty	.254	.306	.382	591	150	33	5	11	11	43	144
Leadoff	.261	.300	.414	249	65	16	2	6	6	13	49
Not Leadoff	.249	.309	.360	342	85	17	3	5	5	30	95
Runners On	.250	.322	.392	408	102	13	3	13	103	45	73
First Base Only	.260	.306	.408	169	44	6	2	5	14	11	29
Scoring Position	.243	.332	.381	239	58	7	1	8	89	34	44
Late Innings, Close	.275	.340	.385	327	90	14	2	6	37	31	72

RBI/Opportunities		
Scoring Position	75 / 359	(21%)
Scoring Position, 2 Out	27 / 165	(16%)
On Third, Less than 2 Out	28 / 65	(43%)
RBI in close games / RBI Total	83 / 114	(73%)

Jeff Robinson
San Francisco Giants

1986: Power, Groundball 1985: Power, Groundball 1984: Finesse, Groundball

	THREE YEARS (84 – 86)										
	G	IP	H	BB	SO	SB	CS	W	L	S	ERA
Totals	106	288.1	303	94	200	30	9	13	18	8	4.15
At Home and on the Road											
Home	49	136.0	142	40	105	9	2	6	5	5	3.71
Road	57	152.1	161	54	95	21	7	7	13	3	4.55
During the Day and and at Night											
Day	52	144.2	159	50	99	13	2	5	8	4	4.48
Night	54	143.2	144	44	101	17	7	8	10	4	3.82
On Grass and on Turf											
Grass	80	209.0	223	64	144	16	6	10	10	6	3.92
Turf	26	79.1	80	30	56	14	3	3	8	2	4.76
By Month											
April	14	44.0	36	21	40	7	0	4	3	1	3.07
May	17	44.2	47	10	36	3	0	1	3	3	4.23
June	19	53.1	61	13	41	5	2	3	5	1	4.56
July	17	46.1	47	16	28	1	2	3	3	1	4.27
August	18	48.0	53	15	21	6	1	2	1	0	4.87
Sept/Oct	21	52.0	59	19	34	8	4	0	3	2	3.81

	vs. Opponent Batters THREE YEARS (84 – 86)										
	Ave.	OBP	SLG	AB	H	2B	3B	HR	RBI	BB	SO
Totals	.271	.328	.382	1119	303	45	7	22	133	94	200
Pitching vs. Left and Right-handed Batters											
Left	.301	.361	.445	571	172	28	6	14	69	54	79
Right	.239	.294	.318	548	131	17	1	8	64	40	121
Situational											
Bases Empty	.250	.304	.357	655	164	26	4	12	12	48	114
Leadoff	.258	.292	.352	287	74	15	0	4	4	14	42
Not Leadoff	.245	.312	.361	368	90	11	4	8	8	34	72
Runners On	.300	.362	.418	464	139	19	3	10	121	46	86
First Base Only	.307	.348	.397	189	58	9	1	2	7	10	33
Scoring Position	.295	.370	.433	275	81	10	2	8	114	36	53
Late Innings, Close	.247	.286	.357	182	45	3	1	5	19	9	44

RBI/Opportunities		
Scoring Position	97 / 398	(24%)
Scoring Position, 2 Out	38 / 157	(24%)
On Third, Less than 2 Out	41 / 89	(46%)
RBI in close games / RBI Total	85 / 133	(64%)

Gary Roenicke
New York Yankees

	THREE YEARS (84 – 86)										
	Ave.	OBP	SLG	AB	H	2B	3B	HR	RBI	BB	SO
Totals	.230	.353	.403	687	158	33	1	28	105	129	108
Batting vs. Left and Right-handed Pitchers											
Left	.238	.372	.428	432	103	20	1	20	76	91	66
Right	.216	.320	.361	255	55	13	0	8	29	38	42
At Home and on the Road											
Home	.248	.377	.454	335	83	12	0	19	60	68	52
Road	.213	.330	.355	352	75	21	1	9	45	61	56
Facing Groundball Pitchers and Flyball Pitchers											
Groundball	.238	.353	.437	302	72	10	1	16	49	53	45
Flyball	.223	.353	.377	385	86	23	0	12	56	76	63
Facing Finesse Pitchers and Power Pitchers											
Finesse	.233	.348	.418	335	78	14	0	16	57	58	40
Power	.227	.357	.389	352	80	19	1	12	48	71	68
On Grass and on Turf											
Grass	.240	.366	.429	574	138	27	0	27	96	112	88
Turf	.177	.285	.274	113	20	6	1	1	9	17	20
During the Day and at Night											
Day	.217	.326	.412	226	49	6	1	12	38	37	36
Night	.236	.366	.399	461	109	27	0	16	67	92	72
By Month											
April	.165	.306	.297	91	15	3	0	3	13	18	11
May	.295	.429	.464	112	33	8	1	3	13	26	23
June	.286	.372	.514	105	30	6	0	6	19	15	14
July	.224	.332	.394	165	37	4	0	8	27	27	24
August	.168	.327	.328	125	21	8	0	4	17	28	19
Sept/Oct	.247	.358	.427	89	22	4	0	4	16	15	17
Situational											
Bases Empty	.205	.327	.350	380	78	14	1	13	13	67	65
Leadoff	.189	.299	.277	159	30	5	0	3	3	24	18
Not Leadoff	.217	.347	.403	221	48	9	1	10	10	43	47
Runners On	.261	.384	.469	307	80	19	0	15	92	62	43
First Base Only	.263	.395	.444	133	35	6	0	6	15	27	13
Scoring Position	.259	.375	.489	174	45	13	0	9	77	35	30
Late Innings, Close	.206	.394	.299	97	20	3	0	2	12	29	11

RBI/Opportunities		
Scoring Position	61 / 257	(24%)
Scoring Position, 2 Out	22 / 130	(17%)
On Third, Less than 2 Out	24 / 48	(50%)
RBI in close games / RBI Total	69 / 105	(66%)

Ron Roenicke
Philadelphia Phillies

THREE YEARS (84 – 86)										
Ave.	OBP	SLG	AB	H	2B	3B	HR	RBI	BB	SO
Totals .252	.389	.379	428	108	23	2	9	57	98	84
Batting vs. Left and Right-handed Pitchers										
Left .311	.426	.432	132	41	7	0	3	18	28	26
Right .226	.372	.355	296	67	16	2	6	39	70	58
At Home and on the Road										
Home .270	.425	.428	222	60	13	2	6	30	61	46
Road .233	.347	.325	206	48	10	0	3	27	37	38
Facing Groundball Pitchers and Flyball Pitchers										
Groundball .279	.398	.400	190	53	11	0	4	23	39	37
Flyball .231	.381	.355	238	55	12	2	5	34	59	47
Facing Finesse Pitchers and Power Pitchers										
Finesse .263	.388	.397	232	61	13	0	6	28	48	40
Power .240	.390	.357	196	47	10	2	3	29	50	44
On Grass and on Turf										
Grass .247	.374	.374	190	47	10	1	4	21	39	37
Turf .256	.400	.382	238	61	13	1	5	36	59	47
During the Day and at Night										
Day .221	.355	.314	172	38	7	0	3	24	37	33
Night .273	.411	.422	256	70	16	2	6	33	61	51
By Month										
April .000	.000	.000	0	0	0	0	0	0	0	0
May .275	.326	.325	40	11	2	0	0	8	3	8
June .320	.445	.495	103	33	7	1	3	14	24	18
July .195	.330	.280	82	16	2	1	1	17	17	14
August .220	.412	.320	50	11	2	0	1	5	17	13
Sept/Oct .242	.387	.386	153	37	10	0	4	13	37	31
Situational										
Bases Empty .250	.388	.411	236	59	15	1	7	7	53	50
Leadoff .283	.400	.435	92	26	8	0	2	2	18	16
Not Leadoff .229	.380	.396	144	33	7	1	5	5	35	34
Runners On .255	.390	.339	192	49	8	1	2	50	45	34
First Base Only .260	.393	.411	73	19	6	1	1	7	16	7
Scoring Position .252	.388	.294	119	30	2	0	1	43	29	27
Late Innings, Close .258	.390	.323	93	24	4	1	0	18	22	17

RBI/Opportunities		
Scoring Position	42 / 192	(22%)
Scoring Position, 2 Out	18 / 76	(24%)
On Third, Less than 2 Out	17 / 38	(45%)
RBI in close games / RBI Total	45 / 57	(79%)

Ron Romanick
California Angels

1986: Finesse, Groundball   1985: Finesse, Flyball   1984: Finesse, Flyball

THREE YEARS (84 – 86)										
G	IP	H	BB	SO	SB	CS	W	L	S	ERA
Totals 82	531.0	574	167	189	35	18	31	29	0	4.24
At Home and on the Road										
Home 45	297.2	325	91	102	17	11	16	16	0	4.02
Road 37	233.1	249	76	87	18	7	15	13	0	4.51
During the Day and and at Night										
Day 22	139.0	149	50	56	18	5	8	6	0	3.95
Night 60	392.0	425	117	133	17	13	23	23	0	4.34
On Grass and on Turf										
Grass 69	453.2	478	144	155	24	17	27	22	0	3.93
Turf 13	77.1	96	23	34	11	1	4	7	0	6.05
By Month										
April 13	86.1	96	35	36	10	2	7	3	0	4.69
May 17	119.1	112	39	38	1	3	8	5	0	3.62
June 18	118.0	129	29	42	8	6	6	10	0	3.74
July 14	97.1	90	32	24	4	5	7	3	0	3.61
August 10	46.2	78	23	21	5	0	0	4	0	7.52
Sept/Oct 10	63.1	69	9	28	7	2	3	4	0	4.26

vs. Opponent Batters										
THREE YEARS (84 – 86)										
Ave.	OBP	SLG	AB	H	2B	3B	HR	RBI	BB	SO
Totals .279	.332	.429	2057	574	94	10	65	243	167	189
Pitching vs. Left and Right-handed Batters										
Left .278	.324	.427	1123	312	55	7	33	136	82	86
Right .281	.340	.431	934	262	39	3	32	107	85	103
Situational										
Bases Empty .284	.336	.439	1212	344	62	6	38	38	92	107
Leadoff .294	.335	.460	528	155	26	4	18	18	32	47
Not Leadoff .276	.336	.423	684	189	36	2	20	20	60	60
Runners On .272	.326	.415	845	230	32	4	27	205	75	82
First Base Only .277	.336	.427	405	112	14	1	15	34	34	33
Scoring Position .268	.317	.405	440	118	18	3	12	171	41	49
Late Innings, Close .320	.347	.475	181	58	8	1	6	19	8	18

RBI/Opportunities		
Scoring Position	149 / 596	(25%)
Scoring Position, 2 Out	53 / 268	(20%)
On Third, Less than 2 Out	64 / 108	(59%)
RBI in close games / RBI Total	163 / 243	(67%)

Ed Romero
Boston Red Sox

THREE YEARS (84 – 86)										
Ave.	OBP	SLG	AB	H	2B	3B	HR	RBI	BB	SO
Totals .240	.301	.294	841	202	34	1	3	75	73	62
Batting vs. Left and Right-handed Pitchers										
Left .225	.296	.289	325	73	18	0	1	22	33	20
Right .250	.304	.297	516	129	16	1	2	53	40	42
At Home and on the Road										
Home .231	.290	.299	428	99	18	1	3	31	35	28
Road .249	.312	.288	413	103	16	0	0	44	38	34
Facing Groundball Pitchers and Flyball Pitchers										
Groundball .258	.313	.318	400	103	16	1	2	38	32	26
Flyball .224	.290	.272	441	99	18	0	1	37	41	36
Facing Finesse Pitchers and Power Pitchers										
Finesse .242	.293	.297	491	119	22	1	1	46	34	34
Power .237	.312	.289	350	83	12	0	2	29	39	28
On Grass and on Turf										
Grass .246	.304	.299	725	178	28	1	3	68	62	54
Turf .207	.281	.259	116	24	6	0	0	7	11	8
During the Day and at Night										
Day .236	.289	.278	259	61	8	0	1	20	20	18
Night .242	.306	.301	582	141	26	1	2	55	53	44
By Month										
April .247	.356	.315	89	22	6	0	0	11	14	5
May .205	.250	.214	112	23	1	0	0	6	6	7
June .262	.316	.301	103	27	4	0	0	10	7	5
July .212	.281	.255	137	29	6	0	0	13	14	19
August .270	.314	.342	222	60	11	1	1	21	15	16
Sept/Oct .230	.297	.298	178	41	6	0	2	14	17	10
Situational										
Bases Empty .229	.296	.287	484	111	20	1	2	2	44	38
Leadoff .246	.310	.338	207	51	11	1	2	2	17	21
Not Leadoff .217	.286	.249	277	60	9	0	0	0	27	17
Runners On .255	.307	.303	357	91	14	0	1	73	29	24
First Base Only .241	.283	.277	137	33	5	0	0	1	7	10
Scoring Position .264	.321	.318	220	58	9	0	1	72	22	14
Late Innings, Close .298	.372	.366	131	39	9	0	0	12	16	14

RBI/Opportunities		
Scoring Position	69 / 324	(21%)
Scoring Position, 2 Out	32 / 157	(20%)
On Third, Less than 2 Out	26 / 51	(51%)
RBI in close games / RBI Total	42 / 75	(56%)

Pete Rose
Cincinnati Reds

THREE YEARS (84 – 86)										
Ave.	OBP	SLG	AB	H	2B	3B	HR	RBI	BB	SO
Totals .262	.364	.314	1016	266	35	6	2	105	156	93
Batting vs. Left and Right-handed Pitchers										
Left .261	.353	.311	161	42	6	1	0	12	23	14
Right .262	.366	.315	855	224	29	5	2	93	133	79
At Home and on the Road										
Home .260	.368	.310	493	128	19	3	0	53	76	43
Road .264	.361	.317	523	138	16	3	2	52	80	50
Facing Groundball Pitchers and Flyball Pitchers										
Groundball .244	.351	.285	480	117	16	2	0	48	76	40
Flyball .278	.376	.340	536	149	19	4	2	57	80	53
Facing Finesse Pitchers and Power Pitchers										
Finesse .246	.338	.288	586	144	16	3	1	53	76	47
Power .284	.398	.349	430	122	19	3	1	52	80	46
On Grass and on Turf										
Grass .299	.381	.363	278	83	8	2	2	31	37	24
Turf .248	.358	.295	738	183	27	4	0	74	119	69
During the Day and at Night										
Day .273	.371	.325	348	95	8	2	2	42	54	32
Night .256	.361	.308	668	171	27	4	0	63	102	61
By Month										
April .248	.343	.288	153	38	4	1	0	12	22	11
May .271	.373	.347	170	46	8	1	1	19	25	20
June .267	.373	.316	206	55	6	2	0	23	33	14
July .225	.335	.265	204	46	6	1	0	20	33	17
August .253	.329	.280	150	38	4	0	0	17	17	17
Sept/Oct .323	.442	.414	133	43	7	1	1	14	26	14
Situational										
Bases Empty .243	.330	.283	626	152	18	2	1	1	75	58
Leadoff .242	.329	.293	215	52	8	0	1	1	26	19
Not Leadoff .243	.330	.277	411	100	10	2	0	0	49	39
Runners On .292	.415	.364	390	114	17	4	1	104	81	35
First Base Only .277	.340	.328	137	38	3	2	0	4	13	13
Scoring Position .300	.449	.383	253	76	14	2	1	100	68	22
Late Innings, Close .308	.409	.367	169	52	4	3	0	16	27	20

RBI/Opportunities		
Scoring Position	92 / 380	(24%)
Scoring Position, 2 Out	42 / 168	(25%)
On Third, Less than 2 Out	30 / 63	(48%)
RBI in close games / RBI Total	70 / 105	(67%)

Jerry Royster
San Diego Padres

THREE YEARS (84 – 86)

	Ave.	OBP	SLG	AB	H	2B	3B	HR	RBI	BB	SO
Totals	.250	.322	.357	733	183	38	4	11	78	80	117
Batting vs. Left and Right-handed Pitchers											
Left	.273	.350	.398	447	122	29	3	7	43	55	56
Right	.213	.276	.294	286	61	9	1	4	35	25	61
At Home and on the Road											
Home	.251	.320	.372	347	87	22	1	6	39	36	54
Road	.249	.323	.345	386	96	16	3	5	39	44	63
Facing Groundball Pitchers and Flyball Pitchers											
Groundball	.264	.335	.363	397	105	16	4	5	48	44	59
Flyball	.232	.306	.351	336	78	22	0	6	30	36	58
Facing Finesse Pitchers and Power Pitchers											
Finesse	.259	.323	.367	417	108	24	3	5	38	40	55
Power	.237	.319	.345	316	75	14	1	6	40	40	62
On Grass and on Turf											
Grass	.243	.308	.340	530	129	26	2	7	53	50	84
Turf	.266	.356	.404	203	54	12	2	4	25	30	33
During the Day and at Night											
Day	.275	.337	.370	276	76	14	3	2	32	26	43
Night	.234	.313	.350	457	107	24	1	9	46	54	74
By Month											
April	.194	.206	.258	93	18	4	1	0	8	2	10
May	.271	.338	.398	133	36	12	1	1	19	14	17
June	.271	.381	.364	118	32	8	0	1	13	21	28
July	.255	.325	.353	102	26	4	0	2	7	11	13
August	.234	.296	.372	145	34	6	1	4	13	13	33
Sept/Oct	.261	.348	.366	142	37	4	1	3	18	19	16
Situational											
Bases Empty	.226	.297	.345	447	101	23	3	8	8	45	73
Leadoff	.219	.291	.354	237	52	11	0	7	7	24	38
Not Leadoff	.233	.303	.333	210	49	12	3	1	1	21	35
Runners On	.287	.359	.378	286	82	15	1	3	70	35	44
First Base Only	.267	.331	.371	116	31	4	1	2	6	10	14
Scoring Position	.300	.376	.382	170	51	11	0	1	64	25	30
Late Innings, Close	.217	.314	.312	138	30	5	1	2	16	20	18

RBI/Opportunities

Scoring Position	61 / 242	(25%)
Scoring Position, 2 Out	29 / 116	(25%)
On Third, Less than 2 Out	21 / 39	(54%)
RBI in close games / RBI Total	41 / 78	(53%)

Bruce Ruffin
Philadelphia Phillies

1986: Finesse, Groundball   1985: Did not play   1984: Did not play

THREE YEARS (84 – 86)

	G	IP	H	BB	SO	SB	CS	W	L	S	ERA
Totals	21	146.1	138	44	70	16	6	9	4	0	2.46
At Home and on the Road											
Home	12	87.2	82	25	36	5	3	6	2	0	2.16
Road	9	58.2	56	19	34	11	3	3	2	0	2.91
During the Day and and at Night											
Day	7	48.2	43	13	25	5	0	2	1	0	1.66
Night	14	97.2	95	31	45	11	6	7	3	0	2.86
On Grass and on Turf											
Grass	5	37.0	30	8	18	5	0	3	1	0	1.22
Turf	16	109.1	108	36	52	11	6	6	3	0	2.88
By Month											
April	0	0.0	0	0	0	0	0	0	0	0	0.00
May	0	0.0	0	0	0	0	0	0	0	0	0.00
June	1	6.1	7	1	5	1	0	0	0	0	4.26
July	6	45.0	42	14	18	2	3	3	2	0	3.00
August	6	43.1	35	10	24	6	0	4	1	0	1.45
Sept/Oct	8	51.2	54	19	23	7	3	2	1	0	2.61

vs. Opponent Batters
THREE YEARS (84 – 86)

	Ave.	OBP	SLG	AB	H	2B	3B	HR	RBI	BB	SO
Totals	.251	.306	.346	549	138	30	2	6	44	44	70
Pitching vs. Left and Right-handed Batters											
Left	.138	.216	.250	80	11	1	1	2	9	8	24
Right	.271	.322	.362	469	127	29	1	4	35	36	46
Situational											
Bases Empty	.252	.308	.342	325	82	16	2	3	3	25	45
Leadoff	.213	.265	.277	141	30	6	0	1	1	10	14
Not Leadoff	.283	.340	.391	184	52	10	2	2	2	15	31
Runners On	.250	.304	.353	224	56	14	0	3	41	19	25
First Base Only	.275	.321	.382	102	28	8	0	1	6	7	13
Scoring Position	.230	.290	.328	122	28	6	0	2	35	12	12
Late Innings, Close	.281	.314	.391	64	18	4	0	1	11	4	6

RBI/Opportunities

Scoring Position	31 / 157	(20%)
Scoring Position, 2 Out	9 / 72	(13%)
On Third, Less than 2 Out	16 / 31	(52%)
RBI in close games / RBI Total	34 / 44	(77%)

Vern Ruhle
California Angels

1986: Finesse, Groundball 1985: Finesse, Groundball 1984: Power, Groundball

THREE YEARS (84 – 86)

	G	IP	H	BB	SO	SB	CS	W	L	S	ERA
Totals	98	263.0	297	66	137	21	9	4	22	6	4.38
At Home and on the Road											
Home	41	118.2	128	27	61	12	4	2	7	5	4.85
Road	57	144.1	169	39	76	9	5	2	15	1	3.99
During the Day and and at Night											
Day	30	86.1	92	16	39	9	3	2	4	0	3.54
Night	68	176.2	205	50	98	12	6	2	18	6	4.79
On Grass and on Turf											
Grass	63	175.1	194	46	83	10	7	3	16	4	4.11
Turf	35	87.2	103	20	54	11	2	1	6	2	4.93
By Month											
April	13	35.0	37	14	21	4	0	1	3	1	3.34
May	9	24.2	19	6	17	0	1	0	1	1	2.92
June	10	45.0	59	15	25	5	3	1	4	0	5.20
July	20	58.1	79	10	25	6	2	1	7	0	5.71
August	22	54.1	57	15	25	2	2	1	4	2	4.64
Sept/Oct	24	45.2	46	6	24	4	1	0	3	2	3.15

vs. Opponent Batters
THREE YEARS (84 – 86)

	Ave.	OBP	SLG	AB	H	2B	3B	HR	RBI	BB	SO
Totals	.285	.329	.400	1041	297	37	2	26	131	66	137
Pitching vs. Left and Right-handed Batters											
Left	.271	.318	.369	501	136	14	1	11	45	34	64
Right	.298	.340	.428	540	161	23	1	15	86	32	73
Situational											
Bases Empty	.253	.292	.360	609	154	20	0	15	15	31	79
Leadoff	.279	.309	.388	258	72	10	0	6	6	10	34
Not Leadoff	.234	.281	.339	351	82	10	0	9	9	21	45
Runners On	.331	.379	.456	432	143	17	2	11	116	35	58
First Base Only	.344	.378	.457	186	64	6	0	5	12	8	23
Scoring Position	.321	.379	.455	246	79	11	2	6	104	27	35
Late Innings, Close	.234	.314	.291	141	33	2	0	2	16	16	24

RBI/Opportunities

Scoring Position	92 / 341	(27%)
Scoring Position, 2 Out	28 / 144	(19%)
On Third, Less than 2 Out	40 / 72	(56%)
RBI in close games / RBI Total	71 / 131	(54%)

Bill Russell
Los Angeles Dodgers

THREE YEARS (84 – 86)

	Ave.	OBP	SLG	AB	H	2B	3B	HR	RBI	BB	SO
Totals	.260	.321	.311	647	168	29	2	0	50	58	56
Batting vs. Left and Right-handed Pitchers											
Left	.297	.369	.350	317	94	15	1	0	25	37	21
Right	.224	.273	.273	330	74	14	1	0	25	21	35
At Home and on the Road											
Home	.255	.327	.287	314	80	10	0	0	27	34	20
Road	.264	.316	.333	333	88	19	2	0	23	24	36
Facing Groundball Pitchers and Flyball Pitchers											
Groundball	.262	.322	.309	301	79	12	1	0	20	26	25
Flyball	.257	.320	.312	346	89	17	1	0	30	32	31
Facing Finesse Pitchers and Power Pitchers											
Finesse	.263	.320	.305	377	99	16	0	0	29	32	21
Power	.256	.322	.319	270	69	13	2	0	21	26	35
On Grass and on Turf											
Grass	.262	.329	.308	477	125	22	0	0	41	48	37
Turf	.253	.298	.318	170	43	7	2	0	9	10	19
During the Day and at Night											
Day	.282	.340	.347	213	60	10	2	0	15	20	15
Night	.249	.312	.293	434	108	19	0	0	35	38	41
By Month											
April	.282	.357	.323	124	35	5	0	0	9	14	3
May	.239	.290	.315	92	22	3	2	0	6	7	11
June	.286	.341	.336	119	34	6	0	0	15	10	9
July	.283	.350	.315	127	36	4	0	0	10	13	9
August	.198	.253	.253	91	18	5	0	0	6	7	16
Sept/Oct	.245	.304	.309	94	23	6	0	0	4	7	8
Situational											
Bases Empty	.251	.299	.311	395	99	20	2	0	0	26	31
Leadoff	.286	.326	.346	133	38	6	1	0	0	7	7
Not Leadoff	.233	.285	.294	262	61	14	1	0	0	19	24
Runners On	.274	.354	.310	252	69	9	0	0	50	32	25
First Base Only	.291	.345	.336	110	32	5	0	0	3	8	8
Scoring Position	.261	.360	.289	142	37	4	0	0	47	24	17
Late Innings, Close	.268	.300	.289	142	38	3	0	0	10	6	14

RBI/Opportunities

Scoring Position	46 / 219	(21%)
Scoring Position, 2 Out	20 / 91	(22%)
On Third, Less than 2 Out	19 / 39	(49%)
RBI in close games / RBI Total	37 / 50	(74%)

Jeff Russell
Texas Rangers

1986: Power, Groundball   1985: Power, Groundball   1984: Finesse, Flyball

THREE YEARS (84 – 86)											
	G	IP	H	BB	SO	SB	CS	W	L	S	ERA
Totals	83	325.2	345	123	199	37	14	14	26	2	4.67
At Home and on the Road											
Home	37	149.1	167	50	93	21	7	8	7	1	4.76
Road	46	176.1	178	73	106	16	7	6	19	1	4.59
During the Day and and at Night											
Day	13	57.2	63	19	39	7	4	2	5	0	5.15
Night	70	268.0	282	104	160	30	10	12	21	2	4.57
On Grass and on Turf											
Grass	52	188.1	206	72	111	21	9	7	16	2	4.73
Turf	31	137.1	139	51	88	16	5	7	10	0	4.59
By Month											
April	5	24.0	30	12	11	3	1	1	3	0	3.75
May	6	29.0	30	9	20	1	1	1	2	0	4.97
June	11	56.0	54	17	27	4	3	2	4	0	3.70
July	15	48.2	49	16	28	4	3	2	4	0	4.44
August	26	90.2	97	43	49	14	2	6	8	1	5.16
Sept/Oct	20	77.1	85	26	64	11	4	2	5	1	5.12

vs. Opponent Batters										
THREE YEARS (84 – 86)										
	Ave.	OBP	SLG	AB	H	2B	3B	HR	RBI	BB	SO
Totals	.271	.337	.418	1272	345	63	8	36	172	123	199
Pitching vs. Left and Right-handed Batters											
Left	.293	.366	.450	587	172	38	3	16	85	68	88
Right	.253	.312	.391	685	173	25	5	20	87	55	111
Situational											
Bases Empty	.259	.323	.397	711	184	33	4	19	19	64	113
Leadoff	.273	.317	.405	311	85	10	2	9	9	20	47
Not Leadoff	.247	.328	.390	400	99	23	2	10	10	44	66
Runners On	.287	.353	.446	561	161	30	4	17	153	59	86
First Base Only	.327	.383	.500	208	68	11	2	7	19	17	29
Scoring Position	.263	.337	.414	353	93	19	2	10	134	42	57
Late Innings, Close	.171	.260	.247	158	27	6	0	2	3	18	31

RBI/Opportunities		
Scoring Position	113 / 482	(23%)
Scoring Position, 2 Out	56 / 217	(26%)
On Third, Less than 2 Out	35 / 78	(45%)
RBI in close games / RBI Total	118 / 172	(69%)

John Russell
Philadelphia Phillies

THREE YEARS (84 – 86)										
	Ave.	OBP	SLG	AB	H	2B	3B	HR	RBI	BB	SO
Totals	.240	.301	.429	630	151	41	3	24	94	55	208
Batting vs. Left and Right-handed Pitchers											
Left	.246	.333	.426	256	63	20	1	8	33	32	78
Right	.235	.277	.430	374	88	21	2	16	61	23	130
At Home and on the Road											
Home	.290	.348	.521	334	97	26	3	15	61	30	108
Road	.182	.248	.324	296	54	15	0	9	33	25	100
Facing Groundball Pitchers and Flyball Pitchers											
Groundball	.287	.342	.494	320	92	26	2	12	51	27	91
Flyball	.190	.258	.361	310	59	15	1	12	43	28	117
Facing Finesse Pitchers and Power Pitchers											
Finesse	.263	.309	.471	357	94	26	3	14	57	23	93
Power	.209	.290	.374	273	57	15	0	10	37	32	115
On Grass and on Turf											
Grass	.210	.305	.395	124	26	8	0	5	12	16	44
Turf	.247	.300	.437	506	125	33	3	19	82	39	164
During the Day and at Night											
Day	.244	.307	.442	197	48	16	1	7	35	17	61
Night	.238	.298	.423	433	103	25	2	17	59	38	147
By Month											
April	.226	.317	.340	53	12	3	0	1	5	6	22
May	.217	.379	.478	46	10	3	0	3	7	12	23
June	.253	.311	.470	83	21	9	0	3	17	6	28
July	.260	.289	.449	127	33	6	0	6	23	6	38
August	.261	.302	.435	138	36	13	1	3	13	9	34
Sept/Oct	.213	.276	.404	183	39	7	2	8	29	16	63
Situational											
Bases Empty	.206	.272	.381	344	71	22	1	12	12	29	127
Leadoff	.196	.263	.364	143	28	10	1	4	4	12	48
Not Leadoff	.214	.279	.393	201	43	12	0	8	8	17	79
Runners On	.280	.334	.486	286	80	19	2	12	82	26	81
First Base Only	.317	.363	.516	126	40	7	0	6	14	9	34
Scoring Position	.250	.314	.463	160	40	12	2	6	68	17	47
Late Innings, Close	.248	.280	.410	117	29	4	0	5	13	6	48

RBI/Opportunities		
Scoring Position	54 / 221	(24%)
Scoring Position, 2 Out	27 / 106	(25%)
On Third, Less than 2 Out	18 / 40	(45%)
RBI in close games / RBI Total	47 / 94	(50%)

Mark Salas
Minnesota Twins

THREE YEARS (84 – 86)										
	Ave.	OBP	SLG	AB	H	2B	3B	HR	RBI	BB	SO
Totals	.266	.305	.418	638	170	17	9	17	75	36	72
Batting vs. Left and Right-handed Pitchers											
Left	.268	.348	.341	41	11	1	1	0	7	5	7
Right	.266	.302	.424	597	159	27	8	17	68	31	65
At Home and on the Road											
Home	.274	.311	.462	329	90	15	7	11	39	19	39
Road	.259	.298	.372	309	80	13	2	6	36	17	33
Facing Groundball Pitchers and Flyball Pitchers											
Groundball	.278	.309	.422	320	89	12	8	6	40	16	32
Flyball	.255	.301	.415	318	81	16	1	11	35	20	40
Facing Finesse Pitchers and Power Pitchers											
Finesse	.296	.321	.468	348	103	16	4	12	48	14	27
Power	.231	.287	.359	290	67	12	5	5	27	22	45
On Grass and on Turf											
Grass	.259	.305	.350	243	63	10	0	4	26	15	24
Turf	.271	.305	.461	395	107	18	9	13	49	21	48
During the Day and at Night											
Day	.246	.281	.430	207	51	10	2	8	22	10	24
Night	.276	.316	.413	431	119	18	7	9	53	26	48
By Month											
April	.270	.308	.480	100	27	2	2	5	18	6	10
May	.286	.325	.375	112	32	3	2	1	12	7	14
June	.300	.347	.389	90	27	2	0	2	11	6	12
July	.243	.292	.351	111	27	7	1	1	9	8	14
August	.186	.221	.340	97	18	3	3	2	12	4	10
Sept/Oct	.305	.331	.547	128	39	11	1	6	13	5	12
Situational											
Bases Empty	.242	.280	.390	356	86	18	4	9	9	18	38
Leadoff	.204	.242	.357	157	32	5	2	5	5	8	13
Not Leadoff	.271	.310	.417	199	54	13	2	4	4	10	25
Runners On	.298	.336	.454	282	84	10	5	8	66	18	34
First Base Only	.375	.395	.508	120	45	6	2	2	9	3	10
Scoring Position	.241	.295	.414	162	39	4	3	6	57	15	24
Late Innings, Close	.248	.291	.358	109	27	2	2	2	14	6	18

RBI/Opportunities		
Scoring Position	46 / 217	(21%)
Scoring Position, 2 Out	22 / 104	(21%)
On Third, Less than 2 Out	15 / 40	(38%)
RBI in close games / RBI Total	55 / 75	(73%)

Angel Salazar
Kansas City Royals

THREE YEARS (84 – 86)										
	Ave.	OBP	SLG	AB	H	2B	3B	HR	RBI	BB	SO
Totals	.212	.234	.280	472	100	24	4	0	36	11	84
Batting vs. Left and Right-handed Pitchers											
Left	.298	.307	.384	151	45	11	1	0	15	2	17
Right	.171	.200	.231	321	55	13	3	0	21	9	67
At Home and on the Road											
Home	.217	.235	.275	207	45	8	2	0	16	2	31
Road	.208	.233	.283	265	55	16	2	0	20	9	53
Facing Groundball Pitchers and Flyball Pitchers											
Groundball	.204	.225	.246	211	43	7	1	0	11	5	32
Flyball	.218	.241	.307	261	57	17	3	0	25	6	52
Facing Finesse Pitchers and Power Pitchers											
Finesse	.228	.243	.292	281	64	16	1	0	20	4	42
Power	.188	.220	.262	191	36	8	3	0	16	7	42
On Grass and on Turf											
Grass	.202	.225	.259	193	39	9	1	0	11	6	36
Turf	.219	.240	.294	279	61	15	3	0	25	5	48
During the Day and at Night											
Day	.149	.164	.211	161	24	4	3	0	16	2	35
Night	.244	.269	.315	311	76	20	1	0	20	9	49
By Month											
April	.182	.217	.264	110	20	5	2	0	7	4	20
May	.231	.263	.278	108	25	5	0	0	9	3	16
June	.203	.203	.278	79	16	4	1	0	5	0	15
July	.182	.203	.260	77	14	6	0	0	3	2	16
August	.268	.276	.357	56	15	3	1	0	7	1	9
Sept/Oct	.238	.256	.262	42	10	1	0	0	5	1	8
Situational											
Bases Empty	.198	.226	.264	273	54	16	1	0	0	7	44
Leadoff	.200	.220	.267	120	24	8	0	0	0	3	16
Not Leadoff	.196	.231	.261	153	30	8	1	0	0	4	28
Runners On	.231	.244	.302	199	46	8	3	0	36	4	40
First Base Only	.198	.207	.233	86	17	1	1	0	2	1	19
Scoring Position	.257	.271	.354	113	29	7	2	0	34	3	21
Late Innings, Close	.216	.216	.235	51	11	1	0	0	3	0	7

RBI/Opportunities		
Scoring Position	31 / 150	(21%)
Scoring Position, 2 Out	11 / 69	(16%)
On Third, Less than 2 Out	14 / 22	(64%)
RBI in close games / RBI Total	20 / 36	(56%)

Joe Sambito
Boston Red Sox

1986: Power, Flyball   1985: Power, Groundball   1984: Finesse, Flyball

THREE YEARS (84 – 86)

	G	IP	H	BB	SO	SB	CS	W	L	S	ERA
Totals	93	103.0	114	40	59	9	3	2	0	12	4.81
At Home and on the Road											
Home	49	61.1	58	18	31	4	2	1	0	6	3.52
Road	44	41.2	56	22	28	5	1	1	0	6	6.70
During the Day and and at Night											
Day	32	29.2	41	14	18	1	2	1	0	3	8.19
Night	61	73.1	73	26	41	8	1	1	0	9	3.44
On Grass and on Turf											
Grass	62	60.1	71	19	42	1	3	2	0	12	5.07
Turf	31	42.2	43	21	17	8	0	0	0	0	4.43
By Month											
April	6	2.2	2	0	0	1	0	0	0	1	3.37
May	18	15.0	15	4	8	0	1	1	0	3	4.20
June	21	29.1	28	13	16	3	1	0	0	2	3.99
July	20	24.1	34	9	15	1	1	0	0	3	5.55
August	14	16.0	21	9	9	3	0	1	0	2	7.31
Sept/Oct	14	15.2	14	5	11	1	0	0	0	1	3.45

vs. Opponent Batters
THREE YEARS (84 – 86)

	Ave.	OBP	SLG	AB	H	2B	3B	HR	RBI	BB	SO
Totals	.284	.348	.418	402	114	22	1	10	76	40	59
Pitching vs. Left and Right-handed Batters											
Left	.182	.283	.226	137	25	6	0	0	18	18	34
Right	.336	.384	.517	265	89	16	1	10	58	22	25
Situational											
Bases Empty	.274	.332	.409	186	51	11	1	4	4	15	23
Leadoff	.244	.306	.372	78	19	2	1	2	2	6	12
Not Leadoff	.296	.350	.435	108	32	9	0	2	2	9	11
Runners On	.292	.362	.426	216	63	11	0	6	72	25	36
First Base Only	.229	.304	.337	83	19	3	0	2	4	9	15
Scoring Position	.331	.396	.481	133	44	8	0	4	68	16	21
Late Innings, Close	.250	.291	.350	80	20	2	0	2	13	4	13

RBI/Opportunities

Scoring Position	60 / 202	(30%)
Scoring Position, 2 Out	19 / 84	(23%)
On Third, Less than 2 Out	24 / 50	(48%)
RBI in close games / RBI Total	14 / 76	(18%)

Scott Sanderson
Chicago Cubs

1986: Finesse, Flyball   1985: Finesse, Flyball   1984: Finesse, Flyball

THREE YEARS (84 – 86)

	G	IP	H	BB	SO	SB	CS	W	L	S	ERA
Totals	80	431.1	405	88	280	25	25	22	22	1	3.55
At Home and on the Road											
Home	39	217.1	187	50	151	14	9	13	10	0	3.35
Road	41	214.0	218	38	129	11	16	9	12	1	3.74
During the Day and and at Night											
Day	50	274.2	239	60	196	16	14	15	12	0	3.37
Night	30	156.2	166	28	84	9	11	7	10	1	3.85
On Grass and on Turf											
Grass	58	326.1	303	68	226	18	19	18	16	0	3.31
Turf	22	105.0	102	20	54	7	6	4	6	1	4.29
By Month											
April	11	72.1	62	12	42	3	5	5	3	0	2.74
May	17	95.2	89	21	63	3	4	5	1	0	3.20
June	9	60.1	45	14	43	0	2	1	5	0	3.43
July	14	76.1	72	16	55	6	9	5	4	0	3.42
August	14	76.1	91	18	45	8	5	2	7	0	5.78
Sept/Oct	15	50.1	46	7	32	5	0	4	2	1	2.32

vs. Opponent Batters
THREE YEARS (84 – 86)

	Ave.	OBP	SLG	AB	H	2B	3B	HR	RBI	BB	SO
Totals	.250	.287	.395	1617	405	80	18	39	163	88	280
Pitching vs. Left and Right-handed Batters											
Left	.246	.287	.406	896	220	45	12	25	85	56	136
Right	.257	.288	.380	721	185	35	6	14	78	32	144
Situational											
Bases Empty	.249	.286	.397	1025	255	53	12	25	25	54	183
Leadoff	.253	.282	.391	427	108	25	5	8	8	17	57
Not Leadoff	.246	.290	.401	598	147	28	7	17	17	37	126
Runners On	.253	.289	.390	592	150	27	6	14	138	34	97
First Base Only	.269	.301	.402	264	71	13	2	6	20	10	31
Scoring Position	.241	.281	.381	328	79	14	4	8	118	24	66
Late Innings, Close	.235	.270	.319	119	28	1	0	3	8	6	16

RBI/Opportunities

Scoring Position	100 / 411	(24%)
Scoring Position, 2 Out	32 / 186	(17%)
On Third, Less than 2 Out	49 / 85	(58%)
RBI in close games / RBI Total	128 / 163	(79%)

Billy Sample
Atlanta Braves

THREE YEARS (84 – 86)

	Ave.	OBP	SLG	AB	H	2B	3B	HR	RBI	BB	SO
Totals	.263	.307	.355	828	218	36	2	12	62	52	82
Batting vs. Left and Right-handed Pitchers											
Left	.289	.336	.396	439	127	21	1	8	35	29	37
Right	.234	.274	.308	389	91	15	1	4	27	23	45
At Home and on the Road											
Home	.248	.292	.336	432	107	22	2	4	21	24	49
Road	.280	.324	.376	396	111	14	0	8	41	28	33
Facing Groundball Pitchers and Flyball Pitchers											
Groundball	.260	.307	.345	411	107	22	2	3	26	27	39
Flyball	.266	.307	.365	417	111	14	0	9	36	25	43
Facing Finesse Pitchers and Power Pitchers											
Finesse	.255	.288	.341	487	124	19	1	7	26	21	43
Power	.276	.334	.375	341	94	17	1	5	36	31	39
On Grass and on Turf											
Grass	.263	.306	.341	674	177	28	2	7	45	41	72
Turf	.266	.314	.416	154	41	8	0	5	17	11	10
During the Day and at Night											
Day	.271	.317	.422	166	45	8	1	5	17	10	10
Night	.261	.305	.338	662	173	28	1	7	45	42	72
By Month											
April	.242	.283	.323	99	24	0	1	2	7	6	9
May	.345	.376	.462	171	59	8	0	4	15	10	19
June	.212	.270	.307	179	38	6	1	3	15	13	15
July	.165	.202	.211	109	18	5	0	0	3	4	16
August	.320	.363	.402	169	54	11	0	1	12	12	12
Sept/Oct	.248	.297	.366	101	25	6	0	2	10	7	11
Situational											
Bases Empty	.265	.311	.359	543	144	24	0	9	9	32	50
Leadoff	.255	.300	.366	298	76	12	0	7	7	18	28
Not Leadoff	.278	.324	.351	245	68	12	0	2	2	14	22
Runners On	.260	.301	.347	285	74	12	2	3	53	20	32
First Base Only	.299	.326	.354	127	38	4	0	1	3	5	10
Scoring Position	.228	.283	.342	158	36	8	2	2	50	15	22
Late Innings, Close	.229	.281	.293	140	32	7	1	0	11	11	17

RBI/Opportunities

Scoring Position	45 / 221	(20%)
Scoring Position, 2 Out	14 / 97	(14%)
On Third, Less than 2 Out	22 / 51	(43%)
RBI in close games / RBI Total	42 / 62	(68%)

Rafael Santana
New York Mets

THREE YEARS (84 – 86)

	Ave.	OBP	SLG	AB	H	2B	3B	HR	RBI	BB	SO
Totals	.246	.294	.296	1075	264	41	2	3	69	74	114
Batting vs. Left and Right-handed Pitchers											
Left	.267	.329	.319	408	109	13	1	2	25	38	43
Right	.232	.272	.282	667	155	28	1	1	44	36	71
At Home and on the Road											
Home	.229	.280	.276	510	117	19	1	1	33	36	57
Road	.260	.307	.313	565	147	22	1	2	36	38	57
Facing Groundball Pitchers and Flyball Pitchers											
Groundball	.246	.294	.303	508	125	19	2	2	36	34	55
Flyball	.245	.295	.289	567	139	22	0	1	33	40	59
Facing Finesse Pitchers and Power Pitchers											
Finesse	.246	.286	.298	601	148	25	0	2	40	33	60
Power	.245	.304	.293	474	116	16	2	1	29	41	54
On Grass and on Turf											
Grass	.241	.287	.295	743	179	32	1	2	49	47	80
Turf	.256	.310	.298	332	85	9	1	1	20	27	34
During the Day and at Night											
Day	.212	.262	.255	415	88	13	1	1	28	28	40
Night	.267	.314	.321	660	176	28	1	2	41	46	74
By Month											
April	.176	.239	.235	102	18	3	0	1	7	9	14
May	.205	.242	.238	122	25	4	0	0	3	5	17
June	.252	.301	.282	163	41	5	0	0	15	12	10
July	.254	.298	.283	205	52	6	0	0	7	13	21
August	.294	.325	.360	272	80	15	0	1	20	12	17
Sept/Oct	.227	.302	.299	211	48	8	2	1	17	23	25
Situational											
Bases Empty	.258	.300	.310	632	163	26	2	1	1	36	78
Leadoff	.268	.309	.327	269	72	12	2	0	0	15	25
Not Leadoff	.251	.294	.298	363	91	14	0	1	1	21	53
Runners On	.228	.286	.275	443	101	15	0	2	68	38	36
First Base Only	.262	.284	.318	195	51	5	0	2	5	6	10
Scoring Position	.202	.288	.242	248	50	10	0	0	63	32	26
Late Innings, Close	.234	.284	.261	184	43	5	0	0	5	13	28

RBI/Opportunities

Scoring Position	62 / 335	(19%)
Scoring Position, 2 Out	20 / 171	(12%)
On Third, Less than 2 Out	31 / 63	(49%)
RBI in close games / RBI Total	48 / 69	(70%)

Dan Schatzeder
Philadelphia Phillies

1986: Finesse, Flyball   1985: Finesse, Flyball   1984: Finesse, Flyball

THREE YEARS (84 – 86)

	G	IP	H	BB	SO	SB	CS	W	L	S	ERA
Totals	115	328.2	294	102	200	32	9	16	17	2	3.20
At Home and on the Road											
Home	62	190.0	155	51	124	19	2	12	7	1	2.32
Road	53	138.2	139	51	76	13	7	4	10	1	4.41
During the Day and and at Night											
Day	48	127.0	123	36	67	6	2	8	9	0	3.97
Night	67	201.2	171	66	133	26	7	8	8	2	2.72
On Grass and on Turf											
Grass	30	82.2	90	26	42	5	2	3	8	1	5.12
Turf	85	246.0	204	76	158	27	7	13	9	1	2.56
By Month											
April	19	35.2	42	12	22	0	1	0	2	0	5.30
May	22	58.1	51	14	27	2	2	4	2	1	2.78
June	20	61.1	41	17	43	6	1	3	2	0	1.76
July	18	57.0	50	18	37	3	0	2	2	1	3.32
August	16	60.0	53	18	28	8	2	3	5	0	3.30
Sept/Oct	20	56.1	57	23	43	13	3	4	4	0	3.67

vs. Opponent Batters
THREE YEARS (84 – 86)

	Ave.	OBP	SLG	AB	H	2B	3B	HR	RBI	BB	SO
Totals	.240	.298	.383	1223	294	52	9	35	129	102	200
Pitching vs. Left and Right-handed Batters											
Left	.244	.286	.302	262	64	10	1	1	27	16	50
Right	.239	.301	.406	961	230	42	8	34	102	86	150
Situational											
Bases Empty	.244	.305	.395	750	183	33	7	22	22	65	121
Leadoff	.238	.284	.392	311	74	14	2	10	10	20	42
Not Leadoff	.248	.320	.396	439	109	19	5	12	12	45	79
Runners On	.235	.286	.366	473	111	19	2	13	107	37	79
First Base Only	.230	.268	.380	213	49	7	2	7	17	11	33
Scoring Position	.238	.300	.354	260	62	12	0	6	90	26	46
Late Innings, Close	.222	.303	.355	203	45	5	2	6	17	24	25

RBI/Opportunities

Scoring Position	74 / 347	(21%)
Scoring Position, 2 Out	28 / 152	(18%)
On Third, Less than 2 Out	29 / 71	(41%)
RBI in close games / RBI Total	67 / 129	(52%)

Calvin Schiraldi
Boston Red Sox

1986: Power, Flyball   1985: Power, Flyball   1984: Power, Groundball

THREE YEARS (84 – 86)

	G	IP	H	BB	SO	SB	CS	W	L	S	ERA
Totals	40	94.2	99	36	92	12	2	6	5	9	4.28
At Home and on the Road											
Home	15	29.2	39	6	30	6	0	3	2	2	4.25
Road	25	65.0	60	30	62	6	2	3	3	7	4.29
During the Day and and at Night											
Day	17	39.0	41	14	42	6	1	3	1	3	3.46
Night	23	55.2	58	22	50	6	1	3	4	6	4.85
On Grass and on Turf											
Grass	27	63.1	61	22	59	7	2	5	3	6	2.84
Turf	13	31.1	38	14	33	5	0	1	2	3	7.18
By Month											
April	2	6.2	9	2	2	0	0	1	0	0	6.75
May	2	7.0	6	7	8	0	1	0	0	0	3.86
June	5	12.0	26	2	10	4	0	1	1	0	12.75
July	4	12.2	10	6	12	2	1	0	0	0	0.71
August	12	20.1	11	3	24	1	0	2	1	6	1.33
Sept/Oct	15	36.0	37	16	36	5	0	2	3	3	4.00

vs. Opponent Batters
THREE YEARS (84 – 86)

	Ave.	OBP	SLG	AB	H	2B	3B	HR	RBI	BB	SO
Totals	.270	.342	.434	366	99	16	4	12	50	36	92
Pitching vs. Left and Right-handed Batters											
Left	.253	.322	.418	182	46	4	1	8	22	18	38
Right	.288	.361	.451	184	53	12	3	4	28	18	54
Situational											
Bases Empty	.279	.343	.431	197	55	8	2	6	6	17	45
Leadoff	.310	.363	.548	84	26	2	0	6	6	7	14
Not Leadoff	.257	.328	.345	113	29	6	2	0	0	10	31
Runners On	.260	.340	.438	169	44	8	2	6	44	19	47
First Base Only	.269	.338	.463	67	18	4	0	3	7	7	16
Scoring Position	.255	.342	.422	102	26	4	2	3	37	12	31
Late Innings, Close	.207	.258	.390	82	17	3	0	4	10	6	28

RBI/Opportunities

Scoring Position	30 / 138	(22%)
Scoring Position, 2 Out	11 / 61	(18%)
On Third, Less than 2 Out	13 / 24	(54%)
RBI in close games / RBI Total	22 / 50	(44%)

Dave Schmidt
Chicago White Sox

1986: Finesse, Groundball 1985: Finesse, Groundball   1984: Power, Groundball

THREE YEARS (84 – 86)

	G	IP	H	BB	SO	SB	CS	W	L	S	ERA
Totals	143	248.1	244	69	159	22	5	16	18	25	3.04
At Home and on the Road											
Home	74	132.1	123	31	82	14	2	10	8	17	2.99
Road	69	116.0	121	38	77	8	3	6	10	8	3.10
During the Day and and at Night											
Day	29	43.0	40	9	31	2	1	2	3	2	2.93
Night	114	205.1	204	60	128	20	4	14	15	23	3.07
On Grass and on Turf											
Grass	120	208.0	197	52	133	18	5	14	16	21	2.99
Turf	23	40.1	47	17	26	4	0	2	2	4	3.35
By Month											
April	18	33.2	34	5	26	5	2	1	1	1	4.01
May	20	36.2	42	13	18	8	1	1	5	2	3.93
June	24	50.1	42	10	37	2	1	4	1	3	2.15
July	31	41.1	32	13	24	1	0	1	3	10	1.74
August	29	41.1	45	11	29	3	1	5	4	7	2.40
Sept/Oct	21	45.0	49	17	25	3	0	4	4	2	4.40

vs. Opponent Batters
THREE YEARS (84 – 86)

	Ave.	OBP	SLG	AB	H	2B	3B	HR	RBI	BB	SO
Totals	.257	.309	.380	948	244	37	11	19	113	69	159
Pitching vs. Left and Right-handed Batters											
Left	.248	.310	.377	464	115	19	10	7	54	41	76
Right	.267	.308	.382	484	129	18	1	12	59	28	83
Situational											
Bases Empty	.267	.303	.434	509	136	25	6	16	16	25	78
Leadoff	.249	.269	.364	217	54	10	3	3	3	6	33
Not Leadoff	.281	.327	.486	292	82	15	3	13	13	19	45
Runners On	.246	.315	.317	439	108	12	5	3	97	44	81
First Base Only	.243	.287	.284	148	36	4	1	0	2	7	30
Scoring Position	.247	.328	.333	291	72	8	4	3	95	37	51
Late Innings, Close	.269	.323	.351	350	94	12	1	5	43	28	58

RBI/Opportunities

Scoring Position	88 / 401	(22%)
Scoring Position, 2 Out	42 / 192	(22%)
On Third, Less than 2 Out	29 / 74	(39%)
RBI in close games / RBI Total	58 / 113	(51%)

Bill Schroeder
Milwaukee Brewers

THREE YEARS (84 – 86)

	Ave.	OBP	SLG	AB	H	2B	3B	HR	RBI	BB	SO
Totals	.237	.280	.422	621	147	28	0	29	69	29	174
Batting vs. Left and Right-handed Pitchers											
Left	.270	.311	.505	196	53	7	0	13	28	11	58
Right	.221	.265	.384	425	94	21	0	16	41	18	116
At Home and on the Road											
Home	.221	.266	.359	326	72	12	0	11	24	13	92
Road	.254	.295	.492	295	75	16	0	18	45	16	82
Facing Groundball Pitchers and Flyball Pitchers											
Groundball	.257	.306	.413	327	84	9	0	14	40	18	92
Flyball	.214	.250	.432	294	63	19	0	15	29	11	82
Facing Finesse Pitchers and Power Pitchers											
Finesse	.258	.301	.435	329	85	16	0	14	36	16	73
Power	.212	.255	.408	292	62	12	0	15	33	13	101
On Grass and on Turf											
Grass	.238	.283	.416	522	124	24	0	23	55	27	142
Turf	.232	.260	.455	99	23	4	0	6	14	2	32
During the Day and at Night											
Day	.207	.257	.369	203	42	9	0	8	18	12	67
Night	.251	.291	.447	418	105	19	0	21	51	17	107
By Month											
April	.214	.260	.443	70	15	1	0	5	15	5	29
May	.292	.330	.490	96	28	7	0	4	9	4	31
June	.186	.245	.279	86	16	2	0	2	4	6	26
July	.204	.257	.367	98	20	4	0	4	11	3	22
August	.281	.312	.514	146	41	7	0	9	15	6	33
Sept/Oct	.216	.258	.392	125	27	7	0	5	15	5	33
Situational											
Bases Empty	.261	.304	.483	348	91	20	0	19	19	16	97
Leadoff	.319	.364	.546	141	45	11	0	7	7	8	32
Not Leadoff	.222	.261	.440	207	46	9	0	12	12	8	65
Runners On	.205	.250	.344	273	56	8	0	10	50	13	77
First Base Only	.274	.308	.387	124	34	5	0	3	9	3	32
Scoring Position	.148	.205	.309	149	22	3	0	7	41	10	45
Late Innings, Close	.253	.296	.394	99	25	5	0	3	11	7	25

RBI/Opportunities

Scoring Position	31 / 202	(15%)
Scoring Position, 2 Out	11 / 91	(12%)
On Third, Less than 2 Out	14 / 40	(35%)
RBI in close games / RBI Total	49 / 69	(71%)

Ken Schrom
Cleveland Indians

1986: Finesse, Flyball 1985: Finesse, Flyball 1984: Finesse, Flyball

	THREE YEARS (84 - 86)										
	G	IP	H	BB	SO	SB	CS	W	L	S	ERA
Totals	88	503.2	537	149	210	41	19	28	30	0	4.66
At Home and on the Road											
Home	51	301.0	314	81	130	21	10	20	17	0	4.43
Road	37	202.2	223	68	80	20	9	8	13	0	5.02
During the Day and and at Night											
Day	27	167.0	193	33	82	14	10	10	10	0	4.63
Night	61	336.2	344	116	128	27	9	18	20	0	4.68
On Grass and on Turf											
Grass	45	265.0	289	81	113	24	11	14	15	0	4.72
Turf	43	238.2	248	68	97	17	8	14	15	0	4.60
By Month											
April	9	54.2	55	17	15	5	4	4	3	0	4.77
May	12	64.1	74	13	34	2	2	2	3	0	5.18
June	17	114.2	99	37	45	7	3	10	4	0	2.98
July	17	105.1	115	31	46	9	3	6	9	0	4.78
August	15	75.0	96	21	36	9	4	1	6	0	5.64
Sept/Oct	18	89.2	98	30	34	9	3	5	5	0	5.42

	vs. Opponent Batters THREE YEARS (84 - 86)										
	Ave.	OBP	SLG	AB	H	2B	3B	HR	RBI	BB	SO
Totals	.275	.327	.453	1953	537	103	7	77	244	149	210
Pitching vs. Left and Right-handed Batters											
Left	.296	.348	.467	1071	317	50	5	41	134	90	97
Right	.249	.300	.437	882	220	53	2	36	110	59	113
Situational											
Bases Empty	.275	.329	.470	1198	329	63	6	53	53	89	120
Leadoff	.271	.339	.470	494	134	29	3	21	21	45	48
Not Leadoff	.277	.321	.470	704	195	34	3	32	32	44	72
Runners On	.275	.323	.426	755	208	40	1	24	191	60	90
First Base Only	.294	.345	.450	347	102	21	0	11	32	25	36
Scoring Position	.260	.306	.407	408	106	19	1	13	159	35	54
Late Innings, Close	.261	.325	.391	138	36	6	0	4	11	12	17

RBI/Opportunities		
Scoring Position	132 / 540	(24%)
Scoring Position, 2 Out	37 / 216	(17%)
On Third, Less than 2 Out	60 / 105	(57%)
RBI in close games / RBI Total	159 / 244	(65%)

Rick Schu
Philadelphia Phillies

	THREE YEARS (84 - 86)										
	Ave.	OBP	SLG	AB	H	2B	3B	HR	RBI	BB	SO
Totals	.260	.327	.407	653	170	33	6	17	54	62	128
Batting vs. Left and Right-handed Pitchers											
Left	.284	.347	.488	250	71	16	4	9	22	23	43
Right	.246	.315	.357	403	99	17	2	8	32	39	85
At Home and on the Road											
Home	.267	.339	.397	292	78	18	4	4	24	33	54
Road	.255	.316	.416	361	92	15	2	13	30	29	74
Facing Groundball Pitchers and Flyball Pitchers											
Groundball	.295	.354	.488	322	95	20	3	12	30	27	57
Flyball	.227	.301	.329	331	75	13	3	5	24	35	71
Facing Finesse Pitchers and Power Pitchers											
Finesse	.290	.335	.427	335	97	19	3	7	23	22	49
Power	.230	.319	.387	318	73	14	3	10	31	40	79
On Grass and on Turf											
Grass	.203	.275	.342	187	38	6	1	6	13	17	44
Turf	.283	.348	.433	466	132	27	5	11	41	45	84
During the Day and at Night											
Day	.263	.328	.488	213	56	11	2	11	26	21	42
Night	.259	.326	.368	440	114	22	4	6	28	41	86
By Month											
April	.409	.435	.682	22	9	0	0	2	3	1	6
May	.205	.273	.284	88	18	4	0	1	3	8	25
June	.270	.340	.355	141	38	8	2	0	10	13	23
July	.326	.385	.484	95	31	6	0	3	6	8	16
August	.276	.328	.520	127	35	4	3	7	20	10	25
Sept/Oct	.217	.300	.356	180	39	11	1	4	12	22	33
Situational											
Bases Empty	.275	.336	.427	400	110	22	3	11	11	34	75
Leadoff	.288	.354	.473	146	42	10	1	5	5	12	18
Not Leadoff	.268	.326	.402	254	68	12	2	6	6	22	57
Runners On	.237	.312	.375	253	60	11	3	6	43	28	53
First Base Only	.259	.308	.438	112	29	4	2	4	10	7	18
Scoring Position	.220	.315	.326	141	31	7	1	2	33	21	35
Late Innings, Close	.193	.270	.263	114	22	2	0	2	4	9	22

RBI/Opportunities		
Scoring Position	31 / 197	(16%)
Scoring Position, 2 Out	16 / 97	(16%)
On Third, Less than 2 Out	12 / 25	(48%)
RBI in close games / RBI Total	21 / 54	(39%)

Don Schulze
Cleveland Indians

1986: Finesse, Groundball 1985: Finesse, Groundball 1984: Finesse, Groundball

	THREE YEARS (84 - 86)										
	G	IP	H	BB	SO	SB	CS	W	L	S	ERA
Totals	58	267.2	329	81	111	22	9	11	20	0	5.38
At Home and on the Road											
Home	29	152.2	173	37	54	11	6	5	10	0	4.48
Road	29	115.0	156	44	57	11	3	6	10	0	6.57
During the Day and and at Night											
Day	21	80.1	116	23	28	10	4	3	6	0	6.50
Night	37	187.1	213	58	83	12	5	8	14	0	4.90
On Grass and on Turf											
Grass	49	234.2	287	70	94	16	8	9	15	0	5.18
Turf	9	33.0	42	11	17	6	1	2	5	0	6.82
By Month											
April	7	34.1	43	11	16	2	1	4	0	0	4.19
May	13	62.0	68	19	23	6	1	2	6	0	5.52
June	10	41.2	71	15	12	7	3	1	6	0	8.64
July	9	30.1	35	12	12	2	1	1	2	0	5.04
August	7	31.1	36	5	11	4	1	1	2	0	3.45
Sept/Oct	12	68.0	76	19	37	1	2	2	4	0	4.90

	vs. Opponent Batters THREE YEARS (84 - 86)										
	Ave.	OBP	SLG	AB	H	2B	3B	HR	RBI	BB	SO
Totals	.302	.353	.443	1090	329	56	7	28	162	81	111
Pitching vs. Left and Right-handed Batters											
Left	.330	.374	.470	581	192	29	5	14	88	42	42
Right	.269	.329	.413	509	137	27	2	14	74	39	69
Situational											
Bases Empty	.292	.340	.409	607	177	23	3	14	14	41	62
Leadoff	.307	.348	.444	270	83	12	2	7	7	16	29
Not Leadoff	.279	.334	.380	337	94	11	1	7	7	25	33
Runners On	.315	.368	.487	483	152	33	4	14	148	40	49
First Base Only	.300	.346	.460	213	64	13	3	5	19	13	24
Scoring Position	.326	.383	.507	270	88	20	1	9	129	27	25
Late Innings, Close	.234	.330	.468	77	18	1	1	5	12	11	8

RBI/Opportunities		
Scoring Position	114 / 363	(31%)
Scoring Position, 2 Out	36 / 149	(24%)
On Third, Less than 2 Out	49 / 86	(57%)
RBI in close games / RBI Total	118 / 162	(73%)

Rod Scurry
New York Yankees

1986: Power, Groundball 1985: Power, Groundball 1984: Power, Groundball

	THREE YEARS (84 - 86)										
	G	IP	H	BB	SO	SB	CS	W	L	S	ERA
Totals	109	146.0	113	82	144	13	7	7	9	9	3.08
At Home and on the Road											
Home	52	69.1	48	44	71	5	3	3	4	7	2.47
Road	57	76.2	65	38	73	8	4	4	5	2	3.64
During the Day and and at Night											
Day	39	46.0	45	32	48	2	4	1	6	2	3.33
Night	70	100.0	68	50	96	11	3	6	3	7	2.97
On Grass and on Turf											
Grass	47	68.0	55	44	70	6	3	1	5	4	3.57
Turf	62	78.0	58	38	74	7	4	6	4	5	2.65
By Month											
April	15	16.0	16	9	15	1	0	0	2	1	4.50
May	16	24.2	19	13	17	3	1	0	1	2	3.28
June	17	25.2	17	14	28	2	2	1	2	2	2.81
July	14	19.1	12	8	15	2	2	2	1	0	1.40
August	22	27.1	23	14	28	0	2	1	2	1	2.30
Sept/Oct	25	33.0	26	24	41	5	0	3	1	3	4.09

	vs. Opponent Batters THREE YEARS (84 - 86)										
	Ave.	OBP	SLG	AB	H	2B	3B	HR	RBI	BB	SO
Totals	.215	.321	.319	530	114	17	7	8	76	82	144
Pitching vs. Left and Right-handed Batters											
Left	.199	.306	.311	161	32	3	3	3	27	24	57
Right	.222	.328	.322	369	82	14	4	5	49	58	87
Situational											
Bases Empty	.192	.277	.258	287	55	7	3	2	2	33	83
Leadoff	.179	.263	.228	123	22	6	0	0	0	14	41
Not Leadoff	.201	.288	.280	164	33	1	3	2	2	19	42
Runners On	.243	.369	.391	243	59	10	4	6	74	49	61
First Base Only	.191	.276	.298	94	18	5	1	1	5	11	25
Scoring Position	.275	.421	.450	149	41	5	3	5	69	38	36
Late Innings, Close	.232	.338	.314	185	43	6	3	1	24	29	44

RBI/Opportunities		
Scoring Position	56 / 235	(24%)
Scoring Position, 2 Out	27 / 126	(21%)
On Third, Less than 2 Out	16 / 37	(43%)
RBI in close games / RBI Total	35 / 76	(46%)

Ray Searage
Chicago White Sox

1986: Power, Flyball   1985: Power, Flyball   1984: Power, Flyball

THREE YEARS (84 – 86)	G	IP	H	BB	SO	SB	CS	W	L	S	ERA
Totals	100	127.1	118	68	101	10	4	4	6	8	3.32
At Home and on the Road											
Home	49	75.0	83	43	61	6	1	4	4	3	4.20
Road	51	52.1	35	25	40	4	3	0	2	5	2.06
During the Day and and at Night											
Day	39	41.1	47	29	26	2	0	0	2	3	5.66
Night	61	86.0	71	39	75	8	4	4	4	5	2.20
On Grass and on Turf											
Grass	83	109.1	109	64	88	10	3	4	5	7	3.54
Turf	17	18.0	9	4	13	0	1	0	1	1	2.00
By Month											
April	11	12.0	17	7	12	1	1	0	3	2	8.25
May	6	7.0	12	7	6	0	0	0	1	0	9.00
June	12	13.0	18	6	8	2	0	1	0	0	8.31
July	8	12.1	11	6	8	0	0	0	0	0	2.92
August	26	36.0	30	20	29	3	2	0	1	1	1.75
Sept/Oct	37	47.0	30	22	38	4	1	3	1	5	1.15

vs. Opponent Batters THREE YEARS (84 – 86)	Ave.	OBP	SLG	AB	H	2B	3B	HR	RBI	BB	SO
Totals	.247	.342	.354	477	118	22	1	9	59	68	101
Pitching vs. Left and Right-handed Batters											
Left	.233	.324	.320	150	35	8	1	1	21	21	42
Right	.254	.350	.370	327	83	14	0	8	38	47	59
Situational											
Bases Empty	.286	.365	.411	224	64	16	0	4	4	27	41
Leadoff	.250	.322	.356	104	26	5	0	2	2	10	20
Not Leadoff	.317	.401	.458	120	38	11	0	2	2	17	21
Runners On	.213	.322	.304	253	54	6	1	5	55	41	60
First Base Only	.240	.315	.340	100	24	4	0	2	4	11	21
Scoring Position	.196	.326	.281	153	30	2	1	3	51	30	39
Late Innings, Close	.243	.332	.319	185	45	5	0	3	20	24	49

RBI/Opportunities		
Scoring Position	44 / 242	(18%)
Scoring Position, 2 Out	16 / 112	(14%)
On Third, Less than 2 Out	17 / 45	(38%)
RBI in close games / RBI Total	20 / 59	(34%)

Bob Sebra
Montreal Expos

1986: Finesse, Flyball   1985: Power, Flyball   1984: Did not play

THREE YEARS (84 – 86)	G	IP	H	BB	SO	SB	CS	W	L	S	ERA
Totals	24	111.2	108	39	79	18	3	5	7	0	4.27
At Home and on the Road											
Home	12	58.2	53	19	39	7	1	2	3	0	3.99
Road	12	53.0	55	20	40	11	2	3	4	0	4.58
During the Day and and at Night											
Day	7	29.0	29	14	18	9	0	0	1	0	4.97
Night	17	82.2	79	25	61	9	3	5	6	0	4.03
On Grass and on Turf											
Grass	9	36.1	39	14	29	3	1	2	3	0	5.45
Turf	15	75.1	69	25	50	15	2	3	4	0	3.70
By Month											
April	0	0.0	0	0	0	0	0	0	0	0	0.00
May	0	0.0	0	0	0	0	0	0	0	0	0.00
June	1	5.0	5	4	1	3	0	0	0	0	3.60
July	7	18.0	23	11	16	1	0	1	3	0	9.00
August	6	41.0	41	7	26	9	2	2	1	0	3.73
Sept/Oct	10	47.2	39	17	36	5	1	2	3	0	3.02

vs. Opponent Batters THREE YEARS (84 – 86)	Ave.	OBP	SLG	AB	H	2B	3B	HR	RBI	BB	SO
Totals	.252	.317	.407	428	108	21	3	13	51	39	79
Pitching vs. Left and Right-handed Batters											
Left	.266	.358	.460	237	63	12	2	10	30	31	40
Right	.236	.262	.340	191	45	9	1	3	21	8	39
Situational											
Bases Empty	.252	.305	.374	262	66	15	1	5	5	19	50
Leadoff	.241	.287	.417	108	26	8	1	3	3	7	16
Not Leadoff	.260	.317	.344	154	40	7	0	2	2	12	34
Runners On	.253	.335	.458	166	42	6	2	8	46	20	29
First Base Only	.305	.349	.559	59	18	4	1	3	8	4	9
Scoring Position	.224	.328	.402	107	24	2	1	5	38	16	20
Late Innings, Close	.189	.295	.351	37	7	3	0	1	4	5	6

RBI/Opportunities		
Scoring Position	29 / 148	(20%)
Scoring Position, 2 Out	10 / 70	(14%)
On Third, Less than 2 Out	14 / 19	(74%)
RBI in close games / RBI Total	37 / 51	(73%)

Larry Sheets
Baltimore Orioles

THREE YEARS (84 – 86)	Ave.	OBP	SLG	AB	H	2B	3B	HR	RBI	BB	SO
Totals	.271	.323	.471	682	185	26	1	36	112	50	111
Batting vs. Left and Right-handed Pitchers											
Left	.136	.231	.250	44	6	2	0	1	8	6	14
Right	.281	.330	.486	638	179	24	1	35	104	44	97
At Home and on the Road											
Home	.280	.327	.451	357	100	16	0	15	59	23	60
Road	.262	.319	.492	325	85	10	1	21	53	27	51
Facing Groundball Pitchers and Flyball Pitchers											
Groundball	.264	.319	.431	341	90	13	1	14	47	25	62
Flyball	.279	.328	.510	341	95	13	0	22	65	25	49
Facing Finesse Pitchers and Power Pitchers											
Finesse	.298	.332	.524	433	129	15	1	27	71	20	61
Power	.225	.310	.378	249	56	11	0	9	41	30	50
On Grass and on Turf											
Grass	.272	.324	.465	596	162	23	1	30	101	44	96
Turf	.267	.323	.512	86	23	3	0	6	11	6	15
During the Day and at Night											
Day	.274	.316	.492	197	54	10	0	11	33	12	35
Night	.270	.326	.462	485	131	16	1	25	79	38	76
By Month											
April	.309	.356	.559	68	21	3	1	4	12	5	5
May	.326	.371	.589	129	42	7	0	9	29	9	23
June	.257	.287	.393	140	36	4	0	5	26	13	21
July	.214	.287	.321	84	18	3	0	2	7	8	12
August	.270	.315	.582	122	33	5	0	11	26	8	25
Sept/Oct	.252	.291	.388	139	35	4	0	5	12	7	25
Situational											
Bases Empty	.255	.306	.408	368	94	17	0	13	13	24	71
Leadoff	.293	.357	.457	140	41	8	0	5	5	8	24
Not Leadoff	.232	.289	.377	228	53	9	0	8	8	16	47
Runners On	.290	.343	.545	314	91	9	1	23	99	26	40
First Base Only	.284	.322	.537	162	46	2	0	13	27	9	18
Scoring Position	.296	.364	.553	152	45	7	1	10	72	17	22
Late Innings, Close	.190	.261	.352	105	20	2	0	5	12	10	27

RBI/Opportunities		
Scoring Position	58 / 209	(28%)
Scoring Position, 2 Out	19 / 86	(22%)
On Third, Less than 2 Out	24 / 38	(63%)
RBI in close games / RBI Total	67 / 112	(60%)

John Shelby
Baltimore Orioles

THREE YEARS (84 – 86)	Ave.	OBP	SLG	AB	H	2B	3B	HR	RBI	BB	SO
Totals	.232	.266	.359	992	230	32	11	24	106	45	190
Batting vs. Left and Right-handed Pitchers											
Left	.227	.261	.361	374	85	13	2	11	32	16	69
Right	.235	.269	.358	618	145	19	9	13	74	29	121
At Home and on the Road											
Home	.206	.237	.311	472	97	15	1	11	42	19	94
Road	.256	.293	.402	520	133	17	10	13	64	26	96
Facing Groundball Pitchers and Flyball Pitchers											
Groundball	.225	.258	.351	444	100	9	7	11	52	20	79
Flyball	.237	.273	.365	548	130	23	4	13	54	25	111
Facing Finesse Pitchers and Power Pitchers											
Finesse	.241	.274	.352	506	122	17	6	9	57	21	71
Power	.222	.258	.366	486	108	15	5	15	49	24	119
On Grass and on Turf											
Grass	.234	.267	.358	864	202	30	7	21	96	39	169
Turf	.219	.259	.367	128	28	2	4	3	10	6	21
During the Day and at Night											
Day	.259	.288	.410	351	91	18	4	9	47	14	59
Night	.217	.254	.331	641	139	14	7	15	59	31	131
By Month											
April	.194	.242	.266	124	24	5	2	0	5	8	25
May	.224	.252	.364	107	24	2	2	3	11	4	18
June	.240	.290	.380	179	43	4	0	7	23	7	34
July	.166	.207	.278	169	28	4	3	3	21	7	36
August	.264	.308	.371	159	42	7	2	2	14	10	31
Sept/Oct	.272	.295	.433	254	69	10	2	9	32	9	46
Situational											
Bases Empty	.217	.252	.335	594	129	12	5	16	16	28	118
Leadoff	.236	.264	.361	296	70	4	3	9	9	11	51
Not Leadoff	.198	.241	.309	298	59	8	2	7	7	17	67
Runners On	.254	.286	.394	398	101	20	6	8	90	17	72
First Base Only	.250	.279	.432	176	44	6	4	6	19	7	34
Scoring Position	.257	.292	.365	222	57	14	2	2	71	10	38
Late Innings, Close	.193	.236	.282	181	35	7	3	1	13	10	35

RBI/Opportunities		
Scoring Position	67 / 300	(22%)
Scoring Position, 2 Out	38 / 147	(26%)
On Third, Less than 2 Out	15 / 47	(32%)
RBI in close games / RBI Total	67 / 106	(63%)

Pat Sheridan
Detroit Tigers

THREE YEARS (84 – 86)	Ave.	OBP	SLG	AB	H	2B	3B	HR	RBI	BB	SO
Totals	.259	.322	.375	923	239	42	7	17	89	86	186
Batting vs. Left and Right-handed Pitchers											
Left	.194	.240	.276	98	19	3	1	1	5	5	32
Right	.267	.332	.387	825	220	39	6	16	84	81	154
At Home and on the Road											
Home	.256	.320	.382	442	113	26	3	8	44	42	85
Road	.262	.324	.368	481	126	16	4	9	45	44	101
Facing Groundball Pitchers and Flyball Pitchers											
Groundball	.242	.299	.341	425	103	15	3	7	44	34	81
Flyball	.273	.342	.404	498	136	27	4	10	45	52	105
Facing Finesse Pitchers and Power Pitchers											
Finesse	.276	.333	.418	555	153	28	6	13	66	49	92
Power	.234	.306	.310	368	86	14	1	4	23	37	94
On Grass and on Turf											
Grass	.261	.325	.367	452	118	18	3	8	44	44	101
Turf	.257	.319	.382	471	121	24	4	9	45	42	85
During the Day and at Night											
Day	.274	.337	.418	263	72	8	3	8	37	25	57
Night	.253	.316	.358	660	167	34	4	9	52	61	129
By Month											
April	.260	.323	.363	146	38	6	3	1	11	14	22
May	.228	.295	.386	189	43	7	1	7	21	18	41
June	.300	.348	.459	170	51	10	1	5	16	12	30
July	.256	.295	.321	156	40	6	2	0	13	9	28
August	.264	.363	.328	125	33	5	0	1	12	19	26
Sept/Oct	.248	.318	.372	137	34	8	0	3	16	14	39
Situational											
Bases Empty	.265	.326	.385	533	141	21	5	11	11	47	103
Leadoff	.189	.247	.283	180	34	3	1	4	4	14	36
Not Leadoff	.303	.366	.436	353	107	18	4	7	7	33	67
Runners On	.251	.317	.362	390	98	21	2	6	78	39	83
First Base Only	.257	.298	.401	152	39	12	2	2	13	9	24
Scoring Position	.248	.327	.336	238	59	9	0	4	65	30	59
Late Innings, Close	.264	.331	.354	144	38	7	3	0	9	14	31

RBI/Opportunities		
Scoring Position	58 / 335	(17%)
Scoring Position, 2 Out	24 / 151	(16%)
On Third, Less than 2 Out	22 / 59	(37%)
RBI in close games / RBI Total	66 / 89	(74%)

Bob Shirley
New York Yankees

1986: Finesse, Flyball   1985: Finesse, Flyball   1984: Finesse, Flyball

THREE YEARS (84 – 86)	G	IP	H	BB	SO	SB	CS	W	L	S	ERA
Totals	128	328.2	330	104	167	10	17	8	12	5	3.67
At Home and on the Road											
Home	65	204.1	199	60	103	6	12	7	6	3	3.00
Road	63	124.1	131	44	64	4	5	1	6	2	4.78
During the Day and and at Night											
Day	47	104.2	102	38	64	5	6	3	5	1	3.96
Night	81	224.0	228	66	103	5	11	5	7	4	3.54
On Grass and on Turf											
Grass	113	307.1	287	92	153	10	16	8	10	5	3.05
Turf	15	21.1	43	12	14	0	1	0	2	0	12.66
By Month											
April	18	33.1	48	14	18	2	2	0	2	0	6.75
May	13	44.1	37	21	24	2	2	1	1	0	3.05
June	28	75.0	80	23	31	1	4	2	3	1	4.44
July	18	52.2	70	16	28	3	3	1	4	0	5.30
August	27	57.2	57	13	29	0	3	0	1	0	2.81
Sept/Oct	24	65.2	38	17	37	2	3	4	1	4	1.10

vs. Opponent Batters THREE YEARS (84 – 86)	Ave.	OBP	SLG	AB	H	2B	3B	HR	RBI	BB	SO
Totals	.266	.321	.394	1242	330	53	14	26	147	104	167
Pitching vs. Left and Right-handed Batters											
Left	.223	.274	.311	367	82	10	5	4	34	26	82
Right	.283	.340	.429	875	248	43	9	22	113	78	85
Situational											
Bases Empty	.245	.303	.357	695	170	30	6	12	12	56	91
Leadoff	.258	.301	.389	298	77	11	2	8	8	17	36
Not Leadoff	.234	.304	.332	397	93	19	4	4	4	39	55
Runners On	.293	.343	.441	547	160	23	8	14	135	48	76
First Base Only	.362	.423	.555	218	79	10	4	8	23	22	21
Scoring Position	.246	.290	.365	329	81	13	4	6	112	26	55
Late Innings, Close	.236	.290	.319	191	45	5	1	3	20	16	21

RBI/Opportunities		
Scoring Position	96 / 438	(22%)
Scoring Position, 2 Out	40 / 193	(21%)
On Third, Less than 2 Out	39 / 84	(46%)
RBI in close games / RBI Total	71 / 147	(48%)

Eric Show
San Diego Padres

1986: Power, Flyball   1985: Finesse, Flyball   1984: Finesse, Flyball

THREE YEARS (84 – 86)	G	IP	H	BB	SO	SB	CS	W	L	S	ERA
Totals	91	576.0	496	245	339	38	36	36	25	0	3.17
At Home and on the Road											
Home	45	275.2	239	119	182	15	21	17	13	0	3.40
Road	46	300.1	257	126	157	23	15	19	12	0	2.97
During the Day and and at Night											
Day	26	171.1	163	72	94	11	10	10	8	0	3.68
Night	65	404.2	333	173	245	27	26	26	17	0	2.96
On Grass and on Turf											
Grass	66	405.0	366	173	254	26	25	27	19	0	3.60
Turf	25	171.0	130	72	85	12	11	9	6	0	2.16
By Month											
April	14	96.1	70	33	62	6	5	5	4	0	2.62
May	18	116.0	96	60	82	14	6	8	4	0	3.18
June	17	105.1	92	59	58	3	10	7	6	0	3.93
July	13	80.0	75	34	50	6	5	5	3	0	3.04
August	17	96.2	86	32	41	5	5	7	4	0	2.98
Sept/Oct	12	81.2	77	27	46	4	5	4	4	0	3.20

vs. Opponent Batters THREE YEARS (84 – 86)	Ave.	OBP	SLG	AB	H	2B	3B	HR	RBI	BB	SO
Totals	.236	.318	.360	2103	496	73	10	56	193	245	339
Pitching vs. Left and Right-handed Batters											
Left	.272	.361	.401	1112	302	44	8	28	103	155	124
Right	.196	.267	.314	991	194	29	2	28	90	90	215
Situational											
Bases Empty	.248	.328	.383	1274	316	51	5	37	37	144	201
Leadoff	.247	.316	.411	543	134	21	4	20	20	52	86
Not Leadoff	.249	.336	.363	731	182	30	1	17	17	92	115
Runners On	.217	.303	.324	829	180	22	5	19	156	101	138
First Base Only	.231	.304	.364	390	90	9	2	13	31	38	59
Scoring Position	.205	.302	.289	439	90	13	3	6	125	63	79
Late Innings, Close	.256	.335	.402	199	51	4	2	7	14	24	23

RBI/Opportunities		
Scoring Position	115 / 602	(19%)
Scoring Position, 2 Out	39 / 306	(13%)
On Third, Less than 2 Out	51 / 86	(59%)
RBI in close games / RBI Total	156 / 193	(81%)

Ruben Sierra
Texas Rangers

THREE YEARS (84 – 86)	Ave.	OBP	SLG	AB	H	2B	3B	HR	RBI	BB	SO
Totals	.264	.302	.476	382	101	13	10	16	55	22	65
Batting vs. Left and Right-handed Pitchers											
Left	.253	.269	.434	99	25	4	1	4	15	4	11
Right	.269	.315	.491	283	76	9	9	12	40	18	54
At Home and on the Road											
Home	.238	.256	.459	172	41	2	6	8	31	5	38
Road	.286	.339	.490	210	60	11	4	8	24	17	27
Facing Groundball Pitchers and Flyball Pitchers											
Groundball	.241	.282	.432	162	39	6	5	5	21	10	23
Flyball	.282	.318	.509	220	62	7	5	11	34	12	42
Facing Finesse Pitchers and Power Pitchers											
Finesse	.266	.297	.491	218	58	5	7	10	29	11	30
Power	.262	.309	.457	164	43	8	3	6	26	11	35
On Grass and on Turf											
Grass	.249	.286	.438	297	74	7	8	11	42	16	53
Turf	.318	.359	.612	85	27	6	2	5	13	6	12
During the Day and at Night											
Day	.222	.256	.444	72	16	2	1	4	12	4	7
Night	.274	.313	.484	310	85	11	9	12	43	18	58
By Month											
April	.000	.000	.000	0	0	0	0	0	0	0	0
May	.000	.000	.000	0	0	0	0	0	0	0	0
June	.193	.228	.358	109	21	4	1	4	7	4	25
July	.241	.297	.500	58	14	1	4	2	8	5	8
August	.330	.374	.582	91	30	6	4	3	17	7	12
Sept/Oct	.290	.316	.492	124	36	2	1	7	23	6	20
Situational											
Bases Empty	.244	.275	.484	213	52	9	6	10	10	8	39
Leadoff	.222	.250	.333	81	18	4	1	1	1	3	12
Not Leadoff	.258	.290	.576	132	34	5	5	9	9	5	27
Runners On	.290	.335	.467	169	49	4	4	6	45	14	26
First Base Only	.358	.419	.507	67	24	4	0	2	5	7	10
Scoring Position	.245	.281	.441	102	25	0	4	4	40	7	16
Late Innings, Close	.329	.355	.603	73	24	5	3	4	8	2	13

RBI/Opportunities		
Scoring Position	34 / 135	(25%)
Scoring Position, 2 Out	14 / 66	(21%)
On Third, Less than 2 Out	13 / 25	(52%)
RBI in close games / RBI Total	34 / 55	(62%)

Ted Simmons
Atlanta Braves

THREE YEARS (84 – 86)	Ave.	OBP	SLG	AB	H	2B	3B	HR	RBI	BB	SO
Totals	.248	.308	.356	1152	286	56	4	20	153	99	86
Batting vs. Left and Right-handed Pitchers											
Left	.257	.313	.404	401	103	25	2	10	63	32	28
Right	.244	.306	.330	751	183	31	2	10	90	67	58
At Home and on the Road											
Home	.236	.292	.342	559	132	24	1	11	75	44	49
Road	.260	.323	.369	593	154	32	3	9	78	55	37
Facing Groundball Pitchers and Flyball Pitchers											
Groundball	.235	.298	.324	549	129	29	1	6	77	53	32
Flyball	.260	.318	.385	603	157	27	3	14	76	46	54
Facing Finesse Pitchers and Power Pitchers											
Finesse	.267	.327	.377	660	176	36	2	11	93	60	37
Power	.224	.283	.327	492	110	20	2	9	60	39	49
On Grass and on Turf											
Grass	.241	.304	.343	951	229	47	1	16	122	85	75
Turf	.284	.326	.418	201	57	9	3	4	31	14	11
During the Day and at Night											
Day	.255	.292	.365	353	90	17	2	6	50	19	20
Night	.245	.315	.352	799	196	39	2	14	103	80	66
By Month											
April	.232	.304	.274	164	38	4	0	1	18	17	12
May	.268	.319	.374	198	53	11	2	2	26	15	14
June	.221	.269	.318	217	48	12	0	3	26	14	13
July	.262	.316	.440	248	65	13	2	9	41	19	22
August	.251	.330	.374	179	45	10	0	4	29	21	18
Sept/Oct	.253	.313	.315	146	37	6	0	1	13	13	7
Situational											
Bases Empty	.226	.282	.326	619	140	28	2	10	10	46	48
Leadoff	.213	.262	.324	272	58	15	0	5	5	17	19
Not Leadoff	.236	.297	.329	347	82	13	2	5	5	29	29
Runners On	.274	.337	.390	533	146	28	2	10	143	53	38
First Base Only	.281	.329	.372	199	56	13	1	1	9	11	17
Scoring Position	.269	.342	.401	334	90	15	1	9	134	42	21
Late Innings, Close	.216	.278	.345	232	50	12	0	6	41	21	21

RBI/Opportunities		
Scoring Position	115 / 448	(26%)
Scoring Position, 2 Out	48 / 220	(22%)
On Third, Less than 2 Out	38 / 89	(43%)
RBI in close games / RBI Total	119 / 153	(78%)

Doug Sisk
New York Mets

1986: Finesse, Groundball 1985: Finesse, Groundball 1984: Power, Groundball

THREE YEARS (84 – 86)	G	IP	H	BB	SO	SB	CS	W	L	S	ERA
Totals	133	221.1	220	125	89	11	13	9	10	18	3.46
At Home and on the Road											
Home	66	106.1	100	56	43	6	3	2	5	8	2.88
Road	67	115.0	120	69	46	5	10	7	5	10	3.99
During the Day and and at Night											
Day	55	91.1	107	51	38	3	3	3	3	5	4.43
Night	78	130.0	113	74	51	8	10	6	7	13	2.77
On Grass and on Turf											
Grass	95	159.0	158	86	66	7	7	5	7	12	3.00
Turf	38	62.1	62	39	23	4	6	4	3	6	4.62
By Month											
April	20	32.0	29	23	13	3	1	2	2	3	3.09
May	18	26.2	27	14	15	2	2	0	1	2	4.39
June	29	53.2	37	22	18	4	1	2	4	7	2.52
July	29	47.0	60	24	19	2	3	1	3	4	5.17
August	19	33.1	34	21	12	0	3	1	0	0	2.43
Sept/Oct	18	28.2	33	21	12	0	3	3	0	2	3.14

vs. Opponent Batters THREE YEARS (84 – 86)	Ave.	OBP	SLG	AB	H	2B	3B	HR	RBI	BB	SO
Totals	.264	.366	.326	834	220	34	3	4	102	125	89
Pitching vs. Left and Right-handed Batters											
Left	.254	.369	.328	378	96	17	1	3	46	67	28
Right	.272	.364	.325	456	124	17	2	1	56	58	61
Situational											
Bases Empty	.254	.357	.303	393	100	15	2	0	0	60	46
Leadoff	.239	.352	.272	184	44	4	1	0	0	32	21
Not Leadoff	.268	.362	.330	209	56	11	1	0	0	28	25
Runners On	.272	.374	.347	441	120	19	1	4	102	65	43
First Base Only	.235	.342	.289	166	39	6	0	1	5	22	14
Scoring Position	.295	.394	.382	275	81	13	1	3	97	43	29
Late Innings, Close	.231	.348	.263	376	87	9	0	1	29	62	44

RBI/Opportunities		
Scoring Position	89 / 403	(22%)
Scoring Position, 2 Out	35 / 182	(19%)
On Third, Less than 2 Out	30 / 69	(43%)
RBI in close games / RBI Total	38 / 102	(37%)

Joel Skinner
New York Yankees

THREE YEARS (84 – 86)	Ave.	OBP	SLG	AB	H	2B	3B	HR	RBI	BB	SO
Totals	.239	.285	.323	439	105	15	2	6	45	28	115
Batting vs. Left and Right-handed Pitchers											
Left	.229	.282	.266	188	43	4	0	1	16	14	44
Right	.247	.286	.367	251	62	11	2	5	29	14	71
At Home and on the Road											
Home	.219	.252	.288	219	48	7	1	2	19	9	61
Road	.259	.315	.359	220	57	8	1	4	26	19	54
Facing Groundball Pitchers and Flyball Pitchers											
Groundball	.243	.295	.314	169	41	5	2	1	16	12	46
Flyball	.237	.278	.330	270	64	10	0	5	29	16	69
Facing Finesse Pitchers and Power Pitchers											
Finesse	.257	.294	.375	253	65	11	2	5	30	13	60
Power	.215	.272	.253	186	40	4	0	1	15	15	55
On Grass and on Turf											
Grass	.239	.283	.320	372	89	14	2	4	41	23	99
Turf	.239	.292	.343	67	16	1	0	2	4	5	16
During the Day and at Night											
Day	.255	.279	.369	157	40	7	1	3	24	5	44
Night	.230	.288	.298	282	65	8	1	3	21	23	71
By Month											
April	.171	.222	.220	41	7	0	1	0	4	2	11
May	.237	.316	.316	38	9	0	0	1	3	2	7
June	.221	.264	.279	86	19	5	0	0	7	5	22
July	.204	.246	.426	54	11	3	0	3	8	3	19
August	.219	.256	.288	73	16	2	0	1	6	4	27
Sept/Oct	.293	.344	.361	147	43	5	1	1	17	12	29
Situational											
Bases Empty	.255	.305	.327	251	64	8	2	2	2	17	68
Leadoff	.229	.315	.313	96	22	5	0	1	1	11	25
Not Leadoff	.271	.298	.335	155	42	3	2	1	1	6	43
Runners On	.218	.257	.319	188	41	7	0	4	43	11	47
First Base Only	.162	.194	.222	99	16	3	0	1	3	4	23
Scoring Position	.281	.323	.427	89	25	4	0	3	40	7	24
Late Innings, Close	.159	.196	.205	44	7	2	0	0	1	2	15

RBI/Opportunities		
Scoring Position	34 / 115	(30%)
Scoring Position, 2 Out	12 / 47	(26%)
On Third, Less than 2 Out	10 / 22	(45%)
RBI in close games / RBI Total	26 / 45	(58%)

Jim Slaton
Detroit Tigers

1986: Finesse, Flyball 1985: Finesse, Flyball 1984: Finesse, Flyball

THREE YEARS (84 – 86)	G	IP	H	BB	SO	SB	CS	W	L	S	ERA
Totals	97	424.2	484	159	170	13	21	17	26	3	4.79
At Home and on the Road											
Home	50	232.0	240	72	94	8	7	9	11	1	4.15
Road	47	192.2	244	87	76	5	14	8	15	2	5.56
During the Day and and at Night											
Day	31	128.0	156	46	55	4	10	5	5	0	5.20
Night	66	296.2	328	113	115	9	11	12	21	3	4.61
On Grass and on Turf											
Grass	84	362.0	411	136	141	10	16	11	23	2	4.85
Turf	13	62.2	73	23	29	3	5	6	3	1	4.45
By Month											
April	15	68.1	73	19	31	2	5	6	1	0	4.08
May	17	86.2	102	42	29	8	5	3	8	0	5.40
June	12	61.0	70	31	20	1	3	1	5	0	4.72
July	17	65.0	82	21	20	1	2	1	6	1	5.12
August	20	83.2	89	22	40	0	2	4	2	1	4.20
Sept/Oct	16	60.0	68	24	30	1	4	2	4	1	5.25

vs. Opponent Batters THREE YEARS (84 – 86)	Ave.	OBP	SLG	AB	H	2B	3B	HR	RBI	BB	SO
Totals	.291	.351	.464	1666	484	93	11	58	226	159	170
Pitching vs. Left and Right-handed Batters											
Left	.294	.366	.455	841	247	45	8	25	117	99	79
Right	.287	.336	.473	825	237	48	3	33	109	60	91
Situational											
Bases Empty	.288	.352	.460	943	272	45	6	35	35	88	96
Leadoff	.299	.356	.473	412	123	21	6	13	13	35	36
Not Leadoff	.281	.348	.450	531	149	24	0	22	22	53	60
Runners On	.293	.351	.469	723	212	48	5	23	191	71	74
First Base Only	.327	.356	.512	346	113	21	2	13	35	16	33
Scoring Position	.263	.347	.430	377	99	27	3	10	156	55	41
Late Innings, Close	.285	.375	.431	130	37	11	1	2	16	19	12

RBI/Opportunities		
Scoring Position	134 / 538	(25%)
Scoring Position, 2 Out	55 / 257	(21%)
On Third, Less than 2 Out	50 / 94	(53%)
RBI in close games / RBI Total	142 / 226	(63%)

Don Slaught
Texas Rangers

THREE YEARS (84 – 86)	Ave.	OBP	SLG	AB	H	2B	3B	HR	RBI	BB	SO
Totals	.269	.311	.414	1066	287	61	9	25	123	56	155
Batting vs. Left and Right-handed Pitchers											
Left	.305	.340	.486	331	101	21	3	11	55	17	52
Right	.253	.298	.381	735	186	40	6	14	68	39	103
At Home and on the Road											
Home	.299	.344	.445	521	156	38	4	10	56	33	69
Road	.240	.279	.383	545	131	23	5	15	67	23	86
Facing Groundball Pitchers and Flyball Pitchers											
Groundball	.273	.315	.419	494	135	22	4	14	61	20	63
Flyball	.266	.307	.409	572	152	39	5	11	62	36	92
Facing Finesse Pitchers and Power Pitchers											
Finesse	.303	.340	.468	601	182	36	6	17	76	30	62
Power	.226	.274	.344	465	105	25	3	8	47	26	93
On Grass and on Turf											
Grass	.271	.313	.420	722	196	37	5	20	88	35	105
Turf	.265	.308	.401	344	91	24	4	5	35	21	50
During the Day and at Night											
Day	.284	.322	.467	229	65	12	3	8	32	11	28
Night	.265	.308	.399	837	222	49	6	17	91	45	127
By Month											
April	.275	.319	.433	171	47	7	1	6	24	9	21
May	.188	.245	.313	144	27	4	1	4	15	8	16
June	.287	.342	.434	136	39	13	2	1	14	12	17
July	.317	.352	.533	167	53	13	4	5	19	7	23
August	.258	.297	.359	198	51	11	0	3	22	10	35
Sept/Oct	.280	.310	.412	250	70	13	1	6	29	10	43
Situational											
Bases Empty	.262	.298	.416	622	163	41	5	15	15	27	96
Leadoff	.259	.298	.368	239	62	19	2	1	1	13	34
Not Leadoff	.264	.299	.446	383	101	22	3	14	14	14	62
Runners On	.279	.328	.410	444	124	20	4	10	108	29	59
First Base Only	.325	.377	.487	191	62	9	2	6	18	11	22
Scoring Position	.245	.292	.352	253	62	11	2	4	90	18	37
Late Innings, Close	.291	.324	.446	175	51	7	1	6	25	8	23

RBI/Opportunities		
Scoring Position	79 / 334	(24%)
Scoring Position, 2 Out	31 / 156	(20%)
On Third, Less than 2 Out	31 / 60	(52%)
RBI in close games / RBI Total	78 / 123	(63%)

Zane Smith
Atlanta Braves

1986: Power, Groundball 1985: Power, Groundball 1984: Power, Groundball

THREE YEARS (84 – 86)	G	IP	H	BB	SO	SB	CS	W	L	S	ERA
Totals	83	371.2	360	198	240	57	23	18	26	1	3.85
At Home and on the Road											
Home	44	206.1	204	104	140	24	10	9	12	1	3.79
Road	39	165.1	156	94	100	33	13	9	14	0	3.92
During the Day and and at Night											
Day	22	108.1	109	57	70	17	6	5	9	0	3.74
Night	61	263.1	251	141	170	40	17	13	17	1	3.90
On Grass and on Turf											
Grass	60	281.1	277	144	177	36	18	14	19	1	3.97
Turf	23	90.1	83	54	63	21	5	4	7	0	3.49
By Month											
April	14	51.2	38	20	36	5	0	3	3	0	2.79
May	16	65.1	65	35	54	13	3	3	5	0	3.86
June	13	77.0	80	42	46	15	5	4	4	0	3.04
July	12	72.2	62	37	50	8	7	3	5	0	3.72
August	5	28.2	36	20	10	1	4	0	4	0	6.28
Sept/Oct	23	76.1	79	44	44	15	4	5	5	1	4.60

vs. Opponent Batters – THREE YEARS (84 – 86)	Ave.	OBP	SLG	AB	H	2B	3B	HR	RBI	BB	SO
Totals	.264	.359	.368	1364	360	79	12	13	161	198	240
Pitching vs. Left and Right-handed Batters											
Left	.247	.297	.316	215	53	10	1	1	22	15	61
Right	.267	.370	.378	1149	307	69	11	12	139	183	179
Situational											
Bases Empty	.268	.366	.372	725	194	44	7	6	6	110	116
Leadoff	.274	.358	.390	336	92	21	3	4	4	42	52
Not Leadoff	.262	.373	.357	389	102	23	4	2	2	68	64
Runners On	.260	.350	.363	639	166	35	5	7	155	88	124
First Base Only	.248	.313	.326	242	60	8	1	3	11	20	36
Scoring Position	.267	.371	.385	397	106	27	4	4	144	68	88
Late Innings, Close	.241	.361	.293	133	32	7	0	0	13	25	25

RBI/Opportunities		
Scoring Position	132 / 560	(24%)
Scoring Position, 2 Out	48 / 244	(20%)
On Third, Less than 2 Out	49 / 101	(49%)
RBI in close games / RBI Total	106 / 161	(66%)

Nate Snell
Baltimore Orioles

1986: Finesse, Groundball 1985: Finesse, Groundball 1984: Power, Flyball

THREE YEARS (84 – 86)	G	IP	H	BB	SO	SB	CS	W	L	S	ERA
Totals	82	180.1	177	53	77	3	6	6	4	5	3.14
At Home and on the Road											
Home	43	98.0	95	23	43	1	5	3	0	2	2.57
Road	39	82.1	82	30	34	2	1	3	4	3	3.83
During the Day and and at Night											
Day	30	64.0	68	25	27	3	2	2	1	1	3.37
Night	52	116.1	109	28	50	0	4	4	3	4	3.02
On Grass and on Turf											
Grass	68	148.1	148	40	64	3	5	5	3	3	2.97
Turf	14	32.0	29	13	13	0	1	1	1	2	3.94
By Month											
April	8	19.0	12	6	6	0	1	0	1	0	1.42
May	14	50.1	34	11	25	0	1	2	0	2	2.32
June	17	32.2	34	12	15	0	2	2	0	1	2.48
July	13	26.2	32	9	6	0	1	1	1	1	5.40
August	9	14.0	14	5	3	0	1	0	1	1	2.57
Sept/Oct	21	37.2	51	10	22	3	0	1	1	0	4.30

vs. Opponent Batters – THREE YEARS (84 – 86)	Ave.	OBP	SLG	AB	H	2B	3B	HR	RBI	BB	SO
Totals	.259	.312	.371	684	177	29	3	14	88	53	77
Pitching vs. Left and Right-handed Batters											
Left	.277	.326	.399	303	84	12	2	7	32	23	24
Right	.244	.300	.349	381	93	17	1	7	56	30	53
Situational											
Bases Empty	.246	.297	.346	370	91	16	0	7	7	26	42
Leadoff	.237	.270	.397	156	37	7	0	6	6	7	17
Not Leadoff	.252	.316	.308	214	54	9	0	1	1	19	25
Runners On	.274	.329	.401	314	86	13	3	7	81	27	35
First Base Only	.266	.297	.410	139	37	3	1	5	12	6	15
Scoring Position	.280	.351	.394	175	49	10	2	2	69	21	20
Late Innings, Close	.291	.362	.466	103	30	3	0	5	15	12	10

RBI/Opportunities		
Scoring Position	63 / 248	(25%)
Scoring Position, 2 Out	19 / 99	(19%)
On Third, Less than 2 Out	28 / 61	(46%)
RBI in close games / RBI Total	32 / 88	(36%)

Ray Soff
St. Louis Cardinals

1986: Finesse, Groundball 1985: Did not play 1984: Did not play

THREE YEARS (84 – 86)	G	IP	H	BB	SO	SB	CS	W	L	S	ERA
Totals	30	38.1	37	13	22	3	1	4	2	0	3.29
At Home and on the Road											
Home	11	14.2	15	6	9	1	0	1	2	0	3.68
Road	19	23.2	22	7	13	2	1	3	0	0	3.04
During the Day and and at Night											
Day	8	10.1	12	2	7	1	0	0	1	0	6.10
Night	22	28.0	25	11	15	2	1	4	1	0	2.25
On Grass and on Turf											
Grass	6	6.2	7	0	4	0	0	1	0	0	5.40
Turf	24	31.2	30	13	18	3	1	3	2	0	2.84
By Month											
April	0	0.0	0	0	0	0	0	0	0	0	0.00
May	0	0.0	0	0	0	0	0	0	0	0	0.00
June	0	0.0	0	0	0	0	0	0	0	0	0.00
July	6	6.0	3	4	6	1	0	0	0	0	0.00
August	9	11.0	15	4	7	2	0	0	0	0	4.91
Sept/Oct	15	21.1	19	5	9	0	1	4	2	0	3.38

vs. Opponent Batters – THREE YEARS (84 – 86)	Ave.	OBP	SLG	AB	H	2B	3B	HR	RBI	BB	SO
Totals	.255	.313	.434	145	37	10	2	4	17	13	22
Pitching vs. Left and Right-handed Batters											
Left	.271	.338	.390	59	16	4	0	1	4	6	10
Right	.244	.295	.465	86	21	6	2	3	13	7	12
Situational											
Bases Empty	.289	.365	.513	76	22	8	0	3	3	9	13
Leadoff	.226	.351	.419	31	7	3	0	1	1	6	5
Not Leadoff	.333	.375	.578	45	15	5	0	2	2	3	8
Runners On	.217	.253	.348	69	15	2	2	1	14	4	9
First Base Only	.214	.241	.250	28	6	1	0	0	0	1	3
Scoring Position	.220	.261	.415	41	9	1	2	1	14	3	6
Late Innings, Close	.250	.304	.423	52	13	4	1	1	3	4	7

RBI/Opportunities		
Scoring Position	12 / 52	(23%)
Scoring Position, 2 Out	3 / 20	(15%)
On Third, Less than 2 Out	7 / 10	(70%)
RBI in close games / RBI Total	4 / 17	(24%)

Julio Solano
Houston Astros

1986: Power, Flyball — 1985: Finesse, Flyball — 1984: Power, Flyball

THREE YEARS (84 – 86)	G	IP	H	BB	SO	SB	CS	W	L	S	ERA
Totals	67	116.1	104	53	71	13	7	6	6	0	3.95
At Home and on the Road											
Home	35	55.2	50	31	39	7	2	4	3	0	4.04
Road	32	60.2	54	22	32	6	5	2	3	0	3.86
During the Day and at Night											
Day	14	27.1	21	14	18	3	2	1	1	0	3.29
Night	53	89.0	83	39	53	10	5	5	5	0	4.15
On Grass and on Turf											
Grass	18	31.0	25	11	16	2	3	1	2	0	4.06
Turf	49	85.1	79	42	55	11	4	5	4	0	3.90
By Month											
April	8	12.0	17	5	5	1	1	1	0	0	5.25
May	9	24.2	25	13	20	1	3	3	2	0	5.47
June	13	24.2	20	12	13	3	2	0	1	0	4.01
July	9	15.1	11	3	7	1	0	0	0	0	1.17
August	10	13.2	9	4	9	3	0	1	2	0	2.63
Sept/Oct	18	26.0	22	16	17	4	1	1	1	0	4.15

vs. Opponent Batters

THREE YEARS (84 – 86)	Ave.	OBP	SLG	AB	H	2B	3B	HR	RBI	BB	SO
Totals	.242	.327	.403	429	104	28	1	13	48	53	71
Pitching vs. Left and Right-handed Batters											
Left	.229	.318	.343	175	40	9	1	3	15	23	23
Right	.252	.333	.445	254	64	19	0	10	33	30	48
Situational											
Bases Empty	.235	.316	.412	238	56	13	1	9	9	26	40
Leadoff	.310	.384	.630	100	31	11	0	7	7	11	14
Not Leadoff	.181	.266	.254	138	25	2	1	2	2	15	26
Runners On	.251	.341	.393	191	48	15	0	4	39	27	31
First Base Only	.348	.392	.565	69	24	9	0	2	5	4	9
Scoring Position	.197	.315	.295	122	24	6	0	2	34	23	22
Late Innings, Close	.278	.375	.574	54	15	4	0	4	9	9	12

RBI/Opportunities
Scoring Position	31 / 188	(16%)
Scoring Position, 2 Out	11 / 96	(11%)
On Third, Less than 2 Out	11 / 33	(33%)
RBI in close games / RBI Total	18 / 48	(38%)

Mario Soto
Cincinnati Reds

1986: Power, Flyball — 1985: Power, Flyball — 1984: Power, Flyball

THREE YEARS (84 – 86)	G	IP	H	BB	SO	SB	CS	W	L	S	ERA
Totals	88	599.0	490	237	466	90	32	35	32	0	3.76
At Home and on the Road											
Home	45	307.1	262	137	257	49	19	19	17	0	4.30
Road	43	291.2	228	100	209	41	13	16	15	0	3.18
During the Day and at Night											
Day	28	205.2	155	76	174	21	11	13	7	0	3.06
Night	60	393.1	335	161	292	69	21	22	25	0	4.12
On Grass and on Turf											
Grass	27	178.0	138	58	128	26	10	9	9	0	3.24
Turf	61	421.0	352	179	338	64	22	26	23	0	3.98
By Month											
April	16	114.2	92	39	82	12	10	8	4	0	2.75
May	17	119.2	77	53	93	17	7	9	6	0	3.16
June	15	98.1	76	44	73	13	5	3	5	0	3.48
July	14	92.1	91	37	73	21	5	4	8	0	4.78
August	16	97.0	92	35	72	19	4	4	9	0	4.92
Sept/Oct	10	77.0	62	29	73	8	1	7	0	0	3.86

vs. Opponent Batters

THREE YEARS (84 – 86)	Ave.	OBP	SLG	AB	H	2B	3B	HR	RBI	BB	SO
Totals	.223	.299	.376	2194	490	87	18	71	245	237	466
Pitching vs. Left and Right-handed Batters											
Left	.223	.319	.387	1105	246	42	10	40	127	155	221
Right	.224	.278	.365	1089	244	45	8	31	118	82	245
Situational											
Bases Empty	.219	.284	.364	1386	304	55	11	41	41	122	282
Leadoff	.232	.291	.421	565	131	25	8	22	22	47	109
Not Leadoff	.211	.280	.324	821	173	30	3	19	19	75	173
Runners On	.230	.322	.399	808	186	32	7	30	204	115	184
First Base Only	.247	.317	.423	312	77	14	1	13	31	31	64
Scoring Position	.220	.326	.383	496	109	18	6	17	173	84	120
Late Innings, Close	.211	.302	.316	285	60	7	1	7	23	36	46

RBI/Opportunities
Scoring Position	144 / 692	(21%)
Scoring Position, 2 Out	58 / 324	(18%)
On Third, Less than 2 Out	54 / 107	(50%)
RBI in close games / RBI Total	186 / 245	(76%)

Chris Speier
Chicago Cubs

THREE YEARS (84 – 86)	Ave.	OBP	SLG	AB	H	2B	3B	HR	RBI	BB	SO
Totals	.234	.291	.360	531	124	26	1	13	56	42	93
Batting vs. Left and Right-handed Pitchers											
Left	.247	.304	.402	174	43	7	1	6	21	15	25
Right	.227	.284	.339	357	81	19	0	7	35	27	68
At Home and on the Road											
Home	.227	.291	.333	273	62	12	1	5	31	24	48
Road	.240	.290	.386	258	62	14	0	8	25	18	45
Facing Groundball Pitchers and Flyball Pitchers											
Groundball	.242	.299	.375	240	58	12	1	6	26	20	34
Flyball	.227	.284	.347	291	66	14	0	7	30	22	59
Facing Finesse Pitchers and Power Pitchers											
Finesse	.215	.254	.342	298	64	15	1	7	28	15	42
Power	.258	.335	.382	233	60	11	0	6	28	27	51
On Grass and on Turf											
Grass	.246	.314	.352	281	69	12	0	6	30	28	51
Turf	.220	.263	.368	250	55	14	1	7	26	14	42
During the Day and at Night											
Day	.233	.293	.328	296	69	14	1	4	29	25	51
Night	.234	.287	.400	235	55	12	0	9	27	17	42
By Month											
April	.290	.378	.419	31	9	1	0	1	4	5	4
May	.177	.271	.242	62	11	1	0	1	2	7	15
June	.218	.258	.361	119	26	5	0	4	16	7	23
July	.223	.285	.353	139	31	7	1	3	9	11	23
August	.244	.294	.386	127	31	9	0	3	17	9	21
Sept/Oct	.302	.339	.415	53	16	3	0	1	8	3	7
Situational											
Bases Empty	.219	.275	.335	310	68	16	1	6	6	24	59
Leadoff	.221	.261	.366	131	29	8	1	3	3	7	24
Not Leadoff	.218	.286	.313	179	39	8	0	3	3	17	35
Runners On	.253	.311	.394	221	56	10	0	7	50	18	34
First Base Only	.250	.308	.405	84	21	4	0	3	7	6	13
Scoring Position	.255	.314	.387	137	35	6	0	4	43	12	21
Late Innings, Close	.282	.375	.443	131	37	6	0	5	16	20	20

RBI/Opportunities
Scoring Position	36 / 186	(19%)
Scoring Position, 2 Out	17 / 87	(20%)
On Third, Less than 2 Out	14 / 29	(48%)
RBI in close games / RBI Total	36 / 56	(64%)

Bob Stanley
Boston Red Sox

1986: Finesse, Groundball 1985: Finesse, Groundball 1984: Finesse, Groundball

THREE YEARS (84 – 86)	G	IP	H	BB	SO	SB	CS	W	L	S	ERA
Totals	171	276.2	298	75	152	8	7	21	22	48	3.58
At Home and on the Road											
Home	84	138.1	165	36	76	3	6	11	11	22	4.55
Road	87	138.1	133	39	76	5	1	10	11	26	2.60
During the Day and at Night											
Day	59	90.0	92	19	44	1	4	6	6	15	3.60
Night	112	186.2	206	56	108	7	3	15	16	33	3.57
On Grass and on Turf											
Grass	145	234.2	248	65	132	6	6	18	16	42	3.72
Turf	26	42.0	50	10	20	2	1	3	6	6	2.79
By Month											
April	25	54.2	45	8	28	0	2	1	5	8	2.47
May	32	47.1	51	15	23	2	2	3	3	14	3.99
June	33	54.0	52	17	29	1	0	7	3	12	4.00
July	28	44.2	39	17	31	1	2	6	3	6	2.42
August	33	51.2	82	14	25	2	1	2	7	3	5.40
Sept/Oct	20	24.1	29	4	16	2	0	2	1	5	2.59

vs. Opponent Batters

THREE YEARS (84 – 86)	Ave.	OBP	SLG	AB	H	2B	3B	HR	RBI	BB	SO
Totals	.275	.322	.399	1082	298	45	7	25	173	75	152
Pitching vs. Left and Right-handed Batters											
Left	.278	.343	.396	533	148	23	2	12	92	56	65
Right	.273	.300	.403	549	150	22	5	13	81	19	87
Situational											
Bases Empty	.238	.271	.356	550	131	23	3	12	12	24	96
Leadoff	.254	.292	.433	224	57	12	2	8	8	12	35
Not Leadoff	.227	.257	.304	326	74	11	1	4	4	12	61
Runners On	.314	.371	.444	532	167	22	4	13	161	51	56
First Base Only	.344	.376	.467	180	62	8	1	4	13	8	13
Scoring Position	.298	.369	.432	352	105	14	3	9	148	43	43
Late Innings, Close	.259	.313	.383	629	163	24	3	16	108	52	92

RBI/Opportunities
Scoring Position	130 / 524	(25%)
Scoring Position, 2 Out	41 / 209	(20%)
On Third, Less than 2 Out	58 / 113	(51%)
RBI in close games / RBI Total	128 / 173	(74%)

John Stefero
Baltimore Orioles

	Ave.	OBP	SLG	AB	H	2B	3B	HR	RBI	BB	SO
THREE YEARS (84 – 86)											
Totals	.233	.321	.300	120	28	2	0	2	13	16	25
Batting vs. Left and Right-handed Pitchers											
Left	.167	.167	.167	6	1	0	0	0	0	0	1
Right	.237	.328	.307	114	27	2	0	2	13	16	24
At Home and on the Road											
Home	.200	.263	.300	70	14	1	0	2	9	6	14
Road	.280	.393	.300	50	14	1	0	0	4	10	11
Facing Groundball Pitchers and Flyball Pitchers											
Groundball	.262	.338	.344	61	16	2	0	1	6	7	12
Flyball	.203	.304	.254	59	12	0	0	1	7	9	13
Facing Finesse Pitchers and Power Pitchers											
Finesse	.240	.313	.253	75	18	1	0	0	3	8	17
Power	.222	.333	.378	45	10	1	0	2	10	8	8
On Grass and on Turf											
Grass	.227	.312	.300	110	25	2	0	2	13	14	21
Turf	.300	.417	.300	10	3	0	0	0	0	2	4
During the Day and at Night											
Day	.216	.326	.297	37	8	0	0	1	6	6	11
Night	.241	.319	.301	83	20	2	0	1	7	10	14
By Month											
April	.333	.429	.583	12	4	0	0	1	4	2	5
May	.071	.133	.071	14	1	0	0	0	0	1	8
June	.000	.000	.000	0	0	0	0	0	0	0	0
July	.500	.500	.500	2	1	0	0	0	0	0	1
August	.238	.313	.333	42	10	1	0	1	5	5	8
Sept/Oct	.240	.345	.260	50	12	1	0	0	4	8	3
Situational											
Bases Empty	.266	.347	.281	64	17	1	0	0	0	8	12
Leadoff	.375	.400	.417	24	9	1	0	0	0	1	3
Not Leadoff	.200	.319	.200	40	8	0	0	0	0	7	9
Runners On	.196	.292	.321	56	11	1	0	2	13	8	13
First Base Only	.148	.148	.185	27	4	1	0	0	1	0	4
Scoring Position	.241	.395	.448	29	7	0	0	2	12	8	9
Late Innings, Close	.273	.360	.455	22	6	1	0	1	4	3	4

RBI/Opportunities		
Scoring Position	8 / 45	(18%)
Scoring Position, 2 Out	5 / 20	(25%)
On Third, Less than 2 Out	1 / 6	(17%)
RBI in close games / RBI Total	11 / 13	(85%)

Dave Stewart
Oakland A's

1986: Power, Flyball   1985: Power, Flyball   1984: Power, Flyball

	G	IP	H	BB	SO	SB	CS	W	L	S	ERA
THREE YEARS (84 – 86)											
Totals	115	439.2	436	197	296	49	14	16	25	4	4.59
At Home and on the Road											
Home	63	253.2	250	107	182	35	6	8	14	1	4.51
Road	52	186.0	186	90	114	14	8	8	11	3	4.69
During the Day and and at Night											
Day	36	150.2	134	74	105	18	5	7	10	1	3.70
Night	79	289.0	302	123	191	31	9	9	15	3	5.04
On Grass and on Turf											
Grass	90	364.1	355	164	245	42	10	14	21	4	4.55
Turf	25	75.1	81	33	51	7	4	2	4	0	4.78
By Month											
April	18	46.1	54	26	33	8	0	0	8	2	6.80
May	17	48.2	51	20	30	4	3	3	1	1	4.44
June	23	80.2	77	34	47	8	1	1	3	1	4.69
July	21	72.2	69	38	43	7	1	4	3	0	5.20
August	17	91.1	83	34	69	8	5	4	3	0	3.65
Sept/Oct	19	100.0	102	45	74	14	4	4	7	0	3.96

	Ave.	OBP	SLG	AB	H	2B	3B	HR	RBI	BB	SO
vs. Opponent Batters											
THREE YEARS (84 – 86)											
Totals	.257	.335	.417	1696	436	78	14	55	212	197	296
Pitching vs. Left and Right-handed Batters											
Left	.271	.357	.429	861	233	39	8	27	114	121	136
Right	.243	.312	.405	835	203	39	6	28	98	76	160
Situational											
Bases Empty	.262	.328	.437	987	259	47	10	35	35	91	176
Leadoff	.251	.309	.400	415	104	16	5	12	12	33	68
Not Leadoff	.271	.342	.463	572	155	31	5	23	23	58	108
Runners On	.250	.344	.389	709	177	31	4	20	177	106	120
First Base Only	.292	.399	.412	257	75	11	1	6	19	44	30
Scoring Position	.226	.312	.376	452	102	20	3	14	158	62	90
Late Innings, Close	.229	.319	.354	223	51	8	1	6	23	31	29

RBI/Opportunities		
Scoring Position	131 / 612	(21%)
Scoring Position, 2 Out	42 / 277	(15%)
On Third, Less than 2 Out	52 / 112	(46%)
RBI in close games / RBI Total	120 / 212	(57%)

Sammy Stewart
Boston Red Sox

1986: Power, Flyball   1985: Power, Groundball   1984: Power, Flyball

	G	IP	H	BB	SO	SB	CS	W	L	S	ERA
THREE YEARS (84 – 86)											
Totals	143	286.1	262	161	180	21	11	16	12	22	3.65
At Home and on the Road											
Home	73	161.1	129	99	110	5	8	9	4	12	2.85
Road	70	125.0	133	62	70	16	3	7	8	10	4.68
During the Day and and at Night											
Day	44	81.1	93	45	42	10	4	4	3	6	5.20
Night	99	205.0	169	116	138	11	7	12	9	16	3.03
On Grass and on Turf											
Grass	122	250.1	220	140	158	15	10	15	11	19	3.52
Turf	21	36.0	42	21	22	6	1	1	1	3	4.50
By Month											
April	23	47.1	36	25	32	4	2	6	2	4	2.28
May	21	42.2	33	20	24	3	0	2	0	1	2.74
June	20	32.2	31	23	11	4	1	1	3	2	4.68
July	21	44.2	41	23	32	2	3	1	1	6	3.02
August	27	65.0	56	34	42	3	2	4	1	5	3.05
Sept/Oct	31	54.0	65	36	39	5	5	2	5	4	6.17

	Ave.	OBP	SLG	AB	H	2B	3B	HR	RBI	BB	SO
vs. Opponent Batters											
THREE YEARS (84 – 86)											
Totals	.249	.346	.376	1052	262	37	5	29	164	161	180
Pitching vs. Left and Right-handed Batters											
Left	.264	.389	.373	469	124	20	2	9	64	98	72
Right	.237	.308	.379	583	138	17	3	20	100	63	108
Situational											
Bases Empty	.247	.341	.383	519	128	22	2	15	15	73	79
Leadoff	.276	.363	.458	225	62	7	2	10	10	31	39
Not Leadoff	.224	.323	.327	294	66	15	0	5	5	42	40
Runners On	.251	.350	.370	533	134	15	3	14	149	88	101
First Base Only	.247	.332	.399	198	49	4	1	8	18	25	35
Scoring Position	.254	.360	.352	335	.85	11	2	6	131	63	66
Late Innings, Close	.240	.325	.348	371	89	8	1	10	48	48	61

RBI/Opportunities		
Scoring Position	117 / 513	(23%)
Scoring Position, 2 Out	49 / 239	(21%)
On Third, Less than 2 Out	43 / 93	(46%)
RBI in close games / RBI Total	74 / 164	(45%)

Kurt Stillwell
Cincinnati Reds

	Ave.	OBP	SLG	AB	H	2B	3B	HR	RBI	BB	SO
THREE YEARS (84 – 86)											
Totals	.229	.309	.258	279	64	6	1	0	26	30	47
Batting vs. Left and Right-handed Pitchers											
Left	.244	.363	.279	86	21	3	0	0	7	16	14
Right	.223	.282	.249	193	43	3	1	0	19	14	33
At Home and on the Road											
Home	.219	.298	.245	151	33	4	0	0	12	15	29
Road	.242	.322	.273	128	31	2	1	0	14	15	18
Facing Groundball Pitchers and Flyball Pitchers											
Groundball	.240	.325	.293	150	36	6	1	0	14	18	23
Flyball	.217	.289	.217	129	28	0	0	0	12	12	24
Facing Finesse Pitchers and Power Pitchers											
Finesse	.231	.313	.261	134	31	4	0	0	7	16	29
Power	.228	.304	.255	145	33	2	1	0	19	14	18
On Grass and on Turf											
Grass	.212	.291	.222	99	21	1	0	0	9	11	12
Turf	.239	.318	.278	180	43	5	1	0	17	19	35
During the Day and at Night											
Day	.206	.308	.216	102	21	1	0	0	8	14	25
Night	.243	.309	.282	177	43	5	1	0	18	16	22
By Month											
April	.286	.348	.286	21	6	0	0	0	1	2	6
May	.158	.304	.237	38	6	1	1	0	3	8	10
June	.140	.229	.140	43	6	0	0	0	1	5	11
July	.235	.291	.275	51	12	2	0	0	7	4	8
August	.261	.338	.290	69	18	2	0	0	6	8	6
Sept/Oct	.281	.339	.298	57	16	1	0	0	8	3	6
Situational											
Bases Empty	.212	.308	.237	160	34	4	0	0	0	20	31
Leadoff	.153	.256	.181	72	11	2	0	0	0	8	18
Not Leadoff	.261	.350	.284	88	23	2	0	0	0	12	13
Runners On	.252	.310	.286	119	30	2	1	0	26	10	16
First Base Only	.171	.209	.195	41	7	1	0	0	2	2	7
Scoring Position	.295	.360	.333	78	23	1	1	0	26	8	9
Late Innings, Close	.189	.232	.226	53	10	2	0	0	8	3	12

RBI/Opportunities		
Scoring Position	25 / 109	(23%)
Scoring Position, 2 Out	13 / 54	(24%)
On Third, Less than 2 Out	6 / 20	(30%)
RBI in close games / RBI Total	18 / 26	(69%)

Tim Stoddard
New York Yankees

1986: Power, Flyball   1985: Power, Flyball   1984: Power, Flyball

THREE YEARS (84 – 86)	G	IP	H	BB	SO	SB	CS	W	L	S	ERA
Totals	156	246.2	214	151	210	40	9	16	16	8	4.01
At Home and on the Road											
Home	85	126.2	101	73	109	18	3	12	7	4	3.77
Road	71	120.0	113	78	101	22	6	4	9	4	4.28
During the Day and and at Night											
Day	78	124.1	115	80	110	20	4	10	5	4	4.78
Night	78	122.1	99	71	100	20	5	6	11	4	3.24
On Grass and on Turf											
Grass	119	186.1	153	114	167	27	6	14	11	7	3.67
Turf	37	60.1	61	37	43	13	3	2	5	1	5.07
By Month											
April	18	23.2	15	14	18	3	0	3	2	0	2.28
May	28	41.0	42	31	46	11	2	1	2	2	4.83
June	37	57.1	41	38	43	8	1	2	3	3	2.98
July	26	47.0	42	27	40	9	3	3	5	2	2.68
August	26	52.1	46	25	41	5	3	4	2	1	5.33
Sept/Oct	21	25.1	28	16	22	4	0	3	2	0	6.39

vs. Opponent Batters

THREE YEARS (84 – 86)	Ave.	OBP	SLG	AB	H	2B	3B	HR	RBI	BB	SO
Totals	.237	.344	.379	902	214	36	10	24	138	151	210
Pitching vs. Left and Right-handed Batters											
Left	.250	.366	.407	388	97	15	8	10	60	75	65
Right	.228	.327	.358	514	117	21	2	14	78	76	145
Situational											
Bases Empty	.241	.331	.389	457	110	18	4	14	14	62	106
Leadoff	.251	.345	.390	195	49	10	1	5	5	28	39
Not Leadoff	.233	.321	.389	262	61	8	3	9	9	34	67
Runners On	.234	.356	.369	445	104	18	6	10	124	89	104
First Base Only	.199	.286	.340	156	31	5	4	3	13	18	30
Scoring Position	.253	.389	.384	289	73	13	2	7	111	71	74
Late Innings, Close	.252	.357	.407	305	77	10	5	9	44	52	69

RBI/Opportunities		
Scoring Position	99 / 445	(22%)
Scoring Position, 2 Out	36 / 213	(17%)
On Third, Less than 2 Out	38 / 77	(49%)
RBI in close games / RBI Total	65 / 138	(47%)

Jeff Stone
Philadelphia Phillies

THREE YEARS (84 – 86)	Ave.	OBP	SLG	AB	H	2B	3B	HR	RBI	BB	SO
Totals	.295	.342	.395	698	206	14	13	10	45	44	128
Batting vs. Left and Right-handed Pitchers											
Left	.322	.381	.443	115	37	4	2	2	5	10	22
Right	.290	.334	.386	583	169	10	11	8	40	34	106
At Home and on the Road											
Home	.326	.373	.445	362	118	6	8	7	29	26	63
Road	.262	.308	.342	336	88	8	5	3	16	18	65
Facing Groundball Pitchers and Flyball Pitchers											
Groundball	.310	.347	.413	281	87	7	5	4	20	14	48
Flyball	.285	.339	.384	417	119	7	8	6	25	30	80
Facing Finesse Pitchers and Power Pitchers											
Finesse	.301	.334	.390	408	123	8	5	6	22	18	61
Power	.286	.353	.403	290	83	6	8	4	23	26	67
On Grass and on Turf											
Grass	.258	.293	.320	194	50	6	0	2	8	8	42
Turf	.310	.361	.425	504	156	8	13	8	37	36	86
During the Day and at Night											
Day	.303	.367	.415	195	59	3	2	5	17	20	36
Night	.292	.332	.388	503	147	11	11	5	28	24	92
By Month											
April	.300	.364	.467	60	18	0	2	2	5	6	10
May	.200	.223	.200	100	20	0	0	0	3	3	22
June	.313	.363	.428	166	52	5	4	2	12	12	24
July	.273	.342	.394	66	18	3	1	1	5	6	11
August	.300	.349	.475	120	36	3	3	4	9	5	21
Sept/Oct	.333	.373	.398	186	62	3	3	1	11	12	40
Situational											
Bases Empty	.299	.351	.385	481	144	9	7	6	6	33	84
Leadoff	.274	.328	.333	234	64	4	2	2	2	17	47
Not Leadoff	.324	.372	.433	247	80	5	5	4	4	16	37
Runners On	.286	.323	.419	217	62	5	6	4	39	11	44
First Base Only	.361	.398	.518	83	30	4	3	1	5	5	12
Scoring Position	.239	.278	.358	134	32	1	3	3	34	6	32
Late Innings, Close	.261	.305	.378	111	29	2	1	3	7	5	27

RBI/Opportunities		
Scoring Position	29 / 165	(18%)
Scoring Position, 2 Out	8 / 73	(11%)
On Third, Less than 2 Out	12 / 26	(46%)
RBI! in close games / RBI Total	28 / 45	(62%)

Franklin Stubbs
Los Angeles Dodgers

THREE YEARS (84 – 86)	Ave.	OBP	SLG	AB	H	2B	3B	HR	RBI	BB	SO
Totals	.215	.284	.392	646	139	13	4	31	77	61	173
Batting vs. Left and Right-handed Pitchers											
Left	.215	.235	.340	144	31	3	0	5	12	4	28
Right	.215	.297	.406	502	108	10	4	26	65	57	145
At Home and on the Road											
Home	.244	.314	.431	311	76	6	2	16	42	33	82
Road	.188	.255	.355	335	63	7	2	15	35	28	91
Facing Groundball Pitchers and Flyball Pitchers											
Groundball	.269	.322	.492	309	83	6	3	19	48	24	65
Flyball	.166	.249	.300	337	56	7	1	12	29	37	108
Facing Finesse Pitchers and Power Pitchers											
Finesse	.243	.302	.421	354	86	11	2	16	51	30	81
Power	.182	.262	.356	292	53	2	2	15	26	31	92
On Grass and on Turf											
Grass	.210	.277	.375	480	101	9	2	22	57	45	132
Turf	.229	.304	.440	166	38	4	2	9	20	16	41
During the Day and at Night											
Day	.224	.292	.407	214	48	5	2	10	25	21	47
Night	.211	.279	.384	432	91	8	2	21	52	40	126
By Month											
April	.145	.206	.339	62	9	0	0	4	10	5	28
May	.252	.325	.486	107	27	3	2	6	15	11	32
June	.274	.355	.519	135	37	3	0	10	21	17	25
July	.227	.281	.409	154	35	3	2	7	17	11	36
August	.138	.198	.202	94	13	0	0	2	2	7	29
Sept/Oct	.191	.269	.298	94	18	4	0	2	12	10	23
Situational											
Bases Empty	.222	.262	.405	365	81	6	2	19	19	19	81
Leadoff	.270	.289	.466	148	40	3	1	8	8	4	23
Not Leadoff	.189	.245	.364	217	41	3	1	11	11	15	58
Runners On	.206	.309	.374	281	58	7	2	12	58	42	92
First Base Only	.259	.306	.431	116	30	2	0	6	12	8	36
Scoring Position	.170	.310	.333	165	28	5	2	6	46	34	56
Late Innings, Close	.217	.346	.377	106	23	1	2	4	12	20	32

RBI/Opportunities		
Scoring Position	37 / 233	(16%)
Scoring Position, 2 Out	15 / 111	(14%)
On Third, Less than 2 Out	13 / 34	(38%)
RBI in close games / RBI Total	52 / 77	(68%)

Marc Sullivan
Boston Red Sox

THREE YEARS (84 – 86)	Ave.	OBP	SLG	AB	H	2B	3B	HR	RBI	BB	SO
Totals	.196	.263	.273	194	38	6	0	3	18	14	47
Batting vs. Left and Right-handed Pitchers											
Left	.178	.265	.277	101	18	1	0	3	9	10	24
Right	.215	.260	.269	93	20	5	0	0	9	4	23
At Home and on the Road											
Home	.231	.286	.363	91	21	3	0	3	13	5	23
Road	.165	.243	.194	103	17	3	0	0	5	9	24
Facing Groundball Pitchers and Flyball Pitchers											
Groundball	.173	.221	.272	81	14	2	0	2	5	4	17
Flyball	.212	.291	.274	113	24	4	0	1	13	10	30
Facing Finesse Pitchers and Power Pitchers											
Finesse	.169	.224	.185	124	21	2	0	0	6	8	28
Power	.243	.329	.429	70	17	4	0	3	12	6	19
On Grass and on Turf											
Grass	.204	.280	.293	157	32	5	0	3	18	13	39
Turf	.162	.184	.189	37	6	1	0	0	0	1	8
During the Day and at Night											
Day	.221	.293	.294	68	15	2	0	1	8	6	14
Night	.183	.246	.262	126	23	4	0	2	10	8	33
By Month											
April	.167	.211	.167	18	3	0	0	0	1	1	5
May	.326	.400	.419	43	14	1	0	1	7	3	8
June	.042	.042	.042	24	1	0	0	0	0	0	8
July	.115	.148	.231	26	3	0	0	1	3	1	7
August	.103	.212	.207	29	3	3	0	0	0	3	10
Sept/Oct	.259	.333	.352	54	14	2	0	1	7	6	9
Situational											
Bases Empty	.171	.233	.228	123	21	4	0	1	1	9	29
Leadoff	.179	.233	.214	56	10	2	0	0	0	4	17
Not Leadoff	.164	.233	.239	67	11	2	0	1	1	5	12
Runners On	.239	.313	.352	71	17	2	0	2	17	5	18
First Base Only	.115	.207	.154	26	3	1	0	0	0	3	5
Scoring Position	.311	.373	.467	45	14	1	0	2	17	2	13
Late Innings, Close	.278	.409	.444	18	5	0	0	1	6	2	4

RBI/Opportunities		
Scoring Position	14 / 64	(22%)
Scoring Position, 2 Out	11 / 37	(30%)
On Third, Less than 2 Out	2 / 7	(29%)
RBI in close games / RBI Total	10 / 18	(56%)

Dale Sveum
Milwaukee Brewers

THREE YEARS (84 – 86)

	Ave.	OBP	SLG	AB	H	2B	3B	HR	RBI	BB	SO
Totals	.246	.316	.366	317	78	13	2	7	35	32	63
Batting vs. Left and Right-handed Pitchers											
Left	.271	.366	.438	96	26	8	1	2	12	14	15
Right	.235	.293	.335	221	52	5	1	5	23	18	48
At Home and on the Road											
Home	.226	.317	.346	159	36	7	0	4	17	20	29
Road	.266	.316	.386	158	42	6	2	3	18	12	34
Facing Groundball Pitchers and Flyball Pitchers											
Groundball	.232	.316	.329	155	36	7	1	2	20	17	25
Flyball	.259	.324	.401	162	42	6	1	5	15	15	38
Facing Finesse Pitchers and Power Pitchers											
Finesse	.229	.302	.370	192	44	8	2	5	17	20	35
Power	.272	.338	.360	125	34	5	0	2	18	12	28
On Grass and on Turf											
Grass	.238	.312	.363	256	61	9	1	7	26	27	52
Turf	.279	.333	.377	61	17	4	1	0	9	5	11
During the Day and at Night											
Day	.260	.328	.337	104	27	2	0	2	12	11	22
Night	.239	.311	.380	213	51	11	2	5	23	21	41
By Month											
April	.000	.000	.000	0	0	0	0	0	0	0	0
May	.385	.420	.554	65	25	6	1	1	12	4	14
June	.196	.240	.289	97	19	3	0	2	8	6	16
July	.304	.340	.393	56	17	2	0	1	7	9	14
August	.190	.292	.333	42	8	1	1	1	1	6	5
Sept/Oct	.158	.262	.281	57	9	1	0	2	7	7	14
Situational											
Bases Empty	.235	.297	.358	179	42	2	1	6	6	16	36
Leadoff	.205	.256	.329	73	15	0	0	3	3	5	17
Not Leadoff	.255	.325	.377	106	27	2	1	3	3	11	19
Runners On	.261	.340	.377	138	36	11	1	1	29	16	27
First Base Only	.230	.319	.361	61	14	3	1	1	4	8	13
Scoring Position	.286	.356	.390	77	22	8	0	0	25	8	14
Late Innings, Close	.264	.310	.283	53	14	1	0	0	6	4	9

RBI/Opportunities

Scoring Position	22 / 104	(21%)
Scoring Position, 2 Out	14 / 52	(27%)
On Third, Less than 2 Out	5 / 15	(33%)
RBI in close games / RBI Total	21 / 35	(60%)

Bill Swift
Seattle Mariners

1986: Finesse, Groundball 1985: Finesse, Groundball 1984: Did not play

THREE YEARS (84 – 86)

	G	IP	H	BB	SO	SB	CS	W	L	S	ERA
Totals	52	236.0	279	103	110	27	14	8	19	0	5.11
At Home and on the Road											
Home	26	122.0	149	52	61	15	4	4	9	0	4.94
Road	26	114.0	130	51	49	12	10	4	10	0	5.29
During the Day and and at Night											
Day	13	54.2	74	21	24	7	2	2	4	0	5.27
Night	39	181.1	205	82	86	20	12	6	15	0	5.06
On Grass and on Turf											
Grass	20	88.1	100	42	36	8	9	3	9	0	5.71
Turf	32	147.2	179	61	74	19	5	5	10	0	4.75
By Month											
April	7	18.2	17	17	14	4	1	0	0	0	3.86
May	7	26.0	40	8	13	2	2	0	3	0	6.58
June	10	52.0	58	18	18	9	5	3	2	0	5.02
July	6	29.1	43	12	14	1	1	1	4	0	6.14
August	9	54.0	53	26	21	6	1	2	4	0	4.33
Sept/Oct	13	56.0	68	22	30	5	4	2	6	0	5.14

vs. Opponent Batters

THREE YEARS (84 – 86)

	Ave.	OBP	SLG	AB	H	2B	3B	HR	RBI	BB	SO
Totals	.298	.373	.406	935	279	50	6	13	126	103	110
Pitching vs. Left and Right-handed Batters											
Left	.345	.422	.484	516	178	37	4	9	77	66	46
Right	.241	.310	.310	419	101	13	2	4	49	37	64
Situational											
Bases Empty	.291	.361	.406	508	148	28	3	8	8	47	53
Leadoff	.271	.354	.418	225	61	13	1	6	6	27	28
Not Leadoff	.307	.366	.396	283	87	15	2	2	2	20	25
Runners On	.307	.387	.407	427	131	22	3	5	118	56	57
First Base Only	.295	.357	.398	166	49	11	0	2	8	15	21
Scoring Position	.314	.405	.414	261	82	11	3	3	110	41	36
Late Innings, Close	.275	.348	.400	80	22	2	1	2	3	7	9

RBI/Opportunities

Scoring Position	102 / 368	(28%)
Scoring Position, 2 Out	37 / 155	(24%)
On Third, Less than 2 Out	41 / 65	(63%)
RBI in close games / RBI Total	89 / 126	(71%)

Scott Terry
Cincinnati Reds

1986: Power, Flyball 1985: Did not play 1984: Did not play

THREE YEARS (84 – 86)

	G	IP	H	BB	SO	SB	CS	W	L	S	ERA
Totals	28	55.2	66	32	32	9	3	1	2	0	6.14
At Home and on the Road											
Home	14	31.1	40	13	16	4	2	1	1	0	4.88
Road	14	24.1	26	19	16	5	1	0	1	0	7.77
During the Day and and at Night											
Day	11	29.1	42	12	16	3	2	1	1	0	7.67
Night	17	26.1	24	20	16	6	1	0	1	0	4.44
On Grass and on Turf											
Grass	7	15.2	19	8	10	2	0	0	1	0	8.04
Turf	21	40.0	47	24	22	7	3	1	1	0	5.40
By Month											
April	5	8.1	7	5	4	3	1	0	0	0	1.08
May	7	16.1	20	8	11	3	0	0	1	0	8.82
June	6	8.1	12	5	4	0	1	0	1	0	4.32
July	6	16.0	21	11	9	3	1	0	0	0	7.87
August	1	2.0	1	0	1	0	0	0	0	0	0.00
Sept/Oct	3	4.2	5	3	3	0	0	1	0	0	5.79

vs. Opponent Batters

THREE YEARS (84 – 86)

	Ave.	OBP	SLG	AB	H	2B	3B	HR	RBI	BB	SO
Totals	.300	.387	.455	220	66	4	3	8	40	32	32
Pitching vs. Left and Right-handed Batters											
Left	.343	.410	.500	108	37	2	3	3	18	13	15
Right	.259	.366	.411	112	29	2	0	5	22	19	17
Situational											
Bases Empty	.266	.365	.330	109	29	2	1	1	1	17	18
Leadoff	.319	.418	.383	47	15	0	0	1	1	8	5
Not Leadoff	.226	.324	.290	62	14	2	1	0	0	9	13
Runners On	.333	.409	.577	111	37	2	2	7	39	15	14
First Base Only	.389	.421	.630	54	21	0	2	3	8	3	5
Scoring Position	.281	.400	.526	57	16	2	0	4	31	12	9
Late Innings, Close	.296	.375	.333	27	8	1	0	0	1	4	2

RBI/Opportunities

Scoring Position	23 / 90	(26%)
Scoring Position, 2 Out	11 / 43	(26%)
On Third, Less than 2 Out	6 / 15	(40%)
RBI in close games / RBI Total	12 / 40	(30%)

Mickey Tettleton
Oakland A's

THREE YEARS (84 – 86)

	Ave.	OBP	SLG	AB	H	2B	3B	HR	RBI	BB	SO
Totals	.233	.336	.367	498	116	23	1	14	55	77	131
Batting vs. Left and Right-handed Pitchers											
Left	.235	.335	.425	179	42	10	0	8	21	27	47
Right	.232	.337	.335	319	74	13	1	6	34	50	84
At Home and on the Road											
Home	.236	.344	.350	263	62	10	1	6	24	43	70
Road	.230	.327	.387	235	54	13	0	8	31	34	61
Facing Groundball Pitchers and Flyball Pitchers											
Groundball	.254	.361	.391	248	63	14	1	6	25	41	66
Flyball	.212	.311	.344	250	53	9	0	8	30	36	65
Facing Finesse Pitchers and Power Pitchers											
Finesse	.239	.321	.396	293	70	14	1	10	36	36	75
Power	.224	.356	.327	205	46	9	0	4	19	41	56
On Grass and on Turf											
Grass	.236	.335	.376	415	98	20	1	12	44	62	111
Turf	.217	.340	.325	83	18	3	0	2	11	15	20
During the Day and at Night											
Day	.271	.372	.380	192	52	6	0	5	21	30	49
Night	.209	.314	.359	306	64	17	1	9	34	47	82
By Month											
April	.125	.250	.167	48	6	2	0	0	3	8	6
May	.182	.259	.364	22	4	1	0	1	5	3	6
June	.320		.467	75	24	5	0	2	7	10	15
July	.223	.336	.306	121	27	4	0	2	10	19	37
August	.185	.283	.370	81	15	3	0	4	15	11	26
Sept/Oct	.265	.372	.430	151	40	8	1	5	15	26	41
Situational											
Bases Empty	.234	.334	.406	278	65	10	1	12	12	40	72
Leadoff	.269	.368	.556	108	29	7	0	8	8	16	23
Not Leadoff	.212	.313	.312	170	36	3	1	4	4	24	49
Runners On	.232	.338	.318	220	51	13	0	2	43	37	59
First Base Only	.260	.324	.302	96	25	4	0	0	3	9	21
Scoring Position	.210	.348	.331	124	26	9	0	2	40	28	38
Late Innings, Close	.215	.279	.354	79	17	2	0	3	7	7	19

RBI/Opportunities

Scoring Position	36 / 184	(20%)
Scoring Position, 2 Out	10 / 75	(13%)
On Third, Less than 2 Out	17 / 36	(47%)
RBI in close games / RBI Total	27 / 55	(49%)

Tim Teufel
New York Mets

THREE YEARS (84 – 86)

	Ave.	OBP	SLG	AB	H	2B	3B	HR	RBI	BB	SO
Totals	.258	.339	.393	1281	331	74	7	28	142	156	185
Batting vs. Left and Right-handed Pitchers											
Left	.251	.335	.365	499	125	26	2	9	45	65	56
Right	.263	.342	.410	782	206	48	5	19	97	91	129
At Home and on the Road											
Home	.252	.324	.395	651	164	34	4	17	88	70	101
Road	.265	.355	.390	630	167	40	3	11	54	86	84
Facing Groundball Pitchers and Flyball Pitchers											
Groundball	.252	.333	.380	648	163	35	0	16	74	79	94
Flyball	.265	.345	.406	633	168	39	7	12	68	77	91
Facing Finesse Pitchers and Power Pitchers											
Finesse	.261	.326	.408	713	186	44	2	19	82	70	80
Power	.255	.354	.373	568	145	30	5	9	60	86	105
On Grass and on Turf											
Grass	.258	.350	.370	565	146	35	2	8	52	81	90
Turf	.258	.330	.411	716	185	39	5	20	90	75	95
During the Day and at Night											
Day	.268	.347	.424	403	108	23	2	12	59	51	58
Night	.254	.335	.378	878	223	51	5	16	83	105	127
By Month											
April	.251	.338	.372	199	50	12	0	4	32	25	26
May	.274	.352	.397	237	65	7	2	6	31	28	40
June	.267	.335	.430	221	59	22	1	4	23	22	22
July	.255	.342	.337	196	50	8	1	2	19	28	26
August	.279	.372	.434	219	61	11	1	7	15	33	34
Sept/Oct	.220	.291	.378	209	46	14	2	5	22	20	37
Situational											
Bases Empty	.238	.326	.387	705	168	38	5	19	19	86	114
Leadoff	.270	.339	.468	248	67	17	1	10	10	25	28
Not Leadoff	.221	.319	.344	457	101	21	4	9	9	61	86
Runners On	.283	.355	.399	576	163	36	2	9	123	70	71
First Base Only	.337	.375	.481	264	89	21	1	5	17	16	28
Scoring Position	.237	.340	.330	312	74	15	1	4	106	54	43
Late Innings, Close	.245	.347	.358	212	52	9	0	5	27	32	35

RBI/Opportunities

Scoring Position	98 / 447	(22%)
Scoring Position, 2 Out	31 / 170	(18%)
On Third, Less than 2 Out	46 / 91	(51%)
RBI in close games / RBI Total	92 / 142	(65%)

Bob Tewksbury
New York Yankees

1986: Finesse, Groundball   1985: Did not play   1984: Did not play

THREE YEARS (84 – 86)

	G	IP	H	BB	SO	SB	CS	W	L	S	ERA
Totals	23	130.1	144	31	49	1	3	9	5	0	3.31
At Home and on the Road											
Home	10	59.2	64	13	22	0	2	4	1	0	2.56
Road	13	70.2	80	18	27	1	1	5	4	0	3.95
During the Day and and at Night											
Day	10	59.2	61	11	22	1	1	4	3	0	3.17
Night	13	70.2	83	20	27	0	2	5	2	0	3.44
On Grass and on Turf											
Grass	19	111.0	123	28	36	1	3	8	4	0	3.24
Turf	4	19.1	21	3	13	0	0	1	1	0	3.72
By Month											
April	4	27.0	27	4	10	0	1	2	1	0	3.33
May	4	18.2	29	3	9	1	1	2	1	0	5.30
June	6	29.1	35	6	8	0	0	1	0	0	2.45
July	3	17.2	20	5	7	0	0	1	2	0	4.08
August	0	0.0	0	0	0	0	0	0	0	0	0.00
Sept/Oct	6	37.2	33	13	15	0	1	3	1	0	2.63

vs. Opponent Batters

THREE YEARS (84 – 86)

	Ave.	OBP	SLG	AB	H	2B	3B	HR	RBI	BB	SO
Totals	.282	.325	.397	511	144	21	7	8	48	31	49
Pitching vs. Left and Right-handed Batters											
Left	.254	.288	.383	264	67	6	5	6	22	13	21
Right	.312	.363	.413	247	77	15	2	2	26	18	28
Situational											
Bases Empty	.283	.327	.433	293	83	18	4	6	6	17	31
Leadoff	.308	.333	.429	133	41	8	1	2	2	5	13
Not Leadoff	.263	.322	.438	160	42	10	3	4	4	12	18
Runners On	.280	.322	.349	218	61	3	3	2	42	14	18
First Base Only	.292	.327	.385	96	28	1	1	2	5	3	11
Scoring Position	.270	.319	.320	122	33	2	2	0	37	11	7
Late Innings, Close	.265	.297	.353	34	9	1	1	0	1	2	0

RBI/Opportunities

Scoring Position	36 / 161	(22%)
Scoring Position, 2 Out	19 / 70	(27%)
On Third, Less than 2 Out	14 / 32	(44%)
RBI in close games / RBI Total	33 / 48	(69%)

Bob Thigpen
Chicago White Sox

1986: Finesse, Flyball   1985: Did not play   1984: Did not play

THREE YEARS (84 – 86)

	G	IP	H	BB	SO	SB	CS	W	L	S	ERA
Totals	20	35.2	26	12	20	2	0	2	0	7	1.77
At Home and on the Road											
Home	10	16.2	10	5	10	0	0	1	0	5	1.08
Road	10	19.0	16	7	10	2	0	1	0	2	2.37
During the Day and and at Night											
Day	6	12.0	9	5	7	1	0	0	0	3	1.50
Night	14	23.2	17	7	13	1	0	2	0	4	1.90
On Grass and on Turf											
Grass	15	28.1	22	12	16	1	0	1	0	5	1.91
Turf	5	7.1	4	0	4	1	0	1	0	2	1.23
By Month											
April	0	0.0	0	0	0	0	0	0	0	0	0.00
May	0	0.0	0	0	0	0	0	0	0	0	0.00
June	0	0.0	0	0	0	0	0	0	0	0	0.00
July	0	0.0	0	0	0	0	0	0	0	0	0.00
August	10	19.1	12	11	10	1	0	0	0	3	0.93
Sept/Oct	10	16.1	14	1	10	1	0	2	0	4	2.76

vs. Opponent Batters

THREE YEARS (84 – 86)

	Ave.	OBP	SLG	AB	H	2B	3B	HR	RBI	BB	SO
Totals	.205	.277	.268	127	26	3	1	1	12	12	20
Pitching vs. Left and Right-handed Batters											
Left	.170	.254	.189	53	9	1	0	0	4	6	8
Right	.230	.293	.324	74	17	2	1	1	8	6	12
Situational											
Bases Empty	.185	.243	.277	65	12	3	0	1	1	5	10
Leadoff	.222	.250	.370	27	6	1	0	1	1	1	5
Not Leadoff	.158	.238	.211	38	6	2	0	0	0	4	5
Runners On	.226	.310	.258	62	14	0	1	0	11	7	10
First Base Only	.238	.333	.238	21	5	0	0	0	0	3	3
Scoring Position	.220	.298	.268	41	9	0	1	0	11	4	7
Late Innings, Close	.205	.230	.301	83	17	3	1	1	9	2	13

RBI/Opportunities

Scoring Position	11 / 55	(20%)
Scoring Position, 2 Out	3 / 23	(13%)
On Third, Less than 2 Out	4 / 13	(31%)
RBI in close games / RBI Total	9 / 12	(75%)

Andres Thomas
Atlanta Braves

THREE YEARS (84 – 86)

	Ave.	OBP	SLG	AB	H	2B	3B	HR	RBI	BB	SO
Totals	.252	.268	.367	341	86	17	2	6	34	8	51
Batting vs. Left and Right-handed Pitchers											
Left	.265	.270	.381	147	39	9	1	2	12	1	17
Right	.242	.266	.356	194	47	8	1	4	22	7	34
At Home and on the Road											
Home	.203	.233	.275	138	28	5	1	1	11	6	16
Road	.286	.293	.429	203	58	12	1	5	23	2	35
Facing Groundball Pitchers and Flyball Pitchers											
Groundball	.293	.314	.463	147	43	9	2	4	18	5	21
Flyball	.222	.232	.294	194	43	8	0	2	16	3	30
Facing Finesse Pitchers and Power Pitchers											
Finesse	.254	.260	.384	177	45	10	2	3	19	2	20
Power	.250	.276	.348	164	41	7	0	3	15	6	31
On Grass and on Turf											
Grass	.217	.238	.264	235	51	6	1	1	19	7	34
Turf	.330	.336	.594	106	35	11	1	5	15	1	17
During the Day and at Night											
Day	.245	.261	.358	106	26	10	1	0	13	3	19
Night	.255	.271	.370	235	60	7	1	6	21	5	32
By Month											
April	.286	.333	.429	14	4	2	0	0	2	1	0
May	.333	.358	.490	51	17	5	0	1	5	2	8
June	.268	.268	.482	56	15	1	1	3	6	0	5
July	.316	.337	.506	79	25	7	1	2	11	3	15
August	.149	.163	.170	47	7	1	0	0	3	1	10
Sept/Oct	.191	.200	.202	94	18	1	0	0	7	1	13
Situational											
Bases Empty	.249	.261	.384	185	46	9	2	4	4	3	34
Leadoff	.250	.250	.397	68	17	4	0	2	2	0	11
Not Leadoff	.248	.267	.376	117	29	5	2	2	2	3	23
Runners On	.256	.276	.346	156	40	8	0	2	30	5	17
First Base Only	.294	.294	.353	68	20	1	0	1	3	0	6
Scoring Position	.227	.263	.341	88	20	7	0	1	27	5	11
Late Innings, Close	.250	.308	.350	60	15	3	0	1	7	5	8

RBI/Opportunities

Scoring Position	24 / 125	(19%)
Scoring Position, 2 Out	14 / 55	(25%)
On Third, Less than 2 Out	7 / 24	(29%)
RBI in close games / RBI Total	19 / 34	(56%)

Gorman Thomas
Milwaukee Brewers

THREE YEARS (84 – 86)

	Ave.	OBP	SLG	AB	H	2B	3B	HR	RBI	BB	SO
Totals	.198	.324	.395	907	180	27	2	49	136	170	258
Batting vs. Left and Right-handed Pitchers											
Left	.185	.338	.409	276	51	8	0	18	49	65	74
Right	.204	.318	.388	631	129	19	2	31	87	105	184
At Home and on the Road											
Home	.187	.313	.379	433	81	12	1	23	63	80	126
Road	.209	.334	.409	474	99	15	1	26	73	90	132
Facing Groundball Pitchers and Flyball Pitchers											
Groundball	.190	.314	.361	415	79	15	1	18	52	76	116
Flyball	.205	.333	.423	492	101	12	1	31	84	94	142
Facing Finesse Pitchers and Power Pitchers											
Finesse	.227	.344	.412	524	119	18	2	25	75	95	128
Power	.159	.296	.371	383	61	9	0	24	61	75	130
On Grass and on Turf											
Grass	.208	.353	.419	399	83	13	1	23	58	90	118
Turf	.191	.300	.376	508	97	14	1	26	78	80	140
During the Day and at Night											
Day	.188	.321	.376	229	43	7	0	12	36	44	62
Night	.202	.325	.401	678	137	20	2	37	100	126	196
By Month											
April	.231	.370	.432	199	46	4	0	12	35	43	51
May	.155	.257	.323	155	24	5	0	7	22	23	42
June	.216	.349	.375	88	19	2	0	4	14	25	28
July	.229	.337	.543	140	32	5	0	13	25	23	36
August	.168	.282	.335	167	28	4	0	8	20	27	53
Sept/Oct	.196	.323	.361	158	31	7	2	5	20	29	48
Situational											
Bases Empty	.218	.332	.436	440	96	17	2	25	25	74	125
Leadoff	.239	.345	.497	197	47	10	1	13	13	31	52
Not Leadoff	.202	.322	.387	243	49	7	1	12	12	43	73
Runners On	.180	.317	.355	467	84	10	0	24	111	96	133
First Base Only	.203	.308	.391	197	40	4	0	11	23	29	56
Scoring Position	.163	.323	.330	270	44	6	0	13	88	67	77
Late Innings, Close	.137	.256	.261	153	21	4	0	5	18	25	46

RBI/Opportunities

Scoring Position	67 / 413	(16%)
Scoring Position, 2 Out	19 / 174	(11%)
On Third, Less than 2 Out	31 / 81	(38%)
RBI in close games / RBI Total	74 / 136	(54%)

Milt Thompson
Philadelphia Phillies

THREE YEARS (84 – 86)

	Ave.	OBP	SLG	AB	H	2B	3B	HR	RBI	BB	SO
Totals	.276	.330	.353	580	160	15	3	8	33	44	109
Batting vs. Left and Right-handed Pitchers											
Left	.173	.202	.185	81	14	1	0	0	3	3	18
Right	.293	.350	.381	499	146	14	3	8	30	41	91
At Home and on the Road											
Home	.295	.345	.390	292	86	10	3	4	17	21	56
Road	.257	.315	.316	288	74	5	0	4	16	23	53
Facing Groundball Pitchers and Flyball Pitchers											
Groundball	.259	.309	.384	282	73	8	1	2	16	19	52
Flyball	.292	.350	.389	298	87	7	2	6	17	25	57
Facing Finesse Pitchers and Power Pitchers											
Finesse	.291	.329	.363	292	85	8	2	3	20	15	47
Power	.260	.331	.344	288	75	7	1	5	13	29	62
On Grass and on Turf											
Grass	.295	.337	.370	305	90	10	2	3	15	16	53
Turf	.255	.322	.335	275	70	5	1	5	18	28	56
During the Day and at Night											
Day	.242	.303	.300	190	46	3	1	2	12	16	43
Night	.292	.344	.379	390	114	12	2	6	21	28	66
By Month											
April	.194	.250	.258	62	12	1	0	1	4	5	13
May	.198	.244	.259	81	16	2	0	1	4	4	17
June	.286	.348	.429	21	6	0	0	1	4	2	3
July	.333	.333	.410	39	13	1	1	0	1	0	10
August	.319	.339	.398	113	36	5	2	0	8	2	27
Sept/Oct	.292	.368	.371	264	77	6	0	5	12	31	39
Situational											
Bases Empty	.267	.321	.362	389	104	12	2	7	7	28	73
Leadoff	.289	.335	.377	204	59	7	1	3	3	12	37
Not Leadoff	.243	.307	.346	185	45	5	1	4	4	16	36
Runners On	.293	.348	.335	191	56	3	1	1	26	16	36
First Base Only	.310	.356	.381	84	26	1	1	1	3	6	11
Scoring Position	.280	.342	.299	107	30	2	0	0	23	10	25
Late Innings, Close	.315	.377	.387	111	35	5	0	1	8	10	24

RBI/Opportunities

Scoring Position	23 / 146	(16%)
Scoring Position, 2 Out	8 / 68	(12%)
On Third, Less than 2 Out	11 / 18	(61%)
RBI in close games / RBI Total	26 / 33	(79%)

Dickie Thon
Houston Astros

THREE YEARS (84 – 86)

	Ave.	OBP	SLG	AB	H	2B	3B	HR	RBI	BB	SO
Totals	.253	.312	.348	546	138	19	3	9	51	47	103
Batting vs. Left and Right-handed Pitchers											
Left	.259	.323	.344	340	88	12	1	5	28	33	53
Right	.243	.293	.354	206	50	7	2	4	23	14	50
At Home and on the Road											
Home	.231	.294	.322	286	66	11	3	3	22	25	50
Road	.277	.331	.377	260	72	8	0	6	29	22	53
Facing Groundball Pitchers and Flyball Pitchers											
Groundball	.234	.297	.295	278	65	11	0	2	21	26	58
Flyball	.272	.326	.403	268	73	8	3	7	30	21	45
Facing Finesse Pitchers and Power Pitchers											
Finesse	.255	.318	.369	306	78	13	2	6	29	28	49
Power	.250	.304	.321	240	60	6	1	3	22	19	54
On Grass and on Turf											
Grass	.261	.322	.338	157	41	3	0	3	19	15	40
Turf	.249	.307	.352	389	97	16	3	6	32	32	63
During the Day and at Night											
Day	.250	.323	.355	172	43	3	0	5	21	19	36
Night	.254	.306	.345	374	95	16	3	4	30	28	67
By Month											
April	.245	.310	.311	106	26	5	1	0	9	9	26
May	.216	.280	.338	74	16	4	1	1	4	7	13
June	.192	.224	.219	73	14	2	0	0	2	3	19
July	.341	.363	.466	88	30	5	0	2	9	3	11
August	.214	.290	.345	84	18	0	1	3	14	9	13
Sept/Oct	.281	.360	.380	121	34	3	0	3	13	16	21
Situational											
Bases Empty	.263	.310	.344	323	85	11	0	5	5	22	59
Leadoff	.285	.327	.361	144	41	5	0	2	2	9	24
Not Leadoff	.246	.297	.330	179	44	6	0	3	3	13	35
Runners On	.238	.313	.354	223	53	8	3	4	46	25	44
First Base Only	.194	.255	.245	98	19	2	0	1	3	7	21
Scoring Position	.272	.356	.440	125	34	6	3	3	43	18	23
Late Innings, Close	.282	.364	.359	78	22	0	0	2	5	10	20

RBI/Opportunities

Scoring Position	38 / 172	(22%)
Scoring Position, 2 Out	18 / 86	(21%)
On Third, Less than 2 Out	13 / 26	(50%)
RBI in close games / RBI Total	24 / 51	(47%)

Andre Thornton
Cleveland Indians

THREE YEARS (84 – 86)

	Ave.	OBP	SLG	AB	H	2B	3B	HR	RBI	BB	SO
Totals	.248	.337	.434	1449	360	53	0	72	253	203	221
Batting vs. Left and Right-handed Pitchers											
Left	.261	.374	.460	433	113	14	0	24	74	80	59
Right	.243	.321	.423	1016	247	39	0	48	179	123	162
At Home and on the Road											
Home	.281	.364	.499	727	204	30	0	43	154	102	91
Road	.216	.311	.368	722	156	23	0	29	99	101	130
Facing Groundball Pitchers and Flyball Pitchers											
Groundball	.264	.345	.434	705	186	27	0	31	125	93	112
Flyball	.234	.334	.434	744	174	26	0	41	128	110	109
Facing Finesse Pitchers and Power Pitchers											
Finesse	.247	.315	.441	826	204	34	0	42	138	85	108
Power	.250	.364	.425	623	156	19	0	30	115	118	113
On Grass and on Turf											
Grass	.256	.346	.453	1240	318	43	0	67	232	179	190
Turf	.201	.286	.321	209	42	10	0	5	21	24	31
During the Day and at Night											
Day	.259	.356	.455	440	114	17	0	23	90	71	70
Night	.244	.329	.425	1009	246	36	0	49	163	132	151
By Month											
April	.183	.278	.314	153	28	5	0	5	23	20	34
May	.227	.332	.355	273	62	8	0	9	33	45	40
June	.244	.315	.481	258	63	7	0	18	45	29	40
July	.237	.329	.393	257	61	10	0	10	47	36	43
August	.281	.371	.495	303	85	11	0	18	55	45	38
Sept/Oct	.298	.376	.532	205	61	12	0	12	50	28	26
Situational											
Bases Empty	.230	.323	.411	742	171	20	0	38	38	101	114
Leadoff	.218	.296	.363	399	87	13	0	15	15	44	63
Not Leadoff	.245	.354	.466	343	84	7	0	23	23	57	51
Runners On	.267	.351	.458	707	189	33	0	34	215	102	107
First Base Only	.258	.323	.425	325	84	12	0	14	34	29	41
Scoring Position	.275	.372	.487	382	105	21	0	20	181	73	66
Late Innings, Close	.274	.383	.500	212	58	6	0	14	46	40	31

RBI/Opportunities

Scoring Position	147 / 543	(27%)
Scoring Position, 2 Out	54 / 244	(22%)
On Third, Less than 2 Out	54 / 108	(50%)
RBI in close games / RBI Total	175 / 253	(69%)

Mark Thurmond
Detroit Tigers

1986: Finesse, Groundball 1985: Finesse, Groundball 1984: Finesse, Groundball

THREE YEARS (84 – 86)

	G	IP	H	BB	SO	SB	CS	W	L	S	ERA
Totals	110	439.1	468	143	163	44	18	28	27	5	3.73
At Home and on the Road											
Home	59	235.2	249	66	96	21	10	14	16	3	3.59
Road	51	203.2	219	77	67	23	8	14	11	2	3.89
During the Day and and at Night											
Day	38	148.1	152	56	53	6	8	7	8	0	4.07
Night	72	291.0	316	87	110	38	10	21	19	5	3.56
On Grass and on Turf											
Grass	88	342.1	368	110	126	25	14	22	22	5	3.65
Turf	22	97.0	100	33	37	19	4	6	5	0	3.99
By Month											
April	14	70.2	72	26	30	7	1	3	5	0	3.57
May	13	53.1	64	21	20	7	3	4	4	1	6.41
June	20	89.1	108	26	26	5	3	4	7	0	4.84
July	18	61.2	68	27	25	10	1	4	4	0	3.65
August	22	85.1	74	24	30	7	6	9	2	1	1.58
Sept/Oct	23	79.0	82	19	32	8	4	4	5	3	3.19

vs. Opponent Batters
THREE YEARS (84 – 86)

	Ave.	OBP	SLG	AB	H	2B	3B	HR	RBI	BB	SO
Totals	.276	.332	.383	1693	468	59	8	35	187	143	163
Pitching vs. Left and Right-handed Batters											
Left	.229	.289	.293	314	72	6	1	4	32	26	47
Right	.287	.342	.403	1379	396	53	7	31	155	117	116
Situational											
Bases Empty	.265	.298	.364	1037	275	27	3	23	23	48	100
Leadoff	.264	.295	.373	432	114	5	0	14	14	19	50
Not Leadoff	.266	.301	.357	605	161	22	3	9	9	29	50
Runners On	.294	.380	.413	656	193	32	5	12	164	95	63
First Base Only	.334	.385	.438	290	97	14	2	4	20	24	24
Scoring Position	.262	.376	.393	366	96	18	3	8	144	71	39
Late Innings, Close	.209	.252	.317	139	29	5	2	2	8	8	18

RBI/Opportunities

Scoring Position	126 / 535	(24%)
Scoring Position, 2 Out	54 / 243	(22%)
On Third, Less than 2 Out	48 / 95	(51%)
RBI in close games / RBI Total	140 / 187	(75%)

Jay Tibbs
Montreal Expos

1986: Finesse, Groundball 1985: Finesse, Groundball 1984: Finesse, Groundball

THREE YEARS (84 – 86)

	G	IP	H	BB	SO	SB	CS	W	L	S	ERA
Totals	84	509.0	484	186	255	26	23	23	27	0	3.73
At Home and on the Road											
Home	44	276.0	249	94	138	9	9	12	14	0	3.52
Road	40	233.0	235	92	117	17	14	11	13	0	3.98
During the Day and and at Night											
Day	25	156.0	133	53	68	12	2	7	8	0	3.40
Night	59	353.0	351	133	187	14	21	16	19	0	3.88
On Grass and on Turf											
Grass	20	107.2	109	48	42	8	6	2	9	0	4.76
Turf	64	401.1	375	138	213	18	17	21	18	0	3.45
By Month											
April	11	77.1	61	33	44	4	2	3	4	0	2.91
May	13	69.1	75	32	27	8	3	3	4	0	5.32
June	11	63.2	66	27	37	4	4	2	5	0	4.52
July	13	72.2	59	29	30	6	4	3	4	0	3.34
August	20	126.1	123	29	67	0	8	5	8	0	3.13
Sept/Oct	16	99.2	100	36	50	4	2	7	2	0	3.79

vs. Opponent Batters
THREE YEARS (84 – 86)

	Ave.	OBP	SLG	AB	H	2B	3B	HR	RBI	BB	SO
Totals	.255	.321	.367	1897	484	85	19	30	194	186	255
Pitching vs. Left and Right-handed Batters											
Left	.269	.334	.384	1011	272	53	12	13	98	101	119
Right	.239	.305	.349	886	212	32	7	17	96	85	136
Situational											
Bases Empty	.240	.309	.355	1122	269	51	12	18	18	110	167
Leadoff	.259	.316	.357	487	126	25	1	7	7	41	71
Not Leadoff	.225	.303	.353	635	143	26	11	11	11	69	96
Runners On	.277	.338	.386	775	215	34	7	12	176	76	88
First Base Only	.277	.318	.418	347	96	19	3	8	29	20	34
Scoring Position	.278	.353	.360	428	119	15	4	4	147	56	54
Late Innings, Close	.250	.341	.309	152	38	6	0	1	11	20	16

RBI/Opportunities

Scoring Position	133 / 587	(23%)
Scoring Position, 2 Out	54 / 267	(20%)
On Third, Less than 2 Out	52 / 107	(49%)
RBI in close games / RBI Total	142 / 194	(73%)

Wayne Tolleson
New York Yankees

THREE YEARS (84 – 86)

	Ave.	OBP	SLG	AB	H	2B	3B	HR	RBI	BB	SO
Totals	.263	.324	.325	1136	299	34	12	4	70	100	169
Batting vs. Left and Right-handed Pitchers											
Left	.273	.335	.363	366	100	12	6	3	28	34	62
Right	.258	.318	.306	770	199	22	6	1	42	66	107
At Home and on the Road											
Home	.277	.336	.338	588	163	17	8	1	42	52	78
Road	.248	.311	.310	548	136	17	4	3	28	48	91
Facing Groundball Pitchers and Flyball Pitchers											
Groundball	.245	.313	.300	527	129	18	4	1	30	51	79
Flyball	.279	.333	.346	609	170	16	8	3	40	49	90
Facing Finesse Pitchers and Power Pitchers											
Finesse	.272	.323	.329	633	172	15	4	3	36	48	86
Power	.252	.324	.320	503	127	19	6	1	34	52	83
On Grass and on Turf											
Grass	.271	.334	.333	969	263	29	11	3	63	91	134
Turf	.216	.260	.275	167	36	5	1	1	7	9	35
During the Day and at Night											
Day	.269	.330	.338	308	83	11	2	2	29	29	47
Night	.261	.321	.320	828	216	23	10	2	41	71	122
By Month											
April	.283	.363	.371	159	45	7	2	1	16	21	18
May	.249	.315	.289	201	50	3	1	1	7	18	38
June	.218	.289	.282	206	45	8	1	1	7	21	26
July	.318	.387	.357	154	49	3	0	1	17	17	21
August	.268	.298	.348	198	53	6	5	0	10	9	33
Sept/Oct	.261	.311	.321	218	57	7	3	0	13	14	33
Situational											
Bases Empty	.278	.340	.335	684	190	20	8	1	1	62	109
Leadoff	.265	.339	.328	287	76	5	5	1	1	32	47
Not Leadoff	.287	.342	.340	397	114	15	3	0	0	30	62
Runners On	.241	.299	.310	452	109	14	4	3	69	38	60
First Base Only	.262	.304	.322	214	56	6	2	1	6	13	28
Scoring Position	.223	.294	.298	238	53	8	2	2	63	25	32
Late Innings, Close	.270	.339	.347	196	53	3	3	2	12	20	30

RBI/Opportunities

Scoring Position	57 / 347	(16%)
Scoring Position, 2 Out	23 / 165	(14%)
On Third, Less than 2 Out	19 / 43	(44%)
RBI in close games / RBI Total	48 / 70	(69%)

Jim Traber
Baltimore Orioles

THREE YEARS (84 – 86)

	Ave.	OBP	SLG	AB	H	2B	3B	HR	RBI	BB	SO
Totals	.253	.318	.451	233	59	7	0	13	46	20	35
Batting vs. Left and Right-handed Pitchers											
Left	.189	.289	.351	37	7	0	0	2	9	3	7
Right	.265	.324	.469	196	52	7	0	11	37	17	28
At Home and on the Road											
Home	.287	.369	.533	122	35	3	0	9	26	14	20
Road	.216	.260	.360	111	24	4	0	4	20	6	15
Facing Groundball Pitchers and Flyball Pitchers											
Groundball	.267	.331	.492	120	32	3	0	8	21	10	12
Flyball	.239	.305	.407	113	27	4	0	5	25	10	23
Facing Finesse Pitchers and Power Pitchers											
Finesse	.277	.313	.489	141	39	3	0	9	28	7	19
Power	.217	.325	.391	92	20	4	0	4	18	13	16
On Grass and on Turf											
Grass	.249	.318	.435	209	52	6	0	11	41	20	33
Turf	.292	.320	.583	24	7	1	0	2	5	0	2
During the Day and at Night											
Day	.254	.297	.522	67	17	3	0	5	19	5	6
Night	.253	.326	.422	166	42	4	0	8	27	15	29
By Month											
April	.000	.000	.000	0	0	0	0	0	0	0	0
May	.000	.000	.000	0	0	0	0	0	0	0	0
June	.000	.000	.000	0	0	0	0	0	0	0	0
July	.326	.388	.721	43	14	2	0	5	15	4	5
August	.279	.341	.481	104	29	3	0	6	20	7	13
Sept/Oct	.186	.268	.279	86	16	2	0	2	11	9	17
Situational											
Bases Empty	.212	.285	.381	118	25	5	0	5	5	10	20
Leadoff	.220	.304	.340	50	11	3	0	1	1	4	9
Not Leadoff	.206	.270	.412	68	14	2	0	4	4	6	11
Runners On	.296	.351	.522	115	34	2	0	8	41	10	15
First Base Only	.340	.369	.642	53	18	1	0	5	11	3	8
Scoring Position	.258	.316	.419	62	16	1	0	3	30	7	7
Late Innings, Close	.400	.422	.425	40	16	1	0	0	8	2	6

RBI/Opportunities

Scoring Position	24 / 92	(26%)
Scoring Position, 2 Out	12 / 51	(24%)
On Third, Less than 2 Out	10 / 14	(71%)
RBI in close games / RBI Total	28 / 46	(61%)

Alex Trevino
Los Angeles Dodgers

THREE YEARS (84 – 86)

	Ave.	OBP	SLG	AB	H	2B	3B	HR	RBI	BB	SO
Totals	.242	.312	.369	631	153	39	1	13	73	63	88
Batting vs. Left and Right-handed Pitchers											
Left	.235	.309	.332	268	63	12	1	4	22	28	43
Right	.248	.314	.397	363	90	27	0	9	51	35	45
At Home and on the Road											
Home	.246	.305	.374	313	77	22	0	6	37	27	43
Road	.239	.318	.365	318	76	17	1	7	36	36	45
Facing Groundball Pitchers and Flyball Pitchers											
Groundball	.259	.325	.397	340	88	21	1	8	42	34	39
Flyball	.223	.296	.337	291	65	18	0	5	31	29	49
Facing Finesse Pitchers and Power Pitchers											
Finesse	.233	.297	.329	374	87	22	1	4	40	33	49
Power	.257	.333	.428	257	66	17	0	9	33	30	39
On Grass and on Turf											
Grass	.245	.321	.372	444	109	24	1	10	52	48	60
Turf	.235	.291	.364	187	44	15	0	3	21	15	28
During the Day and at Night											
Day	.260	.329	.413	254	66	16	1	7	27	25	33
Night	.231	.301	.340	377	87	23	0	6	46	38	55
By Month											
April	.243	.282	.324	37	9	3	0	0	0	2	7
May	.266	.329	.344	128	34	7	0	1	13	11	16
June	.238	.335	.417	151	36	12	0	5	15	22	24
July	.223	.291	.281	121	27	4	0	1	16	12	20
August	.202	.269	.404	94	19	7	0	4	13	9	15
Sept/Oct	.280	.330	.420	100	28	6	1	2	16	7	6
Situational											
Bases Empty	.236	.314	.375	331	78	20	1	8	8	37	47
Leadoff	.288	.350	.472	125	36	8	0	5	5	11	11
Not Leadoff	.204	.293	.316	206	42	12	1	3	3	26	36
Runners On	.250	.309	.363	300	75	19	0	5	65	26	41
First Base Only	.292	.331	.383	120	35	8	0	1	5	7	12
Scoring Position	.222	.296	.350	180	40	11	0	4	60	19	29
Late Innings, Close	.299	.346	.444	144	43	12	0	3	20	10	12

RBI/Opportunities

Scoring Position	49 / 242	(20%)
Scoring Position, 2 Out	25 / 106	(24%)
On Third, Less than 2 Out	13 / 39	(33%)
RBI in close games / RBI Total	50 / 73	(68%)

Manny Trillo
Chicago Cubs

THREE YEARS (84 – 86)

	Ave.	OBP	SLG	AB	H	2B	3B	HR	RBI	BB	SO
Totals	.247	.304	.324	1004	248	47	3	8	80	81	120
Batting vs. Left and Right-handed Pitchers											
Left	.249	.304	.311	289	72	12	0	2	20	22	38
Right	.246	.303	.329	715	176	35	3	6	60	59	82
At Home and on the Road											
Home	.231	.285	.316	468	108	25	0	5	40	35	59
Road	.261	.320	.330	536	140	22	3	3	40	46	61
Facing Groundball Pitchers and Flyball Pitchers											
Groundball	.266	.326	.360	470	125	27	1	5	42	41	57
Flyball	.230	.284	.292	534	123	20	2	3	38	40	63
Facing Finesse Pitchers and Power Pitchers											
Finesse	.247	.290	.330	612	151	27	3	6	48	36	69
Power	.247	.324	.314	392	97	20	0	2	32	45	51
On Grass and on Turf											
Grass	.245	.301	.331	709	174	37	0	8	60	57	92
Turf	.251	.310	.305	295	74	10	3	0	20	24	28
During the Day and at Night											
Day	.249	.306	.360	506	126	28	2	8	45	43	57
Night	.245	.301	.287	498	122	19	1	0	35	38	63
By Month											
April	.273	.359	.384	172	47	10	0	3	13	23	20
May	.236	.285	.311	148	35	4	2	1	8	9	16
June	.228	.316	.287	101	23	6	0	0	4	12	12
July	.259	.303	.339	174	45	5	0	3	17	11	22
August	.241	.278	.306	232	56	10	1	1	20	13	26
Sept/Oct	.237	.288	.305	177	42	12	0	0	18	13	24
Situational											
Bases Empty	.228	.288	.319	589	134	29	2	7	7	48	74
Leadoff	.272	.335	.403	191	52	11	1	4	4	18	21
Not Leadoff	.206	.265	.279	398	82	18	1	3	3	30	53
Runners On	.275	.325	.330	415	114	18	1	1	73	33	46
First Base Only	.335	.362	.382	170	57	8	0	0	5	6	16
Scoring Position	.233	.302	.294	245	57	10	1	1	68	27	30
Late Innings, Close	.222	.292	.281	185	41	8	0	1	18	20	28

RBI/Opportunities

Scoring Position	64 / 330	(19%)
Scoring Position, 2 Out	26 / 159	(16%)
On Third, Less than 2 Out	28 / 48	(58%)
RBI in close games / RBI Total	54 / 80	(68%)

Steve Trout
Chicago Cubs

1986: Finesse, Groundball 1985: Finesse, Groundball 1984: Finesse, Groundball

THREE YEARS (84 – 86)

	G	IP	H	BB	SO	SB	CS	W	L	S	ERA
Totals	93	491.2	531	200	194	36	41	27	21	0	3.84
At Home and on the Road											
Home	51	267.1	289	118	109	16	17	14	9	0	4.11
Road	42	224.1	242	82	85	20	24	13	12	0	3.53
During the Day and and at Night											
Day	65	348.0	367	137	143	22	23	19	13	0	3.72
Night	28	143.2	164	63	51	14	18	8	8	0	4.13
On Grass and on Turf											
Grass	68	362.1	384	159	149	23	29	19	14	0	3.92
Turf	25	129.1	147	41	45	13	12	8	7	0	3.62
By Month											
April	15	97.0	89	26	30	1	10	8	2	0	2.69
May	15	82.0	73	34	30	4	3	5	5	0	3.62
June	15	85.2	96	37	41	5	8	5	2	0	3.99
July	14	75.1	91	34	34	6	6	4	4	0	4.66
August	16	73.0	93	36	32	8	7	3	2	0	4.07
Sept/Oct	18	78.2	89	33	27	12	7	2	6	0	4.35

vs. Opponent Batters

THREE YEARS (84 – 86)

	Ave.	OBP	SLG	AB	H	2B	3B	HR	RBI	BB	SO
Totals	.285	.353	.368	1861	531	69	11	21	197	200	194
Pitching vs. Left and Right-handed Batters											
Left	.302	.363	.361	288	87	12	1	1	31	26	33
Right	.282	.352	.369	1573	444	57	10	20	166	174	161
Situational											
Bases Empty	.286	.349	.374	1036	296	37	6	14	14	98	109
Leadoff	.321	.375	.423	471	151	19	4	7	7	40	50
Not Leadoff	.257	.328	.333	565	145	18	2	7	7	58	59
Runners On	.285	.358	.361	825	235	32	5	7	183	102	85
First Base Only	.289	.355	.371	356	103	14	0	5	14	35	36
Scoring Position	.281	.361	.354	469	132	18	5	2	169	67	49
Late Innings, Close	.286	.375	.367	98	28	6	1	0	10	14	11

RBI/Opportunities

Scoring Position	162 / 659	(25%)
Scoring Position, 2 Out	50 / 279	(18%)
On Third, Less than 2 Out	80 / 144	(56%)
RBI in close games / RBI Total	146 / 197	(74%)

Ed Vande Berg
Los Angeles Dodgers

1986: Power, Groundball 1985: Power, Groundball 1984: Power, Groundball

THREE YEARS (84 – 86)

	G	IP	H	BB	SO	SB	CS	W	L	S	ERA
Totals	186	269.1	319	114	147	13	13	11	18	10	4.14
At Home and on the Road											
Home	91	123.1	155	55	70	5	7	5	9	5	4.38
Road	95	146.0	164	59	77	8	6	6	9	5	3.95
During the Day and and at Night											
Day	49	76.0	68	24	46	5	1	1	4	3	2.61
Night	137	193.1	251	90	101	8	12	10	14	7	4.75
On Grass and on Turf											
Grass	87	133.2	153	57	65	9	5	6	7	4	3.77
Turf	99	135.2	166	57	82	4	8	5	11	6	4.51
By Month											
April	30	29.2	27	20	20	2	0	1	2	3	2.12
May	31	66.1	74	20	38	1	4	3	3	1	2.98
June	32	63.1	79	26	29	4	6	2	5	2	4.69
July	28	42.2	63	14	19	0	0	3	5	2	6.54
August	33	37.2	42	19	21	3	3	1	3	2	5.02
Sept/Oct	32	29.2	34	15	20	3	0	1	0	0	3.03

vs. Opponent Batters

THREE YEARS (84 – 86)

	Ave.	OBP	SLG	AB	H	2B	3B	HR	RBI	BB	SO
Totals	.298	.363	.448	1071	319	53	9	30	162	114	147
Pitching vs. Left and Right-handed Batters											
Left	.248	.340	.348	310	77	11	4	4	41	44	43
Right	.318	.373	.489	761	242	42	5	26	121	70	104
Situational											
Bases Empty	.303	.357	.464	519	157	29	5	15	15	42	72
Leadoff	.301	.360	.464	226	68	13	3	4	4	19	30
Not Leadoff	.304	.354	.485	293	89	16	2	11	11	23	42
Runners On	.293	.368	.433	552	162	24	4	15	147	72	75
First Base Only	.308	.360	.436	211	65	9	0	6	18	17	28
Scoring Position	.284	.373	.431	341	97	15	4	9	129	55	47
Late Innings, Close	.345	.446	.525	200	69	10	1	8	43	37	23

RBI/Opportunities

Scoring Position	114 / 497	(23%)
Scoring Position, 2 Out	33 / 215	(15%)
On Third, Less than 2 Out	48 / 98	(49%)
RBI in close games / RBI Total	92 / 162	(57%)

Max Venable
Cincinnati Reds

	Ave.	OBP	SLG	AB	H	2B	3B	HR	RBI	BB	SO
THREE YEARS (84 – 86)											
Totals	.246	.296	.363	353	87	21	4	4	32	26	48
Batting vs. Left and Right-handed Pitchers											
Left	.172	.235	.172	29	5	0	0	0	4	3	4
Right	.253	.302	.380	324	82	21	4	4	28	23	44
At Home and on the Road											
Home	.249	.298	.343	181	45	8	3	1	14	13	20
Road	.244	.294	.384	172	42	13	1	3	18	13	28
Facing Groundball Pitchers and Flyball Pitchers											
Groundball	.289	.329	.456	149	43	10	3	3	17	10	19
Flyball	.216	.272	.294	204	44	11	1	1	15	16	29
Facing Finesse Pitchers and Power Pitchers											
Finesse	.269	.290	.410	212	57	15	3	3	23	7	20
Power	.213	.304	.291	141	30	6	1	1	9	19	28
On Grass and on Turf											
Grass	.259	.296	.422	116	30	8	1	3	13	7	20
Turf	.241	.296	.333	237	57	13	3	1	19	19	28
During the Day and at Night											
Day	.203	.248	.281	128	26	5	1	1	8	8	16
Night	.271	.323	.409	225	61	16	3	3	24	18	32
By Month											
April	.300	.364	.500	10	3	2	0	0	0	1	3
May	.194	.242	.226	31	6	1	0	0	2	2	3
June	.260	.327	.400	50	13	5	1	0	3	5	4
July	.237	.299	.325	80	19	5	1	0	3	7	14
August	.265	.304	.373	83	22	3	0	2	10	5	12
Sept/Oct	.242	.280	.394	99	24	5	2	2	14	6	12
Situational											
Bases Empty	.241	.295	.385	195	47	11	4	3	3	14	25
Leadoff	.240	.287	.387	75	18	2	0	3	3	4	11
Not Leadoff	.242	.300	.383	120	29	9	4	0	0	10	14
Runners On	.253	.297	.335	158	40	10	0	1	29	12	23
First Base Only	.333	.354	.365	63	21	2	0	0	1	2	7
Scoring Position	.200	.264	.316	95	19	8	0	1	28	10	16
Late Innings, Close	.250	.333	.317	104	26	3	2	0	7	12	15

RBI/Opportunities

Scoring Position	25 / 130	(19%)
Scoring Position, 2 Out	9 / 59	(15%)
On Third, Less than 2 Out	9 / 17	(53%)
RBI in close games / RBI Total	22 / 32	(69%)

Bob Walk
Pittsburgh Pirates

1986: Finesse, Groundball 1985: Power, Groundball 1984: Power, Flyball

	G	IP	H	BB	SO	SB	CS	W	L	S	ERA
THREE YEARS (84 – 86)											
Totals	55	210.2	197	86	128	16	13	10	12	2	3.67
At Home and on the Road											
Home	28	86.2	79	27	55	7	3	3	8	2	4.05
Road	27	124.0	118	59	73	9	10	7	4	0	3.41
During the Day and and at Night											
Day	17	62.1	60	28	35	7	5	3	4	1	4.33
Night	38	148.1	137	58	93	9	8	7	8	1	3.40
On Grass and on Turf											
Grass	12	43.2	37	17	29	2	4	2	2	0	3.09
Turf	43	167.0	160	69	99	14	9	8	10	2	3.83
By Month											
April	6	17.2	9	6	13	0	2	0	0	1	1.53
May	11	20.2	17	10	12	1	1	2	2	0	3.92
June	8	26.2	28	15	16	1	2	1	2	1	4.39
July	8	39.1	34	13	27	3	2	3	3	0	3.20
August	10	65.0	66	21	33	8	5	4	2	0	3.46
Sept/Oct	12	41.1	43	21	27	3	1	1	3	0	4.79

	Ave.	OBP	SLG	AB	H	2B	3B	HR	RBI	BB	SO
vs. Opponent Batters											
THREE YEARS (84 – 86)											
Totals	.253	.327	.379	780	197	29	8	18	90	86	128
Pitching vs. Left and Right-handed Batters											
Left	.263	.341	.373	407	107	12	6	7	34	50	57
Right	.241	.311	.386	373	90	17	2	11	56	36	71
Situational											
Bases Empty	.248	.312	.368	475	118	15	6	10	10	42	73
Leadoff	.294	.321	.446	204	60	7	3	6	6	14	21
Not Leadoff	.214	.290	.310	271	58	8	3	4	4	28	52
Runners On	.259	.348	.397	305	79	14	2	8	80	44	55
First Base Only	.271	.326	.398	133	36	8	0	3	8	10	25
Scoring Position	.250	.363	.395	172	43	6	2	5	72	34	30
Late Innings, Close	.302	.397	.472	106	32	3	0	5	24	18	16

RBI/Opportunities

Scoring Position	61 / 256	(24%)
Scoring Position, 2 Out	24 / 114	(21%)
On Third, Less than 2 Out	25 / 57	(44%)
RBI in close games / RBI Total	73 / 90	(81%)

Chico Walker
Chicago Cubs

	Ave.	OBP	SLG	AB	H	2B	3B	HR	RBI	BB	SO
THREE YEARS (84 – 86)											
Totals	.252	.307	.339	115	29	3	2	1	8	10	26
Batting vs. Left and Right-handed Pitchers											
Left	.263	.300	.316	19	5	1	0	0	0	1	4
Right	.250	.308	.344	96	24	2	2	1	8	9	22
At Home and on the Road											
Home	.260	.345	.340	50	13	2	1	0	4	7	10
Road	.246	.275	.338	65	16	1	1	1	4	3	16
Facing Groundball Pitchers and Flyball Pitchers											
Groundball	.328	.354	.426	61	20	2	2	0	6	3	12
Flyball	.167	.258	.241	54	9	1	0	1	2	7	14
Facing Finesse Pitchers and Power Pitchers											
Finesse	.288	.333	.409	66	19	1	2	1	7	5	10
Power	.204	.273	.245	49	10	2	0	0	1	5	16
On Grass and on Turf											
Grass	.234	.311	.297	64	15	2	1	0	5	8	13
Turf	.275	.302	.392	51	14	1	1	1	3	2	13
During the Day and at Night											
Day	.243	.313	.343	70	17	2	1	1	7	8	16
Night	.267	.298	.333	45	12	1	1	0	1	2	10
By Month											
April	.000	.000	.000	0	0	0	0	0	0	0	0
May	.000	.000	.000	2	0	0	0	0	0	0	1
June	.083	.077	.083	12	1	0	0	0	1	0	5
July	.000	.000	.000	0	0	0	0	0	0	0	0
August	.000	.000	.000	0	0	0	0	0	0	0	0
Sept/Oct	.277	.339	.376	101	28	3	2	1	7	10	20
Situational											
Bases Empty	.288	.365	.409	66	19	3	1	1	1	8	12
Leadoff	.250	.325	.333	36	9	3	0	0	0	4	7
Not Leadoff	.333	.412	.500	30	10	0	1	1	1	4	5
Runners On	.204	.226	.245	49	10	0	1	0	7	2	14
First Base Only	.217	.304	.304	23	5	0	1	0	1	0	8
Scoring Position	.192	.233	.192	26	5	0	0	0	6	2	6
Late Innings, Close	.143	.174	.143	21	3	0	0	0	1	1	5

RBI/Opportunities

Scoring Position	6 / 44	(14%)
Scoring Position, 2 Out	1 / 18	(6%)
On Third, Less than 2 Out	3 / 9	(33%)
RBI in close games / RBI Total	4 / 8	(50%)

Denny Walling
Houston Astros

	Ave.	OBP	SLG	AB	H	2B	3B	HR	RBI	BB	SO
THREE YEARS (84 – 86)											
Totals	.289	.338	.429	976	282	54	7	23	134	77	85
Batting vs. Left and Right-handed Pitchers											
Left	.230	.278	.252	135	31	3	0	0	15	9	23
Right	.298	.348	.458	841	251	51	7	23	119	68	62
At Home and on the Road											
Home	.294	.337	.416	493	145	29	5	7	65	35	40
Road	.284	.340	.443	483	137	25	2	16	69	42	45
Facing Groundball Pitchers and Flyball Pitchers											
Groundball	.297	.344	.397	468	139	25	2	6	57	35	35
Flyball	.281	.333	.459	508	143	29	5	17	77	42	50
Facing Finesse Pitchers and Power Pitchers											
Finesse	.322	.362	.462	541	174	28	6	12	88	37	25
Power	.248	.310	.389	435	108	26	1	11	46	40	60
On Grass and on Turf											
Grass	.296	.347	.453	287	85	13	1	10	43	23	25
Turf	.286	.335	.419	689	197	41	6	13	91	54	60
During the Day and at Night											
Day	.312	.362	.494	231	72	18	0	8	37	19	18
Night	.282	.331	.409	745	210	36	7	15	97	58	67
By Month											
April	.333	.379	.442	120	40	7	0	2	15	10	8
May	.277	.308	.385	148	41	11	1	1	18	7	14
June	.216	.296	.336	134	29	5	1	3	15	16	10
July	.271	.356	.410	210	57	11	0	6	32	24	23
August	.324	.356	.490	210	68	9	4	6	32	11	17
Sept/Oct	.305	.341	.487	154	47	11	1	5	22	9	13
Situational											
Bases Empty	.289	.325	.425	539	156	37	3	10	10	28	45
Leadoff	.277	.302	.446	195	54	14	2	5	5	7	22
Not Leadoff	.297	.337	.413	344	102	23	1	5	5	21	23
Runners On	.288	.354	.434	437	126	17	4	13	124	49	40
First Base Only	.301	.332	.455	176	53	7	1	6	16	8	10
Scoring Position	.280	.367	.421	261	73	10	3	7	108	41	30
Late Innings, Close	.241	.315	.333	195	47	6	0	4	20	22	24

RBI/Opportunities

Scoring Position	95 / 357	(27%)
Scoring Position, 2 Out	33 / 142	(23%)
On Third, Less than 2 Out	40 / 77	(52%)
RBI in close games / RBI Total	86 / 134	(64%)

Gene Walter
San Diego Padres

1986: Power, Groundball   1985: Power, Groundball   1984: Did not play

THREE YEARS (84 – 86)	G	IP	H	BB	SO	SB	CS	W	L	S	ERA
Totals	72	120.0	101	57	102	11	6	2	4	4	3.52
At Home and on the Road											
Home	35	64.2	50	30	49	8	5	1	2	3	2.78
Road	37	55.1	51	27	53	3	1	1	2	1	4.39
During the Day and and at Night											
Day	23	35.0	27	20	28	3	0	0	2	1	3.09
Night	49	85.0	74	37	74	8	6	2	2	3	3.71
On Grass and on Turf											
Grass	50	87.2	70	42	69	8	5	1	4	3	3.29
Turf	22	32.1	31	15	33	3	1	1	0	1	4.18
By Month											
April	6	15.1	10	6	20	2	2	0	0	0	2.35
May	11	11.1	11	5	11	1	0	1	0	0	3.97
June	13	15.2	19	9	20	1	1	1	1	0	5.17
July	8	13.2	8	7	9	1	0	0	0	0	2.63
August	18	33.2	38	15	24	3	1	0	3	3	5.08
Sept/Oct	16	30.1	15	15	18	3	2	0	0	1	1.78

vs. Opponent Batters

THREE YEARS (84 – 86)	Ave.	OBP	SLG	AB	H	2B	3B	HR	RBI	BB	SO
Totals	.231	.323	.327	437	101	17	2	7	51	57	102
Pitching vs. Left and Right-handed Batters											
Left	.154	.286	.183	104	16	3	0	0	10	18	38
Right	.255	.335	.372	333	85	14	2	7	41	39	64
Situational											
Bases Empty	.212	.303	.278	245	52	7	0	3	3	31	55
Leadoff	.235	.336	.286	98	23	2	0	1	1	14	23
Not Leadoff	.197	.280	.272	147	29	5	0	2	2	17	32
Runners On	.255	.347	.391	192	49	10	2	4	48	26	47
First Base Only	.275	.348	.362	80	22	1	0	2	5	9	17
Scoring Position	.241	.346	.411	112	27	9	2	2	43	17	30
Late Innings, Close	.205	.336	.341	88	18	4	1	2	12	18	26

RBI/Opportunities

Scoring Position	37 / 168	(22%)
Scoring Position, 2 Out	11 / 79	(14%)
On Third, Less than 2 Out	15 / 35	(43%)
RBI in close games / RBI Total	14 / 51	(27%)

U.L. Washington
Pittsburgh Pirates

THREE YEARS (84 – 86)	Ave.	OBP	SLG	AB	H	2B	3B	HR	RBI	BB	SO
Totals	.227	.288	.301	498	113	15	8	2	37	44	91
Batting vs. Left and Right-handed Pitchers											
Left	.224	.267	.333	174	39	9	2	2	17	11	37
Right	.228	.299	.284	324	74	6	6	0	20	33	54
At Home and on the Road											
Home	.184	.248	.261	207	38	7	3	1	18	18	40
Road	.258	.317	.330	291	75	8	5	1	19	26	51
Facing Groundball Pitchers and Flyball Pitchers											
Groundball	.222	.278	.281	221	49	4	3	1	16	18	38
Flyball	.231	.296	.318	277	64	11	5	1	21	26	53
Facing Finesse Pitchers and Power Pitchers											
Finesse	.243	.294	.302	305	74	9	3	1	13	22	47
Power	.202	.280	.301	193	39	6	5	1	24	22	44
On Grass and on Turf											
Grass	.274	.321	.350	197	54	6	3	1	15	14	39
Turf	.196	.267	.269	301	59	9	5	1	22	30	52
During the Day and at Night											
Day	.235	.314	.329	170	40	4	3	2	13	20	35
Night	.223	.274	.287	328	73	11	5	0	24	24	56
By Month											
April	.333	.355	.333	30	10	0	0	0	1	1	4
May	.224	.274	.308	107	24	5	2	0	13	8	18
June	.290	.360	.390	100	29	6	2	0	9	11	15
July	.244	.321	.358	123	30	2	3	2	11	14	23
August	.111	.191	.136	81	9	2	0	0	1	8	17
Sept/Oct	.193	.217	.228	57	11	0	1	0	2	2	14
Situational											
Bases Empty	.197	.245	.273	300	59	7	5	2	2	19	63
Leadoff	.232	.273	.312	125	29	4	3	0	0	7	25
Not Leadoff	.171	.225	.246	175	30	3	2	2	2	12	38
Runners On	.273	.350	.343	198	54	8	3	0	35	25	28
First Base Only	.300	.378	.338	80	24	3	0	0	1	10	14
Scoring Position	.254	.331	.347	118	30	5	3	0	34	15	14
Late Innings, Close	.184	.264	.214	98	18	1	1	0	6	11	22

RBI/Opportunities

Scoring Position	32 / 164	(20%)
Scoring Position, 2 Out	10 / 71	(14%)
On Third, Less than 2 Out	13 / 36	(36%)
RBI in close games / RBI Total	22 / 37	(59%)

Claudell Washington
New York Yankees

THREE YEARS (84 – 86)	Ave.	OBP	SLG	AB	H	2B	3B	HR	RBI	BB	SO
Totals	.274	.347	.455	1086	298	51	8	43	134	120	203
Batting vs. Left and Right-handed Pitchers											
Left	.265	.331	.398	226	60	14	2	4	26	23	48
Right	.277	.351	.470	860	238	37	6	39	108	97	155
At Home and on the Road											
Home	.275	.341	.459	556	153	25	4	23	72	55	90
Road	.274	.353	.451	530	145	26	4	20	62	65	113
Facing Groundball Pitchers and Flyball Pitchers											
Groundball	.278	.354	.450	533	148	25	5	19	64	65	93
Flyball	.271	.340	.459	553	150	26	3	24	70	55	110
Facing Finesse Pitchers and Power Pitchers											
Finesse	.263	.337	.423	659	173	31	3	23	64	74	109
Power	.293	.362	.504	427	125	20	5	20	70	46	94
On Grass and on Turf											
Grass	.278	.348	.458	799	222	35	5	33	102	85	147
Turf	.265	.344	.446	287	76	16	3	10	32	35	56
During the Day and at Night											
Day	.275	.367	.509	338	93	18	2	19	56	47	70
Night	.274	.338	.430	748	205	33	6	24	78	73	133
By Month											
April	.271	.362	.477	199	54	12	1	9	25	28	40
May	.314	.388	.500	210	66	13	1	8	30	26	34
June	.288	.338	.489	139	40	6	2	6	15	11	25
July	.286	.351	.479	234	67	12	3	9	28	23	47
August	.204	.293	.315	162	33	3	0	5	16	20	26
Sept/Oct	.268	.327	.444	142	38	5	1	6	20	12	31
Situational											
Bases Empty	.281	.342	.480	708	199	35	5	32	32	62	130
Leadoff	.268	.333	.492	370	99	18	1	21	21	35	69
Not Leadoff	.296	.351	.467	338	100	17	4	11	11	27	61
Runners On	.262	.357	.407	378	99	16	3	11	102	58	73
First Base Only	.273	.331	.460	150	41	6	2	6	17	13	24
Scoring Position	.254	.371	.373	228	58	10	1	5	85	45	49
Late Innings, Close	.248	.323	.398	206	51	5	1	8	28	24	48

RBI/Opportunities

Scoring Position	78 / 329	(24%)
Scoring Position, 2 Out	35 / 184	(19%)
On Third, Less than 2 Out	28 / 48	(58%)
RBI in close games / RBI Total	96 / 134	(72%)

Bill Wegman
Milwaukee Brewers

1986: Finesse, Flyball   1985: Finesse, Groundball   1984: Did not play

THREE YEARS (84 – 86)	G	IP	H	BB	SO	SB	CS	W	L	S	ERA
Totals	38	216.0	234	46	88	9	10	7	12	0	5.00
At Home and on the Road											
Home	21	122.1	133	17	55	7	5	3	5	0	4.93
Road	17	93.2	101	29	33	2	5	4	7	0	5.09
During the Day and and at Night											
Day	9	52.1	61	5	26	3	4	0	3	0	4.47
Night	29	163.2	173	41	62	6	6	7	9	0	5.17
On Grass and on Turf											
Grass	34	193.2	207	43	77	9	8	6	9	0	5.02
Turf	4	22.1	27	3	11	0	2	1	3	0	4.84
By Month											
April	4	24.1	26	8	6	2	1	0	1	0	4.07
May	7	54.1	53	10	18	1	5	0	4	0	4.96
June	5	33.2	34	4	18	1	0	2	1	0	5.61
July	5	27.2	28	6	8	0	1	0	3	0	5.53
August	7	43.0	45	7	21	1	4	1	1	0	4.40
Sept/Oct	10	42.0	48	11	17	4	0	3	2	0	5.36

vs. Opponent Batters

THREE YEARS (84 – 86)	Ave.	OBP	SLG	AB	H	2B	3B	HR	RBI	BB	SO
Totals	.277	.317	.460	846	234	40	5	35	111	46	88
Pitching vs. Left and Right-handed Batters											
Left	.271	.316	.451	472	128	20	1	21	61	31	46
Right	.283	.319	.471	374	106	20	4	14	50	15	42
Situational											
Bases Empty	.262	.307	.453	523	137	22	3	24	24	29	55
Leadoff	.270	.305	.484	215	58	8	1	12	12	11	20
Not Leadoff	.256	.308	.432	308	79	14	2	12	12	18	35
Runners On	.300	.333	.471	323	97	18	2	11	87	17	33
First Base Only	.275	.319	.444	153	42	8	0	6	14	8	16
Scoring Position	.324	.346	.494	170	55	10	2	5	73	9	17
Late Innings, Close	.284	.314	.478	67	19	5	1	2	5	3	7

RBI/Opportunities

Scoring Position	64 / 206	(31%)
Scoring Position, 2 Out	30 / 100	(30%)
On Third, Less than 2 Out	21 / 32	(66%)
RBI in close games / RBI Total	89 / 111	(80%)

Chris Welsh
Cincinnati Reds

1986: Finesse, Groundball 1985: Finesse, Groundball 1984: Did not play

	G	IP	H	BB	SO	SB	CS	W	L	S	ERA
THREE YEARS (84 – 86)											
Totals	49	215.2	264	65	71	22	8	8	14	0	4.55
At Home and on the Road											
Home	22	112.0	128	33	36	12	5	5	7	0	4.34
Road	27	103.2	136	32	35	10	3	3	7	0	4.77
During the Day and and at Night											
Day	8	33.2	42	10	16	7	0	0	5	0	4.54
Night	41	182.0	222	55	55	15	8	8	9	0	4.55
On Grass and on Turf											
Grass	26	83.0	109	22	30	7	4	4	3	0	4.12
Turf	23	132.2	155	43	41	15	6	4	11	0	4.82
By Month											
April	0	0.0	0	0	0	0	0	0	0	0	0.00
May	1	4.2	5	0	1	1	0	0	0	0	1.93
June	12	61.2	66	15	22	9	2	3	4	0	3.06
July	9	44.0	49	18	13	3	4	2	1	0	3.27
August	14	52.0	78	15	24	5	1	2	5	0	7.27
Sept/Oct	13	53.1	66	17	11	4	1	1	4	0	4.89

vs. Opponent Batters

	Ave.	OBP	SLG	AB	H	2B	3B	HR	RBI	BB	SO
THREE YEARS (84 – 86)											
Totals	.307	.358	.464	861	264	49	5	20	114	65	71
Pitching vs. Left and Right-handed Batters											
Left	.228	.278	.352	193	44	10	1	4	27	14	25
Right	.329	.381	.472	668	220	39	4	16	87	51	46
Situational											
Bases Empty	.302	.359	.436	463	140	27	1	11	11	38	36
Leadoff	.274	.333	.443	201	55	10	0	8	8	15	10
Not Leadoff	.324	.379	.431	262	85	17	1	3	3	23	26
Runners On	.312	.357	.455	398	124	22	4	9	103	27	35
First Base Only	.325	.364	.422	166	54	9	2	1	9	7	13
Scoring Position	.302	.353	.478	232	70	13	2	8	94	20	22
Late Innings, Close	.289	.400	.447	38	11	0	0	2	6	7	4

RBI/Opportunities

Scoring Position	77 / 295	(26%)
Scoring Position, 2 Out	37 / 152	(24%)
On Third, Less than 2 Out	24 / 45	(53%)
RBI in close games / RBI Total	66 / 114	(58%)

Ed Whitson
San Diego Padres

1986: Power, Flyball 1985: Finesse, Flyball 1984: Finesse, Flyball

	G	IP	H	BB	SO	SB	CS	W	L	S	ERA
THREE YEARS (84 – 86)											
Totals	92	460.1	521	145	265	35	16	30	25	0	4.54
At Home and on the Road											
Home	43	230.1	251	60	130	17	10	16	11	0	3.91
Road	49	230.0	270	85	135	18	6	14	14	0	5.17
During the Day and and at Night											
Day	25	115.1	150	22	80	8	2	5	10	0	5.54
Night	67	345.0	371	123	185	27	14	25	15	0	4.20
On Grass and on Turf											
Grass	70	348.1	400	110	197	24	12	24	20	0	4.39
Turf	22	112.0	121	35	68	11	4	6	5	0	4.98
By Month											
April	14	66.1	72	26	31	4	1	4	6	0	4.07
May	12	53.0	70	20	37	6	4	5	3	0	6.28
June	15	71.1	81	21	41	3	3	7	3	0	3.91
July	17	97.0	94	26	45	8	3	8	4	0	3.34
August	17	94.2	116	28	60	8	1	3	6	0	5.89
Sept/Oct	17	78.0	88	24	51	6	4	3	3	0	4.15

vs. Opponent Batters

	Ave.	OBP	SLG	AB	H	2B	3B	HR	RBI	BB	SO
THREE YEARS (84 – 86)											
Totals	.287	.338	.431	1817	521	84	17	48	228	145	265
Pitching vs. Left and Right-handed Batters											
Left	.284	.340	.428	978	278	44	8	27	121	83	127
Right	.290	.336	.434	839	243	40	9	21	107	62	138
Situational											
Bases Empty	.277	.334	.410	1027	284	46	8	25	25	84	152
Leadoff	.291	.340	.433	453	132	22	6	10	10	32	61
Not Leadoff	.265	.329	.392	574	152	24	2	15	15	52	91
Runners On	.300	.343	.458	790	237	38	9	23	203	61	113
First Base Only	.323	.360	.515	371	120	15	4	16	44	21	53
Scoring Position	.279	.330	.408	419	117	23	5	7	159	40	60
Late Innings, Close	.228	.299	.354	79	18	4	0	2	6	8	11

RBI/Opportunities

Scoring Position	146 / 545	(27%)
Scoring Position, 2 Out	41 / 232	(18%)
On Third, Less than 2 Out	67 / 115	(58%)
RBI in close games / RBI Total	147 / 228	(64%)

Alan Wiggins
Baltimore Orioles

	Ave.	OBP	SLG	AB	H	2B	3B	HR	RBI	BB	SO
THREE YEARS (84 – 86)											
Totals	.257	.331	.315	1170	301	34	12	3	66	128	97
Batting vs. Left and Right-handed Pitchers											
Left	.302	.369	.392	378	114	23	1	3	19	40	24
Right	.236	.313	.278	792	187	11	11	0	47	88	73
At Home and on the Road											
Home	.249	.331	.315	594	148	20	5	3	30	72	44
Road	.266	.344	.576	153	14	7	0	36	56	53	
Facing Groundball Pitchers and Flyball Pitchers											
Groundball	.260	.332	.308	624	162	17	5	1	32	66	60
Flyball	.255	.330	.322	546	139	17	7	2	34	62	37
Facing Finesse Pitchers and Power Pitchers											
Finesse	.262	.322	.323	679	178	22	8	1	36	58	58
Power	.251	.343	.303	491	123	12	4	2	30	70	39
On Grass and on Turf											
Grass	.250	.324	.305	928	232	24	9	3	50	101	70
Turf	.285	.357	.351	242	69	10	3	0	16	27	27
During the Day and at Night											
Day	.241	.315	.301	319	77	10	3	1	24	36	26
Night	.263	.337	.320	851	224	24	9	2	42	92	71
By Month											
April	.168	.236	.200	185	31	6	0	0	5	17	14
May	.331	.410	.382	178	59	2	2	1	14	24	11
June	.227	.291	.247	194	44	4	0	0	8	18	23
July	.255	.328	.325	212	54	8	2	1	16	23	19
August	.286	.376	.386	210	60	6	6	1	12	28	15
Sept/Oct	.277	.338	.340	191	53	8	2	0	11	18	15
Situational											
Bases Empty	.243	.319	.302	839	204	24	8	3	3	89	77
Leadoff	.243	.316	.298	510	124	16	3	2	2	52	45
Not Leadoff	.243	.323	.307	329	80	8	5	1	1	37	32
Runners On	.293	.361	.347	331	97	10	4	0	63	39	20
First Base Only	.310	.367	.352	145	45	6	0	0	2	13	6
Scoring Position	.280	.357	.344	186	52	4	4	0	61	26	14
Late Innings, Close	.253	.343	.285	158	40	2	0	1	10	22	15

RBI/Opportunities

Scoring Position	60 / 280	(21%)
Scoring Position, 2 Out	22 / 139	(16%)
On Third, Less than 2 Out	29 / 48	(60%)
RBI in close games / RBI Total	41 / 66	(62%)

Rob Wilfong
California Angels

	Ave.	OBP	SLG	AB	H	2B	3B	HR	RBI	BB	SO
THREE YEARS (84 – 86)											
Totals	.222	.270	.314	812	180	26	5	13	79	52	119
Batting vs. Left and Right-handed Pitchers											
Left	.185	.236	.296	81	15	1	1	2	12	6	24
Right	.226	.274	.316	731	165	25	4	11	67	46	95
At Home and on the Road											
Home	.218	.267	.323	372	81	15	0	8	38	24	54
Road	.225	.273	.307	440	99	11	5	5	41	28	65
Facing Groundball Pitchers and Flyball Pitchers											
Groundball	.245	.293	.332	380	93	12	3	5	43	27	52
Flyball	.201	.250	.299	432	87	14	2	8	36	25	67
Facing Finesse Pitchers and Power Pitchers											
Finesse	.234	.274	.340	462	108	14	4	9	50	26	53
Power	.206	.264	.280	350	72	12	1	4	29	26	66
On Grass and on Turf											
Grass	.225	.273	.325	677	152	23	3	13	66	44	96
Turf	.207	.257	.259	135	28	3	2	0	13	8	23
During the Day and at Night											
Day	.200	.252	.300	260	52	4	2	6	24	19	39
Night	.232	.279	.321	552	128	22	3	7	55	33	80
By Month											
April	.259	.343	.397	116	30	6	2	2	15	15	10
May	.247	.299	.341	170	42	5	1	3	17	13	26
June	.229	.263	.301	166	38	4	1	2	16	7	27
July	.207	.233	.300	140	29	5	1	2	12	4	21
August	.246	.267	.341	126	31	6	0	2	10	4	21
Sept/Oct	.106	.192	.170	94	10	0	0	2	9	9	14
Situational											
Bases Empty	.189	.237	.306	477	90	19	2	11	11	27	64
Leadoff	.211	.261	.340	194	41	8	1	5	5	11	25
Not Leadoff	.173	.220	.283	283	49	11	1	6	6	16	39
Runners On	.269	.316	.325	335	90	7	3	2	68	25	55
First Base Only	.235	.267	.257	136	32	3	0	0	4	22	
Scoring Position	.291	.352	.372	199	58	4	3	2	68	21	33
Late Innings, Close	.236	.276	.326	144	34	5	1	2	14	7	18

RBI/Opportunities

Scoring Position	63 / 265	(24%)
Scoring Position, 2 Out	29 / 107	(27%)
On Third, Less than 2 Out	24 / 46	(52%)
RBI in close games / RBI Total	41 / 79	(52%)

Curtis Wilkerson
Texas Rangers

THREE YEARS (84 – 86)

	Ave.	OBP	SLG	AB	H	2B	3B	HR	RBI	BB	SO
Totals	.244	.284	.294	1080	264	33	9	1	63	55	177
Batting vs. Left and Right-handed Pitchers											
Left	.229	.303	.281	249	57	9	2	0	14	25	42
Right	.249	.278	.298	831	207	24	7	1	49	30	135
At Home and on the Road											
Home	.241	.282	.282	515	124	13	4	0	30	26	80
Road	.248	.286	.306	565	140	20	5	1	33	29	97
Facing Groundball Pitchers and Flyball Pitchers											
Groundball	.262	.296	.308	546	143	16	3	1	33	26	87
Flyball	.227	.272	.281	534	121	17	6	0	30	29	90
Facing Finesse Pitchers and Power Pitchers											
Finesse	.255	.286	.314	624	159	22	6	1	32	24	90
Power	.230	.281	.268	456	105	11	3	0	31	31	87
On Grass and on Turf											
Grass	.243	.283	.288	886	215	24	8	0	49	45	146
Turf	.253	.286	.325	194	49	9	1	1	14	10	31
During the Day and at Night											
Day	.234	.270	.281	231	54	6	1	0	16	10	39
Night	.247	.288	.298	849	210	27	8	0	47	45	138
By Month											
April	.162	.219	.182	148	24	3	0	0	7	11	30
May	.298	.323	.372	188	56	10	2	0	10	7	31
June	.279	.312	.311	222	62	5	1	0	17	9	38
July	.225	.267	.272	191	43	3	3	0	10	10	28
August	.233	.272	.267	150	35	3	1	0	5	8	23
Sept/Oct	.243	.291	.331	181	44	9	2	1	14	10	27
Situational											
Bases Empty	.246	.283	.296	700	172	22	5	1	1	33	117
Leadoff	.257	.295	.305	292	75	6	4	0	0	14	51
Not Leadoff	.238	.273	.289	408	97	16	1	1	1	19	66
Runners On	.242	.286	.292	380	92	11	4	0	62	22	60
First Base Only	.266	.298	.312	154	41	5	1	0	2	4	22
Scoring Position	.226	.279	.279	226	51	6	3	0	60	18	38
Late Innings, Close	.283	.312	.337	166	47	7	1	0	10	6	30

RBI/Opportunities

Scoring Position	58 / 302	(19%)
Scoring Position, 2 Out	28 / 161	(17%)
On Third, Less than 2 Out	22 / 44	(50%)
RBI in close games / RBI Total	43 / 63	(68%)

Jerry Willard
Oakland A's

THREE YEARS (84 – 86)

	Ave.	OBP	SLG	AB	H	2B	3B	HR	RBI	BB	SO
Totals	.253	.324	.385	707	179	28	1	21	99	75	142
Batting vs. Left and Right-handed Pitchers											
Left	.205	.278	.259	112	23	3	0	1	13	11	39
Right	.262	.333	.408	595	156	25	1	20	86	64	103
At Home and on the Road											
Home	.263	.332	.389	357	94	12	0	11	53	36	77
Road	.243	.316	.380	350	85	16	1	10	46	39	65
Facing Groundball Pitchers and Flyball Pitchers											
Groundball	.254	.321	.390	362	92	16	0	11	56	36	60
Flyball	.252	.327	.380	345	87	12	1	10	43	39	82
Facing Finesse Pitchers and Power Pitchers											
Finesse	.264	.335	.436	397	105	18	1	16	61	42	64
Power	.239	.310	.319	310	74	10	0	5	38	33	78
On Grass and on Turf											
Grass	.250	.319	.365	584	146	19	0	16	78	60	117
Turf	.268	.348	.480	123	33	9	1	5	21	15	25
During the Day and at Night											
Day	.248	.310	.353	266	66	10	0	6	35	25	48
Night	.256	.333	.404	441	113	18	1	15	64	50	94
By Month											
April	.194	.268	.278	36	7	3	0	0	2	4	6
May	.151	.292	.264	53	8	0	0	2	5	11	9
June	.276	.360	.422	185	51	12	0	5	29	24	32
July	.284	.333	.381	134	38	5	1	2	11	10	34
August	.228	.277	.317	123	28	2	0	3	20	9	24
Sept/Oct	.267	.333	.455	176	47	6	0	9	32	17	37
Situational											
Bases Empty	.255	.322	.381	388	99	14	1	11	11	37	82
Leadoff	.294	.372	.448	163	48	5	1	6	6	19	33
Not Leadoff	.227	.284	.333	225	51	9	0	5	5	18	49
Runners On	.251	.327	.389	319	80	14	0	10	88	38	60
First Base Only	.261	.309	.472	142	37	9	0	7	21	10	25
Scoring Position	.243	.340	.322	177	43	5	0	3	67	28	35
Late Innings, Close	.279	.355	.418	122	34	5	0	4	23	14	19

RBI/Opportunities

Scoring Position	60 / 266	(23%)
Scoring Position, 2 Out	20 / 111	(18%)
On Third, Less than 2 Out	22 / 39	(56%)
RBI in close games / RBI Total	51 / 99	(52%)

Frank Williams
San Francisco Giants

1986: Finesse, Groundball 1985: Power, Groundball 1984: Power, Groundball

THREE YEARS (84 – 86)

	G	IP	H	BB	SO	SB	CS	W	L	S	ERA
Totals	146	231.2	188	107	178	23	18	14	9	4	3.22
At Home and on the Road											
Home	73	115.2	73	56	95	8	8	5	4	2	2.49
Road	73	116.0	115	51	83	15	10	9	5	2	3.96
During the Day and and at Night											
Day	69	105.0	72	50	78	13	8	5	4	2	2.83
Night	77	126.2	116	57	100	10	10	9	5	2	3.55
On Grass and on Turf											
Grass	108	167.2	125	78	132	16	14	9	7	3	3.01
Turf	38	64.0	63	29	46	7	4	5	2	1	3.80
By Month											
April	15	20.0	21	17	15	3	1	0	1	1	6.30
May	14	23.2	15	16	23	1	0	1	0	1	3.42
June	28	47.0	41	15	41	5	5	8	2	0	2.87
July	21	35.0	27	17	22	3	3	0	0	1	2.31
August	38	61.2	52	24	46	6	4	4	3	1	4.09
Sept/Oct	30	44.1	32	18	31	5	5	1	3	0	1.62

vs. Opponent Batters

THREE YEARS (84 – 86)

	Ave.	OBP	SLG	AB	H	2B	3B	HR	RBI	BB	SO
Totals	.228	.324	.293	823	188	26	3	7	99	107	178
Pitching vs. Left and Right-handed Batters											
Left	.301	.324	.399	366	110	21	3	3	46	55	54
Right	.171	.268	.208	457	78	5	0	4	53	52	124
Situational											
Bases Empty	.241	.326	.303	439	106	16	1	3	3	49	99
Leadoff	.271	.336	.333	192	52	10	1	0	0	18	41
Not Leadoff	.219	.318	.279	247	54	6	0	3	3	31	58
Runners On	.214	.322	.281	384	82	10	2	4	96	58	79
First Base Only	.185	.284	.233	146	27	2	1	1	3	17	26
Scoring Position	.231	.345	.311	238	55	8	1	3	93	41	53
Late Innings, Close	.234	.336	.274	252	59	7	0	1	23	37	61

RBI/Opportunities

Scoring Position	83 / 357	(23%)
Scoring Position, 2 Out	33 / 163	(20%)
On Third, Less than 2 Out	40 / 69	(58%)
RBI in close games / RBI Total	43 / 99	(43%)

Mitch Williams
Texas Rangers

1986: Power, Flyball 1985: Did not play 1984: Did not play

THREE YEARS (84 – 86)

	G	IP	H	BB	SO	SB	CS	W	L	S	ERA
Totals	80	98.0	69	79	90	8	5	8	6	8	3.58
At Home and on the Road											
Home	39	52.0	38	37	44	2	1	3	3	5	3.46
Road	41	46.0	31	42	46	6	4	5	3	3	3.72
During the Day and and at Night											
Day	18	17.2	16	13	18	3	1	3	0	1	3.57
Night	62	80.1	53	66	72	5	4	5	6	7	3.59
On Grass and on Turf											
Grass	67	81.2	56	69	68	6	4	6	5	8	3.20
Turf	13	16.1	13	10	22	2	1	2	1	0	5.51
By Month											
April	7	7.0	7	5	5	3	1	1	0	0	5.14
May	11	12.1	4	4	15	1	0	2	0	1	0.00
June	16	19.0	18	13	26	2	1	3	1	1	3.32
July	13	20.0	17	18	15	0	2	1	1	1	4.05
August	18	27.1	13	22	18	2	0	1	2	4	2.96
Sept/Oct	15	12.1	10	17	11	0	1	0	2	1	7.30

vs. Opponent Batters

THREE YEARS (84 – 86)

	Ave.	OBP	SLG	AB	H	2B	3B	HR	RBI	BB	SO
Totals	.202	.366	.330	342	69	14	3	8	43	79	90
Pitching vs. Left and Right-handed Batters											
Left	.203	.331	.322	118	24	5	0	3	15	19	29
Right	.201	.382	.335	224	45	9	3	5	28	60	61
Situational											
Bases Empty	.184	.361	.316	158	29	5	2	4	4	40	43
Leadoff	.203	.368	.362	69	14	2	0	3	3	15	18
Not Leadoff	.169	.357	.281	89	15	3	2	1	1	25	25
Runners On	.217	.369	.342	184	40	9	1	4	39	39	47
First Base Only	.282	.393	.437	71	20	5	0	2	7	9	16
Scoring Position	.177	.356	.283	113	20	4	1	2	32	30	31
Late Innings, Close	.211	.364	.314	175	37	7	1	3	27	37	48

RBI/Opportunities

Scoring Position	26 / 190	(14%)
Scoring Position, 2 Out	11 / 91	(12%)
On Third, Less than 2 Out	12 / 33	(36%)
RBI in close games / RBI Total	30 / 43	(70%)

Reggie Williams
Los Angeles Dodgers

THREE YEARS (84 – 86)	Ave.	OBP	SLG	AB	H	2B	3B	HR	RBI	BB	SO
Totals	.279	.331	.375	312	87	14	2	4	32	23	61
Batting vs. Left and Right-handed Pitchers											
Left	.291	.351	.383	175	51	9	2	1	13	15	31
Right	.263	.306	.365	137	36	5	0	3	19	8	30
At Home and on the Road											
Home	.276	.329	.353	156	43	7	1	1	12	12	29
Road	.282	.333	.397	156	44	7	1	3	20	11	32
Facing Groundball Pitchers and Flyball Pitchers											
Groundball	.294	.340	.375	136	40	6	1	1	15	10	23
Flyball	.267	.325	.375	176	47	8	1	3	17	13	38
Facing Finesse Pitchers and Power Pitchers											
Finesse	.278	.324	.364	162	45	6	1	2	19	10	21
Power	.280	.339	.387	150	42	8	1	2	13	13	40
On Grass and on Turf											
Grass	.293	.339	.383	222	65	10	2	2	21	15	42
Turf	.244	.313	.356	90	22	4	0	2	11	8	19
During the Day and at Night											
Day	.258	.308	.340	97	25	5	0	1	11	7	24
Night	.288	.342	.391	215	62	9	2	3	21	16	37
By Month											
April	.167	.167	.167	6	1	0	0	0	0	0	0
May	.275	.293	.353	51	14	4	0	0	3	4	10
June	.369	.406	.492	65	24	6	1	0	9	4	12
July	.250	.256	.368	76	19	3	0	2	10	1	17
August	.241	.349	.315	54	13	1	0	1	5	8	8
Sept/Oct	.267	.333	.350	60	16	1	0	1	5	6	14
Situational											
Bases Empty	.269	.303	.349	186	50	8	2	1	1	9	38
Leadoff	.324	.380	.380	71	23	4	0	0	0	1	15
Not Leadoff	.235	.285	.330	115	27	4	2	1	1	8	23
Runners On	.294	.371	.413	126	37	6	0	3	31	14	23
First Base Only	.309	.345	.509	55	17	5	0	2	5	3	10
Scoring Position	.282	.388	.338	71	20	1	0	1	26	11	13
Late Innings, Close	.278	.316	.407	54	15	4	0	1	6	3	11

RBI/Opportunities		
Scoring Position	24 / 113	(21%)
Scoring Position, 2 Out	12 / 48	(25%)
On Third, Less than 2 Out	8 / 23	(35%)
RBI in close games / RBI Total	20 / 32	(63%)

Carl Willis
Cincinnati Reds

1986: Power, Flyball   1985: Finesse, Flyball   1984: Finesse, Groundball

THREE YEARS (84 – 86)	G	IP	H	BB	SO	SB	CS	W	L	S	ERA
Totals	57	91.2	108	44	37	8	3	2	6	2	5.60
At Home and on the Road											
Home	29	49.0	62	24	23	3	2	2	3	1	6.61
Road	28	42.2	46	20	14	5	1	0	3	1	4.43
During the Day and and at Night											
Day	20	32.2	40	19	11	6	1	0	1	1	6.34
Night	37	59.0	68	25	26	2	2	2	5	1	5.19
On Grass and on Turf											
Grass	22	36.2	43	16	16	3	1	0	3	0	4.91
Turf	35	55.0	65	28	21	5	2	2	3	2	6.05
By Month											
April	7	10.0	14	3	5	1	1	1	0	1	5.40
May	4	3.2	7	2	1	0	0	0	0	0	19.64
June	12	20.1	23	5	6	3	1	1	1	0	4.43
July	11	17.1	20	12	6	0	0	0	2	0	4.15
August	12	19.1	28	13	10	3	0	0	2	0	8.38
Sept/Oct	11	21.0	16	9	9	1	1	0	1	1	3.00

vs. Opponent Batters THREE YEARS (84 – 86)	Ave.	OBP	SLG	AB	H	2B	3B	HR	RBI	BB	SO
Totals	.301	.376	.468	359	108	25	4	9	62	44	37
Pitching vs. Left and Right-handed Batters											
Left	.299	.380	.467	157	47	9	1	2	24	20	15
Right	.302	.373	.515	202	61	16	3	7	38	24	22
Situational											
Bases Empty	.316	.376	.463	177	56	7	2	5	5	16	20
Leadoff	.359	.438	.577	78	28	4	2	3	3	11	8
Not Leadoff	.283	.324	.374	99	28	3	0	2	2	5	12
Runners On	.286	.376	.473	182	52	18	2	4	57	28	17
First Base Only	.276	.329	.474	76	21	7	1	2	7	6	6
Scoring Position	.292	.405	.472	106	31	11	1	2	50	22	11
Late Innings, Close	.337	.411	.530	83	28	8	1	2	7	10	9

RBI/Opportunities		
Scoring Position	43 / 177	(24%)
Scoring Position, 2 Out	11 / 59	(19%)
On Third, Less than 2 Out	18 / 42	(43%)
RBI in close games / RBI Total	21 / 62	(34%)

Frank Wills
Cleveland Indians

1986: Power, Flyball   1985: Power, Flyball   1984: Finesse, Flyball

THREE YEARS (84 – 86)	G	IP	H	BB	SO	SB	CS	W	L	S	ERA
Totals	60	200.1	204	97	120	15	12	11	18	5	5.62
At Home and on the Road											
Home	32	113.1	105	53	69	10	9	7	7	4	4.76
Road	28	87.0	99	44	51	5	3	4	11	1	6.72
During the Day and and at Night											
Day	16	56.2	48	33	33	1	1	3	5	3	4.29
Night	44	143.2	156	64	87	14	11	8	13	2	6.14
On Grass and on Turf											
Grass	36	89.1	99	40	56	3	3	5	10	3	5.94
Turf	24	111.0	105	57	64	12	9	6	8	2	5.35
By Month											
April	1	1.0	1	0	1	0	0	0	0	0	0.00
May	0	0.0	0	0	0	0	0	0	0	0	0.00
June	5	27.0	23	19	16	0	3	3	1	0	5.00
July	13	56.2	51	37	34	6	2	2	5	1	5.40
August	21	57.2	69	25	32	3	4	1	6	1	5.77
Sept/Oct	20	58.0	60	16	37	6	3	5	6	3	6.05

vs. Opponent Batters THREE YEARS (84 – 86)	Ave.	OBP	SLG	AB	H	2B	3B	HR	RBI	BB	SO
Totals	.268	.348	.430	760	204	36	3	27	118	97	120
Pitching vs. Left and Right-handed Batters											
Left	.285	.380	.443	411	117	23	3	12	63	65	67
Right	.249	.309	.415	349	87	13	0	15	55	32	53
Situational											
Bases Empty	.266	.348	.411	406	108	13	2	14	14	50	74
Leadoff	.287	.380	.443	174	50	7	1	6	6	26	31
Not Leadoff	.250	.323	.388	232	58	6	1	8	8	24	43
Runners On	.271	.348	.452	354	96	23	1	13	104	47	46
First Base Only	.319	.388	.486	144	46	9	0	5	16	15	19
Scoring Position	.238	.323	.429	210	50	14	1	8	88	32	27
Late Innings, Close	.306	.368	.396	111	34	7	0	1	14	12	19

RBI/Opportunities		
Scoring Position	74 / 315	(23%)
Scoring Position, 2 Out	22 / 135	(16%)
On Third, Less than 2 Out	34 / 58	(59%)
RBI in close games / RBI Total	72 / 118	(61%)

Jim Winn
Pittsburgh Pirates

1986: Power, Groundball   1985: Finesse, Groundball   1984: Power, Groundball

THREE YEARS (84 – 86)	G	IP	H	BB	SO	SB	CS	W	L	S	ERA
Totals	89	182.1	181	78	103	24	5	7	11	4	4.29
At Home and on the Road											
Home	41	80.0	78	31	54	8	3	2	2	0	4.39
Road	48	102.1	103	47	49	16	2	5	9	4	4.22
During the Day and and at Night											
Day	32	62.1	65	30	38	5	1	2	4	1	4.33
Night	57	120.0	116	48	65	19	4	5	7	3	4.28
On Grass and on Turf											
Grass	27	50.0	41	29	25	3	1	3	3	3	3.96
Turf	62	132.1	140	49	78	21	4	4	8	1	4.42
By Month											
April	9	8.2	6	1	8	0	1	0	0	1	2.08
May	12	24.1	21	11	17	0	1	2	1	1	4.07
June	19	52.0	53	14	24	7	1	1	4	1	3.29
July	16	27.0	33	19	10	1	0	2	2	0	6.00
August	13	36.1	37	17	28	14	2	1	3	0	4.95
Sept/Oct	20	34.0	31	16	16	2	0	1	1	1	4.50

vs. Opponent Batters THREE YEARS (84 – 86)	Ave.	OBP	SLG	AB	H	2B	3B	HR	RBI	BB	SO
Totals	.262	.338	.361	692	181	22	1	15	80	78	103
Pitching vs. Left and Right-handed Batters											
Left	.280	.354	.397	307	86	9	0	9	36	35	44
Right	.247	.326	.332	385	95	13	1	6	44	43	59
Situational											
Bases Empty	.240	.298	.348	391	94	10	1	10	10	30	54
Leadoff	.209	.267	.288	163	34	1	0	4	4	11	22
Not Leadoff	.263	.320	.390	228	60	9	1	6	6	19	32
Runners On	.289	.386	.379	301	87	12	0	5	70	48	49
First Base Only	.316	.355	.412	114	36	2	0	3	6	7	14
Scoring Position	.273	.402	.358	187	51	10	0	2	64	41	35
Late Innings, Close	.345	.431	.540	87	30	2	0	5	10	13	13

RBI/Opportunities		
Scoring Position	60 / 295	(20%)
Scoring Position, 2 Out	19 / 129	(15%)
On Third, Less than 2 Out	27 / 60	(45%)
RBI in close games / RBI Total	37 / 80	(46%)

Herm Winningham
Montreal Expos

THREE YEARS (84 – 86)

	Ave.	OBP	SLG	AB	H	2B	3B	HR	RBI	BB	SO
Totals	.239	.299	.338	524	125	13	9	7	37	47	130
Batting vs. Left and Right-handed Pitchers											
Left	.270	.282	.351	74	20	0	0	2	7	2	25
Right	.233	.302	.336	450	105	13	9	5	30	45	105
At Home and on the Road											
Home	.185	.277	.254	260	48	3	6	1	16	34	67
Road	.292	.323	.420	264	77	10	3	6	21	13	63
Facing Groundball Pitchers and Flyball Pitchers											
Groundball	.225	.292	.292	236	53	5	4	1	13	23	63
Flyball	.250	.305	.375	288	72	8	5	6	24	24	67
Facing Finesse Pitchers and Power Pitchers											
Finesse	.257	.305	.387	261	67	10	6	4	21	20	53
Power	.221	.293	.289	263	58	3	3	3	16	27	77
On Grass and on Turf											
Grass	.234	.284	.321	137	32	2	2	2	7	10	44
Turf	.240	.304	.344	387	93	11	7	5	30	37	86
During the Day and at Night											
Day	.225	.298	.344	218	49	3	4	5	13	24	50
Night	.248	.300	.333	306	76	10	5	2	24	23	80
By Month											
April	.230	.338	.328	61	14	0	0	2	6	10	13
May	.261	.356	.426	115	30	4	3	3	8	17	26
June	.232	.259	.304	112	26	3	1	1	6	4	37
July	.333	.340	.511	45	15	1	2	1	7	2	11
August	.188	.244	.263	80	15	2	2	0	2	6	15
Sept/Oct	.225	.275	.270	111	25	3	1	0	8	8	28
Situational											
Bases Empty	.241	.296	.356	323	78	9	5	6	6	25	74
Leadoff	.301	.345	.444	133	40	6	2	3	3	9	25
Not Leadoff	.200	.262	.295	190	38	3	3	3	3	16	49
Runners On	.234	.304	.308	201	47	4	4	1	31	22	56
First Base Only	.256	.287	.356	90	23	2	2	1	4	4	22
Scoring Position	.216	.316	.270	111	24	2	2	0	27	18	34
Late Innings, Close	.239	.308	.321	109	26	4	1	1	7	11	29

RBI/Opportunities

Scoring Position	27 / 164	(16%)
Scoring Position, 2 Out	7 / 68	(10%)
On Third, Less than 2 Out	14 / 32	(44%)
RBI in close games / RBI Total	26 / 37	(70%)

Bobby Witt
Texas Rangers

1986: Power, Flyball   1985: Did not play   1984: Did not play

THREE YEARS (84 – 86)

	G	IP	H	BB	SO	SB	CS	W	L	S	ERA
Totals	31	157.2	130	143	174	44	4	11	9	0	5.48
At Home and on the Road											
Home	16	90.0	69	69	94	20	2	6	3	0	4.00
Road	15	67.2	61	74	80	24	2	5	6	0	7.45
During the Day and and at Night											
Day	8	42.2	29	46	66	14	1	3	3	0	5.91
Night	23	115.0	101	97	108	30	3	8	6	0	5.32
On Grass and on Turf											
Grass	28	140.1	118	131	155	40	3	10	8	0	5.58
Turf	3	17.1	12	12	19	4	1	1	1	0	4.67
By Month											
April	4	21.1	11	24	27	6	1	2	0	0	3.80
May	6	28.2	25	29	14	6	2	0	4	0	7.53
June	6	31.0	31	27	37	9	1	2	2	0	6.39
July	4	17.0	15	18	21	6	0	1	3	0	8.47
August	5	25.2	23	22	34	8	0	2	0	0	3.86
Sept/Oct	6	34.0	25	23	41	9	0	4	0	0	3.71

vs. Opponent Batters
THREE YEARS (84 – 86)

	Ave.	OBP	SLG	AB	H	2B	3B	HR	RBI	BB	SO
Totals	.223	.374	.369	583	130	31	0	18	88	143	174
Pitching vs. Left and Right-handed Batters											
Left	.248	.409	.382	314	78	21	0	7	49	86	81
Right	.193	.330	.353	269	52	10	0	11	39	57	93
Situational											
Bases Empty	.215	.368	.364	302	65	15	0	10	10	71	84
Leadoff	.248	.412	.414	133	33	4	0	6	6	36	40
Not Leadoff	.189	.332	.325	169	32	11	0	4	4	35	44
Runners On	.231	.380	.374	281	65	16	0	8	78	72	90
First Base Only	.248	.363	.429	105	26	4	0	5	13	19	33
Scoring Position	.222	.389	.341	176	39	12	0	3	65	53	57
Late Innings, Close	.400	.409	.500	20	8	2	0	0	2	1	4

RBI/Opportunities

Scoring Position	57 / 290	(20%)
Scoring Position, 2 Out	23 / 145	(16%)
On Third, Less than 2 Out	20 / 41	(49%)
RBI in close games / RBI Total	63 / 88	(72%)

George Wright
Montreal Expos

THREE YEARS (84 – 86)

	Ave.	OBP	SLG	AB	H	2B	3B	HR	RBI	BB	SO
Totals	.214	.257	.311	969	207	41	7	13	78	55	154
Batting vs. Left and Right-handed Pitchers											
Left	.186	.240	.271	295	55	14	1	3	22	22	56
Right	.226	.264	.328	674	152	27	6	10	56	33	98
At Home and on the Road											
Home	.197	.241	.303	452	89	13	4	9	37	24	78
Road	.228	.270	.317	517	118	28	3	4	41	31	76
Facing Groundball Pitchers and Flyball Pitchers											
Groundball	.229	.269	.334	515	118	24	3	8	49	27	78
Flyball	.196	.243	.284	454	89	17	4	5	29	28	76
Facing Finesse Pitchers and Power Pitchers											
Finesse	.230	.264	.343	539	124	27	2	10	45	23	85
Power	.193	.247	.270	430	83	14	5	3	33	32	69
On Grass and on Turf											
Grass	.214	.252	.316	752	161	31	5	12	65	37	115
Turf	.212	.272	.290	217	46	10	2	1	13	18	39
During the Day and at Night											
Day	.222	.269	.278	248	55	9	1	1	13	16	43
Night	.211	.252	.322	721	152	32	6	12	65	39	111
By Month											
April	.205	.232	.281	171	35	5	1	2	10	6	22
May	.169	.221	.225	160	27	4	1	1	8	11	21
June	.254	.329	.381	63	16	3	1	1	5	6	11
July	.177	.239	.252	147	26	8	0	1	12	11	26
August	.273	.310	.440	216	59	11	2	7	26	12	31
Sept/Oct	.208	.238	.288	212	44	10	2	1	17	9	43
Situational											
Bases Empty	.211	.248	.322	568	120	29	5	8	8	27	86
Leadoff	.194	.218	.347	222	43	15	2	5	5	7	28
Not Leadoff	.223	.267	.306	346	77	14	3	3	3	20	58
Runners On	.217	.268	.294	401	87	12	2	5	70	28	68
First Base Only	.234	.269	.337	184	43	5	1	4	11	7	29
Scoring Position	.203	.266	.258	217	44	7	1	1	59	21	39
Late Innings, Close	.240	.276	.324	204	49	4	2	3	19	11	28

RBI/Opportunities

Scoring Position	55 / 297	(19%)
Scoring Position, 2 Out	19 / 127	(15%)
On Third, Less than 2 Out	23 / 55	(42%)
RBI in close games / RBI Total	51 / 78	(65%)

Ricky Wright
Texas Rangers

1986: Power, Groundball   1985: Power, Groundball   1984: Power, Groundball

THREE YEARS (84 – 86)

	G	IP	H	BB	SO	SB	CS	W	L	S	ERA
Totals	34	61.2	69	37	36	5	1	1	2	0	5.25
At Home and on the Road											
Home	17	30.2	32	15	18	2	0	1	1	0	3.52
Road	17	31.0	37	22	18	3	1	0	1	0	6.97
During the Day and and at Night											
Day	9	19.1	11	6	11	2	1	0	0	0	2.79
Night	25	42.1	58	31	25	3	0	1	2	0	6.38
On Grass and on Turf											
Grass	28	52.0	56	29	30	4	1	1	2	0	4.85
Turf	6	9.2	13	8	6	1	0	0	0	0	7.45
By Month											
April	6	11.0	12	6	8	2	1	1	0	0	5.73
May	13	28.2	29	15	12	2	0	0	1	0	5.34
June	4	3.1	9	5	2	0	0	0	0	0	8.10
July	0	0.0	0	0	0	0	0	0	0	0	0.00
August	2	3.1	6	1	3	0	0	0	0	0	8.10
Sept/Oct	9	15.1	13	10	11	1	0	0	1	0	3.52

vs. Opponent Batters
THREE YEARS (84 – 86)

	Ave.	OBP	SLG	AB	H	2B	3B	HR	RBI	BB	SO
Totals	.290	.385	.395	238	69	13	0	4	35	37	36
Pitching vs. Left and Right-handed Batters											
Left	.324	.400	.437	71	23	5	0	1	14	9	13
Right	.275	.379	.377	167	46	8	0	3	21	28	23
Situational											
Bases Empty	.279	.375	.423	111	31	7	0	3	3	17	18
Leadoff	.308	.390	.519	52	16	5	0	2	2	7	8
Not Leadoff	.254	.362	.339	59	15	2	0	1	1	10	10
Runners On	.299	.395	.370	127	38	6	0	1	32	20	18
First Base Only	.224	.321	.245	49	11	1	0	0	1	7	5
Scoring Position	.346	.440	.449	78	27	5	0	1	31	13	13
Late Innings, Close	.314	.415	.486	35	11	3	0	1	5	6	5

RBI/Opportunities

Scoring Position	30 / 109	(28%)
Scoring Position, 2 Out	14 / 52	(27%)
On Third, Less than 2 Out	7 / 12	(58%)
RBI in close games / RBI Total	15 / 35	(43%)

Butch Wynegar
New York Yankees

	Ave.	OBP	SLG	AB	H	2B	3B	HR	RBI	BB	SO
THREE YEARS (84 – 86)											
Totals	.240	.348	.335	945	227	32	2	18	106	159	99
Batting vs. Left and Right-handed Pitchers											
Left	.249	.356	.391	345	86	18	2	9	47	58	46
Right	.235	.344	.303	600	141	14	0	9	59	101	53
At Home and on the Road											
Home	.238	.345	.330	488	116	17	2	8	47	81	47
Road	.243	.352	.341	457	111	15	0	10	59	78	52
Facing Groundball Pitchers and Flyball Pitchers											
Groundball	.235	.342	.280	460	108	12	0	3	41	75	46
Flyball	.245	.354	.388	485	119	20	2	15	65	84	53
Facing Finesse Pitchers and Power Pitchers											
Finesse	.249	.339	.340	526	131	22	1	8	57	73	53
Power	.229	.360	.329	419	96	10	1	10	49	86	46
On Grass and on Turf											
Grass	.242	.346	.322	810	196	25	2	12	83	131	87
Turf	.230	.360	.415	135	31	7	0	6	23	28	12
During the Day and at Night											
Day	.202	.303	.273	297	60	9	0	4	26	43	34
Night	.258	.368	.364	648	167	23	2	14	80	116	65
By Month											
April	.243	.323	.354	144	35	7	0	3	19	17	19
May	.209	.322	.342	225	47	6	0	8	36	38	20
June	.317	.396	.409	186	59	6	1	3	20	25	15
July	.168	.256	.242	149	25	6	1	1	11	18	15
August	.293	.436	.374	123	36	7	0	1	14	32	16
Sept/Oct	.212	.367	.263	118	25	0	0	2	6	29	14
Situational											
Bases Empty	.239	.338	.310	507	121	16	1	6	6	76	49
Leadoff	.228	.315	.301	206	47	6	0	3	3	26	23
Not Leadoff	.246	.353	.316	301	74	10	1	3	3	50	26
Runners On	.242	.360	.365	438	106	16	1	12	100	83	50
First Base Only	.255	.329	.361	208	53	8	1	4	13	23	16
Scoring Position	.230	.384	.370	230	53	8	0	8	87	60	34
Late Innings, Close	.232	.333	.316	190	44	4	0	4	20	29	23

RBI/Opportunities

Scoring Position	71 / 356	(20%)
Scoring Position, 2 Out	32 / 157	(20%)
On Third, Less than 2 Out	28 / 70	(40%)
RBI in close games / RBI Total	67 / 106	(63%)

Marvell Wynne
San Diego Padres

	Ave.	OBP	SLG	AB	H	2B	3B	HR	RBI	BB	SO
THREE YEARS (84 – 86)											
Totals	.250	.291	.334	1278	319	49	16	9	94	75	174
Batting vs. Left and Right-handed Pitchers											
Left	.242	.293	.326	347	84	10	5	3	23	25	60
Right	.252	.290	.337	931	235	39	11	6	71	50	114
At Home and on the Road											
Home	.273	.313	.375	645	176	32	8	6	57	38	89
Road	.226	.268	.292	633	143	17	8	3	37	37	85
Facing Groundball Pitchers and Flyball Pitchers											
Groundball	.262	.302	.353	634	166	27	8	5	50	37	74
Flyball	.238	.280	.315	644	153	22	8	4	44	38	100
Facing Finesse Pitchers and Power Pitchers											
Finesse	.261	.309	.353	736	192	30	7	8	55	51	83
Power	.234	.266	.308	542	127	19	9	1	39	24	91
On Grass and on Turf											
Grass	.253	.291	.362	505	128	23	7	6	41	28	80
Turf	.247	.291	.316	773	191	26	9	3	53	47	94
During the Day and at Night											
Day	.252	.292	.365	417	105	22	5	5	33	25	58
Night	.249	.291	.319	861	214	27	11	4	61	50	116
By Month											
April	.279	.320	.393	140	39	6	2	2	6	9	16
May	.239	.278	.302	205	49	6	2	1	12	11	25
June	.304	.345	.374	257	78	11	2	1	24	16	26
July	.248	.281	.357	319	79	18	4	3	24	15	46
August	.186	.235	.229	236	44	2	1	2	14	15	38
Sept/Oct	.248	.299	.380	121	30	6	5	0	14	9	23
Situational											
Bases Empty	.255	.290	.351	824	210	30	11	9	9	40	110
Leadoff	.291	.318	.402	470	137	21	8	5	5	18	56
Not Leadoff	.206	.255	.282	354	73	9	3	4	4	22	54
Runners On	.240	.293	.304	454	109	19	5	0	85	35	64
First Base Only	.222	.273	.297	185	41	8	3	0	7	13	25
Scoring Position	.253	.306	.309	269	68	11	2	0	78	22	39
Late Innings, Close	.248	.296	.351	262	65	12	3	3	25	18	37

RBI/Opportunities

Scoring Position	74 / 360	(21%)
Scoring Position, 2 Out	32 / 181	(18%)
On Third, Less than 2 Out	27 / 55	(49%)
RBI in close games / RBI Total	64 / 94	(68%)

Steve Yeager
Seattle Mariners

	Ave.	OBP	SLG	AB	H	2B	3B	HR	RBI	BB	SO
THREE YEARS (84 – 86)											
Totals	.217	.276	.283	448	97	10	1	6	50	39	85
Batting vs. Left and Right-handed Pitchers											
Left	.235	.285	.320	281	66	9	0	5	34	21	50
Right	.186	.261	.222	167	31	1	1	1	16	18	35
At Home and on the Road											
Home	.235	.280	.278	234	55	4	0	2	27	15	41
Road	.196	.272	.290	214	42	6	1	4	23	24	44
Facing Groundball Pitchers and Flyball Pitchers											
Groundball	.209	.271	.262	206	43	2	0	3	15	18	45
Flyball	.223	.280	.302	242	54	8	1	3	35	21	40
Facing Finesse Pitchers and Power Pitchers											
Finesse	.213	.268	.259	263	56	4	0	2	18	21	43
Power	.222	.286	.319	185	41	4	1	4	32	18	42
On Grass and on Turf											
Grass	.217	.271	.278	295	64	7	1	3	29	23	56
Turf	.216	.285	.294	153	33	3	0	3	21	16	29
During the Day and at Night											
Day	.270	.317	.322	152	41	6	1	0	21	12	28
Night	.189	.255	.264	296	56	4	0	6	29	27	57
By Month											
April	.187	.219	.242	91	17	2	0	1	9	4	23
May	.193	.279	.272	114	22	3	0	2	5	14	21
June	.297	.358	.419	74	22	3	0	2	15	7	10
July	.250	.311	.263	80	20	1	0	0	13	8	17
August	.145	.203	.194	62	9	0	0	1	7	5	10
Sept/Oct	.259	.286	.370	27	7	1	1	0	1	1	4
Situational											
Bases Empty	.193	.259	.257	269	52	3	1	4	4	24	48
Leadoff	.182	.250	.291	110	20	1	1	3	3	10	19
Not Leadoff	.201	.266	.233	159	32	2	0	1	1	14	29
Runners On	.251	.300	.324	179	45	7	0	2	46	15	37
First Base Only	.265	.306	.353	68	18	6	0	0	2	4	15
Scoring Position	.243	.297	.306	111	27	1	0	2	44	11	22
Late Innings, Close	.240	.293	.280	75	18	0	0	1	10	6	12

RBI/Opportunities

Scoring Position	39 / 158	(25%)
Scoring Position, 2 Out	13 / 65	(20%)
On Third, Less than 2 Out	17 / 27	(63%)
RBI in close games / RBI Total	26 / 50	(52%)

Rich Yett
Cleveland Indians

1986: Power, Flyball   **1985: Power, Flyball**   **1984: Did not play**

	G	IP	H	BB	SO	SB	CS	W	L	S	ERA
THREE YEARS (84 – 86)											
Totals	40	79.0	85	39	50	3	5	5	3	1	5.24
At Home and on the Road											
Home	21	39.1	48	18	32	0	5	3	1	0	5.49
Road	19	39.2	37	21	18	3	0	2	2	1	4.99
During the Day and and at Night											
Day	10	10.1	9	8	8	0	0	0	0	1	6.97
Night	30	68.2	76	31	42	3	5	5	3	0	4.98
On Grass and on Turf											
Grass	34	72.1	78	34	47	2	5	5	3	1	4.98
Turf	6	6.2	7	5	3	1	0	0	0	0	8.10
By Month											
April	4	5.0	7	2	3	1	0	0	0	1	7.20
May	11	15.1	16	7	12	1	0	2	0	0	4.11
June	7	10.2	12	6	9	0	3	1	0	0	4.22
July	6	18.1	20	7	10	1	1	1	1	0	6.38
August	6	13.0	18	8	5	0	1	0	1	0	9.00
Sept/Oct	6	16.2	12	9	11	0	0	1	1	0	2.16

vs. Opponent Batters

	Ave.	OBP	SLG	AB	H	2B	3B	HR	RBI	BB	SO
THREE YEARS (84 – 86)											
Totals	.275	.354	.427	309	85	15	1	10	51	39	50
Pitching vs. Left and Right-handed Batters											
Left	.266	.337	.379	169	45	8	1	3	21	19	23
Right	.286	.374	.486	140	40	7	0	7	30	20	27
Situational											
Bases Empty	.235	.301	.380	179	42	6	1	6	6	17	32
Leadoff	.182	.280	.318	66	12	1	1	2	2	9	9
Not Leadoff	.265	.314	.416	113	30	5	0	4	4	8	23
Runners On	.331	.420	.492	130	43	9	0	4	45	22	18
First Base Only	.308	.357	.462	52	16	2	0	2	5	4	8
Scoring Position	.346	.455	.513	78	27	7	0	2	40	18	10
Late Innings, Close	.283	.371	.491	53	15	2	0	3	14	7	10

RBI/Opportunities

Scoring Position	34 / 128	(27%)
Scoring Position, 2 Out	16 / 64	(25%)
On Third, Less than 2 Out	12 / 26	(46%)
RBI in close games / RBI Total	22 / 51	(43%)

Mike Young
Baltimore Orioles

	Ave.	OBP	SLG	AB	H	2B	3B	HR	RBI	BB	SO
THREE YEARS (84 – 86)											
Totals	.260	.348	.443	1220	317	54	4	54	175	155	304
Batting vs. Left and Right-handed Pitchers											
Left	.259	.333	.436	424	110	17	2	18	53	42	87
Right	.260	.357	.447	796	207	37	2	36	122	113	217
At Home and on the Road											
Home	.274	.371	.479	570	156	28	1	29	81	83	136
Road	.248	.328	.412	650	161	26	3	25	94	72	168
Facing Groundball Pitchers and Flyball Pitchers											
Groundball	.248	.336	.449	593	147	26	3	29	85	74	146
Flyball	.271	.360	.439	627	170	28	1	25	90	81	158
Facing Finesse Pitchers and Power Pitchers											
Finesse	.282	.365	.476	634	179	38	2	27	91	77	140
Power	.235	.330	.408	586	138	16	2	27	84	78	164
On Grass and on Turf											
Grass	.264	.352	.452	1040	275	41	2	50	154	131	245
Turf	.233	.329	.394	180	42	13	2	4	21	24	59
During the Day and at Night											
Day	.225	.308	.373	378	85	18	1	12	38	44	100
Night	.276	.366	.475	842	232	36	3	42	137	111	204
By Month											
April	.243	.368	.351	111	27	6	0	2	11	21	30
May	.251	.364	.400	175	44	14	0	4	21	29	44
June	.241	.311	.403	191	46	5	1	8	28	20	55
July	.242	.312	.430	207	50	9	3	8	23	20	61
August	.291	.402	.643	182	53	10	0	18	48	32	35
Sept/Oct	.274	.345	.421	354	97	10	0	14	44	33	79
Situational											
Bases Empty	.246	.330	.437	671	165	25	2	33	33	77	171
Leadoff	.259	.332	.485	274	71	8	0	18	18	24	63
Not Leadoff	.237	.328	.403	397	94	17	2	15	15	53	108
Runners On	.277	.370	.452	549	152	29	2	21	142	78	133
First Base Only	.289	.386	.472	235	68	14	1	9	21	35	48
Scoring Position	.268	.359	.436	314	84	15	1	12	121	43	85
Late Innings, Close	.230	.343	.410	200	46	9	0	9	37	34	57

RBI/Opportunities		
Scoring Position	100 / 445	(22%)
Scoring Position, 2 Out	42 / 220	(19%)
On Third, Less than 2 Out	31 / 62	(50%)
RBI in close games / RBI Total	114 / 175	(65%)

Joel Youngblood
San Francisco Giants

	Ave.	OBP	SLG	AB	H	2B	3B	HR	RBI	BB	SO
THREE YEARS (84 – 86)											
Totals	.258	.334	.365	883	228	35	1	19	103	96	157
Batting vs. Left and Right-handed Pitchers											
Left	.267	.335	.351	285	76	12	0	4	26	29	48
Right	.254	.333	.371	598	152	23	1	15	77	67	109
At Home and on the Road											
Home	.244	.324	.333	427	104	17	0	7	48	50	80
Road	.272	.343	.395	456	124	18	1	12	55	46	77
Facing Groundball Pitchers and Flyball Pitchers											
Groundball	.249	.304	.337	442	110	21	0	6	48	33	77
Flyball	.268	.361	.392	441	118	14	1	13	55	63	80
Facing Finesse Pitchers and Power Pitchers											
Finesse	.296	.359	.408	493	146	25	0	10	57	46	69
Power	.210	.302	.310	390	82	10	1	9	46	50	88
On Grass and on Turf											
Grass	.259	.333	.365	636	165	26	1	13	75	70	119
Turf	.255	.335	.364	247	63	9	0	6	28	26	38
During the Day and at Night											
Day	.252	.328	.366	413	104	21	1	8	50	46	75
Night	.264	.339	.364	470	124	14	0	11	53	50	82
By Month											
April	.231	.306	.256	121	28	3	0	0	12	13	22
May	.257	.336	.367	109	28	4	1	2	8	10	22
June	.284	.361	.423	194	55	6	0	7	26	23	30
July	.280	.367	.433	164	46	7	0	6	23	22	27
August	.225	.280	.307	218	49	9	0	3	23	17	42
Sept/Oct	.286	.378	.403	77	22	6	0	1	11	11	14
Situational											
Bases Empty	.236	.307	.348	488	115	16	0	13	13	48	88
Leadoff	.297	.350	.420	219	65	9	0	6	6	18	30
Not Leadoff	.186	.272	.290	269	50	7	0	7	7	30	58
Runners On	.286	.366	.385	395	113	19	1	6	90	48	69
First Base Only	.285	.331	.380	158	45	6	0	3	9	11	28
Scoring Position	.287	.387	.388	237	68	13	1	3	81	37	41
Late Innings, Close	.286	.365	.379	206	59	8	1	3	28	25	45

RBI/Opportunities		
Scoring Position	73 / 328	(22%)
Scoring Position, 2 Out	30 / 154	(19%)
On Third, Less than 2 Out	29 / 59	(49%)
RBI in close games / RBI Total	66 / 103	(64%)

IV

ESSAYS

HOW PROJECT SCORESHEET CHANGED MY LIFE

by Donald A. Yeager

Certain dates in history are etched in everyone's mind: July 4, 1776, December 7, 1941, October 12, 1492. For me, two more can be added to that list: September 20, 1983 and June 10, 1986.

Let me explain. I live in a town just outside of Rochester, N.Y. which is best described as suburban/rural. For years, I was forced to sit back and clench my teeth as the more densely populated city and suburbs were wired for Cable TV. They had everything: sports (especially baseball—almost everyday), movies, even reruns. I had nothing. But then it changed. On September 20, 1983, the cable system was finally turned on to my home, and the first thing I watched was a meaningless, late season day/night doubleheader between the Reds and the Braves. Heaven!

I had fully expected to be watching baseball every night from that point on. But as the 1984 and 1985 seasons wore on, and the thrill of cable wore off, I found my attention span for baseball waning. In spite of the fact that I loved the game, its history, its nuances, the stats, I just couldn't sit still for an entire game on TV. I was constantly changing channels—a few innings of this game, a few innings of another, and so on.

Which brings me to epic date number two: June 10, 1986. It was on this night that I scored my first ballgame for Project Scoresheet.

I first learned of Project Scoresheet in the 1986 *Baseball Abstract.* The whole concept sounded intriguing; it was unique, complete, and above all, it would provide even more numbers for Bill James, Craig Wright, Pete Palmer, and others to analyze and expound upon.

I wrote to John Dewan, the Project's director, and received my instruction packet in mid-May. I started to study. After reading everything over, my initial reaction was one of fear. Could anything be this hard? Would I have to back out of this thing before I had even started? Well, I was determined to give it a try. After numerous re-readings, I reluctantly decided I was ready.

11:00 PM EDT, JUNE 10, 1986
Atlanta Braves at San Francisco Giants

I chose this game because the rest of my family would be in bed: NO interruptions. Looking back, what I remember most about scoring that game was the constant referral back to the instruction sheets, my dependence on the replay, and my increased awareness of everything the announcers were saying. When it finally ended, I felt relief, and silly as it may sound, a sense of accomplishment.

I didn't realize it immediately, but I was hooked! I couldn't wait to do another game. A week went by before I scored my second game, but as I did more, that interval grew shorter, and like any learned skill, it did become easier. I still have to refer to the instructions occasionally, even after forty-six games. But I love it! I'm reborn. I feel like a complete baseball nut now!

Scoring for Project Scoresheet has had a profound affect on my ability to watch baseball. For one, it makes me pay attention. Who fielded the ball hit to the gap in right-center? Who are the umpires? What was the temperature at gametime? Not all of these things are mentioned in a regular and orderly manner by the announcers. You have to watch and listen for them. When I tried to score a game from the radio, I found it to be nearly impossible. As rich a tradition as this is, too many vital pieces of information are left out in these broadcasts. At least on TV, I can see what happens, and if I miss something, hope for the replay.

Primarily, however, scoring for the Project makes me want to watch baseball because I enjoy using the scoring system, a system which I find absolutely ingenious. No more squiggly lines drawn on a tiny diamond with no room for numbers. Everything is taken into account. As I see it, the system is nearly perfect. To confirm my opinion, I need only look back at a completed scoresheet. The letters and numbers are immediately transformed into visual images of shortstops fielding pop fouls down the thirdbase line (6/FL) or Fenway Park "Green Monster" singles (S7/F7D).

All of which leaves me to ponder the future. What if I bought one of those new TV sets that can monitor three or four channels simultaneously, one in each corner of the screen? And what if two or three more superstations sprang up on Cable and started televising an entire team's schedule? To these possibilities, I can only exclaim, "Holy Cow!"

Editor's note—While certainly a very personal account, Mr. Yeager's story emphasizes the increased enjoyment and awareness of baseball one enjoys when scoring the game—using any scoring system. Patterns of play and strategy emerge, and a deeper understanding of the game develops.

I can certainly commiserate with him on his attempt to score games from radio broadcasts. While away from home last season, I was scoring a Chicago game off my local radio station. During the middle-innings, the radio and television announcers trade places, and the famous baseball personality with the same initials as "Holy Cow" took over. With a runner on first, he gave the following account of the next batter's fate:

"There's a groundball . . . out at second, out at first!"

I could only be sure that it was a groundball doubleplay. Fortunately, the play was described more fully the hitter's next time up.

Don't let this shake you. Others around the country assure me that some radio broadcasts are typically quite good. Most of the time, the Cubs' are, and Don Zminda scores nearly all of the White Sox games from taped radio broadcasts with excellent results.

I guess my point is that if a game is broadcast—in any fashion—it can be enjoyed more by scoring it. Give it a try!
—Mark Podrazik

WINS, LOSSES AND RUNS SCORED

By Carmen J. Corica

We can learn much by looking at the win-loss records of baseball teams. Daily and weekly publications break these records down into home-road, grass-turf, day-night and so on. But the most indicative win-loss breakdown is in the margin of victory: that is, a team's record in games won by one run, two runs and so on.

We can tell much about the quality of a team by its record in games won by three or more runs. Teams with winning percentages over .500 in games decided by three or more runs are the better teams. A winning record in close games—one-run games—can be a result of luck. In a close game, any kind of break can win it or lose it. A bad bounce, an umpire's call or the weather conditions can have a big effect on who wins a 3–2 ballgame. In games won by three runs or more, a team must do many things to win, and a bad bounce is unlikely to change the outcome.

In football, the NFL champion Chicago Bears won games by scores of 44–7 and 20–0. Their ability to blow teams out made them one of the best in the league. The same can be said about the 1986 World Series champion New York Mets, who won games 8–1 and 11–0. The statistics will prove this out.

Starting at the bottom, the two worst records in the National League belonged to the Chicago Cubs and Pittsburgh Pirates. The Cubs lost 90 games and the Pirates lost 98. The Pirates' record, whether it is broken down into one-run games or three-run games, home or away, turf or grass, Tuesdays or Thursdays, or any other way you choose, comes out rather dismally. The Pirates make a fine argument for being the worst National League team of 1986. The Cubs, division winners just two short years ago, had a worse record than every other National League team except the Pirates. But the Cubs, in games decided by one run, played .509 ball.

The other National League teams that were over .500 in one-run games were Atlanta, San Diego, Montreal, Philadelphia, Houston and New York. This group can be divided in two: New York, Houston and Philadelphia had overall records above .500 for the season; San Diego, Atlanta and Chicago finished below .500 for the season.

In games decided by four or more runs, the Phillies had a winning percentage of .537, the Astros .608 and the Mets .679. The Braves went .373, the Cubs .392 and the Padres .458.

It is clear that not just the best teams have good records in one-run games. But if a team is good, it will dominate the games in which there is an easy winner. The National League teams that played better than .500 in games decided by three or more runs had an overall winning percentage of .576. The teams that played below .500 in games won by three or more runs had an overall winning percentage of .445. The good teams win games decided by three or more runs; anybody can win the close ones.

The American League teams score more runs. While just more than 46 percent of the National League games

were decided by three or more runs, almost 54 percent of the American League games were decided by three or more. With more scoring being done in the American League, there were more games decided by bigger margins, but the pattern of wins and losses was the same.

Just as in the senior circuit, the American League had six teams that did better than .500 in games decided by one run: Boston at .706, California at .636, Baltimore at .541, Milwaukee at .531, Cleveland at .526 and Texas at .519. Once again, the division champions, Boston and California, were among these teams, but so were Milwaukee and Baltimore. The Orioles finished the season 16 games under .500. In games decided by three runs or more, the Orioles played .424 ball and the Brewers played .427 ball. The Indians, Rangers, Red Sox and Angels combined for a .532 record in games decided by three or more runs. There were no American League teams that finished above .500 in games decided by three or more runs and had a seasonal record below .500.

The good teams do more than beat the bad teams; they beat them up. The Red Sox beat the Mariners by scores of 12–2, 11–5, 9–4 and 7–3. The Red Sox not only won those games by more than a field goal, they made it very difficult to tie the game with one or two swings of the bat. That is the mark of a good team.

At the end of May, the Texas Rangers were leading the American League West by a game over Kansas City and by 1 1/2 games over California. By mid-June, the Rangers' lead over the Royals had increased to four games and over the Angels to two games. On June 22, the Angels went into Arlington, Tex., for a three-game series with the Rangers and swept to take over first place by a game.

Listening to the California announcers, we were led to believe that the Texas Rangers would now begin to fold and take their rightful place with the also-rans at the bottom of the division. The talent on the team was overlooked. The Rangers were so bad in 1985, they couldn't be taken seriously in 1986. In June, that was all taken for granted, but in September, the praises were heard for manager Bobby Valentine and the wonderful job all the young talent was doing in Texas. The praise was as late as it was justified. The truth is we should have known during the June series that the Texas Rangers were for real.

The Rangers were .500 in one-run games at the end of June and .550 in games decided by three or more runs. This told us that we were watching a team that had the ability to win in a big way. By June 22, the Rangers had played 76 games, so we're not talking about a two-week span in which any club can get hot; we're talking about almost half a schedule. As a rule, teams don't change drastically from one half of the season to the other. The Rangers should have been taken much more seriously in June.

In the National League, by the end of May, the closest challenger to the Mets was Montreal. The Expos were six games back. By July 1, the lead was extended to 9 1/2 games and the race for first place was almost over. The battle in the East from then on was for second.

By looking at team victories in games decided by three or more runs, we would have had a clue as to which team would finish second. At the All-Star break, the Expos had a 4 1/2-game lead on Philadelphia but had won 17 games by three or more runs. At the same time, the Phillies had won 19 by the same margin. No other team besides the Mets had more wins in three-run games than the Phillies. By the season's end, the Phillies were the second best team in the East.

Fans always are comparing teams by batting average, the ability to hit home runs and pitching staffs. Those things help to win pennants, but the only statistic that really serves to capture division titles and pennants are wins—although the 1981 Cincinnati Reds might argue otherwise. A team's batting average, home runs, stolen bases and so on will give some indication of a team's quality. In order to really see how good a team is, we should look at its ability to smash, blast, ravage, wreck, overwhelm and otherwise put a serious damper on the opposing team's day.

Team records by margin of victory: American League

In games decided by:	1 run	2 runs	3 runs	4 runs	5+ runs	1–2 runs	3+runs
Boston	24–10 .706	22–13 .629	12–13 .480	7–11 .389	30–19 .612	46–23 .667	49–43 .533
New York	22–24 .478	22–10 .688	12–10 .545	11–5 .688	23–23 .500	44–34 .564	46–38 .548
Detroit	21–22 .488	11–22 .333	18–9 .667	8–6 .571	29–18 .617	32–42 .432	55–33 .625
Toronto	22–25 .468	15–22 .405	17–9 .654	9–3 .750	23–17 .575	37–47 .440	49–29 .628
Cleveland	20–18 .526	18–12 .600	13–11 .542	8–16 .333	25–21 .543	38–30 .559	46–48 .489
Milwaukee	26–23 .531	16–14 .533	11–11 .500	7–9 .438	17–27 .386	42–37 .532	35–47 .427
Baltimore	20–17 .541	14–19 .424	9–18 .333	8–10 .444	22–25 .468	34–36 .486	39–53 .424
California	28–16 .636	13–12 .520	13–21 .382	13–8 .619	25–13 .568	41–28 .594	51–42 .548
Texas	28–26 .519	13–13 .500	15–4 .789	10–6 .625	21–26 .447	41–39 .513	46–36 .561
Kansas City	24–25 .490	12–4 .462	10–12 .455	7–13 .350	23–22 .511	36–39 .480	40–47 .460
Oakland	22–29 .431	15–10 .600	12–15 .444	11–15 .423	16–17 .485	37–39 .487	39–47 .453
Chicago	23–29 .442	14–14 .500	11–16 .407	9–14 .391	15–17 .469	37–43 .463	35–47 .427
Minnesota	20–27 .426	8–10 .444	11–17 .393	13–7 .650	19–30 .388	28–37 .431	43–54 .443
Seattle	17–26 .395	12–22 .353	12–10 .545	11–9 .550	15–28 .349	29–48 .377	38–47 .447
Total games	317	205	176	132	303	522	611

Team records by margin of victory: National League

In games decided by:	1 run	2 runs	3 runs	4 runs	5+ runs	1–2 runs	3+runs
New York	29–20 .592	23–9 .719	20–8 .714	9–8 .529	27–9 .750	52–29 .642	56–25 .691
Philadelphia	34–26 .567	15–12 .556	8–12 .400	13–7 .650	16–18 .471	49–38 .563	37–37 .500
St. Louis	28–32 .467	17–16 .515	14–9 .609	5–6 .455	15–19 .441	45–48 .484	34–34 .500
Montreal	34–28 .548	15–16 .484	11–13 .458	5–6 .455	13–20 .394	49–44 .527	29–39 .426
Chicago	29–28 .509	11–18 .379	10–13 .435	5–11 .313	15–20 .429	40–46 .465	30–44 .405
Pittsburgh	16–37 .302	14–18 .438	8–14 .364	8–11 .421	18–18 .500	30–55 .355	34–43 .442
Houston	34–27 .557	16–10 .615	15–9 .625	14–7 .667	17–13 .567	50–37 .575	46–29 .613
Cincinnati	26–26 .500	21–14 .600	15–9 .625	10–8 .556	14–19 .424	47–40 .540	39–36 .520
San Francisco	30–30 .500	11–16 .407	9–14 .391	10–9 .526	23–10 .697	41–46 .471	42–33 .560
San Diego	32–30 .516	8–19 .296	12–13 .480	7–7 .500	15–19 .441	40–49 .449	34–49 .466
Los Angeles	28–38 .424	10–9 .526	8–14 .364	12–12 .500	15–16 .484	38–47 .447	35–42 .455
Atlanta	26–24 .520	14–18 .438	13–15 .464	7–13 .350	12–19 .387	40–42 .488	32–47 .405
Total games	346	175	143	105	200	521	448

Team records by runs scored: National League

Record when they scored:	0 runs	1 runs	2 runs	3 runs	4 runs	5 runs	6 runs	7 runs	8+ runs
New York	0–4 .000	1–11 .083	6–13 .316	7–10 .412	22–8 .733	19–3 .864	15–2 .882	11–1 .917	27–2 .931
Philadelphia	0–7 .000	3–11 .071	7–16 .304	7–9 .438	13–12 .520	17–11 .607	11–4 .733	8–4 .667	20–1 .952
St. Louis	0–13 .000	4–14 .222	8–20 .286	12–21 .364	13–7 .650	10–2 .833	7–2 .778	9–3 .750	16–0 1.000
Montreal	0–11 .000	3–23 .115	4–22 .154	6–15 .286	10–11 .476	8–5 .615	9–4 .692	9–2 .818	22–5 .815
Chicago	0–10 .000	2–16 .111	4–22 .154	6–15 .286	10–11 .476	8–5 .615	9–4 .692	9–2 .818	22–5 .815
Pittsburgh	0–10 .000	0–17 .000	3–24 .111	8–13 .381	17–18 .486	6–12 .333	8–0 1.000	5–1 .833	17–3 .850
Houston	0–6 .000	4–15 .211	6–18 .250	17–12 .586	18–6 .750	12–4 .750	16–3 .842	7–2 .778	16–0 1.000
Cincinnati	0–7 .000	0–18 .000	7–12 .368	7–14 .333	10–7 .588	14–6 .700	16–8 .667	15–4 .765	19–0 1.000
San Francisco	0–12 .000	3–16 .158	8–11 .421	11–15 .423	12–11 .522	5–7 .417	11–4 .923	12–1 .913	21–2 .913
San Diego	0–9 .000	1–15 .063	7–22 .241	8–16 .333	14–9 .609	13–8 .619	5–5 .500	10–3 .769	16–1 .941
Los Angeles	0–14 .000	4–15 .211	8–16 .333	7–14 .333	10–14 .417	8–7 .533	14–5 .737	8–2 .800	14–2 .875
Atlanta	0–10 .000	1–18 .053	4–21 .190	8–18 .308	20–9 .690	7–9 .438	7–2 .778	10–1 .909	15–1 .937
Total games Lg Avg W/L%:	113 .121	215 .121	284 .254	276 .391	295 .586	207 .638	171 .738	136 .809	240 .921

Team records by runs scored: American League

Record when they scored:	0 runs	1 runs	2 runs	3 runs	4 runs	5 runs	6 runs	7 runs	8+ runs
Boston	0–11 .000	0–16 .000	5–12 .294	12–8 .600	0–6 .600	10–10 .500	11–3 .786	14–0 1.000	34–0 1.000
New York	0–9 .000	0–10 .000	4–13 .235	12–18 .400	11–10 .524	14–4 .778	7–1 .875	8–4 .667	34–3 .919
Detroit	0–5 .000	1–15 .063	7–17 .292	5–8 .385	10–14 .417	13–5 .722	12–3 .800	10–6 .625	29–2 .935
Toronto	0–6 .000	1–16 .059	3–10 .231	7–16 .304	7–9 .438	10–7 .588	19–5 .792	12–4 .750	27–3 .900
Cleveland	0–4 .000	0–14 .000	1–14 .067	8–23 .258	5–4 .556	12–7 .632	18–4 .818	10–3 .769	30–5 .857
Milwaukee	0–6 .000	3–21 .125	5–18 .217	8–15 .348	11–7 .611	18–7 .720	8–5 .615	8–3 .727	16–2 .889
Baltimore	0–13 .000	2–14 .125	4–14 .222	6–20 .231	11–13 .458	13–6 .684	6–4 .600	7–3 .700	24–2 .923
California	0–10 .000	0–8 .000	5–12 .294	10–15 .400	11–12 .478	14–7 .667	16–2 .889	9–3 .750	27–1 .964
Texas	0–4 .000	2–16 .111	7–20 .259	8–12 .400	10–11 .476	10–2 .833	13–4 .765	12–3 .750	25–3 .893
Kansas City	0–12 .000	4–17 .190	8–22 .267	3–10 .231	7–12 .368	12–8 .600	14–4 .778	9–1 .900	19–0 1.000
Oakland	0–6 .000	3–13 .188	5–15 .250	4–12 .250	13–16 .448	11–12 .478	13–6 .684	7–4 .636	20–2 .909
Chicago	0–13 .000	1–19 .050	3–18 .143	10–18 .357	14–6 .700	12–5 .706	8–5 .615	7–2 .778	17–4 .810
Minnesota	0–13 .000	1–19 .050	3–19 .136	4–12 .250	8–8 .500	10–9 .526	8–4 .667	13–4 .765	24–5 .828
Seattle	0–13 .000	2–14 .125	0–18 .000	7–10 .412	7–15 .318	11–16 .407	8–7 .533	8–1 .889	24–1 .960
Total games Lg Avg W/L%	123 .000	232 .086	282 .213	301 .346	277 .484	275 .618	218 .739	175 .766	383 .914

ALL OR NOTHING—THE 1986 AMERICAN LEAGUE

by Alan Boodman

As of mid June, this past season was well on its way to being remembered as the year of the homer. Tony Kubek (and others) were certain that there was something funny with the baseballs, and they had the stats to prove it. After all, they said, how else do you explain Kirby Puckett? Eight players in the American League, led by Wally Joyner, were on a pace to hit 40 or more homers, 4 more were heading for 35–40, and how do you explain that? And if you could, then how about people like Rance Mulliniks, Rick Dempsey, Darnell Coles and Ken Griffey? These guys aren't your typical power hitters, yet all of them—and many others—were heading for a 20 HR season. According to the July 7 issue of *The Sporting News,* 1986 was becoming the most prolific year for homeruns since expansion to 26 teams.

Of course, a month or so later, the rabbit was dead. Only one player (Jesse Barfield) managed 40 homers, and only four others reached the 35 mark. Not shabby figures to be sure, but not quite the onslaught of power that had been forseen earlier in the season. Yes, the rabbit may have died, but it left behind one of its cousins—strikeouts—in record numbers.

There were 13,058 K's in the AL in 1986—an increase of 10.9% over 1985. This represents the largest one-season percentage increase in strikeouts since the real pitchers returned from WW II in 1946. The average number of strikeouts per team in the American League was 932.7 in 1986. This was not a record, for it was exceeded for 5 consecutive years in the '60's (1964–68). But it should be noted that pitchers had to hit for themselves during these years. In 1985, NL pitchers struck out about 35% of the time. In that same year, AL designated hitters K'd at about half that rate. Using these facts, we can estimate that the average AL team in 1986 would have struck out about 1025 times had pitchers been forced to see how the other half lived. This would have been a record.

Speaking of records, the Seattle Mariners came within 55 of establishing an all-time record for batter's strikeouts in a season. They finished with 1148, good for third place, behind the 1970 Padres (1164), and the 1968 Mets (1203). Both of these clubs received sizable contributions (strikeout-wise) from their pitching staffs. The Padres' hurlers K'd 161 times in 370 AB (43.5%); Mets' pitchers added 236 in 437 AB (56.0%). The Mariners, of course, did not benefit from this kind of assistance in their pursuit of this unenviable record. Had the DH not been employed, the Mariners would have easily topped the 1200 mark, and likely outdistanced the '68 Mets.

So, who is to blame for this plethora of strikeouts in the American League? It doesn't seem likely that the umpires have expanded the strike zone. It has been observed in recent years that the AL strike zone has moved lower, and now resembles its NL counterpart. This is due, it would seem, to the discarding of the external chest protectors from the home plate umpires. This now gives them a better look at lower pitches, and has caused the AL to cease being a high-pitch league. This, however, did not take place in one season, rather it has been a gradual change which finally was completed this year. It is difficult then to see how this change alone could cause such a dramatic increase in strikeouts in such a short period of time.

No, the primary reason for this explosion would seem to be the recent introduction of a fairly large group of young power hitters into the AL, and in particular, the 1986 rookie crop. There were three players in the AL in 1986 who made a serious run at Bobby Bonds' record of 189 K's in a season—2 of these being rookies—and a total of 10 struck out more than 130 times. Altogether, 27 players reached the century mark in K's—nearly 2 per team, which established yet another dubious record. During a season, we expect to see a certain amount of people strike out 100–200 times, and perhaps a couple more up near 150. But until this season, only 29 players in history had managed to whiff 150 times in a season. This year, the AL had five, and two others barely missed.

The following chart includes all American League players who K'd 100 times in 1986, and shows the number of runs they created (RC) as figured by the stolen-base method, and the number of runs they created per 26 outs (RC/G).

PLAYER	RC	RC/G	PLAYER	RC	RC/G
Incaviglia	79.5	5.08	Canseco	85.7	4.81
Deer	77.0	5.56	Presley	84.0	4.78
Tartabull	84.2	5.75	Lr. Parrish	82.4	6.36
Balboni	66.6	4.38	McDowell	83.1	4.97
Barfield	117.0	7.13	Baylor	78.4	4.52
Jacoby	90.1	5.63	D. Henderson	58.3	5.26
P. Bradley	92.8	6.44	Kittle	45.2	4.14
Pettis	68.2	4.29	Gaetti	101.7	6.01
Kingman	60.7	3.54	Gagne	53.5	3.82
Snyder	61.0	5.18	Gibson	83.4	6.59
Moseby	81.5	4.70	Winfield	90.6	5.58
Pagliarulo	73.2	4.95	Da. Evans	79.6	5.35
Dw. Evans	93.6	6.16	Thomas	36.6	3.67
Jackson	64.5	5.25			

Notice how good most of these guys are? The AL averaged 4.61 runs/game in 1986, and 21 of these 27 players on this chart exceeded this figure. This is not really surprising, as 72% of all players striking out over 100 times (in the AL) in a season exceeded their league average in RC/G from 1982 to 1986. A logical reason for this is: Bad players don't get a chance to strike out 100 times. Unless you're really good at it (remember Dave Nicholson?), you need 400 or more at-bats to reach 100 K's. Players who cannot create a sufficient number of runs will not be able to keep a starting job long enough to reach 100 strikeouts, unless they compensate with a high level of defensive skill.

So, are these strikeouts necessarily bad? In the 1986 *Baseball Abstract,* Bill James (in the comment on Dave Kingman) determined that K's have only a slight negative run value in comparison with other types of outs; certainly no reason to panic if your favorite player happens to swing and miss a lot. Players who strike out a lot can generally atone for it by hammering a good deal of home runs. It is rare in this era to see players like Don Mattingly and Joe DiMaggio, who combine good power with the ability to make frequent contact.

Therefore, these recent trends in the AL—homers up, strikeouts way up, batting averages down some, triples way down—shouldn't give us cause for much alarm, yet there was a time some years ago when these same patterns emerged, and suffered because of it. I refer to the 1950's.

Baseball during this decade degenerated into a mass of homeruns and strikeouts. As this happened, other forms of offense (2B, 3B, SB) declined noticeably until the offenses of most teams were indistinguishable from each other. Attendance suffered, as the game ceased to be a contest of managerial strategies or diverse offensive philosophies, and baseball seemed to be at its height of boredom. Certainly nobody today is complaining about baseball being boring, and attendance is booming, but do these trends today perhaps presage a return to duller times? The chart which follows shows the changes in offensive statistics over two different eight year periods in American League history: 1951–58 and 1979–86.

	'51–'58	'79–'86
Strikeouts	up 31.4%	up 29.1%
Home Runs	up 26.0%	up 14.2%
Doubles	down 11.6%	down 0.3%
Triples	down 17.0%	down 14.6%
Stolen Bases	down 14.7%	down 1.7%
Batting Avg.	down 3.1%	down 3.0%
	(8 points)	(8 points)

I have stated that I believe that the reason for the strikeout problem is the sudden influx of young power hitters who have yet to learn patience and/or the major league strike zone. But what about these other trends? Stolen bases have dropped by about 10/team since the mid 1970's. As homers continue to rise (if they do), SB should continue to fall; why risk losing a baserunner if homeruns are so prevalent? It's just as easy to score from first on a homer as from 2nd (or 3rd). In this repect, HR & SB could be said to have an inverse relationship. Batting average should decline along with stolen bases. As batters swing for the fences, they tend to make less contact overall, and other types of hits decline.

The decline in triples is a bit more mysterious. 3/4 of the decline took place in 1986. The biggest dropoffs were by Toronto (53 3B in 1985, 35 in 1986), Detroit (45–30), Boston (31–21), Baltimore (22–13), and New York (31–23). These five account for a decline of 60 triples from '85 to '86 —the AL fell off exactly 60 triples from '85 to '86—so this may not be a league-wide trend.

It's impossible to predict with any accuracy what 1987 will hold in store, but we're now at the point where records will be broken each year homeruns or strikeouts go higher. With speedsters like Rickey Henderson in the league, it's hard to see how stolen bases could keep declining, but the fact is that stolen bases were at higher levels before Rickey came into the league. And I know this sounds strange, but if it weren't for the Cleveland Indians, batting averages would have been even lower. If the Indians had maintained their .265 1985 batting average, instead of hitting .284(!) as they did, the 1986 AL batting average might not have reached .260. I know they're a young improving team, but if the Indians have to save the league, the league's in trouble. I think that if these trends continue, we could be entering an era very similar to the 1950's, and, just as it was then, baseball may be the worse off for it.

THE PYTHAGOREAN THEORY REVISITED

By Tom Henry

I

No sport makes better use of its off-season to remain a part of the sporting public's consciousness than does baseball. As soon as the World Series is gaveled to a close by the hooves of the mounted police, the barroom debates begin anew, the past season is dissected, would-be general managers begin addressing weaknesses, and the fans start singing the timeless refrain, "Wait 'til next year."

Cubs fans spent the better part of the 1985–86 off-season predicting a return to the glorious heights of 1984 —if only the pitching staff remained healthy. While not exactly injury-free, the Cubs got more innings from Rick Sutcliffe and Dennis Eckersly in 1986 than in 1984 (remember, they were acquired in mid-season 1984) and they got more innings out of Scott Sanderson as well. Of the Big Four in '84, only Steve Trout pitched less last season. Nevertheless, the staff allowed 52 more runs in 1986 than in 1985, and a whopping 123 more than in 1984, all of which can be attributed to what some folks thought might be the best starting rotation in the National League. Here are their comparative statistics.

	IP	H	ER	BB	SO	W-L	ERA
1984 Big Four	641.1	620	220	158	393	47–21	3.09
1985 Not-So-Big Four	708.1	721	357	254	452	25–43	4.54

The Cubs also scored 82 fewer runs than in 1984—and friends, if your offense is down 82 runs and your defense is up 123, you've got problems.

This winter, Yankee fans are declaring that the Steinbrenners are sure to win it all in 1987—if only they can find another starting pitcher under the age of 35. After all, Guidry is sure to bounce back (they say), and Rhoden won 15 games for the Pirates, for Chrissakes! Blue Jays fans need only wish for a return to form by Dave Stieb to re-establish their supremacy in the Al East. Royals fans are convinced that the young pitchers who were so good in 1985 can't be as bad as they were in '86, Cardinals fans feel the same way about their offense, and Dodgers fans look forward to seeing Pedro Guerrero play again. The Reds look good and have a bunch of kids coming up with Pete to teach them, the Phillies just need another starting pitcher and maybe a catcher, and the Mets just may not lose a game all season!

The development of sabermetric theories has given many fans still more opportunities to reflect on what happened in the past year and to try to get a glimpse of the future. One of the new tools keeping the winter chatter lively is the Pythogorean Theory, which hypothesizes that a team's won-lost record is directly related to the number of runs the team scores and the number of runs it gives up. While that might not seem particularly novel, it is a useful tool to evaluate which teams performed as might be expected and which teams were either overachievers or underachievers by notable margins.

The Pythagorean theory is expressed in a simple mathematical formula:

$$\frac{R^2}{(R^2 + OR^2)}$$

The formula gives you a Won-Lost percentage which can easily be translated into a team's projected record. For example, the Minnesota Twins scored 741 runs last season and allowed 839. Using the formula, you come up with a .438 Won-Lost percentage. When applied to a 162 game season, this works out to a 71–91 record, exactly what the Twins posted last season.

In fact, in 1986, 24 of the 26 major-league teams came within four games of their projected record using the formula (see chart). Only San Fransisco and Pittsburgh missed by a big margin, and both of them were on the down side. Pittsburgh was 13 games worse in the final standings then could have been expected; the Giants, who shocked the baseball world with an 83-79 finish, actually missed by eight games what might have been.

If the theory has any validity, those records could mean that both teams (barring major off-season overhauls, Guerrero-type injuries, etc.) might be expected to perform considerably better in the upcoming year than they did last year.

II

Precedents do exist for the above, most recently for the Boston Red Sox. Roger Clemens' team, a mediocre 81–81 in 1985 and generally relegated to the bottom half of the AL East in the 1986 pre-season prognostication, really was not a bad ball club. Using the formula, the Sox projected record in 1985 was a rather nifty 90–72. They just didn't play up to that mark. The same formula indicates that the Red Sox should have been 91–70 last year, virtually the same record. They exceeded that projection by four games to finish 95–66.

This lends some credence to the idea that the difference between the two teams was largely intangible: Baylor's leadership for the entire season, Seaver's steadying hand for a half-season (particularly in July and August when the pitching staff was shorthanded) and so on. It is true that Jim Rice and Marty Barrett had better seasons, but it is also true that Rich Gedman, Bill Buckner and Tony Armas all fell short of their 1985 offensive production. In fact, the Bosox scored six fewer runs last year than in 1985. And while Clemens had a career year, the pitching staff as a whole allowed just 24 fewer runs during 1986 than 1985, certainly not enough to account for a 15 game improvement in the win column.

Cleveland also looked like a team with a chance to improve last season. The Tribe finished 60–102 in '85, eight games short of their projected record. While the difference was not enough to rank the team as a contender for anything higher than fifth place, there were some indications that the team had a chance to move up, especially with the powerful, young offense that seemed to be a good candidate for improvement. The rest is history. The Indians had a modest, 20-run improvement from the pitching staff, but improved its offensive production by 102 runs over 1985, finishing over .500 for the first time since 1981.

A look at the 1983 Cubs is instructive as well. The team finished 71–91, but projected to be eight games better at 79–83. Still not the stuff of pennants, but with the additions of Bobby Dernier, Gary Matthews and Scott Sanderson during the off-season (at a cost of Bill Campbell, Craig Lefferts and Carmelo Martinez), the mid-season acquisitions of Sutcliffe and Eckersley, and "one-more-time" years from Ron Cey and Larry Bowa, the Cubs climbed to the top.

III

If every team improved the following year the way those mentioned did, Giant fans might be icing the champagne already. Alas, it isn't so. Panic, dumb moves by management, injuries, and other such twists of fate still work to the detriment of theory. Take the Pirates. They've had three underachieving years in a row—by significant margins. There has got to be a reason for that. They are not a good team, but they should not have been as bad as they've ended up, either.

Still, the fact remains that Pittsburgh is far and away the one team in the major leagues to consistently diverge from its projected won-lost records. In fact, Pittsburgh has been 32 games total off the mark over the past three seasons. The Bucs won 13 fewer than they should have in 1984, six fewer in 1985, and 13 fewer last year. The second place team in the divergence standings is the New York Mets, who have missed the mark by 16 games total over the past three years. Nearly all of that came in 1984, a season with which we will deal later. Even more importantly, the Mets have won 16 more games than could have been expected in that time, while the Bucs are in the minus column for their 32.

The Pirates recent history is one filled with costly mistakes, some of commission and others of omission. The Pirates finished 84–78 in both 1982 and 1983, and led the National League East by 2 1/2 games as recently as August 3, 1983. They were not winning any pennants, but they were not finishing last either.

The offense in 1983 had tailed off badly, dropping 64 runs from 1982, primarily because Dave Parker had reached his nadir in Pittsburgh while Jason Thompson had started down the slow road to the end of the line. Good years from Lary McWilliams, John Candelaria, Rick Rhoden, Kent Tekulve and rookies Jose DeLeon, Lee Tunnell, and Cecilio Guante meant that the pitching staff was able to offset the decline in offense, and the Bucs held their own.

Still, in 1984, the Pirates pitching was superb. They lead the National League with a 3.11 ERA, allowing only 567 runs. The team scored 615 runs and when those numbers are plugged into the Pythagorean formula, they work out to an 88–74 record. This would have been good enough for a third place in the N.L. East. Instead, they went 75–87 and finished last.

The 1985 season was a nightmare. Front office and clubhouse chaos were the norm. The team finished 57–104 (six games off what the Pythagorean Theory indicates they could have finished). In either case, they were awful.

Kemp, Hendrick and Lezcano combined for a batting average of .234, with 7 homers and only 55 RBIs. Keeping the Pirates afloat was the unlikely combination of veteran Bill Almon, who hit .270 and played just about everywhere, and the bionically-reconstructed righthander Rick Reuschel, who went 14–8 with a 2.27 ERA while the rest of the staff fizzled.

Time to back up the truck. Hendrick, Candelaria and Al Holland went to the Angels. Bill Madlock, hitting in the .250 range for the second straight season, went to the Dodgers. First baseman Sid Bream, outfielders Mike Brown and R.J. Reynolds, and pitchers Bob Kipper and Pat Clements came in return, and all played extensively in 1986. Barry Bonds was given on-the-job training. All were young and not a part of the team's earlier demise, yet the 1986 season was still one of underachievement. A club that could have gone 77–85 finished 64–98, but this time they did it with a bunch of kids who can be expected to improve, rather than with codgers and gripers like Kemp, Madlock, Thompson, Hendrick and Candelaria.

Clements has since been packaged with Rick Rhoden to the funny farm at Yankee Stadium, but the Pirates picked up young pitchers Doug Drabek and Brian Fisher in return. The jury is still out on Drabek, but Fisher has proven (in 1985) that he can be successful. He has also proven (in 1986) that he can be unsuccessful, but you have to like his long range chances a whole lot better than those of Rhoden, who is 34.

Finally, things are beginning to make some sense again in Pittsburgh. Unless something bizarre happens between the time this is written (December) and opening day, the Pirates could be a "surprisingly" improved team in 1987.

IV

Even assuming this, the Pirates are probably not an immediate threat to the contenders in the National League East. However, amazing though it may seem, the Giants might not be a one-year phenomenon in the West.

Anyone who spent time in Candlestick Park in 1985 knew that the Giants' biggest problem was an anemic offense. The club had several players who went through unspeakable seasons at the plate, and San Francisco came in dead last in the league, and in all of baseball, scoring only 556 runs. The miserable attack masked a nearly one-run-per-game improvement from the Giants pitching staff, and the team grabbed onto last place early in the campaign and never let go. The difference in 1986 was that the pitching continued to improve while the offense returned to its 1984 level, scoring 698 runs, or 142 more than the year before. That kind of offense, when combined with the 618 runs the Giants allowed (4th best in the league) worked out to a projected won-lost record of 91–71.

Houston, on the other hand, projected out to a 92–70 mark, only one game better than San Francisco; the Reds projected only to 83–79. The reason the Giants finished third was that their record was eight games worse than it projected to be. Meanwhile, the Reds finished three games better than projected, and the Astros four games better. So, the Giants, who might have finished second, just one game out, finished third instead, 13 games behind the Astros. However, this closer look would seem to say that, unless the Giants do something stupid or the offense returns to hibernation or Mike Krukow rediscovers that he has been a .500 pitcher all of his life, the Giants will have a chance to move up without doing much of anything before opening day.

One key to that happening will be the bullpen.

V

As there are teams every year that differ from performance norms on the low side, so there are also those that finish with records far superior to what could have been expected.

The most dramatic of those teams was the 1984 edition of the New York Mets when folks like Dwight Gooden, Ron Darling, Sid Fernandez and Doug Sisk were rookies. The Mets that year could have been a sub-.500 team instead of giving the Cubs a run for the Eastern Division championship. The Mets actually were outscored during the season, but finished 90–72. This was a truly remarkable turnaround from the team's last-place finish in 1983, and fully 12 games better than they had any right to expect.

The arrivals of Gooden, Darling and Fernandez, along with the emergence of Walt Terrell, gave the Mets a young and talented starting rotation, but one that also was prone to inconsistency. Even Gooden was sometimes hittable early in the season. When the Mets won, they won close games. When they lost, they got killed, especially early in the season. Some examples follow.

Bill Deane of Pleasant Valley, New York reported in the 1985 edition of *The Bill James Baseball Abstract* that the Mets put together an 18–12 record from April 2 through May 12, 1984, even though they were outscored 147–107. They were outscored in their 12 losses 110–31, but they gave up just 32 runs in their 18 wins. During that period, relievers Jesse Orosco and Doug Sisk combined for three victories, nine saves and a 1.36 ERA.

In July, they ran off a 21–4 streak, including a 13–1 mark in one-run games. They scored 133 runs while giving up 91, projecting a 17–8 record. Orosco picked up three wins and eight saves in 12 appearances during that stretch.

During those two periods of time, the Mets were 39–16 when, by Pythagorean rights, they should have been closer to 28–27, or eleven games worse. As good as the starting pitching was, the relief duo of Orosco and Sisk was the difference. The Mets played 32 games decided by two runs or less during these two streaks, and they had a incredible 30–2 record. That just doesn't happen. Credit the bullpen.

For the year, Orosco was 10–6 with 31 saves and a 2.59 ERA. Sisk was 1–3 with 15 saves and an ERA of 2.09 before shoulder problems sidelined him; lefty Tom Gorman chipped in with a 6–0 record and a 2.97 ERA in middle relief.

The experience of the Mets bullpen in 1984 is instructive because other teams that substantially outperformed their projections in recent years also had monster bullpens. That is especially true of teams that had a legitimate role in pennant races.

Surprisingly, one of those teams is the more recent underperforming Giants. Back in 1982, the Giants ran up a record of 87–75, eight games better than their projected

79–83 mark. Again, the bullpen was the difference. Greg Minton had an outstanding season, compiling a 10–4 record, 30 saves and a 1.83 ERA. Gary Lavelle was 10–7 with eight saves and a 2.67 ERA. Al Holland, Jim Barr and Fred Breining enjoyed productive years in middle and long relief, helping to overcome the inconsistency displayed by one of the youngest starting rotations in the major leagues that year.

Strong bullpens also helped Kansas City in 1983 and 1984, San Diego in 1984, and Cincinnati and California an 1985 to log substantially better records than otherwise might have been expected.

Of course, Dan Quisenberry was the biggest reason for the Kansas City experience. Quiz had a total of 89 saves in 1983–84 (45 and 44 respectively), but he had a lot of help. Mike Armstrong (10–7, 3.86 ERA) was a solid set-up man in 1983, while Mark Huismann and Joe Beckwith were reliable in long and middle relief in 1984, helping the young starting staff that year.

The Padres ended up in the World Series in 1984 largely because of a typical Goose Gossage performance, but he also had help. Craig Lefferts, who had been obtained from the Cubs, took some of the pressure off the Goose and had the best year of his career to date. The bullpen depth is important here because San Diego actually had the second best Pythagorean record in the NL West in 1984. Houston had the best, projecting to 89–73, while the Padres projected only 87–75. Nevertheless, with a strong pen, the Padres played five games over their projection while the Astros, with an inconsistent bullpen (only 29 team saves despite good ERAs), missed their projection by a full nine games.

It happened again in 1985. The Reds were not nearly as good on paper as they were on the field that year. Cincinnati finished second to Los Angeles with an 89–72 record, seven games above projections. A big year in relief from Ted Power (8–6, 2.70, 27 saves), and a smashing rookie debut from lefty John Franco (12–3, 2.18, 12 saves) meant that the Reds had a bullpen unlike any since the days of the Big Red Machine in the mid-70's. Tom Hume helped as well, picking up three saves and a 3.26 ERA after having posted a 5.64 ERA the year before.

California long had been noted for having a firestarter corps in the bullpen prior to 1985. No lead was considered safe until that season. Finally, the Angels hit paydirt not once, not twice, but three times.

The big find, of course, was Donnie Moore, obtained via the free agency compensation draft from Atlanta. Moore, a journeyman who had enjoyed a decent 1984 season with the Braves, put together his career best—31 saves and 1.92 ERA. The second find was rookie Stu Cliburn, who went 9–3 with a 2.09 ERA and added six saves. Lefty Pat Clements, who went to Pittsburgh late in the season, was 5–0 with a 3.34 ERA before the deal.

When all was said and done, the Angels were 90–72, one game behind division-winning Kansas City, and six games better in the standings than projected.

VI

It would appear that a strong case could be made that a team that substantially underperforms one year can be expected to make an improvement the following season, particularly if it can put together a decent bullpen. The examples previously discussed provide such evidence, but, of course, there are no absolutes. While the overachievers listed above all had first-class bullpens, a couple of other recent teams that did much better than anticipated (the Phillies and the A's in 1982) didn't have much. Moreover, while most of the teams who underachieved one year made substantial improvements the following year, the above-mentioned 1984 Astros improved only slightly, largely due to a complete collapse of the bullpen.

For 1987, the Pirates, who are doing their best to make a myth of the Pythagorean theory, have taken the first step in that direction by giving Brian Fisher a chance. San Fran-sisco experimented with Scott Garrelts in the starting rotation last season, after he had an eye-popping 1985 rookie year exclusively in relief.

They found out that he is a better relief pitcher than starter, and will probably use him in short relief in 1987. If he can repeat what he did in 1985, and can get some help from Jeff Robinson, Greg Minton, Mark Davis or someone else, the Giants are likely to be a major factor all season. That is particularly true if Jeffrey Leonard can rebound and play a full season, and if Chris Brown's physical problems can be overcome.

We will know in October, when we can again examine the prescience of Pythagoras.

PYTHAGOREAN THEORY WORKSHEET

NL West TEAM	R	OR	1984 PROJ.	ACTUAL	DIFF	R	OR	1985 PROJ.	ACTUAL	DIFF	R	OR	1986 PROJ.	ACTUAL	DIFF
Atlanta	632	655	78–84	80–82	+2	632	781	64–98	66–96	+2	615	719	68–93	72–89	+4
Cincinnati	627	747	67–95	70–92	+3	677	666	82–79	89–72	+7	732	717	83–79	86–76	+3
Houston	693	630	89–73	80–82	−9	706	691	83–79	83–79	0	654	569	92–70	96–66	+4
Los Angeles	580	600	78–84	79–83	+1	682	579	94–68	95–67	+1	638	679	76–86	73–89	−3
San Diego	686	634	87–75	92–70	+5	650	622	85–77	83–79	−2	656	723	73–89	74–88	+1
San Francisco	682	807	67–95	66–96	−1	556	674	66–96	62–100	−4	698	618	91–71	83–79	−8

NL East TEAM	R	OR	1984 PROJ.	ACTUAL	DIFF	R	OR	1985 PROJ.	ACTUAL	DIFF	R	OR	1986 PROJ.	ACTUAL	DIFF
Chicago	762	658	92–69	96–65	+4	686	729	76–85	77–84	+1	680	781	69–91	70–90	+1
Montreal	593	585	82–79	78–83	−4	633	636	80–81	84–77	+4	637	688	74–87	78–83	+4
New York	652	676	78–84	90–72	+12	695	568	97–65	98–64	+1	783	578	105–57	108–54	+3
Philadelphia	720	690	84–78	81–81	−3	667	673	80–82	75–87	−5	739	713	83–78	86–75	+3
Pittsburgh	615	567	88–74	75–87	−13	568	708	63–98	57–104	−6	663	700	77–85	64–98	−13
St.Louis	652	645	82–80	84–78	+2	747	572	102–60	101–61	−1	601	611	79–82	79–82	0

AL West TEAM	R	OR	1984 PROJ.	ACTUAL	DIFF	R	OR	1985 PROJ.	ACTUAL	DIFF	R	OR	1986 PROJ.	ACTUAL	DIFF
California	696	697	81–81	81–81	0	732	703	84–78	90–72	+6	786	684	92–70	92–70	0
Chicago	679	736	74–88	74–88	0	736	720	83–79	85–77	+2	644	699	74–88	72–90	−2
Kansas City	673	686	79–83	84–78	+5	687	639	87–75	91–71	+4	654	673	79–83	76–86	−3
Minnesota	673	675	81–81	81–81	0	705	782	73–89	77–85	+4	741	760	78–84	76–86	−2
Oakland	738	796	75–87	77–85	+2	757	787	78–84	77–85	−1	731	760	78–84	76–86	−2
Seattle	682	774	71–91	74–88	+3	719	818	71–91	74–88	+3	718	835	69–93	67–95	−2
Texas	656	714	74–87	69–95	−5	617	685	61–100	62–99	+1	771	743	84–78	87–75	+3

AL East TEAM	R	OR	1984 PROJ.	ACTUAL	DIFF	R	OR	1985 PROJ.	ACTUAL	DIFF	R	OR	1986 PROJ.	ACTUAL	DIFF
Baltimore	681	667	83–79	85–77	+2	818	764	86–75	83–78	−3	708	760	75–87	73–89	−2
Boston	810	764	86–76	86–76	0	800	720	90–72	81–81	−9	794	696	91–70	95–66	+4
Cleveland	761	766	80–82	75–87	−5	729	688	85–76	84–77	−1	798	714	90–72	87–75	−3
Detroit	829	643	101–61	104–58	+3	729	688	85–76	84–77	−1	798	714	90–72	87–75	−3
Milwaukee	641	734	70–91	67–94	−3	690	802	68–96	71–90	+3	667	734	73–88	77–84	+4
New York	758	679	90–72	87–75	−3	839	680	99–62	97–64	−2	797	738	87–75	90–72	+3
Toronto	750	696	87–75	89–73	+2	759	588	101–60	99–62	−2	809	733	89–73	86–76	−3

THE ANALYSIS OF RUN POTENTIAL

by David H. Robinson

It has been recognized for some time that one of the most important pieces of information missing from baseball statistics is a measure relating to what kinds of situations a batter encounters when appearing at the plate, and with what frequencies. For instance, there are 24 possible situations that may occur with regard to the current number of outs and current runners on base. These situations are shown below in Table 1.

Number of Outs	Bases Occupied	Number of Outs	Bases Occupied	Number of Outs	Bases Occupied
0	None	1	None	2	None
0	1st	1	1st	2	1st
0	2nd	1	2nd	2	2nd
0	1st,2nd	1	1st,2nd	2	1st,2nd
0	3rd	1	3rd	2	3rd
0	1st,3rd	1	1st,3rd	2	1st,3rd
0	2nd,3rd	1	2nd,3rd	2	2nd,3rd
0	All	1	All	2	All

Table 1

The first thing needed in analyzing these 24 situations is an idea of how many runs can be expected to score in each case. This idea has been expressed by various authors at different times in the past, including George Lindsey, Pete Palmer, and Charles Pavitt, with each contributing some ideas as to how to proceed. I would like to present some of my own results from some 1985 Project Scoresheet data, in illustrating how an analysis of this type might best make use of the data.

We need to estimate the expected (or average) number of runs to be scored in each of the 24 cases. I decided to work with only one team, the Minnesota Twins, rather than an entire league. There were two reasons for this decision. First of all, the expected number of runs, or "run potential" as I will call it, varies significantly from one team to the next in each situation, so that a separate analysis may be considered appropriate for each team. Secondly, I did not purchase the entire set of 1985 Project Scoresheet data disks, but rather only the disks containing the home games and road games of the Minnesota Twins. So the analysis which follows is restricted to the data for the Twins batters and their opponents in 1985.

I began by tabulating (using a BASIC program written for an IBM PC or compatible) the distribution of runs scored for each of the 24 cases given in Table 1. For a given situation, I counted how many runs scored from that point until the end of the inning, and tabulated those numbers for all 1985 Twins home games and all 1985 Twins road games. I tabulated the home games and road games for the Twins batters, and the home games and road games for the batters of Twins opponents. I separated the home and road games in order to isolate a possible "park effect" of playing in the Metrodome in Minneapolis. The results for Twins batters playing at home are presented below in Table 2, to illustrate the type of tabulation that was done.

Table 2 is a contingency table, presenting the frequency of ocurrence of each combination of outs and bases occupied with the resulting number of runs scored before the end of the inning. Thus the number 502 in the upper left hand corner of the table means that there were 502 times that a batter came to the plate with no outs and nobody on base, and that no runs scored from that point until the end of the inning. It should be noted that in order to keep a degree of independence between the observations in the same row of the table, no situation was tabulated if the same combination of outs and runners on base had already occurred earlier in the same inning.

Tabulation of Runs-Scored Frequencies
1985 Minnesota Twins Home Games

Number of Outs	Bases Occupied	Runs Scored Before the End of the Inning								
		0	1	2	3	4	5	6	7	8
0	None	502	117	58	25	12	6	1	1	1
0	1st	113	36	33	10	5	2	1	0	1
0	2nd	22	23	5	7	5	0	0	0	0
0	1st,2nd	19	8	5	10	2	1	1	0	1
0	3rd	2	7	1	0	1	1	0	0	0
0	1st,3rd	4	8	4	4	3	0	0	0	0
0	2nd,3rd	1	4	5	2	1	0	0	0	0
0	All	1	1	1	3	0	0	0	0	1
1	None	409	46	21	8	4	3	0	1	0
1	1st	173	35	22	7	3	2	0	1	0
1	2nd	54	28	13	4	1	2	0	0	0
1	1st,2nd	41	17	10	5	1	1	0	1	0
1	3rd	11	21	8	1	0	0	0	0	0
1	1st,3rd	16	15	6	6	3	1	0	0	0
1	2nd,3rd	10	12	6	2	2	0	1	0	0
1	All	9	7	2	3	1	2	0	0	0
2	None	347	18	6	1	2	0	0	0	0
2	1st	203	9	11	3	1	0	0	0	0
2	2nd	94	19	6	3	1	0	0	0	0
2	1st,2nd	80	12	6	2	2	0	1	0	0
2	3rd	47	12	3	0	1	0	0	0	0
2	1st,3rd	28	8	5	4	0	0	0	0	0
2	2nd,3rd	21	1	3	1	2	0	0	0	0
2	All	19	2	1	0	2	0	1	0	0

Table 2

The main item of interest in a table such as Table 2, is the average of the tabulated runs scored values in each row. That is, there were 723 values tabulated in the first row of Table 2, for example, and the average of these 723 values is 0.563. This means that on the average, when a batter comes to the plate with no outs and nobody on base, an average of 0.563 runs can be expected to score in the remainder of the inning.

The averages calculated from all 24 of the rows of Table 2 are presented below in Table 3. I shall refer to these average runs-scored values as "Run Potentials" (or RPs).

The averages given in Table 3 are interesting, but not without fault. For instance, the average number of runs

Average Runs-Scored Calculated from Table 2

Bases	Outs	RP	Outs	RP	Outs	RP
None	0	0.563	1	0.305	2	0.110
1st	0	0.876	1	0.531	2	0.194
2nd	0	1.194	1	0.784	2	0.358
1st,2nd	0	1.596	1	0.895	2	0.427
3rd	0	1.500	1	0.976	2	0.349
1st,3rd	0	1.739	1	1.319	2	0.667
2nd,3rd	0	1.846	1	1.333	2	0.643
All	0	2.857	1	1.417	2	0.720

Table 3

scored from having runners on 1st and 3rd with 2 outs is 0.667, while the average number of runs scored from having runners on 2nd and 3rd with 2 outs is only 0.643. Logically, this cannot be true, since surely it is better for a team to have its runners at 2nd and 3rd than it is to have them at 1st and 3rd. The reason for this contradiction in the table lies in what statisticians refer to as "sampling error". The situations with more than one runner on base occur far less frequently than do the situations having nobody on. For example, the case with nobody on and nobody out occurred with the first batter in every inning, for a total of 723 times in the 1985 Twins home games, while the case of having runners at 2nd and 3rd with 2 out occurred only 28 times in the same set of games. These less frequent situations have averages which are far less accurate in representing the true "run potential." Statisticians quantify the relative accuracy of a set of averages, by computing the standard error for each average. The standard errors presented below in Table 4 represent the relative accuracies for the averages in Table 3. The smaller standard errors are indicative of the situations in which the averages from Table 3 are more precise representations of the true run potentials, due to having more observations available for those situations. Had more observations been available for the cases with 2 outs and 2 runners on base, the contradiction in Table 3 would have eventually disappeared.

Standard Errors (SE) for the Averages in Table 3

Bases	Outs	SE	Outs	SE	Outs	SE
None	0	0.040	1	0.038	2	0.024
1st	0	0.091	1	0.067	2	0.041
2nd	0	0.161	1	0.108	2	0.068
1st,2nd	0	0.268	1	0.152	2	0.099
3rd	0	0.435	1	0.118	2	0.091
1st,3rd	0	0.276	1	0.197	2	0.149
2nd,3rd	0	0.296	1	0.245	2	0.237
All	0	0.962	1	0.329	2	0.319

Table 4

In order to improve the estimates of Run Potential for each of the 24 cases, we can again borrow from the science of statistics and use a technique called "least squares regression". However, because the standard errors in Table 4 are so different from each other, we should use a modified technique known as "weighted least squares regression". A separate regression can be computed for the 8 cases in each of the 3 columns of Table 3. The regression procedure computes coefficients B0, B1, B2, and B3 for the following equation:

$$RP = B0 + (B1 \times R1) + (B2 \times R2) + (B3 \times R3)$$

where RP will be the estimated Run Potential for each situation, and R1, R2, and R3 are indicators of whether a runner is on each base. That is,

$$R1 = 1 \text{ if a runner is on 1st,}$$
$$= 0 \text{ if no runner is on 1st;}$$

$$R2 = 1 \text{ if a runner is on 2nd,}$$
$$= 0 \text{ if no runner is on 2nd;}$$

$$R3 = 1 \text{ if a runner is on 3rd,}$$
$$= 0 \text{ if no runner is on 3rd.}$$

The regression equations produced using the data from Table 3 are the following:

0 Outs: RP = 0.562 + 0.332 R1 + 0.629 R2 + 0.809 R3
1 Out : RP = 0.310 + 0.217 R1 + 0.416 R2 + 0.670 R3
2 Outs: RP = 0.107 + 0.096 R1 + 0.241 R2 + 0.300 R3

Equations such as these can be extremely useful for a variety of reasons. For instance, the computed coefficients B1, B2, and B3 can be interpreted as the value (in terms of Run Potential) of having a runner at the corresponding base. Thus, a runner at 1st base with nobody out is worth 0.332 runs, while a runner at 1st base with one out is worth 0.217 runs. These coefficients can also be interpreted as the probability that a runner at that particular base will eventually score a run later in the inning.

The values of B0 in the regression equations represent the value of the current batter and following batters, in terms of Run Potential for the current inning. Thus, when no one is on base, the value of B0 also represents the Run Potential for the current situation. Notice the three values of B0 are extremely close to the average runs scored for the situations at the top of the three columns in Table 3. We can compute the estimated RP for each of the 24 cases, by using the 3 regression equations given above and substituting in 0 or 1 in place of R1, R2, and R3. These values are given below in Table 5. It should be noted that these RPs are derived only from the 1985 Minnesota Twins batting at home in the Metrodome. Ideally, a separate set of RPs should be found for each team batting in each stadium. A more practical goal, however, would be to have a single set of RPs derived from the data for an entire league in a given year, although with so large a sample size, the need for such a regression based approach is lessened.

Notice that the contradiction inherent in the original averages of Table 3 has disappeared in Table 5. These RPs

Run Potentials Calculated from the Regression Equations

Bases	Outs	RP	Outs	RP	Outs	RP
None	0	0.562	1	0.310	2	0.107
1st	0	0.893	1	0.528	2	0.203
2nd	0	1.190	1	0.726	2	0.348
1st,2nd	0	1.522	1	0.943	2	0.444
3rd	0	1.370	1	0.980	2	0.407
1st,3rd	0	1.702	1	1.197	2	0.503
2nd,3rd	0	1.999	1	1.396	2	0.648
All	0	2.331	1	1.613	2	0.744

Table 5

can be considered to be "smoothed" versions of the original averages. It is possible to get some illogical estimates of RPs from regression equations, but it is not nearly as likely to occur as it is when using the raw averages. Thus a regression procedure (in particular, weighted regression) should be considered any time a person wants to estimate Run Potential. Table 6 presents the RPs calculated from all 162 games of the 1985 Minnesota Twins.

Run Potentials—1985 Minnesota Twins—All Games

Bases	Outs	RP	Outs	RP	Outs	RP
None	0	0.487	1	0.262	2	0.087
1st	0	0.842	1	0.501	2	0.172
2nd	0	1.109	1	0.629	2	0.251
1st,2nd	0	1.464	1	0.869	2	0.335
3rd	0	1.483	1	0.968	2	0.335
1st,3rd	0	1.838	1	1.208	2	0.420
2nd,3rd	0	2.105	1	1.335	2	0.499
All	0	2.460	1	1.575	2	0.583

Table 6

By examining these Run Potentials, interesting comparisons can be made. For example, if there are no outs and a runner is on 1st base, should he attempt a steal of 2nd? We can answer this, following the approach of Palmer and Thorn, by comparing the RP of the situation with a runner at 2nd with the RP of having a runner at 1st, with no outs. Assume that the runner has a probability P of successfully stealing 2nd, and a probability of $1 - P$ of being thrown out at 2nd. The RP with the runner at 1st base and no one out is 0.842 (from Table 6). The RP of having the runner at 2nd base with no one out is 1.109. But if the runner were thrown out, the RP would decrease to only 0.262. Then the strategy of attempting to steal 2nd base is a good one only if

$$1.109 * P + 0.262 * (1 - P) > 0.842.$$

From this, we find that the runner should be successful at least 68.5% of the time, if there are no outs. The needed success rates for stealing 2nd, 3rd, or Home with 0, 1, or 2 outs are given below in Table 7. Please remember that these percentages are valid only for the 1985 Minnesota Twins. However, other teams could have their own minimal success rates calculated in a similar way. The calculation of these rates from the data for an entire league would also be interesting.

Minimal Success Rates Needed for Stealing

Base Being Stolen	Number of Outs		
	0	1	2
2nd	68.5%	76.4%	68.5%
3rd	69.4%	61.5%	74.9%
Home	99.7%	75.0%	30.8%

Table 7

What can we tell from a table like this? It's probably just as well that the slow-footed Twins didn't attempt to steal too much in 1985. Their overall stealing percentage was only 60.7% for the year (68 steals in 112 attempts).

This essay has been written to illustrate some possible future directions for sabermetric analysis of Project Scoresheet data. It is hoped that others will try the same or similar analyses for their favorite team, or for an entire league. We now have the capability to produce an "average" which is more representative of a batter's contribution than the traditional batting average, on-base average, or slugging average. I have written BASIC programs to compute various statistics, and I will be glad to share these programs with anyone who has some interest in using them. It is hoped that the computation of averages like these will become more common in the future. With the Project Scoresheet data, many of our common ways of computing baseball statistics can be improved considerably.

THE HERR-McGEE TRAGEDY, AND OTHER DISASTERS OF 1986

By Russ Eagle

I can still remember sliding out of my chair as Jack Clark connected, hitting the floor on my knees as I watched Pedro Guerrero turn toward the wall, and finally leaping as high as an eight-foot ceiling allows when the ball settled into the leftfield seats of Dodger Stadium. The date was October 16, 1985 and the St. Louis Cardinals were National League Champions. They had taken four straight from the Dodgers and despite Vince Coleman's injury, the Redbird offense seemed in high gear. Days later, however, that same offense was reported missing in Kansas City. A year after that, the remains were discovered, buried deep in the National League East, 29–1/2 games behind the New York Mets. In fact, the events which followed Clark's pennant-winning blast were so horrific that St. Louis fans must have thought the Big Dodger in the Sky had spitefully ravaged the Cardinal offense in Biblical fashion.

An overstatement, maybe, but the Cardinals' offensive decline in 1986 was one of historic proportions. They became, I believe, the first team to lead the league in batting average and runs scored in one season and then finish last in both categories the following year. They fell from 101 wins in 1985 to 79 wins in 1986. The 1986 Cards did not have a single .300 hitter. They did not have a 100-RBI man. They didn't even have a 65-RBI man. The '86 Cardinals took it upon themselves to show, once and for all, that stolen bases have very little to do with a good offense, swiping 262 bases while scoring only 601 runs. In 92 of their 161 games in 1986, the Cardinals scored three runs or less. And there's more, much more. I could go on all night reciting similar disasters from 1986, but that's about as much fun as watching highlights of Game 7 from the '85 World Series. Suffice to say, the Cardinal offense in 1986 was offensive only to the St. Louis fans.

Were there other reasons for the collapse? The pitching and defense weren't blameless, as the Redbirds allowed 39 more runs in '86 than they did in '85. But when one remembers that the National League average for runs scored per team increased by 17 runs in '86, the defensive decline is actually only 22 runs. So how about bad luck? If the Cardinals were especially lucky in '85, or especially luckless in '86, that would probably show up when we used Bill James' Pythagorean Theory, which uses the square of runs scored and runs allowed to project winning percentage. Using the theorem, the '85 Cardinals figured to go 102–60 (they were 101–61) while the 1986 team projected to 79–82, which was their actual record. So the Cardinals won as many games as could be expected in both seasons, and luck can be discounted. It's the offensive decline (from 747 runs scored to 601) which has to share most of the blame, about 90% of it.

Let's analyze the club's offense in the two seasons. The 1985 Cardinals had a .355 on-base percentage, easily the top figure in the league. They hit .264 as a team and drew 586 walks. The '86 club had a .309 OBP, with a .236 team batting average and 568 walks. They had only 1838 runners on base as a result of a a hit or walk, compared to 2032 in 1985. Combining these numbers with the runs scored totals, we find that 37% of the runners from 1985 scored, while only 33% of the 1986 runners tallied. The reason for the decline is obvious; the '86 club had absolutely no power, as shown by the decline in slugging percentage from .379 to .327. Home runs were down by 29, which is not terribly important by itself; the Cards have shown in the past that you can win in Busch Stadium without home runs. You cannot win, however, without some punch in your lineup, and the Cards were last in the league in doubles as well as home runs. Even with 48 triples in 1986, the Redbirds were next-to-last in combined doubles and triples with only 264, ahead of only Los Angeles with 246...and the Dodgers hit 130 homers. You can't win in any ballpark without hitting home runs or hitting a lot of doubles, no matter how many bases you steal. Only 25% of all St. Louis hits in 1986 were for extra bases, down from 27% in '85. So the Cardinals were not only getting fewer base hits in 1986, but also had a smaller percentage of extra-base hits.

If we're looking for culprits for this decline, we can start at the top of the lineup, with Vince Coleman and his .301 on-base average. Coleman is a great base stealer, and Coleman is an exciting player. But Coleman is not a good leadoff hitter. In '85 his weakness was less obvious; the Cards led the league in runs scored despite Coleman's .320 OBP. Whitey Herzog, not a stupid man, obviously thought Coleman had potential as a leadoff man, and saw no reason to make a change. But look at 1986. You see just the opposite problem, with the same solution. With the possible exception of the Braves, you now have the worst offense in the league. Batting Vince at the top of the order is costing you runs, especially with Ozzie Smith and his .376 on-base percentage batting seventh or eighth half the time. But you're also 25 games behind the Mets. I don't think Whitey believes that Coleman is a good leadoff hitter at this point. In fact, I'm sure he doesn't. He must feel, however, that Coleman can improve. If he doesn't next year, then Whitey will probably make a change.

So Coleman was partially responsible for the Cardinal decline in '86, but only partially; he was given too much credit in 1985, and too much blame in 1986. But what about the lineup as a whole? Let's look at the lineup production of the 1985 St. Louis Cardinals (See next page).

We've already talked about Coleman, but look at the next three places in the lineup. The number two and three spots were occupied by McGee and Herr for basically the entire year. Both had career years in '85, and while a player can obviously be expected to decline in performance following such a season, this duo's dropoff was extreme. Clark also had a excellent year in '85, although not as out of

517

Bt. Pos	At bats	Runs	Hits	RBI	AVE	Players
1st	688	119	185	47	.269	Coleman
2nd	675	116	229	85	.339	McGee
3rd	620	99	183	109	.295	Herr
4th	598	92	165	108	.276	Clark, Cedeno, Porter
5th	616	88	172	87	.279	Van Slyke, Landrum
6th	621	66	136	87	.219	Pendleton
7th	555	59	146	74	.263	Smith, Porter
8th	552	58	128	66	.232	Smith, Nieto
9th	542	50	102	24	.188	Pitchers

context career-wise as those of Herr and McGee. And when Clark went down, Cedeno stepped in and began hitting like it was 1971 again. When Clark was injured in '86, though, everyone stepped in and no one did the job; Cardinal cleanup hitters hit .256 with 49 RBIs for the 93 games after Jack went out. Clark himself was driving in runs at an even slower rate than that before he was hurt, but that was more the fault of the hitters in front of him, as Jack was being pitched around enough to lead the league in walks at the time of the injury.

The number five spot was also very productive in 1985, with 88 runs scored, 87 RBIs and a .279 average. These numbers were compiled mainly by the rightfield platoon of Andy Van Slyke and Tito Landrum, both of whom had individual offensive winning percentages over .600. The five-spot in '86 fell to 68 runs, 80 RBIs and a .239 average. Van Slyke, the team's best offensive player in '86, hit fifth 30 times, driving in 19 runs. Terry Pendleton, on the other hand, drove in only 20 runs while batting fifth 42 times. It was Pendleton's presence in this spot that was largely responsible for the dropoff in performance. More about that in a minute.

Look back at the chart for 1985. What's the weakest spot? Probably the sixth. Sure, it produced 87 RBIs, but look at the hitters ahead of this spot. The low batting average, combined with the high number of at-bats, suggests a low on-base percentage. The Cardinal sixth-place hitter for most of 1985 was Terry Pendleton, the worst offensive player on the team among the regulars. Amazingly, Pendleton was almost exactly the same player in 1986 that he was in 1985. He improved his base stealing percentage in '86, but otherwise there are no significant differences: his average dropped a point to .239, his slugging percentage remained at .306, and his on-base average fell six points to .279. But he produced these numbers batting sixth in 1985. In 1986 Pendleton batted fifth for over one fourth of the season. There were also ten games where he batted second or third. Because of the decline by the rest of the team, Pendleton was asked to do more in 1986. He responded with basically the same numbers he put up in 1985. In this respect, Pendleton was responsible for a portion of the decline.

Of course the biggest problem is that Pendleton's stats are horrendous for a fifth or sixth place hitter. The situation here is probably the same as suggested earlier with Coleman. Pendleton is a brilliant defensive player who showed hitting promise as a rookie in 1984. He hustles, and Whitey likes hustlers. He's aggressive, and Whitey likes that too. I like him myself, and still think he has potential as an offensive player, but as Bill James wrote in the '86 *Abstract,* his offensive stats at this point are "im-

possible to defend," especially when they're in the middle of the lineup.

The seventh and eight spots held their own in '86, mainly because of Ozzie Smith. Ozzie had basically the same season offensively that he had in '85, with a little less power. In both seasons he hit seventh or eighth a large part of the time, and in '86 he hit over .300 when hitting seventh or eighth. Nieto in '85 and Lavalliere in '86 were basically the same offensively, with Lavalliere having a slight edge. Both hit eighth most of the time. As for the seventh spot, it was mostly Ozzie and Porter in '85, Ozzie, Heath and Lavalliere in '86. The loss of Porter was felt by the Cardinal offense more than a lot of people thought it would be, and not just because Mike Heath was so terrible. Despite his low batting average, Porter walked a lot and hit with pretty good power. His .413 slugging and .335 on-base marks in 1985 made him a valuable offensive performer, with a .606 offensive winning percentage. Porter platooned with Nieto in '85. Heath was platooned with Lavalliere in '86, until the Cards gave up on him. As I said earlier, there's little difference offensively between Nieto and Lavalliere. But while Porter was making a sizable offensive contribution, Heath was horrendous. This decline doesn't really show up if you just look at the number seven spot in the production charts because Porter hit cleanup a lot in '85 after Clark was hurt and Heath didn't hit seventh exclusively either, but the replacement of Porter with Heath in '86 definitely cost the Cardinals on offense.

Now let's look at the lineup production chart for 1986:

Bat. Pos.	At bats	Runs	Hits	RBI	Ave.	Players
1st	667	100	151	33	.226	Coleman
2nd	641	76	164	61	.256	McGee, Smith
3rd	626	70	152	73	.243	McGee, Herr, Van Slyke
4th	607	84	151	72	.249	Clark, Van Slyke, Knicely, etc.
5th	619	68	148	80	.239	Van Slyke, Landrum, Pendleton, Ford
6th	587	57	128	63	.218	Pendleton, Heath
7th	570	61	147	61	.258	Smith, Heath, Lavalliere
8th	551	53	152	58	.276	Smith, Lavalliere
9th	510	32	77	49	.151	Pitchers

Interestingly, the top two averages were compiled by the seventh and eighth spots, causing one to possibly question Whitey's lineup selection. Smith was mainly responsible for those two averages, hitting over .300 in the seventh and eighth spots. Ozzie did hit second 70 times in 1986, but compiled only a .243 average. It just wasn't a good year to be trying to make out a lineup card in the St. Louis dugout. If you look at some of the first and second half breakdowns for 1986, you see that most Cardinal players had a problem with consistency. Ozzie was the only regular with anything resembling a consistent offensive record, and his batting average fell from .296 in the first half to .265 in the second. Other players with differing first and second half batting averages included Coleman (.253, .210), McGee (.237, .292), Herr (.217, .288), Pendleton (.208, .270), Van Slyke (.236, .300) and Landrum (.171, .250). So it's no wonder why it was difficult to come up with a productive and consistent lineup.

On top of these inconsistencies, the Cardinals ran into

a number of injuries in '86. While most were to the pitching staff, injuries to Clark, McGee, Van Slyke, Coleman and Smith kept them out of the lineup at various times in 1986. McGee seemed to have finally found himself offensively in July, and then missed more than a month with an injury. The injuries were no doubt responsible for a lot of the inconsistent seasons turned in during 1986, and of course made it even more difficult to compile a productive batting order.

Injuries aside, the two keys to offense are getting on base and moving runners along, and three of the eight spots in the Cardinal lineup in 1986 (leftfield, third base and catcher) were manned by players who did neither very well. Two of the three spots were filled by the same player in 1985, when they also did not do particularly well. The difference was that in 1985 the Cardinals had five regulars (Smith, Herr, Van Slyke, McGee and Clark) who were so outstanding that the team was able to win without much production from the other spots. Players like Pendleton and Coleman stuck out a lot more now, especially since they were at positions where you generally count on substantial offensive contributions. The career years of Herr-McGee in

1985, along with Jack Clark's sparkling three-fourths of a season, concealed the inadequate production of Pendleton and Coleman, and also possibly gave the Cardinals a false sense of security that led them to release Darrell Porter, who was a productive offensive player. The Mike Heath disaster didn't help, either.

There's no reason not to expect good years from Herr, McGee and Clark in 1987. Herr and McGee finished strong in '86, and Clark has shown before that he can come back from injury. Ozzie and Van Slyke are improving each year, and there's no reason to think they won't continue to do so in '87. The question marks, offensively, remain at catcher, third base and leftfield (this is being written before any off-season trades). It's not unusual for a team to win with no offense at one position. It's rare with two, impossible with three. Pendleton's defense and Coleman's baserunning make them very exciting players to watch, and both have shown potential offensively. But the Cardinals cannot keep putting them in the lineup each day, particularly batting first and sixth, and expect to have a productive offense. It puts too much pressure on the rest of the players. It happened once, in 1985, but it's doubtful that it'll happen again.

BASEBALL AS A MARKOV CHAIN

by Mark D. Pankin

A Markov chain is a type of mathematical model that is well suited to analyzing baseball. The concept of a Markov chain is not new, dating back to 1907, nor is the idea of applying it to baseball, which appeared in mathematical literature as early as 1960. In fact, it is not unusual to see sabermetric analysis that incorporates the fundamental ideas of a Markov chain without formally using the mathematical structure. This type of work typically employs situational analysis and studies the probabilities and effects on expected scoring of moving from one combination of base runners and outs to another. An example is the calculation of break-even probabilities for attempting to steal a base. However, formal Markov chain analysis of baseball is not at all common and is rarely found outside of academic studies. The main reasons for this are 1) most sabermetricians have never heard of Markov chains, 2) obtaining sufficient data has been rather difficult, and 3) a computer is a virtual necessity for serious Markov chain analysis. Project Scoresheet has taken care of the second problem, and the advent of personal computers and advanced software brings the solution to the third problem within the means of many sabermetricians. This essay attempts to do something about the first problem, but none of the mathematical details are presented since that would be inappropriate here.

There are three main sections that follow. The first is a nontechnical description of Markov chains and application of them to baseball. The second section discusses the types of sabermetric analyses that can be performed using Markov chains. The third section descibes some of the author's work with Project Scoresheet data to develop prototype Markov analytical capabilities, and presents examples, which are for illustrative purposes only because of the limited scope of the data, demonstrating the workings of some of the Markov concepts.

A: What are Markov chains and what do they have to do with baseball?

From a mathematical point of view, a Markov chain describes a process that can be considered to be in exactly one of a number of "states" at any given time. A baseball half-inning (the half- will be left out for brevity in the rest of this paper) fits that description if the states are considered the various runners and outs situations. There are 24 such combinations, which are listed below using the notation (runners,outs):

TABLE 1: RUNNERS AND OUTS COMBINATIONS

Runners:	0 (none)	1	2	3	12	13	23	123
0:	(0,0)	(1,0)	(2,0)	(3,0)	(12,0)	(13,0)	(23,0)	(123,0)
Outs 1:	(0,1)	(1,1)	(2,1)	(3,1)	(12,1)	(13,1)	(23,1)	(123,1)
2:	(0,2)	(1,2)	(2,2)	(3,2)	(12,2)	(13,2)	(23,2)	(123,2)

There also is a three out state, and to be technically correct there should be less aggregation of the out states, although this will depend on the problem being analyzed.

The heart of the Markov chain is the analysis of the transitions between the states. The key is the so-called transition matrix that contains the probabilites of moving from any state to any other state. Many of the transitions in baseball are impossible (e.g. the number of outs can never decrease) and have probability equal to zero. The other transitions have probabilities determined by the chances of various baseball events.

For sabermetric purposes, it is useful to have more than one transition matrix. One necessary refinement is to distinguish between transitions ("plays") that change the batter and those that do not. For example, suppose an inning is in the state (1,0) [runner on first, none out] and after the play it is in the state (2,0) [runner on second, none out]. If the batter changed, then the runner scored, most likely on a double. However, if the batter did not change, then the runner on first advanced to second (SB, WP, PB, balk) and no run scored. One way of handling this is to define additional states that indicate whether or not the batter changed, but that proves to be mathematically cumbersome. A better method is to have one transition matrix for plays that change the batter and a second one for plays that do not. In fact, there is no reason to stop at two. When performing strategy analysis, it makes sense to distinguish transitions for which the strategy is in effect from the others. Along these lines, it seems reasonable to establish separate transition matrices for such things as pitchers batting, sacrifice bunts and attempts, stolen bases and caught stealings, intentional walks, and so forth.

Closely associatied with a baseball Markov chain, though strictly speaking not part of it, is the runs after matrix. For each of the 24 runners and outs states listed in Table 1, this matrix records what percentage of the time a specific number of runs scored in the remainder of the inning. For example, after the (0,2) state, there may have been 0 runs 82% of the time, 1 run 14%, 2 runs 2%, etc. From this matrix, it is easy to compute the expected or average number of runs for the rest of the inning. These expected run values for each state are commonly used in situational and strategy analysis to compute break-even probabilities. Note that the expected number of runs after the (0,0) state, in which all innings begin, is the average number of runs per inning. Examples of this matrix may be found in other papers in this book, as well as in *The Hidden Game of Baseball* by Palmer and Thorn.

B. How can Markov chains be used in sabermetrics?

There is a rich mathematical theory of Markov chains, but most of it is not applicable to baseball. (The three out state is an "absorbing" state because once entered, it can't be left. Most of the theory concerns chains without absorbing states.) Perhaps the greatest benefits from considering an inning as a Markov chain come from being able to formulate a large number of complex calculations in terms of matrix notation. The use of matrix algebra, as opposed to keeping track of numerous cases and equations, can greatly simplify the entire analytical process. A spreadsheet program on a personal computer is a natural setting for sabermetric work in general, and these programs with their row and column organization lend themselves naturally to matrix manipulations. The latest versions may have matrix multiplication and matrix inversion commands, which are a virtual necessity for Markov chain analysis. The Markov chain and matrix algebra formulation enables the consideration of a wider range of questions and even makes getting the answers easier.

One fascinating computation that can be performed is to compute from a transition matrix the average or expected number of runs after each of the 24 runners and outs combinations. In particular, the expected runs after the (0,0) state is the average scoring per inning, and in a sense 9 times this number is average scoring per game. The key to this analysis is to start from an "interesting" transition matrix.

If the transition matrix contains only plays in which no strategy was involved (i.e. "hitting away"), then the values obtained are baselines against which strategies can be analyzed. One way of analyzing the strategy is to modify the transition matrix to include the strategy and then compute the expected runs again. For example, if the goal is to determine the effect on scoring of the actual stolen base attempts in a group of games, say for a whole league in a season, then the expected runs computation could be carried starting from a transition matrix without any steal attempts and again starting from the same transition matrix augmented by the steal attempts. Because the expected runs following all situations are calculated, it would be possible to see if the actual strategies increased scoring in some cases, say after (1,2), but not after others, say (1,0), in addition to telling if overall scoring increased or decreased.

Another application of this idea is to evaluate the offensive performance of individual players. Suppose we have a transition matrix for one player by himself. That matrix could be obtained from collecting data on all his plate appearances (and base running events if desired), or it could be estimated from season or career statistics. Calculating the expected runs per inning from that matrix yields an estimate of how much scoring there would be if that player batted (and ran) all the time. Multiplying the runs per inning by nine produces an offensive run average for the player. The player's average could be compared to a league average computed from a transition matrix based on all players.

Markov chain techniques can be used to compare different batting orders. The basic idea is again to compute the expected runs per inning associated with each batting order being analyzed. In this case, the computations are more complicated because nine different transition matrices are involved and how often each player leads off an inning should be accounted for. However, the necessary calculations are feasible, and there are often simplifying assumptions that can be applied to answer specific questions.

A different use of the transition matrix is to study possible differences between ballparks, teams, playing surfaces, etc. The idea is to examine specific transitions that can shed light on the issue. For example, suppose the goal is to determine whether it is harder to score from second base on a single in an astroturf or grass park. Of course, the best way is to go through the play-by-plays from a large of number of suitable games and collect the specific data. However, this may prove to be difficult, and the transition data if available can be of use. In this case, the idea is to examine transitions from a state with a runner on second to a state that was almost certainly reached by a single. This requires first base to be open so short singles can be distinguished from walks, which reduces to a runner on second or runners on second and third. The appropriate transitions are listed below:

TABLE 2: SCORING FROM SECOND ON A SINGLE (I)

| | End State After "single" | |
Start State	Runner on 2nd scored	Did not score
(2,0), (23,0)	(1,0), (0,1)	(13,0), (1,1)
(2,1), (23,1)	(1,1), (0,2)	(13,1), (1,2)
(2,2), (23,2)	(1,2)	(13,2)

In addition, there may be a small number of transitions to three out states that result from singles, but there is no way to distinguish these from other transitions to the three out states. The number of such plays is probably too small to be meaningful in this analysis. A larger problem is that the transitions do not distinguish singles from other plays where the batter reaches first such as errors or fielder's choices. However, since the object is to compare two parks or playing surfaces, it is likely that the proportion of non-singles is similar for both, and the comparison will be valid.

By this point, you may be wondering if anyone would really go to the trouble of doing all of this. The answer is definitely yes. Most, but not all, of this type of work has been done by academic researchers. In some cases, simplifying assumptions were made or a reduced problem was studied. However, more complex analyses also have been performed. The description of the use of Project Scoresheet data that follows shows that elaborate computer facilities are no longer required for Markov chain baseball analysis.

C. Where does Project Scoresheet come in?

The author has been a Project Scoresheet inputter for the past two years. The inputters enter plays from the scoresheets into IBM PC and compatible personal computers using programs supplied by the project director. These programs write data files on floppy diskettes that contain all the information needed to reconstruct the games. The author input 37 Baltimore home games in 1985 and 74 Cincinnati home games in 1986 and kept copies of the data files. All the examples below are drawn from these games and as such form a limited and probably non-representative sample. Thus, any data or conclusions should not be considered to be representative of either league or of major league baseball.

The first step is the extraction from the data files of

the information needed for the transition and runs after matrices: counts of how often each transition took place and how often specific numbers of runs scored after each situation. The author has written a program using the BASIC language for this task. The program keeps track of six different types of transitions: 1) non-pitchers hitting away, 2) pitchers hitting away, 3) intentional walks, 4) sacrifice bunts and attempts, 5) stolen bases and caught stealings, and 6) other transitions that do not change the batter (WP, PB, balk, etc.). In addition, these transitions and the runs after are separated into those for the home team, Baltimore or Cincinnati, and those for the visting teams. The program defines a sacrifice bunt attempt to be any bunt with none out and men on base or any bunt by a pitcher with one out and men on base. Any credited sacrifice hit is counted as such. Because the data files are structured in a way that makes the determination of the score at any point in the game difficult, the definition of sacrifice is not dependent on the game score. The program works fairly quickly processing about 15 games a minute on the author's computer system, and much faster personal computers are currently available.

The BASIC program writes disk files that can be read into the Lotus 1–2–3 spreadsheet program, which is used for the remainder of the analysis. Spreadsheets are an ideal way to manipulate transition data and perform the needed calculations. Commands to multiply and invert matrices are almost a necessity for Markov chains and similar types of computations.

Table 3 below shows for each of the 24 runners and outs combinations 1) how many times each occurred in the observed (from the scoresheets) data, 2) the observed probability of scoring at least one run after the combination (useful for strategy analysis), 3) the observed average runs after, and 4) the average runs after computed from the Markov chain. For the NL (Cincinnati home games) data, two averages are shown, one which excludes the pitchers and one including the pitchers. These averages are calculated only from the hitting away transitions, while the observed averages reflect the effects of all plays. The probability of scoring at least one run is more difficult to calculate from the Markov chain formulation, and it has not been carried out at this time.

It should be noted that the Markov calculations for expected (average) runs after each situation assume all batters have the average transition probabilities. In actuality, each batter has a different transition matrix, which could be accounted for in the Markov calculation, but such a degree of complication is beyond the scope of the current effort. Also, the Markov calculations shown above exclude the effects of intentional walks, sacrifice bunts and attempts, stolen bases and attempts, and other plays that do not change the batter. This can be an advantage when analyzing strategies for the effect on expected runs because these calculations exclude the effects of some primary strategies. For these reasons and others, the observed average runs do not match the Markov calculations. The two are fairly close in many cases for the AL data, but the theoretical calculated values tend to be higher than the observed values for the NL data.

Table 4 summarizes the scoring from second on a single exercise described previously. In both cases, only non-pitcher hitting away transitions are counted.

TABLE 3: OBSERVED AND THEORETICAL SITUATION DATA

37 BALTIMORE HOME GAMES IN 1985 (ALL TEAMS)

Situation	Number	OBSERVED Prob. of runs	OBSERVED Avg. runs	MARKOV Avg. runs
1 (0,0)	691	0.288	0.530	0.536
2 (0,1)	505	0.180	0.323	0.292
3 (0,2)	393	0.079	0.125	0.117
4 (1,0)	171	0.415	0.854	0.910
5 (1,1)	216	0.282	0.583	0.559
6 (1,2)	219	0.100	0.210	0.220
7 (2,0)	46	0.696	1.435	1.253
8 (2,1)	74	0.473	0.689	0.760
9 (2,2)	89	0.270	0.382	0.366
10 (3,0)	4	1.000	2.250	1.557
11 (3,1)	24	0.667	1.333	1.088
12 (3,2)	37	0.297	0.351	0.374
13 (12,0)	42	0.667	1.524	1.380
14 (12,1)	74	0.446	1.014	0.923
15 (12,2)	101	0.277	0.554	0.507
16 (13,0)	16	0.875	1.875	1.736
17 (13,1)	42	0.786	1.524	1.409
18 (13,2)	48	0.292	0.542	0.509
19 (23,0)	8	0.500	0.875	1.820
20 (23,1)	32	0.531	1.156	1.309
21 (23,2)	28	0.143	0.357	0.251
22 (123,0)	16	0.875	1.938	2.118
23 (123,1)	30	0.567	1.133	1.447
24 (123,2)	40	0.250	0.600	0.480
	2946			

74 CINCINNATI HOME GAMES IN 1986 (ALL TEAMS)

Situation	Number	OBSERVED Prob. of runs	OBSERVED Avg. runs	MARKOV Avg. runs no pit.	MARKOV Avg. runs w/pit.
1 (0,0)	1397	0.295	0.515	0.570	0.527
2 (0,1)	1000	0.162	0.259	0.297	0.270
3 (0,2)	804	0.071	0.102	0.114	0.103
4 (1,0)	369	0.472	0.900	1.017	0.955
5 (1,1)	395	0.281	0.532	0.622	0.578
6 (1,2)	408	0.145	0.243	0.281	0.254
7 (2,0)	110	0.609	0.955	1.098	1.034
8 (2,1)	202	0.411	0.678	0.632	0.599
9 (2,2)	246	0.236	0.325	0.360	0.330
10 (3,0)	26	0.923	1.423	1.533	1.498
11 (3,1)	69	0.667	0.942	1.015	0.945
12 (3,2)	125	0.272	0.408	0.373	0.355
13 (12,0)	83	0.735	1.590	1.797	1.703
14 (12,1)	127	0.480	1.087	1.148	1.079
15 (12,2)	194	0.242	0.407	0.514	0.469
16 (13,0)	34	0.824	1.353	1.815	1.748
17 (13,1)	66	0.667	1.045	1.255	1.161
18 (13,2)	77	0.234	0.351	0.451	0.391
19 (23,0)	11	0.818	1.909	1.778	1.715
20 (23,1)	55	0.745	1.455	1.413	1.350
21 (23,2)	57	0.404	0.772	0.726	0.715
22 (123,0)	22	0.955	2.091	2.402	2.282
23 (123,1)	55	0.764	1.764	1.966	1.786
24 (123,2)	73	0.288	0.521	0.751	0.654
	6005				

TABLE 4: SCORING FROM SECOND ON A SINGLE (II)
1985 BALTIMORE GAMES

Start Situation:	(2,0)&(23,0)	(2,1)&(23,1)	(2,2)&(23,2)
End Situations:			
—runner on second scores	(1,0): 4 (0,1): 1	(1,1): 4 (0,2): 1	(1,2): 10
—runner on second does not score	(13,0): 4 (1,1): 0	(13,1): 12 (1,2): 0	(13,2): 2
Scoring percentage:	5/9=.556	5/17=.294	10/12=.833

1986 CINCINNATI GAMES

Start Situation:	(2,0)&(23,0)	(2,1)&(23,1)	(2,2)&(23,2)
End Situations:			
—runner on second scores	(1,0): 6 (0,1): 1	(1,1): 12 (0,2): 0	(1,2): 26
—runner on second does not score	(13,0): 6 (1,1): 2	(13,1): 12 (1,2): 4	(13,2): 6
Scoring percentage:	7/15=.467	12/28=.429	26/32=.813

Because the Orioles and Reds players are involved offensively or defensively in all plays, these transitions can't be considered to be a direct comparison between grass and astroturf. That being said, the above evidence does not support a conclusion that it is easier or harder to score from second on a single in either of the two parks. The only thing shown is the unsurprising observation that runners score from second far more frequently when there are two outs.

Next, the thorny issue of the sacrifice bunt is considered. Because of data limitations the investigation is confined to situations with a runner on first only. For the AL, the no outs situation is the only one for a potential sac try, but in the NL, pitchers will often bunt with one out. These bunts should be evaluated against the objective of increasing the chances of scoring at least one run. In general, the sac bunt reduces overall scoring because it creates an out. One important point is that the probabilities of scoring (at least one run) used are drawn from the observed data, and hence they include the effects of all plays and strategies, including bunts and stolen base tries. That means these probabilities are not the best for the typical type of break-even analysis. Instead, the tables below compare the probabilities of scoring before the bunt, those shown in Table 3 for (1,0) and (1,1), with the probabilities resulting from the outcomes of the actual sacrifice bunt attempts.

TABLE 5: SACRIFICE BUNT ATTEMPT ANALYSIS
BALTIMORE GAMES (bunts with runner on first, no outs)

Ending situation		Number	Percent	Scoring Probability
(0,2)	[Double play]	1	.056	.079
(2,1)	[Sac worked]	14	.778	.473
(12,0)	[Batter safe]	3 — 18	.167	.667

Average probability of scoring after bunt
$$= (.056)(.079) + (.778)(.473) + (.167)(.667) = .483$$
Probability of scoring after (1,0) $\quad = .415$
Net GAIN from sacrifice bunt attempt $\quad = .068$

CINCINNATI GAMES (bunts with runner on first, no outs)

Ending situation		Number	Percent	Scoring Probability
(0,2)	[Double play]	3	.077	.071
(1,1)	[Sac failed]	4	.103	.281
(2,1)	[Sac worked]	28	.718	.411
(12,0)	[Batter safe]	4 — 39	.103	.735

Average probability of scoring after bunt
$$= (.077)(.071) + (.103)(.281) + (.718)(.411)$$
$$+ (.103)(.735) \qquad = .404$$
Probability of scoring after (1,0) $\quad = .472$
Net LOSS from sacrifice bunt attempt $\quad = .068$

CINCINNATI GAMES (bunts with runner on first, one out)

Ending situation		Number	Percent	Scoring Probability
3 out	[Double play]	1	.063	.000
(1,2)	[Sac failed]	3	.188	.145
(2,2)	[Sac worked]	9	.563	.236
(3,1)	[Runner scored, batter reached 3rd on error]	1	.063	1.000 (run scored on bunt)
(12,1)	[Batter safe]	1	.063	.480
(23,1)	[Batter safe, both advance extra base on error]	1 — 16	.063	.745

Average probability of scoring after bunt
$$= (.063)(0) + (.188)(.145) + (.563)(.236) + (.063)(1)$$
$$+ (.063)(.480) + (.063)(.745) \qquad = .299$$
Probability of scoring after (1,1) $\quad = .281$
Net GAIN from sacrifice bunt attempt $\quad = .018$

The number of bunt transitions is not nearly large enough to support any definitive conclusions, but it is still interesting to interpret the above data. The sacrifice bunt as practiced in the games sampled appears to have been a good play. There is a meaningful increase in the probability of scoring at least one run in the AL games, a small increase for the NL one out bunts, and a sizeable decrease for the NL no out bunts. However, all of the NL one out bunts and many if not most of the NL no out bunts are by pitchers. With a pitcher hitting away, the actual probability of scoring after (1,0) or (1,1) is much less than the values shown, which are based on all players. Thus, the NL comparisons are more in favor of the bunt, especially with pitchers batting, than shown, although the exact amount can't be quantified from the data available.

Some caveats are in order. First, the calculations are based on average values. Specific batters will differ from the average to some extent, so any conclusions must be applied with care. A second consideration is that some bunt transitions may not have been tabulated because the scoresheet may have failed to indicate a bunt. This does not affect credited sacrifices, but could affect both failed sacs and sac tries that result in singles. A similar, and perhaps more serious problem, is that the scoresheets do not indicate when a batter tried unsuccessfully to bunt until he had two strikes and then hit away, presumably at a disadvantage. Bunted third strikes are generally recorded and counted as sac try transitions, but there may be some cases where the bunt indication is missing on the scoresheet.

Most sabermetric analysis has denigrated the sacrifice bunt. Although not discussed here, it is almost certain that the sac bunt try decreases total scoring. Much of the published analysis supports the case that the bunt is not a good play to try to score one run. The above supports the opposite, even for non-pitchers, keeping in mind that the data used are obviously limited.

It is tempting to try to use Table 5 to compare bunting on grass and astroturf. It is true that the percentage of failed sac tries is higher for the Cincinnati data, but there is a possible explanation other than the playing surfaces. The NL bunts are mainly the efforts of pitchers, and the AL bunts, of course, are all by non-pitchers. In general, pitchers bunt in sacrifice situations whether or not they are good bunters. However, a non-pitcher who is a poor bunter is rarely asked to bunt. Thus, there is a good chance that the lower success rate in Cincinnati is due to pitchers. What is needed is to isolate the non-pitcher bunts in the NL data, but that was not done for this study.

The final analysis presented concerns the stolen base. Attempted steals are judged against two objectives, increasing the chances of scoring at least one run and increasing the expected number of runs. Because of the relatively small number of transitions, the calculations shown are confined to situations with a runner on first and no other runners. The expected runs shown in Table 6 are the theoretical values computed from the Markov chain for non-pitcher hitting away transitions, which are used because they are generally free of the effects of strategies and certainly are not influenced by stolen bases.

TABLE 6: STOLEN BASE ATTEMPT ANALYSIS
BALTIMORE GAMES (runner on first, no outs)

Ending Situation	Number	Percent	Scoring Probability	Expected Runs
(0,1) [CS]	3	.214	.180	0.292
(2,0) [SB]	10	.714	.696	1.253
(3,0) [SB&E]	1	.071	1.000	1.557
	14	Weighed Avg:	.607	1.069
		Values for (1,0):	.415	0.910
	Gain/loss from SB try:		.192	0.159

[The weighted averages are computed using the method shown in Table 5.]

BALTIMORE GAMES (runner on first, one out)

Ending Situation	Number	Percent	Scoring Probability	Expected Runs
(0,2) [CS]	5	.333	.079	0.117
(2,1) [SB]	10	.667	.473	0.760
	15	Weighed Avg:	.342	0.545
		Values for (1,1):	.282	0.558
	Gain/loss from SB try:		.060	-0.013

BALTIMORE GAMES (runner on first, two out)

Ending Situation	Number	Percent	Scoring Probability	Expected Runs
3 out [CS]	7	.438	.000	0.000
(2,2) [SB]	9	.562	.270	0.366
	16	Weighed Avg:	.152	0.205
		Values for (1,2):	.100	0.219
	Gain/loss from SB try:		.052	-0.014

CINCINNATI GAMES (runner on first, no outs)

Ending Situation	Number	Percent	Scoring Probability	Expected Runs
(0,1) [CS]	11	.324	.162	0.297
(2,0) [SB]	19	.559	.609	1.098
(3,0) [SB&E]	4	.118	.923	1.533
	34	Weighed Avg:	.501	0.890
		Values for (1,0):	.471	1.017
	Gain/loss from SB try:		.030	-0.127

CINCINNATI GAMES (runner on first, one out)

Ending Situation	Number	Percent	Scoring Probability	Expected Runs
(0,2) [CS]	18	.409	.071	0.114
(2,1) [SB]	26	.591	.411	0.632
	44	Weighed Avg:	.272	0.419
		Values for (1,1):	.281	0.621
	Gain/loss from SB try:		-.009	-0.202

CINCINNATI GAMES (runner on first, two out)

Ending Situation	Number	Percent	Scoring Probability	Expected Runs
3 out [CS]	20	.282	.000	0.000
(2,2) [SB]	46	.648	.236	0.360
(3,2) [SB&E]	5	.070	.272	0.373
	71	Weighed Avg:	.172	0.259
		Values for (1,2):	.144	0.280
	Gain/loss from SB try:		.028	-0.021

The scoring probability of 1.000, which means certainty, shown for the (3,0) Baltimore data is based on just four observations. The true probability is a little lower, but that is unlikely to affect the results of this study. One caveat: it is quite possible some plays that should have been scored as caught stealings were instead scored as pick-offs. The tabulation program counts pick-offs as other transitions that do not change the batter, not as stolen base attempts. Thus, the data in Table 6 may have a small bias in favor of the stolen base. With that in mind, readers are invited to draw their own conclusions from Table 6.

While the calculations presented in the above tables may seem tedious and laborious, they were performed rather quickly from a few matrix multiplications that also produced additional information not shown above. Once the transition matrices have been set up in the spreadsheet environment, it is easier to do the computations than to write about them! This is a dramatic illustration of the analytical power that results from the combination of Markov chain techniques and Project Scoresheet data. The author hopes to obtain additional data on disks from the project (the complete 1985 and 1986 seasons should be available) and pursue the types of analysis presented above. He also hopes that this report will stimulate other sabermetricians' interest in the Markov chain concept and that they will be encouraged to break new ground in their own Markov analyses.

THE EFFECTS OF STOLEN BASE ATTEMPTS ON BATTING STATS

By Kevin Hoare

The purpose of this study was to investigate what effects, if any, a stolen base attempt during a batter's plate appearance has on that batter's stats. I hoped by doing this to be able to draw some conclusions as to the value of the stolen base in a team's offense.

To do this, I scoured the Project Scoresheet's 1985 American League Account Form Box Score Book and recorded what happened to the batter during any plate appearance in which there were stolen base attempts. There were 2176 attempts in the AL in 1985 and I recorded data for 2119 (97.4%) of them. The fact that 57 attempts were apparently not accounted for could be due to some failing of my powers of observation or to anomalies between what the official scorer saw and what the Project Scoresheet scorer saw.

Of course, not every stolen base attempt results in a plate appearance by a batter. There were several reasons for this: double steals, the Rickey Henderson strategem of attempting 2 stolen bases while the same batter is at the plate, the runner being caught stealing for the third out (resulting in no plate appearance by the batter), or a pinch-hitter being substituted for the batter after a runner has attempted to steal.

The chart which follows details the data on which I based my conclusions. There are five lines for each team. The first three lines show team statistics at home, on the road and the total during plate appearances where there were stolen base attempts. The fourth line is simply the team's official statistics; the fifth line records how teams batted during plate appearances in which there was not a stolen base attempt.

The column headings are self-explanatory. "SBA" is the number of stolen base attempts. CS/FTO reflects the number of times a runner was caught stealing for the third out without a corresponding plate appearance by the batter (not including DP's where the batter strikes out and the runner is caught stealing).

At the league level, the results look like this:

	Batting Average (BA)	On-Base Average (OBA)	Slugging Average (SA)	Isolated Power (IP)
Without SBAs	.262	.326	.408	.146
With SBA's	.209	.365	.304	.095
% Difference	−20.2%	+12.0%	−25.5%	−34.9%

It was hardly necessary to test the hypothesis that such findings probably didn't result from chance. Nevertheless, I did check, using Student's t and found that one can be 99.95% confident in saying that an SBA during a batter's plate appearance significantly lowers the batter's BA and SA while raising his OBA.

There is an interesting trade-off evident in these findings. Take the case of a runner on first with one out. Do you send him in the hope that he'll steal second and be able to score on a single? If you do and he is successful, he'll probably have to score on a single because you've just decreased the batter's ability to hit for power by 34.9%. In addition, the batter's chance of getting a hit at all is down 20.2%, which makes the hoped-for single considerably less likely. On the other hand, you've now improved the chances by 12% that the batter at the plate will reach base—with the next batter perhaps knocking them both in.

However, if the runner is caught stealing, all you have left is the hope that the batter will now reach first—probably via a walk or a single—to give you a runner on first with two out. It isn't likely he'll do more than that because his ability to hit and his ability to hit for power has been decreased so drastically by the SBA.

To get some idea of whether the increase in on-base average offsets the decrease in batting average and power, I calculated Pete Palmer's Normalized On-Base Plus Slugging (NOPS) for both cases, i.e., both with and without an SBA during the batter's plate appearance. Since NOPS combines OBA and SA to get an index of overall batting effectiveness, it should point out if the trade-off is worthwhile, at least as regards team batting. The third column of the following chart shows what percentage batting improved or worsened when the batter had to contend with an SBA, as opposed to when he didn't.

TEAM	WITHOUT SBAs	WITH SBAs	DIFFERENCE
BAL	109.0	72.7	−36.3
BOS	111.7	147.7	+36.0
CAL	97.0	69.5	−27.5
CHI	92.7	110.6	+18.0
CLE	94.7	68.9	−25.8
DET	101.7	81.6	−20.1
KC	94.9	77.3	−17.6
MIL	92.1	21.9	−70.2
MIN	99.9	86.2	−13.7
NY	111.1	68.0	−43.1
OAK	97.6	118.4	+20.8
SEA	101.4	95.8	−5.6
TEX	91.9	106.9	+15.0
TOR	107.2	69.6	−37.6
LEAGUE	100.2	83.6	−16.6

Although five teams actually improved their hitting during plate appearances when there was an SBA, overall batting effectiveness for the league declined 16.6% when compared to plate appearances when there was no SBA.

However, the fact that an SBA dramatically worsens batting stats does not conversely mean that batting stats improved as dramatically when the batter didn't have to

TEAM	SBA	AB	H	D	T	HR	RBI	SH	SF	HB	BB	IBB	K	AVE	OBA	SLG	CS/FTO
BAL	48	33	8	1	0	0	7	1	0	0	6	1	9	.242	.359	.273	5
	60	38	8	0	0	0	10	0	1	1	15	1	11	.211	.436	.211	3
	108	71	16	1	0	0	17	1	1	1	21	2	20	.225	.404	.239	8
	112	5517	1451	234	22	214	773	31	40	19	604	30	908	.263	.336	.430	—
	0	5446	1453	233	22	214	756	30	39	18	583	28	888	.263	.335	.432	—
BOS	46	29	11	2	0	0	12	0	0	0	11	0	6	.379	.550	.448	4
	43	29	9	1	0	0	9	0	2	0	8	2	9	.310	.436	.345	4
	89	58	20	3	0	0	21	0	2	0	19	2	15	.345	.494	.397	8
	93	5720	1615	292	31	162	760	50	57	30	562	39	816	.282	.347	.429	—
	0	5662	1595	289	31	162	739	50	55	30	543	37	801	.282	.345	.430	—
CAL	71	46	8	2	0	1	8	1	0	0	15	4	10	.174	.377	.283	9
	81	55	10	0	0	1	10	1	1	0	14	0	16	.182	.343	.236	8
	152	101	18	2	0	2	18	2	1	0	29	4	26	.178	.359	.257	17
	157	5442	1364	215	31	153	685	99	35	39	648	51	902	.251	.333	.386	—
	0	5341	1346	213	30	151	667	97	34	39	619	47	876	.252	.332	.388	—
CHI	72	40	10	1	0	2	12	4	2	2	15	0	13	.250	.458	.425	9
	88	60	14	3	0	1	12	5	1	1	10	1	17	.233	.347	.333	11
	160	100	24	4	0	3	24	9	3	3	25	1	30	.240	.397	.370	20
	164	5470	1386	247	37	146	695	59	45	53	471	40	843	.253	.315	.392	—
	0	5370	1362	243	37	143	671	50	42	40	446	39	813	.254	.313	.393	—
CLE	116	81	15	2	0	1	15	0	1	0	15	2	14	.185	.309	.247	15
	88	60	15	2	0	0	14	2	0	1	14	0	17	.250	.400	.283	9
	204	141	30	4	0	1	29	2	1	1	29	2	31	.213	.349	.262	24
	204	5527	1465	254	31	116	689	38	48	15	492	26	817	.265	.324	.385	—
	0	5386	1435	250	31	115	660	36	47	14	463	24	786	.266	.324	.388	—
DET	47	27	4	1	0	0	5	0	4	0	13	1	12	.148	.386	.185	2
	67	50	13	2	1	0	8	0	0	0	9	1	12	.260	.373	.340	7
	114	77	17	3	1	0	13	0	4	0	22	2	24	.221	.379	.286	9
	116	5575	1413	254	45	202	703	40	53	27	526	56	926	.253	.318	.424	—
	0	5498	1396	251	44	202	690	40	49	27	504	54	902	.254	.317	.426	—
KC	99	73	15	3	2	0	11	0	1	1	14	2	17	.205	.337	.301	6
	74	53	12	2	0	0	12	0	0	0	14	1	16	.226	.388	.264	7
	173	126	27	5	2	0	23	0	1	1	28	3	33	.214	.359	.286	13
	176	5500	1384	261	49	154	657	44	41	36	473	57	840	.252	.313	.401	—
	0	5374	1357	256	47	154	634	44	40	35	445	54	807	.253	.312	.404	—
MIL	44	33	3	0	0	0	2	1	0	0	3	1	6	.091	.167	.091	7
	53	35	4	0	0	0	4	0	0	0	14	1	12	.114	.367	.114	4
	97	68	7	0	0	0	6	1	0	0	17	2	18	.103	.282	.103	11
	103	5568	1467	250	44	101	636	54	55	19	462	33	746	.263	.319	.379	—
	0	5500	1460	250	44	101	630	53	55	19	445	31	728	.265	.320	.382	—
MIN	56	45	6	0	1	1	5	0	1	0	6	0	17	.113	.231	.244	3
	51	34	10	3	0	3	6	0	0	0	7	0	13	.294	.415	.529	9
	107	79	16	2	1	3	11	0	1	0	13	0	30	.203	.312	.367	12
	112	5509	1453	282	41	141	678	39	47	31	502	36	779	.264	.326	.407	—
	0	5430	1437	280	40	138	667	39	46	31	489	36	912	.265	.326	.407	—
NY	96	58	13	2	0	1	17	0	4	0	22	5	9	.224	.417	.310	8
	105	71	10	0	0	1	9	0	1	0	22	1	20	.141	.340	.183	7
	201	129	23	2	0	2	26	0	5	0	44	6	29	.178	.376	.240	15
	208	5458	1458	272	31	176	793	48	60	50	620	50	771	.267	.344	.425	—
	0	5329	1435	270	31	174	767	48	55	50	576	44	742	.269	.343	.430	—
OAK	75	48	10	3	0	3	9	0	1	0	16	0	10	.208	.400	.375	6
	95	60	16	5	0	1	15	2	1	0	15	0	17	.267	.408	.400	12
	170	108	26	7	0	3	24	2	2	0	31	0	27	.241	.404	.389	18
	175	5581	1475	230	34	155	690	63	47	16	508	29	861	.264	.325	.401	—
	0	5473	1449	223	34	152	666	61	45	16	477	29	834	.265	.323	.401	—
SEA	66	50	9	3	0	2	10	0	0	0	11	3	18	.180	.328	.360	5
	57	39	9	1	0	2	11	1	1	0	7	0	16	.231	.340	.410	6
	123	89	18	4	0	4	21	1	1	0	18	3	34	.202	.333	.382	11
	129	5521	1410	277	38	171	686	28	41	31	564	36	942	.255	.326	.412	—
	0	5432	1392	273	38	167	665	27	40	31	546	33	908	.256	.326	.413	—
TEX	106	71	18	1	1	3	19	2	0	0	18	4	23	.254	.404	.423	10
	98	72	14	6	0	2	12	1	0	0	13	1	29	.194	.318	.361	11
	204	143	32	7	1	5	31	3	0	0	31	5	52	.224	.362	.392	21
	206	5361	1359	213	41	129	578	34	45	33	530	30	819	.253	.322	.381	—
	0	5218	1327	206	40	124	547	31	45	33	499	25	767	.254	.321	.380	—
TOR	112	78	12	7	0	1	15	0	1	1	20	2	29	.154	.330	.282	12
	105	74	16	4	0	0	14	0	2	0	15	1	24	.216	.341	.270	11
	217	152	28	11	0	1	29	0	3	1	35	3	53	.184	.335	.276	23
	221	5508	1482	281	53	158	714	21	44	30	503	44	807	.269	.331	.425	—
	0	5356	1454	270	53	157	685	21	41	29	468	41	754	.271	.331	.430	—
LEAGUE	2119	1442	302	55	5	24	293	21	25	7	362	35	422	.209	.365	.304	210
	2176	77257	20182	3562	528	2178	9737	648	658	419	7465	557	11777	.261	.327	.406	—
	0	75815	19880	3507	523	2154	9444	627	633	412	7103	522	11355	.262	.326	.408	—

Note: The League entry in the table has only three lines, corresponding to the last three lines of a team entry.

deal with an SBA. Since the average NOPS is 100, we can see that while batting during an SBA decreased the batter's effectiveness by 16.4%, it only improved his effectiveness by 0.2% when there was no SBA. This is, of course, because we are dealing with a much greater number of plate appearances in this case.

There is another factor to consider in assessing the value of the stolen base to team offense. That, of course, is the runner. The point of the exercise is, after all, to score

more runs and not to improve team or player batting stats. It could be argued that while the increase in OBA doesn't offset the decrease in the batter's ability to hit for average and power, perhaps the increase in OBA coupled with advancing of the runner to scoring position does offset the disadvantages the batter experiences.

To examine how SBAs affected team run scoring, I used the Stolen Base version of Bill James' Runs Created formula. In the chart below, the first column shows how many runs a team could be expected to score if they had made the number of SBA's they actually did. The second column shows how many runs a team could be expected to score with no SBA's at all. I derived this column by expanding team batting stats without SBA's to reflect the team's actual number of plate appearances. The third column shows the increase or decrease in runs scored that could be expected to occur if the team had indeed made no attempt to steal at all.

Team	Runs Created w/ SBAs	Runs Created wo/ SBAs	Difference in Runs
BAL	795	800	+4.7
BOS	853	848	−4.1
CAL	695	699	+3.7
CHI	668	670	+1.6
CLE	689	699	+9.1
DET	748	754	+5.7
KC	689	689	+0.3
MIL	674	683	+8.4
MIN	724	731	+6.6
NY	801	803	+1.3
OAK	728	728	−0.4
SEA	742	740	−1.9
TEX	650	653	+2.9
TOR	769	784	+15.1
LEAGUE	10,216	10,274	+57.5

From this we can see that teams would score more runs if they didn't try to steal at all; however, the difference isn't terribly significant. Toronto showed the largest improvement, picking up 15 runs without attempting to steal, while Boston, Oakland, and Seattle all did worse without attempting to steal.

Thus, depending on how one approaches the issue, there are certain conclusions which can be drawn.

If we approach it from the point of view of batting statistics, we can conclude that stolen base attempts definitely affect the batter, bettering his chances of reaching base while worsening his chances of hitting for average and, more seriously, of hitting for power.

When we approach the issue from the point of view of team scoring, we find that stolen bases aren't very meaningful one way or the other. A team would probably score more runs if it made no attempts to steal at all but it would probably not score significantly more.

To conclude then, it seems clear that the question of the value of stolen base attempts needs to be studied not by reference to their effects on the batter or on run production, but by their effects on a team's chances of winning. While much can be inferred from the effects of the SBA on batting stats or run production, it is evident that because of the trade-offs involved, such a strategy needs to be studied situationally to adequately assess just how valuable a tool it is (or can be).

By studying the effects of stolen base attempts on batters, I had hoped to reach a conclusion on how valuable the stolen base attempt is. I now find the issue is too complex to allow for a facile conclusion. However, I believe that this study has shown that if the stolen base attempt is to be used where it will be valuable in an offense, the effects on the batter must objectively be taken into account.

THE DEFENSIVE SPECTRUM AND PAUL MOLITOR

By Kent Kirchstein

In 1981, Paul Molitor appeared destined for greatness. In his first three seasons, he had established himself as one of the best second basemen in baseball, and it seemed he could only get better.

Now, six seasons later, Paul Molitor is considered a quality player who hasn't reached the level of greatness that seemed his destiny. Injuries have hampered his career, but that is not the only thing that has kept him from greatness. The thing that has cost him the most was his being moved from second to third base, with a year in the outfield sandwiched in between.

Molitor was moved from a spot where his hitting ability put him among the elite of the position to a place where a greater premium is placed on hitting ability. His stats had made him one of the best-hitting second basemen in the American League, but with the same stats, he has been only above average at third.

Obviously, it is better to be the best second baseman in the league than an above-average third baseman. It is not so obvious why Molitor is a great-hitting second baseman but only an above average hitter at third. To borrow from Bill James, the defensive spectrum holds the answer:

DH—1B—LF—RF—3B—CF—2B—C—SS—P

This version of the defensive spectrum differs from that presented by James in his *Baseball Abstracts*. He doesn't include catchers or pitchers.

As you move to the left along the spectrum, the defensive value of the position declines. With movement to the right, defensive value increases. A designated hitter offers no defensive value, while shortstops and catchers are the most valuable position players. Because a second baseman is more valuable defensively than a third baseman, the replacement standards as a hitter at second are less demanding. A second baseman's defensive abilities can make up for more offensive liabilities than a third baseman's.

It is quite common to hear a third-base prospect criticized because he lacks power, but how many times do you hear that a second-base prospect lacks power? Power is almost required at third base, but it's merely a bonus at second.

For illustration, let's take two players at opposite ends of the defensive spectrum and give them the following stats: .260 batting average, .300 on-base average, .340 slugging average. Roughly half the starting shortstops in the major leagues are at that offensive level. A DH with the same stats would be a weak hitter and would be replaced, while a shortstop would keep his job in most cases.

Of course, the most important defensive player is the pitcher, who has no offensive replacement level. No matter how poorly a pitcher hits, if he can get outs, he will pitch.

In the same way but to a lesser degree, the offensive standards at second base are lower than they are for third basemen. As Molitor moved from second to third, his defensive value declined.

Assuming Molitor was more valuable at second base, why did the Brewers move him?

By the start of the 1981 season, Molitor had established himself as an injury-prone player. The Brewers claimed that a move to the outfield would extend Molly's career. Also, the Brewers had a feisty player named Jim Gantner, and general manager Harry Dalton wanted him in the lineup. It happened that Gantner was an outstanding defensive second baseman.

In any case, Molitor moved to the outfield and had a dreadful season. Dalton wanted Molitor to play center field, which happened to be Gorman Thomas' position. Thomas, one of the better defensive center-fielders in the American League at the time, did not want to move to right and made his feelings known. When Molitor was slow to progress on defense, he was quickly moved to right field. He had a poor year hitting: .267 average with only two home runs. Finally, despite his move to the so-called safety of the outfield, Molitor was injured and missed 40 games of the strike-shortened season. (It would be interesting to do a study on the safety of second base compared to the outfield. I would think outfielders are injured about as often as second basemen.)

The next season, the Brewers abandoned what they had termed the "great experiment" and moved Molitor to third base, where he has remained.

Judging from his stats, he is a fine hitter when healthy, but he just doesn't have the numbers to stand out at third. Yet Molitor does have the defensive ability to play a position that would allow his offensive ability to stand out—second base. He also is capable of playing shortstop, his position in the minor leagues.

Let's compare Molitor to the Tigers' Lou Whitaker, the best second baseman in the American League, and to the Cubs' Ryne Sandberg, the top second basemen in the National League. Let's also match Molitor with the recognized stars at third in both leagues, the Royals' George Brett and the Phillies' Mike Schmidt. Here are the players' statistics through 1986 in seasonal notation (per 162 games played):

Molitor is better than Sandberg in hits, doubles, triples, runs scored, walks, batting average and on-base average. He tops Whitaker in every category except RBIs, walks and on-base average. Molitor is better than both in runs created.

Now, look at how he compares to Brett and Schmidt, his competition at third. Although he has a better batting average than Schmidt, Molitor is lower in most other categories by far. Brett leaves Molitor behind in every category except stolen bases.

Sandberg and Whitaker are considered superstars and Molitor isn't, and part of the reason is that Sandberg and Whitaker play a key defensive position.

FIGURE 1: Molitor vs. the best at third and second (Seasonal notation: per 162 games played)

	Sandberg	Whitaker	Molitor	Brett	Schmidt
Seasons	4.88	7.92	6.25	10.75	13.01
At-Bats	645	594	664	621	561
Hits	185	167	193	195	150
Runs	101	91	108	100	104
Doubles	31	26	32	40	27
Triples	8	6	7	10	4
Homers	15	12	13	20	38
RBIs	71	66	63	98	107
Walks	50	73	58	65	104
Steals	39	12	37	13	13
AVE	.287	.281	.291	.314	.267
SLG	.430	.406	.419	.507	.532
OBA	.336	.360	.348	.379	.382
Runs created	94	87	97	119	114

Note: Runs created is figured in its simplest form, not including stolen bases.

The move of Molitor to third base boiled down to the need for a spot for Jim Gantner. As it turned out, it was a good move for the team, even if it wasn't for Molitor.

Gantner was an outstanding fielder, better than Molitor, and a pretty darn good hitter for a second baseman. With Cecil Cooper at first, Gantner at second, Robin Yount at shortstop and Molitor at third, the Brewers of 1982 had one of the great infields in baseball history. That year, the Brewers hit 220 home runs and won the pennant.

The move did hurt Molitor because his new position didn't fully use his skills. He also remained injury-prone, and having to learn new positions may have hurt his hitting somewhat.

Now it is 1987, and moving Molitor back to second base would help him and the Brewers, no longer the powerhouse they were in 1982. The Brewers hope youth will bring them back into contention. Gantner is 34 years old and his offensive skills have deteriorated: .274 batting average but with a .313 on-base average and .370 slugging average in 1986. Since the Brewers have no young prospects at second base, Molitor is the logical choice, and he's still only 30. Third base then would be open for Dave Sveum, an erratic but promising player, or the Brewers could find a new third baseman, an easier proposition than finding a good hitter at second.

While Molitor may not be as good as Sandberg at second, his talents would be used to the fullest.

HITTING IN DIFFERENT BASE-OUT SITUATIONS

by Brent MacInnes

This study analyzes differences in hitting in different base-out situations. Using data from the Montreal Expos' 1984, 1985 and 1986 seasons as well as the Expos' opposition in 1984, we have 322 games or over 24,000 plate appearances from which to draw. The players in this study batted .250, had an on-base percentage of .314 and a slugging percentage of .371, approximately two per cent below average across the board. The teams scored 3.80 runs per game, slightly below average for Olympic Stadium. All of these figures should have a negligible effect on the results.

TABLE 1.

Out	Runners 1	2	3	#		AVG	OBP	SLG
0	0	0	0	a	1.	.265	.320	.403
1	0	0	0	b	2.	.231	.285	.334
2	0	0	0	c	3.	.240	.304	.372
0	1	0	0	d	4.	.284	.328	.386
1	1	0	0	e	5.	.272	.311	.385
2	1	0	0	f	6.	.270	.325	.408
0	0	1	0	g	7.	.269	.339	.378
1	0	1	0	h	8.	.253	.364	.378
2	0	1	0	i	9.	.196	.344	.303
0	0	0	1	j	10.	.337	.408	.467
1	0	0	1	k	11.	.268	.409	.415
2	0	0	1	l	12.	.257	.384	.388
0	1	1	0	m	13.	.233	.277	.291
1	1	1	0	n	14.	.229	.282	.341
2	1	1	0	o	15.	.181	.241	.271
0	1	0	1	p	16.	.250	.303	.404
1	1	0	1	q	17.	.333	.401	.422
2	1	0	1	r	18.	.230	.295	.317
0	0	1	1	s	19.	.400	.518	.667
1	0	1	1	t	20.	.321	.516	.482
2	0	1	1	u	21.	.283	.483	.427
0	1	1	1	v	22.	.254	.288	.444
1	1	1	1	w	23.	.277	.317	.348
2	1	1	1	x	24.	.232	.276	.374
	0	0	0		1–3.	.248	.303	.373
	1	0	0		4–6.	.275	.320	.393
	0	1	0		7–9.	.233	.350	.346
	0	0	1		10–12.	.272	.395	.407
	1	1	0		13–15.	.205	.262	.299
	1	0	1		16–18.	.267	.331	.365
	0	1	1		19–21.	.314	.498	.482
	1	1	1		22–24.	.252	.292	.375
Total					1–24.	.250	.314	.371
Scoring Position					7–24.	.240	.337	.353
Above w/two outs					25.	.213	.323	.332

In Table 1, there are 24 base-out situations (3 out situations times 8 base-runner possibilities). The situations are numbered (1–24) to correspond to the letters (a-x) in a commonly used notation. The grouped situations such as 7–9. indicate hitting in a particular situation (in this case, with men on second base only) under all out situations. Situation #25 indicates hitting with two out and men in scoring position. "AVG", "OBP" and "SLG" are batting average, on-base percentage and slugging percentage, respectively with on-base percentage including HP's. Other statistics associated with these states will be introduced as necessary.

One potential problem with a study such as this is to make sure that the plate appearances are uniformly distributed throughout the batting order. For example, if the majority of bases-loaded situations took place with the clean-up hitter at the plate, the performance in this situation would look unusually good. However, this was not the case, as the sample was quite large and randomly distributed, thereby yielding unbiased results.

We begin by examining the lead-off hitter's situation, that with no one on and nobody out. In this situation, both batting average and slugging percentage are up about 8 percent, while on-base percentage is up only about 2 percent. The logical explanation for this is that pitchers try to avoid lead-off walks. In the process, they must sacrifice some power to the batter, as isolated power jumps 15 percent to .138. One and two outs later, batting average, on-base percentage and slugging percentage all drop off significantly, to below average levels. What does remain consistent is the low walk ratio, the lowest of any situations except for hitting with the bases loaded. Isolated power remains slightly above average, indicating that there may well be trade-off between a batter's power and a pitcher's control.

With men on first base only, batting average jumps by 10 per cent. This may be caused by the hole on the right side of the infield. However, the sacrifice also helps to increase the average in this situation because it takes at-bats away from those players who are subpar hitters, primarily pitchers. Sacrifices comprise 10.8 percent of plate appearances with no outs and 2.7 percent one out later. Not coincidentally, batting average is significantly higher (4 percent) with 0 out. Once again, bases on balls fall below normal levels, as they do in any situation where they advance the lead runner. The other mitigating factor in increasing batting average is the double play opportunity. In order to keep the double play in order, the infield must play in closer, thereby allowing more balls to go through. Overall, on-base percentage is up, as the decrease in walks is more than offset by the increase in batting average and the improvement in slugging percentage is strictly a function of a better batting average, as isolated power remains constant.

With men on second base only, the most significant occurrence is the closing of the gap between slugging percentage and on-base percentage. With less than two out, batting average and slugging percentage are slightly above average. However, walks increase from a fairly normal 9.2

percent (actual norm is 8.3 perent) to 14.8 percent to 18.4 percent, predominantly due to the intentional walk (4.5 and 8.1 percent, with one and two outs, respectively). With two out, there were only 161 hits in 1007 plate appearances, but batters were walked 185 times. The normal ratio of hits to walks is 2.7 to 1.0. In situation #9, it is 0.87 to 1.0. The .196 batting average indicates one thing: pitchers only pitch to the batter that they want to in this situation. Situation #9 actually makes on-base percentage higher than slugging percentage in situations #7–9, causing a .062 change.

With no one out and a man on third base, an eye opening .337 batting average was recorded. The primary factor in this increase is the sacrifice fly which occurred at a rate of 17.8 percent. The other factor one must remember is that the infield often plays in. Also, no intentional walks were issued in 125 plate appearances, presumably because setting up and subsequently turning the double play will not stop the runner on third from scoring. One out later, the situation is more in the pitcher's favor. On-base percentage remains as high as for situation #10, but batting average drops. Sacrifice fly rates drop because they attain a greater significance, and rate of significance and success are inversely proportional. It is easy to sacrifice in the early innings as compared to situations where the game is on the line. With two outs, batting average drops to an almost normal level and walks remain high. Overall, these are excellent situations for hitters, as average is up about 9 percent and both on-base percentage and slugging percentage hover around .400.

Hitting with men on first and second base is the poorest of all situations to hit in. The principle reason for this is the ease with which an out is obtained. Force plays are available at three different bases and the sacrifice is difficult to execute as evidenced by rates of 7.5 and 1.4 per cent with none and one out, respectively. As in other situations where they advance runners, bases on balls are low. Isolated power is down, probably because it is much more difficult to double or triple when you have two baserunners directly in front of you. The .181 batting average, .241 on-base percentage and .271 slugging percentage recorded with two out are the worst results of any base-out situation. In 1,613 plate appearances with men on first and second, the batting average was only .205. Also, double play rates are slightly higher than with men on first base (#4–6), at 9.7 and 12.5 percent with none and one out, respectively. Strategies to avoid the double play, such as the hit and run, probably contribute to the low batting average.

With men on first and third, the advantage once again shifts back to the batter. This situation brought the only inconsistent data in the study as the batting average with one out (.333) was much higher than with no one out (.250). As sacrifice fly rates were higher with no one out (15.75%) than with one out (11.7%), the only logical explanation for the results is that the data sample for situation #16 is too small (140 plate appearances). With men on first and third, double play rates are only 5.8 and 8.8 per cent with none and one out, respectively—the lowest rates of all the double play situations. This is mainly due to attempts to throw out runners at the plate, rather than trying for the double play. Overall, batting average and on-base percentage are up moderately, with slugging percentage about normal.

Hitting with men on second and third is the ideal situation, as the highest batting average (.314), slugging percentage (.482), and on-base percentage (.498) were recorded, as well as the best isolated power (.168). Intentional walks run at the rate of 18.5 per cent when there is one out or more, also the highest ratio. In fact, in 464 plate appearances, there were 115 walks and only 97 hits. Besides the sacrifice fly (rates of 10.9 and 10.6%) and playing the infield in, the pitcher is at an absolute disadvantage in this situation. If he tries to eliminate the one run strategies by cutting off the sacrifice fly or by playing the infield in, he is in grave danger of giving up two runs, but the infield defense must play in close enough to hold the baserunners close. As for the high isolated power figure, that is a function, once again, of the offense getting what it is not looking for, presuming that most hitters are looking for a two-run single in this situation.

Finally, hitting with the bases loaded brings results consistent with the factors on both the batter's and pitcher's sides. The batter has the advantage of knowing that he will not be walked (the 5% walk ratio is easily the lowest in any situation) and the sacrifice fly opportunity (rates of 10.8 and 15.0%). The pitcher is throwing in his best double-play situation (rates of 17.6 and 16.1%) and has a force out available at any base. The results are fairly predictable; a normal batting average, a low on-base percentage, and a normal slugging percentage. Once again, the batter trades his bases on balls for increased isolated power.

When hitting with men in scoring position, players batted only .240, had on-base percentages of .337 and slugging percentages of .353. Overall, this is somewhat surprising. Because of such advantages as the sacrifice fly and the altered defense, one would expect to see a higher batting average than the "norm," lying above the batting average with men on first base. Had this happened in one case, it would not be surprising but it happened over the course of four cases (6520 plate appearances). What is not surprising is that on-base percentage is higher here than other situations. Because walks have a much smaller chance of scoring when they are issued with runners already on base, it is easiest to garner a base on balls when men are in scoring position.

Situation #25 is probably the most surprising. In 2990 plate appearances, batters hit only .213 with men in scoring position and two out. Further calculations show that overall batting averages declined—from .268 to .247 to .236—when there were 0, 1 and 2 outs, respectively. Trying to find an explanation for this is difficult. If these findings are fact, do they not imply that a player's batting statistics are distorted by the out situation in which he bats? Over the course of a season, some batters pile up significantly different totals in these categories. To what extent a batter's statistics are shaped by the situation in which he bats is a question as yet unanswered.

The results of this study bring to mind an interesting anecdote from the 1984 World Series. Remember Dick Williams asking Steve Garvey to bunt with men on first and second and no one out? In effect, what he was doing was moving from a situation where the batting average is .223 to one where it is .321. Is there anything that Dick Williams does not know?

THE PROMISE OF '84 — THE REALITY OF '86

by Bill Jensen

For 24 years, the success or failure of the Minnesota Twins rested squarely on the shoulders of Calvin Griffith. It was Calvin who created the pennant contenders of the 60s, the formless teams of the 70s and the promising team of the early 80s. Calvin was neither a fan's owner, a player's owner nor an owner's owner. He was, despite his battles with his son Clark (modern management was the issue), an owner with the Griffith family as his primary consideration. While the "great man" theory may be a corrupt concept of history, it has a lot to offer as a definition of front office management. Players are not born into an organization, nor do they arrive unannounced. They have to be located, drafted, signed, developed, promoted, traded, and released based on the opinions of many but in accordance with the views of the person in charge. Calvin believed this. But simple as it seems, the current Twins management has been unable to make the connection.

The Griffith era ended during the summer of 1984 with the sale of the club to Minneapolis banker Carl Pohlad. In perhaps his finest display of horse trading, Calvin kept in waiting a number of buyers who were anxious to purchase a first place team with promising talent. Pohlad, with considerable financial resources and business acumen, appeared poised to provide the finishing touches necessary to create a pennant winner. It wasn't to be. Following a .500 season in 1984, the Twins slumped to 71 wins last year despite scoring 68 more runs in '86 than in '84. Obvious gaps in the roster have not been filled because of the unsettled condition of the front office.

There are various types of successful baseball organizations, from owner-dominant to general manager-dominant to manager-dominant. Each has a plan. To date, the Twins seem to have unsuccessfully experimented with a variation of the old Cubs College of Coaches.

Attempting to determine who has the final say on trades can lead the observer into a Byzantine bureau of shifting responsibilities.

One of Pohlad's first moves was to elevate Howard Fox, a V.P. under Griffith, to the position of president. Fox had been most famous in Minnesota for a fight with Billy Martin during Martin's coaching stint with the Twins. This said something about Fox's character, but his failings in baseball judgment were immediately obvious. He was joined in 1985 by Andy MacPhail (son of Lee and grandson of Larry), who took over player development. By the summer of '86, Fox and MacPhail were essentially carrying out the same functions.

Meanwhile, Carl's son, Jim (a man who claimed not to know who Billy Martin is) began to make public statements as to the operation and direction of the team. And finally, in 1987, these gentlemen will be joined by Ralph Houk, who needs no introduction, and Bob Gebhard, former director of the Montreal farm system. The differences between the Pohlad front office and the owner-dominant Griffith organization could not be more pronounced. While none of the following difficulties are particularly unusual, they have, in combination, led to decisions stagnating the development of a promising team.

Outside Business Interests

With Calvin it was baseball, baseball and more baseball. Pohlad is here, there and everywhere. So what? That interests outside of baseball have an impact on the operation of a major league franchise is not new to baseball; a few more hit plays for Harry Frazee, and Fenway Park might well have become the house that Ruth re-built. In the case of the Twins, one example will serve to show the undermining of the formation of long-term front office goals. Soon after purchasing the club, Pohlad began scheming with Minneapolis businessman and noted "corporate raider" Irwin Jacobs for control of the Minnesota Vikings. The attempt to take over the football franchise has generated an extended legal battle with the sale of the team likely if Pohlad and Jacobs win. An indifferent attitude toward the operation of the Twins has been the result.

Player Development

In 1984 Pohlad said that the Twins farm system was devoid of talent partly because Calvin had failed to sign the club's high draft choices. He was referring to Bill Swift, Tim Belcher, and Oddibe McDowell, all of whom who were drafted in 1983. You can decide how serious their loss was. The important point is that last December, Pohlad repeated the same sad song and added that help from the farm was not expected soon. What had happened? After Fox eased Griffith's longtime farm director George Brophy out of his job, the front office simply failed to find the talent. Compare Calvin's efforts—Puckett, in the minors, 1982, in the majors, 1984; Hrbek, minors, 1979, majors, 1981; Gaetti, minors, 1979, majors, 1981; Viola, minors, 1981, majors, 1982 —to the current lack of prospects in the present system. Two years of development have been lost, and the claim that Calvin left a bare cupboard has grown stale.

Trades and Acquisitions

A side effect of the inability to recognize talent was the need to rely on outside opinions. Trades have produced two regular players. They are Bert Blyleven, a product of the Griffith organization, and Roy Smalley, who has spent most of his major league career with the Twins. Can Butch Wynegar be far behind? These are players that Fox had at least seen play and were undoubtedly his response to complaints that the '84 pennant race was lost because of a lack of veterans to stablize a young team.

Often the problems have been correctly identified, but the solutions simplistic. Needing a shortstop, a DH, a left-hand bat, and a veteran player, Fox acquired Smalley to do them all.

Needing better starting and relief pitching, Fox fired Billy Gardner, that mad developer of young talent, and hired Oriole pitching coach Ray Miller, who was highly recommended, we were constantly reminded, by Baltimore G.M. Hank Peters. But it turned out that Smalley was unsuccessful in his unique role as shortstop-DH, and Miller had less success with the pitching than Gardner.

A flurry of activity during 1986 by Fox and MacPhail shipped off Ken Schrom, Dave Engle, and Tim Teufel in exchange for Chris Pittaro (you knew someone would believe Sparky), Alex Sanchez, Roy Smith, Billy Beane and others. Nevertheless, there are still openings on the Twins roster.

Beginning with the Steve Howe debacle in '85, Fox and MacPhail turned the bullpen into a halfway house for relief pitchers, as if saying, "Here Ray, see what you can do with these guys." Such notables as Roy Lee Jackson, Frank Pastore, Keith Atherton, Juan Agosto, George Frazier, and Ray Fontenot stepped into the breach and did pretty much what had made them expendable elsewhere. All were veterans. Again the front office liked to have outside confirmation that these were "major leaguers."

By the end of the summer, the Pohlads, alarmed by mediocre management, declining attendance, and unspirited effort, stepped into the picture; they fired Miller (after three months of rumors), kicked Fox upstairs, cleaned house and charted a new and dynamic course. Not quite.

A New Beginning: Almost

The dismissal of Miller set in motion the expected front office reorganization. This admission of failed policies was followed, predictably, by an almost comical period of indecision. A search for a new manager consisted of waiting two months for Jim Frey to turn down the job and for Tom Kelly, the former third base coach and interim manager, to be offered the position and to accept it. Similarly, even though it was obvious that MacPhail had taken over Fox's baseball responsibilities, Pohlad seemed to be reluctant to give him full control without balancing MacPhail's youth (33) with an experienced baseball man; thus the pursuit of Jim Frey and the subsequent hiring of Ralph Houk.

Houk was hired to tell the Twins front office about the Twins' players.

He will do this from Florida on a part time basis. Houk's hiring only makes sense either as a sop to Pohlad or as an admission by MacPhail of his own lack of knowledge about ball players. That the second reason seems to be the case is indicated by MacPhail's almost spur of the moment hiring of Bob Gebhard to be in charge of major league personnel. Fox remains as president with reduced responsibilities. A safe assumption is that after spring training, he and Houk will spend most of their time playing golf in the Sunshine state.

On the field, the hiring of Kelly, at 36 the youngest manager in the majors, may pay the most dividends and create the most difficulties of any recent Twins manager. Kelly was a successful minor league manager in the Griffith farm system and is an organization man of the best type.

His loyalty is strong but not unquestioning. There is no doubt that Kelly will run the team on the field by doing what he feels is necessary to win. He demonstrated this during '86 by ignoring front office directives to play "prospects" and fielding the team he felt could win. After the interim tag was removed, Kelly was successful in naming the coaching staff he wanted, a prerogative that had not been extended to Miller. Kelly's public comments lean toward more aggressiveness on the basepaths and keeping the nucleus of the team together. Both ideas seem unlikely given the current players and the need for management to do "something."

Looked at one way, the front office still seems to be the same muddle it was for the previous two years. Pohlad is involved in most decisions while uncertain that baseball is his sport. Houk, Fox, MacPhail, and Gebhard have overlapping responsibilities, and the manager seems not to understand the limitations of his team. Another view would suggest the following scenario: MacPhail establishes the primary goals for the organization; Gebhard makes the personnel decisions needed to fill out the existing roster; Kelly repeats his minor league success.

A Short Reflection on Calvin

Can the new organization learn from the past? Conditions are rarely the same, but it can be stated that Pohlad-Fox-MacPhail have yet to match Calvin's ability to produce players or make trades. The 1984 team, a post free agency exercise in baseball economics, was Calvin's considered response to the free spending of the time. Along with producing players like Gaetti, Hrbek, Puckett, and Viola, he picked Brunansky off the California bench and acquired Mike Smithson and John Butcher (who combined to win 28 games in '84) for Gary Ward, whose future at the time was uncertain following a serious beaning. By comparison, the new regime's trade of Tim Teufel, an established if not spectacular second baseman, seems to have brought nothing in exchange. In '82, needing a reliever, Calvin traded Smalley and Gary Serum to the Yankees and received Greg Gagne, now the Twins regular shortstop, and Ron Davis. Davis was the set up man for Gossage, had a good fastball, and wanted to be a finisher, all good reasons to give him a shot as the bullpen ace. It didn't work out, but two years ago, arguably, it was not as clear that Davis would fail as it is now. The point is that the reasoning was correct and certainly a much better process than grabbing a bunch of discards and hoping for success.

Interestingly, Calvin faced a similar building job in the early 60s, following the Senators' move to Minnesota.

In RF was Bobby Allison (26 years old), an almost exact match with Tom Brunansky after three years in the majors. At first base there was Harmon Killebrew (25), who had 307 rbi after three years, compared with Kent Hrbek (24), 290 rbi. Third base had some power with Rich Rollins (23 homers) and Gaetti (25). Outfield weaknesses would be alleviated by the arrival of Jimmie Hall in '62; that could be matched with Puckett's arrival in '84. Second base was manned by players who were to be traded and gain fame for alleged altercations—Billy Martin and Tim Teufel. Both pitching staffs had promising lefthanders who were virtually the same size and posted near identical records in their first good years—Jim Kaat and Frank Viola. It was no secret that the '84 team did not have an Earl Battey behind the plate or a Zoilo Versalles at short, but the direction was there. What did Calvin do to produce a World Series team by 1965? He filled in the gaps without ripping the team apart. Turning to the Indians for pitching, he received Jim Perry and Mudcat Grant for nothing. Turning to the farm system, he produced Tony Oliva. Calvin knew what he had, knew what he needed, and produced a team that contended until the dawn of free agency. Whether he could have done it again is a matter of speculation, but it is a matter of record as to where he was heading and that the current ownership has not acquitted itself well with his legacy.

WHY TEAMS WIN AND LOSE: PLAYER PAR-RUN PERFORMANCE IN 1985 & 1986

By Dick Cramer

INTRODUCTION

1986 was a season of exciting performances, and though lacking great pennant races, had the most exciting rounds of post-season play in recent memory. But there was something else special about 1986, something that has escaped all media attention. Under the earth, a giant rolled over in his sleep, and the landscape just isn't the same. In 1986, team fortunes rolled over, in a fashion possibly never seen before. The average difference in wins between the '85 and '86 seasons was +/−11 per club. That is one of the largest—if not the largest—such differences in baseball history.

It is also likely the least cited factor in accounting why 1986 was the first season ever in which each baseball franchise drew at least one-million fans. That achievement could not have been reached without a lot of winners becoming losers or without the doormats becoming challengers. The big winners in '85 drew well thanks to the season-ticket crowd who spent their bucks in the hope of more of the same in '86. The new crop of winners in '86 packed them in by the excitement of their turnarounds, and the results were splendid crowds throughout a season totally lacking in pennant races.

The uniqueness of the 1986 season not only fascinated the fans en masse, but it gave sabermetricians a special opportunity to examine the reasons why teams improve or decline. In a very simplistic way, it seems reasonable that winning teams are those whose players (on average) have better seasons than those on losing teams. Certainly not all players on winning teams have productive or "career" seasons, but neither are all players on losing teams unproductive. How, then, can one account for a team's change in fortune? This report is an attempt to establish why teams win or lose, and it examines the '85 and '86 major league seasons.

The heart of this report are the team tables which are built upon two basic principles:

1) *Teams win games by scoring more runs than they allow.* A rule-of-thumb is that for every 10 runs you score above that which you allow, a loss will be converted into a win. For example, a team scoring 140 runs more than allowed will convert 14 losses into wins, and would finish with a record something like 95–67, or $2 \times 14 = 28$ games above the .500 mark.

2) *An individual player can always be judged against his peers.* Methods exist for quantifying an individual's contribution to a team in terms of the runs he creates. It is quite meaningful to compare a player's run contribution to the league average. This idea, "better or worse than the league average," or "par-runs" for short, is the concept presented

by Pete Palmer in his book with John Thorn, *The Hidden Game.* Hitters who "create" more runs than average are helping win games, as are pitchers and fielders who allow fewer runs than average. This is very useful in determining how individual players contribute to a teams' overall performance, particularly from one year to the next.

TWO STRATEGIC CONSIDERATIONS

Two strategies appear in the evidence surrounding the more successful teams. One is that *offense matters more than defense.* In the two seasons, 1985 and 1986, individual offensive (hitting) par-runs varied from +78.1 to −40.4, or in a different light, from +8 wins to −4. Defense (pitching), however, varied somewhat less, from +63.4 to −30.4 (+6 wins to −3). Moreover, there were 35 individual batting performances of +35 par-runs but only 10 by pitchers, despite the fact that a pitcher can be involved in more plate appearances than a batter, and thus can actually have more chances to excel or fail.

Another reason for placing offense above defense is that offensive performance (i.e., excellence or weakness) is more consistent than defensive performance. Of the 17 players in 1985 and the 18 in 1986 who were +35 par-runs on offense, slightly more than one-half (18) were repeaters from previous seasons. None of the pitchers were repeaters.

A second strategy is that *concentrated strengths are better than balanced strengths.* That is, for purposes of the future, it is more desirable for a team to have one outstanding par-run player than three or four merely good ones, though total par-runs may be the same in either case. A concentrated strength reduces the risks taken when trying to improve a team.

Making random player changes at a position where you are a bit below average already has about as good a chance of improving the team as hurting it. If the first move is disasterous, there are probably plenty of Triple-A players or overpaid benchwarmers who can bring you back to square one. On the other hand, tinkering at a postion where you are +20 par-runs is unlikely to help and can easily put a contending team into the second division.

It would be even more deadly to tinker with a +45 par-run superstar, and the truth is that baseball teams rarely trade or experiment with such players at the peak of their abilities. At least they don't when given a choice. Unusual financial pressure forced Connie Mack to trade a superstar more than once, and that scenario is occasionally seen today with the added pressure of a star player intent on exercising his free agency rights.

Even if you count the early trades before a star showed his true potential, you will find very few +45 performers not with their original team. Among the 54 who had a + 35 par-run rating in either '85 or '86, I am aware of just 11 who are not with the team which originally signed them: Henderson (A's to Yankees), Sandberg (Phillies to Cubs), Guerrero (Indians to Dodgers), Hayes (Indians to Phillies), Parker (Pirates to Reds), Mike Scott (Mets to Astros), Jack Clark (Giants to Cardinals), Hernandez (Cardinals to Mets), Phelps (Royals to Mariners), Leibrandt (Reds to Royals), and Tudor (Red Sox to Pirates to Cardinals).

The reluctance to move a superstar is indicative of *another argument in favor of concentrated strengths: it's virtually a necessity.* Since the rules allow only nine men at a time, to have a reasonable chance of achieving the +140 par-run performance needed to win 95 games and have a chance at a division title, a team almost has to have at least one +35 or better player. In theory, you could have +15 players at every position, but in practice this never happens. (Well, almost never: the 1906 Pirates won a World Championship the hard way and the 1980–81 Astros were similarly balanced.)

READING THE TABLES

There is a pair of tables for each of the 26 teams—one table for each of 1985 and 1986. The presentation is an attempt to demonstrate how each individual player contributed to the overall team showing. As with any balance sheet, there is a "bottom line": for each team-season, a comparison of the *Calculated* team performance in *Runs Scored, Runs Allowed, Wins* and *Losses,* with the *Actual* figures for those categories.

An entry appears for almost every player who batted or pitched for a team in 1985 or 1986. Non-pitchers are categorized by their most common fielding position in order to give a reasonable picture of overall team strength or weakness by position.

The calculation of *Runs Contributed* is conceptually similar to Bill James' runs created. The formula in use here is a variation on the [OBA × SLG] formula which Pete Palmer and I introduced in a 1973 SABR publication, but either version is remarkably accurate for this type of study. (Earnshaw Cook published the first such formula in the early 1960's.)

From left to right, the batters' tables read:

Column 1, *BFP*: This has the usual meaning of the total number of plate appearances by the batter (Batters Facing Pitcher).

Column 2, */Game*: Runs Contributed Per-Game (RPG), in a form which is directly comparable to a pitcher's ERA. It is the number of runs this player would contribute in a typical game with 4 plate appearances. One could add the RPG's for a given lineup to estimate the "run average" (unearned + earned run average) that an opposing pitcher would have. With the DH, the average RPG for the American League is usually near to .500, the average in the NL at about .450. A +35 par-run player would need a full-season RPG of about .700.

Column 3, *Total*: Runs Contributed, computed as the difference in the number of runs the overall league would have scored if this player's batting totals had first

been subtracted from the league totals, the runs being estimated by the formula:

$$R = [(H+BB+HBP) + (0.5\times SB) - CS - (1.5\times GDP)] \times SLG$$

As you would expect intuitively, a player who has contributed 100 runs has had a productive year at the plate, and 75 runs is about average. At the other end of the scale, note that National League "Others"—mostly pitchers—actually contribute negative runs, a consequence of the fact that their rare hits are overbalanced by the plate appearances which their excessive outs take away from their teammates.

Column 4, *vs. LgAv*: Par-runs Versus the League Average is, of course, the most important figure presented. To compute a player's par-runs, I've subtracted from his actual runs contributed the number of runs an average league batter would contribute while using up the same number of outs, computed as:

$$\text{Runs vs. LgAv} = [(AB-H)_{\text{player}}] \times [\text{Runs}/(AB-H)_{\text{league}}]$$

The *Calculated Runs Scored* for a team (listed at the bottom of each table) is given by:

$$\text{Runs}_{\text{team}} = [\text{SUM(LgAv)}] + [(\text{Runs/Innings})_{\text{league}} \times \text{Innings}_{\text{team}}]$$

Column 5, *Unearned Runs vs. LgAv*: This is the fielding column, which expresses only the par-run effect of "par-errors", an infield error somewhat arbitrarily being assigned a scoring effect of 0.5 runs, an outfield or pitcher error 0.3 runs, and a catching error 0.2 runs. These are expressed only as team totals at each postion. (As you can see, differences in errors have little effect on overall team performance; even the Dodgers' antics are costing them only two games in a season).

Regrettably, I had to pass on trying to measure the more important elements of fielding such as "range" and double-play ability. There are many complex problems in measuring these factors, and rather than take the chance of obscuring the central points to be made by these tables, I chose to stay as much as possible with measures enjoying a wider acceptance and understanding.

The pitchers' tables read as follows:

Column 1, *IP.f*: Obviously, Innings Pitched.

Column 2, *Earned Runs vs. LgAv*: The number of earned runs the pitcher yielded compared with the number an average pitcher would have yielded in the same number of innings, given by:

$$\text{ER vs. LgAv} = [(ER/IP)_{\text{league}} * IP_{\text{pitcher}}] - ER_{\text{pitcher}}$$

Column 3, *Expected W-L*: The expected Won-Lost record for this level of pitching skill, taking into account the caliber of the team behind it.

There are obviously other factors which can be brought into play to more accurately view individual player performance such as park effects, or exercising greater control over fielding effectiveness when measuring pitcher performance. As stated earlier, these more complex adjustments have been avoided, lest they obscure the more fundamental and important relationships which are the real focus of this report.

—Dick Cramer

Editors' note: Due to roundoff error, the player data presented in the team tables will not normally total to the value indicated at the bottom of a given column. The roundoff occurs naturally in some instances; a fractional Win or Loss by a pitcher, for example, makes little sense.

—Mark Podrazik & Craig Wright

1985 Baltimore Orioles

| | BATTING Records | BFP | Runs Contributed | | | Unearned Runs | PITCHERS | IP.f | Earned Runs | Expected |
			/Game	Total	vs. Lg Av	vs. Lg Av			vs. Lg Av	W-L
1b	E.MURRAY	677	0.817	123	48.9	-4.0	D.AASE	88.0	3.5	6– 4
							E.BELL	5.2	-0.4	0– 0
2b	A.WIGGINS	335	0.505	41	2.7	-6.0	M.BODDICKER	203.1	1.6	13–10
	R.DAUER	234	0.190	10	-19.9		S.DAVIS	175.0	-7.4	10–10
	L.SAKATA	105	0.296	8	-5.5		K.DIXON	162.0	8.6	11– 7
							M.FLANAGAN	86.0	-9.4	4– 5
3b	F.RAYFORD	372	0.600	56	11.5	1.8	J.HABYAN	2.2	1.2	0– 0
	W.GROSS	264	0.633	39	8.7		B.HAVENS	14.1	-7.4	0– 1
	F.CONNALLY	135	0.481	16	0.4		P.HUFFMAN	4.2	-5.9	0– 1
	T.O'MALLEY	14	-0.213	-1	-3.1		D.MARTINEZ	180.0	-20.1	9–11
							T.MARTINEZ	70.0	-9.8	3– 5
ss	C.RIPKEN	718	0.546	94	11.0	0.9	S.MCGREGOR	204.0	-15.1	11–12
							N.SNELL	100.1	16.2	8– 4
lf	L.LACY	540	0.544	70	7.5	1.2	S.STEWART	129.2	7.7	9– 6
	G.ROENICKE	274	0.586	38	6.4		B.SWAGGERTY	1.2	-0.2	0– 0
							Others	4.0	1.8	0– 0
cf	F.LYNN	508	0.593	72	12.6					
	J.SHELBY	214	0.486	26	-0.0					
rf	M.YOUNG	504	0.666	80	20.7					
	J.DWYER	274	0.527	34	2.6					
c	R.DEMPSEY	420	0.560	56	7.8	0.2				
	A.PARDO	78	-0.005	-1	-12.8					
	J.NOLAN	44	0.083	1	-5.3					
dh	L.SHEETS	360	0.463	41	-2.2	0.2				
	D.FORD	82	0.153	3	-8.5					
	L.HERNANDEZ	22	-0.207	-3	-7.2					
	J.LOWENSTEIN	29	-0.081	-1	-5.5					
	K.PARIS	8	-0.223	-1	-2.5					
	Others	0	-0.223	-0	-0.0	2.6				
	TOTALS	6211		801	68.4	-3.1			-34.9	86– 76

	Runs Scored	Runs Allowed	Won	Lost
CALCULATED	798	767	84	77
ACTUAL	818	764	83	78

Last place was quite a shock for Orioles followers. Not since 1967, the year before Earl Weaver came to Baltimore, have they had a losing record. What happened? Did the Chesapeake Bay dry up, or the South secede again?

Baltimore's 1985 season was also not vintage Orioles. A mediocre veteran pitching staff dragged a strong offensive team down to an uninspiring 83–78 record. Management, it seemed, then decided that the defensive woes were actually problems in the infield (although the pitchers yielded a lot of home runs, and it's asking a lot of a third baseman to flag down those 380-foot drives). They drafted Juan Bonilla and traded their best par-run pitcher of 1985, Sammy Stewart, for a supposed defensive standout, Jackie Gutierrez. They tried them both at second and third base while releasing three above-average but unsung role players: Wayne Gross, Fritz Connally, and Lenn Sakata. More understandably, Rich Dauer was also let go.

The result was a classic example of the nightmare that can result from tinkering with positions where you already have above average performance. Baltimore managed to go from a +20.9 offense plus defense par-run performance at third base in '85 to a −42.2 performance in '86, and at second base from a weak −29.7 to a shocking −48.5, the second worst production by any major league team at any regular position in either 1985 or 1986. The overall swing of 80 par-runs or 8 wins was almost single-handedly responsible for the Orioles' drop of nine in Calculated wins (from 83 to 74), while the modest improvement in pitching par-runs appeared more a result of new blood than improved support for veterans.

Can Baltimore return to contention? Well, as I remarked in the introduction, it's a lot easier to add 20 par-runs in performance to positions that are −20 than those that are +20. Baltimore still has a big man, Eddie Murray, and near big-men in Ripken, Lynn, and Young. The pitching is mediocre but the young arms contributed. If the crippling holes at second base, third base, and catcher can be brought back to average, the Orioles could win 90 games. (As far as I know at the moment, Wayne Gross and Fritz Connally are free agents!) At this writing, the Storm Davis-for-Kennedy move is being criticized, but I would almost always trade a potentially quality pitcher for a potentially quality everyday player. Unfortunately for the Orioles, 90 wins is not likely to win the title in a division with the Yankees, Tigers, and Red Sox.

1986 Baltimore Orioles

| | BATTING Records | BFP | Runs Contributed | | | Unearned Runs | PITCHERS | IP.f | Earned Runs | Expected |
			/Game	Total	vs. Lg Av	vs. Lg Av			vs. Lg Av	W-L
1b	E.MURRAY	578	0.719	93	29.4	-2.7	D.AASE	81.2	10.9	5– 4
	J.TRABER	240	0.542	32	3.2		T.ARNOLD	25.1	1.8	2– 1
							E.BELL	23.1	-2.2	1– 2
2b	J.BONILLA	316	0.289	20	-19.1	1.4	M.BODDICKER	218.1	-12.7	10–14
	A.WIGGINS	270	0.351	24	-8.8		R.BORDI	107.0	-3.4	5– 7
	J.GUTIERREZ	152	0.075	1	-20.4		S.DAVIS	154.0	9.4	9– 8
	R.HUDLER	1	-0.223	0	-0.1		K.DIXON	202.1	-9.1	10–13
	R.JONES	40	0.326	3	-1.5		M.FLANAGAN	172.0	-1.2	9–10
3b	F.RAYFORD	228	0.172	10	-21.7	-11.2	J.HABYAN	26.1	-0.8	1– 2
	T.O'MALLEY	200	0.365	18	-7.2		B.HAVENS	71.0	-3.1	4– 4
	K.PARIS	10	-0.119	-1	-2.4		O.JONES	49.1	1.9	3– 3
	T.DODD	16	0.566	2	0.2		M.KINNUNEN	7.0	-1.8	0– 1
							D.MARTINEZ	6.2	-1.9	0– 1
ss	C.RIPKEN	707	0.612	102	19.1	9.2	T.MARTINEZ	16.0	-2.6	1– 1
							S.MCGREGOR	203.0	-7.8	10–13
lf	L.LACY	537	0.475	61	-3.4	-0.6	N.SNELL	72.1	2.6	4– 4
	L.SHEETS	364	0.500	47	1.3		B.SWAGGERTY	1.0	-1.5	0– 0
	K.GERHART	75	0.253	5	-5.0		Others	3.0	2.4	0– 0
cf	J.SHELBY	428	0.347	40	-17.8					
	J.BENIQUEZ	394	0.555	50	6.0					
rf	F.LYNN	456	0.647	68	16.3					
	M.YOUNG	426	0.464	47	-3.8					
	J.DWYER	188	0.620	28	5.7					
c	R.DEMPSEY	382	0.440	41	-6.3	-0.3				
	J.STEFERO	137	0.372	13	-4.3					
	A.PARDO	51	-0.057	-2	-9.7					
	C.NICHOLS	6	-0.103	-0	-1.2					
	Others	0	-0.103	-0	-0.4	0.0				
	TOTALS	6202		701	-51.9	-4.0			-19.1	75– 87

	Runs Scored	Runs Allowed	Won	Lost
CALCULATED	691	766	74	88
ACTUAL	708	760	73	89

1985 Boston Red Sox

	BATTING Records	BFP	Runs Contributed			Unearned Runs vs. Lg Av	PITCHERS	IP.f	Earned Runs vs. Lg Av	Expected W-L
			/Game	Total	vs. Lg Av					
1b	B.BUCKNER	718	0.544	96	10.9	0.2	O.BOYD	272.1	13.4	18–13
							M.BROWN	3.1	-6.5	0– 1
2b	M.BARRETT	608	0.414	61	-9.7	3.1	M.CLEAR	55.2	2.6	4– 3
	D.STAPLETON	71	0.283	5	-4.0		R.CLEMENS	98.1	9.3	7– 4
							S.CRAWFORD	91.0	3.9	6– 4
3b	W.BOGGS	758	0.882	141	66.7	2.5	J.DORSEY	5.1	-9.5	1– 1
	E.JURAK	14	0.147	0	-1.5		B.HURST	229.1	-9.4	13–13
							B.KISON	92.0	0.4	6– 5
ss	J.GUTIERREZ	297	0.177	13	-25.8	-4.0	T.MCCARTHY	5.0	-3.7	0– 1
	G.HOFFMAN	321	0.520	40	3.9		C.MITCHELL	1.2	-2.2	0– 0
lf	J.RICE	608	0.542	80	10.0	-1.5	A.NIPPER	162.0	1.6	10– 8
							B.OJEDA	157.2	2.6	10– 8
cf	S.LYONS	409	0.446	45	-4.2		B.SELLERS	22.1	1.3	1– 1
	T.ARMAS	410	0.498	55	3.7		B.STANLEY	87.2	12.4	6– 3
	M.GREENWELL	34	1.230	9	5.1		M.TRUJILLO	84.0	-6.3	4– 5
	R.NICHOLS	37	0.222	2	-2.4		R.WOODWARD	26.2	7.3	2– 1
	R.MILLER	51	0.622	7	1.9		Others	72.0	-0.8	4– 4
rf	D.EVANS	744	0.680	115	32.6					
	K.ROMINE	31	0.161	1	-2.6					
c	R.GEDMAN	556	0.673	87	23.8	-0.8				
	M.SULLIVAN	77	0.216	5	-5.6					
	D.SAX	43	0.481	5	0.6					
dh	M.EASLER	631	0.485	75	-0.7	-0.8				
	Others	0	0.485	-0	-0.0	-4.9				
	TOTALS	6418		842	102.5	-6.2			16.2	89– 73

	Runs Scored	Runs Allowed	Won	Lost
CALCULATED	849	737	92	70
ACTUAL	800	720	81	81

Most observers still think the 1986 Red Sox were some kind of fluke. I disagree. While nothing is guaranteed in the AL East, the Red Sox have had two good years in a row and have as good a shot at the division title in 1987 as almost anyone.

Two good years? Well, look at the Red Sox's performances in 1985, good for 92 Calculated wins. So how did they manage just 81 Actual wins? Well, some years you just don't get the breaks. Lots of your hits come when the score is 7–1, or when there are two out and no one on base, and have no effect on whether you win or lose.

"Ah," you may say, "that's clutch performance if you get the hits when they count." I say it's mostly luck. In 1984, the *Elias Baseball Analyst* looked at ten years of data and decided there was unmistakable evidence that clutch hitters exist (and chewing on me a bit in the process). Not many of the statisticians I know were very impressed by Elias' arguments, and, if with ten years' worth of data your argument is at best equivocal, I don't think you have much of a case. For sure, if you're management, you'd better not base roster or lineup changes on that calculation of "clutch"

ability!

Thus, quite correctly, management didn't have to do much going into the start of the 1986 season, except cross their fingers about the pitching. The trades they did make neither helped nor hurt much. (Though Baylor and Easler have very different hitting styles—despite what you may have read to the contrary—their par-run performances were equivalent in both 1985 and 1986.) But the in-season moves were effective in that management recognized and found answers to the problems of injuries and ineffectiveness of Armas, Hoffman, Hurst, and Nipper. Best of all, the luck factor (or whatever it was) followed Baylor to Boston, and in 1986, with about the same overall par-run run performance as 1985, instead of winning eleven fewer games than Calculated the Red Sox won five more.

At the start of the new year, the Red Sox are in as fine a shape as anyone in the AL East except possibly the Yankees and Tigers. They have four big players in Boggs, Rice, Evans, and Clemens. Shoring par-run weaknesses at shortstop (−43), first base (−15), secondary catching (−10) and pitching would give this team a chance at 100 wins.

1986 Boston Red Sox

	BATTING Records	BFP	Runs Contributed			Unearned Runs vs. Lg Av	PITCHERS	IP.f	Earned Runs vs. Lg Av	Expected W-L
			/Game	Total	vs. Lg Av					
1b	B.BUCKNER	681	0.430	74	-11.1	-0.6	O.BOYD	214.1	9.4	14–10
	D.STAPLETON	42	-0.018	-1	-7.3		M.BROWN	57.1	-7.4	3– 4
	P.DODSON	15	1.939	5	3.7		R.CLEMENS	254.0	47.8	20– 9
							S.CRAWFORD	57.1	1.6	4– 3
2b	M.BARRETT	713	0.526	87	4.6	1.4	W.GARDNER	1.0	-0.5	0– 0
							B.HURST	174.1	22.9	13– 7
3b	W.BOGGS	693	0.926	134	65.4	2.1	T.LOLLAR	43.0	-13.1	1– 4
							A.NIPPER	159.0	-21.2	7–11
ss	E.ROMERO	263	0.248	16	-18.0	-4.1	J.SAMBITO	44.2	-3.3	2– 3
	R.QUINONES	215	0.363	19	-8.0		C.SCHIRALDI	51.0	15.7	5– 1
	S.OWEN	147	0.233	9	-10.3		T.SEAVER	104.1	4.4	7– 5
	G.HOFFMAN	26	0.228	1	-1.9		J.SELLERS	82.0	-7.0	4– 5
							B.STANLEY	82.1	-1.8	5– 5
lf	J.RICE	693	0.723	113	36.6	1.2	S.STEWART	63.2	-1.5	4– 4
							M.TRUJILLO	5.2	-3.4	0– 1
cf	T.ARMAS	453	0.419	48	-9.6		R.WOODWARD	35.2	-4.5	2– 2
	K.ROMINE	39	0.385	4	-1.2		Others	4.0	1.9	0– 0
	D.HENDERSON	54	0.200	3	-4.6					
	S.TARVER	26	-0.057	-1	-5.2					
rf	D.EVANS	640	0.711	103	30.5					
	S.LYONS	139	0.385	13	-4.1					
c	R.GEDMAN	509	0.464	59	-4.2	0.7				
	M.SULLIVAN	134	0.214	7	-10.6					
	D.SAX	11	1.592	4	2.4					
dh	D.BAYLOR	687	0.573	94	11.6	0.7				
	M.GREENWELL	40	0.604	5	1.1					
	M.STENHOUSE	34	0.299	3	-0.2					
	Others	1	0.299	1	0.6	-4.0				
	TOTALS	6255		797	60.2	-2.4			40.1	90– 72

	Runs Scored	Runs Allowed	Won	Lost
CALCULATED	799	701	90	71
ACTUAL	794	696	95	66

1985 California Angels

	BATTING Records	BFP	Runs Contributed			Unearned Runs vs. Lg Av	PITCHERS	IP.f	Earned Runs vs. Lg Av	Expected W-L
			/Game	Total	vs. Lg Av					
1b	R.CAREW	518	0.509	62	4.5	0.9	S.CLIBURN	99.0	22.6	8- 3
							D.CORBETT	46.0	-3.8	2- 3
2b	B.GRICH	571	0.470	63	-2.0	5.9	U.LUGO	83.0	4.2	5- 4
	R.WILFONG	243	0.192	13	-18.7		T.MACK	2.1	-2.9	0- 0
	P.KEEDY	4	1.637	2	1.5		K.MCCASKILL	189.2	-11.7	9-12
3b	D.DECINCES	488	0.450	55	-3.1	0.4	D.MOORE	103.0	25.4	8- 3
	J.HOWELL	158	0.321	13	-6.3		R.ROMANICK	195.0	0.8	11-11
							L.SANCHEZ	61.1	-10.8	2- 4
ss	D.SCHOFIELD	496	0.322	41	-20.2	-1.9	J.SLATON	148.1	-3.7	8- 9
	C.GERBER	97	0.233	6	-6.6		D.SMITH	5.0	-1.7	0- 0
	G.POLIDOR	1	4.500	1	0.6		M.WITT	250.0	16.1	15-12
lf	B.DOWNING	620	0.618	89	19.6	1.5	G.ZAHN	37.0	-1.0	2- 2
	D.MILLER	50	0.951	11	5.1		Others	239.0	5.1	14-13
cf	G.PETTIS	516	0.492	64	4.7					
	J.BENIQUEZ	460	0.545	58	6.6					
	D.WHITE	9	0.239	1	-0.3					
rf	R.JACKSON	541	0.646	81	19.0					
	R.JONES	456	0.559	61	7.2					
	M.BROWN	164	0.375	15	-5.6					
	G.HENDRICK	46	-0.044	-0	-6.8					
c	B.BOONE	520	0.318	41	-21.1	0.6				
	J.NARRON	143	0.354	13	-5.4					
dh	D.SCONIERS	116	0.635	17	4.3	0.6				
	R.LINARES	46	0.536	7	0.8					
	Others	0	0.536	-0	-0.0	0.6				
	TOTALS	6263		713	-22.1	8.6			38.7	84- 78

	Runs Scored	Runs Allowed	Won	Lost
CALCULATED	723	698	84	78
ACTUAL	732	703	90	72

In both 1985 and 1986, the Angels had a "balanced team"—one without marked strengths or weaknesses. It's not an easy team with which to make moves, and the Angels have been conservative about addressing even what look like serious, correctable, weaknesses.

Take catching as an example. Bob Boone had one of the lowest offensive par-run two-year totals for 1985 and 1986, but it was actually a marked improvement over 1984, when Boone's "contributions" were −50.4 runs. This performance was historic; only three players in major league history ever turned in −50 performances and none of the others were ever again given 400 plate appearances: Bill Bergen, also a good-field, no-hit catcher, with a .139 batting average in 1909, and two shortstops, Jim Levey in 1933, who never played another major league game, and Sam Dente in 1950, who batted leadoff for the Senators and hence had many more plate appearances. I would guess that Boone's 1984 through 1986 batting performance would be an all-time negative record for a three year period.

The conventional wisdom on Bob Boone, of course, is that his defense makes up for this marked batting deficiency. If you gave him full credit for California's control of the running game as well as points for handling pitchers well, his net worth could approach that of the average American League catcher. However, it would be impossible to shape reality in such a way that he can be considered a positive boon.

But California has a lot more to worry about now than the age and bat of Bob Boone. Their onetime big hitters no longer stir drinks and the team leader in par-runs in both '85 and '86 is a marginal star in his mid-30's: Brian Downing. In 1985 weak hitting at catching and the middle infield held team run-scoring below the American League average, and the team was very lucky to win 90 games. In '86, Joyner's debut and Schofield's development pushed California's offense a bit over the break-even point, and Witt paced an excellent starting rotation. However, so many holes seem to be opening up for 1987 that even in a weak division, the absence of big players will make it very hard for California to repeat.

By the way, did you know that Gary Lucas only hit one batter in the entire 1986 season? (Who, of course, was Rich Gedman, in the LCS, with two out, a two-run lead, and no one on base, up 3 games to 1. . .)

1986 California Angels

| | BATTING Records | BFP | Runs Contributed | | | Unearned Runs | PITCHERS | IP.f | Earned Runs | Expected |
			/Game	Total	vs. Lg Av	vs. Lg Av			vs. Lg Av	W-L
1b	W.JOYNER	674	0.619	97	20.0	-0.6	T.BRYDEN	34.1	-9.1	1– 3
							J.CANDELARIA	91.2	16.5	7– 3
2b	R.WILFONG	316	0.253	20	-21.7	1.4	R.CHADWICK	27.1	-9.3	1– 2
	B.GRICH	366	0.541	45	3.2		M.COOK	9.0	-4.8	0– 1
	G.POLIDOR	20	0.182	1	-1.9		D.CORBETT	78.2	4.5	5– 4
							C.FINLEY	46.1	4.5	3– 2
3b	D.DECINCES	572	0.512	72	2.1	6.3	T.FISCHER	17.0	-0.1	1– 1
	J.HOWELL	175	0.679	27	7.2		K.FORSCH	17.0	-10.1	0– 2
							T.FORSTER	41.0	3.0	3– 2
ss	D.SCHOFIELD	529	0.502	64	1.1	4.3	W.FRASER	4.1	-2.0	0– 0
							G.LUCAS	45.2	5.2	3– 2
lf	B.DOWNING	631	0.693	98	28.6	-0.0	U.LUGO	21.1	0.9	1– 1
	D.MILLER	62	0.215	3	-5.1		K.MCCASKILL	246.1	22.3	17–11
	M.RYAL	34	0.934	7	3.3		D.MOORE	72.2	9.7	5– 3
							R.ROMANICK	106.1	-15.7	5– 7
cf	G.PETTIS	628	0.490	74	0.4		V.RUHLE	47.2	0.1	3– 2
	D.WHITE	57	0.524	8	0.5		J.SLATON	73.1	-12.0	3– 5
							D.SUTTON	207.0	10.0	13–10
rf	R.JONES	470	0.563	63	6.8		M.WITT	269.0	39.8	20–10
	G.HENDRICK	317	0.542	42	3.8		Others	6.0	3.8	1– 0
c	B.BOONE	503	0.280	33	-29.8	-0.1				
	J.NARRON	107	0.258	6	-7.3					
dh	R.JACKSON	517	0.601	71	12.8	-0.1				
	R.BURLESON	312	0.539	38	2.8					
	M.MCLEMORE	6	-0.079	-1	-1.3					
	Others	0	-0.079	-0	-0.0	2.0				
	TOTALS	6296		769	25.5	13.4			57.3	91– 71

	Runs Scored	Runs Allowed	Won	Lost
CALCULATED	779	682	91	71
ACTUAL	786	684	92	70

1985 Chicago White Sox

	BATTING Records	BFP	Runs Contributed			Unearned Runs vs. Lg Av	PITCHERS	IP.f	Earned Runs vs. Lg Av	Expected W-L
			/Game	Total	vs. Lg Av					
1b	G.WALKER	650	0.496	82	1.2	3.7	J.AGOSTO	60.1	3.8	4– 3
	J.DESA	48	0.275	4	-2.6		F.BANNISTER	210.2	-17.0	10–13
							B.BURNS	227.0	4.5	13–12
2b	J.CRUZ	270	0.229	15	-18.9	3.1	E.CORREA	10.1	-3.2	0– 1
	B.LITTLE	223	0.443	24	-1.4		R.DOTSON	52.1	-1.9	3– 3
							B.FALLON	16.0	-3.6	1– 1
3b	T.HULETT	436	0.444	48	-4.6	-10.8	S.FIREOVID	7.0	-0.8	0– 0
	S.FLETCHER	348	0.350	29	-11.0		J.GLEATON	29.2	-5.3	1– 2
							B.JAMES	110.0	24.7	9– 4
ss	O.GUILLEN	513	0.372	49	-15.6	10.0	A.JONES	6.0	1.8	1– 0
							B.LONG	14.0	-9.6	0– 2
lf	R.LAW	427	0.466	50	-1.9	2.4	G.NELSON	145.2	-1.9	8– 8
	T.PACIOREK	133	0.268	9	-7.9		T.SEAVER	238.2	25.9	16–11
	M.RYAL	37	0.063	0	-4.8		D.SPILLNER	91.2	7.2	6– 4
							B.TANNER	27.0	-3.6	1– 2
cf	D.BOSTON	248	0.295	19	-13.3		D.WEHRMEISTER	39.1	3.1	2– 2
	L.SALAZAR	353	0.365	35	-9.2		Others	170.0	-9.7	9–10
	R.NICHOLS	136	0.580	18	3.4					
	M.GILBERT	26	0.470	3	-0.1					
	J.CANGELOSI	4	-0.043	0	-0.2					
rf	H.BAINES	693	0.580	96	16.4					
c	C.FISK	620	0.586	89	14.7	-0.6				
	M.HILL	95	0.072	2	-10.1					
	J.SKINNER	50	0.807	9	3.7					
dh	R.KITTLE	417	0.444	49	-3.8	-0.6				
	O.GAMBLE	184	0.470	21	0.2					
	J.HAIRSTON	175	0.519	22	2.6					
	M.SQUIRES	-	-	-	-					
	Others	-	-	-	-	2.1				
	TOTALS	6086		673	-63.3	9.3			14.3	82– 80

	Runs Scored	Runs Allowed	Won	Lost
CALCULATED	678	718	78	85
ACTUAL	736	720	85	77

Too much was expected of the White Sox in 1986. In 1985, Chicago had won 8 games more than Calculated because they scored some 58 more runs than Calculated, in turn because of very high batting averages with runners on (according to the Chicago Baseball Report). However, there were no +35 players or even any +20 batters, and two of the four best par-run performers, Fisk and Seaver, were veterans with a lot of mileage.

In '86, Chicago continued to hit well with runners on, with 44 more runs Actually scored than Calculated. Unfortunately, the opposition learned that you can defense this offensive capability by not permitting many White Sox batters to reach base, and the White Sox had a woeful offensive par-run total, 50 runs lower than any other 1985 or 1986 team.

If you didn't expect much in '86, you might have seen some signs of mild progress. Ron Hassey, no doubt to the surprise of everyone except his mother, hit at the big player rate of .700 or better in both 1985 and 1986, albeit as a platoon player. Ivan Calderon is a hitting talent based on his 1985 performance with Seattle, and Darryl Boston looked better after his recall. With Walker and Baines the White Sox attack could quickly be back to average, provided the gaping offensive holes, in particular the −40's at shortstop and catcher, can be constructively addressed.

A .500 finish in 1987 would then be plausible, which in the AL West is not far from contention. But if I were running the White Sox, I would roll the dice even more vigorously, looking for those +35 players that might be the nucleus of another Chicago champion. For example, one approach might be to see how much of the Brewers' or Mets' young talent could be pried loose by offering Walker or Baines, or an even more sacreligious suggestion: Ozzie Guillen for almost anyone! (Even Brian Giles swings less, hence more effectively, than Guillen did in '86. . . .)

1986 Chicago White Sox

545

	BATTING Records	BFP	/Game	Total	vs. Lg Av	Unearned Runs vs. Lg Av	PITCHERS	IP.f	Earned Runs vs. Lg Av	Expected W-L
1b	G.WALKER	316	0.658	49	11.9	2.9	J.AGOSTO	4.2	-1.8	0– 0
	R.MORMAN	180	0.418	18	-3.7		N.ALLEN	113.0	4.4	6– 7
							F.BANNISTER	165.1	11.7	9– 9
2b	J.CRUZ	256	0.315	21	-9.2	3.5	S.CARLTON	63.1	3.4	3– 4
	J.PERCONTE	85	0.302	7	-3.9		B.CLARK	8.0	-0.3	0– 1
	B.LITTLE	39	0.105	0	-4.9		J.COWLEY	162.1	5.3	8–10
	B.GILES	11	0.122	0	-1.4		J.DAVIS	105.1	-6.1	5– 7
							B.DAWLEY	97.2	9.3	6– 5
3b	T.HULETT	552	0.315	47	-26.9	0.0	J.DELEON	79.0	10.7	5– 4
	W.TOLLESON	310	0.443	34	-1.8		R.DOTSON	197.0	-28.6	7–15
	D.COCHRANE	68	0.189	3	-6.2		P.FILSON	11.2	-2.6	0– 1
							B.JAMES	58.1	-6.9	2– 4
ss	O.GUILLEN	577	0.252	35	-40.4	2.2	J.MCKEON	33.0	6.3	2– 1
							G.NELSON	114.2	4.2	6– 7
lf	B.BONILLA	271	0.521	33	2.0	-1.5	D.SCHMIDT	92.1	8.8	5– 5
	G.FOSTER	54	0.251	4	-3.8		R.SEARAGE	29.0	11.5	3– 1
	K.WILLIAMS	33	0.017	-0	-5.2		T.SEAVER	72.0	-1.6	3– 5
							B.THIGPEN	35.2	9.5	3– 1
cf	J.CANGELOSI	525	0.446	58	-3.4		Others	5.0	4.3	1– 0
	D.BOSTON	224	0.540	29	2.0					
	R.NICHOLS	150	0.283	10	-8.8					
	S.LYONS	136	0.165	5	-13.0					
rf	H.BAINES	618	0.586	87	13.8					
c	C.FISK	491	0.271	34	-30.9	0.5				
	J.SKINNER	162	0.265	11	-10.5					
	R.KARKOVICE	109	0.496	13	-0.0					
	M.HILL	21	0.099	0	-2.5					
dh	J.HAIRSTON	253	0.504	30	-0.0	0.5				
	R.KITTLE	333	0.381	34	-9.2					
	R.HASSEY	174	0.844	31	13.5					
	R.CRAIG	12	0.284	1	-0.5					
	S.BRADLEY	24	0.309	1	-1.4					
	I.CALDERON	36	0.649	5	1.3					
	L.SALAZAR	8	0.100	0	-0.9					
	Others	2	0.100	-1	-1.3	0.0				
	TOTALS	6030		603	-145.5	8.3			41.5	75– 87

	Runs Scored	Runs Allowed	Won	Lost
CALCULATED	600	696	72	90
ACTUAL	644	699	72	90

1985 Cleveland Indians

BATTING Records	BFP	Runs Contributed /Game	Total	vs. Lg Av	Unearned Runs vs. Lg Av
1b P.TABLER	438	0.385	41	-12.1	-5.4
M.HARGROVE	326	0.511	39	2.4	
2b T.BERNAZARD	579	0.564	77	11.4	-1.8
M.FISCHLIN	69	0.232	4	-4.2	
3b B.JACOBY	662	0.489	80	0.4	2.5
ss J.FRANCO	703	0.452	75	-6.6	-8.9
J.LEMASTER	21	-0.063	-1	-3.9	
lf J.CARTER	523	0.452	60	-4.7	0.3
B.AYALA	81	0.397	8	-1.8	
cf B.BUTLER	666	0.666	102	28.8	
rf G.VUKOVICH	470	0.352	42	-17.3	
O.NIXON	174	0.271	12	-10.1	
C.CASTILLO	198	0.472	24	-0.8	
M.HALL	75	0.601	10	2.1	
c J.WILLARD	334	0.498	41	1.1	0.0
C.BANDO	199	0.069	1	-25.4	
B.BENTON	73	0.101	2	-8.1	
dh A.THORNTON	514	0.422	55	-8.6	0.0
J.WILSON	15	0.636	2	0.6	
Others	0	0.636	-0	-0.0	3.1
TOTALS	6120		675	-56.9	-10.2

PITCHERS	IP.f	Earned Runs vs. Lg Av	Expected W-L
J.BARKLEY	41.0	-5.1	2– 3
R.BEHENNA	19.2	-7.9	0– 2
E.CAMACHO	3.1	-1.5	0– 0
B.CLARK	62.2	-15.1	2– 5
K.CREEL	62.0	-4.5	3– 4
J.EASTERLY	98.2	2.4	6– 5
A.FOWLKES	7.0	-3.8	0– 1
N.HEATON	207.2	-17.4	10–14
J.REED	72.1	0.3	4– 4
J.ROMAN	16.1	-4.5	0– 1
R.ROMERO	64.1	-17.4	2– 5
V.RUHLE	125.0	-2.4	7– 7
D.SCHULZE	94.1	-19.6	3– 7
R.SMITH	62.1	-8.3	3– 4
R.THOMPSON	80.0	-19.2	3– 7
D.VON OHLEN	43.1	6.0	3– 2
T.WADDELL	112.2	-9.1	5– 7
Others	254.0	8.0	15–14
		-119.1	68– 94

	Runs Scored	Runs Allowed	Won	Lost
CALCULATED	669	856	62	100
ACTUAL	729	861	60	102

My wife Libby, who occasionally admits to being a Cleveland Indians fan, is certain that the last thirty-two years of baseball history would have been completely different if Willie Mays had not caught Vic Wertz' drive in the 1954 World Series. Other Indians fans have been heard to suggest that it's the Indians' destiny to win in 1987, since every other AL East club has won a title in the 1980's. I guess reality testing gets a little weak when you haven't been in contention for almost thirty years! (To have six different clubs win a championship in six consecutive years is, of course, unusual. I think the only other instance was from 1914 through 1919 in the eight team National League, when the Cardinals and Pirates were shut out.)

With the wisdom of hindsight, the Indians' strong rebound in 1986 shouldn't have been so surprising. In recent years, Indian management has had deserved success trading today's starting pitchers for tomorrow's regulars. The 1985 team had marked weaknesses in right field, catching, and especially pitching, but the rest of the team was at least average in performance, young, and likely to improve. Management addressed these by rushing a rookie catcher to the majors (which didn't work), shuffling the pitching staff continuously (which worked marvelously), and sending Mel Hall a series of get-well cards (which performed as well as Hallmark might have advertised).

Where to now? Dealing will be risky, because the Indians have an above average regular at nearly every position, meaning that some moves will be as likely to hurt as to help. Yet there is no one on the roster except Andre Thornton who has had a +35 season, and in the AL East it's almost impossible to win without one. Maybe Cory Snyder will develop into a big hitter; all he needs is a better batting eye, and the rookie Dale Murphy was a young hitter who made a similar adjustment. There's no reason not to keep shuffling the pitchers and catchers; only Candiotti and Camacho seem worth holding onto.

1986 Cleveland Indians

| | BATTING Records | BFP | Runs Contributed | | | Unearned Runs | | PITCHERS | IP.f | Earned Runs | Expected |
			/Game	Total	vs. Lg Av	vs. Lg Av				vs. Lg Av	W-L
1b	P.TABLER	508	0.624	73	14.7	0.8		S.BAILES	112.2	-9.7	6– 7
								J.BUTCHER	50.2	-15.5	2– 4
2b	T.BERNAZARD	636	0.674	98	26.2	-4.8		E.CAMACHO	57.1	0.6	4– 3
	D.ROHN	11	0.191	1	-0.9			T.CANDIOTTI	252.1	17.1	17–11
								J.EASTERLY	17.2	-6.8	0– 2
3b	B.JACOBY	641	0.584	89	12.3	-0.7		N.HEATON	74.1	-0.5	5– 4
								D.JONES	18.0	3.4	1– 1
ss	J.FRANCO	636	0.475	73	-3.8	-0.6		J.KERN	27.1	-11.3	1– 2
								P.NIEKRO	210.1	-3.4	13–11
lf	M.HALL	480	0.663	76	18.6	-0.6		D.NOLES	54.2	-5.6	3– 3
	O.NIXON	110	0.538	15	1.7			B.OELKERS	69.0	-4.0	4– 4
	C.SNYDER	433	0.524	60	4.0			R.RITTER	10.0	-2.4	0– 1
	D.CLARK	68	0.625	10	2.0			J.ROMAN	22.0	-5.8	1– 2
	E.WILLIAMS	7	-0.039	-0	-1.3			K.SCHROM	206.0	-8.4	12–11
								D.SCHULZE	84.2	-7.7	4– 5
cf	B.BUTLER	683	0.542	86	7.8			G.SWINDELL	61.2	-0.4	4– 3
								F.WILLS	40.1	-3.3	2– 2
rf	J.CARTER	709	0.693	118	33.2			R.YETT	78.2	-8.5	4– 5
c	A.ALLANSON	323	0.231	18	-23.8	-2.3		OTHERS	6.0	10.8	1– 1
	C.BANDO	290	0.375	25	-9.2						
dh	A.THORNTON	475	0.486	56	-0.8	-2.3					
	C.CASTILLO	217	0.435	24	-3.3						
	F.MULLINS	44	0.158	2	-4.2						
	J.BELL	16	1.342	4	2.6						
	Others	0	1.342	-0	-0.0	-4.5					
	TOTALS	6287		826	75.8	-14.9				-61.6	83– 79

	Runs Scored	Runs Allowed	Won	Lost
CALCULATED	824	825	81	82
ACTUAL	831	841	84	78

1985 Detroit Tigers

	BATTING Records	BFP	Runs Contributed /Game	Runs Contributed Total	Runs Contributed vs. Lg Av	Unearned Runs vs. Lg Av	PITCHERS	IP.f	Earned Runs vs. Lg Av	Expected W-L
1b	D.EVANS	594	0.729	100	31.2	-6.8	J.BERENGUER	95.0	-15.3	4- 7
	D.BERGMAN	157	0.152	5	-15.4		C.CARY	23.2	1.9	1- 1
	B.GARBEY	259	0.395	26	-6.2		W.HERNANDEZ	106.2	17.1	8- 4
	T.LEACH	38	0.237	2	-2.7		A.LOPEZ	86.1	-6.2	4- 5
2b	L.WHITAKER	700	0.680	110	31.3	1.7	J.MORRIS	257.0	23.3	16-12
	D.FLYNN	55	0.226	3	-3.4		R.O'NEAL	94.1	9.4	6- 4
3b	T.BROOKENS	522	0.352	49	-18.0	-8.0	D.PETRY	238.2	20.9	15-11
	C.PITTARO	68	0.358	6	-2.3		B.SCHERRER	66.0	-1.6	3- 4
ss	A.TRAMMELL	677	0.450	76	-4.4	7.2	B.STODDARD	13.1	-3.9	0- 1
	D.BAKER	27	0.075	0	-3.6		W.TERRELL	229.0	7.4	13-12
lf	L.HERNDON	479	0.402	49	-11.4	-1.8	M.WILCOX	39.0	-3.0	2- 2
	N.SIMMONS	281	0.458	32	-2.0		Others	210.0	9.7	13-11
cf	C.LEMON	575	0.574	80	11.2					
rf	K.GIBSON	670	0.801	121	46.8					
c	L.PARRISH	600	0.561	83	11.5	0.6				
	B.MELVIN	87	0.213	5	-6.7					
	M.CASTILLO	87	-0.040	-2	-15.2					
dh	J.GRUBB	184	0.497	22	0.7	0.6				
	O.SANCHEZ	133	0.314	13	-5.2					
	M.LAGA	36	0.077	1	-4.1					
	J.WEAVER	8	0.100	0	-1.0					
	R.KUNTZ	7	-0.017	-0	-1.2					
	S.MADISON	14	-0.120	-1	-2.6					
	W.HERNANDEZ	1	-0.223	-0	-0.3					
	Others	0	-0.223	-0	-0.0	-1.4				
	TOTALS	6259		782	27.2	-7.9			59.8	86- 76

	Runs Scored	Runs Allowed	Won	Lost
CALCULATED	771	692	88	73
ACTUAL	729	688	84	77

Bill James, in his 1986 *Baseball Abstract* put his finger on the main reason why the Tigers didn't come close to repeating in 1985: a marvelous offensive performance by the bench in 1984 was followed by a woeful one in 1985 (rather like the Cardinals in 1985 and 1986, except Whitey's slumpers were regulars, not bench men, and so the Cardinals' tremendous change of form was more damaging).

There were also two regular positions with below average performance, left field and third base, so management brought in new men Darnell Coles and Dave Collins for the '86 season. Coles filled a perennial Tiger weakness, although one odd consequence was that Brookens did a lot of DH'ing. (Really now, wouldn't Nelson Simmons have hit the ball farther and oftener than Brookens?) It was also odd that Pat Sheridan played so much when John Grubb was by far the most effective hitter in the major leagues on a per plate appearance basis.

But the primary problem in 1986 was a shortage of "luck." Despite significant injuries to Gibson, Petry, and Parrish, the Tigers, overall, played well enough to win. They simply didn't hit well with runners on (compare Calculated and Actual Runs Scored) and they fared poorly in close games. That kind of deficiency corrects itself—just compare the Red Sox performances in 1985 and 1986—and if the Tigers can resign their free agents I would expect them to be in the thick of the 1987 race.

Their only weakness, when compared to the Yankees and Red Sox, is that their big hitters do not match up to Henderson and Mattingly, or to Boggs and Rice. However, they can maneuver in left- and center- field without risking much decline in performance, so the Tigers have a good chance to find another big hitter in 1987. (Big hitters are, of course, as much a matter of luck as design—Boggs and Mattingly are as big as they come, and both became regulars only after the lineup incumbent failed!)

1986 Detroit Tigers

| | BATTING Records | BFP | Runs Contributed | | | Unearned Runs vs. Lg Av | | PITCHERS | IP.f | Earned Runs vs. Lg Av | Expected W-L |
			/Game	Total	vs. Lg Av						
1b	D.EVANS	601	0.635	89	18.4	5.7		B.CAMPBELL	55.2	1.8	3– 3
	D.BERGMAN	150	0.399	15	-3.8			C.CARY	31.2	2.7	2– 1
	D.ENGLE	93	0.378	9	-3.2			W.HERNANDEZ	88.2	6.1	6– 4
	M.LAGA	50	0.451	6	-0.7			B.KELLY	20.0	-0.7	1– 1
								E.KING	138.1	10.2	9– 6
2b	L.WHITAKER	651	0.525	82	4.0	2.1		D.LAPOINT	67.2	-11.6	3– 5
								J.LAZORKO	6.2	0.1	0– 0
3b	D.COLES	587	0.585	82	12.4	-3.5		J.MORRIS	267.0	26.9	19–11
	T.BROOKENS	310	0.421	31	-6.4			R.O'NEAL	122.2	-2.1	7– 7
								J.PACELLA	11.0	0.1	1– 1
ss	A.TRAMMELL	653	0.648	98	22.2	1.5		D.PETRY	116.0	-6.2	6– 7
	D.BAKER	30	0.043	0	-3.7			B.SCHERRER	21.0	-7.3	1– 2
								J.SLATON	40.0	0.6	2– 2
lf	D.COLLINS	476	0.439	49	-6.8	2.1		F.TANANA	188.1	0.4	11–10
	L.HERNDON	316	0.456	36	-3.1			W.TERRELL	217.1	-9.2	12–12
	B.FIELDS	47	0.359	4	-1.4			M.THURMOND	51.2	13.0	4– 1
								Others	5.0	2.3	1– 0
cf	C.LEMON	457	0.461	51	-4.4						
rf	K.GIBSON	521	0.771	91	31.3						
	P.SHERIDAN	262	0.414	27	-5.8						
	B.HARPER	41	0.029	-0	-5.9						
c	L.PARRISH	374	0.656	58	13.5	0.3					
	D.LOWRY	174	0.620	24	5.0						
	M.HEATH	103	0.450	12	-1.3						
	M.NOKES	25	0.636	4	0.9						
dh	J.GRUBB	243	1.035	53	27.4	0.3					
	H.SPILMAN	53	0.472	7	-0.3						
	T.TOLMAN	43	0.219	2	-2.7						
	S.MADISON	8	-0.223	-1	-2.2						
	Others	1	-0.223	0	0.4	1.0					
	TOTALS	6269		830	83.4	9.7				27.1	89– 73

	Runs Scored	Runs Allowed	Won	Lost
CALCULATED	830	710	93	69
ACTUAL	798	714	87	75

1985 Kansas City Royals

	BATTING Records	BFP	Runs Contributed /Game	Runs Contributed Total	Runs Contributed vs. Lg Av	Unearned Runs vs. Lg Av	PITCHERS	IP.f	Earned Runs vs. Lg Av	Expected W-L
1b	S.BALBONI	662	0.521	88	5.8	0.9	J.BECKWITH	95.0	0.7	5– 6
2b	F.WHITE	590	0.386	62	-14.7	-3.2	B.BLACK	205.2	-4.3	10–12
							S.FARR	37.2	4.3	2– 2
3b	G.BRETT	665	1.061	144	78.1	3.9	T.FERREIRA	5.2	-2.4	0– 1
	G.PRYOR	125	0.167	4	-11.7		M.GUBICZA	177.1	1.7	9–10
							M.HUISMANN	18.2	4.6	1– 1
ss	O.CONCEPCION	349	0.156	13	-32.4	-4.0	D.JACKSON	208.0	16.8	12–11
	B.BIANCALANA	160	0.218	9	-11.3		M.JONES	64.0	-4.5	3– 4
	J.SCRANTON	4	-0.223	-1	-1.3		M.LACOSS	40.2	-4.3	2– 3
	K.SMITH	-	-	-	-		C.LEIBRANDT	237.2	38.4	16–10
							D.LEONARD	2.0	0.9	0– 0
lf	L.SMITH	498	0.508	63	3.1	-0.6	D.QUISENBERRY	129.0	25.4	9– 5
	L.JONES	169	0.160	6	-15.7		B.SABERHAGEN	235.1	33.4	16–11
	D.LEEPER	35	-0.101	-2	-7.5		Others	9.0	-1.9	0– 1
cf	W.WILSON	642	0.521	83	4.3					
	O.MORENO	75	0.401	8	-1.5					
rf	D.MOTLEY	408	0.280	33	-21.0					
	P.SHERIDAN	234	0.382	23	-6.1					
	D.IORG	138	0.229	8	-10.4					
c	J.SUNDBERG	407	0.403	41	-8.8	0.6				
	J.WATHAN	165	0.361	15	-5.4					
	J.QUIRK	59	0.409	6	-1.4					
dh	H.MCRAE	369	0.559	49	6.2	0.6				
	J.ORTA	330	0.431	35	-4.5					
	Others	10	0.431	4	4.1	2.1				
	TOTALS	6094		690	-52.2	0.3			108.9	87– 75

	Runs Scored	Runs Allowed	Won	Lost
CALCULATED	695	638	87	75
ACTUAL	687	639	91	71

For once the sportswriters were right. As the Royals became one of the most improbable World Champions of history in 1985, there was a lot of grumbling: 'Take George Brett and their pitching away and this is a second division club'. How true. Replace those players with average performers and arithmetic shows that the 1985 Royals would have scored 130 runs fewer than they allowed, for a 68–94 record that would have put them just a few games ahead of Texas. Of course, that fellow Brett had a better year than any player since. He looked a lot like that fellow Brett back in '80.

It ought to have been a great position for rebuilding—replace almost anyone but Brett and the chances are you'll improve. But there's the disadvantage of being World Champions. Those rings make even the Greg Pryors and Darryl Motleys of the world look irreplaceable. So it was that the only changes that the Royals made for 1986 were Salazar for Concepcion and Law for Iorg. The result, of course, was that this time they finished a few games behind Texas and below .500.

There is one team that the current Royals remind me very much of: the New York Yankees of the early 1920's. Like the Royals, those Yankees had one big hitter, an excellent pitching staff, and seven other guys. On the other hand, their hitter turned in consistent seasons of close to +150.0—Ruthian years, I believe they're called. And so soothing was the opiate of consistent success that the Yankees were perfectly content for years with household names like Wally Pipp, Everett Scott, and Whitey Witt in their everyday lineup.

Then the Senators won a couple of pennants, and the Yankees started getting serious. They brought in a little help for Ruth—fellows like Lazzeri, Combs, and Gehrig. The Royals have begun to do so as well, after their fall from grace. Witness the Danny Tartabull trade! Could Bo Jackson be the Lou Gehrig of the next decade? If so, the AL West could quickly turn into Kansas City and the six dwarfs.

Can you imagine future baseball fans talking about the legendary 1988 Royals?

1986 Kansas City Royals

| | BATTING Records | BFP | Runs Contributed | | | Unearned Runs | PITCHERS | IP.f | Earned Runs | Expected |
			/Game	Total	vs. Lg Av	vs. Lg Av			vs. Lg Av	W-L
1b	S.BALBONI	562	0.461	68	-4.4	-4.8	S.BANKHEAD	121.0	-5.9	5- 8
	K.SEITZER	116	0.881	22	10.1		B.BLACK	121.0	13.1	7- 6
							D.CONE	22.2	-3.5	1- 2
2b	F.WHITE	620	0.556	85	9.2	4.2	S.FARR	109.1	12.7	7- 6
	R.JOHNSON	31	0.295	2	-1.8		M.GUBICZA	180.2	10.8	10-10
							A.HARGESHEIMER	13.0	-3.0	0- 1
3b	G.BRETT	529	0.798	93	35.3	0.7	M.HUISMANN	17.1	0.0	1- 1
	G.PRYOR	117	0.015	-2	-18.9		D.JACKSON	185.2	20.1	11-10
	H.PECOTA	34	0.199	1	-2.8		C.LEIBRANDT	231.1	2.3	12-14
ss	A.SALAZAR	313	0.294	23	-18.1	0.1	D.LEONARD	192.2	-5.6	9-13
	B.BIANCALANA	209	0.372	19	-7.3		D.QUISENBERRY	81.1	12.7	5- 4
							B.SABERHAGEN	156.0	0.4	8-10
lf	L.SMITH	568	0.589	79	12.0	-0.3	S.SHIELDS	8.2	2.0	1- 0
	L.JONES	54	0.055	-0	-7.6		Others	4.0	1.9	0- 0
	M.BREWER	20	0.135	1	-2.2					
cf	W.WILSON	675	0.459	77	-7.8					
rf	R.LAW	341	0.491	41	-1.2					
	D.MOTLEY	229	0.202	13	-19.2					
	M.KINGERY	223	0.417	24	-4.8					
	B.JACKSON	91	0.344	8	-3.9					
c	J.SUNDBERG	491	0.355	44	-18.5	1.1				
	J.QUIRK	238	0.334	21	-10.7					
	T.BELL	5	0.065	0	-0.1					
dh	H.MCRAE	299	0.373	28	-10.2	1.1				
	J.ORTA	361	0.461	41	-3.8					
	D.TAYLOR	2	-0.223	-0	-0.6					
	Others	0	-0.223	-0	-0.4	-0.5				
	TOTALS	6128		686	-78.0	1.8			58.2	78- 84

	Runs Scored	Runs Allowed	Won	Lost
CALCULATED	667	685	79	83
ACTUAL	654	673	76	86

1985 Milwaukee Brewers

| | BATTING Records | BFP | Runs Contributed | | | Unearned Runs | | PITCHERS | IP.f | Earned Runs | Expected |
			/Game	Total	vs. Lg Av	vs. Lg Av				vs. Lg Av	W-L
1b	C.COOPER	674	0.504	85	4.4	-4.0		R.BURRIS	170.1	-12.6	8-11
	C.PONCE	66	-0.030	-1	-10.7			J.COCANOWER	116.1	-2.4	6- 7
								D.DARWIN	217.2	8.2	12-12
2b	J.GANTNER	573	0.325	46	-24.2	2.4		R.FINGERS	55.1	-5.5	2- 4
								B.GIBSON	92.1	2.5	5- 5
3b	P.MOLITOR	642	0.568	86	13.2	0.4		M.HAAS	161.2	5.4	9- 9
								T.HIGUERA	212.1	5.8	12-12
ss	E.RILES	495	0.448	53	-4.7	-0.5		J.KERN	11.0	-2.9	0- 1
	E.ROMERO	282	0.365	26	-8.3			P.LADD	45.2	-2.0	2- 3
	B.GILES	65	0.195	3	-5.5			T.LEARY	33.1	0.3	2- 2
								B.LESLEY	6.1	-4.1	0- 1
lf	B.OGLIVIE	394	0.583	54	10.5	-1.2		B.MCCLURE	85.2	-1.6	4- 5
	R.READY	200	0.421	21	-3.2			C.PORTER	13.2	3.3	1- 0
	B.ROBIDOUX	63	0.502	8	0.1			R.SEARAGE	38.0	-7.5	1- 3
cf	R.YOUNT	527	0.590	74	13.4			P.VUCKOVICH	112.2	-17.1	4- 8
	R.MANNING	231	0.267	16	-14.5			R.WAITS	47.0	-12.4	1- 4
	D.LOMAN	70	0.204	4	-5.2			B.WEGMAN	17.2	1.1	1- 1
	M.FELDER	62	0.156	2	-5.9			Others	7.0	5.2	1- 0
	D.JAMES	55	0.302	4	-2.5						
rf	P.HOUSEHOLDER	329	0.495	40	0.2						
	M.BROUHARD	115	0.409	12	-2.4						
	B.CLARK	101	0.211	5	-8.2						
c	C.MOORE	386	0.262	25	-23.6	-1.2					
	B.SCHROEDER	210	0.393	21	-5.1						
	D.HUPPERT	25	-0.125	-2	-5.5						
dh	T.SIMMONS	592	0.500	71	1.5	-1.2					
	R.WAITS	1	-0.223	-0	-0.3						
	Others	0	-0.223	-0	-0.0	-0.4					
	TOTALS	6158		653	-86.4	-5.7				-36.1	73- 89

	Runs Scored	Runs Allowed	Won	Lost
CALCULATED	648	776	68	93
ACTUAL	690	802	71	90

Remember? In 1982 Milwaukee had one of the most crushing lineups in history (recalling that County Stadium is not a hitter's park), especially in the infield. Practically every man was a threat to lead the league in something. Seven of those guys were still there at the end of 1985, and the eighth would be back before the end of 1986. But none of them have led the league in anything for the last four years, and even Robin Yount and Paul Molitor are now over 30.

So the Brewers have been rolling the dice—moving players in and out. It hasn't hurt their chances that the farm system has been producing a lot of talent, but they've also given shots to other teams' disappointments. Paul Householder, Mark Clear, Tim Leary, Rick Cerone, Rob Deer, and Gorman Thomas II all graced their 1986 roster, and as you can see from the numbers they performed much better, collectively, than promotees Robidoux, Braggs, Felder, Sveum, Nieves, Plesac, and Wegman.

Might as well keep shuffling the roster! With no big players—unless another one of the veterans discovers the Fountain of Youth—Milwaukee still has a long way to go to get back into serious contention, and there are not very many positions so strong that an unfortunate trade could be damaging.

1986 Milwaukee Brewers

	BATTING Records	BFP	Runs Contributed /Game	Total	vs. Lg Av	Unearned Runs vs. Lg Av	PITCHERS	IP.f	Earned Runs vs. Lg Av	Expected W-L
1b	C.COOPER	589	0.400	58	-15.8	-1.3	M.BIRKBECK	22.0	-0.8	1– 1
	B.ROBIDOUX	215	0.356	18	-7.7		C.BOSIO	34.2	-10.9	1– 3
	J.ADDUCI	13	0.018	-0	-1.8		M.CLEAR	73.2	16.2	5– 3
							C.CLUTTERBUCK	56.2	-0.7	3– 4
2b	J.GANTNER	542	0.411	54	-12.2	2.8	J.COCANOWER	44.2	-1.3	2– 3
	J.CASTILLO	62	0.113	1	-7.2		D.DARWIN	130.1	9.5	8– 7
							B.GIBSON	26.2	-1.6	1– 2
3b	P.MOLITOR	482	0.569	66	7.9	-12.6	T.HIGUERA	248.1	38.2	16–12
	D.SVEUM	356	0.419	36	-7.8		J.JOHNSON	44.0	7.4	3– 2
							M.KNUDSON	17.2	-6.8	0– 2
ss	E.RILES	588	0.407	57	-14.7	-2.0	T.LEARY	188.1	-0.6	10–12
	E.DIAZ	14	0.246	1	-1.0		B.McCLURE	16.1	0.6	1– 1
	S.KIEFER	6	-0.223	-1	-1.9		J.NIEVES	184.2	-16.3	8–13
lf	G.BRAGGS	232	0.299	18	-12.5	-0.6	D.PLESAC	91.0	12.2	6– 4
	R.READY	89	0.233	5	-6.8		R.SEARAGE	22.0	-6.8	0– 2
							P.VUCKOVICH	32.1	4.0	2– 2
cf	R.YOUNT	595	0.720	96	30.1		B.WEGMAN	198.1	-21.0	8–14
	R.MANNING	227	0.476	27	-1.0		Others	6.0	7.8	1– 0
rf	R.DEER	546	0.663	86	19.9					
	M.FELDER	174	0.380	17	-4.5					
	P.HOUSEHOLDER	90	0.302	7	-4.5					
c	C.MOORE	263	0.413	26	-5.8	-0.1				
	R.CERONE	242	0.406	24	-5.3					
	B.SCHROEDER	237	0.331	21	-10.7					
dh	B.OGLIVIE	384	0.490	45	-0.3	-0.1				
	G.THOMAS	178	0.421	18	-3.5					
	Others	0	0.421	-0	-0.4	1.0				
	TOTALS	6124		680	-67.7	-12.7			29.0	76– 86

	Runs Scored	Runs Allowed	Won	Lost
CALCULATED	672	724	75	86
ACTUAL	667	734	77	84

1985 Minnesota Twins

| BATTING Records | BFP | Runs Contributed | | | Unearned Runs | PITCHERS | IP.f | Earned Runs | Expected |
		/Game	Total	vs. Lg Av	vs. Lg Av			vs. Lg Av	W-L
1b K.HRBEK	666	0.604	95	17.6	2.3	M.BROWN	15.2	-4.8	0- 1
						D.BURTT	28.1	1.0	2- 2
2b T.TEUFEL	496	0.475	57	-0.8	-1.8	J.BUTCHER	207.2	-19.4	9-14
S.LOMBARDOZZI	65	0.820	12	5.6		R.DAVIS	64.2	4.8	4- 3
						F.EUFEMIA	61.2	2.4	4- 3
3b G.GAETTI	608	0.425	66	-10.1	2.5	P.FILSON	95.2	5.1	6- 5
						T.KLAWITTER	9.1	-2.7	0- 1
ss G.GAGNE	322	0.301	25	-15.9	2.3	R.LYSANDER	61.0	-12.9	2- 5
A.ESPINOZA	62	0.224	3	-4.3		M.PORTUGAL	24.1	-3.8	1- 2
R.WASHINGTON	149	0.445	17	-0.9		K.SCHROM	160.2	-15.0	7-11
						M.SMITHSON	257.0	-5.7	13-16
lf M.HATCHER	467	0.374	43	-14.6	0.9	F.VIOLA	250.2	1.4	14-15
R.BUSH	265	0.563	37	4.5		L.WHITEHOUSE	7.1	-5.6	0- 1
						R.YETT	0.1	-0.8	0- 0
cf K.PUCKETT	744	0.487	88	-0.5		Others	188.0	5.6	11-11
rf T.BRUNANSKY	651	0.528	85	7.3					
D.MEIER	126	0.479	14	0.3					
c M.SALAS	382	0.570	53	7.7	-0.2				
T.LAUDNER	182	0.400	19	-3.6					
J.REED	10	0.081	0	-1.3					
dh R.SMALLEY	452	0.551	59	6.7	-0.2				
D.ENGLE	195	0.563	27	3.4					
M.STENHOUSE	209	0.432	22	-2.8					
M.FUNDERBURK	77	0.578	11	2.3					
Others	0	0.578	-0	-0.0	-0.4				
TOTALS	6128	0.5	731		5.4			-50.5	73- 89

	Runs Scored	Runs Allowed	Won	Lost
CALCULATED	729	774	77	85
ACTUAL	705	782	77	85

The Twins have been on a treadmill lately. A few years ago, they picked up some pretty good young players who by now are established regulars, though not necessarily stars. It's tough to move these players because any year now, a Brunansky or a Hrbek could become a big player, just as Puckett did last year. So except for periodically exchanging pitchers with Cleveland (few teams other than Minnesota would consider employing a former Cleveland pitcher), they have not done much. For example, the left field position was a problem in 1985, so they tried to fill it by trading a second baseman. Unfortunately, the result now is two problem positions.

If I were the Twins' management, I'd start shaking things up a bit. It's not like you're breaking up a probable contender, even in the AL West. To the right contender, a Gaetti, Brunansky, Viola, Blyleven, or Smithson could be worth a lot of prospects and suspects, and you don't have to keep the Mickey Hatchers!

Bert Blyleven led the major leagues in home runs last year; he became the first pitcher ever to allow more homeruns than hit by the major league leader. What makes it all the more amazing was that he was still able to turn in an overall plus-pitching performance.

1986 Minnesota Twins

| | BATTING Records | BFP | Runs Contributed | | | Unearned Runs | PITCHERS | IP.f | Earned Runs | Expected |
			/Game	Total	vs. Lg Av	vs. Lg Av			vs. Lg Av	W-L
1b	K.HRBEK	634	0.636	95	20.6	1.5	J.AGOSTO	20.1	-10.6	0– 2
							A.ANDERSON	84.1	-12.9	3– 6
2b	S.LOMBARDOZZI	515	0.395	50	-14.6	2.8	K.ATHERTON	81.2	3.9	5– 4
	C.PITTARO	22	-0.073	-1	-4.5		B.BLYLEVEN	271.2	5.0	16–15
							D.BURTT	2.0	-6.1	0– 1
3b	G.GAETTI	661	0.636	101	23.0	2.1	J.BUTCHER	70.0	-16.5	2– 6
							R.DAVIS	38.2	-21.1	0– 4
ss	G.GAGNE	524	0.443	57	-7.8	-2.0	P.FILSON	6.1	-1.1	0– 0
							R.FONTENOT	16.1	-10.4	0– 2
lf	R.BUSH	402	0.563	54	5.7	1.2	G.FRAZIER	26.2	-0.6	1– 2
	B.BEANE	194	0.200	9	-17.4		N.HEATON	124.1	2.7	7– 7
	M.HATCHER	340	0.415	35	-7.6		R.JACKSON	58.1	2.1	3– 3
							B.LATHAM	16.0	-5.6	0– 1
cf	K.PUCKETT	723	0.758	127	43.5		F.PASTORE	49.1	0.9	3– 3
	M.DAVIDSON	77	0.005	-1	-12.3		M.PORTUGAL	112.2	-1.7	6– 7
							R.SMITH	10.1	-3.2	0– 1
rf	T.BRUNANSKY	655	0.484	79	-2.3		M.SMITHSON	198.0	-13.1	10–13
							F.VIOLA	245.2	-9.0	13–15
c	M.SALAS	285	0.350	25	-10.9	-1.3	Others	6.0	5.8	1– 0
	T.LAUDNER	223	0.561	30	3.3					
	J.REED	185	0.376	17	-6.1					
dh	R.SMALLEY	530	0.564	71	7.7	-1.3				
	A.WOODS	32	0.904	6	2.9					
	R.WASHINGTON	81	0.454	10	-0.5					
	A.ESPINOZA	45	0.144	1	-4.8					
	A.SANCHEZ	17	-0.096	-2	-4.1					
	A.DAVID	5	0.081	0	-0.7					
	Others	1	0.081	-0	-0.3	2.5				
	TOTALS	6151		763	12.6	5.7			-91.5	71– 91

	Runs Scored	Runs Allowed	Won	Lost
CALCULATED	753	826	74	88
ACTUAL	741	839	71	91

1985 New York Yankees

	BATTING Records	BFP	Runs Contributed /Game	Total	vs. Lg Av	Unearned Runs vs. Lg Av		PITCHERS	IP.f	Earned Runs vs. Lg Av	Expected W-L
1b	D.MATTINGLY	727	0.814	135	55.3	4.3		M.ARMSTRONG	14.2	1.8	1– 1
								R.BORDI	98.0	10.1	7– 4
2b	W.RANDOLPH	597	0.500	69	3.7	1.0		M.BYSTROM	41.0	-7.1	2– 3
	R.HUDLER	57	0.001	-0	-8.0			D.COOPER	10.0	-1.4	0– 1
	J.BONILLA	16	-0.039	-0	-2.9			J.COWLEY	159.2	3.5	10– 7
3b	M.PAGLIARULO	435	0.541	58	5.6	-4.5		B.FISHER	98.1	19.3	8– 3
	D.BERRA	118	0.282	9	-6.6			R.GUIDRY	259.0	25.3	19–10
	A.ROBERTSON	136	0.545	17	2.3			J.MONTEFUSCO	7.0	-4.8	0– 1
ss	B.MEACHAM	566	0.285	42	-25.3	0.2		P.NIEKRO	220.0	1.3	14–11
								D.RASMUSSEN	101.2	1.8	7– 5
lf	K.GRIFFEY	487	0.554	65	8.1	0.0		D.RIGHETTI	107.0	16.3	8– 4
	B.SAMPLE	154	0.446	17	-1.1			B.SHIRLEY	109.0	18.2	9– 4
	D.PASQUA	166	0.462	20	-1.3			E.WHITSON	158.2	-12.9	9– 9
cf	R.HENDERSON	654	0.999	138	70.5			Others	59.0	3.2	4– 3
	H.COTTO	60	0.467	7	-0.3						
	O.MORENO	68	0.160	3	-6.3						
	V.MATA	7	-0.039	-0	-1.3						
rf	D.WINFIELD	689	0.567	96	13.2						
c	B.WYNEGAR	375	0.430	39	-4.6	-0.2					
	R.HASSEY	298	0.723	49	15.6						
	J.ESPINO	11	0.567	1	0.2						
dh	D.BAYLOR	564	0.523	72	5.4	-0.2					
	S.BRADLEY	51	0.052	0	-7.1						
	Others	0	0.052	-1	-0.6	1.1					
	TOTALS	6236		835	114.5	1.8				74.4	99– 63

	Runs Scored	Runs Allowed	Won	Lost
CALCULATED	851	660	99	62
ACTUAL	839	660	97	64

Having Mattingly and Henderson on the roster makes the Yankees my winterbook favorite every year. Look at the numbers: together they've averaged about +110 par-runs in 1985 and 1986. If everyone else on the Yankees was an average major leaguer, that +110 would mean a 92–70 record, and as George would probably be the first to tell you, the salary lists suggest that some of the other guys should be better than average too. Winfield is a big player in everything but 1985 and 1986 performance. Dan Pasqua had a terrific rookie year—much better than Joyner, Canseco, Incaviglia, et al. Easler, Randolph, and Pagliarulo also are among the best AL hitters at their respective positions.

If you compare the Yankee Calculated Won and Lost for 1985 and 1986 with those of other AL teams, you'll see that on paper the Yankees have won the last two division titles. Of course, victories only count on the field, and there the Yankees have won more games in the last two years than anyone except the other New York team.

The Yankees are not shy about tackling their weaknesses. During 1986, shortstop and catching were constant problems. Six Yankees played most of their games at shortstop, but the cumulative offensive "production" of −41.9 was about the same as Ozzie Guillen of the White Sox managed by himself. Ultimately Tolleson looks by far the best, but to get Tolleson they had to weaken the catching. Maybe Phil Lombardi can help, because Joel Skinner might make Bob Boone start to look like Johnny Bench.

Even more serious for the 1986 Yankees was an all-round lack of timely hitting, which shows up in these figures as a enormous, 60 par-run difference between Calculated and Actual runs scored. However, I again claim a certain amount of influence here by the luck factor, and so this will doubtless cure itself. (Witness the Red Sox turnaround.)

The pitching finished strongly, and at this writing the Pirates have been kind enough to take on two of the Yankees' weaker par-run pitchers in 1986 in return for three of the four Pirates' top par-run performers. It wouldn't surprise me if the Yankees won the 1987 division title as easily as the Mets won in 1986.

1986 New York Yankees

	BATTING Records	BFP	Runs Contributed /Game	Runs Contributed Total	Runs Contributed vs. Lg Av	Unearned Runs vs. Lg Av	PITCHERS	IP.f	Earned Runs vs. Lg Av	Expected W-L
1b	D.MATTINGLY	742	0.885	146	65.2	5.7	M.ARMSTRONG	8.2	-5.0	0– 1
							B.ARNSBERG	8.0	0.7	1– 0
2b	W.RANDOLPH	601	0.577	80	14.9	-4.8	D.DRABEK	131.2	1.1	8– 7
	B.LITTLE	43	0.118	1	-5.2		B.FISHER	96.2	-8.2	5– 6
							R.GUIDRY	192.1	4.2	12–10
3b	M.PAGLIARULO	565	0.544	76	5.8	0.7	A.HOLLAND	40.2	-4.1	2– 3
	L.HERNANDEZ	23	0.439	3	-0.3		T.JOHN	70.2	9.8	5– 3
							J.MONTEFUSCO	12.1	2.7	1– 0
ss	B.MEACHAM	185	0.262	10	-12.5	-1.3	J.NIEKRO	125.2	-9.7	6– 8
	W.TOLLESON	236	0.423	24	-4.1		S.NIELSEN	56.0	1.0	3– 3
	M.FISCHLIN	116	0.156	3	-11.5		A.PULIDO	30.2	-1.8	2– 2
	P.ZUVELLA	57	-0.042	-2	-9.9		D.RASMUSSEN	202.0	6.7	13–10
	D.BERRA	121	0.402	12	-3.0		D.RIGHETTI	106.2	20.5	8– 4
	I.DEJESUS	5	-0.079	-0	-0.9		R.SCURRY	39.1	2.2	3– 2
							B.SHIRLEY	105.1	-10.1	5– 7
lf	D.PASQUA	332	0.870	63	26.3	0.9	T.STODDARD	49.1	1.9	3– 2
	K.GRIFFEY	219	0.590	31	5.4		B.TEWKSBURY	130.1	12.5	9– 6
	G.ROENICKE	165	0.608	23	5.1		E.WHITSON	37.0	-13.8	1– 3
cf	R.HENDERSON	701	0.726	118	35.4		Others	7.0	3.2	1– 0
	H.COTTO	83	0.163	3	-8.3					
rf	D.WINFIELD	652	0.583	90	13.1					
	C.WASHINGTON	144	0.417	16	-3.2					
c	B.WYNEGAR	226	0.345	19	-9.3	0.1				
	J.SKINNER	174	0.261	10	-12.2					
	R.HASSEY	219	0.653	32	7.8					
	J.ESPINO	40	0.094	1	-4.8					
dh	M.EASLER	546	0.603	76	13.6	0.1				
	R.KITTLE	89	0.488	11	-0.1					
	P.LOMBARDI	41	0.658	6	1.6					
	Others	0	0.658	-0	-0.0	-2.0				
	TOTALS	6325		855	108.9	-0.5			13.9	87– 75

	Runs Scored	Runs Allowed	Won	Lost
CALCULATED	855	733	93	69
ACTUAL	797	738	90	72

1985 Oakland Athletics

BATTING Records	BFP	Runs Contributed /Game	Total	vs. Lg Av	Unearned Runs vs. Lg Av	PITCHERS	IP.f	Earned Runs vs. Lg Av	Expected W-L
1b B.BOCHTE	474	0.609	67	13.0	0.2	K.ATHERTON	104.2	-1.8	6– 6
D.BAKER	396	0.600	55	10.2		T.BIRTSAS	141.1	2.1	8– 7
						C.CODIROLI	226.0	-7.9	12–13
2b D.HILL	436	0.396	43	-7.8	-2.5	T.CONROY	25.1	-0.3	1– 1
M.GALLEGO	93	0.372	9	-2.4		J.HOWELL	98.0	14.1	7– 4
						J.KAISER	16.2	-19.3	1– 3
3b C.LANSFORD	432	0.483	53	0.3	3.2	B.KRUEGER	151.1	-6.3	8– 9
S.KIEFER	71	0.121	3	-7.0		R.LANGFORD	59.0	4.2	4– 3
T.PHILLIPS	178	0.582	25	4.3		S.MCCATTY	85.2	-13.6	4– 6
R.PICCIOLO	104	0.314	8	-5.3		S.MURA	48.0	0.1	3– 3
ss A.GRIFFIN	646	0.353	58	-22.9	-1.9	S.ONTIVEROS	74.2	18.4	6– 2
						J.RIJO	63.2	4.3	4– 3
lf D.COLLINS	418	0.397	42	-9.0	-2.1	T.TELLMANN	21.1	-2.2	1– 1
S.HENDERSON	213	0.515	26	1.3		M.WARREN	49.0	-13.4	1– 4
J.CANSECO	100	0.641	16	3.6		C.YOUNG	46.0	-15.8	1– 4
						Others	247.0	-0.3	14–13
cf D.MURPHY	619	0.498	74	1.7					
rf M.DAVIS	604	0.654	94	23.4					
c M.HEATH	492	0.428	53	-6.0	-0.4				
M.TETTLETON	246	0.436	26	-2.7					
C.O'BRIEN	14	0.709	2	0.8					
dh D.KINGMAN	666	0.447	75	-6.4	-0.4				
D.MEYER	13	-0.168	-1	-3.4					
Others	0	-0.168	-2	-1.7	-0.4				
TOTALS	6215		724	-15.9	-4.3			-37.8	79– 83

	Runs Scored	Runs Allowed	Won	Lost
CALCULATED	727	785	75	87
ACTUAL	757	787	77	85

While the Twins have been on a static treadmill, Oakland makes lots of moves, but they too always seem to wind up in the same place: a bit below .500. Although many folks believe that the Rickey Henderson trade was a good one for both sides, I see it as the prime cause for Oakland's predicament.

Having a player like Henderson gives some stability to your planning, and, of course, he provides you with that most elusive ingredient for a championship team: a genuine superstar. Has there ever been a player of this magnitude traded to another club before his peak? There was that pitcher/outfielder from Boston who also happened to end up with the Yankees, albeit some time ago. Was the trade worth it to the A's? Well, thus far all they have are five players, described as promising, but whose net big-league par-runs turn out negative.

Fellows, if you must cut the payroll, don't go after the big players! It's not the price of star talent that has crippled major league budgets, but rather the price of mediocrity. If Schmidt gets $2 million for hitting 40 homeruns, you don't automatically give $1 million to the guy who hits 20. He is a lot closer in value to a player with 10 homers at the major league minimum $60K than he is to Schmidt. Thought of in the light of supply and demand, you can begin to see how the Schmidts and Hendersons can pay their own way . . . even with multi-million dollar contracts!

Unless Oakland was certain that Henderson was going to use his free agency rights for a change of scenery rather than a trip to the bank, they ought to have kept him at any cost. Combine his future with Jose Canseco's and the A's would really have something to celebrate. As it is, the most they can smile about is that their biggest offensive hole was at dh: the easiest to fill.

1986 Oakland Athletics

	BATTING Records	BFP	Runs Contributed /Game	Runs Contributed Total	Runs Contributed vs. Lg Av	Unearned Runs vs. Lg Av	PITCHERS	IP.f	Earned Runs vs. Lg Av	Expected W-L
1b	B.BOCHTE	473	0.475	54	-2.1	0.1	D.AKERFELDS	5.1	-1.5	0– 0
							J.ANDUJAR	155.1	6.1	9– 8
2b	T.PHILLIPS	532	0.533	67	6.5	-1.4	F.ARROYO	0.0	0.0	0– 0
	D.HILL	366	0.456	40	-4.8		K.ATHERTON	15.1	-2.9	1– 1
	M.GALLEGO	40	0.292	3	-2.3		D.BAIR	45.0	5.9	3– 2
	L.SAKATA	38	0.646	6	1.5		T.BIRTSAS	2.0	-4.1	0– 1
							C.CODIROLI	91.2	1.5	5– 5
3b	C.LANSFORD	640	0.514	80	2.0	4.2	T.DOZIER	6.1	-1.1	0– 0
	M.MCGWIRE	58	0.327	5	-2.7		M.HAAS	72.1	11.6	5– 3
							J.HOWELL	53.1	4.7	3– 3
ss	A.GRIFFIN	649	0.464	72	-5.7	0.8	B.KRUEGER	34.1	-7.1	1– 3
							R.LANGFORD	55.0	-19.5	1– 5
lf	J.CANSECO	682	0.540	91	7.3	-1.5	D.LEIPER	31.2	-2.3	1– 2
	R.TILLMAN	42	0.479	5	-0.3		B.MOONEYHAM	99.2	-3.8	5– 6
	S.HENDERSON	27	-0.213	-4	-8.0		S.ONTIVEROS	72.2	-4.3	4– 5
							E.PLUNK	120.1	-15.2	5– 8
cf	D.MURPHY	400	0.575	53	8.2		J.RIJO	193.2	-10.2	10–12
	S.JAVIER	131	0.337	12	-5.2		R.RODRIGUEZ	16.1	-4.4	0– 1
	R.PETERS	45	0.188	2	-4.1		D.STEWART	149.1	7.3	9– 8
							D.VON OHLEN	15.1	1.1	1– 1
rf	M.DAVIS	533	0.569	75	9.0		C.YOUNG	198.0	15.9	13–10
	D.BAKER	271	0.345	22	-11.3		Others	7.0	4.2	1– 0
c	M.TETTLETON	262	0.505	32	0.8	-0.1				
	J.WILLARD	193	0.521	23	1.6					
	B.BATHE	112	0.184	6	-9.4					
	R.STEINBACH	16	1.146	4	2.2					
dh	D.KINGMAN	604	0.328	57	-24.6	-0.1				
	R.NELSON	10	0.393	1	-0.3					
	W.GROSS	3	0.017	0	-0.2					
	Others	0	0.017	-0	-0.1	-4.0				
	TOTALS	6127		705	-41.9	-1.8			-17.9	78– 84

	Runs Scored	Runs Allowed	Won	Lost
CALCULATED	699	761	75	87
ACTUAL	731	760	76	86

1985 Seattle Mariners

	BATTING Records	BFP	Runs Contributed			Unearned Runs vs. Lg Av		PITCHERS	IP.f	Earned Runs vs. Lg Av	Expected W-L
			/Game	Total	vs. Lg Av						
1b	A.DAVIS	677	0.665	102	28.0	0.2		S.BAROJAS	52.2	-10.7	2- 4
								J.BEATTIE	70.1	-24.6	1- 6
2b	J.PERCONTE	542	0.472	63	-1.3	-3.2		K.BEST	32.1	7.9	3- 1
	H.REYNOLDS	122	0.164	5	-10.5			D.GEISEL	27.0	-6.6	1- 2
								M.LANGSTON	126.2	-18.7	5- 9
3b	J.PRESLEY	625	0.498	79	4.2	2.5		J.LAZORKO	20.1	1.4	1- 1
	D.COLES	71	0.481	8	0.3			J.LEWIS	4.2	-1.9	0- 0
								P.MIRABELLA	13.2	4.3	1- 0
ss	S.OWEN	393	0.457	44	-2.6	2.3		M.MOORE	247.0	18.7	16-12
	D.RAMOS	190	0.193	9	-15.5			M.MORGAN	6.0	-5.2	0- 1
	D.TARTABULL	69	0.890	13	5.9			E.NUNEZ	90.1	10.6	6- 4
								B.SNYDER	35.1	-8.7	1- 3
lf	I.CALDERON	233	0.609	34	7.2	0.3		B.SWIFT	120.2	-8.4	6- 8
	J.MOSES	65	0.051	-0	-9.3			R.THOMAS	93.2	8.1	6- 5
	R.NELSON	2	-0.223	-0	-0.6			D.TOBIK	9.0	-1.9	0- 1
								E.VANDE BERG	67.2	3.2	4- 4
cf	P.BRADLEY	714	0.707	117	35.8			B.WILKINSON	6.0	-6.2	0- 1
	B.BONNELL	117	0.331	10	-5.3			F.WILLS	123.0	-25.4	4-10
								M.YOUNG	218.1	-18.5	10-14
rf	D.HENDERSON	556	0.439	61	-7.6			Others	74.0	1.1	4- 4
	A.COWENS	487	0.432	54	-5.8						
c	B.KEARNEY	326	0.313	26	-15.2	0.2					
	D.SCOTT	205	0.329	18	-8.2						
	D.VALLE	73	0.013	-1	-11.4						
dh	G.THOMAS	574	0.554	77	8.4	0.2					
	K.PHELPS	140	0.655	22	5.0						
	A.CHAMBERS	4	-0.223	-1	-1.3						
	Others	0	-0.223	-0	-0.4	1.1					
	TOTALS	6185		741	-0.2	3.6				-81.5	71- 91

	Runs Scored	Runs Allowed	Won	Lost
CALCULATED	732	810	73	89
ACTUAL	719	818	74	88

At the end of 1985, I said to myself, "the Mariners are going to surprise some people in 1986. Look at all that young batting talent—Bradley, Alvin Davis, Presley, and Calderon, with Tartabull, Henderson, and Coles in the wings. Look at those arms—Moore, Morgan, Young, Langston, Swift, Nunez. This is quality young talent!"

Though probably no one East of the Mississippi noticed, Seattle surprised in 1986. They lost six more games than in 1985 and finished dead last, very much on their own merit. What happened? Bradley, Davis, and Presley all hit about as expected, and the pitching overall was about the same, that is, not very good. Phelps reached big hitter ranking in only 441 plate appearances. Those were not disappointments. Neither were they unexpected.

To catch the immediate problem you have to focus on the middle of the infield. At the end of 1985, the shortstop and secondbaseman were Owens and Perconte—decent hitters and reliable if not gifted fielders. The .164 rpg of a late season rookie named Reynolds dragged the overall par-run performance of the middle infielders below zero to −7.5, not too bad for middle infielders, and there were two rook-

ies of exceptional hitting promise on the horizon in Coles and Tartabull.

I won't even try to understand the rationale for the maneuvers which followed, but the outcome was clear. In 1986, the par-run performance of Seattle second basemen was −30.1, and at shortstop, −54.3, one of the poorest par-run position performances. A team with every position performing at this level, even with average pitching, would finish just a few games ahead of the legendary 1899 Cleveland Spiders, who started the season 17–80, then had their stadium burn down, sending them on an extended road trip during which they lost 51 of their final 54 games.

Of course, the Mariners can't go back to 1985. They can't play Coles because he's in Detroit. They moved Tartabull to the outfield, and now they're trying him in Kansas City. Calderon has moved to Chicago and Henderson to Boston.

What did Seattle get for all this blue chip talent? Not nearly enough, and within 18 months the Mariners have gone from a team of great promise to just another team in search of the answers.

1986 Seattle Mariners

| | BATTING Records | BFP | Runs Contributed | | | Unearned Runs | PITCHERS | IP.f | Earned Runs | Expected |
			/Game	Total	vs. Lg Av	vs. Lg Av			vs. Lg Av	W-L
1b	A.DAVIS	562	0.622	80	16.0	-9.0	J.BEATTIE	40.1	-8.3	1– 3
							K.BEST	35.2	0.5	2– 2
2b	H.REYNOLDS	486	0.278	33	-30.1	-8.4	M.BROWN	15.2	-5.7	0– 1
							S.FIREOVID	21.0	-0.3	1– 1
3b	J.PRESLEY	660	0.468	80	-3.5	5.6	L.GUETTERMAN	76.0	-26.7	1– 7
							M.HUISMANN	80.0	4.1	5– 4
ss	S.OWEN	446	0.343	37	-19.1	-18.1	P.LADD	70.2	2.8	4– 4
	R.QUINONES	131	0.125	4	-14.6		M.LANGSTON	239.1	-18.0	11–16
	D.RAMOS	110	0.073	-0	-15.3		P.MIRABELLA	6.1	-3.1	0– 1
	R.JONES	21	-0.136	-2	-5.3		M.MOORE	266.0	-3.6	14–16
							M.MORGAN	216.1	-8.6	11–13
lf	D.TARTABULL	578	0.635	87	18.3	0.9	E.NUNEZ	21.2	-3.9	1– 2
	M.BRANTLEY	113	0.285	8	-6.7		J.REED	34.2	4.1	2– 2
	I.CALDERON	138	0.319	11	-7.1		B.SWIFT	115.1	-16.5	5– 8
							M.TRUJILLO	41.1	8.2	3– 2
cf	J.MOSES	442	0.367	39	-15.5		M.WILCOX	55.2	-8.2	2– 4
	D.HENDERSON	378	0.651	58	13.1		M.YOUNG	103.2	4.1	6– 6
	B.BONNELL	53	0.051	-0	-7.6		Others	6.0	5.8	1– 0
rf	A.COWENS	87	0.078	1	-11.4					
c	B.KEARNEY	226	0.327	18	-10.2	-0.5				
	S.BRADLEY	217	0.495	26	0.1					
	S.YEAGER	145	0.210	7	-12.1					
	D.VALLE	60	1.072	14	7.3					
dh	P.BRADLEY	614	0.744	101	34.8	-0.5				
	K.PHELPS	441	0.885	83	35.7					
	G.THOMAS	199	0.448	22	-2.9					
	D.HENGEL	66	0.127	2	-7.5					
	R.NELSON	12	0.036	0	-1.8					
	Others	0	0.036	-0	-0.0	6.5				
	TOTALS	6185		709	-45.4	-23.3			-73.3	71– 91

	Runs Scored	Runs Allowed	Won	Lost
CALCULATED	699	841	67	95
ACTUAL	718	835	67	95

1985 Texas Rangers

	BATTING Records	BFP	Runs Contributed			Unearned Runs vs. Lg Av	PITCHERS	IP.f	Earned Runs vs. Lg Av	Expected W-L
			/Game	Total	vs. Lg Av					
1b	P.O'BRIEN	655	0.542	85	9.5	3.0	T.BOGGS	7.0	-5.8	0- 1
	B.STEIN	81	0.305	6	-4.3		G.COOK	40.0	-23.6	0- 5
							J.GUZMAN	32.2	5.0	2- 2
2b	T.HARRAH	521	0.742	87	34.8	1.0	G.HARRIS	113.0	21.0	8- 5
							D.HENRY	21.0	3.7	1- 1
3b	B.BELL	351	0.329	28	-15.2	-1.0	B.HOOTON	124.0	-14.9	5-10
	S.BUECHELE	236	0.256	16	-15.3		C.HOUGH	250.1	23.3	15-14
							M.MASON	179.0	-13.6	7-13
ss	C.WILKERSON	395	0.308	30	-18.5	0.9	D.NOLES	110.1	-11.2	4- 8
	W.TOLLESON	355	0.503	43	2.6		D.ROZEMA	88.0	-0.5	4- 6
	J.KUNKEL	4	0.207	0	-0.3		J.RUSSELL	62.0	-23.5	1- 6
							D.SCHMIDT	85.2	9.4	5- 5
lf	G.WARD	638	0.523	81	5.2	1.5	B.SEBRA	20.1	-7.6	0- 2
	B.JONES	148	0.370	14	-4.5		C.WELSH	76.1	0.1	4- 5
	N.CAPRA	8	-0.071	-0	-1.6		M.WILLIAMS	26.0	5.0	2- 1
							R.WRIGHT	7.2	-0.5	0- 1
cf	O.MCDOWELL	452	0.499	57	1.4		Others	171.0	-30.3	5-14
	G.WRIGHT	393	0.135	11	-41.8					
rf	L.PARRISH	382	0.450	43	-3.7					
	D.WALKER	148	0.261	10	-9.5					
	E.VALENTINE	40	0.253	3	-2.5					
c	D.SLAUGHT	370	0.515	46	1.8	0.6				
	G.BRUMMER	121	0.402	11	-2.9					
	G.PETRALLI	116	0.305	9	-4.6					
	L.PUJOLS	1	4.500	1	0.6					
dh	C.JOHNSON	334	0.573	46	6.7	0.6				
	A.BANNISTER	137	0.475	16	-0.1					
	T.DUNBAR	117	0.202	5	-10.1					
	Others	0	0.202	-0	-0.4	-2.4				
	TOTALS	6003		649	-72.7	4.2			-63.8	63- 99

	Runs Scored	Runs Allowed	Won	Lost
CALCULATED	648	781	67	94
ACTUAL	617	785	62	99

The Texas Rangers deserved their remarkable turnaround. They assessed their situation correctly and showed great courage in shaking up their roster more than any team in baseball. They took advantage of their one strength coming out of the 1985 season: the problems were so obvious that the axe would fall clean.

That is to say, a lot of the move forward was simply addition by subtraction. George Wright's 1985 season of −41.8 was the lowest par-run performance I can recall for an outfielder. Pitchers Cook, Hooton, Noles, Boggs, et cetera, went the way Russell, and Mason would doubtless have gone if they hadn't turned around, after achieving a collective −122.9 par-runs. (Negative team pitching performance is seldom so easily discerned.)

On paper, the Texas Rangers roster today is not very different from that of Oakland, California, or Minnesota—no big players. The difference is that Texas has a wealth of potential big players. They just might wake up one day and find that the outfield of Incaviglia, McDowell, and Sierra is the most productive in baseball. Some young pitchers are also promising, especially Ed Correa and Bobby Witt.

Judging the future of the Rangers is simply a guess as to how many building block talents emerge out of their playpen. The possibilities are indeed exciting.

1986 Texas Rangers

	BATTING Records	BFP	Runs Contributed /Game	Total	vs. Lg Av	Unearned Runs vs. Lg Av	PITCHERS	IP.f	Earned Runs vs. Lg Av	Expected W-L
1b	P.O'BRIEN	641	0.689	100	27.9	2.2	K.BROWN	5.0	0.3	0– 0
							E.CORREA	202.1	-1.1	12–11
2b	T.HARRAH	341	0.419	35	-6.9	-0.7	J.GUZMAN	172.1	-7.0	9–10
	C.WILKERSON	249	0.285	18	-15.3		G.HARRIS	111.1	16.7	8– 4
	J.BROWNE	25	0.813	4	1.8		D.HENRY	19.1	-1.0	1– 1
3b	S.BUECHELE	513	0.428	55	-9.4	2.1	C.HOUGH	230.1	9.9	14–11
							M.LOYND	42.0	-5.5	2– 3
ss	S.FLETCHER	594	0.557	76	7.9	0.8	M.MAHLER	63.0	0.2	4– 3
	J.KUNKEL	13	0.369	1	-0.4		M.MASON	135.0	-2.4	8– 8
							R.MERIDITH	3.0	0.4	0– 0
lf	R.SIERRA	411	0.494	53	0.9	-1.5	D.MOHORCIC	79.0	14.7	6– 3
	G.WARD	418	0.581	56	8.2		D.ROZEMA	10.2	-2.1	0– 1
	B.BROWER	9	-0.193	-1	-2.2		J.RUSSELL	82.0	7.0	5– 4
							M.WILLIAMS	98.0	6.5	6– 5
cf	O.MCDOWELL	643	0.560	86	8.6		B.WITT	157.2	-22.9	7–11
	G.WRIGHT	112	0.203	6	-9.6		R.WRIGHT	39.1	-3.8	2– 2
							Others	3.0	2.4	0– 0
rf	P.INCAVIGLIA	606	0.558	83	8.9					
	B.JONES	23	-0.032	-1	-4.0					
c	D.SLAUGHT	341	0.490	42	-0.4	0.9				
	O.MERCADO	112	0.216	5	-9.0					
	G.PETRALLI	142	0.336	13	-6.1					
dh	L.PARRISH	524	0.643	80	18.4	0.9				
	D.PORTER	178	0.746	31	9.7					
	T.PACIOREK	220	0.385	21	-7.0					
	M.STANLEY	33	0.804	6	2.3					
	Others	0	0.804	-1	-0.6	-0.5				
	TOTALS	6148		768	23.7	4.4			12.3	85– 77

	Runs Scored	Runs Allowed	Won	Lost
CALCULATED	774	733	85	77
ACTUAL	771	743	87	75

1985 Toronto Blue Jays

| | BATTING Records | BFP | Runs Contributed | | | Unearned Runs | PITCHERS | IP.f | Earned Runs | Expected |
			/Game	Total	vs. Lg Av	vs. Lg Av			vs. Lg Av	W-L
1b	W.UPSHAW	557	0.591	79	13.2	-0.5	J.ACKER	86.1	8.8	6– 4
	C.FIELDER	81	0.711	13	4.3		D.ALEXANDER	260.2	20.0	17–12
							B.CAUDILL	69.1	8.9	5– 3
2b	D.GARCIA	627	0.399	63	-14.8	0.3	J.CERUTTI	6.2	-0.9	0– 0
	M.LEE	43	0.009	-1	-7.0		J.CLANCY	128.2	5.2	8– 6
							S.CLARKE	4.0	-0.2	0– 0
3b	R.MULLINIKS	427	0.685	66	19.7	4.6	S.DAVIS	28.0	1.9	2– 1
	G.IORG	312	0.616	45	9.6		T.FILER	48.2	1.4	3– 2
	K.GRUBER	13	0.156	0	-1.3		T.HENKE	40.0	9.4	3– 1
ss	T.FERNANDEZ	618	0.493	73	0.9	-2.6	J.KEY	212.2	26.9	15– 9
							D.LAMP	105.2	9.7	7– 5
							G.LAVELLE	72.2	8.5	5– 3
lf	G.BELL	666	0.618	100	20.8	-1.2	L.LEAL	67.1	-12.0	3– 5
	L.THORNTON	75	0.267	5	-4.9		R.MUSSELMAN	52.1	-1.9	3– 3
	R.SHEPHERD	37	0.005	-0	-5.8		D.STIEB	265.0	49.0	20–10
							Others	6.0	5.8	1– 0
cf	L.MOSEBY	670	0.576	92	13.8					
rf	J.BARFIELD	612	0.771	107	38.4					
c	E.WHITT	465	0.520	60	3.5	0.6				
	B.MARTINEZ	113	0.198	6	-8.8					
	W.AIKENS	24	0.354	2	-0.7					
	G.ALLENSON	34	-0.095	-2	-7.3					
	S.NICOSIA	15	0.253	1	-1.0					
	J.HEARRON	7	-0.039	-0	-1.3					
dh	J.BURROUGHS	227	0.581	30	4.9	0.6				
	A.OLIVER	195	0.310	16	-9.7					
	L.MATUSZEK	166	0.235	10	-11.4					
	C.JOHNSON	83	0.446	9	-0.6					
	M.WEBSTER	1	-0.223	-1	-0.7					
	Others	38	-0.223	3	-2.5	1.1				
	TOTALS	6106		777	51.1	2.9			140.5	97– 65

	Runs Scored	Runs Allowed	Won	Lost
CALCULATED	791	597	100	61
ACTUAL	759	588	99	62

The Blue Jays simply don't impress me as much as the Tigers, Yankees, or Red Sox, and I certainly didn't expect them to repeat in 1986. Their division title in 1985 came on the wave of exceptionally strong pitching: a +140.5 par-run performance. In general, pitchers are not very consistent, and this level of performance is rare; the Met's staffs, universally respected in a pitcher's park and led by Dwight Gooden, performed in 1985 and 1986 at +82.0 and +101.4 levels. On the 1985 Toronto staff, only Stieb and possibly Key were as highly regarded as the Mets pitchers.

The 1985 championship and a complete management reorganization have combined to keep the Toronto roster virtually unchanged over the last two years. In 1986 the offensive performance was little different from that in 1985. Both years, Bell and Barfield led the attack while Moseby and Upshaw were disappointments. However, the pitching staff fell off by some 123 par-runs! Half the difference was Dave Stieb, who dropped 61.0 par-runs, but the rest of the decline was rather evenly distributed. Was there some sort of uniform dip in team defense? It seems unlikely since the regular lineup was identical to the one a year before.

On the other hand, Mark Eichhorn was a most pleasant surprise. Some scoffed when it was learned that Eichhorn had received Cy Young consideration, but I would commend those voters for their perceptiveness. Look through these tables and you'll see that only Roger Clemens had a better par-run total than Eichhorn's +42.8, and then in many more innings. Had Eichhorn been allowed to pitch five more innings, he would have led the American League in ERA, even if he had given up 14 additional earned runs! (For batting titles, a rule allows a man with almost enough plate appearances to win, provided that he would still have the best average after enough hitless at-bats to qualify officially. But for pitchers, there's no theoretical limit on the number of earned runs that might be yielded in a given inning!)

In any division other than the AL East, Toronto would be a favorite, but going into 1987, Boston, New York, and Detroit all look stronger. Nevertheless, more productive years from Stieb, Moseby, and Upshaw, along with infield and catching help, could put Toronto back on top again.

1986 Toronto Blue Jays

| | BATTING Records | BFP | Runs Contributed | | | Unearned Runs | | PITCHERS | IP.f | Earned Runs | Expected |
			/Game	Total	vs. Lg Av	vs. Lg Av				vs. Lg Av	W-L
1b	W.UPSHAW	661	0.522	83	4.6	0.1		J.ACKER	60.0	-1.2	3- 3
								D.ALEXANDER	111.0	-3.5	6- 6
2b	D.GARCIA	446	0.381	42	-14.4	0.0		L.AQUINO	11.1	-2.7	0- 1
	M.LEE	85	0.099	1	-10.3			B.CAUDILL	36.1	-8.1	1- 3
								J.CERUTTI	145.1	0.4	9- 7
3b	R.MULLINIKS	395	0.510	48	0.7	4.2		J.CLANCY	219.1	5.8	14-11
	G.IORG	351	0.385	33	-11.0			S.CLARKE	12.2	-7.1	0- 1
	K.GRUBER	152	0.145	6	-14.9			S.DAVIS	3.2	-5.3	0- 1
ss	T.FERNANDEZ	727	0.571	99	12.3	8.5		M.EICHHORN	157.0	42.8	14- 4
								D.GORDON	21.2	-6.9	1- 2
lf	G.BELL	690	0.688	114	32.3	0.6		T.HENKE	91.1	8.4	6- 4
								J.JOHNSON	88.0	2.8	5- 4
cf	L.MOSEBY	668	0.549	89	8.1			J.KEY	232.0	15.6	15-10
								D.LAMP	73.0	-7.1	4- 4
rf	J.BARFIELD	671	0.806	123	46.1			M.MAHLER	1.0	0.5	0- 0
								J.MUSSELMAN	5.1	-3.5	0- 1
c	E.WHITT	433	0.522	56	2.5	0.5		D.STIEB	205.0	-12.9	11-12
	B.MARTINEZ	185	0.218	10	-14.6			D.WARD	2.0	-2.1	0- 0
	J.HEARRON	26	0.259	2	-1.8			Others	4.0	1.9	0- 0
dh	C.JOHNSON	394	0.575	53	6.9	0.5					
	R.LEACH	266	0.541	35	3.6						
	R.SHEPHERD	73	0.246	5	-5.2						
	C.FIELDER	90	0.161	4	-8.8						
	F.MCGRIFF	5	0.081	0	-0.7						
	Others	0	0.081	-0	-0.0	2.0					
	TOTALS	6318		803	35.6	16.6				17.6	89- 73

	Runs Scored	Runs Allowed	Won	Lost
CALCULATED	799	729	88	75
ACTUAL	809	733	86	76

1985 Atlanta Braves

| BATTING Records | BFP | Runs Contributed | | | Unearned Runs | PITCHERS | IP.f | Earned Runs | Expected |
		/Game	Total	vs. Lg Av	vs. Lg Av			vs. Lg Av	W-L
1b B.HORNER	540	0.580	76	19.6	1.2	L.BARKER	73.2	-22.6	2– 7
G.PERRY	262	0.243	16	-14.2		S.BEDROSIAN	206.2	-5.6	10–12
C.CHAMBLISS	189	0.350	16	-4.4		R.CAMP	127.2	-5.1	6– 8
						J.DEDMON	86.0	-4.7	4– 5
2b G.HUBBARD	512	0.359	46	-8.4	2.1	T.FORSTER	59.1	8.7	4– 2
P.ZUVELLA	210	0.348	18	-4.3		G.GARBER	97.1	-0.2	5– 6
						J.JOHNSON	85.2	-4.8	4– 5
3b K.OBERKFELL	472	0.499	55	6.9	-1.1	R.MAHLER	266.2	3.4	15–15
P.RUNGE	110	0.348	9	-1.5		C.MCMURTRY	45.0	-15.0	1– 4
						P.PEREZ	95.1	-27.0	2– 8
ss R.RAMIREZ	595	0.250	39	-29.5	-8.5	.SCHULER	10.2	-3.7	0– 1
A.THOMAS	19	0.171	1	-1.3		S.SHIELDS	68.0	-11.9	2– 5
						Z.SMITH	147.0	-3.4	8– 9
lf T.HARPER	542	0.471	62	4.3	-1.5	B.SUTTER	88.1	-8.8	4– 6
J.RABB	2	-0.223	-0	-0.6		Others	5.0	5.0	1—0
cf D.MURPHY	712	0.834	129	59.5					
rf C.WASHINGTON	441	0.591	62	15.5					
B.KOMMINSK	343	0.375	32	-5.1					
M.THOMPSON	193	0.500	23	2.9					
A.HALL	57	0.127	1	-5.1					
c R.CERONE	316	0.216	16	-19.5	-0.2				
B.BENEDICT	237	0.177	10	-16.8					
L.OWEN	82	0.389	8	-0.6					
Others	373	0.389	-9	-54.8	-4.5				
TOTALS	6207		611	-57.3	-12.5			-95.7	68– 94

	Runs Scored	Runs Allowed	Won	Lost
CALCULATED	601	767	64	98
ACTUAL	632	781	66	96

The 1985 season was a bitter disappointment to Braves followers. In three years, with virtually the same lineup, they had gone from a division title to 96 losses, all despite having Dale Murphy in the lineup, who as usual had one of the best par-run totals in the league at +59.5, barely second to Pedro Guerrero. Evidently there were severe problems elsewhere, and new management addressed them.

Of course, if you lose 96 games and can't touch Horner or Murphy, and your only blue chip rookie played like Brad Komminsk, your other players are probably not going to be in brisk demand. It does appear as though a good job was done under the circumstances. Addition by subtraction of Barker and Perez and disabling Sutter brought the pitching staff back to mediocrity. Of the many weak positions, the worst was catching at −40.3 par-runs, and here the Braves found the Phillies ready to part with Ozzie Virgil. Rookie Andres Thomas was counted on to help a chronic shortstop weakness, and there was a lot of shuffling of outfielders and hope for comebacks from the other veterans.

Most of these moves were successful. The pitching staff was filled out with veterans Palmer and Alexander and rookie Assenmacher. Ozzie Virgil's batting average was disappointing, but along with pickup Ted Simmons he was a great improvement on his predecessors. Thomas had a good first half, so another shortstop (Zuvella) was passed on to the Yankees for a revived Ken Griffey. Indeed, most of the holdover veterans had decent years. Still, the Braves finished last, because Dale Murphy had a dull year, Rick Mahler the worst par-run pitching performance of the last two years, and the overall shortstop performance was −55.3 par-runs.

That's discouraging. There's been talk of passing on Murphy, to the Mets, for a collection of talents. Unless there's a moneyback guarantee if no Dale Murphy-level talent emerges from the collection, I'd be reluctant. Lose Murphy and you've ruled out a championship for America's Team for the foreseeable future; keep Murphy and there's at least a chance.

1986 Atlanta Braves

	BATTING Records	BFP	Runs Contributed /Game	Total	vs. Lg Av	Unearned Runs vs. Lg Av
1b	B.HORNER	581	0.563	79	16.5	-0.6
	C.CHAMBLISS	138	0.646	20	6.1	
	T.SIMMONS	144	0.473	17	1.1	
2b	G.HUBBARD	488	0.415	49	-3.2	-2.9
	P.RUNGE	10	0.315	1	-0.4	
3b	K.OBERKFELL	596	0.542	74	13.0	6.7
	B.KOMMINSK	5	0.385	0	-0.1	
ss	A.THOMAS	335	0.255	23	-16.9	-7.1
	R.RAMIREZ	530	0.282	38	-24.4	
lf	T.HARPER	298	0.405	29	-3.6	-0.4
	B.SAMPLE	221	0.602	31	7.6	
	G.PERRY	80	0.414	8	-0.8	
cf	D.MURPHY	692	0.638	104	28.5	
rf	O.MORENO	386	0.325	32	-13.4	
	K.GRIFFEY	313	0.712	52	18.4	
	C.WASHINGTON	153	0.502	19	2.1	
	A.HALL	57	0.366	5	-1.1	
	D.MOTLEY	11	0.300	1	-0.5	
c	O.VIRGIL	431	0.490	50	3.6	0.2
	B.BENEDICT	182	0.261	11	-9.7	
	Others	416	0.261	0	-50.3	2.2
	TOTALS	6067		645	-27.4	-2.0

PITCHERS	IP.f	Earned Runs vs. Lg Av	Expected W-L
J.ACKER	95.0	-0.8	5– 6
D.ALEXANDER	117.1	-1.6	6– 7
P.ASSENMACHER	68.1	9.2	5– 3
J.DEDMON	99.2	8.1	6– 5
G.GARBER	78.0	10.2	5– 4
J.JOHNSON	87.0	-12.1	3– 7
R.MAHLER	237.2	-30.9	9–18
C.MCMURTRY	79.2	-9.1	3– 6
E.OLWINE	47.2	1.7	3– 3
D.PALMER	209.2	1.5	11–13
C.PULEO	24.1	2.0	1– 1
S.SHIELDS	12.2	-4.8	0– 1
Z.SMITH	204.2	-7.5	10–13
C.SPECK	28.1	-1.3	1– 2
B.SUTTER	18.2	-1.3	1– 1
D.WARD	16.0	-6.4	0– 2
Others	6.0	4.5	1– 0
		-38.5	71– 91

	Runs Scored	Runs Allowed	Won	Lost
CALCULATED	632	700	73	88
ACTUAL	615	719	72	89

1985 Chicago Cubs

| | BATTING Records | BFP | Runs Contributed | | | Unearned Runs | PITCHERS | IP.f | Earned Runs | Expected |
			/Game	Total	vs. Lg Av	vs. Lg Av			vs. Lg Av	W-L
1b	L.DURHAM	607	0.668	93	30.8	0.5	J.ABREGO	24.0	-7.4	1– 2
	R.HEBNER	128	0.257	9	-6.4		J.BALLER	52.0	0.7	3– 3
							D.BEARD	12.2	-3.9	0– 1
2b	R.SANDBERG	673	0.768	116	48.6	1.4	D.BOTELHO	44.0	-8.4	2– 3
							W.BRUSSTAR	74.1	-20.3	2– 6
3b	R.CEY	564	0.474	66	4.6	-3.9	D.ECKERSLEY	169.1	9.5	11– 8
	D.OWEN	20	0.617	3	0.8		S.ENGEL	51.2	-11.4	2– 4
							R.FONTENOT	154.2	-13.3	8–10
ss	S.DUNSTON	272	0.467	32	2.1	-2.9	G.FRAZIER	76.0	-23.7	2– 7
	L.BOWA	212	0.313	17	-6.2		D.GUMPERT	10.1	0.1	1– 1
	C.SPEIER	240	0.318	20	-6.9		R.MERIDITH	46.1	-4.5	2– 3
							R.PATTERSON	39.0	2.6	3– 2
lf	G.MATTHEWS	362	0.576	48	11.4	0.6	J.PERLMAN	8.2	-7.5	0– 1
	T.BOSLEY	202	0.827	36	16.9		D.RUTHVEN	87.1	-9.2	4– 6
							S.SANDERSON	121.0	6.3	8– 6
cf	B.DERNIER	521	0.386	51	-5.5		L.SMITH	97.2	6.0	6– 5
	D.LOPES	325	0.721	52	20.3		M.SMITH	1.0	0.4	0– 0
	B.HATCHER	178	0.269	13	-7.1		L.SORENSEN	82.1	-6.2	4– 5
	D.JACKSON	11	-0.125	-1	-2.2		R.SUTCLIFFE	130.0	5.9	8– 6
							S.TROUT	140.2	3.1	8– 7
rf	K.MORELAND	667	0.654	99	33.4		Others	25.0	-7.0	1– 2
	G.WOODS	97	0.376	9	-1.2					
	B.DAYETT	27	0.246	2	-1.4					
	C.WALKER	12	-0.122	-1	-2.3					
c	J.DAVIS	536	0.409	56	-3.1	1.0				
	S.LAKE	128	0.009	-0	-16.4					
	Others	395	0.009	-3	-50.9	-2.0				
	TOTALS	6177		716	59.3	-5.3			-88.4	75– 87

	Runs Scored	Runs Allowed	Won	Lost
CALCULATED	711	745	77	85
ACTUAL	686	729	77	84

Because of the overly-friendly confines of their home parks, the Cubs and Red Sox need at least two apparent "big players" to be serious contenders. In 1985 there was one (Ryne Sandberg) and two near misses (Durham and Moreland) plus some super subs in Lopes and Bosley, which might have been enough to contend if the pitching hadn't broken down. The consequences of losing the entire starting rotation show up clearly in the obscure names next to large negative pitching par-run entries. However, even if you remove every negative entry from the Cubs' 1985 pitching par-runs table, then double the positive par-runs of Eckersley, Sanderson, Sutcliffe, and Trout, you still come up with a pitching par-run total of +53.3. Added to the batting and fielding par-runs, this yields 113.6 par-runs or about 92 victories, 9 games in back of the Cardinals. The pitching breakdown was a convenient scapegoat, but the 1985 Cubs could not have won 100 games unless Bob Dernier hit like Willie Mays.

During the winter of 1985–1986, it might have been wise to try to get some good-looking kids for Keith Moreland, whose value was probably at its all-time high, and/or Jody Davis and Ron Cey. Maybe this was attempted unsuccessfully. Anyhow, not much went right for the Cubs in 1986. The 1985 lameness of the starters presaged an ineffectiveness of such uniformity that only Lee Smith had a positive par-run contribution. No one came close to having a big offensive year except part-timer Ron Cey. Even Sandberg dropped 30 par-runs. Only chronic Pirate bad luck kept the Cubs from going from first to last in their division within two seasons.

In the National League East, it's going to be little short of miraculous for the Cubs to return to contention in the near future. They do have some good young players in the infield, but compared to the Mets, or even the Phillies, Expos, and Cardinals, there isn't enough talent. Worse, the veterans are too shopworn and expensive to interest another club.

1986 Chicago Cubs

	BATTING Records	BFP	Runs Contributed /Game	Total	vs. Lg Av	Unearned Runs vs. Lg Av	PITCHERS	IP.f	Earned Runs vs. Lg Av	Expected W-L
1b	L.DURHAM	557	0.623	81	21.5	4.3	J.BALLER	53.2	-9.9	2– 4
							R.DAVIS	20.0	-8.7	0– 2
2b	R.SANDBERG	682	0.532	88	12.7	8.3	F.DIPINO	40.0	-6.5	2– 3
							D.ECKERSLEY	201.0	-19.0	9–13
3b	R.CEY	306	0.782	52	21.3	0.4	R.FONTENOT	56.0	-0.9	3– 3
	M.TRILLO	172	0.538	21	3.5		G.FRAZIER	51.2	-9.7	2– 4
	C.SPEIER	176	0.585	24	5.3		D.GUMPERT	59.2	-4.4	3– 4
	D.LOPES	191	0.833	34	15.3		A.HALL	23.2	-2.2	1– 2
							G.HOFFMAN	84.0	-1.3	5– 5
ss	S.DUNSTON	611	0.401	65	-7.4	-2.9	M.KEOUGH	29.0	-4.0	1– 2
							E.LYNCH	99.2	-0.9	5– 6
lf	G.MATTHEWS	432	0.626	62	16.8	-1.3	G.MADDUX	31.0	-6.2	1– 2
	T.BOSLEY	139	0.530	17	2.6		J.MOYER	87.1	-13.0	4– 6
	B.DAYETT	76	0.538	10	2.2		D.RUTHVEN	10.2	-1.6	0– 1
	R.PALMEIRO	78	0.349	7	-1.8		S.SANDERSON	169.2	-9.0	9–10
							L.SMITH	90.1	6.3	6– 4
cf	B.DERNIER	351	0.320	29	-12.6		R.SUTCLIFFE	176.2	-19.1	8–12
	J.MUMPHREY	339	0.571	45	9.4		S.TROUT	161.0	-18.6	7–11
	D.MARTINEZ	116	0.051	1	-14.3		Others	6.0	6.5	1– 0
	T.FRANCONA	133	0.298	10	-5.5					
rf	K.MORELAND	652	0.429	68	-3.4					
	C.WALKER	112	0.519	14	1.8					
c	J.DAVIS	581	0.441	66	-0.3	1.6				
	S.LAKE	21	0.812	3	1.6					
	M.MARTIN	15	0.044	0	-1.8					
	S.CHRISTMAS	9	-0.044	-0	-1.4					
	Others	378	-0.044	4	-44.8	-1.3				
	TOTALS	6127		702	20.5	9.0			-122.1	69– 93

	Runs Scored	Runs Allowed	Won	Lost
CALCULATED	690	782	70	90
ACTUAL	680	781	70	90

1985 Cincinnati Reds

	BATTING Records	BFP	Runs Contributed /Game	Total	vs. Lg Av	Unearned Runs vs. Lg Av	PITCHERS	IP.f	Earned Runs vs. Lg Av	Expected W-L
1b	P.ROSE	500	0.532	62	14.2	2.6	T.BROWNING	261.1	1.2	15–14
	T.PEREZ	207	0.762	34	14.7		B.BUCHANAN	16.0	-8.6	0– 2
	P.O'NEILL	12	0.572	2	0.4		J.FRANCO	99.0	15.5	7– 4
							T.HUME	80.0	2.9	5– 4
2b	R.OESTER	584	0.499	69	9.0	4.2	A.MCGAFFIGAN	94.1	-1.4	5– 5
	T.FOLEY	98	0.225	6	-5.7		R.MURPHY	3.0	-0.8	0– 0
							F.PASTORE	54.0	-1.5	3– 3
3b	B.BELL	284	0.374	26	-4.5	1.7	T.POWER	80.0	7.9	5– 4
	N.ESASKY	464	0.563	63	14.3		J.PRICE	64.2	-2.2	3– 4
	W.KRENCHICKI	205	0.581	27	7.2		R.ROBINSON	108.1	-4.8	6– 6
	W.ROWDON	11	0.362	1	-0.1		M.SOTO	256.2	0.4	15–14
ss	D.CONCEPCION	620	0.333	50	-16.9	2.7	A.STUPER	99.0	-10.5	5– 6
	T.RUNNELLS	42	0.133	2	-2.9		J.TIBBS	218.0	-8.0	12–13
							C.WILLIS	13.2	-8.5	0– 2
lf	G.REDUS	294	0.710	48	18.2	0.3	Others	6.0	0.4	0– 0
	C.CEDENO	245	0.365	22	-4.4					
	E.DAVIS	131	0.619	21	6.0					
	M.VENABLE	146	0.514	19	3.3					
cf	E.MILNER	520	0.494	62	8.0					
	D.WALKER	54	0.325	5	-1.5					
rf	D.PARKER	694	0.686	112	42.1					
c	D.VAN GORDER	166	0.266	11	-7.0	-0.8				
	B.DIAZ	181	0.404	18	-1.2					
	A.KNICELY	178	0.444	20	0.6					
	D.BILARDELLO	108	0.029	-0	-14.0					
	Others	399	0.029	-7	-55.5	0.0				
	TOTALS	6143		673	24.1	10.7			-18.0	81– 81

	Runs Scored	Runs Allowed	Won	Lost
CALCULATED	680	663	83	79
ACTUAL	677	666	89	72

In Pete Rose's first two years as a manager, the Reds have won six and five games more than Calculated from their par-run performance. Rose has been a remarkable athlete and a successful skipper, but I don't think the Reds can continue to defy the law of averages. To stay in contention, they'll have to play better, and from the looks of things, they will.

In hopes of returning to respectability, the Reds really loaded up on big name veterans during 1985 who mostly were no longer or never were the producers suggested by their reputations. In that category, I'd put Rose, Perez, Oester, Bell, Concepcion, Cedeno, Parker, and Diaz. From that group only Parker, Perez, and Rose himself really produced during 1985, but "with a little bit of luck" the Reds finished a strong second. To bolster a suspect pitching staff for a title run optimistically expected in 1986, the Reds continued the same strategy by trading Redus and his part-time

RPG of .710 for Denny, and a two-for-one to get Gullickson. They didn't look like the right moves, but in 1986 the Reds finished second again after a dreadful start.

What went wrong with the analysis? The veterans performed about as expected; the two new pitchers broke even in par-runs, and a good year by Buddy Bell did not compensate for declines in production by Parker, Oester, Rose, Esasky, and Perez. The intended nucleus of the club was such that this team, expected by many to contend, ought to have had trouble staying out of the cellar.

The Reds' secret weapon was three young outfielders (Davis, Daniels, and Tracy Jones), a young infielder (Larkin), and a young pitcher (Murphy), who, in limited playing time, led the staff with +16.8 par-runs. The three outfielders played at a combined +73 par-run level. If these guys are for real and play every day, the Reds in 1987 could simply blow away the division.

1986 Cincinnati Reds

	BATTING Records	BFP	Runs Contributed			Unearned Runs	PITCHERS	IP.f	Earned Runs	Expected
			/Game	Total	vs. Lg Av	vs. Lg Av			vs. Lg Av	W-L
1b	N.ESASKY	383	0.487	45	3.1	-3.4	T.BROWNING	243.1	-2.6	14–13
	P.ROSE	272	0.340	24	-7.3		S.BUTERA	1.0	0.4	0– 0
	T.PEREZ	228	0.434	24	-1.0		J.DENNY	171.1	-9.3	9–10
							J.FRANCO	101.0	8.7	7– 4
2b	R.OESTER	586	0.416	59	-6.2	-2.2	B.GULLICKSON	244.2	9.0	15–12
	T.RUNNELLS	11	-0.191	-1	-2.6		B.LANDRUM	13.1	-4.5	0– 1
							R.MURPHY	50.1	16.8	5– 1
3b	B.BELL	655	0.605	91	22.8	9.5	T.POWER	129.0	0.2	8– 7
	W.ROWDON	92	0.474	11	0.7		J.PRICE	41.2	-7.8	2– 3
							R.ROBINSON	116.2	6.2	8– 5
ss	K.STILLWELL	315	0.296	23	-13.0	-1.5	M.SMITH	3.1	-3.6	0– 1
	D.CONCEPCION	346	0.374	31	-7.1		M.SOTO	105.0	-11.7	5– 7
	B.LARKIN	169	0.531	22	3.1		S.TERRY	55.2	-15.0	2– 4
							C.WELSH	139.1	-16.5	7– 9
lf	E.DAVIS	487	0.925	97	46.9	-0.4	C.WILLIS	52.1	-4.4	3– 3
	M.VENABLE	168	0.358	16	-3.8		Others	5.0	4.1	1– 0
	T.JONES	96	0.797	17	7.4					
cf	E.MILNER	462	0.544	62	9.8					
	K.DANIELS	207	0.886	39	18.7					
rf	D.PARKER	700	0.556	96	18.5					
c	B.DIAZ	519	0.459	58	0.2	-0.2				
	S.BUTERA	137	0.468	15	0.4					
	D.VAN GORDER	11	-0.158	-1	-3.1					
	Others	399	-0.158	-8	-58.7	-0.8				
	TOTALS	6243		717	28.9	0.9			-30.1	84– 78

	Runs Scored	Runs Allowed	Won	Lost
CALCULATED	709	709	81	81
ACTUAL	732	717	86	76

1985 Houston Astros

	BATTING Records	BFP	Runs Contributed /Game	Total	vs. Lg Av	Unearned Runs vs. Lg Av	PITCHERS	IP.f	Earned Runs vs. Lg Av	Expected W-L
1b	G.DAVIS	390	0.555	53	11.9	-3.0	J.CALHOUN	63.2	7.4	4- 3
	E.CABELL	159	0.402	16	-1.7		B.DAWLEY	81.0	0.3	5- 4
	H.SPILMAN	69	0.005	-0	-9.5		J.DESHAIES	3.0	1.2	0- 0
							F.DIPINO	76.0	-3.7	4- 4
2b	B.DORAN	657	0.614	93	26.8	-0.7	J.HEATHCOCK	56.1	1.5	3- 3
							C.KERFELD	44.1	-2.3	2- 3
3b	P.GARNER	505	0.448	56	1.8	-3.9	B.KNEPPER	241.0	1.1	14-12
	D.WALLING	374	0.453	42	1.6		M.KNUDSON	11.0	-6.6	0- 1
	G.RIVERA	41	0.208	2	-2.5		M.MADDEN	19.0	-1.4	1- 1
	B.PENA	32	0.303	3	-0.8		R.MATHIS	70.0	-19.1	2- 6
							M.ROSS	13.0	-1.8	1- 1
ss	C.REYNOLDS	396	0.411	42	-1.9	4.1	N.RYAN	232.0	-5.5	13-13
	D.THON	272	0.403	28	-2.2		M.SCOTT	221.2	7.4	14-11
							D.SMITH	79.1	11.6	6- 3
lf	J.CRUZ	590	0.585	81	20.0	0.0	J.SOLANO	33.2	0.4	2- 2
	J.PANKOVITS	191	0.392	19	-2.3		Others	216.0	-0.8	13-11
	C.JONES	28	0.211	2	-1.6					
	T.TOLMAN	46	0.086	2	-4.3					
cf	J.MUMPHREY	488	0.476	56	5.0					
	T.GAINEY	42	0.103	1	-3.7					
	E.BULLOCK	26	0.386	3	-0.4					
rf	K.BASS	577	0.481	70	7.1					
	T.PUHL	220	0.588	31	8.5					
c	M.BAILEY	402	0.570	51	12.0	-2.0				
	A.ASHBY	216	0.574	29	6.9					
	J.MIZEROCK	41	0.188	2	-2.8					
	Others	430	0.188	2	-47.1	-1.0				
	TOTALS	6192		682	20.6	-6.5			-10.2	85- 77

	Runs Scored	Runs Allowed	Won	Lost
CALCULATED	680	676	81	81
ACTUAL	706	691	83	79

Houston's 1986 season offers hope for the team without an established "big player" in the everyday lineup. If everybody has a decent year AND two or three regulars approach big seasons AND a pitcher gets really hot AND the other contenders have problems, you can win the division.

Looking at the 1985 table for Houston, there was almost no reason to expect a championship in 1986. The only personnel change was the timely unloading of Joe Niekro's salary onto the Yankees for a promising young pitcher, and the promotion of some other rookies to fill secondary spots on the pitching staff.

The hitters, collectively, performed just as expected. Glenn Davis was up but Bill Doran was down. Denny Walling was up but the shortstops were down. Kevin Bass was up but the catchers were down. The offense added up to +20.6 par-runs in 1985 and -3.9 par-runs in 1986, a relatively even performance.

But the pitching staff par-runs jumped from -10.2 in 1985 (a dreadful performance in the Dome) to +93.7, and the fielding was appreciably tighter, going from -10.2 to +3.8. That's at least ten more wins for a Calculated record of 91-71, and in 1986 no one else in the West won nearly that many games. Although all of the holdover starters—Scott, Ryan, Knepper—improved along with many of the second-line pitchers (suggesting that the team defense might have tightened all around), few would argue with the contention that Mike Scott's "funny pitch" was the critical ingredient in Houston's championship.

Which leads me to a story. Houston was a subscriber to STATS (a baseball statistical/analytical service) for one season, 1984, after which they decided to develop an in-house system after purchasing a computer of their own. Before the final parting from STATS, I was told, "the only thing we really got out of the computer this year was that we convinced Scottie to give up his curveball, because they were hitting .326 off it." (The major league average off all curves is about .225.)

Well, fellows . . . I think you got your money's worth!

1986 Houston Astros

	BATTING Records	BFP	Runs Contributed			Unearned Runs vs. Lg Av	PITCHERS	IP.f	Earned Runs vs. Lg Av	Expected W-L
			/Game	Total	vs. Lg Av					
1b	G.DAVIS	654	0.654	101	30.3	1.5	L.ANDERSEN	64.2	6.7	4– 3
	D.DRIESSEN	29	0.833	5	2.3		J.CALHOUN	26.2	0.0	1– 1
							D.DARWIN	54.1	8.4	4– 2
2b	B.DORAN	642	0.561	83	16.7	-0.8	J.DESHAIES	144.0	7.4	9– 7
	J.PANKOVITS	124	0.475	14	0.4		F.DIPINO	40.1	0.6	2– 2
							T.FUNK	8.1	-2.6	0– 1
3b	D.WALLING	422	0.688	67	22.7	-4.5	M.HERNANDEZ	27.2	-0.6	1– 2
	P.GARNER	347	0.458	39	0.6		M.KEOUGH	35.0	2.4	2– 2
							C.KERFELD	93.2	11.7	6– 4
ss	D.THON	295	0.308	23	-11.8	6.2	B.KNEPPER	258.0	16.5	16–13
	C.REYNOLDS	329	0.308	27	-12.6		M.KNUDSON	42.2	-2.4	2– 3
	B.PENA	34	0.208	1	-2.5		A.LOPEZ	78.0	2.2	4– 4
							M.MADDEN	39.2	-1.6	2– 2
lf	J.CRUZ	536	0.547	69	11.3	2.0	R.MONTALVO	1.0	-0.6	0– 0
	T.PUHL	193	0.351	17	-5.1		C.REYNOLDS	1.0	-2.6	0– 0
	M.MEADOWS	6	0.572	1	0.2		N.RYAN	178.0	7.5	10– 9
							M.SCOTT	275.1	45.6	20–11
cf	B.HATCHER	453	0.425	48	-3.7		D.SMITH	56.0	6.1	4– 3
	T.WALKER	101	0.419	11	-1.0		J.SOLANO	32.0	-13.8	0– 3
	D.LOPES	113	0.362	10	-2.5		Others	5.0	3.1	1– 0
rf	K.BASS	640	0.652	98	29.9					
	T.GAINEY	56	0.753	9	3.6					
	E.BULLOCK	21	-0.171	-2	-4.9					
c	A.ASHBY	361	0.471	41	1.9	-0.0				
	M.BAILEY	182	0.272	12	-8.9					
	J.MIZEROCK	107	0.375	10	-1.3					
	R.WINE	13	0.409	1	-0.2					
	Others	437	0.409	-12	-69.3	-0.3				
	TOTALS	6095		672	-3.9	4.0			94.1	89– 73

	Runs Scored	Runs Allowed	Won	Lost
CALCULATED	671	576	91	71
ACTUAL	654	569	96	66

573

1985 Los Angeles Dodgers

| BATTING Records | BFP | Runs Contributed | | | Unearned Runs | PITCHERS | IP.f | Earned Runs | Expected |
		/Game	Total	vs. Lg Av	vs. Lg Av			vs. Lg Av	W-L
1b G.BROCK	496	0.547	65	12.7	0.5	T.BRENNAN	31.2	-13.4	0- 3
S.BREAM	63	0.205	4	-3.4		B.CASTILLO	68.0	-13.9	2- 5
F.STUBBS	9	0.134	0	-0.8		C.DIAZ	79.1	8.6	5- 3
2b S.SAX	551	0.428	56	-0.6	-7.7	O.HERSHISER	239.2	41.6	18- 8
						B.HOLTON	4.0	-2.4	0- 0
3b D.ANDERSON	262	0.307	20	-7.9	-3.9	R.HONEYCUTT	142.0	2.6	8- 7
B.BAILOR	130	0.217	8	-6.7		K.HOWELL	86.0	-1.7	5- 5
E.CABELL	208	0.496	25	3.2		T.NIEDENFUER	106.1	10.4	7- 5
B.MADLOCK	128	0.808	22	10.4		A.PENA	4.1	-2.3	0- 0
ss M.DUNCAN	620	0.368	59	-8.7	-6.4	D.POWELL	29.1	-5.3	1- 2
B.RUSSELL	192	0.411	20	-0.5		J.REUSS	212.2	15.8	14-10
M.RAMSEY	17	0.135	1	-1.4		F.VALENZUELA	272.1	34.6	19-11
lf P.GUERRERO	581	0.984	117	63.6	-0.3	B.WELCH	167.1	23.8	12- 6
R.REYNOLDS	229	0.391	23	-1.7		Others	26.0	5.4	2- 1
J.GONZALEZ	12	0.396	1	-0.1					
L.MATUSZEK	76	0.491	9	1.5					
A.OLIVER	85	0.301	6	-3.1					
S.PEDERSON	5	-0.223	-0	-1.1					
cf K.LANDREAUX	527	0.466	62	4.9					
R.WILLIAMS	9	0.535	1	0.2					
rf M.MARSHALL	564	0.648	88	28.9					
C.MALDONADO	235	0.339	21	-5.7					
T.WHITFIELD	110	0.444	13	0.2					
R.BRYANT	6	0.461	1	0.0					
c M.SCIOSCIA	525	0.679	78	29.8	-0.2				
S.YEAGER	131	0.160	5	-10.1					
G.REYES	3	0.257	1	0.5					
Others	432	0.257	3	-47.0	-2.0				
TOTALS	6206		708	57.2	-20.0			104.0	94- 68

	Runs Scored	Runs Allowed	Won	Lost
CALCULATED	719	578	96	66
ACTUAL	682	579	95	67

In spite of a team defense that all too often shows why baseball is great family entertainment, the 1985 Dodgers should have been shoo-ins in 1986. Instead, as everyone knows, they barely avoided the historical achievement of receding from first place to last in one season.

The tone was set for the year when Pedro Guerrero snapped his ankle. Since Guerrero was the best hitter in the National League in 1985, this was going to hurt a lot—a loss of +61.8 par-runs. Even if nothing else had gone wrong, the 1986 Astros would have been better than the Guerrero-less 1985 Dodgers, but a lot of other bad things happened to the Dodger offense. The other leading hitters in 1985, Marshall, Scioscia, Madlock, and Brock, all were injured, and perhaps discouraged; almost everyone else sagged. The one shining exception was a most unexpected big year from Steve Sax—almost as good as Tommy Herr's in 1985. Overall, the Dodger offense declined by 101.4 par-runs, almost 90 of which were directly attributable to the Guerrero and Marshall injuries.

But the Dodgers were so strong on paper that they still should have won 86 games and finished second. What hardly anyone seems to have noticed is that the pitching fell off even more: 110.1 par-runs! A lot of attention has been paid to the relief pitching woes, but the starters were the real culprits. It was ironic that Valenzuela was regarded as a leading Cy Young contender as his performance (relative earned run average) dropped 17.4 par-runs. The weak performances of Welch (off 12.5 par-runs), Reuss (off 33.3 par-runs), or Hershiser (off 45.1 par-runs), made the LA staff the biggest pitching disappointment in the National League. The sum of those four declines is −108.3, almost precisely the decline for the entire staff. It is very hard to see why the finger has been pointed only at the relievers, who in fact were the only department on the club who performed as well in 1986 as in 1985.

Can the Dodgers rebound? Their chances rest mostly on the comeback by Guerrero. Improvements by Marshall, Hershiser and the other starting pitchers, or some of the younger players coming on (like Steve Sax) would help, but Guerrero is the straw that stirs LA's future.

1986 Los Angeles Dodgers

BATTING Records	BFP	Runs Contributed /Game	Total	vs. Lg Av	Unearned Runs vs. Lg Av	PITCHERS	IP.f	Earned Runs vs. Lg Av	Expected W-L
1b G.BROCK	367	0.467	43	1.5	-2.0	J.BECKWITH	18.1	-6.4	0– 2
E.CABELL	298	0.334	25	-9.4		C.DIAZ	25.1	-1.5	1– 2
L.SEE	22	0.451	2	-0.0		B.GALVEZ	20.2	-0.5	1– 1
						O.HERSHISER	231.1	-3.5	12–14
2b S.SAX	704	0.702	110	39.1	0.6	B.HOLTON	24.1	-2.0	1– 2
D.ANDERSON	241	0.305	17	-10.0		R.HONEYCUTT	171.0	7.6	10– 9
						K.HOWELL	97.2	-1.7	5– 6
3b B.MADLOCK	421	0.515	52	6.4	-10.1	T.NIEDENFUER	80.0	0.0	4– 5
J.HAMILTON	151	0.235	11	-8.4		A.PENA	70.0	-9.1	3– 5
						D.POWELL	65.1	-4.0	3– 4
ss M.DUNCAN	445	0.333	38	-14.1	-7.8	J.REUSS	74.0	-17.5	2– 6
C.SHIPLEY	31	0.010	-0	-4.3		F.VALENZUELA	269.1	17.2	16–14
						E.VANDE BERG	71.1	2.4	4– 4
lf R.WILLIAMS	338	0.466	37	0.5	-3.1	B.WELCH	235.2	11.3	14–13
F.STUBBS	465	0.436	52	-1.7		Others	4.0	1.7	0– 0
J.GONZALEZ	102	0.340	9	-3.1					
L.MATUSZEK	222	0.550	29	4.9					
R.BRYANT	82	0.655	14	4.6					
P.GUERRERO	64	0.537	9	1.8					
E.AMELUNG	11	-0.174	-1	-2.9					
cf K.LANDREAUX	310	0.422	33	-2.3					
B.RUSSELL	242	0.330	19	-7.7					
C.CEDENO	87	0.314	7	-3.2					
rf M.MARSHALL	362	0.470	44	1.7					
T.WHITFIELD	19	0.072	0	-1.9					
c M.SCIOSCIA	449	0.474	49	2.6	-1.8				
A.TREVINO	233	0.511	28	2.9					
J.FIMPLE	20	0.136	1	-0.6					
Others	415	0.136	10	-40.6	2.7				
TOTALS	6101		639	-44.2	-21.6			-6.1	77– 85

	Runs Scored	Runs Allowed	Won	Lost
CALCULATED	629	701	74	88
ACTUAL	638	679	73	89

1985 Montreal Expos

	BATTING Records	BFP	Runs Contributed /Game	Runs Contributed Total	vs. Lg Av	Unearned Runs vs. Lg Av	PITCHERS	IP.f	Earned Runs vs. Lg Av	Expected W-L
1b	D.DRIESSEN	350	0.427	37	-1.0	-0.2	T.BURKE	120.1	16.0	8– 5
	T.FRANCONA	296	0.387	29	-3.9		S.BUTERA	1.0	0.4	0– 0
	A.GALARRAGA	79	0.175	4	-5.9		J.DOPSON	13.0	-10.8	0– 2
	R.SHINES	54	-0.037	-2	-8.9		E.GLYNN	2.1	-4.1	0– 1
	S.THOMPSON	36	0.381	3	-0.4		D.GRAPENTHIN	7.0	-8.2	0– 1
							B.GULLICKSON	181.1	1.3	10–10
2b	V.LAW	621	0.580	83	21.6	1.4	J.HESKETH	155.1	19.0	10– 7
	U.WASHINGTON	209	0.398	21	-2.2		G.LUCAS	67.2	3.0	4– 4
	A.NEWMAN	32	0.164	1	-2.4		J.O'CONNOR	23.2	-3.6	1– 2
	D.FLYNN	6	0.008	-0	-0.8		D.PALMER	135.2	-1.9	7– 8
	F.MANRIQUE	14	1.133	4	2.1		J.REARDON	87.2	4.0	5– 5
							B.ROBERGE	68.0	1.1	4– 4
3b	T.WALLACH	617	0.469	74	6.5	3.1	S.ROGERS	38.0	-8.8	1– 3
	S.BARNES	26	-0.068	-1	-4.5		D.SCHATZEDER	104.1	-2.4	5– 6
							R.SHINES	1.0	0.4	0– 0
ss	H.BROOKS	652	0.421	70	-1.2	0.6	B.SMITH	222.1	16.7	14–11
							R.ST.CLAIRE	68.2	-2.6	3– 4
lf	T.RAINES	665	0.868	123	60.7	1.8	F.YOUMANS	77.0	9.7	5– 3
	M.DILONE	91	0.124	3	-8.4		Others	88.0	-19.9	3– 7
	R.JOHNSON	5	-0.223	-1	-1.4					
cf	H.WINNINGHAM	345	0.363	32	-5.9					
	M.WEBSTER	234	0.615	35	9.8					
rf	A.DAWSON	570	0.464	69	5.8					
	J.WOHLFORD	142	0.259	10	-6.6					
	D.FROBEL	27	0.072	1	-2.6					
c	M.FITZGERALD	341	0.288	25	-12.8	0.0				
	S.BUTERA	138	0.275	10	-5.2					
	S.NICOSIA	79	0.115	2	-7.3					
	M.O'BERRY	26	0.247	2	-0.8					
	N.YOST	11	0.040	0	-1.4					
	Others	387	0.040	4	-41.3	0.5				
	TOTALS	6053		637	-18.5	7.2			9.3	79– 83

	Runs Scored	Runs Allowed	Won	Lost
CALCULATED	640	642	80	81
ACTUAL	633	636	84	77

Hardly anyone seems to notice how well the Montreal club is being run. In the last two years, they've had an incredible run of crippling injuries and their financial condition is not strong. Yet, they've stayed on the brink of serious contention.

Going into 1985, they took two extreme risks: dealing the popular big player Gary Carter, and playing four former third basemen as their infield. To everyone's surprise, the club started well and stayed in serious contention until the pace set by the Cardinals and Mets became just too strong. They managed this despite the uselessness of pitching aces Steve Rogers and Charlie Lea, and a mediocre offense apart from secondbaseman Vance Law, and Tim Raines—easily the best player in the National League over the past two seasons (a fact not often recognized).

At first look, nothing changed in 1986. The Calculated Won-Lost performance of 80–81 was identical in 1985 and 1986, but it was not for want of constructive moves. Brooks, Fitzgerald, and Youmans contributed four times as many positive par-runs as the man traded for them: Gary Carter.

Pick-up centerfielder Mitch Webster provided a lot of offense, and first baseman Galarraga showed promise. New pitchers Tibbs and McGaffigan pitched more innings than Gullickson with the same par-run performance, but injuries ended the seasons of many key players: Brooks, Fitzgerald, Galarraga, and Hesketh.

Montreal shuffles their roster as much as anyone, and the payoffs of this strategy include Tim Burke, Mitch Webster, and Bob McClure. On the other hand, it's costing them more games than it should to weed out the guys who won't help. George Wright, Dennis Martinez, and Bert Roberge each cost the Expos a game in 1986; Miguel Dilone, Steve Nicosia, and Razor Shines, a game each in 1985.

Two players—Wallach and Reardon—have reputations outweighing their par-run performance, and I would expect Montreal to improve themselves with any trades involving them. One can only hope their overall success in shuffling personnel does not blind them to the absolute importance of holding on to Tim Raines.

1986 Montreal Expos

BATTING Records	BFP	Runs Contributed			Unearned Runs
		/Game	Total	vs. Lg Av	vs. Lg Av
1b A.GALARRAGA	356	0.504	43	3.9	-1.3
W.KRENCHICKI	247	0.349	21	-6.7	
W.JOHNSON	134	0.421	14	-1.4	
J.THOMPSON	69	0.499	8	1.7	
B.MOORE	12	0.008	-0	-1.7	
2b V.LAW	402	0.322	32	-14.2	-2.9
A.NEWMAN	212	0.185	9	-16.0	
C.CANDAELE	110	0.187	5	-8.5	
3b T.WALLACH	539	0.416	56	-4.9	4.6
ss H.BROOKS	338	0.826	62	28.7	-0.8
L.RIVERA	187	0.292	14	-7.9	
T.FOLEY	227	0.441	24	-0.5	
R.GONZALES	28	-0.045	-1	-4.9	
lf T.RAINES	664	0.910	129	64.4	1.1
G.WRIGHT	133	0.195	7	-9.2	
cf M.WEBSTER	645	0.616	92	24.0	
H.WINNINGHAM	204	0.330	17	-6.9	
rf A.DAWSON	546	0.581	77	17.5	
J.WOHLFORD	106	0.439	11	-0.4	
c D.BILARDELLO	212	0.199	11	-15.0	-0.6
M.FITZGERALD	243	0.632	35	9.7	
T.NIETO	72	0.237	4	-4.4	
R.HUNT	53	0.282	4	-2.5	
W.TEJADA	27	0.260	2	-1.5	
Others	407	0.260	6	-45.8	3.2
TOTALS	6173		682	-2.6	3.2

PITCHERS	IP.f	Earned Runs vs. Lg Av	Expected W-L
C.BROWN	11.0	2.5	1– 0
T.BURKE	101.1	8.8	6– 5
J.HESKETH	82.2	-11.9	3– 6
V.LAW	4.0	0.7	0– 0
D.MARTINEZ	98.0	-9.6	4– 7
B.MCCLURE	62.2	4.9	4– 3
A.MCGAFFIGAN	142.2	16.9	9– 6
B.OWCHINKO	15.0	0.2	1– 1
J.PARRETT	20.1	-2.6	1– 1
J.REARDON	89.0	-2.3	4– 5
G.RILEY	8.2	-0.4	0– 1
B.ROBERGE	28.2	-8.2	1– 2
D.SCHATZEDER	59.0	3.4	3– 3
B.SEBRA	91.1	1.7	5– 5
B.SMITH	187.1	-4.7	9–11
R.ST.CLAIRE	19.0	2.8	1– 1
J.TIBBS	190.1	-5.4	9–12
D.TOMLIN	10.1	-1.7	0– 1
S.VALDEZ	25.0	-8.7	0– 2
F.YOUMANS	219.0	4.4	12–12
Others	6.0	0.5	0– 0
		-8.7	76– 86

	Runs Scored	Runs Allowed	Won	Lost
CALCULATED	676	685	80	81
ACTUAL	637	688	78	83

1985 New York Mets

	BATTING Records	BFP	Runs Contributed			Unearned Runs vs. Lg Av	PITCHERS	IP.f	Earned Runs vs. Lg Av	Expected W-L
			/Game	Total	vs. Lg Av					
1b	K.HERNANDEZ	682	0.657	100	34.4	4.7	R.AGUILERA	122.1	4.8	7- 6
							B.BERENYI	13.2	1.5	1- 1
2b	W.BACKMAN	574	0.427	61	0.8	2.8	R.DARLING	248.0	18.9	16-11
	K.CHAPMAN	159	0.094	3	-15.6		S.FERNANDEZ	170.1	14.9	11- 7
							W.GARDNER	12.0	-2.2	0- 1
3b	H.JOHNSON	428	0.426	47	-0.8	2.4	D.GOODEN	276.2	63.4	22- 8
	R.KNIGHT	290	0.171	14	-20.4		T.GORMAN	52.2	-9.0	2- 4
							B.LATHAM	22.2	-1.0	1- 1
ss	R.SANTANA	564	0.297	42	-21.2	-2.9	T.LEACH	55.2	4.2	4- 2
	R.GARDENHIRE	49	0.273	3	-1.8		E.LYNCH	191.0	3.2	11-10
	L.BOWA	22	0.023	0	-2.5		R.MCDOWELL	127.1	10.8	8- 5
							R.MYERS	2.0	0.8	0- 0
lf	G.FOSTER	504	0.578	70	16.7	0.3	R.NIEMANN	4.2	1.9	0- 0
	D.HEEP	305	0.491	36	4.6		J.OROSCO	79.0	7.5	5- 3
	T.PACIOREK	124	0.437	13	-0.1		J.SAMBITO	10.2	-10.7	1- 2
	T.BLOCKER	16	-0.100	-1	-3.0		C.SCHIRALDI	26.1	-15.5	0- 3
	B.BEANE	8	0.332	1	-0.2		D.SISK	73.0	-13.9	3- 5
							Others	6.0	2.4	1- 0
cf	M.WILSON	367	0.525	47	7.6					
	L.DYKSTRA	273	0.455	31	2.3					
rf	D.STRAWBERRY	470	0.870	87	41.6					
	J.CHRISTENSEN	133	0.319	11	-4.1					
	R.STAUB	55	0.661	8	2.7					
c	G.CARTER	633	0.667	96	32.4	1.0				
	R.REYNOLDS	46	0.122	2	-3.9					
	C.HURDLE	97	0.335	8	-2.5					
	Others	444	0.335	13	-36.7	2.0				
	TOTALS	6243		692	30.4	10.3			82.0	93- 69

	Runs Scored	Runs Allowed	Won	Lost
CALCULATED	703	580	94	68
ACTUAL	695	568	98	64

In 1985, the Mets finished a strong second to a surprising Cardinal team. Two judicious drafts and a pair of canny trades put four "big players" on the Met roster—Dwight Gooden, Darryl Strawberry, Keith Hernandez, and Gary Carter (not quite +35, the last two, but very close). Their par-runs total to 171.8, which if everyone else had been average, would have meant 98 Calculated wins. Since the Calculated total was 94, the remainder of the roster held some weaknesses—evident from the tables as the right-handed second base and third-base platooners Chapman and Knight, the shortstop Santana, and the secondary pitchers Sambito, Gorman, Schiraldi, and Sisk, who totaled −106.1 par-runs.

So management bundled two of the problems off to Boston for a fourth starter Ojeda, and sent a suspect to Minnesota for right-handed hitting second baseman Teufel. Knight made a comeback, and a rookie named Mitchell was tried at shortstop and other positions.

In 1986, a lot went poorly for the Mets. Dwight Goo-den fell off 39.2 par-runs, and Gary Carter declined by 22.3 par-runs. (Carter for MVP? C'mon, guys! When Mitchell played shortstop, Gary had a lower RPG and par-run total than every other starting Met!!) George Foster dropped 19.0 par-runs and was released; Fernandez fell by 10.6 par-runs. Collectively, that's −91.1 par-runs, about as bad as losing both Guerrero and Marshall or having McGee and Herr go into a tailspin.

The fact that they succeeded in the face of these declines proves that the greatest strength of the Mets is their depth. They probably have one of the deepest collections of talent since the heyday of the New York Yankees, as evidenced by the fact that ten of them outbatted a strong MVP candidate. In addition, Davey Johnson seems to take care to use his players where they will perform to his and the team's best advantage. Should everything fall into place for the Mets, pity the NL East. It is very easy to construct a scenario in which the 1987 Mets win 110 games and leave the rest of the division far behind.

1986 New York Mets

	BATTING Records	BFP	Runs Contributed /Game	Total	vs. Lg Av	Unearned Runs vs. Lg Av	PITCHERS	IP.f	Earned Runs vs. Lg Av	Expected W-L
1b	K.HERNANDEZ	652	0.753	106	42.8	5.0	R.AGUILERA	141.2	-2.5	9– 7
	D.MAGADAN	21	0.958	4	2.3		R.ANDERSON	49.2	5.5	4– 2
	T.CORCORAN	7	-0.223	-1	-2.0		B.BERENYI	39.2	-11.6	1– 3
							R.DARLING	237.0	23.8	17– 9
2b	W.BACKMAN	440	0.607	60	15.7	-5.7	S.FERNANDEZ	204.1	4.3	13– 9
	T.TEUFEL	318	0.439	34	-1.2		D.GOODEN	250.0	24.2	18– 9
							T.LEACH	6.2	0.8	0– 0
3b	R.KNIGHT	541	0.535	68	11.1	-1.0	E.LYNCH	1.2	0.7	0– 0
	H.JOHNSON	253	0.631	37	9.7		R.MCDOWELL	128.0	9.8	9– 5
							J.MITCHELL	10.0	0.1	1– 0
ss	R.SANTANA	436	0.219	22	-29.1	-2.9	R.MYERS	10.2	-0.6	1– 1
	K.ELSTER	33	0.145	1	-2.9		R.NIEMANN	35.2	-0.3	2– 2
							B.OJEDA	217.1	27.7	16– 7
lf	M.WILSON	415	0.610	60	14.7	0.2	J.OROSCO	81.0	12.4	6– 3
	K.MITCHELL	364	0.613	53	13.3		Others	76.0	7.4	5– 3
	G.FOSTER	256	0.407	28	-2.3					
	L.MAZZILLI	72	0.747	12	4.6					
cf	L.DYKSTRA	498	0.729	80	29.8					
	S.JEFFERSON	27	0.351	2	-0.7					
rf	D.STRAWBERRY	562	0.746	95	36.0					
	D.HEEP	227	0.628	32	8.9					
c	G.CARTER	573	0.516	71	10.1	1.0				
	E.HEARN	151	0.438	16	-0.7					
	J.GIBBONS	22	1.777	7	5.2					
	B.LYONS	10	-0.151	-1	-2.2					
	Others	470	-0.151	-7	-66.1	1.2				
	TOTALS	6348		780	97.0	-2.3			101.7	103– 59

	Runs Scored	Runs Allowed	Won	Lost
CALCULATED	784	588	101	61
ACTUAL	783	578	108	54

1985 Philadelphia Phillies

| | BATTING Records | BFP | Runs Contributed | | | Unearned Runs | | PITCHERS | IP.f | Earned Runs | Expected |
			/Game	Total	vs. Lg Av	vs. Lg Av				vs. Lg Av	W-L
1b	M.SCHMIDT	645	0.787	112	48.0	-1.6		L.ANDERSEN	73.0	-5.9	4- 5
	T.CORCORAN	219	0.279	15	-7.6			S.CARLTON	92.0	2.7	5- 5
	J.WOCKENFUSS	45	0.138	1	-3.9			D.CARMAN	120.1	16.0	8- 5
	A.KNICELY	7	-0.223	-1	-2.0			R.CHILDRESS	33.1	-9.7	1- 3
2b	J.SAMUEL	709	0.510	92	13.2	-0.7		J.DENNY	230.2	-6.0	12-13
3b	R.SCHU	457	0.438	49	-0.5	-3.9		K.GROSS	205.2	4.0	12-11
								C.HUDSON	193.0	-4.0	11-11
ss	S.JELTZ	228	0.182	10	-15.2	-1.5		J.KOOSMAN	99.1	-11.4	4- 7
	L.AGUAYO	200	0.641	29	9.7			S.RAWLEY	198.2	6.3	12-10
	T.FOLEY	171	0.441	18	-0.1			D.RUCKER	79.1	-6.4	4- 5
	D.THOMAS	103	0.355	9	-2.3			D.SHIPANOFF	36.1	1.5	2- 2
	K.GARCIA	3	-0.223	-0	-0.8			F.TOLIVER	25.0	-3.0	1- 2
								P.ZACHRY	12.2	-0.9	1- 1
lf	G.GROSS	205	0.466	23	2.5	-0.3		Others	52.0	3.7	3- 2
	J.RUSSELL	234	0.375	24	-3.6						
cf	V.HAYES	637	0.526	81	13.5						
	G.MADDOX	236	0.323	20	-6.6						
	J.STONE	282	0.398	28	-2.8						
rf	G.WILSON	650	0.433	72	1.0						
c	O.VIRGIL	483	0.508	60	8.0	1.0					
	D.DAULTON	119	0.459	14	0.5						
	B.DIAZ	82	0.240	6	-4.0						
	Others	407	0.240	-2	-51.5	1.5					
	TOTALS	6122		659	-4.6	-5.5				-13.0	81- 81

	Runs Scored	Runs Allowed	Won	Lost
CALCULATED	649	673	79	83
ACTUAL	667	673	75	87

I have been a Phillies fan for over thirty years. If that (now) doesn't automatically imply that I'm a Mike Schmidt fan, then I'll say it: I'm a Mike Schmidt fan.

The treatment he gets from many fans could be construed as an embarrassment to the city of Philadelphia, but it is also interesting to try to understand intellectually. If you listen to a talk-show, Schmidt critics describe him as "inconsistent", an odd observation since Schmidt's season totals, year in and year out, either individually or expressed as par-runs, are as invariant as anyone's.

Another interesting fact is that this year, everyone, including Mike himself, believes he has been more "consistent". So what is "consistent" about this past season? If you look at the numbers for last year, 1986 was strongly different in only two areas: strikeouts and unintentional walks (his first time ever below the 100 mark in either category).

As a first guess, maybe it's the lower number of strikeouts that made Schmitty preceived as more consistent. Yet, consider Glenn Wilson, an outfielder whose "real", that is, par-run, contributions are modest, who strikes out with a frequency similar to Mike Schmidt, but is undeniably a Phillie fan folk hero. No, it can't be strikeouts alone. My guess is that what frustrates fans more than anything is seeing a power hitter take pitches—especially strikes—and especially with runners on base. It was perhaps the fact that Schmidt walked less in '86 which gave the positive impression of greater consistency.

Anyhow, back to the agenda. The Phillies seem to go to so much trouble to accumulate especially promising hitters—the possible +35 par-run hitters of the future—that the farm system has not produced for a decade. Hence Von Hayes, Glenn Wilson, Gary Redus and Milt Thompson, to go with Mike Schmidt, Juan Samuel, and possibly John Russell, Darryl Daulton, Ron Schu, and Jeff Stone. That seems like sound strategy for chasing a team like the Mets; patching holes just won't do the job. In 1986 it paid off, as the big improvement in Hayes and the contributions of Redus and Daulton brought the hitting and the team up to second place. Of course, whenever Schmidt retires, the club will go back to .500 ball.

1986 Philadelphia Phillies

	BATTING Records	BFP	Runs Contributed			Unearned Runs vs. Lg Av	PITCHERS	IP.f	Earned Runs vs. Lg Av	Expected W-L
			/Game	Total	vs. Lg Av					
1b	V.HAYES	690	0.712	110	39.5	-1.3	L.ANDERSEN	12.2	-0.8	1– 1
	F.MELENDEZ	8	0.207	0	-0.6		S.BEDROSIAN	90.1	3.3	6– 4
							J.BITTIGER	14.2	-2.9	1– 1
2b	J.SAMUEL	633	0.522	84	11.6	-7.8	S.CARLTON	83.0	-22.7	3– 7
	L.AGUAYO	146	0.305	12	-5.4		D.CARMAN	134.1	7.4	9– 6
	G.LEGG	20	1.000	4	2.4		R.CHILDRESS	2.2	-0.9	0– 0
							M.FREEMAN	16.0	2.6	1– 1
3b	M.SCHMIDT	657	0.865	122	56.9	4.6	T.GORMAN	11.2	-5.2	0– 1
	R.SCHU	233	0.597	33	7.7		G.GROSS	0.2	0.3	0– 0
							K.GROSS	241.2	-8.3	14–13
ss	S.JELTZ	510	0.314	39	-17.7	2.7	C.HUDSON	144.0	-19.6	7– 9
	T.FOLEY	72	0.607	10	2.9		T.HUME	94.1	9.9	7– 4
							M.JACKSON	13.1	0.5	1– 1
lf	G.REDUS	392	0.611	56	13.7	2.6	R.LERCH	8.0	-3.7	0– 1
	G.GROSS	125	0.447	13	0.4		M.MADDUX	78.0	-14.8	3– 6
							S.RAWLEY	157.2	3.1	10– 8
cf	M.THOMPSON	332	0.423	35	-2.6		D.RUCKER	25.0	-5.7	1– 2
	R.ROENICKE	343	0.563	44	9.7		B.RUFFIN	146.1	20.4	11– 5
	J.STONE	275	0.569	37	7.0		D.SCHATZEDER	29.1	1.1	2– 1
	C.JAMES	48	0.431	5	-0.3		D.STEWART	12.1	-3.9	0– 1
	G.MADDOX	9	0.938	2	1.0		K.TEKULVE	110.0	14.4	8– 4
rf	G.WILSON	639	0.479	76	4.8		F.TOLIVER	25.2	0.6	2– 1
	J.LEFEBVRE	21	-0.041	-1	-4.1		Others	7.0	5.9	1– 0
c	J.RUSSELL	348	0.474	42	2.5	-0.4				
	D.DAULTON	181	0.693	27	9.6					
	R.REYNOLDS	132	0.201	7	-9.2					
	Others	415	0.201	-8	-61.1	-0.8				
	TOTALS	6229		752	68.8	-0.5			-19.0	86– 76

	Runs Scored	Runs Allowed	Won	Lost
CALCULATED	741	692	86	75
ACTUAL	739	713	86	75

1985 Pittsburgh Pirates

	BATTING Records	BFP	Runs Contributed /Game	Total	vs. Lg Av	Unearned Runs vs. Lg Av	PITCHERS	IP.f	Earned Runs vs. Lg Av	Expected W-L
1b	S.BREAM	108	0.533	14	2.7	-2.3	M.BIELECKI	45.2	-4.8	2- 3
	J.THOMPSON	490	0.564	64	14.8		J.DELEON	162.2	-20.1	6-12
	L.MAZZILLI	147	0.679	22	8.5		C.GUANTE	109.0	10.5	6- 6
							R.KRAWCZYK	8.1	-9.7	1- 2
2b	J.RAY	652	0.449	72	2.6	-1.4	L.MCWILLIAMS	126.1	-15.6	5-10
							R.REUSCHEL	194.0	28.4	13- 9
3b	B.MADLOCK	449	0.438	48	0.4	0.3	R.RHODEN	213.1	-20.9	8-16
	J.MORRISON	257	0.332	23	-6.7		D.ROBINSON	95.1	-3.0	4- 6
	D.GONZALEZ	138	0.366	13	-2.5		D.TOMLIN	1.0	0.4	0- 0
							L.TUNNELL	132.1	-6.2	6- 9
ss	S.KHALIFA	367	0.326	30	-8.9	4.8	B.WALK	58.2	-0.6	3- 4
	B.ALMON	274	0.482	32	3.7		J.WINN	75.2	-13.8	2- 6
	J.LEMASTER	65	0.097	2	-6.1		Others	227.0	-4.4	11-15
	T.FOLI	41	0.062	-0	-5.1					
	R.BELLIARD	20	0.081	0	-2.2					
lf	S.KEMP	266	0.406	27	-1.6	-2.7				
	R.REYNOLDS	142	0.674	22	7.7					
cf	J.ORSULAK	436	0.485	51	6.4					
	M.WYNNE	363	0.167	16	-27.1					
	?.LOUCKS	9	1.113	2	1.1					
	T.DAVIS	7	-0.120	-1	-1.5					
rf	G.HENDRICK	277	0.252	18	-13.9					
	M.BROWN	233	0.745	38	16.5					
	S.LEZCANO	153	0.497	18	3.3					
	D.FROBEL	130	0.286	9	-4.5					
c	T.PENA	587	0.310	48	-17.8	0.0				
	J.ORTIZ	76	0.441	8	0.1					
	Others	412	0.441	-0	-50.9	4.5				
	TOTALS	6099		576	-80.9	3.2			-59.8	65- 97

	Runs Scored	Runs Allowed	Won	Lost
CALCULATED	572	710	66	95
ACTUAL	568	708	57	104

In the last three years, the Pirates haven't been very good, and if you look at their Calculated and Actual win totals for 1985 and 1986, they've also been dreadfully (choose one): A) unlucky or B) poor in the clutch.

In 1985, the Pirates' 104 losses and barren farm system certainly qualified them for the "time-tested-proven-veterans-for-tomorrow's-prospects" strategy, and this course was taken throughout the 1985 season. They acquired Mike Brown, Clements, Kipper, Reynolds, and Bream for Madlock, Candelaria, and Hendrick—a pretty decent return. However, they've been surprisingly cautious in moving Tony Pena and Rick Rhoden, two "proven veterans" whose 1985/1986 par-run totals are not as brash as their reputations would leave you to believe.

The Bucs are not as bad a club as the standings suggest, unless you believe that all these guys are "poor in the clutch." Despite a low batting average, Barry Bonds had an outstanding first year (compare his par-runs to those of the AL West homerun heros) and he might quickly develop into the big hitter his dad was. Yet, even with Babe Ruth and Sandy Koufax added to the roster, the 1987 Pirates would probably finish ten games behind the 1987 Mets. If you want to finish first, not second, the National League East is as tough as the American League East.

So I'd keep shuffling the deck, especially in Pittsburgh, because young guys are cheaper anyway, and because after three straight last place finishes, it's unlikely anyone will get upset if a move doesn't pan out.

1986 Pittsburgh Pirates

	BATTING Records	BFP	Runs Contributed			Unearned Runs vs. Lg Av	PITCHERS	IP.f	Earned Runs vs. Lg Av	Expected W-L
			/Game	Total	vs. Lg Av					
1b	S.BREAM	591	0.570	80	16.5	-4.1	M.BIELECKI	148.2	-15.6	7–10
							P.CLEMENTS	61.0	6.2	4– 3
2b	J.RAY	648	0.520	78	10.1	9.0	J.DELEON	16.1	-8.3	0– 2
							S.FANSLER	24.0	-0.1	1– 1
3b	J.MORRISON	593	0.621	88	23.5	0.4	C.GUANTE	78.0	3.2	5– 4
	R.RENTERIA	12	0.290	1	-0.5		B.JONES	37.1	3.4	2– 2
							R.KIPPER	114.0	-3.9	6– 7
ss	R.BELLIARD	350	0.279	23	-16.1	-3.6	R.KRAWCZYK	12.1	-4.9	0– 1
	S.KHALIFA	173	0.175	7	-13.9		L.MCWILLIAMS	122.1	-19.5	5– 9
	U.WASHINGTON	155	0.276	11	-6.8		B.PATTERSON	36.1	-5.0	1– 3
							H.PENA	8.1	-4.6	0– 1
lf	R.REYNOLDS	448	0.521	56	6.8	-1.3	R.REUSCHEL	215.2	-6.0	11–13
	M.BROWN	273	0.268	18	-13.8		R.RHODEN	253.2	24.7	16–12
	B.BONILLA	225	0.392	21	-3.6		D.ROBINSON	69.1	2.6	4– 4
	M.DIAZ	233	0.583	33	7.6		R.SAUVER	12.0	-3.0	0– 1
							J.SMILEY	12.2	-4.8	0– 1
cf	J.ORSULAK	437	0.385	42	-8.1		B.WALK	141.2	-0.5	8– 8
	B.ALMON	230	0.454	26	0.1		J.WINN	88.0	1.3	5– 5
	L.MAZZILLI	120	0.485	14	1.7		Others	4.0	6.7	1– 0
	T.DAVIS	24	-0.101	-1	-4.6					
rf	B.BONDS	484	0.581	67	13.7					
	B.DISTEFANO	42	0.129	2	-3.5					
	S.KEMP	20	0.479	2	0.1					
c	T.PENA	565	0.504	67	6.1	-0.8				
	J.ORTIZ	122	0.555	15	3.0					
	R.RODRIGUEZ	3	-0.223	-0	-0.9					
	Others	409	-0.223	4	-46.3	1.2				
	TOTALS	6157		653	-28.9	0.7			-28.2	77– 85

	Runs Scored	Runs Allowed	Won	Lost
CALCULATED	643	699	75	87
ACTUAL	663	700	64	98

1985 St.Louis Cardinals

	BATTING Records	BFP	Runs Contributed			Unearned Runs vs. Lg Av	PITCHERS	IP.f	Earned Runs vs. Lg Av	Expected W–L
			/Game	Total	vs. Lg Av					
1b	J.CLARK	532	0.779	89	38.4	-3.7	J.ANDUJAR	269.2	5.6	17–13
	M.JORGENSEN	146	0.382	14	-0.4		J.BOEVER	16.1	-1.5	1– 1
	C.CEDENO	82	1.445	23	15.9		G.BOOKER	22.1	-8.1	1– 2
	A.HOWE	3	-0.223	-0	-0.8		B.CAMPBELL	64.1	0.7	4– 3
							D.COX	241.0	19.1	17–10
2b	T.HERR	696	0.683	107	40.6	2.8	K.DAYLEY	65.1	6.1	5– 3
							B.FORSCH	136.0	-4.7	8– 7
3b	T.PENDLETON	602	0.267	40	-27.9	4.5	A.HASSLER	10.0	2.0	1– 0
	I.DEJESUS	78	0.246	5	-3.8		R.HORTON	89.2	6.8	6– 4
	T.LAWLESS	64	0.279	5	-2.5		M.KEOUGH	10.0	-1.0	1– 1
							K.KEPSHIRE	153.1	-19.8	7–10
ss	O.SMITH	615	0.506	74	11.3	-6.4	J.LAHTI	68.1	13.3	6– 2
							P.PERRY	12.1	4.9	1– 0
lf	V.COLEMAN	692	0.481	84	9.1	1.5	J.TUDOR	275.0	50.7	22– 8
	T.LANDRUM	183	0.553	24	5.2		T.WORRELL	21.2	1.6	1– 1
	L.SMITH	115	0.495	13	2.0		Others	13.0	5.2	1– 0
	S.BRAUN	79	0.492	9	1.3					
	B.HARPER	55	0.258	4	-2.6					
cf	W.MCGEE	652	0.783	114	50.3					
rf	A.VAN SLYKE	475	0.607	68	18.1					
	C.FORD	16	1.977	5	4.1					
c	T.NIETO	288	0.267	19	-12.7	1.2				
	D.PORTER	284	0.555	38	7.6					
	R.HUNT	20	-0.020	-0	-2.8					
	M.LAVALLIERE	44	0.118	1	-3.4					
	Others	461	0.118	5	-50.6	10.0				
	TOTALS	6182		741	96.1	9.9			80.7	99– 63

	Runs Scored	Runs Allowed	Won	Lost
CALCULATED	758	571	101	61
ACTUAL	747	572	101	61

The St.Louis Cardinal batters had a historic 1986 season, in several ways: 1) Their last-place team batting average was farther behind the 11th place Pirates than the Pirates were behind the first-place Mets. Ditto, their homerun total and team slugging percentage. 2) They were only the second Cardinal team since 1918 to finish last in runs scored (1958 was the other). 3) The drop in their batting performance of almost 200 (!) par-runs is probably unprecedented for a club that made no significant changes to its starting lineup.

Looking more closely, it is surprising that the drop in batting par-runs was not team-wide. Rather, only half the lineup was affected. In centerfield, McGee lost 57.9 par-runs; at secondbase, Tommy Herr mislaid 39.5; at first base Clark et al dropped 51.7 par-runs, and in leftfield, Vince Coleman and Landrum combined fell-off 33.5 par-runs. The sum total of these declines is an awesome 182.6!

Only the first-base slump had an obvious cause: Jack Clark's injury. The Cardinals' big question for 1987? "Will the real Willie McGee and Tommy Herr please stand up?"

I watched or listened to at least a hundred Cardinal games in both 1985 and 1986, and it certainly was not obvious that McGee or Herr was doing anything different either in 1985 or in 1986. I think the 1985 and 1986 Cardinal seasons were both fantastically large sampling errors, that is, not changes in player skills or intensity, but enormous swings in fortune (luck).

What to do if you're Whitey? There's at least one big hitter, Jack Clark, plus the possibility of Herr and McGee finding more four-leaf clovers. A lot of the Cardinal pitchers have jazzy earned run averages, thanks, I suspect, as much to a brilliant team defense as to park size. Coleman's and Pendleton's offensive liabilities are much more glaring when you finish a bad last in so many offensive categories. Like all the Cardinals, they are colorful and popular, making it hard to experiment. Yet Whitey's never been shy once he makes up his mind, and he has a reputation for trading fan favorites if the right deal comes along.

1986 St.Louis Cardinals

| | BATTING Records | BFP | Runs Contributed | | | Unearned Runs | PITCHERS | IP.f | Earned Runs | Expected |
			/Game	Total	vs. Lg Av	vs. Lg Av			vs. Lg Av	W-L
1b	J.CLARK	279	0.609	39	9.6	3.6	G.BARGAR	27.1	-5.7	1– 2
	C.HURDLE	184	0.354	16	-4.3		J.BOEVER	21.2	4.9	2– 1
	A.KNICELY	100	0.347	9	-2.2		R.BURRIS	82.0	-17.2	2– 7
	J.LINDEMAN	58	0.257	4	-3.0		T.CONROY	115.1	-19.4	4– 9
	M.LAGA	52	0.556	7	1.3		D.COX	220.0	19.8	13–11
							K.DAYLEY	38.2	2.0	2– 2
2b	T.HERR	657	0.457	71	1.1	3.4	B.EARLEY	3.0	1.2	0– 0
							B.FORSCH	230.0	11.9	13–13
3b	T.PENDLETON	626	0.296	47	-26.2	1.8	R.HORTON	100.1	16.4	7– 4
	T.LAWLESS	44	0.469	5	0.5		K.KEPSHIRE	8.0	-0.7	0– 1
	F.MANRIQUE	18	0.172	1	-1.3		J.LAHTI	2.1	1.0	0– 0
							G.MATHEWS	145.1	1.0	7– 9
ss	O.SMITH	609	0.537	76	14.0	7.6	R.OWNBEY	42.2	-0.4	2– 3
	J.OQUENDO	158	0.468	17	0.9		P.PERRY	68.2	-0.7	3– 4
							R.SOFF	38.1	1.8	2– 2
lf	V.COLEMAN	670	0.388	69	-7.4	-0.4	J.TUDOR	219.0	19.4	13–11
	T.LANDRUM	230	0.260	15	-11.9		T.WORRELL	103.2	18.8	7– 4
	J.WHITE	29	0.030	0	-3.2		Others	5.0	4.1	1– 0
cf	W.MCGEE	539	0.400	54	-7.6					
rf	A.VAN SLYKE	470	0.643	71	20.0					
	C.FORD	240	0.469	28	0.9					
	J.MORRIS	108	0.295	8	-4.6					
c	M.LAVALLIERE	350	0.425	30	-8.9	-0.2				
	M.HEATH	216	0.307	17	-8.5					
	S.LAKE	51	0.309	4	-1.9					
	Others	432	0.309	-4	-57.7	-2.3				
	TOTALS	6120		585	-100.3	13.4			58.3	79– 83

	Runs Scored	Runs Allowed	Won	Lost
CALCULATED	579	607	78	83
ACTUAL	601	611	79	82

1985 San Diego Padres

| | BATTING Records | BFP | Runs Contributed | | | Unearned Runs vs. Lg Av | PITCHERS | IP.f | Earned Runs vs. Lg Av | Expected W-L |
			/Game	Total	vs. Lg Av					
1b	S.GARVEY	699	0.459	81	5.3	3.3	L.DELEON	38.2	-2.6	2- 2
							D.DRAVECKY	214.2	15.6	13-10
2b	T.FLANNERY	456	0.547	58	13.4	-4.2	G.GOSSAGE	79.0	15.5	6- 3
	J.ROYSTER	287	0.561	37	8.5		A.HAWKINS	228.2	11.2	14-12
	A.WIGGINS	40	-0.139	-3	-8.5		L.HOYT	210.1	2.9	12-12
							R.JACKSON	40.0	4.0	3- 2
3b	G.NETTLES	515	0.600	71	18.7	3.1	C.LEFFERTS	83.1	2.2	5- 4
	K.BEVACQUA	167	0.473	19	2.0		L.MCCULLERS	35.0	5.0	2- 1
							S.PATTERSON	4.0	-9.4	1- 1
ss	G.TEMPLETON	596	0.496	72	8.9	17.4	E.SHOW	233.0	12.9	14-12
	M.RAMIREZ	63	0.492	8	0.8		T.STODDARD	60.0	-7.1	3- 4
							M.THURMOND	138.1	-5.8	7- 8
lf	C.MARTINEZ	610	0.608	85	23.4	1.2	G.WALTER	22.0	3.8	2- 1
	J.DAVIS	64	0.475	7	0.6		E.WOJNA	42.0	-10.2	1- 3
	M.DILONE	50	0.313	4	-1.5		Others	25.0	-7.0	1- 2
cf	K.MCREYNOLDS	616	0.356	57	-12.1					
	B.BROWN	91	0.036	0	-11.1					
	A.BUMBRY	103	0.173	4	-7.7					
rf	T.GWYNN	671	0.561	87	18.9					
c	T.KENNEDY	565	0.366	53	-10.4	0.4				
	B.BOCHY	120	0.506	16	2.4					
	Others	436	0.506	-15	-68.6	-11.5				
	TOTALS	6149		641	-17.1	9.7			31.0	83- 79

	Runs Scored	Runs Allowed	Won	Lost
CALCULATED	639	615	83	79
ACTUAL	650	622	83	79

Even more than a singles-hitter's batting average, raw speed is the most over-rated commodity in baseball. The 1986 San Diego Padres gave baseball another good example of this fact.

After a 1984 season in which everything blended perfectly (until the World Series), the Padres won eight games fewer in the 1985 regular season. Management decided that team speed was lacking, specifically at second base. Why? Because the only significant roster difference between 1985 and 1984 was the Royster/Flannery platoon combination replacing Wiggins. So they decided to restore the perfect blend of 1984 by drafting a fast second baseman.

Now there have been other secondbase performances where desperation was called for, but the 1985 San Diego platoon was not one of these. Indeed, the secondbasemen produced as much offensively as did any 1985 position. The real offensive declines were right- and centerfield, and the bench.

In 1986 there were some strong individual performances in the outfield, but their total effect was hampered by the emphasis on speed, allowing Marvell Wynne's light bat to steal plate appearances from the best 1985 "RPG bat" on the club: Carlos Martinez (.608). The big offensive disappointments were the veteran infielders, and the best that can be said for Bip Roberts is that it took him a lot more plate appearances to be as bad as Alan Wiggins had been in 1985.

Team speed helps on defense you say? Well, it helped San Diego to a drop of 82 in defensive par-runs, a bigger decline than anyone else except the Dodgers. That is why the Padres won ten games fewer in 1986.

1986 San Diego Padres

| | BATTING Records | BFP | Runs Contributed | | | Unearned Runs | PITCHERS | IP.f | Earned Runs | Expected |
			/Game	Total	vs. Lg Av	vs. Lg Av			vs. Lg Av	W-L
1b	S.GARVEY	584	0.365	57	-11.9	1.5	G.BOOKER	11.0	2.5	1– 0
	T.PYZNARSKI	47	0.296	3	-2.0		D.DRAVECKY	161.1	11.6	10– 8
	D.IORG	109	0.219	7	-7.0		G.GOSSAGE	64.2	-5.3	3– 4
							A.HAWKINS	209.1	-13.6	10–13
2b	T.FLANNERY	432	0.517	51	6.9	0.6	R.HAYWARD	10.0	-5.9	0– 1
	B.ROBERTS	258	0.305	19	-10.6		L.HOYT	159.0	-25.4	6–12
							D.IORG	3.0	-2.8	0– 0
3b	G.NETTLES	400	0.409	42	-4.6	-6.6	J.JONES	18.0	2.4	1– 1
	J.ROYSTER	298	0.442	31	-0.9		D.LAPOINT	61.1	-3.7	3– 4
	R.ASADOOR	60	0.736	10	3.7		C.LEFFERTS	107.2	7.4	7– 5
	M.WASINGER	9	-0.223	-1	-2.3		L.MCCULLERS	136.0	14.1	9– 6
	R.READY	3	-0.223	-0	-0.9		E.SHOW	136.1	11.3	9– 7
							B.STODDARD	23.1	3.6	2– 1
ss	G.TEMPLETON	549	0.313	43	-21.4	4.1	T.STODDARD	45.1	-0.3	2– 3
	G.GREEN	35	0.174	2	-2.8		M.THURMOND	70.2	-21.8	2– 6
							E.VOSBERG	13.2	-4.4	0– 1
lf	J.KRUK	327	0.649	46	14.4	1.1	G.WALTER	98.0	-1.6	5– 6
	C.MARTINEZ	283	0.458	31	0.1		E.WHITSON	75.2	-15.8	2– 6
							E.WOJNA	39.0	2.1	2– 2
cf	K.MCREYNOLDS	641	0.708	103	36.9		Others	5.0	3.1	1– 0
	M.WYNNE	308	0.421	33	-1.9					
rf	T.GWYNN	701	0.707	112	39.8					
c	T.KENNEDY	476	0.471	55	1.5	-0.0				
	B.BOCHY	142	0.621	21	5.6					
	B.SANTIAGO	65	0.545	9	1.7					
	M.PARENT	15	-0.022	-1	-2.5					
	Others	376	-0.022	-2	-49.8	-0.3				
	TOTALS	6118		671	-8.0	0.3			-42.2	75– 87

	Runs Scored	Runs Allowed	Won	Lost
CALCULATED	660	710	76	86
ACTUAL	656	723	74	88

1985 San Francisco Giants

	BATTING Records	BFP	Runs Contributed			Unearned Runs vs. Lg Av	PITCHERS	IP.f	Earned Runs vs. Lg Av	Expected W-L
			/Game	Total	vs. Lg Av					
1b	D.GREEN	321	0.321	26	-9.6	-2.3	V.BLUE	131.0	-12.7	5–10
	D.DRIESSEN	202	0.358	19	-3.8		M.DAVIS	114.1	0.6	6– 7
	S.THOMPSON	114	0.090	2	-11.9		S.GARRELTS	105.2	15.2	7– 5
	G.RAJSICH	110	0.246	7	-4.8		J.GOTT	148.1	-4.8	7–10
							A.HAMMAKER	170.2	-2.9	8–11
2b	M.TRILLO	505	0.285	38	-18.5	0.0	M.KRUKOW	194.2	4.7	10–12
	B.WELLMAN	188	0.262	13	-8.1		D.LAPOINT	206.2	0.4	10–13
	M.WOODARD	93	0.268	7	-3.0		R.MASON	29.2	4.8	2– 1
							G.MINTON	96.2	0.6	5– 6
3b	C.BROWN	482	0.521	60	9.6	1.7	B.MOORE	16.2	0.6	1– 1
							J.ROBINSON	12.1	-2.1	0– 1
ss	J.URIBE	513	0.323	43	-15.1	-0.8	C.WARD	12.1	-1.1	0– 1
	R.ADAMS	130	0.158	6	-9.8		F.WILLIAMS	73.0	-4.9	3– 5
	J.LEMASTER	17	-0.181	-2	-4.1		Others	142.0	0.6	7– 9
lf	J.LEONARD	531	0.312	46	-15.7	-0.9				
	R.DEER	187	0.400	20	-1.6					
cf	D.GLADDEN	561	0.377	54	-7.4					
	R.ROENICKE	170	0.724	27	11.1					
rf	C.DAVIS	551	0.531	69	12.5					
	J.YOUNGBLOOD	263	0.473	29	2.3					
c	B.BRENLY	505	0.443	56	1.0	-1.4				
	A.TREVINO	179	0.417	19	-0.6					
	M.NOKES	55	0.208	3	-3.3					
	Others	378	0.208	9	-34.1	-0.5				
	TOTALS	6055		552	-114.7	-4.2			-1.0	70– 92

	Runs Scored	Runs Allowed	Won	Lost
CALCULATED	540	660	68	94
ACTUAL	556	674	62	100

The Giants' comeback was welcome, but not particularly amazing. New management saw what had to be done and did it. Firstbase and secondbase were special contributors to the Giants' first 100-loss season in history in 1985. They had nothing to lose by changing, but needed to find big players. So they dug as deep in the farm system as necessary until real promise appeared; the kids are a lot better schooled now than they used to be. (Will Clark and Robbie Thompson would later become key parts of the third best team in the National League in 1986.)

When you shuffle, a few guys you pass on are going to take advantage of new chances with other clubs. So it was with Rob Deer and Ron Roenicke, who would have helped more than Maldonado in 1986. Indeed, note that Roenicke had had a .724 big player RPG for the Giants in 1985 but was in the minors when the Phillies got him.

Why do players suddenly play better in other uniforms? One reason might be that they are finally getting a chance to play, but the following story suggests that a lessening of pressure—a fresh start—might be a strong reason itself.

Baseball puts as much mental pressure on athletes as any sport. There is nowhere to hide and there is a lot of time between plays to brood on mistakes. If you're a machinist or a doctor or a secretary, can you imagine having your professional ranking, figured to several decimal places, published in the newspaper each week? I once spent a very pleasant hour watching a game in the intelligent and articulate company of an injured veteran regular whose team had just called up an obscure rookie replacement from AA. Because I was "from the front office" for all of a day (I'd just set up a computer system for the club), he immediately wanted to know "what they really thought" about the new guy. Was he a fill-in or a replacement? This was one of the more pressure-free organizations in the majors!

Of course I had no idea what the front office thinking was, but in case you're wondering, the veteran player's concern was appropriate. The youngster stayed around, played well, and for a while was the starter. Eventually he faded back to the minors, and the veteran had his job back.

For 1987, the Giants now are a team without conspicuous strength or weakness. In other words, they don't have an obvious big hitter, but experimenting to find one could be costly. I think they'll be doing well to stay where they were in the divisional race.

1986 San Francisco Giants

| | BATTING Records | BFP | Runs Contributed | | | Unearned Runs vs. Lg Av | PITCHERS | IP.f | Earned Runs vs. Lg Av | Expected W-L |
			/Game	Total	vs. Lg Av					
1b	W.CLARK	458	0.595	63	14.9	-2.7	J.BERENGUER	73.1	8.3	5– 3
	M.ALDRETE	256	0.537	32	4.8		V.BLUE	156.2	7.7	10– 8
	H.SPILMAN	106	0.668	16	5.1		R.BOCKUS	7.0	0.9	0– 0
	D.DRIESSEN	20	0.466	2	0.1		S.CARLTON	30.0	-4.6	1– 2
	R.LANCELLOTTI	18	0.431	3	0.2		M.DAVIS	84.1	6.8	6– 4
							K.DOWNS	88.1	9.5	6– 4
2b	R.THOMPSON	615	0.436	63	-3.7	-0.1	S.GARRELTS	173.2	11.7	11– 8
	M.WOODARD	90	0.503	11	1.1		J.GOTT	13.0	-5.6	0– 1
							M.GRANT	10.0	0.1	1– 1
3b	C.BROWN	463	0.622	66	18.2	-5.9	C.HENSLEY	7.1	1.0	1– 0
							M.KRUKOW	245.0	18.1	16–11
ss	J.URIBE	517	0.351	46	-13.1	6.2	M.LACOSS	204.1	3.3	12–11
	L.QUINONES	115	0.120	4	-10.8		B.LASKEY	27.1	-1.7	1– 2
	B.WELLMAN	14	0.063	0	-1.7		R.MASON	60.0	-7.2	3– 4
							G.MINTON	68.2	-1.7	4– 4
lf	C.MALDONADO	432	0.448	53	2.2	0.2	T.MULHOLLAND	54.2	-7.4	2– 4
	J.LEONARD	368	0.495	45	3.6		J.ROBINSON	104.1	4.1	6– 5
							F.WILLIAMS	52.1	14.6	4– 1
cf	D.GLADDEN	402	0.536	50	7.6		Others	5.0	6.1	1– 0
	R.KUTCHER	203	0.380	20	-3.5					
rf	C.DAVIS	618	0.613	86	22.5					
	J.YOUNGBLOOD	208	0.496	25	2.2					
c	B.BRENLY	557	0.577	75	15.5	1.6				
	B.MELVIN	289	0.276	21	-13.3					
	B.GULDEN	24	-0.065	-1	-4.5					
	P.OUELLETTE	26	0.037	-1	-3.8					
	Others	409	0.037	6	-44.5	-4.3				
	TOTALS	6208		684	-0.7	-5.1			63.8	90– 72

	Runs Scored	Runs Allowed	Won	Lost
CALCULATED	676	618	87	75
ACTUAL	698	618	83	79

OTHER BASEBALL PUBLICATIONS

by Geoff Beckman

My favorite scene in the movie Jaws is the one in which Roy Scheider first sees the shark. He's seasick, bored and nauseated from having to ladle fish guts into the ocean; when he sees the shark, he blanches, goes over to Robert Shaw and says, very calmly, "You're gonna need a bigger boat." This seems to me a perfect metaphor for Project Scoresheet.

In 1984, when Project Scoresheet began, there were few sabermetricians, no way to get data without hours of labor, and few people willing to listen to you. Now, there are sabermetricians galore, more data than you can shake a bat at, and an audience of thousands of people ready to read the published work—all of a sudden, we need a bigger boat.

One of the solutions to this was this book: a publication that could hold much of this new information. However, some enterprising people found other ways to disseminate this new material in addition to the Project Scoresheet book. Using their scoresheets, computers, and their time, they started publishing team reports, allowing us to benefit from their expertise about their local teams.

What is a team report like? A general definition is that it is a newsletter, published periodically during the year, devoted to statistics and analysis of a particular team. Each has basic statistical breakdowns—home/road, grass/turf, day/night, situational batting. Most also add data on baserunning, fielding, and pitch breakdowns, as well as analytical pieces to explain the above stats.

This definition leaves out the fact that these newsletters are also labors of love. It takes hundreds of hours of work per year to do one, yet most have only a handful of readers, no matter how cheaply-priced or brilliantly-done they are. Making this commitment is certainly not easy, and sabermetrics and baseball fans are the better for it.

These team reports, very simply, are on the cutting edge of sabermetrics. In their photocopied pages are thousands of bits of wisdom: the nuts and bolts that can enlighten and explain to those who want answers. If you want to take a step into this challenging and fascinating world of knowledge, the people to contact are listed below.

BOSTON RED SOX: Readers of the *Baseball Abstract* know that the name Chuck Waseleski means voluminous research and meticulous attention to detail. *The Waseleski Baseball Report* contains a huge amount of information, covering everything except fielding. The final 1986 report has Roger Clemens' and Wade Boggs' seasons broken down both on a pitch-by-pitch basis and on a base-out situational basis. The final issue is $12.50; the full year's subscription price is $50.00. The address is 10 Newton Street, Miller's Falls, MA 01349.

NEW YORK YANKEES: Craig Christmann does only one issue per year, but it is worth waiting for. There are no pitch-by-pitch data, but there are fielding stats and first-half/second-half breakdowns. A house specialty is detailing how current and past Yankees performed against their current teams this year. The price is $12.50; the address is 54 Old Chesnut Ridge Road, Montvale, NJ 07645.

TORONTO BLUE JAYS: Bill James has called David Driscoll "one of the most talented analysts I've run across," (and rightly so). Driscoll's annual Blue Book runs 170 pages, containing every possible type of study. A particular favorite is the "hustle index"—the number of times a player broke up a double play or beat the relay throw. The price is $9.95 from P.O. Box 6493, Station D, London, Ontario N5W 5S5.

CHICAGO WHITE SOX: Sue and John Dewan's *Chicago Baseball Report* features fewer stats than other reports do, but adds a great deal of informed commentary. Don Zminda covers the Sox with matchless zeal, wit and insight. Nobody, arguably including Chicago's front office, understands his subject as well. The final issue has pitch-by-pitch data as well as the best essay on the subject in print. The price is $19.95 for a one-year subscription, including five regular issues and a final report. The address is P.O. Box 46074, Chicago, IL 60646.

CHICAGO CUBS: The format is the same for the north side edition of the *Chicago Baseball Report,* but the commentary is by Mark Podrazik, who is a fine analyst. He is at his best putting events and statistics into an overall framework; his review of the year in the final issue is a comprehensive, thoughtful condensation that is worth the price of the issue alone. (Same price and address as for the White Sox edition.)

SEATTLE MARINERS: In only its first year, the *Seattle Baseball Bulletin* has performed like a veteran. It has all the features (save fielding), as well as many special studies prompted by questions that arise during the year. As a result, Steve Russell's (and his contributors) work is the most startling and challenging of the team reports. The price is $25.00 for the final 1986 issue along with a 1987 subscription; $20.00 for 1987 alone. The address is P.O. Box 221, Redmond, WA 98073.

SABERMETRICS: While not a team report per se—the *Sabermetric Review* is published by an established publisher, has 12 issues per year, and attempts to answer larger, more general questions— it is a fascinating, insightful journal. Edited by Gary Gillette, it contains articles by him and other sabermetricians, including those who publish team reports. A worthy successor to the defunct *Bill James Baseball Abstract Newsletter*. The price is $30.00 for 15 issues; the publisher's address is Meckler Publishing, 11 Ferry Lane West, Westport, CT 06880.

PROJECT SCORESHEET: Edited by yours truly, the *Project Scoresheet Baseball Report* is an attempt to combine *The Sporting News's* form, the team reports' content, and the *Abstract's* style. Written by Project Scoresheet members, it is easily the least technical and most inconsistent effort on the list; but, at its best, I think it's fascinating, witty and iconoclastic. For more objective opinions, you can check out the favorable reviews it has received in *Sabermetric Review* (December 1986) and *Sport* magazine (January 1987). The price is $12.00 for six bi-monthly issues; the address is P.O. Box 181061, Cleveland, OH 44118.

THE PROJECT SCORESHEET SCORING SYSTEM

INTRODUCTION

The Project Scoresheet Scoring System, like all good things, was a group project. The original scoresheet and coding system were designed by Craig Wright, former team sabermetrician for the Texas Rangers. Gary Gillette revised, expanded and redefined the entire system last year. This year, David Nichols redesigned the scoresheet; I rewrote the instructions and introduction. If you like reading comprehensive reference manuals, turn to the section marked INSTRUCTIONS—you'll love what we have. If you'd like to know how and why our system works, first, keep reading.

The problem with 99% of the scoresheets and scoring systems is very simple—they're outdated. A century ago, Henry Chadwick designed a way to list who batted in what order and give enough space to comfortably record whether they had made a hit or an out. Since that didn't use much space, he gave each batter a space to hit in every inning. It made perfect sense to do that—for a while. Then someone else decided to separate outs into "ground outs", "fly outs" and "strike outs". Somebody else decided to list the fielder who had made the outs. Somebody else began recording the way the batter made it around the bases. All of the decisions made sense except one—nobody ever redesigned the basic tools of the trade. Using Chadwick's original scorecard to record the variety of complex information that people now like to record is like using an axe to butter your toast—you don't blame the tool; the person using it is the crazy one.

How do you define the right tool? First you decide what data you want to record and try to find ways to group it so that you could record as much as possible. Second, you look for a way to record the data that lets you read it and see exactly what happened AS IT HAPPENED. If Dykstra walks, steals second while Backman is batting, takes third on a Hernandez grounder and scores on a Carter single, you don't want to have to go back to a box that you've already read (as you do with every available scoresheet) to follow the action. Lastly, you want it to be as easy to read as possible—you want to write as little as possible. What do you do? Here is what one professional did.

1. CLASSIFY. Once a hitter steps into the batter's box,

many things can happen. But if you think about it, you see that they fall into three simple categories:

WHAT HAPPENED BEFORE THE HITTER HIT THE BALL: Did the runner steal? Was he caught? Did someone drop a foul ball that they could have caught? Was there a wild pitch or a passed ball?

WHAT HAPPENED WHEN THE HITTER HIT THE BALL: The two basic questions here are "Did he get on base or get put out?" and "In either case, how did it happen?". Did he get a hit, draw a walk or benefit from an error? Did he strike out? If he hit the ball but got put out, did he hit the ball on the ground or in the air? Who got him out?

WHAT HAPPENED AFTER THE HITTER HIT THE BALL: How far did the runners advance? Was somebody thrown out on the bases? If so, how?

Our first step was dividing the typical box in a scoresheet into three parts, putting the appropriate information into the appropriate area. The method works well in theory —you can read the scoresheet from beginning to end without jumping backwards constantly—but you run into a problem in practice.

2. CONDENSE. If you want to be able to separate every at bat into three parts, you must have larger boxes on your scoresheet. So large, in fact, that you can't give every hitter a space to bat in every inning like the old scoresheets used to do. You run all the way down each column, drawing heavy lines between the boxes when an inning ends, or putting a large number in the upper left corner of the box or whatever method you like. This makes it a little hard to tell in which inning the three-run rally occurred (you actually have to read), but it gives you one tremendous advantage—you can number the boxes and refer to them. Here's a simple example:

Ron Guidry leads Cleveland 2–1 in the eighth. He walks Butler, Franco singles and, with Mel Hall striding to the plate, receives a visit from his manager that results in an early shower. Dave Righetti enters the game—what do you write?

If you use the typical method, you scrawl some reminder of when he entered; with ours, you simply write the number of the box. This saves space, looks better ("30" as opposed to "P Hall—7") and saves wear and tear on your sanity. When Cleveland pinch-hits for Hall (Righetti is a lefty, after all), you'll find it much simpler to enter "Thornton", "PH" and "30" in the boxes provided; when Nixon enters the game the following inning, those little numbers can be a godsend.

3. SIMPLIFY. After you redesign the scoresheet, you look at the codes. The coding system that most people use has been built up over time; the results are naturally slipshod. Some of the most common events have elaborate codes; some incredibly infrequent ones have much simpler ones. The most sensible thing to do would be to rework things—assigning events that happen most frequently the simplest codes—and that is just what we have done. Let's take it step by step:

DID THE BATTER REACH BASE? If you ask people to abbreviate the words "single", "double", "triple", "homer", "walk" and "error", they're likely to write S, D, T, HR, W (or BB) and E. They have two things in common —each is an abbreviation of the way that a hitter can reach base and all are letters. Rule #1 is thus "If the batter made it to first safely, the first thing you write in his box is a letter; if he didn't, the first thing you write is a number". Strikeouts are a special case—the letter K is so universally accepted that we make an exception to the rule.

WHAT KIND OF OUT DID HE MAKE? 99% of the time, it takes two people to turn ground balls into outs and one for flies. Given that, we don't need to write any letters to distinguish between them—so we don't. Rule #2 (with apologies to Paul Revere) is "One number if by air, two if by land".

Consider the fly ball. An infielder catches three kinds of flies—a popup, a line drive and a foul fly. An outfielder catches three kinds of flies—a regular fly, a line drive and a foul fly. Most infielders don't catch fly balls; most outfielders don't catch popups. How can you record the vast majority of outs as simply as possible?

Did you get the answer? If an infielder catches a popup or an outfielder catches a fly, write down only the number. If the ball was foul, write "/FL" after the number. If it was a line drive, write "/L". If it happened to be a sacrifice fly, write "/SF". And if Tony Fernandez goes tearing out into the power alleys to get the ball over his shoulder or Gary Pettis picks off a popup on the pitcher's mound, make a little note in the margin, OK?

By this time, you should have no trouble with ground balls. For a typical grounder, write only the number of the fielders involved. If the ball was a force out (FO), a double play (GDP) or a fielder's choice (FC), write it after the numbers (letters come first only for hits, remember?).

What about stolen bases? How about runner advancement? How do you score a line drive double play? The first two should be obvious—write "SB2" at the top for the first and "2-H" (runner on second scored) on the bottom line for the second. The third is more advanced; this is only an introduction. If you want to dig further into the system, we suggest that you turn the page.

If you would like to get involved with scoring for your favorite team, or or just want to contribute some scoresheets to the Project effort, you can contact John or Sue Dewan at:

PROJECT SCORESHEET
P.O. BOX 46074
CHICAGO, IL 60646
(312) 774–3798

They will put you in touch with your local captain. If you have any comments or suggestions on how to improve the scoring system, write or call Gary Gillette, P.O. Box 10149, Lansing MI 48901, (517) 484–2972.

—Geoff Beckman

INSTRUCTIONS

1. THE AT-BAT BOX AREA

The 54 numbered boxes on the scoresheet represent plate appearances. All scoring is done in the order in which the events occur on the field. Therefore, everything that happens while a particular batter is at bat or as a result of that batter's at-bat is recorded in the same box on the scoresheet. Each box is divided into three parts in order to organize the scoring process:

Use THE TOP LINE to record anything that happens during the at-bat BEFORE the batter reaches base or is put out. This includes balks, wild pitches, passed balls, stolen bases, caught stealings, pick-offs, errors on pick-off plays, and errors on foul fly balls. NOTE: If any of the above plays occurs as the batter strikes out, record them on the bottom line of the box, since the batter is no longer at bat.

Use THE MIDDLE LINE in each box to record the result of the batter's at-bat: hits, walks and most outs and errors. Also use this box to mark the start of each inning by writing the inning number (and circling it) on the far left side of the first batter's box.

Use THE BOTTOM LINE to record what happens as a result of the at-bat. Advances by the runners and runners thrown out on the bases are the most common notations. The baserunning of the batter should only be noted if it isn't obvious—you need not write that the batter reached first on a walk or was retired on a pop-up, but you must record the base he reached on errors, fielder's choices or a throw to another base. Wild pitches, passed balls, stolen bases and other advances would NOT normally be recorded here (see the note above). On errors and fielder's choices, or plays where the batter attempts to take the extra base on a hit or a throw, you must note how far he advanced. If a batter reaches base and is replaced by a pinch runner, you would note that on this line.

The PITCH-RECORDING BOXES are the eight small boxes just to the left of the at-bat boxes. They are OPTIONAL and placed here only for your convenience. If you enjoy scoring games pitch-by-pitch, feel free to use them.

2. THE LINEUP AREA

This portion of the scoresheet is for recording information about the players. You MUST keep a precise record of when a player enters the game, when he leaves it and if and when he changes positions. There are three areas to allow you to do that.

Use the OFFENSIVE IN COLUMN, at the far left, to record the box number of a player's first plate appearance in a game. Use the PLAYER COLUMN to record his name. The DEFENSIVE SECTION has three types of columns that are used to record where a player played in the field. Use the POSITION COLUMN to record his defensive position and the IN COLUMN to record the number of his FIRST defensive appearance (i.e., which opposing player was the first man to bat after he began playing that position). If he switches positions, record his second position and his first defensive appearance in the same way. If he leaves the game, record his LAST defensive appearance in the OUT COLUMN. After the #9 spot, extra lines are provided for use if more than three players are used in any one lineup slot. Since these lines are not next to their appropriate at-bat boxes, record the position that the player bats in the lineup in the "Bats" column when using these extra lines.

Scorers should remember that it is entirely possible for a player to have plate appearances but no defensive appearances (a pinch hitter or designated hitter), defensive appearances but no plate appearances (a late-inning defensive replacement) or neither plate nor defensive appearances (a pinch runner who is replaced by a new player at the start of the next inning) AND that it is not necessary to record defensive in-out information if a player plays the entire game at one position. We encourage you only to use these boxes as it becomes necessary to do so.

The pitching boxes are toward the bottom center. Record the OPPOSING team's starter in the box entitled PITCHER (i.e., if Boston plays Detroit, Jack Morris's name would go on the same side as the Boston hitters). Record the at-bat box number of the first and last batters he faces in the IN and OUT boxes. If more than one pitcher pitches to the same batter, put an ASTERISK next to that OUT number for the first pitcher and the IN number for the second pitcher. This can occur when a pitcher is removed from the game after pitching to a batter but not retiring him or when a team changes pitchers between innings and the last out of the previous inning was a pickoff or caught stealing (so the same batter would lead off next inning). Also record the number of earned runs each pitcher allows, along with Wins, Losses and Saves, in the spaces provided.

The NOTES section of the scoresheet is provided to record any events such as ejections, rain delays, injuries, and protests, as well as allowing room for the scorer to detail any play that is confusing. If you have any doubts about the correct or official scoring of a particular play, or if you feel that the scoring codes cannot adequately describe what happened, please explain it in a note.

The GAME CONDITIONS BOXES are at the top of the scoresheet. Game time refers to YOUR LOCAL TIME (i.e., a Cleveland scorer would code a game in Seattle as beginning at 10:30 PM; a Seattle scorer would write 7:30). The weather data need not be meteorologically precise—if your radio announcer says that it rained in another city that day and "boy, the field is really sloppy", that is enough evidence to let you circle the box marked "soaked" under Field Conditions with confidence.

3. THE SCORING SYSTEM

There are, essentially, only two things that must be recorded—BASES GAINED by the offense and OUTS MADE by the defense. Here are some general notes about each before we get to the specific codes.

You record OUTS by listing every fielder who touched the ball in the process of making an out, and by recording how and where the out was made and (in some cases) what type of out was made. Outs can be recorded on any line in any box, but only certain types of outs will be recorded in certain areas. The top line will contain baserunning (caught stealing, pickoffs, appeal plays) outs only. The middle line contains only the outs that are a DIRECT result of the batter's actions (the batter's outs and all force plays). The bottom line is for all outs on base that are NOT force outs —a caught stealing on a third strike or an out on base (this includes outs where a batter hits safely and is out trying for an extra base).

You account for BASES by recording how each batter reached base and how and when each runner advanced. How batters reach base is recorded on the middle line of the box. Advances by runners while the batter is at the plate are recorded on the top line; advances by the batter and runners after the ball is put into play are recorded on the bottom line.

Some scorers choose to record additional information —we encourage this, but do not require it. If you wish to record more information about hits, turn to section 5— OPTIONAL HIT SCORING SYSTEM. If you wish to chart pitches, section 6—SCORING PITCH BY PITCH— should be consulted.

Use the NOTES section of the scoresheet to record any unusual plays such as interference or obstruction, plays for which the scoring won't fit on the appropriate line (i.e., a lengthy rundown), injuries, ejections, rain delays, protested or suspended games, and anything else you want to record (e.g., pitch-outs, hit-and-run plays).

4. SOME SCORING EXAMPLES AND CLARIFICATIONS

Some plays frequently cause confusion due to their official scoring or to their scoring codes. Here are some explanations that may help in such cases:

ERRORS: The correct scoring of most errors is an "E" followed by the number of the fielder who made the error, then a slash followed by a descriptive code. Examples: "E6/G" means the shortstop booted a grounder; "E3/L" means that the first baseman dropped a line drive. "SB2(2–3(E2))" shows that the catcher made a throwing error on a stolen base attempt, allowing the runner to go to 3B. On some plays, more than one error is made; on other plays in which the ball gets thrown around a lot, the sequence of putouts, assists, errors and advances by runners can be confusing. Code such plays as well as possible on the appropriate lines, but be sure to explain the play fully in the Notes section. Remember that dropped foul fly balls (i.e.,

"FLE7") and pick-off errors, e.g., "POE1 (1–3)", have their own separate codes. On plays where a fielder drops a throw for an error, score an assist to the thrower, such as "6E3". On any play when an error was made, a runner scored and the batter does not receive an RBI, be sure to say so by writing "NO RBI" beside the advancement code on the bottom line of the box (i.e., 2-H, NO RBI).

BUNTS and SACRIFICES: The "B" code is used after a slash to describe all bunt plays except sacrifice hits. Use the "SH" code on bunt plays in which the batter is credited with a sacrifice hit, whether he is retired or not. If the batter attempts to sacrifice but a runner is thrown out instead, record the out normally (it will either be a FO or FC) and note that it was a bunt. Several examples are listed below.

1) Score "S5/B" for a bunt single fielded by the third baseman.
2) Score "23/B" when the batter is out at first attempting to bunt for a base hit.
3) Score "14/SH" if the batter bunts, is put out at 1B (2B covering) and the runner advances (and 1–2 on the bottom line).
4) Score "FC3/SH" if the batter attempts to sacrifice and the first baseman fields the bunt, throws to 3B but fails to get the runner. The batter is credited with a Sacrifice Hit and reaches base on the Fielder's Choice.

INTERFERENCE: On Catcher Interference plays (the most common type of interference), the batter is automatically awarded first base and the catcher is automatically credited with an error. Example: score "C/E2". On other interference plays, score "INT" in the box, record any runner advances, and explain the play with a note below.

FORCE OUTS and FIELDER'S CHOICES: A fielder's choice is any play where a fielder TRIES to put out any runner (other than the batter) who tries (for any reason) to advance on the play; a force out is any play where a fielder SUCCEEDS in putting a runner who is REQUIRED to advance. Thus, all force outs are fielder's choices—but not all fielder's choices are force outs. In fact,

you score a fielder's choice on a play where the fielder fails to retire a runner and the batter reaches base. For scoring purposes, use the "FO" code on any force out (e.g., 64/FO). Use the "FC" code in two situations only:

1) If the batter reaches base and no runners are put out on the play. This happens most frequently on sacrifice bunts when the fielder attempts to get the lead runner and fails (see example under Bunts and Sacrifice Hits).
2) If the batter reaches base and a runner is thrown out attempting to advance when he is not forced to. For example, there is a runner on second only with less than two out and the batter grounds to the shortstop. The SS throws out the runner at 3B and the batter is safe at 1B. Score "FC6" in the middle line and "2X3 (65), B-1" on the bottom line.

PICKOFFS AND CAUGHT STEALINGS: If a runner who is picked off base makes any move at all toward the next base, even if he then begins returning to the base he was at, it is officially scored as a CAUGHT STEALING. In these instances, score the play as a caught stealing; add a note that it resulted from a pickoff. For example, a runner on first is caught off, starts for second, then returns to first when the throw beats him to second and is tagged out. Score the play "CS2 (1343)". A runner who is picked off and makes no move at all to advance is not considered to be caught stealing—score "PO1 (13)" for example. Strikeouts followed by caught stealings are coded "K/DP", with the CS recorded on the bottom line. On pickoffs by the catcher, or on steals of home, the pitcher never gets an assist on a pitch, e.g., PO1 (23) or CSH (2). Pitchers only get assists on direct throws that retire runners, not on legal pitches after which a runner is put out.

STRIKEOUTS or WALKS with WILD PITCHES and PASSED BALLS: If the pitch gets by the catcher after a strike three or a ball four, a wild pitch or passed ball must be scored if the batter reached base after striking out, or if the batter or any runner advanced more than one base after a walk. In these cases, score a "K+" or "W+" or the

PLAYER CODES:

Pitcher	1	Left Fielder	7	
Catcher	2	Center Fielder	8	
First Baseman	3	Right Fielder	9	
Second Baseman	4	Designated Hitter	0	
Third Baseman	5	Pinch-Hitter	PH	
Shortstop	6	Pinch-Runner	PR	

BASERUNNER CODES:

Batter	B
Runner on First	1
Runner on Second	2
Runner on Third	3

ADVANCEMENT CODES:

To First Base	–1
To Second Base	–2
To Third Base	–3
To Home Plate	–H

PLAY SCORING CODES:

		Ground Ball	/G	Fielder's Choice	/FC	Ground Out *	43
Single	S	Line Drive	/L	Force Out	/FO	Unassisted Ground Out *	3/G
Double	D	Foul	/FL	Ground Ball Double Play	/GDP	Fly Out *	8
Triple	T	Bunt	/B	All Other Double Plays	/DP	Foul Out *	2/FL
Home Run	HR	Throw	/TH	Triple Play	/TP	Error *	E6
				Sacrifice Bunt	/SH	Throwing Error *	E5/TH
Passed Ball	PB	Walk	W	Sacrifice Fly	/SF	Foul Ball Error *	FLE2
Wild Pitch	WP	Intentional Walk	IW				
Balk	BK	Strikeout;	K	Caught Stealing/2rd *	CS2(26)	Runner Advanced *	2-H
Stolen Base/2nd	SB2	w/Dropped 3rd Strike	K23	Caught Stealing/3rd *	CS3(25)	Runner Out on Bases *	2XH(92)
Stolen Base/3rd	SB3	w/Batter to First	K+/WP (or PB)	Caught Stealing/Home *	CSH(2)	Pinch Runner/1st	PR1
Stolen Base/Home	SBH	Hit By Pitch	HP	Picked Off/1nd *	PO2(13)	Pinch Runner/2nd	PR2
Double Steal *	SB3;SB2	Catcher's Interference	C/E2	Picked Off/2nd *	PO3(14)	Pinch Runner/3rd	PR3
				Picked Off/3rd *	PO3(15)		

*****IMPORTANT NOTE: The codes listed with an asterisk can be scored in many ways; for the sake of clarity, we have included common examples that MIGHT arise in a game. If the second baseman takes the catcher's throw to second, you would score the caught stealing differently than we have listed it, just as you would not score all ground outs "43".

middle line of the box followed by the "WP" or "PB". Note the advances of the batter and runners on the bottom line. Examples: "K+WP" with "B-1" or "W+PB" with "B-2". If the batter is retired at first after a dropped third strike and no runners advance, score "K23". If the catcher drops the ball but tags out the batter, the "K" will suffice, since the catcher gets credit for a putout on each strikeout anyway.

UNASSISTED GROUNDOUTS: When a player fields a ground ball and either tags a runner out or steps on the base himself, it is ESSENTIAL that you note that it is a groundout—"3/G" for example—so that it CANNOT be mistaken for any type of fly ball. It is possible for an unassisted groundout to be a forceout (4/FO), a fielder's choice (if there is a runner on second only and he tries to move to third on a ground ball to the shortstop, say, score it 6/FC) or a double play. In the latter case, use the GDP symbol to show that the ball was hit on the ground (i.e., 4, 43 GDP).

FINALLY—if you have ANY doubt whatsoever about how the play should be scored, please check with another, reliable source. Please remember that the people who will be entering your scoresheets onto computer will probably not have seen the game or be able to reconstruct the action if you omit information or give a misleading picture. If you simply cannot verify the problem, it is better to say "I didn't see exactly what happened—this is what I think went on" than to pretend that you are sure about something that you are unclear of. Thanks for your help. If you have any questions or comments, please let us know.

5. OPTIONAL HIT SCORING SYSTEM

All traditional baseball scoring systems treat the scoring of outs in much more detail than hits. For instance, a routine ground out can be scored 13, 23, 53, 63, 43, 31 or 3 (unassisted), but a bunt single is scored exactly the same way as a long single in the gap in rightcenter field. Further, traditional scoring systems don't note who fielded a base hit (unless that fielder also made an error) and they never note what kind of hit it was (ground ball, line drive or fly ball).

The trouble with this lack of detail is that it makes answering certain questions impossible. Many analysts have wondered if groundball pitchers have different hit distributions than fly ball pitchers? How many bases do runners advance on singles to left field, as compared to center and right field? How often to batters bunt for a base hit? How many grounders get through grass infields for hits com-

pared to turf infields? How many balls are getting by a fielder in addition to the ones we already know that he catches? Nobody can be sure; if we knew where every hit in a season landed, we could.

Many scorers have already been providing more information on base hits than we require. If you are one of them, we urge you to try this new system. If you are not, maybe you will consider it anyway. In either case, your comments and criticisms are solicited so that we can improve it. PLEASE REMEMBER THAT YOU ARE NOT RE-QUIRED TO USE THIS SYSTEM.

In this system, all hits are still recorded on the middle line of the box. Then, additional elements are added to to provide more information. After you code the hit, record the position number of the player who fields the ball. Obviously, this is not applicable to home runs (unless they are inside-the-park) and ground-rule doubles. A slash comes after the fielder code, then a code to describe the hit (G for ground ball, L for line drive, F for fly ball, and B for bunt). All ground ball hits will have infield location codes; line drive hits that are low enough to be caught by an infielder standing nearby have infield codes; liners too high for infielders to have a chance at them have outfield codes. After that, code where the ball landed. Baserunner advances and errors after hits are scored the same as before.

The hit location codes are based on the position of the base hit relative to the fielder(s). Thus, a hit in rightcenter field is coded 89. A ball through the hole between the third baseman and the shortstop is coded 56. On balls hit to the outfield, add a letter to describe how far it was hit (L for Line, S for Short, D for Deep). You would code a hit between the first baseman and the line 3L; in the left field corner, 7L; a deep fly over the center fielder's head is 8D. A ball hit directly at or through an infielder is coded with his position number followed by "T".

Two final notes: One of the most common mistakes people make with this system is coding balls down the first base line "1L" and balls down the third base line "3L." We humbly beg you not to do this—if you do, it means that some future researcher will have to recode those parts of it. And don't go overboard. We don't expect microscopic analyses that are geometrically precise—we seek only an honest effort by a concerned observer. DON'T WORRY over the difference between a soft liner and a looping fly ball—just knowing that it wasn't a check-swing grounder will help a lot.

HIT CODES:	S	= Single	FIELDER CODES:		DESCRIPTION CODES:	B = Bunt
	D	= Double				G = Ground Ball
	T	= Triple	(Standard #1–9			L = Line Drive
	H or HR	= Home Run	Position Codes)			F = Fly Ball

LOCATION CODES (examples):

INFIELD HITS (Bunts, Ground Balls and occasional Fly Balls)

Between home and pitcher's mound	= 12 (S1/B12)
Inside infield, down 1B line	= 13 (S3/G13)
Inside infield, down 3B line	= 15 (S5/B15)
Past pitcher's mound, right side	= 14 (S4,E4(TH)/G14)
Past pitcher's mound, left side	= 16 (S6,F16)

HITS THROUGH THE INFIELD (Ground Balls and Line Drives)

Down the 1B line	= 3L (D,E9/L3L)
Thru the hole between 1B & 2B	= 34 (S9/G34)
Up the middle (between 2B & SS)	= 46 (S8/L46)
Thru the hole between SS & 3B	= 56 (S,E7/G56)
Down the 3B line	= 5L (D7/G5L)
Directly thru or at infielder	= 1T, 3T, 4T, 5T, 6T (S7/L5T)

OUTFIELD HITS (Line Drives and Fly Balls)

Down the LF line	= 7L (D7/F7L)	In the gap in left center	= 78 (T7/F78)	Short RF (in front of the RF)	= 9S (S9/F9S)
Short LF (in front of the LF)	= 7S (S7/L7S)	Short CF (in front of the CF)	= 8S (S8/L8S)	Deep RF (behind the RF)	= 9D (T9/F9D)
Deep LF (behind the LF)	= 7D (T7/F7D)	Deep CF (behind the CF)	= 8D (H8/F8D)	Down the RF line	= 9L (D9/L9L)
		In the gap in right center	= 89 (D,E8/F89)		

6. OPTIONAL PITCH BY PITCH SCORING SYSTEM

The old proverb "give 'em an inch and they want a mile" seems to apply to scoring, too. Over the last several years, dozens of people (who once protested that they couldn't score games because they didn't have the patience) have asked us when we were going to adapt the scoresheet so that they could record every pitch of every game more easily. If you were one of them, we're happy to oblige. If you aren't—and you wonder how or why anyone would count pitches—we'll try to explain it to you. When a pitcher faces a hitter—whether it's Roger Mason against Mike Schmidt or Roger Clemens versus Mike Gallego—the key to whether the pitcher allows a hit is the count. If the pitcher is behind in the count, he is forced to throw strikes; if he's ahead, the batter must swing at anything close to the plate. Virtually every hitter will hit well when he is ahead in the count and almost any pitcher is unhittable when he is ahead—the good hitters are the men who can work the count in their favor more often and the pitchers are the ones who consistently put hitters in a hole. There are some people who feel that attempting to record the events in a game without also noting the count are missing the important in favor of the trivial—others just find it fascinating to know that Brett Butler will get about 20 pitches thrown to him in a typical game (9 balls, 1 swinging strike, 3 fouls, 4 called strikes and 3 balls put into play) while Cory Snyder averages 14 (10 of which are swinging strikes). You can discover that the 17–8 ace got hitters into an 0–2 count 32% of the time and that the 11–16 journeyman did so only 14%, see when a pitcher is tiring (last time he got the batter out on two pitches—this time it took seven) and decide whether he is making his pitches too fat (hitters batted .519 when they swung at his 2–0 pitch).

Scoring pitch by pitch demands intense concentration—you can't run out for beer and let a friend score for you, carry on much of a conversation during games and one lapse of concentration can ruin an entire evening's work. It definitely isn't for everyone. But, to some people, it is absolutely the only way to score. If you have never tried it, give it a shot—but don't blame us if you get hooked on doing it.

If that prologue intrigued you enough to want to try it, here is the system that we suggest. It is based on discussions with the people in Project Scoresheet who score every game pitch by pitch. YOU ARE NOT REQUIRED TO SCORE PITCH BY PITCH OR TO USE OUR SYSTEM—this is merely a set of guidelines from people who have tried just about everything.

BASICS: There are eight small boxes to the left of the at-bat boxes—we will be entering letter codes to tell us what happened on every pitch. There are two ways to fill the boxes—by going left to right or up and down. We strongly reccommend that you enter left to right, because people read left to right. Here are the codes we recommend:

CALLED STRIKE: C
SWINGING STRIKE: S

FOUL BALL: F
BALL: B
PUT INTO PLAY: X
INTENTIONAL BALL: I
PITCHOUT: P
HIT BY PITCH: H

Most of the codes should be self-explanatory; here are a few notes to help you: If the catcher catches a 2-strike foul tip, it is a SWINGING STRIKE; if he doesn't, it's a foul ball. One of the most basic things to do with the data is computing the percentage of strikes thrown; we keep track of INTENTIONAL BALLS and PITCHOUTS so that we can remove them from the calculations. The term PUT IN PLAY means that the batter made contact with the ball, which resulted in either a hit, an error or an out (i.e., everything but a strikeout, walk or a HIT BY PITCH).

FRILLS: Most scorers feel that, as long as they are recording every pitch, they might as well make notes of when runners try to steal. If you agree, we suggest that you circle the pitch on which the runner tried to steal or was picked off. Some scorers elect to record check swings by adding a small "x" after the code; many don't bother. Some people choose to use other letters or symbols (we think ours is the easiest to remember, but there's no accounting for taste). Some people choose not to use any or all of the symbols; but we disagree with this practice we see no great harm in it. WE DO NOT, however, feel that the PUT IN PLAY symbol is optional. It may seem like wasted effort to record that the batter hit the ball when the at-bat box also tells you that he did; some of us decided not to use it when we started out. But the extra effort involved is minimal and there is virtually no study that you can do where it won't be easier if you do it. Trust us—you'll be glad that you got into the habit when you're counting data from 40 different scoresheets.

HINTS: We suggest that your first pitch by pitch game be one that you attend; most people find it easier to get the hang of the system if they don't have to deal with announcers, commercials or the phone. Try to total the number of pitches that a pitcher throws each inning, breaking them down by balls and strikes and noting them in the margin—having one new bit of tangible knowledge every half-inning seems to give people strength to continue. Try looking for patterns—are hitters swinging at the first pitch? Does the pitcher always try to get the first pitch over? Are hitters waiting the pitcher out or swinging freely?—you never know what you may spot. Once you begin to see what you can do, you should have no problems dealing with the radio announcers.

FINALLY: Some of you have probably already said "Eight boxes can't possibly be enough for every hitter". You're right, it isn't. On the average, there will be one hitter a game who makes the pitcher throw more than eight pitches; when that unlikely event occurs, you can always resort to the NOTES section of the scoresheet. Good luck—if your radio announcer uses the words "Holy Cow!", you'll need it.

Project ScoreSheet

Box 46074 · Chicago IL 60646
1987 Scoring Form

Date

Time

Visitors

Umps: Home

1st
2nd
3rd

Scorer

Home

Off. In	Visiting Players	Defensive Pos In Out

1 2 3 4 5 6 7 8 9

10 11 12 13 14 15 16 17 18

19 20 21 22 23 24 25 26 27

28 29 30 31 32 33 34 35 36

37 38 39 40 41 42 43 44 45

46 47 48 49 50 51 52 53 54

Bats

R H E

1 2 3 4 5 6 7 8 9 10

Home Pitchers	In	Out	ER	W/L Sv

Notes

Visitors

Home

vs.

Date

Scorer

Temperature

40s	50s	60s
70s	80s	90s

| Field | Soaked | Wet | Dry |

Sky

Sunny	Cloudy
Overcast	Night

Precip.

None	Drizzle
Showers	Rain

Home Players

Defensive Pos In Pos In Out

Off. In

1 2 3 4 5 6 7 8 9

10 11 12 13 14 15 16 17 18

19 20 21 22 23 24 25 26 27

28 29 30 31 32 33 34 35 36

37 38 39 40 41 42 43 44 45

46 47 48 49 50 51 52 53 54

Bats

Notes

Visiting Pitchers

| In | Out | ER | W/L Sv |

R H E

1 2 3 4 5 6 7 8 9 10